Pocket Oxford Dictionary, Thesaurus, and Wordpower Guide

Pocket Oxford
Dictionary,
Thesaurus, and
Wordpower Guide

Edited by **Sara Hawker**

OXFORD
UNIVERSITY PRESS

OXFORD
UNIVERSITY PRESS

Great Clarendon Street, Oxford ox2 6DP

Oxford University Press is a department of the University of Oxford.
It furthers the University's objective of excellence in research, scholarship,
and education by publishing worldwide in

Oxford New York

Auckland Bangkok Buenos Aires Cape Town Chennai
Dar es Salaam Delhi Hong Kong Istanbul Karachi Kolkata
Kuala Lumpur Madrid Melbourne Mexico City Mumbai Nairobi
São Paulo Shanghai Singapore Taipei Tokyo Toronto

Oxford is a registered trade mark of Oxford University Press
in the UK and in certain other countries

Published in the United States
by Oxford University Press Inc., New York

First published 2004
Dictionary text first published 2004 as the Oxford Minidictionary, 6th edition;
thesaurus text first published 2003 as the Oxford Mini Thesaurus

British Library Cataloguing in Publication Data

Data available

Library of Congress Cataloging in Publication Data

Data available

ISBN 0–19–8608632

10 9 8 7 6 5 4 3 2 1

Typeset in Nimrod and Arial
by Morton Word Processing Ltd
Printed in Great Britain
by Clays Ltd, Bungay, Suffolk

Contents

Note on trademarks and proprietary status

This dictionary includes some words which have, or are asserted to have, proprietary status as trademarks or otherwise. Their inclusion does not imply that they have acquired for legal purposes a non-proprietary or general significance, nor any other judgement concerning their legal status. In cases where the editorial staff have some evidence that a word has proprietary status this is indicated in the entry for that word by the label trademark but no judgement concerning the legal status of such words is made or implied thereby.

Introduction

....

The *Pocket Oxford Dictionary, Thesaurus, and Wordpower Guide* is a three-in-one resource that has been compiled to provide a range of guidance and help with language in a convenient, compact format. The dictionary and thesaurus texts are arranged in a way that enables quick and easy reference to both, as the top section of each page contains the dictionary text while the lower section gives matching thesaurus entries for many of the words covered by the dictionary.

The dictionary text is derived from the sixth edition of the *Oxford Minidictionary*, which provides up-to-date coverage of the core vocabulary of current English in a crisp, clear, and accessible style. Special notes throughout the text give extra guidance on difficult spellings and tricky points of usage, while pronunciations using a simple respelling system are given for words which might cause problems. The thesaurus text is taken from the *Oxford Mini Thesaurus* and provides lists of alternative words for over 7,500 entries in the dictionary text.

The *Wordpower Guide* is made up of six separate sections on a variety of topics, ranging from commonly confused English words to the countries of the world and collective names for animals and birds.

The *Pocket Oxford Dictionary, Thesaurus, and Wordpower Guide* is an ideal resource for anyone requiring a compact, informative guide to the English language of today.

Structure of the dictionary and thesaurus entries

Headword
Pronunciation (given for difficult words)

DICTIONARY

buoy /boy/ n. a floating object used to mark an area of water. ▶v. **1** keep afloat. **2** (**be buoyed up**) be cheerful and confident.

Typical use

▶ introduces new part of speech

✓ Remember: *u* before *o* in buoy and buoyant.

Spelling note

Plural forms   Sense number

gas n. (pl. **gases** or US **gasses**) **1** an air-like substance which expands to fill any available space. **2** such a substance used as a fuel. **3** US informal petrol. ▶v. (**gassing, gassed**) **1** harm or kill with gas. **2** informal chatter. □ **gas chamber** a room filled with poisonous gas to kill people. **gas mask** a mask used as protection against poison gas. ■ **gassy** adj.

Verb inflections

Label showing how term is used

Label showing where term is used

□ introduces compounds and phrases (in alphabetical order)

Adjective inflections

sad adj. (**sadder, saddest**) **1** unhappy. **2** causing sorrow: *a sad story*. ■ **sadden** v. **sadly** adv. **sadness** n.

Example of use

■ introduces derivatives (in alphabetical order)

Different spelling of headword (both allowed)

bosun (or **bo'sun**) var. of **BOATSWAIN**.

Cross-reference to another dictionary entry

Core synonyms (in small capitals), synonyms closest in meaning to entry word

THESAURUS

benefit n. **1** ADVANTAGE, asset, blessing, boon, plus, plus point, perquisite; *informal* perk. **2** GOOD, well-being, advantage, interest, profit, gain, welfare; convenience, prosperity, good fortune, aid, assistance, help, service, privilege, betterment. **3** AID, allowance, subsidy, grant, payment, assistance; *informal* dole. ■ OPPOSITES disadvantage, detriment.

Label showing level of formality of following synonym(s)

Sense number

Words opposite in meaning to entry word

Pronunciations

....

Pronunciations are given for words which might cause problems but not for words assumed to be familiar. The part of the pronunciation printed in bold is the syllable that is stressed.

List of symbols

vowels	examples	vowels	examples	vowels	examples
a	as in **cat**	ew	as in **few**	oy	as in **boy**
ah	as in **calm**	i	as in **pin**	u	as in **cup**
air	as in **hair**	ɪ	as in **eye**	uh	as in the first part of **ago**
ar	as in **bar**	o	as in **top**		
aw	as in **law**	oh	as in **most**	uu	as in **book**
ay	as in **say**	oi	as in **join**	y	as in **cry**
e	as in **bed**	oo	as in **soon**	yoo	as in **unit**
ee	as in **meet**	oor	as in **poor**	yoor	as in **Europe**
eer	as in **beer**	or	as in **corn**	yr	as in **fire**
er	as in **her**	ow	as in **cow**		

consonants	examples	consonants	examples	consonants	examples
b	as in **bat**	l	as in **leg**	sh	as in **shop**
ch	as in **chin**	m	as in **man**	t	as in **top**
d	as in **day**	n	as in **not**	th	as in **thin**
f	as in **fat**	ng	as in **sing, finger**	*th*	as in **this**
g	as in **get**			v	as in **van**
h	as in **hat**	nk	as in **thank**	w	as in **will**
j	as in **jam**	p	as in **pen**	y	as in **yes**
k	as in **king**	r	as in **red**	z	as in **zebra**
kh	as in **loch**	s	as in **sit**	zh	as in **vision**

Abbreviations used in the dictionary and thesaurus

adj.	adjective	**Naut.**	Nautical
abbrev.	abbreviation	**N. Engl.**	northern English
adv.	adverb	**offens.**	offensive
Austral.	Australian	**pl.**	plural
Chem.	Chemistry	**pl. n.**	plural noun
comb. form	combining form	**possess. pron**	possessive pronoun
conj.	conjunction	**past part.**	past participle
derog.	derogatory	**prep.**	preposition
esp.	especially	**pres. part.**	present participle
exclam.	exclamation	**sing.**	singular
fem.	feminine	**Sc.**	Scottish
Geom.	Geometry	**usu.**	usually
Gk. Myth	Greek Mythology	**v.**	verb
hist.	historical	**var.**	variant
Math.	Mathematics	**vars.**	variants
n.	noun	**aux. v.**	auxiliary verb

Abbreviations that are in common use (such as cm, RC, and USA) appear in the dictionary itself.

a adj. **1** used when mentioning someone or something for the first time; the indefinite article. **2** one single. **3** per: *twice a week*.

AA abbrev. **1** Alcoholics Anonymous. **2** Automobile Association.

aardvark n. an African mammal with a long snout.

aback adv. (**taken aback**) surprised and disconcerted.

abacus n. a frame with rows of wires along which beads are slid, used for counting.

abandon v. **1** leave permanently. **2** give up. ▶ n. lack of inhibition. ■ **abandonment** n.

abandoned adj. wild or uncontrolled.

abase v. humiliate or degrade. ■ **abasement** n.

abashed adj. embarrassed or ashamed.

abate v. become less severe or widespread. ■ **abatement** n.

abattoir /a-buh-twar/ n. a slaughterhouse.

abbey n. a building occupied by a community of monks or nuns.

abbot n. (fem. **abbess**) the head of an abbey.

abbreviate v. shorten a word or phrase. ■ **abbreviation** n.

abdicate v. **1** give up the throne. **2** fail to carry out a duty. ■ **abdication** n.

abdomen n. the part of the body containing the digestive organs. ■ **abdominal** adj.

abduct v. kidnap. ■ **abduction** n. **abductor** n.

aberrant adj. not normal or acceptable.

aberration n. a deviation from what is normal or acceptable.

abet v. (**abetting**, **abetted**) encourage or help in wrongdoing. ■ **abetter** (or **abettor**) n.

abeyance n. (**in abeyance**) in temporary disuse.

abhor v. (**abhorring**, **abhorred**) detest.

abhorrent adj. disgusting; hateful. ■ **abhorrence** n.

abide v. **1** (**abide by**) accept or obey a rule or decision. **2** *informal* put up with.

abiding adj. lasting; enduring.

ability n. (pl. **abilities**) **1** the power to do something. **2** talent.

abject adj. **1** wretched. **2** completely

Thesaurus

abandon v. **1** DESERT, leave, forsake, depart from, leave behind, cast aside, jilt; *informal* run out on. **2** GIVE UP, renounce, relinquish, dispense with, forgo, desist from, forswear. **3** YIELD, surrender, give up, cede, relinquish, abdicate, deliver up, resign. ▶ n. LACK OF RESTRAINT/ INHIBITION, wildness, impulse, impetuosity, immoderation, wantonness. ■ OPPOSITES self-control.

abandoned adj. **1** DESERTED, forsaken, cast aside. **2** RECKLESS, unrestrained, uninhibited, impetuous, wild, careless, wanton.

abashed adj. EMBARRASSED, ashamed, shamefaced, mortified, humiliated, taken aback, disconcerted, nonplussed, discomfited, discomposed, perturbed, confounded, dismayed, dumbfounded, confused, put out of countenance, discountenanced.

abbreviate v. SHORTEN, reduce, cut, cut short/down, contract, condense, compress, abridge, truncate, crop, shrink, constrict, summarize, abstract, precis, synopsize, digest. ■ OPPOSITES expand.

abdicate v. **1** RESIGN, stand down, retire; *informal* quit. **2** GIVE UP, renounce, relinquish, abjure, repudiate, reject, disown, waive, yield, forgo, refuse, abandon, surrender, cast aside.

abduct v. KIDNAP, carry off, run away/off with, make off with, seize, hold as hostage, hold to ransom; *informal* snatch.

aberration n. DEVIATION, anomaly, abnormality, irregularity, variation, freak.

abhorrent adj. DETESTABLE, loathsome, hateful, hated, abominable, repellent, repugnant, repulsive, revolting, disgusting, distasteful, vile, horrible, horrid, heinous, obnoxious, odious, offensive, execrable; *informal* yucky. ■ OPPOSITES delightful, admirable.

abide v. STAND, tolerate, bear, put up with, endure, accept, stomach, brook; *old use* suffer. □ **abide by** KEEP TO, comply with, observe, follow, obey, agree without pride. ■ **abjectly** adv.

abjure v. renounce a belief, claim, etc.

ablaze adj. burning fiercely.

able adj. **1** capable of doing something. **2** talented. ■ **ably** adv.

ablutions pl. n. the act of washing oneself.

abnegate v. renounce or reject.

abnormal adj. not normal. ■ **abnormality** n. **abnormally** adv.

aboard adv. & prep. on board.

abode n. a house or home.

abolish v. put an end to a law or custom. ■ **abolition** n.

abominable adj. causing disgust. ■ **abominably** adv.

abominate v. hate; detest. ■ **abomination** n.

aboriginal adj. existing in a land from its earliest times. ▶ n. (**Aboriginal**) a member of one of the native peoples of Australia.

Aborigine /ab-uh-**ri**-ji-nee/ n. an Australian Aboriginal.

abort v. **1** carry out the abortion of a fetus. **2** bring to an early end as a result of a problem.

abortion n. the deliberate bringing to an end of a human pregnancy.

abortionist n. derog. a person who carries out abortions.

abortive adj. unsuccessful.

abound v. be plentiful.

about prep. & adv. **1** concerning. **2** here and there within a particular area. **3** approximately. □ **about-turn** a complete reversal of direction or policy.

above prep. & adv. **1** at a higher level than. **2** more than. □ **above board** lawful and honest.

abracadabra exclam. said by magicians when performing a trick.

abrasion n. **1** scraping or wearing away. **2** an area of scraped skin.

abrasive adj. **1** able to polish or clean by rubbing or grinding. **2** harsh in manner.

abreast adv. **1** side by side. **2** (**abreast of**) up to date with.

abridge v. shorten a text or film. ■ **abridgement** n.

abroad adv. away from one's home

Thesaurus

to, hold to, conform to, adhere to, stick to, stand by.

ability n. **1** TALENT, competence, competency, proficiency, skill, expertise, expertness, adeptness, aptitude, dexterity, adroitness, qualification, cleverness, flair, gift, knack, savoir faire; *informal* know-how. **2** CAPACITY, capability, potential, potentiality, power, facility, faculty, propensity. ■ OPPOSITES inability.

ablaze adj. **1** ON FIRE, burning, blazing, alight, flaming, aflame; *literary* afire. **2** LIT UP, gleaming, glowing, aglow, illuminated, brilliant, radiant, shimmering, sparkling, flashing, incandescent.

able adj. COMPETENT, capable, talented, skilful, skilled, clever, intelligent, accomplished, gifted, proficient, fit, expert, adept, efficient, effective, qualified, adroit. ■ OPPOSITES incompetent.

abnormal adj. UNUSUAL, strange, odd, peculiar, uncommon, curious, queer, eccentric, extraordinary, unexpected, exceptional, irregular, weird, unnatural, erratic, singular, atypical, anomalous, deviant, deviating, divergent, aberrant; *informal* oddball, off the wall, wacko. ■ OPPOSITES normal.

abolish v. DO AWAY WITH, put an end to, end, stop, terminate, axe, eliminate, eradicate, exterminate, destroy, annihilate, stamp out, obliterate, wipe out, extinguish, quash, expunge, extirpate,

annul, cancel, invalidate, nullify, void, rescind, repeal, revoke, abrogate. ■ OPPOSITES retain.

abominable adj. HATEFUL, loathsome, detestable, odious, obnoxious, base, despicable, contemptible, damnable, cursed, disgusting, revolting, repellent, repulsive, offensive, repugnant, abhorrent, foul, vile, wretched, horrible, nasty, disagreeable, unpleasant, execrable; *informal* yucky, god-awful. ■ OPPOSITES good, admirable.

aboriginal adj. INDIGENOUS, native, original, earliest, first, ancient, primitive, primeval, primordial, autochthonous. ■ OPPOSITES immigrant.

abortive adj. FAILED, unsuccessful, nonsuccessful, vain, futile, useless, worthless, ineffective, ineffectual, fruitless, unproductive, unavailing. ■ OPPOSITES successful.

abound v. BE PLENTIFUL, proliferate, teem, overflow, swarm, thrive, flourish; *informal* be two/ten a penny.

abrasive adj. **1** EROSIVE, eroding, corrosive, chafing, rubbing, coarse, harsh. **2** CAUSTIC, cutting, grating, biting, rough, harsh, irritating, sharp, nasty. ■ OPPOSITES smooth, kind, gentle.

abridge v. SHORTEN, cut down, summarize, condense, precis, abstract, epitomize, synopsize, digest, contract, compress, abbreviate, reduce, decrease, dicountry.

abrogate v. repeal or abolish. ■ **abrogation** n.

abrupt adj. **1** sudden. **2** curt. **3** steep. ■ **abruptly** adv. **abruptness** n.

abscess n. a swelling containing pus.

....

☑ Remember the *s* and *c*: ab*sc*ess.

....

abscond v. leave quickly and secretly.

abseil /ab-sayl/ v. climb down a rock face using a rope fixed at a higher point.

absence n. **1** the state of being absent. **2** lack.

absent adj. not present. ▶v. (**absent oneself**) stay away. □ **absent-minded** forgetful; inattentive.

absentee n. a person who is absent from work etc. ■ **absenteeism** n.

absinthe /ab-sinth/ n. a green liqueur.

absolute adj. **1** complete. **2** not limited or restricted. ■ **absolutely** adv.

absolution n. formal forgiveness of a person's sins.

absolutism n. the principle of government with unrestricted power. ■ **absolutist** n. & adj.

absolve v. clear of guilt or blame.

absorb v. **1** soak up liquid. **2** assimilate information. **3** hold the attention of. ■ **absorption** n.

absorbent adj. able to soak up liquid.

abstain v. **1** stop oneself from doing something. **2** choose not to vote. ■ **abstainer** n. **abstention** n.

abstemious adj. limiting one's intake of food or alcohol.

abstinence n. the avoidance of doing or indulging in something.

abstract adj. **1** having no material existence; theoretical. **2** (of art) not representing things pictorially. ▶v. take out or remove. ▶n. a summary of a book or article. ■ **abstraction** n.

Thesaurus

....

minish, curtail, truncate, lessen, trim. ■ OPPOSITES expand.

abridgement n. **1** SUMMARY, synopsis, precis, abstract, outline, résumé, digest, cut-down version. **2** SHORTENING, cutting, condensation, contraction, reduction, summarization. ■ OPPOSITES expansion.

abrupt adj. **1** SUDDEN, quick, hurried, hasty, swift, rapid, precipitate, headlong, instantaneous, surprising, unexpected, unanticipated, unforeseen. **2** CURT, blunt, brusque, short, terse, brisk, crisp, gruff, unceremonious, rough, rude; *informal* snappish. ■ OPPOSITES gradual, gentle.

abscond v. RUN AWAY, bolt, clear out, flee, make off, escape, take flight, fly, decamp, slip/steal/sneak away, take to one's heels, run for it, make a quick getaway, beat a hasty retreat; *informal* show a clean pair of heels, skedaddle, skip, do a bunk, do a runner.

absent adj. **1** AWAY, off, out, gone, missing, truant. **2** ABSENT-MINDED, distracted, preoccupied, daydreaming, dreaming, dreamy, faraway, blank, empty, vacant, inattentive, vague, absorbed, abstracted, musing, unheeding. ■ OPPOSITES present, attentive.

absent-minded adj. DISTRACTED, preoccupied, absorbed, abstracted, vague, inattentive, forgetful, oblivious, in a brown study, distrait; *informal* scatterbrained. ■ OPPOSITES alert.

absolute adj. **1** COMPLETE, total, utter,

out-and-out, outright, perfect, entire, undivided, unqualified, unadulterated, unalloyed, downright, undiluted, solid, consummate, unmitigated. **2** FIXED, independent, non-relative, non-variable, rigid, established, set, definite. **3** UNLIMITED, unrestricted, unrestrained, unbounded, boundless, infinite, ultimate, total, supreme, unconditional, full, utter, sovereign, omnipotent. ■ OPPOSITES qualified.

absolve v. FORGIVE, pardon, excuse, reprieve, give amnesty to, give dispensation/indulgence to, clear, set free, vindicate.

absorb v. **1** SOAK UP, suck up, draw up/in, take up/in, blot up, mop, sponge up, sop up. **2** TAKE IN, incorporate, assimilate, appropriate, co-opt. **3** OCCUPY, engage, preoccupy, captivate, engross, spellbind, rivet.

absorbent adj. SPONGY, sponge-like, porous, permeable, pervious, penetrable, absorptive, assimilative, receptive. ■ OPPOSITES impervious.

absorbing adj. FASCINATING, gripping, interesting, captivating, engrossing, riveting, spellbinding, intriguing. ■ OPPOSITES boring.

abstain v. REFRAIN, decline, forbear, desist, hold back, keep from, refuse, renounce, avoid, shun, eschew.

abstemious adj. MODERATE, temperate, abstinent, self-denying, austere, sober, self-restrained, ascetic, puritanical. ■ OPPOSITES self-indulgent.

abstruse adj. hard to understand.

absurd adj. completely illogical or ridiculous. ■ **absurdity** n. **absurdly** adv.

abundant adj. **1** plentiful. **2** having plenty of something. ■ **abundance** n. **abundantly** adv.

abuse v. **1** use badly or wrongly. **2** insult. ▶n. **1** ill-treatment or misuse. **2** insulting language.

abusive adj. **1** very insulting. **2** cruel and violent. ■ **abusively** adv.

abut v. (**abutting**, **abutted**) be next to or touching.

abysmal adj. very bad.

abyss n. a very deep hole.

AC abbrev. alternating current.

a/c abbrev. account.

acacia /uh-**kay**-shuh/ n. a tree or shrub with yellow or white flowers.

academic adj. **1** of education or study. **2** of theoretical interest only. ▶n. a teacher or scholar in a university or college. ■ **academically** adv.

academician n. a member of an academy.

academy n. (pl. **academies**) **1** a place for training in a special field. **2** a society of artists or scientists.

accede /uhk-**seed**/ v. agree to a demand or request.

accelerate v. begin to move more quickly. ■ **acceleration** n.

accelerator n. a foot pedal which controls a vehicle's speed.

accent n. **1** a way of pronouncing a language. **2** emphasis. **3** a written mark guiding pronunciation. ▶v. **1** (**accented**) spoken with a particular accent. **2** emphasize.

accentuate v. make more noticeable.

Thesaurus

abstract adj. **1** THEORETICAL, conceptual, notional, intellectual, metaphysical, philosophical. **2** NON-REPRESENTATIONAL, non-realistic, unrealistic. ▶v. EXTRACT, remove, take out/away, separate, detach, draw away, isolate. ▶n. SUMMARY, synopsis, precis, résumé, outline, abridgement, condensation, digest.

abstruse adj. OBSCURE, deep, profound, complex, hidden, esoteric, mysterious, incomprehensible, unfathomable, inscrutable, enigmatic, perplexing, puzzling, recondite, arcane, nebulous. ■ OPPOSITES comprehensible.

absurd adj. RIDICULOUS, foolish, silly, idiotic, stupid, nonsensical, senseless, inane, crazy, ludicrous, funny, laughable, comical, preposterous, farcical, hare-brained, asinine; informal daft. ■ OPPOSITES sensible.

abundance n. PLENTY, plentifulness, profusion, copiousness, amplitude, affluence, lavishness, bountifulness; informal heaps, bags, stacks, loads, tons, oodles. ■ OPPOSITES scarcity.

abundant adj. PLENTIFUL, large, great, huge, ample, well supplied, well provided, profuse, copious, lavish, bountiful, teeming, overflowing, galore. ■ OPPOSITES scarce.

abuse v. **1** MISUSE, misapply, misemploy, mishandle, exploit. **2** MISTREAT, maltreat, ill-use, ill-treat, manhandle, injure, hurt, harm, beat, damage, wrong, oppress, torture. **3** INSULT, swear at, curse, scold, rebuke, upbraid, castigate, reprove, inveigh against, revile, vilify, slander; old use vituperate against. ▶n. **1** MISUSE, misapplication, misemploy-

ment, mishandling, exploitation. **2** MISTREATMENT, maltreatment, ill-use, ill-treatment, manhandling, injury, hurt, harm, beating, damage, wronging, oppression, torture. **3** SWEARING, cursing, scolding, rebuke, upbraiding, castigation, reproval, invective, revilement, vilification, vituperation, defamation, slander, insults, curses, expletives, swear words.

abusive adj. INSULTING, rude, offensive, disparaging, denigratory, derogatory, defamatory, derisive, scornful, vituperative, opprobrious, slanderous, libellous.

abysmal adj. VERY BAD, dreadful, awful, terrible, frightful, atrocious, deplorable, lamentable; informal rotten, appalling, pathetic, pitiful, woeful, lousy, dire, chronic. ■ OPPOSITES excellent.

abyss n. CHASM, gorge, ravine, canyon, crevasse, cavity, void, pit, bottomless pit, hole, gulf, depth.

academic adj. **1** EDUCATIONAL, scholastic, instructional, pedagogical. **2** SCHOLARLY, studious, literary, intellectual, well read, erudite, highbrow, learned, cultured, bookish, pedantic, donnish, cerebral; informal brainy. **3** THEORETICAL, hypothetical, abstract, conjectural, notional, impractical, unrealistic, speculative. ▶n. SCHOLAR, lecturer, don, teacher, tutor, professor, fellow.

accede v. (**accede to**) AGREE TO, consent to, accept, assent to, acquiesce in, endorse, comply with, go along with, concur, grant, yield to.

accelerate v. SPEED UP, go faster, pick up speed, hasten, hurry, quicken.

■ **accentuation** n.

accept v. **1** say yes to. **2** take as true. **3** resign oneself to. ■ **acceptance** n.

acceptable adj. satisfactory. ■ **acceptability** n. **acceptably** adv.

access n. **1** a way in. **2** the right or opportunity to use something or see someone. ▶ v. obtain data from a computer.

accessible adj. able to be reached or used. ■ **accessibility** n. **accessibly** adv.

accession n. **1** the gaining of a position or rank. **2** an addition to a library or museum collection.

accessory n. (pl. **accessories**) **1** a thing added as a supplement or decoration. **2** a person who helps in a crime.

accident n. **1** an unpleasant incident that happens unexpectedly. **2** an incident that happens by chance.

accidental adj. happening by chance. ■ **accidentally** adv.

acclaim v. praise enthusiastically. ▶ n. enthusiastic praise. ■ **acclamation** n.

acclimatize (or **-ise**) v. make or become used to new conditions. ■ **acclimatization** n.

accolade n. a thing given as a special honour or reward.

accommodate v. **1** provide lodging or space for. **2** adapt to.

....

✓ Double c, double m: acco**mm**odate.

....

accommodating adj. willing to do as asked.

accommodation n. a place to live.

Thesaurus

....

■ OPPOSITES decelerate.

accent n. **1** PRONUNCIATION, intonation, enunciation, articulation, inflection, tone, modulation, utterance. **2** STRESS, emphasis, accentuation, force, beat, prominence. **3** EMPHASIS, stress, prominence, importance, accentuation, priority, underlining, underscoring.

accentuate v. EMPHASIZE, stress, highlight, underline, draw attention to, give prominence to, heighten, point up, underscore, accent.

accept v. **1** RECEIVE, take, get, gain, obtain, acquire. **2** ACCEDE TO, agree to, consent to, acquiesce in, concur with, endorse, comply with, go along with, defer to, put up with, recognize, acknowledge, cooperate with, adopt, admit. **3** BELIEVE, trust, credit, be convinced of, have faith in, count/rely on. ■ OPPOSITES reject.

acceptable adj. **1** WELCOME, agreeable, delightful, pleasing, desirable, satisfying, gratifying. **2** SATISFACTORY, good enough, adequate, passable, admissible, tolerable. ■ OPPOSITES unacceptable.

accepted adj. **1** APPROVED, recognized, sanctioned, authorized, received, allowable, acceptable. **2** USUAL, customary, normal, expected, standard, conventional, recognized, acknowledged, established, traditional.

access n. ENTRY, entrance, way in, means of entry/entrance, admittance, admission, approachability, accessibility, approach, means of approach.

accessible adj. **1** ATTAINABLE, reachable, available, approachable, obtainable, achievable; informal get-at-able. **2** APPROACHABLE, available, easy-going, informal, friendly, pleasant, agreeable, obliging, congenial, affable, cordial. ■ OPPOSITES inaccessible.

accessory n. **1** ATTACHMENT, fitment, extra, addition, adjunct, appendage, supplement. **2** ACCOMPLICE, associate, confederate, abetter, helper, assistant, partner. ▶ adj. ADDITIONAL, extra, supplementary, contributory, subsidiary, ancillary, auxiliary, secondary.

accident n. **1** MISHAP, misfortune, misadventure, injury, disaster, tragedy, blow, catastrophe, calamity. **2** CRASH, smash, collision, derailment; informal pile-up, shunt, prang. **3** CHANCE, mere chance, fluke, fate, twist of fate, fortune, good fortune, luck, good luck, fortuity, hazard.

accidental adj. CHANCE, unintentional, unintended, inadvertent, unexpected, unforeseen, unlooked for, fortuitous, unanticipated, unplanned, unpremeditated, uncalculated, unwitting, adventitious. ■ OPPOSITES intentional.

acclaim v. APPLAUD, cheer, celebrate, salute, welcome, approve, honour, praise, commend, hail, extol, eulogize, exalt; formal laud. ▶ n. APPLAUSE, ovation, praise, commendation, approval, approbation, homage, tribute, extolment, cheers, congratulations, plaudits, bouquets, salutes, eulogies; formal laudation.

acclimatize v. ADJUST, adapt, accustom, get used, accommodate, become seasoned, familiarize oneself, become inured.

accommodate v. **1** PUT UP, house, cater for, board, lodge, shelter, give someone a roof over their head, harbour, billet. **2** HELP, assist, aid, oblige,

accompany v. (**accompanying**, **accompanied**) 1 go with. 2 play musical backing for an instrument or voice. ■ **accompaniment** n. **accompanist** n.

accomplice n. a person who helps another commit a crime.

accomplish v. succeed in doing or achieving. ■ **accomplishment** n.

accomplished adj. highly skilled.

accord v. be consistent with. ▶n. agreement in opinion. □ **of one's own accord** willingly.

accordance n. (**in accordance with**) in a way conforming with.

according adv. (**according to**) 1 as stated by. 2 following or agreeing with.

accordingly adv. 1 appropriately. 2 therefore.

accordion n. a musical instrument with bellows and keys or buttons.

accost v. approach and speak to.

account n. 1 a description of an event. 2 a record of money spent and received. 3 a credit arrangement with a bank or firm. ▶v. (**account for**) explain. □ **on account of** because of.

accountable adj. obliged to explain actions or decisions. ■ **accountability** n.

accountant n. a person who keeps or inspects financial accounts. ■ **accountancy** n.

accoutrement /uh-koo-truh-muhnt/ n. an extra item of dress or equipment.

accredited adj. officially authorized.

accretion n. growth or increase by a gradual build-up.

accrue v. (**accruing**, **accrued**) accumulate. ■ **accrual** n.

accumulate v. 1 acquire more and more of. 2 increase. ■ **accumulation** n.

....
✓ Two *c*'s and one *m*: accu*m*ulate.
....

accumulator n. 1 a rechargeable electric cell. 2 a series of bets with the winnings restaked.

accurate adj. with no errors. ■ **accuracy** n. **accurately** adv.

accusative n. (in some languages) the grammatical case used for the object of a verb.

accuse v. charge with committing an offence or crime. ■ **accusation** n. **accuser** n.

accustom v. make or be used to.

Thesaurus
....

meet the needs/wants of, cater for, fit in with, satisfy.

accommodating adj. OBLIGING, co-operative, helpful, considerate, amenable, unselfish, willing, polite, kindly, hospitable, kind, friendly, agreeable.

accommodation n. HOUSING, lodging, board, shelter, place of residence, house, billet, lodgings, quarters; *informal* digs, pad.

accompany v. 1 ESCORT, go with, go along with, keep someone company, attend, usher, show, see, conduct, squire, chaperone, convoy. 2 OCCUR WITH, go with, go together with, go hand in hand with, coexist with, supplement.

accomplice n. PARTNER IN CRIME, associate, accessory, confederate, collaborator, abetter, henchman, fellow conspirator; *informal* sidekick.

accomplish v. ACHIEVE, carry out, fulfil, perform, attain, realize, succeed in, bring off, bring about, effect, execute, effectuate. ■ OPPOSITES fail in.

accomplished adj. SKILLED, skilful, expert, gifted, talented, proficient, adept, masterly, polished, practised, capable, able, competent, experienced, professional, deft, consummate. ■ OPPOSITES incompetent.

accomplishment n. TALENT, ability,

skill, gift, attainment, achievement, capability, proficiency.

accord v. AGREE, concur, fit, correspond, tally, match, conform, harmonize, suit, be in tune. ▶n. AGREEMENT, consensus, unanimity, harmony, rapport, unison, amity, concord. ■ OPPOSITES disagreement.

account n. 1 DESCRIPTION, report, statement, record, narration, narrative, story, recital, explanation, tale, chronicle, history, relation, version. 2 FINANCIAL RECORD, ledger, balance sheet, financial statement, books. 3 BILL, invoice, reckoning, tally, charges, debts. 4 IMPORTANCE, consequence, significance.

accumulate v. 1 GATHER, pile up, build up, collect, amass, increase, augment, cumulate, accrue. 2 AMASS, gather, collect, stockpile, pile up, heap up, store, hoard.

accumulation n. PILE, heap, build-up, mass, collection, store, supply, stockpile, hoard, stock, conglomeration, gathering, growth.

accurate adj. CORRECT, right, true, exact, precise, authentic, factual, truthful, veracious, faultless, reliable, scrupulous, faithful, meticulous, careful, sound, sure, certain, strict; *informal* spot

ace n. **1** a playing card with a single spot. **2** informal an expert. **3** Tennis an unreturnable serve.

acerbic /uh-ser-bik/ adj. sharp and direct. ■ **acerbity** n.

acetate /a-si-tayt/ n. a synthetic textile fibre.

acetic acid /uh-see-tik/ n. the acid that gives vinegar its characteristic taste.

acetone /a-si-tohn/ n. a colourless liquid used as a solvent.

acetylene /uh-set-i-leen/ n. a gas which burns with a bright flame.

ache n. a continuous dull pain. ▶v. suffer from an ache.

achieve v. succeed in doing by effort or skill. ■ **achievable** adj. **achievement** n. **achiever** n.

Achilles heel n. a weak point.

Achilles tendon n. the tendon connecting calf muscles to the heel.

acid n. a substance that turns litmus red, neutralizes alkalis, and dissolves some metals. ▶adj. **1** sour. **2** unkind; cutting. □ **acid rain** rain made acidic by pollution. **acid test** a decisive test of success or value. ■ **acidic** adj. **acidity** n. **acidly** adv.

acknowledge v. **1** admit the truth of. **2** confirm receipt of. **3** express thanks for. ■ **acknowledgement** n.

acme /ak-mi/ n. the height of achievement or excellence.

acne n. a skin condition causing red pimples.

acolyte /ak-uh-lyt/ n. an assistant or follower.

acorn n. the oval nut of the oak tree.

acoustic adj. **1** of sound. **2** not electronically amplified. ▶n. (**acoustics**) the aspects of a room that affect the way sound is carried.

acquaint v. **1** make aware of. **2** (**be acquainted with**) know slightly.

acquaintance n. **1** a person one knows slightly. **2** slight knowledge.

acquiesce v. agree. ■ **acquiescence** n. **acquiescent** adj.

acquire v. buy or obtain.

acquisition n. **1** something acquired. **2** the act of acquiring.

acquisitive adj. eager to acquire things. ■ **acquisitiveness** n.

acquit v. (**acquitting, acquitted**) **1** declare to be not guilty **2** (**acquit oneself**) behave in a particular way. ■ **acquittal** n.

on, bang on. ■ OPPOSITES inaccurate.

accusation n. CHARGE, allegation, indictment, complaint, summons, arraignment, citation, denunciation, imputation; US impeachment.

accuse v. **1** CHARGE, indict, bring/prefer charges against, make allegations against, arraign, prosecute, summons, cite; US impeach. **2** BLAME, hold responsible, denounce, censure, condemn, incriminate, tax; informal point the finger at. ■ OPPOSITES defend.

accustomed adj. **1** USUAL, customary, habitual, regular, established, normal, conventional, expected, routine, familiar, common, fixed, traditional, ordinary, set, prevailing; literary wonted. **2** USED TO, familiar with, habituated, adapted. □ **become/get accustomed** see ADAPT.

ache n. PAIN, soreness, discomfort, hurt, distress, throbbing, twinge, pang, suffering, anguish, smart. ▶v. HURT, be sore, be painful, smart, sting, pound, throb, suffer.

achieve v. **1** SUCCEED IN, accomplish, manage, do successfully, carry out, complete, attain, bring off, effect, perform, conclude, finish, discharge, fulfil, execute, engineer, consummate. **2** GAIN,

obtain, get, acquire, earn, reach, win, score, procure.

acid adj. **1** SHARP, tart, sour, vinegary, tangy, stinging. **2** CAUSTIC, acerbic, sharp, sardonic, scathing, trenchant, vitriolic. ■ OPPOSITES sweet, pleasant.

acknowledge v. **1** ADMIT, concede, accept, agree, confirm, allow, confess, grant, own, affirm, profess. **2** GREET, salute, address, hail, say hello to. **3** ANSWER, reply to, respond to, react to, return. ■ OPPOSITES deny, ignore.

acquaint v. FAMILIARIZE, make familiar, make aware of, inform of, advise of, notify of, apprise of, let know, get up to date, brief, prime; informal fill in on.

acquaintance n. **1** CONTACT, associate, colleague. **2** ASSOCIATION, relationship, contact. **3** FAMILIARITY, awareness, knowledge, experience, understanding, grasp.

acquire v. GET, obtain, buy, purchase, procure, come by, pick up, receive, earn, secure, appropriate; informal get hold of, get one's hands on. ■ OPPOSITES lose.

acquisition n. POSSESSION, gain, purchase, property, prize, addition, accession; informal buy. ■ OPPOSITES loss.

acquit v. CLEAR, find innocent, declare

acre n. a unit of land area equal to 4,840 sq yds (0.405 hectare). ■ **acreage** n.

acrid adj. unpleasantly bitter.

acrimonious adj. angry and bitter. ■ **acrimony** n.

acrobat n. a performer of spectacular gymnastic feats.

acrobatic adj. involving spectacular gymnastic feats. ▶ n. (**acrobatics**) acrobatic feats.

acronym n. a word formed from the first letters of other words, e.g. *laser*.

acropolis n. the citadel of an ancient Greek city.

across prep. & adv. from one side to the other of.

acrostic n. a poem or puzzle in which certain letters in each line form a word or words.

acrylic adj. (of a fabric, paint, etc.) made from **acrylic acid**, a pungent organic acid.

act v. 1 do something. 2 have an effect. 3 behave. 4 (**acting**) temporarily doing another's duties. 5 perform in a play or film. ▶ n. 1 a thing done. 2 a law made by a parliament. 3 a section of a play or opera. 4 a set performance or performing group.

actinium n. a radioactive chemical element.

action n. 1 the process of doing something. 2 a thing done. 3 a lawsuit. 4 a battle.

actionable adj. giving cause for legal action.

activate v. cause to act or work. ■ **activation** n. **activator** n.

active adj. 1 energetic. 2 functioning. ■ **actively** adv.

activist n. a person campaigning for political or social change. ■ **activism** n.

activity n. (pl. **activities**) 1 the state of being active. 2 a pastime or pursuit.

actor n. (fem. **actress**) a person who acts in a play or film.

actual adj. existing in fact or reality. ■ **actuality** n.

actually adv. in truth; really.

actuary n. (pl. **actuaries**) a person who calculates insurance risks and premiums.

Thesaurus

innocent, absolve, set free, free, release, liberate, discharge, reprieve, vindicate, exonerate; *informal* let off; *formal* exculpate. ■ OPPOSITES condemn. □ **acquit oneself** *see* BEHAVE.

acrid adj. PUNGENT, sharp, bitter, harsh, acid, caustic.

acrimonious adj. BITTER, angry, rancorous, caustic, acerbic, scathing, sarcastic, acid, harsh, sharp, cutting, virulent, spiteful, vicious, vitriolic, hostile, venomous, bad-tempered, ill-natured, malicious, waspish. ■ OPPOSITES good-natured.

act v. 1 DO SOMETHING, take action, move, react, take steps. 2 BEHAVE, carry on, conduct oneself, comport oneself. 3 PERFORM, play, appear as, enact, portray, represent, assume the character of, overact; *informal* tread the boards. *See also* PRETEND. 4 FUNCTION, work, operate, have an effect, take effect, serve. ▶ n. 1 DEED, action, feat, exploit, undertaking, effort, enterprise, achievement, step, move, operation, proceeding. 2 LAW, statute, bill, decree, order, enactment, edict. 3 PERFORMANCE, routine, number, turn, item, sketch.

acting adj. TEMPORARY, provisional, interim, stopgap, substitute, stand-in, fill-in, surrogate, deputy, pro tem. ■ OPPOSITES permanent.

action n. 1 DEED, act, feat, exploit, undertaking, process, enterprise, measure, step, effort, endeavour, proceeding, performance, work. 2 ACTIVITY, movement, motion, exertion, drama, liveliness, excitement, vigour, energy, vitality, initiative, exercise, enterprise. 3 STORY, events, incidents, happenings. 4 MECHANISM, works, operation, functioning, working.

activate v. SET OFF, set in motion, operate, start, trigger, initiate, actuate, energize, trip.

active adj. 1 ENERGETIC, lively, sprightly, spry, mobile, vigorous, vital, dynamic, sporty, busy, occupied; *informal* on the go, full of beans. 2 HARD-WORKING, busy, industrious, diligent, tireless, effective, enterprising, involved, enthusiastic, keen, committed, devoted, zealous. 3 OPERATIVE, working, functioning, functional, operating, operational, in action, in operation, live; *informal* up and running. ■ OPPOSITES inactive.

activity n. 1 MOVEMENT, action, bustle, motion, excitement, liveliness, commotion, energy, industry, hurly-burly, animation, life, hustle, stir. 2 HOBBY, pastime, interest, task, job, venture, project, occupation, undertaking, scheme, pursuit.

actual adj. REAL, authentic, genuine, true, factual, verified, realistic, bona fide, definite, existing, current, legitim-

actuate v. **1** activate. **2** motivate.

acumen n. shrewdness.

acupuncture n. the insertion of very thin needles into the skin as a medical treatment. ■ **acupuncturist** n.

acute adj. **1** serious or severe. **2** sharp-witted; shrewd. **3** (of an angle) less than 90°. □ **acute accent** the accent (´). ■ **acutely** adv. **acuteness** n.

AD abbrev. Anno Domini (used in dates counted from the traditional date of Jesus's birth).

adage /ad-ij/ n. a proverb.

adagio /uh-**dah**-ji-oh/ adv. Music in slow time.

adamant adj. refusing to change one's mind.

Adam's apple n. the lump of cartilage at the front of the neck.

adapt v. make or become suitable for a new use or purpose. ■ **adaptation** n.

adaptable adj. able to adapt or be adapted. ■ **adaptability** n.

adaptor (or **adapter**) n. a device for connecting several electric plugs to one socket.

add v. **1** join to or put with something else. **2** put together numbers to find their total value. **3** say as a further remark.

addendum n. (pl. **addenda**) a section added to a book.

adder n. a poisonous snake.

addict n. a person addicted to something.

addicted adj. **1** physically dependent on a substance. **2** devoted to an interest or activity. ■ **addiction** n. **addictive** adj.

addition n. **1** the act of adding. **2** a thing added.

additional adj. added; extra. ■ **additionally** adv.

additive n. a substance added to improve or preserve something.

addled adj. muddled or confused.

address n. **1** the details of where a building is or where someone lives. **2** a speech. ▶ v. **1** write the address on an envelope or parcel. **2** speak to. **3** begin to deal with. ■ **addressee** n.

adduce v. refer to as evidence.

adenoids pl. n. a mass of tissue between the back of the nose and the throat. ■ **adenoidal** adj.

adept adj. very skilled or able.

adequate adj. satisfactory or acceptable. ■ **adequacy** n. **adequately** adv.

adhere v. **1** stick firmly. **2** support a

Thesaurus

ate, indisputable, unquestionable, tangible, certain, truthful, in existence, living, confirmed, corporeal. ■ OPPOSITES imaginary.

acute adj. **1** SERIOUS, urgent, pressing, grave, critical, crucial, precarious. **2** SEVERE, critical, intense. **3** SHARP, piercing, intense, severe, extreme, fierce, excruciating, keen, exquisite, racking, violent, shooting, keen, exquisite, racking. **4** INTELLIGENT, shrewd, sharp, quick, penetrating. *See also* CLEVER. ■ OPPOSITES mild, chronic, dull.

adapt v. **1** GET USED, adjust, get accustomed, habituate oneself, acclimatize, reconcile oneself, attune, accommodate, become hardened, become inured. **2** ALTER, change, modify, adjust, convert, remodel, transform, rebuild, remake, refashion, reshape, reconstruct, tailor.

add v. **1** ATTACH, append, put on, affix, tack on, include, combine. ■ OPPOSITES subtract. □ **add up** TOTAL, count, reckon, tot up.

addict n. ABUSER, user; *informal* junkie, druggy, — freak, —head.

addiction n. DEPENDENCY, craving, habit, compulsion, obsession, enslavement, dedication, devotion.

addition n. **1** INCREASE, enlargement, expansion, supplement, extension, increment, augmentation, gain, adjunct, accessory, addendum, appendage, development, additive, appendix, postscript, afterthought, attachment, annex, amplification, accession; *technical* admixture. **2** ADDING UP, counting, totalling, calculation, reckoning, computation; *informal* totting up. ■ OPPOSITES reduction, subtraction.

additional adj. EXTRA, more, further, added, supplementary, other, new, fresh, increased, spare, supplemental.

address n. **1** LOCATION, whereabouts, place, home, house, residence, dwelling, abode, domicile. **2** SPEECH, talk, lecture, oration, sermon, homily, diatribe, discourse, disquisition, harangue; *literary* philippic. ▶ v. **1** SPEAK TO, talk to, lecture, give a speech to, declaim to, harangue, preach to. **2** GREET, speak to, talk to, engage in conversation, approach, accost, hail, salute; *informal* buttonhole. **3** DIRECT, label, inscribe, superscribe.

adept adj. EXPERT, proficient, clever, accomplished, talented, gifted, practised, masterly. *See also* SKILFUL. ■ OPPOSITES inept.

adequate adj. **1** TOLERABLE, passable, all

a

cause or belief. ■ **adherence** n. **adherent** adj. & n.

adhesion n. the process of sticking to something.

adhesive adj. sticky. ▶ n. an adhesive substance.

ad hoc adj. & adv. created or done for a particular purpose only.

adieu /uh-dyoo/ exclam. goodbye.

ad infinitum adv. endlessly.

adipose adj. (of body tissue) fatty.

adjacent adj. near or next to.

adjective n. a word adding information about a noun. ■ **adjectival** adj.

adjoin v. be next to.

adjourn v. break off a meeting until later. ■ **adjournment** n.

adjudge v. declare to be.

adjudicate v. 1 make a formal judgement. 2 judge a competition. ■ **adjudication** n. **adjudicator** n.

adjunct n. an additional part.

adjure v. command; urge.

adjust v. 1 alter slightly. 2 become used to a new situation. ■ **adjustable** adj.

adjustment n.

adjutant n. an army officer assisting with administrative work.

ad-lib v. (**ad-libbing**, **ad-libbed**) speak without preparing first. ▶ adv. & adj. spoken without preparation.

administer v. 1 organize or put into effect. 2 give or apply a drug or treatment.

administrate v. manage the business affairs of. ■ **administration** n. **administrative** adj. **administrator** n.

admirable adj. deserving respect. ■ **admirably** adv.

admiral n. a naval officer of the highest rank.

admire v. 1 greatly respect. 2 look at with pleasure. ■ **admiration** n.

admissible adj. acceptable or valid. ■ **admissibility** n.

admission n. 1 a confession. 2 the process or fact of being allowed to enter.

admit v. (**admitting**, **admitted**) 1 confess to be true. 2 allow to enter. 3 accept as valid.

Thesaurus

right, average, satisfactory, competent, unexceptional, acceptable, unexceptionable, mediocre, good enough; *informal* OK, so-so. 2 COMPETENT, up to, capable, able, qualified. ■ OPPOSITES inadequate.

adhere v. STICK, cling, bond, attach, bind, fuse.

adherent n. SUPPORTER, follower, devotee, disciple, advocate, fan, upholder, defender, stalwart, partisan.

adjacent adj. NEIGHBOURING, adjoining, bordering, next, close, next door, touching, attached, abutting, contiguous.

adjourn v. BREAK OFF, interrupt, discontinue, postpone, put off, delay, defer, shelve, suspend, prorogue.

adjournment n. INTERRUPTION, break, breaking off, postponement, pause, delay, deferral, deferment, recess, suspension, prorogation.

adjust adj. 1 GET USED TO, become accustomed to, adapt, reconcile oneself, accommodate, acclimatize, habituate oneself, conform. 2 MODIFY, alter, adapt, fix, repair, regulate, put right, put in working order, rectify, change, arrange, amend, set to rights, tune, rearrange, tailor, balance, vary, position, set, refashion, remake, remodel, reorganize.

administer v. 1 MANAGE, direct, run, administrate, control, organize, supervise, oversee, preside over, superintend, regulate, govern, conduct, rule, command. 2 GIVE, dispense, issue, provide, supply, treat with, hand out, deal out, distribute, measure out, dole out. 3 DISPENSE, provide, implement, carry out, mete out, distribute, disburse, bestow, execute.

admirable adj. COMMENDABLE, worthy, praiseworthy, laudable, good, excellent, fine, exemplary, wonderful, great, marvellous, enjoyable, respectable, creditable, pleasing, meritorious, first-rate, first-class, masterly, awe-inspiring, deserving, estimable. ■ OPPOSITES deplorable.

admiration n. APPROVAL, regard, respect, praise, appreciation, commendation, approbation, esteem, awe, veneration, honour. ■ OPPOSITES contempt.

admire v. APPROVE OF, like, respect, appreciate, praise, have a high opinion of, look up to, think highly of, applaud, wonder at, esteem, value, commend, sing someone's praises, love, honour, idolize, revere, venerate, hero-worship, marvel at, be delighted by; *formal* laud. ■ OPPOSITES hate.

admissible adj. ALLOWABLE, allowed, accepted, permitted, permissible, tolerable, justifiable.

admission n. 1 ADMITTANCE, entry, entrance, access, entrée, ingress. 2 ACKNOWLEDGEMENT, acceptance, confession, declaration, disclosure, profession, divulgence, utterance, avowal, revelation, affirmation. ■ OPPOSITES denial.

admittance n. admission to a place.

admittedly adv. it must be admitted that.

admixture n. a mixture.

admonish v. reprimand firmly. ■ **admonition** n.

ad nauseam adv. to a tiresomely excessive degree.

ado n. trouble; fuss.

adobe /uh-**doh**-bi/ n. a kind of clay used as a building material.

adolescent adj. developing from a child into an adult. ▶ n. an adolescent boy or girl. ■ **adolescence** n.

adopt v. **1** bring up another's child as one's own. **2** choose to follow a course of action. ■ **adoption** n.

adoptive adj. related by adoption.

adorable adj. lovable or charming.

adore v. love and respect deeply. ■ **adoration** n.

adorn v. make more attractive; decorate. ■ **adornment** n.

adrenal /uh-**dree**-n'l/ adj. relating to the **adrenal glands**, a pair of glands above the kidneys.

adrenalin (or **adrenaline**) n. a hormone produced by the adrenal glands in response to stress.

adrift adj. & adv. drifting without control.

adroit adj. clever or skilful.

adsorb v. (of a solid) hold a gas or liquid as a thin film on its surface.

adulation n. excessive admiration. ■ **adulatory** adj.

adult n. a fully grown person. ▶ adj. fully grown. ■ **adulthood** n.

adulterate v. make poorer in quality by adding another substance. ■ **adulteration** n.

adulterer n. a person who has committed adultery.

adultery n. sexual unfaithfulness to one's husband or wife. ■ **adulterous** adj.

advance v. **1** move forwards. **2** make or cause to make progress. **3** lend money. ▶ n. **1** a forward movement. **2** an improvement. **3** a loan. **4** (**advances**) romantic or sexual approaches to someone. ■ **advancement** n.

advanced adj. **1** far on in progress or life. **2** not elementary.

advantage n. something that puts one in a favourable position. ☐ **take advantage of 1** exploit. **2** make good use of. ■ **advantageous** adj.

advent n. **1** an arrival. **2** (**Advent**) the

Thesaurus

admit v. **1** ALLOW IN, let in, permit entry to, grant access to. **2** ACKNOWLEDGE, confess, reveal, concede, own up to, declare, make known, accept, disclose, agree, profess, recognize, allow. ■ OPPOSITES exclude, deny.

admonish v. see REPRIMAND.

adolescent adj. TEENAGE, youthful, pubescent, immature, childish, juvenile, puerile, girlish, boyish. ▶ n. TEENAGER, youth, youngster, boy, girl, young person, juvenile.

adopt v. **1** TAKE IN, foster, take care of, take under one's wing. **2** ACCEPT, endorse, approve, support, back, sanction, ratify. **3** EMBRACE, assume, take on, espouse, appropriate, affect.

adore v. LOVE, worship, dote on, cherish, idolize, adulate, revere, venerate, honour, glorify. See also ADMIRE. ■ OPPOSITES hate.

adorn v. DECORATE, embellish, ornament, enhance, beautify, grace, emblazon, bedeck, trim.

adrift adj. **1** DRIFTING, unmoored, unanchored, floating. **2** UNFASTENED, untied, loose, detached. **3** WRONG, amiss, astray, awry, off course.

adult adj. FULLY GROWN, grown up, mature, fully developed, of age, nubile.

■ OPPOSITES immature.

adulterate v. CONTAMINATE, make impure, taint, pollute, debase, degrade, doctor, corrupt, alloy, defile, dilute, thin, water down, weaken.

advance v. **1** MOVE FORWARD, move ahead, go forward, proceed, forge ahead, gain ground, make headway, approach, push forward, press on, press ahead, push on, bear down, make strides. **2** PROGRESS, move forward, go ahead, improve, flourish, thrive, prosper. **3** SPEED UP, bring forward, accelerate, step up, expedite, forward, hurry, hasten. **4** PUT FORWARD, suggest, present, submit, propose, introduce, offer, proffer, adduce, furnish. **5** LEND, pay in advance, loan, provide, supply, proffer. ▶ n. DEVELOPMENT, breakthrough, discovery, finding, progress, improvement, invention.

advanced adj. **1** SOPHISTICATED, modern, latest, up to date. **2** PROGRESSIVE, innovative, original, new, forward-looking, inventive, contemporary, revolutionary, experimental, novel, avant-garde, pioneering, trendsetting, ahead of the times; informal way-out. **3** HIGHER-LEVEL, complex, complicated, difficult, hard. **4** MATURE, grown up, precocious, time before Christmas.

adventure n. an exciting and daring experience. ■ **adventurer** n. **adventurous** adj.

adverb n. a word adding information about an adjective, verb, or other adverb. ■ **adverbial** adj.

adversary n. (pl. **adversaries**) an opponent. ■ **adversarial** adj.

adverse adj. harmful; unfavourable. ■ **adversely** adv.

....
☑ Don't confuse **adverse** with **averse**, which means 'opposed to'.
....

adversity n. (pl. **adversities**) difficulty; misfortune.

advertise v. publicize a product, service, etc. to increase sales, or a job vacancy to encourage applications. ■ **advertiser** n.

advertisement n. a notice or display advertising something.

advice n. guidance or recommendations about future action.

advisable adj. prudent or sensible. ■ **advisability** n.

advise v. **1** give advice about a course of action. **2** inform. ■ **adviser** (or **advisor**) n. **advisory** adj.

advocate n. **1** a person who recommends a policy. **2** a person arguing a case on another's behalf. ▶ v. recommend. ■ **advocacy** n.

adze n. a tool like an axe, with an arched blade.

aegis /ee-jiss/ n. protection or support.

aeolian harp /ee-oh-li-uhn/ n. a stringed instrument that produces musical sounds when wind passes through it.

aeon /ee-on/ (US **eon**) n. an extremely long period of time.

aerate v. introduce air into.

aerial n. a structure for transmitting or receiving radio or television signals. ▶ adj. **1** existing or taking place in the air. **2** by or from aircraft.

aerobatics pl. n. spectacular feats by aircraft in flight. ■ **aerobatic** adj.

aerobics pl. n. vigorous exercises intended to increase oxygen intake. ■ **aerobic** adj.

aerodrome n. a small airport.

Thesaurus

sophisticated, well developed. ■ OPPOSITES backward.

advantage n. **1** BENEFIT, good point, asset, gain, convenience, profit, use, boon, blessing. **2** SUPERIORITY, dominance, edge, upper hand, whip hand, trump card. ■ OPPOSITES disadvantage.

advantageous adj. **1** BENEFICIAL, helpful, useful, of benefit, profitable, valuable, worthwhile. **2** FAVOURABLE, dominant, superior, powerful.

adventure n. **1** EXPLOIT, deed, feat, experience, incident, escapade, venture, undertaking, operation. **2** EXCITEMENT, danger, hazard, risk, precariousness, peril.

adventurous adj. **1** DARING, brave, bold, courageous, heroic, enterprising, intrepid, daredevil, valiant, venturesome, reckless, rash. **2** RISKY, dangerous, exciting, hazardous, challenging, perilous, precarious. ■ OPPOSITES cautious, boring, uneventful.

adverse adj. **1** UNFAVOURABLE, unfortunate, harmful, disadvantageous, inauspicious, unlucky, detrimental, untoward, prejudicial, unpropitious, uncongenial, deleterious, contrary. **2** HOSTILE, unfriendly, antagonistic, negative, disapproving, derogatory, attacking, uncomplimentary, opposing, unkind, unsympathetic, hurtful, unfavourable,

censorious, inimical. ■ OPPOSITES favourable.

adversity n. MISFORTUNE, bad luck, trouble, disaster, sorrow, misery, hard times, tribulation, woe, affliction.

advertise v. PUBLICIZE, promote, market, display, tout, make known, call attention to, merchandise, flaunt, show off, announce, promulgate, proclaim; *informal* push, puff, plug, hype.

advertisement n. COMMERCIAL, promotion, display, publicity, announcement, notice, circular, handout, small ad, leaflet, placard; *informal* ad, advert, plug, puff, blurb.

advice n. GUIDANCE, help, counsel, suggestions, recommendations, hints, pointers, tips, ideas, views, warnings, caution, admonition.

advisable adj. PRUDENT, recommended, sensible, appropriate, expedient, judicious, politic, wise. ■ OPPOSITES inadvisable.

advise v. GIVE GUIDANCE, guide, counsel, enjoin, offer suggestions, caution, instruct, urge, exhort, advocate, warn, encourage, commend, admonish. □ **advise someone of** *see* INFORM.

advocacy n. SUPPORT, backing, promotion, argument for, advising, recommendation.

advocate n. SUPPORTER, proponent,

aerodynamics n. the science concerned with the movement of solid bodies through the air. ■ **aerodynamic** adj.

aerofoil n. a curved structure, such as a wing, designed to give an aircraft lift.

aeronautics n. the study or practice of travel through the air. ■ **aeronautical** adj.

aeroplane n. a powered flying vehicle with fixed wings.

aerosol n. a substance sealed in a container under pressure and released as a fine spray.

aerospace n. the technology and industry concerned with flight.

aesthete /eess-theet/ (US **esthete**) n. a person who appreciates art and beauty.

aesthetic /eess-thet-ik/ (US **esthetic**) adj. **1** concerned with beauty or its appreciation. **2** having a pleasant appearance. ▶ n. (**aesthetics**) the study of beauty and its appreciation. ■ **aesthetically** adv.

aetiology /eet-i-ol-uh-ji/ (US **etiology**) n. the cause of a disease or condition.

afar adv. far away.

affable adj. good-natured and friendly. ■ **affability** n. **affably** adv.

affair n. **1** an event or series of events. **2** a person's responsibility or concern.

3 a temporary sexual relationship.

affect v. **1** make a difference to. **2** pretend to feel, have, etc.

> ✓ Don't confuse **affect** and **effect**: as a verb, **effect** means 'bring about', as in *she effected a cost-cutting exercise*.

affectation n. artificial and pretentious behaviour.

affected adj. showing affectation.

affection n. fondness or liking.

affectionate adj. loving. ■ **affectionately** adv.

affidavit n. a written statement sworn on oath to be true.

affiliate v. link a person or group to a larger organization. ■ **affiliation** n.

affinity n. (pl. **affinities**) **1** a natural liking or sympathy. **2** a close resemblance.

affirm v. state firmly or publicly. ■ **affirmation** n.

affirmative adj. agreeing with or to a statement or request. ▶ n. an affirmative statement or word.

affix v. attach or fasten. ▶ n. a prefix or suffix.

afflict v. cause pain or suffering to. ■ **affliction** n.

affluent adj. wealthy. ■ **affluence** n.

Thesaurus

backer, spokesman, exponent, apologist. ▶ v. ADVISE, recommend, support, back, argue for, urge, favour, endorse, champion.

aesthetic adj. ARTISTIC, tasteful, beautiful, sensitive, in good taste, cultivated. ■ OPPOSITES unfriendly.

affable adj. FRIENDLY, agreeable, pleasant, amiable, good-natured, civil, courteous. ■ OPPOSITES unfriendly.

affair n. **1** EVENT, occurrence, episode, incident, happening, circumstance, case, proceeding, occasion, matter, issue, subject, topic. **2** BUSINESS, concern, activity, responsibility, province, preserve, problem, worry; *informal* lookout. **3** RELATIONSHIP, love affair, romance, involvement, liaison, intrigue, amour, attachment; *informal* carry-on.

affect[1] v. **1** HAVE AN EFFECT ON, influence, act on, change, have an impact on, modify, shape, transform. **2** MOVE, touch, upset, trouble, disturb, concern, perturb, stir, agitate, hit, grieve.

affect[2] v. ADOPT, assume, take on, feign, sham, simulate; *informal* put on. *See also* PRETEND.

affectation n. PRETENCE, affectedness, pretentiousness, pretension, posturing,

artificiality.

affected adj. UNNATURAL, contrived, put on, artificial, mannered, insincere, studied. *See also* PRETENTIOUS. ■ OPPOSITES natural.

affecting adj. MOVING, touching, heartrending, poignant, upsetting, pathetic.

affection n. FONDNESS, liking, love, warmth, devotion, attachment, tenderness, friendship, partiality, amity, warm feelings; *informal* soft spot. ■ OPPOSITES dislike, hatred.

affectionate adj. FOND, loving, caring, devoted, tender, doting, warm, friendly. *See also* LOVING. ■ OPPOSITES cold.

affinity n. **1** LIKING, fondness, closeness, relationship, kinship, like-mindedness, rapport, empathy, understanding; *informal* chemistry. **2** LIKENESS, closeness, similarity, resemblance, correspondence, similitude.

affirm v. STATE, assert, declare, maintain, attest, avow, swear, pronounce, proclaim, aver. ■ OPPOSITES deny.

affirmation n. STATEMENT, assertion, declaration, confirmation, proclamation, pronouncement, oath, attestation, averment. ■ OPPOSITES denial.

a

afford v. **1** have enough money or time for. **2** give or provide.

afforest v. convert land into forest. ■ **afforestation** n.

affray n. a noisy public fight.

affront n. an insult. ▶ v. insult; offend.

aficionado /uh-fi-shuh-**nah**-doh/ n. (pl. **aficionados**) an enthusiastic fan of an activity.

afloat adj. & adv. **1** floating. **2** on a ship or boat.

afoot adv. & adj. going on.

aforementioned adj. mentioned previously.

afraid adj. frightened. □ **I'm afraid** expressing polite regret.

afresh adv. in a new or different way.

African adj. of Africa or its people. ▶ n. an African person.

Afrikaans n. a language of southern Africa derived from Dutch.

Afrikaner n. an Afrikaans-speaking white person in South Africa.

aft adv. & adj. at or towards the rear of a ship or aircraft.

after prep. **1** later than. **2** behind. **3** pursuing. ▶ conj. & adv. in the time following an event. □ **afterbirth** the placenta discharged from the womb after a birth. **after-effect** an effect that occurs after its cause has gone. **aftermath** the results of an unpleasant event. **afternoon** the time between noon and evening. **aftershave** a scented lotion used after shaving. **afterthought** a thing

thought of or added later. **afterwards** at a later time.

again adv. once more; another time.

against prep. **1** in opposition to. **2** in or into contact with.

agar /**ay**-gah/ n. a substance obtained from seaweed, used as a thickener in foods.

agate /**ag**-uht/ n. a form of quartz with bands of colour.

age n. **1** the length of life or existence. **2** a period of history. **3** old age. **4** informal a very long time. ▶ v. (**ageing** or **aging**, **aged**) grow or cause to appear old or older.

aged adj. **1** /**ayjd**/ of a specified age. **2** /**ay**-jid/ old.

ageism n. prejudice on the grounds of age. ■ **ageist** adj.

ageless adj. not ageing or appearing to age.

agency n. **1** an organization providing a particular service. **2** action or intervention.

agenda n. a list of items to be dealt with, esp. at a meeting.

agent n. **1** a person who provides a particular service. **2** a person or thing producing an effect.

agent provocateur /a-zhon pruh-vo-kuh-**ter**/ n. a person who tempts others to do something illegal.

agglomerate v. collect into a mass. ■ **agglomeration** n.

aggrandize (or **-ise**) v. increase the

Thesaurus

affirmative adj. ASSENTING, agreeing, concurring, consenting, positive, approving. ■ OPPOSITES negative.

afflict v. TROUBLE, burden, distress, affect, try, worry, bother, harm, oppress, pain, hurt, torture, plague, rack, torment, beset, harass, wound, bedevil, grieve, pester, annoy, vex.

affluence n. WEALTH, prosperity, riches, fortune, substance, resources. ■ OPPOSITES poverty.

affluent adj. RICH, wealthy, prosperous, well off, well-to-do, moneyed, opulent, comfortable; informal well heeled, loaded. ■ OPPOSITES poor.

afford v. **1** PAY FOR, find enough for, have the means for, spare the price of, meet the expense of, run to, stretch to, spare. **2** see PROVIDE.

afraid adj. **1** FRIGHTENED, scared, terrified, fearful, apprehensive, terror-stricken, timid, intimidated, nervous, alarmed, anxious, trembling, cowardly, panicky, panic-stricken, uneasy, agitated, pusil-

lanimous, faint-hearted, reluctant, craven, diffident, daunted, cowed, timorous; informal chicken, yellow, jittery, windy. **2** SORRY, apologetic, regretful, unhappy. ■ OPPOSITES brave, confident.

aftermath n. AFTER-EFFECTS, consequences, repercussions, results, outcome, end result, upshot.

afterwards adv. LATER, subsequently, then, next, after; formal thereupon. ■ OPPOSITES beforehand.

age n. **1** MATURITY, old age, advancing years, seniority, elderliness; Biology senescence. **2** ERA, epoch, period, time, generation. **3** A LONG TIME, an eternity, aeons, hours, days, months, years; informal yonks. ▶ v. GROW OLD, mature, grow up, ripen, develop, mellow, wither, fade.

aged adj. OLD, elderly, ancient, long in the tooth, superannuated; Biology senescent; informal getting on, over the hill. ■ OPPOSITES young, youthful.

power, status, or wealth of. ■ **aggrandizement** n.

aggravate v. **1** make worse. **2** informal annoy. ■ **aggravation** n.

aggregate n. a whole formed by combining several elements. ▸ adj. formed or calculated by combination or addition. ▸ v. combine or unite. ■ **aggregation** n.

aggression n. hostile or violent behaviour or attitudes.

aggressive adj. showing aggression. ■ **aggressively** adv.

....

☑ Double g, double s: *aggressive*.

....

aggressor n. a person or country that begins hostilities.

aggrieved adj. having a grievance.

aghast adj. filled with horror.

agile adj. able to move quickly and easily. ■ **agility** n.

agitate v. **1** worry; disturb. **2** campaign to arouse public concern. **3** stir briskly. ■ **agitation** n. **agitator** n.

AGM abbrev. annual general meeting.

agnostic n. a person who believes that one cannot know whether or not God exists. ■ **agnosticism** n.

ago adv. before the present.

agog adj. eager and expectant.

agonize (or **-ise**) v. worry greatly.

agonizing (or **-ising**) adj. very painful or worrying.

agony n. (pl. **agonies**) great suffering.

agoraphobia n. abnormal fear of open or public places. ■ **agoraphobic** adj. & n.

agrarian adj. of agriculture.

agree v. (**agreeing**, **agreed**) **1** have the same opinion. **2** consent. □ **agree with 1** be consistent with. **2** be good for.

agreeable adj. **1** pleasant. **2** willing to agree. ■ **agreeably** adv.

agreement n. **1** the sharing of opinion. **2** an arrangement agreed between people. **3** consistency.

agriculture n. the science or practice of farming. ■ **agricultural** adj.

agronomy n. the science of soil management and crop production.

Thesaurus

agent n. REPRESENTATIVE, middleman, go-between, broker, negotiator, intermediary, mediator, emissary, envoy, proxy, factor, trustee, delegate, spokesperson, spokesman, spokeswoman, executor.

aggravate v. **1** MAKE WORSE, worsen, exacerbate, intensify, inflame, exaggerate, make more serious, compound, increase, heighten, magnify, add to. **2** *see* ANNOY. ■ OPPOSITES alleviate, improve.

aggressive adj. **1** HOSTILE, violent, belligerent, combative, attacking, destructive, quarrelsome, warlike, antagonistic, provocative, pugnacious, bellicose, bullying, contentious, jingoistic, militant. **2** ASSERTIVE, forceful, pushy, insistent, vigorous, dynamic, bold, enterprising, energetic, zealous, pushing; *informal* go-ahead, in-your-face. ■ OPPOSITES peaceable, retiring.

aggrieved adj. RESENTFUL, affronted, indignant, angry, distressed, piqued, disturbed; *informal* peeved.

agile adj. NIMBLE, lithe, fit, supple, sprightly, graceful, acrobatic, lively, spry, adroit, deft, quick-moving, limber, in good condition; *informal* nippy. ■ OPPOSITES clumsy, stiff.

agitate v. **1** UPSET, worry, fluster, perturb, disturb, disconcert, trouble, alarm, work up, ruffle, disquiet, unsettle, unnerve, rouse, excite, discomfit, confuse, shake up; *informal* rattle. **2** STIR, whisk, beat, shake, toss, work, churn, froth up, ruffle, ferment. ■ OPPOSITES calm.

agitator n. TROUBLEMAKER, rabble-rouser, agent provocateur, instigator, firebrand, fomenter, revolutionary, demagogue.

agonizing adj. EXCRUCIATING, painful, acute, harrowing, searing, unendurable, torturous.

agony n. SUFFERING, anguish, hurt, torment, torture, distress. *See also* PAIN.

agree v. **1** CONCUR, be of the same mind, comply, see eye to eye. **2** MATCH, correspond, accord, conform, coincide, fit, tally. **3** CONSENT TO, accept, assent to, approve, allow, admit, acquiesce in. ■ OPPOSITES disagree.

agreeable adj. PLEASING, enjoyable, nice, delightful, acceptable, likable, to one's liking, pleasurable. *See also* PLEASANT. ■ OPPOSITES disagreeable.

agreement n. **1** ACCORD, concurrence, harmony, concord, accordance, unity, assent. **2** CONTRACT, deal, compact, settlement, pact, bargain, treaty, covenant, concordat. **3** CORRESPONDENCE, similarity, conformity, match, harmony, accordance, coincidence. ■ OPPOSITES disagreement.

agricultural adj. **1** FARMING, farm, agrarian, pastoral, rural. **2** FARMED, cultivated, planted, productive, tilled.

aground adj. & adv. (of a ship) on the bottom in shallow water.

ague /ay-gyoo/ n. old use an illness involving fever and shivering.

ahead adv. further forward in space or time.

ahoy exclam. Naut. a call to attract attention.

aid n. & v. help.

aide n. an assistant to a political leader. □ **aide-de-camp** a military officer who assists a senior officer.

Aids n. a disease caused by the HIV virus, which breaks down the sufferer's natural defences against infection.

aikido /I-kee-doh/ n. a Japanese martial art.

ail v. cause suffering to.

aileron n. a hinged flap on an aircraft's wing.

ailing adj. in poor health.

ailment n. a minor illness.

aim v. 1 point or direct at a target. 2 try; intend. ▶ n. a purpose or intention.

aimless adj. without purpose. ■ **aimlessly** adv.

ain't contr. informal 1 am not; are not; is not. 2 has not; have not.

air n. 1 the mixture of gases surrounding the earth. 2 a manner or impression. 3 (**airs**) an affected and condescending manner. 4 a tune. ▶ v. 1 express an opinion publicly. 2 expose to fresh or warm air. □ **air bag** a car safety device that fills with air in a collision to pro-

tect the driver. **airbrick** a brick perforated to allow ventilation. **airborne** 1 carried by air. 2 (of an aircraft) flying. **air conditioning** a system that cools the air in a building or vehicle. **aircraft** a machine capable of flight. **aircraft carrier** a warship acting as a base for aircraft. **airfield** an area where aircraft can take off and land. **air force** the branch of the armed forces using aircraft. **air gun** a gun using compressed air to fire pellets. **airlift** an act of transporting supplies by aircraft. **airline** a company providing an air transport service. **airliner** a passenger aircraft. **airlock** 1 a stoppage of the flow in a pipe, caused by an air bubble. 2 an airtight compartment. **airmail** mail carried overseas by aircraft. **airman** a member of an air force. **airplane** US an aeroplane. **airport** an airfield with facilities for passengers and goods. **air raid** an attack by aircraft. **airship** a large aircraft filled with gas that is lighter than air. **airspace** the part of the air above a country. **airstrip** a strip of ground where aircraft can take off and land. **airtight** not allowing air to enter or escape. **airwaves** the radio frequencies used for broadcasting. **airway** 1 a regular route for aircraft. 2 a passage for air into the lungs. **airworthy** (of an aircraft) safe to fly. ■ **airless** adj.

airy adj. (**airier**, **airiest**) 1 well venti-

Thesaurus

■ OPPOSITES urban.

agriculture n. FARMING, cultivation, tillage, husbandry, crofting, agronomy, agronomics, agribusiness.

aground adv. & adj. GROUNDED, beached, ashore, shipwrecked, on the bottom, stranded, stuck, high and dry. ■ OPPOSITES afloat.

aid n. 1 HELP, assistance, support, succour, encouragement, a helping hand, cooperation. 2 CONTRIBUTION, gift, donation, subsidy, loan, debt remission, relief, sponsorship, backing, grant; historical alms. ▶ v. 1 HELP, assist, support, succour, lend a hand, sustain, second. 2 FACILITATE, speed up, hasten, help, encourage, expedite, promote, contribute to, sustain. ■ OPPOSITES hinder.

ailing adj. UNWELL, sick, poorly, sickly, indisposed, infirm; informal under the weather. See also ILL. ■ OPPOSITES healthy.

ailment n. ILLNESS, disease, sickness, disorder, complaint, malady, infirmity, affliction. See also ILLNESS.

aim v. 1 POINT, direct, take aim, train, sight, focus, address, zero in on. 2 INTEND, mean, resolve, wish, aspire, want, plan, propose, seek, try, strive, endeavour. ▶ n. AMBITION, objective, object, end, goal, purpose, intention, intent, plan, target, hope, aspiration, desire, wish, design, direction, focus, dream, destination.

aimless adj. 1 POINTLESS, purposeless, futile, undirected, goalless, objectless. 2 PURPOSELESS, drifting, wandering, undirected, unambitious, undisciplined, wayward. ■ OPPOSITES purposeful.

air n. 1 SKY, atmosphere, airspace; literary heavens, ether. 2 OXYGEN, breath of air, breeze, draught, puff of wind; literary zephyr. 3 APPEARANCE, impression, look, mood, atmosphere, quality, feeling, ambience, character, flavour, demeanour, effect, manner, bearing, tone, aspect, mien. 4 AFFECTATIONS, pretension, pretentiousness, affectedness, airs and graces, posing, posturing. 5 MELODY,

lated. **2** casual; dismissive. ■ **airily** adv.
airiness n.

aisle /rhymes with mile/ n. a passage between rows of seats or between shelves
in a shop.

ajar adv. & adj. (of a door) slightly open.

aka abbrev. also known as.

akimbo adv. with hands on the hips and
elbows turned outwards.

akin adj. related; similar.

alabaster n. a white translucent form
of the mineral gypsum.

à la carte adj. (of a menu) having separately priced dishes.

alacrity n. eager enthusiasm.

alarm n. **1** fear and anxiety. **2** a warning
sound or device. **3** a device to wake
someone at a set time. ▶v. frighten or
disturb.

alarmist n. a person who exaggerates a
danger, causing needless alarm.

alas exclam. an expression of sorrow.

albatross n. a very large seabird.

albeit conj. though.

albino n. (pl. **albinos**) a person or animal without pigment in the skin and
hair.

album n. **1** a blank book for photographs, stamps, etc. **2** a collection of recordings issued as a single item.

albumen n. egg white.

albumin n. a form of protein found in
blood and egg white.

alchemy n. a medieval form of chemistry, attempting to turn other metals

into gold. ■ **alchemist** n.

alcohol n. **1** a colourless liquid which is
the intoxicating ingredient in wine,
beer, etc. **2** drink containing alcohol.

alcoholic adj. of or containing alcohol.
▶n. a person addicted to drinking alcohol. ■ **alcoholism** n.

alcopop n. a ready-mixed fizzy drink
containing alcohol.

alcove n. a recess in a wall.

al dente /al den-tay/ adj. & adv. (of food)
cooked so as to be still firm when
bitten.

alder n. a tree of the birch family, which
bears catkins.

alderman n. hist. a member of an English county or borough council.

ale n. beer.

alert adj. watchful; observant. ▶v. warn
of a danger or problem.

A level n. (in the UK except Scotland)
the higher of the two main levels of the
GCE examination.

alfalfa n. a plant used as fodder for livestock.

alfresco adv. & adj. in the open air.

algae /al-jee, al-gee/ pl. n. simple plants
with no true stems or leaves.

algebra n. a branch of mathematics
using letters and symbols to represent
quantities. ■ **algebraic** adj.

algorithm n. a step-by-step procedure
for calculations.

alias adv. also called. ▶n. a false name.

alibi n. evidence that a person was else-

Thesaurus

tune, song, theme, strain. ▶v. **1** EX-
PRESS, make known, voice, publicize,
broadcast, give vent to, publish, communicate, reveal, proclaim, divulge,
circulate, disseminate, vent, disclose.
2 VENTILATE, aerate, freshen, refresh.

airless adj. STUFFY, close, stifling, suffocating, muggy, unventilated, oppressive, sultry. ■ OPPOSITES airy.

airy adj. **1** WELL VENTILATED, fresh, spacious, uncluttered, light, bright. **2** NON-
CHALANT, casual, light-hearted, breezy,
cheerful, jaunty, flippant, blithe, insouciant; dated gay. ■ OPPOSITES stuffy,
studied.

aisle n. PASSAGE, passageway, gangway,
walkway, corridor, lane, alley.

akin adj. RELATED TO, allied with, connected with, corresponding to, similar to.
■ OPPOSITES unrelated, different.

alacrity n. READINESS, promptness, eagerness, enthusiasm, willingness, haste,
swiftness. ■ OPPOSITES reluctance,
sluggishness.

alarm n. **1** FEAR, apprehension, anxiety,
uneasiness, distress, consternation,
panic, fright, trepidation, disquiet.
2 WARNING SOUND, siren, alert, alarm
bell/signal, danger/distress signal; old
use tocsin. ▶v. FRIGHTEN, scare, panic,
terrify, unnerve, agitate, distress, disturb, startle, shock, upset, worry; informal
put the wind up. ■ OPPOSITES reassure.

alcohol n. DRINK, liquor, spirits; informal
booze, hard stuff, the demon drink, the
bottle, grog, tipple, bevvy.

alcoholic adj. INTOXICATING, strong, in-
ebriating, hard; formal spirituous. ▶n.
DRUNKARD, drunk, hard/heavy drinker,
dipsomaniac, problem drinker, inebriate, tippler, sot, imbiber; informal boozer,
lush, dipso, wino, alky. ■ OPPOSITES
teetotaller.

alert adj. **1** AWARE, alive to, watchful,
vigilant, observant, wary, wide awake,
on one's guard, attentive, on the alert,
sharp-eyed, heedful, circumspect, on
the lookout, on one's toes. **2** SHARP,

where when a crime was committed.

alien adj. **1** foreign. **2** unfamiliar. **3** extraterrestrial. ▶ n. **1** a foreigner. **2** a being from another world.

alienate v. **1** cause to feel isolated. **2** lose the support or sympathy of. ■ **alienation** n.

alight v. step out of a vehicle. ▶ adj. & adv. on fire.

align v. **1** bring into the correct position. **2** ally oneself. ■ **alignment** n.

alike adj. similar. ▶ adv. in a similar way.

alimentary canal n. the passage along which food passes through the body.

alimony n. financial support for a wife or husband after separation or divorce.

alive adj. **1** living. **2** lively.

alkali n. a substance that turns litmus blue and neutralizes acids. ■ **alkaline** adj.

alkaloid n. an organic compound containing nitrogen.

all adj. the whole quantity or extent of. ▶ pron. everything or everyone. ▶ adv. completely. □ **all clear** a signal that danger is over. **all out** using all one's effort. **all right 1** unhurt. **2** satisfactory

or acceptable.

allay v. lessen fears.

allegation n. an unproved accusation.

allege v. state without proof. ■ **alleged** adj. **allegedly** adv.

allegiance n. loyal support.

allegory n. (pl. **allegories**) a story with an underlying meaning. ■ **allegorical** adj. **allegorically** adv.

allegro /uh-lay-groh/ adv. Music briskly.

alleluia var. of HALLELUJAH.

allergen n. a substance causing an allergic reaction.

allergic adj. having or caused by an allergy.

allergy n. (pl. **allergies**) a condition causing an unfavourable reaction to certain substances.

alleviate v. lessen pain or distress. ■ **alleviation** n.

alley n. (pl. **alleys**) **1** a narrow street. **2** a long, narrow area for tenpin bowling or skittles.

alliance n. an association formed for mutual benefit.

allied adj. joined by an alliance.

alligator n. a large reptile similar to a crocodile.

Thesaurus

quick, bright, perceptive, keen, lively, wide awake; *informal* on the ball, quick off the mark. ▶ v. WARN, make aware, caution, advise, forewarn, inform, apprise, notify; *informal* tip off.

alibi n. EXCUSE, defence, justification, explanation, pretext, plea, vindication.

alien adj. FOREIGN, strange, unfamiliar, outlandish, remote, exotic, extraterrestrial. ▶ n. FOREIGNER, stranger, outsider, newcomer, extraterrestrial. ■ OPPOSITES native.

alight[1] v. GET OFF, come down, get down, dismount, disembark, come to rest, land, descend, touch down, settle, perch.

alight[2] adj. **1** ON FIRE, burning, ablaze, blazing, lighted, lit, aflame. **2** LIT UP, shining, bright, illuminated, brilliant.

align v. **1** LINE UP, arrange in line, put in order, straighten, rank, range. **2** ALLY, associate, affiliate, cooperate, side, join, unite, combine, join forces.

alike adj. SIMILAR, like, resembling, indistinguishable, identical, interchangeable, corresponding, matching, the same, twin, uniform. ▶ adv. SIMILARLY, just the same, identically, in a like manner, in the same way. ■ OPPOSITES differently.

alive adj. **1** LIVING, breathing, live, ani-

mate; *informal* alive and kicking, in the land of the living; *old use* quick. **2** *see* ALERT. ■ OPPOSITES dead.

allay v. LESSEN, diminish, reduce, alleviate, calm, assuage, ease, quell, relieve, appease, moderate, mitigate, check, lull, subdue, soothe. ■ OPPOSITES increase, stimulate.

allegation n. CHARGE, accusation, claim, assertion, statement, declaration, testimony, deposition, avowal.

allege v. CLAIM, declare, state, profess, assert, maintain, affirm, avow, attest, contend, aver, lay a charge.

alleged adj. SUPPOSED, claimed, declared, so-called, professed, stated.

allegiance n. LOYALTY, faithfulness, adherence, fidelity, devotion, duty, obedience; *historical* fealty.

allergic adj. **1** HYPERSENSITIVE, sensitive, sensitized, susceptible. **2** AVERSE, opposed, antagonistic, disinclined, hostile, antipathetic, loath.

alleviate v. REDUCE, lessen, diminish, relieve, ease, allay, mitigate, assuage, abate, palliate, lighten, soothe, subdue, temper, ameliorate, check, quell, soften, make lighter. ■ OPPOSITES aggravate.

alliance n. ASSOCIATION, union, coalition, partnership, affiliation, agreement, league, confederation, federation, rela-

alliteration n. the occurrence of the same letter or sound at the start of adjacent words. ■ **alliterative** adj.

allocate v. allot or assign. ■ **allocation** n.

allot v. (**allotting**, **allotted**) distribute; give out as a share.

allotment n. **1** a small plot of land rented for cultivating vegetables etc. **2** an allotted share.

allotrope n. each of the physical forms in which a chemical element can exist.

allow v. **1** permit. **2** set aside for a purpose. **3** admit. **4** (**allow for**) take into account. ■ **allowable** adj.

allowance n. **1** a permitted amount. **2** a sum of money paid regularly. □ **make allowances** be lenient because of mitigating circumstances.

alloy n. a mixture of two or more metals. ▶ v. mix metals to make an alloy.

allspice n. the dried fruit of a Caribbean tree, used as a spice.

allude v. (**allude to**) refer to briefly or indirectly. ■ **allusion** n. **allusive** adj.

allure n. attractiveness or charm.

alluring adj. attractive; tempting.

alluvium n. a fertile deposit left by flood water. ■ **alluvial** adj.

ally n. (pl. **allies**) a person or country that cooperates with another. ▶ v. (**allying**, **allied**) (**ally oneself with**) side with.

alma mater n. the school, college, or university that one once attended.

almanac (or **almanack**) n. **1** a calendar giving important dates and information about the sun, moon, tides, etc. **2** a yearbook of a particular activity.

almighty adj. **1** all-powerful. **2** informal huge.

almond n. an edible oval nut.

almost adv. very nearly.

alms /ahmz/ pl. n. hist. charitable donations to the poor. □ **almshouse** a house providing accommodation for the poor.

aloe n. a tropical plant with fleshy leaves.

aloft adv. high up; upwards.

alone adj. & adv. **1** on one's own. **2** only; exclusively.

along prep. & adv. **1** moving over the length of. **2** extending beside.

alongside prep. close to the side of.

aloof adj. cool and distant. ■ **aloofness** n.

alopecia /a-luh-**pee**-shuh/ n. abnormal hair loss.

aloud adv. in an audible voice.

Thesaurus

tionship, connection, pact, bond, understanding, treaty, marriage, compact, concordat, syndicate, cartel, consortium, bloc, combination, covenant, entente.

allot v. ALLOCATE, assign, apportion, distribute, give out, share out, award, dispense, deal out, ration, divide up, mete out, dole out, dish out.

allow v. **1** PERMIT, let, give permission to, authorize, consent to, sanction, approve, license, enable; informal give the go-ahead to, give the green light to. **2** ADMIT, acknowledge, concede, recognize, grant, confess. ■ OPPOSITES forbid, deny.

allowance n. **1** QUOTA, allocation, ration, portion, share. **2** PAYMENT, subsidy, remittance, grant, contribution. **3** REBATE, discount, deduction, concession, reduction. □ **make allowances (for)** **1** TAKE INTO ACCOUNT, bear in mind, have regard to. **2** EXCUSE, make excuses, forgive, pardon.

alloy n. MIXTURE, blend, amalgam, combination, compound, composite; technical admixture.

allude v. (**allude to**) REFER TO, mention, speak of, touch on, make an allusion to, cite, suggest, hint at; formal advert to.

allure v. ATTRACT, fascinate, charm, seduce, captivate, enchant, bewitch, beguile, tempt, magnetize, lure, entice, cajole, draw, inveigle.

allusion n. REFERENCE, mention, suggestion, citation, hint, intimation.

ally n. ASSOCIATE, colleague, partner, friend, supporter, collaborator, confederate, accomplice, abetter, accessory. ▶ v. JOIN, unite, join forces, combine, merge, go into partnership, band together, form an alliance, team up, link up, affiliate, be in league, cooperate, collaborate, side.

almighty adj. **1** ALL-POWERFUL, supreme, most high, omnipotent. **2** see HUGE, LOUD.

almost adv. NEARLY, just about, close to, not quite, practically, virtually, as good as, approaching, not far from, verging on, well-nigh.

alone adj. & adv. BY ONESELF, on one's own, solitary, apart, unaccompanied, isolated, single, separate, unassisted, solo, lonely, friendless, forlorn, deserted, desolate, lonesome. ■ OPPOSITES accompanied.

aloof adj. DISTANT, unapproachable, remote, stand-offish, unfriendly, unsoci-

alpaca n. a long-haired South American llama.

alpha n. the first letter of the Greek alphabet (Λ, α).

alphabet n. a set of letters in a fixed order representing the sounds of a language. ■ **alphabetical** adj. **alphabetically** adv.

alphabetize (or **-ise**) v. put into alphabetical order.

alpine adj. of or found on high mountains.

already adv. 1 before this time. 2 sooner than expected.

Alsatian n. a German shepherd dog.

also adv. in addition.

altar n. a table used in religious services. □ **altarpiece** a painting behind an altar.

alter v. make or become different. ■ **alteration** n.

altercation n. a noisy dispute.

alternate v. occur in turn repeatedly. ▶ adj. 1 every other. 2 (of two things) repeatedly following and replacing each other. □ **alternating current** an electric current that reverses direction many times a second. ■ **alternately** adv. **alternation** n.

alternative adj. 1 available as another choice. 2 unconventional. ▶ n. a choice or option. ■ **alternatively** adv.

alternator n. a dynamo that generates an alternating current.

although conj. in spite of the fact that.

altimeter n. an instrument in an aircraft showing altitude.

altitude n. height above sea level or ground level.

alto n. (pl. **altos**) the highest adult male or lowest female singing voice.

altogether adv. 1 completely. 2 in total. 3 on the whole.

altruism n. unselfishness. ■ **altruist** n. **altruistic** adj.

aluminium n. a lightweight silvery-grey metal.

always adv. 1 at all times. 2 forever.

Alzheimer's disease /alts-hy-merz/ n. a disease which affects the functioning of the brain.

AM abbrev. amplitude modulation.

am see BE.

a.m. abbrev. before noon.

amalgam n. 1 a blend. 2 an alloy of mercury with another metal.

amalgamate v. combine or unite. ■ **amalgamation** n.

amass v. collect or accumulate.

amateur n. a person who does something as a pastime rather than as a profession.

amateurish adj. unskilful.

amatory adj. to do with love.

Thesaurus

able, reserved, unresponsive, reticent, supercilious, cold, chilly, haughty, formal, inaccessible, detached, undemonstrative, unsympathetic, unforthcoming. ■ OPPOSITES familiar, friendly.

aloud adv. OUT LOUD, clearly, audibly, distinctly, plainly, intelligibly. ■ OPPOSITES silently.

already adv. 1 BY NOW, by this time, previously, before, before now. 2 AS SOON AS THIS, as early as this, so soon, so early.

also adv. IN ADDITION, additionally, moreover, besides, too, to boot, on top of that.

alter v. CHANGE, make different, adjust, adapt, modify, convert, reshape, remodel, remake, vary, amend, revise, transform, emend, edit.

alteration n. CHANGE, adjustment, modification, adaptation, revision, amendment, transformation, conversion, metamorphosis, reorganization, transfiguration.

alternate v. TAKE TURNS, follow each other, rotate, interchange, substitute for each other, replace each other,

oscillate, see-saw.

alternative n. 1 CHOICE, option, preference. 2 SUBSTITUTE, back-up, replacement.

alternatively adv. ON THE OTHER HAND, as an alternative, instead, otherwise, if not, or.

although conjunction THOUGH, even though, even if, despite the fact that, whilst, albeit.

altogether adv. COMPLETELY, totally, entirely, thoroughly, fully, utterly, absolutely, perfectly, quite, wholly.

always adv. 1 EVERY TIME, on every occasion, invariably, consistently, repeatedly, unfailingly. 2 CONTINUALLY, constantly, repeatedly, forever, perpetually, incessantly, eternally. 3 FOREVER, forever and ever, evermore, endlessly, everlastingly, eternally. ■ OPPOSITES never.

amalgamate v. COMBINE, merge, unite, join, blend, integrate, mingle, intermingle, mix, intermix, incorporate, fuse, come together, join forces, coalesce, associate, compound, link up. ■ OPPOSITES split.

amass v. COLLECT, gather, accumulate,

amaze v. astonish. ■ **amazement** n.

Amazon n. a very tall, strong woman.

ambassador n. a diplomat representing their country abroad.

amber n. **1** a hard, clear yellowish resin. **2** a yellowish colour.

ambidextrous adj. able to use either hand equally well.

ambience n. a place's atmosphere.

ambient adj. surrounding.

ambiguous adj. having more than one meaning. ■ **ambiguity** n. **ambiguously** adv.

ambit n. scope or extent.

ambition n. a strong desire to achieve something. ■ **ambitious** adj. **ambitiously** adv.

ambivalent adj. having mixed feelings. ■ **ambivalence** n.

amble v. walk at a leisurely pace.

ambrosia n. something delicious.

ambulance n. a vehicle equipped to carry sick or injured people.

ambush n. a surprise attack by people lying in wait. ▶ v. attack in such a way.

ameba US = AMOEBA.

ameliorate v. make better. ■ **amelioration** n.

amen exclam. so be it (used at the end of a prayer).

amenable adj. cooperative.

amend v. make minor improvements to. □ **make amends** compensate for something. ■ **amendment** n.

amenity n. (pl. **amenities**) a useful or desirable feature of a place.

American adj. of America or the USA. ▶n. an American person. □ **American football** a kind of football played with an oval ball on a field marked with parallel lines.

Americanism n. a word or phrase originating in the USA.

amethyst /am-uh-thist/ n. a violet or purple precious stone.

amiable adj. friendly or likeable. ■ **amiability** n. **amiably** adv.

amicable adj. friendly. ■ **amicably** adv.

Thesaurus

pile up, assemble, store up, hoard.

amateur n. NON-PROFESSIONAL, layman, dabbler, dilettante, enthusiast. ▶ adj. UN-PAID, inexperienced, lay, unqualified. ■ OPPOSITES professional, expert.

amateurish adj. UNPROFESSIONAL, unskilful, untrained, unskilled, incompetent, inexpert, clumsy, crude, bungling, shoddy, unpolished, inept, second-rate, rough and ready. ■ OPPOSITES skilled.

amaze v. ASTONISH, surprise, astound, startle, dumbfound, rock, shock, stagger, stun, bewilder, stupefy, daze, disconcert, confound, awe; informal flabbergast, bowl over.

amazement n. ASTONISHMENT, surprise, bewilderment, wonder, stupefaction, shock.

amazing adj. ASTONISHING, astounding, stunning, staggering, surprising, breathtaking, extraordinary, incredible, remarkable, sensational, phenomenal, prodigious, stupendous, exceptional; informal mind-boggling.

ambassador n. ENVOY, consul, diplomat, emissary, representative, plenipotentiary; old use legate.

ambiguous adj. **1** AMBIVALENT, equivocal, double-edged. **2** OBSCURE, cryptic, vague, unclear, uncertain, indefinite, woolly, indeterminate, confusing, puzzling, perplexing, enigmatic.

ambition n. **1** DRIVE, enterprise, desire, initiative, eagerness, thrust, push, zeal, pushiness, striving, yearning, hankering; informal get-up-and-go, oomph. **2** GOAL, aim, objective, desire, object, intent, purpose, design, target, wish, aspiration, dream, hope, ideal.

ambitious adj. **1** FORCEFUL, enterprising, purposeful, assertive, pushy, aspiring, zealous, enthusiastic, committed, eager, energetic; informal go-ahead, on the make. **2** CHALLENGING, formidable, demanding, difficult, exacting, bold, unrealistic. ■ OPPOSITES aimless, apathetic, easy.

ambivalent adj. EQUIVOCAL, ambiguous, uncertain, doubtful, inconclusive, unclear, unresolved, unsettled, confusing, mixed, conflicting, clashing, opposing, vacillating, two-faced. ■ OPPOSITES unequivocal.

ambush n. TRAP, snare, surprise attack, pitfall, lure; old use ambuscade. ▶ v. LIE IN WAIT FOR, lay a trap for, pounce on, entrap, ensnare, intercept, surprise, waylay, swoop on, decoy; old use ambuscade.

amenable adj. AGREEABLE, accommodating, persuadable, cooperative, tractable, compliant, responsive, willing, acquiescent, adaptable, open-minded, biddable, complaisant, submissive, deferential. ■ OPPOSITES uncooperative.

amend v. **1** ALTER, change, revise, correct, modify, adjust, emend, reorganize, reshape, transform. **2** IMPROVE, remedy, fix, set right, repair, enhance, better, ameliorate, mend.

amenity n. FACILITY, service, convenience, resource, advantage.

a

amid (or **amidst**) prep. in the middle of.

amino acid n. an organic compound found in proteins.

amiss adj. wrong; faulty. □ **take amiss** be offended by.

amity n. friendly relations between people or countries.

ammeter n. an instrument for measuring electric current.

ammonia n. **1** a strong-smelling gas. **2** a solution of ammonia in water.

ammonite n. a fossilized spiral shell of an extinct sea animal.

ammunition n. a supply of bullets and shells.

amnesia n. loss of memory. ■ **amnesiac** adj.

amnesty n. (pl. **amnesties**) a general pardon.

amniocentesis n. (pl. **amniocenteses**) a test for possible fetal abnormality, involving the removal of a sample of amniotic fluid.

amniotic fluid n. the fluid surrounding a fetus before birth.

amoeba /uh-mee-buh/ (US **ameba**) n. (pl. **amoebas** or **amoebae**) a single-celled organism that can change its shape.

amok (or **amuck**) adv. (**run amok**) be out of control.

among (or **amongst**) prep. **1** surrounded by. **2** included in. **3** shared by; between.

amoral adj. not concerned about right or wrong.

amorous adj. showing sexual desire.

amorphous adj. without definite shape.

amortize (or **-ise**) v. gradually pay off a debt.

amount n. **1** the total of something. **2** a quantity. ▶ v. (**amount to**) **1** add up to. **2** be equivalent to.

amp n. informal an amplifier.

ampere /am-pair/ n. a basic unit of electric current.

ampersand n. the sign & (= *and*).

amphetamine n. a drug used as a stimulant.

amphibian n. an animal such as a frog or toad, able to live both on land and in water.

amphibious adj. able to live or operate both on land and in water.

amphitheatre n. a round open building with tiers of seats surrounding a central area.

ample adj. **1** quite enough; plentiful. **2** large. ■ **amply** adv.

amplify v. (**amplifying**, **amplified**) **1** make louder. **2** add details to a story. ■ **amplification** n. **amplifier** n.

amplitude n. great size or extent.

ampoule n. a small sealed capsule containing liquid for injection.

amputate v. cut off a limb. ■ **amputation** n.

amuck var. of AMOK.

amulet n. something worn as protection against evil.

amuse v. **1** make someone laugh or smile. **2** entertain. ■ **amusement** n. **amusing** adj.

an adj. the form of 'a' used before vowel

Thesaurus

amiable adj. FRIENDLY, agreeable, pleasant, charming, likeable, sociable, genial, amicable, congenial, good-natured, well disposed. ■ OPPOSITES unfriendly, disagreeable.

amnesty n. PARDON, general pardon, reprieve, forgiveness, absolution, dispensation, indulgence.

amorous adj. LOVING, passionate, sexual, sexy, erotic, carnal, lustful, affectionate, ardent, fond, enamoured, impassioned; *informal* randy. ■ OPPOSITES unloving, cold.

amorphous adj. FORMLESS, shapeless, structureless, unstructured, unformed, nebulous, vague, ill-organized, indeterminate. ■ OPPOSITES shaped, definite.

amount n. QUANTITY, number, total, aggregate, sum, volume, mass, weight, measure, bulk, extent. □ **amount to** ADD UP TO, total, come to, run to, be equivalent to, equal, correspond to,

approximate to, make.

ample adj. ENOUGH, sufficient, plenty, more than enough, enough and to spare, abundant, considerable, copious, lavish, substantial, bountiful, profuse, liberal, generous, munificent, unstinting; *literary* plenteous. ■ OPPOSITES insufficient.

amplify v. **1** BOOST, increase, intensify, augment, heighten, magnify, supplement. **2** EXPAND, enlarge on, add to, expound on, go into detail about, elaborate on, fill out, make longer, flesh out, develop, extend, lengthen, broaden, explicate, expatiate on, dilate on, supplement.

amputate v. CUT OFF, sever, chop off, saw off, remove, lop off, excise, dismember, truncate, dock, poll.

amuse v. **1** ENTERTAIN, delight, enliven, gladden, cheer, make laugh, please, divert, beguile, regale with, raise a smile sounds.

anabolic steroid n. a synthetic hormone used to build up muscle.

anachronism n. a thing belonging to a period other than the one in which it exists. ■ **anachronistic** adj.

anaconda n. a large South American snake.

anaemia /uh-nee-mi-uh/ (US **anemia**) n. a shortage of red cells or haemoglobin in the blood. ■ **anaemic** adj.

anaerobic adj. not requiring air or oxygen.

anaesthesia /an-iss-thee-ziuh/ (US **anesthesia**) n. insensitivity to pain, esp. as caused by an anaesthetic.

anaesthetic /an-iss-thet-ik/ (US **anesthetic**) n. a drug or gas that stops one feeling pain.

anaesthetist /uh-neess-thuh-tist/ (US **anesthetist**) n. a medical specialist who gives anaesthetics. ■ **anaesthetize** (or **-ise**) v.

anagram n. a word or phrase formed by rearranging the letters of another.

anal /ay-n'l/ adj. of the anus.

analgesic n. a pain-relieving drug.

analogous adj. comparable.

analogue n. an analogous thing. ▶ adj. showing information by means of a dial.

analogy n. (pl. **analogies**) 1 a comparison. 2 a partial similarity.

analyse (US **analyze**) v. 1 examine in

detail. 2 psychoanalyse. ■ **analyst** n.

analysis n. (pl. **analyses**) 1 a detailed examination or study. 2 psychoanalysis.

analytical (or **analytic**) adj. to do with analysis. ■ **analytically** adv.

anarchist n. a person who believes that government should be abolished. ■ **anarchism** n.

anarchy n. complete disorder due to lack of government or control. ■ **anarchic** adj.

anathema /uh-na-thuh-muh/ n. something that one hates.

anathematize (or **-ise**) v. curse.

anatomize (or **-ise**) v. examine the anatomy or structure of.

anatomy n. (pl. **anatomies**) 1 the scientific study of the structure of the body. 2 a detailed analysis. ■ **anatomical** adj. **anatomically** adv.

ancestor n. a person from whom one is descended. ■ **ancestral** adj.

ancestry n. (pl. **ancestries**) a person's ancestors.

anchor n. a heavy metal object for mooring a ship to the sea bottom. ▶ v. 1 moor with an anchor. 2 fix firmly. □ **anchorage** a place where ships may anchor. **anchorman** a person presenting a live TV or radio programme.

anchovy n. (pl. **anchovies**) a small strong-tasting fish.

ancient adj. very old.

Thesaurus

in. 2 OCCUPY, entertain, divert, interest, absorb, engross.

amusement n. 1 LAUGHTER, mirth, hilarity, fun, gaiety, pleasure, delight, enjoyment, merriment. 2 ENTERTAINMENT, interest, diversion, recreation, pastime, hobby, sport, game, pleasure.

amusing adj. see FUNNY, ENJOYABLE.

anaemic adj. PALE, colourless, pallid, ashen, sickly, unhealthy, wan, bloodless, weak, feeble, powerless, ineffective, ineffectual, impotent, vigourless. ■ OPPOSITES healthy, rosy, vigorous.

analogous adj. SIMILAR, comparable, parallel, corresponding, related, matching, equivalent, like, kindred, homologous.

analyse v. 1 BREAK DOWN, dissect, separate out, anatomize, fractionate, test, assay. 2 STUDY, examine, investigate, review, evaluate, interpret, scrutinize, enquire into, dissect.

analysis n. 1 BREAKDOWN, dissection, anatomization, fractionation, assay. 2 STUDY, examination, investigation, enquiry, review, scrutiny, evaluation,

interpretation.

analytical, analytic adj. INVESTIGATIVE, inquisitive, critical, diagnostic, interpretative, enquiring, searching, systematic, questioning, rational, methodical, in depth.

anarchy n. 1 ABSENCE OF GOVERNMENT, lawlessness, nihilism, misrule, misgovernment, mobocracy, revolution. 2 DISORDER, riot, chaos, pandemonium, tumult, mayhem, rebellion, insurrection, mutiny. ■ OPPOSITES order, law.

ancestor n. FOREBEAR, forerunner, forefather, progenitor, predecessor, precursor, antecedent. ■ OPPOSITES descendant, successor.

ancestry n. 1 LINEAGE, descent, parentage, extraction, origin, genealogy, stock, blood, pedigree, derivation. 2 ANTECEDENTS, forebears, forefathers, progenitors, family tree.

anchor n. MAINSTAY, cornerstone, linchpin, bulwark, support. ▶ v. 1 MOOR, berth, make fast, tie up. 2 SECURE, fasten, attach, connect, bind.

ancillary adj. **1** providing support. **2** extra.

and conj. used to connect words, clauses, or sentences.

andante /an-**dan**-tay/ adv. Music in moderately slow time.

andiron n. a metal stand for supporting logs in a fireplace.

androgynous /an-**dro**-ji-nuhss/ adj. partly male and partly female.

android n. a robot with a human appearance.

anecdotal adj. (of a story) not backed up by facts.

anecdote n. a short, entertaining true story.

anemia US = ANAEMIA.

anemone /uh-**nem**-uh-ni/ n. a plant with red, purple, or white flowers.

anesthetic etc. US = ANAESTHETIC etc.

aneurysm /an-yuu-ri-z'm/ n. a swelling of the wall of an artery.

anew adv. **1** in a different way. **2** again.

angel n. **1** a spiritual being acting as a messenger of God. **2** a very kind person. ■ **angelic** adj.

angelica n. the candied stalks of a sweet-smelling plant.

angelus n. a Roman Catholic prayer said at morning, noon, and sunset.

anger n. a strong feeling of displeasure. ▶v. make angry.

angina /an-**jy**-nuh/ (or **angina pectoris**) n. pain in the chest caused by an inadequate blood supply to the heart.

angle n. **1** the space between two lines or surfaces that meet. **2** a position from which something is viewed. **3** a point of view. ▶v. **1** place in a slanting position. **2** present from a certain point of view. **3** fish with a rod and line. **4** try to get something by hinting. ■ **angler** n.

Anglican adj. & n. (a member) of the Church of England. ■ **Anglicanism** n.

anglicize (or **-ise**) v. make English in character.

Anglo- comb. form English or British.

Anglo-Saxon n. **1** a Germanic inhabitant of England between the 5th century and the Norman Conquest. **2** the Old English language.

angora n. soft fabric made from the hair of a long-haired goat or rabbit.

angry adj. (**angrier**, **angriest**) feeling or showing anger. ■ **angrily** adv.

angst n. great anxiety.

angstrom n. a unit of measurement for wavelengths.

anguish n. severe pain or suffering. ■ **anguished** adj.

angular adj. **1** having angles or sharp corners. **2** forming an angle.

anhydrous adj. containing no water.

aniline /an-i-leen/ n. an oily liquid used in making dyes and plastics.

animal n. **1** a living being with sense organs, that can move of its own accord. **2** a mammal, as opposed to a bird, reptile, fish, or insect.

Thesaurus

ancient adj. **1** EARLY, earliest, prehistoric, primeval, primordial, immemorial, bygone. **2** VERY OLD, time-worn, age-old, antique, long-lived, venerable, elderly. **3** OLD-FASHIONED, antiquated, out of date, outmoded, obsolete, archaic, superannuated, antediluvian, atavistic.

ancillary adj. SECONDARY, auxiliary, subsidiary, supplementary, additional, subordinate, extra.

angelic adj. **1** HEAVENLY, seraphic, cherubic, ethereal, beatific, holy, divine, blessed. **2** INNOCENT, pure, virtuous, good, saintly, beautiful, adorable.

anger n. RAGE, fury, wrath, rancour, temper, annoyance, irritability, antagonism, vexation, exasperation, outrage, indignation, spleen, pique, passion, hostility, tantrum; literary ire, choler. ▶v. MAKE ANGRY, infuriate, enrage, madden, incense, outrage, irritate, annoy, exasperate, provoke, antagonize, rile, vex, inflame, aggravate; informal make someone's blood boil, needle, bug, drive crazy. ■ OPPOSITES pacify, placate.

angle n. **1** BEND, corner, fork, nook, niche, recess, elbow. **2** POINT OF VIEW, approach, viewpoint, standpoint, opinion, position, slant. ▶v. **1** TILT, slant, slope, turn, bend. **2** SLANT, distort, skew.

angry adj. FURIOUS, irate, enraged, incensed, maddened, outraged, wrathful, seething, raging, annoyed, irritated, exasperated, fuming, indignant, bitter, irascible, vexed, irked, heated, provoked, raving, wild, fiery, apoplectic, hot-tempered, ill-humoured; informal hot under the collar, mad, up in arms, aerated. ■ OPPOSITES calm, pleased.

anguish n. AGONY, suffering, pain, distress, torment, torture, misery, sorrow, grief, woe, heartache, tribulation. ■ OPPOSITES pleasure, happiness.

angular adj. **1** BENT, crooked, jagged, zigzag, pointed, V-shaped, Y-shaped, forked, bifurcate. **2** BONY, gaunt, spare, scrawny, skinny, lean. ■ OPPOSITES rounded.

animate v. **1** bring life or energy to. **2** make drawings into an animated film. ▶ adj. alive. ■ **animator** n.

animated adj. **1** lively. **2** (of a film) made using animation.

animation n. **1** liveliness. **2** the technique of filming a sequence of drawings to give the appearance of movement.

animism n. the belief that all natural things have a soul.

animosity n. hatred or dislike.

animus n. animosity.

anion n. an ion with a negative charge.

aniseed n. the seed of the **anise plant**, used as a flavouring.

ankle n. the joint connecting the foot with the leg.

anklet n. a chain or band worn round the ankle.

annals pl. n. a historical record of events year by year.

anneal v. toughen metal or glass by heating and slow cooling.

annex v. **1** take possession of. **2** add as an extra part. ▶ n. (also **annexe**) a building attached or near to a main building. ■ **annexation** n.

annihilate v. destroy completely. ■ **annihilation** n.

anniversary n. (pl. **anniversaries**) the date on which an event took place in a previous year.

annotate v. add explanatory notes to. ■ **annotation** n.

announce v. make a public statement about. ■ **announcement** n. **announcer** n.

annoy v. make slightly angry. ■ **annoyance** n.

annual adj. yearly. ▶ n. **1** a plant living

Thesaurus

animal n. **1** CREATURE, beast, brute, organism, being. **2** BRUTE, beast, savage, fiend, barbarian, monster; informal swine. ▶ adj. SENSUAL, carnal, physical, bodily, fleshly, brutish, bestial.

animate v. ENLIVEN, give life to, liven up, cheer up, gladden, brighten up, make lively, revitalize, perk up, inspire, excite, exhilarate, rouse, stir, stimulate, invigorate, fire, move, energize, rejuvenate, revive, encourage, galvanize, urge, arouse, activate, spark, kindle, incite; informal buck up, pep up. ▶ adj. LIVING, alive, live, breathing, conscious, sentient. ■ OPPOSITES inanimate.

animated adj. LIVELY, energetic, excited, enthusiastic, spirited, exuberant, vivacious, bubbling, vibrant, cheerful, bright, ebullient, dynamic, eager, zestful, busy, brisk, active, alive, sprightly, passionate, vigorous, quick. ■ OPPOSITES lethargic, lifeless.

animation n. LIVELINESS, energy, excitement, enthusiasm, passion, dynamism, vitality, vivacity, eagerness, ebullience, exhilaration, zest, exuberance, life, spirit, high spirits, verve, buoyancy, forcefulness, sparkle, briskness, activity, vigour, sprightliness; informal pep, zing. ■ OPPOSITES apathy, lethargy.

animosity n. DISLIKE, enmity, unfriendliness, hostility, resentment, antagonism, hate, hatred, loathing, antipathy, bitterness, spite, bad blood, rancour, venom, ill will, acrimony, vindictiveness, malice, animus, asperity, sourness, malignancy, malignity, odium, acerbity, virulence, sharpness. ■ OPPOSITES goodwill, friendliness.

annex v. SEIZE, take over, conquer, appropriate, acquire, occupy, usurp.

annihilate v. DESTROY, wipe out, exterminate, obliterate, eliminate, eradicate, extirpate, erase, liquidate, raze, extinguish, slaughter, kill off, finish off.

annotate v. COMMENT ON, gloss, add notes to, explain, interpret, elucidate, explicate.

annotation n. NOTE, comment, gloss, footnote, commentary, explanation, interpretation, elucidation, observation.

announce v. **1** MAKE KNOWN, make public, publish, put out, report, state, give out, reveal, declare, disclose, divulge, broadcast, proclaim, advertise, notify of, promulgate, propound, blazon, intimate. **2** INTRODUCE, present, give someone's name, usher in, herald. ■ OPPOSITES suppress.

announcement n. **1** DECLARATION, reporting, proclamation, disclosure, publication, statement, promulgation, notification, advertisement, intimation, revelation. **2** STATEMENT, report, bulletin, message, communiqué.

announcer n. PRESENTER, newsreader, broadcaster, newscaster, reporter, commentator, anchorman, anchor, herald, master of ceremonies, compère, MC.

annoy v. **1** IRRITATE, exasperate, displease, infuriate, anger, madden, vex, provoke, upset, put out, try someone's patience, drive mad, antagonize, irk, gall, nettle, make cross, pique, jar, rub up the wrong way; informal get on someone's nerves, aggravate, bug, peeve, get to. **2** BOTHER, disturb, pester, harass, trouble, fret, worry, plague, for a year or less. **2** a book published once a year. ■ **annually** adv.

annuity n. (pl. **annuities**) a fixed sum of money paid each year.

annul v. (**annulling, annulled**) declare to be no longer valid. ■ **annulment** n.

annular adj. ring-shaped.

Annunciation n. the announcement by the angel Gabriel to the Virgin Mary that she was to be the mother of Jesus.

anode n. an electrode with a positive charge.

anodized (or **-ised**) adj. (of metal) coated with a protective layer by electrolysis.

anodyne adj. bland. ▶n. a painkilling drug.

anoint v. smear or rub with oil as part of a religious ceremony.

anomaly n. (pl. **anomalies**) something differing from what is standard or normal. ■ **anomalous** adj.

anon adv. old use soon.

anonymous adj. having a name that is not publicly known. ■ **anonymity** n. **anonymously** adv.

anorak n. a waterproof jacket with a hood.

anorexia (or **anorexia nervosa**) n. a disorder in which a person refuses to eat because they are afraid of becoming fat. ■ **anorexic** adj. & n.

another adj. & pron. **1** one more. **2** a different.

answer n. **1** something said or written in reaction to a question or statement. **2** the solution to a problem. ▶v. **1** give an answer. **2** (**answer for**) be responsible for. **3** meet a need. □ **answering machine** a machine which answers telephone calls and records callers' messages.

answerable adj. having to account for something.

ant n. a small insect that lives in highly organized groups. □ **anteater** a mammal that feeds on ants and termites.

antacid adj. (of a medicine) reducing excess acid in the stomach.

antagonism n. open hostility.

antagonist n. an opponent or enemy. ■ **antagonistic** adj.

antagonize (or **-ise**) v. make someone hostile.

Antarctic adj. of the region around the South Pole.

ante n. a stake put up by a poker player before receiving cards.

Thesaurus

harry, badger, molest; *informal* bug.

annoyance n. **1** IRRITATION, exasperation, anger, displeasure, vexation, chagrin, pique; *literary* ire. **2** NUISANCE, pest, bother, irritant, trial, offence, provocation; *informal* pain, hassle, pain in the neck, bind, bore.

annoyed adj. IRRITATED, exasperated, cross, displeased, upset, vexed, riled, put out; *informal* miffed, peeved, huffy, in a huff, shirty; *US informal* sore. ■ OPPOSITES pleased.

annoying adj. IRRITATING, infuriating, exasperating, maddening, upsetting, trying, galling, tiresome, grating, troublesome, worrying, vexing, irksome, bothersome, vexatious, wearisome; *informal* aggravating, pestilential.

annul v. NULLIFY, cancel, declare null and void, invalidate, rescind, revoke, repeal, quash, void, negate, abrogate.

anoint v. **1** OIL, apply ointment to, spread over, rub, smear, lubricate, grease. **2** CONSECRATE, bless, sanctify, ordain, hallow.

anomalous adj. ABNORMAL, irregular, atypical, aberrant, deviant, exceptional, unusual, odd, eccentric, bizarre, peculiar, out of the ordinary.

anonymous adj. **1** UNNAMED, unidentified, nameless, unknown, unspecified, incognito, uncredited, unattributed, unsigned. **2** CHARACTERLESS, unremarkable, impersonal, nondescript, boring, dull, uninteresting. ■ OPPOSITES named, known.

answer n. **1** REPLY, response, acknowledgement, rejoinder, retort, riposte; *informal* comeback. **2** SOLUTION, explanation, resolution. **3** DEFENCE, plea, refutation, rebuttal, vindication. ▶v. **1** REPLY TO, respond to, acknowledge, react to, come back, retort, riposte, make a rejoinder, rejoin. **2** SOLVE, explain, resolve. **3** MEET, satisfy, fulfil, suit, measure up to, serve. **4** FIT, match, correspond to, be similar to, conform to, correlate to. □ **answer back** TALK BACK, argue with, be cheeky, contradict, be impertinent. **answer for 1** PAY FOR, suffer for, be punished for, make amends for, atone for. **2** VOUCH FOR, be accountable for, be responsible for, be liable for.

answerable adj. RESPONSIBLE, accountable, liable.

antagonism n. ANIMOSITY, hostility, enmity, antipathy, rancour, opposition, rivalry, friction, conflict, dissension. ■ OPPOSITES friendship.

antecedent n. **1** a thing that comes before another. **2** (**antecedents**) a person's ancestors. ▶ adj. previous.

antechamber n. an anteroom.

antedate v. precede in time.

antediluvian adj. **1** of the time before the biblical Flood. **2** very old-fashioned.

antelope n. a swift deer-like animal.

antenatal adj. before birth; of or during pregnancy.

antenna n. (pl. **antennae**) **1** an insect's feeler. **2** (pl. also **antennas**) an aerial.

anterior adj. at or nearer the front.

anteroom n. a small room leading to a main one.

anthem n. **1** a song chosen by a country to express patriotic feelings. **2** a piece of music to be sung in a religious service.

anther n. the part of a flower's stamen that contains pollen.

anthology n. (pl. **anthologies**) a collection of poems or other pieces of writing or music.

anthracite n. hard coal that burns with little flame and smoke.

anthrax n. a serious disease of sheep and cattle, which can be transmitted to humans.

anthropoid adj. to do with apes resembling humans in form, such as gorillas or chimpanzees.

anthropology n. the study of human origins, societies, and cultures. ■ **anthropological** adj. **anthropologist** n.

anthropomorphic adj. attributing human characteristics to a god or animal. ■ **anthropomorphism** n.

anti- prefix **1** opposed to. **2** preventing or relieving.

antibiotic n. a medicine that kills bacteria.

antibody n. (pl. **antibodies**) a protein produced in the blood in reaction to harmful substances.

anticipate v. **1** be aware of and prepared for a future event. **2** expect or look forward to. ■ **anticipation** n. **anticipatory** adj.

anticlimax n. a disappointing end to exciting events.

anticlockwise adv. & adj. in the opposite direction to the rotation of the hands of a clock.

antics pl. n. foolish behaviour.

anticyclone n. an area of high atmospheric pressure around which air slowly circulates.

antidote n. a medicine taken to counteract a poison.

antifreeze n. a liquid added to water to prevent it from freezing.

antigen n. a harmful substance which causes the body to produce antibodies.

anti-hero n. a central character in a story, film, etc. who is either ordinary or unpleasant.

antihistamine n. a drug used in treating allergies.

antimacassar n. a piece of cloth used to protect the back of a chair from grease and dirt.

antimony n. a silvery-white metallic element.

antipasto n. (pl. **antipasti**) an Italian hors d'oeuvre.

antipathy n. (pl. **antipathies**) strong dislike. ■ **antipathetic** adj.

antiperspirant n. a substance that prevents or reduces sweating.

antiphonal adj. sung or recited alternately between two groups.

Antipodes /an-ti-puh-deez/ pl. n. Australia and New Zealand. ■ **Antipodean** adj. & n.

antiquarian adj. to do with the collection of antiques or rare books.

antiquated adj. old-fashioned or outdated.

antique n. an old and valuable object.

Thesaurus

antagonize v. ANNOY, anger, irritate, alienate, offend, provoke, put out, upset, make an enemy of, arouse hostility in. ■ OPPOSITES pacify.

anthem n. HYMN, psalm, song of praise, chorale, chant, canticle, paean.

anthology n. COLLECTION, compilation, miscellany, selection, treasury, compendium, digest.

anticipate v. **1** EXPECT, predict, forecast, foresee, await, prepare for, reckon on, look for, look forward to. **2** PREVENT, intercept, forestall, pre-empt; informal beat to it, beat to the draw.

anticipation n. **1** EXPECTATION, prediction, preparation, contemplation. **2** EXPECTANCY, hopefulness, hope.

anticlimax n. DISAPPOINTMENT, let-down, damp squib, disillusionment, comedown, bathos.

antics pl. n. PRANKS, capers, escapades, tricks, romps, frolics, clowning, horseplay, skylarking; informal larking about.

antidote n. COUNTERMEASURE, antitoxin, neutralizing agent, cure, remedy, corrective.

antipathy n. DISLIKE, hostility, enmity, opposition, hatred, animosity, antagon-

▶ adj. valuable because of its age.

antiquity n. (pl. **antiquities**) **1** the distant past. **2** an object from the distant past.

anti-Semitism n. prejudice against Jews. ■ **anti-Semitic** adj.

antiseptic adj. preventing the growth of microorganisms that cause disease or infection. ▶n. an antiseptic substance.

antisocial adj. **1** acting in a way that is unacceptable to others. **2** avoiding the company of other people.

antithesis n. (pl. **antitheses**) a person or thing that is the direct opposite of another. ■ **antithetical** adj.

antitoxin n. a substance that neutralizes a toxin.

antler n. each of a pair of branched horns on a male deer.

antonym n. a word opposite in meaning to another.

anus /**ay**-nuhss/ n. the opening at the end of the digestive system through which solid waste leaves the body.

anvil n. an iron block on which metal is hammered and shaped.

anxiety n. (pl. **anxieties**) an anxious feeling or state.

anxious adj. **1** worried or uneasy. **2** very eager. ■ **anxiously** adv.

any adj. & pron. **1** one or some. **2** whichever or whatever one chooses. □ **anybody** anyone. **anyhow 1** anyway. **2** in a careless or disorderly way. **anyone** any person or people. **anything** a thing of any kind. **anyway 1** used to emphasize something just said or to change the subject. **2** nevertheless. **anywhere 1** in or to any place. **2** any place.

AOB abbrev. any other business.

aorta /ay-**or**-tuh/ n. the main artery carrying blood from the heart.

apace adv. literary quickly.

apart adv. **1** separated by a distance. **2** into pieces. □ **apart from** except for.

apartheid /uh-**par**-tayt/ n. the system of racial segregation formerly in force in South Africa.

apartment n. **1** a flat. **2** a set of rooms in a large house.

apathy n. lack of interest or enthusiasm. ■ **apathetic** adj.

ape n. an animal like a monkey but without a tail, e.g. a chimpanzee or gorilla. ▶v. imitate.

aperitif n. an alcoholic drink taken before a meal.

Thesaurus

ism, loathing, repugnance, animus. ■ OPPOSITES liking, affinity.

antiquated adj. OLD-FASHIONED, out of date, outmoded, old, dated, outdated, ancient, aged, archaic, antique, obsolete, antediluvian, outworn, passé, medieval, primitive, primeval, quaint; informal prehistoric, superannuated, past it.

antique adj. **1** ANTIQUARIAN, collectable, vintage, historic, traditional, veteran. **2** see ANTIQUATED. ▶n. COLLECTOR'S ITEM, heirloom, collectable, curiosity, curio, objet d'art, rarity, relic.

antiquity n. CLASSICAL TIMES, former times, bygone age, the past, days gone by, olden days.

antiseptic adj. **1** DISINFECTED, disinfectant, sterile, sterilized, sterilizing, hygienic, sanitized, germ-free, medicated, germicidal, bactericidal. **2** CLINICAL, characterless, anonymous, unexciting, undistinguished.

antisocial adj. **1** UNSOCIABLE, unfriendly, uncommunicative, reserved, withdrawn, retiring, misanthropic, alienated. **2** DISRUPTIVE, disorderly, rude, unruly, nasty, undisciplined, offensive, obnoxious, rebellious, lawless, asocial. ■ OPPOSITES sociable.

antithesis n. OPPOSITE, reverse, converse, inverse, other extreme.

anxiety n. **1** WORRY, concern, apprehension, disquiet, uneasiness, nervousness, dread, stress, tension, tenseness, strain, misgiving, foreboding, fear, uncertainty, fretfulness, agitation, distress, angst. **2** DESIRE, eagerness, longing, keenness, enthusiasm, avidity. ■ OPPOSITES serenity.

anxious adj. **1** WORRIED, concerned, apprehensive, fearful, nervous, nervy, uneasy, disturbed, afraid, perturbed, agitated, alarmed, edgy, troubled, upset, tense, distraught, fraught, overwrought, fretful; informal jittery, on edge. **2** EAGER, keen, longing, desperate, yearning, impatient, intent, avid, desirous; informal dying, itching. ■ OPPOSITES unconcerned, nonchalant.

anyhow adv. **1** IN ANY CASE, in any event, no matter what, at all events. **2** HAPHAZARDLY, carelessly, heedlessly, negligently; informal all over the place.

apathetic adj. UNINTERESTED, indifferent, unenthusiastic, unconcerned, unmotivated, impassive, half-hearted, uninvolved, unresponsive, casual, cool, dispassionate, unfeeling, unemotional, emotionless, phlegmatic, unambitious.

aperture n. an opening, esp. one letting in light.

apex n. the top or highest point.

aphasia /uh-**fay**-zi-uh/ n. inability to understand or produce speech due to brain damage.

aphid /**ay**-fid/ n. a small insect feeding on the sap of plants.

aphorism /af-uh-ri-z'm/ n. a short remark which contains a general truth.

aphrodisiac /af-ruh-**diz**-i-ak/ n. a food, drink, or drug that arouses sexual desire.

apiary n. (pl. **apiaries**) a place where bees are kept. ■ **apiarist** n.

apiece adv. for or by each one.

aplomb /uh-**plom**/ n. calm self-confidence.

apocalypse n. **1** an event involving great destruction. **2** (**the Apocalypse**) the final destruction of the world, as described in the biblical book of Revelation. ■ **apocalyptic** adj.

Apocrypha n. those books of the Old Testament not accepted as part of Hebrew scripture.

apocryphal adj. (of a story) widely circulated but unlikely to be true.

apogee /**ap**-uh-jee/ n. **1** the point in the moon's orbit furthest from the earth. **2** the highest point reached.

apologetic adj. admitting and showing regret for a wrongdoing. ■ **apologetically** adv.

apologize (or **-ise**) v. express regret for a wrongdoing.

apology n. (pl. **apologies**) **1** an expression of regret for a wrongdoing. **2** (**an apology for**) a very poor example of.

apoplectic adj. **1** informal furious. **2** dated of apoplexy.

apoplexy n. (pl. **apoplexies**) dated a stroke.

apostasy /uh-**poss**-tuh-si/ n. abandonment of a belief or principle.

apostate /**ap**-uh-stayt/ n. a person who abandons a belief or principle.

apostle n. **1** (**Apostle**) each of the twelve chief disciples of Jesus. **2** an enthusiastic supporter of an idea or cause. ■ **apostolic** adj.

apostrophe /uh-**poss**-truh-fi/ n. a punctuation mark (') used to indicate either possession or the omission of letters or numbers.

apothecary n. (pl. **apothecaries**) old use a person who prepared and sold medicines.

apotheosis /uh-po-thi-**oh**-siss/ n. (pl. **apotheoses**) **1** the highest level of something. **2** the raising of someone to the rank of a god.

appal v. (**appalling**, **appalled**) horrify.

appalling adj. very bad.

apparatus n. equipment for a particular activity or purpose.

apparel n. clothing.

apparent adj. **1** clearly seen or understood. **2** seeming real, but not necessarily so. ■ **apparently** adv.

Thesaurus

■ OPPOSITES enthusiastic.

apathy n. INDIFFERENCE, lack of interest, lack of enthusiasm, unconcern, impassivity, unresponsiveness. ■ OPPOSITES enthusiasm, passion.

aperture n. OPENING, gap, hole, crack, slit, window, orifice, fissure, breach, eye.

apex n. **1** TOP, peak, summit, tip, head, crest, crown, pinnacle, vertex. **2** HIGH POINT, height, zenith, climax, culmination, apogee, acme. ■ OPPOSITES nadir.

apocryphal adj. UNVERIFIED, unsubstantiated, debatable, questionable, dubious, spurious, mythical, fictitious, untrue, false; informal phoney. ■ OPPOSITES authentic.

apologetic adj. REGRETFUL, sorry, remorseful, contrite, repentant, penitent, conscience-stricken, ashamed, rueful. ■ OPPOSITES unrepentant, impenitent.

apologize v. SAY SORRY, make an apology, express regret, ask forgiveness,

ask for pardon, beg pardon, eat humble pie.

apology n. **1** REGRETS, expression of regret. **2** MOCKERY, travesty, caricature, substitute, poor excuse.

apostle n. EVANGELIST, missionary, spreader of the word, preacher, crusader, teacher, supporter, advocate, propagandist.

appal v. SHOCK, dismay, horrify, sicken, disgust, outrage, astound, alarm, nauseate, revolt.

appalling adj. SHOCKING, horrifying, disgusting, dreadful, awful, frightful, ghastly, dire, hideous, harrowing. See also BAD.

apparatus n. DEVICE, equipment, instrument, contraption, mechanism, appliance, machine, machinery, tackle, gadget, tool, plant; informal gear.

apparel n. CLOTHING, clothes, dress, garments, garb, attire, costume; informal gear.

apparent adj. **1** OBVIOUS, clear, plain,

apparition n. a ghost.

appeal v. **1** make a serious or earnest request. **2** be attractive or interesting. **3** refer a decision to a higher court. ▸ n. **1** an act of appealing. **2** attractiveness or interest.

appear v. **1** become visible. **2** give an impression; seem. ■ **appearance** n.

appease v. pacify someone by agreeing to their demands. ■ **appeasement** n.

appellant n. a person who appeals to a higher court.

append v. add to the end of a document.

appendage n. a thing attached to something larger or more important.

appendectomy n. (pl. **appendectomies**) the surgical removal of the appendix.

appendicitis n. inflammation of the appendix.

appendix n. (pl. **appendices** or **appendixes**) **1** a small tube of tissue attached to the large intestine. **2** a section of additional information at the end of a book.

appertain v. be relevant.

appetite n. **1** desire for food. **2** a liking or inclination.

appetizer (or **-iser**) n. something eaten or drunk to stimulate the appetite.

appetizing (or **-ising**) adj. stimulating the appetite.

applaud v. show approval, esp. by clapping. ■ **applause** n.

apple n. a round fruit with crisp flesh.

appliance n. a device designed for a specific task.

applicable adj. relevant; appropriate. ■ **applicability** n.

applicant n. a person who applies for something.

application n. **1** a formal request. **2** the act of applying something. **3** continued effort. **4** a computer program de-

Thesaurus

evident, recognizable, noticeable, perceptible, manifest, discernible, visible, unmistakable, patent, perceivable. **2** SEEMING, ostensible, superficial, outward. ■ OPPOSITES hidden.

apparition n. GHOST, phantom, spirit, presence, spectre, manifestation, vision, wraith, shade, chimera; *informal* spook; *literary* phantasm.

appeal n. **1** REQUEST, plea, call, application, entreaty, petition, prayer, solicitation, cri de cœur, supplication. **2** ATTRACTION, interest, allure, charm, temptation, fascination, seductiveness. ▸ v. **1** ASK, request, beg, plead, implore, entreat, solicit, call, petition; *literary* beseech. **2** INTEREST, tempt, fascinate, charm, engage, entice, enchant, beguile.

appear v. **1** TURN UP, come into view, come out, emerge, materialize, loom up, arrive, enter, surface, bob up; *informal* show up. **2** OCCUR, materialize, be revealed, be seen, arise, develop, originate, crop up, spring up. **3** SEEM, look, give the impression of, have the appearance of. **4** PERFORM, act, take part, play, come on. ■ OPPOSITES disappear.

appearance n. **1** COMING INTO VIEW, emergence, arrival, advent, materialization, surfacing. **2** LOOK, impression, air, manner, bearing, demeanour, aspect, expression, mien. **3** IMAGE, impression, semblance, guise, pretence. ■ OPPOSITES disappearance.

appease v. **1** PLACATE, pacify, conciliate, mollify, soothe, propitiate. **2** SATISFY, assuage, relieve, blunt, diminish, take the edge off. ■ OPPOSITES provoke.

appendage n. **1** ADDITION, attachment, addendum, adjunct, appurtenance, affix. **2** LIMB, extremity, projection, protuberance.

appendix n. SUPPLEMENT, addition, addendum, postscript, adjunct, codicil, rider, epilogue, extension.

appetite n. **1** HUNGER, taste, relish, desire, palate, stomach. **2** KEENNESS, eagerness, passion, desire, lust, hunger, thirst, yearning, longing, craving, zest, gusto, relish, zeal, hankering, yen, predilection.

appetizing adj. **1** DELICIOUS, mouthwatering, tasty, succulent, palatable; *informal* scrumptious, yummy. **2** INVITING, tempting, appealing, enticing, alluring. ■ OPPOSITES unappetizing.

applaud v. **1** CLAP, cheer, give a standing ovation to; *informal* put one's hands together for, give someone a big hand, bring the house down. **2** PRAISE, admire, express approval of, commend, compliment on, congratulate, salute, acclaim, hail, extol, take one's hat off to. ■ OPPOSITES condemn, criticize.

applause n. **1** CLAPPING, ovation, cheering, bravos, encores, curtain calls. **2** PRAISE, acclaim, admiration, approval, commendation, approbation, accolades, plaudits.

appliance n. DEVICE, gadget, instrument, apparatus, machine, mechanism, tool, implement, contraption.

applicable adj. RELEVANT, appropriate,

signed for a particular purpose.

applicator n. a device for inserting or spreading something.

applied adj. practical rather than theoretical.

appliqué /uh-**plee**-kay/ n. needlework in which fabric shapes are attached to a fabric background.

apply v. (**applying**, **applied**) **1** make a formal request for. **2** bring into operation. **3** be relevant. **4** spread on a surface. **5** (**apply oneself**) concentrate on a task.

appoint v. give a job or role to. ■ **appointee** n.

appointment n. **1** an arrangement to meet. **2** a job.

apportion v. share out.

apposite /ap-puh-zit/ adj. appropriate.

apposition n. Grammar a relationship in which a word or phrase is placed next to another so as to qualify or explain it (e.g. *my friend Sue*).

appraise v. assess the quality or value of. ■ **appraisal** n.

appreciable adj. considerable or noticeable. ■ **appreciably** adv.

appreciate v. **1** recognize the value of. **2** understand fully. **3** be grateful for. **4** rise in value. ■ **appreciation** n. **appreciative** adj.

apprehend v. **1** arrest. **2** grasp the meaning of.

apprehension n. **1** worry or anxiety. **2** understanding.

apprehensive adj. worried or anxious. ■ **apprehensively** adv.

apprentice n. a person learning a trade. ■ **apprenticeship** n.

apprise v. inform.

approach v. **1** come near to. **2** make a proposal or request to. **3** start to deal with a task. ▶n. **1** a way of dealing with something. **2** the act of approaching. **3** a way leading to a place.

approachable adj. easy to talk to.

approbation n. approval.

appropriate adj. suitable; proper. ▶v. **1** take for one's own use. **2** set aside for a special purpose. ■ **appropriately** adv. **appropriation** n.

approval n. **1** the opinion that some-

Thesaurus

pertinent, apposite, apropos. ■ OPPOSITES inapplicable.

applicant n. CANDIDATE, interviewee, competitor, claimant, enquirer, petitioner, supplicant, suitor, postulant.

apply v. **1** USE, employ, exercise, bring to bear, utilize, put into practice, bring into effect. **2** PUT ON, rub on/in, cover with, spread, smear, administer. **3** BE RELEVANT, relate, have a bearing on, be germane, appertain. **4** ENQUIRE AFTER, put in for, request, try for, seek, appeal. □ **apply oneself** MAKE AN EFFORT, be industrious, commit oneself, devote oneself, persevere, persist.

appoint v. **1** SET, fix, arrange, decide on, establish, settle on, determine, ordain, designate. **2** SELECT, name, choose, designate, settle on, plump for, elect, assign, delegate, install as, vote for, co-opt.

appointment n. **1** MEETING, engagement, date, arrangement, interview, rendezvous, assignation, fixture; *literary* tryst. **2** SELECTION, choice, naming, nomination, commissioning, election. **3** JOB, post, position, office, situation, place.

appreciable adj. CONSIDERABLE, substantial, sizeable, significant, goodly.

appreciate v. **1** BE GRATEFUL FOR, be thankful for, be appreciative of, be indebted for. **2** RATE HIGHLY, prize, value, enjoy, admire, approve of, respect,

treasure, hold in high regard, think much of, esteem. **3** RECOGNIZE, realize, acknowledge, see, know, be aware of, understand, comprehend, perceive. **4** INCREASE, rise, grow, go up, gain, mount, soar, escalate. ■ OPPOSITES disparage, ignore, depreciate.

appreciative adj. GRATEFUL, thankful, obliged, indebted, beholden. ■ OPPOSITES ungrateful.

apprehensive adj. WORRIED, uneasy, nervous, frightened, afraid, alarmed, fearful, mistrustful, troubled, concerned; *informal* on edge, jittery. ■ OPPOSITES fearless, unconcerned.

apprentice n. TRAINEE, learner, pupil, student, beginner, novice, probationer, neophyte, cub, tyro; *informal* rookie; *US informal* greenhorn.

approach v. **1** REACH, come/draw near, come/draw close, near, move/advance towards, bear down on. **2** APPEAL TO, make overtures to, proposition, solicit, sound out. **3** SET ABOUT, tackle, begin, start, make a start on, embark on, commence, undertake. **4** COME NEAR/CLOSE TO, compare with, be comparable with, approximate to. ▶n. **1** METHOD, procedure, way, style, attitude, manner, technique, means, mode, modus operandi. **2** APPEAL, application, proposal, overture, proposition. **3** COMING NEAR, advance, arrival, advent. **4** DRIVE, drive-

a

thing is good. **2** official acceptance.

approve v. **1** regard as good or acceptable. **2** officially accept as satisfactory.

approximate adj. almost but not completely accurate. ▶ v. be very similar to.
■ **approximately** adv. **approximation** n.

APR abbrev. annual percentage rate.

après-ski n. social activities following a day's skiing.

apricot n. an orange-yellow fruit like a small peach.

April n. the fourth month.

a priori adj. & adv. based on theoretical reasoning rather than actual observation.

apron n. **1** a garment worn to protect the front of one's clothes. **2** an area on an airfield for manoeuvring or parking aircraft. **3** a strip of stage extending in front of the curtain.

apropos /a-pruh-**poh**/ prep. (**apropos of**) with reference to.

apse n. a recess with a domed or arched roof at the end of a church.

apt adj. **1** appropriate. **2** (**apt to**) tending to. ■ **aptly** adv.

aptitude n. a natural ability.

aqualung n. a portable breathing apparatus for divers.

aquamarine n. a bluish-green precious stone.

aquaplane v. (of a vehicle) slide uncontrollably on a wet surface.

aquarium n. (pl. **aquaria** or **aquariums**) a water-filled glass tank for keeping fish in.

aquatic adj. taking place or living on or in water.

aqua vitae /akwuh **vee**-ty/ n. brandy.

aqueduct n. a structure carrying water across country.

aqueous /ay-kwee-uhss/ adj. of or containing water.

aquifer n. a body of rock that holds water or through which water flows.

aquiline adj. **1** (of a nose) curved like an eagle's beak. **2** like an eagle.

Arab n. a member of a Semitic people of the Middle East and North Africa.
■ **Arabian** n. & adj.

arabesque n. **1** a ballet posture in which one leg is extended backwards and the arms are outstretched. **2** an ornamental design of intertwined lines.

Arabic n. the language of the Arabs.
▶ adj. of the Arabs. □ **Arabic numerals** the numerals 1, 2, 3, 4, etc.

arable adj. (of land) suitable for growing crops.

arachnid n. a creature of a class including spiders, scorpions, mites, and ticks.

arbiter n. **1** a person who settles a dispute. **2** a person who has influence in a certain area.

Thesaurus

way, avenue, access road.

approachable adj. FRIENDLY, open, affable, relaxed, accessible, sympathetic, well disposed. ■ OPPOSITES aloof.

appropriate adj. SUITABLE, fitting, right, apt, timely, applicable, seemly, proper, becoming, correct, well judged, relevant, germane, well suited, pertinent, apposite, opportune, apropos. ▶ v. **1** TAKE OVER, take possession of, seize, confiscate, requisition, commandeer, annex, expropriate, arrogate. **2** STEAL, embezzle, misappropriate, pilfer, purloin, pocket; informal filch, swipe, nick, pinch.

approval n. **1** ADMIRATION, acceptance, praise, liking, support, favour, appreciation, respect, esteem, commendation, approbation. **2** ACCEPTANCE, agreement, endorsement, authorization, confirmation, assent, consent, ratification, sanction, blessing, permission, mandate, concurrence, acquiescence, licence, seal, validation, imprimatur; informal OK, thumbs up, go-ahead, green light. ■ OPPOSITES disapproval, rejec-

tion, refusal.

approve v. **1** BE PLEASED WITH, think well of, like, look on with favour, give one's blessing to, hold in regard/esteem, admire, respect, praise. **2** AGREE TO, accept, consent to, permit, pass, allow, sanction, authorize, bless, support, back, uphold, endorse, ratify, validate, accede to, countenance; informal go along with, rubber-stamp. ■ OPPOSITES disapprove, condemn, refuse, veto.

approximate adj. ROUGH, estimated, near, close, inexact, imprecise, loose.
■ OPPOSITES exact. □ **approximate to** BE CLOSE/NEAR TO, come near to, approach, border on, verge on, resemble, be similar to, roughly equal.

approximately adv. ROUGHLY, about, round about, around, just about, circa, more or less, nearly, close to, near to, in the region/neighbourhood of, approaching, almost, not far off. ■ OPPOSITES precisely.

apt adj. **1** SUITABLE, appropriate, fitting, applicable, apposite, felicitous. **2** LIKELY, inclined, prone, liable, given, disposed.

arbitrary adj. based on random choice. ■ **arbitrarily** adv.

arbitrate v. act as an arbitrator. ■ **arbitration** n.

arbitrator n. a person or body chosen to settle a dispute.

arboreal adj. of or living in trees.

arboretum n. (pl. **arboretums** or **arboreta**) a place where trees are grown for study and display.

arbour (US **arbor**) n. a shady place in a garden, with a canopy of trees or climbing plants.

arc n. **1** a curve forming part of the circumference of a circle. **2** a curving passage through the air. **3** a glowing electrical discharge between two points.

arcade n. **1** a covered passage with arches along one or both sides. **2** a covered walk with shops along the sides.

arcane adj. secret and mysterious.

arch n. **1** a curved structure supporting a bridge, roof, or wall. **2** the inner side of the foot. ▶v. form an arch. ▶adj. affectedly playful or teasing. ▢ **archway** an entrance or passageway under an arch.

arch- comb. form chief, principal, or main.

archaeology (US **archeology**) n. the study of ancient history by examining objects dug up from the ground. ■ **archaeological** adj. **archaeologist** n.

archaic adj. belonging to former or ancient times.

archaism n. an old or old-fashioned word or phrase.

archangel n. an angel of high rank.

archbishop n. a bishop of the highest rank.

archdeacon n. a senior Christian priest.

archer n. a person who shoots with a bow and arrows. ■ **archery** n.

archetype /ar-ki-typ/ n. **1** a typical example. **2** an original model. ■ **archetypal** adj.

archipelago /ar-ki-pel-uh-goh/ n. (pl. **archipelagos** or **archipelagoes**) a group of many islands.

architect n. a person who designs buildings.

architecture n. **1** the design and construction of buildings. **2** the style of a building. ■ **architectural** adj.

architrave n. the frame round a doorway or window.

archive /ar-kyv/ n. a collection of historical documents.

archivist /ar-ki-vist/ n. a person in charge of archives.

Arctic adj. of the regions around the North Pole.

✓ Remember the *c*: Arctic.

ardent adj. enthusiastic or passionate. ■ **ardently** adv.

ardour (US **ardor**) n. enthusiasm or passion.

arduous adj. difficult and tiring.

Thesaurus

■ OPPOSITES inappropriate, unlikely.

aptitude n. TALENT, ability, gift, skill, flair, knack, bent, capability, capacity, faculty.

arbiter n. JUDGE, authority, determiner, controller, director, governor, expert, master, pundit.

arbitrary adj. **1** CAPRICIOUS, unreasonable, whimsical, irrational, illogical, personal, subjective, random, chance, erratic, wilful, unreasoned, inconsistent, unpredictable, unplanned, unjustified. **2** DICTATORIAL, despotic, autocratic, absolute, tyrannical, imperious, domineering, high-handed. ■ OPPOSITES rational, reasoned.

arbitrate v. ADJUDICATE, judge, referee, sit in judgement, mediate, umpire, settle, decide, determine, decide the outcome of.

arbitration n. ADJUDICATION, judgement, settlement, decision, determination, mediation, negotiation, good offices.

arbitrator n. ADJUDICATOR, judge, referee, umpire, arbiter, ombudsman, mediator, negotiator, intermediary, go-between, peacemaker.

arc n. CURVE, bend, bow, crescent, semicircle, half-moon, arch, curvature.

arch¹ n. ARCHWAY, vault, span, bridge. ▶v. CURVE, bend, bow, arc.

arch² adj. PLAYFUL, mischievous, roguish, artful, sly, sliding.

archetype n. PROTOTYPE, example, pattern, model, original, standard, ideal, paradigm, precursor.

architect n. **1** DESIGNER, planner, building consultant, draughtsman. **2** CREATOR, author, engineer, originator, planner, deviser, instigator, founder, prime mover.

ardent adj. PASSIONATE, fervent, impassioned, eager, enthusiastic, intense, keen, zealous, vehement, fierce.

are see BE.

area n. **1** a part of a place, object, or surface. **2** the extent or measurement of a surface. **3** a subject.

arena n. **1** a level area surrounded by seating, for sports and other events. **2** an area of activity.

aren't contr. are not.

arête /uh-ret/ n. a sharp mountain ridge.

argon n. an inert gaseous element.

argot /ar-goh/ n. jargon or slang.

arguable adj. able to be argued or disagreed with. ∎ **arguably** adv.

argue v. **1** exchange conflicting views heatedly. **2** give reasons for an opinion.

argument n. **1** a heated exchange of conflicting views. **2** a set of reasons given in support of an opinion.

argumentative adj. apt to argue.

aria n. a solo in an opera.

arid adj. dry; parched. ∎ **aridity** n.

arise v. (**arising**, **arose**; past part. **arisen**) **1** start to exist or be noticed. **2** occur as a result of. **3** get up.

aristocracy n. (pl. **aristocracies**) the highest social class, consisting of people with hereditary titles. ∎ **aristo-**

crat n. **aristocratic** adj.

arithmetic n. the use of numbers in calculation. ∎ **arithmetical** adj.

ark n. **1** (in the Bible) the ship built by Noah to escape the Flood. **2** a chest housing the holy scrolls in a synagogue. **3** (**Ark of the Covenant**) the chest which contained the laws of the ancient Israelites.

arm n. **1** each of the two upper limbs of the body. **2** a side part of a chair. **3** a branch or division of an organization. **4** (**arms**) weapons. ▸ v. **1** supply with weapons. **2** make a bomb ready to explode. □ **armchair** an upholstered chair with side supports for a person's arms. **armpit** the hollow under the arm at the shoulder.

armada n. a fleet of warships.

armadillo n. (pl. **armadillos**) a mammal of South America, with a body covered in bony plates.

Armageddon n. **1** (in the Bible) the last battle between good and evil before the Day of Judgement. **2** a catastrophic conflict.

armament n. military weapons.

armature n. the rotating coil of a

Thesaurus

∎ OPPOSITES apathetic.

arduous adj. HARD, difficult, demanding, exhausting, laborious, strenuous, tiring, gruelling, punishing, tough, onerous, heavy, rigorous, back-breaking, taxing, Herculean. ∎ OPPOSITES easy, effortless.

area n. **1** REGION, district, environment, vicinity, locality, zone, territory, neighbourhood, environs, terrain, sector, quarter, province, precinct, realm, domain. **2** FIELD, subject, sphere, discipline, sector, realm. **3** SIZE, extent, expanse, measurement, dimensions, space, compass, range, square footage, acreage.

argue v. **1** CLAIM, maintain, hold, reason, insist, contend, declare, assert, demonstrate, make a case, plead, suggest. **2** QUARREL, differ, disagree, fall out, have an argument, bicker, have words, bandy words, fight, squabble, debate, dispute, answer back, object, take exception, wrangle, feud, remonstrate; informal row. **3** DISPUTE, debate, discuss.

argument n. **1** DISAGREEMENT, quarrel, fight, squabble, dispute, difference of opinion, falling-out, altercation, wrangle, conflict, clash, feud, controversy, remonstration; informal row, tiff, set-to, dust-up. **2** CASE, reasoning, reasons,

line of reasoning, grounds, logic, evidence, polemic, argumentation. **3** SUBJECT MATTER, theme, topic, gist, outline, storyline, summary, synopsis, abstract, precis.

argumentative adj. QUARRELSOME, contentious, combative, belligerent, disputatious, litigious.

arid adj. **1** DRY, dried up, waterless, parched, moistureless, scorched, desiccated, barren, infertile, desert, lifeless, sterile. **2** DULL, tedious, dreary, dry, boring, uninteresting, monotonous, flat, vapid, lifeless. ∎ OPPOSITES wet, fertile, interesting.

arise v. **1** COME TO LIGHT, turn/crop up, emerge, occur, begin, come into being. See also APPEAR. **2** RESULT, be caused, originate, follow, proceed, emanate, ensue.

aristocracy n. NOBILITY, peerage, upper class, gentry, high society, elite, ruling class, patriciate; informal upper crust.

aristocratic adj. **1** NOBLE, titled, highborn, blue-blooded, upper-class, patrician. **2** WELL BRED, dignified, refined, courtly, elegant, gracious, haughty, proud.

arm[1] n. **1** INLET, creek, cove, fjord, bay, estuary, firth, sound. **2** BRANCH, department, section, wing, division, sector, dynamo or electric motor.

armistice n. a truce.

armorial adj. of coats of arms.

armour (US **armor**) n. **1** metal coverings formerly worn to protect the body in battle. **2** the tough metal layer covering a military vehicle or ship. ■ **armoured** adj.

armoury (US **armory**) n. (pl. **armouries**) a store or supply of weapons.

army n. (pl. **armies**) **1** an organized military force for fighting on land. **2** a large number.

arnica n. a plant substance used to treat bruises.

aroma n. a pleasant smell. ■ **aromatic** adj.

aromatherapy n. the use of aromatic oils for healing. ■ **aromatherapist** n.

arose past of ARISE.

around adv. & prep. **1** on every side. **2** in or to many places throughout an area. ▶ adv. **1** so as to face in the opposite direction. **2** approximately.

arouse v. **1** bring about a feeling or response. **2** excite sexually. **3** awaken.

arpeggio /ar-pej-ji-oh/ n. (pl. **arpeggios**) the notes of a musical chord played in succession.

arraign /uh-rayn/ v. call before a court to answer a criminal charge. ■ **arraignment** n.

arrange v. **1** put into order. **2** organize. **3** adapt a piece of music. ■ **arrangement** n.

arrant adj. utter; complete.

array n. **1** a display or wide range. **2** an arrangement. **3** literary elaborate clothing. ▶ v. (**be arrayed**) **1** be arranged. **2** be clothed.

arrears pl. n. money owed that should already have been paid.

arrest v. **1** seize and take into custody. **2** stop or delay. **3** (**arresting**) attracting attention. ▶ n. the act of arresting someone.

arrival n. **1** the process of arriving. **2** a person or thing that has arrived.

arrive v. **1** reach a destination. **2** (of a moment) come about. **3** informal become successful.

arrogant adj. exaggerating one's import-

Thesaurus

offshoot, extension.

arm² v. EQUIP, supply, provide, furnish, issue.

armaments pl. n. WEAPONS, guns, arms, firearms, weaponry, munitions, ordnance.

armistice n. CEASEFIRE, truce, peace, treaty, agreement, suspension of hostilities.

armoury n. ARSENAL, arms depot, ammunition dump, magazine, ordnance depot.

army n. **1** ARMED FORCE, troops, soldiers, infantry, land force, soldiery. **2** CROWD, horde, throng, swarm, pack, host, multitude, mob.

aroma n. SMELL, scent, odour, fragrance, perfume, bouquet, savour; literary redolence.

arouse v. **1** INDUCE, prompt, trigger, kindle, provoke, engender, stir up, spark off. **2** WAKE, wake up, awaken, rouse. ■ OPPOSITES allay.

arrange v. **1** PUT IN ORDER, set out, sort, lay out, organize, position, group, sift, align, tidy, file, rank, classify, categorize, array, systematize. **2** FIX, settle on, set up, agree, determine, plan, organize, schedule, bring about, coordinate, make preparations for. **3** SCORE, adapt, set, orchestrate, harmonize. ■ OPPOSITES disturb, cancel.

arrangement n. **1** ORDER, ordering, organization, positioning, grouping, distribution, disposition, system, alignment, filing, marshalling, ranging, spacing, tabulation. **2** AGREEMENT, plan, deal, contract, compact, bargain, pact, understanding, settlement, terms, preparations, provisions. **3** SCORE, orchestration, adaptation, instrumentation, setting, harmonization.

array n. **1** ARRANGEMENT, collection, line-up, formation, presentation, display, exhibition, show, parade, assemblage, muster. **2** DRESS, attire, clothing, garments, garb, finery, apparel. ▶ v. **1** see ARRANGE. **2** CLOTHE, dress, fit out, adorn, garb, rig out, deck, robe, accoutre.

arrest v. **1** TAKE INTO CUSTODY, apprehend, take prisoner, capture, detain, seize, catch, lay hold of; informal pick up, nick, pinch, collar, haul in, nab, bust, run in. **2** STOP, halt, block, end, prevent, obstruct, hinder, impede, interrupt, delay, slow down, bring to a standstill, check, restrain, stem, retard, nip in the bud. ▶ n. APPREHENSION, capture, detention, seizure, taking into custody. ■ OPPOSITES release.

arresting adj. STRIKING, remarkable, extraordinary, impressive, outstanding, unusual, stunning, conspicuous, noticeable. ■ OPPOSITES inconspicuous.

arrival n. **1** COMING, appearance, approach, advent, entrance, entry, occurance or abilities. ■ **arrogance** n. **arrogantly** adv.

arrogate v. take or claim for oneself without justification.

arrow n. **1** a stick with a sharp pointed head, shot from a bow. **2** a sign shaped like this, showing direction.

arrowroot n. a type of edible starch obtained from a plant.

arsenal n. a store of weapons and ammunition.

arsenic n. a brittle grey element with many highly poisonous compounds.

arson n. the criminal act of deliberately setting fire to property. ■ **arsonist** n.

art n. **1** the expression of creative skill in a visual form. **2** paintings, drawings, and sculpture. **3** (**the arts**) creative activities such as painting, music, and drama. **4** a skill. □ **artwork** illustrations to be included in a publication.

artefact (US **artifact**) n. a man-made object.

arteriosclerosis /ar-teer-i-oh-skluh-roh-siss/ n. thickening of the walls of the arteries.

artery n. (pl. **arteries**) **1** any of the tubes carrying blood from the heart around the body. **2** an important transport route. ■ **arterial** adj.

artesian well n. a well bored vertically so that water comes to the surface through natural pressure.

artful adj. crafty. ■ **artfully** adv.

arthritis n. painful inflammation and

stiffness of the joints. ■ **arthritic** adj. & n.

arthropod n. an animal with a segmented body, such as an insect, spider, or crab.

artichoke n. a vegetable consisting of the unopened flower head of a thistle-like plant.

article n. **1** a particular object. **2** a piece of writing in a newspaper or magazine. **3** a clause in a legal document.

articulate adj. fluent and clear in speech. ▶ v. **1** speak or express distinctly or clearly. **2** (**articulated**) having sections connected by a flexible joint or joints. ■ **articulately** adv. **articulation** n.

artifact US = ARTEFACT.

artifice n. clever devices or tricks, esp. as used to deceive.

artificial adj. **1** made as a copy of something natural. **2** not sincere. □ **artificial insemination** the insertion of semen through a syringe into the vagina or womb. **artificial intelligence** the performance by computers of tasks normally requiring human intelligence. ■ **artificiality** n. **artificially** adv.

artillery n. **1** large guns used in warfare on land. **2** a branch of an army using these.

artisan n. a skilled worker who makes things by hand.

artist n. **1** a person who paints or draws. **2** a person who performs any of the

Thesaurus

rence. **2** VISITOR, incomer, guest, immigrant, newcomer, caller. ■ OPPOSITES departure, leaver.

arrive v. **1** COME, appear, enter, get here/there, turn up, get in, put in/make an appearance, drop by/in; *informal* show up, roll in/up, blow in. **2** *see* SUCCEED. ■ OPPOSITES leave, depart.

arrogant adj. HAUGHTY, proud, conceited, self-important, pompous, overbearing, patronizing, superior, high-handed, egotistical, condescending, snobbish, disdainful, imperious, lordly, swaggering, presumptuous, cocky, boastful, supercilious, overweening, blustering, insolent; *informal* stuck up, high and mighty, snooty, uppity. ■ OPPOSITES modest, diffident.

art n. **1** PAINTING, drawing, fine art, design, visual art. **2** SKILL, craft, talent, flair, aptitude, gift, knack, facility, technique, proficiency, expertise, ingenuity, skilfulness, mastery, dexterity, virtuosity, adroitness.

artful adj. CUNNING, sly, wily, clever, shrewd, canny, crafty, devious, tricky, subtle, ingenious, astute, scheming, designing; *informal* smart, foxy, fly. ■ OPPOSITES ingenuous.

article n. **1** THING, object, item, commodity. **2** STORY, piece, item, account, report, feature, column.

articulate adj. FLUENT, eloquent, lucid, expressive, clear, comprehensible, coherent, intelligible, understandable, glib, silver-tongued. ▶ v. ENUNCIATE, say, utter, express, pronounce, vocalize, voice.

articulated adj. HINGED, jointed, segmented, flexible, bendy.

artifice n. TRICKERY, cunning, deceit, deception, craftiness, artfulness, slyness, duplicity, guile, chicanery.

artificial adj. **1** MANUFACTURED, man-made, fabricated, synthetic, imitation, simulated, ersatz. **2** FALSE, affected, fake, unnatural, insincere, forced, sham, contrived, pretended, assumed, creative arts. ■ **artistry** n.

artiste /ar-**teest**/ n. a professional singer or dancer.

artistic adj. **1** having creative skill. **2** to do with art or artists. ■ **artistically** adv.

artless adj. sincere and straightforward. ■ **artlessly** adv.

arty adj. (**artier**, **artiest**) informal interested in the arts, esp. in a pretentious way.

as adv. used in comparisons to refer to extent or amount. ▶ conj. **1** while. **2** in the way that. **3** because. **4** even though. ▶ prep. **1** in the role of. **2** while; when.

asafoetida /ah-suh-**fee**-ti-duh/ n. a strong-smelling resin used in Indian cookery.

asap abbrev. as soon as possible.

asbestos n. a fibrous mineral used in fire-resistant materials.

asbestosis n. a lung disease caused by inhaling asbestos particles.

ascend v. go up; climb or rise.

ascendant adj. rising in power or status. ■ **ascendancy** n.

ascension n. **1** the act of ascending in status. **2** (**the Ascension**) the ascent of Jesus into heaven.

ascent n. **1** an act of ascending. **2** an upward slope.

ascertain v. find out. ■ **ascertainable** adj.

ascetic /uh-**set**-ik/ adj. choosing to live without pleasures or luxuries. ▶ n. an ascetic person. ■ **asceticism** n.

ASCII abbrev. Computing American Standard Code for Information Interchange, a code assigning a different number to each letter and character.

ascorbic acid n. vitamin C.

ascribe v. (**ascribe to**) attribute to. ■ **ascription** n.

aseptic adj. free from harmful bacteria.

asexual adj. without sex or sexual organs. ■ **asexually** adv.

ash n. **1** the powder remaining after something has been burned. **2** a tree with a silver-grey bark.

ashamed adj. feeling shame.

ashen adj. very pale, esp. from shock.

ashlar n. masonry made of large square-cut stones.

ashore adv. to or on the shore.

ashram n. a Hindu religious retreat or community.

Asian adj. of Asia or its people. ▶ n. an Asian person.

Asiatic adj. of Asia.

aside adv. to one side. ▶ n. a remark made so that only certain people will hear.

asinine adj. very silly.

ask v. **1** try to obtain an answer or information from someone. **2** make a request. **3** invite someone.

Thesaurus

put on, mock, unreal, feigned, bogus, pseudo, laboured, hollow, spurious, meretricious; informal phoney. ■ OPPOSITES natural, genuine.

artist n. **1** PAINTER, drawer, sculptor, old master. **2** CRAFTSMAN, craftswoman, expert, master, past master, genius, adept. **3** see PERFORMER.

artistic adj. **1** CREATIVE, imaginative, talented, gifted, accomplished, sensitive, cultured, cultivated. **2** ATTRACTIVE, tasteful, decorative, beautiful, stylish, elegant, graceful, aesthetic, ornamental, exquisite. ■ OPPOSITES ugly.

artistry n. SKILL, art, talent, ability, flair, gift, expertise, creativity, proficiency, craftsmanship, workmanship, brilliance.

ascend v. CLIMB, go/move up, rise, mount, soar, take off, lift off, fly up, levitate, scale. ■ OPPOSITES descend.

ascendancy n. DOMINATION, dominance, control, authority, power, rule, command, supremacy, sway, mastery, sovereignty, the upper hand.

ascent n. CLIMB, rise, hill, slope, incline,

ascension, gradient, ramp. ■ OPPOSITES descent.

ascertain v. FIND OUT, establish, discover, learn, determine, decide, identify, confirm, make certain, get to know, verify, make sure/certain, settle, pin down.

ascribe v. ATTRIBUTE, put down, assign, impute, credit, accredit, chalk up, lay on, blame, charge with.

ashamed adj. **1** EMBARRASSED, shamefaced, sorry, apologetic, sheepish, red-faced, blushing, humiliated, conscience-stricken, remorseful, mortified, crestfallen, discomfited, bashful, contrite, penitent, repentant, rueful, chagrined; informal with one's tail between one's legs. **2** RELUCTANT, loath, unwilling, indisposed. ■ OPPOSITES proud, shameless.

asinine adj. IDIOTIC, stupid, foolish, nonsensical, ridiculous, half-witted, imbecilic, fatuous, moronic; informal batty, nutty, dumb, gormless, daft. ■ OPPOSITES intelligent, sensible.

ask v. **1** QUESTION, inquire, query, quiz,

a

askance adv. with a suspicious or disapproving look.

askew adv. & adj. not straight or level.

asleep adj. & adv. in or into a state of sleep.

asp n. a small poisonous snake.

asparagus n. a vegetable consisting of the shoots of a tall plant.

aspect n. **1** a part or feature of a matter. **2** an appearance or quality. **3** the direction in which a building faces.

aspen n. a poplar tree.

asperity n. harshness of manner.

aspersions pl. n. critical remarks.

asphalt n. a tar-like substance used in surfacing roads or roofs.

asphyxia n. suffocation.

asphyxiate v. suffocate. ■ **asphyxiation** n.

aspic n. a savoury jelly made with meat stock.

aspidistra n. a plant with broad tapering leaves.

aspirant n. a person with ambitions to do or be something.

aspirate v. pronounce with an *h*.

aspiration n. a hope or ambition.

aspire v. have ambitions.

aspirin n. a medicine that relieves pain and reduces fever.

ass n. **1** a donkey. **2** informal a stupid person.

assail v. attack violently.

assailant n. an attacker.

assassin n. a person who assassinates someone.

assassinate v. murder a political or religious leader. ■ **assassination** n.

assault n. & v. (make) a violent attack.

assay n. a test of metal for quality. ▶ v. make an assay of.

assemblage n. **1** a collection or gathering. **2** something made of pieces fitted together.

assemble v. **1** come or bring together. **2** fit together the parts of.

assembly n. (pl. **assemblies**) **1** a group of people gathered together. **2** a body of people with law-making powers. **3** the assembling of parts.

assent n. agreement. ▶ v. agree.

assert v. **1** state confidently. **2** (**assert**

Thesaurus

....

put a question to, interrogate, cross-examine, give the third degree to; *informal* grill, pump. **2** REQUEST, demand, appeal, to apply to, to beg, solicit, implore, plead, seek, supplicate; *literary* beseech. **3** INVITE, summon, bid. ■ OPPOSITES answer.

asleep adj. **1** SLEEPING, fast/sound asleep, in a deep sleep, dozing, resting, slumbering, snoozing, napping, catnapping, reposing, comatose, unconscious, sedated, dormant; *informal* out like a light, dead to the world, kipping; *humorous* in the land of Nod. **2** NUMB, without feeling, deadened. ■ OPPOSITES awake.

aspect n. **1** FEATURE, viewpoint, facet, side, circumstance, angle, characteristic, element, light, standpoint, slant, attribute. **2** APPEARANCE, look, expression, features, air, manner, demeanour, bearing, countenance, mien, visage. **3** DIRECTION, outlook, prospect, orientation, view, exposure, situation, location, position.

asphyxiate v. SUFFOCATE, choke, smother, stifle, strangle, strangulate, throttle.

aspiration n. AIM, desire, objective, ambition, goal, wish, hope, dream, longing, yearning, craving, eagerness, enthusiasm.

aspire v. DESIRE, hope to/for, long for/to, wish to/for, dream of, yearn for/to,

seek, pursue, crave, hunger for.

aspiring adj. WOULD-BE, potential, hopeful, expectant, ambitious, optimistic, wishful, striving.

assail v. ATTACK, assault, set on/upon, fall on, rush, storm; *informal* lay into, tear into, pitch into.

assassin n. MURDERER, killer, executioner, contract killer, liquidator; *informal* hit man; *literary* slayer.

assassinate v. MURDER, kill, execute, eliminate, liquidate; *informal* hit; *literary* slay.

assault v. **1** ATTACK, charge, storm, rush at, set about/on, strike at. **2** STRIKE, hit, attack, beat up, aim blows at; *informal* lay into, pitch into, wade into, do over. **3** MOLEST, rape, sexually assault, interfere with.

assemble v. **1** COME TOGETHER, collect, gather, congregate, meet, convene, join up, flock together, converge, rally round, throng around. **2** BRING/PUT TOGETHER, collect, gather, round up, summon, muster, convoke, mobilize, marshal, rally, amass. **3** CONSTRUCT, build, erect, put together, set up, piece together, fit together, fabricate, manufacture, connect, join. ■ OPPOSITES disperse, dismantle.

assembly n. GATHERING, meeting, crowd, group, congregation, throng, rally, convention, conference, congress, conclave,

oneself) be confident and forceful. **3** exercise one's rights. ■ **assertion** n. **assertive** adj.

assess v. evaluate the value, importance, or quality of. ■ **assessment** n. **assessor** n.

asset n. **1** a useful or valuable thing or person. **2** (**assets**) property owned by a person or company.

assiduous adj. showing great care and thoroughness. ■ **assiduity** n. **assiduously** adv.

assign v. **1** give a task or duty to someone. **2** regard as being caused by.

assignation n. a secret arrangement to meet.

assignment n. a task assigned to some-

one.

assimilate v. **1** take in and understand information. **2** absorb into a larger group. ■ **assimilation** n.

assist v. help. ■ **assistance** n.

assistant n. a person employed to help someone more senior.

assizes n. hist. a county court.

associate v. **1** connect in one's mind. **2** frequently meet or have dealings with. **3** (**associate oneself with**) involved with. ▶n. a work partner or colleague.

association n. **1** a group of people organized for a joint purpose. **2** a connection or link.

assonance n. the rhyming of vowel

Thesaurus

synod; *informal* get-together. *See also* CROWD.

assent n. AGREEMENT, consent, acceptance, approval, permission, sanction, acquiescence, compliance, accord, accordance, approbation. ▶v. AGREE, accept, consent, be willing, comply, approve, acquiesce, concede, concur, give one's permission, submit, yield, accede. ■ OPPOSITES refuse.

assert v. **1** DECLARE, state, maintain, proclaim, pronounce, emphasize, insist on, profess, claim, swear to, stress, affirm, avow, aver. **2** UPHOLD, insist on, stand up for, defend, press/push for, vindicate. □ **assert oneself** BEHAVE CONFIDENTLY, make one's presence felt, stand up for oneself, exert one's influence.

assertive adj. CONFIDENT, self-assured, assured, forceful, pushy, strong-willed, positive, authoritative, dominant, domineering, strong, aggressive, decisive, firm, definite, emphatic, uncompromising, stubborn, opinionated; *informal* bossy.

assess v. JUDGE, evaluate, estimate, gauge, appraise, weigh up, rate, determine, reckon, work out, assay, compute, calculate, fix; *informal* size up.

asset n. ADVANTAGE, benefit, strength, strong point, help, aid, resource, support, blessing, boon, godsend. □ **assets** WEALTH, money, resources, capital, means, property, possessions, belongings, holdings, goods, valuables, reserves, securities, estate, effects; *Law* chattels.

assiduous adj. DILIGENT, industrious, hard-working, persistent, indefatigable, zealous, persevering, sedulous.

assign v. **1** ALLOCATE, allot, distribute, share out, give out, dispense, apportion,

consign. **2** APPOINT, select for, nominate, designate, name, install, delegate, commission. **3** ASCRIBE, put down, attribute, accredit, credit, chalk up. **4** TRANSFER, make over, convey.

assignation n. RENDEZVOUS, date, meeting, appointment; *literary* tryst.

assignment n. **1** TASK, job, duty, mission, responsibility, obligation, charge, commission. **2** ALLOCATION, distribution, allotment, apportionment, dispensation, consignment. **3** TRANSFER, making over, handing down, consignment.

assimilate v. **1** ABSORB, take in, incorporate, ingest, digest. **2** ADAPT, adjust, accustom, become like, acclimatize, blend in, homogenize.

assist v. **1** HELP, help out, aid, support, lend a hand, rally round, cooperate with, collaborate with, work with, play a part, abet, succour. **2** FACILITATE, make easier, boost, further, promote, expedite. ■ OPPOSITES impede, hinder.

assistance n. HELP, aid, support, cooperation, collaboration, succour, a (helping) hand, encouragement, patronage, sponsorship, subsidy, contribution. ■ OPPOSITES hindrance, impedance.

assistant n. **1** DEPUTY, subordinate, second-in-command, auxiliary, righthand man/woman, man/girl Friday, henchman, minion. **2** HELPER, collaborator, associate, partner, colleague, mainstay, accessory, abetter. **3** SHOP/ SALES ASSISTANT, salesperson, salesman, saleswoman, checkout operator, server; *US* clerk.

associate v. **1** LINK, connect, identify, equate, bracket, relate. **2** MIX, socialize, keep company, mingle, fraternize; *informal* hobnob, run/go around, hang out. **3** AFFILIATE, connect, combine, join, sounds.

assorted adj. of various sorts.

assortment n. a varied collection.

assuage /uh-**swayj**/ v. **1** soothe. **2** satisfy a desire.

assume v. **1** accept as true without proof. **2** take responsibility or control. **3** begin to have.

assumption n. a thing assumed to be true.

assurance n. **1** an assertion or promise. **2** self-confidence. **3** life insurance.

assure v. tell confidently; promise.

assured adj. **1** confident. **2** certain; guaranteed. ■ **assuredly** adv.

astatine /**ass**-tuh-teen/ n. an unstable radioactive chemical element.

asterisk n. a symbol (*) used as a pointer to a note.

....

☑ Remember: aster**isk**, not -*ix*.

....

astern adv. behind or towards the rear of a ship or aircraft.

asteroid n. a small rocky planet orbiting the sun.

asthma /**ass**-muh/ n. a medical condition causing difficulty in breathing. ■ **asthmatic** adj. & n.

astigmatism n. a defect in the eye preventing proper focusing. ■ **astigmatic** adj.

astonish v. surprise greatly. ■ **astonishment** n.

astound v. shock or greatly surprise.

astral adj. of the stars.

astray adv. away from the correct course.

astride prep. & adv. with a leg on each side of.

astringent adj. **1** causing body tissue to contract. **2** sharp or severe. ▶ n. an astringent lotion. ■ **astringency** n.

astrology n. the study of the supposed influence of stars and planets on human affairs. ■ **astrologer** n. **astrological** adj.

astronaut n. a person trained to travel in a spacecraft.

astronautics n. the science and technology of space travel.

astronomical adj. **1** of astronomy. **2** informal very large. ■ **astronomically** adv.

astronomy n. the science of stars, planets, and the universe. ■ **astronomer** n.

astrophysics n. the study of the physical nature of stars and planets. ■ **astrophysicist** n.

astute adj. shrewd. ■ **astutely** adv.

asunder adv. literary apart.

Thesaurus

....

attach, band together, team up, ally, incorporate, syndicate. ■ OPPOSITES dissociate.

association n. FEDERATION, affiliation, alliance, partnership, union, confederation, syndicate, coalition, combination, league, fellowship, merger, cartel, consortium, club.

assorted adj. MIXED, varied, various, diverse, miscellaneous, sundry, multifarious, manifold, motley, heterogeneous, variegated; *literary* divers.

assortment n. MIXTURE, collection, range, selection, variety, jumble, miscellany, medley, diversity, melange, farrago, pot-pourri, mishmash, hotchpotch.

assume v. **1** SUPPOSE, presume, think, presuppose, take for granted, believe, suspect, understand, expect, imagine, guess, gather, surmise, fancy. **2** TAKE ON, adopt, take up, acquire, put on, affect, come to have, don. **3** UNDERTAKE, accept, take upon oneself, shoulder, embark on, enter upon. **4** SEIZE, take over, appropriate, commandeer, pre-empt, usurp.

assumption n. SUPPOSITION, presumption, belief, hypothesis, presupposition, theory, suspicion, guess, expectation, conjecture, surmise, premise.

assurance n. **1** SELF-CONFIDENCE, confidence, self-assurance, poise, nerve. **2** GUARANTEE, commitment, word, promise, undertaking, oath, pledge, affirmation.

assure v. **1** DECLARE, give one's word, affirm, guarantee, promise, swear, pledge, certify, vow, attest. **2** ENSURE, make sure/certain, guarantee, confirm, secure, clinch, seal.

assured adj. CONFIDENT, self-confident, self-assured, self-reliant, poised, calm, composed.

astonish v. AMAZE, astound, stagger, stun, surprise, dumbfound, leave speechless, take someone's breath away, take aback, startle, stupefy, daze, bewilder, dazzle; *informal* flabbergast, floor, wow.

astonishing adj. AMAZING, astounding, staggering, surprising, breathtaking, striking, stunning, bewildering, impressive. ■ OPPOSITES unremarkable.

astound v. *see* ASTONISH.

astray adv. & adj. **1** OFF COURSE, lost, off

asylum n. **1** protection from danger, esp. for those who flee their country for political reasons. **2** dated an institution for the mentally ill.

asymmetrical (or **asymmetric**) adj. lacking symmetry. ■ **asymmetrically** adv. **asymmetry** n.

at prep. used to express: **1** location, arrival, or time. **2** a value, rate, or point on a scale. **3** a state or condition. **4** direction towards.

atavistic adj. reverting to something ancient or ancestral. ■ **atavism** n.

ate past of EAT.

atheism n. the belief that God does not exist. ■ **atheist** n.

atherosclerosis n. damage to the arteries caused by a build-up of fatty deposits.

athlete n. **1** a person who is good at sports. **2** a person who takes part in athletics. □ **athlete's foot** a form of ringworm affecting the feet.

athletic adj. **1** fit and good at sport. **2** of athletics. ▶n. (**athletics**) track and field sports. ■ **athletically** adv. **athleticism** n.

atlas n. a book of maps or charts.

atmosphere n. **1** the gases surrounding the earth or another planet. **2** the quality of the air in a place. **3** an overall tone or mood. **4** a unit of pressure. ■ **atmospheric** adj.

atoll n. a ring-shaped coral reef or chain of islands.

atom n. **1** the smallest particle of a chemical element. **2** a very small amount. □ **atom bomb** a bomb deriving its power from the fission of atomic nuclei. ■ **atomic** adj.

atomize (or **-ise**) v. convert into very fine particles or droplets. ■ **atomizer** n.

atonal /ay-toh-n'l/ adj. not written in any musical key.

atone v. (**atone for**) make amends for. ■ **atonement** n.

atrium n. (pl. **atria** or **atriums**) **1** a central hall rising through several storeys. **2** an open central court in an ancient Roman house. **3** each of the two upper cavities of the heart.

atrocious adj. **1** horrifyingly wicked. **2** informal very bad. ■ **atrociously** adv.

atrocity n. (pl. **atrocities**) an extremely wicked or cruel act.

atrophy v. (**atrophying**, **atrophied**) (of part of the body) waste away. ▶n. the process of atrophying.

attach v. **1** fasten or join. **2** attribute. **3** (**attached to**) very fond of.

Thesaurus

the right track, adrift. **2** WRONG, into sin, into wrongdoing, into error; informal off the rails.

astute adj. SHREWD, clever, quick, quick-witted, acute, cunning, intelligent, sly, artful, knowing, canny, ingenious, perceptive, observant, crafty, wily, calculating, perspicacious, sagacious; informal foxy, fly. ■ OPPOSITES stupid, dull.

asylum n. **1** REFUGE, sanctuary, shelter, safety, protection, safe keeping, haven, retreat, harbour, port in a storm. **2** MENTAL HOSPITAL, psychiatric hospital, institution; informal loony bin, madhouse, funny farm.

asymmetrical adj. UNEVEN, irregular, crooked, distorted, lopsided, unbalanced, misshapen, malformed. ■ OPPOSITES symmetrical.

atheist n. UNBELIEVER, disbeliever, non-believer, sceptic, freethinker, heretic, heathen, pagan, infidel. ■ OPPOSITES believer.

athletic adj. **1** MUSCULAR, strong, well built, powerful, fit, active, energetic, sturdy, robust, strapping, wiry, hardy, vigorous, brawny. **2** SPORTING, sports, gymnastics. ■ OPPOSITES puny.

atmosphere n. **1** AIR, sky, aerospace, stratosphere; literary heavens, ether. **2** ENVIRONMENT, climate, mood, feeling, spirit, ambience, surroundings, setting, milieu, character, tone, quality, flavour, vibrations, aura, tenor; informal vibes.

atom n. BIT, particle, scrap, shred, speck, spot, fragment, jot, trace, iota, dot, crumb, grain, morsel; informal smidgen.

atone v. MAKE AMENDS, compensate, pay for, be punished, do penance, answer, pay the penalty/price, make reparations, redeem oneself, redress, expiate.

atrocious adj. **1** WICKED, vicious, brutal, barbaric, evil, dreadful, horrific, horrifying, sickening, abominable, savage, cruel, murderous, frightful, revolting, villainous, heinous, ruthless, monstrous, inhuman, gruesome, hideous, fiendish, diabolical, outrageous, vile. **2** VERY BAD, terrible, appalling, dreadful. ■ OPPOSITES commendable, excellent.

atrocity n. OUTRAGE, crime, offence, horror, abomination, monstrosity, violation, evil.

atrophy v. WASTE AWAY, wither, shrivel, decay, wilt, deteriorate, degenerate, decline.

attach v. **1** FASTEN, stick, affix, join, con-

attaché /uh-**tash**-ay/ n. a member of an ambassador's staff. ☐ **attaché case** a small briefcase for carrying documents.

attachment n. an extra part attached to something.

attack v. 1 take violent action against. 2 criticize fiercely. 3 (in sport) try to score goals or points. ▶ n. 1 an act of attacking. 2 a sudden spell of an illness. ■ **attacker** n.

attain v. succeed in doing. ■ **attainable** adj. **attainment** n.

attar n. a fragrant oil made from rose petals.

attempt v. try. ▶ n. an effort.

attend v. 1 be present at. 2 (**attend to**) deal with or pay attention to. 3 accompany. ■ **attendance** n.

attendant n. 1 a person employed to provide a service. 2 an assistant. ▶ adj. accompanying.

attention n. 1 special care, notice, or consideration. 2 a straight standing position in military drill.

attentive adj. 1 paying attention. 2 considerate; helpful. ■ **attentively** adv. **attentiveness** n.

attenuate v. make thin or weaker. ■ **attenuation** n.

attest v. 1 provide proof of. 2 declare to be true. ■ **attestation** n.

attic n. a space or room inside the roof of a building.

attire n. clothes. ▶ v. (**be attired**) be dressed.

attitude n. 1 a way of thinking. 2 a posture of the body. 3 informal self-confident or hostile behaviour.

attorney n. (pl. **attorneys**) 1 a person

Thesaurus

nect, link, tie, couple, pin, hitch, bond, add, append, annex. 2 PLACE, put, ascribe, assign, attribute, lay, impute, invest with. 3 ASSIGN, appoint, second, allocate, detail. ■ OPPOSITES detach.

attached adj. 1 MARRIED, engaged, spoken for, having a partner. 2 FOND OF, devoted to, having a regard for.

attack v. 1 ASSAULT, set on/upon, beat up, strike, strike at, rush, storm, charge, pounce upon, beset, besiege, beleaguer; informal lay/wade into, let someone have it, do over. 2 CRITICIZE, berate, reprove, censure, rebuke, find fault with, denounce, revile, blame, harangue, vilify, snipe at, fulminate against, impugn, malign, inveigh against, traduce. 3 BEGIN, set about, get/go to work on, get started on, embark on, undertake. ▶ n. 1 ASSAULT, offensive, raid, ambush, sortie, onslaught, charge, strike, invasion, rush, foray, incursion, battery, bombardment. 2 CRITICISM, abuse, censure, outburst, tirade, rebuke, reproval, vilification, diatribe, impugnment, invective. 3 FIT, seizure, bout, spasm, convulsion, paroxysm, stroke.

attacker n. ASSAILANT, aggressor, assaulter, mugger, opponent, raider, critic, detractor, persecutor, slanderer.

attain v. ACHIEVE, accomplish, gain, obtain, get, win, earn, acquire, reach, realize, arrive at, fulfil, succeed in, bring off, grasp, secure, procure.

attempt v. TRY, strive, endeavour, tackle, seek, set out to, venture, aim, undertake, make an effort, bid; informal have a go/shot at, give something a

whirl, have a crack at. ▶ n. TRY, effort, endeavour, venture, undertaking; informal go, shot, crack.

attend v. 1 BE PRESENT, be at, be there/here, appear, put in an appearance, turn up, visit, show, frequent, haunt; informal show up. 2 PAY ATTENTION, listen, concentrate, follow, heed, pay heed, take note, notice, mark, watch. 3 LOOK AFTER, take care of, care for, nurse, tend, see to, mind, minister to. 4 ESCORT, accompany, guard, follow, chaperone, squire, usher, convoy.

attendant n. 1 STEWARD, waiter, waitress, porter, servant. 2 ESCORT, companion, retainer, aide, lady-in-waiting, equerry, chaperone. ▶ adj. RELATED, accompanying, consequent, resulting, concomitant, accessory.

attention n. 1 CONCENTRATION, attentiveness, notice, observation, scrutiny, heed, regard, diligence, thought, thinking, studying. 2 NOTICE, awareness, observation, recognition, regard, consciousness. 3 CARE, treatment, therapy, ministration. 4 OVERTURES, approaches, suit, wooing, compliments, flattery; dated courting.

attentive adj. 1 ALERT, aware, watchful, awake, observant, wide awake, vigilant, intent, mindful, on guard, heedful. 2 CONSIDERATE, thoughtful, conscientious, polite, kind, obliging, accommodating, gallant, chivalrous. ■ OPPOSITES inattentive.

attire n. CLOTHING, dress, clothes, garments, garb, apparel, costume, outfit, wear, ensemble, accoutrements; informal gear, togs, glad rags, rig; old use habit.

who acts for another in legal matters. **2** esp. US a lawyer.

attract v. **1** draw in by offering something interesting or appealing. **2** draw something closer by an unseen force. ■ **attraction** n.

attractive adj. **1** pleasing in appearance. **2** arousing interest. ■ **attractively** adv. **attractiveness** n.

attribute v. (**attribute to**) regard as belonging to or caused by. ▶n. a quality or feature. ■ **attributable** adj. **attribution** n.

attributive adj. Grammar (of an adjective) coming before the word that it describes.

attrition n. gradual wearing down.

attune v. adjust or accustom to a situation.

atypical adj. not typical. ■ **atypically** adv.

aubergine /oh-ber-zheen/ n. a purple vegetable.

auburn n. a reddish-brown colour.

auction n. a public sale where articles are sold to the highest bidder. ▶v. sell at an auction.

auctioneer n. a person who conducts auctions.

audacious adj. daring. ■ **audaciously** adv. **audacity** n.

audible adj. able to be heard. ■ **audibly** adv.

audience n. **1** a group of listeners or spectators. **2** a formal interview.

audio n. sound or the reproduction of sound. □ **audio tape** magnetic tape on which sound can be recorded. **audiovisual** using both sight and sound.

audit n. an official inspection of an organization's accounts. ▶v. (**auditing**, **audited**) make an audit of. ■ **auditor** n.

audition n. a test of a performer's ability for a particular part. ▶v. test or be tested by an audition.

auditorium n. (pl. **auditoriums** or **auditoria**) the part of a theatre or hall in which the audience sits.

auditory adj. of hearing.

au fait /oh fay/ adj. (**au fait with**) having good knowledge of.

auger /aw-ger/ n. a tool for boring holes.

augment v. add to; increase. ■ **augmentation** n.

Thesaurus

attitude n. **1** VIEW, point of view, opinion, viewpoint, outlook, belief, standpoint, frame of mind, position, approach, perspective, reaction, stance, thoughts, ideas. **2** POSITION, pose, stance, bearing, carriage, deportment.

attract v. **1** APPEAL TO, interest, fascinate, charm, entice, captivate, tempt, engage, bewitch, seduce, beguile, lure, allure, inveigle; *informal* turn on. **2** CAUSE, generate, encourage, provoke, incite, stir up. **3** DRAW, pull, magnetize. ■ OPPOSITES repel.

attractive adj. **1** GOOD-LOOKING, beautiful, handsome, pretty, lovely, stunning, striking, gorgeous, irresistible, glamorous, desirable, appealing, captivating, fascinating, charming, adorable, enchanting, alluring, enticing, seductive, bewitching, fetching, prepossessing, winsome; *informal* tasty; *US informal* cute; *old use* comely. **2** APPEALING, agreeable, interesting, tempting, pleasing, inviting. ■ OPPOSITES ugly, uninviting.

attribute n. QUALITY, feature, characteristic, property, mark, sign, trait, indicator, distinction, idiosyncrasy. ▶v. ASCRIBE, assign, put down, accredit, credit, impute, chalk up, lay at the door of.

attrition n. **1** WEAKENING, wearing down, debilitation, sapping, enfeebling.

2 ABRASION, friction, rubbing, corrosion, corroding, erosion, wearing/eating away, grinding, scraping, excoriation.

attune v. ACCUSTOM, adjust, familiarize, adapt, acclimatize.

audacious adj. BOLD, daring, fearless, brave, courageous, adventurous, intrepid, valiant, plucky, reckless, brazen, daredevil; *informal* gutsy. ■ OPPOSITES timid.

audacity n. **1** BOLDNESS, daring, fearlessness, bravery, courage, valour, pluck; *informal* guts. *See also* COURAGE. **2** EFFRONTERY, cheek, impudence, brazenness, impertinence, shamelessness, presumption; *informal* sauce. ■ OPPOSITES timidity.

audible adj. DISCERNIBLE, perceptible, clear, distinct, recognizable, hearable, detectable. ■ OPPOSITES inaudible, faint.

audience n. **1** SPECTATORS, LISTENERS, viewers, onlookers, crowd, gathering, assembly, house, turnout, congregation, gallery. **2** INTERVIEW, meeting, hearing, consultation, discussion, reception.

audit n. INSPECTION, examination, investigation, scrutiny, review, check. ▶v. INSPECT, examine, review, check, scrutinize, investigate, go over/through.

augment v. INCREASE, enlarge, make larger/greater, add to, expand, multi-

au gratin /oh gra-tan/ adj. cooked with a topping of breadcrumbs or grated cheese.

augur /aw-ger/ v. be an omen.

augury /aw-gyoo-ri/ n. (pl. **auguries**) a sign of what will happen in the future.

August n. the eighth month.

august /aw-gust/ adj. inspiring respect.

auk n. a black and white seabird.

aunt n. the sister of one's father or mother or the wife of one's uncle.

au pair n. a foreign girl employed to look after children and help with housework.

aura n. the atmosphere surrounding a place or person.

aural /aw-ruhl/ adj. of the ear. ■ **aurally** adv.

aureole n. a halo.

au revoir /aw ruh-vwar/ exclam. goodbye.

aurora borealis /aw-raw-ruh bo-ri-ay-liss/ n. bands of coloured light seen in the sky near the North Pole; the northern lights.

auscultation n. listening to the sound of the heart or other organs for medical diagnosis.

auspices pl. n. (**under the auspices of**) with the support or protection of.

auspicious adj. suggesting that there is a good chance of success. ■ **auspiciously** adv.

austere adj. **1** severe or strict. **2** very simple or plain. ■ **austerity** n.

Australasian adj. of Australasia, a region made up of Australia, New Zealand, and islands of the SW Pacific.

Australian n. a person from Australia. ▶ adj. of Australia.

authentic adj. of undisputed origin; genuine. ■ **authentically** adv. **authenticity** n.

authenticate v. prove to be authentic. ■ **authentication** n.

author n. **1** a writer of a book etc. **2** the inventor of something. ■ **authorial** adj. **authorship** n.

authoritarian adj. demanding strict obedience to authority.

authoritative adj. **1** reliably true or accurate. **2** commanding and self-confident. ■ **authoritatively** adv.

authority n. (pl. **authorities**) **1** the power to give orders and enforce obedience. **2** a person or body with official power. **3** an expert in a particular field.

authorize (or **-ise**) v. give official per-

Thesaurus

ply, grow, extend, boost, enhance, raise, inflate, heighten, strengthen, intensify, amplify, swell, supplement, magnify. ■ OPPOSITES decrease, diminish.

augur v. BE A SIGN OF, bode, foretell, predict, herald, prophesy, foreshadow, harbinger, portend, forecast, presage.

august adj. DIGNIFIED, solemn, stately, majestic, noble, imposing, impressive, exalted, grand, illustrious. ■ OPPOSITES obscure, insignificant.

auspicious adj. FAVOURABLE, promising, hopeful, encouraging, bright, fortunate, propitious, timely, felicitous. ■ OPPOSITES inauspicious.

austere adj. **1** PLAIN, severe, simple, unadorned, unornamented, stark, subdued, sombre, unembellished. **2** STERN, formal, serious, solemn, severe, cold, distant, aloof, stiff, forbidding, unsmiling, unbending, unyielding, harsh, rigorous, stringent, unrelenting. **3** STRICT, abstemious, disciplined, puritanical, spartan, frugal, ascetic, self-denying, restrained, chaste, celibate, abstinent. ■ OPPOSITES elaborate, genial, immoderate.

authentic adj. **1** GENUINE, real, true, bona fide, actual, legitimate, valid, undisputed; informal the real McCoy. **2** TRUE, accurate, honest, credible, reliable, dependable; informal straight from the horse's mouth. ■ OPPOSITES fake, unreliable.

authenticate v. VERIFY, validate, confirm, substantiate, certify, guarantee, endorse, ratify.

author n. **1** WRITER, composer, novelist, dramatist, playwright, poet, screenwriter, essayist, journalist, reporter, columnist. **2** CREATOR, originator, producer, designer, architect, planner, cause, prime mover, maker, initiator, inventor; literary begetter.

authoritarian adj. DICTATORIAL, tyrannical, strict, domineering, despotic, autocratic, imperious, harsh, Draconian, disciplinarian, dogmatic; informal bossy. ■ OPPOSITES democratic, liberal.

authoritative adj. **1** RELIABLE, accurate, authentic, sound, dependable, factual, definitive, valid, certified. **2** CONFIDENT, self-assured, assertive, commanding, masterful, imposing, arrogant, overbearing, imperious. ■ OPPOSITES unreliable, timid.

authority n. **1** RIGHT, power, jurisdiction, authorization, influence, might, prerogative, rule, command, charge, dominion, sovereignty, supremacy, asmission for. ■ **authorization** n.

autism /aw-ti-z'm/ n. a mental condition characterized by difficulty in communicating with others. ■ **autistic** adj. & n.

auto- comb. form self; own.

autobiography n. (pl. **autobiographies**) an account of a person's life written by that person. ■ **autobiographer** n. **autobiographical** adj.

autocracy n. (pl. **autocracies**) government in which one person has total power.

autocrat n. a ruler with total power. ■ **autocratic** adj.

autocross n. motor racing across country or on rough tracks.

autocue n. trademark a device displaying a presenter's script on a television screen, unseen by the audience.

autograph n. a celebrity's signature. ▶ v. write an autograph on.

autoimmune adj. (of disease) caused by antibodies produced to counteract substances naturally present in the body.

automate v. convert a process or facility so that it can operate automatically. ■ **automation** n.

automatic adj. **1** operating without human control. **2** done without conscious thought. ■ **automatically** adv.

automaton n. (pl. **automata** or **automatons**) a robot.

automobile n. US a car.

automotive adj. to do with motor vehicles.

autonomous adj. self-governing or independent. ■ **autonomy** n.

autopilot n. a device for keeping an aircraft on course automatically.

autopsy n. (pl. **autopsies**) a postmortem.

autumn n. the season between summer and winter. ■ **autumnal** adj.

auxiliary adj. giving help and support. ▶ n. (pl. **auxiliaries**) an auxiliary person or thing. □ **auxiliary verb** a verb used in forming the tenses of other verbs.

avail v. (**avail oneself of**) make use of. ▶ n. use or benefit.

available adj. able to be used or obtained. ■ **availability** n.

avalanche n. a mass of snow and ice pouring down a mountainside.

avant-garde /a-von gard/ adj. (in the arts) new and experimental.

avarice n. greed for wealth. ■ **avaricious** adj.

avenge v. take revenge for. ■ **avenger** n.

avenue n. **1** a broad road. **2** a way of achieving something.

aver v. (**averring**, **averred**) declare to be the case.

average n. **1** the result obtained by adding several amounts together and then dividing the total by the number of amounts. **2** a usual amount or level. ▶ adj. **1** being an average. **2** usual or ordinary.

Thesaurus

cendancy; informal say-so. **2** PERMISSION, authorization, consent, sanction, licence, mandate, warrant. **3** GOVERNMENT, administration, officialdom, management, establishment, bureaucracy; informal powers that be. **4** EXPERT, specialist, master, scholar, pundit, adept.

authorize v. PERMIT, allow, agree to, give permission, consent to, approve, sanction, endorse, back, license, ratify, legalize, certify, countenance, give leave for, warrant, commission; informal give the go-ahead for, give the green light to.

authorized adj. see OFFICIAL.

automatic adj. **1** AUTOMATED, mechanical, mechanized, electronic, self-regulating, self-activating, push-button, programmable, robotic. **2** INSTINCTIVE, spontaneous, involuntary, unconscious, reflex, habitual, natural, unintentional, unthinking, mechanical, conditioned. **3** INEVITABLE, routine, certain, assured. ■ OPPOSITES manual, deliberate.

autonomous adj. INDEPENDENT, free, self-governing, sovereign.

autonomy n. INDEPENDENCE, self-determination, self-sufficiency, individualism, autarchy.

auxiliary adj. SECONDARY, subsidiary, subordinate, ancillary, supporting, additional, extra, reserve, back-up, spare, supplementary, substitute.

available adj. FREE, untaken, obtainable, to hand, handy, procurable, unoccupied, vacant, usable, ready, convenient, accessible, employable. ■ OPPOSITES unavailable, inaccessible.

avarice n. GREED, acquisitiveness, covetousness, materialism, meanness, miserliness. ■ OPPOSITES generosity.

avaricious adj. GREEDY, grasping, covetous, acquisitive, miserly, parsimonious; informal tight-fisted, stingy. ■ OPPOSITES generous.

average adj. **1** NORMAL, typical, ordinary, common, regular, usual, commonplace, everyday, widespread, unexceptional, medium, middling, moderate,

averse adj. (**averse to**) strongly disliking.

....

☑ Don't confuse **averse** with **adverse**, which means 'harmful or unfavourable'.

....

aversion n. a strong dislike.

avert v. **1** turn one's eyes away. **2** prevent from happening.

aviary n. (pl. **aviaries**) a large enclosure for keeping birds in.

aviation n. the activity of operating and flying aircraft.

avid adj. very interested or enthusiastic. ■ **avidly** adv.

avionics n. electronics used in aviation.

avocado n. (pl. **avocados**) a pear-shaped tropical fruit.

avocet n. a wading bird with a long upturned bill.

avoid v. keep away or refrain from. ■ **avoidable** adj. **avoidance** n.

avoirdupois /av-war-dyoo-**pwah**/ n. a system of weights based on a pound of 16 ounces.

avow v. declare. ■ **avowal** n.

avuncular adj. kind and friendly towards a younger person.

await v. wait for.

awake v. (**awaking, awoke**; past part. **awoken**) stop sleeping. ▶ adj. not asleep.

awaken v. **1** awake. **2** stir up a feeling.

award v. give officially as a prize or reward. ▶ n. **1** something awarded. **2** the act of awarding.

aware adj. having knowledge of something. ■ **awareness** n.

awash adj. covered or flooded with water.

away adv. **1** to or at a distance. **2** until disappearing. **3** constantly. ▶ adj. (of a match) played at the opponents' ground.

awe n. great respect mixed with fear. ▶ v. fill with awe.

awesome adj. inspiring awe.

awful adj. **1** very bad or unpleasant. **2** used for emphasis: *an awful lot.* ■ **awfully** adv.

awhile adv. for a short time.

Thesaurus

....

run-of-the-mill. **2** MEDIOCRE, unexceptional, moderate, second-rate, pedestrian, banal. ▶ n. MEAN, midpoint, median, centre, norm, standard, rule, yardstick. ▶ v. EVEN OUT, equalize, normalize, standardize.

averse adj. OPPOSED, hostile, antagonistic, unwilling, disinclined, reluctant, resistant, loath, ill-disposed.

aversion n. DISLIKE, distaste, hatred, repugnance, antipathy, reluctance, unwillingness, evasion, avoidance, shunning. ■ OPPOSITES liking, inclination.

avid adj. KEEN, eager, enthusiastic, fervent, dedicated, ardent, fanatical, zealous, passionate. ■ OPPOSITES apathetic, indifferent.

avoid v. **1** EVADE, elude, hide from, keep away from, keep clear of, shun, ignore, dodge, steer clear of, give a wide berth to, shirk, eschew; *informal* duck. **2** ABSTAIN FROM, circumvent, refrain from, bypass; *informal* skive off. ■ OPPOSITES face, seek.

await v. **1** ANTICIPATE, expect, wait for, hope for, look out for. **2** BE IN STORE FOR, wait for, be ready for, lie ahead for, lie in wait for, be round the corner.

awake adj. **1** WAKEFUL, sleepless, wide awake, insomniac, open-eyed, restless, tossing and turning. **2** AWARE, alert, conscious, attentive, vigilant. ■ OPPOSITES asleep, unaware.

awaken v. **1** WAKE, wake up, awake,

waken, rouse, call, alert. **2** KINDLE, arouse, stimulate, call forth, stir up, excite, revive.

award n. **1** PRIZE, reward, trophy, honour, decoration, medal, badge, cup, grant, scholarship. **2** GIFT, grant, conferment, bestowal, presentation. ▶ v. CONFER, present, give, grant, accord, allot, assign, bestow, endow.

aware adj. CONSCIOUS, alive to, informed, knowledgeable, familiar, acquainted, mindful, heedful, sensitive, responsive, observant, attentive, sensible, conversant, cognizant, versed in. ■ OPPOSITES ignorant, insensitive.

awareness n. CONSCIOUSNESS, perception, realization, knowledge, sense, feeling, understanding, sensitivity, perceptiveness. ■ OPPOSITES ignorance, insensitivity.

awe n. WONDER, amazement, admiration, reverence, veneration, respect, dread, fear.

awesome adj. BREATHTAKING, awe-inspiring, magnificent, stupendous, overwhelming, sublime, majestic, solemn, imposing, dramatic, grand, formidable, marvellous, amazing, staggering, stunning, fearful, impressive; *informal* mind-blowing; *literary* wondrous. *See also* WONDERFUL. ■ OPPOSITES unimpressive.

awful adj. **1** *see* BAD. **2** *see* AWESOME.

awkward adj. **1** hard to do or deal with. **2** causing or feeling embarrassment. **3** inconvenient. **4** clumsy. ■ **awkwardly** adv. **awkwardness** n.

awl n. a pointed tool used for making holes.

awning n. a sheet of canvas on a frame, used for shelter.

awoke past of AWAKE.

awoken past part. of AWAKE.

AWOL /ay-wol/ adj. absent without leave.

awry /uh-ry/ adv. & adj. away from the expected course or position.

axe n. a chopping tool with a heavy blade. ▶ v. suddenly cancel or dismiss.

axiom n. a statement regarded as obviously true. ■ **axiomatic** adj.

axis n. (pl. **axes**) **1** an imaginary line around which an object rotates. **2** a fixed line against which points on a graph are measured.

axle n. a rod on which wheels turn.

ayatollah n. a religious leader in Iran.

aye exclam. old use or dialect yes.

azalea /uh-zay-li-uh/ n. a shrub with brightly coloured flowers.

Aztec n. a member of an American Indian people ruling Mexico before the Spanish conquest in the 16th century.

azure /az-yuur/ n. a bright blue colour, like a cloudless sky.

Thesaurus

awfully adv. **1** VERY, extremely, intensely, deeply, exceedingly; *informal* terribly, dreadfully, ever so; *informal, dated* frightfully. **2** TERRIBLY, badly, dreadfully, appallingly, atrociously, disgracefully, frightfully.

awkward adj. **1** UNWIELDY, cumbersome, unmanageable, inconvenient, bulky. **2** INCONVENIENT, difficult, troublesome, problematic, unhelpful, unsuitable. **3** TRICKY, difficult, perplexing, taxing, puzzling, thorny, troublesome, trying, vexed. **4** UNCOOPERATIVE, unhelpful, disobliging, contrary, obstructive, perverse, troublesome, trying, exasperating, obstinate, stubborn, refractory, intractable; *informal* bloody-minded, bolshie; *US* ornery. **5** CLUMSY, blundering, bungling, ungainly, uncoordinated, inelegant, inexpert, clownish, inept, unskilled, maladroit, gawky, gauche, wooden; *informal* ham-fisted. **6** UNCOMFORTABLE, uneasy, strained, embarrassing, unnatural; *informal* edgy. ■ OPPOSITES convenient, handy, cooperative, graceful, skilful, relaxed.

Bb

BA abbrev. Bachelor of Arts.

baa v. (**baaing, baaed**) (of a sheep or lamb) bleat.

babble v. talk rapidly in a foolish or confused way. ▶n. foolish or confused talk.

babe n. 1 a baby. 2 informal an attractive young woman.

babel n. a confused mixture of voices.

baboon n. a large monkey.

baby n. (pl. **babies**) 1 a very young child or animal. 2 a timid or childish person. ▶adj. small or very young. ■ **babyish** adj.

babysit v. (**babysitting, babysat**) look after a child while the parents are out. ■ **babysitter** n.

baccalaureate /ba-kuh-**lor**-i-uht/ n. an examination taken to qualify for higher education.

baccarat /**bak**-kuh-rah/ n. a gambling card game.

bachelor n. 1 an unmarried man. 2 used in the name of university degrees.

....

☑ There is no *t*: bachelor.

....

bacillus /buh-**sil**-luhss/ n. (pl. **bacilli**) a rod-shaped bacterium.

back n. 1 the rear surface of a person's body from shoulders to hips, or the upper part of an animal's body. 2 the side or part furthest from the front. 3 a defending player in a team game. ▶adv. 1 at or towards the rear. 2 in or into a previous time, position, or state. 3 in return. ▶v. 1 give support to. 2 move backwards. 3 bet money on. 4 (**back on to**) (of a building) have its back facing. ▶adj. 1 at or towards the back. 2 of the past. □ **back down** give in. **back out** withdraw from a commitment. **back-pedal** reverse one's previous action or opinion. **back up 1** support. 2 Computing make a spare copy of data or a disk. ■ **backer** n.

backbencher n. a member of parliament who does not hold a government or opposition post.

backbiting n. spiteful talk about an absent person.

backbone n. the spine.

backchat n. informal cheeky replies.

backdate v. make valid from an earlier date.

backdrop (or **backcloth**) n. a painted cloth at the back of a theatre stage.

backfire v. 1 (of an engine) make a bang due to fuel igniting wrongly. 2 produce an undesired effect.

backgammon n. a board game played with counters and a dice.

background n. 1 the back part of a scene or picture. 2 the circumstances surrounding something.

backhand n. a stroke played with the back of the hand turned forwards.

backhanded adj. indirect or ambiguous.

backhander n. 1 a backhand stroke. 2 informal a bribe.

backlash n. an angry reaction.

Thesaurus

....

babble v. CHATTER, prattle, burble, gabble, jabber, gibber, murmur, mutter; informal waffle, rabbit. ▶n. CHATTER, chat, gabble, prattling, murmur, clamour.

baby n. INFANT, newborn, child; literary babe; technical neonate. ▶adj. TINY, miniature, mini, little, dwarf, diminutive, minute. ▶v. COSSET, pamper, spoil, indulge, coddle, mollycoddle, pet.

babyish adj. CHILDISH, infantile, immature, juvenile, puerile, silly, inane.
■ OPPOSITES mature.

back n. 1 REAR, rear end, stern, tail end, hindquarters, posterior, end. 2 REVERSE, reverse side, other side. ▶adj. 1 REAR, hind, end, hindmost, last. 2 DORSAL, spinal. ▶v. 1 see SUPPORT, UPHOLD. 2 REVERSE, go backwards, move back, back away, back off, retreat, retire, recede, recoil, withdraw, backtrack.

backer n. SUPPORTER, sponsor, promoter, patron, advocate, benefactor, champion, seconder; informal angel.

background n. 1 BACKDROP, setting, surroundings, context, circumstances, conditions, framework, environment. 2 FAMILY, origins, ancestry, upbringing, education, milieu, culture, training,

backlog n. a build-up of work.

backpack n. a rucksack. ■ **backpacker** n. **backpacking** n.

backside n. informal the buttocks.

backslide v. revert to previous bad behaviour.

backstage adv. & adj. behind the stage in a theatre.

backstroke n. a swimming stroke performed on the back.

backtrack v. **1** retrace one's steps. **2** reverse one's opinion.

backward adj. **1** towards the back. **2** having made less than normal progress. ▶ adv. (also **backwards**) **1** towards the back or back towards the starting point. **2** in reverse. ■ **backwardly** adv. **backwardness** n.

backwash n. waves flowing outwards behind a ship.

backwater n. **1** a stretch of stagnant water on a river. **2** a place unaffected by progress.

backwoods pl. n. a remote area.

bacon n. salted or smoked meat from a pig.

bacteria pl. n. (sing. **bacterium**) a group of microscopic organisms, many of which cause disease. ■ **bacterial** adj. **bacteriologist** n. **bacteriology** n.

....

✓ **bacteria** should always be used with a plural verb, e.g. *the bacteria were multiplying.*

....

bad adj. (**worse**, **worst**) **1** poor in quality. **2** unpleasant. **3** severe; serious. **4** wicked. **5** harmful. **6** injured, ill, or diseased. **7** (of food) decayed. ■ **badness** n.

bade past of BID².

badge n. a small flat object worn to show membership or rank.

badger n. a large nocturnal mammal with a black-and-white striped head. ▶ v. pester.

badly adv. (**worse**, **worst**) **1** in an unacceptable way. **2** severely. **3** very much. □ **badly off** poor.

badminton n. a game with rackets in which a shuttlecock is hit across a high net.

Thesaurus

tradition, experience, qualifications, credentials, history. ■ OPPOSITES foreground.

backing n. **1** SUPPORT, encouragement, approval, endorsement, promotion, recommendation, assent, agreement, assistance, help, aid, sponsorship, funding, patronage, subsidy, funds, grant, loan. **2** ACCOMPANIMENT, obbligato.

backlash n. REACTION, recoil, rebound, response, retaliation, counterblast, repercussion, reversal.

backward adj. **1** REVERSE, retreating, rearward, retrograde, regressive, retrogressive. **2** SLOW, late-starting, behind, behindhand, retarded, undeveloped, unprogressive, underdeveloped, disadvantaged, handicapped; *dated* subnormal. **3** SHY, bashful, timid, diffident, hesitant, self-effacing, reticent, unforthcoming, reserved, unassertive, modest, coy, inhibited. ■ OPPOSITES forward, advanced, precocious, confident.

bad adj. **1** POOR, inadequate, unsatisfactory, substandard, inferior, imperfect, defective, deficient, faulty, incompetent, inefficient, incorrect, unsound, useless, worthless, shoddy, abysmal, awful, appalling, disgraceful, atrocious, dreadful, frightful, hopeless, abominable; *informal* lousy, rotten, diabolical, grotty, ropy. **2** UNSUITABLE, unpropitious, unfavourable, inappropriate, adverse, unhelpful,

inconvenient, unlucky, dangerous, harmful, deleterious, detrimental, damaging, unhealthy, risky, injurious, hurtful, destructive. **3** UNPLEASANT, disagreeable, nasty, horrid, horrible, harsh, unwelcome, gloomy, distressing, dreadful, awful, frightful, terrible, foul, appalling, atrocious. **4** SERIOUS, severe, grave, dangerous, disastrous, calamitous, terrible, awful, dreadful, frightful, critical, acute, dire, hideous. **5** IMMORAL, wicked, evil, wrong, corrupt, sinful, vicious, criminal, depraved, villainous, vile, rotten, delinquent, guilty, blameworthy, reprehensible, dishonest, dishonourable, ignoble, base, reprobate. **6** NAUGHTY, mischievous, unruly, wayward, disobedient, disorderly. **7** ROTTEN, decayed, mouldy, off, rancid, tainted, spoiled, sour, decomposing, putrid, contaminated, foul, polluted, mildewed, diseased. **8** REMORSEFUL, regretful, ashamed, guilty, sorry, unhappy, contrite, apologetic, penitent. ■ OPPOSITES good, favourable, fine, fresh.

badge n. EMBLEM, pin, crest, insignia, medal, token, sign, mark, symbol, logo, device, characteristic, trademark; *US* button.

bad-tempered adj. IRRITABLE, shorttempered, quick-tempered, peevish, touchy, prickly, crotchety, irascible, cross, angry, ill-humoured, testy, quar-

baffle v. puzzle. ■ **bafflement** n.

bag n. **1** a flexible container with an opening at the top. **2** (**bags of**) informal plenty of. **3** informal an unpleasant woman. ▶ v. (**bagging, bagged**) **1** put in a bag. **2** informal manage to get.

bagatelle n. **1** a board game in which balls are hit into numbered holes. **2** something unimportant.

bagel /bay-g'l/ n. a ring-shaped bread roll with a heavy texture.

baggage n. luggage.

baggy adj. (**baggier, baggiest**) hanging in loose folds.

bagpipes pl. n. a musical instrument with pipes sounded by wind squeezed from a bag.

baguette /ba-get/ n. a loaf of French bread.

bail n. **1** money pledged as security that an accused person will return for trial. **2** each of two crosspieces resting on the stumps in cricket. ▶ v. **1** free an accused person on payment of bail. **2** (also **bale**) scoop water out of. □ **bail** (or **bale**) **out 1** make an emergency parachute jump from an aircraft. **2** rescue from difficulty.

bailey n. the outer wall of a castle.

bailiff n. a person who delivers writs and seizes property for non-payment of fines or debts.

bailiwick n. an area of authority or interest.

bairn n. Sc. & N. Engl. a child.

bait n. **1** food placed to attract prey. **2** an attraction or inducement. ▶ v. **1** taunt or tease. **2** put bait on or in.

baize n. thick green material used to cover billiard tables.

bake v. cook or harden by dry heat.

baker n. a person whose trade is making bread and cakes. □ **baker's dozen** a group of thirteen. ■ **bakery** n.

baksheesh n. a tip or bribe.

balaclava n. a woollen hat covering the head and neck.

balalaika n. a Russian musical instrument like a guitar.

balance n. **1** an even distribution of weight. **2** proportion. **3** a device for weighing. **4** the difference between credits and debits in an account. **5** an amount still owed after paying part of a debt. ▶ v. **1** be or put in a steady position. **2** compare.

balcony n. (pl. **balconies**) **1** an enclosed platform projecting from the outside of a building. **2** the highest level of seats in a theatre or cinema.

bald adj. **1** having no hair on the head. **2** (of a tyre) with the tread worn away. **3** without details. ■ **baldly** adv. **baldness** n.

balderdash n. nonsense.

balding adj. going bald.

bale (see also **bail**) n. a large, bound quantity of hay, paper, etc. ▶ v. make into bales.

baleful adj. menacing. ■ **balefully** adv.

balk US = **BAULK**.

ball n. **1** a rounded object used in games. **2** a throw or kick of the ball in a game. **3** a rounded part or thing. **4** a formal social gathering for dancing. □ **ball bearing** a ring of small metal balls re-

Thesaurus

relsome, truculent, grumpy, acrimonious, querulous, petulant, gruff, sullen, moody, sulky, disgruntled, grumbling, scowling, churlish, cantankerous, dyspeptic, bilious, crabbed, shrewish; informal snappy, shirty. ■ OPPOSITES good-humoured, affable.

baffle v. **1** BEWILDER, bemuse, mystify, perplex, puzzle, confuse, confound, nonplus, floor; informal flummox, bamboozle, stump. **2** THWART, foil, frustrate, defeat, prevent, check, hinder, block, obstruct.

bag n. HANDBAG, carrier bag, shoulder bag, case, grip, satchel, sack, holdall, rucksack, haversack, reticule. ▶ v. **1** CATCH, capture, shoot, kill, trap, snare, land. **2** GET, gain, acquire, obtain, reserve, secure, get hold of.

baggage n. LUGGAGE, bags, cases, belongings, things, equipment, accoutrements, paraphernalia, impedimenta;

informal gear.

bait n. LURE, attraction, enticement, temptation, incentive, inducement, bribe, decoy, carrot. ▶ v. TEASE, provoke, goad, pester, annoy, harass, plague, torment, persecute, taunt; informal needle, wind up.

balance n. **1** STABILITY, poise, steadiness, equilibrium. **2** CORRESPONDENCE, equivalence, symmetry, equality, parity, equipoise, evenness, proportion. **3** REMAINDER, rest, difference, surplus, excess, residue. **4** SCALES, weighing machine. ▶ v. **1** KEEP BALANCED, poise, steady, stabilize, support. **2** OFFSET, cancel out, counterbalance, match, compensate for, even up, level, equalize, parallel, counterpoise, counteract, neutralize.

bald adj. **1** HAIRLESS, bare, smooth, bald-headed; informal thin on top. **2** BLUNT, frank, plain, straightforward, forthducing friction between moving parts of a machine, or one of these balls. **ballcock** a valve controlling the water level in a cistern. **ballpoint** a pen with a tiny ball as its writing point. **ballroom** a large room for formal dancing.

ballad n. **1** a poem or song telling a story. **2** a slow sentimental song.

ballast n. **1** heavy material carried by a ship to keep it stable. **2** coarse stone used as the base of a railway or road.

ballerina n. a female ballet dancer.

ballet n. an artistic dance form performed to music. ■ **balletic** adj.

ballistics n. the science of missiles and firearms. ◻ **ballistic missile** a missile which is powered when first launched, but falls under gravity on to its target.

balloon n. a rubber bag inflated with air or a lighter gas. ▶ v. swell outwards.

ballot n. a way of voting secretly by means of paper slips placed in a box. ▶ v. (**balloting, balloted**) ask for a secret vote from.

ballyhoo n. informal a fuss.

balm n. **1** a fragrant ointment. **2** something that soothes or heals.

balmy adj. (of the weather) pleasantly warm.

baloney n. informal nonsense.

balsa n. lightweight wood from a tropical American tree.

balsam n. a scented resin used in perfumes and medicines.

baluster n. a short pillar forming part of a series supporting a rail.

balustrade n. a railing supported by balusters.

bamboo n. a giant tropical grass with hollow stems.

bamboozle v. informal **1** mystify. **2** cheat or deceive.

ban v. (**banning, banned**) forbid officially. ▶ n. an official order forbidding something.

banal /buh-**nahl**/ adj. predictable and unoriginal. ■ **banality** n.

banana n. a curved yellow fruit.

band n. **1** a piece of material used as a fastener. **2** a stripe or strip. **3** a range of values or frequencies within a series. **4** a group of musicians. **5** a group of people with a common purpose. ◻ **bandstand** a covered outdoor platform for a band playing music. **bandwagon** an activity or cause that has suddenly become fashionable or popular. ■ **banded** adj.

bandage n. a strip of material for tying round a wound. ▶ v. tie a bandage round.

bandanna (or **bandana**) n. a large coloured handkerchief.

bandit n. a member of a gang of armed robbers.

bandy adj. (of a person's legs) curved outwards at the knees. ▶ v. (**bandying, bandied**) spread an idea or rumour. ◻ **bandy words** exchange angry remarks.

bane n. a cause of great distress or annoyance.

bang n. **1** a sudden loud, sharp noise. **2** a sharp blow. ▶ v. **1** hit or put down noisily. **2** make a bang. ▶ adv. informal exactly: *bang on time*.

banger n. **1** informal a sausage. **2** informal

Thesaurus

right, direct, not beating about the bush, stark, uncompromising, downright, simple, unadorned, unembellished. ■ OPPOSITES hairy.

ball n. SPHERE, globe, orb, globule, spheroid.

ballot n. VOTE, poll, election, referendum, plebiscite.

ban v. PROHIBIT, forbid, veto, outlaw, put a ban on, proscribe, suppress, disallow, interdict, bar, debar, prevent, restrict, exclude, banish, ostracize. ▶ n. PROHIBITION, veto, embargo, boycott, bar, interdict, interdiction, proscription, restriction, taboo, suppression.

banal adj. TRITE, clichéd, hackneyed, commonplace, unoriginal, cliché-ridden, unimaginative, uninspired, stale, boring, dull, everyday, stock, stereotyped, platitudinous, obvious, predictable,

tired, pedestrian, humdrum, prosaic, vapid, fatuous; informal corny, old hat. ■ OPPOSITES interesting, original.

band[1] n. **1** STRIPE, strip, line, belt, bar, streak, border, swathe. **2** BRAID, belt, fillet, sash, tie, ribbon, cord, loop, girdle.

band[2] n. **1** GROUP, troop, crowd, crew, gang, company, body, pack, mob, horde, flock, bunch, gathering, party, throng, society, club, clique, set, association. **2** ENSEMBLE, group, orchestra; informal combo.

bandit n. BRIGAND, outlaw, robber, highwayman, footpad, marauder, desperado, gangster, gunman, pirate, buccaneer, hijacker, plunderer, thief.

bandy[1] adj. BOWED, crooked, curved, bent, bow-legged, misshapen.

bandy[2] v. **1** EXCHANGE, swap, trade, pass, reciprocate. See also ARGUE. **2** SPREAD,

an old car. **3** a loud explosive firework.
bangle n. a bracelet of rigid material.
banish v. **1** send into exile. **2** get rid of;
drive away. ■ **banishment** n.
banisters (or **bannisters**) pl. n. the upright posts and handrail at the side of a
staircase.
banjo n. (pl. **banjos**) a guitar-like musical instrument with a circular body.
bank n. **1** the land alongside a river. **2** a
long, high slope or mass. **3** a row of
lights, switches, etc. **4** an organization
offering financial services, esp. the safe
keeping of money. **5** a stock or supply.
▶ v. **1** make or form into a bank. **2** (of
an aircraft) tilt sideways when turning.
3 place money in a bank. **4** (**bank on**)
rely on. □ **banknote** a piece of paper
money. ■ **banker** n.
bankrupt adj. not having the money to
pay one's debts. ▶ n. a bankrupt person.
▶ v. make bankrupt. ■ **bankruptcy** n.
banner n. a strip of cloth with a slogan
or design, hung up or carried on poles.
banns pl. n. an announcement of a forthcoming marriage.
banquet n. an elaborate formal meal for
many people.
banquette /bang-ket/ n. a padded
bench along a wall.
banshee n. (in Irish legend) a female
spirit whose wailing warns of a death.
bantam n. a small chicken. □ **bantamweight** a weight in boxing between fly-
weight and featherweight.

banter n. friendly teasing. ▶ v. make
friendly teasing remarks.
Bantu n. (pl. **Bantu** or **Bantus**) a member of a large group of indigenous African peoples.

> 🛈 **Bantu** is a very offensive word in
> South African English, especially
> when used of individual black people.

bap n. a soft bread roll.
baptism n. a Christian ceremony in
which a person is sprinkled with or immersed in water as a sign of purification and entry to the Church. ■ **baptis-
mal** adj.
Baptist n. a member of a Protestant
group believing in adult baptism by
total immersion in water.
baptize (or **-ise**) v. **1** perform baptism
on. **2** name or nickname.
bar n. **1** a long rigid piece of wood, metal,
etc. **2** a counter, room, etc. where alcohol is served. **3** a barrier. **4** one of the
short units into which a piece of music
is divided. **5** (**the Bar**) barristers or
their profession. **6** a unit of atmospheric pressure. ▶ v. (**barring**, **barred**)
1 fasten with a bar or bars. **2** forbid or
prevent. ▶ prep. except for. □ **bar code**
a row of printed stripes identifying a
product and its price, readable by a
computer. **barman** (or **barmaid**) a person serving drinks in a pub or bar.
barb n. **1** a backward-pointing part of an

Thesaurus

circulate, pass on, disseminate.
bang n. **1** BOOM, crash, thud, slam,
knock, clash, clap, report, explosion.
2 BLOW, bump, hit, knock, slap, punch,
stroke, cuff, smack, rap; informal whack.
▶ adv. **1** WITH A BANG, crash, thump, thud,
noisily, violently. **2** EXACTLY, precisely,
absolutely, right; informal slap bang.
banish v. **1** EXILE, expel, exclude, deport,
expatriate, ostracize, transport, eject,
evict, outlaw, oust, throw out, proscribe. **2** DISMISS, drive away, dispel,
shut out, eliminate, get rid of, dislodge,
remove, bar, ban, suppress.
bank[1] n. **1** SLOPE, mound, embankment,
hillock, incline, ridge, rise, rampart,
ramp, dyke, pile, mass. **2** EDGE, shore,
brink, side, margin, embankment.
3 ROW, array, collection, display, panel,
rank, tier. ▶ v. TILT, lean, slope, slant,
list, tip, incline.
bank[2] n. STORE, reserve, supply, fund,
stock, hoard, repository, pool, reservoir. ▶ v. DEPOSIT, save, put by, save up,

keep, store, hoard. ■ OPPOSITES withdraw. □ **bank on** see RELY ON.
bankrupt adj. **1** INSOLVENT, ruined,
failed, in liquidation, destitute, penniless; informal broke, bust. **2** MORALLY BANK-
RUPT, deficient, lacking, poor, impoverished, worthless. ■ OPPOSITES solvent.
banner n. FLAG, standard, pennant,
pennon, colours, ensign, banderole,
streamer.
banquet n. FEAST, repast, dinner, meal,
party; informal binge, blowout, spread.
banter n. REPARTEE, joking, badinage,
persiflage, pleasantry, jesting, word-
play.
bar n. **1** BEAM, rod, pole, shaft, stake,
stick, spar, rail, batten, girder, crosspiece. **2** BARRIER, obstacle, obstruction,
impediment, hindrance, check, deterrent, drawback, prohibition, prevention, problem, difficulty. **3** BAND, stripe,
belt, strip, streak, line. **4** CAKE, slab,
chunk, block, piece, wedge, lump,
hunk, nugget, ingot. **5** PUB, public

arrowhead, fish hook, etc. **2** a spiteful remark.

barbarian n. an uncivilized or cruel person.

barbaric adj. **1** savagely cruel. **2** primitive. ∎ **barbarity** n.

barbarous adj. barbaric. ∎ **barbarism** n.

barbecue n. **1** an outdoor meal at which food is grilled over a charcoal fire. **2** a grill used at a barbecue. ▶v. cook on a barbecue.

barbed adj. **1** having a barb. **2** (of a remark) spiteful. ▢ **barbed wire** wire with clusters of sharp points along it.

barber n. a men's hairdresser.

barbican n. a double tower above a gate or drawbridge of a castle or fortified city.

barbiturate n. a sedative drug.

bard n. literary a poet.

bare adj. **1** not clothed. **2** not covered or adorned. **3** only just enough. ▶v. uncover or reveal. **bareback** on horseback without a saddle. **barefaced** done openly and without shame. ∎ **barely** adv.

bargain n. **1** an agreement where each party does something for the other. **2** a thing bought at a low price. ▶v. **1** discuss the terms of an agreement. **2** (**bargain for/on**) expect.

barge n. a long flat-bottomed boat used on canals and rivers. ▶v. **1** move forcefully. **2** (**barge in**) intrude or interrupt

rudely.

baritone n. a man's singing voice between tenor and bass.

barium n. a white metallic element.

bark n. **1** the sharp cry of a dog. **2** the outer layer of a tree. ▶v. **1** give a bark. **2** utter suddenly or fiercely. **3** scrape the skin off one's shin accidentally.

barley n. a type of cereal plant with bristly heads. ▢ **barley sugar** a sweet made of boiled sugar.

bar mitzvah n. a religious ceremony in which a Jewish boy aged 13 takes on the responsibilities of an adult.

barmy adj. (**barmier, barmiest**) informal mad.

barn n. a large farm building used for storing grain etc.

barnacle n. a shellfish which fixes itself to objects under water.

barney n. (pl. **barneys**) informal a noisy quarrel.

barometer n. an instrument that measures atmospheric pressure, used in weather forecasting. ∎ **barometric** adj.

baron n. **1** a man belonging to the lowest rank of the nobility. **2** a powerful businessman. ∎ **baronial** adj.

baroness n. **1** a baron's wife or widow. **2** a woman with the rank of baron.

baronet n. a man who holds a title below that of baron. ∎ **baronetcy** n.

baroque n. an ornate style of architecture, art, and music of the 17th and 18th centuries. ▶adj. ornate in style.

Thesaurus

house, hostelry, inn, tavern; *informal* local, boozer. ▶v. **1** EXCLUDE, ban, banish, keep out, prohibit, forbid, preclude, outlaw, ostracize, proscribe. **2** BLOCK, check, impede, obstruct, prevent, hinder, stop, halt, deter, restrain, arrest, thwart.

barbarian n. SAVAGE, vandal, boor, yahoo, churl, brute, ruffian, hooligan, heathen, pagan, philistine, ignoramus; *informal* yob, yobbo. ▶adj. *see* BARBARIC.

barbaric adj. **1** UNCIVILIZED, primitive, wild, savage, barbarian, uneducated, unsophisticated, crude, brutish. **2** CRUEL, brutal, savage, bestial, barbarous, vicious, ferocious, inhuman. *See also* CRUEL. ∎ OPPOSITES civilized.

bare adj. **1** NAKED, nude, undressed, unclad, uncovered, stripped, unclothed, exposed, denuded; *informal* in the buff, starkers, butt naked; *US informal* buck naked. **2** EMPTY, unfurnished, undecorated, plain, austere, unadorned, vacant. **3** BLEAK, barren, featureless, treeless,

unsheltered, desolate, open. **4** PLAIN, simple, unadorned, unvarnished, unembellished, uncompromising, basic, essential, literal, straightforward, bald, stark, direct, uninterpreted, unelaborated. **5** MERE, basic, essential, minimum, minimal, least, smallest, meagre, scanty, inadequate. ▶v. REVEAL, uncover, expose, lay bare, undress, unmask, unveil, show, disclose, make known, publish, betray. ∎ OPPOSITES conceal.

barely adv. HARDLY, scarcely, just, only just, by the skin of one's teeth, with difficulty.

bargain n. **1** AGREEMENT, deal, pact, contract, arrangement, settlement, treaty, transaction, understanding, promise, pledge, compact, covenant, concordat, engagement, negotiation. **2** GOOD BUY, good deal, special offer, discount, reduction; *informal* snip, giveaway. ▶v. NEGOTIATE, haggle, barter, argue, discuss, deal, trade, traffic, compromise, agree, settle,

barque /bark/ n. a sailing ship

barrack v. shout insults at a performer or speaker. ▶pl. n. (**barracks**) buildings for housing soldiers.

barracuda n. a large, predatory tropical sea fish.

barrage n. 1 a continuous artillery attack. 2 a large number of questions or complaints. 3 an artificial barrier across a river.

barre n. a horizontal bar used for support in ballet exercises.

barrel n. 1 a cylindrical container with flat ends. 2 a tube forming part of a gun, pen, etc. □ **barrel organ** a small organ playing a set tune when a handle is turned.

barren adj. 1 (of land) not fertile. 2 unable to bear young. 3 bleak. ■ **barrenness** n.

barricade n. a makeshift barrier. ▶v. block or defend with a barricade.

barrier n. an obstacle that prevents movement, access, or progress.

barring prep. except for; if not for.

barrister n. a lawyer qualified to argue a case in court.

barrow n. 1 a two-wheeled handcart used by street traders. 2 an ancient burial mound.

barter v. exchange goods or services for other goods or services. ▶n. trading by bartering.

basal /bay-s'l/ adj. forming or belonging to a base.

basalt /ba-sawlt/ n. a dark volcanic rock.

base n. 1 the lowest or supporting part of something. 2 the main place where a person works or stays. 3 a centre of operations. 4 a main element to which others are added. 5 a substance able to react with an acid to form a salt and water. 6 the number on which a system of counting is based. 7 Baseball each of the four points that must be reached in turn to score a run. ▶v. 1 (**base on**) use something as the foundation for. 2 put at a centre of operations. ▶adj. bad or immoral. □ **baseball** a team game played with a bat and ball on a circuit of four bases around all of which a batsman must run to score.

baseless adj. not based on fact; untrue.

basement n. a room or floor below ground level.

bash informal v. hit hard and violently. ▶n. 1 a heavy blow. 2 a party.

bashful adj. shy. ■ **bashfully** adv. **bashfulness** n.

BASIC n. a high-level computer programming language.

basic adj. 1 forming an essential foundation; fundamental. 2 consisting of the minimum needed or offered. ▶n. (**basics**) essential facts or principles. ■ **basically** adv.

basil n. a herb used in cookery.

Thesaurus

promise, pledge, engage. □ **bargain for** EXPECT, allow for, anticipate, be prepared for, take into account. **into the bargain** see MOREOVER.

barrage n. 1 BROADSIDE, gunfire, bombardment, fusillade, salvo, volley, battery, shelling, cannonade. 2 ONSLAUGHT, deluge, torrent, stream, hail, storm, flood, mass, avalanche, abundance, plethora. 3 see BARRIER.

barrel n. CASK, keg, vat, butt, tub, tank, firkin, hogshead.

barren adj. 1 INFERTILE, unproductive, unfruitful, waste, desert, arid, bare, bleak, desolate, lifeless, empty. 2 STERILE, infertile, childless; technical infecund. ■ OPPOSITES fertile.

barricade n. see BARRIER. ▶v. BLOCK OFF, blockade, bar, obstruct, close up, fortify, defend.

barrier n. 1 BAR, fence, railing, barricade, obstruction, blockade, barrage, roadblock, rampart, palisade, bulwark, dam, stockade. 2 OBSTACLE, hindrance, impediment, handicap, difficulty, problem, restriction, check, bar, limitation, drawback, stumbling block.

barter v. BARGAIN, trade, traffic, exchange, swap, deal, haggle.

base¹ n. 1 FOUNDATION, bed, foot, bottom, basis, support, stand, rest, pedestal, prop, plinth, substructure. 2 BASIS, core, fundamentals, essence, essentials, root, heart, source, origin, mainspring. 3 HEADQUARTERS, centre, camp, station, post, starting point, settlement, site. ▶v. 1 FOUND, build, settle, support, ground, rest, derive from, construct, establish. 2 LOCATE, station, centre, post, situate, place, install.

base² adj. IGNOBLE, mean, low, sordid, contemptible, shameful, vulgar, shabby, despicable, unworthy, inferior, corrupt, depraved, vile, dishonourable, disreputable, unprincipled, immoral, evil, wicked, sinful, detestable, degrading. ■ OPPOSITES noble.

bashful adj. SHY, diffident, timid, shrinking, backward, modest, self-effacing, retiring, nervous, self-conscious, re-

basilica n. a large church with two rows of columns and a semicircular apse.

basilisk n. a mythical reptile whose gaze or breath was deadly.

basin n. **1** a round open container for food or liquid. **2** a circular valley or natural depression. **3** an area drained by a river.

basis n. (pl. **bases**) **1** the foundation of a theory or process. **2** a system of proceeding: *they met on a regular basis.*

bask v. lie in warmth and sunlight for pleasure.

basket n. a container for carrying things, made from strips of cane or wire. □ **basketball** a team game in which goals are scored by throwing a ball through a net fixed on a hoop.

Basque n. **1** a member of a people living in the western Pyrenees in France and Spain. **2** the language of the Basques.

bas-relief n. a carving with figures standing out slightly from the background.

bass[1] /bayss/ n. **1** the lowest male singing voice. **2** the deep, low-frequency output of a radio or audio system. **3** a bass guitar or double bass. ▶ adj. of the lowest pitch in music.

bass[2] /bass/ n. (pl. **bass** or **basses**) an edible fish related to the perch.

bassoon n. a large bass woodwind instrument.

bastard n. **1** old use or derog. an illegitimate child. **2** informal an unpleasant person.

baste v. **1** pour fat or juices over meat during cooking. **2** sew together temporarily with loose stitches.

bastion n. **1** a projecting part of a fortification. **2** a stronghold of a particular principle, activity, etc.

bat n. **1** an implement for hitting the ball in sports. **2** a winged mammal active at night. ▶ v. (**batting**, **batted**) **1** (in sport) take the role of hitting rather than throwing the ball. **2** hit with the flat of one's hand. □ **batsman** a player who bats in cricket.

batch n. a quantity of goods produced or dispatched at one time.

bated adj. (**with bated breath**) in great suspense.

....
☑ The spelling is bated, not baited.
....

bath n. **1** a large tub filled with water for washing one's body. **2** an act of washing in a bath. **3** (also **baths**) a public swimming pool. ▶ v. wash in a bath. □ **bathroom** a room containing a bath, washbasin, toilet, etc.

bathe v. **1** soak or wipe gently with liquid to clean or soothe. **2** take a swim. ▶ n. a swim. ■ **bather** n.

bathos /bay-thoss/ n. (in literature) a change in mood from the important and serious to the trivial or ridiculous.

batik /ba-teek/ n. a method of producing designs on cloth by waxing the parts not to be dyed.

batman n. dated (in the armed forces) an officer's personal attendant.

baton n. **1** a thin stick used by the conductor of an orchestra. **2** a short stick passed from runner to runner in a relay race.

battalion n. a large body of troops, forming part of a brigade.

batten n. a long wooden or metal strip for strengthening or securing something.

batter n. a mixture of flour, eggs, and

Thesaurus

served, inhibited, reticent, unforthcoming, hesitant, coy, demure, shamefaced, abashed, sheepish, embarrassed, blushing, uneasy. ■ OPPOSITES confident.

basic adj. **1** FUNDAMENTAL, essential, intrinsic, underlying, primary, elementary, central, key, indispensable, vital, main, principal, chief, crucial, rudimentary. **2** PLAIN, simple, austere, spartan, unadorned, stark, minimal. ■ OPPOSITES luxurious.

basin n. BOWL, dish, pan, vessel, container, receptacle.

basis n. **1** FOUNDATION, base, grounding, support, rest, stand, stay, infrastructure, bottom. **2** STARTING POINT, source, origin, core, essence, beginning, impetus, impulse, material, ingredients, stimulus.

bask v. **1** LIE, laze, relax, sunbathe, lounge, loll. **2** REVEL, wallow, exult, delight, take pleasure, luxuriate, glory, rejoice, enjoy, relish, savour.

bastard n. **1** ILLEGITIMATE CHILD; dated love child; old use natural child. **2** SCOUNDREL, villain, brute, rogue; informal beast; dated cad, blackguard.

batch n. SET, group, lot, cluster, bunch, quantity, collection, accumulation, assemblage, pack, crowd, aggregate, conglomeration.

bathe v. **1** WASH, clean, cleanse, rinse,

milk or water, used in cooking. ▸v. hit repeatedly with hard blows. ▫ **battering ram** a heavy object swung or rammed against a door to break it down.

battery n. (pl. **batteries**) **1** a device containing and supplying electrical power. **2** a series of small cages for the intensive rearing of poultry. **3** Law the crime of physically attacking another person. **4** a group of heavy guns.

battle n. **1** a fight between organized armed forces. **2** a long and difficult struggle. ▸v. fight or struggle with determination. ▫ **battleaxe 1** a large axe used in ancient warfare. **2** informal an aggressive woman. **battlefield** the scene of a battle. **battlement** a parapet with gaps for firing through. **battleship** a large, heavily armoured warship.

batty adj. (**battier**, **battiest**) informal mad.

bauble n. a small, showy trinket or decoration.

baulk (US **balk**) v. **1** (**baulk at**) hesitate to accept. **2** thwart or hinder.

bauxite n. a clay-like rock from which aluminium is obtained.

bawdy adj. (**bawdier**, **bawdiest**) humorously indecent. ■ **bawdiness** n.

bawl v. **1** shout. **2** weep noisily.

bay n. **1** a broad curved inlet of the sea. **2** a Mediterranean shrub whose leaves are used in cookery. **3** a recess in a wall. **4** an area with a particular purpose: *a loading bay*. ▸v. (of a dog) bark or howl loudly. ▸adj. (of a horse) reddish-brown. ▫ **bay window** a window projecting out from a wall.

bayonet n. a long blade fixed to a rifle. ▸v. (**bayoneting**, **bayoneted**) stab with a bayonet.

bazaar n. **1** a market in a Middle Eastern country. **2** a sale of goods to raise funds.

bazooka n. a short-range rocket launcher used against tanks.

B. & B. abbrev. bed and breakfast.

BBC abbrev. British Broadcasting Corporation.

BC abbrev. before Christ (used to indicate that a date is before the Christian era).

be v. (sing. present **am**; **are**; **is**; pl. present **are**; 1st & 3rd sing. past **was**; 2nd sing. past & pl. past **were**; pres. part. **being**; past part. **been**) **1** exist; be present. **2** happen. **3** have a specified state, nature, or role. ▸aux. v. used to form tenses of other verbs.

beach n. an area of sand or pebbles at the edge of the sea. ▸v. bring on to a beach from the water. ▫ **beachcomber** a person who searches beaches for things of value. **beachhead** a fortified position on a beach taken by landing forces.

beacon n. **1** a fire lit on a hill as a sig-

Thesaurus

soak, steep, moisten, wet, immerse. **2** swim, go swimming, take a dip. **3** suffuse, envelop, cover, soak.

baton n. stick, wand, rod, bar, cane, staff, club, truncheon, mace.

batter v. **1** beat, hit, strike, bludgeon, assault, belabour; *informal* bash. *See also* hit. **2** damage, injure, hurt, harm, crush, shatter, exhaust, ruin, destroy, buffet, wear down, wear out, impair, squash, mar, spoil, demolish.

battle n. conflict, fight, fighting, clash, engagement, skirmish, struggle, confrontation, combat, encounter, collision, campaign, war, tussle, scuffle, melee, action, strife, hostilities, fray, crusade; *informal* scrap. ▸v. struggle, fight, contend, compete, contest, combat, feud, quarrel, wrangle, argue, war, cross swords.

battlefield n. battleground, front, battle lines, combat zone, theatre of war, arena.

bawdy adj. ribald, lewd, indecent, salacious, earthy, broad, suggestive, indelicate, naughty, racy, risqué, off

colour, obscene, dirty, filthy, smutty, erotic, prurient, pornographic, coarse, titillating, licentious, lascivious, unseemly, vulgar, Rabelaisian; *informal* blue, raunchy. ■ opposites decent, proper.

bawl v. **1** shout, cry, yell, roar, bellow, thunder, clamour, vociferate; *informal* holler. **2** sob, wail, cry, roar, howl, weep, blubber, squall, snivel, grizzle.

bay[1] n. cove, inlet, gulf, basin, harbour, indentation, sound, arm, bight, creek, firth, fjord, estuary.

bay[2] n. alcove, recess, niche, opening, nook, booth.

bazaar n. **1** market, mart, souk, exchange. **2** fete, fair, sale, jumble sale, bring-and-buy (sale); *US* rummage sale.

be v. **1** exist, live, be alive, breathe. **2** be situated, be located, be positioned, stay, remain, continue, dwell, live, inhabit, be present, attend, persist, survive, endure, last. **3** take place, occur, be due, be planned for, happen, come about, arise, transpire; *literary* come to pass, befall.

nal. **2** a light acting as a signal for ships or aircraft.

bead n. **1** a small piece of glass, stone, etc., threaded in a string with others. **2** a small drop of liquid. ■ **beaded** adj.

beadle n. hist. a parish officer who dealt with minor offenders.

beady adj. (of eyes) small, round, and observant.

beagle n. a small breed of hound.

beak n. **1** a bird's horny projecting jaws. **2** informal a magistrate.

beaker n. **1** a tall plastic cup. **2** a glass container used in laboratories.

beam n. **1** a long piece of timber or metal used as a support in building. **2** a ray of light or particles. **3** a radiant smile. **4** the width of a ship. ▶v. **1** transmit a radio signal. **2** shine brightly. **3** smile radiantly.

bean n. **1** an edible seed growing in long pods on certain plants. **2** the seed of a coffee or cocoa plant.

bear[1] v. (**bearing**, **bore**; past part. **borne**) **1** carry. **2** support a weight. **3** (**bear oneself**) behave in a particular manner. **4** tolerate. **5** give birth to a child. **6** produce fruit or flowers. **7** take a specified direction. □ **bear down on** approach in a purposeful manner. **bear**

out support or confirm. **bear up** remain cheerful in adversity. **bear with** be patient with. ■ **bearable** adj.

bear[2] n. a large mammal with thick fur. □ **bearskin** a tall furry cap worn by certain troops.

beard n. a growth of hair on a man's chin. ▶v. boldly confront. ■ **bearded** adj.

bearing n. **1** a way of standing, moving, or behaving. **2** relevance. **3** a device allowing two parts to rotate or move in contact with each other. **4** direction or position in relation to a fixed point. **5** (**one's bearings**) awareness of one's relative position.

beast n. **1** a large animal. **2** a very cruel or wicked person.

beastly adj. informal very unpleasant. ■ **beastliness** n.

beat v. (**beating**, **beat**; past part. **beaten**) **1** strike repeatedly. **2** defeat or outdo. **3** move or pulsate rhythmically. **4** stir cooking ingredients vigorously. ▶n. **1** a main accent in music or poetry. **2** a regular movement or pulsation. **3** an area patrolled by a police officer. □ **beat it** informal leave. **beat up** attack violently.

beatific /bee-uh-**tif**-ik/ adj. showing

Thesaurus

beach n. SHORE, seashore, sands, sand, seaside, coast, coastline, littoral, margin, foreshore, water's edge, waterfront; *literary* strand.

beached adj. STRANDED, aground, grounded, ashore, high and dry, stuck, cast up, marooned, wrecked, abandoned.

bead n. BALL, pellet, pill, drop, globule.

beaker n. CUP, mug, glass, goblet, tumbler, tankard.

beam n. **1** BAR, spar, rafter, girder, support, boom, plank, board, joist, timber, stanchion, scantling. **2** RAY, shaft, bar, stream, streak, pencil, gleam, glimmer, glow, glint. ▶v. **1** EMIT, radiate, shine, broadcast, transmit, direct, aim. **2** SMILE, grin, laugh, be radiant. ■ OPPOSITES frown.

bear v. **1** HOLD, support, carry, uphold, sustain, prop up, shoulder, take. **2** BRING, carry, transport, convey, fetch, deliver, move, take, transfer; *informal* tote. **3** BE MARKED WITH, display, exhibit, show, present. **4** ENDURE, tolerate, abide, accept, stand, brook, put up with, submit to, suffer, sustain, cope with, live with, stomach, admit, allow, resign oneself to. **5** PRODUCE, yield, give, give

forth, supply, provide. **6** GIVE BIRTH TO, produce, breed, generate; *old use* bring forth. □ **bear out** *see* CONFIRM, SUPPORT.

bear up COPE, survive, endure, manage, keep on, hold out, keep going. **bear with** BE PATIENT WITH, be tolerant towards, make allowances for, tolerate, suffer, indulge.

bearable adj. ENDURABLE, tolerable, supportable, sustainable, sufferable, acceptable, admissible, manageable. ■ OPPOSITES intolerable, unbearable.

bearing n. **1** CARRIAGE, posture, deportment, comportment, gait, demeanour, air, aspect, behaviour, manner, attitude, mien, composure, stance, style. **2** COURSE, direction. **3** RELEVANCE, pertinence, connection, implication, significance, relation, relationship, application, effect, consequence.

beast n. **1** ANIMAL, creature, brute. **2** BRUTE, savage, monster, fiend, devil, sadist, barbarian, wretch; *old use* blackguard.

beat v. **1** HIT, strike, batter, thrash, slap, whip, lash, cuff, cudgel, buffet, cane, scourge, smack, thwack, thump, pound, drub, hammer, flog, chastise; *informal* bash, whack, clout, wallop, lay into, great happiness. ■ **beatifically** adv.

beatify /bi·at·i·fy/ v. (**beatifying, beatified**) (in the RC Church) declare a dead person to be in a state of bliss, the first step towards canonization.

beatitude /bi·at·i·tyood/ n. blessedness.

beautician n. a person whose job is to give beauty treatments.

beautiful adj. **1** very pleasing to the senses. **2** excellent. ■ **beautifully** adv.

beautify v. (**beautifying, beautified**) make beautiful.

beauty n. (pl. **beauties**) **1** a combination of qualities that delights the senses. **2** a beautiful woman. **3** an excellent example.

beaver n. a large rodent that lives partly in water. ▶v. (**beaver away**) informal work hard.

becalmed adj. (of a sailing ship) unable to move through lack of wind.

because conj. for the reason that.

beck n. (**at someone's beck and call**) doing whatever someone asks.

beckon v. make a summoning gesture.

become v. (**becoming, became**; past part. **become**) **1** begin to be. **2** turn into. **3** (**become of**) happen to. **4** (of clothing) suit someone.

becquerel n. a unit of radioactivity.

bed n. **1** a piece of furniture for sleeping on. **2** an area of ground where flowers and plants are grown. **3** a flat base or foundation. ▶v. (**bedding, bedded**) (**bed down**) sleep in an improvised place. □ **bedclothes** sheets, blankets, etc. **bedpan** a container used as a toilet by a bedridden person. **bedridden** confined to bed due to illness or old age. **bedrock 1** a layer of solid rock under soil. **2** the central principles on which something is based. **bedroom** a room for sleeping in. **bedsit** (or **bedsitter**) a rented room combining a bedroom and living room. **bedsore** a sore caused by lying in bed in one position for a long time. **bedspread** a decorative bed covering. **bedstead** the framework of a bed.

bedding n. bedclothes.

bedevil v. (**bedevilling, bedevilled**; US **bedeviling, bedeviled**) cause continual trouble to.

bedlam n. a noisy, confused scene.

Bedouin /bed·oo·in/ n. (pl. **Bedouin**) an Arab living as a nomad in the desert.

bedraggled adj. untidy.

bee n. a winged insect which makes wax and honey. □ **beehive** a structure in which bees are kept. **beeswax** wax

Thesaurus

rough up, knock about, tan, biff. **2** PULSATE, throb, pound, pulse, palpitate, thump, vibrate. **3** DEFEAT, outdo, conquer, surpass, trounce, vanquish, overcome, excel, subdue, master, best, outclass, outdistance, outpace, outwit, quash, worst; informal thrash, lick. **4** WHISK, whip, stir, agitate, blend, mix. **5** FLAP, flutter, quiver, vibrate, tremble. ▶n. **1** PULSE, vibration, throb, throbbing, pounding, palpitation. **2** RHYTHM, stress, accent, pulse, tempo, metre, measure, time. **3** ROUND, rounds, route, circuit, path, track, course, itinerary, way.

beautiful adj. LOVELY, attractive, pretty, gorgeous, ravishing, stunning, handsome, good-looking, elegant, exquisite, charming, delightful, pleasing, picturesque, decorative, scenic, spectacular, superb, fine, glamorous, graceful; literary beauteous, pulchritudinous; old use fair, comely; Sc. & N. Engl. bonny. ■ OPPOSITES ugly.

beautify v. ADORN, embellish, decorate, ornament, bedeck, enhance, improve, prettify, glamorize, smarten, gild; informal do up, doll up, titivate. ■ OPPOSITES spoil.

beauty n. ATTRACTIVENESS, loveliness, prettiness, handsomeness, good looks, allure, appeal, charm, picturesqueness, glamour, elegance, grace, magnificence, radiance, splendour, artistry; literary pulchritude. ■ OPPOSITES ugliness.

because conjunction SINCE, as, for the reason that, in that, seeing that. □ **because of** ON ACCOUNT OF, owing to, due to, as a result of, in view of, by reason of, by virtue of, thanks to.

beckon v. **1** GESTURE, signal, motion, gesticulate, call, summon, bid, invite, encourage. **2** ATTRACT, tempt, pull, draw, allure, entice.

become v. **1** TURN INTO, turn out to be, change into, grow into, develop into, be transformed into, evolve into, metamorphose into. **2** SUIT, flatter, look good on, sit well on, set off, enhance, go well with, grace.

becoming adj. FLATTERING, pretty, attractive, elegant, stylish, chic. ■ OPPOSITES unflattering.

bed n. **1** COUCH, cot, berth; informal the sack, the hay, one's pit. **2** BASE, foundation, bottom, basis, support, substratum, substructure, layer.

bedraggled adj. DISHEVELLED, untidy,

produced by bees to make honeycombs, used in polishes etc. **make a beeline for** hurry straight to.

beech n. a large tree with grey bark and pale wood.

beef n. meat from a cow, bull, or ox. ▶ v. **(beef up)** informal make stronger or larger. □ **beefburger** a fried or grilled cake of minced beef. **beefeater** a warder in the Tower of London.

beefy adj. informal muscular or strong.

been past part. of BE.

beep n. a short, high-pitched sound made by electronic equipment or a vehicle's horn. ▶ v. produce a beep. ■ **beeper** n.

beer n. an alcoholic drink made from malt and hops.

beet n. a plant with a fleshy root, grown as food and for making into sugar.

beetle n. an insect with hard, shiny covers over its wings.

beetroot n. the edible dark red root of a kind of beet.

befall v. **(befalling, befell**; past part. **befallen)** happen to.

befit v. **(befitting, befitted)** be appropriate for.

before prep., conj., & adv. **1** during the time preceding. **2** in front of. **3** rather than.

beforehand adv. in advance.

befriend v. become a friend to.

befuddled adj. muddled or confused.

beg v. **(begging, begged) 1** ask humbly or solemnly for something. **2** ask for food or money as charity.

beget v. **(begetting, begot**; past part. **begotten)** old use **1** father a child. **2** cause.

beggar n. a person who lives by begging for food or money.

beggarly adj. meagre and ungenerous.

begin v. **(beginning, began**; past part. **begun) 1** carry out or experience the first part of an action or activity. **2** come into being. **3** have as its starting point. ■ **beginner** n. **beginning** n.

begonia n. a plant with brightly coloured flowers.

begrudge v. **1** feel envious that someone possesses something. **2** give reluctantly or resentfully.

beguile v. charm or trick.

behalf n. **(on behalf of) 1** in the interests of. **2** as a representative of.

behave v. **1** act in a certain way. **2** (also **behave oneself**) act in a polite or proper way.

unkempt, disordered, muddy, wet, soiled, drenched, soaked, stained, soaking, sodden, soggy, messy, dirty, muddied. ■ OPPOSITES neat, clean.

beef n. BRAWN, muscle, strength, sinew, physique, bulk, burliness, robustness, muscularity.

befall v. HAPPEN, occur, happen to, take place, come about, chance, arise, ensue, follow, transpire; literary come to pass, betide.

before prep. **1** PRIOR TO, ahead of, earlier than, sooner than. **2** IN FRONT OF, in the presence of, in the sight of. ▶ adv. EARLIER, previously, beforehand, in advance, formerly, ahead.

befriend v. **1** MAKE FRIENDS WITH. **2** TAKE UNDER ONE'S PROTECTION, protect, look after, take under one's wing, support, assist, succour.

beg v. **1** ASK FOR MONEY, solicit; informal scrounge, cadge. **2** PLEAD, entreat, ask, request, seek, crave, importune, implore, pray, supplicate, petition, cajole, wheedle; literary beseech.

beggar n. VAGRANT, tramp, down-and-out, derelict, vagabond, mendicant; informal scrounger, sponger, cadger.

begin v. **1** START, commence, set about, start on, set in motion, set going, activate, spark off, embark on, initiate, establish, institute, inaugurate, originate, found, pioneer, open, launch, give rise to, cause, instigate, be the source of. **2** COME INTO BEING, start, commence, arise, emerge, appear, occur, happen, originate, materialize, dawn, spring up. ■ OPPOSITES finish, disappear.

beginner n. NOVICE, learner, trainee, apprentice, student, recruit, tyro, fledgling, neophyte, novitiate; US tenderfoot; informal rookie; US informal greenhorn. ■ OPPOSITES expert, veteran.

beginning n. **1** START, origin, opening, commencement, outset, dawn, birth, inception, starting point, source, emergence, onset, genesis, conception, germ, root, spring. **2** ESTABLISHMENT, foundation, institution, inauguration, opening, creation, introduction. **3** PRELUDE, introduction, preface, opening. ■ OPPOSITES end, conclusion.

begrudge v. GRUDGE, resent, give unwillingly, be jealous of, object to, envy, mind, be dissatisfied with.

beguile v. **1** CHARM, attract, delight, enchant, allure, bewitch, please, entice, seduce, tempt. **2** AMUSE, absorb, engross, engage, divert, entertain, distract, occupy.

behaviour (US **behavior**) n. a way of behaving.

behead v. execute someone by cutting off their head.

behest n. (**at the behest of**) at the request or order of.

behind prep. & adv. **1** at or to the back of. **2** less advanced than others. **3** in support of. **4** responsible for an event or plan. **5** late in doing something. ▶n. informal the buttocks.

behold v. (**beholding, beheld**) old use see or observe.

beholden adj. owing gratitude for a service or favour.

behove v. (**it behoves someone to do**) it is right or necessary for someone to do.

beige n. a pale fawn colour.

being n. **1** existence. **2** the nature of a person. **3** a living creature.

belabour (US **belabor**) v. attack.

belated adj. coming late or too late. ■ **belatedly** adv.

belay v. secure a rope by winding it round something.

belch v. **1** noisily expel wind from the stomach through the mouth. **2** expel smoke or flames with great force. ▶n. an act of belching.

beleaguered adj. **1** under siege. **2** in difficulties; harassed.

belfry n. (pl. **belfries**) the place in a bell tower in which bells are housed.

belie v. (**belying, belied**) **1** fail to give a true idea of. **2** show to be untrue.

belief n. **1** a feeling that something exists or is true. **2** a firmly held opinion. **3** trust or confidence. **4** religious faith.

believe v. **1** accept that something is true or someone is telling the truth. **2** (**believe in**) have faith in the truth or existence of. **3** think or suppose. **4** have religious faith. ■ **believer** n.

Belisha beacon n. a flashing orange ball on a post at each end of a zebra crossing.

belittle v. dismiss as unimportant.

bell n. **1** a metal cup held upside down, that sounds a clear musical note when struck. **2** a device that buzzes or rings to give a signal.

belladonna n. a drug made from deadly nightshade.

belle n. a beautiful woman.

bellicose adj. eager to fight.

belligerent adj. **1** aggressive. **2** engaged in a war. ■ **belligerence** n. **belligerently** adv.

bellow v. **1** give a deep roar of pain or anger. **2** shout very loudly. ▶n. a deep shout or noise.

bellows pl. n. a device used for blowing air into a fire.

belly n. (pl. **bellies**) **1** the abdomen. **2** a person's stomach. ▶v. (**bellying, bel-**

Thesaurus

behalf n. (**on behalf of**) **1** IN THE INTERESTS OF, for the sake of, in support of, for the good of, on account of. **2** REPRESENTING, in the name of, in place of.

behave v. **1** ACT, conduct oneself, perform, operate, function, acquit oneself, comport oneself. **2** BE GOOD, be polite, mind one's manners, be obedient; informal mind one's Ps and Qs.

behaviour n. CONDUCT, actions, demeanour, comportment, manners, ways, activity, functioning, performance, operation; US deportment.

being n. **1** CREATURE, living thing, entity, animal, person, individual, human, mortal. **2** EXISTENCE, life, living, animation, actuality, reality.

belated adj. LATE, overdue, delayed, unpunctual, tardy, behind time, behindhand. ■ OPPOSITES early.

belief n. **1** OPINION, judgement, view, thought, feeling, conviction, way of thinking, theory, notion, impression. **2** TRUST, faith, credence, reliance, assurance, certainty, confidence, security, sureness. **3** FAITH, creed, credo, doctrine, dogma, persuasion, conviction, tenet, teaching, ideology. ■ OPPOSITES doubt.

believe v. **1** ACCEPT, be convinced by, trust, subscribe to, rely on, swear to; informal swallow, buy, fall for, take as gospel. **2** THINK, hold, suppose, reckon, be of the opinion, assume, presume, imagine, consider, conjecture, guess, hypothesize, theorize, maintain, understand, surmise, postulate. ■ OPPOSITES doubt, disbelieve.

believer n. ADHERENT, devotee, follower, supporter, disciple. ■ OPPOSITES sceptic.

belittle n. DISPARAGE, decry, slight, depreciate, deprecate, make light of, underestimate, underrate, undervalue, detract from, denigrate, downgrade, minimize, criticize, scoff at, sneer at. ■ OPPOSITES praise.

belligerent adj. **1** AGGRESSIVE, argumentative, pugnacious, combative, antagonistic, confrontational, disputatious, bellicose, provocative, militant, quarrelsome, hot-tempered, quick-tempered, lied) swell out. ■ **bellyful** n.

belong v. 1 (**belong to**) be the property of. 2 (**belong to**) be a member of. 3 be rightly placed or assigned. 4 fit in a particular place or situation.

belongings pl. n. personal possessions.

beloved adj. dearly loved.

below prep. & adv. at a lower level than.

belt n. 1 a strip of material worn round the waist. 2 a continuous band in machinery that connects two wheels. 3 a strip or encircling area. ▶v. 1 fasten with a belt. 2 informal hit very hard. 3 (**belt up**) informal be quiet. □ **below the belt** unfair.

belying pres. part. of BELIE.

bemoan v. complain about.

bemused adj. confused; bewildered. ■ **bemusement** n.

bench n. 1 a long seat for more than one person. 2 a long work table. 3 (**the bench**) the office of judge or magistrate. □ **benchmark** a standard or point of reference.

bend v. (**bending, bent**) 1 make or be-

come curved. 2 lean or curve the body downwards; stoop. 3 change a rule to suit oneself. ▶n. a curve or turn. ■ **bendy** adj.

beneath prep. & adv. 1 extending or directly underneath. 2 of lower status or worth than.

benediction n. a prayer asking for divine blessing.

benefactor n. a person who gives money or other help. ■ **benefaction** n.

benefice n. the arrangement by which a Christian priest is paid and given accommodation.

beneficent adj. doing good or resulting in good. ■ **beneficence** n.

beneficial adj. favourable or advantageous. ■ **beneficially** adv.

beneficiary n. (pl. **beneficiaries**) a person who benefits from something.

benefit n. 1 advantage or profit. 2 a payment made by the state to someone in need. ▶v. (**benefiting, benefited** or **benefitting, benefitted**) 1 receive an advantage; profit. 2 bring advantage to.

Thesaurus

irascible, captious. 2 WARRING, at war, hostile, battling, combatant, contending, militant, warmongering, warlike, martial. ■ OPPOSITES peaceable.

belong v. 1 BE OWNED BY, be the property of, be held by. 2 BE A MEMBER OF, be part of, be one of, be connected with, be associated with, be affiliated to, be allied to, be included in, be an adherent of. 3 HAVE A PLACE, be supposed to be. 4 BE AT HOME, be suited, be welcome, fit in, be accepted.

belongings pl. n. PROPERTY, possessions, things, effects, goods, chattels, paraphernalia, appurtenances, accoutrements, impedimenta; informal stuff, gear, junk.

beloved adj. LOVED, adored, dear, dearest, cherished, worshipped, treasured, prized, precious, sweet, idolized, darling. ▶n. SWEETHEART, lover, love, girlfriend, boyfriend, inamorata, inamorato; old use paramour.

belt n. 1 GIRDLE, sash, waistband, band, cummerbund, girth; literary cincture. 2 STRIP, stretch, band, stripe, streak, bar, region, zone, area, district, tract, extent. ▶v. HIT, strike, beat, thump, cuff; informal whack, wallop. See also HIT.

bemused adj. BEWILDERED, dazed, confused, stunned, muddled, puzzled, perplexed, baffled, befuddled, stupefied, amazed, astounded, astonished, overwhelmed, disconcerted.

bend v. 1 CURVE, crook, make crooked, arch, bow, twist, flex, warp, fold, contort, mould, shape. 2 TURN, curve, twist, curl, veer, swerve, loop, diverge, deviate, wind, coil, spiral, incurvate. 3 STOOP, lean, crouch, bow, hunch, duck. ▶n. CURVE, corner, turn, twist, arc, angle, loop, coil, spiral, crook, swerve, deflection, deviation, zigzag, dog-leg. ■ OPPOSITES straight.

beneath prep. 1 BELOW, under, underneath, lower than. 2 INFERIOR TO, lower than, subservient to, subordinate to, secondary to. 3 UNWORTHY OF, not proper for, degrading to, undignified for, unsuitable for, inappropriate for, unbecoming for. ■ OPPOSITES above.

benefactor n. HELPER, supporter, sponsor, patron, backer, donor, promoter, subsidizer, subscriber, well-wisher, sympathizer, philanthropist, fairy godmother; informal angel.

beneficial adj. ADVANTAGEOUS, profitable, helpful, useful, worthwhile, valuable, gainful, healthy, rewarding, fruitful, productive, salutary, salubrious, wholesome, improving, serviceable, propitious, promising, favourable, obliging, accommodating, nutritious, nourishing, nurturing. ■ OPPOSITES disadvantageous.

beneficiary n. HEIR, heiress, inheritor, recipient, legatee, payee, assignee, receiver, successor.

benevolent adj. well meaning and kindly. ■ **benevolence** n.

benighted adj. ignorant or primitive.

benign adj. **1** kindly. **2** (of a tumour) not malignant.

bent past & past part. of BEND. ▶ adj. **1** informal dishonest; corrupt. **2** (**bent on**) determined to do. ▶ n. a natural talent.

benzene n. a liquid hydrocarbon found in coal tar and petroleum.

bequeath v. leave property to someone by a will.

bequest n. a legacy.

berate v. scold angrily.

bereaved adj. having recently lost a close relation or friend through their death. ■ **bereavement** n.

bereft adj. **1** (**bereft of**) without. **2** lonely and abandoned.

beret /be-ray/ n. a flat round cap with no peak.

bergamot /ber-guh-mot/ n. an oily substance found in some oranges, used as a flavouring.

beriberi n. a disease caused by a lack of vitamin B_1.

berk n. informal a stupid person.

berry n. (pl. **berries**) a small round juicy fruit without a stone.

berserk adj. out of control; wild and frenzied.

berth n. **1** a place for a ship to moor at a wharf. **2** a bunk on a ship or train. ▶ v. moor in a berth.

beryl n. a transparent pale green, blue, or yellow gemstone.

beryllium n. a lightweight grey metallic element.

beseech v. (**beseeching, besought** or **beseeched**) ask in a pleading way.

beset v. (**besetting, beset**) trouble or worry continuously.

beside prep. **1** at the side of. **2** compared with. **3** (also **besides**) as well as. ▶ adv. (**besides**) as well. □ **beside oneself** frantic with worry.

besiege v. surround a place with armed forces.

besmirch v. damage someone's reputation.

besom /bee-zuhm/ n. a broom made of twigs tied round a stick.

Thesaurus

benefit n. **1** ADVANTAGE, asset, blessing, boon, plus, plus point, perquisite; informal perk. **2** GOOD, well-being, advantage, interest, profit, gain, welfare, convenience, prosperity, good fortune, aid, assistance, help, service, privilege, betterment. **3** AID, allowance, subsidy, grant, payment, assistance; informal dole. ■ OPPOSITES disadvantage, detriment. ▶ v. **1** HELP, profit, be advantageous to, be good for, serve, aid, assist, advance, further, promote, advantage, forward, boost, avail, enhance, improve, better. **2** GAIN, profit, do well, reap benefits/reward, prosper, put to good use, do well out of; informal cash in.

benevolent adj. KIND, kind-hearted, kindly, generous, warm-hearted, caring, benign, amiable, friendly, beneficent, liberal, magnanimous, bountiful, humane, humanitarian, altruistic, philanthropic, compassionate, sympathetic, considerate, thoughtful, obliging, well meaning, helpful. ■ OPPOSITES malicious, unkind.

benign adj. **1** KINDLY, benevolent, kindhearted, kind, generous, cordial, genial, amiable, warm, gentle, tolerant, gracious, friendly, accommodating. **2** FAVOURABLE, auspicious, propitious, opportune, lucky, advantageous, helpful, providential, suitable, appropriate, healthy, wholesome, health-giving, salubrious, pleasant, refreshing, agreeable, mild, temperate, balmy. **3** NON-MALIGNANT, curable, treatable, remediable, innocent, harmless. ■ OPPOSITES unfriendly, unfavourable; malignant.

bent adj. **1** CURVED, crooked, twisted, angled, bowed, arched, warped, distorted, contorted, folded, coiled, buckled, hunched. **2** CORRUPT, dishonest, fraudulent, criminal, untrustworthy, unprincipled, immoral; informal crooked. ▶ n. TENDENCY, inclination, predisposition, leaning, talent, gift, flair, ability, aptitude, penchant, predilection, propensity, proclivity.

bequeath v. LEAVE (IN ONE'S WILL), will, make over, pass on, hand on/down, transfer, donate, give, bestow on, confer on, endow with.

bequest n. LEGACY, inheritance, endowment, settlement, estate, heritage.

bereavement n. DEATH IN THE FAMILY, loss, passing (away), demise, decease.

berserk adj. MAD, crazy, insane, out of one's mind, hysterical, frenzied, crazed, demented, maniacal, manic, frantic, raving, wild, amok, on the rampage; informal off the deep end, ape, bananas, bonkers, spare.

berth n. **1** BUNK, bed, cot, hammock. **2** MOORING, dock, quay, pier. ▶ v. DOCK, moor, land, tie up, make fast.

beseech v. IMPLORE, beg, entreat, plead

besotted adj. infatuated.

besought past & past part. of BESEECH.

bespeak v. (**bespeaking, bespoke**; past part. **bespoken**) be evidence of.

bespoke adj. made to a customer's requirements.

best adj. **1** of the highest quality. **2** most suitable or sensible. ▶ adv. **1** to the highest degree or standard. **2** most suitably or sensibly. ▶ n. (**the best**) that which is of the highest quality. □ **best man** a man chosen by a bridegroom to assist him at his wedding.

bestial adj. savagely cruel or wicked. ■ **bestiality** n.

bestir v. (**bestirring, bestirred**) (**bestir oneself**) rouse oneself to action.

bestow v. award an honour, gift, etc.

bestride v. (**bestriding, bestrode**; past part. **bestridden**) stand astride over.

bet v. (**betting, bet** or **betted**) **1** risk money against someone else's on the outcome of an unpredictable event such as a race. **2** informal feel sure. ▶ n. an act of betting or the money betted.

beta /bee-tuh/ n. the second letter of the Greek alphabet (B, β). □ **beta blocker** a drug used to treat high blood pressure and angina.

betake v. (**betaking, betook**; past part. **betaken**) (**betake oneself to**) go to.

bête noire /bet nwar/ n. (pl. **bêtes noires**) a person or thing that one particularly dislikes.

betide v. literary happen or happen to.

betimes adv. literary early.

betoken v. be a sign of.

betray v. **1** act treacherously towards one's country by helping an enemy. **2** be disloyal to. **3** reveal unintentionally. ■ **betrayal** n. **betrayer** n.

betrothed adj. engaged to be married. ■ **betrothal** n.

better adj. **1** more satisfactory or suitable. **2** recovered from illness or injury. ▶ adv. **1** in a better way. **2** to a greater degree. ▶ n. (**one's betters**) people who are more important or skilled than oneself. ▶ v. **1** improve on. **2** (**better oneself**) improve one's social status. □ **better off** in a more favourable position. **get the better of** defeat.

between prep. & adv. **1** at, across, or in the space or period separating two things. **2** indicating a connection or relationship. **3** shared by; together with.

betwixt prep. & adv. old use between.

bevel n. an edge cut at an angle in wood or glass. ▶ v. (**bevelling, bevelled**; US **beveling, beveled**) cut a bevel on.

beverage n. a drink.

bevy n. (pl. **bevies**) a large group.

bewail v. express great regret or sorrow over.

beware v. be aware of danger.

bewilder v. puzzle or confuse. ■ **bewilderment** n.

bewitch v. **1** cast a spell over. **2** attract

Thesaurus

with, appeal to, call on, supplicate, importune, pray to, ask, petition.

besiege v. **1** LAY SIEGE TO, beleaguer, blockade. **2** SURROUND, mob, crowd round, swarm round, ring, encircle.

best adj. FINEST, greatest, top, foremost, leading, pre-eminent, premier, prime, first, supreme, of the highest quality, superlative, par excellence, unrivalled, second to none, without equal, nonpareil, unsurpassed, peerless, matchless, unparalleled, unbeatable, optimum, optimal, ultimate, ideal, perfect; informal star, number-one. ▶ n. FINEST, top, cream, choice, prime, elite, crème de la crème, flower, jewel in the crown; informal pick of the bunch.

bestial adj. SAVAGE, animal, brutish, brutal, barbaric, cruel, vicious, violent, inhuman, depraved, degenerate. ■ OPPOSITES civilized, humane.

bestow v. CONFER, grant, accord, afford, endow with, vest in, present, award.

bet v. WAGER, gamble, stake, risk, venture, hazard, chance, put/lay money,

speculate; informal have a flutter, have a punt. ▶ n. WAGER, gamble, stake, ante; informal flutter, punt.

betray v. **1** BREAK ONE'S PROMISE TO, be disloyal to, be unfaithful to, break faith with, play someone false, inform on/against, give away, denounce, sell out, stab in the back; informal split on, rat on, peach on, stitch up, do the dirty on, sell down the river, squeal on, grass on, shop, sneak on; US informal finger. **2** REVEAL, disclose, divulge, tell, give away, leak, let slip, let out, blurt out; informal blab, spill.

better adj. **1** SUPERIOR, finer, of higher quality; informal a cut above, streets ahead, head and shoulders above. **2** WELL, healthy, cured, healed, recovered, recovering, on the road to recovery; informal on the mend. ■ OPPOSITES worse, inferior.

beware v. BE ON YOUR GUARD, watch out, look out, mind out, be alert, be on the lookout, keep your eyes open/peeled, keep an eye out, take care, be careful, and delight.

beyond prep. & adv. **1** at or to the further side of. **2** outside the range or limits of. **3** happening or continuing after.

bezel n. a groove holding the glass cover of a watch in place.

bhaji /bah-ji/ n. an Indian dish of vegetables fried in batter.

bi- comb. form **1** two. **2** twice.

biannual adj. occurring twice a year.

bias n. **1** an inclination or prejudice for or against a person or thing. **2** a direction diagonal to the grain of a fabric. **3** (in bowls) a tendency to swerve caused by a bowl's irregular shape.

biased adj. having a bias; prejudiced.

bib n. **1** a piece of cloth or plastic fastened under a child's chin to protect its clothes. **2** the upper front part of an apron or pair of dungarees.

Bible n. **1** the Christian or Jewish scriptures. **2** (**bible**) informal a book seen as authoritative.

biblical adj. of or in the Bible.

bibliography n. (pl. **bibliographies**) **1** a list of the books referred to in a written work. **2** a list of books on a particular subject. ■ **bibliographer** n. **bibliographic** adj.

bibliophile n. a person who collects books.

bicarbonate of soda n. a soluble white powder used in fizzy drinks and in baking.

bicentenary n. (pl. **bicentenaries**) a 200th anniversary. ■ **bicentennial** n. & adj.

biceps n. (pl. **biceps**) a large muscle in the upper arm which flexes the arm and forearm.

bicker v. argue about trivial things.

bicycle n. a two-wheeled vehicle propelled by pedals. ▶ v. ride a bicycle.

bid¹ v. (**bidding**, **bid**) **1** offer a price for something. **2** try to get or do. ▶ n. an act of bidding. ■ **bidder** n. **bidding** n.

bid² v. (**bidding**, **bid** or **bade**; past part. **bid**) **1** say a greeting or farewell to. **2** old use command.

biddable adj. obedient.

bide v. (**bide one's time**) wait patiently for an opportunity.

bidet /bee-day/ n. a low basin for washing one's genital area.

biennial adj. **1** taking place every other year. **2** (of a plant) living for two years.

bier /beer/ n. a platform on which a coffin is placed before burial.

bifocal adj. (of a lens) made in two sections, one for distant and one for close vision. ▶ n. (**bifocals**) a pair of glasses with bifocal lenses.

bifurcate v. split into two branches or forks. ■ **bifurcation** n.

big adj. (**bigger**, **biggest**) **1** large in size, amount, or extent. **2** very important or serious. **3** older or grown-up.

bigamy n. the crime of marrying someone while already married to another person. ■ **bigamist** n. **bigamous** adj.

bigot n. a prejudiced and intolerant person. ■ **bigoted** adj. **bigotry** n.

bijou /bee-zhoo/ adj. small and elegant.

bike n. a bicycle or motorcycle. ■ **biker** n.

bikini n. (pl. **bikinis**) a women's two-piece swimsuit.

bilateral adj. **1** having two sides. **2** involving two parties. ■ **bilaterally** adv.

bilberry n. a small blue edible berry.

Thesaurus

be cautious, have a care, watch your step.

bewilder v. BAFFLE, mystify, bemuse, perplex, puzzle, confuse, nonplus; informal flummox, stump, beat, fox, discombobulate.

bewitch v. CAPTIVATE, enchant, entrance, cast/put a spell on, enrapture, charm, beguile, fascinate, enthral.

bias n. PREJUDICE, partiality, partisanship, favouritism, unfairness, one-sidedness, tendency, inclination, predilection, bigotry, intolerance, discrimination. ▶ v. PREJUDICE, influence, colour, sway, predispose, distort, skew.

biased adj. PREJUDICED, partial, partisan, one-sided, blinkered, jaundiced, distorted, warped, twisted, skewed, bigoted, intolerant, discriminatory. ■ OPPOS-

ITES impartial.

bid v. OFFER, put up, tender, proffer, propose. ▶ n. **1** OFFER, tender, proposal. **2** ATTEMPT, effort, endeavour, try; informal crack, go, shot, stab. □ **bid for** TRY TO GET, go for, make a pitch for, make a bid for.

big adj. LARGE, great, of considerable size, sizeable, substantial, goodly, tall, high, huge, immense, enormous, colossal, massive, mammoth, broad, vast, prodigious, gigantic, giant, monumental, stupendous, gargantuan, man-size, king-size, outsize, considerable; informal whopping, mega, astronomical, humongous, ginormous. ■ OPPOSITES small.

bigot n. DOGMATIST, partisan, sectarian, racist, sexist, chauvinist.

bigoted adj. PREJUDICED, biased, one-

bile n. **1** a bitter fluid produced by the liver. **2** anger or bitterness.

bilge n. **1** the bottom of a ship's hull. **2** informal nonsense.

bilingual adj. written in or able to speak two languages.

bilious adj. affected by sickness.

bill n. **1** a written statement of charges for goods or services. **2** a draft of a proposed law. **3** a programme of entertainment at a theatre or cinema. **4** an advertising poster. **5** US a banknote. **6** a bird's beak. ▶ v. **1** list in a programme. **2** send a statement of charges to. □ **billboard** a hoarding for advertising posters. **billhook** a tool with a curved blade, used for pruning.

billabong n. Austral. a branch of a river forming a backwater or stagnant pool.

billet n. a private house used as lodgings for troops. ▶ v. (**be billeted**) (of a soldier) stay in a private house.

billet-doux /bil-li-doo/ n. (pl. **billets-doux**) a love letter.

billiards n. a game played on a table with pockets at the sides and corners, into which balls are struck with a cue.

billion n. **1** a thousand million. **2** (**billions**) informal very many. ■ **billionth** adj.

billow v. **1** (of smoke, cloud, etc.) roll outward. **2** fill with air and swell out. ▶ n. a large rolling mass of cloud, smoke, etc.

bimbo n. (pl. **bimbos**) informal an attractive but unintelligent woman.

bin n. **1** a container for rubbish. **2** a large storage container. ▶ v. (**binning, binned**) throw away.

binary adj. **1** composed of or involving two things. **2** of a system of numbers with two as its base, using the digits 0 and 1.

bind v. (**binding, bound**) **1** firmly tie, wrap, or fasten. **2** hold together in a united group. **3** place under a legal obligation. **4** (**bind over**) (of a court of law) require someone to do something. **5** enclose the pages of a book in a cover. **6** trim the edge of a piece of material with a fabric strip. ▶ n. informal an annoy-

ing or difficult situation.

binding n. **1** a covering holding the pages of a book together. **2** fabric in a strip, used for binding the edges of material. ▶ adj. (of an agreement) involving a legal obligation.

binge n. informal a bout of uncontrolled eating or drinking.

bingo n. a game in which players mark off randomly called numbers on cards, the winner being the first to mark off all their numbers.

binocular adj. using both eyes. ▶ n. (**binoculars**) an instrument with a separate lens for each eye, for viewing distant objects.

binomial n. an algebraic expression consisting of two terms linked by a plus or minus sign.

biochemistry n. the branch of science concerned with the chemical processes that occur within living things. ■ **biochemical** adj. **biochemist** n.

biodegradable adj. able to be decomposed by bacteria or other living organisms.

biodiversity n. the variety of living things in an environment.

biography n. (pl. **biographies**) an account of a person's life written by someone else. ■ **biographer** n. **biographical** adj.

biology n. the scientific study of living organisms. ■ **biological** adj. **biologist** n.

bionic adj. (of an artificial body part) electronically powered.

biopsy n. (pl. **biopsies**) an examination of tissue taken from a living body.

biorhythm n. a recurring cycle in the functioning of an organism.

biotechnology n. the use of microorganisms in industry and medicine.

bipartisan adj. involving two political parties.

bipartite adj. involving two separate groups.

biped /by-ped/ n. an animal that walks on two feet.

biplane n. an aircraft with two pairs of

Thesaurus

sided, sectarian, discriminatory, opinionated, dogmatic, intolerant, narrow-minded, blinkered, racist, sexist, chauvinistic, jingoistic. ■ OPPOSITES open-minded.

bill n. **1** INVOICE, account, statement; US check; informal tab. **2** DRAFT LAW, proposed legislation, measure. ▶ v. INVOICE,

charge, debit, send a statement to.

billow v. **1** PUFF UP/OUT, balloon (out), swell, fill (out), belly out. **2** SWIRL, spiral, roll, undulate, eddy, pour, flow.

bind v. **1** TIE (UP), fasten (together), hold together, secure, make fast, attach, rope, strap, lash, truss, tether. **2** BANDAGE, dress, cover, wrap, strap up, tape wings, one above the other.

birch n. a slender tree with thin, peeling bark.

bird n. **1** an egg-laying animal with feathers and wings, usu. able to fly. **2** informal a young woman or girlfriend.

birdie n. (pl. **birdies**) Golf a score of one stroke under par at a hole.

biro n. (pl. **biros**) trademark a ballpoint pen.

birth n. **1** the emergence of a baby or other young from its mother's body. **2** the beginning of something. **3** origin or ancestry. □ **birth control** the use of contraceptives. **birthday** the anniversary of the day on which a person was born. **birthmark** a coloured mark on the body, present from birth. **birthright** a right or privilege possessed from birth.

biscuit n. a small, flat, crisp cake.

bisect v. divide into two equal parts.

bisexual adj. sexually attracted to both men and women. ▶ n. a bisexual person. ■ **bisexuality** n.

bishop n. **1** a senior member of the Christian clergy. **2** a chess piece with a top shaped like a mitre.

bishopric n. the position or diocese of a bishop.

bismuth n. a reddish-grey metallic element.

bison n. (pl. **bison**) a shaggy-haired wild ox.

bistro n. (pl. **bistros**) a small, inexpensive restaurant.

bit n. **1** a small piece or quantity. **2** a short time or distance. **3** the mouthpiece of a horse's bridle. **4** a tool for boring or drilling. **5** Computing the smallest unit of information, expressed as either 0 or 1. □ **a bit** rather; slightly.

bitch n. **1** a female dog. **2** informal a spiteful or unpleasant woman. ▶ v. informal make spiteful comments. ■ **bitchiness** n. **bitchy** adj.

bite v. (**biting**, **bit**; past part. **bitten**) **1** cut into with the teeth. **2** (of a tool, tyre, etc.) grip a surface. **3** take effect, with unpleasant consequences. ▶ n. **1** an act of biting or a piece bitten off. **2** informal a quick snack.

biting adj. **1** (of wind) painfully cold. **2** sharply critical.

bitter adj. **1** having a sharp taste; not sweet. **2** resentful. **3** (of a conflict) intense and full of hatred. **4** intensely cold. ▶ n. bitter-tasting beer that is strongly flavoured with hops. ■ **bitterly** adv. **bitterness** n.

bittern n. a marshland bird with a booming call.

bitumen n. a black sticky substance obtained from petroleum. ■ **bituminous** adj.

bivalve n. a mollusc with a hinged double shell, e.g. an oyster or mussel.

bivouac n. a temporary camp without tents. ▶ v. (**bivouacking**, **bivouacked**) stay in a bivouac.

bizarre adj. very strange or unusual.

Thesaurus

up. **3** UNITE, join, bond, knit. ■ OPPOSITES untie, separate.

binding adj. IRREVOCABLE, unalterable, inescapable, unbreakable, contractual, compulsory, obligatory, mandatory.

birth n. **1** CHILDBIRTH, delivery, nativity, birthing; dated confinement. **2** BEGINNING(S), emergence, genesis, dawn, rise, start. **3** ANCESTRY, lineage, blood, descent, parentage, family, extraction, origin, genealogy, stock. ■ OPPOSITES death, demise, end. □ **give birth to** HAVE, bear, produce, be delivered of, bring into the world; US birth; informal drop.

bisect v. CUT IN HALF, halve, divide/cut/split in two, cross, intersect.

bit n. **1** PIECE, portion, segment, section, part, fragment, scrap, shred, crumb, grain, speck, snippet, snatch, spot, drop, pinch, dash, soupçon, morsel, iota, jot, whit, atom, particle, trace, touch, suggestion, hint; informal smidgen, tad. **2** MOMENT, minute, second, (little) while; informal sec, jiffy, mo, tick. ■ OPPOSITES lot. □ **bit by bit** GRADUALLY, little by little, in stages, step by step, piecemeal, slowly.

bite v. **1** SINK ONE'S TEETH INTO, chew, munch, nibble at, gnaw, crunch, champ, tear at. **2** GRIP, hold, get a purchase. **3** TAKE EFFECT, be effective, work, act, have results. ▶ n. **1** CHEW, munch, nibble, gnaw, nip. **2** SNACK, mouthful, refreshments; informal a little something. **3** PIQUANCY, pungency, spiciness, tang, zest, sharpness, tartness; informal kick, punch.

biting adj. see COLD, SCATHING.

bitter adj. **1** ACRID, tart, sour, sharp, acid, unsweetened, harsh, biting, acerbic, astringent, pungent, vinegary, acetous, unpleasant. **2** RESENTFUL, angry, sullen, embittered, sour, sore, rancorous, acerbic, acrimonious, peevish, petulant, spiteful, malicious, vicious, sharp, waspish, piqued, jaundiced, jealous, envious, indignant, morose, begrudging,

blab v. (**blabbing, blabbed**) informal reveal a secret.

black adj. **1** of the very darkest colour. **2** relating to people with dark-coloured skin. **3** (of coffee or tea) without milk. **4** marked by disaster or despair. **5** (of humour) presenting distressing situations in comic terms. **6** hostile. ▶n. **1** black colour. **2** a black person. ▶v. **1** make black. **2** (**black out**) faint. □ **black eye** an area of bruising round the eye. **black economy** unofficial and untaxed business activity. **black hole** a region in space with a gravitational field so strong that no matter or radiation can escape. **black magic** magic involving the summoning of evil spirits. **black market** illegal trading in officially controlled goods. **black pudding** a sausage containing dried pig's blood. **black sheep** a person seen as a disgrace to their family. ■ **blackness** n.

blackball v. exclude from membership of a club.

blackberry n. the dark edible fruit of a prickly shrub.

blackbird n. a type of thrush.

blackboard n. a dark board for writing on with chalk.

blackcurrant n. a small round edible black berry.

blacken v. **1** become or make black. **2** damage someone's reputation.

blackguard /blag-gerd/ n. dated a dishonest or unprincipled man.

blackhead n. a lump of oily matter blocking a pore in the skin.

blackleg n. derog. a person who continues working when fellow workers

are on strike.

blacklist n. a list of people seen as unacceptable or untrustworthy.

blackmail n. the demanding of money from someone in return for not revealing information that could disgrace them. ▶v. use blackmail on. ■ **blackmailer** n.

blackout n. **1** a period when all lights must be turned out during an enemy air raid. **2** a sudden failure of electric lights. **3** a short loss of consciousness.

blacksmith n. a person who makes and repairs things made of iron.

bladder n. a sac in the abdomen which stores urine for excretion.

blade n. **1** the flat cutting edge of a knife or other tool or weapon. **2** the broad flat part of an oar, leaf, etc. **3** a long narrow leaf of grass.

blame v. hold responsible for a fault or wrong. ▶n. responsibility for a fault or wrong. ■ **blameless** adj. **blameworthy** adj.

blanch v. **1** make or become white or pale. **2** immerse vegetables briefly in boiling water.

blancmange /bluh-monzh/ n. a sweet jelly-like dessert made with milk.

bland adj. lacking interesting qualities or features.

blandishments pl. n. flattery intended to persuade or coax.

blank adj. **1** not marked or decorated. **2** not understanding or reacting. ▶n. **1** an empty space. **2** a cartridge containing gunpowder but no bullet. □ **blank verse** poetry that does not rhyme.

blanket n. **1** a warm covering made of

Thesaurus

crabbed. ■ OPPOSITES sweet, happy.

bizarre adj. EXTRAORDINARY, outlandish, eccentric, fantastic, surreal, freakish, grotesque, peculiar, odd, strange, curious, abnormal, weird, unusual, uncommon, outré, unconventional, queer, aberrant, deviant, ludicrous, droll; informal offbeat, oddball, way-out, wacky; informal, dated rum. ■ OPPOSITES ordinary.

black adj. JET, ebony, sable, inky, sooty, pitch-black, pitch-dark, dark, dusky, coal-black, raven; literary Stygian.

blacken v. DARKEN, black, make dark, dirty, smudge, stain, soil, begrime, befoul.

blame v. **1** ACCUSE, hold responsible, condemn, find guilty, find fault with, criticize, censure, reprimand, reproach, admonish, reprove, scold,

upbraid, chide, berate, take to task. **2** ATTRIBUTE, ascribe, impute, pin on. ▶n. **1** RESPONSIBILITY, accountability, guilt, fault, culpability, liability, onus. **2** CRITICISM, condemnation, censure, accusation, incrimination, stricture, reproach, reproof, recrimination, reprimand, castigation, indictment, complaint, berating; informal stick, rap.

blameless adj. INNOCENT, faultless, guiltless, in the clear, irreproachable, unimpeachable, above reproach, upright, moral, virtuous, unoffending, impeccable, stainless, unblemished. ■ OPPOSITES guilty.

bland adj. **1** TASTELESS, insipid, flavourless, mild. **2** DULL, boring, uninspired, uninspiring, unoriginal, unexciting, tedious, nondescript, trite, vapid, mediwoollen material. **2** a thick mass or layer. ▶v. (**blanketing**, **blanketed**) cover with a thick layer.

blare v. & n. (make) a loud, harsh sound.

blarney n. charming or flattering talk.

blasé /blah-zay/ adj. unimpressed with something through over-familiarity.

blaspheme v. speak irreverently about God or sacred things. ■ **blasphemous** adj. **blasphemy** n.

blast n. **1** an explosion, or the rush of air spreading out from it. **2** a strong gust of wind. **3** a loud note of a horn or whistle. ▶v. **1** blow up with explosives. **2** (**blast off**) (of a rocket etc.) take off. **3** produce loud music or noise.

blatant adj. open and unashamed. ■ **blatantly** adv.

 The ending is *-ant*, not *-ent*: blatant.

blather v. chatter foolishly.

blaze n. **1** a large or fierce fire. **2** a bright light or display of colour. **3** an outburst. **4** a white stripe on an animal's face. ▶v. burn or shine fiercely or brightly. □ **blaze a trail 1** mark out a path. **2** pioneer something.

blazer n. a jacket worn by schoolchildren or sports players as part of a uniform.

blazon v. display or describe prominently or vividly.

bleach v. lighten by chemicals or sunlight. ▶n. a chemical used to bleach things and to sterilize drains, sinks, etc.

bleak adj. **1** barren and exposed. **2** dreary and unwelcoming. **3** (of a situation) not hopeful. ■ **bleakly** adv. **bleakness** n.

bleary adj. (**blearier**, **bleariest**) (of the eyes) dull and unfocused. ■ **blearily** adv.

bleat v. **1** (of a sheep or goat) make a weak, wavering cry. **2** speak or complain feebly. ▶n. a bleating sound.

bleed v. (**bleeding**, **bled**) **1** lose blood from the body. **2** draw blood or fluid from. **3** informal drain of money or resources.

bleep n. a short high-pitched sound made by an electronic device. ▶v. make a bleep. ■ **bleeper** n.

blemish n. a small mark or flaw. ▶v. spoil the appearance of.

blench v. flinch suddenly.

Thesaurus

ocre, humdrum, weak. ■ OPPOSITES tangy, interesting.

blank adj. **1** BARE, plain, clean, unmarked, empty, vacant, clear, void, unfilled, spotless. **2** EXPRESSIONLESS, inscrutable, impassive, unresponsive, deadpan, poker-faced, indifferent, vacant, empty, uncomprehending, vacuous, glazed, emotionless, uninterested. **3** EMPTY, vacant, at a loss, nonplussed, confused, baffled, bewildered, lost, dumbfounded, uncomprehending, puzzled, perplexed. ▶n. GAP, void, space, vacancy, emptiness, vacuum, nothingness, vacuity.

blasphemous adj. PROFANE, sacrilegious, irreligious, impious, irreverent, ungodly, godless, sinful, disrespectful, unholy. ■ OPPOSITES reverent.

blasphemy n. **1** SACRILEGE, profanity, impiety, impiousness, irreverence, irreligiousness, profaneness, ungodliness, desecration, unholiness, execration. **2** OATH, curse, swear word, profanity.

blast n. **1** GUST, draught, rush, gale, storm, squall, blow. **2** EXPLOSION, detonation, blowing up, discharge, burst, bang, eruption. ▶v. **1** BLOW UP, blow to pieces, explode, shatter, demolish, burst, ruin. **2** BOOM, roar, blare,

screech, trumpet.

blatant adj. FLAGRANT, glaring, obvious, unconcealed, undisguised, overt, manifest, brazen, shameless, unembarrassed, barefaced, naked, sheer, conspicuous, prominent, obtrusive, apparent, stark, unmistakable, unmitigated, outright, out-and-out. ■ OPPOSITES discreet, inconspicuous.

blaze n. **1** FIRE, conflagration, burning, flame, inferno. **2** BEAM, gleam, glitter, shine, radiance, dazzle, brightness, brilliance, flash, flare. ▶v. **1** BURN, be on fire, be ablaze, flame, catch fire, flare up, burst into flame. **2** SHINE, gleam, glimmer, dazzle, beam, flare, flash, glitter.

bleach v. FADE, blanch, discolour, turn white/pale, etiolate, decolorize, lighten, whiten, peroxide.

bleak adj. **1** DESOLATE, bare, barren, forbidding, exposed, cold, unwelcoming, unsheltered, waste, desert, windswept, windy, arid, uncultivated, wild, dreary, lonely, grim. **2** DISMAL, dreary, gloomy, depressing, melancholy, wretched, hopeless, sombre, discouraging, disheartening, unpromising, comfortless, miserable, cheerless, joyless. ■ OPPOSITES lush, promising.

blend v. **1** mix smoothly. **2** merge well. ▶ n. a mixture.

blender n. an electric device for liquidizing food.

bless v. **1** make holy. **2** call on God to favour. **3** (**be blessed with**) be fortunate in having.

blessed adj. **1** holy. **2** bringing welcome pleasure or relief. ■ **blessedly** adv.

blessing n. **1** God's favour and protection. **2** a prayer for this. **3** something one is very glad of. **4** a person's approval or support.

blew past of **BLOW**.

blight n. **1** a plant disease caused by fungi. **2** a thing that spoils something. ▶ v. **1** infect with blight. **2** spoil.

blimp n. a small airship.

blind adj. **1** unable to see. **2** lacking awareness or judgement. **3** concealed, closed, or blocked off. ▶ v. **1** make blind. **2** cause to stop thinking clearly or sensibly. ▶ n. **1** a screen for a window. **2** something meant to hide one's plans. □ **blindfold** a piece of cloth used to cover a person's eyes and block their sight. ■ **blindly** adv. **blindness** n.

blink v. **1** shut and open the eyes quickly. **2** shine unsteadily. ▶ n. an act of blinking.

blinker n. (**blinkers**) a pair of flaps attached to a horse's bridle to prevent it from seeing sideways. ▶ v. **1** put blinkers on a horse. **2** cause to have a narrow outlook.

blip n. **1** a short high-pitched sound. **2** a flashing point of light on a radar screen. **3** a temporary deviation from an overall trend.

bliss n. perfect happiness. ■ **blissful** adj. **blissfully** adv.

blister n. **1** a small bubble on the skin filled with watery liquid. **2** a similar bubble on a surface. ▶ v. form blisters.

blithe adj. casually indifferent. ■ **blithely** adv.

blitz n. **1** a sudden fierce attack. **2** informal a sudden and concentrated effort. ▶ v.

Thesaurus

bleary adj. BLURRED, blurry, dim, unclear, indistinct, fuzzy, cloudy, clouded, foggy, misty, hazy, filmy, smeary, obscured, fogged, murky, watery, rheumy. ■ OPPOSITES clear.

blemish n. DEFECT, stain, flaw, fault, disfiguration, imperfection, deformity, ugliness, blot, mark, smear, blotch, crack, chip, taint. ▶ v. SPOIL, mar, damage, injure, flaw, mark, stain, taint, impair, disfigure, discolour, tarnish, blot, deface, sully, besmirch.

blend v. **1** MIX, combine, intermix, mingle, amalgamate, unite, commingle, merge, compound, fuse, coalesce, integrate, homogenize, synthesize, meld, alloy; technical admix. **2** HARMONIZE, complement, fit, suit, go with. ▶ n. MIXTURE, mix, combination, amalgam, compound, fusion, union, amalgamation, synthesis, composite, alloy, melange, concoction.

bless v. **1** SANCTIFY, consecrate, hallow, dedicate, anoint, make sacred. **2** GLORIFY, extol, praise, exalt, adore; formal laud. ■ OPPOSITES curse.

blessed adj. **1** SACRED, holy, divine, venerated, consecrated, hallowed, sanctified, beatified, revered. **2** HAPPY, fortunate, blissful, lucky, favoured, joyful, joyous, glad, cheerful, contented; literary blithe. **3** WONDERFUL, marvellous, welcome, longed for. ■ OPPOSITES cursed, wretched.

blessing n. **1** BENEDICTION, consecration, dedication, prayer, grace, thanksgiving, commendation, invocation. **2** APPROVAL, permission, consent, sanction, backing, endorsement, assent, support, concurrence, agreement, encouragement, approbation; informal go-ahead, the green light. **3** GODSEND, boon, gift, favour, benefit, advantage, asset, comfort, convenience, help, bit of luck. ■ OPPOSITES veto.

blight n. **1** DISEASE, plague, pestilence, fungus, infestation, canker, mildew. **2** AFFLICTION, misfortune, plague, disaster, calamity, trouble, ruin, catastrophe, curse, bane, scourge, tribulation, woe. ▶ v. RUIN, destroy, spoil, shrivel, wither, crush, blast, mar.

blind adj. **1** SIGHTLESS, unseeing, visually impaired, visionless, partially sighted, purblind. **2** OBTUSE, blinkered, imperceptive, unaware, insensible, insensitive, unseeing, heedless, careless, unobservant, oblivious, indifferent, neglectful, slow, slow-witted, dense, stupid. **3** UNCRITICAL, unthinking, unreasoning, undiscerning, unreasoned, irrational, indiscriminate, injudicious, partial, prejudiced, biased. ▶ v. **1** MAKE BLIND, deprive of sight, blinker, blindfold. **2** DAZZLE, deceive, delude, beguile, infatuate, confuse, bewilder, hoodwink; informal pull the wool over someone's eyes. ▶ n. SHUTTER, shade, curtain, screen.

bliss n. JOY, ecstasy, delight, rapture, eumake a sudden fierce attack on. **blizzard** n. a severe snowstorm.

bloat v. cause to swell with fluid or gas.

bloater n. a salted smoked herring.

blob n. **1** a drop of a thick liquid. **2** a roundish mass.

bloc n. a group of allied countries with similar political systems.

block n. **1** a solid piece of material with flat surfaces on each side. **2** a large building divided into flats or offices. **3** a group of buildings bounded by four streets. **4** an obstacle. ▶v. prevent movement, flow, or progress in. □ **blockbuster** informal a very successful film or book. **block capitals** plain capital letters.

blockade n. an act of sealing off a place to prevent goods or people from entering or leaving. ▶v. set up a blockade of.

blockage n. an obstruction.

bloke n. informal a man.

blonde adj. (also **blond**) **1** (of hair) fair. **2** having fair hair. ▶n. a woman with blonde hair.

blood n. **1** the red liquid circulating in the arteries and veins. **2** family background. **3** passionate temperament. ▶v. initiate in an activity. □ **bloodbath** a massacre. **blood-curdling** horrifying.

bloodhound a large dog used in tracking scents. **bloodless** without bloodshed. **bloodshed** the killing or wounding of people. **bloodshot** (of eyes) red from dilated blood vessels. **blood sport** a sport involving the killing of animals. **bloodstream** the blood circulating in the body. **bloodthirsty** taking pleasure in killing or violence.

bloody adj. (**bloodier**, **bloodiest**) **1** covered in blood. **2** involving much violence or cruelty. ▶v. (**bloodying**, **bloodied**) cover or stain with blood. □ **bloody-minded** informal deliberately uncooperative.

bloom v. **1** produce flowers. **2** be very healthy. ▶n. **1** a flower. **2** the state or period of blooming. **3** a healthy glow in the complexion.

bloomers pl. n. **1** women's baggy knickers. **2** hist. women's loose-fitting trousers.

blossom n. a flower or a mass of flowers on a tree. ▶v. **1** produce blossom. **2** develop and flourish.

blot n. **1** a spot of ink. **2** a thing that spoils something good. ▶v. (**blotting**, **blotted**) **1** dry with an absorbent material. **2** mark or spoil. **3** (**blot out**) obscure or hide.

Thesaurus

phoria, elation, happiness, pleasure, gladness, blessedness, beatitude, heaven, paradise, seventh heaven. ■ OPPOSITES misery.

bloated adj. SWOLLEN, distended, puffy, puffed up, inflated, enlarged, expanded, dilated.

blob n. DROP, droplet, globule, dollop, gobbet, bubble, ball, bead, daub, blotch, dab, spot, splash, blot, smudge, smear; informal glob.

block v. **1** CLOG, choke, jam, close, obstruct, constrict, stop up, plug, dam, bung up, barricade, bar. **2** HINDER, prevent, obstruct, hamper, impede, bar, frustrate, thwart, check, resist, deter, oppose, arrest, stop, halt, scotch, stonewall. ▶n. **1** BLOCKADE, barrier, barricade, obstacle, bar, hindrance, impediment, obstruction, deterrent, check, stumbling block, difficulty, drawback, hitch. **2** BAR, piece, chunk, hunk, cake, lump, mass, slab, ingot, brick. **3** GROUP, set, batch, section, quantity.

blockage n. OBSTRUCTION, congestion, constriction, stoppage, occlusion, block, impediment, jam, bottleneck.

blood n. **1** GORE, vital fluid; literary lifeblood, ichor. **2** ANCESTRY, lineage, fam-

ily, descent, birth, extraction, pedigree, origin, genealogy, inheritance, stock, race, kinship.

blood-curdling adj. TERRIFYING, horrifying, spine-chilling, chilling, frightening, fearful, dreadful, terrible, horrendous, horrific, appalling, frightful, hair-raising.

bloodshed n. KILLING, carnage, slaughter, murder, massacre, butchery, bloodletting, bloodbath; literary slaying.

bloodthirsty adj. SAVAGE, cruel, murderous, ferocious, homicidal, vicious, brutal, ruthless, barbaric, barbarous, inhuman, sadistic, bloody, slaughterous, violent, warlike, bellicose; old use sanguinary.

bloody adj. **1** BLEEDING, bloodstained, blood-soaked, blood-spattered. **2** SAVAGE, fierce, gory, cruel, slaughterous; old use sanguinary.

bloom n. **1** BLOSSOM, flower, floret. **2** FRESHNESS, radiance, lustre, glow, sheen, flush, perfection, blush, beauty. **3** PERFECTION, prime, heyday, vigour, strength, flourishing. ▶v. **1** FLOWER, blossom, burgeon, bud. **2** FLOURISH, prosper, thrive, be healthy, be happy, do well.

blotch n. a large irregular mark. ■ **blotchy** adj.

blouse n. a woman's shirt-like garment.

blouson /bloo-zon/ n. a short loose-fitting jacket.

blow v. (**blowing, blew;** past part. **blown**) **1** (of wind) move. **2** send out air through pursed lips. **3** play a wind instrument. **4** break or displace with explosives. **5** burst or burn out through pressure or overheating. **6** informal spend money recklessly. **7** informal waste an opportunity. ▶n. **1** an act of blowing. **2** a stroke with the hand or a weapon. **3** a shock or disappointment. □ **blowfly** a large fly which lays its eggs in meat. **blowout** the release of air or gas from a tyre, oil well, etc. **blowtorch** (or **blowlamp**) a portable device producing a hot flame, for burning off paint. **blow up 1** explode. **2** enlarge an image. ■ **blowy** adj.

blowsy (or **blowzy**) adj. (of a woman) plump, untidy, and red-faced.

blub v. (**blubbing, blubbed**) informal sob noisily.

blubber n. the fat of whales and seals. ▶v. informal sob noisily.

bludgeon n. a heavy stick used as a weapon. ▶v. **1** hit with a bludgeon. **2** bully into doing something.

blue adj. **1** of the colour of the sky on a sunny day. **2** informal sad or depressed. **3** informal indecent or pornographic. ▶n. **1** blue colour or material. **2** (**blues**) slow sad music of black American origin. **3** (**the blues**) sadness or depression. □ **bluebell** a plant with blue bell-shaped flowers. **bluebottle** a large bluish fly. **blue-collar** of manual work or workers. **blueprint 1** a technical drawing or plan. **2** a model or prototype. **bluestocking** a serious intellectual woman. **out of the blue** informal unexpectedly. ■ **blueness** n. **bluish** adj.

bluff v. try to deceive someone as to what one can or is going to do. ▶n. **1** an act of bluffing. **2** a steep cliff. ▶adj. frank and direct.

blunder n. a clumsy mistake. ▶v. **1** make a blunder. **2** move clumsily.

blunderbuss n. hist. a gun with a short, wide barrel.

blunt adj. **1** lacking a sharp edge or point. **2** frank and direct. ▶v. make or become blunt. ■ **bluntly** adv.

Thesaurus

blot n. **1** SPOT, smudge, speck, blotch, stain, mark, dot, patch, blob, smear; informal splodge. **2** BLEMISH, imperfection, eyesore, defect, stain, fault, flaw, taint, ugliness. ▶v. MARK, stain, dot, speckle, smudge, spoil, blotch, spot, spatter, bespatter, disfigure; literary besmirch. □ **blot out** OBLITERATE, erase, efface, wipe out, delete, expunge, destroy, obscure, conceal, darken, dim, shadow.

blotchy adj. SPOTTED, speckled, blotted, discoloured, patchy, smudged, uneven, streaked, stained, blotched, spattered.

blow¹ n. WIND, gale, breeze, blast, gust, storm, tempest. ▶v. **1** PUFF, blast, gust, flurry, bluster. **2** WAFT, flutter, buffet, whirl, whisk, sweep, drive, carry, transport, convey. **3** BREATHE, breathe out, exhale, puff, pant, gasp, whistle. **4** SOUND, play, blare, toot, blast. □ **blow over** SUBSIDE, die down, pass, cease, settle, end, vanish. **blow up 1** EXPLODE, shatter, burst, detonate, go off, blast, erupt. **2** INFLATE, pump up, expand, swell, distend, puff up. **3** ENLARGE, magnify, heighten, exaggerate, overstate, embroider, colour, improve on. **4** LOSE ONE'S TEMPER, rage, fume, erupt, go wild; informal blow one's top, hit the roof, fly off the handle.

blow² n. **1** HIT, bang, knock, stroke, slap, smack, punch, buffet, rap, impact, jolt; informal whack, wallop, clout, bash, belt, biff, thwack. **2** AFFLICTION, misfortune, shock, upset, disaster, calamity, catastrophe, grief, disappointment, setback, reversal, bombshell.

blueprint n. DESIGN, plan, draft, prototype, model, pattern, scheme, sketch, diagram, outline, representation, layout.

bluff¹ v. TRICK, deceive, mislead, hoodwink, hoax, take in, dupe, delude, fool, sham, feign, fake, lie; literary cozen. ▶n. BLUSTER, deceit, deception, trickery, fraud, fake, front, facade, pretence, sham, subterfuge, humbug.

bluff² adj. BLUNT, straightforward, frank, candid, outspoken, direct, hearty, rough.

blunder v. **1** MAKE A MISTAKE, slip, err, be in error, miscalculate, misjudge, mismanage, bungle; informal slip up, screw up, botch, blow it, put one's foot in it. **2** STUMBLE, stagger, lurch, flounder, be clumsy. ▶n. ERROR, fault, mistake, slip, miscalculation, misjudgement, false/wrong move, faux pas, oversight, inaccuracy, gaffe; informal slip-up, boo-boo, howler, clanger, boob, cock-up.

blunt adj. **1** DULL, edgeless, unsharpened, unpointed, rounded. **2** DIRECT, frank,

blur v. (**blurring**, **blurred**) make or become less distinct. ▶n. something perceived indistinctly. ■ **blurry** adj.

blurb n. a short description written to promote a book, film, etc.

blurt v. say suddenly and without thinking.

blush v. become red-faced through shyness or embarrassment. ▶n. an act of blushing.

blusher n. a cosmetic used to give a rosy tinge to the cheeks.

bluster v. **1** talk loudly or aggressively but with little effect. **2** blow in gusts. ▶n. loud and empty talk. ■ **blustery** adj.

boa n. **1** a large snake which crushes its prey. **2** a thin stole of feathers or fur.

boar n. (pl. **boar** or **boars**) **1** a wild pig with tusks. **2** a male pig.

board n. **1** a long, thin, flat piece of sawn wood. **2** a rectangular piece of stiff material used as a surface. **3** the decision-making body of an organization. **4** the provision of regular meals in return for payment. ▶v. **1** get on a ship, aircraft, etc. **2** receive meals and accommodation in return for payment. **3** cover or seal with pieces of wood. □ **boarding house** a private house providing meals and accommodation for paying guests. **boarding school** a school in which the pupils live during term time. **boardroom** a room in which a board of directors meets. **on board** on or in a ship, aircraft, etc.

boarder n. a pupil who lives in school during term time.

boast v. **1** talk about oneself with excessive pride. **2** possess a feature that is a source of pride. ▶n. an act of boasting. ■ **boastful** adj. **boastfully** adv.

boat n. a vehicle for travelling on water. ■ **boating** n.

boater n. a flat-topped straw hat.

boatswain /boh-s'n/ n. a ship's officer in charge of equipment and crew.

bob v. (**bobbing**, **bobbed**) move quickly up and down. ▶n. **1** a bobbing movement. **2** a short hairstyle that hangs evenly all round. □ **bobsleigh** a sledge used for racing down an ice-covered run.

bobbin n. a reel for holding thread.

bobble n. a small ball made of strands of wool.

bode v. (**bode well/ill**) be a sign of a good or bad outcome.

bodice n. **1** the upper part of a woman's dress. **2** a woman's sleeveless undergarment.

bodily adj. of the body. ▶adv. by taking

Thesaurus

straightforward, candid, forthright, bluff, outspoken, plain-spoken, unceremonious, undiplomatic, tactless, rude, brusque, curt, abrupt, insensitive; *informal* upfront. ■ OPPOSITES sharp. ▶v. DULL, take the edge off, deaden, weaken, dampen, allay, abate, lessen, appease, impair.

blur v. SMEAR, besmear, smudge, mist, cloud, fog, befog, bedim, blear, becloud, obscure, mask.

blurred adj. INDISTINCT, blurry, hazy, misty, cloudy, foggy, fuzzy, vague, unfocused, unclear, obscure, ill-defined, nebulous, dim, faint, smeary, smudged. ■ OPPOSITES clear.

blurt v. (**blurt out**) SAY, utter, let slip, blab, disclose, reveal, let out, divulge, tell, babble, exclaim; *informal* spill the beans, let the cat out of the bag, give the game away.

blush v. REDDEN, go red/pink, flush, colour, crimson, glow, be ashamed, be embarrassed.

bluster v. **1** BLOW, storm, rage, blast, gust, roar. **2** BOAST, bluff, brag, swagger, show off, vaunt, lord it, hector, bully, domineer, threaten, rant, harangue, be overbearing; *informal* throw one's weight about. ▶n. BOASTING, bravado, bluff, bombast, bragging, braggadocio, hectoring, domineering, swagger.

blustery adj. STORMY, windy, gusty, squally, wild, tempestuous, violent. ■ OPPOSITES calm.

board n. **1** PLANK, beam, panel, slat, timber, sheet, block. **2** FOOD, meals, sustenance, provisions, keep. **3** PANEL, committee, council, directorate. ▶v. **1** GET ON, get aboard/on board, enter, embark, mount. **2** LODGE, stay, live, room, billet.

boast v. **1** BRAG, swank, crow, swagger, vaunt, show off, exaggerate, bluster, blow one's own trumpet, pat oneself on the back; *informal* talk big. **2** POSSESS, have, own, pride oneself on, take pride in, enjoy, benefit from, exhibit, display. ▶n. **1** BRAG, self-praise, vaunt, overstatement; *informal* swank. **2** PRIDE, treasure, joy, gem; *informal* pride and joy, apple of someone's eye.

boastful adj. CONCEITED, bragging, vain, arrogant, cocky, egotistical, proud, swaggering, swollen-headed, blustering, vaunting, braggart, overbearing; *informal* swanky, big-headed; *literary* vainglorious.

hold of a person's body with force.

bodkin n. a thick, blunt needle.

body n. (pl. **bodies**) **1** the physical structure of a person or animal. **2** a corpse. **3** the main part of something. **4** a mass or collection. **5** a group organized for a particular purpose. □ **bodyguard** a person paid to protect an important person. **bodywork** the metal outer shell of a vehicle.

Boer n. a member of the Dutch people who settled in southern Africa.

boffin n. informal a scientist.

bog n. **1** an area of soft, wet, muddy ground. **2** informal a toilet. ▶ v. (**be/get bogged down**) be prevented from making progress. ■ **boggy** adj.

bogey n. (pl. **bogeys**) **1** Golf a score of one stroke over par at a hole. **2** (also **bogy**) a cause of fear or alarm.

boggle v. informal be astonished or baffled.

bogus adj. false.

Bohemian adj. artistic and unconventional.

boil v. **1** (of a liquid) reach a temperature at which it bubbles and turns to vapour. **2** cook in boiling water. ▶ n. **1** the process of boiling. **2** an inflamed pus-filled swelling.

boiler n. a fuel-burning device for heating water.

boisterous adj. noisy, lively, and high-spirited.

bold adj. **1** confident and courageous. **2** (of a colour or design) strong or vivid. **3** (of type) having thick strokes. ■ **boldly** adv. **boldness** n.

bole n. a tree trunk.

bolero n. (pl. **boleros**) **1** /buh-**lair**-oh/ a Spanish dance. **2** /**bol**-uh-roh/ a woman's short open jacket.

boll n. the rounded seed capsule of plants such as cotton.

bollard n. a short thick post.

bolshie (or **bolshy**) adj. informal deliberately uncooperative.

bolster n. a long, firm pillow. ▶ v. support or strengthen.

bolt n. **1** a metal pin that screws into a nut, used to fasten things. **2** a sliding bar used to fasten a door or window. **3** a flash of lightning. **4** a roll of fabric. ▶ v. **1** fasten with a bolt. **2** run away. **3** eat food quickly. □ **bolt-hole** a place into which one can escape.

Thesaurus

■ OPPOSITES modest.

bob v. BOUNCE, dip, jump, nod, leap, hop, jerk, jolt, quiver, wobble, toss, shake, oscillate.

bodily adj. CORPOREAL, physical, carnal, corporal, fleshly, material, substantial, tangible, incarnate.

body n. **1** FIGURE, frame, form, physique, shape, build, anatomy, skeleton, trunk, torso. **2** CORPSE, carcass, remains, relics, mummy; Medicine cadaver; informal stiff. **3** SET, group, band, party, company, crowd, number, assembly, association. **4** ACCUMULATION, collection, quantity, mass, corpus.

bog n. MARSH, swamp, marshland, fen, quagmire, morass, mire, slough, mud. □ **bog down** MIRE, stick, hamper, hinder, obstruct, impede, delay, stall, detain, entangle, ensnare, embroil, swamp, overwhelm.

bogus adj. COUNTERFEIT, fake, sham, false, spurious, forged, fraudulent, artificial, pretended, pretend, pseudo, imitation, mock, inauthentic, supposititious, soi-disant; informal phoney. ■ OPPOSITES genuine.

boil v. **1** BUBBLE, seethe, simmer, stew, heat, cook, effervesce, foam, fizz, steam. **2** RAGE, fume, seethe, storm, rant, rave, fulminate, flare up.

boisterous adj. **1** LIVELY, bouncy, playful, exuberant, frisky, romping, unruly, disorderly, rough, wild, irrepressible, undisciplined, spirited, animated, obstreperous, riotous, rollicking, uproarious, rowdy, noisy; informal rumbustious. **2** ROUGH, choppy, stormy, wild, squally, breezy, turbulent, tempestuous, raging, gusty, blustery. ■ OPPOSITES calm, restrained.

bold adj. **1** DARING, brave, adventurous, dauntless, unafraid, courageous, plucky, intrepid, audacious, fearless, valiant, gallant, hardy, heroic, valorous, undaunted, confident, venturesome, enterprising, daredevil, reckless, resolute. **2** FORWARD, audacious, presumptuous, impudent, pert, impertinent, brazen, shameless, immodest, insolent, brash, cheeky, rude, barefaced, blatant, unashamed; informal saucy. **3** STRIKING, eye-catching, prominent, pronounced, conspicuous, noticeable, emphatic, obvious, vivid, bright, showy, flashy, strong, distinct, marked. ■ OPPOSITES timid, modest, subdued, faint.

bolster n. CUSHION, pillow, support, prop, stay, rest. ▶ v. SUPPORT, prop up, shore up, hold up, reinforce, buttress, strengthen, boost, maintain, build up,

bomb n. **1** a container of explosive or incendiary material. **2** (**the bomb**) nuclear weapons. **3** (**a bomb**) informal a large sum of money. ▶ v. **1** attack with bombs. **2** informal move very quickly. **3** informal fail badly. □ **bombshell** a great surprise or shock.

bombard v. **1** attack with bombs or other missiles. **2** direct a flow of questions or information at. ■ **bombardment** n.

bombardier n. a rank of non-commissioned artillery officer.

bombast n. pompous language with little meaning. ■ **bombastic** adj.

bomber n. **1** an aircraft that drops bombs. **2** a person who plants bombs.

bona fide /boh-nuh fy-di/ adj. genuine.

bonanza n. a sudden supply of riches or good luck.

bond n. **1** a thing used to fasten things together. **2** (**bonds**) physical restraints. **3** a force or feeling that links people. **4** an agreement with legal force. **5** a certificate issued by a government or a public company promising to repay money lent to it at a fixed rate of interest. ▶ v. **1** join securely to something else. **2** establish a relationship based on shared feelings etc.

bondage n. slavery.

bone n. any of the pieces of hard material making up the skeleton in vertebrates. ▶ v. **1** remove the bones from meat or fish. **2** (**bone up on**) informal study a subject intensively.

bonfire n. an open-air fire lit to burn rubbish or as a celebration.

bongo n. (pl. **bongos** or **bongoes**) each of a pair of small drums held between the knees.

bonhomie /bon-uh-mee/ n. good-natured friendliness.

bonnet n. **1** a hat with strings that tie under the chin. **2** the hinged cover over the engine of a motor vehicle.

bonny adj. (**bonnier**, **bonniest**) Sc. & N. Engl. attractive and healthy-looking.

bonsai /bon-sy/ n. the art of growing miniature ornamental trees or shrubs.

bonus n. **1** an extra payment. **2** an unexpected and welcome thing.

bon voyage /bon voy-**yahzh**/ exclam. have a good journey.

bony adj. (**bonier**, **boniest**) **1** containing or resembling bones. **2** so thin that the bones can be seen.

boo exclam. **1** said suddenly to surprise someone. **2** said to show disapproval. ▶ v. (**booing**, **booed**) shout 'boo'.

boob informal n. an embarrassing mistake. ▶ v. make such a mistake.

booby n. (pl. **boobies**) informal a stupid person. □ **booby prize** a prize given to the person who comes last in a contest. **booby trap** an object containing a hidden explosive device.

boogie v. (**boogieing**, **boogied**) informal dance to pop music.

book n. **1** a written or printed work consisting of pages bound in a cover. **2** a main division of a literary work. **3** (**books**) a set of records or accounts. **4** a set of tickets etc. bound together.

Thesaurus

aid, assist, augment.

bolt n. **1** BAR, latch, lock, catch, fastening, pin, peg, rivet, rod. **2** FLASH, streak, flare, shaft, burst. **3** ARROW, dart, missile, projectile, shaft. **4** RUN, dash, sprint, dart, rush, bound, escape. ▶ v. **1** BAR, lock, fasten, secure, rivet, pin, nail, clamp. **2** RUN, dash, sprint, dart, rush, hurtle, hurry, fly, flee, run for it, escape, abscond; informal scarper, do a bunk. **3** GOBBLE, guzzle, wolf, stuff, gulp, cram, devour.

bombard v. **1** SHELL, bomb, blitz, strafe, blast, pound, fire at, attack, assault, assail, batter. **2** BADGER, pester, harass, bother, hound, plague, besiege, beset, assail, importune, belabour.

bombardment n. ASSAULT, attack, bombing, shelling, strafing, blitz, air raid, cannonade, fusillade, barrage, broadside.

bombastic adj. POMPOUS, pretentious, grandiose, grandiloquent, turgid, verbose, ranting, extravagant, magniloquent, blustering, ostentatious, affected, inflated, periphrastic.

bonanza n. WINDFALL, godsend, bonus, boom, plenty, cornucopia, surplus, amplitude, sufficiency.

bond n. **1** CHAIN, fetter, rope, cord, shackle, manacle, tie, restraint, restriction, limitation, harness, straitjacket. **2** LINK, connection, tie, attachment, affinity, union, relation, relationship, closeness, intimacy, nexus, ligature. ▶ v. UNITE, join, bind, connect, link, attach, fasten, secure, stick, glue, fuse, weld, blend, merge.

bondage n. SLAVERY, servitude, enslavement, subjection, captivity, oppression; historical serfdom, vassalage, thraldom. ■ OPPOSITES freedom.

bonus n. **1** GAIN, advantage, extra, plus, benefit, boon. **2** GIFT, gratuity, tip, pres-

▶v. **1** reserve accommodation, a ticket, etc. **2** engage a performer for an event. **3** make an official note of someone who has broken a law or rule. ◻ **bookcase** a cabinet containing shelves for books. **bookkeeping** the keeping of records of financial transactions. **booklet** a small thin book. **bookmaker** a person whose job is taking bets and paying out winnings. **bookmark 1** a strip of paper or leather to mark a place in a book. **2** Computing a record of the address of a file, website, etc. enabling quick access by the user. **bookworm** informal a person who loves reading.

bookie n. informal a bookmaker.

boom n. **1** a loud, deep sound. **2** a period of rapid economic growth. **3** a pivoted beam at the foot of a sail. **4** a movable arm carrying a microphone or film camera. **5** a beam forming a barrier across a harbour mouth. ▶v. **1** make a loud, deep sound. **2** experience rapid economic growth.

boomerang n. a curved flat piece of wood that can be thrown so as to return to the thrower.

boon n. a benefit.

boor n. a rough, bad-mannered person. ■ **boorish** adj.

boost v. help or encourage. ▶n. a source

of help or encouragement.

booster n. **1** a dose of a vaccine that increases or renews the effect of an earlier one. **2** the part of a rocket or spacecraft giving acceleration after lift-off.

boot n. **1** an item of footwear covering the foot and ankle or lower leg. **2** a space at the back of a car for luggage. **3** (**the boot**) informal dismissal from a job. ▶v. **1** kick hard. **2** start up a computer.

bootee n. a baby's woollen shoe.

booth n. **1** a stall or stand for selling goods etc. at a fair or market. **2** a small enclosed cubicle.

bootleg adj. made or distributed illegally. ■ **bootlegger** n. **bootlegging** n.

booty n. valuable stolen goods.

booze informal n. alcoholic drink. ▶v. drink alcohol. ■ **boozer** n. **boozy** adj.

bop v. (**bopping, bopped**) informal dance to pop music.

borax n. a white mineral used in making glass.

border n. **1** a boundary between two countries etc. **2** a decorative band around the edge of something. **3** a flower bed along the edge of a lawn. ▶v. **1** form a border around or along. **2** (**border on**) come close to. ◻ **borderline** a boundary.

Thesaurus

ent, bounty, reward, commission, honorarium; informal perk.

bony adj. THIN, skinny, scrawny, angular, lean, skeletal, emaciated, cadaverous, gaunt, raw-boned. ■ OPPOSITES plump.

book n. VOLUME, tome, work, title, publication, paperback, hardback, folio, edition, copy. ▶v. RESERVE, engage, charter, secure, bag, order, sign up, arrange, organize, schedule, programme.

bookish adj. STUDIOUS, scholarly, scholastic, learned, erudite, highbrow, bluestocking, intellectual, academic, literary, pedantic, impractical; informal brainy, egghead.

booklet n. LEAFLET, pamphlet, brochure, notebook.

boom n. **1** CRASH, bang, report, explosion, blast, rumble, roar, thunder, reverberation. **2** BOOST, surge, increase, upturn, improvement, growth, expansion, spurt, upsurge, success, bonanza, prosperity, advance, popularity, development. ▶v. RESOUND, reverberate, rumble, roar, thunder, bang, blast.

boorish adj. RUDE, crude, loutish, churlish, unrefined, coarse, ill-mannered, impolite, uncouth, gross, oafish, uncul-

tured, philistine, unsophisticated, vulgar, ignorant, indelicate, insensitive; informal yobbish. ■ OPPOSITES refined.

boost v. **1** LIFT, raise, push, thrust, elevate, support, hoist, heave, shove. **2** ENCOURAGE, support, uplift, increase, raise, heighten, promote, further, advance, improve, foster, assist, expand, enlarge, develop, facilitate, sustain; informal hike up, jack up. ▶n. **1** PUSH, shove, lift, thrust, helping hand. **2** IMPETUS, impulse, encouragement, support, increase, expansion, rise, improvement, advance, stimulus; informal shot in the arm.

boot v. KICK, knock, punt.

booth n. **1** STALL, stand, kiosk, counter. **2** CUBICLE, compartment, enclosure, hut, carrel.

booty n. LOOT, plunder, haul, spoils, gains, prizes, profits, takings, pickings, winnings; informal swag, boodle, the goods.

border n. **1** EDGE, perimeter, verge, boundary, limit, margin, periphery, brink, fringe, hem, brim, rim, skirt, surround. **2** FRONTIER, boundary, borderline, limit. ▶v. **1** BE NEXT/ADJACENT

bore¹ v. **1** make someone feel weary and unenthusiastic by being dull. **2** make a hole with a drill or other tool. ▶ n. **1** a tedious person or activity. **2** the hollow part inside a gun barrel. **3** the diameter of this. ■ **boredom** n. **boring** adj.

bore² past part. of BEAR¹.

boric n. of boron.

born adj. **1** existing as a result of birth. **2** having a particular natural ability. □ **born-again** newly converted to Christianity or a particular cause.

borne past part. of BEAR¹.

boron n. a chemical element used in making steel.

borough n. a town with a corporation and privileges granted by a royal charter.

borrow v. take something belonging to someone else with the intention of returning it. ■ **borrower** n.

borstal n. hist. a prison for young offenders.

bosom n. a woman's breast or chest. ▶ adj. (of a friend) very close.

boss n. **1** a person in charge of an employee or organization. **2** a projecting knob. ▶ v. informal give orders in a domineering manner. □ **boss-eyed** cross-eyed.

bossy adj. (**bossier**, **bossiest**) informal tending to give orders. ■ **bossily** adv.

bosun (or **bo'sun**) var. of BOATSWAIN.

botany n. the study of plants. ■ **botanical** adj. **botanist** n.

botch v. informal do badly or carelessly.

both adj. & pron. two people or things regarded together.

bother v. **1** take the trouble to do something. **2** worry, disturb, or upset. ▶ n. **1** trouble and fuss. **2** (**a bother**) a cause of trouble or fuss. ■ **bothersome** adj.

bottle n. a container with a narrow neck, for storing liquids. ▶ v. **1** place in bottles for storage. **2** (**bottle up**) hide one's feelings. □ **bottleneck** a narrow part of a road where congestion occurs.

bottom n. **1** the lowest or furthest point, part, or position. **2** the buttocks. ▶ adj. in the lowest or furthest position. ■ **bottomless** adj.

Thesaurus

TO, be close to, neighbour, adjoin, abut, touch, join, connect, edge, skirt, bound. **2** EDGE, fringe, hem, trim, bind, decorate, rim. □ **border on** VERGE ON, approach, come close to, approximate, be near/similar to, resemble.

bore¹ v. PIERCE, penetrate, drill, puncture, perforate, burrow, tap, tunnel, mine, dig out, sink.

bore² v. BE TEDIOUS TO, weary, tire, fatigue, exhaust, depress, jade, pall on, send to sleep, leave cold, bore to tears, bore to death; informal turn off. ■ OPPOSITES interest, amuse.

boring adj. TEDIOUS, dull, uninteresting, uninspiring, unexciting, unstimulating, monotonous, unvaried, repetitive, dreary, humdrum, commonplace, flat, lacklustre, dry, dry as dust, stale, soporific, dead, soul-destroying, tiring, tiresome, wearisome; informal deadly. ■ OPPOSITES interesting, amusing.

borrow v. **1** ASK FOR THE LOAN OF, beg, be lent, take as a loan, have temporarily, lease, hire; informal cadge, scrounge, bum; US informal mooch. **2** COPY, plagiarize, take, imitate, adopt, appropriate, commandeer, steal, pirate, purloin, help oneself to; informal filch, grab, nick, pinch. ■ OPPOSITES lend.

boss n. HEAD, chief, leader, supervisor, manager, director, employer, superintendent, foreman, overseer, controller, master; informal numero uno, gaffer, governor; US informal head honcho. ▶ v. ORDER ABOUT/AROUND, give orders/commands to, control, bully, push around, domineer, dominate; informal throw one's weight about.

bossy adj. DOMINEERING, overbearing, dictatorial, high-handed, authoritarian, autocratic, tyrannical, despotic, assertive, pushy, imperious, oppressive, bullying, lordly, officious, hectoring. ■ OPPOSITES submissive.

botch v. BUNGLE, make a mess of, do badly, spoil, muff, mismanage, fumble; informal mess/screw up, make a hash of, cock up.

bother v. **1** DISTURB, trouble, worry, pester, harass, annoy, upset, irritate, vex, inconvenience, plague, torment, nag, molest; informal hassle, get in someone's hair. **2** DISTRESS, worry, concern, trouble, perturb, disconcert. ▶ n. **1** NUISANCE, annoyance, irritation, pest, trouble, worry, vexation. **2** TROUBLE, disturbance, commotion, disorder, uproar, fighting, violence, furore, brouhaha.

bottle n. FLASK, container, carafe, pitcher, decanter, flagon, phial, magnum, jeroboam, carboy, demijohn. □ **bottle up** See SUPPRESS (2).

bottleneck n. NARROWING, constriction, obstruction, congestion, blockage, jam,

botulism n. a dangerous form of food poisoning.

boudoir /boo-dwar/ n. a woman's bedroom or small private room.

bouffant /boo-fon/ adj. (of hair) standing out from the head in a rounded shape.

bougainvillea /boo-guhn-vil-li-uh/ n. a tropical plant with brightly coloured bracts.

bough n. a large branch.

bought past & past part. of **BUY**.

boulder n. a large rock.

boulevard n. a wide street.

bounce v. **1** move quickly up or away from a surface after hitting it. **2** move up and down repeatedly. **3** informal (of a cheque) be returned by a bank when there is not enough money in an account to meet it. ▶ n. **1** an act of bouncing. **2** high-spirited self-confidence. ■ **bouncy** adj.

bouncer n. a person employed by a nightclub to control or keep out troublemakers.

bound¹ v. **1** move with leaping strides. **2** form the boundary of. **3** restrict. ▶ n. **1** a leaping movement. **2** a boundary or restriction. ▶ adj. heading in a particular direction. □ **bound to** certain to. **out of bounds** beyond permitted limits.

bound² past & past part. of **BIND**.

boundary n. (pl. **boundaries**) a line marking the limits of an area.

boundless adj. unlimited.

bounteous adj. old use bountiful.

bountiful adj. **1** plentiful. **2** giving generously.

bounty n. (pl. **bounties**) **1** a reward paid for killing or capturing someone. **2** a generous gift. **3** generosity.

bouquet n. **1** a bunch of flowers. **2** the scent of a wine or perfume.

bourbon /ber-buhn/ n. an American whisky made from maize and rye.

bourgeois /boor-zhwah/ adj. to do with the middle class, esp. in being conventional.

bourgeoisie /boor-zhwah-zee/ n. the middle class.

bout n. **1** a period of illness or intense activity. **2** a wrestling or boxing match.

boutique n. a small shop selling fashionable clothes.

bovine adj. **1** of cattle. **2** sluggish or stupid.

bow¹ /rhymes with go/ n. **1** a knot tied with two loops and two loose ends. **2** a weapon for shooting arrows. **3** a rod with horsehair stretched along its length, for playing a violin etc.

bow² /rhymes with cow/ v. **1** bend the head or upper body as a sign of respect.

Thesaurus

hold-up.

bottom n. **1** BASE, foundation, basis, support, substructure, pedestal, substratum, underpinning. **2** LOWEST POINT, foot, base, seat, nadir. **3** UNDERNEATH, underside, lower side, belly. **4** BUTTOCKS, rear end, rear, seat, rump; informal backside, behind, bum, arse, jacksie; US informal butt, fanny; humorous posterior. ■ OPPOSITES top. ▶ adj. LOWEST, deepest, least, last, minimum.

bottomless adj. **1** DEEP, immeasurable, fathomless, unfathomable, unplumbable. **2** UNLIMITED, inexhaustible, infinite, boundless.

bounce v. JUMP, leap, spring, bob, rebound, skip, recoil, ricochet, jounce. ▶ n. SPRINGINESS, spring, elasticity, give, resilience.

bound¹ adj. **1** CERTAIN, sure, definite, very likely, fated, predestined. **2** OBLIGATED, obliged, required, forced, compelled, constrained, duty-bound. **3** TIED, tied up, roped, tethered, fettered, secured. □ **bound for** GOING/TRAVELLING TOWARDS, going to, heading for, making for, off to.

bound² v. LEAP, jump, spring, skip, hop, vault, bounce, hurdle, bob, gambol, romp, prance, caper.

boundary n. FRONTIER, border, limit, edge, dividing line, perimeter, verge, margin, threshold, bounds, periphery, fringe, borderline, brink, extremity.

boundless adj. LIMITLESS, unlimited, infinite, endless, unbounded, unending, never-ending, without end, unrestricted, inexhaustible, immeasurable, incalculable, vast, great, immense. ■ OPPOSITES limited, restricted.

bountiful adj. ABUNDANT, plentiful, ample, superabundant, copious, lavish, profuse, princely; literary plenteous, bounteous. ■ OPPOSITES mean, meagre.

bounty n. **1** REWARD, recompense, remuneration, gratuity, tip, premium, bonus. **2** GENEROSITY, munificence, altruism, largesse, benevolence, kindness, philanthropy.

bouquet n. **1** BUNCH OF FLOWERS, spray, posy, wreath, garland, nosegay, corsage, buttonhole. **2** SMELL, aroma, odour, fragrance, scent, perfume; literary redolence.

2 bend under a heavy weight. **3** give in to pressure. ▸ n. **1** an act of bowing. **2** the front end of a ship.

bowdlerize (or **-ise**) v. remove indecent or offensive material from a text.

bowel n. **1** the intestine. **2** (**bowels**) the innermost parts of something.

bower n. a shady place under trees.

bowl n. **1** a round, deep dish or basin. **2** a rounded, hollow part of an object. **3** a ball used in the game of bowls. **4** (**bowls**) a game in which heavy wooden balls are rolled as close as possible to a small white ball. ▸ v. **1** roll a round object along the ground. **2** Cricket throw the ball towards the batsman. **3** move rapidly and smoothly. **4** (**bowl over**) knock down. **5** (**bowl over**) astonish.

bowler n. **1** Cricket a member of the fielding side who bowls. **2** a player at bowls. **3** a hard black felt hat with a rounded top.

box n. **1** a container with a flat base and sides and a lid. **2** an enclosed area reserved for a group of people in a theatre, sports ground, etc. **3** (**the box**) informal television. **4** an evergreen shrub with glossy leaves and hard wood. ▸ v. **1** put in a box. **2** fight with the fists as a sport. □ **box office** the place at a theatre or cinema where tickets are sold. **box room** a small room used for storage. ▪ **boxing** n.

boxer n. **1** a person who boxes as a sport. **2** a dog with a brown coat and pug-like face. □ **boxer shorts** men's underpants resembling shorts.

boy n. a male child. □ **boyfriend** a person's regular male romantic or sexual partner. ▪ **boyhood** n. **boyish** adj.

boycott v. refuse to have dealings with or trade with. ▸ n. an act of boycotting.

bra n. a woman's undergarment worn to support the breasts.

brace n. **1** (**braces**) a pair of straps that pass over the shoulders and fasten to trousers to hold them up. **2** a strengthening or supporting part. **3** a wire device used to straighten the teeth. **4** (pl. **brace**) a pair. ▸ v. **1** make stronger or firmer with a brace. **2** (**brace oneself**) prepare for something difficult or unpleasant.

bracelet n. an ornamental band or chain worn on the arm.

bracing adj. fresh and invigorating.

bracken n. a tall fern.

bracket n. **1** each of a pair of marks ( ) [ ] { } < > used to enclose words or figures. **2** a category of similar people or things. **3** a right-angled support projecting from a wall. ▸ v. (**bracketing**, **bracketed**) **1** enclose in brackets. **2** place in the same category.

brackish adj. (of water) slightly salty.

bract n. a leaf with a flower in the angle where it meets the stem.

brag v. (**bragging**, **bragged**) boast.

braggart n. a boastful person.

braid n. **1** threads woven into a decorative band. **2** a plait of hair. ▸ v. **1** plait hair. **2** trim with braid.

Braille n. a written language for blind people, using raised dots.

brain n. **1** an organ of soft tissue in the skull, the centre of the nervous system. **2** intellectual ability. □ **brainchild** a particular person's idea or invention. **brainstorm 1** a moment in which one is unable to think clearly. **2** a group discussion to produce ideas. **brainwash** cause someone to completely change their attitudes and beliefs. **brainwave** a sudden clever idea.

Thesaurus

bout n. **1** MATCH, contest, fight, engagement, round, competition, encounter, struggle; informal set-to. **2** ATTACK, spell, fit, period, paroxysm.

bow v. INCLINE THE HEAD/BODY, curtsy, bob, stoop, make obeisance, genuflect, bend the knee, prostrate oneself, kowtow, salaam.

bowl[1] v. (**bowl over**) **1** KNOCK DOWN, bring, down, floor, fell. **2** ASTOUND, amaze, astonish, stagger, dumbfound, stun, surprise; informal flabbergast.

bowl[2] n. BASIN, dish, pan, container, vessel.

box[1] n. CONTAINER, receptacle, crate, case, carton, pack, package, chest, trunk, bin, coffer, casket.

box[2] v. FIGHT, spar, punch, thump, cuff, batter, pummel; informal belt, sock, clout, whack, slug, slam.

boxer n. FIGHTER, pugilist, sparring partner, prizefighter.

boy n. YOUTH, lad, youngster, stripling, schoolboy; informal kid, whippersnapper.

boycott v. **1** SHUN, ostracize, stay away from, avoid, spurn, reject, eschew, send to Coventry, blacklist, blackball. **2** BAN, bar, prohibit, embargo, proscribe, blacklist, debar.

brace v. **1** STRENGTHEN, support, reinforce, shore up, prop up, buttress. **2** STEADY, secure, stabilize, make fast.

brainy adj. (**brainier, brainiest**) informal clever.

braise v. fry food lightly and then stew it slowly in a closed container.

brake n. a device for slowing or stopping a moving vehicle. ▶v. slow or stop a vehicle with a brake.

bramble n. a blackberry bush or similar shrub.

bran n. pieces of grain husk separated from flour after milling.

branch n. **1** a part of a tree growing out from the trunk. **2** a river, road, or railway extending out from a main one. **3** a division of a larger group. ▶v. **1** divide into one or more branches. **2** (**branch out**) extend one's activities.

brand n. **1** a type of product made by a company under a particular name. **2** a mark burned on livestock with hot metal. ▶v. **1** mark with hot metal. **2** mark out as having a particular shameful quality. □ **brand new** completely new.

brandish v. wave something as a threat or in anger or excitement.

brandy n. (pl. **brandies**) a strong alcoholic spirit distilled from wine or fermented fruit juice.

brash adj. aggressively self-confident. ■ **brashness** n.

brass n. **1** a yellow alloy of copper and zinc. **2** a brass memorial plaque. **3** brass wind instruments forming a section of an orchestra.

brasserie /brass-uh-ri/ n. (pl. **brasseries**) an inexpensive French or French-style restaurant.

brassica n. a plant of the cabbage family.

brassiere /braz-i-er/ n. a bra.

brassy adj. (**brassier, brassiest**) **1** like brass. **2** tastelessly showy.

brat n. informal a badly behaved child.

bravado n. boldness intended to impress or intimidate.

brave adj. having or showing courage. ▶n. dated an American Indian warrior. ▶v. face unpleasant conditions with courage. ■ **bravely** adv. **bravery** n.

bravo exclam. well done!

bravura n. great skill and enthusiasm.

brawl n. a noisy fight or quarrel. ▶v. take part in a brawl.

brawn n. physical strength. ■ **brawny** adj.

bray n. the loud, harsh cry of a donkey. ▶v. make such a sound.

brazen adj. bold and shameless. ▶v. (**brazen it out**) endure an awkward situation with an apparent lack of shame. ■ **brazenly** adv.

Thesaurus

3 PREPARE, ready, fortify, tense.

brag v. BOAST, show off, blow one's own trumpet, crow, sing one's own praises.

brain n. **1** CEREBRUM, cerebral matter, encephalon; informal grey matter. **2** INTELLIGENCE, intellect, mind, sense, cleverness, wit, understanding, acumen; informal nous, savvy.

brainy adj. CLEVER, intelligent, bright, brilliant, gifted; informal smart. ■ OPPOSITES stupid.

branch n. **1** BOUGH, limb, stem, twig, shoot, sprig, arm. **2** DEPARTMENT, division, subdivision, section, subsection, part, wing, office. ▶v. FORK, divide, diverge, separate, bifurcate, split, subdivide. □ **branch out** EXTEND, spread out, diversify, expand, proliferate, multiply.

brand n. **1** MAKE, variety, line, trade name, trademark. **2** KIND, type, sort, variety, style, stamp, cast. ▶v. **1** STAMP, mark, burn, scorch, sear, tag, identify. **2** STIGMATIZE, characterize, mark, taint, vilify, disgrace, discredit, denounce.

brandish v. FLOURISH, wave, wield, raise, swing, display, shake, wag, flaunt, show off.

brash adj. BOLD, self-confident, cocky, audacious, assertive, brazen, aggressive, forward, insolent, impudent, bumptious. ■ OPPOSITES meek.

bravado n. BLUSTER, swaggering, arrogance, boldness, audacity, bombast, braggadocio.

brave adj. COURAGEOUS, valiant, fearless, intrepid, plucky, unafraid, heroic, bold, daring, resolute, indomitable, audacious, unshrinking, determined, undaunted, lion-hearted, spirited, dauntless, gallant, valorous, stalwart, doughty, stout-hearted, venturesome, game; informal gutsy, spunky. ■ OPPOSITES cowardly, fearful.

bravery n. COURAGE, courageousness, fearlessness, pluck, pluckiness, intrepidity, boldness, heroism, audacity, daring, nerve, fortitude, resolution, grit, spirit, dauntlessness, mettle, valour, tenacity, doughtiness, hardihood; informal guts, spunk, bottle. ■ OPPOSITES cowardice.

brawl n. FIGHT, scuffle, fracas, rumpus, altercation, clash, free-for-all, tussle, brouhaha, quarrel, wrangle, commotion, uproar, ruckus; informal punch-up, scrap; Law, dated affray. ▶v. see FIGHT.

brazier n. a portable heater holding lighted coals.

brazil nut n. a large three-sided nut from a South American tree.

breach v. 1 make a hole in. 2 break a rule or agreement. ▶ n. 1 a gap made in a wall or barrier. 2 an act of breaking a rule or agreement. 3 a quarrel or disagreement.

bread n. 1 food made of flour, water, and yeast mixed together and baked. 2 informal money. □ **breadwinner** a person who earns money to support their family. **on the breadline** very poor.

breadth n. 1 the distance from side to side of a thing. 2 wide range.

break v. (**breaking, broke**; past part. **broken**) 1 separate into pieces as a result of a blow or strain. 2 stop working. 3 interrupt a sequence or course. 4 fail to observe a rule or agreement. 5 beat a record. 6 soften a fall. 7 suddenly make or become public. 8 (of a boy's voice) deepen at puberty. 9 (of the weather) change suddenly. ▶ n. 1 a pause, gap, or short rest. 2 an instance of breaking, or the point where something is broken. 3 a sudden rush or dash. 4 informal a chance. 5 an uninterrupted series of successful shots in snooker or billiards.

□ **break down 1** stop functioning. 2 lose control of one's emotions. **breakdown 1** a failure or collapse. 2 a careful analysis. **break in 1** force entry to a building. 2 make a horse used to being ridden. **breakneck** dangerously fast. **break out 1** start suddenly. 2 escape. **breakthrough** a sudden important development or success. **break up** (of a gathering or relationship) end or part. **breakwater** a barrier built out into the sea to protect a coast etc. from waves. ■ **breakable** adj.

breakage n. 1 the action of breaking something. 2 a thing that has been broken.

breaker n. a heavy wave that breaks on the shore.

breakfast n. the first meal of the day.

bream n. (pl. **bream**) a freshwater fish.

breast n. 1 either of the two organs on a woman's chest which produce milk after pregnancy. 2 a person's or animal's chest. □ **breastbone** the bone down the centre of the chest. **breast-stroke** a swimming stroke in which the arms are pushed forwards and swept back while the legs are kicked out.

breath n. 1 air taken into or sent out of

Thesaurus

brawny adj. MUSCULAR, powerful, burly, strong, powerfully built, robust, sturdy, strapping, sinewy. ■ OPPOSITES scrawny, puny.

brazen adj. BOLD, shameless, unashamed, unabashed, audacious, defiant, brash, forward, pushy, presumptuous, brassy, impudent, insolent, cheeky, immodest, pert; informal saucy. ■ OPPOSITES reserved, modest.

breach n. 1 BREAK, rupture, split, opening, crack, gap, hole, fissure, rent, fracture, rift, cleft, aperture, gulf, chasm. 2 BREAKING, violation, infringement, contravention, transgression, infraction. 3 BREAKING OFF, severance, estrangement, parting, parting of the ways, rift, split, falling-out, schism, alienation, disaffection, quarrel, discord. ▶ v. 1 BREAK THROUGH, split, rupture, open up, burst through, make a gap in. 2 BREAK, contravene, violate, infringe, transgress against, defy, disobey, flout.

break v. 1 SMASH, crack, shatter, split, burst, fracture, fragment, splinter, crash, snap, rend, tear, divide, sever, separate, part, demolish, disintegrate. 2 VIOLATE, contravene, infringe, breach,

disobey, defy, flout, transgress against. 3 STOP, take a break, pause, rest, discontinue, give up; informal knock off, take five. 4 BEAT, surpass, outdo, better, exceed, outstrip, top, cap. ▶ n. 1 CRACK, hole, gap, opening, chink, split, fissure, tear, rent, gash, rupture, rift, chasm, cleft. 2 INTERVAL, pause, stop, halt, intermission, rest, respite, breathing space, interlude; informal breather, let-up, time out. 3 BREACH, split, rupture, rift, discontinuation, schism, disaffection, alienation. □ **break away** LEAVE, break with, separate from, part company with, detach oneself from, secede from.

break down STOP WORKING, give out, go wrong, malfunction; informal conk out, pack up **break off** END, bring to an end, finish, cease, discontinue, call a halt to, suspend.

breakdown n. 1 STOPPAGE, failure, malfunctioning, seizing up; informal conking out. 2 COLLAPSE, failure, disintegration, foundering, falling through. 3 ANALYSIS, classification, itemization, categorization, explanation, examination, dissection.

breakthrough n. ADVANCE, step/leap forward, leap, quantum leap, discovery, the lungs. **2** an act of breathing in or out. **3** a slight movement of air. □ **breathtaking** amazing or awe-inspiring. **out of breath** panting after exercise. ■ **breathless** adj.

breathalyser (US trademark **Breath-alyzer**) n. a device for measuring the amount of alcohol in a driver's breath. ■ **breathalyse** (US **-yze**) v.

breathe v. **1** take air into the lungs and send it out again. **2** say quietly.

breather n. informal a brief pause for rest.

bred past & past part. of **BREED**.

breech n. the back part of a rifle or gun barrel. □ **breech birth** a birth in which the baby's buttocks or feet are de-livered first.

breeches pl. n. short trousers fastened just below the knee.

breed v. (**breeding**, **bred**) **1** (of animals) mate and produce offspring. **2** keep animals for the purpose of producing young. **3** produce or cause. ▶n. **1** a particular type within a species of animals. **2** a type. ■ **breeder** n.

breeding n. upper-class good manners.

breeze n. a gentle wind. □ **breeze block** a lightweight building block. ■ **breezy** adj.

brethren pl. n. fellow members of a Christian group.

Breton n. a person from Brittany.

breve /breev/ n. Music a note twice as long as a semibreve.

brevity n. **1** concise and exact use of words. **2** shortness of time.

brew v. **1** make beer by soaking, boiling,

and fermentation. **2** make tea or coffee by mixing it with hot water. **3** begin to develop. ▶n. something brewed. ■ **brewer** n.

brewery n. (pl. **breweries**) a place where beer is made.

briar (or **brier**) n. a prickly shrub, esp. a wild rose.

bribe v. dishonestly pay someone to act in one's favour. ▶n. something offered in an attempt to bribe. ■ **bribery** n.

bric-a-brac n. various objects of little value.

brick n. a small rectangular block of fired clay, used in building. ▶v. block or enclose with a wall of bricks. □ **brickbat** a critical remark. **bricklayer** a workman who builds structures with bricks.

bridal adj. of a bride or a newly married couple.

bride n. a woman at the time of her wedding. □ **bridegroom** a man at the time of his wedding. **bridesmaid** a girl or woman who accompanies a bride at her wedding.

bridge n. **1** a structure providing a way across a river, road, etc. **2** the platform on a ship from which the captain directs its course. **3** the upper bony part of the nose. **4** the part on a stringed instrument over which the strings are stretched. **5** a card game played between two pairs of players. ▶v. be or make a bridge over. □ **bridgehead** a strong position gained by an army inside enemy territory.

Thesaurus

find, invention, innovation, development, improvement, revolution.

breast n. BUST, bosom, chest, front, thorax; informal boob, knocker.

breath n. **1** INHALATION, pant, gasp, gulp of air, inspiration, exhalation, expiration. **2** PUFF, waft, gust, breeze.

breathe v. **1** INHALE, EXHALE, respire, puff, pant, gasp, wheeze, gulp. **2** WHISPER, murmur, purr, sigh, say.

breathless adj. OUT OF BREATH, panting, wheezing, wheezy, puffing, gasping, winded, choking.

breathtaking adj. SPECTACULAR, magnificent, impressive, awesome, awe-inspiring, astounding, exciting, astonishing, amazing, thrilling, stunning; informal out of this world.

breed v. **1** REPRODUCE, procreate, multiply, give birth, bring forth young, propagate; literary beget. **2** PRODUCE, bring about, give rise to, create, generate, stir

up, engender, make for, foster, arouse, induce, originate, occasion. ▶n. **1** FAMILY, variety, type, kind, class, strain, stock, line. **2** STOCK, species, race, lineage, extraction, pedigree.

breeze n. BREATH OF WIND, gentle wind, draught, puff of air, gust, flurry, current of air; literary zephyr.

breezy adj. WINDY, blowy, blustery, gusty, squally, fresh.

brevity n. SHORTNESS, briefness, conciseness, concision, terseness, compactness, pithiness, succinctness, economy, curtness, condensation, pointedness.

brew v. **1** MAKE, prepare, infuse, ferment, mash. **2** BE IMMINENT, loom, gather, form, be threatening, be impending, impend. ▶n. DRINK, beverage, liquor, ale, beer, tea, infusion, mixture, potion.

bribe v. CORRUPT, entice, suborn, get at, buy off, pay off; informal grease someone's palm, sweeten, fix, square.

bridle n. the harness used to control a horse. ▶v. **1** put a bridle on. **2** show resentment or anger. □ **bridleway** (or **bridle path**) a path for horse riders or walkers.

brief adj. **1** lasting a short time. **2** using few words. ▶n. **1** a summary of the facts in a case given to a barrister to argue in court. **2** a set of instructions about a task. **3** (**briefs**) short underpants. ▶v. instruct someone about a task. □ **briefcase** a flat case for carrying documents. ■ **briefly** adv.

brier var. of BRIAR.

brig n. a sailing ship with two masts.

brigade n. **1** a large body of troops, forming part of a division. **2** a particular group of people: *the anti-smoking brigade.*

brigadier n. a rank of officer in the army, above colonel.

brigand n. a member of a gang of bandits.

bright adj. **1** giving out or filled with light. **2** (of colour) vivid. **3** intelligent.

4 cheerfully lively. **5** (of prospects) good. ■ **brighten** v. **brightly** adv. **brightness** n.

brilliant adj. **1** very bright or vivid. **2** extremely clever or talented. **3** informal excellent. ■ **brilliance** n. **brilliantly** adv.

brim n. **1** the projecting edge of a hat. **2** the lip of a cup, bowl, etc. ▶v. (**brimming, brimmed**) be full to the point of overflowing.

brimstone n. old use sulphur.

brindle (or **brindled**) adj. (of an animal) brownish with streaks of grey or black.

brine n. salt water. ■ **briny** adj.

bring v. (**bringing, brought**) **1** carry or accompany to a place. **2** cause to be in a particular position or state. **3** begin legal action. □ **bring about** cause to happen. **bring off** achieve. **bring on** cause to occur. **bring out 1** produce and launch. **2** emphasize a feature. **bring up 1** rear a child. **2** raise for discussion.

brink n. **1** the edge of land before a steep slope or a body of water. **2** the verge of

Thesaurus

▶n. INDUCEMENT, enticement, incentive; *informal* backhander, sweetener, graft, kickback.

bridge n. **1** ARCH, span, overpass, flyover, viaduct. **2** BOND, link, tie, connection, cord, binding. ▶v. SPAN, cross, go over, pass over, traverse, extend across, reach across, arch over.

brief adj. **1** CONCISE, short, succinct, to the point, terse, economic, abbreviated, pithy, pointed, curt, crisp, condensed, compressed, sparing, thumbnail, epigrammatic. **2** SHORT-LIVED, short, fleeting, momentary, temporary, impermanent, passing, fading, transitory, ephemeral, transient. ▶v. INSTRUCT, inform, direct, guide, advise, enlighten, prepare, prime; *informal* fill in, put in the picture, give someone the low-down. ▶n. **1** INFORMATION, advice, instructions, directions, guidance, briefing, preparation, priming, intelligence; *informal* lowdown, rundown. **2** ARGUMENT, case, proof, defence, evidence, contention, demonstration.

briefly adv. **1** CONCISELY, succinctly, to the point, tersely, sparingly, economically. **2** FLEETINGLY, temporarily, momentarily, ephemerally. **3** IN SHORT, in brief, to cut a long story short, in a word, in a nutshell, in essence.

briefs pl. n. UNDERPANTS, pants, Y-fronts, knickers, camiknickers; *US* shorts; *informal* panties.

bright adj. **1** SHINING, brilliant, vivid, intense, blazing, dazzling, beaming, sparkling, glittering, gleaming, radiant, glowing, glistening, shimmering, luminous, lustrous, incandescent. **2** VIVID, intense, rich, brilliant, bold, glowing. **3** CLEAR, cloudless, unclouded, sunny, pleasant, clement. **4** INTELLIGENT, clever, sharp, quick-witted, astute, acute, ingenious, resourceful, accomplished; *informal* brainy, smart. **5** PROMISING, optimistic, favourable, hopeful, auspicious, propitious, encouraging, lucky, golden. ■ OPPOSITES dark, dull, stupid.

brighten v. **1** MAKE BRIGHT/BRIGHTER, light up, lighten, illuminate, irradiate; *literary* illumine. **2** CHEER UP, gladden, liven up, enliven, perk up, animate; *informal* buck up, pep up.

brilliant adj. **1** BRIGHT, shining, intense, radiant, beaming, gleaming, sparkling, dazzling, lustrous. **2** CLEVER, intelligent, astute, masterly, inventive, resourceful, discerning; *informal* smart. **3** EXCELLENT, superb, very good, outstanding, exceptional; *informal* brill, smashing. ■ OPPOSITES dull, bad.

brim n. RIM, lip, edge, brink, margin, circumference, perimeter, verge. ▶v. BE FULL, be filled up, be full to capacity, overflow, run over, well over.

bring v. **1** FETCH, carry, bear, take, convey, transport, deliver, lead, guide, conduct, usher, escort. **2** CAUSE, create, a state or situation. ◻ **brinkmanship** the pursuing of a dangerous course of action to the limits of safety before stopping.

briquette n. a block of compressed coal dust used as fuel.

brisk adj. **1** active and energetic. **2** slightly brusque. ■ **briskly** adv.

brisket n. meat from the breast of a cow.

bristle n. a short, stiff hair. ▶v. **1** (of hair or fur) stand upright away from the skin. **2** react angrily. **3** (**bristle with**) be covered with. ■ **bristly** adj.

British adj. of Great Britain.

Briton n. a British person.

brittle adj. hard but easily broken.

broach v. **1** raise a subject for discussion. **2** pierce a container.

broad adj. **1** larger than usual from side to side; wide. **2** large in area or range. **3** without detail. **4** (of an accent) very strong. ◻ **broad bean** a large flat green bean. **broad-minded** not easily shocked. **broadsheet** a large-sized newspaper. **broadside 1** a strongly worded critical attack. **2** hist. a firing of all the guns from one side of a ship. ■ **broaden** v. **broadly** adv.

broadcast v. (**broadcasting, broad-**

cast) **1** transmit by radio or television. **2** make generally known. ▶n. a radio or television programme. ■ **broadcaster** n.

brocade n. a rich fabric woven with a raised pattern.

broccoli n. a vegetable with heads of small green or purplish flower buds.

....

☑ Two c's, one l: broccoli.

....

brochure n. a booklet containing information about a product or service.

broderie anglaise /broh-duh-ri ong-glayz/ n. open embroidery on white cotton or linen.

brogue n. **1** a strong shoe with perforated patterns in the leather. **2** a strong regional accent.

broil v. esp. US grill meat or fish.

broke past of BREAK. ▶adj. informal having no money.

broken past part. of BREAK. ▶adj. (of a language) spoken hesitantly, with many mistakes. ◻ **broken-hearted** overwhelmed with grief.

broker n. a person who buys and sells on behalf of others. ▶v. arrange a deal or plan. ■ **brokerage** n.

produce, result in, engender, give rise to, precipitate, occasion, wreak, effect, contribute to. ◻ **bring in** see EARN. **bring off** see ACHIEVE. **bring up 1** see RAISE (3). **2** see BROACH (2).

brink n. **1** EDGE, verge, margin, limit, rim, extremity, boundary, fringe. **2** VERGE, edge, threshold, point.

brisk adj. **1** QUICK, rapid, fast, swift, speedy, energetic, lively, vigorous, sprightly, spirited. **2** ABRUPT, brusque, no-nonsense, sharp, curt, crisp; informal snappy. ■ OPPOSITES slow, leisurely.

bristle n. HAIR, stubble, whisker, prickle, spine, quill, thorn, barb. ▶v. GROW ANGRY/INDIGNANT, be irritated, bridle, flare up, draw oneself up, rear up.

brittle adj. **1** BREAKABLE, hard, crisp, fragile, frail, delicate; formal frangible. **2** EDGY, nervous, on edge, tense, stiff; informal uptight. ■ OPPOSITES flexible, relaxed.

broach v. **1** PIERCE, puncture, tap, draw off. **2** INTRODUCE, raise, bring up, mention, suggest, open, put forward, propound.

broad adj. **1** WIDE, large, extensive, vast, spacious, expansive, sweeping, boundless, ample, capacious, open. **2** WIDE-

RANGING, wide, general, comprehensive, inclusive, encyclopedic, all-embracing, universal, unlimited. **3** GENERAL, nonspecific, unspecific, imprecise, vague, loose, sweeping. ■ OPPOSITES narrow.

broadcast v. **1** TRANSMIT, relay, send out, put on the air, beam, televise, telecast. **2** ANNOUNCE, make public, report, publicize, publish, advertise, proclaim, air, spread, circulate, disseminate, promulgate. ▶n. PROGRAMME, show, transmission, telecast.

broaden v. **1** WIDEN, make broader, extend, spread, enlarge. **2** EXPAND, widen, enlarge, extend, increase, augment, add to, develop, amplify, swell.

broad-minded adj. OPEN-MINDED, liberal, tolerant, unprejudiced, flexible, unbiased, undogmatic, catholic, fair, progressive, freethinking, enlightened, permissive. ■ OPPOSITES narrow-minded.

brochure n. BOOKLET, catalogue, prospectus, leaflet, pamphlet, handbill, handout, advertisement.

broke adj. PENNILESS, insolvent, bankrupt, poverty-stricken, impoverished, impecunious, destitute, indigent, ruined; informal flat broke, strapped for cash, cleaned out, on one's uppers,

brolly n. (pl. **brollies**) informal an umbrella.

bromide n. a compound of bromine, used in medicine.

bromine n. a dark red liquid chemical element.

bronchial adj. of the tubes leading to the lungs.

bronchitis n. inflammation of the bronchial tubes.

bronco n. (pl. **broncos**) a wild or half-tamed horse of the western US.

brontosaurus n. a huge plant-eating dinosaur.

bronze n. **1** a yellowish-brown alloy of copper and tin. **2** a yellowish-brown colour. **3** an object made of bronze. ▶v. make suntanned.

brooch n. an ornament fastened to clothing with a hinged pin.

brood n. a family of young animals born or hatched at one time. ▶v. **1** think deeply about an unpleasant subject. **2** (of a bird) sit on eggs to hatch them.

broody adj. **1** (of a hen) wishing to hatch eggs. **2** informal (of a woman) wanting to have a baby. **3** thoughtful and unhappy.

brook n. a small stream. ▶v. tolerate.

broom n. **1** a long-handled brush for sweeping. **2** a shrub with yellow flowers. □ **broomstick** the handle of a broom, on which witches are said to fly.

Bros abbrev. brothers.

broth n. thin soup or stock.

brothel n. a house where men visit prostitutes.

brother n. **1** a man or boy in relation to other children of his parents. **2** a male colleague or friend. **3** (pl. also **brethren**) a male fellow Christian or member of a religious order. □ **brother-hood 1** the relationship between brothers. **2** comradeship. **3** a group linked by a shared interest. **brother-in-law** (pl. **brothers-in-law**) the brother of one's wife or husband, or the husband of one's sister. ■ **brotherly** adj.

brought past & past part. of **BRING**.

brow n. **1** the forehead. **2** an eyebrow. **3** the highest point of a hill. ■ **browbeat** intimidate.

brown adj. **1** of the colour of rich soil. **2** suntanned. ▶n. brown colour or material. ▶v. make or become brown. □ **browned off** informal annoyed or resentful. ■ **brownish** adj.

browse v. **1** look at goods or text in a leisurely way. **2** look at information on a computer. **3** (of an animal) feed on leaves, twigs, etc.

browser n. **1** a person or animal that browses. **2** a computer program for navigating the Internet.

bruise n. an area of discoloured skin on the body, caused by a blow. ▶v. cause or develop a bruise.

bruiser n. informal a tough, aggressive person.

brunch n. a meal combining breakfast and lunch.

brunette n. a woman or girl with dark brown hair.

brunt n. the chief impact of something bad.

brush n. **1** an implement with a handle and a block of bristles, hair, or wire. **2** an act of brushing. **3** a brief encounter with something bad. **4** a fox's tail. **5** undergrowth and shrubs. ▶v. **1** clean, smooth, or apply with a brush. **2** touch lightly. **3** (**brush off**) dismiss curtly. **4** (**brush up**) work to regain a former skill.

Thesaurus

skint, stony broke.

broken-hearted adj. GRIEF-STRICKEN, desolate, despairing, devastated, inconsolable, miserable, overwhelmed, wretched, forlorn, woeful, crestfallen.

brood n. OFFSPRING, young, family, clutch, nest, litter, children, youngsters. ▶v. **1** WORRY, agonize, fret, dwell on, meditate, mull over. **2** SIT ON, hatch, incubate.

brook[1] n. STREAM, streamlet, channel, rivulet, runnel; N. Engl. beck; Sc. & N. Engl. burn; US & Austral./NZ creek.

brook[2] v. TOLERATE, stand, bear, allow.

browbeat v. BULLY, force, coerce, intimidate, compel, badger, hector, harangue, terrorize, tyrannize.

brown adj. **1** HAZEL, chestnut, nut-brown, brunette, chocolate, coffee, walnut, ochre, sepia, mahogany, russet, umber, burnt sienna, dun, khaki, beige, tan. **2** TANNED, sunburnt, browned, bronze, bronzed, swarthy. ▶v. GRILL, toast, sear, seal.

browse v. **1** LOOK THROUGH, skim, scan, glance at, thumb through, leaf through, peruse. **2** GRAZE, feed, eat, crop, nibble.

bruise n. CONTUSION, swelling, bump, mark, blemish, welt. ▶v. CONTUSE, injure, blacken, mark, discolour, make black and blue.

brunt n. IMPACT, full force, burden, shock, thrust, violence, pressure, strain, stress, repercussions, consequences.

brusque /bruusk/ adj. abrupt or off-hand. ■ **brusquely** adv.

Brussels sprout n. the edible bud of a variety of cabbage.

brutal adj. savagely violent. ■ **brutality** n. **brutally** adv.

brutalize (or **-ise**) v. **1** make brutal by frequent exposure to violence. **2** treat in a cruel way.

brute n. a violent or savage person or a large, unmanageable animal. ▶ adj. involving physical strength rather than reason: *brute force*. ■ **brutish** adj.

BSc abbrev. Bachelor of Science.

BSE abbrev. bovine spongiform encephalopathy, a fatal brain disease in cattle.

BST abbrev. British Summer Time.

bubble n. **1** a thin sphere of liquid enclosing a gas. **2** an air- or gas-filled cavity. ▶ v. **1** (of a liquid) contain rising bubbles of gas. **2** show great enthusiasm. ■ **bubbly** adj.

bubonic plague n. a form of plague passed on by rat fleas.

buccaneer n. **1** hist. a pirate. **2** a recklessly adventurous person.

buck n. **1** the male of some animals, e.g. deer and rabbits. **2** US & Austral. a dollar. **3** old use a fashionable young man. ▶ v. **1** (of a horse) jump with the back arched. **2** resist or go against. **3** (**buck up**) informal make or become more cheerful. □ **buck teeth** teeth that stick out. **pass the buck** informal shift responsibility to someone else

bucket n. an open container with a handle for carrying liquids. ▶ v. (**bucketing, bucketed**) informal rain heavily.

buckle n. a flat frame with a hinged pin, used as a fastener. ▶ v. **1** fasten with a buckle. **2** crumple under pressure. **3** (**buckle down**) tackle a task with determination.

bucolic /byoo-kol-ik/ adj. of country life; rustic.

bud n. a growth on a plant which develops into a leaf or flower. ▶ v. (**budding, budded**) form a bud or buds.

Buddhism n. a religion based on the teachings of Buddha. ■ **Buddhist** n. & adj.

budding adj. beginning and showing signs of promise.

buddleia n. a shrub with lilac, white, or yellow flowers.

buddy n. (pl. **buddies**) US informal a friend.

budge v. move slightly.

budgerigar n. a small Australian parakeet.

budget n. **1** an estimate of income and spending for a set period. **2** the amount of money available for a purpose. ▶ v. (**budgeting, budgeted**) allow for in a budget. ■ **budgetary** adj.

budgie n. (pl. **budgies**) informal a budgerigar.

buff n. **1** a yellowish-beige colour. **2** informal an expert on a particular subject. ▶ v. polish.

buffalo n. (pl. **buffalo** or **buffaloes**) **1** a wild ox. **2** the North American bison.

buffer n. **1** (**buffers**) shock-absorbing

Thesaurus

brush n. **1** BROOM, sweeper, besom, whisk. **2** ENCOUNTER, clash, confrontation, conflict, skirmish, tussle, fight, engagement. ▶ v. **1** SWEEP, clean, groom, buff. **2** TOUCH, graze, kiss, glance, contact. □ **brush off** *see* REBUFF.

brusque adj. ABRUPT, curt, blunt, short, terse, caustic, gruff, rude, discourteous, impolite. ■ OPPOSITES polite.

brutal adj. SAVAGE, cruel, vicious, sadistic, violent, bloodthirsty, ruthless, callous, murderous, heartless, merciless, pitiless, remorseless, inhuman, barbarous, barbaric, ferocious, wild, brutish, bestial. ■ OPPOSITES gentle.

brute n. **1** ANIMAL, beast, creature. **2** SAVAGE, monster, animal, sadist, barbarian, fiend, devil, lout, oaf, boor; *informal* swine. ▶ adj. CRUDE, rough, mindless, physical, unfeeling.

bubble n. GLOBULE, bead, drop, air pocket. ▶ v. FIZZ, foam, froth, gurgle, effervesce, sparkle, boil, simmer, seethe, percolate.

bubbly adj. **1** FIZZY, foamy, frothy, effervescent, sparkling, sudsy. **2** VIVACIOUS, lively, animated, sparkling, excited, effervescent, bouncy, ebullient, elated.

bucket n. PAIL, pitcher, can, scuttle.

buckle n. **1** CLASP, fastener, clip, catch, fastening, hasp. **2** KINK, warp, distortion, wrinkle, bulge. ▶ v. **1** FASTEN, hook, secure, do up, strap, tie, clasp, clip. **2** BEND, twist, contort, warp, crumple, distort.

bud n. SHOOT, sprout. ▶ v. SPROUT, germinate, shoot, burgeon.

budge v. **1** MOVE, shift, stir, yield, go, proceed. **2** PERSUADE, convince, influence, sway, bend.

budget n. FINANCIAL PLAN, estimate, statement, account, allowance, means, resources. ▶ v. **1** PLAN, allow, set aside, allocate, save. **2** PLAN, schedule, allocate, ration, apportion.

buff[1] v. POLISH, shine, rub, burnish,

devices on a railway track or railway vehicle. **2** a person or thing that lessens the impact of harmful effects.

buffet[1] /boo-fay, buf-fay/ n. **1** a meal in which guests serve themselves. **2** a counter at which snacks are sold.

buffet[2] /buf-fit/ v. (**buffeting**, **buffeted**) (esp. of wind or waves) strike repeatedly and violently.

buffoon n. a ridiculous but amusing person. ▪ **buffoonery** n.

bug n. **1** a small insect. **2** informal a germ or an illness caused by one. **3** a hidden microphone. **4** an error in a computer program or system. ▶v. (**bugging**, **bugged**) **1** hide a microphone in. **2** informal annoy. □ **bugbear** something causing anxiety or irritation.

bugger vulgar n. **1** derog. a person who commits buggery. **2** an unpleasant person or thing. ▶v. practise buggery with.

buggery n. anal sex.

buggy n. (pl. **buggies**) **1** a small open-topped vehicle. **2** a collapsible pushchair.

bugle n. a brass instrument like a small trumpet. ▪ **bugler** n.

build v. (**building**, **built**) **1** construct by putting parts together. **2** (**build up**) increase over time. ▶n. bodily proportions. ▪ **builder** n.

building n. a structure with a roof and walls. □ **building society** an organization that pays interest on members' investments and lends money for mortgages.

built-in adj. included as part of a larger structure.

built-up adj. covered by many buildings.

bulb n. **1** the rounded base of the stem of some plants. **2** a glass ball giving light in an electric lamp.

bulbous adj. round or bulging.

bulge n. a rounded swelling. ▶v. swell or stick out.

bulimia /buu-lim-i-uh/ n. a disorder marked by bouts of overeating, followed by fasting or vomiting. ▪ **bulimic** adj. & n.

bulk n. **1** the mass or size of something large. **2** the greater part. **3** a large mass or shape. □ **bulkhead** a partition in a ship or aircraft. **in bulk** (of goods) in large quantities.

bulky adj. (**bulkier**, **bulkiest**) large and unwieldy.

bull n. **1** an adult male of the cattle group. **2** a male whale or elephant. **3** a bullseye. **4** informal nonsense. **5** an official order issued by the pope. □ **bulldog** a powerful dog with a flat wrinkled face. **bulldozer** a tractor with a device for clearing ground. **bullfighting** the sport of baiting and killing a bull. **bullseye** the centre of the target in archery and darts.

bullet n. a small missile fired from a gun.

Thesaurus

clean.

buff[2] n. FAN, enthusiast, aficionado, devotee, admirer, expert; informal freak, nut.

buffer n. BULWARK, fender, bumper, cushion, guard, safeguard, shield, screen, intermediary.

buffet[1] n. CAFE, cafeteria, snack bar, refreshment counter/stall.

buffet[2] v. BATTER, strike, knock against, hit, bang, beat against.

buffoon n. FOOL, idiot, dolt, nincompoop; informal dope, chump, numbskull, half-wit, nitwit.

bug n. **1** INSECT, flea, mite; informal creepy-crawly, minibeast. **2** GERM, virus, bacterium, microbe, microorganism. **3** ILLNESS, sickness, disease, infection, disorder, upset, complaint; informal lurgy. **4** FAULT, flaw, defect, error, imperfection, failing, obstruction; informal gremlin. ▶v. **1** TAP, wiretap, listen in on, intercept, spy on. **2** see ANNOY.

build v. CONSTRUCT, make, erect, put up/together, assemble, set up, manufacture, fabricate, raise, form. ▶n. PHYSIQUE, body, frame, shape. □ **build up** see INTENSIFY.

building n. STRUCTURE, construction, edifice, pile, erection.

build-up n. GROWTH, increase, expansion, enlargement, accumulation, escalation, development.

bulbous adj. DISTENDED, bulging, swollen, rotund, convex, bloated, spherical, rounded.

bulge v. SWELL, swell out, project, protrude, stick out, balloon, jut out, enlarge, billow, distend, bloat. ▶n. SWELLING, bump, protuberance, protrusion, lump, knob, projection, prominence, distension.

bulk n. **1** SIZE, volume, quantity, weight, extent, mass, substance, magnitude, dimensions, amplitude. **2** MAJORITY, preponderance, greater part, mass, body, generality.

bulky adj. UNWIELDY, awkward, large, big, substantial, massive, immense, voluminous, weighty, ponderous; informal

bulletin n. a short official statement or summary of news.

bullion n. gold or silver in bulk or bars.

bullock n. a castrated bull.

bully n. (pl. **bullies**) a person who intimidates weaker people. ▶v. (**bullying**, **bullied**) intimidate.

bulrush n. a tall waterside plant with a long brown head.

bulwark n. 1 a defensive wall. 2 a ship's side above deck level.

bum n. informal 1 a person's bottom. 2 a lazy or worthless person.

bumble v. act or speak in an awkward or confused way.

bumblebee n. a large hairy bee.

bumf (or **bumph**) n. informal printed information.

bump n. 1 a light blow or collision. 2 a projection on a level surface. ▶v. 1 knock or run into. 2 travel with a jolting movement. 3 (**bump into**) meet by chance. ■ **bumpy** adj.

bumper n. a bar across the front or back of a vehicle to reduce damage in a collision. ▶adj. exceptionally large or successful.

bumpkin n. an unsophisticated country person.

bumptious adj. irritatingly self-assertive.

bun n. 1 a small cake or bread roll. 2 a tight coil of hair at the back of the head.

bunch n. a number of things grouped or held together. ▶v. collect or form into a bunch.

bundle n. 1 a group of things tied or wrapped up together. 2 informal a large amount of money. ▶v. 1 tie or roll up in a bundle. 2 informal push or carry forcibly.

bung n. a stopper for a container. ▶v. 1 (**bung up**) block up. 2 informal put or throw casually.

bungalow n. a one-storeyed house.

bungee jumping n. the sport of leaping from a high place, attached by an elastic cord around the ankles.

bungle v. perform a task clumsily or incompetently. ▶n. a mistake or failure. ■ **bungler** n.

hulking.

bulldoze v. 1 DEMOLISH, flatten, level, raze. 2 FORCE, push, shove, drive, propel.

bulletin n. REPORT, announcement, statement, newsflash, account, message, communiqué, communication, dispatch, notification.

bullish adj. OPTIMISTIC, hopeful, confident, positive, assured, cheerful, sanguine.

bully n. INTIMIDATOR, persecutor, oppressor, browbeater, tyrant, tormentor, bully boy, thug; informal tough. ▶v. INTIMIDATE, coerce, browbeat, oppress, domineer, persecute, torment, pressurize, pressure, terrorize, tyrannize, cow; informal push around.

bulwark n. 1 RAMPART, embankment, fortification, bastion, redoubt, outwork, breastwork. 2 SUPPORT, defence, guard, protection, safeguard.

bumbling adj. CLUMSY, awkward, blundering, incompetent, bungling, inept, inefficient, stumbling, lumbering, foolish.

bump v. 1 HIT, bang, strike, knock, jar, crash into, collide with, smash into. See also HIT. 2 BOUNCE, jolt, shake, jerk, rattle, jounce. ▶n. 1 BANG, crash, thud, thump, knock, smash, collision. 2 LUMP, swelling, contusion, injury, protrusion, bulge, projection, protuberance, hump, knob, distension. □ **bump into** see MEET.

bumpkin n. YOKEL, clodhopper, peasant, rustic, country cousin; US informal hillbilly, hick, hayseed, rube.

bumptious adj. SELF-IMPORTANT, conceited, arrogant, cocky, full of oneself, overconfident, brash, overbearing, puffed up, self-opinionated, egotistical, immodest, boastful, presumptuous, pompous, officious, swaggering, forward, pushy; informal big-headed. ■ OPPOSITES modest.

bumpy adj. 1 ROUGH, uneven, rutted, potholed, pitted, lumpy, knobby. 2 JOLTING, jarring, bouncy, jerky, rough. ■ OPPOSITES smooth.

bunch n. 1 COLLECTION, cluster, batch, set, quantity, bundle, heap, sheaf, clump. 2 BOUQUET, spray, posy, sheaf, corsage, nosegay. 3 GROUP, crowd, party, band, gathering, swarm, gang, flock, mob, knot, cluster, multitude. ▶v. GATHER, cluster, huddle, group, flock, mass, cram, pack, herd, bundle. ■ OPPOSITES disperse.

bundle n. BATCH, pile, collection, heap, stack, bunch, parcel, bale, sheaf, mass, quantity, accumulation. ▶v. 1 TIE, tie up, wrap, bind, fasten together, pack, parcel, roll, truss. 2 PUSH, shove, hurry, hustle, rush, thrust, throw.

bungle v. MAKE A MESS OF, mismanage, spoil, ruin, blunder, muff, mar; informal

bunion n. a painful swelling on the big toe.

bunk n. a narrow shelf-like bed. □ **do a bunk** informal run away.

bunker n. **1** a container for storing fuel. **2** an underground shelter for use in wartime. **3** a hollow filled with sand on a golf course.

bunkum n. informal, dated nonsense.

bunny n. (pl. **bunnies**) informal a rabbit.

Bunsen burner n. a small gas burner used in laboratories.

bunting n. **1** a small songbird. **2** decorative flags.

buoy /boy/ n. a floating object used to mark an area of water. ▶v. **1** keep afloat. **2** (**be buoyed up**) be cheerful and confident.

....
☑ Remember: *u* before *o* in b*uo*y and b*uo*yant.
....

buoyant adj. **1** able to float. **2** cheerful. ■ **buoyancy** n.

burble v. make a continuous murmuring noise. **2** speak at length in a confused way.

burden n. **1** a heavy load. **2** a cause of hardship or distress. ▶v. **1** load heavily. **2** cause hardship or distress to. ■ **burdensome** adj.

bureau /byoor-oh/ n. (pl. **bureaux** or **bureaus**) **1** a writing desk with an angled top. **2** US a chest of drawers. **3** an office for carrying out particular business. **4** a government department.

bureaucracy /byuu-**rok**-ruh-si/ n. (pl. **bureaucracies**) **1** a system of government in which most decisions are taken by unelected officials. **2** overcomplicated administrative procedure.

bureaucrat n. a government official, esp. one who follows guidelines rigidly. ■ **bureaucratic** adj.

burgeon /ber-juhn/ v. grow or increase rapidly.

burger n. a hamburger.

burgher /ber-guh/ n. old use a citizen of a town or city.

burglar n. a person who breaks into a building to steal its contents. ■ **burglary** n. **burgle** v.

burgundy n. (pl. **burgundies**) **1** a red wine. **2** a deep red colour.

burial n. the burying of a dead body.

burlesque n. a comically exaggerated imitation.

burly adj. (**burlier**, **burliest**) (of a man) large and strong.

burn v. (**burning**, **burned** or **burnt**) **1** (of a fire) flame or glow while using up a fuel. **2** harm, damage, or destroy by fire. **3** feel a strong desire or emotion. ▶n. **1** an injury caused by burning. **2** Sc. a stream.

burner n. a part of a cooker, lamp, etc. that gives out a flame.

burning adj. **1** intense. **2** important and urgent.

burnish v. polish by rubbing.

Thesaurus

....

screw up, foul up, mess up, louse up, botch, make a hash of, muck up, cock up.

bungling adj. CLUMSY, incompetent, inept, unskilful, blundering, maladroit; informal ham-fisted, cack-handed.

buoy n. FLOAT, marker, beacon.

buoyant adj. **1** FLOATING, afloat, floatable, light. **2** see CHEERFUL.

burden n. **1** LOAD, weight, cargo, freight. **2** RESPONSIBILITY, duty, obligation, onus, charge, care, worry, anxiety, problem, trouble, difficulty, strain, stress, affliction, weight, trial, tribulation, encumbrance, millstone, cross, albatross. ▶v. **1** LOAD, overload, weigh down, encumber, hamper. **2** TROUBLE, worry, oppress, bother, distress, afflict, torment, strain, tax, overwhelm, saddle, encumber; informal land.

bureau n. **1** AGENCY, office, department, service. **2** DESK, writing desk, writing table.

bureaucracy n. OFFICIALDOM, officials, administration, civil servants, civil service, government, directorate, regulations, paperwork, red tape.

burglar n. HOUSEBREAKER, thief, robber, raider, looter, cat burglar, intruder; US informal second-story man.

burglary n. HOUSEBREAKING, breaking and entering, breaking in, break-in, forced/forcible entry, theft, robbery.

burial n. INTERMENT, burying, entombment, funeral, obsequies; formal exequies. ■ OPPOSITES exhumation.

burly adj. WELL BUILT, muscular, brawny, stout, thickset, stocky, sturdy, big, powerful, strong, strapping, hefty, athletic, tough, husky; informal beefy, hulking. ■ OPPOSITES puny.

burn v. **1** BE ON FIRE, be alight, be ablaze, go up, blaze, be aflame, smoulder, flare, flash, glow, smoke, flicker. **2** SET ON FIRE, set fire to, set alight, ignite, light, kindle, put a match to, incinerate, reduce to ashes, cremate, consume, sear, char, scorch.

burp v. & n. informal (make) a belch.

burr n. **1** a strong pronunciation of the letter *r*. **2** a prickly seed case that clings to clothing and fur.

burrow n. a hole dug by a small animal as a dwelling. ▶v. **1** dig a burrow. **2** hide underneath or delve into something.

bursar n. a person who manages the financial affairs of a college or school.

bursary n. (pl. **bursaries**) a grant for study.

burst v. (**bursting, burst**) **1** break suddenly and violently apart. **2** be very full. **3** move or be opened suddenly and forcibly. **4** suddenly do something as a result of strong emotion. ▶n. **1** an instance of bursting. **2** a sudden brief outbreak.

bury v. (**burying, buried**) **1** put underground. **2** place a dead body in the earth or a tomb. **3** conceal or cover. **4** (**bury oneself**) involve oneself deeply in something.

bus n. (pl. **buses**) a large vehicle carrying customers along a fixed route. ▶v. (**busing, bused** or **bussing, bussed**) transport or travel in a bus.

busby n. (pl. **busbies**) a tall fur hat.

bush n. **1** a shrub. **2** (**the bush**) wild or uncultivated country. □ **bushbaby** a small African mammal with large eyes.

bushel n. **1** a measure of capacity equal to 8 gallons (36.4 litres). **2** US a measure of capacity equal to 64 US pints (35.2 litres).

bushy adj. (**bushier, bushiest**) **1** growing thickly. **2** covered with bushes.

business n. **1** a person's regular occupation. **2** work to be done or matters to be attended to. **3** a person's concern. **4** commercial activity. **5** a commercial organization. □ **businesslike** efficient and practical. **businessman** (or **businesswoman**) a person who works in commerce.

busk v. play music in the street for voluntary donations. ■ **busker** n.

bust n. **1** a woman's breasts. **2** a sculpture of a person's head, shoulders, and chest. ▶v. (**busting, busted** or **bust**) informal burst or break. □ **bust-up** informal a quarrel or fight. **go bust** informal become bankrupt.

bustle v. move energetically or noisily. ▶n. **1** excited activity. **2** hist. a pad or frame worn under a skirt to puff it out.

busy adj. (**busier, busiest**) **1** having a

Thesaurus

burning adj. **1** ON FIRE, blazing, ablaze, aflame, alight, flaring, glowing, smouldering, ignited, flickering, scorching, incandescent; *literary* afire. **2** STINGING, smarting, biting, prickling, irritating, searing, caustic, corrosive, painful. **3** INTENSE, eager, passionate, fervent, ardent, fervid. **4** IMPORTANT, crucial, significant, urgent, pressing, critical, compelling, vital, essential, acute, pivotal.

burnish v. POLISH, shine, brighten, rub, buff, buff up, smooth.

burrow n. TUNNEL, hole, hollow, excavation, lair, den, earth, warren, set. ▶v. DIG, tunnel, excavate, mine, hollow out, gouge out, scoop out.

burst v. **1** SPLIT, break open, rupture, crack, shatter, explode, give way, fracture, disintegrate, fragment, fly open. **2** RUSH, thrust, shove, push, dash, run, erupt, surge.

bury v. **1** INTER, lay to rest, entomb, consign to the grave; *informal* plant. **2** CONCEAL, hide, cover with, submerge, tuck, sink, cup. ■ OPPOSITES exhume.

bush n. **1** SHRUB, thicket, undergrowth, shrubbery. **2** SCRUB, brush, wilds, backwoods; *Austral./NZ* outback.

bushy adj. THICK, shaggy, dense, tangled, hairy, bristly, fuzzy, luxuriant, unruly, untidy, spreading.

business n. **1** OCCUPATION, profession, line, career, job, trade, vocation, work, employment, pursuit, métier. **2** TRADE, commerce, industry, buying and selling, trading, merchandising, trafficking, bargaining, dealing, transactions. **3** COMPANY, firm, enterprise, corporation, concern, organization, venture, shop, establishment, partnership. **4** CONCERN, affair, responsibility, duty, function, task, assignment, obligation, problem. **5** AFFAIR, matter, thing, case, set of circumstances, issue.

businesslike adj. **1** PROFESSIONAL, efficient, organized, methodical, systematic, well ordered, practical, thorough, painstaking, meticulous, correct. **2** ROUTINE, conventional, unimaginative, prosaic, down-to-earth, workaday. ■ OPPOSITES unprofessional, disorganized.

bust[1] n. BREASTS, bosom, chest, torso; *informal* boobs, knockers.

bust[2] v. **1** BREAK, destroy, wreck, rupture, fracture, crack. **2** ARREST, capture, catch, seize; *informal* pinch, nab, collar, nick.

bustle n. ACTIVITY, flurry, stir, restlessness, movement, hustle, hurly-burly, busyness, commotion, tumult, excitegreat deal to do. **2** occupied with an activity. **3** full of activity. ▶v. (**busying, busied**) (**busy oneself**) keep occupied. ◻ **busybody** an interfering person. ■ **busily** adv.

but conj. **1** nevertheless. **2** on the contrary. ▶prep. except; apart from. ▶adv. only.

butane n. a flammable gas used in liquid form as a fuel.

butch adj. informal aggressively masculine.

butcher n. **1** a person who cuts up and sells meat as a trade. **2** a person who kills brutally. ▶v. **1** slaughter or cut up an animal for food. **2** kill brutally. ■ **butchery** n.

butler n. the chief male servant of a house.

butt v. **1** hit with the head or horns. **2** (**butt in**) interrupt. **3** meet end to end. ▶n. **1** an object of criticism or ridicule. **2** a target in archery or shooting. **3** the thicker end of a tool or weapon. **4** a cigarette stub.

butter n. a yellow fatty substance made by churning cream. ▶v. **1** spread with butter. **2** (**butter up**) informal flatter. ◻ **butter bean** a large flat edible bean. **buttermilk** the liquid left after butter has been churned. **butterscotch** a sweet made with butter and brown sugar.

buttercup n. a plant with yellow cup-shaped flowers.

butterfly n. **1** an insect with two pairs of large wings, which feeds on nectar. **2** a swimming stroke in which both arms are raised out of the water together.

buttock n. either of the two round fleshy parts of the body that form the bottom.

button n. **1** a disc sewn on to a garment to fasten it. **2** a knob pressed to operate a piece of equipment. ▶v. fasten with buttons.

buttonhole n. **1** a slit in a garment through which a button is pushed to fasten it. **2** a flower worn in a lapel buttonhole. ▶v. informal stop and detain in conversation.

buttress n. a projecting support of stone or brick built against a wall. ▶v. support or strengthen.

buxom adj. (of a woman) plump and large-breasted.

buy v. (**buying, bought**) **1** get in return for payment. **2** informal accept the truth of. ▶n. a purchase. ■ **buyer** n.

buzz n. **1** a continuous humming sound. **2** the sound of a buzzer or telephone. **3** an atmosphere of excitement and activity. **4** informal a thrill. ▶v. **1** make a humming sound. **2** (**buzz off**) informal go away. **3** have an air of excitement or activity. ◻ **buzzword** informal a technical word that has become fashionable.

buzzard n. a large bird of prey.

buzzer n. an electrical device that makes a buzzing noise as a signal.

by prep. **1** through the action of. **2** indicating the end of a time period. **3** beside. **4** past and beyond. **5** during. ▶adv. so as to go past. ◻ **by and by** before long. **by and large** on the whole.

bye exclam. informal goodbye. ▶n. **1** the

Thesaurus

....

ment, agitation, fuss; informal to-do. ▶v. HURRY, rush, dash, scurry, dart, hasten, scramble, fuss, scamper, flutter; informal tear.

busy adj. **1** ACTIVE, industrious, tireless, energetic, hectic, strenuous, full, bustling, exacting; informal on the go. **2** OCCUPIED, working, engaged, at work, on duty, otherwise engaged; informal tied up. **3** ORNATE, over-elaborate, fussy, over-decorated, cluttered. ■ OPPOSITES idle, simple.

busybody n. MEDDLER, interferer, troublemaker, mischief-maker, gossip, scandalmonger, muckraker; informal snooper, nosy parker.

butt[1] v. KNOCK, strike, shove, ram, bump, push, thrust, prod, poke, jab, thump, buffet. ◻ **butt in** INTERRUPT, intrude, interfere in; informal stick one's nose/oar in.

butt[2] n. TARGET, victim, object, subject, scapegoat, dupe.

butt[3] n. **1** HANDLE, shaft, hilt, haft. **2** STUB, end, remnant, tail end; informal fag end.

buttocks n. CHEEKS, rump, bottom, behind, hindquarters, seat; informal bum, BTM, backside, derrière, arse; US informal butt, fanny; humorous posterior, fundament.

buttonhole v. ACCOST, waylay, importune, detain, grab, catch, take aside.

buttress n. SUPPORT, prop, reinforcement, strut, stanchion, pier. ▶v. STRENGTHEN, support, reinforce, prop up, shore up, brace, underpin, uphold, defend, back up.

buxom adj. BIG-BREASTED, big-bosomed, full-figured, voluptuous, well rounded, Rubenesque, plump, robust, shapely, ample; informal busty, well endowed.

buy v. PURCHASE, pay for, get, acquire, obmoving of a competitor straight to the next round in the absence of an opponent. **2** Cricket a run scored from a ball not hit by the batsman.

by-election n. an election held during a government's term of office to fill a vacant seat.

bygone adj. belonging to the past.

by-law (or **bye-law**) n. a rule made by a local authority, or by a company or society.

byline n. a line in a newspaper naming the writer of an article.

bypass n. **1** a road passing round a town for through traffic. **2** an operation to help the circulation of blood by directing it through a new passage. ▶ v. go past or round.

by-product n. a product produced in the making of something else.

byre n. a cowshed.

bystander n. a person who is present at an event but does not take part.

byte n. a unit of information stored in a computer, equal to eight bits.

byway n. a minor road.

byword n. **1** a notable example of something. **2** a saying.

Thesaurus

tain, come by, procure, invest in. ■ OPPOSITES sell. ▶ n. PURCHASE, acquisition, bargain, deal. ■ OPPOSITES sale.

buzz v. HUM, murmur, drone, whirr, whisper; *literary* susurrate.

bygone adj. PAST, departed, dead, gone, former, previous, one-time, forgotten, lost, old, antiquated, ancient, obsolete, outmoded.

bypass v. **1** GO ROUND, make a detour round, pass round. **2** CIRCUMVENT, avoid, evade, get round, pass over, ignore, skirt, sidestep, miss out, go over the head of, short-circuit, steer clear of; *informal* duck.

bystander n. ONLOOKER, spectator, eyewitness, witness, watcher, viewer, passer-by.

Cc

C (or **c**) n. the Roman numeral for 100. ▶abbrev. **1** Celsius or centigrade. **2** cents. **3** (**c.**) century or centuries. **4** (**c** or **ca.**) (before a date or amount) circa. **5** (ⓒ) copyright. **6** Physics coulombs.

cab n. **1** a taxi. **2** the driver's compartment in a truck, bus, or train.

cabal /kuh-**bal**/ n. a secret political group.

cabaret /kab-uh-ray/ n. entertainment held in a nightclub.

cabbage n. a vegetable with a round mass of green or purple leaves.

cabby n. (pl. **cabbies**) informal a taxi driver.

caber n. a tree trunk thrown in a Scottish Highland sport.

cabin n. **1** a compartment on a ship or in an aircraft. **2** a small hut.

cabinet n. **1** a cupboard with drawers or shelves. **2** (**Cabinet**) a committee of senior government ministers. ◻ **cabinetmaker** a skilled joiner who makes furniture.

cable n. a thick rope of wire or fibre, esp. for carrying electricity or telecommunication signals. ◻ **cable car** a small carriage hung from a moving cable for travelling up and down a mountain. **cable television** a system transmitting television programmes by cable.

cabriolet /kab-ri-oh-lay/ n. a car with a roof that folds down.

cacao /kuh-**kah**-oh/ n. the seeds from which cocoa and chocolate are made.

cache n. a hidden store of things.

cachet /**ka**-shay/ n. the state of being respected or admired; prestige.

cackle n. & v. (make) a noisy clucking cry or laugh.

cacophony /kuh-**kof**-uh-ni/ n. (pl. **cacophonies**) a harsh mixture of sounds. ∎ **cacophonous** adj.

cactus n. (pl. **cacti** or **cactuses**) a plant with thick fleshy stems bearing spines but no leaves.

cad n. dated a dishonourable man. ∎ **caddish** adj.

cadaver n. a corpse.

cadaverous adj. very pale and thin.

caddie (or **caddy**) n. (pl. **caddies**) a person who carries a golfer's clubs. ▶v. (**caddying**, **caddied**) work as a caddie.

caddy n. (pl. **caddies**) a small tin or box.

cadence n. **1** the rise and fall of a person's voice. **2** a sequence of notes ending a musical phrase.

cadenza n. a difficult solo passage in a musical work.

cadet n. a young trainee in the armed services or police.

cadge v. informal ask for or get something to which one is not entitled.

cadmium n. a silvery-white metallic element.

cadre /**kah**-der/ n. a small group of people trained for a particular purpose or at the centre of a political organization.

caecum /**see**-kuhm/ (US **cecum**) n. (pl. **caeca**) a pouch between the small and large intestines.

Caesarean section /si-**zair**-i-uhn/ (US **Cesarean**) n. an operation for delivering a child by cutting through the wall of the mother's abdomen.

caesium /**see**-zi-uhm/ (US **cesium**) n. a soft silvery metallic element.

cafe /**ka**-fay/ n. a small informal restaurant.

Thesaurus

cabin n. **1** HUT, shack, shed, chalet, lodge, shelter, bothy. **2** BERTH, compartment, stateroom, sleeping quarters, saloon, deckhouse.

cable n. ROPE, cord, wire, line, lead, hawser, mooring line, chain, guy.

cache n. HOARD, store, supply, collection, fund; informal stash.

cacophonous adj. DISCORDANT, atonal, dissonant, noisy, raucous, harsh, unmusical. ∎ OPPOSITES harmonious.

cacophony n. DISCORDANCE, dissonance, atonality, noise, racket, din, row, caterwauling, jangle, tumult, stridency, raucousness.

cadaverous adj. CORPSE-LIKE, death-like, gaunt, haggard, drawn, emaciated, skeletal, hollow-eyed, ashen, pale, wan, ghostly.

cadence n. RHYTHM, beat, pulse, tempo,

cafeteria n. a self-service restaurant.

cafetière /ka-fuh-**tyair**/ n. a coffee pot with a plunger to push the grounds to the bottom.

caffeine n. a stimulant found in tea and coffee.

caftan var. of KAFTAN.

cage n. a structure of bars or wires for confining animals. ▶v. enclose in a cage.

cagey (or **cagy**) adj. informal cautiously reluctant to speak. ■ **cagily** adv.

cagoule n. a light hooded waterproof jacket.

cahoots pl. n. (**in cahoots**) informal conspiring together.

caiman (or **cayman**) n. an American reptile like an alligator.

cairn n. a mound of stones built as a memorial or landmark.

cajole v. persuade by using flattery.

Cajun /**kay**-juhn/ adj. of the French-speaking community of Louisiana.

cake n. **1** an item of soft sweet food made from baking a mixture of flour, fat, eggs, and sugar. **2** a flat compact mass of something. ▶v. (of a sticky substance) cover and form a crust on.

calamine n. a pink powder used to make a soothing lotion.

calamity n. (pl. **calamities**) a sudden disastrous event. ■ **calamitous** adj.

calcify v. (**calcifying**, **calcified**) harden by a deposit of calcium salts.

calcium n. a soft grey metallic element.

calculate v. **1** work out using mathematics. **2** intend or plan. ■ **calculation** n.

calculating adj. selfishly scheming or devious.

calculator n. an electronic device for mathematical calculations.

calculus n. **1** the branch of mathematics dealing with rates of variation. **2** a hard deposit formed in the kidney, gall bladder, etc.

caldron US = CAULDRON.

Caledonian adj. of Scotland.

calendar n. a chart showing the days, weeks, and months of a year.

calf n. (pl. **calves**) **1** the young of cattle and of elephants and whales. **2** the back of a person's leg below the knee.

calibrate v. check the accuracy of an instrument by comparing the readings with those of a standard. ■ **calibration** n.

calibre (US **caliber**) n. **1** quality or ability. **2** the diameter of a bullet, shell, or the inside of a gun barrel.

calico n. plain cotton cloth.

californium n. a radioactive metallic element.

caliper (or **calliper**) n. **1** (also **calipers**) a measuring instrument with two hinged legs. **2** a metal support for a person's leg.

caliph /**kay**-lif/ n. hist. a Muslim ruler.

calk US = CAULK.

call v. **1** shout to summon someone or attract their attention. **2** telephone. **3** name or describe as. **4** pay a brief visit. **5** fix a date or time for. ▶n. **1** a shout as a summons or to attract attention. **2** an act of telephoning. **3** a brief visit. **4** a bird or animal's cry. **5** demand or need. □ **call for** require. **call off** cancel. **call on** turn to for help. ■ **caller** n.

calligraphy n. decorative handwriting.

Thesaurus

measure, metre, swing, lilt, intonation, inflection, accent, modulation.

cafe n. CAFETERIA, snack bar, buffet, coffee bar/shop/house, tea room/shop, diner, bistro, restaurant, brasserie.

cage n. PEN, enclosure, pound, coop, lock-up, hutch, aviary. ▶v. (**coop up**) SEE CONFINE.

cagey adj. GUARDED, secretive, cautious, non-committal, wary, careful, chary, wily.

cajole v. COAX, wheedle, beguile, seduce, persuade, flatter, humour, lure, entice, tempt, inveigle; informal sweet-talk, soft-soap, butter up.

cake n. **1** BUN, gateau, pastry. **2** BLOCK, bar, slab, piece, lump, cube, mass, loaf, chunk. ▶v. **1** HARDEN, solidify, thicken, dry, bake, congeal, coagulate, consoli-

date. **2** COVER, coat, plaster, encrust, clog.

calamitous adj. DISASTROUS, catastrophic, devastating, cataclysmic, ruinous, dire, dreadful, terrible, tragic, fatal, wretched, woeful, ghastly, unfortunate.

calamity n. DISASTER, catastrophe, tragedy, misfortune, cataclysm, accident, devastation, misadventure, mischance, mishap, ruin, tribulation, woe.

calculate v. **1** WORK OUT, estimate, determine, compute, count up, figure out, reckon up, evaluate, total. **2** ESTIMATE, gauge, judge, measure, weigh up, reckon, rate. **3** DESIGN, plan, aim, intend.

calculated adj. SEE DELIBERATE.

calculating adj. SEE CRAFTY.

calibre n. **1** QUALITY, worth, stature, dis-

■ **calligrapher** n.

callisthenics (US **calisthenics**) pl. n. gymnastic exercises.

callous adj. insensitive and cruel. ▶ n. (also **callus**) a patch of hardened skin. ■ **calloused** adj. **callousness** n.

callow adj. inexperienced and immature.

calm adj. **1** not nervous, angry, or excited. **2** peaceful and undisturbed. ▶ n. a calm state or period. ▶ v. make or become calm. ■ **calmly** adv. **calmness** n.

Calor gas n. trademark liquefied butane stored under pressure in containers.

calorie n. (pl. **calories**) **1** a unit for measuring how much energy food will produce. **2** a unit of heat.

calorific adj. of heat or calories.

calumniate v. slander.

calumny n. (pl. **calumnies**) slander.

calve v. give birth to a calf.

calves pl. of CALF.

Calvinism n. the form of Protestantism following the teachings of John Calvin. ■ **Calvinist** n.

calypso n. (pl. **calypsos**) a West Indian song improvised on a topical theme.

calyx n. (pl. **calyces** or **calyxes**) the ring of leaves (sepals) covering a flower bud.

cam n. a projecting part on a wheel or shaft changing rotary into to-and-fro motion. □ **camshaft** a shaft with one or more cams attached.

camaraderie n. trust and friendship.

camber n. a slightly arched shape of a horizontal surface, esp. a road.

cambric n. a light white linen or cotton fabric.

camcorder n. a combined video camera and video recorder.

came past of COME.

camel n. a large mammal of desert countries, with either one or two humps on the back.

camellia n. an evergreen flowering shrub.

cameo n. (pl. **cameos**) **1** a piece of jewellery with a head carved in relief on a differently coloured background. **2** a small part in a play or film for a well-known actor.

Thesaurus

tinction, ability, merit, talent, capability, excellence, competence, capacity, endowments, gifts, strengths, scope. **2** BORE, gauge, diameter, size.

call v. **1** CRY, cry out, shout, bellow, exclaim, yell, scream, roar, shriek. **2** TELEPHONE, phone, call up, ring; informal give someone a ring, buzz, give someone a buzz/tinkle. **3** VISIT, pay a visit/call, call on, stop by; informal drop in/by, pop in. **4** CONVENE, summon, assemble, announce, order, convoke. **5** NAME, christen, baptize, entitle, dub, designate, describe as, label, term. **6** SEND FOR, summon, ask for, contact, order, fetch, bid. **7** AWAKEN, wake, arouse, rouse. ▶ n. **1** CRY, shout, exclamation, yell, scream, shriek, roar, bellow. **2** PLEA, request, appeal, order, command, summons. **3** NEED, occasion, reason, cause, justification, grounds, excuse. **4** DEMAND, requirement, request, need, want, requisition. □ **call for** NEED, require, be grounds for, justify, necessitate, demand, entail. **call off** see CANCEL.

calling n. VOCATION, occupation, job, line, line of work, career, profession, métier, business, work, employment, trade, craft, pursuit, province, field.

callous adj. INSENSITIVE, unfeeling, hard, hardened, heartless, hard-hearted, hard-bitten, tough, cold, cool, stony-hearted, cruel, uncaring, unsympathet-

ic, indifferent, unresponsive, dispassionate, unconcerned, unsusceptible, merciless, pitiless, soulless; informal hard-nosed, hard-boiled. ■ OPPOSITES compassionate.

callow adj. IMMATURE, inexperienced, naive, unsophisticated, innocent, uninitiated, raw, green, young, adolescent; informal wet behind the ears. ■ OPPOSITES mature, experienced.

calm adj. **1** COMPOSED, relaxed, collected, cool, controlled, restrained, self-controlled, self-possessed, quiet, tranquil, unruffled, serene, unexcited, unflappable, undisturbed, imperturbable, unemotional, unmoved, impassive, undemonstrative, poised, level-headed, patient, equable, stoical, pacific; informal laid-back, together. **2** STILL, windless, mild, tranquil, balmy, quiet, peaceful, restful, undisturbed, halcyon. ▶ v. **1** SOOTHE, quieten, pacify, hush, tranquillize, mollify, appease, allay, alleviate, assuage. **2** QUIETEN, settle, settle down, die down, still. ▶ n. **1** COMPOSURE, coolness, self-control, tranquillity, serenity, quietness, peace, peacefulness, harmony, restfulness, repose. **2** STILLNESS, tranquillity, serenity, quietness, quietude.

calumny n. SLANDER, libel, defamation, misrepresentation, false accusation, insult, abuse, denigration, vilification, vi-

camera n. a device for taking photographs or recording moving images. □ **in camera** with the press and public excluded.

camiknickers pl. n. a woman's one-piece undergarment combining a camisole and knickers.

camisole n. a woman's loose-fitting undergarment for the upper body.

camomile var. of CHAMOMILE.

camouflage n. **1** clothing etc. used to make soldiers and military equipment blend in with the surroundings. **2** an animal's natural appearance which allows it to blend in with its surroundings. ▶ v. hide by means of camouflage.

camp n. **1** a place where tents are temporarily set up. **2** a complex of buildings for soldiers, holidaymakers, or prisoners. **3** a group supporting a particular party or viewpoint. ▶ adj. informal exaggeratedly effeminate or theatrical. ▶ v. stay in a tent. □ **camp bed** a folding portable bed.

campaign n. **1** a series of military operations in a particular area. **2** an organized course of action to achieve a goal. ▶ v. work towards a goal. ■ **campaigner** n.

campanology n. the art of bell-ringing.

camper n. **1** a person who is camping. **2** (also **camper van**) a large motor vehicle with a living area.

camphor n. a sweet-smelling bitter substance.

campus n. (pl. **campuses**) the grounds and buildings of a university or college.

can¹ aux. v. (past **could**) be able to.

can² n. a cylindrical metal container.

▶ v. (**canning**, **canned**) preserve in a can.

Canadian n. a person from Canada. ▶ adj. of Canada.

canal n. **1** an artificial waterway. **2** a tubular passage in the body.

canalize (or **-ise**) v. **1** convert into a canal. **2** convey through a duct or channel.

canapé /kan-uh-pay/ n. a small piece of bread or pastry with a savoury topping.

canard n. an unfounded rumour.

canary n. (pl. **canaries**) a bright yellow finch with a tuneful song.

cancan n. a lively high-kicking dance performed by women.

cancel v. (**cancelling**, **cancelled**; US **canceling**, **canceled**) **1** decide that a planned event will not happen. **2** end an agreement. **3** (**cancel out**) have an equal but opposite effect on. **4** mark a ticket to show that it has been used. ■ **cancellation** n.

cancer n. **1** a disease caused by uncontrolled growth of abnormal cells. **2** a harmful tumour resulting from this. ■ **cancerous** adj.

candela n. the SI unit of luminous intensity.

candelabrum (or **candelabra**) n. (pl. **candelabra**) a large branched candlestick.

candid adj. truthful and straightforward. ■ **candidly** adv.

candidate n. a person applying for a job, nominated for election, or taking an examination. ■ **candidacy** n.

candied adj. (of fruit) preserved in sugar.

candle n. a stick of wax with a central wick which is burnt to give light.

Thesaurus

tuperation, aspersions, backbiting, detraction, disparagement, deprecation, revilement, obloquy, smear campaign; *informal* mud-slinging.

camouflage n. DISGUISE, mask, screen, cover, protective colouring, cloak, cover-up, front, false front, guise, facade, blind, concealment, masquerade, subterfuge. ▶ v. DISGUISE, hide, conceal, mask, screen, cloak, veil, cover, cover up, obscure.

camp¹ n. ENCAMPMENT, settlement, campsite, camping ground, tents, bivouac, cantonment.

camp² adj. EFFEMINATE, effete, mincing, affected, artificial, mannered, posturing, studied. ■ OPPOSITES macho.

campaign n. **1** BATTLE, war, offensive, expedition, attack, crusade. **2** DRIVE,

push, operation, plan, promotion, strategy, movement, manoeuvre. ▶ v. FIGHT, battle, work, crusade, push, strive, struggle.

cancel v. **1** CALL OFF, scrap, drop, axe, abandon, stop, discontinue. **2** ANNUL, declare void, invalidate, quash, nullify, set aside, retract, negate, countermand, rescind, revoke, repudiate, abrogate, abolish. ■ OPPOSITES confirm. □ **cancel out** COUNTERBALANCE, offset, counteract, neutralize, redeem.

cancer n. MALIGNANT GROWTH, cancerous growth, tumour, malignancy; *technical* carcinoma, sarcoma.

candid adj. FRANK, open, honest, truthful, direct, plain-spoken, blunt, straightforward, straight from the shoulder, outspoken, sincere, forthright, no-

◻ **candlestick** a holder for a candle.

candour (US **candor**) n. frankness.

candy n. (pl. **candies**) US sweets. ◻ **candyfloss** a mass of fluffy spun sugar on a stick. **candy-striped** patterned with alternate stripes of white and another colour.

cane n. **1** the hollow stem of tall reeds, grasses, etc. **2** a stick used as a support or to beat someone. ▸ v. beat with a cane.

canine /kay-nyn/ adj. of dogs. ▸ n. a pointed tooth next to the incisors.

canister n. a cylindrical container.

canker n. **1** a fungal disease of plants. **2** a disease in animals causing open sores.

cannabis n. a drug obtained from the hemp plant.

cannelloni pl. n. rolls of pasta with a savoury filling.

cannibal n. a person who eats human flesh. ▪ **cannibalism** n.

cannibalize (or **-ise**) v. use a machine as a source of spare parts for others.

cannon n. (pl. **cannon** or **cannons**) a large heavy gun. ▸ v. bump heavily into.

cannonade n. continuous heavy gunfire.

cannot contr. can not.

canny adj. (**cannier**, **canniest**) shrewd. ▪ **cannily** adv.

canoe n. a narrow boat propelled with a paddle. ▸ v. (**canoeing**, **canoed**) travel in a canoe. ▪ **canoeist** n.

canon n. **1** a general rule or principle. **2** the authentic set of works of an author or artist. **3** a member of the clergy of a cathedral. ▪ **canonical** adj.

canonize (or **-ise**) v. officially declare to be a saint. ▪ **canonization** n.

canoodle v. informal kiss and cuddle.

canopy n. (pl. **canopies**) a cloth covering held up over a throne or bed.

cant n. **1** insincere talk. **2** the language of a particular group.

can't contr. cannot.

cantaloupe n. a small round melon with orange flesh.

cantankerous adj. bad-tempered and uncooperative.

cantata n. a sung musical composition.

canteen n. **1** a restaurant in a workplace or college. **2** a case of cutlery.

canter n. a horse's pace between a trot and a gallop. ▸ v. move at a canter.

cantilever n. a girder fixed at only one end, used in bridge construction.

canto n. (pl. **cantos**) a section of a long poem.

canton n. a political division of a country, esp. Switzerland.

canvas n. (pl. **canvases** or **canvasses**) **1** a strong coarse cloth. **2** an oil painting on canvas.

canvass v. **1** visit someone to seek their vote in an election. **2** question someone to find out their opinion. ▪ **canvasser** n.

canyon n. a deep gorge.

cap n. **1** a soft hat with a peak. **2** a lid or cover. **3** an upper limit on spending or borrowing. **4** a case of explosive powder for a toy gun. ▸ v. (**capping**, **capped**) **1** put or form a cover on. **2** provide a fitting end to. **3** place a limit on. **4** (**be capped**) be chosen as a member of a national sports team.

capable adj. **1** having the ability to do something. **2** competent and efficient. ▪ **capability** n. **capably** adv.

capacious adj. roomy.

capacitance n. the ability to store

Thesaurus

nonsense, unequivocal, undisguised, bluff, brusque. ▪ OPPOSITES guarded.

candidate n. APPLICANT, contender, nominee, contestant, competitor, runner, entrant, aspirant, possibility.

candour n. FRANKNESS, honesty, truthfulness, openness, directness, bluntness, outspokenness, sincerity, forthrightness.

canny adj. SHREWD, sharp, astute, discerning, penetrating, clever, perspicacious, judicious, wise, sagacious, circumspect. ▪ OPPOSITES foolish.

canopy n. AWNING, shade, sunshade, cover, tarpaulin.

canvass v. **1** SEEK VOTES, solicit votes, campaign, electioneer, drum up support, persuade, convince. **2** INVESTIGATE, survey, find out, enquire into, look into, examine, scrutinize, explore, study, analyse, evaluate. ▸ n. SURVEY, poll, opinion poll, census, investigation, market research.

canyon n. RAVINE, valley, gorge, gully, defile, chasm, gulf, abyss.

capability n. ABILITY, capacity, potential, aptitude, faculty, facility, power, skill, skilfulness, competence, efficiency, effectiveness, proficiency, adeptness.

capable adj. ABLE, competent, effective, efficient, proficient, accomplished, talented, gifted, adept, skilful, experienced, practised, expert, masterly, qualified, adequate, clever, intelligent;

electric charge.

capacitor n. a device used to store electric charge.

capacity n. (pl. **capacities**) **1** the amount that something can contain or produce. **2** the ability to do something. **3** a role or position: *employed in a voluntary capacity.*

caparison v. clothe in rich coverings.

cape n. **1** a short cloak. **2** a coastal promontory.

caper v. skip about in a lively way. ▶ n. **1** a lively skipping movement. **2** informal a light-hearted or dishonest activity. **3** the pickled flower bud of a shrub.

capillarity (or **capillary action**) n. the force which acts on a liquid in a narrow tube to push it up or down.

capillary n. a very fine, hair-like blood vessel or tube.

capital n. **1** the chief city of a country or region. **2** wealth that is owned, invested, lent, or borrowed. **3** a capital letter. **4** the top part of a pillar. ▶ adj. **1** involving the death penalty. **2** (of a letter of the alphabet) large and used to begin sentences and names. **3** informal, dated excellent.

capitalism n. a system in which a country's trade and industry are controlled by private owners. ■ **capitalist** n. & adj.

capitalize (or **-ise**) v. **1** (**capitalize on**) take advantage of. **2** convert into or provide with financial capital. **3** write as or with a capital letter. ■ **capitalization** n.

capitation n. a fee or tax of an equal amount per person.

capitulate v. give in or yield. ■ **capitulation** n.

capon /kay-pon/ n. a castrated domestic cock fattened up for eating.

cappuccino /kap-puh-chee-noh/ n. (pl. **cappuccinos**) coffee made with frothed milk.

caprice /kuh-preess/ n. a sudden change of behaviour.

capricious adj. prone to sudden changes of behaviour. ■ **capriciously** adv.

capsicum n. a sweet pepper.

capsize v. (of a boat) overturn.

capstan n. a broad revolving post used to wind a cable.

capsule n. **1** a small soluble gelatin case containing medicine. **2** a small case or container.

captain n. **1** the person in command of a ship or civil aircraft. **2** a rank of naval officer above commander. **3** a rank of army officer above lieutenant. **4** the leader of a team. ▶ v. be the captain of. ■ **captaincy** n.

caption n. **1** a title or explanation printed with a picture etc. **2** a piece of text appearing with a film or television broadcast.

captious adj. prone to petty fault-finding.

Thesaurus

informal smart. ■ OPPOSITES incapable, incompetent. □ **capable of** UP TO, equal to, inclined to, disposed to, liable to, prone to, likely to.

capacity n. **1** SPACE, room, size, scope, extent, volume, largeness, dimensions, proportions, magnitude, ampleness, amplitude. **2** ABILITY, capability, aptitude, facility, competence, competency, potential, proficiency, skill, talent, accomplishment, cleverness, intelligence. **3** POSITION, role, job, post, office, function, responsibility, appointment, province.

cape[1] n. CLOAK, shawl, wrap, coat, robe, cope.

cape[2] n. HEADLAND, point, promontory, peninsula, neck, tongue.

caper v. FROLIC, romp, skip, gambol, cavort, prance, dance, jig, leap, hop, jump, bound, spring, bounce.

capital n. **1** FIRST CITY, seat of government, metropolis. **2** MONEY, funds, finance, cash, wealth, principal, savings, resources, means, assets, reserves, property, wherewithal. ▶ adj. UPPER-CASE, block.

capitulate v. SURRENDER, yield, give in/ up, back down, submit, concede, throw in the towel/sponge, succumb, cave in, relent, accede, acquiesce. ■ OPPOSITES resist.

caprice n. WHIM, impulse, fancy, vagary, notion, fad, quirk.

capricious adj. FICKLE, unpredictable, impulsive, changeable, inconstant, mercurial, whimsical, volatile, erratic, variable, wayward, fitful, quirky, fanciful, uncertain, irregular, unreliable. ■ OPPOSITES stable, consistent.

capsize v. OVERTURN, turn over, upset, upend, tip over, knock over, keel over, turn turtle, invert.

capsule n. PILL, tablet, caplet, lozenge; *informal* tab.

captain n. **1** COMMANDER, master, officer in charge; *informal* skipper. **2** CHIEF, head, leader, principal; *informal* boss.

captivate v. attract and hold the interest of.

captive n. a person who is held prisoner. ▶ adj. confined. ■ **captivity** n.

captor n. a person who captures another.

capture v. **1** take or get by force. **2** take prisoner. **3** record accurately in words or pictures. **4** cause data to be stored in a computer. ▶ n. the act of capturing.

car n. **1** a motor vehicle for a small number of people. **2** a railway carriage. □ **carport** an open-sided shelter for a car.

carafe /kuh-raf/ n. a glass flask for serving wine or water.

caramel n. **1** sugar or syrup heated until brown. **2** a toffee made with sugar and butter. ■ **caramelize** (or **-ise**) v.

carapace n. the hard upper shell of a tortoise, lobster, etc.

carat n. **1** a unit of weight for precious stones. **2** a measure of the purity of gold.

caravan n. **1** a vehicle equipped for living in, able to be towed by a vehicle or a horse. **2** hist. a group of people travelling together across a desert. ■ **caravanning** n.

caraway n. a plant with aromatic seeds used as a spice.

carbine n. an automatic rifle.

carbohydrate n. an energy-producing substance (e.g. sugar and starch) found in food.

carbolic (or **carbolic acid**) n. a kind of disinfectant.

carbon n. a non-metallic element with two main pure forms (diamond and graphite), found in all organic compounds. □ **carbon copy 1** a copy made with carbon paper. **2** a person or thing identical to another. **carbon dating** a way of finding out the age of an object by measuring how much radioactive carbon is in it. **carbon dioxide** a gas produced by burning carbon and by breathing. **carbon monoxide** a poisonous flammable gas. **carbon paper** thin paper coated with carbon, used to make a copy of a document.

carbonate n. a compound containing carbon and oxygen together with a metal.

carbonated adj. (of a drink) fizzy because it contains dissolved carbon dioxide.

carborundum n. a very hard black substance used for grinding and polishing.

carboy n. a large round bottle with a narrow neck, used for holding acids.

carbuncle n. **1** a severe abscess. **2** a garnet cut in a round shape.

carburettor (US **carburetor**) n. a device in an engine that mixes air with the fuel.

carcass (or **carcase**) n. **1** the dead body of an animal. **2** the structural framework or remains of something.

carcinogen /kar-sin-uh-juhn/ n. a substance that can cause cancer. ■ **carcinogenic** adj.

carcinoma /kar-si-noh-muh/ n. (pl. **carcinomas** or **carcinomata**) a cancerous tumour.

card n. **1** thick, stiff paper or thin cardboard. **2** a piece of card printed with information, greetings, etc. **3** a rectangle of plastic containing information readable by a computer: *a credit card*. **4** a playing card. **5** (**cards**) a game played with playing cards. ▶ v. comb wool with a toothed instrument. □ **cardboard**

Thesaurus

caption n. HEADING, title, wording, head, legend, inscription, description.

captious adj. CRITICAL, criticizing, carping, fault-finding, quibbling, cavilling, hair-splitting; *informal* nit-picking. ■ OPPOSITES forgiving.

captivate v. CHARM, delight, enchant, bewitch, fascinate, dazzle, beguile, entrance, enrapture, attract, hypnotize, mesmerize, enthral, allure, win, infatuate, seduce, ravish, ensnare, steal someone's heart. ■ OPPOSITES repel, bore.

captive adj. IMPRISONED, locked up, caged, incarcerated, jailed, confined, detained, taken prisoner, interned, penned up, captured, ensnared, restrained, in captivity; *informal* under lock and key. ▶ n. PRISONER, detainee, prisoner of war, convict, internee, slave; *informal* jailbird, con.

captivity n. IMPRISONMENT, custody, detention, confinement, internment, incarceration, restraint, committal, bondage, slavery, servitude, enslavement, subjugation, subjection; *historical* thraldom. ■ OPPOSITES freedom.

capture v. CATCH, arrest, apprehend, take prisoner, take into custody, seize, trap, take, lay hold of, take captive; *informal* nab, nick, pinch, collar, lift, bag. ▶ n. ARREST, apprehension, detention, imprisonment, seizure, trapping.

car n. MOTOR CAR, motor, automobile;

stiff paper made from paper pulp. **card sharp** (or **sharper**) a person who cheats at cards.

cardamom n. a spice used in cooking.

cardiac adj. of the heart.

cardigan n. a knitted jumper with buttons down the front.

cardinal n. a leading Roman Catholic clergyman. ▶ adj. most important; chief. □ **cardinal number** a number expressing quantity (1, 2, 3, etc.), rather than order (1st, 2nd, 3rd, etc.).

cardiograph n. an instrument recording heart movements.

cardiology n. the branch of medicine concerned with the heart. ■ **cardiologist** n.

care n. **1** the provision of welfare and protection. **2** serious attention to avoid damage, risk, or error. ▶ v. **1** feel concern or interest. **2** feel affection or liking. **3** (**care for/to do**) like to have or be willing to do. **4** (**care for**) look after.

careen v. (of a ship) tilt to one side.

career n. an occupation undertaken for a long period of a person's life. ▶ v. move swiftly in an uncontrolled way.

careerist n. a person intent on progressing in their career.

carefree adj. free from anxiety or responsibility.

careful adj. **1** taking care to avoid harm or trouble. **2** showing thought and attention. ■ **carefully** adv.

careless adj. not giving enough attention or thought to avoiding harm or mistakes. ■ **carelessly** adv. **carelessness** n.

carer n. a person who cares for a sick, elderly, or disabled person.

caress v. touch or stroke gently or lovingly. ▶ n. a gentle or loving touch.

caret n. a mark (⁁) indicating an insertion in a text.

caretaker n. a person employed to look after a public building.

careworn adj. showing signs of prolonged worry.

cargo n. (pl. **cargoes** or **cargos**) goods carried on a ship, aircraft, or truck.

Caribbean adj. of the Caribbean Sea and its islands.

✓ One *r*, two *b*s: Ca*ribb*ean.

caribou n. (pl. **caribou**) US a reindeer.

caricature n. a portrayal in which a person's characteristics are comically exaggerated. ▶ v. make a caricature of. ■ **caricaturist** n.

caries /kair-eez/ n. decay of a tooth or

Thesaurus

informal wheels; *US informal* auto.

carcass n. **1** BODY, corpse, remains; *Medicine* cadaver; *informal* stiff. **2** FRAME, framework, skeleton, remains, structure, shell, hulk.

cardinal adj. FUNDAMENTAL, basic, main, chief, primary, prime, principal, paramount, key, essential. ■ OPPOSITES unimportant.

care n. **1** WORRY, anxiety, sadness, trouble, stress, unease, distress, disquiet, sorrow, anguish, grief, woe, hardship, tribulation, affliction, responsibility, pressure, strain, burden. **2** CAREFULNESS, attention, thought, regard, thoroughness, conscientiousness, pains, vigilance, accuracy, precision, meticulousness, fastidiousness, punctiliousness, mindfulness, solicitude, forethought, heed. **3** CHARGE, supervision, custody, protection, safe keeping, guardianship, control, management, ministration, wardship.. ▶ v. MIND, be concerned, be interested, worry oneself, bother, trouble, have regard. □ **care for** See LOVE, LOOK AFTER.

career n. PROFESSION, occupation, job, vocation, calling, livelihood, employment, work, métier.

carefree adj. CHEERFUL, light-hearted, happy, nonchalant, unworried, untroubled, cheery, happy-go-lucky, jolly, merry, buoyant, easy-going, relaxed, unconcerned, breezy, jaunty, insouciant, blithe; *informal* upbeat, laid-back. ■ OPPOSITES worried, miserable.

careful adj. **1** CAUTIOUS, alert, attentive, watchful, aware, vigilant, wary, on one's guard, prudent, heedful, circumspect, mindful, observant, chary. **2** CONSCIENTIOUS, painstaking, meticulous, diligent, attentive, accurate, precise, scrupulous, fastidious, punctilious, methodical, organized, systematic, thorough, well organized. ■ OPPOSITES careless.

careless adj. **1** INATTENTIVE, thoughtless, negligent, unthinking, irresponsible, lax, slipshod, sloppy, forgetful, absent-minded, remiss. **2** CURSORY, perfunctory, hasty, inaccurate, disorganized, slapdash, slipshod, sloppy, messy. **3** THOUGHTLESS, unthinking, insensitive, indiscreet, unguarded, ill-considered, reckless, rash, imprudent. ■ OPPOSITES careful.

bone.

carillon /ka-ril-lyuhn/ n. a set of bells sounded by an automatic mechanism.

carmine n. vivid crimson.

carnage n. the killing of a large number of people.

carnal adj. of sexual urges and activities. ■ **carnally** adv.

carnation n. a cultivated plant with pink, red, or white flowers.

carnelian (or **cornelian**) n. a dull red or pink semi-precious stone.

carnival n. a public festival involving a procession and music.

carnivore n. an animal that eats meat. ■ **carnivorous** adj.

carob n. a chocolate substitute made from the pod of an Arabian tree.

carol n. a Christmas hymn. ▶v. (**carolling, carolled**; US **caroling, caroled**) **1** sing carols. **2** sing or say happily.

carotene n. an orange or red substance found in carrots, tomatoes, etc.

carotid artery /kuh-rot-id/ n. either of the two main arteries carrying blood to the head.

carouse /ka-rowz/ v. drink alcohol and enjoy oneself.

carousel n. **1** a merry-go-round at a fair. **2** a rotating device, esp. for baggage at an airport.

carp n. (pl. **carp**) an edible freshwater fish. ▶v. complain continually.

carpel n. the female reproductive organ of a flower.

carpenter n. a person who makes and repairs wooden objects and structures.

■ **carpentry** n.

carpet n. **1** a floor covering of thick woven fabric. **2** a thick, soft layer. ▶v. (**carpeting, carpeted**) **1** cover with a carpet. **2** informal reprimand severely. □ **carpet-bomb** bomb an area intensively.

carpus n. (pl. **carpi**) the group of small bones in the wrist. ■ **carpal** adj.

carriage n. **1** a horse-drawn passenger vehicle. **2** a passenger vehicle in a train. **3** the carrying of goods from one place to another. **4** a person's way of standing or moving. **5** a wheeled support for moving a gun. □ **carriage clock** a portable clock with a handle on top. **carriageway** the part of a road intended for vehicles.

carrier n. **1** a person or thing carrying something. **2** a company transporting goods or people. □ **carrier bag** a bag with handles, for carrying shopping.

carrion n. dead decaying flesh.

carrot n. **1** a tapering orange root vegetable. **2** an incentive.

carry v. (**carrying, carried**) **1** move or take from one place to another. **2** support the weight of. **3** assume responsibility. **4** have as a feature or result. **5** (of a sound or voice) be heard from a distance. **6** approve a proposal by a majority of votes. **7** (**carry oneself**) stand and move in a specified way. □ **be/get carried away** lose self-control. **carry off 1** take away by force. **2** succeed in doing. **carry on** continue. **carry out** perform a task.

Thesaurus

caress v. FONDLE, stroke, smooth, touch, pet, cuddle, pat, nuzzle, kiss, embrace, hug.

caretaker n. JANITOR, superintendent, porter, warden, watchman, keeper, steward, curator, concierge.

cargo n. FREIGHT, payload, load, consignment, contents, goods, merchandise, baggage, shipment, boatload, lorryload, truckload, lading.

caricature n. PARODY, mimicry, lampoon, distortion, burlesque, travesty, cartoon, satire, farce; informal take-off, send-up. ▶v. PARODY, mimic, lampoon, mock, ridicule, distort, satirize, burlesque; informal take off, send up.

carnage n. SLAUGHTER, massacre, mass murder, butchery, bloodbath, bloodshed, holocaust, pogrom.

carnal adj. SEXUAL, sensual, erotic, fleshly, lustful, lewd, lecherous, lascivious, libidinous, coarse, gross, prurient, salacious, lubricious.

carnival n. FESTIVAL, celebration, fair, fiesta, fete, gala, jamboree, festivity, revelry.

carouse v. MAKE MERRY, party, go on a spree, binge, roister, overindulge; informal live it up, paint the town red, go on a bender.

carp v. COMPLAIN, find fault, criticize, quibble, grumble, object, reproach, censure, cavil, nag; informal nit-pick, gripe, go on.

carpenter n. WOODWORKER, cabinetmaker, joiner; informal chippy.

carriage n. **1** COACH, vehicle. **2** BEARING, posture, deportment, comportment, stance, gait, manner, presence, air, demeanour, mien, behaviour, conduct. **3** TRANSPORT, transportation, freight, conveyance, delivery, carrying.

carry v. **1** CONVEY, transport, move, transfer, take, bring, fetch, bear, haul,

cart n. an open, wheeled vehicle for carrying loads. ▶v. **1** transport in a cart. **2** informal carry with difficulty. ▫ **carthorse** a large, strong horse. **cartwheel** a sideways handspring with the arms and legs extended.

carte blanche /kart blahnsh/ n. complete freedom to act as one wishes.

cartel n. a group of manufacturers or suppliers acting together to control prices.

cartilage n. firm, flexible tissue forming part of the skeleton of vertebrates.

cartography n. map-drawing. ■ **cartographer** n.

carton n. a cardboard container.

cartoon n. **1** a humorous drawing. **2** an animated film made from a sequence of drawings. ■ **cartoonist** n.

cartridge n. **1** a container holding film, ink, etc., for inserting into a mechanism. **2** a casing containing a charge and a bullet for a gun. ▫ **cartridge paper** thick, rough-textured drawing paper.

carve v. **1** cut into a hard material to form an object or design. **2** cut cooked meat into slices. ■ **carving** n.

carvery n. (pl. **carveries**) a restaurant where cooked joints are carved as required.

Casanova n. a man who is notorious for seducing women.

cascade n. **1** a waterfall. **2** a falling or hanging mass of something. ▶v. fall like a waterfall.

case n. **1** an instance of something oc-

curring. **2** a lawsuit. **3** a set of arguments supporting one side of a debate or lawsuit. **4** a suitcase. **5** a container. **6** a form of a noun, adjective, or pronoun expressing its role in a sentence. ▶v. enclose in a case.

casement n. a window hinged at the side.

cash n. money in coins or notes. ▶v. **1** give or obtain notes or coins for a cheque. **2** (**cash in**) convert an insurance policy into money. **3** (**cash in on**) informal take advantage of. ▫ **cashpoint** trademark a machine dispensing cash when a special card is inserted.

cashew n. an edible kidney-shaped nut.

cashier n. a person who pays out and receives money in a shop, bank, etc. ▶v. dismiss from the armed forces because of serious wrongdoing.

cashmere n. very fine soft wool.

casing n. a protective cover.

casino n. (pl. **casinos**) a public building or room for gambling.

cask n. a large barrel for storing alcoholic drinks.

casket n. **1** a small ornamental box for valuables. **2** esp. US a coffin.

cassava n. the starchy root of a tropical American tree, used as food.

casserole n. **1** a covered dish for cooking food slowly. **2** a kind of stew cooked slowly. ▶v. cook in a casserole.

cassette n. a sealed case containing audio tape, videotape, etc.

cassock n. a long garment worn by

Thesaurus

shift, transmit, relay, manhandle; informal lug, cart. **2** SUPPORT, bear, sustain, maintain, hold up, shoulder. **3** AFFECT, influence, have an effect on, stimulate, motivate, spur on, drive, impel, urge. **4** INVOLVE, lead to, result in, require, entail, demand. ▫ **carry on** see CONTINUE. **carry out** see DO.

cart n. BARROW, wheelbarrow, handcart, pushcart. ▶v. see CARRY.

carton n. BOX, container, package, case, packet, pack.

cartoon n. **1** CARICATURE, parody, lampoon, burlesque, satire; informal send-up, take-off. **2** ANIMATED FILM, animation, comic strip, photostory.

cartridge n. **1** CASE, container, cylinder, capsule, cassette, magazine. **2** ROUND, shell.

carve v. **1** SCULPT, sculpture, chisel, cut, hew, whittle, form, shape, fashion, mould. **2** ENGRAVE, etch, incise, notch, cut in. **3** SLICE, cut up. ▫ **carve up** see

DIVIDE (3).

cascade n. WATERFALL, falls, shower, fountain, torrent, flood, deluge, outpouring, avalanche, cataract. ▶v. GUSH, pour, surge, spill, overflow, tumble, descend.

case[1] n. **1** SITUATION, occasion, context, circumstances, instance, position, conditions, event, occurrence, predicament, contingency, plight. **2** INSTANCE, example, occurrence, occasion, illustration, specimen. **3** TRIAL, proceedings, lawsuit, action, suit. **4** PATIENT, victim, sufferer, invalid.

case[2] n. CONTAINER, box, receptacle, canister, crate, carton, pack, suitcase, trunk, luggage, baggage.

cash n. MONEY, funds, finance, capital, resources, currency, change, notes, coins, legal tender; informal dough, bread, moolah, readies, the ready. ▶v. EXCHANGE, change, turn into money/cash, realize, encash.

some Christian clergy and choristers.

cassowary n. (pl. **cassowaries**) a large flightless bird.

cast v. **1** throw forcefully. **2** cause to appear on or affect something. **3** direct the eyes or thoughts towards something. **4** register a vote. **5** give a part to an actor or allocate parts in a play or film. **6** shed or discard. **7** shape molten metal in a mould. **8** cause a magic spell to take effect. ▶ n. **1** the actors in a play or film. **2** an object made by casting molten metal. **3** (also **plaster cast**) a bandage stiffened with plaster of Paris to support and protect a broken limb. **4** appearance or character. □ **casting vote** an extra vote used by a chairperson to decide an issue when votes on each side are equal. **cast iron** a hard alloy of iron and carbon cast in a mould. **cast-iron** firm and unchangeable. **cast-off** a discarded garment.

castanets pl. n. two small curved pieces of wood, clicked together in the hand to accompany Spanish dancing.

castaway n. a shipwrecked person.

caste n. each of the Hindu social classes.

castellated adj. having battlements.

castigate v. reprimand severely. ■ **castigation** n.

castle n. a large medieval fortified building.

castor (or **caster**) n. **1** a small swivelling wheel fixed to the legs or base of a piece of furniture. **2** a small container with a perforated top for sprinkling salt, sugar, etc. □ **castor oil** oil from the seeds of an African shrub, used as a laxative. **castor sugar** white sugar in fine granules.

castrate v. remove the testicles of.

■ **castration** n.

casual adj. **1** relaxed and unconcerned. **2** lacking care or thought. **3** not regular; occasional. **4** happening by chance. **5** informal. ■ **casually** adv.

casualty n. (pl. **casualties**) a person killed or injured in a war or accident.

casuistry n. the use of clever but false reasoning. ■ **casuist** n.

cat n. **1** a small furry mammal kept as a pet. **2** a wild animal related to this. □ **catcall** a whistle of disapproval. **catgut** material used for the strings of musical instruments, made of the dried intestines of sheep or horses. **catkin** a spike of small flowers hanging from a willow etc. **catnap** a short nap. **cat's cradle** a game in which patterns are formed in a loop of string held between the fingers of each hand. **catseye** trademark each of a series of reflective studs marking the lanes of a road. **cat's paw** a person used by another to perform an unpleasant task. **catsuit** a woman's close-fitting one-piece garment. **catwalk** a narrow platform along which models walk to display clothes.

cataclysm n. a violent upheaval or disaster. ■ **cataclysmic** adj.

catacomb /kat-uh-koom/ n. an underground cemetery with recesses for tombs.

catafalque n. a decorated wooden support for a coffin.

catalepsy n. a medical condition involving loss of consciousness and the body becoming rigid. ■ **cataleptic** adj. & n.

catalogue (US **catalog**) n. a list of items in systematic order. ▶ v. (**cataloguing**, **catalogued**; US **cataloging**, **cataloged**) list in a catalogue.

Thesaurus

cashier n. TELLER, clerk, banker, treasurer, purser, bursar, controller.

cask n. BARREL, keg, vat, butt, tub, vessel, tun, hogshead, firkin, pipe.

cast v. **1** THROW, toss, fling, pitch, hurl, sling, lob, launch, let fly; informal chuck, heave. **2** EMIT, give off, send out, shed, radiate, diffuse, spread. **3** MOULD, form, fashion, sculpt, model. ▶ n. **1** FIGURE, shape, mould, form, sculpture. **2** SORT, kind, type, style, stamp.

caste n. CLASS, order, rank, level, grade, position, station, place, status, standing, grading.

castle n. FORTRESS, fort, citadel, stronghold, fortification, keep, palace, chateau, tower.

casual adj. **1** INDIFFERENT, careless, lax, unconcerned, uninterested, unenthusiastic, easy-going, nonchalant, offhand, throwaway, relaxed, apathetic, lackadaisical, blasé, insouciant, unprofessional; informal laid-back. **2** SLIGHT, superficial, shallow. **3** TEMPORARY, part-time, freelance, irregular. **4** ACCIDENTAL, chance, unintentional, unplanned, unexpected, unforeseen, unanticipated, fortuitous, serendipitous, incidental. **5** INFORMAL, relaxed, leisure, unceremonious; informal sporty. ■ OPPOSITES diligent, permanent, deliberate, formal.

casualty n. FATALITY, victim, sufferer, dead/wounded/injured person.

cat n. FELINE, tomcat, tom, kitten; informal

catalyse v. cause or speed up a reaction by acting as a catalyst. ■ **catalysis** n.

catalyst n. a substance that speeds up a chemical reaction while remaining unchanged itself.

catalytic converter n. a device in a vehicle's exhaust system for converting pollutant gases into less harmful ones.

catamaran n. a boat with twin parallel hulls.

catapult n. a forked stick with an elastic band attached, for shooting small stones. ▶ v. throw forcefully.

cataract n. 1 a cloudy area on the lens of the eye causing blurred vision. 2 a large waterfall.

catarrh /kuh-tar/ n. excessive mucus in the nose or throat.

catastrophe /kuh-tass-truh-fi/ n. a sudden great disaster. ■ **catastrophic** adj. **catastrophically** adv.

catch v. (**catching**, **caught**) 1 seize and hold something moving. 2 capture. 3 be in time to board a vehicle or see a person etc. 4 surprise someone in the act of doing something. 5 hear or understand. 6 become infected with. ▶ n. 1 an act of catching. 2 a device for fastening a door, window, etc. 3 a hidden problem. 4 an amount of fish caught. □ **catch on** informal 1 become popular. 2 understand. **catch out** discover that

someone has done something wrong.

catchphrase a well-known phrase.

catch-22 a difficult situation in which potential solutions involve unavoidable problems. **catch up** 1 succeed in reaching a person ahead. 2 do tasks that should have been done earlier.

catchword a word or phrase commonly used to sum up a concept.

catching adj. informal infectious.

catchment area n. 1 the area from which a hospital's patients or a school's pupils are drawn. 2 the area from which rainfall flows into a river or lake.

catchy adj. (**catchier**, **catchiest**) (of a tune) appealing and easy to remember.

catechism /kat-i-ki-z'm/ n. a summary of the principles of Christian religion in the form of questions and answers.

catechize (or **-ise**) v. teach by using a catechism.

categorical (or **categoric**) adj. completely clear and direct. ■ **categorically** adv.

categorize (or **-ise**) v. place in a category. ■ **categorization** n.

category n. (pl. **categories**) a class of things with shared characteristics.

cater v. 1 provide food and drink. 2 (**cater for/to**) provide with what is needed or required. ■ **caterer** n.

caterpillar n. 1 the larva of a butterfly

Thesaurus

pussy, pussy cat, puss, kitty, moggie, mog.

catalogue n. LIST, record, register, inventory, index, directory, roll, table, guide, classification, calendar, schedule. ▶ v. LIST, file, classify, categorize, register, record, make an inventory of, alphabetize.

catapult v. LAUNCH, hurl, propel, shoot, fling, fire. See also THROW.

cataract n. WATERFALL, falls, cascade, rapids, torrent, downpour.

catastrophe n. DISASTER, calamity, cataclysm, tragedy, misfortune, blow, mishap, misadventure, reverse, debacle, fiasco, trouble, trial, adversity, affliction.

catch v. 1 GRASP, seize, grab, clutch, grip, hold, pluck, clench, intercept, snare, trap, receive, acquire. 2 CAPTURE, apprehend, arrest, seize, take prisoner, lay hold of, trap, snare; informal collar, nab, pinch, nick. 3 HEAR, understand, follow, grasp, comprehend, make out, take in, discern, perceive, fathom. 4 CONTRACT, get, develop, become infect-

ed by, suffer from, succumb to, go down with. ▶ n. 1 BOLT, lock, fastening, fastener, clasp, hasp, hook, clip, latch, snib. 2 SNAG, disadvantage, drawback, difficulty, hitch, fly in the ointment, stumbling block, trick, snare. 3 YIELD, take, haul, bag, net, prize. □ **catch on** 1 BECOME POPULAR, come into fashion, succeed, become all the rage; informal become trendy. 2 see UNDERSTAND.

catching adj. CONTAGIOUS, infectious, communicable, transmissible, transmittable.

catchy adj. MEMORABLE, popular, haunting, appealing, captivating, melodious, singable.

categorical adj. UNQUALIFIED, unconditional, unequivocal, unambiguous, unreserved, definite, absolute, explicit, emphatic, positive, express, firm, direct, conclusive, decided, forceful, downright, utter, out-and-out. ■ OPPOSITES equivocal, tentative.

category n. CLASS, group, classification, grouping, type, sort, kind, variety, grade, order, rank, division, heading, or moth. **2** (also **caterpillar track** or **tread**) trademark a steel band passing round the wheels of a vehicle for travel on rough ground.

caterwaul /kat-er-wawl/ v. make a shrill wailing noise.

catharsis n. the release of pent-up emotions. ∎ **cathartic** adj.

cathedral n. the principal church of a diocese.

Catherine wheel n. a rotating firework.

catheter n. a tube inserted into the bladder etc. to remove fluid.

cathode n. an electrode with a negative charge. □ **cathode ray tube** a vacuum tube in which beams of electrons produce a luminous image on a fluorescent screen.

catholic adj. **1** including a wide range of things. **2** (**Catholic**) Roman Catholic. ▶ n. (**Catholic**) a Roman Catholic. ∎ **Catholicism** n.

cation /kat-I-uhn/ n. an ion with a positive charge.

cattery n. (pl. **catteries**) a place where cats are kept while their owners are away.

cattle pl. n. cows, bulls, and oxen.

catty adj. spiteful.

caucus n. (pl. **caucuses**) **1** a meeting of a political party's policy-making committee. **2** a group with shared concerns within a larger organization.

caught past & past part. of **CATCH**.

caul n. a membrane enclosing a fetus.

cauldron (US **caldron**) n. a large metal cooking pot.

cauliflower n. a vegetable with a large white flower head.

caulk (US **calk**) n. a waterproof substance for filling cracks and joins.

causal adj. of or being a cause. ∎ **causally** adv. **causality** n.

causation n. the causing of an effect. ∎ **causative** adj.

cause n. **1** a person or thing that produces an effect. **2** a reason for doing something. **3** a principle or movement to support. ▶ v. make happen. □ **cause célèbre** (pl. **causes célèbres**) a matter causing great public interest.

causeway n. a raised road across low or wet ground.

caustic adj. **1** able to burn by chemical action. **2** sarcastic. □ **caustic soda** sodium hydroxide.

cauterize (or **-ise**) v. burn the area around a wound to stop bleeding or prevent infection.

caution n. **1** care taken to avoid danger or mistakes. **2** a formal warning given for a minor offence. ▶ v. **1** warn. **2** give a caution to.

cautionary adj. acting as a warning.

cautious adj. careful to avoid danger or mistakes. ∎ **cautiously** adv.

cavalcade n. a procession.

cavalier n. (**Cavalier**) a supporter of Charles I in the English Civil War. ▶ adj. showing a lack of proper concern.

cavalry n. (pl. **cavalries**) soldiers who

Thesaurus

section, department.

cater v. (**cater for**) **1** FEED, provide food for, provision, serve, cook for; *dated* victual. **2** TAKE INTO ACCOUNT/CONSIDERATION, allow for, bear in mind, make provision for, have regard for.

catholic adj. WIDE, broad, wide-ranging, all-embracing, general, comprehensive, varied, all-inclusive, eclectic, universal. ∎ OPPOSITES narrow.

cattle n. COWS, bovines, livestock, stock, bulls, heifers, calves, bullocks, steers.

cause n. **1** ORIGIN, source, root, beginning, genesis, occasion, mainspring, author, originator, creator, produce, agent, prime mover, maker. **2** REASON, basis, grounds, justification, call, motive, motivation. **3** PRINCIPLE, ideal, belief, conviction, object, end, aim, objective, purpose, charity. ▶ v. **1** BRING ABOUT, produce, create, make happen, give rise to, lead to, result in, provoke, originate, generate, engender, arouse, effect, occa-

sion, precipitate. **2** FORCE, make, compel, induce.

caustic adj. **1** CORROSIVE, acid, corroding, burning, destructive, mordant, acrid. **2** CUTTING, biting, sarcastic, stinging, scathing, virulent, waspish, trenchant, pungent, astringent, acidulous, acrimonious, mordant. ∎ OPPOSITES gentle, mild.

caution n. **1** CARE, carefulness, attention, alertness, wariness, prudence, watchfulness, vigilance, heed, heedfulness, guardedness, circumspection, discretion, forethought, mindfulness. **2** WARNING, reprimand, admonition, injunction; *informal* dressing-down, ticking-off. ▶ v. **1** WARN, advise, urge, counsel, inform, alert, forewarn, admonish. **2** REPRIMAND, admonish, warn, give a warning to, censure; *informal* tell off, tick off.

cautious adj. CAREFUL, wary, prudent, guarded, alert, circumspect, watchful, formerly fought on horseback.

cave n. a natural hollow in a hill or cliff, or underground. ▶v. **1** (**caving**) exploring caves as a sport. **2** (**cave in**) collapse. **3** (**cave in**) give in to demands.

caveat /ka-vi-at/ n. a warning.

cavern n. a large cave.

cavernous adj. huge or gloomy like a cavern.

caviar n. the pickled roe of the sturgeon.

cavil v. (**cavilling**, **cavilled**; US **caviling**, **caviled**) raise petty objections. ▶n. a petty objection.

cavity n. (pl. **cavities**) **1** a hollow space within a solid object. **2** a decayed part of a tooth.

cavort v. jump around excitedly.

caw v. (of a rook or crow) make a harsh cry.

cayenne n. a hot red powder made from dried chillies.

cayman var. of CAIMAN.

CB abbrev. Citizens' Band.

CBE abbrev. Commander of the Order of the British Empire.

cc (or **c.c.**) abbrev. **1** carbon copy. **2** cubic centimetres.

CCTV abbrev. closed-circuit television.

CD abbrev. compact disc.

CD-ROM n. a compact disc used in a computer as a read-only device for data.

cease v. come or bring to an end. ▢ **ceasefire** a temporary truce. **ceaseless** never stopping.

cecum US = CAECUM.

cedar n. a coniferous tree with aromatic wood.

cede v. give up power or territory.

cedilla n. a mark (,) written under the letter *c* to show that it is pronounced like an *s*.

ceilidh /**kay**-li/ n. a social event with Scottish or Irish folk music and dancing.

ceiling n. **1** the upper inside surface of a room. **2** an upper limit.

celandine n. a small yellow-flowered plant.

celebrant n. a person who performs a religious ceremony.

celebrate v. mark an important occasion with festivities. ■ **celebration** n. **celebratory** adj.

celebrated adj. famous.

celebrity n. (pl. **celebrities**) **1** a famous person. **2** fame.

celeriac n. a vegetable with a large edible root.

celerity n. literary speed.

celery n. a vegetable with crisp stalks.

celestial adj. of heaven or the sky.

celibate adj. not marrying or having sex. ■ **celibacy** n.

cell n. **1** a small room for a prisoner, monk, or nun. **2** the smallest unit of a living organism. **3** a small political group. **4** a device for producing electricity by chemical action or light.

cellar n. **1** an underground storage

Thesaurus

vigilant, mindful, shrewd, chary, tactful, non-committal, tentative; *informal* cagey. ■ OPPOSITES incautious, reckless.

cavalier adj. OFFHAND, arrogant, haughty, disdainful, supercilious, insolent, condescending, lofty, patronizing.

cave n. CAVERN, hollow, grotto, pothole, cavity, dugout, underground chamber. ▢ **cave in** *see* COLLAPSE.

cavity n. HOLE, hollow, crater, pit, orifice, gap, dent, aperture.

cease v. STOP, finish, end, bring to a halt, halt, break off, discontinue, conclude, suspend, terminate, desist, leave off, refrain from; *informal* quit, knock off, lay off. ■ OPPOSITES start, begin.

ceaseless adj. UNENDING, endless, constant, continual, continuous, non-stop, perpetual, never-ending, incessant, persistent, relentless, unremitting, interminable, everlasting, untiring, chronic. ■ OPPOSITES intermittent.

celebrate v. **1** ENJOY ONESELF, rejoice,

make merry, revel, party; *informal* go out on the town, paint the town red, whoop it up. **2** COMMEMORATE, remember, honour, observe, make, keep, toast, drink to. **3** PERFORM, officiate at, observe.

celebrated adj. *see* FAMOUS.

celebration n. **1** PARTY, festival, carnival, gala, fete, festivity, revelry, merrymaking, jollification, spree; *informal* bash, shindig, beanfeast, rave-up. **2** COMMEMORATION, remembrance, observance, honouring, keeping.

celebrity n. **1** *see* FAME. **2** FAMOUS PERSON, star, dignitary, luminary, notable, personage; *informal* bigwig, big shot, big noise.

celestial adj. **1** ASTRONOMICAL, cosmic, heavenly, stellar, interstellar, extraterrestrial. **2** DIVINE, heavenly, supernatural, transcendental, godlike, ethereal, sublime, spiritual, immortal, angelic, seraphic, cherubic.

celibacy n. CHASTITY, purity, abstinence, self-denial, asceticism, virginity, bachroom. **2** a stock of wine.

cello /chel-loh/ n. (pl. **cellos**) a large bass instrument of the violin family. ■ **cellist** n.

cellophane n. trademark a thin transparent wrapping material.

cellphone n. a mobile phone.

cellular adj. **1** of or made up of cells. **2** denoting a mobile phone system using short-range radio stations.

cellulite n. fat that builds up under the skin, causing a dimpled effect.

celluloid n. transparent plastic formerly used for cinema film.

cellulose n. a substance in plant tissues, used to make plastics and textiles.

Celsius adj. denoting a scale of temperature on which water freezes at 0° and boils at 100°.

Celt /kelt/ n. a member of an ancient European people or their descendants. ■ **Celtic** adj.

cement n. a powdery substance made by heating lime and clay, used to make mortar and concrete. ▶ v. **1** fix with cement. **2** strengthen.

cemetery n. (pl. **cemeteries**) a large burial ground.

cenotaph n. a memorial to members of the armed forces killed in a war.

censer n. a container for burning incense.

censor n. an official who examines books, films, etc. and bans anything considered offensive or a threat to security. ▶ v. ban unacceptable parts of a book, film, etc. ■ **censorship** n.

....

☑ Don't confuse **censor** with **censure**.

....

censorious adj. severely critical.

censure v. criticize strongly. ▶ n. strong disapproval or criticism.

census n. (pl. **censuses**) an official count of a population.

cent n. a 100th of a dollar or other decimal currency unit.

centaur n. a mythical creature with a man's upper body and a horse's lower body and legs.

centenarian n. a person who is 100 or more years old.

centenary n. (pl. **centenaries**) the 100th anniversary of an event.

centennial n. a centenary.

center US = **CENTRE**.

centigrade adj. measured by the Celsius scale of temperature.

centilitre (US **centiliter**) n. a 100th of a litre.

centimetre (US **centimeter**) n. a 100th of a metre.

centipede n. an insect-like creature with many legs.

central adj. **1** in or near the centre. **2** very important. □ **central heating** heating conducted from a boiler through pipes and radiators. **central nervous system** the brain and spinal cord in vertebrates. ■ **centrality** n. **centrally** adv.

centralize (or **-ise**) v. bring under the control of a central authority. ■ **centralism** n. **centralist** n. & adj. **centralization** n.

centre (US **center**) n. **1** a point or part in the middle of something. **2** a place where an activity takes place. **3** a point from which something spreads or to which something is directed. ▶ v. (**centring**, **centred**; US **centering**, **cen-**

Thesaurus

....

elorhood, spinsterhood, monasticism, monkhood, nunhood, continence, abnegation.

celibate adj. CHASTE, pure, abstinent, virgin, immaculate, continent.

cell n. **1** ENCLOSURE, dungeon, lock-up, cubicle, room, apartment, chamber, stall. **2** CAVITY, compartment, hole, unit.

cement n. ADHESIVE, glue, paste, bonding, binder.

cemetery n. GRAVEYARD, burial ground, churchyard, necropolis.

censor v. EXPURGATE, bowdlerize, cut, delete, edit, remove, make cuts/changes to, amend, prohibit, forbid, ban.

censorious adj. CRITICAL, hypercritical, disapproving, condemnatory, judgemental, moralistic, fault-finding, cap-

tious, carping, cavilling.

censure v. CRITICIZE, blame, disapprove of, denounce, reprove, rebuke, reproach, reprimand, upbraid, berate, scold, chide, reprehend, castigate; informal tell off, tick off, carpet. ▶ n. CRITICISM, blame, condemnation, denunciation, disapproval, reproval, reproof, reproach, rebuke, reprimand, scolding, berating, upbraiding, castigation, obloquy, reprehension, vituperation; informal talking-to, dressing-down.

central adj. **1** MIDDLE, mid, median, mean, mesial. **2** MAIN, chief, principal, foremost, basic, fundamental, key, essential, primary, pivotal, core, focal, cardinal. ■ OPPOSITES side, outer, subordinate.

tered) 1 place in the centre. **2** (**centre on/around**) have as a major concern. □ **centrefold** the two middle pages of a magazine.

centrifugal force n. a force which appears to cause something moving round a centre to fly outwards.

centrifuge n. a machine with a rapidly rotating container, used to separate substances.

centurion n. a commander in the ancient Roman army.

century n. (pl. **centuries**) **1** a period of 100 years. **2** a batsman's score of 100 runs in cricket.

cephalic adj. of the head.

cephalopod n. a mollusc of a group including octopuses and squids.

ceramic adj. made of clay hardened by heat. ▶ n. (**ceramics**) the art of making ceramic objects.

cereal n. **1** a grass producing an edible grain, e.g. wheat. **2** a breakfast food made from this.

cerebellum n. (pl. **cerebellums** or **cerebella**) the part of the brain at the back of the skull.

cerebral adj. **1** of the cerebrum. **2** intellectual. □ **cerebral palsy** a condition involving difficulty in controlling the muscles, caused by brain damage before or at birth.

cerebrum n. (pl. **cerebra**) the main part of the brain.

ceremonial adj. of ceremonies. ■ **ceremonially** adv.

ceremonious adj. done in a grand and formal way. ■ **ceremoniously** adv.

ceremony n. (pl. **ceremonies**) **1** a formal religious or public occasion celebrating an event. **2** the set procedures followed at such occasions. **3** formal behaviour.

cerise /suh-reess/ n. light, clear red.

certain adj. **1** able to be relied on to happen or be the case. **2** feeling sure. **3** specific but not stated.

certainly adv. **1** without doubt; definitely. **2** yes.

certainty n. (pl. **certainties**) **1** the state of being certain. **2** something that is certain.

certifiable adj. able or needing to be certified.

certificate n. an official document recording a fact or event.

certify v. (**certifying**, **certified**) **1** declare in a certificate. **2** officially declare insane.

certitude n. a feeling of certainty.

Thesaurus

centralize v. CONCENTRATE, centre, consolidate, condense, amalgamate, unify, incorporate, streamline, rationalize, focus.

centre n. MIDDLE, middle point, heart, core, nucleus, midpoint, hub, kernel, focus, focal point, pivot, inside, interior. ▶ v. CONCENTRATE, focus, converge, close in, pivot.

ceremonial adj. FORMAL, official, ritual, ritualistic, celebratory, liturgical, stately, dignified, solemn.

ceremonious adj. DIGNIFIED, majestic, imposing, impressive, solemn, stately, formal, courtly, scrupulous, precise, punctilious, deferential, stiff, rigid. ■ OPPOSITES casual.

ceremony n. **1** RITE, service, ritual, sacrament, formality, observance, celebration, commemoration, function, event, parade. **2** FORMALITY, pomp, decorum, formalities, niceties, etiquette, propriety, ritual, attention to detail, protocol, punctiliousness, pageantry, grandeur, ceremonial.

certain adj. **1** SURE, confident, convinced, satisfied, persuaded, assured, unwavering, secure, unshaken. **2** ASSURED, inevitable, definite, destined, in-

escapable, bound to happen, inexorable, unarguable, ineluctable. **3** DEFINITE, sure, sound, reliable, dependable, trustworthy, unquestionable, beyond question, evident, plain, clear, indubitable, undeniable, obvious, undisputed, incontrovertible, incontestable, conclusive, infallible, foolproof; *informal* sure-fire. **4** PARTICULAR, specific, precise, special, individual. ■ OPPOSITES doubtful, possible, unlikely.

certainly adv. DEFINITELY, surely, assuredly, undoubtedly, undeniably, obviously, plainly, clearly.

certainty n. **1** SURENESS, authority, positiveness, confidence, assurance, assuredness, conviction, reliability, conclusiveness, authoritativeness, validity. **2** FACT, inevitability, foregone conclusion, indubitability; *informal* sure thing, dead cert. ■ OPPOSITES uncertainty.

certificate n. CERTIFICATION, authorization, document, licence, warrant, credentials, pass, permit, guarantee, voucher, diploma, qualification, testimonial.

certify v. **1** AUTHENTICATE, document, verify, validate, confirm, bear witness to, attest to, testify to, substantiate, corrob-

cerulean /si-roo-li-uhn/ adj. deep blue like a clear sky.

cervix n. (pl. **cervices**) the narrow passage forming the lower end of the womb. ■ **cervical** adj.

Cesarean US = CAESAREAN.

cesium US = CAESIUM.

cessation n. the act of ceasing.

cession n. ceding of rights or territory.

cesspool (or **cesspit**) n. an underground tank or covered pit for liquid waste and sewage.

cetacean /si-tay-sh'n/ n. a sea mammal of a group including whales and dolphins.

cf abbrev. compare.

CFC abbrev. chlorofluorocarbon, a gas used in refrigerators and aerosols and harmful to the ozone layer.

chador n. a piece of cloth worn by Muslim women around the head and upper body.

chafe v. 1 make or become sore by rubbing. 2 warm by rubbing. 3 become impatient because of restriction.

chafer n. a large flying beetle.

chaff n. husks of grain separated from the seed. ▶ v. tease.

chaffinch n. a pink-breasted finch.

chagrin n. annoyance or shame at having failed.

chain n. 1 a series of connected metal links. 2 a connected series, set, or sequence. ▶ v. fasten or restrain with a chain. □ **chain reaction** a series of events, each caused by the previous one. **chainsaw** a power-driven saw with teeth set on a circular chain.

chair n. 1 a seat for one person, with a back and four legs. 2 the person in charge of a meeting or an organization. ▶ v. act as chairperson of. □ **chairlift** a series of chairs on a moving cable, for carrying passengers up and down a mountain. **chairman** (or **chairwoman**) the person in charge of a meeting or organization. **chairperson** the person in charge of a meeting.

chaise longue /shayz long/ n. (pl. **chaises longues**) a sofa with a backrest at only one end.

chalcedony n. a type of quartz.

chalet /sha-lay/ n. 1 a wooden house with overhanging eaves, found in the Alps. 2 a small wooden cabin used by holidaymakers.

chalice n. a goblet.

chalk n. 1 a white soft limestone. 2 a similar substance made into sticks, used for drawing or writing. ■ **chalky** adj.

challenge n. 1 an invitation to take part in a contest or to prove something. 2 a demanding task or situation. ▶ v. 1 dispute or query something. 2 call on someone to fight or do something difficult. ■ **challenger** n.

chamber n. 1 a large room for formal or public events. 2 each of the houses of a parliament. 3 (**chambers**) rooms used by a barrister. 4 old use a bedroom. 5 a space or cavity. □ **chambermaid** a woman who cleans rooms in a hotel. **chamber music** classical music played by a small group of musicians. **chamber pot** a bowl kept in a bedroom and used as a toilet.

chamberlain n. hist. an officer who managed the household of a monarch or noble.

chameleon /kuh-mee-li-uhn/ n. a small lizard that changes colour according to its surroundings.

chamfer /sham-fer/ v. (**chamfering**, **chamfered**) bevel the edge of.

chamois n. (pl. **chamois**) 1 /sham-wah/ a small European mountain antelope. 2 /sham-mi/ a piece of soft leather for cleaning windows etc.

chamomile (or **camomile**) /kam-uh-

Thesaurus

orate, endorse, vouch for, ratify, warrant. 2 ACCREDIT, license, recognize, authorize, qualify, give a certificate/ diploma to.

cessation n. END, finish, termination, conclusion, halt, pause, break, respite, let-up.

chain n. 1 SHACKLE, fetter, manacle, bonds, coupling, link. 2 SERIES, succession, progression, sequence, string, set, cycle, line, row, concatenation. ▶ v. FASTEN, secure, tie, bind, tether, shackle, fetter, manacle, handcuff, hitch.

chair v. PRESIDE OVER, lead, direct, manage, control, oversee, supervise.

chalky adj. WHITE, pale, wan, pallid, ashen, pasty, waxen, blanched, bleached, colourless.

challenge v. 1 DARE, summon, invite, throw down the gauntlet to, defy. 2 QUESTION, dispute, call into question, protest against, object to, take exception to, disagree with, argue against, contest, oppose, query, demur against, impugn. 3 STIMULATE, test, tax, inspire, excite, arouse, spur on.

challenging adj. STIMULATING, exciting, inspiring, testing, thought-provoking.

myl/ n. a plant with white and yellow flowers.

champ v. munch noisily. □ **champ at the bit** be very impatient.

champagne n. a white sparkling French wine.

champion n. **1** the winner of a sporting contest or other competition. **2** a person who argues or fights for a cause. ▶v. strongly support. ■ **championship** n.

chance n. **1** a possibility of something happening. **2** an opportunity. **3** occurrence without any obvious plan or cause. ▶v. **1** happen or do something by chance. **2** informal risk. □ **on the off chance** just in case.

chancel n. the part of a church near the altar.

chancellor n. **1** a senior state or legal official of various kinds. **2** the head of the government in some European countries. **3** (also **Chancellor of the Exchequer**) (in the UK) the government minister in charge of the country's finances.

Chancery n. a division of the High Court of Justice.

chancy adj. informal risky.

chandelier n. a large hanging light with branches for several light bulbs or candles.

chandler n. a dealer in supplies for ships.

change v. **1** make or become different. **2** exchange for another. **3** move from one to another. **4** exchange a sum of money for the same sum in a different currency or smaller units. ▶n. **1** an act of changing. **2** money returned as the balance of a sum paid. **3** coins as opposed to banknotes. □ **changeling** a child believed to have been exchanged by fairies for the parents' real child. **changeover** a change from one system or situation to another. ■ **changeable** adj. **changeless** adj.

channel n. **1** a stretch of water joining two seas. **2** a passage for water. **3** a means of communication. **4** a band of broadcasting frequencies. ▶v. (**channelling, channelled**; US **channeling, channeled**) direct towards a particular purpose or by a particular route.

Thesaurus

■ OPPOSITES easy.

chamber n. **1** ROOM, cubicle, bedroom, bedchamber, boudoir. **2** CAVITY, compartment, hollow, cell.

champion n. **1** WINNER, prizewinner, medallist, record-breaker, victor, titleholder, conqueror, hero. **2** SUPPORTER, defender, upholder, advocate, backer, patron, protector, vindicator. **3** KNIGHT, hero, warrior, contender, fighter, man-at-arms, paladin. ▶adj. WINNING, victorious, unrivalled, leading, great, supreme, record-breaking. ▶v. DEFEND, support, uphold, stand up for, back, advocate, promote, espouse.

chance n. **1** ACCIDENT, coincidence, luck, fate, destiny, fluke, providence, fortune, serendipity, fortuity. **2** POSSIBILITY, likelihood, prospect, probability, likeliness, odds, conceivability. **3** OPPORTUNITY, time, occasion, turn, opening; informal shot. ▶adj. ACCIDENTAL, unforeseen, unexpected, coincidental, unplanned, lucky, unintended, unintentional, unpremeditated, casual, inadvertent, unanticipated, unforeseeable, random, haphazard, unlooked for, fortuitous, serendipitous, adventitious, fluky. ■ OPPOSITES intentional, deliberate. □ **chance on/upon** MEET, encounter, come across, stumble on; informal bump into, run into.

chancy adj. RISKY, dangerous, hazardous, unsafe, uncertain, precarious, perilous, insecure, speculative, unpredictable; informal dicey, dodgy. ■ OPPOSITES safe.

change v. **1** ALTER, adjust, transform, modify, convert, vary, amend, rearrange, reorganize, remodel, reorder, reform, reconstruct, restyle, recast, tailor, transmute, accustom, metamorphose, transmogrify, permutate, permute. **2** BE CHANGED, alter, be transformed, evolve, develop, move on, mutate, shift, do an about-face, do a U-turn; informal chop and change. **3** EXCHANGE, swap, switch, substitute, replace, trade, interchange, barter, transpose. ▶n. **1** ALTERATION, modification, adaptation, difference, transformation, conversion, variation, development, remodelling, reorganization, rearrangement, reconstruction, shift, transition, metamorphosis, mutation, transmutation, transmogrification, innovation, vicissitude, permutation. **2** EXCHANGE, switch, swap, trade, substitution, interchange, bartering. **3** COINS, silver, small change, cash, petty cash.

changeable adj. VARIABLE, changing, varying, shifting, vacillating, fluctuating, volatile, capricious, wavering, unstable, unsteady, irregular, erratic, unreliable, inconsistent, unpredictable,

chant n. a repeated rhythmic phrase, shouted or sung. ▶v. say, shout, or sing rhythmically.

chaos n. complete disorder and confusion. ■ **chaotic** adj. **chaotically** adv.

chap n. informal a man.

chapatti n. (pl. **chapattis**) (in Indian cookery) a flat cake of wholemeal bread.

chapel n. 1 a small building or room for Christian worship. 2 a part of a large church with its own altar.

chaperone n. an older woman in charge of an unmarried girl at social occasions. ▶v. act as a chaperone to.

chaplain n. a member of the clergy attached to a chapel in a private house or an institution, or to a military unit. ■ **chaplaincy** n.

chapped adj. (of the skin) cracked and sore.

chapter n. 1 a main division of a book. 2 the governing body of a cathedral or other religious community.

char v. (**charring**, **charred**) blacken by burning. ▶n. informal 1 a woman employed to clean a house. 2 tea.

charabanc /sha-ruh-bang/ n. an early form of bus.

character n. 1 the distinctive qualities of a person or thing. 2 strong personal qualities. 3 a person's good reputation.

4 a person in a novel, play, or film. 5 informal an eccentric or amusing person. 6 a printed or written letter or symbol. ■ **characterless** adj.

characteristic adj. typical of a particular person, place, or thing. ▶n. a quality typical of a person or thing. ■ **characteristically** adv.

characterize (or **-ise**) v. 1 describe the character of. 2 be typical of. ■ **characterization** n.

charade /shuh-rahd/ n. 1 an absurd pretence. 2 (**charades**) a game of guessing a word or phrase from acted clues.

charcoal n. a black form of carbon made by burning wood slowly.

charge v. 1 ask an amount as a price. 2 accuse someone formally of something. 3 rush forward, esp. in attack. 4 entrust with a task. 5 store electrical energy in a battery. ▶n. 1 a price asked. 2 a formal accusation against someone brought to trial. 3 responsibility for care or control. 4 a person or thing entrusted to someone's care. 5 a headlong rush forward. 6 electricity existing naturally in a substance. 7 energy stored chemically in a battery. 8 a quantity of explosive. □ **charge card** a credit card issued by a shop. ■ **chargeable** adj.

Thesaurus

fickle, inconstant, mercurial, fluid, fitful, kaleidoscopic, protean, mutable, chequered, vicissitudinous. ■ OPPOSITES constant.

channel n. 1 PASSAGE, sea passage, strait, narrow, neck, waterway, watercourse, fiord. 2 GUTTER, furrow, groove, conduit, duct, culvert, ditch, gully. 3 PATH, route, direction, way, approach, course. 4 MEDIUM, means, agency, vehicle, route. ▶v. CONVEY, conduct, transmit, transport, guide, direct.

chant n. SONG, hymn, chorus, carol, psalm. ▶v. INTONE, recite, sing, cantillate.

chaos n. DISORDER, anarchy, mayhem, bedlam, pandemonium, turmoil, tumult, uproar, disruption, upheaval, confusion, disarray, lawlessness, riot, disorganization. ■ OPPOSITES order.

chaotic adj. ANARCHIC, in chaos, disordered, disorganized, confused, disorderly, unruly, uncontrolled, tumultuous, jumbled, upset, askew, disrupted, in disarray, awry, lawless, riotous, ungovernable, rebellious, orderless, topsy-turvy, haywire, in a shambles,

higgledy-piggledy; *informal* shambolic. ■ OPPOSITES orderly.

character n. 1 PERSONALITY, nature, disposition, temperament, temper, make-up, constitution, cast, attributes, bent, complexion. 2 STRENGTH, honour, integrity, moral fibre, uprightness, rectitude, fortitude, backbone. 3 ECCENTRIC, original, individual, oddity; *informal* oddball, odd fellow, queer fish; *informal, dated* card. 4 PERSON, individual, human being; *informal* fellow, guy, bloke, chap, type, sort, customer. 5 REPUTATION, name, standing, position, status. 6 TYPE, sign, symbol, mark, figure, hieroglyph, cipher, ideogram.

characteristic n. QUALITY, attribute, feature, trait, property, peculiarity, quirk, mannerism, idiosyncrasy, hallmark, trademark. ▶adj. TYPICAL, distinctive, distinguishing, particular, special, individual, peculiar, specific, representative, symbolic, idiosyncratic, symptomatic.

characterize v. PORTRAY, depict, describe, present, identify, draw, brand, typify, delineate, denote, indicate,

chargé d'affaires /shar-zhay da-**fair**/ n. (pl. **chargés d'affaires**) an ambassador's deputy.

charger n. **1** a device for charging a battery. **2** a cavalry horse.

chariot n. a two-wheeled horse-drawn vehicle, used in ancient warfare and racing. ■ **charioteer** n.

charisma /kuh-**riz**-muh/ n. the power to inspire admiration or enthusiasm in other people. ■ **charismatic** adj.

charitable adj. **1** of charity or charities. **2** tolerant in judging others. ■ **charitably** adv.

charity n. (pl. **charities**) **1** an organization set up to help people in need. **2** the giving of money etc. to people in need. **3** tolerance in judging others.

charlatan n. a person falsely claiming to have a skill.

charm n. **1** the power to delight or fascinate. **2** a small ornament worn on a bracelet. **3** an object, act, or saying believed to have magic power. ▶ v. **1** delight greatly. **2** influence by using one's charm. **3** (**charmed**) unusually lucky as if protected by magic. ■ **charmer** n.

charming adj. delightful.

charnel house n. hist. a building in which corpses or bones were kept.

chart n. **1** a table, graph, or diagram. **2** a map for navigation. **3** (**the charts**) a weekly listing of the current best-selling pop records. ▶ v. plot or record on a chart.

charter n. **1** an official document granting or defining rights. **2** a written description of an organization's functions. **3** the hiring of an aircraft, ship, or vehicle. ▶ v. **1** hire an aircraft, ship, or vehicle. **2** grant a charter to. □ **charter flight** a flight by an aircraft chartered for a specific journey.

chartered adj. (of an accountant, engineer, etc.) qualified as a member of a professional body that has a royal charter.

chary adj. cautiously reluctant.

chase v. pursue in order to catch. ▶ n. **1** an act of chasing. **2** (**the chase**) hunting as a sport.

chaser n. informal a strong alcoholic drink taken after a weaker one.

chasm n. a deep crack in the earth.

chassis /**shas**-si/ n. (pl. **chassis** /**shas**-siz/) the base frame of a vehicle.

chaste adj. **1** not having sex outside marriage or at all. **2** demure or modest. ■ **chastity** n.

chasten v. cause to feel subdued or

Thesaurus

specify, designate.

charade n. PRETENCE, travesty, mockery, fake, sham, deception, pose, farce, absurdity, parody, pantomime, play-acting, masquerade.

charge v. **1** ASK IN PAYMENT, ask, ask for, expect, make someone pay, impose, levy, require. **2** ACCUSE OF, arraign, indict, prosecute, impute, blame, incriminate. **3** ATTACK, storm, assault, rush, open fire on, assail, fall on; informal lay into, wade into. **4** ENTRUST, burden, impose on, give, load, encumber, saddle. **5** FILL, load, imbue, instil, suffuse, permeate, pervade. ▶ n. **1** COST, rate, price, amount, fee, payment, expense, outlay, expenditure, levy, toll, terms, dues. **2** ACCUSATION, allegation, indictment, arraignment, impeachment, citation, imputation, blame, incrimination. **3** ATTACK, assault, offensive, storming, raid, strike, onrush, onslaught, sally, incursion, sortie. **4** CARE, custody, responsibility, protection, supervision, safe keeping, keeping, trust, guardianship, surveillance.

charitable adj. **1** GENEROUS, kind, giving, philanthropic, magnanimous, liberal, munificent, bountiful, open-handed, benevolent. **2** LIBERAL, generous, tolerant, understanding, broad-minded, sympathetic. ■ OPPOSITES uncharitable.

charity n. **1** DONATIONS, contributions, handouts, financial assistance, funding, endowments, almsgiving, philanthropy, benefaction. **2** COMPASSION, humanity, goodwill, kindliness, sympathy, love, tolerance, thoughtfulness, generosity, altruism, humanitarianism, benevolence.

charm n. **1** ATTRACTIVENESS, attraction, appeal, allure, fascination, desirability, charisma, lure, delightfulness, captivation, allurement. **2** SPELL, magic words, incantation, sorcery, witchcraft, wizardry. **3** AMULET, trinket, talisman, mascot. ▶ v. DELIGHT, please, attract, captivate, fascinate, win over, bewitch, beguile, enchant, seduce, hypnotize, mesmerize, enthral, intrigue, disarm, enamour, allure, draw. ■ OPPOSITES repel.

chart n. GRAPH, table, diagram, map, plan, blueprint, guide, scheme, tabulation. ▶ v. MAP, map out, plot, graph, delineate, sketch, draft.

chase v. PURSUE, run/go after, follow,

ashamed.

chastise v. reprimand severely. ■ **chastisement** n.

chat v. (**chatting, chatted**) talk in an informal way. ▶n. an informal conversation. ◻ **chat room** an area on the Internet where users can email each other. ■ **chatty** adj.

chateau /sha-toh/ n. (pl. **chateaux**) a large French country house or castle.

chatelaine /sha-tuh-layn/ n. dated a woman in charge of a large house.

chattel n. a personal possession.

chatter v. 1 talk at length about unimportant matters. 2 (of teeth) click together. ▶n. 1 continuous unimportant talk. 2 a series of short high-pitched sounds. ◻ **chatterbox** informal a person who chatters.

chauffeur n. a person employed to drive a car.

chauvinism n. extreme belief in the superiority of one's own cause, group, or sex. ■ **chauvinist** n. & adj. **chauvinistic** adj.

cheap adj. 1 low in price. 2 charging low prices. 3 low in price and quality.

4 worthless because achieved in a regrettable way. ◻ **cheapskate** informal a miserly person. ■ **cheapen** v. **cheaply** adv. **cheapness** n.

cheat v. 1 act dishonestly or unfairly to gain an advantage. 2 deprive of something by deceit. ▶n. 1 a person who cheats. 2 an act of cheating.

check v. 1 examine the accuracy or quality of. 2 stop or slow the progress of. 3 Chess move a piece to a square where it directly attacks the opposing king. ▶n. 1 an act of checking accuracy or quality. 2 an act of checking progress. 3 Chess an act of checking the opposing king. 4 US a restaurant bill. 5 US = CHEQUE. 6 a pattern of small squares. ▶adj. (also **checked**) having a pattern of small squares. ◻ **check in** register at a hotel or airport. **checkmate** Chess a position from which a king cannot escape. **checkout** a point at which goods are paid for in a shop. **check out** settle one's hotel bill before leaving. **checkpoint** a barrier where security checks are carried out on travellers.

Thesaurus

hunt, hound, track, trail, tail.

chasm n. ABYSS, ravine, pit, canyon, opening, void, crater, crevasse, gap, fissure, rift.

chaste adj. 1 CELIBATE, virginal, abstinent, pure, innocent, virtuous, undefiled, moral, immaculate, unmarried. 2 VIRTUOUS, good, pure, innocent, decent, moral, modest, wholesome, upright, righteous, becoming, restrained, unsullied. ■ OPPOSITES promiscuous.

chastity n. CHASTENESS, celibacy, abstinence, virginity, self-restraint, self-denial, virtue, purity, innocence, continence, sinlessness.

chat v. TALK, gossip, chatter, have a conversation with, converse, prattle, jabber. ▶n. TALK, gossip, conversation, heart-to-heart; informal confab, chinwag, natter.

chatty adj. TALKATIVE, garrulous, loquacious, voluble, effusive, gushing, gossipy. ■ OPPOSITES taciturn.

chauvinism n. JINGOISM, prejudice, bigotry, bias, machismo.

cheap adj. 1 INEXPENSIVE, low-cost, low-priced, economical, reasonable, bargain, economy, reduced, marked down, discounted, sale; informal bargain-basement, knock-down. 2 POOR-QUALITY, inferior, shoddy, common, tawdry, tatty, paltry, worthless, second-rate,

gimcrack; informal tacky, trashy. 3 DESPICABLE, contemptible, tasteless, unpleasant, unworthy, mean, low, base, sordid, vulgar. ■ OPPOSITES expensive.

cheapen v. DEGRADE, debase, belittle, demean, devalue, denigrate, discredit, prostitute, lower the tone of.

cheat v. 1 DECEIVE, trick, swindle, take in, defraud, dupe, hoodwink, double-cross, take advantage of, exploit, gull; informal rip off, take for a ride, con, diddle, bamboozle, finagle, bilk, fleece. 2 AVOID, elude, evade, dodge, escape, shun, eschew. ▶n. 1 CHEATER, swindler, fraud, confidence trickster, deceiver, trickster, double-crosser, impostor, crook, hoaxer, rogue, charlatan, mountebank, shark; informal con man, phoney, twister. 2 SWINDLE, fraud, deception, deceit, trick, trickery, ruse, misrepresentation, chicanery, imposture, artifice; informal con, rip-off, fiddle, racket, swizz.

check v. 1 EXAMINE, inspect, look over/at, scrutinize, test, monitor, investigate, probe, enquire into, study; informal give the once-over to. 2 STOP, halt, arrest, bring to a standstill, slow down, brake, obstruct, inhibit, bar, impede, block, retard, curb, delay, thwart. ▶n. 1 EXAMINATION, inspection, scrutiny, test, monitoring, investigation, enquiry, probe, study; informal once-over, going-over.

checkers US = CHEQUERS.

cheek n. **1** either side of the face below the eye. **2** rude or disrespectful behaviour. ▶v. speak rudely to.

cheeky adj. (**cheekier**, **cheekiest**) cheerfully disrespectful. ■ **cheekily** adv. **cheekiness** n.

cheep n. a shrill cry made by a young bird. ▶v. make a cheep.

cheer v. **1** shout for joy or to praise or encourage. **2** (**cheer up**) make or become less miserable. ▶n. **1** a shout of joy, encouragement, or praise. **2** cheerfulness; optimism.

cheerful adj. **1** happy and optimistic. **2** bright and pleasant. ■ **cheerfully** adv. **cheerfulness** n.

cheerless adj. gloomy; depressing.

cheery adj. (**cheerier**, **cheeriest**) happy and optimistic. ■ **cheerily** adv.

cheese n. a food made from the pressed curds of milk. □ **cheesecake** a rich sweet tart made with cream and soft cheese. **cheesecloth** thin, loosely woven cotton cloth. **cheese-paring** meanness with money. ■ **cheesy** adj.

cheetah n. a large swift spotted cat.

chef n. a professional cook.

chef d'oeuvre /shay-**dervr**/ n. (pl. **chefs d'oeuvre**) a masterpiece.

chemical adj. of chemistry or chemicals. ▶n. an artificially prepared or purified substance. ■ **chemically** adv.

chemise /shuh-**meez**/ n. a woman's loose-fitting dress or undergarment.

chemist n. **1** a person authorized to dispense medicinal drugs. **2** a shop where such drugs are dispensed and toiletries etc. are sold. **3** a person engaged in chemical research.

chemistry n. **1** the branch of science concerned with the nature of substances and how they react with each other. **2** attraction or interaction between two people.

chemotherapy /kee-moh-**the**-ruh-pi/ n. the treatment of cancer by the use of drugs.

chenille /shuh-**neel**/ n. a fabric with a velvety pile.

cheque (US **check**) n. a written order to a bank to pay a stated sum from an account. □ **cheque card** a card issued by a bank guaranteeing payment of cheques.

chequered adj. **1** marked with chequers. **2** marked by periods of varied fortune.

chequers (US **checkers**) n. **1** a pattern of alternately coloured squares. **2** (**checkers**) US the game of draughts.

cherish v. **1** protect and care for lovingly. **2** keep in one's mind.

cheroot n. a cigar with both ends open.

2 STOP, stoppage, halt, obstruction, break, slowing down, slowdown, delay, interruption, suspension, hiatus, retardation.

cheek n. IMPUDENCE, impertinence, insolence, effrontery, boldness, audacity, temerity, brazenness; informal brass, neck, gall, lip, sauce.

cheeky adj. IMPUDENT, impertinent, insolent, disrespectful, insulting, impolite, presumptuous, mocking, irreverent, forward, pert; informal saucy; US informal sassy. ■ OPPOSITES respectful.

cheep v. CHIRP, chirrup, tweet, twitter, warble, trill.

cheer v. **1** ACCLAIM, applaud, hail, hurrah, encourage, clap, shout/yell at. **2** MAKE CHEERFUL, please, hearten, gladden, brighten, perk up, comfort, console, buoy up, solace, uplift; informal buck up. ▶n. **1** ACCLAIM, acclamation, applause, hurray, hurrah, ovation, plaudit, shout, shouting, hailing, clapping, encouragement, approval. **2** CHEERFULNESS, happiness, gladness, merriment, glee, mirth, gaiety, joy, pleasure, jubilation, rejoicing, festivity, revelry.

□ **cheer up** BRIGHTEN, liven up, perk up, rally, take heart.

cheerful adj. **1** HAPPY, bright, glad, merry, sunny, joyful, delighted, good-humoured, jolly, animated, buoyant, light-hearted, carefree, gleeful, breezy, cheery, jaunty, perky, smiling, laughing, optimistic, hopeful, positive, in good spirits, sparkling, happy-go-lucky, sprightly, rapturous; informal chirpy; literary blithe. **2** BRIGHT, sunny, cheering, pleasant, agreeable, friendly, happy. ■ OPPOSITES sad, cheerless, dull.

cheerless adj. GLOOMY, miserable, dreary, dull, dismal, depressing, bleak, drab, grim, austere, dark, dingy, desolate, sombre, uninviting, forbidding, melancholy, comfortless, forlorn, joyless, disconsolate, funereal, woeful. ■ OPPOSITES cheerful, bright.

cheery adj. CHEERFUL, happy, bright, merry, glad, in good spirits. See also CHEERFUL. ■ OPPOSITES sad.

chemist n. PHARMACIST, pharmacy; US drugstore; old use apothecary.

chequered adj. MIXED, varied, diverse, diversified, eventful.

cherry n. (pl. **cherries**) **1** a small, round red fruit with a stone. **2** a bright deep red colour.

cherub n. **1** (pl. **cherubim** or **cherubs**) a type of angel, shown in art as a chubby child with wings. **2** (pl. **cherubs**) a beautiful or innocent-looking child. ∎ **cherubic** adj.

chervil n. a herb with an aniseed flavour.

chess n. a board game for two players, the aim being to put the opponent's king into checkmate.

chest n. **1** the upper front surface of a person's body. **2** a large strong box. ◻ **chest of drawers** a piece of furniture consisting of a set of drawers.

chestnut n. **1** an edible brown nut. **2** the tree producing chestnuts. **3** a deep reddish-brown colour. **4** a reddish-brown horse. **5** an old joke or anecdote.

chevron n. a V-shaped symbol.

chew v. bite and work food between the teeth. ∎ **chewy** adj.

chiaroscuro /ki-ah-ruh-**skoor**-oh/ n. the treatment of light and shade in drawing and painting.

chic /sheek/ adj. elegant and fashionable. ▶ n. stylishness and elegance.

chicane /shi-**kayn**/ n. a sharp double bend on a motor-racing track.

chicanery n. trickery.

chick n. a newly hatched young bird.

chicken n. **1** a domestic fowl kept for its eggs or meat. **2** informal a coward. ▶ adj. informal cowardly. ▶ v. (**chicken out**) informal withdraw from cowardice. ◻ **chicken feed** informal a very small sum of money. **chickenpox** a disease causing a fever and itchy inflamed pimples.

chickpea n. a yellowish seed eaten as a vegetable.

chicory n. a plant with edible leaves and a root which can be used instead of coffee.

chide v. scold or rebuke.

chief n. **1** a leader or ruler. **2** the head of an organization. ▶ adj. **1** highest in rank. **2** most important.

chiefly adv. mainly; mostly.

chieftain n. the leader of a people or clan.

chiffon n. a light, see-through fabric.

chignon /**sheen**-yon/ n. a coil of hair arranged on the back of a woman's head.

chihuahua /chi-**wah**-wuh/ n. a very small smooth-haired dog.

chilblain n. a painful swelling caused by exposure to cold.

child n. (pl. **children**) **1** a young human being. **2** a son or daughter. ◻ **childbirth** the act of giving birth to a child. ∎ **childhood** n. **childless** adj.

childish adj. **1** like or appropriate to a child. **2** silly and immature.

childlike adj. simple and innocent.

chill n. **1** an unpleasant feeling of cold-

Thesaurus

....

cherish v. **1** TREASURE, prize, hold dear, love, adore, dote on, idolize, cosset, nurture, look after, protect, value. **2** HAVE, entertain, harbour, cling to, nurture, foster. ∎ OPPOSITES neglect.

chest n. **1** BREAST, thorax, sternum, ribcage. **2** BOX, crate, case, trunk, container, coffer, casket.

chew v. BITE, crunch, gnaw, masticate, champ, grind.

chic adj. STYLISH, fashionable, smart, elegant, modish, voguish.

chief n. **1** CHIEFTAIN, head, headman, ruler, leader, overlord, suzerain. **2** HEAD, ruler, principal, leader, director, manager, supervisor, superintendent, chairman, chairperson, chief executive, proprietor, master, mistress, overseer, foreman, controller, captain, commander; informal boss, kingpin, top dog, big cheese, bigwig, number one, supremo, gaffer, governor. ▶ adj. **1** SUPREME, foremost, principal, highest, leading, pre-eminent, senior, superior, premier, head, directing, grand, top.

2 MAIN, principal, most important, cardinal, key, primary, prime, central, fundamental, predominant, foremost, vital, paramount, uppermost. ∎ OPPOSITES minor, subordinate.

chiefly adv. MAINLY, principally, primarily, in the main, predominantly, especially, particularly, mostly, essentially, on the whole, for the most part, above all.

child n. **1** BOY, GIRL, youngster, young person, infant, baby, toddler, tot, tiny tot, youth, adolescent, kid, juvenile, minor; Sc. bairn; informal kid, nipper, sprog, shaver, brat, guttersnipe. **2** SON, DAUGHTER, offspring, progeny, descendant, scion; Law issue.

childbirth n. LABOUR, delivery, confinement, parturition, accouchement.

childhood n. YOUTH, infancy, babyhood, boyhood, girlhood, adolescence, minority; informal teens, pre-teens.

childish adj. IMMATURE, infantile, juvenile, puerile, irresponsible, foolish, jejune. See also SILLY. ∎ OPPOSITES ness. **2** a feverish cold. ▶v. **1** make cold. **2** frighten. **3** *informal* relax. ▶adj. chilly.

chilli n. (pl. **chillies**) a small hot-tasting pepper.

chilly adj. (**chillier, chilliest**) **1** unpleasantly cold. **2** unfriendly.

chime n. **1** a tuneful ringing sound. **2** a bell or a metal bar used in a set to ring when struck. ▶v. **1** make a tuneful ringing sound. **2** (**chime in**) interrupt with a remark.

chimera /ky-meer-uh/ n. **1** Gk Myth. a female monster with a lion's head, a goat's body, and a serpent's tail. **2** an impossible idea or hope.

chimney n. (pl. **chimneys**) a vertical pipe taking smoke and gases up from a fire or furnace. □ **chimney breast** a projecting part of an inside wall surrounding a chimney. **chimney pot** a pipe at the top of a chimney.

chimp n. *informal* a chimpanzee.

chimpanzee n. an African ape.

chin n. the part of the face below the mouth.

china n. **1** a fine white ceramic material. **2** objects made of china.

chinchilla n. a small squirrel-like South American rodent.

chine n. the backbone of an animal.

Chinese n. (pl. **Chinese**) **1** the language of China. **2** a person from China. ▶adj. of China.

chink n. **1** a narrow opening. **2** a thin beam of light. **3** a high-pitched ringing sound. ▶v. make this sound.

chinoiserie /shin-wah-zuh-ri/ n. Chinese-style objects or decoration.

chinos /chee-nohz/ pl. n. casual trousers made from a smooth cotton fabric.

chintz n. a shiny cotton fabric used for furnishings.

chip n. **1** a small piece cut or broken off from something hard. **2** a mark left by removing such a piece. **3** a strip of deep-fried potato. **4** a microchip. **5** a counter used in gambling. ▶v. (**chipping, chipped**) **1** cut or break a chip from something hard. **2** (**chip in**) *informal* make a contribution. □ **a chip on one's shoulder** *informal* a long-held grievance. **chipboard** board made of compressed wood chips.

chipmunk n. a burrowing squirrel with a striped body.

chipolata n. a small sausage.

chippings pl. n. fragments of stone or wood.

chiropody /ki-rop-uh-di/ n. medical treatment of the feet. ▪ **chiropodist** n.

chiropractic /ky-roh-**prak**-tik/ n. a system of complementary medicine based on manipulation of the joints. ▪ **chiropractor** n.

chirp v. (of a small bird) make a short, high-pitched sound. ▶n. such a sound.

chirpy adj. *informal* cheerful and lively.

chisel n. a tool with a long blade for shaping wood or stone. ▶v. (**chiselling, chiselled**; US **chiseling, chiseled**) cut or shape with a chisel.

chit n. **1** an impudent young woman. **2** a short official note recording a sum owed.

chivalrous adj. polite and gallant, esp. towards women. ▪ **chivalrously** adv. **chivalry** n.

chives pl. n. a herb with thin onion-flavoured leaves.

chivvy v. (**chivvying, chivvied**) nag or pester.

Thesaurus

mature.

childlike adj. INNOCENT, simple, unsophisticated, trusting, gullible, naive, ingenuous, guileless, artless, unaffected, credulous.

chill v. COOL, freeze, refrigerate, make cold/cool. ▶n. **1** COOLNESS, chilliness, coldness, iciness, rawness, frigidity, nip, bite. **2** COLDNESS, coolness, aloofness, unfriendliness, hostility, distance, unresponsiveness.

chilly adj. **1** COLD, cool, icy, freezing, chill, fresh, sharp, biting, raw, brisk, penetrating, wintry, frigid. **2** UNFRIENDLY, cool, cold, aloof, distant, unresponsive, reserved, unsympathetic, unwelcoming, hostile, remote, frigid. ▪ OPPOSITES warm, friendly.

chime v. RING, peal, toll, strike, sound, clang, tinkle, resound. ▶n. PEAL, pealing, ringing, striking, tolling, carillon, tintinabulation.

china n. **1** DISHES, tableware, dinner/tea service. **2** PORCELAIN.

chink n. CRACK, gap, cleft, rift, slit, fissure, crevice, split, opening, aperture, cranny, cavity.

chip n. **1** SHARD, flake, fragment, splinter, paring, sliver, bit, fleck, shred, scrap, snippet. **2** NICK, crack, notch, snick, scratch, splinter, gash, fault, flaw, dent. ▶v. **1** NICK, crack, notch, scratch, splinter, gash, damage, snick. **2** CHISEL, whittle, hew.

chivalrous adj. **1** COURTEOUS, polite, gallant, gentlemanly, gracious, well man-

chloride n. a compound of chlorine with another substance.

chlorinate v. disinfect water with chlorine.

chlorine n. a green gaseous chemical element.

chloroform n. a liquid used as a solvent and formerly as an anaesthetic.

chlorophyll n. a green pigment in plants which allows them to convert sunlight into energy.

chock n. a wedge or block placed against a wheel to prevent it from moving. □ **chock-a-block** informal crammed full.

chocolate n. **1** a dark brown food made from roasted cacao seeds, eaten as a sweet, or made into a drink. **2** a sweet covered with chocolate.

choice n. **1** an act of choosing. **2** the right or ability to choose. **3** a range from which to choose. **4** something chosen. ▶adj. of very good quality.

choir n. **1** an organized group of singers. **2** the part of a church used by a choir.

choke v. **1** prevent someone from breathing by blocking their throat. **2** have trouble breathing. **3** fill or clog up. ▶n. a valve controlling the flow of air into a petrol engine.

choker n. a close-fitting necklace or neckband.

cholera n. an infectious disease causing severe vomiting and diarrhoea.

choleric adj. irritable.

cholesterol n. a substance found in animal tissue, an excess of which is believed to cause disease of the arteries.

chomp v. munch noisily.

choose v. (**choosing**, **chose**; past part. **chosen**) select as being the best of the available alternatives.

choosy adj. (**choosier**, **choosiest**) informal very careful in making a choice.

chop v. (**chopping**, **chopped**) **1** cut into pieces with a knife or axe. **2** hit with a short, downward stroke. ▶n. **1** a downward cutting blow. **2** a thick slice of meat, usu. including a rib.

chopper n. **1** a short large-bladed axe. **2** informal a helicopter.

choppy adj. (of the sea) having many small waves.

chopstick n. each of a pair of thin sticks used as eating utensils in China, Japan, etc.

chop suey n. a Chinese-style dish of meat fried with vegetables.

choral adj. sung by a choir.

chorale n. a simple, stately hymn tune.

chord n. a group of three or more notes sounded together.

chore n. a routine or boring task.

choreograph /ko-ri-uh-grahf/ v. compose the sequence of steps and moves for a dance. ■ **choreographer** n. **choreography** n.

chorister n. a member of a choir.

chortle v. chuckle.

chorus n. (pl. **choruses**) **1** the refrain of a song. **2** something said at the same time by many people. **3** a group of singers or dancers in a musical or opera. ▶v. say the same thing as a group.

chose past of **choose**.

chosen past part. of **choose**.

choux pastry /shoo/ n. light pastry, used for eclairs.

chow n. **1** informal food. **2** a Chinese breed of dog with a tail curled over its back.

chowder n. thick soup containing fish or clams.

Thesaurus

nered, thoughtful, protective. **2** COURT-LY, knightly, courageous, brave, valiant, heroic, daring, intrepid, honourable, just, fair, constant, true, magnanimous. ■ OPPOSITES rude, boorish.

choice n. **1** SELECTION, option, choosing, preference, picking, election, adoption. **2** ALTERNATIVE, option, possibility, solution, answer, way out. **3** VARIETY, range, selection, assortment, mixture, store, supply, display, array, miscellany. ▶adj. BEST, excellent, superior, first-rate, first-class, prize, prime, select, special, exclusive, rare, hand-picked. ■ OPPOS-ITES inferior.

choke v. **1** STRANGLE, asphyxiate, throttle, suffocate, smother, stifle. **2** GAG, gasp, retch, struggle for air, asphyxiate, suffocate. **3** CLOG, congest, jam, block, obstruct, fill up, constrict, plug, stop up.

choose v. SELECT, pick, pick on/out, decide on, opt for, settle on, agree on, fix on, plump for, prefer, designate, elect, single out, adopt, espouse, hand-pick, name, nominate, vote for, show a preference for.

choosy adj. FUSSY, particular, discriminating, exacting, finicky, pernickety, fastidious, hard to please, selective, discerning; informal picky.

chop v. **1** CUT DOWN, fell, hack down, hew, bring down, saw down, lop, split. **2** CUT UP, dice, cube, fragment, crumble. **3** see CUT (2).

choppy adj. ROUGH, turbulent, stormy,

chow mein /mayn/ n. a Chinese-style dish of fried noodles with shredded meat etc.

Christ n. the title given to Jesus.

christen v. name a baby at baptism.

Christendom n. old use the worldwide body of Christians.

Christian adj. of or believing in Christianity. ▶n. a believer in Christianity. □ **Christian name** a forename.

Christianity n. the religion based on the teaching and works of Jesus.

Christmas n. an annual Christian festival celebrating Jesus's birth, held on 25 December.

chromatic adj. **1** (of a musical scale) rising or falling by semitones. **2** of or produced by colour.

chromatography n. a technique for separating a mixture by passing it through a material in which the components move at different rates. ■ **chromatographic** adj.

chrome n. a hard shiny coating made from chromium.

chromium n. a hard white metallic element.

chromosome n. a thread-like structure in a cell nucleus, carrying the genes.

chronic adj. **1** (of an illness etc.) lasting a long time. **2** having a chronic illness or habit. **3** informal very bad. ■ **chronically** adv.

chronicle n. a record of historical events. ▶v. record a series of events. ■ **chronicler** n.

chronological adj. following the order in which things occurred. ■ **chronologically** adv.

chronology n. the arrangement of events in order of occurrence.

chronometer n. an instrument for measuring time.

chrysalis n. (pl. **chrysalises**) **1** an insect pupa, esp. of a butterfly or moth. **2** the hard case enclosing this.

chrysanthemum n. a garden plant with bright flowers.

chubby adj. (**chubbier**, **chubbiest**) plump and rounded.

chuck v. **1** informal throw carelessly. **2** touch playfully under the chin. ▶n. **1** a device holding something in a lathe or a tool in a drill. **2** a cut of beef from the neck to the ribs.

chuckle v. laugh quietly. ▶n. a quiet laugh.

chuff v. (of a steam engine) move with a regular puffing sound.

chuffed adj. informal pleased.

chug v. (**chugging**, **chugged**) (of a vehicle) move slowly with muffled regular sounds.

chum n. informal a close friend. ■ **chummy** adj.

chump n. informal a foolish person.

chunk n. **1** a thick, solid piece. **2** a large amount. ■ **chunky** adj.

church n. **1** a building for public Christian worship. **2** (**Church**) a particular Christian organization. **3** (**the Church**) Christians collectively. □ **churchwarden** a member of a parish congregation assisting with church business. **churchyard** an enclosed area surrounding a church, used for burials.

churlish adj. rude or bad-tempered. ■ **churlishly** adv. **churlishness** n.

churn n. **1** a machine for making butter by shaking milk or cream. **2** a large metal milk can. ▶v. **1** shake milk or cream in a churn to produce butter. **2** (of liquid) move about vigorously. **3** (**churn out**) produce mechanically and in large quantities.

Thesaurus

squally, blustery, tempestuous. ■ OPPOSITES calm.

chorus n. **1** CHOIR, ensemble, choral group, choristers, singers, vocalists. **2** REFRAIN, response.

christen v. BAPTIZE, anoint, name, dub, call, designate, style, term.

chronic adj. **1** PERSISTENT, long-lasting, long-standing, lingering, continual, constant, incessant, deep-rooted, deep-seated, ingrained. **2** HABITUAL, inveterate, confirmed, hardened. **3** BAD, dreadful, appalling, awful, atrocious. ■ OPPOSITES acute.

chronicle n. RECORD, account, history, story, description, calendar, annals, narrative, journal, archive, log. ▶v. RECORD, report, document, set down, relate, tell about, register.

chronological adj. CONSECUTIVE, in sequence, sequential, ordered, historical, serial, progressive.

chubby adj. PLUMP, tubby, flabby, dumpy, paunchy, fleshy, stout, portly, rotund. *See also* FAT. ■ OPPOSITES skinny.

chunk n. LUMP, piece, block, hunk, slab, square, portion, mass, wedge; informal dollop.

church n. PLACE OF WORSHIP, house of God, cathedral, chapel, abbey, minster, temple, tabernacle, mosque, synagogue.

chute n. a sloping channel for moving things to a lower level.

chutney n. (pl. **chutneys**) a spicy sauce made of fruit or vegetables with vinegar and sugar.

CIA abbrev. (in the US) Central Intelligence Agency.

ciabatta /chuh-**bah**-tuh/ n. a flat Italian bread made with olive oil.

ciao /chow/ exclam. hello or goodbye.

cicada /si-**kah**-duh/ n. a chirping insect like a grasshopper.

cicatrix (also **cicatrice**) n. (pl. **cicatrices**) a scar.

CID abbrev. (in the UK) Criminal Investigation Department.

cider n. an alcoholic drink made from fermented apple juice.

cigar n. a cylinder of tobacco in tobacco leaves for smoking.

cigarette n. a cylinder of finely cut tobacco in paper for smoking.

cinch n. informal **1** a very easy task. **2** a certainty.

cinder n. a piece of partly burnt coal or wood.

cine adj. of film-making.

cinema n. **1** a theatre where films are shown. **2** the production of films as an art or industry.

cinematography n. the art of camerawork in film-making. ■ **cinematographer** n.

cinnamon n. a spice made from the bark of an Asian tree.

cipher (or **cypher**) n. **1** a code. **2** an unimportant person or thing.

circa prep. approximately.

circle n. **1** a perfectly round plane figure. **2** a curved upper tier of seats in a theatre. **3** a group with shared interests, friends, etc. ▶v. **1** move or be placed all the way around. **2** draw a line around.

circlet n. a circular band worn on the head.

circuit n. **1** a roughly circular route. **2** a motor-racing track. **3** a system of components forming a complete path for an electric current. **4** a series of sporting events.

circuitous /ser-**kyoo**-i-tuhss/ adj. (of a route) long and indirect.

circuitry n. electric circuits.

circular adj. **1** having the form of a circle. **2** (of an argument) false because using as evidence the point to be proved. ▶n. a letter or leaflet sent to a large number of people.

circulate v. **1** move continuously through a closed system or area. **2** pass from place to place or person to person.

circulation n. **1** movement around something. **2** the continuous movement of blood round the body. **3** the public availability of something. **4** the number of copies sold of a newspaper etc.

circumcise v. cut off the foreskin or clitoris of. ■ **circumcision** n.

circumference n. **1** the boundary of a circle. **2** the distance of this.

circumflex n. the accent (ˆ).

circumlocution n. the use of many words where fewer would do.

circumnavigate v. sail all the way around. ■ **circumnavigation** n.

circumscribe v. restrict; limit.

circumspect adj. cautious; sensible.

Thesaurus

churlish adj. RUDE, impolite, boorish, oafish, ill-mannered, discourteous, surly, curt, sullen, brusque. ■ OPPOSITES polite.

churn v. **1** BEAT, whip up, agitate, stir up, shape up, disturb. **2** SEETHE, foam, boil, froth, swirl, toss, convulse.

cinema n. FILMS, movies, pictures, motion pictures; informal silver screen, big screen.

circle n. **1** RING, disc, round, loop, circumference, ball, globe, sphere, orb. **2** GROUP, circle of friends, set, company, crowd, ring, coterie, clique, assembly, fellowship, class. ▶v. **1** MOVE ROUND, revolve, rotate, orbit, circumnavigate, wheel, gyrate, whirl, pivot, swivel. **2** SURROUND, ring, encircle, enclose, envelop, hedge in, hem in, gird, belt, circumscribe.

circuit n. LAP, round, cycle, loop, circumference, turn, ambit.

circuitous adj. WINDING, indirect, meandering, roundabout, twisting, tortuous, rambling, zigzag, labyrinthine, maze-like, serpentine. ■ OPPOSITES direct.

circular adj. ROUND, spherical, spheroid, ring-shaped, globular, annular. ▶n. PAMPHLET, leaflet, notice, advertisement.

circulate v. **1** SPREAD, spread round, make known, broadcast, publish, distribute, give out, disseminate, propagate, issue, pronounce, advertise; informal put about. **2** MOVE/GO ROUND, flow, revolve, rotate, whirl, gyrate.

circumference n. PERIMETER, border, boundary, periphery, bounds, limits, confines, edge, rim, verge, margin, fringe, outline, skirt, circuit, compass, extremity.

circumstance n. a fact or condition connected with an event or action.

circumstantial adj. (of evidence) suggesting but not proving something.

circumvent v. evade a difficulty.

circus n. (pl. **circuses**) a travelling show with acrobats, trained animals, and clowns.

cirque n. a steep-sided hollow on a mountain.

cirrhosis /si-roh-siss/ n. a liver disease.

cirrus /sir-ruhss/ n. (pl. **cirri**) a high wispy cloud.

cistern n. a water storage tank.

citadel n. a fortress overlooking a city.

cite v. 1 quote as evidence. 2 mention as an example. ■ **citation** n.

citizen n. 1 a person with full rights in a country. 2 an inhabitant of a town or city. ■ **citizenship** n.

citrus n. (pl. **citruses**) a fruit of a group including lemons, oranges, etc. ■ **citric** adj.

city n. (pl. **cities**) 1 a large town, esp. one created by charter and containing a cathedral. 2 (**the City**) the part of London that is a centre of finance and business.

civet /siv-it/ n. 1 a cat native to Africa and Asia. 2 a strong perfume obtained from its glands.

civic adj. of a city or town.

civil adj. 1 of civilians. 2 polite. □ **civil engineer** an engineer who designs roads, bridges, etc. **civil servant** a member of the civil service. **civil service** the departments that carry out the work of the government. **civil war** a war between people of the same country. ■ **civilly** adv.

civilian n. a person not in the armed services or the police force.

civility n. (pl. **civilities**) politeness.

civilization (or **-isation**) n. 1 an advanced stage of social development. 2 the process of achieving this. 3 a civilized nation or area.

civilize (or **-ise**) v. 1 bring to an advanced stage of social development. 2 (**civilized**) polite and good-mannered.

CJD abbrev. Creutzfeldt–Jakob disease, a fatal brain disease.

cl abbrev. centilitre.

clack v. & n. (make) a sharp sound as of a hard object striking another.

clad adj. clothed.

cladding n. a covering or coating on a structure or material.

claim v. 1 assert, without giving proof. 2 demand as one's right. ▶ n. 1 an assertion. 2 a demand for something to which one has a right. ■ **claimant** n.

Thesaurus

circumspect adj. CAUTIOUS, wary, careful, guarded, vigilant, watchful, prudent, suspicious, apprehensive, observant, leery, chary, judicious, politic. ■ OPPOSITES unguarded.

circumstances pl. n. 1 SITUATION, set of affairs, conditions, facts, position, context, occurrence, event, background, particulars, surroundings. 2 STATE, situation, conditions, financial position, plight, predicament, means, resources, station.

circumstantial adj. INDIRECT, incidental, presumed, conjectural, inferential.

citadel n. FORTRESS, fort, fortification, stronghold, bastion, castle, tower, keep, fastness.

citation n. QUOTATION, quote, reference, extract, excerpt, allusion, passage, source.

cite v. QUOTE, mention, refer to, allude to, name, adduce, specify, excerpt, extract.

citizen n. SUBJECT, national, native, passport-holder, resident, inhabitant, denizen, dweller, householder, taxpayer, voter, freeman, freewoman, burgher, burgess.

city n. TOWN, conurbation, metropolis,

urban area, municipality; *informal* concrete jungle, urban sprawl.

civil adj. 1 POLITE, courteous, well mannered, well bred, gentlemanly, ladylike, refined, urbane, polished, cultured, cultivated, cordial, civilized, genial, pleasant. 2 CIVIC, public, municipal, community, local. ■ OPPOSITES rude.

civility n. COURTESY, politeness, courteousness, good manners, graciousness, cordiality, pleasantness, geniality, affability, amiability, urbanity, gallantry. ■ OPPOSITES rudeness.

civilization n. 1 DEVELOPMENT, advancement, progress, enlightenment, culture, cultivation, refinement, sophistication. 2 SOCIETY, culture, community, nation, country, people, way of life.

civilize v. ENLIGHTEN, educate, cultivate, instruct, improve, refine, polish, domesticate, socialize, humanize, edify.

civilized adj. ENLIGHTENED, advanced, developed, cultured, cultivated, educated, sophisticated, refined, sociable, urbane, well behaved. ■ OPPOSITES uncivilized, barbarous.

claim v. 1 DEMAND, request, ask for, lay claim to, require, insist on, command,

clairvoyant n. a person claiming the power to see into the future. ■ **clairvoyance** n.

clam n. a shellfish with a hinged shell. ▶ v. (**clam up**) informal refuse to talk.

clamber v. climb with difficulty.

clammy adj. unpleasantly damp and sticky.

clamour (US **clamor**) n. **1** a loud confused noise. **2** a strong protest or demand. ▶ v. make a clamour. ■ **clamorous** adj.

clamp n. a device for holding something tightly. ▶ v. **1** fasten with a clamp. **2** fit a clamp to the wheel of a car to immobilize it. **3** (**clamp down**) take strict action to prevent something.

clan n. a group of related families.

clandestine adj. done secretly.

clang n. & v. (make) a loud metallic sound.

clanger n. informal a mistake.

clangour (US **clangor**) n. a continuous clanging sound.

clank n. & v. (make) a sharp sound as of pieces of metal striking together.

clap v. (**clapping, clapped**) **1** strike the palms of the hands together repeatedly, esp. to applaud. **2** slap on the back. ▶ n. **1** an act of clapping. **2** a sharp sound of thunder. □ **clapped-out** informal worn out. **claptrap** nonsense

clapper n. the striking part of a bell. □ **clapperboard** hinged boards struck together at the start of filming to synchronize picture and sound machinery.

claret n. a dry red wine.

clarify v. (**clarifying, clarified**) **1** make easier to understand. **2** melt butter to separate out the impurities. ■ **clarification** n.

clarinet n. a woodwind instrument. ■ **clarinettist** n.

clarion adj. loud and clear.

clarity n. clearness.

clash v. **1** come into violent conflict. **2** disagree. **3** look or sound unpleasant together. **4** (of events) occur inconveniently at the same time. ▶ n. an act or sound of clashing.

clasp v. **1** grasp tightly with one's hand. **2** place one's arms tightly around. **3** fasten with a clasp. ▶ n. **1** a device with interlocking parts used for fastening. **2** an act of clasping.

class n. **1** a group of things having a common characteristic. **2** a social rank. **3** a group of students taught together. **4** a lesson. **5** informal impressive stylishness. ▶ v. put in a category. □ **classless** not divided into social classes. **classroom** a room in which a class of students or pupils is taught. ■ **classy** adj. (informal).

classic adj. **1** of recognized high quality. **2** typical. ▶ n. **1** a work of art recognized as being of high quality. **2** (**Classics**) the study of ancient Greek and Latin literature etc. ■ **classicism** n. **classicist** n.

Thesaurus

exact, requisition. **2** PROFESS, maintain, state, declare, assert, aver, allege, protest, insist, contend, hold, avow, affirm, postulate.

clairvoyant noun PSYCHIC, fortune teller, crystal-gazer; medium, spiritualist; telepath.

clamber v. SCRAMBLE, climb, scrabble, scale, ascend, mount, shin, shinny, claw one's way.

clammy adj. MOIST, damp, humid, sweaty, sticky, close, muggy, dank.

clamour n. NOISE, uproar, outcry, racket, row, din, shouts, shouting, yelling, babel, commotion, hubbub, hullabaloo, brouhaha, vociferation. ▶ v. SHOUT, yell, call/cry out, exclaim.

clamp n. VICE, press, brace, clasp, fastener, hasp. ▶ v. GRIP, hold, press, squeeze, clench, fix, secure, make fast.

clandestine adj. SECRET, undercover, surreptitious, furtive, concealed, hidden, underhand, cloak-and-dagger.

clarify v. **1** MAKE CLEAR, explain, clear up, make plain, illuminate, resolve, throw light on, make simple, simplify. **2** PURIFY, refine. ■ OPPOSITES confuse.

clash v. **1** BANG, strike, crash, clang, clatter, rattle, jangle. **2** FIGHT, contend, quarrel, wrangle, do battle, feud, grapple, cross swords. **3** see COINCIDE.

clasp n. **1** CATCH, fastener, fastening, clip, hook, buckle, pin, hasp. **2** EMBRACE, hug, cuddle, hold, grip, grasp. ▶ v. EMBRACE, hug, squeeze, clutch, grip, grasp, hold.

class n. **1** CATEGORY, group, sort, type, kind, set, division, order, rank, classification, grade, section, denomination, species, genus, genre, domain. **2** SOCIAL ORDER/DIVISION, rank, stratum, level, status, standing, station, group, grouping, caste, lineage, pedigree, descent. **3** QUALITY, excellence, distinction, ability, stylishness, elegance, chic. ▶ v. see CLASSIFY.

classic adj. **1** EXCELLENT, memorable, notable, lasting, brilliant, finest, first-

classical adj. **1** of ancient Greek or Latin literature etc. **2** (of music) written in the formal European tradition. ■ **classically** adv.

classify v. (**classifying**, **classified**) **1** divide or arrange according to class. **2** designate as officially secret. ■ **classifiable** adj. **classification** n. **classifier** n.

clatter n. a loud rattling sound as of hard objects striking each other. ▶ v. make a clatter.

clause n. **1** a distinct part of a sentence, with its own verb. **2** a single part of a treaty, law, or contract.

claustrophobia n. extreme fear of being in an enclosed place. ■ **claustrophobic** adj.

clavichord n. an early keyboard instrument.

clavicle n. the collarbone.

claw n. **1** a curved horny nail on an animal's or bird's foot. **2** the pincer of a shellfish. ▶ v. scratch or tear at with a claw or hand.

clay n. sticky earth used for making bricks and pottery. □ **clay pigeon** a piece of baked clay thrown up as a target for shooting.

clean adj. **1** free from dirt or harmful substances. **2** not obscene or immoral. ▶ v. make clean. ■ **cleaner** n. **cleanliness** /klen-li-nuhss/ n. **cleanly** adv.

cleanse v. **1** make clean. **2** rid of something unpleasant or unwanted.

clear adj. **1** easy to see, hear, or understand. **2** leaving or feeling no doubt. **3** transparent. **4** free of marks, obstructions, or anything unwanted. ▶ v. **1** make or become clear. **2** get past or over. **3** prove innocent. **4** give official approval to. □ **clear off** informal go away. **clear out 1** empty. **2** informal leave quickly. **clearway** a main road on which vehicles are not allowed to stop. ■ **clearly** adv.

Thesaurus

rate, first-class, outstanding, exemplary, consummate, masterly, legendary, immortal. **2** TYPICAL, archetypal, definitive, standard, model, stock, prototypical, paradigmatic, copybook. **3** TRADITIONAL, simple, timeless, ageless, enduring, abiding, long-lasting, time-honoured, long-established. ▶ n. MASTERPIECE, master work, great work, standard work.

classical adj. **1** ANCIENT, Greek, Grecian, Hellenic, Attic, Roman, Latin. **2** SERIOUS, symphonic, traditional, highbrow. **3** ELEGANT, balanced, well proportioned, symmetrical, austere, pure, simple, plain, harmonious, restrained.

classification n. CATEGORIZATION, ordering, organization, grouping, arrangement, grading, systemization, codification, tabulation, taxonomy.

classify v. CATEGORIZE, class, arrange, order, sort, organize, group, catalogue, systematize, type, rank, index, file, bracket.

clause n. SECTION, subsection, paragraph, article, item, point, passage, part, heading, provision, proviso, stipulation, note.

claw n. NAIL, talon, pincer, nipper, chela. ▶ v. SCRATCH, tear, scrape, lacerate, rip, maul.

clean adj. **1** UNSTAINED, spotless, unsoiled, unblemished, unsullied, immaculate, speckless, hygienic, sanitary, disinfected, sterile, sterilized, washed, cleansed, laundered, scrubbed. **2** PURE, clear, unpolluted, natural, unadulterated, uncontaminated, untainted. **3** GOOD, upright, virtuous, pure, decent, respectable, moral, upstanding, exemplary, chaste, undefiled. **4** UNUSED, unmarked, blank, untouched, new, vacant, void. **5** FAIR, honest, sporting, sportsmanlike, honourable. ■ OPPOSITES dirty. ▶ v. WASH, cleanse, wipe, sponge, scour, swab, dry-clean, launder, tidy, vacuum, hoover, dust, mop, sweep. ■ OPPOSITES dirty, soil.

cleanse v. WASH, clean, bathe, rinse, disinfect.

clear adj. **1** BRIGHT, cloudless, fine, fair, light, sunny, sunshiny. **2** TRANSPARENT, translucent, limpid, pellucid, crystalline, diaphanous. **3** OBVIOUS, plain, evident, apparent, sure, definite, unmistakable, beyond question, indisputable, patent, manifest, incontrovertible, irrefutable, palpable. **4** COMPREHENSIBLE, plain, intelligible, understandable, lucid, coherent, distinct. **5** OPEN, empty, unobstructed, unimpeded, free, unhindered, unlimited. **6** UNTROUBLED, undisturbed, innocent, guilt-free, guiltless, clean, peaceful, tranquil, serene, sinless, stainless. ■ OPPOSITES cloudy, opaque, vague. ▶ adv. **1** AWAY FROM, at a distance from, apart from, out of contact with. **2** COMPLETELY, entirely, fully, wholly, thoroughly. ▶ v. **1** UNBLOCK, unclog, unstop, clean out, free. **2** EMPTY, vacate, evacuate. **3** ACQUIT, absolve, discharge, let go, exonerate, vindicate, ex-

clearance n. **1** the act of clearing. **2** official authorization. **3** space allowed for one thing to pass another.

clearing n. an open space in a forest.

cleat n. **1** a projection for attaching a rope. **2** a projection on the sole of a shoe.

cleavage n. **1** the space between a woman's breasts. **2** a split.

cleave v. (**cleaving**, **clove** or **cleft** or **cleaved**; past part. **cloven** or **cleft** or **cleaved**) **1** divide; split. **2** (**cleave to**) stick fast or cling to.

cleaver n. a tool for chopping meat.

clef n. Music a symbol on a stave showing the pitch of the notes.

cleft adj. split. ▶ n. a split or crack. ▢ **cleft lip** a split in the upper lip, present from birth. **cleft palate** a split in the roof of the mouth, present from birth.

clematis n. a climbing plant with showy flowers.

clement adj. **1** (of weather) mild. **2** merciful. ■ **clemency** n.

clementine n. a variety of tangerine.

clench v. close one's fist or hold the teeth or muscles together tightly.

clerestory /kleer-stor-i/ n. (pl. **clere-stories**) an upper row of windows in a large church.

clergy n. the body of people ordained for religious duties in the Christian Church. ■ **clergyman** n.

cleric n. a priest or religious leader.

clerical adj. **1** of office work. **2** of the clergy.

clerk n. a person employed to do written work in an office.

clever adj. **1** quick to understand and learn. **2** skilled at doing something.

cliché /klee-shay/ n. an overused phrase or idea. ■ **clichéd** adj.

click n. **1** a short, sharp sound. **2** an act of pressing a button on a computer mouse. ▶ v. **1** make or cause to make a click. **2** press a computer mouse button. **3** informal become friendly.

client n. a person using the services of a professional person or organization.

clientele /klee-on-tel/ n. clients collectively.

cliff n. a steep rock face, esp. on the coast. ▢ **cliffhanger** a story or event that is exciting because its outcome is uncertain.

climate n. the regular weather conditions of an area. ■ **climatic** adj.

Thesaurus

cuse, pardon. **4** JUMP, vault, leap, hop, pass over. **5** AUTHORIZE, sanction, give consent to, approve, permit, allow, pass; informal go-ahead to.

clearance n. **1** CLEARING, removal, emptying, evacuation, eviction, depopulation, withdrawal. **2** GAP, space, headroom, allowance, margin, leeway, room to spare. **3** AUTHORIZATION, permission, consent, sanction, leave, endorsement; informal go-ahead, green light.

clear-cut adj. DEFINITE, specific, precise, explicit, unequivocal.

clearly adv. OBVIOUSLY, plainly, undoubtedly, undeniably, surely, certainly, incontestably, patently, incontrovertibly.

cleave v. SPLIT, crack, lay open, divide, hew, hack, chop/slice up, sever, sunder, rend.

cleft n. SPLIT, crack, fissure, gap, crevice, rift, break, fracture.

clemency n. MERCY, leniency, compassion, kindness, humanity, pity, sympathy, fairness, magnanimity, moderation, indulgence. ■ OPPOSITES ruthlessness.

clench v. GRIP, grasp, clutch, hold, seize, clamp, squeeze.

clergyman n. MINISTER, priest, pastor, preacher, vicar, rabbi, imam, cleric, churchman, churchwoman, man of the cloth, bishop, archbishop, cardinal, prelate, ecclesiastic, divine.

clerical adj. **1** OFFICE, secretarial. **2** ECCLESIASTICAL, spiritual, priestly, episcopal, churchly, pastoral, canonical, rabbinical, sacerdotal, apostolic, prelatic.

clever adj. **1** INTELLIGENT, bright, sharp, quick-witted, quick, gifted, talented, brilliant, able, capable, knowledgeable, educated, sagacious; informal brainy, smart. **2** SHREWD, cunning, ingenious, astute, skilful, skilled, resourceful, wily, inventive, subtle, canny, artful, adroit, guileful; informal foxy; US informal cute. **3** DEXTEROUS, skilful, deft, nimble, handy. ■ OPPOSITES stupid, awkward.

cliché n. HACKNEYED/WELL-WORN PHRASE, platitude, commonplace, banality, truism, saw, maxim; informal old chestnut.

click v. **1** CLINK, clack, snap, tick. **2** BECOME CLEAR, make sense, fall into place, come home to one. **3** TAKE TO EACH OTHER, get on, feel a rapport, be compatible, be on the same wavelength; informal hit it off. **4** BE SUCCESSFUL, prove popular, succeed, be a success, go down well.

client n. CUSTOMER, patron, regular, buyer, purchaser, shopper, consumer, user, patient.

climax n. the most intense, exciting, or important point. ▶v. reach a climax. ■ **climactic** adj.

climb v. go or come up to a higher position. ▶n. **1** an act of climbing. **2** a route up a mountain etc. ■ **climber** n.

clime n. literary a region in terms of its climate.

clinch v. settle conclusively. ▶n. **1** a tight hold in boxing. **2** an embrace.

cling v. (**clinging**, **clung**) (**cling to/on to**) **1** hold on tightly to. **2** stick. ■ **clingy** adj.

clinic n. a place where specialized medical treatment or advice is given.

clinical adj. **1** to do with the treatment of patients. **2** efficient and unemotional. ■ **clinically** adv.

clink n. & v. (make) a sharp ringing sound.

clinker n. the stony remains of burnt coal.

clip n. **1** a device for holding objects together or in place. **2** an act of cutting. **3** an excerpt of a film or broadcast. **4** informal a sharp blow. ▶v. (**clipping**, **clipped**) **1** fasten with a clip. **2** cut with shears or scissors. **3** hit sharply.

clipper n. **1** (**clippers**) a tool for clipping. **2** hist. a fast sailing ship.

clipping n. **1** a piece clipped off. **2** a newspaper cutting.

clique /rhymes with seek/ n. a small exclusive group.

clitoris n. the small sensitive organ just in front of the vagina.

cloak n. a loose sleeveless outer garment. ▶v. cover or hide. □ **cloakroom 1** a room where coats and bags may be left. **2** a room containing a toilet.

clobber informal n. clothing and personal belongings. ▶v. hit hard.

cloche /klosh/ n. a cover for protecting tender plants.

clock n. an instrument indicating time. ▶v. (**clock in/out** or **on/off**) register one's arrival at or departure from work. □ **clockwise** moving in the direction of the hands of a clock. **clockwork** a mechanism with a spring and toothed gearwheels, used to drive a clock etc.

clod n. a lump of earth.

clog n. a shoe with a thick wooden sole. ▶v. (**clogging**, **clogged**) block or become blocked.

cloister n. a covered passage round a courtyard in a convent, monastery, etc.

cloistered adj. **1** having a cloister. **2** sheltered from the outside world.

clone n. an animal or plant created from the cells of another, to which it is genetically identical. ▶v. **1** create as a clone. **2** make an identical copy of.

close adj. **1** near in space or time. **2** very affectionate or intimate. **3** careful and thorough. **4** humid or airless. **5** secretive. ▶adv. so as to be very near. ▶n. **1** a street closed at one end. **2** the grounds surrounding a cathedral. **3** the end of a period of time or an activity. ▶v. **1** move so as to cover an opening. **2** bring two parts of something together. **3** bring or come to an end. □ **closed-circuit television** a television system in which signals are sent by cable to a restricted set of monitors. **close-up** a photograph or film sequence taken at close range. ■ **closely** adv. **closeness** n. **closure** n.

Thesaurus

cliff n. PRECIPICE, rock face, crag, bluff, escarpment, scar, scarp, promontory, tor.

climate n. ATMOSPHERE, mood, environment, temper, spirit, feeling, ambience, aura, ethos.

climax n. CULMINATION, high point, crowning point, height, peak, pinnacle, summit, top, highlight, acme, zenith, apex, apogee, ne plus ultra. ■ OPPOSITES anticlimax, nadir.

climb v. **1** GO UP, ascend, mount, scale, clamber up, shin up. **2** RISE, increase, shoot up, soar. **3** SLOPE UPWARD, incline, bank. ■ OPPOSITES descend. □ **climb down 1** DESCEND, go down, shin down. **2** BACK DOWN, retreat, retract, eat one's words, eat humble pie.

clinch v. COMPLETE, settle, secure, seal, set the seal on, confirm, conclude, assure, cap, close, wind up.

cling v. STICK, adhere, hold, grip, clasp, clutch. □ **cling to** EMBRACE, clutch, hold on to, grasp, grip, cleave to.

clinic n. MEDICAL CENTRE, health centre, infirmary, surgery, sickbay.

clip[1] v. PIN, staple, fasten, fix, attach, hold. ▶n. FASTENER, clasp, pin.

clip[2] v. CUT, crop, trim, snip, shear, prune. ▶n. EXCERPT, cutting, snippet, fragment, portion, bit, passage, section, trailer.

clique n. COTERIE, in-crowd, set, group, gang, faction, band, ring, fraternity.

cloak n. **1** CAPE, robe, wrap, poncho, mantle. **2** COVER, screen, mask, veil, shroud, cloud, shield, disguise. ▶v. HIDE, conceal, cover, screen, mask, veil, shroud, shield, camouflage,

closet n. a cupboard or wardrobe. ▶ adj. secret. ▶ v. (**closeting, closeted**) shut away in private to talk to someone or to be alone.

clot n. **1** a thick mass of a semi-liquid substance, esp. blood. **2** informal a foolish or clumsy person. ▶ v. (**clotting, clotted**) form into clots. □ **clotted cream** thick cream made by heating milk slowly.

cloth n. (pl. **cloths**) **1** woven or felted fabric. **2** a piece of cloth for a particular purpose. **3** (**the cloth**) Christian priests as a group.

clothe v. **1** provide with clothes. **2** (**be clothed in**) be dressed in.

clothes pl. n. things worn to cover the body.

clothing n. clothes as a whole.

cloud n. **1** a white or grey mass of condensed watery vapour floating in the sky. **2** a mass of smoke, dust, etc. **3** a state or cause of gloom or anxiety. ▶ v. **1** become full of clouds. **2** make less clear. **3** become sad or gloomy. □ **cloudburst** a sudden violent rainstorm. ■ **cloudy** adj.

clout informal n. **1** a heavy blow. **2** power or influence. ▶ v. hit hard.

clove¹ n. **1** a dried bud of a tropical tree, used as a spice. **2** any of the divisions making up a compound bulb of garlic etc.

clove² past of CLEAVE. □ **clove hitch** a knot used to fasten a rope round a pole etc.

cloven past part. of CLEAVE. □ **cloven hoof** the divided hoof of animals such as cattle, sheep, etc.

clover n. a flowering plant with three-lobed leaves. □ **in clover** in ease and luxury.

clown n. an entertainer who does comical tricks. ▶ v. act comically or playfully. ■ **clownish** adj.

cloying adj. sickening because excessively sweet or sentimental.

club n. **1** a group who meet for a particular activity. **2** an organization providing benefits for members. **3** a nightclub with dance music. **4** a heavy stick used as a weapon. **5** a club used to hit the ball in golf. **6** (**clubs**) a suit of playing cards, represented by a black trefoil. ▶ v. (**clubbing, clubbed**) **1** (**club together**) combine with others to do

Thesaurus

obscure, disguise.

clog v. OBSTRUCT, block, jam, congest, stop up, plug, dam, bung up, impede, hinder, hamper.

close¹ adj. **1** NEAR, adjacent, neighbouring, in close proximity, adjoining, abutting, hard by. **2** SIMILAR, like, alike, near, comparable, corresponding, akin, parallel. **3** ACCURATE, precise, near, true, faithful, literal, conscientious. **4** INTIMATE, devoted, loving, inseparable, bosom, close-knit, confidential. **5** DENSE, condensed, crowded, compact, packed, solid, tight, cramped, congested, squeezed. **6** HARD-FOUGHT, well matched, evenly matched, sharply contested; informal neck-and-neck, nose-to-nose. **7** CAREFUL, keen, rigorous, thorough, vigilant, alert, concentrated, minute, detailed, intent, assiduous, painstaking, searching. **8** HUMID, muggy, airless, stuffy, suffocating, oppressive, stifling, musty, unventilated; informal fuggy. **9** MEAN, miserly, parsimonious, niggardly, penny-pinching, near; informal tight-fisted, tight, stingy. ■ OPPOSITES distant, remote.

close² v. **1** SHUT, slam, fasten, secure, lock, bolt, bar, latch. **2** SEAL OFF, stop up, obstruct, block, clog, choke. **3** END, bring to an end, conclude, finish, ter-

minate, wind up, adjourn, discontinue. **4** NARROW, lessen, grow smaller, dwindle, reduce. ■ OPPOSITES open.

closet n. CUPBOARD, wardrobe, cabinet, locker, storage room. ▶ v. SHUT AWAY, sequester, cloister, seclude, confine, isolate. ▶ adj. SECRET, undisclosed, hidden, concealed, furtive.

clot n. LUMP, clump, mass, obstruction, thrombus; informal glob. ▶ v. COAGULATE, set, congeal, solidify, thicken, jell, cake, curdle.

cloth n. FABRIC, material, textile, stuff.

clothe v. DRESS, attire, garb, robe, outfit, fit out, turn out, deck out, rig out, drape, accoutre; informal doll up, kit out; old use apparel. ■ OPPOSITES undress.

clothes pl. n. GARMENTS, clothing, dress, attire, apparel, costume, garb, wardrobe, outfit, finery, ensemble, vestments; informal get-up, gear, clobber, togs, weeds; dated raiment.

cloud n. **1** HAZE, pall, shroud, cloak, screen, cover. **2** SHADOW, threat, gloom, darkness.

cloudy adj. **1** OVERCAST, dark, grey, hazy, sombre, leaden, heavy, gloomy, dim, sunless, starless. **2** OPAQUE, murky, muddy, milky, turbid. **3** BLURRED, vague, indistinct, hazy, obscure, confused, muddled, nebulous. ■ OPPOSITES something. **2** go to nightclubs. **3** beat with a club. ■ **clubber** n.

cluck n. a short sound as made by a hen. ▶v. make a cluck.

clue n. a fact that helps solve a mystery or problem.

clump n. **1** a cluster of trees or plants. **2** a mass or lump. ▶v. **1** form into a clump. **2** tread heavily. ■ **clumpy** adj.

clumsy adj. (**clumsier**, **clumsiest**) **1** awkward in movement or performance. **2** difficult to use. ■ **clumsily** adv. **clumsiness** n.

clung past & past part. of CLING.

cluster n. a small close group of similar things. ▶v. form a cluster.

clutch v. grasp tightly. ▶n. **1** a tight grasp. **2** a mechanism for connecting and disconnecting the engine and the transmission system in a vehicle. **3** a group of eggs laid at one time. **4** a brood of chicks.

clutter n. things lying about untidily. ▶v. fill with clutter.

cm abbrev. centimetres.

Co. abbrev. **1** company. **2** county.

c/o abbrev. care of.

co- prefix joint; jointly.

coach n. **1** a long-distance bus. **2** a railway carriage. **3** a horse-drawn carriage. **4** an instructor or trainer in sport. **5** a private tutor. ▶v. train or teach as a coach.

coagulate /koh-ag-yoo-layt/ v. (of a liquid) thicken or become semi-solid. ■ **coagulant** n. **coagulation** n.

coal n. a hard black mineral burnt as fuel. □ **coalfield** a large area rich in underground coal.

coalesce v. form into a mass or whole.

coalition n. a temporary alliance, esp. of political parties.

coarse adj. **1** rough in texture. **2** consisting of large particles. **3** rude or vulgar. □ **coarse fish** any freshwater fish other than salmon and trout. ■ **coarsen** v.

coast n. land next to or near the sea.

Thesaurus

cloudless, clear.

clown n. **1** JESTER, fool, buffoon, harlequin, pierrot. **2** JOKER, comedian, comic, humorist, funny man, prankster, wag, wit.

club¹ n. SOCIETY, group, association, organization, circle, set, league, union, federation, fellowship, fraternity, brotherhood, sisterhood, sorority. □ **club together** COMBINE, join forces, pool resources, divide costs; informal have a whip-round.

club² n. CUDGEL, baton, truncheon, bludgeon, staff; informal cosh. ▶v. see HIT.

clue n. SIGN, lead, hint, indication, indicator, suggestion, pointer, evidence, information, guide, tip, tip-off, suspicion, trace, inkling.

clump n. CLUSTER, bunch, bundle, collection, group, mass, assembly, assemblage.

clumsy adj. **1** AWKWARD, uncoordinated, ungainly, blundering, inept, bungling, bumbling, maladroit, fumbling, lumbering, heavy-handed, unhandy, unskilful, inexpert, graceless, ungraceful; informal cack-handed, ham-fisted, like a bull in a china shop, butterfingered. **2** UNWIELDY, awkward, cumbersome, bulky, heavy, solid, inconvenient, inelegant, ponderous; informal hulking. **3** CRUDE, boorish, crass, inappropriate, ill-judged, tactless, graceless, insensitive, uncouth, inept, gauche, unpolished. ■ OPPOSITES graceful, adroit.

cluster n. BUNCH, clump, group, collection, gathering, crowd, assembly, assemblage, knot. ▶v. GATHER, collect, assemble, congregate, group, come together, flock together.

clutch v. GRIP, grasp, clasp, cling to, hang on to, clench. □ **clutch at** GRAB, seize, catch at, snatch at, claw at, reach for.

clutches pl. n. HANDS, power, control, hold, grip, grasp, claws, possession, keeping, custody.

clutter n. MESS, jumble, litter, disorder, junk, untidiness, chaos, confusion, heap, odds and ends, hotchpotch, tangle. ▶v. LITTER, make untidy, make a mess of, be strewn about, be scattered about; informal mess up.

coach¹ n. BUS, carriage; dated omnibus; historical charabanc.

coach² n. INSTRUCTOR, trainer, teacher, tutor, mentor. ▶v. INSTRUCT, train, teach, tutor, guide, prepare, direct, drill, cram, prime, put someone through their paces.

coagulate v. CONGEAL, clot, thicken, set, gel, solidify, stiffen, curdle.

coalesce v. COMBINE, unite, join together, blend, fuse, amalgamate, integrate, affiliate, commingle.

coalition n. UNION, alliance, league, affiliation, association, federation, bloc, confederacy, amalgamation, merger, conjunction, fusion.

coarse adj. **1** ROUGH, uneven, harsh,

▶v. move easily without using power.
□ **coastguard** an organization or person that keeps watch over coastal waters. ■ **coastal** adj.

coaster n. **1** a small mat for a glass. **2** a ship that trades along the coast.

coat n. **1** a long outer garment with sleeves. **2** an animal's covering of fur or hair. **3** a covering layer. ▶v. cover with a layer. □ **coat of arms** a design on a shield as the emblem of a family or institution.

coating n. a covering layer.

coax v. **1** persuade gently. **2** manipulate carefully.

coaxial /koh-ak-si-uhl/ adj. (of a cable) having two wires, one wrapped around the other but separated by insulation.

cob n. **1** a round loaf of bread. **2** the central part of an ear of maize. **3** a hazelnut. **4** a sturdy short-legged horse.

cobalt n. a silvery-white metallic element.

cobble n. a small round stone used to cover road surfaces. ▶v. (**cobble together**) roughly assemble from available parts. ■ **cobbled** adj.

cobbler n. a person whose job is mending shoes.

cobra n. a poisonous snake native to Africa and Asia.

cobweb n. a spider's web.

cocaine n. a drug used as an illegal stimulant.

coccyx /kok-siks/ n. the bone at the base of the spine.

cochineal /koch-i-neel/ n. red food colouring made from the crushed bodies of an insect.

cock n. **1** a male chicken or game bird. **2** a firing lever in a gun. ▶v. **1** tilt or bend. **2** set a gun ready for firing. □ **cock-a-hoop** extremely pleased.

cockade n. a rosette worn on a hat as a badge.

cockatoo n. a crested parrot.

cockerel n. a young domestic cock.

cockeyed adj. informal **1** crooked. **2** impractical.

cockle n. an edible shellfish.

cockney n. (pl. **cockneys**) **1** a person from the East End of London. **2** the dialect or accent used in this area.

cockpit n. **1** a compartment for the pilot and crew in an aircraft. **2** the driver's compartment in a racing car.

cockroach n. a beetle-like insect.

cocksure adj. arrogantly confident.

cocktail n. **1** a mixed alcoholic drink. **2** a mixture.

cocky adj. (**cockier**, **cockiest**) conceited. ■ **cockily** adv.

cocoa n. **1** a powder made from roasted and ground cacao seeds. **2** a hot drink made from this.

coconut n. the large brown seed of a tropical palm, with edible white flesh.

cocoon n. **1** a silky sheath around a chrysalis. **2** a protective covering. ▶v. wrap in a cocoon.

cod n. (pl. **cod**) a large edible sea fish.

coda n. the final part of a musical composition.

coddle v. treat in an overprotective way.

code n. **1** a system of words, figures, or symbols used to represent others for secrecy. **2** a sequence of numbers dialled to connect a telephone line with another exchange. **3** a set of laws or rules.

codeine n. a painkilling drug.

codex n. (pl. **codices** /koh-di-seez/ or **codexes**) an ancient manuscript text in book form.

codicil n. an addition or alteration to a will.

codify v. (**codifying**, **codified**) organize laws or rules into a system.

co-education n. the education of pupils of both sexes together. ■ **co-educational** adj.

coefficient n. **1** a quantity multiplying

Thesaurus

lumpy, bristly, prickly, gritty, hairy, shaggy, scratchy. **2** RUDE, ill-mannered, uncivil, boorish, loutish, uncouth, crass, churlish. **3** VULGAR, indecent, obscene, crude, smutty, offensive, indelicate, bawdy, immodest, unrefined, earthy, ribald, lewd, improper, foul, prurient, pornographic; informal blue, raunchy. ■ OPPOSITES fine, refined.

coast n. SHORE, seashore, coastline, shoreline, beach, foreshore, seaboard, water's edge; literary strand. ▶v. GLIDE, cruise, freewheel, drift, taxi, sail, skim,

slide.

coat n. **1** JACKET, overcoat. **2** FUR, hair, wool, fleece, hide, pelt. **3** LAYER, covering, coating, overlay, film, patina, veneer, wash, glaze, finish, membrane. ▶v. see COVER.

coax v. CAJOLE, persuade, wheedle, beguile, inveigle, talk into, induce, entice, win over, prevail upon; informal sweettalk, soft-soap.

cocky adj. ARROGANT, conceited, egotistical, vain, swollen-headed, boastful, cocksure, swaggering, brash. ■ OPPOSITES the variable in an algebraic expression. **2** a multiplier or factor that measures a particular property.

coelacanth /seel-uh-kanth/ n. a large sea fish.

coerce v. persuade by using force or threats. ■ **coercion** n. **coercive** adj.

coeval adj. of the same age or date of origin.

coexist v. exist together, esp. harmoniously. ■ **coexistence** n.

C. of E. abbrev. Church of England.

coffee n. **1** a hot drink made from the roasted and ground seeds of a tropical shrub. **2** these seeds.

coffer n. **1** a small chest for holding valuables. **2** (**coffers**) financial resources.

coffin n. a box in which a dead body is buried or cremated.

cog n. a wheel or bar with projections on its edge, which engage with projections on another wheel or bar.

cogent adj. logical and convincing. ■ **cogency** n. **cogently** adv.

cogitate v. think deeply. ■ **cogitation** n.

cognac /kon-yak/ n. French brandy.

cognate adj. connected or related.

cognition n. acquisition of knowledge through thought or perception. ■ **cognitive** adj.

cognizance (or **-isance**) n. knowledge or awareness. ■ **cognizant** adj.

cognoscenti /kon-yuh-shen-ti/ pl. n. people well informed about a particular subject.

cohabit v. live together and have a sexual relationship without being married. ■ **cohabitation** n.

cohere v. hold firmly together; form a whole.

coherent adj. **1** logical and consistent. **2** articulate. ■ **coherence** n. **coherently** adv.

cohesion n. the state of being coherent. ■ **cohesive** adj.

cohort n. **1** a tenth part of an ancient Roman legion. **2** a large group of people.

coiffure /kwah-fyoor/ n. a hairstyle.

coil n. **1** a length of something wound in a spiral. **2** a contraceptive device placed in the womb. ▶v. arrange or form into a coil.

coin n. a flat metal disc used as money. ▶v. **1** make coins by stamping metal. **2** invent a new word or phrase.

coinage n. **1** coins as a whole. **2** the process of making coins. **3** a system of coins in use. **4** a newly invented word or phrase.

coincide v. **1** happen at the same time or place. **2** be the same or similar.

coincidence n. **1** a chance occurrence of events or circumstances at the same time. **2** the fact of two or more things coinciding. ■ **coincidental** adj.

coir /koy-uh/ n. coconut fibre.

coitus n. sexual intercourse. ■ **coital** adj.

coke n. **1** a solid fuel made by heating coal in the absence of air. **2** informal cocaine.

Thesaurus

modest.

code n. **1** CIPHER, secret writing, cryptograph. **2** SYSTEM, laws, rules, regulations, rule book.

coerce v. FORCE, compel, pressure, pressurize, drive, bully, intimidate, frighten, terrorize, browbeat, impel, constrain, oblige; *informal* lean on, twist someone's arm, strong-arm, put the screws on.

coffer n. BOX, chest, case, casket, strongbox, safe, trunk, cabinet.

cogent adj. CONVINCING, persuasive, compelling, forceful, effective, conclusive, indisputable, sound, unanswerable, powerful, strong, weighty, potent, influential, telling, authoritative, well argued. ■ OPPOSITES unconvincing.

coherent adj. LOGICAL, rational, reasoned, consistent, lucid, articulate, systematic, orderly, structured, well structured, well ordered, cohesive, or-

ganized, comprehensible, intelligible, unified, integrated. ■ OPPOSITES incoherent, muddled.

cohort n. TROOP, brigade, squad, squadron, group, company, body, band, legion, column.

coil v. LOOP, wind, spiral, curl, twist, snake, turn, wreathe, entwine, twine, convolute.

coin n. **1** PIECE, bit. **2** CHANGE, small/loose change, silver, copper, coppers, coinage, specie. ▶v. **1** MINT, stamp, mould, die, forge. **2** INVENT, create, make up, devise, conceive, originate, introduce, think/dream up, formulate, concoct, produce, fabricate.

coincide v. **1** OCCUR SIMULTANEOUSLY, fall together, be concurrent, concur, coexist, synchronize, happen together, clash. **2** AGREE, accord, match, correspond, concur, square, tally, harmonize.

coincidence n. CHANCE, accident, luck,

col n. the lowest point between two peaks of a mountain ridge.

colander n. a bowl with holes in it, used for draining food.

cold adj. **1** at a low temperature. **2** not feeling or showing emotion. **3** without preparation. ▶ n. **1** cold weather or surroundings. **2** an infection causing running at the nose and sneezing. □ **cold-blooded 1** (of reptiles and fish) having a body temperature varying with that of the environment. **2** heartless and cruel. **cold sore** an inflamed blister in or near the mouth. **cold turkey** informal unpleasant effects caused by the abrupt withdrawal of an addictive drug. **cold war** the hostility between the countries allied to the Soviet Union and the Western powers after the Second World War. ■ **coldly** adv. **coldness** n.

coleslaw n. a salad of shredded raw cabbage in dressing.

coley n. an edible sea fish.

colic n. severe abdominal pain. ■ **colicky** adj.

collaborate v. work together on an activity. ■ **collaboration** n. **collabora-**tive adj. **collaborator** n.

collage /kol-lahzh/ n. a form of art in which various materials are arranged and stuck to a backing.

collagen n. a protein found in animal tissue.

collapse v. **1** fall down suddenly. **2** fail and come to a sudden end. ▶ n. an instance of collapsing.

collapsible adj. able to be folded down.

collar n. **1** a band of material round the neck of a garment. **2** a band put round the neck of a domestic animal. ▶ v. informal seize or arrest.

collate v. collect and combine texts or information. ■ **collation** n.

collateral n. something promised if one cannot repay a loan. ▶ adj. additional but less important.

colleague n. a person with whom one works.

collect v. **1** bring or come together. **2** buy or find items of a particular kind as a hobby. **3** call for and take away. **4** (**collected**) calm. ■ **collectable** (or **collectible**) adj. & n. **collection** n. **collector** n.

Thesaurus

fluke, fortuity, serendipity.

coincidental adj. ACCIDENTAL, chance, unintentional, unplanned, lucky, casual, fortuitous, serendipitous.

cold adj. **1** CHILLY, cool, freezing, bitter, icy, chill, wintry, frosty, raw, perishing, biting, glacial, numbing, piercing, frigid, inclement, windy, Siberian, crisp, sunless, polar; informal nippy, parky. **2** SHIVERY, shivering, cool, chilly, chilled, freezing, frozen, frozen stiff, frostbitten. **3** DISTANT, reserved, aloof, remote, unfriendly, unresponsive, unfeeling, unemotional, indifferent, dispassionate, stand-offish, frigid, glacial, passionless, unmoved, unexcitable, phlegmatic, lukewarm, apathetic, spiritless, unsympathetic, uncaring, heartless, callous, cold-hearted, stony-hearted, inhospitable. ■ OPPOSITES hot, warm.

cold-blooded adj. RUTHLESS, callous, savage, inhuman, barbaric, heartless, pitiless, merciless, hard-hearted. ■ OPPOSITES kind, humane.

collaborate v. **1** COOPERATE, work together, join forces, join, unite, combine; informal team up, pull together. **2** COL-LUDE, connive, turn traitor, conspire, fraternize; informal help.

collaborator n. **1** CO-WORKER, colleague, associate, fellow worker, part-ner, helper, confederate, accomplice, team mate, co-author; humorous partner in crime. **2** TRAITOR, turncoat, quisling, colluder, fraternizer, conspirator; informal Judas, blackleg.

collapse v. **1** FALL IN/DOWN, cave in, give way, crumple, disintegrate, subside, buckle, tumble down, fall to pieces, come apart, break up, fold up, sink, give in. **2** FAINT, pass out, black out, fall down, lose consciousness, swoon; informal keel over. **3** BREAK DOWN, fail, fold, fall through, founder, come to nothing, crash; informal flop. ▶ n. **1** CAVE-IN, fall-in, subsidence, disintegration, break-up. **2** FAINTING, loss of consciousness, swoon. **3** BREAKDOWN, failure, disintegration, foundering.

collate v. ARRANGE, put in order, order, sort, categorize.

colleague n. CO-WORKER, fellow worker, associate, workmate, partner, collaborator, confederate.

collect v. **1** PUT TOGETHER, gather, accumulate, pile up, assemble, stockpile, amass, store, hoard, put by, save, reserve, heap up, aggregate. **2** COME TO-GETHER, gather, assemble, congregate, converge, mass, flock together, convene, rally. **3** RAISE, gather, solicit, obtain, acquire, secure. **4** FETCH, call for,

collective adj. **1** done by or relating to all the members of a group. **2** taken as a whole. □ **collective noun** a singular noun that refers to a group of individuals (e.g. *staff, family*).

college n. an educational establishment providing higher education or specialized training. ■ **collegiate** adj.

collide v. hit when moving.

collie n. a breed of sheepdog with long hair.

colliery n. (pl. **collieries**) a coal mine.

collision n. an instance of colliding.

colloquial adj. (of language) used in ordinary conversation. ■ **colloquialism** n. **colloquially** adv.

collude v. come to a secret understanding, esp. to cheat or deceive. ■ **collusion** n.

cologne /kuh-**lohn**/ n. a light perfume.

colon n. **1** a punctuation mark (:). **2** the main part of the large intestine. ■ **colonic** adj.

colonel /**ker**-nuhl/ n. a rank of army officer above a lieutenant colonel.

colonial adj. of a colony or colonialism.

colonialism n. the practice of acquiring or maintaining colonies. ■ **colonialist** n. & adj.

colonize (or **-ise**) v. **1** establish a colony in. **2** take over for one's own use. ■ **colonist** n. **colonization** n.

colonnade n. a row of columns.

colony n. (pl. **colonies**) **1** a country under the control of another and occupied by settlers from there. **2** a group of people of one nationality or race living in a foreign place. **3** a community of animals or plants of one kind living close together.

coloration (or **colouration**) n. colouring.

coloratura n. elaborate ornamentation of a vocal melody, e.g. in opera.

colossal adj. extremely large.

colossus n. (pl. **colossi** or **colossuses**) a person or thing of enormous size.

colostomy n. (pl. **colostomies**) an operation in which the colon is shortened and the cut end diverted to an opening in the abdominal wall.

colour (US **color**) n. **1** an object's property of producing different sensations on the eye as a result of the way it reflects or gives out light. **2** one, or any mixture, of the parts into which light can be separated. **3** pigmentation. ▸ v. **1** give a colour to. **2** blush. **3** influence, esp. in a bad way. □ **colour-blind** unable to distinguish between certain colours.

colourant (US **colorant**) n. a dye.

coloured (US **colored**) adj. **1** having a colour or colours. **2** dated or offens. wholly or partly of non-white descent.

colourful (US **colorful**) adj. **1** full of colours. **2** lively and exciting. ■ **colourfully** adv.

colourless (US **colorless**) adj. **1** with-

Thesaurus

go and get, pick up, bring. ■ OPPOSITES disperse.

collected adj. COMPOSED, cool, poised, unperturbed, serene, unruffled, unshaken. *See also* CALM.

collection n. **1** ACCUMULATION, pile, stockpile, store, stock, supply, heap, hoard, mass, conglomeration, array, aggregation. **2** DONATIONS, contributions, gifts, offerings, alms.

collective adj. JOINT, united, combined, shared, common, cooperative, concerted, collaborative, corporate, aggregate. ■ OPPOSITES individual.

college n. UNIVERSITY, polytechnic, institute, college of further education, school, conservatory.

collide v. CRASH, come into collision, bang into, smash into, knock into, run into, slam into, cannon into.

collision n. CRASH, impact, accident, smash, pile-up, bump, scrape, knock, clash, wreck.

colloquial adj. CONVERSATIONAL, infor-mal, casual, familiar, chatty, everyday, idiomatic, demotic, vernacular. ■ OPPOSITES formal.

collusion n. COMPLICITY, connivance, collaboration, secret understanding, plotting, intrigue; *informal* cahoots.

colonize v. OCCUPY, settle, populate, people, subjugate, pioneer, open up, found.

colony n. **1** DEPENDENCY, possession, settlement, territory, province, dominion, protectorate, satellite state. **2** COMMUNITY, group, ghetto, quarter.

colossal adj. ENORMOUS, huge, immense, gigantic, vast, massive, mammoth, gargantuan, monumental, prodigious, monstrous, titanic, mountainous, towering, elephantine, Brobdingnagian. ■ OPPOSITES small.

colour n. **1** HUE, tint, shade, tone, tinge, coloration, colouring, pigmentation, pigment. **2** PINKNESS, rosiness, redness, ruddiness, blush, flush, glow, bloom. ▸ v. **1** TINT, dye, paint, colour-wash, out colour. **2** dull.

colt n. a young male horse.

column n. **1** an upright pillar. **2** a long line of people or vehicles. **3** a vertical division of a page. **4** a regular section of a newspaper or magazine.

columnist n. a journalist who writes a column in a newspaper or magazine.

coma n. long-lasting deep unconsciousness.

comatose adj. in a coma.

comb n. **1** an object with a row of narrow teeth for tidying the hair. **2** a domestic fowl's fleshy crest. ▶v. **1** tidy with a comb. **2** search thoroughly.

combat n. fighting, esp. between armed forces. ▶v. (**combating**, **combated**) take action against. ■**combatant** n. **combative** adj.

combe (or **coomb**) /koom/ n. a short valley.

combination n. **1** the act of combining things. **2** something made up of distinct elements. □ **combination lock** a lock opened using a specific sequence of letters or numbers.

combine v. join or mix together. ▶n. a group acting together for a commercial purpose. □ **combine harvester** a farming machine that reaps and threshes in one operation.

combustible adj. able to catch fire.

combustion n. **1** burning. **2** rapid chemical combination with oxygen, involving the production of heat.

come v. (**coming**, **came**; past part. **come**) **1** move towards or into a place near the speaker. **2** arrive. **3** happen. **4** achieve a specified position. □ **come about** happen. **come across 1** give a particular impression. **2** find by chance. **comeback 1** a return to fame or popularity. **2** a quick reply. **come by** manage to get. **comedown** informal a loss of status. **come into** inherit. **come off** succeed. **come out** (of a fact) become known. **come round 1** recover consciousness. **2** be persuaded. **come to** recover consciousness. **come up** occur. **comeuppance** informal deserved punishment.

comedian n. (fem. **comedienne**) an en-

Thesaurus

tinge, stain, shade, pigment. **2** INFLUENCE, affect, prejudice, distort, bias, slant, taint, sway, pervert, warp.

colourful adj. **1** BRIGHT, vivid, intense, brilliant, vibrant, multi-coloured, deep-coloured, iridescent, psychedelic, gaudy, variegated. **2** VIVID, graphic, lively, interesting, animated, rich, striking, picturesque, stimulating, telling. **3** INTERESTING, eccentric, unusual, flamboyant, dynamic, flashy. ■OPPOSITES colourless, dull.

colourless adj. **1** UNCOLOURED, achromatic, white, bleached, faded. **2** DULL, boring, uninteresting, tame, lifeless, dreary, insipid, lacklustre, characterless, vapid, vacuous. ■OPPOSITES colourful.

column n. **1** PILLAR, post, support, upright, shaft, pilaster, obelisk, caryatid. **2** LINE, row, file, queue, procession, train, rank, string, progression, cavalcade. **3** ARTICLE, piece, item, feature, editorial, leader, leading article.

comb v. **1** GROOM, arrange, tidy, smarten up, spruce up, untangle, curry, dress. **2** SEARCH, hunt through, scour, ransack, rummage, rake, sift, go over with a fine-tooth comb.

combat n. BATTLE, fighting, conflict, hostilities, fight, clash, skirmish, duel, contest, engagement, encounter. ▶v. FIGHT, battle against, oppose, resist, contest,

make a stand against, stand up to, grapple with, struggle against, tackle, withstand, defy, strive against.

combative adj. AGGRESSIVE, belligerent, pugnacious, bellicose, quarrelsome, argumentative, antagonistic, contentious, truculent. ■OPPOSITES conciliatory.

combination n. **1** BLEND, mixture, compound, amalgamation, amalgam, mix, alloy, composite, aggregate, fusion, marriage, synthesis, concoction. **2** UNION, association, alliance, federation, merger, grouping, confederation, confederacy, cooperation, coalition, partnership, league, consortium, syndication.

combine v. **1** JOIN, join forces, unite, form an alliance, get together, cooperate, ally, pool resources, associate, unify, integrate; informal team up, gang together, club together. **2** MIX, blend, add together, fuse, compound, mingle, merge, amalgamate, bind, alloy, bond, incorporate, synthesize, interweave. ■OPPOSITES separate, part.

combustible adj. FLAMMABLE, inflammable, incendiary, explosive. ■OPPOSITES incombustible.

come v. **1** MOVE TOWARDS, approach, advance, draw near, near, reach, bear down on, close in on. **2** ARRIVE, appear, turn up, put in an appearance, materialize; informal show up, fetch up, blow in.

tertainer who makes people laugh.

comedy n. (pl. **comedies**) an amusing film, play, or other entertainment.

comely adj. old use attractive.

comestibles pl. n. food.

comet n. a mass of ice and dust with a long tail, moving around the solar system.

comfort n. **1** a state of physical ease. **2** consolation for grief or anxiety. **3** something giving comfort. ▶v. make less unhappy. ■ **comforter** n.

comfortable adj. **1** giving or enjoying physical comfort. **2** free from financial worry. ■ **comfortably** adv.

comfy adj. (**comfier**, **comfiest**) informal comfortable.

comic adj. **1** causing laughter. **2** of comedy. ▶n. **1** a comedian. **2** a children's magazine with comic strips. □ **comic strip** a sequence of drawings telling an amusing story. ■ **comical** adj. **comically** adv.

comma n. a punctuation mark (,).

command v. **1** give an order. **2** be in charge of a military unit. **3** be in a position to receive. ▶n. **1** an order. **2** authority. **3** a group of officers in control of a particular group or operation. **4** the ability to use or control something.

commandant /kom-muhn-dant/ n. an officer in charge of a force or institution.

commandeer v. officially take possession of.

commander n. **1** a person in command. **2** a rank of naval officer next below captain.

commandment n. a divine rule.

commando n. (pl. **commandos**) a soldier trained for carrying out raids.

commemorate v. honour the memory of. ■ **commemoration** n. **commemorative** adj.

commence v. begin. ■ **commencement** n.

commend v. **1** praise. **2** recommend. ■ **commendable** adj. **commendably** adv. **commendation** n.

Thesaurus

3 BE AVAILABLE, be made, be produced, be on offer. ■ OPPOSITES go, leave. □ **come about** see HAPPEN. **come across** see MEET, FIND. **come clean** see CONFESS.

comedian n. **1** COMIC, stand-up comedian, humorist. **2** WIT, wag, joker, clown, jester; informal laugh; informal, dated card.

comedy n. HUMOUR, joking, funniness, wit, wittiness, fun, farce, hilarity, levity, slapstick, clowning, buffoonery, facetiousness, drollery.

comfort n. **1** EASE, well-being, affluence, contentment, tranquillity, luxury, opulence, serenity, repose, cosiness, plenty, sufficiency. **2** SOLACE, help, support, sympathy, consolation, succour, cheer, condolence, relief, easement, alleviation, gladdening. ▶v. HELP, support, bring comfort to, console, sympathize with, solace, reassure, succour, cheer, soothe, hearten, gladden, assuage. ■ OPPOSITES distress.

comfortable adj. **1** WELL FITTING, snug, loose-fitting, roomy. **2** COSY, homely, snug, relaxing, tranquil. **3** PLEASANT, well off, affluent, prosperous, well-to-do, luxurious, opulent, free from hardship, untroubled, happy, contented. ■ OPPOSITES uncomfortable.

comic adj. FUNNY, humorous, amusing, entertaining, comical, witty, hilarious, farcical, jocular, hysterical, diverting, joking, droll, zany, side-splitting, ridiculous, facetious, whimsical, uproarious, waggish; informal rich, priceless. ■ OPPOSITES serious. ▶n. see COMEDIAN.

command v. **1** ORDER, give orders to, direct, instruct, charge, require, prescribe, ordain, demand, compel, bid, summon, enjoin, adjure. **2** BE IN CHARGE OF, have charge of, control, have control of, lead, head, rule, direct, supervise, manage, govern, preside over, superintend. ▶n. **1** ORDER, instruction, decree, directive, edict, direction, dictate, injunction, requirement, prescription, bidding, mandate, fiat, commandment, precept. **2** CHARGE, control, authority, power, direction, mastery, government, management, supervision, administration, dominion, sway, domination, ascendancy. **3** KNOWLEDGE, grasp, mastery.

commander n. LEADER, head, chief, director, officer-in-charge; informal boss, top dog, kingpin, big cheese. See also CHIEF.

commemorate v. CELEBRATE, remember, honour, salute, mark, memorialize, pay tribute to, pay homage to, immortalize, solemnize.

commence v. BEGIN, start, initiate, originate, embark on, go ahead, inaugurate, launch; informal set the ball rolling, get the show on the road. ■ OPPOSITES finish, end, conclude.

commend v. PRAISE, applaud, speak highly of, acclaim, extol, compliment,

commensurable adj. measurable by the same standard.

commensurate adj. corresponding or in proportion.

comment n. a remark expressing an opinion or reaction. ▶v. express an opinion or reaction.

commentary n. (pl. **commentaries**) **1** the expression of opinions about an event. **2** a broadcast account of an event as it happens. **3** a set of notes on a text.

commentate v. provide a commentary on an event. ■ **commentator** n.

commerce n. the activity of buying and selling.

commercial adj. **1** of or engaged in commerce. **2** intended to make a profit. ▶n. a television or radio advertisement. ■ **commercially** adv.

commercialize (or **-ise**) v. manage in a way designed to make a profit. ■ **commercialization** n.

commiserate v. express sympathy or pity. ■ **commiseration** n.

commission n. **1** an instruction, command, or duty. **2** an order for something to be produced. **3** a group of people given official authority to do something. **4** payment to an agent for selling goods or services. **5** a warrant conferring the rank of military officer. ▶v. **1** order or authorize the production of. **2** bring into working order. **3** (**commissioned**) having the rank of military officer. □ **out of commission** not in use or working order.

commissionaire n. a uniformed door attendant at a hotel, theatre, etc.

commissioner n. **1** a member of a commission. **2** a representative of the highest authority in an area.

commit v. (**committing**, **committed**) **1** carry out a crime etc. **2** bind to a course of action. **3** (**committed**) dedicated to a cause, activity, etc. **4** entrust or consign. **5** send to prison or a psychiatric hospital.

commitment n. **1** dedication to a cause, activity, etc. **2** a promise. **3** an obligation.

....

☑ Two *ms*, but only one *t* in the middle: *commitment*.

....

committal n. the sending of someone to prison or a psychiatric hospital.

committee n. a group of people appointed for a particular function by a larger group.

....

☑ Double *m*, double *t*: *committee*.

....

commode n. a seat with a concealed chamber pot.

commodious adj. spacious.

commodity n. (pl. **commodities**) **1** an article that can be bought and sold. **2** something valuable.

commodore n. **1** a naval rank above captain and below rear admiral. **2** the president of a yacht club.

common adj. **1** occurring, found, or done often; not rare. **2** ordinary. **3** lacking refinement; vulgar. **4** shared. ▶n. a piece of open land for public use. □ **common law** law derived from custom and precedent. **the Common Market** the European Union. **common room** a room in a school or college for students or staff to use outside teaching hours. **common sense** good sense in practical matters. **commonwealth** **1** an independent state. **2** (**the Commonwealth**) an association of the UK and independent states formerly under British rule.

Thesaurus

....

approve of, eulogize; *formal* laud. ■ OPPOSITES criticize.

commendable adj. ADMIRABLE, praiseworthy, laudable, creditable, worthy, estimable, meritorious, reputable, deserving. ■ OPPOSITES reprehensible.

comment v. **1** SAY, observe, state, remark, speak, express an opinion on, interpose, interject, opine. **2** EXPLAIN, annotate, write notes, interpret, elucidate, clarify, shed light on. ▶n. **1** REMARK, opinion, observation, view, statement, reaction, criticism, animadversion. **2** NOTE, annotation, explanation, interpretation, footnote, gloss, expos-

ition, interpolation, marginalia.

commentary n. **1** NARRATION, description, account, review, analysis. **2** ANNOTATION, notes, interpretation, analysis, critique, elucidation, exegesis.

commerce n. BUSINESS, trade, trading, dealing, dealings, financial transactions, buying and selling, merchandising, trafficking.

commercial adj. **1** BUSINESS, trade, profit-making, marketing, mercantile, merchandising, sales. **2** PROFIT-ORIENTATED, materialistic, mercenary, mercantile. ▶n. ADVERTISEMENT, advertising break; *informal* ad, advert, plug.

commoner n. an ordinary person as opposed to an aristocrat.

commonly adv. usually.

commonplace adj. ordinary. ▶n. a cliché.

commotion n. noisy confusion or disturbance.

communal adj. shared or done by a group. ■ **communally** adv.

commune n. a group of people living together and sharing possessions and responsibilities. ▶v. communicate mentally or spiritually.

communicable adj. able to be transmitted to others.

communicant n. a person who receives Holy Communion.

communicate v. 1 share or exchange information. 2 pass on or convey an emotion, disease, etc. 3 (**communicating**) (of two rooms) having a common connecting door.

communication n. 1 the act of communicating. 2 a letter or message. 3 (**communications**) means of travelling or sending information.

communicative adj. willing to talk or give information.

communion n. 1 the sharing of thoughts and feelings. 2 (also **Holy Communion**) the Christian sacrament at which bread and wine are shared.

Thesaurus

commission n. 1 TASK, employment, piece of work, work, duty, charge, mission, responsibility. 2 PERCENTAGE, brokerage, share, fee, compensation; informal cut, rake-off. 3 PERFORMANCE, perpetration, execution, committal. ▶v. 1 ENGAGE, employ, appoint, contract, book, authorize. 2 ORDER, place an order for, contract for, authorize, pay for.

commit v. 1 PERFORM, carry out, perpetrate, execute, enact, effect, do. 2 ENTRUST, trust, deliver, hand over, give, consign, assign, transfer. □ **commit oneself** PROMISE, pledge, engage, bind oneself, obligate oneself, covenant.

commitment n. 1 DEDICATION, involvement in, devotion, zeal, loyalty, allegiance, adherence. 2 PROMISE, pledge, undertaking, vow, assurance, guarantee, covenant. 3 OBLIGATION, duty, responsibility, undertaking, appointment, arrangement, liability, task, engagement, tie.

committed adj. DEDICATED, enthusiastic, devoted, keen, passionate, resolute, earnest, single-minded, whole-hearted, unwavering, ardent, zealous; informal card-carrying. ■ OPPOSITES apathetic.

common adj. 1 ORDINARY, average, normal, conventional, typical, unexceptional, plain, commonplace, run-of-the-mill, simple, habitual, undistinguished, unsurprising, pedestrian, humdrum, everyday, workaday, customary, stock; informal common or garden. 2 WIDESPREAD, general, universal, popular, accepted, prevalent, prevailing, shared, public, communal, collective. 3 VULGAR, coarse, rude, uncouth, unrefined, boorish, churlish, inferior, disreputable, lower-class, plebeian, lowly, proletarian; informal yobbish. ▶n. PARK, heath, parkland.

commonplace adj. ORDINARY, unexceptional, undistinguished, routine, pedestrian, mediocre, dull, uninteresting, humdrum, trite, hackneyed. ■ OPPOSITES remarkable.

commotion n. DISTURBANCE, racket, uproar, disorder, chaos, tumult, clamour, pandemonium, rumpus, hubbub, riot, fracas, hullabaloo, row, furore, brouhaha, confusion, upheaval, disruption, bother, turmoil, agitation, contretemps, excitement, fuss, disquiet, ferment, bustle, hustle and bustle; informal to-do, bedlam, stir, palaver.

communal adj. COMMON, collective, shared, joint, general, public, community, cooperative. ■ OPPOSITES individual, private.

communicable adj. INFECTIOUS, contagious, catching, transmittable, transmissible, transferable.

communicate v. 1 MAKE KNOWN, pass on, convey, spread, impart, get across, publish, transmit, broadcast, announce, report, relay, disseminate, proclaim, promulgate, divulge, disclose, express, mention, reveal, intimate, transfer. 2 GET ONE'S IDEAS/MESSAGE ACROSS, talk, get in touch, converse, confer, correspond, commune, have dealings, interface. 3 TRANSMIT, pass on, spread, give, infect with, transfer. 4 CONNECT, be connected, lead to, adjoin, abut on.

communication n. 1 CONTACT, interaction, getting in touch, link, dissemination, communion. 2 MESSAGE, dispatch, letter, report, statement, news, information, data, intelligence, word.

communicative adj. TALKATIVE, chatty, open, frank, candid, expansive, forthcoming, voluble, loquacious, informative, conversational. ■ OPPOSITES un-

communiqué /kuh-myoo-ni-kay/ n. an official announcement or statement.

communism n. **1** a political system whereby all property is owned by the community. **2** a system of this kind derived from Marxism. ■ **communist** n. & adj.

community n. (pl. **communities**) **1** a group of people living together in one place or having a common religion or race. **2** the people of an area considered as a group; society. **3** similarity of attitudes or interests.

commute v. **1** travel regularly between one's home and place of work. **2** reduce a judicial sentence to a less severe one. ■ **commuter** n.

compact adj. closely and neatly packed together. ▶v. compress. ▶n. **1** a small flat case for face powder. **2** a formal agreement. □ **compact disc** a small disc on which music or other digital information is stored.

companion n. **1** a person with whom one spends time or travels. **2** a thing intended to complement another. □ **companionway** a staircase from a ship's deck down to a lower deck. ■ **companionship** n.

companionable adj. friendly.

company n. (pl. **companies**) **1** a commercial business. **2** being with others in an enjoyable way. **3** a division of an infantry battalion. **4** a group of actors, singers, or dancers.

comparable adj. similar.

comparative adj. **1** involving or measured by comparison. **2** (of an adjective or adverb) expressing a higher degree of a quality (e.g. *braver*). ■ **comparatively** adv.

 comparative, not *-itive*.

compare v. **1** assess the similarity between. **2** be similar to. ■ **comparison** n.

compartment n. a separate section of a structure or container.

compass n. **1** a device showing the direction of magnetic north. **2** a hinged instrument for drawing circles. **3** range or scope.

compassion n. pity and concern. ■ **compassionate** adj.

compatible adj. **1** able to exist or be used together. **2** consistent. ■ **compatibility** n.

compatriot n. a person from the same

Thesaurus

communicative, reserved.

communion n. EMPATHY, rapport, sympathy, affinity, closeness, togetherness, unity, accord, concord, fellowship, harmony, fusion.

commute v. **1** TRAVEL TO AND FROM, travel back and forth, shuttle. **2** LESSEN, reduce, shorten, curtail, mitigate, modify.

compact[1] adj. **1** DENSE, compressed, condensed, packed close, tight-packed, solid, firm, close, consolidated. **2** CONCISE, succinct, terse, brief, condensed, pithy, to the point, epigrammatic, abridged, abbreviated, compendious. **3** SMALL, neat, portable, handy. ■ OPPOSITES loose, rambling, large.

compact[2] n. AGREEMENT, contract, pact, covenant, treaty, alliance, bargain, deal, settlement, entente.

companion n. ESCORT, friend, partner, consort, chaperone, confederate, colleague, associate, ally, crony, comrade. **2** COUNTERPART, fellow, match, twin, complement, mate.

companionship n. FRIENDSHIP, company, fellowship, togetherness, society, camaraderie, intimacy, rapport, comradeship.

company n. **1** BUSINESS, firm, organization, corporation, conglomerate, consortium, concern, enterprise, house, establishment, partnership, syndicate. **2** *see* COMPANIONSHIP. **3** VISITORS, callers, guests. **4** GROUP, band, party, body, association, society, troupe, fellowship, circle, collection, league, crew, guild. **5** ASSEMBLY, gathering, audience, crowd, group, throng.

comparable adj. SIMILAR, like, parallel, analogous, related, equivalent, matching, compatible, commensurable, corresponding, proportionate, proportional, cognate. ■ OPPOSITES dissimilar.

compare v. **1** CONTRAST, make a comparison between, measure against, juxtapose, differentiate, collate. **2** BEAR COMPARISON, be comparable, be the equal of, be on a par, be in the same class, compete, approach, match, come up to; *informal* hold a candle to.

comparison n. **1** CONTRAST, juxtaposition, correlation, distinction, collation, differentiation. **2** RESEMBLANCE, likeness, similarity, correlation, analogy, comparability.

compassionate adj. TENDER, gentle, kindly, soft-hearted, understanding, country.

compel v. (**compelling**, **compelled**) force.

compelling adj. attracting much attention or admiration.

compendious adj. giving much information in a concise way.

compendium n. (pl. **compendiums** or **compendia**) **1** a collection of facts on a subject. **2** a collection of similar items.

compensate v. **1** give a payment to reduce the bad effect of loss, injury, etc. **2** offset something undesirable with an opposite force or effect. ■ **compensation** n.

compère /kom-pair/ n. a person who introduces the acts in a variety show. ▶v. act as a compère for.

compete v. try to gain or win something by defeating others.

competent adj. **1** having the necessary skill or knowledge. **2** satisfactory. ■ **competence** n. **competently** adv.

competition n. **1** the act of competing. **2** an event in which people compete. **3** one's rivals in such an event.

competitive adj. **1** involving competition. **2** keen to be more successful than others. ■ **competitively** adv. **competitiveness** n.

competitor n. a person or organization that competes.

compile v. produce a book, record, etc. by assembling material from other sources. ■ **compilation** n. **compiler** n.

complacent adj. uncritically self-satisfied. ■ **complacency** n. **complacently** adv.

complain v. **1** express dissatisfaction. **2** (**complain of**) state that one is suffering from a symptom. ■ **complainant** n.

complaint n. **1** an act of complaining. **2** an illness.

complaisant adj. willing to please others.

complement n. **1** a thing that completes or improves something. **2** the full number required. ▶v. add to in a way that improves. ■ **complementary** adj.

....

☑ Don't confuse **complement** and **compliment**, which means 'politely congratulate or praise'.

....

complete adj. **1** having all necessary

Thesaurus

sympathetic, humane, pitying, lenient, charitable, benevolent.

compatible adj. **1** WELL SUITED, suited, like-minded, in agreement, in tune, of the same mind, in harmony. **2** CONSISTENT, in keeping, reconcilable, consonant, congruent, congruous. ■ OPPOSITES incompatible.

compel v. FORCE, make, coerce, drive, pressure, pressurize, order, constrain, impel, oblige, press, necessitate, urge; *informal* put the screws on, strong-arm, railroad, bulldoze.

compelling adj. **1** FASCINATING, gripping, enthralling, hypnotic, mesmerizing. **2** CONVINCING, telling, forceful, powerful, weighty, conclusive, irrefutable, cogent. ■ OPPOSITES boring, weak.

compensate v. **1** RECOMPENSE, repay, reimburse, make amends, make up for, atone, redress, make restitution, make reparation, make good, expiate, requite. **2** OFFSET, counterbalance, counteract, balance, cancel out, neutralize, counterpoise, nullify.

compensation n. **1** RECOMPENSE, damages, repayment, reimbursement, indemnification, requital. **2** AMENDS, restitution, redress, atonement, expiation.

compete v. **1** TAKE PART, be a contestant, participate, enter, go in for; *informal*

throw one's hat in the ring. **2** CONTEND, struggle, fight, oppose, rival, be in competition, vie, strive. ■ OPPOSITES cooperate.

competent adj. CAPABLE, able, proficient, skilful, skilled, adept, accomplished, qualified, expert, efficient, effective, trained, workmanlike. ■ OPPOSITES incompetent, inept.

competition n. **1** CONTEST, match, game, heat, tournament, championship, event, meet, quiz, race, rally, trial, challenge. **2** CONTENTION, opposition, rivalry, contest, struggle, vying, strife.

competitive adj. **1** AMBITIOUS, aggressive, combative, antagonistic, hard-fought, keen, cut-throat, lively, contentious. **2** REASONABLE, moderate, fair, comparable, similar, average. ■ OPPOSITES uncompetitive.

competitor n. **1** CONTESTANT, contender, challenger, participant, candidate. **2** RIVAL, opponent, adversary, antagonist, opposition.

compile v. COLLECT, gather, accumulate, amass, assemble, put together, marshal, organize, arrange, collate, anthologize.

complain v. **1** CRITICIZE, make/lodge a complaint, find fault, carp, make a fuss; *informal* kick up a fuss. **2** GRUMBLE, whine, lament, bewail; *informal* moan, gripe, parts. **2** finished. **3** to the greatest degree. ▶v. **1** make complete. **2** fill in a form. ■ **completely** adv. **completion** n.

complex adj. **1** consisting of many parts. **2** hard to understand. ▶n. **1** a group of buildings. **2** an interlinked system. **3** a set of repressed feelings affecting behaviour. ■ **complexity** n.

complexion n. **1** the condition of the skin of a person's face. **2** the general character of something.

compliant adj. **1** excessively obedient. **2** complying with rules. ■ **compliance** n.

complicate v. make complicated.

complicated adj. involving many confusing aspects.

complication n. **1** a factor that complicates something. **2** a secondary disease which makes an existing one worse.

complicity n. involvement in wrong-doing. ■ **complicit** adj.

compliment n. an expression of praise or admiration. ▶v. give a compliment to.

✓ Don't confuse **compliment** with **complement**, which means 'add to in a way that improves'.

complimentary adj. **1** expressing a compliment. **2** free of charge.

comply v. (**complying**, **complied**) act in accordance with a request or law.

component n. a part of a larger whole.

comport v. (**comport oneself**) behave in a particular way.

compose v. **1** create a piece of music or poetry. **2** make up a whole. **3** arrange in an orderly or artistic way. **4** (**composed**) calm and controlled. ■ **composer** n.

Thesaurus

grouch, grouse, bellyache, bitch.

complaint n. **1** GRIEVANCE, criticism, protest, accusation, charge, remonstrance, objection, grumble; *informal* gripe, grouse, moan, beef, whine, whinge. **2** ILLNESS, disease, sickness, ailment, disorder, affliction, malady, infection, malaise. *See also* ILLNESS.

complement n. **1** COMPANION, addition, supplement, accessory, finishing/final touch. **2** AMOUNT, total, allowance, aggregate, load, capacity, quota. ▶v. COMPLETE, round/set off, go well with, add the finishing/final touch to, supplement.

complementary adj. MATCHING, compatible, finishing, perfecting, interdependent, reciprocal.

complete adj. **1** ENTIRE, whole, full, total, intact, comprehensive, undivided, uncut, unshortened, unabridged, unexpurgated. **2** FINISHED, completed, accomplished, achieved, done, concluded, ended, finalized. **3** ABSOLUTE, utter, total, out-and-out, downright, thorough, thoroughgoing, unmitigated, unqualified, sheer, rank, dyed-in-the-wool. ■ OPPOSITES partial. ▶v. **1** FINISH, conclude, end, accomplish, achieve, do, perform, execute, fulfil, effect, discharge, realize, settle, clinch; *informal* wrap up, polish off. **2** ROUND OFF, finish off, make perfect, crown, cap, add the final/finishing touch.

completely adv. TOTALLY, utterly, absolutely, thoroughly, quite, wholly, altogether.

complex adj. **1** COMPLICATED, difficult, in-tricate, convoluted, involved, knotty, puzzling, perplexing, cryptic, problematic, enigmatic, tortuous, labyrinthine; *informal* tricky. **2** COMPOSITE, compound, elaborate, multiple, manifold, heterogeneous, multiplex. ■ OPPOSITES simple, elementary.

complicate v. MAKE DIFFICULT, confuse, make involved/intricate, muddle, jumble, entangle, compound; *informal* snarl up, screw up. ■ OPPOSITES simplify.

complicated adj. see COMPLEX.

complication n. **1** PROBLEM, difficulty, obstacle, snag, drawback, setback. **2** CONFUSION, difficulty, complexity, muddle, intricacy.

compliment n. PRAISE, tribute, admiration, flattery, commendation, congratulations, accolade, honour, plaudits, bouquet, testimonial, eulogy, panegyric, encomium. ▶v. CONGRATULATE, praise, speak highly of, commend, flatter, acclaim, honour, pay tribute to, salute, admire, sing someone's praises, extol, felicitate, eulogize; *formal* laud. ■ OPPOSITES insult, criticize.

complimentary adj. CONGRATULATORY, admiring, approving, appreciative, flattering, commendatory, eulogistic, panegyrical; *formal* laudatory. ■ OPPOSITES insulting, abusive.

comply v. OBEY, conform to, observe, abide by, keep to, adhere to, assent to, consent to, agree with, accord with, acquiesce in, follow, respect, yield, submit, defer to. ■ OPPOSITES disobey, ignore.

component n. PART, piece, element, bit,

composite adj. made up of various parts.

composition n. **1** the way in which something is made up. **2** a work of music, literature, or art. **3** a thing composed of various elements.

compositor n. a typesetter.

compost n. decayed organic material used as a fertilizer.

composure n. calmness.

compote n. fruit cooked in syrup.

compound n. **1** a thing made up of two or more elements. **2** a large open area enclosed by a fence. ▶adj. made up of several parts. ▶v. **1** make up a whole. **2** make worse.

comprehend v. understand.

comprehensible adj. able to be understood.

comprehension n. the act of understanding.

comprehensive adj. including all or nearly all. ▶n. a school providing secondary education for children of all abilities.

compress v. **1** force into a smaller space. **2** squeeze together. ▶n. a pad to reduce inflammation or stop bleeding. ■ **compression** n. **compressor** n.

comprise v. **1** consist of. **2** make up or constitute.

compromise n. an agreement reached by each side making concessions. ▶v. **1** make concessions in order to settle a dispute. **2** expose to danger or scandal by reckless behaviour.

compulsion n. **1** pressure to do something. **2** an irresistible urge.

compulsive adj. **1** resulting from or acting on an irresistible urge. **2** irresistibly exciting.

compulsory adj. required by law or a rule.

compunction a feeling of guilt or

Thesaurus

section, constituent, ingredient, unit, item, module.

compose v. **1** WRITE, make up, create, think up, produce, devise, invent, concoct, compile, fashion, formulate. **2** COMPRISE, form, make up, constitute. **3** CALM, quiet, collect, control, soothe, pacify, assuage, still.

composed adj. *see* CALM.

composition n. **1** STRUCTURE, make-up, organization, layout, configuration, constitution, character, formulation. **2** STORY, article, essay, poem, novel, work of art, piece, work, opus. **3** ARRANGEMENT, proportions, balance, harmony, symmetry.

compound n. BLEND, mixture, amalgam, combination, fusion, alloy, conglomerate, synthesis, medley, hybrid; *technical* admixture. ▶adj. COMPOSITE, blended, complex, fused, conglomerate. ▶v. **1** *see* COMBINE. **2** WORSEN, make worse, add to, exacerbate, aggravate, magnify, intensify, heighten.

comprehend v. UNDERSTAND, grasp, take in, follow, appreciate, see, realize, assimilate, fathom, perceive, discern, apprehend; *informal* twig.

comprehensible adj. UNDERSTANDABLE, clear, straightforward, intelligible, self-explanatory, lucid, explicit, discernible, graspable, fathomable. ■ OPPOSITES incomprehensible.

comprehensive adj. COMPLETE, all-inclusive, full, all-embracing, total, encyclopedic, wholesale, universal, exhaustive, detailed, thorough, extensive, widespread, broad, wide-ranging, far-reaching, blanket, umbrella, catholic. ■ OPPOSITES selective.

compress v. **1** COMPACT, squeeze, press down/together, crush, squash, flatten, cram, condense, constrict, tamp; *informal* jam together. **2** SHORTEN, abbreviate, abridge, reduce, contract, summarize, truncate. ■ OPPOSITES expand.

comprise v. **1** CONSIST OF, include, contain, be composed of, take in, embrace, encompass. **2** MAKE UP, form, constitute, compose.

compromise v. **1** COME TO AN UNDERSTANDING, make concessions, strike a balance, meet halfway, come to terms, make a deal, give and take, find the middle ground, find a happy medium, reach a formula, negotiate a settlement. **2** DAMAGE, injure, undermine, discredit, dishonour, bring into disrepute, shame, embarrass, endanger, jeopardize, imperil, weaken. ▶n. UNDERSTANDING, deal, balance, concession, happy medium, trade-off, middle course, give and take, adjustment.

compulsion n. **1** OBLIGATION, force, constraint, duress, coercion, pressure, oppression. **2** URGE, need, desire, drive, necessity, addiction, preoccupation, obsession.

compulsive adj. **1** UNCONTROLLABLE, obsessive, irresistible, compelling, overwhelming, driving, urgent, besetting. **2** OBSESSIONAL, obsessive, addicted, habitual, incorrigible, incurable, dependent, out of control; *informal* hooked.

shame.

compute v. calculate. ■ **computation** n. **computational** adj.

computer n. an electronic device for storing and processing information.

computerize (or **-ise**) v. convert to a system controlled by or stored on computer.

comrade n. a companion or a fellow member. ■ **comradeship** n.

con informal v. (**conning, conned**) deceive or trick. ▶n. a deception or trick. □ **pros and cons** see PRO.

concatenation n. a connected series.

concave adj. having an outline or surface that curves inwards.

conceal v. hide or keep secret. ■ **concealment** n.

concede v. 1 admit to be true. 2 give up an advantage or right. 3 admit defeat in a contest.

conceit n. 1 excessive pride in oneself.

2 a fanciful idea or figure of speech. ■ **conceited** adj.

conceivable adj. able to be imagined or understood. ■ **conceivably** adv.

conceive v. 1 become pregnant. 2 imagine.

concentrate v. 1 focus all one's attention. 2 gather together at one point. 3 make less dilute. ▶n. a concentrated substance. ■ **concentration** n.

concentration camp n. a camp for holding political prisoners.

concentric adj. (of circles) having the same centre.

concept n. an abstract idea. ■ **conceptual** adj. **conceptualize** (or **-ise**) v.

conception n. 1 the act of conceiving. 2 a concept.

concern v. 1 be about. 2 affect or involve. 3 make anxious. ▶n. 1 anxiety. 2 a matter of interest or importance. 3 a business.

Thesaurus

compulsory adj. OBLIGATORY, mandatory, required, binding, forced, necessary, essential, unavoidable, inescapable, requisite, prescribed, set, statutory, de rigueur, stipulated. ■ OPPOSITES optional.

compunction n. REMORSE, regret, guilt, scruples, qualms, contrition, pangs of conscience, penitence, repentance, contriteness.

compute v. CALCULATE, count, add up, work out, reckon, determine, total, figure out, estimate, tally, measure, evaluate, rate, enumerate, sum.

comrade n. FRIEND, companion, colleague, partner, associate, confederate, co-worker, fellow worker, teammate, ally; informal pal, mate.

con v. DECEIVE, swindle, trick, cheat, mislead, hoodwink, delude; informal bamboozle.

conceal v. 1 HIDE, cover, keep hidden, keep out of sight, obscure, screen, mask, disguise, camouflage, shelter, bury, tuck away. 2 KEEP SECRET, hide, keep dark, cover up, hush up, dissemble; informal keep the lid on. ■ OPPOSITES reveal, expose.

concealed adj. see HIDDEN.

concede v. 1 ADMIT, acknowledge, accept, allow, grant, accede, confess, recognize, own. 2 GIVE UP, yield, surrender, hand over, relinquish, cede. ■ OPPOSITES deny, retain.

conceit n. PRIDE, arrogance, vanity, egotism, self-importance, self-satisfaction, self-admiration, boasting,

swagger, narcissism; literary vainglory. ■ OPPOSITES humility.

conceited adj. PROUD, arrogant, vain, self-important, haughty, immodest, egotistical, egocentric, self-satisfied, smug, cocky, boastful, swollen-headed, swaggering, narcissistic, supercilious, overweening, complacent, bumptious; informal big-headed, stuck up, toffee-nosed, snooty; literary vainglorious. ■ OPPOSITES modest, humble.

conceivable adj. CREDIBLE, believable, thinkable, imaginable, possible, understandable, comprehensible. ■ OPPOSITES inconceivable.

conceive v. 1 BECOME PREGNANT, be impregnated. 2 THINK UP, formulate, create, work out, form, devise, originate, produce, frame, draw up, develop, imagine, dream up, contrive, envisage; informal cook up.

concentrate v. 1 GIVE ONE'S ATTENTION TO, be absorbed in, focus on, be engrossed in, put one's mind to, consider closely. 2 COLLECT, gather, crowd, mass, accumulate, congregate, amass, cluster, converge, rally. 3 CONDENSE, reduce, compress, boil down, distil. ■ OPPOSITES disperse, dilute.

concentrated adj. INTENSIVE, intense, rigorous, vigorous, all-out. ■ OPPOSITES half-hearted.

concern n. 1 WORRY, anxiety, disquiet, distress, apprehension, disturbance, perturbation. 2 INTEREST, importance, relevance, bearing, applicability. 3 AFFAIR, matter of interest, department, in-

concerned adj. anxious.

concerning prep. about.

concert n. a public musical performance.

concerted adj. 1 done jointly. 2 determined.

concertina n. a small musical instrument with bellows and buttons. ▶v. (**concertinaing**, **concertinaed**) compress in folds like those of a concertina.

concerto /kuhn-cher-toh/ n. (pl. **concertos** or **concerti**) a musical composition for an orchestra and a solo instrument.

concession n. 1 a thing given up to settle a dispute. 2 a reduction in price. 3 something granted.

conch n. a shellfish with a spiral shell.

conciliate v. make less hostile or angry. ■ **conciliation** n. **conciliatory** adj.

concise adj. giving information clearly and in few words. ■ **concisely** adv. **concision** n.

conclave n. a private meeting.

conclude v. 1 end. 2 reach an opinion by reasoning. 3 settle an agreement.

conclusion n. 1 an ending. 2 an opinion reached by reasoning.

conclusive adj. decisive or convincing. ■ **conclusively** adv.

concoct v. 1 prepare from ingredients. 2 invent. ■ **concoction** n.

concomitant adj. accompanying or associated.

concord n. agreement; harmony.

concordance n. an index of the important words in a text.

concordant adj. in agreement.

concourse n. a large open area in a public building.

concrete adj. 1 existing in a physical form; not abstract. 2 definite. ▶n. a building material made from gravel, sand, cement, and water. ▶v. cover or fix with concrete.

concubine n. (in some societies) a woman who lives with a man but has lower status than his wife or wives.

concur v. (**concurring**, **concurred**) 1 agree. 2 happen at the same time. ■ **concurrence** n. **concurrent** adj. **concurrently** adv.

concussion n. temporary unconsciousness or confusion caused by a blow on the head. ■ **concussed** adj.

condemn v. 1 express strong disapproval of. 2 sentence to a punishment.

Thesaurus

volvement, business, responsibility, duty, job, task, occupation. 4 BUSINESS, company, firm, enterprise, organization, corporation, establishment. ▶v. 1 AFFECT, be the business of, be relevant to, involve, apply to, be of interest to, touch. 2 WORRY, disturb, trouble, bother, make anxious, perturb, distress.

concerned adj. 1 INVOLVED, implicated, relevant, party to, connected, interested. 2 WORRIED, disturbed, anxious, upset, bothered, apprehensive, uneasy, distressed, perturbed, exercised.

concerning prep. ABOUT, relating to, regarding, as regards, involving, with reference to, with respect to, in the matter of, re, apropos.

concerted adj. JOINT, combined, united, collective, coordinated, collaborative, cooperative, synchronized.

conciliate v. PLACATE, calm down, appease, pacify, mollify, assuage, soothe. ■ OPPOSITES provoke.

concise adj. SUCCINCT, brief, short, compact, condensed, terse, compressed, to the point, pithy, laconic, epigrammatic, synoptic, compendious. ■ OPPOSITES lengthy, wordy.

conclude v. 1 END, finish, come/bring to an end, halt, stop, cease, terminate, discontinue; informal wind up. 2 COME TO A CONCLUSION, deduce, infer, gather, judge, assume, presume, suppose, conjecture, surmise. ■ OPPOSITES start.

conclusion n. 1 END, finish, halt, stop, close, completion, termination, cessation, culmination, discontinuance. 2 DEDUCTION, inference, decision, opinion, judgement, verdict, conviction, assumption, presumption, interpretation, resolution, solution. ■ OPPOSITES beginning.

conclusive adj. DECISIVE, definitive, certain, incontestable, unquestionable, unequivocal, final, clinching, ultimate, categorical, irrefutable, convincing, cogent. ■ OPPOSITES inconclusive.

concoct v. INVENT, devise, think up, dream up, put together, plan, fabricate, formulate, form, hatch, plot, forge, design, fashion, brew; informal cook up.

concrete adj. ACTUAL, real, definite, genuine, factual, substantial, solid, physical, visible, material, tangible, palpable, specific, objective, firm, existing. ■ OPPOSITES abstract, unreal.

concur v. AGREE, assent, acquiesce, accord, be of the same mind. ■ OPPOSITES disagree.

3 force to endure. **4** declare unfit for use. ■ **condemnation** n.

condensation n. water from humid air collecting as droplets on a cold surface.

condense v. **1** make more concentrated. **2** change from a gas or vapour to a liquid. **3** express in fewer words.

condescend v. **1** behave as if one is better than others. **2** do something that one believes to be beneath one. ■ **condescending** adj. **condescension** n.

condiment n. a seasoning for food.

condition n. **1** state as regards appearance, fitness, etc. **2** (**conditions**) circumstances. **3** a state of affairs that must exist before something else is possible. ▶ v. **1** influence. **2** bring into a desired condition. **3** train or accustom.

conditional adj. subject to one or more conditions. ■ **conditionally** adv.

conditioner n. a substance for improving the condition of hair, fabric, etc.

condole v. express sympathy for. ■ **condolence** n.

condom n. a rubber sheath worn on the penis during sex to prevent conception or infection.

condominium n. US a building containing a number of individually owned flats.

condone v. accept or forgive an offence or wrong.

condor n. a large vulture.

conducive adj. (**conducive to**) contributing or helping towards.

conduct n. **1** behaviour. **2** management or direction. ▶ v. **1** organize and carry out. **2** be the conductor of. **3** guide or lead. **4** transmit heat or electricity.

conduction n. the transmission of heat or electricity. ■ **conductive** adj. **conductivity** n.

conductor n. **1** a person who conducts an orchestra or choir. **2** a material that conducts heat or electricity. **3** a person who collects fares on a bus.

conduit n. **1** a channel for liquid. **2** a tube protecting electric wiring.

cone n. **1** an object which tapers from a circular base to a point. **2** the dry fruit of a conifer.

coney n. (pl. **coneys**) a rabbit.

confection n. **1** an elaborate sweet dish. **2** an elaborately constructed thing.

confectioner n. a person who makes or sells confectionery.

confectionery n. sweets and chocolates.

Thesaurus

concurrent adj. SIMULTANEOUS, parallel, coexisting, overlapping, coexistent, coincident, contemporaneous, synchronous, side by side.

condemn v. **1** DENOUNCE, criticize, censure, damn, deplore, berate, reprove, upbraid, castigate, reproach, blame, reprehend, deprecate, disapprove of, disparage, revile, execrate, decry, reprobate; informal slam, slate. **2** SENTENCE, pass sentence on, convict. **3** DAMN, doom, compel, coerce, impel. ■ OPPOSITES praise, acquit.

condense v. **1** SHORTEN, abridge, abbreviate, cut, reduce, compress, curtail, summarize, contract, compact, synopsize, encapsulate. **2** THICKEN, concentrate, reduce, distil, solidify, coagulate. ■ OPPOSITES lengthen.

condescend v. DEIGN, lower oneself, stoop, descend, unbend, humble/demean oneself.

condescending adj. PATRONIZING, supercilious, disdainful, superior, snobbish, lofty, lordly; informal snooty, snotty, toffee-nosed.

condition n. **1** STATE, state of affairs, situation, circumstance, position, predicament, plight, quandary. **2** SHAPE, fitness, health, state of health, order, trim; informal nick, fettle, kilter. **3** RESTRICTION, proviso, provision, stipulation, prerequisite, rule, limitation, terms, limit. **4** DISEASE, illness, disorder, complaint, problem, ailment, malady. ▶ v. TRAIN, accustom, habituate, adapt, influence, mould, determine, govern, educate, inure.

conditional adj. PROVISIONAL, dependent, contingent, qualified, limited, restricted, provisory; informal with strings attached. ■ OPPOSITES unconditional.

condone v. ALLOW, tolerate, excuse, pardon, make allowances for, forgive, overlook, disregard, turn a blind eye to, let pass; informal wink at. ■ OPPOSITES condemn.

conducive adj. CONTRIBUTORY, helpful, favourable, useful, instrumental, advantageous, supportive, beneficial.

conduct n. **1** BEHAVIOUR, actions, habits, practices, bearing, comportment, manners; US deportment. **2** RUNNING, handling, operation, direction, management, organization, administration, control, regulation, guidance, supervision, leadership. ▶ v. **1** BEHAVE, act, acquit, deport, comport. **2** DIRECT, run, manage,

confederacy n. (pl. **confederacies**) an alliance of states.

confederate adj. joined by an agreement or treaty. ▶ n. an accomplice.

confederation n. an alliance.

confer v. (**conferring**, **conferred**) **1** grant a title, degree, etc. **2** have discussions.

conference n. a formal meeting for discussion.

confess v. **1** admit to a crime etc. **2** acknowledge reluctantly. **3** declare one's sins formally to a priest. ■ **confession** n.

confessional n. an enclosed stall in a church for hearing confessions.

confessor n. a priest who hears confessions.

confetti n. bits of coloured paper thrown over a bride and groom.

confidant n. (fem. **confidante**) a person in whom one confides.

confide v. tell someone about a secret or private matter.

confidence n. **1** faith or trust. **2** self-assurance. □ **confidence trick** an act of cheating someone by gaining their trust.

confident adj. feeling confidence. ■ **confidently** adv.

confidential adj. to be kept secret. ■ **confidentiality** n. **confidentially** adv.

configuration n. an arrangement in a particular form.

confine v. **1** restrict to certain limits. **2** keep shut up. ▶ n. (**confines**) boundaries.

confinement n. **1** the state of being confined. **2** dated the time of childbirth.

confirm v. **1** establish the truth of. **2** make definite. **3** administer the religious rite of confirmation to.

confirmation n. **1** the act of confirming. **2** the rite at which a baptized person is admitted as a full member of the Christian Church.

confiscate v. take or seize by authority. ■ **confiscation** n.

conflagration n. a large fire.

conflate v. combine into one.

conflict n. **1** a serious disagreement. **2** an armed struggle. **3** an incompatibility. ▶ v. be incompatible or in opposition.

confluence n. the junction of two

Thesaurus

administer, be in charge of, lead, organize, handle, control, supervise, regulate, preside over. **3** SHOW, guide, lead, escort, accompany, take.

confer v. **1** BESTOW, present, award, grant, give, hand out, invest, accord. **2** TALK, have discussions, exchange views, consult, debate, deliberate, compare notes, converse, seek advice; *informal* put their/your/our heads together.

conference n. MEETING, seminar, discussion, deliberation, convention, council, congress, forum, symposium, colloquium, convocation.

confess v. ADMIT, acknowledge, own up to, make known, disclose, reveal, divulge, accept responsibility, make a clean breast of, unburden oneself, come clean; *informal* spill the beans, get something off one's chest, blurt out, fess up.

confidant n. FRIEND, crony, intimate, familiar, alter ego; *informal* pal, chum, mate.

confide v. CONFESS, reveal, disclose, tell, divulge, admit, unburden oneself, unbosom oneself, open one's heart.

confidence n. **1** BELIEF, reliance, faith, certainty, trust, credence, dependence. **2** SELF-ASSURANCE, self-confidence, self-reliance, self-possession, nerve, poise, courage, boldness, conviction, panache,

composure, mettle, fortitude, verve. ■ OPPOSITES distrust, uncertainty, doubt.

confident adj. **1** CERTAIN, sure, convinced, positive, sanguine. **2** SELF-ASSURED, self-possessed, self-confident, unafraid, fearless, secure, bold, assertive, cocksure. ■ OPPOSITES uncertain.

confidential adj. **1** SECRET, top secret, private, classified, restricted, off the record, suppressed, personal, intimate. **2** CLOSE, trusted, intimate, faithful, reliable, trustworthy.

confine v. **1** ENCLOSE, cage, lock up, imprison, detain, jail, shut up, intern, hold captive, incarcerate, restrain, impound, keep, pen, coop up, box up, immure, wall up. **2** RESTRICT, limit, keep within the limits of, circumscribe, curb. ■ OPPOSITES free.

confirm v. **1** VERIFY, prove, bear out, corroborate, validate, endorse, authenticate, establish, substantiate, give credence to, evidence. **2** RATIFY, endorse, approve, sanction, authorize, underwrite, warrant, accredit. **3** GUARANTEE, assure, affirm, promise, pledge, assert, reassert. ■ OPPOSITES contradict, deny.

confiscate v. SEIZE, impound, take possession of, remove, take away, appropriate, commandeer, expropriate, rivers.

conform v. comply with rules, standards, or conventions. ■ **conformity** n.

conformist n. a person who conforms to rules or custom. ▶ adj. conventional.

confound v. **1** surprise or bewilder. **2** prove wrong.

confront v. **1** meet face to face. **2** face up to a problem. ■ **confrontation** n.

confuse v. **1** make bewildered. **2** make less easy to understand. **3** mistake one for another., ■ **confusion** n.

confute v. prove wrong.

conga n. a dance performed by people in single file.

congeal v. become semi-solid.

congenial adj. agreeable to oneself.

congenital adj. present from birth.

conger n. a large sea eel.

congested adj. **1** very crowded. **2** abnormally full of blood. **3** blocked with mucus. ■ **congestion** n.

conglomerate n. **1** something consisting of a number of different and distinct things. **2** a corporation formed by a merger of separate firms. ■ **conglomeration** n.

congratulate v. express good wishes or praise at the happiness or success of. ■ **congratulation** n. **congratulatory** adj.

congregate v. gather in a crowd.

congregation n. people gathered for religious worship.

congress n. **1** a formal meeting between delegates. **2** (**Congress**) a national law-making body, esp. of the USA. ■ **congressional** adj.

Thesaurus

. . . .

sequester, sequestrate, arrogate.

conflict n. **1** DISPUTE, quarrel, squabble, wrangle, feud, hostility, disagreement, dissension, discord, friction, antagonism, strife, contention; *informal* row. **2** WAR, battle, fight, warfare, clash, engagement, encounter, hostilities, combat, struggle. **3** CLASH, incompatibility, incongruity, mismatch, variance, divergence, inconsistency. ■ OPPOSITES agreement, peace, harmony. ▶ v. CLASH, differ, disagree, be at odds, be in opposition, be at variance, be incompatible, contrast, oppose each other, collide. ■ OPPOSITES agree.

conform v. **1** COMPLY, obey the rules, adapt, adjust, be conventional; *informal* run with the pack, swim with the stream. **2** FIT, match, agree with, correspond to, tally with, square with, accord with. ■ OPPOSITES rebel, differ.

conformity n. **1** CONVENTIONALITY, traditionalism, orthodoxy. **2** COMPLIANCE, obedience, observance, adaptation, adjustment, accommodation.

confront v. FACE, face up to, tackle, stand up to, defy, challenge, take on, resist, attack, assault, accost, waylay, meet head on. ■ OPPOSITES avoid.

confuse v. **1** BEWILDER, puzzle, perplex, bemuse, baffle, mystify, befuddle, disorientate, disorient, agitate, nonplus; *informal* rattle, throw, flummox. **2** MUDDLE, mix up, jumble, tangle up, disorder; *informal* snarl up. **3** MISTAKE, mix/muddle up. ■ OPPOSITES enlighten, simplify.

confused adj. **1** UNCLEAR, hazy, indistinct, foggy, obscure, garbled, incoherent, woolly. **2** MUDDLED, jumbled, untidy, disordered, disorderly, out of order,

chaotic, disorganized, upset, disarranged; *informal* topsy-turvy, at sixes and sevens, higgledy-piggledy. **3** BEWILDERED, disorientated, disoriented, flustered, befuddled, addled, unbalanced, unhinged, demented, at sea, nonplussed; *informal* in a tizzy, discombobulated. ■ OPPOSITES clear, orderly.

confusion n. **1** BEWILDERMENT, perplexity, bafflement, puzzlement, mystification, bemusement, muddle, disorientation, befuddlement, distraction. **2** MUDDLE, jumble, mess, untidiness, disorder, chaos, turmoil, shambles, disorderliness, disorganization, disturbance, fuss, upheaval, commotion, uproar, pandemonium. ■ OPPOSITES clarity, order.

congeal v. SOLIDIFY, coagulate, thicken, clot, set, harden, cake, jell, condense, coalesce, curdle.

congenial adj. AGREEABLE, friendly, pleasant, amiable, amicable, nice, kindly, good-natured, companionable, sympathetic, like-minded, pleasing, understanding, well suited, kindred. ■ OPPOSITES unfriendly, unpleasant.

congenital adj. **1** HEREDITARY, inherited, innate, constitutional, inborn, inbred. **2** INVETERATE, utter, complete, thoroughgoing, dyed-in-the-wool.

congested adj. **1** BLOCKED, clogged, choked, plugged, stopped up. **2** PACKED, jammed, overcrowded, crowded, blocked, obstructed, overflowing, teeming. ■ OPPOSITES clear.

congratulate v. COMPLIMENT, offer good wishes to, wish joy to, praise, felicitate. ■ OPPOSITES criticize.

congregate v. GATHER, assemble, come

congruent adj. **1** in agreement or harmony. **2** Geom. (of figures) identical in form. ■ **congruence** n.

conical adj. cone-shaped.

conifer n. an evergreen tree bearing cones. ■ **coniferous** adj.

conjecture n. & v. (make) a guess.

conjoin v. join.

conjugal adj. of marriage.

conjugate v. give the different forms of a verb. ■ **conjugation** n.

conjunction n. **1** a word used to connect words or clauses (e.g. *and*, *if*). **2** an instance of two or more events occurring together.

conjunctivitis n. inflammation of the membrane connecting the eyeball and eyelid.

conjure v. **1** cause to appear as if by magic. **2** call to the mind.

conjuror (or **conjurer**) n. a performer of seemingly magical tricks.

conk informal v. (**conk out**) (of a machine) break down. ▶ n. a nose.

conker n. the fruit of the horse chestnut tree.

connect v. **1** join or bring together. **2** (**be connected**) be related in some way. **3** (of a train, bus, etc.) arrive in time for passengers to catch another. ■ **connective** adj. **connector** n.

connection n. **1** a link or relationship. **2** (**connections**) influential friends or relatives. **3** a train, bus, etc. that connects.

connive v. (**connive at/in**) secretly allow. ■ **connivance** n.

connoisseur /kon-nuh-ser/ n. an expert judge in matters of taste.

connote v. (of a word) suggest in addition to its primary meaning. ■ **connotation** n.

conquer v. overcome in war or by effort. ■ **conqueror** n. **conquest** n.

conscience n. a person's sense of right and wrong.

conscientious adj. **1** diligent in one's work or duty. **2** of conscience. □ **conscientious objector** a person who refuses to serve in the armed forces for reasons of conscience.

conscious adj. **1** awake and responsive. **2** aware. **3** intentional. ■ **consciously** adv. **consciousness** n.

conscript v. summon for compulsory military service. ▶ n. a conscripted person. ■ **conscription** n.

consecrate v. make or declare sacred. ■ **consecration** n.

consecutive adj. following in unbroken sequence. ■ **consecutively** adv.

consensual adj. involving consent.

Thesaurus

together, collect, mass, group, convene, flock together, converge, meet, crowd, cluster, throng, swarm, rendezvous, muster, rally, foregather. ■ OPPOSITES disperse.

conjecture n. GUESS, suspicion, theory, hypothesis, presumption, presupposition, notion, fancy, surmise, inference; *informal* guesstimate.

connect v. **1** ATTACH, link, fix, couple, affix, clamp, secure, tie, rivet, fuse, solder, weld. **2** ASSOCIATE, link, relate to, equate, identify, bracket, draw a parallel with. ■ OPPOSITES separate.

connection n. **1** ATTACHMENT, fastening, coupling, clamp, joint, clasp. **2** LINK, relationship, association, relation, correspondence, parallel, analogy.

connive v. CONSPIRE, collude, be in collusion with, collaborate, plot, scheme, abet, be a party to, intrigue.

connotation n. NUANCE, undertone, intimation, hint, suggestion, implication, allusion, insinuation, reference.

conquer v. DEFEAT, beat, vanquish, overpower, overthrow, subdue, rout, trounce, subjugate, triumph over, overwhelm, crush, overrun, prevail over,

quell, worst; *informal* thrash, lick. **2** SEIZE, occupy, invade, annex, overrun, win, appropriate. **3** OVERCOME, master, get the better of, surmount, vanquish, quell.

conquest n. **1** VICTORY, beating, defeat, overthrow, overpowering, subjugation, trouncing, rout, triumph, mastery, crushing. **2** OCCUPATION, seizure, takeover, possession, annexation, invasion, overrunning, appropriation. **3** ADMIRER, worshipper, fan, adherent, follower, supporter.

conscience n. MORAL SENSE, morals, principles, ethics, scruples, standards, qualms, reservations, misgivings.

conscientious adj. DILIGENT, careful, meticulous, thorough, attentive, precise, accurate, exact, punctilious, dedicated, hard-working, painstaking, scrupulous, rigorous, detailed. ■ OPPOSITES casual.

conscious adj. **1** AWAKE, aware, alert, sentient, responsive. **2** DELIBERATE, premeditated, intentional, intended, on purpose, calculated, voluntary, studied, knowing, volitional. ■ OPPOSITES unconscious.

consensus n. general agreement.

....

☑ *consensus*, not *-cen-*.

....

consent n. permission or agreement. ▶ v. **1** give permission. **2** agree to do.

consequence n. **1** a result or effect. **2** importance.

consequent adj. resulting. ■ **consequential** adj. **consequently** adv.

conservancy n. (pl. **conservancies**) an organization helping to preserve natural resources.

conservation n. **1** preservation of the natural environment. **2** preservation and repair of historical sites etc. ■ **conservationist** n.

conservative adj. **1** opposed to change. **2** (in politics) favouring free enterprise and private ownership. **3** (**Conservative**) of a particular conservative political party. **4** (of an estimate) deliberately low. ▶ n. **1** a conservative person.

2 (**Conservative**) a member of a Conservative Party. ■ **conservatively** adv. **conservatism** n.

conservatory n. (pl. **conservatories**) a room with a glass roof and walls, attached to a house.

conserve v. protect from harm, decay, etc. ▶ n. jam.

consider v. **1** think carefully about. **2** believe or think. **3** take into account.

considerable adj. great in amount or importance. ■ **considerably** adv.

considerate adj. careful not to harm or inconvenience others. ■ **considerately** adv.

consideration n. **1** careful thought. **2** a fact taken into account when making a decision. **3** thoughtfulness. **4** a payment or reward.

considering prep. taking into account.

consign v. **1** deliver. **2** put or send somewhere.

consignment n. a batch of goods sent.

consist v. (**consist of**) be composed of.

Thesaurus

....

consecrate v. SANCTIFY, bless, make holy/sacred, devote, hallow.

consecutive adj. SUCCESSIVE, succeeding, following, in sequence, sequential, in a row, serial, in turn, progressive, continuous, uninterrupted, unbroken, chronological.

consensus n. AGREEMENT, common consent, consent, unanimity, harmony, unity, concurrence, concord. ■ OPPOSITES disagreement.

consent n. AGREEMENT, assent, acceptance, approval, permission, acquiescence, sanction, compliance, concurrence; *informal* go-ahead, green light. ▶ v. AGREE TO, accept, approve, go along with, acquiesce in, accede to, concede to, yield to, give in to, submit to, comply with, abide by, concur with. ■ OPPOSITES dissent, refuse.

consequence n. **1** RESULT, effect, outcome, aftermath, repercussion, upshot, reverberation, by-product, event, issue, end. **2** IMPORTANCE, significance, note, value, concern, substance, weight, import, moment, portent. ■ OPPOSITES cause.

consequent adj. RESULTING, subsequent, following, ensuing, resultant, consequential, successive, sequential.

conservation n. PRESERVATION, protection, safe keeping, safeguarding, saving, guarding, care, charge, custody, husbandry, upkeep, maintenance. ■ OPPOSITES destruction.

conservative adj. **1** RIGHT-WING, reactionary, Tory; *US* Republican. **2** CONVENTIONAL, traditional, reactionary, orthodox, cautious, prudent, careful, moderate, middle-of-the-road, unadventurous, temperate, stable, unchanging, old-fashioned, hidebound, sober. **3** MODERATE, reasonable, cautious. ■ OPPOSITES radical.

conserve v. PRESERVE, save, keep, protect, take care of, use sparingly, husband, hoard, store up, nurse. ■ OPPOSITES squander, waste.

consider v. **1** THINK ABOUT, weigh up, give thought to, examine, study, ponder, contemplate, deliberate over, mull over, meditate on, ruminate over, chew over, turn over in one's mind. **2** THINK, believe, regard as, deem, hold to be, judge, rate.

considerable adj. **1** SUBSTANTIAL, sizeable, appreciable, tolerable, goodly, fair, reasonable, ample, plentiful, abundant, marked, noticeable, comfortable, decent, great, lavish. **2** DISTINGUISHED, noteworthy, noted, important, significant, influential, illustrious, renowned. ■ OPPOSITES negligible.

considerate adj. THOUGHTFUL, kind, helpful, concerned, attentive, solicitous, kindly, unselfish, compassionate, sympathetic, charitable, patient, generous, obliging, accommodating, neighbourly, altruistic. ■ OPPOSITES thoughtless.

consign v. HAND OVER, give over, deliver,

consistency n. (pl. **consistencies**) **1** being consistent. **2** the degree of thickness of a substance.

consistent adj. **1** regular; unchanging. **2** in agreement; not conflicting. ■ **consistently** adv.

console v. comfort in a time of grief etc. ▶n. **1** a panel containing a set of controls. **2** a machine for playing computerized video games. ■ **consolation** n.

consolidate v. **1** make stronger or more secure. **2** combine. ■ **consolidation** n.

consommé /kuhn-**som**-may/ n. a clear soup.

consonant n. a letter of the alphabet representing a speech sound in which the breath is completely or partly obstructed. ▶ adj. in agreement.

consort n. a wife or husband, esp. of a monarch. ▶v. (**consort with**) associate with.

consortium n. (pl. **consortia** or **consortiums**) an association of several companies.

conspicuous adj. **1** clearly visible. **2** attracting notice. ■ **conspicuously** adv.

conspiracy n. (pl. **conspiracies**) a secret plan by a group to do something unlawful.

conspire v. **1** jointly make secret plans to commit a wrongful act. **2** (of events) combine to produce an effect as though deliberately. ■ **conspirator** n. **conspiratorial** adj.

constable n. a police officer of the lowest rank.

constabulary n. (pl. **constabularies**) a police force.

constant adj. **1** occurring continuously or repeatedly. **2** unchanging. **3** faithful. ▶n. a number or quantity that does not change its value. ■ **constancy** n. **constantly** adv.

constellation n. a group of stars.

consternation n. anxiety or dismay.

constipation n. difficulty in emptying the bowels. ■ **constipated** adj.

constituency n. (pl. **constituencies**) **1** a body of voters who elect a representative. **2** the area represented in this way.

constituent adj. being a part of a whole. ▶n. **1** a voter in a constituency. **2** a constituent part.

constitute v. **1** be a part of a whole.

Thesaurus

send, pass on, transfer, assign, entrust, commend, remit, bequeath.

consignment n. LOAD, batch, delivery, shipment, cargo, container load.

consist v. BE COMPOSED OF, be made up of, comprise, contain, include, incorporate, add up to, involve, embody.

consistent adj. **1** CONSTANT, unchanging, unvarying, undeviating, steady, dependable, steadfast, stable, reliable, faithful, uniform, true to type. **2** COMPATIBLE, conforming to, consonant, agreeing, congruous, accordant. ■ OPPOSITES inconsistent.

consolation n. COMFORT, sympathy, solace, compassion, pity, commiseration, relief, help, support, cheer, encouragement, soothing, assuagement, alleviation.

consolidate v. MAKE STRONGER, strengthen, make secure, secure, make stable, stabilize, reinforce, fortify, cement. ■ OPPOSITES weaken.

consort v. (**consort with**) ASSOCIATE WITH, keep company with, mix with, spend time with, fraternize with, have dealings with; informal hang around with.

conspicuous adj. CLEAR, visible, obvious, evident, apparent, prominent, notable, noticeable, marked, plain, unmistakable, observable, recognizable, discernible, perceptible, distinguishable, manifest, patent, vivid, striking, glaring, blatant, flagrant, obtrusive, showy, bold, ostentatious, eminent. ■ OPPOSITES inconspicuous, unobtrusive.

conspiracy n. PLOT, scheme, plan, stratagem, machinations, cabal, intrigue, collusion, connivance, machination, treason.

conspirator n. PLOTTER, conspirer, schemer, intriguer, colluder, collaborator, confederate, traitor; informal wheeler-dealer.

conspire v. PLOT, scheme, form conspiracy, hatch a plot, intrigue, collude, collaborate, connive, combine, be in league; informal be in cahoots.

constant adj. **1** EVEN, regular, uniform, stable, steady, unchanging, fixed, consistent, invariable, unvarying, sustained, immutable. **2** CONTINUAL, unending, non-stop, sustained, incessant, endless, unceasing, perpetual, persistent, interminable, unflagging, unremitting, relentless, unrelenting. **3** LOYAL, faithful, devoted, dependable, staunch, true, trustworthy, trusty, resolute, steadfast, unwavering, unswerving. ■ OPPOSITES variable, fickle.

2 be or be equivalent to.

constitution n. **1** the principles by which a state is governed. **2** composition or formation. **3** a person's physical or mental state.

constitutional adj. of or in accordance with a constitution. ▶n. dated a walk taken for exercise.

constrain v. compel or oblige.

constraint n. **1** a restriction. **2** strict control of one's behaviour.

constrict v. **1** make or become narrower or tighter. **2** restrict. ■ **constriction** n. **constrictor** n.

construct v. build or put together. ▶n. an idea or theory containing various elements.

construction n. **1** the act or process of constructing. **2** a building or other structure. **3** an interpretation. **4** the arrangement of words in a sentence.

constructive adj. having a useful or helpful effect. ■ **constructively** adv.

construe v. interpret.

consul n. an official representative of a state in a foreign city. ■ **consular** adj.

consulate n. the place where a consul works.

consult v. seek information or advice from. ■ **consultation** n. **consultative** adj.

consultant n. a specialist consulted for professional advice. ■ **consultancy** n.

consume v. **1** eat or drink. **2** use up. **3** (of a fire) destroy. **4** obsess.

consumer n. a person who buys or uses goods or services.

consummate v. /kon-syuu-mayt/ make a marriage or relationship complete by having sex. ▶adj. /kuhn-**sum**-muht/ highly skilled. ■ **consummation** n.

consumption n. **1** the act or process of consuming. **2** dated tuberculosis. ■ **consumptive** adj. & n. (dated).

contact n. **1** physical touching. **2** communication. **3** a person who may be asked for information or help. **4** an electrical connection. ▶v. get in touch with. □ **contact lens** a plastic lens placed on the surface of the eye to correct visual defects.

contagion n. the spreading of a disease by close contact. ■ **contagious** adj.

contain v. **1** have or hold within. **2** control or restrain.

container n. **1** a box, cylinder, etc. for holding something. **2** a large metal box for the transport of goods.

containment n. the keeping of something harmful under control.

contaminate v. pollute. ■ **contamination** n.

contemplate v. **1** gaze at. **2** think about. ■ **contemplation** n. **contemplative** adj.

Thesaurus

consternation n. DISMAY, anxiety, bewilderment, distress, alarm, surprise, astonishment, amazement, confusion, mystification, panic, fear, fright, dread, horror, trepidation, shock, terror, awe.

construct v. BUILD, make, assemble, erect, put up, set up, manufacture, produce, put together, fabricate, fashion, forge, establish, raise, elevate, engineer, form. ■ OPPOSITES demolish.

construction n. **1** BUILDING, assembly, erection, manufacture, fabrication, elevation. **2** STRUCTURE, building, edifice, framework. **3** INTERPRETATION, meaning, reading, explanation, inference.

constructive adj. USEFUL, helpful, productive, practical, positive, valuable, worthwhile, beneficial, creative. ■ OPPOSITES destructive, negative.

consult v. **1** CONFER, discuss, talk, talk over, speak to, exchange views, deliberate; *informal* put heads together, talk turkey. **2** ASK, seek advice from, call in, turn to, take counsel from.

consume v. **1** EAT, drink, swallow, ingest, devour, guzzle; *informal* gobble, tuck into, scoff. **2** USE, utilize, expend, deplete, absorb, exhaust, waste, squander, drain, dissipate.

contact v. COMMUNICATE WITH, get/be in touch with, be in communication with, approach, write to, phone, call, ring up, speak to, reach, get hold of, notify, sound out. ▶n. TOUCH, proximity, exposure, joining, junction, contiguity, tangency.

contagious adj. CATCHING, communicable, transmittable, transmissible, infectious, spreadable, pandemic.

contain v. **1** HOLD, carry, have capacity for, accommodate, seat. **2** INCLUDE, comprise, take in, embrace, incorporate, involve. **3** RESTRAIN, hold in/back, control, keep in check, keep under control, suppress, repress, curb, stifle.

container n. RECEPTACLE, vessel, holder, repository.

contaminate v. ADULTERATE, pollute, debase, defile, corrupt, taint, dirty, infect, foul, spoil, tarnish, sully, soil, stain, befoul.

contemplate v. **1** THINK ABOUT, medi-

contemporaneous adj. existing or occurring at the same time.

contemporary adj. **1** living or occurring at the same time. **2** modern. ▶ n. (pl. **contemporaries**) a person of the same age or living at the same time as another.

contempt n. **1** the feeling that a person or a thing is worthless. **2** disobedience or disrespect to a court of law. ■ **contemptuous** adj. **contemptuously** adv.

contemptible adj. deserving contempt.

content adj. happy or satisfied. ▶ n. **1** (also **contents**) what is contained in something. **2** the subject matter of a speech etc. **3** happiness or satisfaction. ▶ v. satisfy; please. ■ **contented** adj. **contentment** n.

contention n. **1** disagreement. **2** an assertion.

contentious adj. causing disagreement

or controversy.

contest n. a competitive event. ▶ v. **1** compete in or for. **2** challenge or dispute. ■ **contestant** n.

context n. **1** the circumstances surrounding an event etc. **2** the parts that precede and follow a word or passage and clarify its meaning. ■ **contextual** adj.

contiguous adj. adjacent or touching. ■ **contiguity** n.

continent¹ n. **1** any of the world's main land masses. **2** (**the Continent**) the mainland of Europe. ■ **continental** adj.

continent² adj. **1** able to control excretion from the bowels and bladder. **2** self-restrained. ■ **continence** n.

contingency n. (pl. **contingencies**) a possible but unpredictable future event.

contingent adj. **1** subject to chance. **2** (**contingent on**) dependent on. ▶ n. a

Thesaurus

tate over/on, consider, ponder over/on, reflect over/on, muse on, dwell on, deliberate over, ruminate over, cogitate on. **2** ENVISAGE, think about, consider, intend, plan, propose, foresee, expect to. **3** LOOK AT, view, regard, examine, inspect, observe, scrutinize, survey, eye.

contemplative adj. THOUGHTFUL, pensive, reflective, meditative, ruminative, musing, intent, rapt, lost in thought.

contemporary adj. **1** CURRENT, modern, present-day, up to date, latest, fashionable, recent, newest; *informal* trendy, with it. **2** CONTEMPORANEOUS, concurrent, coexistent, coeval, synchronous. ■ OPPOSITES old-fashioned.

contempt n. SCORN, disdain, disgust, loathing, abhorrence, detestation, disrespect, derision, mockery, condescension. *See also* HATRED. ■ OPPOSITES admiration.

contemptible adj. DESPICABLE, detestable, beneath contempt, disgraceful, loathsome, odious, ignominious, lamentable, pitiful, discreditable, low, mean, shameful, abject, unworthy, worthless, base, vile, shabby, cheap, sordid, wretched, degenerate. ■ OPPOSITES admirable.

contemptuous adj. SCORNFUL, disdainful, insulting, disrespectful, derisive, derisory, insolent, mocking, sneering, jeering, belittling, dismissive, condescending, patronizing, haughty, lofty, supercilious, arrogant, superior, snide, imperious; *informal* snooty, high and mighty, snotty; *formal* contumelious. ■ OPPOSITES respectful, admiring.

contend v. **1** COMPETE, oppose, challenge, contest, vie, clash, strive, struggle, grapple, tussle, wrestle. **2** COPE WITH, face, grapple with, take on. **3** STATE, declare, assert, maintain, hold, claim, profess, allege, affirm, aver.

content¹ n. *see* CONTENTMENT. ▶ adj. *see* CONTENTED. ▶ v. *see* SATISFY (2).

content² n. CONSTITUENT, part, ingredient, element.

contented adj. SATISFIED, content, pleased, happy, cheerful, glad, gratified, fulfilled, at ease, at peace, comfortable, relaxed, serene, tranquil, unworried, untroubled, uncomplaining, complacent. ■ OPPOSITES discontented, dissatisfied.

contentment n. SATISFACTION, content, contentedness, happiness, pleasure, cheerfulness, gladness, gratification, fulfilment, relaxation, ease, comfort, peace, serenity, equanimity, tranquillity, complacency. ■ OPPOSITES dissatisfaction.

contest n. **1** *see* COMPETITION. **2** STRUGGLE, conflict, battle, fight, combat, tussle, skirmish. ▶ v. **1** COMPETE FOR, contend for, fight for/over, vie for, battle for, struggle for, tussle over; *informal* make a bid for. **2** CHALLENGE, question, call into question, oppose, doubt, dispute, object to, query, resist.

contestant n. COMPETITOR, entrant, candidate, contender, participant, rival, opponent, adversary, player.

context n. CIRCUMSTANCES, situation, conditions, state of affairs, background, environment, setting, frame of refergroup of people forming part of a larger group.

continual adj. happening constantly or often. ■ **continually** adv.

continue v. **1** keep doing. **2** keep existing or happening. **3** carry on in the same direction. **4** start again. ■ **continuation** n. **continuity** n.

continuous adj. without interruption. ■ **continuously** adv.

continuum n. (pl. **continua**) a continuous sequence in which the elements change gradually.

contort v. twist or bend out of normal shape. ■ **contortion** n.

contortionist n. an entertainer who twists their body into unnatural positions.

contour n. **1** an outline. **2** a line on a map joining points of equal height.

contra- prefix against; opposite.

contraband n. smuggled goods.

contraception n. the use of contraceptives.

contraceptive adj. preventing pregnancy. ▶n. a contraceptive device or drug.

contract n. a legally binding agreement. ▶v. **1** make or become smaller or

shorter. **2** make or arrange by a contract. **3** catch a disease. ■ **contractable** adj. **contractual** adj. **contractor** n.

contractile adj. able to contract or produce contraction.

contraction n. **1** the process of contracting. **2** a shortening of the muscles of the womb during childbirth. **3** a shortened form of a word or words.

contradict v. deny the truth of a statement made by someone by saying the opposite. ■ **contradiction** n. **contradictory** adj.

contraflow n. a flow of traffic in a direction opposite to and alongside the usual flow.

contralto n. (pl. **contraltos**) the lowest female singing voice.

contraption n. a strange machine or device.

contrapuntal adj. of or in counterpoint.

contrariwise adv. in the opposite way.

contrary adj. **1** opposite in nature, direction, or meaning. **2** /kuhn-**trair**-i/ inclined to do the opposite of what is desired. ▶n. (**the contrary**) the opposite.

contrast n. the state of being noticeably

Thesaurus

ence, framework, surroundings, milieu.

contingency n. EVENT, eventuality, incident, happening, occurrence, juncture, accident, chance, possibility, emergency, uncertainty, fortuity.

continual adj. **1** CONSTANT, perpetual, endless, interminable. *See also* CONTINUOUS. **2** FREQUENT, regular, constant, habitual, persistent, recurrent, repeated. ■ OPPOSITES occasional, temporary.

continue v. **1** CARRY ON, go on, keep on, persist, persevere, stay, endure, remain, survive, last, sustain, linger; *informal* stick at. **2** PROLONG, extend, sustain, maintain, protract, perpetuate. **3** RESUME, carry on with, recommence, restart, start again, return to, take up. ■ OPPOSITES stop.

continuous adj. CONSTANT, uninterrupted, non-stop, perpetual, sustained, ceaseless, incessant, relentless, unceasing, unremitting, endless, never-ending, interminable, lasting, everlasting, unbroken. ■ OPPOSITES sporadic, intermittent.

contour n. OUTLINE, silhouette, profile, figure, shape, form, line, curve.

contract n. AGREEMENT, pact, arrangement, settlement, covenant, compact, understanding, treaty, bargain, deal,

convention, concordat, entente. ▶v. **1** GET/BECOME/MAKE SMALLER, shrink, reduce, shrivel, narrow, tighten, draw in, constrict, tense, diminish, decrease, shorten, compress, curtail, concentrate, abbreviate, abridge. **2** AGREE, arrange, come to terms, reach an agreement, negotiate, bargain, strike a bargain, engage, settle, covenant. **3** CATCH, develop, get, become infected with, go down with. ■ OPPOSITES expand.

contradict v. SAY THE OPPOSITE OF, oppose, challenge, counter, be at variance with, clash with, dissent from, rebut, refute, controvert, impugn, confute. ■ OPPOSITES agree.

contradictory adj. OPPOSING, opposite, opposed, conflicting, clashing, contrasting, incompatible, inconsistent, irreconcilable, dissenting, contrary, dissident, antithetical.

contraption n. DEVICE, machine, mechanism, gadget, contrivance, apparatus, appliance; *informal* whatsit, thingamajig, thingamabob, thingummy, whatchamacallit, gizmo, doodah.

contrary adj. **1** OPPOSING, opposite, contradictory, conflicting, contrasting, clashing, incompatible, irreconcilable, inconsistent, incongruous, antithetical.

different when compared. ▶ v. **1** differ noticeably. **2** compare so as to note differences.

contravene v. break a law, treaty, etc. ■ **contravention** n.

contretemps /kon-truh-ton/ n. (pl. **contretemps**) a minor disagreement.

contribute v. **1** give to a common fund or effort. **2** help to cause. ■ **contribution** n. **contributor** n. **contributory** adj.

contrite adj. remorseful. ■ **contritely** adv. **contrition** n.

contrivance n. **1** the act of contriving. **2** a clever device or scheme.

contrive v. **1** make or bring about using skill. **2** manage to do.

contrived adj. artificial; seeming false.

control n. **1** the power to direct, influence, or limit something. **2** a means of limiting or regulating something. **3** a standard for checking the results of an experiment. ▶ v. (**controlling, controlled**) **1** have power over. **2** limit or regulate. ■ **controller** n.

controversial adj. causing contro-

versy. ■ **controversially** adv.

controversy n. (pl. **controversies**) debate or disagreement about a matter which arouses strong opinions.

contusion n. a bruise.

conundrum n. a puzzle or problem.

conurbation n. a large urban area where several towns have merged together.

convalesce v. regain health after illness. ■ **convalescence** n. **convalescent** adj. & n.

convection n. transference of heat within a fluid or gas caused by the tendency of warmer material to rise.

convene v. **1** call together for a meeting. **2** assemble. ■ **convener** (or **convenor**) n.

convenience n. **1** lack of effort or difficulty. **2** a useful device or situation. **3** a public toilet.

convenient adj. **1** fitting in with needs or plans. **2** involving little trouble or effort. ■ **conveniently** adv.

convent n. a building occupied by a

Thesaurus

2 AWKWARD, wilful, perverse, obstinate, stubborn, headstrong, wayward, intractable, unaccommodating, recalcitrant, intransigent, refractory, cantankerous; *informal* pig-headed, cussed, stroppy. ■ OPPOSITES compatible, accommodating.

contrast n. DIFFERENCE, dissimilarity, disparity, distinction, differentiation, divergence, opposition, dissimilitude. ▶ v. **1** COMPARE, set side by side, juxtapose, distinguish, differentiate, discriminate. **2** FORM A CONTRAST, differ, contradict, clash, conflict, be at variance, be contrary, diverge.

contribute v. **1** GIVE, donate, provide, subscribe, present, hand out, supply, grant, endow, bestow, confer, furnish; *informal* chip in. **2** LEAD TO, be conducive to, be instrumental in, help, add to, promote, advance; *informal* have a hand in.

contribution n. **1** DONATION, gift, subscription, offering, present, grant, allowance, subsidy, endowment, handout. **2** PARTICIPATION, input; *informal* one's pennyworth.

contrite adj. PENITENT, repentant, remorseful, regretful, sorry, conscience-stricken, guilt-stricken, chastened, in sackcloth and ashes. ■ OPPOSITES unrepentant.

control n. **1** AUTHORITY, power, charge, management, command, direction, rule, government, supervision, oversight,

regulation, jurisdiction, dominance, mastery, leadership, reign, supremacy, sway, superintendence, guidance. **2** LIMITATION, restriction, regulation, check, restraint, curb, brake. **3** INSTRUMENT, switch, dial, knob, lever. ▶ v. **1** BE IN CHARGE OF, be in control of, manage, head, direct, command, rule, govern, oversee, dominate, preside over, conduct, reign over; *informal* be the boss of, be in the driver's seat, be in the saddle. **2** REGULATE, restrain, keep in check, restrict, curb, hold back, contain, limit, subdue, bridle.

controversial adj. DISPUTED, contentious, at issue, open to question/discussion, disputable, debatable, under discussion, problematical, doubtful, questionable, contended, vexed, moot, tendentious.

controversy n. DISPUTE, argument, debate, disagreement, dissension, contention, altercation, wrangle, wrangling, quarrelling, squabbling, bickering, war of words, polemic.

convalesce v. GET BETTER, recover, recuperate, improve, return to health, be on the mend, regain strength.

convene v. **1** CALL, call together, summon, round up, rally, convoke. **2** ASSEMBLE, gather, meet, collect, congregate, muster.

convenient adj. **1** SUITABLE, suited, appropriate, fitting, fit, favourable, advancommunity of nuns.

convention n. **1** a way in which something is usually done. **2** socially acceptable behaviour. **3** an agreement between countries. **4** a conference. ■ **conventional** adj. **conventionally** adv.

converge v. come to or towards the same point. ■ **convergence** n. **convergent** adj.

conversant adj. (**conversant with**) having knowledge of.

conversation n. an informal talk. ■ **conversational** adj.

converse n. the opposite. ▶ adj. opposite. ▶ v. hold a conversation. ■ **conversely** adv.

convert v. **1** change in form, character, or function. **2** change money or units into another of a different kind. **3** change one's religious faith or other beliefs. ▶ n. a person who has changed their religious faith or other beliefs. ■ **conversion** n.

convertible adj. able to be converted. ▶ n. a car with a folding or detachable roof.

convex adj. having an outline or surface that curves outwards.

convey v. **1** transport or carry. **2** communicate an idea or feeling.

conveyance n. **1** the act of conveying. **2** a means of transport. **3** the transfer of ownership of property. ■ **conveyancing** n.

conveyor belt n. a continuous moving band for transporting objects.

convict v. declare guilty of a criminal offence. ▶ n. a convicted person serving a prison sentence.

conviction n. **1** a firm belief. **2** confidence.

convince v. **1** cause to feel certain that something is true. **2** persuade to do something.

convincing adj. **1** able to convince. **2** (of a victory or a winner) leaving no margin of doubt.

convivial adj. friendly and lively.

convocation n. a large assembly of people.

convoke v. summon to assemble.

convoluted adj. **1** extremely complex. **2** intricately folded or twisted. ■ **convolution** n.

Thesaurus

tageous, opportune, timely, well timed, expedient, useful, serviceable. **2** ACCESSIBLE, nearby, close at hand, handy, at hand, within reach, just round the corner. ■ OPPOSITES inconvenient.

convention n. **1** see ASSEMBLY. **2** PROTOCOL, formality, code, custom, tradition, practice, usage, etiquette, propriety.

conventional adj. **1** ACCEPTED, expected, customary, usual, normal, standard, regular, correct, proper, orthodox, traditional, prevailing, prevalent, conformist, decorous, conservative, formal, ritual. **2** COMMONPLACE, common, run-of-the-mill, everyday, prosaic, routine, stereotyped, pedestrian, hackneyed, unoriginal, clichéd, trite, platitudinous, bourgeois; informal common or garden. ■ OPPOSITES unconventional.

converge v. MEET, intersect, join, merge, unite, come together, become one, coincide, concur. ■ OPPOSITES diverge, separate.

conversant adj. ACQUAINTED WITH, familiar with, knowledgeable about, well versed in, informed about, apprised of, au fait with, experienced in, proficient in, practised in, skilled in; informal well up on.

conversation n. TALK, discussion, chat, dialogue, communication, gossip, exchange of views, conference, tête-à-tête,

discourse, colloquy, intercourse, heart to heart, palaver; informal powwow, confab, chinwag, natter.

convert v. **1** CHANGE, transform, alter, modify, reshape, refashion, remodel, remake, rebuild, reorganize, metamorphose, transfigure, transmogrify, transmute. **2** CONVINCE, persuade, reform, reeducate, baptize, save, proselytize.

convey v. **1** TRANSPORT, carry, bring, fetch, take, move, deliver, bear, shift, transfer, ship, conduct, channel, transmit; informal cart, lug. **2** TRANSMIT, communicate, pass on, send, make known, tell, announce, relate, impart, hand on, dispatch, reveal, disclose.

convict n. PRISONER, criminal, offender, felon, law-breaker, malefactor; informal jailbird, con, old lag. ▶ v. DECLARE/FIND GUILTY, sentence, condemn. ■ OPPOSITES acquit.

conviction n. **1** CONFIDENCE, assurance, belief, certainty, persuasion, firmness, earnestness, certitude. **2** BELIEF, view, principle, opinion, thought, idea, creed, tenet, persuasion. ■ OPPOSITES uncertainty.

convince v. PERSUADE, prove to, satisfy, assure, talk round, bring round, win over, sway.

convincing adj. PERSUASIVE, powerful, plausible, credible, conclusive, cogent,

convolvulus n. a twining plant with trumpet-shaped flowers.

convoy n. a group of ships or vehicles travelling together or under armed protection.

convulse v. 1 suffer convulsions. 2 (**be convulsed**) laugh uncontrollably. ■ **convulsive** adj.

convulsion n. 1 a violent involuntary movement of the body. 2 (**convulsions**) uncontrollable laughter.

coo v. (of a pigeon or dove) make a soft murmuring sound. ▶n. a cooing sound.

cook v. 1 prepare food by heating ingredients. 2 informal alter dishonestly. 3 (**cook up**) informal invent a story. ▶n. a person who cooks.

cooker n. an appliance for cooking food.

cookery n. the practice or skill of cooking.

cookie n. (pl. **cookies**) US a sweet biscuit.

cool adj. 1 fairly cold. 2 unfriendly or unenthusiastic. 3 calm. 4 informal fashionably attractive or impressive. ▶n. 1 low temperature. 2 composure. ▶v. make or become cool. ■ **coolly** adv. **coolness** n.

coolant n. a fluid used for cooling machinery.

coolie n. (pl. **coolies**) dated an unskilled labourer in some Asian countries.

coomb var. of COMBE.

coop n. a cage for poultry. ▶v. (**coop up**) confine in a small space.

cooper n. a person who makes or repairs casks and barrels.

cooperate v. 1 work together towards a common end. 2 comply with a request. ■ **cooperation** n.

cooperative adj. 1 involving cooperation. 2 willing to help. 3 (of a business) owned and run jointly by its members. ▶n. a cooperative business. ■ **cooperatively** adv.

co-opt v. appoint to a committee by the invitation of existing members.

coordinate v. 1 bring the different elements of something complex into an efficient way of working. 2 negotiate with others to work together effectively. ▶n. 1 each of the numbers used to indicate the position of a point. 2 (**coordinates**) matching items of clothing. ■ **coordination** n. **coordinator** n.

coot n. a black waterbird.

cop informal n. a police officer. ▶v. (**copping, copped**) 1 catch or arrest. 2 (**cop out**) avoid doing something that one ought to do.

cope v. deal effectively with something difficult.

copier n. a copying machine.

coping n. the top layer of a brick or stone wall.

copious adj. abundant; plentiful. ■ **copiously** adv.

copper n. 1 a red-brown metallic elem-

Thesaurus

incontrovertible. ■ OPPOSITES unconvincing.

convivial adj. FRIENDLY, genial, cordial, sociable, affable, amiable, congenial, agreeable, jolly, cheerful.

convoy n. GROUP, company, line, fleet, cortège, caravan, assemblage. ▶v. ESCORT, accompany, attend, protect, guard, defend, guide, shepherd, flank.

cook v. PREPARE, make, put together, concoct, improvise.

cool adj. 1 CHILLED, chilly, fresh, refreshing, unheated, breezy, draughty; informal nippy. See also COLD. 2 CALM, relaxed, composed, collected, self-possessed, level-headed, self-controlled, unexcited, unmoved, unperturbed, unruffled, unemotional, placid, serene. 3 ALOOF, distant, reserved, stand-offish, unfriendly, offhand, indifferent, uninterested, undemonstrative, unwelcoming, uncommunicative, chilly, frigid, impassive, dispassionate. 4 SOPHISTICATED, urbane, cosmopolitan, elegant. ■ OPPOSITES warm. ▶v. 1 CHILL, refrigerate, freeze.

2 LESSEN, diminish, reduce, dampen, abate, moderate, temper, soothe, assuage, allay, mollify. ■ OPPOSITES heat, inflame.

cooperate v. WORK TOGETHER, join forces, unite, help each other, act jointly, combine, collaborate, pool resources, conspire, connive, coordinate; informal pull together, pitch in, play ball.

cooperative adj. 1 JOINT, united, shared, unified, combined, concerted, collective, collaborative, coordinated. 2 HELPFUL, of assistance, obliging, accommodating, supportive, responsive, willing. ■ OPPOSITES uncooperative.

coordinate v. ARRANGE, organize, order, integrate, correlate, systematize, synchronize, harmonize.

cope v. MANAGE, succeed, survive, carry on, get through, get on, get by, subsist, come through; informal hack it, make it. □ **cope with** HANDLE, deal with, take care of, contend with, grapple with, struggle with.

copious adj. ABUNDANT, plentiful, ample,

ent. **2** (**coppers**) coins made of copper or bronze. **3** a reddish-brown colour. **4** informal a police officer. □ **copper-bottomed** thoroughly reliable. **copperplate** neat slanting handwriting.

coppice (or **copse**) n. a group of small trees growing together.

copulate v. have sex. ■ **copulation** n.

copy n. (pl. **copies**) **1** a thing made to look like another. **2** a single example of a book, record, etc. **3** matter to be printed in a newspaper etc. ▶v. (**copying**, **copied**) **1** make a copy of. **2** imitate. □ **copyright** the exclusive right to publish or record a work. **copywriter** a person who writes advertising copy.

coquette n. a woman who flirts. ■ **coquetry** n. **coquettish** adj.

coracle n. a small wicker boat.

coral n. **1** a hard substance consisting of the skeletons of certain sea animals. **2** a pinkish-red colour.

cor anglais /kor ong-glay/ n. (pl. **cors anglais**) a woodwind instrument of the oboe family.

corbel n. a stone or wooden support projecting from a wall.

cord n. **1** thin string or rope made from several twisted strands. **2** an electric flex. **3** corduroy. □ **cordless** (of an electrical appliance) working without connection to a mains supply.

cordial adj. **1** warm and friendly. **2** deeply felt. ▶n. a fruit-flavoured drink. ■ **cordiality** n. **cordially** adv.

cordite n. a smokeless explosive.

cordon n. a line or circle of police, soldiers, or guards forming a barrier. ▶v. (**cordon off**) close off by means of a cordon.

cordon bleu /kor-don **bler**/ adj. Cookery of the highest class.

corduroy n. thick cotton fabric with velvety ribs.

core n. **1** the tough central part of various fruits. **2** the central or most import-

ant part. ▶v. remove the core from a fruit.

co-respondent n. the person named in a divorce case as having committed adultery with the respondent.

corgi n. (pl. **corgis**) a short-legged breed of dog.

coriander n. a fragrant herb.

cork n. **1** a light, tough bark of a Mediterranean tree. **2** a bottle stopper made of cork. ▶v. **1** seal with a cork. **2** (**corked**) (of wine) spoilt by a decayed cork. □ **corkage** a charge made by a restaurant for serving wine brought in by a customer. **corkscrew** a device with a spiral rod for pulling corks from bottles.

corm n. an underground storage organ of some plants.

cormorant n. a large black seabird.

corn n. **1** wheat, oats, or maize; grain. **2** a small painful area of thickened skin, esp. on the foot. □ **cornflour** fine flour made from maize.

cornea n. the transparent layer forming the front of the eye.

cornelian var. of CARNELIAN.

corner n. **1** a place or angle where two or more sides or edges meet. **2** a free kick or hit taken from a corner of the field in football or hockey. ▶v. **1** force into a situation from which it is hard to escape. **2** control a market by dominating the supply of a commodity. **3** go round a bend in a road. □ **cornerstone** a vital part; a foundation.

cornet n. **1** a brass instrument like a small trumpet. **2** a cone-shaped wafer holding ice cream.

cornflower n. a blue-flowered plant.

cornice n. a moulding round the wall of a room just below the ceiling.

cornucopia n. **1** an abundant supply. **2** a symbol of plenty consisting of a goat's horn overflowing with flowers and fruit.

Thesaurus

profuse, full, extensive, generous, lavish, superabundant, rich, liberal, bountiful, exuberant, luxuriant, overflowing, abounding; *literary* plenteous, bounteous. ■ OPPOSITES scarce.

copy n. **1** REPRODUCTION, imitation, replica, likeness, representation, twin, counterfeit, forgery, fake, sham. **2** DUPLICATE, facsimile, carbon, carbon copy, photocopy, transcript; *trademark* Xerox, photostat. ▶v. **1** IMITATE, mimic, emulate, mirror, echo, follow, simulate, ape, parrot. **2** DUPLICATE, photocopy, xerox,

photostat. **3** REPRODUCE, replicate, forge, counterfeit.

cord n. STRING, rope, twine, cable, line, ligature.

cordon n. BARRIER, line, chain, ring, picket line. □ **cordon off** CLOSE OFF, fence off, shut off, separate off, isolate, enclose, encircle, surround, picket.

core n. CENTRE, heart, nucleus, nub, kernel, crux, essence, heart of the matter, substance, gist, pith; *informal* nitty-gritty.

corner n. **1** BEND, angle, curve, turn, crook. **2** JUNCTION, turn, intersection,

corny adj. (**cornier**, **corniest**) informal **1** very sentimental. **2** overused.

corolla n. the petals of a flower.

corollary n. (pl. **corollaries**) **1** a proposition that follows logically from another. **2** a direct consequence.

corona n. (pl. **coronae**) a ring of light round the sun or moon.

coronary adj. of the arteries which supply the heart. ▶n. (pl. **coronaries**) a blockage of the flow of blood to the heart.

coronation n. the ceremony of crowning a sovereign.

coroner n. an official who holds inquests into violent, sudden, or suspicious deaths.

coronet n. a small crown.

corpora pl. of CORPUS.

corporal n. a rank of army officer, below sergeant. ▶adj. of the human body. □ **corporal punishment** physical punishment, e.g. caning.

corporate adj. **1** of a business corporation. **2** of or shared by all members of a group.

corporation n. **1** a large company or a group of companies as a unit. **2** a group of people elected to govern a town.

corporeal adj. of the body; physical.

corps /kor/ n. (pl. **corps**) **1** a military unit. **2** an organized group of people.

corpse n. a dead body.

corpulent adj. fat.

corpus n. (pl. **corpora** or **corpuses**) a collection of written texts.

corpuscle n. a blood cell.

corral n. US an enclosure for livestock.

▶v. (**corralling**, **corralled**) put or keep in a corral.

correct adj. **1** free from error; true. **2** following accepted social standards. ▶v. **1** put right. **2** mark errors in a text. ■ **correction** n. **correctly** adv. **correctness** n.

corrective adj. designed to correct something undesirable.

correlate v. have or bring into a dependent relationship. ■ **correlation** n.

correspond v. **1** be similar or equivalent. **2** exchange letters.

correspondence n. **1** similarity. **2** letters sent or received.

correspondent n. **1** a person who writes letters. **2** a journalist reporting on a particular subject.

corridor n. **1** a passage in a building or train, with doors leading into rooms or compartments. **2** a belt of land linking two areas or following a road or river.

corrie n. a round hollow on a mountainside.

corroborate v. confirm or support. ■ **corroboration** n.

corrode v. (of metal etc.) wear or be worn away slowly by chemical action. ■ **corrosion** n. **corrosive** adj.

corrugate v. **1** contract into wrinkles or folds. **2** (**corrugated**) shaped into alternate ridges and grooves. ■ **corrugation** n.

corrupt adj. **1** willing to act dishonestly in return for money etc. **2** evil or immoral. **3** (of a text or computer data) full of errors. ▶v. make corrupt.

corsair n. a pirate.

Thesaurus

crossroads, fork, convergence. **3** NOOK, cranny, recess, crevice, hideaway, niche, cavity, hole; informal hidey-hole. ▶v. TRAP, capture, run to earth, bring to bay.

corpse n. BODY, remains, cadaver, carcass; informal stiff.

correct adj. **1** RIGHT, accurate, true, actual, exact, precise, unerring, faithful, strict, faultless, flawless, confirmed, verified; informal on the mark, spot on, bang on. **2** PROPER, suitable, appropriate, accepted, fit, fitting, seemly, apt, approved, conventional, usual, customary. ■ OPPOSITES wrong. ▶v. **1** RECTIFY, amend, set right, remedy, repair, emend, redress, cure, improve, better. **2** ADJUST, regulate, fix, set, standardize, normalize.

correspond v. **1** AGREE, be in agreement, accord, concur, coincide, conform, match, fit together, square, tally, dovetail, correlate. **2** EXCHANGE LETTERS, write to, communicate, keep in touch/contact.

correspondence n. LETTERS, mail, post, notes, messages.

corroborate v. CONFIRM, verify, bear out, authenticate, validate, certify, endorse, ratify, substantiate, uphold, attest to; informal back up.

corrode v. **1** EAT AWAY, wear away, erode, abrade, destroy, consume, rust, oxidize. **2** WEAR AWAY, rust, deteriorate, disintegrate, crumble, fragment.

corrugated adj. FURROWED, ridged, wrinkled, creased, grooved, crinkled, ribbed, channelled, puckered, fluted.

corrupt adj. **1** DISHONEST, fraudulent, unscrupulous, dishonourable, untrustworthy, venal; informal crooked, bent, shady. **2** IMMORAL, depraved, wicked,

corset n. a tight-fitting undergarment worn to shape or support the body.

cortège /kor-tezh/ n. a funeral procession.

cortex n. (pl. **cortices**) an outer layer of tissue, esp. of the brain. ■ **cortical** adj.

cortisone n. a hormone used to treat inflammation and allergy.

corvette n. a small warship.

cos abbrev. cosine.

cosh n. a heavy stick or bar used as a weapon. ▶ v. hit with a cosh.

cosine n. (in a right-angled triangle) the ratio of the side adjacent to an acute angle to the hypotenuse.

cosmetic adj. **1** intended to improve the appearance. **2** superficial. ▶ n. a cosmetic substance for the face and body.

cosmic adj. of the universe.

cosmology n. the science of the origin and development of the universe. ■ **cosmological** adj. **cosmologist** n.

cosmonaut n. a Russian astronaut.

cosmopolitan adj. **1** made up of people from many different countries. **2** familiar with many different countries.

cosmos n. the universe.

Cossack n. a member of a people of Russia and Ukraine noted for their horsemanship.

cosset v. (**cosseting**, **cosseted**) pamper.

cost v. (**costing**, **cost**) **1** be obtainable for a specific price. **2** involve the loss of. **3** (**costing**, **costed**) estimate the cost of. ▶ n. what something costs.

co-star n. a performer appearing with another of equal importance.

costermonger n. dated a person who sells fruit etc. from a handcart in the street.

costly adj. (**costlier**, **costliest**) **1** expensive. **2** causing suffering or loss.

costume n. **1** a set of clothes typical of a country or historical period. **2** clothes worn by an actor or performer.

cosy (US **cozy**) adj. (**cosier**, **cosiest**)

1 comfortable, warm, and secure. **2** not difficult or demanding. ▶ n. (pl. **cosies**) a cover to keep a teapot etc. hot. ▶ v. (**cosying**, **cosied**) (**cosy up to**) informal try to gain the favour of. ■ **cosily** adv. **cosiness** n.

cot n. **1** a child's bed with high barred sides. □ **cot death** the unexplained death of a baby in its sleep.

coterie /koh-tuh-ri/ n. a small exclusive group.

cottage n. a small house, esp. in the country. □ **cottage cheese** soft, lumpy white cheese. **cottage pie** a dish of minced beef topped with mashed potato.

cotton n. **1** soft white fibres round the seeds of a tropical plant. **2** cloth or thread made from these fibres. ▶ v. (**cotton on**) informal understand. □ **cotton wool** fluffy cotton material for wiping the skin.

cotyledon /ko-ti-lee-duhn/ n. the first leaf growing from a seed.

couch n. a sofa. ▶ v. express in a particular way. □ **couch potato** informal a person who spends a lot of time watching television.

couchette /koo-shet/ n. a railway carriage with seats convertible into beds.

cougar /koo-ger/ US a puma.

cough v. **1** send out air from the lungs with a sudden sharp sound. **2** (**cough up**) informal give money reluctantly. ▶ n. **1** an act or sound of coughing. **2** an illness causing coughing.

could past of CAN.

couldn't contr. could not.

coulomb n. a unit of electric charge.

council n. **1** an assembly meeting regularly for debate and administration. **2** a group of people elected to govern a town or region. □ **council tax** a UK tax charged on households by local authorities. ■ **councillor** n.

counsel n. **1** advice. **2** (pl. **counsel**) a barrister. ▶ v. (**counselling**, **coun-**

Thesaurus

evil, sinful, degenerate, perverted, dissolute, debauched, decadent, abandoned, lascivious, lecherous. ■ OPPOSITES honest, pure. ▶ v. **1** BRIBE, buy, buy off, pay off, suborn, induce, lure, entice; informal grease someone's palm. **2** DEPRAVE, pervert, warp, debauch, lead astray.

cosmic adj. **1** UNIVERSAL, worldwide. **2** VAST, huge, enormous, immense, immeasurable, infinite, limitless.

cosmopolitan adj. **1** INTERNATIONAL,

global, universal. **2** SOPHISTICATED, liberal, urbane, worldly, worldly-wise, well travelled. ■ OPPOSITES parochial.

cost n. **1** PRICE, charge, amount, rate, value, quotation, payment, expense, outlay; informal damage. ▶ v. BE PRICED AT, be worth, come to, fetch, amount to, realize; informal set someone back.

costly adj. **1** EXPENSIVE, dear, exorbitant, extortionate, extravagant; informal steep. **2** DISASTROUS, harmful, ruinous, catastrophic, pyrrhic. ■ OPPOSITES cheap,

selled; US **counseling, counseled**)
1 advise. **2** give professional psychological help to. ■ **counsellor** n.

count v. **1** find the total number of.
2 say numbers in order. **3** include.
4 regard as being. **5** be important.
6 (**count on**) rely on. ▶ n. **1** an act of
counting. **2** a total found by counting.
3 a point to consider. **4** a charge
against an accused person. **5** a foreign
nobleman. □ **countdown 1** the counting of seconds backwards to zero to
launch a rocket. **2** the final moments
before a significant event.

countenance n. a person's face or facial expression. ▶ v. tolerate or allow.

counter n. **1** a long flat surface over
which goods are sold or across which
business is conducted. **2** a small disc
used in board games. ▶ v. speak or act
against. ▶ adv. (**counter to**) **1** in the opposite direction. **2** in opposition to.

counter- prefix **1** against, opposing, or
done in return. **2** corresponding.

counteract v. reduce or prevent the effects of.

counter-attack n. & v. (make) an
attack in response to an opponent's
attack.

counterbalance n. a weight or influence that balances or neutralizes another. ▶ v. act as a counterbalance to.

counterfeit adj. not genuine; forged.
▶ n. a forgery. ▶ v. forge.

counterfoil n. the part of a cheque,
ticket, etc. kept as a record by the person issuing it.

countermand v. cancel an order.

counterpane n. a bedspread.

counterpart n. a person or thing that
corresponds to another.

counterpoint n. **1** the technique of
combining musical melodies. **2** a contrasting idea or theme.

counterproductive adj. having the
opposite of the desired effect.

countersign v. sign a document already signed by another person.

countersink v. (**countersinking,
countersunk**) insert a screw or bolt so
that the head is level with the surface.

countertenor n. the highest male
adult singing voice.

countess n. **1** the wife or widow of a
count or earl. **2** a woman with the rank
of count or earl.

countless adj. too many to be counted.

countrified adj. characteristic of the
country or country life.

country n. (pl. **countries**) **1** a nation
with its own government and territory.
2 areas outside large towns and cities.
□ **countryman** (or **countrywoman**)
1 a person living in the country. **2** a
person from one's own country. **countryside** the land and scenery of a rural
area.

county n. (pl. **counties**) each of the

inexpensive.

cosy adj. COMFORTABLE, snug, restful,
warm, relaxed, homely, sheltered, secure, safe; informal comfy, snug as a bug.
■ OPPOSITES uncomfortable.

counsel n. **1** see ADVICE. **2** see LAWYER.
▶ v. ADVISE, guide, direct, recommend,
warn, admonish, caution.

count v. **1** ADD UP, keep a count of, calculate, work out, total, estimate, reckon
up, enumerate, check, tally, compute,
tell; informal tot up. **2** REGARD, consider,
think, look upon, hold, judge, deem.
3 MATTER, be of account, signify, enter
into consideration, mean anything,
amount to anything, rate. □ **count on**
see RELY ON.

countenance n. FACE, features, expression, look, mien, appearance, visage,
air. ▶ v. see TOLERATE.

counter[1] n. **1** TOP, surface, worktop,
table, checkout, stand. **2** TOKEN, disc,
piece, marker, wafer, man.

counter[2] v. OPPOSE, resist, combat, dispute, argue against, rebut, contradict,

retaliate, ward off, parry; informal hit
back at, come back at.

counteract v. OFFSET, balance, counterbalance, neutralize, act counter to, be
an antidote to, oppose, work against,
thwart, negate, annul, impede, hinder,
invalidate, countervail.

counterbalance v. BALANCE, compensate for, make up for, offset, neutralize,
equalize, set off, undo, counterpoise.

counterfeit adj. FAKE, faked, forged,
copied, imitation, pseudo, fraudulent,
sham, bogus, spurious, feigned, ersatz;
informal phoney. ■ OPPOSITES genuine.
▶ n. FAKE, copy, forgery, imitation, reproduction, fraud, sham. ▶ v. FAKE,
copy, imitate, reproduce, simulate,
feign, falsify, pretend.

counterpart n. EQUIVALENT, equal, opposite number, parallel, complement,
match, twin, mate, fellow, analogue,
correlative, copy, duplicate.

countless adj. INNUMERABLE, incalculable, infinite, immeasurable, endless,
limitless, without limit/end, untold, in-

main administrative areas into which some countries are divided.

coup /koo/ n. (pl. **coups** /kooz/) **1** (also **coup d'état** /koo day-tah/) a sudden violent seizure of power from a government. **2** a successful move.

coup de grâce /koo duh grahss/ n. (pl. **coups de grâce**) a final blow or shot given to kill a wounded person or animal.

coupe /koo-pay, koop/ n. a car with a fixed roof, two doors, and a sloping back.

couple n. **1** two people or things. **2** two people who are married or romantically involved. ▶v. **1** connect or combine. **2** have sex.

couplet n. two successive rhyming lines of verse.

coupling n. a connecting device.

coupon n. **1** a voucher entitling the holder to something. **2** a detachable order form.

courage n. the ability to control fear when facing danger or pain. ■ **courageous** adj. **courageously** adv.

courgette /koor-zhet/ n. a small vegetable marrow.

courier /kuu-ri-er/ n. **1** a messenger carrying goods etc. **2** a person employed to guide and assist tourists.

course n. **1** a direction taken or intended. **2** the way something progresses. **3** a procedure adopted. **4** one of the parts of a meal. **5** a series of lessons. **6** a series

of treatments. **7** an area for racing, golf, or another sport. ▶v. **1** flow. **2** (**coursing**) hunting game, esp. hares, with greyhounds. □ **in** (**the**) **course of 1** in the process of. **2** during. **of course 1** as expected. **2** certainly; yes.

court n. **1** the judge, jury, and law officers who hear legal cases. **2** the place where a law court meets. **3** an area for playing tennis, squash, etc. **4** a courtyard. **5** the residence, advisers, and staff of a sovereign. ▶v. **1** dated try to win the love of. **2** try to win the support of. **3** risk danger etc. □ **court shoe** a woman's shoe with a low-cut upper and no fastening. **court martial** (pl. **court martials** or **courts martial**) a court trying offences against military law. **courtyard** an open area enclosed by walls or buildings.

courteous /ker-ti-uhss/ adj. polite. ■ **courteously** adv. **courtesy** n.

courtesan /kor-ti-zan/ n. a prostitute with upper-class clients.

courtier n. a sovereign's companion or adviser.

courtly adj. dignified and polite.

courtship n. the act or period of courting someone.

couscous /kuuss-kuuss/ n. a North African dish of steamed semolina.

cousin n. (also **first cousin**) a child of one's uncle or aunt. □ **second cousin** a child of one's parent's first cousin.

couture /koo-tyoor/ n. the design and

Thesaurus

exhaustible, boundless, myriad, legion, no end of.

country n. **1** STATE, nation, realm, kingdom, land, territory, power, commonwealth, domain, people, principality. **2** LAND, terrain, landscape, territory, scenery, region, area, district, neighbourhood.

coupon n. VOUCHER, token, ticket, slip, stub, certificate.

courage n. BRAVERY, fearlessness, valour, heroism, intrepidity, pluck, nerve, grit, boldness, daring, audacity, spirit, fortitude, firmness, resolution, tenacity, mettle, determination, lion-heartedness, gallantry, stout-heartedness, dauntlessness, indomitability, hardihood, fibre; *informal* guts, spunk, bottle. ■ OPPOSITES cowardice, fear.

courageous adj. BRAVE, fearless, heroic, bold, daring, plucky, audacious, unshrinking, dauntless, lion-hearted, intrepid, valiant, valorous, gallant, tenacious, indomitable, resolute, deter-

mined, game, spirited, stout-hearted, undaunted, stalwart; *informal* gutsy. ■ OPPOSITES cowardly.

course n. **1** ROUTE, way, track, direction, path, trail, line, road, passage, lane, tack, trajectory, circuit, ambit, orbit. **2** WAY, method, line of action, procedure, process, system, policy, programme, regimen. **3** DURATION, passing, passage, period, lapse, term, span. **4** CLASSES, lectures, curriculum, schedule, syllabus, programme.

court n. **1** LAW COURT, court of law, tribunal, forum, bench, chancery, assizes. **2** ATTENDANTS, household, retinue, entourage, train, suite. **3** HOMAGE, suit, wooing, courtship, respects, blandishments. ▶v. **1** WOO, pursue, run after, go out (with); *informal* date, go steady (with). **2** INVITE, risk, provoke, lead to, cause, bring on, elicit.

courteous adj. POLITE, well mannered, civil, gentlemanly, gracious, mannerly, well bred, civilized, urbane. ■ OPPOSmaking of fashionable clothes. ■ **couturier** n.

cove n. a small bay.

coven /kuv-uhn/ n. a group of witches who meet regularly.

covenant n. a formal agreement.

cover v. **1** put something over or in front of to protect or conceal. **2** spread or extend over. **3** deal with or report on. **4** travel a specified distance. **5** be enough to pay for. **6** protect by insurance. **7** (**cover up**) try to hide a mistake etc. **8** (**cover for**) temporarily do the job of. ▶ n. **1** something that covers or protects. **2** a protective outer part of a book etc. **3** protection by insurance. □ **coverage 1** the treatment of a subject by the media. **2** the extent to which something is covered. **covering letter** an explanatory letter enclosed with goods. **coverlet** a bedspread. **cover-up** an attempt to hide a mistake or crime.

covert adj. done secretly. ▶ n. a thicket in which game can hide. ■ **covertly** adv.

covet v. (**coveting**, **coveted**) long to possess something belonging to someone else. ■ **covetous** adj.

covey /kuv-i/ n. (pl. **coveys**) a small flock of game birds.

cow n. **1** a mature female animal of cattle and of the elephant or whale. **2** informal, derog. a woman. ▶ v. intimidate. □ **cowboy 1** a man on horseback who herds cattle in the western US. **2** informal a dishonest or unqualified tradesman.

coward n. a person who lacks courage. ■ **cowardly** adj. **cowardice** n.

cower v. crouch or shrink in fear.

cowl n. **1** a monk's hood or hooded robe. **2** a covering for a chimney.

cowling n. a removable cover for an engine.

cowrie n. a shellfish with a glossy shell.

cowslip n. a wild plant with small yellow flowers.

cox n. a coxswain. ▶ v. act as a cox for.

coxcomb n. dated a vain and conceited man.

coxswain /kok-suhn/ n. the person who steers a rowing boat.

coy adj. **1** pretending to be shy or modest. **2** reluctant to give details about something. ■ **coyly** adv.

coyote /koy-oh-ti/ n. a North American wolf-like wild dog.

coypu n. a large beaver-like South American rodent.

cozy US = **cosy**.

crab n. a ten-legged shellfish.

crab apple n. a small, sour apple.

crabbed adj. **1** (of writing) hard to read. **2** (also **crabby**) bad-tempered.

Thesaurus

ITES discourteous, rude.

courtier n. ATTENDANT, follower, steward, page, squire, cup-bearer, train-bearer, liegeman.

cove n. BAY, inlet, sound, creek, bight, anchorage; Sc. firth.

cover v. **1** PLACE OVER, spread over, protect, shield, shelter, conceal, coat, extend over, cloak, overlay, blanket, carpet, drape, overlie, overspread, shroud, surface, veil, enclose, mask, screen, obscure, enshroud, house, secrete, bury, hide, submerge, layer, film, mantle, pave, clothe, wrap, swaddle, attire, garb, robe, encase, sheathe. **2** DEAL WITH, involve, take in, contain, encompass, embrace, incorporate, treat, examine, survey. **3** REPORT, write up, describe, tell of, give an account of, give details of, investigate. ▶ n. **1** COVERING, surface, top, lid, cap, screen, layer, coat, coating, carpet, canopy, crust, mantle, blanket, overlay, mask, cloak, veil, film, sheath, shield, veneer, wrapping, housing, cocoon, casing, cladding, skin, tarpaulin, encrustation, rind. **2** DISGUISE, front, camouflage, pretence, facade, false front, smokescreen, window-dressing, pretext, cloak, veil, mask. **3** INSURANCE, protection, compensation, indemnity, indemnification.

covert adj. SECRET, concealed, hidden, surreptitious, furtive, stealthy, private, underground. ■ OPPOSITES overt.

covet v. DESIRE, want, wish for, long/yearn for, crave, hanker after, lust after, thirst for, hunger for, set one's heart on, aspire to, aim for, envy, begrudge.

cowardly adj. FEARFUL, timid, timorous, faint-hearted, spineless, lily-livered, chicken-hearted, craven, base, shrinking, pusillanimous, afraid of one's shadow, submissive, unheroic, unchivalrous, ungallant; informal chicken, yellow, yellow-bellied, gutless, wimpish. ■ OPPOSITES brave, courageous.

cower v. CRINGE, shrink, flinch, draw back, recoil, crouch, wince, slink, blench, quail, quake, tremble, quiver, grovel, skulk.

coy adj. COQUETTISH, arch, kittenish, evasive, shy, modest, unforthcoming, de-

crack n. **1** a line where something has broken but not separated. **2** a sudden sharp blow. **3** a sharp blow. **4** informal a joke. **5** informal an attempt. **6** a strong form of cocaine. ▶ v. **1** break without separating. **2** give way under pressure. **3** make a sudden sharp sound. **4** hit hard. **5** (of a voice) suddenly change in pitch. **6** informal solve. ▶ adj. very good or skilful. □ **crackbrained** informal extremely foolish. **crackdown** a series of severe measures against something. **crack down on** informal take severe measures against. **crackpot** informal eccentric or impractical. **crack up** informal suffer an emotional breakdown.

cracker n. **1** a paper tube making a sharp noise when pulled apart. **2** a small explosive firework. **3** a thin dry biscuit.

crackers adj. informal crazy.

crackle v. & n. (make) a series of slight cracking noises. ■ **crackly** adj.

crackling n. the crisp fatty skin of roast pork.

cradle n. **1** a baby's bed on rockers. **2** a place where something originates. **3** a supporting framework. ▶ v. hold or support gently.

craft n. **1** an activity involving skill with one's hands. **2** skill. **3** (pl. **craft**) a ship or boat. ▶ v. make skilfully.

craftsman n. a worker skilled in a craft. ■ **craftsmanship** n.

crafty adj. (**craftier**, **craftiest**) clever at deceiving people; cunning. ■ **craftily** adv. **craftiness** n.

crag n. a steep or rugged rock face. ■ **craggy** adj.

cram v. (**cramming**, **crammed**) **1** force into too small a space. **2** overfill. **3** study hard for an examination.

cramp n. painful involuntary tightening of a muscle. ▶ v. restrict.

crampon n. a spiked plate fixed to a boot for climbing on ice or rock.

cranberry n. a small sour-tasting red berry.

crane n. **1** a tall machine used for lifting and moving heavy objects. **2** a large wading bird. ▶ v. stretch out one's neck to see something.

cranium n. (pl. **craniums** or **crania**) the skull.

crank n. **1** a right-angled part of an axle or shaft for converting linear to circular motion. **2** an eccentric person. ▶ v. turn a crankshaft or handle. □ **crankshaft** a shaft driven by a crank.

cranny n. (pl. **crannies**) a crevice.

craps n. a gambling game played with two dice.

crash v. **1** (of a vehicle) collide violently with something. **2** (of an aircraft) fall from the sky and hit the land or sea. **3** move loudly and forcefully. **4** Computing fail suddenly. ▶ n. **1** an instance of crashing. **2** a sudden loud noise. ▶ adj. rapid and concentrated. □ **crash helmet** a helmet worn esp. by a motorcyclist to protect the head. **crash-land** (of an aircraft) land roughly in an emergency.

crass adj. very thoughtless and stupid.

Thesaurus

mure, bashful, reticent, diffident, retiring, self-effacing, hesitant, shrinking, withdrawn, timid, prudish, lacking confidence, unsure. ■ OPPOSITES brazen.

crack n. **1** FRACTURE, break, chip, split, fissure, crevice, breach, rupture, rift, chink, gap, cavity, slit, cleft, cranny. **2** ATTEMPT, try, shot, opportunity; informal go, stab. **3** see JOKE. ▶ v. **1** FRACTURE, break, fragment, chip, split, splinter, snap. **2** BREAK DOWN, give way, collapse, yield, succumb; informal go to pieces, come apart at the seams.

cradle n. **1** CRIB, cot, carrycot, bassinet. **2** BIRTHPLACE, source, fount, wellspring, beginnings, nursery. ▶ v. HOLD, rock, nestle, shelter, support.

craft n. **1** SKILL, skilfulness, expertise, ability, mastery, artistry, art, technique, aptitude, dexterity, talent, flair, knack, genius. **2** TRADE, occupation, vocation, calling, pursuit, business, line,

work, employment. **3** VESSEL, ship, boat, aircraft, plane, spacecraft.

crafty adj. CUNNING, artful, calculating, designing, scheming, wily, sly, devious, tricky, foxy, shrewd, astute, canny, sharp, Machiavellian, shifty, guileful, deceitful, duplicitous, insidious, treacherous, fraudulent, underhand; informal crooked. ■ OPPOSITES honest.

crag n. CLIFF, bluff, escarpment, scarp, ridge, peak, pinnacle, tor.

cram v. **1** STUFF, push into, force into, pack in, ram down, press into, squeeze into, compress, compact, condense. **2** see STUDY.

cramped adj. CONFINED, crowded, packed, narrow, small, restricted, limited, uncomfortable, closed in, hemmed in, tight, overfull, squeezed, jammed in, congested. ■ OPPOSITES spacious.

crash v. **1** COLLIDE WITH, bump into, smash into, plough into, pitch into, jolt,

crate n. **1** a wooden box for transporting goods. **2** a container divided into sections for holding bottles. ▸v. pack in a crate.

crater n. a large hollow in the ground or forming the mouth of a volcano.

cravat n. a man's scarf worn tucked inside a shirt.

crave v. **1** feel a strong desire for. **2** old use ask for. ■ **craving** n.

craven adj. cowardly.

craw n. a bird's crop.

crawl v. **1** move forward on the hands and knees or with the body on the ground. **2** move very slowly. **3** (**be crawling with**) be very crowded with. **4** informal behave in a servile way to win favour. ▸n. **1** a crawling movement or pace. **2** an overarm swimming stroke. ■ **crawler** n.

crayfish n. a shellfish like a small lobster.

crayon n. a stick of coloured chalk or wax, used for drawing. ▸v. draw with a crayon or crayons.

craze n. a widespread but short-lived enthusiasm for something.

crazy adj. (**crazier, craziest**) **1** insane. **2** very enthusiastic or fond. **3** very foolish. □ **crazy paving** paving made of irregular pieces. ■ **crazily** adv. **craziness** n.

creak v. & n. (make or move with) a harsh, high sound. ■ **creaky** adj.

cream n. **1** the thick fatty part of milk. **2** something resembling cream in consistency. **3** the very best of a group. **4** a pale yellowish-white colour. ▸v. **1** beat to form a smooth soft paste. **2** (**cream off**) take away the best of. ■ **creamy** adj.

creamery n. (pl. **creameries**) a factory producing butter and cheese.

crease n. **1** a line or ridge made on paper or cloth by folding or pressing. **2** any of a number of lines marked on a cricket pitch at specified places. ▸v. make or develop creases in.

create v. **1** bring into existence. **2** cause to happen; produce. ■ **creation** n. **creator** n.

creative adj. involving the use of the imagination or original ideas in order to create something. ■ **creatively** adv. **creativity** n.

creature n. a living being.

Thesaurus

jar. **2** FALL, topple, tumble, overbalance, pitch, plunge, hurtle, lurch. ▸n. **1** COLLISION, accident, smash, pile-up, bump; *informal* prang, shunt. **2** CLASH, clang, clank, bang, smash, clangour, racket, din, boom, explosion. **3** COLLAPSE, failure, fall, plummet, foundering, ruin, ruination.

crate n. BOX, case, chest, carton, basket, hamper, receptacle.

crater n. HOLE, hollow, pit, cavity, depression, dip, chasm, abyss.

crawl v. **1** CREEP, move on hands and knees, go on all fours, slither, squirm, wriggle, writhe, worm one's way, sneak. **2** FAWN, flatter, grovel, cringe, toady; *informal* suck up.

craze n. TREND, fashion, fad, vogue, enthusiasm, passion, obsession, mania, fixation, whim, fascination, preoccupation, rage, infatuation.

crazy adj. **1** MAD, insane, unbalanced, demented, lunatic, crazed, of unsound mind, deranged, unhinged, touched, berserk; *informal* batty, loony, nuts, nutty, cuckoo, bonkers, mental, round the bend/twist, potty. **2** ABSURD, idiotic, stupid, ridiculous, silly, foolish, peculiar, odd, strange, queer, eccentric, bizarre, weird, fantastic, inane, fatuous, unwise, preposterous; *informal* half-

baked, potty. **3** ENTHUSIASTIC, mad, keen, passionate, smitten, fanatical, devoted, fervent, excited. ■ OPPOSITES sensible, uninterested.

cream n. LOTION, paste, ointment, salve, unguent, liniment, emulsion.

crease n. WRINKLE, furrow, line, fold, crinkle, ridge, corrugation, pucker, ruck, pleat, tuck. ▸v. CRUMPLE, wrinkle, rumple, crinkle, ruck up, pucker, ridge, furrow, corrugate, pleat, tuck.

create v. **1** PRODUCE, originate, generate, design, establish, set up, invent, make, build, construct, develop, initiate, engender, frame, fabricate, erect, found, institute, constitute, inaugurate, shape, form, mould, forge, concoct, hatch. **2** BRING INTO BEING, give birth/life to, father, sire, spawn, procreate; *literary* beget. **3** RESULT IN, make, produce, bring about, give rise to, lead to. ■ OPPOSITES destroy.

creative adj. INVENTIVE, imaginative, original, artistic, inspired, visionary, talented, gifted, resourceful, ingenious, clever, productive, fertile, fecund.

creator n. **1** INVENTOR, originator, author, maker, designer, initiator, deviser, producer, manufacturer, architect, builder, prime mover, parent, generator; *literary* begetter. **2** GOD, the

crèche /kresh/ n. a day nursery.

credence n. belief.

credentials pl. n. **1** qualifications, qualities, etc. indicating a person's suitability for something. **2** documents proving these.

credible adj. able to be believed. ■ **credibility** n. **credibly** adv.

credit n. **1** a system allowing payment for purchases to be deferred. **2** public recognition or praise. **3** a source of pride. **4** an entry in an account recording a sum received. **5** an acknowledgement of a contributor's role at the beginning or end of a film. ▶ v. (**crediting**, **credited**) **1** (**credit with**) attribute something to. **2** believe. **3** add money to an account. □ **credit card** a plastic card allowing the holder to make purchases on credit.

creditable adj. deserving praise. ■ **creditably** adv.

creditor n. a person or company to whom money is owed.

credulous adj. too ready to believe things. ■ **credulity** n.

creed n. **1** a system of religious belief. **2** a set of beliefs or principles.

creek n. **1** an inlet in a shoreline. **2** US a stream.

creep v. (**creeping**, **crept**) **1** move slowly and cautiously. **2** progress or develop gradually. **3** (**creeping**) (of a plant) growing along the ground, a wall, etc. ▶ n. **1** informal an unpleasant person. **2** slow and gradual movement. □ **give one the creeps** informal make one feel disgust or fear. ■ **creeper** n.

creepy adj. (**creepier**, **creepiest**) informal frightening or disturbing.

cremate v. burn a corpse to ashes. ■ **cremation** n.

crematorium n. (pl. **crematoria** or **crematoriums**) a building where the dead are cremated.

crenellated adj. having battlements. ■ **crenellations** pl. n.

Creole /kree-ohl/ n. **1** a descendant of European settlers in the Caribbean or Central or South America. **2** a language formed from a mixture of other languages.

creosote n. a dark brown oil obtained from coal tar.

crêpe n. **1** (also **crape**) /krayp/ a fabric or a type of rubber with a wrinkled surface. **2** /krep/ a thin pancake.

crept past & past part. of CREEP.

crepuscular adj. of or like twilight.

crescendo n. (pl. **crescendos** or **crescendi**) a gradual increase in loudness. ▶ adv. & adj. gradually becoming louder.

crescent n. a narrow curved shape tapering to a point at each end.

cress n. a plant with small leaves, eaten in salads.

crest n. **1** a tuft or outgrowth on a bird's

Thesaurus

Almighty.

creature n. **1** ANIMAL, beast, being, living thing, organism; US informal critter. **2** PERSON, human being, individual, character, soul, mortal; informal fellow. **3** LACKEY, minion, puppet, toady, sycophant, hireling, retainer, dependant, hanger-on, vassal.

credentials pl. n. DOCUMENTS, references, documentation, qualifications, certificate, diploma, testimonial, warrant, licence, permit, card, voucher, passport, letter of introduction.

credible adj. **1** BELIEVABLE, plausible, convincing, likely, conceivable, imaginable, persuasive, tenable. **2** ACCEPTABLE, reliable, trustworthy, dependable. ■ OPPOSITES incredible, untrustworthy.

credit n. **1** PRAISE, acclaim, approval, commendation, acknowledgement, tribute, kudos, glory, recognition, esteem, regard, respect, merit, veneration; formal laudation. **2** FINANCIAL STANDING/STATUS, solvency. ▶ v. **1** BELIEVE, accept, trust, have faith in, rely on, depend on, put confidence in; informal fall for, swallow, buy. **2** ASCRIBE TO, attribute to, assign to, give credit to, accredit to, impute to, chalk up to, put down to.

creditable adj. PRAISEWORTHY, admirable, commendable, laudable, meritorious, exemplary, worthy, respectable, reputable, estimable, honourable, deserving. ■ OPPOSITES discreditable.

credulous adj. GULLIBLE, easily taken in, over-trusting, naive, unsuspicious, uncritical; informal green, wet behind the ears. ■ OPPOSITES suspicious.

creed n. BELIEF, principle, teaching, doctrine, dogma, tenet, catechism, article of faith.

creek n. INLET, bay, cove, estuary, bight; Sc. firth.

creep v. CRAWL, move on hands and knees, go on all fours, slither, squirm, wriggle, writhe, move stealthily, sneak, tiptoe, slink, skulk, worm one's way. ▶ n. SYCOPHANT, toady, fawner, sneak; informal bootlicker.

creepy adj. HORRIFYING, horrific, horrible,

or animal's head. **2** a plume of feathers on a helmet. **3** the top of a ridge, wave, etc. **4** a design above a shield on a coat of arms. □ **crestfallen** sad and disappointed. ■ **crested** adj.

cretin n. **1** informal a stupid person. **2** dated a person who is physically and mentally handicapped. ■ **cretinous** adj.

crevasse n. a deep open crack esp. in a glacier.

crevice n. a narrow opening in a rock or wall.

crew¹ n. **1** the people working on a ship, aircraft, etc. **2** a group working together. ▶ v. act as a member of a crew. □ **crew cut** a very short haircut. **crew neck** a close-fitting round neckline.

crew² past of CROW.

crib n. **1** a child's cot. **2** a rack for animal fodder. **3** informal a translation of a text for use by students. ▶ v. (**cribbing, cribbed**) informal copy dishonestly.

cribbage n. a card game.

crick n. a painful stiff feeling in the neck or back. ▶ v. cause a crick in.

cricket n. **1** an open-air game played with a bat, ball, and wickets, between two teams of 11 players. **2** a brown insect like a grasshopper. ■ **cricketer** n.

cried past & past part. of CRY.

crime n. **1** a serious offence punishable by law. **2** such actions as a whole.

criminal n. a person who has committed a crime. ▶ adj. **1** of crime or a crime. **2** informal disgraceful. ■ **criminality** n. **criminally** adv.

criminology n. the study of crime. ■ **criminologist** n.

crimp v. press into ridges.

crimson n. a deep red colour.

cringe v. **1** cower in fear. **2** feel embarrassment or disgust.

crinkle v. form small creases. ▶ n. a small crease. ■ **crinkly** adj.

crinoline n. a petticoat stiffened with hoops, formerly worn to make a long skirt stand out.

cripple n. old use or offens. a person unable to walk properly through disability or injury. ▶ v. **1** make unable to walk properly. **2** severely damage.

crisis n. (pl. **crises**) a time of severe difficulty or danger.

crisp adj. **1** firm, dry, and brittle. **2** cold and bracing. **3** brisk and decisive. ▶ n. a thin slice of fried potato. □ **crispbread** a thin, crisp biscuit made from rye or wheat. ■ **crisply** adv. **crispness** n. **crispy** adj.

criss-cross adj. with a pattern of crossing lines. ▶ v. form a criss-cross pattern on.

criterion n. (pl. **criteria**) a standard of judgement.

Thesaurus

frightening, scary, terrifying, hair-raising, awful, disturbing, eerie, sinister, weird, nightmarish, macabre, ominous, menacing, threatening, disgusting, repellent, repulsive, revolting.

crest n. **1** COMB, tuft, cockscomb, plume. **2** SUMMIT, top, peak, crown, brow, apex, ridge, heights. **3** BADGE, emblem, regalia, insignia, device, coat of arms, seal, shield, sign, symbol.

crestfallen adj. DOWNCAST, dejected, depressed, glum, downhearted, disheartened, discouraged, dispirited, despondent, disconsolate; informal down in the dumps, in the doldrums. ■ OPPOSITES cheerful.

crevice n. FISSURE, cleft, crack, cranny, split, rift, slit, gash, rent, fracture, opening, gap, hole, interstice.

crick n. PAIN, cramp, twinge, spasm, pang, stiffness.

crime n. **1** OFFENCE, violation, felony, misdemeanour, misdeed, wrong, transgression, fault, injury; old use trespass. **2** LAWBREAKING, illegality, misconduct, wrongdoing, delinquency, villainy, wickedness, evil; Law malfeasance.

criminal adj. **1** UNLAWFUL, illegal, illicit, lawless, felonious, delinquent, indictable, culpable, wrong, villainous, corrupt, evil, wicked, iniquitous, nefarious; informal crooked, bent. **2** DEPLORABLE, scandalous, shameful, reprehensible, senseless, foolish, ridiculous, sinful, immoral. ▶ n. OFFENDER, lawbreaker, wrongdoer, malefactor, felon, delinquent, miscreant, culprit, villain, gangster, racketeer, hoodlum, bandit, transgressor, sinner; informal crook, con, baddy; old use trespasser.

cringe v. COWER, shrink, draw back, quail, flinch, recoil, start, shy, dodge, duck, crouch, wince, tremble, quiver, shake.

cripple v. **1** DISABLE, incapacitate, lame, debilitate, impair, damage, maim, weaken, enfeeble, paralyse. **2** DAMAGE, injure, ruin, destroy, weaken, hamstring, enfeeble, paralyse, bring to a standstill.

crisis n. EMERGENCY, disaster, catastrophe, calamity, predicament, plight, mess, trouble, difficulty, extremity, dilemma, quandary, exigency; informal fix,

☑️ The singular form is **criterion** and the plural form is **criteria**. It's wrong to use **criteria** as a singular, as in *a further criteria needs to be considered*.

critic n. **1** a person who points out faults. **2** a person who assesses literary or artistic works.

critical adj. **1** expressing disapproving comments. **2** assessing a literary or artistic work. **3** having a decisive importance. **4** at a point of danger or crisis. ■ **critically** adv.

criticism n. **1** expression of disapproval. **2** the critical assessment of literary or artistic works.

criticize (or **-ise**) v. **1** express disapproval of. **2** assess a literary or artistic work.

critique n. a critical assessment.

croak n. a deep hoarse sound, like that made by a frog. ▶v. **1** utter a croak. **2** informal die. ■ **croaky** adj.

crochet /kroh-shay/ n. a handicraft in which yarn is looped into a fabric by means of a hooked needle. ▶v. make in this way.

crock n. an earthenware pot or jar.

crockery n. china or earthenware plates, cups, etc.

crocodile n. **1** a large tropical reptile living partly in water. **2** informal a line of schoolchildren walking in pairs. ▢ **crocodile tears** false sorrow.

crocus n. (**crocuses**) a small spring-flowering plant.

croft n. a small rented farm in Scotland. ■ **crofter** n.

croissant /krwass-on/ n. a crescent-shaped flaky bread roll.

crone n. an ugly old woman.

crony n. (pl. **cronies**) informal a close friend or companion.

crook n. **1** a hooked staff. **2** a bend. **3** informal a criminal. ▶v. bend a finger.

crooked adj. **1** not straight. **2** informal dishonest. ■ **crookedly** adv.

croon v. hum, sing, or speak in a soft, low voice. ■ **crooner** n.

crop n. **1** a plant grown for food or other use. **2** a harvest from this. **3** a group of things appearing at one time. **4** a very short hairstyle. **5** a riding crop. **6** a pouch in a bird's throat where food is prepared for digestion. ▶v. (**cropping, cropped**) **1** cut or bite off very short. **2** (**crop up**) occur unexpectedly. **3** produce a crop.

cropper n. (**come a cropper**) informal fall or fail heavily.

croquet /kroh-kay/ n. a game played on a lawn with balls driven through hoops with mallets.

Thesaurus

pickle, scrape.

crisp adj. **1** BRITTLE, breakable, crunchy, crispy, friable. **2** BRISK, decisive, vigorous, brusque, curt, abrupt. ■ OPPOSITES limp, soft, rambling.

criterion n. MEASURE, standard, benchmark, norm, yardstick, scale, touchstone, barometer, exemplar, canon.

critic n. **1** REVIEWER, commentator, pundit, arbiter, judge, evaluator. **2** ATTACKER, fault-finder, detractor, reviler, vilifier, carper, backbiter; *informal* knocker, nit-picker.

critical adj. **1** CENSORIOUS, disapproving, disparaging, derogatory, fault-finding, carping, depreciatory, niggling, cavilling, judgemental, uncomplimentary, scathing, unfavourable, captious; *informal* nit-picking. **2** EVALUATIVE, analytic, interpretative, expository, explanatory, explicative, elucidative, annotative. **3** CRUCIAL, decisive, pivotal, key, important, vital, urgent, pressing. **4** DANGEROUS, grave, serious, risky, perilous, hazardous, precarious. ■ OPPOSITES complimentary, unimportant.

criticism n. **1** CONDEMNATION, censure, disapproval, disparagement, fault-finding, reproof, carping, cavilling, captiousness, animadversion; *informal* nitpicking, brickbats, flak, knocking, slamming. **2** EVALUATION, comment, commentary, assessment, appreciation, appraisal, analysis, interpretation, judgement, elucidation, explication, annotation.

criticize v. FIND FAULT WITH, censure, denounce, condemn, disapprove of, disparage, cast aspersions on, snipe at, impugn, scold, decry, carp at, cavil at, excoriate, animadvert on; *informal* nit-pick, pick holes in, knock, slam, slate, pan, lash, get at, pitch into, rap, flay, hand out brickbats. ■ OPPOSITES praise.

crockery n. DISHES, tableware, pottery, porcelain, china, earthenware.

crook n. **1** see CRIMINAL. **2** BEND, curve, curvature, angle, bow, hook.

crooked adj. **1** see CRIMINAL. **2** BENT, curved, twisted, warped, contorted, angled, bowed, irregular, hooked, flexed, winding, twisting, zigzag, misshapen, out of shape, lopsided, off-centre, meandering, sinuous, tortuous, serpentine.

croquette /kroh-ket/ n. a small ball of potato etc. fried in breadcrumbs.

crosier var. of CROZIER.

cross n. **1** a mark or shape formed by two intersecting lines or pieces (+ or ×). **2** a cross-shaped medal or monument. **3** a thing that has to be endured. **4** a hybrid. **5** a mixture of two things. **6** a pass of the ball across the field in football. ▶v. **1** go or extend across. **2** pass in an opposite or different direction. **3** place crosswise. **4** oppose the wishes of. **5** draw a line or lines across; mark with a cross. **6** mark a cheque so that it must be paid into a named account. **7** pass the ball across the field in football. **8** cause to interbreed. ▶adj. annoyed. □ **at cross purposes** misunderstanding one another. **crossbow** a mechanical bow with a wooden support. **cross-breed** produce an animal by interbreeding. **cross-check** verify figures etc. by an alternative method. **cross-dressing** the wearing of clothing typical of the opposite sex. **cross-examine** question a witness in a court to check a testimony already given. **cross-eyed** having one or both eyes turned inwards. **crossfire** gunfire crossing another line of fire. **cross reference** a reference to another part in the same book. **crossroads** a place where roads cross each other. **cross section** **1** a surface exposed by cutting across something. **2** a representative sample. **crosswise** (or **crossways**) **1** in the form of a cross. **2** diagonally. **crossword** a puzzle consisting of a grid of squares into which intersecting words are written according to clues. ■ **crossly** adv. **crossness** n.

crossing n. **1** a place where roads or railway lines cross. **2** a place to cross a road or railway line.

crotch n. the part of the body between the legs where they join the torso.

crotchet n. a musical note having the value of half a minim.

crotchety adj. irritable.

crouch v. bend the knees and bring the upper body forward and down. ▶n. a crouching position.

croup n. **1** inflammation of the throat in children, causing coughing and breathing difficulties. **2** the rump of a horse.

croupier /kroo-pi-ay/ n. the person in charge of a gambling table at a casino.

crouton /kroo-ton/ n. a small piece of fried or toasted bread as a garnish.

crow n. **1** a large black bird. **2** the cry of a cock. ▶v. (**crowing**, **crowed** or **crew**) **1** (of a cock) make its loud shrill cry. **2** express gloating triumph.

crowbar n. an iron bar with a flattened end, used as a lever.

crowd n. a large group of people. ▶v. **1** fill a space almost completely. **2** move or gather in a crowd.

crown n. **1** a monarch's ceremonial headdress. **2** (**the Crown**) the monarchy or reigning monarch. **3** the top of a hat, person's head, etc. **4** an artificial covering for a tooth. ▶v. **1** place a crown on the head of a new monarch. **2** rest on or form the top of. **3** be the climax of. □ **Crown prince** (or **Crown**

Thesaurus

■ OPPOSITES straight.

crop n. HARVEST, growth, yield, produce, vintage, fruits, gathering, reaping. ▶v. CUT, trim, clip, shear, lop, snip, prune, mow, graze, nibble, browse.

cross n. **1** AFFLICTION, trouble, worry, burden, trial, disaster, tribulation, misfortune, misery, adversity, woe, pain, suffering, catastrophe, calamity. **2** HYBRID, mixture, cross-breed, amalgam, blend, combination, mongrel. ▶v. **1** GO ACROSS, span, stretch/extend across, pass over, bridge, ford, traverse. **2** INTERSECT, meet, join, converge, crisscross, interweave, intertwine. **3** OPPOSE, resist, thwart, frustrate, obstruct, foil, impede, hinder, hamper, check, contradict. ▶adj. ANNOYED, irritated, vexed, bad-tempered, short-tempered, irascible, touchy, fractious, peevish, crotchety, grouchy, querulous, cantanker-

ous, testy, waspish; informal snappy. ■ OPPOSITES pleased, good-humoured. □ **cross out** see DELETE.

crossing n. **1** JUNCTION, crossroads, intersection. **2** PEDESTRIAN/PELICAN CROSSING, underpass, subway, level crossing, bridge, ford, causeway, flyover.

crouch v. SQUAT, bend, duck, stoop, hunch over, hunker, cower, cringe.

crowd n. **1** HORDE, throng, mob, mass, multitude, host, rabble, army, herd, flock, drove, swarm, troupe, pack, press, crush, flood, assembly, gathering, collection, congregation, convention. **2** AUDIENCE, house, turnout, gate, attendance, spectators, viewers, listeners. ▶v. **1** GATHER, cluster, flock, swarm, throng, huddle, concentrate, foregather. **2** PRESS, push, shove, thrust, jostle, elbow, squeeze, pile, pack, cram, jam, bundle, stuff.

princess) the heir to a throne.

crozier (or **crosier**) n. a bishop's hooked staff.

cruces pl. of CRUX.

crucial adj. decisive or critical; very important ■ **crucially** adv.

crucible n. a container in which metals are melted.

crucifix n. a model of a cross with a figure of Jesus on it.

crucifixion n. **1** an act of crucifying someone. **2** (**the Crucifixion**) the killing of Jesus in such a way.

cruciform adj. cross-shaped.

crucify v. (**crucifying**, **crucified**) **1** put to death by nailing or binding to a cross. **2** informal criticize severely.

crude adj. **1** in a natural or raw state. **2** rough or simple. **3** coarse or vulgar. ■ **crudely** adv. **crudity** n.

crudités /kroo-di-tay/ pl. n. mixed raw vegetables to dip in a sauce.

cruel adj. (**crueller**, **cruellest** or **crueler**, **cruelest**) **1** taking pleasure in others' suffering. **2** causing pain or suffering. ■ **cruelly** adv. **cruelty** n.

cruet n. a set of containers for salt, pepper, etc. for use at the table.

cruise v. **1** travel around slowly, esp. by ship. **2** travel at a moderate economical speed. ▶n. a voyage on a ship taken as

a holiday.

cruiser n. **1** a fast warship. **2** a motor boat with a cabin.

crumb n. **1** a small fragment of bread etc. **2** a tiny amount.

crumble v. break or fall apart into small fragments. ▶n. a baked pudding made with fruit and a crumbly topping. ■ **crumbly** adj.

crummy adj. informal bad or unpleasant.

crumpet n. **1** a flat soft yeast cake eaten toasted. **2** informal women as objects of sexual desire.

crumple v. **1** crush so as to become creased. **2** collapse.

crunch v. **1** crush noisily with the teeth. **2** move with a noisy grinding sound. ▶n. **1** a crunching sound. **2** (**the crunch**) informal the crucial point. ■ **crunchy** adj.

crupper n. a strap looped under a horse's tail from the saddle.

crusade n. **1** a medieval Christian military expedition to recover the Holy Land from the Muslims. **2** a campaign for a cause. ▶v. take part in a crusade. ■ **crusader** n.

crush v. **1** press so as to squash, crease, or break up. **2** defeat or subdue completely. ▶n. **1** a crowded mass of people. **2** informal an infatuation.

Thesaurus

crowded adj. FULL, busy, packed, congested, overflowing, teeming, swarming, crammed, thronged, populous; informal jam-packed, full to bursting. ■ OPPOSITES empty.

crown n. **1** ROYALTY, monarchy, monarch, king, queen, emperor, empress. **2** TOP, crest, summit, apex, tip, head, pinnacle. ▶v. **1** INVEST, enthrone, inaugurate, install, induct, anoint. **2** CAP, be the culmination/climax of, round off, complete, perfect, conclude, top off.

crucial adj. IMPORTANT, vital, critical, decisive, pivotal, central, urgent, pressing, high-priority, essential. ■ OPPOSITES unimportant.

crude adj. **1** RAW, unrefined, natural, coarse, unprocessed, unpolished. **2** ROUGH, primitive, rudimentary, rough and ready, unpolished, makeshift, rough-hewn, unskilful, amateurish, clumsy, inartistic, awkward, inept. **3** see VULGAR. ■ OPPOSITES refined.

cruel adj. BRUTAL, savage, barbaric, inhuman, barbarous, vicious, ferocious, fierce, evil, callous, pitiless, fiendish, sadistic, venomous, cold-blooded, ruthless, merciless, unrelenting, implac-

able, remorseless, unfeeling, heartless, malevolent, inhumane, severe, harsh, stern, stony-hearted, hard-hearted, flinty, bestial, tyrannical. ■ OPPOSITES kind, merciful.

cruelty n. BRUTALITY, savagery, savageness, inhumanity, barbarism, barbarousness, viciousness, ferocity, fierceness, callousness, heartlessness, evil, fiendishness, sadism, ruthlessness, pitilessness, relentlessness, severity, harshness, inclemency. ■ OPPOSITES kindness, compassion.

cruise n. TRIP, voyage, sail. ▶v. SAIL, voyage, journey, drift, coast.

crumb n. BIT, fragment, morsel, particle, grain, speck, scrap, snippet, atom, sliver.

crumble v. **1** CRUSH, break up, pulverize, pound, grind, powder, fragment. **2** DISINTEGRATE, fall apart, break down/up, collapse, deteriorate, decompose, rot, rot away, perish.

crumple v. CRUSH, crease, rumple, wrinkle, crinkle, fold, pucker, dent, mangle.

crunch v. BITE, chew, gnaw, masticate, champ, chomp, munch, crush, grind, pulverize.

crust n. a hard outer layer, esp. of bread.
crustacean /kruss-tay-sh'n/ n. an animal with a hard shell, usu. living in water.
crusty adj. (**crustier, crustiest**) 1 having a crust. 2 irritable.
crutch n. 1 a stick with a crosspiece used as a support by a lame person. 2 the crotch.
crux n. (pl. **cruxes** or **cruces**) the most important point under discussion.
cry v. (**crying, cried**) 1 shed tears. 2 shout or scream loudly. 3 (**cry off**) informal fail to keep to an arrangement. ▶n. (pl. **cries**) 1 a period of crying. 2 a loud shout or scream. 3 an animal's call.
cryogenics n. the study of the production and effects of very low temperatures. ■ **cryogenic** adj.
crypt n. an underground room or vault in a church.
cryptic adj. mysterious or obscure in meaning. ■ **cryptically** adv.
cryptogram n. a text written in code.
cryptography n. the art of writing or solving codes.
crystal n. 1 a transparent mineral, esp. quartz. 2 a piece of a solidified substance with symmetrical flat sides. 3 very clear glass.
crystalline adj. 1 of or made of crystal. 2 very clear.
crystallize (or **-ise**) v. 1 form crystals. 2 make or become definite and clear. 3 (**crystallized**) (of fruit) preserved in sugar. ■ **crystallization** n.
CS gas n. tear gas used in the control of riots.
cu. abbrev. cubic.
cub n. 1 the young of a fox, bear, lion,

etc. 2 (also **Cub Scout**) a member of the junior branch of the Scout Association.
cubbyhole n. a very small space or room.
cube n. 1 a solid object with six equal square faces. 2 the product of a number multiplied by itself twice. ▶v. 1 cut into cubes. 2 find the cube of a number. □ **cube root** the number which produces a given number when cubed. ■ **cubic** adj.
cubicle n. a small area partitioned off in a large room.
cubism n. a style of painting in which objects are shown as geometric shapes. ■ **cubist** n. & adj.
cuckold n. a man whose wife has committed adultery.
cuckoo n. a bird that lays its eggs in the nests of other birds.
cucumber n. a long, green fruit eaten in salads.
cud n. food that cattle etc. bring back from the stomach into the mouth for further chewing.
cuddle v. 1 hug lovingly. 2 lie or sit close. ▶n. a gentle hug. ■ **cuddly** adj.
cudgel n. a short thick stick used as a weapon. ▶v. (**cudgelling, cudgelled**; US **cudgeling, cudgeled**) beat with a cudgel.
cue n. 1 a signal for action, esp. to an actor to enter or to begin their speech. 2 a long rod for striking the ball in snooker etc. ▶v. (**cueing** or **cuing, cued**) 1 give a cue to or for. 2 use a cue to strike a ball.
cuff n. 1 the end part of a sleeve. 2 a blow with an open hand. ▶v. strike with an open hand. □ **cufflink** a device

Thesaurus

crusade n. CAMPAIGN, drive, movement, push, struggle, cause, war. ▶v. FIGHT, campaign, work, take up arms, take up a cause.
crush v. 1 SQUASH, squeeze, press, mash, compress, mangle, pound, pulverize, smash, crunch, grind, pulp, break. 2 PUT DOWN, defeat, suppress, subdue, overpower, overwhelm, quash, stamp out, conquer, extinguish. 3 HUMILIATE, mortify, shame, abash, chagrin. ▶n. CROWD, jam, congestion.
crust n. CASING, outer layer, rind, shell, husk, covering, skin, encrustation, scab, concretion.
crusty adj. CRISP, crispy, brittle, hard, well done, friable.
cry v. 1 WEEP, sob, wail, snivel, blubber,

whimper, whine, bawl, howl. 2 CALL OUT, yell, exclaim, screech, bellow, howl. ▶n. 1 SOB, wail, blubbering, keening. 2 CALL, exclamation, scream, screech, yell, shout, bellow, howl.
crypt n. TOMB, vault, burial chamber, sepulchre, catacomb, undercroft.
cryptic adj. MYSTERIOUS, obscure, enigmatic, arcane, esoteric, puzzling, perplexing, secret, concealed, coded, unintelligible, hidden, unclear, veiled. ■ OPPOSITES clear.
cuddle v. HUG, embrace, clasp, fondle, pet, snuggle, nestle, curl up, enfold, nurse, dandle; informal canoodle, neck, smooch.
cudgel n. CLUB, bludgeon, stick, truncheon, blackjack, baton, bat, bastinado;

for fastening together the sides of a shirt cuff. **off the cuff** informal without preparation.

cuisine /kwi-zeen/ n. a style of cooking.

cul-de-sac n. a street closed at one end.

culinary adj. of cooking.

cull v. **1** select and kill animals to reduce numbers. **2** select.

culminate v. reach a climax. ■ **culmination** n.

culottes pl. n. women's short trousers, cut to resemble a skirt.

culpable adj. deserving blame. ■ **culpability** n. **culpably** adv.

culprit n. a person responsible for an offence.

cult n. **1** a system of religious worship. **2** a small, unconventional religious group. **3** something popular among a group.

cultivate v. **1** prepare and use land for crops. **2** grow plants or crops. **3** develop by practice. **4** try to win the friendship or favour of. ■ **cultivation** n. **cultivator** n.

culture n. **1** the arts, customs, etc. of a nation or group. **2** the arts and intellectual achievements as a whole. **3** the artificial growing of cells, bacteria, etc.

4 cells, bacteria, etc. grown artificially. ▶ v. grow cells etc. artificially. ■ **cultured** adj. **cultural** adj. **culturally** adv.

culvert n. a drain under a road.

cum prep. combined with: *a study-cum-bedroom.*

cumbersome adj. heavy and awkward to carry or use.

cumin n. the seeds of a plant, used as a spice.

cummerbund n. a sash worn around the waist.

cumulative adj. increasing by successive additions.

cumulus /kyoo-myuu-luhss/ n. (pl. **cumuli**) cloud forming heaped-up rounded masses on a flat base.

cuneiform /kyoo-ni-form/ n. an ancient writing system using wedge-shaped characters.

cunning adj. **1** skilled at deception. **2** skilful or clever. ▶ n. craftiness. ■ **cunningly** adv.

cup n. **1** a small curved container with a handle for drinking from. **2** a cup-shaped trophy. ▶ v. (**cupping, cupped**) form one's hands into the shape of a cup.

cupboard n. a piece of furniture or

Thesaurus

informal cosh. ▶ v. BLUDGEON, club, beat, strike, pound, pummel, thrash, thump; informal clobber, thwack, cosh.

cue n. SIGNAL, sign, hint, indication, suggestion, reminder, intimation.

culminate v. PEAK, come to/reach a climax, come to an end, come to a head, end, finish, close, conclude, terminate; informal wind up.

culpable adj. GUILTY, in the wrong, at fault, blameworthy, to blame, answerable, wrong, reprehensible, reproachable, sinful. ■ OPPOSITES blameless, innocent.

culprit n. GUILTY PARTY, person responsible, sinner, evil-doer, miscreant, lawbreaker, criminal, delinquent, reprobate, transgressor, malefactor.

cult n. SECT, church, religion, body, denomination, faith, belief, persuasion. **2** CRAZE, fashion, fad, vogue, trend, obsession.

cultivate v. **1** TILL, farm, work, plough, dig, prepare, fertilize. **2** EDUCATE, improve, better, develop, train, civilize, enlighten, refine, elevate, enrich. **3** WOO, court, pursue, ingratiate oneself with, curry favour with; informal butter up, suck up to. **4** FOSTER, develop, pursue, devote oneself to, encourage, support, further, aid.

cultivated adj. see CULTURED.

cultural adj. ARTISTIC, aesthetic, educational, improving, educative, enlightening, intellectual, civilizing, elevating, broadening, developmental.

culture n. **1** CULTIVATION, enlightenment, education, accomplishment, edification, erudition, refinement, polish, sophistication, urbanity, discernment, discrimination, good taste, breeding, politeness, savoir faire. **2** CIVILIZATION, way of life, lifestyle, customs, habits, ways, mores.

cultured adj. ARTISTIC, cultivated, educated, learned, enlightened, intellectual, knowledgeable, highbrow, scholarly, well informed, well read, erudite, accomplished, well versed, refined, genteel, polished, sophisticated, urbane.

cunning adj. **1** CRAFTY, devious, wily, sly, artful, shrewd, astute, knowing, sharp, Machiavellian, deceitful, shifty, guileful; informal tricky, foxy. **2** CLEVER, ingenious, resourceful, inventive, imaginative, skilful, deft, subtle, adroit. ▶ n. **1** CRAFTINESS, artfulness, wiliness, slyness, shrewdness, guile, astuteness, sharpness. **2** CLEVERNESS, ingenuity, resourcefulness, inventiveness, skill, deftsmall recess with a door, used for storage.

cupidity n. greed for money etc.

cupola n. a small dome.

cur n. a mongrel dog.

curare /kyuu-**rah**-ri/ n. a paralysing poison obtained from plants.

curate n. a member of the clergy engaged as assistant to a parish priest. ■ **curacy** n.

curator n. a keeper of a museum or other collection.

curb n. a check or restraint. ▶v. keep in check.

curd (or **curds**) n. a soft, white substance formed when milk coagulates.

curdle v. form or cause to form curds or lumps.

cure v. **1** restore to health. **2** get rid of a disease, problem, etc. **3** preserve by salting, drying, or smoking. ▶n. **1** a remedy. **2** restoration to health. ■ **curable** adj. **curative** adj.

curette n. a surgical instrument for scraping tissue from a body cavity. ■ **curettage** n.

curfew n. **1** a regulation requiring people to remain indoors between specified hours of the night. **2** the time when this begins.

curie n. a unit of radioactivity.

curio n. (pl. **curios**) an unusual and interesting object.

curiosity n. (pl. **curiosities**) **1** a strong desire to know something. **2** a curio.

curious adj. **1** eager to know something. **2** strange; unusual. ■ **curiously** adv.

curl v. form or cause to form a curved or spiral shape. ▶n. something, esp. a lock of hair, in the shape of a spiral or coil. ■ **curly** adj.

curler n. a roller around which hair is wound to curl it.

curlew n. a wading bird with a long curved bill.

curlicue n. a decorative curl or twist.

curling n. a game like bowls played on ice.

curmudgeon n. a bad-tempered person.

currant n. **1** a dried grape. **2** a shrub producing edible berries.

currency n. (pl. **currencies**) **1** a system of money in general use in a country. **2** the state or period of being current.

current adj. **1** happening or being used now. **2** in general use. ▶n. **1** a body of water or air moving in a particular direction. **2** a flow of electricity. ■ **currently** adv.

curriculum n. (pl. **curricula** or **curriculums**) a course of study. □ **curriculum vitae** an outline of a person's qualifications and previous employment. ■ **curricular** adj.

curry n. (pl. **curries**) a dish cooked in a hot, spicy sauce. ▶v. (**currying**, **curried**) **1** (**curried**) made as a curry. **2** groom a horse with a curry comb. □ **curry favour** try to win favour by flattery. **curry comb** an object for grooming horses.

curse n. **1** an appeal to a supernatural power to harm a person or thing. **2** a cause of harm or misery. **3** a swear word. ▶v. **1** use a curse against. **2** (be

Thesaurus

ness, adroitness, finesse, capability.

cup n. **1** MUG, teacup, beaker, tumbler, tankard, wine glass, chalice, goblet. **2** TROPHY, prize, award.

curator n. KEEPER, caretaker, custodian, guardian, conservator, steward.

curb v. RESTRAIN, check, keep in check, control, contain, hold back, repress, suppress, moderate, dampen, put a brake on, impede, retard, subdue, bridle, muzzle. ■ OPPOSITES encourage.

curdle v. CONGEAL, turn, coagulate, clot, solidify, thicken, condense.

cure n. REMEDY, antidote, treatment, therapy, alleviation, medicine, restorative, panacea, corrective. ▶v. **1** HEAL, make better, rehabilitate, remedy, put right, repair, fix, restore, palliate, rectify, relieve. **2** PRESERVE, smoke, salt, dry, kipper, pickle. ■ OPPOSITES aggravate.

curiosity n. INQUISITIVENESS, interest,

questioning, prying, meddling; informal snooping, nosiness.

curious adj. **1** INQUISITIVE, inquiring, interested, searching, querying, questioning, interrogating, puzzled, intrusive, prying, interfering; informal nosy, snooping. **2** see STRANGE. ■ OPPOSITES incurious.

curl v. **1** SPIRAL, coil, bend, twist, wind, loop, twirl, wreathe, meander, snake, corkscrew. **2** CRIMP, perm, crinkle, frizz, wave. ▶n. **1** SPIRAL, twist, coil, whorl, helix. **2** RINGLET, coil, kink, wave, curlicue, corkscrew.

curly adj. CURLED, crimped, kinked, crinkly, wavy, frizzy, permed, fuzzy. ■ OPPOSITES straight.

current adj. PRESENT, present-day, contemporary, up to date, up to the minute, existing, modern, fashionable, popular, prevailing, prevalent, accept-

cursed with be afflicted with. **3** use swear words.

cursive adj. (of writing) written with the characters joined.

cursor n. a movable indicator on a computer screen.

cursory adj. hasty and so not thorough. ■ **cursorily** adv.

curt adj. rudely brief. ■ **curtly** adv.

curtail v. reduce or restrict. ■ **curtailment** n.

curtain n. a piece of material hung as a screen, esp. at a window.

curtsy (or **curtsey**) n. (pl. **curtsies** or **curtseys**) a woman's respectful greeting, made by bending the knees. ▶ v. (**curtsying**, **curtsied**) perform a curtsy.

curvaceous adj. having an attractively curved shape.

curvature n. the fact of being curved.

curve n. a line which gradually turns from a straight course. ▶ v. form a curve. ■ **curvy** adj.

curvilinear adj. contained by or consisting of curved lines.

cushion n. **1** a stuffed bag used for sitting or leaning on. **2** a means of support or protection. ▶ v. **1** protect with a cushion. **2** lessen the impact of.

cushy adj. (**cushier**, **cushiest**) informal easy and undemanding.

cusp n. **1** a pointed end where two curves meet. **2** a point of change, esp. between two astrological signs.

cussed /kuss-id/ adj. informal awkward or annoying.

custard n. a sweet sauce made with milk and eggs or flavoured cornflour.

custodian n. a guardian or keeper.

custody n. **1** protective care. **2** imprisonment. ■ **custodial** adj.

custom n. **1** a traditional way of behaving or acting. **2** regular dealings by customers. **3** (**customs**) duties charged on imported goods.

customary adj. usual. ■ **customarily** adv.

customer n. a person buying goods or services from a shop etc.

Thesaurus

ed, common, general, widespread, rife; *informal* trendy, now, in. ▶ n. FLOW, stream, tide, river, channel, drift, jet, draught, undercurrent, undertow.

curse n. **1** DAMNATION, execration, imprecation, evil eye, malediction, anathema; *informal* jinx. **2** SWEAR WORD, obscenity, oath, profanity, expletive, blasphemy, bad language. ▶ v. **1** PUT A CURSE ON, damn, execrate, put the evil eye on, anathematize. **2** SWEAR, use bad/foul language, utter oaths, blaspheme, be foul-mouthed.

cursory adj. HASTY, rapid, hurried, quick, perfunctory, slapdash, casual, superficial, desultory, fleeting, passing, ephemeral, transient. ■ OPPOSITES thorough.

curt adj. TERSE, abrupt, brusque, blunt, short, sharp, crisp, tart, gruff, uncommunicative, laconic, offhand, rude, summary, impolite, unceremonious, ungracious, uncivil, brief, concise, succinct, pithy, compact; *informal* snappy, snappish. ■ OPPOSITES expansive.

curtail v. REDUCE, shorten, cut, cut back/down, decrease, lessen, diminish, slim down, tighten up, pare down, trim, dock, lop, truncate, abridge, abbreviate, contract, compress, shrink. ■ OPPOSITES lengthen, expand.

curtain n. DRAPE, hanging, blind, screen.

curtsy v. BOW, genuflect, bend the knee, bob, salaam.

curve n. BEND, arch, arc, bow, turn, loop, hook, crescent, spiral, twist, swirl, whorl, corkscrew, curvature, undulation, camber, meander. ▶ v. BEND, arc, arch, bow, turn, swerve, twist, wind, hook, loop, spiral, coil, meander, snake, swirl, bulge, camber, inflect, incurve.

curved adj. BENT, arched, rounded, bowed, twisted, crooked, humped, concave, serpentine, whorled, undulating, meandering, curvy, sinuous. ■ OPPOSITES straight.

cushion n. PILLOW, bolster, pad, headrest, hassock, mat, squab, pillion, scatter cushion, beanbag. ▶ v. **1** PILLOW, bolster, cradle, support, prop up. **2** SOFTEN, lessen, diminish, mitigate, allay, deaden, muffle, stifle.

custody n. **1** CARE, charge, guardianship, keeping, safe keeping, protection, supervision, superintendence, control, tutelage. **2** DETENTION, imprisonment, incarceration, confinement, restraint, constraint, duress.

custom n. **1** HABIT, practice, routine, way, policy, rule, convention, procedure, ritual, ceremony, form, usage, observance, fashion, mode, style. **2** TRADE, business, patronage, support, customers, buyers.

customary adj. USUAL, accustomed, regular, typical, common, habitual, traditional, routine, fixed, set, established, familiar, everyday, prevailing,

cut v. (**cutting, cut**) **1** open or wound with a sharp implement. **2** make, divide, or remove in this way. **3** reduce. **4** go across or through. **5** move to another shot in a film. **6** divide a pack of cards. **7** have a tooth appear through the gum. ▶ n. **1** an act of cutting. **2** an incision or wound. **3** a reduction. **4** a style in which a garment or the hair is cut. **5** a piece of meat cut off. **6** informal a share. □ **cut off** isolated. **cut-throat** ruthless and fierce.

cute adj. **1** charmingly pretty; sweet. **2** informal clever. ■ **cutely** adv. **cuteness** n.

cuticle n. the skin at the base of a nail.

cutlass n. a short curved sword.

cutler n. a maker of cutlery.

cutlery n. knives, forks, and spoons.

cutlet n. **1** a lamb or veal chop from behind the neck. **2** a flat cake of minced meat, nuts, etc., covered in breadcrumbs and fried.

cutting n. **1** an article cut from a newspaper. **2** a piece cut from a plant to grow a new one. **3** a passage cut through high ground for a railway etc. ▶ adj. hurtful. □ **the cutting edge** the most advanced stage.

cuttlefish n. a sea animal like a squid.

CV abbrev. curriculum vitae.

cwt. abbrev. hundredweight.

cyan /sy-uhn/ n. a greenish-blue colour.

cyanide n. a highly poisonous compound.

cyber- comb. form of information technology, the Internet, etc.

cybernetics n. the science of systems of communication and control in machines and living things.

cyberspace n. the hypothetical environment in which communication over computer networks occurs.

cyclamen n. a plant with pink, red, or white flowers.

cycle n. **1** a recurring series of events. **2** a bicycle. ▶ v. ride a bicycle. ■ **cyclist** n.

cyclic (or **cyclical**) adj. occurring in cycles.

cyclone n. **1** a violent wind rotating round a central area. **2** a violent tropical storm. ■ **cyclonic** adj.

cyclotron n. an apparatus for accelerating charged particles in a spiral path.

cygnet n. a young swan.

cylinder n. an object with straight parallel sides and circular ends. ■ **cylindrical** adj.

cymbal n. a musical instrument consisting of a round brass plate struck against another or hit with a stick.

cynic n. a person who believes that people's motives are always selfish. ■ **cynical** adj. **cynically** adv. **cynicism** n.

cynosure /si-nuh-zyoor/ n. a centre of attention.

cypher var. of CIPHER.

cypress n. an evergreen tree.

cyst n. an abnormal sac or cavity in the body, containing fluid.

cystic adj. **1** of cysts. **2** of the bladder or the gall bladder. □ **cystic fibrosis** a hereditary disorder which often results in respiratory infection.

cystitis n. inflammation of the bladder.

cytology n. the study of the structure and function of plant and animal cells. ■ **cytological** adj.

czar var. of TSAR.

Thesaurus

confirmed, normal, ordinary, expected, favourite, popular, stock, well worn; *literary* wonted. ■ OPPOSITES unusual, exceptional.

customer n. BUYER, purchaser, shopper, consumer, patron, client.

cut v. **1** GASH, slash, lacerate, slit, nick, pierce, notch, penetrate, wound, lance, incise, score. **2** CARVE, slice, chop, sever, divide, cleave. **3** SHAPE, fashion, form, mould, chisel, carve, sculpt, chip away, whittle. **4** TRIM, clip, crop, snip, shear, dock, shave, pare, mow. **5** REDUCE, decrease, lessen, lower, diminish, contract, prune, curb, curtail, slash, rationalize, economize on. **6** SHORTEN, abridge, condense, abbreviate, contract, compact, precis, summarize. ▶ n. **1** GASH, laceration, slash, incision, slit. **2** CUTBACK, decrease, reduction, curtailment, contraction. **3** SHARE, portion, proportion, percentage.

cutting adj. WOUNDING, hurtful, caustic, acid, barbed, acrimonious, sarcastic, spiteful, sardonic, vicious, malicious, sharp, trenchant, mordant.

cycle n. **1** SERIES, sequence, succession, round, run, rotation. **2** BICYCLE, bike, tandem, tricycle, monocycle.

cynical adj. SCEPTICAL, pessimistic, doubting, unbelieving, disbelieving, distrustful, suspicious, misanthropic, critical, sardonic, scoffing. ■ OPPOSITES optimistic.

Dd

D (or **d**) n. the Roman numeral for 500. ▶abbrev. (of pre-decimal currency) penny or pence.

dab v. (**dabbing, dabbed**) **1** press lightly with a cloth, sponge, etc. **2** apply with light, quick strokes. ▶n. a small amount lightly applied. □ **dab hand** informal an expert in a particular activity.

dabble v. **1** splash around gently in water. **2** take part in an activity in a casual way.

dacha /da-chuh/ n. a Russian country cottage.

dachshund n. a dog with a long body and very short legs.

dad (or **daddy**) n. informal one's father.

daddy-long-legs n. informal a long-legged flying insect.

dado /day-doh/ n. (pl. **dados**) the lower part of a wall decorated differently from the upper part.

daffodil n. a yellow flower with a long trumpet-shaped centre.

daft adj. informal silly; foolish.

dagger n. a short pointed knife, used as a weapon.

daguerreotype /duh-ger-ruh-typ/ n. an early kind of photograph.

dahlia /day-li-uh/ n. a garden plant with brightly coloured flowers.

daily adj. done, happening, or produced every day or every weekday. ▶adv. every day. ▶n. (pl. **dailies**) informal a daily newspaper.

dainty adj. (**daintier, daintiest**) delicately small and pretty. ■ **daintily** adv. **daintiness** n.

dairy n. (pl. **dairies**) a building where milk and milk products are produced.

dais /day-iss/ n. a low platform for a lectern or throne.

daisy n. (pl. **daisies**) a small flower with many white petals.

dale n. a valley.

dally v. (**dallying, dallied**) **1** waste time. **2** (**dally with**) have a casual relationship with. ■ **dalliance** n.

Dalmatian n. a large white dog with dark spots.

dam n. **1** a barrier built across a river to hold back water. **2** the female parent of an animal. ▶v. (**damming, dammed**) build a dam across.

damage n. **1** physical harm reducing the value or usefulness of something. **2** (**damages**) money as compensation for loss or injury. ▶v. cause harm to.

damask n. a fabric with a pattern woven into it.

dame n. **1** (**Dame**) the title of a woman awarded a knighthood. **2** US informal a woman.

Thesaurus

dab v. PAT, blot, press, touch, smudge, besmear, bedaub. ▶n. **1** PAT, blot, press, touch, smudge. **2** BIT, speck, touch, trace, dash, drop, tinge, suggestion, hint, modicum.

dabble v. **1** PADDLE, dip, splash, slosh. **2** FLIRT WITH, toy with, dally with, dip into.

dabbler n. DILETTANTE, amateur, trifler.

daily adj. **1** EVERYDAY, quotidian, diurnal. **2** COMMON, regular, commonplace, usual, habitual, customary. ▶adv. EVERY DAY, once a day, day after day, day by day, per diem.

dainty adj. **1** PETITE, delicate, neat, exquisite, graceful, elegant, trim, pretty, fine, refined. **2** PARTICULAR, discriminating, fastidious, fussy, finicky, refined, scrupulous, meticulous, squeamish. **3** TASTY, delicious, appetizing, palatable, choice, savoury, flavoursome, luscious, juicy, succulent. ▶n. TITBIT, delicacy, confection, sweetmeat, bonne bouche.

dally v. DAWDLE, loiter, delay, linger, take one's time, loaf, saunter, procrastinate, waste time; informal dilly-dally, hang about; old use tarry. ■ OPPOSITES hurry.

dam n. BARRIER, wall, obstruction, barricade, embankment, barrage, bank, weir. ▶v. BLOCK, obstruct, hold back, check, stop, staunch, stem.

damage n. **1** HARM, injury, destruction, hurt, impairment, defacement, abuse, defilement, vandalism, ruin, devastation, havoc, detriment, mischief, outrage, accident, loss, suffering. **2** COST, charge, expense, bill, total. ▶v. HARM, injure, do damage to, spoil, vandalize, destroy, wreck, ruin, mar, deface, dev-

damn v. **1** (**be damned**) be condemned by God to eternal punishment in hell. **2** strongly criticize. ▶ exclam. expressing anger. ▶ adj. (also **damned**) informal used to emphasize anger. ■ **damnation** n. & exclam.

damnable adj. very bad or unpleasant.

damp adj. slightly wet. ▶ n. moisture. ▶ v. **1** make damp. **2** (**damp down**) control a feeling or situation. ■ **dampness** n.

dampen v. **1** make damp. **2** make less strong or intense. ■ **dampener** n.

damper n. **1** a pad for silencing a piano string. **2** a metal plate regulating the air flow in a chimney.

damsel n. old use a young woman.

damson n. a small purple plum-like fruit.

dance v. **1** move rhythmically to music. **2** move in a quick and lively way. ▶ n. **1** a series of steps and movements performed to music. **2** a social gathering at which people dance. ■ **dancer** n.

dandelion n. a weed with large yellow flowers.

dandle v. gently bounce a young child on one's knees.

dandruff n. flakes of dead skin from the scalp.

dandy n. (pl. **dandies**) a man who is too concerned with looking stylish and fashionable. ■ **dandified** adj.

Dane n. a person from Denmark. ■ **Danish** adj. & n.

danger n. **1** the possibility of suffering harm or injury. **2** a cause of harm.

dangerous adj. likely to cause harm or problems. ■ **dangerously** adv.

dangle v. **1** hang so as to swing freely. **2** offer an incentive. ■ **dangly** adj.

dank adj. damp and cold.

dapper adj. neat in dress and appearance.

dapple v. mark with spots or small patches. □ **dapple grey** (of a horse) grey or white with darker spots.

dare v. **1** have the courage to do. **2** challenge to do. ▶ n. a challenge to do something brave or risky. □ **daredevil** a recklessly daring person.

daring adj. **1** willing to do dangerous things. **2** involving danger. ▶ n. adventurous courage. ■ **daringly** adv.

dark adj. **1** with little or no light. **2** of a deep colour. **3** (of skin, hair, or eyes) brown or black. **4** mysterious. **5** depressing and cheerless. ▶ n. **1** (**the dark**) the absence of light. **2** night. □ **dark horse** a person about whom little is known. **darkroom** a darkened room for developing photographs. ■ **darken** v. **darkly** adv. **darkness** n.

Thesaurus

astate, defile, play havoc with, do mischief to, mutilate, impair, disable, sabotage, warp.

damaging adj. *see* HARMFUL.

damn v. **1** CURSE, execrate, anathematize, imprecate. **2** CRITICIZE, censure, condemn, attack, flay; *informal* pan, slam, knock, blast, take apart, slate. ■ OPPOSITES bless, praise.

damning adj. INCRIMINATING, condemnatory, condemning, implicating, accusatorial.

damp adj. **1** MOIST, soggy, wettish, dank. **2** RAINY, wettish, drizzly, humid, clammy, muggy, misty, foggy, vaporous. ■ OPPOSITES dry. ▶ v. **1** MOISTEN, dampen, sprinkle, humidify. **2** DISCOURAGE, dampen, check, curb, restrain, stifle, inhibit; *informal* put a damper on, pour cold water on. **3** REDUCE, lessen, diminish, decrease, moderate.

dance v. CAPER, trip, jig, skip, prance, cavort, hop, frolic, gambol, jump, leap, romp, bounce, whirl, spin.

dandy n. FOP, man about town; *informal* sharp dresser; *dated* beau, popinjay, blade; *old use* coxcomb.

danger n. **1** RISK, peril, hazard, jeopardy, endangerment, precariousness, insecurity, instability. **2** CHANCE, possibility, threat, risk. ■ OPPOSITES safety.

dangerous adj. **1** RISKY, perilous, unsafe, hazardous, precarious, insecure, exposed, defenceless, uncertain, unsound, critical, alarming; *informal* hairy, chancy. **2** MENACING, threatening, ruthless, nasty, violent, desperate, treacherous, unmanageable, wild, volatile. ■ OPPOSITES safe, harmless.

dangle v. **1** HANG, swing, sway, trail, droop, flap, wave. **2** TEMPT WITH, entice with, lure with, hold out.

dank adj. DAMP, wet, moist, humid, clammy, chilly. ■ OPPOSITES dry.

dappled adj. SPOTTED, marked, mottled, flecked, stippled, freckled, dotted, streaked, patchy, marbled, blotchy, blotched, piebald, motley, brindled, pinto, variegated, particoloured.

dare v. **1** RISK, hazard, venture, have the courage, take the risk, be brave enough, make bold. **2** CHALLENGE, provoke, goad, taunt.

daring adj. BOLD, adventurous, brave, courageous, audacious, intrepid, fearless, undaunted, unshrinking, rash,

darling n. **1** an affectionate form of address. **2** a lovable or popular person. ▶adj. **1** much loved. **2** charming.

darn v. mend knitted material by weaving yarn across it. ▶adj. (also **darned**) informal damn.

dart n. **1** a small pointed missile. **2** (**darts**) an indoor game in which darts are thrown at a target. **3** a sudden run. **4** a tapered tuck in a garment. ▶v. **1** run suddenly. **2** direct a sudden glance. □ **dartboard** a circular target used in the game of darts.

dash v. **1** run or travel in a great hurry. **2** strike or throw with great force. **3** destroy. ▶n. **1** an act of dashing. **2** a small amount added. **3** impressive style; flair. **4** a horizontal stroke (-) in writing. □ **dashboard** the instrument panel in a vehicle.

dashing adj. attractive and stylish.

dastardly adj. wicked and cruel.

data n. **1** facts or statistics used for reference or analysis. **2** information processed by a computer. □ **database** a set of data held in a computer.

> ☑ Although **data** is the plural of Latin **datum**, in everyday English use it is usually treated as a singular noun, taking a singular verb, as in *data was collected over a number of years*.

date n. **1** the day of the month or year as specified by a number. **2** the day or year of an event's occurrence. **3** a social or romantic appointment. **4** a sweet, dark brown, oval fruit. ▶v. **1** establish the date of. **2** mark with a date. **3** (**date back to**) originate from. **4** become or look old-fashioned. **5** informal go on a date or regular dates with. □ **to date** until now.

dated adj. old-fashioned.

dative n. (in certain languages) the case of nouns and pronouns indicating the indirect object.

datum n. (pl. **data**) a piece of information.

daub v. smear with a thick substance. ▶n. **1** a smear. **2** an unskilful painting.

daughter n. a girl or woman in relation to her parents. □ **daughter-in-law** (pl. **daughters-in-law**) the wife of one's son.

daunt v. intimidate or discourage.

dauntless adj. fearless and determined.

dauphin /doh-fan/ n. hist. the eldest son of the King of France.

davit n. a small crane on a ship.

dawdle v. walk slowly; take one's time.

dawn n. **1** the first appearance of light in the morning. **2** the beginning of something. ▶v. **1** (of a day) begin. **2** come into existence. **3** (**dawn on**) become evident to.

Thesaurus

reckless, foolhardy.

dark adj. **1** BLACK, pitch-black, pitch-dark, jet-black, inky, unlit, shadowy, shady, murky, dim, indistinct, dingy, foggy, misty, cloudy, overcast, sunless, gloomy, funereal. **2** DARK-SKINNED, sallow, swarthy, black, olive-skinned, ebony, tanned, bronzed. **3** MOODY, brooding, angry, sullen, dour, glum, morose, sulky, frowning, glowering, forbidding, ominous. **4** EVIL, wicked, villainous, sinful, iniquitous, vile, base, foul, horrible, atrocious, nefarious, fiendish, satanic, damnable. **5** see MYSTERIOUS. ■ OPPOSITES light, pale, happy, cheerful.

darken v. **1** GROW DARK/DARKER, blacken, cloud over, dim, grow dim. **2** MAKE DARK/DARKER, blacken, black, dim, shade, overshadow, eclipse. ■ OPPOSITES lighten, brighten.

darling n. **1** DEAR, dearest, sweetheart, love, beloved, honey. **2** CHARMER, pet, sweetheart; informal sweetie, poppet.

dart n. ARROW, bolt, missile. ▶v. RUSH, dash, bolt, sprint, run, tear, hurtle, fly,

bound, flash, shoot, leap, spring, scuttle, flit; informal scoot, zip, whizz.

dash v. **1** RUSH, run, hurry, race, sprint, tear, speed, fly, dart, bolt, hasten. **2** SHATTER, destroy, ruin, spoil, frustrate, thwart, blight, baulk, check. ▶n. **1** RUSH, bolt, run, race, flight, dart, sprint, sortie, spurt. **2** BIT, pinch, drop, sprinkling, touch, trace, tinge.

dashing adj. DEBONAIR, stylish, lively, spirited, dynamic, energetic, animated, gallant, bold, daring, swashbuckling, dazzling.

data pl. n. INFORMATION, facts, figures, details, statistics, material, input.

date n. **1** DAY, point in time. **2** MEETING, appointment, engagement, rendezvous, assignation; literary tryst. **3** PARTNER, escort, girlfriend, boyfriend; dated beau.

dated adj. OUT OF DATE, outdated, old-fashioned, outmoded, antiquated, passé; informal old hat. ■ OPPOSITES up to date, modern.

daunt v. INTIMIDATE, frighten, overawe, scare, alarm, dismay, unnerve, abash, cow, dishearten, dispirit.

day n. **1** a period of 24 hours. **2** the time between sunrise and sunset. **3** a particular period, esp. of the past. □ **daydream** a series of pleasant distracting thoughts. **daybreak** dawn.

daze v. stun or bewilder. ▶ n. a dazed state.

dazzle v. **1** (of a bright light) blind temporarily. **2** amaze with an impressive quality. ▶ n. blinding brightness.

dB abbrev. decibels.

DC abbrev. direct current.

deacon n. **1** a Christian minister ranking below a priest. **2** (in some Protestant Churches) a lay officer assisting a minister. ■ **deaconess** n.

dead adj. **1** no longer alive. **2** lacking sensation or emotion. **3** lacking activity or excitement. **4** (of equipment) not functioning. **5** complete: *dead silence.* ▶ adv. **1** completely; exactly. **2** informal very. □ **dead end** an end of a road or passage from which no exit is possible. **dead heat** a race in which two or more competitors finish exactly level. **deadline** the latest time or date for completing something. **deadlock** a situation in which no progress can be

made. **deadlocked** in a deadlock. **deadpan** expressionless. ■ **deaden** v.

deadly adj. (**deadlier**, **deadliest**) **1** causing death. **2** informal extremely boring. ▶ adv. **1** as if dead. **2** extremely.

deaf adj. **1** wholly or partially unable to hear. **2** (**deaf to**) unwilling to listen to. ■ **deafen** v. **deafness** n.

deal v. (**dealing**, **dealt**) **1** give out cards to players of a game. **2** (**deal out**) distribute. **3** trade in a product. **4** informal buy and sell illegal drugs. **5** inflict a blow on. ▶ n. **1** an agreement. **2** a particular way of being treated: *a fair deal.* □ **a big deal** informal an important thing. **a good** (or **great**) **deal** a large amount. **deal with 1** take action to put right. **2** cope with. **3** have as a subject. ■ **dealer** n.

dean n. **1** the head of the governing body of a cathedral. **2** the head of a university department etc.

dear adj. **1** much loved. **2** expensive. ▶ n. a lovable person. ▶ adv. at a high cost. ▶ exclam. used in expressions of surprise or dismay. ■ **dearly** adv.

dearth /derth/ n. a scarcity or lack.

death n. **1** the act or fact of dying. **2** the

Thesaurus

dawdle v. LOITER, delay, move slowly, linger, take one's time, waste time, idle, dally, straggle, trail behind, potter about, move at a snail's pace. ■ OPPOSITES hurry, hasten.

dawn n. **1** DAYBREAK, break of day, sunrise, first light, cockcrow. **2** BEGINNING, start, birth, rise, commencement, onset, advent, arrival, appearance, emergence, origin, inception, genesis, unfolding, development. ■ OPPOSITES dusk.

day n. **1** DAYTIME, daylight, daylight hours, broad daylight. **2** PERIOD, time, epoch, age, era, generation.

daze v. STUN, stupefy, confuse, bewilder, befuddle, addle, numb, benumb, paralyse.

dazzle v. **1** BLIND, bedazzle, daze. **2** OVERPOWER, overwhelm, overawe, awe, stagger, fascinate, dumbfound, astonish, amaze.

dead adj. **1** DECEASED, lifeless, gone, passed on/away, departed, no more, late, inanimate, defunct; *informal* done for. **2** OBSOLETE, extinct, outmoded, outdated, lapsed, inactive. **3** DULL, boring, uninteresting, tedious, uneventful, flat, wearisome, humdrum, stale, moribund, vapid. ■ OPPOSITES alive. ▶ adv. COMPLETELY, totally, absolutely, entirely, ut-

terly, thoroughly, categorically.

deaden v. **1** DESENSITIZE, numb, anaesthetize, paralyse, dull. **2** REDUCE, suppress, moderate, blunt, dull, muffle, diminish, mitigate, alleviate, smother, stifle.

deadlock n. STALEMATE, impasse, standoff, standstill, halt, stop.

deadly adj. FATAL, lethal, dangerous, destructive, toxic, poisonous, venomous, virulent, noxious. *See also* HARMFUL. ■ OPPOSITES harmless.

deafening adj. LOUD, ear-splitting, thunderous, resounding, ringing, reverberating.

deal n. **1** AGREEMENT, transaction, arrangement, contract, bargain, understanding, settlement, compact, pact. **2** AMOUNT, quantity, volume. ▶ v. **1** TRADE, do business, buy and sell, traffic. **2** DISTRIBUTE, share out, allocate, divide out, hand out, dole out, apportion, mete out. **3** ADMINISTER, deliver, give, direct, aim. □ **deal with** ATTEND TO, see to, take care of, cope with, handle, manage, tackle.

dealer n. TRADER, broker, retailer, wholesaler, supplier, purveyor, distributor, vendor, tradesman, merchant, trafficker, pedlar.

dear adj. **1** BELOVED, loved, adored, cherstate of being dead. **3** the end of something. □ **death trap** a dangerous building, vehicle, etc. **death-watch beetle** a beetle whose larvae bore into wood.

deathly adj. suggesting death.

debacle /day-bah-k'l/ n. a complete failure or disaster.

debar v. (**debarring, debarred**) prevent from doing something.

debase v. lower in quality or value. ■ **debasement** n.

debatable adj. open to discussion.

debate n. **1** a formal discussion. **2** an argument. ▶ v. **1** discuss. **2** consider.

debauchery n. excessive indulgence in sex, alcohol, and drugs. ■ **debauched** adj.

debenture n. a certificate issued by a company acknowledging that it has borrowed money on which interest is being paid.

debilitate v. weaken. ■ **debilitation** n.

debility n. (pl. **debilities**) physical weakness.

debit n. **1** an entry in an account recording a sum owed. **2** a payment made or owed. ▶ v. (**debiting, debited**) (of a bank) remove money from a customer's account.

debonair adj. confident, stylish, and charming.

debouch v. emerge from a confined space into an open area.

debrief v. question in detail about a completed mission.

debris /deb-ree/ n. scattered broken pieces or rubbish.

debt n. **1** something owed, esp. money. **2** the state of owing something.

debtor n. a person who owes money.

debunk v. reveal a widely held opinion to be false.

debut /day-byoo/ n. a person's first appearance in a role.

debutante /deb-yuh-tahnt/ n. a young upper-class woman making her first formal appearance in society.

decade n. a period of ten years.

decadent adj. immoral and interested only in pleasure. ■ **decadence** n.

decaffeinated adj. with the caffeine removed or reduced.

decagon n. a plane figure with ten straight sides and angles.

decamp v. leave suddenly or secretly.

decant v. pour liquid from one container into another.

decanter n. a bottle into which wine or spirits are decanted.

decapitate v. behead. ■ **decapitation** n.

decathlon n. an athletic contest involving ten events.

decay v. **1** rot. **2** become less powerful or good. ▶ n. the state or process of decaying.

decease n. death.

deceased adj. recently dead.

deceit n. deception. ■ **deceitful** adj. **deceitfully** adv.

Thesaurus

ished, intimate, close, esteemed, respected. **2** EXPENSIVE, costly, overpriced, exorbitant, high-priced; *informal* pricey, steep. ■ OPPOSITES cheap.

dearth n. LACK, scarcity, scarceness, shortage, deficiency, insufficiency, paucity. ■ OPPOSITES abundance.

death n. **1** DYING, demise, end, final exit, passing on/away. **2** KILLING, murder, massacre, slaughter; *literary* slaying. ■ OPPOSITES life.

debacle n. FIASCO, disaster, catastrophe, failure, collapse, ruin, defeat, rout, havoc.

debase v. DEGRADE, devalue, demean, disgrace, dishonour, shame, discredit, cheapen, humble, humiliate, diminish, ruin, soil, sully, vulgarize. ■ OPPOSITES enhance.

debatable adj. ARGUABLE, questionable, open to question, disputable, controversial, contentious, doubtful, open to doubt, dubious, uncertain, unsure, undecided, borderline, moot. ■ OPPOSITES

certain.

debate n. ARGUMENT, dispute, discussion, difference of opinion, altercation, disputation, wrangle, controversy, war of words, polemic. ▶ v. ARGUE, dispute, argue the pros and cons of, discuss, bandy words, wrangle, contend, moot; *informal* kick around.

debauched adj. DEGENERATE, dissipated, dissolute, immoral, abandoned, promiscuous, wanton. ■ OPPOSITES wholesome.

debris n. RUBBLE, wreckage, detritus, rubbish, litter, waste, flotsam, remains, ruin, fragments.

debt n. **1** BILL, account, money owing, score, tally, dues, arrears. **2** OBLIGATION, liability, indebtedness.

decamp v. RUN OFF/AWAY, make off, flee, take off, abscond, escape; *informal* cut and run, skedaddle, vamoose, skip, hightail it, do a moonlight flit.

decay v. **1** ROT, decompose, go bad, putrefy, spoil, perish, corrode. **2** DEGENER-

deceive v. **1** cause to believe something false. **2** be sexually unfaithful to. ■ **deceiver** n.

decelerate v. slow down. ■ **deceleration** n.

December n. the twelfth month.

decennial adj. lasting for or recurring every ten years.

decent adj. **1** following accepted moral standards. **2** of an acceptable quality. **3** informal kind or generous. ■ **decency** n. **decently** adv.

decentralize (or **-ise**) v. transfer from central to local control.

deception n. **1** the act of deceiving. **2** a thing that deceives.

deceptive adj. misleading. ■ **deceptively** adv.

decibel n. a unit for measuring the intensity of sound.

decide v. **1** make up one's mind. **2** settle an issue or contest.

decided adj. definite; unquestionable. ■ **decidedly** adv.

deciduous adj. (of a tree) shedding its leaves annually.

decimal adj. of a system of numbers based on the number ten. ▶ n. a fraction in the decimal system, with figures either side of a full point. □ **decimal place** the position of a digit to the right of a decimal point. **decimal point** a full point placed after the figure representing units in a decimal.

decimate v. kill or destroy a large proportion of. ■ **decimation** n.

decipher v. **1** convert from code into normal language. **2** work out the meaning of.

decision n. **1** a conclusion reached after consideration. **2** the ability to make decisions quickly.

decisive adj. **1** settling an issue quickly. **2** able to make decisions quickly. ■ **decisively** adv. **decisiveness** n.

deck n. **1** a floor of a ship or bus. **2** a pack of cards. **3** a piece of equipment for playing or recording discs or tapes. ▶ v. decorate. □ **deckchair** a folding canvas chair.

declaim v. speak or recite in a dramatic way. ■ **declamation** n. **declamatory** adj.

declare v. **1** announce openly or for-

Thesaurus

ATE, decline, deteriorate, fail, wane, ebb, dwindle, crumble, disintegrate, wither, die, atrophy.

deceit n. DECEPTION, cheating, dishonesty, duplicity, double-dealing, fraud, fraudulence, trickery, subterfuge, untruthfulness, duping, chicanery, underhandedness, cunning, wiliness, dissimulation, pretence, artifice, treachery. ■ OPPOSITES honesty.

deceitful adj. DECEPTIVE, misleading, fraudulent, double-dealing, sneaky, treacherous, untruthful, dishonest, underhand, false, untrustworthy, lying, unfaithful, two-faced, duplicitous, mendacious, insincere, disingenuous, sham, bogus, spurious, perfidious; informal crooked, tricky. ■ OPPOSITES honest.

deceive v. MISLEAD, take in, fool, delude, misguide, lead on, trick, hoodwink, dupe, hoax, swindle, outwit, ensnare, entrap, double-cross, gull; informal con, take for a ride, pull someone's leg, pull a fast one on, bamboozle, diddle.

decelerate v. SLOW DOWN, go slower, reduce speed, brake, put the brakes on, ease up. ■ OPPOSITES accelerate.

decent adj. **1** PROPER, acceptable, respectable, correct, appropriate, seemly, fitting, fit, suitable, modest, becoming, tasteful, decorous, pure. **2** HONEST, trust-

worthy, dependable, respectable, worthy, upright, kind, thoughtful, obliging, helpful, generous, courteous, civil. **3** SUFFICIENT, acceptable, reasonable, adequate, ample. ■ OPPOSITES indecent.

deception n. **1** TRICK, ruse, dodge, subterfuge, fraud, cheat, swindle, sham, pretence, bluff, stratagem, confidence trick, imposture; informal con, scam. **2** see DECEIT.

deceptive adj. **1** MISLEADING, false, illusory, ambiguous, unreliable, wrong, distorted, deceiving, delusive, spurious, treacherous. **2** see DECEITFUL. ■ OPPOSITES genuine.

decide v. **1** COME TO A DECISION, reach/ make a decision, make up one's mind, resolve, choose, come to a conclusion, conclude, commit oneself, opt for, select. **2** JUDGE, adjudicate, arbitrate, make a judgement on, make a ruling, give a verdict.

decided adj. CLEAR, distinct, definite, obvious, certain, marked, pronounced, emphatic, categorical, unequivocal.

decision n. CONCLUSION, resolution, judgement, verdict, pronouncement, determination, outcome, findings.

decisive adj. **1** DETERMINED, resolute, firm, sure, purposeful, unhesitating, unswerving, unwavering, unfaltering, mally. **2** state that one has taxable income or goods. ■ **declaration** n.

declassify v. (**declassifying**, **declassified**) officially declare to be no longer secret.

declension n. the changes in the form of a noun, pronoun, or adjective that identify its grammatical case, number, and gender.

decline v. **1** become smaller, weaker, or worse. **2** politely refuse. ▶ n. a gradual loss of strength, numbers, or value.

declivity n. (pl. **declivities**) a downward slope.

decoction n. the concentrated essence of a substance extracted by boiling.

decode v. **1** convert a coded message into understandable language. **2** convert audio or video signals from analogue to digital. ■ **decoder** n.

décolletage /day-kol-**tahzh**/ n. a low neckline on a woman's garment.

decompose v. decay. ■ **decomposition** n.

decompress v. **1** reduce air pressure in or on. **2** expand compressed computer data to its normal size. ■ **decompression** n.

decongestant n. a medicine that relieves a blocked nose.

decontaminate v. remove dangerous substances from. ■ **decontamination** n.

decor /**day**-kor/ n. the furnishing and decoration of a room.

decorate v. **1** add ornamentation to make more attractive. **2** apply paint or wallpaper to. **3** give an award or medal to. ■ **decoration** n. **decorator** n.

decorative adj. ornamental. ■ **decoratively** adv.

decorous adj. polite and restrained. ■ **decorously** adv.

decorum /di-**kor**-uhm/ n. polite and socially acceptable behaviour.

decoy n. **1** a real or imitation animal used to lure game. **2** a person or thing used to lure someone into a trap. ▶ v. lure by a decoy.

decrease v. make or become smaller or fewer. ▶ n. **1** the amount by which something decreases. **2** the process of

Thesaurus

incisive, emphatic. **2** DECIDING, determining, conclusive, final, critical, crucial, significant, influential. ■ OPPOSITES irresolute, inconclusive.

declaration n. **1** STATEMENT, announcement, proclamation, pronouncement, broadcast, promulgation, edict, notification, manifesto. **2** ASSERTION, protestation, insistence, profession, claim, allegation, avowal, contention, affirmation, swearing, averment.

declare v. STATE, announce, proclaim, make known, assert, pronounce, broadcast, report, trumpet, profess, claim, allege, affirm, maintain, emphasize, swear, insist, avow, attest.

decline v. **1** REFUSE, turn down, reject, say no, rebuff, forgo, send one's regrets; *informal* give the thumbs down to. **2** LESSEN, decrease, dwindle, wane, fade, ebb, fall/taper off, tail off, flag, abate. **3** DETERIORATE, diminish, weaken, fail, degenerate, wither, fade away, sink. ▶ n. DECREASE, reduction, lessening, downturn, downswing, slump, plunge, shrinkage, diminution, ebb, waning, falling-off, deterioration, degeneration, nosedive.

decode v. DECIPHER, unravel, make out, unscramble, solve, explain, interpret, read; *informal* crack, figure out. ■ OPPOSITES encode.

decompose v. ROT, decay, putrefy, go bad, go off, break down, disintegrate, fester.

decor n. DECORATION, furnishings, furbishing, colour scheme, ornamentation.

decorate v. **1** ADORN, ornament, festoon, beautify, prettify, embellish, garnish, trim, enhance, garland. **2** PAINT, wallpaper, paper, renovate, refurbish, furbish; *informal* do up. **3** HONOUR, give a medal to, pin a medal on, confer an award on.

decoration n. **1** ADORNMENT, ornamentation, embellishment, beautification, prettification, enhancement. **2** ORNAMENT, trinket, bauble, frill, flourish, frippery, knick-knack, tinsel, trimming. **3** MEDAL, award, order, badge, star, ribbon, laurel, colours, insignia.

decorative adj. ORNAMENTAL, ornate, fancy, elaborate.

decorous adj. PROPER, seemly, decent, becoming, fitting, tasteful, in good taste, correct, appropriate, suitable, presentable, apt, apposite, polite, well mannered, well behaved, refined, genteel, well bred, respectable, dignified. ■ OPPOSITES indecorous, unseemly.

decorum n. PROPRIETY, decency, correctness, appropriateness, seemliness, respectability, good taste, politeness, courtesy, refinement, breeding, etiquette, protocol, conformity, good form; *informal* the thing to do.

decreasing.

decree n. an official order with the force of law. ▶ v. order by decree.

decrepit adj. worn out or weakened because of age or neglect. ■ **decrepitude** n.

decriminalize (or **-ise**) v. cease to treat as illegal.

decry v. (**decrying**, **decried**) publicly declare to be wrong.

dedicate v. 1 devote to a task or purpose. 2 address a book to a person as a tribute. ■ **dedication** n.

deduce v. arrive at a conclusion by reasoning. ■ **deducible** adj.

deduct v. subtract. ■ **deductible** adj.

deduction n. 1 the act of deducting. 2 an amount deducted. 3 a conclusion drawn by reasoning. ■ **deductive** adj.

deed n. 1 an action performed deliberately. 2 a legal document.

deem v. consider to be.

deep adj. 1 extending or situated far down or in from the top or surface. 2 low-pitched. 3 (of colour) dark. 4 very intense or extreme. 5 difficult to understand. ■ **deepen** v. **deeply** adv.

deer n. (pl. **deer**) a hoofed animal, the male of which usu. has antlers. □ **deerstalker** a cap with peaks in front and behind and ear flaps.

deface v. spoil the surface of.

defame v. damage the good reputation of. ■ **defamation** n. **defamatory** adj.

default n. 1 failure to fulfil an obligation, esp. to repay a loan. 2 a preselected option adopted by a computer program when no alternative is specified. ▶ v. fail to fulfil an obligation. □ **by default** because of a lack of opposition or positive action. ■ **defaulter** n.

defeat v. 1 win a victory over. 2 cause to fail. ▶ n. an act of defeating or the state of being defeated.

Thesaurus

decoy n. LURE, bait, temptation, diversion, distraction, snare, trap, inducement, attraction, enticement. ▶ v. LURE, attract, tempt, seduce, inveigle, draw, lead, ensnare, entrap, snare, trap, trick.

decrease v. 1 LESSEN, reduce, grow less, diminish, drop, fall off, decline, contract, dwindle, shrink, lower, cut down/back, curtail. 2 DIE DOWN, abate, subside, let up, slacken, ebb, wane, taper off, peter out, tail off.. ▶ n. REDUCTION, drop, lessening, decline, falling-off, downturn, cutback, diminution, curtailment, contraction, shrinkage. ■ OPPOSITES increase.

decree n. 1 EDICT, order, law, statute, act, ordinance, regulation, injunction, rule, enactment, command, mandate, proclamation, precept, dictum. 2 RULING, verdict, judgement, decision, finding. ▶ v. ORDAIN, rule, order, command, dictate, lay down, prescribe, pronounce, declare, proclaim, direct, determine, decide, promulgate, enact, adjudge, enjoin.

decrepit adj. DILAPIDATED, battered, ramshackle, derelict, broken-down, rundown, worn out, rickety, antiquated; informal the worse for wear, on its last legs. ■ OPPOSITES sound.

dedicate v. 1 DEVOTE, commit, give, give over, pledge, surrender. 2 INSCRIBE, address, assign, name.

dedicated adj. COMMITTED, devoted, wholehearted, enthusiastic, keen, zealous, single-minded, sworn.

deduce v. CONCLUDE, come to the conclusion that, infer, gather, work out, reason, understand, come to understand, surmise, divine, assume, presume, glean; informal put two and two together; informal suss out.

deduct v. SUBTRACT, take away, take off, withdraw, remove, discount, abstract. ■ OPPOSITES add.

deduction n. 1 CONCLUSION, inference, reasoning, assumption, presumption, findings, result. 2 SUBTRACTION, reduction, decrease, taking off, removal, withdrawal, discount.

deed n. 1 ACT, action, feat, exploit, performance, undertaking, effort, accomplishment, enterprise, achievement, endeavour, stunt. 2 DOCUMENT, title, contract, instrument, indenture.

deep adj. 1 FATHOMLESS, bottomless, yawning, cavernous, profound, unplumbed, abyssal. 2 PROFOUND, extreme, intense, great, deep-seated, deep-rooted, grave. 3 INTENSE, heartfelt, fervent, ardent, impassioned. 4 LOW, low-pitched, bass, rich, powerful, resonant, sonorous, rumbling, booming, resounding. ■ OPPOSITES shallow, light, high.

deface v. SPOIL, disfigure, blemish, mar, deform, ruin, sully, tarnish, damage, mutilate, vandalize, injure, uglify.

defame v. SLANDER, libel, blacken someone's name, cast aspersions on, smear, malign, insult, speak evil of, vilify, traduce, besmirch, drag through the mud, defile, stigmatize, disparage, denigrate.

defeat v. 1 BEAT, conquer, get the better

defeatist n. a person who expects or accepts failure too readily. ■ **defeatism** n.

defecate v. discharge waste matter from the bowels. ■ **defecation** n.

defect n. an imperfection. ▶v. abandon one's country or cause for an opposing one. ■ **defection** n. **defector** n.

defective adj. imperfect or faulty.

defence (US **defense**) n. **1** the act of defending against attack. **2** protective military measures or resources. **3** arguments presented against an accusation or in justification of an action. ■ **defenceless** adj.

defend v. **1** protect from attack. **2** act as a lawyer for the defendant. **3** attempt to justify. ■ **defender** n.

defendant n. a person sued or accused in a court of law.

defensible adj. able to be defended.

defensive adj. **1** intended for defence.

2 sensitive to criticism. ■ **defensively** adv.

defer v. (**deferring, deferred**) **1** put off to a later time. **2** (**defer to**) give in humbly to. ■ **deferment** n. **deferral** n.

deference n. humble respect. ■ **deferential** adj. **deferentially** adv.

defiance n. bold disobedience. ■ **defiant** adj. **defiantly** adv.

deficiency n. (pl. **deficiencies**) **1** a lack or shortage. **2** a failing or shortcoming.

deficient adj. **1** not having enough of a specified thing. **2** inadequate.

deficit n. **1** the amount by which something falls short. **2** an excess of money spent over money earned.

defile v. **1** make dirty. **2** desecrate. ▶n. a narrow gorge or mountain pass.

define v. **1** describe the exact nature of. **2** give the meaning of a word. **3** mark out the limits of.

Thesaurus

of, win a victory over, vanquish, rout, trounce, overcome, overpower, overwhelm, crush, quash, subjugate, subdue, quell; *informal* thrash, wipe the floor with, lick, smash, clobber, zap. **2** BAFFLE, puzzle, perplex, confound, frustrate. **3** REJECT, throw out, outvote. ▶n. CONQUEST, beating, vanquishing, thrashing, rout, overpowering, overthrow, reverse, setback, subjugation, humiliation, failure, repulse; *informal* drubbing, licking.

defect¹ n. FAULT, flaw, imperfection, deficiency, shortcoming, weak spot/point, weakness, mistake, error, failing, inadequacy, omission, absence, snag, kink, deformity, blemish, crack, break, tear, scratch; *informal* bug.

defect² v. DESERT, change sides, go over, apostatize.

defective adj. FAULTY, flawed, imperfect, malfunctioning, broken, in disrepair, inadequate, deficient, incomplete, weak, unsatisfactory, cracked, torn, scratched, insufficient, wanting. ■ OPPOSITES intact.

defence n. **1** PROTECTION, guard, shield, security, safeguard, cover, shelter, fortification, screen, resistance, deterrent. **2** JUSTIFICATION, argument, apology, apologia, vindication, plea, explanation, excuse, extenuation, exoneration.

defenceless adj. VULNERABLE, helpless, exposed, weak, powerless, unguarded, unprotected, unarmed, open to attack, wide open.

defend v. **1** PROTECT, guard, watch over,

safeguard, keep from harm, preserve, secure, shelter, screen, shield, cover, fight for. **2** JUSTIFY, argue for, speak on behalf of, make a case for, give reasons for, plead for, champion, stand up for, explain, exonerate. ■ OPPOSITES attack.

defendant n. ACCUSED, prisoner at the bar, respondent, appellant, litigant.

defensive adj. **1** PROTECTIVE, watchful, shielding, opposing. **2** OVERSENSITIVE, prickly, apologetic, thin-skinned. ■ OPPOSITES offensive.

defer v. POSTPONE, put off, delay, adjourn, hold over, suspend, stay, hold in abeyance, prorogue; *informal* put on ice, shelve.

deference n. RESPECT, reverence, homage, veneration, dutifulness, consideration, regard, attentiveness, attention, thoughtfulness.

defiant adj. CHALLENGING, aggressive, provocative, rebellious, disobedient, uncooperative, insolent, resistant, insubordinate, mutinous, obstinate, headstrong, antagonistic, refractory, contemptuous, scornful, bold, brazen, daring, audacious, truculent, unruly, self-willed.

deficiency n. **1** LACK, shortage, scarcity, scantiness, want, dearth, insufficiency, inadequacy, deficit, absence, paucity. **2** *see* DEFECT¹.

defile v. CORRUPT, contaminate, taint, tarnish, pollute, foul, dirty, soil, sully, pervert, infect, besmirch, desecrate, dishonour.

define v. **1** EXPLAIN, give the meaning of,

definite adj. **1** clearly stated or decided. **2** certain about something. **3** known to be true or real. □ **definite article** the word *the*. ■ **definitely** adv.

....

☑ *-ite*, not *-ate*: defin*ite*.

....

definition n. **1** a statement of the exact meaning of a word. **2** sharpness of outline.

definitive adj. **1** settling something finally with authority. **2** the most accurate of its kind. ■ **definitively** adv.

deflate v. **1** let air or gas out of a tyre etc. **2** make less confident. **3** reduce price levels in an economy. ■ **deflation** n. **deflationary** adj.

deflect v. turn aside. ■ **deflection** n.

deflower v. literary have sex with a woman who is a virgin.

defoliate v. remove the leaves from. ■ **defoliant** n. **defoliation** n.

deforest v. clear of trees. ■ **deforestation** n.

deform v. distort the usual shape of.

deformed adj. misshapen.

deformity n. (pl. **deformities**) **1** a deformed part, esp. of the body. **2** the state of being deformed.

defraud v. deprive of money by using deception.

defray v. provide money to pay a cost.

defrock v. remove the official status of a Christian priest.

defrost v. **1** free of ice. **2** thaw frozen food.

deft adj. quick and skilful. ■ **deftly** adv.

defunct adj. no longer existing or functioning.

defuse v. **1** remove the fuse from an explosive device. **2** reduce the tension in a difficult situation.

....

☑ Don't confuse **defuse** with **diffuse**, meaning 'spread over a wide area'.

....

defy v. (**defying**, **defied**) **1** openly resist or refuse to obey. **2** challenge to do something.

degenerate adj. immoral. ▶n. an immoral person. ▶v. become worse or weaker. ■ **degeneracy** n. **degeneration** n.

degrade v. **1** cause to lose dignity or self-respect. **2** make worse in quality. **3** cause to break down chemically. ■ **degradation** n.

Thesaurus

....

spell out, elucidate, describe, interpret, expound, clarify. **2** MARK OUT/OFF, fix, establish, determine, settle, bound, demarcate, delineate, delimit, circumscribe, describe.

definite adj. **1** SPECIFIC, precise, particular, exact, well defined, clear, clear-cut, explicit, fixed, established, confirmed, determined, express. **2** CERTAIN, sure, decided, positive, settled, guaranteed, assured, conclusive, final. **3** FIXED, marked, delimited, demarcated, circumscribed. ■ OPPOSITES indefinite, uncertain, indeterminate.

definitely adv. CERTAINLY, surely, for sure, without doubt/question, beyond any doubt, undoubtedly, indubitably, positively, absolutely, undeniably, unmistakably, plainly, clearly, obviously, decidedly.

definition n. **1** MEANING, description, elucidation, exposition, interpretation, clarification. **2** SHARPNESS, clearness, clarity, distinctness, focus, precision.

definitive adj. CONCLUSIVE, authoritative, final, decisive, unconditional, unqualified, absolute, categorical, settled, official, ultimate, decided, agreed, standard, complete, correct.

deflect v. TURN ASIDE, turn, divert, parry, fend off, ward off, intercept, glance off, veer, swerve, deviate, switch, avert, sidetrack.

deformed adj. MISSHAPEN, malformed, distorted, contorted, twisted, crooked, crippled, maimed, disfigured, damaged, mutilated, marred, warped, gnarled, mangled, perverted, corrupted, depraved.

defraud v. CHEAT, swindle, rob, trick, fool; *informal* rip off, fleece, con, gyp.

deft adj. DEXTEROUS, nimble, adroit, agile, skilful, skilled, adept, proficient, able, clever, expert, quick. ■ OPPOSITES clumsy, maladroit.

defy v. **1** DISOBEY, disregard, rebel, ignore, flout, deride, slight, scorn; *informal* thumb one's nose at, scoff at, snap one's fingers at. **2** RESIST, stand up to, confront, face, repel, repulse, thwart, frustrate, foil, withstand, brave; *informal* meet head-on. ■ OPPOSITES obey.

degenerate adj. *see* DEBAUCHED. ▶v. DETERIORATE, decline, worsen, decay, rot, regress, fail, fall off, sink, slide, slip; *informal* go to the dogs, go to pot, hit the skids. ■ OPPOSITES improve.

degrade v. **1** DEBASE, discredit, cheapen, belittle, demean, lower, devalue, vitiate, reduce, shame, disgrace, dishonour,

d

degree n. **1** the extent to which something happens or is present. **2** a unit for measuring angles. **3** a stage in a scale, e.g. of temperature. **4** an academic rank awarded by a college or university.

dehumanize (or **-ise**) v. deprive of good human qualities.

dehydrate v. **1** cause to lose a large amount of moisture. **2** remove water from food to preserve it. ■ **dehydration** n.

deify v. (**deifying**, **deified**) worship as a god. ■ **deification** n.

deign /dayn/ v. (**deign to do**) condescend to do.

deity n. (pl. **deities**) a god or goddess.

déjà vu /day-zhah voo/ n. a feeling of having already experienced the present situation.

dejected adj. sad and dispirited.

dejection n. sadness or low spirits.

delay v. **1** make late or slow. **2** postpone. ▶n. **1** the time that someone or something is delayed. **2** the act of delaying.

delectable adj. delightful or delicious. ■ **delectably** adv.

delectation n. pleasure and delight.

delegate n. **1** a person sent to represent others. **2** a member of a committee. ▶v. entrust a task or responsibility to a more junior person.

delete v. **1** remove text. **2** remove data from a computer's memory. ■ **deletion** n.

deleterious adj. harmful.

deliberate adj. **1** intentional. **2** careful and unhurried. ▶v. consider carefully and at length. ■ **deliberately** adv. **deliberation** n.

delicacy n. (pl. **delicacies**) **1** the quality of being delicate. **2** a high-quality or expensive food.

delicate adj. **1** very fine in quality or structure. **2** easily broken or damaged. **3** prone to illness. **4** requiring tact and discretion. ■ **delicately** adv.

delicatessen n. a shop selling cooked

Thesaurus

humble, humiliate, abase, mortify. **2** DEMOTE, downgrade, strip of rank, cashier, unseat, dethrone. ■ OPPOSITES dignify.

degree n. **1** LEVEL, stage, grade, step, rung, point, mark, measure, gradation, limit. **2** EXTENT, measure, magnitude, level, amount, intensity, quality, proportion, ratio.

deign v. CONDESCEND, lower oneself, stoop, think/see fit, deem worthy, consent.

deity n. GOD, goddess, supreme being, divinity, godhead, divine being, demiurge.

dejected adj. DEPRESSED, dispirited, discouraged, disheartened, downhearted, crestfallen, downcast, disappointed, unhappy, sad, miserable, despondent, forlorn, woebegone, disconsolate, morose; *informal* down in the dumps, blue, longfaced. ■ OPPOSITES cheerful.

delay v. **1** POSTPONE, put off, hold over, adjourn, defer, stay, hold in abeyance; *informal* shelve, put on ice, put on the back burner. **2** HOLD UP/BACK, detain, hinder, obstruct, hamper, impede, check, restrain, arrest; *informal* bog down. **3** LINGER, loiter, dawdle, dally, lag/fall behind, procrastinate; *informal* dilly-dally; *old use* tarry. ▶n. **1** POSTPONEMENT, adjournment, deferment, deferral, suspension, stay. **2** HOLD-UP, wait, setback, check, stoppage, halt, interruption, detention, hindrance, obstruction,

impediment.

delegate v. **1** APPOINT, designate, nominate, name, depute, commission, mandate, choose, select, elect, ordain. **2** PASS ON, hand over, transfer, give, entrust, assign, commit. ▶n. REPRESENTATIVE, agent, envoy, legate, emissary.

delegation n. DEPUTATION, legation, mission, commission, embassy.

delete v. ERASE, cross out, rub out, cut out, cancel, edit out, remove, take out, expunge, obliterate, blue-pencil, efface.

deliberate adj. **1** INTENTIONAL, planned, intended, calculated, considered, designed, studied, conscious, purposeful, wilful, premeditated, pre-arranged, preconceived, aforethought. **2** CAREFUL, unhurried, cautious, thoughtful, steady, regular, measured, unwavering, unhesitating, unfaltering, determined, resolute, ponderous, laborious. ■ OPPOSITES unintentional. ▶v. *see* THINK (3).

deliberately adv. INTENTIONALLY, on purpose, purposefully, knowingly, by design, wittingly, consciously, wilfully, premeditatedly, calculatingly; *informal* in cold blood.

delicate adj. **1** FINE, fragile, dainty, exquisite, slender, slight, elegant, graceful, flimsy, wispy, gossamer. **2** FRAIL, sickly, weak, unwell, in poor health, infirm, ailing, debilitated. **3** CAREFUL, sensitive, tactful, discreet, considerate, diplomatic, politic. **4** SUBTLE, subdued, muted, pastel, pale, understated. **5** DIFFImeats, cheeses, and unusual foods.

delicious adj. **1** very pleasant to the taste. **2** delightful. ■ **deliciously** adv.

delight v. **1** please greatly. **2** (**delight in**) take great pleasure in. ▶n. **1** great pleasure. **2** a source of this. ■ **delightful** adj. **delightfully** adv.

delimit v. determine the limits of.

delineate v. describe or indicate precisely. ■ **delineation** n.

delinquent adj. tending to commit crime. ▶n. a delinquent person. ■ **delinquency** n.

delirious adj. **1** suffering from delirium. **2** extremely excited or happy. ■ **deliriously** adv.

delirium n. a disturbed state of mind occurring esp. during a fever.

deliver v. **1** bring and hand over a letter, goods, etc. to someone. **2** save or set free. **3** give a speech, lecture, etc. **4** assist in the birth of. **5** aim a blow. ■ **deliverer** n. **delivery** n.

deliverance n. the process of being saved or set free.

dell n. a small valley.

delphinium n. a tall garden plant with blue flowers.

delta n. **1** the fourth letter of the Greek alphabet (Δ, δ). **2** a triangular area of land where a river has split into several channels just before entering the sea.

delude v. deceive or mislead.

deluge n. **1** a severe flood or heavy fall of rain. **2** a large number of things arriving at the same time. ▶v. **1** overwhelm with a large number of things. **2** flood.

delusion n. a false belief or impression. ■ **delusional** adj.

de luxe adj. of a high quality.

delve v. search deeply.

demagogue n. a political leader appealing to popular desires and prejudices. ■ **demagogic** adj.

demand n. **1** a firm request. **2** (**demands**) pressing requirements. **3** consumers' desire for a particular product or service. ▶v. **1** ask for firmly. **2** need.

Thesaurus

CULT, awkward, tricky, sensitive, critical, precarious; *informal* ticklish, touchy. **6** DEFT, skilled, skilful, expert. ■ OPPOSITES coarse, robust.

delicious adj. **1** APPETIZING, tasty, delectable, mouth-watering, savoury, palatable, luscious, flavoursome, toothsome, ambrosial; *informal* yummy, scrumptious. **2** DELIGHTFUL, enchanting, enjoyable, pleasant, agreeable, charming, pleasurable, entertaining, amusing, diverting. ■ OPPOSITES revolting, disgusting.

delight n. JOY, pleasure, happiness, gladness, bliss, ecstasy, rapture, elation, jubilation, satisfaction, excitement, entertainment, amusement, transports. ▶v. PLEASE, gladden, thrill, cheer, gratify, enchant, excite, transport, captivate, charm, entertain, amuse, divert. ■ OPPOSITES dismay, displease.

delighted adj. *see* HAPPY.

delightful adj. PLEASING, agreeable, enjoyable, pleasant, pleasurable, amusing, entertaining, diverting, gratifying, delectable, enchanting, captivating, entrancing, ravishing, attractive, beautiful, engaging, winning, joyful, exciting, thrilling.

delinquent n. OFFENDER, wrongdoer, lawbreaker, criminal, hooligan, culprit, ruffian, hoodlum, tearaway, miscreant, transgressor, malefactor.

delirious adj. **1** RAVING, incoherent, babbling, irrational, deranged, demented,

unhinged, insane; *informal* off one's head. **2** ECSTATIC, euphoric, carried away, wild with excitement, frantic, transported.

deliver v. **1** DISTRIBUTE, carry, bring, take, transport, convey, send, dispatch, remit. **2** GIVE, give voice to, pronounce, enunciate, announce, proclaim, declare, read, recite, broadcast, promulgate. **3** SET FREE, save, liberate, free, release, rescue, set loose, emancipate, redeem. **4** DIRECT, aim, give, deal, administer, inflict, throw, pitch.

delivery n. **1** DISTRIBUTION, transport, carriage, conveyance, dispatch. **2** CONSIGNMENT, batch, load. **3** ENUNCIATION, articulation, intonation, elocution, utterance, presentation. **4** CHILDBIRTH, labour, confinement, parturition.

deluge n. FLOOD, downpour, inundation, spate, rush. ▶v. FLOOD, inundate, swamp, engulf, drown, submerge, soak, drench, douse, overwhelm.

delusion n. MISCONCEPTION, illusion, fallacy, misapprehension, mistake, misunderstanding, hallucination, fantasy, fancy.

delve v. SEARCH, rummage, dig into, hunt through, investigate, probe, examine.

demand v. **1** ASK FOR, request, insist on, press for, urge, clamour for, claim, lay claim to. **2** EXPECT, impose, insist on, order, requisition. **3** REQUIRE, need, necessitate, involve, want, call for, cry out

demanding adj. requiring much skill or effort.

demarcation n. **1** the fixing of boundaries, esp. of work. **2** a dividing line.

demean v. lower the dignity of.

demeanour (US **demeanor**) n. outward behaviour or bearing.

demented adj. mad or crazy.

dementia n. a serious mental disorder.

demerara sugar n. a kind of light brown sugar.

demesne /di-mayn/ n. hist. land attached to a manor.

demi- prefix half.

demilitarize (or **-ise**) v. remove military forces from. ■ **demilitarization** n.

demise n. **1** death. **2** the end or failure of something.

demo n. (pl. **demos**) informal a demonstration.

demob v. (**demobbing**, **demobbed**) informal demobilize.

demobilize (or **-ise**) v. release from military service. ■ **demobilization** n.

democracy n. (pl. **democracies**) **1** a form of government in which the people have a say in who should hold power. **2** a state governed in such a way. ■ **democrat** n. **democratic** adj. **democratically** adv.

demography n. the statistical study of human populations. ■ **demographic** adj.

demolish v. pull or knock down a building. ■ **demolition** n.

demon n. **1** an evil spirit or devil. **2** an energetic and forceful person. ■ **demoniac** (or **demoniacal**) adj. **demonic** adj. **demonically** adv.

demonstrable adj. clearly apparent or able to be proved. ■ **demonstrably** adv.

demonstrate v. **1** clearly show to exist or be true. **2** show and explain how something works. **3** take part in a public demonstration. ■ **demonstrator** n.

demonstration n. **1** an act of demonstrating. **2** a public meeting or march to protest about an issue.

demonstrative adj. **1** showing one's feelings openly. **2** demonstrating or proving. ■ **demonstratively** adv.

demoralize (or **-ise**) v. dishearten.

demote v. reduce to a less senior position. ■ **demotion** n.

demur v. (**demurring**, **demurred**) raise objections; show reluctance. ▶ n. the act of objecting.

demure adj. reserved, modest, and shy. ■ **demurely** adv.

den n. **1** a wild animal's lair. **2** informal a person's private room.

denationalize (or **-ise**) v. privatize. ■ **denationalization** n.

deniable adj. able to be denied.

denial n. **1** the act of denying. **2** a statement that something is not true.

denier /den-yer/ n. a unit by which the fineness of yarn is measured.

Thesaurus

for. **4** ASK, inquire, question, interrogate. ▶ n. **1** REQUEST, entreaty, claim, requisition. **2** REQUIREMENT, need, necessity, claim, imposition, exigency. **3** INQUIRY, question, interrogation, challenge.

demanding adj. see DIFFICULT.

demean v. DEGRADE, lower, debase, devalue, humble, abase, humiliate, disgrace, shame, belittle.

demeanour n. AIR, appearance, bearing, conduct, behaviour, mien, deportment, carriage, comportment.

demolish v. KNOCK DOWN, pull/tear down, flatten, bring down, raze, level, bulldoze, wreck, topple, dismantle, break up, pulverize. ■ OPPOSITES build.

demonic adj. HELLISH, diabolical, satanic, infernal, evil, wicked, fiendish. ■ OPPOSITES angelic.

demonstrable adj. PROVABLE, verifiable, indisputable, incontrovertible, irrefutable, conclusive, undeniable, unquestionable, confirmable, attestable, evincible.

demonstrate v. **1** SHOW, indicate, display, exhibit, manifest, evince, evidence. **2** PROVE, indicate, show, determine, confirm, validate, verify, establish. **3** PROTEST, march, parade, rally, picket.

demonstration n. **1** EXPLANATION, exposition, illustration, description. **2** INDICATION, confirmation, substantiation, verification, validation, affirmation. **3** PROTEST, march, parade, rally, vigil, lobby, picket; informal demo, sit-in.

demonstrative adj. EMOTIONAL, unrestrained, expressive, open, effusive, expansive, gushing, affectionate, loving, warm. ■ OPPOSITES undemonstrative, reserved.

demoralize v. DISCOURAGE, dishearten, dispirit, depress, crush, shake, undermine. ■ OPPOSITES hearten.

demure adj. MODEST, unassuming, bashful, retiring, shy, meek, diffident, reticent, timid, shrinking, timorous, sober. ■ OPPOSITES brazen.

denial n. **1** CONTRADICTION, repudiation,

denigrate v. criticize unfairly. ■ **denigration** n.

denim n. **1** a hard-wearing cotton twill fabric. **2** (**denims**) jeans made of this.

denizen n. an inhabitant.

denominate v. name.

denomination n. **1** a recognized branch of a church or religion. **2** the face value of a banknote, coin, etc. ■ **denominational** adj.

denominator n. the number below the line in a fraction.

denote v. **1** be a sign of. **2** mean. ■ **denotation** n.

denouement /day-noo-mon/ n. the final outcome of a play, film, etc.

denounce v. publicly declare to be wrong or evil.

dense adj. **1** closely packed together. **2** containing parts crowded closely together. **3** informal stupid. ■ **densely** adv.

density n. (pl. **densities**) the degree to which something is dense.

dent n. a slight hollow made by a blow or pressure. ▶ v. **1** mark with a dent. **2** have a bad effect on.

dental adj. of the teeth or of dentistry.

dentine n. the hard tissue forming the main part of a tooth.

dentist n. a person qualified to treat conditions affecting the teeth and gums. ■ **dentistry** n.

dentition n. the arrangement of the teeth in a species.

denture n. a removable plate or frame holding one or more false teeth.

denude v. make bare or empty.

denunciation n. the act of denouncing.

deny v. (**denying**, **denied**) **1** refuse to admit the truth or existence of. **2** prevent from having.

deodorant n. a substance which prevents unpleasant bodily odours.

deodorize (or **-ise**) v. prevent an unpleasant smell in.

depart v. **1** leave. **2** (**depart from**) do something different from a usual course of action. ■ **departure** n.

departed adj. dead.

department n. a section of a large organization, dealing with a specific area of activity. □ **department store** a large shop selling many types of goods in different departments. ■ **departmental** adj.

depend v. (**depend on**) **1** be determined by. **2** rely on.

dependable adj. reliable. ■ **dependability** n.

Thesaurus

disaffirmation, negation, dissent, abjuration. **2** REFUSAL, rejection, dismissal, veto, repulse; informal thumbs down. ■ OPPOSITES confession.

denigrate v. DISPARAGE, belittle, diminish, deprecate, detract from, decry, defame, slander, libel, cast aspersions on, malign, vilify, besmirch, abuse, revile; informal bad-mouth, put down. ■ OPPOSITES praise.

denomination n. **1** CREED, faith, church, sect, persuasion, communion, order, school. **2** CATEGORY, type, classification, group, grouping.

denote v. BE A SIGN OF, indicate, mean, stand for, signify, represent, symbolize, express, betoken.

denounce v. CONDEMN, attack, criticize, censure, decry, fulminate against, inveigh against, revile, castigate. **2** ACCUSE, inform against, incriminate, implicate, charge, inculpate, indict, impeach.

dense adj. **1** TIGHTLY PACKED, close-packed, crowded, jammed together, crammed, compressed, compacted, closely set. **2** CONCENTRATED, heavy, condensed, thick, viscous, impenetrable, opaque. **3** STUPID, slow-witted, slow,

dull-witted, obtuse, blockheaded; informal thick, dim. ■ OPPOSITES sparse, light, clever.

deny v. **1** REPUDIATE, dispute, reject, contradict, disagree with, disclaim, dissent from, negate, disaffirm, abjure, controvert. **2** REFUSE, reject, turn down, decline, dismiss, repulse, veto; informal give the thumbs down to, give the red light to. ■ OPPOSITES admit, allow, grant.

depart v. **1** LEAVE, go, take one's leave/departure, withdraw, absent oneself, set off, start out, get under way, quit, make an exit, decamp, retire, retreat; informal make tracks, shove off, split, vamoose, hightail it. **2** see DEVIATE.

departed adj. DEAD, deceased, late, gone, passed away/on.

department n. **1** SECTION, division, unit, branch, office, bureau, agency, compartment. **2** AREA OF RESPONSIBILITY, area, concern, sphere, line, province, domain, field, realm, jurisdiction.

departure n. LEAVING, going, starting out, embarkation, escape, exit, withdrawal, retreat, retirement. ■ OPPOSITES arrival.

depend v. **1** BE DEPENDENT ON, turn/hinge on, be subject to, rest on, be contingent

dependant (or **dependent**) n. a person who relies on another for financial support.

dependency n. (pl. **dependencies**) **1** a country or province controlled by another. **2** the state of being dependent.

dependent adj. **1** (**dependent on**) determined by. **2** relying on someone or something for support. **3** (**dependent on**) unable to do without. ▶n. var. of DEPENDANT. ■ **dependence** n.

depict v. represent in a picture or in words. ■ **depiction** n.

depilatory adj. used to remove unwanted hair.

deplete v. reduce the number or quantity of. ■ **depletion** n.

deplorable adj. shockingly bad. ■ **deplorably** adv.

deplore v. feel or express strong disapproval of.

deploy v. **1** bring or move into position for military action. **2** use effectively. ■ **deployment** n.

depopulate v. reduce the population of. ■ **depopulation** n.

deport v. expel a foreigner from a country. ■ **deportation** n.

deportment n. the way a person stands and walks.

depose v. remove from power.

deposit n. **1** a sum of money paid into an account. **2** a first instalment in buying something. **3** a returnable sum paid to cover possible loss or damage of something rented. **4** a layer of collected matter. ▶v. (**depositing, deposited**) **1** put down. **2** entrust for safe keeping. **3** pay as a deposit. **4** leave as a layer. ■ **depositor** n.

depository n. (pl. **depositories**) a place where things are stored.

depot /dep-oh/ n. **1** a place for storing goods. **2** a place where vehicles are housed.

deprave v. corrupt morally. ■ **depravity** n.

deprecate v. express disapproval of. ■ **deprecation** n. **deprecatory** adj.

depreciate v. **1** reduce in value over time. **2** dismiss as unimportant. ■ **depreciation** n.

depredations pl. n. harmful or damaging acts.

depress v. **1** cause to feel very unhappy. **2** reduce the level of activity in. **3** push down. ■ **depressant** n. & adj.

depression n. **1** a mental state involv-

Thesaurus

on, revolve around, be influenced by. **2** RELY ON, count/bank on, trust in, put one's faith in, swear by, be sure of, be supported by.

dependable adj. RELIABLE, trustworthy, trusty, faithful, steady, responsible, sure, stable, unfailing, sound. ■ OPPOSITES unreliable.

dependent adj. **1** DEPENDING ON, conditional on, contingent on, subject to, determined by, connected with, relative to. **2** RELYING ON, supported by, sustained by. **3** RELIANT, helpless, weak, defenceless, vulnerable. ■ OPPOSITES independent.

depict v. PORTRAY, represent, draw, paint, sketch, illustrate, delineate, outline, reproduce, render, describe, set out, relate, detail, narrate, recount, chronicle.

deplete v. EXHAUST, use up, consume, expend, spend, drain, empty, milk. ■ OPPOSITES augment, increase.

deplorable adj. DISGRACEFUL, shameful, reprehensible, scandalous, shocking, dishonourable, discreditable, despicable, contemptible, blameworthy, abominable, lamentable, dire, pitiable, calamitous, base, sordid, vile, execrable, opprobrious. ■ OPPOSITES admirable.

deplore v. **1** See CONDEMN. **2** BE SCANDALIZED BY, be shocked by, be offended by, disapprove of, abhor. ■ OPPOSITES applaud.

deploy v. **1** ARRANGE, position, dispose, distribute, station. **2** USE, utilize, set out/up, bring into play, have recourse to.

deport v. EXPEL, banish, evict, transport, oust, expatriate, extradite.

depose v. UNSEAT, oust, remove, dismiss, dethrone, discharge, cashier; informal sack, fire, give someone the boot/push.

deposit n. **1** DOWN PAYMENT, instalment, retainer, security, pledge, stake. **2** SEDIMENT, accumulation, layer, precipitation, deposition, sublimate, dregs, silt, alluvium. ▶v. **1** BANK, lodge, consign, entrust, store, hoard, stow, put away, lay in; informal squirrel away. **2** PUT, place, lay, drop, let fall; informal dump, park.

depot n. **1** STATION, garage, terminus, terminal. **2** STORE, storehouse, warehouse, repository, depository, magazine, arsenal, cache.

deprave v. CORRUPT, debauch, lead astray, pervert, debase, degrade, defile, pollute, contaminate.

depraved adj. see CORRUPT (2).

ing feelings of great unhappiness. **2** a long slump in an economy or market. **3** a sunken place or hollow. **4** an area of low pressure which may bring rain. ■ **depressive** adj.

deprive v. prevent from having or using something. ■ **deprivation** n.

depth n. **1** the distance from the top or surface down, or from front to back. **2** profound thought. **3** extensive and detailed study. **4** strength of emotion. **5** (**the depths**) the deepest, lowest, or inmost part. □ **depth charge** a charge designed to explode under water.

deputation n. a group of people sent to represent others.

depute v. delegate authority or a task to someone.

deputize (or **-ise**) v. act as a deputy for someone.

deputy n. (pl. **deputies**) a person appointed to act on behalf of another.

derail v. cause a train to leave the tracks. ■ **derailment** n.

derange v. **1** make insane. **2** throw into disorder. ■ **derangement** n.

deregulate v. remove regulations or controls from. ■ **deregulation** n.

derelict adj. left to fall into ruin.

dereliction n. **1** the state of being derelict. **2** (**dereliction of duty**) failure to do one's duty.

deride v. ridicule.

de rigueur /duh ri·ger/ adj. required by etiquette or current fashion.

derision n. scornful ridicule or mockery. ■ **derisive** adj. **derisively** adv.

derisory adj. ridiculously small or inadequate.

derivative adj. lacking originality; copied from another artist, writer, etc. ▶ n. something derived from another source.

derive v. (**derive from**) **1** obtain from. **2** arise or originate from. ■ **derivation** n.

dermatitis n. inflammation of the skin.

dermatology n. the branch of medicine concerned with skin disorders. ■ **dermatologist** n.

derogatory adj. critical or disrespectful.

derrick n. **1** a crane with a pivoted arm. **2** the framework over an oil well.

dervish n. a member of a Muslim religious group known for their wild rituals.

desalinate v. remove salt from seawater. ■ **desalination** n.

descant n. a melody sung or played above a basic melody.

descend v. **1** move, slope, or lead down. **2** (**descend to**) do something shameful. **3** make an attack or unexpected visit. **4** (**be descended from**) have as an ancestor.

descendant n. a person descended from another.

descent n. **1** an act of descending. **2** a downward slope. **3** a person's origin or

Thesaurus

depreciate v. **1** DECREASE IN VALUE, lose value, decline in price. **2** see DISPARAGE.

depress v. **1** SADDEN, make gloomy/despondent, dispirit, dishearten, discourage, weigh down, grieve, oppress, dampen someone's spirits, burden. **2** SLOW DOWN/UP, weaken, lower, reduce, impair, enfeeble, drain, sap, debilitate, devitalize. ■ OPPOSITES cheer.

depressed adj. see SAD.

depression n. **1** SADNESS, unhappiness, despair, gloom, dejection, downheartedness, despondency, melancholy, desolation, moodiness, moroseness, pessimism; informal the dumps, the blues. **2** HOLLOW, indentation, cavity, dip, valley, pit, hole, bowl, excavation, concavity. **3** RECESSION, slump, slowdown, stagnation, decline. ■ OPPOSITES happiness, boom.

deprive v. DISPOSSESS, take away from, strip, deny, expropriate, divest, wrest, rob.

deprived adj. see POOR.

deputize v. TAKE THE PLACE OF, stand in for, act for, do someone's job, substitute for, take over from, replace, cover for, understudy.

deputy n. SUBSTITUTE, representative, stand-in, delegate, envoy, proxy, agent, ambassador, commissioner, legate.

derelict adj. **1** ABANDONED, deserted, neglected, rejected, discarded, forsaken, relinquished, cast off. **2** DILAPIDATED, ramshackle, tumbledown, run-down, broken-down, in disrepair, crumbling, rickety. ▶ n. VAGRANT, beggar, down and out, tramp, outcast; US hobo; informal dosser.

deride v. MOCK, ridicule, jeer at, scoff at, sneer at, make fun of, poke fun at, laugh at, scorn, lampoon, satirize, taunt, insult, rag, tease, chaff, disparage, slight, vilify; informal pooh-pooh.

derogatory adj. DISPARAGING, deprecatory, depreciatory, detracting, disapproving, unflattering, insulting, defamatory. ■ OPPOSITES complimentary.

nationality.

describe v. **1** give a detailed account in words of. **2** mark out or draw a shape.

description n. **1** a spoken or written account. **2** the act of describing. **3** a sort or kind. ■ **descriptive** adj. **descriptively** adv.

descry v. (**descrying**, **descried**) literary catch sight of.

desecrate v. treat something sacred with violent disrespect. ■ **desecration** n.

desegregate v. end racial segregation in. ■ **desegregation** n.

deselect v. reject an existing MP as a candidate in a forthcoming election. ■ **deselection** n.

desert v. **1** leave someone without help or support. **2** leave a place, causing it to appear empty. **3** leave military service without permission. ▶n. a waterless, empty area of land with little or no vegetation. ■ **deserter** n. **desertion** n.

deserts /di-zerts/ pl. n. the reward or punishment that one deserves.

deserve v. be worthy of or entitled to. ■ **deservedly** adv.

deserving adj. worthy of favourable treatment or help.

déshabillé /day-za-bee-yay/ (or **dishabille** /diss-uh-beel/) n. the state of being only partly clothed.

desiccate v. remove the moisture from. ■ **desiccation** n.

desideratum n. (pl. **desiderata**) something needed or wanted.

design n. **1** a plan or drawing that shows how something is to be made. **2** a decorative pattern. **3** underlying purpose or planning. ▶v. **1** produce a design for. **2** intend for a purpose. ■ **designer** n.

designate v. **1** officially assign a status or name to. **2** appoint to a job. ▶adj. appointed to a post but not yet having taken it up. ■ **designation** n.

designing adj. cunning and deceitful.

desirable adj. **1** wished for as being attractive, useful, or necessary. **2** sexually attractive. ■ **desirability** n.

desire n. **1** a strong feeling of wanting something. **2** strong sexual appetite. ▶v. **1** strongly wish for or want. **2** want sexually.

desirous adj. strongly wishing for.

Thesaurus

descend v. **1** GO/COME DOWN, climb down, fall, drop, sink, subside, plunge, plummet, tumble, slump. **2** GET DOWN, get off, alight, disembark, dismount, detrain, deplane. ■ OPPOSITES ascend.

descent n. **1** SLOPE, incline, dip, drop, gradient, declivity, slant. **2** ANCESTRY, parentage, origins, lineage, extraction, heredity, genealogy, succession, stock, line, pedigree, blood, strain. ■ OPPOSITES ascent.

describe v. **1** GIVE DETAILS OF, detail, tell, narrate, put into words, express, recount, relate, report, set out, chronicle, illustrate, characterize, portray, depict. **2** DRAW, mark out, delineate, outline, trace, sketch.

description n. ACCOUNT, statement, report, chronicle, narration, recounting, commentary, explanation, illustration, designation, characterization, portrayal, depiction, elucidation, relation.

descriptive adj. DETAILED, graphic, vivid, striking, expressive, illustrative, depictive, pictorial.

desecrate v. DEFILE, profane, blaspheme, pollute, treat sacrilegiously, contaminate, befoul, infect, debase, degrade, dishonour. ■ OPPOSITES honour.

desert¹ v. **1** ABANDON, forsake, give up, leave, turn one's back on, betray, jilt,

strand, leave stranded, maroon, neglect, shun, relinquish; informal walk out on, leave in the lurch, leave high and dry. **2** ABSCOND, defect, run away, flee, decamp, bolt, depart, quit; informal go AWOL, turn tail, take French leave.

desert² adj. ARID, dry, parched, scorched, torrid. ▶n. WASTELAND, wilderness, barrenness, wilds.

deserted adj. ABANDONED, empty, neglected, vacant, uninhabited, unoccupied, untenanted, desolate, lonely, solitary, godforsaken. ■ OPPOSITES crowded, populous.

deserter n. **1** ABSCONDER, runaway, defector, fugitive, truant, escapee. **2** RENEGADE, turncoat, traitor, betrayer, apostate; informal rat.

deserve v. MERIT, warrant, be worthy of, rate, justify, earn, be entitled to, have a right to, have a claim on.

deserving adj. see WORTHY.

design n. **1** PLAN, blueprint, drawing, sketch, outline, map, plot, diagram, draft, scheme, model. **2** PATTERN, style, arrangement, composition, configuration, shape. **3** INTENTION, aim, purpose, plan, objective, goal, end, target, point, hope, desire, wish, aspiration. ▶v. **1** PLAN, draw, sketch, outline, map out, block out, delineate, draft, depict.

desist v. stop doing.

desk n. **1** a piece of furniture for working on. **2** a counter in a hotel, airport, etc. **3** a section of a news organization. □ **desktop 1** the working surface of a desk. **2** a computer suitable for use at a desk. **3** the working area of a computer screen.

desolate adj. **1** bleak and empty. **2** very unhappy. ▶ v. make very unhappy. ■ **desolation** n.

despair n. complete lack of hope. ▶ v. lose or be without hope.

despatch var. of DISPATCH.

desperado n. (pl. **desperadoes** or **desperados**) dated a desperate or reckless criminal.

desperate adj. **1** feeling or involving despair. **2** done when all else has failed. **3** extremely serious. ■ **desperately** adv. **desperation** n.

✓ desperate, not -parate.

despicable adj. deserving hatred and contempt. ■ **despicably** adv.

despise v. feel contempt or disgust for.

despite prep. in spite of.

despoil v. literary steal valuable possessions from.

despondent adj. sad and dispirited. ■ **despondency** n. **despondently** adv.

despot n. a ruler with total power, esp. a cruel one. ■ **despotic** adj. **despotism** n.

dessert n. the sweet course eaten at the end of a meal. □ **dessertspoon** a spoon between a tablespoon and a teaspoon in size.

destabilize (or **-ise**) v. make unstable.

destination n. the place to which someone or something is going.

destined adj. **1** intended for a particular purpose. **2** bound for a particular destination.

destiny n. (pl. **destinies**) **1** the events that will happen to a person. **2** the hidden power believed to control future events; fate.

d

Thesaurus

2 CREATE, invent, think up, originate, conceive, fashion. **3** INTEND, aim, contrive, plan, tailor, mean, destine.

designer n. CREATOR, inventor, deviser, originator, architect, author.

desire v. **1** WISH FOR, want, long for, yearn for, thirst for, hunger after, crave, ache for, set one's heart on, hanker after, fancy, have a fancy for, covet, aspire to; informal have a yen for. **2** LUST AFTER, burn for; informal have the hots for. ▶ n. **1** WISH, want, fancy, inclination, preference, longing, yearning, craving, eagerness, enthusiasm, hankering, predilection, aspiration. **2** LUST, lustfulness, passion, lechery, sexual appetite, libido, sensuality, sexuality, lasciviousness, salaciousness, libidinousness; informal the hots.

desolate adj. **1** ABANDONED, deserted, barren, uninhabited, unoccupied, lonely, isolated, bare, desert, bleak, depopulated, forsaken, unfrequented, remote, cheerless, dismal, godforsaken. **2** SAD, unhappy, miserable, broken-hearted, wretched, downcast, dejected, downhearted, melancholy, gloomy, depressed, forlorn, disconsolate, despondent, distressed, grieving, bereft. ■ OPPOSITES populous, joyful.

despair n. HOPELESSNESS, depression, dejection, despondency, pessimism, melancholy, gloom, misery, wretchedness, distress, anguish. ▶ v. LOSE HOPE, give

up hope, give up, lose heart, be discouraged, resign oneself.

desperate adj. **1** RECKLESS, rash, foolhardy, risky, hazardous, daring, wild, imprudent, incautious, injudicious, ill-conceived, precipitate. **2** URGENT, pressing, acute, critical, crucial, drastic, serious, grave, dire, extreme, great. **3** BAD, appalling, grave, intolerable, deplorable, lamentable.

despise v. DISDAIN, scorn, hate, detest, loathe, be contemptuous of, abhor, abominate, look down on, deride, spurn, shun, scoff at, jeer at, mock, revile, execrate, undervalue. ■ OPPOSITES admire.

despondent adj. DOWNCAST, miserable, sad, sorrowful, disheartened, discouraged, disconsolate, low-spirited, dispirited, downhearted, in despair, despairing, melancholy, gloomy, glum, morose, woebegone. ■ OPPOSITES cheerful, happy.

despotic adj. AUTOCRATIC, dictatorial, tyrannical, authoritarian, absolute, oppressive, totalitarian, domineering, imperious, arrogant, high-handed, arbitrary.

destination n. JOURNEY'S END, stop, terminus, port of call, goal.

destined adj. **1** BOUND FOR, en route for, heading for/towards, directed towards, scheduled for. **2** FATED, ordained, preordained, predestined, predetermined,

destitute adj. extremely poor. ■ **destitution** n.

destroy v. **1** cause something to cease to exist by badly damaging it. **2** kill an animal by humane means. ■ **destruction** n. **destructive** adj.

destroyer n. **1** a person or thing that destroys. **2** a small, fast warship.

desuetude /dess-wi-tyood/ n. disuse.

desultory /dess-uhl-tuh-ri/ adj. **1** lacking purpose or enthusiasm. **2** going from one subject to another in a half-hearted way. ■ **desultorily** adv.

detach v. **1** disconnect and remove. **2** send a group of soldiers on a separate mission. ■ **detachable** adj.

☑ Only one *t*: de**t**ach, not *-tatch*.

----

detached adj. **1** separate or disconnected. **2** not interested or involved.

detachment n. **1** objectivity. **2** a group of troops, ships, etc. sent on a separate mission.

detail n. **1** a small individual item or fact. **2** small items or facts as a group. **3** a small detachment of troops or police officers. ▸ v. **1** describe item by item. **2** order to undertake a task.

detain v. **1** keep from going somewhere. **2** keep in custody. ■ **detainment** n.

detainee n. a person kept in custody.

detect v. discover the presence of. ■ **detection** n. **detector** n.

detective n. a person whose job is to investigate crimes.

détente /day-**tahnt**/ n. the easing of hostility between countries.

detention n. **1** the detaining of someone. **2** the punishment of being kept in school after hours.

deter v. (**deterring**, **deterred**) discourage from action.

Thesaurus

doomed, certain, sure, bound.

destiny n. **1** FATE, lot, portion, due, future, doom. **2** CHANCE, fortune, predestination, luck, fate, karma, kismet.

destitute adj. PENNILESS, impoverished, poverty-stricken, poor, impecunious, penurious, indigent, insolvent, deprived, down-and-out, beggarly; *informal* on one's uppers, skint. ■ OPPOSITES rich, wealthy.

destroy v. **1** DEMOLISH, wreck, smash, annihilate, knock down, pull down, tear down, level, raze, shatter, dismantle, blow up, wipe out, bomb, torpedo, ruin, spoil, devastate, lay waste to, ravage, wreak havoc on, extinguish, vaporize, extirpate. **2** KILL, slaughter, put to sleep, exterminate, wipe out, massacre, liquidate, decimate. ■ OPPOSITES build, construct.

destruction n. **1** DEMOLITION, annihilation, devastation, levelling, razing, blowing up, wiping out, tearing down, ruination, desolation, ruin, havoc, termination, extinction. **2** KILLING, slaughter, massacre; *literary* slaying.

destructive adj. **1** RUINOUS, devastating, disastrous, catastrophic, calamitous, cataclysmic, fatal, deadly, dangerous, lethal, damaging, noxious, pernicious, injurious, harmful, detrimental, deleterious. **2** NEGATIVE, adverse, unfavourable, contrary, antagonistic, hostile, unfriendly, derogatory, disparaging, disapproving, undermining. ■ OPPOSITES constructive.

desultory adj. HALF-HEARTED, rambling,

aimless, irregular, fitful, haphazard, erratic, inconsistent. ■ OPPOSITES keen.

detach v. DISCONNECT, unfasten, remove, undo, take off, release, unhitch, separate, uncouple, loosen, free, sever, tear off, disengage, part. ■ OPPOSITES join, attach.

detached adj. DISPASSIONATE, impersonal, indifferent, aloof, unconcerned, reserved, remote, cool. ■ OPPOSITES passionate, involved.

detail n. **1** ITEM, point, particular, factor, nicety, fact, element, aspect, circumstance, intricacy, feature, respect, attribute, component, part, unit. **2** UNIT, detachment, task force, patrol.

detailed adj. FULL, comprehensive, exhaustive, thorough, all-inclusive, itemized, precise, exact, specific, meticulous, particularized, blow-by-blow. ■ OPPOSITES general.

detain v. **1** DELAY, hold up/back, keep, slow down/up, hinder, impede, check, retard, inhibit, stay. **2** PUT/KEEP IN CUSTODY, imprison, confine, lock up, jail, incarcerate, intern, restrain, hold, arrest, impound; *informal* collar, nick.

detect v. **1** FIND OUT, discover, turn up, uncover, bring to light, expose, unearth, reveal, unmask, unveil; *informal* track down, ferret out. **2** NOTICE, note, perceive, discern, make out, observe, spot, become aware of, recognize, distinguish, identify, catch, sense, see, smell.

detective n. INVESTIGATOR, police officer; *informal* private eye, sleuth, tec, dick; US

detergent n. a chemical substance used for cleaning.

deteriorate v. become gradually worse. ■ **deterioration** n.

determinant n. a determining factor.

determination n. **1** firmness of purpose. **2** the act of establishing something exactly.

determine v. **1** be the main factor in; control. **2** firmly decide. **3** establish by research or calculation.

determined adj. having firmness of purpose.

deterrent n. a thing that deters or is intended to deter. ■ **deterrence** n.

detest v. dislike intensely. ■ **detestable** adj. **detestation** n.

dethrone v. remove a monarch from power.

detonate v. explode or cause to explode. ■ **detonation** n. **detonator** n.

detour n. a long or roundabout route.

detoxify v. (**detoxifying, detoxified**) remove harmful substances from.

detract v. (**detract from**) cause to seem less valuable or impressive.

detractor n. a person who criticizes someone or something.

detriment n. harm or damage. ■ **detrimental** adj. **detrimentally** adv.

detritus /di-try-tuhss/ n. debris or waste material.

deuce n. the score of 40 all in a game in tennis.

deuterium n. a heavy form of hydrogen.

Deutschmark /doych-mark/ n. a former currency unit in Germany.

devalue v. reduce the value or worth of. ■ **devaluation** n.

devastate v. **1** destroy or ruin. **2** overwhelm with shock or grief. ■ **devastation** n.

devastating adj. **1** very destructive. **2** extremely distressing. **3** informal very impressive or attractive.

develop v. (**developing, developed**) **1** become or make larger, more mature, or more advanced. **2** start to exist, experience, or possess. **3** convert land to a new purpose. **4** treat a film with chemicals to make a visible image. ■ **developer** n. **development** n.

deviant adj. & n. (a person) departing

Thesaurus

informal gumshoe.

detention n. CUSTODY, confinement, imprisonment, incarceration, internment, detainment, arrest, quarantine.

deter v. PREVENT, put off, stop, discourage, talk out of, dissuade, check, restrain, caution, frighten, intimidate, daunt, scare off, warn against, prohibit, hinder, impede, obstruct. ■ OPPOSITES encourage.

deteriorate v. **1** GET WORSE, worsen, decline, degenerate, go downhill, sink, slip, lapse, fall, drop; *informal* go to the dogs, go to pot. **2** DISINTEGRATE, crumble, fall apart, fall to pieces, break up, decay, decompose. ■ OPPOSITES improve.

determination n. FIRMNESS, persistence, resoluteness, tenacity, perseverance, steadfastness, single-mindedness, resolve, drive, fortitude, dedication, backbone, stamina, mettle, conviction, doggedness, stubbornness, intransigence, obduracy, push, thrust, pertinacity; *informal* grit, guts.

determine v. **1** DECIDE, agree on, fix, settle, establish, judge, arbitrate, decree, ordain. **2** FIND OUT, discover, learn, establish, calculate, work out, check, ascertain, verify. **3** AFFECT, influence, act/work on, regulate, decide, condition, direct, control, rule, dictate,

govern, form, shape.

determined adj. FIRM, resolute, purposeful, single-minded, steadfast, tenacious, strong-willed, dedicated, persistent, persevering, dogged, unflinching, tough, assertive, mettlesome, plucky, unwavering, stubborn, obdurate, intransigent, indomitable, inflexible. ■ OPPOSITES irresolute, hesitant.

deterrent n. DISINCENTIVE, inhibition, restraint, discouragement, curb, check, impediment, hindrance, obstacle, block, obstruction, barrier, warning, threat. ■ OPPOSITES incentive.

detest v. LOATHE, hate, abhor, despise, abominate, execrate. ■ OPPOSITES love.

detestable adj. LOATHSOME, abhorrent, hateful, odious, despicable, contemptible, disgusting, repugnant, distasteful, abominable.

detract v. TAKE AWAY FROM, diminish, reduce, lessen, lower, devalue.

detrimental adj. HARMFUL, damaging, injurious, hurtful, destructive, pernicious, deleterious, inimical, prejudicial, unfavourable. ■ OPPOSITES benign.

devastate v. **1** DESTROY, ruin, lay waste to, demolish, wreck, flatten, obliterate, level, raze, annihilate, ravage, despoil, sack. **2** *see* DISMAY.

develop v. **1** GROW, evolve, mature, improve, expand, spread, enlarge, adfrom accepted standards of behaviour. ■ **deviance** n.

deviate v. depart from an established course or normal standards. ■ **deviation** n.

device n. **1** a thing made for a particular purpose. **2** a plan or scheme.

devil n. **1** (**the Devil**) (in Christian and Jewish belief) the most powerful spirit of evil. **2** an evil spirit. **3** a very cruel person. **4** a mischievously clever person. **5** informal a person of a specified type: *the poor devil*. □ **devil-may-care** cheerful and reckless. **devil's advocate** a person who expresses an unpopular opinion to provoke debate. ■ **devilish** adj.

devilled adj. cooked with hot spices.

devilment n. mischief.

devilry n. **1** wickedness. **2** mischief.

devious adj. **1** cunning and underhand. **2** (of a route) indirect. ■ **deviously** adv. **deviousness** n.

devise v. plan or invent.

devoid adj. (**devoid of**) completely lacking in.

devolution n. the transferring of power by central government to local or regional governments.

devolve v. **1** transfer power to a lower level. **2** (**devolve on/to**) (of responsibility) pass to a deputy or successor.

devote v. (**devote to**) give time or resources to.

devoted adj. very loving or loyal.

devotee n. **1** an enthusiast. **2** a follower of a particular religion or god.

devotion n. **1** great love or loyalty. **2** religious worship. **3** (**devotions**) prayers. ■ **devotional** adj.

devour v. **1** eat greedily. **2** (of a force) consume destructively. **3** read quickly and eagerly.

devout adj. **1** deeply religious. **2** earnestly sincere. ■ **devoutly** adv.

dew n. drops of condensed moisture forming on cool surfaces at night. ■ **dewy** adj.

dewlap n. a fold of loose skin hanging from an animal's throat.

dexterity n. skill in performing tasks. ■ **dexterous** (or **dextrous**) adj.

Thesaurus

vance, progress, flourish, prosper, make headway. **2** ELABORATE, unfold, work out, enlarge on, expand, broaden, add to, augment, amplify, dilate on, magnify, supplement, reinforce. **3** ACQUIRE, begin to have, contract, pick up, get. **4** BEGIN, start, come about, follow, happen, result, ensue, break out.

development n. **1** GROWTH, evolution, advance, improvement, expansion, spread, progress, maturing, furtherance, extension, headway. **2** EVENT, turn of events, occurrence, happening, incident, circumstance, situation, issue, outcome, upshot. **3** ESTATE, complex, building, structure, conglomeration.

deviate v. DIVERGE, branch off, turn aside, depart from, make a detour, digress, deflect, differ, vary, change, veer, swerve, wander, bend, drift, stray, tack, slew.

device n. **1** APPLIANCE, gadget, implement, tool, utensil, piece of equipment, apparatus, instrument, machine, contraption, contrivance, invention; informal gizmo. **2** SCHEME, ploy, plan, plot, stratagem, trick, deception, artifice, ruse, dodge, stunt, gambit, subterfuge, manoeuvre, expedient, fraud, imposture. **3** EMBLEM, symbol, insignia, crest, coat of arms, seal, badge, token, motif, design, figure, motto, slogan, legend.

devilish adj. DEMONIC, diabolical, fiend-

ish, satanic, infernal, hellish, demoniacal.

devious adj. **1** CUNNING, underhand, sly, crafty, wily, artful, scheming, designing, calculating, deceitful, dishonest, double-dealing, guileful, treacherous, furtive, secretive; informal slippery, crooked. **2** INDIRECT, roundabout, circuitous, rambling, winding, tortuous, wandering, erratic, digressive. ■ OPPOSITES honest, direct.

devise v. CREATE, invent, originate, concoct, work out, contrive, plan, form, formulate, plot, scheme, compose, frame, construct, think up, fabricate, hatch, put together, prepare.

devoted adj. COMMITTED, faithful, loyal, true, dedicated, staunch, devout, steadfast, constant, unswerving, zealous.

devotee n. FAN, enthusiast, admirer, follower, adherent, disciple, supporter, champion, advocate, fanatic, zealot; informal buff, freak.

devotion n. FAITHFULNESS, loyalty, steadfastness, commitment, staunchness, allegiance, dedication, devoutness, fervour, zeal. ■ OPPOSITES disloyalty, indifference.

devour v. EAT GREEDILY, consume, swallow, gorge oneself on, guzzle down, feast on; informal tuck into, pig out on.

devout adj. PIOUS, religious, godly, churchgoing, reverent, holy, righteous,

dextrose n. a form of glucose.

dhal (or **dal**) n. (in Indian cookery) cooked split pulses.

diabetes n. a disorder in which a lack of insulin results in a failure to absorb sugar and starch properly. ■ **diabetic** adj. & n.

diabolical adj. 1 (or **diabolic**) of or like the Devil. 2 informal very bad. ■ **diabolically** adv.

diachronic adj. concerned with the historical development of a subject.

diaconal adj. of a deacon or deacons.

diacritic n. a sign above or below a letter to show a difference in pronunciation.

diadem n. a jewelled crown.

diaeresis /dy-eer-i-seez/ (US **dieresis**) n. (pl. **diaereses**) a mark (¨) over a vowel to indicate that it is sounded separately.

diagnose v. make a diagnosis of.

diagnosis n. (pl. **diagnoses**) the identification of an illness or problem by examination of the symptoms. ■ **diagnostic** adj.

diagonal adj. 1 (of a line) joining opposite corners of a rectangle or square. 2 slanting. ▶ n. a diagonal line. ■ **diagonally** adv.

diagram n. a simplified drawing showing the appearance or structure of something. ■ **diagrammatic** adj.

dial n. 1 a disc marked to show the time or to indicate a measurement by means of a pointer. 2 a disc with numbered holes on a telephone, turned to make a call. 3 a disc turned to select a setting on a radio, cooker, etc. ▶ v. (**dialling**, **dialled**; US **dialing**, **dialed**) use the dial or buttons on a telephone to call a number.

dialect n. a local form of a language. ■ **dialectal** adj.

dialectic (or **dialectics**) n. a way of investigating the truth of opinions by discussion and logical argument. ■ **dialectical** adj.

dialogue (US **dialog**) n. 1 conversation as a feature of a book, play, etc. 2 a discussion.

dialysis n. (pl. **dialyses**) the purification of a person's blood by filtering it through a membrane.

diamanté /dy-uh-**mon**-tay/ adj. decorated with artificial jewels.

diameter n. 1 a straight line passing from side to side through the centre of a circle or sphere. 2 the length of this.

diametrical adj. 1 (of opposites) complete. 2 of a diameter. ■ **diametric** adj. **diametrically** adv.

diamond n. 1 a very hard, clear precious stone. 2 a figure with four sides of equal length forming two opposite acute angles and two opposite obtuse angles. 3 (**diamonds**) one of the four suits in a pack of cards. ◻ **diamond wedding** the 60th anniversary of a wedding.

diaper n. US a baby's nappy.

diaphanous /dy-af-fuh-nuhss/ adj. delicate and semi-transparent.

diaphragm /dy-uh-fram/ n. 1 a layer of muscle between the lungs and the stomach. 2 a thin contraceptive cap fitting over the cervix.

diarrhoea /dy-uh-ree-uh/ (US **diarrhea**) n. a condition involving frequent liquid bowel movements.

diary n. (pl. **diaries**) a book for keeping a daily record of events, or for noting appointments. ■ **diarist** n.

diatribe n. a violent verbal attack.

dice n. (pl. **dice**; sing. also **die**) a small cube with faces bearing from one to six spots, used in games of chance. ▶ v. 1 cut food into small cubes. 2 (**dice with**) take great risks with.

dicey adj. (**dicier**, **diciest**) informal difficult or risky.

dichotomy /dy-kot-uh-mi/ n. (pl. **di-**

d

Thesaurus

orthodox, saintly. ■ OPPOSITES impious.

dexterity n. DEFTNESS, adroitness, nimbleness, agility, skilfulness, adeptness, expertise, talent, craft, mastery, finesse.

diabolical adj. 1 DEVILISH, demonic, fiendish, satanic, infernal, hellish, demoniacal. 2 VERY BAD, horrible, dreadful, appalling, shocking, outrageous, atrocious.

diagnose v. IDENTIFY, detect, find, determine, recognize, distinguish, isolate, pinpoint.

diagonal adj. CROSSWAYS, crosswise, slanting, slanted, sloping, oblique, angled, cornerways, cornerwise.

diagram n. PLAN, picture, representation, blueprint, sketch, illustration, outline, draft, table, chart, figure.

dialect n. REGIONAL LANGUAGE, vernacular, patois, regionalism, localism, provincialism; informal lingo.

dialogue n. CONVERSATION, talk, chat, communication, debate, argument, exchange of views, discussion, conference, discourse, parley, colloquy, inter-

chotomies) a division or contrast between two things. ■ **dichotomous** adj.

dicky adj. informal not strong, healthy, or working reliably.

dictate v. **1** state or order with the force of authority. **2** say aloud words to be typed or written down. **3** control or determine. ▶ n. an order or command. ■ **dictation** n.

dictator n. a ruler with total power over a country. ■ **dictatorial** adj. **dictatorship** n.

diction n. a person's way of saying or pronouncing words.

dictionary n. (pl. **dictionaries**) a book that lists the words of a language and gives their meaning, or their equivalent in a different language.

dictum n. (pl. **dicta** or **dictums**) **1** a formal announcement. **2** a saying.

did past of **DO**.

didactic adj. intended to teach or give moral instruction.

diddle v. informal cheat or swindle.

didn't contr. did not.

die v. (**dying, died**) **1** stop living. **2** (**die out**) become extinct. **3** become less loud or strong. **4** (**be dying for/to do**) informal be very eager for or to do. ▶ n. **1** (pl. **dies**) a device for cutting or

moulding metal or for stamping a design on to coins etc. **2** sing. of **DICE**. □ **diehard** a person who obstinately resists change.

dieresis US = **DIAERESIS**.

diesel n. **1** an internal-combustion engine in which the heat of compressed air is used to ignite the fuel. **2** a form of petroleum used to fuel diesel engines.

diet n. **1** the food that a person or animal usually eats. **2** a restricted range of food, adopted to lose weight or for medical reasons. **3** a law-making assembly in certain countries. ▶ adj. with reduced fat or sugar content. ▶ v. (**dieting, dieted**) restrict oneself to a diet to lose weight. ■ **dieter** n. **dietary** adj.

dietetics n. the study of diet and its effects on health. ■ **dietetic** adj.

dietitian (or **dietician**) n. an expert on diet and nutrition.

differ v. **1** be unlike. **2** disagree.

difference n. **1** a way in which people or things are unlike each other. **2** the state of being unlike. **3** a disagreement or dispute. **4** the remainder left after one value is subtracted from another.

different adj. **1** not the same as another or each other. **2** separate. **3** new and unusual. ■ **differently** adv.

Thesaurus

locution, palaver; informal powwow, chinwag, rap session.

diary n. JOURNAL, chronicle, account, record, log, history, annals, calendar.

dictate v. **1** READ ALOUD, read out, speak, say, utter, recite. **2** ORDER, command, decree, ordain, direct, enjoin, give orders, order about, impose one's will, domineer, lay down the law; informal boss about, throw one's weight about.

dictator n. ABSOLUTE RULER, despot, autocrat, tyrant, oppressor.

dictatorial adj. TYRANNICAL, oppressive, despotic, overbearing, domineering, repressive, imperious, high-handed, authoritarian, totalitarian, peremptory, dogmatic, arbitrary, fascistic; informal bossy.

diction n. ENUNCIATION, articulation, elocution, pronunciation, intonation, inflection, delivery.

dictum n. UTTERANCE, pronouncement, direction, injunction, statement, dictate, command, order, decree, edict.

die v. **1** EXPIRE, perish, pass on/away, lose one's life, meet one's end, lay down one's life, breathe one's last, be no more, go to one's last resting place; informal give up the ghost, kick the bucket,

bite the dust, be pushing up daisies, croak, turn up one's toes, cash in one's chips, pop off, snuff it, pop one's clogs. **2** COME TO AN END, end, pass, disappear, vanish, fade, decline, ebb, dwindle, melt away, wane, wither, subside. **3** FAIL, break down, halt, stop, lose power. ■ OPPOSITES live.

diehard adj. INTRANSIGENT, inflexible, uncompromising, indomitable, unyielding, rigid, immovable, adamant, dyed-in-the-wool, conservative, reactionary.

differ v. **1** BE DIFFERENT, vary, contrast, diverge, be dissimilar, be distinguishable. **2** DISAGREE, be in dispute, dissent, be at variance, oppose, take issue, contradict, dispute, conflict, clash, quarrel, argue, wrangle, squabble, quibble, altercate. ■ OPPOSITES agree.

difference n. **1** DISSIMILARITY, contrast, distinction, variance, variation, divergence, deviation, contradiction, disparity, imbalance, incongruity, dissimilitude, differentiation, antithesis, nonconformity, contrariety. **2** DIFFERENCE OF OPINION, dispute, disagreement, argument, debate, misunderstanding, quarrel, altercation, wrangle, clash, contretemps, feud, vendetta; informal row, tiff,

differential adj. involving or showing a difference. ▶ n. **1** an agreed difference in wage rates. **2** a gear allowing a vehicle's wheels to revolve at different speeds in cornering.

differentiate v. **1** recognize as different. **2** cause to appear different. ■ **differentiation** n.

difficult adj. **1** needing much effort or skill to do, deal with, or understand. **2** hard to please. ■ **difficulty** n.

diffident adj. lacking self-confidence. ■ **diffidence** n. **diffidently** adv.

diffract v. cause a beam of light to be spread out as a result of passing through a narrow opening or across an edge. ■ **diffraction** n.

diffuse v. **1** spread over a wide area. **2** (of a gas or liquid) become mingled with a substance by movement. ▶ adj. **1** spread out over a large area; not concentrated. **2** not clearly or concisely expressed. ■ **diffusely** adv. **diffuser** n. **diffusion** n.

☑ Don't confuse **diffuse** with **defuse**, which means 'remove the fuse from an explosive device'.

dig v. (**digging**, **dug**) **1** break up and turn over or move earth. **2** remove or move by digging. **3** push or poke sharply. **4** search for. **5** (**dig out/up**) discover facts. ▶ n. **1** an act of digging. **2** an archaeological excavation. **3** a sharp poke. **4** informal a critical remark. **5** (**digs**) informal lodgings. ■ **digger** n.

digest v. **1** break down food in the body so that it can be easily absorbed. **2** reflect on and absorb information. ▶ n. a summary or collection of information. ■ **digestible** adj. **digestion** n.

digestive adj. of or aiding the digestion of food.

digit n. **1** any of the numerals from 0 to 9. **2** a finger, thumb, or toe.

digital adj. **1** of information represented as a series of binary digits, as in a computer. **2** (of a clock) showing the time by displayed digits. ■ **digitally** adv.

digitalis n. a heart stimulant prepared from foxglove leaves.

digitize (or **-ise**) v. convert pictures or sound into a digital form.

d

Thesaurus

set-to. **3** BALANCE, remainder, rest, residue, excess. ■ OPPOSITES similarity.

different adj. **1** DISSIMILAR, contrasting, diverse, disparate, divergent, incompatible, opposed, inconsistent, at variance, at odds, clashing, conflicting, discrepant, unlike. **2** CHANGED, altered, modified, transformed, metamorphosed. **3** VARIOUS, several, many, numerous, sundry, assorted, diverse. **4** UNUSUAL, uncommon, out of the ordinary, distinctive, rare, unique, novel, special, remarkable, singular, noteworthy, unconventional, atypical, strange, odd, bizarre. ■ OPPOSITES similar, ordinary.

difficult adj. **1** HARD, demanding, laborious, onerous, burdensome, tough, strenuous, arduous, exhausting, exacting, tiring, wearisome, back-breaking, painful, oppressive; informal no picnic. **2** COMPLEX, complicated, hard, problematic, intricate, involved, puzzling, baffling, perplexing, knotty, thorny, delicate, obscure, abstruse, enigmatic, abstract, recondite, profound, deep. **3** TROUBLESOME, demanding, tiresome, unmanageable, intractable, perverse, recalcitrant, obstreperous, refractory, fractious, uncooperative, unamenable. **4** INCONVENIENT, ill-timed, unfavourable. ■ OPPOSITES easy, simple.

difficulty n. **1** PROBLEM, complication,

snag, hitch, obstacle, hindrance, hurdle, pitfall, impediment, obstruction, barrier. **2** PROTEST, objection, complaint, gripe, demur, cavil. **3** PREDICAMENT, quandary, dilemma, plight, distress, embarrassment, trouble, straits; informal fix, jam, spot, scrape. **4** HARDSHIP, trial, tribulation, ordeal, exigency.

diffident adj. SHY, modest, bashful, sheepish, unconfident, timid, unassertive, fearful, timorous, shrinking, apprehensive, reserved, withdrawn, hesitant, tentative, reluctant, doubtful, unsure, insecure, unobtrusive, self-effacing, unassuming, humble, meek, distrustful, suspicious. ■ OPPOSITES assertive, bold.

diffuse adj. **1** SPREAD OUT, scattered, dispersed, diffused. **2** WORDY, verbose, long-winded, prolix, discursive, rambling, wandering, meandering, digressive, circumlocutory; informal waffly. ■ OPPOSITES concentrated, concise.

dig v. **1** CULTIVATE, turn over, work, spade, till, harrow, fork over. **2** EXCAVATE, dig out, burrow, mine, quarry, hollow out, scoop out, tunnel, gouge. **3** POKE, nudge, prod, jab, thrust, punch. □ **dig up** EXHUME, unearth, disinter.

digest v. **1** ABSORB, assimilate, break down, dissolve, process, macerate. **2** UNDERSTAND, take in, absorb, compre-

dignified adj. showing dignity.

dignify v. (**dignifying**, **dignified**) make impressive or worthy of respect.

dignitary n. (pl. **dignitaries**) a high-ranking or important person.

dignity n. (pl. **dignities**) **1** the state of being worthy of respect. **2** a calm or serious manner. **3** pride in oneself.

digress v. depart from the main subject temporarily. ■ **digression** n.

dike var. of DYKE.

diktat n. an unpopular decree.

dilapidated adj. in a state of disrepair or ruin. ■ **dilapidation** n.

....
☑ *dil-*, not *del-*: *dil*apidated.
....

dilate v. make or become wider. ■ **dilation** n.

dilatory /di-luh-tri/ adj. **1** slow to act. **2** causing delay.

dilemma n. a situation in which a diffi-cult choice has to be made.

dilettante /di-li-tan-tay/ n. (pl. **dilet-tanti** or **dilettantes**) a person who dabbles in a subject for enjoyment.

diligent adj. careful and conscientious. ■ **diligence** n. **diligently** adv.

dill n. a herb.

dilly-dally v. (**dilly-dallying**, **dilly-dallied**) informal dawdle or be indecisive.

dilute v. **1** make a liquid thinner or weaker by adding water etc. **2** reduce the forcefulness of. ▶ adj. (of a liquid) di-luted. ■ **dilution** n.

dim adj. (**dimmer**, **dimmest**) **1** not shin-ing brightly. **2** indistinct. **3** informal stu-pid. ▶ v. (**dimming**, **dimmed**) make or become less bright or distinct. ■ **dimly** adv. **dimness** n.

dime n. US a 10-cent coin.

dimension n. **1** a measurable extent, such as length, breadth, or height. **2** an aspect or feature. ■ **dimensional** adj.

diminish v. make or become less.

Thesaurus

hend, grasp, master, consider, think about, mull over, weigh up. ▶ n. SUM-MARY, abstract, precis, outline, review, compendium, abridgement, epitome.

dignified adj. FORMAL, grave, solemn, stately, noble, decorous, reserved, cere-monious, courtly, majestic, august, lofty, exalted, regal, lordly, imposing, grand, impressive.

dignitary n. LUMINARY, worthy, notable, VIP, big name, leading light, celebrity, star, lion, pillar of society; informal some-body, bigwig, big shot, big noise, celeb, top brass, lord/lady muck; US informal big wheel.

dignity n. STATELINESS, nobleness, nobil-ity, formality, solemnity, gravity, grav-itas, decorum, propriety, respectability, reserve, courtliness, ceremoniousness, majesty, augustness, loftiness, exalted-ness, regality, grandeur, lordliness, im-pressiveness.

digress v. STRAY FROM THE POINT, get off the subject, go off at a tangent, ramble, wander, deviate, turn aside, depart, drift, meander, maunder; informal lose the thread.

dilapidated adj. RUN-DOWN, ramshackle, broken-down, in ruins, ruined, tumble-down, falling to pieces, falling apart, in disrepair, shabby, battered, rickety, shaky, crumbling, decayed, decrepit, worn out, neglected, uncared for, gone to rack and ruin.

dilate v. ENLARGE, widen, expand. ■ OP-POSITES contract.

dilemma n. DIFFICULTY, problem, quan-dary, predicament, puzzle, plight, trouble, perplexity, confusion, embar-rassment; informal catch-22, a tight spot.
□ **in a dilemma** on the horns of a di-lemma, between the devil and the deep blue sea, between a rock and a hard place, in a cleft stick.

diligent adj. ASSIDUOUS, industrious, con-scientious, hard-working, painstaking, meticulous, thorough, careful, atten-tive, heedful, earnest, studious, perse-vering, persistent, tenacious, zealous, active, busy, untiring, tireless, indefat-igable, dogged, plodding, laborious. ■ OPPOSITES lazy.

dilute v. WATER DOWN, weaken, thin out, cut, adulterate, mix. ■ OPPOSITES con-centrate.

dim adj. **1** DULL, muted, faint, weak, fee-ble, pale, dingy, lustreless. **2** DARK, gloomy, badly lit, poorly lit, dingy, dis-mal. **3** VAGUE, ill-defined, indistinct, un-clear, shadowy, blurred, blurry, fuzzy, imperceptible, obscured, nebulous, bleary, obfuscated. **4** see STUPID. ■ OP-POSITES bright, clear. ▶ v. **1** DIP, turn down, lower. **2** GROW DARKER, darken, cloud over. ■ OPPOSITES brighten.

dimension n. **1** SIZE, extent, length, width, area, volume, capacity, propor-tions. **2** ASPECT, facet, side, feature, element.

diminish v. **1** LESSEN, grow less, de-crease, reduce, shrink, contract, abate, grow weaker, lower, curtail, cut, nar-

diminuendo adv. & adj. Music with a decrease in loudness.

diminution n. a reduction.

diminutive adj. very small. ▶ n. a shortened form of a name, used informally.

dimmer n. a device for varying the brightness of an electric light.

dimple n. a small depression, esp. in the cheeks when one smiles. ▶ v. form or show dimples.

din n. a prolonged loud and unpleasant noise. ▶ v. (**dinning, dinned**) (**din into**) teach someone something by constant repetition.

dinar /dee-nar/ n. the basic unit of money of Serbia, Montenegro, and some African countries.

dine v. eat dinner.

diner n. **1** a person who dines. **2** US a small roadside restaurant.

ding-dong n. **1** the sound of bells ringing. **2** informal a fierce argument or fight.

dinghy n. (pl. **dinghies**) **1** a small open sailing boat. **2** a small inflatable rubber boat.

dingle n. literary a wooded valley.

dingo n. (pl. **dingoes** or **dingos**) a wild Australian dog.

dingy /din-ji/ adj. (**dingier, dingiest**) gloomy and drab.

dinky adj. (**dinkier, dinkiest**) informal attractively small and neat.

dinner n. **1** the main meal of the day. **2** a formal evening meal. ▫ **dinner jacket** a man's jacket worn for formal evening occasions.

dinosaur n. an extinct prehistoric reptile, often of enormous size.

dint n. (**by dint of**) by means of.

diocese /dy-uh-siss/ n. a district for which a bishop is responsible. ■ **diocesan** adj.

diode n. a semiconductor device with two terminals, allowing the flow of current in one direction only.

dioptric adj. of the refraction of light.

dioxide n. an oxide with two atoms of oxygen to one of a metal or other element.

dip v. (**dipping, dipped**) **1** (**dip in/into**) put or lower briefly in or into. **2** move or slope downwards. **3** lower or lower briefly. ▶ n. **1** an act of dipping. **2** a thick sauce in which pieces of food are dipped before eating. **3** a brief swim. **4** a brief downward slope.

diphtheria n. a serious infectious disease causing inflammation of the throat.

diphthong n. a compound vowel sound (as in *coin*).

diploma n. a certificate awarded on completing a course of study.

diplomacy n. **1** the profession or skill of managing international relations. **2** skill and tact in dealing with people.

diplomat n. an official representing a country abroad.

diplomatic adj. **1** of diplomacy. **2** tactful. ■ **diplomatically** adv.

dipper n. a small diving bird.

dipsomania n. alcoholism. ■ **dipsomaniac** n.

diptych /dip-tik/ n. a painting on two hinged panels, forming an altarpiece.

dire adj. **1** very serious or urgent. **2** informal very bad.

direct adj. **1** going straight from one place to another. **2** with nothing or no one in between. **3** frank. **4** clear and ex-

Thesaurus

row, constrict, truncate. **2** SUBSIDE, wane, recede, dwindle, slacken, fade, decline, peter out. **3** DISPARAGE, denigrate, belittle, deprecate, devalue, detract from, cheapen, defame, vilify. ■ OPPOSITES increase, boost.

diminutive adj. SMALL, tiny, little, petite, minute, miniature, microscopic, undersized, dwarfish; *informal* teeny, weeny. ■ OPPOSITES enormous.

din n. NOISE, uproar, row, racket, commotion, hullabaloo, tumult, hubbub, clamour, outcry, shouting, yelling, pandemonium, bedlam, rumpus, brouhaha, babel.

dingy adj. DARK, dull, dim, gloomy, drab, dismal, dreary, cheerless, dusky, sombre, murky, smoggy, dirty, sooty, grimy, discoloured, faded, shabby, worn, seedy, run-down, tacky. ■ OPPOSITES bright.

dip v. **1** GO DOWN, descend, sink, subside, fall, drop, decline, sag, droop. **2** IMMERSE, plunge, submerge, duck, dunk, lower, sink, soak, drench, steep, bathe. ▶ n. **1** SWIM, bathe, plunge, dive, paddle. **2** HOLLOW, hole, basin, concavity, depression, declivity, slope, incline, slant.

diplomacy n. TACTFULNESS, tact, discretion, subtlety, sensitivity, delicacy, politeness, finesse, prudence, judiciousness, cleverness, artfulness, cunning, care, skill.

diplomatic adj. TACTFUL, subtle, discreet, careful, delicate, sensitive, thoughtful, considerate, prudent, judicious, polite, politic, clever, skilful, artful. ■ OPPOSITES tactless.

plicit. ▶adv. in a direct way or by a direct route. ▶v. **1** aim towards. **2** tell or show someone the way. **3** control the operations of. **4** supervise and control a film, play, etc. **5** give an order to. □ **direct current** electric current flowing in one direction only. **direct debit** an arrangement with one's bank for regular payments to be made to a third party. **direct object** the person or thing directly affected by the action of a transitive verb. **direct speech** speech reported by repeating the actual words of a speaker.

direction n. **1** a course along which someone or something moves. **2** a point to which a person faces. **3** control or management. **4** (**directions**) instructions. ■ **directional** adj.

directive n. an official instruction.

directly adv. **1** in a direct way. **2** exactly in a specified position. **3** immediately. ▶conj. as soon as.

director n. **1** a person in charge of an organization or activity. **2** a member of the board managing a company. **3** a person who directs a film, play, etc. ■ **directorial** adj.

directorate n. **1** the board of directors of a company. **2** a section of a government department in charge of a particular activity.

directory n. (pl. **directories**) **1** a book listing names, addresses, and telephone numbers. **2** a computer file listing other files.

dirge n. a mournful song or piece of music.

dirigible n. an airship.

dirk n. a short dagger.

dirndl n. a full, wide skirt.

dirt n. **1** a substance causing something not to be clean. **2** soil. **3** informal excrement. **4** informal scandalous or damaging information.

dirty adj. (**dirtier**, **dirtiest**) **1** covered or marked with dirt. **2** obscene. **3** dishonest; unfair. ▶v. (**dirtying**, **dirtied**) make dirty. ■ **dirtiness** n.

disability n. (pl. **disabilities**) **1** a physical or mental condition that limits a person's movements, senses, or activities. **2** a legal disadvantage.

disable v. **1** limit someone in their movements, senses, or activities. **2** put out of action. ■ **disablement** n.

Thesaurus

dire adj. TERRIBLE, dreadful, awful, appalling, frightful, horrible, atrocious, grim, cruel, disastrous, ruinous, wretched, miserable, woeful, calamitous, catastrophic.

direct adj. **1** STRAIGHT, uncircuitous, unswerving, undeviating. **2** NON-STOP, straight through, through, uninterrupted, unbroken. **3** FRANK, blunt, straightforward, straight to the point, straight, clear, plain, explicit, candid, open, honest, sincere, unambiguous, unequivocal, outspoken, plain-spoken, forthright, matter-of-fact. ▶v. **1** SHOW THE WAY, give directions, guide, steer, lead, conduct, usher, navigate, pilot. **2** BE IN CHARGE OF, lead, run, command, control, supervise, oversee, superintend, regulate, govern, conduct, handle, preside over, mastermind, orchestrate; informal call the shots. **3** AIM AT, address to, intend/mean for, destine for, point at, train on, fix on. **4** COMMAND, order, instruct, charge, bid, enjoin, adjure.

directive n. COMMAND, direction, order, instruction, charge, bidding, injunction, ruling, regulation, dictate, decree, edict, notice, ordinance, prescription, mandate, fiat.

director n. MANAGER, administrator, executive, head, chief, chairperson, leader, governor, president, superintendent, supervisor, overseer; informal boss, kingpin, gaffer.

dirge n. LAMENT, elegy, requiem, funeral song, threnody.

dirt n. **1** GRIME, dust, soot, muck, mud, filth, sludge, slime, ooze, waste, dross, pollution, smudge, stain, tarnish; informal crud, gunge. **2** EARTH, soil, clay, silt, loam. **3** see OBSCENITY.

dirty adj. **1** UNCLEAN, filthy, stained, grimy, soiled, grubby, messy, dusty, mucky, sooty, muddy, bedraggled, slimy, polluted, sullied, foul, smudged, tarnished, defiled, spotted; informal cruddy, yucky, grotty, gungy. **2** OBSCENE, indecent, vulgar, ribald, salacious, smutty, coarse, bawdy, suggestive, prurient, lewd, lascivious, licentious. **3** UNFAIR, unsporting, dishonourable, dishonest, unscrupulous, illegal, deceitful, double-dealing, treacherous; informal crooked. **4** MALEVOLENT, bitter, angry, annoyed, resentful, indignant, offended, smouldering. ▶v. SOIL, stain, muddy, begrime, blacken, mess up, spatter, smudge, smear, spot, splash, sully, pollute, foul, defile; literary besmirch. ■ OPPOSITES clean.

disability n. HANDICAP, infirmity, impairment, affliction, disorder, complaint,

disabled adj. having a physical or mental disability.

disabuse v. cause to realize that a belief is mistaken.

disadvantage n. an unfavourable circumstance or condition. ▶ v. **1** put in an unfavourable position. **2** (**disadvantaged**) in socially or economically deprived circumstances. ∎ **disadvantageous** adj.

disaffected adj. discontented and no longer loyal. ∎ **disaffection** n.

disagree v. **1** have a different opinion. **2** be inconsistent. **3** (**disagree with**) (of food etc.) make slightly unwell. ∎ **disagreement** n.

disagreeable adj. **1** unpleasant. **2** bad-tempered.

disallow v. declare to be invalid.

disappear v. cease to be visible or to exist. ∎ **disappearance** n.

disappoint v. fail to fulfil the hopes of. ∎ **disappointment** n.

disapprobation n. disapproval.

disapprove v. consider a person or thing to be wrong or bad. ∎ **disapproval** n.

disarm v. **1** take weapons away from. **2** (of a country or force) give up or reduce its armed forces or weapons. **3** win over a hostile person. ∎ **disarmament** n.

disarrange v. make untidy.

disarray n. disorder or confusion.

disassociate var. of DISSOCIATE.

disaster n. **1** a sudden event causing great damage or loss of life. **2** a sudden misfortune. ∎ **disastrous** adj. **disastrously** adv.

disavow v. deny any responsibility or

Thesaurus

ailment, illness, malady, disablement.

disable v. INCAPACITATE, impair, damage, injure, cripple, lame, handicap, debilitate, indispose, weaken, enfeeble, render infirm, immobilize, paralyse, hamstring, maim, prostrate, mutilate.

disadvantage n. **1** DRAWBACK, snag, weak point, downside, fly in the ointment, weakness, flaw, defect, fault, handicap, liability, trouble, hindrance, obstacle; informal minus. **2** DETRIMENT, prejudice, harm, damage, loss, injury, hurt. ∎ OPPOSITES advantage.

disaffected adj. ALIENATED, estranged, unfriendly, disunited, dissatisfied, disgruntled, discontented, disloyal, rebellious, mutinous, seditious, hostile, antagonistic; informal up in arms. ∎ OPPOSITES contented.

disagree v. **1** DIFFER, fail to agree, be in dispute, dissent, be at variance/odds, quarrel, argue, bicker, wrangle, squabble, dispute, debate, take issue; informal have words, fall out. **2** BE DIFFERENT, be dissimilar, vary, conflict, clash, contrast, diverge. ∎ OPPOSITES agree.

disagreeable adj. UNPLEASANT, objectionable, disgusting, horrible, nasty, dreadful, hateful, detestable, offensive, repulsive, obnoxious, odious, repellent, revolting, sickening. ∎ OPPOSITES pleasant.

disallow v. REJECT, say no to, refuse, dismiss, forbid, prohibit, veto, embargo, proscribe, rebuff, repel, repudiate, repulse, ban, bar, cancel, disclaim, disown, abjure, disavow.

disappear v. **1** VANISH, pass from sight, be lost to view, fade, recede, dematerialize, evaporate. **2** DIE OUT, come to an end, end, pass away, vanish, expire, perish, fade away, leave no trace, pass into oblivion. ∎ OPPOSITES appear.

disappoint v. LET DOWN, fail, dishearten, depress, dispirit, upset, sadden, dash someone's hopes, dismay, chagrin, disgruntle, disenchant, disillusion, dissatisfy, vex. ∎ OPPOSITES delight.

disappointed adj. SADDENED, let down, disheartened, downhearted, downcast, depressed, despondent, dispirited, disenchanted, disillusioned. ∎ OPPOSITES pleased.

disapproval n. DISAPPROBATION, displeasure, criticism, blame, censure, condemnation, dislike, disfavour, discontent, dissatisfaction, reproach, reproof, remonstration, deprecation, animadversion. ∎ OPPOSITES approval.

disapprove v. FIND UNACCEPTABLE, dislike, deplore, have a poor opinion of, be displeased with, frown on, criticize, look askance at, censure, condemn, denounce, object to, take exception to, reprove, remonstrate, disparage, deprecate; informal take a dim view of, look down one's nose at. ∎ OPPOSITES approve.

disarray n. DISORDER, confusion, untidiness, chaos, mess, muddle, clutter, jumble, mix-up, tangle, shambles, dishevelment; Sc. guddle. ∎ OPPOSITES tidiness.

disaster n. CATASTROPHE, calamity, cataclysm, tragedy, act of God, accident, mishap, misadventure, mischance, stroke of bad luck, heavy blow, shock, adversity, trouble, misfortune, ruin, ruination. ∎ OPPOSITES success.

support for. ■ **disavowal** n.

disband v. (with reference to a group) break up or cause to break up.

disbar v. (**disbarring, disbarred**) expel a barrister from the Bar.

disbelieve v. refuse or be unable to believe. ■ **disbelief** n.

disburse v. pay out money from a fund. ■ **disbursement** n.

disc (US **disk**) n. **1** a flat, thin, round object. **2** (**disk**) a device on which computer data is stored. **3** a layer of cartilage separating vertebrae in the spine. **4** dated a gramophone record. □ **disc jockey** a person who plays recorded pop music on the radio or at a club.

discard v. get rid of as useless or unwanted.

discern v. see or be aware of. ■ **discernible** adj.

discerning adj. having or showing good judgement. ■ **discernment** n.

discharge v. **1** dismiss or allow to leave. **2** send out a liquid, gas, etc. **3** fire a gun or missile. **4** fulfil a responsibility. ▶n. **1** the act of discharging. **2** a substance discharged.

disciple n. **1** one of the original followers of Jesus. **2** a follower of a teacher, leader, etc.

disciplinarian n. a person who enforces strict discipline.

disciplinary adj. of discipline.

discipline n. **1** the training of people to obey rules or a code of behaviour. **2** controlled behaviour resulting from this. **3** a branch of academic study. ▶v. **1** train to be obedient or self-controlled. **2** punish for an offence.

disclaim v. deny responsibility for or knowledge of.

disclaimer n. a statement disclaiming responsibility.

disclose v. reveal; make known. ■ **disclosure** n.

disco n. (pl. **discos**) a club or party at which people dance to pop music.

discolour (US **discolor**) v. make or become stained or otherwise changed in colour. ■ **discoloration** n.

discomfit v. (**discomfiting, discomfited**) make uneasy or embarrassed. ■ **discomfiture** n.

discomfort n. **1** slight pain. **2** slight

Thesaurus

disastrous adj. CATASTROPHIC, cataclysmic, calamitous, devastating, tragic, dire, terrible, shocking, appalling, dreadful, harmful, black, ruinous, unfortunate, unlucky, ill-fated, ill-starred, injurious, detrimental, hapless. ■ OPPOSITES successful.

disbelieve v. REJECT, discount, give no credence to, be incredulous, question, suspect, challenge, scoff at, mistrust, distrust. ■ OPPOSITES believe.

discard v. THROW OUT/AWAY, dispose of, get rid of, jettison, toss out, dispense with, scrap, cast aside, reject, repudiate, abandon, relinquish, forsake, shed; informal have done with, dump, ditch. ■ OPPOSITES keep.

discern v. SEE, notice, observe, perceive, make out, distinguish, detect, recognize, determine.

discernible adj. VISIBLE, noticeable, observable, perceptible, perceivable, detectable, recognizable, apparent, clear, obvious, manifest, conspicuous, patent.

discerning adj. DISCRIMINATING, astute, shrewd, ingenious, clever, perceptive, penetrating, perspicacious, percipient, judicious, sensitive, knowing.

discharge v. **1** EMIT, exude, release, give off, eject, send out, leak, dispense, void, gush, excrete, ooze, belch, secrete,

spew, spit out. **2** DISMISS, expel, get rid of, oust, cashier; informal fire, sack, axe, send packing, give someone the boot, boot out. **3** FIRE, shoot, let off, set off, detonate. **4** SET FREE, free, release, liberate, acquit, clear, absolve, exonerate, pardon, emancipate, exculpate. **5** CARRY OUT, perform, do, accomplish, achieve, fulfil, execute.

disciple n. APOSTLE, follower, supporter, adherent, devotee, advocate, student, pupil, believer, proponent, partisan, votary.

disciplinarian n. MARTINET, authoritarian, hard taskmaster, tyrant, despot, stickler for order, autocrat, dictator, hardliner; informal slave-driver.

discipline n. **1** CONTROL, self-control, self-restraint, strictness, restraint, orderliness, regulation, direction, restriction, limitation, check, curb. **2** PUNISHMENT, correction, chastisement, penalty, reprimand, rebuke, reproof. **3** FIELD OF STUDY, subject, area, course, speciality, specialty. ▶v. **1** CONTROL, restrain, regulate, restrict, govern, limit, check, curb. **2** PUNISH, chastise, correct, penalize, reprimand, rebuke, reprove, castigate.

disclaim v. DENY, renounce, repudiate, reject, refuse, decline, disown, abandon, abjure; informal wash one's hands of.

disclose v. REVEAL, divulge, tell, impart,

anxiety or embarrassment.
discommode v. inconvenience.
disconcert v. unsettle; upset.
disconnect v. **1** break the connection of or between. **2** detach an electrical device from a power supply. ■ **disconnection** n.
disconsolate adj. very unhappy.
discontent n. dissatisfaction. ■ **discontented** adj. **discontentment** n.
discontinue v. stop doing, providing, or making. ■ **discontinuation** n.
discontinuous adj. having intervals or gaps. ■ **discontinuity** n.
discord n. **1** lack of agreement or harmony. **2** harsh and unpleasant noise. ■ **discordant** adj.
discotheque n. a disco.
discount n. a deduction from the usual price. ▶v. **1** reduce the price of. **2** disregard because unlikely.
discourage v. **1** dishearten. **2** prevent by persuasion or showing disapproval. ■ **discouragement** n.
discourse n. **1** communication or debate. **2** a formal discussion of a topic. ▶v. speak or write authoritatively.
discourteous adj. rude and inconsiderate. ■ **discourteously** adv. **discourtesy** n.
discover v. **1** find. **2** gain knowledge or become aware of. **3** be the first to find or observe. ■ **discovery** n.
discredit v. (**discrediting**, **discredited**) **1** harm the good reputation of. **2** cause to seem false or unreliable. ▶n. loss or lack of reputation.
discreditable adj. bringing discredit;

Thesaurus

communicate, broadcast, unveil, leak, let slip, blurt out.
discolour v. STAIN, soil, mark, streak, spot, tarnish, tinge, fade, bleach.
discomfort n. **1** PAIN, ache, soreness, irritation, pang, throb, smart. **2** HARDSHIP, unpleasantness, trouble, distress.
disconcert v. UNSETTLE, shake, disturb, take aback, perturb, ruffle, upset, agitate, worry, discomfit, discompose, confound, throw off balance, distract, confuse, nonplus; *informal* throw, put someone off their stroke, faze, rattle.
disconnect v. UNDO, detach, disengage, uncouple, unfasten, unhook, unhitch, unplug, cut off, break off, sever, part, turn off, switch off. ■ OPPOSITES connect.
disconnected adj. DISJOINTED, confused, garbled, jumbled, mixed up, incoherent, unintelligible, rambling, disordered, wandering.
discontented adj. DISSATISFIED, displeased, disgruntled, unhappy, miserable, disaffected; *informal* fed up, browned off, hacked off, cheesed off.
discord n. **1** DISAGREEMENT, dispute, argument, conflict, friction, strife, opposition, hostility, incompatibility, disunity. *See also* QUARREL. **2** DISHARMONY, dissonance, cacophony. ■ OPPOSITES harmony.
discordant adj. **1** CONFLICTING, differing, contrary, opposed, opposing, opposite, contradictory, contentious, hostile, divergent, incompatible, incongruous. **2** DISSONANT, atonal, tuneless, cacophonous, inharmonious, jangling, grating, jarring, harsh, strident, shrill. ■ OPPOSITES harmonious.
discount n. REDUCTION, price cut, rebate, concession; *informal* mark-down. ▶v. DISREGARD, ignore, dismiss, overlook, pass over, pay no attention to, take no notice of, gloss over, brush off.
discourage v. **1** DISHEARTEN, dispirit, depress, demoralize, deject, disappoint, disenchant, dismay, cast down, frighten, put off, scare, daunt, intimidate, cow, unnerve, unman; *informal* pour cold water on. **2** DISSUADE, put off, deter, talk out of, advise against, urge against, caution against, restrain, inhibit, divert from. **3** OPPOSE, disapprove of, repress, deprecate; *informal* put a damper on. ■ OPPOSITES encourage.
discouragement n. **1** OPPOSITION, disapproval, repression, deprecation. **2** DETERRENT, disincentive, impediment, hindrance, obstacle, barrier, curb, damper, check, restraint, constraint. ■ OPPOSITES encouragement.
discourse n. **1** ADDRESS, speech, lecture, oration, sermon, homily, essay, treatise, dissertation, paper, study, disquisition. **2** *see* CONVERSATION. ▶v. *see* SPEAK, TALK.
discover v. **1** FIND, come across/upon, locate, stumble upon, chance upon, light upon, bring to light, unearth, uncover, turn up; *informal* dig up. **2** FIND OUT, come to know, learn, realize, detect, ascertain, determine, recognize, see, spot, notice, perceive; *informal* get wise to, twig. **3** INVENT, devise, originate, pioneer, conceive of, contrive.
discoverer n. **1** INVENTOR, originator, pioneer, deviser, designer, initiator. **2** FOUNDER, explorer, pioneer.
discovery n. **1** DETECTION, recognition,

shameful.

discreet adj. careful not to attract attention. ■ **discreetly** adv.

....

☑ Don't confuse **discreet** with **discrete**.

....

discrepancy n. (pl. **discrepancies**) a difference between things expected to be the same.

discrete adj. separate and distinct.

discretion n. **1** the quality of being discreet. **2** freedom to decide.

discretionary adj. done or used according to one's judgement.

discriminate v. **1** recognize a difference. **2** treat differently and unfairly on grounds of race, sex, religion, etc. ■ **discrimination** n. **discriminatory** adj.

discriminating adj. having good taste or judgement.

discursive adj. wandering from subject to subject.

discus n. (pl. **discuses**) a heavy disc thrown in athletic contests.

discuss v. **1** talk about so as to reach a decision. **2** talk or write about a topic

in detail. ■ **discussion** n.

disdain n. a feeling of scornful superiority. ▶v. treat with disdain. ■ **disdainful** adj. **disdainfully** adv.

disease n. an illness. ■ **diseased** adj.

disembark v. leave a ship, aircraft, or train. ■ **disembarkation** n.

disembodied adj. (of a sound) coming from a person who cannot be seen.

disembowel v. (**disembowelling**, **disembowelled**; US **disemboweling**, **disemboweled**) cut out the internal organs of.

disenchant v. disillusion. ■ **disenchantment** n.

disenfranchise v. deprive of the right to vote.

disengage v. release or detach. ■ **disengagement** n.

disentangle v. free from being tangled; separate.

disestablish v. deprive a national Church of its official status.

disfavour (US **disfavor**) n. disapproval or dislike.

disfigure v. spoil the appearance of. ■ **disfigurement** n.

disgorge v. eject or cause to pour out.

Thesaurus

....

disclosure, finding, determination, revelation. **2** INNOVATION, invention, breakthrough, finding, find.

discredit v. **1** ATTACK, denigrate, disparage, defame, slur, slander, libel, detract from, cast aspersions on, vilify, bring into disrepute, deprecate, decry, dishonour, devalue, degrade, belittle, disgrace, censure. **2** DISPROVE, invalidate, refute, dispute, challenge, reject, deny.

discreet adj. CAREFUL, circumspect, cautious, wary, guarded, sensitive, prudent, judicious, chary, tactful, reserved, diplomatic, muted, understated, delicate, considerate, politic, wise, sensible, sagacious. ■ OPPOSITES indiscreet, tactless.

discrepancy n. INCONSISTENCY, disparity, deviation, variance, variation, divergence, incongruity, difference, disagreement, dissimilarity, conflict, discordance, gap, lacuna. ■ OPPOSITES similarity.

discretionary adj. OPTIONAL, voluntary, open, open to choice, elective, nonmandatory, unrestricted, volitional. ■ OPPOSITES compulsory.

discriminate v. **1** DISTINGUISH, differentiate, tell the difference, tell apart, separate, discern. **2** BE BIASED AGAINST, show prejudice against/towards, treat

unfairly, treat differently, favour.

discriminating adj. see PERCEPTIVE.

discrimination n. **1** DISCERNMENT, good taste, taste, perception, penetration, perspicacity, shrewdness, astuteness, acumen, judgement, refinement, sensitivity, insight, subtlety, cultivation, artistry. **2** PREJUDICE, bias, intolerance, bigotry, narrow-mindedness, favouritism, chauvinism, racism, sexism, unfairness.

discuss v. TALK OVER, talk/chat about, debate, argue about/over, exchange views about, converse about, deliberate, consider, go into, examine, review, analyse, weigh up, consult about, ventilate; *informal* kick about, thrash out.

discussion n. CONVERSATION, talk, dialogue, chat, argument, dispute, conference, debate, discourse, exchange of views, seminar, consultation, symposium, deliberation, review, analysis; *informal* confab. See also TALK.

disdainful adj. SCORNFUL, contemptuous, derisive, sneering, disparaging, arrogant, proud, supercilious, haughty, superior, lordly, condescending, pompous, snobbish, aloof, indifferent. ■ OPPOSITES respectful.

disease n. see ILLNESS.

diseased adj. UNHEALTHY, unwell, sick,

disgrace n. **1** the loss of the respect of others. **2** a shamefully bad person or thing. ▶ v. bring disgrace on. ■ **disgraceful** adj. **disgracefully** adv.

disgruntled adj. angry or dissatisfied. ■ **disgruntlement** n.

disguise v. **1** conceal the identity of. **2** hide a feeling. ▶ n. **1** a means of concealing one's identity. **2** the state of being disguised.

disgust n. revulsion or strong disapproval. ▶ v. cause disgust in.

dish n. **1** a shallow container for cooking or serving food. **2** a particular kind of prepared food. **3** a shallow, concave object. ▶ v. **1** (**dish out/up**) put food on to plates before a meal. **2** (**dish out**) distribute casually. □ **dishwasher** a machine for washing dishes automatically.

dishabille var. of DÉSHABILLÉ.

disharmony n. lack of harmony.

dishearten v. cause to lose hope or confidence.

dishevelled (US **disheveled**) adj. ruffled and untidy. ■ **dishevelment** n.

dishonest adj. not honest. ■ **dishonestly** adv. **dishonesty** n.

dishonour (US **dishonor**) n. a state of shame or disgrace. ▶ v. **1** bring dishonour to. **2** fail to keep an agreement.

dishonourable (US **dishonorable**) adj. bringing shame or disgrace. ■ **dishonourably** adv.

dishy adj. (**dishier**, **dishiest**) informal sexually attractive.

disillusion n. the disappointing loss of a belief or ideal. ▶ v. cause disillusion in. ■ **disillusionment** n.

Thesaurus

ill, sickly, infected, abnormal, blighted, unsound, cankerous.

disembark v. LAND, arrive, get off, step off, alight, go ashore, deplane, detrain. ■ OPPOSITES embark.

disfigure v. MUTILATE, deface, deform, blemish, scar, spoil, mar, damage, injure, maim, vandalize, ruin, make ugly, uglify.

disgrace n. **1** SHAME, humiliation, dishonour, scandal, ignominy, degradation, discredit, infamy, loss of face, debasement. **2** SCANDAL, black mark, stain, blemish, stigma, blot, smear. ■ OPPOSITES honour.

disgraceful adj. SCANDALOUS, outrageous, shocking, shameful, dishonourable, disreputable, contemptible, despicable, ignominious, reprehensible, improper, unseemly. ■ OPPOSITES admirable.

disgruntled adj. DISSATISFIED, displeased, unhappy, discontented, annoyed, exasperated, irritated, vexed, grumpy, testy, petulant; informal fed up, cheesed off.

disguise v. CAMOUFLAGE, costume, pretence, mask, cover, cloak; informal get-up, smokescreen. ▶ v. **1** DRESS UP, camouflage, cover up, conceal, hide, mask, veil, cloak, shroud. **2** COVER UP, falsify, misrepresent, fake, feign, dissemble, dissimulate, varnish.

disgust n. REVULSION, repugnance, repulsion, aversion, abhorrence, loathing, detestation, distaste, nausea. ▶ v. SICKEN, nauseate, revolt, repel, put off, offend, outrage, shock, appal, scandalize, displease, dissatisfy, annoy, anger; informal turn someone's stomach.

dish n. **1** PLATE, platter, bowl, basin, container, receptacle, salver. **2** FOOD, recipe, fare, concoction, item on the menu. □ **dish up** SERVE, serve up, spoon, ladle, scoop.

dishearten v. DISCOURAGE, dispirit, depress, crush, sadden, disappoint, deter, weigh down; informal put a damper on. ■ OPPOSITES encourage.

dishevelled adj. UNTIDY, rumpled, messy, scruffy, bedraggled, disordered, disarranged, tousled, unkempt, slovenly, uncombed, slatternly, blowsy, frowzy. ■ OPPOSITES tidy, neat.

dishonest adj. UNTRUTHFUL, deceitful, lying, underhand, cheating, fraudulent, false, misleading, dishonourable, unscrupulous, unprincipled, corrupt, deceptive, crafty, cunning, designing, mendacious, double-dealing, two-faced, treacherous, perfidious, unfair, unjust, unethical, disreputable, rascally, knavish, roguish; informal crooked, shady, bent, slippery. ■ OPPOSITES honest.

dishonour n. DISGRACE, shame, humiliation, discredit, blot, blemish, stigma, scandal, infamy, ignominy, disrepute, disfavour, abasement, odium, opprobrium, obloquy. ▶ v. DISGRACE, bring shame to, shame, discredit, degrade, humiliate, sully, stain, stigmatize, insult, abuse, affront, slight, offend.

dishonourable adj. **1** UNPRINCIPLED, unscrupulous, untrustworthy, corrupt, treacherous, perfidious, traitorous, disreputable, discreditable; informal shady; old use blackguardly. **2** DISGRACEFUL, shameful, ignoble, shameless, ignominious, contemptible, blameworthy, despicable, reprehensible, base. ■ OPPOSITES honourable.

disincentive n. a factor discouraging a particular action.

disinclination n. unwillingness.

disinclined adj. reluctant; unwilling.

disinfect v. make free from infection with a disinfectant. ■ **disinfection** n.

disinfectant n. a chemical liquid that destroys bacteria.

disinformation n. information intended to mislead.

disingenuous adj. not sincere.

disinherit v. deprive of an inheritance.

disintegrate v. break up into small parts. ■ **disintegration** n.

disinter v. (**disinterring**, **disinterred**) dig up something buried.

disinterest n. 1 impartiality. 2 lack of interest.

disinterested adj. not influenced by personal feelings; impartial.

··
☑ Don't confuse **disinterested** with **uninterested**, which means 'not interested'.
··

disjointed adj. lacking logical or coherent connection.

disjunction n. a difference between things expected to be similar.

disk US & Computing = **DISC**. □ **disk drive** a device allowing a computer to read from and write to a computer disk.

diskette n. a floppy disk.

dislike v. feel distaste for or hostility towards. ▶ n. 1 distaste or hostility. 2 a thing that is disliked.

dislocate v. 1 displace a bone from its proper position. 2 disrupt. ■ **dislocation** n.

dislodge v. remove from a fixed position.

disloyal adj. not loyal or faithful. ■ **disloyally** adv. **disloyalty** n.

dismal adj. 1 gloomy or depressing. 2 informal very bad. ■ **dismally** adv.

dismantle v. take to pieces.

dismay n. a feeling of discouragement and distress. ▶ v. cause to feel dismay.

Thesaurus

··

disillusion v. DISABUSE, disenchant, shatter someone's illusions, open someone's eyes, set straight, enlighten, disappoint; *informal* make sadder and wiser.

disinclined adj. RELUCTANT, unenthusiastic, unwilling, hesitant, loath, averse, resistant, antipathetic, opposed, recalcitrant, not in the mood.

disinfect v. STERILIZE, sanitize, cleanse, clean, purify, fumigate, decontaminate.

disingenuous adj. INSINCERE, deceitful, feigned, underhand, duplicitous, two-faced, false, untruthful, artful, cunning, wily, scheming, calculating.

disintegrate v. FALL APART, fall to pieces, break up, break apart, shatter, crumble, come apart, crack up, smash, splinter, decompose, decay, rot, dissolve, degenerate, erode, moulder.

disinterested adj. UNBIASED, unprejudiced, impartial, detached, objective, dispassionate, impersonal, open-minded, neutral, fair, just, even-handed. ■ OPPOSITES biased, partial.

disjointed adj. INCOHERENT, rambling, unconnected, disconnected, wandering, disorganized, confused, muddled, jumbled, disordered, aimless, directionless, uncoordinated, fitful, spasmodic, dislocated, discontinuous. ■ OPPOSITES coherent.

dislike v. HAVE NO LIKING FOR, have an aversion to, regard with distaste, feel hostility towards, be unable to stomach, have no taste for, object to, hate, detest, loathe, abominate, abhor, despise, scorn, execrate, shun, have a grudge against. ▶ n. AVERSION, distaste, disapproval, animosity, hostility, antipathy, hate, antagonism, detestation, loathing, disgust, repugnance, enmity, abhorrence, animus.

dislocate v. DISPLACE, put out, disjoint, disengage, disconnect, put out of joint.

disloyal adj. UNFAITHFUL, faithless, false, untrue, inconstant, untrustworthy, treacherous, traitorous, perfidious, disaffected, seditious, subversive, unpatriotic, renegade, apostate, dissident, double-dealing, two-faced, deceitful. ■ OPPOSITES loyal.

disloyalty n. UNFAITHFULNESS, faithlessness, infidelity, breaking of faith, breach of trust, falseness, falsity, inconstancy, untrustworthiness, treachery, treason, perfidiousness, disaffection, sedition, subversion, apostasy, dissidence, double-dealing.

dismal adj. GLOOMY, sad, bleak, miserable, wretched, drab, dreary, dingy, cheerless, desolate, depressing, grim, funereal, uninviting. ■ OPPOSITES cheerful, bright.

dismantle v. TAKE APART, take to pieces, disassemble, pull apart, strip down, tear down, demolish. ■ OPPOSITES assemble.

dismay n. DISAPPOINTMENT, distress, con-

dismember v. tear or cut the limbs from. ■ **dismemberment** n.

dismiss v. **1** order or allow to leave. **2** order an employee to leave a job. **3** treat as unworthy of consideration. ■ **dismissal** n.

dismissive adj. treating something as unworthy of consideration. ■ **dismissively** adv.

dismount v. get off or down from a horse or bicycle.

disobedient adj. not obedient. ■ **disobedience** n.

disobey v. fail or refuse to obey.

disorder n. **1** a lack of order. **2** the disruption of peaceful and law-abiding behaviour. **3** an illness. ■ **disordered** adj. **disorderly** adj.

disorganized (or **-ised**) adj. not properly planned or arranged. ■ **disorganization** n.

disorientate v. cause someone to lose their bearings. ■ **disorientation** n.

disown v. refuse to have anything further to do with.

disparage v. speak critically of. ■ **disparagement** n.

disparate adj. very different in kind. ■ **disparity** n.

dispassionate adj. unemotional and impartial. ■ **dispassionately** adv.

dispatch (or **despatch**) v. **1** send off to a destination or for a purpose. **2** deal with a task quickly. **3** kill. ▶ n. **1** the act of dispatching. **2** an official report on military affairs. **3** a report by a journalist abroad. **4** promptness.

dispel v. (**dispelling**, **dispelled**) make a doubt or feeling disappear.

dispensable adj. not essential.

dispensary n. (pl. **dispensaries**) a room where medicines are dispensed.

Thesaurus

sternation, discouragement, anxiety, apprehension, gloom, horror, agitation. ■ OPPOSITES pleasure, relief. ▶ v. **1** DISCOURAGE, dishearten, dispirit, put off, depress, disappoint, daunt, abash, cast down, devastate. **2** SHOCK, horrify, take aback, startle, alarm, frighten, scare, surprise, disturb, perturb, upset, unsettle, unnerve. ■ OPPOSITES encourage.

dismiss v. **1** BANISH, put away, lay/set aside, reject, drop, put out of one's mind, brush aside, think no more of, spurn, repudiate; informal pooh-pooh. **2** EXPEL, discharge, give notice to, lay off, make redundant, remove, oust, cashier; informal sack, fire, boot out, give the boot/push to, give someone their marching orders, send packing. **3** DISPERSE, send away, disband, let go, release, free, discharge.

disobedient adj. INSUBORDINATE, rebellious, defiant, unruly, wayward, undisciplined, mutinous, recalcitrant, intractable, wilful, refractory, fractious, obdurate, stubborn, obstreperous, disorderly, delinquent, uncontrollable, disruptive, wild, non-compliant, perverse, naughty, mischievous, contrary; formal contumacious. ■ OPPOSITES obedient.

disobey v. DEFY, not comply with, disregard, ignore, oppose, contravene, flout, infringe, resist, overstep, rebel against, transgress, violate; informal fly in the face of.

disobliging adj. UNHELPFUL, uncooperative, unaccommodating, unfriendly, unsympathetic, discourteous, uncivil. ■ OPPOSITES helpful.

disorder n. **1** MESS, untidiness, chaos, muddle, clutter, jumble, confusion, disorderliness, disarray, disorganization, shambles. **2** DISTURBANCE, disruption, riot, tumult, fracas, rumpus, unrest. **3** DISEASE, complaint, affliction, illness, sickness, malady. ■ OPPOSITES tidiness, peace.

disorderly adj. **1** see UNTIDY. **2** see UNDISCIPLINED.

disorganized adj. CONFUSED, disorderly, untidy, chaotic, jumbled, muddled, in disarray, unsystematic, haphazard, random, unorganized, scatterbrained, unmethodical, careless, sloppy, slipshod, slapdash, messy, hit-or-miss, higgledy-piggledy, aimless, unplanned, unstructured; informal shambolic. ■ OPPOSITES organized, systematic.

disown v. RENOUNCE, repudiate, reject, abandon, forsake, disclaim, disavow, deny, disallow, abnegate, disinherit; informal turn one's back on.

disparage v. BELITTLE, slight, deprecate, denigrate, depreciate, dismiss, ridicule, malign, scorn, insult, impugn, vilify, traduce; informal put down, bad-mouth, rubbish. ■ OPPOSITES praise.

disparity n. DISCREPANCY, difference, dissimilarity, contrast, gap, inequality, unevenness, inconsistency, imbalance, incongruity.

dispassionate adj. CALM, level-headed, cool, unflappable, unruffled, collected, nonchalant, sober, equable, serene, unperturbed, detached, objective, disinterested, indifferent. ■ OPPOSITES emotional.

dispensation n. **1** exemption from a rule or requirement. **2** a religious or political system.

dispense v. **1** distribute to a number of people. **2** prepare and supply medicine. **3** (**dispense with**) get rid of or manage without. ∎ **dispenser** n.

disperse v. go or send in different directions or over a wide area. ∎ **dispersal** n. **dispersion** n.

dispirited adj. disheartened or depressed. ∎ **dispiriting** adj.

displace v. **1** move from the proper or usual position. **2** take over the role of. ∎ **displacement** n.

display v. **1** put on show. **2** show. ▶n. **1** a public performance or show. **2** a thing or things displayed.

displease v. annoy or upset.

displeasure n. annoyance.

disport v. (**disport oneself**) enjoy oneself freely.

disposable adj. **1** intended to be thrown away after use. **2** (of income) available for use as required.

disposal n. the act of disposing. □ **at one's disposal** available for one's use.

dispose v. **1** (**dispose of**) get rid of.

2 arrange something. **3** make ready or willing to do something. **4** (**disposed**) having a specified attitude.

disposition n. **1** a person's character. **2** a tendency. **3** the arrangement of something.

dispossess v. deprive of a possession. ∎ **dispossession** n.

disproportionate adj. too large or too small in comparison with something else. ∎ **disproportionately** adv.

disprove v. prove to be false.

disputable adj. open to question.

disputation n. debate or argument.

disputatious adj. fond of arguing.

dispute v. **1** argue about. **2** question the truth of. **3** compete for. ▶n. an argument or disagreement.

disqualify v. (**disqualifying**, **disqualified**) **1** ban from an activity because of a breach of the law or rules. **2** make unsuitable for an activity. ∎ **disqualification** n.

disquiet n. anxiety. ▶v. make anxious.

disquisition n. a long or complex discussion of a subject.

disregard v. pay no attention to. ▶n. lack of attention.

Thesaurus

dispatch v. **1** SEND, post, mail, forward, transmit, consign, remit, convey. **2** see KILL. ▶n. LETTER, message, bulletin, communication, report, account, missive, document.

dispense v. **1** DISTRIBUTE, hand out, share out, measure out, divide out, dole out, allocate, assign, apportion, allot, supply, disburse, bestow, mete out, confer. **2** MAKE UP, prepare, mix, supply. □ **dispense with** OMIT, do without, waive, forgo, give up, relinquish, renounce.

disperse v. **1** GO SEPARATE WAYS, break up, disband, separate, scatter, dissolve, leave, vanish, melt away. **2** DRIVE AWAY, break up, scatter, dissipate, dispel, banish. ∎ OPPOSITES gather.

displace v. **1** REMOVE, dismiss, discharge, depose, dislodge, eject, expel, force out; informal sack, fire. **2** REPLACE, take the place of, take over from, succeed, oust, supersede, supplant.

display v. **1** PUT ON SHOW/VIEW, show, exhibit, present, unveil, set forth, demonstrate, advertise, publicize. **2** MANIFEST, show, evince, betray, show evidence of, reveal, disclose. ∎ OPPOSITES conceal, hide. ▶n. **1** EXHIBITION, show, exhibit, presentation, demonstration, array. **2** SPECTACLE, show, parade, pageant.

displease v. ANNOY, irritate, anger, put

out, dissatisfy, irk, vex, offend, pique, gall, nettle, incense, exasperate, disgust, perturb; informal aggravate.

dispose v. **1** ARRANGE, order, position, place, range, line up, array, marshal, organize, group, rank, regulate. **2** INCLINE, make willing, predispose, make, prompt, lead, induce, motivate. □ **dispose of** see DISCARD.

disposed adj. INCLINED, willing, predisposed, minded, of a mind to, in the mood to, prepared, ready, prone, liable, given, apt.

disprove v. PROVE FALSE, invalidate, refute, negate, confute, rebut, give the lie to, deny, contradict, discredit, controvert, expose, demolish. ∎ OPPOSITES prove.

dispute n. ARGUMENT, quarrel, altercation, clash, wrangle, squabble, feud, disturbance, fracas, brawl; informal row. ▶v. **1** DEBATE, discuss, argue, disagree, clash, quarrel, bicker, wrangle, squabble. **2** QUESTION, call into question, challenge, contest, doubt, deny, object to, oppose, controvert, impugn, gainsay. ∎ OPPOSITES agree.

disqualify v. RULE OUT, bar, exclude, reject, turn down, prohibit, debar, preclude.

disquiet n. UNEASINESS, anxiety, ner-

disrepair n. a poor condition due to neglect.

disreputable adj. not respectable.

disrepute n. the state of having a bad reputation.

disrespect n. lack of respect. ■ **disrespectful** adj. **disrespectfully** adv.

disrobe v. undress.

disrupt v. interrupt or disturb an activity or process. ■ **disruption** n. **disruptive** adj.

dissatisfied adj. not pleased or happy. ■ **dissatisfaction** n.

dissect v. cut up a body or plant in order to study its internal parts. ■ **dissection** n.

dissemble v. hide or disguise one's feelings.

disseminate v. spread widely. ■ **dissemination** n.

dissension n. disagreement within a group.

dissent v. disagree, esp. with a widely or officially held view. ▶ n. disagreement. ■ **dissenter** n.

dissertation n. a long essay.

disservice n. an unhelpful or harmful action.

dissident n. a person opposing official policy. ■ **dissidence** n.

dissimilar adj. not similar; different. ■ **dissimilarity** n.

dissimulate v. hide or disguise one's feelings. ■ **dissimulation** n.

dissipate v. **1** disperse. **2** waste money etc. **3** (**dissipated**) overindulgent in physical pleasures. ■ **dissipation** n.

dissociate v. **1** disconnect or separate. **2** (**dissociate oneself from**) declare that one is not connected with. ■ **dissociation** n.

dissolute adj. overindulgent in physical pleasures.

dissolve v. **1** disperse in a liquid so as to form a solution. **2** close down or end an assembly or agreement. **3** give way to strong emotion. ■ **dissolution** n.

dissonant adj. lacking harmony. ■ **dissonance** n.

dissuade v. persuade or advise not to

d

Thesaurus

vousness, agitation, upset, worry, concern, distress, alarm, fear, fretfulness, dread, foreboding. ■ OPPOSITES calm.

disregard v. IGNORE, pay no attention to, take no notice of, neglect, discount, set aside, brush aside, overlook, turn a blind eye to, pass over, forget, gloss over, make light of, play down, laugh off, skip, snub, cold-shoulder; *informal* pooh-pooh. ■ OPPOSITES attention.

disrepair n. DILAPIDATION, decay, collapse, shabbiness, ruin, deterioration, decrepitude.

disreputable adj. INFAMOUS, notorious, dishonourable, dishonest, unprincipled, villainous, corrupt, unworthy, questionable, unsavoury, contemptible, unscrupulous, despicable, disgraceful, reprehensible, discreditable, shocking, outrageous, scandalous. ■ OPPOSITES reputable.

disrespectful adj. IMPOLITE, discourteous, ill-mannered, rude, uncivil, irreverent, insolent, inconsiderate, impertinent, impudent, cheeky, scornful, contemptuous, insulting, churlish, derisive, uncomplimentary. ■ OPPOSITES respectful.

disrupt v. UPSET, interrupt, break up, throw into disorder, cause turmoil in, disturb, interfere with, throw a spanner in the works, obstruct, impede, hamper, unsettle.

dissatisfaction n. DISCONTENT, dis-

pleasure, disappointment, disapproval, frustration, unhappiness, dismay, disquiet, annoyance, irritation, anger, exasperation, resentment, disgruntlement, malaise, restlessness. ■ OPPOSITES satisfaction.

dissatisfied adj. DISCONTENTED, displeased, disgruntled, unsatisfied, disapproving, disappointed, frustrated, unhappy, angry, vexed, irritated, annoyed, resentful, restless, unfulfilled. ■ OPPOSITES satisfied.

disseminate v. SPREAD, circulate, broadcast, publish, publicize, proclaim, promulgate, propagate, dissipate, scatter, distribute, disperse, diffuse, bruit abroad.

dissident n. DISSENTER, rebel, objector, protestor, nonconformist, recusant, apostate. ■ OPPOSITES conformist.

dissimilar adj. DIFFERENT, distinct, unlike, varying, disparate, unrelated, divergent, deviating, diverse, various, contrasting, mismatched. ■ OPPOSITES similar.

dissipate v. **1** DISPERSE, scatter, drive away, dispel, dissolve. **2** SQUANDER, waste, fritter away, misspend, deplete, use up, consume, run through.

dissipated adj. *see* DEBAUCHED.

dissociate v. SEPARATE, set apart, segregate, isolate, detach, disconnect, sever, divorce. ■ OPPOSITES associate.

dissolve v. **1** LIQUEFY, become liquid,

do. ■ **dissuasion** n.

distaff n. a stick on to which wool etc. is wound for spinning. □ **distaff side** the female side of a family.

distance n. **1** the length of the space between two points. **2** the state of being distant. **3** a far-off point or place. **4** the full length of a race etc. ▶ v. make distant or remote.

distant adj. **1** far away. **2** at a specified distance. **3** aloof. ■ **distantly** adv.

distaste n. dislike.

distasteful adj. unpleasant or offensive.

distemper n. **1** a kind of paint for use on walls. **2** a disease of dogs.

distend v. swell because of internal pressure. ■ **distension** n.

distil (US **distill**) v. (**distilling**, **distilled**) **1** purify a liquid by heating it so that it vaporizes and then condensing the vapour. **2** make spirits in this way. **3** extract the most important aspects of. ■ **distillation** n.

distiller n. a person or company that manufactures spirits. ■ **distillery** n.

distinct adj. **1** noticeably different. **2** clearly perceptible. ■ **distinctly** adv. **distinctness** n.

distinction n. **1** a difference or contrast. **2** outstanding excellence. **3** a special honour or award.

distinctive adj. characteristic of a person or thing and distinct from others. ■ **distinctively** adv. **distinctiveness** n.

distinguish v. **1** recognize or treat as different. **2** manage to see or hear. **3** be a characteristic of. **4** (**distinguish oneself**) make oneself worthy of respect. ■ **distinguishable** adj.

distinguished adj. **1** dignified in appearance. **2** commanding great respect.

distort v. **1** pull or twist out of shape. **2** misrepresent. ■ **distortion** n.

Thesaurus

melt, deliquesce. **2** END, bring to an end, break up, terminate, discontinue, wind up, disband, suspend. **3** BE OVERCOME WITH, break into, collapse into.

dissuade v. PERSUADE AGAINST, advise against, warn against, put off, stop, talk out of, argue out of, discourage from, deter from, divert, turn aside from. ■ OPPOSITES persuade.

distance n. **1** SPACE, extent, interval, gap, separation, span, stretch, measurement, length, width, breadth, depth, range, mileage. **2** ALOOFNESS, reserve, coolness, remoteness, reticence, coldness, stiffness, frigidity, restraint, formality, unresponsiveness, unfriendliness; *informal* stand-offishness. □ **distance oneself** SEPARATE ONESELF, dissociate oneself, keep one's distance, set oneself apart, remove oneself, stay away, keep away, detach oneself, be unfriendly.

distant adj. **1** FAR, faraway, far-off, remote, out of the way, outlying, far-flung, inaccessible. **2** AWAY, off, apart, separated, dispersed, scattered. **3** RESERVED, uncommunicative, remote, aloof, withdrawn, unapproachable, restrained, reticent, cool, cold, stiff, formal, unfriendly, unresponsive, haughty, condescending. ■ OPPOSITES close, friendly.

distasteful adj. DISAGREEABLE, unpleasant, displeasing, undesirable, off-putting, objectionable, offensive, obnoxious, repugnant, disgusting, unsavoury, revolting, nauseating, sickening, loath-some, abhorrent, detestable. ■ OPPOSITES pleasant.

distinct adj. **1** CLEAR, clear-cut, well defined, marked, sharp, decided, visible, perceptible, definite, unmistakable, obvious, recognizable, plain, plain as day, evident, apparent, manifest, patent, unambiguous, palpable, unequivocal. **2** SEPARATE, individual, different, unconnected, contrasting, discrete, disparate, dissimilar, detached, unassociated. ■ OPPOSITES indistinct, vague.

distinction n. **1** CONTRAST, difference, dissimilarity, division, dividing line, separation, differentiation, contradistinction, peculiarity. **2** NOTE, consequence, importance, account, significance, greatness, prestige, eminence, prominence, renown, fame, celebrity, mark, honour, merit, worth, excellence, name, rank, quality, superiority. ■ OPPOSITES similarity, mediocrity.

distinctive adj. DISTINGUISHING, characteristic, typical, individual, particular, special, peculiar, different, uncommon, unusual, remarkable, singular, extraordinary, noteworthy, original, idiosyncratic. ■ OPPOSITES ordinary.

distinguish v. **1** TELL APART, differentiate, discriminate, tell the difference between, decide between, determine. **2** SET APART, single out, separate, characterize, individualize. **3** MAKE OUT, see, perceive, discern, observe, notice, recognize, pick out, espy.

distinguished adj. FAMOUS, renowned, well known, prominent, famed, noted,

distract v. draw away the attention of.

distraction n. **1** a thing that distracts someone's attention. **2** an entertainment. **3** mental agitation.

distraught adj. very worried and upset.

distress n. extreme anxiety, pain, or hardship. ▶v. cause distress to.

distribute v. **1** hand or share out. **2** (**be distributed**) be spread over an area. **3** supply goods to retailers. ■ **distribution** n. **distributive** adj.

distributor n. **1** an agent who supplies goods to retailers. **2** a device in a petrol engine for passing electric current to the spark plugs.

district n. a particular area of a town or region.

distrust n. lack of trust. ▶v. have little trust in. ■ **distrustful** adj. **distrustfully** adv.

disturb v. **1** interrupt the sleep, privacy, etc. of. **2** move something from its place. **3** make anxious. **4** (**disturbed**) having emotional or mental problems. ■ **disturbance** n.

disuse n. the state of not being used. ■ **disused** adj.

ditch n. a narrow trench for drainage. ▶v. informal get rid of.

dither v. be indecisive.

ditto n. (in lists) the same thing again.

ditty n. (pl. **ditties**) a short, simple song.

diuretic n. a drug that causes more urine to be excreted.

diurnal adj. of or in the daytime.

diva /**dee**-vuh/ n. a famous female singer.

d

Thesaurus

notable, illustrious, celebrated, respected, acclaimed, esteemed, legendary. ■ OPPOSITES obscure.

distort v. **1** TWIST, bend, warp, contort, buckle, deform, misshape, mangle, wrench. **2** MISREPRESENT, pervert, twist, falsify, slant, bias, colour, tamper with, alter, change, garble.

distract v. **1** DIVERT, deflect, sidetrack, interrupt, interfere, draw away, turn aside. **2** AMUSE, entertain, divert, beguile, engage, occupy. **3** CONFUSE, bewilder, disturb, fluster, agitate, disconcert, discompose, harass, annoy, trouble; informal hassle.

distracted adj. see DISTRAUGHT.

distraction n. **1** DIVERSION, interruption, disturbance, interference, obstruction. **2** CONFUSION, bewilderment, agitation, befuddlement, harassment. **3** AMUSEMENT, diversion, entertainment, recreation, pastime, divertissement.

distraught adj. DISTRESSED, disturbed, excited, overcome, overwrought, frantic, distracted, beside oneself, wild, hysterical, grief-stricken, mad, maddened, insane, crazed, deranged; informal out of one's mind, worked up. ■ OPPOSITES calm.

distress n. **1** ANGUISH, suffering, pain, agony, affliction, torment, misery, wretchedness, torture, sorrow, grief, sadness, discomfort, heartache, desolation, trouble, worry, anxiety, uneasiness, perturbation, angst. **2** HARDSHIP, adversity, trouble, misfortune, poverty, need, destitution, privation, impoverishment, indigence, penury, beggary, dire straits. ▶v. UPSET, pain, trouble, worry, bother, disturb, perturb, torment, grieve, sadden, make miserable,

vex, shock, scare, alarm. ■ OPPOSITES calm.

distribute v. **1** GIVE OUT, hand out, share out, divide out, dole out, measure out, parcel out, mete out, allocate, allot, issue, dispense, apportion, administer, deal out, dish out, assign, dispose. **2** CIRCULATE, pass around, hand out, deliver, convey, transmit. **3** DISSEMINATE, disperse, scatter, strew, spread, sow, diffuse.

district n. AREA, region, place, locality, neighbourhood, sector, vicinity, quarter, territory, domain, precinct, province, zone, ward, department, parish, community.

distrust v. MISTRUST, be suspicious of, have doubts about, doubt, be wary/chary of, have misgivings about, question, wonder about, suspect, disbelieve; informal be leery of. ■ OPPOSITES trust.

disturb v. **1** INTERRUPT, distract, bother, trouble, intrude on, butt in on, interfere with, harass, plague, pester, hinder; informal hassle. **2** MUDDLE, disorder, disarrange, confuse, throw into confusion; informal jumble up, mess about with. **3** CONCERN, trouble, worry, perturb, upset, fluster, agitate, discomfit, alarm, frighten, dismay, distress, unsettle, ruffle.

disturbed adj. **1** UPSET, troubled, worried, concerned, agitated, alarmed, dismayed, unsettled, ruffled. **2** UNBALANCED, disordered, maladjusted, neurotic, psychotic; informal screwed up.

disused adj. UNUSED, neglected, abandoned, discontinued, obsolete, superannuated, withdrawn, discarded, idle, closed.

ditch n. TRENCH, channel, dyke, canal,

divan n. **1** a bed consisting simply of a base and mattress. **2** a sofa without a back or arms.

dive v. **1** plunge head first into water. **2** swim under water using breathing apparatus. **3** move quickly downwards or under cover. ▶n. **1** an act of diving. **2** informal a disreputable nightclub or bar. ■ **diver** n.

diverge v. separate and go in a different direction. ■ **divergence** n. **divergent** adj.

diverse adj. widely varied.

diversify v. (**diversifying**, **diversified**) **1** make or become more varied. **2** (of a company) expand its range of products or markets. ■ **diversification** n.

diversion n. **1** the diverting of something. **2** an alternative route avoiding a closed road. **3** something intended to distract attention. **4** a recreation.

diversity n. (pl. **diversities**) **1** the state of being varied. **2** a range of different things.

divert v. **1** change the direction or course of. **2** distract. **3** amuse or entertain.

divest v. (**divest of**) strip of.

divide v. **1** separate into parts. **2** cause to disagree. **3** find how many times one number contains another. ▶n. a wide difference between two groups.

dividend n. **1** a sum of money paid to a company's shareholders out of its profits. **2** (**dividends**) benefits.

divider n. **1** a screen dividing a room. **2** (**dividers**) a measuring compass.

divine adj. **1** of God or a god. **2** informal wonderful. ▶v. discover by intuition. ■ **divination** n. **divinely** adv. **diviner** n.

divinity n. (pl. **divinities**) **1** the state of being divine. **2** a god or goddess.

divisible adj. capable of being divided.

division n. **1** the act of dividing. **2** each of the parts into which something is divided. **3** a partition. ■ **divisional** adj.

divisive adj. causing disagreement.

divisor n. a number by which another is to be divided.

divorce n. the legal ending of a mar-

Thesaurus

drain, gutter, gully, moat, furrow, rut. ▶v. THROW OUT, abandon, discard, drop, jettison, scrap, get rid of, dispose of; informal dump.

dive v. PLUNGE, plummet, jump, leap, bound, spring, nosedive, fall, descend, submerge, drop, swoop, dip, pitch, bellyflop.

diverge v. SEPARATE, fork, branch off, radiate, spread out, bifurcate, divide, split, part, go off at a tangent, divaricate, ramify. ■ OPPOSITES converge.

diverse adj. ASSORTED, various, miscellaneous, mixed, varied, diversified, variegated, heterogeneous, different, differing, distinct, unlike, dissimilar, distinctive, contrasting, conflicting.

diversify v. BRANCH OUT, expand, bring variety to, develop, extend, enlarge, spread out, vary, mix, change, transform.

diversion n. **1** DETOUR, deviation, alternative route. **2** AMUSEMENT, entertainment, distraction, fun, relaxation, recreation, pleasure, enjoyment, delight, divertissement.

divert v. **1** DEFLECT, turn aside, change the course of, redirect, draw away, switch, sidetrack. **2** AMUSE, entertain, distract, delight, beguile, give pleasure to, enchant, interest, occupy, absorb, engross.

diverting adj. AMUSING, entertaining, distracting, fun, enjoyable, pleasurable, interesting, absorbing, engrossing. ■ OPPOSITES boring.

divide v. **1** SPLIT, cut up, separate, sever, halve, bisect, sunder, rend, part, segregate, partition, detach, disconnect, disjoin. **2** BRANCH, fork, diverge, split in two. **3** SHARE OUT, allocate, allot, apportion, distribute, dispense, hand out, dole out, measure out, parcel out, carve up. **4** BREAK UP, separate, alienate, split up, disunite, set/pit against one another, set at odds, come between, sow dissension. ■ OPPOSITES unite.

divine¹ adj. **1** HEAVENLY, celestial, holy, angelic, spiritual, saintly, seraphic, sacred, consecrated, godlike, godly, supernatural. **2** LOVELY, beautiful, wonderful, glorious, marvellous, admirable; informal super, stunning. ■ OPPOSITES mortal.

divine² v. FORETELL, predict, foresee, forecast, presage, augur, portend, prognosticate.

divinity n. **1** DIVINE NATURE, divineness, deity, godliness, holiness, sanctity. **2** THEOLOGY, religious studies, religion, scripture.

division n. **1** DIVIDING LINE, boundary, limit, border, partition, demarcation, frontier, margin. **2** SECTION, part, portion, slice, fragment, chunk, component, share, compartment, category, class, group, family, grade. **3** BRANCH, department, section, arm, sector, unit. **4** DISAGREEMENT, conflict, dissension, riage. ▶ v. **1** legally end one's marriage with. **2** detach or dissociate.

divorcee n. a divorced person.

divulge v. reveal information.

Diwali n. a Hindu festival with lights, held in October and November.

DIY n. the activity of doing home decoration and repairs oneself.

dizzy adj. (**dizzier**, **dizziest**) having a sensation of spinning around. ■ **dizzily** adv. **dizziness** n.

DJ n. **1** a disc jockey. **2** a dinner jacket.

djellaba /jel-luh-buh/ n. an Arab cloak.

DNA n. deoxyribonucleic acid, a substance carrying genetic information.

do v. (**does**, **doing**, **did**; past part. **done**) **1** carry out an action or task. **2** act or perform. **3** work on. **4** make or provide. **5** be suitable or acceptable. ▶ aux. v. used in questions, for emphasis, to avoid repeating a verb just used, or to form the past or present tense. ▶ n. (pl. **dos** or **do's**) a party. □ **do away with** informal put an end to. **do-gooder** a well-meaning but interfering person. **do in** informal **1** kill. **2** tire out. **dos and don'ts** rules of behaviour. **do up 1** fasten or wrap. **2** informal renovate.

Dobermann (or **Dobermann pinscher**) n. a large breed of dog with powerful jaws.

docile adj. easy to control; submissive. ■ **docilely** adv. **docility** n.

dock n. **1** an enclosed area of water for the loading, unloading, and repair of ships. **2** the enclosure in a court for a person on trial. **3** a weed with broad leaves. ▶ v. **1** come or bring into a dock. **2** (of a spacecraft) join with another craft in space. **3** deduct money from a person's wages. **4** cut short an animal's tail. □ **dockyard** an area where ships are repaired and built.

docker n. a person who loads and unloads ships.

docket n. a document accompanying goods, listing the contents etc.

doctor n. **1** a person qualified to practise medicine. **2** a person holding a doctorate. ▶ v. **1** tamper with or falsify. **2** add a harmful ingredient to.

doctorate n. the highest degree awarded by a university. ■ **doctoral** adj.

doctrinaire adj. very strict in applying beliefs.

doctrine n. a set of beliefs or principles held by a religious, political, or other group. ■ **doctrinal** adj.

document n. a piece of written, printed, or electronic matter providing information or evidence. ▶ v. record in written or other form. ■ **documentation** n.

documentary adj. **1** consisting of documents. **2** providing a factual report. ▶ n. (pl. **documentaries**) a documentary film.

dodder v. be slow and unsteady. ■ **doddery** adj.

dodecagon n. a plane figure with

Thesaurus

discord, difference of opinion, feud, breach, rupture, split, variance, disunion, estrangement, alienation, schism.

divorce n. BREAK-UP, split, dissolution, annulment, separation, breach, rupture. ▶ v. BREAK UP, split up, separate, part, annul/end the marriage.

dizzy adj. LIGHT-HEADED, giddy, faint, shaky, off balance, reeling, staggering; informal weak at the knees, wobbly, woozy.

do v. **1** PERFORM, carry out, undertake, execute, accomplish, discharge, achieve, implement, complete, finish, bring about, effect, produce, engineer. **2** ACT, behave, conduct oneself, comport oneself. **3** BE ENOUGH, be adequate, suffice, be sufficient, be satisfactory, serve the purpose, fit the bill, pass muster, measure up. **4** GRANT, bestow, render, pay, give, afford. **5** GET ON/ALONG, progress, fare, make out, manage, continue.

docile adj. AMENABLE, compliant, tractable, manageable, accommodating, obedient, pliant, biddable, submissive, dutiful, malleable. ■ OPPOSITES disobedient.

dock[1] n. PIER, quay, wharf, jetty, berth, harbour, port, slipway, marina, waterfront.

dock[2] v. **1** CUT, shorten, crop, lop, truncate. **2** DEDUCT, subtract, remove, take off.

doctor n. PHYSICIAN, medical practitioner, GP, general practitioner, consultant, registrar; informal medic, doc, quack.

doctrine n. CREED, belief, teaching, credo, dogma, conviction, tenet, principle, maxim, axiom, precept, article of faith, canon, theory, thesis, orthodoxy, postulate.

document n. PAPER, form, certificate, record, report, deed, voucher, charter, instrument, licence, parchment, visa, warrant. ▶ v. RECORD, detail, report, register, chart, cite, instance.

twelve sides.

dodge v. **1** avoid by a sudden quick movement. **2** avoid in a cunning way. ▶ n. an act of dodging. ■ **dodger** n.

dodgem n. a small electric car driven at a funfair with the aim of bumping other such cars.

dodgy adj. informal **1** dishonest. **2** risky. **3** not good or reliable.

dodo n. (pl. **dodos** or **dodoes**) a large extinct bird.

doe n. a female deer, hare, or rabbit.

does 3rd person sing. present of **DO**.

doesn't contr. does not.

doff v. remove one's hat when greeting someone.

dog n. **1** a domesticated meat-eating mammal. **2** the male of this, or of a fox or wolf. ▶ v. (**dogging**, **dogged**) follow or affect persistently. □ **dog collar** informal a white upright collar worn by Christian clergy. **dog-eared** having worn or battered corners. **dogfish** a small shark. **dog rose** a wild rose. **dogsbody** informal a person given menial tasks. **in the doghouse** informal in disgrace. ■ **doggy** adj.

doge n. hist. the chief magistrate of Venice or Genoa.

dogged /dog-gid/ adj. persistent. ■ **doggedly** adv.

doggerel n. badly written verse.

doggo adv. (**lie doggo**) informal remain still and quiet to avoid being found.

dogma n. a set of principles intended to be accepted without question.

dogmatic adj. firmly putting forward one's opinions as true. ■ **dogmatically** adv. **dogmatism** n.

doily n. (pl. **doilies**) a small ornamental lace or paper mat.

doldrums pl. n. (**the doldrums**) **1** a state of inactivity or depression. **2** a region of the Atlantic with little or no wind.

dole n. informal unemployment benefit. ▶ v. (**dole out**) distribute.

doleful adj. mournful. ■ **dolefully** adv.

doll n. a small model of a human figure, used as a child's toy. ▶ v. (**be dolled up**) informal be dressed in smart or fancy clothes.

dollar n. the basic unit of money of the US and various other countries.

dollop n. informal a mass of something soft.

dolmen n. a prehistoric tomb with a large flat stone laid on upright ones.

dolour (US **dolor**) n. literary great sorrow. ■ **dolorous** adj.

dolphin n. a small whale with a beak-like snout.

dolt n. a stupid person.

domain n. **1** an area controlled by a ruler or government. **2** an area of activity. **3** a subset of the Internet with addresses sharing a common suffix.

dome n. a rounded roof with a circular base. ■ **domed** adj.

domestic adj. **1** of a home or family. **2** (of an animal) tame and kept by humans. **3** of one's own country. ▶ n. a person employed to do household tasks. ■ **domestically** adv.

domesticate v. tame an animal and keep it as a pet or for farm produce. ■ **domestication** n.

domesticity n. home or family life.

domicile n. the country in which a person lives permanently.

dominant adj. most important or influential. ■ **dominance** n.

Thesaurus

documentary adj. **1** DOCUMENTED, recorded, written, registered. **2** FACTUAL, non-fiction, true-to-life, realistic, real-life.

dodge v. **1** DART, duck, dive, swerve, veer, jump, move aside. **2** EVADE, avoid, elude, fend off, parry, fudge, escape, steer clear of, shun, shirk, deceive, trick. ▶ n. RUSE, ploy, stratagem, trick, subterfuge, wile, deception, manoeuvre, contrivance, expedient; informal wheeze.

dog n. HOUND, bitch, cur, mongrel, tyke, pup, puppy, whelp; informal doggy, pooch, mutt, bow-wow. ▶ v. FOLLOW, pursue, track, shadow, trail, hound, plague, trouble, haunt.

dogged adj. DETERMINED, obstinate, stubborn, tenacious, relentless, single-

minded, unflagging, unwavering, persistent, obdurate, firm, steadfast, staunch.

dogmatic adj. OPINIONATED, peremptory, assertive, insistent, pushy, emphatic, categorical, authoritarian, domineering, imperious, arrogant, overbearing, dictatorial, intolerant, prejudiced, biased.

dole n. BENEFIT, welfare, social security, income support. □ **dole out** see DISTRIBUTE.

doleful adj. MOURNFUL, sad, sorrowful, dejected, depressed, miserable, disconsolate, wretched; informal blue, down in the dumps.

domestic adj. **1** HOME, family, household, private. **2** DOMESTICATED, tame, pet,

dominate v. **1** have a very strong influence over. **2** be the most important or noticeable person or thing in. ■ **domination** n.

domineering adj. arrogant and overbearing.

dominion n. **1** supreme power or control. **2** a ruler's territory.

domino n. (pl. **dominoes**) any of the small oblong pieces marked with 0–6 pips in each half, used in the game of **dominoes**.

don n. a university teacher. ▶ v. (**donning**, **donned**) put on an item of clothing.

donate v. **1** give to a good cause. **2** give blood or an organ for use in treating another person. ■ **donation** n.

done past part. of **DO**.

donkey n. (pl. **donkeys**) a long-eared mammal of the horse family. □ **donkey jacket** a heavy jacket with waterproof material across the shoulders. **donkey's years** informal a very long time.

donor n. a person who donates something.

don't contr. do not.

donut US = **DOUGHNUT**.

doodle v. draw absent-mindedly. ▶ n. a doodled drawing.

doom n. death or another terrible fate. ▶ v. (**be doomed**) be fated to fail or be

destroyed. □ **doomsday** the last day of the world's existence.

door n. a movable barrier at the entrance to a building, room, etc.

dope informal n. **1** an illegal drug. **2** a stupid person. ▶ v. give a drug to.

dopey (or **dopy**) adj. informal **1** half-asleep. **2** stupid.

doppelgänger /dop-puhl-gang-er/ n. a ghost or double of a living person.

dormant adj. temporarily inactive with physical functions slowed down.

dormer n. an upright window set into a sloping roof.

dormitory n. (pl. **dormitories**) a bedroom for a number of people in a school etc.

dormouse n. (pl. **dormice**) a small mouse-like rodent with a bushy tail.

dorsal adj. of or on the back.

dosage n. the size of a dose.

dose n. **1** a quantity of a medicine taken at one time. **2** an amount of radiation received at one time. ▶ v. give a dose of medicine to.

doss v. informal **1** sleep in rough or makeshift conditions. **2** spend time idly. ■ **dosser** n.

dossier n. a collection of documents about a person or event.

dot n. a small round mark. ▶ v. (**dotting**, **dotted**) **1** mark with a dot or dots.

Thesaurus

trained, house-trained; *US* housebroken.

domesticate v. **1** TAME, train, break in, house-train; *US* housebreak. **2** NATURALIZE, acclimatize, habituate, accustom, familiarize, assimilate.

dominant adj. **1** COMMANDING, ruling, controlling, presiding, governing, supreme, ascendant, domineering, most influential, most assertive, authoritative. **2** CHIEF, most important, predominant, main, leading, principal, paramount, pre-eminent, primary, outstanding, prevailing. ■ OPPOSITES submissive, subservient.

dominate v. **1** RULE, govern, control, exercise control over, have the whip hand, command, direct, preside over, have mastery over, domineer, tyrannize, intimidate; *informal* call the shots, have under one's thumb, be in the driver's seat, wear the trousers. **2** OVERLOOK, tower above, stand over, project over, hang over, loom over, bestride.

domineering adj. OVERBEARING, authoritarian, autocratic, imperious, high-handed, peremptory, arrogant, dictatorial, haughty, masterful, forceful, pushy,

tyrannical, despotic, oppressive, iron-fisted; *informal* bossy. ■ OPPOSITES meek, servile.

donate v. GIVE, contribute, present, make a gift of, hand over, grant, subscribe; *informal* chip in, kick in.

donation n. CONTRIBUTION, gift, subscription, present, grant, offering, gratuity, charity, benefaction, largesse.

donor n. CONTRIBUTOR, giver, benefactor, benefactress, supporter, backer, philanthropist; *informal* angel.

doom n. **1** RUIN, ruination, downfall, destruction, disaster, catastrophe, annihilation, extinction, death, termination, quietus. **2** FATE, destiny, fortune, lot, portion. ▶ v. DESTINE, condemn, ordain, preordain, consign, predestine.

doomed adj. DAMNED, cursed, hopeless, accursed, ill-fated, ill-starred, ruined, bedevilled.

door n. **1** DOORWAY, opening, portal, entrance, exit, way out, barrier. **2** ENTRY, entrance, opening, access, gateway, way, path, road, ingress.

dormant adj. **1** SLEEPING, asleep, hibernating, resting, slumbering, inactive,

2 scatter over an area. □ **dot-com** a company doing business on the Internet. **on the dot** informal exactly on time.

dotage n. the period of life when one is old and weak.

dote v. (**dote on**) be excessively fond of. ■ **doting** adj.

dotty adj. informal slightly mad or eccentric.

double adj. **1** consisting of two equal parts or things. **2** of twice the usual size. **3** for use by two people. ▶adv. twice as much. ▶n. **1** a double quantity or thing. **2** a person who looks exactly like another. **3** (**doubles**) a game with two players on each side. ▶v. **1** make or become double. **2** fold or bend over on itself. **3** have two uses or roles. **4** (**double back**) go back in the direction one came from. □ **at the double** very fast. **double bass** the largest and lowest-pitched instrument of the violin family. **double-breasted** (of a coat) having a large overlap at the front. **double chin** a roll of flesh below a person's chin. **double cream** thick cream with a high fat content. **double-cross** betray or deceive. **double dealing** deceitful behaviour. **double-decker** a bus with two levels. **double Dutch** incomprehensible speech. **double entendre** /doo-b'l on-**ton**-druh/ a word or phrase with two meanings, one of which is usu. rude. **double figures** a number from 10 to 99 inclusive. **double glazing** two sheets of glass in a win-

dow, designed to reduce heat loss. **double take** a delayed reaction just after one's first reaction to something unexpected. ■ **doubly** adv.

doublet n. hist. a man's short close-fitting jacket.

doubloon n. hist. a Spanish gold coin.

doubt n. a feeling of uncertainty or disbelief. ▶v. **1** feel uncertain about. **2** question the truth of. ■ **doubter** n.

doubtful adj. **1** feeling uncertain. **2** not known for certain. **3** unlikely. ■ **doubtfully** adv.

doubtless adv. very probably.

douche /doosh/ n. a jet of water applied to part of the body.

dough n. a thick mixture of flour and liquid, for baking into bread or pastry. □ **doughnut** (US **donut**) a small fried cake or ring of sweetened dough. ■ **doughy** adj.

doughty /**dow**-ti/ adj. brave and resolute.

dour adj. stern or gloomy.

douse v. **1** drench with liquid. **2** extinguish a fire or light.

dove n. **1** a stocky bird with a cooing voice. **2** a person who favours a policy of peace and negotiation. □ **dovecote** a shelter for domesticated pigeons.

dovetail n. a wedge-shaped joint interlocking two pieces of wood. ▶v. fit together easily or conveniently.

dowager n. a widow holding a title or property from her late husband.

dowdy adj. not smart or fashionable.

Thesaurus

inert, comatose, quiescent. **2** HIDDEN, latent, potential, untapped, unused. ■ OPPOSITES awake, active.

dose n. **1** AMOUNT, quantity, measure, portion, draught. **2** BOUT, attack, spell.

dot n. SPOT, speck, fleck, point, mark, dab, particle, atom, iota, jot, mote, mite.

dote v. (**dote on**) ADORE, idolize, love, treasure, prize, make much of, lavish affection on, indulge, spoil, pamper.

double adj. **1** DUPLICATE, twinned, twin, paired, in pairs, dual, coupled, twofold. **2** AMBIGUOUS, dual, ambivalent, equivocal, double-edged. ▶n. TWIN, clone, lookalike, doppelgänger, duplicate, replica, copy, facsimile, counterpart, match, mate, fellow; informal spitting image, dead ringer.

double-cross v. BETRAY, cheat, defraud, trick, mislead, deceive, swindle, hoodwink; informal two-time, take for a ride.

doubt v. **1** BE SUSPICIOUS OF, suspect, distrust, mistrust, have misgivings about,

feel uneasy about, call into question, question, query. **2** HAVE DOUBTS, be dubious, be undecided, lack conviction, have scruples. ▶n. **1** DISTRUST, mistrust, suspicion, scepticism, lack of confidence, uneasiness, reservations, misgivings, qualms. **2** UNCERTAINTY, indecision, hesitancy, hesitation, vacillation, wavering, irresolution, lack of conviction. ■ OPPOSITES trust.

doubtful adj. **1** IN DOUBT, uncertain, unsure, improbable, unlikely. **2** DISTRUSTFUL, mistrustful, doubting, suspicious, sceptical, having reservations, apprehensive, uneasy, questioning, unsure, incredulous. **3** UNCERTAIN, dubious, open to question, questionable, debatable, inconclusive, unresolved, unconfirmed. **4** UNCLEAR, dubious, ambiguous, equivocal, obscure, vague, nebulous. **5** SUSPECT, dubious, suspicious, questionable, under suspicion, unreliable, disreputable. ■ OPPOSITES certain.

■ **dowdiness** n.

dowel n. a headless peg for holding together components.

down adv. **1** to, in, or at a lower place or level. **2** to a smaller amount or size. **3** in or into a weaker or worse position or condition. **4** from an earlier to a later point. ▶prep. **1** from a higher to a lower point of. **2** at a point further along. ▶adj. **1** directed or moving downwards. **2** unhappy. **3** (of a computer system) out of action. ▶v. informal **1** knock down. **2** swallow a drink. ▶n. **1** soft fine feathers or hairs. **2** a gently rolling hill. □ **down and out** homeless and without money. **downhill 1** towards the bottom of a slope. **2** into a steadily worsening situation. **downstairs** on or to a lower floor. **downstream** in the direction in which a stream or river flows. **down-to-earth** practical and realistic. **downtown** esp. US in, to, or towards the central area of a city. **down under** informal Australia and New Zealand. ■ **downward** adj. & adv. **downwards** adv.

downbeat adj. **1** gloomy. **2** relaxed and low-key.

downcast adj. **1** (of eyes) looking downwards. **2** dejected.

downfall n. a loss of power or status.

downgrade v. reduce to a lower rank or level.

downhearted adj. sad or discouraged.

download v. copy data from one computer system to another.

downmarket adj. cheap and of poor quality.

downpour n. a heavy fall of rain.

downright adj. & adv. utter; completely as described.

downsize v. reduce the number of staff employed by a company.

Down's syndrome n. a congenital disorder causing mental and physical abnormalities.

downtrodden adj. oppressed.

downy adj. covered with fine soft hair or feathers.

dowry n. (pl. **dowries**) property or money brought by a bride to her husband on their marriage.

dowse /dowz/ v. search for underground water or minerals with a stick which supposedly moves when these are present.

doxology n. (pl. **doxologies**) a prayer praising God.

doyen n. (fem. **doyenne**) the most respected or prominent person in a particular field.

doze v. sleep lightly. ▶n. a short, light sleep.

dozen n. **1** (pl. **dozen**) a group of twelve. **2** (**dozens**) a lot.

dozy adj. feeling drowsy and lazy.

Dr abbrev. (as a title) Doctor.

drab adj. (**drabber**, **drabbest**) dull and uninteresting.

drachm /dram/ n. hist. a unit of measure equivalent to one eighth of an ounce or one eighth of a fluid ounce.

drachma n. a former currency unit in Greece.

draconian adj. very harsh or strict.

draft n. **1** a preliminary version of a piece of writing. **2** a written order to a bank to pay a specified sum. **3** US military conscription. **4** US = DRAUGHT. ▶v. **1** prepare a draft of. **2** US conscript for military service.

draftsman US = DRAUGHTSMAN.

drafty US = DRAUGHTY.

drag v. (**dragging**, **dragged**) **1** pull along with effort. **2** trail along the ground. **3** (of time) pass slowly. **4** (**drag out**) prolong unnecessarily. **5** search the bottom of a lake etc. with hooks or nets. **6** move an image across a computer screen using a mouse. ▶n. **1** the act of dragging. **2** informal a boring or tiresome person or thing. **3** informal women's clothing worn by a man. □ **dragnet** a net drawn through water.

Thesaurus

dour adj. MOROSE, unsmiling, gloomy, sullen, sour, gruff, churlish, uncommunicative, unfriendly, forbidding, grim, stern, austere, severe, harsh, dismal, dreary. ■ OPPOSITES cheerful.

dowdy adj. FRUMPISH, drab, dull, unfashionable, inelegant, unstylish, slovenly, shabby, dingy, untidy, frowzy. ■ OPPOSITES smart.

downcast adj. see DEJECTED.

downright adv. COMPLETELY, totally, absolutely, utterly, thoroughly, really, profoundly, categorically, positively.

downward adj. DECLINING, descending, falling, downhill, going down, earthbound. ■ OPPOSITES upward.

drab adj. **1** DULL, colourless, grey, mousy, dingy, dreary, cheerless, gloomy, sombre, depressing. **2** UNINTERESTING, boring, tedious, dry, dreary, lifeless, lacklustre, uninspired. ■ OPPOSITES bright, interesting.

draft n. **1** OUTLINE, plan, rough version, skeleton, abstract, notes. **2** MONEY

dragon n. a mythical monster that can breathe out fire. □ **dragonfly** a long-bodied insect with two pairs of wings.

dragoon n. a member of any of several British regiments. ▶v. force into doing something.

drain v. **1** draw off or remove liquid from. **2** (of liquid) run off or out. **3** exhaust the strength or resources of. **4** drink the entire contents of. ▶n. **1** a channel or pipe carrying off surplus liquid. **2** a thing that uses up a resource or strength. ■ **drainage** n.

drake n. a male duck.

dram n. a small drink of spirits.

drama n. **1** a play. **2** plays as a literary form. **3** an exciting series of events.

dramatic adj. **1** of drama. **2** sudden and striking. **3** exciting or impressive. ■ **dramatically** adv.

dramatist n. a person who writes plays.

dramatize (or **-ise**) v. **1** present a novel etc. as a play. **2** cause to seem more exciting or serious. ■ **dramatization** n.

drank past of DRINK.

drape v. arrange loosely on or round something. ▶pl. n. (**drapes**) US long curtains.

drastic adj. having a strong or far-reaching effect. ■ **drastically** adv.

draught (US **draft**) n. **1** a current of cool air indoors. **2** an act of drinking or breathing in. **3** old use a medicinal drink. **4** (**draughts**) a game played on a chequered board. ▶adj. **1** (of beer) served from a cask. **2** (of an animal) used for pulling loads. □ **draughtsman** a person who makes detailed technical plans or drawings. ■ **draughty** adj.

draw v. (**drawing**, **drew**; past part. **drawn**) **1** produce a picture or diagram by making lines and marks on paper. **2** pull a vehicle. **3** move in a specified direction. **4** pull curtains shut or open. **5** arrive at a point in time. **6** take out. **7** attract to a place. **8** reach a conclusion. **9** finish a contest or game with an even score. **10** take in a breath. ▶n. **1** a random selection of names or numbers for prizes etc. **2** a game that ends with the scores even. **3** a very attractive or interesting person or thing. □ **drawback** a disadvantage. **drawbridge** a bridge hinged at one end so that it can be raised. **draw in** (of days) become shorter. **draw on** use as a resource. **draw out 1** make something last longer. **2** encourage to talk. **drawstring** a string that can be pulled to close an opening. **draw up 1** come to a halt. **2** prepare a plan or document.

drawer n. **1** a storage compartment made to slide horizontally in and out of

Thesaurus

ORDER, cheque, bill of exchange, postal order.

drag v. **1** PULL, haul, draw, tug, yank, trail, tow, lug. **2** GO ON TOO LONG, go on and on, become tedious, pass slowly, be boring, crawl, creep. □ **drag out** PROTRACT, prolong, draw out, spin out, stretch out, lengthen, extend.

drain v. **1** DRAW OFF, extract, remove, pump out, bleed, milk, tap, filter. **2** FLOW OUT, seep out, leak, trickle, ooze, well out, discharge, exude, effuse. **3** USE UP, exhaust, deplete, consume, sap, bleed, tax, strain. ▶n. TRENCH, channel, duct, sewer, gutter, ditch, culvert, pipe, outlet, conduit.

dramatic adj. **1** THEATRICAL, stage, thespian, dramaturgical. **2** EXCITING, sensational, startling, spectacular, thrilling, tense, suspenseful, electrifying, stirring, affecting. **3** STRIKING, impressive, vivid, breathtaking, moving, affecting, graphic.

dramatist n. PLAYWRIGHT, scriptwriter, screenwriter, dramaturge.

dramatize v. **1** ADAPT, put into dramatic form. **2** EXAGGERATE, make a drama of,

overstate, overdo; *informal* ham it up, lay it on thick.

drape v. COVER, envelope, swathe, blanket, cloak, veil, shroud, decorate, adorn, deck, festoon, array, overlay. ▶n. CURTAIN, drapery, screen, hanging, tapestry, valance.

drastic adj. SEVERE, extreme, strong, vigorous, draconian, desperate, radical, dire, harsh, forceful, rigorous, sharp.

draw v. **1** PULL, haul, drag, tug, yank, tow, trail, lug. **2** ATTRACT, lure, entice, invite, engage, interest, win, capture, captivate, tempt, seduce, fascinate, allure. **3** SKETCH, portray, depict, delineate, make a drawing of, represent, paint, design, trace, map out, chart, mark out. **4** PULL OUT, take out, bring out, extract, withdraw, unsheathe. ▶n. **1** LURE, attraction, pull, enticement, allure, magnetism. **2** LOTTERY, raffle, sweepstake. **3** TIE, dead heat, stalemate. □ **draw on** MAKE USE OF, have recourse to, exploit, employ, rely on. **draw out** EXTEND, protract, prolong, lengthen, drag out, spin out.

drawback n. DISADVANTAGE, catch, proba desk or chest. **2** (**drawers**) dated knickers or underpants.

drawing n. a picture made with a pencil or pen. □ **drawing pin** a pin for fastening paper to a surface. **drawing room** a formal sitting room.

drawl v. speak slowly with prolonged vowels. ▶ n. a drawling accent.

drawn past part. of DRAW. ▶ adj. looking strained from illness or exhaustion.

dray n. a low cart without sides.

dread v. fear greatly. ▶ n. great fear or anxiety.

dreadful adj. extremely bad or serious. ■ **dreadfully** adv.

dreadlocks pl. n. a Rastafarian hairstyle with the hair twisted into tight braids.

dream n. **1** a series of images and feelings occurring in the mind during sleep. **2** a long-held ambition or wish. ▶ v. (**dreaming**, **dreamed** or **dreamt**) **1** have dreams while asleep. **2** think of as possible. **3** (**dream up**) invent. ■ **dreamer** n. **dreamless** adj.

dreamy adj. **1** resembling a dream. **2** tending to daydream.

dreary adj. (**drearier**, **dreariest**) dull, bleak, and depressing. ■ **drearily** adv. **dreariness** n.

dredge v. scoop up mud and objects from the bed of a river etc. ■ **dredger** n.

dregs pl. n. **1** the last drops of liquid and any sediment left in a container. **2** the most worthless parts.

drench v. wet thoroughly.

dress v. **1** put on clothes. **2** (**dress up**) dress in smart clothes or in a special costume. **3** decorate in an attractive way. **4** clean and cover a wound. ▶ n. **1** a woman's or girl's one-piece garment with a bodice and skirt. **2** clothing. □ **dress circle** the first gallery of seats in a theatre. **dress rehearsal** a final rehearsal, in full costume, before a real performance.

dressage /dress-ahzh/ n. controlled movements performed by a horse at the rider's command.

dresser n. **1** a sideboard with shelves above for storing and displaying crockery. **2** a person who dresses in a particular way.

dressing n. **1** a sauce for a salad. **2** a protective covering for a wound. □ **dressing-down** informal a severe reprimand. **dressing gown** a long robe worn after getting out of bed or bathing. **dressing table** a table with a mirror, used while dressing or applying make-up.

dressy adj. (of clothes) smart or formal.

drew past of DRAW.

drey n. a squirrel's nest.

dribble v. **1** (of a liquid) fall slowly in drops or a thin stream. **2** let saliva run from the mouth. **3** (in sport) take the

Thesaurus

lem, snag, difficulty, trouble, flaw, hitch, fly in the ointment, stumbling block, handicap, obstacle, impediment, hindrance, barrier, hurdle, deterrent, nuisance, defect. ■ OPPOSITES benefit.

drawing n. PICTURE, sketch, illustration, portrayal, representation, depiction, composition, study, outline, diagram.

dread n. FEAR, fearfulness, terror, alarm, nervousness, uneasiness, anxiety, apprehension, trepidation, horror, concern, foreboding, dismay, perturbation; informal blue funk, the heebie-jeebies. ▶ v. FEAR, be afraid of, be terrified by, worry about, have forebodings about, shrink from, flinch from; informal have cold feet about.

dreadful adj. **1** TERRIBLE, horrible, frightful, awful, dire, frightening, terrifying, distressing, alarming, shocking, appalling, harrowing, ghastly, fearful, hideous, gruesome, horrendous, calamitous, grievous. **2** NASTY, unpleasant, disagreeable, repugnant, distasteful, odious. ■ OPPOSITES pleasant, agreeable.

dream n. **1** VISION, nightmare, hallucination, fantasy, daydream, reverie, illusion, delusion. **2** AMBITION, aspiration, goal, design, plan, aim, hope, desire, wish, daydream, fantasy. ▶ v. **1** DAY-DREAM, be in a reverie, be in a trance, be lost in thought, muse, be preoccupied. **2** THINK, consider, conceive, suppose, visualize. □ **dream up** THINK UP, invent, concoct, devise, create, hatch; informal cook up.

dreamy adj. DREAMLIKE, vague, dim, hazy, shadowy, misty, faint, indistinct, unclear.

dreary adj. DULL, drab, uninteresting, colourless, lifeless, dry, flat, tedious, boring, humdrum, monotonous, wearisome, routine, unvaried. ■ OPPOSITES interesting.

drench v. SOAK, drown, saturate, flood, inundate, steep, permeate, douse, souse, wet, slosh.

dress n. **1** FROCK, gown, garment, robe. **2** CLOTHES, garments, attire, costume, outfit, ensemble, garb; informal get-up, ball forward with slight touches. ▶n. a thin stream of liquid.

dried past & past part. of **DRY**.

drier var. of **DRYER**.

drift v. **1** be carried slowly by a current of air or water. **2** go slowly or aimlessly. ▶n. **1** a drifting movement. **2** the general meaning of someone's remarks. **3** a mass of snow piled up by the wind. □ **driftwood** pieces of wood floating on the sea or washed ashore.

drifter n. a person who moves aimlessly from place to place.

drill n. **1** a tool or machine for boring holes. **2** training or instruction by means of repeated exercises. **3** (**the drill**) informal the correct procedure. **4** a strong twilled cotton fabric. ▶v. **1** bore a hole with a drill. **2** give training or instruction to.

drily (or **dryly**) adv. in a humorously ironic way.

drink v. (**drinking**, **drank**; past part. **drunk**) **1** swallow liquid. **2** consume alcohol. ▶n. **1** a liquid for drinking. **2** alcohol. ■ **drinker** n.

drip v. (**dripping**, **dripped**) fall or let fall in small drops. ▶n. **1** a small drop of a liquid. **2** an apparatus for slowly passing a substance into a patient's body through a vein. **3** informal an ineffectual person. □ **drip-dry** (of a garment) able to dry without creases if hung up when wet.

dripping n. fat melted from roasting meat.

drive v. (**driving**, **drove**; past part. **driven**) **1** operate a vehicle. **2** carry in a vehicle. **3** carry or urge along. **4** compel to do something. **5** provide the energy to keep a machine in motion. ▶n. **1** a car journey. **2** a short private road leading to a house. **3** an inborn desire. **4** an organized effort to achieve something. **5** determination. ■ **driver** n.

drivel n. nonsense.

drizzle n. light rain falling in fine drops. ▶v. rain lightly.

droll adj. strange and amusing.

dromedary n. (pl. **dromedaries**) an Arabian camel, with one hump.

drone v. **1** make a low humming sound. **2** (**drone on**) speak tediously and at length. ▶n. **1** a low humming sound. **2** a male bee.

drool v. **1** let saliva dribble. **2** informal show great pleasure or desire.

droop v. bend or hang down limply. ■ **droopy** adj.

drop v. (**dropping**, **dropped**) **1** fall or let fall. **2** sink to the ground. **3** make or become lower or less. **4** give up a course of action. **5** set down a passenger or load. ▶n. **1** a small rounded mass of liquid. **2** a small amount of liquid. **3** an act of dropping. **4** an abrupt fall or slope. □ **drop by/in** pay a casual visit. **drop kick** (in rugby) a kick made by dropping a ball and kicking it as it bounces. **drop off** fall asleep. **dropout** a person who has dropped out of a course of study. **drop out** stop partici-

Thesaurus

togs, duds. ▶v. **1** CLOTHE, attire, garb, fit out, turn out, robe, accoutre; old use apparel. **2** BANDAGE, bind up, cover. ■ OPPOSITES undress.

dribble v. **1** DROOL, slaver, slobber; Sc. slabber. **2** DRIP, trickle, leak, run, ooze, seep, exude.

drift v. **1** BE CARRIED ALONG, float, coast, be borne, be wafted. **2** WANDER, roam, rove, meander, stray. **3** PILE UP, accumulate, gather, form heaps, bank up, amass. ▶n. **1** GIST, essence, substance, meaning, significance, import, purport, tenor. **2** PILE, heap, bank, mound, mass, accumulation.

drill v. **1** TRAIN, instruct, coach, teach, exercise, rehearse, ground, inculcate, discipline; informal put someone through their paces. **2** BORE A HOLE IN, pierce, penetrate, puncture, perforate. ▶n. **1** TRAINING, instruction, coaching, teaching, indoctrination. **2** PROCEDURE, routine, practice.

drink v. **1** SWALLOW, sip, gulp down, drain, guzzle, imbibe, quaff, partake of; informal swig, swill, toss off. **2** TAKE ALCOHOL, indulge, imbibe, tipple; informal booze, take a drop, hit the bottle, knock back a few. ▶n. **1** SWALLOW, gulp, sip, draught; informal swill, swig. **2** ALCOHOL, liquor, spirits; informal booze, the hard stuff, hooch.

drip v. DRIBBLE, trickle, drizzle, leak, ooze, splash, sprinkle; informal plop. ▶n. DROP, dribble, splash, trickle, leak, bead.

drive v. **1** OPERATE, steer, handle, guide, direct, manage. **2** MOVE, herd, get going, urge, press, impel, push, round up. **3** FORCE, make, compel, coerce, oblige, impel, pressure, goad, spur, prod. **4** HAMMER, thrust, ram, strike, bang, sink, plunge. ▶n. **1** TRIP, run, outing, journey, jaunt, tour, excursion; informal spin, joyride. **2** ENERGY, determination, enthusiasm, industry, vigour, push, motivation, persistence, keenness, enpating in something.

droplet n. a very small drop of a liquid.

dropper n. a glass tube for measuring out liquid.

droppings pl. n. animal dung.

dropsy n. dated oedema.

dross n. rubbish.

drought /drowt/ n. a very long period of little or no rainfall.

drove past of DRIVE. ▶ n. **1** a flock of animals being driven. **2** a large number of people.

drown v. **1** die or kill through submersion in water. **2** make inaudible by being much louder.

drowsy adj. sleepy. ■ **drowsily** adv. **drowsiness** n.

drubbing n. informal a thorough defeat.

drudge n. a person made to do hard, menial, or dull work. ■ **drudgery** n.

drug n. **1** a substance used as a medicine. **2** an illegal substance taken for its stimulating or other effects. ▶ v. (**drugging**, **drugged**) give or add a drug to. □ **drugstore** US a pharmacy also selling toiletries etc.

Druid n. a priest in the ancient Celtic religion.

drum n. **1** a percussion instrument with a skin stretched across a frame, sounded by being struck. **2** a cylindrical container or part. ▶ v. (**drumming**, **drummed**) **1** play on a drum. **2** make a continuous rhythmic noise. **3** (**drum into**) teach by constant repetition. **4** (**drum up**) try to get support or business. □ **drumstick 1** a stick used for beating a drum. **2** the lower part of a cooked chicken's leg. ■ **drummer** n.

drunk past part. of DRINK. ▶ adj. strongly affected by alcohol. ▶ n. (also **drunkard**) a person who is drunk or often drunk. ■ **drunkenly** adv. **drunkenness** n.

dry adj. (**drier**, **driest**) **1** free from moisture or liquid. **2** serious and boring. **3** (of humour) subtle and understated. **4** (of wine) not sweet. ▶ v. (**drying**, **dried**) **1** make or become dry. **2** preserve by evaporating the moisture from. **3** (**dry up**) (of a supply) decrease and stop. □ **dry-clean** clean a garment with a chemical. **dry ice** white mist produced from solid carbon dioxide, used as a theatrical effect. **dry rot** a fungus causing wood decay. **dry run** informal a rehearsal. ■ **dryness** n.

dryad n. a wood nymph.

Thesaurus

terprise, initiative, aggressiveness, zeal, verve; *informal* get-up-and-go, pizzazz, zip. **3** CAMPAIGN, effort, crusade, push.

drop v. **1** FALL, descend, plunge, dive, plummet, tumble, dip, sink, subside, swoop. **2** DECREASE, fall, lessen, diminish, dwindle, sink, plunge, plummet. **3** LEAVE, finish with, desert, abandon, jilt, reject, discard, renounce, disown; *informal* ditch, chuck, run out on. **4** FALL DOWN, collapse, faint, swoon, drop/fall dead. ■ OPPOSITES rise, increase. ▶ n. **1** DROPLET, globule, bead, bubble, blob, spheroid, oval. **2** BIT, dash, trace, pinch, dab, speck, modicum, dribble, splash, trickle, sprinkle. **3** DECREASE, fall, decline, reduction, cut, lowering, depreciation, slump. **4** INCLINE, slope, descent, declivity, plunge, abyss, chasm, precipice, cliff.

drown v. **1** FLOOD, submerge, inundate, deluge, swamp, engulf, drench. **2** BE LOUDER THAN, muffle, overpower, overwhelm, stifle.

drowsy adj. SLEEPY, tired, lethargic, weary, dozy, dozing, sluggish, somnolent, heavy-eyed; *informal* dopey. ■ OPPOSITES alert.

drug n. **1** MEDICINE, medication, medicament, remedy, cure, panacea; *informal* magic bullet; *dated* physic. **2** NARCOTIC, opiate; *informal* dope, junk. ▶ v. ANAESTHETIZE, tranquillize, sedate, knock out, render unconscious, stupefy, poison, narcotize, befuddle; *informal* dope.

drum v. TAP, beat, rap, knock, tattoo, strike, thrum.

drunk adj. INTOXICATED, inebriated, blind drunk, the worse for drink, under the influence, befuddled, merry, tipsy, incapable, tight; *informal* tiddly, squiffy, plastered, smashed, paralytic, sloshed, blotto, sozzled, drunk as a lord, pie-eyed, three sheets to the wind, well oiled, stewed, pickled, tanked up, steaming, out of it, one over the eight, canned, tired and emotional, legless, bevvied. ■ OPPOSITES sober. ▶ n. DRUNKARD, heavy drinker, alcoholic, dipsomaniac, inebriate; *informal* soak, boozer, alky, lush, wino.

dry adj. **1** ARID, parched, dehydrated, scorched, waterless, moistureless, desiccated, withered, shrivelled, wizened, rainless, torrid, barren, unproductive, sterile. **2** DULL, uninteresting, boring, tedious, dreary, monotonous, tiresome, wearisome, flat, unimaginative, prosaic, humdrum. **3** COOL, cold, indifferent,

dryer (or **drier**) n. a machine or device for drying something.

dryly var. of **DRILY**.

dual adj. consisting of two parts. □ **dual carriageway** a road with two or more lanes in each direction. ■ **duality** n.

dub v. (**dubbing**, **dubbed**) **1** give an unofficial name or nickname to. **2** confer a knighthood on. **3** provide a film with a soundtrack in a different language from the original. ■ **duality** n.

dubbin n. prepared grease for softening and waterproofing leather.

dubiety n. doubt or uncertainty.

dubious adj. **1** hesitating or doubting. **2** not reliable or of certain quality. ■ **dubiously** adv.

ducal adj. of a duke.

ducat /duk-uht/ n. a former European gold coin.

duchess n. **1** a duke's wife or widow. **2** a woman holding a rank equivalent to duke.

duchy n. (pl. **duchies**) the territory of a duke or duchess.

duck n. (pl. **duck** or **ducks**) **1** a waterbird with a broad bill and webbed feet. **2** a female duck. **3** a cricket batsman's score of nought. **4** a quick lowering of the head. ▶ v. **1** lower oneself quickly to avoid being hit or seen. **2** push someone under water. **3** informal avoid a duty. □ **duckboards** wooden slats forming a path over mud etc. **duckling** a young duck.

duct n. **1** a tube or passageway for air, cables, etc. **2** a tube in the body through which fluid passes.

ductile adj. (of a metal) able to be drawn out into a thin wire. ■ **ductility** n.

dud n. informal a thing that fails to work properly.

dude n. US informal a man.

dudgeon n. (**in high dudgeon**) angry or resentful.

due adj. **1** expected at a certain time. **2** needing to be paid; owing. **3** owed or deserving something. ▶ n. **1** (**one's due/dues**) what is owed to or deserved by one. **2** (**dues**) fees. ▶ adv. directly: *due south.* □ **due to 1** caused by. **2** because of.

duel n. hist. **1** a fight between two people to settle a point of honour. **2** a contest between two parties. ▶ v. (**duelling**, **duelled**; US **dueling**, **dueled**) fight a duel.

duet n. a musical composition for two performers.

duff informal adj. worthless or false. ▶ v. (**duff up**) beat up.

duffel coat n. a heavy woollen hooded coat.

duffer n. informal an incompetent or stupid person.

dug past & past part. of **DIG**. ▶ n. an udder or teat.

dugong n. an Asian sea mammal.

dugout n. a low or underground shelter.

duke n. **1** the highest rank of nobleman in Britain and certain other countries. **2** hist. a male ruler of a small independent state. ■ **dukedom** n.

dulcet adj. (of a sound) sweet and soothing.

dulcimer n. a musical instrument with strings struck with hand-held hammers.

dull adj. **1** lacking interest. **2** lacking brightness. **3** slow to understand. ▶ v. make or become dull. ■ **dullness** n. **dully** adv.

dullard n. a stupid person.

duly adv. as is required or expected.

Thesaurus

aloof, unemotional, remote, impersonal. ■ OPPOSITES wet. ▶ v. **1** DRY UP, mop, blot, towel, drain. **2** MAKE DRY, dry up, parch, scorch, dehydrate, sear, desiccate, wither, wilt, shrivel, mummify.

dub v. CALL, name, christen, designate, term, entitle, style, label, tag, nickname, denominate, nominate.

dubious adj. **1** DOUBTFUL, uncertain, unsure, hesitant, undecided, wavering, vacillating, irresolute, suspicious, sceptical; informal iffy. **2** SUSPICIOUS, questionable, suspect, untrustworthy, unreliable, undependable; informal shady, fishy, iffy. ■ OPPOSITES certain, trustworthy.

duck v. **1** BEND, bob down, crouch, stoop, squat, hunch down, hunker down. **2** IM-

MERSE, submerge, dip, plunge, douse, souse, dunk.

duct n. PIPE, tube, conduit, channel, passage, canal, culvert.

due adj. **1** OWING, owed, payable, outstanding, receivable. **2** DESERVED, merited, earned, justified, appropriate, fitting, suitable, right. **3** PROPER, correct, rightful, fitting, appropriate, apt, adequate, ample, satisfactory, requisite, apposite.

dull adj. **1** DRAB, dreary, sombre, dark, subdued, muted, toned down, lacklustre, lustreless, faded, washed out. **2** OVERCAST, cloudy, gloomy, dismal, dreary, dark, leaden, murky, sunless, lowering. **3** UNINTERESTING, boring, tedi-

dumb adj. **1** offens. unable to speak. **2** silent. **3** US informal stupid. ▶v. (**dumb down**) informal make less intellectually challenging. □ **dumb-bell** a short bar with weighted ends, used for exercise. **dumbfound** astonish greatly.

dumdum n. a soft-nosed bullet that expands on impact.

dummy n. (pl. **dummies**) **1** a model of a human being. **2** a model of something used as a substitute. **3** a plastic teat for a baby to suck on. **4** informal a stupid person. □ **dummy run** a practice or trial.

dump n. **1** a site for depositing rubbish or waste. **2** informal an unpleasant or dull place. **3** a temporary store of weapons or provisions. ▶v. **1** deposit as rubbish. **2** put down carelessly. □ **down in the dumps** informal unhappy.

dumpling n. a ball of dough cooked in a stew.

dumpy adj. short and stout.

dun n. a greyish-brown colour.

dunce n. a person slow at learning.

dune n. a mound of drifted sand.

dung n. animal excrement.

dungarees pl. n. a garment consisting of trousers held up by shoulder straps.

dungeon n. an underground prison cell.

dunk v. dip food into a drink or soup before eating it.

duo n. (pl. **duos**) **1** a pair of people or things. **2** a duet.

duodecimal adj. (of a counting system) having twelve as a base.

duodenum /dyoo-uh-**dee**-nuhm/ n. (pl. duodenums or duodena) the part of the small intestine next to the stomach. ■ **duodenal** adj.

dupe v. deceive or trick. ▶n. a duped person.

duple adj. (of rhythm) having two main beats to the bar.

duplex n. US a building divided into two flats.

duplicate adj. **1** exactly like something else. **2** having two corresponding parts. **3** double. ▶n. an exact copy. ▶v. **1** make or be an exact copy of. **2** multiply by two. **3** do again unnecessarily. ■ **duplication** n. **duplicator** n.

duplicity n. deceitfulness. ■ **duplicitous** adj.

durable adj. **1** hard-wearing. **2** (of goods) able to be kept. ■ **durability** n.

duration n. the time during which something continues.

duress n. threats or violence used to force a person to do something.

during prep. **1** throughout. **2** at a point in the course of.

dusk n. the darker stage of twilight.

dusky adj. darkish in colour.

dust n. fine, dry particles of earth or other matter. ▶v. **1** remove dust from the surface of. **2** cover lightly with a powdered substance. □ **dustbin** a large container for household rubbish. **dustman** a man employed to remove household rubbish from dustbins. **dustpan** a container into which dust and waste can be swept. ■ **dusty** adj.

Thesaurus

ous, tiresome, wearisome, dry, monotonous, flat, bland, unimaginative, humdrum, prosaic, vapid. **4** MUTED, muffled, indistinct, feeble, deadened. ■ OPPOSITES bright, interesting.

dumbfound v. ASTOUND, amaze, astonish, startle, surprise, stun, stagger, take aback, bewilder, overwhelm, confound, baffle, confuse, disconcert; informal throw, knock sideways, knock for six.

dummy n. **1** MODEL, mannequin, figure, doll. **2** COPY, reproduction, imitation, representation, sample, substitute, counterfeit, sham. **3** see IDIOT.

dump v. **1** DISPOSE OF, get rid of, discard, throw away/out, scrap, jettison. **2** LEAVE, abandon, desert, walk out on, forsake; informal leave in the lurch. ▶n. **1** TIP, rubbish dump, scrapyard, junkyard. **2** PIGSTY, hovel, slum, shack; informal hole.

dunce n. FOOL, dolt, idiot, ass, ignoramus, imbecile, simpleton; informal

chump, booby, nincompoop, ninny, dunderhead, blockhead, fathead, halfwit, cretin, moron, dummy, numbskull, dimwit, twerp, clot, twit, nitwit.

duplicate n. **1** REPLICA, copy, reproduction, likeness, twin, double, clone, match; informal lookalike, spitting image, dead ringer. **2** COPY, carbon copy, photocopy; trademark photostat, Xerox. ▶adj. MATCHING, twin, identical, corresponding, second, paired. ▶v. **1** COPY, photocopy, reproduce, replicate, clone, photostat, xerox. **2** REPEAT, do again, replicate, perform again.

duplicity n. DECEITFULNESS, doubledealing, dishonesty, two-facedness, trickery, guile, chicanery, artifice.

durable adj. **1** LONG-LASTING, hardwearing, strong, sturdy, tough, resistant, imperishable. **2** LASTING, longlasting, enduring, persistent, abiding, continuing, stable, constant, firm, permanent, unchanging, dependable, reli-

duster n. a cloth for dusting furniture.

Dutch adj. of the Netherlands or its language. ► n. the language of the Netherlands. □ **Dutch courage** confidence gained from drinking alcohol. **go Dutch** share the costs of an outing equally.

dutiable adj. on which customs or other duties must be paid.

dutiful adj. obedient and conscientious. ■ **dutifully** adv.

duty n. (pl. **duties**) **1** a moral or legal obligation. **2** a task required as part of one's job. **3** a tax on the import, export, or sale of goods. □ **on** (or **off**) **duty** engaged (or not engaged) in one's regular work.

duvet /doo-vay/ n. a thick quilt used instead of a top sheet and blankets.

DVD abbrev. digital versatile disc.

dwarf n. (pl. **dwarfs** or **dwarves**) **1** a mythical short human-like being. **2** an abnormally small person. ► v. cause to seem small in comparison.

dwell v. (**dwelling, dwelt** or **dwelled**) **1** live in or at a place. **2** (**dwell on**) think, speak, or write at length about.

dwelling n. a house or other place of residence.

dwindle v. gradually lessen or fade.

dye n. a substance used to colour something. ► v. colour with dye.

dying pres. part. of DIE.

dyke (or **dike**) n. **1** a barrier built to prevent flooding from the sea. **2** a drainage ditch.

dynamic adj. **1** constantly changing or active. **2** full of energy and new ideas. **3** Physics of forces producing motion. ■ **dynamically** adv.

dynamics n. **1** the study of the forces involved in movement. **2** forces which stimulate growth or change. **3** the variations in volume in a musical performance.

dynamism n. the quality of being dynamic.

dynamite n. a high explosive made of nitroglycerine.

dynamo n. (pl. **dynamos**) a machine for converting mechanical energy into electrical energy.

dynasty n. (pl. **dynasties**) a succession of related rulers etc. ■ **dynastic** adj.

dysentery n. a disease causing severe diarrhoea.

dysfunctional adj. **1** not operating properly. **2** unable to deal with normal social relations. ■ **dysfunction** n.

dyslexia n. a condition involving difficulty in reading and spelling. ■ **dyslexic** adj. & n.

dyspepsia n. indigestion. ■ **dyspeptic** adj.

Thesaurus

able. ■ OPPOSITES flimsy, ephemeral.

dusk n. TWILIGHT, sunset, sundown, nightfall, evening, dark.

dust n. **1** DIRT, grime, powder, soot. **2** EARTH, soil, clay, ground, dirt.

dusty adj. **1** DUST-COVERED, dirty, grimy, grubby, unclean, sooty, undusted. **2** POWDERY, chalky, crumbly, sandy, fine, friable.

dutiful adj. CONSCIENTIOUS, obedient, submissive, compliant, deferential, respectful, filial, reverent, reverential, devoted, considerate, thoughtful, pliant, docile. ■ OPPOSITES disrespectful, remiss.

duty n. **1** RESPONSIBILITY, obligation, service, loyalty, allegiance, obedience, faithfulness, respect, deference, fidelity, homage. **2** TASK, job, assignment, requirement, responsibility, obligation,

mission, commission, function, office, charge, role, burden, onus. **3** TAX, levy, tariff, excise, toll, fee, impost.

dwarf v. TOWER OVER, overshadow, dominate, stand head and shoulders above, diminish, minimize.

dwell v. LIVE, reside, stay, lodge, abide; *informal* hang out.

dwindle v. BECOME/GROW LESS, diminish, decrease, lessen, shrink, contract, fade, wane. ■ OPPOSITES increase, grow.

dye n. COLOUR, shade, tint, hue. ► v. COLOUR, tint, stain, pigment, shade.

dynamic adj. ENERGETIC, active, lively, spirited, aggressive, pushy, enthusiastic, driving, eager, motivated, zealous, alive, vigorous, strong, forceful, powerful, high-powered, potent, vital, effective; *informal* go-ahead, go-getting, zippy, peppy.

Ee

E abbrev. **1** East or Eastern. **2** informal the drug Ecstasy. □ **E-number** a code number given to food additives.

each adj. & pron. every one of two or more, regarded separately. ▶ adv. to, for, or by every one of a group.

eager adj. strongly wanting to do or have. ■ **eagerly** adv. **eagerness** n.

eagle n. a large, keen-sighted bird of prey.

ear n. **1** the organ of hearing. **2** an ability to distinguish sounds accurately. **3** the seed-bearing part of corn. □ **eardrum** a membrane in the ear which vibrates in response to sound waves. **earmark** choose for a particular purpose. **earphone** an electrical device worn on the ear to receive communications or listen to a radio. **earring** a piece of jewellery worn on the ear. **earshot** the distance over which one can hear or be heard. **earwig** a small insect with pincers at its rear end.

earl n. a British nobleman between a viscount and a marquess. ■ **earldom** n.

early adj. (**earlier**, **earliest**) & adv. **1** before the usual or expected time. **2** near the beginning of a period or sequence.

earn v. **1** get or deserve in return for work or merit. **2** (of money invested) gain as interest. ■ **earner** n. **earnings** pl. n.

earnest adj. very serious. □ **in earnest** with sincere intent. ■ **earnestly** adv.

earth n. **1** (also **Earth**) the planet we live on. **2** soil. **3** electrical connection to the ground. **4** a fox's den. ▶ v. connect an electrical device to earth. □ **earthquake** a sudden violent movement in the earth's crust. **earthwork** a large defensive bank of soil. **earthworm** a worm that burrows in the soil.

earthen adj. made of earth or of fired clay. □ **earthenware** pottery made of fired clay.

earthly adj. **1** of the earth or human life on the earth. **2** informal used for emphasis: *no earthly reason.*

earthy adj. **1** like soil. **2** direct and unembarrassed about sexual subjects etc.

ease n. **1** absence of difficulty or effort. **2** freedom from anxiety or pain. ▶ v. **1** make or become less severe or intense. **2** move carefully or gradually.

Thesaurus

eager adj. **1** KEEN, enthusiastic, avid, fervent, impatient, zealous, passionate, wholehearted, earnest, diligent, ambitious, enterprising; *informal* bright-eyed and bushy-tailed, raring to go. **2** LONGING, yearning, anxious, intent, agog, wishing, desirous, hopeful, thirsty, hungry, greedy; *informal* dying, itching, hot. ■ OPPOSITES indifferent, apathetic.

early adv. **1** AHEAD OF TIME, too soon, beforehand, before the appointed time, prematurely. **2** IN GOOD TIME, ahead of schedule, before the appointed time. ■ OPPOSITES late. ▶ adj. **1** ADVANCED, forward, premature, untimely, precocious. **2** PRIMITIVE, primeval, prehistoric, primordial. ■ OPPOSITES overdue.

earn v. **1** GET, make, receive, obtain, draw, clear, collect, bring in, take home, gross, net; *informal* pull in, pocket. **2** GAIN, win, attain, merit, achieve, rate, secure, obtain, deserve, be entitled to, be worthy of, warrant.

earnest adj. **1** SERIOUS, solemn, grave, intense, thoughtful, studious, staid, diligent, steady, hard-working, committed, dedicated, assiduous, keen, zealous. **2** SINCERE, fervent, intense, ardent, passionate, heartfelt, wholehearted, enthusiastic, urgent, zealous, fervid, warm. ■ OPPOSITES flippant.

earnings pl. n. INCOME, salary, wage, pay, remuneration, fee, stipend, emolument, honorarium.

earth n. SOIL, clay, loam, turf, clod, dirt, sod, ground.

earthly adj. **1** WORLDLY, temporal, secular, mortal, human, material, materialistic, non-spiritual, mundane, carnal, fleshly, physical, corporeal, gross, sensual, base, sordid, vile, profane. **2** POSSIBLE, feasible, conceivable, imaginable, likely. ■ OPPOSITES spiritual.

earthy adj. **1** UNSOPHISTICATED, down-to-earth, unrefined, homely, simple, plain, unpretentious, natural, uninhibited, rough, robust. **2** CRUDE, bawdy, coarse, ribald, indecent, obscene, indecorous;

easel n. a frame on legs for holding an artist's work.

easement n. a right of way over another's property.

east n. **1** the direction in which the sun rises. **2** the eastern part of a place. ▶ adj. **1** lying towards or facing the east. **2** (of a wind) from the east. ▶ adv. towards the east. ■ **easterly** adj. & adv. **eastward** adj. & adv. **eastwards** adv.

Easter n. the Christian festival celebrating the resurrection of Jesus.

eastern adj. situated in or facing the east.

easterner n. a person from the east of a region.

easy adj. (**easier**, **easiest**) **1** achieved without great effort. **2** free from worry or problems. **3** relaxed and not awkward. □ **easy chair** a large, comfortable chair. **easy-going** relaxed and open-minded. ■ **easily** adv.

eat v. (**eating**, **ate**; past part. **eaten**) **1** chew and swallow food. **2** have a meal. **3** (**eat away**) erode or destroy. **4** (**eat up**) use up resources. ■ **eatable** adj. **eater** n.

eau de cologne /oh duh kuh-**lohn**/ = COLOGNE.

eaves pl. n. the overhanging edge of a roof.

eavesdrop v. (**eavesdropping**, **eavesdropped**) secretly listen to a conversation. ■ **eavesdropper** n.

ebb n. the movement of the tide out to sea. ▶ v. **1** (of the sea) move away from the land. **2** gradually lessen. □ **at a low ebb** in a poor or unhappy state.

ebony n. **1** heavy dark wood from a tropical tree. **2** a deep black colour.

ebullient adj. cheerful and full of energy. ■ **ebullience** n.

EC abbrev. European Community.

eccentric adj. **1** unconventional and strange. **2** not concentric. ▶ n. an eccentric person. ■ **eccentrically** adv. **eccentricity** n.

ecclesiastical adj. of the Christian Church or its clergy.

ECG abbrev. electrocardiogram.

echelon /esh-uh-lon/ n. a level in an organization, profession, etc.

echo n. (pl. **echoes**) **1** a repetition of sound caused by the reflection of sound waves. **2** a reflected radio or radar beam. ▶ v. **1** (of a sound) reverberate or be repeated as an echo. **2** have a continued significance. **3** repeat someone's

Thesaurus

informal blue.

ease n. **1** EFFORTLESSNESS, no difficulty, simplicity, deftness, proficiency, facility, adroitness, dexterity, mastery. **2** COMFORT, contentment, enjoyment, content, affluence, wealth, prosperity, luxury, opulence. **3** PEACE, peacefulness, calmness, tranquillity, composure, serenity, restfulness, quiet, security. ■ OPPOSITES difficulty. ▶ v. **1** LESSEN, mitigate, reduce, lighten, diminish, moderate, ameliorate, relieve, assuage, allay, soothe, palliate, appease. **2** GUIDE, manoeuvre, edge, inch, steer, glide, slip. **3** COMFORT, console, soothe, solace, calm, quieten, pacify. ■ OPPOSITES aggravate.

easy adj. **1** SIMPLE, uncomplicated, straightforward, undemanding, effortless, painless, trouble-free, facile; informal idiot-proof. **2** NATURAL, casual, informal, unceremonious, easy-going, amiable, unconcerned, affable, carefree, nonchalant, composed, urbane, insouciant, suave; informal laid-back. **3** UNTROUBLED, unworried, relaxed, at ease, calm, tranquil, composed, serene, comfortable, contented, secure. **4** MODERATE, steady, regular, undemanding, leisurely, unhurried. ■ OPPOSITES difficult, formal,

uneasy.

easy-going adj. EVEN-TEMPERED, relaxed, carefree, happy-go-lucky, placid, serene, nonchalant, insouciant, tolerant, undemanding, amiable, patient, understanding, imperturbable; informal laid-back, together. ■ OPPOSITES intolerant.

eat v. CONSUME, devour, swallow, chew, munch, gulp down, bolt, wolf, ingest; informal tuck into, put away, scoff. □ **eat away** ERODE, wear away, corrode, gnaw away, dissolve, waste away, rot, decay, destroy.

eavesdrop v. LISTEN IN, spy, monitor, tap, wire-tap, overhear; informal bug, snoop.

ebb v. **1** GO OUT, flow back, retreat, fall back, draw back, recede, abate, subside. **2** see DECLINE.

ebullience n. EXUBERANCE, buoyancy, high spirits, exhilaration, elation, euphoria, high-spiritedness, jubilation, animation, sparkle, vivacity, zest, irrepressibility.

eccentric adj. ODD, strange, queer, peculiar, unconventional, idiosyncratic, quirky, bizarre, weird, outlandish, irregular, uncommon, abnormal, freakish, aberrant, anomalous, capricious, whimsical; informal offbeat, way-out, words.

eclair /i-**klair**/ n. a long cake of choux pastry filled with cream.

eclectic adj. deriving ideas or style from a wide range of sources.

eclipse n. **1** an occasion when one planet, the moon, etc. blocks out the light from another. **2** a sudden loss of significance or power. ▶ v. **1** (of a planet etc.) block the light from or to another. **2** deprive of significance or power.

ecliptic n. the sun's apparent path.

eclogue n. a short pastoral poem.

eco-friendly adj. not harmful to the environment.

E. coli /ee koh-ly/ n. a bacterium which can cause severe food poisoning.

ecology n. the study of the relationships of living things to one another and to their surroundings. ■ **ecological** adj. **ecologist** n.

economic adj. **1** of economics or the economy. **2** profitable.

economical adj. **1** giving good value in relation to resources used or money spent. **2** careful in the use of resources etc. ■ **economically** adv.

economics n. the branch of knowledge concerned with the production, consumption, and transfer of wealth. ■ **economist** n.

economize (or **-ise**) v. spend less.

economy n. (pl. **economies**) **1** the state of a country in terms of the production and consumption of goods and services and the supply of money. **2** careful

management of resources.

ecosystem n. a biological community of interacting living things and their environment.

ecru n. a light beige colour.

ecstasy n. (pl. **ecstasies**) **1** intense happiness. **2** (**Ecstasy**) a hallucinogenic drug. ■ **ecstatic** adj. **ecstatically** adv.

> ☑ No x: -cs- at the beginning and s at the end: ecstasy.

ectopic pregnancy n. a pregnancy in which the fetus develops outside the womb.

ecumenical adj. representing or promoting unity among the different Christian Churches.

eczema /eks-i-muh/ n. a condition causing dry, itchy patches on the skin.

eddy n. (pl. **eddies**) a circular movement of water or air. ▶ v. (**eddying**, **eddied**) move in eddies.

edelweiss /ay-duhl-vyss/ n. an alpine plant.

edema US = OEDEMA.

edge n. **1** the outside limit of an object or area. **2** the sharpened side of a blade. **3** a slight advantage. **4** a sharp or exciting quality. ▶ v. **1** provide with an edge or border. **2** move gradually and carefully. □ **edgeways** (or **edgewise**) with the edge uppermost or towards the viewer. **on edge** tense or irritable.

edging n. a decorative border.

Thesaurus

dotty, nutty, screwy. ▶ n. CHARACTER, oddity, crank; *informal* queer fish, weirdo, oddball, nut, nutter; *US informal* screwball.

echo v. **1** REVERBERATE, resound, ring, repeat, reflect. **2** COPY, imitate, repeat, reproduce, reiterate, mirror, parrot, reflect, parallel, parody, ape.

eclipse v. **1** BLOCK, cover, blot out, obscure, conceal, cast a shadow over, darken, shade, veil, shroud. **2** OUTSHINE, overshadow, dwarf, put in the shade, surpass, exceed, outstrip, transcend.

economical adj. **1** THRIFTY, sparing, careful, prudent, frugal, scrimping, mean, niggardly, penny-pinching, parsimonious; *informal* stingy, tight. **2** CHEAP, inexpensive, reasonable, low-price, low-cost, budget. ■ OPPOSITES extravagant, expensive.

economize v. BUDGET, cut back, scrimp, save, be economical, be sparing, retrench; *informal* cut corners, tighten one's

belt, draw in one's horns.

economy n. **1** WEALTH, resources, financial state. **2** THRIFTINESS, carefulness, prudence, frugality, thrift, care, restraint, meanness, stinginess, miserliness, niggardliness, parsimony, pennypinching, husbandry, conservation.

ecstasy n. BLISS, delight, rapture, joy, joyousness, happiness, elation, euphoria, jubilation, exultation, transports of delight, rhapsodies; *informal* seventh heaven, cloud nine. ■ OPPOSITES misery.

ecstatic adj. BLISSFUL, enraptured, rapturous, joyful, joyous, overjoyed, jubilant, gleeful, exultant, elated, in transports of delight, delirious, in a frenzy of delight, rhapsodic, orgasmic, transported; *informal* on cloud nine, in seventh heaven, over the moon. ■ OPPOSITES miserable.

eddy n. WHIRL, whirlpool, vortex, maelstrom, swirl, countercurrent. ▶ v. SWIRL,

edgy adj. (**edgier**, **edgiest**) tense or irritable. ■ **edgily** adv. **edginess** n.

edible adj. fit to be eaten.

edict n. an official order.

edifice n. a large, impressive building.

edify v. (**edifying**, **edified**) improve the
mind or character of. ■ **edification** n.

edit v. **1** prepare written material for
publication. **2** prepare material for a
film or broadcast.

edition n. **1** a version of a published
text. **2** all the copies of a book etc. issued at one time.

editor n. **1** a person responsible for the
contents of a newspaper etc. or a section of this. **2** a person who edits.

editorial adj. to do with the editing of
material for publication. ▶ n. a newspaper article giving the editor's opinion.

educate v. give intellectual or moral instruction to; teach. ■ **education** n.
educational adj.

Edwardian adj. of the reign of King
Edward VII (1901–10).

EEC abbrev. European Economic Community.

eel n. a snake-like fish.

eerie adj. (**eerier**, **eeriest**) strange and
frightening. ■ **eerily** adv.

efface v. **1** rub off a mark. **2** (**efface
oneself**) make oneself appear inconspicuous.

effect n. **1** a change produced by an action or other cause; a result. **2** operation or effectiveness. **3** (**effects**) personal belongings. **4** (**effects**) the lighting, sound, or scenery used in a play or
film. ▶ v. make happen or bring about.

✓ Don't confuse **affect** and **effect**:
affect is a verb which chiefly means
'make a difference to'.

effective adj. **1** producing an intended
result. **2** operative. **3** fulfilling a function in fact though not officially. ■ **effectively** adv. **effectiveness** n.

effectual adj. effective. ■ **effectually**
adv.

effeminate adj. (of a man) having characteristics regarded as typical of a
woman. ■ **effeminacy** n.

effervescent adj. **1** fizzy. **2** lively and

Thesaurus

whirl, spin, turn, spiral, circulate.

edge n. **1** BORDER, boundary, side, rim,
margin, fringe, outer limit, extremity,
verge, brink, lip, contour, perimeter,
periphery, parameter, ambit. **2** STING,
bite, sharpness, severity, pointedness,
acerbity, acidity, acrimony, virulence,
trenchancy, pungency. **3** ADVANTAGE,
lead, superiority, upper hand, whip
hand, dominance, ascendancy; *informal*
head start. ▶ v. **1** TRIM, hem, border,
fringe, rim, bind, verge. **2** INCH, creep,
sidle, steal, ease, elbow, worm, work,
sidestep.

edgy adj. NERVOUS, nervy, tense, anxious,
apprehensive, on tenterhooks, uneasy,
irritable, touchy, irascible, tetchy; *informal* twitchy, uptight. ■ OPPOSITES calm.

edit v. REVISE, correct, emend, polish,
check, modify, rewrite, rephrase, prepare, adapt, amend, alter.

edition n. **1** ISSUE, number, version,
printing. **2** PRINTING, impression, publication, issue.

educate v. TEACH, instruct, tutor, coach,
school, train, drill, inform, enlighten,
inculcate, prime, indoctrinate, edify,
cultivate, develop, improve, prepare,
rear, nurture, foster.

educated adj. LITERATE, well read, informed, knowledgeable, learned, en-

lightened, erudite, cultivated, refined,
cultured, schooled. ■ OPPOSITES illiterate, ignorant.

education n. **1** TEACHING, schooling, instruction, tuition, training, tutelage, enlightenment, edification, cultivation,
development, improvement, preparation, indoctrination, drilling. **2** LITER-
ACY, knowledge, scholarship, letters,
cultivation, refinement, culture.

eerie adj. UNCANNY, unearthly, ghostly,
mysterious, strange, weird, unnatural,
frightening, chilling, fearful, spine-
chilling, blood-curdling, spectral; *informal*
spooky, scary, creepy.

effect n. **1** RESULT, outcome, consequence, upshot, repercussion, impact,
aftermath, conclusion, issue, fruit. **2** EF-
FECTIVENESS, success, influence, efficacy,
weight, power. **3** SENSE, meaning, drift,
essence, tenor, significance, import,
purport. ▶ v. BRING ABOUT, carry out, execute, initiate, cause, make, create, produce, perform, achieve, accomplish,
complete, fulfil, implement, actuate.

effective adj. **1** SUCCESSFUL, competent,
productive, capable, able, efficient, useful, efficacious, adequate, active.
2 VALID, in force, in operation, operative, active, effectual. **3** FORCEFUL,
powerful, telling, cogent, compelling,
persuasive, convincing, eloquent.

enthusiastic. ■ **effervesce** v. **efferves-cence** n.

effete adj. **1** no longer effective. **2** (of a man) effeminate.

efficacious adj. effective. ■ **efficacy** n.

efficient adj. working productively with no waste of money or effort. ■ **efficiency** n. **efficiently** adv.

effigy n. (pl. **effigies**) a model of a person.

efflorescence n. a high stage of development.

effluent n. liquid waste or sewage.

effluvium n. (pl. **effluvia**) an unpleasant or harmful smell or discharge.

effort n. **1** a vigorous or determined attempt. **2** strenuous exertion. ■ **effortless** adj.

effrontery n. insolence or impertinence.

effusion n. an outpouring.

effusive adj. expressing pleasure or approval in an unrestrained way. ■ **effusively** n.

e.g. abbrev. for example.

egalitarian adj. believing in the principle of equal rights for all. ▶n. an egalitarian person. ■ **egalitarianism** n.

egg n. **1** an oval or round object laid by a female bird, reptile, etc., and containing a cell which can develop into a new organism. **2** an ovum. ▶v. (**egg on**) urge to do something foolish or risky. □ **egghead** informal a very studious person. **eggplant** US an aubergine. ■ **eggy** adj.

ego n. (pl. **egos**) self-esteem.

egocentric adj. self-centred.

egotism (or **egoism**) n. the quality of being excessively conceited or self-centred. ■ **egotist** n. **egotistic** adj. **egotistical** adj.

egregious /i-gree-juhss/ adj. outstandingly bad.

egress n. **1** the act of going out. **2** a way out.

Egyptology n. the study of the ancient Egyptian culture. ■ **Egyptologist** n.

eider n. a large northern sea duck. □ **eiderdown** a quilt filled with down or other soft material.

eight adj. & n. one more than seven; 8 or VIII. ■ **eighth** adj. & n.

eighteen adj. & n. one more than seventeen; 18 or XVIII. ■ **eighteenth** adj. & n.

eighty adj. & n. (pl. **eighties**) ten less than ninety; 80 or LXXX. ■ **eightieth** adj. & n.

einsteinium n. a radioactive element.

eisteddfod /I-steth-vod/ n. a Welsh festival with music and poetry competitions.

either conj. & adv. **1** as the first of two alternatives specified. **2** indicating a link with a previous statement: *she doesn't like him and I don't either.* ▶adj. & pron. **1** one or the other of two. **2** each of two.

ejaculate v. **1** eject semen. **2** dated say suddenly. ■ **ejaculation** n.

eject v. force or throw out. ■ **ejection** n. **ejector** n.

eke v. (**eke out**) **1** use sparingly. **2** make a living with difficulty.

elaborate adj. with many carefully arranged parts. ▶v. **1** develop in detail. **2** add detail to something said. ■ **elaborately** adv. **elaboration** n.

elan n. energy and flair.

Thesaurus

■ OPPOSITES weak, invalid.

effeminate adj. WOMANISH, unmanly, girlish, effete, weak, camp; informal wimpish, sissy, pansy-like. ■ OPPOSITES manly, virile.

efficient adj. WELL ORGANIZED, organized, capable, competent, effective, productive, proficient, adept, skilful, businesslike, workmanlike. ■ OPPOSITES disorganized, incompetent.

effigy n. IMAGE, likeness, statue, statuette, bust, model, dummy, representation, carving.

effort n. **1** EXERTION, force, power, energy, work, application, muscle, labour, striving, endeavour, toil, struggle, strain, stress; informal elbow grease. **2** ATTEMPT, try, endeavour; informal go, shot, crack, stab. **3** ACHIEVEMENT, accomplishment, attainment, creation, result, production, feat, deed, opus.

effrontery n. IMPERTINENCE, insolence, impudence, cheek, audacity, temerity, presumption, gall, rashness, bumptiousness; informal nerve, neck, brass neck.

effusive adj. GUSHING, unrestrained, extravagant, fulsome, lavish, enthusiastic, expansive, profuse, demonstrative, exuberant, verbose, wordy, long-winded; informal over the top, OTT.

egotistic, egotistical adj. EGOCENTRIC, self-absorbed, egoistic, narcissistic, conceited, vain, proud, arrogant, self-important, boastful, superior, bragging, self-admiring.

eject v. **1** EMIT, discharge, expel, cast out, exude, excrete, spew out, disgorge, spout, vomit, ejaculate. **2** EVICT, expel, turn out, put out, remove, oust, banish,

elapse v. (of time) pass.

elastic adj. **1** able to return to normal size or shape after being stretched or squeezed. **2** flexible. ▶ n. elastic cord or fabric. ■ **elasticated** adj. **elasticity** n.

elated adj. very happy and excited. ■ **elation** n.

elbow n. the joint between the forearm and the upper arm. ▶ v. strike or push with one's elbow. □ **elbow grease** informal hard physical work, esp. vigorous cleaning. **elbow room** informal enough space to move or work in.

elder adj. of a greater age. ▶ n. **1** a person older than oneself. **2** a senior figure in a community. **3** a shrub with white flowers and small dark berries (**elderberries**).

elderly adj. old.

eldest adj. oldest.

elect v. **1** choose for a public position by voting. **2** choose to do something. ▶ adj. **1** chosen. **2** elected but not yet in office.

election n. **1** a procedure whereby a person is elected. **2** the act of electing.

electioneering n. campaigning to be elected to a political position.

elective adj. **1** of or appointed by election. **2** optional.

elector n. a person entitled to vote in an election. ■ **electoral** adj.

electorate n. the body of electors in a country or area.

electric adj. **1** of, using, or producing electricity. **2** very exciting. ▶ n. (**electrics**) the electric wiring in a house or vehicle. □ **electric chair** a chair for executing convicted criminals by electrocution.

electrical adj. of, using, or producing electricity. ■ **electrically** adv.

electrician n. a person who installs and repairs electrical equipment.

electricity n. **1** a form of energy resulting from the existence of charged particles. **2** the supply of electric current to a building.

electrify v. (**electrifying**, **electrified**) **1** charge with electricity. **2** convert to the use of electrical power. **3** cause great excitement to. ■ **electrification** n.

electrocardiogram n. a record of the electric current produced by heartbeats.

electroconvulsive adj. (of the treatment of mental illness) using electric shocks applied to the brain.

electrocute v. injure or kill by electric shock. ■ **electrocution** n.

electrode n. a conductor through which electricity enters or leaves something.

electrolysis n. **1** the separation of a liquid into its chemical parts by passing an electric current through it. **2** the removal of hair roots by means of an electric current.

electrolyte n. a liquid or gel that an electric current can pass through.

electromagnet n. a metal core made into a magnet by passing electric current through a surrounding coil.

electromagnetic adj. of electric currents and magnetic fields. ■ **electromagnetism** n.

electromotive adj. producing an electric current.

electron n. a subatomic particle with a negative charge found in all atoms. □ **electron microscope** a very powerful microscope, using electron beams instead of light.

electronic adj. **1** having parts such as microchips and transistors that control and direct electric currents. **2** of electrons or electronics. **3** carried out by a computer. ■ **electronically** adv.

electronics n. **1** the study of the behaviour and movement of electrons.

Thesaurus

deport, exile; *informal* kick out, chuck out, turf out, boot out.

elaborate adj. **1** COMPLICATED, detailed, complex, involved, intricate, studied, painstaking, careful. **2** COMPLEX, detailed, ornate, fancy, showy, fussy, ostentatious, extravagant, baroque, rococo. ■ OPPOSITES simple. □ **elaborate on** EXPAND ON, enlarge on, flesh out, amplify, add detail to, expatiate on.

elastic adj. STRETCHY, stretchable, flexible, springy, pliant, pliable, supple, yielding, rubbery, plastic, resilient. ■ OPPOSITES rigid.

elderly adj. OLD, aging, aged, ancient, superannuated, long in the tooth, past one's prime; *Biology* senescent; *informal* getting on, over the hill. ■ OPPOSITES young, youthful.

elect v. VOTE FOR, cast one's vote for, choose by ballot, choose, pick, select, appoint, opt for, plump for, decide on, designate.

election n. BALLOT, poll, vote, referendum, plebiscite, general election.

electric adj. **1** ELECTRICALLY OPERATED, battery-operated, mains-powered. **2** EXCITING, charged, tense, thrilling, stir-

2 electronic circuits or devices.

electroplate v. coat a metal object with another metal using electrolysis.

elegant adj. **1** graceful and stylish. **2** pleasingly clever but simple. ■ **elegance** n. **elegantly** adv.

elegy n. (pl. **elegies**) a sad poem, esp. a lament for a dead person. ■ **elegiac** adj.

element n. **1** a part, esp. a basic one. **2** a substance that cannot be chemically changed or broken down into other substances. **3** earth, water, air, and fire, formerly believed to make up all matter. **4** a trace. **5** (**the elements**) the weather, esp. when bad. **6** a part that gives out heat in an electric device. □ **in one's element** in a situation in which one feels happy or relaxed. ■ **elemental** adj.

elementary adj. of the most basic aspects of a subject.

elephant n. a very large mammal with a trunk and ivory tusks.

elephantine adj. huge.

elevate v. raise to a higher position or level.

elevation n. **1** the act of elevating. **2** height above a given level. **3** one side of a building.

elevator n. US a lift in a building.

eleven adj. & n. one more than ten; 11 or XI. ■ **eleventh** adj. & n.

elevenses pl. n. informal a mid-morning snack.

elf n. (pl. **elves**) an imaginary small being with magic powers.

elfin adj. (of a face etc.) small and delicate.

elicit v. (**eliciting**, **elicited**) draw out a response.

elide v. omit a sound or syllable when speaking. ■ **elision** n.

eligible adj. **1** satisfying the conditions to do or receive something. **2** desirable as a wife or husband. ■ **eligibility** n.

eliminate v. get rid of. ■ **elimination** n.

elite n. a group regarded as superior and favoured.

elitism n. the favouring of or dominance by a selected group. ■ **elitist** adj. & n.

elixir n. a medicinal or magical potion.

Elizabethan adj. of the reign of Queen Elizabeth I (1558–1603).

elk n. a large deer.

ellipse n. a regular oval.

ellipsis n. (pl. **ellipses**) **1** the omission of words in speech or writing. **2** a set of dots indicating this.

elliptical adj. **1** oval. **2** with a word or words omitted.

elm n. a tall deciduous tree with rough leaves.

elocution n. the skill of clear and expressive speech.

elongate v. lengthen.

elope v. run away secretly to get married. ■ **elopement** n.

eloquence n. fluent or persuasive speaking or writing. ■ **eloquent** adj. **eloquently** adv.

else adv. **1** in addition. **2** different; instead. □ **elsewhere** in or to another

Thesaurus

ring, galvanizing, stimulating, jolting.

electrify v. THRILL, excite, startle, arouse, rouse, stimulate, move, stir, animate, fire, charge, invigorate, galvanize.

elegant adj. STYLISH, graceful, tasteful, artistic, fashionable, cultured, beautiful, lovely, charming, exquisite, polished, cultivated, refined, suave, debonair, modish, dignified, luxurious, sumptuous, opulent. ■ OPPOSITES inelegant.

element n. **1** PART, piece, ingredient, factor, feature, component, constituent, segment, unit, member, subdivision, trace, detail, module. **2** ENVIRONMENT, habitat, medium, milieu, sphere, field, domain, realm, circle, resort, haunt.

elementary adj. **1** BASIC, introductory, preparatory, fundamental, rudimentary, primary. **2** EASY, simple, straightforward, uncomplicated, facile, simplistic. ■ OPPOSITES advanced, difficult.

elevate v. **1** RAISE, lift, hoist, hike.

2 PROMOTE, upgrade, advance, prefer, exalt, aggrandize. ■ OPPOSITES lower, demote.

elevated adj. **1** RAISED, upraised, lifted up, aloft, high up. **2** HIGH, great, grand, lofty, dignified, noble, exalted, magnificent, inflated. **3** LOFTY, exalted, inflated, pompous, bombastic, orotund, fustian.

elf n. FAIRY, pixie, sprite, goblin, hobgoblin, imp, puck, troll.

elicit v. BRING OUT, draw out, obtain, extract, extort, exact, wrest, evoke, derive, educe, call forth.

eligible adj. SUITABLE, fitting, fit, appropriate, proper, acceptable, qualified, worthy, authorized, competent, allowed. ■ OPPOSITES ineligible.

elite n. **1** THE BEST, the pick, the cream, the elect. **2** ARISTOCRACY, nobility, gentry, high society, beau monde; informal beautiful people, jet set.

eloquent adj. ARTICULATE, expressive, well spoken, fluent, silver-tongued,

place. **or else** otherwise; if not.
elucidate v. make clear; explain. ■ **elucidation** n.
elude v. **1** cleverly escape from or avoid. **2** fail to be understood by. **3** be unattainable by. ■ **elusive** adj.
elver n. a young eel.
elves pl. of ELF.
emaciated adj. abnormally thin and weak. ■ **emaciation** n.
email n. the sending of electronic messages from one computer user to another. ▶v. send a message by email.
emanate v. (**emanate from**) issue from a source. ■ **emanation** n.
emancipate v. free from legal, social, or political restrictions. ■ **emancipation** n.
emasculate v. make weaker or less effective. ■ **emasculation** n.
embalm v. treat a corpse to preserve it from decay.
embankment n. a wall or bank built to prevent flooding or to carry a road or railway.
embargo n. (pl. **embargoes**) an official ban, esp. on trade with a particular country. ▶v. (**embargoing, embargoed**) put an embargo on.
embark v. **1** board a ship or aircraft. **2** (**embark on**) begin a new course of action. ■ **embarkation** n.
embarrass v. **1** cause to feel awkward

or ashamed. **2** (**be embarrassed**) be in financial difficulties. ■ **embarrassment** n.

....

✓ Two *r*s, two *s*s: emba*rr*a*ss*.

....

embassy n. (pl. **embassies**) the official residence or offices of an ambassador.
embattled adj. **1** surrounded by enemy forces. **2** beset by difficulties.
embed (or **imbed**) v. (**embedding, embedded**) fix firmly in a surrounding mass.
embellish v. **1** decorate. **2** add false or exaggerated details to a story. ■ **embellishment** n.
ember n. a piece of burning wood or coal in a dying fire.
embezzle v. steal money placed in one's trust. ■ **embezzlement** n. **embezzler** n.
embittered adj. bitter or resentful.
emblazon v. conspicuously display a design on something.
emblem n. a design or symbol as a badge of a nation, group, etc.
emblematic adj. representing a particular quality or idea.
embody v. (**embodying, embodied**) **1** give a tangible or visible form to. **2** include. ■ **embodiment** n.
embolden v. make braver.

Thesaurus

....

smooth-tongued, well expressed, vivid, graphic, pithy, persuasive, glib, forceful, effective, plausible. ■ OPPOSITES inarticulate, tongue-tied.
elude v. AVOID, dodge, evade, lose, escape, duck, flee, circumvent; *informal* shake off, give the slip to, throw off the scent, slip away from.
elusive adj. **1** DIFFICULT TO FIND/CATCH, slippery, evasive; *informal* shifty, cagey. **2** EVASIVE, ambiguous, misleading, equivocal, deceptive, baffling, puzzling, fraudulent.
emaciated adj. THIN, skinny, wasted, skeletal, gaunt, anorexic, starved, scrawny, cadaverous, shrunken, haggard, withered, shrivelled, drawn, pinched, wizened, attenuated, atrophied. ■ OPPOSITES fat.
emancipate v. FREE, set free, liberate, release, let loose, deliver, unchain, discharge, unfetter, unshackle, unyoke; *historical* manumit.
emasculate v. WEAKEN, enfeeble, debilitate, erode, undermine, cripple, pull the teeth of; *informal* water down.

embargo n. BAN, bar, prohibition, stoppage, proscription, restriction, restraint, blockage, check, barrier, obstruction, impediment, hindrance.
embarrass v. MAKE UNCOMFORTABLE/AWKWARD, make self-conscious, upset, disconcert, discomfit, discompose, confuse, fluster, agitate, distress, chagrin, shame, humiliate, abash, mortify, discountenance, nonplus; *informal* show up, put one on the spot.
embed v. INSERT, drive in, hammer in, ram in, sink, implant, plant, set/fix in, root.
embellish v. DECORATE, adorn, ornament, dress up, beautify, festoon, enhance, garnish, trim, gild, varnish, embroider, deck, bedeck, emblazon, bespangle; *informal* tart up.
embezzle v. STEAL, rob, thieve, pilfer, misappropriate, pocket, appropriate, purloin, abstract; *informal* filch, put one's hand in the till, rip off; *formal* peculate.
emblazon v. DECORATE, adorn, ornament, embellish, illuminate, colour, paint.

embolism n. obstruction of an artery by a clot or an air bubble.

emboss v. make a raised design on.

embrace v. **1** hold closely in one's arms as a sign of affection. **2** include or contain. **3** accept or support a change etc. willingly. ▶ n. an act of embracing.

embrocation n. a liquid rubbed on the body to relieve aches.

embroider v. **1** sew decorative needlework patterns on. **2** embellish a story. ■ **embroidery** n.

embroil v. involve in a conflict or difficult situation.

embryo n. (pl. **embryos**) an unborn or unhatched baby or animal in the early stages of development. ■ **embryology** n. **embryonic** adj.

emend v. correct and revise a text. ■ **emendation** n.

emerald n. **1** a bright green precious stone. **2** a bright green colour.

emerge v. **1** come out into view. **2** (of facts) become known. **3** survive a difficult period. ■ **emergence** n. **emergent** adj.

emergency n. (pl. **emergencies**) a serious situation requiring immediate action.

emeritus adj. retired but retaining a title as an honour.

emery board n. a strip of wood or card coated with a hard rough substance and used as a nail file.

emetic adj. & n. (a substance) causing vomiting.

emigrate v. leave one's own country in order to settle permanently in another. ■ **emigrant** n. **emigration** n.

émigré /em-i-gray/ n. an emigrant.

eminence n. **1** the quality of being distinguished and respected. **2** an important person.

eminent adj. **1** distinguished. **2** obvious. ■ **eminently** adv.

emir n. a Muslim ruler.

emirate n. the territory of an emir.

emissary n. (pl. **emissaries**) a person sent on a special diplomatic mission.

emit v. (**emitting**, **emitted**) **1** discharge; send out. **2** make a sound. ■ **emission** n.

emollient adj. softening or soothing.

emolument n. a salary or fee.

emotion n. **1** a strong feeling, such as joy or anger. **2** instinctive feeling as contrasted with reasoning.

emotional adj. **1** of the emotions. **2** arousing or showing emotion. ■ **emotionally** adv.

emotive adj. arousing emotion.

empathize (or **-ise**) v. understand and share the feelings of another.

empathy n. the ability to empathize.

emperor n. the male ruler of an empire.

emphasis n. (pl. **emphases**) **1** special importance or value given to something. **2** stress on a word in speaking.

Thesaurus

emblem n. CREST, insignia, badge, symbol, sign, device, representation, token, image, figure, mark.

embody v. **1** PERSONIFY, represent, symbolize, stand for, typify, exemplify, incarnate, manifest, incorporate, realize, reify. **2** INCORPORATE, combine, bring together, comprise, include, collect, contain, integrate, constitute, consolidate, encompass, assimilate, systematize.

embrace v. **1** TAKE/HOLD IN ONE'S ARMS, hold, hug, cuddle, clasp, squeeze, clutch, seize, grab, enfold, enclasp, encircle; *informal* canoodle with, neck with. **2** WELCOME, accept, take up, espouse, adopt.

emerge v. **1** COME OUT, come into view, appear, become visible, surface, crop up, spring up, materialize, arise, proceed, issue, come forth, emanate. **2** BECOME KNOWN, come out, come to light, become apparent, transpire, come to the fore.

emergency n. CRISIS, difficulty, predicament, danger, accident, quandary,

plight, dilemma, crunch, extremity, exigency; *informal* pickle.

eminence n. IMPORTANCE, greatness, prestige, reputation, fame, distinction, renown, pre-eminence, prominence, illustriousness, rank, standing, note, station, celebrity.

eminent adj. IMPORTANT, great, distinguished, well known, celebrated, famous, renowned, noted, prominent, esteemed, noteworthy, pre-eminent, outstanding, superior, high-ranking, exalted, revered, elevated, august, paramount. ■ OPPOSITES unimportant.

emit v. DISCHARGE, give out/off, throw out, issue, disgorge, vent, vomit, send forth, eject, spew out, emanate, radiate, ejaculate, exude, ooze, leak, excrete.

emotional adj. **1** PASSIONATE, demonstrative, feeling, hot-blooded, warm, responsive, tender, loving, sentimental, ardent, fervent, sensitive, excitable, temperamental, melodramatic. **2** MOVING, touching, affecting, poignant, emotive, tear-jerking, pathetic, heart-rending,

emphasize (or **-ise**) v. give special importance to.

emphatic adj. showing or giving emphasis. ■ **emphatically** adv.

emphysema n. a condition in which the air sacs of the lungs become enlarged, causing breathlessness.

empire n. **1** a group of states ruled over by a single monarch or authority. **2** a large commercial organization controlled by one person or group.

empirical adj. based on observation or experience rather than theory. ■ **empirically** adv. **empiricism** n. **empiricist** n.

emplacement n. a platform for a gun or battery of guns.

employ v. **1** give work to someone and pay them for it. **2** make use of. ■ **employee** n. **employer** n. **employment** n.

emporium n. (pl. **emporia** or **emporiums**) a large shop selling a variety of goods.

empower v. **1** authorize. **2** give strength and confidence to. ■ **empowerment** n.

empress n. **1** a female ruler of an empire. **2** an emperor's wife or widow.

empty adj. (**emptier**, **emptiest**) **1** containing nothing; not filled or occupied. **2** having no real meaning. ▶ v. (**emptying, emptied**) make or become empty. ▶ n. (pl. **empties**) informal an empty bottle or glass. ■ **emptiness** n.

emu n. a flightless Australian bird similar to an ostrich.

emulate v. try to equal or be better than. ■ **emulation** n. **emulator** n.

emulsify v. (**emulsifying, emulsified**) make into or become an emulsion. ■ **emulsification** n. **emulsifier** n.

emulsion n. **1** a smooth liquid in which particles of oil or fat are evenly distributed. **2** a type of paint for walls. **3** a light-sensitive coating for photographic film.

enable v. provide with the ability or means to do something.

enact v. **1** make a bill etc. law. **2** act out a role or play. ■ **enactment** n.

enamel n. **1** a glass-like coating for metal or pottery. **2** the hard outer covering of a tooth. **3** a paint that dries to give a hard coat. ▶ v. (**enamelling, enamelled**; US **enameling, enameled**) coat or decorate with enamel.

enamoured (US **enamored**) adj. fond.

encamp v. settle in a camp.

Thesaurus

soul-stirring, impassioned. ■ OPPOSITES unfeeling.

emotive adj. SENSITIVE, delicate, controversial, touchy, awkward.

emphasis n. **1** STRESS, attention, importance, priority, weight, significance, prominence, urgency, force, insistence, accentuation, pre-eminence, import, mark. **2** ACCENT, stress, accentuation, weight.

emphasize v. LAY/PUT STRESS ON, stress, accent, dwell on, focus on, underline, accentuate, call attention to, highlight, give prominence to, point up, spotlight, insist on, play up, feature, intensify, strengthen, heighten, deepen, underscore. ■ OPPOSITES understate, minimize, play down.

emphatic adj. **1** FORCEFUL, forcible, categorical, unequivocal, definite, decided, certain, determined, absolute, direct, earnest, energetic, vigorous. **2** MARKED, pronounced, decided, positive, definite, distinctive, unmistakable, important, significant, striking, strong, powerful, resounding, telling, momentous. ■ OPPOSITES hesitant.

employ v. **1** HIRE, engage, take on, sign up, put on the payroll, enrol, apprentice, commission, enlist, retain, inden-

ture. **2** USE, make use of, utilize, apply, exercise, bring to bear.

employed adj. **1** WORKING, in work, in employment, in a job. **2** OCCUPIED, busy, engaged, preoccupied. ■ OPPOSITES unemployed, unoccupied.

employee n. WORKER, member of staff, hand, hired hand, hireling, labourer, assistant.

employer n. MANAGER, owner, proprietor, patron, contractor, director; informal gaffer, governor.

empower v. **1** AUTHORIZE, license, certify, accredit, qualify, sanction, warrant, commission, delegate. **2** ALLOW, enable, give strength to, equip.

empty adj. **1** UNFILLED, vacant, unoccupied, hollow, void, uninhabited, bare, desolate, unadorned, barren, blank, clear. **2** MEANINGLESS, futile, ineffective, ineffectual, useless, worthless, insubstantial, fruitless, idle. **3** PURPOSELESS, aimless, hollow, barren, senseless, unsatisfactory, banal, inane, frivolous, trivial, worthless, valueless, profitless. **4** BLANK, expressionless, vacant, deadpan, vacuous, absent. ■ OPPOSITES full. ▶ v. VACATE, clear, evacuate, unload, unburden, void, deplete, sap.

enable v. ALLOW, permit, make possible,

encampment n. a place where a camp is set up.

encapsulate v. **1** enclose in or as if in a capsule. **2** summarize.

encase v. enclose or cover in a case.

encephalitis n. inflammation of the brain.

enchant v. **1** delight. **2** put under a spell. ■ **enchanter** n. **enchantment** n. **enchantress** n.

encircle v. form a circle round.

enclave n. a small territory wholly within the boundaries of another.

enclose v. **1** surround on all sides. **2** place in an envelope with a letter.

enclosure n. **1** an enclosed area. **2** a document etc. placed in an envelope with a letter.

encode v. convert into a coded form. ■ **encoder** n.

encomium n. (pl. **encomiums** or **encomia**) a formal expression of praise.

encompass v. **1** surround. **2** include.

encore /ong-kor/ n. a repeated or additional performance at the end of a concert. ▶ **exclam.** again!

encounter v. unexpectedly meet or be faced with. ▶ n. **1** an unexpected meeting. **2** a confrontation.

encourage v. give confidence, hope, or stimulus to. ■ **encouragement** n.

encroach v. (**encroach on**) gradually intrude on territory, rights, etc. ■ **encroachment** n.

encrust v. cover with a hard crust. ■ **encrustation** n.

encrypt v. convert into code. ■ **encryption** n.

encumber v. be a burden to. ■ **encumbrance** n.

encyclical n. a letter sent by the pope to all Roman Catholic bishops.

encyclopedia (or **encyclopaedia**) n. a book or set of books giving information on many subjects. ■ **encyclopedic** adj.

end n. **1** the final part of something. **2** the furthest part. **3** the stopping of a state or situation. **4** a person's death or downfall. **5** a goal or desired result. ▶ v. **1** come or bring to an end. **2** (**end up**) eventually reach a particular state or place. ◻ **make ends meet** earn just enough money to live on.

endanger v. **1** put in danger. **2** (endan-

Thesaurus

give the means to, equip, empower, facilitate, prepare, entitle, authorize, sanction, permit, license, warrant, validate, accredit, delegate, legalize. ■ OPPOSITES prevent.

enchant v. BEWITCH, hold spellbound, fascinate, charm, captivate, entrance, beguile, enthral, hypnotize, mesmerize, enrapture, delight, enamour.

enchanting adj. BEWITCHING, charming, delightful, attractive, appealing, captivating, irresistible, fascinating, engaging, endearing, entrancing, alluring, winsome, ravishing.

enclose v. **1** SURROUND, circle, hem in, ring, shut in, hedge in, wall in, confine, encompass, encircle, circumscribe, encase, gird. **2** INCLUDE, send with, put in, insert, enfold.

enclosure n. COMPOUND, yard, pen, pound, ring, fold, paddock, stockade, corral, run, sty, cloister, close, kraal.

encompass v. INCLUDE, cover, embrace, contain, comprise, take in, incorporate, envelop, embody.

encounter v. **1** MEET, run into/across, come upon, stumble across, chance upon, happen upon; informal bump into. **2** BE FACED WITH, contend with, confront, tussle with. ▶ n. FIGHT, battle, clash, conflict, confrontation, engagement, skir-

mish, scuffle, tussle, brawl; informal run-in, set-to, brush.

encourage v. **1** CHEER, rally, stimulate, motivate, inspire, stir, incite, hearten, animate, invigorate, embolden; informal buck up. **2** URGE, persuade, prompt, influence, exhort, spur, goad, egg on. **3** PROMOTE, advance, foster, help, assist, support, aid, advocate, back, boost, abet, forward, strengthen. ■ OPPOSITES discourage.

encroach v. TRESPASS, intrude, invade, infringe, infiltrate, overrun, impinge, usurp, appropriate; informal tread on someone's toes, muscle in on, invade someone's space.

encumber v. INCONVENIENCE, constrain, handicap, hinder, impede, obstruct, retard, check, restrain.

encyclopedic adj. COMPREHENSIVE, complete, wide-ranging, all-inclusive, exhaustive, all-embracing, thorough, universal, all-encompassing, compendious, vast.

end n. **1** ENDING, finish, close, conclusion, cessation, termination, completion, resolution, climax, finale, culmination, denouement, epilogue, expiry; informal wind-up, pay-off. **2** EDGE, border, boundary, limit, extremity, margin, point, tip, extent. **3** REMAINDER, remnant, fragment,

gered) in danger of becoming extinct.

endear v. cause to be loved or liked.

endearment n. a word or phrase expressing affection.

endeavour (US **endeavor**) v. try hard to achieve something. ▶n. **1** an attempt to achieve something. **2** hard work.

endemic adj. (of a disease) regularly found in particular people or area.

ending n. an end or final part.

endive n. a plant with bitter leaves, eaten in salads.

endless adj. having or seeming to have no end. ■ **endlessly** adv.

endocrine adj. (of a gland) secreting hormones etc. directly into the blood.

endorphin n. a painkilling hormone in the brain and nervous system.

endorse v. **1** declare approval of. **2** sign a cheque on the back. **3** record an offence on a driving licence. ■ **endorsement** n.

endow v. **1** provide with a permanent income or property. **2** (**be endowed with**) possess a quality or asset. ■ **endowment** n.

endure v. **1** experience and survive pain or hardship. **2** tolerate. **3** last. ■ **endurable** adj. **endurance** n.

enema n. a medical procedure in which fluid is injected into the rectum to empty it.

enemy n. (pl. **enemies**) a person or group opposed or hostile to another.

energetic adj. showing or involving great energy. ■ **energetically** adv.

energize (or **-ise**) v. give energy and enthusiasm to.

energy n. (pl. **energies**) **1** the strength and vitality required to keep active. **2** power derived from physical or chemical resources to provide light, heat, etc. **3** Physics the capacity of matter or radiation to perform work.

Thesaurus

vestige, leftover. **4** AIM, goal, purpose, intention, objective, design, motive, aspiration, intent, object. ■ OPPOSITES beginning, start. ▶v. **1** COME TO AN END, finish, stop, close, cease, conclude, terminate, discontinue, break off, fade away, peter out; *informal* wind up. **2** BRING TO AN END, finish, stop, cease, conclude, close, terminate, break off, complete, dissolve, resolve. ■ OPPOSITES begin, start.

endanger v. THREATEN, put at risk, put in danger, jeopardize, imperil, risk, expose, hazard, compromise. ■ OPPOSITES protect.

endearing adj. CHARMING, adorable, lovable, attractive, engaging, disarming, appealing, winning, sweet, captivating, enchanting, winsome.

endearment n. **1** SWEET TALK, sweet nothings, soft words, blandishments. **2** AFFECTION, love, fondness, liking, attachment.

endeavour v. TRY, attempt, strive, venture, aspire, undertake, struggle, labour, essay; *informal* work at, have a go/stab at.

endless adj. **1** UNENDING, unlimited, infinite, limitless, boundless, continual, perpetual, constant, everlasting, unceasing, unfading, interminable, incessant, measureless, untold, incalculable. **2** CONTINUOUS, unbroken, uninterrupted, never-ending, whole, entire. **3** NON-STOP, interminable, overlong, unremitting, monotonous, boring. ■ OPPOSITES finite, limited.

endorse v. **1** SIGN, countersign, validate, autograph, superscribe, underwrite. **2** APPROVE, support, back, favour, recommend, advocate, champion, subscribe to, uphold, authorize, sanction, ratify, affirm, warrant, confirm, vouch for, corroborate.

endow v. PROVIDE, give, present, confer, bestow, gift, enrich, supply, furnish, award, invest; *literary* endue.

endurance n. **1** STAMINA, staying power, perseverance, tenacity, fortitude, durability, continuance, longevity. **2** TOLERATION, sufferance, forbearance, acceptance, patience, resignation.

endure v. **1** LAST, continue, persist, remain, live on, hold on, survive, abide; *old use* bide, tarry. **2** STAND, bear, put up with, tolerate, suffer, abide, submit to, countenance, brook, stomach, swallow; *informal* stick. ■ OPPOSITES fade.

enemy n. ADVERSARY, opponent, foe, rival, antagonist, competitor. ■ OPPOSITES friend.

energetic adj. **1** ACTIVE, lively, vigorous, strenuous, dynamic, brisk, spirited, animated, vibrant, sprightly, vital, tireless, indefatigable; *informal* zippy, peppy, bright-eyed and bushy-tailed. **2** FORCEFUL, forcible, determined, aggressive, emphatic, driving, powerful, effective, potent. ■ OPPOSITES lethargic.

energy n. VIGOUR, strength, stamina, power, forcefulness, drive, push, exertion, enthusiasm, life, animation, liveliness, vivacity, vitality, spirit, spiritedness, fire, zest, exuberance, buoyancy,

enervate v. cause to feel drained of energy. ■ **enervation** n.

enfant terrible /on-fon te-ree-bluh/ n. (pl. **enfants terribles**) a person whose controversial attitude shocks others.

enfeeble v. weaken.

enfold v. envelop.

enforce v. 1 ensure a law etc. is obeyed. 2 force to happen or be done. ■ **enforceable** adj. **enforcement** n.

enfranchise v. give the right to vote to. ■ **enfranchisement** n.

engage v. 1 involve someone's interest or attention. 2 occupy oneself with. 3 employ. 4 undertake. 5 enter into combat with. 6 move a part of a machine into an operating position.

engaged adj. 1 occupied. 2 in use. 3 having formally agreed to marry.

engagement n. 1 a formal agreement to get married. 2 an appointment. 3 the state of being engaged. 4 a battle.

engaging adj. charming.

engender v. give rise to.

engine n. 1 a machine with moving parts that converts power into motion. 2 a railway locomotive.

engineer n. 1 a person qualified in engineering. 2 a person who maintains or controls an engine or machine. ▶ v.

1 design and build. 2 skilfully arrange for something to occur.

engineering n. the study of the design, building, and use of engines, machines, and structures.

English n. the language of England, used in many varieties throughout the world. ▶ adj. of England.

engorged adj. swollen.

engrave v. carve a design on a hard surface. ■ **engraver** n. **engraving** n.

engross v. absorb all the attention of.

engulf v. surround or cover completely.

enhance v. increase the quality, value, or extent of. ■ **enhancement** n.

enigma n. a mysterious person or thing. ■ **enigmatic** adj. **enigmatically** adv.

enjoin v. instruct or urge to do.

enjoy v. 1 take pleasure in. 2 (**enjoy oneself**) have a pleasant time. 3 possess and benefit from. ■ **enjoyable** adj. **enjoyment** n.

enlarge v. 1 make or become larger. 2 (**enlarge on**) say more about. ■ **enlargement** n.

enlighten v. give greater knowledge and understanding to. ■ **enlightenment** n.

enlist v. 1 enrol or be enrolled in the armed services. 2 secure help from

Thesaurus

verve, dash, sparkle, effervescence, brio, ardour, zeal, passion, might, potency, effectiveness, efficiency, efficacy, cogency; *informal* vim, zip, zing.

enfold v. ENCLOSE, fold, envelop, encircle, swathe, shroud, swaddle.

enforce v. 1 APPLY, carry out, administer, implement, bring to bear, impose, prosecute, execute, discharge, fulfil. 2 FORCE, compel, insist on, require, coerce, necessitate, urge, exact.

engage v. 1 EMPLOY, hire, take on, appoint, enlist, enrol, commission. 2 OCCUPY, absorb, hold, engross, grip, preoccupy, fill. 3 TAKE PART, enter into, become involved in, undertake, embark on, set about, join in, participate in, tackle, launch into. 4 FIT TOGETHER, join together, mesh, intermesh, interconnect. ■ OPPOSITES dismiss.

engender v. CAUSE, produce, create, bring about, give rise to, lead to, arouse, rouse, provoke, excite, incite, whip up, induce, generate, instigate, effect, hatch, occasion, foment; *formal* effectuate.

engine n. MOTOR, mechanism, machine, power source, generator.

engineer v. BRING ABOUT, cause, plan,

plot, contrive, devise, orchestrate, mastermind, originate, manage, control, superintend, direct, conduct, handle, concoct.

engrave v. INSCRIBE, etch, carve, cut, chisel, imprint, impress, mark.

enhance v. ADD TO, increase, heighten, stress, emphasize, strengthen, improve, augment, boost, intensify, reinforce, magnify, amplify, enrich, complement.

enjoy v. 1 TAKE PLEASURE IN, delight in, appreciate, like, love, rejoice in, relish, revel in, savour, lap up, luxuriate in; *informal* fancy. 2 HAVE, possess, benefit from, own, have the advantage of, be blessed with. ■ OPPOSITES dislike. □ **enjoy oneself** HAVE FUN, have a good time, make merry, celebrate, party, have the time of one's life; *informal* have a ball, let one's hair down.

enjoyable adj. ENTERTAINING, amusing, delightful, diverting, satisfying, gratifying, pleasant, lovely, agreeable, pleasurable, fine, good, great, nice. ■ OPPOSITES boring, disagreeable.

enlarge v. MAKE BIGGER/LARGER, expand, extend, add to, augment, amplify, supplement, magnify, multiply, widen, broaden, lengthen, elongate, deepen, someone. ■ **enlistment** n.

enliven v. make more interesting or more lively.

en masse /on mass/ adv. all together.

enmesh v. entangle.

enmity n. (pl. **enmities**) hostility.

ennoble v. give greater dignity to.

ennui /on-wee/ n. boredom.

enormity n. (pl. **enormities**) **1** great wickedness. **2** great size or scale.

enormous adj. very large.

enough adj., pron., & adv. as much or as many as is necessary or desirable.

enquire v. **1** ask. **2** investigate. ■ **enquiry** n.

enrage v. make very angry.

enrapture v. delight greatly.

enrich v. **1** improve the quality or value of. **2** make wealthier. ■ **enrichment** n.

enrol (US **enroll**) v. (**enrolling, enrolled**) officially register as a member or student. ■ **enrolment** n.

en route /on root/ adv. on the way.

ensconce v. establish comfortably or securely.

ensemble /on-som-b'l/ n. **1** a group of performers. **2** a group of items viewed as a whole.

enshrine v. preserve in a form that en-

sures protection and respect.

ensign n. a naval flag.

enslave v. cause to lose freedom of choice or action. ■ **enslavement** n.

ensnare v. catch in or as if in a trap.

ensue v. happen afterwards or as a result.

en suite /on sweet/ adj. & adv. (of a bathroom) next to and accessed via a bedroom.

ensure v. make certain that something will occur or be so.

entail v. involve as a necessary part or consequence.

entangle v. **1** make tangled. **2** involve in complicated circumstances. ■ **entanglement** n.

entente /on-tont/ n. a friendly understanding between states.

enter v. **1** come or go into. **2** begin to be involved in or do. **3** register as a participant in. **4** record information in a book, computer, etc.

enteritis n. inflammation of the intestines.

enterprise n. **1** a project or undertaking. **2** resourcefulness. **3** a business or company.

enterprising adj. showing initiative.

Thesaurus

thicken, distend, dilate, swell, inflate.

enlighten v. INFORM, make aware, advise, instruct, teach, educate, tutor, illuminate, apprise, counsel, edify, civilize, cultivate.

enlist v. **1** ENROL, sign up, conscript, recruit, hire, employ, take on, engage, muster, obtain, secure. **2** JOIN, join up, enrol in, sign up for, enter into, volunteer for.

enliven v. BRIGHTEN UP, cheer up, perk up, hearten, gladden, excite, stimulate, exhilarate, invigorate, revitalize, buoy up, give a boost to, wake up, rouse, refresh; informal jazz up, ginger up, light a fire under.

enormous adj. HUGE, immense, massive, vast, gigantic, colossal, mammoth, astronomic, gargantuan, mountainous, prodigious, tremendous, stupendous, titanic, excessive, Herculean, Brobdingnagian; informal jumbo. ■ OPPOSITES tiny.

enough adj. SUFFICIENT, adequate, ample, abundant. ■ OPPOSITES insufficient, inadequate.

enquire v. see INQUIRE.

enrage v. MADDEN, infuriate, incense, exasperate, provoke, annoy, irritate, inflame, incite, irk, agitate; informal make

someone's hackles rise, make someone's blood boil, get someone's back up, wind up. ■ OPPOSITES placate.

enrapture v. DELIGHT, thrill, captivate, charm, fascinate, enchant, beguile, bewitch, entrance, enthral, transport, ravish; informal blow someone's mind, turn on.

ensue v. FOLLOW, come next/after, result, occur, happen, turn up, arise, transpire, proceed, succeed, issue, derive, stem, supervene; literary come to pass, befall.

ensure v. MAKE CERTAIN, make sure, guarantee, confirm, certify, secure, effect, warrant.

entail v. INVOLVE, require, call for, necessitate, demand, impose, cause, bring about, produce, result in, lead to, give rise to, occasion.

enter v. **1** COME/GO INTO, pass/move into, invade, infiltrate, penetrate, pierce, puncture. **2** BEGIN, start, commence, embark on, engage in, undertake, venture on. **3** TAKE PART IN, participate in, go in for, gain entrance/admittance to. **4** SUBMIT, put forward, present, proffer, register, tender. **5** RECORD, register, put down, note, mark down, document, list, file, log.

entertain v. **1** provide with amusement or enjoyment. **2** offer hospitality to. **3** consider an idea etc. ■ **entertainer** n. **entertainment** n.

enthral (US **enthrall**) v. (**enthralling**, **enthralled**) fascinate and hold the attention of.

enthrone v. ceremonially install a new monarch on a throne. ■ **enthronement** n.

enthuse v. fill with or express great enthusiasm.

enthusiasm n. great enjoyment, interest, or approval. ■ **enthusiastic** adj. **enthusiastically** adv.

enthusiast n. a person who is full of enthusiasm for something.

entice v. attract by offering something pleasant or beneficial. ■ **enticement** n.

entire adj. with no part left out. ■ **entirely** adv.

entirety n. (**in its entirety**) as a whole.

entitle v. **1** give a right to. **2** give a title to a book etc. ■ **entitlement** n.

entity n. (pl. **entities**) a thing existing independently from other things.

entomology n. the study of insects. ■ **entomological** adj. **entomologist** n.

entourage /on-toor-ahzh/ n. the people accompanying an important person.

entr'acte /on-trakt/ n. an interval between acts of a play.

entrails pl. n. intestines.

entrance[1] n. **1** an opening through which one may enter. **2** an act of entering. **3** the right or opportunity to enter.

entrance[2] v. fill with wonder and delight.

Thesaurus

enterprise n. **1** VENTURE, undertaking, project, operation, endeavour, task, effort, plan, scheme, campaign. **2** RESOURCEFULNESS, initiative, drive, push, enthusiasm, zest, energy, vitality, boldness, audacity, courage, imagination, spirit, spiritedness, vigour; informal get-up-and-go, vim, oomph. **3** BUSINESS, firm, industry, concern, operation, corporation, establishment, house.

enterprising adj. RESOURCEFUL, entrepreneurial, energetic, determined, ambitious, purposeful, pushy, adventurous, audacious, bold, daring, active, vigorous, imaginative, spirited, enthusiastic, eager, keen, zealous, vital, courageous, intrepid; informal go-ahead, up-and-coming, peppy.

entertain v. **1** AMUSE, divert, delight, please, charm, cheer, interest, beguile, engage, occupy. **2** PLAY HOST/HOSTESS, receive guests, provide hospitality, have people round, keep company, keep open house, hold/throw a party. **3** CONSIDER, give consideration to, take into consideration, give some thought to, think about/over, contemplate, weigh up, ponder, muse over, bear in mind.

entertainment n. **1** AMUSEMENT, fun, enjoyment, recreation, diversion, distraction, pastime, hobby, sport. **2** SHOW, performance, concert, play, presentation, spectacle, pageant.

enthralling adj. CAPTIVATING, enchanting, spellbinding, fascinating, bewitching, gripping, riveting, charming, delightful, intriguing, mesmerizing, hypnotic.

enthusiasm n. EAGERNESS, keenness, fervour, ardour, passion, zeal, warmth, vehemence, zest, fire, excitement, exuberance, ebullience, avidity, wholeheartedness, commitment, devotion, fanaticism, earnestness. ■ OPPOSITES apathy.

enthusiast n. SUPPORTER, follower, fan, devotee, lover, admirer, fanatic, zealot, aficionado; informal buff, freak.

enthusiastic adj. EAGER, keen, fervent, ardent, passionate, warm, zealous, vehement, excited, spirited, exuberant, ebullient, avid, wholehearted, hearty, committed, devoted, fanatical, earnest; informal mad about. ■ OPPOSITES apathetic, indifferent.

entice v. TEMPT, lure, seduce, inveigle, lead on/astray, beguile, coax, wheedle, cajole, decoy, bait.

entire adj. **1** WHOLE, complete, total, full, continuous, unbroken. **2** INTACT, undamaged, unbroken, sound, unmarked, perfect, unimpaired, unblemished, unspoiled. ■ OPPOSITES partial.

entirely adv. COMPLETELY, absolutely, totally, fully, wholly, altogether, utterly, in every respect, without exception, thoroughly, perfectly.

entitle v. **1** GIVE THE RIGHT TO, make eligible, qualify, authorize, allow, sanction, permit, enable, empower, warrant, enfranchise, accredit. **2** CALL, name, term, style, dub, designate.

entity n. BEING, body, person, creature, individual, organism, object, thing, article, substance, quantity, existence.

entourage n. RETINUE, escort, cortège, train, suite, bodyguard, attendants, companions, followers, associates; informal groupies.

entrails pl. n. INTESTINES, internal organs, bowels, vital organs, viscera; informal

entrant n. a person who joins or takes part in something.

entrap v. (**entrapping, entrapped**) **1** catch in a trap. **2** trick into committing a crime. ■ **entrapment** n.

entreat v. ask earnestly or anxiously. ■ **entreaty** n.

entrée /on-tray/ n. **1** the main course of a meal. **2** a dish served before the main course of a meal. **3** the right to enter a place or social group.

entrench v. establish firmly. ■ **entrenchment** n.

entrepreneur /on-truh-pruh-**ner**/ n. a person who is successful in setting up businesses. ■ **entrepreneurial** adj.

entropy n. a quantity expressing how much of a system's thermal energy is unavailable for conversion into mechanical work.

entrust v. give a responsibility to or put into someone's care.

entry n. (pl. **entries**) **1** the act of entering. **2** an entrance. **3** an item entered in a list etc.

entwine v. wind or twist together.

enumerate v. mention items one by one. ■ **enumeration** n.

enunciate v. **1** pronounce clearly. **2** state precisely. ■ **enunciation** n.

envelop v. (**enveloping, enveloped**) wrap up or surround completely.

envelope n. a flat paper container for a letter etc., with a sealable flap.

enviable adj. desirable and so arousing envy. ■ **enviably** adv.

envious adj. feeling or showing envy. ■ **enviously** adv.

environment n. **1** the surroundings in which a person, animal, or plant lives. **2** the natural world. ■ **environmental** adj. **environmentally** adv.

✓ Don't forget the n: environment.

environmentalist n. a person seeking to protect the environment. ■ **environmentalism** n.

environs pl. n. the surrounding area or district.

envisage v. **1** see as a possibility. **2** imagine.

envoy n. a messenger or representative.

envy n. (pl. **envies**) discontent or resentment aroused by another person's possessions or success. ▶ v. (**envying, envied**) feel envy of.

enzyme n. a substance produced by a living organism and assisting in chemical processes.

eon US = AEON.

epaulette n. an ornamental shoulder piece on a uniform.

ephemera pl. n. items of short-lived interest or use.

ephemeral adj. lasting only for a very short time.

Thesaurus

guts, insides, innards.

entrance n. **1** WAY IN, entry, means of entry/access, access, door, doorway, gate, gateway, drive, driveway, foyer, lobby, porch, threshold, portal. **2** COMING IN, entry, appearance, arrival, introduction, ingress. **3** ADMISSION, entry, permission to enter, right of entry, access, ingress. ■ OPPOSITES departure, exit.

entrant n. **1** NEWCOMER, beginner, new arrival, probationer, trainee, novice, tyro, initiate, neophyte; *informal* cub, rookie; *US informal* greenhorn. **2** CONTESTANT, competitor, participant, player, candidate, applicant, rival, opponent.

entreat v. BEG, implore, plead with, appeal to, petition, solicit, pray, crave, exhort, enjoin, importune, supplicate; *literary* beseech.

entrenched adj. DEEP-SEATED, deep-rooted, rooted, well established, fixed, set, firm, ingrained, unshakeable, immovable, indelible, dyed in the wool.

envelop v. ENFOLD, cover, wrap, swathe, swaddle, cloak, blanket, surround, engulf, encircle, encompass, conceal, hide, obscure.

envelope n. WRAPPER, wrapping, cover, covering, case, casing, jacket, shell, sheath, skin, capsule, holder, container.

enviable adj. EXCITING ENVY, desirable, covetable, worth having, tempting, excellent, fortunate, lucky, favourable.

envious adj. JEALOUS, covetous, desirous, green-eyed, green, grudging, begrudging, resentful, bitter, jaundiced; *informal* green with envy.

environment n. SURROUNDINGS, habitat, territory, domain, medium, element, milieu, situation, location, scene, locale, background, conditions, circumstances, setting, context, atmosphere, ambience, mood.

envisage v. PREDICT, foresee, imagine, visualize, picture, anticipate, envision, contemplate, conceive of, think of, dream of.

envy n. ENVIOUSNESS, jealousy, covetousness, desire, cupidity, longing, resent-

epic n. a long poem, book, or film about heroic actions or figures or covering a long period of time. ▶ adj. **1** of an epic. **2** heroic or on a grand scale.

epicene adj. characteristic of both sexes or neither sex.

epicentre (US **epicenter**) n. the point on the earth's surface directly above the origin of an earthquake.

epicure n. a person who enjoys good food and drink. ■ **epicurean** n. & adj.

epidemic n. a widespread occurrence of an infectious disease in a community.

epidemiology n. the study of the spread and control of diseases. ■ **epidemiologist** n.

epidermis n. the outer layer of the skin.

epidural n. an anaesthetic injected into the space around the spinal cord, esp. during childbirth.

epiglottis n. a flap of cartilage that covers the larynx during swallowing.

epigram n. a short witty saying. ■ **epigrammatic** adj.

epilepsy n. a disorder of the nervous system causing convulsions and loss of consciousness. ■ **epileptic** adj. & n.

epilogue n. a short concluding section of a book or play.

Epiphany n. the Christian festival (6 January) commemorating Jesus's appearance to the Magi.

episcopal adj. of or governed by bishops.

episcopalian adj. & n. (a member) of an episcopal church.

episiotomy n. a cut made at the opening of the vagina during childbirth.

episode n. **1** an event occurring as part of a sequence. **2** each part of a serialized story or programme. ■ **episodic** adj.

epistle n. a letter. ■ **epistolary** adj.

epitaph n. words written in memory of a person who has died.

epithet n. a descriptive word or phrase.

epitome /i-**pit**-uh-mi/ n. a perfect example.

epitomize (or **-ise**) v. be a perfect example of.

epoch n. a period of time in history.

eponymous adj. (of a person) giving their name to something.

equable adj. **1** even-tempered. **2** not varying greatly.

equal adj. **1** the same in quantity, size, value, or status. **2** evenly balanced. **3** (**equal to**) able to deal with. ▶ n. a person or thing that is equal to another. ▶ v. (**equalling**, **equalled**; US **equaling**, **equaled**) **1** be equal to. **2** match or rival. ■ **equality** n. **equally** adv.

equalize (or **-ise**) v. **1** make or become equal. **2** level the score in a match by scoring a goal. ■ **equalization** n. **equalizer** n.

equanimity n. evenness of temper.

Thesaurus

ment, bitterness, resentfulness, discontent, spite, dissatisfaction. ▶ v. BE ENVIOUS OF, be jealous of, covet, be covetous of, begrudge, grudge, resent.

ephemeral adj. FLEETING, short-lived, transitory, transient, momentary, brief, short, temporary, passing, impermanent, evanescent, fugitive. ■ OPPOSITES permanent.

epidemic n. OUTBREAK, pandemic, plague, scourge, upsurge, wave, upswing, upturn, increase, growth, rise, mushrooming. ▶ adj. RIFE, rampant, widespread, extensive, wide-ranging, prevalent, sweeping, predominant.

episode n. **1** PART, instalment, chapter, section, passage, scene. **2** INCIDENT, occurrence, event, happening, experience, adventure, matter, occasion, affair, business, circumstance, interlude.

epitome n. PERSONIFICATION, embodiment, essence, quintessence, archetype, representation, model, typification, example, exemplar, prototype.

epoch n. ERA, age, period, time, date.

equal adj. **1** IDENTICAL, alike, like, comparable, commensurate, the same as, on a par with. **2** EVEN, evenly matched, level pegging, balanced, level, evenly proportioned; informal fifty-fifty, neck and neck. **3** CAPABLE OF, up to, fit for, good enough for, adequate for, sufficient for, suited, ready for. ▶ n. EQUIVALENT, match, parallel, peer, twin, alter ego, counterpart. ▶ v. **1** BE EQUAL/LEVEL WITH, be equivalent to, match, measure up to, equate with, vie with, rival, emulate. **2** MATCH, reach, achieve, parallel, come up to, measure up to.

equality n. **1** SAMENESS, identity, parity, likeness, similarity, uniformity, evenness, levelness, balance, correspondence, comparability. **2** FAIRNESS, justice, justness, impartiality, egalitarianism, equal rights, even-handedness. ■ OPPOSITES inequality.

equanimity n. COMPOSURE, presence of mind, self-control, self-possession,

equate v. consider one thing as equal to another.

equation n. a statement that two mathematical expressions are equal.

equator n. an imaginary line around the earth at equal distances from the North and South Poles. ■ **equatorial** adj.

equerry n. (pl. **equerries**) an officer who assists members of the British royal family.

equestrian adj. of horse riding.

equidistant adj. at equal distances.

equilateral adj. having all sides the same length.

equilibrium n. (pl. **equilibria**) a balanced state.

equine adj. of or like a horse.

equinox n. the time or date (twice each year) when day and night are of equal length. ■ **equinoctial** adj.

equip v. (**equipping**, **equipped**) supply with what is needed.

equipage n. hist. a carriage with its horses and attendants.

equipment n. the items needed for a particular purpose.

equipoise n. equilibrium.

equitable adj. treating everyone equally; fair. ■ **equitably** adv.

equitation n. horse riding.

equity n. 1 fairness and impartiality. 2 (**equities**) stocks and shares not paying a fixed amount of interest.

equivalent adj. equal in value, amount, meaning, etc. ▶n. a person or thing equivalent to another. ■ **equivalence** n.

equivocal adj. ambiguous. ■ **equivocally** adv.

equivocate v. use words ambiguously. ■ **equivocation** n.

era n. a period of history.

eradicate v. remove or destroy completely. ■ **eradication** n.

erase v. remove all traces of. ■ **erasable** adj. **eraser** n. **erasure** n.

ere /air/ prep. & conj. old use before (in time).

erect adj. 1 rigidly upright. 2 (of a body part) enlarged and rigid. ▶v. build. ■ **erection** n.

erectile adj. able to become erect.

erg n. a unit of work or energy.

ergo adv. therefore.

ergonomics n. the study of people's efficiency in their working environment. ■ **ergonomic** adj.

ermine n. 1 a stoat. 2 the stoat's white winter fur.

erode v. gradually wear away. ■ **erosion** n.

erogenous adj. sensitive to sexual stimulation.

erotic adj. of sexual desire or excitement. ■ **erotically** adv.

eroticism n. the quality of being erotic.

err v. 1 make a mistake. 2 do wrong.

Thesaurus

level-headedness, equilibrium, poise, aplomb, sangfroid, calmness, calm, coolness, serenity, placidity, tranquillity, phlegm, imperturbability, unflappability. ■ OPPOSITES anxiety.

equilibrium n. 1 BALANCE, stability, steadiness, evenness, symmetry, equipoise, counterpoise. 2 see EQUANIMITY.

equip v. FIT OUT, rig out, provide, supply, furnish, prepare, stock, arm, attire, array, dress, outfit, accoutre, endow; informal kit out.

equitable adj. FAIR, fair-minded, just, even-handed, right, rightful, proper, reasonable, honest, impartial, unbiased, unprejudiced, open-minded, non-discriminatory, disinterested, dispassionate. ■ OPPOSITES inequitable, unfair.

equivalent adj. EQUAL, identical, similar, the same, alike, like, comparable, corresponding, commensurate, matching, interchangeable, on a par, tantamount, synonymous, homologous. ■ OPPOSITES different, dissimilar.

equivocal adj. AMBIGUOUS, ambivalent, vague, unclear, obscure, roundabout, non-committal, hazy, oblique, evasive, misleading, duplicitous, indeterminate, uncertain. ■ OPPOSITES unequivocal.

era n. AGE, epoch, period, time, eon, generation, stage, cycle, season.

eradicate v. REMOVE, get rid of, wipe out, eliminate, do away with, extirpate, abolish, annihilate, stamp out, obliterate, extinguish, excise, expunge, destroy, kill.

erase v. DELETE, rub out, wipe out, remove, cross out, strike out, blot out, efface, expunge, obliterate, cancel.

erect adj. 1 UPRIGHT, straight, vertical. 2 RIGID, stiff, hard, firm. ▶v. BUILD, construct, put up, assemble, put together, raise, elevate, mount.

erode v. WEAR AWAY, wear, eat away at, corrode, abrade, gnaw away at, grind down, consume, devour, spoil, disintegrate, destroy, excoriate.

erotic adj. AROUSING, stimulating, aphrodisiac, exciting, titillating, seductive,

errand n. a short journey to deliver or collect something.

errant adj. doing something wrong.

erratic adj. uneven or irregular. ■ **erratically** adv.

erratum n. (pl. **errata**) an error in printing or writing.

erroneous adj. incorrect.

error n. **1** a mistake. **2** the state of being wrong.

ersatz adj. used as a poor-quality substitute.

erstwhile adj. former.

erudite adj. learned. ■ **erudition** n.

erupt v. **1** (of a volcano) throw out lava etc. **2** express emotion in a sudden, violent way. ■ **eruption** n.

erythrocyte /i-rith-ruh-syt/ n. a red blood cell.

escalate v. increase in intensity or extent. ■ **escalation** n.

escalator n. a moving staircase.

escalope n. a thin slice of meat coated in breadcrumbs and fried.

escapade n. a daring and adventurous act.

escape v. **1** get free from. **2** succeed in avoiding. **3** fail to be noticed or remembered by. ▶ n. an act or means of escaping. ■ **escapee** n. **escaper** n.

escapement n. a mechanism regulating the movement of a clock or watch.

escapism n. indulging in enjoyable activities so as to ignore unpleasant realities. ■ **escapist** n. & adj.

escapologist n. an entertainer whose act involves breaking free from ropes, handcuffs, etc. ■ **escapology** n.

escarpment n. a steep slope at the edge of an area of high ground.

eschew v. deliberately avoid doing.

escort n. **1** a person, vehicle, or group accompanying another to protect or honour them. **2** a person accompanying a member of the opposite sex to a social event. ▶ v. accompany as an escort.

escritoire /ess-kri-twar/ n. a writing desk with drawers.

escudo n. (pl. **escudos**) a former currency unit of Portugal.

escutcheon n. a shield bearing a coat of arms.

Eskimo n. (pl. **Eskimo** or **Eskimos**) a member of a people inhabiting northern Canada, Alaska, Greenland, and eastern Siberia.

i   Many of the peoples traditionally called **Eskimos** now prefer to call themselves **Inuit**.

esophagus US = OESOPHAGUS.

esoteric adj. intended for or understood by only a few people with specialized knowledge.

ESP abbrev. extrasensory perception.

Thesaurus

sensual, sexy, carnal, salacious, suggestive, pornographic; informal steamy.

err v. BE WRONG, be incorrect, make a mistake, be mistaken, blunder, misjudge, miscalculate, misunderstand, misconstrue, get it wrong, be wide of the mark; informal be barking up the wrong tree, slip up, boob.

errand n. TASK, job, commission, chore, assignment, undertaking, message, charge, mission.

erratic adj. **1** INCONSISTENT, variable, irregular, unstable, unpredictable, unreliable, capricious, whimsical, fitful, wayward, abnormal, eccentric, aberrant, deviant. **2** WANDERING, meandering, wavering, directionless, haphazard. ■ OPPOSITES consistent.

error n. **1** MISTAKE, inaccuracy, miscalculation, blunder, fault, flaw, oversight, misprint, literal, erratum, misinterpretation, misreading, fallacy, misconception, delusion; informal slip-up, boo-boo, boob, howler, typo; informal, dated bloomer. **2** MISCONDUCT, misbehaviour, lawlessness, criminality, delinquency,

sinfulness, evil.

erupt v. **1** EJECT, gush, pour forth, spew, vent, boil over, vomit. **2** BREAK OUT, flare up, blow up, explode.

escalate v. GROW, increase, be stepped up, mushroom, intensify, heighten, accelerate, be extended, be magnified, amplified.

escapade n. STUNT, prank, adventure, caper, romp, frolic, fling, spree, antics; informal lark, scrape, shenanigans.

escape v. **1** GET AWAY, break out, run away, break free, flee, bolt, abscond, decamp, fly, steal away, slip away; informal skedaddle, vamoose, fly the coop, do a bunk, do a runner. **2** AVOID, evade, dodge, elude, circumvent, sidestep, steer clear of, shirk; informal duck, skive (off). **3** LEAK, seep, pour out, gush, spurt, issue, flow, discharge, emanate, drain. ▶ n. **1** BREAKOUT, getaway, flight. **2** AVOIDANCE, evasion, dodging, eluding, elusion, circumvention. **3** LEAK, leakage, seepage, gush, spurt, issue, flow, discharge, outflow, emanation, efflux.

escort n. **1** ENTOURAGE, retinue, attend-

espadrille n. a canvas shoe with a plaited fibre sole.

espalier n. a tree trained against a wall.

especial adj. special; particular.

especially adv. **1** in particular. **2** to a great extent.

Esperanto n. an artificial international language.

espionage n. spying.

esplanade n. a promenade.

espouse v. support or adopt a cause or way of life. ■ **espousal** n.

espresso n. (pl. **espressos**) strong black coffee made by forcing steam through ground coffee.

esprit de corps n. pride and loyalty uniting a group.

espy v. (**espying, espied**) catch sight of.

Esq. abbrev. Esquire, a polite title placed after a man's surname.

essay n. **1** a piece of writing on a particular subject. **2** an attempt. ▶ v. attempt. ■ **essayist** n.

essence n. **1** the quality which makes something what it is. **2** a concentrated extract obtained from a plant etc.

essential adj. **1** absolutely necessary. **2** central to something's nature. ▶ n. (**essentials**) **1** essential things. **2** the

basic elements. □ **essential oil** a natural oil extracted from a plant. ■ **essentially** adv.

establish v. **1** set up on a firm or permanent basis. **2** (**be established**) be settled in a place or role. **3** show to be true.

establishment n. **1** the act of establishing. **2** an organization. **3** (**the Establishment**) the group in society who control policy and resist change.

estate n. **1** a large house with extensive grounds. **2** a residential or industrial area planned as a unit. **3** the money and property owned by a person at the time of their death. □ **estate agent** a person who sells and rents out houses etc. for clients. **estate car** a car with a large storage area behind the seats and a rear door.

esteem n. respect and admiration. ▶ v. respect and admire.

esthete etc. US = **AESTHETE** etc.

estimable adj. worthy of great respect.

estimate n. an approximate judgement of the amount, value, etc. of something. ▶ v. form an estimate of. ■ **estimation** n.

estranged adj. **1** no longer close to or

Thesaurus

ants, train, cortège, bodyguard, protector, convoy, defender, contingent. **2** PARTNER, companion, gigolo, hostess, geisha; informal date; dated beau. ▶ v. **1** ACCOMPANY, guide, conduct, lead, usher, shepherd, guard, protect, safeguard, defend. **2** PARTNER, accompany, take out, go out with, attend on.

esoteric adj. ABSTRUSE, obscure, cryptic, arcane, recondite, abstract, mysterious, hidden, secret, mystic, magical, occult, cabbalistic.

essence n. **1** FUNDAMENTAL NATURE, substance, crux, quintessence, heart, lifeblood, kernel, marrow, pith, reality, actuality; Philosophy quiddity. **2** EXTRACT, concentrate, distillate, tincture, elixir, abstraction.

essential adj. **1** NECESSARY, important, indispensable, vital, crucial, needed, requisite. **2** BASIC, fundamental, chief, intrinsic, inherent, innate, elemental, characteristic, principal, cardinal.
■ OPPOSITES unimportant.

establish v. **1** SET UP, found, institute, form, start, begin, bring about, create, inaugurate, organize, build, construct, install, plant. **2** PROVE, show to be true, show, demonstrate, confirm, attest to, certify, verify, evidence, substantiate,

corroborate, validate, authenticate, ratify. ■ OPPOSITES disprove.

established adj. ACCEPTED, official, proven, settled, conventional, traditional, fixed, entrenched, inveterate, dyed in the wool.

establishment n. **1** FORMATION, foundation, founding, setting up, creation, inception, inauguration, building, construction, organization, installation. **2** RESIDENCE, house, household, home, dwelling, abode, domicile, estate. **3** FIRM, business, company, shop, store, concern, office, factory, organization, enterprise, corporation, conglomerate.

estate n. **1** PROPERTY, landholding, lands, manor, domain. **2** AREA, piece of land, region, tract, development. **3** ASSETS, resources, effects, possessions, belongings, wealth, fortune, property.

esteem v. RESPECT, admire, value, honour, look up to, think highly of, revere, venerate, appreciate, favour, approve of, like, love, cherish, prize, treasure.

estimate v. WORK OUT, calculate, assess, gauge, reckon, weigh up, evaluate, judge, appraise, guess, compute. ▶ n. **1** ESTIMATION, valuation, costing, assessment, appraisal, evaluation. **2** OPINION, estimation, judgement, consideration, friendly with someone. **2** (of someone's husband or wife) no longer living with them. ■ **estrangement** n.

estrogen US = OESTROGEN.

estuary n. (pl. **estuaries**) the mouth of a large river where it becomes affected by tides. ■ **estuarine** adj.

et al. abbrev. and others.

etc. abbrev. et cetera.

et cetera adv. and other similar things.

etch v. **1** produce a picture by engraving a metal plate with acid. **2** make clearly defined. ■ **etching** n.

eternal adj. lasting forever. ■ **eternally** adv.

eternity n. (pl. **eternities**) **1** unending time. **2** informal a very long period of time.

ethanol = ALCOHOL (sense 1).

ether n. **1** a liquid used as an anaesthetic and solvent. **2** the upper regions of the air.

ethereal adj. **1** extremely delicate and light. **2** heavenly or spiritual.

ethic n. **1** a moral principle. **2** (**ethics**) the study of moral principles.

ethical adj. **1** of moral principles. **2** morally correct. ■ **ethically** adv.

ethnic adj. relating to a group of people sharing a common origin, culture, or language. ▢ **ethnic cleansing** the expelling or killing of members of one ethnic or religious group in an area by those of another. ■ **ethnically** adv. **ethnicity** n.

ethnology n. the study of the characteristics of different peoples.

ethos n. the characteristic spirit of a culture, era, or community.

ethylene n. a flammable hydrocarbon gas, present in natural gas and coal gas.

etiolated adj. (of a plant) pale and weak due to a lack of light. ■ **etiolation** n.

etiquette n. the code of polite behaviour in a society.

étude /ay-tyood/ n. a short musical composition or exercise.

etymology n. (pl. **etymologies**) an account of a word's origins and development. ■ **etymological** adj.

EU abbrev. European Union.

eucalyptus n. an evergreen Australasian tree yielding a strong-smelling resin.

Eucharist n. **1** the Christian ceremony commemorating the Last Supper, in which consecrated bread and wine are consumed. **2** this bread and wine.

eugenics n. the science of improving a population by controlled breeding.

eulogy n. (pl. **eulogies**) a speech or piece of writing praising someone. ■ **eulogize** (or **-ise**) v.

eunuch n. a castrated man.

euphemism n. a less direct word used instead of an offensive one. ■ **euphemistic** adj. **euphemistically** adv.

euphony n. pleasantness of sounds, esp. in words.

euphoria n. excited happiness. ■ **euphoric** adj.

Eurasian adj. **1** of mixed European and Asian parentage. **2** of Europe and Asia.

eureka exclam. a cry of joy or satisfaction on the discovery of something.

eurhythmics pl. n. physical exercises to music.

euro n. the single European currency, introduced in 12 countries of the European Union in 2001.

European n. a person from Europe. ▶ adj. of Europe or the European Union. ▢ **European Union** an economic and political association of certain European countries.

Eustachian tube /yoo-stay-sh'n/ n. a passage between the ear and the throat.

euthanasia n. the painless killing of a patient suffering from an incurable illness.

evacuate v. **1** send from a place of danger to a safer place. **2** empty the

Thesaurus

thinking, mind, point of view, viewpoint, feeling, conviction, deduction, conclusion, guess, conjecture, surmise.

estimation n. *see* ESTIMATE.

estrangement n. ALIENATION, parting, separation, divorce, break-up, split, breach, severance, division, hostility, antagonism, antipathy, disaffection.

estuary n. RIVER MOUTH; Sc. firth.

eternal adj. ENDLESS, everlasting, never-ending, without end, immortal, infinite, enduring, deathless, undying, permanent, indestructible, imperishable, im-

mutable, ceaseless, incessant, constant, continuous, unchanging, unremitting, interminable, relentless, perpetual.

eternity n. IMMORTALITY, afterlife, everlasting life, the hereafter, the next world, heaven, paradise, nirvana.

ethical adj. MORAL, honourable, upright, righteous, good, virtuous, decent, principled, honest, just, fair, right, correct, proper, fitting, seemly, high-minded, decorous. ■ OPPOSITES unethical, immoral.

euphoric adj. ELATED, joyful, ecstatic, jubowels. ■ **evacuation** n. **evacuee** n.

evade v. escape or avoid by cleverness or trickery.

evaluate v. assess the amount or value of. ■ **evaluation** n. **evaluator** n.

evanescent adj. quickly fading. ■ **evanescence** n.

evangelical adj. **1** of the teaching of the gospel. **2** of a tradition within Protestant Christianity emphasizing biblical authority. **3** passionately supporting something. ■ **evangelicalism** n.

evangelist n. **1** a person who tries to convert others to Christianity. **2** the writer of one of the four Gospels. ■ **evangelism** n. **evangelistic** adj.

evaporate v. **1** turn from liquid into vapour. **2** disappear. ■ **evaporation** n.

evasion n. the act of evading.

evasive adj. seeking to evade or avoid something. ■ **evasively** adv. **evasiveness** n.

eve n. the day or period of time immediately before an event.

even adj. **1** level. **2** equal in number, amount, or value. **3** regular. **4** equally balanced. **5** placid; calm. **6** (of a number) exactly divisible by two. ▶v. make or become even. ▶adv. used for emphasis: *even less.* ■ **evenly** adv. **evenness** n.

evening n. the period of time at the end of the day.

evensong n. (in the Anglican Church) an evening service.

event n. **1** a thing that happens. **2** a public or social occasion. **3** a contest forming part of a sports competition.

eventful adj. marked by exciting events.

eventual adj. occurring at the end of a process or period of time. ■ **eventually** adv.

eventuality n. (pl. **eventualities**) a possible event.

ever adv. **1** at any time. **2** always. □ **evergreen** a plant having green leaves throughout the year. **everlasting** lasting forever or a very long time. **evermore** forever.

every adj. **1** each without exception.

Thesaurus

bilant, enraptured, rapturous, blissful, exhilarated, gleeful, excited, high-spirited, exalted, buoyant, intoxicated, merry; *informal* on cloud nine, in seventh heaven, over the moon, on a high.

evacuate v. **1** LEAVE, abandon, vacate, move out of, pull out of, quit, withdraw from, retreat from, flee, depart from, go away from, retire from, decamp from, desert, forsake. **2** EXPEL, excrete, eject, discharge, eliminate, void, purge, drain.

evade v. **1** AVOID, dodge, escape from, elude, circumvent, sidestep, shake off, keep out of the way of, keep one's distance from, steer clear of, shun, shirk; *informal* duck, give the slip to, chicken out of. **2** DODGE, avoid, parry, fend off, quibble about, fudge, not give a straight answer to; *informal* duck, cop out of.

evaluate v. ASSESS, put a price on, appraise, weigh up, size up, gauge, judge, rate, estimate, rank, calculate, reckon, measure, determine.

evaporate v. **1** BECOME VAPOUR, vaporize, volatilize. **2** DRY, dry up/out, dehydrate, desiccate, sear, parch. **3** VANISH, fade, disappear, melt away, dissolve, dissipate.

evasive adj. EQUIVOCAL, equivocating, prevaricating, quibbling, indirect, roundabout, circuitous, oblique, cunning, artful, casuistic; *informal* cagey, waffling.

even adj. **1** FLAT, level, smooth, plane, uniform, flush, true. **2** CONSTANT, steady, uniform, consistent, stable, unvarying, unchanging, unwavering, regular, unfluctuating. **3** EQUAL, identical, the same, alike, like, similar, comparable, commensurate, parallel, on a par. ▶adv. **1** YET, still, more so, all the more, all the greater. **2** AT ALL, so much as, hardly, barely, scarcely. ▶v. **1** SMOOTH, level, flatten, make flush. **2** EQUALIZE, make equal, make the same, balance up, standardize, regularize.

evening n. NIGHT, close of day, twilight, dusk, nightfall, sunset, sundown.

event n. **1** OCCASION, affair, business, matter, occurrence, happening, episode, circumstance, fact, eventuality, experience, phenomenon. **2** COMPETITION, contest, fixture, engagement, tournament, game, round, bout, race. **3** END, conclusion, outcome, result, upshot, consequence, effect, aftermath.

eventful adj. BUSY, action-packed, lively, full, active, important, noteworthy, memorable, notable, remarkable, outstanding, fateful, momentous, significant, crucial, historic, critical, decisive, consequential. ■ OPPOSITES uneventful, dull, insignificant.

eventual adj. FINAL, closing, concluding, end, last, ultimate, resulting, resultant, later, ensuing, consequent, subsequent.

eventually adv. IN THE END, ultimately,

2 happening at specified intervals: *every three months.* **3** all possible: *every effort was made.* ◻ **everybody** every person. **everyday 1** daily. **2** ordinary. **everyone** every person. **everything 1** all things. **2** the most important thing. **everywhere** in or to all places.

evict v. expel a tenant legally from a property. ■ **eviction** n.

evidence n. **1** information indicating whether something is true or valid. **2** information presented in a law court to support a case. ▶v. be evidence of. ◻ **in evidence** noticeable.

evident adj. plain or obvious. ■ **evidently** adv.

evil adj. **1** very immoral and wicked. **2** extremely unpleasant. ▶n. **1** extreme wickedness. **2** something harmful or undesirable. ■ **evilly** adv.

evince v. show or indicate.

eviscerate v. disembowel.

evoke v. **1** bring a feeling or image to

the mind. **2** obtain a response. ■ **evocation** n. **evocative** adj.

evolution n. **1** the process by which different kinds of living organism develop from earlier forms. **2** gradual development. ■ **evolutionary** adj.

evolve v. **1** develop gradually. **2** (of an organism) develop by evolution.

ewe n. a female sheep.

ewer n. a large jug.

ex prep. not including. ▶n. informal a former spouse or partner.

exacerbate v. make something bad worse. ■ **exacerbation** n.

exact adj. **1** precise. **2** correct in all details. ▶v. **1** demand and obtain. **2** inflict revenge. ■ **exactness** n.

exacting adj. making great demands on one's endurance or skill.

exactitude n. exactness.

exactly adv. **1** in an exact way. **2** used to express agreement.

exaggerate v. make something seem

Thesaurus

finally, at the end of the day, in the long run, when all is said and done, one day, some day, sooner or later, sometime.

everlasting adj. NEVER-ENDING, endless, without end, eternal, perpetual, undying, immortal, deathless, indestructible, abiding, enduring, infinite, boundless, timeless.

evermore adv. FOREVER, always, for all time, endlessly, without end, ceaselessly, unceasingly, constantly.

evict v. TURN OUT, throw out, eject, expel, remove, oust, dispossess, dislodge; *informal* throw out on the streets, throw someone out on their ear, chuck out, kick/turf out, give the heave-ho to, give the bum's rush to.

evidence n. **1** PROOF, verification, confirmation, substantiation, corroboration, authentication, support, grounds. **2** TESTIMONY, sworn statement, deposition, declaration, allegation, affidavit, attestation.

evident adj. OBVIOUS, clear, apparent, plain, unmistakable, noticeable, conspicuous, perceptible, visible, discernible, transparent, manifest, patent, tangible, palpable, indisputable, incontrovertible, incontestable.

evil adj. **1** WICKED, wrong, bad, immoral, sinful, corrupt, vile, base, depraved, iniquitous, heinous, villainous, nefarious, sinister, reprobate, vicious, atrocious, malevolent, demonic, malicious, devilish, diabolic. **2** BAD, harmful, in-

jurious, destructive, deleterious, pernicious, mischievous, malignant, venomous, noxious. **3** UNFAVOURABLE, adverse, unfortunate, unhappy, disastrous, catastrophic, ruinous, calamitous, unpropitious, inauspicious, dire, woeful. ■ OPPOSITES good. ▶n. **1** WICKEDNESS, wrong, bad, wrongdoing, sin, sinfulness, immorality, vice, iniquity, vileness, baseness, corruption, depravity, villainy, malevolence, devilishness. **2** HARM, hurt, pain, misery, sorrow, suffering, disaster, misfortune, catastrophe, ruin, calamity, affliction, woe. ■ OPPOSITES goodness.

evoke v. BRING ABOUT, cause, produce, bring forth, induce, arouse, excite, awaken, give rise to, stir up, stimulate, kindle, elicit, educe, summon up, call forth, conjure up, invoke, raise.

evolution n. DEVELOPMENT, progress, growth, progression, unrolling, expansion, natural selection, Darwinism.

evolve v. DEVELOP, grow, progress, emerge, mature, expand, unfold, unroll, open out, work out.

exacerbate v. AGGRAVATE, make worse, worsen, intensify; *informal* add fuel to the fire, put salt on the wound.

exact adj. **1** ACCURATE, precise, correct, faithful, close, true, unerring, veracious, literal, strict; *informal* on the nail, spot on, bang on. **2** CAREFUL, precise, meticulous, painstaking, methodical, conscientious, punctilious, rigorous, scrupulous, exacting. ▶v. REQUIRE, degreater than in reality. ■ **exaggeration** n.

exalt v. **1** praise highly. **2** raise to a higher rank.

exaltation n. extreme happiness.

exam n. an examination.

examination n. **1** a detailed inspection. **2** a formal test of knowledge or ability.

examine v. **1** inspect closely. **2** test the knowledge or ability of. ■ **examinee** n. **examiner** n.

example n. **1** a thing typical of its kind or illustrating a general rule. **2** a person or thing worthy of being copied. □ **make an example of** punish as a warning to others.

exasperate v. greatly irritate. ■ **exasperation** n.

excavate v. **1** make a hole by digging. **2** remove earth from an area in order to find buried remains. ■ **excavation** n. **excavator** n.

exceed v. **1** be greater than. **2** go beyond the limit of.

exceedingly adv. extremely.

excel v. (**excelling, excelled**) **1** be very good at. **2** (**excel oneself**) perform exceptionally well.

Excellency n. a form of address for certain high officials of state.

excellent adj. extremely good. ■ **excellence** n. **excellently** adv.

except prep. not including. ▶ v. exclude.

☑ Don't forget the c in **except** and related words.

----

excepting prep. except for.

exception n. a person or thing that is excluded or does not follow a rule. □ **take exception to** object to.

Thesaurus

mand, extract, extort, insist on, request, compel, call for, command, impose, wring, wrest, squeeze.

exacting adj. *see* DIFFICULT.

exaggerate v. OVERSTATE, overemphasize, overstress, overestimate, overvalue, magnify, embellish, amplify, embroider, colour, add colour, overelaborate, aggrandize, overdraw, hyperbolize; *informal* make a mountain out of a molehill, lay it on thick, lay it on with a trowel. ■ OPPOSITES understate, minimize.

exalted adj. **1** HIGH, high-ranking, lofty, grand, eminent, elevated, prestigious, august. **2** ELATED, exultant, jubilant, triumphant, joyful, rapturous, ecstatic, blissful, rhapsodic, transported.

examination n. **1** STUDY, inspection, scrutiny, investigation, review, analysis, research, observation, exploration, consideration, appraisal. **2** CHECK-UP, inspection, observation, assessment. **3** QUESTIONING, cross-questioning, cross-examination.

examine v. **1** LOOK AT/INTO, study, investigate, inquire into, survey, analyse, review, research, explore, sift, probe, check out, consider, appraise, weigh, weigh up, scan, inspect, vet. **2** INSPECT, look at, check over, assess, observe, give a check-up to, scrutinize. **3** PUT QUESTIONS TO, question, interrogate, quiz, test, cross-examine, cross-question; *informal* give the third-degree to, grill, pump.

example n. **1** SAMPLE, specimen, instance, representative, case, case in point, illustration. **2** MODEL, pattern, ideal, standard, paradigm, criterion.

exasperate v. ANGER, infuriate, annoy, irritate, madden, incense, enrage, provoke, irk, vex, gall, pique, try someone's patience; *informal* get on someone's nerves, make someone's blood boil, bug, needle, get to, rile.

excavate v. DIG, dig out, quarry, mine, burrow, hollow out, scoop out, gouge, cut out, unearth.

exceed v. BE GREATER THAN, surpass, beat, outdo, outstrip, outshine, transcend, go beyond, better, pass, top, cap, overshadow, eclipse.

exceedingly adv. EXTREMELY, very, extraordinarily, unusually, tremendously, enormously, vastly, greatly, highly, supremely, hugely, inordinately, superlatively.

excellence n. EMINENCE, merit, pre-eminence, distinction, greatness, fineness, quality, superiority, transcendence, supremacy, value, worth, skill.

excellent adj. VERY GOOD, first-rate, first-class, of a high standard, of high quality, great, fine, distinguished, superior, superb, outstanding, marvellous, eminent, pre-eminent, noted, supreme, admirable, superlative, sterling, worthy, prime, select, model, exemplary, consummate, remarkable; *informal* A1, top-notch, ace, tip-top, super, smashing, brilliant, brill. ■ OPPOSITES poor, inferior.

except prep. WITH THE EXCEPTION OF, excepting, excluding, besides, leaving out, barring, bar, other than, omitting,

exceptionable adj. causing disapproval or offence.

☑️ Don't confuse **exceptionable** and **exceptional**.

exceptional adj. **1** unusual. **2** unusually good. ■ **exceptionally** adv.

excerpt n. a short extract from a film, book, etc.

excess n. **1** an amount more than necessary, allowed, or desirable. **2** (**excesses**) outrageous behaviour. ▶ adj. exceeding a limit.

excessive adj. too much. ■ **excessively** adv.

exchange v. give or receive in place of another thing. ▶ n. **1** the act of exchan-ging. **2** a short conversation. **3** the giving of money for its equivalent in another currency. **4** a building used for trading. **5** a centre where telephone lines are connected. ■ **exchangeable** adj.

exchequer n. a national treasury.

excise n. a tax on certain goods. ▶ v. cut out. ■ **excision** n.

excitable adj. easily excited. ■ **excitability** n. **excitably** adv.

excite v. **1** cause strong feelings of enthusiasm and eagerness in. **2** arouse sexually. **3** cause a feeling or reaction. ■ **excitation** n. **excitement** n. **excitingly** adv.

exclaim v. cry out suddenly.

exclamation n. a sudden cry or re-

Thesaurus

saving, save.

exception n. **1** EXCLUSION, omission. **2** SPECIAL CASE, anomaly, irregularity, peculiarity, oddity, deviation, departure, quirk, freak. □ **take exception** OBJECT, be offended, take offence, resent, take umbrage, demur, disagree, cavil.

exceptional adj. **1** UNUSUAL, uncommon, abnormal, out of the ordinary, atypical, rare, odd, anomalous, singular, peculiar, inconsistent, aberrant, deviant, divergent. **2** UNUSUALLY GOOD, excellent, extraordinary, remarkable, outstanding, special, phenomenal, prodigious. ■ OPPOSITES normal, usual, average.

excerpt n. EXTRACT, quote, citation, quotation, passage, selection, highlight, part, section, fragment, piece, portion.

excess n. **1** SURPLUS, over-abundance, glut, surfeit, superfluity, plethora, superabundance, overkill. **2** REMAINDER, residue, leftovers, overflow, overload. **3** IMMODERATION, lack of restraint, overindulgence, intemperance, debauchery, dissipation, dissolution. ■ OPPOSITES shortage, moderation. ▶ adj. EXTRA, additional, too much, surplus, spare, superfluous, redundant.

excessive adj. TOO MUCH, immoderate, extravagant, lavish, superabundant, unreasonable, undue, uncalled for, extreme, inordinate, unjustifiable, unwarranted, unnecessary, needless, disproportionate, exorbitant, outrageous, intemperate, unconscionable.

exchange v. TRADE, swap, barter, interchange, reciprocate, bandy. ▶ n. TRADE, trade-off, barter, swapping, traffic, dealings, interchange, giving and taking, reciprocity.

excise v. **1** CUT OUT/OFF, remove, eradicate, extirpate; *technical* resect. **2** DELETE, remove, cut out, cross/strike out, erase, expunge, eliminate, blue-pencil, expurgate, bowdlerize.

excitable adj. TEMPERAMENTAL, emotional, highly strung, nervous, edgy, mercurial, volatile, tempestuous, hot-tempered, quick-tempered, hot-headed, passionate, fiery, irascible, testy, moody, choleric. ■ OPPOSITES calm.

excite v. **1** STIMULATE, animate, rouse, arouse, move, thrill, inflame, provoke, stir up, electrify, intoxicate, titillate, discompose; *informal* turn on, get going, work up, wind up. **2** BRING ABOUT, cause, rouse, arouse, awaken, incite, provoke, stimulate, kindle, evoke, stir up, elicit, engender, foment, instigate.

excited adj. AROUSED, animated, stimulated, thrilled, agitated, impassioned, hysterical, frenzied, delirious, enthusiastic, lively, exuberant, exhilarated, overwrought, feverish, wild; *informal* wound up, high, turned on. ■ OPPOSITES calm, indifferent.

excitement n. **1** ANIMATION, enthusiasm, passion, agitation, emotion, exhilaration, anticipation, elation, feverishness, ferment, tumult, discomposure, perturbation. **2** THRILL, adventure, stimulation, pleasure; *informal* kick. **3** AROUSAL, stimulation, awakening, evocation, kindling.

exciting adj. THRILLING, exhilarating, stimulating, gripping, dramatic, stirring, intoxicating, rousing, electrifying, invigorating, spine-tingling, riveting, moving, inspiring, provocative, titillating, sensational. ■ OPPOSITES boring, mark. □ **exclamation mark** a punctuation mark (!) indicating an exclamation. ∎ **exclamatory** adj.

exclude v. **1** prevent from being a part of something. **2** choose not to include for consideration. ∎ **exclusion** n.

exclusive adj. **1** excluding something. **2** restricted to the person, group, or area concerned. **3** catering for a select group. ▶n. a story published in only one newspaper etc. ∎ **exclusively** adv. **exclusivity** n.

excommunicate v. officially bar from the sacraments and services of a Church. ∎ **excommunication** n.

excoriate v. **1** remove part of the skin. **2** criticize severely. ∎ **excoriation** n.

excrement n. waste matter discharged from the bowels.

excrescence n. an abnormal growth on an animal or plant.

excreta n. waste discharged from the body.

excrete v. discharge waste material from the body. ∎ **excretion** n. **excretory** adj.

excruciating adj. **1** very painful. **2** very embarrassing or tedious.

excursion n. a short journey taken for pleasure.

excuse v. **1** justify or defend a fault or offence. **2** release from a duty. **3** forgive. ▶n. a reason put forward to justify a fault or offence. ∎ **excusable** adj.

ex-directory adj. not listed in a telephone directory at one's own request.

execrable adj. extremely bad or unpleasant.

execrate v. loathe. ∎ **execration** n.

execute v. **1** carry out a plan, order, etc. **2** kill a condemned person as a legal punishment. **3** perform an action. ∎ **execution** n. **executioner** n.

executive adj. having the power to put plans, actions, or laws into effect. ▶n. **1** a person or group with managerial responsibilities in a business etc. **2** (**the executive**) the branch of a government responsible for putting plans or laws into effect.

executor n. a person appointed to carry out the terms of a will.

exemplar n. a typical example or model.

exemplary adj. **1** representing the best of its kind. **2** serving as a warning.

exemplify v. (**exemplifying**, **exemplified**) be or give a typical example of.

Thesaurus

uninteresting.

exclaim v. CALL, cry, call/cry out, shout, yell, roar, bellow, shriek, proclaim, utter, vociferate; *dated* ejaculate.

exclamation n. CALL, cry, shout, yell, roar, bellow, shriek, utterance, interjection, expletive; *dated* ejaculation.

exclude v. **1** BAR, debar, keep out, shut out, prohibit, forbid, prevent, disallow, refuse, ban, veto, blackball, proscribe, interdict, stand in the way of. **2** ELIMINATE, rule out, preclude, reject, set aside, omit, pass over, leave out, ignore, repudiate, except. **3** BE EXCLUSIVE OF, not include, not be inclusive of, omit, leave out. ∎ OPPOSITES include.

exclusive adj. **1** SELECT, selective, restrictive, restricted, private, closed, limited, discriminating, cliquish, snobbish, fashionable, chic, elegant, upmarket; *informal* ritzy, posh, swish. **2** NOT INCLUDING, excluding, with the exception of, except for, not counting, leaving out, omitting. ∎ OPPOSITES inclusive.

excommunicate v. EXCLUDE, expel, cast out, banish, eject, remove, bar, debar, proscribe, anathematize, interdict, repudiate.

excrement n. WASTE MATTER, excreta, faeces, stools, droppings, ordure, dung, manure.

excrete v. DEFECATE, urinate, pass, void, discharge, eject, evacuate, expel, eliminate, emit.

excruciating adj. AGONIZING, unbearable, insufferable, harrowing, searing, acute, piercing, racking, torturous, severe, intense.

excusable adj. FORGIVABLE, pardonable, defensible, justifiable, understandable, condonable, venial.

excuse n. **1** EXPLANATION, reason, grounds, justification, defence, apology, vindication, mitigation, mitigating circumstances. **2** PRETEXT, pretence, coverup, front, subterfuge, fabrication, evasion. **3** APOLOGY, travesty, mockery. ▶v. **1** FORGIVE, pardon, absolve, acquit, exonerate, make allowances for, bear with, tolerate, indulge, exculpate. **2** LET OFF, exempt, spare, release, absolve, relieve, free, liberate. ∎ OPPOSITES condemn.

execute v. **1** PUT TO DEATH, kill, carry out a sentence of death. **2** CARRY OUT, accomplish, perform, implement, effect, bring off, achieve, complete, fulfil, enact, enforce, put into effect, do, engineer, prosecute, discharge, realize, attain, render.

■ **exemplification** n.

exempt adj. free from an obligation etc. imposed on others. ▶v. make exempt. ■ **exemption** n.

exercise n. **1** physical activity carried out to improve health and fitness. **2** a task set to practise or test a skill. **3** the use of a power, right, etc. ▶v. **1** use a power, right, etc. **2** engage in or subject to physical exercise. **3** worry or puzzle.

exert v. **1** apply a force, influence, or quality. **2** (**exert oneself**) make an effort. ■ **exertion** n.

exeunt /ek-si-uhnt/ v. a stage direction telling actors to leave the stage.

exfoliate v. **1** shed from a surface in scales or layers. **2** rub the skin with a grainy substance to remove dead cells. ■ **exfoliation** n.

ex gratia /eks gray-shuh/ adv. & adj. (of payment) given as a gift or favour rather than a legal requirement.

exhale v. **1** breathe out. **2** give off va-

pour or fumes. ■ **exhalation** n.

exhaust v. **1** tire out. **2** use up resources completely. ▶n. **1** waste gases expelled from an engine. **2** the device through which such gases are expelled. ■ **exhaustible** adj. **exhaustion** n.

exhaustive adj. covering all aspects fully. ■ **exhaustively** adv.

exhibit v. **1** put on public display. **2** display a quality. ▶n. an object on public display. ■ **exhibition** n. **exhibitor** n.

exhibitionism n. behaviour intended to attract attention. ■ **exhibitionist** n.

exhilarate v. cause to feel very happy or lively. ■ **exhilaration** n.

....

✓ -arate not -erate: exhilarate.

....

exhort v. strongly urge to do something. ■ **exhortation** n.

exhume v. dig up a buried corpse.

exigency n. (pl. **exigencies**) a pressing

Thesaurus

exemplary adj. MODEL, ideal, perfect, excellent, admirable, commendable, faultless, praiseworthy, laudable, honourable, meritorious.

exemplify v. TYPIFY, personify, epitomize, represent, embody, illustrate, show, demonstrate, symbolize.

exempt v. FREE FROM, release from, make an exception for, exclude from, excuse from, absolve from, spare, liberate from, relieve of, discharge from, dismiss from; *informal* let off.

exercise n. **1** ACTIVITY, exertion, effort, action, work, movement, training, gymnastics, sports, aerobics, callisthenics, keep-fit, workout, warm-up, limbering up, drill. **2** EMPLOYMENT, use, application, utilization, implementation, practice, operation, exertion, discharge. ▶v. **1** WORK OUT, train, do exercises, exert oneself, drill. **2** EMPLOY, use, make use of, utilize, apply, implement, exert. **3** WORRY, disturb, trouble, perplex, distress, preoccupy, annoy, make uneasy, perturb, vex.

exert v. **1** EMPLOY, exercise, use, make use of, utilize, apply, wield, bring to bear, set in motion, expend, spend. **2** APPLY ONESELF, make an effort, spare no effort, try hard, do one's best, give one's all, strive, endeavour, struggle, labour, toil, strain, work, push, drive; *informal* put one's back into it.

exhaust v. **1** TIRE, wear out, fatigue, drain, weary, sap, debilitate, prostrate, enfeeble, disable; *informal* knock out,

knacker, fag out; *US informal* poop. **2** USE UP, deplete, consume, finish, expend, run through, waste, squander, dissipate, fritter away; *informal* blow. ■ OPPOSITES invigorate, replenish.

exhausting adj. TIRING, fatiguing, wearing, gruelling, punishing, strenuous, arduous, back-breaking, taxing, laborious, enervating, sapping, debilitating.

exhaustion n. TIREDNESS, fatigue, weariness, weakness, collapse, debility, prostration, faintness, lassitude, enervation.

exhaustive adj. ALL-INCLUSIVE, comprehensive, intensive, all-out, in-depth, total, all-embracing, thorough, encyclopedic, complete, full, thoroughgoing, extensive, profound, far-reaching, sweeping. ■ OPPOSITES perfunctory.

exhibit v. **1** PUT ON DISPLAY, show, display, demonstrate, set out/forth, present, model, expose, air, unveil, flaunt, parade. **2** SHOW, express, indicate, reveal, display, demonstrate, betray, give away, disclose, manifest, evince, evidence.

exhibition n. DISPLAY, show, fair, demonstration, presentation, exposition, spectacle.

exhilarate v. MAKE HAPPY, elate, delight, gladden, brighten, enliven, excite, thrill, animate, invigorate, lift, perk up, stimulate, raise someone's spirits, revitalize, exalt, inspirit; *informal* pep up.

exhilaration n. ELATION, joy, happiness, delight, gladness, high spirits, excitement, gaiety, glee, animation, vivacity,

need or demand. ■ **exigent** adj.
exiguous adj. very small.
exile n. **1** the state of being barred from one's native country. **2** a person who lives in exile. ▶ v. send into exile.
exist v. **1** be real or present. **2** live. ■ **existence** n. **existent** adj.
existential adj. of existence or existentialism.
existentialism n. a philosophical theory emphasizing individuals' freedom to choose their own actions. ■ **existentialist** n. & adj.
exit n. **1** a way out. **2** an act of leaving. ▶ v. (**exiting**, **exited**) go out of or leave a place.
exodus n. a mass departure of people.
ex officio adv. & adj. as a result of one's position or status.
exonerate v. declare free from blame. ■ **exoneration** n.
exorbitant adj. (of a price) unreasonably high. ■ **exorbitantly** adv.
exorcize (or **-ise**) v. drive out an evil spirit from a person or place. ■ **exor-**

cism n. **exorcist** n.
exotic adj. **1** coming from or characteristic of a distant foreign country. **2** strikingly colourful or unusual. ■ **exotically** adv. **exoticism** n.
expand v. **1** make or become larger. **2** (**expand on**) give a fuller account of. ■ **expandable** adj. **expansion** n.
expanse n. a wide continuous area of something.
expansive adj. **1** covering a wide area. **2** relaxed, friendly, and communicative. ■ **expansively** adv.
expatiate /ik-**spay**-shi-ayt/ v. (**expatiate on**) speak or write at length or in detail about.
expatriate n. a person who lives outside their native country.
expect v. **1** regard as likely to happen. **2** regard as likely to do or be something. **3** require or demand as a person's duty. ■ **expectation** n.
expectant adj. **1** filled with anticipation. **2** pregnant. ■ **expectancy** n. **expectantly** adv.

Thesaurus

exaltation, mirth, hilarity.
exhort v. URGE, persuade, press, encourage, prompt, sway, advise, counsel, incite, goad, stimulate, push, entreat, bid, enjoin, admonish, warn.
exile v. BANISH, deport, expatriate, expel, drive out, eject, oust, uproot. ▶ n. **1** BANISHMENT, deportation, expatriation, uprooting, separation. **2** EXPATRIATE, deportee, refugee, displaced person, outcast, pariah.
exist v. **1** LIVE, be, have existence, have being, have life, breathe, draw breath, subsist, be extant, be viable. **2** SURVIVE, live, stay alive, subsist, eke out a living. ■ OPPOSITES die.
existing adj. IN EXISTENCE, existent, extant, living, surviving, remaining, enduring, prevailing, abiding, present, current.
exit n. **1** WAY OUT, door, doorway, gate, gateway, opening, egress, portal. **2** DEPARTURE, withdrawal, leaving, going, retirement, leave-taking, retreat, flight, exodus, farewell, adieu. ■ OPPOSITES entrance, arrival.
exonerate v. ABSOLVE, clear, acquit, discharge, vindicate, exculpate, dismiss, let off, excuse, pardon, justify. ■ OPPOSITES incriminate.
exorbitant adj. EXCESSIVE, unreasonable, extortionate, extreme, immoderate, outrageous, inordinate, preposterous, monstrous, unwarranted, undue,

unconscionable. ■ OPPOSITES moderate.
exotic adj. **1** FOREIGN, tropical, imported, alien, novel, introduced, external, extraneous. **2** STRIKING, outrageous, colourful, extraordinary, sensational, extravagant, unusual, remarkable, astonishing, strange, outlandish, bizarre, peculiar, impressive, glamorous, fascinating, mysterious, curious, different, unfamiliar.
expand v. **1** GROW/BECOME/MAKE LARGER, enlarge, increase in size, swell, inflate, magnify, amplify, add to, distend, lengthen, heighten, broaden, thicken, prolong, stretch, extend, multiply, dilate. **2** OPEN OUT, spread out, unfold, unfurl, unravel, unroll. ■ OPPOSITES contract.
expanse n. AREA, stretch, region, tract, extent, breadth, space, sweep, field, plain, surface, extension.
expansive adj. SOCIABLE, outgoing, friendly, affable, talkative, communicative, uninhibited, open, frank, genial, extrovert, garrulous, loquacious.
expect v. **1** SUPPOSE, assume, believe, imagine, think, presume, surmise, calculate, conjecture; informal reckon. **2** ANTICIPATE, envisage, predict, forecast, await, look for, look forward to, watch for, hope for, contemplate, bargain for, have in prospect. **3** DEMAND, insist on, require, count on, rely on, call for, look for, wish, want, hope for.

expectorant n. a medicine which helps to bring up phlegm, used for coughs.

expectorate v. cough or spit out phlegm.

expedient adj. helping to achieve something, though possibly unfair or immoral. ▶n. a means of achieving something. ■ **expediency** n.

expedite v. help or hasten the progress of.

expedition n. a journey made for a particular purpose. ■ **expeditionary** adj.

expeditious adj. quick and efficient. ■ **expeditiously** adv.

expel v. (**expelling**, **expelled**) **1** force out. **2** force a pupil to leave a school.

expend v. spend or use up a resource.

expendable adj. able to be sacrificed or abandoned to achieve an objective.

expenditure n. **1** the spending of money etc. **2** the amount of money spent.

expense n. **1** the cost of something. **2** (**expenses**) money spent in the course of doing a job etc. **3** something on which money must be spent.

expensive adj. costing a lot of money.

experience n. **1** practical involvement in an activity, event, etc. **2** knowledge or skill gained over time. **3** an event which affects one. ▶v. **1** be involved in. **2** feel an emotion.

experienced adj. having knowledge or skill gained over time.

experiment n. **1** a scientific procedure to find out or prove something. **2** a new course of action with an uncertain outcome. ▶v. **1** perform a scientific experiment. **2** try out new things. ■ **experimental** adj. **experimentally** adv. **experimentation** n.

expert n. & adj. (a person) having great knowledge or skill in a particular area. ■ **expertly** adv.

expertise n. expert skill or knowledge.

Thesaurus

expectant adj. **1** HOPEFUL, eager, anticipating, anticipatory, ready, watchful, in suspense, anxious, on tenterhooks; *informal* keyed up. **2** PREGNANT, expecting, in the family way; *technical* gravid.

expectation n. **1** ASSUMPTION, belief, supposition, presumption, assurance, conjecture, surmise, reckoning, calculation, confidence. **2** PROSPECTS, hopes, outlook, good fortune.

expedient adj. CONVENIENT, useful, pragmatic, advantageous, beneficial, profitable, gainful, practical, desirable, appropriate, suitable, advisable, apt, effective, helpful, politic, judicious, fit, timely, opportune, propitious. ▶n. MEANS, measure, stratagem, plan, scheme, plot, manoeuvre, trick, ploy, ruse, device, artifice, contrivance, invention.

expel v. **1** EVICT, banish, oust, drive out, exile, throw out, cast out, expatriate, deport, proscribe, outlaw; *informal* chuck out, kick out, boot out, turf out, heave out, send packing, give the bum's rush to. **2** DISCHARGE, eject, eliminate, excrete, evacuate, void, belch, spew out.

expend v. SPEND, pay out, lay out, disburse, lavish, squander, waste, fritter away, use up, consume, exhaust, deplete, sap, empty, finish off.

expendable adj. DISPOSABLE, dispensable, replaceable, non-essential, not required, inessential, unimportant. ■ OPPOSITES indispensable.

expense n. COST, price, outlay, payment, expenditure, outgoings, charge, amount, fee, rate, figure, disbursement.

expensive adj. OVERPRICED, exorbitant, steep, costly, dear, high-priced, extortionate, extravagant, lavish. *See also* EXORBITANT. ■ OPPOSITES cheap.

experience n. **1** FAMILIARITY, knowledge, involvement, practice, practical knowledge, participation, contact, acquaintance, exposure, observation, understanding. **2** EVENT, incident, occurrence, happening, affair, episode, adventure, encounter, circumstance, test, trial, case, ordeal. ▶v. HAVE EXPERIENCE OF, undergo, encounter, meet, feel, become familiar with, come into contact with, go through, live through, suffer, sustain.

experienced adj. PRACTISED, proficient, accomplished, skilful, seasoned, trained, expert, competent, adept, capable, knowledgeable, qualified, well versed, professional, mature, veteran, master. ■ OPPOSITES novice.

experiment n. TEST, investigation, trial, trial run, try-out, examination, observation, enquiry, demonstration, venture. ▶v. CONDUCT EXPERIMENTS, carry out tests/trials, conduct research, test, examine, investigate, explore, observe.

experimental adj. TRIAL, exploratory, pilot, tentative, speculative, preliminary, under review.

expert n. AUTHORITY, specialist, professional, master, adept, pundit, maestro, virtuoso, connoisseur; *informal* old hand,

expiate v. make amends for. ■ **expiation** n.

expire v. **1** cease to be valid. **2** die. **3** breathe out air.

expiry n. the end of the period for which something is valid.

explain v. **1** make clear by giving a detailed description. **2** give a reason for. ■ **explanation** n. **explanatory** adj.

expletive n. a swear word.

explicable adj. able to be explained.

explicit adj. clear, detailed, and unambiguous. ■ **explicitly** adv.

explode v. **1** burst or shatter violently. **2** show sudden violent emotion. **3** increase suddenly. **4** show a belief to be false. ■ **explosion** n.

exploit v. **1** make full use of a resource. **2** treat or use unfairly. ▶n. a daring feat. ■ **exploitative** adj. **exploitation** n. **exploiter** n.

explore v. **1** travel through an unfamiliar area in order to learn about it. **2** examine in detail. ■ **exploration** n. **exploratory** adj. **explorer** n.

explosive adj. & n. (a substance) able or likely to explode.

exponent n. **1** a promoter of an idea or theory. **2** a person who does a particular thing skilfully. **3** a raised figure beside a number indicating how many times the number is to be multiplied by itself.

exponential adj. **1** (of an increase) becoming more and more rapid. **2** of a mathematical exponent. ■ **exponentially** adv.

export v. send goods etc. to another country for sale. ▶n. **1** the act of exporting. **2** an exported product. ■ **exportation** n. **exporter** n.

expose v. **1** uncover and make visible

Thesaurus

ace, wizard, buff, pro, dab hand. ▶adj. ACCOMPLISHED, brilliant, competent, adept, master, able, proficient, skilful, experienced, practised, qualified, knowledgeable, capable, specialist, adroit, deft, dexterous, clever; *informal* crack, top-notch, wizard. ■ OPPOSITES incompetent.

expire v. **1** RUN OUT, lapse, finish, end, come to an end, terminate, conclude, discontinue, stop, cease. **2** *see* DIE.

explain v. **1** DESCRIBE, give an explanation of, make clear/plain, teach, illustrate, demonstrate, define, spell out, interpret, clear up, throw light on, clarify, elucidate, explicate, decipher, expound, decode, delineate, expose, resolve, solve, gloss, unravel, unfold; *informal* get across. **2** ACCOUNT FOR, justify, give a reason for, give a justification for, excuse, defend, vindicate, legitimize, rationalize, mitigate.

explanation n. **1** DESCRIPTION, interpretation, elucidation, explication, demonstration, definition, clarification, deciphering, decoding, expounding, illustration, exposure, resolution, solution. **2** ACCOUNT, justification, reason, excuse, defence, apology, vindication, mitigation, apologia.

explanatory adj. EXPOSITORY, descriptive, interpretative, illustrative, demonstrative, elucidatory, exegetic.

expletive n. SWEAR WORD, oath, curse, obscenity, epithet, exclamation, four-letter word, dirty word.

explicit adj. **1** CLEAR, understandable, detailed, crystal-clear, direct, plain, ob-

vious, precise, exact, straightforward, definite, categorical, specific, unequivocal, unambiguous. **2** UNRESTRAINED, unreserved, uninhibited, open, candid, frank, direct, full-frontal, no holds barred. ■ OPPOSITES vague, implicit.

explode v. **1** BLOW UP, detonate, go off, erupt, burst, fly apart, fly into pieces; *informal* go bang. **2** DISPROVE, invalidate, refute, discredit, debunk, repudiate, belie, give the lie to, ridicule; *informal* blow up, blow sky-high, shoot full of holes.

exploit v. **1** MAKE USE OF, use, put to use, utilize, turn/put to good use, profit from/by, turn to account, capitalize on, make capital out of; *informal* milk, cash in on. **2** TAKE ADVANTAGE OF, abuse, impose on, misuse; *informal* take for a ride, walk all over, put one over on. ▶n. FEAT, deed, adventure, stunt, achievement, accomplishment, attainment.

explore v. **1** TRAVEL, tour, range over, traverse, survey, inspect, scout, reconnoitre, prospect. **2** INVESTIGATE, look into, enquire into, consider, examine, scrutinize, research, study, review, take stock of.

explosion n. **1** BLAST, bang, detonation, eruption, discharge, boom, rumble, report, thunder, crash, clap, crack. **2** OUTBURST, flare-up, fit, outbreak, eruption, paroxysm.

explosive adj. **1** VOLATILE, unstable, inflammable, eruptive. **2** TENSE, charged, serious, critical, dangerous, hazardous, overwrought, ugly, volcanic.

exponent n. **1** ADVOCATE, supporter, up-

or unprotected. **2** (**expose to**) make vulnerable to. **3** subject photographic film to light. ■ **exposure** n.

exposé /ik-**spoh**-zay/ n. a report in the media revealing something discreditable.

exposition n. **1** a full account and explanation of a theory. **2** a large exhibition.

expostulate v. disagree strongly. ■ **expostulation** n.

expound v. explain a theory in detail.

express v. **1** convey a feeling etc. by words or gestures. **2** squeeze out liquid or air. ▶ adj. **1** travelling or operating at high speed. **2** stated clearly. ▶ adv. by express train or delivery service. ▶ n. a fast train that stops at few stations. □ **expressway** US an urban motorway. ■ **expressly** adv.

expression n. **1** the act of expressing. **2** a look on someone's face. **3** a word or phrase.

expressionism n. a style of art seeking to express feelings rather than represent objects realistically. ■ **expressionist** n. & adj.

expressive adj. effectively conveying a thought or feeling. ■ **expressively** adv.

expropriate v. take property for public use. ■ **expropriation** n.

expulsion n. the act of expelling.

expunge v. remove completely.

expurgate v. remove unsuitable matter from a text. ■ **expurgation** n.

exquisite adj. **1** very beautiful and delicate. **2** highly refined. **3** intensely felt. ■ **exquisitely** adv.

extant adj. still existing.

extemporize (or **-ise**) v. speak or do without preparation; improvise.

extend v. **1** make larger or longer. **2** reach over or continue for. **3** hold out a part of the body. **4** offer. ■ **extendable** (or **extendible**) adj.

extension n. **1** the act of extending. **2** a part added to something to make it bigger. **3** an additional period of time. **4** a secondary telephone.

extensive adj. large in area, amount, or scope. ■ **extensively** adv.

extensor n. a muscle that extends a part of the body.

extent n. **1** the area covered by something. **2** size or scale. **3** the degree to which something is true.

Thesaurus

holder, backer, defender, champion, spokesperson, promoter, proponent, propagandist. **2** PRACTITIONER, performer, interpreter, player, presenter, executant.

expose v. **1** UNCOVER, bare, lay bare, strip, reveal, denude. **2** REVEAL, show, display, exhibit, make obvious, disclose, manifest, unveil. **3** DISCLOSE, bring to light, reveal, uncover, divulge, let out, denounce, unearth, unmask, detect, betray; *informal* spill the beans on, blow the whistle on. ■ OPPOSITES cover, conceal.

express v. COMMUNICATE, convey, put across/over, utter, voice, air, articulate, state, give vent to, phrase, word, put into words, indicate, show, demonstrate, reveal.

expression n. **1** STATEMENT, utterance, pronouncement, assertion, proclamation, articulation, voicing. **2** WORD, phrase, term, choice of words, turn of phrase, wording, language, phrasing, speech, diction, idiom, style, delivery, intonation; *formal* locution. **3** LOOK, countenance, appearance, air, mien, aspect. **4** FEELING, emotion, passion, intensity, power, force, imagination, artistry, poignancy, depth, spirit, vividness, ardour.

expressionless adj. **1** BLANK, deadpan, inscrutable, emotionless, impassive, poker-faced, straight-faced, vacuous. **2** DULL, dry, boring, wooden, undemonstrative, apathetic, devoid of feeling. ■ OPPOSITES expressive.

expressive adj. **1** ELOQUENT, demonstrative, emotional, suggestive, telling, vivid. **2** PASSIONATE, intense, emotional, moving, poignant, striking, eloquent, vivid, evocative, artistic, sympathetic. ■ OPPOSITES expressionless, unemotional.

expressly adv. **1** ABSOLUTELY, explicitly, clearly, plainly, distinctly, specifically, unequivocally, precisely. **2** SPECIALLY, especially, particularly, solely, specifically, singularly.

extend v. **1** EXPAND, increase, enlarge, lengthen, widen, broaden, stretch, draw out, elongate. **2** INCREASE, widen, add to, expand, augment, enhance, develop, supplement, amplify. **3** PROLONG, increase, lengthen, protract, drag out, stretch out, spin out. **4** OFFER, give, proffer, present, hold out, confer, advance, impart. **5** CONTINUE, stretch, carry on, run on, last, unroll, range. ■ OPPOSITES contract, curtail.

extensive adj. **1** LARGE, sizeable, substantial, spacious, considerable, vast,

extenuating adj. making an offence less serious or more forgivable.

exterior adj. of the outside. ▶ n. an outer surface or structure.

exterminate v. destroy completely. ■ **extermination** n. **exterminator** n.

external adj. of or on the outside. ■ **externally** adv.

externalize (or **-ise**) v. express a thought etc. in words or actions.

extinct adj. **1** (of a species etc.) having no living members. **2** (of a volcano) not having erupted in recorded history. ■ **extinction** n.

extinguish v. **1** put out a fire or light. **2** put an end to. ■ **extinguisher** n.

extirpate v. search out and destroy. ■ **extirpation** n.

extol v. (**extolling**, **extolled**) praise enthusiastically.

extort v. obtain by force or threats. ■ **extortion** n.

extortionate adj. (of a price) much too high. ■ **extortionately** adv.

extra adj. added to an existing or usual amount. ▶ adv. **1** to a greater extent than usual. **2** in addition. ▶ n. **1** an additional item. **2** a person employed as one of a crowd in a film.

extra- prefix **1** outside. **2** beyond the scope of.

extract v. **1** take out or obtain by force or effort. **2** obtain a substance etc. by a special method. **3** select a passage from a book, film, etc. ▶ n. **1** a short passage from a text, film, etc. **2** the concentrated active ingredient of a substance. ■ **extractor** n.

extraction n. **1** the act of extracting. **2** ancestry or ethnic origin.

extra-curricular adj. done in addition to the normal curriculum.

extradite v. hand over an accused person for trial in the country where the crime was committed. ■ **extradition** n.

extramarital adj. occurring outside marriage.

extramural adj. for students who are not full-time members of a university.

extraneous adj. unrelated or irrelevant.

extraordinary adj. **1** very unusual or remarkable. **2** (of a meeting) held for a special reason. ■ **extraordinarily** adv.

extrapolate v. use a fact valid for one situation to make conclusions about a different situation. ■ **extrapolation** n.

extrasensory perception n. the supposed ability to perceive things by means other than the known senses.

extraterrestrial adj. of or from outside the earth or its atmosphere.

extravagant adj. **1** spending money or using resources excessively. **2** exceeding what is reasonable. ■ **extravagance** n. **extravagantly** adv.

Thesaurus

immense. **2** BROAD, wide, wide-ranging, comprehensive, thorough, complete, all-embracing, inclusive. ■ OPPOSITES small, limited.

extent n. **1** LENGTH, area, expanse, stretch, range, scope. **2** BREADTH, range, scope, degree, comprehensiveness, completeness, thoroughness.

exterior n. OUTSIDE, surface, front, covering, facade, shell, skin. ▶ adj. OUTER, outside, outermost, outward, external, surface, superficial. ■ OPPOSITES interior.

exterminate v. KILL, destroy, annihilate, eradicate, extirpate, abolish, eliminate; informal wipe out, bump off.

extinguish v. **1** PUT OUT, blow out, quench, smother, douse, snuff out, dampen down, stifle, choke off. **2** DESTROY, kill, end, remove, annihilate, wipe out, eliminate, abolish, eradicate, erase, expunge, suppress, extirpate. ■ OPPOSITES light, kindle.

extol v. PRAISE, sing someone's praises, applaud, acclaim, pay tribute to, commend, exalt, congratulate, compliment, celebrate, glorify, eulogize; formal laud. ■ OPPOSITES condemn.

extra adj. **1** ADDITIONAL, further, supplementary, supplemental, added, subsidiary, auxiliary, ancillary, other, accessory. **2** SPARE, surplus, left over, excess, redundant, superfluous, reserve, unused.

extract v. **1** PULL OUT, draw out, take out, pluck out, wrench out, prise out, tear out, uproot, withdraw. **2** EXTORT, exact, force, coerce, elicit, wring, wrest, squeeze. ▶ n. **1** CONCENTRATE, essence, distillate, juice, solution, decoction. **2** EXCERPT, passage, cutting, clipping, abstract, citation, selection, quotation, fragment.

extraordinary adj. **1** EXCEPTIONAL, unusual, rare, uncommon, unique, singular, outstanding, striking, remarkable, phenomenal, marvellous, wonderful, signal, peculiar, unprecedented. **2** AMAZING, surprising, unusual, remarkable, strange, astounding, odd. **3** ODD, strange, curious, bizarre, unconventional, weird. ■ OPPOSITES ordinary,

extravaganza n. a lavish spectacular entertainment.

extreme adj. **1** to the highest degree. **2** highly unusual. **3** very severe or serious. **4** not moderate. **5** furthest from the centre or a given point. ▶n. **1** either of two abstract things that are as different from each other as possible. **2** the most extreme degree. ■ **extremely** adv.

extremist n. a person holding extreme views. ■ **extremism** n.

extremity n. (pl. **extremities**) **1** the furthest point or limit. **2** (**extremities**) the hands and feet. **3** severity. **4** extreme hardship.

extricate v. free from a difficulty. ■ **extrication** n.

extrinsic adj. coming from outside.

extrovert n. a lively, sociable person.

extrude v. thrust or force out. ■ **extrusion** n.

exuberant adj. lively and cheerful. ■ **exuberance** n.

exude v. **1** discharge or be discharged slowly and steadily. **2** display a quality strongly and openly.

exult v. show or feel triumphant joy. ■ **exultant** adj. **exultation** n.

eye n. **1** the organ of sight. **2** something compared to an eye in shape, position, etc. ▶v. (**eyeing**, **eyed**) look at closely or with interest. □ **eyeball** the round part of the eye within the eyelids. **eyebrow** the strip of hair on the ridge above the eye socket. **eyelash** each of the hairs on the edges of the eyelids. **eyelet** a small round hole through which a lace can be threaded. **eyelid** either of the two folds of skin which cover the eye when closed. **eye-opener** informal an unexpectedly revealing event or situation. **eyeshadow** a cosmetic applied to the skin around the eyes. **eyesight** a person's ability to see. **eyesore** a very ugly thing. **eye tooth** a canine tooth. **eyewitness** a person who has seen something happen. **see eye to eye** have similar views; be in full agreement.

eyrie /eer-i/ n. an eagle's nest.

Thesaurus

commonplace.

extravagant adj. **1** SPENDTHRIFT, profligate, wasteful, lavish, reckless, imprudent, excessive, improvident, prodigal, thriftless. **2** EXAGGERATED, excessive, unrestrained, outrageous, immoderate, preposterous, absurd, irrational, reckless, wild; informal over-the-top, OTT. **3** EXORBITANT, excessive, unreasonable, extortionate, inordinate, immoderate, expensive, steep, dear, costly, overpriced. ■ OPPOSITES thrifty, restrained.

extreme adj. **1** GREAT, greatest, acute, intense, severe, highest, utmost, maximum, supreme, high, ultimate, exceptional, extraordinary. **2** SEVERE, harsh, Draconian, stringent, drastic, strict, stern, unrelenting, relentless, unbending, uncompromising, unyielding. **3** FANATICAL, immoderate, intemperate, militant, radical, intransigent, extremist, exaggerated, excessive, unreasonable, overzealous. ■ OPPOSITES moderate. ▶n. MAXIMUM, highest point, pinnacle, climax, acme, zenith, apex, ne plus ultra.

extremely adv. VERY, exceedingly, exceptionally, intensely, greatly, acutely, utterly, excessively, inordinately, markedly, extraordinarily, uncommonly, severely, terribly; informal awfully.

extrovert adj. OUTGOING, extroverted, sociable, friendly, social, lively, cheerful, effervescent, exuberant. ■ OPPOSITES introverted.

exuberant adj. **1** ELATED, exhilarated, cheerful, sparkling, full of life, animated, lively, high-spirited, spirited, buoyant, effervescent, vivacious, excited, ebullient, exultant, enthusiastic, irrepressible, energetic, vigorous, zestful; informal upbeat, bouncy. **2** PROFUSE, luxuriant, lush, thriving, abundant, superabundant, prolific, teeming, lavish, copious, rich, plentiful, abounding, overflowing, rank. ■ OPPOSITES depressed, meagre.

exultant adj. JOYFUL, overjoyed, jubilant, triumphant, delighted, ecstatic, cock-a-hoop, gleeful, enraptured, transported.

eyeful n. **1** LOOK, good look, view, stare, gaze; informal load, gander, butcher's, shufti. **2** VISION, dream, beauty, dazzler; informal stunner, knockout, sight for sore eyes, bobby-dazzler.

eyesore n. BLEMISH, blot, scar, blight, disfigurement, defacement, defect, monstrosity, carbuncle, atrocity, disgrace, ugliness.

eyewitness n. WITNESS, observer, onlooker, bystander, passer-by, spectator, watcher, viewer, beholder.

Ff

F abbrev. Fahrenheit.

FA abbrev. Football Association.

fable n. a story with a moral or based on myth.

fabled adj. **1** famous. **2** mythical.

fabric n. **1** cloth. **2** the essential structure of a building etc.

fabricate v. **1** invent untrue facts. **2** construct. ■ **fabrication** n.

fabulous adj. **1** great; extraordinary. **2** informal excellent. **3** mythical. ■ **fabulously** adv.

facade n. **1** the front of a building. **2** a misleading outward appearance.

face n. **1** the front of the head. **2** an expression on this. **3** a grimace. **4** a surface. **5** an aspect. ▶ v. **1** have the face or front towards. **2** confront. **3** put a facing on. □ **facecloth** a small cloth for washing one's face. **faceless** remote and impersonal. **facelift** an operation to remove wrinkles by tightening the skin of the face. **lose** (or **save**) **face** suffer (or avoid) humiliation.

facet n. **1** one side of something with many sides. **2** an aspect.

facetious adj. treating serious issues with inappropriate humour. ■ **facetiously** adv. **facetiousness** n.

facia var. of FASCIA.

facial adj. of the face. ▶ n. a beauty treatment for the face.

facile adj. **1** produced without careful thought. **2** too simple.

facilitate v. make easy or easier. ■ **facilitation** n. **facilitator** n.

facility n. (pl. **facilities**) **1** a building, service, etc. provided for a particular purpose. **2** a natural ability or skill.

facing n. **1** a piece of material sewn to an inside edge of a garment to strengthen it. **2** an outer layer on a wall.

facsimile n. **1** an exact copy of a document. **2** a fax.

fact n. a thing known to be true. □ **the facts of life** information about sexual matters. **in fact** in reality.

faction n. a small dissenting group within a larger group. ■ **factional** adj. **factious** adj.

factitious adj. not genuine.

factor n. **1** a circumstance contributing to a result. **2** a number or quantity that when multiplied with another produces a given number or expression.

factory n. (pl. **factories**) a building

Thesaurus

fabric n. **1** CLOTH, material, textile, stuff. **2** STRUCTURE, make-up, framework, frame, constitution, essence.

fabricate v. **1** ASSEMBLE, construct, build, make, manufacture, erect, put together, form, produce, fashion, frame, shape. **2** MAKE UP, invent, concoct, think up, hatch, devise, trump up, coin.

fabulous adj. **1** see MARVELLOUS. **2** MYTHICAL, legendary, fantastical, imaginary, fictional, fictitious, unreal, made up, fanciful, apocryphal.

face n. **1** COUNTENANCE, visage, physiognomy, features, lineaments; informal mug, clock, dial, phizog, phiz. **2** EXPRESSION, look, demeanour, air, aspect. ▶ v. **1** LOOK ON TO, overlook, look towards, give on to, be opposite to. **2** ENCOUNTER, meet, confront, withstand, cope with, deal with, brazen out, defy, brave, oppose; informal get to grips with, meet head-on. **3** DRESS, finish, polish, smooth, level, coat, surface, clad, veneer.

■ OPPOSITES evade.

facet n. ASPECT, feature, characteristic, factor, element, angle, side, point, part.

facetious adj. FLIPPANT, jocular, frivolous, light-hearted, tongue-in-cheek, waggish, jocose. ■ OPPOSITES serious.

facile adj. **1** INSINCERE, superficial, glib, shallow, slick, urbane, suave, bland. **2** EASY, simple, uncomplicated, unchallenging.

facility n. **1** EASE, effortlessness, skill, adroitness, smoothness, fluency, slickness. **2** AMENITY, resource, service, benefit, convenience, equipment, aid, opportunity.

fact n. **1** TRUTH, actuality, reality, certainty, certitude. **2** DETAIL, particular, information, point, item, factor, element, feature, circumstance, specific. ■ OPPOSITES falsehood.

faction n. GROUP, section, side, party, band, set, ring, division, contingent, lobby, camp, bloc, clique, coalition, conwhere goods are made or assembled.

factotum n. a person employed to do a wide variety of tasks.

factual adj. based on or containing facts. ■ **factually** adv.

faculty n. (pl. **faculties**) **1** a mental or physical power. **2** a university department concerned with a particular subject.

fad n. **1** a craze. **2** a fussy like or dislike. ■ **faddy** adj.

fade v. **1** gradually disappear. **2** lose or cause to lose colour.

faeces /fee-seez/ (US **feces**) pl. n. excrement. ■ **faecal** adj.

fag n. informal **1** a tiring or tedious task. **2** a cigarette.

faggot n. **1** a ball of seasoned chopped liver etc., baked or fried. **2** (US **fagot**) a bundle of sticks tied together.

Fahrenheit adj. denoting a scale of temperature on which water freezes at 32° and boils at 212°.

faience /fy-ahns/ n. painted glazed earthenware.

fail v. **1** be unsuccessful in a task or examination. **2** neglect to do. **3** stop working properly. **4** become weaker. **5** desert or let down. ▶ n. a mark too low to pass an examination. ■ **failure** n.

failing n. a weakness or fault. ▶ prep. if not.

fain adv. old use gladly.

faint adj. **1** not clearly perceived. **2** slight. **3** about to faint. ▶ v. briefly lose consciousness. □ **faint-hearted** timid. ■ **faintly** adv. **faintness** n.

fair adj. **1** treating people equally. **2** just or appropriate. **3** quite large in size or amount. **4** moderately good. **5** light in colour. **6** (of wind) favourable. ▶ adv. in a fair way. ▶ n. **1** a funfair. **2** a gathering for the sale of goods. **3** an exhibition to promote a particular product. □ **fairground** an outdoor area where a funfair is held. **fairway** a part of a golf course between a tee and a green. ■ **fairness** n.

Thesaurus

federacy, coterie, caucus, cabal, junta, ginger group, splinter group, pressure group; informal gang, crew.

factor n. ELEMENT, part, component, ingredient, constituent, point, detail, item, facet, aspect, feature, characteristic, consideration, influence, circumstance, thing, determinant.

factual adj. REAL, realistic, true, fact-based, true-to-life, truthful, authentic, genuine, accurate, sure, exact, precise, honest, faithful, literal, matter-of-fact, verbatim, word-for-word, objective, unbiased, unprejudiced, unvarnished, unadorned, unadulterated, unexaggerated. ■ OPPOSITES untrue, fictitious.

fad n. CRAZE, mania, enthusiasm, vogue, fashion, trend, mode, fancy, whim.

fade v. **1** GROW PALE, lose colour, become paler, become bleached, become washed out, dull, dim, lose lustre. **2** GROW LESS, dwindle, diminish, decline, die away, disappear, vanish, die, peter out, dissolve, melt away, grow faint, wane, fail, evanesce. ■ OPPOSITES increase.

fail v. **1** NOT SUCCEED, be unsuccessful, fall through, be frustrated, break down, be defeated, be in vain, collapse, founder, misfire, meet with disaster, come to grief, come to nothing, run aground, go astray; informal come a cropper, bite the dust, fizzle out, miss the mark, not come up to scratch. **2** GO BANKRUPT, collapse, crash, go under, become insolvent, go into receivership, cease trading,

be closed, close down; informal fold, flop, go bust, go broke. **3** LET DOWN, desert, neglect, abandon, forsake, disappoint. **4** OMIT, neglect, forget, be unable. ■ OPPOSITES succeed.

failing n. FAULT, shortcoming, weakness, imperfection, defect, flaw, blemish, frailty, foible, drawback. ■ OPPOSITES strength.

failure n. **1** FIASCO, vain attempt, defeat, debacle, blunder; informal botch, flop, washout. **2** LOSER, incompetent, nonachiever, disappointment, ne'er-do-well; informal no-hoper, dud, flop, washout. **3** OMISSION, neglect, negligence, dereliction, remissness, delinquency. ■ OPPOSITES success.

faint adj. **1** INDISTINCT, unclear, obscure, dim, pale, faded, bleached. **2** SOFT, muted, indistinct, low, weak, feeble, subdued, stifled, whispered. **3** SLIGHT, small, remote, vague, minimal. **4** DIZZY, giddy, light-headed, muzzy, weak, weak-headed, vertiginous; informal woozy. ■ OPPOSITES clear, loud. ▶ v. LOSE CONSCIOUSNESS, black out, pass out, collapse, swoon; informal keel over, conk out, flake out.

fair¹ adj. **1** JUST, impartial, unbiased, unprejudiced, objective, even-handed, disinterested, dispassionate, equitable, detached, above board, lawful, legal, legitimate, proper, square; informal on the level. **2** REASONABLE, tolerable, passable, satisfactory, respectable, decent, good-

fairing n. a streamlining structure added to a vehicle, boat, etc.

fairly adv. **1** justly. **2** moderately.

fairy n. (pl. **fairies**) a small imaginary being with magical powers. ▫ **fairy godmother** a person who comes to the aid of someone in difficulty. **fairy lights** small electric lights used as decorations.

fait accompli n. a thing that has been done and cannot now be altered.

faith n. **1** complete trust or confidence. **2** strong religious belief. **3** a system of religious belief. ▫ **faith healing** healing achieved by religious faith and prayer.

faithful adj. **1** loyal. **2** true to the facts or the original. ■ **faithfully** adv. **faithfulness** n.

faithless adj. disloyal.

fake adj. not genuine. ▶ n. a fake person or thing. ▶ v. **1** make a copy or imitation of. **2** pretend.

fakir n. a Muslim or Hindu holy man who lives by begging.

falcon n. a fast-flying bird of prey.

falconry n. the keeping and training of birds of prey. ■ **falconer** n.

fall v. (**falling**, **fell**; past part. **fallen**) **1** move downwards quickly and without control. **2** collapse to the ground. **3** hang or slope down. **4** become less or lower. **5** become. **6** be captured or defeated in a battle. ▶ n. **1** an act of falling. **2** a thing which has fallen. **3** (**falls**) a waterfall. **4** a drop in size or number. **5** US autumn. ▫ **fall for** informal **1** fall in love with. **2** be tricked by. **fallout** airborne radioactive debris. **fall out** quarrel. **fall through** fail.

fallacy n. (pl. **fallacies**) **1** a mistaken belief. **2** unsound reasoning. ■ **fallacious** adj.

fallible adj. capable of making mistakes. ■ **fallibility** n.

Fallopian tube n. either of two tubes connecting the ovaries to the uterus.

fallow adj. (of farmland) left unplanted for a period.

false adj. **1** not true or correct. **2** fake; artificial. **3** disloyal. ■ **falsely** adv. **falseness** n. **falsity** n.

Thesaurus

ish, moderate, average, middling, adequate, sufficient, ample, so-so. **3** BLOND/BLONDE, light, yellow, golden, flaxen, light brown, strawberry blonde. **4** BEAUTIFUL, pretty, lovely, attractive, good-looking; Sc. & N. Engl. bonny; literary beauteous; old use comely. **5** FINE, dry, bright, clear, sunny, cloudless, unclouded. ■ OPPOSITES unfair, ugly.

fair² n. **1** EXHIBITION, display, show, exhibit, exposition, expo. **2** FESTIVAL, carnival, fete, gala.

fairly adv. **1** JUSTLY, equitably, impartially, even-handedly, without prejudice, objectively. **2** REASONABLY, quite, pretty, passably, tolerably, moderately, satisfactorily, rather, somewhat, adequately.

faith n. **1** TRUST, belief, confidence, conviction, credence, reliance, credit, optimism, hopefulness. **2** RELIGION, church, denomination, belief, creed, persuasion, teaching, doctrine, sect. ■ OPPOSITES mistrust.

faithful adj. **1** LOYAL, devoted, constant, dependable, true, reliable, trustworthy, staunch, unswerving, unwavering, steadfast, dutiful, dedicated, committed. **2** ACCURATE, true, exact, precise, close, strict, unerring; informal spot on, bang on. ■ OPPOSITES unfaithful, inaccurate.

fake adj. **1** SHAM, imitation, false, counterfeit, forged, fraudulent, bogus, spurious, pseudo, mock, simulated, artificial,

synthetic, reproduction, ersatz; informal phoney. **2** ASSUMED, affected, feigned, put on, pseudo, insincere; informal phoney. ■ OPPOSITES genuine. ▶ n. **1** SHAM, imitation, forgery, counterfeit, copy, reproduction, hoax. **2** FRAUD, charlatan, impostor, hoaxer, cheat, humbug, mountebank, quack; informal phoney.

fall v. **1** DROP, descend, come/go down, sink, plummet, cascade, gravitate. **2** FALL DOWN/OVER, collapse, fall in a heap, trip, trip over, stumble, slip, tumble, slide, topple over, keel over, go head over heels, take a spill. **3** DECREASE, dwindle, go down, grow less, diminish, plummet, depreciate, slump, deteriorate. ▶ n. **1** TUMBLE, trip, spill, stumble, slide, collapse. **2** DOWNFALL, demise, collapse, ruin, failure, decline, deterioration, destruction, overthrow. **3** DECREASE, lessening, cut, dip, reduction, depreciation, slump. ▫ **fall apart** see DISINTEGRATE. **fall back on** RESORT TO, have recourse to, call into play, call upon, make use of, use, employ, rely on.

fallacy n. MISCONCEPTION, false notion, error, mistake, misapprehension, miscalculation, delusion, misjudgement.

false adj. **1** UNTRUE, untruthful, fictitious, inaccurate, misleading, invented, concocted, fabricated, incorrect, wrong, faulty, erroneous, unfounded, invalid,

falsehood n. **1** the state of being un-true. **2** a lie.

falsetto n. (pl. **falsettos**) a high-pitched voice above one's natural range.

falsify v. (**falsifying, falsified**) alter so as to mislead. ■ **falsification** n.

falter v. **1** lose strength or momentum. **2** move or speak hesitantly.

fame n. the state of being famous. ■ **famed** adj.

familial adj. of a family.

familiar adj. **1** well known. **2** often en-countered. **3** (**familiar with**) having knowledge of. **4** friendly. ▶ n. a spirit supposedly attending and obeying a witch. ■ **familiarity** n. **familiarly** adv.

familiarize (or **-ise**) v. give someone knowledge or understanding. ■ **famil-iarization** n.

family n. (pl. **families**) **1** a group consist-ing of parents and their children. **2** a person's children. **3** a group of related people or things.

famine n. extreme scarcity of food.

famished adj. informal very hungry.

famous adj. **1** known about by many people. **2** informal excellent. ■ **famously** adv.

fan n. **1** a hand-held or mechanical de-vice creating a cooling current of air. **2** an enthusiastic admirer or supporter. ▶ v. (**fanning, fanned**) **1** drive a cur-rent of air towards. **2** strengthen a be-lief etc. **3** spread out from a central point. ☐ **fan belt** a belt driving the fan that cools a vehicle's engine.

fanatic n. a person with excessive en-thusiasm for something. ■ **fanatical** adj. **fanatically** adv. **fanaticism** n.

fancier n. a person who keeps or breeds a particular type of animal.

fanciful adj. **1** imaginary. **2** very un-

Thesaurus

forged, fraudulent, spurious. **2** TREACH-EROUS, disloyal, unfaithful, faithless, traitorous, two-faced, double-dealing, untrustworthy, deceitful, untrue, de-ceiving, deceptive, duplicitous, dishon-ourable, perfidious, dishonest, hypocrit-ical, unreliable, unsound, lying, menda-cious. ■ OPPOSITES true, loyal, faithful.

falsehood n. LIE, untruth, false state-ment, fib, falsification, fabrication, in-vention, piece of fiction, fairy story, exaggeration; informal whopper. ■ OPPOS-ITES truth.

falsify v. ALTER, doctor, tamper with, forge, counterfeit, distort, pervert, adul-terate.

falter v. **1** HESITATE, waver, delay, drag one's feet, vacillate, shilly-shally, blow hot and cold, be undecided, sit on the fence, oscillate, fluctuate, hum and haw, haver. **2** STAMMER, stutter, speak haltingly.

fame n. RENOWN, celebrity, eminence, notability, note, distinction, promin-ence, mark, esteem, importance, great-ness, account, pre-eminence, glory, honour, illustriousness, stardom, repu-tation, repute, notoriety, infamy. ■ OP-POSITES obscurity.

familiar adj. **1** WELL KNOWN, known, rec-ognized, accustomed, common, custom-ary, everyday, ordinary, commonplace, frequent, habitual, usual, repeated, stock, routine, mundane, run-of-the-mill, conventional, household; informal common or garden. **2** OVERFAMILIAR, pre-sumptuous, disrespectful, forward, bold, impudent, impertinent, intrusive,

pushy. ■ OPPOSITES unfamiliar. ☐ **fa-miliar with** ACQUAINTED WITH, know-ledgeable about, informed about, expert in, conversant with, well up on, au fait with, at home with, no stranger to, au courant with.

family n. **1** HOUSEHOLD, ménage, clan, tribe. **2** CHILDREN, offspring, progeny, brood, descendants; informal kids; Law issue, scions. **3** ANCESTRY, extraction, parentage, pedigree, birth, background, descent, lineage, genealogy, line, blood-line, stock, dynasty, house, forebears, forefathers.

famine n. **1** STARVATION, hunger, lack of food. **2** SCARCITY, shortage, insuffi-ciency, lack, want, dearth, paucity, defi-ciency.

famished adj. STARVING, starved, raven-ous, hungry, undernourished.

famous adj. WELL KNOWN, renowned, cele-brated, famed, noted, prominent, not-able, eminent, great, pre-eminent, dis-tinguished, esteemed, respected, vener-able, illustrious, acclaimed, honour-able, exalted, glorious, remarkable, popular, legendary. ■ OPPOSITES un-known, obscure.

fan n. ADMIRER, follower, devotee, enthusi-ast, aficionado, disciple, adherent, sup-porter, backer, champion; informal buff, freak, nut, groupie.

fanatic n. **1** EXTREMIST, zealot, militant, activist, partisan, bigot, sectarian. **2** DE-VOTEE, addict, enthusiast, fan, lover.

fanatical adj. **1** EXTREMIST, extreme, zeal-ous, radical, militant, sectarian, bigot-ed, dogmatic, prejudiced, intolerant, usual or creative. ■ **fancifully** adv.

fancy v. (**fancying**, **fancied**) **1** informal want or want to do. **2** informal find sexually attractive. **3** imagine; think. ▶ adj. (**fancier**, **fanciest**) elaborate or highly decorated. ▶ n. (pl. **fancies**) **1** a brief feeling of attraction. **2** imagination. **3** an unfounded belief. □ **fancy dress** a costume representing a historical character, animal, etc., worn for a party.

fanfare n. a short ceremonious tune played on trumpets.

fang n. **1** a long sharp tooth. **2** a snake's tooth which injects poison.

fantasia n. an improvised musical composition.

fantasize (or -**ise**) v. daydream. ■ **fantasist** n.

fantastic adj. **1** hard to believe. **2** strange or exotic. **3** informal excellent. ■ **fantastically** adv.

fantasy n. (pl. **fantasies**) **1** the imagining of things that do not exist in reality. **2** a daydream. **3** a type of fiction involving magic and adventure.

far adv. **1** at, to, or by a great distance. **2** by a great deal. ▶ adj. **1** distant. **2** extreme. □ **the Far East** China, Japan, and other countries of east Asia. **farfetched** exaggerated or unlikely.

farad n. the basic unit of electrical capacitance.

farce n. **1** a comedy involving ridiculous situations. **2** an absurd event. ■ **farcical** adj. **farcically** adv.

fare n. **1** the price charged to a passenger on public transport. **2** a range of food. ▶ v. perform in a specified way.

farewell exclam. old use goodbye. ▶ n. an act of leaving or saying goodbye.

farinaceous adj. starchy.

farm n. an area of land and its buildings used for growing crops and rearing animals. ▶ v. **1** grow crops or keep livestock as one's livelihood. **2** breed or grow commercially. **3** (**farm out**) subcontract work to others. ■ **farmer** n.

farrago /fuh-**rah**-goh/ n. (pl. **farragos** or **farragoes**) a confused mixture.

farrier n. a person who shoes horses.

farrow n. a litter of pigs. ▶ v. give birth to piglets.

farther, **farthest** vars. of FURTHER, FURTHEST.

farthingale n. a hooped petticoat.

fascia (or **facia**) /**fay**-shuh/ n. **1** a signboard on a shopfront. **2** a vehicle's dashboard. **3** a covering for a mobile phone.

fascinate v. interest or charm greatly. ■ **fascination** n.

fascism /**fash**-i-z'm/ n. a right-wing sys-

Thesaurus

narrow-minded, partisan, rabid. **2** ENTHUSIASTIC, eager, keen, fervent, passionate, obsessive, immoderate, frenzied, frenetic; informal wild, gung-ho.

fanciful adj. **1** UNREAL, imaginary, illusory, made up, fantastic, romantic, mythical, legendary, fairy-tale. **2** IMAGINATIVE, inventive, whimsical, capricious, visionary, impractical.

fancy n. **1** DESIRE, urge, wish, want, yearning, longing, inclination, bent, hankering, impulse, fondness, liking, love, partiality, preference, taste, predilection, relish, penchant; informal yen, itch. **2** IMAGINATION, creativity, conception, images, visualizations. ▶ v. **1** HAVE AN IDEA, think, guess, believe, suppose, reckon, suspect, conjecture, surmise. **2** FIND ATTRACTIVE, be attracted to, be infatuated by, take to, desire, lust after; informal go for, be wild/mad about, have taken a shine to. ▶ adj. ORNATE, elaborate, ornamented, decorative, embellished, intricate, lavish, ostentatious, showy, luxurious, sumptuous; informal jazzy, snazzy, ritzy.

fantastic adj. **1** FANCIFUL, imaginary, unreal, illusory, romantic, make-believe,

extravagant, irrational, wild, mad, absurd, incredible, strange, eccentric, whimsical. **2** STRANGE, weird, queer, peculiar, outlandish, eccentric, bizarre, grotesque, freakish, fanciful, quaint, exotic, elaborate, ornate, intricate, rococo, baroque. **3** see MARVELLOUS. ■ OPPOSITES ordinary.

fantasy n. **1** IMAGINATION, fancy, creativity, invention, originality, vision, myth, romance. **2** SPECULATION, fancy, daydreaming, reverie, flight of fancy, fanciful notion, dream, daydream, pipe dream.

far adv. A LONG WAY, a great distance, a good way, afar. ▶ adj. FARAWAY, far-flung, distant, remote, out of the way, far removed, outlying, inaccessible. ■ OPPOSITES near.

farcical adj. RIDICULOUS, ludicrous, absurd, laughable, preposterous, nonsensical, silly, foolish, asinine.

farewell n. GOODBYE, adieu, leavetaking, parting, send-off, departure, departing. ▶ exclamation GOODBYE, so long, adieu, au revoir, see you, see you later; informal cheerio, cheers.

far-fetched adj. IMPROBABLE, unlikely,

tem of government characterized by extreme nationalistic beliefs. ■ **fascist** n. & adj.

fashion n. **1** a popular trend, esp. in dress. **2** the production and marketing of new styles of clothing etc. **3** a way of doing something. ▶ v. make or shape.

fashionable adj. in or adopting a currently popular style. ■ **fashionably** adv.

fast adj. **1** moving or able to move at high speed. **2** taking place or done at high speed. **3** (of a clock etc.) ahead of the correct time. **4** firmly fixed. ▶ adv. **1** quickly. **2** firmly or securely. ▶ v. go without food. ▶ n. a period of fasting.

fasten v. **1** close or do up securely. **2** fix or hold in place. ■ **fastener** n.

fastidious adj. **1** attentive to detail. **2** very concerned about cleanliness. ■ **fastidiously** adv. **fastidiousness** n.

fastness n. a secure place well protected by natural features.

fat n. **1** an oily substance found in animals. **2** this, or a similar substance made from plants, used in cooking. ▶ adj. (**fatter**, **fattest**) **1** having too much fat. **2** informal large; substantial. ■ **fatness** n. **fatten** v. **fatty** adj.

fatal adj. causing death or disaster. ■ **fatally** adv.

fatalism n. the belief that all events are decided in advance by a supernatural power. ■ **fatalist** n. **fatalistic** adj.

fatality n. (pl. **fatalities**) a death caused by an accident or disease, or occurring in war.

fate n. **1** a power believed to control all events. **2** the unavoidable events or outcome of a person's life. ▶ v. (**be fated**) be destined to happen in a particular way.

fateful adj. having important, often unpleasant, consequences.

father n. **1** a male parent. **2** a founder or

Thesaurus

implausible, remote, incredible, unbelievable, doubtful, dubious, unconvincing, strained, laboured, fanciful, unrealistic; *informal* hard to take/swallow. ■ OPPOSITES likely.

fascinate v. CAPTIVATE, enchant, beguile, bewitch, infatuate, enthral, enrapture, entrance, hold spellbound, rivet, transfix, mesmerize, hypnotize, lure, allure, tempt, entice, draw, tantalize, charm, attract, intrigue, delight, absorb, engross. ■ OPPOSITES bore, repel.

fashion n. **1** STYLE, vogue, trend, latest thing, taste, mode, craze, rage, fad, convention, custom, practice. **2** CLOTHES, design, couture; *informal* rag trade. **3** WAY, manner, style, method, system, mode, approach. ▶ v. MAKE, build, construct, manufacture, create, devise, shape, form, mould, forge, hew, carve.

fashionable adj. STYLISH, in fashion, up to date, up to the minute, contemporary, modern, voguish, in vogue, modish, popular, all the rage, trendsetting, latest, smart, chic, elegant; *informal* trendy, natty, with it, ritzy. ■ OPPOSITES unfashionable.

fast adj. **1** QUICK, rapid, swift, speedy, brisk, hurried, breakneck, hasty, accelerated, flying, express, fleet; *informal* nippy. **2** LOYAL, devoted, faithful, steadfast, firm, staunch, constant, lasting, unchanging, unwavering, enduring. **3** LICENTIOUS, promiscuous, dissolute, loose, wanton. **4** WILD, dissipated, debauched, dissolute, promiscuous, intemperate, immoderate, unrestrained,

reckless, profligate, extravagant. ■ OPPOSITES slow. ▶ adv. **1** QUICKLY, rapidly, swiftly, speedily, briskly, hastily, hurriedly, in a hurry, post-haste, expeditiously; *informal* hell for leather, like a shot, like a bat out of hell, lickety-split. **2** FIRMLY, tightly, securely, immovably, fixedly.

fasten v. **1** BOLT, lock, secure, chain, seal. **2** ATTACH, fix, affix, clip, pin, tack, stick. **3** TIE, bind, tether, hitch, anchor, lash. **4** DIRECT, aim, point, focus, fix, concentrate, rivet, zero in.

fastidious adj. FUSSY, finicky, overparticular, critical, hard to please, overcritical, hypercritical; *informal* choosy, picky, pernickety. ■ OPPOSITES easygoing.

fat adj. **1** PLUMP, stout, overweight, obese, heavy, large, solid, corpulent, tubby, chubby, portly, rotund, pudgy, flabby, pot-bellied, gross, paunchy, bloated, dumpy, bulky, fleshy, stocky, well fed, massive, elephantine; *informal* beefy, roly-poly. **2** SUBSTANTIAL, large, major, sizeable, significant, considerable. ■ OPPOSITES thin, lean.

fatal adj. **1** MORTAL, deadly, lethal, terminal, final, incurable. **2** RUINOUS, disastrous, destructive, catastrophic, calamitous, cataclysmic. **3** CRITICAL, fateful, decisive, crucial, pivotal, determining, momentous, important.

fatalism n. STOICISM, resignation, acceptance.

fatality n. DEATH, casualty, mortality, loss.

originator. **3** a title of certain priests. ▶v. be the father of. ☐ **father-in-law** (pl. **fathers-in-law**) the father of one's husband or wife. **fatherland** a person's native country. ■ **fatherhood** n. **fatherless** adj. **fatherly** adj.

fathom n. a measure of the depth of water, equal to 1.8 m. ▶v. understand.

fatigue n. **1** tiredness. **2** brittleness in metal etc. caused by repeated stress. **3** (**fatigues**) loose-fitting military clothing. ▶v. make very tired.

fatuous adj. silly and pointless. ■ **fatuously** adv.

fatwa n. an authoritative ruling on a point of Islamic law.

faucet n. US a tap.

fault n. **1** a defect or mistake. **2** responsibility for a mistake etc. **3** a break in the layers of rock of the earth's crust. ▶v. find defects in. ☐ **at fault** responsible for a mistake etc. ■ **faultless** adj. **faulty** adj.

faun n. a Roman god of woods and fields, with a man's body and a goat's horns and legs.

fauna n. the animals of a particular region or period.

faux pas /foh pah/ n. (pl. **faux pas**) an embarrassing social blunder.

favour (US **favor**) n. **1** approval or liking. **2** an act of kindness beyond what is due. **3** favouritism. ▶v. **1** regard or treat with favour. **2** work to the advantage of.

favourable (US **favorable**) adj. **1** expressing approval or agreement. **2** advantageous or helpful. ■ **favourably** adv.

favourite (US **favorite**) adj. preferred to all others. ▶n. **1** a favourite person or thing. **2** the competitor expected to win.

favouritism (US **favoritism**) n. unfairly generous treatment of one person or group.

fawn n. **1** a young deer in its first year.

Thesaurus

fate n. **1** DESTINY, providence, predestination, predetermination, kismet, chance, one's lot in life, the stars. **2** FUTURE, outcome, issue, upshot, end.

father n. MALE PARENT, paterfamilias, patriarch; *informal* dad, daddy, pop, poppa, pa, old boy, old man; *informal, dated* pater.

fathom v. UNDERSTAND, comprehend, grasp, perceive, divine, penetrate, search out, get to the bottom of, ferret out.

fatigue n. TIREDNESS, weariness, exhaustion, lethargy, prostration, lassitude, debility, listlessness, enervation. ▶v. TIRE, tire out, weary, exhaust, wear out, drain, prostrate, enervate; *informal* take it out of, do in, whack, fag out; *US informal* poop.

fatuous adj. SILLY, foolish, stupid, senseless, nonsensical, idiotic, puerile, brainless, mindless, asinine, vacuous, moronic, witless. ■ OPPOSITES sensible.

fault n. **1** DEFECT, flaw, imperfection, blemish, failing, weakness, weak point, deficiency, snag, error, mistake, inaccuracy, blunder, oversight. **2** MISDEED, wrongdoing, offence, misdemeanour, sin, vice, misconduct, lapse, indiscretion, transgression, peccadillo; *old use* trespass. ▶v. FIND FAULT WITH, criticize, complain about, censure, quibble about, find lacking, impugn; *informal* pick holes in. ☐ **at fault** TO BLAME, in the wrong, culpable, responsible, accountable, answerable, blameworthy.

faultless adj. **1** PERFECT, flawless, without fault, unblemished, impeccable, correct, exemplary, model. **2** INNOCENT, blameless, guiltless, above reproach, irreproachable, pure, sinless, unsullied. ■ OPPOSITES imperfect.

faulty adj. **1** MALFUNCTIONING, defective, broken, out of order, damaged, unsound; *informal* on the blink, kaput. **2** DEFECTIVE, flawed, unsound, wrong, inaccurate, incorrect, erroneous, fallacious, impaired, weak, invalid. ■ OPPOSITES working, correct.

favour n. **1** SERVICE, good turn, kindness, courtesy, good deed. **2** APPROVAL, approbation, good will, esteem, kindness, benevolence, friendliness. **3** BACKING, support, patronage, aid, assistance, championship. ▶v. **1** APPROVE OF, advocate, recommend, support, back, endorse, sanction. **2** BE TO THE ADVANTAGE OF, be advantageous to, benefit, help, assist, aid, advance, abet, succour. ■ OPPOSITES oppose.

favourable adj. **1** APPROVING, good, enthusiastic, well disposed, commendatory. **2** ADVANTAGEOUS, in one's favour, beneficial, on one's side, helpful, good, hopeful, promising, fair, auspicious, propitious, opportune, timely, encouraging, conducive, convenient, suitable, fitting, appropriate. **3** GOOD, pleasing, agreeable, successful, positive. ■ OPPOSITES unfavourable.

favourite adj. BEST-LOVED, most-liked, favoured, preferred, chosen, ideal, treas-

2 a light brown colour. ▶v. try to gain favour by using flattery.

fax n. **1** a copy of a document which has been scanned and sent electronically. **2** a machine for sending and receiving faxes. ▶v. send by fax.

faze v. informal unsettle.

FBI abbrev. (in the US) Federal Bureau of Investigation.

FC abbrev. Football Club.

fealty n. hist. loyalty or allegiance.

fear n. an unpleasant emotion caused by the threat of danger, pain, or harm. ▶v. **1** be afraid of. **2** (**fear for**) be anxious about.

fearful adj. **1** showing or causing fear. **2** informal very great. ■ **fearfully** adv.

fearless adj. feeling no fear; brave. ■ **fearlessly** adv.

fearsome adj. frightening.

feasible adj. able to be done; possible. ■ **feasibility** n. **feasibly** adv.

feast n. **1** a large meal marking a special occasion. **2** an annual religious celebration. ▶v. **1** have a feast. **2** eat heartily.

feat n. an act requiring great courage, skill, or strength.

feather n. any of the structures growing from a bird's skin, with a partly hollow shaft fringed with fine strands. ▶v. turn an oar so that the blade passes through the air edgeways. □ **featherweight** a weight in boxing between bantamweight and lightweight. ■ **feathered** adj. **feathery** adj.

feature n. **1** a distinctive element or aspect. **2** a distinctive part of the face. **3** a newspaper article or a broadcast on a particular topic. **4** the main film showing at a cinema. ▶v. **1** have as a feature. **2** be a feature of or in.

febrile adj. **1** feverish. **2** overactive and excitable.

February n. the second month.

....

✓ -ruary, not -uary: February.

....

feces US = **FAECES**.

feckless adj. **1** lacking purpose. **2** irresponsible.

fecund adj. fertile. ■ **fecundity** n.

fed past & past part. of **FEED**. □ **fed up** informal annoyed and resentful.

federal adj. of a system in which several states unite under a central authority but are independent in internal affairs. ■ **federalism** n. **federalist** n. & adj. **federally** adv.

federate v. unite as a federation.

federation n. **1** a group of states united on a federal basis. **2** a group organized like a federation.

Thesaurus

....

ured, pet, well liked. ▶n. FIRST CHOICE, pick, beloved, darling, idol, god, goddess, jewel; informal teacher's pet, blue-eyed boy.

fear n. **1** FEARFULNESS, fright, terror, alarm, panic, trepidation, apprehensiveness, dread, nervousness, timidity, disquiet, trembling, anxiety, worry, unease, agitation, concern, foreboding, misgiving, doubt, angst, quaking, quivering, consternation, dismay, shivers, tremors; informal funk, blue funk, butterflies. **2** LIKELIHOOD, probability, chance, prospect, possibility. ▶v. BE AFRAID OF, be scared of, dread, live in fear of, go in terror of, take fright at, shudder at, shrink from, quail at, tremble at, have cold feet.

fearful adj. **1** AFRAID, frightened, scared, terrified, apprehensive, alarmed, uneasy, nervous, tense, panicky, timid, faint-hearted, timorous, diffident, intimidated, hesitant, trembling, quaking, quivering, cowering, cowardly, pusillanimous; informal jumpy, jittery. **2** TERRIBLE, dreadful, appalling, frightful, ghastly, horrific, horrible, horrendous, shocking, awful, hideous, atrocious, monstrous, dire, grim, unspeakable, gruesome, distressing, harrowing, fearsome, alarming. ■ OPPOSITES fearless.

fearless adj. UNAFRAID, brave, courageous, intrepid, valiant, gallant, plucky, lion-hearted, stout-hearted, heroic, bold, daring, confident, game, audacious, indomitable, doughty, undaunted, unflinching, unshrinking, unabashed; informal gutsy, spunky. ■ OPPOSITES fearful, cowardly.

fearsome adj. see FEARFUL (2).

feasible adj. PRACTICABLE, possible, achievable, doable, likely, attainable, workable, accomplishable, realizable, viable, reasonable, realistic, within reason; informal doable. ■ OPPOSITES impractical, impossible.

feast n. **1** BANQUET, dinner, repast, junket, revels; informal blowout, spread, bash, beanfeast, beano. **2** FEAST DAY, festival, saint's day, holy day, holiday, fete, gala, festivity. ▶v. EAT ONE'S FILL OF, gorge on, indulge in; informal stuff one's face with, stuff oneself with.

feat n. DEED, act, action, exploit, achieve-

fee n. a sum payable for professional services or to be allowed to do something.

feeble adj. **1** weak. **2** unconvincing. ■ **feebleness** n. **feebly** adv.

feed v. (**feeding, fed**) **1** give food to. **2** eat. **3** supply with material, power, etc. **4** pass gradually through a confined space. ▶ n. **1** an act of feeding. **2** food for domestic animals. □ **feedback 1** comments about a product or a person's performance. **2** the return of part of the output of an amplifier to its input, causing a whistling sound.

feeder n. **1** a thing that feeds or supplies something. **2** a minor route linking outlying districts with the main route.

feel v. (**feeling, felt**) **1** be aware of or examine by touch. **2** give a sensation when touched. **3** experience an emotion or sensation. **4** have a belief or opinion. ▶ n. **1** an act of touching. **2** the sense of touch. **3** a sensation or impression. □ **feel like** wish to have or do.

feeler n. **1** a long slender organ of touch in some animals. **2** a suggestion made to gauge opinion.

feeling n. **1** an emotional state or reaction. **2** (**feelings**) the emotional side of a person's character. **3** the ability to feel. **4** the sensation of touching or being touched. **5** a belief or opinion.

feet pl. of **FOOT**.

feign v. pretend.

feint n. a pretended attack in boxing or fencing. ▶ v. make a feint. ▶ adj. (of paper) printed with faint ruled lines.

feisty /fy-sti/ adj. spirited and lively.

feldspar (or **felspar**) n. a white or red mineral.

felicitations pl. n. congratulations.

felicitous adj. appropriate or well chosen.

felicity n. (pl. **felicities**) **1** great happiness. **2** an appropriate or well-chosen feature.

feline adj. of a cat or cats. ▶ n. an animal of the cat family.

fell¹ past of **FALL**.

fell² v. cut or knock down. ▶ n. a hill or stretch of high moorland in northern England.

fellow n. **1** a man or boy. **2** a person in the same situation as another. **3** a thing of the same kind as another. **4** a member of a learned society or governing body of a college.

fellowship n. **1** friendliness and companionship. **2** a society. **3** the position of a fellow of a college or society.

Thesaurus

ment, accomplishment, performance, attainment, manoeuvre, move, stunt.

feather n. PLUME, quill, pinion, plumule, pinna, plumage, down, hackles.

feature n. **1** ASPECT, characteristic, facet, side, point, attribute, quality, property, trait, mark, hallmark, trademark, peculiarity, idiosyncrasy. **2** ARTICLE, piece, item, report, story, column. ▶ v. **1** PRESENT, give prominence to, promote, star, spotlight, highlight, emphasize, accentuate, play up. **2** PLAY A PART, have a place, have prominence.

federation n. CONFEDERATION, confederacy, league, alliance, coalition, union, syndicate, association, amalgamation, combination, entente, fraternity.

feeble adj. **1** WEAK, weakly, weakened, frail, infirm, sickly, puny, delicate, slight, failing, ailing, helpless, powerless, debilitated, decrepit, doddering, tottering, enfeebled, enervated, effete, etiolated. **2** INADEQUATE, ineffectual, ineffective, weak, indecisive, wishy-washy. **3** UNCONVINCING, unsuccessful, ineffective, ineffectual, poor, weak, futile, tame, paltry, slight. ■ OPPOSITES strong.

feed v. **1** NOURISH, sustain, cater for, provide for, wine and dine. **2** EAT, take nourishment, graze, browse. **3** GIVE, supply, provide, furnish.

feel v. **1** TOUCH, stroke, caress, fondle, handle, finger, manipulate, paw, maul. **2** BE AWARE OF, notice, be conscious of, perceive, observe, be sensible of. **3** EXPERIENCE, undergo, have, know, go through, bear, endure, suffer. **4** THINK, believe, consider, be of the opinion, hold, judge, deem. □ **feel for** SYMPATHIZE WITH, be sorry for, pity, empathize with, feel compassion for, be moved by, weep for, grieve for, commiserate with.

feeling n. **1** SENSATION, sense, perception, awareness, consciousness. **2** IDEA, suspicion, funny feeling, impression, notion, inkling, hunch, apprehension, presentiment, premonition, foreboding. **3** SYMPATHY, pity, compassion, understanding, concern, sensitivity, tenderness, commiseration, empathy, fellow-feeling.

felicitous adj. **1** APT, well chosen, well expressed, well put, fitting, suitable, appropriate, pertinent, apposite, germane. **2** HAPPY, joyful, fortunate, lucky, successful, prosperous. ■ OPPOSITES inappropriate, unfortunate.

fell v. **1** CUT DOWN, chop down, saw down.

felon n. a person who has committed a serious crime. ■ **felony** n.

felspar var. of FELDSPAR.

felt[1] n. cloth made by rolling and pressing damp wool.

felt[2] past & past part. of FEEL.

female adj. **1** of the sex that can bear offspring or produce eggs. **2** (of a plant or flower) having a pistil but no stamens. **3** (of a fitting) made hollow to allow insertion of another part. ▶ n. a female person, animal, or plant.

feminine adj. **1** having qualities associated with women. **2** female. ■ **femininity** n.

feminism n. a movement supporting equal rights for women. ■ **feminist** n. & adj.

femme fatale /fam fuh-**tahl**/ n. (pl. **femmes fatales**) an attractive and seductive woman.

femur n. (pl. **femurs** or **femora**) the thigh bone. ■ **femoral** adj.

fen n. a low-lying marshy or flooded area of land.

fence n. **1** a barrier made of wire or wood enclosing an area. **2** informal a dealer in stolen goods. ▶ v. **1** surround with a fence. **2** practise the sport of fencing. ■ **fencer** n.

fencing n. **1** the sport of fighting with blunted swords. **2** fences or material for fences.

fend v. **1** (**fend for oneself**) provide for oneself. **2** (**fend off**) ward off.

fender n. **1** a low frame around a fireplace. **2** a cushioning device hung over a ship's side to protect against impact.

3 US the bumper of a vehicle.

feng shui /feng shoo-i, fung shway/ n. an ancient Chinese system of designing buildings and arranging objects to ensure a favourable flow of energy.

fennel n. an aniseed-flavoured plant.

fenugreek n. a plant with seeds used as a spice.

feral adj. wild.

ferment v. **1** undergo or cause to undergo fermentation. **2** stir up unrest. ▶ n. unrest.

fermentation n. the chemical breakdown of a substance by bacteria, yeast, etc.

fern n. a flowerless plant with feathery green leaves.

ferocious adj. very fierce or violent. ■ **ferociously** adv. **ferocity** n.

ferret n. a domesticated polecat. ▶ v. (**ferreting**, **ferreted**) search for in a place or container.

ferric (or **ferrous**) adj. of or containing iron.

Ferris wheel n. a funfair ride consisting of a large upright revolving wheel.

ferrule n. a metal cap for strengthening the end of a stick etc.

ferry n. (pl. **ferries**) a boat for transporting passengers and goods. ▶ v. (**ferrying**, **ferried**) carry by ferry or other transport.

fertile adj. **1** producing abundant vegetation or crops. **2** able to conceive young or produce seed. **3** productive or inventive. ■ **fertility** n.

fertilize (or **-ise**) v. **1** introduce sperm or pollen into an egg or plant. **2** add fer-

Thesaurus

2 KNOCK DOWN, bring down, knock out; informal deck, floor, lay out.

fellow n. MAN, male, boy, person, individual; informal guy, bloke, chap, character, customer, codger.

feminine adj. WOMANLY, girlish, ladylike, soft, delicate, leaven, tender, graceful, refined, modest; informal girly. ■ OPPOSITES masculine.

fence n. BARRIER, railing, rail, paling, wall, hedge, barricade, rampart, stockade, palisade. ▶ v. **1** ENCLOSE, surround, encircle, circumscribe, encompass. **2** SHUT IN, confine, pen, separate off, secure, imprison.

fend v. **1** (**fend for oneself**) PROVIDE FOR ONESELF, take care of oneself, get by, look after oneself, support oneself, survive. **2** (**fend off**) WARD OFF, stave off, parry, turn aside, keep off, divert, deflect, avert, defend oneself against,

guard against, forestall.

ferment n. **1** FERMENTATION AGENT, yeast, mould, bacteria, leaven, leavening. **2** FRENZY, furore, fever, tumult, commotion, uproar, agitation, turbulence, stir, confusion, fuss, brouhaha, hubbub, stew, hurly-burly, racket, imbroglio. ▶ v. **1** UNDERGO FERMENTATION, foam, froth, bubble, effervesce, seethe, boil, rise, work. **2** EXCITE, inflame, agitate, incite.

ferocious adj. **1** FIERCE, savage, brutal, brutish, ruthless, cruel, pitiless, merciless, vicious, barbarous, violent, barbaric, inhuman, inexorable, bloodthirsty, murderous, wild, untamed, predatory, rapacious. **2** INTENSE, very great, fierce, extreme, acute. ■ OPPOSITES gentle.

ferry v. CARRY, transport, convey, run, ship, shuttle, chauffeur.

tilizer to. ■ **fertilization** n.
fertilizer (or **-iser**) n. a substance added to soil to increase its fertility.
fervent adj. very passionate. ■ **fervency** n. **fervently** adv.
fervid adj. fervent.
fervour (US **fervor**) n. intense and passionate feeling.
fester v. **1** become septic. **2** (of ill feeling) become worse.
festival n. **1** a day or period of celebration. **2** a series of concerts, films, etc.
festive adj. of or suitable for a festival.
festivity n. **1** joyful celebration. **2** (**festivities**) activities or events celebrating a special occasion.
festoon n. a hanging chain of flowers or ribbons. ▶v. decorate with festoons.
feta n. a salty Greek cheese.
fetch v. **1** go for and bring back. **2** sell for a particular price. **3** (**fetching**) attractive.
fete /fayt/ n. an outdoor public event to raise funds for charity, involving entertainment and the sale of goods. ▶v. honour or entertain lavishly.
fetid (or **foetid**) adj. smelling very unpleasant.
fetish n. **1** an object worshipped for its supposed magical powers. **2** a form of

sexual desire in which pleasure is gained from a particular object.
fetlock n. the joint of a horse's leg between the knee and the hoof.
fetter n. **1** a shackle for the ankles. **2** a restriction. ▶v. **1** restrain with fetters. **2** restrict.
fettle n. condition: *in fine fettle.*
fetus (or **foetus**) n. (pl. **fetuses**) an unborn baby of a mammal. ■ **fetal** adj.
feud n. & v. (take part in) a long-lasting and bitter dispute.
feudalism n. a medieval social system involving a strict hierarchy in which lower orders held lands from and worked and fought for higher orders. ■ **feudal** adj.
fever n. **1** an abnormally high body temperature. **2** a state of nervous excitement. ■ **fevered** adj. **feverish** adj.
few adj., pron., & n. **1** (**a few**) a small number of. **2** not many.

☑ Be careful to distinguish between **fewer** and **less**. Use **fewer** with plural nouns, as in *there are fewer people here today*; use **less** with nouns referring to things that can't be counted, as in *there is less blossom on this tree.*

Thesaurus

fertile adj. **1** FRUITFUL, productive, rich, fecund. **2** INVENTIVE, creative, original, ingenious, resourceful, productive, visionary, constructive. ■ OPPOSITES sterile.
fertilize v. **1** ADD FERTILIZER TO, feed, enrich, mulch, dress, compost, top-dress. **2** IMPREGNATE, inseminate, make pregnant, fecundate.
fertilizer n. PLANT FOOD, manure, dung, compost, dressing, top-dressing, bonemeal, guano, marl.
fervent adj. PASSIONATE, ardent, impassioned, intense, vehement, heartfelt, emotional, fervid, emotive, warm, devout, sincere, eager, zealous, earnest, enthusiastic, excited, animated, spirited; *literary* perfervid. ■ OPPOSITES apathetic, unemotional.
fervour n. PASSION, ardour, intensity, vehemence, emotion, warmth, devoutness, sincerity, eagerness, zeal, enthusiasm, earnestness, excitement, animation, spirit, vigour. ■ OPPOSITES apathy, indifference.
fester v. **1** SUPPURATE, run, discharge, ulcerate, rot, decay, go bad, go off, decompose, disintegrate, gather, come to a head. **2** RANKLE, chafe, cause bitterness/

resentment, gnaw.
festival n. **1** SAINT'S DAY, holy day, feast day, holiday, anniversary, day of observance. **2** CARNIVAL, gala day, fete, celebrations, festivities.
festive adj. JOYFUL, joyous, happy, jolly, merry, jovial, light-hearted, cheerful, cheery, jubilant, convivial, gleeful, mirthful, uproarious, rollicking, backslapping, celebratory, carnival, sportive, festal.
festoon v. GARLAND, wreathe, hang, drape, decorate, adorn, ornament, array, deck, bedeck, swathe, beribbon. ▶n. GARLAND, wreath, chaplet, lei, swathe, swag.
fetch v. **1** GET, go and get, bring, carry, deliver, convey, transport, escort, conduct, lead, usher in. **2** SELL FOR, realize, go for, bring in, yield, earn, cost, afford.
fetching adj. ATTRACTIVE, charming, enchanting, sweet, winsome, captivating, fascinating, alluring.
feud n. VENDETTA, conflict, quarrel, argument, hostility, enmity, strife, discord, bad blood, animosity, grudge, antagonism, estrangement, unfriendliness, schism.
fever n. FEVERISHNESS, high temperature,

fey adj. **1** unworldly and vague. **2** able to see into the future.

fez n. (pl. **fezzes**) a flat-topped conical red hat worn by some Muslim men.

ff. abbrev. following pages.

fiancé n. (fem. **fiancée**) a person to whom one is engaged to be married.

fiasco n. (pl. **fiascos**) a ridiculous or humiliating failure.

fiat n. an official order.

fib n. a trivial lie. ▶v. (**fibbing, fibbed**) tell a fib. ■ **fibber** n.

fibre (US **fiber**) n. **1** a thread or strand from which a plant or animal tissue, mineral, or textile is formed. **2** a substance formed of fibres. **3** roughage. **4** strength of character. □ **fibreglass** a reinforced plastic material containing glass fibres. **fibre optics** the use of thin flexible glass fibres to send information in the form of light. ■ **fibrous** adj.

fibril n. a small fibre.

fibroid adj. consisting of fibrous tissue. ▶n. a benign fibroid tumour in the womb.

fibrositis n. inflammation of fibrous connective tissue in the body, causing stiffness and pain.

fibula n. (pl. **fibulae** or **fibulas**) the outer of the two bones between the knee and the ankle.

fickle adj. changeable in one's loyalties. ■ **fickleness** n.

fiction n. **1** literature describing imaginary events and people. **2** an invented story. ■ **fictional** adj.

fictitious adj. imaginary or invented.

fiddle informal n. **1** a violin. **2** an act of fraud. ▶v. **1** handle something restlessly or nervously. **2** falsify expenses etc. □ **fiddlesticks** nonsense. ■ **fiddler** n.

fiddly adj. informal complicated and awkward.

fidelity n. **1** faithfulness. **2** accuracy in a copy or reproduction.

fidget v. (**fidgeting, fidgeted**) make small movements through nervousness or impatience. ▶n. a person who fidgets. ■ **fidgety** adj.

fiduciary adj. held or given in trust. ▶n. (**fiduciaries**) a trustee.

fief /feef/ n. hist. an estate of land held on condition of feudal service.

field n. **1** an enclosed area of land for crops or grazing animals. **2** a piece of land used for a sport. **3** an area rich in a natural product. **4** a subject of study or area of activity. **5** the participants in a race etc. ▶v. **1** Cricket & Baseball attempt to catch or stop the ball after it has been hit. **2** select to play in a game or to stand in an election. □ **field day** an opportunity to do something without being hindered. **field events** athletic sports other than races. **field glasses** binoculars. **field marshal** the highest rank of army officer. **fieldwork** practical research done outside a laboratory or office. ■ **fielder** n.

fiend n. **1** an evil spirit. **2** a very cruel

Thesaurus

delirium; formal pyrexia.

feverish adj. **1** FEVERED, febrile, hot, burning. **2** FRENZIED, excited, frenetic, agitated, nervous, overwrought, frantic, distracted, worked up, flustered, impatient, passionate.

few adj. **1** NOT MANY, hardly any, scarcely any, one or two, a handful of, a sprinkling of, a couple of, few and far between, infrequent, sporadic, irregular. **2** SCARCE, rare, negligible, scant, thin on the ground. ■ OPPOSITES many.

fiasco n. FAILURE, disaster, debacle, catastrophe, mess, farce; informal flop, washout.

fibre n. THREAD, strand, tendril, filament, fibril.

fickle adj. CAPRICIOUS, unpredictable, mercurial, changeable, variable, volatile, inconstant, unstable, vacillating, unsteady, unfaithful, faithless, undependable, inconsistent, irresolute, flighty, giddy, erratic, fitful, irregular, mutable. ■ OPPOSITES constant, stable.

fiction n. **1** STORY TELLING, narration, romance, fable, fantasy, legend. **2** FABRICATION, lie, piece of fiction, untruth, falsehood, invention, concoction, fib; informal cock and bull story, whopper. ■ OPPOSITES fact.

fictional adj. FICTITIOUS, invented, made up, imaginary, unreal, non-existent, make-believe, fabricated, mythical, fanciful. ■ OPPOSITES real, actual.

fictitious adj. **1** INVENTED, made up, imaginary, imagined, untrue, false, apocryphal. **2** FALSE, bogus, sham, counterfeit, fake, fabricated, spurious, concocted. ■ OPPOSITES true, genuine.

fidelity n. FAITHFULNESS, loyalty, devotedness, devotion, allegiance, commitment, constancy, trustworthiness, dependability, reliability, staunchness, obedience. ■ OPPOSITES disloyalty.

fidget v. **1** MOVE RESTLESSLY, wriggle, squirm, twitch, jiggle; informal have ants in one's pants. **2** FIDDLE WITH, play with, fuss with.

person. **3** informal an enthusiast: *an exercise fiend.*

fiendish adj. **1** very cruel. **2** very difficult. ■ **fiendishly** adv.

fierce adj. **1** violent or aggressive. **2** powerful. ■ **fiercely** adv. **fierceness** n.

fiery adj. (**fierier, fieriest**) **1** consisting of or like fire. **2** quick-tempered or passionate.

fiesta n. (in Spanish-speaking countries) a religious festival.

fife n. a small high-pitched flute.

fifteen adj. & n. one more than fourteen; 15 or XV. ■ **fifteenth** adj. & n.

fifth adj. & n. next after fourth.

fifty adj. & n. (pl. **fifties**) ten less than sixty; 50 or L. □ **fifty-fifty** with equal shares or chances. ■ **fiftieth** adj. & n.

fig n. a soft, sweet fruit with many seeds.

fight v. (**fighting, fought**) **1** take part in a violent physical struggle. **2** strive to overcome or prevent. **3** try hard to obtain or do. ▶ n. an act of fighting.

fighter n. **1** a person or animal that fights. **2** a military aircraft designed for attack.

figment n. a thing that exists only in the imagination.

figurative adj. not using words literally. ■ **figuratively** adv.

figure n. **1** a number or numerical symbol. **2** a person's body shape. **3** a well-known person. **4** a geometric shape. **5** a diagram or drawing. ▶ v. **1** play an important part. **2** US informal think; suppose. **3** (**figured**) patterned. □ **figurehead 1** a carved statue at the front of an old-fashioned sailing ship. **2** a leader without real power. **figure of speech** a word or phrase used in a non-literal sense.

figurine n. a statuette.

filament n. **1** a slender thread. **2** a fine wire giving off light in an electric light bulb.

filbert n. a hazelnut.

filch v. informal steal.

file n. **1** a folder or box for keeping loose papers. **2** a set of computer data stored under a single name. **3** a line of people or things one behind another. **4** a tool

Thesaurus

fidgety adj. RESTLESS, restive, on edge, uneasy, nervous, nervy, twitchy; *informal* jittery, jumpy, like a cat on hot bricks.

field n. **1** PASTURE, meadow, grassland, paddock, sward; *literary* lea, mead, greensward; *old use* glebe. **2** AREA, area of activity, sphere, province, department, subject, discipline, line, speciality, domain, territory, regime. **3** RANGE, scope, limits, confines, purview.

fiend n. **1** DEVIL, demon, evil spirit. **2** BRUTE, monster, savage, beast, barbarian, sadist, ogre; *old use* blackguard.

fiendish adj. WICKED, cruel, savage, brutal, brutish, barbaric, barbarous, inhuman, vicious, bloodthirsty, ferocious, ruthless, heartless, pitiless, merciless, black-hearted, unfeeling, malevolent, villainous, odious, malignant, devilish, diabolical, demonic, satanic.

fierce adj. **1** FEROCIOUS, savage, wild, vicious, bloodthirsty, dangerous, brutal, cruel, murderous, menacing, threatening, slaughterous, terrible, grim, tigerish, wolfish, feral. **2** PASSIONATE, intense, ardent, impassioned, fervent, fiery, uncontrolled, fervid. **3** KEEN, strong, intense, relentless, cut-throat. ■ OPPOSITES gentle, mild.

fight v. **1** ATTACK/ASSAULT EACH OTHER, hit each other, come to blows, exchange blows, grapple, scuffle, brawl, box, skirmish, tussle, collide, spar, joust, clash, wrestle, battle, do battle, give battle, war, wage war, go to war, make war, take up arms, combat, engage, meet; *informal* scrap. **2** QUARREL, argue, feud, bicker, squabble, fall out, wrangle, dispute, be at odds, disagree, battle, altercate. **3** OPPOSE, contest, take a stand against, object to, resist, defy, withstand, struggle against, take issue with. ▶ n. **1** BRAWL, scuffle, tussle, skirmish, struggle, fracas, battle, engagement, clash, conflict, combat, contest, encounter, exchange, brush; *informal* set-to, scrap, punch-up, dust-up; *Law, dated* affray. **2** QUARREL, disagreement, difference of opinion, dispute, argument, altercation, feud. □ **fight back 1** DEFEND ONESELF, put up a fight, retaliate, counter-attack. **2** SUPPRESS, repress, check, curb, restrain, contain, bottle up. **fight off** WARD OFF, beat off, stave off, repel, repulse, hold at bay, resist.

figurative adj. METAPHORICAL, symbolic, allegorical, non-literal, representative, emblematic, imagistic. ■ OPPOSITES literal.

figure n. **1** NUMBER, numeral, digit, integer, sum, value, symbol, cipher. **2** COST, price, amount, value, total, sum, aggregate. **3** SHAPE, form, outline, silhouette. **4** BODY, physique, build, frame, torso, proportions. **5** DIAGRAM, illustration, picture, drawing, sketch, chart, plan, map.

with a rough surface for smoothing.
▶ v. **1** place in a file. **2** place on record.
3 walk one behind the other. **4** smooth
with a file.

filial adj. of a son or daughter.

filibuster n. prolonged speaking which
obstructs progress in a law-making assembly.

filigree n. ornamental work of fine gold
or silver wire.

filings pl. n. small particles rubbed off by
a file.

Filipino n. (pl. **Filipinos**) a person from
the Philippines. ▶ adj. of the Philippines.

fill v. **1** make or become full. **2** block up a
hole etc. **3** appoint a person to a vacant
post. **4** occupy time. ▶ n. (**one's fill**) as
much as one wants or can bear. □ **fill in
1** complete a form. **2** inform more fully
of a matter. **3** act as a substitute. **fill
out 1** put on weight. **2** complete a form.

filler n. something used to fill a gap or to
increase bulk.

fillet n. a boneless piece of meat or fish.
▶ v. (**filleting, filleted**) remove the
bones from a fish.

filling n. a substance used to fill something. ▶ adj. (of food) leaving one feeling
full. □ **filling station** a petrol station.

fillip n. a stimulus or boost.

filly n. (pl. **fillies**) a young female horse.

film n. **1** a thin, flexible strip of light-
sensitive material for photographs or
motion pictures. **2** a story or event recorded by a camera and shown in a cinema or on television. **3** a thin layer covering a surface. ▶ v. make a film of.

filmy adj. thin and almost transparent.

filo n. pastry in the form of very thin
sheets.

filter n. **1** a device or substance for holding back unwanted material in a liquid
or gas passing through it. **2** a screen
which absorbs some of the light passing
through it. ▶ v. **1** pass through a filter
to remove unwanted material. **2** move
gradually in or out.

filth n. **1** disgusting dirt. **2** obscene language or material. ■ **filthy** adj.

filtrate n. a filtered liquid. ■ **filtration** n.

fin n. **1** a flattened projection on the body
of a fish, dolphin, etc., used for swimming and balancing. **2** a projection on
an aircraft etc. to improve stability.

final adj. **1** coming at the end; last. **2** allowing no dispute. ▶ n. **1** the last game
in a tournament, deciding the overall
winner. **2** (**finals**) examinations at the
end of a degree course. ■ **finality** n.
finally adv.

finale /fi-nah-li/ n. the last part of a
piece of music or entertainment.

finalist n. a competitor in a final.

finalize (or **-ise**) v. complete a plan or
agreement.

Thesaurus

▶ v. **1** APPEAR, feature, play a part, be
featured, be conspicuous. **2** BE LIKELY, be
probable, be understandable, make
sense. □ **figure out 1** see CALCULATE.
2 see UNDERSTAND.

file[1] n. **1** FOLDER, portfolio, box, document
case, filing cabinet. **2** DOSSIER, information, documents, records, data, particulars, case notes. ▶ v. RECORD, enter,
store, categorize, classify, put in place,
put in order, put on record, pigeonhole.

file[2] n. LINE, column, row, string, chain,
queue. ▶ v. WALK/MARCH IN A LINE, march,
parade, troop, stream.

fill v. **1** OCCUPY ALL OF, crowd, overcrowd,
congest, cram, pervade. **2** PACK, load,
stack, supply, furnish, provide, replenish, restock, refill. **3** STOP UP, block up,
plug, seal, bung up, close, clog. **4** CARRY
OUT, execute, perform, complete, fulfil.

film n. **1** MOVIE, picture, motion picture,
video; informal flick. **2** LAYER, coat, coating, covering, cover, dusting, sheet,
blanket, skin, tissue, membrane, pel-
licle. **3** HAZE, mist, cloud, blur, veil,
murkiness.

filter n. STRAINER, sieve, riddle, sifter, colander, gauze, netting. ▶ v. STRAIN, sieve,
sift, riddle, filtrate, clarify, purify,
clear, refine.

filth n. DIRT, muck, grime, mud, sludge,
mire, slime, excrement, dung, manure,
ordure, sewage, rubbish, refuse, garbage, trash, contamination, pollution;
informal crud, gunge.

filthy adj. DIRTY, unclean, mucky, muddy,
slimy, murky, squalid, foul, nasty,
polluted, contaminated, unwashed,
grubby, dirt-encrusted, black, black-
ened, begrimed, rotten, decaying,
smelly, fetid, putrid, faecal. ■ OPPOS-
ITES clean, spotless.

final adj. **1** LAST, closing, concluding, finishing, terminal, end, ultimate, even-
tual, endmost. **2** ABSOLUTE, conclusive,
irrevocable, unalterable, incontrovertible, indisputable, decisive, definite, definitive, settled. ■ OPPOSITES first.

finale n. END, finish, close, conclusion,
climax, culmination, denouement, last
act, final scene, final curtain, epilogue;
informal wind-up.

finance n. **1** the management of money. **2** money to support an enterprise. **3** (**finances**) the money held by an organization etc. ▶v. fund. ∎ **financial** adj. **financially** adv.

financier n. a person who manages the finances of large organizations.

finch n. a small bird.

find v. (**finding**, **found**) **1** discover. **2** learn. **3** declare a verdict. **4** reach; obtain. ▶n. a valuable or interesting discovery. ◻ **find out** discover information. ∎ **finder** n.

finding n. a conclusion reached after an inquiry etc.

fine adj. **1** of very high quality. **2** satisfactory. **3** in good health. **4** (of the weather) bright and free from rain. **5** thin. **6** consisting of small particles. **7** delicate or complex. **8** subtle. ▶n. a sum of money to be paid as a punishment. ▶v. punish by a fine. ∎ **finely** adv. **fineness** n.

finery n. showy clothes.

finesse n. **1** elegant or delicate skill. **2** tact.

finger n. **1** each of the four jointed parts attached to either hand (five, if the thumb is included). **2** a small measure

of alcohol in a glass. ▶v. touch or feel with the fingers. ◻ **fingerboard** a flat strip on the neck of a stringed instrument, against which the strings are pressed to vary the pitch. **fingerprint** an impression of the ridges on the pad of a finger, used for identification.

finial n. an ornament at the end of a roof etc.

finicky adj. **1** fussy. **2** excessively detailed or elaborate.

finish v. **1** bring or come to an end. **2** eat or drink the whole or the remainder of. **3** reach the end of a race etc. **4** (**finish off**) kill or completely defeat. **5** complete or put the final touches to. ▶n. **1** an end or final stage. **2** the way in which a manufactured article is finished.

finite /fy-nyt/ adj. limited.

Finn n. a person from Finland. ∎ **Finnish** n. & adj.

fiord var. of **FJORD**.

fir n. an evergreen coniferous tree.

fire n. **1** the state of burning. **2** an instance of destructive burning. **3** wood or coal burnt to provide heat. **4** a gas or electric heater. **5** passion. **6** the firing of guns. ▶v. **1** send a bullet, missile,

Thesaurus

finalize v. COMPLETE, conclude, settle, decide, agree on, work out, tie up, wrap up, put the finishing touches to, clinch, sew up.

finance n. **1** MONEY MATTERS, financial affairs, economics, commerce, business, investment, banking, accounting. **2** MONEY, funds, cash, resources, assets, capital, wealth, wherewithal, revenue, stock. ▶v. PAY FOR, fund, back, support, subsidize, underwrite, capitalize, guarantee, provide capital for.

financial adj. MONETARY, fiscal, pecuniary, economic, budgetary.

find v. **1** DISCOVER, come across, chance upon, stumble on, light on, bring to light, turn up, happen upon, come up with, hit upon, uncover, unearth, locate, lay one's hands on, encounter. **2** OBTAIN, get, achieve, attain, acquire, gain, earn, procure. **3** REALIZE, discover, learn, conclude, detect, observe, notice, note, perceive.

finding n. DECISION, conclusion, verdict, judgement, pronouncement, decree, order, recommendation.

fine adj. **1** EXCELLENT, first-class, first-rate, great, exceptional, outstanding, admirable, superior, magnificent, splendid, quality, beautiful, exquisite, choice, se-

lect, prime, supreme, rare; *informal* A1, top-notch; *informal, dated* top-hole. **2** FAIR, dry, bright, clear, cloudless, sunny, balmy, clement. **3** SHEER, light, lightweight, thin, flimsy, diaphanous, filmy, chiffony, gossamer, gauze-like, gauzy, transparent, translucent, airy, ethereal. **4** ELEGANT, stylish, expensive, smart, chic, fashionable, modish, high-fashion, lavish. **5** ALL RIGHT, satisfactory, acceptable, agreeable, convenient, suitable; *informal* OK.

finish v. **1** COMPLETE, conclude, accomplish, carry out, execute, discharge, deal with, do, get done, fulfil, achieve, attain, end, close, bring to a conclusion, finalize, terminate, round off, put the finishing touches to; *informal* wind up, wrap up, sew up, polish off, knock off. **2** STOP, cease, give up, suspend, have done with, discontinue. **3** USE, use up, consume, exhaust, empty, deplete, drain, expend, dispatch, dispose of. ∎ OPPOSITES start, begin. ▶n. **1** END, completion, conclusion, close, closing, cessation, final act, finale, accomplishment, fulfilment, achievement, consummation, execution. **2** SURFACE, veneer, coating, texture, glaze, lustre, gloss, polish, shine, patina.

etc. from a gun or other weapon. **2** informal dismiss from a job. **3** supply fuel to. **4** stimulate. **5** bake pottery in a kiln. □ **firearm** a rifle, pistol, or shotgun. **firebrand** a person who causes trouble and unrest. **firebreak** a strip of open space to stop a fire from spreading. **fire brigade** an organized body of people employed to put out fires. **firedog** a metal support for logs in a fireplace. **fire engine** a vehicle carrying firefighters and their equipment. **fire escape** a staircase or ladder used to escape from a burning building. **firefighter** a person whose job is to put out fires. **firefly** a kind of beetle which glows in the dark. **fireman** a male firefighter. **fireplace** a recess at the base of a chimney for a domestic fire. **fireside** the area round a fireplace. **firewall** a part of a computer system that blocks unauthorized access. **firework** a device containing chemicals that explode to produce spectacular effects. **firing squad** a group ordered to shoot a condemned person.

firm adj. **1** not giving way or sinking under pressure. **2** solidly in place. **3** (of a grip etc.) steady and strong. **4** showing determination and strength of character. **5** fixed or definite. ▶v. make firm. ▶adv. firmly. ▶n. a business organization. ■ **firmly** adv. **firmness** n.

firmament n. the heavens; the sky.

first adj. & n. **1** coming before all others in time, order, or importance. **2** before doing something else. □ **at first** at the beginning. **first aid** emergency medical help given before full treatment is available. **first class** excellent. **first-degree** (of burns) affecting only the surface of the skin. **first-hand** directly from the original source. **first name** a personal name. **first-rate** excellent. ■ **firstly** adv.

firth n. a narrow inlet of the sea, esp. in Scotland.

fiscal adj. of government revenue.

fish n. (pl. **fish** or **fishes**) **1** a cold-blooded animal with gills and fins, living in water. **2** the flesh of fish as food. ▶v. **1** try to catch fish. **2** pull or take out of water or a container. **3** try to elicit by subtle means. □ **fishmeal** ground dried fish used as a fertilizer or animal feed. **fisherman** a person who catches fish for a living or for sport. **fishmonger** a person selling fish for food. **fishnet** an open mesh fabric.

fishery n. (pl. **fisheries**) a place where fish are reared for food, or caught in numbers.

Thesaurus

finite adj. LIMITED, restricted, bounded, delimited, demarcated, subject to limitations, determinate, measurable, countable. ■ OPPOSITES infinite.

fire n. **1** BLAZE, conflagration, inferno, flames, combustion. **2** GUNFIRE, sniping, bombardment, flak, shelling, barrage, fusillade, salvo. **3** PASSION, intensity, ardour, zeal, energy, spirit, vivacity, sparkle, vigour, fervour, enthusiasm. ▶v. **1** SET FIRE TO, set on fire, set alight, set ablaze, light, ignite, kindle, put a match to. **2** SHOOT, let off, discharge, trigger. **3** STIMULATE, animate, arouse, rouse, stir up, excite, enliven, inflame, inspire, motivate, incite, galvanize, electrify, impassion. **4** DISMISS, discharge, get rid of, oust, depose, cashier; informal give someone their marching orders, show someone the door, sack, give someone the sack, axe, give someone the bullet.

firebrand n. TROUBLEMAKER, agitator, radical, rabble-rouser, demagogue, tubthumper.

fireproof adj. NON-FLAMMABLE, noninflammable, fire-resistant, flame-resistant, flame-retardant, incombustible, unburnable, heatproof. ■ OPPOS-ITES inflammable.

firm[1] adj. **1** HARD, hardened, stiff, rigid, inflexible, unyielding, inelastic, resistant, solid, solidified, compacted, compressed, condensed, dense, close-grained, congealed, frozen, set, jelled, stony. **2** SETTLED, fixed, decided, definite, established, unalterable, unchangeable. **3** STRONG, vigorous, sturdy, powerful. **4** CONSTANT, unchanging, enduring, abiding, durable, deep-rooted, long-standing, long-lasting, steady, stable, staunch. **5** DETERMINED, resolute, decided, resolved, unfaltering, unwavering, unflinching, unswerving, unyielding, unbending, inflexible, obstinate, stubborn, obdurate, strict, intransigent, unmalleable. ■ OPPOSITES soft.

firm[2] n. BUSINESS, company, concern, establishment, organization, corporation, conglomerate, partnership; informal outfit.

first adj. **1** INITIAL, earliest, original, introductory, opening, primitive, premier, primordial, primeval. **2** BASIC, fundamental, rudimentary, key, cardinal, primary, beginning. ■ OPPOSITES last. ▶adv. **1** AT FIRST, to begin with, at the

fishy adj. **1** of or like fish. **2** informal arousing suspicion.

fissile adj. **1** able to undergo nuclear fission. **2** (of rock) easily split.

fission n. the act of splitting, esp. of an atomic nucleus with the release of much energy.

fissure n. a long, narrow crack.

fist n. a tightly closed hand. □ **fisticuffs** fighting with the fists. ■ **fistful** n.

fistula n. a tubular ulcer or passage in the body.

fit adj. (**fitter**, **fittest**) **1** of a suitable quality, standard, or type. **2** in good health. ▶ v. (**fitting**, **fitted**) **1** be the right shape and size for. **2** be able to occupy a particular position or space. **3** fix into place. **4** provide with. **5** try on and alter. ▶ n. **1** the way something fits. **2** a sudden attack of convulsions or loss of consciousness. **3** a sudden outburst of emotion or action. ■ **fitness** n.

fitful adj. occurring irregularly. ■ **fitfully** adv.

fitment n. a fixed item of furniture.

fitter n. **1** a person who assembles or installs machinery. **2** a person who fits clothes.

fitting n. **1** (**fittings**) items fixed in a building but removable when the owner moves. **2** an occasion of a garment being fitted. ▶ adj. appropriate. ■ **fittingly** adv.

five adj. & n. one more than four; 5 or V.

fiver n. informal a five-pound note.

fix v. **1** attach or position securely. **2** repair. **3** decide or settle on. **4** make arrangements for. **5** make permanent. **6** (**fix on**) direct the eyes etc. steadily toward. **7** informal influence a result etc. dishonestly. ▶ n. **1** an act of fixing. **2** informal a difficult situation. **3** informal a dose of a narcotic drug to which one is addicted. □ **fix up 1** organize. **2** informal provide with. ■ **fixedly** adv. **fixer** n.

fixated adj. obsessed.

fixation n. an obsession.

fixative n. a substance used to fix, protect, or stabilize something.

fixity n. the state of being permanent.

fixture n. **1** a piece of equipment etc. which is fixed in position. **2** a sporting event taking place on a particular date.

fizz v. produce bubbles of gas with a hissing sound. ▶ n. **1** the sound of fizzing. **2** informal a bubbly drink. **3** liveliness. ■ **fizziness** n. **fizzy** adj.

fizzle v. **1** make a weak hissing sound. **2** (**fizzle out**) end feebly.

fjord (or **fiord**) /fyord, fee-ord/ n. a long, narrow inlet of the sea between high cliffs, esp. in Norway.

fl. abbrev. **1** floruit. **2** fluid.

flab n. informal excess fat on the body.

flabbergasted adj. informal very surprised.

flabby adj. (**flabbier**, **flabbiest**) fat and floppy. ■ **flabbiness** n.

flaccid adj. soft and limp.

flag n. **1** a piece of cloth attached to a pole or rope as a symbol or signal. **2** a flagstone. ▶ v. (**flagging**, **flagged**)

Thesaurus

beginning, at the outset, initially. **2** FIRSTLY, before anything else, first and foremost, in the first place.

fish v. GO FISHING, angle, cast, trawl.

fishy adj. SUSPICIOUS, dubious, questionable, doubtful, suspect, odd, queer, peculiar, strange, not quite right; informal funny, shady, not kosher.

fit[1] adj. **1** WELL, healthy, in good health, in shape, in good shape, in good trim, in good condition, strong, robust, hale and hearty, sturdy, hardy, vigorous. **2** CAPABLE, able, competent, good enough, adequate, ready, prepared, satisfactory, qualified, trained, equipped, worthy, eligible; informal up to scratch. **3** FITTING, proper, seemly, decent, right, decorous, correct, apt, appropriate, suitable, apposite, relevant, pertinent. ▶ v. **1** AGREE WITH, be in agreement with, accord with, concur with, correspond with, match, tally with, suit, go with, conform to, dovetail with, be consonant with, be congruent with. **2** JOIN, connect, put together, put in place, fix, arrange, insert, adjust, shape.

fit[2] n. **1** CONVULSION, spasm, paroxysm, seizure, attack. **2** BOUT, burst, outburst, outbreak.

fix v. **1** FASTEN, secure, attach, connect, join, couple, stick, glue, cement, pin, nail, screw, bolt, clamp, bind, tie, pinion, anchor, plant, embed, establish, position, station. **2** DECIDE ON, settle, set, agree on, arrange, arrive at, determine, establish, name, specify. **3** REPAIR, mend, put right, patch up, put to rights, restore, adjust, rectify, sort out, see to. ▶ n. PREDICAMENT, difficulty, quandary, plight, dilemma, trouble, muddle, mess, corner, tricky situation, tight spot; informal pickle, jam, hole, scrape, spot of bother.

fixation n. OBSESSION, preoccupation, compulsion, complex, mania, monomania; informal hang-up, thing.

1 mark for attention. 2 (**flag down**) signal to a driver to stop. 3 become tired or less enthusiastic. □ **flagship** 1 an admiral's ship. 2 the most important product of an organization. **flagstone** a large paving stone.

flagellate v. whip. ■ **flagellation** n.

flageolet /fla-juh-lay/ n. a small wind instrument.

flagon n. a large bottle or jug for wine, cider, etc.

flagrant adj. very obvious and unashamed. ■ **flagrantly** adv.

flail v. thrash or swing about wildly. ▶n. a tool or machine formerly used for threshing grain.

flair n. 1 a natural ability or talent. 2 stylishness.

flak n. 1 anti-aircraft fire. 2 strong criticism.

flake n. a small, flat, thin piece of something. ▶v. 1 come off in flakes. 2 separate into flakes. 3 (**flake out**) informal fall asleep or drop from exhaustion. ■ **flakiness** n. **flaky** adj.

flambé /flom-bay/ v. (**flambéing, flambéed**) cover food with spirits and set it alight briefly.

flamboyant adj. 1 very confident and lively. 2 garish. ■ **flamboyance** n. **flamboyantly** adv.

flame n. 1 a hot, glowing stream of burning gas produced by something on fire. 2 an orange-red colour. ▶v. 1 give off flames. 2 (of the face) become bright red. □ **old flame** informal a former lover.

flamenco n. a Spanish style of singing and dancing.

flamingo n. (pl. **flamingos** or **flamingoes**) a wading bird with pink feathers and long legs.

flammable adj. easily set on fire. ■ **flammability** n.

flan n. an open pastry or sponge case with a filling.

flange n. a projecting flat rim. ■ **flanged** adj.

flank n. 1 a side, esp. of the body between the ribs and hip. 2 the left or right side of a group. ▶v. be on either side of.

flannel n. 1 a soft fabric with a raised surface. 2 (**flannels**) trousers made of flannel. 3 a facecloth. 4 informal evasive and meaningless talk. ▶v. (**flannelling, flannelled**) informal talk evasively and meaninglessly.

flannelette n. a cotton fabric resembling flannel.

flap v. (**flapping, flapped**) 1 move up and down or from side to side. 2 informal be agitated. ▶n. 1 a piece of something attached on one side only to cover an opening. 2 a single flapping movement. 3 informal a panic.

flapjack n. a soft biscuit made with oats.

flare n. 1 a sudden blaze. 2 a device producing a very bright flame as a signal or marker. 3 a gradual widening towards the hem of a garment. 4 (**flares**) trousers which widen from the knees down. ▶v. 1 blaze suddenly. 2 suddenly become stronger or violent. 3 gradually become wider at one end.

flash v. 1 shine with a bright but brief or irregular light. 2 move or send swiftly. 3 display or be displayed briefly, repeatedly, or ostentatiously. ▶n. 1 a sudden brief burst of bright light. 2 a camera attachment producing a flash of light. 3 a sudden or brief occurrence. 4 a coloured patch on a uniform. ▶adj. informal ostentatiously stylish or expensive. □ **flashback** a scene in a film or novel set in a time earlier than the main story. **flash flood** a sudden local flood. **flash in the pan** a sudden but brief success. **flashlight** an electric torch. **flashpoint** 1 a point at which anger or violence flares up. 2 the temperature at which a vapour ignites.

flashing n. a strip of metal sealing the joins of a roof.

flashy adj. (**flashier, flashiest**) ostentatiously attractive or impressive.

Thesaurus

fizz v. BUBBLE, effervesce, froth, sparkle, foam, fizzle, sputter.

fizzy adj. BUBBLY, bubbling, sparkling, effervescent, gassy, carbonated.

flag[1] n. STANDARD, ensign, banner, pennant, streamer, bunting, colours, pennon, gonfalon.

flag[2] v. 1 TIRE, become tired/weary, weaken, grow weak, lose one's strength. 2 FADE, decline, fail, wane, diminish, ebb, decrease, taper off.

flagrant adj. OBVIOUS, glaring, blatant, overt, outrageous, shameless, disgraceful, shocking, scandalous, terrible, dreadful.

flair n. 1 ABILITY, capability, aptitude, facility, skill, talent, gift, knack, bent, genius. 2 STYLE, panache, dash, elan, good taste, discrimination, discernment.

flap v. FLUTTER, beat, thresh, thrash, wave, wag, agitate, waggle, swing, shake, oscillate.

■ **flashily** adv.

flask n. **1** a bottle with a narrow neck. **2** a vacuum flask.

flat adj. (**flatter, flattest**) **1** level and even. **2** not sloping. **3** lacking liveliness or interest. **4** no longer fizzy. **5** (of a battery) having used up its charge. **6** (of a charge or price) fixed. **7** definite and firm. **8** (of musical sound) below true pitch. **9** (of a note) lower by a semitone. ▶ adv. **1** so as to be flat. **2** informal definitely; absolutely. **3** (**flat out**) as fast or as hard as possible. ▶ n. **1** a flat part or area. **2** a musical note that is a semitone lower, or a sign indicating this. **3** a set of rooms forming an individual home within a larger building. □ **flatfish** a sea fish with a flattened body and both eyes on the upper side. **flatmate** a person with whom one shares a flat. **flat race** a horse race over a course with no jumps. ■ **flatly** adv. **flatness** n. **flatten** v.

flatter v. **1** compliment insincerely. **2** cause to feel honoured. **3** make appear attractive. ■ **flatterer** n. **flattery** n.

flatulent adj. suffering from a build-up of gas in the intestines or stomach. ■ **flatulence** n.

flaunt v. display proudly or obviously.

☑ Don't confuse **flaunt** with **flout**, which means 'openly fail to follow a rule'.

flautist n. a flute player.

flavour (US **flavor**) n. **1** the distinctive taste of a food or drink. **2** a particular quality. ▶ v. give flavour to. ■ **flavourless** adj.

flavouring (US **flavoring**) n. a substance used to give flavour to food or drink.

flaw n. **1** a mark or fault that spoils something. **2** a weakness or mistake. ■ **flawed** adj. **flawless** adj.

flax n. **1** a blue-flowered plant. **2** textile fibre made from flax.

flaxen adj. (of hair) pale yellow.

flay v. **1** strip the skin from. **2** criticize harshly.

flea n. a small jumping bloodsucking insect. □ **flea market** a street market selling second-hand goods.

fleck n. a very small patch or particle. ▶ v. mark with flecks.

fledged adj. (of a young bird) having wing feathers large enough for flight.

fledgling (or **fledgeling**) n. a young bird that has just learned to fly.

flee v. (**fleeing, fled**) run away.

fleece n. **1** the wool coat of a sheep. **2** a

Thesaurus

flash v. **1** GLARE, beam, gleam, shine out, glint, sparkle, flicker, shimmer, twinkle, glimmer, glisten, scintillate, coruscate. **2** SHOW OFF, flaunt, flourish, display, exhibit.

flat adj. **1** LEVEL, horizontal, levelled, even, smooth, unbroken, plane. **2** STRETCHED OUT, prone, spreadeagled, prostrate, supine, recumbent. **3** DEFLATED, punctured, burst, collapsed, ruptured. **4** MONOTONOUS, boring, dull, tedious, uninteresting, lifeless, dead, lacklustre, bland, insipid, vapid, prosaic. **5** OUTRIGHT, direct, out-and-out, definite, positive, downright, firm, conclusive, utter, complete, categorical, unconditional.

flatten v. **1** LEVEL, level out/off, even out, smooth, compress, trample, press down, crush, squash, compact. **2** DEMOLISH, tear down, knock down, raze, raze to the ground. **3** KNOCK SOMEONE OFF THEIR FEET, knock to the ground, floor, prostrate, fell.

flatter v. COMPLIMENT, praise, sing someone's praises, praise to excess, praise to the skies, pay court to, pay blandishments to, fawn upon, cajole, humour, flannel, wheedle; informal sweet-talk, soft-soap, butter up, lay it on thick, play up to. ■ OPPOSITES insult.

flattering adj. **1** COMPLIMENTARY, adulatory, fulsome, laudatory, honeyed, sugary, ingratiating, cajoling. **2** ENHANCING, becoming. ■ OPPOSITES unflattering.

flattery n. PRAISE, adulation, fulsomeness, unctuousness, fawning, puffery, cajolery, wheedling, compliments, blandishments, honeyed words; informal sweet talk, soft soap, flannel.

flaunt v. SHOW OFF, parade, display, exhibit, draw attention to, make a show of, wave, dangle, brandish.

flavour n. **1** TASTE, savour, tang, relish. **2** FLAVOURING, seasoning, tastiness, tang, relish, piquancy, spiciness, zest. **3** ATMOSPHERE, spirit, essence, nature, character, soul, quality, feel, feeling, ambience, tone, style.

flaw n. **1** SHORTCOMING, defect, imperfection, fault, failing, blemish, weakness, weak spot, foible. **2** DEFECT, fault, crack, chip, fracture, break, crevice, fissure, rent, split, tear. ■ OPPOSITES strength.

flawless adj. **1** PERFECT, impeccable, faultless. **2** UNBLEMISHED, perfect, soft, warm fabric with a pile, or a garment made from this. ▶v. informal swindle. ■ **fleecy** adj.

fleet n. **1** a group of ships, vehicles, or aircraft travelling together or having the same owner. **2** a navy. ▶adj. fast and nimble.

fleeting adj. passing quickly; brief. ■ **fleetingly** adv.

flesh n. **1** the soft substance in the body consisting of muscle and fat. **2** the soft part of a fruit or vegetable. **3** (**the flesh**) the physical aspects of the body. ▶v. (**flesh out**) make more detailed. □ **in the flesh** in person.

fleshly adj. of the body and its needs.

fleshy adj. (**fleshier**, **fleshiest**) **1** plump. **2** soft and thick.

fleur-de-lis (or **fleur-de-lys**) /fler-duh-lee/ n. (pl. **fleurs-de-lis**) a design of a lily with three petals.

flew past of FLY.

flex v. **1** bend a limb or joint. **2** tighten a muscle. ▶n. a flexible insulated cable for carrying electric current. □ **flexitime** a system allowing flexible working hours. ■ **flexion** n.

flexible adj. **1** able to bend easily. **2** easily changed; adaptable. ■ **flexibility** n. **flexibly** adv.

flibbertigibbet n. a frivolous person.

flick n. **1** a sudden sharp movement up and down or from side to side. **2** (**the flicks**) informal the cinema. ▶v. move, hit, or remove with a flick.

flicker v. **1** shine or burn unsteadily. **2** appear briefly. **3** make small, quick movements. ▶n. **1** a flickering movement or light. **2** a brief occurrence.

flier var. of FLYER.

flight n. **1** the act of flying. **2** a journey through air or space. **3** the path of something through the air. **4** the act of running away. **5** a group of flying birds or aircraft. **6** a series of steps. **7** the tail of an arrow or dart. □ **flight deck 1** the cockpit of a large aircraft. **2** the deck of an aircraft carrier, used as a runway. **flightless** unable to fly.

flighty adj. unreliable and frivolous.

flimsy adj. (**flimsier**, **flimsiest**) **1** fragile. **2** light and thin. **3** unconvincing. ■ **flimsily** adv. **flimsiness** n.

flinch v. **1** make a quick, nervous movement from fear or pain. **2** (**flinch from**) avoid through fear or anxiety.

fling v. (**flinging**, **flung**) throw or move forcefully. ▶n. **1** a short period of enjoyment. **2** a short sexual relationship.

flint n. **1** a hard grey rock. **2** a piece of flint or a metal alloy, used to produce a spark. □ **flintlock** an old type of gun. ■ **flinty** adj.

flip v. (**flipping**, **flipped**) **1** turn over,

Thesaurus

blemish-free, unmarred, unimpaired. **3** PERFECT, whole, intact, sound, undamaged, unbroken. ■ OPPOSITES imperfect, flawed.

flee v. RUN AWAY, run off, make off, fly, take flight, beat a hasty retreat, bolt, abscond, retreat, depart hastily, make a quick exit, run for it, make a run for it, take off, take to one's heels, decamp, escape, make one's getaway, vanish; *informal* do a disappearing act, cut and run, beat it, skedaddle, split, scram, light out, scarper, do a bunk, do a runner.

fleeting adj. BRIEF, short-lived, transient, momentary, rapid, swift, transitory, ephemeral, temporary, impermanent, here today and gone tomorrow, evanescent, fugitive, vanishing, flying, passing, flitting. ■ OPPOSITES lasting.

flesh n. MUSCLE, tissue, meat, brawn, body.

flexible adj. **1** BENDABLE, pliable, pliant, elastic, plastic, springy, mouldable, rubbery. **2** SUPPLE, agile, limber, lithe, lissom, double-jointed. **3** ADAPTABLE, adjustable, changeable, open to change, variable, open, open-ended, provisional, mutable. **4** COOPERATIVE, accommodating, tractable, compliant, manageable, amenable, malleable, biddable, docile, submissive, yielding. ■ OPPOSITES inflexible, rigid.

flick v. **1** STRIKE, hit, whip, rap, tap, touch. **2** CLICK, switch, snap, flip, jerk. □ **flick through** SKIM, glance over/through, browse through, thumb through.

flight n. **1** AVIATION, flying, air transport, aeronautics. **2** FLOCK, group, skein, bevy, covey, migration.

flimsy adj. **1** INSUBSTANTIAL, fragile, frail, slight, makeshift, rickety, shaky, jerry-built, ramshackle, gimcrack. **2** THIN, light, fine, delicate, lightweight, sheer, filmy, diaphanous, transparent, gossamer, gauzy. **3** FEEBLE, weak, poor, inadequate, thin, unconvincing, transparent, implausible, unsatisfactory, trivial, shallow, paltry. ■ OPPOSITES strong.

flinch v. DRAW BACK, shrink back, pull back, start back, recoil, withdraw, shy away, cringe, cower, quail, crouch, wince, blench. □ **flinch from** SHIRK, evade, avoid, shy away from, dodge, throw, or move with a sudden, quick movement. **2** informal lose one's self-control. ▶n. a flipping movement. ▶adj. flippant.

flippant adj. not showing proper seriousness or respect. ■ **flippancy** n. **flippantly** adv.

flipper n. **1** a sea animal's broad, flat limb used in swimming. **2** each of two flat rubber attachments worn on the feet for underwater swimming.

flirt v. **1** behave as if trying to attract someone sexually but without serious intentions. **2** (**flirt with**) show a casual interest in. ▶n. a person who flirts. ■ **flirtation** n. **flirtatious** adj.

flit v. (**flitting, flitted**) move quickly and lightly. ▶n. informal an act of leaving one's home in secrecy.

flitter v. flit about.

float v. **1** rest or move on the surface of a liquid. **2** move or be held up in the air. **3** put forward a suggestion. **4** offer the shares of a company for sale. **5** allow a currency to have a variable rate of exchange. ▶n. **1** a thing designed to float on water. **2** a vehicle carrying a display in a procession. **3** a sum of money for minor expenses or giving change. ■ **floaty** adj.

floatation var. of FLOTATION.

flocculent adj. like tufts of wool.

flock n. **1** a number of birds or animals together. **2** a large number or crowd. **3** a congregation. **4** wool or cotton refuse used as stuffing. ▶v. gather or move in a flock. □ **flock wallpaper** wallpaper with a raised pattern made from powdered cloth.

floe n. a sheet of floating ice.

flog v. (**flogging, flogged**) **1** beat with a whip or stick. **2** informal sell.

flood n. **1** an overflow of a large amount of water over dry land. **2** an overwhelming quantity or outpouring. **3** the rising of the tide. ▶v. **1** cover or become covered with flood water. **2** (of a river) overflow its banks. **3** arrive in very large numbers.

floodlight n. a large lamp with a broad, powerful beam. ▶v. (**floodlighting, floodlit**) light up with floodlights.

floor n. **1** the lower surface of a room. **2** a storey of a building. **3** (**the floor**) the right to speak in a debate. ▶v. **1** provide with a floor. **2** informal knock down. **3** informal baffle. □ **floor show** a cabaret.

flooring n. material for a floor.

floozy (or **floozie**) n. (pl. **floozies**) informal a promiscuous or sexually provocative woman.

flop v. (**flopping, flopped**) **1** hang loosely. **2** sit or lie down heavily. **3** informal fail totally. ▶n. **1** a flopping movement. **2** informal a total failure.

floppy adj. not firm or rigid. □ **floppy disk** a flexible disk for storing computer data.

flora n. (pl. **floras** or **florae**) the plants of an area or period.

floral adj. of flowers.

floret n. **1** each of the small flowers of a composite flower. **2** each of the flowering stems of a head of cauliflower or broccoli.

florid adj. **1** red or flushed. **2** over-elaborate.

Thesaurus

duck, baulk at.

fling v. THROW, hurl, toss, pitch, cast, launch, catapult, propel, send flying, let fly, shy, lob; informal chuck, heave.

flippant adj. FRIVOLOUS, glib, offhand, impertinent, insouciant, impudent, irreverent, superficial, carefree, thoughtless, shallow, cheeky, pert; informal flip. ■ OPPOSITES serious.

flirt v. CHAT UP, make eyes at, toy with, lead on, trifle with, dally with, tease. ▶n. COQUETTE, tease, vamp, heartbreaker, trifler, philanderer.

flirtatious adj. PROVOCATIVE, teasing, coquettish, playful, amorous, philandering, come-hither.

float v. **1** STAY AFLOAT, be buoyant, sail, bob, glide, drift, slip. **2** MOVE AIMLESSLY, drift, wander, meander; US informal bum around. ■ OPPOSITES sink.

flock n. **1** HERD, drove. **2** FLIGHT, bevy, gaggle, skein. **3** CROWD, gathering, assembly, group, company, collection, congregation, throng, mass, host, multitude, troop, convoy.

flog v. WHIP, lash, horsewhip, flay, flagellate, birch, scourge, belt, cane, strap, thrash, beat, whack, wallop, chastise, trounce; informal tan someone's hide.

flood n. **1** DELUGE, torrent, inundation, spate, overflow, flash flood. **2** ABUNDANCE, superabundance, profusion, glut, surfeit, plethora, superfluity; informal tons, heaps, loads. ▶v. **1** INUNDATE, deluge, pour over, immerse, submerge, swamp, drown, engulf, saturate. **2** OVERSUPPLY, saturate, overfill, glut, overwhelm. ■ OPPOSITES trickle.

floor n. STOREY, level, tier, deck.

flop v. **1** COLLAPSE, slump, drop, fall, tum-

florin n. a former British coin worth two shillings.

florist n. a person who sells flowers. ■ **floristry** n.

floruit v. used to indicate when a historical figure lived or was most active.

floss n. **1** untwisted silk thread. **2** a soft thread used to clean between the teeth.

flotation (or **floatation**) n. the act of floating, esp. of a company's shares.

flotilla n. a small fleet.

flotsam n. wreckage floating on the sea. □ **flotsam and jetsam** useless or discarded objects.

flounce v. move in an angry or impatient way. ▶ n. **1** a flouncing movement. **2** a wide frill.

flounder v. **1** stagger clumsily in mud or water. **2** have difficulty doing something. ▶ n. a small edible flatfish.

flour n. a powder produced by grinding grain, esp. wheat. ■ **floury** adj.

flourish v. **1** grow vigorously. **2** be successful. **3** wave about in a noticeable way. ▶ n. **1** an unrestrained gesture. **2** an ornamental curve in handwriting. **3** a fanfare.

flout v. openly fail to follow a rule etc.

✓ Don't confuse **flout** with **flaunt**, which means 'display proudly or obviously'.

flow v. **1** move steadily and continuously in a stream. **2** move or proceed smoothly and steadily. **3** hang loosely. ▶ n. **1** the act of flowing. **2** a steady, continuous stream. □ **flow chart** a diagram showing a sequence of stages in a process.

flower n. **1** the part of a plant from which the seed or fruit develops, usu. brightly coloured or decorative. **2** the best of a group. ▶ v. produce flowers. □ **flowerpot** a container for growing plants in. ■ **flowered** adj.

flowery adj. **1** full of flowers. **2** elaborate.

flown past part. of FLY.

flu n. influenza.

fluctuate v. vary irregularly. ■ **fluctuation** n.

flue n. a passage for smoke and waste gases in a chimney or for conveying heat.

fluent adj. **1** speaking or writing in a clear and natural manner. **2** smoothly graceful and easy. ■ **fluency** n. **fluently** adv.

fluff n. a soft mass of fibres or down. ▶ v. **1** make fuller and softer by shaking or patting. **2** informal fail to do properly. ■ **fluffiness** n. **fluffy** adj.

fluid n. a liquid. ▶ adj. **1** able to flow easily. **2** not stable. **3** graceful. □ **fluid ounce** one twentieth of a pint (approx. 0.028 litre). ■ **fluidity** n.

Thesaurus

ble, droop, sag, dangle. **2** FAIL, be unsuccessful, be a disaster, miss the mark, founder, fall flat; *informal* bomb, go down like a lead balloon, go to the wall. ■ OPPOSITES succeed.

florid adj. **1** RED, ruddy, flushed, high-coloured, rubicund, rubescent, erubescent. **2** FLOWERY, over-elaborate, verbose, purple, grandiloquent. ■ OPPOSITES pale, plain.

flounder v. **1** THRASH, struggle, blunder, stumble, fumble, grope. **2** STRUGGLE, falter, be in difficulties, be confused, be in the dark, be out of one's depth.

flourish v. **1** BRANDISH, wave, wield, swing, hold aloft, display, exhibit, flaunt, show off, parade, vaunt. **2** THRIVE, grow, do well, develop, burgeon, bloom, blossom, bear fruit, flower, succeed, prosper.

flout v. DEFY, disdain, scorn, show contempt for, scoff at, mock, laugh at, deride, ridicule, sneer at. ■ OPPOSITES obey, observe.

flow v. **1** MOVE, course, run, go along, proceed, glide, stream, ripple, swirl,

surge, sweep, roll, whirl, rush, drift, slide, trickle, gurgle. **2** GUSH, stream, well, spurt, spout, squirt, spew, jet, spill, leak, seep, ooze, drip. ▶ n. **1** CURRENT, course, drift, stream, tide, spate. **2** GUSH, stream, outflow, outpouring, welling.

flower n. **1** BLOOM, blossom, floweret, floret, annual, perennial. **2** BEST, finest, pick, cream, elite.

fluctuate v. **1** RISE AND FALL, go up and down, see-saw, yo-yo, be unstable, vary, change, alter, swing, oscillate, ebb and flow, undulate. **2** WAVER, vacillate, hesitate, change one's mind, blow hot and cold, hum and haw, shilly-shally, alternate, veer, teeter, totter.

fluent adj. **1** ARTICULATE, eloquent, silver-tongued, smooth-spoken, voluble. **2** SMOOTH, flowing, fluid, natural, effortless, graceful, elegant, mellifluous, euphonious. ■ OPPOSITES inarticulate.

fluff n. DOWN, fuzz, lint, nap, pile, dust.

fluid adj. **1** LIQUID, liquefied, gaseous, gassy, melted, molten, running, flowing, uncongealed. **2** SMOOTH, fluent,

fluke n. **1** a lucky chance occurrence. **2** a parasitic worm. **3** the barbed arm of an anchor. **4** a lobe of a whale's tail.

flume n. **1** an artificial water channel. **2** a water slide.

flummery n. empty talk or compliments.

flummox v. informal baffle.

flung past & past part. of FLING.

flunk v. informal fail an examination.

flunkey (or **flunky**) n. (pl. **flunkeys** or **flunkies**) **1** a uniformed servant. **2** a person who does menial work.

fluorescent adj. **1** giving off bright light when exposed to radiation such as ultraviolet light. **2** vividly colourful. ■ **fluoresce** v. **fluorescence** n.

fluoridate v. add fluoride to. ■ **fluoridation** n.

fluoride n. a compound of fluorine added to water supplies or toothpaste to reduce tooth decay.

fluorine n. a poisonous gaseous element.

fluorite (or **fluorspar**) n. a colourless mineral.

flurry n. (pl. **flurries**) **1** a swirling mass of snow, leaves, etc. **2** a sudden spell of activity or excitement.

flush v. **1** make or become red; blush. **2** clean or remove by passing large quantities of water through. **3** force into the open. ▶n. **1** a blush. **2** a rush of emotion. **3** an act of flushing. ▶adj. **1** level with another surface. **2** informal having plenty of money.

fluster v. make agitated or confused. ▶n. a flustered state.

flute n. **1** a wind instrument consisting of a tube held sideways with holes along its length. **2** a tall, narrow wine glass. **3** an ornamental groove.

flutter v. **1** fly unsteadily by flapping the wings quickly and lightly. **2** move with a light trembling motion. **3** (of the heart) beat irregularly. ▶n. **1** a fluttering movement. **2** a state of nervous excitement. **3** informal a small bet.

fluvial adj. of rivers.

flux n. **1** continuous change. **2** a flow. **3** a substance mixed with a solid to lower the melting point.

fly[1] v. (**flies**, **flying**, **flew**; past part. **flown**) **1** (of a winged creature or aircraft) move through the air. **2** control the flight of or transport in an aircraft. **3** move quickly through the air. **4** go or move quickly. **5** flutter in the wind. **6** (of a flag) be displayed on a flagpole. **7** (**fly into**) suddenly go into a rage or temper. **8** (**fly at**) attack. **9** old use run away. ▶n. (pl. **flies**) **1** (also **flies**) an opening at the crotch of a pair of trousers, closed with a zip or buttons. **2** a flap of material covering the opening of a tent. □ **flying buttress** a buttress slanting upwards from a separate support. **flying fish** a tropical fish with wing-like fins for gliding above the water. **flying saucer** a disc-shaped flying craft supposedly piloted by aliens. **flying squad** a division of a police force capable of reaching an incident quickly. **fly-tipping** the illegal dumping of waste.

fly[2] n. (pl. **flies**) a two-winged flying insect. □ **flyblown** contaminated by contact with flies. **fly in the ointment** a minor irritation that spoils something. **fly on the wall** an unnoticed observer.

flyer (or **flier**) n. **1** a person or thing that flies. **2** a small handbill advertising something.

FM abbrev. frequency modulation.

foal n. a young horse or related animal. ▶v. give birth to a foal.

foam n. **1** a mass of small bubbles. **2** a substance containing many small bubbles. **3** lightweight spongy rubber or plastic. ▶v. form or produce foam. ■ **foamy** adj.

Thesaurus

flowing, graceful, elegant, effortless, easy, natural. **3** FLEXIBLE, open to change, adaptable, not fixed, adjustable, variable, mutable. **4** UNSTABLE, likely to change, unsteady, fluctuating, shifting. ▶n. LIQUID, gas, solution.

flush v. **1** BLUSH, turn red, redden, colour, colour up, crimson, burn up, flame up, glow, suffuse with colour. **2** WASH OUT, rinse out, cleanse, hose down, swab. **3** EXPEL, eject.

fluster v. AGITATE, ruffle, unsettle, upset, bother, put on edge, panic, disconcert, discompose, confuse, throw off balance, confound, nonplus; informal hassle, rattle, faze, throw into a tizz.

flutter v. **1** BEAT, flap, quiver, agitate, vibrate, ruffle. **2** BAT, flicker, flit. **3** FLAP, wave, flop, ripple, quiver, shiver, tremble.

fly v. **1** SOAR, take wing, take to the air, wing, wing its way, hover, swoop. **2** DISPLAY, show, exhibit, wave, hoist, raise, hang out. **3** DASH, race, rush, tear, bolt, zoom, dart, speed, hurry, career, hasten; informal hare off, be off like a shot. **4** FLEE, run away, bolt, take flight, make off, abscond, beat a retreat, run for it,

fob n. **1** a chain attached to a watch. **2** a tab on a key ring. ▶v. **(fobbing, fobbed) (fob off)** try to deceive into accepting excuses or something inferior.

focal adj. of or at a focus.

fo'c'sle var. of FORECASTLE.

focus n. (pl. **focuses** or **foci**) **1** the centre of interest or activity. **2** clear visual definition. **3** the point at which an object must be situated for a lens etc. to produce a clear image of it. **4** a point where rays or sound waves etc. meet. ▶v. **(focusing, focused** or **focussing, focussed) 1** bring into focus. **2** adjust the focus of. **3** concentrate. □ **focus group** a group assembled to assess a new product, policy, etc. ■ **focuser** n.

fodder n. food for animals.

foe n. an enemy.

foetid var. of FETID.

foetus var. of FETUS.

fog n. a thick mist. ▶v. **(fogging, fogged) 1** cover or become covered with mist. **2** confuse. □ **foghorn** a device making a loud, deep sound as a warning to ships in fog. ■ **foggy** adj.

fogey (or **fogy**) n. (pl. **fogeys** or **fogies**) an old-fashioned person.

foible n. a minor weakness or eccentricity.

foil v. prevent someone from doing something; thwart. ▶n. **1** a very thin flexible sheet of metal. **2** a person or thing emphasizing another's qualities by contrast. **3** a long, thin fencing sword with a button on its point.

foist v. **(foist on)** impose an unwelcome person or thing on.

fold v. **1** bend something over on itself so that one part of it covers another. **2** wrap. **3** clasp in one's arms. **4** informal go out of business. **5** mix an ingredient gently into another. ▶n. **1** a folded part or thing. **2** a line produced by folding. **3** a pen for sheep.

folder n. a folding cover or wallet for loose papers.

foliage n. leaves.

foliate adj. decorated with leaves.

folio n. (pl. **folios**) **1** a sheet of paper folded once to form two leaves of a book. **2** a book made up of such sheets.

folk pl. n. **1** (also **folks**) informal people. **2** (**one's folks**) one's family. **3** traditional music. ▶adj. (of music etc.) in the traditional style of a country or region. □ **folklore** the traditional beliefs and stories of a community.

folksy adj. traditional and homely. ■ **folksiness** n.

follicle n. a small cavity containing a hair root. ■ **follicular** adj.

follow v. **1** go or come after. **2** go along a route. **3** be a logical consequence. **4** occur as a result of. **5** act according to an instruction or example. **6** understand or pay close attention to. **7** (**follow up**) investigate further. □ **follow suit** do the same as someone else. ■ **follower** n.

Thesaurus

decamp, make one's escape; *informal* cut and run, skedaddle, scarper, do a bunk.

foam v. FROTH, froth up, bubble, fizz, cream, lather, spume, effervesce. ▶n. FROTH, bubbles, fizz, head, spume, lather, effervescence, suds.

focus n. **1** CENTRE, central point, focal point, centre of attention, core, hub, pivot, magnet, cynosure. **2** FOCAL POINT, point of conversion. ▶v. AIM, fix, concentrate, bring to bear, zero in on, zoom in on, centre, pinpoint, rivet.

foe n. ENEMY, opponent, adversary, rival, antagonist, combatant, contestant. ■ OPPOSITES friend.

fog n. MIST, smog, haze, murk, murkiness, gloom; *informal* pea-souper.

foggy adj. **1** MISTY, smoggy, dark, grey, dim, overcast, murky, hazy, gloomy. **2** VAGUE, indistinct, cloudy, hazy, unclear, obscure, befuddled, confused, muddled, dazed. ■ OPPOSITES clear.

foible n. WEAKNESS, weak point, failing, shortcoming, flaw, blemish, defect, frailty, quirk, idiosyncrasy; *informal* hang-up.

foil v. THWART, frustrate, stop, baffle, defeat, check, checkmate, circumvent, counter, baulk, disappoint, impede, obstruct, hamper, hinder.

fold n. **1** LAYER, pleat, overlap, turn, gather, crease, knife-edge. **2** WRINKLE, pucker, furrow, crinkle, crows feet. ▶v. **1** DOUBLE UP, turn under, turn up, bend, tuck, crease, gather, pleat, crimp, crumple. **2** WRAP, enfold, clasp, embrace, envelop, hug, squeeze. **3** FAIL, collapse, go out of business, go bankrupt, crash, go to the wall; *informal* go bust, go under, flop.

folk n. PEOPLE, populace, population, citizenry, general public, public, clan, tribe.

follow v. **1** GO/COME BEHIND, walk behind, go with, escort, accompany, keep pace with, attend, chase, pursue, run after, trail, shadow, hunt, stalk, track, dog, hound; *informal* tread on someone's heels,

following prep. coming after or as a result of. ▶ n. a group of supporters or admirers. ▶ adj. next in time or order.

folly n. (pl. **follies**) **1** foolishness. **2** a foolish act. **3** an ornamental building with no practical purpose.

foment v. stir up conflict.

fond adj. **1** (**fond of**) having an affection or liking for. **2** affectionate. **3** (of a hope) unlikely to be fulfilled. ■ **fondly** adv. **fondness** n.

fondant n. a paste of sugar and water, used to make sweets and as icing.

fondle v. stroke lovingly.

fondue n. a dish of melted cheese etc. into which pieces of food are dipped.

font n. **1** a large stone bowl in a church holding water for baptism. **2** (also **fount**) a size and design of printing type.

fontanelle n. a soft area between the bones of the skull in a baby or fetus.

food n. any substance that people or animals eat or drink or that plants absorb to maintain life and growth. □ **foodstuff** a substance used as food.

fool n. **1** a foolish person. **2** a cold dessert made of puréed fruit and cream. ▶ v. **1** trick or deceive. **2** (**fool about/around**) act in a joking or silly way. ■ **foolery** n.

foolhardy adj. bold in a reckless way. ■ **foolhardiness** n.

foolish adj. silly or unwise. ■ **foolishly** adv. **foolishness** n.

foolproof adj. unable to go wrong or be wrongly used.

foolscap n. a large size of paper.

foot n. (pl. **feet**) **1** the part of the leg below the ankle. **2** a lower end; a base. **3** the end of a bed etc. **4** a unit of length equal to 12 inches (30.48 cm). **5** a basic unit of metre in poetry. ▶ v. informal pay a bill. □ **foot-and-mouth disease** a contagious viral disease of livestock. **footbridge** a bridge for pedestrians. **footfall** the sound of footsteps. **foothill** a low hill at the base of a mountain or range. **foothold 1** a place where one can put a foot down securely when climbing. **2** a secure position as a basis for progress. **footlights** spotlights along the front of a stage. **footloose** free to do as one pleases. **footman** a uniformed manservant. **footnote** a note printed at the bottom of a page. **footpath** a path for people to walk along. **footprint** the mark left by a foot

Thesaurus

tail, tag after. **2** OBEY, observe, comply with, heed, conform to, pay attention to, stick to, adhere to, note, have regard to, mind, be guided by, accept, yield to. **3** RESULT FROM, arise from, be consequent on, develop from, ensue from, emanate from, issue from, proceed from, spring from, flow from. **4** UNDERSTAND, comprehend, take in, see, grasp, fathom, get, catch on to, appreciate. **5** BE A FOLLOWER OF, be a supporter of, be interested in, be devoted to, support, keep abreast of, keep up to date with. □ **follow through** CONTINUE, complete, bring to completion, see something through. **follow up** INVESTIGATE, research, find out about, look into, check out, pursue.

following adj. NEXT, ensuing, succeeding, subsequent, successive. ▶ n. SUPPORTERS, backers, fans, admirers, devotees, public, audience, adherents, patrons.

foment v. INCITE, instigate, stir up, provoke, excite, arouse, encourage, initiate, agitate. *See also* STIMULATE.

fond adj. **1** ADORING, devoted, loving, affectionate, caring, warm, tender, amorous, doting, indulgent. **2** FOOLISH, naive, deluded, delusory, absurd, vain, empty.

■ OPPOSITES hostile.

fondle v. CARESS, stroke, pat, pet, cuddle, hug, nuzzle.

food n. NOURISHMENT, sustenance, nutriment, subsistence, diet, fare, menu, bread, board, provender, cooking, cuisine, foodstuffs, refreshments, edibles, meals, provisions, rations, stores, commons, comestibles, solids; *informal* nosh, grub, eats, chow, scoff; *dated* victuals.

fool n. **1** IDIOT, dolt, dunce, ass, ignoramus, imbecile, simpleton; *informal* chump, booby, nincompoop, ninny, dunderhead, blockhead, fathead, half-wit, cretin, moron, dummy, numbskull, dimwit, twerp, clot, twit, nitwit. **2** DUPE, butt, laughing stock, gull, easy mark, cat's paw; *informal* stooge, sucker, pushover, sap, fall guy, mug. ▶ v. **1** TRICK, deceive, hoax, make a fool of, dupe, take in, mislead, hoodwink, bluff, delude, beguile, gull; *informal* con, bamboozle, kid, have on. **2** PRETEND, make believe, feign, put on an act, sham, fake.

foolish adj. SILLY, stupid, idiotic, senseless, brainless, dense, moronic, half-witted, doltish, imprudent, incautious, injudicious, irresponsible, mad, crazy, unwise, ill-advised, ill-considered; *informal* dotty, batty, nutty, dippy, screwy, or shoe on the ground. **footsore** having sore feet from much walking. **footstep** a step taken in walking. **footstool** a low stool for resting the feet on when sitting. **footwear** shoes, boots, etc. **footwork** the manner of moving one's feet in dancing and sport.

footage n. **1** part of a cinema or television film. **2** length measured in feet.

football n. **1** a team game involving kicking a ball, in particular (in the UK) soccer or (in the US) American football. **2** a large ball used in football. ■ **footballer** n.

footing n. **1** a secure grip with one's feet. **2** the basis on which something is established or operates.

footling adj. trivial.

fop n. a man overly concerned with his clothes and appearance. ■ **foppish** adj.

for prep. **1** relating to. **2** in favour or on behalf of. **3** so as to get, have, or do. **5** in place of. **6** in the direction of. **7** over a period or distance. ▶ conj. literary because.

forage v. search for food. ▶ n. fodder.

foray n. **1** a sudden attack or advancing move. **2** a brief attempt to become involved in a new activity.

forbear v. (**forbearing**, **forbore**; past part. **forborne**) refrain from.

forbearing adj. patient or tolerant. ■ **forbearance** n.

forbid v. (**forbidding**, **forbade**; past part. **forbidden**) **1** refuse to allow. **2** order not to do.

forbidding adj. appearing unfriendly or threatening.

force n. **1** physical strength or energy. **2** Physics a measurable influence causing movement. **3** violence used to obtain or achieve something. **4** influence or power. **5** an organized group of soldiers, police, etc. ▶ v. **1** move using force. **2** achieve or produce by effort. **3** make someone do something against their will. □ **forcemeat** finely chopped seasoned meat used as a stuffing. **in force 1** in great strength or numbers. **2** in effect.

forceful adj. powerful and confident. ■ **forcefully** adv. **forcefulness** n.

forceps pl. n. pincers used in surgery etc.

forcible adj. done by force. ■ **forcibly** adv.

ford n. a shallow place in a river where it can be crossed. ▶ v. cross at a ford.

fore adj. in or at the front. □ **to the fore** in or to a prominent position.

forearm n. the arm from the elbow to the wrist. ▶ v. (**be forearmed**) be prepared in advance for danger or attack.

forebear n. an ancestor.

foreboding n. a feeling that something bad will happen.

forecast v. predict a future event. ▶ n. a prediction. ■ **forecaster** n.

forecastle (or **fo'c's'le**) /fohk-s'l/ n. the front part of a ship below the deck.

foreclose v. take possession of a property because the occupant has failed to keep up the mortgage payments. ■ **foreclosure** n.

Thesaurus

daft, potty, barmy. ■ OPPOSITES wise, sensible.

foolproof adj. INFALLIBLE, certain, sure, guaranteed, safe, dependable, trustworthy, never-failing.

forbid v. PROHIBIT, ban, bar, debar, outlaw, veto, proscribe, disallow, preclude, interdict, exclude, rule out, stop. ■ OPPOSITES allow.

forbidden adj. PROHIBITED, out of bounds, banned, outlawed, vetoed, proscribed, taboo, debarred, interdicted.

forbidding adj. **1** STERN, harsh, grim, hard, tough, hostile, unfriendly, disagreeable, nasty, mean, repellent, offputting. **2** FRIGHTENING, ominous, threatening, menacing, sinister, daunting, foreboding. ■ OPPOSITES friendly.

force n. **1** POWER, strength, vigour, energy, potency, muscle, might, effort, impact, exertion, pressure, stamina, vitality, stimulus, dynamism. **2** COERCION, duress, compulsion, pressure, constraint, enforcement, violence; informal arm-twisting. **3** PERSUASIVENESS, validity, weight, effectiveness, influence, power, strength, vehemence, efficacy; informal punch, bite. **4** DETACHMENT, unit, squad, squadron, battalion, division, regiment, army, patrol. ▶ v. **1** COMPEL, coerce, make, bring pressure on, use force on, pressure, pressurize, impel, drive, oblige, necessitate, constrain, urge, press-gang; informal use strong-arm tactics on, put the squeeze on. **2** DRIVE, push, propel, thrust, shove, press. **3** WREST, extract, extort, wring, drag.

forceful adj. **1** POWERFUL, vigorous, strong, potent, dynamic, energetic, assertive. **2** PERSUASIVE, telling, convincing, compelling, effective, cogent, impressive, valid. ■ OPPOSITES weak, unconvincing.

forecast v. PREDICT, foretell, foresee,

forecourt n. an open area in front of a building.

forefather n. an ancestor.

forefinger n. the finger next to the thumb.

forefoot n. (pl. **forefeet**) an animal's front foot.

forefront n. the leading position.

foregather v. assemble.

forego var. of **FORGO**.

foregoing adj. preceding.

foregone conclusion n. a predictable result.

foreground n. the part of a view or picture nearest to the observer.

forehand n. (in tennis etc.) a stroke played with the palm of the hand facing forwards.

forehead n. the part of the face above the eyebrows.

foreign adj. **1** of a country or language other than one's own. **2** of other countries. **3** coming from outside. **4** (**foreign to**) not known to or typical of. ■ **foreigner** n.

✓ Single r: foreign is an exception to the *i* before e rule.

foreknowledge n. awareness of something before it happens.

foreleg n. an animal's front leg.

forelock n. a lock of hair just above the forehead.

foreman (or **forewoman**) n. **1** a worker who supervises others. **2** a person who is head of a jury and speaks on its behalf.

foremost adj. highest in importance or position. ▶ adv. in the first place.

forename n. a first name.

forenoon n. the morning.

forensic adj. **1** of the use of scientific methods in the investigation of crime. **2** of a court of law.

foreplay n. sexual activity preceding intercourse.

forerunner n. a person or thing coming before and influencing someone or something else.

foresee v. (**foreseeing, foresaw**; past part. **foreseen**) be aware of beforehand. ■ **foreseeable** adj.

foreshadow v. be a warning of.

foreshore n. the part of a shore between the highest and lowest levels reached by the sea.

foreshorten v. portray an object as closer than it really is.

foresight n. the ability to predict and prepare for future needs.

foreskin n. the roll of skin covering the end of the penis.

forest n. a large area covered thickly with trees. ■ **forested** adj.

forestall v. prevent or delay by taking action first.

forestry n. the science or practice of planting and managing forests. ■ **forester** n.

foretaste n. a sample of something that lies ahead.

foretell v. (**foretelling, foretold**) predict.

forethought n. careful planning for the future.

Thesaurus

prophesy, forewarn, prognosticate, augur, divine, guess, conjecture, speculate, calculate. ▶ n. PREDICTION, prophecy, guess, prognostication, augury, prognosis, conjecture, projection.

foregoing adj. PRECEDING, prior, previous, former, above, aforesaid, antecedent, anterior.

foreign adj. **1** OVERSEAS, distant, remote, alien, exotic. **2** STRANGE, unfamiliar, unknown, exotic, outlandish, odd, peculiar, curious. **3** IRRELEVANT, unrelated, not pertinent, unconnected, inappropriate, extraneous, outside, extrinsic, inapposite. ■ OPPOSITES domestic, native, familiar.

foreigner n. ALIEN, non-native, immigrant, incomer, newcomer, stranger, outsider. ■ OPPOSITES native.

foremost adj. LEADING, principal, premier, top, first, primary, front, para-

mount, chief, main, most important, supreme, highest.

forerunner n. PREDECESSOR, precursor, antecedent, ancestor, forefather, harbinger, herald, usher, advance guard.

foreshadow v. FOREBODE, bode, presage, augur, portend, indicate, show, signify, point to, prefigure, promise.

foresight n. FAR-SIGHTEDNESS, perspicacity, anticipation, forethought, presence of mind, preparedness, readiness, prescience, provision, discernment, care, caution.

forest n. WOODLAND, wood, woods, trees, plantation.

forestall v. PRE-EMPT, anticipate, intercept, thwart, frustrate, stave off, ward off, fend off, prevent, avert, hinder, impede, obstruct; *informal* steal a march on, get ahead of.

foretell v. **1** PREDICT, forecast, prophesy,

forever adv. **1** for all future time. **2** continually.

forewarn v. warn in advance.

forewent past of FOREGO.

foreword n. an introduction in a book.

forfeit v. lose property or a right as a penalty for wrongdoing. ▶n. something lost as a penalty for wrongdoing. ▶adj. forfeited. ■ **forfeiture** n.

forge v. **1** make or shape a metal object by heating and hammering. **2** make a fraudulent copy of. **3** move forward gradually or steadily. ▶n. **1** a blacksmith's workshop. **2** a furnace for heating metal. ■ **forger** n. **forgery** n.

forget v. (**forgetting**, **forgot**; past part. **forgotten**) **1** fail to remember. **2** no longer think of. **3** (**forget oneself**) behave inappropriately. □ **forget-me-not** a plant with small blue flowers. ■ **forgettable** adj.

forgetful adj. tending not to remember. ■ **forgetfully** adv. **forgetfulness** n.

forgive v. (**forgiving**, **forgave**; past part. **forgiven**) stop feeling angry or resentful towards or about. ■ **forgivable** adj.

forgiveness n.

forgo (or **forego**) v. (**forgoing**, **forwent**; past part. **forgone**) go without.

fork n. **1** a small pronged implement for lifting or holding food. **2** a large pronged tool for digging or lifting. **3** a point where a road etc. divides into two parts. **4** either of two such parts. ▶v. **1** divide into two parts. **2** take one route or the other at a fork. **3** dig or lift with a fork. **4** (**fork out**) informal pay money. □ **forklift truck** a vehicle with a forked device for lifting and carrying loads. ■ **forked** adj.

forlorn adj. very sad and lonely. □ **forlorn hope** a desperate enterprise. ■ **forlornly** adv.

form n. **1** shape or structure. **2** a way in which a thing exists. **3** a type or variety. **4** the way something is usually done. **5** a document with blank spaces for information. **6** a school class or year. **7** a person's mood, state of health, etc. ▶v. **1** create. **2** constitute. **3** establish or develop. ■ **formless** adj.

formal adj. **1** suitable for official or im-

foresee, forewarn, prognosticate, augur, divine. **2** PRESAGE, augur, forebode, portend, foreshadow, prefigure, point to, indicate, betoken.

forethought n. FORESIGHT, farsightedness, anticipation, provision, circumspection, prudence, judiciousness, care, precaution.

forever adv. ALWAYS, evermore, ever, for all time, until the end of time, eternally, perpetually; *informal* till the cows come home, till hell freezes over, for keeps, for good and all.

forfeit n. FINE, penalty, confiscation, damages, loss, relinquishment. ▶v. GIVE UP, hand over, relinquish, be stripped of.

forge v. **1** BEAT INTO SHAPE, hammer out, shape, form, fashion, mould, cast, found, make, manufacture, frame, construct, create. **2** FAKE, fabricate, falsify, counterfeit, copy, imitate.

forgery n. FAKE, counterfeit, sham, fraud, imitation, reproduction; *informal* phoney.

forget v. **1** FAIL TO REMEMBER, lose track of, overlook, let slip. **2** DISREGARD, put out of one's mind, ignore, let bygones be bygones. **3** LEAVE BEHIND, omit to take, overlook. ■ OPPOSITES remember.

forgetful adj. **1** ABSENT-MINDED, vague, apt to forget, abstracted, amnesiac. **2** NEGLECTFUL, negligent, careless, heed-

less, unmindful, inattentive, lax, remiss, oblivious.

forgive v. PARDON, excuse, absolve, exonerate, acquit, let off, let bygones be bygones, bury the hatchet, bear no malice, harbour no grudge; *informal* let someone off the hook.

forgiveness n. PARDON, amnesty, reprieve, absolution, exoneration, acquittal, remission, clemency, tolerance, compassion, exculpation, indulgence, leniency.

forgiving adj. MERCIFUL, lenient, magnanimous, understanding, compassionate, humane, clement, soft-hearted, forbearing, tolerant, mild. ■ OPPOSITES unforgiving.

forgo v. DO/GO WITHOUT, waive, renounce, sacrifice, relinquish, abjure, surrender, cede, abandon, yield, abstain from, refrain from, eschew, forswear.

fork v. BRANCH, branch off, diverge, bifurcate, divide, split, separate, go separate ways, divaricate.

forlorn adj. UNHAPPY, sad, miserable, wretched, pathetic, woebegone, disconsolate, lonely, cheerless, desolate, pitiable, pitiful, uncared for.

form n. **1** SHAPE, formation, configuration, structure, construction, conformation, arrangement, appearance, exterior. **2** APPEARANCE, shape, character, guise, description, manifestation, sembportant occasions. **2** officially recognized. **3** arranged in a precise way. ■ **formalize** (or **-ize**) v. **formally** adv.

formaldehyde /for-mal-di-hyd/ n. a colourless gas used in solution as a preservative and disinfectant.

formalin n. a solution of formaldehyde in water.

formalism n. excessive concern with rules and outward form.

formality n. (pl. **formalities**) **1** the rigid following of rules or customs. **2** a thing done simply to follow customs or rules.

format n. **1** the way something is arranged. **2** the shape and size of a book. **3** a structure for the processing etc. of computer data. ▶ v. (**formatting**, **formatted**) put into a format.

formation n. **1** the act of forming. **2** a structure or arrangement.

formative adj. influencing development.

former adj. **1** having been previously. **2** in the past. **3** referring to the first of two things mentioned.

formerly adv. in the past.

formic acid n. an acid in the fluid discharged by some ants.

formidable adj. causing fear or respect. ■ **formidably** adv.

formula n. (pl. **formulae** or **formulas**) **1** a set of symbols showing chemical constituents or expressing a mathematical relationship. **2** a fixed form of words used in particular situations. **3** a list of ingredients. **4** a classification of racing car. ■ **formulaic** adj.

formulate v. **1** create or devise. **2** express precisely. ■ **formulation** n.

fornicate v. have sex outside marriage. ■ **fornication** n. **fornicator** n.

forsake v. (**forsaking**, **forsook**; past part. **forsaken**) **1** abandon. **2** give up.

forsooth adv. old use indeed.

forswear v. (**forswearing**, **forswore**; past part. **forsworn**) **1** agree to give up or do without. **2** (usu. **be forsworn**) commit perjury.

forsythia /for-sy-thi-uh/ n. a shrub with bright yellow flowers.

fort n. a fortified building.

Thesaurus

lance. **3** TYPE, kind, sort, variety, species, genre, kidney, genus. **4** STRUCTURE, organization, order, planning, symmetry, proportion, orderliness, framework, format. **5** CONDITION, fitness, health, shape, trim, fettle. **6** APPLICATION, document, paper, sheet of paper. ▶ v. **1** MAKE, fashion, shape, model, mould, forge, construct, build, assemble, put together, set up, erect, produce, concoct. **2** DEVISE, formulate, think up, plan, draw up, frame, hatch, forge, develop, organize, dream up. **3** BRING ABOUT, set up, establish, found, organize, institute, inaugurate. **4** TAKE SHAPE, appear, materialize, show, become visible, come into being. **5** ACQUIRE, get into, contract, develop, get, pick up, grow into.

formal adj. **1** CORRECT, proper, conventional, reserved, aloof, remote, precise, exact, punctilious, stiff, unbending, inflexible, stand-offish, prim, stuffy, strait-laced. **2** OFFICIAL, set, fixed, conventional, standard, regular, customary, approved, prescribed, pro forma, legal, lawful, ceremonial, ritual. **3** ORDERLY, arranged, symmetrical, regular, methodical. ■ OPPOSITES informal.

formation n. **1** ARRANGEMENT, pattern, order, grouping, configuration, structure, format, layout, disposition, design. **2** ESTABLISHMENT, setting up, institution, founding, creation, inaugur-

ation. **3** COMPOSITION, make-up, constitution, organization.

former adj. **1** PREVIOUS, ex-, prior, preceding, earlier, late, sometime, erstwhile, one-time, foregoing, antecedent, anterior, ci-devant, quondam. **2** EARLIER, past, long past, bygone, long departed, long gone, old, ancient, of yore.

formidable adj. **1** INTIMIDATING, daunting, alarming, frightening, terrifying, horrifying, dreadful, awesome, fearsome, menacing, threatening, dangerous; informal scary. **2** STRONG, powerful, impressive, mighty, great, redoubtable, terrific, indomitable, invincible. **3** DIFFICULT, hard, taxing, arduous, onerous, tough, colossal, challenging, overwhelming, staggering. ■ OPPOSITES weak, easy.

formula n. **1** FORM OF WORDS, set expression, wording, rubric, formulary. **2** RECIPE, prescription, method, blueprint, procedure, convention, modus operandi, ritual, principles, rules, precepts, rubric.

formulate v. **1** DRAW UP, work out, plan, map out, prepare, compose, devise, think up, conceive, create, invent, coin, design. **2** DEFINE, state clearly, set down, frame, give form to, specify, itemize, detail, indicate, systematize.

forsake v. **1** DESERT, abandon, leave, quit, jilt, throw over, cast off, discard, repudiate, reject, disown; informal leave

forte /for-tay/ n. a thing for which someone has a particular talent. ▶ adv. Music loudly.

forth adv. **1** out and forwards. **2** onwards in time.

forthcoming adj. **1** about to happen or appear. **2** willing to reveal information.

forthright adj. direct and outspoken.

forthwith adv. without delay.

fortify v. (**fortifying**, **fortified**) **1** strengthen against attack. **2** invigorate or encourage. **3** increase the alcoholic content or nutritious value of. ■ **fortification** n.

fortissimo adv. Music very loudly.

fortitude n. courage when facing pain or trouble.

fortnight n. a period of two weeks. ■ **fortnightly** adj. & adv.

fortress n. a fortified building or town.

fortuitous adj. **1** happening by chance. **2** lucky. ■ **fortuitously** adv.

fortunate adj. lucky. ■ **fortunately** adv.

fortune n. **1** chance as a force affecting people's lives. **2** luck. **3** (**fortunes**) the success or failure of a person or undertaking. **4** a large amount of money. □ **fortune-teller** a person who predicts future events in people's lives.

forty adj. & n. (pl. **forties**) ten less than fifty; 40 or XL. □ **forty winks** informal a short sleep. ■ **fortieth** adj. & n.

forum n. a meeting or opportunity for an exchange of views.

forward adv. & adj. **1** in the direction that one is facing or moving. **2** towards a successful end. **3** ahead in time. **4** in or near the front. ▶ adj. bold or presumptuous. ▶ n. an attacking player in a sport. ▶ v. send a letter etc. on to a further destination. ■ **forwards** adv.

forwent past of FORGO.

fossil n. the remains of a prehistoric plant or animal that have become hardened into rock. □ **fossil fuel** a fuel such as coal or gas, formed from the remains of animals and plants. ■ **fossilize** (or **-ise**) v.

foster v. **1** encourage the development of. **2** bring up a child that is not one's own.

fought past & past part. of FIGHT.

Thesaurus

in the lurch, leave flat. **2** GIVE UP, renounce, relinquish, forgo, turn one's back on, repudiate, have done with, discard, set aside.

forthcoming adj. **1** FUTURE, coming, expected, prospective, imminent, impending. **2** COMMUNICATIVE, informative, talkative, expansive, voluble, chatty, loquacious, open.

forthright adj. DIRECT, frank, open, candid, blunt, outspoken, plain-speaking, plain-spoken, straightforward, honest. ■ OPPOSITES evasive.

fortify v. **1** BUILD DEFENCES ROUND, protect, secure, garrison, cover, guard, buttress, shore up. **2** STRENGTHEN, invigorate, energize, revive, embolden, give courage to, encourage, cheer, hearten, buoy up, reassure, make confident, brace, sustain.

fortitude n. STRENGTH, firmness, courage, nerve, grit, backbone, bravery, pluck, mettle, fearlessness, valour, intrepidity, stout-heartedness, forbearance, tenacity, perseverance, resolution, resoluteness, determination. ■ OPPOSITES cowardice.

fortunate adj. LUCKY, blessed, favoured, in luck, having a charmed life, happy, felicitous, prosperous, well off, successful, flourishing; informal sitting pretty, born with a silver spoon in one's mouth, jammy.

fortune n. **1** WEALTH, affluence, treasure, opulence, prosperity, riches, property, assets, means, possessions. **2** HUGE AMOUNT, mint, king's ransom; informal packet, bundle, bomb, pile. **3** CHANCE, accident, luck, coincidence, happy chance, fortuity, serendipity, contingency, providence. ■ OPPOSITES pittance.

fortune-teller n. SEER, soothsayer, prophet, prophetess, augur, diviner, sibyl, oracle, clairvoyant, astrologer.

forward adj. **1** ONWARD, advancing, progressing, progressive, frontal. **2** ADVANCED, well advanced, early, premature, precocious. **3** FRONT, at the front/fore, fore, frontal, foremost, head, leading, advance. **4** BOLD, brash, brazen, audacious, presumptuous, cocky, familiar, assertive, confident, overweening, aggressive, pushy, thrusting, pert, impudent, impertinent, cheeky, insolent; informal brass-necked, fresh. ▶ adv. **1** TOWARDS THE FRONT, onward, onwards, on, ahead, forth. **2** OUT, into view, into the open, into public view. ▶ v. **1** SEND ON, pass on, dispatch, transmit, post, mail, ship, freight, deliver. **2** ADVANCE, further, hasten, speed up, hurry along, accelerate, expedite, step up, aid, assist, help, encourage, foster, promote, favour, support, back, give backing to.

foster v. **1** ENCOURAGE, promote, further,

foul adj. **1** having a disgusting smell or taste. **2** very bad. **3** against the rules of a sport. **4** polluted. ▶n. an action that breaks the rules of a sport. ▶v. **1** make foul or dirty. **2** (in sport) commit a foul against. **3** (**foul up**) make a mistake with. **4** entangle or jam. ■ **foully** adv.

found[1] past & past part. of FIND.

found[2] v. **1** establish an institution etc. **2** (**be founded on**) be based on. **3** melt and mould metal to make an object.

foundation n. **1** the lowest weight-bearing part of a building. **2** an underlying basis. **3** the act of founding an institution etc. **4** an institution. **5** a cream applied as a base for other make-up.

founder n. a person who founds an institution etc. ▶v. **1** (of a ship) sink. **2** (of a plan etc.) fail.

foundling n. an infant abandoned by its parents.

foundry n. (pl. **foundries**) a workshop or factory for casting metal.

fount n. **1** a source. **2** literary a spring or fountain. **3** var. of FONT (sense 2).

fountain n. **1** a decorative structure pumping out a jet of water. **2** a source. □ **fountainhead** a source. **fountain pen** a pen with a container supplying ink to the nib.

four adj. & n. one more than three; 4 or IV. □ **four-poster** a bed with four posts supporting a canopy. **foursome** a group of four people. **four-wheel drive** a vehicle with a system providing power directly to all four wheels. ■ **fourfold** adj. & adv.

fourteen adj. & n. one more than thirteen; 14 or XIV. ■ **fourteenth** adj. & n.

fourth adj. & n. **1** next after third. **2** a quarter. ■ **fourthly** adv.

fowl n. a domesticated bird kept for its eggs or meat.

fox n. **1** a wild animal with a bushy tail and a reddish coat. **2** informal a sly or crafty person. ▶v. informal baffle or deceive. □ **foxglove** a tall plant with flowers shaped like the fingers of gloves. **foxhole** a hole in the ground used by troops as a shelter. **foxhound** a hound trained to hunt foxes in packs. **foxtrot** a ballroom dance with slow and quick steps. ■ **foxy** adj.

foyer /foy-ay/ n. a large entrance hall in a hotel, theatre, etc.

fracas /fra-kah/ n. (pl. **fracas**) a noisy disturbance or quarrel.

fraction n. **1** a number that is not a whole number. **2** a very small part or amount. ■ **fractional** adj. **fractionally** adv.

fractious adj. **1** bad-tempered. **2** difficult to control. ■ **fractiously** adv. **fractiousness** n.

fracture n. **1** the cracking or breaking

Thesaurus

stimulate, boost, advance, forward, cultivate, foment, help, aid, assist, support, uphold, back, give backing to, facilitate. **2** BRING UP, rear, raise, care for, look after, take care of, mother, parent. **3** CHERISH, harbour, hold, entertain, nurse, nourish, nurture, sustain.

foul adj. **1** DISGUSTING, revolting, repulsive, nauseating, sickening, loathsome, odious, abominable, offensive, nasty. **2** EVIL-SMELLING, stinking, high, rank, fetid; literary mephitic, noisome. **3** IMPURE, contaminated, polluted, adulterated, infected, tainted, defiled, filthy, dirty, unclean. **4** BLASPHEMOUS, profane, obscene, vulgar, offensive, coarse, filthy, dirty, indecent, indelicate, smutty, salacious, suggestive, off colour, low, ribald, lewd, scatological; informal blue. **5** ABHORRENT, detestable, hateful, loathsome, despicable, contemptible, offensive, odious, disgusting, revolting, dishonourable, disgraceful, base, low, mean, sordid, vile, wicked, heinous, execrable, iniquitous, nefarious, infamous. **6** UNFAIR, dishonourable, dishonest, underhand, unsportsmanlike, unsporting, dirty, unprincipled, unscrupulous, immoral, fraudulent; informal crooked. ▶v. DIRTY, soil, stain, blacken, muddy, begrime, smear, spatter, besmear, defile, pollute, contaminate, taint, sully; literary besmirch.

found v. ESTABLISH, set up, institute, originate, initiate, bring into being, create, start, inaugurate, constitute, endow, organize, develop.

foundation n. **1** BASE, bottom, substructure, bedrock, substratum, underpinning. **2** BASIS, groundwork, principles, fundamentals, rudiments. **3** ESTABLISHMENT, founding, institution, inauguration, initiation, constitution, endowment.

founder n. ESTABLISHER, builder, constructor, maker, initiator, institutor, beginner, inventor, discoverer, framer, designer, architect, creator, author, originator, organizer, developer, generator, prime mover, father, patriarch.

fountain n. **1** SPRAY, jet, spout, well, fount, stream, fountainhead. **2** SOURCE, of something. **2** a break, esp. in a bone. ▶ v. break.

fragile adj. **1** easily broken or damaged. **2** delicate. ■ **fragility** n.

fragment n. **1** a small part broken off. **2** an incomplete part. ▶ v. break into fragments. ■ **fragmentary** adj. **fragmentation** n.

fragrance n. a pleasant, sweet smell. ■ **fragrant** adj.

frail adj. **1** weak. **2** fragile. ■ **frailty** n.

frame n. **1** a rigid structure surrounding a picture etc. or supporting something. **2** a person's body. **3** a basis. **4** a single picture in a series forming a cinema or video film. **5** a single game of snooker. ▶ v. **1** put or form a frame around. **2** develop a plan etc. **3** informal produce false evidence against. □ **frame of mind** a particular mood. **framework** a supporting structure.

franc n. a unit of money in Switzerland (formerly also in France and Belgium).

franchise n. **1** authorization to use or sell a company's products. **2** the right to vote in public elections. ▶ v. grant a franchise to.

francium n. an unstable radioactive metallic element.

Franco- comb. form French.

frank adj. **1** honest and direct. **2** open or undisguised. ▶ v. mark a letter etc. to indicate that postage has been paid. ■ **frankly** adv. **frankness** n.

frankfurter n. a smoked sausage.

frankincense n. a sweet-smelling gum burnt as incense.

frantic adj. **1** wildly agitated. **2** hurried and confused. ■ **frantically** adv.

fraternal adj. of a brother or brothers.

fraternity n. (pl. **fraternities**) **1** a group with a common interest. **2** friendship and support in a group.

fraternize (or **-ise**) v. be on friendly terms. ■ **fraternization** n.

fratricide n. the killing of one's brother or sister. ■ **fratricidal** adj.

Frau /frow/ n. a title for a German married woman.

fraud n. **1** criminal deception to gain money or goods. **2** a person intending to deceive. ■ **fraudster** n. **fraudulence** n. **fraudulent** adj.

fraught adj. **1** (**fraught with**) filled with.

Thesaurus

fount, fountainhead, origin, wellspring, commencement, beginning, cause, birth, genesis, root, mainspring, derivation, inception, inspiration.

fractious adj. BAD-TEMPERED, cross, irritable, ill-humoured, ill-natured, petulant, testy, querulous, touchy, irascible, sulky, sullen, morose; informal snappish.

fracture n. BREAK, breakage, rupture, split, crack, fissure, cleft, rift, rent, chink, crevice, gap, opening, aperture. ▶ v. BREAK, crack, split, snap, rupture, splinter.

fragile adj. **1** FLIMSY, breakable, frail, delicate, insubstantial, brittle, dainty, fine. **2** ILL, unwell, sickly, ailing, delicate, weak, infirm. ■ OPPOSITES strong.

fragment n. PIECE, part, particle, shred, chip, shard, sliver, splinter, scrap, bit, snip, snippet, wisp, tatter, remnant, remainder, fraction. ▶ v. see BREAK.

fragmentary adj. INCOMPLETE, partial, piecemeal, disconnected, broken, disjointed, discontinuous, uneven, incoherent, scrappy, bitty, sketchy, unsystematic. ■ OPPOSITES complete, whole.

fragrance n. SCENT, smell, perfume, aroma, bouquet, balm, balminess; literary redolence.

fragrant adj. SWEET-SMELLING, sweet-scented, aromatic, scented, perfumed, balmy, odorous, odoriferous; literary redo-

lent. ■ OPPOSITES smelly.

frail adj. **1** FRAGILE, breakable, delicate, easily broken; formal frangible. **2** WEAK, infirm, ill, unwell, sickly, ailing, delicate, slight, slender, puny, unsound. ■ OPPOSITES strong, robust.

frame n. **1** STRUCTURE, framework, foundation, body, chassis, skeleton, scaffolding, shell, casing, support. **2** BODY, physique, build, figure, shape, size, carcass. **3** MOUNT, mounting, setting, border. ▶ v. **1** FORMULATE, put together, draw up, plan, think up, draft, map out, shape, compose, form, devise, create, establish, conceive. **2** INCRIMINATE, fabricate charges/evidence against; informal fit up.

framework n. **1** see FRAME. **2** ORDER, organization, frame, scheme, fabric.

frank adj. **1** CANDID, direct, straightforward, plain, plain-spoken, straight, outspoken, blunt, open, sincere, honest, truthful, artless, guileless, explicit, downright. **2** OPEN, obvious, transparent, patent, undisguised, manifest, unmistakable, evident, noticeable, visible. ■ OPPOSITES evasive.

frantic adj. DISTRAUGHT, overwrought, panic-stricken, panicky, beside oneself, at one's wits' end, frenzied, wild, hysterical, frenetic, berserk, worked up, fraught, distracted, agitated, distressed, out of control, uncontrolled, unhinged,

2 causing or feeling anxiety.

Fräulein /froy-lyn/ n. a title for a young German woman.

fray v. **1** (of a fabric, rope, or cord) unravel or become worn at the edge. **2** (of a person's nerves or temper) show the effects of strain. ▶ n. a battle, fight, or other conflict.

frazzle n. informal an exhausted state. ■ **frazzled** adj.

freak n. **1** an abnormal person, thing, or event. **2** informal a person obsessed with a particular interest. ▶ v. informal behave or cause to behave wildly and irrationally. ■ **freakish** adj. **freaky** adj.

freckle n. a small light brown spot on the skin. ■ **freckled** adj. **freckly** adj.

free adj. (**freer**, **freest**) **1** not under the control of anyone else. **2** not confined, obstructed, or fixed. **3** not busy or taken up. **4** not in use. **5** (**free of/from**) not subject to or affected by. **6** costing nothing. **7** (**free with**) using or giving without restraint. ▶ adv. at no cost. ▶ v. set free. □ **freebooter** a pirate. **free fall** downward movement under the force of gravity. **freehand** drawn by hand without the aid of a ruler etc. **freehold** permanent ownership of land or property with the freedom to sell it when one wishes. **free house** a pub not controlled by a brewery. **freelance 1** working for various companies rather than permanently employed by one. **2** (also **freelancer**) a freelance worker. **freeloader** informal a person who takes advantage of other people's generosity. **free radical** a highly reactive molecule with an unpaired electron. **free-range** referring to farming in which animals are kept in natural conditions and may move around freely. **freestyle** having few restrictions on the style or technique to be used. **freeway** US a dual carriageway. **freewheel** ride a bicycle without pedalling. ■ **freely** adv.

freebie n. informal a thing given free of charge.

freedom n. **1** the right to act or speak freely. **2** the state of being free. **3** a special privilege or right of access.

Thesaurus

mad, crazed, out of one's mind, maniacal. ■ OPPOSITES calm.

fraud n. **1** FRAUDULENCE, sharp practice, cheating, swindling, crookedness, embezzlement, trickery, deceit, double-dealing, duplicity, treachery, chicanery, imposture, skulduggery; informal monkey business. **2** RUSE, trick, deception, swindle, hoax, subterfuge, wile, stratagem, artifice. **3** IMPOSTOR, fake, sham, cheat, cheater, swindler, trickster, charlatan, quack, mountebank; informal phoney, con man.

fraudulent adj. DISHONEST, cheating, swindling, criminal, deceitful, double-dealing, duplicitous, unscrupulous, dishonourable; informal crooked, shady, sharp. ■ OPPOSITES honest.

fraught adj. **1** FILLED WITH, full of, attended by, teeming with, accompanied by. **2** ANXIOUS, distraught, overwrought, agitated, worked up, distracted, distressed.

fray v. **1** UNRAVEL, wear, wear thin, wear out/away, become threadbare, become tattered/ragged. **2** STRAIN, tax, overtax, irritate, put on edge, make edgy/tense.

freak n. **1** ABERRATION, abnormality, oddity, irregularity, monster, monstrosity, mutant, malformation. **2** ODDITY, peculiar person; informal queer fish, odd bod, oddball, weirdo, nutcase, nut. **3** FAN, enthusiast, fanatic, addict, aficionado, devotee; informal buff, fiend, nut. ▶ adj.

ABNORMAL, unusual, aberrant, atypical, exceptional, unaccountable, unpredictable, unforeseeable, bizarre, queer, odd, unparalleled, fluky.

free adj. **1** FREE OF CHARGE, complimentary, for nothing, without charge, gratis, at no cost, for free, on the house. **2** AVAILABLE, unoccupied, at leisure, with time on one's hands, with time to spare. **3** UNOCCUPIED, empty, vacant, available, spare, untaken, uninhabited. **4** INDEPENDENT, self-governing, autonomous, sovereign, emancipated, democratic, enfranchised. **5** AT LIBERTY, at large, loose, on the loose, unconfined, unchained, unrestrained, unshackled, unfettered. **6** UNOBSTRUCTED, unimpeded, clear, unblocked, unhampered. **7** FAMILIAR, overfamiliar, bold, assertive, presumptuous, cocky, forward, cheeky, impudent. ▶ v. **1** SET FREE, release, let go, set at liberty, liberate, turn loose, untie, unchain, unfetter, unshackle, uncage, unleash, deliver. **2** RESCUE, release, extricate, get loose, disentangle, disengage, disencumber. **3** EXEMPT, make exempt, excuse, except, relieve. □ **free of/from** WITHOUT, devoid of, lacking in, exempt from, not liable to, safe from, immune to, unaffected by, clear of, unencumbered by, relieved of, released from, rid of.

freedom n. **1** LIBERTY, emancipation, re-

Freemason n. a member of an organization established for mutual help, which holds secret ceremonies. ■ **Freemasonry** n.

freesia n. a plant with fragrant flowers.

freeze v. (**freezing**, **froze**; past part. **frozen**) **1** change or be changed from a liquid to a solid as a result of extreme cold. **2** become blocked or rigid with ice. **3** be or make very cold. **4** preserve by storing at a very low temperature. **5** become motionless. **6** keep or stop at a fixed level or in a fixed state. ▶ n. **1** an act of freezing. **2** a period of very cold weather. □ **freeze-dry** preserve by rapid freezing and removing the ice in a vacuum.

freezer n. a refrigerated cabinet for preserving food at very low temperatures.

freight n. **1** transport of goods in bulk. **2** goods transported in bulk. ▶ v. transport goods.

freighter n. a large ship or aircraft designed to carry freight.

French adj. of France or its people or language. ▶ n. the language of France. □ **French bread** white bread in a long, crisp loaf. **French fries** chips. **French horn** a brass instrument with a coiled tube. **French polish** a kind of wood polish producing a high gloss. **French windows** a pair of glazed doors in an outside wall.

frenetic adj. fast, energetic, and disorganized. ■ **frenetically** adv.

frenzy n. (pl. **frenzies**) a state of uncontrolled excitement or wild behaviour. ■ **frenzied** adj.

frequency n. (pl. **frequencies**) **1** the rate at which something occurs or is repeated. **2** the state of being frequent. **3** the number of cycles per second of a sound, light, or radio wave. **4** the particular waveband at which radio signals are transmitted.

frequent adj. **1** occurring or done many times at short intervals. **2** doing something often. ▶ v. visit a place often. ■ **frequently** adv.

fresco n. (pl. **frescoes** or **frescos**) a painting done on wet plaster on a wall or ceiling.

fresh adj. **1** new. **2** (of food) recently made or obtained. **3** not faded or stale. **4** (of water) not salty. **5** (of the wind) cool and fairly strong. **6** pleasantly clean and cool. **7** full of energy. **8** informal over-familiar. □ **freshman** (or **fresher**) a first-year college or university student. **freshwater** of or found in fresh water; not of the sea. ■ **freshen** v. **freshener** n. **freshly** adv. **freshness** n.

fret v. (**fretting**, **fretted**) be constantly or visibly anxious. ▶ n. each of the ridges on the fingerboard of a guitar etc.

fretful adj. anxious or irritated. ■ **fretfully** adv.

Thesaurus

lease, deliverance, independence, autonomy, sovereignty, self-government, enfranchisement; *historical* manumission. **2** SCOPE, latitude, flexibility, wide margin, elbow room, licence, facility, free rein. **3** NATURALNESS, openness, lack of reserve, informality, lack of ceremony, spontaneity. ■ OPPOSITES captivity.

freeze v. **1** ICE OVER/UP, glaciate, solidify, harden. **2** CHILL, cool, make cold, deep-freeze. **3** STAND STILL, stop dead, stop in one's tracks, go rigid, become motionless. **4** FIX, hold, peg, suspend.

freezing adj. BITTERLY COLD, chilling, frosty, glacial, arctic, wintry, raw, biting, piercing, penetrating, cutting, numbing, Siberian.

freight n. CARGO, load, consignment, lading, merchandise, goods.

frenzy n. MADNESS, mania, insanity, wild excitement, wildness, hysteria, agitation, distraction, fit, seizure, paroxysm, outburst, spasm.

frequent adj. **1** MANY, numerous, several, repeated, recurrent, persistent, continuing, quite a lot/few. **2** REGULAR, habitual, common, customary, usual, familiar, everyday, continual, constant, incessant. ▶ v. VISIT, attend, haunt, patronize; *informal* hang out at.

fresh adj. **1** NATURAL, unprocessed, raw, newly harvested, crisp, unwilted, undried, uncured. **2** NEW, brand new, recent, latest, up to date, modern, newfangled, innovative, different, original, novel, unusual, unconventional, unorthodox. **3** ENERGETIC, vigorous, invigorated, lively, vibrant, spry, sprightly, bright, alert, bouncing, refreshed, rested, restored, revived, fresh as a daisy; *informal* full of beans, bright-eyed and bushy-tailed. **4** ADDITIONAL, more, further, extra, supplementary. **5** HEALTHY, clear, bright, wholesome, blooming, glowing, fair, rosy, pink, ruddy. **6** CLEAR, bright, cool, crisp, sparkling, pure, clean, refreshing. **7** FAMILIAR, over-familiar, forward, presumptuous, cocky, bold, audacious, brazen, cheeky, impudent, impertinent, insolent, disres-

fretsaw n. a narrow saw used for fret-work.

fretwork n. decorative patterns cut in wood.

friable adj. easily crumbled.

friar n. a member of certain religious orders of men.

friary n. (pl. **friaries**) a building occupied by friars.

fricassée /fri-kuh-say/ n. a dish of pieces of meat in a white sauce.

friction n. **1** the resistance encountered by one surface when moving over another. **2** the action of one surface rubbing against another. **3** conflict or disagreement. ■ **frictional** adj.

Friday n. the day before Saturday.

fridge n. a refrigerator.

fried past & past part. of **FRY**.

friend n. **1** a person that one likes and knows well. **2** a supporter of a cause or organization. ■ **friendship** n.

☑ *-ie-*, not *-ei-*: friend.

friendly adj. (**friendlier**, **friendliest**) **1** treating someone as a friend; on good terms. **2** kind and pleasant. **3** not harmful to a specified thing. ▶ n. (pl. **friendlies**) a game not forming part of a serious competition. ■ **friendliness** n.

frieze n. a band of decoration around a wall.

frigate n. a kind of fast warship.

fright n. **1** a sudden strong feeling of fear. **2** a shock.

frighten v. **1** cause to be afraid. **2** drive away by fear. ■ **frightening** adj.

frightful adj. **1** very unpleasant, serious, or shocking. **2** informal awful; extreme. ■ **frightfully** adv.

Thesaurus

pectful; *informal* brass-necked. ■ OPPOSITES stale, old, tired.

fret v. WORRY, be upset, be distressed, be anxious, agonize, pine, brood, mope, fuss, complain, grumble, whine.

friction n. **1** ABRASION, attrition, rubbing, chafing, scraping, rasping. **2** DISSENSION, dissent, disagreement, discord, strife, conflict, contention, dispute, argument, quarrelling, bickering, squabbling, hostility, rivalry, animosity, antagonism, resentment, bad feeling. ■ OPPOSITES harmony.

friend n. COMPANION, crony, bosom friend, comrade, playmate, soul mate, intimate, confidante, alter ego, ally, acquaintance, associate, familiar, shadow; *informal* pal, chum, mate; *US informal* buddy. ■ OPPOSITES enemy.

friendless adj. ALONE, companionless, by oneself, lone, lonely, lonesome, with no one to turn to, solitary, with no ties, unattached, single, forlorn, unpopular, unloved, forsaken, deserted, ostracized, abandoned.

friendliness n. AMIABILITY, affability, geniality, warmth, affection, cordiality, conviviality, sociability, neighbourliness, bonhomie, good nature, gregariousness, approachability, amenability, benevolence. ■ OPPOSITES hostility.

friendly adj. **1** AMIABLE, affable, warm, genial, agreeable, companionable, cordial, convivial, sociable, hospitable, comradely, neighbourly, outgoing, approachable, accessible, communicative, open, unreserved, easy-going, good-

natured, kindly, benign, amenable, well disposed, sympathetic, benevolent; *informal* chummy, matey. **2** AMICABLE, close, cordial, congenial, intimate, familiar, peaceable, conciliatory. ■ OPPOSITES unfriendly.

friendship n. **1** CLOSE RELATIONSHIP, companionship, intimacy, rapport, affinity, attachment, alliance, harmony, fellowship, mutual understanding, amity, comradeship. **2** FRIENDLINESS, affability, amiability, warmth, geniality, cordiality, neighbourliness, good-naturedness, kindliness.

fright n. **1** FEAR, terror, alarm, horror, dread, fearfulness, apprehension, trepidation, consternation, dismay, disquiet, nervousness, panic; *informal* blue funk, jitters, heebie-jeebies, willies. **2** SCARE, shock, shivers.

frighten v. SCARE, terrify, startle, alarm, terrorize, give a shock to, shock, panic, appal, throw into a panic, unnerve, unman, intimidate, cow, daunt, dismay, make someone's blood run cold, freeze someone's blood; *informal* scare the living daylights out of, scare stiff, scare someone out of their wits, scare witless, make someone's hair stand on end, make someone's hair curl, throw into a blue funk, make someone jump out of their skin, spook, put the wind up.

frightful adj. **1** DREADFUL, terrible, horrible, horrid, hideous, ghastly, gruesome, grisly, macabre, grim, dire, abhorrent, odious, revolting, repulsive, loathsome, fearful, fearsome, terrifying, alarming, shocking, harrowing, appall-

frigid adj. **1** very cold. **2** sexually unresponsive. ■ **frigidity** n.

frill n. **1** a strip of gathered or pleated material used as a decorative edging. **2** (**frills**) unnecessary extra features. ■ **frilled** adj. **frilly** adj.

fringe n. **1** a decorative edging of threads on clothing etc. **2** the front part of someone's hair cut so as to hang over the forehead. **3** the outer part of something. ▶adj. not part of the mainstream. ▶v. give or form a fringe to. □ **fringe benefit** an additional benefit.

frippery n. (pl. **fripperies**) a showy or unnecessary ornament.

frisbee n. trademark a plastic disc for skimming through the air as an outdoor game.

frisk v. **1** feel over to search for hidden weapons or drugs. **2** skip or move playfully.

frisky adj. (**friskier**, **friskiest**) playful and lively. ■ **friskily** adv. **friskiness** n.

frisson /free-son/ n. a thrill.

fritter v. waste time or money on trivial things. ▶n. a piece of food coated in batter and deep-fried.

frivolous adj. **1** not having any serious purpose or value. **2** carefree and not serious. ■ **frivolity** n. **frivolously** adv.

frizz v. (of hair) form into a mass of tight curls. ▶n. a mass of tight curls. ■ **frizzy** adj.

frock n. a dress. □ **frock coat** a man's double-breasted, long-skirted coat.

frog n. a tailless amphibian with long hind legs for leaping. □ **frogman** a

diver with a rubber suit, flippers, and breathing equipment. **frogmarch** force someone to walk while pinning their arms from behind. **frogspawn** a mass of frogs' eggs surrounded by transparent jelly.

frolic v. (**frolicking**, **frolicked**) play or move about in a cheerful, lively way. ▶n. a playful action.

from prep. **1** indicating the starting point, source, or cause. **2** indicating separation, removal, or prevention.

fromage frais /from-ahzh fray/ n. a smooth soft cheese.

frond n. the leaf or leaf-like part of a palm, fern, etc.

front n. **1** the part of an object that presents itself to view or that is normally seen first. **2** the position directly ahead. **3** the furthest position reached by an army. **4** the forward edge of an advancing mass of air. **5** a particular situation. **6** a false appearance or way of behaving. **7** a cover for secret activities. ▶adj. of or at the front. ▶v. **1** have the front towards. **2** place or be at the front of. **3** provide with a front of a specified type. **4** act as a front for. □ **frontage 1** the front of a building. **2** a strip of land next to a street or waterway. **frontbencher** a member of the cabinet or shadow cabinet, who sits in the foremost seats in the House of Commons. **front line** the part of an army closest to the enemy. **front runner** the contestant most likely to win. ■ **frontal** adj. **frontally** adv.

Thesaurus

ing, daunting, unnerving. **2** DISAGREEABLE, unpleasant, dreadful, horrible, terrible, awful, ghastly, insufferable, unbearable, annoying, irritating. **3** VERY BAD, terrible, dreadful, awful, ghastly, nasty.

frigid adj. **1** COLD, icy, distant, austere, aloof, remote, unapproachable, forbidding, stiff, formal, unbending, cool, unfeeling, unemotional, unfriendly, hostile, unenthusiastic. **2** PASSIONLESS, cold, unresponsive, passive. **3** VERY COLD, bitterly cold, freezing, frozen, icy, frosty, chilly, wintry, arctic, glacial, Siberian, polar, gelid.

fringe n. **1** BORDER, frill, ruffle, gathering, trimming, tassels, edging. **2** OUTER EDGE, edge, border, perimeter, periphery, margin, rim, limits, outskirts, verge.

frisky adj. LIVELY, bouncy, active, playful, spirited, romping, rollicking, sportive,

in high spirits, high-spirited, exuberant, joyful, sprightly, perky, jaunty; informal full of beans; literary frolicsome.

frivolity n. **1** LIGHT-HEARTEDNESS, gaiety, levity, fun, silliness, foolishness. **2** EMPTY-HEADEDNESS, frivolousness, giddiness, flightiness, dizziness, flippancy, silliness, zaniness.

frivolous adj. **1** SILLY, flighty, foolish, dizzy, facetious, flippant, senseless, giddy, light-hearted, merry, superficial, shallow, empty-headed, feather-brained. **2** FLIPPANT, ill-considered, inane, facetious, superficial, shallow; informal flip. ■ OPPOSITES serious.

frolic v. GAMBOL, cavort, skip, frisk, caper, cut capers, dance, leap, romp, trip, prance, hop, jump, bounce, rollick, sport, curvet. ▶n. ROMP, lark, antics, caper, escapade, prank, revels, spree, high jinks.

front n. **1** FACE, facade, frontage, fore,

frontier n. **1** a border separating two countries. **2** the extreme limit of settled land.

frontispiece n. an illustration facing the title page of a book.

frost n. **1** small white ice crystals on grass etc. **2** a period of cold weather when frost forms. ▶ v. cover with or as if with frost.

frostbite n. injury to body tissues caused by exposure to extreme cold. ■ **frostbitten** adj.

frosted adj. (of glass) having a semi-transparent textured surface.

frosting n. US icing.

frosty adj. (**frostier**, **frostiest**) **1** very cold with frost forming on surfaces. **2** cold and unfriendly. ■ **frostily** adv. **frostiness** n.

froth n. a mass of small bubbles. ▶ v. form or contain froth. ■ **frothy** adj.

frown v. **1** wrinkle one's brow in disapproval or thought. **2** (**frown on**) disapprove of. ▶ n. a frowning expression.

frowsty adj. warm and stuffy.

frowzy (or **frowsy**) adj. scruffy and dingy.

froze past of FREEZE.

frozen past part. of FREEZE.

fructose n. a sugar found in honey and fruit.

frugal adj. sparing with money or food. ■ **frugality** n. **frugally** adv.

fruit n. **1** a fleshy part of a plant that contains seed and can be eaten as food. **2** the seed-bearing part of any plant. **3** the result of work or activity. ▶ v. produce fruit. □ **bear fruit** have good results. **fruit machine** a coin-operated gambling machine.

fruiterer n. a person who sells fruit.

fruitful adj. producing a lot of fruit or good results. ■ **fruitfully** adv. **fruitfulness** n.

fruition n. the fulfilment of a plan or project.

fruitless adj. failing to achieve the desired results. ■ **fruitlessly** adv.

fruity adj. (**fruitier**, **fruitiest**) **1** like or containing fruit. **2** (of a voice) deep and rich. ■ **fruitiness** n.

frump n. a dowdy woman. ■ **frumpy** adj.

frustrate v. **1** prevent from progressing or succeeding. **2** cause to feel dissatisfied. ■ **frustration** n.

fry[1] v. (**frying**, **fried**) cook in hot fat or oil. ■ **fryer** n.

fry[2] pl. n. young fish.

ft abbrev. foot or feet.

fuchsia /fyoo-shuh/ n. a plant with drooping pink flowers.

fuddled adj. confused or dazed.

fuddy-duddy n. (pl. **fuddy-duddies**) informal an old-fashioned person.

fudge n. **1** a soft sweet made of sugar, butter, and milk. **2** an attempt to pres-

Thesaurus

forepart, foremost part, forefront, foreground, anterior. **2** HEAD, top, lead, beginning. **3** FRONT LINE, vanguard, van, firing line. **4** COVER, blind, facade, disguise, pretext, mask. ■ OPPOSITES back. ▶ adj. LEADING, lead, first, foremost. □ **front on** FACE TOWARDS, look out on, overlook, lie opposite to.

frontier n. BORDER, boundary, limit, edge, rim, bounds, confines, marches.

frosty adj. **1** FREEZING, frozen, cold, glacial, frigid, arctic, icy, wintry, bitter. **2** UNFRIENDLY, cold, unwelcoming, unenthusiastic, icy, glacial.

froth n. FOAM, fizz, lather, head, scum, effervescence, bubbles, suds, spume.

frown v. **1** SCOWL, glare, glower, knit one's brows, lower, lour; informal look daggers at, give a dirty look to. **2** DISAPPROVE OF, view with dislike/disfavour, dislike, not take kindly to, not think much of, take a dim view of, look askance at.

frugal adj. THRIFTY, economical, sparing, careful, prudent, abstemious, scrimping, niggardly, cheese-paring, penny-

pinching, miserly, parsimonious; informal stingy. ■ OPPOSITES extravagant, spendthrift.

fruitful adj. **1** FERTILE, fecund, potent, abundant, flourishing, lush, copious, bountiful; literary bounteous. **2** USEFUL, worthwhile, productive, well spent, profitable, advantageous, beneficial, rewarding, gainful, successful, effective. ■ OPPOSITES barren, futile, fruitless.

fruition n. FULFILMENT, realization, materialization, achievement, attainment, success, completion, consummation, actualization, perfection, maturation, maturity, ripening.

fruitless adj. FUTILE, useless, vain, in vain, to no avail, worthless, pointless, abortive, to no effect, idle, ineffectual, ineffective, inefficacious, unproductive, unrewarding, profitless, unsuccessful, unavailing. ■ OPPOSITES fruitful, productive.

frustrate v. **1** DISCOURAGE, dishearten, dispirit, depress, dissatisfy, make discontented, anger, annoy, vex, irritate, embitter, irk. **2** DEFEAT, thwart, obent an issue in a vague way. ▶ v. present in a vague way.

fuel n. **1** material burnt to produce heat or power. **2** something that stirs up argument or emotion. ▶ v. (**fuelling, fuelled**; US **fueling, fueled**) provide with fuel.

fug n. informal a warm, stuffy atmosphere. ■ **fuggy** adj.

fugitive n. a person who has escaped from captivity or is in hiding. ▶ adj. fleeting.

fugue /fyoog/ n. a musical composition in which a short melody is successively repeated by different voices or instruments.

fulcrum n. the point of support on which a lever turns.

fulfil (US **fulfill**) v. (**fulfilling, fulfilled**) **1** achieve something desired or promised. **2** meet a requirement. **3** (**fulfil oneself**) fully develop one's abilities. ■ **fulfilment** n.

full adj. **1** holding as much or as many as possible. **2** (**full of**) having a lot of. **3** complete. **4** rounded. **5** (of flavour etc.) strong or rich. ▶ adv. **1** directly. **2** very. ◻ **fullback** (in soccer etc.) a defender who plays at the side. **full-blooded** wholehearted. **full-blown** fully developed. **full moon** the moon

when its whole disc is illuminated. **full-scale** (of a model etc.) of the same size as the thing represented. **full stop** a punctuation mark (.) used at the end of a sentence or an abbreviation. **full time 1** the end of a sports match. **2** (**full-time**) working for the whole of the available time. ■ **fully** adv. **fullness** n.

fulminate v. express strong protest. ■ **fulmination** n.

fulsome adj. **1** excessively flattering. **2** of large size or quantity.

fumble v. **1** use the hands clumsily. **2** deal with clumsily. ▶ n. an act of fumbling.

fume n. a strong-smelling gas or vapour. ▶ v. **1** send out fumes. **2** feel great anger.

fumigate v. disinfect with chemical fumes. ■ **fumigation** n.

fun n. light-hearted pleasure. ◻ **funfair** a gathering of rides, sideshows, etc. for public entertainment. **make fun of** laugh at in a mocking way.

function n. **1** a purpose or natural activity of a person or thing. **2** a large or formal social event. **3** Math. a quantity whose value depends on the varying values of others. ▶ v. **1** work or operate. **2** (**function as**) fulfil the purpose of.

Thesaurus

struct, impede, hamper, hinder, check, block, counter, foil, baulk, forestall, disappoint, baffle, stymie, stop, cripple, spoil, circumvent.

fudge v. EVADE, dodge, avoid, skirt, duck, hedge, prevaricate.

fuel v. SUPPLY WITH FUEL, fire, stoke up, charge, power.

fugitive n. ESCAPEE, runaway, deserter, refugee, renegade. ▶ adj. TRANSIENT, transitory, fleeting, ephemeral, passing, impermanent, momentary, short-lived, short, brief, evanescent, fugacious.

fulfil v. **1** ACCOMPLISH, achieve, carry out, execute, perform, discharge, complete, implement, finish, conclude, effect; formal effectuate. **2** SATISFY, realize, attain, consummate. **3** CONFORM TO, satisfy, fill, answer, meet, comply with, obey.

full adj. **1** FILLED UP, filled, filled to the brim, brimming, overflowing, filled to capacity. **2** CROWDED, packed, crammed, solid with people, chock-a-block, chockfull; informal jam-packed. **3** SATISFIED, sated, gorged, replete, glutted, cloyed. **4** COMPLETE, entire, whole, comprehensive, thorough, exhaustive, detailed, all-inclusive, all-encompassing, exten-

sive, unabridged. **5** BAGGY, voluminous, loose-fitting, capacious. **6** RICH, deep, resonant, loud, strong; informal fruity. ■ OPPOSITES empty, incomplete.

fully adv. COMPLETELY, entirely, wholly, totally, thoroughly, in all respects, utterly, amply, satisfactorily.

fumble v. **1** FAIL TO CATCH, miss, drop, mishandle, misfield. **2** GROPE, feel about, search blindly, scrabble about/around.

fume v. BE ENRAGED, seethe, boil, be livid, rage, rant and rave, be furious, be incensed, flare up; informal be up in arms, get hot under the collar, fly off the handle, foam at the mouth, get all steamed up, flip one's lid, blow one's top.

fumes pl. n. VAPOUR, gas, exhaust, smoke, pollution, smog, fog.

fun n. **1** AMUSEMENT, entertainment, recreation, relaxation, enjoyment, pleasure, diversion, play, playfulness, tomfoolery, buffoonery, distraction, good time, jollification, merrymaking, junketing; informal living it up, skylarking. **2** MERRIMENT, gaiety, mirth, laughter, hilarity, glee, cheerfulness, gladness, jollity, joy, high spirits, zest. ■ OPPOSITES misery.

functional adj. **1** of a function. **2** practical and useful rather than decorative. **3** working or operating. ∎ **functionality** n. **functionally** adv.

functionary n. (pl. **functionaries**) an official.

fund n. **1** a sum of money for a special purpose. **2** (**funds**) financial resources. **3** a large stock. ▶v. provide with money.

fundamental adj. of basic importance. ▶n. a basic rule or principle. ∎ **fundamentally** adv.

fundamentalism n. strict following of the basic teachings of a religion. ∎ **fundamentalist** n. & adj.

funeral n. a ceremony in which a dead person is buried or cremated. □ **funeral director** an undertaker.

funerary adj. of or used for a funeral.

funereal adj. solemn or mournful.

fungicide n. a chemical that destroys fungus. ∎ **fungicidal** adj.

fungus n. (pl. **fungi**) an organism without leaves or flowers that grows on other plants or on decaying matter (e.g. a mushroom or mould). ∎ **fungal** adj.

funicular adj. (of a railway) operating by cable up and down a steep slope.

funk n. a style of dance music with a strong rhythm.

funky adj. (**funkier, funkiest**) informal **1** having a strong dance rhythm. **2** stylish and modern.

funnel n. **1** a tube with a wide top for pouring liquid or powder into small openings. **2** a chimney on a ship or steam engine. ▶v. (**funnelling, funnelled**; US **funneling, funneled**) move through a funnel or narrow space.

funny adj. (**funnier, funniest**) **1** causing amusement. **2** strange. □ **funny bone** informal the part of the elbow over which a very sensitive nerve passes. ∎ **funnily** adv.

fur n. **1** the short, soft hair of some animals. **2** the skin of an animal with fur on it. **3** a deposit formed by hard water on the inside of a kettle etc. ▶v. (**furring, furred**) coat with a deposit. ∎ **furriness** n. **furry** adj.

furbish v. renovate.

furious adj. **1** extremely angry. **2** intense or energetic. ∎ **furiously** adv.

furl v. roll up neatly and securely.

furlong n. an eighth of a mile.

furlough /fer-loh/ n. leave of absence.

furnace n. an enclosed chamber for heating material to very high temperatures.

furnish v. **1** equip with furniture. **2** supply or provide.

Thesaurus

□ **make fun of** RIDICULE, deride, mock, scoff at, sneer at, taunt, jeer at, lampoon, parody; informal send up, rib, take off.

function n. **1** ROLE, capacity, responsibility, duty, task, job, post, situation, office, occupation, employment, business, charge, province, capacity, activity, operation, mission. **2** SOCIAL EVENT, gathering, affair, reception, party; informal do, beanfeast. ▶v. WORK, go, run, be in working order, operate.

functional adj. **1** PRACTICAL, useful, serviceable, utilitarian, working, workaday, hard-wearing. **2** WORKING, in working order, going, running, operative, in commission.

fund n. RESERVE, collection, pool, kitty, endowment, foundation, grant, investment, capital, savings. ▶v. FINANCE, pay for, back, subsidize, stake, endow, support.

fundamental adj. BASIC, rudimentary, elemental, underlying, primary, cardinal, initial, original, prime, first, principal, chief, key, central, structural, organic, inherent, intrinsic, vital, essential, important, indispensable, necessary. ∎ OPPOSITES unimportant.

fundamentally adv. BASICALLY, at heart, at bottom, deep down, essentially, intrinsically.

funds pl. n. MONEY, ready money, cash, hard cash, capital, the wherewithal, means, assets, resources, savings; informal dough, bread, dosh.

funny adj. **1** AMUSING, comical, comic, humorous, hilarious, entertaining, witty, diverting, laughable, hysterical, riotous, side-splitting, jocular, droll, absurd, rich, facetious, ludicrous, ridiculous, farcical, risible, silly, slapstick, waggish. **2** PECULIAR, odd, strange, curious, queer, bizarre, mysterious, suspicious, dubious; informal weird. ∎ OPPOSITES serious.

furious adj. **1** ENRAGED, very angry, raging, infuriated, livid, fuming, boiling, incensed, inflamed, frenzied, indignant, mad, maddened, wrathful, beside oneself, in high dudgeon; informal hot under the collar, up in arms, foaming at the mouth. **2** VIOLENT, fierce, wild, intense, vehement, unrestrained, tumultuous, tempestuous, stormy, turbulent, boisterous. ∎ OPPOSITES calm.

furnishings pl. n. furniture and fittings.

furniture n. the movable objects used to make a room or building suitable for living or working in.

furore /fyoo-ror-i/ (US **furor**) n. an outbreak of public anger or excitement.

furrier n. a person who deals in furs.

furrow n. **1** a long, narrow trench cut in the ground. **2** a groove. ▶v. make a furrow in.

further adv. (also **farther**) **1** at, to, or over a greater distance. **2** at or to a more advanced stage. **3** in addition. ▶adj. **1** (also **farther**) more distant in space. **2** additional. ▶v. help the progress of. □ **further education** education below degree level for people above school age.

furtherance n. the advancement of a plan or interest.

furthermore adv. in addition.

furthest (or **farthest**) adj. & adv. at or to the greatest distance.

furtive adj. secretively trying to avoid notice. ■ **furtively** adv.

fury n. (pl. **furies**) **1** extreme anger. **2** extreme violence.

furze n. gorse.

fuse v. **1** combine to form a whole. **2** melt something so as to join it with something else. **3** (of an electrical appliance) stop working when a fuse melts. **4** fit an appliance with a fuse. ▶n. **1** a strip of wire that melts and breaks an electric circuit if the current goes beyond a safe level. **2** a length of material lit to explode a bomb or firework. **3** a device in a bomb controlling the timing of the explosion. ■ **fusible** adj.

fuselage /fyoo-zuh-lahzh/ n. the main body of an aircraft.

fusilier /fyoo-zi-leer/ n. a soldier of certain regiments.

fusillade /fyoo-zi-layd/ n. a series of shots fired at the same time or one after the other.

fusion n. the act of fusing, esp. of atomic nuclei with the release of much energy.

fuss n. **1** unnecessary excitement or activity. **2** a vigorous protest. ▶v. show unnecessary concern.

fussy adj. (**fussier**, **fussiest**) **1** hard to please. **2** full of unnecessary detail. ■ **fussily** adv. **fussiness** n.

fustian n. a thick twilled cotton.

fusty adj. **1** smelling stale or damp. **2** old-fashioned.

futile adj. pointless. ■ **futility** n.

Thesaurus

furnish v. **1** PROVIDE WITH FURNITURE, fit out, outfit, appoint. **2** SUPPLY, provide, give, present, offer, equip, grant, bestow, endow, provision.

furniture n. FURNISHINGS, house fittings, effects, movables, appointments; *Law* chattels.

furore n. COMMOTION, uproar, disturbance, hullabaloo, turmoil, tumult, brouhaha, tempest, stir, excitement, outburst, outcry; *informal* to-do.

furrow n. **1** GROOVE, trench, channel, rut, trough, ditch, seam, hollow. **2** CREASE, line, wrinkle, crinkle, corrugation, crow's foot.

further adj. ADDITIONAL, more, extra, supplementary, other, new, fresh. ▶adv. FURTHERMORE, moreover, what's more, also, besides, additionally, as well to, boot, on top of that, over and above that, by the same token. ▶v. ADVANCE, forward, facilitate, aid, assist, help, lend a hand to, promote, back, contribute to, encourage, foster, champion.

furthest adj. FARTHEST, furthermost, most distant, most remote, outermost, outmost, extreme, uttermost, ultimate.

furtive adj. SECRETIVE, secret, stealthy, surreptitious, clandestine, sneaky, sneaking, hidden, disguised, shifty, skulking, covert, cloaked, conspiratorial, sly, underhand, under the table, wily. ■ OPPOSITES open, above board.

fury n. **1** ANGER, rage, wrath, madness, passion, frenzy; *literary* ire. **2** FIERCENESS, violence, ferocity, intensity, force, power, severity, turbulence, tempestuousness.

fuse v. COMBINE, amalgamate, join, put together, unite, blend, intermix, intermingle, merge, coalesce, integrate, meld, compound, agglutinate, weld, solder. ■ OPPOSITES separate.

fuss n. FLUSTER, agitation, excitement, bother, commotion, stir, confusion, uproar, tumult, upset, worry; *informal* palaver, storm in a teacup, flap, tizzy, stew. ▶v. BE WORRIED/AGITATED, worry, rush about, dash about; *informal* get worked up, be in a tizzy, flap, be in a stew, make a big thing out of it.

fussy adj. **1** PARTICULAR, over-particular, finicky, pernickety, fastidious, hard to please, difficult, exacting, demanding, selective, discriminating, faddish; *informal* choosy, picky, faddy, nit-picking. **2** CLUTTERED, busy, over-decorated, ornate, overdone, over-elaborate, rococo, over-embellished.

futile adj. USELESS, vain, in vain, to no

futon /foo-ton/ n. a padded mattress that can be rolled up.

future n. **1** time still to come. **2** what may happen in time still to come. **3** a prospect of success. ▶ adj. existing or occurring in the future.

futuristic adj. **1** with very modern technology or design. **2** set in the future.

fuzz n. a frizzy mass of hair or fibre.

fuzzy adj. (**fuzzier**, **fuzziest**) **1** frizzy. **2** not clear. ■ **fuzzily** adv. **fuzziness** n.

Thesaurus

. . . .

avail, ineffectual, unsuccessful, unproductive, unprofitable, abortive, unavailing, inefficacious, barren, impotent, hollow. ■ OPPOSITES fruitful.

future n. **1** TIME TO COME, time ahead, hereafter, coming times. **2** PROSPECTS, chances, expectations, anticipation, outlook, likely success/advancement.

▶ adj. FORTHCOMING, coming, impending, approaching, prospective, expected, planned, destined, awaited.

fuzzy adj. **1** DOWNY, down-covered, frizzy, woolly, furry, fleecy, fluffy, linty, napped. **2** OUT OF FOCUS, unfocused, blurred, blurry, indistinct, unclear, misty, distorted, ill-defined, bleary.

Gg

G (or **g**) abbrev. **1** giga-. **2** grams. **3** gravity. ▶ symb. Physics the acceleration due to gravity.

gabble v. talk quickly and indistinctly.

gaberdine (or **gabardine**) n. a smooth, hard-wearing cloth for making raincoats.

gable n. the triangular upper part of a wall at the end of a ridged roof. ■ **gabled** adj.

gad v. (**gadding, gadded**) (**gad about/around**) informal go from place to place in search of pleasure. ▫ **gadabout** a person who gads about.

gadfly n. a fly that bites livestock.

gadget n. a small mechanical device. ■ **gadgetry** n.

Gaelic /ga-lik, gay-lik/ n. a language spoken in parts of Ireland and western Scotland.

gaff n. a hooked stick for landing large fish.

gaffe n. an embarrassing blunder.

gaffer informal n. **1** a boss. **2** an old man.

gag n. **1** a piece of cloth put over a person's mouth to silence them. **2** a joke. ▶ v. (**gagging, gagged**) **1** put a gag on. **2** choke or retch.

gaga adj. informal senile.

gage US = GAUGE.

gaggle n. **1** a flock of geese. **2** informal a disorderly group.

gaiety n. light-hearted and cheerful mood or behaviour.

gaily adv. **1** cheerfully. **2** thoughtlessly. **3** colourfully.

gain v. **1** obtain or secure. **2** reach. **3** (**gain on**) come closer to someone or something pursued. **4** increase in weight, speed, value, etc. **5** (of a clock) become fast. ▶ n. **1** a thing gained. **2** an increase in wealth or value.

gainful adj. paid; profitable. ■ **gainfully** adv.

gainsay v. (**gainsaying, gainsaid**) deny or contradict.

gait n. a manner of walking or running.

gaiter n. a covering for the ankle and lower leg.

gala n. **1** a festive entertainment or performance. **2** a sports event, esp. a swimming competition.

galaxy n. (pl. **galaxies**) **1** a system of millions or billions of stars. **2** (**the Galaxy**) the galaxy including the sun and the earth. ■ **galactic** adj.

gale n. **1** a very strong wind. **2** an outburst of laughter.

gall /gawl/ n. **1** bold and impudent behaviour. **2** bitterness or cruelty. **3** annoyance; irritation. **4** a sore made by rubbing. **5** an abnormal growth on

Thesaurus

gadget n. APPLIANCE, apparatus, device, contrivance, mechanism, instrument, tool, implement, invention, contraption; informal widget, gizmo.

gaffe n. MISTAKE, blunder, slip, indiscretion, faux pas, solecism, gaucherie; informal clanger, howler, boo-boo, boob; informal, dated bloomer.

gag n. JOKE, witticism, jest, quip, funny remark, hoax, prank; informal crack, wisecrack.

gaiety n. **1** CHEERFULNESS, light-heartedness, merriment, glee, happiness, high spirits, gladness, delight, joy, joyfulness, joyousness, pleasure, exuberance, elation, jollity, hilarity, mirth, joviality, liveliness, animation, vivacity, effervescence, buoyancy, sprightliness, exultation; literary blitheness. **2** COLOURFULNESS, brightness, sparkle, brilliance, glitter, showiness, gaudiness, garishness. ■ OPPOSITES gloom.

gain v. **1** OBTAIN, get, acquire, secure, procure, attain, build up, achieve, arrive at, come to have, win, capture, pick up, net, reap, gather. **2** INCREASE IN, add on, get more of. **3** CATCH UP WITH, get nearer to, close in on, narrow the gap between, overtake, come up to, approach. **4** REACH, arrive at, get to, come to, attain. ▶ n. **1** INCREASE, addition, rise, augmentation, increment, accumulation, accretion. **2** PROFIT, earnings, income, advantage, benefit, reward, yield, return, winnings, proceeds, dividend, interest, emolument; informal pickings.

gainful adj. PROFITABLE, rewarding, remunerative, lucrative, productive, beneficial, fruitful, advantageous, worthplants and trees. ▶v. annoy; irritate. □ **gall bladder** an organ beneath the liver, storing bile. **gallstone** a small hard mass forming in the gall bladder.

gallant adj. **1** brave. **2** chivalrous. ■ **gallantry** n.

galleon n. hist. a large sailing ship.

gallery n. (pl. **galleries**) **1** a building for displaying works of art. **2** a balcony in a theatre or church. **3** a long room or passage.

galley n. (pl. **galleys**) **1** hist. a sailing ship with several banks of oars. **2** a kitchen in a ship or aircraft.

Gallic adj. of France or the French.

gallium n. a soft metallic element.

gallivant v. informal go from place to place seeking pleasure.

gallon n. a measure for liquids, equal to eight pints (4.55 litres).

gallop n. **1** a horse's fastest pace. **2** a ride on a horse at a gallop. ▶v. (**galloping, galloped**) **1** go at the pace of a gallop. **2** go fast.

gallows pl. n. a structure with a noose for hanging criminals.

galore adj. in abundance: *there were prizes galore.*

galoshes pl. n. rubber overshoes.

galvanize (or **-ise**) v. **1** shock or excite into action. **2** (**galvanized**) (of iron or steel) coated with zinc.

gambit n. an action or remark intended to gain an advantage.

gamble v. **1** play games of chance for money. **2** bet money. **3** risk in the hope of gaining something. ▶n. an act of gambling. ■ **gambler** n.

gambol v. (**gambolling, gambolled**; US **gamboling, gamboled**) run or jump about playfully.

game n. **1** a form of play or sport. **2** a

period of play, ending in a final result. **3** wild mammals or birds hunted for sport or food. ▶adj. eager and willing. ▶v. play at games of chance for money. □ **gamekeeper** a person employed to breed and protect game. **gamesmanship** the art of winning games by making one's opponent feel less confident. ■ **gamely** adv.

gamete n. a reproductive cell.

gamine adj. (of a girl) having a mischievous, boyish charm.

gamma n. the third letter of the Greek alphabet (Γ, γ). □ **gamma rays** electromagnetic radiation of shorter wavelength than X-rays.

gammon n. cured ham.

gammy adj. informal lame or injured.

gamut n. the whole range or scope.

gamy (or **gamey**) adj. (of meat) having the strong flavour or smell of game when it is high.

gander n. **1** a male goose. **2** informal a look.

gang n. an organized group, esp. of criminals or manual workers. ▶v. (**gang up**) join together against someone.

gangling (or **gangly**) adj. tall, thin, and awkward.

ganglion n. (pl. **ganglia** or **ganglions**) **1** a mass of nerve cells. **2** a swelling on a tendon.

gangplank n. a movable plank used to board or leave a ship.

gangrene n. the death of body tissue. ■ **gangrenous** adj.

gangster n. a member of a gang of violent criminals.

gangway n. **1** a passage between rows of seats. **2** a movable bridge linking a ship to the shore.

gannet n. **1** a large seabird. **2** informal a

Thesaurus

while, useful.

gait n. WALK, step, stride, pace, tread, manner of walking, bearing, carriage.

gale n. STORM, tempest, hurricane, squall, tornado, cyclone, typhoon.

gallant adj. **1** CHIVALROUS, gentlemanly, courtly, courteous, polite, attentive, gracious, considerate, thoughtful, obliging, deferential. **2** BRAVE, courageous, valiant, bold, daring, plucky, fearless, intrepid, dashing, heroic, lion-hearted, mettlesome. ■ OPPOSITES discourteous, cowardly.

galvanize v. ELECTRIFY, shock, stir, startle, jolt, arouse, awaken, spur, prod, stimulate, invigorate, fire, animate, vitalize, energize, thrill, inspire.

gamble v. **1** BET, wager, lay a bet, place a wager, stake, game, try one's luck; *informal* punt, have a flutter. **2** TAKE A CHANCE/RISK, speculate, venture; *informal* stick one's neck out, go out on a limb, take a flier.

game n. **1** PASTIME, diversion, recreation, entertainment, amusement, sport, play, distraction, frolic, romp, fun, merriment. **2** MATCH, contest, tournament, meeting, event, round, bout. **3** BUSINESS, line, trade, occupation, profession, industry, activity, calling. **4** WILD ANIMALS, quarry, prey, big game.

gang n. GROUP, band, company, crowd, gathering, pack, horde, mob, herd.

gangly adj. LANKY, rangy, skinny, angugreedy person.

gantry n. (pl. **gantries**) an overhead structure supporting equipment such as railway signals.

gaol var. of JAIL.

gap n. **1** a break or hole. **2** a space or interval. ■ **gappy** adj.

gape v. **1** be or become wide open. **2** stare with one's mouth open wide in amazement.

garage n. **1** a building for storing a vehicle. **2** an establishment selling fuel or repairing and selling vehicles.

garb n. clothing. ▶ v. (**be garbed**) be clothed.

garbage n. rubbish.

garble v. confuse or distort a message etc.

garden n. **1** a piece of ground next to a house, with a lawn or flowers. **2** (**gardens**) ornamental public grounds. ▶ v. work in a garden. ■ **gardener** n.

gargantuan adj. enormous.

gargle v. wash one's throat with a liquid that is kept there by breathing out through it.

gargoyle n. a grotesque face or figure carved on the gutter of a building.

garish /gair-ish/ adj. unpleasantly bright and showy. ■ **garishly** adv.

garland n. a wreath of flowers and leaves. ▶ v. decorate with a garland.

garlic n. a plant of the onion family with

a divided bulb, used in cookery. ■ **garlicky** adj.

garment n. an item of clothing.

garner v. gather or collect.

garnet n. a red semi-precious stone.

garnish v. decorate food. ▶ n. a decoration for food.

garret n. an attic.

garrison n. a body of troops in a fortress or town. ▶ v. provide a town with a garrison.

garrotte (US **garrote**) v. kill by strangulation. ▶ n. a wire or cord used for garrotting.

garrulous adj. extremely talkative.

garter n. a band worn around the leg to keep up a stocking or sock.

gas n. (pl. **gases** or US **gasses**) **1** an airlike substance which expands to fill any available space. **2** such a substance used as a fuel. **3** US informal petrol. ▶ v. (**gassing, gassed**) **1** harm or kill with gas. **2** informal chatter. □ **gas chamber** a room filled with poisonous gas to kill people. **gas mask** a mask used as protection against poison gas. ■ **gassy** adj.

gaseous adj. of or like a gas.

gash n. a long deep cut. ▶ v. make a gash in.

gasket n. a sheet or ring of rubber sealing a joint in an engine etc.

gasoline n. US petrol.

gasp v. draw in breath suddenly or with

Thesaurus

lar, spindly, awkward.

gangster n. RACKETEER, crook, criminal, hoodlum, Mafioso, gang member, mobster, robber, brigand, bandit, desperado, thug; informal tough; US informal hood.

gap n. **1** OPENING, hole, aperture, cavity, space, break, breach, break, fracture, rift, fissure, rent, cleft, chink, crack, crevice, divide, cranny, orifice, interstice. **2** PAUSE, break, intermission, interval, interlude, lull, respite, breathing space, rest, suspension, hiatus, recess. **3** OMISSION, blank, lacuna, void, vacuity. **4** DIFFERENCE, disparity, inconsistency, incompatibility, disagreement, divergence, breach, discrepancy, distance, division.

gape v. **1** STARE, gaze, goggle, ogle; informal gawk, rubberneck. **2** OPEN WIDE, open up, yawn, part, split, crack.

garb n. CLOTHES, garments, clothing, dress, attire, apparel, costume, outfit, wear, uniform, vestments, livery, trappings; informal gear, get-up, togs, rig-out, duds; old use habit. ▶ v. CLOTHE, dress, attire, array, robe, cover, outfit, fit; informal

kit out, rig out; old use apparel.

garbage n. WASTE, rubbish, refuse, litter, debris, junk, filth, detritus, scraps, leftovers, remains, slops.

garble v. DISTORT, twist, warp, slant, doctor, falsify, pervert, corrupt, misstate, misquote, misreport, misrepresent, misinterpret, misunderstand.

garish adj. FLASHY, flash, showy, loud, gaudy, lurid, bold, glaring, brassy, tinselly, vivid, tawdry, tasteless, in poor taste, vulgar. ■ OPPOSITES tasteful, sober.

garner v. GATHER, collect, accumulate, heap, pile up, amass, stack up, assemble, hoard, stockpile, deposit, husband, reserve, save, preserve.

garrison n. **1** FORCE, detachment, unit, brigade, platoon, squadron. **2** BARRACKS, base, fort, fortress, fortification, stronghold, camp, encampment, citadel. ▶ v. STATION, post, assign, position, billet, send in.

garrulous adj. TALKATIVE, chatty, verbose, loquacious, long-winded, effusive; informal mouthy, gabby. ■ OPPOSITES difficulty. ▶ n. a sudden intake of breath.

gastric adj. of the stomach.

gastro-enteritis n. inflammation of the stomach and intestines.

gastronomy n. the art of cooking and eating good food. ■ **gastronomic** adj.

gastropod n. a mollusc, e.g. a snail, with a single muscular foot.

gate n. **1** a hinged barrier in a wall, fence, etc. **2** an exit from an airport building to an aircraft. **3** the number of people paying to attend a sports event. □ **gatecrash** go to a party without an invitation. **gateway 1** an opening closed by a gate. **2** a means of entry or access.

gateau n. (pl. **gateaus** or **gateaux**) a cake with layers of cream or fruit.

gather v. **1** come or bring together. **2** collect plants or fruit for food. **3** increase in speed, force, etc. **4** infer; understand. **5** pull fabric into folds by drawing thread through it. ▶ n. a small fold in fabric, made by gathering.

gathering n. an assembled group.

gauche /gohsh/ adj. socially awkward.

gaucho /gow-choh/ n. (pl. **gauchos**) a South American cowboy.

gaudy adj. (**gaudier, gaudiest**) excessively or tastelessly bright or showy.

■ **gaudily** adv. **gaudiness** n.

gauge (US **gage**) n. **1** an instrument for measuring the amount or level of something. **2** a measure of thickness, size, etc. **3** the distance between the rails of a railway track. ▶ v. estimate, measure, or judge.

✓ gau-, not gua-: *gauge*

gaunt adj. lean and haggard.

gauntlet n. a glove with a long wide cuff. □ **run the gauntlet** go through an intimidating crowd or experience. **throw down the gauntlet** set a challenge.

gauze n. **1** a thin transparent fabric. **2** a fine wire mesh. ■ **gauzy** adj.

gave past of GIVE.

gavel n. a small hammer used by an auctioneer or judge to call for attention or order.

gawky adj. awkward and ungainly.

gawp v. informal stare in a stupid or rude manner.

gay adj. **1** homosexual. **2** dated lighthearted and carefree. **3** dated brightly coloured. ▶ n. a homosexual person.

gaze v. look steadily and intently. ▶ n. a steady intent look. ■ **gazer** n.

Thesaurus

taciturn.

gash v. CUT, slash, tear, lacerate, wound, gouge, incise, slit, rend, split, rent, nick, cleave.

gasp v. PANT, puff, puff and blow, blow, catch one's breath, gulp, choke, fight for breath, wheeze; informal huff and puff.

gate n. BARRIER, door, gateway, doorway, access, entrance, exit, opening, turnstile, passage, egress, portal, wicket, postern.

gather v. **1** COME TOGETHER, collect, assemble, congregate, meet, group, cluster, mass, crowd, flock together, convene, foregather, muster, converge, accumulate. **2** CALL TOGETHER, summon, assemble, collect, convene, round up, muster, marshal. **3** COLLECT, accumulate, assemble, amass, store, garner, stockpile, heap up, pile up, stack up, hoard; informal stash away. **4** UNDERSTAND, be given to understand, believe, hear, learn, infer, deduce, conclude, come to the conclusion, surmise, assume. **5** HARVEST, pick, collect, reap, glean, garner, cull, pluck. **6** INCREASE, grow, rise, build, expand, enlarge, swell, extend, intensify, deepen, heighten, thicken.

■ OPPOSITES disperse.

gathering n. ASSEMBLY, congregation, company, collection, group, crowd, band, throng, mass, horde, meeting, convention, conclave, rally, congress, convocation.

gauche adj. AWKWARD, clumsy, ungainly, bumbling, maladroit, lumbering, inept, inelegant, unpolished, graceless, unsophisticated, uncultured, uncultivated.

■ OPPOSITES sophisticated, adroit.

gaudy adj. see GARISH.

gauge n. **1** SIZE, measure, extent, degree, capacity, magnitude, height, width, thickness, span, bore. **2** MEASURE, basis, standard, guide, guideline, touchstone, yardstick, benchmark, criterion, rule, norm, example, model, pattern, exemplar, sample, test, indicator.

gaunt adj. **1** HAGGARD, drawn, cadaverous, skeletal, emaciated, skinny, skin and bone, spare, bony, angular, lanky, lean, raw-boned, spindly, pinched, hollow-cheeked, scrawny, scraggy, wasted, shrivelled, withered. **2** BLEAK, barren, desolate, bare, dreary, dismal, forlorn, grim, stern, harsh, forbidding.

■ OPPOSITES fat, lush.

gazebo /guh-zee-boh/ n. (pl. **gazebos** or **gazeboes**) a summer house with a wide view.

gazelle n. a small antelope.

gazette n. a journal or newspaper.

gazetteer n. a list of place names.

gazump v. informal offer or accept a higher price for a house after a lower price has already been accepted.

GB abbrev. **1** Great Britain. **2** (also **Gb**) gigabytes.

GBH abbrev. grievous bodily harm.

GCE abbrev. General Certificate of Education.

GCSE abbrev. General Certificate of Secondary Education.

GDP abbrev. gross domestic product.

gear n. **1** a set of toothed wheels working together to alter the relation between the speed of an engine and the speed of the driven parts. **2** a particular setting of these. **3** informal equipment or clothing. ▶ v. **1** design or adjust the gears in a machine. **2** (**gear up**) equip or prepare. □ **gearbox** a set of gears with its casing. **in** (or **out of**) **gear** with a gear (or no gear) engaged.

gecko n. (pl. **geckos** or **geckoes**) a tropical lizard.

geese pl. of GOOSE.

Geiger counter /gy-ger/ n. a device for measuring radioactivity.

geisha /gay-shuh/ n. (pl. **geisha** or **geishas**) a Japanese hostess trained to entertain men.

gel /jel/ n. a jelly-like substance. ▶ v. make or become firm.

gelatin (or **gelatine**) n. a clear substance obtained from animal bones, used to make jelly, glue, and photo-

graphic film. ■ **gelatinous** adj.

geld v. castrate.

gelding n. a castrated horse.

gelignite n. a high explosive made from nitroglycerine.

gem n. **1** a precious stone. **2** an outstanding person or thing.

gender n. **1** each of the classes into which nouns are placed in some languages, usu. masculine, feminine, and neuter. **2** the state of being male or female (with reference to social or cultural differences).

gene n. a distinct sequence of DNA by which offspring inherit parental characteristics.

genealogy n. (pl. **genealogies**) **1** a line of descent. **2** the study of lines of descent. ■ **genealogical** adj. **genealogist** n.

genera pl. of GENUS.

general adj. **1** affecting or concerning all or most people or things. **2** involving only the main features; not detailed. ▶ n. an army officer ranking above lieutenant general. □ **general anaesthetic** an anaesthetic causing a loss of consciousness. **general election** an election of parliamentary representatives from the whole country. **general practitioner** a doctor treating patients in a local community rather than at a hospital. **in general 1** usually. **2** as a whole. ■ **generally** adv.

generality n. (pl. **generalities**) **1** a general statement. **2** the state of being general. **3** the majority.

generalize (or **-ise**) v. **1** make a general statement. **2** make generally available or applicable. ■ **generalization** n.

Thesaurus

gaze v. STARE, gape, take a good look, look fixedly, goggle, stand agog, watch in wonder, ogle, eye, contemplate; informal gawk, rubberneck, give the once-over.

gear n. **1** EQUIPMENT, tools, kit, apparatus, implements, tackle, appliances, utensils, supplies, accessories, paraphernalia, accoutrements, contrivances, trappings; informal stuff. **2** BELONGINGS, possessions, things, luggage, baggage, kit, effects, goods, paraphernalia, impedimenta; Law chattels.

genealogy n. FAMILY TREE, ancestry, pedigree, line, lineage, descent, parentage, birth, derivation, extraction, family, strain, stock, bloodline, heritage, roots.

general adj. **1** USUAL, customary, com-

mon, ordinary, normal, standard, regular, everyday, typical, conventional, habitual, run-of-the-mill. **2** COMMON, accepted, widespread, shared, broad, wide, prevalent, prevailing, universal, popular, public, generic, extensive. **3** UNIVERSAL, blanket, comprehensive, all-inclusive, across-the-board, broad-ranging, broad, sweeping, indiscriminate, catholic, encyclopedic. **4** MIXED, assorted, miscellaneous, diversified, variegated, composite, heterogeneous. **5** BROAD, loose, rough, approximate, non-specific, vague, ill-defined, indefinite, inexact, imprecise. ■ OPPOSITES unusual, specific, detailed.

generally adv. **1** USUALLY, in general, as a rule, normally, ordinarily, almost always, customarily, habitually, typical-

generate v. create or produce.

generation n. **1** all of the people born and living at about the same time. **2** the average period in which a person grows up and has children of their own. **3** a single stage in the descent of a family. ■ **generational** adj.

generator n. a machine converting mechanical energy into electricity.

generic adj. **1** of a whole class or genus. **2** (of goods) having no brand name. ■ **generically** adv.

generous adj. **1** giving freely. **2** kind. **3** large or plentiful. ■ **generosity** n. **generously** adv.

genesis n. the origin of something.

genetic adj. of genes or genetics. ▶ n. (**genetics**) the study of heredity and inherited characteristics. □ **genetically modified** containing genetic material artificially altered to produce a desired characteristic. **genetic engineering** the alteration of an animal's or plant's characteristics by manipulating its DNA. **genetic fingerprinting** the analysis of DNA to identify individuals. ■ **genetically** adv. **geneticist** n.

genial adj. friendly and cheerful. ■ **geniality** n. **genially** adv.

genie n. a spirit in Arabian folklore.

genital adj. of human or animal reproductive organs. ▶ pl. n. (**genitals** or **genitalia**) the external reproductive organs.

genitive n. the grammatical case showing possession.

genius n. (pl. **geniuses**) **1** exceptional natural ability. **2** a person with this.

genocide n. the deliberate killing of a very large number of people from a particular ethnic group or nation.

genre /zhon-ruh/ n. a style of art or literature.

genteel adj. affectedly polite and refined.

gentian /jen-sh'n/ n. a plant with deep blue flowers.

Gentile n. a person who is not Jewish.

gentility n. polite and refined behaviour.

gentle adj. **1** mild or kind; not rough or violent. **2** not harsh or severe. ■ **gentleness** n. **gently** adv.

gentleman n. **1** a courteous or honourable man. **2** a man of good social position. ■ **gentlemanly** adj.

gentrify v. (**gentrifying**, **gentrified**) renovate a district so that it conforms to middle-class taste.

gentry n. people of the class next below the nobility.

genuflect v. lower one's body briefly by

Thesaurus

ly, regularly, for the most part, mainly, by and large, on average, on the whole, in most cases, in the main. **2** COMMONLY, widely, extensively, popularly, universally.

generate v. CAUSE, give rise to, produce, make, bring into being, create, engender, originate, initiate, occasion, arouse, whip up, propagate.

generosity n. LIBERALITY, kindness, magnanimity, benevolence, munificence, open-handedness, bounty, hospitality, charitableness, lavishness.

generous adj. **1** LIBERAL, kind, magnanimous, benevolent, munificent, beneficent, bountiful, hospitable, open-handed, charitable, ungrudging, lavish, unstinting, free-handed, princely; *literary* bounteous. **2** NOBLE, magnanimous, high-minded, honourable, good, unselfish, altruistic, unprejudiced, disinterested. **3** ABUNDANT, liberal, plentiful, lavish, ample, rich, copious, superabundant, overflowing. ■ OPPOSITES mean, selfish, meagre.

genial adj. AMIABLE, affable, friendly, sociable, congenial, amicable, convivial, good-humoured, good-natured, agree-

able, warm, pleasant, cordial, amenable, well disposed, cheerful, cheery, kind, kindly, benign, happy, sunny, jovial, easy-going, sympathetic. ■ OPPOSITES unfriendly.

genius n. **1** BRILLIANT PERSON, mental giant, prodigy, virtuoso, master, mastermind, maestro, intellectual, intellect, expert, adept; *informal* brain, Einstein. **2** BRILLIANCE, intelligence, cleverness, capability, flair, talent, aptitude, ability, capacity, endowment.

genteel adj. **1** RESPECTABLE, refined, patrician, ladylike, gentlemanly, well bred, aristocratic, noble, blue-blooded, well born. **2** POLITE, well mannered, courteous, mannerly, civil, gracious, decorous, courtly, polished, cultivated, stylish, elegant. ■ OPPOSITES uncouth.

gentle adj. **1** TENDER, kind, kindly, humane, benign, merciful, lenient, compassionate, tender-hearted, placid, sweet-tempered, mild, serene, soft, quiet, tranquil, still, peaceful, pacific, meek, dove-like. **2** MILD, moderate, light, temperate, soft, balmy. **3** SOFT, light, smooth, soothing. **4** PLACID, docile, tame, biddable, tractable, manageable, bending one knee, esp. as a sign of respect. ■ **genuflection** n.

genuine adj. truly what it is said to be.
■ **genuinely** adv.

genus n. (pl. **genera**) a category in the classification of animals and plants.

geocentric adj. **1** having the earth as a centre. **2** measured or viewed from the earth's centre.

geode n. **1** a cavity lined with crystals. **2** a rock containing this.

geodesy n. the study of the earth's shape and area.

geography n. **1** the study of the earth's physical features and how people relate to these. **2** the features and arrangement of a place. ■ **geographer** n. **geographical** (or **geographic**) adj. **geographically** adv.

geology n. **1** the study of the earth's physical structure and substance. **2** the geological features of a district. ■ **geological** adj. **geologically** adv. **geologist** n.

geometry n. the branch of mathematics dealing with points, lines, surfaces, and solids. ■ **geometric** (or **geometrical**) adj. **geometrically** adv.

Georgian adj. of the time of Kings George I–IV (1714–1830).

geranium n. a flowering garden plant.

gerbil n. a desert rodent with long hind legs.

geriatric adj. of old people. ▶ n. **1** an old person. **2** (**geriatrics**) the branch of medicine dealing with the health and care of old people.

germ n. **1** a microorganism causing disease. **2** a part of an organism capable of developing into a new one. **3** a basis from which a thing may develop.

German n. **1** a person from Germany. **2** the language of Germany, Austria, and parts of Switzerland. ▶ adj. of Germany or its language. □ **German measles** rubella. **German shepherd** a

large breed of dog often used as guard dogs.

germane adj. relevant.

Germanic adj. **1** of the language family including English, German, Dutch, and the Scandinavian languages. **2** of Germans or Germany.

germanium n. a grey crystalline element.

germinate v. begin or cause to grow. ■ **germination** n.

gerontology n. the study of old age and old people.

gerrymander v. alter the boundaries of an electoral constituency so as to favour one party.

gerund n. a noun formed from a verb, in English ending in *-ing*.

Gestapo n. the German secret police under Nazi rule.

gestation n. **1** the growth of a baby in the womb. **2** the development of an idea over time.

gesticulate v. gesture dramatically in place of or to emphasize speech. ■ **gesticulation** n.

gesture n. **1** a movement of part of the body to convey a meaning. **2** something done to convey one's feelings or intentions. ▶ v. make a gesture.

get v. (**getting, got**) **1** come to have or hold; receive. **2** succeed in achieving. **3** experience or suffer. **4** fetch. **5** bring or come into a specified state or position. **6** catch or thwart. **7** persuade or induce. **8** begin to be or do. **9** travel by a form of transport. □ **get across** make or be understood. **getaway** an escape. **get by** manage to survive. **get off** informal escape punishment. **get on 1** make progress. **2** be friendly. **3** informal grow old. **get over** recover from. **get round** persuade. **get through 1** make contact by telephone. **2** make or be understood. **get-together** a social gathering. **get-up** informal an outfit.

Thesaurus

meek, easily handled, broken, trained, schooled. **5** GRADUAL, slight, easy, imperceptible. ■ OPPOSITES cruel, fierce, rough.

genuine adj. **1** REAL, authentic, true, pure, actual, bona fide, veritable, sound, pukka, sterling, legitimate, lawful, legal, valid, original, unadulterated, unalloyed; *informal* kosher, honest-to-goodness. **2** SINCERE, truthful, honest, frank, candid, open, natural, unaffected, artless, ingenuous; *informal* upfront. ■ OPPOSITES fake, insincere.

germ n. **1** MICROBE, microorganism, bacillus, bacterium, virus; *informal* bug. **2** BEGINNING, start, genesis, seed, embryo, root, bud, origin, source, fount, fountain, rudiment.

gesture n. SIGNAL, motion, sign, wave, indication, gesticulation. ▶ v. GESTICULATE, signal, make a sign, motion, wave, indicate.

get v. **1** ACQUIRE, obtain, come by, come into possession of, secure, procure, buy, purchase. **2** RECEIVE, be sent, be given. **3** GO FOR, fetch, bring, collect, carry,

geyser n. a hot spring intermittently sending a jet of water and steam into the air.

ghastly adj. **1** causing great horror. **2** very pale. **3** informal very unpleasant. ■ **ghastliness** n.

ghee n. clarified butter used in Indian cooking.

gherkin n. a small pickled cucumber.

ghetto n. (pl. **ghettos** or **ghettoes**) a part of a city occupied by a minority group.

ghost n. **1** an apparition of a dead person. **2** a faint trace. ▶v. write as a ghost writer. □ **ghost town** a town with few or no remaining inhabitants. **ghost writer** a person who writes a book etc. for another person, who is the named author. ■ **ghostly** adj.

ghoul n. **1** an evil spirit. **2** a person excessively interested in death or disaster. ■ **ghoulish** adj.

GI n. (pl. **GIs**) a private soldier in the US army.

giant n. **1** an imaginary being of superhuman size. **2** an unusually large person, animal, or plant. ▶adj. very large.

gibber v. speak rapidly and unintelligibly.

gibberish n. unintelligible speech or writing.

gibbet n. hist. a gallows.

gibbon n. a long-armed SE Asian ape.

gibe var. of JIBE.

giblets pl. n. the liver, heart, etc. of a chicken, turkey, or other bird.

giddy adj. (**giddier, giddiest**) **1** having or causing a feeling of whirling and being about to fall. **2** not interested in serious things. ■ **giddiness** n.

gift n. **1** a thing given without payment. **2** a natural talent. ▶v. **1** give as a gift. **2** (**gifted**) having exceptional talent.

gig n. **1** esp. hist. a light two-wheeled horse-drawn carriage. **2** informal a live performance by a musician.

gigabyte n. Computing a unit of information equal to one thousand million bytes.

gigantic adj. very large.

giggle v. laugh in a nervous or silly manner. ▶n. a nervous or silly laugh. ■ **giggly** adj.

gigolo /jig-uh-loh/ n. (pl. **gigolos**) a man

Thesaurus

transport, convey. **4** EARN, be paid, make, bring in, clear, gross, net, take home, pocket; informal pull in. **5** CAPTURE, seize, arrest, apprehend, take, trap, lay hold of, grab, bag, take captive, grasp; informal collar, nab, nick. **6** UNDERSTAND, comprehend, grasp, see, fathom, work out, follow; informal make head or tail of, catch on, get the hang of. **7** PERSUADE, induce, coax, talk into, wheedle into, prevail upon, influence, sway, convince, win over. **8** BECOME, grow, come to be, turn. ■ OPPOSITES lose. □ **get ahead** SUCCEED, do well, make good, be successful, prosper, flourish, rise in the world. **get at 1** FIND FAULT WITH, pick on, criticize, carp, nag, taunt. **2** SUGGEST, mean, imply, hint, intend, lead up to. **get by** SURVIVE, cope, manage, subsist, exist, get along, fare, make both ends meet; informal keep one's head above water, make out. **get out of** AVOID, dodge, evade, shirk, escape.

getaway n. ESCAPE, flight, breakout, break, absconding.

ghastly adj. **1** TERRIBLE, horrible, frightful, dreadful, awful, horrid, horrendous, hideous, shocking, grim, gruesome, terrifying, frightening. **2** LOATHSOME, odious, nasty, contemptible, dreadful, appalling, foul. **3** VERY BAD, serious, grave, critical, unforgivable,

awful, terrible.

ghost n. **1** APPARITION, spectre, spirit, phantom, wraith, shade; informal spook; literary phantasm. **2** SUGGESTION, hint, trace, glimmer, shadow, impression, semblance.

ghostly adj. SPECTRAL, phantom, ghostlike, wraithlike, unearthly, supernatural, other-worldly, illusory, insubstantial, shadowy, eerie, creepy, scary, weird, uncanny; informal spooky; literary phantasmal.

giant n. COLOSSUS, behemoth, man mountain, titan, Goliath. ▶adj. GIGANTIC, enormous, huge, colossal, immense, vast, mammoth, gargantuan, titanic, elephantine, prodigious, stupendous, Brobdingnagian; informal jumbo.

gibe n. see JIBE.

giddy adj. DIZZY, faint, light-headed, unsteady, reeling, vertiginous; informal woozy.

gift n. **1** PRESENT, offering, donation, contribution, grant, bonus, largesse, boon, gratuity, benefaction, bequest, legacy, inheritance, endowment. **2** TALENT, aptitude, flair, facility, knack, bent, ability, faculty, capacity, capability, skill, attribute, expertise, genius, mind for.

gifted adj. TALENTED, brilliant, clever, bright, intelligent, ingenious, sharp, paid by a woman to be her escort or lover.

gild v. cover thinly with gold. ▪ **gilding** n.

gill /jil/ n. a quarter of a pint.

gills /gilz/ pl. n. **1** the organ with which a fish breathes. **2** the plates on the underside of a mushroom.

gilt adj. covered thinly with gold. ▶ n. **1** a thin layer of gold on a surface. **2** a gilt-edged investment. □ **gilt-edged** (of an investment) very safe.

gimbals /jim-buhlz/ pl. n. a device for keeping instruments horizontal on a ship.

gimcrack /jim-krak/ adj. showy but poorly made.

gimlet /gim-lit/ n. a small tool with a screw-tip for boring holes.

gimmick n. a trick or device intended to attract attention. ▪ **gimmicky** adj.

gin n. an alcoholic spirit flavoured with juniper berries.

ginger n. **1** a hot spice made from the root of a SE Asian plant. **2** a light reddish-yellow colour. □ **gingerbread** cake flavoured with ginger. ▪ **gingery** adj.

gingerly adv. cautiously.

gingham /ging-uhm/ n. cotton cloth with a checked pattern.

gingivitis /jin-ji-vy-tiss/ n. inflammation of the gums.

ginseng n. a plant whose root is credited with various medicinal properties.

Gipsy var. of GYPSY.

giraffe n. a large African animal with a very long neck and legs.

gird v. literary encircle with a belt or band.

girder n. a metal beam supporting a structure.

girdle n. **1** a belt. **2** a corset. ▶ v. encircle or surround.

girl n. **1** a female child. **2** a young woman. □ **girlfriend 1** a person's regular female romantic or sexual partner. **2** a woman's female friend. ▪ **girlhood** n. **girlish** adj.

giro n. (pl. **giros**) a system in which a payment is electronically transferred from one bank or post office account to another.

girth n. **1** the measurement around the middle of something. **2** a band attached to a saddle and fastened around a horse's belly.

gist /jist/ n. the general meaning of a speech or text.

give v. (**giving**, **gave**; past part. **given**) **1** cause to have, get, or experience. **2** do an action or make a sound. **3** state information. **4** (**give off/out**) send out a smell, heat, etc. **5** bend under pressure. ▶ n. the ability to bend under pressure. □ **give and take** willingness to compromise on both sides. **give away** reveal something secret. **giveaway** informal **1** a free gift. **2** an inadvertent revelation. **give in** admit defeat. **give out** stop operating. **give rise to** make happen. **give up 1** cease one's efforts. **2** stop doing regularly. **3** hand over. **give way 1** collapse. **2** allow other traffic to go first.

given adj. **1** specified or stated. **2** (**given to**) inclined to. ▶ prep. taking into account. ▶ n. an established fact. □ **given name** a first name.

g

Thesaurus

able, accomplished, capable, masterly, skilled, adroit, proficient, expert; informal smart. ▪ OPPOSITES inept.

gigantic adj. see HUGE.

giggle v. TITTER, snigger, snicker, chuckle, chortle, laugh, cackle; informal tee-hee.

gingerly adv. CAUTIOUSLY, warily, carefully, attentively, heedfully, vigilantly, watchfully, guardedly, prudently, circumspectly, judiciously, suspiciously, hesitantly, reluctantly, timidly, timorously. ▪ OPPOSITES recklessly.

girl n. **1** YOUNG WOMAN, female, young lady, miss; Sc. & N. Engl. lass, lassie; informal chick, bird, filly; US informal babe, broad; Austral./NZ informal sheila. **2** GIRL-FRIEND, lover, sweetheart, mistress, inamorata.

girth n. CIRCUMFERENCE, perimeter, size,

bulk, measure.

gist n. ESSENCE, substance, drift, sense, crux, significance, idea, import, core, quintessence, nucleus, kernel, nub, pith, marrow, burden.

give v. **1** PRESENT, hand, hand over, bestow, donate, contribute, confer, turn over, award, grant, accord, leave, will, bequeath, make over, entrust, consign, vouchsafe. **2** PROVIDE, supply, furnish, proffer, offer. **3** PRODUCE, yield, afford, result in. **4** CAUSE, be a source of, make, create. **5** LET OUT, utter, emit, issue, voice. □ **give away** REVEAL, disclose, divulge, let slip, leak, let out, expose, uncover. **give in** GIVE UP, surrender, admit defeat, concede, yield, capitulate, submit, comply, succumb, retreat; informal quit. **give off** EMIT, send out, throw out, discharge, exude, release, vent,

gizmo n. (pl. **gizmos**) informal a gadget.

gizzard n. a muscular part of a bird's stomach for grinding food.

glacé /gla-say/ adj. preserved in sugar.

glacial adj. **1** of ice and glaciers. **2** very cold.

glaciation n. the formation of glaciers.

glacier n. a slowly moving mass of ice.

glad adj. (**gladder, gladdest**) **1** pleased; delighted. **2** causing happiness. ■ **gladden** v. **gladly** adv. **gladness** n.

glade n. an open space in a forest.

gladiator n. a man trained to fight at public shows in ancient Rome. ■ **gladiatorial** adj.

gladiolus n. (pl. **gladioli** or **gladioluses**) a tall plant with sword-shaped leaves.

glamour (US **glamor**) n. an attractive and exciting quality. ■ **glamorize** (or **-ise**) v. **glamorous** adj.

....
☑ Remember that **glamorous** drops the *u* of **glamour**.
....

glance v. **1** look briefly. **2** strike and bounce off at an angle. ▶n. a brief look.

gland n. an organ of the body which secretes particular chemical substances. ■ **glandular** adj.

glare v. **1** stare angrily. **2** shine with a dazzling light. **3** (**glaring**) very obvious. ▶n. **1** an angry stare. **2** dazzling light.

glass n. **1** a hard brittle transparent substance. **2** a drinking container made of glass. **3** (**glasses**) a pair of lenses in a frame that rests on the nose and ears, used to correct eyesight. **4** a mirror. **5** a barometer. □ **glass ceiling** an imaginary barrier to progress in a profession. **glasshouse** a greenhouse. ■ **glassy** adj.

glaucoma n. a condition causing gradual loss of sight.

glaze v. **1** fit or cover with glass. **2** cover with a glaze. **3** (of the eyes) lose brightness and animation. ▶n. a shiny surface or coating.

glazier n. a person whose job is to fit glass into windows.

gleam v. shine brightly with reflected light. ▶n. **1** a faint or brief light. **2** a brief or faint show of a quality.

glean v. **1** collect from various sources. **2** hist. gather leftover grain after a harvest. ■ **gleanings** pl. n.

glebe n. hist. a piece of land allocated to a clergyman and providing income.

glee n. triumph or delight. ■ **gleeful** adj.

Thesaurus
....

produce. **give up** STOP, cease, leave off, desist from, swear off, renounce, abandon, discontinue, forswear; informal quit, cut out, chuck.

glad adj. **1** HAPPY, pleased, delighted, thrilled, gratified, overjoyed, elated, satisfied, contented; informal over the moon, tickled pink, chuffed. **2** WILLING, eager, ready, prepared, happy, pleased. **3** WELCOME, joyful, cheering, happy, cheerful, pleasing, gratifying. ■ OPPOSITES unhappy, reluctant.

gladden v. MAKE HAPPY, delight, cheer, cheer up, hearten, brighten up, raise someone's spirits, please, elate, buoy up, give a lift to; informal buck up. ■ OPPOSITES sadden.

glamorous adj. **1** ALLURING, dazzling, smart, elegant, beautiful, lovely, attractive, charming, fascinating, exciting, beguiling, bewitching, enchanting, entrancing, irresistible, tantalizing. **2** EXCITING, fascinating, stimulating, thrilling, glossy, glittering; informal ritzy, glitzy. ■ OPPOSITES dowdy, boring.

glamour n. **1** BEAUTY, loveliness, attractiveness, allure, attraction, elegance, charm, fascination. **2** EXCITEMENT, allure, charm, fascination, enchantment,

captivation, magic, spell.

glance v. LOOK QUICKLY/HURRIEDLY, take a quick look, glimpse, catch a glimpse, peek, peep, sneak a look.

glare v. **1** SCOWL, glower, frown, look threateningly, look daggers, give someone dirty looks, lour. **2** DAZZLE, beam, flare, blaze, flame.

glaring adj. **1** DAZZLING, blazing, flaring. **2** OBVIOUS, conspicuous, manifest, overt, patent, visible, flagrant, blatant, outrageous, egregious, gross.

glass n. TUMBLER, flute, schooner, balloon, goblet, beaker.

glasses pl. n. SPECTACLES, eyeglasses, bifocals, sunglasses, monocle, lorgnette, pince-nez, field glasses, binoculars, opera glasses.

glassy adj. **1** SHINY, glossy, smooth, mirror-like, clear, transparent, translucent, limpid, pellucid. **2** GLAZED, blank, expressionless, empty, vacant, deadpan, vacuous, fixed, unmoving, lifeless, motionless.

glaze v. VARNISH, coat, polish, enamel, lacquer, gloss, burnish. ▶n. GLOSS, lustre, finish, lacquer, enamel.

gleam v. SHINE, radiate, flash, glow, glint, flare, glisten, glitter, beam, shimmer,

gleefully adv.

glen n. a narrow valley.

glib adj. articulate but insincere or shallow. ■ **glibly** adv.

glide v. **1** move with a smooth, quiet motion. **2** fly without power or in a glider. ▶ n. an act of gliding.

glider n. a light aircraft with no engine.

glimmer v. shine faintly with a wavering light. ▶ n. **1** a faint or wavering light. **2** a faint sign of a quality.

glimpse n. a brief or partial view. ▶ v. see briefly or partially.

glint v. give out small flashes of light. ▶ n. a small flash of light.

glisten v. (of something wet) shine or sparkle.

glitch n. informal a sudden problem or fault.

glitter v. **1** sparkle. **2** (**glittering**) impressively successful. ▶ n. **1** sparkling light. **2** tiny pieces of sparkling material for decoration. ■ **glittery** adj.

glitz n. informal superficial glamour. ■ **glitzy** adj.

gloaming n. literary twilight.

gloat v. be smug or pleased about one's own success or another's failure.

global adj. **1** worldwide. **2** of or affecting an entire group. □ **global warming** the gradual increase in the temperature of the earth's atmosphere due to increased levels of carbon dioxide etc. ■ **globally** adv.

globalize (or **-ise**) v. operate worldwide. ■ **globalization** n.

globe n. **1** a spherical or rounded object. **2** a spherical model of the earth with a map on the surface.

globetrotter n. informal a person who travels widely. ■ **globetrotting** n. & adj.

globule n. a small round drop. ■ **globular** adj.

globulin n. a protein found in blood serum.

glockenspiel /glok-uhn-shpeel/ n. a musical instrument consisting of metal bars struck with hammers.

gloom n. **1** partial or total darkness. **2** depression or despair. ■ **gloomily** adv. **gloomy** adj.

glorify v. (**glorifying**, **glorified**) **1** represent as admirable. **2** cause to seem more important than in reality. **3** praise and worship God. ■ **glorification** n.

glorious adj. **1** having or bringing glory. **2** strikingly beautiful or impressive.

Thesaurus

glimmer, sparkle, twinkle, scintillate. ▶ n. **1** BEAM, flash, glow, shaft, ray, flare, glint. **2** LUSTRE, glow, shine, gloss, sheen, brightness, flash, brilliance, coruscation.

glee n. MIRTH, merriment, gaiety, delight, joy, joyfulness, joyousness, gladness, happiness, pleasure, jollity, hilarity, jocularity, joviality, exhilaration, high spirits, cheerfulness, exaltation, elation, exuberance, liveliness, verve, triumph; literary blitheness.

glib adj. SMOOTH-TALKING, fast-talking, slick, smooth, fluent, smooth-tongued, silver-tongued, plausible, talkative, voluble, loquacious, unctuous, having the gift of the gab; informal sweet-talking. ■ OPPOSITES tongue-tied, inarticulate.

glimpse v. CATCH SIGHT OF, catch a glimpse of, spot, spy, discern, make out, distinguish, notice, observe, sight, espy, descry. ▶ n. GLANCE, brief look, peek, peep, look, sight, view.

glint v. SHINE, sparkle, flash, twinkle, glitter, glimmer, blink, gleam, wink, shimmer, glisten, dazzle, scintillate.

glisten v. SHINE, shimmer, sparkle, twinkle, flicker, glint, blink, wink, gleam, flash, scintillate, coruscate.

glitter v. SPARKLE, twinkle, flicker, blink, wink, shimmer, glimmer, glint, flash, gleam. ▶ n. **1** SPARKLE, twinkle, flicker, blink, winking. **2** SHOWINESS, flashiness, glamour, ostentation, pageantry, splendour, fanfare; informal razzle-dazzle, glitz, pizzazz.

gloat v. RELISH, revel in, glory in, rejoice in, exult in, triumph over, crow about; informal rub it in.

global adj. **1** WORLDWIDE, universal, international, planetary. **2** GENERAL, comprehensive, all-encompassing, exhaustive, encyclopedic, thorough, total, with no exceptions, across-the-board.

globule n. BEAD, drop, ball, droplet, pearl, particle.

gloom n. **1** DIMNESS, darkness, dark, blackness, murkiness, shadowiness, shadiness, dullness, obscurity, dusk, twilight. **2** SADNESS, melancholy, unhappiness, sorrow, woe, grief, despondency, misery, dejection, glumness, desolation, depression, despair, pessimism, hopelessness. ■ OPPOSITES light, cheer.

gloomy adj. **1** DARK, overcast, cloudy, dull, sunless, dim, shadowy, black, unlit, murky, sombre, dismal, dreary, shady, dingy. **2** SAD, melancholy, unhappy, miserable, sorrowful, despondent, woebegone, disconsolate, dejected,

■ **gloriously** adv.

glory n. (pl. **glories**) **1** fame and honour. **2** beauty or splendour. **3** a beautiful or splendid thing. **4** praise and worship of God. ▶v. (**glorying**, **gloried**) (**glory in**) take great pride or pleasure in.

gloss n. **1** the shine on a smooth surface. **2** a type of paint drying to a shiny finish. **3** a translation or explanation. ▶v. **1** (**gloss over**) try to conceal a fault etc. **2** provide a gloss for. ■ **glossy** adj.

glossary n. (pl. **glossaries**) a list of words and their meanings.

glottis n. the part of the larynx made up of the vocal cords and the opening between them. ■ **glottal** adj.

glove n. a covering for the hand with separate parts for each finger.

glow v. **1** give out steady light without flame. **2** have a warm or flushed look.

3 show or feel great pleasure. ▶n. a glowing state. □ **glow-worm** a kind of beetle that gives out light.

glower /glow-er/ v. & n. (a) scowl.

glucose n. a form of sugar found in fruit juice.

glue n. a sticky substance used for joining things. ▶v. (**gluing** or **glueing**, **glued**) join with glue.

glum adj. (**glummer**, **glummest**) dejected; morose. ■ **glumly** adv.

glut n. an excessive supply. ▶v. (**glutting**, **glutted**) supply to excess.

gluten n. a protein found in cereal grains.

glutinous adj. like glue in texture; sticky.

glutton n. **1** a greedy person. **2** a person who is eager for something. ■ **gluttonous** adj. **gluttony** n.

glycerine (US **glycerin**) n. a thick sweet

Thesaurus

downcast, downhearted, glum, dispirited, desolate, depressed, blue, pessimistic, morose; *informal* down in the mouth. ■ OPPOSITES bright, cheerful.

glorious adj. **1** ILLUSTRIOUS, celebrated, noble, famous, famed, renowned, distinguished, honoured, eminent, magnificent, excellent, majestic, splendid, resplendent, supreme, triumphant, sublime, victorious. **2** BEAUTIFUL, bright, sunny, brilliant, perfect. **3** MARVELLOUS, splendid, wonderful, delightful, enjoyable, pleasurable, fine, excellent, great; *informal* fab, terrific.

glory n. **1** EXALTATION, worship, adoration, honour, reverence, extolment, veneration, thanksgiving. **2** DISTINCTION, fame, kudos, renown, honour, prestige, acclaim, illustriousness, credit, accolade, recognition; *formal* laudation. **3** SPLENDOUR, resplendence, magnificence, grandeur, majesty, pomp, pageantry, beauty. ■ OPPOSITES disgrace. □ **glory in** EXULT IN, rejoice in, take pleasure in, be proud of, delight in, revel in, boast about, crow about, gloat about.

gloss n. **1** SHINE, sheen, lustre, gleam, brightness, brilliance, sparkle, polish, shimmer, burnish. **2** FRONT, facade, disguise, mask, semblance, camouflage, show, veneer, surface. □ **gloss over** EVADE, avoid, smooth over, conceal, hide, cover up, disguise, mask, veil, whitewash.

glossy adj. SHINING, shiny, gleaming, bright, smooth, lustrous, glistening, brilliant, polished, burnished, glazed,

silky, silken, sleek, waxed. ■ OPPOSITES dull, lustreless.

glow v. **1** GLEAM, shine, glimmer, smoulder, shed a glow, light up. **2** BLUSH, flush, redden, grow pink, go scarlet, colour, crimson, radiate, thrill, tingle. ▶n. **1** GLEAM, glimmer, luminosity, incandescence, phosphorescence, lambency. **2** BRIGHTNESS, vividness, colourfulness, brilliance, radiance, splendour, richness. **3** BLUSH, rosiness, flush, pinkness, redness, crimson, reddening, scarlet, bloom.

glower v. SCOWL, stare angrily, glare, frown, give someone black/dirty looks, look daggers, lour. ■ OPPOSITES smile.

glowing adj. **1** LUMINOUS, bright, vivid, brilliant, radiant, rich, smouldering, incandescent, phosphorescent, aglow, lambent. **2** FAVOURABLE, enthusiastic, complimentary, laudatory, adulatory, ecstatic, rhapsodic, eulogistic, panegyrical; *informal* rave.

glue n. ADHESIVE, gum, fixative, paste, cement, epoxy resin, mucilage. ▶v. STICK, paste, gum, fix, affix, cement, bond, seal.

glum adj. GLOOMY, melancholy, sad, despondent, miserable, dejected, downcast, downhearted, dispirited, depressed, in low spirits; *informal* down in the mouth. ■ OPPOSITES cheerful.

glut n. SURPLUS, excess, surfeit, overabundance, superabundance, oversupply, overprovision, saturation, superfluity. ■ OPPOSITES dearth.

glutinous adj. STICKY, viscous, tacky, mucous, gummy, adhesive, viscid, liquid used in medicines etc.

glycerol n. glycerine.

GM abbrev. genetically modified.

gm abbrev. grams.

GMT abbrev. Greenwich Mean Time.

gnarled adj. knobbly or twisted.

gnash v. grind one's teeth together.

gnat n. a small biting fly.

gnaw v. **1** bite at persistently. **2** cause persistent anxiety or pain.

gnome n. an imaginary being like a very small man.

gnomic adj. concise and clever but difficult to understand.

gnomon n. the rod of a sundial.

gnostic adj. of or having mystical knowledge.

GNP abbrev. gross national product.

gnu /noo/ n. a large heavy antelope.

GNVQ abbrev. General National Vocational Qualification.

go v. (**goes**, **going**, **went**; past part. **gone**) **1** move to or from a place. **2** pass into or be in a particular state. **3** extend. **4** come to an end. **5** disappear or be used up. **6** (of time) pass. **7** engage in a specified activity. **8** have a particular outcome. **9** function. **10** match. **11** fit into or be regularly kept in. **12** make a specified sound. ▸ n. (pl. **goes**) informal **1** an attempt. **2** a turn to do something. **3** energy. □ **go-ahead** informal permission to proceed. **go back on** fail to keep a promise. **go-between** an intermediary or negotiator. **go-cart** (or **go-kart**) a small lightweight racing car. **go for 1** choose. **2** attack. **go-getter** informal an energetically enterprising person. **go into** investigate. **go off 1** explode. **2** (of food) become stale or bad. **3** informal begin to dislike. **go out 1** be extinguished. **2** carry on a regular romantic relationship with someone. **go round** be enough for everyone.

goad n. **1** a pointed stick for driving cattle. **2** a stimulus to action. ▸ v. provoke to action.

goal n. **1** (in soccer, rugby, etc.) a framework into or over which the ball has to be sent to score. **2** an act of scoring. **3** an aim or desired result. □ **goalkeeper** (in soccer, hockey, etc.) a player whose job is to keep the ball out of the goal. **goalpost** either of the two upright posts of a goal.

goalie n. informal a goalkeeper.

goat n. an animal with horns, sometimes kept for milk.

goatee n. a small pointed beard like that of a goat.

gobble v. **1** eat hurriedly and noisily. **2** (of a turkey) make a swallowing sound in the throat.

gobbledegook n. informal pompous or unintelligible language.

goblet n. a drinking glass with a foot and a stem.

goblin n. a mischievous ugly elf.

Thesaurus

glue-like, mucilaginous.

gluttonous adj. GREEDY, voracious, insatiable, ravenous, gormandizing; informal piggish, hoggish.

gnaw v. CHEW, munch, bite, nibble, masticate, worry.

go v. **1** MOVE, proceed, progress, walk, pass, travel, journey, repair. **2** LEAVE, go away, depart, withdraw, retire, set off, set out, decamp; informal beat it, scram. **3** WORK, be in working order, function, operate, be operative, run, perform. **4** BECOME, grow, get, come to be, turn. **5** BELONG, have a place, fit in, be located, be situated, be found, lie, stand. **6** STOP, cease, disappear, vanish, be no more, fade away, melt away. **7** TURN OUT, work out, fare, progress, develop, result, end, end up, eventuate. **8** MATCH, go together, be compatible, blend, suit each other, complement each other, harmonize, accord, be in accord. ▸ n. TRY, attempt, turn, opportunity, effort, bid, endeavour, essay; informal shot, stab, crack, whirl, whack. □ **go down 1** SINK, submerge, founder, go under. **2** DECREASE, fall, drop, be reduced, decline, plummet. **go far** DO WELL, be successful, succeed, make progress, get on, get ahead, make a name for oneself, advance; informal set the world on fire. **go in for** ENGAGE IN, take part in, participate in, practise, pursue, take up, adopt, espouse, embrace. **go off 1** EXPLODE, detonate, blow up, erupt, burst; informal go bang. **2** GO BAD, go stale, go sour, be rotten.

goad n. STIMULUS, incentive, incitement, inducement, stimulation, impetus, motivation, pressure, spur, jolt, prod, poke. ▸ v. PROMPT, stimulate, induce, motivate, spur, urge, chivvy.

go-ahead n. PERMISSION, authorization, assent, consent, sanction, leave, confirmation, imprimatur; informal green light, OK, okay, thumbs up. ▸ adj. ENTERPRISING, ambitious, pioneering, progressive; informal up-and-coming, go-getting.

goal n. AIM, objective, end, purpose, ambition, target, design, intention, intent,

God n. **1** (in Christianity and some other religions) the creator and supreme ruler of the universe. **2** (**god**) a super-human being or spirit. □ **God-fearing** earnestly religious.

godchild n. a person in relation to a godparent.

god-daughter n. a female godchild.

goddess n. a female god.

godfather n. **1** a male godparent. **2** the male leader of an illegal organization.

godforsaken adj. lacking any merit or attraction.

godhead n. **1** (**the Godhead**) God. **2** divine nature.

godly adj. very religious.

godmother n. a female godparent.

godparent n. a person who promises to be responsible for a child's religious education.

godsend n. a very helpful or welcome thing.

godson n. a male godchild.

goes 3rd person sing. present of GO.

goggle v. stare with wide open eyes. ▶ n. (**goggles**) close-fitting protective glasses.

going n. the condition of the ground as suitable for horse racing or walking. ▶ adj. **1** existing or available. **2** (of a price) current. □ **going concern** a thriving business.

goitre /goy-ter/ n. a swollen neck resulting from an enlarged thyroid gland.

gold n. **1** a yellow precious metal. **2** a deep yellow colour. **3** coins or articles made of gold. □ **goldfish** a small orange carp often kept in ponds and tanks. **gold leaf** gold beaten into a very thin sheet. **gold rush** a rush of people to a place where gold has been discovered. **goldsmith** a person who makes gold articles.

golden adj. **1** made of or like gold. **2** very happy and prosperous. **3** excellent. □ **golden boy** (or **golden girl**) informal a very popular or successful young man or woman. **golden hand-shake** informal a payment given on re-dundancy or early retirement. **golden jubilee** the 50th anniversary of an im-portant event. **golden wedding** the 50th anniversary of a wedding.

golf n. an outdoor game in which a small ball is struck with a club into a series of small holes. ■ **golfer** n.

golliwog n. a soft doll with a black face and fuzzy hair.

gonad n. a bodily organ producing gam-etes.

gondola n. a boat with high-pointed ends and a single oar, used on canals in Venice.

gondolier n. a person who propels a gondola.

gone past part. of GO.

gong n. **1** a metal disc that makes a res-onant sound when struck. **2** informal a medal or award.

gonorrhoea /gon-uh-**ree**-uh/ (US **gon-orrhea**) n. a sexually transmitted dis-ease.

goo n. informal a sticky or slimy substance. ■ **gooey** adj.

good adj. (**better**, **best**) **1** having the right qualities; of a high standard. **2** be-having in a way that is morally right, polite, or obedient. **3** enjoyable or satis-fying. **4** appropriate. **5** beneficial. **6** thorough. ▶ n. **1** that which is right or of benefit. **2** (**goods**) products or possessions. **3** (**goods**) freight. □ **good faith** honesty or sincerity of intention. **good-for-nothing** worthless. **Good Fri-day** the Friday before Easter Sunday, commemorating the Crucifixion of Jesus. **goodwill 1** friendly feeling. **2** the popularity of a business as a sale-able asset. **make good 1** compensate for loss or damage. **2** fulfil a promise. ■ **goodness** n.

goodbye exclam. used to express good

Thesaurus

aspiration, ideal.

go-between n. INTERMEDIARY, mediator, middleman, liaison, contact, messen-ger, agent, broker, medium, dealer, fac-tor, pander.

godforsaken adj. DESOLATE, dismal, dreary, bleak, wretched, miserable, gloomy, deserted, abandoned, forlorn, neglected, remote, backward, in the back of beyond.

godless adj. ATHEISTIC, agnostic, scepti-cal, faithless, pagan, heathen, ungodly, impious, irreligious, unrighteous, sin-ful, wicked, evil, depraved.

godsend n. PIECE OF GOOD FORTUNE, stroke of luck, blessing, boon, windfall, bonanza, gift, benediction. ■ OPPOSITES curse.

goggle v. STARE, gape, gaze, ogle; informal gawk, rubberneck.

good adj. **1** VIRTUOUS, moral, ethical, righteous, right-minded, right-thinking, honourable, upright, honest, high-minded, noble, worthy, admirable, estimable, exemplary. **2** SATISFACTORY, acceptable, passable, tolerable, wishes when parting or ending a conversation.

goody n. (or **goodie**) (pl. **goodies**) informal **1** a good person in a story etc. **2** (**goodies**) pleasant things, esp. to eat. □ **goody-goody** a person who behaves well to impress others.

goose n. (pl. **geese**) **1** a large waterbird with webbed feet. **2** a female goose. □ **gooseflesh** (or **goose pimples**) small raised bumps on the skin caused by cold or fear. **goose step** a marching step with the legs kept straight.

gooseberry n. **1** an edible berry with a hairy skin. **2** informal a third person in the company of two lovers.

gopher n. a burrowing American rodent.

gore n. **1** blood from a wound. **2** a triangular part of a garment, sail, etc. ▶ v. pierce with a horn or tusk.

gorge n. a narrow valley or ravine. ▶ v. eat greedily.

gorgeous adj. **1** beautiful. **2** informal very

pleasant.

gorgon n. **1** a mythical monster able to turn people to stone. **2** an intimidating woman.

gorilla n. a large powerful ape.

gormless adj. informal stupid.

gorse n. a yellow-flowered prickly shrub.

gory adj. **1** involving bloodshed. **2** covered in blood.

gosling n. a young goose.

gospel n. **1** the teachings of Jesus. **2** (**Gospel**) any of the first four books of the New Testament. **3** something absolutely true. **4** a style of black American religious singing.

gossamer n. a fine piece of cobweb. ▶ adj. very fine or flimsy.

gossip n. **1** casual talk about other people. **2** a person who likes gossip. ▶ v. (**gossiping**, **gossiped**) engage in gossip.

got past & past part. of GET.

Gothic adj. **1** of the style of architecture

Thesaurus

adequate, fine, excellent; informal great, hunky-dory, OK. **3** WELL BEHAVED, well mannered, obedient, manageable, tractable, malleable. **4** CORRECT, right, proper, fitting, suitable, appropriate, decorous, seemly. **5** COMPETENT, capable, able, accomplished, skilful, efficient, adept, proficient, expert, excellent, first-rate; informal top-notch, tip-top, A1. **6** FINE, healthy, sound, robust, strong, vigorous. **7** KIND, kindly, kind-hearted, good-hearted, friendly, obliging, well disposed, charitable, gracious, sympathetic, benevolent, altruistic, benign. **8** WHOLESOME, healthy, nutritious, nutritional, beneficial. **9** DELICIOUS, tasty, appetizing; informal scrumptious, yummy. **10** VALID, legitimate, genuine, authentic, sound, bona fide. **11** CONSIDERABLE, substantial, goodly, sizeable, large, sufficient, ample; informal tidy. **12** FINE, fair, mild, clear, bright, cloudless, sunny, calm, balmy, tranquil, clement, halcyon. ■ OPPOSITES bad. ▶ n. **1** BENEFIT, advantage, gain, profit, interest, well-being, welfare. **2** VIRTUE, goodness, righteousness, morality, ethics, rectitude, honour, uprightness, honesty, integrity, probity, worth, merit.

goodbye exclamation FAREWELL, adieu, au revoir; informal bye, bye-bye, see you later, see you, so long, ciao, cheerio, cheers, ta-ta.

good-humoured adj. AMIABLE, affable,

easy-going, genial, cheerful, cheery, happy, pleasant, good-tempered. ■ OPPOSITES grumpy.

good-looking adj. ATTRACTIVE, handsome, pretty, lovely, beautiful, personable, well favoured; old use comely, fair.

goodly adj. CONSIDERABLE, substantial, sizeable, significant, large, great, ample, sufficient; informal tidy. ■ OPPOSITES paltry.

good-natured adj. KIND, kindly, kind-hearted, warm-hearted, generous, benevolent, charitable, friendly, helpful, accommodating, amiable, tolerant.

goods pl. n. PROPERTY, belongings, possessions, effects, things, paraphernalia, chattels, movables, appurtenances, trappings, accoutrements; informal stuff, gear.

gorge n. CHASM, canyon, ravine, abyss, defile, pass, cleft, crevice, rift, fissure.

gorgeous adj. **1** BEAUTIFUL, attractive, lovely, good-looking, sexy; informal stunning. **2** SPLENDID, magnificent, superb, grand, impressive, sumptuous, imposing, dazzling, brilliant, glittering, breathtaking.

gory adj. BLOODY, bloodstained, horrific, violent, bloodthirsty, brutal, murderous, savage.

gossip n. **1** RUMOURS, scandal, tittle-tattle, hearsay, whispering campaign; informal mud-slinging, dirt. **2** GOSSIP-MONGER, rumour-monger, scandalmonger, busybody, babbler, chatterer, pratcommon in western Europe in the 12th–16th centuries. **2** very gloomy or horrifying.

gouache /goo-ash/ n. **1** a method of painting using watercolours thickened with glue. **2** paint of this kind.

gouge v. cut out roughly. ▶n. a chisel with a concave blade.

goulash n. a rich Hungarian stew of meat and vegetables.

gourd n. a hard-skinned fleshy fruit of a climbing plant, esp. when hollowed and used as a container.

gourmand n. a person who enjoys eating.

gourmet /gor-may/ n. a person knowledgeable about good food.

gout n. a disease causing swollen painful joints.

govern v. **1** conduct the policy and affairs of a state etc. **2** control or influence. ■ **governance** n. **governor** n.

governess n. a woman employed to teach children in a private household.

government n. **1** the governing body of a state. **2** the system by which a state is governed. ■ **governmental** adj.

gown n. **1** a long dress. **2** a protective overgarment. **3** an official robe.

GP abbrev. general practitioner.

grab v. (**grabbed**, **grabbing**) seize suddenly and roughly. ▶n. a sudden attempt to seize.

grace n. **1** elegance of movement. **2** polite respect. **3** (**graces**) attractive behaviour. **4** unearned favour, esp. from God. **5** a period allowed to do something. **6** a short prayer of thanks for a meal. ▶v. **1** honour by one's presence. **2** be an ornament to. ■ **graceful** adj. **gracefully** adv. **gracefulness** n. **graceless** adj.

gracious adj. polite, kind, and pleasant, esp. to those of lower status. ■ **graciously** adv.

gradation n. **1** a scale of successive stages. **2** a stage in a such a scale.

grade n. **1** a level of rank or quality. **2** a mark indicating the quality of a student's work. **3** US a class in school. ▶v. arrange in or allocate to grades. ☐ **make the grade** informal succeed.

gradient n. **1** a slope. **2** the degree to which ground slopes.

Thesaurus

tler. ▶v. SPREAD RUMOURS, chat, chit-chat, blather, blether, talk, tattle, babble, gabble, prattle, prate; informal chin-wag, jaw, yack.

gouge v. DIG, incise, chisel, gash, scoop, hollow.

govern v. **1** RULE, reign over, be in power over, exercise control over, hold sway over, preside over, administer, lead, be in charge of, control, command, direct, order, guide, manage, conduct, oversee, supervise, superintend, pilot, steer. **2** CONTROL, restrain, keep in check, check, curb, hold back, keep back, rein in, bridle, subdue, constrain, arrest, contain. **3** DETERMINE, decide, sway, rule, influence, have an influence on, be a factor in.

government n. ADMINISTRATION, regime, parliament, ministry, executive, rule, leadership, command, direction, control, guidance, management, conduct, supervision, superintendence.

gown n. DRESS, frock, garment, costume, garb, habit.

grab v. **1** GRASP, clutch, grip, clasp, lay hold of, catch hold of, take hold of, fasten upon; informal collar. **2** SEIZE, snatch, pluck, snap up, appropriate, capture; informal bag, nab.

grace n. **1** ELEGANCE, refinement, charm, attractiveness, beauty, loveliness, pol-

ish, suaveness, culture, cultivation, good taste, taste, tastefulness, smoothness, suppleness, fluidity. **2** MANNERS, courtesy, decency, consideration, tact, breeding, decorum, propriety. **3** FAVOUR, good will, generosity, kindness, kindliness, indulgence, benefaction, mercy, mercifulness, compassion, clemency. **4** BLESSING, prayer, thanksgiving, thanks, benediction. ▶v. ADORN, decorate, ornament, embellish, enhance, beautify, prettify, set off, deck.

graceful adj. ELEGANT, refined, smooth, agile, flowing, nimble, cultured, cultivated, polished, suave, charming, appealing, attractive, beautiful, lovely; old use comely. ■ OPPOSITES inelegant.

gracious adj. **1** COURTEOUS, cordial, kindly, kind-hearted, warm-hearted, benevolent, friendly, amiable, considerate, affable, pleasant, polite, civil, well mannered, chivalrous, charitable, indulgent, obliging, accommodating, beneficent, benign. **2** ELEGANT, tasteful, comfortable, luxurious. **3** MERCIFUL, compassionate, gentle, mild, humane, clement.

grade n. **1** LEVEL, degree, stage, echelon, rank, standing, station, position, order, class. **2** CATEGORY, class, classification, type, brand. **3** GRADIENT, slope, incline, hill, rise, bank, declivity. ▶v. CLASSIFY,

gradual adj. **1** taking place in stages over time. **2** (of a slope) not steep. ■ **gradually** adv.

graduate n. a person awarded a first academic degree. ▶v. **1** successfully complete a degree or course. **2** arrange or mark out in gradations. **3** change gradually. ■ **graduation** n.

graffiti n. writings or drawings on a surface in a public place.

··

☑ In Italian, **graffiti** is a plural noun, but in English it is generally treated as a normal singular noun.

··

graft n. **1** a shoot from one plant inserted into another to form a new growth. **2** a piece of living bodily tissue transplanted surgically. **3** hard work. ▶v. **1** insert or transplant as a graft. **2** work hard.

Grail n. (in medieval legend) the cup or bowl used by Jesus at the Last Supper.

grain n. **1** cultivated cereal used as food. **2** a single seed of a cereal. **3** a small, hard particle. **4** a unit of weight. **5** the arrangement of fibres in wood etc. □ **against the grain** contrary to one's instinct. ■ **grainy** adj.

gram (or **gramme**) n. one thousandth of a kilogram.

grammar n. **1** the whole system and structure of a language. **2** knowledge and use of the rules of grammar. **3** a book on grammar.

··

☑ -ar, not -er: grammar.

··

grammatical adj. conforming to the rules of grammar. ■ **grammatically** adv.

gramophone n. dated a record player.

grampus n. (pl. **grampuses**) a dolphin-like sea animal.

gran n. informal one's grandmother.

granary n. (pl. **granaries**) a storehouse for grain.

grand adj. **1** large and impressive. **2** ambitious in scale. **3** of the highest importance or rank. **4** informal excellent. ▶n. **1** informal a thousand dollars or pounds. **2** a grand piano. □ **grand piano** a large piano with a horizontal body and strings. **grand slam** the winning of all the major championships in a sport in the same year. **grandstand** the main stand at a sports ground. ■ **grandly** adv.

grandad n. informal one's grandfather.

grandchild n. a child of one's son or daughter.

granddaughter n. the daughter of one's son or daughter.

grandeur n. **1** splendour and impressiveness. **2** high rank or social status.

grandfather n. the father of one's father or mother. □ **grandfather clock** a clock in a tall wooden case.

grandiloquent adj. using pompous language.

grandiose adj. impressive or ambitious in scale.

grandma n. informal one's grandmother.

grandmother n. the mother of one's father or mother.

grandpa n. informal one's grandfather.

grandparent n. a grandmother or

Thesaurus

··

class, categorize, sort, group, order, brand, size, rank, evaluate, rate, value, range, graduate.

gradient n. SLOPE, incline, hill, rise, bank, acclivity, declivity, grade.

gradual adj. PROGRESSIVE, regular, steady, even, moderate, slow, measured, unhurried, step-by-step, successive, continuous, systematic. ■ OPPOSITES sudden, abrupt.

gradually adv. SLOWLY, steadily, moderately, evenly, bit by bit, little by little, by degrees, step by step, inch by inch, piece by piece, drop by drop.

graduate v. **1** TAKE A DEGREE, receive one's degree, become a graduate. **2** MARK OFF, measure off, divide into degrees, grade, calibrate. **3** MOVE UP, progress, advance, gain promotion, be promoted.

graft n. **1** SHOOT, bud, scion, new growth, slip, sprout, splice. **2** TRANSPLANT, implant, implantation.

grain n. **1** PARTICLE, granule, bit, piece, scrap, crumb, fragment, morsel, speck, trace, scintilla, mite, iota. **2** TEXTURE, weave, fibre, pattern, nap.

grand adj. **1** IMPRESSIVE, imposing, magnificent, splendid, superb, striking, palatial, stately, large, monumental, majestic. **2** SPLENDID, sumptuous, lavish, luxurious, magnificent, opulent, princely. **3** GREAT, noble, aristocratic, distinguished, august, illustrious, eminent, elevated, esteemed, celebrated, preeminent, leading, prominent, notable, renowned, famous. ■ OPPOSITES unimpressive, lowly.

grandiose adj. **1** OVERAMBITIOUS, ambitious, extravagant, high-flown, highgrandfather.

grandson n. the son of one's son or daughter.

grange n. a country house with farm buildings attached.

granite n. a very hard grey rock.

granny (or **grannie**) n. (pl. **grannies**) informal one's grandmother. □ **granny flat** a self-contained part of a house suitable for an elderly relative to live in.

grant v. **1** agree to give or allow. **2** give formally or legally. **3** admit to be true. ▶ n. a sum of money given from public funds for a particular purpose. □ **take for granted 1** fail to appreciate. **2** assume to be true.

granulated adj. in the form of granules.

granule n. a small particle or grain. ■ **granular** adj.

grape n. a green or purple berry, used for making wine. □ **grapevine 1** a vine bearing grapes. **2** (**the grapevine**) the spreading of information through talk or rumour.

grapefruit n. a large round yellow citrus fruit.

graph n. a diagram showing the relation between variable quantities.

graphic adj. **1** of visual art, esp. drawing, engraving, or lettering. **2** giving vividly explicit detail. ▶ n. **1** a pictorial image or symbol on a computer screen. **2** (**graphics**) the use of designs or pictures to illustrate books etc. □ **graphic equalizer** a device for controlling the strength and quality of selected frequency bands. ■ **graphically** adv.

graphite n. a form of carbon.

graphology n. the study of handwriting. ■ **graphologist** n.

grapnel n. a grappling hook.

grapple v. wrestle. □ **grappling hook** (or **iron**) a device with iron claws for dragging or grasping.

grasp v. **1** seize and hold firmly. **2** understand fully. **3** (**grasping**) greedy. ▶ n. **1** a firm grip. **2** understanding.

grass n. **1** a short plant with long narrow leaves. **2** ground covered with grass. **3** informal cannabis. **4** informal an informer. ▶ v. **1** cover with grass. **2** informal act as an informer. □ **grasshopper** a jumping insect that makes a chirping sound. **grass roots** ordinary people in an organization or society, rather than the leaders. ■ **grassy** adj.

grate v. **1** shred food by rubbing it on a grater. **2** make an unpleasant scraping sound. **3** have an irritating effect. ▶ n. a metal frame keeping fuel in a fireplace.

grateful adj. feeling or showing gratitude. ■ **gratefully** adv.

grater n. a device having a surface covered with sharp-edged holes, used for grating food.

gratify v. (**gratifying**, **gratified**) **1** give pleasure or satisfaction. **2** satisfy a wish. ■ **gratification** n.

grating n. a screen of parallel or crossed

Thesaurus

sounding, pompous, flamboyant, pretentious; informal OTT. **2** GRAND, impressive, magnificent, imposing, striking, splendid, superb, stately, majestic. ■ OPPOSITES modest.

grant v. **1** AGREE TO, consent to, assent to, accede to, permit, give one's permission for, allow, concede, accord, vouchsafe. **2** ACKNOWLEDGE, concede, accept, cede, yield, go along with. ▶ n. AWARD, endowment, contribution, donation, allowance, subsidy, allocation, allotment, gift, present, subvention, sponsorship, honorarium, bursary.

granule n. GRAIN, particle, fragment, crumb, bit, scrap, molecule, atom, mite, iota, jot.

graphic adj. VIVID, striking, expressive, descriptive, illustrative, lively, forcible, detailed, well defined, well drawn, telling, effective, cogent, clear, lucid, explicit. ■ OPPOSITES dull.

grapple v. **1** FIGHT WITH, wrestle with, struggle with, tussle with, clash with, engage with, close with, battle with, combat with, brawl with. **2** TACKLE, face, cope with, deal with, handle, manage, confront, address oneself to, attack, get down to, come to grips with.

grasp v. **1** GRIP, clutch, hold, clasp, clench, grab, snatch, get/take hold of, seize. **2** UNDERSTAND, comprehend, follow, see, take in, realize, perceive; informal get, get the picture, get the drift, catch on.

grasping adj. GREEDY, acquisitive, avaricious, rapacious, covetous, mean, parsimonious, niggardly, penny-pinching, selfish, possessive; informal grabby, tightfisted, stingy. ■ OPPOSITES generous.

grate v. **1** SHRED, pulverize, mince, grind, granulate, triturate. **2** RASP, scrape, jar, scratch, grind, creak, rub, grit. **3** IRRITATE, annoy, jar on, irk, vex, gall, rankle with, anger, rile, exasperate, chafe, rub up the wrong way; informal set someone's teeth on edge, get on someone's nerves, aggravate.

bars over an opening.

gratis adv. & adj. free of charge.

gratitude n. appreciation of kindness; thankfulness.

gratuitous adj. without reason. ■ **gratuitously** adv.

gratuity n. (pl. **gratuities**) a tip given to a waiter etc.

grave n. a hole dug to bury a corpse. ▶ adj. **1** giving cause for alarm or concern. **2** solemn. □ **gravestone** a stone slab marking a grave. **graveyard** a burial ground. ■ **gravely** adv.

grave accent /grahv/ n. the accent (`).

gravel n. small stones, used for paths etc.

gravelly adj. **1** made of gravel. **2** rough-sounding.

graven adj. engraved.

gravitate v. be drawn towards.

gravitation n. movement towards a centre of gravity. ■ **gravitational** adj.

gravity n. **1** the force that attracts a body towards the centre of the earth. **2** seriousness. **3** solemnity.

gravy n. (pl. **gravies**) a sauce made from the fat and juices from cooked meat. □ **gravy train** informal an easy way of making money.

gray US = GREY.

graze v. **1** eat grass in a field. **2** injure by scraping the skin. **3** touch lightly in passing. ▶ n. a grazed area on the skin.

grease n. a fatty or oily substance. ▶ v. smear or lubricate with grease. □ **greasepaint** make-up used by actors. ■ **greasy** adj.

great adj. **1** considerably above average in size, intensity, ability, quality, or importance. **2** informal excellent. **3** (**great-**) (of a family relationship) one generation removed in ancestry or descent. ■ **greatness** n.

greatly adv. very much.

Thesaurus

grateful adj. THANKFUL, appreciative, obliged, indebted, obligated, beholden, filled with gratitude. ■ OPPOSITES ungrateful.

gratify v. PLEASE, make happy, delight, give pleasure to, gladden, satisfy, thrill; informal warm the cockles of the heart.

gratitude n. GRATEFULNESS, thankfulness, thanks, appreciation, thanksgiving, indebtedness, acknowledgement, recognition, sense of obligation. ■ OPPOSITES ingratitude.

gratuitous adj. **1** UNPROVOKED, unjustified, groundless, without cause, without reason, unfounded, baseless, uncalled for, unwarranted, unmerited, needless, unnecessary, superfluous. **2** FREE, complimentary, voluntary, unpaid, unrewarded, unasked for, without charge, at no cost.

gratuity n. TIP, bonus, gift, present, donation, reward, recompense, largesse.

grave adj. **1** SOLEMN, serious, earnest, sober, sombre, severe, unsmiling, long-faced, stony-faced, grim-faced, grim, gloomy, preoccupied, thoughtful, pensive, subdued, muted, quiet, dignified, sedate, dour, staid. **2** SERIOUS, important, significant, weighty, momentous, urgent, pressing, vital, crucial, life-and-death, acute, pivotal, perilous, hazardous, dangerous, threatening. ■ OPPOSITES carefree, trivial.

graveyard n. CEMETERY, burial ground, churchyard, memorial park, necropolis, charnel house; informal boneyard; US informal potter's field.

gravitate v. **1** MOVE TOWARDS, head towards, be drawn to, be pulled towards, be attracted to, drift towards, lean towards, incline towards. **2** SINK, fall, drop, descend, precipitate, be precipitated, settle.

gravity n. **1** SOLEMNITY, seriousness, earnestness, sobriety, sombreness, severity, grimness, thoughtfulness, pensiveness, sedateness, dignity, dourness, staidness. **2** SERIOUSNESS, importance, momentousness, weightiness, acuteness, criticalness, consequence, perilousness, peril, hazard, danger.

graze v. **1** BRUSH, touch, rub, glance off, shave, skim, kiss. **2** SCRAPE, abrade, skin, scratch, chafe, bark, scuff, bruise, contuse.

greasy adj. **1** FATTY, fat, oily, buttery, oleaginous, sebaceous, adipose. **2** SLIPPERY, slippy, slimy. **3** SLIMY, oily, unctuous, smooth, smooth-tongued, glib, suave, slick, fawning, ingratiating, grovelling, sycophantic, toadying, flattering, gushing; informal smarmy.

great adj. **1** LARGE, big, extensive, vast, immense, boundless, unlimited, huge, spacious, enormous, gigantic, colossal, mammoth, monstrous, prodigious, tremendous, stupendous. **2** MAJOR, main, most important, leading, chief, principal, capital, paramount, primary. **3** IMPRESSIVE, grand, magnificent, imposing, splendid, majestic, glorious, sumptuous. **4** PROMINENT, eminent, pre-eminent, distinguished, illustrious, august, cele-

grebe n. a diving bird.

Grecian adj. of ancient Greece, esp. its architecture.

greed n. excessive desire for food, wealth, or power. ■ **greedily** adv. **greedy** adj.

Greek n. **1** a person from Greece. **2** the ancient or modern language of Greece. ▶ adj. of Greece or its language.

green adj. **1** of a colour between blue and yellow, as of grass. **2** covered with grass. **3** (**Green**) concerned with protecting the environment. **4** inexperienced or naive. ▶ n. **1** green colour. **2** a piece of public grassy land. **3** (**greens**) green vegetables. **4** (**Green**) a supporter of a Green political party. □ **green belt** an area of open land round a city, on which building is restricted. **green card** (in the US) a permit allowing a foreigner to live and work permanently in the US. **green fingers** informal skill in growing plants. **greenfly** a green aphid. **greengage** a sweet greenish plum-like fruit. **greengrocer** a person selling fruit and vegetables. **green light** permission to go ahead with a project. **Green Paper** a preliminary report of government proposals. **green room** a room in a theatre used by performers when not on stage. **greenstick fracture** a partial break in a bone. ■ **greenish** adj. **greenness** n.

greenery n. green leaves or plants.

greenhouse n. a glass building for protecting young plants from cold weather. □ **greenhouse effect** the tendency of atmospheric temperature to rise because certain gases absorb infrared radiation from the earth. **greenhouse gas** a gas that contributes to the greenhouse effect.

greet v. **1** meet with friendliness or expressions of welcome. **2** react to in a particular way. ■ **greeting** n.

gregarious adj. **1** fond of company. **2** living in flocks or colonies.

gremlin n. a mischievous sprite regarded as responsible for mechanical faults.

grenade n. a small bomb thrown by hand or launched mechanically.

grenadier n. hist. a soldier armed with grenades.

grew past of GROW.

grey (US **gray**) adj. **1** of a colour between black and white, as of ash. **2** (of weather) cloudy and dull. **3** lacking interest or character. ▶ n. grey colour. ▶ v. (of hair) become grey. □ **grey area** a situation that does not fit easily into existing categories. **greyhound** a swift, slender breed of dog used in racing. **grey matter** informal the brain. ■ **greyish** adj. **greyness** n.

grid n. **1** a grating. **2** a network of crossed lines forming a series of squares. **3** a network of cables or pipes. □ **gridiron 1** a frame of metal bars for

Thesaurus

brated, renowned, noted, notable, noteworthy, famous, famed, leading, top, high, high-ranking, noble. **5** GIFTED, talented, outstanding, remarkable, exceptional, first-rate, incomparable, expert, skilful, skilled, able, masterly, adept, proficient, adroit; informal crack, ace. **6** EXCELLENT, enjoyable, marvellous, wonderful, first-class, first-rate, fine, very good, admirable; informal fab, super.

greatly adv. VERY MUCH, considerably, to a great extent, extremely, exceedingly, vastly, enormously, immensely, tremendously, hugely, markedly, mightily, remarkably, abundantly.

greed n. **1** GLUTTONY, voraciousness, voracity, ravenousness, insatiability; informal hoggishness, piggishness. **2** AVARICE, acquisitiveness, rapacity, covetousness, cupidity, miserliness, parsimony; informal tight-fistedness. **3** DESIRE, eagerness, avidity, hunger, hankering, craving, longing, enthusiasm, impatience.

greedy adj. **1** GLUTTONOUS, voracious,

ravenous, ravening, famished, gourmandizing, insatiable, omnivorous; informal piggish, hoggish, gutsy; old use esurient. **2** AVARICIOUS, acquisitive, grasping, rapacious, grabbing, covetous, miserly, hoarding, niggardly, close-fisted, parsimonious; informal grabby, money-grubbing, tight-fisted. **3** EAGER, hungry, avid, desirous, anxious, impatient, enthusiastic, longing, craving. ■ OPPOSITES generous.

greenhouse n. HOTHOUSE, glasshouse, conservatory.

greet v. SAY HELLO TO, address, salute, hail, nod to, wave to, raise one's hat to, acknowledge, accost, receive, meet, welcome.

greeting n. HELLO, salute, salutation, address, nod, wave, acknowledgement, welcome.

greetings pl. n. GOOD WISHES, best wishes, regards, kind regards, congratulations, compliments, respects.

grey adj. **1** CLOUDY, overcast, dull, dark, sunless, gloomy, dim, dreary, dismal, grilling food over an open fire. **2** a field for American football. **gridlock** a traffic jam affecting a network of intersecting streets.

griddle n. an iron plate for cooking food.

grief n. deep sorrow.

grievance n. a cause for complaint.

grieve v. suffer or cause grief.

grievous adj. very severe or serious. □ **grievous bodily harm** the offence of deliberately inflicting serious physical injury. ■ **grievously** adv.

griffin (or **gryphon**) n. a mythical creature with an eagle's head and wings and a lion's body.

griffon n. **1** a small dog like a terrier. **2** a vulture.

grill n. **1** a device on a cooker for directing heat downwards. **2** food cooked using a grill. ▶v. **1** cook with a grill. **2** informal interrogate.

grille n. a grating.

grim adj. (**grimmer**, **grimmest**) **1** very serious or gloomy. **2** depressing or unappealing. ■ **grimly** adv. **grimness** n.

grimace n. a twisted facial expression, showing disgust, pain, or amusement. ▶v. make a grimace.

grime n. ingrained dirt. ■ **grimy** adj.

grin v. (**grinning**, **grinned**) smile broadly. ▶n. a broad smile.

grind v. (**grinding**, **ground**) **1** crush into small particles or powder. **2** sharpen or smooth by friction. **3** rub together gratingly. **4** (**grind down**) oppress cruelly. ▶n. hard dull work. □ **grindstone** a revolving disc for sharpening or polishing metal objects.

grip v. (**gripping**, **gripped**) **1** hold firmly. **2** hold the attention of. ▶n. **1** a firm hold. **2** understanding. **3** a part by which something is held.

gripe v. informal grumble. ▶n. **1** informal a trivial complaint. **2** pain in the stomach or intestines.

grisly adj. (**grislier**, **grisliest**) causing horror or revulsion.

grist n. grain to be ground. □ **grist to the mill** useful experience or knowledge.

gristle n. tough inedible tissue in meat. ■ **gristly** adj.

grit n. **1** particles of stone or sand. **2** courage and determination. ▶v. (**grit-**

Thesaurus

cheerless, depressing, misty, foggy, murky. **2** DULL, uninteresting, boring, characterless, anonymous, colourless. **3** UNCLEAR, doubtful, uncertain, indistinct, mixed.

grief n. SORROW, mourning, mournfulness, bereavement, lamentation, misery, sadness, anguish, pain, distress, agony, suffering, affliction, heartache, heartbreak, broken-heartedness, heaviness of heart, trouble, woe, tribulation, desolation, trial, despondency, dejection, despair, remorse, regret. ■ OPPOSITES joy, delight.

grievance n. **1** COMPLAINT, protest, charge, moan, axe to grind, bone to pick; informal grouse, gripe, beef. **2** INJUSTICE, unfairness, injury, damage, hardship, offence, affront, insult.

grieve v. **1** MOURN, lament, be sorrowful, sorrow, be sad, weep and wail, cry, sob, suffer, ache, be in anguish, be distressed, bemoan, bewail; informal eat one's heart out. **2** HURT, wound, pain, sadden, break someone's heart, upset, distress, cause suffering to, crush. ■ OPPOSITES rejoice.

grim adj. **1** STERN, forbidding, fierce, formidable, threatening, ferocious, menacing, harsh, sombre, cross, crabbed, churlish, morose, surly, ill-tempered, sour, implacable, cruel, ruthless, merci-

less. **2** RESOLUTE, determined, firm, decided, obstinate, adamant, unyielding, unwavering, unfaltering, unshakeable, obdurate, inflexible, unrelenting, relentless, inexorable, dead set. **3** DREADFUL, horrible, horrendous, terrible, horrid, dire, ghastly, awful, appalling, frightful, shocking, unspeakable, harrowing, grisly, hideous, gruesome, macabre. ■ OPPOSITES amiable.

grimy adj. DIRTY, grubby, stained, soiled, dusty, sooty, muddy, filthy, besmeared; literary besmirched. ■ OPPOSITES clean.

grind v. **1** CRUSH, pound, pulverize, mill, powder, granulate, crumble, mash, smash, triturate, kibble, levigate. **2** SHARPEN, file, whet, smooth, polish, sand. **3** GNASH, grit, grate, scrape, rasp. □ **grind down** OPPRESS, persecute, illtreat, torture, torment, harass, harry.

grip v. **1** GRASP, clutch, hold, clasp, clench, take/lay hold of, grab, seize, catch, latch on to. **2** ABSORB, engross, rivet, spellbind, hold spellbound, entrance, fascinate, enthral, hold, catch, mesmerize, hypnotize, compel. ▶n. **1** GRASP, clutch, clasp, clench, handshake, clinch. **2** UNDERSTANDING, comprehension, awareness, perception.

grisly adj. GRUESOME, frightful, horrifying, horrid, grim, horrendous, awful, dreadful, terrible, fearful, disgusting,

ting, **gritted**) **1** clench the teeth with determination. **2** spread grit on an icy road. ■ **grittiness** n. **gritty** adj.

grizzle v. informal cry fretfully.

grizzled adj. grey-haired.

grizzly bear n. a large brown bear.

groan v. **1** make a deep sound of pain or despair. **2** make a low creaking sound. ▶n. a groaning sound.

grocer n. a person selling food and household goods.

grocery n. (pl. **groceries**) **1** a grocer's shop. **2** (**groceries**) items of food sold in a grocer's shop or supermarket.

grog n. spirits mixed with water.

groggy adj. dazed and unsteady. ■ **groggily** adv.

groin n. **1** the area between the abdomen and the thigh. **2** a curved edge formed by two intersecting roof arches. **3** US = GROYNE.

grommet n. **1** a protective metal ring or eyelet. **2** a tube implanted in the eardrum to drain the ear.

groom v. **1** brush and clean the coat of an animal. **2** prepare or train for a particular activity. ▶n. **1** a person employed to take care of horses. **2** a bridegroom.

groove n. **1** a long, narrow channel. **2** a spiral track in a record. **3** a fixed routine. ■ **grooved** adj.

grope v. feel about with the hands.

gross adj. **1** unattractively large. **2** vulgar. **3** informal very unpleasant. **4** (of income etc.) without deductions; total. ▶v. produce or earn as gross profit. ▶n. (pl. **gross**) twelve dozen. ■ **grossly** adv. **grossness** n.

grotesque adj. comically or repulsively ugly or distorted. ▶n. a grotesque figure or image. ■ **grotesquely** adv.

grotto n. (pl. **grottoes** or **grottos**) a small cave.

grouch n. informal **1** a grumpy person. **2** a complaint. ■ **grouchy** adj.

ground[1] n. **1** the solid surface of the earth. **2** land or soil of a specified kind. **3** an area of land or sea with a specified use. **4** (**grounds**) an area of enclosed land surrounding a large house. **5** (**grounds**) good reasons for doing something. **6** (**grounds**) coffee dregs. ▶v. **1** ban or prevent from flying. **2** (**be grounded in**/**on**) have as a basis. □ **ground-breaking** innovative; pioneering. **groundnut** a peanut. **ground rent** rent paid by the owner of a building to the owner of the land on which it is built. **groundsheet** a waterproof sheet spread on the ground inside a tent. **groundsman** a person employed to look after a sports ground. **groundswell** a build-up of public opinion. **groundwork** preliminary or basic work.

ground[2] past & past part. of GRIND.

grounding n. basic training or instruc-

Thesaurus

hideous, repulsive, revolting, repugnant, repellent, macabre, spine-chilling, sickening, appalling, loathsome, abhorrent, odious, abominable. ■ OPPOSITES pleasant.

grit n. **1** GRAVEL, sand, dust, dirt. **2** PLUCK, courage, bravery, mettle, backbone, spirit, gameness, fortitude, toughness, determination, resolution, tenacity; informal guts, spunk, bottle.

groan v. **1** MOAN, cry, call out, sigh, murmur, whine, whimper. **2** COMPLAIN, grumble, object, lament; informal moan, grouse, gripe, beef, bellyache, bitch. **3** CREAK, grate, squeak, screech.

groove n. **1** CHANNEL, furrow, trench, trough, canal, gouge, rut, gutter, cutting, cut, score, rabbet, rebate. **2** RUT, routine, habit, treadmill, daily grind.

grope v. **1** FEEL, fumble, move blindly, pick. **2** FUMBLE FOR, fish for, scrabble for, cast about for, search for, hunt for, look for.

gross adj. **1** OBESE, massive, huge, immense, colossal, big, large, overweight, fat, corpulent, bloated, bulky, lumpish, cumbersome, unwieldy; informal hulking. **2** COARSE, crude, vulgar, obscene, rude, lewd, ribald, bawdy, dirty, filthy, smutty, earthy, risqué, indecent, indelicate, improper, unseemly, impure, offensive, sexual, sensual, pornographic; informal blue. **3** BOORISH, loutish, oafish, coarse, vulgar, crass, ignorant, unrefined, unsophisticated, uncultured, uncultivated, undiscriminating, tasteless, insensitive, unfeeling, imperceptive, callous; informal yobbish. **4** FLAGRANT, blatant, glaring, outrageous, shocking, serious, egregious, manifest, obvious, plain, apparent. **5** TOTAL, whole, entire, aggregate, before deductions, before tax. ▶v. EARN, make, bring in, take home, rake in.

grotesque adj. **1** BIZARRE, weird, outlandish, freakish, strange, odd, peculiar, unnatural, surreal, macabre, queer, fantastic, fanciful, ridiculous, ludicrous, absurd, incongruous, preposterous, extravagant. **2** DISTORtion in a subject.

groundless adj. not based on any good reason.

group n. **1** a number of people or things gathered or classed together. **2** a band of pop musicians or singers. ▶v. place in or form a group or groups.

grouse n. **1** (pl. **grouse**) a game bird. **2** a complaint. ▶v. grumble.

grout n. a paste for filling gaps between tiles. ▶v. fill between tiles with grout.

grove n. a group of trees.

grovel v. (**grovelling, grovelled**; US **groveling, groveled**) **1** crouch or crawl on the ground. **2** act humbly to obtain forgiveness or favour.

grow v. (**growing, grew**; past part. **grown**) **1** (of a living thing) develop and get bigger. **2** cultivate a crop. **3** in-crease in size or amount. **4** become gradually or increasingly. **5** (**grow up**) become adult. **6** (**grow on**) gradually start to appeal to. □ **grown-up** (an) adult. ■ **grower** n.

growl v. (of a dog) make a low hostile sound in the throat. ▶n. a growling sound.

growth n. **1** the process of growing. **2** something that has grown or is grow-ing. **3** a tumour.

groyne (US **groin**) n. a low wall built out into the sea to prevent erosion.

grub n. **1** the larva of an insect. **2** informal food. ▶v. (**grubbing, grubbed**) dig shallowly in soil.

grubby adj. (**grubbier, grubbiest**) dirty. ■ **grubbiness** n.

grudge n. a long-lasting feeling of re-

Thesaurus

TED, misshapen, twisted, deformed, mal-formed, misproportioned. ■ OPPOSITES normal.

ground n. **1** EARTH, floor, terra firma; in-formal deck. **2** SOIL, earth, dirt, land, ter-rain, clay, turf, loam, clod, sod, dust. **3** PITCH, stadium, field, arena, park. *See also* GROUNDS. ▶v. **1** BASE, establish, set-tle, set, found. **2** TEACH, instruct, train, tutor, coach, educate, drill, school, pre-pare, familiarize with, acquaint with, inform.

groundless adj. WITHOUT BASIS, baseless, without foundation, unfounded, unsup-ported, imaginary, illusory, false, unsubstantiated, unwarranted, unjusti-fied, unjustifiable, uncalled for, unpro-voked, without cause/reason, unreason-able, irrational, illogical, empty, idle, chimerical.

grounds pl. n. **1** SURROUNDINGS, land, property, estate, acres, lawns, gardens, park, parkland, area, domain, holding, territory. **2** REASON, cause, basis, base, foundation, justification, call, rationale, argument, premise, occasion, factor, ex-cuse, pretext, motive, inducement. **3** DREGS, deposit, lees, sediment, pre-cipitate, settlings, grouts.

group n. **1** SET, lot, category, classifica-tion, class, batch, family, species, genus, bracket. **2** COMPANY, band, party, body, gathering, congregation, assem-bly, collection, bunch, cluster, crowd, flock, pack, troop, gang, batch. **3** FAC-TION, set, coterie, clique, circle. **4** SOCI-ETY, association, league, guild, circle, club, work party. ▶v. **1** CLASSIFY, class, categorize, sort, grade, rank, bracket. **2** ASSEMBLE, collect, gather together, ar-range, organize, marshal, range, line up, dispose. **3** COLLECT, gather, assem-ble, cluster. **4** GET TOGETHER, band to-gether, associate, consort.

grouse v. COMPLAIN, grumble, groan, pro-test; informal moan, gripe, bellyache, beef, bitch, grouch, whinge.

grovel v. **1** ABASE ONESELF, toady, fawn, flatter, curry favour, humble oneself, kowtow, bow and scrape, lick someone's boots; informal crawl, butter someone up. **2** PROSTRATE ONESELF, fall on one's knees, crawl, creep, kneel, slither.

grow v. **1** GET BIGGER, get larger, get tall-er, stretch, lengthen, heighten, enlarge, extend, expand, spread, thicken, widen, fill out, swell, increase, multiply. **2** DE-VELOP, sprout, shoot up, spring up, ger-minate, bud, burgeon, flourish, thrive, pullulate. **3** FLOURISH, thrive, prosper, succeed, progress, make progress, make headway, advance, improve, expand. **4** ARISE, originate, stem, issue, spring. **5** BECOME, come to be, get to be, get, turn, wax. **6** PRODUCE, cultivate, farm, propagate, raise. ■ OPPOSITES shrink.

grown-up n. ADULT, grown man, man, grown woman, woman, mature man/ woman.

growth n. **1** INCREASE, expansion, en-largement, development, augmentation, proliferation, multiplication, extension, evolution, magnification, amplification, growing, deepening, heightening, widening, thickening, broadening, swelling, aggrandizement. **2** DEVELOP-MENT, maturation, germination, bur-geoning, sprouting, shooting up, bloom-ing, vegetation, pullulation. **3** EXPANsentiment or ill will. ▶ v. **1** be unwilling to give or allow. **2** resent. ■ **grudgingly** adv.

gruel n. thin porridge.

gruelling (US **grueling**) adj. very tiring.

gruesome adj. causing repulsion or horror.

gruff adj. **1** (of a voice) rough and low. **2** abrupt in manner. ■ **gruffly** adv. **gruffness** n.

grumble v. **1** complain in a bad-tempered way. **2** rumble. ▶ n. a complaint.

grumpy adj. bad-tempered and sulky. ■ **grumpily** adv. **grumpiness** n.

grunge n. a style of rock music with a raucous guitar sound. ■ **grungy** adj.

grunt v. & n. (make) a low, short sound.

gryphon var. of GRIFFIN.

G-string n. a skimpy pair of knickers consisting of a narrow strip of cloth attached to a waistband.

gite /zheet/ n. a small holiday house in France.

guano /gwah-noh/ n. the excrement of seabirds, used as fertilizer.

guarantee n. **1** a formal promise to do something or that a product is of a specified quality. **2** something offered as security. ▶ v. give a guarantee for.

guarantor n. a person or organization that gives a guarantee.

guard v. **1** watch over in order to protect or control. **2** take precautions. ▶ n. **1** a person or group guarding or keeping watch. **2** a defensive posture or device. **3** a state of vigilance. **4** an official who rides on and is in general charge of a train.

guarded adj. cautious.

guardian n. **1** a defender or protector. **2** a person legally responsible for someone unable to manage their own affairs. ■ **guardianship** n.

guava /gwah-vuh/ n. a tropical fruit.

gudgeon n. **1** a small freshwater fish. **2** a pivot or socket.

guerrilla (or **guerilla**) n. a member of a small independent group fighting against the government or regular forces.

guess v. estimate or suppose without enough information to be sure. ▶ n. an estimate. □ **guesswork** guessing.

Thesaurus

SION, rise, progress, success, advance, advancement, improvement, headway. **4** TUMOUR, lump, cancer, swelling, excrescence, intumescence, tumefaction.

grubby adj. DIRTY, filthy, unwashed, grimy, messy, soiled, scruffy, shabby, untidy, unkempt, slovenly, sordid, squalid; informal mucky, cruddy, gungy. ■ OPPOSITES clean.

grudge n. RESENTMENT, spite, malice, bitterness, ill will, pique, umbrage, grievance, hard feelings, rancour, malevolence, venom, hatred, dislike, aversion, animosity, animus. ▶ v. **1** BEGRUDGE, give unwillingly, give reluctantly. **2** RESENT, mind, take ill, begrudge, envy, be jealous of.

gruelling adj. EXHAUSTING, tiring, fatiguing, wearying, taxing, demanding, trying, arduous, hard, laborious, back-breaking, strenuous, punishing, crushing, draining, difficult, harsh, severe, grinding, stiff, brutal, relentless, unsparing, inexorable.

gruesome adj. GRISLY, ghastly, frightful, horrible, horrifying, horrid, horrendous, awful, dreadful, grim, terrible, fearful, hideous, disgusting, repulsive, revolting, repugnant, repellent, macabre, spine-chilling, sickening, appalling, shocking, abominable, loathsome, abhorrent, odious.

grumble v. COMPLAIN, groan, protest, object, find fault, carp, whine; informal moan, grouse, gripe, bellyache, beef, bitch, grouch, whinge.

grumpy adj. BAD-TEMPERED, surly, churlish, crotchety, tetchy, crabby, crusty, ill-natured, bearish; informal grouchy. ■ OPPOSITES good-humoured.

guarantee n. **1** WARRANTY, warrant, covenant, bond, contract, guaranty. **2** PLEDGE, promise, assurance, word, word of honour, oath, bond. ▶ v. **1** UNDERWRITE, sponsor, back, support, provide collateral for, vouch for, provide surety for. **2** PROMISE, pledge, give a pledge, give an assurance, give one's word, swear.

guard v. **1** DEFEND, shield, safeguard, stand guard over, protect, watch over, cover, patrol, police, preserve, save, conserve, secure, screen, shelter. **2** BEWARE, keep watch, be alert, take care, be on the lookout; informal keep an eye out, keep one's eyes peeled/skinned. ▶ n. **1** DEFENDER, guardian, bodyguard, custodian, sentry, sentinel, watchman, nightwatchman, lookout, scout, watch, picket, garrison, escort, convoy, patrol; informal minder. **2** WARDER, jailer, keeper; informal screw.

guarded adj. CAREFUL, cautious, circumspect, wary, chary, reluctant, non-

guest n. **1** a person invited to someone's house or to a social occasion. **2** a visiting speaker or performer. **3** a person staying at a hotel. □ **guest house** a private house offering accommodation to paying guests.

guffaw n. a loud, deep laugh. ▶v. give a loud, deep laugh.

guidance n. advice or information to solve a problem.

guide n. **1** a person who advises or shows the way to others. **2** a thing helping a person make a decision. **3** a book of information. **4** a structure or marking to direct the movement or position of something. ▶v. **1** act as a guide to. **2** (**guided**) directed by remote control or internal equipment. □ **guidebook** a book of information about a place. **guideline** a general rule or principle.

guild n. **1** a medieval association of craftsmen or merchants. **2** an association of people for a common purpose.

guilder n. a former currency unit of the Netherlands.

guile n. sly or cunning intelligence.

■ **guileless** adj.

guillotine n. **1** a machine for beheading people. **2** a machine for cutting paper or metal. ▶v. execute by guillotine.

guilt n. **1** the fact of having committed an offence. **2** a feeling of having done something wrong. ■ **guiltless** adj.

guilty adj. (**guiltier, guiltiest**) **1** responsible for a specified wrongdoing. **2** having or showing guilt. ■ **guiltily** adv.

guinea n. a former British coin worth 21 shillings.

guinea pig n. **1** a small domestic rodent. **2** a person or thing used as a subject for experiment.

guise n. an external form or appearance.

guitar n. a stringed musical instrument. ■ **guitarist** n.

gulf n. **1** a deep inlet of the sea with a narrow mouth. **2** a deep ravine. **3** a wide difference in opinion.

gull n. a long-winged seabird.

gullet n. the passage by which food passes from the mouth to the stomach.

gullible adj. easily deceived. ■ **gullibility** n.

Thesaurus

committal, reticent, restrained, reserved, discreet, prudent; *informal* cagey.

guess n. CONJECTURE, surmise, estimate, hypothesis, guesswork, theory, reckoning, judgement, supposition, feeling, assumption, inference, prediction, speculation, notion; *informal* guesstimate. ▶v. **1** CONJECTURE, surmise, estimate, reckon, hypothesize, postulate, predict, speculate. **2** SUPPOSE, believe, think, imagine, judge, consider, feel, suspect, dare say, fancy, divine, deem, surmise, reckon.

guest n. **1** VISITOR, caller, company. **2** RESIDENT, boarder, lodger, patron, tenant.

guidance n. **1** DIRECTION, leadership, management, auspices, control, handling, conduct, government, charge, rule, teaching, instruction. **2** ADVICE, counselling, counsel, direction, recommendation, suggestion, tip, hint, pointer, intelligence, information, instruction.

guide v. **1** LEAD, lead the way, conduct, show, usher, shepherd, direct, show the way, pilot, steer, escort, accompany, convoy, attend. **2** CONTROL, direct, manage, steer, command, be in charge of, govern, rule, preside over, superintend, supervise, handle, regulate, manipulate, manoeuvre. **3** ADVISE, give advice to, counsel, give counselling to, make suggestions/recommendations to, give

someone pointers/tips, inform, instruct. ▶n. **1** ESCORT, chaperone, leader, courier, pilot, usher, attendant, director. **2** ADVISER, counsellor, mentor, tutor, teacher, guru, confidant. **3** GUIDEBOOK, handbook, manual, ABC, instructions, key, catalogue.

guile n. CUNNING, duplicity, craftiness, artfulness, craft, wiliness, artifice, foxiness, slyness, deception, deceit, underhandedness, double-dealing, sharp practice, trickery, trickiness, treachery, chicanery, skulduggery, fraud, gamesmanship, knavery. ■ OPPOSITES candour.

guilty adj. **1** TO BLAME, blameworthy, culpable, blameable, at fault, responsible, in the wrong, convicted, criminal, reproachable, condemnable, erring, errant, wrong, delinquent, offending, sinful, wicked, evil, unlawful, illegal, illicit, reprehensible, felonious. **2** REMORSEFUL, ashamed, conscience-stricken, shamefaced, regretful, contrite, repentant, penitent, rueful, sheepish, hangdog, guilt-ridden, abashed. ■ OPPOSITES innocent, unrepentant.

guise n. **1** COSTUME, clothes, likeness, outfit, dress, appearance, style. **2** PRETENCE, disguise, screen, cover, blind, appearance, form.

gulf n. **1** BAY, cove, inlet, bight. **2** CHASM, abyss, hollow, pit, hole, opening, rift,

gully n. (pl. **gullies** or **gulleys**) **1** a ravine formed by the action of water. **2** a gutter or drain.

gulp v. **1** swallow food or drink quickly or in large mouthfuls. **2** swallow noisily from nervousness etc. ▶ n. **1** an act of gulping. **2** a large mouthful of liquid hastily drunk.

gum n. **1** the firm area of flesh around the roots of the teeth. **2** a sticky substance produced by some trees. **3** glue. **4** chewing gum. ▶ v. (**gumming**, **gummed**) cover or fasten with glue. □ **gumboot** dated a wellington boot. **gumdrop** a firm, jelly-like sweet. ■ **gummy** adj.

gumption n. informal resourcefulness.

gun n. **1** a weapon that fires shells or bullets from a metal tube. **2** a device for discharging something in a required direction. ▶ v. (**gunning**, **gunned**) (**gun down**) shoot with a gun. □ **gunman** a man who uses a gun to commit a crime. **gunpowder** an explosive mixture of saltpetre, sulphur, and charcoal. **gunship** a heavily armed helicopter. **gunsmith** a person who makes and sells small firearms. **jump the gun** informal act before the proper time.

gunge n. informal unpleasantly sticky and messy matter.

gunnel var. of GUNWALE.

gunner n. **1** a person who operates a gun. **2** a British artillery soldier.

gunnery n. the manufacture or firing of heavy guns.

gunrunner n. a person engaged in smuggling firearms. ■ **gunrunning** n.

gunwale (or **gunnel**) /gun-n'l/ n. the upper edge of a boat's side.

gurdwara n. a Sikh temple.

gurgle v. & n. (make) a bubbling sound.

Gurkha n. a Nepalese soldier serving in a regiment of the British army.

guru n. **1** a Hindu spiritual teacher. **2** an influential teacher or popular expert.

gush v. **1** flow in a strong, fast stream. **2** express approval in an unrestrained way. ▶ n. a strong, fast stream.

gusset n. a piece of material sewn into a garment to strengthen or enlarge a part of it.

gust n. a brief, strong rush of wind. ▶ v. blow in gusts. ■ **gusty** adj.

gusto n. enjoyment or vigour.

gut n. **1** the stomach. **2** the intestine. **3** (**guts**) informal courage and determination. ▶ v. (**gutting**, **gutted**) **1** take out the internal organs of a fish. **2** remove or destroy the internal parts of. ▶ adj. informal instinctive.

gutsy adj. (**gutsier**, **gutsiest**) informal brave and determined.

gutter n. **1** a shallow trough round a roof, or a channel beside a road, for carrying away rainwater. **2** (**the gutter**) a very poor environment. ▶ v. (of a flame) flicker and burn unsteadily. □ **guttersnipe** a scruffy child who spends most of their time on the street.

Thesaurus

cleft, fissure, split, crevice, gully, canyon, gorge, ravine.

gullible adj. CREDULOUS, trustful, overtrustful, easily deceived, easily taken in, unsuspecting, unsuspicious, ingenuous, naive, innocent, simple, inexperienced, green, foolish, silly; informal wet behind the ears. ■ OPPOSITES cynical, suspicious.

gulp v. **1** SWALLOW, quaff, toss off, drain one's glass; informal swig, swill. **2** BOLT, wolf, gobble, guzzle, devour; informal tuck into. **3** FIGHT BACK, suppress, stifle, smother, choke back, strangle. ▶ n. SWALLOW, mouthful, draught; informal swig.

gunman n. ARMED ROBBER, sniper, gangster, terrorist, assassin, murderer, killer, bandit; informal gunslinger, hit man, hired gun, trigger man, gunfighter; US informal hood.

gurgle v. BUBBLE, murmur, babble, burble, lap, splash, tinkle, plash, purl.

gush v. **1** STREAM, rush, spout, spurt, surge, jet, well, pour, burst, cascade, flood, flow, run, issue, emanate. **2** BE EFFUSIVE, enthuse, wax lyrical, bubble over, get carried away, fuss, babble, prattle, jabber, gabble, blather, chatter, make too much, overstate the case. ▶ n. STREAM, outpouring, spurt, jet, spout, rush, burst, surge, cascade, flood, torrent, spate, freshet.

gusto n. ZEST, enthusiasm, relish, zeal, fervour, verve, enjoyment, delight, exhilaration, pleasure, appreciation, liking, fondness, appetite, savour, taste. ■ OPPOSITES apathy, indifference.

gut n. STOMACH, belly, abdomen, bowels, colon, intestines, entrails, vital organs, viscera; informal insides, innards. ▶ v. **1** EVISCERATE, disembowel, dress, clean, draw. **2** STRIP, ransack, empty, plunder, loot, rob, rifle, ravage, sack, clear out, destroy, devastate, lay waste.

guts pl. n. COURAGE, bravery, valour, nerve, fortitude, pluck, mettle, spirit, boldness, audacity, daring, hardiness,

guttural adj. (of a speech sound) produced in the throat.

guy n. **1** informal a man. **2** an effigy of Guy Fawkes burnt on 5 November. **3** a rope fixed to the ground to secure a tent etc. ▶v. ridicule.

guzzle v. eat or drink greedily.

gybe (US **jibe**) Sailing v. change course by swinging the sail across a following wind. ▶n. an act of gybing.

gym n. **1** a gymnasium. **2** a place with facilities for improving physical fitness. **3** gymnastics.

gymkhana n. a horse-riding competition.

gymnasium n. (pl. **gymnasiums** or **gymnasia**) a room equipped for gymnastics and other physical exercise.

gymnast n. a person trained in gymnastics.

gymnastics n. exercises involving physical agility and flexibility. ■ **gymnastic** adj.

gynaecology /gy-ni-**kol**-uh-ji/ (US **gynecology**) n. the branch of medicine concerned with conditions and diseases specific to women. ■ **gynaecological** adj. **gynaecologist** n.

gyp n. informal pain; discomfort.

gypsum n. a chalk-like mineral used for plaster of Paris and in building.

Gypsy (or **Gipsy**) n. (pl. **Gypsies**) a member of a travelling people.

gyrate v. move in a circle or spiral. ■ **gyration** n. **gyratory** adj.

gyrocompass n. a navigation compass using a gyroscope.

gyroscope n. a device consisting of a disc rotating on an axis, used to maintain stability or a fixed direction.

Thesaurus

toughness, forcefulness, will power, tenacity; *informal* grit, gumption, spunk, bottle.

gutter n. DRAIN, sewer, sluice, culvert, conduit, pipe, duct, channel, trench, trough, ditch, furrow.

guttural adj. HUSKY, throaty, gruff, gravelly, growly, harsh, croaking, rasping, deep, low, rough, thick, croaky.

gyrate v. ROTATE, revolve, wheel round, turn round, circle, whirl, pirouette, twirl, swirl, spin, swivel.

Hh

ha abbrev. hectares.

habeas corpus n. an order requiring an arrested person to be brought to court.

haberdasher n. a dealer in sewing goods. ■ **haberdashery** n.

habit n. **1** something that a person does often. **2** informal an addiction. **3** a long, loose garment worn by a monk or nun.

habitable adj. suitable to live in.

habitat n. the natural environment of an animal or plant.

habitation n. a house or home.

habitual adj. **1** done often. **2** usual. ■ **habitually** adv.

habituate v. accustom.

hacienda n. (in Spanish-speaking countries) a large estate with a house.

hack v. **1** cut with rough or heavy blows. **2** gain unauthorized access to computer data. ▶ n. **1** a rough cut or blow. **2** a journalist producing dull, unoriginal work. **3** a horse for ordinary riding. □ **hacking cough** a dry, frequent cough. **hacksaw** a saw with a narrow blade set in a frame. ■ **hacker** n.

hackles pl. n. hairs along an animal's back, raised in anger.

hackneyed adj. unoriginal and dull.

had past & past part. of HAVE.

haddock n. (pl. **haddock**) an edible sea fish.

hadn't contr. had not.

haematology /hee-muh-**tol**-uh-ji/ (US **hematology**) n. the study of blood. ■ **haematologist** n.

haemoglobin /hee-muh-**gloh**-bin/ (US **hemoglobin**) n. a red protein transporting oxygen in the blood.

haemophilia /hee-muh-**fi**-li-uh/ (US **hemophilia**) n. a condition in which failure of the blood to clot properly causes heavy bleeding. ■ **haemophiliac** n.

haemorrhage /**hem**-uh-rij/ (US **hemorrhage**) n. heavy bleeding. ▶ v. bleed heavily.

haemorrhoid /**hem**-uh-royd/ (US **hemorrhoid**) n. a swollen vein at or near the anus.

hafnium n. a hard metallic element.

haft n. the handle of a knife, axe, etc.

hag n. an ugly old woman.

haggard adj. looking exhausted and unwell.

haggis n. a Scottish dish made from offal mixed with suet and oatmeal.

haggle v. bargain over a price.

haiku /**hy**-koo/ n. (pl. **haiku** or **haikus**) a Japanese poem of 17 syllables.

hail n. **1** pellets of frozen rain falling in showers. **2** a large number of bullets, questions, etc. ▶ v. **1** fall as hail. **2** call out to. **3** welcome or acclaim. **4** (**hail from**) have one's home in. □ **hailstone** a pellet of hail.

hair n. **1** any of the fine thread-like

Thesaurus

habit n. **1** CUSTOM, practice, wont, procedure, way, routine, matter of course, style, pattern, convention, policy, mode, rule. **2** TENDENCY, propensity, predisposition, proclivity, penchant, leaning, bent, inclination, custom, practice, quirk. **3** ADDICTION, dependence, weakness, obsession, fixation. **4** COSTUME, dress, garb, attire, clothes, clothing, garments, apparel, livery, uniform.

habitable adj. INHABITABLE, liveable in, usable, fit to live in, fit to occupy, tenantable. ■ OPPOSITES uninhabitable.

habitual adj. **1** USUAL, customary, accustomed, regular, normal, set, fixed, established, routine, common, ordinary, familiar, traditional; literary wonted.

2 PERSISTENT, constant, continual, repeated, recurrent, perpetual, non-stop, continuous, frequent. **3** CONFIRMED, addicted, chronic, inveterate, hardened, ingrained. ■ OPPOSITES unaccustomed, infrequent, occasional.

hackneyed adj. BANAL, trite, overused, overworked, tired, worn out, time-worn, stale, clichéd, platitudinous, unoriginal, commonplace, common, run-of-the-mill, unimaginative, pedestrian, prosaic, stock, conventional; informal corny, old hat, played out. ■ OPPOSITES fresh, original.

haggard adj. GAUNT, drawn, pinched, hollow-cheeked, scraggy, scrawny, withered, exhausted, ghost-like, deathstrands growing from the skin. **2** strands of hair. □ **hairdresser** a person who cuts and styles hair. **hairdo** informal the style of a person's hair. **hairgrip** a flat hairpin. **hairline 1** the edge of a person's hair. **2** (of a crack) very thin. **hairpin** a U-shaped pin for fastening the hair. **hairpin bend** a sharp U-shaped bend. **hair-raising** very frightening.

hairy adj. (**hairier, hairiest**) **1** covered with hair. **2** informal alarming and difficult. ■ **hairiness** n.

hajj n. a pilgrimage made by Muslims to Mecca.

haka n. a ceremonial Maori war dance.

hake n. (pl. **hake**) an edible sea fish.

halal adj. (of meat) prepared according to Muslim law.

halcyon /hal-si-uhn/ adj. (of a past time) happy and peaceful.

hale adj. strong and healthy.

half n. (pl. **halves**) **1** either of two equal parts into which something is divided. **2** informal half a pint of beer. ▶ adj. & pron. an amount equal to a half. ▶ adv. **1** to the extent of half. **2** partly. □ **at half mast** (of a flag) flown halfway down its mast as a sign of mourning. **half-and-half** in equal parts. **halfback** a player between the forwards and fullbacks. **half board** bed, breakfast, and an evening meal at a hotel etc. **half-brother** (or **sister**) a brother (or sister) with whom one has only one parent in common. **half-caste** offens. a person of mixed race. **half-hearted** not very enthusiastic. **half-life** the time taken for radioactivity to fall to half its original value. **half nelson** a wrestling hold. **half-term** a short holiday halfway through a school term. **half-timbered** having walls with a timber frame and a brick

or plaster filling. **half-time** an interval between two halves of a sports match. **half-volley** (in sport) a strike or kick of the ball immediately after it bounces. **halfway** at or to a point equal in distance between two others. **half-witted** informal stupid.

halfpenny /hayp-ni/ n. (pl. **halfpennies; halfpence**) a former British coin worth half a penny.

halibut n. (pl. **halibut**) a large edible flatfish.

halitosis n. unpleasant-smelling breath.

hall n. **1** the room or space inside the front entrance of a house. **2** a large room or building for meetings, concerts, etc. **3** a large country house.

hallelujah (or **alleluia**) exclam. God be praised.

hallmark n. **1** an official mark stamped on articles of gold, silver, or platinum to certify their purity. **2** a distinctive feature. ▶ v. stamp with a hallmark.

hallo var. of HELLO.

hallowed adj. made holy.

Halloween (or **Hallowe'en**) n. 31 October, the eve of All Saints' Day.

hallucinate v. see something which is not actually present. ■ **hallucination** n. **hallucinatory** adj.

hallucinogen n. a drug causing hallucinations. ■ **hallucinogenic** adj.

halo n. (pl. **haloes** or **halos**) a circle of light, esp. one round the head of a holy figure.

halogen n. any of a group of elements including fluorine, chlorine, and iodine.

halon n. a gas composed of halogens, used to put out fires.

halt v. bring or come to a sudden stop. ▶ n. **1** a temporary stop. **2** a minor stopping place on a railway.

Thesaurus

like, wan, pallid, ghastly, cadaverous, peaked, drained, careworn, emaciated, wasted, thin. ■ OPPOSITES plump.

hail v. **1** GREET, salute, acknowledge, lift one's hat to. **2** SIGNAL, make a sign, flag, flag down, wave down, call, shout to. **3** see ACCLAIM.

hair n. **1** LOCKS, tresses, shock of hair, mop of hair, head of hair. **2** COAT, fur, pelt, hide, wool, fleece, mane.

hair-raising adj. SPINE-CHILLING, bloodcurdling, terrifying, horrifying, petrifying, frightening, alarming, shocking, exciting, thrilling; informal scary, creepy.

hairy adj. HIRSUTE, woolly, shaggy, bushy, fuzzy, bristly, fleecy, downy, bearded,

unshaven, bewhiskered, stubbly.

half-hearted adj. LUKEWARM, unenthusiastic, apathetic, indifferent, uninterested, unconcerned, cool, listless, unemotional, lacklustre, dispassionate, cursory, perfunctory, superficial, passive, neutral. ■ OPPOSITES enthusiastic.

hallmark n. MARK, trademark, stamp, sign, badge, device, symbol, indicator, indication.

hallucinate v. IMAGINE THINGS, see things, have hallucinations, dream, fantasize, be delirious; informal be on a trip.

hallucination n. ILLUSION, delusion, figment of the imagination, vision, fantasy, apparition, dream, mirage, chi-

halter n. a strap round a horse's head for leading or holding it.

halting adj. slow and hesitant.

halve v. **1** divide into two equal parts. **2** reduce by half.

halves pl. of HALF.

halyard n. a rope for raising and lowering a sail or flag.

ham n. **1** salted or smoked meat from a pig's thigh. **2** (**hams**) the thighs and buttocks. **3** a poor actor. **4** informal an amateur radio operator. ▶v. (**hamming**, **hammed**) informal overact. □ **ham-fisted** informal clumsy.

hamburger n. a flat cake of minced beef.

hamlet n. a small village.

hammer n. **1** a tool with a head for driving in nails etc. **2** a metal ball attached to a wire, thrown in an athletic contest. ▶v. **1** hit repeatedly. **2** impress on someone's mind by constant repetition.

hammock n. a hanging bed of canvas or rope mesh.

hamper n. **1** a lidded basket for food etc. on a picnic. **2** a box containing food and drink as a gift. ▶v. prevent the free movement or progress of.

hamster n. a small domesticated rodent.

hamstring n. a tendon at the back of the knee. ▶v. (**hamstringing**, **hamstrung**) **1** cripple by cutting the hamstrings. **2** severely restrict.

hand n. **1** the part of the arm below the wrist. **2** a pointer on a clock, dial, etc.

3 (**hands**) power or control. **4** help. **5** a manual worker. **6** informal a round of applause. **7** the cards dealt to a player in a card game. **8** a unit of measurement of a horse's height. ▶v. give or pass. □ **at hand** near. **handbag** a small bag for everyday personal items. **handball 1** a game in which the ball is hit with the hand in a walled court. **2** Soccer illegal touching of the ball with the hand or arm. **handbill** a printed notice distributed by hand. **handbook** a book giving basic information. **handcuff** put handcuffs on. **handcuffs** a pair of lockable linked metal rings for securing a prisoner's wrists. **handful 1** a quantity that fills the hand. **2** a small number or amount. **3** informal a person hard to deal with or control. **handout 1** a sum of money etc. given to a needy person. **2** a piece of printed information given free of charge. **handshake** an act of shaking a person's hand. **handstand** an act of balancing upside down on one's hands. **handwriting 1** writing by hand with a pen or pencil. **2** a style of this. **on hand** available. **out of hand** out of control. **to hand** within reach.

handicap n. **1** something that makes progress difficult. **2** dated a physical or mental disability. **3** a disadvantage given to a superior competitor in sports to make the chances more equal. **4** the number of strokes by which a golfer normally exceeds par for a course. ▶v. (**handicapping**, **handicapped**) act as a handicap to.

Thesaurus

mera, delirium, phantasmagoria.

halt v. **1** COME TO A HALT, stop, come to a stop/standstill, pull up, draw up, wait. **2** FINISH, stop, cease, break off, call it a day, desist, discontinue; informal knock off, down tools. **3** BLOCK, arrest, terminate, stop, curb, put an end/stop to, bring to an end, crush, frustrate, obstruct, baulk, impede, hold back. ▶n. STOP, stoppage, cessation, close, end, standstill, pause, interval, interlude, intermission, break, hiatus, respite, rest.

hammer v. BEAT, batter, pound, pummel, hit, strike, cudgel, slap, bludgeon, club; informal wallop, clobber.

hamper v. HINDER, obstruct, impede, hold back, inhibit, retard, slow down, hold up, restrain, block, check, frustrate, thwart, foil, curb, interfere with, throw a spanner in the works, cramp, restrict, bridle, handicap, stymie, hamstring,

shackle, fetter, encumber, trammel, cumber. ■ OPPOSITES expedite.

hand n. **1** FIST, palm; informal mitt, paw, duke. **2** POINTER, indicator, needle. **3** WORKER, workman, employee, operative, hired hand, labourer, artisan. ▶v. GIVE, pass, pass over, hand over, deliver, present. □ **hand on/down** PASS ON/DOWN, bequeath, will, give, transfer. **hand out** DISTRIBUTE, give out, pass out, deal out, dole out, mete out, dispense, apportion, disseminate, disburse, dish out.

handicap n. **1** DISABILITY, impairment, abnormality, disadvantage, defect. **2** IMPEDIMENT, disadvantage, hindrance, obstruction, obstacle, encumbrance, check, block, curb, barrier, stumbling block, constraint, restriction, limitation, drawback, shortcoming. ■ OPPOSITES advantage. ▶v. DISADVANTAGE, put at a disadvantage, impede, hinder, im-

handkerchief n. (pl. **handkerchiefs** or **handkerchieves**) a square of material for wiping the nose.

handle v. **1** feel or move with the hands. **2** control. **3** cope with. ▶ n. a part by which a thing is held, carried, or controlled. □ **handlebar** the steering bar of a bicycle or motorbike.

handler n. a person in charge of a trained animal.

handsome adj. **1** good-looking. **2** striking and impressive. **3** (of an amount) large. ■ **handsomely** adv.

handy adj. (**handier, handiest**) **1** useful. **2** convenient. □ **handyman** a person who does domestic repairs etc. ■ **handily** adv.

hang v. (**hanging, hung** except in sense 2) **1** suspend or be suspended from above. **2** (past & past part. **hanged**) kill by suspending from a rope tied round the neck. **3** (of a garment) drape in a particular way. □ **hangman** an executioner who hangs condemned people. **hangnail** a piece of torn skin at the base of a fingernail. **hang out** informal spend time

relaxing.

hangar n. a building for aircraft.

hangdog adj. shamefaced.

hanger n. a shaped piece of wood, plastic, etc. to hang a garment on.

hang-glider n. an unpowered flying apparatus consisting of a framework from which the pilot is suspended in a harness. ■ **hang-gliding** n.

hanging n. a decorative piece of fabric hung on a wall.

hangover n. a headache and other after-effects from drinking too much alcohol.

hank n. a coil or length of wool etc.

hanker v. feel a longing.

hanky (or **hankie**) n. (pl. **hankies**) informal a handkerchief.

Hanukkah n. a Jewish festival of lights held in December.

haphazard adj. lacking order; random. ■ **haphazardly** adv.

hapless adj. unlucky.

happen v. **1** take place; occur. **2** (**happen on**) find by chance. **3** (**happen to**) be experienced by. **4** (**happen to**) be-

Thesaurus

pair, hamper, obstruct, check, block, encumber, curb, trammel, bridle, hold back, constrain, restrict, limit.

handiwork n. **1** HANDICRAFT, craft, craftsmanship. **2** ACTION, achievement, work, doing, creation, design, product, production, result.

handle v. **1** TOUCH, feel, hold, finger, grasp, grip, pick up, lift, pat, caress, stroke, fondle, poke, maul; informal paw. **2** COPE WITH, deal with, treat, manage, control. **3** BE IN CHARGE OF, control, manage, administer, direct, guide, conduct, supervise, take care of. **4** DRIVE, steer, operate, manoeuvre. **5** DEAL IN, trade in, traffic in, market, sell, stock, carry. ▶ n. SHAFT, grip, handgrip, hilt, haft, knob, stock, helve.

handsome adj. **1** GOOD-LOOKING, attractive, personable; informal dishy. **2** ATTRACTIVE, good-looking, lovely, elegant, fine, personable, well formed, well proportioned, stately, dignified. **3** GENEROUS, magnanimous, liberal, lavish, considerable, sizeable, large, ample, abundant, plentiful; literary bounteous. ■ OPPOSITES ugly.

handy adj. **1** TO HAND, at hand, within reach, available, accessible, near, nearby, close, at one's fingertips, convenient; informal on tap. **2** USEFUL, helpful, practicable, practical, serviceable, functional, expedient, easy-to-use, neat, con-

venient. **3** DEFT, dexterous, nimble-fingered, adroit, proficient, adept, skilful, skilled, expert, clever/good with one's hands. ■ OPPOSITES inaccessible, useless, inept.

hang v. **1** BE SUSPENDED, dangle, swing, sway, be pendent. **2** SEND TO THE GALLOWS, send to the gibbet, execute; informal string up. **3** STICK UP, attach, fix, fasten on, paste, glue, cement. **4** ADORN, decorate, deck, ornament, drape, cover, furnish. □ **hang about/around** WAIT, linger, loiter, dally, waste time; old use tarry. **hang back** HOLD BACK, stay back, stay in the background, be reluctant, hesitate, recoil, demur, shrink back. **hang on** WAIT, hold on, stop, stay, remain, persevere.

hang-up n. FIXATION, preoccupation, obsession, phobia, problem; informal thing, bee in one's bonnet.

hanker v. (**hanker after/for**) LONG FOR, have a longing for, yearn for, crave, desire, hunger for, thirst for, be bent on, covet, want, wish for, set one's heart on, pine for, lust after; informal be itching for, be dying for, have a yen for.

haphazard adj. UNPLANNED, random, indiscriminate, undirected, unforeseen, chaotic, chance, unsystematic, unorganized, unmethodical, orderless, aimless, irregular, slapdash, thrown together, careless, casual, hit-or-miss.

come of: *what happened to the money?*

happy adj. (**happier**, **happiest**) **1** feeling or showing pleasure. **2** fortunate. □ **happy-go-lucky** cheerfully unconcerned. ■ **happily** adv. **happiness** n.

harangue v. criticize aggressively.

harass v. **1** subject to constant interference or bullying. **2** make attacks on. ■ **harassment** n.

....

☑ Only one *r*: harass.

....

harbinger /har-bin-jer/ n. a sign or herald of something.

harbour (US **harbor**) n. a place on the coast for ships to moor. ▶v. **1** keep a thought etc. secretly in one's mind. **2** shelter.

hard adj. **1** solid, firm, and rigid. **2** requiring effort. **3** not showing weakness. **4** (of information) precise and true. **5** harsh or unpleasant. **6** done with force. **7** (of drink) strongly alcoholic.

8 (of a drug) very addictive. **9** (of water) containing mineral salts. ▶adv. **1** with effort or force. **2** so as to be firm. □ **hardbitten** tough and cynical. **hardboard** stiff board made of compressed wood pulp. **hard-boiled 1** (of an egg) boiled until solid. **2** (of a person) tough and cynical. **hard copy** a printed version of data held in a computer. **hard disk** (or **hard drive**) a rigid magnetic disk with a large data storage capacity. **hard-headed** tough and realistic. **hard-hearted** unfeeling. **hard sell** aggressive selling. **hard shoulder** a strip of road alongside a motorway for use in an emergency. **hardship** poverty. **hard up** informal short of money. **hardware 1** the machinery, wiring, etc. of a computer. **2** tools and household implements. **hardwood** wood from broadleaved trees such as oaks or beeches, as opposed to that of conifers. ■ **harden** v. **hardness** n.

hardly adv. **1** scarcely. **2** only with great

Thesaurus

....

■ OPPOSITES methodical, systematic.

hapless adj. UNLUCKY, unfortunate, out of luck, ill-starred, forlorn, wretched, unhappy, woebegone; *informal* down on one's luck. ■ OPPOSITES lucky.

happen v. TAKE PLACE, occur, come about, present itself, arise, materialize, appear, come into being, chance, arrive, transpire, crop up, develop, eventuate, supervene; *literary* come to pass.

happening n. OCCURRENCE, event, incident, occasion, affair, circumstance, action, case, phenomenon, eventuality, episode, experience, adventure, scene, proceedings, chance.

happiness n. CHEERFULNESS, cheeriness, merriment, gaiety, good spirits, high spirits, light-heartedness, joy, joyfulness, glee, joviality, carefreeness, enjoyment, gladness, delight, exuberance, elation, ecstasy, bliss, blissfulness, euphoria, transports; *literary* blitheness. ■ OPPOSITES unhappiness, sadness.

happy adj. **1** CHEERFUL, cheery, merry, in good/high spirits, joyful, joyous, lighthearted, jovial, gleeful, buoyant, carefree, untroubled, smiling, glad, delighted, elated, ecstatic, blissful, euphoric, overjoyed, exuberant, in seventh heaven, floating/walking on air; *informal* over the moon, on cloud nine, on top of the world; *dated* gay; *literary* blithe. **2** GLAD, pleased, delighted, contented, satisfied, gratified, thrilled. **3** LUCKY, fortunate, advantageous, favourable, bene-

ficial, opportune, helpful, timely, convenient, welcome, propitious, auspicious, felicitous, fortuitous. **4** APPROPRIATE, fitting, apt, fit, good, right, proper, seemly. ■ OPPOSITES unhappy, sad, displeased, unfortunate.

harangue n. LECTURE, tirade, diatribe, speech, talk, sermon, exhortation, declamation, oration, address, homily, peroration; *informal* spiel.

harass v. **1** BOTHER, pester, annoy, exasperate, worry, fret, disturb, agitate, provoke, badger, hound, torment, plague, persecute, harry, tease, bait, nag, molest, bedevil; *informal* hassle, give someone a hard time, drive someone up the wall. **2** HARRY, attack repeatedly, raid, beleaguer, press hard, oppress.

harassed adj. STRESSED, under pressure, distraught, under stress, strained, worried, careworn, troubled, vexed, agitated, fretting; *informal* hassled. ■ OPPOSITES carefree.

harbour n. **1** PORT, anchorage, dock, haven, marina. **2** REFUGE, shelter, haven, sanctuary, retreat, asylum, sanctum, covert. ▶v. **1** SHELTER, give shelter to, house, lodge, put up, take in, billet, provide refuge for, shield, protect, conceal, hide, secrete. **2** NURSE, maintain, nurture, hold on to, cherish, cling to, retain, entertain.

hard adj. **1** FIRM, solid, compact, compacted, compressed, condensed, dense, rigid, stiff, unyielding, resistant, inflexdifficulty.

hardy adj. (**hardier**, **hardiest**) capable of surviving difficult conditions. ■ **hardiness** n.

hare n. a field animal like a large rabbit. ▶ v. run very fast. □ **hare-brained** ill-judged.

harebell n. a plant with blue bell-shaped flowers.

harelip n. offens. a cleft lip.

harem /hah-reem/ n. **1** the women's quarters of a Muslim household. **2** the women living in a harem.

hark v. **1** literary listen. **2** (**hark back**) recall an earlier period.

harlequin n. a character in traditional pantomime with a colourful diamond-patterned costume. ▶ adj. in varied colours; variegated.

harlot n. old use a prostitute.

harm n. **1** deliberate injury. **2** damage. ▶ v. cause harm to. ■ **harmful** adj. **harmless** adj.

harmonica n. a mouth organ.

harmonium n. a musical instrument like a small organ.

harmonize (or **-ise**) v. **1** add notes to a melody to produce harmony. **2** make or be harmonious. ■ **harmonization** n.

harmony n. (pl. **harmonies**) **1** the combination of musical notes to produce chords with a pleasing effect. **2** the

ible, unpliable, tough, strong, stony, unmalleable, close-packed, rock-like. **2** STRENUOUS, arduous, heavy, tiring, fatiguing, exhausting, back-breaking, laborious, rigorous, exacting, formidable, tough, difficult, uphill, toilsome, Herculean. **3** DIFFICULT, complicated, complex, involved, intricate, puzzling, perplexing, baffling, knotty, thorny, bewildering, insoluble, enigmatic, unfathomable, incomprehensible. **4** HARSH, severe, stern, hard-hearted, cold, unfeeling, unsympathetic, grim, ruthless, oppressive, tyrannical, pitiless, merciless, unrelenting, unsparing, callous, cruel, vicious, implacable, obdurate, unyielding, unjust, unfair. **5** UNPLEASANT, grim, harsh, difficult, disagreeable, uncomfortable, intolerable, unendurable, unbearable, insupportable, distressing, painful, disastrous, calamitous. **6** FORCEFUL, violent, heavy, strong, powerful, fierce, harsh, sharp. ■ OPPOSITES soft, easy.

harden v. **1** SOLIDIFY, become hard, set, stiffen, cake, congeal, clot, coagulate, bake, anneal. **2** TOUGHEN, make insensitive/unfeeling, deaden, numb, benumb.

hard-hitting adj. TOUGH, uncompromising, unsparing, strongly worded, vigorous, straight-talking, blunt, frank, critical; informal pulling no punches.

hardly adv. SCARCELY, barely, only just, just, almost not, with difficulty, with effort. ■ OPPOSITES fully.

hardship n. ADVERSITY, deprivation, privation, want, need, destitution, poverty, austerity, desolation, misfortune, distress, suffering, affliction, pain, misery, wretchedness, tribulation, trials, burdens, calamity, catastrophe, disaster, ruin, ruination, torment, torture; literary travail. ■ OPPOSITES ease, comfort.

hardy adj. HEALTHY, fit, strong, robust, sturdy, tough, rugged, vigorous, in good condition, resilient, lusty, stalwart, hale and hearty, fit as a fiddle, sound in body and limb, in fine fettle, in good kilter. ■ OPPOSITES delicate.

harm n. **1** HURT, injury, pain, suffering, trauma, destruction, loss, ruin, havoc, adversity, disservice, abuse, damage, mischief, detriment, defacement, defilement, impairment. **2** EVIL, badness, wrongdoing, wrong, wickedness, vice, iniquity, sin, sinfulness, immorality, nefariousness. ▶ v. HURT, injure, wound, inflict pain/suffering on, abuse, maltreat, ill-treat, ill-use, molest, do violence to, destroy, damage, do mischief to, deface, defile, impair, spoil, mar, blemish.

harmful adj. **1** HURTFUL, injurious, wounding, abusive, detrimental, damaging, deleterious, disadvantageous, destructive, dangerous, pernicious, noxious, baneful, toxic. **2** BAD, evil, wicked, malign, corrupting, subversive. ■ OPPOSITES harmless.

harmless adj. **1** SAFE, innocuous, non-toxic, mild, non-irritant. **2** INOFFENSIVE, innocuous, unoffending, innocent, blameless, gentle. ■ OPPOSITES harmful, dangerous.

harmonious adj. **1** MELODIOUS, tuneful, musical, harmonizing, sweet-sounding, mellifluous, dulcet, euphonious, symphonious, consonant. **2** PEACEFUL, peaceable, friendly, amicable, cordial, amiable, agreeable, congenial, united, co-operative, in harmony, in tune, attuned, in accord, compatible, sympathetic. ■ OPPOSITES discordant, hostile.

harmonize v. **1** BE IN ACCORD, coincide, agree, correspond, tally, be in unison, quality of forming a pleasing combination. **3** agreement; peace. ■ **harmonic** adj. **harmonious** adj. **harmoniously** adv.

harness n. **1** a set of straps and fastenings by which a horse is controlled. **2** a similar set for attaching a parachute etc. ▶v. **1** fit with a harness. **2** control and make use of a resource.

harp n. a musical instrument with strings in a triangular frame. ▶v. (**harp on**) talk persistently about. ■ **harpist** n.

harpoon n. a spear-like missile for catching whales etc. ▶v. spear with a harpoon.

harpsichord n. a keyboard instrument.

harpy n. (pl. **harpies**) a cruel or greedy woman.

harridan n. a bossy or aggressive old woman.

harrier n. **1** a hound used for hunting hares. **2** a bird of prey.

harrow n. a heavy frame with spikes for breaking up soil. ▶v. **1** draw a harrow over. **2** (**harrowing**) very distressing.

harry v. (**harrying**, **harried**) harass.

harsh adj. **1** rough or jarring to the senses. **2** cruel or severe. ■ **harshly**

adv. **harshness** n.

hart n. an adult male deer.

harvest n. **1** the process or period of gathering in crops. **2** the season's yield or crop. ▶v. gather as a harvest. ■ **harvester** n.

has 3rd person sing. present of HAVE. □ **has-been** informal a person who is no longer important.

hash n. **1** a dish of chopped reheated meat. **2** hashish. □ **make a hash of** informal make or do badly.

hashish n. cannabis.

hasn't contr. has not.

hasp n. a hinged metal plate fitted over a metal loop as part of a fastening.

hassle informal n. **1** annoying inconvenience. **2** harassment. ▶v. harass or bother.

hassock n. a cushion for kneeling on in church.

haste n. hurry.

hasten v. **1** hurry. **2** cause to happen sooner.

hasty adj. (**hastier, hastiest**) hurried; rushed. ■ **hastily** adv.

hat n. a shaped covering for the head.

Thesaurus

be congruent, be of one mind. **2** RECONCILE, settle differences, restore harmony to, make peaceful, patch up, negotiate peace between, heal the breach, pour oil on troubled waters.

harmony n. **1** AGREEMENT, accord, accordance, concordance, concurrence, unanimity, cooperation, unity, unison, oneness, amicability, good will, amity, affinity, rapport, sympathy, like-mindedness, friendship, fellowship, comradeship, peace, peacefulness. **2** COMPATIBILITY, congruity, consonance, concord, coordination, blending, balance, symmetry, suitability. **3** TUNE, melody, tunefulness, melodiousness, mellifluousness, euphony. ■ OPPOSITES disagreement, incongruity, dissonance.

harrowing adj. DISTRESSING, agonizing, excruciating, traumatic, heart-rending, heartbreaking, painful, racking, afflicting, chilling, disturbing, vexing, alarming, perturbing, unnerving, horrifying, terrifying.

harsh adj. **1** ABRUPT, brusque, blunt, curt, gruff, short, surly, concise, clipped, impolite, discourteous, uncivil, ungracious. **2** CRUEL, brutal, savage, barbarous, hard-hearted, despotic, tyrannical, ruthless, unfeeling, merciless, pitiless, relentless, unrelenting, inhuman. **3** SEVERE, stringent, stern, grim, austere,

uncompromising, inflexible, punitive, draconian. **4** GRATING, jarring, grinding, rasping, strident, jangling, raucous, ear-piercing, discordant, dissonant, unharmonious. **5** ROUGH, coarse, guttural, hoarse, croaking, raucous, strident, gravelly. **6** BLEAK, grim, desolate, stark, severe, austere, barren, rough, wild, bitter, inhospitable, comfortless, spartan. **7** GARISH, gaudy, glaring, bold, loud, flashy, showy, crass, crude, vulgar. ■ OPPOSITES lenient, gentle.

harvest n. REAPING, crop, yield, produce, vintage, ingathering. ▶v. GATHER, gather in, reap, glean, pick, pluck, collect, amass, accumulate, garner.

hassle v. ANNOY, badger, harass, hound, pester, bother, trouble, worry, torment, plague; informal give someone a hard time. ▶n. TROUBLE, bother, inconvenience, annoyance, nuisance, harassment, difficulty, problem, struggle, fight, quarrel, altercation, disagreement, dispute, wrangle, tussle.

haste n. SPEED, swiftness, rapidity, rapidness, quickness, fastness, briskness, urgency, alacrity, promptness, dispatch, expeditiousness, promptitude, expedition, celerity, fleetness.

hasty adj. **1** SWIFT, rapid, quick, fast, speedy, hurried, hurrying, running, prompt, expeditious, brisk, urgent,

□ **hat-trick** three successes of the same kind, esp. in sports.

hatch n. a small opening in a floor, wall, or roof allowing access. ▸v. **1** come out or cause to come out from an egg. **2** devise a plot. **3** shade with close parallel lines. □ **hatchback** a car with a back door that opens upwards.

hatchet n. a small axe. □ **bury the hatchet** end a quarrel.

hate v. feel intense dislike for. ▸n. intense dislike.

hateful adj. arousing hate.

hatred n. extreme hate.

haughty adj. (**haughtier**, **haughtiest**) arrogant and contemptuous of others. ▪ **haughtily** adv. **haughtiness** n.

haul v. pull or drag with effort. ▸n. a quantity of something obtained, esp. illegally.

haulage n. the commercial transport of goods.

haulier n. a person or company transporting goods by road.

haunch n. **1** the buttock and thigh. **2** a leg and loin of meat.

haunt v. **1** (of a ghost) appear regularly at or to. **2** frequent. **3** persist disturbingly in the mind. ▸n. a place often visited by a particular person.

haute couture /oht kuu-**tyoor**/ n. high fashion.

haute cuisine /oht kwi-**zeen**/ n. high-quality cookery.

have v. (**has**, **having**, **had**) **1** possess. **2** experience. **3** (**have to**) be obliged to. **4** suffer from. **5** cause to be or be done. **6** place, hold, or keep. ▸aux. v. used with a past participle to form past tenses. □ **have on** informal try to fool someone.

haven n. a place of safety.

haven't contr. have not.

haversack n. a strong bag carried on the back or over the shoulder.

havoc n. widespread destruction or

Thesaurus

fleet. **2** QUICK, short, brief, rushed, short-lived, fleeting, transitory, cursory, perfunctory, superficial, slight. **3** HURRIED, rushed, impetuous, reckless, rash, foolhardy, precipitate, impulsive, headlong, thoughtless, heedless, careless, ill-conceived. ▪ OPPOSITES slow, cautious.

hatch v. **1** INCUBATE, brood, sit on, cover. **2** DEVISE, concoct, contrive, plan, scheme, design, invent, formulate, originate, conceive, dream up, think up; informal cook up.

hate v. **1** LOATHE, detest, abhor, dislike, despise, abominate, execrate, have an aversion to, feel hostile towards, be unable to stand/bear, view with dislike, be sick of, be tired of, shudder at, be repelled by, recoil from. **2** BE RELUCTANT, be loath, be unwilling, feel disinclined, be sorry, dislike, not have the heart, shy away from, flinch from. ▪ OPPOSITES love, relish.

hateful adj. DETESTABLE, loathsome, abhorrent, abominable, despicable, execrable, odious, revolting, repugnant, repellent, disgusting, obnoxious, offensive, insufferable, horrible, unpleasant, nasty, disagreeable, foul, vile, heinous. ▪ OPPOSITES admirable.

hatred n. HATE, loathing, detestation, abhorrence, dislike, aversion, hostility, ill will, enmity, animosity, antagonism, antipathy, animus, revulsion, repugnance, odium, rancour, grudge, execration, abomination. ▪ OPPOSITES love.

haughty adj. ARROGANT, proud, conceited, self-important, egotistical, vain, swollen-headed, overweening, overbearing, pompous, smug, presumptuous, condescending, supercilious, lofty, patronizing, snobbish, imperious, boastful, scornful, lordly, high-handed; informal snooty, on one's high horse, high and mighty, stuck up, hoity-toity, uppity, uppish. ▪ OPPOSITES modest, humble.

haul v. DRAG, pull, tug, draw, heave, trail, lug, tow, take in tow, cart, carry, convoy, ship.

haunt v. **1** FREQUENT, visit regularly, patronize; informal hang out in. **2** OBSESS, prey on someone's mind, prey on, torment, plague, disturb, trouble, worry, oppress, burden, beset, harry, weigh on, come back to, stay with.

have v. **1** OWN, possess, keep, keep for one's use, use, hold, retain. **2** GET, be given, receive, accept, obtain, acquire, procure, secure, gain. **3** CONTAIN, include, comprise, embrace, take in, incorporate, embody. **4** EXPERIENCE, undergo, go through, encounter, meet, find, be subjected to, submit to, suffer from, endure, tolerate, put up with. **5** FEEL, entertain, have/keep/bear in mind, harbour, foster, nurse, cherish. **6** GIVE BIRTH TO, bear, deliver, be delivered of, bring into the world, bring forth. □ **have had it** BE FINISHED, be out, be defeated, have lost, have no chance, have no hope. **have to** MUST, have got to, be bound to, be obliged to, be forced great disorder.

haw n. a hawthorn berry.

hawk n. **1** a bird of prey. **2** a person who favours aggressive policies in foreign affairs. ▶v. **1** offer goods for sale in the street. **2** clear one's throat noisily. □ **hawk-eyed** keen-sighted. ■ **hawkish** adj.

hawser n. a thick rope or cable for mooring or towing a ship.

hawthorn n. a thorny shrub or tree with small red berries.

hay n. grass cut and dried for use as fodder. □ **hay fever** an allergy to pollen or dust. **haystack** (or **hayrick**) a large packed pile of hay.

haywire adj. informal out of control.

hazard n. a danger. ▶v. **1** dare to say. **2** put at risk. ■ **hazardous** adj.

haze n. a thin mist.

hazel n. **1** a tree bearing small round nuts (**hazelnuts**). **2** a rich reddish-brown colour.

hazy adj. (**hazier**, **haziest**) **1** covered by a haze. **2** vague or unclear. ■ **hazily** adv.

HB abbrev. (of a pencil lead) hard black.

H-bomb n. a hydrogen bomb.

he pron. **1** the male previously mentioned. **2** a person or animal of unspecified sex.

☑️ The use of **he** to refer to any person, male or female, is considered outdated and sexist by many. Using **he or she** can be clumsy, so **they** is often used instead, as in everyone needs to feel that they matter.

head n. **1** the part of the body containing the brain, mouth, and sense organs. **2** the mind or intellect. **3** a person in charge. **4** the front or top part of something. **5** a person or animal considered as a unit. **6** something shaped like a head. **7** (**heads**) the side of a coin bearing the image of a head. **8** pressure of water or steam in an enclosed space. ▶adj. chief. ▶v. **1** be or act as the head of. **2** give a heading to. **3** move in a specified direction. **4** (**head off**) obstruct and turn aside. **5** Soccer hit the ball with the head. □ **come to a head** reach a crisis. **headache 1** a continuous pain in the head. **2** informal a cause of worry. **headdress** an ornamental covering for the head. **headgear** hats, helmets, etc. **headhunt** approach someone already employed elsewhere to fill a vacant post. **headland** a promontory. **headlight** a powerful light at the front of a vehicle etc. **headline** a heading in a newspaper. **headlines** a summary of broadcast news. **headlong 1** with the head first. **2** in a rush. **headmaster** (or **headmistress**) a male (or female) head teacher. **head-on 1** involving the front of a vehicle. **2** involving direct confrontation. **headphones** a pair of earphones. **headquarters** the place from which an organization or military operation is directed. **headstone** a stone slab set up at the head of a grave. **headstrong** wilful and determined. **headway** progress. **headwind** a wind blowing from directly in front. ■ **headless** adj.

header n. Soccer a heading of the ball.

Thesaurus

to, be compelled to.

haven n. REFUGE, shelter, sanctuary, asylum, retreat, sanctum, sanctum sanctorum, covert.

havoc n. **1** DEVASTATION, destruction, damage, ruination, ruin, rack and ruin, despoliation, waste, gutting, wreckage, desolation, disaster, catastrophe, cataclysm. **2** CHAOS, disorder, confusion, disruption, disorganization, mayhem; informal shambles.

hazard n. **1** DANGER, peril, risk, jeopardy, threat, menace. **2** CHANCE, accident, luck, contingency, fortuity, fortuitousness. ▶v. **1** RISK, put at risk, endanger, expose to danger, imperil, put in jeopardy, jeopardize. **2** VENTURE, put forward, proffer, offer, submit, advance, volunteer.

hazardous adj. DANGEROUS, risky, perilous, fraught with danger/risk, chancy, uncertain, unpredictable, precarious, parlous, unsafe, insecure; informal dicey, hairy, tricky. ■ OPPOSITES safe.

haze n. MIST, mistiness, fog, cloud, cloudiness, smog, vapour.

hazy adj. **1** MISTY, foggy, cloudy, smoggy, overcast. **2** VAGUE, indefinite, blurred, fuzzy, faint, confused, muddled, unclear, obscure, dim, indistinct, ill-defined. ■ OPPOSITES clear.

head n. **1** SKULL, cranium; informal nut, bonce; informal, dated conk, noodle, noddle. **2** MIND, intelligence, intellect, brain, brains, mentality, wit, sense, wisdom, reasoning, rationality, understanding. **3** LEADER, chief, commander, director, manager, superintendent, controller, administrator, supervisor, principal, captain. **4** FRONT, fore, forefront, van,

heading n. **1** a title at the top of a section of a text. **2** a direction or bearing.

heady adj. (**headier**, **headiest**) **1** intoxicating. **2** having an exciting effect.

heal v. make or become healthy again.
■ **healer** n.

health n. **1** the state of being free from illness. **2** mental or physical condition. □ **health farm** an establishment where people try to improve their health by dieting, exercise, etc. **health visitor** a nurse who visits chronically ill patients etc. at home.

healthy adj. (**healthier**, **healthiest**) **1** having or helping towards good health. **2** sensible or desirable.
■ **healthily** adv. **healthiness** n.

heap n. **1** a pile of a substance or of a number of objects. **2** informal a large amount or number. ▶v. **1** put in or form a heap. **2** load heavily with.

hear v. (**hearing**, **heard**) **1** perceive a sound with the ear. **2** be told of. **3** (**hear from**) be contacted by. **4** listen to. **5** judge a legal case. □ **hearsay** information received which may be unreliable. ■ **hearer** n.

hearing n. **1** the ability to hear. **2** an opportunity to state one's case: *a fair hearing*. **3** an act of listening to evidence. □ **hearing aid** a small device worn by a partially deaf person, which amplifies sounds.

hearse /herss/ n. a vehicle for conveying the coffin at a funeral.

heart n. **1** the muscular organ that pumps the blood around the body. **2** the central or innermost part. **3** capacity for love or compassion. **4** courage or enthusiasm. **5** a shape representing a heart. **6** (**hearts**) one of the four suits in a pack of playing cards. □ **at heart** in one's real nature. **break someone's heart** make someone deeply sad. **by heart** memorized thoroughly. **heartache** worry or grief. **heart attack** (or **heart failure**) a sudden failure of the heart to function normally. **heartbeat** a pulsation of the heart. **heartburn** indigestion felt as a burning sensation in the chest. **heartfelt** deeply felt. **heart-rending** very distressing. **heart-searching** examination of one's feelings and motives. **heart-throb** informal a very attractive famous man. **heart-to-heart** (of a conversation) intimate. **heart-warming** emotionally uplifting.

heartbreak n. extreme distress.

vanguard. ▶v. **1** LEAD, be at the head of, be in charge of, be in command/control of, command, control, run, supervise, rule, govern, guide. **2** MAKE FOR, go to, go in the direction of, aim for, set out for, start out for, go towards, steer towards, make a beeline for. □ **head off** DIVERT, intercept, deflect, turn aside, block off, cut off, forestall.

headlong adv. **1** HEAD FIRST, head on, on one's head. **2** HASTILY, hurriedly, impatiently, without thinking, rashly, recklessly, wildly, prematurely, carelessly, precipitately, heedlessly. ■ OPPOSITES cautiously.

headquarters n. CENTRE OF OPERATIONS, base, command post, main office/branch, head office.

heal v. **1** CURE, make well, make better, remedy, treat, mend, restore, regenerate. **2** RECUPERATE, get better/well, mend, be cured, be on the mend, improve, be restored. **3** RECONCILE, patch up, settle, set right, put right, harmonize, conciliate.

health n. **1** HEALTHINESS, fitness, wellbeing, good condition, good shape, soundness, robustness, strength, vigour, fine fettle, salubrity. **2** STATE OF HEALTH, constitution, physical state, shape, condition, form, tone.

healthy adj. **1** IN GOOD HEALTH, fit, in good condition, robust, strong, vigorous, hardy, flourishing, blooming, hale and hearty, hale; *informal* in the pink. **2** HEALTH-GIVING, beneficial, invigorating, bracing, stimulating, refreshing, nutritious, nourishing, wholesome, good for one. ■ OPPOSITES unhealthy.

heap n. **1** PILE, stack, mound, mass, stockpile, accumulation, collection, agglomeration, conglomeration, hoard, store, stock, supply. **2** A LOT, lots, a great deal, abundance, plenty, a mint; *informal* oodles, loads, tons, pots, stacks, lashings. ▶v. PILE UP, stack, amass, stockpile, mound, accumulate, collect, assemble, hoard, store, stock up, set aside, lay by.

hear v. **1** TAKE IN, catch, perceive, overhear; *informal* get, latch on to. **2** BE INFORMED, be told of, be made aware, receive information, find out, discover, learn, gather, pick up, hear tell, get wind of. **3** TRY, judge, pass judgement on, adjudicate, examine, investigate, inquire into, consider.

hearing n. INQUIRY, trial, inquest, investigation, review.

heart n. **1** PASSION, love, affection, emo-

■ **heartbreaking** adj. **heartbroken** adj.

hearten v. make more cheerful or confident.

hearth n. the floor of a fireplace.

heartless adj. unfeeling. ■ **heartlessly** adv.

hearty adj. (**heartier**, **heartiest**) **1** enthusiastic and friendly. **2** strong and healthy. **3** heartfelt. **4** (of a meal or appetite) large. ■ **heartily** adv.

heat n. **1** the quality of being hot. **2** a source of heat. **3** energy produced by the movement of molecules. **4** strength of feeling. **5** a preliminary round in a race or contest. ▶ v. **1** make or become hot. **2** (**heated**) angry. □ **heatstroke** a condition caused by overexposure to sun. **heatwave** a period of unusually hot weather. **on heat** (of a female mammal) ready to mate. ■ **heatedly** adv.

heater n. a device supplying heat.

heath n. an area of open uncultivated land covered with heather, gorse, etc.

heathen n. a person who does not belong to a widely held religion.

heather n. a shrub with small purple flowers.

heating n. equipment used to provide heat.

heave v. (**heaving**, **heaved** or Naut. **hove**) **1** lift or drag with great effort. **2** produce a sigh noisily. **3** informal throw. **4** rise and fall. **5** try to vomit. ▶ n. an act of heaving.

heaven n. **1** (in various religions) the place where God or the gods live. **2** (**the heavens**) literary the sky. **3** informal a place or state of extreme happiness.

heavenly adj. **1** of heaven. **2** of the sky. **3** informal wonderful. □ **heavenly body** a planet, star, etc.

heavy adj. (**heavier**, **heaviest**) **1** of great weight. **2** thick or dense. **3** of more than the usual size, amount, or force. **4** doing something to excess. **5** forceful. **6** requiring physical effort. **7** serious or difficult. □ **heavy-hearted** sad. **heavy industry** industry producing heavy machinery and materials. **heavy metal** a type of loud rock

Thesaurus

tions, feelings. **2** TENDERNESS, compassion, sympathy, empathy, humanity, responsiveness, fellow feeling, goodwill, kindness, kindliness. **3** SPIRIT, enthusiasm, keenness, eagerness, liveliness. **4** ESSENCE, crux, substance, core, quintessence.

heartache n. SORROW, grief, sadness, anguish, pain, hurt, agony, suffering, misery, wretchedness, despair, desolation, woe, despondency; literary dolour. ■ OPPOSITES happiness.

heartbreaking adj. SAD, pitiful, tragic, poignant, painful, agonizing, distressing, affecting, grievous, bitter, cruel, harsh, tear-jerking, harrowing, excruciating.

hearten v. CHEER, raise someone's spirits, revitalize, energize, invigorate, animate, exhilarate, uplift, elate, comfort, encourage, buoy up; informal buck up, give someone a shot in the arm.

heartfelt adj. DEEPLY FELT, deep, profound, wholehearted, sincere, earnest, honest, devout, genuine, unfeigned, ardent, fervent, passionate, warm, enthusiastic, eager.

heartless adj. UNFEELING, unsympathetic, unkind, uncaring, unmoved, untouched, cold, cold-hearted, cold-blooded, hard-hearted, cruel, harsh, stern, hard, brutal, merciless, pitiless, ruthless. ■ OPPOSITES compassionate.

heat n. **1** HOTNESS, warmth, warmness,

torridness, torridity, sultriness, calefaction. **2** PASSION, warmth, intensity, vehemence, ardour, fervour, fervency, zeal, eagerness, animation, earnestness, excitement, agitation. ■ OPPOSITES cold. ▶ v. **1** WARM, warm up, make hot/warm, reheat, cook. **2** GROW HOT/WARM, become hotter/warmer.

heated adj. VEHEMENT, passionate, fierce, angry, furious, stormy, tempestuous, frenzied, raging, intense, impassioned, violent, animated, inflamed, enraged.

heathen n. UNBELIEVER, infidel, pagan, disbeliever, atheist, heretic, idolater/idolatress. ▶ adj. PAGAN, godless, infidel, heathenish, irreligious, idolatrous, atheistic, heretical.

heave v. **1** LIFT, haul, tug, raise, hoist. **2** THROW, cast, toss, fling, hurl, let fly, pitch; informal sling, chuck. **3** VOMIT, be sick, gag, retch; US get sick; informal throw up, puke.

heaven n. **1** PARADISE, the next life, the hereafter, the life to come, the next world, the afterlife, nirvana. **2** ECSTASY, bliss, rapture, joy, happiness, contentment, seventh heaven. **3** SKY, skies; literary firmament, empyrean, ether. ■ OPPOSITES hell.

heavenly adj. **1** CELESTIAL, divine, angelic, seraphic, cherubic, beatific, blessed, holy, god-like, immortal, paradisiacal. **2** DELIGHTFUL, pleasurable, enjoyable, music. **heavyweight 1** the heaviest weight in boxing etc. **2** informal an influential person. ■ **heavily** adv. **heaviness** n.

Hebrew n. **1** a member of an ancient people living in what is now Israel and Palestine. **2** the language of the Hebrews. ■ **Hebraic** adj.

heckle v. interrupt a public speaker with comments or abuse. ■ **heckler** n.

hectare n. a unit of area, 10,000 sq m (2.471 acres).

hectic adj. full of frantic activity. ■ **hectically** adv.

hector v. talk to in a bullying way.

hedge n. a barrier of closely growing bushes. ▶v. **1** surround with a hedge. **2** avoid making a definite statement or decision. □ **hedgehog** a small mammal with a spiny coat. **hedgerow** bushes and trees bordering a field.

hedonism n. the pursuit of pleasure. ■ **hedonist** n. **hedonistic** adj.

heed v. pay attention to. □ **pay** (or **take**) **heed** pay careful attention. ■ **heedless** adj. **heedlessly** adv.

heel n. **1** the back part of the foot below the ankle. **2** the part of a shoe supporting the heel. ▶v. **1** renew the heel on a shoe. **2** (of a ship) tilt to one side.

hefty adj. (**heftier**, **heftiest**) large, heavy, and powerful.

hegemony /hi-**jem**-uh-ni, hi-**gem**-uh-ni/ n. dominance of one group or state over another.

Hegira /hej-**iruh**/ n. Muhammad's flight from Mecca (AD 622).

heifer /**hef**-fer/ n. a young cow.

height n. **1** the measurement from head to foot or from base to top. **2** the distance above ground or sea level. **3** the quality of being tall or high. **4** a high place. **5** the most intense part. **6** an extreme example. ■ **heighten** v.

heinous /**hay**-nuhss, **hee**-nuhss/ adj. very wicked.

marvellous, wonderful, gratifying, blissful, rapturous, sublime, glorious, divine. **3** BEAUTIFUL, exquisite, perfect, superb, ravishing, enchanting, alluring. ■ OPPOSITES hellish.

heavy adj. **1** WEIGHTY, bulky, hefty, big, large, substantial, massive, enormous, unwieldy, cumbersome, burdensome. **2** ONEROUS, burdensome, oppressive, difficult, unbearable, intolerable. **3** HARD, forceful, strong, severe, harsh, intense, sharp. **4** OVERWEIGHT, fat, stout, obese, tubby, corpulent, paunchy, lumbering, bulky; informal hulking. **5** SEVERE, intense, serious, grave. ■ OPPOSITES light.

heavy-handed adj. see CLUMSY.

hectic adj. BUSY, active, frantic, frenetic, frenzied, bustling, flurried, fast and furious, turbulent, tumultuous, confused, exciting, excited, wild. ■ OPPOSITES leisurely.

hedge n. **1** HEDGEROW, row of bushes, quickset, barrier, screen, protection, windbreak. **2** SAFEGUARD, guard, protection, shield, cover, insurance. ▶v. **1** SURROUND, enclose, encircle, circle, border, edge, skirt. **2** EQUIVOCATE, prevaricate, be vague/ambivalent, be non-committal, dodge the question/issue, beat about the bush, sidestep the question/issue, temporize, quibble, hum and haw; US informal waffle.

heed n. ATTENTION, attentiveness, notice, note, regard, mindfulness, mind, respect, consideration, thought, care, caution, watchfulness, wariness, chariness. ▶v. PAY HEED/ATTENTION TO, attend to, take notice/note of, notice, note, bear in mind, be mindful of, mind, mark, take into account, follow, obey, adhere to, observe, take to heart, be alert to, be cautious of, watch out for.

heedful adj. ATTENTIVE, careful, mindful, cautious, prudent, circumspect, wary, observant, watchful, vigilant, alert, on guard. ■ OPPOSITES heedless.

heedless adj. INATTENTIVE, unheeding, careless, incautious, unmindful, regardless, unthinking, thoughtless, unwary, oblivious, unobservant, negligent, neglectful, rash, reckless, foolhardy, precipitate. ■ OPPOSITES heedful.

heft v. LIFT, lift up, raise, hoist, hike up, heave, boost.

hefty adj. **1** HEAVY, bulky, big, large, stout, massive, huge, muscular, brawny, strapping, sturdy, solidly built, strong; informal beefy, hulking. **2** SUBSTANTIAL, sizeable, huge, colossal, expensive. ■ OPPOSITES light.

height n. **1** HIGHNESS, altitude, loftiness, elevation, tallness, stature. **2** TOP, mountain top, hilltop, summit, peak, crest, crown, pinnacle, apex, vertex, apogee. **3** PEAK, zenith, apex, culmination, crowning point, climax, consummation, perfection.

heighten v. **1** RAISE, make higher, lift, elevate. **2** MAKE GREATER, intensify, raise, increase, add to, build up, augment, boost, strengthen, amplify, mag-

heir /air/ n. (fem. **heiress**) a person entitled to inherit property or a rank. □ **heirloom** a valuable object that has belonged to a family for several generations.

held past & past part. of HOLD.

helical adj. like a helix.

helicopter n. an aircraft with horizontally revolving overhead blades.

heliport n. a landing place for helicopters.

helium n. a light colourless gas that does not burn.

helix n. (pl. **helices**) a spiral.

hell n. **1** (in various religions) a place of punishment for the wicked after death. **2** a state or place of great suffering. □ **hell-bent** recklessly determined. **hell for leather** as fast as possible. ■ **hellish** adj.

hello (or **hallo, hullo**) exclam. used as a greeting or to attract attention.

helm n. a tiller or wheel for steering a ship or boat. □ **helmsman** a person who steers a boat.

helmet n. a hard or padded protective hat.

help v. **1** make a task etc. easier for someone. **2** improve or ease. **3** serve with food or drink. **4** (**help oneself**) take without asking first. **5** (**can/could not help**) cannot or could not stop oneself doing. ▶ n. **1** the act of helping. **2** a

person or thing that helps. □ **helpline** a telephone service providing help with problems. ■ **helper** n.

helpful adj. **1** ready to give help. **2** useful. ■ **helpfully** adv. **helpfulness** n.

helping n. a portion of food served.

helpless adj. **1** unable to manage without help. **2** uncontrollable. ■ **helplessly** adv. **helplessness** n.

helter-skelter adj. & adv. in disorderly haste. ▶ n. a spiral slide round a tower at a fair.

hem n. the edge of a piece of cloth or clothing turned under and sewn. ▶ v. (**hemming, hemmed**) **1** turn under and sew the edge of. **2** (**hem in**) surround and restrict.

hematology etc. US = HAEMATOLOGY etc.

hemisphere n. **1** a half of a sphere. **2** a half of the earth. ■ **hemispherical** adj.

hemlock n. a poisonous plant.

hemp n. a plant with coarse fibres used to make rope, cloth, etc., and from which the drug cannabis is made.

hen n. a female bird, esp. of a domestic fowl. □ **hen night** (or **hen party**) an all-female celebration held for a woman about to get married. **henpecked** (of a man) nagged by his wife.

hence adv. **1** for this reason. **2** from now.

henceforth (or **henceforward**) adv.

Thesaurus

nify, aggravate, enhance. ■ OPPOSITES lower.

heinous adj. ABOMINABLE, atrocious, abhorrent, odious, detestable, loathsome, hateful, wicked, monstrous, horrible, ghastly, shocking, flagrant, contemptible, reprehensible, despicable.

hellish adj. **1** DEMONIC, diabolical, devilish, fiendish, satanic, infernal. **2** UNPLEASANT, nasty, disagreeable, horrible, horrid, awful.

help v. **1** ASSIST, aid, give someone a (helping) hand, lend a hand, guide, be of service to, be useful to, succour, befriend. **2** SUPPORT, back, contribute to, promote, boost. **3** SOOTHE, relieve, ameliorate, alleviate, mitigate, assuage, cure, heal, improve, ease. ▶ n. **1** ASSISTANCE, aid, service, helping hand, guidance, benefit, advantage, support, backing, succour. **2** RELIEF, alleviation, amelioration, mitigation, remedy, cure, improvement, ease, corrective, balm. **3** SERVANT, maid, worker, hired help; informal daily. □ **help oneself to** TAKE, appropriate, commandeer, steal, make

free with; informal walk off with, pinch, nick.

helper n. ASSISTANT, aide, deputy, adjutant, second-in-command, auxiliary, right-hand man/woman, henchman, colleague, associate, co-worker, partner, ally, collaborator.

helpful adj. **1** USEFUL, of use, of service, beneficial, valuable, advantageous, constructive, practical, productive, instrumental. **2** SUPPORTIVE, kind, friendly, obliging, accommodating, cooperative, sympathetic, considerate, caring, neighbourly, charitable, benevolent. ■ OPPOSITES useless, unhelpful.

helping n. PORTION, serving, ration, piece, plateful, amount, share.

helpless adj. **1** WEAK, feeble, disabled, incapable, infirm, debilitated, powerless, dependent, unfit, invalid, bedridden, paralysed; informal laid up. **2** DEFENCELESS, unprotected, vulnerable, exposed, abandoned, destitute, forlorn, desolate. ■ OPPOSITES independent.

hem n. BORDER, edge, edging, trim, trimming, fringe, frill, flounce, valance. ▶ v.

from this or that time on.
henchman n. a follower or assistant.
henna n. a reddish-brown dye made from a shrub. ■ **hennaed** adj.
henry n. (pl. **henries** or **henrys**) Physics the SI unit of inductance.
hepatic adj. of the liver.
hepatitis n. inflammation of the liver.
heptagon n. a plane figure with seven sides. ■ **heptagonal** adj.
heptathlon n. an athletic contest involving seven events. ■ **heptathlete** n.
her pron. used as the object of a verb or preposition to refer to a female previously mentioned. ▶ adj. belonging to her.
herald n. **1** hist. a person who carried official messages and made announcements. **2** a sign of something to come. ▶ v. be a herald of.
heraldry n. the system by which coats of arms are devised and regulated. ■ **heraldic** adj.
herb n. a plant used for flavouring or in medicine. ■ **herbal** adj.
herbaceous /her-bay-shuhss/ adj. soft-stemmed. □ **herbaceous border** a garden border containing esp. perennial flowering plants.
herbalism n. the study or practice of using plants in medicine. ■ **herbalist** n.
herbicide n. a substance used to destroy plants.
herbivore n. an animal that feeds on plants. ■ **herbivorous** adj.
Herculean adj. requiring or having great strength or effort.
herd n. **1** a large group of animals living or kept together. **2** a large crowd of people. ▶ v. **1** move in a group. **2** look after livestock. □ **herdsman** the owner or keeper of a herd of animals.
here adv. **1** in, at, or to this place or position. **2** at this time or point. □ **hereabouts** near this place. **hereafter 1** from now on. **2** (**the hereafter**) life after death. **hereby** by this means. **herein** in this document etc. **hereto** to this. **herewith** with this.
hereditary adj. of or by inheritance.
heredity n. inheritance of characteristics from parents.
heresy n. (pl. **heresies**) a belief or opinion contrary to traditional religious doctrine.
heretic n. a person believing in a heresy. ■ **heretical** adj.
heritage n. valued things such as historic buildings, passed down from previous generations.
hermaphrodite n. a person, animal, or plant having both male and female sex organs or characteristics.
hermetic adj. airtight. ■ **hermetically** adv.
hermit n. a person living in solitude, esp. for religious reasons.
hermitage n. the home of a hermit.
hernia n. a condition in which part of an organ protrudes through the wall of the cavity containing it.
hero n. (pl. **heroes**) **1** a person admired for their courage or actions. **2** the chief male character in a story. ■ **heroism** n.
heroic adj. very brave. ▶ n. (**heroics**) brave or dramatic behaviour. ■ **heroically** adv.

Thesaurus

1 BIND, edge, trim, fringe. **2** BORDER, edge, skirt, surround, encircle, circle, enclose, encompass. **3** SHUT IN, hedge in, close in, pen in, confine, constrain, restrict, limit, trap, keep within bounds.
herd n. FLOCK, pack, mob, crowd, throng, swarm, press, multitude. ▶ v. DRIVE, round up, assemble, collect, muster, shepherd, guide, lead, force, urge, goad.
hereditary adj. **1** GENETIC, congenital, innate, inborn, inherent, family, inbred, transmissible, transferable. **2** INHERITED, handed down, bequeathed, willed, transferred, transmitted, family, ancestral.
heresy n. APOSTASY, dissent, nonconformity, unorthodoxy, free thinking, dissidence, scepticism, agnosticism, atheism, heterodoxy, revisionism, idolatry, paganism.

heretic n. DISSENTER, apostate, unbeliever, sceptic, agnostic, atheist, nonconformist, free thinker, renegade, revisionist, schismatic, pagan, idolater, recusant.
heretical adj. DISSIDENT, sceptical, nonconformist, atheistical, agnostic, free-thinking, unorthodox, heterodox, renegade, revisionist, schismatic, pagan, idolatrous, recusant. ■ OPPOSITES orthodox.
heritage n. HISTORY, tradition, background, ancestry, lineage, descent, family, extraction, heredity, birth.
hermit n. RECLUSE, solitary, anchorite, anchoress, eremite, stylite.
heroic adj. **1** BRAVE, courageous, valiant, intrepid, fearless, gallant, valorous, stout-hearted, lion-hearted, bold, daring, undaunted, dauntless, manly, vir-

heroin n. a highly addictive illegal drug.

heroine n. 1 a woman admired for her courage or achievements. 2 the chief female character in a story.

heron n. a long-legged wading bird.

herpes /her-peez/ n. a viral disease causing blisters.

Herr n. (pl. **Herren**) a title for a German man.

herring n. (pl. **herring** or **herrings**) an edible fish. □ **herringbone** a pattern of columns of short slanting parallel lines.

hers possess. pron. belonging to her.

....

☑ No apostrophe: he*rs*.

....

herself pron. 1 used when a female who performs an action is also affected by it. 2 she or her personally.

hertz n. (pl. **hertz**) the SI unit of frequency.

hesitant adj. slow to act or speak through indecision or reluctance. ■ **hesitancy** n. **hesitantly** adv.

hesitate v. 1 pause indecisively. 2 be reluctant to do. ■ **hesitation** n.

hessian n. a strong, coarse fabric of hemp or jute.

heterodox adj. not following traditional standards or beliefs.

heterogeneous adj. varied. ■ **heterogeneity** n.

heterosexual adj. sexually attracted to people of the opposite sex. ▶ n. a heterosexual person. ■ **heterosexuality** n.

hew v. (**hewing**, **hewed**, past part. **hewn** or **hewed**) chop or cut with an axe etc.

hex n. a magic spell or curse.

hexagon n. a plane figure with six sides. ■ **hexagonal** adj.

hexagram n. a six-pointed star formed by two intersecting triangles.

hexameter n. a line of verse made up of six metrical feet.

heyday n. the period of a person's greatest success, energy, etc.

HGV abbrev. heavy goods vehicle.

hiatus /hy-ay-tuhss/ n. (pl. **hiatuses**) a pause or gap in a sequence.

hibernate v. spend the winter in a sleep-like state. ■ **hibernation** n.

Hibernian adj. Irish. ▶ n. an Irish person.

hibiscus n. a plant with large brightly coloured flowers.

hiccup (or **hiccough**) n. 1 a gulping sound in the throat. 2 a minor setback. ▶ v. (**hiccuping**, **hiccuped**) make the sound of a hiccup.

hide v. (**hiding**, **hid**; past part. **hidden**) 1 put or keep out of sight. 2 conceal oneself. 3 keep secret. ▶ n. 1 a concealed shelter for observing wildlife. 2 the skin of an animal. □ **hidebound** unwilling to change because of convention. **hideout** a hiding place.

hideous adj. very ugly. ■ **hideously** adv.

Thesaurus

....

ile, doughty, chivalrous. **2** LEGENDARY, mythological, classic, classical, fabulous. **3** EPIC, Homeric, grandiloquent, high-flown, high-sounding, extravagant, grandiose, bombastic, rhetorical, pretentious, turgid, magniloquent, orotund, elevated. ■ OPPOSITES cowardly.

heroism n. BRAVERY, courage, courageousness, valour, intrepidity, fearlessness, gallantry, stout-heartedness, lionheartedness, boldness, daring, dauntlessness, doughtiness, manliness, virility, mettle, spirit, fortitude, chivalry.

hesitant adj. **1** UNCERTAIN, unsure, doubtful, dubious, sceptical, irresolute, indecisive, vacillating, wavering, oscillating, shilly-shallying, stalling, delaying, disinclined, unwilling, half-hearted, lacking confidence, diffident, timid, shy. **2** RELUCTANT, unwilling, disinclined, diffident, having qualms about. ■ OPPOSITES determined, decisive.

hesitate v. **1** DELAY, pause, hang back, wait, be uncertain, be unsure, be doubtful, be indecisive, vacillate, waver, dither, shilly-shally, dally, stall, temporize, dilly-dally. **2** BE RELUCTANT, be unwilling, be disinclined, shrink from, hang back from, think twice about, baulk at, demur from, scruple to, have misgivings about, be diffident about. **3** STAMMER, stumble, falter, fumble for words, hum and haw.

hew v. **1** CHOP, hack, axe, cut, saw, fell, lop, sever, trim, prune. **2** CARVE, sculpt, sculpture, shape, fashion, form, model, whittle, chip, hammer, chisel, roughhew.

hidden adj. **1** OUT OF SIGHT, secret, unseen, not visible, not on view, covered, concealed, masked, shrouded, unrevealed. **2** SECRET, obscure, indistinct, indefinite, unclear, vague, cryptic, mysterious, covert, concealed, under wraps, abstruse, arcane, recondite, clandestine, ulterior, unfathomable, inexplicable, occult, mystical. ■ OPPOSITES obvious.

hide v. **1** CONCEAL ONESELF, go into hiding,

hideousness n.

hiding n. a severe beating.

hierarchy n. (pl. **hierarchies**) a system ranking people or things one above the other according to status or importance. ■ **hierarchical** adj.

hieroglyphics pl. n. a form of writing consisting of pictorial symbols. ■ **hieroglyphic** adj.

hi-fi adj. of high fidelity. ▶ n. (pl. **hi-fis**) a set of high-fidelity equipment.

higgledy-piggledy adv. & adj. in disorder.

high adj. **1** extending far upwards. **2** of a specified height. **3** far above ground or sea level. **4** large or greater in amount, value, size, etc. **5** at the peak. **6** great in status. **7** (of a sound) not deep or low. **8** informal under the influence of drugs or alcohol. **9** (of food) beginning to go bad. ▶ n. **1** a high level. **2** an area of high atmospheric pressure. **3** informal a euphoric state. ▶ adv. at or to a high or specified level. □ **highbrow** intellectual or refined. **higher education** education at university etc. **high fidelity** the reproduction of sound with little distortion. **high-handed** using authority arrogantly. **highland** (also **highlands**) an area of high or mountainous land. **high-rise** (of a building) with many storeys. **high school** a secondary school. **high seas** the areas of the sea

not under the control of any one country. **high season** the busiest time for a hotel etc. **high-spirited** lively and cheerful. **high street** the main shopping street of a town. **high tea** a meal eaten in the late afternoon or early evening. **high-tech** involving advanced technology. **high tide** (or **high water**) the tide when at its highest level. **high time** at or past the time when something should have happened.

highlight n. **1** an outstanding part of an event etc. **2** a bright area in a picture. **3** a dyed light streak in the hair. ▶ v. **1** draw attention to. **2** create highlights in.

highly adv. **1** to a high degree. **2** favourably. □ **highly strung** nervous and easily upset.

Highness n. (**His**, **Your**, etc. **Highness**) a title given to a royal person.

highway n. **1** a main road. **2** a public road. □ **highwayman** (in the past) a man who held up and robbed travellers.

hijack v. illegally seize control of a vehicle, aircraft, etc. while it is travelling. ▶ n. an act of hijacking. ■ **hijacker** n.

hike n. **1** a long walk. **2** a sharp increase. ▶ v. **1** go on a hike. **2** raise. ■ **hiker** n.

hilarious adj. very funny. ■ **hilariously** adv. **hilarity** n.

hill n. a raised area of land, lower than a mountain. ■ **hilly** adj.

Thesaurus

take cover, find a hiding place, lie low, keep out of sight, secrete oneself, go to ground, go underground, cover one's tracks; informal hole up. **2** STOW AWAY, secrete, store away, lock up; informal stash. **3** OBSCURE, block, obstruct, darken, eclipse, cloud. **4** KEEP SECRET, keep dark, withhold, conceal, suppress, mask, veil, shroud, camouflage, disguise, hush up; informal keep mum about, keep under one's hat. ■ OPPOSITES reveal.

hideous adj. **1** UGLY, unsightly, grotesque, monstrous, repulsive, repellent, revolting, gruesome, disgusting, grim, ghastly, macabre. **2** AWFUL, horrible, horrific, horrendous, horrifying, frightful, shocking, dreadful, outrageous, monstrous, appalling, terrible, terrifying, heinous, abominable, foul, vile, odious, loathsome, contemptible, execrable. ■ OPPOSITES beautiful.

hiding n. BEATING, thrashing, whipping, caning, spanking, flogging, drubbing, battering; informal licking, walloping, tanning, whaling, lathering.

hierarchy n. SOCIAL ORDER, ranking,

grading, class system, pecking order.

high adj. **1** TALL, lofty, elevated, soaring, towering, steep. **2** HIGH-RANKING, leading, top, powerful, important, prominent, eminent, principal, chief, influential, distinguished, notable, illustrious, exalted. **3** INTENSE, strong, powerful, extreme, forceful, vigorous, potent, violent. **4** DRUGGED, intoxicated, inebriated, delirious, hallucinating; informal stoned, on a trip, turned on. ■ OPPOSITES low.

highbrow n. INTELLECTUAL, scholar, genius, mastermind; informal egghead, brain, brainbox. ▶ adj. INTELLECTUAL, scholarly, bookish, cultured, cultivated, educated, sophisticated; informal brainy. ■ OPPOSITES lowbrow.

high-handed adj. AUTOCRATIC, tyrannical, despotic, domineering, oppressive, overbearing, imperious, haughty, lordly; informal bossy.

hike v. **1** WALK, march, tramp, trek, trudge, plod, ramble, wander, backpack. **2** HITCH UP, pull up, jack up, lift up. **3** RAISE, increase, add to, put up, jack up. ▶ n. **1** WALK, march, tramp, trek,

hillock n. a small hill.

hilt n. the handle of a sword or dagger. ☐ **to the hilt** completely.

him pron. used as the object of a verb or preposition to refer to a male previously mentioned.

himself pron. **1** used when a male who performs an action is also affected by it. **2** he or him personally.

hind adj. situated at the back. ▶ n. a female deer.

hinder v. delay or obstruct. ■ **hindrance** n.

Hindi n. a language of northern India.

hindmost adj. furthest back.

hindsight n. understanding of a situation or event after it has happened.

Hindu n. (pl. **Hindus**) a follower of Hinduism.

Hinduism n. a major religion of the Indian subcontinent.

Hindustani n. a group of languages of NW India.

hinge n. a movable joint or mechanism by which a door, lid, etc. opens and closes. ▶ v. **1** attach with a hinge. **2** (**hinge on**) depend on.

hint n. **1** a slight or indirect suggestion. **2** a slight trace. **3** a piece of practical information. ▶ v. suggest indirectly.

hinterland n. the remote areas of a country away from the coast.

hip n. **1** the projection of the pelvis on each side of the body. **2** the fruit of a rose.

hip hop n. a style of popular music fea-

turing rap with an electronic backing.

hippo n. (pl. **hippo** or **hippos**) a hippopotamus.

hippopotamus n. (pl. **hippopotamuses** or **hippopotami**) a large African river mammal with a thick skin.

hippy (or **hippie**) n. (pl. **hippies**) a person with long hair and unconventional clothes.

hire v. **1** have or grant the temporary use of in return for payment. **2** employ. ▶ n. the act of hiring. ☐ **hireling** a hired helper. **hire purchase** a system of buying by payment in instalments.

hirsute /her-syoot/ adj. hairy.

his adj. & possess. pron. belonging to a male previously mentioned.

Hispanic adj. of Spain or a Spanish-speaking country.

hiss v. **1** make a sharp sound as of the letter s, esp. in disapproval. **2** whisper urgently. ▶ n. a hissing sound.

histamine n. a substance released by cells in allergic and inflammatory reactions.

histology n. the study of animal or plant tissues. ■ **histologist** n.

historian n. an expert in history.

historic adj. important in history, or likely to be seen as such in the future.

historical adj. **1** of history. **2** belonging to or set in the past. ■ **historically** adv.

history n. (pl. **histories**) **1** the study of past events. **2** the past. **3** the past events connected with someone or something. **4** a record of past events.

Thesaurus

ramble, trudge, wander.

hilarious adj. VERY FUNNY, extremely amusing, comical, uproarious, humorous, entertaining, side-splitting; informal priceless.

hill n. **1** ELEVATION, heights, hillock, hilltop, knoll, hummock, mound, mount, fell, ridge. **2** SLOPE, incline, rise, gradient, ramp, acclivity, declivity.

hinder v. IMPEDE, hamper, hold back, interfere with, delay, hold up, slow down, retard, obstruct, inhibit, handicap, hamstring, block, interrupt, check, trammel, forestall, curb, baulk, thwart, frustrate, baffle, foil, stymie, stop, bring to a halt, arrest, defer, abort, prevent, debar. ■ OPPOSITES facilitate.

hindrance n. IMPEDIMENT, obstacle, obstruction, interference, handicap, block, restraint, interruption, check, bar, barrier, drawback, snag, difficulty, stumbling block, encumbrance, curb, stoppage, trammel, deterrent, preven-

tion, debarment. ■ OPPOSITES aid, help.

hinge v. (**hinge on**) DEPEND ON, turn on, hang on, be contingent on, pivot on, revolve around, rest on, centre on.

hint n. **1** CLUE, inkling, suggestion, innuendo, tip-off, insinuation, implication, indication, mention, allusion, intimation, whisper, a word to the wise. **2** TIP, pointer, advice, help, suggestion. **3** TOUCH, trace, suggestion, dash, soupçon, sprinkling, tinge, whiff, breath, taste, scent. ▶ v. SUGGEST, insinuate, imply, indicate, mention, allude to, intimate, let it be known, signal, refer to, make a reference to.

hire v. **1** RENT, lease, charter, engage. **2** APPOINT, sign on, take on, engage, employ, secure someone's services, enlist, contract with.

historic adj. FAMED, notable, famous, celebrated, renowned, momentous, significant, important, consequential, memorable, remarkable, outstanding,

histrionic adj. excessively dramatic. ▶n. (**histrionics**) exaggerated behaviour.

hit v. (**hitting, hit**) **1** strike with one's hand or a tool, bat, etc. **2** come into sudden and forceful contact with. **3** strike a target. **4** cause harm or distress to. ▶n. **1** an instance of hitting or being hit. **2** a success. □ **hit it off** informal like one another. **hit list** a list of people to be killed. **hitman** a person paid to kill someone.

hitch v. **1** move with a jerk. **2** fasten with a rope. **3** informal travel by hitchhiking. ▶n. **1** a temporary difficulty. **2** a kind of knot. □ **get hitched** informal get married. **hitchhike** travel by getting lifts in passing vehicles.

hither adv. to or towards this place.

hitherto adv. until this time.

HIV abbrev. human immunodeficiency virus (causing Aids).

hive n. **1** a beehive. **2** (**hives**) an allergic rash of round itchy weals. ▶v. (**hive off**) separate from a larger group.

HM abbrev. Her (or His) Majesty or Majesty's.

HMS abbrev. Her or His Majesty's Ship.

HNC abbrev. Higher National Certificate.

HND abbrev. Higher National Diploma.

hoard n. a store of something valued. ▶v. build up a store of. ■ **hoarder** n.

✓ Don't confuse **hoard** with **horde**, which means 'a large crowd'.

hoarding n. a large board for displaying advertisements.

hoar frost n. a feathery frost.

hoarse adj. (of a voice) rough and harsh. ■ **hoarsely** adv. **hoarseness** n.

hoary adj. **1** having grey hair. **2** old and unoriginal.

hoax n. & v. (deceive with) a humorous or cruel trick. ■ **hoaxer** n.

hob n. the flat top part of a cooker, with hotplates or burners.

hobble v. **1** walk with difficulty or painfully. **2** strap together the legs of a horse to limit its movement. ▶n. a hobbling walk.

hobby n. (pl. **hobbies**) an activity done regularly in one's leisure time for pleasure. □ **hobby horse 1** a child's toy consisting of a stick with a model of a horse's head. **2** a person's favourite topic.

hobgoblin n. a mischievous imp.

hobnail n. a heavy-headed nail for the soles of boots. ■ **hobnailed** adj.

hobnob v. (**hobnobbing, hobnobbed**) informal socialize with important people.

hobo n. (pl. **hoboes** or **hobos**) US a homeless person.

Hobson's choice n. a choice of taking what is offered or nothing at all.

hock n. **1** the middle joint in the back leg of a four-legged animal. **2** a dry white German wine. ▶v. informal pawn.

hockey n. a game played with hooked sticks and a small hard ball.

hocus-pocus n. meaningless talk used

Thesaurus

extraordinary, epoch-making, red-letter.

historical adj. DOCUMENTED, recorded, factual, chronicled, archival, authentic, actual, attested, verified, confirmed.

history n. **1** ANNAL, records, chronicles, account, study, tale, saga, narrative, recital, reports, memoirs, biography. **2** LIFE STORY, background, antecedents, experiences, adventures, fortunes. **3** THE PAST, former times, bygone days, yesterday, the old days, the good old days, time gone by, antiquity.

hit v. **1** STRIKE, smack, slap, punch, box, cuff, buffet, thump, batter, pound, pummel, thrash, hammer, bang, knock, club, swat; informal whack, wallop, bash, belt, clout, clip, clobber, sock, biff, swipe. **2** RUN INTO, collide with, bang into, smash into, crash into, knock into, bump, meet head-on.

hoard v. STORE, store up, stock up, stockpile, put by, put away, lay by, lay in, set aside, pile up, stack up, stow away, husband, save, buy up, accumulate, amass, heap up, collect, gather, squirrel away, garner. ▶n. STORE, stockpile, supply, reserve, fund, cache, reservoir, accumulation, heap, pile, mass, aggregation, conglomeration; informal stash.

hoarse adj. CROAKY, croaking, gruff, rough, throaty, harsh, husky, gravelly, rasping, guttural, raucous, cracked. ■ OPPOSITES smooth.

hoax n. PRACTICAL JOKE, joke, prank, jest, trick, ruse, deception, fraud, imposture, cheat, swindle; informal con, fast one, spoof, scam. ▶v. TRICK, fool, deceive, hoodwink, delude, bluff, dupe, take in, cheat, swindle, defraud, gull; informal con, pull a fast one on, pull the wool over someone's eyes, take for a ride, spoof.

hobble v. WALK WITH DIFFICULTY, limp, falter, shuffle, totter, stagger, reel; Sc. hirple.

to deceive.

hod n. **1** a V-shaped trough on a pole for carrying mortar or bricks. **2** a container for storing coal.

hodgepodge US = HOTCHPOTCH.

hoe n. a gardening tool with a thin metal blade. ▶v. use a hoe to cut through earth or weeds.

hog n. a castrated male pig reared for slaughter. ▶v. (**hogging**, **hogged**) informal take or hoard selfishly.

Hogmanay n. (in Scotland) New Year's Eve.

hoick v. informal lift or pull with a jerk.

hoi polloi pl. n. the ordinary people.

hoist v. haul or lift up. ▶n. an apparatus for hoisting.

hoity-toity adj. snobbish.

hokum n. informal **1** nonsense. **2** overused or sentimental material in a film etc.

hold v. (**holding**, **held**) **1** grasp, carry, or support. **2** keep or detain. **3** have, own, or occupy. **4** contain or be able to contain. **5** stay or keep at a certain level. **6** arrange and take part in. **7** regard in a specified way. ▶n. **1** a grip. **2** a place where one can grip while climbing. **3** a degree of control. **4** a storage space in the lower part of a ship or aircraft. ▫ **hold on** wait. **2** keep going in adversity. **hold out 1** resist adversity.

2 continue to be sufficient. **hold up 1** delay. **2** rob using the threat of violence. **hold-up 1** a delay. **2** a robbery carried out with the threat of violence. **no holds barred** without restrictions. ■ **holder** n.

holdall n. a large soft bag.

holding n. **1** land held by lease. **2** (**holdings**) stocks and property owned by someone.

hole n. **1** a hollow space or opening in an object or surface. **2** informal an awkward or unpleasant place or situation. ▶v. **1** make a hole in. **2** Golf hit the ball into a hole. ■ **holey** adj.

holiday n. an extended period of leisure. ▶v. spend a holiday.

holistic adj. treating the whole person rather than just the symptoms of a disease. ■ **holism** n.

hollow adj. **1** having empty space inside. **2** sunken. **3** echoing. **4** worthless. ▶n. **1** a hole or sunken place. **2** a small valley. ▶v. make hollow.

holly n. an evergreen shrub with prickly leaves and red berries.

hollyhock n. a tall plant with large showy flowers.

holmium n. a soft metallic element.

holocaust n. destruction or slaughter on a mass scale.

Thesaurus

hobby n. INTEREST, pursuit, pastime, diversion, recreation, relaxation, sideline, divertissement, entertainment, amusement.

hold v. **1** CLASP, clutch, grasp, grip, clench, seize, cling to. **2** BEAR, carry, take, support, hold up, buttress, keep up, sustain, prop up, brace, suspend. **3** DETAIN, hold in custody, confine, impound, constrain, lock up, imprison, put behind bars, incarcerate. **4** KEEP, maintain, occupy, engage, involve, absorb, engross, monopolize, catch, arrest, fascinate, rivet. **5** CONTAIN, take, accommodate, have room for. **6** CALL, convene, assemble, conduct, run, preside over, officiate at. ▶n. **1** GRIP, grasp, clutch, clasp. **2** CONTROL, grip, power, dominance, influence, mastery, dominion, authority, ascendancy. ▫ **hold out** STAND FAST, stand firm, resist, withstand, maintain one's position, stay put. **hold up** DELAY, hinder, impede, obstruct, retard, slow down, set back, stop, bring to a halt, prevent.

holder n. **1** OWNER, possessor, bearer, proprietor, keeper, custodian, purchaser, incumbent, occupier. **2** CONTAIN-

ER, case, casing, receptacle, stand, cover, covering, housing, sheath.

hole n. **1** OPENING, aperture, gap, orifice, space, breach, break, fissure, crack, rift, puncture, perforation, cut, incision, split, gash, rent, slit, vent, notch. **2** PIT, crater, excavation, mine, shaft, dugout, cave, cavern, pothole, depression, hollow, chamber, pocket, cavity, dip.

holiness n. SANCTITY, sanctitude, saintliness, sacredness, divineness, divinity, godliness, blessedness, spirituality, religiousness, piety, righteousness, goodness, virtue, purity, sanctimoniousness.

hollow adj. **1** EMPTY, vacant, not filled, not solid, hollowed out. **2** SUNKEN, deepset, indented, depressed, concave, caved in, cavernous, incurvate. **3** MUFFLED, muted, low, dull, deep, rumbling, flat, dead, sepulchral. **4** WORTHLESS, valueless, empty, profitless, fruitless, unprofitable, pointless, meaningless, insignificant, specious, pyrrhic. **5** INSINCERE, false, dissembling, deceitful, sham, untrue, spurious. ▶n. INDENTATION, depression, concavity, dent, dip, dint, dimple, hole, crater, cavern, pit,

hologram n. a three-dimensional photographic image. ■ **holographic** adj.

holograph n. a manuscript handwritten by its author.

holster n. a holder for a handgun.

holy adj. (**holier**, **holiest**) **1** dedicated to God or a religious purpose. **2** morally and spiritually good. ■ **holiness** n.

homage n. honour shown to someone in public.

home n. **1** the place where one lives. **2** an institution for people needing professional care. ▶ adj. **1** of one's home or country. **2** (of a match) played on a team's own ground. ▶ adv. **1** to or at one's home. **2** to the intended position. ▶ v. **1** (of an animal) return by instinct to its territory. **2** (**home in on**) move or be aimed towards. □ **homeland** a person's native land. **home page** the main page of an individual's or organization's Internet site. **homesick** sad because one is missing one's home. **home truth** an unpleasant fact about oneself. **homework** school work to be done at home. ■ **homeless** adj. **homelessness** n. **homeward** adj. & adv. **homewards** adv.

homely adj. **1** simple but comfortable. **2** unsophisticated.

homeopathy (or **homoeopathy**) n. a system of treating diseases by tiny doses of substances that would normally produce symptoms of the disease. ■ **homeopath** n. **homeopathic** adj.

homicide n. the killing of another person. ■ **homicidal** adj.

homily n. (pl. **homilies**) a moralizing talk.

hominid n. a member of a family of primates including humans and their prehistoric ancestors.

homogeneous /hom-uh-jee-ni-uhss/ adj. **1** alike. **2** made up of parts of the same kind. ■ **homogeneity** n.

homogenize (or **-ise**) v. treat milk so that the cream does not separate.

homograph (or **homonym**) n. a word with the same spelling as another.

homophobia n. hatred or fear of homosexuals. ■ **homophobic** adj.

homophone n. a word with the same pronunciation as another.

Homo sapiens n. the species to which modern humans belong.

homosexual adj. sexually attracted to people of one's own sex. ▶ n. a homosexual person. ■ **homosexuality** n.

hone v. sharpen.

honest adj. **1** truthful and sincere. **2** fairly earned. ■ **honesty** n.

honestly adv. **1** in an honest way. **2** really (used for emphasis).

honey n. (pl. **honeys**) a sweet, sticky

Thesaurus

cavity, well, trough.

holocaust n. **1** DEVASTATION, destruction, inferno, conflagration, demolition. **2** GENOCIDE, mass murder, annihilation, massacre, carnage, slaughter, extermination, butchery, ethnic cleansing.

holy adj. **1** DEVOUT, God-fearing, pious, spiritual, religious, righteous, good, virtuous, moral, saintly, saintlike, sinless, pietistic. **2** SACRED, blessed, blest, sanctified, consecrated, hallowed, sacrosanct, dedicated, venerated, divine, religious. ■ OPPOSITES impious.

home n. **1** HOUSE, residence, habitation, dwelling, abode, domicile. **2** HOMELAND, birth place, native land, fatherland, motherland, country of origin. **3** HABITAT, environment, natural element, territory, ground, haunts, domain, abode. □ **home in on** AIM AT, focus on, focus attention on, concentrate on, pinpoint, zero in on, zoom in on.

homeless adj. OF NO FIXED ABODE, destitute, derelict, without a roof over one's head, down-and-out, vagrant, itinerant, nomadic, dispossessed, rootless.

homely adj. **1** COMFORTABLE, cosy, snug, welcoming, informal, relaxed, modest, unassuming, unpretentious, simple, natural, plain. **2** PLAIN, unattractive, ugly, plain-featured, ill-favoured; informal not much to look at, short on looks. ■ OPPOSITES grand, beautiful.

homicide n. MURDER, manslaughter, killing, slaughter, assassination, patricide, matricide, infanticide; literary slaying.

homily n. SERMON, lecture, speech, address, discourse, lesson, talk, oration.

honest adj. **1** PRINCIPLED, upright, honourable, ethical, moral, righteous, right-minded, virtuous, good, worthy, decent, law-abiding, high-minded, upstanding, just, fair, truthful, incorruptible, true, trustworthy, trusty, reliable, conscientious, scrupulous, reputable, dependable, loyal, faithful, veracious. **2** TRUTHFUL, frank, candid, direct, forthright, straightforward, open, genuine, plain-speaking, matter-of-fact, outspoken, blunt, undisguised, unfeigned, unequivocal. ■ OPPOSITES dishonest.

honestly adv. **1** LAWFULLY, legally, legitimately, fairly, by fair means, honourably, decently, ethically, morally, withfluid made by bees from nectar. □ **honeybee** the common bee. **honeycomb** a structure of six-sided wax compartments made by bees to store honey and eggs. **honeydew 1** a sweet, sticky substance produced by small insects feeding on plants. **2** a type of melon with sweet green flesh. **honeymoon 1** a holiday taken by a newly married couple. **2** an initial period of goodwill. **honeysuckle** a climbing shrub with fragrant flowers.

honeyed adj. (of words) soothing.

honk n. **1** the cry of a goose. **2** the sound of a car horn. ▶v. make a honk.

honorarium n. (pl. **honorariums** or **honoraria**) a voluntary payment for services offered without charge.

honorary adj. **1** given as an honour. **2** (of a position or its holder) unpaid.

honour (US **honor**) n. **1** great respect. **2** a privilege. **3** a clear sense of what is morally right. **4** an award given as a reward for achievement. **5** (**honours**) a university course of a higher level than an ordinary one. ▶v. **1** regard or treat with great respect. **2** keep an agreement.

honourable (US **honorable**) adj. **1** bringing or worthy of honour. **2** having high moral standards. ■ **honourably** adv.

hood n. **1** a covering for the head and neck. **2** a folding waterproof cover of a vehicle or pram. **3** US a car bonnet. **4** informal a gangster or gunman. ■ **hooded** adj.

hoodlum n. a gangster or hooligan.

hoodoo n. a run or cause of bad luck.

hoodwink v. deceive or trick.

hoof n. (pl. **hoofs** or **hooves**) the horny part of the foot of a horse, cow, etc. ■ **hoofed** adj.

hook n. **1** a curved device for catching hold of things or hanging things on. **2** a curved cutting instrument. **3** a short punch made with the elbow bent. ▶v. **1** be or become attached with a hook. **2** (**hook up**) link to electronic equipment. **3** catch with a hook. □ **hookworm** an intestinal worm with hook-like mouthparts. ■ **hooked** adj.

hookah n. an oriental tobacco pipe with a long tube to draw the smoke through water.

hooligan n. a violent young trouble-maker. ■ **hooliganism** n.

hoop n. **1** a rigid circular band. **2** a large ring used as a toy. **3** a metal croquet arch. ■ **hooped** adj.

hoopla n. a game in which rings are thrown to encircle a prize.

hoopoe n. a crested bird.

hooray exclam. hurrah.

hoot n. **1** a low sound made by owls or a hooter. **2** a short laugh or mocking shout. **3** informal an amusing person or thing. ▶v. make a hoot.

hooter n. a siren, steam whistle, or horn.

Hoover n. trademark a vacuum cleaner. ▶v. (**hoover**) vacuum.

hooves pl. of HOOF.

hop v. (**hopping**, **hopped**) **1** jump along on one foot. **2** (of an animal) jump along with all feet at once. **3** informal

Thesaurus

out corruption; *informal* on the level, on the straight and narrow. **2** SPEAKING TRUTHFULLY, truthfully, to be honest, speaking frankly, in all sincerity, candidly, openly, plainly, in plain language, to someone's face, without dissembling; *informal* straight out, straight up, Scout's honour.

honorary adj. NOMINAL, titular, in name only, unofficial, ex officio, complimentary, unpaid.

honour n. **1** HONESTY, uprightness, integrity, ethics, morals, high principles, righteousness, virtue, rectitude, goodness, decency, probity, worthiness, worth, fairness, justness, justice, truthfulness, trustworthiness, reliability, dependability, faithfulness, fidelity. **2** GLORY, prestige, renown, fame, illustriousness, notability, esteem, distinction, credit, kudos. **3** ACCLAIM, acclam-

ation, applause, accolades, tributes, homage, praise, compliments, eulogy, paeans, adoration, reverence, adulation. ▶v. **1** ESTEEM, respect, hold in esteem, have a high regard for, admire, defer to, revere, venerate, worship, adore, idolize. **2** ACCLAIM, applaud, pay homage to, pay tribute to, lionize, cheer, praise, eulogize. **3** FULFIL, discharge, carry out, observe, keep, be true to, live up to.

honourable adj. HONEST, upright, ethical, moral, principled, upstanding, righteous, right-minded, virtuous, good, decent, worthy, fair, just, true, truthful, trustworthy, trusty, reliable, dependable, faithful.

hook v. **1** FASTEN, secure, fix, close the clasp. **2** SNARE, trap, ensnare, entrap, enmesh.

hooligan n. THUG, vandal, lout, rowdy,

move or go quickly. ▶n. **1** a hopping movement. **2** a short journey. **3** a plant used to flavour beer. ◻ **hopscotch** a children's game of hopping into and over marked squares. **on the hop** informal unprepared.

hope n. **1** a feeling that something wanted may happen. **2** a cause for hope. **3** something hoped for. ▶v. expect and want to happen. ■ **hopeful** adj.

hopefully adv. **1** in a hopeful way. **2** it is to be hoped that.

hopeless adj. **1** without hope. **2** very bad or unskilful. ■ **hopelessly** adv.

hopper n. a tapering container that empties its contents at the bottom.

horde n. a large group or crowd.

··
☑ Don't confuse **horde** with **hoard**, which means 'a store of something valued'.
··

horizon n. **1** the line at which the earth's surface and the sky appear to meet. **2** the limit of a person's understanding or interests.

horizontal adj. parallel to the horizon. ■ **horizontally** adv.

hormone n. a substance produced by a living thing to stimulate cells or tissues into action. ■ **hormonal** adj.

horn n. **1** a hard bony growth on the heads of cattle, sheep, etc. **2** the substance of a horn. **3** a wind instrument shaped like a cone or wound into a spiral. **4** an instrument sounding a warning. ◻ **hornpipe** a lively solo dance traditionally performed by sailors. ■ **horned** adj.

hornblende n. a dark mineral present in many rocks.

hornet n. a large wasp.

horny adj. (**hornier**, **horniest**) **1** of or like horn. **2** informal sexually aroused.

horology n. **1** the study and measurement of time. **2** the making of clocks and watches.

horoscope n. a forecast of events based on the positions of stars.

horrendous adj. very unpleasant or horrifying. ■ **horrendously** adv.

horrible adj. **1** causing horror. **2** very unpleasant. ■ **horribly** adv.

horrid adj. horrible.

horrific adj. causing horror. ■ **horrifically** adv.

horrify v. (**horrifying**, **horrified**) fill with horror.

horror n. **1** intense fear and shock or disgust. **2** a thing causing this. **3** great

Thesaurus

delinquent, ruffian, mugger, hoodlum, tearaway; informal yob, yobbo, tough, yahoo.

hoop n. RING, band, circle, loop, wheel, girdle.

hop v. JUMP, leap, bound, spring, vault, bounce, skip, caper, dance, frisk.

hope n. EXPECTATION, hopefulness, expectancy, anticipation, desire, longing, wish, wishing, craving, yearning, aspiration, ambition, dream, belief, assurance, confidence, assumption, conviction, faith, trust, optimism. ▶v. BE HOPEFUL OF, expect, anticipate, look forward to, await, contemplate, desire, long, wish, crave, yearn, aspire, be ambitious, dream, believe, assume, have confidence, be convinced, rely on, count on, trust in. ■ OPPOSITES despair.

hopeful adj. **1** FULL OF HOPE, expectant, optimistic, confident, positive, assured, buoyant, sanguine. **2** ENCOURAGING, promising, heartening, reassuring, gladdening, optimistic, favourable, auspicious, propitious, cheerful, bright, pleasant, rosy. ■ OPPOSITES hopeless.

hopefully adv. **1** WITH HOPE, full of hope, expectantly, optimistically, confidently, with assurance, buoyantly, sanguinely.

2 IT IS TO BE HOPED THAT, with luck, all being well, if all goes well, probably, conceivably, feasibly.

hopeless adj. **1** WITHOUT HOPE, despairing, in despair, desperate, pessimistic, dejected, downhearted, despondent, demoralized, disconsolate, downcast, wretched, forlorn, suicidal, woebegone. **2** IMPOSSIBLE, impracticable, futile, useless, vain, pointless, worthless, unattainable, unachievable, no-win. **3** POOR, incompetent, inadequate, inferior, ineffective, ineffectual; informal no good, useless. ■ OPPOSITES hopeful, accomplished.

horde n. CROWD, throng, mob, mass, group, multitude, host, army, pack, gang, troop, drove, crew, band, flock, swarm, gathering, assembly.

horrible adj. **1** AWFUL, dreadful, terrible, horrid, horrifying, terrifying, frightful, fearful, horrendous, shocking, gruesome, hideous, grim, ghastly, harrowing, disgusting, revolting, repulsive, loathsome, abhorrent, detestable, hateful, abominable. **2** DISAGREEABLE, nasty, unpleasant, obnoxious, odious, awful, dreadful, ghastly, frightful, appalling, insufferable, objectionable, vile.

dismay.

hors d'oeuvre /or derv/ n. a small savoury first course of a meal.

horse n. a four-legged mammal used for riding and for pulling heavy loads. ▶v. **(horse around/about)** informal fool about. □ **horsebox** a vehicle or trailer for transporting horses. **horse chestnut 1** a large tree producing nuts (conkers). **2** a conker. **horsefly** a large biting fly. **horseman** (or **horsewoman**) a rider on horseback. **horseplay** boisterous play. **horsepower** a unit measuring the power of an engine. **horseradish** a plant with a hot-tasting root used to make a sauce. **horseshoe** a U-shaped iron shoe for a horse. **on horseback** mounted on a horse.

horsey (or **horsy**) adj. **1** of or like a horse. **2** very keen on horses.

horticulture n. the art of garden cultivation. ■ **horticultural** adj. **horticulturist** n.

hose n. **1** a flexible tube conveying water. **2** hosiery. ▶v. wash or spray with a hose.

hosiery n. stockings, socks, and tights.

hospice n. a home for the care of the terminally ill.

hospitable adj. friendly and welcoming. ■ **hospitably** adv.

hospital n. an institution for the treatment and care of sick or injured people.

hospitality n. friendly and generous treatment of guests etc.

hospitalize (or **-ise**) v. admit to hospital for treatment. ■ **hospitalization** n.

host n. **1** a person who receives or entertains guests. **2** the presenter of a television or radio programme. **3** a place holding an event to which others are invited. **4** an animal or plant on or in which a parasite lives. **5** a large number of people or things. ▶v. act as host at or for.

hostage n. a person held captive to try to ensure that a demand or condition is met.

hostel n. a place providing cheap food and lodging for a particular group.

hostelry n. (pl. **hostelries**) old use an inn or pub.

hostess n. a female host.

hostile adj. **1** unfriendly. **2** of a military enemy. **3** opposed.

hostility n. **1** hostile behaviour. **2** (**hostilities**) acts of warfare.

hot adj. (**hotter**, **hottest**) **1** having a high temperature. **2** feeling or producing an uncomfortable sensation of heat. **3** very exciting or intense. **4** currently popular or interesting. ▶v. (**hotting**, **hotted**) (**hot up**) informal become more exciting or intense. □ **hotbed** a place where a particular activity happens or flourishes. **hot-blooded** passionate. **hot dog** a hot sausage served in a bread roll. **hotfoot** in eager haste. **hothead** a rash or quick-tempered per-

Thesaurus

■ OPPOSITES pleasant.

horrify v. SHOCK, appal, outrage, scandalize, disgust, revolt, repel, nauseate, sicken, offend, dismay; informal turn off.

horror n. **1** TERROR, fear, fearfulness, alarm, fright, dread, awe, panic, trepidation, apprehensiveness, uneasiness, nervousness, dismay, consternation. **2** ABHORRENCE, abomination, loathing, hate, detestation, repulsion, revulsion, disgust, distaste, aversion, hostility, antipathy, animosity.

horse n. STEED, mount, hack, cob, nag; informal gee-gee.

horseman, horsewoman n. RIDER, equestrian, jockey, horse soldier, cavalryman, dragoon, cavalier, cowboy, cowgirl.

horseplay n. CLOWNING, fooling, tomfoolery, buffoonery, pranks, antics, capers, high jinks, rough and tumble, skylarking; informal shenanigans, monkey business.

hospitable adj. WELCOMING, generous,

open-handed, sociable, friendly, bountiful, neighbourly, kind, warm, helpful. ■ OPPOSITES inhospitable.

hospital n. CLINIC, infirmary, health centre, medical centre, sanatorium, nursing home, hospice, sick bay.

host n. **1** PROPRIETOR, proprietress, landlord, landlady, innkeeper, hotel-keeper, hotelier. **2** PRESENTER, compère, master of ceremonies, MC, anchorman, anchorwoman.

hostage n. CAPTIVE, prisoner, pawn, pledge, security.

hostile adj. **1** OPPOSED, antagonistic, averse, ill-disposed, against, inimical; informal anti. **2** AGGRESSIVE, angry, belligerent, bellicose, warlike, warring, militant, antagonistic, unfriendly, unkind, unsympathetic, malevolent, malicious, spiteful, wrathful. **3** ADVERSE, unfavourable, inauspicious, unpropitious, disadvantageous. ■ OPPOSITES favourable, friendly.

hostility n. **1** ANTAGONISM, opposition, ill

son. **hothouse 1** a heated greenhouse. **2** an environment encouraging rapid development. **hotline** a direct telephone line set up for a specific purpose. **hotplate** a flat heated surface on an electric cooker. ∎ **hotly** adv.

hotchpotch (US **hodgepodge**) n. a confused mixture.

hotel n. an establishment providing rooms and meals for travellers and tourists.

hotelier n. a person who owns or manages a hotel.

houmous var. of HUMMUS.

hound n. a hunting dog. ▶v. harass.

hour n. **1** a period of 60 minutes, one of the 24 parts of a day. **2** a point in time. **3** a period set aside for a particular purpose or activity. ◻ **hourglass** a device with two connected glass bulbs containing sand that takes an hour to fall from the upper to the lower bulb. ∎ **hourly** adj. & adv.

houri /hoor-i/ n. a beautiful young woman.

house n. **1** a building for people to live in, or for a specific purpose. **2** a business. **3** a group into which pupils are divided for games etc. **4** a law-making assembly. **5** a dynasty. **6** a style of fast popular dance music. ▶v. **1** provide accommodation or storage space for. **2** enclose. ◻ **house arrest** detention in one's own house. **houseboat** a boat that people can live in. **housebound** unable to leave one's house because of illness or old age. **housebreaking** breaking into a building to commit a crime. **housecoat** a woman's dressing gown. **household** a house and its occu-

pants. **householder** a person who owns or rents a house. **housekeeper** a person employed to manage a household. **housemaster** (or **housemistress**) a teacher in charge of a house at a boarding school. **house-proud** very concerned with the appearance of one's home. **house-train** train a pet to urinate and defecate outside the house. **house-warming** a party celebrating a move to a new home. **housewife** a woman whose main occupation is looking after her family and the home. **housework** cleaning, cooking, etc. done in running a home. **on the house** at the management's expense.

housing n. **1** houses and flats. **2** a rigid case for a piece of equipment.

hove Naut. past of HEAVE.

hovel n. a small dirty or run-down house.

hover v. **1** remain in one place in the air. **2** wait close by. **3** remain at or near a particular level. ◻ **hovercraft** a vehicle that travels over land or water on a cushion of air.

how adv. **1** in what way or by what means. **2** in what condition. **3** to what extent or degree. **4** the way in which.

howdah n. a seat for riding on the back of an elephant.

however adv. **1** nevertheless; despite this. **2** in whatever way or to whatever extent.

howitzer n. a short gun firing shells at a high angle.

howl n. & v. (make) a long wailing cry or sound.

howler n. informal a stupid mistake.

hoyden n. dated a girl who acts in a

Thesaurus

will, aversion, animosity, enmity. **2** AGGRESSION, belligerence, anger, bellicosity, militancy, antagonism, unfriendliness, unkindness, malevolence, spite, malice, wrath. ∎ OPPOSITES friendship.

hot adj. **1** HEATED, very warm, boiling, boiling hot, piping hot, scalding, red-hot, sizzling, steaming, scorching, roasting, searing, blazing hot, sweltering, blistering, baking, oven-like, torrid, sultry. **2** SPICY, peppery, piquant, fiery, pungent, sharp, biting, acrid. **3** VIOLENT, furious, heated, fierce, ferocious, stormy, tempestuous, savage. ∎ OPPOSITES cold, mild.

hot-headed adj. HOT-TEMPERED, quick-tempered, short-tempered, fiery, excitable, volatile, hasty, rash, impetuous, impulsive, reckless, foolhardy, wild,

unruly.

house n. **1** RESIDENCE, home, dwelling, abode, domicile, habitation; informal pad, gaff. **2** FAMILY, clan, line, dynasty, lineage, ancestry. ▶v. **1** ACCOMMODATE, lodge, put up, take in, have room for, sleep, shelter, harbour. **2** COVER, sheathe, protect, shelter, guard, contain, keep.

household n. FAMILY, home, house, ménage, establishment. ▶adj. DOMESTIC, family, ordinary, everyday, common, usual, run-of-the-mill.

hover v. **1** FLOAT, fly, be suspended, hang, drift, be wafted, flutter. **2** LINGER, loiter, hang about, wait, stay. **3** VACILLATE, fluctuate, oscillate, alternate, seesaw; Sc. swither.

however adv. NEVERTHELESS, be that as it

high-spirited or wild way.

h.p. (or **HP**) abbrev. **1** hire purchase. **2** horsepower.

HQ abbrev. headquarters.

HRH abbrev. Her (or His) Royal Highness.

HRT abbrev. hormone replacement therapy.

HTML n. Hypertext Markup Language.

hub n. **1** the central part of a wheel. **2** the centre of an activity. □ **hubcap** a cover for the hub of a wheel.

hubbub n. a confused noise of a crowd.

hubris /hyoo-briss/ n. excessive pride or self-confidence.

huddle v. **1** crowd together. **2** curl one's body into a small space. ▶n. a close group or mass.

hue n. a colour or shade.

hue and cry n. a strong public outcry.

huff v. (**huff and puff**) **1** breathe out noisily. **2** show one's annoyance. ▶n. a fit of annoyance. ■ **huffy** adj. **huffily** adv.

hug v. (**hugging**, **hugged**) **1** hold tightly in one's arms. **2** keep close to. ▶n. an embrace.

huge adj. very large. ■ **hugely** adv.

hula hoop n. trademark a large hoop spun round the body.

hulk n. **1** an old ship stripped of its fittings. **2** a large or clumsy person or thing.

hulking adj. informal very large or clumsy.

hull n. **1** the main body of a ship. **2** the outer covering of a fruit or seed. **3** the cluster of leaves on a strawberry. ▶v.

remove the hulls from.

hullabaloo n. informal an uproar.

hullo var. of HELLO.

hum v. (**humming**, **hummed**) **1** make a low continuous sound. **2** sing with closed lips. **3** informal be in a state of great activity. ▶n. a low continuous sound.

human adj. **1** of people. **2** showing the better qualities of people. ▶n. (also **human being**) a person. □ **humankind** people as a whole. **human resources** the section of an organization dealing with training, recruitment, etc. **human rights** basic rights to which all people are entitled, e.g. freedom. ■ **humanly** adv.

humane adj. showing concern and kindness. ■ **humanely** adv.

humanism n. a system of thought believing that people are able to live their lives without the need for religious beliefs. ■ **humanist** n. & adj.

humanitarian adj. concerned with human welfare. ■ **humanitarianism** n.

humanity n. (pl. **humanities**) **1** people as a whole. **2** the condition of being human. **3** sympathy and kindness. **4** (**humanities**) arts subjects.

humanize (or **-ise**) v. make more pleasant or suitable for people.

humble adj. **1** having a low opinion of one's importance. **2** of low rank. **3** not large or elaborate. ▶v. cause to seem less important. ■ **humbly** adv.

Thesaurus

may, nonetheless, notwithstanding, anyway, anyhow, regardless, despite that, still, yet, just the same, though.

howl v. BAY, yowl, ululate, yelp, wail, bawl, scream, bellow, caterwaul, cry.

hub n. **1** PIVOT, axis, nave. **2** CENTRE, middle, core, heart, focus, focal point.

huddle v. **1** CROWD, throng, press, pack, cluster, cram, herd, squeeze, gather, congregate. **2** CURL UP, snuggle, cuddle, nestle, hunch up. ▶n. GATHERING, crowd, cluster, pack, press.

hue n. **1** COLOUR, tone, shade, tint, tinge, dye. **2** COMPLEXION, cast, aspect, light.

hug v. **1** EMBRACE, cuddle, take in one's arms, hold close, enfold in one's arms, clasp/press to one's bosom, squeeze, snuggle against. **2** KEEP CLOSE TO, stay near, follow closely.

huge adj. ENORMOUS, immense, great, massive, colossal, vast, prodigious, gigantic, giant, gargantuan, mammoth, monumental, monstrous, elephantine, bulky, extensive, mountainous, titanic,

Brobdingnagian, Herculean; *informal* jumbo. ■ OPPOSITES tiny.

hulk n. **1** WRECK, shipwreck, derelict, ruin, shell, skeleton, hull, frame. **2** OAF, lout, lump, lubber.

hull n. FRAMEWORK, body, frame, skeleton, structure, casing, covering.

hum v. **1** MURMUR, drone, vibrate, thrum, buzz, whirr, purr. **2** SING, croon, whisper, mumble.

human adj. **1** MORTAL, physical, bodily, fleshly, carnal, corporal. **2** KIND, kindly, considerate, understanding, sympathetic, compassionate, approachable, humane, accessible. **3** FLESH AND BLOOD, fallible, weak, frail, vulnerable, erring.

humane adj. KIND, kindly, kind-hearted, good, good-natured, compassionate, understanding, considerate, sympathetic, forgiving, merciful, lenient, forbearing, gentle, tender, mild, benign, clement, benevolent, charitable, generous, magnanimous, approachable, accessible. ■ OPPOSITES cruel, inhumane.

humbug n. **1** false or misleading talk or behaviour. **2** a boiled peppermint sweet.

humdrum adj. dull or ordinary.

humerus n. (pl. **humeri**) the bone in the upper arm.

humid adj. (of the air or weather) damp and warm. ■ **humidity** n.

humidify v. (**humidifying**, **humidified**) increase the level of moisture in air. ■ **humidifier** n.

humiliate v. cause to feel ashamed or stupid. ■ **humiliation** n.

humility n. the quality of being humble.

hummock n. a small hill or mound.

hummus (or **houmous**) n. a paste made from ground chickpeas and sesame seeds.

humorist n. a writer or speaker noted for being amusing.

humour (US **humor**) n. **1** the quality of being amusing. **2** a state of mind. ▶v. agree with the wishes of someone to keep them happy. ■ **humorous** adj. **humorously** adv. **humourless** adj.

hump n. **1** a rounded projecting part. **2** a lump on a person's back caused by an abnormal curve of the spine. ▶v. informal lift or carry with difficulty. ■ **humped** adj.

humus /hyoo-muhss/ n. a substance found in soil, formed from dead leaves and plants.

hunch v. raise one's shoulders and bend the top of one's body forward. ▶n. a belief based on a feeling rather than evidence. □ **hunchback** offens. a person with an abnormal hump on their back.

hundred adj. & n. ten more than ninety; 100 or C. □ **hundredweight** **1** a unit of weight equal to 112 lb (about 50.8 kg). **2** US a unit of weight equal to 100 lb (about 45.4 kg). ■ **hundredfold** adj. & adv. **hundredth** adj. & n.

hung past & past part. of HANG. ▶adj. **1** having no political party with an overall majority. **2** (of a jury) unable to agree on a verdict. □ **hungover** suffering from a hangover.

hunger n. **1** a feeling of discomfort caused by lack of food. **2** a strong desire. ▶v. (**hunger after/for**) have a strong desire for. □ **hunger strike** refusal to eat as a means of protest.

h

Thesaurus

humble adj. **1** MODEST, unassuming, self-effacing, meek, unassertive, unpretentious, unostentatious, servile, docile, submissive, obsequious, subservient, deferential, over-respectful, slavish, sycophantic. **2** COMMON, ordinary, simple, poor, low-born, of low birth, low-ranking, low, lowly, inferior, plebeian, proletarian, base, mean, unrefined, vulgar, unimportant, insignificant, inconsequential, undistinguished, ignoble. ▶v. **1** HUMILIATE, mortify, subdue, chasten, shame, put to shame, abash, degrade. **2** DEFEAT, crush, trounce, rout, break, conquer, vanquish, overwhelm, bring someone to their knees.

humdrum adj. COMMONPLACE, routine, run-of-the-mill, unvaried, unvarying, ordinary, everyday, mundane, monotonous, repetitious, dull, uninteresting, boring, tedious, banal, tiresome, wearisome. ■ OPPOSITES remarkable.

humiliate v. MORTIFY, shame, humble, put to shame, make ashamed, disgrace, embarrass, discomfit, chasten, subdue, deflate, abash, debase, abase, degrade, crush, demean; informal take someone down a peg or two, make someone eat humble pie, put down, show up; US make someone eat crow.

humiliation n. MORTIFICATION, loss of pride, humbling, disgrace, loss of face, slap in the face, dishonour, indignity, discredit, embarrassment, discomfiture, affront, abasement, debasement, degradation; informal put-down.

humility n. HUMBLENESS, lack of pride, modesty, meekness, self-effacement, unpretentiousness, unobtrusiveness, diffidence, servility, submissiveness, obsequiousness, subservience, deference, sycophancy. ■ OPPOSITES arrogance, pride.

humorous adj. FUNNY, comic, comical, entertaining, witty, jocular, amusing, hilarious, side-splitting, rib-tickling, farcical, facetious, ridiculous, ludicrous, absurd, droll, tongue-in-cheek. ■ OPPOSITES serious.

humour n. **1** FUNNINESS, comic side, funny side, comical aspect, comedy, farce, jocularity, hilarity, ludicrousness, absurdness, absurdity, drollness. **2** COMEDY, jokes, joking, jests, jesting, wit, wittiness, witticisms, waggishness, pleasantries, buffoonery; informal gags, wisecracks. **3** MOOD, temper, temperament, frame of mind, state of mind, disposition, spirits.

hump n. PROTRUSION, protuberance, projection, bulge, swelling, lump, bump, knob, hunch, mass, nodule, node, intumescence, tumefaction. ▶v. **1** HUNCH, arch, curve, curl up, crook. **2** CARRY,

hungry adj. (**hungrier, hungriest**) feeling hunger. ■ **hungrily** adv.

hunk n. **1** a large piece cut or broken off. **2** informal a good-looking man.

hunt v. **1** chase and kill a wild animal for sport or food. **2** search. **3** (**hunt down**) chase and capture. ▶ n. **1** an act of hunting. **2** a group who hunt animals as a sport. ■ **hunter** n.

hurdle n. **1** an upright frame to be jumped over in a race. **2** an obstacle or difficulty. **3** a portable fencing panel. ■ **hurdler** n.

hurl v. throw with great force.

hurly-burly n. busy and noisy activity.

hurrah (or **hooray, hurray**) exclam. used to express joy or approval.

hurricane n. a severe storm with a violent wind. □ **hurricane lamp** an oil lamp with the flame protected by a glass tube.

hurry v. (**hurrying, hurried**) **1** move or act quickly, or cause to do so. **2** do too quickly. ▶ n. great haste. ■ **hurriedly** adv.

hurt v. (**hurting, hurt**) **1** cause pain or injury to. **2** feel pain. **3** cause distress to. ▶ n. injury or pain. ■ **hurtful** adj.

hurtle v. move at great speed.

husband n. a married man in relation to his wife. ▶ v. use resources carefully.

husbandry n. **1** farming. **2** careful use of resources.

hush v. **1** make or become quiet. **2** (**hush up**) prevent from becoming generally known. ▶ n. a silence.

husk n. the dry outer covering of some fruits or seeds.

husky adj. (**huskier, huskiest**) **1** (of a voice) low and slightly hoarse. **2** big and strong. ▶ n. (pl. **huskies**) a powerful dog used for pulling sledges. ■ **huskily** adv. **huskiness** n.

hussy n. (pl. **hussies**) dated an impudent or immoral girl or woman.

hustings n. the political meetings, campaigns, and speeches before an election.

hustle v. push or move roughly. ▶ n. busy movement and activity.

hut n. a small simple house or shelter.

Thesaurus

lift, lug, heave, shoulder, hoist.

hunch n. **1** FEELING, presentiment, premonition, intuition, sixth sense, suspicion, inkling, impression, idea. **2** see HUMP.

hunger n. **1** HUNGRINESS, lack of food, starvation, ravenousness, emptiness, famine, voracity, greediness. **2** LONGING, craving, yearning, desire, want, need, thirst, appetite, hankering, lust; informal itch.

hungry adj. **1** FAMISHED, famishing, ravenous, starving, starved, half-starved, empty, greedy, voracious; dated sharpset. **2** LONGING, yearning, craving, in need/want of, eager, keen, desirous of, covetous of. ■ OPPOSITES full.

hunt v. **1** CHASE, give chase, pursue, stalk, track, trail, follow, shadow, hound, tail. **2** SEARCH FOR, look for, seek, try to find, scour for, forage for, fish for, rummage for, scrabble for.

hurdle n. **1** FENCE, barrier, railing, rail, wall, hedge, hedgerow, bar, barricade. **2** OBSTACLE, barrier, hindrance, impediment, obstruction, stumbling block, snag, complication, difficulty, handicap.

hurl v. THROW, fling, pitch, cast, toss, heave, fire, launch, let fly, shy, propel, project, dart, catapult; informal sling, chuck.

hurried adj. **1** QUICK, rapid, fast, swift, speedy, hasty, breakneck. **2** HASTY, quick, swift, rushed, cursory, superfi-

cial, perfunctory, offhand, passing, fleeting, transitory. ■ OPPOSITES slow.

hurry v. **1** MOVE QUICKLY, hurry up, be quick, make haste, hasten, speed, lose no time, press on, push on, run, dash, rush; informal go hell for leather, get a move on, put one's foot down, step on it, get cracking, shake a leg, go like a bat out of hell, hightail it, hotfoot it. **2** SPEED UP, quicken, hasten, accelerate, expedite, urge on, drive on, push on, goad, prod, hustle. ■ OPPOSITES dawdle, delay.

hurt v. **1** BE SORE, be painful, cause pain, ache, smart, sting, nip, throb, tingle, burn. **2** INJURE, wound, bruise, cut, scratch, lacerate, maim, damage, mutilate, disable, incapacitate, impair, debilitate. **3** UPSET, sadden, grieve, wound, distress, pain, cut to the quick, sting, offend, give offence to, discompose. **4** HARM, damage, spoil, blight, mar, blemish, impair.

hurtful adj. **1** UPSETTING, wounding, injurious, distressing, unkind, nasty, mean, spiteful, malicious, cutting, cruel, mischievous, offensive. **2** HARMFUL, damaging, injurious, detrimental, deleterious, destructive, prejudicial, ruinous, inimical.

husband n. SPOUSE, partner, consort, groom, bridegroom; informal hubby, old man, other half.

hush v. SILENCE, quieten, quieten down,

hutch n. a box with a wire mesh front, for keeping rabbits etc.

hyacinth n. a plant with fragrant bell-shaped flowers.

hyaena var. of HYENA.

hybrid n. **1** the offspring of two plants or animals of different species or varieties. **2** something made by combining two different elements.

hybridize (or **-ise**) v. produce hybrids. ■ **hybridization** n.

hydrangea /hy-**drayn**-juh/ n. a shrub with white, blue, or pink flowers.

hydrant n. a water pipe with a nozzle to which a fire hose can be attached.

hydrate n. a chemical compound of water and another substance. ▶v. cause to absorb or combine with water. ■ **hydration** n.

hydraulic adj. of or operated by a liquid moving in a confined space under pressure. ▶n. (**hydraulics**) the study of the use of liquids moving under pressure to provide mechanical force. ■ **hydraulically** adv.

hydrocarbon n. a compound of hydrogen and carbon.

hydrochloric acid n. a corrosive acid containing hydrogen and chlorine.

hydrodynamics n. the study of the forces acting on or generated by liquids. ■ **hydrodynamic** adj.

hydroelectric adj. using flowing water to generate electricity.

hydrofoil n. a boat with a structure that lifts the hull clear of the water at speed.

hydrogen n. a highly flammable gas which is the lightest chemical element. □ **hydrogen bomb** a nuclear bomb whose power comes from the fusion of hydrogen nuclei.

hydrolysis n. the chemical breakdown of a compound due to reaction with water.

hydrometer n. an instrument for measuring the density of liquids.

hydrophobia n. **1** extreme fear of water, esp. as a symptom of rabies. **2** rabies.

hydroponics n. the growing of plants in sand, gravel, or liquid, with added nutrients but without soil.

hydrotherapy n. therapeutic exercises in water.

hydrous adj. containing water.

hyena (or **hyaena**) n. a doglike African mammal.

hygiene n. the practice of keeping oneself and one's surroundings clean to prevent disease. ■ **hygienic** adj. **hygienically** adv. **hygienist** n.

hymen n. the membrane partially closing the opening of the vagina, usu. broken when a woman or girl first has sex.

hymn n. a religious song of praise.

hype informal n. excessive or exaggerated publicity. ▶v. publicize in an excessive or exaggerated way.

hyper- prefix **1** over; above. **2** excessively.

hyperactive adj. abnormally active.

hyperbola /hy-**per**-buh-luh/ n. (pl. **hyperbolas** or **hyperbolae**) a symmetrical curve formed when a cone is cut by a plane nearly parallel to the cone's axis.

hyperbole /hy-**per**-buh-li/ n. statements that are deliberately exaggerated for effect.

hyperlink n. a link from a hypertext document to another location.

hypermarket n. a very large supermarket.

hypersonic adj. of speeds more than five times that of sound.

hypertension n. abnormally high blood pressure.

hypertext n. a software system allowing users to move quickly between related documents or sections of text.

hyperventilate v. breathe at an abnormally rapid rate. ■ **hyperventilation** n.

hyphen n. the sign (-) used to join words together or to divide a word into parts between one line and the next. ■ **hyphenate** v. **hyphenation** n.

hypnosis n. the practice of causing a person to enter a state in which they respond very readily to suggestions or commands. ■ **hypnotic** adj. **hypnotically** adv.

hypnotism n. hypnosis. ■ **hypnotist** n. **hypnotize** (or **-ise**) v.

Thesaurus

shush, shut up. ▶n. QUIET, quietness, silence, stillness, still, peace, calm, tranquillity.

hustle v. **1** PUSH, shove, thrust, crowd, jostle, elbow, nudge, shoulder. **2** see HURRY. **3** COERCE, force, impel, pressure, badger, urge, goad, prod, spur, propel.

hut n. SHED, lean-to, shack, cabin, shanty, hovel; Sc. bothy.

hygiene n. CLEANLINESS, sanitation, public health, sanitary measures.

hygienic adj. SANITARY, clean, germ-free, disinfected, sterilized, sterile, aseptic, unpolluted, uncontaminated, healthy,

hypo- prefix **1** under. **2** below normal.

hypoallergenic adj. unlikely to cause an allergic reaction.

hypochondria n. constant and excessive anxiety about one's health. ■ **hypochondriac** n.

hypocrisy n. behaviour in which a person pretends to have higher standards than is the case.

hypocrite n. a person guilty of hypocrisy. ■ **hypocritical** adj. **hypocritically** adv.

hypodermic adj. used to inject a drug etc. beneath the skin. ▶ n. a hypodermic syringe.

hypotension n. abnormally low blood pressure.

hypotenuse /hy-**pot**-uh-nyooz/ n. the longest side of a right-angled triangle, opposite the right angle.

hypothermia n. the condition of having an abnormally low body temperature.

hypothesis n. (pl. **hypotheses**) a proposed explanation based on limited evidence, used as a basis for further investigation.

hypothetical adj. based on an imagined or possible situation rather than fact. ■ **hypothetically** adv.

hysterectomy n. (pl. **hysterectomies**) an operation to remove all or part of the womb.

hysteria n. extreme or uncontrollable emotion or excitement. ■ **hysterical** adj. **hysterically** adv.

hysterics pl. n. **1** wildly emotional behaviour. **2** informal uncontrollable laughter.

Hz abbrev. hertz.

Thesaurus

pure. ■ OPPOSITES dirty, unsanitary.

hypnotic adj. MESMERIC, mesmerizing, sleep-inducing, soporific, somniferous, numbing, sedative, stupefacient.

hypnotize v. **1** PUT UNDER, put out, send into a trance, mesmerize, put to sleep. **2** FASCINATE, bewitch, entrance, beguile, spellbind, magnetize.

hypocrisy n. INSINCERITY, falseness, sanctimoniousness, falsity, deceptiveness, deceit, deceitfulness, deception, dishonesty, duplicity, imposture, cant, two-facedness, double-dealing, pretence, Pharisaism, pietism. ■ OPPOSITES sincerity.

hypocritical adj. FALSE, insincere, sanctimonious, fraudulent, deceitful, deceptive, dishonest, untruthful, lying, dissembling, duplicitous, two-faced, double-dealing, untrustworthy, perfidious, specious, spurious; informal phoney.

hypothesis n. THEORY, thesis, theorem, proposition, axiom, premise, postulate, supposition, assumption, presumption, conjecture, speculation.

hypothetical adj. ASSUMED, presumed, theoretical, putative, speculative, conjectured, imagined, notional, academic.

hysteria n. HYSTERICS, frenzy, loss of control, agitation, panic, alarm, distress, madness, delirium; informal the screaming habdabs.

hysterical adj. **1** FRENZIED, in a frenzy, frantic, out of control, berserk, beside oneself, distracted, distraught, overwrought, agitated, in a panic, mad, crazed, delirious, raving. **2** VERY FUNNY/AMUSING, hilarious, uproarious, side-splitting, comical, farcical, screamingly funny. ■ OPPOSITES calm.

Ii

I pron. used by a speaker to refer to himself or herself. ▶ n. (also **i**) the Roman numeral for one.

iambic adj. (of verse) having one short syllable followed by one long syllable.

Iberian adj. of the peninsula consisting of modern Spain and Portugal.

ibex n. (pl. **ibexes**) a wild mountain goat.

ibid. adv. in the book just mentioned.

ice n. **1** frozen water. **2** an ice cream. ▶ v. **1** decorate with icing. **2** become covered with ice. □ **break the ice** start a conversation on first meeting. **ice age** a period when ice covered much of the earth's surface. **iceberg** a large mass of ice floating in the sea. **icebox** a freezing compartment in a refrigerator. **ice cream** a frozen dessert made with milk fat. **ice skate** a boot with a blade attached to the sole, for gliding over ice.

ichthyology /ik-thi-ol-uh-ji/ n. the study of fish. ■ **ichthyologist** n.

icicle n. a hanging, tapering piece of ice.

icing n. a mixture of powdered sugar with liquid or fat, used to coat cakes.

icon n. **1** (also **ikon**) a sacred painting of a holy figure. **2** a greatly admired person. **3** a symbol on a computer screen of a program or option. ■ **iconic** adj.

iconoclast n. a person who attacks established customs and values. ■ **iconoclastic** adj.

icy adj. (**icier**, **iciest**) **1** covered with ice. **2** very cold. **3** very unfriendly. ■ **icily** adv. **iciness** n.

ID abbrev. identification or identity.

idea n. **1** a thought or suggestion about a possible course of action. **2** a mental impression. **3** a belief.

ideal adj. most suitable; perfect. ▶ n. **1** a person or thing regarded as perfect. **2** an aim, principle, or standard. ■ **ideally** adv.

idealism n. the belief that ideals can be achieved. ■ **idealist** n. **idealistic** adj.

idealize (or **-ise**) v. regard or present as better than in reality.

identical adj. **1** exactly alike. **2** the same. ■ **identically** adv.

identify v. (**identifying**, **identified**) **1** prove or recognize as being a specified person or thing. **2** feel understanding or empathy. **3** associate closely. ■ **identifiable** adj. **identification** n.

identikit n. trademark a picture of a want-

ice n. FROZEN WATER, frost, icicle, iceberg, glacier, rime.

icy adj. **1** FREEZING, chill, chilly, frigid, frosty, biting, raw, bitter, arctic, glacial, Siberian, polar, gelid. **2** FROZEN, ice-bound, frosty, rimy, glassy, slippery, slippy. **3** COLD, cool, frigid, frosty, stiff, aloof, distant, unfriendly, unresponsive, uncommunicative, reserved, reticent, restrained.

idea n. **1** CONCEPT, thought, conception, conceptualization, image, abstraction, perception, notion. **2** THOUGHT, theory, view, viewpoint, opinion, feeling, outlook, belief, judgement, conclusion. **3** IMPRESSION, feeling, notion, suspicion, inkling. **4** ESTIMATION, approximation, guess, surmise; informal guesstimate. **5** PLAN, design, aim, scheme, intention, objective, object, purpose, end, goal, target.

ideal adj. **1** PERFECT, consummate, supreme, absolute, complete, flawless, exemplary, classic, archetypal, model, quintessential. **2** UNATTAINABLE, utopian, unreal, impracticable, imaginary, ivory-towered, romantic, visionary, fanciful. ▶ n. **1** ARCHETYPE, prototype, model, pattern, exemplar, paradigm, example, criterion, yardstick. **2** PRINCIPLE, standard, moral value, morals, ethics.

idealistic adj. IMPRACTICAL, utopian, perfectionist, visionary, romantic, quixotic, unrealistic; informal starry-eyed. ■ OPPOSITES practical, realistic.

ideally adv. IN A PERFECT WORLD, all things being equal, theoretically, hypothetically, in theory.

identical adj. **1** THE SAME, the very same, one and the same, selfsame. **2** ALIKE, like, similar, much the same, indistinguishable, corresponding, matching, twin. ■ OPPOSITES different.

identify v. **1** RECOGNIZE, single out, pick out, spot, point out, pinpoint, discern, distinguish, name; informal put the finger ed person, put together from witnesses' selections of typical facial features.

identity n. (pl. **identities**) **1** the fact of being who or what a person or thing is. **2** a close similarity.

ideogram n. a symbol used to represent the idea of a thing rather than the sounds of a word.

ideology n. (pl. **ideologies**) a system of ideas forming the basis of an economic or political theory. ■ **ideological** adj.

idiocy n. (pl. **idiocies**) very stupid behaviour.

idiom n. a phrase whose meaning is different from the meanings of the individual words.

idiomatic adj. using expressions natural to a native speaker.

idiosyncrasy n. (pl. **idiosyncrasies**) a person's particular way of behaving or thinking. ■ **idiosyncratic** adj.

....

☑ The ending is -asy, not -acy: idiosyncrasy.

....

idiot n. a stupid person. ■ **idiotic** adj.

idiotically adv.

idle adj. **1** avoiding work; lazy. **2** not working or in use. **3** having no purpose or effect. ▶ v. **1** spend time doing nothing. **2** (of an engine) run slowly while out of gear. ■ **idleness** n. **idler** n. **idly** adv.

idol n. **1** a statue or picture of a god that is worshipped. **2** a greatly admired person.

idolatry n. worship of idols. ■ **idolater** n. **idolatrous** adj.

idolize (or -**ise**) v. admire or love greatly or excessively.

idyll /ˈi-dil/ n. **1** a very happy or peaceful situation. **2** a short poem describing a picturesque scene. ■ **idyllic** adj. **idyllically** adv.

i.e. abbrev. that is.

if conj. **1** on the condition or in the event that. **2** whether.

iffy adj. informal **1** uncertain. **2** of doubtful quality.

igloo n. a dome-shaped Eskimo house built from blocks of snow.

igneous adj. (of rock) formed from

Thesaurus

....

on. **2** ESTABLISH, find out, ascertain, diagnose, select, choose. **3** ASSOCIATE, connect, think of in connection with. **4** RELATE TO, empathize with, sympathize with, have a rapport with, respond to, feel for.

identity n. **1** NAME, specification. **2** PERSONALITY, self, selfhood, individuality, ego, distinctiveness, singularity, uniqueness. **3** IDENTIFICATION, recognition, naming. **4** SAMENESS, interchangeability, likeness, similarity, closeness, accordance.

ideology n. DOCTRINE, creed, credo, teaching, dogma, theory, thesis, tenets, beliefs, opinions, principles, convictions, attitudes.

idiocy n. STUPIDITY, foolishness, absurdity, inanity, fatuity, fatuousness, asininity, lunacy, craziness, insanity, dumbness, daftness. ■ OPPOSITES sense.

idiom n. **1** PHRASE, expression, locution, turn of phrase, set phrase, fixed expression. **2** LANGUAGE, style of speech, speech, talk, usage, parlance, vernacular, jargon, patois; informal lingo.

idiomatic adj. COLLOQUIAL, informal, vernacular, natural.

idiosyncrasy n. PECULIARITY, oddity, eccentricity, trait, singularity, mannerism, quirk, habit, characteristic, speciality, quality, feature.

idiot n. FOOL, dolt, ass, ignoramus, imbecile, simpleton; informal chump, booby, nincompoop, ninny, dunderhead, blockhead, fathead, halfwit, cretin, moron, dummy, numbskull, dimwit, twerp, clot, twit, nitwit.

idiotic adj. STUPID, foolish, senseless, absurd, fatuous, inane, asinine, unintelligent, half-witted, hare-brained, lunatic, crazy, insane, mad, moronic, dumb, irrational, nonsensical, ridiculous, daft. ■ OPPOSITES sensible.

idle adj. **1** LAZY, indolent, slothful, sluggish, apathetic, torpid, slow, shiftless, loafing. **2** INOPERATIVE, not in operation, inactive, out of action, unused, mothballed. **3** EMPTY, unoccupied, vacant, unfilled. **4** GROUNDLESS, baseless, worthless, futile, vain. **5** TRIVIAL, unimportant, insignificant, trifling, superficial, shallow, foolish, inane, fatuous. ■ OPPOSITES industrious, busy. ▶ v. **1** WHILE, loaf, lounge, loiter, dawdle, fritter, dally, potter. **2** DO NOTHING, laze, loaf, be inactive, mark time, kill time, shirk, slack, vegetate, take it easy, rest on one's oars.

idol n. **1** GOD, icon, effigy, image, graven image, fetish, likeness. **2** HERO, heroine, favourite, darling, pet, beloved, star, superstar, apple of one's eye; informal blue-eyed boy/girl.

idolize v. **1** WORSHIP, bow down before,

solidified molten rock.

ignite v. catch or set on fire.

ignition n. **1** the act of igniting. **2** the mechanism igniting the fuel in an engine.

ignoble adj. dishonourable.

ignominy n. public disgrace. ■ **ignominious** adj. **ignominiously** adv.

ignoramus n. (pl. **ignoramuses**) an ignorant person.

ignorant adj. **1** lacking knowledge. **2** informal not polite. ■ **ignorance** n.

ignore v. **1** deliberately take no notice of. **2** fail to consider.

iguana n. a large tropical lizard.

ikon var. of ICON (sense 1).

ileum n. the lowest part of the small intestine.

ilk n. (**of that ilk**) of that type.

ill adj. **1** not in full health. **2** poor in quality. **3** harmful, hostile, or unfavourable. ▶ adv. **1** badly or wrongly. **2** only with difficulty. ▶ n. **1** a problem or misfortune. **2** harm. □ **ill-advised** unwise. **ill at ease** uncomfortable or embarrassed. **ill-gotten** obtained illegally or unfairly. **ill-mannered** having bad manners. **ill-treat** treat cruelly. **ill will** hostility.

illegal adj. against the law. ■ **illegality** n. **illegally** adv.

illegible adj. not clear enough to be read. ■ **illegibility** n.

illegitimate adj. **1** not allowed by law or rules. **2** born of parents not married to each other. ■ **illegitimacy** n.

illicit adj. forbidden by law or rules. ■ **illicitly** adv.

Thesaurus

glorify, exalt, revere, deify. **2** HERO-WORSHIP, worship, adulate, adore, love, look up to, admire, dote on, lionize, revere, venerate.

ignite v. **1** SET FIRE TO, light, set on fire, set alight, fire, kindle, inflame, touch off, put a match to. **2** CATCH FIRE, catch, burst into flames, burn up, burn, flame up, kindle. ■ OPPOSITES extinguish.

ignominious adj. **1** SHAMEFUL, dishonourable, disgraceful, humiliating, mortifying, discreditable, disreputable, undignified, infamous, ignoble, inglorious, scandalous, abject, sorry, base. **2** CONTEMPTIBLE, despicable, offensive, vile, wicked, base, low. ■ OPPOSITES glorious.

ignorance n. UNFAMILIARITY, unconsciousness, lack of knowledge, inexperience, greenness, innocence; literary nescience. ■ OPPOSITES knowledge.

ignorant adj. **1** UNAWARE OF, unfamiliar with, unconscious of, unacquainted with, uninformed about, unconversant with, unenlightened about, inexperienced in, blind to, unschooled in, naive about, innocent about; informal in the dark about. **2** UNEDUCATED, unschooled, illiterate, unlettered, uninformed, unknowledgeable, unintelligent, stupid, benighted. ■ OPPOSITES knowledgeable.

ignore v. **1** DISREGARD, pay no attention to, take no notice of, brush aside, pass over, shrug off, shut one's eyes to, be oblivious to, turn a blind eye to, turn a deaf ear to. **2** SLIGHT, spurn, cold-shoulder, look right through, look past, turn one's back on, send to Coventry, cut, cut dead. ■ OPPOSITES acknowledge.

ill adj. **1** SICK, unwell, not well, poorly, ailing, sickly, infirm, feeling bad, afflicted, indisposed, out of sorts, diseased, bedridden, invalided, weak, feeble, off colour; informal under the weather, laid up, queasy, funny, seedy; informal, dated queer. **2** HOSTILE, unfriendly, antagonistic, acrimonious, belligerent, bellicose, unkind, spiteful, rancorous, malicious, resentful, malevolent, bitter. **3** BAD, infamous, notorious, wicked, nefarious, vile, evil, foul, sinful, corrupt, depraved, degenerate. ▶ adv. BADLY, unfavourably, with disfavour, with disapproval, with hostility, unkindly, maliciously, spitefully.

ill-advised adj. UNWISE, ill-considered, imprudent, incautious, injudicious, ill-judged, impolitic, misguided, foolish, foolhardy, rash, hasty, overhasty, short-sighted, thoughtless, careless, reckless.

illegal adj. UNLAWFUL, illegitimate, illicit, lawless, criminal, felonious, actionable, unlicensed, unauthorized, unsanctioned, unwarranted, unofficial, outlawed, banned, forbidden, barred, prohibited, proscribed, contraband, black-market, under the counter, bootleg. ■ OPPOSITES legal.

illegible adj. INDECIPHERABLE, unreadable, unintelligible, scrawled, scribbled, unclear, obscure, squiggly. ■ OPPOSITES legible.

illegitimate adj. **1** ILLEGAL, illicit, unlawful, lawless, criminal, unauthorized, unsanctioned, irregular, invalid. **2** BORN OUT OF WEDLOCK; dated love, born on the wrong side of the blanket; old use bastard, natural. **3** UNSOUND, illogical, in-

illiterate adj. **1** unable to read or write. **2** uneducated. ■ **illiteracy** n.

illness n. a disease or period of being ill.

illogical adj. not logical. ■ **illogicality** n. **illogically** adv.

illuminate v. **1** light up. **2** explain or make clear. ■ **illumination** n.

illumine v. illuminate.

illusion n. **1** a false idea or belief. **2** a thing that seems to be something it is not.

illusionist n. a magician.

illusory (or **illusive**) adj. not real.

illustrate v. **1** provide a book etc. with pictures. **2** make clear by using examples etc. **3** act as an example of. ■ **illustration** n. **illustrative** adj. **illustrator** n.

illustrious adj. famous and admired.

image n. **1** a picture or statue. **2** a picture seen on a screen, through a lens, or in a mirror. **3** a picture in the mind. **4** a general impression presented to the public.

imaginary adj. existing only in the imagination.

imagination n. **1** the part of the mind that imagines things. **2** the ability to be creative or solve problems. ■ **imaginative** adj. **imaginatively** adv.

imagine v. **1** form a mental picture of. **2** suppose; assume. **3** believe something unreal to exist. ■ **imaginable** adj.

imago /i-may-goh/ n. (pl. **imagos** or **imagines** /i-may-ji-neez/) the fully developed adult stage of an insect.

imam n. the person who leads prayers in a mosque.

Thesaurus

valid, incorrect, spurious. ■ OPPOSITES legitimate.

ill-fated adj. UNLUCKY, luckless, unfortunate, hapless, unhappy, doomed, blighted, ill-starred, ill-omened.

ill-judged adj. see ILL-ADVISED.

illness n. SICKNESS, ailment, disease, complaint, malady, disorder, affliction, disability, attack, indisposition, infection, contagion, ill health, poor health.

illogical adj. UNSOUND, fallacious, unproved, invalid, specious, unreasonable, unreasoned, fallible, untenable, unscientific, casuistic, sophistic, inconsistent, incorrect, wrong, absurd, preposterous, meaningless, senseless. ■ OPPOSITES logical.

ill-treat v. TREAT BADLY, abuse, harm, injure, damage, handle roughly, mishandle, ill-use, maltreat, misuse; informal knock about.

illuminating adj. INSTRUCTIVE, informative, enlightening, explanatory, revealing, helpful.

illusion n. **1** DELUSION, misapprehension, misconception, deception, false/mistaken impression, fallacy, error, misjudgement, fancy. **2** HALLUCINATION, figment of the imagination, spectre, phantom, mirage, fantasy, will-o'-the-wisp; literary phantasm.

illusory adj. FALSE, mistaken, deceptive, delusory, delusional, delusive, fallacious, erroneous, misleading, untrue, specious, unreal, imagined, imaginary, fancied, non-existent, fanciful, notional, chimerical, dreamlike. ■ OPPOSITES genuine.

illustrate v. **1** ADD PICTURES TO, adorn, decorate, ornament, embellish. **2** DEM-ONSTRATE, exemplify, show, point up, instance, make plain/clear, clarify, bring home, emphasize, interpret.

illustration n. **1** PICTURE, drawing, sketch, figure, plate, artwork. **2** EXAMPLE, demonstration, typical case, case in point, instance, specimen, sample, exemplar, analogy.

image n. **1** LIKENESS, representation, painting, picture, portrait, effigy, figure, statue, sculpture, bust. **2** DOUBLE, twin, replica, clone, copy, reproduction, counterpart, doppelgänger; informal spit, spitting image, ringer, dead ringer. **3** FIGURE OF SPEECH, conceit, trope, expression.

imaginary adj. UNREAL, non-existent, illusory, fanciful, unsubstantial, chimerical, notional, assumed, supposed, suppositious, fictitious, fictional, mythical, mythological, made up, invented, hallucinatory, ghostly, spectral, dreamlike, visionary, shadowy; literary phantasmic. ■ OPPOSITES real, actual.

imagination n. **1** CREATIVITY, vision, inspiration, inventiveness, originality, innovation, ingenuity, insight, fancifulness. **2** ILLUSION, figment of the imagination, fancy, vision, dream, unreality.

imaginative adj. CREATIVE, inventive, original, innovative, visionary, inspired, fanciful, resourceful, ingenious, enterprising, clever, whimsical. ■ OPPOSITES unimaginative.

imagine v. **1** PICTURE, visualize, see in the mind's eye, envision, envisage, conjure up, dream about, dream up, think up, conceive, fantasize about, conceptualize, plan, scheme, project. **2** ASSUME, presume, expect, suppose, think, be-

imbalance n. a lack of balance.

imbecile n. informal a stupid person.

imbed var. of EMBED.

imbibe v. **1** drink alcohol. **2** absorb ideas.

imbroglio /im-broh-li-oh/ n. (pl. **imbroglios**) a confused or complicated situation.

imbue v. fill with a feeling or quality.

IMF abbrev. International Monetary Fund.

imitate v. **1** follow as a model. **2** copy. ■ **imitation** n. **imitative** adj. **imitator** n.

immaculate adj. **1** completely clean or tidy. **2** free from flaws or mistakes. ■ **immaculately** adv.

immanent adj. present throughout; inherent. ■ **immanence** n.

immaterial adj. not important or relevant.

immature adj. **1** not fully developed. **2** childish. ■ **immaturity** n.

immeasurable adj. too large, extensive, or extreme to measure. ■ **im-**

measurably adv.

immediate adj. **1** occurring or done at once. **2** nearest in time, space, or relationship. ■ **immediacy** n. **immediately** adv.

immemorial adj. existing for longer than can be remembered.

immense adj. very large or great. ■ **immensely** adv. **immensity** n.

immerse v. **1** dip or cover completely in a liquid. **2** involve deeply in an activity. ■ **immersion** n.

immersion heater n. an electric device placed in a water tank to heat the water.

immigrate v. come to live permanently in a foreign country. ■ **immigrant** n. **immigration** n.

imminent adj. about to happen. ■ **imminence** n. **imminently** adv.

immobile adj. **1** not moving. **2** not able to move. ■ **immobility** n. **immobilize** (or **-ise**) v.

Thesaurus

lieve, be of the opinion that, take it, gather, fancy, judge, deem, infer, deduce, conjecture, surmise, guess, reckon, suspect, realize.

imbue v. FILL, impregnate, inject, inculcate, instil, ingrain, inspire, permeate, charge.

imitate v. **1** COPY, emulate, simulate, mirror, follow someone's example, take after, follow, follow suit, take a page from someone's book, follow in someone's footsteps, echo. **2** MIMIC, ape, impersonate, do an impression of, parody, mock, caricature, burlesque, travesty; informal send up, take off, spoof, do.

imitation n. **1** COPY, reproduction, forgery, fake, counterfeit, resemblance, emulation, duplication, likeness, replica, simulation. **2** MIMICKING, mimicry, aping, impersonation, impression, parody, mockery, caricature, burlesque, travesty; informal send-up, take-off, spoof. ▶ adj. ARTIFICIAL, simulated, synthetic, man-made, mock, sham, fake, reproduction, pseudo, ersatz; informal phoney.

immature adj. **1** UNRIPE, undeveloped, unformed, imperfect, unfinished, incomplete, half-grown, crude, raw, green, unfledged, untimely. **2** CHILDISH, juvenile, adolescent, infantile, babyish, puerile, callow, jejune, inexperienced, green; informal wet behind the ears. ■ OPPOSITES mature.

immediate adj. **1** INSTANT, instantaneous, prompt, swift, speedy, sudden, abrupt. **2** NEAR, nearest, next, next-door,

close, closest, adjacent, adjoining, abutting, contiguous, proximate. **3** CURRENT, present, existing, actual, existent, extant, urgent, pressing. ■ OPPOSITES delayed, distant.

immediately adv. RIGHT AWAY, right now, straight away, at once, instantly, now, this minute, directly, promptly, without delay; informal before you can say Jack Robinson, pronto.

immense adj. HUGE, vast, massive, enormous, gigantic, colossal, giant, great, extensive, infinite, immeasurable, illimitable, monumental, tremendous, prodigious, elephantine, monstrous, titanic, Brobdingnagian; informal mega, ginormous. ■ OPPOSITES tiny, minute.

immerse v. **1** SUBMERGE, plunge, dip, dunk, duck, sink, souse, soak, drench, imbue, saturate. **2** ABSORB, engross, occupy, engage, preoccupy, involve, engulf, lose oneself in.

immigrant n. SETTLER, alien, incomer, non-native, new arrival, migrant, naturalized citizen, expatriate.

imminent adj. IMPENDING, approaching, close, fast-approaching, at hand, near, coming, forthcoming, on the way, about to happen, upon us, in the offing, on the horizon, in the air, brewing, threatening, menacing, looming. ■ OPPOSITES distant.

immobile adj. UNMOVING, motionless, immovable, still, static, at rest, stationary, at a standstill, stock-still, dormant, rooted, fixed to the spot, rigid, frozen,

immoderate adj. excessive.

immolate v. sacrifice by burning.

immoral adj. not following accepted standards of morality. ■ **immorality** n.

immortal adj. **1** living forever. **2** deserving to be remembered forever. ■ **immortality** n. **immortalize** (or **-ise**) v.

immovable adj. **1** unable to be moved. **2** unable to be changed. ■ **immovably** adv.

immune adj. **1** resistant to an infection. **2** not affected. **3** exempt. ■ **immunity** n. **immunize** (or **-ise**) v. **immunization** n.

immunodeficiency n. failure of the body's ability to resist infection.

immunology n. the study of immunity to infection. ■ **immunological** adj. **immunologist** n.

immure v. confine or imprison.

immutable adj. unchanging or unchangeable. ■ **immutability** n.

imp n. **1** a small devil. **2** a mischievous child. ■ **impish** adj.

impact n. **1** an act of one object hitting another. **2** a noticeable effect. ▶ v. **1** hit another object. **2** have a strong effect. **3** press firmly.

impair v. weaken or damage. ■ **impairment** n.

impala n. (pl. **impala**) an African antelope with lyre-shaped horns.

impale v. pierce with a sharp object.

impalpable adj. **1** unable to be felt by touch. **2** not easily understood.

impart v. **1** communicate information. **2** give a quality.

impartial adj. not favouring one more than another. ■ **impartiality** n. **impartially** adv.

impassable adj. impossible to travel along or over.

impasse /am-pahss/ n. a deadlock.

impassioned adj. filled with or showing great emotion.

Thesaurus

stiff, riveted, like a statue; *technical* immotile, immotive.

immobilize v. STOP, halt, bring to a standstill, paralyse, put out of action, inactivate, disable, cripple, freeze, transfix.

immodest adj. BOLD, brazen, forward, impudent, unblushing, shameless, wanton, improper, indecent, cheeky.

immoral adj. BAD, wicked, evil, unprincipled, dishonest, unethical, sinful, impure, corrupt, iniquitous, depraved, vile, base, degenerate, debauched, abandoned, dissolute, villainous, nefarious, reprobate, indecent, lewd, licentious, pornographic, unchaste, bawdy, of easy virtue. ■ OPPOSITES ethical, chaste.

immortal adj. **1** UNDYING, eternal, deathless, everlasting, never-ending, endless, imperishable, timeless, indestructible, unfading, perennial, evergreen, perpetual, lasting, enduring, constant, abiding, immutable, indissoluble; *literary* sempiternal. **2** FAMOUS, celebrated, renowned. ■ OPPOSITES mortal.

immortalize v. COMMEMORATE, memorialize, eternalize, eternize, perpetuate, exalt, glorify; *formal* laud.

immovable adj. **1** FIXED, set fast/firm, fast, firm, secure, stable, rooted, riveted, moored, anchored, stuck, jammed, stiff, unbudgeable. **2** MOTIONLESS, unmoving, stationary, still, stock-still, at a standstill, dead still, statue-like. **3** FIRM, adamant, steadfast, unwavering, unswerving, resolute, determined, tenacious, stubborn, dogged, obdurate, inflexible, unyielding, unbending, uncompromising, unshakeable, inexorable.

immune adj. NOT SUBJECT TO, not liable to, protected from, safe from, unsusceptible to, secure against, exempt from, clear of, free from, absolved from, released from, excused from, relieved of, spared from, exempted from, unaffected by, resistant to, proof against. ■ OPPOSITES liable, susceptible.

immunize v. INOCULATE, vaccinate, protect, shield, safeguard.

impact n. **1** COLLISION, crash, contact, smash, striking, clash, bump, knock, bang, jolt, thump, whack, thwack, slam, smack, slap. **2** INFLUENCE, effect, impression, results, consequences, repercussions.

impair v. WEAKEN, lessen, decrease, reduce, blunt, diminish, enfeeble, debilitate, enervate, damage, mar, spoil, injure, harm, hinder, disable, impede, undermine, vitiate. ■ OPPOSITES improve, enhance.

impart v. PASS ON, convey, communicate, transmit, relate, tell, make known, report, disclose, reveal, divulge, proclaim, broadcast.

impartial adj. UNBIASED, unprejudiced, disinterested, objective, detached, neutral, equitable, even-handed, fair, fairminded, open-minded, non-partisan, without fear or favour, with no axe to grind. ■ OPPOSITES biased, partisan.

impartiality n. DETACHMENT, disinterest, objectivity, neutrality, fairness, evenhandedness, justness, lack of bias,

impassive adj. not feeling or showing emotion.

impatient adj. 1 lacking patience or tolerance. 2 restlessly eager. ■ **impatience** n. **impatiently** adv.

impeach v. charge a public official with serious misconduct. ■ **impeachment** n.

impeccable adj. faultless. ■ **impeccably** adv.

impecunious adj. having little or no money.

impedance n. the total resistance of an electric circuit to the flow of alternating current.

impede v. hinder.

impediment n. 1 a hindrance. 2 a defect in a person's speech.

impel v. (**impelling**, **impelled**) drive or urge to do something.

impending adj. imminent.

impenetrable adj. impossible to get through or into or to understand.

imperative adj. 1 essential or vital.

2 giving or expressing a command. ▶ n. an essential thing.

imperceptible adj. too slight to be seen or felt. ■ **imperceptibly** adv.

imperfect adj. 1 faulty or incomplete. 2 (of a tense) referring to a past action not yet completed. ■ **imperfection** n. **imperfectly** adv.

imperial adj. 1 of an empire or an emperor. 2 (of measures) using a non-metric system formerly used in the UK.

imperialism n. a policy of extending a country's power and influence by establishing colonies etc. ■ **imperialist** n. & adj.

imperil v. (**imperilling**, **imperilled**; US **imperiling**, **imperiled**) endanger.

imperious adj. expecting unquestioning obedience. ■ **imperiously** adv.

impermeable adj. not allowing fluid to pass through.

impersonal adj. 1 not showing or influenced by personal feelings. 2 lacking human feelings. ■ **impersonally** adv.

Thesaurus

open-mindedness.

impassable adj. 1 CLOSE, blocked, obstructed, unnavigable, untraversable, impenetrable. 2 INSURMOUNTABLE, insuperable, unconquerable.

impatient adj. 1 EAGER, keen, anxious, avid, desirous, yearning, longing. 2 RESTLESS, restive, excitable, agitated, nervous, edgy, impetuous. 3 ABRUPT, brusque, terse, short, irritated, angry, testy, short-tempered, quick-tempered, curt, querulous, peevish, intolerant; *informal* snappy. ■ OPPOSITES patient.

impede v. HINDER, obstruct, hamper, handicap, block, check, curb, bar, hold back, hold up, delay, interfere with, disrupt, retard, slow, slow down, brake, restrain, thwart, frustrate, baulk, stop, throw a spanner in the works. ■ OPPOSITES facilitate.

impediment n. HINDRANCE, obstruction, obstacle, handicap, block, stumbling block, check, encumbrance, bar, barrier, curb, brake, restraint, drawback, difficulty, snag, setback.

impel v. URGE, press, exhort, force, oblige, constrain, necessitate, require, demand, make, apply pressure, pressure, pressurize, spur, goad, incite, prompt, chivvy, persuade, inspire.

impending adj. see IMMINENT.

impenetrable adj. 1 IMPERVIOUS, impermeable, solid, dense, thick, hard, closed, sealed, resistant, waterproof, tight, unpierceable. 2 IMPASSABLE, in-

accessible, thick, dense, overgrown. 3 INCOMPREHENSIBLE, baffling, puzzling, abstruse, obscure, inexplicable, unfathomable, recondite, inscrutable, enigmatic.

imperceptible adj. UNNOTICEABLE, unobtrusive, unapparent, slight, small, gradual, subtle, faint, fine, inconsequential, tiny, minute, minuscule, microscopic, infinitesimal, undetectable, indistinguishable, indiscernible, invisible, indistinct, unclear, obscure, vague, indefinite, shadowy, inaudible, muffled, impalpable. ■ OPPOSITES obvious.

imperceptibly adv. UNNOTICEABLY, unobtrusively, unseen, gradually, slowly, subtly, undetectably, little by little, bit by bit.

imperfect adj. 1 FAULTY, flawed, defective, blemished, damaged, broken, impaired. 2 DEFICIENT, inadequate, insufficient, rudimentary, limited, patchy, sketchy. ■ OPPOSITES flawless.

imperfection n. 1 FAULT, flaw, defect, blemish, deformity, crack, break, scratch, cut, tear, stain, spot. 2 FAILING, foible, deficiency, weakness, weak point, shortcoming, fallibility, frailty, infirmity, peccadillo.

imperious adj. OVERBEARING, overweening, domineering, peremptory, highhanded, assertive, commanding, authoritative, lordly, masterful, dictatorial, tyrannical. ■ OPPOSITES humble.

impersonal adj. 1 OBJECTIVE, detached,

impersonate v. pretend to be another person. ■ **impersonation** n. **impersonator** n.

impertinent adj. not showing proper respect. ■ **impertinence** n. **impertinently** adv.

imperturbable adj. unable to be upset.

impervious adj. 1 impermeable. 2 (**impervious to**) unable to be affected by.

impetigo /im-pi-ty-goh/ n. a contagious skin infection.

impetuous adj. acting or done quickly and without thought. ■ **impetuously** adv.

impetus n. a driving or moving force.

impinge v. (**impinge on**) have an effect or impact on.

impious adj. irreverent.

implacable adj. 1 unwilling to be reconciled. 2 unstoppable. ■ **implacably** adv.

implant v. 1 insert tissue or a device into the body. 2 fix an idea in the mind. ▶ n. something implanted. ■ **implantation** n.

implausible adj. improbable or unconvincing. ■ **implausibly** adv.

implement n. a tool. ▶ v. put into effect. ■ **implementation** n.

implicate v. 1 show to be involved in a crime. 2 (**be implicated in**) be partly responsible for.

implication n. 1 something implied. 2 a possible effect. 3 the fact of being implicated.

implicit adj. 1 implied but not stated. 2 total and unquestioning. ■ **implicitly** adv.

implode v. collapse violently inwards. ■ **implosion** n.

implore v. beg earnestly.

imply v. (**implying**, **implied**) 1 suggest rather than state directly. 2 suggest as a possible effect.

Thesaurus

disinterested, dispassionate, neutral, unbiased, unprejudiced, fair, equitable, even-handed. 2 COLD, cool, aloof, frigid, stiff, rigid, wooden, starchy, stilted, stuffy, businesslike, bureaucratic, matter-of-fact. ■ OPPOSITES biased.

impersonate v. IMITATE, mimic, personate, ape, mock, parody, caricature, masquerade as, burlesque, pose as, pass oneself off as; *informal* take off, do.

impertinent adj. INSOLENT, impudent, cheeky, rude, impolite, unmannerly, ill-mannered, uncivil, coarse, uncouth, crude, discourteous, disrespectful, bold, brazen, audacious, presumptuous, forward, pert, brash, shameless; *informal* saucy, brass-necked, fresh, flip. ■ OPPOSITES polite.

imperturbable adj. SELF-POSSESSED, composed, collected, calm, cool, tranquil, serene, unexcitable, unflappable, even-tempered, easy-going, unruffled, at ease, untroubled, undismayed, unmoved, nonchalant. ■ OPPOSITES nervous, excitable.

impetuous adj. 1 IMPULSIVE, hasty, impatient, excitable, headstrong, rash, reckless, foolhardy, wild, uncontrolled, eager, enthusiastic, spontaneous, passionate, ardent, zealous. 2 HASTY, precipitate, impulsive, spontaneous, impromptu, spur-of-the-moment, unthinking, unplanned, ill-considered, unreasoned, heedless, reckless, rash. ■ OPPOSITES cautious.

impetus n. 1 MOMENTUM, energy, force, power, propulsion, motion. 2 STIMULUS,

motivation, incentive, inducement, inspiration, encouragement, influence, push, urging, pressing, spur, goading, goad, instigation, actuation.

impinge v. (**impinge on**) 1 ENCROACH ON, infringe, intrude on, invade, trespass on, violate, usurp, make inroads on, obtrude on. 2 AFFECT, have an effect on, have a bearing on, impress, touch, exert influence on, bear upon.

implausible adj. UNLIKELY, improbable, hard to believe, incredible, unbelievable, unimaginable, inconceivable, debatable, questionable, doubtful. ■ OPPOSITES plausible.

implement n. TOOL, utensil, appliance, instrument, gadget, device, apparatus, contrivance; *informal* gizmo. ▶ v. CARRY OUT, fulfil, execute, perform, discharge, accomplish, achieve, realize, put into effect, bring about, effect, enforce.

implicate v. INCRIMINATE, involve, compromise, accuse, charge, blame, entangle, impeach, inculpate. ■ OPPOSITES absolve.

implication n. 1 INCRIMINATION, involvement, connection, entanglement, embroilment, association. 2 SUGGESTION, inference, insinuation, innuendo, hint, allusion, reference, assumption, presumption.

implicit adj. 1 IMPLIED, indirect, inferred, unspoken, undeclared, unexpressed, unstated, tacit, understood, suggested. 2 ABSOLUTE, complete, total, wholehearted, utter, unqualified, unconditional, unreserved, unquestioning, firm, stead-

☑ Don't confuse **imply** and **infer**. If you **imply** something, you are suggesting it though not saying it directly. If you **infer** something from a statement, you come to the conclusion that this is what was meant.

impolite adj. not having or showing good manners.

impolitic adj. unwise.

imponderable adj. difficult or impossible to assess.

import v. bring goods etc. into a country from abroad. ▶ n. **1** an imported article. **2** meaning. **3** importance. ■ **importation** n. **importer** n.

important adj. **1** having a great effect or of great value. **2** having great authority or influence. ■ **importance** n. **importantly** adv.

importunate adj. very persistent.

importune v. bother with persistent requests.

impose v. **1** introduce a tax, restriction, etc. **2** force something to be accepted. **3** (**impose on**) take unfair advantage

of. ■ **imposition** n.

imposing adj. impressive.

impossible adj. **1** not able to occur, exist, or be done. **2** very hard to deal with. ■ **impossibility** n. **impossibly** adv.

impostor (or **imposter**) n. a person who pretends to be someone else in order to deceive others.

impotent adj. **1** helpless or powerless. **2** (of a man) unable to achieve an erection. ■ **impotence** n.

impound v. **1** seize and take legal possession of. **2** shut up in an enclosure.

impoverish v. **1** make poor. **2** make worse in quality.

impracticable adj. not able to be done.

impractical adj. not sensible or realistic. ■ **impracticality** n.

imprecation n. a spoken curse.

imprecise adj. not exact.

impregnable adj. unable to be captured or broken into.

impregnate v. **1** saturate with a substance. **2** make pregnant. ■ **impregnation** n.

Thesaurus

fast. ■ OPPOSITES explicit.

implore v. BEG, appeal to, entreat, plead with, ask, pray, request, solicit, supplicate, importune, press, crave, plead for, appeal for; *literary* beseech.

imply v. INSINUATE, hint, suggest, intimate, make out, give to understand, signal, indicate.

impolite adj. *see* RUDE.

important adj. **1** SIGNIFICANT, crucial, of great consequence/import, far-reaching, critical, pivotal, momentous, substantial, weighty, valuable, serious, grave, urgent, of great moment, consequential, salient, chief, main, principal, major, of concern, of interest, relevant, of value, necessary, essential. **2** EMINENT, prominent, pre-eminent, leading, foremost, outstanding, distinguished, esteemed, notable, noteworthy, of note, influential, of influence, powerful, high-ranking, high-level, top-level, prestigious. ■ OPPOSITES unimportant.

importunate adj. PERSISTENT, insistent, dogged, unremitting, relentless, pertinacious, pressing, urgent, demanding, exacting, clamorous, entreating, solicitous, imprecatory.

importune v. BEG, implore, plead with, appeal to, call upon, supplicate, petition, press; *literary* beseech.

impose v. **1** ENFORCE, apply, exact, levy, charge, lay on, set, establish, fix, or-

dain, introduce, promulgate, decree. **2** FORCE, inflict, foist, thrust, obtrude.

imposing adj. IMPRESSIVE, striking, grand, splendid, majestic, august, lofty, stately.

impossible adj. **1** NOT POSSIBLE, out of the question, inconceivable, unthinkable, unimaginable, impracticable, unattainable, unachievable, unobtainable, beyond one, hopeless. **2** UNBELIEVABLE, incredible, absurd, ludicrous, ridiculous, preposterous, outlandish. **3** UNMANAGEABLE, intractable, recalcitrant, wayward, exasperating, infuriating. ■ OPPOSITES possible, plausible.

impostor n. DECEIVER, pretender, fake, fraud, sham, charlatan, mountebank, hoodwinker, bluffer, trickster, cheat, cheater, swindler, confidence man/woman, rogue; *informal* con man/woman, con artist.

impracticable adj. IMPOSSIBLE, out of the question, unfeasible, unworkable, unattainable, unrealizable, unsuitable. ■ OPPOSITES feasible, possible.

impractical adj. **1** USELESS, ineffective, ineffectual, unrealistic, impossible, unviable. **2** UNREALISTIC, idealistic, romantic, quixotic, starry-eyed. ■ OPPOSITES practical.

imprecise adj. **1** INEXACT, approximate, estimated, rough, inaccurate, incorrect. **2** VAGUE, loose, hazy, blurred, indefinite,

impresario n. (pl. **impresarios**) an organizer of theatrical or musical productions.

impress v. **1** cause to feel admiration. **2** make a mark on something with a stamp etc. **3** (**impress on**) emphasize an idea in the mind of.

impression n. **1** an idea, feeling, or opinion. **2** an effect produced on someone. **3** an imitation of a person or thing, done to entertain. **4** a mark made by pressing.

impressionable adj. easily influenced.

Impressionism n. a style of art depicting the visual impression of a moment or mood. ■ **Impressionist** n. & adj.

impressive adj. arousing admiration through size, quality, or skill. ■ **impressively** adv. **impressiveness** n.

imprint v. **1** make a mark on an object by pressure. **2** have an effect on. ▶ n. **1** a mark made by pressure. **2** a publisher's name etc. in a book.

imprison v. put or keep in prison. ■ **imprisonment** n.

improbable adj. not likely to be true or to happen. ■ **improbability** n. **improbably** adv.

impromptu adj. & adv. done without being planned or rehearsed.

improper adj. **1** not conforming to rules or standards. **2** not modest or decent. ■ **improperly** adv. **impropriety** n.

improve v. make or become better. ■ **improvement** n.

improvident adj. not providing for future needs.

improvise v. **1** invent and perform drama, music, etc. without planning in advance. **2** make from whatever is available. ■ **improvisation** n.

imprudent adj. not careful; rash.

impudent adj. not showing proper respect. ■ **impudence** n. **impudently** adv.

Thesaurus

woolly, confused, ambiguous, equivocal. ■ OPPOSITES precise.

impregnate v. SUFFUSE, permeate, imbue, penetrate, fill, infuse, pervade, soak, steep, saturate, drench, inundate.

impress v. **1** MAKE AN IMPRESSION/IMPACT ON, move, sway, influence, affect, stir, rouse, excite, inspire, galvanize. **2** STAMP, imprint, print, mark, engrave, emboss.

impression n. **1** EFFECT, influence, impact, sway, hold, power, control. **2** MARK, indentation, dent, hollow, outline, stamp, imprint. **3** FEELING, sense, sensation, awareness, perception, notion, idea, thought, belief, opinion, conviction, suspicion, inkling, intuition, hunch, funny feeling. **4** IMPERSONATION, imitation, mimicry, parody, caricature, take-off, send-up, burlesque, travesty.

impressionable adj. SUGGESTIBLE, susceptible, persuadable, receptive, responsive, sensitive, open, gullible, ingenuous, pliable, malleable, mouldable.

impressive adj. IMPOSING, striking, magnificent, splendid, moving, touching, affecting, stirring, rousing, exciting, powerful, inspiring. ■ OPPOSITES ordinary, unexciting.

imprison v. PUT IN PRISON, send to prison, jail, lock up, take into custody, put under lock and key, put away, incarcerate, confine, shut in/up, intern, detain, constrain, immure; informal send down.

imprisonment n. CUSTODY, incarceration, internment, confinement, detention, restraint; informal porridge.

improbable adj. UNLIKELY, doubtful, questionable, dubious, implausible, far-fetched, unconvincing, unbelievable, incredible, ridiculous, ludicrous, preposterous. ■ OPPOSITES probable.

impromptu adj. UNREHEARSED, ad lib, unprepared, extempore, extemporized, extemporaneous, spontaneous, improvised, unscripted, unpremeditated, unstudied; informal off-the-cuff, off the top of one's head, on the spur of the moment. ■ OPPOSITES rehearsed.

improper adj. **1** UNSEEMLY, unbecoming, indecorous, unfitting, indiscreet, injudicious. **2** INDECENT, off colour, indelicate, risqué, suggestive, smutty, obscene, lewd, pornographic; informal blue. **3** INCORRECT, inaccurate, wrong, erroneous, false, fallacious. ■ OPPOSITES proper.

improve v. **1** MAKE BETTER, better, ameliorate, mend, amend, reform, rehabilitate, set/put right, correct, rectify, help, advance, upgrade, revamp, modernize; informal give something a facelift. **2** GET/GROW BETTER, advance, come along, make headway, develop, progress, make progress, pick up, perk up, take a turn for the better, take on a new lease of life, rally, look up. **3** GET BETTER, recuperate, be on the mend, turn the corner, recover, gain strength, convalesce. ■ OPPOSITES worsen.

improvident adj. UNTHRIFTY, thriftless, spendthrift, wasteful, prodigal, extravagant, uneconomical, shiftless. ■ OPPOSITES thrifty.

improvise v. **1** EXTEMPORIZE, ad-lib; infor-

impugn /im-pyoon/ v. express doubts about the truth or honesty of.

impulse n. **1** a sudden urge to do something. **2** a driving force. **3** a pulse of electrical energy. ■ **impulsion** n. **impulsive** adj. **impulsively** adv.

impunity n. freedom from punishment or harm.

impure adj. **1** mixed with another substance. **2** morally wrong. ■ **impurity** n.

impute v. attribute a fault to someone. ■ **imputation** n.

in prep. **1** enclosed, surrounded, or inside. **2** during or within a period of time. **3** having as a state or quality. **4** included or involved. **5** indicating the language or medium used. ▶ adv. **1** so as to be enclosed, surrounded, or inside. **2** present at one's home or office. **3** expressing arrival. ▶ adj. informal fashionable. □ **in-house** within an organization. **in-law** a relative by marriage. **the ins and outs** informal all the details.

in. abbrev. inches.

inability n. the state of being unable to do something.

in absentia adv. while not present.

inaccessible adj. **1** unable to be reached. **2** difficult to understand.

inaccurate adj. not accurate. ■ **inaccuracy** n. **inaccurately** adv.

inaction n. lack of action.

inactive adj. not active or working. ■ **inactivity** n.

inadequate adj. **1** not enough or not good enough. **2** unable to deal with a situation. ■ **inadequacy** n. **inadequately** adv.

inadmissible adj. not allowable.

inadvertent adj. unintentional. ■ **inadvertently** adv.

☑ *-ent*, not *-ant*: inadvert*ent*.

inalienable adj. not able to be taken or given away.

inane adj. lacking sense; silly. ■ **inanely** adv. **inanity** n.

inanimate adj. **1** not alive. **2** showing

Thesaurus

mal speak off the cuff, play it by ear, make it up as you go along, wing it. **2** THROW/PUT TOGETHER, contrive, devise, concoct, rig, jury-rig.

impudent adj. IMPERTINENT, insolent, cheeky, bold, audacious, brazen, cocky, pert, presumptuous, forward, bumptious, impolite, rude, disrespectful, ill-mannered, unmannerly, ill-bred, shameless, immodest; *informal* saucy, brass-necked.

impulse n. **1** DRIVE, urge, instinct, appetite, proclivity. **2** STIMULUS, inspiration, stimulation, incitement, incentive, inducement, motivation.

impulsive adj. **1** HASTY, sudden, quick, precipitate, impetuous, impromptu, spontaneous, snap, ill-considered, unplanned, unpremeditated, thoughtless, rash, reckless. **2** IMPETUOUS, rash, reckless, spontaneous, instinctive, passionate, intuitive, emotional, foolhardy, madcap, devil-may-care. ■ OPPOSITES deliberate, cautious.

impure adj. **1** ADULTERATED, debased, contaminated, polluted, tainted, infected, dirty, foul, unclean, filthy, sullied, defiled, unwholesome, poisoned, feculent. **2** LEWD, lustful, obscene, indecent, lecherous, ribald, smutty, pornographic, improper, crude, vulgar, coarse, gross. ■ OPPOSITES pure.

inaccessible adj. UNREACHABLE, out of reach, cut off, beyond reach, un-

approachable, impenetrable, unattainable, out of the way, isolated, lonely, remote, godforsaken, off the beaten track. ■ OPPOSITES accessible.

inaccurate adj. **1** INCORRECT, wrong, erroneous, faulty, inexact, imprecise, out. **2** WRONG, false, not true, erroneous, fallacious, not right, imperfect, flawed, defective, unsound, unreliable, wide of the mark; *informal* full of holes. ■ OPPOSITES accurate.

inactive adj. **1** IMMOBILE, motionless, inert, stationary, idle, sluggish, slow, indolent, lazy, lifeless, slothful, lethargic, stagnant, vegetating, dilatory, torpid. **2** INOPERATIVE, idle, out of service, unused, out of use, unoccupied, mothballed, unemployed. **3** DORMANT, quiescent, latent, passive.

inadequate adj. **1** INSUFFICIENT, not enough, too little, too few, lacking, found wanting, deficient, short, in short supply, meagre, scanty, scant, niggardly, scarce, sparse, skimpy, sketchy, incomplete. **2** INCAPABLE, incompetent, unfit, ineffective, ineffectual, inefficient, unskilful, inexpert, inept; *informal* not up to scratch. ■ OPPOSITES adequate.

inadvertent adj. ACCIDENTAL, unintentional, chance, unpremeditated, unplanned, unconscious, uncalculated, unwitting, involuntary. ■ OPPOSITES deliberate.

no sign of life.

inapplicable adj. not relevant or appropriate.

inappropriate adj. unsuitable. ■ **inappropriately** adv.

inarticulate adj. **1** unable to express one's ideas clearly. **2** not expressed in words.

inasmuch adv. (**inasmuch as**) **1** to the extent that. **2** considering that.

inattentive adj. not paying attention.

inaudible adj. unable to be heard. ■ **inaudibly** adv.

inaugurate v. **1** begin or introduce a system etc. **2** establish someone in office or mark the opening of a building etc. with a ceremony. ■ **inaugural** adj. **inauguration** n.

inboard adv. & adj. (of an engine) inside a boat.

inborn adj. existing from birth.

inbred adj. **1** produced by inbreeding. **2** inborn.

inbreeding n. breeding from closely related people or animals.

incalculable adj. too great to be calculated or estimated.

incandescent adj. glowing with heat. ■ **incandescence** n.

incantation n. words said as a magic spell.

incapable adj. **1** not able to do something. **2** not able to care for oneself.

incapacitate v. prevent from functioning.

incapacity n. inability to do something.

incarcerate v. imprison. ■ **incarceration** n.

incarnate adj. in human or physical form.

incarnation n. **1** a god, spirit, or quality in human form. **2** (**the Incarnation**) (in Christian belief) God as Jesus Christ.

incendiary adj. **1** (of a bomb) designed to cause fire. **2** tending to stir up conflict. ▶ n. (pl. **incendiaries**) an incendiary bomb.

incense n. a substance burnt to produce a sweet smell. ▶ v. make very angry.

incentive n. something that encourages action or effort.

inception n. the beginning of something.

incessant adj. never stopping. ■ **incessantly** adv.

incest n. sex between very closely related people. ■ **incestuous** adj.

inch n. a unit of length equal to one twelfth of a foot (2.54 cm). ▶ v. move

Thesaurus

inadvisable adj. UNWISE, ill-advised, ill-judged, misguided, injudicious, imprudent, foolish, impolitic, inexpedient. ■ OPPOSITES shrewd.

inanimate adj. **1** LIFELESS, without life, dead, inert, insentient, insensate, extinct, defunct. **2** APATHETIC, spiritless, lazy, inactive, listless, lethargic, sluggish, torpid. ■ OPPOSITES living.

inappropriate adj. UNSUITABLE, unfitting, out of place, out of keeping, unseemly, unbecoming, improper, indecorous, inapposite, incongruous, out of keeping, inexpedient, inadvisable, injudicious, infelicitous, untimely. ■ OPPOSITES appropriate.

inarticulate adj. **1** UNINTELLIGIBLE, incomprehensible, incoherent, unclear, indistinct, blurred, muffled, mumbled, muttered. **2** POORLY SPOKEN, faltering, hesitating, halting, stumbling, stuttering, stammering. **3** UNSPOKEN, unuttered, unexpressed, unvoiced, wordless, silent, mute, dumb, speechless, voiceless, soundless, taciturn, tongue-tied. ■ OPPOSITES articulate.

inattentive adj. **1** NEGLECTFUL, negligent, remiss, forgetful, careless, thoughtless, heedless, indifferent, unconcerned, inconsiderate. **2** DISTRACTED, preoccupied, absent-minded, daydreaming, wool-gathering, lost in thought; *informal* in a world of one's own, miles away, with one's head in the clouds, in a brown study. ■ OPPOSITES attentive.

inauspicious adj. UNPROPITIOUS, unpromising, unlucky, unfortunate, unhappy, infelicitous, unfavourable, ill-omened, ominous, ill-fated, ill-starred, untoward, untimely. ■ OPPOSITES auspicious.

incapable adj. **1** INCOMPETENT, ineffective, ineffectual, inadequate, inefficacious, unfit, unfitted, unqualified, inept, inapt, useless, feeble; *informal* not up to scratch. **2** UNABLE TO, not capable of, lacking the ability to. ■ OPPOSITES capable.

inception n. BEGINNING, commencement, start, starting point, outset, opening, debut, inauguration, initiation, institution, birth, dawn, origin, rise; *informal* kick-off. ■ OPPOSITES end.

incessant adj. UNCEASING, ceaseless, non-stop, endless, unending, never-ending, everlasting, eternal, constant, slowly and carefully.

inchoate adj. not fully formed or developed.

incidence n. **1** the rate of occurrence of something. **2** Physics the meeting of a line or ray with a surface.

incident n. an event, esp. a violent one.

incidental adj. **1** occurring as a result of something else. **2** minor or unimportant. □ **incidental music** background music in a film.

incidentally adv. **1** by the way. **2** in an incidental way.

incinerate v. destroy by burning. ■ **incineration** n. **incinerator** n.

incipient adj. beginning to happen or develop.

incise v. make a cut in a surface. ■ **incision** n.

incisive adj. **1** showing clear thought and understanding. **2** quick and direct.

incisor n. a narrow-edged front tooth.

incite v. urge to act violently or unlawfully. ■ **incitement** n.

incivility n. rudeness.

inclement adj. (of the weather) unpleasantly cold or wet.

inclination n. **1** a tendency to act in a

particular way. **2** an interest or liking. **3** a slope or slant.

incline v. **1** (**be inclined to**) tend or be willing to. **2** (**be inclined**) have a particular tendency or talent. **3** lean or bend. ▶ n. a slope.

include v. **1** have as part of a whole. **2** make or treat as part of a whole. ■ **inclusion** n.

inclusive adj. **1** including everything expected or required. **2** between the limits stated.

incognito /in-kog-nee-toh/ adj. & adv. with one's true identity concealed.

incoherent adj. **1** hard to understand. **2** not logical or well-organized. ■ **incoherence** n. **incoherently** adv.

income n. money received as wages, interest, etc.

incoming adj. coming in.

incommunicado adj. & adv. not able to communicate with other people.

incomparable adj. without an equal in quality. ■ **incomparably** adv.

incompatible adj. not able to exist, be used, or to live or work together. ■ **incompatibility** n.

incompetent adj. lacking the skill to

Thesaurus

continual, perpetual, continuous, uninterrupted, unbroken, unremitting, on-going, persistent, recurrent. ■ OPPOSITES intermittent.

incident n. **1** EVENT, happening, occurrence, episode, experience, proceeding, adventure, occasion, circumstance, fact, matter. **2** DISTURBANCE, commotion, scene, row, fracas, contretemps, skirmish, clash, conflict, confrontation, brush.

incidental adj. **1** ACCIDENTAL, by chance, chance, random, fortuitous. **2** RELATED, connected, associated, accompanying, attendant, concomitant, contingent. **3** SECONDARY, subsidiary, subordinate.

incise v. CUT, cut into, make an incision in, slit, slit open, gash, slash, notch, nick, furrow.

incite v. **1** INSTIGATE, provoke, foment, whip up, stir up, prompt. **2** ENCOURAGE, urge, egg on, goad, spur on, prod, stimulate, drive on, excite, arouse, agitate, inflame, stir up, provoke. ■ OPPOSITES discourage.

inclination n. **1** TENDENCY, leaning, propensity, proclivity, predisposition, weakness, penchant, predilection, partiality, preference, affinity, attraction, fancy, liking, fondness, affection, love. **2** BEND, bow, nod, lowing, stooping.

incline v. **1** TEND, lean, swing, veer, have a preference for, be attracted to, have an affinity for. **2** BEND, slope, slant, bank, cant, bevel, tilt, lean, tip, list, deviate. ▶ n. SLOPE, gradient, hill, drop, declivity, descent, ascent, rise. □ **be inclined to** HAVE A TENDENCY TO, be liable to, be likely to, be predisposed to.

include v. **1** CONTAIN, hold, take in, admit, incorporate, embrace, encompass, comprise, embody, comprehend, subsume. **2** ADD, insert, allow for, put in, enter, introduce, count in, take account of, build in, number, incorporate. ■ OPPOSITES exclude.

incoherent adj. UNCONNECTED, disconnected, disjointed, disordered, confused, mixed up, muddled, jumbled, scrambled, rambling, wandering, discursive, illogical, unintelligible, hard to follow, garbled, inarticulate, mumbled, muttered, stuttered, stammered. ■ OPPOSITES coherent.

income n. SALARY, pay, earnings, wages, remuneration, takings, profits, revenue, gains, proceeds, means.

incomparable adj. BEYOND COMPARE, inimitable, unequalled, matchless, nonpareil, unrivalled, peerless, unparalleled, unsurpassed, superlative, supreme, transcendent.

do something. ■ **incompetence** n.
incomplete adj. not complete.
incomprehensible adj. not able to be understood.
inconceivable adj. extremely unlikely. ■ **inconceivably** adv.
inconclusive adj. not leading to a firm conclusion.
incongruous adj. out of place. ■ **incongruity** n. **incongruously** adv.
inconsequential adj. not important.
inconsiderable adj. small in size, amount, etc.
inconsiderate adj. not thinking of others' feelings or wishes.

inconsistent adj. not consistent. ■ **inconsistency** n.
inconsolable adj. not able to be comforted.
inconstant adj. **1** frequently changing. **2** not faithful.
incontestable adj. indisputable.
incontinent adj. unable to control the excretion of one's urine or faeces. ■ **incontinence** n.
incontrovertible adj. undeniable or indisputable. ■ **incontrovertibly** adv.
inconvenience n. slight trouble or difficulty. ▶ v. cause inconvenience to. ■ **inconvenient** adj.

Thesaurus

incompatible adj. **1** UNSUITED, mismatched, like chalk and cheese, ill-assorted, incongruous, antagonistic, conflicting, antipathetic, discordant. **2** CLASHING, discordant, jarring, inharmonious. **3** CONTRARY TO, differing from, at odds with, inconsistent with, in opposition to, diametrically opposed to. ■ OPPOSITES compatible.

incompetent adj. **1** INCAPABLE, inept, inefficient, ineffectual, unqualified, unable, unfitted, unsuitable, useless, inadequate, deficient. **2** INEXPERT, unskilful, inept, bungling, awkward, maladroit, clumsy, floundering, gauche; informal botched. ■ OPPOSITES competent.

incomplete adj. **1** UNFINISHED, partial, unaccomplished, undone, undeveloped, unexecuted, unperformed. **2** IMPERFECT, broken, defective, lacking, wanting, deficient. **3** SHORTENED, deficient, curtailed, abridged, expurgated, bowdlerized. ■ OPPOSITES complete.

incomprehensible adj. **1** UNINTELLIGIBLE, too difficult/hard, complicated, complex, involved, intricate; informal over one's head. **2** ILLEGIBLE, indecipherable, unintelligible, unreadable. ■ OPPOSITES intelligible, clear.

inconceivable adj. UNIMAGINABLE, unthinkable, incomprehensible, incredible, unbelievable, implausible, impossible, out of the question, preposterous, ridiculous, ludicrous. ■ OPPOSITES plausible.

inconclusive adj. INDEFINITE, indeterminate, indecisive, undetermined, open to question, open to doubt, vague, unsettled, unresolved, questionable, ambiguous, equivocal, unestablished; informal up in the air. ■ OPPOSITES conclusive.

incongruous adj. OUT OF PLACE, inappropriate, incompatible, discordant, jarring, out of keeping, inconsistent, contrary, unsuited, at odds, in opposition, opposed, conflicting, irreconcilable, strange, odd, absurd, unsuitable. ■ OPPOSITES appropriate, suitable.

inconsequential adj. INSIGNIFICANT, negligible, unimportant, trivial, trifling, petty; informal piddling. ■ OPPOSITES important.

inconsiderate adj. THOUGHTLESS, unthinking, uncaring, heedless, unmindful, regardless, undiscerning, insensitive, tactless, uncharitable, unkind, ungracious, selfish, self-centred, egotistical. ■ OPPOSITES considerate.

inconsistent adj. **1** INCOMPATIBLE, out of keeping, out of place, contrary, at odds, at variance, in opposition, conflicting, in conflict, irreconcilable, discordant, discrepant. **2** UNSTABLE, unsteady, changeable, erratic, irregular, unpredictable, capricious, fickle, whimsical, mercurial, volatile. ■ OPPOSITES consistent.

inconspicuous adj. UNOBTRUSIVE, unnoticeable, indistinct, ordinary, plain, run-of-the-mill, unremarkable, undistinguished, unostentatious, unimposing, hidden, insignificant, quiet, retiring, unassuming, in the background; informal low-key. ■ OPPOSITES noticeable, conspicuous.

inconvenience n. **1** TROUBLE, bother, disruption, disturbance, vexation, worry, annoyance, disadvantage, difficulty, embarrassment. **2** AWKWARDNESS, unwieldiness, cumbersomeness, unhandiness. ▶ v. DISTURB, bother, trouble, worry, disrupt, put out, impose upon, burden, distract, annoy, discommode.

inconvenient adj. **1** AWKWARD, unsuitable, inappropriate, inopportune, disadvantageous, inexpedient, disturbing, troublesome, bothersome, tiresome,

incorporate v. **1** include as part of a whole. **2** form a company into a corporation. ■ **incorporation** n.

incorrect adj. not true, accurate, or following accepted standards. ■ **incorrectly** adv.

incorrigible adj. having bad habits that cannot be changed.

incorruptible adj. **1** too honest to take bribes. **2** not subject to death or decay.

increase v. make or become greater in size, amount, or intensity. ▶n. a rise in amount, size, or intensity. ■ **increasingly** adv.

incredible adj. impossible or hard to believe. ■ **incredibly** adv.

incredulous adj. unwilling or unable to believe something. ■ **incredulity** n. **incredulously** adv.

increment n. an increase in a number or amount. ■ **incremental** adj.

incriminate v. cause to appear guilty of a crime.

incubate v. **1** hatch eggs by keeping them warm. **2** cause bacteria etc. to develop by maintaining a suitable temperature. ■ **incubation** n. **incubator** n.

inculcate v. fix an idea etc. in the mind by repetition.

incumbent adj. **1** necessary as a duty. **2** currently holding office. ▶n. the holder of an office.

incur v. (**incurring**, **incurred**) bring something unwelcome on oneself.

incurable adj. not able to be cured. ■ **incurably** adv.

incursion n. a sudden or brief invasion.

indebted adj. **1** grateful. **2** owing money.

indecent adj. not conforming with accepted standards of behaviour or propriety. □ **indecent assault** sexual as-

Thesaurus

vexatious, annoying, embarrassing, ill-timed, untimely, unseasonable. **2** UN-WIELDY, cumbersome, awkward, unmanageable, difficult. ■ OPPOSITES convenient.

incorporate v. **1** INCLUDE, embrace, absorb, embody, assimilate, subsume. **2** MERGE, coalesce, fuse, blend, mix, amalgamate, combine, unite, integrate, unify, compact. ■ OPPOSITES exclude.

incorrect adj. **1** WRONG, inaccurate, erroneous, wide of the mark. **2** MISTAKEN, inaccurate, faulty, inexact, untrue, false, fallacious, non-factual, flawed; informal full of holes. **3** IMPROPER, unsuitable, indecorous, inappropriate, lacking in propriety, unseemly, ungentlemanly, unladylike. ■ OPPOSITES correct.

incorrigible adj. INVETERATE, irredeemable, hardened, dyed-in-the-wool, incurable, irreformable, hopeless, beyond hope, beyond redemption, impenitent, uncontrite, unrepentant, obdurate, habitual, shameless.

incorruptible adj. **1** VIRTUOUS, honest, upright, honourable, moral, ethical, trustworthy, straight, unbribable, high-principled. **2** IMPERISHABLE, indestructible, indissoluble, everlasting, non-biodegradable. ■ OPPOSITES venal, corrupt.

increase v. **1** GROW, become greater/larger/bigger, expand, extend, multiply, intensify, heighten, mount, escalate, mushroom, snowball, swell, wax. **2** ADD TO, enhance, build up, enlarge, augment, expand, extend, spread, heighten, raise, intensify, strengthen, magnify,

proliferate, inflate, step up. ■ OPPOS-ITES decrease. ▶n. GROWTH, rise, enlargement, expansion, extension, increment, addition, development, intensification, escalation, heightening, boost, augmentation, snowballing, mushrooming, strengthening, magnification, inflation. ■ OPPOSITES decrease.

incredible adj. **1** UNBELIEVABLE, hard to believe, beyond belief, far-fetched, inconceivable, unimaginable, unthinkable, impossible, implausible, highly unlikely, improbable, absurd, preposterous, questionable, dubious, doubtful, fictitious, mythical. **2** EXTRAORDINARY, wonderful, great, supreme, tremendous, marvellous, amazing, astounding, prodigious, awe-inspiring, awesome, superhuman; informal fantastic, fab, magic. ■ OPPOSITES credible.

incredulous adj. DISBELIEVING, unbelieving, sceptical, cynical, distrusting, distrustful, mistrusting, mistrustful, doubtful, doubting, dubious, unconvinced, suspicious, uncertain. ■ OPPOS-ITES credulous.

incriminate v. IMPLICATE, involve, inculpate, inform against, charge, blame, pin the blame on, accuse, indict, impeach, arraign, stigmatize, blacken someone's name; informal point the finger at, finger, rat on, grass on.

incumbent adj. **1** BINDING, obligatory, mandatory, necessary, compulsory. **2** CURRENT, existing, present, in office, in power.

incur v. BRING UPON ONESELF, expose oneself to, lay oneself open to, provoke, be sault that does not involve rape. **indecent exposure** the crime of showing one's genitals in public. ■ **indecency** n. **indecently** adv.

indecipherable adj. not able to be read or understood.

indecisive adj. not decisive. ■ **indecision** n.

indeed adv. used to emphasize a statement.

indefatigable adj. never tiring.

indefensible adj. not able to be justified or defended.

indefinable adj. not able to be defined exactly.

indefinite adj. **1** not clearly defined; vague. **2** lasting for an unknown length of time. □ **indefinite article** the word *a* or *an*. ■ **indefinitely** adv.

indelible adj. **1** (of ink or a mark) unable to be removed. **2** unable to be forgotten. ■ **indelibly** adv.

indelicate adj. **1** tactless. **2** slightly indecent.

indemnity n. (pl. **indemnities**) **1** insurance against legal responsibility for one's actions. **2** compensation for damage or loss. ■ **indemnify** v.

indent v. **1** form hollows or notches in. **2** begin a line of writing further from the margin than the other lines. **3** place a written order for goods. ■ **indentation** n.

indenture n. a formal contract, esp. of apprenticeship.

independent adj. **1** free from outside control or influence. **2** self-governing. **3** having enough money to support oneself. **4** not connected; separate. ■ **independence** n. **independently** adv.

....

☑️ *-ent*, not *-ant*: independ*ent*.

....

indescribable adj. too extreme or unusual to be described. ■ **indescribably** adv.

indestructible adj. unable to be destroyed.

indeterminate adj. not exactly known or defined.

index n. (pl. **indexes** or **indices**) **1** an alphabetical list of names, subjects, etc., with references. **2** a sign or measure of something. **3** a number indicating the current level of prices, wages,

Thesaurus

....

liable to, contract, meet with, experience.

incurable adj. **1** UNTREATABLE, inoperable, beyond cure, fatal, terminal, irremediable. **2** *see* INCORRIGIBLE.

indecent adj. **1** IMPROPER, suggestive, indelicate, impure, risqué, off colour, ribald, bawdy, foul, vulgar, gross, crude, obscene, dirty, smutty, coarse, lewd, lascivious, salacious, licentious, pornographic, scatological; *informal* blue, raunchy. **2** UNSEEMLY, improper, inappropriate, unsuitable, unacceptable, offensive, outrageous. ■ OPPOSITES proper, seemly.

indecisive adj. IRRESOLUTE, hesitant, in two minds, wavering, vacillating, ambivalent, undecided, uncertain, unresolved, sitting on the fence, blowing hot and cold.

indefatigable adj. TIRELESS, untiring, unflagging, persistent, tenacious, dogged, assiduous, industrious, indomitable, relentless, unremitting.

indefensible adj. **1** INEXCUSABLE, unjustifiable, unpardonable, unforgivable, inexpiable. **2** UNTENABLE, insupportable, flawed, faulty, implausible, specious, unarguable.

indefinite adj. **1** VAGUE, unclear, imprecise, inexact, ambiguous, ambivalent,

equivocal, confused, evasive. **2** INDETERMINATE, unspecified. **3** BLURRED, ill-defined, indistinct, fuzzy, hazy, dim, vague, obscure. ■ OPPOSITES definite.

indemnify v. INSURE, underwrite, guarantee, protect, secure, make secure, give security to, endorse.

independence n. **1** SELF-GOVERNMENT, autonomy, self-determination, sovereignty, freedom, home rule, autarchy. **2** FREEDOM, liberty, self-sufficiency, self-reliance.

independent adj. **1** SELF-GOVERNING, autonomous, free, self-determining, sovereign, non-aligned, neutral, autarchic. **2** FREETHINKING, bold, liberated, individualistic, unconventional, unrestrained, untrammelled, unfettered, unconstrained. **3** SEPARATE, unconnected, unrelated, unattached, distinct, individual. ■ OPPOSITES subservient, biased, related.

indescribable adj. INEXPRESSIBLE, undefinable, beyond words/description, incommunicable, ineffable, unutterable, incredible, extraordinary, remarkable, prodigious.

indestructible adj. UNBREAKABLE, imperishable, durable, enduring, infrangible, inextinguishable, perennial, deathless, undying, immortal, endless,

etc. compared with a previous level.
4 Math. an exponent. ▶v. record in or provide with an index. □ **index finger** the forefinger. ■ **indexation** n.

Indian n. **1** a person from India. **2** an American Indian. ▶adj. of India or American Indians. □ **Indian ink** deep black ink used in drawing. **Indian summer** dry, warm weather in autumn. **India rubber** natural rubber.

indicate v. **1** point out. **2** be a sign of. **3** state briefly. ■ **indication** n. **indicative** adj.

indicator n. **1** a thing that indicates a state or level. **2** a flashing light on a vehicle showing that it is about to pull out or turn.

indict /in-dyt/ v. formally accuse or charge with a serious crime. ■ **indictable** adj. **indictment** n.

indifferent adj. **1** having no interest or sympathy. **2** not very good. ■ **indifference** n. **indifferently** adv.

indigenous adj. native.

indigent adj. very poor.

indigestible adj. difficult or impossible to digest.

indigestion n. discomfort caused by difficulty in digesting food.

indignation n. annoyance caused by unfair treatment. ■ **indignant** adj. **indignantly** adv.

indignity n. (pl. **indignities**) humiliating treatment.

indigo n. a dark blue colour or dye.

indirect adj. **1** not direct. **2** (of taxation) charged on goods etc. rather than income or profits. □ **indirect object** a person or thing that is affected by the action of a transitive verb but is not the main object. ■ **indirectly** adv.

indiscreet adj. revealing things that should remain private. ■ **indiscretion** n. **indiscreetly** adv.

indiscriminate adj. done or acting without careful judgement. ■ **indiscriminately** adv.

indispensable adj. essential.

....

☑ *-able*, not *-ible*: indispens*able*.

....

Thesaurus

everlasting. ■ OPPOSITES fragile.

indeterminate adj. UNFIXED, indefinite, undetermined, unspecified, unknown, uncertain, unpredictable, uncounted, uncalculated.

index n. KEY, guide, directory, catalogue, table of contents.

indicate v. **1** SHOW, demonstrate, exhibit, display, manifest, evince, express, make known, tell, state, reveal, disclose, register, record, signal, denote, betoken, suggest, imply. **2** POINT TO/AT, designate, specify.

indication n. **1** SIGN, symptom, mark, manifestation, signal, omen, augury, portent, warning, hint. **2** SHOW, demonstration, exhibition, display, manifestation, revelation, disclosure.

indicator n. **1** POINTER, needle, marker, meter, display. **2** INDEX, guide, mark, sign, signal, symbol, signpost.

indifferent adj. **1** UNCONCERNED, apathetic, heedless, uncaring, uninterested, unimpressed, aloof, detached, distant, cold, cool, impassive, dispassionate, unresponsive, unemotional, emotionless, unmoved, unexcited, unfeeling, unsympathetic, callous. **2** MEDIOCRE, middling, moderate, fair, not bad, passable, adequate, barely adequate, average, ordinary, commonplace, undistinguished, uninspired; *informal* so-so, OK. ■ OPPOSITES enthusiastic.

indigenous adj. NATIVE, original, aboriginal, autochthonous.

indignant adj. ANGRY, angered, irate, furious, incensed, infuriated, annoyed, irritated, wrathful, enraged, exasperated, heated, riled, in a temper, in high dudgeon, provoked, piqued, disgruntled, fuming, livid, mad, seeing red; *informal* miffed, in a huff, up in arms, huffy, narked.

indirect adj. **1** CIRCUITOUS, roundabout, wandering, meandering, winding, curving, tortuous, zigzag, divergent, deviant. **2** OBLIQUE, digressive, long-drawn-out, rambling, circumlocutory, periphrastic, allusive, implicit, implied. **3** BACKHANDED, devious, insidious, underhand, sneaky, surreptitious. ■ OPPOSITES direct.

indiscreet adj. IMPRUDENT, unwise, incautious, injudicious, ill-advised, ill-judged, ill-thought-out, ill-considered, foolish, impolitic, careless, unwary, hasty, rash, reckless, impulsive, precipitate, foolhardy, tactless, insensitive, undiplomatic.

indiscriminate adj. **1** UNSELECTIVE, undiscriminating, uncritical, careless, aimless, hit-or-miss, haphazard, random, unsystematic, unmethodical, sweeping, general, broad-based, wholesale. **2** JUMBLED, mixed, haphazard, motley, miscellaneous, diverse, varied,

indisposed adj. **1** slightly unwell. **2** unwilling. ■ **indisposition** n.

indisputable adj. undeniable. ■ **indisputably** adv.

indissoluble adj. unable to be destroyed; lasting.

indistinct adj. not clear or sharp. ■ **indistinctly** adv.

indistinguishable adj. not identifiable as different.

indium n. a soft metallic element.

individual adj. **1** single; separate. **2** of or for one person. **3** striking or unusual. ▶ n. a single person or item as distinct from a group. ■ **individuality** n. **individually** adv.

individualism n. the quality of being independent in thought and action. ■ **individualist** n.

indivisible adj. unable to be divided.

indoctrinate v. force to accept a set of beliefs. ■ **indoctrination** n.

indolent adj. lazy. ■ **indolence** n.

indomitable adj. impossible to defeat or subdue.

indoor adj. situated, done, or used inside a building. ▶ adv. (**indoors**) into or inside a building.

indubitable adj. impossible to doubt. ■ **indubitably** adv.

induce v. **1** persuade. **2** bring about. **3** bring on labour in childbirth by drugs etc.

inducement n. a thing that persuades someone to do something.

induct v. introduce formally to a post or organization.

inductance n. a process by which a change in the current of an electric circuit produces an electromotive force.

induction n. **1** the act of inducting. **2** reasoning in which a general rule is drawn from particular examples. **3** the passing of electricity or magnetism from one object to another without them touching. ■ **inductive** adj.

indulge v. **1** (**indulge in**) allow oneself something enjoyable. **2** satisfy a desire. **3** allow someone to do or have what they want. ■ **indulgence** n. **indulgent** adj. **indulgently** adv.

industrial adj. of or for industry. ▢ **industrial action** a strike or similar protest by workers. **industrial estate** an area of land developed for factories and businesses. **industrial relations** relations between management and workers. ■ **industrially** adv.

industrialism n. a system in which industry is the basis of the economy.

industrialist n. a person who owns or controls a manufacturing business.

industrialize (or **-ise**) v. develop industries in a country or region on a wide

Thesaurus

confused, mongrel, chaotic, thrown together; *informal* higgledy-piggledy. ■ OPPOSITES systematic.

indispensable adj. ESSENTIAL, vital, crucial, imperative, key, necessary, requisite, needed, important, urgent, pressing, high-priority, fundamental. ■ OPPOSITES superfluous.

indisputable adj. INCONTESTABLE, incontrovertible, undeniable, irrefutable, unquestionable, indubitable, beyond dispute/question, beyond the shadow of a doubt, unassailable, certain, sure, positive, definite, absolute, final, conclusive. ■ OPPOSITES debatable.

indistinct adj. **1** BLURRED, fuzzy, out of focus, bleary, hazy, misty, shadowy, dim, obscure, indefinite, indistinguishable, barely perceptible. **2** MUFFLED, muted, low, muttered, mumbled, slurred. ■ OPPOSITES distinct.

indistinguishable adj. IDENTICAL, alike, very similar, interchangeable, the same; *informal* like two peas in a pod. ■ OPPOSITES different.

individual adj. **1** SINGLE, separate, lone, sole, solitary, distinct, distinctive, particular, specific, peculiar, isolated. **2** CHARACTERISTIC, distinctive, peculiar, personal, personalized, own, private, special, singular, original, unique, idiosyncratic.

indolent adj. LAZY, idle, slothful, lethargic, slow-moving, slack, lackadaisical, apathetic, listless, inert, torpid. ■ OPPOSITES active.

induce v. **1** PERSUADE, talk into, get, prevail upon, move, prompt, inspire, instigate, influence, press, urge, incite, encourage, impel, motivate, inveigle, coax, wheedle. **2** BRING ABOUT, bring on, cause, produce, effect, create, give rise to, generate, originate, engender, occasion, set in motion, develop, lead to.

inducement n. INCENTIVE, encouragement, attraction, bait, carrot, lure, reward, incitement, stimulus, spur, goad, impetus, motive, provocation; *informal* come-on.

indulge v. PAMPER, spoil, coddle, mollycoddle, cosset, pander to, humour, go along with, baby, pet.

indulgent adj. PERMISSIVE, easy-going, compliant, fond, doting, forbearing, scale. ■ **industrialization** n.

industrious adj. hard-working. ■ **industriously** adv.

industry n. (pl. **industries**) **1** the manufacture of goods in factories. **2** a branch of commercial activity. **3** hard work.

inebriated adj. drunk.

inedible adj. not fit for eating.

ineffable adj. too great or extreme to be described.

ineffective adj. not producing any or the desired effect. ■ **ineffectively** adv.

ineffectual adj. **1** ineffective. **2** not forceful enough to do something. ■ **ineffectually** adv.

inefficient adj. not efficient. ■ **inefficiency** n. **inefficiently** adv.

inelegant adj. not elegant or graceful.

ineligible adj. not eligible.

ineluctable adj. unable to be resisted or avoided.

inept adj. lacking skill. ■ **ineptitude** n.

inequality n. (pl. **inequalities**) lack of equality.

inequitable adj. unfair; unjust. ■ **inequity** n.

inert adj. **1** lacking the ability or strength to move or act. **2** without active chemical properties.

inertia /i-ner-shuh/ n. **1** a tendency to do nothing or to remain unchanged. **2** a property by which matter remains still or continues moving unless acted on by an external force.

inescapable adj. unavoidable.

inessential adj. not essential.

inestimable adj. too great to be measured.

inevitable adj. certain to happen. ■ **inevitability** n. **inevitably** adv.

Thesaurus

compassionate, humane, kind, understanding, sympathetic, liberal, forgiving, lenient, merciful, clement. ■ OPPOSITES intolerant.

industrious adj. HARD-WORKING, diligent, assiduous, conscientious, sedulous, laborious, steady, busy, active, bustling, energetic, on the go, vigorous, determined, dynamic, indefatigable, tireless, persistent, pertinacious, zealous, productive. ■ OPPOSITES idle, lazy.

industry n. **1** MANUFACTURING, production, fabrication, construction, business, trade, field, line, craft. **2** INDUSTRIOUSNESS, diligence, assiduity, application, activity, energy, vigour, effort, determination, dynamism, tirelessness, persistence, zeal, pertinacity, productiveness, sedulousness, sedulity, conscientiousness.

ineffective adj. **1** UNAVAILING, useless, to no avail, ineffectual, worthless, unsuccessful, futile, fruitless, unproductive, profitless, abortive, inadequate, inefficient, inefficacious, impotent, able, feeble, weak, incompetent, inept, lame, barren, sterile. **2** INCOMPETENT, inept, unproductive, inadequate, ineffectual, feeble, weak, impotent. ■ OPPOSITES effective.

inelegant adj. **1** AWKWARD, clumsy, ungainly, ungraceful, graceless. **2** UNREFINED, uncultured, uncultivated, unpolished, unsophisticated, unfinished, gauche, crude, uncouth, ill-bred, coarse, vulgar. ■ OPPOSITES graceful, refined.

ineligible adj. UNSUITABLE, unqualified, unfit, unfitted, inappropriate, unequipped, unacceptable, undesirable,

disqualified. ■ OPPOSITES eligible.

inept adj. **1** INCOMPETENT, incapable, unskilled, inexpert, clumsy, awkward, maladroit, heavy-handed; informal cack-handed. **2** INAPPROPRIATE, badly timed, inapt, unsuitable, infelicitous. ■ OPPOSITES competent, appropriate.

inequality n. DISPARITY, imbalance, lack of balance, disproportion, variation, variability, difference, discrepancy, contrast, dissimilarity, unevenness, incongruity. ■ OPPOSITES equality.

inequitable adj. UNFAIR, unjust, prejudiced, biased, discriminatory, partisan, partial, preferential, one-sided, intolerant, bigoted. ■ OPPOSITES fair.

inert adj. **1** UNMOVING, inactive, motionless, immobile, still, stock-still, stationary, static, lifeless, inanimate, unconscious, out cold, comatose, dormant, dead. **2** IDLE, inactive, indolent, slack, lazy, slothful, dull, sluggish, lethargic, stagnant, languid, lackadaisical, listless, torpid. ■ OPPOSITES active.

inertia n. INERTNESS, inactivity, inaction, motionlessness, immobility, stagnation, passivity, stasis, idleness, indolence, laziness, sloth, slothfulness, dullness, sluggishness, lethargy, languor, listlessness, torpor. ■ OPPOSITES activity.

inescapable adj. UNAVOIDABLE, inevitable, unpreventable, inexorable, assured, certain, bound to happen, ineludible, ineluctable. ■ OPPOSITES avoidable.

inestimable adj. IMMEASURABLE, measureless, incalculable, priceless, precious, invaluable, unparalleled, supreme, superlative.

inexact adj. not exact.

inexcusable adj. too bad to be justified or tolerated.

inexhaustible adj. available in unlimited quantities.

inexorable adj. impossible to stop or prevent. ■ **inexorably** adv.

inexpensive adj. cheap.

inexperience n. lack of experience. ■ **inexperienced** adj.

inexpert adj. lacking skill or knowledge.

inexplicable adj. unable to be explained. ■ **inexplicably** adv.

inexpressible adj. too intense to be expressed in words.

in extremis adv. 1 in a very difficult situation. 2 at the point of death.

inextricable adj. impossible to separate. ■ **inextricably** adv.

infallible adj. incapable of being wrong. ■ **infallibly** adv.

infamous adj. well known for a bad quality or deed. ■ **infamy** n.

infancy n. 1 early childhood or babyhood. 2 an early stage of development.

infant n. a very young child or baby.

infanticide n. the killing of an infant.

infantile adj. 1 of infants. 2 childish.

infantry n. soldiers who fight on foot.

infatuated adj. feeling an intense passion for someone. ■ **infatuation** n.

infect v. 1 affect or contaminate with an organism causing disease. 2 cause to share a feeling.

infection n. 1 the process of infecting. 2 an infectious disease.

infectious adj. 1 (of a disease) able to be transmitted through the environment. 2 likely to spread infection. 3 likely to spread to others.

infer v. (**inferring**, **inferred**) work out from available information; conclude. ■ **inference** n.

....
☑ On the difference between **imply** and **infer**, see the note at **IMPLY**.
....

inferior adj. lower in status or quality. ▶ n. an inferior person. ■ **inferiority** n.

infernal adj. 1 of hell. 2 informal very

Thesaurus

inevitable adj. UNAVOIDABLE, unpreventable, inexorable, inescapable, fixed, settled, irrevocable, fated, destined, predestined, ordained, decreed, out of one's hands, assured, certain, bound/ sure to happen, for sure, necessary, ineluctable. ■ OPPOSITES avoidable.

inexhaustible adj. UNLIMITED, limitless, illimitable, infinite, boundless, endless, never-ending, unrestricted, bottomless, measureless, copious, abundant. ■ OPPOSITES limited.

inexpensive adj. *see* CHEAP.

inexperienced adj. UNTRAINED, untutored, unqualified, undrilled, unpractised, amateur, unskilled, uninitiated, uninformed, ignorant, unacquainted, unversed, naive, unsophisticated, unfledged, untried, unseasoned, new, callow, immature, fresh, green, raw; *informal* wet behind the ears.

inexplicable adj. UNEXPLAINABLE, unaccountable, incomprehensible, beyond comprehension, unintelligible, unfathomable, baffling, puzzling, mysterious, strange, weird, abstruse, enigmatic, inscrutable. ■ OPPOSITES understandable.

infallible adj. 1 UNFAILING, foolproof, dependable, trustworthy, reliable, sure, certain; *informal* sure-fire. 2 UNERRING, unfailing, error-free, faultless, flawless, impeccable, unimpeachable, perfect. ■ OPPOSITES fallible.

infamous adj. NOTORIOUS, disreputable, ill-famed, of ill-repute, iniquitous, ignominious, dishonourable, discreditable, villainous, wicked, evil, vile, nefarious.

infant n. BABY, little child, little one, tot, toddler; *Sc.* bairn.

infantile adj. CHILDISH, babyish, puerile, immature, juvenile, adolescent. ■ OPPOSITES mature.

infatuated adj. BESOTTED, enamoured, captivated, bewitched, beguiled, spellbound, fascinated, enraptured, carried away, obsessed, swept off one's feet, smitten.

infatuation n. PASSING FANCY, crush, fancy, passion, obsession, fixation, craze, mania.

infect v. 1 CONTAMINATE, pollute, taint, blight, spoil, mar. 2 INFLUENCE, affect, imbue, infuse, stimulate, inspire, corrupt, pervert.

infectious adj. 1 CONTAGIOUS, infective, communicable, transmittable, transmissible, catching, spreading. 2 GERM-LADEN, pestilential, contaminating, toxic, noxious, virulent, poisonous. 3 CATCHING, spreading, contagious, communicable, irresistible, compelling.

infer v. DEDUCE, conclude, work out, derive, reason, gather, understand, presume, conjecture, surmise, theorize, hypothesize; *informal* figure, suss.

inferior adj. 1 LOWER, lesser, subordinate, junior, secondary, subsidiary, an-

annoying.

inferno n. (pl. **infernos**) a large uncontrollable fire.

infertile adj. **1** unable to bear young. **2** (of land) unable to produce crops. ■ **infertility** n.

infest v. be present in a place in large numbers, so as to cause damage or disease. ■ **infestation** n.

infidel n. old use a person who does not believe in a religion.

infidelity n. (pl. **infidelities**) unfaithfulness to one's sexual partner.

infighting n. conflict within a group.

infiltrate v. secretly and gradually gain access to a group etc. ■ **infiltration** n. **infiltrator** n.

infinite adj. **1** limitless. **2** very great or very many. ■ **infinitely** adv.

infinitesimal adj. very small. ■ **infinitesimally** adv.

infinitive n. the basic uninflected form of a verb.

infinity n. (pl. **infinities**) **1** the state of being infinite. **2** a very great number or amount.

infirm adj. physically weak. ■ **infirmity** n.

infirmary n. (pl. **infirmaries**) a hospital.

inflame v. **1** provoke or intensify strong feeling. **2** cause inflammation in.

inflammable adj. easily set on fire.

inflammation n. redness, swelling, heat, and pain in a part of the body.

inflammatory adj. arousing strong feeling or anger.

inflatable adj. able to be inflated. ▶ n. an object that is inflated before use.

inflate v. **1** expand by filling with air or gas. **2** increase by a large amount; exaggerate.

inflation n. **1** the act of inflating. **2** a general increase in prices. ■ **inflationary** adj.

inflect v. **1** (of a word) change in form to show a grammatical function or quality. **2** vary the tone or pitch of the voice. ■ **inflection** n.

inflexible adj. **1** not able to be altered. **2** unwilling to change or compromise. **3** not able to be bent.

inflict v. cause something painful or unpleasant to be suffered. ■ **infliction** n.

inflorescence n. the complete flower head of a plant.

influence n. **1** the power or ability to affect beliefs or actions. **2** a person or thing with such ability or power. ▶ v. have an influence on. ■ **influential** adj.

influenza n. a viral infection causing

Thesaurus

cillary, minor, subservient, lowly, humble, servile, menial. **2** FAULTY, imperfect, defective, substandard, low-quality, low-grade, shoddy, cheap, reject, gimcrack; informal grotty. **3** SECOND-RATE, indifferent, mediocre, incompetent, poor, bad, awful. ■ OPPOSITES superior.

infernal adj. HELLISH, diabolical, devilish, demonic, demoniac, fiendish, satanic.

infest v. SPREAD THROUGH, overrun, take over, pervade, permeate, penetrate, infiltrate, invade, swarm over, beset, plague.

infidelity n. UNFAITHFULNESS, adultery, cheating, cuckoldry, affair, liaison, intrigue, amour.

infinite adj. **1** BOUNDLESS, unbounded, unlimited, limitless, without end, vast. **2** COUNTLESS, without number, numberless, innumerable, immeasurable, incalculable, untold, uncountable, inestimable, indeterminate, vast, enormous, stupendous, prodigious. **3** UNLIMITED, boundless, endless, unending, never-ending, inexhaustible, interminable, absolute, total. ■ OPPOSITES limited.

infinity n. LIMITLESSNESS, boundlessness, unlimitedness, endlessness, infinitude.

infirm adj. FEEBLE, enfeebled, weak, frail, debilitated, decrepit, disabled, in poor health, failing, ailing, doddery, lame, crippled. ■ OPPOSITES fit.

inflame v. INCITE, excite, arouse, rouse, stir up, work up, whip up, agitate, fire, ignite, kindle, foment, impassion, provoke, stimulate, actuate. ■ OPPOSITES cool.

inflammable adj. FLAMMABLE, combustible, burnable, ignitable, incendiary. ■ OPPOSITES incombustible.

inflate v. **1** BLOW UP, pump up, puff up/ out, dilate, distend, swell, aerate. **2** EXAGGERATE, increase, extend, amplify, augment, expand, intensify. ■ OPPOSITES deflate.

inflexible adj. **1** RIGID, stiff, non-flexible, unbendable, unyielding, taut, hard, firm, inelastic, unmalleable. **2** UNCHANGEABLE, unalterable, immutable, unvarying, firm, fixed, hard and fast, uncompromising, stringent, rigorous, inexorable. **3** ADAMANT, firm, immovable, unaccommodating, stubborn, dyed-in-the-wool, obdurate, obstinate, intractable, unbending, intolerant, relentless, merciless, pitiless, uncompromising, inexorable, steely, ironfever, aches, and catarrh.

influx n. an arrival of large numbers of people or things.

inform v. **1** give information to. **2** (**inform on**) reveal someone's criminal activity to the police. **3** (**informed**) showing knowledge or understanding. **4** be an essential principle of. ▪ **informant** n. **informer** n.

informal adj. **1** relaxed or unofficial. **2** casual. ▪ **informality** n. **informally** adv.

information n. facts or knowledge provided or learned. ◻ **information technology** the study or use of computers and telecommunications for storing and sending information.

informative adj. providing useful information.

infrared adj. of or using electromagnetic radiation with a wavelength just greater than that of red light.

infrastructure n. the basic structures and facilities (e.g. roads or power) needed for the operation of a society or organization.

infrequent adj. not frequent. ▪ **infrequently** adv.

infringe v. **1** break a law or agreement. **2** intrude on a right or privilege. ▪ **infringement** n.

infuriate v. make angry.

infuse v. **1** spread throughout. **2** soak tea or herbs to extract the flavour. ▪ **infuser** n. **infusion** n.

ingenious adj. clever and inventive. ▪ **ingeniously** adv. **ingenuity** n.

ingenuous adj. innocent and unsuspecting. ▪ **ingenuously** adv.

ingest v. take in as food.

Thesaurus

willed. ▪ OPPOSITES flexible.

inflict v. ADMINISTER, deal out, mete out, serve out, deliver, apply, lay on, impose, levy, exact, wreak.

influence n. EFFECT, impact, control, sway, ascendancy, power, mastery, agency, guidance, domination, rule, supremacy, leadership, direction, pressure. ▶v. **1** AFFECT, have an effect on, impact on, sway, bias, incline, motivate, determine, guide, control, change, alter, transform. **2** PERSUADE, induce, impel, incite, manipulate, prompt.

influential adj. **1** POWERFUL, important, leading, authoritative, controlling, dominant, predominant, prestigious. **2** INSTRUMENTAL, guiding, significant, important, persuasive, telling, meaningful. ▪ OPPOSITES unimportant.

influx n. RUSH, inflow, inundation, flood, invasion, intrusion, incursion, ingress, convergence.

inform v. **1** TELL, let know, advise, apprise, notify, announce to, impart to, relate to, communicate to, acquaint, brief, instruct, enlighten, make conversant, send word to; *informal* put in the picture, fill in, clue in, put wise, spill the beans to, tip off, tip the wink to, give the inside story to. **2** DENOUNCE, betray, incriminate, inculpate; *informal* blab on, rat on, squeal on, tell on, blow the whistle on, put the finger on, finger, sell down the river, snitch on, peach on, grass on.

informal adj. **1** CASUAL, unceremonious, unofficial, simple, unpretentious, everyday, relaxed, easy. **2** COLLOQUIAL, vernacular, non-literary, simple, natural, unofficial, unpretentious; *informal* slangy. ▪ OPPOSITES formal.

information n. **1** DATA, facts. **2** KNOWLEDGE, intelligence, news, notice, word, advice, counsel, instruction, enlightenment, tidings, message, report, communiqué, communication; *informal* info, gen, low-down, dope, inside story, bumf, dirt.

informative adj. INSTRUCTIVE, illuminating, enlightening, edifying, educational, revealing, telling, communicative, newsy, chatty, gossipy. ▪ OPPOSITES uninformative.

informed adj. KNOWLEDGEABLE, well briefed, posted, abreast of the facts, well versed, primed, up to date, au fait, au courant.

informer n. INFORMANT, betrayer, traitor, Judas, whistle-blower; *informal* grass, nark, snout, rat, squealer, stool pigeon, canary, snitch, peacher.

infrequent adj. RARE, occasional, irregular, sporadic, uncommon, unusual, exceptional, few and far between, intermittent; *informal* once in a blue moon. ▪ OPPOSITES frequent.

infringe v. BREAK, disobey, violate, contravene, transgress, breach, disregard, take no notice of, defy, flout.

ingenious adj. CLEVER, intelligent, shrewd, astute, sharp, bright, talented, brilliant, masterly, resourceful, inventive, creative, original, subtle, crafty, wily, cunning, skilful, adroit, deft, capable; *informal* smart. ▪ OPPOSITES stupid, unimaginative.

ingenuous adj. OPEN, sincere, honest, frank, candid, direct, forthcoming, art-

inglenook n. a space on either side of a large fireplace.

inglorious adj. causing shame.

ingot n. a rectangular block of metal.

ingrained adj. **1** (of a habit or belief) firmly established. **2** (of dirt) deeply embedded.

ingratiate v. (**ingratiate oneself**) gain favour by flattery or trying to please.

ingratitude n. a lack of gratitude.

ingredient n. any of the substances combined to make a dish.

ingress n. **1** the act of entering. **2** a place or means of access.

ingrown (or **ingrowing**) adj. (of a toenail) having grown into the flesh.

inhabit v. live in or occupy. ■ **inhabitable** adj. **inhabitant** n.

inhalant n. a medicine that is inhaled.

inhale v. breathe in air, smoke, etc. ■ **inhalation** n.

inhaler n. a device for inhaling a drug to relieve asthma.

inherent adj. existing in something as a permanent or essential quality. ■ **inherently** adv.

inherit v. (**inheriting**, **inherited**) **1** receive property or a title from someone when they die. **2** have a characteristic passed on from one's parents or ancestors. ■ **inheritance** n.

inhibit v. **1** hinder or prevent. **2** cause to feel inhibitions.

inhibition n. a feeling preventing one from acting naturally.

inhospitable adj. **1** (of a place) harsh and difficult to live in. **2** unwelcoming.

inhuman (or **inhumane**) adj. cruel and barbaric.

inimical adj. harmful; hostile.

inimitable adj. impossible to imitate. ■ **inimitably** adv.

iniquity n. (pl. **iniquities**) great injustice. ■ **iniquitous** adj.

initial adj. occurring at the beginning; first. ▶n. the first letter of a name or word. ▶v. (**initialling**, **initialled**; US **initialing**, **initialed**) mark with one's initials. ■ **initially** adv.

initiate v. **1** cause a process etc. to begin. **2** admit to a group with a formal ceremony. **3** introduce to a new activity. ■ **initiation** n.

initiative n. **1** the ability to act independently. **2** the opportunity to act before others do. **3** a new approach to a problem.

inject v. **1** introduce a drug etc. into the

Thesaurus

less, guileless, simple, naive, innocent, genuine, unaffected, trustful, trusting, truthful, unsuspicious. ■ OPPOSITES insincere, artful.

ingratiating adj. SYCOPHANTIC, toadying, fawning, unctuous, obsequious, servile, crawling, flattering, wheedling; informal bootlicking.

inhabit v. LIVE IN, dwell in, reside in, occupy, lodge in, tenant, make one's home in, settle in, people, populate.

inhabitant n. RESIDENT, dweller, occupant, habitant, settler, native, tenant, occupier.

inherent adj. **1** INTRINSIC, innate, built-in, inseparable, essential, basic, fundamental, ingrained. **2** INBORN, inbred, innate, hereditary, inherited, in the family, congenital, familial.

inherit v. BE LEFT, be willed, be bequeathed, come into, fall heir to, succeed to, accede to, assume, take over.

inheritance n. LEGACY, bequest, endowment, birthright, heritage, patrimony.

inhibit v. IMPEDE, hold back, prevent, stop, hamper, hinder, obstruct, interfere with, curb, check, restrict, restrain, constrain, bridle, rein in, baulk, frustrate, arrest. ■ OPPOSITES assist, encourage.

inhibited adj. SHY, reticent, self-conscious, reserved, constrained, repressed, embarrassed, tongue-tied, subdued, withdrawn; informal uptight. ■ OPPOSITES uninhibited.

inhibition n. **1** OBSTRUCTION, prevention, stopping, hindrance, hampering, impediment, curb, check, restriction, restraint, frustration, arrest. **2** SHYNESS, reticence, reserve, self-consciousness, repression, constraint, embarrassment.

inhospitable adj. **1** UNWELCOMING, unfriendly, unsociable, unsocial, antisocial, uncivil, discourteous, ungracious, ungenerous, cool, cold, chilly, aloof, unkind, unsympathetic, ill-disposed, hostile, inimical, xenophobic. **2** BLEAK, bare, uninviting, barren, desolate, lonely, empty, forbidding, hostile. ■ OPPOSITES hospitable.

initial adj. FIRST, beginning, starting, commencing, opening, early, prime, primary, elementary, introductory, inaugural, foundational, inceptive. ■ OPPOSITES final.

initiate v. **1** BEGIN, start, commence, open, institute, inaugurate, get under way, set in motion, lay the foundations of, launch, actuate, instigate, trigger off, originate, pioneer, sow the seeds of;

body with a syringe. **2** introduce a different quality. ■ **injection** n.

injudicious adj. unwise.

injunction n. a court order stating that someone must or must not do something.

injure v. **1** do physical harm to; wound. **2** damage or impair. ■ **injury** n.

injurious adj. harmful.

injustice n. **1** lack of justice. **2** an unjust act.

ink n. coloured liquid for writing, drawing, or printing. ▶ v. apply ink to. ■ **inky** adj.

inkling n. a slight suspicion.

inland adj. & adv. in or into the interior of a country.

inlay v. (**inlaying, inlaid**) ornament by embedding pieces of a different material in a surface. ▶ n. inlaid decoration or material.

inlet n. **1** a narrow inland extension of the sea etc. **2** a way in.

in loco parentis adv. & adj. in the place of a parent.

inmate n. a person living in a prison or other institution.

inmost adj. innermost.

inn n. a pub, esp. in the country.

innards pl. n. informal internal organs or parts.

innate adj. inborn; natural. ■ **innately** adv.

inner adj. **1** inside; close to the centre. **2** mental or spiritual. **3** private. ◻ **inner city** an area in or near the centre of a city.

innermost adj. **1** furthest in. **2** most private.

innings n. (pl. **innings**) (in cricket) a batsman's or side's turn at batting.

innocent adj. **1** not guilty. **2** without experience of evil or sexual matters. **3** not intended to cause harm. ▶ n. an innocent person. ■ **innocence** n. **innocently** adv.

innocuous adj. harmless. ■ **innocuously** adv.

innovate v. introduce something new. ■ **innovation** n. **innovative** adj. **innovator** n.

innuendo n. (pl. **innuendoes** or **innuendos**) a remark indirectly referring to something.

innumerable adj. too many to be counted; very many.

Thesaurus

informal start the ball rolling. **2** TEACH, instruct, coach, tutor, school, train, prime, drill, bruise, indoctrinate. ■ OPPOSITES finish.

initiative n. ENTERPRISE, resourcefulness, inventiveness, resource, originality, creativity, drive, push, dynamism, ambition, ambitiousness, verve, dash, leadership; informal get-up-and-go, pep, zip.

injunction n. COMMAND, instruction, order, ruling, direction, directive, dictate, dictum, mandate, enjoinment, admonition, precept, ultimatum.

injure v. HURT, harm, damage, wound, maim, cripple, lame, disable, mutilate, deform, mangle, impair, weaken, enfeeble, blight, blemish.

injurious adj. HARMFUL, hurtful, damaging, deleterious, detrimental, disadvantageous, unfavourable, destructive, pernicious, ruinous, disastrous, calamitous, malignant. ■ OPPOSITES harmless, innocuous.

injury n. **1** HARM, hurt, wounding, damage, impairment, affliction. **2** WOUND, sore, cut, bruise, gash, laceration, abrasion, lesion, contusion, trauma.

injustice n. UNFAIRNESS, unjustness, inequity, bias, prejudice, favouritism, partiality, one-sidedness, discrimin-

ation, partisanship, intolerance. ■ OPPOSITES justice.

inkling n. HINT, clue, intimation, suggestion, indication, whisper, suspicion, insinuation, notion, glimmering; informal the foggiest idea, the foggiest.

innate adj. INBORN, inbred, congenital, hereditary, inherited, inherent, intrinsic, ingrained, natural, native, indigenous.

inner adj. INTERIOR, inside, central, middle, further in. ■ OPPOSITES outer.

innocence n. **1** GUILTLESSNESS, blamelessness, irreproachability, clean hands. **2** SIMPLENESS, ingenuousness, naivety, guilelessness, openness, credulity, inexperience, gullibility. ■ OPPOSITES guilt.

innocent adj. **1** NOT GUILTY, guiltless, blameless, clear, in the clear, above suspicion, above reproach, unimpeachable, irreproachable. **2** HARMLESS, innocuous, safe, unobjectionable, inoffensive, playful. **3** SIMPLE, naive, ingenuous, unsophisticated, artless, guileless, childlike, frank, open, trustful, trusting, credulous, inexperienced, unworldly, green, gullible; informal wet behind the ears. ■ OPPOSITES guilty.

innocuous adj. **1** SAFE, harmless, non-poisonous. **2** INOFFENSIVE, harmless, un-

innumerate adj. without a basic knowledge of mathematics.

inoculate v. vaccinate. ■ **inoculation** n.

 One *n*, one *c*: inoculate.

inoperable adj. unable to be cured by a medical operation.

inoperative adj. not working or taking effect.

inopportune adj. occurring at an inconvenient time.

inordinate adj. unusually large; excessive. ■ **inordinately** adv.

inorganic adj. **1** not coming from a living organism. **2** not containing carbon.

inpatient n. a hospital patient staying day and night during treatment.

input n. **1** something put in or contributed. **2** the act of inputting data. ▶v. (**inputting**, **input**) put data into a computer.

inquest n. an official inquiry, esp. by a coroner into the cause of a death.

inquire v. investigate; enquire. ■ **inquiry** n.

inquisition n. a long period of intensive questioning. ■ **inquisitor** n.

inquisitive adj. **1** curious. **2** prying. ■ **inquisitively** adv.

inroad n. a gradual entry into or effect on a place or situation.

insalubrious adj. seedy; unwholesome.

insane adj. **1** seriously mentally ill. **2** very foolish. ■ **insanely** adv. **insanity** n.

insanitary adj. dirty and unhygienic.

insatiable adj. impossible to satisfy. ■ **insatiably** adv.

inscribe v. **1** write or carve words on a surface. **2** write a dedication to someone in a book.

inscription n. words inscribed.

inscrutable adj. impossible to interpret. ■ **inscrutably** adv.

insect n. a small invertebrate animal with six legs and a segmented body.

insecticide n. a substance for killing insects.

insectivorous adj. feeding on insects.

insecure adj. **1** not confident. **2** not firmly fixed.

inseminate v. introduce semen into. ■ **insemination** n.

insensible adj. unconscious.

insensitive adj. not sensitive. ■ **insensitively** adv. **insensitivity** n.

inseparable adj. unable to be separated or treated separately. ■ **inseparably** adv.

insert v. place, fit, or add into. ▶n. a loose page or section in a magazine. ■ **insertion** n.

inset n. a thing inserted. ▶v. (**insetting**,

Thesaurus

objectionable, unexceptionable, mild, peaceful, bland, commonplace, insipid.

innuendo n. INSINUATION, implication, suggestion, hint, overtone, allusion, inkling, imputation, aspersion.

innumerable adj. VERY MANY, numerous, countless, untold, incalculable, numberless, unnumbered, infinite, myriad; *informal* umpteen, masses, oodles. ■ OPPOSITES few.

inquire v. ASK, make inquiries about, investigate, question, query, research, look into, examine, explore, probe, scan, scrutinize, study.

inquiry n. **1** INVESTIGATION, examination, exploration, probe, review, search, scrutiny, scrutinization, inspection, study, interrogation. **2** QUESTION, query.

inquisitive adj. INQUIRING, questioning, probing, scrutinizing, curious, burning with curiosity, interested, intrusive, meddlesome, prying; *informal* nosy, nosy-parker, snooping, snoopy. ■ OPPOSITES uninterested.

insane adj. MAD, crazy, deranged, demented, unhinged, out of one's mind, non

compos mentis; *informal* not all there, bonkers, cracked, batty, bats, cuckoo, loony, loopy, nuts, nutty, screwy, bananas, off one's rocker, round the bend, barmy, crackers, off one's trolley. ■ OPPOSITES sane.

inscrutable adj. ENIGMATIC, impenetrable, unreadable, cryptic, deadpan, sphinx-like, poker-faced. ■ OPPOSITES transparent.

insecure adj. **1** VULNERABLE, open to attack, defenceless, unprotected, unguarded, exposed, in danger, dangerous, perilous, hazardous. **2** UNCONFIDENT, lacking confidence, timid, diffident, uncertain, unsure, doubtful, hesitant, anxious, fearful, apprehensive, worried. ■ OPPOSITES secure.

insensitive adj. **1** IMPERVIOUS TO, immune to, oblivious to, unmoved by, indifferent to, proof against, insusceptible to, unaffected by, unreactive to. **2** HEARTLESS, uncaring, unfeeling, callous, tactless, thick-skinned, unconcerned, unsympathetic. ■ OPPOSITES sensitive.

inset) insert.

inshore adj. & adv. at sea but close or towards the shore.

inside n. **1** the inner side, part, or surface of something. **2** (**insides**) informal the stomach and bowels. ▶adj. on or in the inside. ▶prep. & adv. **1** situated or moving within. **2** informal in prison. **3** in less than a specified time. □ **inside out** with the inner surface turned outwards. **know inside out** know very thoroughly.

insider n. a person in an organization who has information not known to those outside it.

insidious adj. developing gradually and with harmful effect. ■ **insidiously** adv.

insight n. intuitive understanding of the truth about people or situations.

insignia n. (pl. **insignia**) a badge or symbol indicating rank or office.

insignificant adj. of little or no importance or value. ■ **insignificance** n. **insignificantly** adv.

insinuate v. **1** suggest something bad indirectly. **2** move oneself gradually into a favourable position. ■ **insinuation** n.

insipid adj. **1** lacking flavour. **2** dull.

insist v. **1** demand or state forcefully. **2** (**insist on**) persist in doing.

insistent adj. **1** insisting. **2** repeatedly demanding attention. ■ **insistence** n. **insistently** adv.

in situ adv. & adj. in the original position.

insolent adj. rude and disrespectful. ■ **insolence** n. **insolently** adv.

insoluble adj. **1** impossible to solve. **2** unable to be dissolved.

insolvent adj. unable to pay one's debts. ■ **insolvency** n.

insomnia n. inability to sleep. ■ **insomniac** n.

insouciant adj. unconcerned. ■ **insouciance** n.

inspect v. **1** look at closely. **2** visit officially to check on standards. ■ **inspection** n.

Thesaurus

insert v. DRIVE IN, push in, put in, press in, stick in, thrust in, work in, slide in, slip in, tuck in, pop in. ▶n. INSERTION, inset, supplement, circular, advertisement, ad.

inside n. **1** INTERIOR, inner part, contents. **2** STOMACH, abdomen, gut, intestines, viscera, entrails, bowels, vital organs. ▶adj. INTERIOR, inner, internal, innermost, inward, on the inside, intramural.

insidious adj. SURREPTITIOUS, sneaky, cunning, crafty, stealthy, subtle, artful, Machiavellian, sly, wily, slick, deceitful, deceptive, underhand, doubledealing, duplicitous, dishonest, insincere, treacherous, perfidious; informal tricky. ■ OPPOSITES straightforward.

insignificant adj. UNIMPORTANT, trivial, trifling, negligible, inconsequential, of no consequence, not worth mentioning, nugatory, meagre, paltry, scanty, petty, insubstantial, flimsy, irrelevant, immaterial, peripheral. ■ OPPOSITES significant, important.

insincere adj. UNTRUTHFUL, dishonest, deceptive, not candid, not frank, disingenuous, dissembling, dissimulating, pretended, devious, hypocritical, deceitful, duplicitous, underhand, doubledealing, false, faithless, disloyal, treacherous, two-faced, lying, mendacious, evasive, shifty, slippery. ■ OPPOSITES sincere.

insinuate v. IMPLY, hint, whisper, suggest, indicate, give the impression, intimate, mention.

insist v. **1** BE FIRM, stand one's ground, stand firm, make a stand, be resolute, be determined, be emphatic, not take no for an answer, brook no refusal. **2** MAINTAIN, assert, state, declare, contend, pronounce, proclaim, avow, aver, vow, swear, stress, reiterate.

insistent adj. FIRM, emphatic, determined, resolute, tenacious, persistent, unyielding, obstinate, dogged, unrelenting, unremitting, relentless, inexorable, importunate.

insolence n. IMPERTINENCE, impudence, cheek, cheekiness, rudeness, disrespect, incivility, insubordination, contempt, abuse, offensiveness, audacity, boldness, brazenness, brashness, pertness, forwardness, effrontery, insults; informal gall, chutzpah; informal sauce, backchat.

insolent adj. IMPERTINENT, impudent, cheeky, rude, ill-mannered, disrespectful, insubordinate, contemptuous, insulting, abusive, offensive, audacious, bold, brash, brazen, pert, forward; informal saucy, fresh, lippy; US informal sassy. ■ OPPOSITES respectful.

insoluble adj. **1** UNSOLVABLE, baffling, unfathomable, indecipherable, perplexing, complicated, intricate, involved, impenetrable, inscrutable, enigmatic, obscure, mystifying, inexplicable, unanswerable, incomprehensible, mysterious. **2** INDISSOLUBLE.

inspector n. **1** a person who inspects. **2** a police officer ranking below a chief inspector.

inspiration n. **1** the process of being inspired. **2** an inspiring person or thing. **3** a sudden clever idea. ∎ **inspirational** adj.

inspire v. **1** fill with the urge to do something. **2** create a feeling in a person.

instability n. lack of stability.

install v. **1** place in position ready for use. **2** establish in a new place or role. ∎ **installation** n.

instalment (US **installment**) n. **1** each of several payments made over a period of time. **2** each of the parts of a serial.

instance n. a particular example or occurrence. ▶ v. give as an example.

instant adj. **1** immediate. **2** (of food) processed to allow quick preparation. ▶ n. **1** a precise moment of time. **2** a very short time. ∎ **instantly** adv.

instantaneous adj. instant. ∎ **instantaneously** adv.

instead adv. as an alternative.

instep n. the middle part of the foot.

instigate v. **1** cause to happen or begin. **2** encourage to do. ∎ **instigation** n.

instil (US **instill**) v. (**instilling, instilled**) gradually establish in someone's mind.

instinct n. **1** an inborn tendency. **2** a natural ability. ∎ **instinctive** adj. **instinctively** adv.

institute n. an organization for the promotion of science, education, etc. ▶ v. begin or establish.

institution n. **1** an important organiza-

insolvent adj. BANKRUPT, ruined, penniless, impoverished, penurious, impecunious; *informal* gone bust, in the red, broke, strapped for cash.

inspect v. EXAMINE, check, go over, look over, survey, scrutinize, vet, audit, study, pore over, view, scan, observe, investigate, assess, appraise; *informal* give the once-over to.

inspection n. EXAMINATION, check, check-up, survey, scrutiny, view, scan, observation, investigation, probe, assessment, appraisal; *informal* once-over, look-see.

inspector n. EXAMINER, checker, scrutinizer, scrutineer, auditor, surveyor, observer, investigator, overseer, supervisor, assessor, appraiser, critic.

inspiration n. **1** STIMULUS, stimulation, motivation, fillip, encouragement, influence, muse, goad, spur, incitement, arousal. **2** CREATIVITY, originality, inventiveness, genius, insight, vision, afflatus. **3** BRIGHT IDEA, revelation, illumination, enlightenment.

inspire v. **1** STIMULATE, motivate, encourage, influence, rouse, stir, goad, energize, galvanize, animate. **2** AROUSE, excite, touch off, spark off, ignite, kindle, give rise to, produce, bring about, prompt, instigate.

instability n. **1** UNSTEADINESS, unsoundness, shakiness, frailty, flimsiness, insubstantiality. **2** IMPERMANENCE, temporariness, transience, inconstancy. **3** CAPRICIOUSNESS, volatility, changeableness, flightiness, vacillation, wavering, fitfulness, oscillation. ∎ OPPOSITES stability.

install v. **1** PUT IN, insert, put in place, position, place, fix, locate, situate, sta-

tion, lodge. **2** INVEST, ordain, establish, initiate, ensconce, induct, institute. ∎ OPPOSITES remove.

instalment n. PART, portion, section, segment, chapter, episode, division.

instance n. CASE, case in point, example, illustration, occasion, occurrence. ▶ v. CITE, mention, name, specify, quote, adduce.

instant adj. **1** INSTANTANEOUS, immediate, prompt, rapid, sudden, abrupt. **2** PRE-PREPARED, ready-prepared, ready-mixed, pre-cooked. ▶ n. MOMENT, minute, second, split second, trice, twinkling, twinkling of an eye, flash; *informal* jiffy, tick, shake.

instigate v. **1** BRING ABOUT, start, initiate, generate, actuate, incite, provoke, inspire, foment, kindle, stir up, whip up. **2** INCITE, encourage, egg on, urge, prompt, goad, prod, induce, impel, constrain, press, persuade, prevail upon, sway, entice. ∎ OPPOSITES discourage.

instigator n. INCITER, prime mover, motivator, agitator, fomenter, troublemaker, mischief-maker, ringleader, leader.

instil v. IMBUE, infuse, inculcate, introduce, inject, implant, insinuate, ingrain, indoctrinate, teach, drill, arouse.

instinct n. **1** NATURAL FEELING, tendency, inclination, intuition, sixth sense, inner prompting. **2** TALENT, gift, ability, capacity, faculty, aptitude, knack, bent, trait, characteristic.

instinctive adj. **1** AUTOMATIC, reflex, mechanical, spontaneous, involuntary, impulsive, intuitive, unthinking, unpremeditated. **2** INBORN, inbred, innate, inherent, natural, intuitive, untaught, tion or public body. **2** a home providing care for people with special needs. **3** an established law or custom. ■ **institutional** adj.

institutionalize (or **-ise**) v. **1** establish as a feature. **2** place in a residential institution.

instruct v. **1** direct or order. **2** teach. ■ **instruction** n. **instructional** adj. **instructor** n.

instructive adj. useful and informative.

instrument n. **1** a tool or implement for precise work. **2** a measuring device. **3** a device for producing musical sounds.

instrumental adj. **1** acting as a means. **2** performed on musical instruments. ■ **instrumentalist** n.

insubordinate adj. disobedient. ■ **insubordination** n.

insubstantial adj. lacking solidity.

insufferable adj. intolerable. ■ **insufferably** adv.

insufficient adj. not enough. ■ **insufficiency** n. **insufficiently** adv.

insular adj. **1** narrow-minded. **2** of an island. ■ **insularity** n.

insulate v. **1** cover or line with material to prevent heat, sound, etc. being conducted. **2** protect from something unpleasant. ■ **insulation** n. **insulator** n.

insulin n. a hormone regulating glucose levels in the blood.

insult v. speak to or treat in a way that offends. ▶ n. an insulting remark or act.

Thesaurus

unlearned. ■ OPPOSITES learned.

institute v. **1** BEGIN, start, commence, set in motion, put into operation, initiate. **2** FOUND, establish, launch, bring into being, set up, constitute, organize, develop, create, originate, pioneer. ▶ n. INSTITUTION, establishment, organization, foundation, society, association, league, guild, consortium.

institutional adj. **1** ORGANIZED, established, bureaucratic, accepted, orthodox, conventional, customary, formal, systematic, methodical, orderly. **2** UNIFORM, same, unvarying, unvaried, unchanging, monotonous, bland, dull, insipid. **3** COLD, cheerless, clinical, dreary, drab, unwelcoming, uninviting, impersonal, formal, forbidding.

instruct v. **1** TELL, order, direct, command, bid, charge, enjoin, demand, require. **2** TEACH, educate, tutor, coach, train, school, drill, ground, prepare, prime, guide, inform, enlighten, discipline, edify.

instruction n. **1** TEACHING, education, tutoring, tutelage, coaching, training, schooling, drilling, grounding, preparation, priming, guidance, information, enlightenment, edification, lessons, classes, lectures. **2** DIRECTIVE, direction, briefing, order, command, charge, injunction, requirement, ruling, mandate, decree, edict.

instructive adj. INFORMATIVE, educational, educative, enlightening, illuminating, revealing, useful, helpful, edifying, uplifting, informational, cultural, academic, didactic, doctrinal.

instructor n. TEACHER, schoolmaster, schoolmistress, educator, lecturer, professor, tutor, coach, trainer, adviser, counsellor, guide, mentor.

instrument n. IMPLEMENT, tool, appliance, apparatus, mechanism, utensil, gadget, contrivance, device, aid.

instrumental adj. HELPFUL, of use, of help, of assistance, useful, of service, contributory, active, involved, influential, significant, important, valuable, beneficial.

insubordinate adj. DEFIANT, rebellious, mutinous, disobedient, refractory, recalcitrant, undisciplined, ungovernable, uncontrollable, unmanageable, unruly, disorderly, seditious, riotous, insurgent, contumacious. ■ OPPOSITES obedient.

insufferable adj. INTOLERABLE, unbearable, unendurable, insupportable, impossible, dreadful, excruciating, grim, outrageous. ■ OPPOSITES bearable.

insufficient adj. INADEQUATE, deficient, in short supply, scarce, meagre, scant, scanty, too small/few/little, not enough, lacking, wanting, at a premium. ■ OPPOSITES sufficient.

insular adj. **1** ISOLATED, detached, separate, solitary, insulated, self-sufficient. **2** NARROW, narrow-minded, illiberal, prejudiced, biased, bigoted, provincial, blinkered, parochial, limited, restricted. ■ OPPOSITES broad-minded.

insulate v. **1** COVER, wrap, encase, enwrap, envelop, pad, cushion, seal, heatproof, soundproof. **2** SEPARATE, segregate, isolate, detach, cut off, keep apart, exclude, sequester, protect, shield.

insult n. SLIGHT, affront, gibe, snub, barb, slur, dig, abuse, disparagement, depreciation, impugnment, revilement, insolence, rudeness, aspersions. ▶ v. OFFEND, affront, slight, hurt someone's feelings,

insuperable adj. impossible to overcome.

insupportable adj. intolerable.

insurance n. **1** the act or business of insuring. **2** money paid to insure someone or something. **3** a safeguard.

insure v. **1** pay money to receive financial compensation in the event of damage to or loss of property, life, etc. **2** ensure. ■ **insurer** n.

insurgent n. a rebel. ▶ adj. rebellious.

insurmountable adj. too great to be overcome.

insurrection n. a violent revolt.

intact adj. not damaged.

intake n. **1** an amount taken in. **2** a set of people entering a school etc. at a particular time.

intangible adj. **1** not solid or real. **2** vague and abstract.

integer n. a whole number.

integral adj. necessary to make a whole complete.

integrate v. **1** combine to form a whole. **2** make or be accepted as part of a group. ■ **integration** n.

integrity n. **1** the quality of being honest and fair. **2** the state of being whole or unified.

intellect n. the power of reasoning and understanding.

intellectual adj. **1** of or appealing to the intellect. **2** having a highly developed intellect. ▶ n. an intellectual person. ■ **intellectually** adv.

intelligence n. **1** the ability to gain and apply knowledge and skills. **2** secret information obtained about an enemy.

intelligent adj. having a high level of intelligence. ■ **intelligently** adv.

intelligentsia n. intellectual or highly educated people.

intelligible adj. able to be understood. ■ **intelligibility** n. **intelligibly** adv.

intend v. **1** have as one's aim or plan.

Thesaurus

hurt, abuse, injure, wound, mortify, humiliate, disparage, discredit, depreciate, impugn, slur, revile. ■ OPPOSITES compliment.

insuperable adj. INSURMOUNTABLE, impassable, overwhelming, invincible, unconquerable, unassailable.

insure v. ASSURE, indemnify, cover, underwrite, guarantee, warrant.

intact adj. WHOLE, complete, entire, perfect, in one piece, sound, unbroken, undamaged, unblemished, faultless, flawless. ■ OPPOSITES damaged.

intangible adj. **1** IMPALPABLE, untouchable, incorporeal, phantom, spectral, ghostly. **2** INDEFINABLE, indescribable, vague, subtle, unclear, obscure, mysterious. ■ OPPOSITES tangible.

integral adj. **1** ESSENTIAL, necessary, indispensable, requisite, basic, fundamental, inherent, intrinsic, innate. **2** ENTIRE, complete, whole, total, full, intact, unified, integrated, undivided. ■ OPPOSITES peripheral, fragmented.

integrate v. JOIN, unite, combine, amalgamate, consolidate, blend, incorporate, coalesce, fuse, merge, intermix, mingle, commingle, assimilate, homogenize, mesh, harmonize, concatenate. ■ OPPOSITES separate.

integrity n. **1** HONESTY, uprightness, rectitude, righteousness, virtue, probity, morality, honour, goodness, decency, truthfulness, fairness, sincerity, candour. **2** UNITY, wholeness, entirety, completeness, totality, cohesion, solidarity.

■ OPPOSITES dishonesty.

intellect n. INTELLIGENCE, understanding, reason, comprehension, mind, brain, thought, sense, judgement.

intellectual adj. **1** MENTAL, cerebral, academic, rational, logical. **2** INTELLIGENT, academic, well educated, well read, erudite, learned, bookish, donnish, highbrow, scholarly, studious. ▶ n. INTELLECT, genius, thinker, mastermind, academic, don, man/woman of letters, bluestocking, highbrow, pedant; *informal* egghead, bookworm.

intelligence n. **1** INTELLECT, mind, brain, brainpower, mental capacity, aptitude, reason, understanding, comprehension, acumen, wit, cleverness, brightness, sharpness, brilliance, quickness of mind, discernment, alertness, perception, perspicacity, penetration, sense, brains, sagacity; *informal* grey matter, nous. **2** INFORMATION, news, notice, notification, knowledge, account, advice, rumour, facts, data, reports, tidings; *informal* gen, low-down, dope. **3** SPYING, observation, information collection, investigation, surveillance.

intelligent adj. CLEVER, bright, sharp, brilliant, quick, quick-witted, perceptive, penetrating, discerning, sagacious, thinking, well informed, educated, knowledgeable, enlightened; *informal* brainy, smart.

intelligentsia pl. n. INTELLECTUALS, academics, literati, cognoscenti, illuminati, highbrows, pedants, the enlightened.

2 plan a particular role, use, or meaning for.

intense adj. 1 extreme. 2 very earnest or serious. ■ **intensify** v. **intensity** n.

intensive adj. 1 very thorough or concentrated. 2 aiming to achieve maximum results within a limited area or time. □ **intensive care** special medical treatment of a dangerously ill patient. ■ **intensively** adv.

intent n. intention or purpose. ▶adj. 1 (**intent on**) determined to do. 2 showing concentrated attention. ■ **intently** adv.

intention n. an aim or plan.

intentional adj. deliberate. ■ **intentionally** adv.

inter v. (**interring, interred**) bury a dead body.

interact v. act so as to affect each other. ■ **interaction** n. **interactive** adj.

inter alia adv. among other things.

interbreed v. (**interbreeding, interbred**) breed with an animal of a different race or species.

intercede v. intervene on behalf of another.

intercept v. stop and prevent from continuing to a destination. ■ **interception** n. **interceptor** n.

intercession n. the act of interceding.

interchange v. 1 (of two people) exchange things. 2 put each of two things in the other's place. ▶n. 1 the act of interchanging. 2 a road junction on several levels. ■ **interchangeable** adj.

intercom n. an electrical device allowing one-way or two-way communication.

interconnect v. connect with each other.

intercontinental adj. of or travelling between continents.

intercourse n. 1 dealings between people. 2 sexual intercourse.

interdenominational adj. involving more than one religious denomination.

interdependent adj. dependent on each other.

interdict n. an order forbidding something.

interdisciplinary adj. involving more than one branch of knowledge.

interest n. 1 the state of wanting to

Thesaurus

intelligible adj. UNDERSTANDABLE, comprehensible, clear, lucid, plain, explicit, unambiguous, legible, decipherable, straightforward, meaningful. ■ OPPOSITES unintelligible, incomprehensible.

intemperate adj. IMMODERATE, self-indulgent, excessive, inordinate, extreme, extravagant, unreasonable, outrageous. ■ OPPOSITES moderate.

intend v. MEAN, plan, have in mind/view, propose, aim, resolve, be resolved, be determined, expect, purpose, contemplate, think of.

intense adj. 1 ACUTE, fierce, severe, extreme, harsh, strong, powerful, potent, vigorous, great, profound, deep, concentrated, consuming. 2 EARNEST, ardent, eager, keen, enthusiastic, zealous, excited, impassioned, passionate, fervent, burning, fervid, consuming, vehement, fanatical. 3 NERVOUS, nervy, tense, overwrought, fraught, highly strung, emotional. ■ OPPOSITES mild.

intensify v. STRENGTHEN, increase, deepen, heighten, enhance, add to, fuel, build up, reinforce, magnify, fan, extend, boost, augment, escalate, step up, aggravate, exacerbate, worsen, inflame, raise. ■ OPPOSITES reduce, decrease.

intensive adj. CONCENTRATED, in-depth, thorough, exhaustive, all-out, thoroughgoing, total, all-absorbing, high-

powered, unremitting, comprehensive. ■ OPPOSITES cursory.

intent adj. 1 CONCENTRATED, concentrating, fixed, steady, steadfast, absorbed, attentive, engrossed, focused, occupied, preoccupied, rapt, enrapt, wrapped up, observant, watchful, alert, earnest, committed, intense. 2 SET ON, bent on, committed to, firm about, determined to, resolved to; *informal* hell-bent on.

intention n. 1 AIM, purpose, objective, goal, intent, end, end in view, target, aspiration, wish, ambition, plan, design, resolve, resolution, determination. 2 PREMEDITATION, design, plan, calculation, preconception.

intentional adj. INTENDED, deliberate, meant, done on purpose, wilful, purposeful, planned, calculated, designed, premeditated, preconceived, predetermined, pre-arranged, considered, weighed up, studied. ■ OPPOSITES accidental, inadvertent.

inter v. BURY, entomb, consign to the grave, lay to rest; *informal* put six feet under.

intercept v. CUT OFF, stop, deflect, head off, catch, check, arrest, block, obstruct, impede, interrupt, thwart.

intercourse n. 1 DEALINGS, trade, traffic, commerce, association, communication, connection, contact, correspond-

know about something or someone.
2 the quality of making someone curious or attentive. **3** a subject about which one is concerned or enthusiastic. **4** money paid for the use of money lent. **5** advantage: *in my own interest.* **6** a share in a business. ▶v. **1** make curious or attentive. **2** (**interested**) not impartial.

interface n. **1** a point where two things interact. **2** a device or program enabling a user to communicate with a computer, or for connecting two items of hardware or software.

interfere v. **1** prevent the progress or operation of something. **2** become involved in something without being asked. **3** (**interfere with**) sexually molest.

interference n. **1** the act of interfering. **2** disturbance to radio signals.

interferon n. a protein preventing a virus from reproducing.

intergalactic adj. between galaxies.

interim n. the time between two events. ▶adj. temporary.

interior adj. inner. ▶n. **1** the inner part. **2** the internal affairs of a country.

interject v. say suddenly as an interruption. ■ **interjection** n.

interlace v. weave together.

interlink v. link together.

interlock v. (of two parts) fit together.

interloper n. an intruder.

interlude n. **1** a period of time that contrasts with what goes before or after. **2** an interval.

intermarry v. (**intermarrying**, **intermarried**) (of people of different races, religions, etc.) marry each other. ■ **intermarriage** n.

intermediary n. (pl. **intermediaries**) a person who tries to settle a dispute.

intermediate adj. **1** coming between two things in time, place, etc. **2** having more than basic knowledge or skills.

interment n. burial.

intermezzo /in-ter-met-zoh/ n. (pl. **intermezzi** or **intermezzos**) a short piece of music.

interminable adj. seemingly endless. ■ **interminably** adv.

Thesaurus

ence, congress, communion. **2** SEX, sexual intercourse, sexual relations, copulation, lovemaking, coitus, coition, carnal knowledge, sexual congress, congress, intimacy.

interest n. **1** ATTENTIVENESS, attention, absorption, engrossment, heed, regard, notice, scrutiny, curiosity, inquisitiveness. **2** CURIOSITY, attraction, appeal, fascination, charm, allure. **3** CONCERN, importance, consequence, import, moment, significance, note, relevance, weight, gravity. **4** PASTIME, hobby, activity, diversion, amusement, pursuit, relaxation; *informal* thing, scene. **5** SHARE, stake, portion, claim, investment, involvement, participation, stock, equity. ▶v. ATTRACT, absorb, hold/engage someone's interest, engross, fascinate, rivet, grip, captivate, amuse, intrigue, arouse curiosity in, concern. ■ OPPOSITES bore.

interested adj. **1** ATTENTIVE, intent, absorbed, engrossed, curious, fascinated, riveted, gripped, captivated, intrigued. **2** CONCERNED, involved, implicated. **3** PARTIAL, involved, partisan, biased, prejudiced. ■ OPPOSITES uninterested, disinterested.

interesting adj. ABSORBING, engrossing, fascinating, riveting, gripping, compelling, compulsive, spellbinding, captivating, appealing, engaging, amusing,

entertaining, stimulating, thought-provoking, diverting, exciting, intriguing. ■ OPPOSITES boring, uninteresting.

interfere v. **1** HINDER, inhibit, impede, obstruct, get in the way of, check, block, hamper, handicap, cramp, frustrate, trammel, thwart, baulk. **2** MEDDLE WITH, butt into, pry into, intrude into, intervene in, get involved in, tamper with, intercede in; *informal* poke one's nose into, horn in, stick one's oar in.

interim adj. TEMPORARY, provisional, pro tem, stopgap, caretaker, acting, make-shift, improvised.

interior adj. INNER, internal, inside, inward. ▶n. **1** INSIDE, inner part, centre, middle, nucleus, core, heart. **2** HINTERLAND, centre, heartland. ■ OPPOSITES exterior.

interject v. INTRODUCE, interpose, interpolate, add, insinuate, intersperse.

interlude n. INTERVAL, intermission, break, pause, recess, rest, respite, halt, stop, stoppage, breathing space, delay, wait, hiatus.

intermediary n. MEDIATOR, go-between, broker, agent, middleman, arbitrator, negotiator.

intermediate adj. HALFWAY, in-between, middle, in the middle, mid, midway, intervening, interposed, transitional, medial, median, intermediary.

intermission n. a pause or interval.

intermittent adj. happening at irregular intervals. ■ **intermittently** adv.

intern n. US a junior doctor receiving training in a hospital. ▶v. confine as a prisoner. ■ **internee** n. **internment** n.

internal adj. **1** of the inside. **2** inside the body. **3** of affairs and activities within a country. **4** used within an organization. □ **internal-combustion engine** an engine generating power by the explosion of fuel and air inside the engine. ■ **internally** adv.

internalize (or **-ise**) v. make part of one's behaviour or thinking.

international adj. **1** between nations. **2** agreed on or used by all or many nations. ▶n. a match between teams from different countries. ■ **internationally** adv.

internecine /in-ter-nee-syn/ adj. (of conflict) happening between members of a group.

Internet n. an international information network linking computers.

interplay n. interaction.

interpolate /in-ter-puh-layt/ v. **1** insert. **2** interject. ■ **interpolation** n.

interpose v. **1** place or insert between one thing and another. **2** intervene between parties.

interpret v. **1** explain the meaning of. **2** translate aloud the words of a person speaking a different language. **3** understand as having a particular meaning. ■ **interpretable** adj. **interpretation** n. **interpreter** n.

interracial adj. involving different races.

interregnum n. a period between regimes when normal government is suspended.

interrelated adj. related to each other.

interrogate v. question closely or aggressively. ■ **interrogation** n. **interrogator** n.

interrogative adj. in the form of a question or used in questions.

interrupt v. **1** stop a person speaking by saying or doing something. **2** break the continuity of. ■ **interruption** n.

intersect v. divide or cross by passing or lying across. ■ **intersection** n.

intersperse v. scatter among or place between other things.

interstate adj. between states.

interval n. **1** a period of time between two events. **2** a pause. **3** a pause between parts of a play etc. **4** a difference in musical pitch.

Thesaurus

interminable adj. ENDLESS, never-ending, everlasting, incessant, ceaseless, unlimited, infinite, boundless, countless, untold, innumerable, incalculable, immeasurable, indeterminable.

intermittent adj. FITFUL, spasmodic, irregular, sporadic, occasional, periodic, cyclic, recurrent, recurring, broken, discontinuous, on and off, erratic. ■ OPPOSITES continuous.

internal adj. **1** INNER, inside, inward, interior. **2** DOMESTIC, home, civil, interior, in-house, local. ■ OPPOSITES external, foreign.

international adj. WORLDWIDE, cosmopolitan, global, universal, intercontinental, multinational.

interpolate v. INSERT, interject, interpose, introduce, add, inject, insinuate, put in, work in, intercalate.

interpret v. **1** TRANSLATE, transliterate, transcribe, paraphrase. **2** EXPLAIN, elucidate, expound, explicate, clarify, make clear, illuminate, shed light on, gloss, simplify, spell out. **3** DECODE, decipher, solve, crack, unravel, untangle. **4** UNDERSTAND, take, take to mean, read.

interrogate v. QUESTION, put/pose questions to, examine, cross-examine, give the third degree to, inquire of, quiz, probe; *informal* put the screws on, pump, grill.

interrogation n. QUESTIONING, cross-examination, inquisition, investigation, grilling, probing, inquiry; *informal* the third degree.

interrogative adj. INQUISITIVE, questioning, quizzical, inquiring, curious, investigative, inquisitorial, probing.

interrupt v. **1** CUT IN ON, break in on, barge in on, intrude on, butt in on, disturb, heckle, interfere with; *informal* chime in on, horn in on, muscle in on, chip in on. **2** SUSPEND, discontinue, break, break off, hold up, delay, lay aside, leave off, postpone, stop, put a stop to, halt, bring to a halt/standstill, cease, end, cancel, sever.

interruption n. **1** INTERFERENCE, disturbance, intrusion, butting in, obtrusion; *informal* horning in. **2** SUSPENSION, discontinuance, breaking off, postponement, delay, stopping, halt, cessation. **3** INTERMISSION, interval, interlude, break, pause, recess, gap, hiatus.

intersect v. **1** CUT ACROSS/THROUGH, cut in two, divide, bisect. **2** CROSS, crisscross, meet, connect.

intervene v. **1** become involved in a situation to improve or control it. **2** occur between events. ■ **intervention** n.

interview n. a formal conversation with someone designed to elicit information or assess their suitability for a post. ▶ v. hold an interview with. ■ **interviewee** n. **interviewer** n.

interweave v. (**interweaving, interwove**, past part. **interwoven**) weave or become woven together.

intestate adj. not having made a valid will.

intestine n. the long tubular organ leading from the end of the stomach to the anus. ■ **intestinal** adj.

intimate¹ /in-ti-muht/ adj. **1** close and friendly. **2** private and personal. **3** having a sexual relationship. **4** (of knowledge) detailed. ▶ n. a close friend. ■ **intimacy** n. **intimately** adv.

intimate² /in-ti-mayt/ v. state indirectly. ■ **intimation** n.

intimidate v. frighten, esp. into doing something. ■ **intimidation** n.

into prep. **1** to a point on or within. **2** expressing a change or result. **3** in the direction of. **4** concerning. **5** expressing division.

intolerable adj. unable to be endured. ■ **intolerably** adv.

intonation n. the rise and fall of the voice in speaking.

intone v. say with little intonation.

intoxicate v. **1** make drunk. **2** exhilarate. ■ **intoxicant** n. **intoxication** n.

intractable adj. **1** hard to deal with. **2** stubborn.

intramural adj. forming part of normal university or college studies.

intransigent adj. stubborn. ■ **intransigence** n.

intransitive adj. (of a verb) not taking a

Thesaurus

intersection n. JUNCTION, interchange, crossroads, roundabout, spaghetti junction.

interval n. **1** INTERLUDE, interim, intervening time, time, period, meantime, meanwhile, wait, space. **2** INTERMISSION, break, half-time, pause, lull, respite, breather, breathing space, gap, hiatus, delay.

intervene v. **1** COME/OCCUR BETWEEN, occur, happen, arise, take place, ensue, supervene, succeed; literary come to pass. **2** INTERCEDE, mediate, arbitrate, negotiate, step in, involve oneself, come into, interpose, interfere, intrude.

interview n. **1** APPRAISAL, evaluation, discussion, meeting, talk, dialogue. **2** AUDIENCE, question and answer session, exchange, dialogue, colloquy, interlocution. ▶ v. TALK TO, have a discussion/dialogue with, hold a meeting with, confer with, question, put questions to, sound out, examine, interrogate, cross-examine, evaluate.

interweave v. **1** WEAVE, intertwine, twine, twist, interlace, braid, plait. **2** INTERMINGLE, mingle, interlink, intermix, mix, blend, interlock, knit, connect, associate.

intimate¹ adj. **1** CLOSE, near, dear, nearest and dearest, cherished, bosom, familiar, confidential, warm, friendly, comradely, amicable. **2** INFORMAL, warm, cosy, friendly, comfortable, snug. **3** PERSONAL, private, confidential, secret, privy. ■ OPPOSITES distant.

intimate² v. **1** ANNOUNCE, make known,

state, tell, inform, communicate, impart. **2** IMPLY, suggest, let it be known, hint, insinuate, give an inkling that, indicate, signal; informal tip someone the wink.

intimidate v. FRIGHTEN, terrify, scare, alarm, terrorize, overawe, awe, cow, subdue, daunt, domineer, browbeat, bully, tyrannize, coerce, compel, bulldoze, pressure, pressurize, threaten; informal push around, lean on, twist someone's arm.

intolerable adj. UNBEARABLE, unendurable, beyond endurance, insufferable, insupportable, not to be borne, more than flesh and blood can stand, impossible, painful, excruciating, agonizing, too much to bear.

intolerant adj. BIGOTED, illiberal, narrow-minded, narrow, parochial, provincial, insular, small-minded, prejudiced, biased, partisan, one-sided, warped, twisted, fanatical, chauvinistic, jingoistic, racist, xenophobic, sexist, ageist, homophobic.

intonation n. PITCH, tone, timbre, cadence, lilt, inflection, accentuation, emphasis, stress.

intoxicate v. **1** INEBRIATE, make drunk, befuddle, fuddle, stupefy. **2** EXHILARATE, elate, thrill, invigorate, animate, enliven, excite, arouse, captivate, enrapture.

intoxicated adj. see DRUNK.

intractable adj. **1** UNMANAGEABLE, ungovernable, uncontrollable, stubborn, obstinate, obdurate, perverse, disobedidirect object.

intrauterine adj. within the womb.

intravenous adj. within or into a vein or veins. ■ **intravenously** adv.

intrepid adj. fearless.

intricate adj. very complicated. ■ **intricacy** n. **intricately** adv.

intrigue v. **1** arouse the curiosity of. **2** plot secretly. ▶ n. **1** a plot. **2** a secret love affair. ■ **intriguing** adj.

intrinsic adj. forming part of the basic nature of something. ■ **intrinsically** adv.

introduce v. **1** bring into use. **2** present someone by name to another. **3** bring to someone's attention for the first time. **4** insert. **5** occur at the start of. ■ **introduction** n. **introductory** adj.

introspection n. examination of one's own thoughts or feelings. ■ **introspective** adj.

introvert n. a shy, introspective person.

■ **introverted** adj.

intrude v. come into a place or situation where one is unwelcome or uninvited. ■ **intrusion** n. **intrusive** adj.

intruder n. a person who enters a place illegally.

intuition n. the ability to understand or know something without conscious reasoning. ■ **intuitive** adj.

Inuit /in-yuu-it/ n. (pl. **Inuit** or **Inuits**) a member of a people of northern Canada and parts of Greenland and Alaska.

....
ⓘ **Inuit** is the official term in Canada and many of the peoples traditionally called **Eskimos** prefer it.
....

inundate v. **1** flood. **2** overwhelm.

inure v. accustom to something unpleasant.

invade v. **1** enter a country so as to conquer or occupy it. **2** enter in large num-

Thesaurus

ent, indomitable, refractory, recalcitrant, insubordinate, rebellious, wild, unruly, rowdy. ■ OPPOSITES manageable, compliant.

intricate adj. **1** TANGLED, entangled, ravelled, twisted, knotty, convoluted, involute, maze-like, labyrinthine, winding, serpentine, circuitous, sinuous, fancy, elaborate, ornate, Byzantine, rococo. **2** COMPLEX, complicated, difficult, involved, perplexing, puzzling, thorny, mystifying, enigmatic, obscure. ■ OPPOSITES simple.

intrigue v. **1** INTEREST, absorb, arouse someone's curiosity, attract, draw, pull, rivet someone's attention, rivet, fascinate, charm, captivate, divert, pique, titillate. **2** PLOT, conspire, scheme, connive, manoeuvre, machinate, devise. ■ OPPOSITES bore. ▶ n. PLOT, conspiracy, collusion, cabal, scheme, ruse, stratagem, wile, dodge, artifice, manoeuvre, machination, trickery, sharp practice, double-dealing.

intrinsic adj. INHERENT, inborn, inbred, congenital, natural, native, indigenous, constitutional, built-in, ingrained, implanted, basic, fundamental, elemental, essential, true, genuine, real, authentic.

introduce v. **1** PRESENT, make known, acquaint, make acquainted, announce, give an introduction to. **2** PREFACE, precede, lead into, commence, start off, begin. **3** BRING IN, bring into being, originate, launch, inaugurate, institute, initiate, establish, found, set in motion, organize, develop, start, begin, com-

mence, usher in, pioneer. **4** INSERT, inject, interject, interpose, interpolate, intercalate, add, bring, infuse, instil.

introduction n. FOREWORD, preface, front matter, preamble, prologue, prelude, exordium, lead-in; *informal* intro, prelims. ■ OPPOSITES afterword.

introductory adj. **1** PREFATORY, preliminary, precursory, lead-in, initiatory, opening, initial, starting. **2** PREPARATORY, elementary, basic, basal, rudimentary, fundamental, initiatory. ■ OPPOSITES closing.

introspective adj. INWARD-LOOKING, inner-directed, introverted, self-analysing, self-examining, subjective, contemplative, reflective, meditative, musing, pensive, brooding, preoccupied, navel-gazing.

intrude v. **1** INTERRUPT, push/thrust oneself in, gatecrash, barge in, encroach, butt in, interfere, obtrude. **2** ENCROACH ON, invade, impinge on, infringe on, trespass on, obtrude on, violate.

intruder n. **1** BURGLAR, housebreaker, thief, raider, invader, prowler, trespasser. **2** UNWELCOME GUEST/VISITOR, gatecrasher, interloper, infiltrator.

intuition n. **1** INSTINCT, sixth sense, divination, presentiment, clairvoyance, second sight, extrasensory perception, ESP. **2** FEELING, feeling in one's bones, hunch, inkling, presentiment, foreboding.

inundate v. **1** FLOOD, deluge, overrun, swamp, submerge, engulf, drown, cover, saturate, soak. **2** OVERWHELM, bers. **3** intrude on.

invalid n. a person weak or disabled by illness or injury. ▶adj. not valid. ■ **invalidity** n.

invalidate v. make invalid.

invaluable adj. very useful.

invariable adj. never changing. ■ **invariably** adv.

invasion n. an act of invading. ■ **invasive** adj.

invective n. abusive language.

inveigh /in-vay/ v. (**inveigh against**) speak or write about with great hostility.

inveigle /in-vay-g'l/ v. persuade by trickery or flattery.

invent v. **1** create or design something new. **2** make up a false story, name, etc.

■ **invention** n. **inventive** adj. **inventor** n.

inverse adj. opposite.

invert v. put upside down or in the opposite position or order. □ **inverted comma** a quotation mark. ■ **inversion** n.

invertebrate n. an animal having no backbone.

invest v. **1** use money or spend time or effort in order to earn a profit or achieve a result. **2** provide with a quality. **3** confer a rank or office on. ■ **investment** n. **investor** n.

investigate v. **1** carry out a systematic inquiry into. **2** research. ■ **investigation** n. **investigative** adj. **investigator** n.

Thesaurus

overpower, overburden, swamp, bog down, glut.

inure v. HARDEN, toughen, season, temper, habituate, familiarize, accustom, naturalize, acclimatize.

invade v. **1** ATTACK, assail, assault, overrun, occupy, storm, take over, descend upon, make inroads on, raid, plunder. **2** INTRUDE ON, obtrude on, encroach on, infringe on, trespass on, burst in on, violate. ■ OPPOSITES withdraw.

invalid adj. **1** INOPERATIVE, legally void, null, null and void, void, not binding, nullified, revoked, rescinded, abolished. **2** UNJUSTIFIED, unsubstantiated, unwarranted, untenable, illogical, irrational, unscientific, false, faulty, fallacious, spurious, unacceptable, inadequate, unconvincing, ineffectual, unsound, weak, useless, worthless.

invaluable adj. PRICELESS, beyond price, inestimable, precious, costly, worth its weight in gold, worth a king's ransom. ■ OPPOSITES worthless.

invariable adj. UNCHANGING, changeless, unchangeable, constant, unvarying, unvaried, invariant, unalterable, immutable, fixed, stable, set, steady, unwavering, static, uniform, regular, consistent. ■ OPPOSITES varied.

invariably adv. ALWAYS, every/each time, on every occasion, at all times, without fail/exception, regularly, consistently, repeatedly, habitually, unfailingly, infallibly, inevitably.

invasion n. **1** OVERRUNNING, occupation, incursion, offensive, attack, assailing, assault, raid, foray, onslaught, plundering. **2** INTRUSION, obtrusion, encroachment, infringement, breach, infraction, trespass, violation.

inveigle v. PERSUADE, talk into, cajole, wheedle, coax, beguile, tempt, decoy, lure, entice, seduce, deceive; *informal* sweet-talk.

invent v. **1** ORIGINATE, create, innovate, discover, design, devise, contrive, formulate, think up, conceive, come up with, hit upon, compose, frame, coin. **2** MAKE UP, fabricate, concoct, hatch, trump up, forge; *informal* cook up.

invention n. **1** ORIGINATION, creation, innovation, discovery, design, contrivance, construction, coinage; *informal* brainchild. **2** INVENTIVENESS, originality, creativity, creativeness, imagination, artistry, inspiration, ingenuity, resourcefulness, genius.

inventive adj. ORIGINAL, creative, innovational, imaginative, artistic, inspired, ingenious, resourceful, innovative, gifted, talented, skilful, clever. ■ OPPOSITES unimaginative.

inventor n. ORIGINATOR, creator, innovator, discoverer, author, architect, designer, deviser, developer, initiator, coiner, father, prime mover, maker, framer, producer.

inventory n. LIST, listing, checklist, catalogue, record, register, tally, account, description, statement.

inverse adj. OPPOSITE, converse, contrary, reverse, counter.

invert v. TURN UPSIDE DOWN, upturn, overturn, upset, turn turtle, capsize.

invest v. **1** PUT/SINK MONEY INTO, lay out money on, provide capital for, fund, subsidize. **2** SPEND, expend, lay out, put in, use up, devote, contribute, donate, give. **3** VEST, endow, confer, bestow, grant, entrust, give, place.

investigate v. INQUIRE INTO, make in-

investiture n. the act or ceremony of investing a person with an office etc.

inveterate adj. 1 habitual. 2 firmly established.

invidious adj. likely to cause resentment.

invigilate v. supervise examination candidates. ■ **invigilator** n.

invigorate v. give strength or energy to.

invincible adj. too powerful to be defeated or overcome. ■ **invincibility** n.

inviolable adj. unable to be attacked or dishonoured.

inviolate adj. free from injury or violation.

invisible adj. unable to be seen. ■ **invisibility** n. **invisibly** adv.

invite v. 1 ask someone to come somewhere or do something. 2 ask for. 3 risk provoking. ■ **invitation** n.

inviting adj. tempting or attractive.

in vitro adj. & adv. in a test tube or elsewhere outside a living organism.

invocation n. the act of invoking.

invoice n. a bill for goods or services. ▶v. send an invoice to.

invoke v. 1 appeal to as an authority. 2 call on a god or spirit.

involuntary adj. 1 done without conscious control. 2 done against someone's will. ■ **involuntarily** adv.

involve v. 1 have as a necessary part or result. 2 cause to participate. ■ **involvement** n.

involved adj. 1 connected on an emotional or personal level. 2 complicated.

invulnerable adj. not vulnerable.

Thesaurus

quiries about, go/look into, research, probe, explore, search, scrutinize, study, examine, inspect, consider, sift, analyse; *informal* check out, suss out.

investigation n. INQUIRY, fact-finding, search, scrutinization, scrutiny, research, probe, exploration, study, survey, review, examination, inspection, consideration, sifting, analysis, inquest, hearing, questioning, inquisition.

inveterate adj. CONFIRMED, habitual, inured, hardened, chronic, die-hard, deep-dyed, dyed-in-the-wool, long-standing, addicted, incorrigible, hardcore.

invidious adj. 1 DISCRIMINATORY, unfair, prejudicial, slighting, offensive, objectionable, deleterious, detrimental. 2 UNPLEASANT, awkward, unpopular, repugnant, hateful. ■ OPPOSITES pleasant, fair.

invigorate v. REVITALIZE, energize, fortify, strengthen, put new strength/life/heart in, brace, refresh, rejuvenate, enliven, liven up, animate, exhilarate, perk up, stimulate, motivate, rouse, excite, wake up, galvanize, electrify; *informal* pep up. ■ OPPOSITES tire.

invincible adj. 1 UNCONQUERABLE, undefeatable, unbeatable, unassailable, invulnerable, indestructible, impregnable, indomitable, unyielding, unflinching, dauntless. 2 INSUPERABLE, unsurmountable, overwhelming, overpowering. ■ OPPOSITES vulnerable.

inviolable adj. INALIENABLE, untouchable, unalterable, sacrosanct, sacred, holy, hallowed.

invisible adj. UNSEEABLE, out of sight, undetectable, imperceptible, indiscern-

ible, indistinguishable, unseen, unnoticed, unobserved, hidden, concealed, inconspicuous, unnoticeable.

invite v. 1 ASK, bid, summon, request someone's company/presence. 2 ASK FOR, request, call for, solicit, look for, seek, appeal for, petition, summon. 3 CAUSE, bring on, bring upon oneself, induce, provoke.

inviting adj. ATTRACTIVE, appealing, pleasant, agreeable, delightful, engaging, tempting, enticing, alluring, irresistible, ravishing, seductive. ■ OPPOSITES repellent.

invocation n. CALL, prayer, request, petition, appeal, supplication, entreaty, solicitation, imploring, importuning; *literary* beseeching.

invoke v. CALL FOR, call up, pray for, request, supplicate, entreat, solicit, beg, implore, importune, call on, petition, appeal to; *literary* beseech.

involuntary adj. 1 REFLEXIVE, reflex, automatic, mechanical, unconditioned, spontaneous, instinctive, instinctual, unconscious, unthinking, unintentional, uncontrolled. 2 UNWILLING, against one's will/wishes, reluctant, grudging, forced, coerced, coercive, compelled, compulsory, obligatory. ■ OPPOSITES deliberate, voluntary.

involve v. 1 ENTAIL, imply, mean, denote, betoken, connote, require, necessitate, presuppose. 2 INCLUDE, count in, cover, embrace, take in, number, incorporate, encompass, comprise, contain, comprehend. 3 INTEREST, be of interest to, absorb, engage, engage/hold someone's attention, rivet, grip, occupy, engross. ■ OPPOSITES preclude, exclude.

inward adj. **1** directed or going towards the inside. **2** mental or spiritual. ▶ adv. (also **inwards**) towards the inside.

iodine n. a chemical element used in solution as an antiseptic.

iodize (or **-ise**) v. treat or impregnate with iodine.

ion n. an electrically charged atom that has lost or gained an electron. ■ **ionic** adj.

ionize (or **-ise**) v. convert into an ion or ions.

ionosphere n. a layer of the atmosphere containing a high concentration of ions.

iota n. a very small amount.

IOU n. a signed document acknowledging a debt.

ipso facto adv. by that very fact.

IQ abbrev. intelligence quotient.

IRA abbrev. Irish Republican Army.

irascible adj. bad-tempered.

irate adj. very angry.

ire n. anger.

iridescent adj. shimmering with many colours. ■ **iridescence** n.

iridium n. a hard metallic element.

iris n. **1** the coloured part of the eyeball, with the pupil in the centre. **2** a plant with large bright flowers.

Irish n. the language of Ireland. ▶ adj. of Ireland or Irish.

irk v. annoy. ■ **irksome** adj.

iron n. **1** a strong magnetic metallic element. **2** an implement with a flat base heated for smoothing clothes.

3 (**irons**) fetters or handcuffs. ▶ v. **1** smooth clothes with an iron. **2** (**iron out**) solve problems. □ **ironmonger** a person selling tools and other hardware.

irony n. (pl. **ironies**) **1** the expression of meaning through the use of language which normally means the opposite. **2** a situation that appears opposite to what one expects. ■ **ironic** adj. **ironical** adj. **ironically** adv.

irradiate v. **1** expose to radiation. **2** illuminate. ■ **irradiation** n.

irrational adj. not logical or reasonable. ■ **irrationally** adv.

irreconcilable adj. **1** incompatible. **2** not able to be resolved.

irredeemable adj. unable to be saved or put right.

irrefutable adj. impossible to disprove.

irregular adj. **1** not regular in shape, arrangement, or occurrence. **2** contrary to a rule or standard. ■ **irregularity** n.

irrelevant adj. not relevant. ■ **irrelevance** n. **irrelevantly** adv.

....

✓ *-ant*, not *-ent*: irrelev*ant*.

....

irreparable adj. impossible to put right or repair. ■ **irreparably** adv.

irreplaceable adj. impossible to replace.

irrepressible adj. not able to be restrained.

irreproachable adj. beyond criticism;

Thesaurus

involved adj. COMPLICATED, difficult, intricate, complex, elaborate, confused, confusing, mixed up, jumbled, tangled, entangled, convoluted, knotty, tortuous, labyrinthine, Byzantine.

iota n. BIT, mite, speck, atom, jot, whit, particle, fraction, morsel, grain; *informal* smidgen.

ironic adj. **1** SATIRICAL, mocking, derisive, scornful, sardonic, wry, double-edged, sarcastic; *informal* sarky. **2** PARADOXICAL, incongruous.

irrational adj. ILLOGICAL, unreasonable, groundless, unsound, implausible, absurd, ridiculous, silly, foolish, senseless, nonsensical, muddled, confused, ludicrous, preposterous, crazy, demented, insane. ■ OPPOSITES rational.

irrefutable adj. INCONTROVERTIBLE, incontestable, indisputable, undeniable, unquestionable, beyond question, indubitable, beyond doubt, conclusive, decisive, definite.

irregular adj. **1** ASYMMETRIC, unsymmetrical, uneven, broken, jagged, ragged, serrated, crooked, curving, craggy. **2** UNEVEN, unsteady, shaky, fitful, variable, erratic, spasmodic, wavering, fluctuating, aperiodic. **3** INCONSISTENT, sporadic, variable, inconstant, desultory, haphazard, intermittent, occasional. **4** OUT OF ORDER, against the rules, unofficial, unorthodox, unconventional, abnormal.

irrelevant adj. IMMATERIAL, unrelated, unconnected, inapposite, inapt, inapplicable, non-germane, inappropriate, extraneous, beside the point, not to the point, out of place; *informal* nothing to do with it, neither here nor there.

irreparable adj. BEYOND REPAIR, past mending, irreversible, irrevocable, irretrievable, irrecoverable, irremediable, incurable, ruinous.

irreplaceable adj. PRICELESS, invaluable, precious, unique, worth its weight blameless or faultless.

irresistible adj. too tempting or powerful to be resisted. ■ **irresistibly** adv.

....

☑ *-ible*, not *-able*: irresist*ible*.

....

irresolute adj. uncertain.

irrespective adj. (**irrespective of**) regardless of.

irresponsible adj. not showing a proper sense of responsibility. ■ **irresponsibly** adv.

irretrievable adj. not able to be improved or set right.

irreverent adj. disrespectful. ■ **irreverence** n. **irreverently** adv.

irreversible adj. impossible to alter or undo. ■ **irreversibly** adv.

irrevocable adj. irreversible or unalterable. ■ **irrevocably** adv.

irrigate v. supply water to land or crops by means of channels. ■ **irrigation** n.

irritable adj. easily annoyed or angered. ■ **irritability** n. **irritably** adv.

irritate v. **1** make annoyed. **2** cause inflammation in a part of the body. ■ **irritant** n. **irritation** n.

is see **BE**.

isinglass n. gelatin obtained from fish.

Islam n. the Muslim religion. ■ **Islamic** adj.

island n. a piece of land surrounded by water. ■ **islander** n.

isle n. an island.

islet n. a small island.

isn't contr. is not.

isobar n. a line on a map connecting points with the same atmospheric pressure.

isolate v. **1** place apart or alone. **2** extract a substance in a pure form. ■ **isolation** n.

isolationism n. a policy of remaining

Thesaurus

....

in gold, rare.

irrepressible adj. **1** INEXTINGUISHABLE, unquenchable, uncontainable, uncontrollable, unstoppable, unreserved, unchecked, unbridled. **2** BUOYANT, effervescent, ebullient, vivacious, animated, spirited, lively.

irresistible adj. **1** OVERWHELMING, overpowering, compelling, irrepressible, forceful, potent, imperative, urgent. **2** FASCINATING, alluring, enticing, seductive, captivating, enchanting, ravishing, tempting, tantalizing.

irresolute adj. UNCERTAIN, unsure, doubtful, dubious, undecided, indecisive, unresolved, undetermined, unsettled, vacillating, wavering, hesitant, hesitating, tentative, in two minds, oscillating. ■ OPPOSITES resolute.

irresponsible adj. **1** UNDEPENDABLE, unreliable, untrustworthy, careless, rash, reckless, flighty, giddy, scatterbrained, erratic, hare-brained, feather-brained. **2** THOUGHTLESS, ill-considered, unwise, imprudent, injudicious, careless, reckless, foolhardy, immature. ■ OPPOSITES sensible.

irreverent adj. **1** DISRESPECTFUL, impertinent, insolent, impudent, rude, cheeky, discourteous, impolite, uncivil. **2** IMPIOUS, irreligious, heretical, sacrilegious, ungodly, blasphemous, profane. ■ OPPOSITES respectful.

irrevocable adj. UNALTERABLE, unchangeable, irreversible, fixed, settled, fated, immutable, predetermined, predestined.

irrigation n. WATERING, wetting, spraying, sprinkling, moistening, soaking, flooding, inundating.

irritable adj. BAD-TEMPERED, ill-tempered, ill-humoured, irascible, cross, edgy, testy, touchy, crabbed, peevish, petulant, cantankerous, grumpy, grouchy, crusty, dyspeptic, choleric, splenetic; *informal* snappish, snappy. ■ OPPOSITES good-humoured, cheerful.

irritate v. **1** ANNOY, vex, provoke, irk, nettle, get on someone's nerves, exasperate, infuriate, anger, enrage, incense, make someone's hackles rise, ruffle, disturb, put out, bother, pester, try someone's patience, rub up the wrong way; *informal* aggravate, peeve, get someone's goat, get someone's back up, get up someone's nose, drive up the wall, drive bananas. **2** CHAFE, fret, rub, pain, hurt, inflame, aggravate.

irritation n. **1** IRRITABILITY, annoyance, impatience, vexation, exasperation, indignation, crossness, ill temper, anger, fury, rage, wrath, displeasure; *informal* aggravation; *literary* ire. **2** SOURCE OF ANNOYANCE, annoyance, irritant, pest, nuisance, thorn in the flesh; *informal* pain in the neck, pain.

isolate v. SET APART, segregate, cut off, separate, detach, abstract, quarantine, keep in solitude, sequester, insulate.

isolated adj. **1** ALONE, solitary, lonely, separated, exiled, forsaken, forlorn. **2** REMOTE, out of the way, off the beaten track, outlying, secluded, hidden, unfrequented, lonely, desolate, godforsaken.

apart from the political affairs of other countries. ■ **isolationist** n.

isomer n. each of two or more compounds with the same formula but a different arrangement of atoms.

isosceles /I-soss-i-leez/ adj. (of a triangle) having two sides of equal length.

isotherm n. a line on a map connecting points with the same temperature.

isotope n. each of two or more forms of the same element that contain equal numbers of protons but different numbers of neutrons.

ISP abbrev. Internet service provider.

Israelite /iz-ruh-lyt/ n. a member of the ancient Hebrew nation.

issue n. **1** an important topic to be resolved. **2** the act of issuing. **3** each of a regular series of publications. ▶v. **1** supply or give out. **2** formally send out or make known. **3** come or flow out. □ **at issue** under discussion.

isthmus /iss-muhss/ n. (pl. **isthmuses**) a narrow strip of land with sea on either side, linking two larger areas of land.

IT abbrev. information technology.

it pron. **1** a thing previously mentioned or easily identified. **2** an animal or child of unspecified sex. **3** used to identify a person: *it's me.* **4** used as a subject in statements about time, distance, or weather: *it is raining.*

Italian n. **1** a person from Italy. **2** the language of Italy. ▶adj. of Italy or Italian.

italic adj. (of a typeface) sloping. ▶n.

(also **italics**) an italic typeface.

italicize (or **-ise**) v. print in italics.

itch n. an uncomfortable sensation that causes a desire to scratch. ▶v. **1** have an itch. **2** informal feel an impatient desire. ■ **itchy** adj.

item n. an individual article or unit.

itemize (or **-ise**) v. present as a list of items.

iterate v. do or say repeatedly. ■ **iteration** n. **iterative** adj.

itinerant adj. travelling.

itinerary n. (pl. **itineraries**) a planned route or journey.

its adj. of a thing previously mentioned; belonging to it.

....

☑ Don't confuse the possessive **its** (as in *turn the camera on its side*) with the form **it's** (short for either **it is** or **it has**, as in *it's my fault* or *it's been raining*).

....

itself pron. **1** used when a thing which performs an action is also affected by it. **2** used to emphasize a particular thing mentioned.

ITV abbrev. Independent Television.

IUD abbrev. intrauterine device, a contraceptive fitted inside the womb.

IVF abbrev. in vitro fertilization.

ivory n. (pl. **ivories**) **1** a hard creamy-white substance forming the tusks of an elephant etc. **2** the creamy-white colour of ivory. □ **ivory tower** a privileged position that is remote from normal difficulties.

ivy n. an evergreen climbing plant.

Thesaurus

....

3 SINGLE, solitary, unique, random, unrelated, unusual, uncommon, exceptional, abnormal, atypical, untypical, anomalous, freak.

issue n. **1** MATTER, matter in question, point at issue, question, subject, topic, affair, problem, bone of contention, controversy, argument. **2** RESULT, outcome, decision, upshot, end, conclusion, consequence, termination, effect, denouement. **3** EDITION, number, printing, print run, impression, copy, instalment, version. **4** ISSUING, issuance, publication, circulation, distribution, supplying, supply, dissemination, sending out, delivery. ▶v. **1** PUT OUT, give out, deal out, send out, distribute, circulate, release, disseminate, announce, pro-

claim, broadcast. **2** COME OUT/FORTH, emerge, emanate, appear, pour out/forth, exude, gush, seep, ooze.

itch v. **1** TINGLE, prickle, tickle, be irritated, be itchy. **2** LONG, have a longing, yearn, hanker, pine, ache, burn, hunger, thirst, lust, desire greatly, crave. ▶n. **1** TINGLING, irritation, itchiness, prickling, tickling; *Medicine* formication, paraesthesia. **2** GREAT DESIRE, longing, yearning, craving, hankering, ache, burning, hunger, thirst, lust; *informal* yen.

item n. **1** ARTICLE, thing, piece of merchandise, artefact, product. **2** POINT, detail, matter, consideration, particular, feature, circumstance, aspect, element, ingredient.

Jj

J abbrev. joules.

jab v. (**jabbing**, **jabbed**) poke roughly with something pointed. ▶ n. **1** a rough poke. **2** informal an injection.

jabber v. talk quickly but unintelligibly.

jack n. **1** a device for lifting a vehicle off the ground. **2** a playing card next below a queen. **3** a connection between two pieces of electrical equipment. **4** a small ball aimed at in bowls. ▶ v. (**jack up**) raise with a jack.

jackal n. a wild dog of Africa and Asia.

jackass n. **1** a stupid person. **2** a male ass.

jackboot n. a military boot reaching to the knee.

jackdaw n. a small grey-headed crow.

jacket n. **1** a short coat. **2** an outer covering. **3** the skin of a potato.

jackknife n. a large folding knife. ▶ v. (of an articulated vehicle) bend into a V-shape in a skid.

jackpot n. a large cash prize in a game or lottery.

Jacobean adj. of the reign of James I of England (1603–1625).

Jacobite n. a supporter of the deposed James II and his descendants.

jacuzzi /juh-**koo**-zi/ n. (pl. **jacuzzis**) trademark a large bath with jets of water.

jade n. **1** a green precious stone. **2** a green colour.

jaded adj. tired and bored.

jagged adj. with rough, sharp projections.

jaguar n. a large cat of Central and South America.

jail (or **gaol**) n. prison. ▶ v. put in jail. ■ **jailer** n.

Jainism n. an Indian religion. ■ **Jain** n.

jalopy /juh-**lop**-i/ n. (pl. **jalopies**) informal an old, battered car.

jam v. (**jamming**, **jammed**) **1** pack tightly into a space. **2** block a road through crowding. **3** become stuck. **4** block a radio transmission by causing interference. ▶ n. **1** an instance of being blocked. **2** informal a difficult situation. **3** a thick spread made from fruit and sugar.

jamb n. a side post of a door or window.

jamboree n. a lavish or noisy party.

jangle v. **1** make a ringing metallic sound. **2** (of one's nerves) be set on edge. ▶ n. a jangling sound.

janitor n. a caretaker.

January n. the first month.

Japanese n. (pl. **Japanese**) **1** a person from Japan. **2** the language of Japan. ▶ adj. of Japan or Japanese.

japanned adj. coated with a black glossy varnish.

japonica n. a shrub with bright red flowers.

jar n. a cylindrical glass or pottery container. ▶ v. (**jarring**, **jarred**) **1** strike with a painful jolt. **2** have an unpleasant effect.

jardinière /zhar-din-**yair**/ n. an ornamental plant pot or stand.

jargon n. words used by a particular group and hard for others to understand.

jasmine n. a shrub with sweet-smelling

Thesaurus

jab n. POKE, prod, dig, nudge, elbow, thrust, stab, bump, tap, punch; informal sock, biff.

jacket n. CASING, case, encasement, sheath, sheathing, envelope, cover, covering, wrapping, wrapper, wrap.

jaded adj. TIRED, weary, fatigued, worn out, exhausted, spent; informal played out, bushed, fagged out, done in, fagged out; US informal pooped. ■ OPPOSITES fresh.

jagged adj. SERRATED, toothed, notched, sawtooth, indented, nicked, pointed, snaggy, spiked, barbed, uneven, rough, ridged, ragged, craggy, broken, cleft.

■ OPPOSITES smooth.

jam v. **1** WEDGE, sandwich, insert, force, ram, thrust, push, stick, press, cram, stuff. **2** CRAM, pack, crowd, squeeze, crush. **3** BECOME STUCK, stick, stall, halt, stop. ▶ n. **1** TRAFFIC JAM, hold-up, obstruction, congestion, bottleneck, stoppage, gridlock. **2** PREDICAMENT, plight, straits, trouble, quandary; informal fix, pickle, hole, spot, tight spot, scrape, spot of bother.

jar v. **1** GRATE, rasp, scratch, squeak, screech. **2** GRATE ON, irritate, disturb, upset, discompose, irk, annoy, nettle, flowers.

jasper n. a reddish-brown quartz.

jaundice n. **1** yellowing of the skin due to a bile disorder. **2** bitterness or resentment. ■ **jaundiced** adj.

jaunt n. a short trip for pleasure.

jaunty adj. lively and self-confident. ■ **jauntily** adv.

javelin n. a long spear thrown in a sport.

jaw n. **1** the upper and lower bony structures forming the framework of the mouth. **2** (**jaws**) the gripping parts of a tool. ▶ v. informal talk at length.

jay n. a bird of the crow family.

jaywalk v. cross a road without regard for the traffic. ■ **jaywalker** n.

jazz n. a type of music characterized by improvisation.

JCB n. trademark a mechanical excavator.

jealous adj. **1** envious of someone's success. **2** resentful of someone seen as a sexual rival. **3** very protective of one's possessions. ■ **jealousy** n.

jeans pl. n. denim trousers.

jeep n. trademark a sturdy four-wheel drive vehicle.

jeer v. make rude mocking remarks at. ▶ n. a rude mocking remark.

Jehovah n. the name of God in some translations of the Bible.

jejune adj. **1** simplistic. **2** dull.

jell (or **gel**) v. **1** (of jelly etc.) set. **2** take definite form.

jelly n. (pl. **jellies**) **1** a dessert made of a sweet, flavoured liquid set with gelatin. **2** a substance of a similar consistency. □ **jellyfish** a sea animal with a soft body.

jemmy n. (pl. **jemmies**) a short crowbar.

jenny n. (pl. **jennies**) a female donkey.

jeopardize (or **-ise**) v. endanger.

jeopardy n. danger.

jerk n. a sharp, sudden movement or pull. ▶ v. move or pull with a jerk. ■ **jerkily** adv. **jerky** adj.

jerkin n. a sleeveless jacket.

jerry-built adj. badly or hastily built.

jerrycan n. a large flat-sided can for liquids.

jersey n. (pl. **jerseys**) **1** a knitted garment with sleeves. **2** a soft knitted fabric.

jest n. a joke. ▶ v. speak in a joking way.

jester n. a clown at a medieval court.

Jesuit n. a member of a Roman Catholic order of priests.

jet n. **1** a stream of liquid or gas forced out of a small opening. **2** an aircraft powered by jet engines. **3** a hard black mineral. **4** a glossy black colour. ▶ v. (**jetting**, **jetted**) **1** spurt out in a jet. **2** travel by jet aircraft. □ **jet engine** an aircraft engine providing propulsion by ejecting a high-speed jet of gas from burning fuel. **jet lag** extreme tiredness felt after a long flight. **jet ski** trademark a small vehicle which skims across the surface of water.

jetsam n. unwanted material thrown

Thesaurus

vex. **3** CLASH, conflict, be in opposition, be at variance, be at odds.

jargon n. CANT, slang, argot, idiom, usage, vernacular, dialect, patois; informal lingo.

jaundiced adj. CYNICAL, pessimistic, sceptical, distrustful, suspicious, misanthropic, bitter, resentful, jealous, envious.

jaunt n. TRIP, outing, excursion, expedition, tour, holiday, break, airing, stroll, ramble.

jaunty adj. SPRIGHTLY, bouncy, buoyant, lively, breezy, perky, frisky, merry, blithe, carefree, joyful. See also HAPPY.

jazzy adj. FLASHY, fancy, stylish, smart, gaudy; informal flash, snazzy.

jealous adj. **1** ENVIOUS, begrudging, grudging, resentful, green with envy, green-eyed, covetous, desirous, emulous. **2** SUSPICIOUS, possessive, distrustful, mistrustful, doubting, insecure. **3** PROTECTIVE, vigilant, watchful, heedful, mindful, careful, solicitous, on guard, wary. ■ OPPOSITES trusting.

jeer v. MOCK, ridicule, deride, taunt, gibe, scorn, cry down, hector, barrack, boo, hiss, tease, scoff at, laugh at, sneer at; informal knock. ■ OPPOSITES cheer.

jeopardy n. RISK, danger, endangerment, peril, hazard, precariousness, insecurity, vulnerability, threat, menace. ■ OPPOSITES safety.

jerk v. **1** PULL, yank, tug, wrench, tweak, pluck. **2** JOLT, lurch, bump, jump, bounce, jounce. ▶ n. **1** PULL, yank, tug, wrench, tweak. **2** JOLT, lurch, bump, start, jar. **3** see IDIOT.

jerky adj. **1** SPASMODIC, fitful, convulsive, twitchy, shaking, shaky, tremulous, uncontrolled. **2** JOLTING, lurching, bumpy, bouncy, jouncing, rough; informal jumpy. ■ OPPOSITES smooth.

jester n. **1** COMIC, comedian, humorist, wag, wit. **2** FOOL, clown, buffoon, merry andrew, harlequin, pantaloon.

jet n. **1** STREAM, gush, spurt, spout, spray, rush, fountain, spring. **2** NOZZLE, spout, from a ship and washed ashore.

jettison v. throw or drop from an aircraft or ship.

jetty n. (pl. **jetties**) a landing stage or small pier.

Jew n. a person whose religion is Judaism and who is of ancient Hebrew descent. ■ **Jewish** adj.

jewel n. **1** a precious stone cut or set as an ornament. **2** a highly valued person or thing. ■ **jewelled** (US **jeweled**) adj.

jewellery (US **jewelry**) n. personal ornaments such as necklaces or rings. ■ **jeweller** n.

Jewry n. Jews as a group.

jib n. **1** a triangular sail in front of a mast. **2** the projecting arm of a crane. ▶v. (**jibbing**, **jibbed**) **1** (**jib at**) be unwilling to do or accept. **2** refuse to go on.

jibe (or **gibe**) n. **1** an insulting remark. **2** US = GYBE. ▶v. **1** make jibes. **2** US = GYBE.

jiffy n. informal a moment.

jig n. **1** a lively dance. **2** a device that holds something and guides the tools working on it. ▶v. (**jigging**, **jigged**) **1** dance a jig. **2** move quickly up and down.

jiggery-pokery n. informal dishonest behaviour.

jiggle v. rock or shake lightly.

jigsaw n. **1** a picture cut into interlocking pieces that have to be fitted together. **2** a machine saw with a fine blade.

jihad n. (among Muslims) a war or struggle against unbelievers.

jilt v. break off a relationship with a lover.

jingle n. **1** a light ringing sound. **2** a short memorable slogan etc. ▶v. make or cause to make a jingle.

jingoism n. excessive support for one's country. ■ **jingoistic** adj.

jinx n. a person or thing that brings bad luck. ■ **jinxed** adj.

jitters pl. n. informal nervousness. ■ **jittery** adj.

jive n. a lively dance to swing music. ▶v. dance the jive.

job n. **1** a paid position of employment. **2** a task. ▶v. (**jobbing**, **jobbed**) do casual work. ◻ **jobcentre** (in the UK) a government office giving out information about available jobs. **job lot** a batch of articles sold or bought at one time. ■ **jobless** adj.

jockey n. (pl. **jockeys**) a professional rider in horse races. ▶v. struggle to gain or achieve.

jockstrap n. a support or protection for a man's genitals.

jocose adj. humorous.

jocular adj. humorous. ■ **jocularity** n.

jocund adj. cheerful.

jodhpurs pl. n. trousers worn for horse riding that fit closely below the knee.

jog v. (**jogging**, **jogged**) **1** run at a steady, gentle pace. **2** continue in a steady, uneventful way. **3** knock slightly. **4** trigger one's memory. ▶n. **1** a period of jogging. **2** a slight knock. ■ **jogger** n.

Thesaurus

nose, sprinkler, sprinkler head, spray, rose, atomizer. ▶v. SHOOT, gush, spurt, spout, well, rush, spray, squirt, spew, stream, surge, flow, issue.

jetty n. PIER, wharf, quay, harbour, dock, breakwater, mole, groyne.

jewel n. GEM, gemstone, precious stone, stone, brilliant; informal sparkler, rock.

jib v. BALK AT, recoil from, shrink from, stop short of, refuse.

jibe v. TAUNT, sneer, jeer, mocking, sneering, scoffing, scorn, derision, ridicule, teasing, sarcasm; informal dig.

jilt v. REJECT, cast aside, discard, throw over, leave, forsake; informal ditch, dump, give the brush-off, give the heave-ho, give the elbow.

jingle v. **1** CLINK, chink, jangle, rattle, clank. **2** TINKLE, ding, go ding-dong, go ting-a-ling, ring, chime. ▶n. DITTY, chorus, refrain, short song, limerick, piece of doggerel, carol, melody, tune, catchy tune.

job n. **1** WORK, piece of work, task, undertaking, chore, assignment, venture, enterprise, activity, business, affair. **2** OCCUPATION, profession, trade, employment, vocation, calling, career, field of work, means of livelihood, métier, pursuit, position, post, situation, appointment. **3** DUTY, task, chore, errand, responsibility, concern, role, charge, office, commission, capacity, contribution.

jobless adj. UNEMPLOYED, without employment, out of work, without work, workless, idle, inactive, unoccupied. ■ OPPOSITES employed.

jocular adj. HUMOROUS, funny, witty, comic, comical, facetious, joking, jesting, playful, roguish, waggish, whimsical, droll, jocose, teasing, tongue-in-cheek, sportive, amusing, entertaining, diverting, hilarious, farcical, laughable.

joggle v. shake slightly.

join v. **1** link or become linked to. **2** unite to form a whole. **3** become a member or employee of. **4** (**join up**) enlist in the armed forces. **5** come into the company of. ▶n. a place where things join.

joiner n. a person who makes the wooden parts of a building. ■ **joinery** n.

joint n. **1** a join. **2** a structure in the body joining two bones. **3** a large piece of meat. **4** informal a place of a specified kind. **5** informal a cannabis cigarette. ▶adj. shared, held, or made by two or more people. ▶v. **1** connect with a joint. **2** cut into joints. □ **out of joint** **1** dislocated. **2** in disorder. ■ **jointly** adv.

joist n. a beam supporting part of the structure of a building.

jojoba /hoh-hoh-buh/ n. an oil extracted from the seeds of a shrub, used in cosmetics.

joke n. **1** something said or done to cause laughter. **2** informal a ridiculously inadequate person or thing. ▶v. make jokes. ■ **jokey** adj.

joker n. **1** a person who jokes. **2** a playing card used as a wild card.

jollification n. merrymaking.

jollity n. **1** lively and cheerful activity. **2** the quality of being jolly.

jolly adj. (**jollier**, **jolliest**) **1** happy and cheerful. **2** lively and entertaining. ▶v. (**jollying**, **jollied**) informal encourage in a friendly way. ▶adv. informal very.

jolt v. **1** push or shake abruptly and roughly. **2** shock into taking action. ▶n. **1** an act of jolting. **2** a shock.

josh v. informal tease playfully.

joss stick n. a thin stick of incense.

jostle v. push roughly.

jot v. (**jotting**, **jotted**) write quickly. ▶n. a very small amount.

jotter n. a small notebook.

joule n. a unit of energy.

journal n. **1** a newspaper or magazine. **2** a diary.

journalese n. informal a clichéd style of writing.

journalist n. a person who writes for a newspaper etc. or prepares features to be broadcast. ■ **journalism** n.

journey n. (pl. **journeys**) an act of trav-

Thesaurus

■ OPPOSITES serious.

jog v. **1** GO JOGGING, run slowly, dogtrot, trot, canter, lope. **2** NUDGE, prod, poke, push, elbow, tap. **3** STIMULATE, activate, stir, arouse, prompt.

join v. **1** FASTEN, attach, tie, bind, couple, connect, unite, link, splice, yoke, knit, glue, cement, fuse, weld, solder. **2** JOIN FORCES WITH, team up with, band together with, cooperate with, collaborate with, affiliate with. **3** ENLIST, sign up, enrol, become a member of, enlist in, sign up for, enrol in. **4** ADJOIN, conjoin, abut on, border, border on, touch, meet, verge on, reach to, extend to. ■ OPPOSITES detach, leave.

joint n. JOIN, junction, juncture, intersection, nexus, knot, seam, coupling. ▶adj. COMMON, shared, joined, mutual, combined, collective, cooperative, allied, united, concerted, consolidated. ■ OPPOSITES separate.

jointly adv. TOGETHER, in combination, in conjunction, as one, mutually, in partnership, cooperatively, in cooperation, in league, in collusion; informal in cahoots.

joke n. **1** JEST, witticism, quip, yarn, pun, sally; informal wisecrack, crack, gag, funny. **2** PRACTICAL JOKE, prank, trick, hoax, jape; informal leg-pull, lark. **3** LAUGHING STOCK, butt, figure of fun, target, fair

game, Aunt Sally. ▶v. **1** TELL JOKES, crack jokes, jest, banter, quip, wisecrack. **2** FOOL, fool around, tease, pull someone's leg; informal kid, have someone on.

jolly adj. MERRY, joyful, joyous, jovial, happy, glad, mirthful, gleeful, cheerful, cheery, carefree, buoyant, lively, bright, light-hearted, jocund, sprightly, elated, exuberant, exhilarated, jubilant, high-spirited, sportive, playful; informal chirpy; dated gay; literary blithe. ■ OPPOSITES miserable.

jolt v. **1** BUMP AGAINST, knock against, bump into, bang into, collide with, jostle, push, shove, elbow, nudge, jar. **2** BUMP, bounce, jounce, start, jerk, lurch, jar. **3** UPSET, disturb, perturb, shake, shake up, shock, stun, disconcert, discompose, disquiet, startle, surprise, astonish, amaze, stagger.

jostle v. **1** BUMP AGAINST, knock against, bump into, bang into, collide with, jolt, push, shove, elbow. **2** PUSH, thrust, shove, press, squeeze, elbow, force.

jot n. IOTA, whit, bit, scrap, fraction, atom, grain, particle, morsel, mite, speck, trace, trifle, tinge; informal smidgen, tad.

journal n. **1** DIARY, daybook, notebook, commonplace book, log, logbook, chronicle, record, register. **2** PERIODICAL, magazine, trade magazine, review, pub-

elling from one place to another. ▶v.
travel.

journeyman n. a skilled worker employed by another.

joust v. (of medieval knights) fight on horseback with lances.

jovial adj. cheerful and friendly. ■ **joviality** n. **jovially** adv.

jowl n. the lower part of the cheek.

joy n. 1 great happiness. 2 a cause of joy. ■ **joyful** adj. **joyfully** adv. **joyless** adj.

joyous adj. very happy. ■ **joyously** adv.

joyride n. informal a fast ride in a stolen vehicle. ■ **joyrider** n. **joyriding** n.

joystick n. 1 the control column of an aircraft. 2 a lever controlling the movement of an image on a screen.

JP abbrev. Justice of the Peace.

jubilant adj. happy and triumphant. ■ **jubilation** n.

jubilee n. a special anniversary.

Judaism n. the religion of the Jews.

■ **Judaic** adj.

judder v. shake noisily or violently. ▶n. an act of juddering.

judge n. 1 a public officer who decides cases in a law court. 2 a person who decides who has won a competition. 3 a person able to give an opinion. ▶v. 1 form an opinion about. 2 decide a case in a law court. 3 decide the winner of.

judgement (or **judgment**) n. 1 the ability to make sound decisions. 2 a judge's decision.

judgemental (or **judgmental**) adj. 1 of judgement. 2 excessively critical.

judicial adj. of a law court or judge. ■ **judicially** adv.

judiciary n. (pl. **judiciaries**) judges as a group.

judicious adj. having or done with good judgement. ■ **judiciously** adv.

judo n. a sport of unarmed combat.

Thesaurus

lication. 3 NEWSPAPER, paper, daily newspaper, daily, weekly newspaper, weekly, gazette.

journalist n. REPORTER, newspaperman/woman, newsman/woman, news hound, pressman/woman, feature writer, columnist, correspondent, contributor, commentator, reviewer, editor, sub-editor; informal stringer, sub.

journey n. TRIP, expedition, excursion, travels, tour, trek, voyage, cruise, safari, peregrination, roaming, roving, globetrotting, odyssey, pilgrimage, outing, jaunt. ▶v. see TRAVEL.

jovial adj. JOLLY, jocular, jocose, jocund, happy, cheerful, cheery, glad, in good spirits, merry, mirthful, buoyant, animated, convivial, sociable, cordial; informal chirpy; dated gay; literary blithe. ■ OPPOSITES miserable.

joy n. 1 DELIGHT, pleasure, gladness, enjoyment, gratification, happiness, rapture, glee, ecstasy, elation, rejoicing, exultation, jubilation, euphoria, ravishment, transport, felicity. 2 SOURCE OF JOY, treasure, prize, gem, jewel, pride and joy, delight. 3 SUCCESS, satisfaction, good fortune, luck, achievement. ■ OPPOSITES misery.

joyful adj. 1 OVERJOYED, elated, beside oneself, thrilled, delighted, pleased, gratified, happy, glad, gleeful, jubilant, ecstatic, exultant, euphoric, enraptured; informal over the moon, in seventh heaven, on cloud nine, tickled pink; literary blithe. 2 GLAD, happy, good, pleasing, cheering, gratifying, heart-warming.

3 JOYOUS, happy, cheerful, merry, festive, celebratory; dated gay. ■ OPPOSITES unhappy.

judge v. 1 ADJUDICATE, adjudge, umpire, referee, arbitrate, mediate. 2 ASSESS, appraise, evaluate, weigh up, size up, gauge, examine, review, criticize, diagnose. 3 ESTIMATE, assess, reckon, guess, surmise; informal guesstimate. 4 CONSIDER, believe, think, form the opinion, deduce, gather, conclude. ▶n. 1 MAGISTRATE, sheriff, His/Her/Your Honour, m'lud; informal beak. 2 APPRAISER, assessor, evaluator, critic, expert. 3 ADJUDICATOR, umpire, referee, arbiter, arbitrator, mediator.

judgement n. 1 DISCERNMENT, acumen, shrewdness, common sense, good sense, sense, perception, perspicacity, percipience, penetration, discrimination, wisdom, judiciousness, prudence, sagacity, understanding, intelligence, powers of reasoning. 2 VERDICT, decision, adjudication, ruling, finding, opinion, conclusion, decree, sentence. 3 OPINION, view, belief, conviction, estimation, evaluation, assessment, appraisal.

judicial adj. 1 JUDICIARY, juridical, judicatory, legal. 2 JUDGELIKE, impartial, unbiased, critical, analytical, discriminating, discerning, perceptive.

judicious adj. WISE, prudent, politic, sagacious, shrewd, astute, sensible, common-sense, sound, well advised, well considered, well judged, considered, thoughtful, expedient, practical, discerning, discriminating, in-

jug n. a container with a handle and a lip, for holding and pouring liquids.

juggernaut n. a large heavy vehicle.

juggle v. 1 continuously toss and catch several objects, keeping one or more in the air at any time. 2 do several things at the same time. ■ **juggler** n.

jugular n. any of several large veins in the neck.

juice n. 1 the liquid in fruit, vegetables, or meat. 2 (**juices**) fluid produced by the stomach. ▶ v. extract the juice from.

juicy adj. (**juicier**, **juiciest**) 1 full of juice. 2 informal exciting or scandalous.

ju-jitsu n. a Japanese sport of unarmed combat.

jukebox n. a coin-operated machine playing musical recordings.

julep n. a sweet drink made from sugar syrup.

julienne n. a portion of vegetables cut into thin strips.

July n. the seventh month.

jumble n. 1 an untidy collection. 2 items for a jumble sale. ▶ v. mix up in a confused way. □ **jumble sale** a sale of second-hand goods.

jumbo n. (pl. **jumbos**) informal 1 a very large person or thing. 2 (also **jumbo jet**) a very large airliner.

jump v. 1 push oneself off the ground with one's legs and feet. 2 cross by jumping. 3 make a sudden involuntary movement from surprise. 4 (**jump at**) accept eagerly. 5 pass abruptly from one subject or state to another. ▶ n. 1 an act of jumping. 2 a large or sudden increase. 3 an obstacle to be jumped. □ **jump leads** a pair of cables for recharging a battery in a vehicle by connecting it to the battery in another. **jumpsuit** a one-piece garment of trousers and a top. **jump the queue** move ahead of one's proper place in a queue.

jumper n. 1 a pullover. 2 a person or animal that jumps.

jumpy adj. (**jumpier**, **jumpiest**) informal anxious and uneasy.

junction n. 1 a point where things meet or join. 2 a place where roads or railway lines meet.

juncture n. 1 a particular point in time. 2 a join.

June n. the sixth month.

jungle n. 1 an area of thick tropical forest and tangled vegetation. 2 a bewildering or competitive situation.

junior adj. 1 of or for younger people. 2 of or for schoolchildren aged 7–11. 3 younger. 4 low or lower in status. ▶ n. a junior person.

juniper n. an evergreen shrub.

junk n. 1 informal useless or worthless articles. 2 a flat-bottomed sailing boat

Thesaurus

formed, intelligent, clever, enlightened, logical, rational, discreet, careful, cautious, circumspect, diplomatic; informal smart. ■ OPPOSITES foolish, ill-advised.

jug n. PITCHER, carafe, decanter, jar, urn, crock, vessel, receptacle, container.

juggle v. CHANGE AROUND, alter, tamper with, falsify, fake, manipulate, manoeuvre, rig, massage; informal fix, doctor, cook.

juice n. EXTRACT, sap, secretion, liquid, liquor, fluid, serum.

juicy adj. 1 SUCCULENT, moist, lush, sappy, watery, wet, flowing. 2 RACY, risqué, spicy, sensational, thrilling, fascinating, colourful, exciting, vivid. ■ OPPOSITES dry, dull.

jumble v. DISORGANIZE, muddle, confuse, disarrange, disorder, dishevel, tangle, shuffle, mix, mix up, mingle, put in disarray, make a shambles of, throw into chaos. ▶ n. CLUTTER, muddle, confusion, litter, mess, hodgepodge, hotchpotch, mishmash, confused heap, miscellany, motley collection, mixture, medley, gallimaufry, farrago.

jump v. 1 SPRING, leap, bound, hop, bounce, skip, caper, gambol, frolic, frisk, cavort. 2 LEAP OVER, vault, pole-vault, hurdle, clear, go over, sail over. 3 START, flinch, jerk, recoil, twitch, quiver, shake, wince; informal jump out of one's skin. 4 SET UPON, mug, pounce on, fall on, swoop down on, attack, assault. ▶ n. 1 SPRING, leap, vault, bound, hop, bounce, skip. 2 HURDLE, fence, rail, hedge, obstacle, barrier, gate. 3 GAP, break, hiatus, interruption, space, lacuna, breach, interval. 4 START, flinch, jerk, twitch, quiver, shake, wince.

jumpy adj. NERVOUS, nervy, edgy, on edge, agitated, fidgety, anxious, uneasy, restive, tense, alarmed, apprehensive, panicky; informal jittery. ■ OPPOSITES calm.

junction n. 1 JOIN, joint, juncture, link, bond, connection, seam, joining, coupling, linking, welding, union. 2 CROSSROADS, crossing, intersection, interchange.

juncture n. POINT, point in time, time, stage, period, critical point, crucial moment, moment of truth, turning point, used in China. □ **junk food** unhealthy food. **junk mail** unwanted advertising material sent by post.

junket n. **1** a dish of sweetened curds of milk. **2** informal an extravagant trip or party.

junkie n. informal a drug addict.

junta n. a group ruling a country after taking power by force.

jurisdiction n. **1** the official power to make legal decisions. **2** the extent of this.

jurisprudence n. the theory of law.

jurist n. an expert in law.

juror n. a member of a jury.

jury n. (pl. **juries**) a group of people required to attend a legal case and give a verdict on the basis of the evidence presented.

just adj. **1** right and fair. **2** deserved. ▶ adv. **1** exactly. **2** exactly or nearly at that moment. **3** very recently. **4** barely.

5 only. ■ **justly** adv.

justice n. **1** just behaviour or treatment. **2** the administration of law. **3** a judge or magistrate. □ **Justice of the Peace** a non-professional magistrate.

justifiable adj. able to be shown to be right or reasonable. ■ **justifiably** adv.

justify v. (**justifying, justified**) **1** show to be right or reasonable. **2** be a good reason for. **3** adjust lines of type to form straight edges at both sides. ■ **justification** n.

jut v. (**jutting, jutted**) protrude.

jute n. rough fibre from the stems of a tropical plant, used for ropes etc.

juvenile adj. **1** of young people or animals. **2** childish. ▶ n. a young person or animal. □ **juvenile deliquent** a young person who regularly commits criminal acts.

juxtapose v. place close together. ■ **juxtaposition** n.

Thesaurus

crisis, crux, extremity.

junior adj. YOUNGER, subordinate, lesser, lower, minor, secondary, inferior. ■ OPPOSITES senior, older.

junk n. RUBBISH, refuse, litter, scrap, waste, garbage, trash, debris, leavings, leftovers, remnants, cast-offs, rejects, odds and ends, bric-a-brac, oddments. ▶ v. THROW OUT, throw away, discard, get rid of, dispose of, scrap; informal dump.

just adj. **1** FAIR, fair-minded, equitable, even-handed, impartial, unbiased, objective, neutral, disinterested, unprejudiced, open-minded. **2** VALID, sound, well founded, well grounded, justified, justifiable, warrantable, defensible, reasonable. ■ OPPOSITES unjust, undeserved.

justice n. **1** JUSTNESS, fairness, fair play, fair-mindedness, equitableness, equity, even-handedness, impartiality, lack of bias, objectivity, neutrality, disinterestedness, lack of prejudice, open-mindedness. **2** VALIDITY, justification, soundness, reasonableness. **3** AMENDS,

recompense, redress, compensation, reparation, requital, retribution, penalty, punishment. **4** JUDGE, magistrate, informal beak.

justifiable adj. VALID, sound, well founded, lawful, legitimate, legal, tenable, right, defensible, supportable, sustainable, warrantable, reasonable, within reason, sensible, acceptable, plausible, vindicable.

justify v. **1** GIVE GROUNDS FOR, give reasons for, show just cause for, explain, account for, give an explanation for, rationalize, defend, stand up for, uphold. **2** WARRANT, substantiate, bear out, show to be reasonable, prove to be right, confirm.

jut v. STICK OUT, project, protrude, poke out, bulge out, overhang, beetle.

juvenile adj. **1** YOUNG, junior, minor. **2** CHILDISH, puerile, infantile, immature, inexperienced, callow, green, unsophisticated, naive; informal wet behind the ears.

Kk

K abbrev. **1** kelvins. **2** kilobytes. **3** informal thousand.

kaftan (or **caftan**) n. a long, loose tunic or robe.

kaiser n. hist. the German or Austrian Emperor.

Kalashnikov n. a type of rifle or sub-machine gun.

kale n. a type of cabbage.

kaleidoscope /kuh-**ly**-duh-skohp/ n. a tube containing coloured fragments whose reflections produce changing patterns when the tube is turned. ■ **kaleidoscopic** adj.

kamikaze /ka-mi-**kah**-zi/ n. (in the Second World War) a Japanese aircraft loaded with explosives and deliberately crashed on its target. ▶ adj. reckless or suicidal.

kangaroo n. a large Australian marsupial with strong hind legs for leaping. □ **kangaroo court** a court set up unofficially to try someone seen as guilty.

kaolin n. a fine white clay, used for making china and in medicine.

kapok n. a fluffy fibre used as padding.

kaput /kuh-**puut**/ adj. informal broken.

karaoke /ka-ri-**oh**-ki/ n. an entertainment in which people sing popular songs to pre-recorded backing tracks.

karate /kuh-**rah**-ti/ n. an oriental system of unarmed combat using the hands and feet to deliver and block blows.

karma n. (in Hinduism and Buddhism) the sum of a person's actions seen as affecting their future lives.

kayak /**ky**-ak/ n. a light covered canoe.

kebab n. pieces of meat etc. cooked on a skewer.

kedge n. a small anchor.

kedgeree n. a dish of smoked fish, rice, and hard-boiled eggs.

keel n. a structure running along the base of a ship. ▶ v. (**keel over**) **1** capsize. **2** fall over.

keen adj. **1** eager and enthusiastic. **2** sharp. **3** quick to understand. **4** highly developed. ■ **keenly** adv. **keenness** n.

keep v. (**keeping**, **kept**) **1** have or stay in possession of. **2** retain for use in the future. **3** store in a regular place. **4** continue in a specified condition, position, or activity. **5** fulfil a promise. **6** cause to be late. **7** provide food etc. for. ▶ n. **1** food and other essentials for living. **2** the strongest or central tower of a castle. □ **keep on** continue. **keepsake** a small item kept in memory of the person who gave it. **keep up 1** move at the same rate as another. **2** continue.

keeper n. **1** a person who manages or looks after something or someone. **2** a goalkeeper or wicketkeeper.

keeping n. care or custody. □ **in** (or **out**

Thesaurus

keen adj. **1** EAGER, enthusiastic, willing, avid, earnest, intent, diligent, assiduous, conscientious, zealous, fervent, fervid, impatient, yearning; informal raring to, itching to. **2** FOND OF, devoted to, eager for, hungry for, thirsty for. **3** ACUTE, sharp, discerning, perceptive, sensitive, discriminating. **4** ASTUTE, sharp, quick-witted, sharp-witted, shrewd, perceptive, penetrating, perspicacious, clever, bright, intelligent, brilliant, wise, canny, sagacious; informal brainy, smart; formal sapient. ■ OPPOSITES apathetic, stupid.

keep v. **1** CARRY ON, continue, maintain, persist, persevere. **2** HOLD ON TO, keep hold of, retain; informal hang on to. **3** SAVE UP, accumulate, store, hoard, amass, pile up, collect, garner. **4** LOOK AFTER, keep in good order, tend, mind, maintain, keep up, manage, superintend. **5** PROVIDE FOR, support, maintain, sustain, subsidize, feed, nurture. **6** KEEP TO, abide by, comply with, fulfil, carry out, keep faith with, stand by, stick to, make good, honour, obey, observe; formal effectuate. **7** OBSERVE, hold, celebrate, commemorate, respect, ritualize, solemnize. **8** KEEP BACK, hold back, hold up, delay, detain, retard, hinder, obstruct, impede, hamper, constrain, check, block. □ **keep at** PERSIST, persevere, be persistent, be pertinacious, carry on, keep going, continue, work away, see it through; informal stick at it, stay the distance, hang on in there. **2** KEEP ON AT, of) **keeping** in (or out of) harmony.

keg n. a small barrel.

kelp n. a type of seaweed.

kelvin n. a unit of temperature.

kennel n. **1** a shelter for a dog. **2** (**kennels**) a boarding or breeding establishment for dogs.

kept past & past part. of KEEP.

keratin n. a protein forming the basis of hair, nails, and horns.

kerb n. a stone edging to a pavement.

kerchief n. a piece of fabric worn over the head.

kerfuffle n. informal a commotion or fuss.

kernel n. **1** the softer part inside the shell of a nut, seed, or fruit stone. **2** the seed and husk of a cereal. **3** the central part of something.

kerosene n. a light fuel oil distilled from petroleum.

kestrel n. a small falcon.

ketch n. a two-masted sailing boat.

ketchup n. a thick tomato sauce.

kettle n. a container with a lid, spout, and handle, for boiling water. □ **kettledrum** a large bowl-shaped drum with adjustable pitch.

key n. **1** a piece of shaped metal for opening or closing a lock or turning a screw, peg, etc. **2** a lever pressed down by the finger on a piano etc. **3** a button on a panel for operating a typewriter or computer. **4** a thing providing access or understanding. **5** an explanatory list of the symbols in a map etc. **6** a group of related notes forming a musical scale. ▶adj. of central importance. ▶v. **1** enter data using a computer keyboard. **2** (**be keyed up**) be tense or excited. □ **keynote 1** a central theme. **2** the note on which a musical key is based. **keypad** a set of buttons for operating an electronic device or telephone. **key ring** a metal ring for holding keys together in a bunch. **keystone 1** the central stone at the top of an arch, locking the whole together. **2** the central part of a policy or system. **keyword 1** a significant

word mentioned in an index. **2** a word used in a computer system to indicate a document's content.

keyboard n. **1** a set of keys on a computer, typewriter, or piano etc. **2** an electronic musical instrument with keys arranged as on a piano. ▶v. key data. ■ **keyboarder** n.

keyhole n. a hole for a key in a lock. □ **keyhole surgery** surgery carried out through a very small incision.

kg abbrev. kilograms.

KGB abbrev. the secret police of the former Soviet Union.

khaki n. a dull brownish-yellow colour.

khan n. a title given to rulers and officials in central Asia.

kHz abbrev. kilohertz.

kibbutz n. (pl. **kibbutzim**) a communal farming settlement in Israel.

kick v. **1** strike or propel forcibly with the foot. **2** informal give up a habit. **3** (of a gun) spring back when fired. **4** (**kick in**) come into effect. ▶n. **1** an act of kicking. **2** informal the strong effect of alcohol. **3** informal a thrill. □ **kick-off** the start of a football match. **kick-start 1** start a motorcycle engine with a downward thrust of a pedal. **2** stimulate.

kid n. **1** informal a child or young person. **2** a young goat. ▶adj. made of leather from a kid's skin. ▶v. (**kidding, kidded**) informal fool into believing something.

kidnap v. (**kidnapping, kidnapped**; US **kidnaping, kidnaped**) take by force and hold captive for a ransom. ▶n. an act of kidnapping. ■ **kidnapper** n.

kidney n. (pl. **kidneys**) each of a pair of organs that remove waste products from the blood and produce urine.

kill v. **1** cause the death of. **2** put an end to. **3** pass time. ▶n. **1** an act of killing. **2** an animal or animals killed by a hunter. □ **killjoy** a person who spoils the enjoyment of others. ■ **killer** n.

kiln n. an oven for hardening or drying

Thesaurus

keep after, go on at, chivvy, badger, harp on at, nag, harass. **keep back** WITHHOLD, keep secret, keep hidden, hide, conceal, suppress.

keeper n. **1** JAILER, warder, warden, guard, custodian, sentry; informal screw. **2** CURATOR, conservator, attendant, caretaker, steward, superintendent, overseer, administrator.

keepsake n. MEMENTO, souvenir, remembrance, reminder, token of remem-

brance, relic, favour.

kernel n. **1** SEED, nut, grain, germ. **2** NUB, nucleus, core, centre, heart, marrow, pith, substance, essence, essential part, gist, quintessence; informal nitty-gritty, nuts and bolts.

key n. **1** ANSWER, solution, explanation, guide, clue, cue, pointer, interpretation, explication, clarification, exposition. **2** TONE, pitch, timbre, tonality.

kick v. **1** BOOT, punt. **2** RECOIL, spring

pottery etc.

kilo n. (pl. **kilos**) a kilogram.

kilobyte n. Computing 1,024 bytes.

kilocalorie n. 1,000 calories.

kilogram n. 1,000 grams.

kilohertz n. 1,000 hertz.

kilojoule n. 1,000 joules.

kilometre (US **kilometer**) n. 1,000 metres.

kilovolt n. 1,000 volts.

kilowatt n. 1,000 watts.

kilt n. a knee-length skirt of pleated tartan cloth, traditionally worn by men as part of Scottish Highland dress.

kimono n. (pl. **kimonos**) a loose Japanese robe worn with a sash.

kin (or **kinsfolk**) pl. n. one's relations. □ **kinship** blood relationship. ■ **kinsman** n. **kinswoman** n.

kind n. a class of similar people or things. ▶ adj. considerate and generous. □ **in kind 1** in the same way. **2** (of payment) in goods etc. instead of money. **kind-hearted** kind. ■ **kindness** n.

kindergarten n. a nursery school.

kindle v. **1** light a flame. **2** arouse an emotion.

kindling n. small sticks used for lighting fires.

kindly adv. **1** in a kind way. **2** please (used in a polite request). ▶ adj. kind. ■ **kindliness** n.

kindred pl. n. one's relatives. ▶ adj. similar in kind.

kinetic adj. of or resulting from motion. ■ **kinetically** adv.

king n. **1** the male ruler of a country. **2** the best or most important person or thing. **3** a playing card ranking next below an ace. **4** the most important chess piece. □ **kingfisher** a colourful diving bird. **kingpin** an indispensable person or thing. **king-size** (or **king-sized**) extra large.

kingdom n. **1** a country ruled by a king or queen. **2** each of the three divisions in which natural objects are classified.

kink n. **1** a sharp twist in something straight. **2** a flaw. **3** a peculiar characteristic. ▶ v. form a kink.

kinky adj. (**kinkier**, **kinkiest**) **1** having kinks or twists. **2** informal having to do with unusual sexual behaviour.

kiosk /kee-ossk/ n. a booth from which

Thesaurus

back. **3** GIVE UP, stop, abandon, leave off, desist from; informal quit.

kill v. **1** TAKE SOMEONE'S LIFE, murder, do away with, do to death, slaughter, butcher, massacre, assassinate, liquidate, wipe out, destroy, erase, eradicate, exterminate, dispatch, put to death, execute; informal bump off, do in, knock off, top; literary slay. **2** DESTROY, put an end to, ruin, extinguish, scotch, quell. **3** EXHAUST, overtire, tire out, fatigue, wear out, debilitate, enervate, prostrate, tax, overtax, strain; informal fag out. **4** HURT, cause pain, cause discomfort, be uncomfortable, be painful.

killer n. MURDERER, slaughterer, butcher, assassin, liquidator, destroyer, exterminator, executioner, gunman; informal hit man; literary slayer.

killing n. **1** MURDER, manslaughter, homicide, slaughter, butchery, massacre, bloodshed, carnage, liquidation, destruction, extermination, execution. **2** FINANCIAL SUCCESS, bonanza, fortune, windfall, gain, profit, booty, coup; informal bomb, clean-up.

killjoy n. SPOILSPORT, dampener, damper; informal wet blanket, party-pooper.

kin n. RELATIVES, relations, family, connections, folks, people, kindred, kith and kin, kinsfolk, kinsmen, kinswomen.

kind[1] n. **1** SORT, type, variety, brand, class, category, genus, species. **2** NATURE, character, manner, aspect, disposition, humour, style, stamp, mould.

kind[2] adj. KIND-HEARTED, kindly, generous, charitable, giving, benevolent, magnanimous, big-hearted, warm-hearted, altruistic, philanthropic, humanitarian, humane, tender-hearted, soft-hearted, gentle, mild, lenient, merciful, clement, pitying, forbearing, patient, tolerant, sympathetic, compassionate, understanding, considerate, helpful, thoughtful, good, nice, pleasant, benign, friendly, genial, congenial, amiable, amicable, cordial, courteous, gracious, good-natured, warm, affectionate, loving, indulgent, obliging, accommodating, neighbourly; informal decent; literary bounteous. ■ OPPOSITES unkind, nasty.

kindle v. **1** LIGHT, set alight, set on fire, set fire to, ignite, start, torch. **2** STIMULATE, rouse, arouse, excite, stir, awaken, inspire, inflame, incite, induce, provoke, actuate, activate, touch off. ■ OPPOSITES extinguish.

kindred adj. **1** RELATED, connected, of the same blood, of the same family, consanguineous, cognate. **2** LIKE, similar, resembling, corresponding, matching, congenial, allied.

kink n. **1** TWIST, bend, coil, corkscrew, curl, twirl, knot, tangle, entanglement.

newspapers, tickets, etc. are sold, or containing a public telephone.

kip n. informal a sleep.

kipper n. a smoked herring.

kirk n. Sc. a church.

kismet n. fate.

kiss v. touch with the lips. ▶ n. a touch with the lips. □ **kiss of life** mouth-to-mouth resuscitation. **kissogram** a novelty greetings message delivered with a kiss.

kit n. a set of equipment or clothes for a specific purpose. ▶ v. (**kitting, kitted**) (**kit out**) provide with appropriate clothing or equipment.

kitchen n. a room where food is prepared and cooked. □ **kitchenette** n. a small kitchen. **kitchen garden** a garden for vegetables, fruit, and herbs.

kite n. **1** a light frame with fabric stretched over it, flown in the wind at the end of a long string. **2** a bird of prey. □ **Kitemark** trademark an official mark on goods approved by the British Standards Institution.

kith n. (**kith and kin**) one's relations.

kitsch n. art, objects, or design regarded as tastelessly bright or too sentimental.

kitten n. **1** a young cat. **2** the young of certain other animals, e.g. the rabbit.

kitty n. (pl. **kitties**) a fund of money for use by a number of people.

kiwi n. (pl. **kiwis**) a flightless New Zealand bird. □ **kiwi fruit** a fruit with hairy skin and green flesh.

kJ abbrev. kilojoules.

klaxon n. trademark a vehicle horn or a hooter.

kleptomania n. a recurring urge to steal. ■ **kleptomaniac** n. & adj.

km abbrev. kilometres.

knack n. a skill at performing a task.

knacker n. a person who disposes of dead or unwanted animals. ▶ v. informal wear out.

knapsack n. a small rucksack.

knave n. **1** old use a dishonest man. **2** (in cards) a jack.

knead v. **1** work dough or clay with the hands. **2** massage as if kneading.

knee n. **1** the joint between the thigh and the lower leg. **2** the upper surface of a sitting person's thigh. ▶ v. (**kneeing, kneed**) hit with the knee. □ **kneecap 1** the bone in front of the knee joint. **2** shoot in the knee as a punishment. **knee-jerk** automatic and unthinking. **knees-up** informal a lively party.

kneel v. (**kneeling, knelt** or US **kneeled**) fall or rest on the knees.

knell n. the sound of a bell rung solemnly for a death or funeral.

knew past of KNOW.

knickerbockers pl. n. loose-fitting trousers or knickers gathered at the knee or calf.

knickers pl. n. women's or girls' underpants.

knick-knack n. a cheap ornament.

knife n. (pl. **knives**) a cutting instrument with a blade fixed in a handle. ▶ v. stab with a knife.

knight n. **1** (in the Middle Ages) a man of noble rank with a duty to fight for his king. **2** a man awarded a title and entitled to use 'Sir' in front of his name. **3** a chess piece shaped like a horse's head. ▶ v. give the title of knight to. ■ **knighthood** n.

knit v. (**knitting, knitted** or **knit**) **1** make a garment by looping yarn together with long blunt needles or a machine. **2** join together. **3** tighten one's eyebrows in a frown. ■ **knitter** n. **knitting** n.

Thesaurus

2 FLAW, defect, imperfection, hitch, snag, difficulty, complication.

kinky adj. **1** QUIRKY, peculiar, odd, strange, queer, bizarre, eccentric, idiosyncratic, weird, outlandish, unconventional, unorthodox, whimsical, capricious, fanciful. **2** PERVERTED, warped, deviant, unnatural, abnormal, depraved, degenerate, lascivious, licentious, lewd, sadistic, masochistic.

kit n. **1** EQUIPMENT, apparatus, set of tools, tools, implements, instruments, utensils, tackle, supplies, paraphernalia, accoutrements, effects, trappings, appurtenances; informal gear, stuff. **2** OUTFIT, clothing, dress, uniform, colours; informal

rig-out, gear, strip. □ **kit out** EQUIP, supply, provide, fit out, fix up, furnish, outfit, deck out, rig out, arm, accoutre.

knack n. TALENT, aptitude, gift, flair, bent, forte, ability, capability, capacity, expertise, expertness, skill, genius, facility, propensity, dexterity, ingenuity, proficiency, competence, handiness.

knead v. WORK, manipulate, press, squeeze, massage, rub, form, shape.

kneel v. GET DOWN ON ONE'S KNEES, fall to one's knees, genuflect, bow, bow down, stoop, make obeisance, kowtow.

knife n. BLADE, cutting tool. ▶ v. STAB, pierce, run through, impale, bayonet, transfix, cut, slash, lacerate, wound. *See*

knob n. **1** a rounded lump. **2** a ball-shaped handle or switch. ■ **knobbly** adj.

knock v. **1** strike a surface noisily to attract attention. **2** collide with. **3** cause to move or fall with a blow. **4** make a hole, dent, etc. with a blow. **5** informal criticize. ▶n. **1** a sudden short sound made by a blow. **2** a blow. **3** a setback. □ **knock-down** informal (of a price) very low. **knock-kneed** having legs that curve inwards at the knee. **knock off** informal **1** stop work. **2** produce a piece of work quickly. **knock-on effect** an effect or result affecting other things. **knockout 1** an act of knocking someone out. **2** a tournament in which the loser in each round is eliminated. **3** informal a very impressive person or thing. **knock out 1** make unconscious. **2** informal greatly impress. **3** eliminate from a competition.

knocker n. a hinged device for knocking on a door.

knoll n. a small hill.

knot n. **1** a fastening made by tying a piece of string, rope, etc. **2** a tangled mass in hair, wool, etc. **3** a hard mass in wood at the point where the trunk and a branch join. **4** a small group of people. **5** a unit of speed of ships, aircraft, or winds. ▶v. **(knotting, knotted) 1** fasten with a knot. **2** tangle.

knotty adj. **(knottier, knottiest) 1** full of knots. **2** very complex.

know v. **(knowing, knew**; past part. **known) 1** be aware of as a result of observing, asking, or being informed. **2** be certain. **3** be familiar with. **4** have a good command of a language etc. **5** **(known as)** called or referred to as. □ **be in the know** have secret information. **know-how** practical knowledge or skill.

knowing adj. suggesting that one has secret knowledge. ■ **knowingly** adv.

knowledge n. **1** information or awareness gained through experience or education. **2** the sum of what is known.

 Remember the *d*: knowle*d*ge.

knowledgeable (or **knowledgable**) adj. intelligent and well informed. ■ **knowledgeably** adv.

knuckle n. **1** a finger joint. **2** a joint of an animal's leg as meat. ▶v. **1** **(knuckle down)** apply oneself seriously to a task. **2** **(knuckle under)** submit. □ **knuckleduster** a metal device worn over the knuckles to increase the effect of blows.

koala n. a bear-like tree-dwelling Australian marsupial.

kohl n. a black powder used as eye make-up.

kookaburra n. a large, noisy, Australasian kingfisher.

k

Thesaurus

also WOUND.

knit v. **1** LOOP, weave, interweave, crochet. **2** LINK, bind, unite, draw together, ally.

knob n. **1** DOORKNOB, handle, door handle, switch, on/off switch. **2** BUMP, bulge, swelling, lump, knot, node, nodule, pustule, growth, tumour, protuberance, tumescence.

knock v. **1** TAP, rap, bang, pound, hammer. **2** STRIKE, hit, slap, smack, box, punch, cuff, buffet, thump, thwack, batter, pummel. **3** KNOCK INTO, bang into, bump into, collide with, run into, crash into, crash against, smash into, dash against, jolt. **4** CRITICIZE, find fault with, take apart, take to pieces, pick holes in, run down, carp at, cavil at, deprecate, belittle, disparage, censure, condemn.

knot n. LOOP, twist, bend, intertwinement, interlacement, ligature. ▶v. TIE, loop, bind, secure, tether, lash, leash.

know v. **1** BE AWARE OF, notice, perceive, realize, be conscious of, be cognizant of, sense, recognize; *informal* latch on to.

2 HAVE KNOWLEDGE OF, understand, comprehend, apprehend, be conversant with, be familiar with, be acquainted with. **3** BE FAMILIAR WITH, be acquainted with, experience, undergo, go through. **4** HAVE MET, be acquainted with, have dealings with, associate with, be friends with, socialize with, fraternize with, be intimate with, be close to, be on good terms with.

know-how n. KNOWLEDGE, expertise, skill, proficiency, mastery, technique, ability, capability, competence, dexterity, adeptness, adroitness.

knowing adj. **1** ASTUTE, shrewd, perceptive, meaningful, well informed, significant, eloquent, expressive. **2** AWARE, astute, shrewd, perceptive, sophisticated, worldly, worldly-wise. **3** CONSCIOUS, intentional, intended, deliberate, wilful, purposeful, calculated, on purpose, by design.

knowledge n. **1** LEARNING, erudition, scholarship, letters, education, enlightenment, wisdom. **2** UNDERSTANDING,

kopek (or **kopeck**) n. a unit of money of Russia and some other countries, equal to 100th of a rouble.

Koran n. the sacred book of Islam.

kosher /koh-sher/ adj. **1** (of food) prepared according to Jewish law. **2** informal genuine and legitimate.

kowtow v. be excessively meek and obedient.

kph abbrev. kilometres per hour.

Kremlin n. the Russian government.

krill pl. n. small shrimp-like crustaceans that are eaten by whales etc.

krona n. the basic unit of money of Swe-den (pl. **kronor**) or Iceland (pl. **kronur**).

krone n. (pl. **kroner**) the basic unit of money of Denmark and Norway.

krugerrand n. a South African gold coin.

krypton n. an inert, odourless, gaseous chemical element.

kt abbrev. knots.

kudos n. praise and honour.

kumquat n. a small orange-like fruit.

kung fu n. a Chinese martial art.

Kurd n. a member of a people of SW Asia. ■ **Kurdish** adj.

kV abbrev. kilovolts.

kW abbrev. kilowatts.

Thesaurus

grasp, comprehension, apprehension, cognition, adeptness, skill, expertise, proficiency; *informal* know-how. **3** AC-QUAINTANCESHIP, familiarity, conversance.

knowledgeable adj. **1** WELL INFORMED, informed, educated, learned, erudite, scholarly, well read, cultured, culti-vated, enlightened. **2** HAVING A KNOW-LEDGE OF, acquainted with, familiar with, experienced in, expert in, conversant with, having an understanding of. ■ OPPOSITES ill-informed.

known adj. RECOGNIZED, acknowledged, admitted, declared, proclaimed, avowed, confessed, published, revealed.

k

L (or **l**) n. the Roman numeral for 50. ▶abbrev. **1** Lake. **2** large. **3** learner driver. **4** (**l**) litres.

lab n. informal a laboratory.

label n. a piece of card, fabric, etc. attached to an object and giving information about it. ▶v. (**labelling, labelled;** US **labeling, labeled**) **1** attach a label to. **2** put in a category.

labia pl. n. the inner and outer folds of the vulva.

labial adj. of the lips or the labia.

laboratory n. (pl. **laboratories**) a room or building equipped for scientific work.

laborious adj. requiring or showing much effort. ■ **laboriously** adv.

labour (US **labor**) n. **1** work. **2** workers as a group. **3** (**Labour** or **the Labour Party**) a left-wing political party. **4** the process of childbirth. ▶v. **1** do hard physical work. **2** move or do with difficulty. **3** (**labour under**) be misled by a mistaken belief. □ **labour the point** explain something at excessive length.

labourer (US **laborer**) n. a person doing unskilled manual work.

Labrador n. a large breed of dog.

laburnum n. a tree with hanging clusters of yellow flowers.

labyrinth n. a complicated network of passages. ■ **labyrinthine** adj.

lace n. **1** a fine open fabric made by looping thread in patterns. **2** a cord used to fasten a shoe or garment. ▶v. **1** fasten with a lace or laces. **2** twist or tangle together. **3** add alcohol to a drink or dish.

lacerate v. tear the flesh or skin. ■ **laceration** n.

lachrymose /lak-ri-mohss/ adj. tearful.

lack n. the state of being without or not having enough of something. ▶v. be without or without enough of.

lackadaisical adj. lacking enthusiasm and thoroughness.

Thesaurus

label n. **1** IDENTIFICATION TAG, tag, ticket, tab, sticker, marker, docket. **2** EPITHET, name, nickname, title, sobriquet, designation, denomination, description, characterization. ▶v. **1** ATTACH LABELS TO, tag, tab, ticket, stamp, mark, put stickers on, docket. **2** DESCRIBE, designate, identify, classify, class, categorize, brand, call, name, term, dub.

laborious adj. **1** HARD, heavy, difficult, arduous, strenuous, fatiguing, tiring, wearying, wearisome, tedious. **2** PAINSTAKING, careful, meticulous, diligent, assiduous, industrious, hard-working, scrupulous, persevering, pertinacious, zealous. **3** LABOURED, strained, forced. ■ OPPOSITES easy, natural.

labour n. **1** WORK, employment, job, toil, exertion, effort, industry, industriousness, hard work, hard labour, drudgery, slog, donkey work, sweat of one's brow; literary travail. **2** TASK, job, chore, undertaking, commission, assignment, charge, venture. **3** EMPLOYEES, workers, workmen, workforce, working people, hands, labourers. **4** CHILDBIRTH, birth, parturition, delivery, contractions, labour pains; literary travail; dated confinement. ▶v. WORK HARD, work away, toil, slave away, drudge, grub away, plod on/away, grind/sweat away, struggle, exert oneself, work like a slave, work one's fingers to the bone, work like a Trojan; literary travail.

laboured adj. **1** DIFFICULT, strained, forced, heavy, awkward. **2** CONTRIVED, affected, studied, stiff, strained, stilted, forced, unnatural, artificial, overdone, overworked, heavy, ponderous, ornate, elaborate, over-elaborate, intricate, convoluted, complex, laborious.

labyrinth n. MAZE, warren, network, convolution, entanglement.

labyrinthine adj. **1** MAZE-LIKE, meandering, winding, wandering, twisting, circuitous, tangled. **2** INTRICATE, complex, complicated, involved, tortuous, convoluted, tangled, entangled, confusing, puzzling, perplexing, mystifying, bewildering.

lacerate v. CUT, tear, gash, slash, cut open, rip, rend, mangle, mutilate, hurt, wound, injure, maim.

lack n. ABSENCE, want, need, deprivation, deficiency, privation, dearth, insufficiency, shortage, scarcity, scarceness,

lackey n. (pl. **lackeys**) **1** a servant. **2** a servile or obsequious person.

lacklustre (US **lackluster**) adj. **1** lacking energy or inspiration. **2** (of the hair or eyes) not shining.

laconic adj. using few words. ■ **laconically** adv.

lacquer n. **1** a hard glossy varnish. **2** a substance sprayed on hair to keep it in place. ▶ v. coat with lacquer.

lacrosse n. a team game in which a ball is thrown, carried, and caught using sticks with a net at the end.

lactate v. (of a female mammal) produce milk. ■ **lactation** n.

lactic acid n. an acid present in sour milk and produced in the muscles during exercise.

lactose n. a sugar present in milk.

lacuna n. (pl. **lacunae** or **lacunas**) a gap or missing portion.

lacy adj. (**lacier**, **laciest**) of or like lace.

lad n. informal a boy or young man.

ladder n. **1** a set of bars or steps between two uprights, used for climbing up. **2** a series of stages by which progress can be made. **3** a strip of unravelled fabric in tights or stockings. ▶ v. make a ladder in tights or stockings.

laden adj. loaded.

ladle n. a long-handled spoon with a cup-shaped bowl. ▶ v. serve or transfer with a ladle.

lady n. (pl. **ladies**) **1** a woman. **2** a woman of a high social position. **3** (**Lady**) a title used by peeresses and the wives and widows of knights. **4** a well-mannered woman. □ **ladybird** a small flying beetle, usu. red with black spots. **lady-in-waiting** a woman who accompanies and looks after a queen or princess. **ladylike** well-mannered.

Your/Her Ladyship a respectful way of referring to or addressing a Lady.

lag v. (**lagging**, **lagged**) **1** fall behind. **2** cover a water tank etc. with insulating material. ▶ n. a period of time between two events.

lager n. a light fizzy beer.

laggard n. a person who lags behind others.

lagging n. insulating material for lagging a water tank etc.

lagoon n. a stretch of salt water separated from the sea by a sandbank or coral reef.

laid past & past part. of LAY¹. □ **laid-back** informal relaxed and easy-going.

lain past part. of LIE¹.

lair n. **1** a wild animal's resting place. **2** a hiding place.

laird n. (in Scotland) a landowner.

laissez-faire /less-ay-**fair**/ n. a policy of not interfering in the course of things.

laity n. people who do not belong to the clergy.

lake n. a large area of water surrounded by land.

lam v. (**lamming**, **lammed**) informal hit hard.

lama n. a Tibetan or Mongolian Buddhist monk.

lamb n. **1** a young sheep. **2** a mild-mannered or gentle person. ▶ v. give birth to a lamb.

lambaste (or **lambast**) v. criticize harshly.

lame adj. **1** walking with difficulty because of an injured leg or foot. **2** unconvincing and feeble. ▶ v. make lame. ■ **lamely** adv. **lameness** n.

lamé /**lah**-may/ n. fabric with interwoven gold or silver threads.

Thesaurus

paucity. ▶ v. BE LACKING, be without, have need of, need, stand in need of, require, want, be short of, be deficient in, miss.

laconic adj. BRIEF, concise, terse, succinct, short, elliptical, crisp, pithy, to the point, incisive, abrupt, blunt, curt. ■ OPPOSITES verbose.

laden adj. LOADED, burdened, heavily laden, weighed down, weighted, encumbered, hampered, oppressed, taxed.

lady n. **1** WOMAN, female. **2** NOBLEWOMAN, gentlewoman, aristocrat.

ladylike adj. GENTEEL, refined, well bred, cultivated, polished, decorous, proper, correct, respectable, well mannered, courteous, polite, civil, gracious; informal

posh. ■ OPPOSITES coarse.

lag v. FALL BEHIND, fall back, trail, not keep pace, bring up the rear, loiter, linger, dally, straggle, dawdle, hang back, delay, move slowly, drag one's feet.

laid-back adj. RELAXED, at ease, easy, leisurely, unhurried, casual, easygoing, free and easy, informal, nonchalant, unexcitable, imperturbable, unflappable. ■ OPPOSITES tense.

lair n. **1** TUNNEL, dugout, hollow, cave, haunt. **2** RETREAT, hideaway, refuge, sanctuary, sanctum, sanctum sanctorum.

lake n. POND, tarn, pool, reservoir, lagoon; Sc. loch; US bayou.

lame adj. **1** LIMPING, hobbling, halting,

lament n. **1** an expression of grief. **2** a song or poem expressing grief. ▶v. feel or express grief or regret for. ■ **lamentation** n.

lamentable adj. very bad or regrettable. ■ **lamentably** adv.

laminate v. **1** cover with a protective layer. **2** make by sticking layers together. ▶n. laminated material.

lamp n. a device for giving light.

lampoon v. publicly mock or ridicule. ▶n. a mocking attack.

lamprey n. (pl. **lampreys**) an eel-like jawless fish.

lance n. a long spear. ▶v. prick or cut open with a sharp instrument. □ **lance corporal** an army rank below corporal.

lancet n. a pointed two-edged knife used in surgery.

land n. **1** the part of the earth's surface not covered by water. **2** an area of ground in terms of its ownership or use. **3** ground or soil used for farming. **4** a country or state. ▶v. **1** put or go ashore. **2** come or bring down to the ground. **3** informal succeed in obtaining or achieving. **4** informal put or end up in a difficult situation. **5** informal inflict a blow. □ **landfall** arrival at land on a sea or air journey. **landfill 1** the disposal of waste material by burying it. **2** buried waste material. **landlocked** surrounded by land. **landlubber** informal

a person unfamiliar with the sea or sailing. **landmark 1** an object or feature easily seen from a distance. **2** an event marking an important stage.

landslide 1 (also **landslip**) a fall of earth or rock from a mountain or cliff. **2** an overwhelming majority of votes. ■ **landward** adv. & adj. **landwards** adv.

landed adj. owning much land.

landing n. **1** a place where people and goods can be landed from a boat. **2** a level area at the top of a staircase. □ **landing stage** a platform for coming ashore from a boat.

landlord (or **landlady**) n. **1** a person who rents out property or land. **2** a person who owns or runs a pub.

landscape n. **1** all the visible features of an area of land. **2** a picture of an area of countryside. ▶v. improve the aesthetic appearance of a piece of land.

lane n. **1** a narrow road. **2** a division of a road for a single line of traffic. **3** a strip of track or water for each of the competitors in a race. **4** a course followed by ships or aircraft.

language n. **1** human communication through the structured use of words. **2** a particular system or style of this. **3** a system of symbols and rules for writing computer programs.

languid adj. lacking energy or vigour. ■ **languidly** adv.

Thesaurus

crippled, game, disabled, incapacitated, defective; informal gammy. **2** WEAK, feeble, thin, flimsy, unconvincing, unsatisfactory, inadequate, insufficient, deficient, defective, ineffectual.

lament v. **1** MOURN, grieve, sorrow, wail, moan, groan, cry, sob, complain, keen, ululate, howl, beat one's breast. **2** COMPLAIN ABOUT, bemoan, deplore, bewail.

lamentable adj. **1** DEPLORABLE, regrettable, tragic, wretched, woeful, sorrowful, distressing, grievous. **2** MISERABLE, pitiful, poor, meagre, low, unsatisfactory, inadequate; informal measly.

lamp n. LANTERN, table lamp, standard lamp, night light, light bulb, headlight, headlamp, sidelight, fog light, fog lamp.

land n. **1** DRY LAND, ground, solid ground, earth, terra firma. **2** GROUND, fields, open space, expanse, stretch, tract. **3** PROPERTY, ground, acres, estate, realty, real estate. **4** COUNTRY, nation, fatherland, motherland, state, realm, province, territory, district, region, area, domain. ▶v. **1** TOUCH DOWN, alight,

make a landing, come in to land. **2** MAKE A LANDING, bring down, put down, take down. **3** BERTH, dock, reach the shore, come ashore, disembark, debark. **4** DEAL, deliver, give, inflict; informal fetch.

landlady, landlord n. **1** PUBLICAN, pubowner, innkeeper, hotel keeper, hotelier, host, mine host. **2** OWNER, proprietor, lessor, householder, freeholder.

landscape n. COUNTRYSIDE, scene, scenery, outlook, view, aspect, prospect, vista, panorama, perspective.

landslide n. **1** AVALANCHE, landslip, rockfall. **2** DECISIVE VICTORY, runaway victory, overwhelming majority.

language n. **1** SPEECH, speaking, talking, words, vocabulary, utterances, verbal expression, verbalization, vocalization, communication, conversation, discourse, interchange. **2** TONGUE, speech, parlance, mother tongue, native tongue; informal lingo.

languid adj. LANGUISHING, listless, languorous, lackadaisical, spiritless, lacking energy, lethargic, torpid, idle, in-

languish v. **1** become weak or feeble. **2** be forced to remain in an unpleasant place.

languor n. pleasurable tiredness or inactivity. ■ **languorous** adj.

lank adj. (of hair) long, limp, and straight.

lanky adj. tall and thin.

lanolin n. a fatty substance from sheep's wool, used in ointments.

lantern n. a lamp with a transparent case protecting the flame or bulb.

lanthanum n. a metallic element.

lanyard n. **1** a rope used on a ship for securing sails etc. **2** a cord for hanging a whistle or similar object round the neck or shoulder.

lap n. **1** the flat area between the waist and knees of a seated person. **2** one circuit of a racetrack. **3** a part of a journey. ▶v. (**lapping**, **lapped**) **1** take up liquid with the tongue. **2** (**lap up**) accept with obvious pleasure. **3** (of water) wash against something with a gentle sound. **4** overtake a competitor in a race to become one lap ahead. □ **lapdog** a small pampered pet dog. **laptop** a portable microcomputer.

laparoscope n. a fibre-optic instrument inserted through the abdominal wall to view the internal organs.

■ **laparoscopy** n.

lapel n. a flap folded back on each side of a coat etc. below the collar.

lapidary adj. of the cutting or polishing of stones and gems.

lapis lazuli n. a blue semi-precious stone.

Lapp n. a member of a people of the extreme north of Scandinavia.

┌─┐
│i│ The people themselves prefer to be
└─┘ called **Sami**.

lapse n. **1** a brief failure of concentration, memory, etc. **2** a decline in standard. **3** an interval of time. ▶v. **1** (of a right or agreement) become invalid because not used or renewed. **2** cease to follow the rules of a religion. **3** pass gradually into an inferior state.

larch n. a deciduous coniferous tree.

lard n. fat from a pig, used in cooking. ▶v. **1** insert strips of bacon in meat before cooking. **2** add technical or obscure expressions to talk or writing.

larder n. a room or large cupboard for storing food.

large adj. of great size or extent. □ **at large 1** escaped or not yet captured. **2** as a whole. ■ **largely** adv.

largesse (or **largess**) /lar-**zhess**/ n.

Thesaurus

active, inert, indolent, lazy, sluggish, slow-moving, unenthusiastic, apathetic, indifferent. ■ OPPOSITES energetic, vigorous.

languish v. DROOP, flag, wilt, wither, fade, fail, weaken, decline, go into a decline, go downhill, waste away. **2** WASTE AWAY, rot, decay, wither away, be abandoned, be neglected, be forgotten, be disregarded. ■ OPPOSITES thrive.

languor n. LISTLESSNESS, lethargy, torpor, idleness, inactivity, inertia, indolence, laziness, sluggishness, sleepiness, drowsiness, somnolence, dreaminess, relaxation. ■ OPPOSITES vigour.

lank adj. LIFELESS, lustreless, limp, straggling, straight, long.

lanky adj. TALL, spindly, gangling, gangly, lean, thin, angular, scraggy, bony, gaunt, raw-boned, gawky, rangy; informal weedy. ■ OPPOSITES sturdy.

lap n. **1** CIRCUIT, circle, loop, orbit, round, compass, ambit. **2** ROUND, tour, section, stage.

lapse n. **1** SLIP, error, mistake, blunder, failing, fault, failure, omission, oversight, negligence, dereliction; informal slip-up. **2** INTERVAL, gap, pause, intermis-sion, interlude, lull, hiatus, break, passage. **3** DECLINE, downturn, fall, falling, falling away, slipping, drop, deterioration, worsening, degeneration, backsliding. ▶v. **1** DECLINE, fall, fall off, drop, go downhill, deteriorate, worsen, degenerate, go to pot. **2** BECOME VOID, become invalid, expire, run out, terminate, become obsolete. **3** SLIDE, slip, drift, sink, subside, submerge.

larder n. PANTRY, storage room, storeroom, store, still room, cooler, scullery.

large adj. **1** BIG, great, of considerable size, sizeable, substantial, goodly, tall, high, huge, immense, enormous, colossal, massive, mammoth, vast, prodigious, gigantic, giant, monumental, stupendous, gargantuan, man-size, king-size, giant-size, outsize, considerable; informal jumbo, whopping. **2** BURLY, big, heavy, bulky, thickset, powerfully built, heavy-set, chunky, strapping, hefty, ample, fat, obese, corpulent; informal hulking. **3** ABUNDANT, copious, plentiful, ample, liberal, generous. **4** WIDE, wide-ranging, large-scale, broad, extensive, far-reaching, sweeping, comprehensive, exhaustive. ■ OPPOSITES

1 generosity. **2** money or gifts given generously.

lariat n. a lasso.

lark n. **1** a brown bird that sings in flight. **2** an amusing adventure or escapade. ▶ v. behave playfully.

larva n. (pl. **larvae**) an immature form of an insect that undergoes metamorphosis. ■ **larval** adj.

laryngitis n. inflammation of the larynx.

larynx n. (pl. **larynges**) the part of the throat containing the vocal cords.

lasagne /luh-**zan**-yuh/ n. a dish of strips of pasta layered with meat and cheese sauces.

lascivious /luh-**siv**-i-uhss/ adj. feeling or showing sexual desire. ■ **lasciviousness** n.

laser n. a device producing an intense narrow beam of light.

lash v. **1** beat with a whip or stick. **2** beat against. **3** (**lash out**) launch a verbal or physical attack. **4** (of an animal) move its tail quickly to and fro. **5** fasten securely with a rope. ▶ n. **1** a blow with a whip or stick. **2** the flexible part of a whip. **3** an eyelash.

lashings pl. n. informal a large amount.

lass (or **lassie**) n. Sc. & N. Engl. a girl or young woman.

lassitude n. weariness or lack of energy.

lasso /luh-**soo**/ n. (pl. **lassos**) a rope with a noose for catching cattle. ▶ v. (**lassoing**, **lassoed**) catch with a lasso.

last adj. **1** coming after all others in time or order. **2** most recent. **3** lowest in importance. **4** only remaining. ▶ adv. on the last occasion before the present.

▶ n. **1** the last person or thing. **2** the only remaining part. **3** a foot-shaped block used in making or repairing a shoe. ▶ v. **1** continue. **2** survive or endure. **3** (of resources etc.) be enough for a specified length of time. □ **at** (**long**) **last** in the end; eventually. **last post** a military bugle call sounded at sunset and at military funerals. **the last straw** the final thing making a situation unbearable. **last word 1** a final statement. **2** the most modern or advanced example of something. ■ **lastly** adv.

latch n. **1** a bar with a catch and lever for fastening a door or gate. **2** a type of door lock which can only be opened from the outside with a key. ▶ v. fasten with a latch. □ **on the latch** closed but not locked.

late adj. **1** arriving or happening after the proper or usual time. **2** far on in the day or night or a period. **3** (**the late**) (of a person) dead. **4** (**latest**) most recent. ▶ adv. **1** after the proper or usual time. **2** far on in the day or night or a period. **3** (**later**) in the near future. □ **of late** recently. ■ **lateness** n.

lately adv. recently.

latent adj. existing but not yet developed, apparent, or active. ■ **latency** n.

lateral adj. of, at, to, or from the side or sides. ■ **laterally** adv.

latex n. **1** a milky fluid in some plants, esp. the rubber tree. **2** a similar synthetic product used to make coatings etc.

lath n. (pl. **laths**) a thin, flat strip of wood.

Thesaurus

small. □ **at large** AT LIBERTY, free, unconfined, unrestrained, roaming, on the loose, on the run, fugitive.

largely adv. TO A LARGE EXTENT, to a great degree, chiefly, for the most part, mostly, mainly, in the main, principally, in great measure.

lascivious adj. LEWD, lecherous, lustful, licentious, promiscuous, libidinous, prurient, salacious, lubricious, concupiscent, debauched, depraved, degenerate, dissolute, dissipated.

lash v. WHIP, horsewhip, scourge, birch, switch, flog, flail, flagellate, thrash, beat, strike, batter, hammer; informal wallop, whack.

last¹ adj. **1** FINAL, closing, concluding, ending, finishing, terminating, ultimate, terminal. **2** HINDMOST, rearmost, at

the end, at the back, final, aftermost. **3** LEAST LIKELY, most unlikely, least suitable, least wanted, least favourite. **4** LATEST, most recent.

last² v. **1** CONTINUE, go on, carry on, remain, persist, keep on. **2** SURVIVE, exist, live, subsist, hold on, hold out. **3** LAST LONG, wear well, stand up to wear, keep, endure.

late adj. **1** BEHIND SCHEDULE, behind, not on time, tardy, overdue, delayed, dilatory, slow. **2** DECEASED, dead, departed, defunct, non-extant. **3** FORMER, previous, preceding, past, prior. ■ OPPOSITES punctual.

latent adj. DORMANT, quiescent, inactive, passive, hidden, unrevealed, concealed, unapparent, indiscernible, imperceptible, invisible, covert, undeveloped, un-

lathe n. a machine for shaping pieces of wood by turning them against a cutting tool.

lather n. **1** froth from soap and water. **2** heavy frothy sweat on a horse's coat. ▶v. form or cover with a lather.

Latin n. the language of the ancient Romans. ▶adj. of Latin. □ **Latin America** the parts of the American continent where Spanish or Portuguese is the national language.

latitude n. **1** the distance of a place north or south of the equator. **2** a region. **3** freedom of action or thought.

latrine n. a communal toilet in a camp or barracks.

latter adj. **1** nearer to the end than to the beginning. **2** recent. **3** (**the latter**) the second of two people or things to be mentioned. □ **latter-day** modern or contemporary. ■ **latterly** adv.

lattice n. a structure of strips crossing each other.

laudable adj. deserving praise.

laudanum n. a solution of opium formerly used as a sedative.

laudatory adj. expressing praise.

laugh v. make the sounds and movements that express great amusement. **2** (**laugh at**) make fun of. ▶n. **1** an act of laughing. **2** (**a laugh**) informal a cause

of laughter. □ **laughing stock** a person who is ridiculed by everyone.

laughable adj. ridiculous.

laughter n. the act or sound of laughing.

launch v. **1** move a boat into the water. **2** send a rocket etc. into the air. **3** start an enterprise or introduce a new product. ▶n. **1** an act of launching. **2** a large motor boat.

launder v. **1** wash and iron clothes etc. **2** informal pass illegally obtained money through a bank or business to conceal its origin.

launderette n. a place with coin-operated washing machines and dryers for public use.

laundry n. (pl. **laundries**) **1** clothes etc. for washing. **2** a place where clothes etc. are laundered.

laurel n. **1** an evergreen shrub. **2** (**laurels**) honour or praise.

lava n. flowing or hardened molten rock from a volcano.

lavatory n. (pl. **lavatories**) a toilet.

lavender n. **1** a shrub with fragrant purple flowers. **2** a light purple colour.

lavish adj. **1** very rich, elaborate, or luxurious. **2** generous. ▶v. give or spend in large quantities. ■ **lavishly** adv.

law n. **1** a rule or system of rules estab-

Thesaurus

realized, potential, possible. ■ OPPOSITES evident.

lateral adj. SIDEWISE, sideways, sidelong, sideward, edgewise, edgeways, indirect, oblique, slanting.

latitude n. **1** PARALLEL. **2** SCOPE, freedom of action, freedom, liberty, free play, carte blanche, leeway, elbow room, licence, indulgence. ■ OPPOSITES longitude, restriction.

latter adj. **1** LAST-MENTIONED, second-mentioned, second of the two, second. **2** LATER, hindmost, closing, end, concluding, final. ■ OPPOSITES former.

laudable adj. PRAISEWORTHY, commendable, admirable, worthy of admiration, meritorious, deserving, creditable, worthy, estimable, of note, noteworthy, exemplary, excellent. ■ OPPOSITES shameful.

laugh v. CHUCKLE, chortle, guffaw, giggle, titter, snigger, tee-hee, burst out laughing, roar/hoot with laughter, shake/be convulsed with laughter, split one's sides, be rolling in the aisles, be doubled up; informal be in stitches, die laughing, be creased up, fall about, crack up, break up. □ **laugh at** MOCK,

ridicule, deride, scoff at, jeer at, sneer at, make fun of, poke fun at, make a fool of, lampoon, satirize, taunt, tease; informal send up, take the mickey out of.

laughter n. LAUGHING, chuckling, chortling, guffawing, giggling, tittering, sniggering, amusement, entertainment, humour, mirth, merriment, gaiety, hilarity, glee, light-heartedness; literary blitheness.

launch v. **1** FIRE, discharge, propel, project, send forth, throw, cast, hurl, let fly, blast off. **2** SET IN MOTION, get going, begin, start, commence, embark upon, initiate, instigate, institute, inaugurate, establish, set up, organize, introduce, usher in.

lavatory n. TOILET, WC, ladies, gents, public convenience, cloakroom, powder room, privy, urinal, latrine; US bathroom, washroom, rest room; Nautical head; informal loo, lav, little girls' room, little boys' room, bog, khazi; US informal can, john; dated water closet.

lavish adj. **1** COPIOUS, abundant, superabundant, plentiful, profuse, prolific, unlimited. **2** EXTRAVAGANT, excessive, immoderate, wasteful, squandering, lished by authority. **2** a statement that a particular phenomenon always occurs if certain conditions are present. ◻ **law-abiding** obeying the law. **law court** a place where legal cases or trials are heard. **lawsuit** a claim brought to a law court to be decided.

lawful adj. allowed by or obeying the law or rules. ■ **lawfully** adv.

lawless adj. not obeying the law. ■ **lawlessness** n.

lawn n. **1** an area of mown grass in a garden or park. **2** a fine linen or cotton fabric. ◻ **lawnmower** a machine for cutting grass.

lawrencium n. a radioactive metallic element.

lawyer n. a person who practises law.

lax adj. not strict, severe, or careful. ■ **laxity** n.

laxative n. a medicine causing the bowels to empty.

lay¹ v. (**laying, laid**) **1** put down carefully. **2** put down and set in position for use. **3** assign or place. **4** (of a female bird etc.) produce an egg. ▶ n. the appearance of an area of land. ▶ adj. **1** not having an official position in the Church. **2** non-professional or non-specialist. ◻ **layabout** a person who does little or no work. **lay-by** (pl. **lay-bys**) an area at the side of a road where vehicles may stop. **lay off 1** discharge a worker because of a shortage of work. **2** informal stop doing something. **lay on** provide. **layout** the way in which something is laid out. **lay out 1** arrange according to a plan. **2** prepare a body for burial. **lay up** put out of action through illness or injury.

> ☑ Don't confuse **lay**, 'put something down' and **lie**, 'recline on a flat surface'. The past tense and past participle of **lay** is **laid** (*they laid the carpet*); the past tense of **lie** is **lay** (*he lay on the floor*) and the past participle is **lain** (*she had lain awake for hours*).

lay² past of **LIE¹**.

layer n. **1** a sheet or thickness of material covering a surface. **2** a person or thing that lays something. ▶ v. arrange or cut in a layer or layers.

Thesaurus

profligate, prodigal, thriftless, improvident, intemperate, unrestrained. **3** GENEROUS, liberal, bountiful, open-handed, unstinting, free, munificent, extravagant. **4** LUXURIANT, lush, gorgeous, sumptuous, costly, opulent, pretentious, showy. ▶ v. HEAP, shower, pour, deluge, give freely, give generously, bestow freely, waste, squander, dissipate.

law n. **1** STATUTE, regulation, rule, enactment, act, decree, edict, command, order, ordinance, commandment, directive, pronouncement, covenant. **2** PRINCIPLE, precept, standard, criterion, formula, tenet, doctrine, canon. **3** GENERALIZATION, general truth, axiom, maxim, truism. **4** LITIGATION, legal action, legal proceedings, lawsuit.

law-abiding adj. LAWFUL, righteous, honest, honourable, upright, upstanding, good, virtuous, orderly, peaceable, peaceful, dutiful, duteous, obedient, compliant, complying. ■ OPPOSITES lawless.

lawful adj. **1** LEGAL, legitimate, licit, just, valid, permissible, allowable, rightful, proper, constitutional, legalized, sanctioned, authorized, warranted, approved, recognized. **2** see LAW-ABIDING. ■ OPPOSITES illegal.

lawless adj. **1** WITHOUT LAW AND ORDER, anarchic, disorderly, ungoverned, unruly, insurrectionary, insurgent, revolutionary, rebellious, insubordinate, riotous, mutinous, seditious, terrorist. **2** UNLAWFUL, illegal, law-breaking, illicit, illegitimate, criminal, felonious, miscreant, transgressing, violating. ■ OPPOSITES orderly, legal.

lawyer n. SOLICITOR, legal practitioner, legal adviser, barrister, advocate, counsel, Queen's Counsel, QC; *informal* brief; *US* attorney.

lax adj. SLACK, slipshod, negligent, neglectful, remiss, careless, heedless, unmindful, inattentive, casual, easygoing, lenient, permissive, indulgent, overindulgent, complaisant, overtolerant.

laxative n. PURGATIVE, aperient, cathartic, senna, ipecacuanha, castor oil.

lay v. **1** SET, deposit, plant, settle, position. **2** POSITION, set out, arrange, dispose. **3** ATTRIBUTE, assign, ascribe, allocate, allot, impute. **4** IMPOSE, inflict, encumber, saddle, tax, charge, burden, apply. ◻ **lay aside** PUT ASIDE, put to one side, keep, save, store. **lay down 1** SURRENDER, relinquish, give up, yield, cede, turn over. **2** SET DOWN, stipulate, prescribe, order, command, ordain, postulate, demand, proclaim, assert, maintain. **lay in** STOCK UP WITH/ON, stockpile, store, accumulate, amass, heap up,

layette n. a set of clothing etc. for a newborn child.

laze v. spend time idly.

lazy adj. (**lazier**, **laziest**) **1** unwilling to work or use energy. **2** showing a lack of effort or care. ■ **lazily** adv. **laziness** n.

lb abbrev. pounds (in weight).

lbw abbrev. Cricket leg before wicket.

lea n. literary an area of grassy land.

leach v. remove a soluble substance from soil by the action of water passing through it.

lead[1] v. (**leading**, **led**) **1** cause to go with one. **2** be a route or means of access. **3** (**lead to**) result in. **4** influence. **5** be in charge of. **6** be ahead of or superior to a competitor. **7** have a particular way of life. **8** (**lead up to**) come before or result in. **9** (**lead on**) deceive into believing something. ▶ n. **1** the initiative in an action. **2** a position of advantage. **3** the chief part in a play or film. **4** a clue. **5** a strap or cord for leading a dog. **6** a wire conveying electric current. □ **leading question** a question worded to prompt the answer wanted.

lead[2] n. **1** a heavy grey metallic element. **2** the part of a pencil that makes a mark.

leaded adj. framed or covered with lead.

leaden adj. **1** heavy or slow. **2** dull grey.

leader n. **1** a person or thing that leads. **2** a newspaper article giving the editor's opinion. ■ **leadership** n.

leaf n. (pl. **leaves**) **1** a flat green structure growing from the stem or root of a plant. **2** a single sheet of paper. **3** metal in the form of very thin foil. **4** a hinged or detachable part of a table. ▶ v. (**leaf through**) turn over pages, reading them quickly or casually. □ **leaf mould** soil or compost consisting of decayed leaves. ■ **leafy** adj.

leaflet n. **1** a printed sheet of paper giving information. **2** a small leaf. ▶ v. (**leafleted**, **leafleting**) distribute leaflets to.

league n. **1** a group of people or countries united for a purpose. **2** a group of sports clubs which play each other over a period for a championship. **3** a class of quality or excellence. □ **in league** plotting with another or others.

Thesaurus

layabout n. GOOD-FOR-NOTHING, ne'er-do-well, do-nothing, idler, loafer, lounger, shirker, wastrel, sluggard, laggard; informal waster, skiver.

layman n. AMATEUR, non-professional, dilettante.

laze v. IDLE, do nothing, loaf, lounge, lounge about, loll around, waste time, fritter away time.

laziness n. IDLENESS, indolence, slothfulness, sloth, inactivity, inertia, lethargy, languor, remissness, laxity.

lazy adj. IDLE, indolent, slothful, workshy, inactive, inert, sluggish, lethargic, languorous, listless, torpid, slow-moving, remiss, negligent, lax. ■ OPPOSITES industrious.

lead v. **1** GUIDE, show someone the way, conduct, lead the way, usher, escort, steer, pilot. **2** CAUSE, induce, prompt, move, incline, dispose, predispose, persuade, sway, influence, prevail upon, bring round. **3** BE AT THE HEAD OF, be at the front of, head. **4** COMMAND, direct, govern, rule, manage, be in charge of, regulate, preside over, head, supervise, superintend, oversee; informal head up. **5** BE IN THE LEAD, be in front, be out in front, be ahead, be first, come first, precede. **6** HAVE, live, pass, spend, experience, undergo. ▶ n. **1** LEADING POSITION/PLACE, first place, advance position, van, vanguard. **2** MARGIN, gap, interval. **3** EXAMPLE, model, pattern, standard of excellence. **4** LEADING ROLE, star/starring role, star part, title role, principal part. **5** LEASH, tether, rein, cord, rope, chain. □ **lead off** BEGIN, start, start off, commence, open; informal kick off. **lead to** CAUSE, result in, bring on, call forth, provoke, contribute to. **lead up to** PREPARE THE WAY FOR, pave the way for, open the way for, do the groundwork for, work round/up to, make overtures about, make advances about, hint at, approach the subject of, introduce the subject of.

leader n. **1** RULER, head, chief, commander, director, governor, principal, captain, manager, superintendent, supervisor, overseer, foreman, kingpin; informal boss, number one, skipper, gaffer, guv'nor. **2** PACESETTER, pacemaker, trendsetter, front runner, innovator, pioneer, trailblazer, pathfinder, groundbreaker, originator. ■ OPPOSITES follower, supporter.

leading adj. CHIEF, main, most important, principal, foremost, supreme, paramount, dominant, superior, first-rate, greatest, best, outstanding, pre-eminent; informal number-one. ■ OPPOSITES subordinate, minor.

leak v. **1** accidentally allow contents to pass through a hole or crack. **2** (of liquid, gas, etc.) pass accidentally through a hole or crack. **3** disclose secret information. ▶ n. **1** a hole or crack through which contents leak. **2** an instance of leaking. ■ **leakage** n. **leaky** adj.

lean v. (**leaning, leaned** or **leant**) **1** be in or put into a sloping position. **2** (**lean against/on**) rest against. **3** (**lean on**) rely on for support. ▶ adj. **1** (of a person) thin. **2** (of meat) with little fat. **3** (of a period) difficult and unprofitable. □ **lean-to** (pl. **lean-tos**) a small building sharing a wall with a larger one.

leaning n. a tendency or preference.

leap v. (**leaping, leaped** or **leapt**) **1** jump suddenly or a long way. **2** (**leap at**) accept eagerly. ▶ n. an act of leaping. □ **leap year** a year with 366 days, occurring once every four years.

leapfrog n. a game in which players vault over others who are bending down. ▶ v. (**leapfrogging, leapfrogged**) **1** perform such a vault. **2** overtake others to reach a leading position.

learn v. (**learning, learned** or **learnt**) **1** gain knowledge of or skill in. **2** become aware of. **3** memorize. ■ **learner** n.

learned adj. having gained much knowledge by study.

learning n. knowledge gained through study.

lease n. a contract by which one party lets land, property, etc. to another for a specified time. ▶ v. let or rent on lease. ■ **leasehold** n.

leash n. a dog's lead.

least adj. & pron. smallest in amount, extent, or significance. ▶ adv. to the smallest extent or degree. □ **at least 1** not less than. **2** if nothing else. **3** anyway.

leather n. a material made from the skin of an animal by tanning or a

Thesaurus

leaflet n. PAMPHLET, booklet, brochure, handbill, flyer, bill, circular; *informal* advert.

league n. ALLIANCE, confederation, confederacy, federation, union, association, coalition, combine, consortium, affiliation, guild, corporation, conglomerate, cooperative, partnership, fellowship, syndicate, band, group.

leak n. **1** DRIP, leaking, leakage, escape, seeping, seepage, oozing, percolation, discharge. **2** OPENING, crack, crevice, chink, fissure, puncture, cut, gash, slit, rent, break, rift. **3** DISCLOSURE, divulgence, revelation, uncovering. ▶ v. **1** ESCAPE, drip out, seep out/through, ooze out, exude, discharge, issue, gush out. **2** DISCLOSE, divulge, reveal, make known, make public, impart, pass on, relate, give away, let slip; *informal* let the cat out of the bag, spill the beans about, take the lid off.

lean v. **1** BE SUPPORTED, be propped up, recline, repose. **2** INCLINE, bend, slant, tilt, be at an angle, slope, bank, list, heel. **3** INCLINE TOWARDS, tend towards, have a tendency towards, have a propensity for, have a proclivity for, have a preference for, be attracted to, have a liking for, gravitate towards, have an affinity with. **4** DEPEND ON, be dependent on, rely on, count on, pin one's faith on, have faith in, trust, have every confidence in.

leaning n. TENDENCY, inclination, bent, proclivity, propensity, penchant, predisposition, predilection, proneness, partiality, preference, bias, attraction, liking, fondness, taste.

leap v. **1** JUMP, bound, bounce, hop, skip, romp, caper, spring, frolic, frisk, cavort, gambol, dance. **2** JUMP OVER, jump, vault over, vault, spring over, bound over, hurdle, clear, cross over, sail over. **3** INCREASE RAPIDLY, soar, rocket, skyrocket, shoot up, escalate, mount.

learn v. **1** ACQUIRE A KNOWLEDGE OF, gain an understanding of, acquire skill in, become competent in, grasp, master, take in, absorb, assimilate, pick up. **2** LEARN BY HEART, get by heart, memorize, commit to memory, become word-perfect in, get off pat. **3** DISCOVER, find out, detect, become aware of, gather, hear, be informed, have it brought to one's attention, understand, ascertain, discern, perceive, get word of, get wind of.

learned adj. ERUDITE, scholarly, well educated, knowledgeable, well read, widely read, well versed, well informed, lettered, cultured, intellectual, academic, literary, bookish; *informal* brainy. ■ OPPOSITES ignorant.

learner n. BEGINNER, trainee, apprentice, pupil, student, novice, tyro, neophyte, initiate; *informal* rookie; *US informal* greenhorn. ■ OPPOSITES veteran.

lease v. **1** RENT, hire, charter. **2** LET, let out, rent, rent out, hire, hire out, similar process.

leathery adj. having a tough, hard texture like leather.

leave v. (**leaving, left**) **1** go away from. **2** stop living at or working for. **3** allow to remain. **4** bequeath. **5** entrust to. **6** deposit something to be collected or attended to. ▶n. **1** time when one has permission to be absent from work or duty. **2** permission. □ **leave out** fail to include.

leaven /lev-uhn/ n. a substance added to dough to make it ferment and rise. ▶v. **1** add leaven to. **2** improve.

leaves pl. of LEAF.

lecher n. a lecherous man. ■ **lechery** n.

lecherous adj. showing sexual desire in an offensive way.

lecithin n. a substance used as a food emulsifier and stabilizer.

lectern n. a stand with a sloping top from which a speaker can read while standing.

lecture n. **1** an educational talk. **2** a lengthy reprimand. ▶v. **1** give a lecture or lectures. **2** reprimand. ■ **lecturer** n.

led past & past part. of LEAD¹.

ledge n. a narrow horizontal projection or shelf.

ledger n. a book of financial accounts.

lee n. **1** shelter from wind or weather given by an object. **2** the side sheltered from the wind. □ **leeway** the available amount of freedom to move or act. ■ **leeward** adj. & adv.

leech n. a small bloodsucking worm.

leek n. a long, thin vegetable related to the onion.

leer v. look in a lustful or unpleasant way. ▶n. a lustful or unpleasant look.

lees pl. n. sediment in wine.

left¹ adj. & adv. of, on, or towards the side which is to the west when facing north. ▶n. **1** (**the left**) the left-hand side or direction. **2** a left turn. **3** a left-wing group or party. □ **left-handed** using or done with the left hand. **left-wing** radical, reforming, or socialist.

left² past & past part. of LEAVE. □ **left-overs** food remaining after the rest has been used.

leg n. **1** each of the limbs on which a person or animal moves and stands. **2** a long, thin support of a chair, table, etc. **3** a section of a journey, race, etc. □ **leg it** informal run away.

Thesaurus

sublet.

leash n. **1** LEAD, rein, tether, rope, cord, chain. **2** REIN, curb, control, check, restraint, hold.

leathery adj. **1** WRINKLED, wizened, weather-beaten, rough, rugged, coriaceous. **2** TOUGH, hard, hardened.

leave¹ v. **1** DEPART, go away, go, withdraw, retire, take oneself off, exit, take one's leave, make off, pull out, quit, be gone, decamp, disappear, say one's farewells/goodbyes; informal push off, shove off, cut, split, vamoose, do a bunk. **2** SET OFF, set sail. **3** ABANDON, desert, forsake, give up, discard, turn one's back on, leave in the lurch; informal quit. **4** LEAVE BEHIND, forget, mislay. **5** ASSIGN, allot, consign, hand over, give over, refer, commit, entrust. **6** BEQUEATH, will, endow, hand down, transfer, convey. **7** CAUSE, leave behind, produce, generate, result in. □ **leave out** MISS OUT, omit, fail to include, overlook.

leave² n. **1** PERMISSION, consent, authorization, sanction, warrant, dispensation, concession, indulgence. **2** HOLIDAY, vacation, break, time off, furlough, sabbatical, leave of absence; informal hols, vac. **3** LEAVING, leave-taking, departure, parting, withdrawal, exit, farewell, goodbye, adieu.

lecherous adj. LUSTFUL, promiscuous, carnal, sensual, licentious, lascivious, lewd, salacious, libertine, libidinous, lubricious, concupiscent, debauched, dissolute, wanton, intemperate, dissipated, degenerate, depraved; informal horny, raunchy. ■ OPPOSITES chaste.

lecture n. **1** TALK, speech, address, discourse, disquisition, lesson, sermon, homily. **2** SCOLDING, reprimand, rebuke, reproof, reproach, remonstration, upbraiding, berating, tirade, diatribe; informal dressing-down, telling-off, talking-to. ▶v. **1** TEACH, tutor in, instruct in, give instruction in, give lessons in. **2** SCOLD, reprimand, rebuke, reprove, reproach, remonstrate with, upbraid, berate, castigate.

lecturer n. TEACHER, college teacher, tutor, reader, instructor, academic, academician.

ledge n. SHELF, sill, mantel, mantelpiece, mantelshelf, projection, protrusion, overhang, ridge, step.

leer v. OGLE, look lasciviously at, look suggestively at, eye, wink at, watch, stare, goggle, sneer, smirk grin; informal give someone the glad eye, give someone the once-over.

left adj. **1** LEFT-HAND, sinistral; Nautical port; Heraldry sinister. **2** LEFT-WING, leftist, so-

legacy n. (pl. **legacies**) something left to someone in a will, or handed down by a predecessor.

legal adj. of, required, or permitted by law. □ **legal aid** payment from public funds towards the cost of legal action. **legal tender** accepted methods of payment such as coins or banknotes. ■ **legality** n. **legalize** (or **-ise**) v. **legally** adv.

legate n. a representative of the Pope.

legatee n. a person who receives a legacy.

legation n. 1 a diplomatic minister and staff. 2 the official residence of a diplomat.

legato adv. & adj. Music in a smooth, flowing manner.

legend n. 1 a traditional story from the past which may or may not be true. 2 a very famous person. 3 an inscription, caption, or key.

legendary adj. 1 described in legends. 2 famous.

legerdemain /lej-er-di-**mayn**/ n. 1 skilful use of the hands when doing conjuring tricks. 2 trickery.

leggings pl. n. women's tight-fitting stretchy trousers.

legible adj. clear enough to read. ■ **legibility** n. **legibly** adv.

legion n. 1 a division of the ancient Roman army. 2 a great number. ▶ adj. great in number.

legionnaire n. a member of a legion.

□ **legionnaires' disease** a form of bacterial pneumonia.

legislate v. make laws. ■ **legislative** adj. **legislator** n.

legislation n. laws as a whole.

legislature n. the law-making body of a state.

legitimate adj. 1 allowed by the law or rules. 2 justifiable. 3 (of a child) born of parents married to each other. ■ **legitimacy** n. **legitimately** adv. **legitimize** (or **-ise**) v.

legume n. a plant bearing seeds in pods. ■ **leguminous** adj.

leisure n. time spent not working. □ **at leisure 1** not busy; free. **2** in an unhurried way. ■ **leisured** adj.

leisurely adj. & adv. without hurry.

leitmotif (or **leitmotiv**) /**lyt**-moh-teef/ n. a frequently repeated theme in a musical or literary composition.

lemming n. a short-tailed Arctic rodent, noted for its periodic mass migrations.

lemon n. 1 a pale yellow citrus fruit with acidic juice. 2 a pale yellow colour.

lemonade n. a lemon-flavoured drink.

lemur n. a primate with a pointed snout, found in Madagascar.

lend v. (**lending**, **lent**) **1** allow someone the temporary use of something. **2** give someone money under an agreement to pay it back later. **3** add a quality to. **4** (**lend itself to**) be suitable for. ■ **lender** n.

Thesaurus

cialist, radical, progressive, liberal, communist, communistic. ■ OPPOSITES right.

leg n. **1** LOWER LIMB, limb, member, shank; informal stump, peg, pin. **2** SUPPORT, upright, prop, brace, underpinning. **3** PART, portion, segment, section, bit, stretch, stage, lap.

legal adj. **1** LAWFUL, legitimate, licit, legalized, valid, right, proper, sound, permissible, permitted, allowable, allowed, above board, admissible, acceptable, authorized, sanctioned, licensed; informal legit. **2** JUDICIAL, juridical, forensic. ■ OPPOSITES illegal.

legalize v. MAKE LEGAL, decriminalize, legitimize, legitimatize, validate, ratify, permit, allow, admit, accept, authorize, sanction, warrant, license.

legend n. MYTH, saga, epic, folk tale, folk story, traditional story, tale, story, narrative, fable, romance.

legendary adj. **1** MYTHICAL, heroic, traditional, fabled, fictitious, fictional, storybook, romantic, fanciful, fantastical, fabulous. **2** CELEBRATED, acclaimed, illustrious, famous, famed, renowned, well known, popular, immortal.

legitimate adj. **1** LEGAL, lawful, licit, within the law, going by the rules; informal legit. **2** LAWFUL, rightful, genuine, authentic, real, true, proper, correct, authorized, sanctioned, warranted, acknowledged, recognized, approved. **3** VALID, sound, admissible, acceptable, well founded, justifiable, reasonable, plausible, credible, believable, reliable, logical, rational. ■ OPPOSITES illegitimate, illegal.

legitimize v. LEGALIZE, pronounce lawful, declare legal, legitimate, decriminalize, validate, permit, warrant, authorize, sanction, license, give the stamp of approval to.

leisure n. FREE TIME, spare time, idle hours, inactivity, time off, relaxation, recreation, freedom, holiday, vacation, breathing space, respite; informal R & R,

length n. **1** the measurement or extent from end to end. **2** the amount of time occupied by something. **3** the quality of being long. **4** a stretch or piece of something. **5** a degree of effort: *go to great lengths*. □ **at length 1** in detail. **2** after a long time. **lengthways** (or **lengthwise**) in a direction parallel with a thing's length. ■ **lengthen** v.

lengthy adj. (**lengthier**, **lengthiest**) very long. ■ **lengthily** adv.

lenient adj. not strict; merciful. ■ **leniency** n. **leniently** adv.

lens n. **1** a piece of transparent curved material that concentrates or disperses light rays, used in cameras, spectacles, etc. **2** the transparent part of the eye that focuses light on to the retina.

Lent n. (in the Christian Church) the period immediately before Easter.

lent past & past part. of LEND.

lentil n. a pulse or edible seed.

leonine adj. of or like a lion.

leopard n. a large spotted cat, found in Africa and Asia.

leotard n. a close-fitting, stretchy garment worn by dancers, gymnasts, etc.

leper n. **1** a person with leprosy. **2** a person shunned by others.

leprechaun n. (in Irish folklore) a small, mischievous sprite.

leprosy n. a contagious disease which affects the skin and can cause deformities. ■ **leprous** adj.

lesbian n. a homosexual woman. ▶ adj. of lesbians. ■ **lesbianism** n.

lese-majesty /leez/ n. the insulting of a ruler; treason.

lesion n. a part of an organ or tissue which has been damaged.

less adj. & pron. **1** a smaller amount of. **2** fewer in number. ▶ adv. to a smaller extent. ▶ prep. minus. ■ **lessen** v.

☑ For the difference between **less** and **fewer**, see the note at FEW.

lessee n. a person who holds the lease of a property.

lesser adj. not so great or important as the other or the rest.

lesson n. **1** a period of learning or teaching. **2** a thing learned. **3** a thing acting as a warning or encouragement. **4** a passage from the Bible read aloud.

lessor n. a person who leases a property to another.

lest conj. for fear that.

let v. (**letting**, **let**) **1** allow. **2** used to express an intention, suggestion, order, or assumption: *let's try*. **3** allow someone to use a room or property in return for payment. ▶ n. **1** a period during which a room or property is rented. **2** (in tennis etc.) a situation in which a point is not counted and is played for again. □ **let alone** not to mention. **let down** fail to support or help. **let go** stop holding on to or allow to go free. **let off 1** cause a gun, firework, etc. to fire or explode. **2** choose not to punish. **3** excuse. **let up** informal become less intense.

lethal adj. able to cause death.

Thesaurus

time to kill.

leisurely adj. UNHURRIED, relaxed, easy, easy-going, gentle, comfortable, restful, slow, lazy, lingering; informal laid-back. ■ OPPOSITES hurried.

lend v. **1** LOAN, give someone the loan of, let someone have the use of, advance. **2** IMPART, add, give, bestow, confer, provide, supply, furnish. ■ OPPOSITES borrow.

length n. **1** DISTANCE, extent, linear measure, span, reach. **2** PERIOD, stretch, duration, term, span. **3** PIECE, portion, section, measure, segment, swatch.

lengthen v. **1** MAKE LONGER, elongate, let down. **2** GROW LONGER, get longer, draw out, stretch. **3** PROLONG, make longer, increase, extend, expand, protract, stretch out, draw out. ■ OPPOSITES shorten.

lengthy adj. LONG, long-lasting, prolonged, extended, protracted, long-

drawn-out. ■ OPPOSITES short.

lenient adj. MERCIFUL, clement, sparing, moderate, compassionate, humane, forbearing, tolerant, liberal, magnanimous, indulgent, kind, gentle, easy-going, mild. ■ OPPOSITES severe.

less adj. SMALLER, slighter, not so much, not so great. ▶ pron. A SMALLER AMOUNT, not so much. ▶ adv. TO A LESSER DEGREE, to a smaller extent, not so much. ▶ prep. MINUS, subtracting, excepting, without.

lessen v. **1** GROW LESS, abate, decrease, diminish, subside, moderate, slacken, die down, let up, ease off, tail off, ebb, wane. **2** RELIEVE, soothe, allay, assuage, alleviate, palliate, ease, dull, deaden, blunt, take the edge off. ■ OPPOSITES increase.

lesson n. **1** CLASS, period of instruction, exercise, schoolwork, homework, assignment, task. **2** EXAMPLE, warning, deterrent, message, moral, precept.

lethargy n. lack of energy and enthusiasm. ■ **lethargic** adj. **lethargically** adv.

letter n. **1** a symbol representing a speech sound. **2** a written communication sent by post or messenger. **3** the precise terms of something. **4** (**letters**) literature. ▶v. inscribe letters on. □ **letter box** a slot in a door through which letters etc. are delivered. **letterhead** a printed heading on stationery.

lettuce n. a plant whose leaves are eaten in salads.

leucocyte /loo-koh-syt/ n. a white blood cell.

leukaemia /loo-kee-mi-uh/ (US **leukemia**) n. a disease in which too many white blood cells are produced.

levee /lev-i/ n. an embankment built against flooding.

level n. **1** a horizontal line or surface. **2** a position on a scale. **3** a height from the ground or another base. **4** an instrument to test a horizontal line. ▶adj. **1** having a flat, horizontal surface. **2** having the same relative height or position as someone or something else. ▶v. (**levelling**, **levelled**; US **leveling**, **leveled**) **1** make or become level. **2** aim a gun etc. □ **level crossing** a place where a railway and road cross at the same level. **level-headed** sensible. **on the level** honest.

lever n. **1** a bar on a pivot, used to move

a load with one end when pressure is applied to the other. **2** a handle used to operate a mechanism. ▶v. lift or move with a lever.

leverage n. **1** the exertion of force by means of a lever. **2** the power to influence.

leveret n. a young hare.

leviathan /li-vy-uh-thuhn/ n. a very large or powerful thing.

levitate v. rise or cause to rise and hover in the air. ■ **levitation** n.

levity n. humorous treatment of a serious matter.

levy n. (pl. **levies**) **1** the imposing of a tax, fee, or fine. **2** a sum of money raised by a levy. ▶v. (**levying**, **levied**) impose a levy.

lewd adj. crude and offensive in a sexual way.

lexical adj. of words.

lexicography n. the writing of dictionaries. ■ **lexicographer** n.

lexicon n. **1** a vocabulary. **2** a dictionary.

liability n. (pl. **liabilities**) **1** the state of being liable. **2** a debt. **3** a person or thing likely to cause embarrassment or trouble.

liable adj. **1** responsible by law. **2** (**liable to**) subject by law to. **3** (**liable to do**) likely to do.

liaise v. **1** cooperate on a matter. **2** act

Thesaurus

let v. **1** ALLOW, permit, give permission to, give leave to, authorize, sanction, grant, license, assent to, consent to, agree to; *informal* give the thumbs up to, give the go-ahead to, give the green light to. **2** LET OUT, rent, rent out, lease, hire, sublet. □ **let down** FAIL, disappoint, disillusion, forsake, abandon, desert, leave, betray, leave in the lurch. **let off 1** EXPLODE, detonate. **2** ACQUIT, release, discharge, reprieve, absolve, exonerate, pardon, forgive, exempt, spare. **let up** LESSEN, abate, decrease, diminish, subside, moderate, slacken, die down, ease off, tail off, ebb, wane.

let-down n. DISAPPOINTMENT, disillusionment, fiasco, anticlimax; *informal* washout.

lethal adj. FATAL, deadly, mortal, death-dealing, murderous, poisonous, toxic, dangerous, virulent, noxious, destructive, disastrous, calamitous, ruinous. ■ OPPOSITES harmless.

lethargic adj. SLUGGISH, inactive, slow, slothful, torpid, listless, languid, apathetic, passive, weary, enervated, fa-

tigued, sleepy, indolent, dull, comatose. ■ OPPOSITES energetic.

lethargy n. SLUGGISHNESS, inertia, inactivity, slowness, sloth, idleness, torpor, torpidity, lifelessness, dullness, listlessness, languor, languidness, apathy, passivity, weariness, lassitude, fatigue, sleepiness, drowsiness, somnolence, narcosis. ■ OPPOSITES energy.

letter n. **1** CHARACTER, sign, symbol. **2** MESSAGE, note, line, missive, epistle, dispatch.

level adj. **1** FLAT, smooth, even, uniform, plane, flush, horizontal. **2** EVEN, uniform, regular, consistent, constant, stable, steady, unchanging, unvarying, unfluctuating. **3** EQUAL, on a level, close together, neck and neck, level-pegging, side by side, on a par, with nothing to choose between them. ▶n. **1** HEIGHT, highness, altitude, elevation. **2** LEVEL OF ACHIEVEMENT, position, rank, standing, status, station, degree, grade, stage, standard. **3** LAYER, stratum, bed. ▶v. **1** LEVEL OUT, make level, even off, even out, make flat, flatten, smooth, smooth as a link.

liaison n. **1** communication and cooperation. **2** a sexual relationship.

> ☑ Remember the second *i*: lia*i*son.

liana n. a tropical climbing plant.

liar n. a person who tells lies.

libation n. a drink poured as an offering to a god.

libel n. the crime of publishing a false statement that harms a person's reputation. ▶ v. (**libelling**, **libelled**; US **libeling**, **libeled**) publish something false about. ■ **libellous** adj.

liberal adj. **1** willing to respect and accept behaviour or opinions different from one's own. **2** (in politics) favouring moderate social reform. **3** (of an interpretation) not strict. **4** generous. ■ **liberally** adv.

liberalize (or **-ise**) v. make less strict. ■ **liberalization** n.

liberate v. **1** set free. **2** (**liberated**) free from social conventions. ■ **liberation** n. **liberator** n.

libertarian n. a person believing in very limited state intervention in people's lives. ■ **libertarianism** n.

libertine n. a man who leads an immoral life.

liberty n. (pl. **liberties**) **1** freedom. **2** a right or privilege. □ **at liberty** permitted to do something. **take liberties** behave with undue freedom or familiarity.

libido n. (pl. **libidos**) sexual desire.

librarian n. a person in charge of or assisting in a library.

library n. (pl. **libraries**) **1** a building or room containing a collection of books etc. for consulting or borrowing. **2** a private collection of books.

libretto n. (pl. **libretti** or **librettos**) the words of an opera.

lice pl. of LOUSE.

licence (US **license**) n. **1** an official permit to own, use, or do something. **2** freedom to do as one wishes.

> ☑ *licence* is the spelling for the noun, *license* for the verb; in US English the *-ense* spelling is used for both.

license v. grant a licence to or for.

licensee n. the holder of a licence.

licentiate /ly-sen-shi-uht/ n. the holder

Thesaurus

out, plane. **2** RAZE, raze to the ground, pull down, knock down, tear down, demolish, flatten, bulldoze, lay waste, destroy.

liable adj. **1** RESPONSIBLE, accountable, answerable, chargeable, blameworthy, at fault, censurable. **2** EXPOSED, open, subject, susceptible, vulnerable, in danger of, at risk of. **3** APT, likely, inclined, tending, disposed, predisposed, prone.

liar n. FIBBER, perjurer, falsifier, false witness, fabricator, deceiver, spinner of yarns.

libel n. DEFAMATION, denigration, vilification, disparagement, aspersions, calumny, slander, false report, traducement, obloquy, abuse, slur, smear; *formal* derogation, calumniation. ▶ v. DEFAME, vilify, blacken someone's name, denigrate, disparage, cast aspersions on, slander, traduce, abuse, revile, malign, slur, smear, fling mud at; *formal* derogate, calumniate.

libellous adj. DEFAMATORY, denigratory, vilifying, disparaging, derogatory, slanderous, false, misrepresentative, traducing, abusive, reviling, malicious, scurrilous, muckraking.

liberal adj. **1** ABUNDANT, copious, ample, plentiful, lavish, profuse, munificent, bountiful, rich, handsome, generous. **2** GENEROUS, magnanimous, open-handed, unsparing, unstinting, lavish, munificent, bountiful, big-hearted, kind, philanthropic, charitable, altruistic, unselfish; *literary* bounteous. **3** UNPREJUDICED, unbiased, unbigoted, impartial, disinterested, broad-minded, enlightened, catholic, indulgent, permissive. **4** LOOSE, flexible, free, general, inexact, imprecise. **5** ADVANCED, forward-looking, progressive, reformist, radical, latitudinarian. ■ OPPOSITES conservative.

liberate v. SET FREE, free, release, let out, let go, discharge, set loose, unshackle, unfetter, unchain, deliver, rescue, emancipate, unyoke; *historical* manumit.

liberty n. **1** FREEDOM, independence, autonomy, sovereignty, self-government, self-rule. **2** LIBERATION, freeing, release, discharge, deliverance, emancipation; *historical* manumission. □ **at liberty** FREE, loose, on the loose, at large, unconfined.

licence n. **1** PERMIT, certificate, credentials, document, documentation, pass. **2** PERMISSION, leave, liberty, freedom, consent, authority, authorization, sanction, approval, warranty.

license v. **1** GRANT A LICENCE TO, authorof a certificate of competence in a particular profession.

licentious adj. sexually immoral.

lichen /ly-kuhn/ n. a plant resembling moss which grows on rocks, walls, and trees.

lick v. **1** pass the tongue over. **2** move lightly and quickly. **3** informal totally defeat. ▶ n. **1** an act of licking. **2** informal a quick application of something. **3** informal a fast pace.

licorice US = LIQUORICE.

lid n. **1** a removable or hinged cover for a container. **2** an eyelid.

lie¹ v. (**lying**, **lay**; past part. **lain**) **1** be in or take up a horizontal position on a supporting surface. **2** be in a particular state. **3** be found or situated. ▶ n. the direction or position in which something lies. ☐ **lie-in** a prolonged stay in bed in the morning. **lie low** avoid attention.

✓ Don't confuse **lay** and **lie**: see the note at LAY¹.
---

lie² n. a deliberately false statement. ▶ v. (**lying**, **lied**) tell a lie or lies.

liege /leej/ n. hist. **1** a feudal lord. **2** a vassal or subject.

lien /leen, lee-uhn/ n. the right to hold another person's property until a debt is paid.

lieu /loo/ n. (**in lieu**) instead.

lieutenant /lef-ten-uhnt/ n. **1** a deputy or substitute acting for a superior. **2** a

rank of officer in the army and navy.

life n. (pl. **lives**) **1** the ability of animals and plants to function and grow. **2** the existence of an individual. **3** a particular type or aspect of people's existence. **4** living things and their activity. **5** vitality or energy. ☐ **lifebelt** a ring of buoyant material to keep a person afloat. **lifeboat 1** a boat for rescuing people at sea. **2** a small boat on a ship for emergency use. **life cycle** the series of changes in the life of an organism. **lifeguard** a person employed to rescue bathers in difficulty. **life jacket** a buoyant or inflatable jacket for keeping a person afloat. **lifelike** exactly like a real person or thing. **lifeless 1** dead or apparently dead. **2** without living things. **3** lacking energy. **lifeline 1** a rope thrown to rescue someone in difficulty in water. **2** a thing essential for continued existence. **lifelong** lasting all one's life. **life sciences** the sciences concerned with living organisms, e.g. biology. **lifestyle** the way in which a person lives. **life-support** (of medical equipment) keeping the body functioning after serious illness or injury. **lifetime** the length of time that a person lives or a thing lasts.

lift v. **1** raise or be raised. **2** pick up and move to a different position. **3** formally end a legal restriction. **4** (**lift off**) (of a spacecraft etc.) take off. ▶ n. **1** an apparatus for moving people or things between different levels of a building etc.

Thesaurus

ize, warrant, accredit, charter, franchise. **2** GIVE PERMISSION TO, permit, allow, grant leave to, entitle, give the freedom to, sanction, give one's approval to, empower. ■ OPPOSITES ban.

lid n. COVER, top, cap, cork, stopper, plug.

lie¹ n. UNTRUTH, falsehood, fib, white lie, fabrication, made-up story, trumped-up story, invention, piece of fiction, falsification, falsity, fairy story, cock and bull story, dissimulation, departure from the truth; informal terminological inexactitude, tall tale, whopper. ▶ v. TELL A LIE, perjure oneself, fib, fabricate, invent/make up a story, falsify, dissemble, dissimulate, prevaricate, depart from the truth, be economical with the truth, bear false witness.

lie² v. **1** RECLINE, be recumbent, be prostrate, be supine, be prone, be stretched out, sprawl, rest, repose, relax, lounge, loll. **2** BE, be situated, be located, be placed, be positioned, be found. ☐ **lie**

in CONSIST, be inherent, inhere, be present, exist, reside. **lie low** HIDE, go into hiding, hide out, conceal oneself, keep out of sight, keep a low profile, take cover, go to earth, go to ground, go underground; informal hole up.

life n. **1** EXISTENCE, being, animation, aliveness, viability. **2** LIVING THINGS, living beings, living creatures, human/animal/plant life, fauna, flora. **3** PERSON, human being, individual, mortal, soul. **4** LIFETIME, days, duration of life, course of life, lifespan, time on earth, existence, career; informal one's born days.

lifeless adj. **1** DEAD, deceased, gone, cold, defunct. **2** BARREN, sterile, bare, desolate, stark, arid, unproductive, uncultivated, empty, uninhabited, unoccupied. **3** SPIRITLESS, lacking vitality, lacklustre, apathetic, uninspired, colourless, dull, flat, stiff, wooden, tedious, uninspiring. ■ OPPOSITES alive, lively.

2 an act of lifting. **3** a free ride in another person's vehicle. **4** a feeling of increased cheerfulness. □ **lift-off** the vertical take-off of a spacecraft etc.

ligament n. a band of tissue connecting bones or cartilages.

ligature n. a cord for tying up a bleeding artery.

light n. **1** the natural form of energy that makes things visible. **2** a source of this. **3** a device producing a flame or spark. **4** understanding or enlightenment. ▸ v. (**lighting**, **lit**; past part. **lit** or **lighted**) **1** provide with light. **2** ignite or be ignited. **3** (**light up**) make or become lively or happy. **4** (**light on**) discover by chance. ▸ adj. **1** having a lot of light. **2** (of a colour) pale. **3** of little weight; not heavy. **4** not strongly or heavily built. **5** relatively low in density or amount. **6** not serious or profound. □ **bring** (or **come**) **to light** make (or become) widely known. **in the light of** taking something into consideration. **light-fingered** prone to steal. **light-headed** dizzy and slightly faint. **light-hearted** amusing and entertaining. **lighthouse** a tower with a powerful light to guide ships at sea. **light industry** industry producing small or light articles. **lightship** a moored ship with a light, acting as a lighthouse. **light-**

weight 1 a weight in boxing etc. between featherweight and welterweight. **2** informal a person of little importance. **light year** the distance light travels in one year, nearly 6 million million miles. **make light of** treat as unimportant. ■ **lighten** v. **lightly** adv. **lightness** n.

lighter n. **1** a device for lighting cigarettes. **2** a flat-bottomed barge used to transfer goods to and from ships in harbour.

lighting n. **1** equipment for producing light. **2** the effect of lights.

lightning n. the discharge of electricity between a cloud and the ground or within a cloud, accompanied by a bright flash. ▸ adj. very quick.

✓ The spelling is *lightning*, not *-tening*.

---

lights pl. n. the lungs of certain animals used as food.

lignite n. soft brown coal.

like prep. **1** similar to. **2** in the manner of. **3** in a way appropriate to. **4** such as. ▸ conj. informal **1** in the same way that. **2** as if. ▸ n. **1** (**the like**) things of the same kind. **2** (**likes**) the things one likes. ▸ adj. similar. ▸ v. **1** find agreeable or satisfactory. **2** wish for; want.

Thesaurus

lifelike adj. TRUE-TO-LIFE, realistic, photographic, faithful, authentic, exact, vivid, graphic, natural. ■ OPPOSITES unrealistic.

lift v. **1** PICK UP, uplift, hoist, heave up, raise, raise up, heft. **2** REMOVE, raise, withdraw, revoke, cancel, annul, void, countermand, relax, end, stop, terminate. **3** STEAL, thieve, rob, pilfer, purloin, pocket, take, appropriate; informal filch, swipe, pinch, nick.

light¹ n. **1** ILLUMINATION, luminescence, luminosity, shining, gleaming, brightness, brilliance, blaze, glare, incandescence, effulgence, refulgence, lambency, radiance, lustre. **2** DAYLIGHT, daylight hours, daytime, day, hours of sunlight. **3** ASPECT, angle, slant, approach, viewpoint, point of view. ▸ v. **1** SET BURNING, set fire to, set a match to, ignite, kindle. **2** ILLUMINATE, brighten, lighten, irradiate, flood with light, floodlight; literary illumine. ▸ adj. **1** FULL OF LIGHT, bright, well lit, well illuminated, sunny. **2** LIGHT-COLOURED, light-toned, pale, pastel, whitish, faded, bleached.

light² adj. **1** LIGHTWEIGHT, underweight, portable. **2** thin, flimsy, insubstantial, delicate, floaty, gossamer. **3** GENTLE, slight, delicate, soft, weak, faint, indistinct. **4** MODERATE, easy, simple, undemanding, untaxing, effortless, facile; informal cushy. **5** LIGHT-HEARTED, entertaining, diverting, recreational, amusing, humorous, funny, frivolous, superficial, trivial, trifling. ■ OPPOSITES heavy.

lighten¹ v. MAKE LIGHTER, lessen, reduce, ease, alleviate, mitigate, allay, relieve, assuage, ameliorate. ■ OPPOSITES increase.

lighten² v. **1** BECOME LIGHTER, grow brighter, brighten. **2** MAKE LIGHTER, make brighter, brighten, light up, illuminate, shed light on, cast light on, irradiate. ■ OPPOSITES darken.

lightly adv. **1** SLIGHTLY, thinly, softly, gently. **2** SPARINGLY, sparsely, slightly. **3** AIRILY, carelessly, heedlessly, uncaringly, indifferently, thoughtlessly, flippantly, frivolously, slightingly.

like¹ v. **1** BE FOND OF, have a liking for, be attracted to, be keen on, love, adore, have a soft spot for. **2** ENJOY, be keen on, find/take pleasure in, be partial to,

likeable (or **likable**) adj. pleasant; easy to like.

likelihood n. a probability.

likely adj. (**likelier**, **likeliest**) **1** probable. **2** promising. ▶ adv. probably.

liken v. (**liken to**) point out the resemblance of someone or something to.

likeness n. **1** resemblance. **2** a portrait or representation.

likewise adv. **1** also. **2** similarly.

liking n. **1** a fondness. **2** (**one's liking**) one's taste.

lilac n. **1** a shrub with fragrant purple or white blossom. **2** a pale purple colour.

lilt n. **1** a rise and fall of the voice when speaking. **2** a gentle rhythm in a tune. ■ **lilting** adj.

lily n. a plant with large flowers on a tall stem.

limb n. **1** an arm, leg, or wing. **2** a large branch of a tree.

limber adj. supple. ▶ v. (**limber up**) warm up in preparation for exercise.

limbo n. **1** an uncertain period of waiting. **2** (pl. **limbos**) a West Indian dance in which the dancer bends back to pass under a bar.

lime n. **1** a white alkaline substance used as a building material or fertilizer. **2** a round green citrus fruit. **3** a bright green colour. **4** a tree with heart-shaped leaves. □ **limelight** the focus of public attention. **limestone** a hard rock composed mainly of calcium carbonate.

limerick n. a humorous five-line poem.

limit n. **1** a point beyond which something does not or may not pass. **2** a restriction on size or amount. ▶ v. put a limit on. □ **off limits** out of bounds. ■ **limitation** n. **limitless** adj.

limousine n. a large, luxurious car.

Thesaurus

love, adore, find agreeable, delight in, relish, revel in; *informal* get a kick from. **3** WISH, want, desire, prefer, had sooner, had rather. ■ OPPOSITES dislike.

like² adj. SIMILAR, comparable, corresponding, resembling, analogous, parallel, equivalent, of a kind, identical, matching, akin. ■ OPPOSITES dissimilar. ▶ prep. **1** IN THE SAME WAY AS, in the manner of, in a similar way to, after the fashion of, along the lines of. **2** TYPICAL OF, characteristic of, in character with. ▶ n. EQUAL, match, counterpart, fellow, twin, mate, parallel, peer, compeer.

likeable adj. PLEASANT, nice, friendly, agreeable, amiable, genial, charming, engaging, pleasing, appealing, winning, attractive, winsome, lovable, adorable. ■ OPPOSITES unpleasant.

likelihood n. LIKELINESS, probability, good chance, chance, prospect, good prospect, possibility.

likely adj. **1** PROBABLE, possible, to be expected, on the cards, odds-on. **2** APT, inclined, tending, liable, prone. **3** SUITABLE, appropriate, fit, fitting, acceptable, proper, right, qualified, relevant, reasonable. **4** PROMISING, talented, gifted; *informal* up-and-coming. ■ OPPOSITES unlikely.

liken v. COMPARE, equate, analogize, draw an analogy between, draw a parallel between, parallel, correlate, associate, link.

likeness n. **1** RESEMBLANCE, similarity, sameness, similitude, correspondence, analogy. **2** GUISE, semblance, appearance, outward form, form, shape, character. **3** PICTURE, drawing, sketch, painting, portrait, photograph, study, representation, image, bust, statue, statuette, sculpture.

liking n. FONDNESS, love, affection, desire, preference, partiality, penchant, bias, weakness, weak spot, soft spot, appreciation, taste, predilection, fancy, inclination, bent, leaning, affinity, proclivity, propensity, proneness, tendency. ■ OPPOSITES dislike, aversion.

limb n. **1** ARM, leg, wing, member, extremity, appendage. **2** BRANCH, bough.

limelight n. FOCUS OF ATTENTION, public attention, public notice, public eye, public recognition, publicity, fame, renown, celebrity, stardom, notability, eminence, prominence, spotlight.

limit n. **1** BOUNDARY, border, bound, frontier, edge, perimeter, confines, periphery. **2** MAXIMUM, ceiling, limitation, restriction, curb, check, restraint. ▶ v. **1** PLACE A LIMIT ON, restrict, curb, check, keep within bounds, hold in check, restrain, confine, control, ration, reduce. **2** RESTRICT, curb, restrain, constrain, hinder, impede, hamper, trammel, check.

limitation n. **1** RESTRICTION, curb, restraint, constraint, qualification, control, check, hindrance, impediment, obstacle, obstruction, bar, barrier, block, deterrent. **2** INABILITY, incapability, incapacity, defect, frailty, weakness.

limited adj. RESTRICTED, scanty, sparse, cramped, narrow, basic, minimal, little,

limp v. walk with difficulty because of an injured leg or foot. ▶ n. a limping walk. ▶ adj. not stiff or firm. ■ **limply** adv.

limpet n. a shellfish that clings tightly to rocks.

limpid adj. (of a liquid or the eyes) clear.

linchpin n. **1** a pin through the end of an axle keeping a wheel in position. **2** a person or thing vital to an enterprise.

linctus n. thick liquid cough medicine.

line n. **1** a long, narrow mark. **2** a length of cord, wire, etc. **3** a row or series of people or things. **4** a row of words. **5** a course or channel. **6** a telephone connection. **7** a railway track or route. **8** a series of military defences. **9** a wrinkle. **10** an area of activity. **11** (**lines**) the words of an actor's part. ▶ v. **1** be positioned at intervals along. **2** (**line up**) arrange in a row. **3** (**lined**) marked with lines. **4** cover the inner surface of. □ **line dancing** country and western dancing in which a line of dancers follow a set pattern of steps. **linesman** (in sport) an official who assists the referee or umpire in deciding whether the ball is out of play.

lineage /lin-i-ij/ n. ancestry.

lineal adj. of or in a line.

linear adj. **1** arranged in or extending along a straight line. **2** consisting of lines. **3** progressing from one stage to another in steps.

linen n. **1** cloth made of flax. **2** household articles such as sheets, formerly made of linen.

liner n. **1** a large passenger ship. **2** a removable lining.

ling n. **1** an edible sea fish. **2** heather.

linger v. **1** be slow or reluctant to leave. **2** (**linger over**) spend a long time over.

lingerie /lan-zhuh-ri/ n. women's underwear.

lingua franca n. (pl. **lingua francas**) a common language used among speakers whose native languages are different.

lingual adj. **1** of the tongue. **2** of speech or language.

linguist n. **1** a person skilled in foreign languages. **2** a person who studies linguistics.

linguistic adj. of language. ▶ n. (**linguistics**) the study of language. ■ **linguistically** adv.

liniment n. an ointment to relieve pain or bruising.

lining n. a layer of material covering the inside of something.

link n. **1** a connection. **2** a means of contact. **3** a loop in a chain. ▶ v. make or suggest a link with or between. ■ **linkage** n.

lino n. informal linoleum.

linoleum n. a smooth covering for floors.

linseed n. the seeds of the flax plant, used to make oil.

lint n. **1** fluff from cloth or yarn. **2** a fabric for dressing wounds.

Thesaurus

inadequate, insufficient. ■ OPPOSITES ample, boundless.

limitless adj. **1** INFINITE, endless, never-ending, interminable, immense, vast, extensive, measureless. **2** UNLIMITED, boundless, unbounded, illimitable, infinite, endless, unceasing, interminable, inexhaustible, constant, perpetual.

limp adj. **1** FLOPPY, drooping, droopy, soft, flaccid, flabby, loose, slack. **2** TIRED, fatigued, weary, exhausted, worn out, lethargic, enervated, feeble, frail, puny, debilitated. **3** WEAK, characterless, ineffectual, insipid, wishy-washy, vapid; informal wet. ■ OPPOSITES stiff.

line n. **1** RULE, bar, score, underline, underscore, stroke, slash. **2** BAND, stripe, strip, belt, seam. **3** FURROW, wrinkle, crease, crow's foot, groove, scar. **4** OUTLINE, contour, configuration, shape, figure, delineation, silhouette, profile. **5** BOUNDARY, boundary line, limit, border, borderline, frontier, edge, margin, perimeter, periphery. **6** ROW,

queue, procession, column, file, string, chain, array; informal crocodile. **7** LINEAGE, descent, ancestry, parentage, family, extraction, heritage, stock, strain, race, breed. **8** ROPE, string, cord, cable, wire, thread, twine, strand, filament. ▶ v. BORDER, edge, fringe, bound, skirt, hem, rim, verge. □ **line up** FORM A LINE, get into rows/columns, file, form a queue, queue up, group together, fall in.

linger v. **1** STAY, remain, wait around, hang around, dawdle, loiter, dally, take one's time; informal dilly-dally; old use tarry. **2** PERSIST, continue, remain, stay, hang around, be protracted, endure.

link n. **1** CHAIN RING, loop, connection, connective, coupling, joint, knot. **2** COMPONENT, constituent, element, part, piece, member, division. **3** CONNECTION, relationship, relatedness, association, tie-up. **4** BOND, tie, attachment, connection, relationship, association, affiliation,

lintel n. a horizontal support across the top of a door or window.

lion n. a large cat of Africa and NW India.

lionize (or **-ise**) v. treat as a celebrity.

lip n. **1** either of the two fleshy parts forming the edges of the mouth opening. **2** the edge of a container or opening. **3** informal cheeky talk. □ **lip-read** understand speech from watching a speaker's lip movements. **lipstick** a cosmetic for colouring the lips.

liposuction n. removal of fat from under the skin by suction, used in cosmetic surgery.

liquefy v. (**liquefying**, **liquefied**) make or become liquid. ■ **liquefaction** n.

....
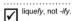 liquefy, not -ify.
....

liqueur /li-**kyoor**/ n. a strong, sweet alcoholic spirit.

liquid n. a substance such as water or oil that flows freely. ▶ adj. **1** in the form of a liquid. **2** (of assets) held in or easily converted into cash.

liquidate v. **1** wind up a company and divide the assets among its creditors. **2** convert assets into cash. **3** informal kill. ■ **liquidation** n.

liquidity n. the availability of liquid assets to a market or company.

liquidize (or **-ise**) v. reduce solid food to a liquid. ■ **liquidizer** n.

liquor n. **1** alcoholic drink. **2** liquid produced in cooking.

liquorice (US **licorice**) n. a black substance used as a sweet and in medicine.

lira n. (pl. **lire**) the basic unit of money of Turkey and formerly of Italy.

lisp n. a speech defect in which s and z are pronounced like th. ▶ v. speak with a lisp.

lissom adj. slim and supple.

list n. **1** a number of connected items or names written as a series. **2** an instance of a ship listing. ▶ v. **1** make a list of. **2** include in a list. **3** (of a ship) lean over to one side.

listen v. **1** give one's attention to a sound. **2** make an effort to hear something. **3** (**listen in**) listen to a private conversation. **4** respond to advice or a request. ■ **listener** n.

listeria n. a type of bacterium causing food poisoning.

listless adj. lacking energy or enthusiasm. ■ **listlessly** adv.

lit past & past part. of **LIGHT**.

litany n. (pl. **litanies**) **1** a series of prayers. **2** a boring recital.

liter US = **LITRE**.

literal adj. using or interpreting words in their usual or most basic sense; not metaphorical. ■ **literally** adv.

literary adj. of literature.

literate adj. able to read and write. ■ **literacy** n.

literati pl. n. educated people interested

Thesaurus
....

mutual interest. ▶ v. **1** CONNECT, fasten together, attach, bind, unite, couple, yoke. **2** JOIN, connect, associate, relate, bracket. ■ OPPOSITES detach, separate.

lip n. EDGE, rim, brim, margin, border, verge, brink.

liquid n. FLUID, liquor, solution, juice, sap.

liquidate v. **1** CONVERT TO CASH, cash, cash in, sell off, sell up, realize. **2** KILL, murder, put to death, do away with, assassinate, put an end to, eliminate, dispatch, finish off, destroy, obliterate; informal do in, bump off, wipe out.

liquidize v. BLEND, crush, purée, pulverize, process.

list¹ n. CATALOGUE, inventory, record, register, roll, file, index, directory, listing, enumeration, table, tabulation, schedule, syllabus, calendar, programme, series. ▶ v. NOTE DOWN, write down, record, register, set down, enter, itemize, enumerate, catalogue, file, tabulate, schedule, chronicle, classify, alphabetize.

list² v. LEAN, lean over, tilt, tip, heel, heel over, careen, cant, incline, slant, slope.

listen v. PAY ATTENTION TO, be attentive to, hear, attend, hark, give ear to, lend an ear to, hang on someone's words, keep one's ears open, prick up one's ears; informal be all ears, pin back one's ears.

listless adj. LANGUID, lethargic, languishing, enervated, lackadaisical, spiritless, lifeless, inactive, inert, indolent, apathetic, passive, dull, heavy, sluggish, slothful, limp, languorous, torpid, supine, indifferent, uninterested, impassive. ■ OPPOSITES energetic.

literal adj. WORD-FOR-WORD, verbatim, line-for-line, exact, precise, faithful, close, strict, undeviating, accurate, true.

literary adj. **1** WELL READ, widely read, educated, well educated, scholarly, learned, intellectual, cultured, erudite, bookish, studious, lettered. **2** FORMAL, poetic.

in literature.

literature n. **1** written works regarded as having artistic merit. **2** books and printed information on a particular subject.

lithe /lyth/ adj. slim and supple.

lithium n. a metallic element.

lithography n. printing from a flat metal surface treated so that ink sticks only where required. ■ **lithograph** n.

litigant n. a person involved in a lawsuit.

litigate v. take a dispute or claim to a law court. ■ **litigation** n.

litigious adj. fond of litigation.

litmus n. a dye turned red by acids and blue by alkalis.

litotes /ly-toh-teez/ n. ironical understatement (e.g. *I shan't be sorry* for *I shall be glad*).

litre (US **liter**) n. a metric unit of capacity equal to 1,000 cubic centimetres (1.76 pints).

litter n. **1** rubbish left in a public place. **2** a number of young born to an animal at one time. **3** material to absorb a cat's excrement. **4** straw used as animal bed-

ding. **5** hist. an enclosed bed or seat carried by men or animals. ▶ v. make untidy with scattered articles.

little adj. **1** small in size, amount, or degree. **2** young or younger. ▶ n. & pron. not much. ▶ adv. **1** (**a little**) to a small extent. **2** hardly or not at all.

littoral adj. of or by the seashore.

liturgy n. (pl. **liturgies**) a set form of public worship. ■ **liturgical** adj.

live[1] v. **1** be or remain alive. **2** spend one's life in a particular way. **3** have one's home in a place or with a person. **4** obtain the things necessary for staying alive. **5** (**live on**) eat as a major part of one's diet. **6** (**live down**) succeed in making others forget something embarrassing.

live[2] adj. **1** living. **2** (of a broadcast) transmitted at the time of occurrence. **3** connected to an electric current. **4** able to explode.

livelihood n. a means of earning or obtaining the necessities of life.

lively adj. (**livelier**, **liveliest**) full of energy or activity. ■ **liveliness** n.

liven v. (**liven up**) make or become more

Thesaurus

literate adj. **1** ABLE TO READ AND WRITE, educated, schooled. **2** EDUCATED, well educated, well read, scholarly, learned, intellectual, erudite, cultured, cultivated, knowledgeable, well informed. **3** WELL WRITTEN, stylish, polished, articulate, lucid, eloquent.

literature n. **1** WRITTEN WORKS, writings, printed works, published works, letters. **2** PRINTED MATTER, brochure, leaflet, pamphlet, circular, information, data, facts; *informal* bumf.

lithe adj. AGILE, flexible, supple, limber, loose-limbed, pliant, pliable, lissom.

litigation n. LAWSUIT, legal case, case, legal dispute, legal contest, legal action, legal proceedings, suit, suit at law.

litter n. **1** RUBBISH, debris, refuse, junk, odds and ends, fragments, detritus, flotsam; *US* trash, garbage. **2** BROOD, young, offspring, progeny, family. **3** STRETCHER, portable bed/couch, palanquin. ▶ v. MAKE UNTIDY, mess up, make a mess of, clutter up, throw into disorder, disarrange; *informal* make a shambles of.

little adj. **1** SMALL, short, slight, petite, tiny, wee, miniature, mini, diminutive, minute, infinitesimal, microscopic, minuscule, young, dwarf, midget, pygmy, bantam; *informal* teeny, teeny-weeny, pint-sized. **2** UNIMPORTANT, insignificant, minor, trivial, trifling, petty,

paltry, inconsequential, negligible, nugatory. **3** HARDLY ANY, small, scant, meagre, skimpy, sparse, insufficient, exiguous; *informal* piddling. ■ OPPOSITES big, important. ▶ adv. HARDLY, barely, scarcely, not much, only slightly, only just.

liturgy n. RITUAL, worship, service, ceremony, rite, observance, celebration, office, sacrament.

live adj. **1** ALIVE, living, having life, breathing, animate, vital, existing, existent; *informal* in the land of the living. **2** NOT PRERECORDED, unedited, with an audience. **3** CHARGED, connected, active, switched on. **4** CURRENT, topical, active, prevalent, important, of interest, lively, vital, pressing, burning, pertinent, controversial, debatable, unsettled. ■ OPPOSITES dead.

livelihood n. LIVING, subsistence, means of support, income, keep, maintenance, sustenance, upkeep, work, employment, occupation, trade, profession, career.

lively adj. **1** FULL OF LIFE, active, animated, energetic, alive, vigorous, alert, spirited, high-spirited, vivacious, enthusiastic, keen, cheerful, buoyant, sparkling, bouncy, perky, sprightly, spry, frisky, agile, nimble; *informal* chirpy, chipper, peppy. **2** BRISK, quick, rapid, swift, speedy, vigorous. **3** ANIlively.

liver n. a large organ in the abdomen producing bile.

livery n. (pl. **liveries**) **1** a special uniform. **2** a distinctive design and colour scheme used on a company's vehicles or products. ■ **liveried** adj.

lives pl. of LIFE.

livestock n. farm animals.

livid adj. **1** informal very angry. **2** appearing dark and inflamed.

living n. **1** a way or style of life. **2** an income, or the means of earning it. ▶ adj. alive. □ **living room** a room for general everyday use.

lizard n. a four-legged reptile with a long tail.

llama /lah-muh/ n. a South American animal related to the camel.

load n. **1** a thing or quantity carried. **2** a weight or source of pressure. **3** (**a load/loads of**) informal a lot of. **4** the amount of work to be done by a person. ▶ v. **1** put a load on or in. **2** insert something into a device so that it will operate. **3** put ammunition into a gun. **4** (**loaded**) biased towards a particular outcome.

loaf n. (pl. **loaves**) a quantity of bread

shaped and baked in one piece. ▶ v. idle one's time away. ■ **loafer** n.

loam n. a fertile soil.

loan n. **1** a sum of money lent. **2** the act of lending. ▶ v. lend. □ **loan shark** informal a moneylender charging very high rates of interest.

loath adj. unwilling.

loathe v. feel hatred or disgust for. ■ **loathsome** adj.

lob v. (**lobbing**, **lobbed**) throw or hit in a high arc. ▶ n. a lobbed ball.

lobby n. (pl. **lobbies**) **1** an open area inside the entrance of a public building. **2** a group trying to influence politicians on a particular issue. ▶ v. (**lobbying**, **lobbied**) try to influence a politician on an issue. ■ **lobbyist** n.

lobe n. a flat rounded part or projection.

lobelia n. a garden plant with blue or scarlet flowers.

lobotomy n. (pl. **lobotomies**) an operation involving cutting into part of the brain.

lobster n. a shellfish with large pincers.

local adj. of or affecting a particular place or part. ▶ n. **1** a person who lives in a particular place. **2** informal a pub near a person's home. ■ **locally** adv.

Thesaurus

MATED, spirited, stimulating, heated, enthusiastic, forceful. **4** BUSY, crowded, bustling, hectic, swarming, teeming, astir, buzzing, thronging. ■ OPPOSITES apathetic.

liven v. (**liven up**) ENLIVEN, put some life into, brighten up, cheer up, perk up, put some spark into, add some zest to, give a boost to, animate, vitalize, vivify; informal pep up, hot up.

living adj. ALIVE, live, having life, breathing, animate, vital, existing, existent; informal in the land of the living. ▶ n. LIVELIHOOD, subsistence, means of support, income, keep, maintenance, sustenance, upkeep, job, work, employment, occupation.

load n. **1** CARGO, freight, charge, burden, lading, contents, consignment, shipment, lorryload, shipload, busload. **2** BURDEN, onus, weight, responsibility, duty, charge, obligation, tax, strain, trouble, worry, encumbrance, affliction, oppression, handicap, trial, tribulation, cross, millstone, albatross, incubus. ▶ v. **1** FILL, fill up, lade, freight, charge, pack, pile, heap, stack, stuff, cram. **2** BURDEN, weigh down, weight, saddle, charge, tax, strain, encumber, hamper, handicap, overburden, overwhelm,

oppress, trouble, worry. **3** PRIME, charge, fill. **4** WEIGHT, add weight to, bias, rig.

loaf v. LAZE, lounge, do nothing, idle, lie around, hang about, waste time, fritter away time, take things easy, twiddle one's thumbs, sit on one's hands.

loan n. ADVANCE, credit, mortgage. ▶ v. LEND, advance, give credit, give on loan, let out.

loath adj. RELUCTANT, unwilling, disinclined, not in the mood, against, averse, opposed, resisting. ■ OPPOSITES eager.

loathe v. HATE, detest, abhor, despise, abominate, have an aversion to, not be able to bear, dislike, shrink from, recoil from, feel repugnance towards, be unable to stomach, execrate. ■ OPPOSITES like, love.

loathing n. HATRED, hate, detestation, abhorrence, aversion, abomination, repugnance, disgust, revulsion, odium, antipathy, dislike, ill will, enmity, execration.

loathsome adj. HATEFUL, detestable, abhorrent, odious, repugnant, disgusting, repulsive, revolting, nauseating, abominable, vile, nasty, obnoxious, horrible, offensive, disagreeable, despicable, contemptible, reprehensible, execrable;

locale /loh-kahl/ n. a place where something happens.

locality n. (pl. **localities**) **1** an area or neighbourhood. **2** the position of something.

localize (or **-ise**) v. restrict to a particular place. ■ **localization** n.

locate v. **1** discover the exact place of. **2** (**be located**) be situated.

location n. **1** a place where something is located. **2** the act of locating. **3** a place outside a studio where a film etc. is made.

loch n. (in Scotland) a lake or inlet of the sea.

loci pl. of LOCUS.

lock n. **1** a device for keeping a door or lid fastened etc., operated by a key. **2** a section of a canal with gates at each end allowing the water level to be changed. **3** a wrestling hold. **4** the turning of a vehicle's front wheels. **5** a coil or hanging piece of a person's hair. **6** (**locks**) a person's hair. ▶ v. **1** fasten with a lock. **2** shut in by locking a door. **3** make or become fixed. □ **lockjaw** tetanus. **lockout** the exclusion of employees from their workplace during a dispute. **locksmith** a person who makes and repairs locks. **lock-up 1** a makeshift jail. **2** non-residential premises that can be locked up, esp. a garage. ■ **lockable** adj.

locker n. a small lockable cupboard.

locket n. a small ornamental case worn on a chain round the neck.

locomotion n. movement from one place to another.

locomotive n. a powered railway vehicle for pulling trains. ▶ adj. of locomotion.

locum n. a doctor or priest standing in for another who is temporarily away.

locus n. (pl. **loci**) **1** a particular position or place. **2** Math. a curve etc. formed by all the points satisfying a particular condition.

locust n. a large destructive tropical grasshopper.

lode n. a vein of metal ore. □ **lodestar** the pole star. **lodestone** a piece of magnetic iron ore used as a magnet.

lodge n. **1** a small house at the gates of a large house with grounds. **2** a porter's room at the entrance of a large building. **3** a small house where people stay while hunting, shooting, etc. **4** a branch of certain organizations. **5** a beaver's den. ▶ v. **1** present a complaint, appeal, etc. **2** fix or be fixed in a place. **3** live as a lodger.

lodger n. a person who pays rent to live in a property with the owner.

lodging n. **1** temporary accommodation. **2** (**lodgings**) a rented room or rooms in the same house as the owner.

loft n. **1** a room or space under a roof. **2** a large, open flat in a converted building. **3** a gallery in a church or hall. ▶ v. kick, hit, or throw a ball high into the air.

lofty adj. (**loftier**, **loftiest**) **1** very tall. **2** noble. **3** haughty and aloof. ■ **loftily** adv.

Thesaurus

informal yucky.

local n. **1** LOCAL PERSON, native, inhabitant, resident, parishioner. **2** PUB, public house, bar, inn, tavern; informal watering hole, boozer.

locale n. PLACE, site, spot, position, location, venue, area, neighbourhood, locality, setting, scene.

locality n. **1** VICINITY, surrounding area, area, neighbourhood, district, region, environs, locale. **2** LOCATION, position, place, whereabouts, bearings; technical locus.

localize v. CONFINE, restrict, contain, limit, circumscribe, delimit.

locate v. **1** FIND, find out, discover, identify, pinpoint, detect, uncover, track down, run to earth, unearth, hit upon, come across, reveal, pin down. **2** SITUATE, site, position, place, put, build, establish, station, set, fix, settle.

location n. POSITION, place, situation,

whereabouts, bearings, site, spot, point, scene, setting, venue, locale; technical locus.

lock v. **1** BOLT, fasten, bar, secure, make secure, padlock. **2** JAM, become immovable, become rigid. ▶ n. BOLT, catch, fastener, clasp, bar, hasp.

locker n. CUPBOARD, compartment, cabinet, cubicle, storeroom, storage room.

lodge v. **1** BOARD, have lodgings, put up, reside, dwell, sojourn, stop; informal have digs. **2** REGISTER, submit, put forward, place, file, lay, put on record, record. **3** BECOME FIXED, become embedded, become implanted, stick, become caught, come to rest.

lofty adj. **1** TOWERING, soaring, tall, high, elevated, sky-high, sky-scraping. **2** ARROGANT, haughty, proud, self-important, conceited, overweening, disdainful, supercilious, condescending, patronizing, lordly, snobbish, scornful, con-

log n. **1** a piece cut from the trunk or a branch of a tree. **2** an official record of the voyage of a ship or aircraft. ▶v. (**logging, logged**) **1** enter facts in a log. **2** (**log in/on** or **out/off**) begin (or finish) using a computer system. **3** cut down trees for commercial use. □ **logbook 1** a log of a ship or aircraft. **2** a document recording details of a vehicle and its owner.

loganberry n. a red soft fruit, similar to a raspberry.

logarithm n. each of a series of numbers set out in tables, used to simplify calculations.

loggerheads pl. n. (**at loggerheads**) in strong disagreement.

logic n. **1** the science or a method of reasoning. **2** good reasoning. ■ **logician** n.

logical adj. **1** following the rules of logic. **2** showing clear, sound reasoning. **3** reasonable. ■ **logically** adv.

logistics n. the detailed organization of a large and complex exercise. ■ **logistical** adj.

logo n. (pl. **logos**) a design or symbol used as an emblem.

loin n. the part of the body between the ribs and the hip bones. □ **loincloth** a piece of cloth worn round the hips.

loiter v. stand around idly. ■ **loiterer** n.

loll v. **1** sit, lie, or stand in a relaxed way. **2** hang loosely.

lollipop n. a large boiled sweet on the end of a stick.

lollop v. (**lolloped, lolloping**) move with clumsy bounding steps.

lolly n. (pl. **lollies**) informal **1** a lollipop. **2** money.

lone adj. solitary.

lonely adj. (**lonelier, loneliest**) **1** sad because one has no friends or company. **2** (of time) spent alone. **3** (of a place) remote. ■ **loneliness** n.

loner n. a person who prefers to be alone.

lonesome adj. US lonely.

long adj. **1** of great or a particular length. **2** (of odds) reflecting a low probability. ▶adv. **1** for a long time. **2** throughout a specified period of time. ▶v. have a strong wish. □ **as** (or **so**) **long as** provided that. **long face** an unhappy expression. **longhand** ordinary handwriting as opposed to shorthand, typing, etc. **long-haul** involving transport over a long distance. **long johns** informal close-fitting underpants with long legs. **long-range 1** able to travel long distances. **2** of a period of time far in the future. **long shot** a scheme or guess very unlikely to succeed. **long-sighted** unable to see things clearly if they are close to the eyes. **long-standing** having existed for a long time. **long-suffering** bearing problems or annoyance patiently. **long-term** of or for a long time. **long wave** a radio wave of a wavelength above a kilometre and a frequency below 300 kHz. **longways** lengthways. **long-winded** long and boring.

longevity /lon-jev-i-ti/ n. long life.

longing n. a strong wish. ■ **longingly** adv.

Thesaurus

temptuous, insulting, cavalier; *informal* high and mighty, stuck up, snooty, toffee-nosed, uppity. **3** NOBLE, exalted, grand, sublime, imposing, esoteric. ■ OPPOSITES low, modest, base.

log n. **1** BLOCK, piece, chunk, billet, stump, trunk, branch, bole. **2** LOGBOOK, record, register, journal, diary, daybook, chart, account, tally.

logic n. **1** LINE OF REASONING, reasoning, argument, argumentation. **2** REASON, sound judgement, judgement, wisdom, sense, good sense, common sense, rationale, relevance, coherence.

logical adj. **1** REASONED, well reasoned, rational, sound, cogent, coherent, clear, consistent, relevant. **2** MOST LIKELY, likeliest, plausible, obvious. **3** REASONING, thinking, straight-thinking, rational, consistent. ■ OPPOSITES illogical.

loiter v. HANG AROUND/ABOUT, linger, wait, skulk, loaf, lounge, idle, waste time,

dawdle, take one's time, go at a snail's pace, dally, stroll, saunter, delay, loll.

lone adj. SINGLE, solitary, sole, unaccompanied.

lonely adj. **1** FRIENDLESS, companionless, lonesome, forlorn, forsaken, abandoned, rejected, isolated, outcast, sad, unhappy, despondent. **2** DESOLATE, barren, isolated, out of the way, remote, secluded, off the beaten track, deserted, uninhabited, unfrequented, unpopulated, godforsaken. ■ OPPOSITES popular, crowded.

long¹ adj. **1** LENGTHY, extended, extensive, stretched out, spread out. **2** PROLONGED, lengthy, protracted, extended, long-drawn-out, spun out, dragged out, interminable. ■ OPPOSITES short.

long² v. (**long for**) WISH FOR, desire, want, yearn for, crave, hunger for, thirst for, covet, lust after, hope for, dream of, pine for, eat one's heart out over, have

longitude n. the distance east or west of the Greenwich meridian, measured in degrees.

longitudinal adj. **1** extending lengthwise. **2** of longitude. ■ **longitudinally** adv.

loo n. informal a toilet.

loofah n. the dried inner parts of a tropical fruit, used as a bath sponge.

look v. **1** direct one's eyes. **2** seem. **3** face. ▶n. **1** an act of looking. **2** appearance. **3** (**looks**) a person's facial appearance. □ **look after** take care of. **lookalike** a person who looks very similar to another. **look down on** think that one is better than. **look for** try to find. **look into** investigate. **look on** watch without getting involved. **look out** be vigilant. **lookout 1** a place from which to keep watch. **2** a person keeping watch. **3** (**one's lookout**) informal one's own concern. **look up 1** improve. **2** search for and find information. **3** informal visit or contact. **look up**

to admire and respect.

loom n. a machine for weaving cloth. ▶v. **1** appear as a vague and threatening shape. **2** (of an unfavourable event) seem ominously close.

loop n. **1** a curve that bends round and crosses itself. **2** an endless strip of tape or film. ▶v. form into or have the shape of a loop. □ **loophole** a means of evading a rule or contract. **loop the loop** fly an aircraft in a vertical circle.

loose adj. **1** not firmly fixed in place. **2** not tied up or shut in. **3** (of a garment) not fitting tightly. **4** not dense or compact. **5** not exact. ▶v. unfasten or set free. □ **at a loose end** with nothing to do. **loose box** a stall for a horse. **loose-leaf** with each page removable. **on the loose** having escaped from being shut in or tied up. ■ **loosely** adv. **loosen** v. **looseness** n.

loot n. property taken from an enemy or stolen by thieves. ▶v. steal goods from a place during a war or riot. ■ **looter** n.

Thesaurus

a fancy for, hanker for/after; informal itch for, have a yen for.

longing n. wish, desire, wanting, yearning, craving, hunger, thirst, covetousness, lust, hope, dream, aspiration, pining, fancy, urge, hankering; informal itch, yen.

look v. **1** see, take a look, glance, fix one's gaze, focus, observe, view, regard, eye, take in, watch, examine, study, inspect, scan, scrutinize, survey, check, contemplate, consider, pay attention to, run the eyes over, peep, peek, glimpse, gaze, stare, gape, ogle; informal take a gander, have a squint, gawp, rubberneck, take a butcher's, take a dekko, take a shufti; US informal eyeball. **2** seem, seem to be, appear, appear to be, give every appearance/indication of being, look to be, strike someone as being. **3** face, overlook, front, front on, give on to. ▶n. **1** sight, glance, observation, view, examination, study, inspection, scan, survey, peep, peek, glimpse, gaze, stare, gape, ogle; informal eyeful, gander, look-see, once-over, squint, butcher's, dekko, shufti. **2** expression, face, countenance, features, mien. □ **look after** take care of, care for, attend to, tend, mind, keep an eye on, watch, sit with, nurse, take charge of, supervise, protect, guard. **look down on** regard with contempt, scorn, disdain, hold in disdain, sneer at, spurn, disparage, despise; informal look down one's nose at,

turn up one's nose at. **look for** search for, hunt for, seek, look around for, cast about for, forage for.

loom v. **1** appear, emerge, become visible, take shape, materialize, reveal itself. **2** be imminent, impend, be close, be ominously close, threaten, menace.

loop n. coil, hoop, noose, circle, ring, oval, spiral, curl, twirl, whorl, twist, convolution. ▶v. form a hoop with, make a circle with, bend into spirals/ whorls.

loophole n. let-out clause, means of avoidance, means of escape, escape clause, escape route, ambiguity, omission.

loose adj. **1** at large, at liberty, free, on the loose, unconfined, untied, unchained, untethered, unsecured, unshackled, unfastened, unrestricted, freed, let go, liberated, released, set loose. **2** wobbly, not secure, insecure, rickety, unsteady, movable. **3** untied, unpinned, hanging free, flowing, floppy. **4** loose-fitting, easy-fitting, generously cut, slack, baggy, saggy, sloppy. **5** inexact, imprecise, vague, indefinite, ill-defined, broad, general, non-specific. □ **let loose** set free, unloose, turn loose, set loose, untie, unchain, untether, unfasten, detach, unleash, let go, release, free, liberate.

loosen v. **1** slacken, slack, unstick, work loose, work free. **2** loose, relax, slacken, weaken, lessen, moderate.

lop v. (**lopping**, **lopped**) cut off a branch from a tree.

lope v. run with a long bounding stride.

lop-eared adj. with drooping ears.

lopsided adj. with one side lower or smaller than the other.

loquacious adj. talkative. ■ **loquacity** n.

lord n. **1** a nobleman. **2** (**Lord**) a title given to certain British peers or high officials. **3** a master or ruler. **4** (**Lord**) a name for God or Jesus. □ **lord it over** act in an arrogant and bullying way towards. **Your/His Lordship** a form of address to a judge, bishop, or nobleman.

lore n. a body of traditions and knowledge.

lorgnette /lor-nyet/ n. a pair of glasses held by a long handle.

lorry n. (pl. **lorries**) a large vehicle for transporting goods.

lose v. (**losing**, **lost**) **1** have taken away from one; cease to have. **2** become unable to find. **3** fail to win. **4** waste time or an opportunity. **5** (**lose oneself in**) become deeply involved in. □ **lose heart** become discouraged. **lose out** not get a fair chance or advantage. ■ **loser** n.

loss n. **1** the act of losing. **2** a person or thing lost. **3** sadness after losing a valued person or thing. **4** a person or thing badly missed when lost. □ **at a loss** uncertain or puzzled. **loss-leader** a product sold at a loss to attract customers.

lot pron. & adv. (**a lot/lots**) informal a large number or amount. ▶ n. **1** an item for sale at an auction. **2** informal a group of people or things. **3** a piece of paper chosen at random from a number of marked pieces as a method of deciding something. **4** a person's situation in life. **5** a plot of land. □ **the lot** informal the whole number or quantity.

lotion n. a medicinal or cosmetic liquid put on the skin.

lottery n. (pl. **lotteries**) **1** a means of raising money by selling numbered tickets and giving prizes to the holders of numbers drawn at random. **2** something whose success is controlled by luck.

lotus n. **1** a large water lily. **2** a mythical fruit.

loud adj. **1** making a lot of noise. **2** easily heard. **3** garish. ▶ adv. with much noise. □ **loudhailer** an electronic megaphone. **loudspeaker** a device that converts electrical impulses into sound. ■ **loudly** adv. **loudness** n.

Thesaurus

■ OPPOSITES tighten. □ **loosen up** RELAX, ease up/off; informal let up, hang loose, lighten up.

loot n. BOOTY, spoils, plunder, haul, stolen goods, pillage, prize; informal swag, the goods, hot goods, boodle. ▶ v. PLUNDER, pillage, rob, burgle, steal from, ransack, sack, maraud, ravage, despoil.

lop v. CUT OFF, chop, chop off, hack off, prune, sever, clip, dock, crop, remove, detach.

lose v. **1** MISLAY, misplace, fail to keep/retain, fail to keep sight of, drop, forget. **2** BE DEPRIVED OF, suffer the loss of. **3** ESCAPE FROM, evade, elude, dodge, give the slip to, shake off, throw off, throw off the scent, duck, get rid of. **4** SUFFER DEFEAT, be defeated, be the loser, be worsted, get/have the worst of it, be beaten, be conquered, be vanquished, be trounced, come off second-best, fail, come to grief, meet one's Waterloo; informal come a cropper.

loser n. RUNNER-UP, also-ran, the defeated, the vanquished, failure, born loser; informal flop, dud, non-starter, no-hoper, washout. ■ OPPOSITES winner, success.

loss n. **1** MISLAYING, misplacement, drop-

ping, forgetting. **2** LOSING, deprivation, privation, forfeiture, bereavement, disappearance, waste, squandering, dissipation. **3** CASUALTY, fatality, dead, death toll, number killed. **4** DEFICIT, debit, debt, lack of profit, deficiency, losing, depletion.

lost adj. **1** MISSING, strayed, gone missing/astray, mislaid, misplaced, vanished, disappeared, forgotten. **2** STRAY, astray, off course, off-track, disorientated, having lost one's bearings, adrift, going round in circles, at sea. **3** MISSED, passed, forfeited, neglected, wasted, squandered, dissipated, gone by the board; informal down the drain.

lotion n. CREAM, salve, ointment, moisturizer, balm, emollient, lubricant, unguent, liniment, embrocation, pomade, hand lotion, body lotion.

lottery n. DRAW, raffle, sweepstake, game of chance, gamble, drawing of lots, bingo, tombola.

loud adj. **1** BLARING, booming, noisy, deafening, resounding, reverberant, sonorous, stentorian, roaring, thunderous, tumultuous, clamorous, head-splitting,

lough /lok/ n. (in Ireland) a loch.

lounge v. lie, sit, or stand in a relaxed way. ▶n. **1** a sitting room. **2** a waiting room at an airport etc. □ **lounge suit** a man's suit for ordinary day wear.

lour (or **lower**) v. (of the sky) look dark and threatening.

louse n. **1** (pl. **lice**) a small parasitic insect. **2** (pl. **louses**) informal an unpleasant person.

lousy adj. (**lousier**, **lousiest**) **1** informal very bad. **2** infested with lice.

lout n. a rude or aggressive man or boy. ■ **loutish** adj.

louvre /loo-ver/ (US **louver**) n. each of a set of slanting slats fixed at intervals to allow air or light through.

lovable (or **loveable**) adj. inspiring love or affection.

love n. **1** very strong affection. **2** very strong affection and sexual attraction. **3** great liking. **4** a person or thing that one loves. **5** (in tennis etc.) a score of zero. ▶v. **1** feel love for. **2** like very much. □ **love affair** a romantic or sexual relationship between two people who are not married to each other. **lovelorn** unhappy because of unrequited love. **make love** have sex. ■ **loveless** adj. **lover** n. **lovingly** adv.

lovely adj. (**lovelier**, **loveliest**) **1** very beautiful. **2** informal very pleasant. ■ **loveliness** n.

low adj. **1** not high or tall or far above the ground. **2** below average in amount or strength. **3** lacking importance or quality. **4** (of a sound) deep or quiet. **5** depressed. **6** dishonourable. ▶n. **1** a

Thesaurus

ear-splitting, ear-piercing, piercing, strident, harsh, raucous. **2** BRASH, brazen, bold, loud-mouthed, vociferous, raucous, aggressive, pushy, coarse, crude, rough, crass, vulgar, brassy. **3** GARISH, gaudy, flashy, bold, flamboyant, lurid, glaring, showy, obtrusive, vulgar, tawdry, tasteless, meretricious; informal flash, kitsch, camp, tacky, naff. ■ OPPOSITES quiet.

lounge v. LAZE, lie, lie around, recline, relax, take it easy, sprawl, slump, loll, repose, loaf, idle, loiter, hang about, linger, skulk, waste time; informal hang out. ▶n. SITTING ROOM, drawing room, living room, parlour.

lousy adj. **1** VERY BAD, poor, incompetent, inadequate, unsatisfactory, inferior, careless, second-rate, terrible, miserable; informal rotten, no-good, poxy, duff. **2** DIRTY, low, mean, base, despicable, contemptible, hateful, detestable, loathsome, vile, wicked, vicious.

lout n. BOOR, oaf, dolt, churl, bumpkin, yahoo, barbarian; informal yob, yobbo, slob, clodhopper; US informal lummox.

lovable adj. ADORABLE, dear, sweet, cute, charming, lovely, likeable, attractive, delightful, captivating, enchanting, engaging, bewitching, pleasing, appealing, winsome, winning, endearing, warmhearted, cuddly. ■ OPPOSITES hateful, loathsome.

love v. **1** BE IN LOVE WITH, be fond of, feel affection for, be attracted to, be attached to, care fore, hold dear, adore, think the world of, dote on, worship, idolize, treasure, prize, cherish, be devoted to, desire, want, be infatuated with, lust after, long for, yearn for, adulate; informal fancy, have a crush on, lech after, have the hots for, be soft on. **2** LIKE, have a liking for, have a weakness for, be partial to, have a soft spot for, be addicted to, enjoy, find enjoyment in, relish, savour, appreciate, take pleasure in, delight in; informal get a kick out of, have a thing about. ■ OPPOSITES hate. ▶n. **1** AFFECTION, fondness, care, concern, attachment, regard, warmth, intimacy, devotion, adoration, passion, ardour, desire, lust, yearning, infatuation, adulation. **2** LIKING FOR, weakness for, partiality for, enjoyment of, appreciation of, delight in, relish, passion for. **3** BELOVED, loved one, true love, love of one's life, dear, dearest, dear one, darling, sweetheart, sweet, sweet one, angel, lover, inamorato/inamorata.

love affair n. AFFAIR, romance, relationship, liaison, amour, intrigue, affair of the heart, affaire de cœur.

lovely adj. **1** BEAUTIFUL, pretty, attractive, good-looking, glamorous, handsome, sweet, fair, charming, adorable, enchanting, engaging, bewitching, winsome, seductive, ravishing; old use comely. **2** DELIGHTFUL, pleasant, nice, agreeable, pleasing, marvellous, wonderful; informal fabulous, terrific. ■ OPPOSITES ugly, horrible.

lover n. **1** BOYFRIEND, girlfriend, mistress, lady-love, other man, other woman, beau, loved one, beloved, sweetheart, inamorato/inamorata; informal bit on the side, bit of fluff, toy boy, fancy man, fancy woman; old use paramour. **2** ADMIRER, devotee, fan, enthusiast, aficionado; informal buff, freak.

loving adj. AFFECTIONATE, fond, devoted,

low point. **2** an area of low atmospheric pressure. ▶ adv. at or into a low point. ▶ v. (of a cow) moo. □ **lowbrow** not intellectual or cultured. **the low-down** the important facts. **low-key** not elaborate or showy. **lowland** (also **lowlands**) low-lying country. **low-rise** (of a building) having few storeys. **low season** the least busy time for a hotel etc.

lower[1] adj. less high. ▶ v. **1** make or become lower. **2** move downwards. □ **lower case** small letters as opposed to capitals.

lower[2] var. of LOUR.

lowly adj. (**lowlier**, **lowliest**) low in status or importance.

loyal adj. firm and constant in one's support. ■ **loyally** adv. **loyalty** n.

loyalist n. a person who remains loyal to the established ruler or government.

lozenge n. **1** a diamond-shaped figure.

2 a tablet sucked to soothe a sore throat.

LP abbrev. long-playing record.

LSD n. a powerful hallucinogenic drug.

Ltd abbrev. Limited.

lubricant n. a lubricating substance.

lubricate v. oil or grease machinery so that it moves easily. ■ **lubrication** n.

lubricious adj. lewd.

lucerne n. alfalfa.

lucid adj. **1** easy to understand. **2** able to think clearly. ■ **lucidity** n. **lucidly** adv.

luck n. **1** good or bad things that happen by chance. **2** good fortune. ■ **luckless** adj.

lucky adj. (**luckier**, **luckiest**) having, bringing, or resulting from good luck. □ **lucky dip** a game in which small prizes are hidden in a container for people to pick out at random. ■ **luckily** adv.

lucrative adj. making a large profit.

Thesaurus

caring, adoring, doting, solicitous, demonstrative, tender, warm, warm-hearted, friendly, kind, sympathetic, charitable, cordial, amiable, amorous, ardent, passionate.

low adj. **1** SHORT, small, little, squat, stubby, stunted, truncated, dwarfish, knee-high. **2** SPARSE, meagre, scarce, scanty, scant, few, little, deficient, inadequate, paltry, measly, trifling, reduced, depleted, diminished. **3** DEPRESSED, dejected, despondent, disheartened, downhearted, downcast, gloomy, glum, unhappy, sad, miserable, blue, morose, moody, heavy-hearted, forlorn; *informal* fed up, down in the mouth, down in the dumps, brassed off, cheesed off. **4** LOW-GRADE, inferior, substandard, below par, second-rate, deficient, defective, wanting, lacking, inadequate, mediocre, unacceptable, worthless. **5** UNFAVOURABLE, poor, bad, adverse, hostile, negative.

lower[1] adj. **1** LESSER, lower-level, lower-grade, subordinate, junior, inferior, minor, secondary. **2** CHEAPER, reduced, decreased, lessened, cut, slashed, curtailed, pruned. ■ OPPOSITES higher.

lower[2] v. **1** LET DOWN, take down, haul down, drop, let fall, let sink. **2** SOFTEN, quieten, hush, tone down, muffle, turn down, mute. **3** DEGRADE, debase, demean, downgrade, discredit, devalue, dishonour, disgrace, belittle, humble, humiliate, disparage. **4** REDUCE, bring down, decrease, lessen, cut, slash, curtail, prune. **5** ABATE, die down, subside,

let up, moderate, slacken, dwindle, lessen, ebb, fade away, wane, taper off, lull. ■ OPPOSITES raise.

lowly adj. **1** HUMBLE, low-born, low-ranking, plebeian, peasant, poor, common, ordinary, inferior, subordinate. **2** ORDINARY, simple, plain, commonplace, run-of-the-mill, modest, unambitious, unpretentious, unaspiring. ■ OPPOSITES aristocratic, exalted.

loyal adj. FAITHFUL, true, true-hearted, tried and true, trusted, trustworthy, trusty, true-blue, steadfast, staunch, dependable, reliable, devoted, dutiful, patriotic, constant, unchanging, unwavering, unswerving, firm, stable. ■ OPPOSITES disloyal, treacherous.

loyalty n. FAITHFULNESS, fidelity, allegiance, trueness, true-heartedness, trustiness, trustworthiness, steadfastness, staunchness, dependability, reliability, devotion, duty, patriotism, constancy; *historical* fealty. ■ OPPOSITES disloyalty, treachery.

lucid adj. **1** CLEAR, clear-cut, crystal-clear, comprehensible, intelligible, understandable, plain, simple, direct, straightforward, graphic, explicit. **2** SANE, rational, in one's right mind, in possession of one's faculties, of sound mind, compos mentis, sensible, clear-headed. ■ OPPOSITES confusing.

luck n. **1** FATE, fortune, destiny, chance, fortuity, accident, hazard, serendipity. **2** GOOD LUCK, good fortune, stroke of luck, success, prosperity, advantage, advantageousness, felicity; *informal* lucky

lucre /loo-ker/ n. money.

Luddite n. a person opposed to new technology.

ludicrous adj. ridiculous. ■ **ludicrously** adv.

lug v. (**lugging, lugged**) carry or drag with great effort. ▶ n. **1** informal an ear. **2** a projection on an object for carrying it or fixing it in place.

luge n. a light toboggan.

luggage n. suitcases or other bags for a traveller's belongings.

lugubrious adj. sad; gloomy.

lukewarm adj. **1** only slightly warm. **2** unenthusiastic.

lull v. **1** calm or send to sleep. **2** cause to feel deceptively safe or confident. ▶ n. a period of quiet or inactivity.

lullaby n. (pl. **lullabies**) a soothing song to send a child to sleep.

lumbago n. lower back pain.

lumbar adj. of the lower back.

lumber n. **1** disused articles of furniture. **2** US timber sawn into planks. ▶ v. **1** informal give an unwanted responsibility to. **2** move slowly and awkwardly. □ **lumberjack** a person who fells and cuts up trees.

luminary n. (pl. **luminaries**) an inspiring or influential person.

luminescence n. light given off by a substance that has not been heated. ■ **luminescent** adj.

luminous adj. giving off light, esp. in the dark. ■ **luminosity** n.

lump n. **1** an irregular hard or solid mass. **2** a swelling under the skin. ▶ v. casually treat as alike. ■ **lumpy** adj.

lumpectomy n. (pl. **lumpectomies**) an operation to remove a lump from the breast.

lunacy n. **1** insanity. **2** great stupidity.

lunar adj. of or like the moon. □ **lunar month** the period between one new moon and the next (roughly 29½ days).

lunatic n. **1** a mentally ill person. **2** a very foolish person.

lunch n. a midday meal. ▶ v. eat lunch.

luncheon n. lunch. □ **luncheon voucher** a voucher given to employees, exchangeable for food at restaurants and shops.

lung n. either of the pair of organs in the chest into which air is drawn in breathing.

lunge n. **1** a sudden forward movement of the body. **2** a long rein on which a horse is made to move round its trainer. ▶ v. make a lunge.

lupin n. a plant with spikes of tall flowers.

lupine adj. of or like a wolf.

Thesaurus

break.

lucky adj. **1** FORTUNATE, blessed with good luck, favoured, born under a lucky star, charmed, successful, prosperous, happy, advantaged; informal jammy. **2** FORTUITOUS, fortunate, providential, advantageous, timely, opportune, expedient, auspicious, propitious. ■ OPPOSITES unlucky.

lucrative adj. PROFITABLE, profit-making, moneymaking, paying, high-income, well paid, high-paying, gainful, remunerative, productive, fat, fruitful, rewarding, worthwhile. ■ OPPOSITES unprofitable.

ludicrous adj. ABSURD, ridiculous, laughable, risible, comic, comical, farcical, silly, crazy, nonsensical, odd, outlandish, eccentric, incongruous, preposterous. ■ OPPOSITES sensible.

lull v. SOOTHE, quiet, hush, silence, calm, still, quell, assuage, allay, ease, alleviate, pacify. ▶ n. RESPITE, interval, break, hiatus, let-up, calm, calmness, stillness, quiet, quietness, tranquillity, silence, hush.

lumber v. CLUMP, stump, plod, trudge, stamp, shuffle, shamble, stumble, waddle, lurch.

lumbering adj. AWKWARD, clumsy, heavy-footed, blundering, bumbling, inept, maladroit, ungainly, like a bull in a china shop, ungraceful, lumpish, ponderous; informal clodhopping. ■ OPPOSITES graceful, agile.

luminous adj. ILLUMINATED, shining, bright, brilliant, radiant, dazzling, glowing, effulgent, luminescent, phosphorescent, vivid, resplendent.

lump n. **1** CHUNK, wedge, hunk, piece, mass, cake, nugget, ball, dab, pat, clod, gobbet, wad, clump, cluster, mound; informal gob. **2** BUMP, swelling, bruise, bulge, protuberance, growth, carbuncle, tumour, tumescence, node.

lunacy n. INSANITY, madness, mental illness/derangement, dementia, dementedness, loss of reason, unsoundness of mind, mania, frenzy, psychosis; informal craziness. ■ OPPOSITES sanity.

lunatic n. MANIAC, madman, madwoman, imbecile, idiot, psychopath; informal loony, nut, nutter, nutcase, head case, headbanger, psycho; US informal screwball.

lunge v. **1** SPRING, jump, leap, bound,

lurch n. a sudden unsteady movement. ▶v. make a lurch. □ **leave in the lurch** leave in a difficult situation.

lure v. entice. ▶n. **1** a bait used in fishing or hunting. **2** an enticement.

lurid adj. **1** unpleasantly bright in colour. **2** vividly shocking. ■ **luridly** adv.

lurk v. wait in hiding to attack someone.

luscious adj. **1** rich and sweet in taste. **2** sexually attractive.

lush adj. **1** growing thickly and strongly. **2** luxurious. ■ **lushly** adv. **lushness** n.

lust n. **1** strong sexual desire. **2** a strong desire. ▶v. feel lust. ■ **lustful** adj.

lustre (US **luster**) n. **1** a soft glow or shine. **2** prestige. ■ **lustrous** adj.

lusty adj. (**lustier**, **lustiest**) healthy and strong. ■ **lustily** adv.

lute n. a guitar-like instrument with a rounded body. ■ **lutenist** n.

luxuriant adj. growing thickly and strongly. ■ **luxuriance** n. **luxuriantly** adv.

luxuriate v. take pleasure in something enjoyable.

luxurious adj. very comfortable or elegant and expensive. ■ **luxuriously** adv.

luxury n. (pl. **luxuries**) **1** comfortable and expensive living or surroundings. **2** an item that is expensive and enjoyable but not essential.

lychee n. a fruit with sweet white flesh and rough skin.

lychgate n. a roofed gateway to a churchyard.

Lycra n. trademark an elastic fibre or fabric.

lye n. an alkaline solution used for cleaning.

lying pres. part. of LIE¹, LIE².

lymph n. a colourless fluid containing white blood cells. □ **lymph gland** each of a number of small swellings where lymph is filtered. ■ **lymphatic** adj.

lymphoma n. (pl. **lymphomas** or **lymphomata**) cancer of the lymph glands.

lynch v. (of a mob) kill someone for an alleged crime without a legal trial.

lynx n. a wild cat.

Thesaurus

dash, charge, pounce, dive. **2** STAB, jab, poke, thrust at, pitch into, lash out at, take a swing at, aim a blow at; *informal* take a swipe at.

lurch v. STAGGER, sway, reel, weave, stumble, totter.

lure v. ENTICE, cajole, attract, induce, inveigle, decoy, draw, lead, allure, tempt, seduce, beguile, ensnare.

lurid adj. **1** BRILLIANT, glaring, flaming, dazzling, glowing, intense, vivid, showy, gaudy. **2** SENSATIONAL, melodramatic, exaggerated, extravagant, graphic, explicit, unrestrained, shocking, startling. ■ OPPOSITES muted, restrained.

lurk v. SKULK, lie in wait, lie low, hide, conceal oneself, take cover, crouch, sneak, slink, prowl, steal, tiptoe.

luscious adj. JUICY, sweet, succulent, mouth-watering, tasty, appetizing, delectable, palatable, toothsome, nectarlike; *informal* scrumptious, yummy.

lush adj. **1** LUXURIANT, abundant, profuse, exuberant, dense, thick, riotous, overgrown, prolific, rank, flourishing, verdant, green. **2** LUXURIOUS, sumptuous, grand, palatial, opulent, lavish, elaborate, extravagant; *informal* plush, ritzy.

lustful adj. LECHEROUS, lascivious, lewd, libidinous, licentious, salacious, prurient, concupiscent, wanton, unchaste, hot-blooded, passionate, sensual, sexy; *informal* horny, randy. ■ OPPOSITES chaste.

lusty adj. **1** HEALTHY, strong, vigorous, robust, hale and hearty, hearty, energetic, lively, blooming, rugged, sturdy, tough, stalwart, brawny, hefty, husky, burly, solidly built, powerful, virile, red-blooded. **2** LOUD, vigorous, hearty, powerful, forceful.

luxuriant adj. **1** LUSH, abundant, profuse, exuberant, dense, thick, riotous, overgrown, prolific, teeming, verdant. **2** ORNATE, elaborate, fancy, adorned, decorated, embellished, embroidered, extravagant, flamboyant, ostentatious, showy, baroque, rococo.

luxurious adj. OPULENT, affluent, sumptuous, expensive, rich, costly, de luxe, lush, grand, splendid, magnificent, lavish, well appointed, comfortable, extravagant, ornate, fancy; *informal* plush, ritzy, swanky, posh. ■ OPPOSITES spartan, plain.

luxury n. **1** LUXURIOUSNESS, opulence, affluence, sumptuousness, grandeur, splendour, magnificence, lavishness, lap of luxury, bed of roses. **2** EXTRA, non-essential, frill, extravagance, indulgence, treat, refinement. ■ OPPOSITES simplicity, necessity.

lying n. UNTRUTHFULNESS, fabrication, fibbing, perjury, falseness, falsity, dishonesty, mendacity, storytelling, dissimulation, dissembling, prevarication, deceit, guile; *informal* crookedness. ▶adj. UN-

lyre n. an ancient musical instrument like a small U-shaped harp.

lyric n. **1** (also **lyrics**) the words of a song. **2** a lyric poem. ▶adj. (of poetry) expressing the writer's emotions.

lyrical adj. (of literature or music) expressing the writer's emotions imaginatively. □ **wax lyrical** talk in a highly enthusiastic way. ■ **lyrically** adv.

lyricist n. a person who writes lyrics.

Thesaurus

TRUTHFUL, fabricating, false, dishonest, mendacious, dissimulating, dissembling, prevaricating, deceitful, guileful, duplicitous, double-dealing, two-faced; *informal* crooked. ■ OPPOSITES truthful.

lyrical adj. RHAPSODIC, effusive, rapturous, ecstatic, euphoric, carried away, emotional, impassioned, deeply felt, expressive, passionate, personal. ■ OPPOSITES unenthusiastic.

Mm

M (or **m**) n. the Roman numeral for 1,000. ▶ abbrev. **1** medium. **2** motorway. **3** (**m**) metres. **4** (**m**) miles. **5** (**m**) millions.

MA abbrev. Master of Arts.

ma'am n. madam.

mac n. informal a mackintosh.

macabre adj. disturbing and horrifying because concerned with death and injury.

macadam n. broken stone used in surfacing roads. ■ **macadamized** adj.

macaroni n. narrow tubes of pasta.

macaroon n. a biscuit made with almonds.

macaw n. a parrot of Central and South America.

mace n. **1** a ceremonial staff. **2** a spice.

macerate v. soften by soaking. ■ **maceration** n.

Mach /mak/ n. used with a numeral to indicate the ratio of a moving body to the speed of sound.

machete /muh-**shet**-i/ n. a broad, heavy knife.

Machiavellian /ma-ki-uh-**vel**-i-uhn/ adj. cunning and underhand.

machinations pl. n. plots and scheming.

machine n. **1** a device with several parts, using mechanical power to perform a particular task. **2** an efficient group of influential people. ▶ v. make or work on with a machine. □ **machine gun** an automatic gun firing bullets in rapid succession. **machine-readable** in a form that a computer can process.

machinery n. **1** machines, or the parts of a machine. **2** a system or structure.

machinist n. a person who operates a machine.

machismo /muh-**kiz**-moh/ n. aggressive male pride.

macho /ma-choh/ adj. aggressively masculine.

mackerel n. (pl. **mackerel**) an edible sea fish.

mackintosh (or **macintosh**) n. a waterproof coat.

macramé /muh-**krah**-may/ n. the craft of knotting cord in patterns.

macro n. a single instruction that expands to a set to perform a particular computing task.

macrobiotic adj. (of diet) consisting of organic unprocessed foods.

macrocosm n. the whole of a complex structure.

mad adj. (**madder**, **maddest**) **1** insane. **2** very foolish. **3** frantic. **4** informal very enthusiastic. **5** informal angry. □ **mad cow disease** BSE. ■ **madden** v. **madly** adv. **madness** n.

madam n. a polite form of address for a woman.

Madame /muh-**dam**/ n. (pl. **Mesdames**) a title for a French woman.

madcap adj. reckless.

madder n. a red dye.

Thesaurus

macabre adj. GRUESOME, grisly, grim, gory, morbid, ghastly, hideous, horrific, horrible, horrifying, horrendous, frightening, frightful, fearsome, shocking, dreadful.

machine n. APPLIANCE, apparatus, instrument, tool, device, contraption, gadget, mechanism, engine, motor, vehicle, car, bicycle, motor cycle, aeroplane.

machismo n. MASCULINITY, manliness, virility, toughness, male chauvinism, sexism.

mad adj. **1** INSANE, deranged, crazy, demented, of unsound mind, crazed, lunatic, non compos mentis, unbalanced, unhinged, unstable, distracted, manic, frenzied, raving, distraught, frantic, hysterical, delirious, psychotic; informal not quite right, mad as a hatter, mad as a March hare, foaming at the mouth, off one's head, out of one's mind, off one's nut, nuts, nutty, off one's rocker, round the bend, raving mad, batty, bonkers, crackpot, cuckoo, loopy, loony, bananas, loco, dippy, screwy, with a screw loose, off the wall, not all there, not right upstairs, barmy, crackers, round the twist, not the full shilling, off one's trolley. **2** see ANGRY. **3** FOOLISH, insane, stupid, lunatic, foolhardy, idiotic, crackbrained, irrational, unreasonable, illogical, senseless, nonsensical, absurd, impractical, silly,

made past & past part. of MAKE.

Madeira n. a fortified wine from Madeira. □ **Madeira cake** a rich sponge cake.

Mademoiselle /ma-duh-mwah-zel/ n. (pl. **Mesdemoiselles**) a title for an unmarried French woman.

Madonna n. (**the Madonna**) the Virgin Mary.

madrigal n. a song for several unaccompanied voices.

maelstrom /mayl-struhm/ n. **1** a powerful whirlpool. **2** a confused situation.

maestro /my-stroh/ n. (pl. **maestros**) a famous and talented man, esp. a classical musician.

Mafia n. **1** an international criminal organization originating in Sicily. **2** (**mafia**) a powerful, secretly influential group.

magazine n. **1** a periodical containing articles and pictures. **2** a chamber holding cartridges in a gun. **3** a store for arms or ammunition.

magenta n. a purplish crimson.

maggot n. a larva of a fly or other insect.

Magi /may-jI/ pl. n. the three wise men from the East who brought gifts to the infant Jesus.

magic n. **1** the supposed use of mysterious or supernatural powers to influence events. **2** conjuring tricks. **3** a mysterious or wonderful quality. ▸ adj. having supernatural powers. ■ **magical** adj. **magically** adv.

magician n. **1** a person with magic powers. **2** a conjuror.

magisterial adj. **1** authoritative. **2** of a magistrate.

magistrate n. an official with authority to judge minor cases and hold preliminary hearings. ■ **magistracy** n.

magma n. molten rock under the earth's crust.

magnanimous adj. generous or forgiving. ■ **magnanimity** n.

magnate n. a wealthy and influential person.

magnesia n. a medicinal compound of magnesium.

magnesium n. a metallic element which burns with a bright white flame.

magnet n. **1** a piece of iron that attracts objects containing iron and points north and south when suspended. **2** a powerful attraction.

magnetic adj. **1** having the property of a magnet. **2** very attractive. □ **magnetic tape** tape used in recording sound, pictures, or computer data. ■ **magnetically** adv.

magnetism n. **1** the properties and effects of magnets and magnetic substances. **2** the ability to attract and

Thesaurus

inane, asinine, ludicrous, wild, unwise, imprudent, preposterous. **4** see ENTHUSIASTIC. ■ OPPOSITES sane, sensible.

madden v. ANGER, infuriate, enrage, incense, exasperate, irritate, inflame, annoy, provoke, upset, agitate, vex, irk, pique, gall, make someone's hackles rise, make someone's blood boil; informal make someone see red, get someone's back up.

madman n. MANIAC, lunatic, psychopath; informal loony, nut, nutter, nutcase, head case, headbanger, psycho; US informal screwball.

madness n. INSANITY, craziness, dementia, mental illness, derangement, dementedness, instability of mind, unsoundness of mind, lunacy, distraction, mania, frenzy, psychosis. ■ OPPOSITES sanity, calm.

magazine n. PERIODICAL, journal, publication, supplement, colour supplement; informal glossy.

magic n. **1** SORCERY, witchcraft, wizardry, enchantment, spell-working, necromancy, the supernatural, occultism, the occult, black magic, black art, voodoo, hoodoo, thaumaturgy. **2** SLEIGHT OF HAND, legerdemain, conjuring, illusion, prestidigitation, deception, trickery, juggling. ▸ adj. **1** MAGICAL, enchanting, entrancing, spellbinding, fascinating, captivating, charming, glamorous, magnetic, irresistible, hypnotic. **2** MARVELLOUS, wonderful, excellent; informal terrific, fab, brilliant, brill.

magician n. SORCERER, sorceress, witch, wizard, warlock, enchanter, enchantress, spell-worker, spell-caster, necromancer, thaumaturge.

magnanimity n. GENEROSITY, charitableness, charity, benevolence, beneficence, open-handedness, kindness, bigheartedness, munificence, bountifulness, largesse, altruism, philanthropy, unselfishness, selflessness, selfsacrifice, mercy, leniency. ■ OPPOSITES meanness, selfishness.

magnanimous adj. GENEROUS, charitable, benevolent, beneficent, openhanded, big-hearted, great-hearted, kind, kindly, munificent, bountiful, libcharm people.

magnetize (or **-ise**) v. make magnetic.

magneto /mag-nee-toh/ n. (pl. **magnetos**) a small electric generator using a magnet.

magnificent adj. **1** very attractive and impressive. **2** very good. ■ **magnificence** n. **magnificently** adv.

magnify v. (**magnifying**, **magnified**) **1** make something appear larger than it is with a lens or microscope. **2** make larger or stronger. **3** old use praise. ■ **magnification** n.

magnitude n. **1** great size or importance. **2** size.

magnolia n. a tree with large white or pink flowers.

magnum n. (pl. **magnums**) a wine bottle of twice the standard size.

magpie n. a black and white bird with a long tail.

Magyar n. **1** a member of the predominant people in Hungary. **2** the Hungarian language.

maharaja (or **maharajah**) n. hist. an Indian prince.

maharani n. hist. a maharaja's wife or widow.

mahatma n. (in India) a holy person or sage.

mah-jong (or **mah-jongg**) n. a Chinese game played with small rectangular tiles.

mahogany n. hard reddish-brown wood.

mahout /muh-howt/ n. an elephant driver or keeper.

maid (or **maidservant**) n. a female servant.

maiden n. old use a girl or young woman, esp. a virgin. ▶adj. **1** (of an older woman) unmarried. **2** first of its kind. □ **maiden name** the surname of a married woman before her marriage. **maiden over** an over in cricket in which no runs are scored.

mail n. **1** letters etc. sent by post. **2** email. **3** hist. armour made of linked metal rings. ▶v. send by post or email. □ **mail order** the buying or selling of goods by post. **mailshot** a piece of advertising material sent to a large number of addresses.

maim v. injure so that part of the body is permanently damaged.

main adj. greatest or most important. ▶n. a chief water or gas pipe or electricity cable. □ **in the main** on the whole. **mainframe** a large computer. **mainland** the main area of land of a country, not including islands. **mainspring** the most important or influential part. **mainstay** a thing on which something depends or is based. **mainstream** the ideas, attitudes, etc. shared by most people. ■ **mainly** adv.

maintain v. **1** cause to continue in the same state. **2** regularly check and repair. **3** support financially. **4** assert.

maintenance n. **1** the act of maintain-

Thesaurus

eral, altruistic, philanthropic, noble, unselfish, selfless, self-sacrificing, ungrudging, unstinting, forgiving, merciful, lenient, indulgent. ■ OPPOSITES mean.

magnificent adj. **1** SPLENDID, resplendent, grand, grandiose, impressive, imposing, striking, glorious, superb, majestic, august, noble, stately, exalted, awe-inspiring, royal, regal, kingly, princely, sumptuous, opulent, luxurious, lavish, rich, brilliant, radiant, elegant, gorgeous; informal ritzy, posh. **2** EXCELLENT, masterly, skilful, virtuoso, splendid, impressive, fine, marvellous, wonderful. ■ OPPOSITES ordinary, poor.

magnify v. **1** AUGMENT, enlarge, expand, amplify, intensify, heighten, deepen, broaden, widen, dilate, boost, enhance. **2** EXAGGERATE, overstate, overdo, overemphasize, overplay, dramatize, colour, embroider, embellish, enhance, inflate, make a mountain out of a molehill.

■ OPPOSITES minimize.

magnitude n. SIZE, extent, measure, proportions, dimensions, volume, weight, quantity, mass, bulk, amplitude, capacity.

mail n. POST, letters, packages, parcels, correspondence.

main adj. HEAD, chief, principal, leading, foremost, most important, central, prime, premier, primary, supreme, predominant, pre-eminent, paramount, cardinal, crucial, vital, critical, pivotal, urgent. ■ OPPOSITES minor.

mainly adv. FOR THE MOST PART, mostly, in the main, on the whole, largely, by and large, to a large extent, to a great degree, predominantly, chiefly, principally, substantially, overall, in general, generally, usually, commonly, as a rule.

maintain v. **1** CONTINUE, keep going, keep up, keep alive, keep in existence, carry on, preserve, conserve, prolong, perpetuate, sustain. **2** KEEP IN GOOD CONDITION, keep in repair, keep up, coning. **2** financial support given to one's former husband or wife after divorce.

maisonette n. a flat on two storeys of a larger building.

maize n. a cereal plant with rows of large grains on a cob.

majestic adj. impressively grand or beautiful. ■ **majestically** adv.

majesty n. (pl. **majesties**) **1** impressive beauty or grandeur. **2** (**His, Your,** etc. **Majesty**) a title given to a king or queen or their wife or widow.

major adj. **1** important or serious. **2** main. **3** Music (of a scale) having intervals of a semitone between the 3rd and 4th, and 7th and 8th notes. ▶ v. (**major in**) US specialize in a subject at college. □ **major general** a rank of army officer above brigadier.

majority n. (pl. **majorities**) **1** the greater number. **2** the number of votes by which one party or candidate in an election defeats the opposition. **3** the age when a person becomes an adult in law.

make v. (**making, made**) **1** form by combining parts. **2** cause to happen or exist. **3** force to do something. **4** constitute. **5** be suitable as. **6** estimate or decide on. **7** earn money. **8** arrive at or achieve. **9** (**make it**) be successful. ▶ n. a brand of goods. □ **make-believe** fantasy or pretence. **make do** manage with something unsatisfactory. **make for** move towards. **make off** leave hurriedly. **make off with** steal. **make out 1** manage to see, hear, or understand. **2** claim or pretend. **make over 1** transfer ownership of. **2** give a new image to. **makeshift** temporary and improvised. **make-up 1** cosmetics. **2** the composition of something. **make up 1** put together from parts or ingredients. **2** invent. **3** compensate. **4** be reconciled after a quarrel. **5** apply cosmetics to. **makeweight** something added to make up a required weight. ■ **maker** n.

malachite n. a green mineral.

Thesaurus

serve, preserve, keep intact, care for, take good care of, look after. **3** SUPPORT, provide for, keep, finance, feed, nurture, nourish, sustain. **4** INSIST ON, hold to, declare, assert, state, announce, affirm, avow, profess, claim, allege, contend, aver.

maintenance n. **1** UPKEEP, repairs, preservation, conservation, care. **2** ALIMONY, support, allowance, keep, upkeep, subsistence.

majestic adj. REGAL, royal, kingly, queenly, princely, imperial, noble, lordly, august, exalted, awesome, elevated, lofty, stately, dignified, distinguished, magnificent, grand, splendid, resplendent, glorious, impressive, imposing, marvellous, superb, proud.

major adj. **1** GREATEST, best, most important, leading, foremost, chief, main, outstanding, first-rate, notable, eminent, pre-eminent, supreme. **2** IMPORTANT, significant, crucial, vital, great, weighty, paramount, utmost, prime. **3** SERIOUS, radical, complicated. ■ OPPOSITES minor.

majority n. **1** LARGER PART/NUMBER, greater part/number, most, more than half, bulk, mass, main body, preponderance, lion's share. **2** LEGAL AGE, coming-of-age, seniority, adulthood, manhood, womanhood, maturity, age of consent. ■ OPPOSITES minority.

make v. **1** BUILD, construct, assemble, put together, put up, erect, manufacture, produce, fabricate, create, form, fashion, model, mould, shape, forge. **2** FORCE TO, compel to, coerce into, press into, drive into, pressure into, pressurize into, oblige to, require to, prevail upon to, dragoon into, impel to, constrain to, urge to; informal railroad into, put the heat on, put the screws on, use strong-arm tactics on. **3** CAUSE, create, give rise to, produce, bring about, generate, engender, occasion, effect. **4** CREATE, appoint, designate, name, nominate, select, elect, vote in, install, invest, ordain, assign. **5** GAIN, acquire, obtain, get, realize, secure, win, earn, net, gross, clear, bring in, take home, pocket. **6** PREPARE, get ready, put together, concoct, cook; informal whip up. **7** COME TO, add up to, total, amount to. **8** GIVE, deliver, utter, give voice to, enunciate, recite, pronounce. **9** BE, act as, serve as, constitute, perform the function of, play the part of, represent, embody. ▶ n. BRAND, label, sort, type, variety, style, mark, marque.

make-believe n. PRETENCE, fantasy, daydreaming, dreaming, fabrication, play-acting, charade, masquerade. ▶ adj. PRETENDED, feigned, made up, fantasy, dream, imagined, imaginary, unreal, fictitious, mock, sham, pretend.

maker n. MANUFACTURER, builder, constructor, producer, creator, fabricator,

maladjusted adj. unable to cope with normal social situations.

maladministration n. bad or corrupt management of business etc. affairs.

maladroit adj. clumsy.

malady n. (pl. **maladies**) an illness.

malaise n. a feeling of unease, illness, or low spirits.

malapropism n. the mistaken use of a word in place of a similar-sounding one.

malaria n. a disease causing recurrent fever. ■ **malarial** adj.

Malay n. **1** a member of a people inhabiting Malaysia and Indonesia. **2** the language of the Malays.

malcontent n. a dissatisfied and rebellious person.

male adj. **1** of the sex that can fertilize or inseminate the female. **2** (of a plant or flower) having stamens but not a pistil. **3** (of a fitting) for insertion into a corresponding part. ▶n. a male person, animal, or plant.

malediction n. a curse.

malefactor n. a wrongdoer.

malevolent adj. wishing harm to others. ■ **malevolence** n.

malfeasance n. misconduct.

malformation n. the state of being abnormally shaped. ■ **malformed** adj.

malfunction v. fail to function normally. ▶n. such a failure.

malice n. the desire to harm someone. ■ **malicious** adj. **maliciously** adv.

malign /muh-**lyn**/ adj. harmful or evil. ▶v. say unpleasant things about.

malignant adj. **1** malevolent. **2** (of a tumour) cancerous. ■ **malignancy** n.

malinger v. pretend to be ill to avoid work. ■ **malingerer** n.

mall /mawl/ n. **1** a large enclosed shopping area. **2** a sheltered walk.

mallard n. a kind of wild duck.

malleable adj. **1** able to be hammered or pressed into shape. **2** easily influenced. ■ **malleability** n.

mallet n. **1** a hammer with a large wooden head. **2** a wooden stick with a head used in croquet or polo.

mallow n. a plant with pink or purple flowers.

malmsey n. a strong, sweet wine.

malnutrition n. poor health caused by not having enough food, or not enough of the right food. ■ **malnourished** adj.

malodorous adj. smelling very unpleasant.

malpractice n. illegal or unethical professional behaviour.

malt n. **1** barley or other grain soaked in water then dried. **2** whisky made with malt.

maltreat v. treat cruelly. ■ **maltreatment** n.

mamba n. a poisonous snake.

mammal n. a warm-blooded animal that produces milk and bears live young. ■ **mammalian** adj.

mammary adj. of the breasts.

mammography n. the use of X-rays to detect tumours in the breasts.

mammoth n. a large extinct elephant. ▶adj. huge.

man n. (pl. **men**) **1** an adult human male. **2** a person. **3** human beings. **4** a piece used in a board game. ▶v. (**manning**, **manned**) provide a place etc. with people to work in or defend it. ☐ **manhandle 1** move an object with effort. **2** push or drag roughly. **manhole** a covered opening through which a person can enter a sewer etc. **manhood 1** the state or period of being a man. **2** the men of a country. **3** qualities associated with men. **man-hour** one

Thesaurus

author, architect, framer.

makeshift adj. STOPGAP, make-do, provisional, temporary, rough and ready, substitute, improvised, standby, jerry-built, thrown together.

malice n. MALEVOLENCE, maliciousness, malignity, malignancy, evil intentions, ill will, ill feeling, animosity, animus, hostility, enmity, bad blood, hatred, hate, spite, spitefulness, vindictiveness, rancour, bitterness, grudge, venom, spleen, defamation; informal bitchiness, cattiness. ■ OPPOSITES benevolence.

malicious adj. MALEVOLENT, malign, malignant, evil, evil-intentioned, ill-natured, hostile, spiteful, baleful, vin-

dictive, rancorous, bitter, venomous, pernicious, hurtful, destructive, defamatory; informal bitchy, catty. ■ OPPOSITES friendly.

malign v. SLANDER, libel, defame, smear, blacken someone's name/character, vilify, speak ill of, spread lies about, cast aspersions on, misrepresent, traduce, denigrate, calumniate. ■ OPPOSITES praise.

malnutrition n. UNDERNOURISHMENT, lack of food, starvation, famine, anorexia.

maltreat v. TREAT BADLY, ill-treat, ill-use, mistreat, misuse, abuse, handle/treat roughly, bully, injure, harm, hurt, molest.

hour's work by one person. **mankind** human beings as a whole. **man-made** made or caused by human beings. **man-power** the number of people available for work. **manservant** a male servant. **manslaughter** the crime of killing a person without meaning to do so.

manacle n. a shackle for the wrists or ankles. ■ **manacled** adj.

manage v. **1** be in charge of an organization or people. **2** succeed in doing. **3** be able to cope. **4** control the use of money or resources. ■ **manageable** adj.

management n. **1** the act of managing. **2** the managers of an organization.

manager n. (fem. **manageress**) a person who manages staff, an organization, etc. ■ **managerial** adj.

manatee n. a large plant-eating sea mammal.

mandarin n. **1** (**Mandarin**) the official form of the Chinese language. **2** a powerful official. **3** a small citrus fruit.

mandate n. an official order or authority to do something. ▶ v. give authority to do something.

mandatory adj. compulsory.

mandible n. a jaw or jaw-like part.

mandolin n. a musical instrument like a lute.

mandrake n. a plant with a forked fleshy root.

mandrel n. a shaft holding work in a lathe.

mane n. a growth of long hair on the neck of a horse or lion.

maneuver US = MANOEUVRE.

manful adj. brave or determined. ■ **manfully** adv.

manganese n. a hard metallic element.

mange n. a skin disease in some animals. ■ **mangy** adj.

manger n. a long trough from which horses etc. feed.

mangetout /monzh-too/ n. a variety of pea eaten with the pod.

mangle n. a machine with rollers for wringing out wet laundry. ▶ v. destroy or damage by tearing or crushing.

mango n. (pl. **mangoes** or **mangos**) a tropical fruit.

mangrove n. a tropical tree growing in swamps.

mania n. **1** mental illness involving periods of wild excitement. **2** an extreme enthusiasm.

maniac n. **1** a person who behaves very wildly or violently. **2** informal a person with an extreme enthusiasm. ■ **maniacal** adj.

manic adj. **1** of or affected by mania. **2** showing wild excitement or energy. ■ **manically** adv.

manicure n. a cosmetic treatment of the hands and nails. ▶ v. give a manicure to. ■ **manicurist** n.

manifest adj. clear and obvious. ▶ v. **1** show or display. **2** appear or become noticeable. ▶ n. a list of the cargo, crew,

Thesaurus

maltreatment n. ILL-TREATMENT, ill use, mistreatment, abuse, rough handling, mishandling, manhandling, bullying, injury, harm.

manage v. **1** BE IN CHARGE OF, run, be head of, head, direct, control, preside over, lead, govern, rule, command, superintend, supervise, oversee, administer, organize, conduct, handle, guide, be at the helm of; informal head up. **2** SUCCEED IN, contrive, engineer, bring about/off, achieve, accomplish, effect. **3** COPE, deal with the situation, get along/on, carry on, survive, make do.

manageable adj. **1** EASY, doable, practicable, possible, feasible, viable. **2** CONTROLLABLE, governable, tractable, pliant, compliant, docile, accommodating, amenable, yielding, submissive. ■ OPPOSITES unmanageable.

management n. **1** MANAGERS, employers, owners, proprietors, directors, board of directors, board, directorate,

executives, administration; informal bosses, top brass. **2** RUNNING, charge, care, direction, leadership, control, governing, ruling, command, superintendence, supervision, administration.

mandatory adj. OBLIGATORY, compulsory, binding, required, requisite, essential, imperative, necessary. ■ OPPOSITES voluntary.

mangle v. MUTILATE, hack, cut about, lacerate, maul, tear at, rend, butcher, disfigure, deform.

mangy adj. **1** SCABBY, scaly, diseased. **2** SHABBY, moth-eaten, worn, shoddy, dirty, mean, squalid, filthy, seedy; informal grotty.

manhandle v. **1** HANDLE ROUGHLY, push, pull, shove, maul, mistreat, ill-treat, abuse, injure, damage, beat, batter; informal knock about, rough up. **2** HEAVE, haul, push, shove, pull, tug, manoeuvre; informal hump.

mania n. **1** FRENZY, violence, wildness,

or passengers of a ship or aircraft. ■ **manifestation** n. **manifestly** adv.

manifesto n. (pl. **manifestos**) a public declaration of policy.

manifold adj. many and various. ▶ n. a pipe with several openings, esp. in an engine.

manikin n. a very small person.

Manila n. strong brown paper.

manipulate v. **1** handle or control skilfully. **2** control or influence in a clever or underhand way. ■ **manipulation** n. **manipulative** adj. **manipulator** n.

manly adj. (**manlier, manliest**) **1** brave or strong. **2** suitable for a man. ■ **manliness** n.

mannequin n. a dummy used to display clothes in a shop.

manner n. **1** a way in which something is done or happens. **2** a person's behaviour towards others. **3** (**manners**) polite behaviour. **4** a kind or sort.

mannered adj. **1** behaving in a specified way. **2** artificial and affected.

mannerism n. a distinctive gesture or way of speaking.

mannerly adj. well-mannered; polite.

manoeuvre /muh-**noo**-ver/ (US **maneuver**) n. **1** a skilful movement. **2** a carefully planned scheme. **3** (**manoeuvres**) a large-scale military exercise. ▶ v. **1** perform manoeuvres. **2** guide skilfully or craftily. ■ **manoeuvrable** adj.

manor n. a large country house with lands. ■ **manorial** adj.

manqué /**mong**-kay/ adj. having never become what one might have been: *an actor manqué.*

manse n. a house provided for a church minister in Scotland.

mansion n. a large, impressive house.

mantelpiece n. the shelf above a fireplace.

mantilla n. a lace scarf worn over the hair and shoulders.

mantis n. (pl. **mantis** or **mantises**) a long-bodied predatory insect.

mantle n. **1** a loose cloak. **2** a cover or covering. **3** a role or responsibility passed on to another person.

mantra n. a word or sound repeated to aid concentration when meditating.

manual adj. **1** of, done, or operated by the hands. **2** working with the hands. ▶ n. a book giving instructions or information. ■ **manually** adv.

manufacture v. **1** make on a large scale with machinery. **2** invent a story. ▶ n. the process of manufacturing. ■ **manufacturer** n.

manure n. animal dung used for fertiliz-

Thesaurus

hysteria, raving, derangement, dementia. **2** OBSESSION, compulsion, fixation, fetish, fascination, preoccupation, passion, enthusiasm, urge.

maniac n. *see* MADMAN.

manifest adj. OBVIOUS, clear, plain, apparent, patent, noticeable, perceptible, visible, transparent, conspicuous, unmistakable, distinct, blatant, glaring.

manifestation n. **1** DISPLAY, show, exhibition, demonstration, presentation, exposition, illustration, exemplification, indication, declaration, expression, profession. **2** EVIDENCE, proof, testimony, substantiation, sign, indication, mark, symbol, token, symptom.

manifold adj. MULTIFARIOUS, multiple, numerous, many, several, multitudinous, various.

manipulate v. **1** HANDLE, wield, ply, work. **2** INFLUENCE, control, use to one's advantage, exploit, manoeuvre, direct, guide, pull the strings. **3** JUGGLE, massage, falsify, doctor, tamper with, fiddle with, tinker with.

manipulator n. HANDLER, wielder, operator.

mankind n. MAN, homo sapiens, the human race, the human species, humankind, human beings, humans, people.

manly adj. MASCULINE, all-male, macho, virile, strong, robust, vigorous, muscular, powerful, well built, strapping, sturdy, rugged, tough. ■ OPPOSITES effeminate.

manner n. **1** WAY, means, method, system, approach, technique, procedure, process, methodology, routine, practice, fashion, mode, style, habit, custom. **2** AIR, appearance, demeanour, aspect, mien, bearing, deportment, cast, behaviour, conduct. **3** KIND, sort, type, variety, form, nature, breed, brand, stamp, class, category.

mannerism n. HABIT, characteristic, trait, idiosyncrasy, peculiarity, foible, quirk.

manoeuvre n. **1** MOVEMENT, move, measure. **2** TRICK, stratagem, tactic, machination, manipulation, artifice, subterfuge, device, dodge, ploy, ruse, scheme, plan, plot, intrigue; *informal* wangle. ▶ v. **1** MOVE, work, negotiate, steer, guide, direct, manipulate. **2** SCHEME, intrigue, plot, use trickery/artifice, maing land.

manuscript n. **1** a handwritten book, document, etc. **2** an author's text before printing.

Manx adj. of the Isle of Man.

many pron. & adj. a large number of. ▶ n. the majority of people.

Maori /mow-ri/ n. (pl. **Maori** or **Maoris**) a member of the aboriginal people of New Zealand.

map n. a diagram of an area showing physical features, cities, roads, etc. ▶ v. (**mapping, mapped**) **1** make a map of. **2** (**map out**) plan in detail.

maple n. a tree with five-pointed leaves.

mar v. (**marring, marred**) spoil the appearance or quality of.

maraca n. a container filled with small beans etc., shaken as a musical instrument.

marathon n. **1** a long-distance running race. **2** a long, difficult task.

maraud v. make a raid in search of things to steal. ■ **marauder** n.

marble n. **1** a hard form of limestone, usu. with coloured streaks, which is polished and used in sculpture and building. **2** a small ball of coloured glass used as a toy.

marbled adj. having coloured streaks like marble.

March n. the third month.

march v. **1** walk in time and with regular paces or in an organized column. **2** walk purposefully. **3** force to walk quickly. ▶ n. **1** an act of marching. **2** a piece of music written to accompany marching. **3** (**Marches**) border regions. ■ **marcher** n.

marchioness /mar-shuh-**ness**/ n. **1** the wife or widow of a marquess. **2** a woman with the rank of marquess.

mare n. the female of a horse or related animal.

margarine n. a butter substitute made from vegetable oils or animal fats.

margin n. **1** an edge or border. **2** the blank border on each side of the print on a page. **3** an amount above or below a given level.

marginal adj. **1** of or in a margin. **2** slight; unimportant. ■ **marginally** adv.

marginalize (or **-ise**) v. cause to feel less important.

marguerite n. a large daisy.

marigold n. a plant with yellow or orange flowers.

marijuana /ma-ri-**hwah**-nuh/ n. cannabis.

marina n. a harbour for yachts and small boats.

marinade n. a flavoured liquid in which food is soaked before cooking. ▶ v. marinate.

marinate v. soak in a marinade.

marine adj. of the sea or shipping. ▶ n. a soldier trained to serve on land or sea.

mariner n. a sailor.

marionette n. a puppet worked by strings.

marital adj. of marriage.

maritime adj. **1** of shipping or other activity taking place at sea. **2** living or found in or near the sea.

marjoram n. a herb.

mark n. **1** a small area on a surface different in colour from the rest. **2** something indicating position. **3** a symbol. **4** a sign of a quality or feeling. **5** a characteristic feature. **6** a point awarded for a correct answer or a piece of work. **7** a particular model of a vehicle or machine. **8** a Deutschmark. ▶ v. **1** make a mark on. **2** write a word or symbol on an object to identify it. **3** in-

Thesaurus

chinate; *informal* pull strings.

manufacture v. MAKE, produce, mass-produce, build, construct, assemble, put together, create, fabricate, turn out, process, form, fashion, model, mould, shape, forge.

manufacturer n. MAKER, producer, builder, constructor, creator, fabricator, factory owner, industrialist, captain of industry.

many adj. A LOT OF, lots of, numerous, innumerable, a large/great number of, countless, scores of, myriad, great quantities of, multitudinous, multiple, copious, abundant. ■ OPPOSITES few.

mar v. SPOIL, detract from, impair, damage, ruin, wreck, disfigure, blemish, scar, deface, harm, hurt, injure, deform, mutilate, maim, mangle. ■ OPPOSITES enhance.

marauder n. RAIDER, plunderer, pillager, looter, ravager, robber, pirate, brigand, freebooter.

march n. WALK, step, pace, stride, tramp, hike, demonstration, parade, procession; *informal* demo.

margin n. **1** EDGE, side, verge, border, perimeter, boundary, limits, periphery, brim. **2** LEEWAY, latitude, scope, room, room for manoeuvre, space, allowance, extra, surplus.

marginal adj. SLIGHT, small, tiny, mindicate the position of. **4 (mark out)** distinguish. **5** acknowledge an event. **6** give a mark to a piece of work. **7** pay attention to. **8** (in team games) stay close to an opponent to prevent them getting or passing the ball. □ **mark time** march on the spot. **quick off the mark** fast in responding.

marked adj. clearly noticeable. ■ **markedly** adv.

marker n. **1** an object used to indicate a position or route. **2** a broad felt-tip pen.

market n. **1** a place or gathering for the sale of food, livestock, etc. **2** demand for a particular product or service. ▶ v. (**marketing, marketed**) advertise or promote. □ **market garden** a place where produce is grown for sale. **on the market** offered for sale. ■ **marketable** adj.

marking n. **1** an identifying mark. **2** a pattern of marks on an animal.

marksman n. a person skilled in shooting. ■ **marksmanship** n.

marl n. soil consisting of clay and lime.

marmalade n. a preserve made from oranges.

marmoset n. a small tropical American monkey.

maroon n. a dark brownish-red colour. ▶ v. (**be marooned**) be abandoned alone in a remote place.

marquee n. a large tent for special events.

marquess n. a nobleman ranking

above an earl.

marquetry n. inlaid work made from pieces of coloured wood.

marquis n. (in some European countries) a nobleman ranking above a count.

marram grass n. a coarse grass growing on sand.

marriage n. **1** the formal union of a man and a woman as husband and wife. **2** a combination. ■ **marriageable** adj.

marrow n. **1** a long vegetable. **2** a soft fatty substance in the cavities of bones.

marry v. (**marrying, married**) **1** become the husband or wife of. **2** join in marriage. **3** join together.

marsh n. an area of low-lying waterlogged land. ■ **marshy** adj.

marshal n. **1** an officer of the highest rank in some armed forces. **2** an official responsible for supervising public events. ▶ v. (**marshalling, marshalled**; US **marshaling, marshaled**) assemble in order.

marshmallow n. a spongy sweet made from sugar, egg white, and gelatin.

marsupial n. a mammal whose young are carried and suckled in a pouch.

mart n. a market.

martial adj. of war. □ **martial arts** sports which originated as forms of self-defence or attack. **martial law** government by the military forces of a country.

Thesaurus

ute, low, minor, insignificant, minimal, negligible.

maritime adj. NAVAL, marine, nautical, seafaring, seagoing.

mark n. **1** STAIN, blemish, blot, smear, trace, spot, speck, dot, blotch, smudge, bruise, scratch, scar, dent, pit, pock, chip, notch, nick, line, score, cut, incision, gash; *informal* splotch. **2** MARKER, guide, pointer, landmark, direction post, signpost, milestone, waymark. **3** SIGN, symbol, indication, symptom, feature, token, badge, emblem, evidence, proof, clue, hint. ▶ v. **1** STAIN, smear, smudge, scratch, scar, dent, chip, notch, score, cut, gash. **2** PUT ONE'S NAME ON, initial, label, tag, stamp, brand, earmark. **3** CORRECT, assess, evaluate, appraise, grade. **4** CELEBRATE, commemorate, honour, observe, recognize, acknowledge, solemnize.

marked adj. PRONOUNCED, decided, striking, clear, glaring, blatant, unmistakable, remarkable, prominent, signal,

conspicuous, noticeable. ■ OPPOSITES inconspicuous.

maroon v. ABANDON, forsake, leave behind, desert, strand, leave stranded, leave isolated.

marriage n. **1** MARRIED STATE, matrimony, holy matrimony, wedlock, conjugal bond, union, match. **2** MARRIAGE CEREMONY, wedding, wedding ceremony, nuptials. **3** ALLIANCE, union, merger, unification, amalgamation, combination, affiliation, association, connection, coupling; *informal* hook-up.

marry v. BE MARRIED, wed, be wed, become man and wife, become espoused; *informal* tie the knot, walk down the aisle, take the plunge, get spliced, get hitched, get yoked.

marsh n. MARSHLAND, bog, peat bog, swamp, swampland, morass, mire, quagmire, quag, slough, fen, fenland; US bayou.

marshal v. GATHER TOGETHER, assemble, collect, muster, draw up, line up, align,

martinet n. a person who enforces strict discipline.

martyr n. **1** a person who is killed because of their beliefs. **2** a person who exaggerates their difficulties to gain sympathy. ▶v. make a martyr of. ■ **martyrdom** n.

marvel v. (**marvelling, marvelled**; US **marveling, marveled**) feel wonder. ▶n. a person or thing causing wonder.

marvellous (US **marvelous**) adj. **1** causing great wonder. **2** very good. ■ **marvellously** adv.

Marxism n. the political and economic theories of Karl Marx. ■ **Marxist** n. & adj.

marzipan n. a sweet paste made with ground almonds.

mascara n. a cosmetic for darkening the eyelashes.

mascot n. a person or thing supposed to bring good luck.

masculine adj. **1** of men. **2** having qualities associated with men. ■ **masculinity** n.

mash n. a soft mass made by crushing a substance. ▶v. crush or beat to a mash.

mask n. a covering worn over the face as a disguise or protection. ▶v. **1** cover with a mask. **2** conceal or disguise.

masochism `n. pleasure derived from suffering pain. ■ **masochist** n. **masochistic** adj.

mason n. a builder and worker in stone.

masonry n. stonework.

masque /mahsk/ n. hist a dramatic entertainment with masked actors.

masquerade n. a pretence. ▶v. pretend to be someone or something.

mass n. **1** a body of matter with no definite shape. **2** a large group of people or things. **3** (**the masses**) ordinary people. **4** (**masses**) a large amount. **5** the quantity of matter which a body contains. **6** (**Mass**) a Christian service of the Eucharist. ▶v. gather into a mass. □ **mass-produced** produced in large quantities using machinery.

massacre n. a brutal slaughter of a large number of people. ▶v. brutally kill a large number of people.

massage n. rubbing and kneading of the body to relieve tension or pain. ▶v. **1** give a massage to. **2** manipulate figures to give a more acceptable result.

masseur n. (fem. **masseuse**) a person who provides massage professionally.

massif n. a compact group of mountains.

massive adj. large and heavy or solid. ■ **massively** adv.

mast n. a tall upright post, esp. one carrying a boat's sail or sails.

mastectomy n. (pl. **mastectomies**) an operation to remove a breast.

master n. **1** a man in a position of authority, control, or ownership. **2** a person skilled in a particular activity. **3** a male schoolteacher. **4** a university degree above a first degree. **5** an original recording etc. from which copies are made. **6** a title placed before the name of a boy. ▶adj. **1** highly skilled. **2** main. ▶v. **1** gain complete knowledge or skill in. **2** gain control of. □ **master key** a key that opens several different locks.

mastermind 1 a person who plans and directs a complex scheme. **2** be the

Thesaurus

set/put in order, arrange, deploy, dispose.

martial adj. MILITANT, warlike, combative, belligerent, bellicose, aggressive, pugnacious.

marvel n. WONDER, amazing thing, prodigy, sensation, spectacle, phenomenon, miracle. □ **marvel at** BE AMAZED BY, be filled with amazement at, be awed by, be full of wonder at, wonder at.

marvellous adj. **1** AMAZING, astounding, astonishing, awesome, breathtaking, sensational, remarkable, spectacular, stupendous, phenomenal, prodigious, miraculous, extraordinary; literary wondrous. **2** EXCELLENT, splendid, wonderful, magnificent, superb, glorious, great; informal super, fantastic, terrific, smashing., fabulous, awesome, ace, mean, bad, wicked

masculine adj. MALE, manly, manlike, virile, all-male, robust, vigorous, muscular, strapping, rugged, macho. ■ OPPOSITES feminine.

mash v. CRUSH, pulp, purée, smash, squash, pound, beat. ▶n. PULP, mush, paste, purée, slush, pap.

mask n. DISGUISE, guise, concealment, cover, cover-up, cloak, camouflage, veil, screen, front, false front, facade, blind, semblance, false colours, pretence. ▶v. DISGUISE, hide, conceal, cover up, obscure, cloak, camouflage, veil, screen.

mass n. **1** CONCENTRATION, conglomeration, aggregation, assemblage, collection. **2** MAJORITY, greater part, major part, most, bulk, main body, preponderance. ▶adj. WHOLESALE, universal, widespread, general, large-scale, extensive, pandemic, popular. ▶v. AMASS, accumumastermind of. **masterpiece** a work of outstanding skill.

masterful adj. **1** powerful and able to control others. **2** very skilful. ■ **masterfully** adv.

masterly adj. very skilful.

mastery n. **1** complete knowledge or great skill. **2** control or superiority.

mastic n. **1** gum from a Mediterranean tree. **2** a putty-like substance used in building.

masticate v. chew.

mastiff n. a dog of a large, strong breed.

mastitis n. inflammation of the breast or udder.

mastoid n. a projecting part of the bone behind the ear.

masturbate v. stimulate the genitals with the hand. ■ **masturbation** n.

mat n. **1** a piece of decorative or protective material placed on the floor or other surface. **2** a thick layer of hairy or woolly material.

matador n. a bullfighter.

match n. **1** a contest in a game or sport. **2** a person or thing equal to another in quality. **3** an exact or near equivalent to another. **4** a marriage or possible marriage partner. **5** a short stick tipped with a substance that ignites when rubbed on a rough surface. ▶ v. **1** correspond. **2** be equal to. **3** place in competition with another. □ **matchmaker** a person who tries to arrange marriages or relationships between others.

mate n. **1** informal a friend. **2** a fellow member or occupant. **3** an animal's sexual partner. **4** an officer on a merchant ship. **5** checkmate. ▶ v. (of animals) come together in order to breed.

material n. **1** the matter from which something is or can be made. **2** items needed for creating something. **3** cloth. ▶ adj. **1** of physical objects rather than the mind or spirit. **2** essential or relevant. ■ **materially** adv.

materialism n. a strong interest in material possessions rather than spiritual values. ■ **materialist** n. **materialistic** adj.

materialize (or **-ise**) v. **1** become fact; happen. **2** appear suddenly.

maternal adj. **1** of or like a mother. **2** related through one's mother. ■ **maternally** adv.

maternity n. motherhood. ▶ adj. of or for pregnant women.

Thesaurus

late, assemble, gather, collect, draw together, join together.

massacre v. *see* KILL.

massage v. RUB, knead, pummel, work, manipulate.

master n. LORD, overlord, ruler, overseer, superintendent, director, manager, controller, governor, commander, captain, chief, head, headman, principal, owner, employer; *informal* boss, top dog, big cheese. ▶ v. **1** CONQUER, vanquish, defeat, overcome, overpower, subdue, subjugate, govern, quell, quash, suppress, control, curb, check, bridle, tame. **2** LEARN, become proficient in, grasp; *informal* get the hang of, get clued up about.

masterful adj. AUTHORITATIVE, powerful, controlling, domineering, dictatorial, overbearing, overweening, imperious, peremptory, high-handed, arrogant, haughty. ■ OPPOSITES weak.

masterly adj. EXPERT, adept, clever, skilful, deft, adroit, skilled, dexterous, accomplished, polished; *informal* ace. ■ OPPOSITES inept.

mastermind v. DIRECT, manage, plan, organize, arrange, engineer, conceive, devise, forge, originate, initiate, think up, come up with; *informal* be the brains behind.

masterpiece n. MAGNUM OPUS, masterwork, chef-d'œuvre, work of art, creation, pièce de resistance.

match v. **1** COMPLEMENT, blend with, harmonize with, go with, tone with, coordinate with, team with, tally with, correspond to, accord with. **2** BE EQUAL TO, be a match for, measure up to, rival, vie with, compete with, compare with. **3** PAIR UP, mate, couple, unite, join, combine, link, ally; *informal* hitch up, yoke.

matching adj. CORRESPONDING, equivalent, parallel, analogous, complementary, the same, paired, twin, coupled, double, duplicate, identical, like. ■ OPPOSITES different.

mate n. **1** FRIEND, companion, comrade, crony; *informal* pal, chum; *US informal* buddy. **2** ASSISTANT, helper, apprentice, subordinate. ▶ v. BREED, copulate, couple.

material n. **1** MATTER, substance, stuff, medium, constituent elements. **2** FABRIC, cloth, stuff, textile. **3** DATA, information, facts, facts and figures, evidence, details. ▶ adj. CORPOREAL, physical, bodily, fleshly, tangible, substantial, concrete.

materialize v. **1** COME INTO BEING, hap-

mathematics n. the study of numbers, quantities, and space. ■ **mathematical** adj. **mathematically** adv. **mathematician** n.

maths (US **math**) n. mathematics.

matinee /mat-i-nay/ n. an afternoon performance in a theatre or cinema.

matins n. a service of morning prayer.

maître d'hôtel /may-truh doh-**tel**/ n. (pl. **maîtres d'hôtel**) a head waiter.

matriarch n. a female head of a family or tribe. ■ **matriarchal** adj. **matriarchy** n.

matricide n. **1** the killing of one's mother. **2** a person who kills their mother.

matriculate v. enrol at a college or university. ■ **matriculation** n.

matrimony n. marriage. ■ **matrimonial** adj.

matrix n. (pl. **matrices** or **matrixes**) **1** an environment in which something develops. **2** a mould in which something is cast. **3** a grid-like array of elements.

matron n. **1** a woman in charge of medical and living arrangements at a school. **2** a dignified or sedate married woman. **3** dated a woman in charge of nursing at a hospital. ■ **matronly** adj.

matt (or **matte**) adj. not shiny.

matted adj. (of hair or fur) tangled into a thick mass.

matter n. **1** physical substance or material. **2** a situation to be dealt with. **3** a problem. ▶v. be important. □ **matter-of-fact** unemotional and practical.

mattress n. a fabric case filled with soft, firm, or springy material for sleeping on.

maturation n. the act of maturing.

mature adj. **1** fully grown. **2** like a sensible adult. ▶v. **1** become mature. **2** (of an insurance policy) reach the end of

its term and so become payable. ■ **maturely** adv. **maturity** n.

matzo n. (pl. **matzos**) a wafer of unleavened bread.

maudlin adj. sentimental and full of self-pity.

maul v. **1** wound by scratching and tearing. **2** treat roughly.

maunder v. talk in a rambling way.

mausoleum n. a building housing a tomb or tombs.

mauve n. a pale purple colour.

maverick n. an unconventional, independent-minded person.

mawkish adj. sentimental in a sickly way.

maxim n. a sentence expressing a general truth or rule of behaviour.

maximize (or **-ise**) v. make as great as possible.

maximum n. (pl. **maxima** or **maximums**) the greatest amount or size possible. ▶adj. greatest in amount or size. ■ **maximal** adj.

May n. **1** the fifth month. **2** (**may**) the hawthorn or its blossom. □ **mayfly** a short-lived insect living near water. **maypole** a decorated pole for dancing round on the first day of May.

may aux. v. (past **might**) expressing possibility, permission, or a wish.

maybe adv. perhaps.

Mayday n. an international radio distress signal used by ships and aircraft.

mayhem n. violent disorder.

mayonnaise n. a dressing made from egg yolks, oil, and vinegar.

mayor n. the elected head of a city or borough council. ■ **mayoral** adj. **mayoralty** n.

mayoress n. **1** the wife of a mayor. **2** a woman elected as mayor.

maze n. a network of paths and walls or hedges through which one has to find a

Thesaurus

pen, occur, come about, take place; *literary* come to pass. **2** APPEAR, turn up, become visible, come into view, come into sight, show oneself/itself, come to light, emerge.

matrimonial adj. MARITAL, conjugal, connubial, nuptial, spousal.

matter n. **1** MATERIAL, substance, stuff. **2** AFFAIR, business, proceeding, situation, circumstance, event, happening, occurrence, incident, occasion, experience. **3** SUBJECT, topic, issue, question, point, case. ▶v. BE OF IMPORTANCE, be of consequence, make a difference, signify, be relevant, carry weight, count.

mature adj. **1** ADULT, grown up, grown, fully grown, full-grown, of age. **2** RIPE, ripened, mellow, ready, seasoned. ▶v. GROW UP, develop fully, become adult, reach adulthood, come of age.

maverick n. NONCONFORMIST, rebel, dissenter, dissident, individualist, free spirit, bohemian, eccentric. ■ OPPOSITES conformist.

maxim n. APHORISM, proverb, adage, saw, saying, axiom, precept, epigram, gnome.

maximum n. MOST, utmost, uttermost, upper limit, ceiling, top, summit, peak, apogee, acme. ▶adj. HIGHEST, greatest, way.

MB (or **Mb**) abbrev. megabytes.

MBA abbrev. Master of Business Administration.

MBE abbrev. Member of the Order of the British Empire.

MC abbrev. Master of Ceremonies.

MD abbrev. **1** Doctor of Medicine. **2** Managing Director.

ME abbrev. myalgic encephalomyelitis, a medical condition causing aches and prolonged tiredness.

me pron. the form of 'I' used when the speaker or writer is the object of a verb or preposition.

☑ It's wrong to use *me* as the subject of a verb, as in *John and me went to the shops*; in this case use *I* instead.

mead n. an alcoholic drink made from honey and water.

meadow n. a field of grass.

meagre (US **meager**) adj. small in quantity. ■ **meagreness** n.

meal n. **1** a regular occasion when food is eaten. **2** the food eaten on such an occasion. **3** coarsely ground grain.

mealy adj. of or like meal. □ **mealy-mouthed** unwilling to speak frankly.

mean v. (**meaning**, **meant**) **1** intend.

2 (of a word) have as its explanation in the same language or its equivalent in another. **3** have as a result. **4** be of specified importance. ▶adj. **1** unwilling to give or share. **2** unkind. **3** aggressive. **4** poor in quality or appearance. **5** dated of a low social class. **6** calculated as a mean. **7** in the middle of two extremes. ▶n. **1** the average value of a set of quantities. **2** something in the middle of two extremes. ■ **meanly** adv. **meanness** n.

meander v. **1** follow a winding course. **2** wander in an aimless way. ▶n. a winding bend of a river or road.

meaning n. **1** what is meant. **2** a sense of purpose. ■ **meaningful** adj. **meaningless** adj.

means n. **1** a thing or method for achieving a result. **2** financial resources. □ **by all means** of course. **by no means** certainly not. **means test** an official investigation of a person's finances to find out their eligibility for welfare benefits.

meantime adv. (**in the meantime**) meanwhile.

meanwhile adv. **1** in the period of time between two events. **2** at the same time.

measles n. an infectious disease causing fever and a red rash.

m

Thesaurus

biggest, largest, topmost, most, utmost, supreme. ■ OPPOSITES minimum.

mayhem n. HAVOC, disorder, confusion, chaos, bedlam.

meadow n. FIELD, grassland, pasture, paddock, lea.

meagre adj. PALTRY, sparse, scant, scanty, spare, inadequate, insufficient, insubstantial, skimpy, miserly, niggardly, pathetic; *informal* stingy. ■ OPPOSITES abundant.

mean[1] v. **1** INDICATE, signify, express, convey, denote, designate, stand for, represent, symbolize, portend, connote, imply, purport, suggest, allude to, intimate, hint at, insinuate, drive at. **2** INTEND, have in mind, have in view, contemplate, set out, aim, aspire, desire, want, wish. **3** INVOLVE, entail, lead to, result in, give rise to, bring about, cause.

mean[2] adj. **1** MISERLY, niggardly, parsimonious, close-fisted, penny-pinching, grasping, greedy, avaricious, ungenerous, illiberal, close, near; *informal* stingy, tight, tight-fisted, mingy. **2** NASTY, disagreeable, unpleasant, unfriendly, offensive, obnoxious, cross, ill-natured, bad-tempered, irritable, churlish, surly,

cantankerous, crotchety, crabbed. **3** LOW, lowly, low-born, humble, modest, common, ordinary, base, proletarian, plebeian, obscure. ■ OPPOSITES generous, kind, noble.

meander v. WIND, zigzag, snake, curve, turn, bend.

meaning n. **1** DEFINITION, explanation, interpretation, elucidation, explication. **2** SIGNIFICANCE, point, value, worth, consequence, account.

meaningful adj. **1** SIGNIFICANT, important, serious, sincere, in earnest. **2** POINTED, significant, suggestive, eloquent, expressive, pregnant. ■ OPPOSITES meaningless.

meaningless adj. **1** SENSELESS, unintelligible, incomprehensible, incoherent. **2** POINTLESS, senseless, purposeless, motiveless, irrational. **3** EMPTY, futile, pointless, aimless, valueless, worthless, trivial, insignificant. ■ OPPOSITES meaningful.

means pl. n. WAY, method, expedient, process, mode, manner, agency, medium, instrument, channel, avenue, course.

meanwhile adv. **1** IN THE MEANTIME, for

measly adj. informal meagre.

measure v. **1** find the size, amount, etc. of something by comparing it with a standard. **2** be of a specified size. **3 (measure out)** take an exact quantity of. **4 (measure up)** reach the required standard. ▶ n. **1** a course of action. **2** a proposal for a law. **3** a standard unit used in measuring. **4** a measuring device marked with such units. **5 (a measure of)** a certain amount of. ■ **measurable** adj. **measurably** adv.

measured adj. **1** slow and regular in rhythm. **2** carefully considered.

measurement n. **1** the act of measuring. **2** a size etc. found by measuring.

meat n. animal flesh as food.

meaty adj. (**meatier**, **meatiest**) **1** like or full of meat. **2** brawny. **3** substantial or satisfying.

mechanic n. a skilled worker who repairs and maintains machinery.

mechanical adj. **1** of or operated by machinery. **2** done without conscious thought. ■ **mechanically** adv.

mechanics n. **1** the study of motion and forces producing motion. **2** working parts. **3** the practical aspects of something.

mechanism n. **1** a piece of machinery. **2** the way something works or happens.

mechanize (or **-ise**) v. equip with machinery. ■ **mechanization** n.

medal n. an inscribed metal disc awarded for achievement or to mark an event.

medallion n. a pendant shaped like a medal.

medallist (US **medalist**) n. a person awarded a medal.

meddle v. interfere in something that is not one's concern. ■ **meddler** n. **meddlesome** adj.

media n. **1** television, radio, and newspapers as the means of mass communication. **2** pl. of MEDIUM.

mediaeval var. of MEDIEVAL.

medial adj. situated in the middle. ■ **medially** adv.

median adj. situated in the middle. ▶ n. a median value or line.

mediate v. try to settle a dispute between two other parties. ■ **mediation** n. **mediator** n.

medic n. informal a doctor or medical student.

medical adj. of the science of medicine. ▶ n. an examination to assess a person's physical health. ■ **medically** adv.

medicament n. a medicine.

medicate v. **1** give medicine to. **2 (medicated)** containing a medicinal substance.

medication n. **1** a medicine. **2** treatment with medicines.

medicinal adj. having healing properties. ■ **medicinally** adv.

medicine n. **1** the science or practice of the treatment and prevention of disease. **2** a substance taken to treat or prevent disease. □ **medicine man** a witch doctor.

Thesaurus

the time being, for now, for the moment, in the interim, in the interval. **2** AT THE SAME TIME, simultaneously, concurrently, coincidentally.

measure n. **1** SIZE, dimension, proportions, magnitude, amplitude, mass, bulk, volume, capacity, quantity, weight. **2** RULE, ruler, tape measure, gauge, meter, scale, level, yardstick. **3** SHARE, portion, division, allotment, part, piece, quota, lot, ration, percentage; informal rake-off. **4** ACTION, act, course, course of action, deed, proceeding, procedure, step, means, expedient. ▶ v. CALCULATE, compute, estimate, quantify, weigh, size, evaluate, rate, assess, appraise, gauge, measure out, determine, judge, survey.

measured adj. CAREFULLY CHOSEN, selected with care, well thought out, studied, calculated, planned, considered, deliberate, reasoned.

mechanical adj. **1** AUTOMATED, auto-

matic, machine-driven, motor-driven, power-driven. **2** AUTOMATIC, unthinking, unconscious, unfeeling, unemotional, cold, involuntary, instinctive, routine, habitual. ■ OPPOSITES manual.

mechanism n. **1** MACHINE, apparatus, appliance, tool, device, instrument, contraption, contrivance. **2** PROCESS, procedure, system, operation, method, means, medium, agency, channel.

meddle v. INTERFERE, butt in, intrude, intervene, interlope, pry, nose; informal stick one's nose in, horn in, snoop.

mediate v. ARBITRATE, negotiate, conciliate, intervene, intercede, interpose, moderate, umpire, referee, act as peacemaker, reconcile, restore harmony, make peace, bring to terms, step in.

mediator n. ARBITRATOR, arbiter, negotiator, go-between, middleman, intermediary, honest broker, peacemaker, intervenor, interceder, moderator, umpire, referee, judge, adjudicator, con-

medieval (or **mediaeval**) adj. of the Middle Ages.

mediocre adj. of average or fairly low quality. ■ **mediocrity** n.

meditate v. **1** focus one's mind for spiritual purposes or relaxation. **2** think carefully. ■ **meditation** n. **meditative** adj. **meditatively** adv.

Mediterranean adj. of the Mediterranean Sea or the countries around it.

medium n. (pl. **media** or **mediums**) **1** a means of doing or communicating something. **2** a substance through which something acts or is conveyed. **3** (pl. **mediums**) a person claiming to communicate between the dead and the living. **4** the middle state between two extremes. ▶ adj. between two extremes. □ **medium wave** a radio wave of a frequency between 300 kHz and 3 mHz.

medlar n. a small apple-like fruit.

medley n. (pl. **medleys**) **1** a varied mixture. **2** various musical excerpts performed as a continuous piece.

medulla n. a separate inner region of an organ or tissue.

meek adj. quiet, gentle, and obedient. ■ **meekly** adv. **meekness** n.

meerschaum /meer-shawm/ n. a tobacco pipe with a white clay bowl.

meet v. (**meeting, met**) **1** come together with someone at the same place and time. **2** be introduced to or encounter for the first time. **3** touch or join. **4** experience. **5** (**meet with**) receive a reaction. **6** satisfy a requirement. ▶ n. a meeting for races or fox hunting. ▶ adj. old use suitable or proper.

meeting n. **1** an organized gathering for a discussion etc. **2** a situation in which people come together.

mega adj. informal **1** huge. **2** excellent.

megabyte n. a unit of information equal to 1,048,576 bytes.

megahertz n. (pl. **megahertz**) a unit of frequency equal to one million hertz.

megalith n. a large stone forming a prehistoric monument or part of one. ■ **megalithic** adj.

megalomania n. **1** obsession with power. **2** the false belief that one has great power. ■ **megalomaniac** n. & adj.

megaphone n. a large cone-shaped device for amplifying the voice.

megawatt n. a unit of power equal to one million watts.

melamine n. a hard plastic used for laminated coatings.

melancholy n. deep sadness or depression. ▶ adj. sad or depressed.

melanin n. a dark pigment in the hair

Thesaurus

ciliator, reconciler.

medicinal adj. MEDICAL, therapeutic, curative, healing, remedial, restorative, health-giving, analeptic.

medicine n. **1** MEDICATION, medicament, drug, remedy, cure; old use physic. **2** MEDICAL SCIENCE, practice of medicine, healing art.

mediocre adj. **1** INDIFFERENT, average, middle-of-the-road, middling, ordinary, commonplace, pedestrian, run-of-the-mill, tolerable, passable, adequate, uninspired, undistinguished, unexceptional; informal SO-SO, fair-to-middling, no great shakes, nothing to write home about. **2** INFERIOR, second-rate, second-class, low-grade, poor, shabby, minor. ■ OPPOSITES exceptional.

meditate v. CONTEMPLATE, think about/over, muse on/about, ponder on/over, consider, concentrate on, reflect on, deliberate about/on, ruminate about/on/over, brood over, mull over, be in a brown study over.

meditation n. CONTEMPLATION, thought, musing, pondering, consideration, reflection, deliberation, rumination.

medium n. **1** MEDIAN, mid-point, middle, centre point, average, norm, standard, middle course, compromise, happy medium, golden mean. **2** MEANS, agency, channel, avenue, vehicle, organ, instrument. ▶ adj. MIDDLE, mean, medial, median, midway, midpoint, intermediate.

meek adj. DOCILE, modest, humble, unassuming, unpretentious, submissive, yielding, unresisting, patient, long-suffering, forbearing, resigned, gentle, peaceful, compliant, acquiescent, deferential, weak, timid, frightened, spineless, spiritless; informal weak-kneed. ■ OPPOSITES assertive.

meet v. **1** ENCOUNTER, come face to face with, make contact with, run into, run across, come across, come upon, chance upon, happen upon, light upon; informal bump into. **2** COME TOGETHER, abut, adjoin, join, link up, unite, connect, touch, converge, intersect. **3** GATHER, assemble, come together, foregather, congregate, convene, muster, rally, convoke. ■ OPPOSITES avoid.

meeting n. **1** ENCOUNTER, contact, assignation, rendezvous; literary tryst. **2** GATHERING, assembly, conference, congregation, convention, convocation, con-

and skin.

melanoma n. a malignant skin cancer.

meld v. blend.

melee /mel-ay/ n. **1** a confused fight. **2** a disorderly crowd.

mellifluous adj. sweet-sounding.

mellow adj. **1** pleasantly smooth or soft in sound, taste, or colour. **2** relaxed and good-humoured. ▶v. make or become mellow.

melodeon n. a small accordion or organ.

melodious adj. tuneful.

melodrama n. **1** a sensational play with exciting events. **2** dramatic events or behaviour. ■ **melodramatic** adj. **melodramatically** adv.

melody n. (pl. **melodies**) **1** a tune. **2** the main part in harmonized music. ■ **melodic** adj. **melodically** adv.

melon n. a large round fruit.

melt v. **1** make or become liquid by heating. **2** gradually disappear. □ **meltdown** an accident in a nuclear reactor in which the fuel overheats and melts the core.

member n. **1** a person belonging to a group or society. **2** a part of a structure. ■ **membership** n.

membrane n. a thin flexible skin-like tissue. ■ **membranous** adj.

memento n. (pl. **mementos** or **mementoes**) an object kept as a reminder.

memo n. (pl. **memos**) a memorandum.

memoir /mem-war/ n. a written account of events etc. one remembers.

memorable adj. worth remembering or easy to remember. ■ **memorably** adv.

memorandum n. (pl. **memoranda** or **memorandums**) **1** a note sent from one person to another in an organization. **2** a note written as a reminder.

memorial n. an object commemorating a person or event. ▶adj. in memory of someone.

memorize (or **-ise**) v. learn by heart.

memory n. (pl. **memories**) **1** the ability to remember things. **2** a thing remembered. **3** a computer's equipment or capacity for storing data. □ **in memory of** so as to commemorate.

men pl. of **MAN**.

menace n. **1** a dangerous or troublesome person or thing. **2** a threatening quality. ▶v. threaten.

ménage /may-nahj/ n. the members of a household.

menagerie n. a small zoo.

mend v. **1** restore to the correct or working condition. **2** improve a bad situ-

Thesaurus

clave; *informal* get-together. **3** ABUTMENT, junction, conjunction, union, convergence, confluence, concourse, intersection. **4** MEET, race meeting, athletics meeting, sports meeting.

melancholy adj. DESPONDENT, dejected, depressed, down, downhearted, downcast, disconsolate, glum, gloomy, sunk in gloom, miserable, dismal, dispirited, low, in low spirits, in the doldrums, blue, mournful, lugubrious, woeful, woebegone, doleful, sorrowful, unhappy, heavy-hearted, low-spirited, sombre, pessimistic; *informal* down in the dumps, down in the mouth. ■ OPPOSITES cheerful.

mellifluous adj. SWEET, sweet-sounding, sweet-toned, dulcet, honeyed, mellow, soft, soothing, smooth, silvery, euphonious, musical.

mellow adj. **1** MATURE, well matured, soft, juicy, tender, luscious, sweet. **2** GENTLE, easy-going, pleasant, kindly, kind-hearted, amicable, amiable, good-natured, affable, gracious. **3** GENIAL, jovial, jolly, cheerful, happy, merry.

melodious adj. MELODIC, musical, tuneful, harmonious, lyrical, dulcet, sweet, sweet-sounding, sweet-toned, silvery,

silvery-toned, euphonious. ■ OPPOSITES discordant.

melodramatic adj. THEATRICAL, stagy, overdramatic, histrionic, oversensational, extravagant, exaggerated, overdone, overemotional; *informal* actressy, camp, hammy.

melody n. TUNE, air, strain, music, refrain, theme, song.

melt v. DISSOLVE, deliquesce, thaw, unfreeze, defrost, soften, fuse.

member n. **1** ADHERENT, associate, fellow, subscriber. **2** ORGAN, limb, appendage, extremity.

memorable adj. UNFORGETTABLE, not to be forgotten, momentous, significant, historic, notable, noteworthy, important, consequential, remarkable, outstanding, extraordinary, striking, impressive, distinctive, distinguished. ■ OPPOSITES forgettable.

memorial n. MONUMENT, statue, plaque, shrine, tombstone.

memorize v. COMMIT TO MEMORY, remember, learn by heart, get by heart, learn off, learn, learn by rote.

memory n. **1** RECOLLECTION, remembrance, powers of recall, recall, powers of retention, retention. **2** COMMEMORation. □ **on the mend** improving.

mendacious adj. untruthful. ■ **mendacity** n.

mendicant adj. living by begging. ▶n. a beggar.

menhir /men-heer/ n. a tall stone set up in prehistoric times.

menial adj. (of work) unskilled and lacking status. ▶n. a person with a menial job.

meningitis n. inflammation of the membranes enclosing the brain and spinal cord.

meniscus n. (pl. **menisci**) **1** the curved surface of a liquid in a tube. **2** a lens convex on one side and concave on the other.

menopause n. the period in a woman's life when menstruation gradually stops. ■ **menopausal** adj.

menorah n. a large branched candlestick used in Jewish worship.

menstruate v. discharge blood from the lining of the womb each month. ■ **menstrual** adj. **menstruation** n.

mensuration n. measurement, esp. in geometry.

mental adj. **1** having to do with the mind. **2** informal mad. □ **mental age** a person's mental ability expressed as the age at which an average person reaches that ability. ■ **mentally** adv.

mentality n. (pl. **mentalities**) a typical way of thinking.

menthol n. a substance in peppermint oil used as a decongestant. ■ **mentholated** adj.

mention v. refer to briefly or by name. ▶n. a reference to someone or something.

mentor n. an experienced person acting as an adviser.

menu n. **1** a list of dishes available. **2** a list of options on a computer screen.

meow var. of MIAOW.

MEP abbrev. Member of the European Parliament.

mercantile adj. of trade.

mercenary adj. motivated by the desire to make money. ▶n. (pl. **mercenaries**) a professional soldier hired by a foreign army.

mercerized (or **-ised**) adj. (of cotton) treated with a glossy substance that adds strength.

merchandise n. goods for sale. ▶v. promote the sale of.

merchant n. a trader who sells goods in large quantities. □ **merchant bank** a bank dealing in commercial loans and investment. **merchantman** (or **merchant ship**) a ship carrying merchandise. **merchant navy** a country's commercial shipping.

merchantable adj. saleable.

merciful adj. **1** showing mercy. **2** giving relief from suffering. ■ **mercifully** adv.

mercurial adj. **1** tending to change

Thesaurus

ATION, remembrance, honour, tribute.

menace n. THREAT, danger, hazard, jeopardy. ▶v. THREATEN, intimidate, frighten, scare, alarm, terrify, bully, browbeat, cow, terrorize.

mend v. **1** REPAIR, fix, put back together, patch up, restore, rehabilitate, renew, renovate, make whole, make well, cure, heal. **2** GET BETTER, recover, recuperate, improve, be well, be cured. **3** PUT RIGHT, set straight, rectify, put in order, correct, amend, emend, improve.

menial adj. LOWLY, humble, low-grade, low-status, unskilled, routine, humdrum, boring, dull. ▶n. SERVANT, domestic, drudge, underling, lackey, flunkey; informal dogsbody, skivvy.

mentality n. **1** CAST OF MIND, frame of mind, turn of mind, way of thinking, mind, psychology, mental attitude, outlook, character, disposition, make-up. **2** INTELLECT, intellectual capabilities, intelligence, IQ, brainpower, brains, mind, comprehension, understanding; informal grey matter.

mention v. **1** REFER TO, allude to, touch on, speak briefly of, hint at. **2** SAY, state, name, cite, quote, call attention to, adduce. **3** TELL, speak about/of, utter, communicate, let someone know, disclose, divulge, breathe a word of, reveal, intimate, whisper; informal let on about. ▶n. REFERENCE, allusion, observation, remark, statement, announcement, indication.

mentor n. ADVISER, counsellor, guide, guru, spiritual leader, confidant, teacher, tutor, coach, instructor.

mercenary adj. MONEY-ORIENTED, grasping, greedy, acquisitive, avaricious, covetous, bribable, venal; informal money-grubbing.

merchandise n. GOODS, wares, stock, commodities, produce, vendibles.

merchant n. TRADER, dealer, trafficker, wholesaler, broker, seller, salesman/woman/person, vendor, retailer, shopkeeper, distributor.

merciful adj. LENIENT, clement, compassionate, pitying, forgiving, forbearing, mood suddenly. **2** of mercury.

mercury n. a heavy liquid metallic element.

mercy n. (pl. **mercies**) **1** pity or forgiveness shown towards someone in one's power. **2** something to be grateful for. □ **at the mercy of** in the power of. ■ **merciless** adj. **mercilessly** adv.

mere adj. **1** no more or no better than what is specified. **2** (**the merest**) the slightest. ▶n. literary a lake. ■ **merely** adv.

meretricious adj. superficially attractive but having no real value.

merge v. **1** combine into a whole. **2** blend gradually.

merger n. a merging of two organizations into one.

meridian n. a circle passing at the same longitude through a given place on the earth's surface and the poles.

meringue /muh-**rang**/ n. beaten egg whites and sugar baked until crisp.

merino n. (pl. **merinos**) a soft wool obtained from a breed of sheep with a long fleece.

merit n. **1** excellence. **2** a good point or quality. ▶v. (**meriting**, **merited**) deserve.

meritocracy n. (pl. **meritocracies**) a

society in which power is held by those with the greatest ability.

meritorious adj. deserving reward or praise.

merlin n. a small falcon.

mermaid n. a mythical sea creature with a woman's head and body and a fish's tail instead of legs.

merry adj. (**merrier**, **merriest**) **1** cheerful and lively. **2** informal slightly drunk. □ **merry-go-round** a revolving platform with model horses or cars on which people ride for amusement. **merrymaking** cheerful celebration. ■ **merrily** adj. **merriment** n.

mescaline n. a hallucinogenic drug.

Mesdames pl. of **MADAME**.

Mesdemoiselles pl. of **MADEMOISELLE**.

mesh n. **1** material made of a network of wire or thread. **2** the spacing of the strands of a net. ▶v. **1** be in harmony. **2** become entangled. **3** (of a gearwheel) lock together with another.

mesmerize (or -**ise**) v. completely capture the attention of.

meson n. an unstable elementary particle.

mess n. **1** a dirty or untidy state. **2** a state of confusion or difficulty. **3** a

Thesaurus

sparing, humane, mild, soft-hearted, tender-hearted, kind, sympathetic, liberal, tolerant, generous, beneficent, benignant. ■ OPPOSITES merciless, cruel.

merciless adj. UNMERCIFUL, ruthless, relentless, inexorable, harsh, pitiless, unforgiving, unsparing, unpitying, implacable, barbarous, inhumane, inhuman, hard-hearted, heartless, callous, cruel, unsympathetic, unfeeling, illiberal, intolerant, rigid, severe, stern. ■ OPPOSITES merciful, compassionate.

mercy n. LENIENCY, clemency, compassion, pity, charity, forgiveness, forbearance, quarter, humanity, humaneness, mildness, soft-heartedness, tender-heartedness, kindness, sympathy, liberality, tolerance, generosity, beneficence, benignancy. ■ OPPOSITES severity, cruelty.

mere adj. NOTHING MORE THAN, no better than, no more important than, just a, only a, pure and simple.

merge v. **1** JOIN TOGETHER, join forces, amalgamate, unite, combine, incorporate, coalesce, team up. **2** BLEND, fuse, mingle, mix, intermix, homogenize. ■ OPPOSITES separate.

merit n. **1** EXCELLENCE, goodness, quality,

worth, worthiness, value. **2** GOOD POINT, strong point, advantage, asset, plus. ▶v. DESERVE, be deserving of, earn, be worthy of, be worth, be entitled to, have a right to, have a claim to, warrant, rate, incur.

merriment n. CHEERFULNESS, gaiety, high-spiritedness, high spirits, buoyancy, carefreeness, levity, sportiveness, joy, joyfulness, joyousness, jolliness, jollity, rejoicing, conviviality, festivity, merrymaking, revelry, mirth, glee, gleefulness, laughter, hilarity, amusement, fun. ■ OPPOSITES misery.

merry adj. CHEERFUL, cheery, in good spirits, high-spirited, light-hearted, buoyant, carefree, sportive, joyful, joyous, rejoicing, jolly, jocund, convivial, festive, mirthful, gleeful, happy, glad, laughing; dated gay; literary frolicsome. ■ OPPOSITES miserable.

mesh n. **1** NETTING, net, tracery, web, lattice, latticework, lacework, trellis, reticulation. **2** TANGLE, entanglement, web, snare, trap. ▶v. **1** BE ENGAGED, connect, interlock. **2** HARMONIZE, fit together, go together, coordinate, match, be on the same wavelength, dovetail.

place where members of the armed forces eat and relax. ▶v. **1** make untidy or dirty. **2** (**mess about/around**) behave in a silly or playful way.

message n. **1** a spoken or written communication. **2** a significant point or central theme.

messenger n. a person who carries a message.

Messiah n. **1** the prophesied deliverer of the Jewish nation. **2** Jesus regarded by Christians as this. ■ **messianic** adj.

Messieurs pl. of **Monsieur**.

Messrs pl. of **Mr**.

messy adj. (**messier, messiest**) **1** untidy or dirty. **2** confused and difficult. ■ **messily** adv. **messiness** n.

met past & past part. of **meet**.

metabolism n. the process by which food is used for growth or energy. ■ **metabolic** adj.

metabolize (or **-ise**) v. process by metabolism.

metacarpus n. (pl. **metacarpi**) the set of bones between the wrist and fingers.

metal n. **1** a hard, shiny, solid material which conducts electricity and heat. **2** broken stone used in making roads. ■ **metallic** adj.

metalled adj. (of a road) having a hard surface.

metallurgy n. the study of metals. ■ **metallurgist** n.

metamorphic adj. (of rock) changed by heat, pressure, etc.

metamorphosis n. (pl. **metamorph-**

oses) a change in form or nature. ■ **metamorphose** v.

metaphor n. a figure of speech in which a word or phrase is used to represent or stand for something else (e.g. *food for thought*). ■ **metaphorical** adj. **metaphorically** adv.

metaphysics n. philosophy concerned with the nature of existence, truth, and knowledge. ■ **metaphysical** adj.

metatarsus n. (pl. **metatarsi**) the set of bones between the ankle and the toes.

mete v. (**mete out**) deal out justice, punishment, etc.

meteor n. a small body of matter from outer space appearing as a streak of light.

meteoric adj. **1** of meteors or meteorites. **2** (of success) very rapid.

meteorite n. a meteor that has fallen to earth.

meteorology n. the study of atmospheric conditions for weather forecasting. ■ **meteorological** adj. **meteorologist** n.

meter n. **1** a device that measures and records the quantity, degree, or rate of something. **2** US = **metre**. ▶v. measure with a meter.

methadone n. a powerful painkilling drug.

methane n. a flammable gas.

methanol n. a poisonous flammable alcohol, used as a solvent.

method n. **1** a way of doing something. **2** orderliness.

Thesaurus

mesmerize v. **1** HYPNOTIZE, put into a trance, put under. **2** HOLD SPELLBOUND, spellbind, entrance, enthral, bewitch, captivate, enchant, fascinate, grip, magnetize, hypnotize.

mess n. **1** DISORDER, untidiness, disarray, dirtiness, filthiness, clutter, shambles, litter, jumble, muddle, chaos, confusion, disorganization, turmoil. **2** PLIGHT, predicament, tight spot, tight corner, difficulty, trouble, quandary, dilemma, muddle, mix-up, confusion, imbroglio; *informal* jam, fix, pickle, stew, hole. **3** MUDDLE, bungle; *informal* botch, screw-up, cock-up. □ **mess up 1** DIRTY, befoul, litter, pollute, clutter up, disarrange, throw into disorder, dishevel; *literary* besmirch. **2** BUNGLE, muff, make a mess of, mar, spoil, ruin; *informal* botch, make a hash of, muck up, foul up, screw up, cock up, make a muck of.

message n. **1** COMMUNICATION, piece of information, news, word, tidings, note,

memorandum, letter, missive, bulletin, communiqué, dispatch, memo. **2** MEANING, import, idea, point, purport, intimation, theme, moral.

messenger n. MESSAGE-BEARER, courier, errand boy/girl, runner, envoy, emissary, agent, go-between, harbinger, herald.

messy adj. UNTIDY, disordered, dirty, filthy, grubby, slovenly, cluttered, littered, muddled, in a muddle, chaotic, confused, disorganized, sloppy, in disarray, disarranged, dishevelled, unkempt; *informal* shambolic. ■ OPPOSITES orderly.

metamorphosis n. TRANSFORMATION, transfiguration, change, alteration, conversion, changeover, mutation, transmutation, sea change; *informal* transmogrification.

method n. **1** PROCEDURE, technique, system, practice, modus operandi, process, approach, way, course of action,

methodical adj. orderly or systematic. ■ **methodically** adv.

Methodist n. a member of a Protestant group originating in the 18th century. ▶ adj. of Methodists or their beliefs. ■ **Methodism** n.

methodology n. (pl. **methodologies**) a system of methods used in a particular field.

meths n. informal methylated spirit.

methyl n. a chemical unit derived from methane.

methylated spirit n. a form of alcohol used as a solvent or fuel.

meticulous adj. careful and precise. ■ **meticulously** adv. **meticulousness** n.

métier /may-ti-ay/ n. **1** a trade or profession. **2** one's special ability.

metre (US **meter**) n. **1** a metric unit of length, equal to 100 cm (approx. 39.37 inches). **2** the rhythm in poetry.

metric adj. of or using the metric system. □ **metric system** the decimal measuring system based on the metre, litre, and gram. **metric ton** a unit of weight equal to 1,000 kg (2,205 lb).

metrical adj. of or in poetic metre.

metricate v. convert to a metric system. ■ **metrication** n.

metro n. (pl. **metros**) an underground railway.

metronome n. a device for indicating tempo while practising music.

metropolis n. the main city of a country or region. ■ **metropolitan** adj.

mettle n. spirit and strength of character.

mew v. (of a cat or gull) make a high-pitched cry. ▶ n. a mewing cry.

mews n. (pl. **mews**) a row of houses converted from stables.

mezzanine n. a floor extending over only part of the area of a building, between two full floors.

mezzo /met-zoh/ (or **mezzo-soprano**) n. (pl. **mezzos**) a female singer with a voice pitched between soprano and contralto.

mezzotint n. a method of engraving.

mg abbrev. milligrams.

MHz abbrev. megahertz.

miaow (or **meow**) n. & v. (make) the cry of a cat.

miasma n. an unpleasant or unhealthy atmosphere.

mica /my-kuh/ n. a mineral found as tiny shiny scales in rocks.

mice pl. of MOUSE.

microbe n. a microorganism. ■ **microbial** adj.

microbiology n. the study of microorganisms.

microchip n. a miniature electronic circuit made from a tiny wafer of silicon.

microclimate n. the climate of a very small area.

microcosm n. a thing representing something much larger.

microfiche (or **microfilm**) n. a piece of film containing greatly reduced photographs of the pages of a book etc.

microlight n. a very small, light aircraft for one or two people.

micrometer n. an instrument for measuring small distances or thicknesses.

micron n. one millionth of a metre.

microorganism n. a microscopic organism.

microphone n. an instrument for changing sound waves into electrical energy which is then amplified or transmitted.

microprocessor n. an integrated circuit which can function as the main part of a computer.

microscope n. an instrument for magnifying very small objects.

microscopic adj. **1** so small as to be visible only with a microscope. **2** of a microscope. ■ **microscopically** adv.

microsurgery n. complex surgery performed using very small instruments and a microscope.

microwave n. **1** an electromagnetic wave with a wavelength in the range 0.001–0.3 m. **2** an oven that uses microwaves to cook or heat food.

mid adj. in the middle.

midday n. noon.

midden n. a heap of dung or rubbish.

middle adj. **1** at an equal distance from

Thesaurus

scheme, plan, rule, arrangement, form, style, manner, mode. **2** ORDER, orderliness, sense of order, organization, arrangement, structure, form, planning, plan, design, purpose, pattern, regularity. ■ OPPOSITES disorder.

methodical adj. ORDERLY, well ordered, organized, systematic, structured, logical, well regulated, planned, efficient, businesslike, scientific. ■ OPPOSITES disorganized.

meticulous adj. CONSCIENTIOUS, careful, scrupulous, punctilious, painstaking, demanding, exacting, thorough, perfecthe edges or ends of something. **2** medium in rank, quality, etc. ▶n. **1** a middle point or position. **2** informal the waist and stomach. □ **middle-aged** in the period of life between about 45 and 60. **Middle Ages** the period of European history from about 1000 to 1453. **middle class** the social class between the upper and working classes. **Middle East** the area stretching from the Mediterranean to Pakistan. **middleman** a person who buys goods from producers and sells them to consumers. **middleweight** a weight in boxing etc. above welterweight.

middling adj. average in size, amount, or rank.

midfield n. the central part of a sports field.

midge n. a small biting insect.

midget n. a very small person or thing.

Midlands pl. n. the inland counties of central England. ■ **Midland** adj.

midnight n. 12 o'clock at night.

midriff n. the front of the body between the chest and the waist.

midshipman n. a low-ranking officer in the Royal Navy.

midst n. the middle.

midway adv. halfway.

midwife n. a nurse trained to assist at childbirth.

mien /meen/ n. a person's look or manner.

might aux. v. **1** used to express possibility. **2** used politely in questions and requests. ▶n. great power or strength.

mightn't contr. might not.

mighty adj. (**mightier**, **mightiest**) powerful or strong. ▶adv. informal very. ■ **mightily** adv.

migraine n. a severe headache.

migrant n. **1** a migrating animal. **2** a worker who travels to find work. ▶adj. migrating or having migrated.

migrate v. **1** (of an animal) move from one area to another according to the seasons. **2** move to settle in a new area to find work. ■ **migration** n. **migratory** adj.

mike n. informal a microphone.

milch adj. (of a cow) giving or kept for milk.

mild adj. **1** gentle. **2** not severe, harsh, or extreme. **3** not strong in flavour. **4** (of weather) fairly warm. ■ **mildly** adv. **mildness** n.

mildew n. a coating of tiny fungi on plants or damp material. ■ **mildewed** adj.

mile n. a unit of length equal to 1,760 yds (approx. 1.609 km). □ **mileage** a number of miles covered. **mileometer** var. of **MILOMETER**. **milestone 1** a stone showing the distance to a particular place. **2** a significant event or stage.

milieu /mee-lyer/ n. (pl. **milieux** or **milieus**) a person's social environment.

militant adj. prepared to take aggressive action in support of a cause. ▶n. a militant person. ■ **militancy** n.

militarism n. belief in the value of military strength. ■ **militaristic** adj.

military adj. of soldiers or the armed forces. ▶n. (**the military**) the armed

Thesaurus

tionist, fastidious, particular. ■ OPPOSITES careless, slapdash.

microscopic adj. INFINITESIMAL, minuscule, tiny, minute. ■ OPPOSITES huge, massive.

middle adj. MID, mean, medium, medial, median, midway, halfway, central, equidistant, intermediate, intermediary. ▶n. MEAN, median, mid-point, halfway point, centre, dead centre.

middling adj. AVERAGE, medium, ordinary, fair, moderate, adequate, passable, tolerable, mediocre, indifferent, run-of-the-mill, unexceptional, unremarkable; informal fair-to-middling, so-so.

might n. FORCE, power, strength, mightiness, powerfulness, forcefulness, potency, toughness, robustness, sturdiness, muscularity.

mighty adj. **1** FORCEFUL, powerful, strong, potent, tough, robust, sturdy, muscular,

strapping, vigorous, energetic. **2** HUGE, massive, vast, enormous, colossal, giant, gigantic, monumental, mountainous, towering. ■ OPPOSITES puny, tiny.

migrant adj. MIGRATORY, wandering, drifting, nomadic, itinerant, peripatetic, vagrant.

mild adj. **1** TENDER, gentle, soft, soft-hearted, tender-hearted, sensitive, sympathetic, compassionate, humane, warm, forgiving, conciliatory, forbearing, placid, meek, docile, calm, tranquil, serene, peaceful, peaceable, good-natured, amiable, affable, genial, easy, easy-going, mellow. **2** GENTLE, soft, moderate, warm, balmy. **3** BLAND, insipid, tasteless. ■ OPPOSITES cruel, harsh, spicy.

milieu n. ENVIRONMENT, surroundings, background, setting, scene, location, sphere, element.

forces. ■ **militarily** adv.

militate v. (**militate against**) be a powerful factor in preventing.

☑ Don't confuse **militate** with **mitigate**, which means 'make less severe or serious'.

militia n. a military force made up of trained civilians.

milk n. **1** a white fluid produced by female mammals to feed their young. **2** cows' milk as a food and drink for humans. ▶v. **1** draw milk from. **2** exploit or defraud. **3** take full advantage of. □ **milk float** an electric van for delivering milk to houses. **milkman** a man who delivers milk to houses. **milkshake** a cold drink made from milk whisked with ice cream. **milksop** a timid person. **milk tooth** a temporary tooth in a child or young mammal. ■ **milky** adj.

mill n. **1** a building equipped with machinery for grinding grain into flour. **2** a device for grinding a specified substance. **3** a building fitted with machinery for manufacturing. ▶v. **1** grind in a mill. **2** (**milled**) (of a coin) having ribbed markings on the edge. **3** (**mill about/around**) move around in a confused mass. □ **millstone 1** each of a pair of circular stones used for grinding grain. **2** a burden of responsibility.

millennium n. (pl. **millennia** or **millenniums**) a period of a thousand years.

☑ Two *l*s, two *n*s: mil*l*en*n*ium.

miller n. a person who owns or works in a grain mill.

millet n. a type of cereal grass.

millibar n. a unit for measuring atmospheric pressure.

milligram (or **milligramme**) n. one thousandth of a gram.

millilitre (US **milliliter**) n. one thousandth of a litre.

millimetre (US **millimeter**) n. one thousandth of a metre.

milliner n. a person who makes or sells women's hats. ■ **millinery** n.

million n. **1** one thousand thousand; 1,000,000. **2** (**millions**) informal very many. ■ **millionth** adj. & n.

millionaire n. a person who has more than one million pounds or dollars.

millipede n. a small invertebrate animal with many legs.

millisecond n. one thousandth of a second.

milometer (or **mileometer**) n. an instrument on a vehicle for recording the number of miles travelled.

milt n. the semen of a male fish.

mime n. the use of gestures and expressions only to tell a story or convey feelings. ▶v. use mime to act out.

mimic v. (**mimicking, mimicked**) imitate the voice or behaviour of another person. ▶n. a person skilled in mimicking. ■ **mimicry** n.

mimosa n. an acacia tree with yellow flowers.

minaret n. a slender tower on or by a mosque.

mince v. **1** cut meat into very small pieces. **2** walk in an affected way with short, quick steps. ▶n. minced meat. □ **mincemeat** a mixture of dried fruit, sugar, etc. **mince pie** a small pie containing mincemeat. **not mince (one's) words** voice one's disapproval directly. ■ **mincer** n.

mind n. **1** the faculty of consciousness

Thesaurus

militant adj. AGGRESSIVE, combative, pugnacious, fighting, warring, combating, contending, embattled, in arms, belligerent, bellicose. ▶n. ACTIVIST, extremist, partisan.

military adj. ARMY, service, soldierly, soldier-like, armed, martial. ▶n. ARMY, armed forces, services, militia, soldiery, navy, air force, marines.

militate v. (**militate against**) OPERATE AGAINST, go against, count against, tell against, weigh against, be detrimental to, be disadvantageous to, be to the disfavour of, be counter to the interests of, conflict with the interests of.

milk v. **1** DRAW, draw off, express, siphon,

tap, drain, extract. **2** EXPLOIT, take advantage of, impose on, bleed, suck dry.

milky adj. WHITE, milk-white, whitish, creamy, pearly, nacreous, ivory, alabaster, off-white, clouded, cloudy.

mill n. FACTORY, plant, foundry, works, workshop, shop, industrial centre. ▶v. GRIND, pulverize, pound, crush, powder, crunch, granulate; *technical* comminute, triturate. □ **mill about/around** MOVE AROUND, wander around, meander, amble, crowd, swarm, throng.

mimic v. **1** IMPERSONATE, give an impersonation of, imitate, copy, ape, caricature, parody; *informal* take off. **2** RESEMBLE, look like, have/take on the appear-

and thought. **2** a person's intellect or memory. **3** a person's attention or will. ▶v. **1** be distressed or annoyed by. **2** remember or take care to do. **3** watch out for. **4** look after or take care of temporarily. **5** (**minded**) inclined to think in a particular way. ■ **minder** n.

mindful adj. conscious or aware of something.

mindless adj. **1** acting or done without thought. **2** simple and repetitive. ■ **mindlessly** adv.

mine[1] possess. pron. belonging to or associated with me.

mine[2] n. **1** a hole or passage dug in the earth for extracting coal etc. **2** an abundant source. **3** a type of bomb placed on or in the ground or water. ▶v. **1** obtain coal etc. from a mine. **2** lay explosive mines on or in. □ **minefield 1** an area planted with explosive mines. **2** a situation presenting hidden dangers. **mine-sweeper** a warship equipped for detecting and removing explosive mines.

miner n. a person who works in a mine.

mineral n. an inorganic natural substance. □ **mineral water** water which contains dissolved mineral salts.

■ **mineralogy** n.

minestrone /mi-ni-stroh-ni/ n. an Italian soup containing vegetables and pasta.

mingle v. **1** mix together. **2** move around and chat at a party etc.

mini adj. very small of its kind.

miniature adj. much smaller than normal. ▶n. a small-scale portrait, copy, or model. ■ **miniaturize** (or **-ise**) v.

minibus n. a small bus for about twelve people.

minicab n. a taxi available for hire but only when ordered in advance.

minidisc n. a disc similar to a small CD but able to record sound or data as well as play it back.

minim n. a musical note lasting as long as two crotchets.

minimal adj. of a minimum amount, quantity, or degree. ■ **minimally** adv.

minimalism n. the use of simple basic design forms. ■ **minimalist** adj. & n.

minimize (or **-ise**) v. **1** reduce to a minimum. **2** represent as less important than in reality.

minimum n. (pl. **minima** or **minimums**) the smallest amount or extent possible. ▶adj. smallest in amount or extent.

Thesaurus

ance of, echo, mirror, simulate. ▶n. MIMICKER, impersonator, impressionist, imitator, parodist, copyist, parrot, ape.

mince v. CHOP/CUT INTO TINY PIECES, grind, crumble, hash.

mind n. **1** BRAIN, head, seat of intellect, psyche, ego, subconscious. **2** BRAINPOWER, powers of thought, intellect, intellectual capabilities, mentality, intelligence, powers of reasoning, brain, brains, wits, understanding, comprehension, sense, ratiocination; *informal* grey matter. **3** OPINION, way of thinking, thoughts, outlook, view, viewpoint, point of view, belief, judgement, attitude, feeling, sentiment. **4** GENIUS, intellect, intellectual, thinker; *informal* brain, egghead. ▶v. **1** BE OFFENDED BY, take offence at, object to, care about, be bothered by, be upset by, be affronted by, resent, dislike, disapprove of, look askance at. **2** TAKE HEED OF, heed, pay heed to, pay attention to, attend to, concentrate on, listen to, note, mark, observe, respect, obey, follow, comply with, adhere to. **3** LOOK AFTER, take care of, attend to, tend, have charge of, keep an eye on, watch. □ **never mind** DO NOT BOTHER ABOUT, pay no attention to, do not worry about, disregard, forget, do

not take into consideration, do not give a second thought to.

mindful adj. PAYING ATTENTION TO, heedful of, watchful of, careful of, wary of, chary of, cognizant of, aware of, conscious of, alert to, alive to, sensible of. ■ OPPOSITES heedless.

mindless adj. STUPID, foolish, senseless, witless, empty-headed, unintelligent, dull, slow-witted, obtuse; *informal* birdbrained, dumb, dopey, moronic. ■ OPPOSITES intelligent.

mine n. **1** COLLIERY, pit, quarry, lode, vein, deposit, coal mine. **2** SOURCE, reservoir, repository, store, storehouse, wealth. ▶v. EXCAVATE, quarry for, dig for, dig up, extract, unearth.

mingle v. **1** MIX, blend, combine, compound, homogenize, unite, join, amalgamate, fuse. **2** CIRCULATE, socialize, hobnob, fraternize, meet people. ■ OPPOSITES separate.

miniature adj. SMALL-SCALE, scaled down, mini, midget, baby, toy, pocket, dwarf; *informal* pint-sized. ■ OPPOSITES giant.

minimal adj. MINIMUM, least, smallest, slightest, nominal, token. ■ OPPOSITES maximum.

minimize v. **1** KEEP AT/TO A MINIMUM, reduce, decrease, curtail, cut back on,

minion n. a lowly worker or unimportant follower.

miniskirt n. a very short skirt.

minister n. **1** the head of a government department. **2** a senior diplomatic representative. **3** a member of the clergy. ▶v. (**minister to**) attend to the needs of. ■ **ministerial** adj.

ministrations pl. n. the providing of help or care.

ministry n. (pl. **ministries**) **1** a government department headed by a minister. **2** a period of government under one Prime Minister. **3** the work of a minister of religion.

mink n. a small stoat-like animal farmed for its fur.

minnow n. a small fish.

minor adj. **1** not important or serious. **2** Music (of a scale) having intervals of a semitone between the 2nd and 3rd, 5th and 6th, and 7th and 8th notes. ▶n. a person under the age of full legal responsibility.

minority n. (pl. **minorities**) **1** the smaller number or part. **2** a small group differing from the majority in race, religion, etc.

minster n. a large church.

minstrel n. a medieval singer or musician.

mint n. **1** a fragrant herb. **2** the flavour of mint. **3** a peppermint sweet. **4** a place where money is coined. ▶v. make coins. □ **in mint condition** as good as new. ■ **minty** adj.

minuet n. a slow ballroom dance.

minus prep. **1** with the subtraction of. **2** falling below zero by a specific number of degrees. **3** informal lacking. ▶adj. **1** (before a number) below zero. **2** (after a grade) slightly below. ▶n. (also **minus sign**) the symbol −.

minuscule adj. very tiny.

....

☑ -u-, not -i- in the middle: min*u*scule.

....

minute[1] /min-it/ n. **1** one sixtieth of an hour or degree. **2** a very short time. **3** (**minutes**) a written summary of the points discussed at a meeting. ▶v. record in the minutes.

minute[2] /my-nyoot/ adj. **1** very small. **2** precise and careful. ■ **minutely** adv.

minutiae /mi-nyoo-shi-ee/ pl. n. small or precise details.

minx n. a cheeky girl or young woman.

miracle n. **1** a welcome event so extraordinary that it is believed to be the work of God, a saint, etc. **2** a remarkable event or thing. ■ **miraculous** adj. **miraculously** adv.

mirage n. an optical illusion caused by atmospheric conditions.

mire n. a stretch of swampy ground.

mirror n. a surface which reflects a clear image. ▶v. reflect.

mirth n. laughter. ■ **mirthful** adj. **mirthless** adj.

misadventure n. a mishap or accident.

misanthrope n. a person who dislikes and avoids other people. ■ **misan-**

Thesaurus

....

prune, slash. **2** BELITTLE, make light of, decry, discount, play down, deprecate, depreciate, underestimate, underrate. ■ OPPOSITES maximize, exaggerate.

minimum n. LOWEST LEVEL, bottom level, bottom, depth, nadir, least, lowest, slightest. ▶adj. MINIMAL, lowest, smallest, littlest, least, least possible, slightest. ■ OPPOSITES maximum.

minion n. LACKEY, flunkey, henchman, creature, toady, underling, hireling, servant, stooge, dependant, hanger-on, parasite.

minor adj. LESSER, insignificant, unimportant, inconsequential, inferior, trivial, negligible, trifling, lightweight, subordinate. ■ OPPOSITES major.

mint n. FORTUNE, small fortune, vast sum, king's ransom; *informal* pile, stack, heap, packet, bundle. ▶adj. BRAND NEW, as new, unused, perfect, unblemished, undamaged, fresh. ▶v. STAMP, punch, die,

cast, strike, coin, make, manufacture, produce.

minute adj. TINY, minuscule, microscopic, miniature, diminutive, Lilliputian, little, small. ■ OPPOSITES gigantic, huge.

minutely adv. IN DETAIL, exhaustively, meticulously, punctiliously, painstakingly, closely.

miracle n. WONDER, marvel, prodigy, phenomenon.

miraculous adj. SUPERNATURAL, fantastic, magical, inexplicable, unaccountable, preternatural, superhuman, phenomenal, prodigious, wonderful, remarkable, extraordinary, incredible, amazing; *literary* wondrous.

mire n. MARSH, bog, swamp, morass, quagmire, quag, slough, fen, fenland; US bayou. ▶v. SINK, sink down, bog down, stick in the mud.

mirror v. REFLECT, imitate, emulate,

thropic adj. **misanthropy** n.

misapprehension n. a mistaken belief.

misappropriate v. dishonestly take for one's own use. ■ **misappropriation** n.

misbehave v. behave badly.

miscalculate v. calculate wrongly. ■ **miscalculation** n.

miscarriage n. the birth of a fetus before it can survive independently.

miscarry v. (**miscarrying, miscarried**) **1** have a miscarriage. **2** (of a plan) fail.

miscellaneous adj. consisting of many different kinds.

miscellany n. (pl. **miscellanies**) a collection of different things.

mischance n. bad luck.

mischief n. **1** playful misbehaviour. **2** harm or trouble.

mischievous adj. **1** full of mischief.

2 intended to cause trouble. ■ **mischievously** adv.

☑ The ending is *-ous*, not *-ious*: mischievous.

misconception n. a mistaken idea or belief.

misconduct n. bad behaviour.

misconstrue v. interpret wrongly. ■ **misconstruction** n.

miscreant n. a wrongdoer.

misdeed n. a wrongful act.

misdemeanour (US **misdemeanor**) n. a minor wrongdoing.

miser n. a person who hoards money and spends as little as possible. ■ **miserliness** n. **miserly** adj.

miserable adj. **1** very unhappy. **2** causing unhappiness. ■ **miserably** adv.

misery n. (pl. **miseries**) **1** great unhap-

simulate, copy, follow, mimic, echo, ape, parrot, impersonate.

mirth n. GAIETY, merriment, high spirits, cheerfulness, cheeriness, hilarity, glee, laughter, jocularity.

misapprehension n. MISUNDERSTANDING, misinterpretation, misconstruction, misreading, misjudgement, misconception, the wrong idea, a false impression, delusion.

misappropriate v. EMBEZZLE, steal, thieve, swindle, pocket, help oneself to; *informal* nick, pinch; *formal* peculate.

misbehave v. BEHAVE BADLY, be bad, be naughty, be disobedient, get up to mischief, misconduct oneself, be guilty of misconduct, be bad-mannered, show bad/poor manners, be rude, fool around; *informal* carry on, act up.

misbehaviour n. MISCONDUCT, bad behaviour, disorderly conduct, badness, naughtiness, mischief, mischievousness, delinquency, misdeed, misdemeanour, bad/poor manners, rudeness; *informal* carrying on, acting up, shenanigans.

miscalculate v. CALCULATE WRONGLY, make a mistake, go wrong, err, blunder, be wide of the mark; *informal* slip up, make a boo-boo, boob.

miscarriage n. **1** FAILURE, foundering, ruination, non-fulfilment, misfiring, breakdown, mismanagement, perversion, thwarting, frustration. **2** SPONTANEOUS ABORTION, termination.

miscarry v. **1** HAVE A MISCARRIAGE, abort, lose the baby. **2** GO WRONG, go awry, go amiss, be unsuccessful, fail, misfire,

founder, come to nothing, come to grief, meet with disaster, fall through, be ruined, fall flat. ■ OPPOSITES succeed.

miscellaneous adj. VARIED, assorted, mixed, diverse, sundry, variegated, diversified, motley, multifarious, jumbled, confused, indiscriminate, heterogeneous.

miscellany n. ASSORTMENT, mixture, mixed bag, variety, collection, medley, pot-pourri, conglomeration, jumble, confusion, mix, mishmash, hotchpotch, hodgepodge, pastiche, patchwork, farrago, gallimaufry.

mischief n. **1** MISCHIEVOUSNESS, naughtiness, badness, bad behaviour, misbehaviour, misconduct, pranks, wrongdoing, delinquency; *informal* monkey business, shenanigans. **2** HARM, hurt, injury, damage, disruption, trouble.

mischievous adj. **1** NAUGHTY, bad, badly behaved, misbehaving, disobedient, troublesome, vexatious, playful, rascally, roguish, delinquent; *literary* frolicsome. **2** PLAYFUL, teasing, impish, roguish, waggish, arch. ■ OPPOSITES well behaved.

misconception n. see MISAPPREHENSION.

miserable adj. **1** UNHAPPY, sorrowful, dejected, depressed, downcast, downhearted, down, despondent, disconsolate, desolate, wretched, glum, gloomy, dismal, blue, melancholy, low-spirited, mournful, woeful, woebegone, sad, doleful, forlorn, crestfallen; *informal* down in the mouth, down in the dumps. **2** WRETCHED, mean, poor, shabby, squalid, filthy, foul, sordid, seedy, dipiness. **2** a cause of this. **3** informal a constantly miserable person.

misfire v. **1** (of a gun) fail to fire properly. **2** (of an engine) fail to ignite the fuel correctly. **3** fail to produce the intended result.

misfit n. a person whose behaviour etc. sets them apart from others.

misfortune n. **1** bad luck. **2** an unfortunate event.

misgivings pl. n. feelings of doubt or worry.

misguided adj. showing bad judgement.

mishap n. an unlucky accident.

misinform v. give wrong information to. ■ **misinformation** n.

misinterpret v. interpret wrongly. ■ **misinterpretation** n.

misjudge v. **1** form a wrong opinion of. **2** estimate wrongly.

mislay v. (**mislaying**, **mislaid**) lose temporarily.

mislead v. (**misleading**, **misled**) give a wrong impression or wrong information to.

mismanage v. manage something badly

or wrongly. ■ **mismanagement** n.

misnomer n. a wrongly applied name or description.

misogynist /mi-soj-uh-nist/ n. a man who hates women. ■ **misogyny** n.

misplace v. **1** put in the wrong place. **2** (**misplaced**) unwise or inappropriate.

misprint n. a mistake in printed text.

misquote v. quote inaccurately.

misread v. (**misreading**, **misread**) read or interpret wrongly.

misrepresent v. give a misleading account of. ■ **misrepresentation** n.

misrule n. **1** bad government. **2** disorder.

Miss n. a title for an unmarried woman or girl.

miss v. **1** fail to hit or reach. **2** be too late for. **3** fail to see or hear. **4** fail to be present at. **5** avoid. **6** (**miss out**) omit. **7** notice or feel the loss or absence of. ▶ n. a failure to hit or reach something.

missile n. an object thrown or fired at a target.

missing adj. lost or absent.

Thesaurus

lapidated. **3** MEAGRE, paltry, scanty, low, poor, niggardly, pathetic. **4** UNPLEASANT, disagreeable, displeasing, uncomfortable, wet, rainy, stormy. ■ OPPOSITES happy.

miserly adj. MEAN, niggardly, parsimonious, close-fisted, penny-pinching, cheese-paring, penurious, grasping, greedy, avaricious, ungenerous, illiberal, close, near; informal stingy, mingy, tight, tight-fisted, money-grabbing; US informal cheap. ■ OPPOSITES generous.

misery n. **1** DISTRESS, wretchedness, hardship, suffering, affliction, anguish, torment, torture, agony, pain, discomfort, deprivation, poverty, grief, sorrow, heartbreak, despair, depression, dejection, desolation, gloom, melancholy, woe, sadness, unhappiness. **2** MISFORTUNE, trouble, adversity, affliction, ordeal, pain, sorrow, burden, load, blow, trial, tribulation, woe, torment, catastrophe, calamity, disaster. ■ OPPOSITES happiness.

misfortune n. **1** BAD LUCK, ill luck, ill fortune, poor/hard luck, accident, misadventure, mischance. **2** MISHAP, trouble, setback, reverse, adversity, misadventure, blow, failure, accident, disaster, tragedy, affliction, sorrow, misery, woe, trial, tribulation, catastrophe, calamity.

misgiving n. QUALM, doubt, reservation,

suspicion, apprehension, unease, uncertainty.

misguided adj. MISTAKEN, deluded, erroneous, fallacious, wrong, unwarranted, uncalled for, misplaced, ill-advised, unwise, injudicious, imprudent, foolish.

mishap n. ACCIDENT, trouble, setback, reverse, adversity, misadventure, misfortune, stroke of bad luck, blow, disaster, trial, tribulation, catastrophe, calamity.

mislay v. LOSE, misplace, lose track of, miss, be unable to find. ■ OPPOSITES find.

mislead v. MISINFORM, misdirect, delude, take in, deceive, fool, hoodwink, lead astray, throw off the scent, send on a wild-goose chase; informal lead up the garden path, take for a ride, pull the wool over someone's eyes.

misleading adj. see DECEPTIVE.

miss v. **1** FAIL TO ATTEND, be too late for, absent oneself from, skip, be absent from, play truant from, take French leave from. **2** FAIL TO SEIZE/GRASP, let slip, let go, pass up, overlook, disregard. **3** REGRET THE ABSENCE/LOSS OF, feel the loss of, feel nostalgic for, long to see, long for, pine for, yearn for, ache for.

misshapen adj. DEFORMED, malformed, ill-proportioned, misproportioned, out of shape, twisted, distorted, contorted, warped, curved, crooked, wry, bent,

mission n. **1** an important task or assignment. **2** a group sent on a mission. **3** a strongly felt aim or calling. **4** the headquarters of a group of missionaries.

missionary n. (pl. **missionaries**) a person sent to teach others about Christianity. ▶ adj. of a missionary or a religious mission.

missive n. a letter.

misspell v. (**misspelling**, **misspelt** or **misspelled**) spell wrongly.

mist n. tiny water droplets in the air or on a surface. ▶ v. cover or become covered with mist.

mistake n. **1** a thing that is incorrect. **2** an error of judgement. ▶ v. (**mistaking**, past part. **mistaken**) **1** be wrong about. **2** (**mistake for**) confuse with.

mister var. of **Mr**.

mistletoe n. a plant with white berries, growing on trees.

mistral n. a strong north-westerly wind in southern France.

mistress n. **1** a woman in a position of authority or control. **2** a woman having a sexual relationship with a man married to someone else. **3** a female school-teacher.

mistrial n. a trial made invalid through a mistake in proceedings.

mistrust v. have no trust in. ▶ n. lack of trust.

misty adj. (**mistier**, **mistiest**) **1** covered with mist. **2** indistinct.

misunderstand v. (**misunderstanding**, **misunderstood**) fail to understand correctly. ■ **misunderstanding** n.

misuse v. **1** use wrongly. **2** treat badly. ▶ n. wrong use.

mite n. **1** a tiny animal like a spider. **2** a small child or animal. **3** a very small amount.

mitigate v. make less severe or serious.

hunchbacked.

missing adj. LOST, mislaid, misplaced, nowhere to be found, absent, not present, gone, gone astray, unaccounted for. ■ OPPOSITES present.

mission n. **1** ASSIGNMENT, commission, task, job, errand, sortie, operation, work, chore, undertaking, duty, charge, trust. **2** VOCATION, calling, pursuit, goal, aim, quest. **3** DELEGATION, deputation, commission, legation.

mistake n. ERROR, fault, inaccuracy, slip, blunder, miscalculation, misunderstanding, oversight, gaffe, faux pas, solecism, misapprehension; informal slip-up, boo-boo, howler, boob; informal, dated bloomer. ▶ v. GET WRONG, misunderstand, misapprehend, misinterpret, misconstrue, misread. □ **be mistaken** BE WRONG, be in error, be at fault, be under a misapprehension, be misinformed, be misguided, be wide of the mark, be barking up the wrong tree, get the wrong end of the stick. **mistake for** TAKE FOR, mix up with, confuse with, misinterpret as.

mistakenly adv. BY MISTAKE, wrongly, in error, erroneously, incorrectly, falsely, fallaciously, misguidedly. ■ OPPOSITES correctly.

mistreat v. MALTREAT, treat badly, ill-treat, ill-use, misuse, abuse, mishandle, harm, hurt, molest; informal beat up, rough up.

mistress n. LOVER, girlfriend, partner, lady-love, kept woman, inamorata; old use paramour, concubine.

mistrust v. FEEL MISTRUSTFUL OF, distrust, feel distrustful of, have doubts about, be suspicious of, suspect, have reservations about, have misgivings about, be wary of, have no confidence in, question, doubt, lack faith in. ■ OPPOSITES trust.

misty adj. HAZY, foggy, cloudy, blurred, fuzzy, dim, indistinct, vague, obscure, nebulous. ■ OPPOSITES clear.

misunderstand v. MISAPPREHEND, misinterpret, misconstrue, misread, get the wrong idea, receive a false impression; informal get the wrong end of the stick, be barking up the wrong tree.

misunderstanding n. **1** MISAPPREHENSION, mistake, error, mix-up, misinterpretation, misconstruction, misreading, misconception, misbelief, the wrong idea, a false impression; informal the wrong end of the stick. **2** DISAGREEMENT, difference of opinion, falling-out, clash of views, dispute, quarrel, argument, squabble, conflict; informal spat, scrap, tiff.

misuse v. **1** PUT TO WRONG USE, misapply, misemploy, abuse, squander, waste, dissipate. **2** MALTREAT, mistreat, treat badly, ill-treat, ill-use, abuse, mishandle, manhandle, harm, hurt, bully, molest, beat up, rough up. ▶ n. **1** WRONG USE, misapplication, misemployment, abuse, squandering, waste, dissipation. **2** MISUSAGE, malapropism, barbarism, catachresis. **3** MALTREATMENT, mistreat-

■ **mitigation** n.

☑ Don't confuse **mitigate** with **militate**: **militate against** means 'be a powerful factor in preventing'.

mitre (US **miter**) n. **1** a bishop's pointed headdress. **2** a joint between two pieces of wood cut to form a right angle. ▶v. join with a mitre joint.

mitt n. a mitten.

mitten n. a glove with a single section for all four fingers.

mix v. **1** combine or be combined. **2** make by mixing ingredients. **3** (**mix up**) confuse. **4** meet people socially. ▶n. a mixture. ■ **mixer** n. **mixture** n.

mizzen (or **mizzenmast**) n. the mast behind a ship's main mast.

ml abbrev. millilitres.

mm abbrev. millimetres.

MMR abbrev. measles, mumps, and rubella (a vaccination given to children).

mnemonic /ni-mon-ik/ n. a pattern of words etc. used to aid the memory.

moan n. **1** a low mournful sound. **2** a trivial complaint. ▶v. **1** make a moan. **2** grumble.

moat n. a wide water-filled ditch round a castle or town.

mob n. **1** a disorderly crowd. **2** informal a group. ▶v. (**mobbing, mobbed**) crowd round in an unruly way.

mobile adj. able to move or be moved easily. ▶n. **1** a decorative structure hung so as to turn freely in the air. **2** (also **mobile phone**) a portable phone. ■ **mobility** n.

mobilize (or **-ise**) v. organize troops for active service. ■ **mobilization** n.

moccasin n. a soft flat shoe.

mocha /mok-uh/ n. a drink of coffee and chocolate.

mock v. **1** tease scornfully. **2** imitate in an unkind way. ▶adj. not genuine or real. □ **mock-up** a model for testing or study.

mockery n. (pl. **mockeries**) **1** ridicule. **2** an absurd or worthless version of something.

mode n. **1** a way of doing something. **2** a style in clothes, art, etc.

Thesaurus

ment, ill-treatment, ill use, abuse, rough handling, mishandling, man-handling, bullying, injury, harm, molesting.

mitigate v. ALLEVIATE, reduce, diminish, lessen, weaken, attenuate, allay, assuage, palliate, appease, soothe, relieve, ease, soften, temper, mollify, lighten, still, quieten, quiet, tone down, moderate, modify, extenuate, calm, lull, pacify, placate, tranquillize. ■ OPPOSITES aggravate.

mix v. **1** BLEND, combine, mingle, compound, homogenize, alloy, merge, unite, join, amalgamate, fuse, coalesce, interweave. **2** SOCIALIZE, mingle, associate with others, meet people. ▶n. MIXTURE, blend, combination, compound, alloy, merger, union, amalgamation, fusion. □ **mix up 1** CONFUSE, muddle up, mistake, scramble. **2** INVOLVE, implicate, entangle, embroil, forged, draw into, incriminate.

mixed adj. **1** ASSORTED, varied, miscellaneous, diverse, diversified, motley, heterogeneous. **2** HYBRID, cross-bred, inter-bred, mongrel. **3** AMBIVALENT, equivocal, unsure, uncertain. ■ OPPOSITES homogeneous.

mixture n. **1** COMPOUND, blend, mix, brew, combination, concoction, alloy. **2** ASSORTMENT, variety, melange, collection, medley, pot-pourri, conglomeration, jumble, mix, mishmash, hotch-potch, pastiche, farrago, mixed bag. **3** CROSS, cross-breed, mongrel, hybrid.

moan n. GROAN, lament, lamentation, wail, whimper, whine. ▶v. **1** GROAN, wail, whimper, whine. **2** COMPLAIN, whine, carp; informal grouse, gripe, grouch, whinge, beef.

mob n. CROWD, horde, multitude, rabble, mass, body, throng, host, gang, gathering, assemblage. ▶v. CROWD AROUND, swarm around, surround, besiege, jostle.

mobile adj. **1** ABLE TO MOVE, moving, walking, motile, ambulatory. **2** TRANSPORTABLE, portable, travelling, peripatetic, locomotive. **3** EXPRESSIVE, animated, ever-changing, changeable. ■ OPPOSITES immobile.

mobilize v. **1** MUSTER, rally, marshal, assemble, call to arms, organize, make ready, prepare, ready. **2** GET READY, prepare, ready oneself.

mock v. RIDICULE, jeer at, sneer at, deride, scorn, make fun of, poke fun at, laugh at, tease, taunt, twit, chaff, gibe at, insult; informal rag, kid, rib, take the mickey out of. ▶adj. IMITATION, artificial, simulated, synthetic, ersatz, so-called, fake, sham, false, spurious, bogus, counterfeit, forged, pseudo, pretended.

mockery n. **1** RIDICULE, jeering, derision, contempt, scorn, disdain, gibe, insult; informal ribbing. **2** PARODY, travesty, cari-

model n. **1** a three-dimensional copy of a person or thing, usu. on a smaller scale. **2** something used as an example. **3** a person or thing seen as an excellent example of a quality. **4** a person employed to pose for an artist or to display clothes by wearing them. ▶v. (**modelling, modelled**; US **modeling, modeled**) **1** make a model of. **2** (**model on**) use as an example for. **3** work as a model.

modem n. a device connecting a computer to a telephone line.

moderate adj. **1** medium. **2** not extreme. ▶n. a person with moderate views. ▶v. make or become moderate. ■ **moderately** adv. **moderation** n.

moderator n. **1** an arbitrator. **2** a Presbyterian minister presiding over a church assembly.

modern adj. **1** of the present or recent times. **2** involving up-to-date techniques or equipment. ■ **modernity** n. **modernize** (or **-ise**) v.

modernism n. modern ideas, methods, or styles. ■ **modernist** n. & adj.

modest adj. **1** unassuming in the estimation of one's abilities. **2** moderate or small. **3** avoiding indecency. ■ **modestly** adv. **modesty** n.

modicum n. a small amount.

modify v. (**modifying, modified**) make small changes to. ■ **modification** n.

modish adj. fashionable.

modulate v. **1** regulate. **2** vary in tone or pitch.

module n. **1** each of a set of parts or units that can be used to create a more complex structure. **2** a unit forming part of a course of study etc. ■ **modular** adj.

modus operandi n. a way of doing something.

mogul n. an important or powerful person.

mohair n. a yarn made from the hair of the angora goat.

moiety /moy-it-ee/ n. (pl. **moieties**) a half.

moist adj. slightly wet; damp. ■ **moisten** v.

moisture n. water or other liquid making something damp.

moisturize (or **-ise**) v. make the skin less dry. ■ **moisturizer** n.

molar n. a grinding tooth at the back of

---

cature, lampoon, burlesque.

mocking adj. SNEERING, derisive, derisory, contemptuous, scornful, disdainful, sardonic, insulting, satirical.

model n. **1** REPLICA, representation, mock-up, copy, dummy, imitation, facsimile, image. **2** PROTOTYPE, archetype, type, mould, original, pattern, design, paradigm, sample, example, exemplar. **3** STYLE, design, mode, form, mark, version, type, variety, kind, sort. **4** IDEAL, paragon, perfect example, perfect specimen, exemplar, epitome, nonpareil, acme.

moderate adj. **1** MIDDLE-OF-THE-ROAD, non-radical. **2** REASONABLE, within reason, within due limits, fair, just. **3** NOT GIVEN TO EXCESSES, restrained, controlled, temperate, sober, steady. **4** AVERAGE, middling, ordinary, fair, fairish, modest, tolerable, passable, adequate. ▶v. **1** ABATE, let up, die down, calm down, lessen, decrease, diminish, slacken. **2** LESSEN, decrease, diminish, mitigate, alleviate, allay, assuage, ease, palliate.

moderately adv. QUITE, rather, somewhat, fairly, reasonably, to a certain degree, to some extent, within reason, within limits.

modern adj. **1** CONTEMPORARY, present-day, present, current, twenty-first-century, existing, existent. **2** UP TO DATE, up to the minute, fashionable, in fashion, in, in style, in vogue, voguish, modish, the latest, new, newfangled, fresh, advanced, progressive; *informal* trendy, with it. ■ OPPOSITES old-fashioned.

modernize v. MAKE MODERN, update, bring up to date, renovate, remodel, remake, redo, refresh, revamp, rejuvenate; *informal* do over.

modest adj. **1** SELF-EFFACING, humble, unpretentious, unassuming, free from vanity. **2** SHY, bashful, self-conscious, diffident, reserved, retiring, reticent, quiet, coy, embarrassed, blushing, timid, fearful, meek. **3** MODERATE, fair, tolerable, passable, adequate, satisfactory, acceptable, unexceptional, small, limited. ■ OPPOSITES conceited, grand.

modesty n. **1** LACK OF VANITY, humility, self-effacement, lack of pretension, unpretentiousness. **2** SHYNESS, bashfulness, self-consciousness, reserve, reticence, timidity, meekness.

modify v. ALTER, change, adjust, adapt, revise, recast, reform, reshape, refashion, rework, remould, redo, revamp, reorganize, refine, transform.

moist adj. WET, damp, clammy, humid,

the mouth.

molasses n. a thick brown liquid obtained from raw sugar.

mold etc. US = MOULD etc.

mole n. **1** a small burrowing mammal with dark fur. **2** a spy within an organization. **3** a small dark patch on the skin. **4** a pier or breakwater. □ **molehill** a small mound of earth thrown up by a mole.

molecule n. a group of atoms forming the smallest unit that can take part in a chemical reaction. ■ **molecular** adj.

molest v. **1** pester or harass. **2** assault sexually. ■ **molestation** n. **molester** n.

mollify v. (**mollifying**, **mollified**) lessen the anger of.

mollusc (US **mollusk**) n. an animal with a soft body and often an external shell.

mollycoddle v. pamper.

Molotov cocktail n. a bomb made of a bottle of flammable liquid.

molt US = MOULT.

molten adj. made liquid by heat.

molybdenum /muh-lib-duh-nuhm/ n. a brittle metallic element.

moment n. **1** an exact point or brief period of time. **2** importance.

momentary adj. very brief or short-lived. ■ **momentarily** adv.

momentous adj. very important.

momentum n. impetus gained by movement or progress.

monarch n. a king, queen, emperor, or empress. ■ **monarchical** adj.

monarchist n. a supporter of monarchy.

monarchy n. (pl. **monarchies**) **1** government by a monarch. **2** a state ruled by a monarch.

monastery n. (pl. **monasteries**) a community of monks living under religious vows.

monastic adj. of monks or nuns or their communities.

Monday n. the day before Tuesday.

monetarism n. the theory that inflation is best controlled by limiting the supply of money. ■ **monetarist** n. & adj.

monetary adj. of money or currency.

money n. **1** current coins and banknotes. **2** wealth. **3** payment or financial gain. **4** (**moneys** or **monies**) sums of money.

moneyed adj. wealthy.

Mongol n. **1** a person from Mongolia. **2** (**mongol**) offens. a person with Down's syndrome.

mongoose n. (pl. **mongooses**) a small carnivorous mammal of Africa and Asia.

mongrel n. a dog of no particular breed.

monitor n. **1** a person or device that monitors something. **2** a television used to view a picture from a camera or a display from a computer. **3** a school pupil with special duties. ▶ v. keep under observation.

monk n. a man belonging to a religious community.

monkey n. (pl. **monkeys**) **1** a small primate, usu. with a long tail and living in trees. **2** a mischievous child. ▶ v. (**monkeying**, **monkeyed**) **1** (**monkey about/around**) behave in a silly way. **2** (**monkey with**) tamper with. □ **monkey wrench** a spanner with large adjustable jaws.

mono n. monophonic sound.

mono- comb. form one; single.

Thesaurus

dank, rainy, drizzly, dewy, soggy, succulent, juicy, soft, spongy.

moisture n. WATER, liquid, wetness, wet, dampness, damp, humidity, dankness, rain, dew, drizzle, perspiration, sweat.

molest v. PESTER, annoy, plague, torment, harass, badger, harry, persecute, bother, worry, trouble, provoke; informal bug, needle, hassle.

mollify v. CALM DOWN, pacify, placate, appease, soothe, quiet. ■ OPPOSITES enrage.

moment n. **1** SHORT TIME, minute, second, instant; informal tick, jiffy. **2** POINT IN TIME, time, instant, minute, juncture, stage.

momentary adj. BRIEF, short, short-lived, fleeting, passing, transient, transitory, ephemeral, evanescent,

temporary, impermanent. ■ OPPOSITES lengthy.

momentous adj. CRUCIAL, critical, vital, decisive, pivotal, serious, grave, important, significant, consequential, fateful, historic; informal earth-shattering. ■ OPPOSITES insignificant.

momentum n. IMPETUS, impulse, propulsion, thrust, push, driving power, drive, power, energy, force.

money n. CASH, hard cash, ready money, finance, capital, funds, banknotes, currency, coin, coinage, silver, copper, legal tender, specie; informal wherewithal, dough, bread, dosh, brass, lolly, spondulicks, the ready, readies, loot, the necessary, shekels, tin, gelt, moolah, filthy lucre; US informal mazuma.

monitor n. DETECTOR, scanner, recorder,

monochrome adj. done in black and white or in tones of one colour.

monocle n. a single lens worn at one eye.

monocular adj. of or for one eye.

monoculture n. the cultivation of only one crop in an area.

monogamy n. the practice of having only one husband or wife at a time. ■ **monogamous** adj.

monogram n. a motif of two or more interwoven letters, usu. a person's initials. ■ **monogrammed** adj.

monograph n. a scholarly text on a single subject.

monolith n. a large single upright block of stone. ■ **monolithic** adj.

monologue n. a long speech.

monomania n. an obsession with one thing. ■ **monomaniac** n.

monophonic adj. (of sound reproduction) using only one channel of transmission.

monoplane n. an aircraft with one pair of wings.

monopolize (or **-ise**) v. dominate or take control of.

monopoly n. (pl. **monopolies**) the complete possession or control of something, esp. the supply of a product or service, by one person or organization.

monorail n. a railway in which the track consists of a single rail.

monosodium glutamate n. a compound used to add flavour to food.

monosyllable n. a word of one syllable. ■ **monosyllabic** adj.

monotheism n. the belief that there is a single god. ■ **monotheist** n. **mono-**

theistic adj.

monotone n. a level unchanging tone of voice.

monotonous adj. dull because lacking in variety or variation. ■ **monotonously** adv. **monotony** n.

monoxide n. an oxide with one atom of oxygen.

Monsieur /muh-syer/ n. (pl. **Messieurs**) a form of address for a French man.

monsoon n. **1** a seasonal wind in the Indian subcontinent and SE Asia. **2** the rainy season accompanying this.

monster n. **1** a large, frightening imaginary creature. **2** a very cruel person. ▶ adj. very large.

monstrosity n. (pl. **monstrosities**) **1** a very large and ugly object. **2** an evil act.

monstrous adj. **1** very large and ugly or frightening. **2** very evil or wrong. ■ **monstrously** adv.

montage /mon-tahzh/ n. a picture or film made by putting together pieces from other pictures or films.

month n. **1** each of the twelve periods into which a year is divided. **2** a period of 28 days. ■ **monthly** adj. & adv.

monument n. **1** a statue or structure built to commemorate a person or event. **2** a structure or site of historical importance.

monumental adj. **1** very large or impressive. **2** acting as a monument.

moo v. (of a cow) make a long, deep sound. ▶ n. (pl. **moos**) such a sound.

mooch v. informal pass one's time in a bored or listless way.

m

Thesaurus

security camera, observer, watchdog, overseer, supervisor, invigilator. ▶ v. OBSERVE, scan, record, survey, follow, keep an eye on, keep track of, check, oversee, supervise, invigilate.

monopolize v. **1** CORNER, control, take over, have sole rights in. **2** DOMINATE, take over, not let anyone else take part in. ■ OPPOSITES share.

monotonous adj. UNVARYING, lacking/ without variety, unchanging, repetitious, all the same, uniform, routine, humdrum, run-of-the-mill, commonplace, mechanical, uninteresting, unexciting, prosaic, wearisome, dull, boring, tedious, tiresome. ■ OPPOSITES varied, interesting.

monster n. **1** FIEND, beast, brute, barbarian, savage, villain, ogre, devil, demon. **2** MONSTROSITY, malformation, abortion,

freak, freak of nature, mutant.

monstrous adj. **1** MALFORMED, unnatural, abnormal, grotesque, gruesome, repellent, freakish, mutant. **2** OUTRAGEOUS, shocking, disgraceful, scandalous, atrocious, heinous, evil, abominable, terrible, horrible, dreadful, hideous, foul, vile, nasty, ghastly, odious, loathsome, intolerable, contemptible, despicable, vicious, cruel, savage. ■ OPPOSITES lovely.

monument n. **1** MEMORIAL, statue, shrine, reliquary, sepulchre, mausoleum, cairn, obelisk, dolmen, cromlech, megalith. **2** COMMEMORATION, memorial, remembrance, reminder, testament, witness, token.

monumental adj. **1** GREAT, huge, enormous, immense, vast, exceptional, extraordinary, tremendous, stupen-

mood n. **1** a temporary state of mind. **2** a fit of bad temper or depression.

moody adj. (**moodier**, **moodiest**) **1** having sudden changes of mood. **2** gloomy or sulky. ■ **moodily** adv.

moon n. **1** the natural satellite of the earth. **2** a natural satellite of any planet. ▶ v. behave in a dreamy manner. □ **moonscape** a rocky landscape like that of the moon. **moonshine 1** foolish ideas. **2** US illegally made alcoholic drink. **moonstone** a white semi-precious stone.

moonlight n. the light of the moon. ▶ v. (**moonlighting**, **moonlighted**) informal do a second job without declaring it for tax purposes. ■ **moonlit** adj.

Moor n. a member of a NW African Muslim people. ■ **Moorish** adj.

moor n. a stretch of high, open uncultivated land. ▶ v. fasten a boat to the shore or to an anchor. □ **moorhen** a small black waterbird. **mooring** (or **moorings**) a place or the ropes for mooring a boat.

moose (pl. **moose**) = **ELK**.

moot adj. uncertain or undecided: *a moot point.*

mop n. **1** a bundle of thick strings or a sponge on a stick, used for wiping floors. **2** a thick mass of hair. ▶ v. (**mopping**, **mopped**) clean or soak up by wiping.

mope v. be listless and unhappy.

moped n. a light motorcycle.

moraine n. a mass of rocks etc. deposited by a glacier.

moral adj. **1** concerned with the principles of right and wrong behaviour. **2** following accepted standards of behaviour. ▶ n. **1** a moral lesson learned from a story or experience. **2** (**morals**)

standards of good behaviour. □ **moral support** encouragement. **moral victory** a defeat that can be interpreted as a victory because one has done the right thing. ■ **morally** adv.

morale n. the level of confidence and spirits of a person or group.

moralist n. a person who teaches or promotes morality.

morality n. (pl. **moralities**) **1** moral principles or behaviour. **2** the extent to which an action is right or wrong.

moralize (or **-ise**) v. comment on moral matters in a disapproving way.

morass n. **1** a boggy area. **2** a complicated situation.

moratorium n. (pl. **moratoriums** or **moratoria**) a temporary ban on an activity.

morbid adj. **1** having a strong interest in death and disease. **2** of disease. ■ **morbidity** n. **morbidly** adv.

mordant adj. (of wit) sharply sarcastic. ▶ n. a substance combining with a dye to fix it.

more n. & pron. a greater or additional amount or degree. ▶ adv. **1** to a greater extent. **2** again. □ **moreover** besides.

mores /mor-ayz/ pl. n. the customs and conventions of a community.

morgue n. a mortuary.

moribund adj. at the point of death.

Mormon n. a member of the Church of Jesus Christ of Latter-Day Saints.

morning n. the part of the day before noon. □ **morning sickness** nausea occurring during early pregnancy.

morocco n. leather made from goatskin.

moron n. informal a stupid person. ■ **moronic** adj.

morose adj. sullen and ill-tempered.

Thesaurus

dous, prodigious, staggering. **2** MASSIVE, impressive, striking, remarkable, magnificent, awe-inspiring, marvellous, majestic, stupendous, prodigious.

mood n. HUMOUR, temper, disposition, frame of mind, state of mind, spirit, tenor, vein.

moody adj. TEMPERAMENTAL, changeable, unpredictable, volatile, mercurial, unstable, unsteady, erratic, fitful, impulsive, capricious.

moon v. LANGUISH, idle, mope, daydream, be in a reverie, be in a brown study.

moot adj. DEBATABLE, open to question, open, doubtful, disputable, arguable, contestable, controversial, unresolved, undecided.

moral n. LESSON, teaching, message, meaning, significance, point.

morale n. CONFIDENCE, heart, spirit, hope, hopefulness, optimism, determination, zeal.

morality n. MORALS, moral code, moral standards, ethics, principles of right and wrong, standards/principles of behaviour.

morbid adj. GRUESOME, grisly, macabre, hideous, dreadful, horrible, unwholesome. ■ OPPOSITES wholesome.

more adv. TO A GREATER EXTENT, further, longer, some more. ▶ pron ADDITIONAL AMOUNT/NUMBER, greater quantity/part, addition, supplement, extra, increase, increment. ■ OPPOSITES less.

■ **morosely** adv.

morphine n. a painkilling drug obtained from opium.

morphology n. the study of forms of living organisms or words. ■ **morphological** adj.

morris dancing n. traditional English folk dancing performed in costumes decorated with ribbons and bells.

Morse code n. a code in which letters are represented by long and short sounds or flashes of light.

morsel n. a small piece of food.

mortal adj. **1** subject to death. **2** causing death. **3** lasting until death. ▶n. a human being. ■ **mortally** adv.

mortality n. **1** the state of being mortal. **2** death. **3** the death rate.

mortar n. **1** a mixture of lime, cement, sand, and water for holding bricks or stones together. **2** a bowl in which substances are crushed with a pestle. **3** a short cannon. □ **mortar board** an academic cap with a flat square top.

mortgage n. **1** a legal agreement by which a person takes out a loan using their house as security. **2** the amount of money lent in a mortgage. ▶v. transfer a property to a creditor as security for a loan.

mortgagee n. the lender in a mortgage.

mortgagor n. the borrower in a mortgage.

mortician n. an undertaker.

mortify v. (**mortifying**, **mortified**) **1** embarrass or humiliate. **2** subdue physical urges by self-discipline. ■ **mortification** n.

mortise (or **mortice**) n. a hole or recess in one part designed to receive a projection in another so that the two are held together. □ **mortise lock** a lock set into the framework of a door.

mortuary n. (pl. **mortuaries**) a place where dead bodies are kept until burial or cremation.

mosaic n. a picture or pattern made with small coloured pieces of stone, tile, or glass.

Moslem var. of **Muslim**.

mosque n. a Muslim place of worship.

mosquito n. (pl. **mosquitoes**) a small bloodsucking fly.

moss n. a small green plant forming a dense growth in damp habitats. ■ **mossy** adj.

most n. & pron. **1** greatest in amount or degree. **2** the majority of. ▶adv. **1** to the greatest extent. **2** very.

mostly adv. on the whole; mainly.

MOT n. a compulsory annual safety test of vehicles of more than a specified age.

motel n. a roadside hotel for motorists.

motet n. a short religious choral work.

moth n. an insect like a butterfly, usu. active at night. □ **mothball** a small ball of camphor for keeping moths away from stored clothes.

mother n. **1** a female parent. **2** (**Mother**) the title of the head of a convent. ▶v. look after kindly and protectively. □ **motherboard** a printed circuit board containing the main components of a computer. **mother-in-law** (pl. **mothers-in-law**) the mother of one's husband or wife. **motherland** one's native country. **mother-of-pearl** a pearly substance lining the shells of oysters. **mother tongue** one's native language. ■ **motherhood** n. **motherless** adj. **motherly** adj.

motif n. **1** a single or repeated image forming a design. **2** a recurring feature or theme.

motion n. **1** an act or the process of moving. **2** a formal proposal put to a meeting. **3** an emptying of the bowels. ▶v. direct with a gesture. □ **motion pic-**

Thesaurus

moreover adv. BESIDES, furthermore, further, what is more, in addition, also, as well, into the bargain, to boot.

moron n. FOOL, idiot, dolt, dunce, ass, ignoramus, imbecile, simpleton; *informal* chump, booby, nincompoop, ninny, dunderhead, blockhead, fathead, halfwit, cretin, dummy, numbskull, dimwit, twerp, clot, twit, nitwit; *US informal* schmuck.

morsel n. BITE, nibble, bit, crumb, grain, particle, fragment, piece, scrap, segment, soupçon, taste.

mortal adj. **1** TEMPORAL, transient, ephemeral, passing, impermanent, per-

ishable, human, earthly, worldly, corporeal, fleshly. **2** DEADLY, irreconcilable, sworn, bitter, out and out, implacable, unrelenting, remorseless. ■ OPPOSITES immortal.

mortify v. HUMILIATE, humble, bring low, disgrace, shame, abash, chasten, degrade, abase, deflate, crush, discomfit, embarrass.

mostly adv. FOR THE MOST PART, on the whole, in the main, largely, mainly, chiefly, predominantly.

mother n. FEMALE PARENT, materfamilias, matriarch; *informal* mum, mummy, ma, mam, mammy, old lady, old woman; *US*

ture a cinema film. ∎ **motionless** adj.

motivate v. **1** provide with a motive. **2** stimulate the interest of. ∎ **motivation** n.

motive n. a person's reason for doing something. ▸ adj. producing motion.

motley adj. varied or assorted.

motocross n. cross-country racing on motorcycles.

motor n. **1** a machine supplying motive power. **2** informal a car. ▸ adj. giving or producing motion. ▸ v. travel by car. □ **motorbike** a motorcycle. **motorcade** a procession of vehicles. **motor vehicle** a road vehicle powered by an engine. **motorway** a road designed for fast long-distance traffic. ∎ **motorized** (or **-ised**) adj.

motorcycle n. a two-wheeled vehicle powered by a motor. ∎ **motorcyclist** n.

motorist n. a car driver.

mottled adj. marked with patches of a different colour.

motto n. (pl. **mottoes** or **mottos**) a short sentence or phrase expressing a belief or aim.

mould (US **mold**) n. **1** a container into which a liquid is poured to set in a desired shape. **2** a distinctive style or character. **3** a furry growth of tiny fungi on a damp surface. ▸ v. **1** form an object of a particular shape out of a soft substance. **2** influence the development of.

moulder (US **molder**) v. decay.

moulding (US **molding**) n. a decorative strip of wood, stone, or plaster.

mouldy (US **moldy**) adj. covered with mould.

moult (US **molt**) v. shed feathers, hair, or skin before new growth. ▸ n. a period of moulting.

mound n. **1** a raised mass of earth. **2** a small hill. **3** a heap.

mount v. **1** climb up or on to. **2** get up on an animal etc. to ride it. **3** increase in number or intensity. **4** organize. **5** fix in place or on a support. ▸ n. **1** a support or setting. **2** a horse for riding. **3** (in names) a mountain.

mountain n. **1** a very high, steep hill. **2** a large pile or quantity. □ **mountain bike** a sturdy bicycle with broad deep-treaded tyres.

mountaineering n. the sport or activity of climbing mountains. ∎ **mountaineer** n.

mountainous adj. **1** having many mountains. **2** huge.

mourn v. feel deep sorrow about the death or loss of. ∎ **mourner** n.

mournful adj. very sad or depressing. ∎ **mournfully** adv.

mourning n. **1** the expression of deep

Thesaurus

informal mom, mommy; informal, dated mater.

motherly adj. MATERNAL, protective, comforting, caring, loving, affectionate, fond, warm, tender.

motion n. MOBILITY, locomotion, movement, moving, travel, travelling, progress, passing, passage, flow, action, activity.

motionless adj. UNMOVING, stock-still, at a standstill, stationary, immobile, immovable, static, at rest, frozen, inert, lifeless. ∎ OPPOSITES mobile.

motivate v. MOVE, cause, lead, persuade, prompt, actuate, drive, impel, spur, induce, provoke, incite, inspire.

motive n. MOTIVATION, reason, rationale, grounds, cause, basis, occasion, incentive, inducement, incitement, influence, stimulus, spur, goad; informal what makes one tick.

motley adj. ASSORTED, varied, miscellaneous, mixed, diverse, diversified, variegated.

mottled adj. BLOTCHED, blotchy, speckled, spotted, streaked, marbled, flecked, freckled, dappled, stippled; informal splotchy.

motto n. MAXIM, aphorism, adage, saying, saw, axiom, truism, precept, epigram, proverb.

mould v. SHAPE, form, fashion, model, create, design, carve, sculpt, chisel, forge.

mouldy adj. MILDEWED, blighted, musty, fusty, decaying, rotting, rotten, bad, spoiled.

mound n. HILLOCK, knoll, rise, hummock, tump, embankment, bank, dune.

mount v. **1** ASCEND, go up, climb up, clamber up, make one's way up, scale. **2** INCREASE, grow, escalate, intensify. **3** STAGE, put on, install, prepare, organize, arrange, set in motion, get up. ∎ OPPOSITES descend.

mountain n. PEAK, mount, height, elevation, eminence, pinnacle, fell, alp; Sc. ben.

mountainous adj. HILLY, high, highland, steep, lofty, towering, soaring, alpine, rocky.

mourn v. GRIEVE, sorrow, keen, lament, bewail, bemoan.

mournful adj. SAD, sorrowful, doleful,

sorrow for someone who has died. **2** black clothes worn in a period of mourning.

mouse n. (pl. **mice**) **1** a small rodent with a long tail. **2** a quiet, timid person. **3** (pl. also **mouses**) a small hand-held device controlling the cursor on a computer screen.

moussaka n. a Greek dish of minced lamb and aubergines.

mousse n. **1** a dish made with whipped cream or egg white. **2** a light substance for styling hair.

moustache (US **mustache**) n. a strip of hair on the upper lip.

mousy adj. **1** of a light brown colour. **2** timid.

mouth n. **1** the opening in the body through which food is taken and sounds are made. **2** an opening or entrance. **3** the place where a river enters the sea. ▸v. **1** move the lips as if to form words. **2** say insincerely. □ **mouth organ** a small instrument played by blowing and sucking. **mouthpiece** a part of a musical instrument, telephone, etc. put in or against the mouth. **mouthwash** an antiseptic liquid for rinsing the mouth. ■ **mouthful** n.

movable adj. able to be moved.

move v. **1** go or cause to go in a specified direction or manner. **2** change position. **3** change the place where one lives. **4** take or cause to take action.

5 make progress. **6** provoke emotion in. ▸n. **1** an act of moving. **2** a purposeful action. **3** a player's turn in a board game.

movement n. **1** an act or the process of moving. **2** a group with a shared cause. **3** (**movements**) a person's activities during a particular period. **4** a main division of a musical work.

movie n. US a cinema film.

moving adj. arousing sadness or sympathy. ■ **movingly** adv.

mow v. (**mowing**, **mowed**; past part. **mowed** or **mown**) **1** cut down or trim grass or hay. **2** (**mow down**) kill by gunfire or by knocking down with a vehicle. ■ **mower** n.

mozzarella /mot-suh-**rel**-luh/ n. a firm white Italian cheese.

MP abbrev. Member of Parliament.

mpg abbrev. miles per gallon.

mph abbrev. miles per hour.

Mr n. a title used before a man's name.

Mrs n. a title used before a married woman's name.

MS abbrev. **1** (pl. **MSS**) manuscript. **2** multiple sclerosis.

Ms n. a title used before a married or unmarried woman's name.

MSc abbrev. Master of Science.

Mt abbrev. Mount.

much pron. a large amount. ▸adv. **1** to a great extent. **2** often.

mucilage /**mew**-sil-ij/ n. a sticky solution extracted from plants, used esp. in

m

Thesaurus

gloomy, sombre, melancholy, lugubrious, funereal, dejected, depressed, downcast, miserable, woeful, unhappy. ■ OPPOSITES cheerful.

mouth n. **1** LIPS, jaws, maw, muzzle; informal trap, chops, kisser, gob. **2** OPENING, entrance, entry, inlet, door, doorway, gateway, hatch, aperture, orifice.

mouthful n. BITE, swallow, nibble, sip, sup, taste, drop, bit, piece, morsel, sample.

mouthpiece n. SPOKESMAN, spokeswoman, spokesperson, negotiator, intermediary, mediator, agent, representative.

move v. **1** GO, walk, march, proceed, progress, advance. **2** CARRY, transport, transfer, transpose, change over, shift, switch. **3** TAKE ACTION, act, do something, get moving. **4** MOVE HOUSE, relocate, move away, leave. **5** AFFECT, touch, impress, upset, disturb, disquiet, agitate, make an impression on, have an impact on. **6** PROVOKE, incite, actu-

ate, rouse, excite, urge, incline, stimulate, motivate, influence, persuade, lead, prompt, cause, impel, induce. **7** PROPOSE, put forward, advocate, recommend, urge, suggest. ▸n. **1** MOVEMENT, motion, moving, action, activity, gesture, gesticulation. **2** ACTION, act, deed, measure, step, tack, manoeuvre, tactic, stratagem, ploy, ruse, trick. **3** TURN, go. □ **get a move on** HURRY UP, make haste, speed up, move faster, get moving; informal get cracking, make it snappy, step on it, shake a leg.

movement n. **1** MOVING, carrying, transportation, transferral, shifting. **2** MOVE, motion, action, activity, gesture, gesticulation. **3** MECHANISM, machinery, works, workings, action. **4** CAMPAIGN, crusade, drive, group, party, organization, coalition, front.

moving adj. **1** AFFECTING, touching, emotive, emotional, poignant, stirring, arousing, upsetting, disturbing. **2** MOVABLE, mobile, motile, unfixed. **3** DRIVING, adhesives.

muck n. **1** dirt or rubbish. **2** manure. ▶v. **1 (muck up)** informal spoil. **2 (muck about/around)** informal behave in a silly way. **3 (muck out)** clean a stable. □ **muckraking** the searching out and publicizing of scandal. ■ **mucky** adj.

mucous adj. of or covered with mucus.

mucus n. a slimy substance coating the lining of many body cavities and organs.

mud n. wet, soft earth. □ **mudguard** a curved cover above a wheel of a bicycle or motorcycle to protect against spray from the road. ■ **muddy** adj.

muddle v. **1** bring into a disordered state. **2** confuse. **3 (muddle along/through)** cope more or less satisfactorily. ▶n. a muddled state.

muesli /myooz-li/ n. a mixture of oats, dried fruit, and nuts, eaten with milk.

muezzin /moo-ez-zin/ n. a man who calls Muslims to prayer.

muff n. a tube-shaped furry covering for the hands.

muffin n. **1** a flat bread roll eaten toasted with butter. **2** a small cake.

muffle v. **1** wrap or cover for warmth. **2** make a sound quieter.

muffler n. a scarf.

mufti n. civilian clothes when worn by military or police staff.

mug n. **1** a large cylindrical cup with a handle. **2** informal the face. **3** informal a stupid or gullible person. ▶v. **(mugging, mugged) 1** attack and rob someone in a public place. **2 (mug up)** informal learn or study a subject quickly and intensively. ■ **mugger** n.

muggy adj. **(muggier, muggiest)** (of the weather) unpleasantly warm and humid.

mulberry n. a dark red or white fruit similar to a loganberry.

mulch n. a mass of leaves, bark, etc.

spread around a plant for protection or to enrich the soil. ▶v. cover with mulch.

mule n. **1** the offspring of a male donkey and a female horse. **2** a light backless shoe.

mulish adj. stubborn.

mull v. **1 (mull over)** think about at length. **2** heat wine with sugar and spices.

mullah n. a Muslim learned in Islamic theology and law.

mullet n. (pl. **mullet**) an edible sea fish.

mullion n. a vertical bar between the panes in a window.

multi- comb. form many.

multicultural adj. of or involving several cultural or ethnic groups.

multifarious adj. very varied.

multilateral adj. involving three or more participants.

multimedia n. a computer system providing video and audio material as well as text.

multinational adj. involving several countries. ▶n. a company operating in several countries.

multiple adj. having or involving several parts or elements. ▶n. a number divisible by another a certain number of times without a remainder. □ **multiple sclerosis** see SCLEROSIS.

multiplex n. a cinema with several separate screens.

multiplicand n. a number to be multiplied by another.

multiplicity n. (pl. **multiplicities**) a large number or variety.

multiplier n. a number by which another number is to be multiplied.

multiply v. **(multiplying, multiplied) 1** add a number to itself a specified number of times. **2** increase in number or quantity. ■ **multiplication** n.

multiracial adj. of or involving people

Thesaurus

dynamic, impelling, motivating, stimulating, inspirational.

mow v. CUT, trim, crop, clip, scythe, shear.

muck n. **1** DIRT, grime, filth, mud, slime, sludge, scum, mire; informal gunk, gunge. **2** DUNG, manure, ordure, excrement, guano, droppings, faeces. □ **muck up** BUNGLE, muff, make a mess of, mess up, mar, spoil, ruin, foul up; informal botch, screw up.

muddle v. **1** MIX UP, get confused, confuse, jumble, scramble, throw into disorder, get into a tangle, make a mess of,

mess up. **2** BEWILDER, disorientate, confuse, befuddle, daze, perplex, puzzle, baffle, nonplus, confound.

muddy v. **1** DIRTY, begrime, soil. **2** MAKE UNCLEAR, cloud, confuse, mix up, jumble, scramble, get into a tangle.

muffle v. **1** WRAP UP, cover up, swathe, swaddle, envelop, cloak. **2** DEADEN, dull, dampen, stifle, smother, suppress, soften, quieten, mute.

mug v. ASSAULT, attack, beat up, knock down, rob; informal rough up, do over.

muggy adj. CLOSE, stuffy, sultry, oppressive, airless, humid, clammy, sticky.

of many races.

multitude n. a large number of people or things.

multitudinous adj. very numerous.

mum informal n. one's mother. ▶ adj. (**keep mum**) remain silent so as not to reveal a secret.

mumble v. say something indistinctly. ▶ n. indistinct speech.

mumbo-jumbo n. informal complicated but meaningless language.

mummify v. (**mummifying, mummified**) preserve a body as a mummy. ■ **mummification** n.

mummy n. (pl. **mummies**) **1** informal one's mother. **2** (in ancient Egypt) a body preserved for burial by embalming and wrapping in bandages.

mumps pl. n. a disease causing swelling of the glands at the sides of the face.

munch v. eat steadily and noisily.

mundane adj. **1** dull or routine. **2** worldly.

municipality n. (pl. **municipalities**) a town or district with its own local government. ■ **municipal** adj.

munificent adj. very generous. ■ **munificence** n.

munitions pl. n. weapons, ammunition, etc.

muon n. an unstable elementary particle.

mural n. a painting done directly on a wall.

murder n. the illegal deliberate killing of one person by another. ▶ v. kill illegally and deliberately. ■ **murderer** n. **murderous** adj.

murk n. darkness or fog.

murky adj. **1** dark and gloomy. **2** dirty or cloudy. **3** dishonest and secret.

murmur n. **1** something said quietly. **2** a low continuous noise. ▶ v. **1** say something quietly. **2** make a murmur.

muscle n. **1** a band of tissue in the body that can contract to move a part of the body. **2** power or strength. ▶ v. (**muscle in**) informal interfere in another's affairs.

Muscovite n. a person from Moscow.

muscular adj. **1** of the muscles. **2** having well-developed muscles. □ **muscular dystrophy** a condition in which the muscles gradually get weaker and waste away. ■ **muscularity** n.

muse n. a woman who is a creative artist's inspiration. ▶ v. be deep in thought.

museum n. a building in which objects of interest or importance are stored and displayed.

mush n. **1** a soft, wet mass. **2** excessive sentimentality. ■ **mushy** adj.

mushroom n. an edible fungus with a domed head on a stalk. ▶ v. increase or develop rapidly.

music n. **1** vocal or instrumental sounds combined in a pleasing way. **2** the art of writing or playing music. **3** the written signs representing music.

musical adj. **1** of or accompanied by music. **2** fond of or skilled in music. **3** pleasant-sounding. ▶ n. a play or film with singing and dancing. ■ **musically** adv.

musician n. a person who plays a mu-

■ OPPOSITES fresh.

multiple adj. SEVERAL, many, numerous, various, collective, manifold. ■ OPPOSITES single.

multiply v. **1** BREED, reproduce. **2** INCREASE, grow, accumulate, augment, proliferate, spread.

multitude n. CROWD, assembly, throng, host, horde, mass, mob, legion, army.

munch v. CHEW, champ, chomp, masticate, crunch, eat.

mundane adj. COMMON, ordinary, everyday, workaday, usual, prosaic, pedestrian, routine, customary, regular, normal, typical, commonplace, banal, hackneyed, trite, stale, platitudinous. ■ OPPOSITES extraordinary.

municipal adj. CIVIC, civil, city, metropolitan, urban, town, borough.

murder n. KILLING, manslaughter, homicide, slaughter, assassination, butch-

ery, carnage, massacre; literary slaying. ▶ v. see KILL.

murderer n. KILLER, slaughterer, cutthroat, assassin, butcher; literary slayer.

murderous adj. FATAL, lethal, deadly, mortal, homicidal, savage, barbarous, brutal, bloodthirsty.

murky adj. DARK, dim, gloomy, dirty, muddy, dingy, dull, cloudy, turbid, opaque. ■ OPPOSITES clear.

murmur n. **1** WHISPER, undertone, mutter, mumble. **2** BABBLE, burble, whisper, purl, rustle, buzzing, drone. ▶ v. **1** WHISPER, speak in an undertone, speak sotto voce, mutter, mumble. **2** BABBLE, burble, whisper, purl, rustle, buzz, drone.

muscular adj. BRAWNY, strapping, powerfully built, solidly built, hefty, sturdy, rugged, burly; informal beefy. ■ OPPOSITES weak, puny.

muse v. THINK, meditate, ruminate, consical instrument or writes music.

musicology n. the study of the history and theory of music.

musk n. a strong-smelling substance produced by a type of male deer, used in perfumes. ■ **musky** adj.

musket n. hist. a light gun with a long barrel.

Muslim (or **Moslem**) n. a follower of Islam. ▶ adj. of Muslims or Islam.

muslin n. thin cotton cloth.

mussel n. a small shellfish with a dark shell.

must aux. v. expressing obligation, insistence, or certainty. ▶ n. informal something that should not be missed.

mustache US = MOUSTACHE.

mustang n. a small wild horse of the south-western US.

mustard n. a hot-tasting paste made from the crushed seeds of a plant.

muster v. **1** bring troops together. **2** (of people) gather together. **3** summon up a feeling. ▢ **pass muster** be satisfactory.

mustn't contr. must not.

musty adj. having a stale or mouldy smell. ■ **mustiness** n.

mutable adj. liable to change. ■ **mutability** n.

mutagen n. something causing genetic mutation.

mutant adj. resulting from or showing the effect of mutation. ▶ n. a mutant form.

mutate v. undergo mutation.

mutation n. **1** the process of changing in form. **2** a change in genetic structure resulting in a variant form. **3** a mutant.

mute adj. **1** not speaking. **2** dated unable to speak. ▶ n. **1** dated a person who is unable to speak. **2** a device used to muffle the sound of a musical instrument. ▶ v. **1** deaden or muffle the sound of. **2** reduce the intensity of. ■ **mutely** adv.

mutilate v. severely injure or damage,

esp. by cutting off a part. ■ **mutilation** n.

mutiny n. (pl. **mutinies**) an open rebellion against authority, esp. by soldiers or sailors. ▶ v. (**mutinying**, **mutinied**) engage in mutiny. ■ **mutineer** n. **mutinous** adj.

mutter v. **1** say quietly and indistinctly. **2** talk or grumble in private. ▶ n. something muttered.

mutton n. the flesh of sheep as food.

mutual adj. **1** felt or done by two or more people to the other or others. **2** shared by two or more people. ■ **mutuality** n. **mutually** adv.

muzzle n. **1** the nose and mouth of an animal. **2** a guard fitted over an animal's muzzle to stop it biting. **3** the open end of a firearm's barrel. ▶ v. **1** put a muzzle on. **2** prevent from expressing opinions freely.

muzzy adj. (**muzzier**, **muzziest**) **1** dazed or confused. **2** blurred.

MW abbrev. **1** medium wave. **2** megawatts.

my adj. belonging to me.

myalgia n. muscle pain.

mycelium n. (pl. **mycelia**) a network of fine threads forming part of a fungus.

mycology n. the study of fungi.

myelin n. a substance forming a sheath around nerve fibres.

mynah n. an Asian or Australasian bird, some kinds of which can mimic human speech.

myopia n. short-sightedness. ■ **myopic** adj.

myriad n. a very great number.

myrrh /mer/ n. a fragrant gum resin used in perfumes and incense.

myrtle n. an evergreen shrub with white flowers and purple berries.

myself pron. **1** used when the speaker is also the person affected by an action. **2** I or me personally.

Thesaurus

template, reflect, deliberate, day dream, be in a reverie.

musical adj. TUNEFUL, melodic, melodious, harmonious, mellifluous, dulcet, euphonious.

muster v. ASSEMBLE, bring together, call/gather together, call up, summon, rally, mobilize, round up, marshal, convoke, collect.

musty adj. MOULDY, mildewed, fusty, decaying, stale, stuffy, airless, damp, dank.

mutation n. CHANGE, variation, alteration, modification, transformation,

metamorphosis, evolution, transmutation, transfiguration.

mute adj. SILENT, speechless, wordless, unspeaking, taciturn, uncommunicative; informal mum. ▶ v. see MUFFLE (2).

muted adj. SOFT, softened, subdued, subtle, discreet, toned down, quiet, understated.

mutinous adj. REBELLIOUS, insurgent, insurrectionary, revolutionary, subversive, seditious, traitorous, insubordinate, disobedient, riotous, unruly, restive, contumacious, refractory; informal bolshie.

mysterious adj. difficult or impossible to understand or explain. ■ **mysteriously** adv.

mystery n. (pl. **mysteries**) **1** something that remains unexplained. **2** secrecy. **3** a story dealing with a puzzling crime.

mystic n. a person who seeks to know God through contemplation and prayer. ▶ adj. mystical. ■ **mysticism** n.

mystical adj. **1** having a spiritual significance beyond human understanding. **2** inspiring a sense of mystery and awe.

mystify v. (**mystifying, mystified**) utterly bewilder. ■ **mystification** n.

mystique n. an air of secrecy or mystery.

myth n. **1** a traditional story of early history or explaining a natural event, esp. involving supernatural beings. **2** an imaginary person or thing. ■ **mythical** adj.

mythology n. myths. ■ **mythological** adj.

myxomatosis n. a highly infectious and usually fatal disease of rabbits.

Thesaurus

mutiny n. REBELLION, revolt, insurrection, insurgence, insurgency, uprising, rising, revolution, disobedience, defiance, insubordination.

mysterious adj. ENIGMATIC, impenetrable, inscrutable, incomprehensible, inexplicable, unexplainable, unfathomable, unaccountable, dark, obscure, arcane, abstruse, cryptic, unknown, recondite, secret, preternatural, supernatural, uncanny, mystical, peculiar, strange, weird, curious, bizarre, undisclosed, mystifying, baffling, puzzling, perplexing, bewildering.

mystery n. ENIGMA, puzzle, secret, riddle, conundrum, question, question mark, closed book, unexplored ground, terra incognita.

mystic, mystical adj. SPIRITUAL, paranormal, transcendental, other-worldly, supernatural, preternatural, occult, metaphysical.

mystify v. CONFUSE, bewilder, confound, perplex, baffle, nonplus, puzzle, elude, escape; *informal* stump, beat, bamboozle.

myth n. **1** LEGEND, saga, tale, story, fable, folk tale, allegory, parable, fairy story/tale. **2** FANTASY, delusion, invention, fabrication, untruth, lie.

mythical adj. **1** LEGENDARY, mythological, fabled, chimerical, fabulous, fantastical, fairy-tale, storybook, fictitious, allegorical. **2** IMAGINED, imaginary, pretend, make-believe, unreal, fictitious, invented, fabricated, made up, untrue. ■ OPPOSITES real.

Nn

N abbrev. **1** North or Northern. **2** newtons.

Naafi n. a shop or canteen run by the Navy, Army, and Air Force Institutes.

naan var. of NAN (sense 2).

nab v. (**nabbing**, **nabbed**) informal **1** catch a wrongdoer. **2** take suddenly.

nadir n. the lowest point.

naevus /nee-vuhss/ (US **nevus**) n. (pl. **naevi**) a birthmark.

naff adj. informal lacking taste or style.

nag v. (**nagging**, **nagged**) **1** harass constantly to do something. **2** be constantly worrying or painful to. ▶ n. **1** a person who nags. **2** informal a horse.

naiad /ny-ad/ n. (in Greek mythology) a water nymph.

nail n. **1** a small metal spike with a flat head, used to join pieces of wood together. **2** a thin hard layer over the tip of a finger or toe. ▶ v. **1** fasten with a nail or nails. **2** informal catch or arrest a suspected criminal.

naive /ny-eev/ adj. lacking experience or judgement. ■ **naively** adv. **naivety** n.

naked adj. **1** without clothes. **2** without coverings. **3** not hidden; open. □ **the naked eye** the eyes unassisted by a microscope etc. ■ **nakedness** n.

namby-pamby adj. feeble or cowardly.

name n. **1** a word or words by which someone or something is known or referred to. **2** a famous person. **3** a reputation. ▶ v. **1** give a name to. **2** identify. **3** specify. **4** appoint. □ **namesake** a person or thing with the same name as another.

namely adv. that is to say.

nan n. **1** informal one's grandmother. **2** (also **naan**) a soft flat Indian bread.

nanny n. (pl. **nannies**) a woman employed to look after a child in its own home.

nanosecond n. one thousand millionth of a second.

nanotechnology n. technology on an atomic or molecular scale.

nap n. **1** a short sleep during the day. **2** short raised fibres on the surface of fabric. ▶ v. (**napping**, **napped**) have a short sleep.

napalm /nay-pahm/ n. a jelly-like form of petrol used in firebombs.

nape n. the back of the neck.

naphtha /naf-thuh/ n. a flammable oil.

naphthalene n. a strong-smelling substance used in mothballs.

napkin n. a piece of cloth or paper used at meals to protect clothes or wipe the lips.

nappy n. (pl. **nappies**) a piece of material worn by a baby to absorb and retain urine and faeces.

narcissism n. excessive interest in oneself and one's appearance. ■ **narcissistic** adj.

narcissus n. (pl. **narcissi** or **narcissuses**) a daffodil with pale outer petals.

narcosis n. a drug-induced state of drowsiness.

narcotic n. **1** an addictive drug affecting mood or behaviour. **2** a drug caus-

Thesaurus

nadir n. THE LOWEST POINT, rock bottom, the depths, all-time low, as low as one can get; informal the pits. ■ OPPOSITES zenith.

nag v. SCOLD, carp, pick on, keep on at, harp on at, henpeck, bully, upbraid, berate, chivvy, criticize, find fault with, complain to, grumble to. ▶ n. SHREW, scold, harpy, termagant, carper, caviller, complainer, grumbler.

naive adj. INNOCENT, artless, childlike, simple, ingenuous, guileless, trusting, unsophisticated, unworldly, jejune, natural, unaffected, unpretentious, frank, open, candid. ■ OPPOSITES worldly.

naked adj. STARK NAKED, nude, in the

nude, bare, stripped, unclothed, undressed, uncovered, undraped, disrobed, au naturel; informal in the buff, butt naked, starkers; US informal buck naked. ■ OPPOSITES clothed.

name n. DESIGNATION, title, label, tag, cognomen, denomination, appellation, sobriquet, epithet, first name, given name, surname, family name, maiden name, nickname, pet name, stage name, pseudonym, alias; informal moniker, handle. ▶ v. CHRISTEN, baptize, call, entitle, label, style, term, title, denominate, dub.

nameless adj. UNNAMED, untitled, unlabelled, untagged, anonymous, unidening drowsiness. ▶ adj. of narcotics.

narrate v. **1** tell a story. **2** provide a commentary for. ■ **narration** n. **narrator** n.

narrative n. an account of something; a story. ▶ adj. of or forming a narrative.

narrow adj. **1** of small width in comparison to length. **2** limited in extent, amount, or scope. ▶ v. become or make narrower. □ **narrow-minded** intolerant. ■ **narrowly** adv.

narwhal n. an Arctic whale with a spirally twisted tusk.

nasal adj. of the nose. ■ **nasally** adv.

nascent adj. just coming into existence.

nasturtium n. a garden plant with orange, yellow, or red flowers.

nasty adj. (**nastier**, **nastiest**) **1** unpleasant. **2** spiteful. ■ **nastily** adv. **nastiness** n.

natal adj. of the place or time of one's birth.

nation n. a large group sharing the same culture, language, or history, and inhabiting a particular state or area.

national adj. **1** having to do with a nation. **2** owned or supported by the state. ▶ n. a citizen of a particular country. ■ **nationally** adv.

nationalism n. **1** patriotic feeling. **2** belief in political independence for a particular country. ■ **nationalist** n. & adj. **nationalistic** adj.

nationality n. (pl. **nationalities**) **1** the status of belonging to a particular na-

tion. **2** an ethnic group.

nationalize (or **-ise**) v. transfer from private to state ownership. ■ **nationalization** n.

native n. **1** a person born in a specified place. **2** a local inhabitant. ▶ adj. **1** associated with a person's place of birth. **2** (of a plant or animal) growing or living naturally in a place. **3** in a person's character.

Nativity n. (**the Nativity**) the birth of Jesus.

NATO abbrev. North Atlantic Treaty Organization.

natter v. & n. informal chat.

natural adj. **1** of or produced by nature; not made or caused by humans. **2** born with a particular skill or quality. **3** relaxed and unaffected. ▶ n. a person with an inborn gift or talent. □ **natural gas** gas occurring naturally underground, used as fuel. **natural history** the study of animals and plants. ■ **naturally** adv.

naturalism n. realism in art or literature. ■ **naturalistic** adj.

naturalist n. an expert in natural history.

naturalize (or **-ise**) v. **1** make a foreigner a citizen of a country. **2** introduce a plant or animal into a region where it is not native. ■ **naturalization** n.

nature n. **1** the physical world, including plants, animals, and all things not made by people. **2** the typical qualities or characteristics of a person or thing. **3** a kind or sort.

Thesaurus

tified, undesignated, unspecified.

nap n. SHORT SLEEP, catnap, doze, light sleep, rest, lie-down; informal snooze, forty winks, shut-eye, kip.

narrate v. TELL, relate, recount, recite, unfold, chronicle, describe, detail, portray, sketch out, rehearse, repeat.

narrator n. REPORTER, describer, chronicler, annalist, storyteller, raconteur.

narrow adj. **1** SLENDER, thin, slim, slight, spare, attenuated, tapering. **2** LIMITED, restricted, select, exclusive. ■ OPPOSITES wide.

narrow-minded adj. INTOLERANT, illiberal, reactionary, close-minded, unreasonable, prejudiced, bigoted, biased, discriminatory, jaundiced, parochial, provincial, insular, small-minded, petty-minded, petty, mean-spirited, prudish, strait-laced. ■ OPPOSITES broad-minded.

nasty adj. UNPLEASANT, disagreeable, distasteful, horrible, vile, foul, hateful, loathsome, revolting, disgusting, odi-

ous, obnoxious, repellent, repugnant, ugly, offensive, objectionable, squalid, dirty, filthy, impure, polluted, tainted, unpalatable, unsavoury, unappetizing, evil-smelling, foul-smelling, stinking, rank, fetid, malodorous; literary mephitic, noisome. ■ OPPOSITES pleasant.

nation n. COUNTRY, land, state, kingdom, empire, realm, republic, commonwealth, people, race, tribe, society.

national adj. NATIONWIDE, countrywide, state, coast-to-coast, widespread, comprehensive, general. ▶ n. CITIZEN, subject, native.

native adj. **1** INBORN, inherent, innate, intrinsic, instinctive, intuitive, natural, congenital, hereditary. **2** INDIGENOUS, home-grown, domestic, local.

natural adj. **1** ORGANIC, pure, unrefined, unmixed, whole, plain, real, chemical-free, additive-free. **2** NATIVE, inborn, inherent, innate, intrinsic, instinctive, intuitive, congenital, hereditary, inherited, ingrained. **3** GENUINE, real, authen-

naturism n. nudism. ■ **naturist** n.
naught pron. old use nothing.
naughty adj. (**naughtier**, **naughtiest**)
1 disobedient; badly behaved. **2** informal
mildly indecent. ■ **naughtiness** n.
nausea /naw-zi-uh/ n. **1** a feeling of
sickness. **2** disgust.
nauseate v. cause to feel sick or disgusted.
nauseous adj. affected with or causing
nausea.
nautical adj. of sailors or navigation.
□ **nautical mile** a unit of 1,852 m
(approx. 2,025 yds).
nautilus n. (pl. **nautiluses** or **nautili**) a
mollusc with a spiral shell.
naval adj. of a navy.
nave n. the central part of a church.
navel n. the small hollow in a person's
stomach where the umbilical cord was
cut at birth.
navigable adj. able to be used by boats
and ships.
navigate v. **1** plan and direct the route
of a ship, aircraft, etc. **2** sail or travel
over. ■ **navigation** n. **navigator** n.
navvy n. (pl. **navvies**) dated a labourer
employed in building a road etc.
navy n. (pl. **navies**) **1** the branch of a
country's armed services which fights
at sea. **2** a dark blue colour.
Nazi /naht-si/ n. (pl. **Nazis**) hist. a member of the far-right National Socialist
German Workers' Party.
NB abbrev. note well.

NE abbrev. north-east or north-eastern.
Neanderthal /ni-an-der-tahl/ n. an extinct human living in Europe between
about 120,000 and 35,000 years ago.
neap tide n. a tide when there is least
difference between high and low water.
near adv. **1** at or to a short distance in space
or time. **2** almost. ▶ prep. **1** a short distance from. **2** on the verge of. ▶ adj. **1** at
a short distance away. **2** close to being:
a near disaster. **3** closely related. ▶ v.
approach. ■ **nearness** n.
nearby adj. & adv. not far away.
nearly adv. very close to; almost.
neat adj. **1** tidy or carefully arranged.
2 clever but simple. **3** undiluted.
■ **neaten** v. **neatly** adv. **neatness** n.
nebula n. (pl. **nebulae** or **nebulas**) a
cloud of gas or dust in space.
nebulous adj. not clearly defined;
vague.
necessarily adv. as a necessary result;
unavoidably.
necessary adj. **1** needing to be done or
present; essential. **2** unavoidable. ▶ n.
(**necessaries**) essential items.

....

☑ One *c*, two *s*'s: necessary.

....

necessitate v. make necessary.
necessitous adj. poor.
necessity n. (pl. **necessities**) **1** the
fact of being necessary. **2** something
essential. **3** a situation requiring a

Thesaurus
....

tic, simple, unaffected, unpretentious,
spontaneous, artless, ingenuous, candid, open, frank, relaxed, unstudied.
■ OPPOSITES unnatural.
nature n. **1** NATURAL FORCES, creation, the
environment, the earth, mother earth,
landscape, scenery. **2** KIND, sort, type,
variety, description, category, class,
classification. **3** TEMPERAMENT, temper,
personality, disposition, humour,
mood, outlook.
naughty adj. MISCHIEVOUS, badly behaved,
misbehaving, disobedient, defiant, unruly, roguish, wayward, delinquent, undisciplined, unmanageable, ungovernable, fractious, refractory, perverse,
errant. ■ OPPOSITES well behaved.
nausea n. SICKNESS, vomiting, retching,
gagging, biliousness, queasiness, faintness.
nauseous adj. **1** SICK, queasy, unwell,
indisposed, off colour; informal green
about the gills. **2** DISGUSTING, revolting,
repulsive, repellent, repugnant, offen-

sive, loathsome, abhorrent, odious.
nautical adj. MARITIME, naval, marine,
seagoing, seafaring.
navigable adj. NEGOTIABLE, passable,
traversable, clear, unobstructed.
near adj. **1** CLOSE, nearby, alongside, at
close range/quarters, accessible, within
reach, close/near at hand, at hand,
neighbouring, adjacent, adjoining, bordering, contiguous, proximate. **2** AP-
PROACHING, coming, imminent, forthcoming, in the offing, impending, looming. ■ OPPOSITES distant.
nearly adv. ALMOST, virtually, next to,
close to, well-nigh, about, just about,
practically, roughly, approximately, not
quite.
neat adj. **1** TIDY, orderly, well ordered, in
good order, spick and span. **2** SMART,
spruce, trim, tidy, dapper, well
groomed, well turned out. **3** ADROIT,
skilful, expert, practised, dexterous,
deft, accurate, precise, nimble, agile.
■ OPPOSITES untidy.

particular course of action.

neck n. **1** the part connecting the head to the rest of the body. **2** a narrow connecting or end part. □ **neck and neck** level in a race. **necklace** a piece of jewellery worn round the neck. **neckline** the edge of a woman's garment at or below the neck.

necromancy n. prediction of the future by supposedly communicating with dead people. ■ **necromancer** n.

necrosis n. the death of cells in the body.

nectar n. **1** a sweet fluid produced by flowers and made into honey by bees. **2** a delicious drink.

nectarine n. a kind of peach with a smooth skin.

née /nay/ adj. born (used in giving a married woman's maiden name).

need v. **1** want something because it is essential. **2** be obliged or required to. ▶ n. **1** a situation in which something is necessary or must be done. **2** something needed. **3** the state of being very poor.

needful adj. necessary.

needle n. **1** a very thin pointed piece of metal used in sewing. **2** a long thin rod used in knitting. **3** the end of a hypodermic syringe. **4** a stylus for playing records. **5** a thin pointer on a dial, compass, etc. **6** the thin, stiff leaf of a fir or pine tree. ▶ v. informal deliberately annoy. □ **needlework** sewing or embroidery.

needless adj. unnecessary. ■ **needlessly** adv.

needy adj. (**needier**, **neediest**) very poor.

nefarious adj. wicked or criminal.

negate v. **1** stop or undo the effect of.

2 deny the existence of. ■ **negation** n.

negative adj. **1** showing the absence rather than the presence of something. **2** expressing denial, disagreement, or refusal. **3** not hopeful or favourable. **4** (of a quantity) less than zero. **5** of the kind of electric charge carried by electrons. ▶ n. **1** a negative word or statement. **2** a photograph showing light and shade or colours reversed from those of the original, from which positive prints may be made. ■ **negatively** adv. **negativity** n.

neglect v. **1** fail to give proper care or attention to. **2** fail to do something. ▶ n. the act of neglecting or the state of being neglected. ■ **neglectful** adj.

negligee /neg-li-zhay/ n. a woman's light, flimsy dressing gown.

negligence n. lack of proper care and attention. ■ **negligent** adj.

negligible adj. so small or unimportant as to be not worth considering.

negotiate v. **1** try to reach an agreement by discussion. **2** bring about by discussion. **3** find a way over or through. ■ **negotiable** adj. **negotiation** n. **negotiator** n.

Negro n. (pl. **Negroes**) a black person.

ℹ️ The term **Negro** is now regarded as old-fashioned and offensive; it is better to use **black** instead.

---

neigh n. a high-pitched cry made by a horse. ▶ v. make this cry.

neighbour (US **neighbor**) n. a person living next or very near to another. ▶ v. be next or very near to. ■ **neighbourly** adj.

neighbourhood (US **neighborhood**) n. a district.

neither adj. & pron. not either. ▶ adv.

Thesaurus

necessary adj. NEEDED, needful, essential, required, requisite, vital, indispensable, imperative, mandatory, de rigueur, obligatory, compulsory. ■ OPPOSITES unnecessary.

need v. REQUIRE, necessitate, demand, call for, have occasion for, want, lack, be without. ▶ n. REQUIREMENT, want, wish, demand, prerequisite, requisite, essential, desideratum.

needless adj. UNNECESSARY, uncalled for, gratuitous, undesired, unwanted, pointless, useless, dispensable, expendable, inessential. ■ OPPOSITES necessary.

negative adj. PESSIMISTIC, defeatist, gloomy, gloom-laden, cynical, jaundiced, critical, fault-finding, complain-

ing, unhelpful, uncooperative. ■ OPPOSITES positive.

neglect v. **1** FAIL TO LOOK AFTER, fail to provide for, abandon, forsake, leave alone. **2** LET SLIDE, skimp on, shirk, be remiss about, be lax about, not attend to, leave undone, procrastinate about. ▶ n. NEGLIGENCE, neglectfulness, remissness, carelessness, heedlessness, slackness, laxity, laxness, dereliction. ■ OPPOSITES care, attention.

negligent adj. NEGLECTFUL, remiss, lax, careless, inattentive, heedless, thoughtless, unmindful, uncaring, forgetful, indifferent, offhand, cursory, slack, sloppy, slapdash, slipshod, procrastinating, dilatory. ■ OPPOSITES attentive.

1 not either. **2** not also.

nemesis /nem-i-siss/ n. (pl. **nemeses**) a means of deserved and unavoidable downfall.

neoclassical adj. of the revival of a classical style in the arts.

Neolithic adj. of the later part of the Stone Age.

neologism n. a new word.

neon n. an inert gaseous element used in fluorescent lighting.

neonatal adj. of newborn children.

neophyte n. a novice.

nephew n. a son of one's brother or sister.

nephritis n. inflammation of the kidneys.

nepotism n. favouritism shown to relatives or friends, esp. by giving them jobs.

neptunium n. a radioactive metallic element.

nerd n. informal an unfashionable person obsessed with a particular interest.

nerve n. **1** a fibre transmitting impulses of sensation between the brain or spinal cord and other parts of the body. **2** steadiness and courage. **3** (**nerves**) nervousness. **4** informal cheeky boldness. ▶ v. (**nerve oneself**) brace oneself for a demanding situation. □ **get on someone's nerves** informal irritate someone.

nervous adj. **1** easily frightened or worried. **2** anxious. **3** of the nerves. ■ **nervously** adv. **nervousness** n.

nervy adj. (**nervier, nerviest**) nervous or tense.

nest n. **1** a structure made by a bird for laying eggs and sheltering its young. **2** a place where an animal or insect breeds or shelters. **3** a set of similar objects designed to fit inside each other. ▶ v. **1** use or build a nest. **2** fit an object inside a larger one. □ **nest egg** a sum of money saved for the future.

nestle v. **1** settle comfortably within or against something. **2** (of a place) lie in a sheltered position.

nestling n. a bird too young to leave the nest.

net n. **1** a material made of twine or cord woven or tied together to form small open squares. **2** a piece or structure of net for catching fish, surrounding a goal, etc. **3** (**the Net**) the Internet. ▶ v. (**netting, netted**) **1** catch in a net. **2** acquire as net profit. ▶ adj. (also **nett**) **1** remaining after tax or expenses have been deducted. **2** (of a weight) not including packaging. □ **netball** a team game in which a ball has to be thrown into a high net.

nether adj. lower.

netting n. net.

nettle n. a plant with leaves covered in stinging hairs. ▶ v. annoy.

network n. **1** a system of crossing or connecting railways, lines, etc. **2** a group of interconnected broadcasting stations, computers, etc. **3** a group of people who contact each other to exchange information. ▶ v. interact with others to exchange information.

neural adj. of nerves.

neuralgia n. intense pain along a nerve. ■ **neuralgic** adj.

neurology n. the study of the nervous system. ■ **neurological** adj. **neurologist** n.

neurosis n. (pl. **neuroses**) a mental illness involving depression, anxiety, or obsessive behaviour.

neurotic adj. **1** of or caused by neurosis. **2** informal excessively sensitive, anxious, or obsessive.

Thesaurus

negligible adj. TRIVIAL, trifling, insignificant, of no account, paltry, petty, tiny, minute, small, minor, inconsequential, inappreciable, imperceptible. ■ OPPOSITES significant.

negotiate v. BARGAIN, drive a bargain, hold talks, confer, debate, discuss, discuss terms, discuss a settlement, consult together, parley, haggle.

neighbourhood n. DISTRICT, area, region, locality, part, quarter, precinct, community; informal neck of the woods, stamping ground.

neighbouring adj. ADJACENT, adjoining, bordering, abutting, contiguous, nearby, near, very near, close/near at hand, not far away, in the vicinity.

nervous adj. ON EDGE, edgy, tense, strained, anxious, nervy, agitated, worried, fretful, uneasy, disquieted, on tenterhooks, fidgety, ruffled, flustered, apprehensive, fearful, frightened, scared, with one's heart in one's mouth, quaking, trembling, shaking, shaky; informal jittery, twitchy, jumpy, in a state, uptight, wired. ■ OPPOSITES calm.

nestle v. SNUGGLE, curl up, huddle together, cuddle up, nuzzle.

net n. NETTING, fishnet, mesh, latticework, lattice, openwork, webbing, tracery. ▶ v. CATCH, trap, snare, ensnare, entangle, enmesh, bag.

nettle v. IRRITATE, provoke, ruffle, annoy,

neuter adj. **1** (of a noun) not masculine or feminine. **2** (of an animal or plant) having no sexual or reproductive organs. ▶ v. castrate or spay an animal.

neutral adj. **1** not supporting either side in a dispute or war. **2** lacking noticeable or strong qualities. ▶ n. **1** a neutral state or person. **2** a position of a gear mechanism in which the engine is disconnected from the driven parts. ■ **neutrality** n. **neutrally** adv.

neutralize (or **-ise**) v. make ineffective. ■ **neutralization** n.

neutrino n. (pl. **neutrinos**) a subatomic particle with a mass close to zero and no electric charge.

neutron n. a subatomic particle of about the same mass as a proton but without an electric charge. □ **neutron bomb** a nuclear bomb that kills people but does little harm to property.

never adv. **1** not ever. **2** not at all.

nevermore adv. never again.

nevertheless adv. in spite of that.

nevus US = **NAEVUS**.

new adj. **1** made, introduced, discovered, or experienced recently. **2** not previously used or owned. **3** (**new to/at**) not used to or experienced at. **4** replacing a former one of the same kind. ▶ adv. newly. □ **New Age** a movement concerned with alternative approaches to spirituality, medicine, etc. **newcomer** a person who has recently arrived or is new to an activity. **newfangled** derog. newly developed and unfamiliar. **new moon** the moon when it appears as a thin crescent. **New Testament** the second part of the Christian Bible. **new year** the first days of January. **New**

Year's Day 1 January. ■ **newness** n.

newel n. **1** the central pillar of a winding staircase. **2** the top or bottom post of a stair rail.

newly adv. **1** recently. **2** again. □ **newlywed** a recently married person.

news n. **1** new information about recent events. **2** (**the news**) a broadcast or published news report. □ **newsagent** a shopkeeper who sells newspapers, magazines, etc. **newscaster** a newsreader. **newsflash** a brief item of important news, interrupting other radio or television programmes. **newsgroup** a group of Internet users who exchange email on a shared interest. **newsletter** a bulletin issued periodically to the members of a society etc. **newspaper** a daily or weekly publication containing news and articles. **newsprint** cheap, low-quality paper used for newspapers. **newsreader** a person who reads the news on radio or television. **newsworthy** important enough to report as news.

newt n. a small lizard-like animal that can live in water or on land.

newton n. a unit of force.

next adj. nearest in position or time. ▶ adv. **1** immediately afterwards. **2** following in the specified order. ▶ n. the next person or thing. □ **next door** in or to the next house or room. **next of kin** one's closest living relative or relatives.

nexus n. (pl. **nexus** or **nexuses**) a connection or series of connections.

NHS abbrev. National Health Service.

NI abbrev. **1** National Insurance. **2** Northern Ireland.

niacin = **NICOTINIC ACID**.

nib n. the pointed end part of a pen.

Thesaurus

incense, exasperate, irk, vex, pique, bother, pester, harass, torment, plague.

neurotic adj. UNSTABLE, maladjusted, obsessive, phobic, fixated, compulsive, oversensitive, hysterical, irrational. ■ OPPOSITES stable.

neuter adj. ASEXUAL, sexless, unsexed. ▶ v. CASTRATE, geld, emasculate, spay, dress; *informal* fix, doctor.

neutral adj. IMPARTIAL, unbiased, unprejudiced, open-minded, non-partisan, even-handed, disinterested, non-aligned, dispassionate, objective, detached, uninvolved, uncommitted. ■ OPPOSITES biased, partisan.

neutralize v. COUNTERACT, cancel, nullify, negate, annul, undo, invalidate, frustrate, be an antidote to.

new adj. MODERN, recent, advanced, state-

of-the-art, present-day, contemporary, current, latest, up to date, up to the minute, new-fashioned, modish, brand new, newly arrived, modernist, ultra-modern, avant-garde, futuristic, new-fangled. ■ OPPOSITES old.

newcomer n. ARRIVAL, incomer, immigrant, settler, stranger, outsider, foreigner, intruder, interloper; *informal* johnny-come-lately.

news pl. n. INFORMATION, facts, data, report, story, news item, news flash, account, statement, announcement, press release, communiqué, message, bulletin, dispatch, disclosure, revelation, word, talk, the latest; *informal* gen, info.

newspaper n. PAPER, gazette, journal, tabloid, broadsheet, weekly, scandal sheet; *informal* rag.

nibble v. take small quick or gentle bites at. ▶ n. a small bite of food.

nice adj. **1** pleasant. **2** good-natured. **3** subtle or precise: *a nice distinction*. ■ **nicely** adv. **niceness** n.

nicety n. (pl. **niceties**) **1** a fine detail. **2** accuracy.

niche n. **1** a shallow recess in a wall. **2** a job or role to which one is suited.

nick n. **1** a small cut. **2** (**the nick**) informal prison or a police station. **3** informal condition: *in good nick*. ▶ v. **1** make a nick in. **2** informal steal. **3** informal arrest. □ **in the nick of time** only just in time.

nickel n. **1** a metallic element used in alloys. **2** US a five-cent coin.

nickname n. a familiar or amusing name for a person or thing. ▶ v. give a nickname to.

nicotine n. a poisonous oily liquid found in tobacco.

nicotinic acid n. a vitamin of the B complex.

niece n. a daughter of one's brother or sister.

niggardly adj. not generous; meagre.

nigger n. offens. a black person.

niggle v. **1** worry or annoy slightly. **2** criticize in a petty way. ■ **niggly** adj.

nigh adv., prep., & adj. old use near.

night n. **1** the time from sunset to sunrise. **2** an evening until bedtime. □ **nightcap** a hot or alcoholic drink taken at bedtime. **nightclub** a club open at night, with a bar and music. **nightdress** (or **nightgown**) a loose garment worn by a woman or girl in bed. **nightfall** dusk. **nightjar** a nocturnal bird with a harsh cry. **nightlife** entertainment available at night. **night school** instruction provided in the evening. **nightshade** a plant with poisonous berries. **nightshirt** a long shirt worn in bed. **nightspot** informal a nightclub. ■ **nightly** adj. & adv.

nightie n. informal a nightdress.

nightingale n. a small thrush with a tuneful song.

nightmare n. **1** a frightening dream. **2** a very unpleasant experience. ■ **nightmarish** adj.

nihilism n. the belief that nothing has any value. ■ **nihilist** n. **nihilistic** adj.

nil n. nothing; zero.

nimble adj. quick and agile. ■ **nimbly** adv.

nimbus n. (pl. **nimbi** or **nimbuses**) **1** a rain cloud. **2** a halo.

nincompoop n. a stupid person.

nine adj. & n. one less than ten; 9 or IX. □ **ninepins** a game of skittles played with nine pins. ■ **ninth** adj. & n.

nineteen adj. & n. one more than eighteen; 19 or XIX. ■ **nineteenth** adj. & n.

ninety adj. & n. ten less than one hundred; 90 or XC. ■ **ninetieth** adj. & n.

ninny n. (pl. **ninnies**) informal a foolish person.

niobium n. a metallic element.

nip v. (**nipping, nipped**) **1** pinch, squeeze, or bite sharply. **2** informal go quickly. ▶ v. **1** an act of nipping. **2** a sharp coldness. **3** a small quantity or sip of spirits.

nipple n. a small projection in the centre of each breast.

nippy adj. (**nippier, nippiest**) informal **1** quick; nimble. **2** chilly.

nirvana n. (in Buddhism) a state of perfect happiness.

Nissen hut n. a tunnel-shaped hut of corrugated iron.

nit n. informal the egg of a human head louse. □ **nit-picking** petty criticism.

nitrate n. a substance formed from nitric acid.

nitric acid n. a very corrosive acid containing nitrogen.

nitrogen n. a gaseous element forming about 78 per cent of the earth's atmosphere.

nitroglycerine (or **nitroglycerin**) n. a powerful explosive.

nitrous oxide n. a gas used as an anaesthetic.

nitty-gritty n. informal the most important details of a matter.

nitwit n. informal a foolish person.

no adj. not any. ▶ exclam. used to refuse or disagree. ▶ adv. not at all. □ **no-man's-land** an area between two opposing armies that is not controlled by either. **no**

Thesaurus

next adj. **1** FOLLOWING, succeeding, successive, subsequent, later, ensuing. **2** NEIGHBOURING, adjacent, adjoining, bordering, contiguous. ■ OPPOSITES previous.

nice adj. **1** GOOD, pleasant, enjoyable, pleasurable, agreeable, delightful, marvellous. **2** FINE, ultra-fine, subtle, min-

ute, precise, exact, accurate, strict, close. ■ OPPOSITES unpleasant, rough.

nicety n. FINER POINT, subtlety, nuance, detail.

niggardly adj. MEAN, miserly, parsimonious, penny-pinching, cheese-paring; informal tight-fisted, stingy. ■ OPPOSITES generous.

one no person.

no. abbrev. number.

nobble v. informal try to influence by underhand methods.

nobelium n. a radioactive metallic element.

nobility n. **1** the quality of being noble. **2** the aristocracy.

noble adj. **1** belonging to the aristocracy. **2** having fine personal qualities. **3** magnificent; impressive. ▶n. a nobleman or noblewoman. □ **nobleman** (or **noble-woman**) a member of the aristocracy. ■ **nobly** adv.

nobody pron. no person. ▶n. (pl. **no-bodies**) an unimportant person.

nocturnal adj. done or active at night. ■ **nocturnally** adv.

nocturne n. a short romantic piece of music.

nod v. (**nodding, nodded**) **1** lower and raise one's head briefly to show agreement or as a greeting or signal. **2** let one's head fall forward when drowsy or asleep. **3** (**nod off**) informal fall asleep. ▶n. an act of nodding.

node n. **1** a point in a network where lines cross or branch. **2** the part of a plant stem from which a leaf grows. **3** a small mass of distinct tissue in the body. ■ **nodal** adj.

nodule n. a small swelling or lump. ■ **nodular** adj.

noggin n. informal a small quantity of alcoholic drink.

noise n. **1** a sound or series of sounds, esp. a loud or unpleasant one. **2** disturbances that accompany and interfere with an electrical signal. ■ **noiseless** adj.

noisome adj. having a very unpleasant smell.

noisy adj. (**noisier, noisiest**) full of or making a lot of noise. ■ **noisily** adv.

nomad n. a member of a people that travels from place to place to find fresh pasture for its animals. ■ **nomadic** adj.

nom de plume n. (pl. **noms de plume**) a writer's pseudonym.

nomenclature n. a system of names used in a particular subject.

nominal adj. **1** in name but not in reality. **2** (of a fee) very small. □ **nominal value** the face value of a coin etc. ■ **nominally** adv.

nominate v. **1** put forward as a candidate for a job, award, etc. **2** specify a time or place for an event formally. ■ **nomination** n. **nominee** n.

nominative n. the grammatical case used for the subject of a verb.

non- prefix not.

nonagenarian n. a person between 90 and 99 years old.

non-aligned adj. not allied with a major world power.

nonchalant adj. calm and relaxed. ■ **nonchalance** n. **nonchalantly** adv.

non-committal adj. not showing what one thinks or which side one supports. ■ **non-committally** adv.

nonconformist n. **1** a person who does not follow accepted ideas or behaviour. **2** (**Nonconformist**) a member of a Protestant Church which does not follow the beliefs of the established Church of England.

non-contributory adj. (of a pension) funded by regular payments by the employer, not the employee.

nondescript adj. lacking special or interesting features.

none pron. **1** not any. **2** no one. ▶adv. not at all: *none the wiser.* □ **nonetheless**

Thesaurus

nimble adj. AGILE, lithe, sprightly, spry, graceful, skilful, deft. ■ OPPOSITES clumsy.

nippy adj. ICY, chilly, bitter, raw, piercing, stinging. ■ OPPOSITES warm.

no adv. ABSOLUTELY NOT, under no circumstances, by no means, never; informal not on your life, no way, nope.

noble adj. **1** ARISTOCRATIC, patrician, blue-blooded, titled, landed. **2** NOBLE-MINDED, magnanimous, generous, self-sacrificing, honourable, virtuous, brave. ■ OPPOSITES common, dishonourable.

nod v. INCLINE, bob, bow, dip, duck.

noise n. SOUND, din, hubbub, clamour, racket, row, uproar, tumult, commo-

tion, rumpus, pandemonium. ■ OPPOS-ITES silence.

noisy adj. **1** ROWDY, clamorous, boisterous, obstreperous, turbulent; informal rackety. **2** LOUD, blaring, blasting, deafening, ear-splitting. ■ OPPOSITES quiet.

nomad n. ITINERANT, traveller, migrant, wanderer, transient, vagabond, vagrant, tramp.

nominal adj. **1** IN NAME ONLY, titular, formal, theoretical, self-styled, purported, supposed. **2** TOKEN, symbolic, minimal, trivial, insignificant.

nominate v. NAME, propose, put forward, submit, present, recommend; informal put up.

nonchalant adj. SELF-POSSESSED, impernevertheless.

nonentity n. (pl. **nonentities**) an unimportant person or thing.

non-event n. a very disappointing or uninteresting event.

non-existent adj. not real or present. ■ **non-existence** n.

nonplussed adj. surprised and confused.

nonsense n. **1** words that make no sense. **2** foolish ideas or behaviour. ■ **nonsensical** adj.

non sequitur n. a statement or conclusion that does not follow from the previous statement.

non-starter n. informal something that has no chance of succeeding.

non-stop adj. & adv. **1** without stopping. **2** having no stops on the way to a destination.

noodles pl. n. long, thin strips of pasta.

nook n. a sheltered or hidden place.

noon n. 12 o'clock in the day.

noose n. a loop with a knot which tightens as the rope or wire is pulled.

nor conj. & adv. and not; and not either.

norm n. **1** (**the norm**) the usual or standard thing. **2** a required or acceptable standard.

normal adj. usual, typical, or expected. ▶ n. the normal state or condition. ■ **normality** n. **normally** adv.

north n. **1** the direction on the left-hand side of a person facing east. **2** the northern part of a place. ▶ adj. **1** lying towards or facing the north. **2** (of a wind) from the north. ▶ adv. towards the north. ■ **northerly** adj. & adv. **north-**

ward adj. & adv. **northwards** adv.

north-east n. the direction or region halfway between north and east. ▶ adj. & adv. **1** towards or facing the north-east. **2** (of a wind) from the north-east. ■ **north-easterly** adj. & adv. **north-eastern** adj.

northern adj. situated in or facing the north. □ **northern lights** the aurora borealis.

northerner n. a person from the north of a region.

north-west n. the direction or region halfway between north and west. ▶ adj. & adv. **1** towards or facing the north-west. **2** (of a wind) from the north-west. ■ **north-westerly** adj. & adv. **north-western** adj.

nose n. **1** the part of the face containing the nostrils, used in breathing and smelling. **2** the front end of an aircraft, car, etc. **3** the sense of smell. **4** a talent for finding something. ▶ v. **1** thrust the nose against something. **2** look around or pry. **3** move forward slowly. □ **nosebag** a bag of fodder hung from a horse's head. **nosedive** a steep downward plunge by an aircraft. **nosegay** a posy of flowers.

nosh n. informal food.

nostalgia n. longing for the happy times of the past. ■ **nostalgic** adj.

nostril n. either of the two external openings in the nose.

nostrum n. **1** an ineffective medicine prepared by an unqualified person. **2** a favourite scheme or method.

nosy adj. (**nosier**, **nosiest**) informal very

Thesaurus

turbable, calm, cool, collected, cool as a cucumber, unconcerned, indifferent, blasé, casual, offhand, carefree, insouciant, easy-going, careless; informal laid-back. ■ OPPOSITES anxious.

nonplus v. TAKE ABACK, stun, dumbfound, confound, astound, astonish, amaze, surprise, disconcert, stump, confuse, bewilder, embarrass, fluster; informal faze, flummox, floor.

nonsense n. RUBBISH, balderdash, drivel, gibberish, blather, trash, claptrap; informal twaddle, waffle, tripe, bilge, bull, tosh, bosh, gobbledegook, mumbo-jumbo, poppycock, stuff and nonsense, flannel; informal, dated bunkum, tommyrot. ■ OPPOSITES sense.

nonsensical adj. MEANINGLESS, incomprehensible, unintelligible, senseless, foolish, absurd, silly, inane, stupid, ridiculous, ludicrous, preposterous,

hare-brained, irrational, idiotic, insane; informal crazy, crackpot, nutty, wacky. ■ OPPOSITES sensible.

non-stop adj. INCESSANT, unceasing, ceaseless, constant, continuous, continual, unbroken, unfaltering, steady, unremitting, relentless, persistent, endless, never-ending, unending, interminable.

nook n. CORNER, cranny, recess, alcove, niche, opening, cavity, crevice, gap.

normal adj. **1** USUAL, standard, average, common, ordinary, natural, general, commonplace, conventional, typical, regular, routine, run-of-the-mill, everyday, accustomed, habitual, prevailing, popular, accepted, acknowledged. **2** WELL ADJUSTED, well balanced, rational, compos mentis, sane. ■ OPPOSITES abnormal.

normally adv. USUALLY, ordinarily, as a

inquisitive or prying.

not adv. used to express a negative.

notable adj. worthy of notice. ▶n. a famous or important person. ■ **notably** adv.

notary n. (pl. **notaries**) a lawyer authorized to draw up and witness the signing of contracts etc.

notation n. a system of written symbols representing numbers, amounts, musical notes, etc.

notch n. **1** a V-shaped cut or indentation. **2** a point on a scale. ▶v. **1** make notches in. **2** (**notch up**) score or achieve.

note n. **1** a brief record written as an aid to memory. **2** a short written message or document. **3** a banknote. **4** a single musical sound of a particular pitch and length, or a symbol representing this. **5** a particular quality: *a note of scorn*. ▶v. **1** notice. **2** write down. ▢ **notebook** a small book for writing notes in. **notepaper** paper for writing letters on. **take note** pay attention.

noted adj. well known.

noteworthy adj. interesting or important.

nothing pron. **1** not anything. **2** something unimportant or uninteresting. **3** nought; no amount. ▶adv. not at all. ▢ **for nothing 1** for no payment or charge. **2** to no purpose. **nothing for it** no alternative.

notice n. **1** the fact of being aware or paying attention. **2** warning that something is going to happen. **3** a formal statement that one is going to leave a job or end an agreement. **4** a sheet or placard displayed to give information. **5** a short published review. ▶v. become aware of. ▢ **take notice (of)** pay attention (to).

noticeable adj. easily seen or noticed. ■ **noticeably** adv.

notifiable adj. (of a disease) that must be reported to the health authorities.

notify v. (**notifying, notified**) inform someone formally about something. ■ **notification** n.

notion n. **1** an idea or belief. **2** an understanding.

notional adj. hypothetical. ■ **notionally** adv.

notorious adj. famous for something bad. ■ **notoriety** n. **notoriously** adv.

notwithstanding prep. in spite of.

Thesaurus

rule, as a general rule, generally, in general, mostly, commonly, habitually.

nose n. SNOUT, muzzle, bill, beak, proboscis; *informal* snoot, hooter, conk; *US informal* schnozz.

nosy adj. INQUISITIVE, curious, interfering, meddlesome, intrusive; *informal* snooping, snoopy.

notable adj. **1** NOTEWORTHY, remarkable, outstanding, important, significant, momentous, memorable, unforgettable, pronounced, marked, striking, impressive, uncommon, unusual, particular, special, extraordinary. **2** NOTED, of note, distinguished, eminent, pre-eminent, well known, prominent, illustrious, great, famous, famed, renowned, celebrated, acclaimed. ■ OPPOSITES insignificant.

note n. **1** RECORD, account, entry, item, notation, comment, jotting, inscription. **2** LETTER, message, memorandum, memo, epistle, missive, communication. **3** FOOTNOTE, annotation, commentary, gloss, marginalia, explanation, explication, exposition, exegesis. **4** DISTINCTION, eminence, pre-eminence, illustriousness, greatness, prestige, fame, renown. **5** TONE, intonation, inflection, sound, indication, hint, element. ▶v. **1** WRITE DOWN, jot down, mark down,

enter, mark, record, register. **2** TAKE NOTE OF, take notice of, see, observe, perceive, behold, detect, take in.

noted adj. NOTABLE, distinguished, eminent, pre-eminent, well known, prominent, illustrious, great, famous, famed, renowned, celebrated, acclaimed. ■ OPPOSITES unknown.

notice n. **1** ATTENTION, attentiveness, heed, note, observation, cognizance, regard, consideration, watchfulness, vigilance. **2** BULLETIN, poster, handbill, bill, circular, leaflet, pamphlet, advertisement. ▶v. SEE, note, take note of, observe, perceive, discern, detect, behold, spot, distinguish, make out, take heed of, heed, pay attention to, take notice of, mark, regard. ■ OPPOSITES overlook.

noticeable adj. OBSERVABLE, visible, discernible, perceptible, detectable, distinguishable, distinct, evident, obvious, apparent, manifest, patent, plain, clear, conspicuous, unmistakable, pronounced, striking, blatant. ■ OPPOSITES imperceptible.

notify v. INFORM, tell, advise, acquaint, apprise, warn, alert, caution.

notion n. IDEA, belief, opinion, thought, impression, view, conviction, concept, assumption, presumption, hypothesis,

▶ adv. nevertheless.

nougat /noo-gah/ n. a sweet made from sugar or honey, nuts, and egg white.

nought n. the figure 0. ▶ pron. nothing.

noun n. a word referring to a person, place, or thing.

nourish v. **1** provide with the food etc. necessary for growth and health. **2** cherish a feeling.

nourishment n. the food etc. necessary for life, growth, and good health.

nous /nowss/ n. informal common sense.

nouveau riche /noo-voh reesh/ n. people who have recently become rich and display their wealth in an obvious or tasteless way.

nova n. (pl. **novae** or **novas**) a star that suddenly becomes brighter for a short time.

novel n. a fictitious story of book length. ▶ adj. new and unusual.

novelette n. a short esp. romantic novel.

novelist n. a person who writes novels.

novelty n. (pl. **novelties**) **1** the quality of being novel. **2** a small toy or ornament.

November n. the eleventh month.

novice n. **1** a person new to and lacking experience in a job or situation. **2** a person who has entered a religious order but has not yet taken their vows.

now adv. **1** at the present time. **2** immediately. ▶ conj. as a result of the fact. □ **nowadays** at the present time, in contrast with the past. **now and again** (or **then**) from time to time.

nowhere adv. not anywhere. ▶ pron. no place.

noxious adj. harmful, poisonous, or very unpleasant.

nozzle n. a spout controlling a stream of liquid or gas.

nuance /nyoo-ahnss/ n. a slight difference in meaning or expression.

nub n. **1** the central point of a matter. **2** a small lump.

nubile adj. (of a young woman) sexually mature and attractive.

nuclear adj. **1** of a nucleus. **2** using energy released in the fission or fusion of atomic nuclei. □ **nuclear family** a couple and their children, as a basic unit of society.

nucleic acid n. either of two complex organic substances, DNA and RNA, present in all living cells.

nucleus n. (pl. **nuclei**) **1** the central and most important part of an object or group. **2** the positively charged central core of an atom. **3** a structure in a cell containing the genetic material.

nude adj. wearing no clothes. ▶ n. a naked human figure as a subject in art. ■ **nudity** n.

nudge v. **1** prod with one's elbow to attract attention. **2** touch or push gently. ▶ n. a light prod or push.

nudist n. a person who goes naked wherever possible. ■ **nudism** n.

nugget n. a small lump of precious metal found in the earth.

nuisance n. an annoying person or thing.

nuke v. informal attack with nuclear weapons.

null adj. having the value zero. □ **null and void** having no legal force. ■ **nullity** n.

nullify v. (**nullifying**, **nullified**) **1** make

Thesaurus

theory, postulation, apprehension, understanding.

notorious adj. INFAMOUS, ill-famed, disreputable, dishonourable, of ill repute, well known, prominent, scandalous, opprobrious, legendary.

nourishing adj. NUTRITIOUS, nutritive, wholesome, healthy, health-giving, healthful, beneficial, good for one. ■ OPPOSITES unhealthy.

nourishment n. FOOD, nutriment, nutrition, sustenance, subsistence, provisions; informal grub, chow, scoff; dated victuals.

novel adj. NEW, fresh, different, original, unusual, rare, unique, imaginative, unconventional, innovative, groundbreaking, trailblazing, modern, advanced.

novice n. BEGINNER, newcomer, apprentice, trainee, learner, probationer, student, pupil, recruit, neophyte, tyro, initiate; informal rookie; US informal greenhorn.

now adv. AT PRESENT, at the present time, at this time, at the moment, for the time being, currently.

noxious adj. UNWHOLESOME, unhealthy, poisonous, toxic, harmful, injurious, malignant, detrimental, deleterious. ■ OPPOSITES innocuous.

nuance n. SHADE, shading, gradation, subtlety, nicety, refinement, degree.

nucleus n. CORE, kernel, centre, heart, nub.

nude adj. see NAKED.

nudge v. POKE, jab, prod, dig, jog, elbow, touch, push, shove.

legally invalid. **2** cancel out the effect of. ■ **nullification** n.

numb adj. **1** (of a part of the body) having no sensation. **2** lacking the power to feel, think, or react. ▶v. make numb. ■ **numbly** adv. **numbness** n.

number n. **1** a quantity or value expressed by a word or symbol. **2** a quantity. **3** (**a number of**) several. **4** a single issue of a magazine. **5** a song, dance, or other musical item. ▶v. **1** amount to. **2** give a number to. **3** count. □ **number plate** a sign on the front and rear of a vehicle showing its registration number. ■ **numberless** adj.

numeral n. a symbol or word representing a number.

numerate adj. having a good basic knowledge of arithmetic. ■ **numeracy** n.

numerator n. the number above the line in a fraction.

numerical adj. of a number or series of numbers. ■ **numerically** adv.

numerous adj. many.

numismatics n. the study of coins and medals.

nun n. a woman belonging to a female religious community.

nuncio n. (pl. **nuncios**) a diplomatic representative of the pope.

nunnery n. (pl. **nunneries**) a convent.

nuptial adj. of marriage or weddings. ▶n. (**nuptials**) a wedding.

nurse n. **1** a person trained to care for sick or injured people. **2** dated a person employed to look after young children. ▶v. **1** act as nurse to. **2** hold carefully. **3** harbour a belief or feeling. **4** feed a baby at the breast. □ **nursing home** a private home providing accommodation and health care for elderly people.

nursery n. (pl. **nurseries**) **1** a room for children. **2** a nursery school. **3** a place where plants are grown for sale. □ **nurseryman** a worker in or owner of a plant nursery. **nursery rhyme** a traditional song or poem for children. **nursery school** a school for children between three and five.

nurture v. **1** care for and encourage the growth or development of. **2** have a hope or belief for a long time. ▶n. the act of nurturing.

nut n. **1** a fruit consisting of a hard shell around an edible kernel. **2** the kernel of such a fruit. **3** a small flat metal ring for screwing on to a bolt. **4** informal a mad or fanatical person. **5** informal the head. ▶adj. (**nuts**) informal mad. □ **in a nutshell** in the fewest possible words. **nutcase** informal a mad or foolish person. **nuthatch** a small climbing bird. ■ **nutty** adj.

nutmeg n. a spice.

nutrient n. a substance essential for life and growth.

nutriment n. nourishment.

nutrition n. **1** the process of eating or taking nourishment. **2** the study of this. ■ **nutritional** adj.

nutritious adj. nourishing.

nuzzle v. rub or push against gently with the nose.

NVQ abbrev. National Vocational Qualification.

NW abbrev. north-west or north-western.

nylon n. a strong, light, synthetic fibre.

nymph n. **1** a mythological spirit in the form of a beautiful young woman. **2** an immature form of an insect.

nymphomania n. uncontrollable sexual desire in a woman. ■ **nymphomaniac** n.

NZ abbrev. New Zealand.

Thesaurus

nuisance n. PEST, bother, plague, irritant, annoyance, trouble, burden, problem, difficulty, worry; informal drag. ■ OPPOSITES blessing.

numb adj. WITHOUT FEELING, deadened, benumbed, insensible, insensate, dull, anaesthetized, dazed, stunned, stupefied, paralysed, immobilized, frozen. ▶v. DEADEN, dull, anaesthetize, benumb, daze, stun, stupefy, paralyse, immobilize, freeze.

number n. **1** FIGURE, digit, numeral, cipher, character, symbol, unit, integer. **2** TOTAL, aggregate, score, tally, count, sum. ▶v. COUNT, add up, enumerate,

total, calculate, compute, reckon, tell, estimate, assess.

numerous adj. MANY, a lot, lots, innumerable, myriad, multitudinous, several, quite a few, various, diverse. ■ OPPOSITES few.

nurse v. **1** TAKE CARE OF, care for, look after, tend, attend to, minister to. **2** SUCKLE, breast-feed, feed, wet-nurse.

nurture v. FEED, nourish, provide for, care for, take care of, tend, attend to, bring up, rear, look after, support, foster, parent.

nutritious adj. see NOURISHING.

nuzzle v. NOSE, nudge, prod, push.

Oo

oaf n. a stupid or clumsy man.

oak n. a large tree producing acorns and a hard wood. □ **oak apple** a growth which forms on oak trees, caused by wasp larvae. ■ **oaken** adj.

OAP abbrev. old-age pensioner.

oar n. a pole with a flat blade used to row a boat.

oasis n. (pl. **oases**) **1** a fertile place in a desert where water rises to ground level. **2** a pleasant area or period in the midst of a difficult situation.

oast house n. a building with a kiln for drying hops.

oat n. **1** a hardy cereal plant. **2** (**oats**) the edible grain of this. □ **oatcake** a savoury oatmeal biscuit. **oatmeal** ground oats.

oath n. (pl. **oaths**) **1** a solemn promise, esp. that something is true. **2** a swear word.

obdurate adj. stubborn. ■ **obduracy** n.

OBE abbrev. Officer of the Order of the British Empire.

obedient adj. willing to do what one is told. ■ **obedience** n. **obediently** adv.

obeisance n. **1** humble respect. **2** a bow or curtsy.

obelisk n. a stone pillar tapering to a point, set up as a monument.

obese adj. very fat. ■ **obesity** n.

obey v. **1** carry out the orders of. **2** behave in accordance with a law etc.

obfuscate v. make unclear or hard to understand. ■ **obfuscation** n.

obituary n. (pl. **obituaries**) a short biography of someone published in a newspaper when they die.

object n. **1** a physical thing that can be seen and touched. **2** a person or thing to which an action or feeling is directed. **3** a purpose. **4** a noun acted on by a transitive verb or by a preposition. ▶ v. express disapproval or opposition. ■ **objection** n. **objector** n.

objectionable adj. unpleasant or offensive.

objective adj. **1** not influenced by personal feelings or opinions. **2** having actual existence outside the mind. **3** of a case of nouns and pronouns used for the object of a transitive verb or a preposition. ▶ n. a goal or aim. □ **object lesson** a clear practical example of a principle or ideal. ■ **objectively** adv. **objectivity** n.

Thesaurus

oaf n. LOUT, blunderer, bungler, boor, churl, bumpkin, yokel, brute, galoot; *informal* clodhopper; *US informal* lummox.

oath n. **1** VOW, promise, pledge, avowal, affirmation, attestation, bond, word of honour, word. **2** CURSE, swear word, expletive, blasphemy, profanity, imprecation, malediction, obscenity, epithet, four-letter word, dirty word.

obedient adj. COMPLIANT, acquiescent, biddable, dutiful, deferential, respectful, tractable, amenable, malleable, governable, well trained, submissive, docile, meek, subservient, obsequious, servile. ■ OPPOSITES disobedient.

obese adj. *see* FAT.

obey v. **1** ABIDE BY, comply with, adhere to, observe, conform to, respect, acquiesce in, consent to, agree to, follow. **2** PERFORM, carry out, execute, put into effect, fulfil, act upon. ■ OPPOSITES disobey.

object n. **1** THING, article, body, entity, item, device, gadget; *informal* thingamajig, thingamabob, thingummy, whatchamacallit, whatsit. **2** OBJECTIVE, aim, goal, target, end, ambition, purpose, design, intent, intention, idea, point. ▶ v. PROTEST, demur, beg to differ, remonstrate, expostulate, take exception, argue against, oppose, be in opposition to, complain about.

objection n. PROTEST, protestation, complaint, demurral, opposition, remonstration, remonstrance, expostulation, dissatisfaction, disapproval, grievance, scruple, qualm; *informal* niggle. ■ OPPOSITES approval.

objectionable adj. OFFENSIVE, obnoxious, unpleasant, disagreeable, nasty, disgusting, repulsive, repellent, abhorrent, repugnant, revolting, loathsome, hateful, detestable, reprehensible, deplorable, insufferable, intolerable, despicable, contemptible, odious, vile, obscene, foul, horrible, horrid, noxious.

objet d'art /ob-zhay dar/ n. (pl. **objets d'art**) a small decorative or artistic object.

oblation n. an offering made to a god.

obligated adj. obliged or compelled.

obligation n. **1** something one must do because of a law, agreement, promise, etc. **2** the state of being obliged to do something.

obligatory adj. compulsory.

oblige v. **1** make someone do something by law, necessity, or because it is their duty. **2** perform a service or favour for. **3** (**be obliged**) be grateful.

obliging adj. willing to do a service; helpful. ■ **obligingly** adv.

oblique /uh-bleek/ adj. **1** at an angle; slanting. **2** not explicit or direct. ■ **obliquely** adv.

obliterate v. destroy or cover completely. ■ **obliteration** n.

oblivion n. **1** the state of being unaware. **2** the state of being forgotten or completely destroyed.

oblivious adj. unaware.

oblong adj. rectangular in shape. ▶n. an oblong shape.

obloquy /ob-luh-kwi/ n. **1** strong public criticism. **2** disgrace.

obnoxious adj. very unpleasant.

oboe n. a woodwind instrument of treble pitch with a double reed. ■ **oboist** n.

obscene adj. **1** dealing with sexual matters in an offensive or disgusting way. **2** (of an amount) unacceptably large. ■ **obscenely** adv. **obscenity** n.

obscure adj. **1** not known about or well known. **2** hard to understand or see. ▶v. hide or make unclear. ■ **obscurely** adv. **obscurity** n.

obsequies /ob-si-kwiz/ pl. n. funeral rites.

obsequious adj. excessively obedient or respectful. ■ **obsequiously** adv. **obsequiousness** n.

observance n. behaving in accordance

Thesaurus

■ OPPOSITES agreeable.

objective adj. UNBIASED, unprejudiced, impartial, neutral, uninvolved, nonpartisan, disinterested, detached, dispassionate, even-handed, equitable, fair, just, open-minded. ■ OPPOSITES subjective. ▶n. OBJECT, aim, goal, target, end, ambition, aspiration, intent, intention, purpose, design, plan, scheme, plot.

obligatory adj. COMPULSORY, mandatory, enforced, necessary, essential, required, requisite, imperative, de rigueur, unavoidable, inescapable. ■ OPPOSITES voluntary.

oblige v. **1** COMPEL, require, necessitate, obligate, impel, force, constrain, press, pressure, pressurize. **2** DO SOMEONE A FAVOUR, do someone a kindness, do someone a service, help, accommodate, meet someone's wants/needs, put oneself out for, indulge, assist.

obliging adj. see HELPFUL (2).

oblique adj. **1** SLANTING, slanted, sloping, italic, sloped, inclined, at an angle, angled, tilted, listing, diagonal. **2** INDIRECT, implied, roundabout, circuitous, circumlocutory, ambiguous, evasive, backhanded. ■ OPPOSITES direct.

obliterate v. ERASE, eradicate, efface, blot out, rub out, wipe out, expunge, delete, destroy, annihilate, eliminate, extirpate, decimate, liquidate, demolish.

oblivious adj. HEEDLESS OF, unmindful of, unaware of, unconscious of, insensible of, ignorant of, blind to, unobservant of, deaf to, inattentive to, neglectful of, forgetful of, absent-minded, careless of, unconcerned with, abstracted, preoccupied, absorbed, far away. ■ OPPOSITES conscious.

obscene adj. INDECENT, pornographic, off colour, risqué, lewd, salacious, smutty, lecherous, lascivious, licentious, prurient, lubricious, ribald, scatological, scabrous, bawdy, suggestive, vulgar, dirty, filthy, foul, coarse, gross, vile, nasty, offensive, immoral, impure, immodest, shameless, unchaste, improper, unwholesome, erotic, carnal, sexy; *informal* raunchy, blue. ■ OPPOSITES decent.

obscenity n. **1** INDECENCY, lewdness, salaciousness, lasciviousness, licentiousness, prurience, lubricity, ribaldry, scabrousness, bawdiness, suggestiveness, vulgarity, dirtiness. **2** CURSE, oath, swear word, expletive, imprecation, blasphemy, epithet, profanity, fourletter word, dirty word.

obscure adj. **1** UNCLEAR, indeterminate, opaque, abstruse, recondite, unexplained, concealed, hidden, arcane, enigmatic, deep, cryptic, mysterious, puzzling, perplexing, confusing, involved, unfathomable, incomprehensible, impenetrable, vague, indefinite, hazy, uncertain, doubtful, dubious, ambiguous, equivocal. **2** INDISTINCT, vague, shadowy, hazy, blurred, fuzzy, cloudy. **3** LITTLE KNOWN, unknown, unheard of, undistinguished, insignificant, inconspicuous, minor, unimportant, unrecognized, unwith a law, rule, or ritual.

observant adj. quick to notice things.

observation n. **1** the close watching of someone or something. **2** the ability to notice important details. **3** a remark. ■ **observational** adj.

observatory n. (pl. **observatories**) a building equipped for observing the stars and planets.

observe v. **1** notice. **2** watch carefully. **3** make a remark. **4** obey a law or rule. **5** celebrate a festival. ■ **observable** adj. **observer** n.

obsess v. preoccupy to a disturbing extent.

obsession n. **1** the state of being obsessed. **2** a persistent thought. ■ **obsessional** adj. **obsessive** adj. **obsessively** adv.

obsolescent adj. becoming obsolete. ■ **obsolescence** n.

obsolete adj. no longer produced or used; out of date.

obstacle n. a thing that obstructs progress.

obstetrics n. the branch of medicine concerned with childbirth. ■ **obstetric** adj. **obstetrician** n.

obstinate adj. **1** stubbornly refusing to change one's mind. **2** (of a problem) hard to deal with. ■ **obstinacy** n. **obstinately** adv.

obstreperous adj. noisy and unruly.

obstruct v. **1** be in the way of. **2** stop or hinder progress. ■ **obstruction** n. **obstructive** adj.

obtain v. **1** come into possession of; get. **2** be established or usual. ■ **obtainable** adj.

obtrude v. become noticeable in an unwelcome way.

obtrusive adj. noticeable in an unwel-

Thesaurus

sung. ■ OPPOSITES clear, famous.

obsequious adj. SERVILE, subservient, submissive, slavish, menial, abject, fawning, grovelling, cringing, toadying, truckling, sycophantic, ingratiating, unctuous, oily, Uriah Heepish; informal bootlicking.

observant adj. ALERT, sharp-eyed, sharp, eagle-eyed, attentive, vigilant, wide awake, watchful, heedful, on the lookout, on guard, mindful, intent, aware, conscious; informal beady-eyed, not missing a thing/trick, on the ball. ■ OPPOSITES inattentive.

observation n. **1** SCRUTINY, scrutinization, watch, monitoring, surveillance, inspection, attention, consideration, study, review, examination. **2** REMARK, comment, statement, utterance, pronouncement, declaration.

observe v. **1** SEE, catch sight of, notice, note, perceive, discern, detect, espy, behold, watch, view, spot, witness; informal get a load of. **2** KEEP, obey, adhere to, abide by, heed, follow, comply with, conform to, acquiesce in, consent to, accept, respect, defer to. **3** CARRY OUT, perform, execute, discharge, fulfil. **4** CELEBRATE, keep, recognize, commemorate, mark, remember, solemnize.

observer n. WATCHER, looker-on, onlooker, witness, eyewitness, spectator, bystander, beholder, viewer, spotter.

obsess v. PREOCCUPY, haunt, have a hold on, possess, consume, engross, have a grip on, grip, dominate, rule, control, be on someone's mind, prey on, plague, torment, hound, bedevil.

obsession n. PREOCCUPATION, fixation, consuming passion, mania, enthusiasm, infatuation, compulsion, phobia, complex, fetish, craze; informal bee in one's bonnet, hang-up.

obsessive adj. EXCESSIVE, overdone, consuming, compulsive, besetting, gripping, haunting.

obsolete adj. OUTWORN, discarded, discontinued, extinct, bygone, outmoded, antiquated, out of date, superannuated, old-fashioned, behind the times, old, dated, antique, archaic, ancient, antediluvian, time-worn, past its prime. ■ OPPOSITES current.

obstacle n. BAR, barrier, obstruction, impediment, hindrance, hurdle, barricade, blockade, stumbling block, blockage, curb, check, snag, difficulty, catch, drawback. ■ OPPOSITES advantage, aid.

obstinate adj. STUBBORN, mulish, pigheaded, wilful, self-willed, strongminded, perverse, refractory, recalcitrant, contumacious, unmanageable, firm, steadfast, unyielding, inflexible, unbending, immovable, intransigent, intractable, uncompromising, persistent, tenacious, dogged, single-minded. ■ OPPOSITES amenable, tractable.

obstruct v. BLOCK, barricade, bar, cut off, shut off, choke, clog, hold up, bring to a standstill, stop, halt, hinder, impede, hamper, interfere with, frustrate, thwart, stymie, baulk, inhibit, curb, hamstring, encumber. ■ OPPOSITES clear, facilitate.

obtain v. **1** GET, get hold of, acquire, come by, procure, secure, gain, earn, come way.

obtuse adj. **1** annoyingly slow to understand. **2** (of an angle) more than 90° and less than 180°. **3** blunt.

obverse n. **1** the side of a coin or medal bearing the head or main design. **2** the opposite.

obviate v. remove a need or difficulty.

obvious adj. **1** easily seen or understood; clear. **2** predictable. ■ **obviously** adv.

ocarina n. an egg-shaped wind instrument.

occasion n. **1** a particular event, or the time at which it happens. **2** a special event. **3** a suitable time. **4** reason or cause. ▶ v. cause.

 Two c's and one s: occasion.

occasional adj. happening or done from time to time. ■ **occasionally** adv.

occidental adj. of the countries of the West.

occlude v. close up or block. □ **occluded front** a weather front produced when a cold front catches up with a warm front, so that the warm air in between rises. ■ **occlusion** n.

occult n. (**the occult**) supernatural beliefs, practices, or events. ▶ adj. of the occult.

occupant n. a person occupying a place or job. ■ **occupancy** n.

occupation n. **1** a job or profession. **2** the act of occupying or state of being occupied. **3** a way of spending time.

occupational adj. of a job or profession. □ **occupational therapy** the use of particular activities as an aid to recovery from illness.

occupy v. (**occupying**, **occupied**) **1** live or work in. **2** enter and take control of a place. **3** fill a space, time, or position. **4** keep busy. ■ **occupier** n.

occur v. (**occurring**, **occurred**) **1** happen. **2** be found or present. **3** (**occur to**) come into the mind of. ■ **occurrence** n.

ocean n. a very large expanse of sea. ■ **oceanic** adj.

oceanography n. the study of the sea.

ocelot n. a wild cat found in South and Central America.

ochre /oh-ker/ (US **ocher**) n. a light yellowish brown.

o'clock adv. used to specify the hour when telling the time.

octagon n. a plane figure with eight sides. ■ **octagonal** adj.

octane n. a liquid hydrocarbon present

Thesaurus

achieve, attain, get one's hands on, seize, grab, pick up. **2** BE IN FORCE, be effective, exist, stand, prevail, hold, be the case, reign, rule, hold sway.

obtrusive adj. NOTICEABLE, conspicuous, obvious, unmistakable, blatant, flagrant, bold, audacious, intrusive. ■ OPPOSITES unobtrusive.

obtuse adj. see STUPID.

obvious adj. CLEAR, plain, visible, noticeable, perceptible, discernible, detectable, recognizable, evident, apparent, manifest, palpable, patent, conspicuous, unconcealed, overt, pronounced, transparent, prominent, unmistakable, indisputable, undeniable; *informal* sticking out like a sore thumb, sticking out a mile, as plain as the nose on your face. ■ OPPOSITES imperceptible, inconspicuous.

occasion n. **1** TIME, juncture, point, situation, instance, case, circumstance. **2** EVENT, incident, occurrence, happening, episode, affair, experience. ▶ v. CAUSE, give rise to, bring about, result in, lead to, prompt, provoke, produce, create, generate, engender.

occasional adj. INFREQUENT, intermittent, irregular, sporadic, odd, rare, cas-

ual, incidental. ■ OPPOSITES regular, habitual.

occasionally adv. NOW AND THEN, now and again, from time to time, sometimes, at times, every so often, once in a while, on occasion, periodically, at intervals, irregularly, sporadically, infrequently, intermittently, off and on.

occupation n. **1** JOB, profession, business, employment, employ, career, calling, vocation, trade, craft, line, field, province, area. **2** OCCUPANCY, tenancy, tenure, residence, inhabitancy, habitation, possession, holding. **3** INVASION, seizure, takeover, conquest, capture, overthrow, subjugation, subjection.

occupy v. **1** LIVE IN, inhabit, reside in, dwell in, tenant, have one's residence/abode in, make one's home in. **2** FILL, fill up, take up, use up, utilize, cover. **3** INVADE, overrun, seize, take over.

occur v. **1** HAPPEN, take place, come about, materialize, transpire, arise, crop up, turn up, eventuate; *literary* come to pass, befall. **2** BE FOUND, be met with, be present, exist, obtain, appear, present itself, show itself, manifest itself.

occurrence n. **1** HAPPENING, event, inciin petrol.

octave n. **1** a series of eight musical notes occupying the interval between (and including) two notes. **2** the interval between two such notes.

octavo n. (pl. **octavos**) a size of book page formed by folding each printed sheet into eight leaves.

octet n. **1** a group of eight voices or musicians. **2** a piece of music for an octet.

October n. the tenth month.

octogenarian n. a person between 80 and 89 years old.

octopus n. (pl. **octopuses**) a sea animal with eight tentacles.

ocular adj. of, for, or by the eyes.

oculist n. a doctor who treats eye diseases or defects.

OD v. (**OD'ing**, **OD'd**) informal take an overdose of a drug.

odd adj. **1** unusual or unexpected; strange. **2** (of a number) having a remainder of one when divided by two. **3** occasional. **4** separated from a pair or set. □ **oddment** an item or piece left over from a larger piece or set. ■ **oddly** adv. **oddness** n.

oddity n. (pl. **oddities**) **1** the quality of being strange. **2** a strange person or thing.

odds pl. n. **1** the ratio between the amount placed as a bet and the money which would be received if the bet was won. **2** the chances of something happening. □ **at odds** in conflict or disagreement. **odds and ends** various articles or remnants. **odds-on** very likely to win, succeed, or happen.

ode n. a poem addressed to a person or thing or celebrating an event.

odious adj. very unpleasant.

odium n. widespread hatred or disgust.

odometer n. a milometer.

odoriferous adj. smelly.

odour (US **odor**) n. a smell. ■ **odorous**

adj. **odourless** adj.

odyssey n. (pl. **odysseys**) a long eventful journey.

oedema /i-dee-muh/ (US **edema**) n. excess fluid in the tissues of the body.

oesophagus /ee-sof-fuh-guhss/ (US **esophagus**) n. (pl. **oesophagi** or **oesophaguses**) the tube connecting the throat to the stomach.

oestrogen /ee-struh-juhn/ (US **estrogen**) n. a hormone which develops and maintains female physical and sexual characteristics.

of prep. **1** helping to form; made up from. **2** belonging to; involving. **3** indicating measurement, value, or age.

off adv. **1** away from a place. **2** so as to be separated. **3** so as to finish or be discontinued. **4** not working or connected. ▶ prep. **1** away from. **2** so as to be separated from. **3** informal having a temporary dislike of. ▶ adj. (of food) no longer fresh. □ **offbeat** informal unconventional. **off colour** slightly unwell. **offcut** a piece of wood, fabric, etc. left after cutting a larger piece. **offhand 1** rudely casual or abrupt. **2** without previous thought. **off-licence** a shop selling alcoholic drink to be drunk elsewhere. **offline** not connected to a computer. **offload** unload. **off-putting** unpleasant or unsettling. **offset** counteract by having an equal and opposite force or effect. **offshoot** a thing that develops from something else. **offside** (in football etc.) in a position on the field where playing the ball is not allowed. **off-white** a white colour with a grey or yellow tinge.

offal n. the internal organs of an animal used as food.

offence (US **offense**) n. **1** an illegal act. **2** a feeling of hurt or annoyance.

offend v. **1** cause someone to feel hurt or annoyed. **2** do something illegal.

Thesaurus

dent, circumstance, affair, episode, proceedings, adventure. **2** EXISTENCE, appearance, instance, manifestation, materialization.

odd adj. **1** STRANGE, eccentric, queer, peculiar, idiosyncratic, unconventional, outlandish, weird, bizarre, freakish; informal offbeat, wacky, freaky. **2** OCCASIONAL, casual, temporary, part-time, seasonal, periodic, irregular, miscellaneous. **3** RANDOM, irregular, periodic, haphazard, chance, fortuitous. **4** UNMATCHED, unpaired, left over, spare, remaining, surplus, superfluous, lone,

single, solitary, sole. ■ OPPOSITES normal, ordinary.

odious adj. ABHORRENT, offensive, repugnant, disgusting, repulsive, repellent, revolting, foul, vile, unpleasant, disagreeable, loathsome, detestable, hateful, despicable, contemptible. ■ OPPOSITES delightful.

odour n. AROMA, smell, scent, perfume, fragrance, bouquet, essence, stench, stink; informal niff, pong; literary redolence.

offence n. **1** CRIME, illegal act, wrongdoing, wrong, misdemeanour, misdeed, peccadillo, sin, transgression, short-

■ **offender** n.

offensive adj. **1** causing offence. **2** used in attack. ▶n. a campaign to attack or achieve something. ■ **offensively** adv.

offer v. **1** present for acceptance, rejection, or consideration. **2** express willingness to do something for someone. ▶n. **1** an expression of willingness to do or give something. **2** an amount of money offered. **3** a specially reduced price.

offering n. a gift or contribution.

offertory n. (pl. **offertories**) **1** the offering of the bread and wine at Holy Communion. **2** a collection of money at a Christian church service.

office n. **1** a room or building used for business or clerical work. **2** a position of authority. **3** the holding of an official position.

officer n. a person holding a position of authority, esp. in the armed services.

official adj. of or authorized by an authority or public organization. ▶n. a person holding public office or having official duties. ■ **officially** adv.

officiate v. **1** act as an official in charge of something. **2** perform a religious ceremony.

officious adj. asserting authority in an overbearing way. ■ **officiously** adv.

offspring n. (pl. **offspring**) a person's child or children, or the young of an animal.

often adv. **1** frequently. **2** in many cases.

ogle v. stare at in a lecherous way.

ogre n. **1** (in folklore) a man-eating giant. **2** a terrifying person.

oh exclam. expressing surprise, disappointment, joy, etc.

ohm /ohm/ n. a unit of electrical resistance.

oil n. **1** a thick, sticky liquid obtained from petroleum. **2** a thick liquid which does not dissolve in water. **3** oil paint. ▶v. treat or coat with oil. □ **oilfield** an area where oil is found beneath the ground or the seabed. **oil paint** paint made from pigment mixed with oil. **oil rig** a structure providing a stable base

Thesaurus

coming, fault, lapse; *Law* malfeasance. **2** ANNOYANCE, anger, indignation, exasperation, wrath, displeasure, disapproval, dislike, animosity, resentment; *literary* ire.

offend v. **1** GIVE OFFENCE TO, affront, upset, displease, annoy, anger, incense, exasperate, vex, pique, put out, gall, irritate, provoke, ruffle, disgruntle, rankle with, outrage, insult, slight, humiliate; *informal* put someone's back up. **2** COMMIT A CRIME, break the law, do wrong, sin, go astray, fall from grace, err, transgress.

offender n. WRONGDOER, culprit, criminal, lawbreaker, miscreant, delinquent, sinner, transgressor, malefactor.

offensive adj. **1** HURTFUL, wounding, abusive, affronting, displeasing, annoying, exasperating, vexing, galling, irritating, provocative, objectionable, outrageous, insulting, rude, discourteous, uncivil, impolite. **2** DISAGREEABLE, unpleasant, nasty, foul, vile, objectionable, odious, abominable, detestable, loathsome, repugnant, disgusting, obnoxious, repulsive, repellent. ■ OPPOSITES complimentary.

offer v. **1** PUT FORWARD, propose, advance, submit, propound, suggest, recommend. **2** VOLUNTEER ONE'S SERVICES, volunteer, offer one's service, offer assistance/help, make oneself available.

offering n. CONTRIBUTION, donation, subscription, gift, present, handout.

offhand adj. CASUAL, unceremonious, cavalier, careless, indifferent, perfunctory, cursory, abrupt, brusque, discourteous, uncivil, impolite, rude.

office n. **1** PLACE OF BUSINESS, base, workplace. **2** POST, position, role, place, situation, station, function, responsibility, obligation, charge, tenure.

official adj. AUTHORIZED, accredited, approved, validated, authenticated, certified, endorsed, sanctioned, licensed, recognized, accepted, legitimate, legal, lawful, bona fide, proper, ex cathedra; *informal* kosher. ■ OPPOSITES unofficial.

officiate v. TAKE CHARGE, be in charge, preside, oversee, superintend, conduct, run, take the chair.

officious adj. OVERZEALOUS, interfering, intrusive, meddlesome, importunate, forward, obtrusive, self-important, opinionated, dictatorial, domineering, pushy; *informal* nosy. ■ OPPOSITES self-effacing.

offset v. COUNTERBALANCE, counteract, countervail, balance, balance out, cancel out, neutralize, compensate for, make up for, make good.

offshoot n. BRANCH, subsidiary, adjunct, appendage.

offspring n. CHILDREN, family, progeny, young, descendants, heirs, successors, spawn; *informal* kids; *Law* issue.

often adv. FREQUENTLY, a lot, many a time,

above water for drilling for and extracting oil. **oilskin 1** heavy cotton cloth waterproofed with oil. **2** (**oilskins**) clothing made of oilskin. ■ **oily** adj.

ointment n. a cream rubbed on the skin for medicinal purposes.

OK (or **okay**) informal adj. satisfactory. ▶ adv. in a satisfactory way.

okapi /oh-kah-pi/ n. (pl. **okapi** or **okapis**) a large African mammal of the giraffe family.

okra n. the long seed pods of a tropical plant, eaten as a vegetable.

old adj. **1** having lived or existed for a long time. **2** former. **3** showing signs of age. **4** of a specified age. □ **old age** the later part of normal life. **old-fashioned** no longer current or modern. **Old Testament** the first part of the Christian Bible. **old wives' tale** a traditional belief now thought to be incorrect.

oleaginous /oh-li-aj-i-nuhss/ adj. **1** oily. **2** excessively flattering.

oleander /oh-li-an-der/ n. a flowering evergreen shrub of warm countries.

olfactory adj. of the sense of smell.

oligarchy n. (pl. **oligarchies**) **1** a small group governing a state. **2** a state governed by such a group. ■ **oligarch** n.

oligarchic adj.

olive n. **1** a small oval fruit with bitter flesh which yields **olive oil**, or the tree producing this fruit. **2** a greyish-green colour. ▶ adj. **1** greyish-green. **2** (of skin) yellowish brown. □ **olive branch** an offer to restore friendly relations.

ombudsman n. an official appointed to investigate complaints against public organizations.

omega n. the last letter of the Greek alphabet (Ω, ω).

omelette n. a dish of beaten eggs cooked in a frying pan.

omen n. an event seen as a sign of future good or bad luck.

ominous adj. suggesting that something bad is going to happen. ■ **ominously** adv.

omit v. (**omitting, omitted**) **1** leave out or exclude. **2** fail to do. ■ **omission** n.

omnibus n. **1** a book or programme containing several works or programmes previously published or broadcast separately. **2** dated a bus.

omnipotent adj. having unlimited or very great power. ■ **omnipotence** n.

omnipresent adj. present everywhere. ■ **omnipresence** n.

Thesaurus

repeatedly, again and again, time and again, time after time, over and over, over and over again, {day in, day out}; literary oft, oft-times. ■ OPPOSITES seldom, never.

oily adj. **1** GREASY, fatty, buttery. **2** SMOOTH, smooth-talking, flattering, fulsome, glib, unctuous, subservient, servile, oleaginous.

ointment n. CREAM, lotion, emollient, salve, balm, liniment, embrocation, unguent, gel.

old adj. **1** OLDER, elderly, aged, advanced in years, long in the tooth, mature, grey-haired, grizzled, hoary, past one's prime, ancient, decrepit, senile, venerable, senior; Biology senescent; informal getting on, past it, over the hill. **2** OUT OF DATE, outdated, old-fashioned, outmoded, passé, archaic, obsolete, extinct, antiquated, antediluvian, superannuated; informal old hat. **3** BYGONE, past, early, earlier, primeval, primordial, prehistoric. **4** AGE-OLD, long-standing, long-lived, long-established, time-honoured, enduring, lasting. **5** EX-, former, previous, one-time, sometime, erstwhile, quondam. ■ OPPOSITES young.

old age n. OLDNESS, elderliness, age, declining years, advanced years, winter/autumn of one's life, twilight years, senility, dotage; Biology senescence.

old-fashioned adj. OUT OF FASHION, outmoded, unfashionable, out of style, out of date, outdated, dated, out, dead, old-time, behind the times, past, bygone, passé, archaic, obsolescent, obsolete, ancient, antiquated, superannuated, antediluvian, old-fangled; informal old hat, not with it. ■ OPPOSITES up to date, fashionable.

omen n. PORTENT, sign, token, foretoken, harbinger, premonition, forewarning, warning, prediction, forecast, prophecy, augury.

ominous adj. THREATENING, menacing, minatory, black, dark, gloomy, heavy, sinister, bad, unpromising, unpropitious, pessimistic, inauspicious, unfavourable, unlucky. ■ OPPOSITES auspicious.

omission n. **1** EXCLUSION, exception, deletion, erasure, elimination, expunction. **2** NEGLECT, negligence, dereliction, forgetfulness, oversight, disregard, default, failure.

omit v. **1** LEAVE OUT, exclude, except, miss out, miss, fail to mention, pass over, drop; informal give something a miss.

omniscient /om-**ni**-si-uhnt/ adj. knowing everything. ■ **omniscience** n.

omnivorous adj. eating both plants and meat.

on prep. **1** (also **on to**) into contact with, or aboard. **2** about; concerning. **3** as a member of. **4** stored in or broadcast by. **5** in the course of. **6** at a point in time. ▶ adv. **1** in contact with or covering something. **2** with continued movement or action. **3** taking place or being presented. **4** functioning. □ **oncoming** approaching. **ongoing** still in progress.

online controlled by or connected to a computer.

once adv. **1** on one occasion only. **2** formerly. ▶ conj. as soon as. □ **at once 1** immediately. **2** at the same time. **once upon a time** at some time in the past. **once-over** informal a rapid inspection or search.

oncogene n. a gene that transforms a gene into a cancer cell.

oncology n. the study and treatment of tumours.

one n. & adj. **1** the lowest cardinal number; 1 or I. **2** single, or a single person or thing. **3** a certain. **4** the same. ▶ pron. **1** used to refer to a person or thing previously mentioned. **2** used to refer to the speaker or to represent people in general. □ **one-sided 1** unfairly biased. **2** very unequal. **one-upmanship** informal the technique of gaining an advantage over someone else. **one-way** allowing movement in one direction only.

onerous /**oh**-nuh-ruhss/ adj. involving much effort and difficulty.

oneself pron. **1** used when 'one' is the subject of the verb and is also affected by it. **2** used to emphasize 'one'.

onion n. a vegetable with a bulb having a strong taste and smell.

onlooker n. a spectator.

only adv. **1** and no one or nothing more besides. **2** no longer ago than. ▶ adj. **1** single or solitary. **2** alone deserving consideration. ▶ conj. informal except that.

onomatopoeia /on-uh-mat-uh-**pee**-uh/ n. the formation of a word from the sound of the thing described. ■ **onomatopoeic** adj.

onset n. a beginning.

onslaught n. a fierce attack.

onto var. of on to (see **ON**).

onus /**oh**-nuhss/ n. a responsibility.

onward adv. & adj. in a continuing forward direction. ■ **onwards** adv.

onyx n. a semi-precious stone with layers of different colours.

oodles pl. n. informal a very great number or amount.

ooze v. **1** slowly seep out. **2** exude. ▶ n. wet mud or slime.

opal n. an iridescent gemstone.

opalescent adj. iridescent like an opal.

opaque adj. **1** impossible to see through. **2** difficult to understand. ■ **opacity** n.

op. cit. adv. in the work already mentioned.

open adj. **1** not closed, fastened, or restricted. **2** not covered or protected. **3** (**open to**) likely to be affected by. **4** expanded or unfolded. **5** undisguised. **6** not concealing thoughts or feelings. **7** not finally settled. ▶ v. **1** make or become open. **2** formally begin or establish. ▶ n. (**the open**) fresh air or open countryside. □ **in the open** not secret. **opencast** (of mining) near the surface, rather than from shafts. **open-ended** with no limit decided in advance. **open-handed** generous. **open house** a situation in which all visitors are welcome. **open letter** a letter addressed to a particular person but published in a newspaper. **open-plan** having few or no dividing walls. **open prison** a prison with the minimum of restrictions on prisoners' movements. **open verdict** a verdict that a person's death is suspicious but that the cause is unknown. ■ **opener** n. **openly** adv. **openness** n.

Thesaurus

2 FORGET TO, neglect to, fail to, leave undone, overlook, skip.

omnipotent adj. ALL-POWERFUL, almighty, supreme, pre-eminent, invincible.

onerous adj. ARDUOUS, strenuous, difficult, hard, burdensome, crushing, back-breaking, taxing, demanding, exacting, wearing, wearisome, fatiguing. ■ OPPOSITES easy.

ongoing adj. IN PROGRESS, current, progressing, advancing, successful, developing, evolving, growing, extant.

onset n. START, beginning, commencement, inception, outbreak; informal kick-off. ■ OPPOSITES end.

onslaught n. ASSAULT, attack, charge, storming, sortie, sally, raid, foray, push, thrust, drive, blitz.

onus n. BURDEN, weight, load, responsibility, liability, obligation, duty, charge, encumbrance.

open adj. **1** NOT SHUT, not closed, unlocked, unbolted, unlatched, unbarred,

opening n. **1** a gap. **2** a beginning, or a ceremony marking this. **3** an opportunity.

opera n. **1** a play set to music for singers and musicians. **2** pl. of OPUS. □ **opera glasses** small binoculars for use at a theatre. ■ **operatic** adj.

operable adj. **1** able to be operated. **2** able to be treated by surgery.

operate v. **1** function. **2** control the functioning of a machine or the activities of an organization. **3** perform a surgical operation. □ **operating system** the software supporting a computer's basic functions.

operation n. **1** the act of operating. **2** an act of surgery performed on a patient. **3** an organized action involving a number of people.

operational adj. **1** in or ready for use. **2** of the functioning of an organization.

operative adj. **1** functioning. **2** of surgery. ▶ n. **1** a worker. **2** a secret agent.

operator n. **1** a person who operates equipment or a machine. **2** a person who works at the switchboard of a telephone exchange.

operetta n. a short opera on a light theme.

ophthalmic adj. of the eye and its diseases. □ **ophthalmic optician** an optician qualified to prescribe and supply glasses etc. and to detect eye diseases.

ophthalmology /off-thal-**mol**-uh-ji/ n. the study of disorders and diseases of the eye. ■ **ophthalmologist** n.

opiate n. a drug containing opium.

opine v. state as one's opinion.

opinion n. **1** a personal view not necessarily based on fact or knowledge. **2** a formal statement of advice from an expert.

opinionated adj. tending to put forward one's views forcefully.

opium n. an addictive drug made from the juice of a poppy.

opossum n. a small tree-dwelling marsupial.

opponent n. **1** a person who competes with or fights another. **2** a person who disagrees with something.

opportune adj. occurring at an especially appropriate time.

opportunist n. a person who exploits opportunities as and when they arise, esp. unscrupulously. ■ **opportunism** n. **opportunistic** adj.

opportunity n. (pl. **opportunities**) a favourable time or situation for doing something.

Thesaurus

unfastened, unsecured, ajar, wide open, agape, gaping, yawning. **2** UNCOVERED, topless, unsealed. **3** EXPOSED, unsheltered, wide, wide open, extensive, broad, spacious, sweeping, airy, uncrowded, uncluttered, undeveloped. **4** FRANK, candid, honest, forthright, direct, blunt, plain-spoken, downright. **5** OBVIOUS, clear, noticeable, visible, apparent, evident, manifest, overt, conspicuous, patent, unconcealed, unhidden, undisguised, blatant, flagrant. **6** WIDE OPEN TO, allowing of, permitting, vulnerable to, exposed to, susceptible to, liable to, at the mercy of, an easy target for. **7** UNBIASED, unprejudiced, non-partisan, impartial, objective, disinterested, dispassionate, detached. ▶ v. **1** THROW OPEN, unlock, unbolt, unlatch, unbar, unfasten. **2** UNWRAP, undo, untie, unseal. ■ OPPOSITES close.

opening n. **1** GAP, aperture, space, hole, orifice, vent, slot, breach, crack, split, fissure, cleft, crevice, chink, interstice, rent, rupture. **2** VACANCY, position, job, opportunity, chance; *informal* break, lucky break.

operate v. **1** FUNCTION, work, go, run, perform, act. **2** MANAGE, run, work, use,

utilize, employ, handle, be in charge of. **3** PERFORM AN OPERATION, perform surgery; *informal* put under the knife.

operational adj. OPERATIVE, workable, in operation, working, in working order, functioning, functional, going, in use, usable, in action, ready for action.

operative adj. **1** IN OPERATION, in force, effective, valid. **2** OPERATIONAL, workable, working, functioning, functional, usable. ▶ n. WORKER, workman, machinist, operator, mechanic, factory hand/ employee.

opinion n. POINT OF VIEW, view, viewpoint, belief, thought, thinking, way of thinking, standpoint, theory, judgement, estimation, feeling, sentiment, impression, notion, assumption, conception, conviction, persuasion, creed, dogma.

opponent n. OPPOSITION, rival, adversary, opposer, contestant, competitor, enemy, foe, antagonist, contender, dissenter, disputant. ■ OPPOSITES ally.

opportune adj. ADVANTAGEOUS, favourable, auspicious, propitious, good, lucky, happy, timely, well timed, fortunate, providential, felicitous, convenient, expedient, suitable, apt, fitting,

oppose v. **1** disagree with and try to prevent or resist. **2** compete with or fight. **3** (**opposed**) (of two or more things) contrasting or conflicting. **4** (**opposing**) opposite.

opposite adj. **1** facing. **2** completely different. **3** being the other of a contrasted pair. ▶n. an opposite person or thing. ▶adv. & prep. in an opposite position to something.

opposition n. **1** resistance or disagreement. **2** a group of opponents. **3** (**the Opposition**) the main party in parliament opposing the one in power. **4** a contrast or opposite.

oppress v. **1** treat harshly and unfairly. **2** distress or make anxious. ■ **oppression** n. **oppressor** n.

oppressive adj. **1** harsh and unfair. **2** causing distress or anxiety. **3** (of weather) close and sultry.

opprobrious adj. highly critical.

opprobrium n. **1** harsh criticism. **2** disgrace as a result of bad behaviour.

opt v. make a choice. □ **opt out 1** choose not to participate. **2** (of a school or hospital) withdraw from local authority control.

optic adj. of the eye or vision.

optical adj. of vision, light, or optics. □ **optical fibre** a thin glass fibre through which light can be transmitted. ■ **optically** adv.

optician n. a person qualified to prescribe and supply glasses etc. and to detect eye diseases.

optics n. the study of vision and the behaviour of light.

optimal adj. best or most favourable.

optimism n. hopefulness and confidence about the future. ■ **optimist** n. **optimistic** adj. **optimistically** adv.

optimize (or **-ise**) v. make the best use of.

optimum adj. most likely to lead to a favourable outcome. ▶n. (pl. **optima** or **optimums**) the most favourable conditions for growth or success.

option n. **1** a thing that is or may be chosen. **2** the freedom or right to choose. **3** a right to buy or sell something at a specified price within a set time.

optional adj. not compulsory. ■ **optionally** adv.

optometry n. the occupation of measuring eyesight, prescribing lenses, and detecting eye disease. ■ **optometrist** n.

Thesaurus

relevant, pertinent. ■ OPPOSITES unfavourable.

opportunity n. CHANCE, good time, golden opportunity, favourable time/occasion/moment, right set of circumstances, appropriate time; *informal* break.

oppose v. BE HOSTILE TO, take a stand against, stand up to, take issue with, take on, contradict, counter, argue against, counter-attack, confront, resist, withstand, defy, fight, put up a fight against, combat, fly in the face of. ■ OPPOSITES support.

opposite adj. **1** FACING, face to face with; *informal* eyeball to eyeball with. **2** OPPOSING, differing, different, unlike, contrary, reverse, contradictory, conflicting, clashing, discordant, dissident, at variance, incompatible, irreconcilable, antipathetic, poles apart.

opposition n. **1** HOSTILITY, dislike, disapproval, resistance, defiance. **2** OPPONENT, opposing side, other side/team, rival, adversary, competition, antagonist, enemy, foe.

oppress v. SUBJUGATE, enslave, suppress, crush, subdue, quash, quell, bring someone to their knees, tyrannize, repress, abuse, maltreat, persecute, rule with a rod of iron, trample on, trample underfoot, ride roughshod over.

oppressed adj. ENSLAVED, crushed, subdued, repressed, persecuted, subjugated, maltreated, misused, browbeaten, downtrodden, disadvantaged, underprivileged.

oppression n. SUBJUGATION, subduing, tyranny, suppression, persecution, abuse, maltreatment, cruelty, brutality, injustice, ruthlessness, harshness.

oppressive adj. **1** TYRANNICAL, despotic, Draconian, iron-fisted, high-handed, repressive, domineering, harsh, crushing, cruel, brutal, ruthless, merciless, pitiless, unjust. **2** MUGGY, close, airless, stuffy, stifling, suffocating, sultry, torrid. ■ OPPOSITES lenient.

oppressor n. TYRANT, despot, autocrat, persecutor, bully, iron hand, slavedriver, hard taskmaster, dictator, scourge.

optimistic adj. POSITIVE, sanguine, hopeful, confident, bullish, cheerful, buoyant; *informal* upbeat. ■ OPPOSITES pessimistic.

optimum adj. **1** MOST FAVOURABLE, best, most advantageous, most appropriate, ideal, perfect. **2** PEAK, top, best, perfect, ideal, flawless, superlative, optimal.

option n. CHOICE, freedom of choice, al-

opulent adj. ostentatiously luxurious. ■ **opulence** n. **opulently** adv.

opus n. (pl. **opuses** or **opera**) a separate musical composition or set of compositions.

or conj. **1** used to link alternatives. **2** otherwise.

oracle n. **1** (in ancient Greece or Rome) a priest or priestess who acted as a channel for prophecy from the gods. **2** an authority which is always correct.

oracular adj. **1** of an oracle. **2** hard to interpret.

oral adj. **1** spoken rather than written. **2** of or done by the mouth. ▶n. a spoken examination. ■ **orally** adv.

orange n. **1** a large round citrus fruit with reddish-yellow rind. **2** a bright reddish-yellow colour.

orang-utan (or **orang-utang**) n. a large ape with reddish hair.

oration n. a formal speech.

orator n. a skilful public speaker.

oratorio n. (pl. **oratorios**) a musical work on a religious theme for orchestra and voices.

oratory n. formal public speaking, esp. when inspiring. ■ **oratorical** adj.

orb n. **1** a sphere. **2** a golden globe with a cross on top, carried by a monarch.

orbit n. **1** the regularly repeated course of a planet, spacecraft, etc. around a star or planet. **2** an area of activity or influence. ▶v. (**orbiting**, **orbited**) move in orbit round.

orbital adj. **1** of an orbit or orbits. **2** (of a road) passing round the outside of a town.

orchard n. a piece of land planted with fruit trees.

orchestra n. a large group of musicians with string, woodwind, brass, and percussion sections. ■ **orchestral** adj.

orchestrate v. **1** arrange music for performance by an orchestra. **2** direct a situation to produce a desired effect. ■ **orchestration** n.

orchid n. a plant with unusually shaped flowers.

ordain v. **1** make someone a priest or minister. **2** order officially.

ordeal n. a prolonged painful or horrific experience.

order n. **1** the arrangement of people or things according to a particular sequence or method. **2** a state in which everything is in its correct place. **3** a state in which the laws regulating public behaviour are followed. **4** a command. **5** a request for something to be supplied. **6** the set procedure followed in a court, religious service, etc. **7** a rank, kind, or quality. **8** a religious community living according to particular rules. **9** a classifying category of plants and animals. ▶v. **1** give a command. **2** request that something be supplied. **3** arrange methodically. □ **in order 1** in the correct condition for use. **2** suitable in the circumstances. **out of order** not functioning.

orderly adj. **1** neatly arranged. **2** well behaved. ▶n. (pl. **orderlies**) **1** a hospital attendant. **2** a soldier assisting an officer. ■ **orderliness** n.

ordinal number n. a number express-

Thesaurus

ternative, other possibility, preference.

optional adj. NON-COMPULSORY, not required, voluntary, discretionary, at one's discretion, elective. ■ OPPOSITES compulsory.

opulent adj. **1** LUXURIOUS, sumptuous, lavishly appointed; informal plush, plushy, ritzy. **2** AFFLUENT, wealthy, rich, well off, well-to-do, moneyed, prosperous; informal well heeled, rolling in it. ■ OPPOSITES spartan, poor.

orbit n. **1** REVOLUTION, circle, circuit, cycle, rotation. **2** SPHERE, sphere of influence, range, reach, scope, ambit, sweep, domain.

ordeal n. TRIAL, test, tribulation, suffering, affliction, distress, agony, anguish, torture, torment, calamity, trouble, nightmare.

order n. **1** ORDERLINESS, neatness, tidiness, trimness, harmony. **2** METHOD, or-

ganization, system, plan, uniformity, regularity, symmetry, pattern. **3** CONDITION, state, shape, situation. **4** ARRANGEMENT, grouping, system, organization, form, structure, disposition, classification, categorization, codification, series, sequence, progression, succession, layout, set-up. **5** COMMAND, direction, directive, instruction, decree, edict, injunction, law, rule, regulation, ordinance, stipulation, dictate. **6** REQUEST, call, requirement, requisition, demand, booking, reservation, commission. **7** BROTHERHOOD, sisterhood, community. ▶v. **1** GIVE THE ORDER TO, command, instruct, direct, bid, enjoin. **2** PUT IN/PLACE AN ORDER FOR, request, call for, requisition, book, reserve, contract for, apply for, send away for.

orderly adj. **1** IN ORDER, neat, tidy, trim, shipshape, shipshape and Bristol fashing order (1st, 2nd, 3rd, etc.), rather than quantity (1, 2, 3, etc.).

ordinance n. an official order.

ordinand n. a candidate for ordination.

ordinary adj. normal or usual. ■ **ordinarily** adv.

ordination n. the ordaining of someone as a priest or minister.

ordnance n. **1** large guns mounted on wheels. **2** military equipment and stores.

ordure n. dung.

ore n. naturally occurring material from which a metal or mineral can be extracted.

oregano /o-ri-gah-noh/ n. a herb.

organ n. **1** a body part with a particular function. **2** a keyboard instrument with rows of pipes supplied with air from bellows, or one producing similar sounds electronically. **3** a newspaper which puts forward particular views. ■ **organist** n.

organic adj. **1** of or derived from living matter. **2** produced without artificial chemicals such as fertilizers. **3** of a bodily organ or organs. **4** (of development or change) continuous or natural. ■ **organically** adv.

organism n. an individual animal, plant, or life form.

organization (or **-isation**) n. **1** the act of organizing. **2** a systematic arrangement or approach. **3** an organized

group with a particular purpose, e.g. a business. ■ **organizational** adj.

organize (or **-ise**) v. **1** arrange in an orderly way. **2** make arrangements for. ■ **organizer** n.

orgasm n. a climax of sexual excitement.

orgy n. (pl. **orgies**) **1** a wild party. **2** excessive indulgence in a specified activity. ■ **orgiastic** adj.

orient n. (**the Orient**) the countries of the East. ▶v. (also **orientate**) **1** position in relation to the points of a compass. **2** (**orient oneself**) find one's position in relation to unfamiliar surroundings. **3** tailor to meet particular needs. ■ **oriental** adj. **orientation** n.

orienteering n. the sport of finding one's way across country with a map and compass.

orifice n. an opening in the body.

origami /o-ri-gah-mi/ n. the Japanese art of folding paper into decorative shapes.

origin n. **1** the point where something begins. **2** a person's social background or ancestry.

original adj. **1** existing from the beginning. **2** produced by an artist, author, etc. rather than copied. **3** inventive or novel. ▶n. the earliest form of something, from which copies can be made. ■ **originality** n. **originally** adv.

originate v. bring or come into being.

Thesaurus

ion, in apple-pie order. **2** ORGANIZED, well organized, methodical, systematic, efficient, businesslike. **3** WELL BEHAVED, disciplined, quiet, peaceful, controlled, restrained. ■ OPPOSITES disorderly.

ordinary adj. **1** USUAL, normal, standard, typical, stock, common, customary, habitual, accustomed, everyday, quotidian, regular, routine, established, settled, fixed, prevailing, humdrum; *literary* wonted. **2** RUN-OF-THE-MILL, common, conventional, standard, typical, average, commonplace, workaday, humdrum, unremarkable, unexceptional, undistinguished, unmemorable, pedestrian, prosaic, unpretentious, modest, plain, simple. ■ OPPOSITES unusual.

organization n. **1** ARRANGEMENT, regulation, coordination, systematization, categorization, administration, running, management. **2** COMPANY, firm, concern, operation, corporation, institution, group, consortium, conglomerate, combine, syndicate, federation, confederation, association, body.

organize v. **1** ARRANGE, dispose, regulate, marshal, put in order, put straight, coordinate, systematize, methodize, standardize, collocate, group, sort, sort out, classify, categorize, catalogue, codify, tabulate. **2** BE RESPONSIBLE FOR, be in charge of, take care of, administrate, run, manage, lick/knock into shape, see to.

orientate v. **1** FIND ONE'S BEARINGS, get the lie of the land, establish one's location. **2** ADAPT, adjust, accommodate, familiarize, acclimatize, find one's feet. **3** DIRECT, guide, lead, point someone in the direction of, turn.

orifice n. OPENING, hole, vent, aperture, gap, space, breach, break, rent, slot, slit, cleft, cranny, fissure, crevice, rift, crack, chink.

origin n. **1** SOURCE, basis, base, derivation, root, roots, provenance, etymology, genesis, spring, wellspring, fountain, fountainhead. **2** DESCENT, ancestry, pedigree, lineage, heritage, parentage, extraction, beginnings.

■ **origination** n. **originator** n.

ormolu n. a gold-coloured alloy of copper, zinc, and tin.

ornament n. **1** an object designed to add beauty to something. **2** decorative items as a whole. ■ **ornamental** adj. **ornamentation** n.

ornate adj. highly decorated.

ornithology n. the study of birds. ■ **ornithological** adj. **ornithologist** n.

orphan n. a child whose parents are dead. ▶ v. **(be orphaned)** (of a child) be made an orphan.

orphanage n. a home which cares for orphans.

orthodontics n. the treatment of irregularities in the teeth. ■ **orthodontic** adj. **orthodontist** n.

orthodox adj. **1** of or holding traditional or generally accepted beliefs. **2** conventional; normal. □ **Orthodox Church** the Christian Church in Greece and eastern Europe. ■ **orthodoxy** n.

orthography n. the conventional spelling system of a language. ■ **orthographic** adj.

orthopaedics (US **orthopedics**) n. the branch of medicine concerned with bones or muscles. ■ **orthopaedic** adj.

oscillate v. move or swing back and forth. ■ **oscillation** n.

osier /oh-zi-er/ n. a willow with long flexible shoots.

osmium n. a hard metallic element.

osmosis n. a process by which molecules pass through a membrane from a less concentrated solution into a more concentrated one. ■ **osmotic** adj.

osprey n. (pl. **ospreys**) a large fish-eating bird of prey.

osseous adj. consisting of or turned into bone.

ossify v. (**ossifying**, **ossified**) **1** turn into bone. **2** stop developing. ■ **ossification** n.

ostensible adj. apparently true, but not necessarily so. ■ **ostensibly** adv.

ostentation n. showy display intended to impress. ■ **ostentatious** adj. **ostentatiously** adv.

osteopathy n. a system of complementary medicine involving manipulation of bones and muscles. ■ **osteopath** n.

ostracize (or **-ise**) v. exclude from a society or group. ■ **ostracism** n.

ostrich n. a large flightless African bird.

other adj. & pron. **1** used to refer to a person or thing different from one already mentioned or known. **3** alternative of two. **4** those not already mentioned. □ **otherwise 1** in different circumstances. **2** in other respects. **3** in a different way.

otiose adj. serving no practical purpose.

Thesaurus

original adj. **1** ABORIGINAL, indigenous, early, earliest, first, primary, primordial, primal, primeval, primitive, autochthonous. **2** INNOVATIVE, innovatory, inventive, new, novel, fresh, creative, imaginative, individual, ingenious, unusual, unconventional, unorthodox, unprecedented, ground-breaking. ■ OPPOSITES unoriginal, derivative.

originate v. **1** ARISE, stem, spring, result, derive, start, begin, commence. **2** GIVE BIRTH TO, set in motion, set up, invent, dream up, conceive, discover, initiate, create, formulate, inaugurate, pioneer, introduce, establish, found, evolve, develop, generate.

ornament n. **1** KNICK-KNACK, trinket, bauble, gewgaw, accessory, decoration, frill, whatnot, doodah. **2** DECORATION, adornment, embellishment, trimming, garnish, garnishing.

ornamental adj. DECORATIVE, attractive, showy, embellishing, ornamenting.

ornate adj. ELABORATE, over-elaborate, decorated, embellished, adorned, ornamented, fancy, fussy, busy, ostentatious, showy, baroque, rococo; *informal*

flash. ■ OPPOSITES plain.

orthodox adj. **1** DOCTRINAL, of the faith, of the true faith, sound, conservative, correct, faithful, true, devoted, strict, devout. **2** CONVENTIONAL, accepted, approved, correct, proper, conformist, established, traditional, usual, regular. ■ OPPOSITES unconventional.

ostensible adj. APPARENT, seeming, professed, outward, alleged, claimed, purported, pretended, feigned, supposed. ■ OPPOSITES genuine.

ostentation n. SHOWINESS, show, conspicuousness, obtrusiveness, loudness, extravagance, flamboyance, gaudiness, flashiness, pretentiousness, affectation, exhibitionism; *informal* swank.

ostentatious adj. SHOWY, conspicuous, obtrusive, loud, extravagant, flamboyant, gaudy, flashy, pretentious, affected, overdone; *informal* flash, swanky. ■ OPPOSITES unobtrusive.

ostracize v. COLD-SHOULDER, give someone the cold shoulder, send to Coventry, exclude, shut out, shun, spurn, avoid, boycott, repudiate, cast out, reject, blackball, blacklist. ■ OPPOSITES

otter n. a fish-eating water mammal.

ottoman n. (pl. **ottomans**) a low padded seat without a back or arms.

ought aux. v. **1** expressing duty, advisability, or a desired state. **2** expressing probability.

Ouija board /wee-juh/ n. trademark a board marked with letters and signs, to which a pointer moves, supposedly in answer to questions at a seance.

ounce n. **1** a unit of weight of one sixteenth of a pound (approx. 28 g). **2** a very small amount.

our adj. of or belonging to us.

ours possess. pron. belonging to us.

ourselves pron. **1** the form of 'we' used when oneself and another person or people are the subject of the verb and are also affected by it. **2** we or us personally.

oust v. force from a position of power.

out adv. **1** moving away from a place. **2** away from one's home or place of work. **3** outdoors. **4** so as to be revealed, heard, or known. **5** at or to an end. **6** so as to be extinguished. **7** away from the land. ▸ adj. **1** not possible. **2** unconscious. **3** (of the ball in tennis etc.) not in the playing area. ▸ v. informal reveal the homosexuality of. □ **out and out** absolute. **out of date** no longer current, valid, or fashionable.

outback n. the remote, sparsely populated part of Australia.

outboard adj. (of a motor) attached to the outside of a boat.

outbreak n. a sudden or violent occurrence of war, disease, etc.

outbuilding n. a smaller building in the grounds of a main building.

outburst n. a sudden release of strong emotion.

outcast n. a person rejected by their society or social group.

outclass v. be far better than.

outcome n. a consequence.

outcrop n. a part of a rock formation visible on the surface.

outcry n. (pl. **outcries**) a strong expression of public disapproval.

outdistance v. leave a pursuer far behind.

outdo v. (**outdoes**, **outdoing**, **outdid**; past part. **outdone**) do better than.

outdoor adj. done, situated, or used in the open air. ■ **outdoors** adv.

outer adj. **1** outside. **2** further from the centre or the inside. ■ **outermost** adj.

outface v. defeat someone by confronting them boldly.

outfit n. a set of clothes worn together.

outflank v. **1** move round the side of an enemy. **2** outwit.

outgoing adj. **1** friendly and confident. **2** leaving a job or position. ▸ n. (**outgoings**) regular expenditure.

outgrow v. (**outgrowing**, **outgrew**; past part. **outgrown**) **1** grow too big for. **2** leave behind or cease to be interested in as one matures.

outhouse n. a smaller building attached or close to a house.

outing n. a short trip taken for pleasure.

outlandish adj. strange or unfamiliar.

outlast v. last longer than.

outlaw n. a person who has broken the law and remains at large. ▸ v. make illegal.

outlay n. an amount of money spent.

outlet n. **1** a pipe or hole for water or gas to escape. **2** a point from which goods are sold. **3** a means of expressing

Thesaurus

welcome.

other adj. **1** DIFFERENT, unlike, variant, dissimilar, distinct, separate, alternative. **2** MORE, additional, further, extra.

outbreak n. ERUPTION, flare-up, upsurge, outburst, start, rash.

outburst n. BURST, explosion, eruption, outbreak, flare-up, attack, fit, spasm, paroxysm.

outcome n. RESULT, upshot, issue, product, conclusion, after-effect, aftermath, wake; informal pay-off.

outdated adj. OUT OF DATE, out of fashion, old-fashioned, unfashionable, outmoded, dated, passé, behind the times, antiquated, archaic, obsolete. ■ OPPOSITES modern.

outdo v. SURPASS, top, exceed, excel, get the better of, outstrip, outshine, eclipse, overshadow, outclass, overcome, beat, defeat.

outer adj. **1** OUTSIDE, outermost, outward, exterior, external, surface, superficial. **2** OUTLYING, distant, remote, faraway, peripheral, fringe, perimeter. ■ OPPOSITES inner.

outgoing adj. **1** EXTROVERT, demonstrative, affectionate, warm, friendly, genial, cordial, affable, communicative, sociable, open, expansive, talkative, gregarious, approachable. **2** RETIRING, departing, withdrawing, ex-, former. ■ OPPOSITES reserved, incoming.

outlandish adj. STRANGE, unfamiliar, unknown, unheard of, odd, unusual, extraordinary, peculiar, queer, curious, one's energy, emotions, etc.

outline n. **1** a sketch or diagram showing the shape of an object. **2** the outer edges of an object. **3** a summary. ▶v. **1** draw the outer edge or shape of. **2** summarize.

outlook n. **1** a person's attitude to life. **2** a view. **3** what is likely to happen in the future.

outlying adj. situated far from a centre.

outmoded adj. old-fashioned.

outnumber v. be more numerous than.

outpace v. go faster than.

outpatient n. a patient attending a hospital for treatment without staying overnight.

outpost n. **1** a small military camp at a distance from the main army. **2** a remote settlement.

output n. the amount of power, energy, work, etc. produced. ▶v. (**outputting, output** or **outputted**) (of a computer) produce data.

outrage n. **1** extreme shock and anger. **2** a very cruel, wicked, or shocking act. ▶v. cause to feel outrage.

outrageous adj. **1** shockingly bad or excessive. **2** very bold and unusual. ■ **outrageously** adv.

outré /oo-tray/ adj. unusual and rather shocking.

outrider n. a person in a vehicle or on horseback escorting another vehicle.

outrigger n. a float fixed parallel to a canoe or small ship to aid stability.

outright adv. **1** totally. **2** openly. **3** immediately. ▶adj. **1** open and direct. **2** complete.

outrun v. (**outrunning, outran**; past part. **outrun**) run faster or further than.

outset n. the beginning.

outside n. the external side, part, or surface. ▶adj. **1** on or near the outside. **2** not of or from a particular group. ▶prep. & adv. **1** situated or moving beyond the boundaries of. **2** not being a member of. □ **an outside chance** a remote possibility.

outsider n. **1** a person who does not belong to a particular group. **2** a competitor thought to have little chance of success.

outsize adj. very large.

outskirts pl. n. the outer parts of a town or city.

outsource v. arrange for work to be done outside a company.

outspoken adj. very frank.

outstanding adj. **1** very good. **2** clearly noticeable. **3** not yet dealt with or paid. ■ **outstandingly** adv.

outstrip v. (**outstripping, outstripped**)

Thesaurus

singular, eccentric, quaint, bizarre, grotesque, preposterous, weird; *informal* freaky, wacky, far out, off-the-wall. ■ OPPOSITES ordinary.

outline n. **1** THUMBNAIL SKETCH, rough idea, quick rundown, abbreviated version, summary, synopsis, main points, bones, bare bones. **2** CONTOUR, silhouette, profile, lineaments, delineation, configuration, perimeter, circumference.

outlook n. **1** POINT OF VIEW, viewpoint, view, perspective, attitude, frame of mind, standpoint, slant, angle, interpretation, opinion. **2** VISTA, view, prospect, panorama, aspect.

outlying adj. OUTER, outermost, out of the way, remote, distant, far-flung, peripheral, isolated, inaccessible, off the beaten track.

output n. PRODUCTION, product, productivity, yield, harvest, crop.

outrage n. **1** ATROCITY, crime, horror, enormity, brutality. **2** OFFENCE, affront, insult, injury, abuse, scandal, desecration, violation. **3** ANGER, fury, rage, indignation, wrath, annoyance, shock, resentment, horror.

outrageous adj. **1** INTOLERABLE, insufferable, insupportable, unendurable, unbearable, impossible, exasperating, offensive, maddening, distressing. **2** ATROCIOUS, heinous, abominable, wicked, vile, foul, monstrous, horrible, horrid, dreadful, terrible, horrendous, hideous, ghastly, unspeakable, gruesome.

outside adj. **1** OUTER, outermost, outward, exterior, external. **2** OUTDOOR, out of doors. **3** UNLIKELY, improbable, slight, slender, slim, small, faint, negligible, marginal, remote, distant, vague. ■ OPPOSITES inside.

outsider n. ALIEN, stranger, foreigner, outlander, immigrant, incomer, newcomer, parvenu/parvenue, arriviste, interloper, intruder, gatecrasher, outcast, misfit.

outskirts pl. n. VICINITY, neighbourhood, environs, outlying districts, fringes, margin, periphery, borders, boundary, suburbs.

outspoken adj. CANDID, frank, forthright, direct, straightforward, plainspoken, explicit, blunt. ■ OPPOSITES diplomatic.

1 move faster than and overtake. **2** surpass.

outvote v. defeat by gaining more votes.

outward adj. & adv. **1** on or from the outside. **2** out or away from a place. ■ **outwardly** adv. **outwards** adv.

outweigh v. be greater or more important than.

outwit v. (**outwitting**, **outwitted**) defeat by cunning or ingenuity.

ova pl. of **ovum**.

oval adj. having a rounded and slightly elongated outline. ▶ n. an oval object or shape.

ovary n. (pl. **ovaries**) **1** a female reproductive organ in which eggs are produced. **2** the base of the reproductive organ of a flower. ■ **ovarian** adj.

ovate adj. oval.

ovation n. a long, enthusiastic round of applause.

oven n. an enclosed compartment in which things are cooked or heated.

over prep. **1** extending upwards from or above. **2** so as to cover or protect. **3** expressing movement across. **4** beyond and falling or hanging from. **5** expressing length of time. **6** higher or more than. **7** expressing authority or control. ▶ adv. **1** expressing movement across an area. **2** beyond and falling or hanging from a point. **3** finished. **4** repeatedly. ▶ n. Cricket a sequence of six balls bowled from one end of the pitch.

over- prefix **1** excessively. **2** over; above.

overall adj. & adv. including everything; taken as a whole. ▶ n. (also **overalls**) a loose-fitting garment worn over ordinary clothes for protection.

overarm adj. & adv. (of an arm action) made with the hand brought forward and down from above shoulder level.

overawe v. impress someone so much

that they are silent or nervous.

overbalance v. fall due to loss of balance.

overbearing adj. unpleasantly overpowering.

overblown adj. pretentious.

overboard adv. from a ship into the water. ▢ **go overboard** be very or too enthusiastic.

overcast adj. cloudy.

overcharge v. charge too high a price.

overcoat n. a long, warm coat.

overcome v. (**overcoming**, **overcame**; past part. **overcome**) **1** succeed in dealing with a problem. **2** defeat. **3** (**be overcome**) be overwhelmed by an emotion.

overdo v. (**overdoes**, **overdoing**, **overdid**; past part. **overdone**) **1** do excessively or in an exaggerated way. **2** use too much of. **3** cook for too long.

overdose n. a dangerously large dose of a drug. ▶ v. take an overdose.

overdraft n. an arrangement with a bank allowing one to take out more money than one's account holds.

overdrawn adj. (of a bank account) having had more money taken out of it than it holds.

overdrive n. **1** a mechanism providing an extra gear above top gear. **2** a state of great activity.

overdue adj. not having arrived, happened, or been done by the expected or required time.

overestimate v. form too high an estimate of. ▶ n. an estimate which is too high.

overflow v. **1** flow over the edge of a container. **2** be too full or crowded. ▶ n. **1** an excess or surplus. **2** an outlet for excess water.

overgrown adj. **1** covered with weeds.

Thesaurus

outstanding adj. **1** EXCELLENT, remarkable, exceptional, superlative, preeminent, eminent, well known, notable, noteworthy, distinguished, important, famous, famed, renowned, celebrated, great. **2** UNPAID, unsettled, owing, due. ■ OPPOSITES unexceptional.

outwardly adv. **1** EXTERNALLY, on the outside. **2** ON THE SURFACE, superficially, on the face of it, to all appearances, as far as one can see, to all intents and purposes, apparently, evidently.

outwit v. GET THE BETTER OF, be cleverer than, outsmart, outmanoeuvre, steal a march on, trick, dupe, make a fool of; informal put one over on, pull a fast one on.

overall adj. COMPREHENSIVE, universal, all-embracing, inclusive, all-inclusive, general, sweeping, complete, blanket, umbrella, global. ▶ adv. ON THE WHOLE, in general, generally speaking.

overawe v. INTIMIDATE, daunt, disconcert, abash, dismay, frighten, alarm, scare, terrify, terrorize.

overcome v. CONQUER, defeat, vanquish, beat, prevail over, get the better of, triumph over, best, worst, trounce, rout, master, overpower, overwhelm, overthrow, subdue, subjugate, quell, quash, crush; informal thrash, lick, clobber, whip. ▶ adj. OVERWHELMED, emotional, moved, affected, speechless, at a loss for

2 grown too large.

overhaul v. **1** examine and repair. **2** overtake. ▶n. an act of examining and repairing.

overhead adv. & adj. above one's head. ▶n. (**overheads**) expenses incurred in running a business etc.

overhear v. (**overhearing**, **overheard**) hear accidentally.

overjoyed adj. very happy.

overkill n. too much of something.

overland adj. & adv. by land.

overlap v. (**overlapping**, **overlapped**) **1** extend over so as to partly cover. **2** partly coincide in time. ▶n. an overlapping part or amount.

overleaf adv. on the other side of the page.

overload v. **1** load too heavily. **2** put too great a demand on. ▶n. an excessive amount.

overlook v. **1** fail to notice. **2** ignore a fault. **3** have a view of from above.

overly adv. excessively.

overnight adv. & adj. during or for a night.

overpass n. a bridge by which a road crosses another.

overpower v. **1** defeat with greater strength. **2** overwhelm.

overrate v. rate more highly than is deserved.

overreach v. (**overreach oneself**) fail through being too ambitious.

overreact v. react more strongly than is justified. ■ **overreaction** n.

override v. (**overriding**, **overrode**; past part. **overridden**) **1** overrule. **2** interrupt the action of an automatic device. **3** be more important than.

overrule v. reject or disallow by using one's higher authority.

overrun v. (**overrunning**, **overran**; past part. **overrun**) **1** spread over or occupy in large numbers. **2** exceed a limit.

overseas adv. & adj. in or to a foreign country.

oversee v. (**overseeing**, **oversaw**; past part. **overseen**) supervise. ■ **overseer** n.

overshadow v. **1** cast a shadow over. **2** appear more important or successful than.

overshoot v. (**overshooting**, **overshot**) go past an intended place or limit.

oversight n. an unintentional failure to notice or do something.

overspill n. people who move from an overcrowded area to live elsewhere.

oversteer v. (of a car) tend to turn more sharply than intended.

overstep v. (**overstepping**, **overstepped**) go beyond a limit.

overt adj. done or shown openly. ■ **overtly** adv.

overtake v. (**overtaking**, **overtook**; past part. **overtaken**) **1** catch up with and pass while travelling in the same direction. **2** suddenly affect.

overthrow v. (**overthrowing**, **overthrew**; past part. **overthrown**) remove from power by force. ▶n. a removal from power.

overtime n. time worked in addition to normal working hours.

overtone n. a subtle or additional quality or implication.

overture n. **1** an orchestral piece at the beginning of a musical work. **2** an approach towards opening negotiations or establishing a relationship.

overturn v. **1** turn over and come to rest upside down, or cause do this.

Thesaurus

words; informal bowled over.

overdue adj. **1** LATE, behind schedule, delayed, belated, tardy, unpunctual. **2** UNPAID, owed, owing, outstanding, unsettled, in arrears.

overflow v. FLOW OVER, run over, spill over, brim over, well over, pour forth, stream forth, discharge, surge, debouch.

overhead adv. ABOVE, up above, high up, up in the sky, on high, aloft.

overlook v. **1** FAIL TO NOTICE, miss, leave, neglect; informal slip up on. **2** LEAVE UNDONE, ignore, disregard, omit, neglect, forget. **3** LOOK OVER, look on to, front on to, have/afford a view of, command a view of.

overpowering adj. OVERWHELMING, burdensome, weighty, unbearable, unendurable, intolerable, shattering; informal mind-blowing.

overriding adj. MOST IMPORTANT, predominant, principal, primary, paramount, chief, main, major, foremost, central.

oversight n. **1** CARELESSNESS, inattention, neglect, inadvertence, laxity, dereliction, omission. **2** MISTAKE, error, slip, blunder, gaffe, fault, omission, lapse.

overt adj. OBVIOUS, noticeable, undisguised, unconcealed, apparent, plain, manifest, patent, open, public, blatant, conspicuous. ■ OPPOSITES covert.

overtake v. PASS, get past, go past, go by, overhaul, leave behind, outstrip, go

2 abolish or reverse a decision, system, etc.

overview n. a general review.

overweening adj. showing too much confidence or pride.

overwhelm v. **1** bury beneath a huge mass. **2** overpower. **3** have a strong emotional effect on.

overwrought adj. very worried or nervously excited.

oviduct n. the tube through which an ovum passes from an ovary.

oviparous adj. egg-laying.

ovoid adj. egg-shaped.

ovulate v. discharge ova from the ovary. ■ **ovulation** n.

ovule n. the part of the ovary of a plant that after fertilization becomes the seed.

ovum n. (pl. **ova**) a female reproductive cell, which can develop into an embryo if fertilized by a male cell.

owe v. (**owing, owed**) **1** be required to pay or repay money etc. in return for something received. **2** have something because of: *I owe him my life.*

owing adj. yet to be paid. □ **owing to** because of.

owl n. a bird of prey with large eyes, active at night. ■ **owlish** adj.

own adj. & pron. belonging to or done by the person specified. ▶ v. **1** possess.

2 admit to be the case. **3** (**own up**) confess to a wrongdoing. ■ **owner** n. **ownership** n.

ox n. (pl. **oxen**) **1** a cow or bull. **2** a castrated bull, used for pulling heavy loads.

oxide n. a compound of oxygen and another element.

oxidize (or **-ise**) v. combine with oxygen. ■ **oxidation** n. **oxidization** n.

oxyacetylene adj. (of welding or cutting) using a very hot flame produced by mixing acetylene and oxygen.

oxygen n. a gaseous element forming about 20 per cent of the earth's atmosphere and essential to life.

oxygenate v. supply or treat with oxygen.

oxymoron n. a figure of speech in which apparently contradictory terms appear together (e.g. *a deafening silence*).

oyster n. an edible shellfish. □ **oystercatcher** a wading bird.

oz abbrev. ounces.

ozone n. a strong-smelling, poisonous form of oxygen. □ **ozone hole** an area of the ozone layer where the ozone is greatly reduced. **ozone layer** a layer in the earth's stratosphere containing much ozone, absorbing ultraviolet radiation.

Thesaurus

faster than.

overthrow v. *see* OVERCOME.

overtone n. IMPLICATION, innuendo, hint, suggestion, insinuation, association, connotation, undercurrent, nuance.

overwhelm v. **1** OVERCOME, move, make emotional, daze, dumbfound, shake, take aback, leave speechless, stagger. **2** INUNDATE, flood, deluge, engulf, submerge, swamp, bury, overload, overbur-

den, snow under.

overwhelming adj. **1** UNCONTROLLABLE, irrepressible, irresistible, overpowering. **2** VAST, massive, great, large.

owe v. BE IN DEBT, be indebted, be under an obligation, be obligated, be beholden.

own v. POSSESS, have in one's possession, have, keep, retain, maintain, hold, enjoy. □ **own up** *see* CONFESS.

Pp

p abbrev. **1** page. **2** penny or pence.

PA abbrev. **1** personal assistant. **2** public address.

p.a. abbrev. per annum.

pace n. **1** a single step when walking or running. **2** rate of movement or change. ▶v. **1** walk steadily or to and fro. **2** measure a distance by pacing. **3** (**pace oneself**) do something at a controlled and steady rate. □ **pacemaker 1** an artificial device for regulating the heart muscle. **2** a runner who sets the pace for another.

pachyderm /pak-i-derm/ n. a large thick-skinned mammal, e.g. an elephant.

pacific adj. peaceful.

pacifism n. the belief that disputes should be settled without the use of war and violence. ∎ **pacifist** n. & adj.

pacify v. (**pacifying, pacified**) **1** make less angry or upset. **2** establish peace in a country. ∎ **pacification** n.

pack n. **1** a cardboard or paper container and the items in it. **2** a set of playing cards. **3** a group of dogs or wolves. ▶v. **1** fill a bag with items needed for travel. **2** put or cram items into a container. **3** cover or surround with something crammed tightly. □ **pack in** informal stop doing. **pack off** informal send away. ∎ **packer** n.

package n. **1** something wrapped in paper or packed in a box. **2** a set of proposals offered or agreed as a whole. ▶v. **1** put into a box or wrapping. **2** present in an attractive way. □ **package holiday** a holiday whose price covers transport and accommodation.

packet n. **1** a small container or plastic bag in which goods are packed. **2** (**a packet**) informal a large sum of money.

pact n. a formal agreement.

pad n. **1** a piece of soft or absorbent material. **2** the fleshy underpart of an animal's foot. **3** a number of sheets of blank paper fastened together at one edge. **4** a flat surface for helicopter take-off and landing or for rocket-launching. ▶v. (**padding, padded**) **1** fill or cover with a pad. **2** lengthen a speech etc. with unnecessary material. **3** walk with soft, steady steps.

padding n. soft material used to pad or stuff something.

paddle n. a short oar with a broad blade. ▶v. **1** propel with a paddle. **2** walk with bare feet in shallow water.

paddock n. a small field or enclosure for horses.

padlock n. a detachable lock hanging by a hinged hook through a ring on the object fastened. ▶v. secure with a padlock.

padre /pah-dray/ n. a chaplain in the armed services.

paean /pee-uhn/ n. a song of praise or triumph.

paediatrics /pee-di-at-riks/ (US **pediatrics**) n. the branch of medicine concerned with children's diseases. ∎ **paediatric** adj. **paediatrician** n.

paedophile /pee-duh-fyl/ (US **pedophile**) n. a person who is sexually attracted to children. ∎ **paedophilia** n.

paella /py-el-uh/ n. a Spanish dish of rice, seafood, etc.

pagan n. a person holding religious be-

Thesaurus

pace n. **1** STEP, stride. **2** GAIT, walk, tread. **3** SPEED, swiftness, fastness, quickness, rapidity, velocity.

pacify v. CALM DOWN, placate, conciliate, propitiate, appease, mollify, soothe, tranquillize, quieten. ∎ OPPOSITES enrage.

pack n. **1** PACKET, container, package, carton. **2** BACKPACK, rucksack, knapsack, kitbag, satchel. ▶v. **1** FILL, store, stow, load, bundle, stuff, cram. **2** FILL, crowd, throng, mob, cram, jam, press

into, squeeze into.

packed adj. FULL, filled to capacity, crowded, thronged, mobbed, crammed, jammed, brimful, chock-full, chock-a-block, jam-packed.

pact n. AGREEMENT, treaty, deal, contract, settlement, bargain, compact, covenant, bond, concordat, entente.

pad n. **1** PADDING, wadding, stuffing, buffer. **2** CUSHION, pillow, bolster. **3** NOTEPAD, writing pad, notebook, jotter, memo pad. ▶v. PACK, stuff, fill, line, liefs other than those of established religions. ▸ adj. of pagans or their beliefs. ■ **paganism** n.

page n. **1** a leaf of a book etc. **2** one side of this. **3** a young male attendant in a hotel. **4** a young boy attending a bride. **5** hist. a boy in training for knighthood. ▸v. **1** (**page through**) leaf through. **2** summon over a public address system or by a pager.

pageant /paj-uhnt/ n. a public entertainment performed in elaborate or historical costumes. ■ **pageantry** n.

pager n. a radio device that bleeps or vibrates to summon the wearer.

pagoda n. a Hindu or Buddhist temple or other sacred building.

paid past & past part. of **PAY**.

pail n. a bucket.

pain n. **1** strong physical discomfort caused by illness or injury. **2** mental suffering. **3** (**pains**) great care or trouble. ▸v. cause pain to. □ **painkiller** a medicine for relieving pain. ■ **painful** adj. **painfully** adv. **painless** adj. **painlessly** adv.

painstaking adj. very careful and thorough.

paint n. a coloured substance spread over a surface to give a decorative or protective coating. ▸v. **1** apply paint to. **2** apply a liquid to a surface with a brush. **3** produce a picture with paint.

4 describe. ■ **painting** n.

painter n. **1** a person who paints as an artist or decorator. **2** a rope attached to a boat's bow for tying it up.

pair n. **1** a set of two things or people. **2** an article consisting of two parts: *a pair of scissors*. ▸v. **1** connect to form a pair. **2** (**pair off/up**) form a couple.

paisley n. an intricate pattern of curved shapes like feathers.

pajamas US = **PYJAMAS**.

pal n. informal a friend.

palace n. an official residence of a monarch, archbishop, etc.

palaeography /pa-li-*og*-ruh-fi/ (US **paleography**) n. the study of ancient writing and manuscripts.

Palaeolithic /pa-li-uh-**li**-thik/ (US **Paleolithic**) adj. of the early phase of the Stone Age.

palaeontology /pa-li-on-**tol**-uh-ji/ (US **paleontology**) n. the study of fossil animals and plants. ■ **palaeontologist** n.

palatable adj. **1** pleasant to taste. **2** acceptable.

palate n. **1** the roof of the mouth. **2** the sense of taste.

palatial /puh-**lay**-sh'l/ adj. of or like a palace; grand.

palaver n. informal a lengthy, boring fuss.

pale adj. **1** light in colour. **2** (of the face) having less colour than normal. ▸v.

Thesaurus

cushion, protect.

paddle v. ROW, pull, oar, scull, pole, punt.

paddock n. FIELD, meadow, enclosure, yard, pen, pound, corral.

pagan n. UNBELIEVER, heathen, infidel, idolater, pantheist, polytheist. ▸ adj. HEATHEN, infidel, idolatrous, pantheistic, polytheistic.

pageantry n. SPECTACLE, magnificence, pomp, splendour, grandeur, glamour, theatricality, show, showiness; informal pizzazz.

pain n. **1** SORENESS, hurt, ache, aching, agony, throb, throbbing, smarting, twinge, pang, spasm, cramp, discomfort, irritation, tenderness. **2** SUFFERING, hurt, sorrow, grief, heartache, sadness, unhappiness, distress, misery, wretchedness, anguish, affliction, woe.

pained adj. HURT, aggrieved, reproachful, offended, insulted, upset, unhappy, distressed; informal miffed.

painful adj. **1** SORE, hurting, aching, throbbing, smarting, tender, inflamed, agonizing, excruciating. **2** DISAGREEABLE,

unpleasant, nasty, distressing, disquieting, disturbing, miserable, wretched, agonizing, harrowing.

painless adj. **1** PAIN-FREE, without pain. **2** EASY, simple, trouble-free, effortless, plain sailing; informal as easy as pie, as easy as falling off a log, child's play, a cinch. ■ OPPOSITES painful, difficult.

painstaking adj. CAREFUL, thorough, assiduous, conscientious, meticulous, punctilious, sedulous, scrupulous. ■ OPPOSITES careless.

painting n. PICTURE, illustration, portrayal, depiction, delineation, representation, likeness.

pair n. COUPLE, duo, brace, two, twosome, matched set, matching set. □ **pair off** ARRANGE/GROUP IN PAIRS, pair up, put together, get together, join up, link up, team up.

palatable adj. **1** TASTY, appetizing, pleasant-tasting, flavoursome, delicious, mouth-watering, savoury; informal scrumptious, yummy. **2** AGREEABLE, pleasant, pleasing, pleasurable, nice, attractive, acceptable, satisfactory.

1 become pale. **2** seem less important. □ **beyond the pale** outside the bounds of acceptable behaviour.

palette n. **1** a board on which an artist mixes paints. **2** a range of colours used. □ **palette knife** a knife with a blunt, flexible blade for applying paint or smoothing soft substances.

palindrome n. a word or phrase that reads the same backwards as forwards.

paling n. **1** a fence made from stakes. **2** a stake.

palisade n. a fence of stakes or iron railings.

pall /pawl/ n. **1** a cloth spread over a coffin. **2** a dark cloud of smoke, dust, etc. ▶v. become less appealing through familiarity. □ **pall-bearer** a person helping to carry or escorting a coffin at a funeral.

palladium n. a rare metallic element.

pallet n. **1** a straw mattress or makeshift bed. **2** a portable platform on which goods can be moved or stacked.

palliate v. **1** make the symptoms of a disease less severe. **2** make something bad less serious. ■ **palliative** adj.

pallid adj. pale, esp. from illness. ■ **pallor** n.

pally adj. informal friendly.

palm n. **1** an evergreen tree of warm regions, with a crown of long leaves. **2** the inner surface of the hand. ▶v. **1** hide in the hand. **2** (**palm off**) informal persuade someone to accept something by deception. □ **palmtop** a computer small enough to be held in one hand.

palmistry n. the prediction of a person's future by examining their hand. ■ **palmist** n.

palomino n. (pl. **palominos**) a pale golden horse with a white mane and tail.

palpable adj. able to be touched or felt. ■ **palpably** adv.

palpate v. medically examine by touch.

palpitate v. **1** (of the heart) beat rapidly. **2** shake; tremble. ■ **palpitation** n.

palsy n. (pl. **palsies**) dated paralysis. ■ **palsied** adj.

paltry adj. **1** (of an amount) very small. **2** trivial.

pampas n. vast treeless plains in South America.

pamper v. treat very indulgently.

pamphlet n. a small booklet or leaflet.

pamphleteer n. a writer of pamphlets.

pan n. **1** a metal container for cooking food in. **2** the bowl of a toilet. ▶v. (**panning**, **panned**) **1** informal criticize severely. **2** swing a film camera to give a panoramic effect or follow a subject. **3** wash gravel in a bowl to separate out gold.

pan- comb. form all or whole.

panacea /pan-uh-**see**-uh/ n. a solution or remedy for all difficulties or diseases.

panache /puh-**nash**/ n. a confident stylish manner.

panama n. a straw hat.

pancake n. a thin, flat cake of fried batter.

pancreas n. a gland behind the stomach producing insulin. ■ **pancreatic** adj.

panda n. a large black and white bear-like mammal.

pandemic adj. (of a disease) occurring over a whole country or a wide area.

pandemonium n. uproar.

pander v. (**pander to**) indulge an immoral or distasteful desire or habit.

pane n. a single sheet of glass in a window or door.

panegyric /pa-ni-**ji**-rik/ n. a speech or text in praise of someone or something.

panel n. **1** a section of a door, vehicle, garment, etc. **2** a small group assem-

Thesaurus

■ OPPOSITES unpalatable.

palatial adj. LUXURIOUS, imposing, splendid, grand, magnificent, stately, majestic, opulent, sumptuous, plush. ■ OPPOSITES humble.

pale adj. **1** WHITE, white-faced, colourless, anaemic, wan, drained, pallid, pasty, peaky, ashen, waxen, as white as a sheet/ghost, deathly pale. **2** LIGHT, pastel, muted, low-key, restrained, faded, bleached, washed out, etiolated. **3** DIM, faint, weak, feeble, thin. ■ OPPOSITES dark. ▶v. GROW/BECOME PALE, go/turn white, blanch, lose colour.

pallid adj. see PALE.

palpable adj. TANGIBLE, feelable, touchable, solid, concrete. ■ OPPOSITES intangible.

paltry adj. **1** SMALL, meagre, trifling, minor, insignificant, trivial, derisory; informal piddling, measly. **2** WORTHLESS, despicable, contemptible, miserable, wretched, sorry, puny. ■ OPPOSITES considerable.

pamper v. SPOIL, cosset, indulge, overindulge, humour, coddle, mollycoddle.

pamphlet n. LEAFLET, booklet, brochure, circular.

panache n. STYLE, verve, flamboyance,

bled to investigate or decide on a matter. ■ **panelled** (US **paneled**) adj. **panellist** (US **panelist**) n.

panelling (US **paneling**) n. wooden panels as a wall covering.

pang n. a sudden sharp pain or painful emotion.

panic n. **1** sudden uncontrollable fear. **2** a frenzied hurry to do something. ▶ v. (**panicking**, **panicked**) feel panic. ■ **panic-stricken** adj. **panicky** adj.

panjandrum n. a self-important official.

pannier n. **1** a bag fitted on the back of a bicycle or motorcycle. **2** a basket carried by a donkey etc.

panoply n. an impressive display.

panorama n. a view of a wide area or sequence of events. ■ **panoramic** adj.

pan pipes pl. n. a musical instrument made from a row of short pipes.

pansy n. **1** a plant with brightly coloured flowers. **2** offens. an effeminate or homosexual man.

pant v. breathe with short, quick breaths.

pantaloons pl. n. baggy trousers gathered at the ankles.

pantechnicon n. a large van for transporting furniture.

pantheism n. the belief that God is present in all things. ■ **pantheist** n. **pantheistic** adj.

pantheon n. **1** all the gods of a people or religion. **2** an ancient temple dedicated to all the gods.

panther n. a black leopard.

panties pl. n. informal women's underpants.

pantile n. a curved roof tile.

pantograph n. a device for copying a plan etc. on any scale.

pantomime n. a theatrical entertainment based on a fairy tale.

pantry n. (pl. **pantries**) a small room or cupboard for storing food, crockery, etc.

pants pl. n. **1** underpants or knickers. **2** US trousers.

pap n. **1** bland soft food suitable for babies or invalids. **2** undemanding reading matter or entertainment.

papacy n. (pl. **papacies**) the position or period of office of the pope.

papal adj. of the pope or papacy.

paparazzo /pa-puh-**rat**-zoh/ n. (pl. **paparazzi**) a freelance photographer who pursues celebrities to get photographs of them.

papaya /puh-**py**-uh/ n. a tropical fruit with orange flesh.

paper n. **1** material manufactured in thin sheets from wood pulp, used for writing on, wrapping, etc. **2** a document. **3** a newspaper. **4** an essay. **5** a set of examination questions. ▶ v. cover with wallpaper. □ **paperback** a book bound in flexible card. **paperweight** a small, heavy object for keeping loose papers in place. **paperwork** routine work involving written documents.

papier mâché /pa-pi-ay **mash**-ay/ n. a mixture of paper and glue that becomes hard when dry.

paprika n. a powdered spice made from red peppers.

papyrus n. (pl. **papyri** or **papyruses**) a material made in ancient Egypt from the stem of a water plant, used for writing or painting on.

par n. Golf the number of strokes required by a first-class player for a hole or course. □ **above** (or **below** or **under**) **par** above (or below) the usual or expected level. **on a par with** equal to.

parable n. a story told to illustrate a moral.

parabola n. a curve resembling the path of an object that is thrown into the air and falls back down. ■ **parabolic** adj.

paracetamol n. a drug used to reduce pain and fever.

parachute n. a cloth canopy used to slow the descent of a person or object dropping from a great height. ▶ v. drop by parachute. ■ **parachutist** n.

parade n. **1** a public procession. **2** a formal assembly of troops. **3** an ostentatious display. **4** a public square, promenade, or row of shops. ▶ v. **1** march in a parade. **2** display ostentatiously.

Thesaurus

zest, dash, flourish, brio, elan; informal pizzazz.

pander v. GRATIFY, indulge, humour, give in to, please, satisfy, cater for.

panic n. ALARM, fright, fear, terror, horror, agitation, hysteria. ▶ v. BE ALARMED, take fright, be terrified/horrified, be agitated, be hysterical, lose one's nerve, overreact.

panoramic adj. WIDE, extensive, sweeping, bird's-eye, comprehensive.

pant v. PUFF, huff and puff, blow, gasp, wheeze.

paper n. **1** NEWSPAPER, magazine, journal, gazette, broadsheet, tabloid; informal rag. **2** ESSAY, article, work, dissertation,

paradigm /pa-ruh-dym/ n. a typical example or model.

paradise n. **1** heaven. **2** a very pleasant or beautiful place or state.

paradox n. a statement that seems to contradict itself, but may in fact be true. ■ **paradoxical** adj. **paradoxically** adv.

paraffin n. a flammable substance obtained from petroleum or shale, used as fuel.

paragliding n. a sport in which a person glides with a wide parachute after jumping from or being hauled to a height.

paragon n. a model of excellence or of a particular quality.

paragraph n. a distinct section of a piece of writing, begun on a new line.

parakeet n. a small parrot.

parallax n. an apparent difference in an object's position when viewed from different points.

parallel adj. **1** (of lines or planes) side by side and having the same distance continuously between them. **2** existing at the same time or in a similar way. ▶n. **1** a person or thing similar to another. **2** a comparison. **3** a line of latitude. ▶v. (**paralleling, paralleled**) **1** be parallel to. **2** be similar to.

parallelogram n. a plane figure with four straight sides and opposite sides parallel.

paralyse (US **paralyze**) v. affect with paralysis.

paralysis n. (pl. **paralyses**) **1** the loss of the power of movement. **2** inability to act or function. ■ **paralytic** adj.

paramedic n. a person who is trained to do medical work but is not a fully qualified doctor.

parameter n. a limit defining the scope of a process or activity.

paramilitary adj. organized like a military force.

paramount adj. more important than anything else.

paramour n. old use a lover.

paranoia n. **1** a mental condition in which a person has delusions of persecution or grandeur. **2** unjustified mistrust of others. ■ **paranoid** adj.

paranormal adj. beyond the scope of scientific knowledge.

parapet n. a low wall along the edge of a bridge, balcony, etc.

paraphernalia n. miscellaneous equipment.

paraphrase v. express using different words. ▶n. a rewording of a passage.

paraplegia /pa-ruh-plee-juh/ n. paralysis of the legs and lower body. ■ **paraplegic** adj. & n.

parapsychology n. the study of mental phenomena such as telepathy or hypnosis.

paraquat n. a poisonous weedkiller.

parasite n. **1** an organism living in or on another. **2** a person living off others. ■ **parasitic** adj.

parasol n. a light umbrella used to give shade from the sun.

paratroops pl. n. troops trained to parachute into an attack. ■ **paratrooper** n.

parboil v. partly cook by boiling.

parcel n. **1** something wrapped in paper in order to be carried or sent by post. **2** a quantity or amount of something. ▶v. (**parcelling, parcelled**; US **parceling, parceled**) **1** wrap as a parcel. **2** divide into portions.

parched adj. **1** dried out through heat. **2** informal very thirsty.

parchment n. **1** hist. writing material made from animal skin. **2** paper treated to resemble this.

pardon n. **1** forgiveness. **2** a cancella-

Thesaurus

treatise, thesis, monograph, study, report.

parade n. PROCESSION, progression, cavalcade, spectacle, pageant, array. ▶v. **1** MARCH, go in columns, file by. **2** DISPLAY, show off, exhibit, show, demonstrate, make a show of, flaunt.

paradox n. CONTRADICTION, inconsistency, incongruity, anomaly, enigma, puzzle, absurdity, oxymoron.

paradoxical adj. SELF-CONTRADICTORY, inconsistent, incongruous, anomalous, enigmatic, puzzling, absurd.

parallel adj. **1** SIDE BY SIDE, equidistant, collateral. **2** SIMILAR, like, resembling,

analogous, comparable, equivalent, corresponding, matching. ▶n. COUNTERPART, equivalent, analogue, match, duplicate, equal. ▶v. BE SIMILAR TO, be like, resemble, be analogous to, correspond to, compare with, bear a resemblance to, be comparable/equivalent to.

paralyse v. IMMOBILIZE, numb, deaden, dull, incapacitate, debilitate, disable, cripple.

paralysis n. IMMOBILITY, powerlessness, lack of feeling, numbness, palsy, incapacity, debilitation; Medicine paresis.

parameter n. LIMIT, limitation, limiting factor, restriction, specification, guidetion of the punishment for an offence. ▶v. (**pardoning, pardoned**) **1** forgive. **2** give an offender a pardon. ■ **pardonable** adj.

pare v. **1** trim the edges of. **2** gradually reduce.

parent n. **1** a father or mother. **2** an organization owning or controlling subsidiary ones. ■ **parental** adj. **parenthood** n. **parenting** n.

parentage n. the identity and origins of one's parents.

parenthesis /puh-ren-thi-siss/ n. (pl. **parentheses**) **1** a word or phrase added as an explanation or aside. **2** (**parentheses**) a pair of round brackets (). ■ **parenthetic** adj. **parenthetical** adj.

pariah n. an outcast.

parietal bone n. either of two bones forming part of the skull.

parings pl. n. thin strips pared off something.

parish n. **1** a district with its own church and clergy. **2** the smallest unit of local government in rural areas. ■ **parishioner** n.

parity n. equality.

park n. **1** a large public garden in a town. **2** the enclosed land of a country house. **3** an area devoted to a specified purpose. **4** an area for parking vehicles. ▶v. stop and leave a vehicle temporarily.

parka n. a windproof hooded jacket.

Parkinson's disease n. a progressive disease causing trembling and muscular rigidity.

parky adj. informal chilly.

parlance n. a particular way of using words.

parley n. (pl. **parleys**) a meeting between enemies to settle a dispute. ▶v. (**parleying, parleyed**) hold a parley.

parliament n. an assembly making the laws in a country. ■ **parliamentarian** n. **parliamentary** adj.

parlour (US **parlor**) n. **1** dated a sitting room. **2** a shop providing particular goods or services.

parlous adj. precarious.

Parmesan n. a hard Italian cheese.

parochial adj. **1** of a parish. **2** having a narrow outlook. ■ **parochialism** n.

parody n. (pl. **parodies**) a piece of writing etc. that imitates the style of another so as to be amusing. ▶v. (**parodying, parodied**) produce a parody of.

parole n. the release of a prisoner before the end of their sentence, on the condition of good behaviour. ▶v. release on parole.

paroxysm n. a sudden attack or outburst.

parquet /par-kay/ n. flooring composed of wooden blocks arranged in a pattern.

parricide n. the killing of one's own parent.

parrot n. a tropical bird with a hooked bill, some kinds of which can copy human speech. ▶v. (**parroting, parroted**) repeat mechanically.

parry v. (**parrying, parried**) **1** ward off a weapon or blow. **2** evade a question.

parse v. analyse a sentence in terms of grammar.

parsimony n. extreme reluctance to spend money. ■ **parsimonious** adj.

parsley n. a herb with crinkly or flat leaves.

parsnip n. a long tapering cream-coloured root vegetable.

parson n. an Anglican parish priest.

parsonage n. a parson's house.

part n. **1** a piece combining with others to make up a whole. **2** some but not all of something. **3** an acting role. **4** a person's contribution to a situation. ▶v. **1** separate or be separated. **2** (**part with**) give up possession of. ▶adv. partly. □ **in good part** without taking offence. **part of speech** a category in which a word is placed according to its grammatical function, e.g. noun, verb,

Thesaurus

lines, framework.

parched adj. DRIED UP/OUT, dry, baked, burned, scorched, seared, desiccated, dehydrated, withered, shrivelled.

pardon n. **1** FORGIVENESS, forbearance, indulgence, clemency, lenience, leniency, mercy. **2** FREE PARDON, reprieve, release, acquittal, absolution, amnesty, exoneration, exculpation. ▶v. **1** EXCUSE, condone, let off. **2** REPRIEVE, release, acquit, absolve, exonerate, exculpate.

pardonable adj. FORGIVABLE, excusable,

allowable, condonable, understandable, minor, slight, venial. ■ OPPOSITES inexcusable.

parentage n. FAMILY, birth, origins, extraction, ancestry, lineage, descent, heritage, pedigree.

parliament n. LEGISLATIVE ASSEMBLY, congress, senate, chamber, house, convocation, diet.

parody n. LAMPOON, spoof, send-up, satire, pastiche, caricature, mimicry, take-off, burlesque. ▶v. LAMPOON, satir-

partake v. (**partaking**, **partook**; past part. **partaken**) **1** (**partake in**) participate in. **2** (**partake of**) eat or drink.

partial adj. **1** not complete or whole. **2** favouring one side in a dispute. **3** (**partial to**) having a liking for. ■ **partiality** n. **partially** adv.

participate v. take part. ■ **participant** n. **participation** n.

participle n. a word formed from a verb (e.g. *burning*, *burnt*) and used in compound tenses or as an adjective or noun. ■ **participial** adj.

particle n. a tiny portion of matter.

particular adj. **1** of an individual member of a group or class. **2** more than is usual. **3** very careful or concerned about something. ▶ n. a detail. □ **in particular** especially. ■ **particularly** adv.

parting n. **1** an act of leaving someone. **2** a line of scalp visible when the hair is combed in different directions.

partisan n. **1** a strong supporter. **2** a guerrilla. ▶ adj. prejudiced.

partition n. **1** a structure dividing a space or room. **2** division into parts. ▶ v. divide into parts or with a partition.

partly adv. to some extent.

partner n. **1** each of two or more people who are involved in an undertaking. **2** either of two people doing something as a pair. **3** either member of a couple having a sexual or romantic relationship. ▶ v. be the partner of. ■ **partnership** n.

partook past of PARTAKE.

partridge n. a game bird.

parturition n. the act of giving birth.

party n. (pl. **parties**) **1** a social gathering. **2** an organized political group. **3** a group taking part in an activity or trip. **4** one side in an agreement or dispute. □ **party line** a policy officially adopted by a political party. **party wall** a wall shared by two adjoining buildings or rooms.

parvenu n. derog. a person who has recently become wealthy or famous.

pascal n. a unit of pressure.

paschal /pass-kuhl/ adj. **1** of Easter.

Thesaurus

ize, caricature, mimic, take off, send up, burlesque.

parry v. WARD OFF, fend off, stave off, turn aside, avert, deflect, block, rebuff, repel, repulse, hold at bay.

part n. **1** PORTION, division, section, segment, bit, piece, fragment, scrap, slice, fraction, chunk. **2** SECTION, area, region, sector, quarter, territory, neighbourhood. **3** FUNCTION, role, job, task, work, responsibility, capacity, participation. **4** ROLE, character. ▶ v. **1** DIVIDE, separate, split, break up, sever, disjoin. **2** LEAVE, go away, say goodbye, say one's goodbyes, separate; *informal* split, push off, hit the road.

partial adj. **1** PART, in part, limited, incomplete, imperfect, fragmentary. **2** BIASED, prejudiced, partisan, one-sided, discriminatory, preferential, unjust, unfair. ■ OPPOSITES complete, impartial. □ **be partial to** see LIKE¹ (2).

participate v. TAKE PART IN, join in, engage in, play a part in, contribute to, be involved in, share in, have a hand in.

participation n. PART, contribution, association, involvement, partaking.

particle n. **1** BIT, piece, speck, spot, atom, molecule. **2** IOTA, jot, whit, grain, bit, scrap, shred, morsel, atom, hint, touch, trace, suggestion.

particular adj. **1** SPECIFIC, individual,

single, distinct, precise. **2** SPECIAL, especial, singular, peculiar, exceptional, unusual, uncommon, notable, noteworthy, remarkable. **3** FASTIDIOUS, discriminating, selective, fussy, painstaking, meticulous, punctilious, demanding, critical, finicky; *informal* pernickety, choosy, picky. ■ OPPOSITES general, careless.

particularly adv. **1** ESPECIALLY, specially, singularly, peculiarly, distinctly, markedly, exceptionally, unusually, amazingly, uncommonly. **2** IN PARTICULAR, specifically, explicitly, expressly, specially, especially.

partisan n. **1** GUERRILLA, resistance fighter, underground fighter. **2** SUPPORTER, adherent, devotee, backer, follower, disciple. ▶ adj. *see* PARTIAL (2).

partition v. DIVIDE, divide up, subdivide, separate, separate off, screen off, wall off, fence off.

partly adv. IN PART, partially, not wholly, not fully, half, somewhat, to some extent/degree, in some measure, fractionally, slightly. ■ OPPOSITES completely.

partnership n. **1** ASSOCIATION, cooperation, collaboration, alliance, union, affiliation, fellowship, companionship. **2** COLLABORATION, collusion, connivance, conspiracy.

party n. **1** GATHERING, function, reception,

2 of Passover.

pass v. **1** move or go onward, past, through, or across. **2** change from one state to another. **3** transfer. **4** kick, hit, or throw the ball to a teammate. **5** (of time) go by. **6** spend time. **7** be successful in an examination. **8** declare to be satisfactory. **9** approve a proposal etc. by voting. ▶ n. **1** an act of passing. **2** a success in an examination. **3** a permit to enter a place. **4** a route over or through mountains. **5** informal a sexual advance. □ **pass away** die. **pass off as** pretend that something is something else. **pass out** become unconscious. **pass up** refrain from taking an opportunity. **password** a secret word or phrase used to gain admission.

passable adj. **1** just satisfactory. **2** able to be travelled along or on. ■ **passably** adv.

passage n. **1** the act of passing. **2** a way through something. **3** a journey by sea. **4** the right to pass through. **5** a short section from a text etc. □ **passageway** a corridor or walled access between buildings or rooms.

passé /pass-ay/ adj. old-fashioned.

passenger n. a person travelling in a vehicle, ship, or aircraft, other than the driver, pilot, or crew.

passer-by n. (pl. **passers-by**) a person who happens to be walking past something or someone.

passim adv. at various places throughout a text.

passing adj. done quickly and casually.

passion n. **1** very strong emotion. **2** intense sexual love. **3** great enthusiasm. **4** (**the Passion**) the suffering and death of Jesus on the cross. ■ **passionate** adj. **passionately** adv.

passive adj. **1** accepting what happens without resistance. **2** (of a verb) in which the subject undergoes the action of the verb. ■ **passively** adv. **passivity** n.

Passover n. a Jewish spring festival commemorating the liberation of the Israelites from slavery in Egypt.

passport n. an official document certifying the holder's identity and citizenship and entitling them to travel abroad.

past adj. **1** gone by in time and no longer existing. **2** (of time) that has gone by. ▶ n. **1** a past period or the events in it. **2** a person's previous experiences. ▶ prep. **1** beyond in time or space. **2** in front of or from one side to the other of. **3** beyond the scope or power of. ▶ adv. going past or beyond. □ **past master** an expert.

pasta n. dough formed into various

Thesaurus

celebration, festivity, at-home, soirée, bacchanal; informal do, bash, shindig, rave-up. **2** POLITICAL PARTY, alliance, association, grouping, faction, camp, set, caucus.

pass v. **1** GO, move, proceed, progress, drive, run, travel, roll, flow, course. **2** GO PAST, move past, go/get ahead of, go by, overtake, outstrip. **3** HAND OVER, reach, let someone have, give, transfer. **4** ELAPSE, go by, proceed, progress, advance. **5** SPEND, occupy, fill, take up, use, employ, while away. **6** GAIN A PASS IN, get through, be successful in, succeed in, pass muster in. **7** VOTE FOR, accept, approve, adopt, authorize, ratify. ▶ n. PERMIT, warrant, authorization, licence, passport, visa, safe conduct, exeat. □ **pass for** BE TAKEN FOR, be accepted as, be mistaken for. **pass out** FAINT, collapse, black out, keel over, swoon.

passable adj. **1** ADEQUATE, all right, tolerable, fair, acceptable, satisfactory, mediocre, middling, ordinary, average, run-of-the-mill, not too bad, unexceptional, indifferent. **2** OPEN, clear, crossable, traversable, navigable, unblocked, unobstructed.

passage n. **1** PASSING, progress, advance, process, flow, course. **2** JOURNEY, voyage, transit, trek, crossing, trip, tour. **3** PASSAGEWAY, corridor, hall, hallway, entrance hall, entrance, vestibule, lobby. **4** EXTRACT, excerpt, quotation, citation, section, verse.

passer-by n. BYSTANDER, onlooker, witness, spectator.

passion n. **1** INTENSITY, fervour, ardour, zeal, vehemence, fire, emotion, feeling, zest, eagerness, excitement, animation. **2** FASCINATION, keen interest, obsession, fixation, craze, mania.

passionate adj. **1** IMPASSIONED, intense, fervent, fervid, ardent, zealous, vehement, fiery, emotional, heartfelt, animated. **2** ARDENT, aroused, desirous, hot, sexy, amorous, sensual, erotic, lustful. ■ OPPOSITES apathetic, frigid.

passive adj. **1** INACTIVE, unassertive, uninvolved, unresisting, yielding, submissive, compliant, pliant, acquiescent, quiescent, resigned, obedient, tractable, malleable. **2** IMPASSIVE, emotionless, unshapes and cooked in boiling water.

paste n. **1** a soft, moist substance. **2** a glue. **3** a hard substance used in making imitation gems. ▶v. coat or stick with paste. □ **pasteboard** cardboard.

pastel n. **1** a crayon made of powdered pigments. **2** a picture drawn with pastels. **3** a pale shade of a colour.

pasteurize (or **-ise**) v. sterilize by heating. ■ **pasteurization** n.

pastiche /pa-steesh/ n. a work in the style of another artist.

pastille n. a small sweet or lozenge.

pastime n. an activity done regularly for enjoyment.

pastor n. a minister in charge of a church or congregation.

pastoral adj. **1** of or used for the keeping of sheep or cattle. **2** of country life. **3** of spiritual and moral guidance.

pastrami /pass-trah-mi/ n. seasoned smoked beef.

pastry n. (pl. **pastries**) **1** a dough of flour, fat, and water, used for making pies etc. **2** a cake of sweet pastry with a filling.

pasture n. grassy land suitable for grazing cattle or sheep. ▶v. put animals to graze in a pasture. ■ **pasturage** n.

pasty¹ /pass-ti/ n. (pl. **pasties**) a folded pastry case filled with meat and vegetables.

pasty² /pay-sti/ adj. unhealthily pale.

pat v. (**patted**, **patting**) tap quickly and gently with the flat of the hand. ▶n. **1** an act of patting. **2** a mass of a soft substance. ▶adj. too quick or easy and not convincing. □ **off pat** perfectly memorized.

patch n. **1** a piece of material used to mend a hole or strengthen a weak point. **2** a small area differing from its

surroundings. **3** a small plot of land. **4** informal a period of time. **5** a cover worn over an injured eye. ▶v. mend with a patch. □ **patch up** informal **1** repair quickly or temporarily. **2** settle a dispute. **patchwork** needlework in which small pieces of cloth are joined to make a pattern.

patchy adj. **1** existing in small, isolated areas. **2** uneven in quality.

pâté /pa-tay/ n. a rich savoury paste of meat etc.

patella n. (pl. **patellae**) the kneecap.

patent n. a licence giving someone the sole right to make, use, or sell their invention. ▶adj. **1** obvious. **2** patented. ▶v. obtain a patent for. □ **patent leather** glossy varnished leather. ■ **patently** adv.

paternal adj. **1** of or like a father. **2** related through one's father. ■ **paternally** adv.

paternalism n. the policy of protecting the people one has control over, but also of restricting their freedom. ■ **paternalistic** adj.

paternity n. the state or fact of being a father.

path n. **1** a way laid down for or made by walking. **2** the course along which a person or thing moves. **3** a course of action.

pathetic adj. **1** arousing pity. **2** informal completely inadequate. ■ **pathetically** adv.

pathological adj. **1** of or caused by a disease. **2** informal compulsive. ■ **pathologically** adv.

pathology n. the study of diseases. ■ **pathologist** n.

pathos n. a quality arousing pity or sadness.

Thesaurus

moved, unresponsive, undemonstrative, dispassionate, detached, distant, remote, aloof, indifferent. ■ OPPOSITES active.

past adj. **1** GONE BY, gone, bygone, elapsed, over, ended, former, long ago. **2** FORMER, previous, prior, erstwhile, one-time, sometime, foregoing, ex-. ■ OPPOSITES present.

pastel adj. PALE, soft, delicate, muted, subdued, faint, low-key. ■ OPPOSITES vivid.

pastime n. HOBBY, leisure activity, sport, game, recreation, diversion, amusement, entertainment, distraction, relaxation.

pastoral adj. RURAL, country, rustic, sim-

ple, idyllic, innocent, Arcadian, agricultural, bucolic, georgic.

pasture n. PASTURAGE, grazing, grassland, grass, field, meadow.

patch n. **1** COVER, covering, pad, shield. **2** PLOT, area, piece, tract, parcel. ▶v. COVER, mend, repair, fix, sew up, stitch.

patent adj. OBVIOUS, clear, plain, evident, apparent, manifest, transparent, conspicuous, blatant, unmistakable.

path n. **1** PATHWAY, footpath, footway, track, trail, towpath, walk. **2** COURSE, route, circuit, track, orbit, trajectory.

pathetic adj. **1** PITEOUS, pitiful, moving, touching, poignant, affecting, heartbreaking, heart-rending, sad, wretched, mournful, woeful. **2** LAMENTABLE, deplor-

patience n. **1** the ability to accept delay or trouble calmly. **2** a card game for one player.

patient adj. showing patience. ▶n. a person receiving medical treatment. ■ **patiently** adv.

patina n. **1** a green film on bronze. **2** a sheen on a surface produced by age and polishing.

patio n. (pl. **patios**) a paved outdoor area by a house.

patisserie n. a shop where cakes etc. are sold.

patois /pat-wah/ n. (pl. **patois**) a dialect.

patriarch n. **1** the male head of a family or tribe. **2** a high-ranking bishop in certain Churches. ■ **patriarchal** adj. **patriarchy** n.

patricide n. **1** the killing of one's father. **2** a person who kills their father.

patrimony n. (pl. **patrimonies**) property inherited from one's father or male ancestor.

patriot n. a person who strongly supports their country. ■ **patriotic** adj. **patriotism** n.

patrol v. (**patrolling, patrolled**) keep watch over an area by regularly walking or travelling around it. ▶n. **1** a person or group sent to patrol an area. **2** the act of patrolling.

patron n. **1** a person giving financial or other support to a cause. **2** a regular customer of a hotel etc. □ **patron saint** a saint believed to protect a particular place or group. ■ **patronage** n.

patronize (or **-ise**) v. **1** treat someone in a way that suggests they are inferior. **2** be a regular customer of.

patronymic n. a name derived from that of a father or ancestor.

patter v. make a repeated light tapping sound. ▶n. **1** a pattering sound. **2** fast continuous talk.

pattern n. **1** a repeated decorative design. **2** a regular sequence of actions or events. **3** a model, design, or set of instructions for making something. **4** an example to follow. **5** a sample of cloth etc. ■ **patterned** adj.

patty n. (pl. **patties**) a small pie or pasty.

paucity n. scarcity or lack of something.

paunch n. a protruding stomach.

pauper n. a very poor person.

pause n. a temporary stop. ▶v. stop temporarily.

pave v. cover a piece of ground with flat stones or bricks. ■ **paving** n.

pavement n. a raised path at the side of a road.

pavilion n. **1** a building at a sports ground for changing and taking refreshments. **2** a summer house in a park etc.

Thesaurus

able, miserable, wretched, feeble, pitiful, woeful, poor, contemptible, inadequate, unsatisfactory, worthless.

pathological adj. COMPULSIVE, obsessive, inveterate, chronic, habitual, hardened, confirmed.

patience n. **1** CALMNESS, composure, even-temperedness, equanimity, serenity, tranquillity, restraint, imperturbability, tolerance, indulgence, forbearance, endurance, resignation, stoicism, fortitude. **2** PERSEVERANCE, persistence, endurance, tenacity, assiduity, diligence, staying power, indefatigability, doggedness, singleness of purpose.
■ OPPOSITES impatience.

patient adj. UNCOMPLAINING, serene, calm, composed, even-tempered, tranquil, restrained, imperturbable, tolerant, accommodating, long-suffering, forbearing, indulgent, resigned, stoical, unflappable; informal cool.

patriotic adj. NATIONALIST, nationalistic, chauvinistic, flag-waving, jingoistic.

patrol v. MAKE THE ROUNDS OF, range, police, keep watch on, guard, keep guard on, monitor. ▶n. **1** PATROLLING, round, policing, watch, guard, monitoring. **2** SENTRY, guard, watchman, watch, nightwatchman, policeman, policewoman.

patron n. **1** SPONSOR, backer, benefactor, benefactress, promoter, friend; informal angel. **2** CUSTOMER, client, shopper, regular, frequenter.

patronize v. **1** LOOK DOWN ON, talk down to, condescend to, treat condescendingly, treat scornfully/contemptuously, be snobbish to. **2** BE A CUSTOMER OF, be a client of, frequent, shop at, buy from, do business with, deal with, trade with.

patronizing adj. CONDESCENDING, supercilious, superior, haughty, lofty, lordly, snobbish; informal snooty, toffee-nosed.

pattern n. **1** DECORATION, design, motif, ornamentation, device, figure. **2** PLAN, guide, blueprint, model, design, template, instructions.

pause v. STOP, halt, cease, discontinue, take a break, desist, rest, hold back, delay, hesitate, waver; informal take a breather. ▶n. BREAK, halt, stoppage, ces-

paw n. an animal's foot having claws and pads. ▶v. feel or scrape with a paw or hoof.

pawn n. **1** a chess piece of the smallest size and value. **2** a person used by others for their own purposes. ▶v. leave an item with a pawnbroker as security for money lent. ◻ **pawnbroker** a person licensed to lend money in exchange for an item left with them. **pawnshop** a pawnbroker's shop.

pawpaw n. a papaya.

pay v. (**paying**, **paid**) **1** give someone money for work or goods. **2** give a sum of money owed. **3** result in a profit or advantage. **4** suffer as a result of an action. **5** give attention etc. to. **6** make a visit to. ▶n. money paid for work. ◻ **payload** an explosive warhead carried by an aircraft or missile. **pay-off** informal a payment made as a bribe or on leaving a job. **pay off 1** dismiss with a final payment. **2** informal yield good results. **payroll** a list of a company's employees and their wages or salaries. ■ **payable** adj. **payment** n.

PAYE abbrev. pay as you earn, a system whereby tax is deducted from wages before payment.

payee n. a person to whom money is paid.

payola n. US bribery in return for the unofficial promotion of a product in the media.

PC abbrev. **1** personal computer. **2** police constable. **3** politically correct; political correctness.

PE abbrev. physical education.

pea n. a round green seed in a pod, eaten as a vegetable.

peace n. **1** freedom from noise or anxiety. **2** freedom from war.

peaceable adj. **1** avoiding conflict. **2** peaceful. ■ **peaceably** adv.

peaceful adj. **1** free from noise or anxiety. **2** not involving war or violence. ■ **peacefully** adv. **peacefulness** n.

peach n. **1** a round juicy fruit with a rough stone inside. **2** a pinkish-orange colour.

peacock n. a colourful bird with long tail feathers that can be fanned out in display.

peahen n. the female of the peacock.

peak n. **1** the pointed top of a mountain. **2** a stiff brim at the front of a cap. **3** the point of highest activity, achievement, etc. ▶v. reach a highest point. ▶adj. maximum. ■ **peaked** adj.

peaky adj. pale from illness or tiredness.

peal n. **1** the loud ringing sound of a bell or bells. **2** a loud sound of thunder or laughter. **3** a set of bells. ▶v. ring or sound loudly.

peanut n. **1** the oval edible seed of a South American plant. **2** (**peanuts**) informal a very small sum of money.

pear n. a rounded fruit tapering towards the stalk.

pearl n. a small, hard, shiny white gem formed within the shell of an oyster. ■ **pearly** adj.

peasant n. a poor smallholder or farm labourer. ■ **peasantry** n.

Thesaurus

sation, interruption, lull, respite, stay, discontinuation, gap, interlude, intermission, interval, rest, hesitation, delay.

pay v. **1** SETTLE UP WITH, remunerate, reimburse, recompense. **2** PAY OUT, spend, expend, lay out, part with, disburse, hand over, remit, render; informal shell out, fork out, cough up. **3** MAKE MONEY, be profitable, make a profit, be remunerative, make a return. **4** REPAY, be advantageous to, be of advantage to, be of benefit to, be beneficial to, be profitable to, be worthwhile to. ▶n. PAYMENT, salary, wages, earnings, fee, remuneration, recompense, reimbursement, reward, stipend, emoluments.

payment n. **1** SETTLEMENT, discharge, clearance, squaring, liquidation. **2** see PAY. **3** INSTALMENT, premium, amount, remittance.

peace n. **1** TRANQUILLITY, peacefulness,

serenity, calm, calmness, composure, placidity, rest, repose, contentment. **2** HARMONY, peaceableness, peacefulness, accord, concord, amity, amicableness, goodwill, friendship, cordiality. **3** TREATY, truce, agreement, armistice, cessation of hostilities, non-aggression, ceasefire. ■ OPPOSITES anxiety, war.

peaceable adj. PEACE-LOVING, non-violent, easy-going, placid, gentle, mild, good-natured, even-tempered, amiable, amicable, pacific, pacifist, dovelike, dovish. ■ OPPOSITES aggressive.

peaceful adj. TRANQUIL, restful, quiet, calm, still, serene, composed, placid, reposeful, undisturbed, untroubled, unworried, anxiety-free. ■ OPPOSITES noisy, agitated.

peacemaker n. CONCILIATOR, mediator, arbitrator, pacifier, appeaser, peacemonger.

peak n. **1** TOP, summit, crest, pinnacle,

peat n. decomposed vegetable matter formed in boggy ground, used in gardening or as fuel. ■ **peaty** adj.

pebble n. a small, smooth, round stone. □ **pebble dash** mortar mixed with small pebbles, used to coat exterior walls. ■ **pebbly** adj.

pecan n. a smooth pinkish-brown nut.

peccadillo n. (pl. **peccadilloes** or **peccadillos**) a minor fault.

peccary n. (pl. **peccaries**) a small pig-like mammal.

peck v. **1** strike or bite with the beak. **2** kiss lightly and quickly. ▶ n. an act of pecking.

peckish adj. informal hungry.

pectin n. a substance present in fruits, used to set jam.

pectoral adj. of, in, or on the breast or chest. ▶ n. a pectoral fin or muscle.

peculiar adj. **1** strange or odd. **2** (**peculiar to**) belonging only to. ■ **peculiarity** n. **peculiarly** adv.

pecuniary adj. of or in money.

pedagogue n. a teacher. ■ **pedagogy** n.

pedal n. a lever operated by the foot. ▶ v. (**pedalling**, **pedalled**; US **pedaling**, **pedaled**) move a bicycle by working the pedals.

....

☑ Don't confuse **pedal** with **peddle**, which means 'sell goods'.

....

pedalo n. (pl. **pedalos** or **pedaloes**) a small pedal-operated pleasure boat.

pedantic adj. excessively concerned with minor details or rules. ■ **pedant** n. **pedantry** n.

peddle v. **1** sell goods by going from place to place. **2** sell illegal drugs.

peddler var. of PEDLAR.

pederast n. a man who has sexual intercourse with boys.

pedestal n. the base supporting a statue or column etc.

pedestrian n. a person walking rather than travelling in a vehicle. ▶ adj. dull.

pediatrics etc. US = PAEDIATRICS etc.

pedicure n. a cosmetic treatment for the feet and toenails.

pedigree n. **1** an animal's record of descent. **2** a person's ancestry.

pediment n. the triangular part above the entrance of a classical building.

pedlar (or **peddler**) n. **1** a travelling trader who sells small goods. **2** a person who sells illegal drugs.

pedometer n. an instrument for estimating the distance travelled on foot.

pee informal v. urinate. ▶ n. **1** an act of urinating. **2** urine.

peek v. & n. peep.

peel v. **1** remove the skin from a fruit or vegetable. **2** remove a thin covering or layer from. **3** (of a surface) come off in small pieces. ▶ n. the outer skin of a fruit or vegetable. ■ **peeler** n. **peelings** pl. n.

peep v. **1** look quickly or secretly. **2** (**peep out**) be just visible. ▶ n. **1** a quick or secret look. **2** a glimpse. □ **peephole** a small hole in a door through which callers can be seen. **peeping Tom** a furtive voyeur.

peer v. look with difficulty or concentration. ▶ n. **1** a member of the nobility in Britain or Ireland. **2** a person of the same age, status, etc. as another specified person.

Thesaurus

mountain, hill, height, alp. **2** HEIGHT, high point, climax, culmination, zenith, acme, meridian, apogee, prime, heyday. ■ OPPOSITES nadir.

peculiar adj. **1** STRANGE, odd, queer, funny, curious, unusual, abnormal, eccentric, unconventional, bizarre, weird, quaint, outlandish, out of the way, grotesque, freakish, offbeat, droll, comical; informal far out, way-out. **2** CHARACTERISTIC, distinctive, distinct, individual, distinguishing, special, unique, idiosyncratic. ■ OPPOSITES ordinary.

peculiarity n. **1** STRANGENESS, oddness, queerness, abnormality, eccentricity, unconventionality, bizarreness, weirdness, outlandishness, grotesqueness, freakishness. **2** CHARACTERISTIC, feature, quality, property, trait, attribute, mark, stamp, hallmark.

pedantic adj. PRECISE, exact, scrupulous, over-scrupulous, punctilious, meticulous, overnice, perfectionist, formalist, dogmatic, literalist, literalistic, quibbling, hair-splitting, casuistic, casuistical, pettifogging; informal nit-picking.

pedestal n. BASE, support, stand, foundation, pillar, column, plinth.

pedestrian n. WALKER, person on foot, hiker, footslogger. ▶ adj. **1** PEDESTRIANIZED, for pedestrians. **2** PLODDING, unimaginative, uninspired, unexciting, dull, flat, prosaic, turgid, stodgy, mundane, humdrum, banal, run-of-the-mill, commonplace, ordinary, mediocre. ■ OPPOSITES inspired.

peek v. PEEP, glance, sneak a look, cast a brief look, look hurriedly; look; informal

peerage n. **1** the rank of peer or peeress. **2** peers as a whole.

peeress n. **1** a woman holding the rank of a peer. **2** a peer's wife or widow.

peerless adj. better than all others.

peevish adj. irritable. ■ **peevishly** adv.

peg n. **1** a pin or bolt used for hanging things on or fastening something. **2** a clip for holding clothes on a line. ▶v. (**pegging, pegged**) **1** fix, attach, or mark with a peg or pegs. **2** fix a price etc. at a particular level. □ **off the peg** (of clothes) ready-made.

pejorative adj. expressing contempt or disapproval.

Pekinese n. (pl. **Pekinese**) a small dog with long hair, short legs, and a snub nose.

pelican n. a waterbird with a long bill and a throat pouch. □ **pelican crossing** a pedestrian crossing with traffic lights operated by pedestrians.

pellagra n. a disease involving inflamed skin, diarrhoea, etc., caused by an inadequate diet.

pellet n. **1** a small compressed mass of a substance. **2** a piece of small shot.

pell-mell adj. & adv. in a confused or rushed way.

pellucid adj. very clear.

pelmet n. a strip of wood or fabric fitted above a window to conceal curtain fittings.

pelt v. **1** hurl missiles at. **2** (**pelt down**) fall very heavily. ▶n. an animal skin with the fur or wool still on it. □ (**at**) **full pelt** as fast as possible.

pelvis n. the bony frame at the base of the spine to which the legs are attached. ■ **pelvic** adj.

pen n. **1** an instrument for writing or drawing with ink. **2** a small enclosure for farm animals. **3** a female swan. ▶v. (**penning, penned**) **1** write or compose. **2** put or keep in a pen or restricted space. □ **penfriend** a person with whom one forms a friendship by exchanging letters. **pen name** a name used by a writer instead of their real name.

penal adj. of the use of punishment as part of the legal system.

penalize (or **-ise**) v. **1** give a penalty or punishment to. **2** put in an unfavourable position.

penalty n. (pl. **penalties**) a punishment for breaking a law, rule, or contract.

penance n. an act done as a punishment for or acknowledgement of wrongdoing.

pence pl. of PENNY.

penchant /pon-shon/ n. a strong liking.

pencil n. an instrument for writing or drawing, consisting of a stick of wood with a graphite core. ▶v. (**pencilling, pencilled**; US **penciling, penciled**) write, draw, or mark with a pencil.

pendant n. a piece of jewellery hung from a chain around the neck.

pendent (or **pendant**) adj. hanging down.

pending adj. waiting to be decided or settled. ▶prep. until.

pendulous adj. hanging loosely.

pendulum n. a weight hung from a fixed point so that it can swing freely, used to regulate a clock's mechanism.

penetrate v. **1** force a way into or through. **2** understand or gain insight into. **3** (**penetrating**) (of a sound) clearly heard above other sounds. ■ **penetration** n.

penguin n. a flightless seabird of the southern hemisphere.

penicillin n. an antibiotic.

peninsula n. a long piece of land projecting into the sea. ■ **peninsular** adj.

penis n. the male organ used for urinating and having sex.

penitent adj. feeling regret for having done wrong. ▶n. a penitent person. ■ **penitence** n. **penitential** adj.

Thesaurus

take a gander, have a look-see.

peephole n. APERTURE, opening, spyhole, judas, slit, crack, chink, crevice, fissure.

peer[1] v. LOOK CLOSELY, try to see, narrow one's eyes, screw up one's eyes, squint.

peer[2] n. **1** NOBLE, nobleman, aristocrat, lord, patrician. **2** COMPEER, fellow, equal, match, like, co-equal.

peeve v. IRRITATE, annoy, anger, vex, provoke, upset, exasperate, irk, pique, nettle, get on someone's nerves, rub up the wrong way; *informal* aggravate, miff, nark.

penalize v. PUNISH, discipline, fine, correct. ■ OPPOSITES reward.

penalty n. PENANCE, fine, forfeit, sentence, mulct.

penance n. ATONEMENT, reparation, amends, mortification.

penchant n. LIKING, fondness, preference, taste, partiality, inclination, bent, proclivity, predilection.

pending adj. IMMINENT, impending, on the way, coming, approaching, forthcoming, near, nearing, close, close at hand,

penitentiary n. (pl. **penitentiaries**) US a prison.

pennant n. a long, tapering flag.

penniless adj. without money.

pennon n. a pennant.

penny n. (pl. **pennies**; **pence**) **1** a British bronze coin worth one hundredth of a pound. **2** a former coin worth one twelfth of a shilling. □ **penny-farthing** an early type of bicycle with a large front wheel and small rear wheel. **penny-pinching** miserly.

pension¹ n. a regular payment made to retired people, widows, etc., either by the state or from an investment fund. ▶v. (**pension off**) dismiss with a pension. ■ **pensionable** adj. **pensioner** n.

pension² /pon-syon/ n. a small hotel in Europe.

pensive adj. deep in thought. ■ **pensively** adv.

pentagon n. a plane figure with five sides.

pentagram n. a five-pointed star.

pentathlon n. an athletic contest involving five events.

Pentecost n. a Christian festival celebrating the descent of the Holy Spirit on the disciples of Jesus.

penthouse n. a flat on the top floor of a tall building.

penultimate adj. last but one.

penumbra n. (pl. **penumbrae** or **penumbras**) the partially shaded outer part of a shadow.

penury n. extreme poverty. ■ **penurious** adj.

peony n. (pl. **peonies**) a plant grown for its showy flowers.

people pl. n. **1** human beings. **2** the ordinary citizens of a country. **3** (pl. **peoples**) the members of a particular nation, community, or ethnic group. ▶v. fill with people.

pep informal n. liveliness. ▶v. (**pepping**, **pepped**) (**pep up**) make more lively. □ **pep talk** a talk intended to make someone feel more courageous or enthusiastic.

pepper n. **1** a hot-tasting seasoning made from peppercorns. **2** the fruit of a tropical American plant. ▶v. **1** sprinkle with pepper. **2** (**pepper with**) scatter in large amounts over or through. **3** hit repeatedly with small missiles or gunshot. ■ **peppery** adj.

peppercorn n. the dried berry of a plant, ground to make pepper. □ **peppercorn rent** a very low or nominal rent.

peppermint n. **1** a plant producing an aromatic oil. **2** a sweet flavoured with peppermint oil.

pepperoni n. beef and pork sausage seasoned with pepper.

pepsin n. the chief digestive enzyme in the stomach.

peptic adj. of digestion.

per prep. **1** for each. **2** (**as per**) in accordance with. □ **per annum** for each year. **per capita** for each person. **per cent** in or for every hundred. **per se** by or in itself.

perambulate v. walk or travel from place to place. ■ **perambulation** n.

perambulator n. a pram.

perceive v. **1** become aware of through the senses. **2** regard as.

percentage n. **1** a rate or amount in each hundred. **2** a proportion or share, esp. of profits.

perceptible adj. able to be perceived. ■ **perceptibly** adv.

perception n. the ability to perceive,

Thesaurus

in the offing.

penetrate v. **1** PIERCE, bore, perforate, stab, prick, gore, spike. **2** PERMEATE, pervade, fill, imbue, suffuse, seep through, saturate.

penitent adj. REPENTANT, contrite, regretful, remorseful, sorry, apologetic, rueful, ashamed, abject, sorrowful. ■ OPPOSITES unrepentant.

penniless adj. IMPECUNIOUS, penurious, impoverished, indigent, poor, poverty-stricken, destitute, bankrupt, hard up; informal broke, skint. ■ OPPOSITES wealthy.

pensive adj. THOUGHTFUL, reflective, lost in thought, contemplative, meditative, cogitative, ruminative, absorbed, preoccupied.

people n. **1** PERSONS, individuals, human beings, humans, mortals, living souls, {men, women, and children}. **2** RACE, tribe, clan, nation, country, population, populace. **3** THE GENERAL PUBLIC, the public, the masses, the rank and file, commonalty, the mob, the multitude, the hoi polloi.

perceive v. **1** SEE, catch sight of, spot, observe, glimpse, notice, make out, discern, behold, espy, detect, witness, remark. **2** DISCERN, appreciate, recognize, be aware of, be conscious of, know, grasp, understand, comprehend, apprehend, see, sense.

perceptible adj. PERCEIVABLE, discern-

or the act of perceiving.

perceptive adj. having or showing insight. ■ **perceptively** adv.

perch n. **1** a branch, bar, etc. on which a bird rests or roosts. **2** a high seat. **3** (pl. **perch**) an edible freshwater fish. ▶v. **1** sit or rest somewhere. **2** place or balance somewhere.

percipient adj. perceptive. ■ **percipience** n.

percolate v. **1** filter, esp. through small holes. **2** prepare coffee in a percolator. ■ **percolation** n.

percolator n. a device for making coffee, consisting of a pot in which boiling water is circulated through ground coffee held in a small chamber.

percussion n. musical instruments that are played by being struck or shaken.

perdition n. eternal damnation.

peregrinations pl. n. old use travels.

peregrine n. a falcon.

peremptory adj. insisting on immediate attention or obedience. ■ **peremptorily** adv.

perennial adj. **1** lasting for a long time or forever. **2** (of a plant) living for several years. **3** constantly recurring. ▶n. a perennial plant. ■ **perennially** adv.

perestroika /pe-ri-stroy-kuh/ n. (in the former USSR) the economic and political reforms introduced during the 1980s.

perfect adj. **1** without faults or defects. **2** complete; total. ▶v. make perfect. ■ **perfection** n. **perfectly** adv.

perfectionism n. refusal to accept any standard short of perfection. ■ **perfectionist** n.

perfidious adj. deceitful and disloyal. ■ **perfidy** n.

perforate v. pierce and make a hole or holes in. ■ **perforation** n.

perforce adv. necessarily; unavoidably.

perform v. **1** carry out or complete an action or function. **2** present entertainment to an audience. ■ **performance** n. **performer** n.

perfume n. **1** a sweet-smelling liquid for applying to the body. **2** a pleasant smell. ▶v. give a pleasant smell to. ■ **perfumery** n.

perfunctory adj. done with a minimum of effort or thought. ■ **perfunctorily** adv.

Thesaurus

ible, noticeable, detectable, distinguishable, appreciable, visible, observable, distinct, palpable, tangible. ■ OPPOSITES imperceptible.

perception n. **1** DISCERNMENT, appreciation, recognition, awareness, grasp, consciousness, knowledge, understanding, comprehension, apprehension, notion, conception, idea, sense. **2** PERSPICACITY, discernment, perceptiveness, understanding, discrimination, insight, intuition, feeling, sensitivity.

perceptive adj. PENETRATING, astute, shrewd, discerning, perspicacious, percipient, understanding, discriminating, intuitive, responsive, sensitive. ■ OPPOSITES obtuse.

perch n. POLE, rod, branch, roost, rest. ▶v. SIT, rest, roost, settle, alight, land.

peremptory adj. IMPERIOUS, high-handed, overbearing, dogmatic, autocratic, dictatorial, domineering, arbitrary, tyrannical, despotic, arrogant.

perfect adj. **1** FLAWLESS, faultless, unmarred, ideal, impeccable, consummate, immaculate, exemplary, superb, superlative, supreme, excellent, complete, full, whole, entire. **2** EXACT, precise, accurate, faithful, strict; informal spot on. **3** ABSOLUTE, complete, out-and-out, thorough, thoroughgoing, down-

right, utter, sheer, consummate, unmitigated, unqualified. ▶v. MAKE PERFECT, render faultless/flawless, polish, refine, complete, consummate, put the finishing touches to.

perfection n. **1** PERFECTING, polishing, refinement, completion, consummation. **2** FLAWLESSNESS, faultlessness, impeccability, immaculateness, exemplariness, superbness.

perfidious adj. TREACHEROUS, traitorous, treasonous, false, untrue, disloyal, faithless, unfaithful, deceitful. ■ OPPOSITES faithful.

perform v. **1** DO, carry out, execute, discharge, conduct, effect, bring about, bring off, accomplish, achieve, fulfil, complete. **2** ACT, play, appear. **3** FUNCTION, work, operate, run, go.

performance n. **1** EXECUTION, discharge, accomplishment, achievement, fulfilment. **2** SHOW, production, entertainment, act, presentation; informal gig.

performer n. ACTOR/ACTRESS, player, entertainer, artist, artiste, Thespian, musician, singer, dancer.

perfume n. **1** SMELL, fragrance, aroma, scent, bouquet; literary redolence. **2** FRAGRANCE, scent, eau de Cologne, cologne.

perfunctory adj. CURSORY, superficial, desultory, mechanical, automatic, rou-

pergola n. an arched framework for climbing plants.

perhaps adv. possibly; maybe.

pericardium n. (pl. **pericardia**) the membrane enclosing the heart.

perigee n. the point in the moon's orbit when it is nearest to the earth.

peril n. serious danger. ■ **perilous** adj. **perilously** adv.

perimeter n. the outer edge or boundary of something.

perinatal adj. of the time immediately before and after birth.

period n. **1** a length or portion of time. **2** a lesson in a school. **3** a flow of blood each month from the lining of a woman's womb. **4** a full stop. ▶ adj. belonging to a past historical time.

periodic adj. occurring at intervals. □ **periodic table** a table of all the chemical elements.

periodical adj. periodic. ▶ n. a magazine etc. published at regular intervals. ■ **periodically** adv.

peripatetic adj. travelling from place to place.

periphery n. (pl. **peripheries**) **1** the outer limits of an area or object. **2** the less important part of a subject or group. ■ **peripheral** adj.

periphrasis n. (pl. **periphrases**) indirect language.

periscope n. a tube attached to a set of mirrors, by which one can see things that are above or behind something else.

perish v. **1** die. **2** be destroyed. **3** rot. **4 (perishing)** informal very cold.

perishable adj. (of food) likely to rot quickly.

peritoneum /pe-ri-tuh-**nee**-uhm/ n. (pl. **peritoneums** or **peritonea**) the membrane lining the abdominal cavity.

peritonitis n. inflammation of the peritoneum.

periwinkle n. a plant with flat five-petalled flowers.

perjure v. **(perjure oneself)** commit perjury.

perjury n. the offence of deliberately telling a lie in court when under oath.

perk v. **(perk up)** make or become more cheerful or lively. ▶ n. informal a benefit to which an employee is entitled.

perky adj. **(perkier, perkiest)** cheerful and lively. ■ **perkily** adv.

perm n. a chemical treatment giving hair a long-lasting curly style. ▶ v. treat hair with a perm.

permafrost n. a layer of soil beneath the surface that remains frozen throughout the year.

permanent adj. lasting for a long time or forever. ■ **permanence** n. **permanently** adv.

permeable adj. allowing liquids or gases to pass through. ■ **permeability** n.

permeate v. spread throughout.

permissible adj. allowable.

tine, sketchy, brief, hasty, hurried, rapid, fleeting, quick, fast, offhand, casual, indifferent, careless, inattentive. ■ OPPOSITES careful, thorough.

perhaps adv. MAYBE, possibly, it is possible that, conceivably, feasibly, for all one knows, it could be; *literary* peradventure, perchance.

peril n. DANGER, jeopardy, risk, hazard, menace, threat. ■ OPPOSITES safety.

perilous adj. DANGEROUS, risky, precarious, hazardous, chancy, threatening, unsafe. ■ OPPOSITES safe.

perimeter n. BOUNDARY, border, frontier, limits, outer limits, confines, edge, margin, fringe, periphery.

period n. SPACE, spell, interval, term, stretch, span, age, era, epoch, aeon.

periodic adj. PERIODICAL, recurrent, recurring, repeated, cyclical, cyclic, regular, intermittent, occasional, infrequent, sporadic.

peripheral adj. **1** OUTER, on the edge/outskirts, surrounding, neighbouring.

2 MINOR, lesser, secondary, subsidiary, ancillary, unimportant, superficial, irrelevant. ■ OPPOSITES central.

perish v. **1** DIE, lose one's life, be killed, lay down one's life, meet one's death, breathe one's last, draw one's last breath; *informal* bite the dust, kick the bucket. **2** GO BAD, go off, go sour, rot, decay, decompose.

perk v. **(perk up)** CHEER UP, brighten up, take heart; *informal* buck up, pep up.

perk n. BENEFIT, advantage, bonus, dividend, extra, plus, perquisite; *informal* freebie.

permanent adj. LASTING, long-lasting, stable, fixed, established, everlasting, perpetual, eternal, enduring, perennial, abiding, constant, persistent, unending, endless, never-ending, immutable, unchangeable, unalterable, invariable. ■ OPPOSITES impermanent.

permeate v. SPREAD THROUGH, pass through, pervade, saturate, fill, diffuse through, extend throughout, imbue,

permission n. the act of allowing someone to do something.

permissive adj. allowing freedom of behaviour, esp. in sexual matters. ■ **permissiveness** n.

permit v. (**permitting, permitted**) **1** give permission to or for. **2** make possible. ▶ n. an official document giving permission to do something.

permutation n. each of several possible ways of ordering or arranging a number of things.

pernicious adj. harmful.

pernickety adj. informal fussy.

peroration n. the concluding part of a speech.

peroxide n. a chemical used to bleach hair.

perpendicular adj. at an angle of 90° to a line or surface. ▶ n. a perpendicular line.

perpetrate v. carry out a bad or illegal action. ■ **perpetration** n. **perpetrator** n.

perpetual adj. **1** never ending or changing. **2** very frequent. ■ **perpetually** adv.

perpetuate v. cause to continue for a long time. ■ **perpetuation** n.

perpetuity n. the state of lasting forever.

perplex v. puzzle greatly. ■ **perplexity** n.

perquisite n. a special right or privilege given as a result of one's position.

perry n. an alcoholic drink made from fermented pears.

persecute v. **1** treat badly over a long period. **2** persistently harass. ■ **persecution** n. **persecutor** n.

persevere v. continue in spite of difficulty or lack of success. ■ **perseverance** n.

persimmon n. a tropical fruit.

persist v. **1** continue doing something in spite of difficulty or opposition. **2** continue to exist. ■ **persistence** n. **persistent** adj. **persistently** adv.

person n. (pl. **people** or **persons**) **1** an individual human being. **2** an individual's body. **3** Grammar a category used in classifying pronouns or verb forms according to whether they indicate the speaker (**first person**), the person spoken to (**second person**), or a third party (**third person**). □ **in person**

Thesaurus
. . . .

penetrate, infiltrate, percolate through.

permissible adj. PERMITTED, allowable, admissible, acceptable, tolerated, authorized, sanctioned, legal, lawful, legitimate, licit, within bounds; informal legit. ■ OPPOSITES forbidden.

permission n. AUTHORIZATION, sanction, leave, licence, dispensation, empowerment, allowance, consent, assent, acquiescence, agreement, approval, approbation, tolerance, sufferance; informal green light, go-ahead, thumbs up.

permissive adj. LIBERAL, tolerant, broad-minded, open-minded, easygoing, indulgent, lenient, live-and-let-live, overindulgent, lax, unprescriptive. ■ OPPOSITES intolerant, strict.

permit v. GIVE PERMISSION, allow, let, authorize, give leave, sanction, grant, license, consent to, assent to, acquiesce in, agree to, approve of, tolerate, countenance, suffer, brook; informal give the green light to, give the go-ahead to, give the thumbs up to. ■ OPPOSITES forbid.
▶ n. LICENCE, authorization, warrant, sanction, pass, passport.

perpetual adj. **1** EVERLASTING, eternal, never-ending, unending, endless, undying, perennial, permanent, lasting, abiding, persisting, enduring, constant, unfailing, unchanging, unvarying, in-

variable; literary perdurable. **2** INCESSANT, unceasing, ceaseless, unending, endless, non-stop, continuous, uninterrupted, unbroken, unremitting. **3** INTERMINABLE, persistent, frequent, continual, recurrent, repeated; informal eternal.

perpetuate v. KEEP ALIVE, keep going, keep up, preserve, conserve, sustain, maintain, continue.

perplex v. PUZZLE, baffle, mystify, stump, bewilder, confound, confuse, nonplus, disconcert, dismay, dumbfound; informal bamboozle.

persecute v. OPPRESS, tyrannize, abuse, mistreat, maltreat, ill-treat, molest, afflict, torment, torture, victimize, martyr.

persevere v. PERSIST, go on, keep on, keep at, keep going, continue, carry on, struggle, work, hammer away, be tenacious, be persistent, be pertinacious, be resolute, be purposeful, be obstinate, be insistent, be intransigent, be patient, be diligent; informal plug away. ■ OPPOSITES give up.

persist v. see PERSEVERE.

persistent adj. **1** PERSEVERING, tenacious, pertinacious, determined, resolute, purposeful, obstinate, stubborn, insistent, intransigent, obdurate, intractable, patient, diligent. **2** CONSTANT, actually present.

persona n. (pl. **personas** or **personae**) the aspect of a person's character that is presented to others.

personable adj. having a pleasant appearance and manner.

personage n. an important or famous person.

personal adj. **1** belonging to or affecting a particular person. **2** done by a particular person rather than someone else. **3** concerning a person's private life. **4** of a person's body. □ **personal computer** a computer designed for use by one person. **personal organizer** a loose-leaf notebook with a diary and address section. **personal pronoun** each of the pronouns (*I, you, he, she*, etc.) that show person, gender, number, and case. ■ **personally** adv.

personality n. (pl. **personalities**) **1** the qualities that form a person's character. **2** qualities that make someone interesting or popular. **3** a celebrity.

personalize (or **-ise**) v. **1** design to suit or identify as belonging to a particular person. **2** cause an issue to be concerned with personalities or feelings.

personify v. (**personifying, personified**) **1** represent in human form or as having human characteristics. **2** be an example of a quality. ■ **personification** n.

personnel pl. n. employees; staff.

perspective n. **1** the art of drawing things so as to give an effect of solidity and relative distance. **2** a particular way of seeing something. **3** understanding of the relative importance of things.

perspex n. trademark a tough transparent plastic.

perspicacious adj. quickly gaining insight into things. ■ **perspicacity** n.

perspicuous adj. expressing things clearly. ■ **perspicuity** n.

perspire v. sweat. ■ **perspiration** n.

persuade v. cause to do or believe something by reasoning.

persuasion n. **1** the act or a means of persuading. **2** a belief or set of beliefs.

persuasive adj. **1** good at persuading. **2** providing sound reasoning. ■ **persuasively** adv.

pert adj. attractively lively or cheeky.

pertain v. be related or relevant.

pertinacious adj. persistent. ■ **pertinacity** n.

pertinent adj. relevant. ■ **pertinence** n. **pertinently** adv.

perturb v. make anxious. ■ **perturbation** n.

peruse v. read carefully. ■ **perusal** n.

Thesaurus

continual, continuous, continuing, interminable, incessant, unceasing, endless, unremitting, unrelenting, relentless, non-stop. ■ OPPOSITES irresolute, intermittent.

person n. INDIVIDUAL, human being, human, creature, living soul, soul, mortal.

personable adj. PLEASANT, agreeable, amiable, affable, likeable, charming, nice, attractive, presentable, good-looking. ■ OPPOSITES disagreeable.

personal adj. **1** INDIVIDUAL, private, confidential, secret, one's own business. **2** PERSONALIZED, individual, idiosyncratic, characteristic, unique, peculiar. **3** INSULTING, slighting, derogatory, disparaging, pejorative, offensive. ■ OPPOSITES public, general.

personality n. **1** NATURE, disposition, character, temperament, temper, make-up, psyche. **2** FORCE OF PERSONALITY, character, charisma, magnetism, powers of attraction, charm. **3** CELEBRITY, VIP, household name, dignitary, notable, personage, luminary, worthy.

personally adv. FOR MY PART, for myself, from my own point of view, as far as I am concerned.

personification n. EMBODIMENT, incarnation, epitome, quintessence, essence, symbol, representation, image.

personnel n. STAFF, employees, workers, workforce, labour force, manpower, human resources, liveware.

perspective n. **1** OUTLOOK, view, viewpoint, point of view, standpoint, stance, angle, slant, attitude. **2** VIEW, vista, bird's-eye view, prospect, scene, outlook, panorama, aspect, sweep.

persuade v. PREVAIL UPON, induce, convince, win over, talk into, bring round, influence, sway, prompt, coerce, inveigle, cajole, wheedle; *informal* sweet-talk, soft-soap. ■ OPPOSITES discourage.

persuasive adj. EFFECTIVE, effectual, convincing, cogent, plausible, compelling, forceful, eloquent, weighty, influential, telling. ■ OPPOSITES ineffective.

pertain v. BE CONNECTED, relate, be relevant, have relevance, concern, apply to, be pertinent to, have reference to, have a bearing upon.

pertinent adj. RELEVANT, appropriate, suitable, fitting, fit, apt, apposite, to the point, applicable, material, germane,

pervade v. spread or be present throughout. ■ **pervasive** adj.

perverse adj. 1 deliberately choosing to behave in an unacceptable way. 2 contrary to what is accepted or expected. ■ **perversely** adv. **perversity** n.

pervert v. 1 divert from the correct or intended meaning or course. 2 lead into abnormal or unacceptable sexual behaviour. ▶n. a person with abnormal or unacceptable sexual behaviour. ■ **perversion** n.

pervious adj. allowing water to pass through.

peseta n. a former currency unit of Spain.

peso n. a currency unit of several South American countries.

pessary n. (pl. **pessaries**) a small soluble block inserted into the vagina to treat infection.

pessimism n. lack of hope or confidence in the future. ■ **pessimist** n. **pessimistic** adj. **pessimistically** adv.

pest n. a destructive insect or other animal that attacks plants, crops, etc.

pester v. trouble with persistent requests or interruptions.

pesticide n. a substance for destroying insects or other pests.

pestilence n. old use a deadly epidemic disease. ■ **pestilential** adj.

pestle n. a heavy tool with a rounded end for crushing things in a mortar.

pesto n. a sauce of basil, pine nuts, Parmesan cheese, and olive oil, served with pasta.

pet n. 1 a tame animal kept for company and pleasure. 2 a person treated with special favour. ▶adj. 1 of or kept as a pet. 2 favourite or particular. ▶v. (**petting, petted**) 1 stroke or pat an animal. 2 caress sexually.

petal n. each of the segments forming the outer part of a flower.

peter v. (**peter out**) come to an end gradually.

petite adj. small and dainty.

petition n. a formal written request signed by many people. ▶v. present a petition to.

petrel n. a seabird.

Thesaurus

to the purpose, apropos. ■ OPPOSITES irrelevant.

perturb v. DISTURB, make anxious, worry, alarm, trouble, upset, disquiet, discompose, disconcert, vex, bother, agitate, unsettle, fluster, ruffle, harass. ■ OPPOSITES reassure.

pervade v. SPREAD THROUGH, permeate, fill, pass through, suffuse, diffuse through, imbue, infuse, penetrate, infiltrate, percolate.

pervasive adj. PERVADING, permeating, prevalent, extensive, ubiquitous, omnipresent, rife, widespread, universal, suffusive.

perverse adj. CONTRARY, wayward, troublesome, difficult, awkward, unreasonable, disobedient, unmanageable, uncontrollable, rebellious, wilful, headstrong, capricious, stubborn, obstinate, obdurate, pertinacious, mulish, pigheaded, wrong-headed, querulous, fractious, intractable, refractory, intransigent, contumacious; informal bolshie, stroppy.

perversion n. 1 DISTORTION, misuse, misrepresentation, falsification, misinterpretation, misconstruction. 2 DEVIATION, aberration, abnormality, irregularity, unnaturalness, corruption, vice, debauchery, depravity; informal kinkiness.

pervert v. 1 MISAPPLY, misuse, distort,

garble, warp, twist, misinterpret, misconstrue. 2 LEAD ASTRAY, corrupt, warp, deprave, debauch, debase, degrade. ▶n. DEVIANT, deviate, degenerate, debauchee; informal perv.

perverted adj. DEPRAVED, debauched, debased, corrupt, deviant, abnormal, aberrant, warped, distorted, twisted, sick, unhealthy, immoral, evil, vile; informal kinky.

pessimist n. PROPHET OF DOOM, cynic, defeatist, fatalist, alarmist, doubter, doubting Thomas; informal doom merchant, gloom merchant. ■ OPPOSITES optimist.

pessimistic adj. GLOOMY, gloom-ridden, cynical, defeatist, fatalistic, hopeless, distrustful, alarmist, doubting, suspicious, bleak, resigned, depressed, despondent, dejected, despairing. ■ OPPOSITES optimistic.

pest n. NUISANCE, bother, irritant, thorn in the flesh, problem, trouble, worry, inconvenience, trial, tribulation, the bane of one's life; informal pain, pain in the neck.

pester v. BADGER, hound, irritate, annoy, bother, irk, nag, harass, chivvy, torment, plague, bedevil, harry; informal bug, hassle.

pet n. FAVOURITE, darling, idol, apple of one's eye; informal blue-eyed boy/girl; US informal fair-haired boy/girl. ▶v. STROKE,

petrify v. (**petrifying**, **petrified**)
1 change organic matter into stone.
2 paralyse with fear. ■ **petrifaction** n.

petrochemical n. a chemical obtained from petroleum and natural gas.

petrol n. refined petroleum used as fuel in vehicles.

petroleum n. an oil found in layers of rock and refined to produce fuels.

petticoat n. a woman's undergarment in the form of a skirt.

pettifogging adj. petty; trivial.

pettish adj. childishly sulky.

petty adj. (**pettier**, **pettiest**) **1** unimportant; trivial. **2** small-minded. **3** minor. □ **petty cash** money kept in an office for small payments. **petty officer** a rank of naval officer. ■ **pettiness** n.

petulant adj. sulky or bad-tempered. ■ **petulance** n. **petulantly** adv.

petunia n. a plant with white, purple, or red funnel-shaped flowers.

pew n. a long bench with a back in a church.

pewter n. a grey alloy of tin with copper and antimony.

pfennig n. a former currency unit of Germany.

PG abbrev. (in film classification) parental guidance.

pH n. a measure of the acidity or alkalinity of a substance.

phalanx n. (pl. **phalanxes**) a group of people or things, esp. a body of troops or police officers.

phallus n. (pl. **phalli** or **phalluses**) a penis. ■ **phallic** adj.

phantasm n. an illusion.

phantasmagoria n. a sequence of dreamlike images.

phantom n. a ghost.

pharaoh /fair-oh/ n. a ruler in ancient Egypt.

pharmaceutical adj. of medicinal drugs.

pharmacist n. a person qualified to prepare and dispense medicinal drugs.

pharmacology n. the study of the uses and effects of drugs. ■ **pharmacological** adj. **pharmacologist** n.

pharmacopoeia /far-muh-kuh-pee-uh/ n. an official list of medicinal drugs with their effects.

pharmacy n. (pl. **pharmacies**) **1** a place where medicinal drugs are prepared or sold. **2** the preparation and dispensing of medicinal drugs.

pharynx n. (pl. **pharynges** /fa-rin-jeez/) the cavity behind the nose and mouth.

phase n. a distinct stage in a process of change or development. ▶ v. **1** carry out in gradual stages. **2** (**phase in/out**) gradually introduce or withdraw.

PhD abbrev. Doctor of Philosophy.

pheasant n. a long-tailed game bird.

phenomenal adj. excellent. ■ **phenomenally** adv.

phenomenon n. (pl. **phenomena**) **1** a fact or situation observed to exist or happen. **2** a remarkable person or thing.

. . . .

☑ The plural of **phenomenon** is **phenomena**. Don't use **phenomena** as a singular form.

. . . .

pheromone n. a chemical released by an animal and causing a response in others of its species.

phial n. a small bottle.

philander v. (of a man) have numerous sexual relationships with women. ■ **philanderer** n.

Thesaurus

caress, fondle, pat.

peter v. (**peter out**) FADE, wane, ebb, diminish, taper off, come to nothing, die out, fail, fall through, come to a halt, come to an end.

petition n. APPEAL, request, entreaty, supplication, plea, prayer, application, suit. ▶ v. APPEAL TO, request, ask, apply to, entreat, beg, plead with, make a plea to; *literary* beseech.

petrify v. **1** TERRIFY, frighten, horrify, fill with fear, panic, alarm, scare someone out of their wits, paralyse, stun, stupefy, transfix. **2** TURN TO STONE, fossilize, calcify, ossify.

petulant adj. QUERULOUS, complaining, peevish, fretful, impatient, cross, irrit-

able, moody, crabbed, crabby, crotchety, touchy, bad-tempered, irascible, sulky; *informal* snappish, ratty.

phantom n. GHOST, apparition, spectre, shade, spirit, revenant, wraith, shadow; *informal* spook; *literary* phantasm.

phenomenal adj. EXTRAORDINARY, remarkable, exceptional, singular, uncommon, unheard of, unique, unusual, unparalleled, unprecedented, amazing, astonishing, astounding, marvellous, prodigious, sensational, miraculous; *informal* mind-blowing.

phenomenon n. **1** FACT, experience, occurrence, happening, event, incident, episode. **2** MARVEL, prodigy, rarity, wonder, sensation, miracle, nonpareil.

philanthropy n. the practice of helping people in need. ■ **philanthropic** adj. **philanthropist** n.

philately n. stamp collecting. ■ **philatelist** n.

philistine n. a person who is not interested in culture.

philology n. the study of languages. ■ **philological** adj. **philologist** n.

philosophical adj. **1** of philosophy. **2** calm in difficult circumstances. ■ **philosophically** adv.

philosophize (or **-ise**) v. theorize.

philosophy n. (pl. **philosophies**) **1** the study of the fundamental nature of knowledge, reality, and existence. **2** a set or system of beliefs. ■ **philosopher** n.

philtre (US **philter**) n. a love potion.

phlegm /flem/ n. mucus in the nose and throat.

phlegmatic /fleg-mat-ik/ adj. calm and unemotional.

phlox n. a flowering garden plant.

phobia n. an extreme or irrational fear. ■ **phobic** adj. & n.

phoenix /fee-niks/ n. a mythological bird said to burn itself and be born again from its ashes.

phone n. a telephone. ▶v. telephone. □ **phonecard** a prepaid telephone allowing calls to be made on a public telephone. **phone-in** a broadcast during which listeners or viewers join in by telephone.

phonetic adj. **1** of or representing speech sounds. **2** (of spelling) closely matching the sounds represented. ▶n. (**phonetics**) the study of speech sounds. ■ **phonetically** adv.

phoney (or **phony**) informal adj. (**phonier**, **phoniest**) not genuine. ▶n. (pl. **phoneys** or **phonies**) a phoney person or thing.

phonograph n. US a record player.

phosphate n. a compound of phosphorus.

phosphorescent adj. luminous. ■ **phosphorescence** n.

phosphorus n. a yellowish waxy element which glows in the dark and ignites in air.

photo n. (pl. **photos**) a photograph. □ **photo finish** a finish of a race so close that the winner has to be decided from a photograph. **photofit** a picture of a person made up of separate photographs of facial features. **photogenic** looking attractive in photographs.

photocopy n. (pl. **photocopies**) a photographic copy of a document etc. ▶v. (**photocopying**, **photocopied**) make a photocopy of. ■ **photocopier** n.

photoelectric cell n. a device generating an electric current when light falls on it.

photograph n. a picture made with a camera. ▶v. take a photograph of. ■ **photographer** n. **photographic** adj. **photography** n.

photon n. an indivisible unit of electromagnetic radiation.

photosensitive adj. responding to light.

photostat n. trademark **1** a type of photocopier. **2** a copy made by a photostat.

photosynthesis n. the process by which green plants use sunlight to form nutrients from carbon dioxide and water. ■ **photosynthesize** (or **-ise**) v.

phrase n. **1** a small group of words

Thesaurus

philanthropic adj. BENEVOLENT, beneficent, benignant, charitable, almsgiving, generous, kind, munificent, bountiful, liberal, open-handed, giving, helping; *literary* bounteous. ■ OPPOSITES selfish.

philistine adj. UNCULTURED, uncultivated, uneducated, unenlightened, unread, ignorant, boorish, barbaric.

philosophical adj. **1** THOUGHTFUL, reflective, pensive, meditative, contemplative. **2** CALM, composed, cool, collected, self-possessed, serene, tranquil, stoical, impassive, phlegmatic, unperturbed, imperturbable, dispassionate, unruffled, patient, resigned, rational, logical, realistic, practical.

philosophy n. **1** THOUGHT, thinking, reasoning, logic, wisdom. **2** BELIEFS, convictions, ideology, ideas, doctrine, tenets, values, principles, attitude, view, viewpoint, outlook.

phlegmatic adj. CALM, cool, composed, collected, serene, tranquil, placid, impassive, imperturbable, dispassionate, philosophical. ■ OPPOSITES excitable.

phobia n. AVERSION, fear, dread, horror, terror, dislike, hatred, loathing, detestation, distaste, antipathy, revulsion, repulsion; *informal* thing, hang-up.

phone v. TELEPHONE, call, give someone a call, ring, ring up; *informal* buzz, get on the blower to.

phoney adj. BOGUS, sham, counterfeit, imitation, spurious, mock, ersatz, fake, forged, feigned, simulated, make-believe, false, fraudulent. ■ OPPOSITES genuine.

photograph n. PHOTO, snap, snapshot,

forming a unit. **2** a group of musical notes forming a distinct unit. ▶ v. put into a particular form of words. ■ **phrasal** adj.

phraseology n. (pl. **phraseologies**) a particular form or use of words.

phrenology n. the study of the shape of a person's skull as a supposed indication of their character.

phylum n. (pl. **phyla**) a category used in classifying animals.

physical adj. **1** of the body. **2** of things that can be seen, heard, or touched. **3** of physics or the operation of natural forces. □ **physical education** instruction in physical exercise and games. **physical geography** the study of the earth's natural features. **physical sciences** the sciences studying inanimate natural objects. ■ **physically** adv.

physician n. a person qualified to practise medicine.

physics n. the study of the nature and properties of matter and energy. ■ **physicist** n.

physiognomy n. (pl. **physiognomies**) a person's face.

physiology n. the study of the way in which living organisms function. ■ **physiological** adj. **physiologist** n.

physiotherapy n. the treatment of an injury etc. by massage and exercise. ■ **physiotherapist** n.

physique n. the shape and size of a person's body.

pi n. the ratio of a circle's circumference to its diameter (about 3.14).

pianissimo adv. & adj. Music very softly.

piano n. (pl. **pianos**) a musical instrument with strings struck by hammers when keys are pressed. ▶ adv. & adj. Music softly. ■ **pianist** n.

pianoforte n. formal a piano.

piazza /pi-at-zuh/ n. a public square or marketplace.

picador n. a bullfighter on horseback.

picaresque adj. of fiction dealing with the adventures of a dishonest but appealing hero.

piccalilli n. a pickle of chopped vegetables and hot spices.

piccolo n. (pl. **piccolos**) a small flute.

pick v. **1** take hold of and lift or remove from its place. **2** select. ▶ n. **1** an act or the right of selecting. **2** informal the best of a group. **3** (also **pickaxe**) a tool with a pointed iron bar fixed at right angles to its handle, for breaking up hard ground etc. □ **pick holes in** find fault with. **pick a lock** open a lock with something other than a key. **pick off** single out and shoot. **pick on** single out for unfair treatment. **pickpocket** a person who steals from people's pockets. **pickup 1** a small truck with low sides. **2** an act of picking up a person or goods. **3** a device converting sound vibrations into electrical signals for amplification. **pick up 1** lift up. **2** go to collect. **3** improve or increase. **4** casually get to know someone as a sexual overture. ■ **picker** n.

picket n. **1** a person or group standing outside a workplace to dissuade others from entering during a strike. **2** a pointed wooden stake driven into the ground. ▶ v. (**picketing, picketed**) act as a picket outside a workplace.

pickings pl. n. profits or gains.

pickle n. **1** vegetables or fruit preserved in vinegar or brine. **2** (**a pickle**) informal a difficult situation. ▶ v. preserve in vinegar or brine.

picnic n. an informal meal eaten outdoors. ▶ v. (**picnicking, picnicked**) have a picnic. ■ **picnicker** n.

Thesaurus

picture, likeness, shot, print, slide, transparency.

photographic adj. **1** PICTORIAL, in photographs. **2** DETAILED, graphic, exact, accurate, precise.

phrase n. EXPRESSION, idiom, remark, saying, utterance, witticism, tag. ▶ v. PUT INTO WORDS, put, word, express, formulate, couch, frame.

phraseology n. PHRASING, wording, words, choice of words, language, vocabulary, terminology.

physical adj. MATERIAL, substantial, solid, concrete, tangible, palpable, visible, real, bodily, non-mental, corporeal, corporal. ■ OPPOSITES mental,

spiritual.

physician n. DOCTOR, medical practitioner, general practitioner, GP, specialist, consultant; informal doc, medic, medico, quack.

physique n. BODY, build, shape, frame, form, figure.

pick v. **1** CHOOSE, select, opt for, plump for, single out, hand-pick, decide upon, settle upon, fix upon, prefer, favour, elect. **2** HARVEST, gather, collect, take in, pluck, pull, cull. ▶ n. **1** CHOICE, selection, option, preference. **2** BEST, choicest, prime, cream, flower, prize. □ **pick on** BULLY, victimize, tyrannize, torment, persecute, harass, hound, taunt. **pick**

pictograph n. a picture representing a word or phrase.

pictorial adj. of or using pictures. ■ **pictorially** adv.

picture n. **1** a painting, drawing, or photograph. **2** an image. **3** (**the pictures**) the cinema. ▶ v. **1** show in a picture. **2** imagine.

picturesque adj. attractive in a quaint or charming way.

pidgin n. a simple form of a language with elements taken from local languages.

pie n. a baked dish of ingredients topped with pastry. □ **pie chart** a diagram representing quantities as sections of a circle.

piebald adj. (of a horse) having irregular patches of two colours.

piece n. **1** a portion or part. **2** an item forming part of a set. **3** a musical, literary, or artistic work. **4** a small object used in a board game. ▶ v. (**piece together**) assemble from individual parts. □ **piecemeal** done in a gradual and inconsistent way. **piecework** work paid for according to the amount produced.

pièce de résistance /pyess duh ray-**ziss**-tonss/ n. the most impressive feature.

pied adj. having two or more different colours.

pied-à-terre /pyay-dah-**tair**/ n. (pl. **pieds-à-terre**) a small flat or house for occasional use.

pier n. a structure built out into the sea, used as a landing stage or promenade.

pierce v. **1** make a hole in or through with a sharp object. **2** force a way through. **3** (**piercing**) very sharp, cold, or high-pitched.

piety n. (pl. **pieties**) the quality of being deeply religious.

piffle n. informal nonsense.

pig n. **1** a domestic or wild mammal with a flat snout. **2** informal a greedy or dirty person. □ **pig-headed** stubborn. **pig iron** oblong blocks of crude iron from a smelting furnace. **pigsty** an enclosure for pigs. **pigtail** a length of hair worn in a plait at the back or on each side of the head. ■ **piglet** n.

pigeon n. a plump bird with a cooing voice.

pigeonhole n. each of a set of small compartments where letters etc. may be left. ▶ v. place in a particular category.

piggery n. (pl. **piggeries**) a farm or enclosure where pigs are kept.

piggy adj. like a pig. □ **piggyback** a ride on someone's back and shoulders. **piggy bank** a money box shaped like a pig.

pigment n. a colouring matter. ■ **pigmentation** n.

pigmy var. of PYGMY.

pike n. **1** (pl. **pike**) a large predatory freshwater fish. **2** a spear with a long wooden shaft.

pilaf (or **pilau**) n. a dish of rice with

up IMPROVE, get better, recover, rally, perk up, be on the mend, make headway, make progress, take a turn for the better.

picture n. **1** PAINTING, drawing, sketch, oil painting, watercolour, print, canvas, delineation, portrait, portrayal, illustration, likeness, representation, similitude, semblance. **2** see PHOTOGRAPH. ▶ v. **1** SEE IN ONE'S MIND/MIND'S EYE, imagine, call to mind, visualize, see, evoke. **2** PAINT, draw, sketch, depict, delineate, portray, illustrate, reproduce, represent.

picturesque adj. **1** BEAUTIFUL, pretty, lovely, attractive, scenic, charming, quaint, pleasing, delightful. **2** VIVID, graphic, colourful, impressive, striking. ■ OPPOSITES ugly.

pie n. PASTRY, tart, tartlet, pasty, quiche.

piece n. **1** PART, bit, section, segment, length, quantity, unit, slice, chunk, lump, hunk, wedge, remnant, scrap, snippet. **2** FRAGMENT, smithereens, shard, shred, tatter. **3** SHARE, slice, portion, allotment, allocation, quota, percentage, fraction. □ **piece together** PUT TOGETHER, assemble, join up, fit together, unite.

piecemeal adv. PIECE BY PIECE, bit by bit, gradually, in stages, in steps, little by little, by degrees, in fits and starts.

pier n. **1** JETTY, quay, wharf, dock, landing, landing place, promenade. **2** SUPPORT, upright, pillar, post, column, pile, piling, buttress.

pierce v. PENETRATE, puncture, perforate, prick, stab, spike, enter, pass through, transfix, bore, drill.

piercing adj. **1** SHREWD, sharp, keen, searching, alert, penetrating, perceptive, probing. **2** SHRILL, penetrating, ear-splitting, high-pitched, loud. **3** SEVERE, sharp, stabbing, shooting, penetrating, intense, fierce, excruciating, agonizing, exquisite.

spices, meat, etc.

pilaster n. a rectangular column projecting from a wall.

pilchard n. a small edible fish.

pile n. **1** a number of things lying one on top of another. **2** informal a large amount. **3** a large imposing building. **4** a heavy post driven into the ground to support foundations. **5** the surface of a carpet or fabric, consisting of many small projecting threads. **6** (**piles**) haemorrhoids. ▶v. **1** place things one on top of the other. **2** (**pile up**) accumulate. □ **pile-up** informal a crash involving several vehicles.

pilfer v. steal small items of little value.

pilgrim n. a person who travels to a holy place for religious reasons. ■ **pilgrimage** n.

pill n. **1** a small piece of solid medicine for swallowing whole. **2** (**the Pill**) a contraceptive pill. □ **pillbox 1** a small round hat. **2** a small, partly underground concrete fort.

pillage v. & n. plunder.

pillar n. an upright structure used as a support for a building. □ **pillar box** a red cylindrical postbox.

pillion n. a seat for a passenger behind a motorcyclist.

pillory n. (pl. **pillories**) a wooden frame with holes for the head and hands, in which offenders were formerly locked and exposed to public abuse. ▶v. (**pillorying, pilloried**) ridicule publicly.

pillow n. a cushion to support the head when lying down. ▶v. rest one's head as if on a pillow.

pilot n. **1** a person who operates an aircraft's flying controls. **2** a person qualified to steer ships into or out of a harbour. **3** something done as a test before being introduced more widely. ▶v. (**piloting, piloted**) **1** act as a pilot of an aircraft or ship. **2** test a project before introducing it more widely. □ **pilot light** a small gas burner kept alight permanently to light a larger burner.

pimiento n. (pl. **pimientos**) a red sweet pepper.

pimp n. a man who controls prostitutes and takes a percentage of their earnings. ▶v. act as a pimp.

pimple n. a small inflamed spot on the skin. ■ **pimply** adj.

PIN (or **PIN number**) abbrev. personal identification number.

pin n. **1** a thin pointed piece of metal with a round head, used as a fastener. **2** a short metal rod or peg. ▶v. (**pinning, pinned**) **1** attach or fasten with a pin or pins. **2** hold someone firmly so they are unable to move. **3** (**pin down**) force someone to be definite or give details. **4** (**pin on**) fix blame on. □ **pinball** a game in which small balls are propelled across a sloping board to strike targets. **pin money** a small sum of money for spending on everyday items. **pinpoint** locate exactly. **pins and needles** a tingling sensation. **pinstripe** a very narrow pale stripe in dark cloth. **pin-up** a poster of an attractive person.

pinafore n. **1** a collarless sleeveless dress worn over a blouse or jumper. **2** an apron.

pince-nez /panss-nay/ n. a pair of glasses with a nose clip instead of earpieces.

pincer n. **1** (**pincers**) a metal tool with blunt jaws for gripping and pulling things. **2** a front claw of a lobster etc.

Thesaurus

piety n. PIOUSNESS, religiousness, holiness, godliness, devoutness, devotion, veneration, reverence, religious duty, spirituality, sanctity, religious zeal. ■ OPPOSITES impiety.

pile n. **1** HEAP, bundle, stack, mound, mass, accumulation, collection, assemblage, store, stockpile, hoard, load, mountain. **2** GREAT DEAL, a lot, lots, quantity, abundance, mountain; informal heap, ocean, stacks, oodles, scuds. ▶v. **1** HEAP, stack. **2** ACCUMULATE, amass, collect, gather, stockpile, hoard, store up, assemble, lay by/in. **3** FORM PILES, form heaps, heap up, amass, accumulate.

pile-up n. CRASH, collision, smash, smash-up, accident, road accident.

pill n. TABLET, capsule, pellet, lozenge, bolus.

pillage v. PLUNDER, rob, raid, loot, maraud, sack, ransack, ravage, lay waste, despoil. ▶n. PLUNDER, robbery, raiding, looting, marauding, sacking, ransacking, ravaging, rapine, despoiling, laying waste, spoliation, depredation.

pillory v. STIGMATIZE, cast a slur on, denounce, hold up to shame, hold up to ridicule, ridicule, heap scorn on; informal show up.

pilot n. **1** AIRMAN/AIRWOMAN, aviator, flier, captain, commander, co-pilot. **2** NAVIGATOR, guide, steersman, helmsman. ▶v. FLY, drive, operate, navigate, guide, steer, control, handle, manoeuvre.

pimple n. SPOT, pustule, boil, swelling, papule; informal zit.

p

pinch v. **1** grip flesh tightly between the finger and thumb. **2** hurt by being too tight. **3** informal steal. ▶n. **1** an act of pinching. **2** a very small amount. □ **at a pinch** if absolutely necessary. **feel the pinch** experience financial hardship.

pine v. **1** become weak because of grief etc. **2** (**pine for**) miss someone intensely. ▶n. an evergreen coniferous tree with needle-shaped leaves. □ **pine marten** a dark brown weasel-like mammal.

pineapple n. a large juicy tropical fruit.

ping n. & v. (make) a short high-pitched ringing sound. □ **ping-pong** informal table tennis.

pinion n. **1** the outer part of a bird's wing. **2** a small cogwheel. ▶v. tie or hold the arms or legs of.

pink adj. pale red. ▶n. **1** pink colour. **2** (**the pink**) informal the best condition. **3** a plant with sweet-smelling flowers. ▶v. **1** cut a zigzag edge on. **2** (of an engine) make rattling sounds when running imperfectly.

pinnacle n. **1** a high pointed rock. **2** a small turret. **3** the most successful point.

pint n. a liquid measure equal to one eighth of a gallon (0.568 litre).

pioneer n. **1** a person who explores or settles in a new region. **2** a person who develops a new idea or technique. ▶v. be a pioneer of.

pious adj. **1** deeply religious. **2** pretending to be good or religious. ■ **piously** adv.

pip n. **1** a small seed in a fruit. **2** a short high-pitched sound. **3** a star on an army officer's uniform, showing rank. ▶v. (**be pipped**) informal be only just defeated.

pipe n. **1** a tube through which water, gas, oil, etc. can flow. **2** a narrow tube with a bowl at one end for smoking tobacco. **3** a wind instrument. **4** (**pipes**) bagpipes. ▶v. **1** send through a pipe. **2** play a tune on a pipe. **3** say in a high voice. □ **pipe down** informal be quiet. **pipe dream** an unrealistic hope or scheme. **piping hot** very hot. ■ **piper** n.

pipeline n. a long pipe for carrying oil, gas, etc. over a distance. □ **in the pipeline** being developed.

pipette n. a thin tube for transferring or measuring small quantities of liquid.

piquant adj. having a pleasantly sharp or spicy taste. ■ **piquancy** n.

pique /peek/ n. resentment arising from hurt pride. ▶v. **1** stimulate interest. **2** (**be piqued**) feel resentful.

piquet /pee-kay/ n. a card game for two players.

piranha /pi-rah-nuh/ n. a freshwater fish with very sharp teeth.

pirate n. a person who attacks and robs ships at sea. ▶v. reproduce a film, recording, etc. for profit without permission. ■ **piracy** n. **piratical** adj.

pirouette n. (in ballet) an act of spinning on one foot. ▶v. perform a pirouette.

pistachio /pi-sta-shi-oh/ n. (pl. **pistachios**) a nut with a green kernel.

piste /peest/ n. a ski run.

pistil n. the female organs of a flower.

pistol n. a small gun.

piston n. a sliding disc or cylinder in-

Thesaurus

pin v. **1** ATTACH, fasten, affix, fix, stick, tack, nail. **2** PINION, hold, press, restrain, constrain, hold fast, immobilize, pin down.

pinch v. **1** NIP, tweak, squeeze, compress. **2** see STEAL.

pinched adj. DRAWN, haggard, worn, peaky, pale, wan, strained, stressed, drained. ■ OPPOSITES healthy.

pinnacle n. PEAK, height, culmination, high point, acme, zenith, climax, crowning point, summit, apex, vertex, apogee. ■ OPPOSITES nadir.

pinpoint v. IDENTIFY, discover, distinguish, locate, spot, home in on, put one's finger on.

pioneer n. **1** SETTLER, colonist, colonizer, explorer. **2** DEVELOPER, innovator, ground-breaker, trailblazer, founder, founding father, architect. ▶v. DEVELOP, introduce, launch, instigate, initiate, institute, originate, create, open up, blaze a trail, break new ground.

pious adj. **1** RELIGIOUS, holy, godly, spiritual, devout, devoted, dedicated, reverent, God-fearing, righteous, faithful. **2** SANCTIMONIOUS, hypocritical, self-righteous, unctuous, pietistic, holier-than-thou, goody-goody. ■ OPPOSITES impious.

pipe n. TUBE, cylinder, conduit, main, duct, channel, pipeline, drainpipe. ▶v. CONVEY, duct, channel, transmit, bring in, siphon.

piquant adj. **1** SPICY, flavoursome, peppery, tangy, pungent, sharp, tart, zesty, biting, stinging. **2** STIMULATING, intriguing, interesting, fascinating, alluring, side a tube, esp. as part of an engine or pump.

pit n. **1** a large hole in the ground. **2** a coal mine. **3** a sunken area. **4** an area at the side of a track where racing cars are refuelled etc. **5** (**the pits**) informal a very bad place or situation. ▶ v. (**pitting**, **pitted**) **1** (**pit against**) set in competition with. **2** make a hollow in the surface of.

pitch n. **1** an area of ground where outdoor team games are played. **2** the extent to which a sound is high or low. **3** the steepness of a roof. **4** a particular level of intensity. **5** a form of words used to persuade. **6** a place where a street seller or performer is stationed. **7** a sticky black substance. ▶ v. **1** throw roughly. **2** fall heavily. **3** set at a particular musical pitch. **4** aim at a particular level, target, or audience. **5** set up a tent. **6** (**pitch in**) informal join in enthusiastically. **7** (of a ship) rock from side to side or from front to back. **8** (**pitched**) (of a roof) sloping. ▫ **pitch-black** (or **pitch-dark**) completely dark. **pitched battle** a fierce fight involving many people. **pitchfork** a long-handled fork for lifting hay.

pitchblende n. a mineral containing radium.

pitcher n. a large jug.

piteous adj. deserving or arousing pity. ■ **piteously** adv.

pitfall n. a hidden danger or difficulty.

pith n. spongy white tissue in stems or fruits.

pithy adj. **1** full of pith. **2** (of language or style) concise and expressive.

pitiful adj. **1** deserving or arousing pity. **2** very small or poor. ■ **pitifully** adv.

pitiless adj. showing no pity.

piton /pee-ton/ n. a peg used in rock climbing.

pitta n. a type of flat bread, hollow inside.

pittance n. a very small amount of money.

pituitary gland n. a gland at the base of the brain controlling growth and development.

pity n. (pl. **pities**) **1** a feeling of sorrow for another's suffering. **2** a cause for regret. ▶ v. (**pitying**, **pitied**) feel pity for.

pivot n. a central point or shaft on which a mechanism turns or is balanced. ▶ v. (**pivoting**, **pivoted**) turn on a pivot.

pivotal adj. **1** of a pivot. **2** of central importance.

pixel n. any of the tiny areas of light on a display screen making up an image.

pixelate v. divide an image into pixels.

pixie (or **pixy**) n. (pl. **pixies**) (in fairy tales etc.) a tiny being with pointed ears.

pizza n. a flat base of dough baked with a savoury topping.

pizzeria n. a pizza restaurant serving pizzas.

pizzicato adv. & adj. plucking the strings of a violin etc. instead of using the bow.

placard n. a sign or notice.

placate v. make less angry. ■ **placatory** adj.

Thesaurus

racy, salty, provocative. ■ OPPOSITES insipid.

pirate n. FREEBOOTER, marauder, raider; historical privateer; old use buccaneer, corsair.

pit n. ABYSS, chasm, crater, hole, cavity, excavation, quarry, coal mine, mine, diggings, working.

pitch v. **1** THROW, cast, fling, hurl, toss, lob, launch; informal chuck, heave, bung. **2** PUT UP, set up, erect, raise. **3** FALL HEADLONG, fall, tumble, topple, plunge, dive. ▶ n. **1** FIELD, ground, park, stadium, arena, playing field. **2** LEVEL, point, degree, height, extent, intensity. ▫ **pitch in** HELP, assist, lend a hand, join in, participate, play a part, do one's bit, cooperate, collaborate.

piteous adj. PITIFUL, pitiable, pathetic, distressing, affecting, moving, sad, heart-rending, heartbreaking, poignant,

emotional, emotive.

pitfall n. TRAP, snare, catch, stumbling block, hazard, peril, danger, difficulty.

pitiful adj. **1** see PITEOUS. **2** CONTEMPTIBLE, despicable, poor, sorry, miserable, inadequate, worthless, woeful, lamentable; informal pathetic.

pitiless adj. MERCILESS, ruthless, relentless, cruel, severe, harsh, heartless, callous, brutal, inhuman, inhumane, cold-hearted, hard-hearted, unfeeling, uncaring, unsympathetic. ■ OPPOSITES merciful.

pity n. **1** COMMISERATION, condolence, sympathy, compassion, fellow feeling, understanding, forbearance, distress, sadness, emotion, mercy, clemency, kindness. **2** SHAME, crying shame, misfortune, sad thing, sin. ▶ v. FEEL SORRY FOR, commiserate with, feel sympathy for, sympathize with, feel for.

place n. **1** a particular position or area. **2** a portion of space occupied by or set aside for someone or something. **3** a position in a sequence. **4** a person's status, or a right arising from this. ▶ v. **1** put in a particular position or situation. **2** give a specified position in a sequence. **3** make an order for goods etc. □ **out of place** inappropriate or incongruous. **take place** occur.

placebo /pluh-see-boh/ n. (pl. **placebos**) a medicine prescribed for the mental benefit of the patient rather than for any physical effect.

placement n. **1** the act of placing. **2** a temporary job undertaken for work experience.

placenta n. (pl. **placentae** or **placentas**) an organ in the womb of a pregnant mammal supplying nourishment to the fetus.

placid adj. not easily upset or excited. ■ **placidity** n. **placidly** adv.

placket n. an opening in a garment, covering fastenings or for access to a pocket.

plagiarize (or **-ise**) v. take someone else's work etc. and pretend it is one's own. ■ **plagiarism** n. **plagiarist** n.

plague n. **1** a very serious infectious disease. **2** a very large number of destructive animals or insects. ▶ v.

1 cause continual trouble to. **2** pester.

plaice n. (pl. **plaice**) an edible flatfish.

plaid /plad/ n. tartan fabric.

plain adj. **1** simple or ordinary. **2** without a pattern. **3** easy to see or understand. **4** (of language) direct. **5** not attractive. ▶ adv. informal used for emphasis: *plain stupid*. ▶ n. a large area of flat land with few trees. □ **plain clothes** ordinary clothes rather than uniform. **plain sailing** easy progress. **plainsong** unaccompanied medieval church music for several voices. ■ **plainly** adv. **plainness** n.

plaintiff n. a person bringing a case against another in a court of law.

plaintive adj. sounding sad. ■ **plaintively** adv.

plait n. a single length of hair or rope made up of three or more intertwined strands. ▶ v. form into a plait or plaits.

plan n. **1** a proposal for doing or achieving something. **2** an intention. **3** a map or diagram. ▶ v. (**planning**, **planned**) **1** decide on and arrange in advance. **2** intend. **3** draw a plan of a proposed building etc. ■ **planner** n.

plane n. **1** a completely flat surface. **2** a level of existence or thought. **3** an aeroplane. **4** a tool for smoothing wood by cutting shavings from it. **5** a tall tree with a peeling bark. ▶ adj. completely

Thesaurus

pivot n. AXIS, fulcrum, axle, swivel, spindle, central shaft.

placate v. CALM, pacify, soothe, appease, conciliate, propitiate, mollify.

place n. **1** LOCATION, spot, scene, setting, position, site, situation, venue, area, region, whereabouts; *technical* locus. **2** POSITION, status, grade, rank, station, standing, footing, role, niche. ▶ v. **1** PUT, position, set/lay down, deposit, rest, settle, station, situate. **2** ORDER, rank, grade, group, arrange, sort, class, classify, categorize, bracket.

placid adj. **1** STILL, calm, peaceful, at peace, pacific, tranquil, motionless, smooth, unruffled, undisturbed. **2** CALM, cool, composed, self-possessed, serene, tranquil, equable, even-tempered, peaceable, easy-going, unmoved, undisturbed, unperturbed, imperturbable, unexcited, unexcitable, unruffled, unemotional; *informal* unflappable. ■ OPPOSITES excitable, bustling.

plagiarize v. COPY, pirate, poach, borrow, reproduce, appropriate; *informal* rip off, crib.

plague n. **1** CONTAGION, disease, pesti-

lence, sickness, epidemic, pandemic. **2** MULTITUDE, host, swarm, influx, infestation. ▶ v. AFFLICT, cause suffering to, torture, torment, bedevil, trouble.

plain adj. **1** CLEAR, crystal-clear, obvious, evident, apparent, manifest, transparent, patent, unmistakable. **2** CLEAR-CUT, simple, straightforward, uncomplicated, comprehensible, intelligible, understandable, lucid, unambiguous. **3** SIMPLE, austere, stark, severe, basic, ordinary, unsophisticated, spartan. **4** UNATTRACTIVE, ugly, unprepossessing, unlovely, homely. ■ OPPOSITES obscure, fancy, attractive. ▶ adv. DOWNRIGHT, utterly, completely, totally, thoroughly, positively, incontrovertibly, unquestionably, simply.

plaintive adj. MOURNFUL, doleful, melancholy, sad, sorrowful, unhappy, disconsolate.

plan n. **1** PLAN OF ACTION, scheme, system, procedure, method, programme, schedule, project, way, means, strategy, tactics, formula. **2** SCALE DRAWING, blueprint, layout, sketch, diagram, chart, map, illustration, representation, delinflat. ▶ v. smooth with a plane.

planet n. a large round mass in space orbiting round a star. ■ **planetary** adj.

planetarium n. (pl. **planetariums** or **planetaria**) a building in which images of stars and planets are projected on to a domed ceiling.

plangent adj. loud and mournful.

plank n. a long, flat piece of timber.

plankton n. tiny organisms living in the sea or fresh water.

plant n. **1** a living thing that absorbs substances through its roots and makes nutrients in its leaves by photosynthesis. **2** a factory. **3** machinery used in manufacturing. **4** a person sent to a group as a spy. **5** a thing put among someone's belongings to incriminate them. ▶ v. **1** place a seed, bulb, etc. in the ground to grow. **2** place in a specified position. **3** send or place as a plant. ■ **planter** n.

plantain n. **1** a low-growing plant. **2** a type of banana.

plantation n. **1** an estate on which coffee, tobacco, etc. is grown. **2** an area in which trees have been planted.

plaque n. **1** a commemorative plate fixed to a wall. **2** a sticky deposit on teeth, encouraging the growth of bacteria.

plasma n. **1** the colourless fluid part of blood. **2** a type of gas.

plaster n. **1** a mixture of lime, sand, water, etc. used for coating walls. **2** (also **plaster of Paris**) a white paste of gypsum and water that hardens when dry, used for making moulds and casts. **3** a sticky strip of material for covering wounds. ▶ v. **1** apply plaster to. **2** coat thickly. □ **plasterboard** board made of plaster set between two sheets of paper, used to line interior walls and ceilings. ■ **plasterer** n.

plastic n. a chemically produced material that can be moulded to a permanent shape. ▶ adj. **1** made of plastic. **2** easily shaped. □ **plastic surgery** surgery performed to repair or reconstruct parts of the body. ■ **plasticity** n.

plasticine n. trademark a soft modelling material.

plate n. **1** a flat dish for holding food. **2** bowls, cups, etc. made of gold or silver. **3** a thin, flat piece of metal, glass, etc. **4** a printed photograph or illustration in a book. ▶ v. coat a metal object with a different metal. □ **plate glass** thick glass for windows and doors.

plateau /plat-oh/ n. (pl. **plateaux** or **plateaus**) **1** an area of level high ground. **2** a state of little change following a period of progress.

platelet n. a disc-shaped cell fragment in blood, involved in clotting.

platen n. **1** a plate in a printing press holding the paper against the type. **2** the roller in a typewriter against which the paper is held.

platform n. **1** a raised level area on which people or things can stand. **2** the stated policy of a political party.

platinum n. a precious silvery-white metallic element.

platitude n. a remark used too often to be interesting. ■ **platitudinous** adj.

platonic adj. friendly and affectionate but not sexual.

platoon n. a subdivision of a company of soldiers.

platter n. a large flat serving dish.

platypus n. (pl. **platypuses**) an egg-laying Australian mammal with a duck-like bill.

plaudits pl. n. praise.

plausible adj. seeming reasonable or probable. ■ **plausibility** n. **plausibly** adv.

Thesaurus

eation. ▶ v. **1** ARRANGE, organize, line up, schedule, programme. **2** MAKE PLANS, intend, aim, propose, mean, purpose, contemplate, envisage, foresee.

plane adj. FLAT, level, horizontal, even, flush, smooth, regular, uniform.

plant n. **1** FLOWER, vegetable, herb, shrub, weed. **2** MACHINERY, equipment, apparatus; informal gear. **3** FACTORY, works, foundry, mill, workshop, shop, yard. ▶ v. **1** IMPLANT, set out, sow, scatter. **2** PLACE, position, set, situate.

plaster v. COVER THICKLY, spread, coat, smear, overlay, bedaub.

plastic adj. **1** MOULDABLE, malleable,

workable, ductile, pliant, pliable, supple, flexible, soft. **2** FALSE, artificial, synthetic, spurious, sham, bogus; informal phoney.

plate n. **1** DISH, platter, dinner plate, side plate. **2** PLAQUE, tablet, sign, brass. **3** ILLUSTRATION, picture, photograph, print, lithograph. **4** SHEET, panel, slab.

platform n. **1** DAIS, rostrum, podium, stage, stand. **2** PROGRAMME, policy, manifesto, plan, objectives, principles, tenets.

platitude n. TRUISM, hackneyed expression, commonplace, stock expression, trite phrase, banality, bromide, inanity.

play v. **1** take part in games for enjoyment. **2** compete against in a sport or contest. **3** act the role of. **4** perform a piece of music on an instrument. **5** move a piece or display a playing card in a game. **6** make a CD, tape, etc. produce sounds. **7** move or flicker over a surface. ▶ n. **1** games taken part in for enjoyment. **2** the performing of a sports match. **3** action or operation. **4** a piece of writing performed by actors. **5** freedom of movement. □ **playboy** a wealthy man who spends his time seeking pleasure. **play down** disguise the importance of. **playgroup** a regular play session for pre-school children. **playhouse** a theatre. **playing card** each of a set of pieces of card used in various games. **playmate** a friend with whom a child plays. **play off against** bring one person into conflict with another for one's own advantage. **play on** exploit a weakness. **playpen** a portable enclosure for a young child to play in. **play up** **1** emphasize the importance of. **2** informal cause problems. **playwright** a person who writes plays. ■ **player** n.

playful adj. **1** fond of games and amusement. **2** for amusement; not serious. ■ **playfully** adv. **playfulness** n.

plaza n. a public square.

plc (or **PLC**) abbrev. public limited company.

plea n. **1** an emotional request. **2** a formal statement by or on behalf of a defendant or prisoner.

plead v. (**pleading**, **pleaded** or US or Sc. **pled**) **1** make an emotional request. **2** argue in support of. **3** state formally in court whether one is guilty or not guilty of an offence. **4** present as an excuse.

pleasant adj. **1** satisfactory and enjoyable. **2** likeable. ■ **pleasantly** adv. **pleasantness** n.

pleasantry n. (pl. **pleasantries**) a friendly or humorous remark.

please v. **1** cause to feel happy and satisfied. **2** wish: *do as you please.* **3** (**please oneself**) consider only one's own wishes. ▶ adv. used in polite requests.

pleased adj. feeling or showing pleasure and satisfaction.

pleasurable adj. enjoyable; pleasing.

Thesaurus

platter n. SERVING PLATE, salver, plate, dish, tray.

plausible adj. BELIEVABLE, credible, convincing, persuasive, likely, probable, conceivable, imaginable, tenable, cogent, reasonable. ■ OPPOSITES unlikely, implausible.

play v. **1** AMUSE ONESELF, entertain oneself, enjoy oneself, have fun, play games, frolic, frisk, gambol, romp, cavort. **2** PLAY THE PART OF, act, act the part of, perform, portray, represent, execute. **3** PERFORM, carry out, execute, do, accomplish. **4** TAKE PART IN, participate in, engage in, be involved in. **5** COMPETE AGAINST, contend against, oppose, take on, challenge, vie with, rival. ▶ n. **1** AMUSEMENT, entertainment, recreation, diversion, leisure, enjoyment, fun, merrymaking, revelry. **2** MOVEMENT, freedom of movement, free motion, slack, give. □ **play at** PRETEND TO BE, give the appearance of, assume/affect the role of; *informal* make like. **play down** MAKE LIGHT OF, make little of, gloss over, minimize, diminish, set little store by, underrate, underestimate, undervalue, think little of; *informal* soft-pedal.

player n. **1** COMPETITOR, contestant, participant, team member, sportsman/ sportswoman. **2** ACTOR/ACTRESS, performer, entertainer, artist, artiste, trouper, Thespian. **3** PERFORMER, musician, instrumentalist, artist, artiste, virtuoso.

playful adj. **1** FUN-LOVING, full of fun, high-spirited, frisky, skittish, coltish, sportive, mischievous, impish, puckish; *literary* frolicsome. **2** IN FUN, joking, jesting, humorous, facetious, waggish, tongue-in-cheek, arch, roguish. ■ OPPOSITES serious.

plea n. **1** APPEAL, entreaty, supplication, petition, prayer, request, solicitation, suit, invocation. **2** EXCUSE, pretext, claim, vindication.

plead v. **1** APPEAL TO, beg, entreat, implore, petition, supplicate, importune, pray to, solicit, request, ask earnestly; *literary* beseech. **2** PUT FORWARD, state, assert, argue, claim, allege.

pleasant adj. **1** PLEASING, pleasurable, agreeable, enjoyable, entertaining, amusing, delightful, satisfying, gratifying, nice, good, fine. **2** AGREEABLE, friendly, amiable, affable, genial, likeable, nice, good-humoured, charming, engaging, winning, delightful. ■ OPPOSITES unpleasant.

please v. **1** GIVE PLEASURE TO, be agreeable to, make pleased/happy/glad etc.,

■ **pleasurably** adv.

pleasure n. **1** a feeling of satisfaction and enjoyment. **2** a source of this.

pleat n. a fold in fabric, held by stitching at the top or side. ▶v. form into pleats.

pleb n. informal, derog. a member of the lower social classes.

plebeian /pli-bee-uhn/ adj. lower-class or unsophisticated.

plebiscite /pleb-i-syt/ n. a referendum.

plectrum n. (pl. **plectrums** or **plectra**) a small piece of plastic etc. for plucking the strings of a musical instrument.

pled US or Sc. past part. of PLEAD.

pledge n. **1** a solemn promise. **2** a valuable item given as a guarantee that a debt will be paid etc. **3** a token of love or loyalty. ▶v. **1** make a solemn promise. **2** give as a pledge.

plenary adj. (of a meeting at a conference etc.) attended by all participants.

plenipotentiary n. (pl. **plenipotentiaries**) a person given full power by a government to act on its behalf.

plenitude n. an abundance.

plentiful adj. existing in large amounts. ■ **plentifully** adv.

plenty pron. a large or sufficient amount or quantity. ■ **plenteous** adj.

plethora n. an excessive amount.

pleurisy n. inflammation of the membrane round the lungs.

pliable adj. **1** easily bent. **2** easily influenced or persuaded. ■ **pliability** n.

pliant adj. pliable. ■ **pliancy** n.

pliers pl. n. pincers with flat surfaces for gripping small objects.

plight n. a dangerous or difficult situation. ▶v. (**plight one's troth**) make a solemn promise to marry.

plimsoll n. a light rubber-soled canvas shoe.

Plimsoll line n. a mark on a ship's side showing the legal water level when loaded.

plinth n. a slab forming the base of a column, statue, etc.

plod v. (**plodding, plodded**) **1** walk with heavy slow steps. **2** work slowly and steadily.

plonk informal v. set down heavily or carelessly. ▶n. cheap wine.

plop n. a sound like that of a small object dropping into water. ▶v. (**plopping, plopped**) fall with a plop.

plot n. **1** a secret plan to do something illegal or harmful. **2** the story in a play, novel, or film. **3** a small piece of land. ▶v. (**plotting, plotted**) **1** secretly plan an illegal or harmful act. **2** mark a route or position on a map or graph. ■ **plotter** n.

plough (US **plow**) n. a large implement for turning over and cutting furrows in soil. ▶v. **1** turn soil with a plough. **2** progress with difficulty.

ploy n. a cunning act.

***

Thesaurus

gladden, delight, cheer up, charm, divert, entertain, amuse. **2** WANT, wish, see fit, will, like, desire, be inclined, prefer. ■ OPPOSITES displease.

pleased adj. HAPPY, glad, cheerful, delighted, thrilled, elated, contented, satisfied, gratified, fulfilled; informal over the moon, chuffed.

pleasure n. HAPPINESS, gladness, delight, joy, enjoyment, entertainment, amusement, diversion, satisfaction, gratification, fulfilment, contentment.

pledge n. **1** PROMISE, word, word of honour, vow, assurance, undertaking, oath, covenant, warrant. **2** SECURITY, surety, guarantee, collateral. ▶v. **1** PROMISE, give one's word, vow, give an undertaking, undertake, take an oath, swear, vouch, engage, contract. **2** MORTGAGE, put up as collateral, guarantee, plight, pawn.

plentiful adj. ABUNDANT, copious, ample, profuse, lavish, liberal, generous, large, huge, bumper, infinite. ■ OPPOSITES scanty.

plenty n. PLENTIFULNESS, affluence, prosperity, wealth, opulence, luxury, abundance, copiousness, fruitfulness, profusion; literary plenteousness. □ **plenty of** ENOUGH, sufficient, a good deal of, a great deal of, masses of; informal lots of, heaps of, stacks of, piles of.

plethora n. OVER-ABUNDANCE, superabundance, excess, superfluity, surplus, surfeit, glut. ■ OPPOSITES dearth.

pliable adj. **1** FLEXIBLE, bendable, bendy, pliant, elastic, supple, stretchable, ductile, plastic. **2** MALLEABLE, compliant, docile, biddable, tractable, manageable, governable, controllable, amenable. ■ OPPOSITES rigid, obdurate.

plot n. **1** PIECE OF GROUND, parcel, patch, allotment; US lot. **2** CONSPIRACY, intrigue, stratagem. **3** ACTION, theme, subject, story line, story, scenario, thread. ▶v. **1** MAP OUT, draw, draw a diagram of, draw the layout of, make a blueprint/chart of, sketch out, outline. **2** TAKE PART IN A PLOT, scheme, conspire, participate in a conspiracy, connive, intrigue, form

pluck v. **1** take hold of and quickly remove from its place. **2** pull out or at. **3** pull the feathers from a bird's carcass. ▸ n. courage.

plucky adj. (**pluckier**, **pluckiest**) determined and brave. ■ **pluckily** adv.

plug n. **1** a piece of solid material tightly blocking a hole. **2** a device with metal pins that fit into holes in a socket to make an electrical connection. ▸ v. (**plugging**, **plugged**) **1** block a hole. **2** (**plug in**) connect an electrical appliance to the mains by means of a socket. **3** informal promote something by mentioning it publicly. **4** (**plug away**) informal work steadily.

plum n. **1** an oval, usu. reddish-purple fruit. **2** a reddish-purple colour. ▸ adj. informal highly desirable.

plumage n. a bird's feathers.

plumb v. **1** measure or test with a plumb line. **2** explore or experience fully. **3** connect an appliance etc. to water and drainage pipes. ▸ n. a weight attached to a plumb line. ▸ adv. informal exactly. □ **plumb line** a cord with a weight attached to it, used to find the depth of water or test whether an upright surface is vertical.

plumber n. a person who fits and repairs plumbing.

plumbing n. the system of pipes, fittings, etc. for the water supply, heating, and sanitation in a building.

plume n. **1** a long, soft feather. **2** a long cloud of smoke. ■ **plumed** adj.

plummet v. (**plummeting**, **plummeted**) fall steeply or rapidly.

plump adj. **1** full and rounded in shape. **2** rather fat. ▸ v. **1** (**plump up**) make or become plump. **2** (**plump for**) decide on. ■ **plumpness** n.

plunder v. enter a place by force and steal goods from it. ▸ n. **1** the act of plundering. **2** goods obtained by plundering.

plunge v. **1** fall suddenly. **2** jump or dive quickly. **3** push or thrust quickly. ▸ n. an act of plunging.

plunger n. a device that works with a plunging movement.

pluperfect adj. (of a tense) referring to an action completed earlier than some past point of time.

plural adj. **1** more than one in number. **2** (of a word or form) referring to more than one. ▸ n. a plural word or form. ■ **plurality** n.

plus prep. with the addition of. ▸ adj. **1** more than the amount indicated. **2** above zero. ▸ n. **1** the symbol +. **2** informal an advantage. ▸ conj. also.

plush n. fabric with a long, soft nap. ▸ adj. informal expensively luxurious.

plutocracy n. (pl. **plutocracies**) government by the wealthy. ■ **plutocrat** n.

plutonium n. a radioactive metallic element.

ply n. (pl. **plies**) a layer or strand of a material. ▸ v. (**plying**, **plied**) **1** work steadily with a tool or at one's job. **2** (of a ship etc.) travel regularly over a route. **3** (**ply with**) keep presenting with food etc. □ **plywood** board made of layers of wood glued together.

PM abbrev. Prime Minister.

p.m. abbrev. after noon.

PMT abbrev. premenstrual tension.

pneumatic /nyoo-mat-ik/ adj. containing or operated by air or gas under pressure.

pneumonia /nyoo-moh-ni-uh/ n. inflammation of one or both lungs.

PO abbrev. Post Office.

poach v. **1** simmer in a small amount of liquid. **2** hunt or catch game or fish illegally. **3** unfairly entice customers, workers, etc. away from someone else. ■ **poacher** n.

pocket n. **1** a small bag sewn into or on clothing. **2** an isolated group or area. **3** an opening at the corner or side of a billiard table. ▸ v. (**pocketing**, **pocketed**) **1** put into one's pocket. **2** take dishonestly. □ **out of pocket** having made a loss. **pocket money** a small regular allowance given to children by their parents.

Thesaurus

an intrigue.

plough v. TILL, work, cultivate, break up, turn up.

ploy n. DODGE, ruse, scheme, trick, stratagem, manoeuvre, move.

plummet v. FALL, fall headlong, plunge, hurtle, nosedive, dive, drop.

plump adj. CHUBBY, well rounded, of ample proportions, rotund, buxom, stout, fat, obese, corpulent, fleshy, portly, tubby, dumpy, roly-poly, well covered; informal podgy. ■ OPPOSITES slim, skinny.

plunder v. ROB, pillage, loot, raid, ransack, strip, fleece, lay waste, despoil, maraud, sack, rape. ▸ n. LOOT, booty, spoils, prize, pillage, ill-gotten gains; informal swag.

plunge v. **1** THRUST, stick, jab, push, drive. **2** DIVE, nosedive, jump, plummet,

pockmarked adj. marked by hollow scars.

pod n. a long narrow seed case.

podgy adj. informal rather fat.

podium n. (pl. **podiums** or **podia**) a small platform.

poem n. a piece of imaginative writing in verse.

poet n. a person who writes poems. □ **Poet Laureate** a poet appointed by the British monarch to write poems for important occasions.

poetic (or **poetical**) adj. of or like poetry. ■ **poetically** adv.

poetry n. **1** poems as a whole or as a form of literature. **2** a quality of beauty or emotional power.

po-faced adj. informal serious and disapproving.

pogrom n. an organized massacre of an ethnic group.

poignant adj. arousing a sense of sadness or regret. ■ **poignancy** n. **poignantly** adv.

poinsettia n. a plant with large scarlet bracts.

point n. **1** a tapered, sharp end. **2** a particular place or moment. **3** an item, detail, or idea. **4** the advantage or purpose of something. **5** a particular feature or quality. **6** a unit of scoring, value, or measurement. **7** a dot. **8** a promontory. **9** (**points**) a movable pair of rails at a junction of two railway lines. **10** an electrical socket. ▶ v. **1** direct someone's attention by extending one's finger. **2** aim or face in a particular direction. **3** (**point out**) make someone aware of. **4** fill the joints of brickwork with mortar. □ **beside the point** irrelevant. **point-blank 1** at very close range. **2** in a blunt and very direct way. **point of view** a particular attitude or opinion. **to the point** relevant.

pointed adj. **1** tapering to a point. **2** (of a remark or look) expressing a clear message. ■ **pointedly** adv.

pointer n. **1** a thing that points to something. **2** a dog that on scenting game stands rigid looking towards it.

pointing n. mortar used to fill the joints of brickwork.

pointless adj. having little or no purpose. ■ **pointlessly** adv.

poise n. **1** a graceful way of holding the body. **2** a calm and confident manner. ▶ v. be or cause to be balanced.

poison n. a substance that causes death or injury when swallowed or absorbed. ▶ v. **1** harm or kill with poison. **2** put poison on or in. **3** have a harmful effect on. ■ **poisoner** n. **poisonous** adj.

Thesaurus

drop, fall, descend.

plush adj. LUXURIOUS, luxury, sumptuous, lavish, gorgeous, opulent, rich, costly; informal ritzy, classy. ■ OPPOSITES plain.

pocket n. POUCH, compartment, receptacle. ▶ adj. SMALL, little, miniature, compact, concise, abridged, potted. ▶ v. MISAPPROPRIATE, steal, thieve, purloin; informal lift, pinch, nick, filch, swipe, snaffle.

poet n. VERSIFIER, rhymester, sonneteer, balladeer, lyricist, bard, minstrel.

poetic adj. IMAGINATIVE, creative, figurative, symbolic, flowery.

poignant adj. MOVING, affecting, touching, tender, emotional, sentimental, heartfelt, sad, sorrowful, tearful, tearjerking, evocative.

point n. **1** TIP, top, extremity, prong, spike, tine. **2** PROMONTORY, headland, head, foreland, cape, bluff. **3** PLACE, position, location, situation, site, spot, area, locality. **4** TIME, juncture, stage, period, moment, instant. **5** MAIN POINT, central point, essential point, focal point, salient point, keynote, heart of the matter, essence, nub, core, pith, marrow, meat, crux. **6** MEANING, significance, signification, import, essence, gist, substance, drift, thrust, burden, theme, tenor, vein. **7** AIM, purpose, object, objective, goal, intention, reason for, use, utility. **8** CHARACTERISTIC, trait, attribute, quality, feature, property, predisposition, streak, peculiarity, idiosyncrasy. ▶ v. DIRECT, aim, level, train. □ **point out** CALL ATTENTION TO, draw attention to, indicate, show, specify, designate, identify, mention, allude to.

pointed adj. **1** SHARP, sharp-edged, edged; formal cuspidate, acicular. **2** CUTTING, trenchant, biting, incisive, penetrating, forceful, telling, significant.

pointless adj. FUTILE, useless, in vain, unavailing, to no purpose, valueless, unproductive, senseless, absurd, foolish, nonsensical, stupid, silly. ■ OPPOSITES useful.

poise n. COMPOSURE, equanimity, self-possession, aplomb, self-assurance, calmness, coolness, serenity, dignity, imperturbability, suaveness, urbanity; informal cool. ▶ v. BALANCE, steady, position, support.

poised adj. **1** COMPOSED, serene, self-possessed, self-assured, calm, cool, imperturbable, unruffled, unflappable.

P

poke v. **1** push a finger or pointed object into. **2** search or pry. **3** push or stick out. ▸ n. an act of poking.

poker n. **1** a metal rod for prodding an open fire. **2** a gambling card game. □ **poker face** a blank expression.

poky adj. (**pokier**, **pokiest**) small and cramped.

polar adj. **1** of or near the North or South Pole. **2** having an electrical or magnetic field. **3** completely opposite. □ **polar bear** a large white Arctic bear. ■ **polarity** n.

polarize (or **-ise**) v. **1** divide into two groups with completely opposite views. **2** restrict the vibrations of a light wave to one direction. **3** give magnetic or electric polarity to. ■ **polarization** n.

Polaroid n. trademark **1** a material that polarizes light passing through it, used in sunglasses. **2** a camera that produces a finished print rapidly after each exposure.

Pole n. a person from Poland.

pole n. **1** a long, thin rod or post. **2** either of the two points (**North Pole** or **South Pole**) at opposite ends of the earth's axis. **3** either of the two opposite points of a magnet. **4** the positive or negative terminal of an electric cell or battery. ▸ v. push a boat along with a pole. □ **poles apart** having nothing in common. **pole position** the most favourable starting position in a motor race. **Pole Star** a star located in the part of the sky above the North Pole.

polecat n. **1** a dark brown weasel-like animal. **2** US a skunk.

polemic n. a strong verbal or written attack. ■ **polemical** adj.

polenta n. maize flour or a dough made from this.

police n. an official body of people employed by a state to prevent crime and keep public order. ▸ v. keep law and order in an area. □ **police state** a country in which political police secretly watch and control citizens' activities. ■ **policeman** n. **policewoman** n.

policy n. (pl. **policies**) **1** a course of action adopted or proposed. **2** a contract of insurance.

polio (or **poliomyelitis**) n. an infectious disease causing temporary or permanent paralysis.

Polish n. the language of Poland. ▸ adj. of Poland.

polish v. **1** make smooth and shiny by rubbing. **2** refine or improve. **3** (**polish off**) finish quickly. ▸ n. **1** a substance used to polish something. **2** an act of polishing. **3** shiny appearance. **4** refinement or elegance. ■ **polisher** n.

polite adj. **1** respectful and considerate. **2** civilized or well bred. ■ **politely** adv. **politeness** n.

politic adj. sensible and wise in the circumstances.

Thesaurus

2 READY, prepared, all set, standing by, waiting. ■ OPPOSITES flustered.

poison n. **1** VENOM, toxin. **2** BLIGHT, contagion, cancer, canker, malignancy, corruption, pollution. ▸ v. **1** CONTAMINATE, pollute, blight, spoil. **2** CORRUPT, warp, pervert, deprave, defile, debauch.

poisonous adj. VENOMOUS, deadly, fatal, lethal, noxious. ■ OPPOSITES non-toxic.

poke v. JAB, prod, dig, elbow, nudge, push, thrust, shove, stick.

poky adj. CONFINED, cramped, narrow, cell-like, small, little, tiny. ■ OPPOSITES spacious.

pole n. POST, upright, pillar, stanchion, standard, support, prop, rod, shaft, mast.

police n. POLICE FORCE, police officers, constabulary; informal the cops, the fuzz, the law, the boys in blue, the (Old) Bill, the rozzers, the force, the pigs, the filth. ▸ v. GUARD, keep guard over, keep watch on, protect, keep in order, control, keep under control, regulate.

police officer n. POLICEMAN, POLICE-WOMAN, constable, PC, WPC; US patrolman, trooper; informal cop, bobby, copper, rozzer.

policy n. PLAN, scheme, programme, schedule, code, system, approach, procedure, guideline, theory.

polish v. **1** WAX, buff, rub up, burnish, shine. **2** PERFECT, refine, improve, brush up, touch up, finish off.

polished adj. **1** WAXED, buffed, burnished, shining, shiny, glossy, gleaming, lustrous, glassy, slippery. **2** REFINED, cultivated, civilized, well bred, polite, well mannered, genteel, courtly, urbane, suave, sophisticated. **3** EXPERT, accomplished, masterly, skilful, proficient, adept, impeccable, flawless, faultless, perfect, consummate, outstanding, remarkable. ■ OPPOSITES dull, gauche, inexpert.

polite adj. **1** WELL MANNERED, mannerly, courteous, civil, respectful, deferential, well behaved, well bred, genteel, polished, tactful, diplomatic. **2** WELL BRED, civilized, cultured, refined, polished,

political adj. **1** of the government or public affairs of a country. **2** of politics. □ **political correctness** the avoidance of language or behaviour that could offend certain groups. ■ **politically** adv.

politician n. an elected political representative.

politics n. **1** the activities concerned with governing a country or area. **2** a set of political beliefs.

polity n. (pl. **polities**) **1** a form of government. **2** a society.

polka n. a lively dance for couples.

poll n. **1** the process of voting in an election. **2** a record of the number of votes cast. ▶ v. **1** record the opinion or vote of. **2** receive a specified number of votes. □ **poll tax** a tax paid at the same rate by every adult.

pollard v. cut off the top and branches of a tree to encourage new growth.

pollen n. a powder produced by the male part of a flower, containing the fertilizing agent. □ **pollen count** a measure of the amount of pollen in the air.

pollinate v. fertilize with pollen. ■ **pollination** n.

pollster n. a person who carries out opinion polls.

pollute v. make dirty with harmful or poisonous substances. ■ **pollutant** n. **pollution** n.

polo n. a game like hockey, played on horseback. □ **polo neck** a high turned-over collar on a sweater.

polonium n. a radioactive metallic element.

poltergeist n. a ghost said to throw objects about.

polyandry n. the practice of having more than one husband at the same time.

polychromatic (or **polychrome**) adj. multicoloured.

polyester n. a synthetic fibre or resin.

polyethylene n. polythene.

polygamy n. the practice of having more than one wife or husband at the same time. ■ **polygamist** n. **polygamous** adj.

polyglot adj. knowing or using several languages.

polygon n. a figure with three or more straight sides. ■ **polygonal** adj.

polygraph n. a lie detector.

polyhedron n. (pl. **polyhedra** or **polyhedrons**) a solid with many sides. ■ **polyhedral** adj.

polymath n. a person with knowledge of many subjects.

polymer n. a substance with a molecular structure formed from many identical small molecules bonded together.

polymerize (or **-ise**) v. combine to form a polymer.

polyp n. **1** a simple sea animal which remains fixed in the same place. **2** a small lump projecting from a mucous membrane.

polyphony n. the combination of a number of harmonizing melodies. ■ **polyphonic** adj.

polystyrene n. a light synthetic material, used esp. as packaging.

polytechnic n. hist. a college offering courses up to degree level (now called a 'university').

polytheism n. the belief in more than one god. ■ **polytheistic** adj.

polythene n. a tough, light, flexible plastic.

polyunsaturated adj. (of a fat) not associated with the formation of cholesterol in the blood.

polyurethane n. a synthetic resin used in paint etc.

pomander n. a ball of sweet-smelling substances.

pomegranate n. a round tropical fruit with many seeds.

pommel /pum·m'l/ n. **1** the upward projecting front part of a saddle. **2** a knob on the hilt of a sword.

pomp n. splendid display and ceremony.

pompom n. a small woollen ball attached to a garment for decoration.

pompous adj. ostentatiously or foolishly self-important. ■ **pomposity** n. **pompously** adv.

poncho n. (pl. **ponchos**) ▶ a garment

Thesaurus

genteel, urbane, sophisticated, elegant, courtly. ■ OPPOSITES rude.

politic adj. WISE, prudent, sensible, advisable, judicious, well judged, sagacious, expedient, shrewd, astute, discreet, tactful, diplomatic. ■ OPPOSITES unwise.

political adj. **1** GOVERNMENTAL, ministerial, public, civic, administrative, bur-

eaucratic. **2** FACTIONAL, partisan, bipartisan, power, status.

poll n. **1** VOTE, ballot, canvass, headcount. **2** RETURNS, count, tally. ▶ v. **1** REGISTER, record, return, get, gain. **2** BALLOT, canvass, question, interview, survey, sample.

pollute v. CONTAMINATE, adulterate, infect, taint, poison, dirty, soil, befoul, made of a thick piece of cloth with a slit for the head.

pond n. a small area of still water.

ponder v. consider carefully.

ponderous adj. moving slowly and heavily. ■ **ponderously** adv.

pong n. & v. informal (give off) a stink.

pontiff n. the Pope.

pontificate v. speak pompously and at length.

pontoon n. **1** a card game. **2** a flat-bottomed boat supporting a temporary bridge. **3** a bridge supported by pontoons.

pony n. (pl. **ponies**) a horse of a small breed. □ **ponytail** a hairstyle in which the hair is drawn back and tied at the back of the head.

poodle n. a dog with a curly coat.

pool n. **1** a small area of still water. **2** (also **swimming pool**) an artificial pool for swimming in. **3** a shallow patch of liquid on a surface. **4** a shared fund or supply. **5** a game resembling snooker. **6** (**the pools**) a form of gambling on the results of football matches. ▶ v. put into a common fund; share.

poop n. a raised deck at the back of a ship.

poor adj. **1** having little money. **2** of a low standard or quality. **3** deserving sympathy.

poorly adv. in a poor way. ▶ adj. unwell.

pop v. (**popping**, **popped**) **1** make a sudden short explosive sound. **2** go or put somewhere quickly. ▶ n. **1** a sudden short explosive sound. **2** informal a soft fizzy drink. **3** (also **pop music**) modern popular music with a strong melody and beat. ▶ adj. **1** of pop music. **2** made intellectually accessible to the general public. □ **popcorn** maize kernels heated until they burst open.

pope n. the head of the Roman Catholic Church.

poplar n. a tall, slender tree.

poplin n. a cotton fabric.

poppadom n. a thin circular piece of Indian bread fried until crisp.

popper n. informal a press stud.

poppy n. a plant with large bright flowers.

poppycock n. informal nonsense.

populace n. the general public.

popular adj. **1** liked by many people. **2** of or for the general public. ■ **popularity** n. **popularly** adv.

popularize (or **-ise**) v. **1** make popular. **2** make accessible or interesting to the general public.

populate v. form the population of.

population n. the inhabitants of a place.

populous adj. densely populated.

Thesaurus

foul. ■ OPPOSITES purify.

pomp n. CEREMONY, ritual, display, pageantry, show, spectacle, splendour, grandeur, magnificence, majesty.

pompous adj. SELF-IMPORTANT, presumptuous, imperious, overbearing, grandiose, affected, pretentious, arrogant, vain, haughty, proud, conceited, egotistic, supercilious, condescending, patronizing; informal uppity, uppish. ■ OPPOSITES humble.

ponder v. THINK ABOUT, give thought to, consider, reflect on, mull over, contemplate, meditate on, deliberate about/on, dwell on, brood on/over, ruminate about/on/over, puzzle over, cogitate about/on, weigh up, review.

pontificate v. HOLD FORTH, expound, declaim, preach, lay down the law, sound off, dogmatize, sermonize; informal preachify.

poor adj. **1** PENNILESS, hard up, badly off, poverty-stricken, needy, deprived, in need, needful, in want, indigent, impoverished, impecunious, destitute, penurious, beggared, in straitened circumstances, in the red, on one's beam-ends;

informal broke, flat broke, on one's uppers, skint, stony broke. **2** INFERIOR, unsatisfactory, below standard, below par, imperfect, bad, low-grade, inadequate, deficient, insufficient, sparse, scanty, meagre, scarce, skimpy, paltry, miserable. **3** UNFORTUNATE, wretched, pitiable, pitiful, unlucky, luckless, unhappy, hapless, ill-fated, ill-starred. ■ OPPOSITES rich.

populace n. THE GENERAL PUBLIC, the public, the people, the population, the common people, the masses.

popular adj. **1** WELL LIKED, liked, favoured, in favour, favourite, well received, approved, admired, accepted. **2** PUBLIC, general, civic. **3** CURRENT, prevalent, prevailing, accepted, recognized, widespread, universal, general, common, customary, usual, standard, stock, conventional. ■ OPPOSITES unpopular.

popularity n. **1** FAVOUR, approval, approbation, admiration, acceptance. **2** DEMAND, fashionableness, vogue.

populate v. **1** INHABIT, dwell in, occupy, people. **2** SETTLE, colonize, people.

porcelain n. fine china.

porch n. a covered shelter over the entrance of a building.

porcine adj. of or like a pig.

porcupine n. an animal covered with long protective spines.

pore n. a tiny opening in the skin or another surface. ▶v. (**pore over**) study closely.

pork n. the flesh of a pig as food.

porn n. informal pornography.

pornography n. pictures, writing, or films intended to arouse sexual excitement. ■ **pornographer** n. **pornographic** adj.

porous adj. having tiny spaces through which liquid or air may pass. ■ **porosity** n.

porpoise n. a small whale.

porridge n. a dish of oats or oatmeal boiled with water or milk.

port n. **1** a town or city with a harbour. **2** a harbour. **3** an opening for boarding or loading a ship or for firing a gun from a tank etc. **4** a socket in a computer network into which a device can be plugged. **5** a strong, sweet dark red wine. **6** the left-hand side of a ship or aircraft. □ **porthole** a small window in the side of a ship or aircraft.

portable adj. able to be carried. ■ **portability** n.

portal n. a large impressive doorway or gate.

portcullis n. a strong grating lowered to block a castle's gateway.

portend v. be a portent of.

portent n. a sign or warning of a future event. ■ **portentous** adj.

porter n. **1** a person employed to carry luggage or goods or move hospital equipment or patients. **2** a doorkeeper of a large building.

portfolio n. (pl. **portfolios**) **1** a thin, flat case for drawings, maps, etc. **2** a set of investments. **3** a government minister's area of responsibility.

portico n. (pl. **porticoes** or **porticos**) a roof supported by columns forming a porch.

portion n. **1** a part or share. **2** an amount of food for one person. ▶v. divide into portions and share out.

portly adj. rather fat.

portmanteau /port-**man**-toh/ n. (pl. **portmanteaus** or **portmanteaux**) a large travelling bag.

portrait n. **1** a picture of a person. **2** a description.

portray v. show or describe in a work of art or literature. ■ **portrayal** n.

Portuguese n. (pl. **Portuguese**) **1** a person from Portugal. **2** the language of Portugal and Brazil. ▶adj. of Portugal. □ **Portuguese man-of-war** a jellyfish.

pose v. **1** present or be a problem, question, etc. **2** sit or stand in a particular position to be photographed, painted, etc. **3** (**pose as**) pretend to be. ▶n. **1** a position adopted to be photographed, painted, etc. **2** a way of behaving intended to impress or mislead.

poser n. **1** a poseur. **2** a puzzling question or problem.

Thesaurus

population n. INHABITANTS, residents, community, people, citizenry, populace, society.

populous adj. DENSELY POPULATED, heavily populated, thickly populated, over-populated, crowded, packed, teeming. ■ OPPOSITES deserted.

pore n. OPENING, orifice, hole, outlet.

pornographic adj. OBSCENE, indecent, erotic, dirty, smutty, filthy, salacious, lewd, prurient; informal porno, blue.

porous adj. ABSORBENT, permeable, penetrable, pervious, spongy, sponge-like. ■ OPPOSITES impermeable.

port n. HARBOUR, harbourage, haven, anchorage, dock, mooring, marina.

portable adj. TRANSPORTABLE, movable, conveyable, easily carried, lightweight, compact, handy, manageable.

portend v. BE A SIGN OF, be a warning of, point to, be an omen of, herald, bode, augur, presage, forebode, foreshadow, foretell.

portion n. **1** HELPING, serving, piece, quantity. **2** SHARE, division, quota, part, bit, allocation, allotment, piece; informal cut, whack.

portly adj. STOUT, plump, fat, corpulent, obese, tubby, stocky. ■ OPPOSITES slim.

portrait n. PORTRAYAL, representation, likeness, image, study, depiction.

portray v. **1** PAINT, draw a picture of, draw, sketch, depict, represent, delineate. **2** DESCRIBE, depict, characterize, put into words.

pose v. **1** SIT, model, take up a position. **2** ARRANGE, position, lay out, set out, dispose, place, put, locate, situate. **3** STRIKE AN ATTITUDE, posture, put on an act, play-act, attitudinize, put on airs, show off. **4** PRESENT, set, create, cause, give rise to. ▶n. **1** POSTURE, stance, position, attitude. **2** ACT, pretence, facade, front, masquerade, attitudinizing,

poseur n. a person who behaves in a way intended to impress.

posh adj. informal **1** very elegant or luxurious. **2** upper-class.

posit v. (**positing, posited**) put forward as a basis for argument.

position n. **1** a place where someone or something is or should be. **2** a way in which someone or something is placed or arranged. **3** a situation. **4** a job. **5** a person's status. **6** a point of view. ▶ v. place or arrange. ■ **positional** adj.

positive adj. **1** expressing agreement or permission. **2** hopeful or favourable. **3** not allowing doubt; certain. **4** (of a test) showing the presence of something. **5** (of a quantity) greater than zero. **6** of the kind of electric charge opposite to that carried by electrons. ▶ n. a positive quality. □ **positive discrimination** the policy of employing members of groups which suffer discrimination. ■ **positively** adv.

positron n. a particle with the same mass as an electron but a positive charge.

posse /poss-i/ n. **1** US hist. a body of men summoned by a sheriff to enforce the law. **2** informal a group or gang.

possess v. **1** have as belonging to one. **2** dominate or have complete power over. ■ **possessor** n.

possession n. **1** the state of possessing something. **2** a thing owned.

possessive adj. **1** demanding someone's total attention and love. **2** unwilling to share one's possessions. **3** Grammar expressing possession. □ **possessive pronoun** a pronoun showing possession (e.g. *mine*). ■ **possessively** adv.

possible adj. capable of existing, happening, or being done. ■ **possibility** n. **possibly** adv.

possum n. an opossum.

post n. **1** an upright piece of timber or metal used as a support or marker. **2** the official service or system for delivering letters and parcels. **3** letters and parcels sent or delivered. **4** a place where someone is on duty or where an activity is carried out. **5** a job. ▶ v. **1** send via the postal system. **2** put up a notice. **3** send to a place to take up a job or duty. □ **keep posted** keep informed. **postbox** a large public box into which letters are put for sending by post. **postcard** a card for sending a message by post without an envelope. **postcode** a group of letters and numbers in a postal address to assist the sorting of mail. **postman** (or **post-**

Thesaurus

affectation, airs.

poser¹ n. VEXED QUESTION, enigma, dilemma, puzzle, mystery, conundrum.

poser² n. POSEUR, attitudinizer, posturer, play-actor, impostor, exhibitionist, show-off; informal phoney.

posh adj. **1** LUXURIOUS, luxury, sumptuous, opulent, lavish, rich, fancy; informal plushy, ritzy, swanky. **2** UPPER-CLASS, aristocratic, upmarket, fancy; informal upper-crust.

position n. **1** SITUATION, location, site, place, spot, area, locality, locale, scene, setting. **2** POSTURE, stance, attitude, pose, bearing. **3** STATE, condition, situation, circumstance, predicament, plight, pass. **4** POINT OF VIEW, viewpoint, opinion, way of thinking, outlook, attitude, stand, standpoint, stance. **5** POST, job, situation, appointment, role, office, place, capacity, duty. **6** PLACE, level, grade, grading, rank, status, standing. ▶ v. PLACE, locate, situate, put, arrange, set, settle, dispose, array.

positive adj. **1** CONFIDENT, optimistic, assured, assertive, firm, forceful, determined, resolute; informal upbeat. **2** GOOD, favourable, effective, promising, encouraging, heartening, auspicious, propitious. **3** CONSTRUCTIVE, productive, helpful, practical, useful, beneficial. ■ OPPOSITES negative.

possess v. **1** OWN, be the owner of, have, be the possessor of, count among one's possessions, have to one's name, hold, be blessed with, enjoy, be endowed with, be gifted with. **2** INFLUENCE, control, dominate, have mastery over, bewitch, enchant, put under a spell, obsess.

possessions pl. n. BELONGINGS, things, property, assets, luggage, baggage, personal effects, goods and chattels, accoutrements, paraphernalia, appendages, impedimenta.

possessive adj. **1** ACQUISITIVE, greedy, grasping, covetous, selfish. **2** OVERPROTECTIVE, clinging, controlling, dominating, jealous.

possibility n. FEASIBILITY, practicability, attainability, likelihood, potentiality, conceivability, probability.

possible adj. **1** FEASIBLE, able to be done, practicable, doable, attainable, achievable, realizable, within reach; informal on. **2** LIKELY, potential, conceivable, imagin-

woman) a person employed to deliver or collect post. **postmark** an official mark stamped on a letter or parcel, giving the date of posting. **postmaster** (or **postmistress**) a person in charge of a post office. **post office** a building where postal business is carried on.

post- prefix after.

postage n. the charge for sending something by post.

postal adj. of or sent by post.

post-date v. **1** put a date later than the actual one on a cheque etc. **2** occur later than.

poster n. a large picture or notice used for decoration or advertisement.

poste restante /pohst ress-tuhnt/ n. a post office department where letters are kept until collected by the addressee.

posterior adj. at or nearer the back. ▸ n. a person's bottom.

posterity n. future generations.

postern n. a back or side entrance.

postgraduate n. a person studying for a higher degree.

post-haste adv. with great speed.

posthumous adj. happening, awarded, or published after the person involved has died. ■ **posthumously** adv.

post-mortem n. **1** an examination of a dead body to find out the cause of death. **2** an analysis of an event after it has occurred.

post-natal adj. after childbirth.

postpone v. arrange for something to take place later than first planned. ■ **postponement** n.

postprandial adj. after a meal.

postscript n. a remark added at the end of a letter.

postulant n. a candidate wishing to enter a religious order.

postulate v. assume to be true, as a basis for a theory or discussion. ■ **postulation** n.

posture n. the way in which a person holds their body. ▸ v. behave in a way intended to impress or mislead. ■ **postural** adj.

posy n. (pl. **posies**) a small bunch of flowers.

pot n. **1** a rounded container for storage or cooking. **2** informal cannabis. ▸ v. (**potting, potted**) **1** plant in a pot. **2** preserve food in a pot. **3** (**potted**) in a short, understandable form. **4** strike a billiard ball into a pocket. □ **pot belly** a large protruding stomach. **pot luck** a situation of taking a chance that whatever is available will be acceptable. **potsherd** a broken piece of earthenware. **potshot** a shot aimed at random.

potable adj. drinkable.

potash n. a compound of potassium.

potassium n. a soft metallic element.

potato n. (pl. **potatoes**) a vegetable with starchy white flesh that grows underground as a tuber.

poteen n. illegally distilled whisky.

potent adj. **1** having great power, influence, or effect. **2** (of a man) able to achieve an erection. ■ **potency** n.

potentate n. a monarch or ruler.

potential adj. capable of becoming or developing into something. ▸ n. qualities that may be developed. ■ **potentiality** n. **potentially** adv.

pothole n. **1** a deep underground cave. **2** a hole in a road surface. □ **potholing** exploring potholes as a sport.

potion n. a drink with healing, magical, or poisonous powers.

Thesaurus

able, probable, credible, tenable. ■ OPPOSITES impossible.

possibly adv. **1** PERHAPS, maybe, for all one knows, very likely. **2** CONCEIVABLY, by any means, by any chance, at all.

post n. STAKE, upright, pole, shaft, prop, support, column, stanchion, standard, stock, picket, pillar, palisade, baluster, newel. ▸ v. **1** PUT UP, stick, stick up, pin, pin up, tack, tack up, attach, affix, hang, display. **2** ANNOUNCE, make known, advertise, publish, publicize, circulate, broadcast.

poster n. PLACARD, bill, notice, public notice, sticker, advertisement, announcement, bulletin; informal advert.

postpone v. DEFER, put off, put back, delay, hold over, adjourn, shelve, table, pigeonhole; informal put on ice, put on the back burner. ■ OPPOSITES advance.

postscript n. PS, subscript, afterthought, afterword, addendum, appendix, codicil, supplement.

posture n. **1** POSITION, pose, attitude, carriage, bearing, stance. **2** ATTITUDE, position, point of view, viewpoint, opinion, outlook, stand, standpoint, stance, angle, slant. ▸ v. POSE, strike an attitude, put on an act, act, play-act, attitudinize, show off.

potent adj. POWERFUL, forceful, strong, vigorous, mighty, influential, authoritative, commanding, compelling, dominant, energetic, dynamic, convincing, cogent, effective, persuasive, eloquent; literary puissant. ■ OPPOSITES impotent.

pot-pourri /poh-poor-i/ n. (pl. **pot-pourris**) **1** a scented mixture of dried petals and spices. **2** a mixture.

pottage n. old use soup or stew.

potter v. do minor pleasant tasks in a relaxed way. ▶n. a person who makes pottery.

pottery n. (pl. **potteries**) **1** articles made of baked clay. **2** the craft of making pottery.

potty adj. informal foolish; mad. ▶n. (pl. **potties**) a bowl for a child to use as a toilet.

pouch n. **1** a small flexible bag. **2** a pocket of skin in which certain animals carry their young.

pouffe n. a large firm cushion used as a seat.

poult n. a young chicken or game bird.

poulterer n. a person who sells poultry.

poultice n. a moist mass put on the skin to reduce inflammation.

poultry n. chickens, turkeys, ducks, and geese.

pounce v. move suddenly so as to seize or attack. ▶n. an act of pouncing.

pound n. **1** a unit of weight equal to 16 oz avoirdupois (0.454 kg), or 12 oz troy (0.373 kg). **2** the basic unit of money of the UK. **3** a place where stray dogs or illegally parked vehicles are kept until claimed. ▶v. **1** hit heavily again and again. **2** run with heavy steps. **3** beat or throb with a strong regular rhythm. **4** crush to a powder or paste.

poundage n. a charge made per pound in weight or value.

pour v. **1** flow or cause to flow. **2** rain heavily. **3** come or go in large numbers.

pout v. push out one's lips. ▶n. a pouting expression.

poverty n. **1** the state of being very poor. **2** lack or scarcity of a quality etc.

POW abbrev. prisoner of war.

powder n. **1** a mass of fine dry particles. **2** a cosmetic in this form. ▶v. sprinkle or cover with powder. □ **powder room** a women's toilet. ■ **powdery** adj.

power n. **1** the ability to do something. **2** influence or control. **3** right or authority. **4** a country of international influence and military strength. **5** strength or force. **6** energy produced by mechanical, electrical, or other means. **7** the product of a number multiplied by itself a certain number of times. ▶v. supply with power. □ **power of attorney** the authority to act for another person in legal or financial matters. **power station** a building where electricity is generated. ■ **powerful** adj. **powerfully** adv. **powerless** adj.

p. & p. abbrev. postage and packing.

pp abbrev. **1** (**pp.**) pages. **2** per procurationem (used when signing a letter on someone else's behalf).

PR abbrev. **1** proportional representation. **2** public relations.

practicable adj. able to be done. ■ **practicability** n.

Thesaurus

potential adj. BUDDING, embryonic, developing, promising, prospective, likely, possible, probable. ▶n. PROMISE, possibilities, capability, capacity, ability, aptitude.

potion n. DRINK, beverage, brew, concoction, mixture, draught, elixir, philtre.

potter v. DAWDLE, loiter, dally, dilly-dally; informal mess about/around.

pouch n. BAG, purse, wallet, container.

pounce v. SWOOP ON, spring on, lunge at, leap at, jump at/on, set upon, ambush, take by surprise, take unawares, attack suddenly.

pound¹ v. **1** CRUSH, beat, pulverize, powder, smash, mash, grind; technical comminute, triturate. **2** BEAT, pulsate, pulse, throb, thump, pump, palpitate.

pound² n. COMPOUND, enclosure, pen, yard.

pour v. **1** GUSH, rush, stream, flow, course, spout, jet, spurt. **2** LET FLOW, decant, splash, spill.

poverty n. PENNILESSNESS, neediness, need, want, hardship, deprivation, indigence, impoverishment, impecuniousness, destitution, penury, privation, beggary. **2** DEFICIENCY, dearth, shortage, scarcity, paucity, insufficiency, lack, want, meagreness. ■ OPPOSITES wealth.

powder v. DUST, sprinkle, scatter, strew.

powdery adj. POWDER-LIKE, fine, dusty, chalky, floury, friable, granulated, ground, crushed, pulverized.

power n. **1** ABILITY, capability, capacity, faculty, potential, potentiality. **2** STRENGTH, force, might, weight. **3** CONTROL, authority, mastery, domination, dominance, rule, command, ascendancy, supremacy, dominion, sway.

powerful adj. **1** STRONG, sturdy, strapping, stout, robust, vigorous, tough. **2** INFLUENTIAL, dominant, authoritative, commanding, forceful, strong, vigorous, potent. **3** FORCEFUL, strong, effective, cogent, compelling, convincing, persuasive, eloquent, impressive. ■ OPPOSITES weak.

practical adj. **1** involving the actual doing or use of something rather than theory. **2** likely to be successful or useful. **3** skilled at making or doing things. **4** almost complete; virtual. □ **practical joke** a humorous trick played on someone. ■ **practicality** n. **practically** adv.

practice n. **1** the action rather than the theory of doing something. **2** the usual way of doing something. **3** the business of a doctor, dentist, or lawyer. **4** the doing of something repeatedly to improve one's skill.

☑ **practice** is the spelling for the noun, and in America for the verb as well; **practise** is the British spelling for the verb.

practise (US **practice**) v. **1** do something repeatedly to improve one's skill. **2** do something regularly. **3** be working in a particular profession. **4** (**practised**) expert or experienced.

practitioner n. a person who practises a profession.

pragmatic adj. dealing with things in a practical and sensible way. ■ **pragmatically** adv. **pragmatism** n. **pragmatist** n.

prairie n. a large open area of grassland, esp. in North America. □ **prairie dog** a

North American rodent that lives in burrows.

praise v. **1** express approval of or admiration for. **2** express thanks to or respect for a deity. ▶ n. the expression of approval or admiration. ■ **praiseworthy** adj.

praline n. a sweet substance made from nuts boiled in sugar.

pram n. a wheeled vehicle for a baby, pushed by a person on foot.

prance v. move with high steps.

prang v. informal crash a vehicle.

prank n. a mischievous act.

prankster n. a person fond of playing pranks.

prat n. informal a stupid person.

prattle v. chatter in a foolish or trivial way. ▶ n. foolish or trivial talk.

prawn n. an edible shellfish like a large shrimp.

pray v. **1** say a prayer. **2** wish or hope strongly for something.

prayer n. **1** a request for help or expression of thanks made to God or a god. **2** an earnest hope or wish.

pre- prefix before.

preach v. **1** give a religious talk to a group. **2** recommend a course of action. **3** give moral advice in an annoying or boring way. ■ **preacher** n.

preamble n. an introduction or opening

Thesaurus

powerless adj. WEAK, feeble, impotent, helpless, unfit, ineffectual, inadequate, paralysed, disabled, incapacitated, debilitated. ■ OPPOSITES powerful, strong.

practicable adj. FEASIBLE, possible, viable, workable, doable, achievable, attainable, accomplishable. ■ OPPOSITES theoretical.

practical adj. **1** APPLIED, empirical, pragmatic, workaday, hands-on. **2** FUNCTIONAL, useful, utilitarian, sensible. **3** BUSINESSLIKE, sensible, down-to-earth, pragmatic, realistic, hard-headed; informal hard-nosed. ■ OPPOSITES impractical.

practically adv. ALMOST, nearly, virtually, all but, in effect; informal pretty nearly/well.

practice n. **1** ACTION, operation, application, effect, exercise, use. **2** TRAINING, preparation, study, exercise, drill, workout, rehearsal. **3** PROCEDURE, method, system, usage, tradition, convention.

practise v. **1** PERFORM, carry out, do, execute, follow, pursue, observe. **2** REHEARSE, go through, run through, go

over, work at, polish, refine. **3** WORK IN, have a career in, pursue a career in, engage in.

praise v. **1** EXPRESS ADMIRATION FOR, applaud, acclaim, express approval of, cheer, compliment, congratulate, commend, pay tribute to, extol, sing the praises of, eulogize; formal laud. **2** WORSHIP, glorify, honour, exalt, adore, pay tribute to, give thanks to; formal laud. ■ OPPOSITES condemn. ▶ n. **1** APPROBATION, applause, acclaim, approval, acclamation, compliments, congratulations, commendation, tributes, accolades, plaudits, eulogy, panegyric, encomium; formal laudation. **2** WORSHIP, glory, honour, devotion, exaltation, adoration.

praiseworthy adj. COMMENDABLE, laudable, admirable, estimable, creditable, deserving, meritorious, worthy, excellent, exemplary, sterling, fine.

prance v. **1** LEAP, spring, jump, skip, cavort, caper, frisk, gambol. **2** PARADE, strut, swagger; informal swank.

prank n. TRICK, practical joke, joke, hoax, caper, stunt; informal lark.

statement.

pre-arrange v. arrange beforehand.

precarious adj. **1** likely to tip or fall. **2** unsafe or uncertain. ■ **precariously** adv.

precaution n. something done in advance to avoid problems or danger. ■ **precautionary** adj.

precede v. come, go, or happen before in time or order.

precedence n. the state of coming before others in order or importance.

precedent n. a previous case taken as an example to be followed in a similar situation.

precept n. a general rule of behaviour.

precinct n. **1** an area closed to traffic in a town. **2** the area around a place or building, often enclosed by a wall. **3** US each of the electoral or policing districts of a city or town.

precious adj. **1** having great value. **2** greatly loved or valued. **3** affectedly refined.

precipice n. a very steep rock face or cliff.

precipitate v. **1** cause an undesirable event to happen suddenly or too soon. **2** cause to move suddenly and with force. **3** cause a substance to be deposited in solid form from a solution. **4** cause vapour to condense and fall as rain, snow, etc. ▶ adj. rash or hasty. ▶ n. a substance precipitated from a solution.

precipitation n. **1** rain, snow, sleet, or hail. **2** the act of precipitating.

precipitous adj. very steep.

precis /pray-si/ n. (pl. **precis**) a summary. ▶ v. make a precis of.

precise adj. **1** clear and detailed. **2** careful about details and accuracy. **3** particular. ■ **precisely** adv. **precision** n.

preclude v. prevent something from happening.

precocious adj. having developed certain abilities etc. earlier than usual. ■ **precocity** n.

precognition n. foreknowledge by paranormal means.

preconceived adj. (of an idea) formed before having full knowledge or evidence. ■ **preconception** n.

precondition n. a condition that must be fulfilled beforehand.

precursor n. a forerunner.

pre-date v. exist or occur at a date earlier than.

predator n. a predatory animal.

predatory adj. (of an animal) killing others for food.

Thesaurus

pray v. **1** OFFER PRAYERS TO, say prayers to. **2** APPEAL FOR, beg for, petition for, solicit, plead for.

prayer n. DEVOTION, communion, litany, collect.

preach v. **1** GIVE A SERMON, sermonize, spread the gospel, evangelize. **2** LECTURE, pontificate, moralize, harangue, sermonize.

preacher n. MINISTER, parson, clergyman, churchman, cleric, missionary, revivalist, evangelist, televangelist.

precarious adj. RISKY, hazardous, insecure, unstable, shaky, tricky, perilous, dangerous, touch-and-go; informal dicey, hairy. ■ OPPOSITES safe.

precaution n. **1** PREVENTIVE MEASURE, preventative measure, safety measure, safeguard, provision. **2** FORESIGHT, foresightedness, forethought, prudence, far-sightedness, anticipation, circumspection, caution, care, attentiveness, chariness, wariness.

precede v. **1** GO BEFORE, come before, go/come ahead of, lead, usher in. **2** LEAD TO, lead up to, antedate, antecede, usher in, herald, pave the way for. ■ OPPOSITES follow.

precedence n. RANK, seniority, superiority, pre-eminence, eminence, supremacy, primacy, ascendancy.

precedent n. PREVIOUS CASE, prior case, previous instance, prior instance, pattern, model, example, exemplar, paradigm, criterion, yardstick, standard.

precious adj. **1** VALUABLE, costly, expensive, dear, priceless, rare, choice. **2** VALUED, cherished, prized, treasured, favourite, dear, beloved, adored, revered, venerated.

precipitate v. HASTEN, accelerate, expedite, speed up, push forward, bring on, trigger. ▶ adj. HURRIED, rapid, swift, speedy, headlong, abrupt, sudden, unexpected, breakneck, precipitous.

precipitous adj. **1** STEEP, sheer, perpendicular, abrupt, high. **2** see PRECIPITATE.

precise adj. **1** EXACT, literal, actual, close, faithful, strict, express, minute, accurate, correct. **2** EXACT, very, actual, particular, specific, distinct. ■ OPPOSITES imprecise.

preclude v. PREVENT, prohibit, make impossible, rule out, eliminate, debar, interdict, block, bar, impede.

precocious adj. ADVANCED, ahead, forward, gifted, brilliant, quick, smart. ■ OPPOSITES backward.

predecease v. die before another person.

predecessor n. a person who held a job or office before the current holder.

predestination n. the belief that everything has been decided in advance by God or fate.

predicament n. a difficult situation.

predicate n. the part of a sentence or clause containing a verb and stating something about the subject. ■ **predicative** adj.

predict v. state that an event will happen in the future. ■ **predictable** adj. **predictably** adv. **prediction** n. **predictive** adj. **predictor** n.

predilection n. a special liking.

predispose v. make likely to be, do, or think something. ■ **predisposition** n.

predominant adj. **1** present as the main part. **2** having the greatest power. ■ **predominance** n. **predominantly** adv. **predominate** v.

pre-eminent adj. better than all others; outstanding. ■ **pre-eminence** n.

pre-empt v. **1** take action to prevent something happening. **2** prevent from saying something by speaking first. ■ **pre-emption** n. **pre-emptive** adj.

preen v. **1** (of a bird) tidy and clean its feathers with its beak. **2** attend to and admire one's appearance. **3** (**preen oneself**) feel very self-satisfied.

prefabricated adj. (of a building) made in sections for easy assembly on site.

preface n. an introduction to a book. ▶ v. say or do something to introduce a book, speech, etc.

prefect n. **1** a senior pupil in a school who has some authority over other pupils. **2** an administrative official in certain countries. ■ **prefecture** n.

prefer v. (**preferring, preferred**) **1** like better than another or others. **2** put forward a formal accusation.

preferable adj. more desirable. ■ **preferably** adv.

preference n. **1** a greater liking for one alternative over another or others. **2** a thing preferred. **3** favour shown to one person over others.

preferential adj. favouring a particular person or group. ■ **preferentially** adv.

preferment n. promotion.

prefix n. a letter or group of letters placed at the beginning of a word to alter its meaning. ▶ v. add a prefix to.

pregnant adj. **1** having a child or young developing in the womb. **2** full of meaning. ■ **pregnancy** n.

Thesaurus

preconception n. PRECONCEIVED IDEA, assumption, presupposition, presumption, prejudgement, prejudice, bias.

predatory adj. **1** HUNTING, predacious, rapacious, raptorial. **2** EXPLOITATIVE, greedy, acquisitive, rapacious, wolfish, vulturine.

predecessor n. PRECURSOR, forerunner, antecedent, ancestor, forefather, forebear, progenitor. ■ OPPOSITES successor, descendant.

predestine v. FATE, predetermine, destine, foreordain, predestinate.

predicament n. DIFFICULT SITUATION, plight, tight corner, mess, emergency, crisis, dilemma, quandary, trouble; informal jam, hole, fix, pickle, scrape, tight spot.

predict v. FORECAST, foretell, prophesy, foresee, divine, prognosticate, forewarn, forebode, portend, presage, augur.

predictable adj. FORESEEABLE, expected, anticipated, probable, likely, certain, sure; informal on the cards.

predilection n. LIKING, fondness, preference, love, partiality, taste, weakness, penchant, fancy, inclination, leaning. ■ OPPOSITES dislike.

predominate v. BE DOMINANT, be in control, rule, hold ascendancy, hold sway, have the upper hand, carry most weight.

pre-eminent adj. OUTSTANDING, leading, foremost, chief, excellent, distinguished, prominent, eminent, important, superior, unrivalled, unsurpassed. ■ OPPOSITES undistinguished.

preface n. INTRODUCTION, foreword, preamble, prologue, prelude, front matter, proem, exordium, prolegomenon; informal prelims, intro. ▶ v. PRECEDE, prefix, introduce, begin, open, launch.

prefer v. LIKE BETTER, favour, fancy, be more partial to, incline towards, choose, select, pick, opt for, go for, plump for, single out.

preferable adj. BETTER, superior, more desirable, more suitable.

preference n. **1** CHOICE, first choice, first option, liking, fancy, desire, wish, inclination, partiality, predilection, leaning, bias, bent. **2** PREFERENTIAL TREATMENT, favour, precedence, priority, advantage.

preferential adj. SPECIAL, better, advantageous, favoured, privileged, partial, partisan.

prehensile adj. (of an animal's limb or tail) able to grasp things.

prehistoric adj. of the period before written records.

prejudge v. form a judgement before knowing all the facts.

prejudice n. **1** an opinion not based on reason or experience. **2** dislike or unfair behaviour based on such opinions. ▶v. **1** give rise to prejudice in. **2** cause harm to.

prejudicial adj. harmful to rights etc.

prelate n. a high-ranking member of the clergy.

preliminary adj. happening before or preparing for a main action or event. ▶n. (pl. **preliminaries**) a preliminary action or event.

prelude n. **1** an action or event acting as an introduction to something more important. **2** an introductory piece of music.

premarital adj. before marriage.

premature adj. occurring or done before the usual or proper time. ■ **prematurely** adv.

premeditated adj. planned in advance. ■ **premeditation** n.

premenstrual adj. occurring before menstruation.

premier adj. first in importance, order, or position. ▶n. a Prime Minister or other head of government. ■ **premiership** n.

premiere n. the first performance of a play, film, etc.

premise (or **premiss**) n. a statement or idea forming the basis for a theory or argument.

premises pl. n. the building and land occupied by a business.

premium n. (pl. **premiums**) **1** an amount paid for an insurance policy. **2** a sum added to a usual price or charge. □ **at a premium 1** scarce and in demand. **2** above the usual price.

premonition n. a feeling that something is about to happen. ■ **premonitory** adj.

preoccupy v. (**preoccupying**, **preoccupied**) fill the mind of completely. ■ **preoccupation** n.

preparation n. **1** the act of preparing. **2** something done to prepare for an event or undertaking. **3** a substance prepared for use.

preparatory adj. done so as to prepare for something. □ **preparatory school** a private school for pupils aged 7 to 13.

prepare v. **1** make ready for use.

Thesaurus

pregnant adj. **1** HAVING A BABY/CHILD, expectant, expecting, in the family way, with child, enceinte; *informal* preggers, with a bun in the oven, in the club; *technical* gravid. **2** MEANINGFUL, significant, eloquent, expressive, suggestive, pointed, telling.

prejudice n. BIAS, discrimination, partisanship, partiality, preference, onesidedness, chauvinism, bigotry, narrow-mindedness, intolerance, unfairness, unjustness, racism, sexism, ageism, heterosexism. ▶v. BE PREJUDICIAL TO, be disadvantageous to, damage, injure, harm, hurt, mar, spoil, impair, undermine.

prejudiced adj. BIASED, discriminatory, partisan, partial, one-sided, jaundiced, chauvinistic, bigoted, intolerant, narrow-minded, unfair, unjust, racist, sexist, ageist. ■ OPPOSITES impartial.

prejudicial adj. DETRIMENTAL, deleterious, unfavourable, damaging, injurious, harmful, hurtful, inimical. ■ OPPOSITES beneficial.

preliminary adj. INTRODUCTORY, prefatory, prior, precursory, opening, initial, beginning, preparatory, initiatory. ■ OPPOSITES final.

prelude n. **1** PRECURSOR, forerunner, curtain-raiser, harbinger, herald, preliminary, introduction, start, beginning. **2** INTRODUCTION, preface, prologue, preamble, proem, exordium, prolegomenon; *informal* intro.

premature adj. TOO SOON, too early, early, untimely, overhasty, precipitate, impulsive, impetuous, rash. ■ OPPOSITES overdue.

premeditated adj. PLANNED, pre-planned, pre-arranged, intentional, intended, deliberate, calculated, wilful. ■ OPPOSITES spontaneous.

premier n. HEAD OF GOVERNMENT, president, prime minister, PM. ▶ adj. LEADING, foremost, chief, principal, head, top, first, highest, main.

premonition n. FOREBODING, presentiment, intuition, feeling, hunch, suspicion, sneaking suspicion, misgiving, apprehension, fear, feeling in one's bones, funny feeling.

preoccupied adj. LOST IN THOUGHT, deep in thought, in a brown study, absorbed, engrossed, pensive, absent-minded, distracted, abstracted, distrait, oblivious, faraway, rapt.

preparation n. **1** ARRANGEMENT, provi-

2 make or get ready to do or deal with something. **3** (**prepared**) willing.

preponderance n. the state of being greater in number. ■ **preponderant** adj. **preponderate** v.

preposition n. a word used with a noun or pronoun to show place, position, time, or method. ■ **prepositional** adj.

prepossessing adj. attractive.

preposterous adj. utterly absurd or ridiculous. ■ **preposterously** adv.

prepuce /pree-pyooss/ n. the foreskin.

prerequisite n. something that must exist or happen before something else can exist or happen.

prerogative n. a right or privilege.

presage v. be an omen of. ▶ n. an omen.

Presbyterian adj. of a Protestant Church governed by elders of equal rank. ▶ n. a member of a Presbyterian Church. ■ **Presbyterianism** n.

presbytery n. (pl. **presbyteries**) **1** an administrative body in a Presbyterian Church. **2** the house of an RC priest.

prescient /press-i-uhnt/ adj. having knowledge of events before they happen. ■ **prescience** n.

prescribe v. **1** recommend and permit the use of a medicine etc. **2** state officially that something should be done.

☑ Don't confuse **prescribe** with **proscribe**, which means 'forbid'.

---

prescription n. a doctor's written instruction stating that a patient may be issued with a medicine.

prescriptive adj. stating what should be done.

presence n. **1** the state of being present. **2** an impressive manner or appearance. **3** a person or thing that seems to be present but is not seen. □ **presence of mind** the ability to act quickly and sensibly in a crisis.

present¹ adj. **1** being or occurring in a particular place. **2** existing or occurring now. ▶ n. the present time.

present² v. **1** give formally at a ceremony. **2** introduce and appear in a broadcast. **3** be the cause of a problem. **4** give a particular impression. ▶ n. a gift. ■ **presentation** n. **presenter** n.

presentable adj. clean or smart enough to be seen in public.

presentiment n. a feeling that something unpleasant is going to happen.

presently adv. **1** soon. **2** now.

preservative n. a substance used to prevent food or wood from decaying.

preserve v. **1** keep in its original or existing state. **2** keep safe from harm. **3** treat food to prevent it from decaying. ▶ n. **1** jam. **2** something seen as reserved for a particular person or group. ■ **preservation** n. **preserver** n.

preset v. (**presetting**, **preset**) set the controls of an electrical device before it

---

Thesaurus

sion, preparatory measure, necessary step, groundwork, spadework. **2** COACH-ING, training, grooming, priming. **3** MIX-TURE, compound, concoction, composition, tincture.

prepare v. **1** GET READY, make ready, arrange, develop, put together, assemble, draw up, produce, construct, compose, concoct, fashion, work up. **2** REVISE, study, cram, do homework; informal swot. **3** COACH, train, groom, prime.

preposterous adj. ABSURD, ridiculous, foolish, ludicrous, farcical, asinine, senseless, unreasonable, crazy, insane, outrageous, unbelievable, incredible, unthinkable. ■ OPPOSITES sensible.

prerequisite adj. NECESSARY, needed, required, called for, essential, requisite, vital, indispensable, imperative, obligatory, mandatory. ▶ n. REQUIREMENT, necessity, essential, requisite, precondition, condition, sine qua non; informal must.

prescribe v. **1** ADVISE, recommend, commend, suggest. **2** LAY DOWN, require,

stipulate, specify, decree, order, command, ordain, enjoin.

presence n. **1** EXISTENCE, being. **2** COM-PANY, proximity, neighbourhood, vicinity, closeness, nearness. **3** MAGNETISM, aura, charisma, personality, attraction, poise. ■ OPPOSITES absence.

present¹ adj. **1** EXISTING, existent, extant. **2** PRESENT-DAY, existing, current, contemporary. **3** IN ATTENDANCE, nearby, near, available, at hand, ready. ■ OP-POSITES absent. ▶ n. TODAY, now, here and now, the present moment, the time being.

present² v. **1** GIVE, hand over, confer, bestow, donate, award, grant, accord. **2** INTRODUCE, make known, announce. **3** PUT ON, produce, perform, stage, mount.

present³ n. GIFT, donation, offering, contribution, gratuity, handout, presentation, award, bounty, benefaction; informal freebie, pressie.

presentable adj. WELL GROOMED, smartly dressed, tidily dressed, tidy, spruce, is used.

preside v. be in charge of a meeting, court, etc.

president n. **1** the elected head of a republic. **2** the head of an organization. ■ **presidency** n. **presidential** adj.

press v. **1** move into contact with something by using steady force. **2** push something to operate a device. **3** apply pressure to something to flatten or shape it. **4** move in a particular direction by pushing. **5** (**press on/ahead**) continue in one's action. **6** forcefully put forward an opinion or claim. **7** try hard to persuade. **8** (**be pressed for**) have too little of. ▶ n. **1** a device for flattening or shaping something. **2** a printing press. **3** newspapers or journalists as a whole. □ **press conference** a meeting with a number of journalists. **press-gang** force into doing something. **press into service** put to a particular use as a makeshift measure. **press stud** a small fastener with two parts that fit together when pressed. **press-up** an exercise in which a person lies on the floor and raises their body by pressing down on their hands.

pressing adj. urgent.

pressure n. **1** steady force applied to an object. **2** the use of persuasion or threats. **3** stress. **4** the force per unit area applied by a fluid against a surface. ▶ v. pressurize. □ **pressure cooker** an airtight pot for cooking food quickly under steam pressure. **pressure group** a group that tries to influence public policy in the interest of a particular cause.

pressurize (or **-ise**) v. **1** persuade or force into doing something. **2** keep the air pressure in an aircraft cabin the same as it is at ground level.

prestige n. respect and admiration resulting from achievements, high quality, etc.

prestigious adj. having or bringing prestige.

presto adv. & adj. Music quickly.

prestressed adj. (of concrete) strengthened by rods or wires inside it.

presumably adv. as may be presumed.

presume v. **1** suppose to be true. **2** be bold enough to do something that one should not do. **3** (**presume on**) take advantage of someone's kindness, friendship, etc. ■ **presumption** n.

presumptuous adj. behaving too confidently. ■ **presumptuously** adv.

presuppose v. **1** require as a precondition. **2** assume to be the case. ■ **presupposition** n.

pretence (US **pretense**) n. **1** an act of pretending. **2** a claim to have or be something.

Thesaurus

of smart appearance, fit to be seen.

preserve v. CONSERVE, protect, care for, safeguard, guard, defend, shield, save, keep, maintain, perpetuate, uphold. ■ OPPOSITES neglect.

preside v. BE IN CHARGE OF, control, direct, run, conduct, supervise, govern, rule.

press v. **1** DEPRESS, push down, force down, bear down on. **2** CRUSH, squeeze, compress, mash, reduce. **3** SMOOTH OUT, flatten, iron. **4** URGE, entreat, exhort, implore, put pressure on, pressurize, force, compel, coerce. ▶ n. NEWSPAPERS, the media, journalists, reporters, Fleet Street.

pressing adj. see URGENT.

pressure n. **1** FORCE, weight, heaviness, compression. **2** COERCION, compulsion, force, constraint, duress. **3** STRAIN, stress, tension, burden, load, weight, trouble; informal hassle. ▶ v. PUT PRESSURE ON, pressurize, press, force, compel, coerce, constrain, bulldoze, dragoon.

prestige n. STATUS, kudos, standing, stature, importance, reputation, fame,

renown, esteem, influence, authority, supremacy, eminence, superiority, predominance.

prestigious adj. IMPORTANT, prominent, impressive, high-ranking, reputable, respected, esteemed, eminent, distinguished, of high standing, well known, celebrated, illustrious, renowned, famous.

presume v. **1** ASSUME, take for granted, take it, take as read, suppose, presuppose, believe, think, imagine, judge, guess, surmise, conjecture, hypothesize, infer, deduce. **2** HAVE THE TEMERITY, have the audacity, be so bold as, have the effrontery, go so far as, venture, dare.

presumptuous adj. OVERCONFIDENT, cocksure, arrogant, egotistical, conceited, bold, audacious, forward, pushy, insolent, impudent, bumptious; informal too big for one's boots.

pretence n. **1** FALSE SHOW, show, semblance, appearance, false front, guise, facade, masquerade, mask, veneer, cover, charade. **2** PRETEXT, false excuse, guise,

pretend v. **1** make it seem that something is the case when in fact it is not. **2** (**pretend to**) claim to have. ■ **pretender** n.

pretension n. **1** a claim to have or be something. **2** pretentiousness.

pretentious adj. trying to appear more important or better than one actually is. ■ **pretentiousness** n.

preternatural adj. beyond what is normal or natural. ■ **preternaturally** adv.

pretext n. a false reason used to justify an action.

prettify v. (**prettifying**, **prettified**) make something seem pretty.

pretty adj. (**prettier**, **prettiest**) attractive in a delicate way. ▶ adv. informal to a certain extent. ■ **prettily** adv. **prettiness** n.

pretzel n. a knot-shaped salted biscuit.

prevail v. **1** be more powerful than. **2** (**prevail on**) persuade. **3** be widespread or current.

prevalent adj. widespread in a particular area. ■ **prevalence** n.

prevaricate v. avoid giving a direct answer. ■ **prevarication** n.

prevent v. stop something from happening or someone from doing something. ■ **preventable** adj. **prevention** n.

preventive (or **preventative**) adj. designed to prevent something.

previous adj. coming before in time or order. ■ **previously** adv.

prey n. **1** an animal hunted and killed by another for food. **2** a victim. ▶ v. (**prey on**) **1** hunt and kill for food. **2** take advantage of or cause distress to.

price n. **1** the amount of money for which something is bought or sold. **2** something unwelcome that must be done to achieve something. ▶ v. decide the price of.

priceless adj. **1** very valuable. **2** informal very amusing.

prick v. **1** pierce slightly. **2** cause to have a slight prickling feeling. ▶ n. a mark, hole, or pain caused by pricking.

Thesaurus

sham, ruse, wile, trickery, lie, falsehood. **3** PRETENTIOUSNESS, display, ostentation, affectation, showiness, flaunting, posturing.

pretend v. **1** PUT ON AN ACT, act, play-act, put it on, dissemble, sham, feign, fake, dissimulate, make believe, put on a false front, posture, go through the motions. **2** CLAIM, make believe, purport, affect, profess, make out, fabricate.

pretender n. CLAIMANT, claimer, aspirant.

pretentious adj. AFFECTED, ostentatious, showy, pompous, artificial, mannered, high-flown, high-sounding, flowery, grandiose, elaborate, extravagant, flamboyant, grandiloquent, bombastic, orotund; informal highfalutin. ■ OPPOSITES plain, simple.

pretty adj. LOVELY, attractive, good-looking, nice-looking, personable, prepossessing, appealing, charming, delightful, engaging, pleasing, winning, nice, winsome, as pretty as a picture; Sc. & N. Engl. bonny; US informal cute; old use fair, comely. ■ OPPOSITES ugly. ▶ adv. QUITE, rather, fairly, somewhat, moderately, reasonably; informal kind of.

prevail v. WIN, triumph, be victorious, carry the day, conquer, overcome, gain mastery.

prevalent adj. **1** PREVAILING, current, frequent, usual, common, general, widespread, pervasive, universal, set, established, accepted, popular, fashionable,

in fashion, in style, in vogue. **2** WIDESPREAD, extensive, frequent, usual, endemic, universal, ubiquitous, rampant, rife. ■ OPPOSITES uncommon.

prevaricate v. BE EVASIVE, shilly-shally, dodge the issue, hedge, beat about the bush, equivocate, quibble, hum and haw.

prevent v. PUT A STOP TO, halt, arrest, avert, nip in the bud, fend off, turn aside, stave off, ward off, block, check, hinder, impede, hamper, obstruct, baulk, foil, thwart, frustrate, forestall, inhibit, hold back, restrain, prohibit, bar, deter. ■ OPPOSITES encourage.

preventative, preventive adj. PRECAUTIONARY, protective, deterrent, prophylactic.

previous adj. **1** FORMER, ex-, past, sometime, one-time, erstwhile, quondam. **2** PRECEDING, foregoing, earlier, prior, above, precursory, antecedent, anterior. ■ OPPOSITES following.

previously adv. FORMERLY, earlier on, before, until now, hitherto, heretofore, once, at one time, in the past, in years gone by.

price n. **1** COST, asking price, charge, fee, payment, rate, amount, figure, value, valuation, bill. **2** RESULT, cost, penalty, sacrifice, forfeit, forfeiture, punishment. ▶ v. FIX/SET THE PRICE OF, cost, value, rate, evaluate, assess, estimate, appraise, assay.

priceless adj. **1** INVALUABLE, precious,

□ **prick up one's ears 1** (of an animal) make the ears stand erect. **2** begin to pay attention.

prickle n. **1** a small thorn or a pointed spine. **2** a tingling feeling. ▶v. have a tingling feeling.

prickly adj. **1** having prickles. **2** easily offended or annoyed.

pride n. **1** pleasure or satisfaction gained from achievements, qualities, or possessions. **2** a source of this. **3** self-respect. **4** a group of lions. ▶v. (**pride oneself on**) be proud of. □ **pride of place** the most noticeable or important position.

priest n. **1** a member of the clergy. **2** (fem. **priestess**) a person who performs ceremonies in a non-Christian religion. ■ **priesthood** n. **priestly** adj.

prig n. a self-righteous person. ■ **priggish** adj.

prim adj. showing prudish disapproval of anything improper. ■ **primly** adv.

prima ballerina n. the chief female dancer in a ballet company.

primacy n. the fact of being most important.

prima donna n. **1** the chief female singer in an opera. **2** a temperamental self-important person.

prima facie /pry-muh **fay**-shi-ee/ adj. & adv. Law accepted as correct until proved otherwise.

primal adj. **1** primitive; primeval. **2** fundamental.

primary adj. **1** most important. **2** earliest in time or order. **3** of education for children below the age of 11. ▶n. (pl. **primaries**) (in the US) a preliminary election to select delegates or candidates. □ **primary colour** each of the colours blue, red, and yellow, from which all other colours can be obtained by mixing. ■ **primarily** adv.

primate n. **1** a mammal of an order including monkeys, apes, and humans. **2** an archbishop.

prime adj. **1** most important. **2** excellent. **3** (of a number) that can be divided only by itself and one. **4** a time of greatest strength, success, etc. ▶v. **1** make ready for use or action. **2** provide with information in preparation for something. □ **prime minister** the head of a government.

primer n. **1** a substance painted on a surface as a base coat. **2** a book giving a basic introduction to a subject.

primeval adj. of the earliest times in history.

primitive adj. **1** of the earliest times in history or stages in development. **2** simple or crude.

primogeniture n. a system by which an eldest son inherits all his parents' property.

primordial adj. primeval.

primrose n. a pale yellow spring flower.

primula n. a kind of primrose.

Thesaurus

rare, incomparable, expensive, costly, rich, dear, irreplaceable, treasured, prized. **2** *see* HILARIOUS. ■ OPPOSITES worthless.

prick v. PIERCE, puncture, perforate, stab, nick, gash, slit, bore, spike.

prickle n. **1** THORN, needle, barb, spike, spine, spur. **2** TINGLE, tingling, sting, stinging, smarting, itching. ▶v. TINGLE, sting, smart, itch.

pride n. **1** SELF-ESTEEM, self-respect, ego, amour propre, self-worth, self-image, feelings, sensibilities. **2** CONCEIT, vanity, arrogance, haughtiness, self-love, self-importance, egotism, presumption, hauteur, superciliousness, disdain; *informal* big-headedness. **3** SATISFACTION, gratification, pleasure, joy, delight. ■ OPPOSITES humility. ▶v. BE PROUD OF, take pride in, take satisfaction in, congratulate oneself on, revel in, glory in, exult in, boast about, brag about, crow about.

priest n. CLERGYMAN, cleric, man/woman of the cloth, man/woman of God, father,

padre.

prim adj. PROPER, demure, formal, precise, stuffy, starchy, strait-laced, prudish, prissy, old-maidish, priggish, puritanical.

primarily adv. BASICALLY, essentially, in essence, fundamentally, in the first place, first and foremost, chiefly, mainly, in the main, principally, mostly, for the most part, on the whole, predominantly, predominately.

primary adj. **1** PRIME, chief, main, principal, leading, predominant, most important, paramount, basic, fundamental, elemental, rudimentary, essential. **2** EARLIEST, original, initial, beginning, first, opening. ■ OPPOSITES secondary.

prime adj. **1** *see* PRIMARY. **2** TOP-QUALITY, highest, top, best, first-class, high-grade, grade A, superior, choice, select. ▶n. BEST PART, peak, pinnacle, best days, height, zenith, acme, culmination, apex, heyday, full flowering.

primitive adj. **1** ANCIENT, earliest, primeval, primordial, primal, pristine.

prince n. a son or other close male relative of a monarch.

princely adj. **1** of or suitable for a prince. **2** (of a sum of money) generous.

princess n. **1** a daughter or other close female relative of a monarch. **2** a prince's wife or widow.

principal adj. most important; main. ▶ n. **1** the most important person in an organization or group. **2** the head of a school or college. **3** a sum of money lent or invested, on which interest is paid. ■ **principally** adv.

....

☑️ Don't confuse **principal** and **principle**, a noun meaning 'a truth or general law'.

....

principality n. (pl. **principalities**) a state ruled by a prince.

principle n. **1** a truth or general law used as a basis for a theory or system of belief. **2** (**principles**) beliefs governing one's behaviour. **3** a general scientific law. ■ **in principle** in theory. **on principle** because of one's moral beliefs.

print v. **1** produce a book etc. by a process involving the transfer of words or pictures to paper. **2** produce a photographic print from a negative. **3** write words clearly without joining the letters. **4** mark with a coloured design. ▶ n. **1** printed words. **2** a mark where something has pressed or touched a surface. **3** a printed picture, design, or fabric. **4** a photograph printed on paper from a negative or transparency.

□ **printed circuit** an electronic circuit with thin strips of conducting material on an insulating board. **printing press** a machine for printing from type or plates. **printout** a page of printed material from a computer's printer. ■ **printer** n.

prior adj. coming before in time, order, or importance. ▶ n. (fem. **prioress**) **1** the person next in rank below an abbot (or abbess). **2** the head of a priory.

prioritize (or **-ise**) v. **1** treat as most important. **2** decide the order of importance of tasks.

priority n. (pl. **priorities**) **1** the state of being more important. **2** a thing seen as more important than others. **3** the right to go before other traffic.

priory n. (pl. **priories**) a monastery or nunnery governed by a prior or prioress.

prise (US **prize**) v. force open or apart.

prism n. **1** a transparent object with triangular ends, used to separate white light into colours. **2** a solid geometric figure whose ends are parallel and of the same size and shape. ■ **prismatic** adj.

prison n. a building used to confine criminals or people awaiting trial.

prisoner n. **1** a person kept in prison. **2** a person captured and kept confined.

prissy adj. prim.

pristine adj. in its original and unspoilt condition.

privacy n. a state in which one is not watched or disturbed by others.

private adj. **1** for or belonging to a par-

P

Thesaurus

2 CRUDE, simple, rudimentary, undeveloped, unrefined, rough, unsophisticated, rude. **3** UNCIVILIZED, barbarian, barbaric, savage, wild. ■ OPPOSITES advanced.

principal adj. **1** FOREMOST, chief, leading, pre-eminent, most important, most influential, dominant, controlling, ruling, in charge. **2** MAJOR, main, chief, leading, key, primary, prime, paramount. ▶ n. **1** HEAD TEACHER, headmaster, headmistress, head, rector, master, dean. **2** LEADING PLAYER/PERFORMER, leading man/lady, lead, star.

principle n. **1** THEORY, basis, fundamental, essence, assumption, rule, law, canon, tenet, code, maxim, axiom, dictum, postulate. **2** MORALS, ethics, integrity, uprightness, righteousness, probity, rectitude, honour, conscience, scruples.

print v. **1** SET IN PRINT, send to press, publish, issue, run off, put to bed. **2** IMPRINT, stamp, mark. ▶ n. **1** TYPE, letters, lettering, typeface, newsprint. **2** COPY, reproduction, replica.

prior adj. EARLIER, previous, anterior. ■ OPPOSITES subsequent. □ **prior to** BEFORE, until, up to, earlier than, preceding.

priority n. **1** FIRST/PRIME CONCERN, most important thing. **2** PRECEDENCE, preference, urgency.

prison n. JAIL, lock-up, penal institution, place of detention, place of confinement, dungeon; US penitentiary, correctional facility; informal nick, clink, cooler, slammer, stir, jug; US informal can, pen; informal, dated chokey.

prisoner n. CONVICT, captive, detainee, internee, hostage; informal con, lag, lifer, jailbird.

ticular person or group only. **2** not to be made known. **3** not provided or owned by the state. **4** not connected with a person's work. **5** where one will not be disturbed; secluded. ▶ n. a soldier of the lowest rank. ■ **privately** adv.

privation n. lack of food and other essentials.

privatize (or **-ise**) v. transfer from state to private ownership. ■ **privatization** n.

privet n. a shrub with small dark green leaves.

privilege n. a special right or advantage for a particular person or group. ■ **privileged** adj.

....

☑ There's no *d*: privi*lege*.

....

privy adj. (**privy to**) sharing in the knowledge of a secret. ▶ n. (pl. **privies**) an outside toilet.

prize n. a thing given to a winner or to mark an outstanding achievement. ▶ adj. **1** having been awarded a prize. **2** excellent. ▶ v. **1** value highly. **2** US = PRISE.

pro n. (pl. **pros**) **1** informal a professional. **2** (**pros and cons**) arguments for and against something.

pro- prefix in favour of.

proactive adj. creating or controlling a situation rather than just responding to it. ■ **proactively** adv.

probable adj. likely to happen or be the case. ■ **probability** n. **probably** adv.

probate n. the official process of proving that a will is valid.

probation n. **1** a system whereby an offender is not sent to prison subject to a period of good behaviour under supervision. **2** a period of training and testing a new employee. ■ **probationary** adj. **probationer** n.

probe n. **1** a blunt surgical instrument for exploring a wound etc. **2** an investigation. **3** an unmanned exploratory spacecraft. ▶ v. **1** examine with a probe. **2** investigate closely.

probity /proh-bi-ti/ n. honesty.

problem n. something difficult to deal with or understand. ■ **problematic** adj. **problematical** adj.

proboscis /pruh-boss-iss/ n. (pl. **probosces** or **proboscises**) **1** a long, flexible nose. **2** an insect's elongated sucking mouthpart.

procedure n. **1** an established or official way of doing something. **2** a series of actions done in a certain way. ■ **procedural** adj.

proceed v. **1** begin a course of action. **2** go on to do. **3** continue. **4** move forward.

proceedings pl. n. **1** a series of activ-

Thesaurus

....

p

pristine adj. UNMARKED, unblemished, unspoilt, spotless, immaculate, clean, in mint/perfect condition. ■ OPPOSITES dirty, spoilt.

private adj. **1** CONFIDENTIAL, secret, unofficial, off-the-record, in camera, closet, privileged; informal hush-hush. **2** PERSONAL, intimate, secret. **3** SECLUDED, secret, remote, out of the way, quiet. **4** RESERVED, retiring, self-contained, uncommunicative, diffident, secretive. ■ OPPOSITES public, open, extrovert.

privileged adj. **1** ADVANTAGED, socially advantaged, favoured, elite, indulgent, spoilt. **2** CONFIDENTIAL, private, off-the-record, secret, classified, top secret; informal hush-hush. ■ OPPOSITES disadvantaged, public.

prize n. TROPHY, medal, award, accolade, reward, premium, honour, laurels, palm, bays. ▶ adj. PRIZEWINNING, award-winning, winning, champion. ▶ v. VALUE, treasure, cherish, hold dear, esteem, hold in high regard.

probable adj. LIKELY, most likely, odds-on, expected, anticipated, predictable,

foreseeable, on the cards, credible, quite possible, possible. ■ OPPOSITES improbable.

probably adv. IN ALL PROBABILITY, in all likelihood, as likely as not, it is to be expected that, perhaps.

probe n. INVESTIGATION, scrutiny, inquest, exploration, examination, study. ▶ v. **1** FEEL, feel around, prod, poke, explore. **2** INVESTIGATE, scrutinize, inquire into, examine, study, research, analyse.

problem n. **1** DIFFICULTY, complication, trouble, mess, predicament, plight, dilemma, quandary; informal pickle, can of worms. **2** PUZZLE, poser, enigma, riddle, conundrum; informal teaser, brain-teaser.

problematic adj. **1** PROBLEMATICAL, difficult, troublesome, complicated, puzzling, knotty, thorny, ticklish, tricky; informal dodgy. **2** DOUBTFUL, uncertain, unsettled, questionable, open to question, debatable, arguable. ■ OPPOSITES straightforward.

procedure n. **1** COURSE OF ACTION, plan of action, policy, system, method, methodology, modus operandi, technique, ities. **2** a lawsuit.

proceeds pl. n. money obtained from an event or activity.

process n. **1** a series of actions to achieve an end. **2** a natural series of changes. ▶v. **1** perform a series of actions to change or preserve something. **2** deal with using an established procedure. ■ **processor** n.

procession n. a number of people or vehicles moving forward in an orderly line.

proclaim v. announce publicly. ■ **proclamation** n.

proclivity n. (pl. **proclivities**) a tendency or inclination.

procrastinate v. postpone action. ■ **procrastination** n.

procreate v. produce young. ■ **procreation** n.

procurator fiscal n. (in Scotland) a local coroner and public prosecutor.

procure v. obtain. ■ **procurement** n.

procurer n. a person who obtains a prostitute for another person.

prod v. (**prodding, prodded**) **1** poke. **2** prompt or remind to do something. ▶n. **1** a poke. **2** a prompt or reminder. **3** a pointed implement.

prodigal adj. wasteful or extravagant.

prodigious adj. impressively large. ■ **prodigiously** adv.

prodigy n. (pl. **prodigies**) **1** a young person with exceptional abilities. **2** an amazing or unusual thing.

produce v. **1** make, manufacture, or create. **2** cause to happen or exist. **3** show or provide for consideration. **4** administer the financing of a film or the staging of a play. **5** supervise the making of a recording. ▶n. things that have been produced or grown. ■ **producer** n. **production** n.

product n. **1** a thing produced. **2** a number obtained by multiplying.

productive adj. producing or achieving a great deal.

productivity n. the efficiency with which things are produced.

profane adj. **1** not holy or religious. **2** not reverent. ▶v. treat irreverently. ■ **profanity** n.

profess v. **1** claim to have, feel, or be. **2** declare one's faith in a religion.

profession n. **1** a job requiring special training and a formal qualification. **2** a body of people engaged in this. **3** a declaration.

means, practice, operation, strategy. **2** STEP, process, measure, move, operation, transaction.

proceed v. **1** MAKE ONE'S WAY, go, advance, carry on, move on, press on, progress. **2** ARISE, originate, spring, stem, come, derive, result, follow, ensue, emanate, issue, flow.

proceedings pl. n. **1** ACTIVITIES, events, action, process, affairs, doings, happenings. **2** CASE, lawsuit, litigation, trial. **3** MINUTES, report, account, record, transactions.

proceeds pl. n. TAKINGS, profits, returns, receipts, income, earnings.

process n. **1** METHOD, system, technique, means, practice, way, procedure. **2** DEVELOPMENT, evolution, changes, stages, steps.

procession n. **1** PARADE, march, column, file, train, cortège, cavalcade, motorcade. **2** STREAM, steady stream, succession, series, sequence, run.

proclaim v. **1** ANNOUNCE, declare, make known, give out, notify, circulate, advertise, publish, broadcast, promulgate. **2** PRONOUNCE, announce, declare to be.

procrastinate v. DELAY, postpone action, defer action, be dilatory, use delaying tactics, stall, temporize, play for

time, play a waiting game, dally, dilly-dally, drag one's feet/heels.

prod v. **1** POKE, jab, dig, nudge, elbow, butt, push, shove, thrust. **2** see URGE.

prodigious adj. IMPRESSIVE, striking, startling, extraordinary, remarkable, exceptional, amazing, staggering, stupendous, phenomenal, miraculous. ■ OPPOSITES small, unexceptional.

prodigy n. CHILD GENIUS, wonder child, wunderkind, gifted child, wonder, marvel, phenomenon, sensation.

produce v. **1** MAKE, manufacture, create, construct, build, fabricate, put together, assemble, turn out, compose, originate, prepare, develop, fashion. **2** PRESENT, offer, set forth, proffer, advance, show, exhibit, demonstrate, disclose, reveal. **3** YIELD, bear, give, bring forth, supply, provide, furnish. **4** GIVE BIRTH TO, bring forth, bear, breed, give life to, bring into the world, procreate. **5** MOUNT, stage, put on, present. ▶n. YIELD, crops, harvest, output.

product n. **1** COMMODITY, artefact, goods, wares, merchandise. **2** RESULT, outcome, effect, consequence, upshot, fruit, spin-off, legacy.

productive adj. **1** FERTILE, fruitful, fecund, rich, high-yielding. **2** PROLIFIC, en-

professional adj. **1** of or belonging to a profession. **2** doing something as a job rather than as a hobby. **3** competent. ▶n. a professional person. ■ **professionalism** n. **professionally** adv.

professor n. a university academic of the highest rank. ■ **professorial** adj.

proffer v. offer.

proficient adj. competent; skilled. ■ **proficiency** n.

profile n. **1** an outline of a person's face seen from the side. **2** a short descriptive article about someone. **3** the extent to which a person or organization attracts notice.

profit n. **1** a financial gain. **2** advantage; benefit. ▶v. (**profiting, profited**) benefit, esp. financially.

profitable adj. **1** making a profit. **2** useful. ■ **profitability** n. **profitably** adv.

profiteering n. the making of a large profit in an unfair way.

profligate adj. **1** extravagant or wasteful. **2** dissolute. ▶n. a profligate person. ■ **profligacy** n.

profound adj. **1** very great. **2** showing or needing great knowledge, understanding, or thought. ■ **profoundly** adv.

profundity n.

profuse adj. plentiful. ■ **profusely** adv. **profusion** n.

progenitor n. an ancestor.

progeny n. offspring.

progesterone n. a hormone that stimulates the womb to prepare for pregnancy.

prognosis n. (pl. **prognoses**) a forecast, esp. of the likely course of an illness. ■ **prognostic** adj.

prognosticate v. forecast. ■ **prognostication** n.

programme (US **program**) n. **1** a planned series of events. **2** a radio or television broadcast. **3** a set of related measures with a long-term aim. **4** a sheet or booklet giving details about a play, concert, etc. **5** (**program**) a series of software instructions to control the operation of a computer. ▶v. **1** (**program**) (**programming, programmed**; US **programing, programed**) provide a computer with a program. **2** arrange according to a plan. ■ **programmer** n.

progress n. **1** forward movement. **2** development or improvement. ▶v. move forward or develop. ■ **progression** n.

Thesaurus

ergetic, vigorous, efficient, effective, valuable. ■ OPPOSITES sterile, unproductive.

profess v. DECLARE, announce, proclaim, assert, state, utter, affirm, avow, aver.

profession n. **1** CAREER, job, calling, business, vocation, occupation, line of work, métier, position, situation. **2** DECLARATION, announcement, proclamation, assertion, statement, affirmation, avowal, averment.

professional adj. **1** SKILLED, skilful, proficient, expert, adept, competent, efficient, experienced. **2** SKILFUL, expert, adept, masterly, excellent, fine, polished, finished. **3** NON-AMATEUR, paid. ■ OPPOSITES amateurish, amateur.

proffer v. OFFER, tender, present, extend, give, submit, volunteer, suggest. ■ OPPOSITES withdraw.

profile n. **1** OUTLINE, silhouette, contour, lines, shape, form, figure. **2** SHORT BIOGRAPHY, sketch, thumbnail sketch, portrait, vignette.

profit n. **1** TAKINGS, proceeds, gain, yield, return, receipts, income, earnings, winnings. **2** GAIN, benefit, advantage, good, value, use, avail. ■ OPPOSITES loss. ▶v. BENEFIT, be of benefit to, be of advantage to, be of use/value to, serve, help, be helpful to, assist, aid, stand in good stead.

profitable adj. **1** MONEY-MAKING, commercial, gainful, remunerative, paying, lucrative. **2** BENEFICIAL, advantageous, rewarding, helpful, productive, useful, worthwhile, valuable. ■ OPPOSITES unprofitable.

profound adj. **1** SERIOUS, weighty, deep, learned, discerning, penetrating, thoughtful, philosophical, erudite, wise, sagacious. **2** SINCERE, intense, keen, great, extreme, deep, heartfelt. **3** FAR-REACHING, radical, extensive, exhaustive, thoroughgoing. ■ OPPOSITES shallow, superficial.

profuse adj. **1** COPIOUS, prolific, abundant, liberal, effusive, lavish, extravagant, inordinate. **2** LUXURIANT, plentiful, lush, rich, exuberant, riotous, rank, rampant. ■ OPPOSITES meagre.

programme n. **1** AGENDA, calendar, schedule, syllabus, list of events, order of the day. **2** PRODUCTION, presentation, show, performance, broadcast. **3** SYLLABUS, prospectus, schedule, list, curriculum, literature.

progress n. **1** FORWARD MOVEMENT, headway, advance, passage, advancement, progression. **2** PROGRESSION, improvement, betterment, upgrading, development, growth. ▶v. **1** GO FORWARD, move

progressive adj. **1** happening gradually. **2** favouring new ideas or social reform. ■ **progressively** adv.

prohibit v. (**prohibiting**, **prohibited**) forbid. ■ **prohibition** n.

prohibitive adj. **1** forbidding something. **2** (of a price) too high.

project n. **1** a piece of work planned with a particular aim. **2** a piece of work involving research. ▶v. **1** estimate. **2** plan. **3** stick out beyond something else. **4** make light or an image fall on a surface. **5** present an image of oneself to others.

projectile n. a missile.

projection n. **1** a forecast based on present trends. **2** the projecting of an image etc. **3** a thing that sticks out. ■ **projectionist** n.

projector n. a device for projecting slides or film on to a screen.

prolapse n. a condition in which an organ of the body has slipped from its normal position.

proletariat n. workers or working-class people. ■ **proletarian** adj. & n.

proliferate v. reproduce or grow rapidly. ■ **proliferation** n.

prolific adj. producing things in abundance. ■ **prolifically** adv.

prolix adj. (of speech or writing) long and boring. ■ **prolixity** n.

prologue (US **prolog**) n. an introduction to a book, play, etc.

prolong v. cause to last longer. ■ **prolongation** n.

prom n. **1** a promenade by the sea. **2** a promenade concert.

promenade n. **1** a paved public walk along a seafront. **2** a leisurely walk, ride, or drive. □ **promenade concert** a concert of classical music at which part of the audience stands.

prominent adj. **1** important; famous. **2** sticking out. **3** conspicuous. ■ **prominence** n. **prominently** adv.

promiscuous adj. having many sexual relationships. ■ **promiscuity** n.

promise n. **1** an assurance that one will do something or that something will happen. **2** potential excellence. ▶v. **1** make a promise. **2** give good grounds for expecting.

promising adj. showing signs of future success.

promissory note n. a written signed promise to pay a stated sum.

promontory n. (pl. **promontories**) high

Thesaurus

forward/on, make one's way, advance, go on, continue, proceed, push forward, forge ahead. **2** MAKE PROGRESS, get better, improve, recover, recuperate. ■ OPPOSITES regress.

progressive adj. **1** INCREASING, growing, intensifying, accelerating, escalating. **2** MODERN, advanced, radical, reforming, innovative, revolutionary, forward-looking, enlightened, avant-garde; *informal* go-ahead. ■ OPPOSITES conservative, reactionary.

prohibit v. **1** FORBID, ban, bar, disallow, proscribe, veto, interdict, outlaw. **2** PREVENT, stop, rule out, preclude, make impossible, hinder, impede, hamper, obstruct, restrict, constrain. ■ OPPOSITES allow.

prohibitive adj. EXORBITANT, steep, extortionate, excessive, preposterous, high-priced, high-cost, sky-high.

project n. SCHEME, plan, programme, enterprise, undertaking, venture, activity, operation, campaign. ▶v. **1** PLAN, propose, map out, devise, design, outline. **2** LAUNCH, discharge, propel, hurl, throw, cast, fling, shoot. **3** JUT OUT, protrude, extend, stick out, stand out, hang over, obtrude.

proliferate v. INCREASE, multiply, extend, expand, burgeon, accelerate, escalate, rocket, snowball, mushroom. ■ OPPOSITES decrease.

prolong v. LENGTHEN, make longer, elongate, extend, stretch out, draw out, drag out, protract, spin out.

prominent adj. **1** PROTRUDING, protuberant, jutting, projecting, standing out, bulging. **2** CONSPICUOUS, noticeable, obvious, unmistakable, obtrusive, eye-catching, striking. **3** EMINENT, important, pre-eminent, distinguished, notable, noted, illustrious, celebrated, well known, famous, renowned, leading. ■ OPPOSITES inconspicuous.

promiscuous adj. DISSOLUTE, dissipated, fast, licentious, loose, profligate, abandoned, immoral, debauched, wanton, of easy virtue, unchaste. ■ OPPOSITES chaste.

promise v. **1** GIVE ONE'S WORD, give an undertaking, give one's assurance, swear, vow, pledge, contract. **2** AUGUR, indicate, denote, signify, be a sign of, show signs of, suggest, betoken, presage. ▶n. **1** WORD, undertaking, assurance, guarantee, commitment, vow, oath, pledge, bond, contract, covenant. **2** POTENTIAL, flair, talent, ability, aptitude, capability, capacity.

land jutting out into the sea.

promote v. **1** aid the progress of a cause or aim. **2** publicize a product. **3** raise to a higher rank or office. ■ **promoter** n. **promotion** n.

prompt v. **1** cause to happen or to do. **2** tell an actor a word they have forgotten. ▸ n. an act of prompting. ▸ adj. done or acting without delay. ▸ adv. punctually. ■ **prompter** n. **promptly** adv.

promulgate v. make widely known. ■ **promulgation** n.

prone adj. **1** likely to suffer from or do. **2** lying face downwards.

prong n. each of the projecting pointed parts of a fork.

pronoun n. a word used instead of a noun to indicate someone or something already mentioned or known, e.g. *I*, *this*.

pronounce v. **1** make the sound of a word or part of a word. **2** declare or announce. ■ **pronouncement** n. **pronunciation** n.

....

☑ **pronunciation** does not have an *o* in the middle.

....

pronounced adj. noticeable.

proof n. **1** evidence proving that something is true. **2** a copy of printed material for making corrections before final printing. ▸ adj. resistant to: *damp-proof*. ☐ **proofread** read printed proofs and mark any errors.

prop n. **1** a pole or beam used as a temporary support. **2** a portable object used on the set of a play or film. ▸ v. (**propping, propped**) support with or as if with a prop.

propaganda n. false or exaggerated information used to promote a political cause etc.

propagate v. **1** produce a new plant from a parent plant. **2** promote an idea etc. widely. ■ **propagation** n. **propagator** n.

propane n. a gas present in natural gas, used as fuel.

propel v. (**propelling, propelled**) drive or push forwards. ■ **propellant** n.

propeller n. a revolving shaft with angled blades, for propelling a ship or aircraft.

propensity n. (pl. **propensities**) a tendency.

Thesaurus

....

promising adj. ENCOURAGING, hopeful, favourable, auspicious, propitious, optimistic, bright. ■ OPPOSITES unfavourable, hopeless.

promontory n. HEADLAND, point, cape, foreland, bluff, cliff, precipice, overhang, height, projection, prominence.

promote v. **1** ELEVATE, advance, move up, upgrade, prefer, aggrandize. **2** ADVANCE, further, assist, aid, help, contribute to, foster, boost. **3** ADVERTISE, publicize, push, puff, beat the drum for; *informal* plug, give a plug to/for, hype. ■ OPPOSITES demote, obstruct.

promotion n. **1** UPGRADING, elevation, advancement, preferment, aggrandizement. **2** ADVANCEMENT, furtherance, furthering, assistance, aid, help, contribution, fostering, boosting. **3** ADVERTISING, publicity, hard sell, puff; *informal* plug, hype, hyping.

prompt adj. **1** IMMEDIATE, instant, instantaneous, swift, rapid, speedy, quick, fast, expeditious, early, punctual, in good time, timely. **2** SWIFT, rapid, speedy, quick, fast, ready, willing, eager. ▸ v. **1** CAUSE, make, encourage, move, induce, urge, incite, impel, spur on, motivate, stimulate, inspire, provoke. **2** REMIND, jog someone's memory, refresh someone's memory, cue, help out.

pronounce v. **1** ENUNCIATE, articulate, say, utter, sound, voice, vocalize. **2** ANNOUNCE, declare, proclaim, assert, affirm, rule, decree.

pronounced adj. **1** MARKED, noticeable, obvious, evident, conspicuous, striking, distinct, unmistakable. **2** DECIDED, definite, clear, strong, positive, distinct. ■ OPPOSITES slight.

pronunciation n. ENUNCIATION, articulation, accent, saying, uttering, utterance, sounding, voicing, vocalization.

proof n. EVIDENCE, demonstration, substantiation, corroboration, confirmation, attestation, testimony, certification, verification, authentication, validation. ▸ adj. IMPERVIOUS, impenetrable, resistant, repellent.

prop n. SUPPORT, upright, brace, buttress, stay, bolster, stanchion, truss, column, post, rod, pole, shaft. ▸ v. LEAN, rest, set, lay, stand, balance, steady. ☐ **prop up** HOLD UP, shore up, bolster up, buttress, support, brace, underpin, reinforce, strengthen.

propaganda n. PUBLICITY MATERIAL, publicity, promotion, advertising, advertisement, information, agitprop.

propagate v. **1** GROW, breed, multiply, reproduce. **2** SPREAD, communicate, circulate, disseminate, transmit, distrib-

proper adj. **1** deserving the description; genuine. **2** appropriate or correct. **3** very respectable. **4** (**proper to**) belonging exclusively to. □ **proper name** (or **proper noun**) a name for a person, place, or organization. ■ **properly** adv.

property n. (pl. **properties**) **1** a thing or things belonging to someone. **2** a building and the land belonging to it. **3** a quality or characteristic.

prophecy n. (pl. **prophecies**) a prediction about what will happen.

prophesy v. (**prophesying**, **prophesied**) predict.

prophet n. **1** a person regarded as being sent by God to teach people. **2** a person who predicts the future.

prophetic adj. **1** accurately predicting the future. **2** of a prophet or prophecy.

prophylactic adj. intended to prevent disease. ▶ n. a preventive medicine.

propinquity n. nearness.

propitiate v. win or regain the favour of. ■ **propitiation** n. **propitiatory** adj.

propitious adj. favourable.

proponent n. a person proposing a theory or plan.

proportion n. **1** a part or share of a whole. **2** relative size or amount. **3** the correct relation between things. **4** (**proportions**) dimensions.

proportional (or **proportionate**) adj. corresponding in size or amount to something else. □ **proportional representation** an electoral system in which parties gain seats in proportion to the number of votes cast for them. ■ **proportionally** adv.

proposal n. **1** a plan or suggestion. **2** the act of proposing. **3** an offer of marriage.

propose v. **1** put forward an idea for consideration. **2** nominate for a post. **3** make an offer of marriage to someone.

proposition n. **1** a statement expressing an opinion. **2** a plan of action. ▶ v. informal ask someone to have sex with one.

propound v. put forward an idea for consideration.

proprietary adj. **1** of an owner or ownership. **2** (of a product) marketed under a registered trade name.

proprietor n. the owner of a business. ■ **proprietorial** adj.

propriety n. (pl. **proprieties**) correctness of behaviour.

propulsion n. the act of propelling.

pro rata adj. proportional. ▶ adv. proportionally.

prorogue /pruh-rohg/ v. suspend a session of parliament without dissolving it.

prosaic adj. ordinary or unimaginative. ■ **prosaically** adv.

Thesaurus

ute, broadcast, publish, publicize, proclaim, promulgate.

propel v. MOVE, set in motion, push forward, drive, thrust forward, force, impel.

propensity n. see TENDENCY.

proper adj. **1** SUITABLE, fitting, appropriate, apt. **2** CORRECT, right, accepted, established, orthodox, conventional, formal. **3** SEEMLY, decorous, respectable, decent, refined, genteel, formal, conventional, orthodox, strict, punctilious. ■ OPPOSITES improper.

property n. **1** POSSESSIONS, belongings, things, goods, effects, chattels, assets, resources. **2** REAL ESTATE, buildings, land. **3** QUALITY, attribute, characteristic, feature, power, peculiarity, idiosyncrasy, quirk.

prophecy n. PREDICTION, forecast, prognostication, divination, augury.

prophesy v. PREDICT, foretell, forecast, foresee, forewarn of, presage, prognosticate, divine, augur.

prophet n. SEER, soothsayer, diviner, clairvoyant, prophesier, oracle, augur, sibyl, Cassandra.

proportion n. **1** RATIO, distribution, relative amount/number, relationship. **2** PORTION, part, segment, share, quota, division, percentage, fraction, measure; informal cut. **3** BALANCE, symmetry, harmony, correspondence, congruity, agreement.

proportional adj. PROPORTIONATE, corresponding, commensurate, equivalent, comparable. ■ OPPOSITES disproportionate.

proposal n. SCHEME, plan, project, programme, motion, bid, proposition, presentation, suggestion, recommendation, tender, terms.

propose v. **1** PUT FORWARD, advance, offer, proffer, present, submit, tender, propound, suggest, recommend, advocate. **2** INTEND, mean, plan, have in mind, aim, purpose. **3** NOMINATE, name, put forward, put up, suggest, recommend.

proprieties pl. n. ETIQUETTE, social niceties, protocol, civilities, formalities, rules of conduct, accepted behaviour,

proscenium n. (pl. **prosceniums** or **proscenia**) the part of a stage in front of the curtain.

proscribe v. forbid.

☑ Don't confuse **proscribe** with **prescribe**.

prose n. ordinary written or spoken language.

prosecute v. **1** take legal proceedings against someone for a crime. **2** continue a course of action. ■ **prosecution** n. **prosecutor** n.

proselyte /pross-i-lyt/ n. a convert from one religion to another. ■ **proselytize** (or **-ise**) v.

prospect n. **1** the possibility of something occurring. **2** (**prospects**) chances for success. ▶v. search for mineral deposits. ■ **prospector** n.

prospective adj. likely to happen or be in the future.

prospectus n. (pl. **prospectuses**) a booklet giving details of a school etc. or a share offer.

prosper v. succeed or flourish.

prosperous adj. rich and successful.

■ **prosperity** n.

prostate n. a gland surrounding the neck of the bladder in male mammals.

prosthesis n. (pl. **prostheses**) an artificial body part. ■ **prosthetic** adj.

prostitute n. a person who has sex for payment. ▶v. **1** offer as a prostitute. **2** put one's abilities to an unworthy use. ■ **prostitution** n.

prostrate adj. **1** lying stretched with one's face downwards. **2** overcome with distress or exhaustion. ▶v. **1** (**prostrate oneself**) throw oneself flat on the ground. **2** (**be prostrated**) be overcome with distress or exhaustion. ■ **prostration** n.

protagonist n. **1** the leading character in a drama, novel, etc. **2** a supporter of a cause etc.

protean adj. able to change or adapt.

protect v. keep safe from harm or injury. ■ **protection** n. **protector** n.

protectionism n. the policy of shielding a country's industries from foreign competition by taxing imports. ■ **protectionist** n. & adj.

protective adj. serving or wishing to protect. ■ **protectively** adv.

Thesaurus

good manners, good form, the done thing, punctilio.

proprietor n. OWNER, possessor, title-holder, deed-holder, landowner, landlord/landlady.

prosaic adj. UNIMAGINATIVE, ordinary, uninspired, commonplace, dull, tedious, boring, dry, humdrum, mundane, pedestrian, lifeless, spiritless, stale, bland, vapid, banal, hackneyed, trite, insipid, monotonous, flat. ■ OPPOSITES imaginative.

prosecute v. **1** CHARGE, prefer charges against, bring an action against, try, bring to trial, put on trial, sue, bring a suit against, interdict, arraign. **2** CARRY ON, conduct, direct, engage in, work at, proceed with, continue with.

prospect n. **1** LIKELIHOOD, likeliness, hope, expectation, anticipation, chance, chances, odds, probability, possibility. **2** VIEW, vista, outlook, perspective, panorama, scene, spectacle. ▶v. EXPLORE, search, inspect, survey, examine, check out.

prospective adj. FUTURE, to-be, soon-to-be, intended, expected, would-be, potential, possible, likely, hoped for, looked for, awaited, anticipated.

prospects pl. n. POTENTIAL, promise, possibilities, expectations, scope.

prosper v. DO WELL, get on well, thrive, flourish, be successful, succeed, get ahead, progress, advance, get on in the world, make headway, make good, become rich, be in clover. ■ OPPOSITES fail.

prosperity n. AFFLUENCE, wealth, riches, prosperousness, success, good fortune, ease, plenty, the good life, luxury. ■ OPPOSITES hardship.

prosperous adj. WELL OFF, well-to-do, affluent, wealthy, rich, successful, moneyed, opulent, in clover; informal well heeled, in the money, on Easy Street. ■ OPPOSITES poor.

prostitute n. CALL GIRL, whore; informal tart, pro, working girl, member of the oldest profession, tom; US informal hooker, hustler; dated loose woman, woman of ill repute, streetwalker, woman of the streets, fallen woman; old use courtesan, strumpet, harlot, trollop, wench.

prostrate adj. PRONE, lying down, flat, stretched out, horizontal, procumbent. ▶v. KNOCK FLAT, flatten, knock down, floor, level.

protect v. **1** KEEP SAFE, save, safeguard, shield, preserve, defend, shelter, secure. **2** GUARD, mount/stand guard on, defend, secure, watch over, look after, take care of. ■ OPPOSITES endanger.

protectorate n. a state that is controlled and protected by another.

protégé /prot-i-zhay/ n. (fem. **protégée**) a person who is guided and supported by a more experienced person.

protein n. a substance which forms part of body tissues and is an important part of the diet.

☑ **protein** is an exception to the usual rule of *i* before *e* except after *c*.

pro tem adv. & adj. for the time being.

protest n. a statement or action expressing disapproval or objection. ▶ v. **1** express an objection. **2** state strongly. ■ **protestation** n. **protester** n.

Protestant n. a member of any of the Western Christian Churches which are separate from the Roman Catholic Church. ■ **Protestantism** n.

protocol n. **1** the system of rules governing formal occasions. **2** the accepted code of behaviour in a situation. **3** a draft of a treaty.

proton n. a subatomic particle with a positive electric charge.

protoplasm n. the material comprising the living part of a cell.

prototype n. a first or earlier form from which others are developed.

protozoan n. a single-celled microscopic animal.

protracted adj. lasting longer than usual or expected.

protractor n. an instrument for measuring angles.

protrude v. stick out from a surface. ■ **protrusion** n.

protuberance n. a protruding part. ■ **protuberant** adj.

proud adj. **1** feeling pride. **2** giving cause for pride. **3** slightly projecting from a surface. ■ **proudly** adv.

prove v. (**proving**, **proved**; past part. **proved** or **proven**) **1** show by evidence or argument that something is true or exists. **2** show or be seen to be.

provenance n. the place of origin of something.

provender n. animal fodder.

proverb n. a short saying stating a general truth or piece of advice.

proverbial adj. **1** referred to in a proverb. **2** well known.

provide v. **1** make available for use; supply. **2** (**provide for**) make enough preparation for. ■ **provider** n.

provided (or **providing**) conj. on the condition that.

Thesaurus

protection n. **1** SAFE KEEPING, safety, care, charge, keeping, preservation, defence, security. **2** SAFEGUARD, shield, barrier, buffer, screen, cover.

protective adj. **1** PROTECTING, safeguarding, shielding, covering. **2** CAREFUL, watchful, vigilant, paternal/maternal, fatherly/motherly, overprotective, possessive, clinging.

protector n. DEFENDER, champion, bodyguard, guardian, guardian angel.

protest v. **1** OBJECT, raise objections, take issue, make/take a stand, put up a fight, take exception, complain, demur, remonstrate, make a fuss, demonstrate; *informal* kick up a fuss, beef. **2** DECLARE, announce, profess, proclaim, assert, affirm, argue, attest, maintain, insist on, avow, aver. ▶ n. OBJECTION, opposition, exception, complaint, disapproval, disagreement, dissent, demurral, remonstration, protestation, fuss, outcry, demonstration.

protocol n. ETIQUETTE, rules of conduct, code of behaviour, conventions, formalities, customs, propriety, proprieties, decorum, manners, courtesies, civilities, good form, politesse.

protract v. PROLONG, extend, stretch out, draw out, lengthen, make longer, drag out, spin out, keep going, continue. ■ OPPOSITES curtail, shorten.

proud adj. **1** PLEASED, glad, happy, satisfied, gratified, content, appreciative. **2** ARROGANT, conceited, vain, self-important, egotistical, boastful, haughty, disdainful, scornful, supercilious, snobbish, imperious, overbearing, overweening, high-handed; *informal* high and mighty, stuck up, snooty, toffee-nosed. **3** GRATIFYING, satisfying, happy, memorable, notable, red-letter, glorious, marvellous. ■ OPPOSITES ashamed, humble.

prove v. ESTABLISH, determine, demonstrate, show beyond doubt, validate, substantiate, corroborate, verify, authenticate, confirm. ■ OPPOSITES disprove.

proverb n. SAYING, adage, maxim, saw, axiom, aphorism, dictum, apophthegm.

proverbial adj. LEGENDARY, notorious, infamous, famous, famed, renowned, well known, acknowledged, accepted, traditional, time-honoured.

provide v. **1** SUPPLY, furnish, equip, accommodate, provision, outfit. **2** GIVE, bring, afford, present, offer, accord,

providence n. **1** the protective care of God or of nature. **2** the state of being provident.

provident adj. careful in planning for the future.

providential adj. happening at a favourable time. ■ **providentially** adv.

province n. **1** a main administrative division of a country. **2** (**the provinces**) the whole of a country outside the capital. **3** an area of knowledge or responsibility.

provincial adj. **1** of a province or the provinces. **2** unsophisticated or narrow-minded. ▶ n. a person who lives in the provinces.

provision n. **1** the act of providing. **2** something provided. **3** (**provisions**) supplies of food and drink. **4** a condition in a legal document.

provisional adj. arranged temporarily. ■ **provisionally** adv.

proviso /pruh-vy-zoh/ n. (pl. **provisos**) a condition attached to an agreement.

provoke v. **1** cause a strong reaction. **2** deliberately annoy or anger. **3** stir up to do something. ■ **provocation** n. **provocative** adj.

provost n. the head of certain colleges and schools.

prow n. the pointed front part of a ship.

prowess n. skill or expertise.

prowl v. move about in a stealthy or restless way. ■ **prowler** n.

proximity n. nearness. ■ **proximate** adj.

proxy n. (pl. **proxies**) **1** the authority to represent someone else, esp. in voting. **2** a person authorized to act on behalf of another.

prude n. a person who is easily shocked by sexual matters. ■ **prudery** n. **prudish** adj.

prudent adj. showing thought for the future. ■ **prudence** n. **prudently** adv.

prune n. a dried plum. ▶ v. trim a shrub etc. by cutting away dead or unwanted parts.

prurient adj. showing excessive interest in sexual matters. ■ **prurience** n.

pry v. (**prying**, **pried**) enquire too intrusively into a person's private affairs.

Thesaurus

yield, impart, lend. □ **provide for** SUPPORT, maintain, keep, sustain, take care of, care for, look after.

provided conjunction PROVIDING THAT, on condition that, if, as long as, given, with the provision/proviso that, contingent upon, on the assumption that.

provident adj. FAR-SIGHTED, prudent, judicious, shrewd, cautious, careful, thrifty, canny, economical, frugal.

provincial adj. **1** LOCAL, small-town, rural, country. **2** UNSOPHISTICATED, parochial, limited, small-minded, insular, inward-looking, illiberal, narrow, narrow-minded, inflexible, bigoted, prejudiced, intolerant. ■ OPPOSITES metropolitan, sophisticated.

provisional adj. PROVISORY, temporary, interim, stopgap, transitional, to be confirmed, conditional, tentative, contingent, pro tem. ■ OPPOSITES permanent, definite.

provisions pl. n. SUPPLIES, stores, groceries, food and drink, foodstuffs, staples, rations, provender, eatables, edibles, comestibles; *literary* viands; *dated* victuals.

proviso n. CONDITION, stipulation, provision, clause, rider, qualification, restriction, reservation, limitation.

provocative adj. **1** PROVOKING, annoying, irritating, exasperating, galling, infuriating, maddening, vexing, insulting; *informal* aggravating. **2** SEDUCTIVE, sexy, tempting, suggestive, arousing, exciting, alluring, erotic, titillating.

provoke v. **1** ANNOY, anger, incense, enrage, irritate, exasperate, infuriate, madden, pique, nettle, vex, harass, irk, gall, affront, insult; *informal* make someone's blood boil, aggravate. **2** INCITE, rouse, stir, move, stimulate, motivate, excite, inflame, prompt, induce, spur, goad, prod, egg on. ■ OPPOSITES allay, pacify.

prowess n. SKILL, skilfulness, expertise, facility, ability, capability, talent, genius, adroitness, adeptness, aptitude, competence, proficiency; *informal* know-how.

prowl v. ROAM, range, move stealthily, slink, skulk, steal, sneak, stalk.

proxy n. REPRESENTATIVE, deputy, substitute, agent, delegate, surrogate.

prudent adj. **1** WISE, well judged, judicious, sagacious, sage, shrewd, sensible, circumspect, far-sighted, politic. **2** CAUTIOUS, careful, discreet, wary, vigilant, heedful, thrifty, economical, canny, sparing, frugal, provident. ■ OPPOSITES imprudent.

prudish adj. PRIGGISH, prim, prim and proper, strait-laced, prissy, puritan, puritanical, stuffy, starchy, Victorian, Grundyish, old-maid, old-maidish, schoolmarmish; *informal* goody-goody.

PS abbrev. postscript.

psalm /sahm/ n. a song or poem praising God.

psalter /sawl-ter/ n. a copy of the Book of Psalms in the Bible.

psephology /se-fol-uh-ji/ n. the study of trends in voting.

pseudo /syoo-doh/ adj. fake.

pseudonym /syoo-duh-nim/ n. a false name, esp. one used by an author.

psoriasis /suh-ry-uh-siss/ n. a skin condition causing itchy, scaly patches.

psyche /sy-ki/ n. the human soul, mind, or spirit.

psychedelic /sy-kuh-del-ik/ adj. **1** (of a drug) producing hallucinations. **2** having bright colours or an abstract pattern.

psychiatry /sy-ky-uh-tri/ n. the study and treatment of mental illness. ■ **psychiatric** adj. **psychiatrist** n.

psychic /sy-kik/ adj. **1** of or possessing abilities that cannot be explained by science. **2** of the mind. ▶ n. a person claiming to have psychic powers. ■ **psychically** adv.

psychoanalyse (US **-yze**) v. treat using psychoanalysis.

psychoanalysis n. a method of treating mental illnesses by investigating the unconscious elements of the mind. ■ **psychoanalyst** n.

psychology n. **1** the study of the human mind and its functions. **2** a person's mental characteristics. ■ **psychological** adj. **psychologically** adv. **psychologist** n.

psychopath n. a person with a serious mental illness causing violent behaviour. ■ **psychopathic** adj.

psychosis n. (pl. **psychoses**) a severe mental illness in which a person loses contact with reality. ■ **psychotic** adj.

psychosomatic adj. (of a physical illness) caused or made worse by a mental factor such as stress.

psychotherapy n. the treatment of mental illness by psychological rather than medical means. ■ **psychotherapist** n.

PT abbrev. physical training.

Pt abbrev. **1** Part. **2** (**pt**) pint. **3** (**pt.**) point.

PTA abbrev. parent-teacher association.

ptarmigan /tar-mi-guhn/ n. a grouse of northern regions.

pterodactyl /te-ruh-dak-til/ n. an extinct reptile with wings.

PTO abbrev. please turn over.

pub n. a building licensed to serve alcoholic drinks.

puberty n. the period during which adolescents reach sexual maturity.

pubescence n. the time when puberty begins. ■ **pubescent** adj.

pubic adj. of the lower abdomen.

public adj. **1** of, for, or known to people in general. **2** provided by the state rather than an independent company. ▶ n. (**the public**) **1** ordinary people in general. **2** a group with a particular interest. □ **public address system** a system of microphones and loudspeakers for amplifying speech or music. **public house** a pub. **public relations** the business of maintaining a good public image for an organization or famous person. **public school** (in the UK) a private fee-paying secondary school. **public servant** a person working for the state or for local government. ■ **publicly** adv.

publican n. a person who owns or manages a pub.

publication n. **1** the act of publishing. **2** a published book etc.

publicity n. **1** attention given to someone or something by the media. **2** information used for advertising.

publicize (or **-ise**) v. **1** make widely known. **2** advertise. ■ **publicist** n.

Thesaurus

■ OPPOSITES permissive.

prune v. CUT, lop, chop, clip, snip, remove.

pry v. BE INQUISITIVE, interfere, meddle, intrude, be nosy, be a busybody; *informal* stick/poke one's nose in, stick one's oar in, snoop; *Austral./NZ informal* stickybeak.

pseudonym n. ASSUMED NAME, alias, false name, nom de plume, pen-name, stage name, professional name, sobriquet, nickname, nom de guerre.

psychological adj. MENTAL, of the mind, cerebral, psychic, psychical.

pub n. BAR, public house, tavern, inn; *informal* local, boozer.

puberty n. PUBESCENCE, adolescence, young adulthood, teenage years, teens.

public adj. **1** POPULAR, general, common, universal, widespread. **2** KNOWN, widely known, acknowledged, overt, obvious, plain, in circulation, published, publicized. **3** PROMINENT, well known, important, eminent, respected, influential, prestigious, famous. ■ OPPOSITES private. ▶ n. PEOPLE, population, country, nation, community, citizens, populace, the masses, the multitude, the mob, the hoi polloi.

publish v. **1** produce a book etc. for public sale. **2** print in a book or newspaper. ■ **publisher** n.

puce n. a purple-brown colour.

puck n. a hard rubber disc used in ice hockey.

pucker v. gather into wrinkles. ▶n. a wrinkle.

pudding n. **1** a cooked dessert. **2** a savoury dish made with suet and flour. **3** a kind of sausage.

puddle n. a small pool of rainwater or other liquid.

puerile /pyoor-yl/ adj. childishly silly.

puerperal fever n. fever caused by infection of the womb after childbirth.

puff n. **1** a short amount of air or smoke blown out. **2** an act of drawing quickly on a cigarette etc. **3** a light pastry case. ▶v. **1** breathe in repeated short gasps. **2** move with short, noisy puffs of air or steam. **3** smoke a cigarette etc. **4** (**puff out/up**) swell or cause to swell. □ **puffball** a ball-shaped fungus. **puff pastry** light flaky pastry.

puffin n. a seabird with a large bright bill.

puffy adj. (**puffier**, **puffiest**) swollen. ■ **puffiness** n.

pug n. a small dog with a flat nose and wrinkled face.

pugilist n. a boxer. ■ **pugilistic** adj.

pugnacious adj. quick to argue or fight. ■ **pugnaciously** adv. **pugnacity** n.

puke v. & n. informal vomit.

pukka adj. **1** genuine. **2** informal excellent.

pull v. **1** apply force to something so as to move it towards oneself. **2** move steadily or with effort. **3** strain a muscle etc. **4** inhale deeply while smoking. ▶n. **1** an act of pulling. **2** a deep drink of something or a deep breath of smoke from a cigarette etc. **3** a force or attraction. □ **pull off** informal succeed in doing. **pull out** withdraw. **pull through** recover from a serious illness or injury. **pull up** (of a vehicle) stop.

pullet n. a young hen.

pulley n. (pl. **pulleys**) a wheel around which a rope etc. passes, used in lifting things.

pullover n. a knitted garment for the upper body.

pulmonary adj. of the lungs.

pulp n. **1** a soft, wet mass of crushed material. **2** the soft fleshy part of a fruit. ▶v. crush into a pulp. ▶adj. (of writing) popular and badly written. ■ **pulpy** adj.

pulpit n. a raised platform in a church from which a preacher speaks.

pulsar n. a star emitting regular pulses of radio waves.

pulsate v. expand and contract rhythmically. ■ **pulsation** n.

pulse n. **1** the regular throbbing of the arteries as blood is sent through them. **2** a single vibration or short burst of sound, light, etc. **3** the edible seeds of various plants of the pea family. ▶v. pulsate.

pulverize (or **-ise**) v. crush to fine particles.

puma n. a large American wild cat.

pumice /pum-iss/ n. solidified lava, used to remove hard skin.

Thesaurus

publication n. **1** PUBLISHING, production, issuing, issuance. **2** BOOK, newspaper, magazine, periodical, journal, daily, weekly, monthly, quarterly, booklet, brochure, leaflet, pamphlet, handbill.

publicize v. **1** MAKE PUBLIC, make known, announce, publish, broadcast, distribute, disseminate, promulgate. **2** GIVE PUBLICITY TO, promote, advertise, puff, puff up, push, beat the drum for; informal hype, plug. ■ OPPOSITES conceal.

publish v. **1** PRODUCE, issue, print, bring out. **2** see PUBLICIZE.

pucker v. SCREW UP, wrinkle, crease, furrow, knit, crinkle, corrugate.

puerile adj. CHILDISH, immature, infantile, juvenile, adolescent, foolish, silly, inane, asinine. ■ OPPOSITES mature.

puff n. GUST, blast, whiff, breath, flurry, draught. ▶v. **1** PANT, blow, gasp, gulp. **2** SWELL, distend, inflate, dilate, bloat.

pugnacious adj. BELLIGERENT, bellicose, combative, aggressive, antagonistic, argumentative, disputatious, hostile, threatening, irascible, ill-tempered, bad-tempered. ■ OPPOSITES peaceable.

pull v. **1** HAUL, drag, draw, trail, tow, tug. **2** STRAIN, sprain, wrench, stretch, tear, dislocate, damage. ■ OPPOSITES push. □ **pull back** WITHDRAW, retreat, draw back, fall back. **pull down** KNOCK DOWN, demolish, raze, level, destroy, bulldoze. **pull oneself together** REGAIN ONE'S COMPOSURE/CALM, get a grip on oneself; informal snap out of it. **pull out** WITHDRAW, retreat from, leave, abandon, give up, quit.

pulp n. PURÉE, mush, mash, pap, triturate. ▶v. CRUSH, squash, mash, purée, pulverize, triturate.

pulsate v. BEAT, throb, vibrate, pulse, palpitate, pound, thud, thump, drum.

p

pummel v. (**pummelling, pummelled;** US **pummeling, pummeled**) strike repeatedly with the fists.

pump n. **1** a device for moving liquid, gas, or air. **2** a plimsoll. ▶v. **1** move with a pump. **2** fill with liquid, gas, etc. **3** move vigorously up and down.

pumpkin n. a large round orange fruit.

pun n. a joke that uses a word or words with more than one meaning. ▶v. (**punning, punned**) make a pun.

punch v. **1** strike with the fist. **2** press a key on a machine. **3** pierce a hole in a material. ▶n. **1** a blow with the fist. **2** a device for cutting holes or impressing a design. **3** a drink of wine or spirits mixed with fruit juices etc. ▫ **punch-drunk** dazed by a series of punches. **punchline** the final part of a joke, providing the humour.

punctilious adj. showing great attention to detail or correct behaviour.

punctual adj. happening or doing something at the appointed time. ■ **punctuality** n. **punctually** adv.

punctuate v. **1** interrupt at intervals. **2** put punctuation marks in.

punctuation n. the marks, such as full stop and comma, used in writing to separate sentences and to make meaning clear.

puncture n. a small hole made by a sharp object. ▶v. make a puncture in.

pundit n. an expert.

pungent adj. having a strong taste or smell. ■ **pungency** n.

punish v. impose a penalty on someone for an offence. ■ **punishment** n.

punitive adj. intended as punishment.

punk n. **1** a loud, fast form of rock music with aggressive lyrics and behaviour. **2** an admirer of punk music.

punnet n. a small container for fruit.

punt n. a long, narrow, flat-bottomed boat moved with a long pole. ▶v. travel in a punt.

punter n. informal **1** a person who places a bet. **2** a customer.

puny adj. (**punier, puniest**) small and weak.

pup n. **1** a puppy. **2** a young wolf, seal, or rat.

pupa /pyoo-puh/ n. (pl. **pupae**) an insect in the form between larva and adult.

pupate v. become a pupa.

pupil n. **1** a person who is taught by another. **2** the dark opening in the centre of the iris of the eye.

puppet n. **1** a model of a person or animal moved either by strings or by a hand inside it. **2** a person under the control of another. ■ **puppetry** n.

puppy n. (pl. **puppies**) a young dog.

purchase v. buy. ▶n. **1** the act of buying. **2** a thing bought. **3** firm contact or grip. ■ **purchaser** n.

Thesaurus

pulse n. BEAT, rhythm, throb, throbbing, vibration, pulsation, pounding, thud, thumping, thump, drumming. ▶v. *see* PULSATE.

pump v. **1** DRIVE, force, push, send. **2** QUESTION, quiz, interrogate, cross-examine; *informal* grill.

punch v. STRIKE, hit, knock, thump, thwack, box, jab, cuff, slug, smash, slam, batter, pound, pummel; *informal* sock, biff, bash, bop, wallop, whack, clout.

punctilious adj. CAREFUL, scrupulous, meticulous, conscientious, exact, precise, particular, strict, nice, finicky, fussy. ■ OPPOSITES careless.

punctual adj. ON TIME, on the dot, prompt, in good time, when expected, timely, well timed. ■ OPPOSITES late.

puncture n. HOLE, perforation, flat, prick, rupture, cut, nick, slit, leak. ▶v. MAKE A HOLE IN, hole, perforate, pierce, bore, prick, penetrate, rupture, cut, nick, slit.

pungent adj. **1** SHARP, acrid, acid, sour, biting, stinging, burning, bitter, tart, tangy, spicy, highly flavoured, aromatic, piquant, peppery, hot, fiery. **2** CAUSTIC, acid, biting, cutting, sharp, incisive, scathing, pointed, acrimonious, trenchant, mordant. ■ OPPOSITES bland, mild.

punish v. **1** DISCIPLINE, teach someone a lesson, penalize, chastise, smack, slap, beat, cane, whip, flog, lash, scourge. **2** MALTREAT, mistreat, abuse, manhandle, damage, harm.

punishing adj. ARDUOUS, demanding, taxing, strenuous, hard, exhausting, fatiguing, wearing, tiring, gruelling, uphill, back-breaking.

punitive adj. **1** PENAL, disciplinary, corrective, correctional. **2** HARSH, severe, stiff, cruel, savage.

puny adj. WEAK, weakly, frail, feeble, undersized, underdeveloped, stunted, small, slight, little. ■ OPPOSITES strong.

pupil n. SCHOOLBOY/GIRL, schoolchild, scholar, student.

puppet n. **1** MARIONETTE, string puppet, glove puppet, finger puppet. **2** TOOL, instrument, cat's-paw, pawn, creature,

purdah n. the practice in certain Muslim and Hindu societies of screening women from men or strangers.

pure adj. **1** not mixed with any other substance. **2** innocent or good. **3** complete; nothing but. **4** theoretical rather than practical. ■ **purely** adv. **purity** n.

purée /pyoor-ay/ n. pulped fruit or vegetables. ▶v. make a purée of.

purgative adj. having a strongly laxative effect. ▶n. a laxative.

purgatory n. (pl. **purgatories**) (in RC belief) a place of suffering inhabited by the souls of sinners making amends before going to heaven.

purge v. **1** rid of undesirable people or things. **2** empty one's bowels as a result of taking a laxative. ▶n. **1** an act of purging. **2** dated a laxative.

purify v. (**purifying**, **purified**) make pure. ■ **purification** n. **purifier** n.

purist n. an adherent of traditional rules in language, style, etc.

puritan n. a person with strong moral beliefs who is critical of the behaviour of others. ■ **puritanical** adj.

purl n. a knitting stitch.

purlieus /per-lyooz/ pl. n. the area surrounding a place.

purloin v. steal.

purple n. a colour between red and blue.

purport v. appear to be or do, esp. falsely. ▶n. meaning. ■ **purportedly** adv.

purpose n. **1** the reason for an action or for existence. **2** strong determination. ▶v. intend. □ **on purpose** intentionally. ■ **purposeful** adj. **purposefully** adv.

purposely adv. on purpose.

purr v. (of a cat) make a low continuous sound of contentment. ▶n. a purring sound.

purse n. **1** a small pouch for carrying money. **2** US a handbag. ▶v. pucker one's lips.

purser n. a ship's officer who keeps the accounts.

pursuance n. the carrying out of a plan etc.

pursue v. **1** follow in order to catch or attack. **2** try to achieve a goal. **3** engage in an activity. **4** continue to investigate or discuss. ■ **pursuer** n.

....
☑ pur-, not per-: pursue.
....

pursuit n. **1** the act of pursuing. **2** a leisure activity.

purulent adj. of or containing pus.

purvey v. supply food or drink as one's business. ■ **purveyor** n.

pus n. a thick yellowish liquid produced in infected tissue.

push v. **1** apply force to something so as to move it away from oneself. **2** move forward by using force. **3** urge to great-

Thesaurus

dupe, mouthpiece; *informal* poodle.

purchase v. *see* BUY. ▶n. **1** ACQUISITION, order, investment; *informal* buy. **2** GRIP, hold, foothold, footing, toehold, support, grasp, leverage.

pure adj. **1** UNALLOYED, unmixed, unadulterated, uncontaminated, flawless, perfect, genuine, real, true. **2** CLEAN, clear, fresh, unpolluted, untainted, unadulterated, uncontaminated, uninfected, wholesome, natural. **3** VIRGINAL, chaste, maidenly, virtuous, undefiled, unsullied. **4** STAINLESS, spotless, unsullied, unblemished, impeccable, immaculate, blameless, sinless. **5** SHEER, utter, absolute, downright, out-and-out, complete, total, perfect, unmitigated, unqualified. ■ OPPOSITES adulterated, polluted, immoral.

purely adv. ENTIRELY, completely, totally, wholly, solely, only, simply, just, merely.

purge v. **1** CLEANSE, clear, purify, make pure. **2** REMOVE, clear out, expel, eject, dismiss, oust, depose, eradicate, root out, weed out.

purify v. MAKE PURE, clean, cleanse, decontaminate, filter, refine, disinfect, sterilize, sanitize, fumigate. ■ OPPOSITES contaminate.

puritanical adj. PRUDISH, prim, priggish, prissy, puritan, ascetic, austere, straitlaced, narrow-minded, rigid, stiff. ■ OPPOSITES broad-minded.

purpose n. **1** REASON, point, basis, motivation, cause, justification. **2** AIM, intention, object, objective, goal, end, target, ambition, aspiration, desire, wish, hope. **3** DETERMINATION, resolution, resolve, firmness, steadfastness, single-mindedness, persistence, perseverance, tenacity, doggedness. ▶v. *see* INTEND.

purposeful adj. DETERMINED, resolute, resolved, firm, steadfast, single-minded, persistent, tenacious, dogged, unfaltering, unwavering. ■ OPPOSITES aimless.

purposely adv. ON PURPOSE, intentionally, deliberately, by design, wilfully, wittingly, knowingly, consciously.

pursue v. **1** GO AFTER, run after, follow, chase, hunt, stalk, track, trail, shadow; *informal* tail. **2** PROCEED WITH, go on with, er effort. **4** informal sell an illegal drug. ▶ n. **1** an act of pushing. **2** a great effort. □ **pushchair** a folding chair on wheels, in which a young child can be pushed along. ■ **pusher** n.

pushy adj. (**pushier, pushiest**) very self-assertive or ambitious.

pusillanimous adj. cowardly.

puss (or **pussy**) n. informal a cat. □ **pussyfoot** act cautiously.

pustule n. a small pimple containing pus. ■ **pustular** adj.

put v. (**putting, put**) **1** move or bring into a particular position or state. **2** express or phrase. **3** throw a shot or weight as a sport. □ **put down 1** suppress by force. **2** kill a sick animal. **put off 1** postpone. **2** discourage or cause to feel dislike. **put on 1** organize an event. **2** gain weight. **put out** annoy or inconvenience. **put up** accommodate for a short time. **put up with** tolerate.

putative adj. reputed.

putrefy v. (**putrefying, putrefied**) rot. ■ **putrefaction** n. **putrescent** adj.

putrid adj. rotting and foul-smelling.

putt v. strike a golf ball gently so that it rolls into or near a hole. ▶ n. a stroke of this kind. ■ **putter** n.

putty n. a soft paste that sets hard, used for sealing glass in window frames.

puzzle v. **1** confuse because hard to understand. **2** think hard about a problem. ▶ n. **1** a toy or problem designed to test mental skills. **2** a difficult question or problem. ■ **puzzlement** n.

PVC abbrev. polyvinyl chloride, a type of plastic.

pygmy (or **pigmy**) n. (pl. **pygmies**) a member of an African people of very short stature.

pyjamas (US **pajamas**) pl. n. a jacket and loose trousers for sleeping in.

pylon n. a tall metal structure carrying electricity cables.

pyramid n. a structure with a square or triangular base and sloping sides that meet in a point at the top. ■ **pyramidal** adj.

pyre n. a large pile of wood for the ritual burning of a dead body.

pyretic adj. of or producing fever.

Pyrex n. trademark a hard heat-resistant glass.

pyrites /py-ry-teez/ n. a shiny yellow mineral that is a compound of iron and sulphur.

pyromania n. a strong urge to set fire to things. ■ **pyromaniac** n.

pyrotechnics pl. n. a firework display, or the art of staging these. ■ **pyrotechnic** adj.

pyrrhic /pir-rik/ adj. (of a victory) won at too great a cost to have been worthwhile.

python n. a large snake that crushes its prey.

Thesaurus

follow, keep/carry on with, continue with, continue, persist in. **3** WORK AT, engage in, follow, practise, prosecute, apply oneself to.

push v. **1** SHOVE, thrust, propel, drive, ram, butt, jostle. **2** URGE, press, egg on, spur on, prod, goad, incite, impel, dragoon, force, coerce, constrain, browbeat, strong-arm. **3** PROMOTE, advertise, publicize, puff, puff up, boost, beat the drum for; informal plug, hype. □ **push around** BULLY, ride roughshod over, browbeat, tyrannize, intimidate, domineer.

pushy adj. ASSERTIVE, self-assertive, aggressive, forceful, forward, bold, brash, bumptious, presumptuous, cocksure, overconfident; informal bossy. ■ OPPOSITES submissive.

put v. **1** PLACE, lay, set down, deposit, position, rest, stand, locate, situate, settle, install. **2** LAY, present, bring forward, forward, submit, tender, offer, proffer, put forward, set forth, advance. □ **put**

about SPREAD, bandy about, circulate, disseminate, make public, make known, give out, publicize, broadcast, propagate, announce, bruit. **put away** IMPRISON, confine, lock up, shut away/ up. **put down 1** PUT TO SLEEP, put out of its misery, destroy, do away with, kill; US euthanize. **2** SNUB, disparage, deprecate, belittle, denigrate, deflate, slight, humiliate, crush, mortify. **put out 1** INCONVENIENCE, trouble, bother, impose upon, discommode, incommode. **2** EXTINGUISH, quench, douse, stamp out.

puzzle v. PERPLEX, baffle, stump, beat, mystify, confuse, bewilder, nonplus, stagger, dumbfound, daze, confound; informal flummox.

puzzling adj. DIFFICULT, hard, unclear, perplexing, knotty, baffling, enigmatic, abstruse, mystifying, bewildering, unfathomable, inexplicable, incomprehensible, beyond one, above one's head. ■ OPPOSITES clear.

Qq

Q abbrev. question.

QC abbrev. Queen's Counsel.

QED abbrev. quod erat demonstrandum, used to say that something proves the truth of one's claim.

qua /kway, kwah/ conj. in the capacity of.

quack n. **1** the harsh sound made by a duck. **2** a person who falsely claims to have medical knowledge. ▶v. (of a duck) make a quack.

quad n. **1** a quadrangle. **2** a quadruplet. □ **quad bike** a motorcycle with four large tyres, for off-road use.

quadrangle n. a square or rectangular courtyard enclosed by buildings.

quadrant n. **1** a quarter of a circle or of its circumference. **2** hist. an instrument for measuring altitude in astronomy and navigation.

quadraphonic adj. (of sound reproduction) using four channels.

quadratic adj. Math. involving the second and no higher power of an unknown quantity or variable.

quadrilateral n. a four-sided figure. ▶ adj. having four straight sides.

quadrille n. a square dance.

quadriplegia n. paralysis of all four limbs. ■ **quadriplegic** adj. & n.

quadruped n. a four-footed animal.

quadruple adj. **1** having four parts or elements. **2** four times as much. ▶v. multiply by four.

quadruplet n. each of four children born at one birth.

quaff /kwoff/ v. drink heartily.

quagmire n. a bog or marsh.

quail n. a small game bird. ▶v. feel or show fear.

quaint adj. attractively unusual or old-fashioned. ■ **quaintly** adv.

quake v. shake or tremble.

Quaker n. a member of the Religious Society of Friends, a Christian movement rejecting set forms of worship.

qualification n. **1** the act of qualifying. **2** a pass in an examination or the completion of a course. **3** a statement limiting the meaning of another statement.

qualify v. (**qualifying**, **qualified**) **1** meet the necessary standard or conditions to be entitled to something. **2** become officially recognized as able to do a particular job. **3** limit the meaning of a statement etc. ■ **qualifier** n.

qualitative adj. of or measured by quality.

quality n. (pl. **qualities**) **1** excellence or the degree of this. **2** a distinctive feature.

qualm /kwahm/ n. a feeling of doubt about one's actions.

quandary n. (pl. **quandaries**) a state of uncertainty.

quango n. (pl. **quangos**) a semi-public organization with senior appointments made by the government.

Thesaurus

quail v. FLINCH, shrink, recoil, shy away, pull back, draw back, cower, cringe, shudder, shiver, tremble, shake, quake, blench, blanch.

quake v. SHAKE, tremble, quiver, shiver, shudder, rock, vibrate, pulsate, throb.

qualification n. **1** CERTIFICATION, training, competence, competency, accomplishment, eligibility, acceptability, suitableness, preparedness, fitness, proficiency, skilfulness, adeptness, capability, aptitude, skill, ability, attribute, endowment. **2** MODIFICATION, limitation, restriction, reservation, stipulation, allowance, adaptation, adjustment, condition, proviso, provision, caveat.

qualified adj. **1** TRAINED, certificated, equipped, prepared, competent, accomplished, proficient, skilled, skilful, adept, practised, experienced, expert, capable, able. **2** MODIFIED, limited, conditional, restricted, bounded, contingent, confined, circumscribed, reserved, guarded, equivocal.

qualify v. **1** CERTIFY, license, empower, authorize, allow, permit, sanction, warrant, fit, equip. **2** COUNT, be considered, be designated, be eligible, meet the requirements of. **3** MODIFY, limit, make conditional, restrict.

quality n. **1** DEGREE OF EXCELLENCE, standard, grade, level, sort, type, variety, kind. **2** FEATURE, trait, attribute, characteristic, aspect, property, peculiarity.

quantify v. (**quantifying**, **quantified**) express or measure the quantity of. ■ **quantifiable** adj.

quantitative adj. of or measured by quantity.

quantity n. (pl. **quantities**) 1 an amount or number. 2 a large number or amount. □ **quantity surveyor** a person who calculates the amount and cost of materials needed for building work.

quantum leap n. a sudden large increase or advance.

quantum theory n. a theory of matter and energy based on the idea that energy exists in indivisible units.

quarantine n. a period of isolation for people or animals that have been exposed to an infectious disease. ▶ v. put in quarantine.

quark n. any of a group of subatomic particles believed to form protons, neutrons, etc.

quarrel n. 1 an angry argument. 2 a reason for disagreement. ▶ v. (**quarrelling**, **quarrelled**; US **quarreling**, **quarreled**) have a quarrel. ■ **quarrelsome** adj.

quarry n. (pl. **quarries**) 1 a place where stone etc. is dug out of the earth. 2 a person or animal being chased or hunted. ▶ v. (**quarrying**, **quarried**) take stone etc. from a quarry.

quart n. a quarter of a gallon, approx. 1.13 litres.

quarter n. 1 each of four equal parts of something. 2 three months. 3 fifteen minutes. 4 a particular part of a town or city. 5 a US or Canadian coin worth 25 cents. 6 (**quarters**) rooms or lodg-

ings. 7 mercy shown to an opponent. ▶ v. 1 divide into quarters. 2 (**be quartered**) be lodged. □ **quarterdeck** the part of a ship's upper deck near the stern. **quarter-final** a match of a competition preceding the semi-final. **quartermaster** a regimental officer in charge of accommodation and supplies.

quarterly adj. & adv. produced or occurring once every three months. ▶ n. (pl. **quarterlies**) a quarterly publication.

quartet n. 1 a group of four playing music or singing together. 2 music for a quartet.

quarto n. (pl. **quartos**) a size of book page resulting from folding a sheet into four leaves.

quartz n. a hard mineral.

quasar /kway-zar/ n. a galaxy giving off enormous amounts of energy.

quash v. 1 reject as invalid. 2 put an end to.

quasi- /kway-zy/ comb. form seemingly.

quatrain n. a verse of four lines.

quaver v. (of a voice) tremble. ▶ n. 1 a tremble in a voice. 2 a musical note with the value of half a crotchet. ■ **quavery** adj.

quay /kee/ n. a platform in a harbour for loading and unloading ships. □ **quayside** a quay and the area around it.

queasy adj. (**queasier**, **queasiest**) feeling sick. ■ **queasiness** n.

queen n. 1 the female ruler of a country. 2 a king's wife. 3 the best or most important woman or thing. 4 a playing card ranking next below a king. 5 the most powerful chess piece. 6 a repro-

Thesaurus q

qualm n. DOUBT, misgiving, scruple, hesitation, hesitancy, reluctance, anxiety, apprehension, disquiet, uneasiness, concern.

quantity n. NUMBER, amount, total, aggregate, sum, quota, weight, capacity, mass, volume, bulk, extent, length, area.

quarrel n. ARGUMENT, fight, disagreement, difference of opinion, dispute, disputation, squabble, altercation, wrangle, misunderstanding, feud, vendetta; informal row, spat, scrap, tiff. ▶ v. ARGUE, have a fight, fight, dispute, squabble, bicker, spar, wrangle, have a misunderstanding, fall out; informal row, have a row. ■ OPPOSITES agree.

quarrelsome adj. ARGUMENTATIVE, belligerent, disputatious, contentious, pugnacious, combative, ready for a fight, bellicose, litigious, hot-tempered, iras-

cible, choleric, irritable. ■ OPPOSITES peaceable.

quarry n. PREY, victim, prize.

quarter n. 1 DISTRICT, area, region, part, side, neighbourhood, locality, zone. 2 MERCY, leniency, clemency, compassion, pity. ▶ v. PUT UP, house, board, billet, accommodate, lodge, install.

quarters pl. n. ACCOMMODATION, billet, residence, dwelling, abode, domicile, habitation, lodgings, rooms, barracks; informal digs, pad.

quash v. 1 ANNUL, declare null and void, nullify, invalidate, void, cancel, overrule, override, overthrow, reject, set aside, reverse, revoke, rescind, repeal. 2 CRUSH, put down, squash, quell, subdue, suppress, repress, quench, extinguish, stamp out, put a stop to, end, terminate, defeat, destroy. ■ OPPOSITES validate.

ductive bee, ant, etc. **7** informal a homosexual man. □ **queen mother** the widow of a king and mother of the sovereign. ■ **queenly** adj.

queer adj. **1** strange; odd. **2** derog. homosexual. ▶ n. derog. a homosexual. □ **queer someone's pitch** informal spoil someone's plans or chances.

quell v. suppress.

quench v. **1** satisfy thirst. **2** put out a fire.

quern n. a hand mill for grinding grain.

querulous adj. complaining petulantly. ■ **querulously** adv.

query n. (pl. **queries**) a question, esp. one expressing doubt. ▶ v. (**querying**, **queried**) raise a query.

quest n. a long search.

question n. **1** a sentence requesting information. **2** a doubt. **3** a problem needing to be solved. ▶ v. **1** ask questions of. **2** express doubt about. □ **in question** being discussed or disputed. **out of the question** not possible. **question mark** a punctuation mark (?) indicating a question.

questionable adj. open to doubt.

questionnaire n. a set of printed questions for a survey.

queue n. a line of people or vehicles waiting for something. ▶ v. (**queuing** or **queueing**, **queued**) wait in a queue.

quibble n. a minor objection. ▶ v. raise a minor objection.

quiche /keesh/ n. a baked flan with a savoury filling.

quick adj. **1** moving fast. **2** taking a short time. **3** intelligent or alert. **4** (of temper) easily roused. ▶ n. the tender flesh below a fingernail or toenail. □ **quicklime** = LIME (sense 1). **quicksand** loose wet sand that sucks in anything resting on it. **quicksilver** mercury. **quickstep** a fast foxtrot. ■ **quicken** v. **quickly** adv. **quickness** n.

quid n. (pl. **quid**) informal one pound in money.

quid pro quo n. (pl. **quid pro quos**) a favour given in return for another.

quiescent adj. inactive. ■ **quiescence** n.

quiet adj. **1** making little or no noise. **2** calm and tranquil. **3** discreet. ▶ n. absence of noise or disturbance. □ **on the quiet** informal secretly. ■ **quieten** v. **quietly** adv. **quietness** n.

quietude n. calmness and quiet.

quiff n. an upright tuft of hair.

quill n. **1** a large feather. **2** a pen made from this. **3** a spine of a porcupine or

Thesaurus

quaver v. QUIVER, vibrate, tremble, shake, waver.

queasy adj. SICK, nauseated, ill, indisposed, dizzy, sick to one's stomach.

queer adj. **1** ODD, strange, unusual, extraordinary, funny, curious, peculiar, weird, outlandish, singular, eccentric, unconventional, unorthodox, atypical, abnormal, irregular, anomalous, deviant, offbeat; informal off-the-wall. **2** SUSPICIOUS, suspect, irregular, questionable, dubious, doubtful; informal fishy, shady.

quell v. **1** ALLAY, lull, quiet, silence, calm, soothe, appease, assuage, abate, deaden, dull, pacify. **2** see QUASH (2).

quench v. **1** SATISFY, slake, sate, satiate. **2** EXTINGUISH, put out, snuff out, blow out, douse.

quest n. **1** SEARCH, seeking, pursuit, chase, hunt. **2** ADVENTURE, expedition, journey, voyage, exploration, crusade.

question n. **1** QUERY, enquiry, interrogation. **2** ISSUE, problem, matter, point, subject, topic, theme, bone of contention. ▶ v. **1** ASK QUESTIONS OF, interrogate, cross-examine, quiz, interview, sound out, examine; informal grill, pump. **2** CALL INTO QUESTION, query, raise doubts about, throw doubt on, have suspicions about, challenge.

questionable adj. OPEN TO QUESTION/ DOUBT, doubtful, dubious, uncertain, debatable, in dispute, arguable, controversial, controvertible. ■ OPPOSITES indisputable.

queue n. LINE, row, column, file, chain, string, train, succession, sequence, series, concatenation.

quibble n. CRITICISM, complaint, protest, objection, niggle, cavil, nicety. ▶ v. CAVIL, carp, pettifog, split hairs, chop logic; informal nit-pick.

quick adj. **1** FAST, rapid, speedy, swift, fleet, express. **2** PROMPT, without delay, immediate, instantaneous, expeditious. **3** BRIEF, brisk, fleeting, momentary, hasty, hurried, cursory, perfunctory. **4** QUICK-WITTED, sharp-witted, alert, intelligent. ■ OPPOSITES slow, long.

quicken v. **1** BECOME/GROW FASTER, speed up, accelerate, hurry, hasten. **2** see AROUSE.

quiet adj. **1** SILENT, hushed, noiseless, soundless, peaceful. **2** SOFT, low, inaudible. **3** PEACEFUL, sleepy, undisturbed, unfrequented, secluded, isolated, out of the way, off the beaten track. ■ OPPOSITES noisy.

hedgehog.

quilt n. a padded bed covering.

quilted adj. made of two layers of fabric filled with padding.

quin n. informal a quintuplet.

quince n. a hard yellowish fruit.

quinine n. a bitter compound formerly used to treat malaria.

quinsy n. an abscess on a tonsil.

quintessence n. **1** a perfect or most typical example. **2** a refined extract of a substance. ■ **quintessential** adj. **quintessentially** adv.

quintet n. **1** a group of five playing music or singing together. **2** music for a quintet.

quintuple adj. **1** having five parts or elements. **2** five times as much.

quintuplet n. each of five children born at one birth.

quip n. a witty remark. ▶v. (**quipping**, **quipped**) make a quip.

quire n. 25 sheets of paper.

quirk n. **1** a peculiar habit in a person's behaviour. **2** a strange thing happening by chance. ■ **quirky** adj.

quisling n. a traitor collaborating with an occupying force.

quit v. (**quitting**, **quitted** or **quit**) **1** leave. **2** resign from a job. **3** informal, esp. US cease.

quite adv. **1** completely. **2** to a certain extent.

quits adj. on equal terms because a debt or score has been settled.

quiver v. shake or vibrate with a slight rapid motion. ▶n. **1** a quivering movement or sound. **2** a case for carrying arrows.

quixotic adj. idealistic and impractical.

quiz n. (pl. **quizzes**) a game or competition involving a set of questions as a test of knowledge. ▶v. (**quizzing**, **quizzed**) interrogate.

quizzical adj. showing mild or amused puzzlement. ■ **quizzically** adv.

quoit /koyt/ n. a ring thrown to land over a peg in the game of **quoits**.

quondam /kwon-dam/ adj. former.

quorate /kwor-uht/ adj. (of a meeting) having a quorum.

quorum /kwor-uhm/ n. a minimum number of people that must be present at a meeting to make it valid.

quota n. **1** a limited quantity allowed. **2** a fixed share.

quotable adj. worth quoting.

quotation n. a passage or price quoted. □ **quotation mark** each of a set of punctuation marks, (' ' or " "), enclosing quoted words.

quote v. **1** repeat something spoken or written by another person. **2** give an estimated price.

quoth v. old use said.

quotidian /kwuh-tid-i-uhn/ adj. daily.

quotient /kwoh-shuhnt/ n. a result obtained by dividing one quantity by another.

q.v. abbrev. used to direct a reader to another part of a book for further information.

Thesaurus

quieten v. **1** SILENCE, hush, shush, quiet, still; informal shut up. **2** ALLAY, soothe, calm (down), appease, lull, pacify, mollify, palliate.

quit v. **1** GIVE UP, stop, cease, leave off, abandon, abstain from, desist from. **2** LEAVE, depart from, vacate, walk out on.

quite adv. **1** COMPLETELY, fully, entirely, totally, wholly, absolutely, in all respects. **2** FAIRLY, relatively, moderately, reasonably, to some extent/degree, rather, somewhat.

quiver v. TREMBLE, shiver, vibrate, qua-ver, quake, shudder, pulsate, convulse, palpitate.

quota n. SHARE, allowance, allocation, portion, ration, part, slice, measure, proportion; informal cut, whack.

quotation n. **1** CITATION, reference, quote, allusion, excerpt, extract, selection, passage, line. **2** ESTIMATE, estimated price, quote, cost, charge, figure.

quote v. **1** REPEAT, iterate, recite, reproduce. **2** CITE, give, name, instance, mention, refer to, make reference to, allude to, specify, identify. **3** ESTIMATE FOR, price, set a price for.

Rr

R abbrev. **1** Regina or Rex. **2** (**R.**) River.

r abbrev. **1** radius. **2** right.

rabbi n. (pl. **rabbis**) a Jewish religious leader. ■ **rabbinical** adj.

rabbit n. a burrowing mammal with long ears and a short tail. ▶v. (**rabbiting, rabbited**) informal chatter.

rabble n. a disorderly crowd.

rabid adj. **1** fanatical. **2** affected with rabies.

rabies n. a dangerous disease of dogs etc. that can be transmitted through saliva to humans.

raccoon (or **racoon**) n. an American mammal with a black face and striped tail.

race n. **1** a competition to determine the fastest over a set course. **2** each of the major divisions of humankind, based on particular physical characteristics. **3** a subdivision of a species. ▶v. **1** compete in a race or have a race with. **2** move or operate at full or excessive speed. □ **racecourse** a ground or track for horse or dog racing. **racetrack 1** a racecourse. **2** a track for motor racing. ■ **racer** n.

raceme n. a flower cluster with separate flowers along a central stem.

racial adj. of or based on race. ■ **racially** adv.

racialism n. racism. ■ **racialist** n. & adj.

racism n. **1** the belief that certain races are better than others. **2** discrimination against or hostility towards other races. ■ **racist** n. & adj.

rack n. **1** a framework for holding or storing things. **2** hist. a frame on which a person was tortured by being stretched. **3** a bar with cogs or teeth that engage with those on a wheel. ▶v. (or **wrack**) cause great pain to. □ **go to rack and ruin** fall into a bad condition. **rack one's brains** think very hard.

racket n. **1** (also **racquet**) a bat with a stringed frame, used in tennis etc. **2** a loud unpleasant noise. **3** informal a dishonest scheme for obtaining money.

racketeer n. a person who makes money through dishonest activities. ■ **racketeering** n.

raconteur /ra-kon-ter/ n. a person who tells stories in an entertaining way.

racoon var. of RACCOON.

racy adj. (**racier**, **raciest**) lively and exciting, esp. in a sexual way.

radar n. a system for detecting aircraft, ships, etc. by means of reflected radio waves.

radial adj. **1** arranged in lines coming out from a common central point. **2** (of a tyre) in which fabric layers run at right angles to the circumference of the tyre. ■ **radially** adv.

radiant adj. **1** shining or glowing brightly. **2** showing joy or health. **3** (of heat) transmitted by radiation. ■ **radiance** n. **radiantly** adv.

radiate v. **1** (of energy) be sent out in rays or waves. **2** spread out from a central point.

radiation n. **1** the act of radiating. **2** energy sent out as electromagnetic waves or subatomic particles.

Thesaurus

rabble n. MOB, horde, swarm, crowd, throng.

race¹ n. **1** CONTEST, competition, chase, pursuit, relay. **2** CHANNEL, waterway, watercourse, sluice, spillway. ▶v. **1** RUN AGAINST, compete against, be pitted against. **2** RUN, sprint, dash, dart, bolt, speed, hare, fly, tear, zoom, accelerate, career.

race² n. ETHNIC GROUP, people, bloodline, stock, line, lineage, breed, strain.

racial adj. RACE-RELATED, ethnic, ethnological.

racism n. RACIALISM, racial discrimination, racial prejudice/bigotry, chauvinism, xenophobia.

racist n. RACIALIST, bigot. ▶adj. RACIALIST, discriminatory, prejudiced, bigoted, intolerant, illiberal.

rack n. FRAME, framework, stand, form, trestle, structure, holder, shelf.

racket n. **1** NOISE, din, row, commotion, disturbance, uproar, hubbub, hullabaloo, clamour, pandemonium, tumult.

radiant adj. **1** SHINING, bright, illuminated, brilliant, luminous, luminescent, lustrous. **2** JOYFUL, happy, elated, ecstatic, delighted, pleased. See also HAPPY.

radiator n. **1** a metal device that radiates heat, esp. one filled with hot water pumped in through pipes. **2** a cooling device in a vehicle.

radical adj. **1** of the basic nature of something; fundamental. **2** supporting complete political or social reform. ▶ n. a person holding radical views. ■ **radically** adv.

radicchio /ra-dee-ki-oh/ n. (pl. **radicchios**) a variety of chicory with dark red leaves.

radicle n. a developing plant root.

radii pl. of **RADIUS**.

radio n. (pl. **radios**) **1** the sending and receiving of electromagnetic waves carrying sound messages. **2** broadcasting in sound. **3** a device for receiving radio broadcasts, or for sending and receiving radio messages. ▶ v. (**radioing, radioed**) send by radio.

radioactive adj. giving out harmful radiation or particles. ■ **radioactivity** n.

radiocarbon n. a radioactive form of carbon used in carbon dating.

radiography n. the production of images by X-rays or other radiation. ■ **radiographer** n.

radiology n. the study and use of X-rays and similar radiation in medicine. ■ **radiologist** n.

radiotherapy n. the treatment of disease using X-rays or similar radiation. ■ **radiotherapist** n.

radish n. a plant with a crisp, hot-tasting root eaten raw.

radium n. a radioactive metallic element.

radius n. (pl. **radii** or **radiuses**) **1** a straight line from the centre to the circumference of a circle. **2** the length of this. **3** the thicker of the two bones in the forearm.

radon n. a radioactive gaseous element.

RAF abbrev. Royal Air Force.

raffia n. fibre from the leaves of a palm tree, used for hats, baskets, etc.

raffish adj. slightly disreputable.

raffle n. a lottery with goods as prizes. ▶ v. offer as a prize in a raffle.

raft n. **1** a flat floating structure used as a boat. **2** a large amount.

rafter n. a beam forming part of the internal framework of a roof.

rag n. **1** a piece of old cloth. **2** (**rags**) old torn clothes. **3** informal a low-quality newspaper. **4** a programme of entertainments by students in aid of charity. ▶ v. (**ragging, ragged**) tease.

ragamuffin n. a person in ragged, dirty clothes.

rage n. violent anger. ▶ v. **1** feel or express rage. **2** continue with great force. □ **all the rage** temporarily very popular or fashionable.

ragged adj. **1** (of clothes) old and torn. **2** rough or irregular.

raglan adj. (of a sleeve) continuing in one piece up to the neck.

ragout /ra-goo/ n. a stew of meat and vegetables.

ragtime n. an early form of jazz, played esp. on the piano.

raid n. **1** a sudden attack on people or premises. **2** a surprise visit by police to arrest suspects or seize illegal goods. ▶ v. make a raid on. ■ **raider** n.

rail n. **1** a fixed horizontal bar. **2** each of the two metal bars forming a railway track. **3** railways as a means of transport. ▶ v. **1** provide or enclose with a rail or rails. **2** (**rail against/at**) complain strongly about. □ **railing** a fence made of rails. **railroad 1** US a railway. **2** informal force into doing something. **railway 1** a track made of rails along which trains run. **2** a system of transport using these.

Thesaurus

■ OPPOSITES dark, gloomy.

radiate v. SEND OUT/FORTH, give off/out, emit, emanate, scatter, disperse, diffuse, spread, shed.

radical adj. **1** FUNDAMENTAL, basic, rudimentary, elementary, elemental, constitutional. **2** THOROUGH, complete, total, entire, absolute, utter, comprehensive, exhaustive, sweeping, far-reaching, profound, drastic. **3** EXTREMIST, extreme, immoderate, revolutionary, rebel, rebellious, militant. ■ OPPOSITES superficial, moderate.

raffle n. LOTTERY, draw, sweepstake, sweep, tombola.

rage n. FURY, anger, wrath, high dudgeon, frenzy, madness; literary ire. ▶ v. BE FURIOUS, be infuriated, be angry, seethe, be beside oneself, lose one's temper, boil over, rant, rave, storm, fume, fulminate; informal blow one's top, flip one's lid, freak out.

ragged adj. **1** TATTERED, threadbare, frayed, the worse for wear, torn, rent, in holes, worn to shreds, falling to pieces. **2** JAGGED, uneven, irregular, notched, serrated, saw-toothed, craggy. ■ OPPOSITES smart.

raid n. SURPRISE ATTACK, assault, onslaught, invasion, incursion, thrust,

raiment n. old use clothing.

rain n. **1** condensed moisture from the atmosphere falling in separate drops. **2** (**rains**) falls of rain. ▶v. **1** fall as rain. **2** fall in large quantities. ◻ **rainbow** an arch of colours in the sky, caused by the sun shining through water droplets in the atmosphere. **raincoat** a coat made from water-resistant fabric. **rainfall** the amount of rain falling. **rainforest** a dense tropical forest with consistently heavy rainfall. ■ **rainy** adj.

raise v. **1** lift or move upwards or into an upright position. **2** increase the amount or level of. **3** cause to be heard, felt, or considered. **4** collect money. **5** bring up a child. **6** (**raise to**) multiply a quantity to a specified power. ▶n. US an increase in salary.

raisin n. a partially dried grape.

Raj n. the period of British rule in India.

raja (or **rajah**) n. hist. an Indian king or prince.

rake n. **1** a pole with prongs at the end for collecting fallen leaves, smoothing soil, etc. **2** a fashionable, wealthy, but immoral man. **3** the angle at which something slopes. ▶v. **1** collect or smooth with a rake. **2** scratch with a sweeping movement. **3** sweep with gunfire etc. **4** search through. **5** (**rake up**) revive the memory of something best forgotten. **6** set at a sloping angle.

rakish adj. dashing but slightly disreputable in appearance.

rally v. (**rallying**, **rallied**) **1** bring or come together again for united action. **2** recover in health or strength. ▶n. (pl. **rallies**) **1** a mass meeting held as a protest or in support of a cause. **2** a long-distance driving competition over roads or rough country. **3** a recovery. **4** a long exchange of strokes in tennis etc.

RAM abbrev. Computing random-access memory.

ram n. **1** an adult male sheep. **2** a striking or plunging device. ▶v. (**ramming**, **rammed**) hit or push with force. ◻ **ram raid** a robbery in which a shop window is rammed with a vehicle. **ramrod** a rod formerly used to ram down the charge of a firearm.

Ramadan n. the ninth month of the Muslim year, during which Muslims fast from dawn to sunset.

ramble v. **1** walk for pleasure in the countryside. **2** talk in a confused way and at length. ▶n. a country walk for pleasure. ■ **rambler** n.

ramekin /ra-mi-kin/ n. a small individual baking dish.

ramifications pl. n. complex results of an action or event.

ramify v. (**ramifying**, **ramified**) branch out.

ramp n. a slope joining two levels.

rampage v. rush around in a wild, violent way. ▶n. a period of wild, violent behaviour.

rampant adj. **1** flourishing or spreading uncontrollably. **2** (of an animal in heraldry) standing on its left hind leg with its forelegs in the air.

Thesaurus

sortie, sally. ▶v. **1** ATTACK, assault, invade, assail, storm, rush, set upon, descend upon, swoop down. **2** PLUNDER, pillage, loot, rifle, forage, ransack, steal from.

rain n. RAINFALL, precipitation, raindrops, drizzle, shower, rainstorm, cloudburst, torrent, downpour, deluge. ▶v. POUR, pour/come down, precipitate; informal rain cats and dogs, come down in buckets.

rainy adj. WET, showery, drizzly, damp.

raise v. **1** LIFT, lift up, raise aloft, elevate, uplift, hoist, heave up. **2** INCREASE, put up, escalate, inflate, heighten, augment, amplify, intensify; informal step up, hike, jack up. **3** BRING UP, rear, nurture, educate. ■ OPPOSITES lower.

rally v. **1** COME/GET TOGETHER, assemble, group, band together, convene, unite. **2** CALL/BRING TOGETHER, assemble, summon, round up, muster, marshall, mobilize. **3** RECOVER, recuperate, revive, get well/well, improve, perk up. ▶n. MEETING, gathering, assembly, convention, convocation.

ram v. **1** FORCE, cram, stuff, compress, jam, squeeze, thrust, tamp. **2** STRIKE, hit, run into, crash into, collide with, bump, slam.

ramble v. **1** WALK, hike, wander, stroll, amble, roam, range, rove, traipse. **2** DIGRESS, wander, gabble; informal rattle on, rabbit on, witter on.

rambling adj. **1** DIGRESSIVE, wandering, roundabout, circuitous, periphrastic, disconnected, disjointed, maundering, long-winded, verbose, wordy, prolix. **2** SPRAWLING, spreading, unsystematic, straggling. ■ OPPOSITES concise.

ramification n. CONSEQUENCE, aftermath, outcome, result, upshot, issue, sequel, complication, implication.

ramp n. SLOPE, incline, gradient, rise,

rampart n. a defensive wall having a broad top with a walkway.

ramshackle adj. in a very bad condition.

ran past of RUN.

ranch n. a large cattle farm in America. ∎ **rancher** n.

rancid adj. smelling or tasting of stale fat.

rancour (US **rancor**) n. bitter feeling or resentment. ∎ **rancorous** adj.

rand n. the basic unit of money of South Africa.

random adj. done or happening without order, purpose, or planning. ∎ **randomly** adv. **randomness** n.

randy adj. (**randier**, **randiest**) informal sexually excited.

rang past of RING.

range n. 1 the limits between which something varies. 2 a set of things of the same general type. 3 the distance over which a sound, missile, etc. can travel. 4 a line of mountains or hills. 5 a large open area for grazing or hunting. 6 an area for testing military equipment or for shooting practice. ▶v. 1 vary between particular limits. 2 arrange in order. 3 travel over or cover a wide area.

ranger n. a keeper of a park, forest, or area of countryside.

rangy adj. tall and slim.

rank n. 1 a position within the armed forces or an organization. 2 a row of people or things. 3 high social position. 4 (**the ranks**) ordinary soldiers rather than officers. ▶v. 1 give a rank to.

2 hold a specified rank. 3 arrange in a row or rows. ▶adj. 1 foul-smelling. 2 growing too thickly. 3 complete: *a rank amateur*. □ **rank and file** the ordinary members of an organization.

rankle v. cause continuing resentment.

ransack v. go hurriedly through a place stealing or searching for things.

ransom n. a sum of money demanded or paid for the release of a captive. ▶v. demand or pay a ransom for.

rant v. speak in a loud, forceful way.

rap v. (**rapping**, **rapped**) 1 strike sharply. 2 informal criticize sharply. ▶n. 1 a quick, sharp knock or blow. 2 informal criticism. 3 a type of popular music in which words are spoken rapidly and rhythmically over an instrumental backing. ∎ **rapper** n.

rapacious adj. very greedy. ∎ **rapacity** n.

rape v. (of a man) force someone to have sex with him against their will. ▶n. 1 an act of raping. 2 a plant with oil-rich seeds.

rapid adj. quick. ▶pl. n. (**rapids**) a part of a river where the water flows very fast. ∎ **rapidity** n. **rapidly** adv.

rapier n. a thin, light sword.

rapist n. a man who commits rape.

rapport /rap-por/ n. a close and harmonious relationship.

rapprochement /ra-prosh-mon/ n. a renewal of friendly relations.

rapt adj. fascinated or totally absorbed.

rapture n. great joy. ∎ **rapturous** adj.

rare adj. 1 not occurring or found very often. 2 unusually good. 3 (of meat)

Thesaurus

acclivity.

rampage v. RUN RIOT, run amok, charge, tear, storm, go berserk. ▶n. UPROAR, furore, mayhem, turmoil.

rampant adj. OUT OF CONTROL/HAND, unrestrained, unchecked, unbridled, widespread, pandemic, epidemic. ∎ OPPOSITES controlled.

random adj. HAPHAZARD, chance, accidental, fortuitous, serendipitous, adventitious, arbitrary, hit-or-miss, indiscriminate, sporadic, stray, spot, casual, unsystematic, unmethodical, disorganized, unplanned, undirected. ∎ OPPOSITES systematic.

range n. 1 SCOPE, compass, limits, bounds, confines, radius, span, scale, gamut, reach, sweep, extent, area, field, orbit, province, domain, latitude. 2 ASSORTMENT, variety, kind, sort, type, class, rank, order, genus, species. ▶v.

1 EXTEND, stretch, reach, cover, go, run, pass, fluctuate between, vary between. 2 ROAM, rove, ramble, traverse, travel over, wander, meander, amble, stroll, stray, drift.

rank[1] n. 1 GRADE, level, echelon, stratum, class, status, position, station. 2 NOBILITY, aristocracy, eminence, distinction. ▶v. 1 CLASSIFY, class, categorize, grade. 2 HAVE A RANK, be graded, be placed, be positioned.

rank[2] adj. 1 see LUSH. 2 see SMELLY.

rankle v. FESTER, annoy, anger, irk, vex, irritate, rile, chafe, gall, embitter; *informal* get someone's goat.

ransack v. 1 see PLUNDER. 2 see SEARCH.

rapid adj. QUICK, fast, swift, speedy, fleet, hurried, hasty, expeditious, express, brisk, lively, prompt, precipitate. ∎ OPPOSITES slow.

rapport n. AFFINITY, bond, empathy,

lightly cooked, so that the inside is still red. ■ **rarely** adv. **rarity** n.

rarebit (or **Welsh rarebit**) n. a dish of melted cheese on toast.

rarefied adj. **1** (of air) of lower pressure than usual. **2** understood by only a limited group.

....

☑ -*ref*-, not -*rif*-: rarefied.

....

raring adj. informal very eager: *raring to go*.

rascal n. a mischievous person. ■ **rascally** adj.

rash adj. acting or done without considering the possible results. ▶n. an area of red spots or patches on the skin. ■ **rashly** adv.

rasher n. a slice of bacon.

rasp n. **1** a coarse file. **2** a harsh, grating noise. ▶v. **1** (of a rough surface) scrape. **2** make a rasping noise.

raspberry n. **1** an edible red soft fruit. **2** informal a rude sound made with the tongue and lips to express contempt.

Rastafarian n. a member of a Jamaican religious movement which worships Haile Selassie, former Emperor of Ethiopia. ■ **Rastafarianism** n.

rat n. **1** a rodent like a large mouse. **2** informal an unpleasant or disliked person. ▶v. (**ratting**, **ratted**) (**rat on**) informal inform on. □ **the rat race** informal a fiercely competitive way of life.

ratatouille /ra-tuh-**too**-i/ n. a dish of stewed onions, courgettes, tomatoes, etc.

ratchet n. a bar or wheel with a set of angled teeth in which a cog etc. fits, allowing movement in one direction only.

rate n. **1** a measure, quantity, or frequency measured against another. **2** a speed. **3** a fixed price or charge. **4** (**rates**) a local tax on land and buildings paid by a business. ▶v. **1** assign a value to according to a particular scale. **2** regard in a certain way. **3** be worthy of. □ **at any rate** whatever happens. ■ **rateable** (or **ratable**) adj.

rather adv. **1** (**would rather**) would prefer. **2** to some extent. **3** on the contrary or more precisely.

ratify v. (**ratifying**, **ratified**) confirm an agreement etc. formally. ■ **ratification** n.

rating n. **1** a classification based on quality or standard. **2** (**ratings**) the estimated audience of a broadcast. **3** a non-commissioned sailor.

ratio n. (pl. **ratios**) the relationship between two amounts, showing the number of times one value contains the other.

ratiocination n. logical reasoning.

ration n. a fixed allowance of food, fuel, etc. ▶v. limit the supply of food, fuel, etc.

rational adj. **1** based on reason or logic. **2** able to think sensibly or logically. ■ **rationality** n. **rationally** adv.

rationale /ra-shuh-**nahl**/ n. the reasons

Thesaurus

....

sympathy, understanding.

rapture n. JOY, ecstasy, elation, exaltation, exhilaration, bliss, euphoria, rhapsody, enchantment, delight.

rare adj. **1** UNUSUAL, uncommon, out of the ordinary, exceptional, atypical, singular, remarkable, unique. **2** INFREQUENT, few and far between, scarce, sparse, sporadic, scattered. ■ OPPOSITES common.

rascal n. **1** IMP, scamp, scallywag, mischief-maker, little devil. **2** SCOUNDREL, rogue, ne'er-do-well, good-for-nothing, wastrel, reprobate; dated cad; informal creep, rat; informal, dated rotter; old use blackguard.

rash adj. RECKLESS, impetuous, hasty, impulsive, bold, madcap, audacious, brash, daredevil, foolhardy, foolish, harum-scarum, devil-may-care, headstrong, hot-headed, incautious, careless, heedless, thoughtless, unthinking, imprudent, injudicious. ■ OPPOSITES

prudent.

rate n. **1** PERCENTAGE, ratio, proportion, scale, degree, standard. **2** PACE, stride, gait, motion, speed, tempo, velocity, measure. ▶v. **1** JUDGE, assess, appraise, evaluate, value, measure, weigh up, grade, rank, adjudge. **2** REGARD AS, consider, deem, reckon, account.

rather adv. **1** SOONER, preferably, more readily. **2** QUITE, fairly, a bit, a little, slightly, somewhat; informal sort of, kind of, pretty.

ratify v. CONFIRM, endorse, sign, sanction, warrant, approve, authorize, validate. ■ OPPOSITES revoke.

ratio n. PROPORTION, comparative size/extent, correlation, correspondence, percentage, fraction, quotient.

ration n. ALLOWANCE, quota, allotment, portion, share, measure, part, lot, amount, helping, proportion, percentage. ▶v. LIMIT, restrict, control, conserve, budget.

for a course of action or a belief.

rationalism n. the belief that opinions and actions should be based on reason rather than on religious belief or emotions. ■ **rationalist** n.

rationalize (or **-ise**) v. **1** try to find a logical reason for. **2** make more efficient. ■ **rationalization** n.

rattan n. the thin, pliable stems of a palm, used to make furniture.

rattle v. **1** make or move with a rapid series of short, sharp sounds. **2** informal make nervous or irritated. **3** (**rattle off**) say or do quickly. ▶ n. **1** a rattling sound. **2** a device or toy that makes this. □ **rattlesnake** an American viper with horny rings on the tail that produce a rattling sound.

raucous adj. loud and harsh. ■ **raucously** adv.

raunchy adj. (**raunchier, raunchiest**) informal sexually direct.

ravage v. do great damage to. ▶ n. (**ravages**) damage.

rave v. **1** talk angrily or incoherently. **2** speak or write about enthusiastically. ▶ n. a very large event with dancing to fast electronic music.

raven n. a large black crow. ▶ adj. (of hair) glossy black.

ravenous adj. very hungry. ■ **ravenously** adv.

ravine n. a deep, narrow gorge.

ravioli pl. n. small square pasta cases

with a savoury filling.

ravish v. **1** dated rape. **2** (**ravishing**) very beautiful.

raw adj. **1** not cooked. **2** not yet processed. **3** new and inexperienced. **4** (of the skin) red and painful from being rubbed. **5** (of the weather) cold and damp. □ **raw deal** unfair treatment. **rawhide** untanned leather. ■ **rawness** n.

ray n. **1** a narrow line or beam of light or other radiation. **2** a large flat fish.

rayon n. a synthetic fibre or fabric made from viscose.

raze v. completely destroy a building etc.

razor n. an instrument with a sharp blade for shaving.

razzmatazz n. informal noisy, showy, and exciting activity or display.

R & B abbrev. rhythm and blues.

RC abbrev. Roman Catholic.

R & D abbrev. research and development.

RE abbrev. religious education.

re prep. with regard to.

reach v. **1** stretch out an arm to touch or grasp something. **2** be able to touch. **3** arrive at; get as far as. **4** achieve. **5** make contact with. ▶ n. **1** the distance over which someone or something can reach. **2** a stretch of river between two bends.

react v. cause or undergo a reaction. ■ **reactive** adj.

reaction n. **1** something done or experi-

Thesaurus

rational adj. SENSIBLE, reasonable, logical, sound, intelligent, wise, judicious, sagacious, prudent, circumspect, politic, astute, shrewd, perceptive, well advised, well grounded. ■ OPPOSITES irrational.

rationalize v. **1** EXPLAIN AWAY, account for, make excuses, make plausible, try to vindicate/justify. **2** STREAMLINE, trim, make cuts in, cut back on, retrench on.

rattle v. **1** BANG, knock, rap, clatter, clang, clank, jangle, clink. **2** DISCONCERT, disturb, fluster, upset, shake, perturb, faze, discompose, discomfit.

raucous adj. STRIDENT, piercing, ear-splitting, shrill, screeching, harsh, sharp, grating, rasping, discordant, dissonant, jarring. ■ OPPOSITES soft, quiet.

ravage v. DEVASTATE, lay waste, ruin, wreak havoc on, destroy, level, raze, demolish.

rave v. **1** RANT AND RAVE, rage, storm, fulminate, explode in anger; informal fly off the handle, flip one's lid. **2** RHAPSODIZE

OVER, enthuse about, praise to the skies, gush over.

ravenous adj. STARVING, starved, famished, ravening, wolfish, voracious, insatiable, insatiate.

ravishing adj. BEAUTIFUL, lovely, stunning, gorgeous, dazzling, radiant, enchanting, bewitching, charming. ■ OPPOSITES hideous.

raw adj. **1** UNCOOKED, fresh. **2** UNREFINED, crude, green, coarse, unprocessed, unprepared, untreated. **3** INEXPERIENCED, untrained, unskilled, untutored, new, callow, immature, green; informal wet behind the ears. **4** COLD, chilly, freezing, bitter, biting, nippy, piercing, penetrating. ■ OPPOSITES cooked, processed.

ray n. BEAM, shaft, streak, stream, gleam, glint, flash, glimmer.

raze v. TEAR/PULL DOWN, knock down, level, bulldoze, flatten, demolish, ruin, wreck.

reach v. **1** STRETCH, extend, hold out, thrust out, stick out. **2** GET AS FAR AS, get to, arrive at, come to. **3** CONTACT, get in enced as a result of an event. **2** a bad response by the body to a drug etc. **3** a process in which substances interact causing chemical or physical change.

reactionary adj. opposing political or social progress or reform. ▶ n. (pl. **reactionaries**) a reactionary person.

reactor n. an apparatus for producing nuclear energy.

read v. (**reading**, **read**) **1** understand the meaning of written or printed words or symbols. **2** speak written or printed words aloud. **3** interpret in a particular way. **4** (**read into**) think that something has a meaning that it may not possess. **5** (of an instrument) show a measurement. ▶ n. informal a book that is interesting to read. ■ **readable** adj.

reader n. **1** a person who reads. **2** a book containing extracts of texts for teaching. **3** a device producing a readable image from a microfiche. **4** a senior university lecturer. ☐ **readership** the readers of a publication as a group.

readjust v. **1** adjust again. **2** adapt to a changed situation. ■ **readjustment** n.

ready adj. (**readier**, **readiest**) **1** pre-

pared. **2** available for immediate use. **3** easily obtained. **4** willing. **5** quick. ▶ n. (**readies** or **the ready**) informal cash. ▶ v. (**readying**, **readied**) prepare. ■ **readily** adv. **readiness** n.

reagent /ri-ay-juhnt/ n. a substance used to produce a chemical reaction.

real adj. **1** actually existing or occurring. **2** not artificial; genuine. **3** worthy of the description. ☐ **real estate** US buildings or land.

realign v. change to a different position or state. ■ **realignment** n.

realism n. **1** the acceptance of a situation as it is. **2** the accurate and true representation of things. ■ **realist** n. **realistic** adj. **realistically** adv.

reality n. (pl. **realities**) **1** the state of things as they actually exist. **2** a thing that is real. **3** the state of being real.

realize (or **-ise**) v. **1** become aware of as a fact. **2** achieve a wish or plan. **3** convert property etc. into money by selling it. ■ **realization** n.

really adv. **1** in fact. **2** very. ▶ exclam. expressing interest, surprise, doubt, etc.

realm n. **1** a kingdom. **2** a field of activity or interest.

Thesaurus

touch with, get hold of, get through to, communicate with. ▶ n. SCOPE, range, compass, latitude, ambit, orbit, sphere, area.

react v. **1** HAVE A REACTION/RESPONSE TO, respond. **2** BEHAVE, act, conduct oneself, proceed, operate, function, cope.

reactionary adj. ULTRA-CONSERVATIVE, conservative, obscurantist, diehard, rightist, right-wing, Colonel-Blimpish. ■ OPPOSITES progressive.

read v. **1** PERUSE, study, scan, pore over, scrutinize; informal wade through, dip into. **2** INTERPRET, construe, decipher, deduce, understand, comprehend. **3** REGISTER, record, display, show, indicate.

readable adj. **1** LEGIBLE, easy to read, decipherable, clear, intelligible, understandable, comprehensible. **2** ENJOYABLE, entertaining, interesting, stimulating. ■ OPPOSITES unreadable.

readily adv. **1** WILLINGLY, gladly, happily, cheerfully, eagerly. **2** EASILY, without difficulty, effortlessly. ■ OPPOSITES reluctantly.

ready adj. **1** FINISHED, completed, prepared, organized. **2** PREPARED, equipped, organized, all set, in a fit state; informal fit. **3** WITHIN REACH, available, on hand, present, near, near at hand, accessible,

handy, convenient, on call, at one's fingertips; informal on tap. **4** ABOUT TO, on the verge/brink of, in danger of, liable to, likely to. **5** EAGER, prepared, enthusiastic, anxious, keen; informal psyched up, geared up.

real adj. **1** ACTUAL, existent, factual, non-fictitious. **2** AUTHENTIC, genuine, bona fide; informal pukka, kosher. **3** SINCERE, heartfelt, earnest, fervent, unfeigned, unaffected, honest, truthful. ■ OPPOSITES imaginary, false.

realistic adj. **1** PRACTICAL, pragmatic, rational, down-to-earth, matter-of-fact, sensible, no-nonsense, commonsensical, level-headed, hard-headed, businesslike, hard-boiled, sober, unromantic, unsentimental, with both feet on the ground. **2** LIFELIKE, true-to-life, true, faithful, close, representational, graphic, naturalistic, authentic, genuine. ■ OPPOSITES unrealistic.

reality n. **1** REAL WORLD, actuality, physical existence, corporeality, substantiality, materiality. **2** FACT, actuality, truth. ■ OPPOSITES fantasy.

realize v. **1** UNDERSTAND CLEARLY, grasp, take in, know, comprehend, apprehend, appreciate, recognize, perceive, discern, conceive; informal latch on, twig. **2** FULFIL, achieve, accomplish, bring

ream n. **1** 500 sheets of paper. **2** (**reams**) a large quantity.

reap v. **1** cut a crop as harvest. **2** receive as a result of one's actions. ■ **reaper** n.

reappear v. appear again. ■ **reappearance** n.

rear n. the back part. ▶adj. at the back. ▶v. **1** bring up and care for children. **2** breed animals. **3** (of an animal) raise itself upright on its hind legs. **4** extend to a great height. ☐ **rear admiral** a naval rank below vice admiral. **rearguard** a body of troops protecting the rear of the main force. ■ **rearward** adj. & adv. **rearwards** adv.

rearm v. arm again. ■ **rearmament** n.

rearrange v. arrange in a different way. ■ **rearrangement** n.

reason n. **1** a cause or explanation. **2** the ability to think, understand, and draw conclusions. **3** (**one's reason**) one's sanity. **4** what is right or practical. ▶v. **1** think, understand, and draw conclusions. **2** (**reason with**) persuade by giving reasons.

reasonable adj. **1** fair and sensible. **2** appropriate. **3** fairly good. **4** not too expensive. ■ **reasonably** adv.

reassess v. reconsider. ■ **reassessment** n.

reassure v. cause to feel less worried or afraid. ■ **reassurance** n.

rebate n. a partial refund.

rebel n. a person who rebels. ▶v. (**rebelling, rebelled**) **1** fight against an established government or ruler. **2** oppose authority or accepted behaviour. ■ **rebellion** n. **rebellious** adj.

reboot v. start up a computer again.

rebound v. bounce back after impact. ▶n. a ball or shot that rebounds. ☐ **on the rebound** while still upset after the ending of a romantic relationship.

rebuff v. reject in an abrupt or unkind way. ▶n. an act of rebuffing.

rebuke v. reprimand. ▶n. a reprimand.

about, bring off, bring to fruition, consummate, effect, perform, execute, actualize, reify; *formal* effectuate. **3** MAKE, clear, acquire, gain, bring in, obtain, earn.

realm n. KINGDOM, country, land, state, province, empire, domain, monarchy, principality.

reap v. **1** CUT, crop, harvest, gather in, bring in, take in. **2** REALIZE, receive, obtain, get, acquire, secure, procure.

rear[1] v. **1** BRING UP, raise, care for, nurture, parent, educate, train, instruct. **2** RAISE, lift up, hold up, elevate, upraise.

rear[2] n. BACK, back part, hind part, back end, tail, tail end. ■ OPPOSITES front.

reason n. **1** GROUNDS, cause, basis, motive, motivation, impetus. **2** EXPLANATION, justification, argument, case, defence, vindication, apologia, rationalization, excuse, apology. **3** REASONING, intellect, intelligence, intellectuality, mind, judgement, logic, rationality, thought, understanding, apprehension, comprehension, ratiocination. **4** SANITY, mind, soundness of mind, senses. ▶v. **1** THINK, think straight, use one's mind, use one's brain/head, analyse, cogitate, cerebrate, intellectualize, ratiocinate; *informal* put on one's thinking cap. **2** USE LOGIC ON, argue with, debate with, dispute with, try to persuade, plead with.

reasonable adj. **1** LOGICAL, practical, rational, sensible, intelligent, wise, sound, judicious, advisable, well

thought out, tenable, plausible. **2** OPEN TO REASON, fair, just, equitable, impartial, dispassionate, unbiased, disinterested. **3** MODERATE, low, modest, cheap, within one's means. **4** TOLERABLE, passable, acceptable, average; *informal* OK. ■ OPPOSITES unreasonable.

reasoned adj. LOGICAL, rational, well thought out, clear, systematic, methodical, organized, well expressed, well presented.

reassure v. PUT ONE'S MIND AT REST, put at ease, restore/give confidence to, encourage, hearten, buoy up, cheer up.

rebel n. REVOLUTIONARY, revolutionist, insurrectionist, insurgent, mutineer. ▶v. MUTINY, riot, revolt, rise up, rise up in arms, take to the streets. ■ OPPOSITES conform.

rebellion n. **1** REVOLT, revolution, insurrection, uprising, rising, mutiny. **2** DEFIANCE, disobedience, resistance, dissent, nonconformity, heresy, apostasy, schism, recusancy.

rebellious adj. **1** DEFIANT, disobedient, unruly, ungovernable, unmanageable, turbulent, disorderly, intractable, recalcitrant, incorrigible; *formal* contumacious. **2** REVOLUTIONARY, insurrectionary, insurgent, mutinous. ■ OPPOSITES obedient.

rebound v. **1** BOUNCE BACK, recoil, ricochet, boomerang. **2** MISFIRE, backfire, come back on, redound on.

rebuff n. REJECTION, repudiation, discouragement, snub, slight; *informal* brush-off,

rebus n. a puzzle in which a word is represented by pictures and letters.

rebut v. (**rebutting**, **rebutted**) claim or prove to be false. ■ **rebuttal** n.

recalcitrant adj. unwilling to cooperate. ■ **recalcitrance** n.

recall v. **1** remember. **2** cause one to think of. **3** order someone to return. ▶n. the act of recalling.

recant v. withdraw a former opinion or belief.

recap v. (**recapping**, **recapped**) recapitulate. ▶n. a recapitulation.

recapitulate v. give a summary of. ■ **recapitulation** n.

recapture v. **1** capture again. **2** experience again.

recce /rek-ki/ n. informal a reconnaissance.

recede v. **1** move back or further away. **2** diminish. **3** slope backwards.

receipt n. **1** the act of receiving. **2** a written confirmation that something has been paid for or received.

receive v. **1** be given or paid. **2** accept or take in. **3** experience or meet with. **4** greet or welcome.

receiver n. **1** an apparatus that converts broadcast signals into sound or images. **2** the part of a telephone that converts electrical signals into sounds. **3** a person appointed to manage the financial affairs of a bankrupt business. ▢ **receivership** the state of being managed by an official receiver.

recent adj. having happened or been done shortly before the present. ■ **recently** adv.

receptacle n. a container.

reception n. **1** the act of receiving. **2** a reaction to something. **3** a formal social occasion. **4** the area in a hotel, office, etc. where visitors are greeted. **5** the quality of broadcast signals received.

receptionist n. a person who greets and deals with visitors to an office, hotel, etc.

receptive adj. willing to consider new ideas.

receptor n. a bodily organ or cell that responds to a stimulus and transmits a signal to a nerve.

recess n. **1** a small space set back in a wall etc. **2** a break between sessions of a parliament, law court, etc. ▶v. set a light etc. back into a wall or surface.

recession n. a temporary decline in economic activity.

recessive adj. (of a gene) appearing in offspring only if a contrary gene is not also inherited.

recidivist n. a person who persistently relapses into crime. ■ **recidivism** n.

recipe n. **1** a list of ingredients and instructions for preparing a dish. **2** something likely to lead to a particular outcome.

recipient n. a person who receives something.

reciprocal adj. **1** given or done in return. **2** affecting two parties equally. ■ **reciprocally** adv. **reciprocity** n.

reciprocate v. respond to an action with a similar one.

recital n. **1** a musical performance. **2** a listing of facts etc.

Thesaurus

slap in the face. ▶v. REJECT, refuse, turn down, turn away, spurn, brush off, repudiate, snub, slight.

rebuke v. REPRIMAND, tell off, scold, chide, admonish, reproach, reprove, remonstrate with, lecture, reprehend, berate, upbraid, castigate, take to task; informal bawl out, tick off, tear off a strip, carpet. ■ OPPOSITES praise.

recalcitrant adj. INTRACTABLE, refractory, unmanageable, ungovernable, disobedient, insubordinate, defiant, contrary, wayward; informal bolshie, bloody-minded. ■ OPPOSITES compliant.

recall v. **1** SUMMON BACK, call back, bring back. **2** see REMEMBER.

receive v. **1** BE IN RECEIPT OF, accept delivery of, accept, take into one's possession. **2** UNDERGO, experience, meet with, encounter, be subjected to, bear, suffer. **3** WELCOME, greet, entertain, be at home

to. ■ OPPOSITES give, send.

recent adj. **1** NEW, fresh, novel, latest, late, modern, contemporary, latter-day, current, up to date. **2** OCCURRING/ APPEARING RECENTLY, not long past.

recently adv. LATELY, of late, latterly, in recent times, not along ago.

receptacle n. CONTAINER, holder, repository.

receptive adj. OPEN, open to suggestions, flexible, willing, perceptive, sensitive, alert, bright, quick, keen. ■ OPPOSITES unresponsive.

recess n. **1** ALCOVE, niche, nook, corner, cavity, bay, oriel. **2** BREAK, respite, rest, interval, intermission, holiday, time off, vacation.

recession n. DOWNTURN, depression, slump. ■ OPPOSITES boom.

recipe n. DIRECTIONS, instructions, guide, method, system, procedure.

recitative /re-si-tuh-**teev**/ n. a passage in an opera sung in a rhythm like that of ordinary speech.

recite v. 1 repeat aloud from memory. 2 state facts in order. ■ **recitation** n.

reckless adj. without thought or care for the results of an action. ■ **recklessly** adv. **recklessness** n.

reckon v. 1 calculate. 2 have as an opinion. 3 (**reckon on**) rely on. 4 (**reckon with** or **without**) take (or fail to take) into account.

reclaim v. 1 recover possession of. 2 make waste land usable. ■ **reclamation** n.

recline v. lean or lie back in a relaxed position.

recluse n. a person who avoids other people. ■ **reclusive** adj.

recognizance /ri-**cog**-niz-uhns/ n. a pledge to a law court to observe a condition.

recognize (or **-ise**) v. 1 know from having encountered before. 2 accept as genuine, legal, or valid. 3 show official appreciation of. ■ **recognition** n. **recognizable** adj.

recoil v. 1 suddenly move back in fear,
horror, or disgust. 2 (of a gun) suddenly move backwards after firing. 3 (**recoil on**) have an unpleasant effect on. ▶ n. the act of recoiling.

recollect v. remember. ■ **recollection** n.

recommend v. 1 suggest as suitable for a purpose or role. 2 make appealing or desirable. ■ **recommendation** n.

recompense v. 1 compensate. 2 pay for work. ▶ n. compensation.

reconcile v. 1 restore friendly relations between. 2 find a satisfactory way of dealing with opposing facts, ideas, etc. 3 (**reconcile to**) cause to accept an unwelcome situation. ■ **reconciliation** n.

recondite adj. obscure and little known.

recondition v. renovate.

reconnaissance /ri-**kon**-ni-suhnss/ n. military observation of an area to gain information.

reconnoitre /rek-uh-**noy**-ter/ (US **reconnoiter**) v. make a reconnaissance of.

reconsider v. consider again, with a view to changing a decision. ■ **reconsideration** n.

Thesaurus

reciprocal adj. MUTUAL, shared, common, exchanged, give and take, complementary, corresponding, correlative.

reciprocate v. RETURN, requite, repay, give back.

recital n. 1 PERFORMANCE, concert, show. 2 ACCOUNT, report, telling, relation, description, detailing, rendering, record, chronicle.

recite v. SAY, repeat, read aloud, deliver, declaim, speak, render.

reckless adj. RASH, careless, thoughtless, incautious, heedless, unheeding, regardless, daredevil, devil-may-care, madcap, harum-scarum, wild, precipitate, headlong, hasty, irresponsible, hare-brained, foolhardy, imprudent, unwise, indiscreet, mindless, negligent. ■ OPPOSITES cautious.

reckon v. 1 BE OF THE OPINION, think, believe, suppose, assume. 2 COUNT, calculate, add up, compute, total, tally, put a figure on, give a figure to.

reclaim v. HAVE RETURNED, get back, take back, regain, retrieve, recover.

recline v. LIE DOWN, be recumbent, rest, repose, loll, lounge, sprawl, stretch out.

recluse n. HERMIT, anchorite, eremite, solitary, lone wolf, loner.

recognize v. 1 KNOW, know again, identify, place, spot, recall, recollect, remember, call to mind. 2 REALIZE, see, be aware of, be conscious of, perceive, discern, appreciate, understand, apprehend, acknowledge, accept, own, admit, concede, allow, grant, confess. 3 ACKNOWLEDGE, accept, admit, concede, allow, grant, endorse, sanction, approve, validate, ratify, uphold.

recoil v. DRAW BACK, jump back, pull back, shrink, shy away, flinch, start, wince, cower, quail.

recollect v. REMEMBER, recall, call to mind, think of, summon up, place; informal put one's finger on. ■ OPPOSITES forget.

recommend v. ADVOCATE, commend, put in a good word for, speak favourably of, endorse, approve, vouch for, suggest, offer, put forward, propose, advance.

recommendation n. COMMENDATION, endorsement, suggestion, tip, hint, proposal, good word, favourable mention, praise; informal plug.

reconcile v. REUNITE, bring together, restore harmony between, make peace between, bring to terms, pacify, appease, placate, propitiate, mollify. ■ OPPOSITES estrange, quarrel.

reconnaissance n. SURVEY, exploration, scouting, probe, inspection, ob

reconstitute v. **1** change the form of an organization. **2** restore dried food to its original state by adding water. ∎ **reconstitution** n.

reconstruct v. **1** construct again. **2** act out a past event. ∎ **reconstruction** n.

record n. **1** a permanent account kept for evidence or information. **2** previous behaviour or performance. **3** a list of a person's previous criminal convictions. **4** the best officially recognized performance of its kind. **5** a disc carrying recorded sound in grooves. ▸v. **1** make a record of. **2** convert sound etc. into permanent form in order to be reproduced later. **3** indicate or register as a measurement. □ **off the record** not made as an official statement.

recorder n. **1** a person or thing that records. **2** a barrister serving as a part-time judge. **3** a simple woodwind instrument.

recount[1] v. tell in detail.

recount[2] v. count again. ▸n. an act of recounting.

recoup v. recover a loss.

recourse n. **1** a source of help in a difficult situation. **2** (**recourse to**) the use of a particular source of help.

recover v. **1** return to health. **2** regain possession or control of. ∎ **recovery** n.

recreation n. enjoyable leisure activity. ∎ **recreational** adj.

recrimination n. an accusation in response to another.

recruit v. take on someone to serve in the armed forces or work for an organization. ▸n. a newly recruited person. ∎ **recruitment** n.

rectangle n. a plane figure with four straight sides and four right angles, and with unequal adjacent sides. ∎ **rectangular** adj.

rectify v. (**rectifying**, **rectified**) **1** put right. **2** convert alternating current to direct current. ∎ **rectification** n.

rectilinear adj. within or moving in a straight line or lines.

rectitude n. correct behaviour.

recto n. (pl. **rectos**) a right-hand page of an open book.

rector n. **1** a priest in charge of a parish. **2** the head of certain universities, colleges, and schools.

rectory n. (pl. **rectories**) the house of a rector.

rectum n. (pl. **rectums** or **recta**) the final section of the large intestine, ending at the anus. ∎ **rectal** adj.

recumbent adj. lying down.

recuperate v. **1** recover from illness. **2** regain. ∎ **recuperation** n. **recuperative** adj.

recur v. (**recurring**, **recurred**) happen

Thesaurus

servation; *informal* recce.

reconnoitre v. SURVEY, see how the land lies, spy out, take stock of, explore, scout, investigate, scrutinize, scan, inspect, observe; *informal* recce, check out.

reconsider v. RETHINK, review, re-examine, re-evaluate, reassess, think again, think twice, have second thoughts, change one's mind.

reconstruct v. REBUILD, remake, reassemble, refashion, recreate, remodel, revamp, renovate, recondition.

record n. **1** DOCUMENT, register, log, log-book, file, official report/account, chronicle, documentation, minutes, notes, annals, archives. **2** DISC, album, single, recording, release; *informal* platter. ▸v. **1** PUT ON RECORD, set down, write down, put in writing, take down, put down, enter, make a note of, document. **2** REGISTER, read, indicate, show, display.

recount v. DESCRIBE, detail, enumerate, list, specify, itemize, cite, particularize, catalogue.

recover v. **1** GET BACK, win back, regain, recoup, retrieve, reclaim, repossess, re-

deem, recuperate, recapture. **2** GET BETTER, get well, recuperate, convalesce, heal, get back on one's feet, feel oneself again, improve, mend, pick up, perk up, rally, revive, pull through, bounce back. ∎ OPPOSITES deteriorate.

recovery n. **1** RECOUPING, regaining, retrieval, reclamation, repossession, recapture. **2** RECUPERATION, convalescence, healing, rallying, revival.

recreation n. **1** RELAXATION, leisure, refreshment, amusement, entertainment, distraction, diversion. **2** ACTIVITY, pastime, hobby, diversion, distraction.

recrimination n. COUNTER-ACCUSATION, countercharge, counter-attack, retaliation, reprisal.

recruit v. ENLIST, enrol, sign up, draft, conscript, levy, engage, obtain, acquire, procure, take on, round up, muster. ▸n. **1** DRAFTEE, conscript. **2** NEWCOMER, initiate, beginner, learner, trainee, novice, apprentice.

rectify v. PUT/SET RIGHT, right, correct, amend, emend, remedy, repair, fix, make good.

rectitude n. RIGHTEOUSNESS, virtue, honagain or repeatedly. ■ **recurrence** n. **recurrent** adj.

recusant n. a person who refuses to obey an authority or rule.

recycle v. convert waste into a reusable form. ■ **recyclable** adj.

red adj. (**redder, reddest**) **1** of the colour of blood or fire. **2** (of hair) reddish-brown. **3** informal communist. ▶ n. **1** red colour or material. **2** informal a communist. □ **in the red** overdrawn. **redcurrant** a small edible red berry. **red-handed** in the act of doing something wrong. **redhead** a person with red hair. **red herring** a misleading clue or distraction. **red-hot 1** so hot as to glow red. **2** very exciting or recent. **red-letter day** an important or memorable day. **red light** a signal to stop. **red-light district** an area with many brothels, strip clubs, etc. **red tape** complicated official rules which hinder progress. **redwood** a giant coniferous tree with reddish wood. **see red** informal become very angry. ■ **redden** v. **reddish** adj. **redness** n.

redeem v. **1** make up for the faults of. **2** save from sin. **3** fulfil a promise. **4** buy back. **5** exchange a coupon for goods or money. ■ **redemption** n.

redeploy v. assign to a new place or task. ■ **redeployment** n.

redolent adj. (**redolent of/with**) **1** strongly suggestive of. **2** smelling of. ■ **redolence** n.

redouble v. increase or intensify.

redoubtable adj. formidable.

redound v. (**redound to**) contribute greatly to a person's credit.

redress v. set right. ▶ n. reparation or amends.

reduce v. **1** make or become less. **2** change to a different or simpler form. **3** bring to a particular state or condition. ■ **reducible** adj. **reduction** n.

redundant adj. **1** no longer needed or useful. **2** unemployed because one's job is no longer needed. ■ **redundancy** n.

reed n. **1** a water or marsh plant with hollow stems. **2** a piece of thin cane or metal in certain wind instruments which vibrates to produce the sound.

reedy adj. (of a voice) high and thin in tone.

reef n. **1** a ridge of rock or coral near the surface of the sea. **2** a strip in a sail that can be drawn in to reduce the area exposed to the wind. ▶ v. take in a reef or reefs of a sail. □ **reef knot** a secure double knot.

reefer n. **1** informal a cannabis cigarette. **2** a thick double-breasted jacket.

reek v. smell strongly. ▶ n. a strong unpleasant smell.

reel n. **1** a cylinder on which something is wound. **2** a lively Scottish or Irish folk dance. ▶ v. **1** (**reel in**) bring towards one by turning a reel. **2** (**reel off**) say rapidly and with ease. **3** stagger.

refectory n. (pl. **refectories**) a room for meals in a college or religious institution.

refer v. (**referring, referred**) (**refer to**) **1** mention. **2** turn to for information. **3** pass to an authority or specialist for

Thesaurus

our, integrity, principle, probity, uprightness, good character, decency, honesty.

recuperate v. *see* RECOVER.

recur v. REOCCUR, happen/occur again, come back, return, reappear, be repeated, happen repeatedly.

recurrent adj. RECURRING, repeated, repetitive, reiterative, periodic, cyclical, regular, habitual, continual, frequent, intermittent, chronic.

recycle v. REUSE, reprocess, salvage, save.

redden v. GO RED, blush, flush, colour, colour up, crimson.

redeem v. **1** EXCHANGE, cash in, convert, turn in, trade in. **2** SAVE, deliver from sin, turn from sin, convert, purge/absolve of sin.

redolent adj. **1** EVOCATIVE, suggestive, reminiscent. **2** SWEET-SMELLING, fragrant, scented, perfumed, aromatic.

reduce v. **1** MAKE SMALLER, lessen, lower, decrease, diminish, cut, curtail, contract, shorten, abbreviate, moderate, dilute, alleviate, abate. **2** BRING TO, bring to the point of, force to, drive to. **3** DEMOTE, downgrade, lower, lower in rank/status, humble. **4** LOWER/CUT IN PRICE, lower, make cheaper, cheapen, cut, mark down, slash, discount, put on sale. ■ OPPOSITES increase.

reduction n. **1** LESSENING, lowering, decrease, diminution, cut, contraction, abbreviation, moderation, dilution, alleviation, abatement. **2** DISCOUNT, deduction, cut, markdown, concession, allowance. **3** DEMOTION, downgrading, lowering, humbling.

redundant adj. SURPLUS TO REQUIREMENTS, not required, unnecessary, inessential, unwanted, surplus, supernumerary.

a decision. ■ **referral** n.

referee n. **1** an official who supervises a game to ensure that players keep to the rules. **2** a person who provides a reference for a person applying for a job. ▶ v. (**refereeing, refereed**) be a referee of.

reference n. **1** the act of referring. **2** a mention of a source of information in a book etc. **3** a letter testifying to someone's suitability for a job. □ **with** (or **in**) **reference to** in relation to.

referendum n. (pl. **referendums** or **referenda**) a vote by a country's electorate on a single political issue.

refill v. fill again. ▶ n. an act of refilling.

refine v. **1** remove unwanted substances from. **2** improve by making minor changes. **3** (**refined**) well educated and elegant. ■ **refinement** n.

refinery n. (pl. **refineries**) a factory where a substance is refined.

refit v. (**refitting, refitted**) replace or repair fittings in a ship etc. ▶ n. an act of refitting.

reflate v. expand the output of an economy after deflation. ■ **reflation** n. **reflationary** adj.

reflect v. **1** throw back heat, light, or sound from a surface. **2** (of a mirror) show an image of. **3** (**reflect well/badly on**) give a good or bad impression of. **4** think seriously.

reflection n. **1** the act of reflecting. **2** a reflected image. **3** a sign. **4** a source of shame or blame. **5** serious thought.

reflective adj. **1** providing a reflection. **2** thoughtful. ■ **reflectively** adv.

reflector n. something that reflects light or heat.

reflex n. an action done without conscious thought as a response to something. ▶ adj. **1** done as a reflex. **2** (of an angle) more than 180°.

reflexive adj. Grammar referring back to the subject of a clause or verb, e.g. *myself* in *I hurt myself.*

reflexology n. a system of massage of points on the feet used to relieve tension and treat illness. ■ **reflexologist** n.

reform v. **1** improve by making changes. **2** cause to improve behaviour. ▶ n. the act of reforming. ■ **reformation** n. **reformer** n. **reformist** adj. & n.

refract v. (of water, air, or glass) make a ray of light change direction when it enters at an angle. ■ **refraction** n. **refractive** adj. **refractor** n.

refractory adj. **1** stubborn or difficult to control. **2** (of a disease) not responding to treatment. **3** heat-resistant.

refrain v. (**refrain from**) stop oneself from doing something. ▶ n. the part of a song that is repeated at the end of each verse.

Thesaurus

reel v. **1** STAGGER, lurch, sway, stumble, totter, wobble, falter, waver, pitch, roll. **2** FEEL GIDDY/DIZZY, feel confused, be shaken, be in shock, be upset.

refer v. **1** CONSULT, turn to, look at, look up, have recourse to. **2** PASS, hand on, send on, transfer, remit, direct. **3** MENTION, make mention of, make reference to, allude to, touch on, speak of, cite, hint at; *formal* advert to. **4** APPLY TO, be relevant to, have relevance to, concern, relate to, belong to.

referee n. UMPIRE, judge, adjudicator, arbitrator, arbiter, mediator; *informal* ref.

reference n. **1** MENTION, allusion, citation, hint. **2** REGARD, respect, relation, bearing, relevance, pertinence. **3** SOURCE, citation, authority, bibliography. **4** TESTIMONIAL, recommendation, good word, credentials.

refine v. PURIFY, rarefy, clarify, clear, cleanse, strain, sift, filter, distil, process.

refined adj. **1** PURIFIED, pure, rarefied, clarified, clear, filtered, distilled, processed. **2** CULTIVATED, cultured, polished, civilized, civil, gracious, stylish, elegant, sophisticated, urbane, courtly, well mannered, well bred, gentlemanly, ladylike, genteel. ■ OPPOSITES crude.

refinement n. **1** PURIFICATION, processing, distillation, filtration. **2** CULTIVATION, culture, taste, discrimination, polish, finish, civility, grace, graciousness, style, elegance, finesse, sophistication, urbanity, courtliness, good breeding, politeness, good manners, gentility. **3** SUBTLETY, nicety, nuance, fine point.

reflect v. **1** THROW BACK, cast back, send back, give back, scatter, diffuse. **2** MIRROR, echo. **3** THINK, consider, mull over, contemplate, deliberate, ponder, meditate, muse, ruminate, cogitate, brood.

reflection n. **1** IMAGE, mirror image, echo. **2** THINKING, thought, consideration, contemplation, deliberation, meditation, rumination, cogitation. **3** OPINION, thought, view, idea, impression, comment, findings.

reform v. IMPROVE, make better, ameliorate, amend, mend, rectify, correct, rehabilitate, change, make over, revamp,

refresh v. **1** give new energy to. **2** prompt someone's memory. **3** (**refreshing**) pleasantly new or different. ■ **refreshingly** adv.

refreshment n. **1** a snack or drink. **2** the giving of new energy.

refrigerate v. make food or drink cold so as to chill or preserve it. ■ **refrigeration** n.

refrigerator n. an appliance for storing food and drink at a low temperature.

☑ No *d* in the middle: refrig*erator*, not *-ridg-*.

refuge n. **1** shelter from danger or trouble. **2** a safe place.

refugee n. a person forced to leave their country because of war or persecution.

refulgent adj. literary shining.

refund v. pay back. ▶ n. a repayment of a sum of money.

refurbish v. redecorate and improve a building or room. ■ **refurbishment** n.

refuse[1] /ri-fyooz/ v. state that one is unwilling to do or accept something. ■ **refusal** n.

refuse[2] /ref-yooss/ n. waste material.

refute v. prove wrong. ■ **refutation** n.

☑ **refute** means 'prove wrong'; it does not mean simply 'deny'.

regain v. **1** get back after loss. **2** get back to a place.

regal adj. of or like a monarch. ■ **regality** n. **regally** adv.

regale v. feed or entertain well.

regalia n. the distinctive clothing and objects of royalty or other rank or office, used at formal occasions.

regard v. **1** think of in a particular way. **2** look steadily at. ▶ n. **1** concern or care. **2** high opinion; respect. **3** a steady gaze. **4** (**regards**) best wishes. □ **as regards** concerning. **with** (or **in**) **regard to** concerning.

regarding prep. concerning.

regardless adv. **1** (**regardless of**) without concern for. **2** despite what is happening.

regatta n. a series of boat or yacht races.

regency n. (pl. **regencies**) a period of rule by a regent.

regenerate v. **1** bring new life or strength to. **2** grow new tissue. ■ **regeneration** n. **regenerative** adj.

Thesaurus

renovate. **2** MEND ONE'S WAYS, change for the better, turn over a new leaf, improve; *informal* go straight.

refrain v. DESIST, abstain, hold back, forbear, forgo, do without, avoid, eschew, cease, stop, give up, leave off, renounce; *informal* quit.

refresh v. **1** FRESHEN, invigorate, revitalize, revive, brace, fortify, enliven, perk up, stimulate, energize, exhilarate, rejuvenate, regenerate, breathe new life into, inspirit. **2** STIMULATE, prompt, prod, jog, activate, rouse, arouse. ■ OPPOSITES weary.

refreshing adj. FRESHENING, invigorating, revitalizing, reviving, bracing, stimulating, exhilarating, energizing.

refuge n. **1** SHELTER, safety, security, protection, asylum, sanctuary. **2** PLACE OF SAFETY, shelter, haven, retreat, bolthole, sanctuary, harbour.

refund v. GIVE BACK, return, repay, pay back, reimburse, make good, restore, replace. ▶ n. REPAYMENT, reimbursement.

refuse[1] v. TURN DOWN, decline, say no to, reject, spurn, rebuff, repudiate; *informal* pass up, knock back. **2** DECLINE, be unwilling, baulk at, demur at, avoid, resist, protest at. ■ OPPOSITES accept.

refuse[2] n. RUBBISH, waste, debris, litter,

dross, dregs, leavings, sweepings; *US* garbage, trash; *informal* junk.

refute v. PROVE WRONG, disprove, negate, invalidate, discredit.

regain v. GET BACK, win back, recover, recoup, retrieve, reclaim, repossess, redeem, recuperate, take back, retake, recapture.

regal adj. ROYAL, majestic, noble, proud, kingly, queenly, princely, fit for a king/queen/prince/princess.

regard v. **1** WATCH, look at, gaze at, keep an eye on, stare at, observe, view, study, scrutinize, eye, mark, behold. **2** LOOK UPON, view, consider, contemplate, think of, weigh up, mull over, reflect on, deliberate on. ▶ n. **1** LOOK, gaze, stare, observation, scrutiny. **2** HEED, attention, notice, consideration, thought, mind. **3** RESPECT, esteem, admiration, approval, approbation, favour.

regarding prep. WITH/IN REGARD TO, as regards, as to, with reference to, on the subject/matter of, apropos, concerning, about, respecting.

regardless adv. (**regardless of**) WITHOUT REGARD TO, disregarding, unmindful of, heedless of, without consideration of, indifferent to, negligent of.

regards pl. n. BEST/GOOD WISHES, greet-

regent n. a person appointed to rule while the monarch is too young or unfit to rule, or is absent.

reggae /reg-gay/ n. a West Indian style of music with a strong beat.

regicide n. **1** the killing of a king. **2** a person who kills a king.

regime /ray-zheem/ n. **1** a government. **2** a system of doing something.

regimen n. a course of medical treatment, diet, or exercise.

regiment n. a permanent unit of an army. ▶ v. organize according to a strict system. ■ **regimental** adj. **regimentation** n.

Regina n. the reigning queen (used in referring to lawsuits).

region n. **1** an area of a country or the world. **2** an administrative district. **3** a part of the body. □ **in the region of** approximately. ■ **regional** adj.

register n. **1** an official list. **2** a part of the range of a voice or musical instrument. **3** the level of formality of writing or speech. ▶ v. **1** enter in a register. **2** express an opinion or emotion. **3** become aware of. **4** (of a measuring instrument) show a reading. □ **register office** a local government building where civil marriages are performed and births, marriages, and deaths are recorded. ■ **registration** n.

registrar n. **1** an official responsible for keeping official records. **2** a hospital doctor who is training to be a specialist.

registry n. (pl. **registries**) a place where official records are kept. □ **registry office** a register office.

regress v. return to an earlier or less advanced state. ■ **regression** n. **regressive** adj.

regret n. a feeling of sorrow or disappointment about something one has done or should have done. ▶ v. (**regretting, regretted**) feel regret about. ■ **regretful** adj. **regretfully** adv.

regrettable adj. giving rise to regret. ■ **regrettably** adv.

regular adj. **1** following or arranged in an evenly spaced pattern or sequence. **2** done, happening, or doing something frequently. **3** following an accepted standard. **4** belonging to a country's permanent armed forces. **5** (of a figure) having all sides and all angles equal. ▶ n. a regular customer, soldier, etc. ■ **regularity** n. **regularly** adv.

regularize (or **-ise**) v. **1** make regular. **2** make a temporary situation legal or official.

regulate v. **1** control the rate or speed of a machine or process. **2** control by rules. ■ **regulator** n. **regulatory** adj.

regulation n. **1** a rule. **2** the act of regulating.

Thesaurus

ings, salutations, respects, compliments.

regenerate v. RENEW, breathe new life into, restore, invigorate, refresh, revitalize, revive, revivify, rejuvenate.

regiment v. ORGANIZE, order, control, discipline, keep a tight rein on, bring into line, rule with a rod of iron.

region n. AREA, province, territory, division, section, sector, zone, tract, part, quarter, locality.

register n. LIST, listing, roll, roster, index, directory, catalogue. ▶ v. **1** RECORD, put on record, enter, set down, chronicle, write down, take down, note, minute, list, catalogue. **2** READ, record, indicate, show, display. **3** SHOW, express, display, exhibit, evince, betray, reveal, manifest, demonstrate, reflect. **4** MAKE AN IMPRESSION, get through, sink in, penetrate, have an effect.

regret v. **1** FEEL SORRY/CONTRITE ABOUT, feel remorse about, wish undone, repent, rue. **2** LAMENT, bemoan, be upset/disappointed about, mourn, grieve over, weep over, fret about, pine over,

deplore. ▶ n. **1** SORROW, remorse, contrition, repentance, pangs of conscience, compunction, ruefulness, self-reproach, penitence. **2** DISAPPOINTMENT, lamentation, grief, mourning, pining. ■ OPPOSITES satisfaction.

regretful adj. SORRY, apologetic, remorseful, contrite, rueful, repentant, conscience-stricken, penitent. ■ OPPOSITES unrepentant.

regrettable adj. DEPLORABLE, reprehensible, disgraceful, blameworthy, unfortunate, unwelcome, ill-advised.

regular adj. **1** USUAL, normal, customary, habitual, routine, typical, everyday, daily, unvarying, common, average, commonplace. **2** RHYTHMIC, steady, even, uniform, constant, consistent, orderly. **3** REAL, thorough, absolute, utter, complete. ■ OPPOSITES occasional, erratic.

regulate v. **1** CONTROL, direct, guide, govern, rule, manage, order, organize, conduct, run, supervise, oversee, superintend, monitor. **2** ADJUST, balance, set, synchronize, modulate.

regulation n. **1** CONTROL, direction,

regulo n. trademark used before a number to indicate a temperature setting in a gas oven.

regurgitate v. **1** bring swallowed food up again to the mouth. **2** repeat facts without understanding them. ■ **regurgitation** n.

rehabilitate v. help back to normal life after imprisonment or illness. ■ **rehabilitation** n.

rehash v. reuse old ideas or material. ▶ n. an act of rehashing.

rehearse v. **1** practise a play etc. for later public performance. **2** state points made many times before. ■ **rehearsal** n.

reign v. rule as monarch. ▶ n. a monarch's period of rule.

reimburse v. repay money to a person. ■ **reimbursement** n.

rein n. **(reins)** **1** long, narrow straps attached to a bridle, used to control a horse. **2** the power to direct and control. ▶ v. **1** control with reins. **2** **(rein in/back)** restrain.

reincarnate v. **(be reincarnated)** be born again in another body. ■ **reincarnation** n.

reindeer n. (pl. **reindeer** or **reindeers**) a deer with large antlers, found in cold northern regions.

reinforce v. **1** make stronger. **2** strengthen a military force with additional personnel. ■ **reinforcement** n.

reinstate v. restore to a former position. ■ **reinstatement** n.

reiterate v. say again or repeatedly. ■ **reiteration** n.

reject v. refuse to accept. ▶ n. a rejected person or thing. ■ **rejection** n.

rejig v. **(rejigging, rejigged)** rearrange.

rejoice v. feel or show great joy.

rejoin v. **1** join again. **2** retort.

rejoinder n. a retort.

rejuvenate v. make more lively or youthful. ■ **rejuvenation** n.

relapse v. **1** become ill again after a period of improvement. **2** return to a worse state. ▶ n. an act of relapsing.

relate v. **1** give an account of. **2** **(relate to)** have to do with. **3** **(relate to)** feel sympathy with.

related adj. belonging to the same family, group, or type; connected.

relation n. **1** a connection between people or things. **2** **(relations)** people's feelings and behaviour towards each other. **3** a relative. **4** **(relations)** sexual intercourse. □ **in relation to** in connection with. ■ **relationship** n.

guidance, government, rule, management, administration, organization, supervision. **2** RULE, ruling, order, directive, act, law, decree, statute, edict, ordinance.

rehearsal n. PRACTICE, preparation, trial performance, run-through, going-over.

rehearse v. PRACTISE, try out, run through, go over.

reign v. **1** BE KING/QUEEN, sit on the throne, occupy the throne, wear the crown, wield the sceptre. **2** BE IN POWER, govern, rule, be in charge/control, administer, hold sway. ▶ n. **1** MONARCHY, sovereignty. **2** POWER, government, rule, command, control, administration, charge.

rein v. **(rein in)** CHECK, curb, restrain, constrain, hold back, restrict, control, bridle.

reinforce v. **1** STRENGTHEN, fortify, bolster up, shore up, buttress, prop up, brace, support, back up, uphold, stress, underline, emphasize. **2** AUGMENT, increase, add to, supplement.

reiterate v. REPEAT, say again, go over again, belabour, dwell on, harp on, hammer away at.

reject v. **1** REFUSE, turn down, decline, say no to, spurn, rebuff, repudiate, veto, deny; *informal* pass up, knock back, give the thumbs down to. **2** CAST OUT, cast aside, discard, jettison, renounce, abandon, forsake, scrap, exclude, eliminate. ■ OPPOSITES accept. ▶ n. **1** SUBSTANDARD ARTICLE, discard, second. **2** FAILURE, outcast, derelict; *informal* dropout.

rejoice v. BE JOYFUL, be happy, be pleased, be glad, be delighted, be elated, be overjoyed, be jubilant, be euphoric, exult. ■ OPPOSITES mourn.

rejoinder n. ANSWER, response, reply, riposte, retort; *informal* comeback.

relapse v. LAPSE, regress, retrogress, revert, backslide, fall away, go backwards, slip back, degenerate. ▶ n. LAPSE, regression, retrogression, reversion, backsliding, recidivism.

relate v. **1** RECOUNT, tell, narrate, describe, report, impart, communicate, recite, rehearse, present, detail, delineate, chronicle, set forth. **2** CONNECT, associate, link, correlate, ally, couple, join. **3** APPLY TO, be relevant to, have relevance to, concern, refer to, have reference to, pertain to, bear on.

related adj. **1** CONNECTED, interconnect-

relative adj. **1** considered in relation to something else. **2** existing only in comparison to something else. **3** Grammar referring to an earlier noun or clause. ▶n. a person connected by blood or marriage. ■ **relatively** adv.

relativity n. **1** the state of being relative. **2** Physics a description of matter, energy, space, and time according to Einstein's theories.

relax v. **1** make or become less tense. **2** rest from work; do something recreational. **3** make a rule less strict. ■ **relaxation** n.

relay n. **1** a group engaged in a task for a time and then replaced by a similar group. **2** a race between teams, each team member in turn covering part of the total distance. **3** an electrical device activating a circuit. **4** a device to receive and transmit a signal. ▶v. receive and pass on or transmit again.

release v. **1** set free. **2** allow to move freely. **3** make information, a film, or a recording available to the public. ▶n. **1** the act of releasing. **2** a film or recording released to the public.

relegate v. place in a lower rank or position. ■ **relegation** n.

relent v. **1** abandon or moderate a harsh intention or cruel treatment. **2** become less intense.

relentless adj. **1** never stopping or weakening. **2** harsh or inflexible. ■ **relentlessly** adv.

relevant adj. connected or appropriate to the current matter. ■ **relevance** n.

reliable adj. able to be relied on. ■ **reliability** n. **reliably** adv.

reliance n. dependence on or trust in someone or something. ■ **reliant** adj.

relic n. **1** something surviving from an earlier time. **2** a part of a holy person's body or belongings kept after their death.

relief n. **1** a feeling of relaxation after anxiety. **2** alleviation of pain. **3** a break in a tense or boring situation. **4** help

Thesaurus

ed, associated, linked, correlated, allied, affiliated, accompanying, concomitant, akin. **2** OF THE SAME FAMILY, connected, akin, kindred, agnate, cognate, consanguineous. ■ OPPOSITES unrelated.

relation n. **1** CONNECTION, association, link, tie-in, correlation, alliance, bond, relationship, interdependence. **2** RELATIVE, family member, kinsman, kinswoman, connection, kin.

relationship n. **1** see RELATION. **2** FRIENDSHIP, love affair, affair, liaison.

relative adj. **1** COMPARATIVE, comparable, respective, correlative, parallel, corresponding. **2** PROPORTIONATE, in proportion, proportional, commensurate. ▶n. see RELATION (2).

relax v. **1** LOOSEN, slacken, weaken, lessen, let up, reduce, diminish. **2** BECOME LESS TENSE/STIFF/RIGID, loosen, slacken. **3** MODERATE, make less strict/formal, soften, ease. **4** LOOSEN UP, ease up/off; informal unwind, take it easy, let it all hang out, hang loose. ■ OPPOSITES tense, tighten.

relaxation n. **1** LOOSENING, slackening, weakening, letting up. **2** LESSENING, reduction, easing off, abatement. **3** LEISURE, recreation, enjoyment, amusement, entertainment, pleasure, refreshment, rest.

relay v. PASS ON, hand on, communicate, send, transmit, broadcast, spread, circulate.

release v. **1** SET FREE, free, let go, set/

turn loose, let out, liberate, untie, undo, unloose, unbind, unchain, unfetter, unshackle, extricate, deliver, emancipate; historical manumit. **2** MAKE PUBLIC, make known, issue, break, announce, reveal, divulge, unveil, present, disclose, publish, broadcast, put out, circulate, disseminate, distribute, spread. ■ OPPOSITES imprison, suppress.

relent v. SOFTEN, become merciful/lenient, show mercy/pity, give quarter, capitulate, yield, give way, give in, unbend, come round, forbear, change one's mind.

relentless adj. **1** UNCEASING, unrelenting, unremitting, persistent, unswerving, persevering, unflagging, unfaltering, unstoppable, incessant. **2** HARSH, ruthless, merciless, pitiless, remorseless, unforgiving, implacable, inexorable, cruel, grim, hard, hard-hearted, cold-hearted, fierce, strict, obdurate, unyielding, inflexible, unbending. ■ OPPOSITES lenient.

relevant adj. APPLICABLE, pertinent, apposite, material, appurtenant, to the point/purpose, germane, admissible, appropriate, apt, fitting. ■ OPPOSITES irrelevant.

reliable adj. **1** TRUSTWORTHY, dependable, trusty, true, faithful, devoted, steady, steadfast, constant, unfailing, certain, sure. **2** WELL FOUNDED, well grounded, sound, trustworthy, dependable, credible, authentic, genuine. ■ OPPOSITES given to people in need. **5** a person or group replacing another on duty. **6** a carving in which the design stands out from the surface. □ **relief map** a map showing hills and valleys by shading.

relieve v. **1** bring relief to. **2** replace someone on duty. **3** take a responsibility from. **4** bring military support for a place under siege. **5** (**relieve oneself**) urinate or defecate.

religion n. **1** the belief in and worship of a God or gods. **2** a particular system of this.

religious adj. **1** of or believing in a religion. **2** very careful or regular. ■ **religiously** adv.

relinquish v. give up. ■ **relinquishment** n.

reliquary n. (pl. **reliquaries**) a container for holy relics.

relish n. **1** great enjoyment. **2** a highly flavoured sauce or pickle. ▶v. enjoy greatly.

relocate v. move to a different place. ■ **relocation** n.

reluctant adj. unwilling and hesitant. ■ **reluctance** n. **reluctantly** adv.

rely v. (**relying, relied**) (**rely on**) **1** trust or have faith in. **2** be dependent on.

remain v. **1** stay. **2** continue to be. **3** be left over.

remainder n. **1** a remaining part, number, or amount. **2** the number left over when one quantity does not exactly divide into another.

remains pl. n. **1** things remaining. **2** archaeological relics. **3** a dead body.

remand v. send a defendant to await trial, either on bail or in jail. □ **on remand** in jail awaiting trial.

remark v. **1** say as a comment. **2** notice. ▶n. a comment.

remarkable adj. extraordinary or striking. ■ **remarkably** adv.

remedial adj. **1** intended as a remedy. **2** for children with learning difficulties.

remedy n. (pl. **remedies**) **1** a medicine or treatment for a disease or injury. **2** a means of putting a matter right. ▶v. (**remedying, remedied**) put right.

Thesaurus

unreliable.

relic n. **1** ANCIENT/HISTORICAL OBJECT, artefact, antique, heirloom. **2** VESTIGE, trace, survivor, remnant.

relief n. **1** ALLEVIATION, mitigation, assuagement, palliation, ease, appeasement, abatement. **2** AID, help, assistance, succour. **3** RESPITE, remission, interruption, break, variation, diversion; *informal* let-up. ■ OPPOSITES intensification.

relieve v. **1** ALLEVIATE, mitigate, assuage, allay, soothe, soften, palliate, appease, ease, dull, abate, reduce, lessen, diminish. **2** BRING AID TO, aid, help, assist, rescue, save, succour. **3** BRING RESPITE TO, interrupt, break up, vary, lighten. ■ OPPOSITES aggravate.

religious adj. **1** CHURCH, holy, divine, theological, doctrinal, spiritual, sectarian. **2** CHURCHGOING, God-fearing, godly, pious, devout. **3** SCRUPULOUS, conscientious, meticulous, zealous, strict, rigid, rigorous. ■ OPPOSITES irreligious.

relinquish v. GIVE UP, renounce, resign, abdicate, surrender, sign away. ■ OPPOSITES retain.

relish n. ENJOYMENT, delight, pleasure, satisfaction, gratification, appreciation, liking, zest, gusto. ▶v. ENJOY, delight in, like, love, adore, appreciate, revel in, luxuriate in. ■ OPPOSITES dislike.

reluctant adj. UNWILLING, disinclined, hesitant, unenthusiastic, grudging,

loath, averse, slow, chary. ■ OPPOSITES eager.

rely v. (**rely on**) DEPEND ON, count on, bank on, trust, lean on, be confident/sure of, swear by.

remain v. **1** BE LEFT, be left over, stay behind, survive, last, abide, endure, prevail. **2** WAIT, stay, linger; *informal* stay put; *old use* tarry. **3** STAY, continue to be, persist in being.

remainder n. REMNANT, residue, leavings, dregs, residuum, balance, surplus, excess, superfluity.

remains pl. n. **1** REMNANTS, leftovers, leavings, scraps, residue, debris, detritus. **2** RELICS, reliquiae, fragments, shards. **3** CORPSE, dead body, body, carcass; *Medicine* cadaver; *informal* stiff.

remark v. **1** MENTION, say, state, declare, pronounce, assert, observe. **2** NOTE, notice, observe, mark, perceive, discern. ▶n. COMMENT, statement, utterance, declaration, pronouncement, observation, reference, opinion.

remarkable adj. OUT OF THE ORDINARY, extraordinary, unusual, uncommon, conspicuous, singular, notable, noteworthy, memorable, signal, rare, exceptional, outstanding, striking, impressive, considerable, pre-eminent, significant, important, momentous, phenomenal, wonderful. ■ OPPOSITES ordinary, commonplace.

remedy n. **1** CURE, treatment, medicine,

remember v. **1** have in or bring to one's mind someone or something from the past. **2** not fail to do something necessary. ■ **remembrance** n.

remind v. cause to remember. ■ **reminder** n.

reminisce v. think or talk about the past. ■ **reminiscence** n.

reminiscent adj. tending to remind one of something.

remiss adj. negligent.

remission n. **1** the cancellation of a debt or charge. **2** the reduction of a prison sentence for good behaviour. **3** a temporary period during which an illness becomes less severe.

remit v. (**remitting, remitted**) **1** cancel a debt or punishment. **2** send money in payment. **3** refer a matter for decision to an authority. ▶ n. a task assigned to someone.

remittance n. money sent in payment.

remnant n. a small remaining quantity.

remonstrate v. make a protest. ■ **remonstration** n.

remorse n. deep regret or guilt for one's wrongdoing. ■ **remorseful** adj.

remorseless adj. **1** without remorse. **2** relentless. ■ **remorselessly** adv.

remote adj. **1** far away in space or time; at a distance. **2** not closely connected or related. **3** (of a possibility) slight. **4** unfriendly and aloof. ■ **remotely** adv. **remoteness** n.

remould (US **remold**) v. **1** mould again. **2** put a new tread on a worn tyre. ▶ n. a remoulded tyre.

remove v. **1** take off or away. **2** get rid of. **3** dismiss from a post. ▶ n. the extent to which two things are separated. ■ **removable** adj. **removal** n. **remover** n.

remunerate v. pay for work. ■ **remuneration** n. **remunerative** adj.

Thesaurus

medication, medicament, therapy, antidote, restorative, nostrum, panacea. **2** CORRECTIVE, solution, redress, panacea. ▶ v. **1** CURE, heal, treat, counteract, control. **2** RECTIFY, solve, set to rights, put right, redress, fix, sort out.

remember v. **1** RECALL, call to mind, recollect, think of, keep/bear in mind, not forget. **2** REMINISCE ABOUT, look/think back on, hark back to, summon up. ■ OPPOSITES forget.

remind v. CAUSE TO REMEMBER, jog/refresh someone's memory, prompt.

reminiscent adj. EVOCATIVE, suggestive, redolent.

remiss adj. NEGLIGENT, neglectful, lax, slack, slipshod, sloppy, careless, forgetful, inattentive, heedless, thoughtless, unthinking, culpable, delinquent. ■ OPPOSITES careful, diligent.

remission n. **1** CANCELLATION, revocation, repeal, rescinding. **2** EASING, moderation, abatement, lessening, decrease, dwindling, wane, waning, ebb, ebbing, subsidence.

remit v. **1** CANCEL, revoke, repeal, rescind, stop, halt. **2** EASE, moderate, abate, lessen, decrease, dwindle, wane, ebb, subside. **3** SEND, dispatch, forward, transmit, post, mail.

remnant n. **1** REMAINDER, residue, balance, remains, vestiges. **2** PIECE, fragment, scrap.

remonstrate v. (**remonstrate with**) TAKE ISSUE WITH, argue with, dispute with, protest to, complain to, expostulate with.

remorse n. REGRET, sorrow, contrition, penitence, repentance, guilty conscience, guilt, shame, self-reproach, ruefulness, pangs of conscience, compunction.

remorseful adj. SORRY, regretful, contrite, apologetic, penitent, repentant, guilt-ridden, conscience-stricken, ashamed, chastened, rueful. ■ OPPOSITES unrepentant.

remorseless adj. see RELENTLESS.

remote adj. **1** DISTANT, far, far-off, faraway, out of the way, outlying, inaccessible, off the beaten track, isolated, secluded, lonely, godforsaken. **2** UNLIKELY, improbable, implausible, negligible, insignificant, doubtful, dubious, slight, slender, slim, small, poor. **3** ALOOF, distant, detached, withdrawn, reserved, uncommunicative, unapproachable, stand-offish, cool, haughty, uninvolved, indifferent, unconcerned. ■ OPPOSITES near, likely, friendly.

removal n. **1** DISMISSAL, eviction, ejection, expulsion, ousting, dislodgement, deposition. **2** TAKING AWAY, withdrawal, deprivation, abolition. **3** DELETION, elimination, erasure, effacing, obliteration.

remove v. **1** TAKE AWAY, carry away, move, shift, convey, transfer, transport. **2** DISMISS, get rid of, eject, expel, cast out, oust, throw out, dislodge, relegate, unseat, depose, displace; informal sack, fire. **3** TAKE OFF, pull off, strip off; informal peel off. **4** DELETE, eliminate, erase, rub out, cross out, strike out, blue-pencil,

Renaissance n. **1** the revival of classical styles in art and literature in the 14th–16th centuries. **2** (**renaissance**) a revival of interest in something.

renal adj. of the kidneys.

rend v. (**rending, rent**) tear.

render v. **1** provide a service, help, etc. **2** present for payment. **3** cause to become. **4** interpret or perform artistically. **5** melt down fat.

rendezvous /ron-day-voo/ n. (pl. **rendezvous**) a prearranged meeting or meeting place. ▶v. meet at an agreed time and place.

rendition n. a performance of a dramatic or musical work.

renegade n. a person who deserts and betrays a group, cause, etc.

renege /ri-nayg/ v. fail to keep a promise or agreement.

renew v. **1** begin again after an interruption. **2** give fresh life or strength to. **3** extend the period of validity of a licence etc. **4** replace something broken or worn out. ■ **renewal** n.

rennet n. a substance to curdle milk in making cheese.

renounce v. formally give up.

renovate v. restore to a good state of repair. ■ **renovation** n.

renown n. fame. ■ **renowned** adj.

rent¹ n. a regular payment for the use of property or land. ▶v. pay or receive rent for.

rent² past & past part. of REND. ▶n. a large tear in a piece of fabric.

rental n. **1** an amount paid as rent. **2** the act of renting.

renunciation n. the act of renouncing.

reorganize (or **-ise**) v. change the organization of. ■ **reorganization** n.

reorient v. **1** change the focus of. **2** (**reorient oneself**) find one's bearings again.

rep n. informal a representative.

repair v. **1** restore to a good condition; mend. **2** (**repair to**) go to a place. ▶n. **1** the act or result of repairing. **2** the condition of an object. ■ **repairer** n.

reparation n. **1** the making of amends for a wrong. **2** (**reparations**) compensation for war damage paid by a defeated state.

repartee n. quick, witty comments or replies.

repast n. a meal.

repatriate v. send someone back to their own country. ■ **repatriation** n.

repay v. (**repaying, repaid**) pay back. ■ **repayable** n. **repayment** n.

repeal v. officially cancel a law. ▶n. the act of repealing.

Thesaurus

efface, obliterate. **5** TAKE OUT, pull out, uproot, eradicate, extirpate, destroy, exterminate, annihilate. **6** CUT OFF, amputate, lop off, chop off, excise.

remunerative adj. PROFITABLE, moneymaking, paying, lucrative, gainful, financially rewarding, rich.

render v. **1** MAKE, cause to be/become, leave. **2** GIVE, contribute, make available, provide, supply, furnish. **3** PRESENT, send in, submit, tender. **4** ACT, perform, play, execute, interpret.

rendezvous n. APPOINTMENT, date, engagement, meeting, assignation.

renegade n. DEFECTOR, deserter, turncoat, traitor, apostate, revolutionary, rebel, mutineer.

renege v. GO BACK ON ONE'S WORD, break one's promise, default, back out, welsh, pull out; informal cop out. ■ OPPOSITES honour.

renounce v. **1** RELINQUISH, give up, resign, abdicate, surrender, sign away, waive, forego. **2** DISOWN, repudiate, cast off, discard, reject, disinherit, wash one's hands of, spurn, shun. **3** ABSTAIN FROM, give up, desist from, swear off, eschew. ■ OPPOSITES embrace.

renovate v. MODERNIZE, recondition, refurbish, rehabilitate, overhaul, revamp, remodel, repair, redecorate, refit; informal do up, fix up.

renown n. FAME, repute, acclaim, celebrity, distinction, illustriousness, eminence, pre-eminence, prominence, mark, note, consequence, prestige.

renowned adj. FAMOUS, famed, well known, of repute, acclaimed, celebrated, distinguished, illustrious, eminent, pre-eminent, prominent, noted, notable, of note, of consequence, prestigious. ■ OPPOSITES obscure.

rent¹ n. RENTAL, payment, hire fee. ▶v. **1** LEASE, hire, charter. **2** LET, lease, hire, hire/let out, farm out.

rent² n. TEAR, rip, split, gash, slash, hole, perforation, break, crack, fracture, crevice, fissure, cleft.

repair v. **1** MEND, fix, put right, restore, adjust, regulate, overhaul. **2** PUT RIGHT, make good, rectify, correct, redress, compensate for.

repay v. **1** PAY BACK, refund, reimburse, recompense, remunerate, square accounts with, settle up with. **2** GET BACK AT, hit back, retaliate against, get even

repeat v. **1** say or do again. **2** (**repeat itself**) occur again in the same way. ▶n. a repeated broadcast. ■ **repeatedly** adv.

repel v. (**repelled, repelling**) **1** drive or force back or away. **2** disgust. **3** (of a substance) be able to keep something out.

repellent adj. **1** able to repel a particular thing. **2** causing disgust. ▶n. a substance used to deter insects or to make something repel water.

repent v. feel or express remorse about something. ■ **repentance** n. **repentant** adj.

repercussions pl. n. the consequences of an event or action.

repertoire /rep-er-twar/ n. the works known or regularly performed by a performer or company.

repertory n. (pl. **repertories**) **1** the performance by a company of various plays, operas, etc. at regular intervals. **2** a repertoire.

repetition n. **1** the act of repeating. **2** a thing that repeats another.

repetitious adj. repetitive.

repetitive adj. repeated many times or too much. ■ **repetitively** adv.

repine v. literary be unhappy.

replace v. **1** provide or be a substitute for. **2** put back in place. ■ **replacement** n.

replay v. play again or back. ▶n. an act of replaying.

replenish v. fill up a supply again after some has been used. ■ **replenishment** n.

replete adj. **1** well supplied. **2** very full with food.

replica n. an exact copy.

replicate v. make a replica of. ■ **replication** n. **replicator** n.

reply v. (**replying, replied**) answer or respond. ▶n. (pl. **replies**) an answer.

report v. **1** give an account of. **2** make a formal complaint about. **3** present oneself on arrival. **4** be responsible to a manager. ▶n. **1** a spoken or written account. **2** a teacher's written assessment of a pupil's progress. **3** the sound of an explosion or gunfire.

Thesaurus

with, settle the score with; *informal* get one's own back on.

repeal v. REVOKE, rescind, abrogate, annul, nullify, make void, void, invalidate, quash, set aside, cancel, countermand, retract, overrule, override, reverse.

repeat v. **1** SAY AGAIN, restate, retell, reiterate, recapitulate, recap, echo, parrot, quote. **2** DO AGAIN, redo, duplicate, replicate.

repeated adj. RECURRENT, frequent, continual, incessant, constant, endless.

repel v. **1** REPULSE, drive back, push back, thrust back, force back, beat back, ward off, fend off, keep at bay, keep at arm's length. **2** REVOLT, disgust, sicken, nauseate, make someone sick, turn someone's stomach, be repugnant to, make someone's flesh creep; *informal* give someone the creeps. ■ OPPOSITES welcome, attract.

repellent adj. REPULSIVE, revolting, disgusting, sickening, nauseating, distasteful, repugnant, abhorrent, offensive, obnoxious, loathsome, off-putting, hateful, vile, nasty, odious, abominable, horrible, horrid, foul, heinous, obscene. ■ OPPOSITES attractive.

repent v. BE SORRY, be contrite, be conscience-stricken, reproach oneself, be ashamed, regret, rue, be penitent.

repentant adj. PENITENT, sorrowful, apologetic, regretful, contrite, rueful, remorseful, conscience-stricken, guilt-ridden, ashamed. ■ OPPOSITES unashamed, impenitent.

repercussion n. EFFECT, result, consequence, reverberation, backlash.

repetitive adj. RECURRENT, unchanging, unvaried, monotonous, humdrum, tedious, boring, mechanical, automatic; *informal* samey.

replace v. **1** PUT BACK, return, restore. **2** TAKE THE PLACE OF, succeed, supersede, follow after, come after, supplant, substitute for, stand in for, act for, fill in for, cover for.

replacement n. SUCCESSOR, substitute, stand-in, fill-in, locum, understudy, proxy, surrogate.

replenish v. REFILL, top up, fill up, recharge, reload.

replica n. COPY, carbon copy, duplicate, facsimile, model, reproduction, imitation, dummy.

reply v. ANSWER, respond, write back, rejoin, retort, return, riposte, come back, counter. ▶n. ANSWER, response, acknowledgement, rejoinder, retort, return, riposte; *informal* comeback.

report n. **1** ACCOUNT, statement, record, exposition. **2** ARTICLE, piece, story, write-up, communiqué, dispatch, bulletin. **3** EXPLOSION, bang, boom, crack, crash. ▶v. **1** ANNOUNCE, pass on, commu-

reportage /rep-or-*tahzh*/ n. the reporting of news.

reporter n. a person who reports news for a newspaper or broadcasting company.

repose n. a state of calm or peace. ▶v. rest; lie.

repository n. (pl. **repositories**) a place or container for storage.

repossess v. take back goods etc. when the required payments are not made. ■ **repossession** n.

reprehend v. reprimand.

reprehensible adj. deserving condemnation.

represent v. 1 be entitled to act and speak on behalf of. 2 be an example of. 3 constitute. 4 describe in a particular way. 5 depict in a work of art. 6 be a symbol of.

representation n. 1 the act of representing. 2 an image, model, etc. 3 (**representations**) statements made as an appeal or protest.

representative adj. 1 typical of a class or group. 2 consisting of people chosen to represent a wider group. ▶n. 1 a person chosen to represent others. 2 an agent of a firm who visits potential clients to sell its products.

repress v. 1 bring under control by force. 2 restrain or suppress a thought or feeling. ■ **repression** n. **repressive** adj.

reprieve v. cancel the punishment of. ▶n. 1 an act of reprieving. 2 a short rest from difficulty.

reprimand n. a formal expression of disapproval. ▶v. give a reprimand to.

reprint v. print again. ▶n. a copy of a book that has been reprinted.

reprisal n. an act of retaliation.

reproach v. express disapproval of or disappointment with. ▶n. an act of reproaching. ■ **reproachful** adj. **reproachfully** adv.

Thesaurus

nicate, relay, relate, tell, recount, give an account of, set forth, document, narrate, describe, delineate, detail, divulge, disclose, circulate. 2 TELL ON, inform on, accuse, make a charge/complaint against; *informal* squeal on, rat on, grass on. 3 PRESENT ONESELF, be present, appear, arrive, come, turn up, clock in/on; *informal* show up.

reporter n. JOURNALIST, newsman, newswoman, pressman, correspondent, writer, broadcaster, announcer, presenter; *informal* newshound, hack.

reprehensible adj. BLAMEWORTHY, culpable, erring, errant, wrong, bad, shameful, disgraceful, discreditable, dishonourable, objectionable, unpardonable, indefensible, unjustifiable, inexcusable. ■ OPPOSITES praiseworthy.

represent v. 1 STAND FOR, symbolize, personify, epitomize, typify, embody, incorporate, exemplify. 2 DEPICT, portray, delineate, illustrate, picture, denote, paint, draw, sketch, exhibit, show, display, evoke. 3 ACT FOR, appear for, speak for, be the representative of.

representation n. DEPICTION, portrayal, portrait, delineation, illustration, picture, painting, drawing, sketch, image, model.

representative adj. 1 TYPICAL, archetypal, exemplary, characteristic, indicative, illustrative. 2 ELECTED, elective, chosen, delegated. ▶n. 1 SPOKESMAN, spokeswoman, spokesperson, agent, deputy, proxy. 2 MEMBER OF PARLIAMENT,

MP, Member, deputy, councillor.

repress v. 1 SUBJUGATE, conquer, vanquish, overpower, overcome, crush, master, dominate, domineer, bully, intimidate, oppress. 2 HOLD/KEEP BACK, hold in, bite back, restrain, suppress, keep in check, check, inhibit, bottle up, silence, muffle, stifle, smother.

repressed adj. 1 SUBJUGATED, oppressed, tyrannized. 2 RESTRAINED, suppressed, muffled, smothered. 3 INHIBITED, withdrawn, restrained.

repression n. 1 OPPRESSION, dictatorship, authoritarianism, tyranny, despotism, domination, coercion, suppression, subjugation. 2 HOLDING BACK, biting back, restraint, suppression, smothering, stifling.

repressive adj. TYRANNICAL, despotic, dictatorial, authoritarian, oppressive, coercive, suppressive, harsh, severe, strict, cruel.

reprieve v. POSTPONE/CANCEL PUNISHMENT OF, grant a stay of execution to, let off, spare, pardon, let off the hook, show clemency to.

reprimand v. REBUKE, scold, chide, reproach, reprove, lecture, admonish, berate, upbraid, castigate, correct, take to task, haul over the coals; *informal* tell off, give someone a dressing-down, bawl out, tick off. ▶n. REBUKE, scolding, chiding, reproach, reproof, admonition, berating, upbraiding, castigation, tonguelashing; *informal* talking-to, telling-off, dressing-down, bawling-out, ticking-off,

reprobate n. an immoral or unprincipled person.

reproduce v. 1 produce a copy of. 2 produce again. 3 produce offspring. ■ **reproduction** n. **reproductive** adj.

reproof n. a reprimand.

reprove v. reprimand.

reptile n. a cold-blooded vertebrate animal with scaly skin. ■ **reptilian** adj.

republic n. a state in which power is held by the people's representatives, with an elected president rather than a monarch.

republican adj. of or supporting the principles of a republic. ▶ n. a person in favour of republican government.

repudiate v. 1 reject or disown. 2 deny the truth of. ■ **repudiation** n.

repugnant adj. very distasteful or unpleasant. ■ **repugnance** n.

repulse v. 1 drive back an attacking enemy. 2 reject or rebuff.

repulsion n. 1 a feeling of intense dislike or disgust. 2 a force by which objects tend to move away from each other.

repulsive adj. arousing disgust. ■ **repulsively** adv.

reputable adj. having a good reputation.

reputation n. the opinion generally held about someone or something.

repute n. reputation, esp. when good. ▶ v. (**be reputed**) be said or thought to be. ■ **reputedly** adv.

request n. 1 an act of asking for something. 2 a thing asked for. ▶ v. ask for or ask someone to do something.

requiem n. 1 a Mass for the souls of the dead. 2 music for this.

require v. 1 need for a purpose. 2 order or expect to do something.

requirement n. something needed.

requisite adj. necessary on account of circumstances or rules. ▶ n. something needed.

requisition n. an official order allowing property or materials to be taken and used. ▶ v. officially take or use, esp. during a war.

Thesaurus

wigging. ■ OPPOSITES commendation.

reprisal n. RETALIATION, revenge, vengeance, retribution, redress, requital, recrimination, an eye for an eye; informal tit for tat.

reproach v. & n. see REPRIMAND.

reproachful adj. DISAPPROVING, disappointed, critical, censorious, admonitory, condemnatory, disparaging, reproving, castigatory. ■ OPPOSITES approving.

reproduce v. 1 COPY, duplicate, replicate, photocopy, recreate, redo, remake, imitate, follow, emulate, echo, mirror, parallel, match, mimic, ape. 2 BREED, procreate, bear young, produce offspring, give birth, multiply, propagate, proliferate, spawn.

reproduction n. 1 COPY, duplicate, replica, facsimile, imitation, print. 2 BREEDING, procreation, propagation, proliferation.

repudiate v. DISOWN, reject, cast off, cut off, abandon, forsake, desert, discard, renounce, disavow, abjure, turn one's back on, have nothing to do with, wash one's hands of. ■ OPPOSITES embrace.

repugnant adj. ABHORRENT, revolting, repulsive, repellent, disgusting, sickening, nauseating, disagreeable, distasteful, offensive, objectionable, obnoxious, loathsome, off-putting, hateful, despicable, reprehensible, contemptible, abominable, horrible, horrid, foul,

nasty, vile, ugly, odious, heinous. ■ OPPOSITES agreeable.

repulsive adj. see REPUGNANT.

reputable adj. RESPECTABLE, respected, well thought of, esteemed, estimable, of good repute, worthy, creditable, reliable, dependable, conscientious, trustworthy, above board, legitimate, upright, virtuous, good, excellent. ■ OPPOSITES disreputable.

reputation n. REPUTE, standing, name, character, position, status, station.

request n. ENTREATY, appeal, petition, plea, application, demand, solicitation, call, suit. ▶ v. ASK FOR, solicit, seek, apply for, put in for, call for, beg for, plead for, pray for, petition, implore, sue for, supplicate for, requisition, demand, desire; literary beseech.

require v. 1 NEED, have need of, lack, be short of, want, wish, desire, crave, miss. 2 CALL FOR, demand, necessitate, involve, take.

required adj. COMPULSORY, obligatory, mandatory, prescribed, recommended, requisite, set, essential, necessary, vital. ■ OPPOSITES optional.

requirement n. NEED, want, lack, must, necessity, demand, prerequisite, requisite, precondition, specification, qualification, sine qua non, stipulation.

requisite adj. see REQUIRED.

requisition n. 1 APPLICATION, order, claim, request, call, demand. 2 COMMAN-

requite v. return a favour or service.

rescind v. cancel a law etc.

rescue v. save from danger or distress. ▶ n. an act of rescuing. ■ **rescuer** n.

research n. the study of materials and sources to discover facts. ▶ v. carry out research into a subject or for a book etc. ■ **researcher** n.

resemble v. be like. ■ **resemblance** n.

resent v. feel bitter or angry about. ■ **resentful** adj. **resentfully** adv. **resentment** n.

reservation n. **1** the act of reserving. **2** an arrangement whereby something is reserved. **3** an area of land set aside for native people. **4** doubt.

reserve v. **1** keep for future use. **2** arrange for a room, seat, etc. to be kept for a particular person. **3** retain. ▶ n. **1** a supply of something available for use if required. **2** a military force kept to reinforce others or for use in an emergency. **3** an extra player in a team, serving as a possible substitute. **4** an area of land set aside for wildlife or for a native people. **5** a lack of warmth or openness. **6** the lowest acceptable price for an item sold at auction.

reserved adj. slow to reveal emotion.

reservist n. a member of a reserve force.

reservoir n. **1** a lake used as a source of water supply. **2** a container for a supply of fluid.

reshuffle v. change the roles or positions of government ministers. ▶ n. act of reshuffling.

reside v. **1** live in a particular place. **2** (of a right or power) belong.

residence n. **1** the fact of residing. **2** the place where a person lives.

resident n. **1** a person living somewhere on a long-term basis. **2** a guest in a hotel. ▶ adj. living somewhere on a long-term basis.

residential adj. **1** designed for living in. **2** providing accommodation.

residue n. what is left over after the

Thesaurus

DEERING, appropriation, possession, occupation, seizure, confiscation. ▶ v. **1** APPLY FOR, order, put in a claim for, request, call for, demand. **2** COMMANDEER, appropriate, take over, take possession of, occupy, seize, confiscate.

rescue v. SAVE, come to someone's aid, free, set free, release, liberate, emancipate, get out, extricate, redeem, salvage, relieve. ▶ n. DELIVERANCE, freeing, release, liberation, emancipation, extrication, redemption, salvage, relief.

research n. EXPERIMENT, assessment, study, tests, investigation, experimentation, fact-finding, testing, exploration. ▶ v. DO TESTS ON, investigate, inquire into, look into, probe, explore, analyse, study, examine.

resemblance n. LIKENESS, similarity, semblance, sameness, uniformity, correspondence, comparability, affinity, closeness, nearness, agreement, congruity, concurrence, conformity.

resemble v. BE LIKE, look like, bear a resemblance to, be similar to, remind one of, take after, echo, mirror, parallel, favour.

resent v. TAKE OFFENCE/UMBRAGE AT, take exception to, take amiss, be annoyed/angry at, begrudge, feel bitter about, dislike. ■ OPPOSITES welcome.

resentful adj. AGGRIEVED, offended, indignant, irritated, displeased, annoyed, angry, irate, incensed, piqued, in high dudgeon, grudging, bitter, embittered, wounded; informal in a huff.

resentment n. OFFENCE, indignation, irritation, displeasure, annoyance, anger, pique, grudgingness, bitterness, animosity, hostility, hard feelings; literary ire.

reservation n. **1** BOOKING, engagement, appointment. **2** CONDITION, stipulation, qualification, proviso, provision, qualm, scruple, hesitancy, doubt.

reserve v. **1** PUT/SET/LAY ASIDE, put away, keep back, keep, withhold, conserve, save, retain, store, hoard, stockpile; informal hang on to. **2** BOOK, engage, arrange for, charter, hire. ▶ n. **1** STORE, stock, supply, reservoir, pool, cache, fund, stockpile, accumulation, backlog, hoard. **2** ALOOFNESS, detachment, distance, remoteness, formality, coolness, coldness, frigidity, reticence, unapproachability, uncommunicativeness, shyness, diffidence, taciturnity. **3** PRESERVE, reservation, sanctuary, park.

reserved adj. ALOOF, detached, remote, formal, unemotional, undemonstrative, cool, cold, frigid, reticent, unapproachable, uncommunicative, unsociable, unfriendly, unresponsive, unforthcoming, shy, retiring, diffident, secret, secretive, taciturn, silent. ■ OPPOSITES outgoing.

reside v. (**reside in**) LIVE IN, dwell in, stay in, inhabit, occupy.

residence n. HOUSE, home, dwelling,

main part has gone. ■ **residual** adj.

resign v. **1** voluntarily leave a job. **2** (**resign oneself** or **be resigned**) accept that something bad cannot be avoided. ■ **resignation** n.

resilient adj. **1** able to spring back into shape after bending, stretching, etc. **2** able to recover quickly from difficulty or distress. ■ **resilience** n.

resin n. **1** a sticky substance produced by some trees. **2** a synthetic substance used in plastics etc. ■ **resinous** adj.

resist v. **1** withstand. **2** try to prevent or fight against. **3** refrain from something tempting. ■ **resistance** n. **resistant** adj.

resistor n. a device that resists the passage of an electric current.

resolute adj. determined. ■ **resolutely** adv.

resolution n. **1** a firm decision. **2** a formal expression of opinion by a law-making body. **3** determination. **4** the solving of a problem etc. **5** the degree to which detail is visible in an image.

resolve v. **1** find a solution to. **2** decide firmly on a course of action. **3** separate into constituent parts. ▶ n. determination.

resonant adj. **1** deep, clear, and ringing. **2** tending to prolong sounds. ■ **resonance** n.

resonate v. make a deep, clear, ringing sound.

resort v. (**resort to**) adopt a course of action to solve a problem. ▶ n. **1** a place visited for holidays or recreation. **2** a course of action.

resound v. be filled with a ringing or echoing sound.

resource n. **1** (**resources**) a stock or supply of materials or assets. **2** something to be used to help achieve an aim. **3** (**resources**) personal qualities for dealing with difficult circumstances.

resourceful adj. quick and clever at overcoming difficulties. ■ **resourcefully** adv. **resourcefulness** n.

respect n. **1** admiration for someone because of their qualities or achievements. **2** regard for the feelings or rights of others. **3** a particular aspect or point. ▶ v. have respect for. ■ **respectful** adj. **respectfully** adv.

Thesaurus

domicile, habitation, quarters, lodgings; *informal* pad.

resident n. INHABITANT, occupant, householder, denizen, occupier.

residue n. REMAINDER, remnant, residuum, rest, surplus, extra, excess, remains, leftovers, dregs, lees.

resign v. **1** GIVE NOTICE, hand in one's notice, leave; *informal* quit. **2** RENOUNCE, relinquish, give up, abdicate, surrender, cede.

resilient adj. **1** ELASTIC, springy, rubbery, whippy, flexible, pliant, supple, pliable, plastic. **2** TOUGH, strong, hardy, quick to recover, difficult to keep down, irrepressible.

resist v. **1** WITHSTAND, be proof against, repel. **2** STOP, halt, prevent, check stem, curb, obstruct, hinder, impede, block, thwart, frustrate, inhibit, restrain.

resistant adj. PROOF AGAINST, impervious to, unaffected by, immune to.

resolute adj. DETERMINED, resolved, decided, firm, fixed, set, intent, steadfast, constant, earnest, staunch, bold, courageous, serious, purposeful, deliberate, inflexible, unyielding, unwavering, unfaltering, unhesitating, unswerving, unflinching, obstinate, obdurate, strong-willed, dogged, persevering, persistent, tenacious, relentless, unshakeable, dedicated. ■ OPPOSITES irresolute.

resolution n. **1** RESOLVE, determination, firmness, intentness, steadfastness, constancy, staunchness, boldness, courage, seriousness, purposefulness, obstinacy, obduracy, will power, doggedness, perseverance, persistence, tenacity, staying power, dedication. **2** MOTION, declaration, decree, verdict, judgement. **3** SOLVING, solution, answer, sorting out, working out, unravelling, disentanglement, cracking.

resolve v. **1** DECIDE, make up one's mind, determine, settle on, undertake. **2** SOLVE, answer, sort out, work out, clear up, fathom, unravel, disentangle, crack. ▶ n. *see* RESOLUTION.

resort v. FALL BACK ON, turn to, have recourse to, look to, make use of, use, avail oneself of, bring into play/service, exercise. ▶ n. **1** HOLIDAY/TOURIST CENTRE, centre, spot, retreat. **2** RECOURSE, source of help, expedient, alternative, choice, possibility, hope.

resound v. REVERBERATE, resonate, echo, ring.

resource n. **1** ASSET, reserve, reservoir, store, stock, supply, pool, fund, stockpile. **2** RESOURCEFULNESS, initiative, ingenuity, talent, inventiveness, quick-wittedness, cleverness, native wit, ability, capability.

respect n. **1** ESTEEM, high regard, re-

respectable adj. **1** regarded by society as proper or correct. **2** adequate or acceptable. ■ **respectability** n. **respectably** adv.

respective adj. belonging to each as an individual.

respectively adv. separately and in the order mentioned.

respiration n. the act of breathing.

respirator n. **1** an apparatus worn over the face to prevent the breathing in of smoke, dust, etc. **2** an apparatus for giving artificial respiration.

respiratory adj. of respiration.

respire v. breathe.

respite n. rest or relief from something difficult or unpleasant.

resplendent adj. impressively bright and colourful.

respond v. say or do in reply or as a reaction.

respondent n. a defendant in a lawsuit.

response n. an answer or reaction.

responsibility n. (pl. **responsibilities**) **1** the state of being responsible. **2** a thing required to be done as part of a job or legal obligation.

responsible adj. **1** obliged to do something or care for someone. **2** being the cause of something and so deserving blame or credit for it. **3** able to be trusted; reliable. **4** (of a job) involving important duties. **5** having to report to a senior person. ■ **responsibly** adv.

responsive adj. responding readily.

rest v. **1** stop work or movement in order to relax or recover one's strength. **2** place or be placed in a specified position. **3** remain in a specified state: *rest assured*. **4** (**rest on**) depend or be based on. **5** (**rest with**) (of power etc.) belong to. **6** (of a matter) be left without further action. ▶ n. **1** a period of resting. **2** a motionless state. **3** an object used to hold or support something. **4** the remaining part or group.

restaurant n. a place where people pay to eat meals cooked on the premises.

restaurateur /ress-tuh-ruh-**ter**/ n. the owner or manager of a restaurant.

 There is no *n*: resta*u*r*ateur*.

restful adj. relaxing.

gard, high opinion, admiration, approval, appreciation, veneration, reverence, deference, honour, praise, homage. **2** ASPECT, facet, feature, way, sense, characteristic, particular, point, detail. ▶ v. ESTEEM, have a high opinion of, think highly of, admire, approve of, appreciate, venerate, revere, honour, praise. ■ OPPOSITES despise.

respectable adj. **1** REPUTABLE, of good repute, upright, honest, honourable, trustworthy, above board, worthy, decent, good, virtuous, admirable, well bred, proper, decorous. **2** REASONABLE, fairly good, fair, considerable, ample, sizable, substantial; *informal* not to be sneezed at. ■ OPPOSITES disreputable, paltry.

respective adj. INDIVIDUAL, separate, personal, own, particular, specific.

respects pl. n. REGARDS, best wishes, greetings, compliments, remembrances.

respite n. REST, break, interval, intermission, recess, lull, pause, hiatus, halt, relief, relaxation; *informal* breather, let-up.

respond v. **1** ANSWER, reply to, say in response to, acknowledge. **2** SAY IN RESPONSE, answer, reply, rejoin, retort, return, riposte, come back, counter.

response n. ANSWER, reply, acknow-

ledgement, rejoinder, retort, return, riposte; *informal* comeback. ■ OPPOSITES question.

responsibility n. **1** DUTY, charge, onus, task, role, liability, accountability, answerability. **2** BLAME, fault, guilt, culpability.

responsible adj. **1** IN CHARGE/CONTROL OF, at the helm of, accountable for, liable for. **2** ACCOUNTABLE, answerable, to blame, blameworthy, at fault, guilty, culpable. **3** SENSIBLE, level-headed, rational, reasonable, sound, stable, reliable, dependable, trustworthy, competent, conscientious, hard-working, industrious. ■ OPPOSITES irresponsible.

responsive adj. QUICK TO REACT, reactive, receptive, forthcoming, sensitive, perceptive, sympathetic, susceptible, impressionable, open, alive, awake, aware, sharp.

rest n. **1** REPOSE, relaxation, leisure, ease, inactivity, respite, time off, breathing space, sleep, slumber. **2** BREAK, interval, interlude, intermission, lull, pause, time off. **3** STAND, base, holder, support, prop, shelf. ▶ v. **1** TAKE A REST, relax, sit down, lie down, go to bed, sleep, take a nap, nap, catnap, doze, slumber; *informal* take it easy. **2** BE SUPPORTED BY, be propped up by, lie on,

restitution n. **1** the restoration of something lost or stolen to its proper owner. **2** payment for injury or loss.

restive adj. restless; impatient.

restless adj. unable to rest or relax. ■ **restlessly** adv. **restlessness** n.

restorative adj. able to restore health or strength. ▶ n. a restorative medicine or drink.

restore v. **1** return to a previous condition, place, or owner. **2** repair or renovate. **3** bring back a previous practice, situation, etc. ■ **restoration** n. **restorer** n.

restrain v. **1** keep under control. **2** stop from moving or acting freely. ■ **restraint** n.

restrict v. **1** put a limit on. **2** stop from moving or acting freely. ■ **restriction** n. **restrictive** adj.

result n. **1** a thing caused or produced by something else. **2** information obtained by experiment or calculation. **3** a final score or mark in a contest or examination. ▶ v. **1** occur as a result. **2** (**result in**) have as a result.

resultant adj. occurring as a result.

resume v. **1** begin again or continue after an interruption. **2** return to a seat. ■ **resumption** n.

résumé /rez-yuu-may/ n. **1** a summary. **2** US a curriculum vitae.

resurgent adj. becoming stronger or more popular again. ■ **resurgence** n.

resurrect v. **1** restore to life. **2** revive a practice etc. ■ **resurrection** n.

resuscitate v. revive from unconsciousness. ■ **resuscitation** n.

retail n. the sale of goods to the general public. ▶ v. sell or be sold to the public. ■ **retailer** n.

retain v. **1** keep possession of. **2** absorb and hold. **3** keep in place. **4** secure the services of.

retainer n. a fee paid in advance to secure someone's services.

retaliate v. make an attack in return for a similar attack. ■ **retaliation** n. **retaliatory** adj.

retard v. hold back the development or progress of. ■ **retardation** n.

retarded adj. offens. less developed mentally than is usual for one's age.

retch v. make the sound and movement

Thesaurus

be laid on, recline on, stand on, sit on. **3** DEPEND, rely, hang, hinge, be based, be founded.

restful adj. QUIET, calm, tranquil, relaxed, peaceful, placid, still, languid, undisturbed, unhurried, sleepy. ■ OPPOSITES hectic.

restless adj. **1** SLEEPLESS, wakeful, tossing and turning, fitful. **2** UNEASY, ill at ease, on edge, agitated. **3** UNSETTLED, roaming, roving, wandering, itinerant, travelling, nomadic, peripatetic.

restore v. **1** RENOVATE, repair, fix, mend, set to rights, recondition, rehabilitate, refurbish, rebuild, reconstruct, remodel, revamp, redecorate, touch up; *informal* do up, fix up. **2** RETURN, give back, hand back, send back. **3** REESTABLISH, reinstitute, reinstate, reinstall, reimpose.

restrain v. CONTROL, keep under control, check, hold in check, curb, keep within bounds, subdue, suppress, repress, contain, smother, stifle, bottle up, rein in; *informal* keep the lid on.

restraint n. **1** CONSTRAINT, check, curb, block, hindrance, impediment, deterrent, inhibition. **2** SELF-RESTRAINT, self-control, self-discipline, moderation, temperateness, prudence, judiciousness.

restrict v. HINDER, impede, hamper, retard, handicap, cramp. **2** LIMIT, set/impose limits on, keep under control, regulate, control, moderate.

restriction n. CONSTRAINT, limitation, control, check, curb, regulation, condition, provision, proviso, stipulation, qualification, demarcation.

result n. **1** OUTCOME, consequence, issue, upshot, sequel, effect, repercussion, end, conclusion, termination, aftermath, product, by-product, fruits. **2** ANSWER, solution. ▶ v. FOLLOW, ensue, issue, develop, stem, evolve, emerge, emanate, occur, happen, come about, eventuate. □ **result in** END IN, culminate in, finish in, terminate in.

resume v. CARRY ON, continue, recommence, begin again, reopen, reinstitute.

resurrect v. RAISE FROM THE DEAD, restore to life, bring back to life, revive, breathe new life into, give new life to.

retain v. **1** KEEP, keep possession/hold of, hold on to, hang on to, preserve, maintain. **2** HIRE, employ, engage, commission, keep on the payroll.

retaliate v. TAKE/EXACT/WREAK REVENGE, avenge oneself, exact retribution, give as good as one gets, get one's own back, get back at, make reprisals, get even with, even the scores, settle a score.

retard v. SLOW DOWN, slow up, hold back, set back, hold up, delay, hinder, hamof vomiting.

retention n. the act of retaining.

retentive adj. able to retain facts easily.

rethink v. (**rethinking**, **rethought**) reconsider.

reticent adj. not revealing one's thoughts or feelings. ■ **reticence** n.

retina n. (pl. **retinas** or **retinae**) a layer at the back of the eyeball that is sensitive to light.

retinue n. a group of assistants accompanying an important person.

retire v. 1 stop working because one has reached a particular age. 2 withdraw. 3 go to bed. ■ **retirement** n.

retiring adj. shy.

retort v. make a sharp or witty reply. ▶n. 1 a sharp or witty reply. 2 a container or furnace for carrying out a chemical process on a large scale. 3 a glass container with a long neck, used in distilling.

retouch v. improve a painting or photograph with slight alterations.

retrace v. go back over or follow a route.

retract v. 1 draw or be drawn back. 2 withdraw an accusation etc. ■ **retractable** adj. **retraction** n.

retractile adj. able to be retracted.

retreat v. 1 (of an army) withdraw from attacking enemy forces. 2 move back from a difficult situation. ▶n. 1 an act of retreating. 2 a quiet or secluded place.

retrench v. reduce costs or spending. ■ **retrenchment** n.

retrial n. a second or further trial.

retribution n. severe punishment inflicted as revenge.

retrieve v. 1 get or bring back. 2 extract information from a computer. 3 improve a bad situation. ■ **retrieval** n.

retriever n. a dog of a breed used to retrieve game.

retro adj. imitative of a style from the recent past.

retroactive adj. taking effect from a date in the past.

retrograde adj. moving backwards or to a worse state.

retrogressive adj. returning to an earlier and worse state. ■ **retrogression** n.

retrospect n. (**in retrospect**) when looking back on a past event.

retrospective adj. 1 looking back on or dealing with past events. 2 retroactive. ■ **retrospectively** adv.

retroussé /ruh-troo-say/ adj. (of a nose) turned up at the tip.

retsina n. a Greek wine flavoured with resin.

return v. 1 come or go back. 2 give, send, or put back. 3 feel, say, or do the same thing in response. 4 give a verdict. 5 yield a profit. 6 elect to office. ▶n. 1 an act of returning. 2 a profit. 3 a ticket allowing travel to a place and back again.

Thesaurus

per, obstruct, impede, decelerate, put a brake on, check, arrest, interfere with, interrupt, thwart, frustrate. ■ OPPOSITES expedite.

reticent adj. see RESERVED.

retire v. 1 GIVE UP WORK, stop working, be pensioned off; *informal* be put out to grass. 2 WITHDRAW, go out, depart, exit, leave, absent oneself. 3 GO TO BED, go to sleep, turn in, call it a day; *informal* hit the sack.

retiring adj. SHY, diffident, bashful, self-effacing, shrinking, unassuming, reserved, reticent, timid, timorous, nervous, modest, demure. ■ OPPOSITES brash.

retract v. 1 DRAW IN, pull in, pull back. 2 TAKE BACK, withdraw, revoke, repeal, rescind, annul, cancel, abrogate, disavow, abjure, renounce, recant, disclaim, backtrack on, renege on.

retreat v. 1 WITHDRAW, pull back, fall back, back off, give way/ground, decamp, depart, leave, flee, take flight,

turn tail, beat a retreat, beat a hasty retreat. 2 GO BACK, recede, ebb. ▶n. 1 WITHDRAWAL, pulling back, departure, flight, evacuation. 2 REFUGE, haven, shelter, sanctuary, sanctum sanctorum, hideaway, resort, asylum.

retribution n. REPRISAL, retaliation, revenge, vengeance, punishment, justice, nemesis, reckoning, requital, an eye for an eye, tit for tat.

retrieve v. GET BACK, recover, regain, win back, recoup, redeem, reclaim, repossess, recapture, salvage, rescue.

retrograde adj. RETROGRESSIVE, backwards, deteriorating, declining, on the wane.

retrospect n. (**in retrospect**) ON REFLECTION, on looking/thinking back, with hindsight.

return v. 1 GO BACK, come back, reappear, reoccur, come again, come round again. 2 GIVE BACK, send back, take back, carry back, put back, replace, restore, reinstate, reinstall. 3 RE-

reunion n. a social gathering of people who have not seen each other for some time.

reunite v. bring or come together again.

reuse v. use again. ■ **reusable** adj.

Rev. abbrev. Reverend.

rev informal n. a revolution of an engine. ▶v. (**revving, revved**) increase the running speed of an engine.

revamp v. alter something so as to improve it.

Revd abbrev. Reverend.

reveal v. **1** make known. **2** allow something hidden to be seen.

reveille /ri-val-li/ n. a signal sounded to wake up soldiers.

revel v. (**revelling, revelled;** US **reveling, reveled**) **1** enjoy oneself in a lively way. **2** (**revel in**) gain great pleasure from. ▶n. (**revels**) lively celebrations. ■ **reveller** n. **revelry** n.

revelation n. **1** the act of revealing. **2** a surprising thing.

revenge n. something harmful done in return for an injury or wrong. ▶v. (**be revenged**) inflict revenge.

revenue n. the income received by an organization, or by a state from taxes.

reverberate v. **1** be repeated as an echo. **2** have continuing effects. ■ **reverberation** n.

revere v. respect or admire deeply.

reverence n. deep respect. ■ **reverent** adj. **reverential** adj.

reverend adj. a title given to Christian ministers.

reverie n. a daydream.

reverse v. **1** move backwards. **2** make something the opposite of what it was. **3** turn the other way round or inside out. **4** cancel a judgement. ▶adj. opposite in direction, order, etc. ▶n. **1** a change of direction or action. **2** the opposite. **3** a setback. ■ **reversal** n. **reversible** adj.

revert v. return to a previous state, practice, etc. ■ **reversion** n.

review n. **1** a formal examination or reconsideration. **2** a critical assessment of a book etc. **3** a report of events. **4** a ceremonial inspection of military or naval forces. ▶v. carry out or write a review of. ■ **reviewer** n.

revile v. criticize in a rude or scornful

Thesaurus

ciprocate, repay, requite, send/give in response to. ▶n. **1** HOMECOMING, reappearance, reoccurrence. **2** REPLACEMENT, restoration, reinstatement, reinstallation. **3** PROFIT, yield, gain, income, revenue, interest. ■ OPPOSITES departure.

reveal v. **1** SHOW, display, exhibit, expose to view. **2** BRING TO LIGHT, uncover, expose to view, lay bare, unearth, unveil, unmask. **3** DISCLOSE, divulge, tell, let out, let on, let slip, give away, give out, leak, betray, make known/public, broadcast, publicize, publish, proclaim. ■ OPPOSITES conceal, hide.

revel v. CELEBRATE, make merry, have a party, party, carouse, roister. □ **revel in** DELIGHT IN, take pleasure in, bask in, rejoice in, relish, savour, gloat over, luxuriate in, wallow in.

revelation n. DISCLOSURE, divulgence, telling, leak, betrayal, broadcasting, publicizing, communication, publishing, proclamation.

revelry n. CELEBRATIONS, festivities, jollification, merrymaking, carousal.

revenge n. VENGEANCE, retaliation, retribution, reprisal, redress, an eye for an eye. ▶v. TAKE REVENGE FOR, avenge, retaliate, exact retribution for, take reprisals for, requite.

revenue n. INCOME, return, yield, interest, profits, returns, receipts, proceeds, takings. ■ OPPOSITES expenditure.

reverberate v. RESOUND, echo, ring, vibrate.

revere v. LOOK UP TO, think highly of, admire, respect, esteem, defer to, honour, venerate, exalt, put on a pedestal, idolize. ■ OPPOSITES despise.

reverence n. ESTEEM, admiration, respect, deference, honour, veneration, worship, homage, adoration, devotion, awe, exaltation. ■ OPPOSITES scorn.

reverent adj. REVERENTIAL, admiring, respectful, deferential, adoring, loving, devoted, awed, submissive, humble, meek.

reversal n. **1** TURNAROUND, turnabout, about-face, volte-face, U-turn, change of heart, about-turn. **2** CHANGE, exchange, trading, trade-off, swapping. **3** OVERTURN, overthrow, revocation, repeal, rescinding, annulment, invalidation.

reverse v. **1** TURN ROUND, put back to front, turn upside down, upend, invert. **2** MOVE/DIRECT BACKWARDS, back. **3** CHANGE, exchange, trade, swap. **4** SET ASIDE, overturn, overthrow, revoke, repeal, rescind, annul, nullify, declare null and void, void, invalidate, quash. ▶adj. REVERSED, backwards, inverted, transposed, turned round. ▶n. **1** OPPOSITE, contrary, converse, antithesis.

way.

revise v. **1** examine and alter. **2** reread previous work in preparation for an examination. ■ **revision** n.

revivalism n. the promotion of a revival of religious faith. ■ **revivalist** n. & adj.

revive v. **1** restore to consciousness, health, or strength. **2** start doing or using again. ■ **revival** n.

revivify v. (**revivifying**, **revivified**) give new life or strength to.

revoke v. make a decree, law, etc. no longer valid. ■ **revocation** n.

revolt v. **1** rebel against an authority. **2** cause to feel disgust. ▶ n. an act of rebellion or defiance.

revolution n. **1** the overthrow of a government by force, in favour of a new system. **2** a dramatic and far-reaching change. **3** a single movement around a central point.

revolutionary adj. **1** involving dramatic change. **2** of or engaged in political revolution. ▶ n. (pl. **revolutionaries**) a person who starts or supports a political revolution.

revolutionize (or **-ise**) v. change completely.

revolve v. **1** move in a circle around a central point. **2** move in an orbit around.

revolver n. a type of pistol.

revue n. a theatrical show with a series of items.

revulsion n. strong disgust.

reward n. a thing given in recognition of service, effort, or achievement. ▶ v. give a reward to or for.

rewire v. provide with new electric wiring.

Rex n. a reigning king.

RFC abbrev. Rugby Football Club.

rhapsodize (or **-ise**) v. express great enthusiasm.

rhapsody n. (pl. **rhapsodies**) **1** an expression of great enthusiasm. **2** a piece of music in one extended movement. ■ **rhapsodic** adj.

rhenium n. a metallic element.

rheostat n. a device for varying the resistance in an electrical circuit.

rhesus factor n. a substance in red blood cells which can cause disease in a newborn baby.

rhesus monkey n. a small southern Asian monkey.

rhetoric n. **1** effective or persuasive public speaking. **2** persuasive but insincere language.

Thesaurus

2 OTHER SIDE, back, rear, underside, flip side. **3** REVERSAL, upset, setback, failure, misfortune, mishap, disappointment, blow.

review n. **1** STUDY, analysis, survey, examination, scrutiny, assessment, appraisal. **2** CRITICISM, critique, notice, assessment, evaluation, rating. ▶ v. **1** ANALYSE, examine, study, survey, scrutinize, assess, appraise. **2** CRITICIZE, evaluate, judge, comment on, weigh up, discuss.

revise v. **1** AMEND, emend, correct, alter, change, edit, rewrite, redraft, rework, update, revamp. **2** GO OVER, reread, run through, study; *informal* bone up on, swot up on.

revival n. RESUSCITATION, resurrection, rebirth, renaissance, comeback, restoration, reintroduction.

revive v. **1** BRING ROUND, resuscitate, give artificial respiration to, save, restore to health; *informal* give the kiss of life to. **2** REFRESH, restore, cheer up, comfort, enliven, revitalize.

revoke v. REPEAL, rescind, abrogate, countermand, annul, nullify, declare null and void, void, invalidate, quash. ■ OPPOSITES enact.

revolt v. **1** RISE UP, take to the streets, take up arms, rebel, mutiny. **2** REPEL, disgust, sicken, nauseate, turn someone's stomach, be repugnant to, make someone's flesh creep, put off, offend, shock.

revolting adj. *see* REPELLENT.

revolution n. **1** REBELLION, revolt, insurrection, uprising, rising, insurgence, coup, putsch. **2** DRASTIC CHANGE, metamorphosis, sea change, upheaval, upset, transformation. **3** ROTATION, single turn, whirl, round, spin, wheel.

revolutionary adj. **1** REBELLIOUS, insurrectionary, mutinous, seditious, subversive, extremist. **2** PROGRESSIVE, radical, innovative, new, novel, avant-garde, experimental, different, drastic. ▶ n. REBEL, insurgent, insurrectionist.

revolve v. GO ROUND, turn round, rotate, spin, circle, orbit, gyrate, whirl.

revulsion n. REPULSION, disgust, nausea, distaste, aversion, repugnance, abhorrence, loathing. ■ OPPOSITES delight.

reward n. RECOMPENSE, payment, remuneration, bonus, bounty, present, gift, tip, gratuity, prize. ■ OPPOSITES punishment. ▶ v. RECOMPENSE, pay, remunerate, give a bonus to, tip.

rhetorical adj. **1** intended to impress. **2** (of a question) asked to make a statement rather than to obtain an answer. ■ **rhetorically** adv.

rheumatism n. a disease causing inflammation and pain in the joints and muscles. ■ **rheumatic** adj.

rheumatoid adj. of or resembling rheumatism.

rhinestone n. an imitation diamond.

rhino n. (pl. **rhino** or **rhinos**) informal a rhinoceros.

rhinoceros n. (pl. **rhinoceros** or **rhinoceroses**) a large thick-skinned mammal with one or two horns on the nose.

rhizome n. an underground stem bearing both roots and shoots.

rhodium n. a metallic element.

rhododendron n. a shrub with large clusters of flowers.

rhombus n. (pl. **rhombuses** or **rhombi**) a parallelogram with four straight equal sides forming two opposite acute angles and two opposite obtuse angles. ■ **rhomboid** adj. & n.

rhubarb n. a plant with thick red stems cooked and eaten as a fruit.

rhyme n. **1** a word that has or ends with the same sound as another. **2** similarity of sound between words or the endings of words. **3** a short poem with rhyming lines. ▶ v. have or end with the same sound.

....

✓ Remember the first *h*, following the *r*, in *rhyme* and *rhythm*.

....

rhythm n. **1** a strong, regular repeated pattern of sound or movement. **2** a

regularly recurring sequence of events. ❑ **rhythm and blues** a type of music that is a combination of blues and jazz. ■ **rhythmic** adj. **rhythmical** adj. **rhythmically** adv.

rib n. **1** each of a series of bones curving round the chest. **2** a curved structure forming part of a boat's framework. **3** a pattern of ridges in knitting. ▶ v. (**ribbing**, **ribbed**) informal tease.

ribald adj. humorous in a coarse way. ■ **ribaldry** n.

riband n. old use a ribbon.

ribbon n. **1** a long, narrow strip of fabric, for tying or decoration. **2** a long, narrow strip.

riboflavin n. vitamin B_2.

rice n. the grains of a cereal plant grown for food on wet land in warm countries.

rich adj. **1** having a great deal of money or assets. **2** plentiful. **3** having something in large amounts. **4** (of a colour, sound, or smell) pleasantly deep and strong. **5** (of soil) fertile. ▶ pl. n. (**riches**) wealth. ■ **richness** n.

richly adv. **1** in a rich way. **2** fully.

Richter scale /rik-ter/ n. a scale for measuring the severity of an earthquake.

rick n. **1** a stack of hay etc. **2** a slight sprain or strain. ▶ v. strain slightly.

rickets n. a bone disease of children caused by lack of vitamin D.

rickety adj. likely to collapse.

rickshaw n. a light two-wheeled vehicle pulled by a person walking or riding a bicycle.

ricochet /ri-kuh-shay/ v. (**ricocheting**, **ricocheted**) rebound off a surface. ▶ n. a shot or hit that ricochets.

Thesaurus
....

rewarding adj. SATISFYING, fulfilling, enriching, edifying, beneficial, profitable, advantageous, productive, valuable.

rhetoric n. BOMBAST, grandiloquence, magniloquence, hyperbole, pomposity, verbosity, prolixity, turgidity.

rhetorical adj. POMPOUS, high-flown, flamboyant, showy, flowery, florid, oratorical, declamatory, bombastic, grandiloquent, magniloquent, hyperbolical, verbose, long-winded, prolix, turgid, periphrastic.

rhythm n. BEAT, cadence, tempo, pulse, metre, pattern.

ribald adj. BAWDY, risqué, smutty, vulgar, coarse, earthy, off colour, rude, naughty, racy, suggestive, indecent, indelicate. *See also* OBSCENE.

rich adj. **1** WEALTHY, affluent, well off,

well-to-do, prosperous, moneyed, propertied; *informal* well heeled, filthy rich, loaded, made of money, rolling in it/money, flush, worth a packet/bundle, on Easy Street. **2** OPULENT, expensive, costly, precious, valuable, priceless, beyond price, lavish, luxurious, lush, sumptuous, palatial, splendid, superb, resplendent, elegant, fine, exquisite, magnificent, grand, gorgeous. **3** WELL PROVIDED, well supplied, well stocked, abounding, overflowing, replete, rife. **4** FERTILE, productive, fecund, fruitful, lush. **5** CREAMY, fatty, heavy. ■ OPPOSITES poor, plain, barren.

riches pl. n. WEALTH, affluence, prosperity, money, capital, property, treasure, assets, resources.

richly adv. **1** EXPENSIVELY, lavishly, lux-

ricotta n. a soft white Italian cheese.

rictus n. a fixed grimace or grin.

rid v. (**ridding, rid**) **1** (**rid of**) free of an unwanted person or thing. **2** (**be/get rid of**) be freed or relieved of.

riddance n. (**good riddance**) expressing relief at being rid of someone or something.

riddle n. **1** a cleverly worded question asked as a game. **2** a puzzling person or thing. **3** a coarse sieve. ▶v. (**be riddled**) **1** have many holes. **2** be filled with something undesirable.

ride v. (**riding, rode**; past part. **ridden**) **1** sit on and control the movement of a horse, bicycle, etc. **2** travel in a vehicle. **3** be carried or supported by. ▶n. **1** an act of riding. **2** a roller coaster, roundabout, etc. ridden at a fair or amusement park. **3** a path for horse riding.

rider n. **1** a person who rides a horse, bicycle, etc. **2** an additional condition or statement.

ridge n. **1** a long narrow hilltop. **2** a narrow raised band. **3** a long region of high pressure. **4** the edge formed where the two slopes of a roof meet at the top. ■ **ridged** adj.

ridicule n. mockery or derision. ▶v. make fun of.

ridiculous adj. causing mockery or derision; absurd. ■ **ridiculously** adv.

rife adj. **1** widespread. **2** (**rife with**) full of.

riff n. a short repeated phrase in jazz etc.

riffle v. turn over pages quickly and casually.

riff-raff n. people considered socially unacceptable.

rifle n. a gun with a long barrel. ▶v. search through something hurriedly.

rift n. **1** a crack, split, or break. **2** a serious break in friendly relations. □ **rift valley** a steep-sided valley formed by subsidence of the earth's surface.

rig v. (**rigging, rigged**) **1** fit sails and rigging on a boat. **2** set up a device or structure. **3** arrange dishonestly to gain an advantage. ▶n. **1** the arrangement of a boat's sails and rigging. **2** an apparatus for a particular purpose. **3** an oil rig.

rigging n. the system of ropes etc. supporting a ship's masts and sails.

right adj. **1** of, on, or towards the side which is to the east when facing north. **2** morally good or justified. **3** factually correct. **4** most appropriate. **5** in a satisfactory, sound, or normal condition. **6** informal complete: *a right idiot*. ▶adv. **1** on or to the right side. **2** completely. **3** exactly; directly. **4** correctly. ▶n. **1** that which is morally right. **2** an entitlement to have or do something. **3** (**the right**) the right-hand side or direction. **4** a right turn. **5** a right-wing group or party. ▶v. **1** restore to a normal or upright position. **2** correct or make amends for. □ **by rights** if things were fair or correct. **in one's own right** as a result of one's own qualifications or efforts. **right angle** an angle of

uriously, sumptuously, palatially, splendidly, superbly, magnificently. **2** FULLY, in full measure, well, thoroughly, completely, amply, utterly. ■ OPPOSITES meanly.

rid v. DO AWAY WITH, remove, get rid of, dispense with, eliminate, dump, dispose of, unload, expel, eject, weed out, clear, cleanse, purge, purify.

riddle n. PUZZLE, poser, conundrum, brain-teaser, problem, enigma, mystery, question.

ride v. **1** SIT ON, mount, be mounted on, bestride, manage, control. **2** TRAVEL, go, move, progress. ▶n. **3** TRIP, outing, journey, jaunt; *informal* spin.

ridicule n. DERISION, mockery, laughter, scorn, jeering, gibing, teasing, taunting, chaff, banter, badinage, raillery, satire, sarcasm, irony; *informal* kidding, ribbing, ragging. ▶v. DERIDE, mock, laugh at, scoff at, scorn, jeer at, gibe at, make fun of, poke fun at, make a fool of, tease,

taunt, chaff; *informal* kid, rib, rag, take the mickey out of, send up.

ridiculous adj. **1** ABSURD, comical, funny, laughable, hilarious, humorous, droll, farcical, facetious, ludicrous, risible, derisory. **2** POINTLESS, senseless, foolish, inane, fatuous, nonsensical, mindless. **3** UNBELIEVABLE, incredible, outrageous, preposterous, shocking, monstrous. ■ OPPOSITES sensible.

rife adj. WIDESPREAD, common, prevalent, predominant, general, extensive, ubiquitous, universal, global, rampant.

rifle v. (**rifle through**) RANSACK, rummage through, go through, rake through, search.

rift n. **1** SPLIT, break, breach, fissure, cleft, crevice, gap, crack, cranny, slit. **2** DISAGREEMENT, fight, falling-out, breach, division, estrangement, schism, split, alienation, quarrel, altercation, conflict, feud; *informal* row.

rig[1] v. **1** (**rig out**) CLOTHE, dress, attire, ac-

90°, as in a corner of a square. **right away** immediately. **right-handed** using or done with the right hand. **right-hand man** an indispensable assistant. **right of way 1** the legal right to go through another's property. **2** a public path through another's property. **3** the right to proceed before another vehicle. **right-wing** conservative or reactionary. ■ **rightly** adv.

righteous adj. morally right or justifiable. ■ **righteousness** n.

rightful adj. **1** having a right to something. **2** just; fitting. ■ **rightfully** adv.

rigid adj. **1** unable to bend. **2** strict or inflexible. ■ **rigidity** n. **rigidly** adv.

rigmarole n. a long, complicated procedure.

rigor mortis n. stiffening of the body after death.

rigour (US **rigor**) n. **1** thoroughness and accuracy. **2** strictness or severity. **3** (**rigours**) harsh conditions. ■ **rigorous** adj. **rigorously** adv.

rile v. informal annoy.

rill n. a small stream.

rim n. an edge or border, esp. of something circular. ▶ v. (**rimming, rimmed**) provide with a rim.

rime n. literary frost.

rind n. a tough outer layer on fruit, cheese, or bacon.

ring¹ n. **1** a small circular band worn on a finger. **2** a circular band, object, or mark. **3** an enclosed space in which a sport or show takes place. **4** a group working together illegally or secretly. ▶ v. **1** surround. **2** draw a circle round. ◻ **ringleader** a person who leads others in crime or causing trouble. **ringlet** a corkscrew-shaped curl of hair. **ringworm** a skin disease causing small circular itchy patches.

ring² v. (**ringing, rang;** past part. **rung**) **1** make a clear resonating sound. **2** (**ring with**) echo with a sound. **3** call by telephone. **4** (**ring off**) end a telephone call. **5** call for attention by sounding a bell. ▶ n. **1** an act of ringing. **2** a loud clear sound or tone. **3** a telephone call. **4** a quality conveyed by words: *a ring of truth.*

rink n. **1** an enclosed area of ice for skating etc. **2** a smooth enclosed floor for roller skating.

rinse v. wash with clean water to remove soap or dirt. ▶ n. **1** an act of rinsing. **2** a mouthwash. **3** a liquid for conditioning or colouring the hair.

riot n. **1** a violent disturbance by a crowd. **2** a confused combination or display. **3** informal a very amusing person

Thesaurus

coutre, array, deck, bedeck, drape. **2** (**rig up**) PUT TOGETHER, erect, assemble, throw together, cobble together.

rig² v. FALSIFY, fake, tamper with, doctor, engineer, manipulate.

right adj. **1** JUST, fair, equitable, impartial, good, upright, righteous, virtuous, proper, moral, ethical, honourable, honest, principled, lawful, legal. **2** CORRECT, accurate, unerring, exact, precise, valid; *informal* on the mark; *informal* spot on, bang on. **3** SUITABLE, appropriate, fit, proper, desirable, ideal, opportune, favourable, convenient, propitious. **4** RIGHT-HAND, dextral; *Nautical* starboard; *Heraldry* dexter. **5** CONSERVATIVE, right-wing, Tory, reactionary. ■ OPPOSITES wrong, left. ▶ n. **1** LAWFULNESS, legality, goodness, righteousness, virtue, virtuousness, integrity, rectitude, propriety, justice, justness, fairness, equity, equitableness. **2** PREROGATIVE, privilege, authority, power, licence, permission, entitlement. ▶ v. PUT TO RIGHTS, sort out, straighten out, rectify, fix, put in order, repair.

righteous adj. GOOD, virtuous, upright, moral, ethical, law-abiding, honest, honourable, pure, noble, God-fearing. ■ OPPOSITES sinful.

rigid adj. **1** STIFF, hard, taut, inflexible, unbendable, unbending, unyielding, inelastic, non-pliant. **2** STRICT, severe, stern, stringent, rigorous, austere, spartan, harsh, inflexible, intransigent, uncompromising. ■ OPPOSITES flexible.

rigorous adj. **1** METICULOUS, painstaking, thorough, laborious, scrupulous, conscientious, nice, exact, precise, accurate. **2** HARSH, severe, bad, bleak, extreme, inclement. ■ OPPOSITES slapdash, mild.

rim n. BRIM, edge, lip, circumference, border, verge, margin, brink.

rind n. OUTER LAYER, peel, skin, husk, crust.

ring¹ n. **1** BAND, circle, loop, circuit, halo, disc, round. **2** ARENA, enclosure, area. **3** GANG, syndicate, cartel, association, league. ▶ v. CIRCLE, encircle, circumscribe, encompass, loop, gird, enclose, surround, hem in, fence in, seal off.

ring² n. **1** RINGING, tolling, peal, pealing, knell, chime, clang, tinkle. **2** CALL, telephone call, phone call; *informal* phone, buzz. ▶ v. **1** TOLL, peal, sound, chime, or thing. ▶ v. take part in a riot. □ **run riot** behave in a violent and uncontrolled way. ■ **rioter** n. **riotous** adj.

RIP abbrev. rest in peace (used on graves).

rip v. (**ripping, ripped**) **1** tear or become torn. **2** pull forcibly away. **3** move rapidly. ▶ n. a long tear. □ **let rip** informal act or speak without restraint. **ripcord** a cord pulled to open a parachute. **rip-off** informal an overpriced article. **rip off** informal **1** cheat someone. **2** steal.

ripe adj. **1** ready for harvesting and eating. **2** (of a cheese) fully matured. **3** (**ripe for**) ready for. **4** (of age) advanced. ■ **ripen** v. **ripeness** n.

riposte n. a quick reply.

ripple n. **1** a small wave. **2** a feeling or effect that spreads through someone or something. ▶ v. form ripples.

rise v. (**rising, rose**; past part. **risen**) **1** come or go up. **2** get up from lying, sitting, or kneeling. **3** increase in number, size, intensity, etc. **4** (of land) slope upwards. **5** (of the sun etc.) appear above the horizon. **6** reach a higher rank or position. **7** rebel. **8** (of a river) have its source. ▶ n. **1** an act of rising. **2** an upward slope. **3** a pay increase.

risible adj. causing laughter. ■ **risibly** adv.

risk n. **1** the possibility of being exposed to danger or loss. **2** a person or thing causing this. ▶ v. **1** expose to danger or loss. **2** act in such a way that something bad could happen.

risky adj. (**riskier, riskiest**) involving risk. ■ **riskily** adv. **riskiness** n.

risotto n. (pl. **risottos**) a dish of rice cooked in stock with other ingredients.

risqué /riss-kay/ adj. slightly indecent.

rissole n. a small cake of minced meat, coated in breadcrumbs and fried.

rite n. a ritual.

ritual n. a religious or solemn ceremony involving a set series of actions. ▶ adj. of or done as a ritual. ■ **ritualistic** adj. **ritually** adv.

rival n. a person or thing competing with or equal to another. ▶ v. (**rivalling, rivalled**; US **rivaling, rivaled**) be comparable to. ■ **rivalry** n.

riven adj. torn apart.

river n. **1** a large natural flow of water. **2** a large quantity of a flowing substance.

rivet n. a short bolt for holding together two metal plates. ▶ v. (**riveting, riveted**) **1** fasten with a rivet or rivets. **2** (**be riveted**) be completely engrossed.

rivulet n. a small stream.

RN abbrev. Royal Navy.

Thesaurus

ding, ding-dong, clang, tinkle. **2** CALL, telephone, phone; informal buzz.

rinse v. WASH, wash out, clean, sluice, flush, drench.

riot n. STREET FIGHT, commotion, disturbance, uproar, tumult, melee, scuffle, fracas, fray, brawl, free-for-all, uprising, insurrection. ▶ v. RUN RIOT, rampage, go on the rampage, run wild/amok, go berserk, fight, brawl, take to the streets.

riotous adj. **1** DISORDERLY, uncontrollable, ungovernable, unmanageable, rowdy, wild, violent, brawling, lawless, anarchic, rebellious, mutinous. **2** LOUD, noisy, boisterous, uproarious, rollicking, orgiastic. **3** HILARIOUS, funny, uproarious, side-splitting. ■ OPPOSITES peaceable.

ripe adj. **1** MATURE, developed, full grown, ready to eat, ready, mellow, seasoned, tempered. **2** READY, fit, suitable, right. ■ OPPOSITES immature.

ripen v. MATURE, come to maturity, develop, mellow.

riposte n. RETORT, rejoinder, reply, response, sally; informal comeback.

rise v. **1** ARISE, come/go up, move up, ascend, climb up. **2** RISE UP, tower, soar, loom, rear up. **3** GO UP, get higher, increase, soar, rocket, escalate. **4** STAND UP, get to one's feet, get up, jump up. **5** GET UP, get out of bed, wake up, surface. ■ OPPOSITES fall. ▶ n. **1** INCLINE, elevation, slope, acclivity, rising ground, hillock, hill. **2** INCREASE, escalation, upsurge, upswing.

risk n. **1** CHANCE, possibility. **2** DANGER, peril, jeopardy. ▶ v. **1** PUT AT RISK, endanger, imperil, jeopardize. **2** TAKE THE RISK OF, chance, venture. **3** BET, gamble, hazard, chance, venture.

risky adj. DANGEROUS, hazardous, perilous, unsafe, precarious, touch-and-go, tricky, uncertain; informal chancy, dicey, dodgy.

rite n. RITUAL, ceremony, ceremonial, observance, service, sacrament, celebration, performance, act, practice, tradition, convention, formality, procedure, usage.

rival n. OPPONENT, opposition, adversary, antagonist, contestant, competitor, challenger, contender. ■ OPPOSITES ally. ▶ v. COMPETE WITH, vie with, match, equal, emulate, measure up to, compare with, parallel. ▶ adj. OPPOSING, compet-

RNA n. ribonucleic acid, a substance in living cells which carries instructions from DNA.

road n. **1** a wide track with a hard surface for vehicles to travel on. **2** a way to achieving a particular outcome. □ **road hog** informal a reckless or inconsiderate motorist. **road rage** violent anger caused by conflict with another driver. **roadway 1** a road. **2** the part of a road intended for vehicles. **roadworks** repairs to roads. **roadworthy** (of a vehicle) fit to be used on the road.

roadie n. informal a person who sets up equipment for a touring pop or rock group.

roadster n. an open-top sports car.

roam v. wander.

roan adj. (of a horse) having a dark coat interspersed with white hairs.

roar n. **1** a long, deep sound as made by a lion, engine, etc. **2** a loud sound of laughter. ▶v. **1** make a roar. **2** laugh loudly. **3** (esp. of a vehicle) move very fast.

roaring adj. informal complete: *a roaring success*.

roast v. **1** cook meat etc. in an oven or over a fire. **2** process coffee beans etc. with intense heat. **3** make or become very warm. ▶adj. (of food) having been roasted. ▶n. a roast joint of meat.

rob v. (**robbing**, **robbed**) **1** steal from by force or threat of force. **2** unfairly deprive of. ■ **robber** n. **robbery** n.

robe n. a long loose outer garment for formal or ceremonial occasions. ▶v. dress in a robe.

robin n. a red-breasted songbird.

robot n. a machine capable of carrying out a complex series of actions auto-

matically. ■ **robotic** adj.

robotics n. the study of the design, construction, and use of robots.

robust adj. **1** sturdy. **2** healthy. **3** forceful.

rock n. **1** the hard material of the earth's crust. **2** a mass of this. **3** a hard sweet in the form of a cylindrical stick. **4** a form of loud popular music with a strong beat. **5** a rocking movement. ▶v. **1** move to and fro or from side to side. **2** shock or distress greatly. □ **on the rocks** informal **1** in difficulties and likely to fail. **2** (of a drink) served with ice cubes. **rock and roll** a type of popular dance music with a strong beat and simple melodies. **rock bottom** the lowest possible level. **rock plant** a plant that grows on or among rocks.

rocker n. **1** a person who performs or likes rock music. **2** a curved piece of wood on which something may rock.

rockery n. (pl. **rockeries**) a bank of rocks and soil planted with rock plants.

rocket n. **1** a cylindrical missile or spacecraft propelled by a stream of burning gases. **2** a firework that shoots into the air and explodes. **3** informal a severe reprimand. ▶v. (**rocketing**, **rocketed**) move or increase very rapidly.

rocketry n. the design and construction of rockets.

rocky adj. (**rockier**, **rockiest**) **1** of rock. **2** full of rocks. **3** unsteady or unstable.

rococo adj. of an ornate style of furniture or architecture of the 18th century.

rod n. **1** a thin straight bar of wood, metal, etc. **2** a fishing rod.

rode past of RIDE.

rodent n. a mammal of a group with

Thesaurus

ing, in competition, contending, in conflict, conflicting.

rivalry n. OPPOSITION, competition, competitiveness, vying, contention, conflict.

road n. STREET, thoroughfare, highway.

roam v. WANDER, rove, ramble, meander, drift, range, travel, walk, tramp, traverse, trek, peregrinate.

roar v. BELLOW, yell, bawl, shout, howl, thunder, shriek, scream, cry, bay.

rob v. STEAL FROM, burgle, burglarize, hold up, break into, mug, defraud, swindle, cheat, mulct; informal rip off, diddle, bilk, do out of.

robber n. BURGLAR, thief, mugger, pilferer, housebreaker, looter, raider, bandit, brigand, pirate, highwayman.

robbery n. THEFT, burglary, stealing,

housebreaking, larceny, pilfering, embezzlement, misappropriation, swindling, fraud, mugging, hold-up, break-in, raid; informal filching.

robe n. **1** VESTMENT, habit, costume, gown. **2** DRESSING GOWN, housecoat, wrapper, peignoir.

robust adj. STURDY, tough, rugged, strong, healthy, vigorous, hale and hearty, muscular, powerful, strapping, burly. ■ OPPOSITES weak.

rock¹ v. **1** MOVE TO AND FRO, swing, sway, roll, lurch, pitch. **2** STUN, shock, stagger, astound, astonish, dumbfound, shake, take aback.

rock² n. BOULDER, stone.

rocky¹ adj. ROCK-STREWN, stony, pebbly, rough.

large front teeth.

rodeo n. (pl. **rodeos**) a contest or entertainment in which cowboys show their skills.

roe n. **1** the eggs of a fish, eaten as food. **2** (pl. **roe** or **roes**) a small deer.

roentgen /runt-yuhn/ n. a unit of ionizing radiation.

rogue n. **1** a dishonest or mischievous person. **2** an elephant living apart from the herd.

roguish adj. playfully mischievous.

roister v. enjoy oneself or celebrate noisily.

role n. **1** an actor's part. **2** a person's or thing's function.

roll v. **1** move by turning over and over. **2** move on wheels or with a smooth, wave-like motion. **3** (of a ship, aircraft, etc.) sway from side to side. **4** turn something flexible over and over on itself to form a cylinder or ball. **5** flatten with a roller. **6** (of a deep sound) reverberate. ▶ n. **1** a cylinder formed by rolling flexible material. **2** a rolling movement. **3** a reverberating sound. **4** a very small loaf of bread. **5** an official list or register of names. □ **roll-call** the reading aloud of a list of names to check who is present. **rolled gold** a thin coating of gold on another metal. **rolling pin** a cylinder for rolling out dough. **rolling stock** locomotives, carriages, and other railway vehicles. **rollmop** a rolled uncooked pickled herring fillet. **roll-on roll-off** (of a ferry) in which vehicles are driven directly on and off.

roller n. **1** a rotating cylinder used to move, flatten, or spread something. **2** a small cylinder on which hair is wound to produce curls. **3** a long swelling wave. □ **roller coaster** a railway at a fairground with a steep, twisting track. **roller skate** a boot with wheels, for gliding across a hard surface.

rollicking adj. very lively and amusing.

roly-poly n. a pudding of suet pastry spread with jam, rolled up, and steamed or baked. ▶ adj. informal plump.

ROM abbrev. Computing read-only memory.

Roman adj. of ancient Rome or its empire or people. ▶ n. **1** an inhabitant of Rome. **2** (**roman**) plain upright type. □ **Roman Catholic** (a member of) the part of the Christian Church which has the Pope as its head **Roman numeral** each of the letters used as numbers in the ancient Roman system.

romance n. **1** a feeling of excitement associated with love. **2** a love affair. **3** a book or film dealing with love. **4** a feeling of mystery and excitement. **5** (**Romance**) the group of languages descended from Latin. ▶ v. try to gain the love of.

Romanesque adj. of a style of architecture common in Europe c.900–1200.

romantic adj. **1** of love or romance. **2** showing or expecting life in an unrealistic and idealized way. **3** (**Romantic**) of Romanticism. ▶ n. **1** a romantic person. **2** (**Romantic**) a writer or artist of the Romantic movement. ■ **romantically** adv.

Romanticism n. a literary and artistic movement which emphasized creative inspiration and emotion.

romanticize (or **-ise**) v. regard or represent as more appealing than in reality.

Romany n. (pl. **Romanies**) **1** the language of the Gypsies. **2** a Gypsy.

romp v. **1** play about roughly and energetically. **2** informal do something easily.

rondeau n. (pl. **rondeaux**) a short poem with the opening words used as a refrain.

rondo n. (pl. **rondos**) a piece of music

Thesaurus

rocky² adj. UNSTEADY, unstable, shaky, tottering, teetering, wobbly. ■ OPPOSITES steady, stable.

rod n. BAR, stick, pole, baton, staff.

rogue n. VILLAIN, scoundrel, rascal, reprobate, swindler, fraudster, cheat, deceiver, confidence trickster, charlatan, mountebank, sharper, wretch, ne'er-do-well, wastrel, good-for-nothing, crook; informal, dated rotter, bounder; dated cad; old use blackguard.

role n. **1** PART, character, representation, portrayal. **2** CAPACITY, function, position, place, situation, job, post, task.

roll v. **1** GO ROUND, turn, turn round, rotate, revolve, spin, whirl, wheel. **2** FURL, coil, fold. **3** PASS, go, flow, travel. **4** FLATTEN, level, smooth, even, press down, crush. ▶ n. **1** TURN, rotation, revolution, spin, whirl. **2** SPOOL, reel, bobbin, cylinder. **3** REGISTER, list, file, index, roster, directory, catalogue.

romance n. **1** FANTASY, fancy, whimsy, fabrication, glamour, mystery, legend, fairy tale, idyll. **2** LOVE AFFAIR, affair, liaison, attachment, intrigue, courtship, amour.

romantic adj. **1** LOVING, amorous, passionate, fond, tender, sentimental, sloppy; informal mushy, soppy. **2** UNREALISwith a recurring theme.

rood screen n. a screen separating the nave from the chancel of a church.

roof n. (pl. **roofs**) the upper covering of a building, vehicle, etc. ▶v. cover with a roof.

rook n. **1** a bird of the crow family. **2** a chess piece that can move in any direction.

rookery n. (pl. **rookeries**) a colony of rooks.

room n. **1** a part of a building enclosed by walls, a floor, and a ceiling. **2** space for holding things or moving in. **3** scope.

roomy adj. (**roomier, roomiest**) having plenty of space.

roost n. a place where birds regularly settle to rest. ▶v. (of a bird) settle for rest.

rooster n. a male domestic fowl.

root n. **1** the part of a plant below ground, which collects water and nourishment. **2** the embedded part of hair, a tooth, etc. **3** the basic cause or origin. **4** (**roots**) family, ethnic, or cultural origins. **5** a number that when multiplied by itself one or more times gives a specified number. ▶v. **1** cause to establish roots. **2** (**be rooted**) stand still through fear or wonder. **3** (**root out/up**) find and get rid of. **4** (of an animal) turn up the ground with its snout in search of food. **5** (**root for**) informal support enthusiastically. **6** rummage. □ **take root** become established. ▪ **rootless** adj.

rope n. **1** strong thick cord. **2** (**the ropes**) informal the established procedure. ▶v. **1** catch, tie, or fence off with rope. **2** (**rope in**) persuade to take part in something. □ **on the ropes** in a state of near collapse.

rosary n. (pl. **rosaries**) **1** (in the RC Church) a set series of prayers. **2** a string of beads for keeping count of prayers said.

rose[1] n. **1** a fragrant flower growing on a prickly bush. **2** a warm pink colour. □ **rosewood** a dark fragrant wood of a tropical tree, used for making furniture.

rose[2] past of RISE.

rosé /roh-zay/ n. light pink wine.

rosemary n. an evergreen shrub with leaves used as a herb.

rosette n. a round badge made of ribbon.

rosin n. a kind of resin.

roster n. a list of people's names and their turns of duty etc.

rostrum n. (pl. **rostra** or **rostrums**) a platform for standing on to make a speech, conduct an orchestra, etc.

rosy adj. (**rosier, rosiest**) **1** pink. **2** promising.

rot v. (**rotting, rotted**) break down as a result of bacterial action. ▶n. **1** the process or state of rotting. **2** informal nonsense.

rota n. a list showing times and names for people to take their turn to perform duties.

rotary adj. **1** rotating. **2** having a rotating part or parts.

rotate v. **1** move in a circle round a central point. **2** arrange or be dealt with in a regularly recurring order. ▪ **rotation** n. **rotatory** adj.

rote n. regular repetition of something to be learned.

rotisserie n. a rotating spit for roasting meat.

rotor n. the rotating part of a machine.

rotten adj. **1** decayed. **2** corrupt. **3** informal very bad.

Thesaurus

TIC, idealistic, visionary, utopian, starry-eyed, optimistic, hopeful. **3** FASCINATING, mysterious, glamorous, exotic, exciting. ▶n. DREAMER, visionary, idealist, utopian. ▪ OPPOSITES realist.

room n. **1** SPACE, area, territory, expanse, extent, volume, elbow room. **2** SCOPE, capacity, margin, leeway, latitude, occasion, opportunity.

roomy adj. SPACIOUS, commodious, capacious, voluminous, ample, generous, sizeable, large, broad, wide, extensive. ▪ OPPOSITES cramped.

root n. **1** ROOTSTOCK, tuber, tap root; Botany rhizome, radicle. **2** SOURCE, origin, starting point, basis, foundation, beginnings, seat, cause, reason, rationale, oc-

casion; formal radix. ▶v. TAKE ROOT, grow roots, become established, set.

rope n. CORD, cable, line, strand, hawser.

roster n. LIST, listing, rota, roll, register, schedule, agenda, calendar, directory, index, table.

rot v. **1** DECOMPOSE, decay, crumble, disintegrate, corrode, perish. **2** GO BAD, spoil, go sour, putrefy, fester; informal go off. ▶n. **1** DECOMPOSITION, decay, disintegration, corrosion, putrefaction, mould, blight. **2** RUBBISH, nonsense, claptrap, drivel; informal bosh, twaddle, poppycock, guff, tosh, codswallop; informal, dated bunkum, bunk.

rotary adj. ROTATING, rotational, revolving, rotatory, turning, gyrating,

Rottweiler n. a large powerful breed of dog.

rotund adj. rounded and plump. ■ **rotundity** n.

rotunda n. a round building or room.

rouble (or **ruble**) n. the basic unit of money of Russia.

rouge n. a cosmetic for colouring the cheeks.

rough adj. **1** not smooth or level. **2** not gentle. **3** (of weather or the sea) wild and stormy. **4** plain and basic. **5** harsh in sound or taste. **6** unsophisticated. **7** not detailed; approximate. **8** informal difficult and unpleasant. ▶ n. **1** a basic version. **2** long grass at the edge of a golf course. ▶ v. **1** (**rough out**) make a rough version of. **2** (**rough it**) informal live with only very basic necessities. **3** (**rough up**) informal beat up. □ **rough and ready** basic but effective. **rough and tumble** a competitive situation without rules. **rough diamond** a person of good character but lacking manners or education. ■ **roughen** v. **roughly** adv. **roughness** n.

roughage n. indigestible material in cereals, vegetables, and fruit.

roughshod adj. (**ride roughshod over**) fail to consider the wishes or feelings of.

roulette n. a gambling game in which a ball is dropped on to a revolving wheel with numbered compartments.

round adj. **1** curved, circular, cylindrical, or spherical. **2** (of a number) expressed in convenient units rather than exactly. ▶ n. **1** a circular shape or piece.

2 a route by which a number of people or places are visited in turn. **3** a regular sequence of activities. **4** each of a sequence of stages in a sports contest. **5** a song for several voices, each singing the same theme but starting one after another. **6** the amount of ammunition needed to fire one shot. ▶ adv. **1** in a circle or curve. **2** so as to include a whole area or group. **3** so as to turn in the opposite direction. **4** so as to surround. ▶ prep. **1** on every side of. **2** so as to encircle. ▶ v. **1** pass and go round. **2** make a figure less exact but more convenient. **3** make or become round in shape. □ **round off** complete. **round robin** a tournament in which each competitor plays in turn against every other. **round trip** a journey to a place and back again. **round-up** a summary. **round up** collect into one place. **roundworm** a parasitic worm with a rounded body. ■ **roundness** n.

roundabout n. **1** a road junction with a circular island round which traffic has to move in one direction. **2** a large revolving device in a playground. **3** a merry-go-round. ▶ adj. indirect.

roundel n. a small disc.

rounders n. a ball game in which players run round a circuit after hitting the ball with a bat.

Roundhead n. hist. a supporter of Parliament in the English Civil War.

roundly adv. **1** in a firm or thorough way. **2** in a circular shape.

rouse v. **1** wake. **2** stir to action or excitement.

Thesaurus

gyratory, spinning, whirling.

rotate v. **1** GO ROUND, move round, turn, revolve, spin, whirl, swivel, reel, wheel, gyrate. **2** ALTERNATE, take turns, take in turn.

rotten adj. **1** BAD, off, mouldy, mouldering, spoiled, tainted, sour, rancid, rank, decaying, decomposed, putrid, putrescent, festering, fetid, stinking. **2** NASTY, foul, mean, bad, dirty, filthy, contemptible, despicable. ■ OPPOSITES fresh, kind.

rough adj. **1** UNEVEN, irregular, bumpy, broken, stony, rugged, craggy, lumpy, nodulous. **2** BOISTEROUS, rowdy, disorderly, wild, violent, savage. **3** TURBULENT, tumultuous, choppy. **4** STORMY, squally, wild, tempestuous, wintry. **5** COARSE, crude, uncouth, vulgar, unrefined, loutish, boorish, churlish, brutish, ill-mannered, unmannerly, impol-

ite, discourteous, uncivil. **6** HARSH, severe, hard, tough, difficult, unpleasant, disagreeable, nasty, cruel. **7** ROUGH AND READY, hasty, quick, cursory, crude, incomplete, rudimentary, basic. **8** APPROXIMATE, inexact, imprecise, vague, hazy. **9** ILL, sick, unwell, unhealthy, below par, off colour. ■ OPPOSITES smooth, exact.

round adj. **1** CIRCULAR, ring-shaped, cycloid, discoid, disk-like, cylindrical, spherical, spheroid, ball-shaped, globe-like, convex, curved. **2** WELL ROUNDED, ample, rotund, chubby, buxom, roly-poly, tubby, portly, stout, corpulent, fat, obese; informal podgy. ▶ n. **1** SUCCESSION, sequence, series, cycle. **2** CIRCUIT, course, beat, routine, schedule. **3** STAGE, level, division, lap, heat. ▶ v. GO ROUND, travel round, sail round, circumnavigate.

rout n. **1** a disorderly retreat. **2** a decisive defeat. ▶ v. defeat decisively.

route n. a way taken in getting from a starting point to a destination.

routine n. **1** a regular procedure. **2** a set sequence in a performance. ▶ adj. performed as part of a regular procedure. ■ **routinely** adv.

roux /roo/ n. (pl. **roux**) a mixture of butter and flour used in making sauces.

rove v. wander. ■ **rover** n.

row[1] /roh/ n. **1** a number of people or things in a line. **2** a period of rowing. ▶ v. propel a boat with oars.

row[2] /row/ n. **1** an angry quarrel. **2** a loud noise. ▶ v. quarrel angrily.

rowan n. a small tree with red berries.

rowdy adj. (**rowdier**, **rowdiest**) noisy and disorderly. ▶ n. (pl. **rowdies**) a rowdy person. ■ **rowdily** adv. **rowdiness** n.

rowlock /rol-luhk/ n. a fitting on the side of a boat for holding an oar.

royal adj. **1** of or having the status of a king or queen or a member of their family. **2** splendid. ▶ n. informal a member of the royal family. □ **royal blue** a deep, vivid blue. ■ **royally** adv.

royalist n. a person supporting the principle of having a king or queen.

royalty n. (pl. **royalties**) **1** people of royal status. **2** the status of a king or queen. **3** a sum paid to the author of a book for each copy sold or to a composer for each performance of a work.

rpm abbrev. revolutions per minute.

RSI abbrev. repetitive strain injury.

RSPCA abbrev. Royal Society for the Pre-

vention of Cruelty to Animals.

RSVP abbrev. répondez s'il vous plaît; please reply.

rub v. (**rubbing**, **rubbed**) **1** move one's hand, a cloth, etc. back and forth over a surface while pressing against it. **2** dry, smooth, or make sore by rubbing. **3** (**rub out**) erase pencil marks with a rubber. ▶ n. **1** an act of rubbing. **2** an ointment for rubbing on the skin.

rubber n. **1** a tough elastic substance made from a tropical plant or from chemicals. **2** a piece of this for erasing pencil marks. **3** a unit of play in the card game bridge. □ **rubber-stamp** approve automatically without proper consideration. ■ **rubbery** adj.

rubbish n. **1** waste material. **2** nonsense.

rubble n. rough fragments of stone, brick, etc.

rubella n. a viral disease with symptoms like mild measles.

rubidium n. a soft metallic element.

ruble var. of ROUBLE.

rubric n. **1** a document heading. **2** a set of instructions.

ruby n. (pl. **rubies**) **1** a deep red precious stone. **2** a deep red colour. □ **ruby wedding** the 40th anniversary of a wedding.

ruche /roosh/ n. a frill or pleat. ■ **ruched** adj.

ruck n. **1** Rugby a loose scrum. **2** a tightly packed crowd. ▶ v. (**ruck up**) make or form creases or folds.

rucksack n. a bag carried on the back.

ructions pl. n. informal angry protests or

Thesaurus

roundabout adj. INDIRECT, circuitous, meandering, winding, tortuous, discursive, oblique, circumlocutory, periphrastic. ■ OPPOSITES direct.

rouse v. **1** WAKE, wake up, rise, call, get up. **2** STIR UP, excite, incite, egg on, induce, impel, inflame, agitate, whip up, galvanize, stimulate. ■ OPPOSITES calm, pacify.

rout v. DEFEAT, trounce, worst, conquer, subjugate, overthrow, crush, beat; informal lick, thrash, give someone a pasting. ■ OPPOSITES victory.

route n. COURSE, way, itinerary, road, path.

routine n. **1** PATTERN, procedure, practice, custom, habit, programme, schedule, formula, method, system, order. **2** ACT, performance, piece; informal spiel. ▶ adj. USUAL, normal, everyday, workaday, common, ordinary, typical, cus-

tomary, habitual, scheduled, conventional, standard. ■ OPPOSITES unusual.

row[1] n. LINE, column, queue, procession, chain, string; informal crocodile.

row[2] n. **1** ARGUMENT, dispute, disagreement, falling-out, controversy, quarrel, squabble, fight, conflict, altercation, wrangle; informal set-to, tiff. **2** NOISE, din, clamour, commotion, rumpus, uproar, tumult, hubbub, pandemonium.

rowdy adj. UNRULY, disorderly, noisy, boisterous, loud, obstreperous, wild, rough, unrestrained, lawless. ■ OPPOSITES quiet.

royal adj. KINGLY, queenly, kinglike, queenlike, princely, regal, monarchical, sovereign.

rub v. **1** MASSAGE, knead, stroke, caress, fondle. **2** SCRUB, scour, wipe, clean. **3** CHAFE, pinch. □ **rub out** ERASE, wipe off, efface, obliterate, expunge, remove.

trouble.

rudder n. a hinged upright piece of wood or metal at the back of a boat or aircraft, used for steering.

ruddy adj. (**ruddier, ruddiest**) reddish.

rude adj. **1** impolite or bad-mannered. **2** referring to sex in an offensive way. **3** (of health) good. **4** dated roughly made. ∎ **rudely** adv. **rudeness** n.

rudiment n. **1** (**rudiments**) the basic facts of a subject. **2** an undeveloped part.

rudimentary adj. **1** basic or elementary. **2** not highly or fully developed.

rue v. bitterly regret.

rueful adj. expressing regret. ∎ **ruefully** adv.

ruff n. **1** a starched frill worn round the neck. **2** a ring of feathers or hair round the neck of a bird or mammal.

ruffian n. a violent person.

ruffle v. **1** disturb the smooth surface of. **2** upset the composure of. ▸ n. a gathered frill.

rug n. **1** a small carpet. **2** a thick blanket.

rugby n. a team game played with an oval ball that may be kicked or carried.

rugged adj. **1** rocky or uneven. **2** (of a man) having strong, attractive features. ∎ **ruggedly** adv.

rugger n. informal rugby.

ruin n. **1** destruction. **2** (also **ruins**) the damaged remains of a building. **3** the complete loss of a person's money and property. ▸ v. **1** destroy. **2** make bankrupt or very poor. ∎ **ruination** n.

ruinous adj. **1** disastrous or destructive. **2** in ruins.

rule n. **1** a statement of what must be done or not done. **2** authority and control. **3** a ruler for measuring with. ▸ v. **1** have authority and control over. **2** decide or state with legal authority. **3** make lines on paper. □ **as a rule** usually. **rule of thumb** a rough guide. **rule out** exclude.

ruler n. **1** a person who rules. **2** a straight strip of plastic, wood, etc. for drawing straight lines or measuring distances.

Thesaurus

rubbish n. **1** WASTE, refuse, litter, lumber, junk, debris, detritus, dross, rubble, sweepings, leavings, dregs, offscourings; US garbage, trash. **2** see NONSENSE.

rude adj. **1** ILL-MANNERED, bad-mannered, mannerless, impolite, discourteous, impertinent, insolent, impudent, uncivil, disrespectful, churlish, curt, brusque, blunt, offhand, short, offensive. **2** VULGAR, coarse, indelicate, smutty, dirty, naughty, risqué, ribald, bawdy, licentious; informal blue. **3** PRIMITIVE, crude, rudimentary, rough, rough-hewn, simple. ∎ OPPOSITES polite.

rudimentary adj. **1** ELEMENTARY, basic, fundamental, introductory, early, primitive, crude, rough, simple. **2** UNDEVELOPED, immature, incomplete, vestigial.

rudiments pl. n. BASICS, fundamentals, beginnings, elements, essentials, foundation; informal nuts and bolts.

rueful adj. REGRETFUL, apologetic, sorry, remorseful, contrite, repentant, penitent, woebegone, woeful, plaintive.

ruffle v. **1** RUMPLE, dishevel, tousle, disarrange, discompose, disorder, derange, tangle, mess up; informal muss up. **2** FLUSTER, agitate, harass, upset, disturb, discompose, perturb, unsettle, disconcert, worry, alarm, trouble, confuse, rattle, shake up. ∎ OPPOSITES smooth, soothe.

rugged adj. **1** ROUGH, uneven, irregular, bumpy, rocky, stony, broken up, jagged, craggy. **2** WRINKLED, furrowed, lined, gnarled, weather-beaten, leathery. **3** TOUGH, hardy, robust, sturdy, strong, vigorous, stalwart, hale and hearty, muscular, brawny. ∎ OPPOSITES smooth, flimsy.

ruin n. **1** DESTRUCTION, devastation, wreckage, demolition, disintegration, decay, disrepair. **2** RUINATION, loss, failure, bankruptcy, insolvency, penury, impoverishment, indigence, destitution, calamity, disaster. ▸ v. **1** DESTROY, devastate, lay waste, raze, demolish, damage, spoil, wreak havoc on. **2** BANKRUPT, make insolvent, impoverish, pauperize. ∎ OPPOSITES save.

ruined adj. IN RUINS, ruinous, dilapidated, decaying, in disrepair, derelict, ramshackle, decrepit.

ruinous adj. **1** DISASTROUS, devastating, calamitous, catastrophic, cataclysmic, dire, injurious, damaging, crippling. **2** see RUINED.

rule n. **1** RULING, law, regulation, statute, ordinance, tenet, order, decree, commandment, directive. **2** PRINCIPLE, precept, standard, axiom, maxim. **3** GOVERNMENT, administration, jurisdiction, reign, authority, control, direction, mastery, leadership, command. ▸ v. **1** PRESIDE OVER, govern, control, dominate, direct, administer, manage, regulate. **2** ORDER, decree, direct, pronounce,

ruling n. an authoritative decision or statement.

rum n. an alcoholic spirit made from sugar cane or molasses. ▶adj. informal, dated peculiar.

rumba n. a ballroom dance.

rumble v. **1** make a low continuous sound. **2** informal find out the truth about. ▶n. a rumbling sound.

rumbustious adj. informal boisterous.

ruminant n. a mammal that chews the cud.

ruminate v. **1** think deeply. **2** chew the cud. ■ **rumination** n. **ruminative** adj.

rummage v. search in a disorderly way. ▶n. an act of rummaging.

rummy n. a card game.

rumour (US **rumor**) n. a story spread among a number of people which is unconfirmed or may be false. ▶v. (**be rumoured**) be spread as a rumour.

rump n. the hind part of the body of a mammal or the lower back of a bird.

rumple v. make untidy.

rumpus n. (pl. **rumpuses**) a noisy disturbance.

run v. (**running, ran**; past part. **run**) **1** move at a speed faster than walking. **2** move smoothly. **3** (of a bus, train, etc.) travel on a particular route. **4** be in charge of. **5** continue or proceed. **6** function or cause to function. **7** (of a liquid) flow or spread. **8** stand as a candidate in an election. **9** smuggle goods. ▶n. **1** an act or spell of running. **2** a journey or route. **3** a continuous period or sequence. **4** an enclosed area in which animals or birds may run freely. **5** (**the run of**) unrestricted use of or access to a place. **6** a point scored in cricket or baseball. **7** a ladder in tights etc. □ **in** (or **out of**) **the running** in (or no longer in) with a chance of success. **on the run** escaping. **run down 1** criticize. **2** reduce in size or resources. **run-down 1** in a poor or neglected state. **2** tired and rather unwell. **run into** meet by chance. **run off** produce a copy on a machine. **run-of-the-mill** ordinary. **run out** use up or be used up. **run over** knock down with a vehicle. **run up** allow it fall, score, etc. to build up. **run-up** the period of preparation before an important event. **runway** a strip of hard ground where aircraft take off and land.

rune n. a letter of an ancient Germanic alphabet. ■ **runic** adj.

rung[1] n. a horizontal bar on a ladder.

rung[2] past part. of **RING**[2].

runner n. **1** a person or animal that runs. **2** a messenger. **3** a rod, groove, or roller on which something slides. **4** a creeping shoot of a plant which can take root. **5** a long, narrow rug. □ **runner-up** (pl. **runners-up**) a competitor or team coming second in a contest.

runny adj. (**runnier, runniest**) **1** semiliquid. **2** (of the nose) producing mucus.

runt n. the smallest animal in a litter.

rupee n. the basic unit of money of India, Pakistan, etc.

rupture v. **1** break or burst suddenly. **2** suffer an abdominal hernia. ▶n. **1** an instance of rupturing. **2** an abdominal hernia.

rural adj. of, in, or like the countryside.

ruse n. a trick or deception.

rush v. **1** move or act with great speed or

Thesaurus

make a judgement, judge, adjudge, adjudicate, lay down, decide, determine, resolve, settle, establish. □ **rule out** see EXCLUDE (2).

ruling n. JUDGEMENT, adjudication, finding, verdict, resolution, decree, pronouncement.

rumour n. REPORT, story, whisper, word, news, tidings, gossip, hearsay, talk. ▶v. SAY, report.

run v. **1** RACE, rush, hasten, hurry, dash, sprint, bolt, dart, gallop, career along, tear along, charge along, speed along, jog along; informal scoot, hare, step on it, hotfoot it. **2** MOVE, go, get along, travel. **3** GLIDE, course, roll, slide. **4** OPERATE, be in operation, be valid, be current, continue. **5** GO, continue, proceed, extend, stretch. **6** FLOW, issue, stream, pour,

gush, cascade, spurt, jet, trickle, leak. **7** OWN, operate, conduct, carry on, direct, manage, administer, be in charge of, control, head, lead, look after, organize, coordinate, supervise, superintend, oversee. ▶n. **1** JOG, sprint, dash, gallop, canter, headlong rush, scamper. **2** DRIVE, ride, trip, outing, excursion, jaunt, short journey; informal spin. **3** SPELL, stretch, streak, chain, string, round, cycle, sequence, series, succession. □ **run after** see PURSUE. **run into** see MEET.

runner n. **1** RACER, sprinter, hurdler, harrier, jogger, athlete. **2** BRANCH, shoot, offshoot, tendril.

rupture n. BREAK, fracture, crack, split, burst, rent, tear, rift, fissure. ▶v. **1** BREAK, fracture, crack, split, breach, haste. **2** produce, deal with, or transport with urgent haste. **3** dash towards in a sudden attack. ▶n. **1** a sudden quick movement. **2** a very busy spell of activity. **3** a sudden strong feeling. **4** a water plant used in making baskets etc. □ **rush hour** a time at the start and end of the working day when traffic is at its heaviest.

rusk n. a biscuit for babies.

russet n. a reddish-brown colour.

rust n. a reddish-brown flaky coating formed on iron exposed to moisture. ▶v. be affected with rust.

rustic adj. **1** of or like life in the country. **2** simple and charming.

rustle v. **1** make or move with a soft crackling sound. **2** steal cattle, horses, or sheep. **3** (**rustle up**) informal produce food or a drink quickly. ▶n. a rustling sound. ■ **rustler** n.

rusty adj. **1** affected by rust. **2** (of knowledge or a skill) weakened by lack of recent practice.

rut n. **1** a deep track made by wheels. **2** a habitual dull pattern of behaviour. **3** an annual period of sexual activity in deer etc., when males fight for access to the females. ▶v. (**rutting**, **rutted**) engage in such activity.

ruthless adj. having no pity; hard and determined. ■ **ruthlessly** adv. **ruthlessness** n.

rye n. **1** a cereal plant. **2** whisky made from rye. □ **ryegrass** a grass used for animal fodder.

Thesaurus

burst, rend, tear, puncture. **2** SEVER, cut off, break off, disrupt, breach.

rural adj. COUNTRY, rustic, bucolic, pastoral, agricultural, agrarian, Arcadian. ■ OPPOSITES urban.

rush v. HURRY, hasten, run, race, dash, sprint, bolt, dart, gallop, career, tear, charge, speed, scurry, scamper; informal step on it, get a move on, hotfoot it. ▶n. **1** ONSLAUGHT, attack, assault, charge. **2** SURGE, flow, gush, stream, flood. **3** HURRY, haste, speed, swiftness, rapidity, dispatch.

rushed adj. HURRIED, hasty, speedy, quick, fast, swift, rapid, expeditious, prompt.

rustle v. **1** SWISH, whisper, whoosh.

2 STEAL, purloin, plunder, abduct, kidnap; informal filch.

rusty adj. **1** RUSTED, corroded, oxidized. **2** WEAK, below par, unpractised, out of practice, neglected, not what it was.

rut n. **1** FURROW, groove, track, crack, hollow, hole, pothole. **2** HUMDRUM EXISTENCE, routine job, boring routine, treadmill, dead end.

ruthless adj. MERCILESS, pitiless, relentless, unrelenting, remorseless, unforgiving, unsparing, inexorable, implacable, heartless, cold-hearted, unfeeling, hard, harsh, severe, grim, cruel, vicious, brutal, barbarous, callous, savage, fierce, ferocious. ■ OPPOSITES compassionate.

Ss

S abbrev. **1** South or Southern. **2** (**s**) seconds.

SA abbrev. **1** South Africa. **2** South Australia.

sabbath n. a day for rest and religious worship.

sabbatical n. paid leave granted to a university teacher for study or travel.

sable n. a marten native to Japan and Siberia, hunted for its thick brown fur.

sabotage /sab-uh-tahzh/ v. deliberately destroy or damage. ▶ n. the act of sabotaging. ■ **saboteur** n.

sabre (US **saber**) n. a curved sword.

sac n. a hollow, flexible bag-like structure.

saccharin n. a synthetic sugar substitute.

saccharine adj. excessively sweet or sentimental.

sacerdotal adj. of priests.

sachet /sa-shay/ n. a small sealed packet.

sack n. **1** a large bag made of strong fabric, paper, or plastic. **2** (**the sack**) informal dismissal from employment. ▶ v. **1** informal dismiss from employment. **2** (in the past) attack, steal from, and destroy a place. □ **sackcloth** (also **sacking**) a coarse fabric woven from flax or hemp.

sacral /say-kruhl/ adj. of the sacrum.

sacrament n. any of the symbolic religious ceremonies in the Christian Church. ■ **sacramental** adj.

sacred adj. **1** connected with a god or goddess or a religion and greatly respected. **2** religious. □ **sacred cow** a long-standing idea, custom, etc. regarded as above criticism.

sacrifice n. **1** the killing of an animal or person or giving up of a possession as an offering to a god or goddess. **2** an animal, person, etc. offered in this way. **3** an act of giving up something valued for the sake of something else. ▶ v. give as a sacrifice. ■ **sacrificial** adj.

sacrilege n. disrespect to something sacred or highly valued. ■ **sacrilegious** adj.

sacristan n. a person in charge of a sacristy.

sacristy n. (pl. **sacristies**) a room in a church where sacred objects are kept.

sacrosanct adj. too important or valuable to be changed or questioned.

sacrum n. (pl. **sacra** or **sacrums**) a triangular bone between the two hip bones.

sad adj. (**sadder**, **saddest**) **1** unhappy. **2** causing sorrow: *a sad story.* ■ **sadden** v. **sadly** adv. **sadness** n.

Thesaurus

sabotage n. DAMAGE, destruction, vandalism, disruption, ruining, wrecking. ▶ v. DAMAGE, destroy, wreck, ruin, impair, incapacitate, cripple, vandalize, disrupt, throw a spanner in the works; *informal* foul up.

sack n. **1** BAG, pack. **2** DISMISSAL, discharge, redundancy; *informal* the boot, the chop, the push, the axe. ▶ v. **1** DISCHARGE, dismiss, declare redundant; *informal* kick out, give someone their marching orders, boot out, give someone the sack/boot/push/chop, give someone the old heave-ho, give someone their cards. **2** see PLUNDER.

sacred adj. **1** HOLY, blessed, blest, hallowed, consecrated, sanctified. **2** RELIGIOUS, spiritual, devotional, church, churchly, ecclesiastical. ■ OPPOSITES profane.

sacrifice n. **1** GIVING UP, renunciation, abandonment, surrender, relinquishment, yielding, ceding, forfeiture. **2** OFFERING, gifts, oblation. ▶ v. **1** GIVE UP, forgo, renounce, abandon, surrender, relinquish, yield, cede, forfeit. **2** OFFER UP, offer, immolate.

sacrilege n. DESECRATION, profanity, blasphemy, impiety, irreverence, irreligion, godlessness, disrespect. ■ OPPOSITES piety.

sad adj. **1** UNHAPPY, miserable, sorrowful, gloomy, melancholy, blue, mournful, woebegone, wretched, dejected, downcast, despondent, in low spirits, low-spirited, low, downhearted, depressed, doleful, glum, cheerless, dispirited, disconsolate, heartbroken, broken-hearted, sick at heart, grief-stricken, grieving; *informal* down, down in the dumps, down

saddle n. **1** a seat on a bicycle or motorcycle or fastened on the back of a horse for riding. **2** a joint of meat consisting of the two loins. ▶v. **1** put a saddle on a horse. **2** burden with a task.

saddler n. a person who makes, repairs, or deals in equipment for horses.

sadism n. pleasure felt from hurting or humiliating other people. ■ **sadist** n. **sadistic** adj.

safari n. (pl. **safaris**) an expedition to observe or hunt animals in their natural environment. □ **safari park** an area of parkland where animals are kept in the open and may be observed by visitors.

safe adj. **1** protected from danger or risk. **2** not leading to harm. **3** giving security. ▶n. a strong cabinet with a complex lock for storing valuables. □ **safe conduct** protection from arrest or harm. ■ **safely** adv.

safeguard n. a measure taken to protect or prevent something. ▶v. protect.

safety n. the condition of being safe. □ **safety belt** a seat belt. **safety pin** a pin with a point bent back to the head and held in a guard when closed. **safety valve** a valve that opens automatically to relieve excessive pressure.

saffron n. a yellow spice.

sag v. (**sagging**, **sagged**) sink or droop gradually. ■ **saggy** adj.

saga n. a long story.

sagacious adj. wise. ■ **sagacity** n.

sage n. **1** a herb. **2** a very wise man. ▶adj. wise. ■ **sagely** adv.

sago n. starchy granules obtained from a palm, cooked with milk as a pudding.

said past & past part. of SAY.

sail n. **1** a piece of fabric spread on a mast to catch the wind and propel a boat or ship. **2** a trip in a sailing boat. **3** a flat board attached to the arm of a windmill. ▶v. **1** travel in a ship or boat. **2** begin a voyage. **3** direct or control a boat. **4** move smoothly. **5** (**sail through**) informal succeed easily at. □ **sailboard** a board with a mast and a sail, used in windsurfing. **sailcloth 1** strong fabric for sails. **2** a similar fabric for hard-wearing clothes. **sailing boat** (or **sailboat**) a boat with sails.

sailor n. a member of a ship's crew.

saint n. **1** a holy person venerated by the Church after death. **2** a very good or kind person. ■ **sainthood** n. **saintliness** n. **saintly** adj.

sake[1] n. (**for the sake of**) **1** so as to get

Thesaurus

in the mouth, in the pits. **2** UNFORTUNATE, unhappy, sorrowful, miserable, sorry, depressing, upsetting, distressing, dispiriting, heartbreaking, heartrending, pitiful, pitiable, grievous, tragic, disastrous, calamitous. **3** SORRY, wretched, deplorable, lamentable, regrettable, unfortunate, pitiful, pitiable, pathetic, shameful, disgraceful. ■ OPPOSITES happy.

sadden v. CAST DOWN, deject, depress, dishearten, dispirit, dampen someone's spirits, cast a gloom upon, desolate, upset, distress, grieve, break someone's heart, make someone's heart bleed. ■ OPPOSITES cheer.

sadness n. UNHAPPINESS, misery, sorrow, gloom, melancholy, wretchedness, dejection, despondency, low spirits, depression, dolefulness, glumness, cheerlessness, broken-heartedness, grief, heartache. ■ OPPOSITES happiness.

safe adj. **1** SAFE AND SOUND, secure, protected, sheltered, guarded, defended, free from harm/danger, out of harm's way. **2** UNHARMED, all right, alive and well, well, unhurt, uninjured, unscathed, undamaged, out of danger; informal OK, out of the woods. **3** CAUTIOUS, circumspect, prudent, unadventurous,

conservative, timid, unenterprising. **4** HARMLESS, innocuous, non-toxic, non-poisonous, wholesome. ■ OPPOSITES dangerous. ▶n. STRONGBOX, safety-deposit box, safe-deposit box, cash box, repository, depository, locker, vault, crypt.

safeguard n. PROTECTION, defence, preventive, precaution, security, surety. ▶v. PROTECT, look after, defend, guard, preserve, secure. ■ OPPOSITES endanger, jeopardize.

safety n. **1** SAFENESS, security, secureness, soundness, impregnability. **2** RELIABILITY, dependability, responsibility, trustworthiness. **3** SHELTER, sanctuary, refuge.

sag v. SINK, subside, slump, curve down, droop.

saga n. EPIC, chronicle, legend, history, romance.

sail v. **1** CRUISE, ride the waves, go by water, go on a sea voyage, voyage. **2** SET SAIL, embark, put to sea, leave port/dock, raise sail, put off, shove off. **3** STEER, captain, pilot, navigate.

sailor n. SEAMAN, seafarer, mariner, salt, sea dog, boatman, yachtsman/woman; informal matelot; informal, dated tar, Jack Tar.

or keep. **2** out of consideration for.

sake² /sah-ki/ n. a Japanese alcoholic drink made from rice.

salaam /suh-lahm/ n. a low bow with the hand touching the forehead, used as a gesture of respect by Muslims.

salacious adj. containing too much sexual detail.

salad n. a cold dish of raw vegetables.

salamander n. an animal resembling a newt.

salami n. (pl. **salami** or **salamis**) a type of spicy preserved sausage.

salary n. (pl. **salaries**) a fixed regular payment made by an employer to an employee. ■ **salaried** adj.

sale n. **1** the exchange of something for money. **2** (**sales**) the activity or profession of selling. **3** a period in which goods are sold at reduced prices. **4** a public event at which goods are sold. □ **salesman** (or **saleswoman** or **salesperson**) a person whose job is to sell goods. ■ **saleable** (or **salable**) adj.

salient adj. most noticeable or important. ▶ n. a piece of land or fortification jutting out to form an angle.

saline adj. containing salt. ■ **salinity** n.

saliva n. a watery liquid produced in the mouth. ■ **salivary** adj.

salivate v. produce saliva. ■ **salivation** n.

sallow adj. (of the complexion) yellowish.

sally n. (pl. **sallies**) **1** a sudden charge out of a place surrounded by an enemy. **2** a witty reply. ▶ v. (**sallying**, **sallied**) (**sally forth**) set out.

salmon n. (pl. **salmon**) a large edible fish with pink flesh.

salmonella n. a bacterium causing food poisoning.

salon n. **1** a place where a hairdresser, beautician, etc. works. **2** a reception room in a large house.

saloon n. **1** a public room, esp. on a ship. **2** a car with a separate boot.

salsa n. **1** a Latin American dance performed to music combining jazz and rock. **2** a spicy sauce.

salt n. **1** sodium chloride, a white substance in the form of crystals, used to season and preserve food. **2** a chemical compound of an acid and a metal. ▶ v. season or preserve with salt. □ **salt cellar** a container for salt. **saltpetre** (US **saltpeter**) potassium nitrate. **take with a pinch** (or **grain**) **of salt** recognize as untrue or exaggerated. **worth one's salt** competent. ■ **saltiness** n. **salty** adj.

salubrious adj. good for the health.

salutary adj. producing a beneficial effect.

salutation n. a greeting.

salute n. **1** a gesture of respect or acknowledgement. **2** a raising of a hand to the head, made as a formal military gesture of respect. ▶ v. make a salute to.

salvage v. **1** rescue a ship or its cargo from loss at sea. **2** save from being lost or destroyed. ▶ n. **1** the act of salvaging. **2** salvaged cargo.

salvation n. the saving of someone from harm or (in Christian belief) from the consequences of sin.

salve n. **1** a soothing ointment. **2** something that soothes an uneasy conscience. ▶ v. soothe.

salver n. a tray.

salvo n. (pl. **salvos** or **salvoes**) **1** a simultaneous firing of a number of guns. **2** a sudden series of aggressive statements or acts.

sal volatile /sal vuh-**lat**-i-li/ n. a scented solution used as a remedy for faintness.

Samaritan n. a kind or helpful person.

Thesaurus

saintly adj. SAINTLIKE, sainted, holy, godly, pious, God-fearing, religious, devout, blessed, virtuous, righteous, good, innocent, sinless, blameless, pure, angelic. ■ OPPOSITES ungodly.

sake n. WELL-BEING, welfare, behalf, benefit, advantage, interest, gain, profit, consideration, regard, concern, account, respect.

salary n. PAY, wages, earnings, remuneration, fee, emolument, stipend, honorarium.

sale n. SELLING, marketing, trade, traffic, vending, bargaining. □ **on sale** FOR SALE, in stock, on the market, purchasable, available, obtainable.

salubrious adj. HEALTHY, health-giving, beneficial, good for one's health, wholesome, salutary, refreshing, invigorating, bracing. ■ OPPOSITES unhealthy.

salute n. **1** GREETING, salutation, address, welcome. **2** TRIBUTE, testimonial, honour, homage, recognition, acknowledgement. ▶ v. **1** GREET, address, hail, acknowledge, pay one's respects to. **2** PAY TRIBUTE TO, pay homage to, honour, recognize, acknowledge; *informal* take one's hat off to.

salvage n. **1** RESCUE, saving, recovery, reclamation, salvation. **2** WASTE MATER-

samba n. a Brazilian dance.

same adj. **1** exactly alike. **2** referring to a person or thing already mentioned. ▶ pron. the person or thing already mentioned. ▶ adv. in the same way. ■ **sameness** n.

Sami pl. n. the Lapps of northern Scandinavia.

samosa n. a triangular fried Indian pastry containing spiced vegetables or meat.

samovar n. a Russian tea urn.

sampan n. a small boat used in the Far East.

samphire n. a seashore plant with edible fleshy leaves.

sample n. **1** a small part or quantity intended to show what the whole is like. **2** a specimen. ▶ v. **1** take a sample or samples of. **2** take an extract from one musical recording and use it as part of another.

sampler n. a piece of embroidery showing a person's skill at various stitches.

samurai /sam-uh-ry/ n. (pl. **samurai**) hist. a member of a powerful Japanese military class.

sanatorium n. (pl. **sanatoriums** or **sanatoria**) **1** a place for the care of people with a long-term illness or convalescents. **2** a place in a boarding school for sick pupils.

sanctify v. (**sanctifying**, **sanctified**) make or declare holy. ■ **sanctification** n.

sanctimonious adj. making a show of being morally superior.

sanction n. **1** a penalty for disobeying a rule or to coerce a state to conform on an issue. **2** permission or approval. ▶ v. give permission for.

sanctity n. (pl. **sanctities**) **1** holiness. **2** supreme importance.

sanctuary n. (pl. **sanctuaries**) **1** a place of safety. **2** a nature reserve. **3** a holy place.

sanctum n. (pl. **sanctums**) a sacred or private place.

sand n. **1** very fine particles of crushed rock. **2** (**sands**) a wide area of sand. ▶ v. **1** smooth with sandpaper or a sander. **2** sprinkle with sand. □ **sandbag** a bag of sand, used to protect against floods etc. **sandbank** a deposit of sand forming a shallow area in the sea or a river. **sandblast** roughen or clean with a jet of sand driven by compressed air or steam. **sandcastle** a model of a castle built out of sand. **sandpaper** paper with a coating of sand or another rough substance, used for smoothing surfaces. **sandstone** rock formed from compressed sand. **sandstorm** a strong desert wind carrying clouds of sand.

sandal n. a shoe with a partly open upper part or straps.

sandalwood n. a fragrant wood.

sander n. a power tool used for smoothing a surface.

sandwich n. two pieces of bread with a filling between them. ▶ v. **1** insert something between two people or things.

Thesaurus

IAL, scrap, remains. ▶ v. RESCUE, save, recover, retrieve, reclaim, get back.

salvation n. REDEMPTION, deliverance, saving, rescue. ■ OPPOSITES damnation, destruction.

same adj. **1** IDENTICAL, the very same, selfsame, one and the same, the very. **2** EXACTLY SIMILAR, identical, alike, duplicate, twin, indistinguishable, interchangeable, corresponding, equivalent. **3** UNCHANGING, unchanged, unvarying, unvaried, invariable, constant, consistent, uniform. ■ OPPOSITES different.

sample n. **1** SPECIMEN, example, instance, illustration, exemplification, representative type, model, pattern. **2** CROSS-SECTION, sampling, test. ▶ v. TRY, try out, test, examine, inspect, taste.

sanctify v. CONSECRATE, make holy/sacred, bless, hallow, dedicate, set apart.

sanctimonious adj. SELF-RIGHTEOUS, holier-than-thou, pietistic, unctuous, smug, mealy-mouthed, hypocritical, Pharisaic, Tartuffian; informal goody-goody.

sanction n. **1** AUTHORIZATION, warrant, accreditation, licence, endorsement, permission, consent, approval, backing, support, seal/stamp of approval, approbation, acceptance; informal thumbs up, go-ahead, the green light. **2** PENALTY, punishment, penalization, penance, sentence. ▶ v. AUTHORIZE, warrant, accredit, license, endorse, permit, allow, consent to, back, support, approve, accept; informal give the thumbs up to, give the green light to, OK. ■ OPPOSITES reject.

sanctity n. **1** SACREDNESS, holiness, inviolability. **2** HOLINESS, godliness, saintliness, spirituality, religiosity, piety, devoutness, devotion, righteousness, goodness, virtue, purity.

sanctuary n. **1** REFUGE, haven, shelter, retreat, hideout, hiding place. **2** HOLY

2 squeeze two things together.

sandy adj. (**sandier**, **sandiest**) **1** covered in or consisting of sand. **2** light yellowish brown.

sane adj. **1** not mad. **2** sensible.

sang past of SING.

sangfroid /song-frwah/ n. calmness in difficult situations.

sangria n. a Spanish drink of red wine, lemonade, and fruit.

sanguinary adj. involving much bloodshed.

sanguine adj. optimistic.

sanitarium n. US a sanatorium.

sanitary adj. **1** of sanitation. **2** hygienic. □ **sanitary towel** a pad worn to absorb menstrual blood.

sanitation n. arrangements to protect public health, esp. the provision of clean drinking water and the disposal of sewage.

sanitize (or **-ise**) v. **1** make hygienic. **2** make something unpleasant seem more acceptable.

sanity n. the condition of being sane.

sank past of SINK.

Sanskrit n. an ancient language of India.

sap n. the liquid in plants, carrying food to all parts. ▶v. (**sapping**, **sapped**) gradually weaken.

sapling n. a young tree.

sapper n. a military engineer who lays or finds and defuses mines.

sapphire n. **1** a blue precious stone. **2** a bright blue colour.

saprophyte n. a plant or fungus living on decaying matter.

sarcasm n. the use of irony to mock or convey contempt. ■ **sarcastic** adj. **sarcastically** adv.

sarcophagus n. (pl. **sarcophagi**) a stone coffin.

sardine n. a young pilchard or similar small fish.

sardonic adj. mocking. ■ **sardonically** adv.

sari n. (pl. **saris**) a length of fabric draped round the body, worn by women from the Indian subcontinent.

sarong n. a length of fabric wrapped round the body and tucked at the waist or armpits.

sartorial adj. of clothing or style of dress.

SAS abbrev. Special Air Service.

sash n. **1** a strip of cloth worn over one shoulder or round the waist. **2** a frame holding the glass in a window. □ **sash window** a window with two sashes which can be slid up and down to open it.

SAT abbrev. standard assessment task.

sat past & past part. of SIT.

Satan n. the Devil.

satanic adj. of Satan or the worship of Satan.

satanism n. the worship of Satan. ■ **satanist** n. & adj.

satchel n. a bag with a shoulder strap, for carrying school books.

sated adj. fully satisfied.

satellite n. **1** an artificial object placed in orbit round a planet to collect information or for communication. **2** a natural object orbiting a planet. ▶adj. (of a

Thesaurus

PLACE, church, temple, shrine, altar, sanctum. **3** PRESERVE, reserve, wildlife reserve, reservation. **4** SAFETY, safe keeping, protection, shelter, security, immunity.

sane adj. **1** OF SOUND MIND, in one's right mind, compos mentis, rational, lucid, in possession of one's faculties; informal all there. **2** SENSIBLE, reasonable, balanced, judicious, responsible, prudent, wise, advisable. ■ OPPOSITES insane.

sanguine adj. OPTIMISTIC, confident, assured, hopeful, buoyant, cheerful, spirited. ■ OPPOSITES gloomy.

sanitary adj. HYGIENIC, clean, germ-free, antiseptic, aseptic, sterile, unpolluted, salubrious, healthy.

sanity n. **1** SANENESS, soundness of mind, mental health, reason, rationality, lucidity. **2** SENSE, sensibleness, common sense, good sense, reasonableness, ra-

tionality, soundness, judiciousness, prudence, wisdom, advisability.

sap n. **1** FLUID, moisture, juice, secretion. **2** VIGOUR, energy, vitality, vivacity, enthusiasm, spirit; informal pep, zip, oomph. ▶v. DRAIN, enervate, exhaust, weaken, enfeeble, debilitate, devitalize..

sarcasm n. DERISION, scorn, mockery, ridicule, irony, satire, trenchancy, acerbity, asperity, mordancy, bitterness, spitefulness.

sarcastic adj. DERISIVE, derisory, scornful, mocking, sneering, jeering, scoffing, taunting, ironic, sardonic, satirical, caustic, trenchant, acerbic, acrimonious, mordant, bitter, spiteful; informal sarky.

sardonic adj. DRY, wry, derisory, cynical, ironic, sarcastic, caustic, trenchant, acerbic, mordant, bitter.

satanic adj. DIABOLICAL, fiendish, devilcountry etc.) dependent on another. □ **satellite dish** a bowl-shaped aerial for receiving satellite television. **satellite television** television in which the signals are broadcast via satellite.

satiate /say-shi-ayt/ v. satisfy fully. ■ **satiation** n. **satiety** n.

satin n. a smooth, glossy fabric. ■ **satiny** adj.

satire n. **1** the use of humour, irony, etc. to criticize or ridicule. **2** a play, novel, etc. using satire. ■ **satirical** adj. **satirically** adv. **satirist** n.

satirize (or **-ise**) v. criticize using satire.

satisfactory adj. acceptable. ■ **satisfactorily** adv.

satisfy v. (**satisfying, satisfied**) **1** fulfil the needs or wants of. **2** meet a demand, desire, or need. ■ **satisfaction** n.

satsuma n. a variety of tangerine.

saturate v. **1** soak thoroughly. **2** supply a market beyond the point at which there is demand for a product. ■ **saturation** n.

Saturday n. the day before Sunday.

saturnine adj. gloomy or brooding in appearance or manner.

satyr /sat-er/ n. a woodland god in classical mythology, with a goat's ears, legs, and tail.

sauce n. **1** a thick liquid served with food to add moistness and flavour. **2** informal impudence. □ **saucepan** a deep cooking pan with a long handle.

saucer n. a shallow dish on which a cup stands.

saucy adj. (**saucier, sauciest**) informal **1** cheeky. **2** sexually suggestive. ■ **saucily** adv.

sauerkraut /sow-er-krowt/ n. chopped pickled cabbage.

sauna /saw-nuh/ n. a small room used as a hot-air or steam bath.

saunter v. stroll. ▶ n. a stroll.

sausage n. a short tube of minced meat encased in a skin.

sauté /soh-tay/ v. (**sautéing, sautéed** or **sautéd**) fry quickly in shallow oil.

savage adj. **1** fierce and violent. **2** cruel and vicious. **3** uncivilized or primitive. ▶ n. a primitive and uncivilized person. ▶ v. attack fiercely and maul. ■ **savagely** adv. **savagery** n.

savannah n. a grassy plain in tropical regions.

save v. **1** keep safe or rescue from harm or danger. **2** store for future use. **3** set aside money in this way. **4** prevent the scoring of a goal. ▶ n. an act of preventing a goal. ■ **saver** n.

saveloy n. a smoked pork sausage.

Thesaurus

ish, demonic, demoniac, demoniacal, hellish, infernal, accursed, wicked, evil, sinful, iniquitous, malevolent, vile, foul.

satire n. **1** TAKE-OFF, spoof, send-up, burlesque, parody, travesty, caricature, lampoon, pasquinade. **2** MOCKERY, ridicule, irony, sarcasm.

satirical adj. MOCKING, ridiculing, taunting, ironic, sarcastic, sardonic, caustic, biting, cutting.

satirize v. MOCK, ridicule, hold up to ridicule, take off, send up, deride, make fun of, poke fun at, parody, lampoon, burlesque, travesty, criticize, censure.

satisfaction n. FULFILMENT, gratification, pleasure, enjoyment, delight, happiness, pride, comfort, content, contentment, smugness. ■ OPPOSITES dissatisfaction.

satisfactory adj. ADEQUATE, all right, acceptable, fine, good enough, sufficient, competent, up to standard, up to the mark, up to par, up to scratch, passable, average; informal OK, okay. ■ OPPOSITES unsatisfactory.

satisfy v. **1** SATIATE, sate, slake, quench. **2** FULFIL, gratify, appease, assuage,

meet, indulge, content. **3** CONVINCE, persuade, assure, reassure, remove/dispel doubts, put someone's mind at rest. ■ OPPOSITES frustrate.

saturate v. WET THROUGH, wet, soak, drench, souse, steep, douse, permeate, imbue, pervade, suffuse.

sauce n. **1** RELISH, dressing, condiment, flavouring. **2** see INSOLENCE.

saucy adj. IMPUDENT, cheeky, impertinent, insolent, rude, disrespectful, audacious, presumptuous, bold, brash; informal fresh. ■ OPPOSITES demure, polite.

saunter v. STROLL, amble, wander, meander, walk, promenade; informal mosey.

savage adj. **1** VICIOUS, ferocious, fierce, brutal, cruel, bloody, murderous, bloodthirsty, inhuman, harsh, grim, terrible, merciless, ruthless, pitiless, sadistic, barbarous. **2** UNTAMED, wild, undomesticated, feral. **3** UNCIVILIZED, uncultivated, barbarous, barbaric, wild, primitive. ■ OPPOSITES mild, tame. ▶ n. BARBARIAN, wild man/woman, primitive, heathen. ▶ v. MAUL, lacerate, mangle, tear to pieces, attack.

save v. RESCUE, free, set free, liberate, deliver, snatch, bail out, salvage, re-

s

savings pl. n. money saved.

saviour (US **savior**) n. a person who saves someone from danger or harm.

savoir faire /sav-war fair/ n. the ability to act appropriately in social situations.

savour (US **savor**) v. **1** enjoy the taste of food or drink. **2** enjoy or appreciate fully. ▶ n. a flavour or smell.

savoury (US **savory**) adj. (of food) salty or spicy rather than sweet.

saw[1] n. **1** a cutting tool with a jagged blade. **2** a proverb or wise saying. ▶ v. (**sawing**, **sawed**; past part. **sawn** or US **sawed**) **1** cut with a saw. **2** move back and forward.

saw[2] past of SEE.

sax n. informal a saxophone.

saxophone n. a metal wind instrument. ■ **saxophonist** n.

say v. (**saying**, **said**) **1** speak words. **2** convey or express information. **3** suggest as an example or theory. ▶ n. an opportunity to state one's opinion or to influence events.

saying n. a well-known expression or proverb.

scab n. **1** a crust forming over a cut or wound. **2** derog. a person who refuses to take part in a strike. ■ **scabby** adj.

scabbard n. a cover for the blade of a sword or dagger.

scabies n. a skin disease causing itching, caused by a mite.

scabrous adj. **1** covered with scabs. **2** indecent.

scaffold n. **1** a platform used formerly for public executions. **2** a structure of scaffolding.

scaffolding n. a structure of planks and metal poles, used while working on a building.

scald v. **1** burn with very hot liquid or steam. **2** heat a liquid to near boiling point. ▶ n. a burn caused by scalding.

scale n. **1** each of the overlapping plates protecting the skin of fish and reptiles. **2** a dry flake of skin. **3** a white deposit formed in a kettle etc. by hard water. **4** tartar on teeth. **5** an ordered range of values for measuring or grading something. **6** relative size or extent. **7** (**scales**) an instrument for weighing. **8** a fixed series of notes in a system of music. ▶ v. **1** climb. **2** represent in proportion to the size of the original. **3** remove scale or scales from. ■ **scaly** adj.

scalene adj. (of a triangle) having unequal sides.

scallop n. **1** an edible shellfish with two hinged fan-shaped shells. **2** each of a series of small curves as a decorative edging. ■ **scalloped** adj.

scallywag n. informal a mischievous person.

scalp n. the skin covering the top and back of the head. ▶ v. cut the scalp from.

scalpel n. a surgeon's knife with a small blade.

scam n. informal a dishonest scheme.

scamp n. informal a mischievous person.

Thesaurus

deem. **2** PROTECT, safeguard, guard, keep, keep safe, shield, screen, preserve, conserve. **3** PREVENT, obviate, forestall, spare, make unnecessary, rule out. **4** PUT ASIDE, set aside, put by, put away, lay by, keep, reserve, conserve, salt away, stockpile, store, hoard.

savings pl. n. CAPITAL, assets, resources, reserves, funds, nest egg.

saviour n. RESCUER, liberator, deliverer, emancipator, champion, knight in shining armour, Good Samaritan, friend in need.

savour n. TASTE, flavour, tang, relish, smack, smell, aroma, fragrance. ▶ v. TASTE, enjoy, appreciate, delight in, take pleasure in, relish, revel in.

savoury adj. **1** APPETIZING, mouthwatering, fragrant, flavoursome, palatable, tasty, delicious, delectable, luscious, toothsome; informal scrumptious. **2** SALTY, piquant, tangy. ■ OPPOSITES unpalatable, sweet.

say v. **1** MENTION, voice, pronounce, put into words, give utterance to, give voice to, vocalize. **2** STATE, remark, announce, affirm, assert, maintain, declare, allege, profess, avow, aver, opine; informal come out with. **3** ESTIMATE, judge, guess, hazard a guess, predict, speculate, conjecture, surmise, imagine, assume, suppose, presume. **4** PROPOSE, advance, bring forward, offer, introduce, adduce, plead.

saying n. PROVERB, maxim, aphorism, axiom, adage, saw, epigram, dictum, gnome, apothegm, platitude, cliché.

scaffold n. **1** SCAFFOLDING, frame, framework, gantry. **2** GALLOWS, gibbet.

scale[1] n. **1** PLATE, flake; technical lamella, lamina, squama. **2** COATING, coat, crust, encrustation, limescale, fur.

scale[2] n. **1** PROGRESSION, succession, sequence, series, ranking, register, ladder, hierarchy; informal pecking order. **2** EXTENT, scope, range, degree, reach.

scamper v. run with quick light steps.

scampi pl. n. small lobster-like shellfish.

scan v. (**scanning, scanned**) **1** look at all parts of quickly. **2** move a detector or beam across. **3** convert a document etc. into digital form for storing or processing on a computer. **4** analyse the metre of a line of verse. **5** (of verse) follow metrical rules. ▶ n. an act of scanning. ■ **scanner** n.

scandal n. **1** an action or event causing outrage. **2** outrage or gossip arising from this. ■ **scandalous** adj. **scandalously** adv.

scandalize (or **-ise**) v. shock or outrage.

Scandinavian adj. of the countries of Scandinavia, esp. Norway, Sweden, and Denmark.

scandium n. a soft metallic element.

scansion n. the rhythm of a line of verse.

scant adj. barely enough.

scanty adj. (**scantier, scantiest**) too little in quantity or amount. ■ **scantily** adv.

scapegoat n. a person blamed for the wrongdoings of others.

scapula n. (pl. **scapulae** or **scapulas**) the shoulder blade. ■ **scapular** adj.

scar n. a mark left where a wound has healed. ▶ v. (**scarring, scarred**) mark or be marked with a scar.

scarab n. a beetle treated as sacred in ancient Egypt.

scarce adj. **1** available in quantities insufficient to meet demand. **2** rare. ■ **scarcity** n.

scarcely adv. **1** only just. **2** surely or probably not.

scare v. frighten or be frightened. ▶ n. **1** a fright. **2** a period of general alarm. □ **scarecrow** a figure set up to scare birds away from crops. **scaremongering** the spreading of alarming rumours.

scarf n. (pl. **scarves** or **scarfs**) a length or square of fabric worn around the neck or head.

scarify v. (**scarifying, scarified**) **1** make shallow cuts in. **2** rake out unwanted material from a lawn.

scarlet n. a bright red colour. □ **scarlet fever** an infectious disease causing fever and a scarlet rash.

Thesaurus

▶ v. CLIMB, ascend, go up, clamber, mount, clamber up. □ **scale down** REDUCE, cut down, cut back on, decrease, lessen, lower.

scaly adj. FLAKY, scurfy, rough, scabrous.

scamp n. RASCAL, rogue, imp, devil, monkey, scallywag, mischief-maker, troublemaker, prankster, tyke.

scan v. **1** STUDY, examine, scrutinize, survey, inspect, take stock of, search, scour, sweep. **2** SKIM, look over, glance over, run one's eye over, read through, leaf through, thumb through.

scandal n. **1** DISGRACE, shame, dishonour, disrepute, discredit, odium, opprobrium, censure, obloquy. **2** SLANDER, libel, calumny, defamation, aspersion, gossip, malicious rumours, dirt, muckraking, smear campaign.

scandalous adj. **1** DISGRACEFUL, shameful, dishonourable, outrageous, shocking, monstrous, disreputable, improper, unseemly, discreditable, infamous, opprobrious, sordid. **2** SLANDEROUS, libellous, defamatory, scurrilous, malicious.

scant adj. LITTLE, minimal, limited, insufficient, inadequate, deficient. ■ OPPOSITES abundant.

scanty adj. MEAGRE, scant, sparse, small, paltry, slender, negligible, skimpy, thin, poor, insufficient, inadequate, deficient, limited, restricted, exiguous. ■ OPPOSITES ample, copious.

scapegoat n. WHIPPING BOY, Aunt Sally; informal fall guy; US informal patsy.

scar n. **1** MARK, blemish, blotch, discoloration, cicatrix, disfigurement, defacement. **2** DAMAGE, trauma, shock, injury, suffering, upset. ▶ v. **1** MARK, blemish, blotch, discolour, disfigure, deface. **2** DAMAGE, traumatize, shock, injure, upset.

scarce adj. **1** IN SHORT SUPPLY, short, meagre, scant, scanty, sparse, paltry, not enough, too little, insufficient, deficient, inadequate, lacking, at a premium, exiguous. **2** RARE, infrequent, few and far between, seldom seen/found, sparse, uncommon, unusual. ■ OPPOSITES plentiful, abundant.

scarcely adv. HARDLY, barely, only just.

scarcity n. **1** DEARTH, shortage, undersupply, paucity, meagreness, sparseness, insufficiency, deficiency, inadequacy, lack, exiguity. **2** RARITY, rareness, infrequency, sparseness, uncommonness.

scare v. FRIGHTEN, alarm, startle, make fearful, make nervous, terrify, terrorize, petrify, horrify, appal, shock, intimidate, daunt, awe, cow, panic, put the fear of God into, scare stiff, make someone's blood run cold, make

scarp n. a steep slope.

scary adj. (**scarier**, **scariest**) informal frightening. ∎ **scarily** adv.

scathing adj. harshly critical.

scatological adj. obsessed with excrement. ∎ **scatology** n.

scatter v. **1** throw in various random directions. **2** separate and move off in different directions. □ **scatterbrained** (or **scatty**) disorganized and forgetful.

scavenge v. **1** search for and collect anything usable from waste. **2** (of an animal) search for dead animals as food. ∎ **scavenger** n.

scenario n. (pl. **scenarios**) **1** a written outline of a film, novel, etc. **2** a possible sequence of future events.

scene n. **1** the place where an incident occurs. **2** a view or landscape as seen by a spectator. **3** an incident. **4** a sequence of continuous action in a play, film, etc. **5** a display of emotion or anger. **6** a specified area of activity or interest. □ **behind the scenes** out of public view.

scenery n. **1** the features of a landscape. **2** the background used to represent a place on a stage or film set.

scenic adj. picturesque.

scent n. **1** a pleasant smell. **2** perfume. **3** a trail left by an animal, indicated by its smell. ▶ v. **1** give a pleasant smell to. **2** detect by smell. **3** sense the imminence of.

sceptic /skep-tik/ (US **skeptic**) n. a sceptical person. ∎ **scepticism** n.

sceptical adj. not easily convinced; having doubts. ∎ **sceptically** adv.

sceptre /sep-ter/ (US **scepter**) n. a staff carried by a monarch on ceremonial occasions.

schedule n. a programme or timetable of intended events. ▶ v. **1** plan for something to happen at a particular time. **2** (**scheduled**) (of a flight) forming part of a regular service rather than specially chartered.

schema n. (pl. **schemata** or **schemas**) an outline of a plan or theory.

schematic adj. (of a diagram) outlining the main features; simplified. ∎ **schematically** adv. **schematize** (or **-ise**) v.

scheme n. **1** a systematic plan of work or action. **2** an ordered system or pattern. ▶ v. make secret plans. ∎ **schemer** n.

Thesaurus

someone's flesh creep, make someone's hair stand on end; informal scare the pants off, put the wind up. ▶ n. FRIGHT, alarm, start, fearfulness, nervousness, terror, horror, shock, panic.

scathing adj. VIRULENT, savage, fierce, ferocious, brutal, stinging, biting, mordant, trenchant, caustic, vitriolic, withering, scornful, harsh, severe, stern. ∎ OPPOSITES mild.

scatter v. **1** DISSEMINATE, diffuse, spread, sow, sprinkle, strew, broadcast, fling, toss, throw. **2** BREAK UP, disperse, disband, separate, dissolve. ∎ OPPOSITES gather, assemble.

scavenge v. SEARCH, look for, hunt, forage for, rummage for.

scenario n. PLOT, outline, synopsis, summary, precis, rundown, storyline, structure, scheme, plan, sequence of events.

scene n. **1** PLACE, location, site, position, spot, setting, locale, whereabouts, arena, stage. **2** EVENT, incident, happening, situation, episode, affair, moment, proceeding. **3** FUSS, exhibition, outburst, commotion, to-do, row, upset, tantrum, furore, brouhaha.

scenery n. **1** VIEW, outlook, landscape, vista, panorama, prospect. **2** SET, stage set, setting, background, backdrop.

scenic adj. PICTURESQUE, pretty, beautiful, pleasing.

scent n. **1** AROMA, perfume, fragrance, smell, bouquet, odour; literary redolence. **2** TRACK, trail, spoor.

sceptic n. QUESTIONER, doubter, agnostic, unbeliever, doubting Thomas, disbeliever, dissenter, scoffer, cynic.

sceptical adj. DOUBTING, doubtful, dubious, questioning, distrustful, mistrustful, suspicious, hesitant, disbelieving, misbelieving, incredulous, unconvinced, scoffing, cynical. ∎ OPPOSITES certain, convinced.

scepticism n. DOUBT, doubtfulness, dubiety, agnosticism, distrust, mistrust, suspicion, hesitancy, disbelief, misbelief, incredulity, cynicism.

schedule n. PLAN, scheme, timetable, programme, diary, calendar, itinerary, agenda. ▶ v. ARRANGE, timetable, organize, plan, programme, book.

scheme n. **1** PLAN, programme, project, course of action, system, procedure, strategy, design, tactics, contrivance. **2** ARRANGEMENT, system, organization, disposition, schema. **3** PLOT, ruse, ploy, stratagem, manoeuvre, machinations, intrigue, conspiracy; informal game, racket. ▶ v. PLOT, conspire, intrigue, manoeuvre, plan, lay plans.

scherzo /skair-tsoh/ n. (pl. **scherzos** or **scherzi**) a lively piece of music.

schism /ski-z'm/ n. a division into opposing groups through a deep difference in belief or opinion. ■ **schismatic** adj.

schist /shist/ n. a rock consisting of different layers of minerals.

schizoid /skit-soyd/ adj. having a mental condition similar to schizophrenia.

schizophrenia n. a mental disorder whose symptoms include withdrawal from reality into fantasy. ■ **schizophrenic** adj. & n.

schmaltz n. informal excessive sentimentality. ■ **schmaltzy** adj.

schnapps n. a strong alcoholic drink.

scholar n. **1** a person studying at an advanced level. **2** the holder of a scholarship. ■ **scholarliness** n. **scholarly** adj.

scholarship n. **1** academic study. **2** a grant made to support a student's education.

scholastic adj. of schools or education.

school n. **1** an educational institution. **2** a group of artists, philosophers, etc. sharing similar ideas. **3** a large group of fish or sea mammals. ▶ v. educate or train.

schooner n. **1** a sailing ship. **2** a large sherry glass.

sciatica /sy-at-ik-uh/ n. pain in the back, hip, and thigh.

science n. the study or knowledge of the physical and natural world based on observation and experiment. ■ **scientific** adj. **scientifically** adv.

scientist n. a person who studies or is an expert in science.

scimitar /sim-i-ter/ n. a short curved sword.

scintilla n. a trace.

scintillating adj. **1** sparkling. **2** brilliant and exciting.

scion /sy-uhn/ n. **1** a plant shoot cut off for grafting. **2** a descendant.

scissors pl. n. a cutting tool with two crossing pivoted blades.

sclerosis n. **1** abnormal hardening of body tissue. **2** (in full **multiple sclerosis**) a serious disease of the nervous system that can cause paralysis.

scoff v. **1** speak about scornfully. **2** informal eat greedily.

scold v. angrily rebuke.

sconce n. a candle holder attached to a wall.

scone n. a small plain cake, usu. eaten buttered.

scoop n. **1** a utensil resembling a spoon, with a short handle and a deep bowl. **2** informal a piece of news printed by one newspaper before its rivals. ▶ v. **1** pick up or hollow out with a scoop. **2** pick up in a quick, smooth movement. **3** informal print a piece of news before rival newspapers.

scooter n. **1** a light motorcycle. **2** a child's toy consisting of a footboard on two wheels and a long steering handle, moved by pushing one foot against the ground.

scope n. **1** the range of a subject, activity, etc. **2** opportunity.

scorch v. **1** burn on the surface. **2** (**scorching**) very hot.

Thesaurus

scheming adj. CALCULATING, designing, conniving, wily, crafty, cunning, sly, artful, slippery, underhand, duplicitous, devious, Machiavellian; informal tricky. ■ OPPOSITES ingenuous, honest.

schism n. DIVISION, breach, split, rift, break, rupture, separation, severance, detachment, discord, disagreement.

scholar n. MAN/WOMAN OF LETTERS, learned person, academic, highbrow, intellectual, pundit, savant; informal bookworm, egghead.

scholarly adj. LEARNED, erudite, academic, well read, intellectual, highbrow, scholastic, literary, studious, bookish, lettered. ■ OPPOSITES ignorant.

scholarship n. **1** LEARNING, knowledge, education, erudition, letters. **2** GRANT, fellowship, endowment, bursary.

school n. **1** EDUCATIONAL INSTITUTION, academy. **2** SCHOOL OF THOUGHT, outlook, persuasion, opinion, point of view, belief, faith, creed. ▶ v. EDUCATE, teach, instruct, train, coach, drill, discipline, direct, guide, prepare, prime, verse.

scientific adj. SYSTEMATIC, methodical, orderly, regulated, controlled, exact, precise, mathematical.

scintillating adj. SPARKLING, dazzling, vivacious, effervescent, lively, animated, ebullient, bright, brilliant, witty, exciting, stimulating, invigorating. ■ OPPOSITES dull, boring.

scoff v. JEER AT, mock at, sneer at, gibe at, taunt, laugh at, ridicule, poke fun at, make a fool of, make sport of, rag, revile, deride, belittle, scorn, knock; informal pooh-pooh.

scold v. see REPRIMAND.

scoop n. **1** LADLE, spoon, dipper. **2** EXCLUSIVE STORY, revelation, exposé. □ **scoop out** HOLLOW OUT, gouge out, dig, excav-

score n. **1** the number of points, goals, runs, etc. achieved in a game. **2** (pl. **score**) a set of twenty. **3** a written representation of a piece of music. ►v. **1** gain a point, goal, etc. in a game. **2** record the score during a game. **3** cut a mark on a surface. **4** (**score out**) cross out text. **5** arrange a piece of music. ■ **scorer** n.

scorn n. open contempt or disdain. ►v. **1** express scorn for. **2** reject with scorn. ■ **scornful** adj. **scornfully** adv.

scorpion n. a creature related to the spiders, with pincers and a poisonous sting at the end of its tail.

Scot n. a person from Scotland.

Scotch adj. Scottish. ►n. whisky made in Scotland.

....

☑ Use **Scotch** only to refer to things: people are **Scots** or **Scottish**.

....

scotch v. put an end to a rumour.

scot-free adv. without punishment or injury.

Scots adj. Scottish. ►n. the form of English used in Scotland.

Scottish adj. of Scotland or its people.

scoundrel n. a dishonest person.

scour v. **1** clean by rubbing with something rough. **2** search thoroughly.

scourge n. **1** hist. a whip. **2** a cause of great suffering. ►v. **1** hist. whip. **2** cause suffering to.

scout n. a person sent ahead to gather information about the enemy. ►v. **1** search. **2** act as a scout.

scowl n. a bad-tempered expression. ►v. make a scowl.

scrabble v. grope around with one's fingers to find or hold on to something.

scraggy adj. thin and bony.

scram v. (**scramming**, **scrammed**) informal go away quickly.

scramble v. **1** move quickly and awkwardly, using hands as well as feet. **2** muddle. **3** put a transmission into a form intelligible only with a decoding device. **4** stir and cook beaten eggs. **5** (of fighter aircraft) take off immediately in an emergency. ►n. **1** an act of scrambling. **2** a motorcycle race over rough ground. ■ **scrambler** n.

scrap n. **1** a small piece. **2** (**scraps**) uneaten food left after a meal. **3** waste metal etc. discarded for reprocessing. **4** informal a short fight or quarrel. ►v. (**scrapping**, **scrapped**) **1** discard as useless or unwanted. **2** informal have a short fight or quarrel. □ **scrapbook** a book for sticking cuttings, drawings, etc. in.

Thesaurus

....

ate. **scoop up** GATHER UP, pick up, lift.

scope n. **1** EXTENT, range, sphere, area, field, realm, compass, orbit, reach, span, sweep, confine, limit. **2** OPPORTUNITY, freedom, latitude, capacity.

scorch v. BURN, singe, char, sear, discolour, blacken.

score n. **1** NUMBER OF POINTS/GOALS, total, result, outcome. **2** NOTCH, mark, scratch, scrape, groove, cut, nick, chip, gouge. ►v. **1** WIN, gain, achieve, chalk up, notch up. **2** MAKE A NOTCH IN, mark, scratch, scrape, groove, cut, nick, chip, gouge.

scorn n. CONTEMPT, contemptuousness, disdain, haughtiness, disparagement, derision, mockery, contumely. ►v. **1** BE CONTEMPTUOUS, hold in contempt, look down on, disdain, disparage, slight, deride, mock, scoff at, sneer at. **2** REBUFF, spurn, shun, refuse, reject, turn down.

scornful adj. CONTEMPTUOUS, disdainful, haughty, supercilious, disparaging, slighting, scathing, derisive, mocking, scoffing, sneering, contumelious. ■ OPPOSITES respectful.

scoundrel n. VILLAIN, rogue, rascal, miscreant, reprobate, scapegrace, good-for-nothing, ne'er-do-well, wastrel; dated cad; informal, dated rotter, bounder.

scour[1] v. SCRUB, rub, clean, cleanse, abrade, wash, wipe, polish, buff, burnish.

scour[2] v. SEARCH, comb, go over, look all over, ransack, hunt through, rake through, rummage through, leave no stone unturned.

scourge n. BANE, curse, affliction, plague, trial, torment, torture, suffering, burden, cross to bear, thorn in one's flesh/side, nuisance, pest, punishment, penalty.

scout n. LOOKOUT, outrider, spy. ►v. RECONNOITRE, make a reconnaissance of, spy out, survey, inspect, investigate, examine, scan.

scowl v. FROWN, glower, glare, lower, look daggers. ►n. FROWN, glower, glare, black look, dirty look.

scraggy adj. see SCRAWNY.

scramble v. **1** CLAMBER, climb, crawl. **2** HURRY, hasten, rush, race, scurry. **3** MIX UP, jumble, tangle, throw into confusion, disorganize. ►n. **1** CLAMBER, climb, trek. **2** HURRY, rush, race, scurry.

scrap n. **1** FRAGMENT, piece, bit, snippet, remnant, leftover, tatter, morsel, par-

scrape v. 1 drag a hard or sharp implement across a surface. 2 rub against a rough surface. 3 just manage to achieve. ▶n. 1 an act or sound of scraping. 2 an injury or mark caused by scraping. 3 informal an embarrassing or difficult situation.

scrapie n. a disease of sheep causing loss of coordination.

scrappy adj. disorganized or incomplete.

scratch v. 1 mark or wound with something sharp or pointed. 2 rub part of the body with one's fingernails to relieve itching. 3 withdraw from a competition. 4 cancel or abandon. ▶n. a mark or wound made by scratching. ▶adj. assembled from whatever is available. □ **from scratch** from the very beginning. **scratch card** a card with sections which may be scraped to reveal whether a prize has been won. **up to scratch** up to the required standard. ■ scratchy adj.

scrawl v. write in a hurried, careless way. ▶n. scrawled handwriting.

scrawny adj. (**scrawnier**, **scrawniest**) thin and bony.

scream v. make a loud, piercing cry, esp. of fear or pain. ▶n. 1 a screaming cry or sound. 2 informal a very funny person or thing.

scree n. a mass of small loose stones on a mountainside.

screech n. a loud, harsh cry or sound. ▶v. make a screech.

screed n. a long speech or piece of writing.

screen n. 1 an upright partition used to divide a room or hide something. 2 the flat front surface of a television, VDU, etc., on which images and data are displayed. 3 a blank surface on to which films are projected. ▶v. 1 conceal or protect with a screen. 2 show or broadcast a film or television programme. 3 test for the presence or absence of a disease. □ **screenplay** the script of a film. **screen saver** a computer program which replaces an unchanging screen display with a moving image.

screw n. 1 a metal pin with a spiral ridge round its length, turned and pressed into a surface to join things together. 2 a propeller. 3 informal a prison warder. ▶v. 1 fasten or tighten with a screw or screws. 2 rotate so as to attach or remove. 3 informal swindle. □ **screwdriver** a tool for turning screws. **screw up** 1 crush into a tight mass. 2 informal cause to go wrong. 3 informal make emotionally disturbed.

scribble v. write or draw carelessly or hurriedly. ▶n. something scribbled.

scribe n. (in the past) a person who copied out documents.

scrimmage n. a confused struggle.

scrimp v. economize; save.

script n. 1 the written text of a play, film, or broadcast. 2 handwriting as distinct from print. ▶v. write a script for.

scripture (or **scriptures**) n. the sacred writings of Christianity or another religion. ■ scriptural adj.

scroll n. 1 a roll of parchment or paper. 2 an ornamental design in the shape of this. ▶v. move text up or down on a computer screen.

scrotum n. (pl. **scrota** or **scrotums**) the pouch of skin containing the testicles.

scrounge v. informal try to get something without paying or working for it. ■ scrounger n.

scrub v. (**scrubbing**, **scrubbed**) 1 rub

Thesaurus s

ticle, sliver. 2 WASTE, junk, rubbish. ▶v. THROW AWAY, get rid of, discard, toss out, abandon, jettison, dispense with, shed; informal ditch, junk. ■ OPPOSITES keep, preserve.

scrape v. 1 SCOUR, rub, scrub, abrade, remove, erase, grate, rasp, grind, file, sandpaper. 2 GRAZE, scratch, skin, cut, lacerate, bark. ▶n. GRAZE, scratch, abrasion, cut, laceration, wound.

scratch v. SCRAPE, abrade, graze, score, cut, lacerate. ▶n. SCRAPE, abrasion, graze, cut, laceration, wound, mark, line.

scream v. SHRIEK, howl, shout, cry out, call out, yell, screech, wail, squawk,

bawl; informal holler. ▶n. SHRIEK, howl, shout, yell, cry, screech, wail, squawk.

screen n. 1 SHIELD, protection, shelter, guard, safeguard, buffer. 2 COVER, cloak, veil, mask, camouflage, disguise, facade, front, blind. 3 SIEVE, riddle, strainer, colander, filter. ▶v. 1 PARTITION OFF, divide off, screen off. 2 SHELTER, shield, protect, guard, safeguard. 3 VET, check, test, examine, investigate, scan.

scribble v. DASH OFF, jot down, scrawl.

scrimp v. SKIMP, economize, be frugal, be thrifty, husband one's resources, tighten one's belt, draw in one's horns.

script n. 1 HANDWRITING, writing, hand, pen, calligraphy. 2 TEXT, book, libretto, hard to clean. **2** informal cancel. ▶ n. **1** an act of scrubbing. **2** vegetation consisting mainly of bushes and small trees. **3** land covered with scrub.

scruff n. the back of the neck.

scruffy adj. (**scruffier**, **scruffiest**) shabby and untidy. ■ **scruffily** adv.

scrum n. **1** (also **scrummage**) Rugby a formation in which players push against each other with heads down and the ball is thrown in. **2** informal a disorderly crowd.

scrumptious adj. informal delicious.

scrumpy n. strong cider made in the west of England.

scrunch v. crush or squeeze into a tight mass.

scruple n. a feeling of doubt as to whether an action is morally right. ▶ v. be reluctant to do something one thinks may be wrong.

scrupulous adj. very careful and thorough. ■ **scrupulously** adv.

scrutinize (or **-ise**) v. examine closely and thoroughly.

scrutiny n. (pl. **scrutinies**) careful examination.

scuba-diving n. swimming underwater using an aqualung.

scud v. (**scudding**, **scudded**) move quickly, driven by the wind.

scuff v. **1** scrape a shoe etc. against something. **2** mark by scuffing.

scuffle n. a short, confused fight or struggle. ▶ v. engage in a scuffle.

scull n. **1** each of a pair of small oars used by a single rower. **2** a light boat propelled by a single rower. ▶ v. row with sculls.

scullery n. (pl. **sculleries**) a room for washing dishes and other household work.

sculpt v. carve or shape.

sculpture n. **1** the art of making figures and shapes by carving or shaping stone, wood, metal, etc. **2** a work made in this way. ▶ v. make by sculpture. ■ **sculptor** (fem. **sculptress**) n. **sculptural** adj.

scum n. **1** a layer of dirt or froth on the surface of a liquid. **2** informal a worthless person.

scupper n. a hole in a ship's side to drain water from the deck. ▶ v. **1** sink a ship deliberately. **2** informal spoil or ruin.

scurf n. flakes of skin.

scurrilous adj. insulting and abusive.

scurry v. (**scurrying**, **scurried**) move hurriedly with short, quick steps.

scurvy n. a disease caused by a lack of vitamin C.

scut n. the short tail of a hare, rabbit, or deer.

scuttle n. a metal container used to fetch and store coal. ▶ v. **1** scurry. **2** sink a ship deliberately.

scythe n. a tool with a long curved blade, for cutting long grass.

SE abbrev. **1** south-east. **2** south-eastern.

sea n. **1** the area of salt water surrounding the land masses of the earth. **2** a particular area of this. **3** a vast ex-

Thesaurus

score, lines, words, manuscript.

scrounge v. BEG, borrow; informal sponge, cadge, bum; US informal mooch.

scrounger n. BEGGAR, borrower, parasite; informal sponger, cadger, freeloader.

scrub v. RUB, scour, clean, cleanse, wipe.

scruffy adj. UNTIDY, unkempt, dishevelled, ungroomed, ill-groomed, shabby, down at heel, ragged, tattered, slovenly, messy, slatternly, sluttish. ■ OPPOSITES smart.

scruple v. HAVE QUALMS ABOUT, hesitate to, think twice about, balk at, demur about, be reluctant to, recoil from, shrink from, waver about, vacillate about.

scruples pl. n. QUALMS, compunction, hesitation, second thoughts, doubt, misgivings, uneasiness, reluctance, restraint, wavering, vacillation.

scrupulous adj. **1** METICULOUS, careful, painstaking, thorough, rigorous, strict, conscientious, punctilious, exact, precise, fastidious. **2** HONEST, honourable, upright, righteous, right-minded, moral, ethical. ■ OPPOSITES careless, unscrupulous.

scrutinize v. EXAMINE, study, inspect, survey, scan, look over, investigate, go over, peruse, probe, inquire into, sift, analyse, dissect.

scrutiny n. EXAMINATION, study, inspection, perusal, investigation, exploration, probe, inquiry, analysis, dissection; informal going-over.

sculpture n. STATUE, statuette, bust, figure, figurine. ▶ v. SCULPT, chisel, model, fashion, shape, cast, carve, cut, hew.

scum n. **1** FILM, crust, algae, filth, dirt. **2** LOWEST OF THE LOW, dregs of society, riff-raff, rabble.

scupper v. **1** SINK, submerge. **2** RUIN, defeat, demolish, wreck, smash.

scurrilous adj. ABUSIVE, insulting, offensive, disparaging, defamatory, slanderpanse. □ **at sea** confused. **seaboard** the coast. **sea change** a great or remarkable transformation. **seafaring** travelling by sea. **seafood** shellfish and sea fish as food. **seagoing** of or for sea voyages. **seagull** a gull. **sea horse** a small sea fish that swims upright and has a horse-like head. **sea lion** a large seal. **seaman** a sailor. **seaplane** an aircraft designed to land on and take off from water. **seascape** a view or picture of the sea. **seasick** suffering from nausea caused by the motion of a ship. **seaside** a beach area, esp. as a holiday resort. **sea urchin** a sea animal with a round spiny shell. **seaweed** large algae growing in the sea. **seaworthy** (of a boat) in good enough condition to sail on the sea. ▪ **seaward** adj. & adv. **seawards** adv.

seal n. **1** a device or substance used to join things or prevent fluid passing through. **2** a piece of wax with a design stamped into it, attached to a document. **3** a confirmation or guarantee. **4** a sea mammal with flippers and a streamlined body. ▸ v. **1** fasten or close securely. **2** coat so as to prevent fluid passing through. **3** make definite; conclude.

sealant n. material used to make something airtight or watertight.

seam n. **1** a line where two pieces of fabric are sewn together. **2** an underground layer of coal etc. ▸ v. join with a seam.

seamless adj. smooth and without obvious joins. ▪ **seamlessly** adv.

seamstress n. a woman who sews, esp. as a job.

seamy adj. (**seamier**, **seamiest**) immoral; sordid.

seance /say-onss/ n. a meeting at which people attempt to make contact with the dead.

sear v. burn or scorch.

search v. **1** try to find. **2** examine thoroughly in order to find something. **3** (**searching**) investigating deeply. ▸ n. an act of searching. □ **search engine** a computer program for finding data etc. on a database or network. **searchlight** a powerful outdoor light with a movable beam. ▪ **searcher** n. **searchingly** adv.

season n. **1** each of the four divisions of the year marked by particular weather and daylight hours. **2** a period of the year when a particular activity takes place. ▸ v. **1** add salt etc. to food. **2** dry wood for use as timber. **3** (**seasoned**) experienced. □ **in season 1** (of fruit etc.) ready to eat. **2** (of a female mammal) ready to mate. **season ticket** a ticket allowing travel or admission within a particular period.

seasonable adj. usual for a particular season.

seasonal adj. **1** of a particular season. **2** changing according to the season. ▪ **seasonally** adv.

seasoning n. salt or spices added to food to improve the flavour.

seat n. **1** a thing made or used for sitting on. **2** the buttocks. **3** a place in an elected parliament or council. **4** a site or location. **5** a large country house. ▸ v. **1** cause to sit. **2** have seats for. □ **seat belt** a belt used to secure someone in the seat of a vehicle or aircraft.

Thesaurus

ous, gross, foul, scandalous.

scurry v. HURRY, hasten, make haste, rush, race, dash, run, sprint, scuttle, scamper, scramble.

seal n. **1** EMBLEM, symbol, insignia, badge, crest, token, mark, monogram. **2** SEALANT, sealer, adhesive. ▸ v. **1** FASTEN, secure, shut, close up. **2** MAKE AIRTIGHT, make watertight, close, shut, cork, stopper. **3** SECURE, clinch, settle, decide, complete. □ **seal off** CLOSE OFF, shut off, cordon off, fence off.

seam n. **1** JOINT, join, junction. **2** LAYER, stratum, vein, lode.

sear v. BURN, singe, scorch, char, dry up, wither, discolour, brown.

search v. **1** GO THROUGH, look through, hunt through, rummage through, forage through, rifle through, scour, ransack, comb, go through with a finetooth comb, sift through, turn upside down, turn inside out, leave no stone unturned in. **2** LOOK FOR, seek, hunt for, look high and low for, cast around for, ferret about for, scout out. **3** EXAMINE, inspect, check; informal frisk. ▸ n. **1** HUNT, rummage, forage, ransacking. **2** EXPLORATION, quest, probe.

season n. PERIOD, time, time of year, spell, term. ▸ v. **1** FLAVOUR, add flavouring to, spice, add spices to; informal pep up, add zing to. **2** MATURE, age, mellow, prime, prepare.

seasonable adj. OPPORTUNE, timely, well timed, appropriate, suitable, apt.

seasoned adj. EXPERIENCED, practised, well versed, established, long-serving, veteran, hardened, battle-scarred,

sebaceous /si-bay-shuhss/ adj. producing oil or fat.

secateurs pl. n. pruning clippers for use with one hand.

secede v. withdraw from an alliance or federation. ■ **secession** n.

secluded adj. **1** (of a place) sheltered and private. **2** having little contact with others.

seclusion n. privacy.

second[1] adj. & n. **1** that is number two in a sequence. **2** lower in position, rank, or importance. **3** (**seconds**) goods of inferior quality. **4** an attendant at a duel or boxing match. ▶ v. formally support a proposal etc. □ **second best** not quite as good as the best. **second class** next or inferior to first class in quality etc. **second-degree** (of burns) causing blistering but not permanent scars. **second-hand 1** having had a previous owner. **2** learned from others. **second nature** a habit that has become instinctive. **second-rate** of poor quality. **second sight** the supposed ability to foresee the future. **second thoughts** a change of opinion after reconsideration. **second wind** fresh energy enabling one to continue with an activity. ■ **secondly** adv.

second[2] n. one-sixtieth of a minute.

second[3] /si-kond/ v. temporarily move a worker to another job or role. ■ **secondment** n.

secondary adj. **1** coming after or less important than something primary. **2** of education for children from the age of 11 to 16 or 18. ■ **secondarily** adv.

secret adj. kept from or not known by others. ▶ n. **1** something secret. **2** a method of achieving something. ■ **secrecy** n. secretly adv.

secretariat n. a government office or department.

secretary n. (pl. **secretaries**) **1** a person employed to type letters, keep records, etc. **2** an administrative official of an organization etc. **3** the chief assistant of a government minister. □ **Secretary of State** (in the UK) the head of a major government department. ■ **secretarial** adj.

secrete v. **1** (of a cell, gland, etc.) produce and discharge a substance. **2** hide. ■ **secretion** n. **secretory** adj.

secretive adj. inclined to hide one's feelings or withhold information. ■ **secretively** adv.

Thesaurus

■ OPPOSITES inexperienced.

seat n. **1** CHAIR, bench, settle, stool, stall. **2** HEADQUARTERS, location, site, base, centre, hub, heart. **3** BUTTOCKS, bottom, rump, hindquarters; *informal* behind, backside, bum; *US informal* butt, tail, fanny; *humorous* posterior. ▶ v. **1** PLACE, position, put, situate, deposit. **2** HOLD, take, have room for, accommodate.

secluded adj. SHELTERED, concealed, hidden, private, solitary, lonely, sequestered, retired, out of the way, remote, isolated, off the beaten track, tucked away, cut-off. ■ OPPOSITES accessible.

seclusion n. PRIVACY, solitude, retreat, retirement, withdrawal, sequestration, isolation, concealment, hiding, secrecy.

second[1] adj. **1** SECONDARY, lower, subordinate, lesser, lower-grade, inferior. **2** ADDITIONAL, extra, further. ▶ n. ASSISTANT, attendant, helper, supporter, backer, right-hand man/woman. ▶ v. SUPPORT, give one's support to, back, approve, give one's approval to, endorse, promote.

second[2] n. MOMENT, instant, trice, twinkling, twinkling of an eye; *informal* sec, jiffy, tick, two shakes of a lamb's tail, two shakes.

secondary adj. **1** LESSER, subordinate, minor, ancillary, subsidiary, nonessential, unimportant. **2** NON-PRIMARY, derived, derivative, indirect, resulting, resultant. **3** RESERVE, back-up, relief, auxiliary, extra, alternative, subsidiary. ■ OPPOSITES primary.

second-hand adj. USED, pre-owned, worn, nearly new, handed down, hand-me-down; *informal, dated* reach-me-down. ▶ adv. AT SECOND HAND, indirectly. ■ OPPOSITES directly.

second-rate adj. SECOND-CLASS, low-class, inferior, lesser, substandard, poor-quality, low-quality, low-grade, shoddy, rubbishy, tawdry. ■ OPPOSITES first-rate, excellent.

secret adj. **1** CONFIDENTIAL, private, unrevealed, undisclosed, under wraps, unpublished, untold, unknown; *informal* hush-hush. **2** HIDDEN, concealed, camouflaged, disguised, clandestine, furtive, conspiratorial, undercover, surreptitious, stealthy, cloak-and-dagger, covert. ■ OPPOSITES open, obvious.

secrete[1] v. DISCHARGE, emit, excrete, exude, ooze, leak, give off, send out. ■ OPPOSITES absorb.

secrete[2] v. HIDE, conceal, cover up, stow away, sequester, cache; *informal* stash away. ■ OPPOSITES reveal.

s

sect n. a small religious or political group with different beliefs from those of a larger group to which they belong.

sectarian adj. of a sect or group.

section n. **1** any of the parts into which something is divided. **2** a distinct group. **3** a cross section. ▶v. **1** divide into sections. **2** commit to a psychiatric hospital. ■ **sectional** adj.

sector n. **1** a distinct area or part. **2** a part of a circle between two lines drawn from its centre to its circumference.

secular adj. not religious or spiritual.

secure adj. **1** certain to remain safe. **2** fixed or fastened so as not to give way, become loose, etc. **3** free from fear or anxiety. ▶v. **1** make secure. **2** obtain. ■ **securely** adv.

security n. (pl. **securities**) **1** the state of being or feeling secure. **2** the safety of a state or organization. **3** a valuable item given as a guarantee that one will repay a loan.

sedan n. **1** hist. an enclosed chair carried between two horizontal poles. **2** US a car for four or more people.

sedate adj. calm and unhurried. ▶v. give a sedative to. ■ **sedately** adv. **sedation** n.

sedative adj. making someone calm or sleepy. ▶n. a sedative drug.

sedentary adj. **1** involving little exercise. **2** tending to spend much time seated.

sedge n. a grass-like marsh plant.

sediment n. **1** matter that settles to the bottom of a liquid. **2** material carried and deposited by water or wind. ■ **sedimentary** adj.

sedition n. actions or speech inciting rebellion. ■ **seditious** adj.

seduce v. **1** persuade to do something unwise. **2** tempt into sexual activity. ■ **seducer** n. **seduction** n. **seductive** adj.

sedulous adj. dedicated and careful.

see v. (**seeing, saw**; past part. **seen**) **1** perceive with the eyes. **2** experience. **3** realize or deduce. **4** think of in a particular way. **5** meet. **6** meet regularly as a boyfriend or girlfriend. **7** guide or lead to a place. ▶n. the district or position of a bishop or archbishop. □ **see off** escort to the point of departure. **see to 1** deal with. **2** ensure that.

Thesaurus

secretive adj. SECRET, reticent, uncommunicative, unforthcoming, reserved, taciturn, silent, quiet, tight-lipped, close-mouthed, close, playing one's cards close to one's chest; *informal* cagey. ■ OPPOSITES open.

secretly adv. IN SECRET, confidentially, privately, behind closed doors, in camera, sub rosa.

sectarian adj. BIGOTED, prejudiced, doctrinaire, partisan, narrow-minded, insular, hidebound, extreme, fanatic, fanatical. ■ OPPOSITES tolerant.

section n. PART, segment, division, department, component, piece, portion, bit, slice, fraction, fragment.

sector n. **1** PART, division, area, branch, department, category, field. **2** ZONE, quarter, district, area, region.

secular adj. LAY, non-religious, non-spiritual, non-church, laical, temporal, worldly, earthly. ■ OPPOSITES holy, religious.

secure adj. **1** SAFE, free from danger, out of harm's way, invulnerable, unharmed, undamaged, protected, sheltered, shielded. **2** FASTENED, closed, shut, locked, sealed. **3** STABLE, fixed, steady, strong, sturdy, solid. **4** UNWORRIED, at ease, comfortable, confident, assured. ▶v. **1** MAKE SAFE, make sound,

fortify, strengthen, protect. **2** FASTEN, close, shut, lock, bolt, chain, seal. **3** ACQUIRE, obtain, gain, get, get hold of, procure, get possession of, come by; *informal* get one's hands on, land.

sedate¹ v. GIVE A SEDATIVE TO, put under sedation, tranquillize.

sedate² adj. **1** CALM, tranquil, placid, dignified, formal, decorous, proper, demure, sober, earnest, staid, stiff. **2** SLOW, slow-moving, leisurely, measured, deliberate, dignified. ■ OPPOSITES exciting, fast.

sedative n. TRANQUILLIZER, calmative, depressant, sleeping pill, narcotic, opiate; *informal* downer. ▶adj. CALMING, tranquillizing, soothing, relaxing, assuaging, lenitive, soporific, narcotic.

sedentary adj. SITTING, seated, deskbound, desk, inactive. ■ OPPOSITES active.

sediment n. DREGS, lees, grounds, deposit, residue, precipitate, settlings.

seduce v. **1** PERSUADE TO HAVE SEX; *informal* have one's (wicked) way with, take advantage of; *dated* debauch. **2** ATTRACT, lure, tempt, entice, beguile, ensnare.

seductive adj. ATTRACTIVE, alluring, appealing, inviting, tempting, enticing, beguiling, provocative, exciting, arousing, sexy.

seed n. **1** a small object produced by a plant, from which a new plant may grow. **2** the beginning of a feeling, process, etc. **3** old use semen. **4** any of the stronger competitors in a sports tournament who are kept from playing each other in the early rounds. ▶v. **1** sow with seeds. **2** remove the seeds from. **3** make a competitor a seed in a tournament.

seedling n. a young plant raised from seed.

seedy adj. (**seedier**, **seediest**) sordid or disreputable. ■ **seediness** n.

seek v. (**seeking**, **sought**) **1** try to find or obtain. **2** try or want to do.

seem v. give the impression of being. ■ **seemingly** adv.

seemly adj. respectable or in good taste.

seen past part. of SEE.

seep v. flow or leak slowly through a substance. ■ **seepage** n.

seer n. a person supposedly able to foresee the future.

see-saw n. a long plank balanced on a fixed support, on which children sit at each end and move up and down by pushing the ground with their feet. ▶v. repeatedly change between two states or positions.

seethe v. **1** boil or churn. **2** be filled with great but unexpressed anger.

segment n. each of the parts into which something is divided. ▶v. divide into segments.

segregate v. keep separate from others. ■ **segregation** n.

seine /sayn/ n. a fishing net which hangs vertically from floats.

seismic /syz-mik/ adj. of earthquakes.

seismograph n. an instrument for measuring and recording earthquakes.

seismology n. the study of earthquakes. ■ **seismologist** n.

seize v. **1** take hold of suddenly and forcibly. **2** take possession of by force or by right. **3** (**seize on**) take eager advantage of. **4** (**seize up**) become jammed.

....

☑ **seize** is an exception to the usual rule of *i* before *e* except after *c*.

....

seizure n. **1** the act of seizing. **2** a stroke or an epileptic fit.

seldom adv. not often.

select v. carefully choose as the best or most suitable. ▶adj. **1** carefully chosen. **2** used by or made up of wealthy people. ■ **selector** n.

Thesaurus

....

see v. **1** MAKE OUT, catch sight of, glimpse, spot, notice, observe, view, perceive, discern, espy, descry, distinguish, identify, recognize. **2** WATCH, look at, view. **3** UNDERSTAND, grasp, get, comprehend, follow, take in, know, realize, get the drift of, make out, fathom. **4** FIND OUT, discover, learn, ascertain, determine, ask, enquire, make enquiries, investigate. **5** FORESEE, predict, forecast, anticipate, envisage, picture, visualize. □ **see about** SEE TO, deal with, attend to, cope with, look after, take care of. **see through** NOT BE TAKEN IN BY, be wise to, get the measure of, penetrate; *informal* have someone's number.

seed n. **1** OVULE, pip, kernel, stone, germ. **2** SOURCE, origin, root, cause, reason.

seek v. **1** SEARCH FOR, look for, be on the lookout for, be after, hunt for, be in quest of, be in pursuit of. **2** ASK FOR, request, solicit, entreat, beg for.

seem v. APPEAR, appear to be, have the appearance of being, give the impression of being, look, look like, look to be, have the look of.

seep v. OOZE, leak, exude, drip, drain, percolate.

see-saw v. FLUCTUATE, go from one extreme to the other, swing, oscillate.

seethe v. **1** BOIL, bubble, fizz, foam, froth, ferment, churn. **2** BE FURIOUS, be livid, be incensed, storm, fume.

segment n. SECTION, part, division, component, piece, portion, slice, wedge.

segregate v. SEPARATE, set apart, isolate, cut off, sequester, ostracize, discriminate against. ■ OPPOSITES amalgamate.

segregation n. SEPARATION, setting apart, isolation, dissociation, sequestration, discrimination, apartheid, partition.

seize v. **1** GRAB, grab hold of, take hold of, grasp, take a grip of, grip, clutch at. **2** CONFISCATE, impound, commandeer, appropriate, sequester, sequestrate. **3** SNATCH, abduct, take captive, kidnap, hijack.

seizure n. **1** CONFISCATION, commandeering, appropriation, sequestration. **2** SNATCHING, abduction, kidnapping, hijacking.

seldom adv. RARELY, hardly ever, scarcely ever, infrequently, only occasionally; *informal* once in a blue moon. ■ OPPOSITES frequently.

select v. CHOOSE, pick, hand-pick, single

selection n. **1** the act of selecting. **2** things selected. **3** a range from which to choose.

selective adj. **1** of selection. **2** tending to choose carefully. **3** affecting some things and not others. ■ **selectively** adv. **selectivity** n.

selenium n. a chemical element.

self n. (pl. **selves**) **1** a person's essential being that distinguishes them from others. **2** a person's particular nature.

self- comb. form of, to, or by oneself or itself.

self-assurance n. confidence. ■ **self-assured** adj.

self-centred adj. obsessed with oneself and one's affairs.

self-confidence n. trust in one's abilities and qualities. ■ **self-confident** adj.

self-conscious adj. nervous or awkward from knowing that one is being observed.

self-contained adj. **1** complete in itself. **2** (of accommodation) having its own facilities. **3** independent.

self-control n. the ability to control one's emotions and behaviour. ■ **self-controlled** adj.

self-denial n. not allowing oneself to

have things that one wants.

self-determination n. the right of a country to run its own affairs.

self-evident adj. obvious.

self-interest n. one's personal interest or advantage.

selfish adj. concerned mainly with one's own needs or wishes. ■ **selfishly** adv. **selfishness** n.

selfless adj. unselfish.

self-made adj. having become successful or rich by one's own efforts.

self-possessed adj. calm, confident, and in control of one's feelings. ■ **self-possession** n.

self-raising adj. (of flour) having baking powder already added.

self-respect n. pride and confidence in oneself.

self-righteous adj. certain that one is correct or morally superior.

selfsame adj. (**the selfsame**) the very same.

self-satisfied adj. smugly pleased with oneself. ■ **self-satisfaction** n.

self-seeking adj. concerned only with one's own welfare and interests.

self-service adj. (of a shop etc.) in which customers select goods and pay at a checkout.

Thesaurus

out, opt for, decide on, settle on, prefer, favour. ▶adj. **1** CHOICE, hand-picked, prime, first-rate, first-class, finest, best, high-quality, top-quality. **2** EXCLUSIVE, elite, limited, privileged, cliquey, cliquish; *informal* posh. ■ OPPOSITES inferior.

selection n. **1** CHOICE, pick, option. **2** VARIETY, assortment, anthology, miscellany, collection, range.

selective adj. PARTICULAR, discriminating, discriminatory, discerning, fussy, careful, cautious; *informal* choosy, picky.

self-centred adj. EGOCENTRIC, egotistical, self-absorbed, self-seeking, wrapped up in oneself, selfish, narcissistic.

self-confidence n. SELF-ASSURANCE, confidence, poise, self-reliance, self-dependence, self-possession, aplomb, composure, sangfroid.

self-conscious adj. AWKWARD, shy, diffident, bashful, blushing, timorous, nervous, timid, retiring, shrinking, ill at ease, embarrassed, uncomfortable. ■ OPPOSITES confident.

self-control n. SELF-RESTRAINT, restraint, self-discipline, will power, strength of will.

self-important adj. POMPOUS, vain, conceited, arrogant, swollen-headed, egotis-

tical, presumptuous, overbearing, overweening, haughty, swaggering, strutting. ■ OPPOSITES humble.

self-indulgence n. SELF-GRATIFICATION, lack of self-restraint, intemperance, immoderation, excess, pleasure-seeking, sensualism, dissipation.

selfish adj. SELF-SEEKING, self-centred, egocentric, egotistic, egoistic, self-interested, self-regarding, self-absorbed; *informal* looking out for number one. ■ OPPOSITES unselfish, selfless.

selfless adj. UNSELFISH, altruistic, generous, self-sacrificing, self-denying, magnanimous, liberal, ungrudging. ■ OPPOSITES selfish.

self-respect n. SELF-ESTEEM, self-regard, pride in oneself, pride in one's abilities, belief in one's worth, faith in oneself, amour propre.

self-righteous adj. SANCTIMONIOUS, pious, holier-than-thou, pietistic, too good to be true, Pharisaic, unctuous, mealy-mouthed; *informal* goody-goody. ■ OPPOSITES humble.

self-sacrifice n. SELF-DENIAL, selflessness, unselfishness, altruism.

self-seeking adj. SELF-INTERESTED, opportunistic, ambitious, mercenary, out

self-styled adj. using a description or title that one has given oneself.

self-sufficient adj. able to do or produce what one needs without outside help. ■ **self-sufficiency** n.

self-willed adj. obstinately doing what one wishes.

sell v. (**selling**, **sold**) **1** exchange goods etc. for money. **2** deal in goods etc. **3** (of goods) achieve sales. **4** (**sell out**) sell all of one's stock. **5** (**sell up**) sell one's house or business. **6** persuade someone of the merits of. **7** (**sell out**) abandon one's principles. ■ **seller** n.

Sellotape n. trademark transparent adhesive tape.

selvedge (or **selvage**) n. an edge on woven fabric that prevents it from unravelling.

selves pl. of SELF.

semantic adj. to do with meaning. ▶(**semantics**) n. the study of the meaning of words. ■ **semantically** adv.

semaphore n. a system of signalling with the arms.

semblance n. the way something looks or seems.

semen n. the liquid containing sperm that is produced by males.

semester n. a half-year term in a school or university.

semi- prefix **1** half. **2** partly.

semibreve n. a musical note equal to four crotchets.

semicircle n. a half of a circle. ■ **semicircular** adj.

semicolon n. a punctuation mark (;).

semiconductor n. a solid that conducts electricity in certain conditions.

semi-detached adj. (of a house) joined to another house on one side.

semi-final n. (in sport) a match or round preceding the final. ■ **semifinalist** n.

seminal adj. **1** strongly influencing later developments. **2** of semen.

seminar n. **1** a meeting for discussion or training. **2** a small group of university students meeting to discuss topics with a teacher.

seminary n. (pl. **seminaries**) a training college for priests or rabbis.

semi-precious adj. (of minerals) used as gems but less valuable than precious stones.

semiquaver n. a musical note equal to half a quaver.

Semite n. a member of the group of peoples including the Jews and Arabs. ■ **Semitic** adj.

semitone n. half a tone in music.

semolina n. the hard grains left after flour is milled, used in puddings and pasta.

senate n. **1** the smaller but higher lawmaking body in the US and other countries. **2** the governing body of a university or college.

senator n. a member of a senate.

send v. (**sending**, **sent**) **1** cause to go or be taken to a destination. **2** cause to move sharply or quickly. **3** cause to be in a specified state. □ **send for** order to come or be brought. **send up** informal ridicule by imitation.

senile adj. having a loss of mental abilities because of old age. ■ **senility** n.

senior adj. **1** of or for older people. **2** of or for schoolchildren above the age of about 11. **3** older. **4** high or higher in status. ▶n. a senior person. □ **senior citizen** an elderly person. ■ **seniority** n.

senna n. a laxative prepared from the dried pods of a tropical tree.

sensation n. **1** a feeling resulting from something that happens to or comes into contact with the body. **2** a vague awareness. **3** a widespread reaction of excited interest, or a person or thing

Thesaurus

for what one can get, fortune-hunting, gold-digging; *informal* on the make, looking out for number one. ■ OPPOSITES altruistic.

sell v. **1** PUT UP FOR SALE, put on sale, dispose of, vend, auction off, trade, barter, trade in, deal in, traffic in, stock, market, handle, peddle, hawk. **2** BOUGHT, be purchased, go, move, be in demand. **3** RETAIL, go for, be, be found for. **4** GET ACCEPTANCE FOR, win approval for, get support for, get across, promote. ■ OPPOSITES buy.

seller n. VENDOR, retailer, salesman/woman/person, shopkeeper, trader, merchant, dealer, agent, representative, rep.

semblance n. APPEARANCE, show, air, guise, pretence, facade, front, veneer, mask, cloak, disguise, camouflage, pretext.

send v. **1** DISPATCH, forward, mail, post, remit. **2** THROW, fling, hurl, cast, let fly, propel, project. **3** DRIVE, make, cause someone to be/become. ■ OPPOSITES receive. □ **send for** CALL FOR, summon, request, order.

senile adj. DODDERING, decrepit, failing, in

causing it.

sensational adj. causing or trying to cause great public interest and excitement. ■ **sensationalism** n. **sensationalist** adj. **sensationally** adv.

sense n. **1** any of the powers of sight, smell, hearing, taste, and touch, by which the body perceives things. **2** a feeling that something is the case. **3** awareness or sensitivity. **4** a sensible and practical attitude. **5** a meaning. ▶ v. **1** perceive by a sense. **2** be vaguely aware of. □ **make sense** be understandable or sensible.

senseless adj. **1** unconscious. **2** lacking meaning, purpose, or common sense.

sensibility n. (pl. **sensibilities**) the ability to respond emotionally.

sensible adj. having or showing common sense. ■ **sensibly** adv.

sensitive adj. **1** quick to detect or be affected by slight changes. **2** appreciating the feelings of others. **3** easily offended or upset. **4** secret or controversial. ■ **sensitively** adv. **sensitivity** n.

sensitize (or **-ise**) v. make sensitive or

aware.

sensor n. a device for detecting or measuring a physical property.

sensory adj. of sensation or the senses.

sensual adj. of the physical senses as a source of pleasure. ■ **sensuality** n. **sensually** adv.

sensuous adj. **1** of the senses rather than the intellect. **2** attractive or pleasing physically. ■ **sensuously** adv.

sent past & past part. of SEND.

sentence n. **1** a set of words that is complete in itself, conveying a statement, question, etc. **2** a punishment given to someone found guilty by a court. ▶ v. declare the punishment decided for an offender.

sententious adj. making pompous comments on moral issues.

sentient adj. able to perceive or feel things. ■ **sentience** n.

sentiment n. **1** an opinion or feeling. **2** sentimentality.

sentimental adj. showing or having excessive feelings of tenderness, sadness, or nostalgia. ■ **sentimentality** n. **sentimentally** adv.

Thesaurus

one's dotage, in one's second childhood; *informal* past it.

senior adj. **1** HIGH-RANKING, higher-ranking, superior. **2** OLDER, elder. ■ OPPOSITES junior.

sensation n. **1** FEELING, sense, awareness, consciousness, perception, impression. **2** STIR, excitement, agitation, commotion, furore, scandal.

sensational adj. **1** SPECTACULAR, stirring, exciting, startling, staggering, dramatic, amazing, shocking, scandalous, lurid. **2** MARVELLOUS, superb, excellent, exceptional, remarkable; *informal* fabulous, fab, out of this world.

sense n. **1** FEELING, sensation, faculty, sensibility. **2** APPRECIATION, awareness, understanding, comprehension. **3** COMMON SENSE, practicality, wisdom, sagacity, sharpness, discernment, perception, wit, intelligence, cleverness, understanding, reason, logic, brains, nous. **4** MEANING, definition, import, signification, significance, implication, nuance, drift, gist, purport, denotation. ▶ v. FEEL, get the impression of, be aware of, be conscious of, observe, notice, perceive, discern, grasp, pick up, suspect, divine, intuit.

senseless adj. **1** NONSENSICAL, stupid, foolish, silly, inane, idiotic, mindless, unintelligent, unwise, irrational, il-

logical, meaningless, pointless, absurd, ludicrous, fatuous, asinine, moronic, imbecilic. **2** UNCONSCIOUS, insensible, out cold, out, stunned, numb, numbed, insensate. ■ OPPOSITES wise.

sensible adj. PRACTICAL, realistic, down-to-earth, wise, prudent, judicious, sagacious, shrewd, discerning, perceptive, intelligent, clever, reasonable, rational, logical. ■ OPPOSITES foolish.

sensitive adj. **1** DELICATE, fine, soft, fragile. **2** RESPONSIVE, receptive, perceptive, discerning, discriminatory, sympathetic, understanding, empathetic. **3** PROBLEMATIC, difficult, delicate, ticklish. ■ OPPOSITES resilient, impervious, uncontroversial. □ **sensitive to** RESPONSIVE TO, easily affected by, susceptible to, reactive to, sentient of.

sensual adj. **1** PHYSICAL, carnal, bodily, fleshly, animal, voluptuous, epicurean, sybaritic. **2** VOLUPTUOUS, sexual, sexy, erotic. ■ OPPOSITES spiritual.

sensuous adj. PLEASING, pleasurable, gratifying, aesthetic.

sentence n. **1** JUDGEMENT, verdict, ruling, decision, decree. **2** PRISON SENTENCE, jail sentence, prison term; *informal* time, porridge. ▶ v. IMPOSE A SENTENCE ON, pass judgement on, penalize, punish, condemn, doom.

sentiment n. **1** EMOTION, emotionalism,

sentinel n. a sentry.

sentry n. (pl. **sentries**) a soldier stationed to keep guard or control access to a place.

sepal n. each of the leaf-like parts of a flower surrounding the petals.

separate adj. forming a unit by itself. ▶v. **1** set, move, or keep apart. **2** stop living together as a couple. **3** divide. ■ **separable** adj. **separately** adv. **separation** n.

✓ The middle is *-par-*, not *-per-*: se**par**ate.

separatist n. a member of a group favouring separation and independence from a larger group. ■ **separatism** n.

sepia n. a reddish-brown colour.

sepsis n. the presence in tissues of harmful bacteria.

September n. the ninth month.

septet n. a group of seven playing music or singing together.

septic adj. infected with bacteria. □ **septic tank** an underground tank in which sewage decomposes before draining into the soil.

septicaemia (US **septicemia**) n. blood poisoning caused by bacteria.

septuagenarian n. a person between 70 and 79 years old.

sepulchral adj. gloomy.

sepulchre /sep-uhl-ker/ (US **sepulcher**) n. a stone tomb.

sequel n. **1** a book, film, etc. continuing the story of an earlier one. **2** something taking place after or as a result of an earlier event.

sequence n. **1** an order in which related things follow each other. **2** a set of related things following each other in a particular order.

sequential adj. following in a logical sequence. ■ **sequentially** adv.

sequester v. **1** isolate. **2** sequestrate.

sequestrate v. take legal possession of assets until a debt has been paid. ■ **sequestration** n.

sequin n. a small, shiny disc for decorating clothes. ■ **sequinned** adj.

sequoia n. a redwood tree.

seraglio /si-rah-li-oh/ n. (pl. **seraglios**) a harem.

seraph n. (pl. **seraphim** or **seraphs**) a type of angel associated with light and purity. ■ **seraphic** adj.

serenade n. a piece of music sung or played by a man to the woman he loves, outdoors and at night. ▶v. sing or play a serenade for.

serendipity n. the fortunate occurrence of events by chance. ■ **serendipitous** adj.

serene adj. calm and peaceful. ■ **serenely** adv. **serenity** n.

serf n. (in the feudal system) an agricultural labourer tied to working on a particular estate.

serge n. a hard-wearing fabric.

sergeant n. **1** a non-commissioned officer in the army or air force above corporal. **2** a police officer ranking below an inspector.

serial adj. **1** of or forming part of a series. **2** repeatedly committing the same offence: *a serial killer.* ▶n. a story published or broadcast in regular instal-

Thesaurus

finer feelings, tender feelings, tenderness, softness. **2** FEELINGS, attitude, belief, opinion, view, point of view.

sentimental adj. **1** ROMANTIC, emotional, mawkish, maudlin; *informal* mushy, slushy, schmaltzy, corny, soppy. **2** NOSTALGIC, emotional, affectionate, loving, tender, warm.

sentiments pl. n. FEELING, attitude, belief, thoughts, way of thinking, opinion, view, point of view, idea, judgement.

sentry n. GUARD, lookout, watch, watchman, sentinel.

separate adj. **1** INDIVIDUAL, distinct, different, particular, autonomous, independent. **2** UNCONNECTED, distinct, different, disconnected, unrelated, detached, divorced, divided, discrete. ▶v. **1** DISCONNECT, detach, sever, uncouple, divide, sunder. **2** DIVIDE, come between,

stand between, keep apart, partition. **3** PART, part company, go their/your/ our separate ways, go different ways, diverge, split, divide. **4** BREAK UP, split up, part, become estranged, divorce. ■ OPPOSITES join, unite.

separately adv. **1** APART, individually, independently, autonomously. **2** INDIVIDUALLY, one by one, one at a time, singly, severally, independently.

septic adj. INFECTED, festering, poisoned, putrefying, putrefactive, putrid.

sequel n. FOLLOW-UP, development, result, consequence, outcome, issue, upshot.

sequence n. CHAIN, course, cycle, series, progression, succession, set, arrangement, order, pattern.

serene adj. CALM, composed, tranquil, peaceful, placid, still, quiet, unperments. □ **serial number** an identification number given to a manufactured item. ■ **serially** adv.

serialize (or **-ise**) v. publish or broadcast as a serial. ■ **serialization** n.

series n. (pl. **series**) **1** a number of similar things coming one after another. **2** a sequence of related television or radio programmes.

serious adj. **1** needing careful consideration or action. **2** solemn or thoughtful. **3** sincere and in earnest. **4** dangerous or severe. ■ **seriously** adv. **seriousness** n.

sermon n. a talk on a religious or moral subject, esp. during a church service.

sermonize (or **-ise**) v. give moral advice.

serpent n. a large snake.

serpentine adj. winding or twisting.

serrated adj. having a jagged edge. ■ **serration** n.

serried adj. placed or standing close together.

serum n. (pl. **sera** or **serums**) the thin liquid which separates out when blood clots.

servant n. a person employed to do domestic work in a household or for a person.

serve v. **1** perform duties or services for. **2** be employed as a member of the armed forces. **3** spend a period in a job or in prison. **4** present food or drink to someone. **5** attend to a customer. **6** ful-

fil a purpose. **7** hit the ball in tennis etc. to begin play for each point of a game. ▶n. an act of serving in tennis etc.

server n. **1** a person or thing that serves. **2** a computer or program managing access to a resource or service in a network.

service n. **1** the act of serving. **2** a period of employment with an organization. **3** an act of assistance. **4** a religious ceremony. **5** a system supplying a public need. **6** a department run by the state. **7** (**the services**) the armed forces. **8** a set of matching crockery. **9** a serve in tennis etc. **10** a routine inspection and maintenance of a vehicle etc. ▶v. **1** perform maintenance on. **2** provide services for. **3** pay interest on a debt. □ **service area** a roadside area with a service station, toilets, etc. for motorists. **serviceman** (or **servicewoman**) a member of the armed forces. **service provider** a company which provides access to the Internet. **service road** a road running parallel to a main road, giving access to houses, shops, etc. **service station** a garage selling petrol, oil, etc.

serviceable adj. **1** in working order. **2** useful and hard-wearing.

serviette n. a table napkin.

servile adj. excessively willing to serve or please others. ■ **servility** n.

servitude n. the state of being a slave

turbed, imperturbable, undisturbed, unruffled, unworried, unexcited, unexcitable, unflappable. ■ OPPOSITES excitable, turbulent.

series n. SUCCESSION, progression, sequence, chain, course, string, train, run, cycle, set, row, arrangement, order.

serious adj. **1** SOLEMN, earnest, unsmiling, thoughtful, preoccupied, pensive, grave, sombre, sober, long-faced, dour, stern, grim, poker-faced. **2** IMPORTANT, significant, consequential, of consequence, momentous, weighty, far-reaching, urgent, pressing, crucial, vital, life-and-death. **3** ACUTE, grave, bad, critical, grievous, dangerous, perilous. **4** EARNEST, in earnest, sincere, honest, genuine, firm, resolute, resolved, determined, fervent. ■ OPPOSITES cheerful, minor, trivial.

sermon n. HOMILY, address, oration, lecture, preaching, teaching.

servant n. DOMESTIC, help, domestic

help, maid, handyman, menial, drudge, scullion, retainer, attendant, lackey; *informal* char; *dated* charwoman.

serve v. **1** HAVE/HOLD A PLACE ON, be on, perform duties, carry out duties. **2** ACT AS, do duty as, function as, do the work of, be suitable for. **3** DISH UP, give out, distribute, set out, present, provide. **4** ATTEND TO, look after, take care of, assist.

service n. **1** GOOD TURN, assistance, help, advantage, benefit. **2** WORK, employment, labour, duty, business. **3** CEREMONY, ritual, rite, sacrament. **4** SERVICING, overhaul, check, maintenance, repair. ▶v. CHECK, go over, overhaul, maintain, repair.

serviceable adj. **1** FUNCTIONAL, utilitarian, practical, useful, durable, hard-wearing, tough, strong. **2** USABLE, of use, functioning, operative, repairable. ■ OPPOSITES impractical, unusable.

servile adj. **1** MENIAL, low, lowly, humble, mean, base. **2** SUBSERVIENT, obsequious, or completely subject to someone more powerful.

sesame n. a tropical plant grown for its oil-rich seeds.

session n. 1 a period devoted to a particular activity. 2 a meeting of a council, court, etc. to conduct its business.

set v. (**setting**, **set**) 1 put in a specified place, position, or state. 2 give someone a task. 3 decide on or fix a time, value, etc. 4 establish as an example or record. 5 adjust a device as required. 6 prepare a table for a meal. 7 make or become solid, semi-solid, or fixed. 8 (of the sun etc.) appear to move towards and below the earth's horizon. ▶ n. 1 a number of things or people grouped together. 2 the way something is set. 3 a radio or television receiver. 4 a group of games counting as a unit towards a match in tennis etc. 5 a collection of scenery used for a scene in a play or film. ▶ adj. 1 fixed or established beforehand. 2 (**set on**) determined to do. □ **set about** start doing. **set aside** temporarily stop using land for growing crops. **setback** a problem that delays progress. **set off 1** begin a journey. 2 cause a bomb or alarm to go off. **set out 1** begin a journey. 2 intend.

set square a right-angled triangular drawing instrument. **set up 1** place or erect in position. 2 establish. 3 informal cause an innocent person to appear guilty.

sett n. a badger's burrow.

settee n. a sofa.

setter n. a breed of dog trained to stand rigid on scenting game.

setting n. 1 the way or place in which something is set. 2 a set of crockery and cutlery laid for one person.

settle v. 1 resolve a dispute or problem. 2 adopt a more steady or secure lifestyle. 3 make one's home in a new place. 4 become or make calmer or quieter. 5 begin to feel at ease in a new situation. 6 sit or rest comfortably or securely. 7 pay a debt. 8 (**settle for**) resign oneself to accepting. ▶ n. a wooden bench with a high back and arms. ■ **settlement** n. **settler** n.

seven adj. & n. one more than six; 7 or VII. ■ **seventh** adj. & n.

seventeen adj. & n. one more than sixteen; 17 or XVII. ■ **seventeenth** adj. & n.

seventy adj. & n. (pl. **seventies**) ten less than eighty; 70 or LXX. ■ **seventieth** adj. & n.

Thesaurus

sycophantic, fawning, toadying, grovelling, submissive; *informal* bootlicking. ■ OPPOSITES assertive.

serving n. HELPING, portion, plateful.

session n. 1 PERIOD, time, spell, stretch. 2 MEETING, sitting, assembly, conference, discussion.

set[1] v. 1 PUT, place, lay, lay down, deposit, position, rest, locate, lodge, situate, station; *informal* stick, park, plonk. 2 FIX, embed, insert, lodge, mount, arrange, install. 3 ADJUST, regulate, synchronize, coordinate, harmonize, calibrate, rectify, set right. 4 STYLE, fix, arrange, curl, wave. 5 SOLIDIFY, stiffen, thicken, jell, harden, cake, congeal, coagulate. 6 DECIDE ON, fix, fix on, agree on, appoint, name, specify, stipulate, determine, designate, select, choose, arrange, schedule.

set[2] n. 1 COLLECTION, group, assemblage, series, batch, array, assortment, selection. 2 STAGE SET, setting, scenery, backdrop.

set[3] adj. 1 FIXED, prescribed, scheduled, specified, determined, arranged, appointed, established, decided, agreed. 2 READY, prepared, equipped, primed; *informal* fit, geared up. ■ OPPOSITES vari-

able, unprepared.

setback n. REVERSAL, reverse, upset, check, hitch, hold-up, hindrance, impediment, obstruction, disappointment, misfortune, blow. ■ OPPOSITES breakthrough.

setting n. 1 ENVIRONMENT, surroundings, milieu, background, location, place, site. 2 STAGE SETTING, set, scene, stage, scenery, backdrop. 3 MOUNT, frame.

settle v. 1 MAKE ONE'S HOME, set up home, take up residence, put down roots, establish oneself, go to live, move to, emigrate to. 2 ESTABLISH/FOUND A COLONY, colonize, occupy, people, inhabit, populate. 3 CALM DOWN, quieten down, be quiet, be still, relax. 4 LIGHT, land, come down, descend, repose, rest. 5 RESOLVE, clear up, patch up, reconcile, conclude, bring to an end. 6 PUT IN ORDER, order, arrange, set to rights, straighten out, organize, regulate, adjust, clear up. ■ OPPOSITES agitate, rise. □ **settle for** COMPROMISE ON, accept, agree to, accede to, acquiesce in. **settle on** DECIDE ON, agree on, determine, confirm, arrange, fix, choose, appoint, select.

settlement n. 1 COMMUNITY, colony, village, hamlet, encampment, outpost.

sever v. cut off or break off. ■ **severance** n.

several adj. & pron. more than two but not many. ▸ adj. separate or respective. ■ **severally** adv.

severe adj. **1** (of something bad or difficult) very great. **2** strict or harsh. **3** very plain in style or appearance. ■ **severely** adv. **severity** n.

sew v. (**sewing, sewed**; past part. **sewn** or **sewed**) join or repair by making stitches with a needle and thread.

sewage /soo-ij/ n. waste water and excrement conveyed in sewers.

sewer /soo-er/ n. an underground pipe for sewage. ■ **sewerage** n.

sex n. **1** either of the two main categories (male and female) into which living things are divided. **2** the fact of being male or female. **3** sexual intercourse. ▸ v. determine the sex of.

sexagenarian n. a person between 60 and 69 years old.

sexism n. prejudice or discrimination on the basis of sex. ■ **sexist** adj. & n.

sexless adj. **1** not sexually attractive or active. **2** neither male nor female.

sextant n. an instrument for measuring angles and distances, used in navigation and surveying.

sextet n. **1** a group of six playing music or singing together. **2** music for a sextet.

sexton n. a person who looks after a church and churchyard.

sextuplet n. each of six children born at one birth.

sexual adj. **1** of sex or physical attraction or contact. **2** of the sexes. **3** (of reproduction) involving the fusion of male and female cells. □ **sexual intercourse** sexual contact in which a man puts his erect penis into a woman's vagina. ■ **sexually** adv.

sexuality n. (pl. **sexualities**) **1** capacity for sexual feelings. **2** a person's sexual preference.

sexy adj. (**sexier, sexiest**) **1** sexually attractive or exciting. **2** sexually aroused. **3** informal exciting or appealing. ■ **sexily** adv. **sexiness** n.

shabby adj. (**shabbier, shabbiest**) **1** worn out or scruffy. **2** mean and unfair. ■ **shabbily** adv. **shabbiness** n.

shack n. a roughly built hut.

shackle n. (**shackles**) a pair of rings connected by a chain, used to fasten a prisoner's wrists or ankles. ▸ v. **1** put shackles on. **2** restrain; limit.

shade n. **1** relative darkness and cool-

Thesaurus

2 RESOLUTION, reconciliation, conclusion, agreement, contract, pact, compact.

settler n. COLONIST, colonizer, pioneer, immigrant.

sever v. **1** CUT OFF, chop off, lop off, hack off, break off, tear off. **2** DIVIDE, split, cleave, dissect, halve. **3** BREAK OFF, discontinue, suspend, dissolve, end, terminate, stop, cease, conclude. ■ OPPOSITES join, maintain.

several adj. SOME, a number of, a few.

severe adj. **1** HARSH, hard, stringent, rigorous, unsparing, relentless, merciless, ruthless, painful, sharp, caustic, biting, cutting, scathing, serious, extreme. **2** EXTREME, very bad, serious, grave, acute, critical, dire, dangerous, perilous. **3** FIERCE, strong, violent, intense, powerful, forceful. **4** STERN, grim, cold, chilly, austere, forbidding, dour, disapproving, unsmiling, sombre, grave, sober, serious. **5** AUSTERE, stark, spartan, ascetic, plain, simple, modest, bare, unadorned, unembellished, restrained, functional, classic. ■ OPPOSITES mild, friendly, ornate.

sew v. STITCH, seam, embroider, mend, darn.

sex n. **1** SEXUALITY, sexual attraction, sexual chemistry, sexual desire, desire, sex drive, sexual appetite, libido. **2** FACTS OF LIFE, sexual reproduction, reproduction; informal the birds and the bees. **3** SEXUAL INTERCOURSE, making love, intimacy, coitus, coition, coupling, copulation, carnal knowledge, mating, fornication. **4** GENDER.

sexuality n. **1** SEX, gender, sexual characteristics. **2** SEXUAL DESIRE, sexual appetite, sexiness, carnality, physicalness, eroticism, lust, sensuality, voluptuousness. **3** SEXUAL ORIENTATION, sexual preferences.

sexy adj. **1** EROTIC, titillating, suggestive, arousing, exciting, stimulating. **2** AROUSING, provocative, seductive, sensuous, slinky. **3** ATTRACTIVE, alluring, seductive, shapely.

shabby adj. **1** DILAPIDATED, broken-down, run down, tumbledown, ramshackle, in disrepair, scruffy, dingy, seedy, squalid, tatty; informal tacky. **2** WORN, worn out, threadbare, ragged, frayed, tattered, faded, scruffy, tatty, the worse for wear. **3** CONTEMPTIBLE, despicable, rotten, dishonourable, disreputable, mean, base, low, dirty, odious, shameness caused by shelter from direct sunlight. **2** a colour, esp. with regard to how light or dark it is. **3** a variety. **4** a slight amount. **5** a lampshade. **6 (shades)** informal sunglasses. **7** literary a ghost. ▶v. **1** screen from direct light. **2** cover or reduce the light of. **3** darken parts of a drawing etc. **4** change gradually.

shadow n. **1** a dark area produced by an object coming between light rays and a surface. **2** partial or complete darkness. **3** sadness or gloom. **4** a slight trace. **5** a person who constantly accompanies or secretly follows another. ▶v. **1** cast a shadow over. **2** follow and observe secretly. □ **shadow-boxing** boxing against an imaginary opponent as a form of training. **Shadow Cabinet** members of the main opposition party in Parliament holding posts corresponding to those of the government Cabinet. ■ **shadowy** adj.

shady adj. (**shadier, shadiest**) **1** giving or situated in shade. **2** informal of doubtful honesty or legality.

shaft n. **1** the long, narrow handle of a tool or body of an arrow etc. **2** a ray or beam. **3** a narrow vertical or sloping passage. **4** each of the two poles between which a horse is harnessed to a

vehicle. **5** a rotating rod transmitting mechanical power in a machine.

shag n. **1** coarse tobacco. **2** a cormorant. ▶adj. (of a carpet) with a long, rough pile.

shaggy adj. (**shaggier, shaggiest**) **1** (of hair or fur) long, thick, and untidy. **2** having shaggy hair or fur.

shah n. a title of the former king of Iran.

shake v. (**shaking, shook;** past part. **shaken**) **1** move quickly and jerkily up and down or to and fro. **2** tremble. **3** shock or disturb. **4** (**shake off**) get rid of. ▶n. an act of shaking. □ **shake hands** clasp right hands on meeting, parting, or as a sign of agreement. **shake up 1** stir into action. **2** make major changes to. ■ **shaker** n.

shaky adj. (**shakier, shakiest**) **1** shaking; unsteady. **2** not safe or certain. ■ **shakily** adv.

shale n. soft rock that splits easily.

shall aux. v. **1** used with I and we to express the future tense. **2** expressing determination or an order.

shallot n. a small onion.

shallow adj. **1** not deep. **2** not thinking or thought out seriously. ▶n. (**shallows**) a shallow area of water. ■ **shallowness** n.

sham n. a thing that is not as good or

Thesaurus

ful, ignoble, unworthy, cheap, shoddy. ■ OPPOSITES smart.

shackle v. CHAIN, fetter, put in irons, manacle, tie up, bind, tether, hobble, handcuff.

shade n. **1** SHADINESS, shadow, shadowiness, shadows, shelter, cover. **2** COLOUR, hue, tone, tint, tinge. **3** NUANCE, degree, gradation, difference, variety. ■ OPPOSITES light. ▶v. **1** SHUT OUT THE LIGHT FROM, block off, shield, shut out; cast a shadow over, screen, darken, dim. **2** COVER, obscure, hide, conceal, veil, curtain.

shadow n. **1** see SHADE. **2** SILHOUETTE, outline, shape. **3** A TRACE, a hint, a suggestion, a suspicion, a ghost.

shadowy adj. **1** SHADY, shaded, dim, dark, gloomy, murky, crepuscular, tenebrous. **2** INDISTINCT, indeterminate, indefinite, unclear, vague, nebulous, ill-defined. ■ OPPOSITES bright, clear, distinct.

shady adj. **1** see SHADOWY. **2** DISREPUTABLE, suspicious, suspect, questionable, dishonest, dishonourable, untrustworthy, devious, shifty, slippery, underhand, unscrupulous; informal crooked, tricky, fishy. ■ OPPOSITES

honest.

shaft n. **1** POLE, stick, rod, staff, shank, stem, handle, upright. **2** RAY, beam, gleam, streak, pencil. **3** PASSAGE, duct, tunnel, well, flue.

shaggy adj. HAIRY, hirsute, long-haired, rough, coarse, matted, tangled, unkempt, untidy. ■ OPPOSITES sleek.

shake v. **1** ROCK, bump, jolt, bounce, roll, sway, judder, swing, jar, oscillate, wobble, rattle, vibrate, jerk, joggle, jounce. **2** SHIVER, tremble, quiver, quake, shudder. **3** JIGGLE, joggle, jolt, jerk, rattle, agitate, jounce. **4** AGITATE, upset, distress, shock, alarm, disturb, perturb, fluster, unsettle, discompose, disquiet, disconcert, unnerve, ruffle; informal rattle.

shaky adj. **1** TREMBLING, tremulous, quivering, quivery, unsteady, wobbly, weak, tottering, teetering, doddering, staggering. **2** INFIRM, unsound, unwell, ill, below par, indisposed, light-headed, dizzy, faint; informal under the weather. **3** QUESTIONABLE, dubious, tenuous, flimsy, weak, unsound, unreliable. ■ OPPOSITES steady, sound.

shallow adj. **1** FRIVOLOUS, foolish, uningenuine as it seems to be. ▶ adj. not genuine; false. ▶ v. (**shamming, shammed**) pretend.

shaman /shay-muhn/ n. (in some societies) a person believed to be able to contact good and evil spirits.

shamble v. walk in a slow, shuffling way.

shambles n. informal a state of complete disorder.

shame n. **1** embarrassment or distress arising from awareness that one has done something wrong or foolish. **2** loss of respect. **3** a cause of shame. **4** a cause for regret. ▶ v. cause to feel ashamed. □ **shamefaced** showing shame. ■ **shameful** adj. **shamefully** adv. **shameless** adj.

shammy n. (pl. **shammies**) informal chamois leather.

shampoo n. **1** a liquid soap for washing the hair. **2** a similar substance for cleaning a carpet etc. **3** an act of washing something with shampoo. ▶ v. (**shampooing, shampooed**) wash or clean with shampoo.

shamrock n. a clover-like plant.

shandy n. (pl. **shandies**) beer mixed with lemonade or ginger beer.

shank n. **1** the lower part of the leg. **2** the shaft of a tool.

shan't contr. shall not.

shanty n. (pl. **shanties**) **1** a small roughly built hut. **2** a sailors' traditional song. □ **shanty town** a settlement in or near a town where people live in shanties.

shape n. **1** the form of something produced by its outline. **2** a particular condition: *in poor shape*. **3** structure or orderly arrangement. ▶ v. **1** give a shape to. **2** have a great influence on. **3** (**shape up**) develop in a particular way. ■ **shapeless** adj.

shapely adj. having an attractive shape.

shard n. a piece of broken pottery, glass, etc.

share n. **1** a part of a larger amount which is divided among or contributed by a number of people. **2** any of the equal parts into which a company's wealth is divided, entitling the holder to a proportion of the profits. ▶ v. **1** have or give a share of. **2** have or use jointly. □ **shareholder** an owner of

Thesaurus

telligent, unthinking, trivial, insincere, superficial. **2** SUPERFICIAL, unsubstantial, trifling, trivial, petty, empty, meaningless. ■ OPPOSITES serious, deep.

sham v. FAKE, pretend, feign, counterfeit, put on, simulate, affect, imitate. ▶ n. **1** COUNTERFEIT, fake, forgery, copy, imitation, hoax, pretence, simulation. **2** IMPOSTOR, fake, fraud, pretender, masquerader, dissembler, charlatan; informal phoney. ▶ adj. PRETEND, feigned, artificial, synthetic, ersatz, fake, pseudo, contrived, simulated, affected, put on, insincere, false, bogus, spurious; informal phoney. ■ OPPOSITES genuine.

shamble v. SHUFFLE, hobble, limp, falter, totter, dodder.

shambles pl. n. CHAOS, muddle, mess, confusion, disorder, disarray, disorganization, anarchy; informal disaster area.

shame n. **1** HUMILIATION, ignominy, mortification, loss of face, remorse, guilt, compunction, embarrassment, discomfort, discomposure. **2** DISGRACE, dishonour, scandal, discredit, degradation, ignominy, disrepute, infamy, odium, opprobrium. **3** PITY, misfortune, bad luck, ill luck, source of regret. ■ OPPOSITES pride, honour.

shamefaced adj. **1** ASHAMED, embarrassed, guilty, conscience-stricken, re-

morseful, contrite, penitent, regretful, humiliated, mortified, shamed, sheepish; informal with one's tail between one's legs. **2** SHY, bashful, timid, shrinking, coy. ■ OPPOSITES unrepentant.

shameful adj. **1** DISGRACEFUL, base, mean, low, vile, outrageous, shocking, dishonourable, unbecoming, unworthy, discreditable, deplorable, despicable, contemptible, reprehensible, scandalous, atrocious, heinous. **2** SHAMING, humiliating, mortifying, embarrassing; informal blush-making. ■ OPPOSITES admirable.

shameless adj. **1** UNASHAMED, without shame, unabashed, uncontrite, impenitent. **2** BRAZEN, impudent, bold, brash, forward, audacious, immodest, unseemly, improper, unbecoming, indecorous, wanton, abandoned, indecent. ■ OPPOSITES modest.

shape n. **1** FORM, figure, configuration, formation, conformation, contour, outline, silhouette, profile, outward form, external appearance. **2** GUISE, form, appearance, likeness, look, semblance, image, aspect. **3** CONDITION, state, health, trim, fettle. ▶ v. FORM, fashion, make, mould, model, cast, frame, block, carve, sculpt.

shapeless adj. **1** AMORPHOUS, formless, unformed, unshaped, unfashioned, unshares in a company. ■ **sharer** n.

shark n. **1** a large, usu. predatory sea fish with a triangular fin. **2** informal a person who exploits or swindles others.

sharp adj. **1** having a cutting or piercing edge or point. **2** tapering to a point or edge. **3** sudden and noticeable. **4** clear and definite. **5** producing a sudden, piercing feeling. **6** quick to understand, notice, or respond. **7** unscrupulous. **8** (of a taste or smell) strong and slightly bitter. **9** above true or normal pitch in music. ▶ adv. **1** precisely. **2** suddenly or abruptly. ▶ n. a musical note raised by a semitone, or the sign showing this. ☐ **sharp practice** dishonest business dealings. **sharpshooter** a person skilled in shooting. ■ **sharpen** v. **sharpener** n. **sharply** adv. **sharpness** n.

shatter v. **1** break violently into pieces. **2** destroy. **3** upset greatly.

shave v. **1** remove hair by cutting it off close to the skin with a razor. **2** cut a thin slice from something. **3** pass very close to. ▶ n. an act of shaving. ■ **shaver** n.

shaven adj. shaved.

shaving n. a thin strip cut off a surface.

shawl n. a large piece of fabric worn over the shoulders or wrapped round a baby.

she pron. the female previously mentioned.

sheaf n. (pl. **sheaves**) **1** a bundle of grain stalks. **2** a bundle of papers.

shear v. (**shearing**, **sheared**; past part. **shorn** or **sheared**) **1** cut off or trim with shears. **2** break off because of strain. ▶ pl. n. (**shears**) a cutting implement like very large scissors. ■ **shearer** n.

sheath n. (pl. **sheaths**) **1** a cover for the blade of a knife or sword. **2** a condom.

sheathe v. **1** put a sword etc. into a sheath. **2** encase in a close-fitting cover.

shed n. a simple building used for storage or to shelter animals. ▶ v. (**shedding**, **shed**) **1** have leaves, hair, etc. fall off naturally. **2** give off light. **3** accidentally drop or spill.

sheen n. a soft shine on a surface.

sheep n. (pl. **sheep**) a grass-eating mammal with a thick woolly coat. ☐ **sheepdog** a dog trained to guard and herd sheep. **sheepskin** a sheep's skin with the wool on.

sheepish adj. embarrassed or shy. ■ **sheepishly** adv.

sheer adj. **1** nothing but; absolute. **2** vertical or almost vertical. **3** (of a fabric) very thin. ▶ adv. vertically. ▶ v. change course quickly.

sheet n. **1** a large piece of cotton or

Thesaurus

developed, embryonic. **2** FORMLESS, badly cut, sack-like, ill-proportioned, inelegant.

shapely adj. WELL FORMED, well proportioned, elegant, curvaceous, curvy.

share n. ALLOWANCE, ration, allocation, division, quota, allotment, portion, part, lot, measure, helping, serving; informal cut, rake-off, piece of the cake, piece of the action, whack. ▶ v. **1** DIVIDE, split, have in common, go halves in; informal go fifty-fifty in, go Dutch. **2** DISTRIBUTE, divide, apportion, parcel out, deal out, dole out, give out.

sharp adj. **1** EDGED, razor-edged, keen, cutting, serrated, knife-like, pointed, needle-like, barbed, spiky. **2** STEEP, sheer, abrupt, precipitous, vertical. **3** SUDDEN, abrupt, rapid, unexpected. **4** INTENSE, acute, keen, piercing, cutting, extreme, severe, stabbing, shooting, stinging. **5** PUNGENT, biting, bitter, acid, sour, tart, vinegary. **6** HARSH, curt, brusque, bitter, hard, cutting, scathing, caustic, biting, barbed, acrimonious, trenchant, venomous, malicious, vitriolic, hurtful, unkind, cruel. **7** INTELLI-GENT, bright, clever, quick. **8** KEEN, acute, quick, ready, knowing, shrewd, discerning, perceptive, penetrating; informal smart. ■ OPPOSITES blunt.

sharpen v. PUT AN EDGE ON, edge, whet, hone, strop, grind.

shatter v. **1** SMASH, break, break into pieces, splinter, fracture, pulverize, crush, crack; informal bust. **2** DESTROY, demolish, wreck, ruin, dash, blight, wipe out, devastate; informal torpedo.

shave v. **1** CUT OFF, trim, snip off, crop. **2** PARE, plane, shear. **3** BRUSH, graze, touch, scrape, rub.

sheath n. CASE, casing, cover, covering, envelope, wrapper.

shed[1] n. HUT, outhouse, lean-to, shack.

shed[2] v. **1** LET FALL, let drop, cast off, slough off. **2** TAKE OFF, remove, strip off, doff. **3** SEND FORTH, radiate, disperse, scatter.

sheen n. SHINE, lustre, gleam, sparkle, gloss, burnish, polish, patina.

sheer adj. **1** UTTER, complete, thoroughgoing, total, absolute, veritable, downright, out-and-out, unqualified, unconditional, unmitigated, unalloyed, unother fabric, used to cover a bed. **2** a broad thin piece of metal, glass, paper, etc. **3** an expanse of water, flame, etc. **4** a rope attached to the lower corner of a sail to hold and adjust it.

sheikh (or **sheik**) /shayk/ n. a Muslim or Arab leader. ■ **sheikhdom** n.

shekel n. the basic unit of money of Israel.

shelf n. (pl. **shelves**) **1** a flat length of wood etc. fixed horizontally for displaying or storing things. **2** a ledge of rock. □ **shelf life** the time for which an item to be sold remains fresh or usable.

shell n. **1** the hard outer covering of an egg, nut kernel, or an animal such as a shellfish or turtle. **2** a metal case filled with explosive, fired from a large gun. **3** an outer structure or framework, esp. when hollow. ▶v. **1** fire explosive shells at. **2** remove the shell or pod from. **3** (**shell out**) informal pay a sum of money. □ **shellfish** an edible water animal that has a shell. **shell shock** a mental condition that can be caused by exposure to battle conditions.

shellac n. a resin used in varnish.

shelter n. **1** a place giving protection from bad weather or danger. **2** protection. ▶v. **1** provide with shelter. **2** find or take shelter.

shelve v. **1** put on a shelf. **2** postpone or cancel. **3** slope downwards.

shelving n. shelves.

shepherd n. a person who looks after sheep. ▶v. guide. □ **shepherd's pie** a dish of minced meat topped with mashed potato. ■ **shepherdess** n.

sherbet n. a sweet fizzing powder eaten alone or made into a drink.

sheriff n. **1** (in England and Wales) the

chief executive officer of the Crown in a county. **2** (in Scotland) a judge. **3** US an elected officer in a county, responsible for keeping the peace.

Sherpa n. (pl. **Sherpa** or **Sherpas**) a member of a Himalayan people of Nepal and Tibet.

sherry n. (pl. **sherries**) a strong wine.

shiatsu /shi-at-soo/ n. a Japanese therapy in which pressure is applied with the hands to points on the body.

shibboleth n. a long-standing belief or principle held by a group, but generally thought of as outdated.

shied past & past part. of **SHY**.

shield n. **1** a broad piece of armour held for protection against blows or missiles. **2** a sporting trophy shaped like a shield. **3** a person or thing acting as a barrier or screen. ▶v. protect.

shift v. **1** move or change from one position to another. **2** transfer blame etc. **3** informal move quickly. ▶n. **1** a slight change in position or direction. **2** a period of time worked by a group of workers who start work as another group finishes. **3** a straight dress without a waist.

shiftless adj. lazy and lacking ambition.

shifty adj. informal dishonest or untrustworthy.

Shiite /shee-yt/ n. a follower of one of the two main branches of Islam.

shilling n. a former British coin worth one twentieth of a pound or 12 pence.

shilly-shally v. (**shilly-shallying**, **shilly-shallied**) be indecisive.

shimmer v. shine with a soft wavering light. ▶n. a soft wavering light or shine.

shin n. the front of the leg below the

Thesaurus

adulterated. **2** STEEP, abrupt, sharp, precipitous, vertical. **3** DIAPHANOUS, transparent, see-through, translucent, fine, thin. ■ OPPOSITES gradual, thick.

sheet n. **1** BEDSHEET, bedlinen. **2** PIECE, pane, panel, plate, slab. **3** PIECE OF PAPER, leaf, page, folio. **4** EXPANSE, stretch, span, reach, sweep, covering, blanket, carpet.

shell n. **1** CARAPACE, case, casing, husk, pod, integument. **2** BULLET, grenade, shot, shrapnel. **3** FRAMEWORK, frame, structure, chassis, hull, skeleton. ▶v. BOMB, bombard, blitz, strafe, fire on.

shelter n. **1** PROTECTION, shield, cover, screen, safety, security, defence. **2** REFUGE, sanctuary, retreat, haven, harbour. ▶v. **1** PROTECT, shield, screen, safe-

guard, provide refuge/sanctuary from, guard, harbour, conceal, hide. **2** TAKE SHELTER, take refuge, seek protection, seek refuge/sanctuary. ■ OPPOSITES expose.

sheltered adj. **1** SHADY, shaded, protected, screened, shielded, secluded. **2** QUIET, withdrawn, retired, isolated, protected, cloistered, reclusive.

shepherd v. ESCORT, conduct, usher, convoy, guide, marshal, steer.

shift v. MOVE, carry, transfer, switch, reposition, rearrange. ▶n. **1** MOVE, movement, transference, switch, repositioning. **2** STINT, spell/period of work.

shifty adj. EVASIVE, slippery, devious, duplicitous, deceitful, underhand, untrustworthy, double-dealing, dishonest, wily, knee. ▶v. (**shinning**, **shinned**) climb quickly up or down by gripping with the arms and legs.

shindig n. informal a large, lively party.

shine v. (**shining**, **shone** or **shined**) **1** give out or reflect light. **2** direct a torch etc. somewhere. **3** be very good at something. **4** (past & past part. **shined**) polish. ▶n. brightness. □ **take a shine to** informal develop a liking for. ■ **shiny** adj.

shingle n. **1** a mass of small rounded pebbles, esp. on a beach. **2** a wooden roof tile. **3** (**shingles**) a disease with a rash of painful blisters.

Shinto n. a Japanese religion involving the worship of ancestors and nature spirits.

ship n. a large boat for transporting people or goods by sea. ▶v. (**shipping**, **shipped**) transport on a ship or by other means. □ **shipment 1** the act of transporting goods. **2** an amount of goods shipped. **shipping** ships as a whole. **shipshape** orderly and neat. **shipwreck** the sinking or breaking up of a ship at sea. **shipwrecked** having suffered a shipwreck. **shipyard** a place where ships are built and repaired. ■ **shipper** n.

shire n. a county. □ **shire horse** a heavy powerful horse.

shirk v. avoid work or a duty. ■ **shirker** n.

shirt n. a garment for the upper body, with sleeves and buttons down the front.

shirty adj. informal angry or annoyed.

shiver v. shake slightly, esp. from fear or cold. ▶n. a shivering movement. ■ **shivery** adj.

shoal n. **1** a large number of fish swimming together. **2** an area of shallow water. **3** a submerged sandbank. ▶v. (of fish) form shoals.

shock n. **1** a sudden upsetting or surprising experience. **2** surprise and distress caused by such an experience. **3** a serious medical condition caused by loss of blood, severe injury, etc. **4** a violent shaking movement caused by an impact, earthquake, etc. **5** a sudden discharge of electricity through the body. **6** a thick mass of hair. ▶v. **1** surprise and upset. **2** outrage or disgust.

shocking adj. **1** causing outrage or disgust. **2** informal very bad. ■ **shocker** n. **shockingly** adv.

shoddy adj. badly made or done. ■ **shoddily** adv.

shoe n. **1** a covering for the foot with a stiff sole. **2** a horseshoe. ▶v. (**shoeing**, **shod**) fit with a shoe or shoes. □ **on a shoestring** with only a very small amount of money. **shoehorn** a curved implement for easing one's heel into a shoe. **shoe tree** a shaped block for keeping a shoe in shape.

shone past & past part. of SHINE.

shoo exclam. a word said to drive away animals. ▶v. drive away.

shook past of SHAKE.

shoot v. (**shooting**, **shot**) **1** kill or wound with a bullet or arrow. **2** fire a gun etc. **3** move suddenly and rapidly. **4** (in sport) kick, hit, or throw

Thesaurus

crafty, artful, sly, scheming, contriving. ■ OPPOSITES honest.

shimmer v. GLISTEN, glint, flicker, twinkle, sparkle, gleam, glow, scintillate, dance.

shine v. **1** GLEAM, glow, glint, sparkle, twinkle, flicker, glitter, glisten, shimmer, flash, dazzle, beam, radiate, illuminate, luminesce, incandesce. **2** POLISH, burnish, buff, wax, gloss. **3** EXCEL, be expert, be brilliant, be very good, be outstanding. ▶n. **1** LIGHT, brightness, gleam, glow, glint, sparkle, twinkle, flicker, glitter, glisten, shimmer, flash, dazzle, glare, beam, radiance, illumination, luminescence, luminosity, lambency, effulgence. **2** POLISH, burnish, gleam, gloss, lustre, sheen, patina.

shiny adj. SHINING, polished, burnished, gleaming, glossy, satiny, lustrous. ■ OPPOSITES dull.

shirk v. AVOID, evade, dodge, sidestep, shrink from, shun, get out of, play truant from; informal funk, skive off.

shirker n. SLACKER, truant, absentee, malingerer, layabout, loafer, idler; informal skiver.

shiver v. TREMBLE, quiver, shake, shudder, quaver, quake, vibrate. ▶n. TREMBLE, quiver, shake, quaver, shudder.

shock n. **1** IMPACT, blow, collision, crash, dash, jolt, bump, jar, jerk. **2** BLOW, upset, bombshell, bolt from the blue, disturbance, rude awakening, source of distress, revelation; informal eye-opener. ▶v. APPAL, horrify, scandalize, outrage, repel, revolt, disgust, nauseate, sicken, offend, traumatize, make someone's blood run cold, distress, upset, perturb, disturb, disquiet, unsettle, astound, dumbfound, stagger, amaze, astonish, stun.

S

the ball etc. in an attempt to score. **5** film or photograph. **6** send out shoots. ▶n. a new part growing from a plant. □ **shooting star** a small, rapidly moving meteor. **shooting stick** a walking stick with a handle that unfolds to form a seat. ■ **shooter** n.

shop n. **1** a building where goods or services are sold. **2** a workshop. ▶v. (**shopping, shopped**) **1** go to a shop or shops to buy goods. **2** (**shop around**) look for the best available price for goods. **3** informal inform on. □ **shop floor** the part of a factory where production is carried out. **shoplifter** a person who steals goods from a shop. **shop-soiled** dirty or damaged from being displayed in a shop. **shop steward** a trade union official elected by workers as their representative. **talk shop** discuss one's work in a social setting. ■ **shopper** n. **shopping** n.

shore n. the land along the edge of a sea, lake, etc. ▶v. (**shore up**) support or prop up with a beam.

shorn past part. of SHEAR.

short adj. **1** of a small length in space or time. **2** small in height. **3** (**short of/on**) not having enough of. **4** rude and abrupt. **5** (of odds in betting) reflecting a high probability. **6** (of pastry) crumbly.

▶adv. not as far as expected or required. ▶n. **1** informal a small drink of spirits. **2** (**shorts**) short trousers reaching to the knees or thighs. ▶v. short-circuit. □ **shortbread** (or **shortcake**) a rich, crumbly biscuit. **short-change** cheat, esp. by giving insufficient change. **short circuit** a fault in an electrical circuit when the current flows along a shorter route than it should do. **short-circuit** cause to suffer a short circuit. **shortcoming** a fault or defect. **short cut** a quicker route or method. **shortfall** an amount by which something is less than what is required. **shorthand** a method of rapid writing using abbreviations and symbols. **short-handed** without enough staff. **shortlist** a list of selected candidates from which a final choice is made. **short shrift** abrupt or unsympathetic treatment. **short-sighted** unable to see things clearly unless they are close to the eyes. **2** lacking foresight. **short wave** a radio wave of a frequency of about 3 to 30 megahertz. ■ **shorten** v. **shortness** n.

shortage n. a lack or insufficiency.

shortening n. fat used to make pastry.

shortly adv. **1** in a short time; soon. **2** abruptly or sharply.

shot past & past part. of SHOOT. ▶n.

Thesaurus

shoddy adj. POOR-QUALITY, inferior, second-rate, tawdry, rubbishy, trashy, junky, gimcrack, cheapjack, jerry-built; informal tacky, tatty, rubbish. ■ OPPOS-ITES quality.

shoot v. **1** HIT, shoot down, bring down, pick off, bag, fell, kill; informal plug, zap; literary slay. **2** FIRE, discharge, launch, let fly, send forth. **3** RACE, dash, sprint, charge, dart, fly, hurtle, bolt, streak, flash, whisk, run, speed. **4** BUD, burgeon, sprout, germinate, appear, spring up. ▶n. BUD, offshoot, slip, scion, sucker, sprout, branch, twig, sprig, cutting, graft.

shop n. STORE, retail outlet, retailer, establishment, emporium, trading post.

shore[1] n. SEASHORE, seaside, beach, coast, seaboard, waterside, foreshore; literary strand.

shore[2] v. (**shore up**) PROP UP, support, hold up, underpin, strengthen, brace, buttress.

short adj. **1** SMALL, little, slight, petite, tiny, squat, dwarfish, diminutive, dumpy, Lilliputian; Sc. wee; informal pint-sized, pocket-sized, knee-high to a

grasshopper. **2** BRIEF, concise, succinct, to the point, compact, terse, summary, crisp, pithy, epigrammatic, abridged, abbreviated, condensed, summarized, contracted, curtailed, truncated. **3** SHORT-LIVED, momentary, temporary, brief, impermanent, short-term, cursory, fleeting, passing, transitory, transient, ephemeral, fugacious, evanescent. **4** DEFICIENT, lacking, wanting, insufficient, inadequate, scarce, scanty, meagre, sparse, tight, low. **5** CURT, sharp, abrupt, blunt, brusque, terse, gruff, surly, testy, tart, rude, discourteous, uncivil, impolite. ■ OPPOSITES tall, long, plentiful.

shortage n. DEARTH, scarcity, lack, deficiency, insufficiency, paucity, deficit, inadequacy, shortfall, want, poverty. ■ OPPOSITES abundance.

shortcoming n. DEFECT, fault, flaw, imperfection, failing, blunt, drawback, weakness, weak point, foible, frailty, infirmity. ■ OPPOSITES strength.

shorten v. ABBREVIATE, condense, abridge, cut, cut down, contract, compress, reduce, lessen, decrease, dimin-

1 the firing of a gun etc. **2** (in sport) a hit, stroke, or kick of the ball as an attempt to score. **3** informal an attempt. **4** a photograph. **5** (pl. **shot**) a ball of stone or metal fired from a large gun. **6** tiny lead pellets used in a shotgun. **7** informal a small drink of spirits. **8** informal an injection. ▶adj. **1** woven with different colours to give a contrasting effect. **2** (**shot through with**) filled with. □ **like a shot** informal without hesitation. **shotgun** a gun for firing small shot at short range. **shot put** an athletic contest in which a heavy round ball is thrown as far as possible.

should aux. v. **1** expressing duty or obligation, or a possible or probable future event. **2** expressing a polite request, opinion, or hope.

shoulder n. the joint between the upper arm or forelimb and the main part of the body. ▶v. **1** take on a responsibility. **2** push aside with one's shoulder. □ **shoulder blade** either of the large, flat, triangular bones at the top of the back.

shouldn't contr. should not.

shout v. **1** speak or call out very loudly. **2** (**shout down**) prevent from speaking or being heard by shouting. ▶n. a loud cry or call.

shove v. **1** push roughly. **2** put somewhere carelessly or roughly. **3** (**shove off**) informal go away. ▶n. a strong push.

shovel n. a tool resembling a spade for moving earth, snow, etc. ▶v. (**shovel-**ling, **shovelled**; US **shoveling**, **shoveled**) move with a shovel.

show v. (**showing**, **showed**; past part. **shown** or **showed**) **1** be or make visible. **2** offer for inspection or viewing. **3** present an image of. **4** lead or guide. **5** treat in a particular way. **6** demonstrate or prove. ▶n. **1** a theatrical performance or light entertainment programme. **2** a competition involving the public display of animals, plants, etc. **3** an impressive or pleasing sight. **4** an outward display, esp. when misleading. □ **show business** theatre, films, television, etc. as a profession or industry. **showdown** a final confrontation intended to settle a dispute. **showjumping** the sport of riding horses over a course of obstacles in an arena. **showman** the manager or presenter of a circus, fair, etc. **show off 1** boastfully display one's abilities etc. **2** display. **showpiece** an outstanding example of its type. **showroom** a room used to display goods for sale. **show up 1** reveal as being bad or faulty. **2** informal humiliate or embarrass.

shower n. **1** a brief fall of rain or snow. **2** a large number of things that fall or arrive together. **3** a device producing a spray of water under which one stands to wash oneself. **4** an act of washing oneself in a shower. ▶v. **1** fall or make things fall in a shower. **2** give a great number of things to. **3** wash in a shower. ■ **showery** adj.

Thesaurus

ish, curtail, duck, trim, pare down. ■ OPPOSITES extend.

shortly adv. SOON, in a short while, in a little while, presently, before long, directly; informal before you can say Jack Robinson.

short-sighted adj. **1** MYOPIC, near-sighted. **2** IMPRUDENT, injudicious, unwise, ill-advised, thoughtless, unthinking, heedless, rash, incautious.

shot n. **1** CRACK, bang, report, blast, explosion, gunfire. **2** PELLET, bullet, slug, projectile, ammunition. **3** PHOTOGRAPH, photo, snap, snapshot.

shout v. CRY OUT, call out, yell, roar, howl, bellow, scream, bawl, call at the top of one's voice, raise one's voice; informal holler. ■ OPPOSITES whisper.

shove v. PUSH, thrust, drive, force, shoulder, elbow, jostle, jolt.

shovel n. SPADE, scoop. ▶v. SCOOP UP, dig, excavate, spade.

show v. **1** BE VISIBLE, be seen, be in view, appear, put in an appearance. **2** EXHIBIT, display, present, demonstrate, set forth, uncover, reveal. **3** INDICATE, express, manifest, reveal, make known, make plain, make obvious, evince, evidence, disclose, betray, divulge. **4** DEMONSTRATE, point out, explain, expound, teach, instruct in, give instructions in, tutor in, indoctrinate in. **5** ESCORT, accompany, usher, conduct, attend, guide, lead, direct, steer. **6** APPEAR, put in an appearance, make an appearance, turn up, come, arrive, be present. ■ OPPOSITES conceal. ▶n. **1** DISPLAY, array, arrangement, exhibition, presentation, exposition, spectacle. **2** EXHIBITION, demonstration, display, exposition, presentation. **3** PERFORMANCE, production; informal gig. **4** APPEARANCE, outward appearance, air, guise, semblance, pretence, illusion, pose, affectation, profession.

shower n. **1** FALL, drizzle, flurry, sprinkling. **2** ABUNDANCE, profusion, plethora,

showy adj. ostentatiously bright or colourful. ■ **showily** adv.

shrank past of SHRINK.

shrapnel n. small metal fragments from an exploding shell or bomb.

shred n. **1** a strip of material torn or cut from something. **2** a very small amount. ▶v. (**shredding**, **shredded**) tear or cut into shreds. ■ **shredder** n.

shrew n. a small mouse-like mammal with a pointed snout.

shrewd adj. having or showing good judgement. ■ **shrewdly** adv. **shrewdness** n.

shriek v. & n. (make) a piercing sound or cry.

shrill adj. high-pitched and piercing. ■ **shrillness** n. **shrilly** adv.

shrimp n. (pl. **shrimp** or **shrimps**) a small edible shellfish.

shrine n. a holy or revered place.

shrink v. (**shrinking**, **shrank**; past part. **shrunk** or (esp. as adj.) **shrunken**) **1** become or make smaller. **2** move back or away in fear or disgust. ▶n. informal a psychiatrist. ■ **shrinkage** n.

shrivel v. (**shrivelling**, **shrivelled**; US **shriveling**, **shriveled**) wrinkle and shrink through loss of moisture.

shroud n. **1** a length of cloth in which a dead person is wrapped for burial. **2** a thing covering or hiding something.

▶v. cover or hide.

shrub n. a woody plant smaller than a tree. ■ **shrubby** adj.

shrubbery n. (pl. **shrubberies**) an area planted with shrubs.

shrug v. (**shrugging**, **shrugged**) **1** raise one's shoulders briefly as a sign of indifference or ignorance. **2** (**shrug off**) treat as unimportant. ▶n. an act of shrugging.

shrunk (or **shrunken**) past part. of SHRINK.

shudder v. tremble or shake violently. ▶n. an act of shuddering.

shuffle v. **1** walk without lifting one's feet clear of the ground. **2** rearrange a pack of cards. **3** (**shuffle off**) avoid a responsibility. ▶n. an act of shuffling.

shun v. (**shunning**, **shunned**) avoid or reject.

shunt v. push or pull a train from one set of tracks to another.

shut v. (**shutting**, **shut**) **1** move into position to block an opening. **2** (**shut in/out**) keep in or out by closing a door etc. **3** prevent access to. **4** (referring to a shop etc.) stop operating for business. **5** close a book, curtains, etc. □ **shut down** cease business or operation. **shut off** stop from flowing or working. **shut up** informal stop talking.

shutter n. **1** a pair of hinged panels that

Thesaurus

flood, deluge. ▶v. **1** DELUGE, inundate, overwhelm. **2** LAVISH, pour, load, heap.

show-off n. EXHIBITIONIST, extrovert, bragger, braggart, boaster; US informal blowhard.

showy adj. OSTENTATIOUS, flamboyant, elaborate, fancy, pretentious, overdone, glittering. ■ OPPOSITES restrained.

shred n. **1** SCRAP, fragment, wisp, sliver, bit, piece, remnant, snippet, tatter. **2** TRACE, iota, whit, particle, atom, modicum, scrap, speck. ▶v. CUT UP, tear up, rip up, grate.

shrewd adj. ASTUTE, sharp, clever, intelligent, alert, quick-witted, discerning, perspicacious, perceptive, discriminating, wise, sagacious, far-seeing, canny, cunning, artful, crafty, wily, calculating; informal smart. ■ OPPOSITES stupid.

shriek v. SCREAM, screech, squeal, yell, howl, shout, cry out, call out, whoop, wail; informal holler.

shrill adj. HIGH-PITCHED, high, sharp, piercing, ear-piercing, penetrating, ear-splitting, screeching, shrieking.

shrine n. **1** HOLY PLACE, temple, church. **2** MEMORIAL, monument, cenotaph.

3 RELIQUARY, burial chamber, tomb, sepulchre.

shrink v. GET/BECOME/GROW SMALLER, contract, diminish, lessen, reduce, dwindle, narrow, decline, fall off, drop off, shrivel. ■ OPPOSITES expand, increase. □ **shrink from** DRAW BACK, pull back, back away, shy away, recoil, retreat, withdraw, flinch, cringe, wince.

shrivel v. DRY UP, wither, desiccate, dehydrate, wrinkle, pucker up.

shroud n. COVER, covering, pall, cloak, mantle, blanket, cloud, veil, screen. ▶v. COVER, enshroud, swathe, envelop, cloak, blanket, cloud, veil, screen, conceal, hide.

shrug v. (**shrug off**) DISREGARD, take no notice of, not trouble about, dismiss, gloss over, play down, make light of, minimize.

shuffle v. **1** SHAMBLE, hobble, limp, drag one's feet. **2** MIX, intermix, shift about, rearrange, reorganize, jumble.

shun v. AVOID, evade, eschew, steer clear of, shy away from, recoil from, keep away from, keep one's distance from, cold-shoulder, give a wide berth to.

can be closed over a window. **2** a device that opens and closes to expose the film in a camera. ▶v. close the shutters of.

shuttle n. **1** a form of transport travelling regularly between two places. **2** a bobbin carrying the weft thread in weaving. ▶v. **1** travel regularly between places. **2** transport in a shuttle. □ **shuttlecock** a light cone-shaped object, struck with rackets in badminton.

shy adj. nervous or timid in the company of others. ▶v. (**shying, shied**) **1** (of a horse) suddenly turn aside in fright. **2** (**shy from**) avoid through nervousness. **3** throw. ■ **shyly** adv. **shyness** n.

SI abbrev. Système International, the international system of units of measurement.

Siamese adj. of Siam, the former name of Thailand. □ **Siamese cat** a breed of cat with pale fur and darker face, paws, and tail. **Siamese twins** twins whose bodies are joined at birth.

sibilant adj. making a hissing sound.

sibling n. a brother or sister.

sibyl n. an ancient Greek or Roman prophetess.

sic adv. written exactly as it stands in the original.

sick adj. **1** physically or mentally ill. **2** wanting to vomit. **3** (**sick of**) bored by or annoyed with. **4** informal (of humour) dealing with unpleasant subjects in an offensive way.

sicken v. **1** disgust or shock. **2** become ill.

sickle n. a short-handled tool with a curved blade.

sickly adj. (**sicklier, sickliest**) **1** often ill. **2** looking unhealthy. **3** so bright or sweet as to cause sickness. **4** excessively sentimental.

sickness n. **1** the state of being ill. **2** an illness or disease. **3** nausea or vomiting.

side n. **1** a position to the left or right of an object, place, or central point. **2** either of the halves into which something is divided. **3** a surface of an object, esp. one that is not the top, bottom, front, or back. **4** each of the lines forming the boundary of a plane figure. **5** a part near the edge of something. **6** a person or group opposing another or others in a dispute or contest. **7** a particular aspect. ▶adj. additional or less important. ▶v. (**side with/against**) support or oppose in a conflict or dispute. □ **on the side** informal **1** in addition to one's regular job. **2** as a secret additional sexual relationship. **sideboard** a piece of furniture with cupboards and drawers for crockery, glasses, etc. **sideboards** (or **sideburns**) a strip of hair growing down each side of a man's face. **side effect** a secondary, usu. bad effect of a drug. **sidelong** to or from one side; sideways. **side-saddle** (of a rider) sitting with both feet on the same side of the horse. **sideshow** a small show or stall at a fair etc. **sidestep** **1** avoid by stepping sideways. **2** avoid dealing with or discussing. **sidetrack** distract. **sidewalk** US a pavement. **sideways** to, towards, or from the side.

sideline n. **1** an activity done in add-

Thesaurus

. . . .

■ OPPOSITES seek.

shut v. CLOSE, draw to, pull to, fasten, bar, lock, secure, seal. ■ OPPOSITES open. □ **shut in** see IMPRISON. **shut out** EXCLUDE, leave out, omit, keep out, bar, debar, ostracize, blackball, banish, exile, outlaw. **shut up** KEEP QUIET, be quiet, keep silent, hold one's tongue; informal keep mum, pipe down, keep one's trap shut.

shy adj. BASHFUL, diffident, reserved, reticent, retiring, self-effacing, withdrawn, timid, timorous, fearful, nervous, hesitant, wary, suspicious, chary, unconfident, self-conscious, embarrassed, abashed, modest. ■ OPPOSITES brash, confident.

sick adj. **1** UNWELL, ill, ailing, indisposed, poorly, below par, out of sorts, laid up, on the sick list; informal under the weather. **2** NAUSEATED, queasy, bilious; infor-

mal green about the gills. **3** TIRED, weary, bored, jaded, surfeited, satiated, glutted; informal fed up, have had something up to here. **4** MORBID, macabre, ghoulish, gruesome, sadistic, perverted, cruel. ■ OPPOSITES well. □ **be sick** VOMIT, throw up; informal spew, puke.

sicken v. **1** MAKE SICK, nauseate, turn someone's stomach, make someone's gorge rise, revolt, disgust, repel, shock, appal. **2** TAKE/FALL ILL, become ill, become infected, contract, be stricken. ■ OPPOSITES recover.

sickening adj. see REPELLENT, ANNOYING.

sickly adj. **1** UNHEALTHY, in poor health, ill, delicate, frail, weak, feeble, puny. **2** SENTIMENTAL, cloying, mawkish, maudlin, slushy, mushy, syrupy; informal schmaltzy, soppy. ■ OPPOSITES healthy.

sickness n. **1** ILLNESS, disease, disorder, ailment, complaint, affliction, malady, ition to one's main job. **2** either of the two lines along the longer sides of a sports field or court. **3** (**the sidelines**) a position of watching a situation rather than being directly involved. ▶v. remove from an influential position.

sidereal /sy-**deer**-i-uhl/ adj. of the stars or their apparent positions in the sky.

siding n. a short track beside a railway, where trains are left.

sidle v. walk in a stealthy or timid way.

siege n. a military operation in which forces surround a town and cut off its supplies.

sienna n. a brownish earth used as a pigment.

sierra n. a chain of mountains with jagged peaks.

siesta n. an afternoon rest or nap.

sieve n. a piece of mesh held in a frame, used for straining solids from liquids or separating coarser from finer particles. ▶v. put through a sieve.

sift v. **1** sieve. **2** examine carefully to select what is important.

sigh v. let out a long, deep, breath expressing sadness, relief, etc. ▶n. an act of sighing.

sight n. **1** the ability to see. **2** the act of seeing. **3** the distance within which someone can see. **4** a thing seen or worth seeing. **5** informal a person or thing that looks ridiculous or unattractive. **6** a device looked through to aim a gun or see with a telescope etc. ▶v. manage to see or glimpse. □ **sight-read** perform music without previous study of the score. ■ **sighted** adj. **sightless** adj.

sightseeing n. visiting places of interest. ■ **sightseer** n.

sign n. **1** an indication that something exists, is occurring, or may occur. **2** a signal, gesture, or notice giving information or an instruction. **3** a symbol or word representing something in algebra, music, etc. **4** each of the twelve divisions of the zodiac. ▶v. **1** write one's name on something to authorize it. **2** use gestures to give instructions. □ **sign on 1** commit oneself to a job. **2** register as unemployed. **signpost** n. a sign on a post, giving the direction and distance to a nearby place. **sign up** commit oneself to a course, job, etc.

signal n. **1** a gesture, action, or sound giving information or an instruction. **2** a device that indicates whether a road or railway is clear. **3** an electrical impulse or radio wave sent or received. ▶v. (**signalling**, **signalled**; US **signaling**, **signaled**) **1** give a signal. **2** indicate by means of a signal. ▶adj. noteworthy. □ **signal box** a building beside a railway track from which signals, points, etc. are controlled.

signatory n. (pl. **signatories**) a person who has signed an agreement.

signature n. a person's name written in a distinctive way, used in signing something. □ **signature tune** a tune announcing a particular television or radio programme.

signet ring n. a ring with an engraved design.

significance n. **1** importance. **2** the meaning of something. ■ **significant**

Thesaurus

infirmity, indisposition; *informal* bug. **2** NAUSEA, queasiness, biliousness.

side n. **1** EDGE, border, verge, boundary, margin, rim, fringe, skirt, flank, brink, brim, periphery. **2** PART, quarter, section, sector, neighbourhood. **3** ASPECT, angle, facet, point of view, viewpoint, view, opinion, standpoint, position, slant. **4** CAMP, faction, caucus, party, wing, splinter group, sect. □ **side with** TAKE SOMEONE'S SIDE, be on someone's side, take someone's part, support, give one's support to, back, give one's backing to, join with, favour.

sidelong adj. SIDE, sideways, oblique, indirect, covert. ■ OPPOSITES overt.

sidetrack v. DIVERT, deflect, distract, lead away from.

sideways adv. **1** SIDE FIRST, edgeways, edgewise. **2** OBLIQUELY, indirectly, sidelong.

sieve n. STRAINER, filter, colander, riddle, screen.

sift v. **1** FILTER, strain, riddle, screen. **2** EXAMINE, scrutinize, study, investigate, analyse, review.

sigh v. BREATHE OUT, exhale. □ **sigh for** YEARN FOR, long for, weep for, mourn for.

sight n. **1** EYESIGHT, vision, power of sight. **2** RANGE OF VISION, field of vision, view. **3** VIEW, glimpse, look. ▶v. CATCH SIGHT OF, see, behold, spot, make out, descry, espy, perceive, observe, discern.

sign n. **1** INDICATION, symptom, hint, suggestion, trace, mark, clue, manifestation, token, evidence, proof. **2** SIGNPOST, notice, placard, board, marker. **3** GESTURE, signal, motion, movement, wave, gesticulation. **4** SYMBOL, mark, cipher, code, hieroglyph. ▶v. **1** WRITE, inscribe, autograph, initial. **2** *see* SIGNAL.

adj. **significantly** adv.

signify v. (**signifying, signified**) **1** be a sign of; mean. **2** make known. ∎ **signification** n.

Sikh /seek/ n. a follower of a religion that developed from Hinduism. ∎ **Sikhism** n.

silage /sy-lij/ n. grass or green crops stored in a silo without being dried, used as animal feed.

silence n. complete absence of sound or speech. ▶v. make silent.

silencer n. a device for reducing the noise made by a gun or exhaust system.

silent adj. **1** without sound. **2** not speaking or not spoken aloud. ∎ **silently** adv.

silhouette n. a dark shadow or outline seen against a lighter background. ▶v. show as a silhouette.

silica n. a compound of silicon occurring as quartz and found in sandstone.

silicate n. a compound of silica.

silicon n. a non-metallic element, used to make electronic circuits. ◻ **silicon chip** a microchip.

silicone n. a synthetic substance made from silicon.

silk n. a fine, soft shiny fibre produced by silkworms, made into thread or fabric. ◻ **silkworm** a caterpillar that spins a silk cocoon. ∎ **silken** adj. **silky** adj.

sill n. a shelf or ledge at the foot of a window or doorway.

silly adj. (**sillier, silliest**) lacking common sense or judgement. ∎ **silliness** n.

silo n. (pl. **silos**) **1** a tower on a farm for storing grain. **2** a pit or airtight structure for storing silage. **3** an underground chamber in which a guided missile is kept ready for firing.

silt n. fine sand or clay deposited by running water. ▶v. (**silt up**) fill or block with silt.

silvan var. of SYLVAN.

silver n. **1** a shiny greyish-white precious metal. **2** a shiny grey-white colour. **3** coins or articles made of silver or of a metal resembling silver. ◻ **silverfish** a small wingless insect. **silver jubilee** the 25th anniversary of an important event. **silverside** a joint of beef from the outside of the leg. **silver wedding** the 25th anniversary of a wedding. ∎ **silvery** adj.

SIM card n. a smart card in a mobile phone carrying an identification

Thesaurus

signal v. **1** SIGN, give a sign to, indicate, beckon, gesture, motion, gesticulate, nod. **2** BE A SIGN OF, mark signify, designate. ▶n. SIGN, indicator, cue, indication, token, evidence, hint.

significance n. **1** MEANING, sense, import, signification, purport, point, gist, essence, implications. **2** IMPORTANCE, consequence, momentousness, magnitude, seriousness.

significant adj. **1** MEANINGFUL, eloquent, expressive, pregnant, knowing. **2** IMPORTANT, of importance, of consequence, momentous, of moment, weighty, material, impressive, serious, vital, critical. ∎ OPPOSITES insignificant.

signify v. **1** BE A SIGN OF, indicate, mean, denote, suggest, point to, portend. **2** MEAN, denote, represent, symbolize, stand for. **3** MATTER, be of importance, be of consequence, be important, be significant, be of significance, carry weight, count.

silence n. **1** QUIET, quietness, hush, still, stillness, peace, peacefulness, tranquillity, noiselessness, soundlessness. **2** SPEECHLESSNESS, wordlessness, dumbness, muteness, taciturnity, reticence, uncommunicativeness. ∎ OPPOSITES noise. ▶v. **1** QUIET, quieten, hush, still, calm, pacify, subdue, quell. **2** MUFFLE, deaden, abate, extinguish.

silent adj. **1** QUIET, hushed, still, peaceful, tranquil, noiseless, soundless. **2** SPEECHLESS, unspeaking, voiceless, dumb, mute, taciturn, reticent, uncommunicative, mum, tight-lipped, tongue-tied; *informal* struck dumb. **3** UNSPOKEN, wordless, unvoiced, unsaid, unexpressed, unpronounced, tacit, implicit, understood, implied. ∎ OPPOSITES noisy, loquacious.

silhouette n. OUTLINE, contour, profile, delineation, form, shape.

silky adj. SILKEN, smooth, sleek, velvety, diaphanous.

silly adj. **1** UNINTELLIGENT, stupid, foolish, idiotic, brainless, witless, unwise, imprudent, thoughtless, reckless, foolhardy, irresponsible, mad, erratic, unstable, scatterbrained, feather-brained, flighty, frivolous, giddy, fatuous, inane, immature, childish, naive; *informal* crazy, dotty, scatty, loopy, screwy, daft. **2** SENSELESS, stupid, foolish, mindless, idiotic, unwise, imprudent, inadvisable, injudicious, misguided, impractical, pointless, meaningless, inappropriate, illogical, irrational, unreasonable, thoughtless, reckless, foolhardy, irresponsible, erratic, hare-brained, absurd, ridiculous, ludicrous, laugh-

number and storing personal data.
simian adj. of or like apes or monkeys.
similar adj. alike but not identical. ■ **similarity** n. **similarly** adv.
simile /sim-i-li/ n. a figure of speech in which one thing is compared to another.
similitude n. similarity.
simmer v. **1** stay or cause to stay just below boiling point. **2** be in a state of barely suppressed anger or excitement. **3** (**simmer down**) become calmer.
simper v. smile coyly. ▶ n. a coy smile.
simple adj. **1** easily understood or done. **2** plain and basic. **3** composed of a single element; not compound. **4** of very low intelligence. ■ **simplicity** n. **simply** adv.
simpleton n. a foolish or gullible person.
simplify v. (**simplifying, simplified**) make easier to do or understand. ■ **simplification** n.
simplistic adj. over-simplified. ■ **simplistically** adv.

simulate v. **1** imitate. **2** produce a computer model of. **3** pretend to feel. ■ **simulation** n. **simulator** n.
simultaneous adj. occurring or done at the same time. ■ **simultaneity** n. **simultaneously** adv.
sin n. an act that breaks a religious or moral law. ▶ v. (**sinning, sinned**) commit a sin. ▶ abbrev. sine. ■ **sinner** n.
since prep. from a specified time or event until the present. ▶ conj. **1** from the time that. **2** because. ▶ adv. from the time mentioned until the present.
sincere adj. without pretence or deceit. ■ **sincerely** adv. **sincerity** n.
sine n. (in a right-angled triangle) the ratio of the side opposite a particular acute angle to the hypotenuse.
sinecure /sin-i-kyoor/ n. a paid job requiring little or no work.
sinew n. a piece of tough fibrous tissue joining muscle to bone. ■ **sinewy** adj.
sinful adj. wicked. ■ **sinfully** adv. **sinfulness** n.
sing v. (**singing, sang**; past part. **sung**)

Thesaurus

able, risible, farcical, preposterous, fatuous, asinine; *informal* half-baked, crazy, screwy, daft. ■ OPPOSITES sensible.
similar adj. LIKE, alike, resembling, close, much the same, comparable, corresponding, analogous, parallel, equivalent, kindred, approximate. ■ OPPOSITES dissimilar, different.
similarity n. RESEMBLANCE, likeness, sameness, similitude, comparability, correspondence, analogy, parallel, parallelism, equivalence, approximation, closeness, affinity, kinship. ■ OPPOSITES dissimilarity, difference.
similarly adv. LIKEWISE, in the same way, in like matter, correspondingly, by the same token.
simmer v. BOIL, cook, bubble, stew, poach, seethe.
simple adj. **1** EASY, uncomplicated, straightforward, uninvolved, effortless, manageable, elementary, facile; *informal* like falling off a log, a piece of cake, a cinch, easy-peasy, no sweat. **2** CLEAR, plain, intelligible, comprehensible, understandable, lucid, direct, straightforward, uncomplicated, uninvolved. **3** PLAIN, classic, clean-cut, unelaborate, unadorned, undecorated. **4** SIMPLEMINDED, feeble-minded, retarded, backward, slow-witted, slow, dull-witted. ■ OPPOSITES difficult, complex, ornate.
simplify v. MAKE SIMPLE/SIMPLER, make

easy/easier to understand, make plainer, clarify, decipher, disentangle, explain, paraphrase, translate. ■ OPPOSITES complicate.
simplistic adj. OVERSIMPLE, oversimplified, facile, shallow, superficial, naive.
simply adv. **1** CLEARLY, plainly, intelligibly, lucidly, directly, straightforwardly. **2** PLAINLY, unfussily, without clutter, austerely, starkly, spartanly, with restraint, naturally, casually.
simultaneous adj. CONCURRENT, contemporaneous, concomitant, coinciding, coincident, synchronous, coexistent, parallel.
sin n. WRONG, wrongdoing, act of evil/wickedness, crime, offence, misdeed, misdemeanour, transgression, error, lapse, fall from grace; *old use* trespass. ■ OPPOSITES virtue. ▶ v. COMMIT A SIN, do wrong, offend, commit an offence, transgress, misbehave, go astray, stray from the straight and narrow, go wrong, fall from grace.
sincere adj. **1** GENUINE, real, true, honest, unfeigned, unaffected, bona fide, wholehearted, heartfelt, serious, earnest, fervent. **2** HONEST, above board, trustworthy, frank, candid, straightforward, plain-dealing, no-nonsense, genuine, artless, guileless, ingenuous; *informal* upfront. ■ OPPOSITES insincere.
sincerely adv. **1** WITH ALL SINCERITY, wholeheartedly, with all one's heart,

1 make musical sounds with the voice. **2** perform a song. **3** make a whistling sound. ◻ **sing-song 1** a rising and falling rhythm in a person's voice. **2** informal an informal gathering for singing. ■ **singer** n.

singe v. burn slightly. ▶n. a slight burn.

single adj. **1** one only. **2** designed for one person. **3** consisting of one part. **4** individual and distinct. **5** unmarried or not involved in a stable relationship. **6** (of a ticket) valid for an outward journey only. ▶n. **1** a single person or thing. **2** a record or CD with one song on each side. **3** (**singles**) a game or contest for individual players. ▶v. (**single out**) choose from a group. ◻ **single-handed** done without help from others. **single market** an association of countries trading with few or no restrictions. **single-minded** concentrating on one particular aim. **single parent** a person bringing up a child or children without a partner. ■ **singly** adv.

singlet n. a sleeveless vest.

singleton n. a single person or thing.

singular adj. **1** very good; remarkable. **2** (of a word or form) referring to just one person or thing. ▶n. the singular form of a word. ■ **singularity** n. **singularly** adv.

sinister adj. seeming evil or dangerous.

sink v. (**sinking**, **sank**; past part. **sunk**) **1** go down below the surface of liquid. **2** go or cause to go to the bottom of the sea. **3** move slowly downwards. **4** decrease in amount or strength. **5** cause something sharp to go through a surface. **6** (**sink in**) be understood. **7** invest money. ▶n. a fixed basin with taps and an outflow pipe.

sinker n. a weight used to keep a fishing line beneath the water.

sinuous adj. **1** curving. **2** gracefully swaying.

sinus /sy-nuhss/ n. a hollow space in the bones of the face that connects with the nostrils.

sinusitis n. inflammation of a sinus.

sip v. (**sipping**, **sipped**) drink in small mouthfuls. ▶n. a small mouthful of liquid.

siphon n. a tube for transferring liquid from one container to another, using air pressure to maintain the flow. ▶v. **1** draw off by means of a siphon. **2** (**siphon off**) take small amounts of money over time.

sir n. **1** a polite form of address to a man. **2** the title of a knight or baronet.

sire n. **1** an animal's male parent. **2** old use a respectful form of address to a king. ▶v. be the male parent of.

siren n. **1** a device that makes a long loud warning sound. **2** an attractive but dangerous woman.

sirloin n. the best part of a loin of beef.

sirocco n. (pl. **siroccos**) a hot wind blowing from Africa to southern Europe.

sisal n. fibre made from a tropical plant, used for ropes or matting.

sissy n. (pl. **sissies**) informal an effeminate

Thesaurus

earnestly, fervently. **2** GENUINELY, really, truly, in truth, without pretence, honestly, in good faith.

sinful adj. WRONG, evil, wicked, bad, iniquitous, criminal, immoral, corrupt, nefarious, unrighteous, ungodly, irreligious, irreverent, profane, blasphemous, impious, sacrilegious. ■ OPPOSITES virtuous.

sing v. CAROL, trill, warble, pipe, quaver, croon, chant, yodel.

singe v. SCORCH, burn, sear, blacken, char.

single adj. **1** ONE, sole, lone, solitary, unique, isolated, by itself, exclusive. **2** INDIVIDUAL, particular, separate, distinct. **3** UNMARRIED, unwed, unwedded, wifeless/husbandless, spouseless, partnerless, unattached, free. ◻ **single out** SEPARATE OUT, set apart, put to one side, pick, choose, select, fix on, decide on.

single-handed adv. BY ONESELF, alone, on one's own, solo, independently, unaided, unassisted, without help.

single-minded adj. UNSWERVING, unwavering, undeviating, fixed, devoted, dedicated, committed, determined, dogged, tireless, purposeful, obsessive, monomaniacal.

singular adj. **1** EXTRAORDINARY, exceptional, rare, unusual, unique, remarkable, outstanding, notable, noteworthy, striking, conspicuous, distinctive. **2** STRANGE, unusual, odd, peculiar, curious, queer, bizarre, weird, abnormal, atypical. ■ OPPOSITES ordinary.

sinister adj. **1** EVIL-LOOKING, villainous, malevolent, menacing, threatening, frightening. **2** EVIL, wicked, bad, criminal, base, vile, vicious, cruel, malicious, malign. **3** OMINOUS, inauspicious, portentous. ■ OPPOSITES innocent.

sink v. **1** GO UNDER, submerge, founder, capsize. **2** FALL, drop, descend, go down, or weak person.

sister n. **1** a woman or girl in relation to other children of her parents. **2** a female friend or colleague. **3** a nun. **4** a senior female nurse. □ **sisterhood 1** a feeling of closeness between women. **2** a group of women with a shared aim. **sister-in-law** (pl. **sisters-in-law**) the sister of one's wife or husband, or the wife of one's brother. ■ **sisterly** adj.

sit v. (**sitting**, **sat**) **1** be or put in a position with one's body resting on the buttocks. **2** be in a particular position or state. **3** pose for a portrait. **4** be a member of a committee etc. **5** (of a parliament, law court, etc.) be carrying on its business. **6** take an examination.

sitar n. a long-necked Indian lute.

sitcom n. informal a situation comedy.

site n. a place where something is, was, or will be located. ▶ v. establish or build in a particular place.

sitter n. **1** a person who sits for an artist. **2** a babysitter.

sitting n. **1** a period of posing for a portrait. **2** a period of time when a group are served a meal. **3** a period of time when a law court etc. is carrying on its business. □ **sitting room** a room for sitting and relaxing in. **sitting tenant** a tenant who has the legal right to remain living in a property.

situate v. put in a particular place.

situation n. **1** a set of circumstances. **2** the location and surroundings of a place. **3** a job. □ **situation comedy** a comedy series in which the same characters are involved in amusing situations. ■ **situational** adj.

six adj. & n. one more than five; 6 or VI. ■ **sixth** adj. & n.

sixteen adj. & n. one more than fifteen; 16 or XVI. ■ **sixteenth** adj. & n.

sixty adj. & n. (pl. **sixties**) ten more than fifty; 60 or LX. ■ **sixtieth** adj. & n.

size n. **1** the overall measurements or extent of something. **2** each of the series of standard measurements in which articles are made. **3** a sticky solution used to glaze paper, stiffen textiles, etc. ▶ v. (**size up**) assess.

sizeable (or **sizable**) adj. fairly large.

sizzle v. (of food) make a hissing sound when being fried.

skate n. **1** an ice skate or roller skate. **2** an edible flatfish. ▶ v. **1** move on skates. **2** (**skate over**) refer only briefly to a problem. □ **skateboard** a narrow board with wheels fixed to the bottom, for riding on while standing up. ■ **skater** n.

skedaddle v. informal leave quickly.

skein n. a loosely coiled bundle of yarn.

skeletal adj. **1** of the skeleton. **2** very thin.

skeleton n. **1** a framework of bone or cartilage supporting or containing an animal's body. **2** a supporting structure. ▶ adj. comprising an essential or minimum number: *a skeleton staff*. □ **skeleton key** a key designed to fit many locks.

skeptic US = SCEPTIC.

sketch n. **1** a rough drawing. **2** a short humorous scene in a comedy show. **3** a brief account. ▶ v. make a sketch of.

sketchy adj. not thorough or detailed. ■ **sketchily** adv.

skew v. **1** suddenly change direction or move at an angle. **2** make biased or distorted. □ **skewbald** (of a horse) having patches of white and brown.

skewer n. a long piece of wood or metal for holding pieces of food together dur-

Thesaurus

go lower, plunge, plummet, slump. ■ OPPOSITES float, rise.

sinner n. WRONGDOER, evil-doer, criminal, offender, miscreant, transgressor, reprobate; *old use* trespasser.

sit v. **1** SIT DOWN, take a seat, settle down, be seated; *informal* take the load/weight off one's feet. **2** BE PLACED, be positioned, be situated, rest, perch, stand. **3** BE CONVENED, meet, assemble, be in session.

site n. LOCATION, situation, position, place, locality, setting, scene. ▶ v. *see* SITUATE.

situate v. PLACE, position, locate, site, put, install, station, establish, set up.

situation n. **1** PLACE, position, location,

site, setting, milieu, environment. **2** CIRCUMSTANCES, affairs, state of affairs, condition, case, predicament, plight; *informal* kettle of fish, ball game. **3** POST, position, place, job, employment.

size n. DIMENSIONS, measurements, proportions, bigness, largeness, magnitude, vastness, bulk, area, expanse, extent.

sketch n. **1** DRAWING, outline, diagram, plan, representation, delineation. **2** OUTLINE, summary, abstract, precis, skeleton, bones, bare bones, draft, plan. **3** SKIT, act, scene. ▶ v. DRAW, rough out, outline, represent, delineate, depict.

sketchy adj. **1** PRELIMINARY, provisional, unfinished, unrefined, unpolished, ing cooking. ▶v. hold or pierce with a skewer.

ski n. (pl. **skis**) each of a pair of long, narrow pieces of plastic etc. attached to boots for travelling over snow. ▶v. (**skiing**, **skied**) travel on skis. ∎ **skier** n.

skid v. (**skidding**, **skidded**) slide sideways in an uncontrolled way. ▶n. an act of skidding.

skiff n. a light rowing boat.

skilful (US **skillful**) adj. having or showing skill. ∎ **skilfully** adv.

....
☑ There is only one *l* in the middle in British English: *skilful*.
....

skill n. the ability to do something well. ∎ **skilled** adj.

skillet n. a frying pan.

skim v. (**skimming**, **skimmed**) **1** remove a substance from the surface of a liquid. **2** glide. **3** read quickly. □ **skimmed milk** milk from which the cream has been removed.

skimp v. spend less money, time, etc. than is really needed.

skimpy adj. (**skimpier**, **skimpiest**) **1** meagre. **2** (of clothes) short and revealing.

skin n. **1** the thin layer of tissue forming the outer covering of the body. **2** the skin of a dead animal used for clothing etc. **3** an outer layer. ▶v. (**skinning**, **skinned**) remove the skin from. □ **skin diving** swimming under water without a diving suit, using an aqualung and flippers. **skinflint** informal a miser. **skinhead** a young person of a group with very short shaved hair.

skinny adj. (**skinnier**, **skinniest**) very thin.

skint adj. informal having little or no money.

skip v. (**skipping**, **skipped**) **1** move lightly, jumping from one foot to the other. **2** jump repeatedly over a rope turned over the head and under the feet. **3** omit or miss. ▶n. **1** a skipping movement. **2** a large open container for bulky refuse.

skipper n. informal a captain.

skirmish n. a short spell of fighting. ▶v. take part in a skirmish.

skirt n. a woman's garment hanging from the waist, or this part of a coat or dress. ▶v. **1** go round or past the edge of. **2** avoid dealing with. □ **skirting board** a wooden board along the base of the wall of a room.

skit n. a short comedy sketch.

skittish adj. lively and unpredictable.

skittle n. **1** (**skittles**) a game played with wooden pins set up at the end of an alley to be bowled down with a ball. **2** a pin used in skittles.

skive v. informal avoid work or a duty by staying away or leaving early. ∎ **skiver** n.

skulduggery n. underhand behaviour.

Thesaurus

....

rough, crude. **2** LIGHT, superficial, cursory, perfunctory, meagre, scrappy, skimpy, bitty, insufficient, inadequate, imperfect, incomplete. ∎ OPPOSITES detailed.

skilful adj. SKILLED, able, good, accomplished, adept, competent, efficient, adroit, deft, dexterous, masterly, expert, first-rate, experienced, trained, practised, professional, talented, gifted, clever; informal smart. ∎ OPPOSITES incompetent.

skill n. SKILFULNESS, ability, accomplishment, adeptness, competence, efficiency, adroitness, deftness, dexterity, aptitude, expertise, expertness, art, finesse, experience, professionalism, talent, cleverness; informal smartness. ∎ OPPOSITES incompetence.

skilled adj. *see* SKILFUL.

skim v. GLIDE OVER, move lightly over, brush, graze. □ **skim through** READ QUICKLY, glance at, scan, run one's eye over, flip through, leaf through, thumb through.

skimp v. BE SPARING, be economical, economize, be frugal, be mean, be parsimonious, be niggardly, scrimp, cut corners; informal be stingy. ∎ OPPOSITES lavish.

skin n. **1** INTEGUMENT, epidermis, cuticle, corium, derma. **2** HIDE, pelt, fleece, fell, integument, tegument. **3** PEEL, rind, hull, husk. **4** FILM, coating, coat, layer, crust.

skinny adj. THIN, thin as a rake, scraggy, scrawny, emaciated, skeletal; informal skin and bone. *See also* THIN.

skip v. **1** BOUND, jump, leap, spring, hop, bounce, dance, caper, prance, trip, cavort, gambol, frisk, bob. **2** OMIT, leave out, miss out, pass over, bypass, skim over.

skirmish n. BATTLE, fight, clash, conflict, encounter, confrontation, engagement, tussle, scrimmage, fracas.

skirt v. **1** GO ROUND, move round, walk round, circle, circumnavigate. **2** EVADE,

skulk v. loiter stealthily.

skull n. the bony framework surrounding the brain. □ **skullcap** a small cap without a peak.

skunk n. a black-and-white striped mammal able to spray foul-smelling liquid.

sky n. (pl. **skies**) the upper atmosphere seen from the earth. □ **skydiving** the sport of jumping from an aircraft and performing acrobatic movements before landing by parachute. **skylark** a lark that sings while in flight. **skylight** a window set in a roof or ceiling. **skyscraper** a very tall building.

slab n. a broad, flat piece of something solid.

slack adj. **1** not taut or tight. **2** not busy. **3** careless or lazy. ▶ n. **1** a slack part of a rope. **2** (**slacks**) casual trousers. **3** coal dust. ▶ v. **1** decrease in intensity or speed. **2** informal work slowly. ■ **slacken** v. **slacker** n. **slackness** n.

slag n. **1** stony waste left when metal has been smelted. **2** informal, derog. a promiscuous woman. ▶ v. (**slagging, slagged**) (**slag off**) informal criticize or insult. □ **slag heap** a mound of waste material from a mine.

slain past part. of SLAY.

slake v. satisfy a thirst. □ **slaked lime** a substance produced by combining lime with water.

slalom n. a skiing or canoeing race following a winding course.

slam v. (**slamming, slammed**) **1** shut forcefully and loudly. **2** put or hit with great force. **3** informal criticize severely. ▶ n. a noise of slamming.

slander n. the crime of making false statements that damage a person's reputation. ▶ v. make false and harmful statements about. ■ **slanderous** adj.

slang n. very informal language used esp. in speech and by a particular group.

slant v. **1** slope. **2** present information from a particular point of view. ▶ n. **1** a slope. **2** a point of view. ■ **slantwise** adv.

slap v. (**slapping, slapped**) **1** hit with the palm of one's hand or a flat object. **2** place quickly or carelessly. ▶ n. an act of slapping. ▶ adv. informal suddenly and forcefully. □ **slapdash** hurried and careless. **slapstick** comedy based on deliberately clumsy actions.

slash v. **1** cut with a sweeping stroke. **2** informal reduce greatly. ▶ n. **1** a cut made with a sweeping stroke. **2** a slanting line (/) used between alternatives.

slat n. a thin, narrow piece of wood etc.

slate n. a greyish rock easily split into smooth, flat plates, used as roofing material and formerly for writing on. ▶ v. informal criticize severely.

slattern n. old use a dirty, untidy woman. ■ **slatternly** adj.

slaughter n. the killing of farm animals

Thesaurus

avoid, dodge, steer clear of, sidestep, circumvent, bypass.

skittish adj. PLAYFUL, lively, frisky, sportive; *literary* frolicsome.

sky n. ATMOSPHERE, air, airspace; *literary* the heavens, the firmament, the blue, the (wide) blue yonder, the welkin.

slab n. HUNK, piece, chunk, lump, slice, wedge, portion.

slack adj. **1** LOOSE, baggy, bagging, easy, hanging, flapping. **2** SLOW, quiet, inactive, sluggish. **3** LAX, negligent, remiss, neglectful, careless, inattentive, offhand, slapdash, slipshod, sloppy, disorderly, disorganized, tardy. ▶ v. IDLE, shirk, be inactive, be lazy, be indolent, be neglectful.

slacker n. IDLER, shirker, loafer, dawdler, layabout, malingerer, good-for-nothing, clock-watcher.

slam v. BANG, thump, crash, smash, dash, hurt, fling, throw.

slander n. DEFAMATION, misrepresentation, calumny, libel, aspersions, vilification, verbal abuse, muckraking,

smear campaigning, backbiting, obloquy, disparagement, denigration. ▶ v. DEFAME, blacken someone's name, libel, cast aspersions on, malign, vilify, verbally abuse, smear, slur, backbite, disparage, denigrate, decry, run down, calumniate.

slanderous adj. DEFAMATORY, libellous, damaging, abusive, muckraking, malicious, backbiting, disparaging, denigrating. ■ OPPOSITES complimentary.

slang n. **1** COLLOQUIALISM, informal language, lingo. **2** JARGON, cant, argot; *informal* gobbledegook, technospeak, mumbo-jumbo.

slant v. **1** SLOPE, tilt, be askew, lean, dip, shelve, list. **2** GIVE A SLANT TO, give a bias to, bias, angle, distort, twist. ▶ n. **1** SLOPE, tilt, dip, leaning, inclination, shelving, listing. **2** BIAS, leaning, onesidedness, prejudice, angle, distortion, twist.

slanting adj. SLANTED, aslant, at an angle, sloping, italic, oblique, tilting, tilted, askew, leaning, dipping, on an for food or of people violently or in large numbers. ▶ v. kill in this way. □ **slaughterhouse** a place where animals are killed for food.

Slav n. a member of a group of peoples in central and eastern Europe.

slave n. **1** hist. a person owned by another and forced to obey them. **2** a person strongly influenced or controlled by something. ▶ v. work very hard. □ **slave-driver** informal a person who makes other people work very hard. ■ **slavery** n.

slaver v. let saliva run from the mouth.

slavish adj. showing no originality. ■ **slavishly** adv.

Slavonic n. the group of languages including Russian and Polish.

slay v. (**slaying, slew**; past part. **slain**) old use kill. ■ **slayer** n.

sleazy adj. (**sleazier, sleaziest**) **1** immoral or dishonest. **2** squalid. ■ **sleaze** n. **sleaziness** n.

sled n. US a sledge.

sledge n. a vehicle on runners for travelling over snow. ▶ v. ride on a sledge.

sledgehammer n. a large, heavy hammer.

sleek adj. **1** smooth and glossy. **2** looking wealthy and smart.

sleep n. a state of rest in which the eyes are closed and the mind unconscious. ▶ v. (**sleeping, slept**) **1** be asleep. **2** (**sleep in**) remain asleep later than usual. **3** have sleeping accommodation

for. □ **sleeping bag** a padded bag to sleep in. **sleepwalk** walk around while asleep. ■ **sleepless** adj.

sleeper n. **1** a beam on which a railway track rests. **2** a ring or bar worn in a pierced ear to keep the hole from closing. **3** a train with carriages fitted with beds or berths.

sleepy adj. (**sleepier, sleepiest**) **1** needing or ready for sleep. **2** without much activity. ■ **sleepily** adv. **sleepiness** n.

sleet n. rain containing snow. ▶ v. fall as sleet. ■ **sleety** adj.

sleeve n. **1** the part of a garment covering the arm. **2** a protective cover. □ **up one's sleeve** secret but ready for use. ■ **sleeveless** adj.

sleigh n. a sledge pulled by horses or reindeer.

sleight /slyt/ n. (**sleight of hand**) skilful use of the hands when performing conjuring tricks.

slender adj. **1** gracefully thin. **2** barely enough.

slept past & past part. of SLEEP.

sleuth /slooth/ n. informal a detective.

slew[1] v. turn or slide uncontrollably.

slew[2] past of SLAY.

slice n. **1** a thin, broad piece of food cut from a larger portion. **2** a share. **3** a utensil for lifting food. **4** a sliced stroke or shot. ▶ v. **1** cut into slices. **2** hit a ball so that it spins and curves as it travels.

Thesaurus

incline, shelving, listing, diagonal.

slap v. SMACK, strike, hit, cuff; informal wallop, clout, whack, biff, belt, sock.

slapdash adj. see CARELESS.

slaughter v. KILL, butcher, massacre, murder, put to death, do to death, put to the sword; literary slay. See also KILL. ▶ n. MASSACRE, murder, butchery, killing, bloodshed, carnage.

slave n. historical serf, vassal; old use bondsman/woman. ▶ v. TOIL, drudge, slog, labour, grind, work one's fingers to the bone, work day and night, work like a Trojan.

slavery n. ENSLAVEMENT, bondage, servitude, subjugation; historical serfdom, vassalage, thrall, thraldom. ■ OPPOSITES freedom.

slavish adj. **1** SERVILE, subservient, obsequious, sycophantic, deferential, grovelling, fawning, cringing, menial, abject. **2** IMITATIVE, unoriginal, uninspired, unimaginative.

slay v. KILL, murder, slaughter, put to

death, do to death, assassinate, do away with; informal rub out.

sleek adj. SMOOTH, glossy, shiny, lustrous, silken, silky, satiny, burnished.

sleep v. BE ASLEEP, slumber, doze, nap, drowse; informal snooze, crash, have forty winks, be in the land of Nod. ■ OPPOSITES wake up. ▶ n. SLUMBER, doze, nap, rest, siesta, drowse; informal snooze, forty winks, a bit of shut-eye.

sleepiness n. DROWSINESS, tiredness, somnolence, somnolency, languor, languidness, lethargy, sluggishness, inactivity, lassitude, torpor, torpidity.

sleepless adj. WITHOUT SLEEP, wakeful, insomniac, restless, disturbed.

sleepy adj. **1** DROWSY, tired, somnolent, languorous, lethargic, sluggish, inactive, heavy, torpid, comatose. **2** INACTIVE, quiet, peaceful, slow-moving, slumberous. ■ OPPOSITES alert.

slender adj. **1** SLIM, thin, slight, lean, svelte, silken, willowy, sylphlike. **2** SMALL, slight, slim, faint, remote, feeble,

slick adj. **1** smooth and efficient. **2** self-confident but insincere. **3** smooth and glossy or slippery. ▶n. a patch of oil. ▶v. make hair flat and smooth.

slide v. (**sliding, slid**) **1** move along a smooth surface while remaining in contact with it. **2** move smoothly or unobtrusively. ▶n. **1** a structure with a smooth sloping surface for sliding down. **2** a piece of glass on which an object is placed for viewing under a microscope. **3** a piece of photographic film for viewing with a projector. **4** a hairgrip. □ **sliding scale** a scale of fees, wages, etc., that varies according to particular conditions.

slight adj. **1** small in degree. **2** lacking depth; trivial. **3** slender. ▶v. insult by treating disrespectfully. ▶n. an insult. ∎ **slightly** adv.

slim adj. (**slimmer, slimmest**) **1** gracefully thin. **2** small in width. **3** very slight. ▶v. (**slimming, slimmed**) make or become thinner. □ **slimline** slender in design. ∎ **slimmer** n.

slime n. an unpleasantly moist, slippery substance.

slimy adj. (**slimier, slimiest**) **1** like or covered by slime. **2** informal insincerely flattering.

sling n. **1** a loop of fabric used to support or lift something. **2** a strap or loop for hurling small missiles. ▶v. (**slinging, slung**) **1** hang or carry loosely. **2** informal throw carelessly.

slink v. (**slinking, slunk**) move quietly and stealthily.

slinky adj. graceful and curvy.

slip v. (**slipping, slipped**) **1** lose one's balance and slide. **2** slide out of position or one's grasp. **3** gradually worsen. **4** (**slip up**) make a careless error. **5** move or place quietly, quickly, or secretly. **6** elude. ▶n. **1** an act of slipping. **2** a minor mistake. **3** a petticoat. **4** a small piece of paper. **5** a mixture of clay and water for decorating pottery. □ **give someone the slip** informal escape from someone. **slipped disc** a displaced disc between vertebrae in the spine. **slip road** a road entering or leaving a motorway. **slipshod** careless or disorganized. **slipstream** a current of air or water driven back by a revolving propeller or jet engine. **slipway** a slope on which boats are launched or landed, or built and repaired.

slipper n. a light indoor shoe.

slippery adj. **1** difficult to hold or stand on because smooth or wet. **2** not trustworthy.

slit n. a long, narrow cut or opening. ▶v.

Thesaurus

flimsy, tenuous, fragile. ∎ OPPOSITES fat.

sleuth n. DETECTIVE, investigator, private investigator; informal private eye, dick; US informal gumshoe.

slice n. PIECE, portion, segment, sliver, wedge, chunk, hunk; informal wodge. ▶v. CUT UP/THROUGH, carve, chop, divide, cleave, sever.

slick adj. **1** WELL ORGANIZED, streamlined, efficient, smooth, polished. **2** GLIB, smooth, fluent, plausible, specious. **3** SUAVE, urbane, sophisticated, polished, glib, smooth, efficient, professional, smart, sharp, shrewd.

slide v. SLIP, skid, slither, skate, skim, glissade, glide.

slight adj. **1** SMALL, little, tiny, minute, inappreciable, imperceptible, subtle, modest. **2** SLIM, slender, small, spare, delicate, frail. ▶v. SNUB, insult, affront, rebuff, give the cold shoulder to, cold-shoulder, keep at arm's length, disregard, ignore, neglect, take no notice of, disdain, scorn. ▶n. SNUB, insult, affront, rebuff, scorn, disdain; informal slap in the face.

slightly adv. A LITTLE, a bit, somewhat, rather, to some degree. ∎ OPPOSITES very.

slim adj. **1** SLENDER, thin, slight, lean, narrow, svelte, willowy, sylphlike. **2** SLIGHT, small, slender, faint, remote, feeble, flimsy, tenuous, fragile. ∎ OPPOSITES fat. ▶v. LOSE WEIGHT, shed weight, diet, go on a diet.

slime n. SLUDGE, muck, ooze, mud; informal goo, gunk.

slimy adj. **1** SLUDGY, mucky, oozy, muddy, slippery, sticky, viscous, mucous. **2** OILY, unctuous, obsequious, sycophantic, servile, grovelling.

sling v. TOSS, fling, throw, cast, hurl, pitch, shy, lob; informal chuck, heave.

slink v. SKULK, lurk, sneak, creep, steal, slip, slide.

slip v. **1** SKID, slither, lose one's footing, lose one's balance. **2** FALL, slide, drop. **3** STEAL, slide, creep, sneak, slink. **4** GO DOWN, decline, decrease, lessen, depreciate, sink, slump, plummet. ▶n. **1** SLIP-UP, mistake, error, blunder, miscalculation, oversight; informal boo-boo, boob; informal, dated bloomer. **2** UNDERSKIRT, petticoat. □ **slip up** MAKE A MISTAKE, blunder, make a blunder, miscalculate, err;

s

(**slitting**, **slit**) make a slit in.
slither v. slide unsteadily.
sliver n. a small sharp piece.
slob n. informal a lazy, untidy person.
slobber v. slaver or dribble.
sloe n. a small sour bluish-black fruit.
slog v. (**slogging**, **slogged**) **1** work hard. **2** move with effort. **3** hit hard. ▶ n. a period of hard work or travelling.
slogan n. a short, memorable phrase used in advertising or as a motto.
sloop n. a sailing boat with one mast.
slop v. (**slopping**, **slopped**) spill or overflow. ▶ pl. n. (**slops**) **1** waste liquid. **2** unappetizing semi-liquid food.
slope n. a surface with one end or side at a higher level than another. ▶ v. **1** form a slope. **2** (**slope off**) informal leave unobtrusively.
sloppy adj. (**sloppier**, **sloppiest**) **1** containing too much liquid. **2** careless or disorganized. ■ **sloppily** adv. **sloppiness** n.
slosh v. (of liquid) move with a splashing sound.
slot n. **1** a long, narrow opening into which something may be inserted. **2** a place in an arrangement etc. ▶ v. (**slotting**, **slotted**) fit something into a slot.

□ **slot machine** a fruit machine or vending machine.
sloth /slohth/ n. **1** laziness. **2** a slow-moving tropical American mammal. ■ **slothful** adj.
slouch v. stand, move, or sit in a drooping way. ▶ n. a drooping posture.
slough[1] /slow/ n. a swamp.
slough[2] /sluf/ v. cast off old or dead skin.
slovenly adj. **1** untidy. **2** careless. ■ **slovenliness** n.
slow adj. **1** not moving or able to move quickly. **2** taking a long time. **3** (of a clock etc.) showing a time earlier than the correct time. **4** not quick to understand or learn. ▶ v. reduce speed. □ **slowcoach** informal a slow or lazy person. **slow-worm** a lizard without legs. ■ **slowly** n. **slowness** n.
sludge n. thick, soft mud.
slug n. **1** a small creature like a snail without a shell. **2** a bullet. **3** a small amount of an alcoholic drink. ▶ v. (**slugging**, **slugged**) informal hit hard.
sluggard n. a lazy person.
sluggish adj. **1** slow-moving. **2** not lively or alert. ■ **sluggishly** adv. **sluggish-**

Thesaurus

informal make a boo-boo, screw up, boob; *informal, dated* make a bloomer.
slippery adj. **1** GREASY, oily, slimy, icy, glassy, smooth, soapy; *informal* slippy, skiddy. **2** SHIFTY, devious, deceitful, duplicitous, crafty, cunning, sneaky, treacherous, perfidious, two-faced, dishonest, false, unreliable, untrustworthy; *informal* tricky, foxy.
slit v. CUT, split open, slash, gash, rip, make an incision in, tear, rend, pierce. ▶ n. CUT, split, slash, gash, rip, incision, tear, rent, fissure, opening.
slither v. SLIDE, slip, skid.
sliver n. CHIP, flake, splinter, shred, fragment, scrap.
slobber v. SLAVER, drool, salivate, dribble, splutter.
slog v. (**slog away**) WORK, labour, toil, slave, drudge, plough.
slogan n. MOTTO, logo, catchword, jingle, rallying cry, shibboleth.
slop v. SPILL, overflow, splash, slosh, splatter, spatter.
slope v. DROP AWAY, fall away, slant, incline, lean, tilt, dip. ▶ n. SLANT, inclination, angle, skew, tilt, dip, gradient.
sloping adj. SLANTING, oblique, leaning, inclined, angled, italic, askew, tilting, dipping. ■ OPPOSITES level.
sloppy adj. **1** WATERY, wet, soggy,

splashy, slushy, sludgy. **2** CARELESS, slapdash, slipshod, disorganized, unmethodical, untidy, messy, slovenly. ■ OPPOSITES meticulous.
slot n. **1** SLIT, crack, hole, opening, aperture, groove, notch. **2** PLACE, position, niche, space, opening, time, period.
sloth n. LAZINESS, indolence, idleness, sluggishness, inertia, inactivity, lethargy, langour, slothfulness, torpor.
slothful adj. LAZY, indolent, idle, workshy, sluggish, inert, inactive, lethargic, languorous, torpid. ■ OPPOSITES industrious.
slovenly adj. SLATTERNLY, untidy, dirty, unclean, messy, unkempt, dishevelled, bedraggled, tousled, rumpled. ■ OPPOSITES tidy.
slow adj. **1** SLOW-MOVING, unhurried, leisurely, measured, deliberate, ponderous, creeping, dawdling, loitering, lagging, laggard, sluggish, snail-like, tortoise-like. **2** BACKWARD, retarded, slow-witted, dull-witted, dull, unintelligent, stupid, thick, dense; *informal* dumb, dopey. **3** TIME-CONSUMING, protracted, drawn-out, prolonged, interminable. ■ OPPOSITES quick, bright. ▶ v. **1** REDUCE SPEED, decelerate, put the brakes on. **2** HOLD BACK, keep back, delay, detain, restrain.
slowly adv. AT A SLOW PACE, without

ness n.

sluice /slooss/ n. **1** a sliding gate controlling a flow of water. **2** a channel for surplus water. ▶ v. rinse with water.

slum n. a squalid house or district.

slumber v. sleep. ▶ n. a sleep.

slump v. **1** sit or lean heavily and limply. **2** decline greatly. ▶ n. a sudden fall in prices or demand.

slung past & past part. of SLING.

slunk past & past part. of SLINK.

slur v. (**slurring, slurred**) **1** speak in an unclear way. **2** perform a group of musical notes in a flowing way. ▶ n. **1** an insulting remark or accusation. **2** a curved line indicating that notes are to be slurred.

slurp v. eat or drink with a loud sucking sound.

slurry n. a semi-liquid mixture of manure, cement, or coal and water.

slush n. **1** partially melted snow or ice. **2** informal sentimental talk or writing. □ **slush fund** a reserve of money for illegal purposes. ▪ **slushy** adj.

slut n. a slovenly or promiscuous woman. ▪ **sluttish** adj.

sly adj. **1** cunning and deceitful. **2** (of a remark etc.) suggesting secret knowledge. □ **on the sly** secretly. ▪ **slyly** adv. **slyness** n.

smack n. **1** a slap. **2** the sound of this. **3** a loud kiss. **4** a sailing boat with one mast. ▶ v. **1** slap. **2** part the lips noisily. □ **smack of 1** taste of. **2** suggest the presence of.

small adj. **1** of less than normal size. **2** not large. **3** young. **4** unimportant. ▶ n. (**smalls**) informal underwear. □ **smallholding** a small farm. **small hours** the early hours of the morning after midnight. **small-minded** narrow-minded. **smallpox** a viral disease with blisters that leave permanent scars. **small talk** polite conversation about unimportant matters. ▪ **smallness** n.

smarmy adj. informal excessively and insincerely polite and friendly.

smart adj. **1** neat and stylish. **2** fashionable and upmarket. **3** intelligent. **4** quick. ▶ v. **1** give a sharp, stinging pain. **2** feel annoyed. □ **smart card** a plastic card on which information is stored in electronic form. ▪ **smarten** v. **smartly** adv. **smartness** n.

smash v. **1** break violently into pieces. **2** hit or collide with forcefully. **3** destroy or ruin. ▶ n. **1** an act or sound of smashing. **2** informal a very successful song, film, etc.

smashing adj. informal excellent.

smattering n. **1** a small amount. **2** a slight knowledge.

smear v. **1** coat or mark with a greasy or sticky substance. **2** damage the reputation of. ▶ n. **1** a greasy or sticky

Thesaurus

hurrying, unhurriedly, at a leisurely pace, steadily, ploddingly, taking one's time, in one's own good time, with heavy steps, at a snail's pace.

sluggish adj. INACTIVE, inert, heavy, lifeless, apathetic, listless, lethargic, languid, languorous, torpid, phlegmatic, indolent, lazy, slothful, drowsy, sleepy. ▪ OPPOSITES energetic.

slump n. PLUNGE, nosedive, collapse, fall, falling-off, drop, downturn, downswing, slide, decline, decrease, lowering, devaluation, depreciation, depression. ▶ v. **1** COLLAPSE, sink, fall, subside. **2** PLUMMET, plunge, nosedive, fall, drop, go down, slide, decline, decrease, devalue. ▪ OPPOSITES rise.

slur n. INSULT, slight, aspersion, imputation, affront, defamation, slander, libel, misrepresentation, smear, stain, stigma.

sly adj. **1** CUNNING, crafty, wily, artful, conniving, scheming, devious, underhand, shrewd, astute; informal tricky, foxy, smart. **2** ROGUISH, impish, mischievous, playful, arch, knowing.

smack n. & v. SLAP, blow, hit, whack, thump, cuff, punch, spank, buffet, rap, bang; informal wallop, clout, belt, sock.

small adj. **1** LITTLE, tiny, petite, slight, minute, miniature, pocket-size, mini, minuscule, diminutive, undersized, puny; informal pint-sized, teeny, teeny-weeny, teensy-weensy; Sc. wee. **2** SLIGHT, minor, unimportant, trifling, trivial, insignificant, inconsequential, inappreciable. **3** HUMBLE, modest, lowly, simple, unpretentious, poor, inferior. **4** NARROW, narrow-minded, mean, petty. ▪ OPPOSITES big, large.

smart adj. **1** WELL DRESSED, well turned out, fashionably dressed, fashionable, stylish, modish, elegant, chic, neat, spruce, trim; informal natty, snappy, out of a bandbox. **2** CLEVER, bright, intelligent, gifted, sharp, quick-witted, nimble-witted, shrewd, ingenious. **3** BRISK, quick, fast, swift, lively, energetic, spirited, vigorous, jaunty; informal cracking, spanking. ▪ OPPOSITES scruffy. ▶ v. STING, nip, burn, bite, pain.

smash v. **1** BREAK, shatter, crash, shiver,

mark. **2** a false accusation.

smell n. **1** the ability to perceive things by means of the organs in the nose. **2** a quality sensed by this. **3** an act of smelling. ▶v. (**smelling, smelt** or **smelled**) **1** perceive the smell of. **2** give off an odour. ■ **smelly** adj.

smelt v. heat and melt ore to extract metal.

smidgen (or **smidgin**) n. informal a tiny amount.

smile v. turn up the corners of one's mouth to show pleasure, amusement, or friendliness. ▶n. an act of smiling.

smirch v. discredit.

smirk v. smile smugly. ▶n. a smug smile.

smite v. (**smiting, smote**; past part. **smitten**) **1** old use hit hard. **2** (**be smitten**) be strongly attracted to someone.

smith n. **1** a worker in metal. **2** a blacksmith.

smithereens pl. n. informal small pieces.

smithy n. (pl. **smithies**) a blacksmith's workshop.

smock n. a loose dress, shirt, or overall.

smog n. dense smoky fog or haze.

smoke n. **1** a visible vapour produced by a burning substance. **2** an act of smoking tobacco. ▶v. **1** give out smoke. **2** breathe the smoke of tobacco or a drug in and out. **3** preserve meat or fish by exposure to smoke. □ **smoke-screen** a thing designed to disguise or conceal activities. ■ **smokeless** adj. **smoker** n. **smoky** adj.

smolder US = SMOULDER.

smooch v. informal kiss and cuddle.

smooth adj. **1** having an even and regular surface. **2** moving without jerks. **3** without difficulties. **4** charming but possibly insincere. **5** not harsh or bitter. ▶v. make smooth. ■ **smoothly** adv. **smoothness** n.

smorgasbord n. a meal consisting of a range of savoury items.

smote past of SMITE.

smother v. **1** suffocate. **2** put out a fire by covering it. **3** cover entirely. **4** suppress.

smoulder (US **smolder**) v. **1** burn slowly with smoke but no flame. **2** feel strong and barely hidden anger etc.

SMS abbrev. Short Message Service, used to send and receive text messages on mobile phones.

smudge v. make or become blurred or smeared. ▶n. a smudged mark. ■ **smudgy** adj.

smug adj. (**smugger, smuggest**) irritatingly pleased with oneself. ■ **smugly** adv. **smugness** n.

Thesaurus

pulverize, splinter, crack. **2** CRASH, collide, wreck. **3** DESTROY, ruin, shatter, devastate.

smattering n. BIT, modicum, dash, rudiments, elements.

smear v. **1** SPREAD, daub, slap, plaster. **2** SMUDGE, streak, blur. **3** SULLY, tarnish, blacken, taint, stain, slur, defame, defile, vilify, slander, libel, calumniate. ▶n. **1** DAUB, spot, patch; informal splotch. **2** SMUDGE, streak. **3** TAINT, stain, slur, blot.

smell v. **1** SCENT, sniff, get a sniff of; informal get a whiff of. **2** HAVE A BAD SMELL, stink, be stinking, reek, be malodorous; informal stink to high heaven, pong, whiff, hum. ▶n. **1** ODOUR, scent, aroma, perfume, fragrance, bouquet; literary redolence. **2** STINK, stench, reek; informal pong, whiff, hum.

smelly adj. SMELLING, evil-smelling, foul-smelling, stinking, high, malodorous, fetid, rank; informal ponging, humming, whiffy; literary noisome, mephitic.

smirk v. LEER, sneer, simper, grin.

smitten adj. TAKEN WITH, infatuated with, enamoured of, attracted by, charmed by, captivated by, enchanted by, beguiled by; informal bowled over by.

smog n. HAZE, fog, pollution.

smoke v. **1** SMOULDER, reek. **2** CURE, dry, preserve.

smoky adj. SMOKE-FILLED, hazy, foggy, smoggy, reeky, murky.

smooth adj. **1** EVEN, level, flat, plane, flush, unwrinkled. **2** CALM, still, tranquil, flat, glassy, mirror-like. **3** EASY, effortless, trouble-free, simple, plain sailing. **4** STEADY, regular, rhythmic, uninterrupted, flowing, fluid. **5** SMOOTH-TONGUED, suave, urbane, sophisticated, courteous, gracious, glib, persuasive, slick, oily, ingratiating, unctuous; informal smarmy. ■ OPPOSITES rough. ▶v. **1** LEVEL, even, flatten, plane, press down, steamroll. **2** EASE, make easy/easier, facilitate, clear the way for, pave the way for, open the door for, expedite, assist, aid, help, help along.

smother v. **1** SUFFOCATE, stifle, asphyxiate, choke. **2** OVERWHELM, shower, inundate, envelop, surround, cocoon.

smoulder v. **1** SMOKE, reek. **2** SEETHE, fume, burn, boil, foam, rage.

smudge n. MARK, spot, smear, streak, stain, blotch, blot, blur, smut; informal

smuggle v. **1** move goods illegally into or out of a country. **2** convey secretly. ■ **smuggler** n.

smut n. **1** a small flake of soot or dirt. **2** indecent writing, pictures, etc. ■ **smutty** adj.

snack n. a small or casual meal.

snaffle n. a type of horse's bit. ▶v. informal secretly take.

snag n. **1** an unexpected difficulty. **2** a jagged projection. **3** a small tear. ▶v. (**snagging**, **snagged**) catch or tear on a snag.

snail n. a mollusc with a spiral shell.

snake n. a reptile with no legs and a long slender body. ▶v. move with a twisting motion. ■ **snaky** adj.

snap v. (**snapping**, **snapped**) **1** break with a sharp cracking sound. **2** open or close with a brisk movement or sharp sound. **3** (**snap up**) quickly buy. **4** say quickly and irritably. **5** take a snapshot of. ▶n. **1** an act or sound of snapping. **2** a snapshot. ▶adj. done on the spur of the moment. □ **snapdragon** a plant with brightly coloured flowers that have a mouth-like opening. **snapshot** an informal photograph.

snapper n. an edible sea fish.

snappy adj. (**snappier**, **snappiest**) informal **1** irritable. **2** stylish. □ **make it snappy** do it quickly.

snare n. a trap with a loop of wire that pulls tight. ▶v. catch in a snare.

snarl v. **1** growl with bared teeth. **2** say aggressively. **3** (**snarl up**) entangle. ▶n. an act or sound of snarling. □ **snarl-up** informal a traffic jam.

snatch v. seize quickly or eagerly. ▶n. **1** an act of snatching. **2** a fragment.

snazzy adj. (**snazzier**, **snazziest**) informal stylish.

sneak v. **1** go, do, or obtain furtively. **2** informal report another's wrongdoings. **3** (**sneaking**) (of a feeling) persisting in one's mind. ▶n. informal a telltale. ■ **sneakily** adv. **sneaky** adj.

sneaker n. a soft shoe worn for sports or casual occasions.

sneer n. a scornful smile or remark. ▶v. smile or speak in a scornful way.

sneeze v. suddenly expel air from the nose and mouth. ▶n. an act of sneezing.

snicker v. & n. = SNIGGER.

snide adj. disrespectful or mocking in an indirect way.

sniff v. **1** draw in air audibly through the nose. **2** smell by sniffing. **3** (**sniff around**) informal investigate secretly. ▶n. an act of sniffing. ■ **sniffer** n.

sniffle v. sniff slightly or repeatedly. ▶n. an act of sniffling.

snifter n. informal a small quantity of an alcoholic drink.

snigger n. & v. (give) a half-suppressed laugh.

snip v. (**snipping**, **snipped**) cut with scissors using small, quick strokes. ▶n. **1** an act of snipping. **2** informal a bargain.

snipe n. (pl. **snipe** or **snipes**) a wading

Thesaurus

splotch.

smug adj. SELF-SATISFIED, complacent, pleased with oneself, superior, proud of oneself, conceited.

snack n. LIGHT MEAL, bite, nibbles, titbit, bite to eat, little something.

snag n. **1** CATCH, drawback, hitch, stumbling block, obstacle, disadvantage, inconvenience, problem, complication. **2** RIP, tear, run, hole. ▶v. CATCH, rip, tear.

snap v. **1** BREAK, fracture, splinter, separate, come apart, crack. **2** CRACK, click, crackle. **3** BITE, gnash, nip. **4** SPEAK SHARPLY/BRUSQUELY, bark, snarl, growl; informal jump down someone's throat, fly off the handle at.

snappy adj. **1** IRRITABLE, irascible, cross, touchy, testy, crabbed, crotchety, grumpy, grouchy, peppery. **2** SMART, fashionable, stylish, chic, modish, dapper; informal natty, trendy. ■ OPPOSITES peaceable, slovenly.

snare v. TRAP, ensnare, catch, get hold of, seize, capture. ▶n. TRAP, gin, springe, net, noose.

snatch v. **1** SEIZE, grab, take hold of, pluck. **2** GRAB, steal, make off with, appropriate; informal nab, swipe. **3** KIDNAP, abduct, grab, take as hostage.

sneak v. **1** CREEP, skulk, lurk, prowl, steal, slip, slide, slink, sidle. **2** TELL TALES ON, inform on, report; informal tell on, grass on, squeal on, peach on.

sneaking adj. SECRET, private, hidden, concealed, unexpressed, unvoiced, undisclosed, undivulged, unconfessed, unavowed.

sneer v. **1** CURL ONE'S LIP, smirk, snicker, snigger. **2** SCOFF AT, scorn, be contemptuous of, hold in contempt, disdain, mock, jeer at, gibe at, ridicule, deride, taunt, insult, slight. ▶n. **1** SMIRK, snicker. **2** JEER, jibe, taunt, insult, slight.

sniff v. **1** SNUFFLE, inhale, breathe in. **2** SMELL, catch the scent of, scent; informal get a whiff of.

bird with a long bill. ▶v. **1** fire shots from a hiding place at long range. **2** criticize in a sly or petty way. ■ **sniper** n.

snippet n. a small piece.

snivel v. (**snivelling**, **snivelled**; US **sniveling**, **sniveled**) **1** cry. **2** complain in a whining way.

snob n. a person who greatly respects social status or wealth and who looks down on people of a lower class. ■ **snobbery** n. **snobbish** adj.

snog informal v. (**snogging**, **snogged**) kiss. ▶n. a kiss.

snood n. a hairnet worn over a woman's hair at the back.

snooker n. a game played with cues on a billiard table.

snoop v. informal pry. ■ **snooper** n.

snooty adj. (**snootier**, **snootiest**) informal superior towards others. ■ **snootily** adv.

snooze informal n. a nap. ▶v. have a nap.

snore n. a snorting sound made whilst asleep. ▶v. make such sounds.

snorkel n. a tube for a swimmer to breathe through while under water. ▶v. (**snorkelling**, **snorkelled**; US **snorkeling**, **snorkeled**) swim with a snorkel.

snort n. an explosive sound made by forcing breath through the nose. ▶v. **1** make a snort. **2** informal inhale cocaine.

snout n. an animal's projecting nose and mouth.

snow n. frozen water vapour in the atmosphere falling in light white flakes and settling as a white layer. ▶v. **1** fall as snow. **2** (**be snowed under**) be overwhelmed with work etc. □ **snowboarding** the sport of sliding downhill over snow on a single short, broad ski. **snowdrift** a bank of deep snow heaped up by the wind. **snowdrop** a plant bearing drooping white flowers in late winter. **snowman** a human figure made of compressed snow. **snowplough** (US **snowplow**) a device or vehicle for clearing roads of snow. ■ **snowy** adj.

snowball n. a ball of packed snow for throwing. ▶v. increase rapidly in size or importance.

snub v. (**snubbing**, **snubbed**) ignore or reject scornfully. ▶n. an act of snubbing. ▶adj. (of the nose) short and turned up at the end.

snuff v. **1** put out a candle. **2** (**snuff it**) informal die. ▶n. powdered tobacco for sniffing up the nostril.

snuffle v. breathe with noisy sniffs. ▶n. a snuffling sound.

snug adj. (**snugger**, **snuggest**) **1** cosy. **2** close-fitting. ▶n. a small, cosy room in a pub. ■ **snugly** adv.

snuggle v. settle into a warm, comfortable position.

so adv. **1** to such a great extent. **2** to the same extent. **3** similarly. **4** thus. ▶conj. **1** therefore. **2** (**so that**) with the result or aim that. □ **so-and-so** informal **1** a person or thing whose name the speaker does not know. **2** a person who is disliked. **so-called** wrongly called by the name or term specified.

soak v. **1** make something thoroughly wet by leaving it in liquid. **2** (of a liquid) spread throughout. **3** (**soak up**) absorb. ▶n. **1** an act of soaking. **2** informal a heavy drinker.

soap n. **1** a substance used with water

Thesaurus

snigger v. SNICKER, sneer, smirk, titter, giggle, chortle.

snip v. CUT, cut into, nick, slit, notch, incise, snick. ▶n. **1** CUT, nick, slit, notch, incision, snick. **2** BARGAIN, value for money; informal good buy, cheap buy, giveaway, steal.

snippet n. BIT, piece, scrap, fragment, particle, shred, snatch.

snivel v. **1** WEEP, cry, sob, whimper; informal blub, blubber. **2** SNIFFLE, snuffle, run at the nose, have a runny nose.

snobbish adj. SNOBBY, arrogant, proud, condescending, haughty, disdainful, supercilious, patronizing; informal snooty, uppity, stuck up, hoity-toity, toffee-nosed.

snoop v. PRY, spy, interfere, meddle; informal poke one's nose in. ▶n. BUSYBODY, interferer, meddler; informal snooper, nosy parker; Austral./NZ informal stickybeak.

snooze v. DOZE, nap, catnap, drowse, sleep, slumber; informal take forty winks, have a kip, kip. ▶n. DOZE, nap, catnap, siesta, sleep, slumber; informal forty winks, informal kip.

snub v. IGNORE, disregard, take no notice of, shun, rebuff, repulse, spurn, slight, give the cold shoulder to, cold-shoulder, insult, affront; informal give the brush-off to, give the go-by, put down.

snug adj. **1** COSY, comfortable, warm, homelike, homely, sheltered; informal comfy. **2** CLOSE-FITTING, tight, skin-tight. ■ OPPOSITES bleak, loose.

snuggle v. NESTLE, cuddle (up), curl up, nuzzle.

for washing. **2** informal a soap opera. ▶ v. wash with soap. □ **soap opera** a television or radio serial dealing with the daily lives of a group of characters. ■ **soapy** adj.

soar v. **1** rise high into the air. **2** increase rapidly.

sob v. (**sobbing**, **sobbed**) **1** cry with loud gasps. **2** say while sobbing. ▶ n. an act of sobbing.

sober adj. **1** not drunk. **2** serious. **3** (of a colour) not bright. ▶ v. make or become sober. ■ **soberly** adv. **sobriety** n.

sobriquet (or **soubriquet**) /soh-bri-kay/ n. a nickname.

soccer n. a form of football played with a round ball which may not be handled during play except by the goalkeepers.

sociable adj. **1** enjoying the company of others. **2** marked by friendliness. ■ **sociability** n. **sociably** adv.

social adj. **1** of society and its organization. **2** needing the company of others. **3** (of an activity) in which people meet for pleasure. **4** (of animals) living in organized communities. ▶ n. a social gathering. □ **social security** money provided by the state for people with little or no income. **social services** services provided by the state such as education and medical care. **social worker** a person whose job is to help and advise people with family or financial problems. ■ **socially** adv.

socialism n. a political and economic theory that a country's transport, resources, and chief industries should be owned or controlled by the state. ■ **socialist** n. & adj.

socialite n. a person who mixes in fashionable society.

socialize (or **-ise**) v. mix socially with others.

society n. (pl. **societies**) **1** people living together in an ordered community. **2** a community of people. **3** fashionable and wealthy people. **4** an organization or club. **5** the company of other people.

sociology n. the study of human society. ■ **sociological** adj. **sociologist** n.

sock n. **1** a knitted garment for the foot and lower leg. **2** informal a hard blow. ▶ v. informal hit forcefully.

socket n. a hollow or device into which something fits.

sod n. grass-covered ground, or a piece of this.

soda n. **1** carbonated water. **2** a compound of sodium.

sodden adj. soaked through.

sodium n. a soft silver-white metallic element. □ **sodium chloride** the chemical name for salt.

sodomy n. anal intercourse. ■ **sodomite** n.

sofa n. a long padded seat with a back and arms.

soft adj. **1** easy to mould, cut, compress, or fold. **2** not rough in texture. **3** quiet and gentle. **4** (of light or colour) not

Thesaurus

soak v. **1** DRENCH, wet through, saturate, make sopping. **2** STEEP, immerse, souse.

soaking adj. SOAKED, soaked to the skin, wet through, drenched, sodden, saturated, sopping wet, dripping wet, wringing wet, streaming wet. ■ OPPOSITES parched.

soar v. **1** FLY, take flight, take off, ascend, climb, rise. **2** RISE, go up, increase, climb rapidly, spiral. ■ OPPOSITES plummet.

sob v. WEEP, cry, shed tears, blubber, snivel, howl, bawl; Sc. greet; informal boohoo.

sober adj. **1** NOT DRUNK, abstemious, teetotal, abstinent, temperate; informal on the wagon, dry. **2** SERIOUS, solemn, thoughtful, grave, earnest, calm, composed, sedate, staid, dignified, steady, level-headed, self-controlled, strict, puritanical. **3** DISPASSIONATE, objective, rational, logical, well considered, circumspect, lucid, clear. **4** DARK, sombre, quiet, restrained, drab, severe, austere.

■ OPPOSITES drunk.

sociable adj. FRIENDLY, affable, cordial, social, neighbourly, companionable, gregarious, convivial, communicative, genial, clubbable, outgoing, approachable, accessible. ■ OPPOSITES unsociable, unfriendly.

social adj. **1** COMMUNITY, civil, civic, public, societal. **2** ENTERTAINMENT, recreation, amusement. **3** see SOCIABLE. ■ OPPOSITES individual.

socialize v. BE SOCIABLE/SOCIAL, mix, mingle, keep company, fraternize, consort, hobnob, get together, get out and about.

society n. **1** MANKIND, humanity, civilization, the public, the general public, the people, the population, the world at large, the community. **2** COMMUNITY, group, culture, civilization. **3** HIGH SOCIETY, polite society, aristocracy, gentry, nobility, upper classes, the elite, the smart set, beau monde, haut monde; informal the upper crust, the top drawer, harsh. **5** not strict. **6** (of a drink) not alcoholic. **7** (of a drug) not likely to cause addiction. **8** (of water) free from mineral salts. □ **softball** a form of baseball played with a larger, softer ball. **soft fruit** a small fruit without a stone. **soft furnishings** curtains, cushions, rugs, etc. **soft-hearted** kind and compassionate. **soft option** an easy alternative. **software** computer programs. **softwood** wood from coniferous trees. ■ **softly** adv. **softness** n.

soften v. make or become soft or softer. ■ **softener** n.

soggy adj. (**soggier**, **soggiest**) very wet and soft.

soigné /swun-yay/ adj. elegant and well groomed.

soil n. **1** the upper layer of the earth. **2** a nation's territory. ▶v. make dirty.

soirée /swah-ray/ n. an evening social gathering.

sojourn /so-juhn/ n. a temporary stay. ▶v. stay temporarily.

solace n. comfort in time of distress. ▶v. give solace to.

solar adj. of the sun or its rays. □ **solar plexus** a network of nerves at the pit of the stomach. **solar system** the sun with the planets etc. in orbit around it.

solarium n. (pl. **solariums** or **solaria**) a room equipped with sunbeds.

sold past & past part. of SELL.

solder n. a soft alloy for joining metals. ▶v. join with solder. □ **soldering iron** a tool for melting and applying solder.

soldier n. a person serving in an army. ▶v. **1** serve as a soldier. **2** (**soldier on**) informal keep trying.

sole n. **1** the underside of the foot. **2** a section forming the underside of a piece of footwear. **3** an edible flatfish. ▶v. put a sole on a shoe. ▶adj. **1** one and only. **2** belonging or restricted to one person or group. ■ **solely** adv.

solecism /sol-i-si-z'm/ n. **1** a grammatical mistake. **2** an instance of bad manners or incorrect behaviour.

solemn adj. **1** formal and dignified. **2** serious. ■ **solemnity** n. **solemnly** adv.

solemnize (or **-ise**) v. perform or mark with a ceremony.

solenoid n. a coil of wire which becomes magnetic when an electric current is passed through it.

solicit v. (**soliciting**, **solicited**) **1** ask for something from someone. **2** approach someone and offer one's services as a prostitute. ■ **solicitation** n.

solicitor n. a lawyer who advises clients and instructs barristers.

solicitous adj. concerned about a person's well-being. ■ **solicitously** adv. **solicitude** n.

solid adj. **1** firm and stable in shape. **2** strongly built. **3** not hollow or having spaces or gaps. **4** consisting of the same substance throughout. **5** (of time) uninterrupted. **6** reliable. **7** three-dimensional. ▶n. a solid substance, object, or food. ■ **solidity** n. **solidly** adv.

Thesaurus

toffs, nobs, swells. **4** ASSOCIATION, club, group, band, circle, body, fraternity, brotherhood, sisterhood, league, union, alliance, federation.

sodden adj. see SOAKING.

soft adj. **1** PLIABLE, pliant, supple, elastic, flexible, ductile, malleable, plastic, mushy, squashy, pulpy, doughy, spongy; informal gooey. **2** SMOOTH, velvety, cushiony, fleecy, downy, furry, silky, silken, satin; informal like a baby's bottom. **3** LOW, dim, shaded, subdued, muted, mellow. **4** HUSHED, whispered, murmured, stifled, inaudible, low, quiet, mellow, melodious, mellifluous. **5** EASY-GOING, tolerant, forgiving, forbearing, lenient, indulgent, permissive, liberal, lax. ■ OPPOSITES firm, hard.

soften v. **1** EASE, cushion, temper, mitigate, assuage. **2** ABATE, moderate, lessen, diminish, calm down. **3** MODERATE, temper, tone down.

soggy adj. SOAKING, saturated, sodden,

sopping wet, soft, boggy, swampy, miry, waterlogged, over-moist.

soil[1] n. EARTH, ground, clay, dirt, land.

soil[2] v. DIRTY, stain, muddy, spot, smear, splash, smudge, sully, taint, blot; literary besmirch.

soldier n. FIGHTER, serviceman, servicewoman, warrior, trooper; informal cannon fodder.

solemn adj. **1** SERIOUS, grave, important, formal, profound. **2** DIGNIFIED, ceremonious, stately, majestic, imposing, impressive, grand. **3** SOMBRE, serious, unsmiling, pensive, thoughtful, gloomy, glum, grim. **4** EARNEST, sincere, honest, genuine, committed, heartfelt. ■ OPPOSITES frivolous.

solicit v. **1** ASK FOR, request, apply for, seek, beg, plead for, crave. **2** WORK AS A PROSTITUTE, engage in prostitution, make sexual advances; informal hustle.

solicitous adj. CONCERNED, caring, attentive, considerate, anxious, worried,

solidarity n. agreement and support resulting from shared interests, feelings, etc.

solidify v. (**solidifying, solidified**) make or become solid. ■ **solidification** n.

soliloquy n. (pl. **soliloquies**) a speech in a play made by a character while alone.

solitaire n. **1** a game for one person played on a board with pegs. **2** a single gem in a piece of jewellery.

solitary adj. **1** alone. **2** isolated. **3** single.

solitude n. the state of being alone.

solo n. (pl. **solos**) a song, dance, or piece of music by or for one performer. ▶ adj. & adv. for or done by one person.

soloist n. the performer of a solo.

solstice n. either of the two times in the year, midsummer and midwinter, when the sun reaches its highest or lowest point in the sky at noon.

soluble adj. **1** able to be dissolved. **2** able to be solved. ■ **solubility** n.

solution n. **1** a way of solving a problem. **2** the correct answer to a puzzle. **3** a mixture formed when a substance is dissolved in a liquid. **4** the process of dissolving.

solve v. find an answer to a problem etc.

solvent adj. **1** having more money than one owes. **2** able to dissolve other substances. ▶ n. a liquid used to dissolve other substances. ■ **solvency** n.

somatic adj. of the body rather than the mind.

sombre (US **somber**) adj. dark and gloomy.

sombrero n. (pl. **sombreros**) a broad-brimmed hat.

some adj. **1** an unspecified amount or number of. **2** unknown or unspecified. **3** approximately. **4** considerable. **5** expressing admiration. ▶ pron. a certain amount or number of people or things. □ **somebody** someone. **somehow** in an unknown or unspecified way. **someone 1** an unknown or unspecified person. **2** a person of importance. **something** an unspecified or unknown thing or amount. **sometime 1** at an unspecified or unknown time. **2** former. **sometimes** occasionally. **somewhat** to some extent. **somewhere** in or to an unspecified or unknown place.

somersault n. a movement in which a person turns head over heels and finishes on their feet. ▶ v. perform a somersault.

somnambulism n. sleepwalking.

Thesaurus

nervous, uneasy, apprehensive.

solid adj. **1** FIRM, hard, thick, dense, concrete, compact, compressed, condensed. **2** STURDY, substantial, strong, sound, stout, durable, well built, well constructed, stable. **3** SOUND, well founded, well grounded, concrete, valid, reasonable, logical, cogent, weighty, authoritative, convincing, plausible, reliable. **4** SENSIBLE, level-headed, down-to-earth, decent, law-abiding, upright, upstanding, worthy. **5** STAID, worthy, sound, unexciting, unimaginative, uninspired. **6** FINANCIALLY SOUND, solvent, creditworthy, in good standing, in the black, secure. **7** CONTINUOUS, uninterrupted, unbroken, undivided. ■ OPPOSITES liquid, flimsy, unreliable.

solidarity n. UNITY, union, unanimity, singleness of purpose, like-mindedness, team spirit, camaraderie, harmony, esprit de corps.

solidify v. HARDEN, go hard, set, jell, congeal, cake. ■ OPPOSITES liquefy.

solitary adj. **1** LONELY, lonesome, companionless, friendless, antisocial, unsocial, unsociable, withdrawn, reclusive, cloistered, introverted, hermitic. **2** REMOTE, out of the way, isolated, se-

cluded, hidden, concealed, private, unfrequented, unvisited, desolate. **3** LONE, single, sole, alone, by oneself/itself. ▶ n. LONER, lone wolf, recluse, hermit, eremite, anchorite, stylite, coenobite.

solitude n. LONELINESS, remoteness, isolation, seclusion, privacy, retirement, desolation.

solution n. **1** ANSWER, result, key, resolution, solving, resolving, explanation, clarification, elucidation, unravelling, unfolding. **2** SUSPENSION, emulsion, mixture, mix, blend, compound.

solve v. FIND THE SOLUTION TO, answer, find the answer to, resolve, work out, figure out, fathom, find the key to, decipher, clear up, get to the bottom of, unravel, disentangle, unfold; informal crack.

solvent adj. FINANCIALLY SOUND, debt-free, creditworthy, in the black, viable. ■ OPPOSITES insolvent.

sombre adj. **1** DARK, dark-coloured, dull, dull-coloured, drab, dingy. **2** GLOOMY, depressed, sad, melancholy, dismal, doleful, mournful, joyless, cheerless, lugubrious, funereal, sepulchral. ■ OPPOSITES bright, cheerful.

somehow adv. BY SOME MEANS, in some way, in one way or other, no matter

■ **somnambulist** n.

somnolent adj. sleepy. ■ **somnolence** n.

son n. a boy or man in relation to his parents. □ **son-in-law** (pl. **sons-in-law**) the husband of one's daughter.

sonar n. a system for detecting objects under water by giving out sound pulses.

sonata n. a piece of music for a solo instrument, often with a piano accompaniment.

son et lumière /son ay loo-mee-air/ n. a night-time entertainment dramatizing a historical event with lighting and sound effects.

song n. **1** a set of words set to music. **2** singing. □ **songbird** a bird with a musical song. **songster** (fem. **songstress**) a singer.

sonic adj. of or using sound waves. □ **sonic boom** a loud noise caused by the shock wave from an object travelling faster than the speed of sound. ■ **sonically** adv.

sonnet n. a poem of 14 lines.

sonorous adj. (of a sound) deep and full. ■ **sonority** n. **sonorously** adv.

soon adv. **1** in or after a short time. **2** (**sooner**) rather. □ **sooner or later** eventually.

soot n. a black powdery substance pro-

duced when coal, wood, etc. is burnt. ■ **sooty** adj.

soothe v. **1** calm. **2** relieve pain or discomfort.

soothsayer n. a prophet.

sop n. a thing given or done to pacify someone. ▶ v. (**sopping**, **sopped**) (**sop up**) soak up liquid.

sophist n. a person who uses clever but false arguments. ■ **sophism** n. **sophistry** n.

sophisticated adj. **1** having experience and taste in matters of culture or fashion. **2** highly developed and complex. ■ **sophistication** n.

soporific adj. causing drowsiness or sleep.

sopping adj. wet through.

soppy adj. (**soppier**, **soppiest**) informal too sentimental. ■ **soppily** adv.

soprano n. (pl. **sopranos**) the highest singing voice.

sorbet /sor-bay/ n. a water ice.

sorcerer n. (fem. **sorceress**) a person who practises magic. ■ **sorcery** n.

sordid adj. **1** dishonest or immoral. **2** very dirty and unpleasant. ■ **sordidly** adv. **sordidness** n.

sore adj. painful or aching. ▶ n. a sore place on the body. □ **sore point** a cause of distress or annoyance. ■ **soreness** n.

sorely adv. extremely; badly.

Thesaurus

how, come what may, by fair means or foul, by hook or by crook; informal come hell or high water.

sometimes adv. OCCASIONALLY, on occasion, on occasions, now and then, now and again, from time to time, once in a while, every so often, off and on.

somnolent adj. SLEEPY, drowsy, half asleep, heavy-eyed, dozy, groggy, comatose; informal dopey.

sonorous adj. DEEP, rich, full, round, resonant, resounding, booming, ringing, reverberating, vibrating, pulsating.

soon adv. SHORTLY, in a short time, in a little while, before long, in a minute, in a moment, any minute, in the near future, in a twinkling, in the twinkling of an eye; informal before you can say Jack Robinson, pronto, in two shakes of a lamb's tail.

soothe v. EASE, assuage, alleviate, allay, moderate, mitigate, temper, palliate, soften, lessen, reduce. ■ OPPOSITES aggravate.

sophisticated adj. **1** WORLDLY-WISE, worldly, experienced, seasoned, suave, urbane, cultured, cultivated, polished,

refined, elegant, stylish, cosmopolitan, blasé. **2** ADVANCED, highly developed, ultra-modern, complex, complicated, elaborate, intricate. ■ OPPOSITES unsophisticated, crude.

soppy adj. MAWKISH, maudlin, sentimental, overemotional, sloppy; informal slushy, mushy, schmaltzy, corny.

sorcerer n. MAGICIAN, wizard, enchanter, warlock, necromancer, magus, thaumaturgist.

sorcery n. MAGIC, witchcraft, witchery, wizardry, necromancy, black art, enchantment, thaumaturgy.

sordid adj. **1** FILTHY, dirty, foul, unclean, grimy, sooty, soiled, stained, mucky, squalid, shabby, seedy, seamy, slummy, sleazy. **2** VILE, foul, base, low, debased, degenerate, dishonourable, disreputable, despicable, ignominious, ignoble, abhorrent, abominable. **3** MEAN, greedy, avaricious, covetous, grasping, mercenary, miserly, niggardly; informal stingy. ■ OPPOSITES clean.

sore adj. **1** PAINFUL, in pain, aching, hurting, tender, inflamed, raw, smarting, stinging, burning, irritated, bruised,

S

sorghum n. a cereal grown for grain and animal feed.

sorrel n. 1 a sharp-tasting herb. 2 a light reddish-brown colour.

sorrow n. 1 deep distress caused by loss or disappointment. 2 a cause of this. ■ **sorrowful** adj. **sorrowfully** adv.

sorry adj. (**sorrier**, **sorriest**) 1 feeling sympathy for another's misfortune. 2 feeling regret. 3 wretched or pitiful.

sort n. 1 a kind or category. 2 informal a person with a specified nature. ▶ v. 1 arrange in groups. 2 separate from a mixed group. 3 (**sort out**) resolve a problem or difficulty.

sortie n. 1 an attack by troops from a defended position. 2 a flight by a single aircraft on a military operation.

SOS n. 1 an international distress signal. 2 an urgent appeal for help.

sot n. a habitual drunkard.

sotto voce /sot-toh voh-chay/ adv. & adj. in a quiet voice.

soubriquet var. of SOBRIQUET.

soufflé n. a light baked dish made with beaten egg whites.

sough /sow, suf/ v. make a moaning or whistling sound.

sought past & past part. of SEEK.

souk /sook/ n. an Arab market.

soul n. 1 the spiritual or immortal element of a person. 2 a person's inner nature. 3 emotional energy or power. 4 a perfect example of a particular quality: *the soul of discretion.* 5 a person. 6 a kind of music with elements of gospel and rhythm and blues.

soulful adj. expressing deep emotion. ■ **soulfully** adv.

soulless adj. lacking character, interest, or emotion.

sound n. 1 vibrations travelling through air or water and sensed by the ear. 2 a thing that can be heard. 3 a strait. ▶ v. 1 make or cause to make a sound. 2 utter. 3 give a specified impression. 4 (**sound off**) express one's opinions forcefully. 5 find out the depth of a lake etc. using a line, pole, or sound echoes. 6 (**sound out**) question someone as to their opinions. ▶ adj. 1 in good condition. 2 based on solid judgement. 3 (of sleep) deep. □ **sound barrier** the point at which an aircraft reaches the speed of sound. **sound bite** a short memorable extract from a speech or interview. **sounding board** a person or group used to test ideas or opinions. **soundproof** preventing sound getting in or out. **soundtrack** the sound accompaniment to a film. ■ **soundly** adv.

soup n. a liquid dish of meat, fish, or ve-

Thesaurus

wounded, injured. 2 DISTRESSED, upset, resentful, aggrieved, offended, hurt, pained, annoyed, angry, irritated, irked, nettled; *informal* peeved. ▶ n. WOUND, scrape, abrasion, cut, laceration, graze, boil, abscess, swelling.

sorrow n. 1 SADNESS, unhappiness, grief, misery, distress, heartache, heartbreak, anguish, suffering, pain, woe, affliction, wretchedness, dejection, heaviness of heart, desolation, depression, disconsolateness, mourning. 2 TROUBLE, worry, woe, misfortune, affliction, trial, tribulation. ■ OPPOSITES joy. ▶ v. BE SAD, feel sad, be miserable, suffer, be wretched, be dejected, be heavy of heart, pine, weep.

sorrowful adj. UNHAPPY, sad, heartbroken, wretched, woebegone, tearful, miserable, dejected, desolated, depressed, disconsolate, mournful, doleful, melancholy, lugubrious. ■ OPPOSITES happy.

sorry adj. 1 REGRETFUL, apologetic, repentant, penitent, remorseful, contrite, ashamed, conscience-stricken, guilt-ridden, in sackcloth and ashes, compunctious. 2 SYMPATHETIC, pitying, full of pity, compassionate, moved, commiserative, empathetic. ■ OPPOSITES glad, unsympathetic, unrepentant.

sort n. 1 KIND, type, variety, class, category, style, group, set, genre, genus, family, order, breed, make, brand, stamp. 2 PERSON, individual, soul; *informal* fellow, guy, bloke, chap, character, customer. ▶ v. CLASSIFY, class, categorize, catalogue, grade, rank, group, divide, arrange, order, put in order, organize, assort, systematize, methodize. □ **sort out** CLEAR UP, put straight, put right, solve, find a solution to.

sortie n. SALLY, foray, charge, rush, onrush, raid, attack.

soul n. 1 SPIRIT, psyche, inner self, true being, vital force, animating principle. 2 PERSON, human being, individual, creature.

sound[1] n. 1 NOISE, utterance, cry. 2 HEARING, distance, earshot, range. ▶ v. 1 RESOUND, reverberate, resonate. 2 PRONOUNCE, utter, voice, enunciate, articulate, vocalize. 3 APPEAR, seem, give/create the impression that, strike someone that, give every indication that.

sound[2] adj. 1 HEALTHY, in good health, in

getables. ▶v. (**soup up**) informal increase the power of a car or engine. □ **soup kitchen** a place where free food is served to homeless or poor people.

soupçon /soop-son/ n. a very small quantity.

sour adj. **1** having a sharp taste. **2** tasting or smelling stale. **3** resentful or angry. ▶v. make or become sour. ■ **sourly** adv. **sourness** n.

source n. **1** a place, person, or thing from which something comes or is obtained. **2** a place where a river begins. **3** a person, book, etc. providing information.

souse v. **1** soak in or drench with. **2** pickle.

south n. **1** the direction on the right-hand side of a person facing east. **2** the southern part of a place. ▶adj. **1** lying towards or facing the south. **2** (of a wind) from the south. ▶adv. towards the south. ■ **southerly** adj. & adv. **southward** adj. & adv. **southwards** adv.

south-east n. the direction or region halfway between south and east. ▶adj. & adv. **1** towards or facing the south-east. **2** (of a wind) from the south-east. ■ **south-easterly** adj. & adv. **south-eastern** adj.

southern adj. situated in or facing the south.

southerner n. a person from the south of a region.

south-west n. the direction or region halfway between south and west. ▶adj. & adv. **1** towards or facing the south-

west. **2** (of a wind) from the south-west. ■ **south-westerly** adj. & adv. **south-western** adj.

souvenir n. a thing kept as a reminder of a person, place, or event.

sou'wester n. a waterproof hat with a broad flap at the back.

sovereign n. **1** a king or queen who is the supreme ruler of a country. **2** a former British gold coin worth one pound sterling. ▶adj. **1** having supreme power. **2** (of a state) independent. ■ **sovereignty** n.

Soviet n. a citizen of the former Soviet Union. ▶adj. of the former Soviet Union.

sow[1] /soh/ v. (**sowing, sowed**; past part. **sown** or **sowed**) **1** plant seed by scattering it on or in the earth. **2** plant an area with seed. **3** give rise to.

sow[2] /sow/ n. an adult female pig.

soya n. a plant producing an edible bean high in protein.

sozzled adj. informal very drunk.

spa n. **1** a mineral spring with health-giving properties. **2** a place with a spa.

space n. **1** unoccupied ground or an area of this. **2** the boundless expanse in which all things exist and move. **3** the universe beyond the earth's atmosphere. **4** a blank between written words or characters. **5** an interval of time. ▶v. **1** position items at a distance from one another. **2** (**spaced out**) informal dazed. □ **spacecraft** a vehicle for travelling in space. **spaceship** a manned spacecraft.

Thesaurus

. . . .

good condition, physically fit, hale and hearty, undamaged, unimpaired, in good shape, in fine fettle. **2** STURDY, substantial, solid, well constructed, intact, whole, undamaged, unimpaired. **3** WELL FOUNDED, well grounded, solid, valid, reasonable, logical, cogent, weighty, authoritative, convincing, plausible, reliable. **4** SOLVENT, creditworthy, in good financial standing, in the black, solid, secure. **5** THOROUGH, complete, without reserve, unqualified, out-and-out, drastic, severe. ■ OPPOSITES unhealthy, flimsy, insolvent.

sound[3] v. PLUMB, fathom. □ **sound out** INVESTIGATE, conduct a survey of, research, explore, look into, examine, probe, canvass.

sour adj. **1** ACID, acidy, acid-like, acetic, acidulous, tart, bitter, sharp, vinegary, pungent. **2** TURNED, curdled, fermented, rancid, bad. **3** EMBITTERED, nasty, un-

pleasant, disagreeable, bad-tempered, ill-tempered, ill-natured, sharp-tongued, irritable, crotchety, cross, crabbed, testy, touchy, peevish, churlish, grumpy; informal grouchy, snappish. ■ OPPOSITES sweet, fresh, amiable.

source n. **1** ORIGIN, derivation, commencement, beginning, start, rise, cause, wellspring, fountainhead, provenance, author, originator; literary begetter. **2** WELLSPRING, well head, headspring. **3** REFERENCE, authority.

sovereign n. RULER, monarch, king, queen, emperor, empress, tsar, crowned head, potentate. ▶adj. **1** SUPREME, absolute, unlimited, chief, paramount, principal, dominant, predominant, ruling. **2** INDEPENDENT, autonomous, self-ruling, self-governing.

sow v. SCATTER, spread, broadcast, disperse, strew, bestrew, disseminate, distribute.

spacious adj. having plenty of space. ■ **spaciousness** n.

spade n. **1** a tool for digging, with a broad metal blade on a long handle. **2** (**spades**) one of the four suits in a pack of playing cards. □ **spadework** hard preparatory work.

spaghetti pl. n. pasta in long strands.

span n. **1** extent from side to side. **2** the length of time for which something lasts. **3** a part of a bridge between the uprights supporting it. ▶v. (**spanning, spanned**) extend across or over.

spangle n. a small piece of decorative glittering material. ■ **spangled** adj.

Spaniard n. a person from Spain.

spaniel n. a dog with a long silky coat and drooping ears.

Spanish n. the main language of Spain and of much of Central and South America. ▶adj. of Spain or Spanish.

spank v. slap on the buttocks.

spanking adj. **1** brisk: *a spanking pace*. **2** informal impressive.

spanner n. a tool for gripping and turning a nut or bolt.

spar n. a strong pole used for a mast or yard on a ship. ▶v. (**sparring, sparred**) **1** make the motions of boxing but without force, as a form of training. **2** argue without hostility.

spare adj. **1** additional to what is required. **2** not currently in use or occupied. **3** thin. ▶n. an extra thing kept in case another is lost, broken, etc. ▶v. **1** give something of which one has enough to someone. **2** refrain from killing or harming. □ **to spare** left over.

sparing adj. not wasteful; economical. ■ **sparingly** adv.

spark n. **1** a fiery particle. **2** a flash of light produced by an electrical discharge. **3** a small but concentrated amount. ▶v. **1** produce sparks. **2** give rise to; provoke. □ **spark plug** a device which ignites the explosive mixture in an internal-combustion engine.

sparkle v. **1** shine with flashes of light. **2** be lively and witty. **3** (**sparkling**) (of drink) fizzy. ▶n. a sparkling light. ■ **sparkly** adj.

sparkler n. a hand-held firework that gives out sparks.

sparrow n. a small brown and grey bird.

sparse adj. thinly scattered. ■ **sparsely** adv. **sparsity** n.

spartan adj. lacking in comfort or luxury.

spasm n. **1** a sudden involuntary contraction of a muscle. **2** a sudden spell of an activity or sensation.

Thesaurus

space n. **1** ROOM, expanse, extent, capacity, area, volume, spaciousness, scope, elbow room, latitude, margin, leeway. **2** GAP, interval, opening, interstice, break. **3** TIME, duration, period, span, stretch, interval. **4** OUTER SPACE, the universe, the galaxy, the solar system, infinity. ▶v. PLACE AT INTERVALS, arrange, line up, range, order, interspace, set apart.

spacious adj. ROOMY, commodious, capacious, sizable, ample, large, big, extensive, broad, wide, expansive, vast. ■ OPPOSITES small.

span n. **1** LENGTH, extent, reach, stretch, spread, distance. **2** TIME, duration, period, space, stretch, interval. ▶v. EXTEND OVER, stretch across, cover, range over, bridge, cross, traverse, pass over, arch over, vault over.

spare adj. **1** EXTRA, additional, reserve, supplementary, auxiliary, surplus, supernumerary. **2** FREE, leisure, unoccupied. **3** LEAN, thin, slim, slender, skinny, skin and bone, wiry, lank. ▶v. **1** AFFORD, part with, give, provide, dispense with, do without, manage without, get along without. **2** BE MERCIFUL TO,

show mercy to, be lenient to, deal leniently with, pardon, leave unpunished; informal let off, go easy on.

sparing adj. ECONOMICAL, frugal, thrifty, careful, prudent, parsimonious, niggardly; informal stingy, tight-fisted. ■ OPPOSITES extravagant.

spark n. FLICKER, flash, flare, glint. ▶v. SET OFF, spark off, start off, trigger off, touch off, precipitate, provoke, stir up, incite.

sparkle v. **1** TWINKLE, flicker, shimmer, flash, glitter, glint, shine, gleam, glow, coruscate. **2** BE VIVACIOUS, be lively, be animated, be ebullient, be effervescent, be witty, be brilliant. ▶n. **1** TWINKLE, flicker, shimmer, flash, glitter, glint, shining, gleam, glow, coruscation. **2** VIVACITY, liveliness, life, animation, energy, vitality, spirit, enthusiasm, dash, panache; informal pizzazz, vim, zip, zing.

sparse adj. SCANTY, meagre, slight, light, sparing, inadequate, few and far between; informal thin on the ground. ■ OPPOSITES abundant.

spartan adj. AUSTERE, harsh, frugal, stringent, rigorous, strict, severe, bleak, grim, ascetic, abstemious, self-

spasmodic adj. **1** occurring or done in brief, irregular bursts. **2** caused by a spasm or spasms. ■ **spasmodically** adv.

spastic adj. **1** of or affected by muscle spasm. **2** offens. of cerebral palsy. ▶n. offens. a person with cerebral palsy. ■ **spasticity** n.

....

ℹ Say *person with cerebral palsy* rather than **spastic**, which many people find offensive.

....

spat[1] past & past part. of SPIT.

spat[2] n. **1** informal a petty quarrel. **2** a cloth covering formerly worn over the instep and ankles.

spate n. **1** a large number of similar things coming one after another. **2** a sudden flood.

spatial adj. of space. ■ **spatially** adv.

spatter v. spray or splash with drops or spots. ▶n. a spray or splash.

spatula n. an implement with a broad, flat, blunt blade for mixing or spreading.

spawn v. **1** (of a fish, frog, etc.) release or deposit eggs. **2** give rise to. ▶n. the eggs of fish, frogs, etc.

spay v. sterilize a female animal by removing the ovaries.

speak v. (**speaking**, **spoke**; past part. **spoken**) **1** say something. **2** communicate or be able to communicate in a specified language. **3** suggest or be a sign of. □ **speak up for** speak in defence of.

speaker n. **1** a person who speaks. **2** a person who makes a speech. **3** a loudspeaker.

spear n. **1** a weapon with a pointed tip and a long shaft. **2** a pointed stem of asparagus or broccoli. ▶v. pierce with a pointed object. □ **spearhead 1** a person or group leading an attack or movement. **2** lead an attack or movement.

spearmint n. a type of mint used in cooking.

spec n. (**on spec**) informal without any preparation or plan.

special adj. **1** better than or different from what is usual. **2** for a particular purpose or person. ■ **specially** adv.

specialist n. an expert in a particular field. ■ **specialism** n.

speciality n. (pl. **specialities**) a subject or skill in which someone is an expert.

specialize (or **-ise**) v. **1** be or become a specialist. **2** (**be specialized**) be adapted for a special function. ■ **specialization** n.

species n. (pl. **species**) a group of animals or plants able to breed with each other.

specific adj. **1** clearly defined or identified. **2** precise and clear. ▶n. (**specifics**) precise details. ■ **specifically** adv.

specification n. **1** the act of specify-

Thesaurus

....

denying. ■ OPPOSITES luxurious.

spasm n. **1** CONTRACTION, convulsion, cramp, twitch. **2** FIT, paroxysm, convulsion, attack, bout, seizure, outburst, access.

spasmodic adj. INTERMITTENT, fitful, irregular, sporadic, erratic, occasional, periodic, recurring, recurrent. ■ OPPOSITES regular.

spate n. RUSH, flood, deluge, torrent, outpouring, outbreak, cluster.

spatter v. SPLASH, spray, shower, bespatter, daub.

speak v. **1** UTTER, voice, express, say, pronounce, articulate, enunciate, state, discourse upon, tell. **2** ADDRESS, talk to, converse with, communicate with, have a discussion with, chat with, have a chat with, have a word with, accost; *informal* have a chinwag with, chew the fat/rag with, pass the time of day with. □ **speak for 1** REPRESENT, act for, act on behalf of, intercede for. **2** SUPPORT, uphold, defend, stand up for, advocate.

speak out SPEAK BOLDLY, speak frankly, speak openly, speak one's mind, sound off, stand up and be counted.

speaker n. PUBLIC SPEAKER, lecturer, orator, declaimer, haranguer, demagogue; *informal* tub-thumper, spieler.

spearhead n. VANGUARD, van, forefront, driving force. ▶v. LEAD, head, set in motion, initiate, launch, pioneer.

special adj. **1** EXCEPTIONAL, remarkable, unusual, rare, out of the ordinary, extraordinary, singular, distinctive, notable, outstanding, unique. **2** SPECIFIC, particular, individual, distinctive, exact, precise, definite. **3** ESPECIAL, extra special, particular, exceptional, out of the ordinary. **4** SIGNIFICANT, momentous, memorable, festive, gala, red-letter. ■ OPPOSITES ordinary.

specialist n. EXPERT, authority, professional, consultant, master.

speciality n. **1** SPECIALTY, area of specialization, field of study. **2** DISTINCTIVE FEATURE, forte, métier, talent, gift, claim to fame.

species n. SORT, kind, type, variety,

ing. **2** a detailed description of the design and materials used to make something.

specify v. (**specifying, specified**) state or identify clearly and definitely.

specimen n. **1** an individual animal, plant, etc. used as an example for study or display. **2** a sample for medical testing.

specious adj. seeming reasonable, but actually wrong.

speck n. a tiny spot or particle.

speckle n. a small spot or patch of colour. ■ **speckled** adj.

specs pl. n. informal spectacles.

spectacle n. **1** a visually striking performance or display. **2** (**spectacles**) a pair of glasses.

spectacular adj. very impressive or dramatic. ▶n. a spectacular performance or event. ■ **spectacularly** adv.

spectator n. a person who watches a game, incident, etc.

spectral adj. **1** of or like a ghost. **2** of the spectrum.

spectre (US **specter**) n. **1** a ghost. **2** a possible unwelcome occurrence.

spectrum n. (pl. **spectra**) **1** a band of colours produced by separating light into parts with different wavelengths. **2** a range of sound waves or other types of wave. **3** a range of beliefs, qualities, etc.

speculate v. **1** form a theory without firm evidence. **2** invest in stocks, property, etc. in the hope of making a profit. ■ **speculation** n. **speculative** adj. **speculator** n.

speculum n. (pl. **specula**) a medical instrument for widening openings in the body to allow inspection.

speech n. **1** the expression of thoughts and feelings using spoken language. **2** a formal talk given to an audience. **3** a manner of speaking.

speechless adj. unable to speak due to shock or emotion.

speed n. **1** the rate at which someone or something moves or operates. **2** rapidity of movement or action. **3** informal an amphetamine drug. ▶v. (**speeding, speeded** or **sped**) **1** move quickly. **2** (**speed up**) move or work more quickly. **3** drive at a speed greater than the legal limit. □ **speedboat** a fast motor boat. **speedometer** a device in a vehicle indicating its speed. **speedway** a form of motorcycle racing on a

Thesaurus

class, category, group, genus, breed, genre.

specific adj. **1** WELL DEFINED, clear-cut, unambiguous, unequivocal, exact, precise, explicit, express, detailed. **2** PARTICULAR, specified, fixed, set, determined, distinct, definite. ■ OPPOSITES vague, general.

specify v. STATE, mention, name, stipulate, define, set out, itemize, designate, detail, list, spell out, enumerate, particularize, catalogue, be specific about.

specimen n. SAMPLE, representative, example, illustration, instance, type, exhibit.

specious adj. MISLEADING, deceptive, fallacious, unsound, casuistic, sophistic.

speck n. **1** SPOT, fleck, dot, speckle, stain, mark, smudge, blemish. **2** PARTICLE, bit, piece, atom, iota, grain, trace.

speckled adj. MOTTLED, flecked, spotted, dotted, dappled, brindled, stippled.

spectacle n. **1** SIGHT, vision, scene, picture. **2** DISPLAY, show, exhibition, pageant, parade, extravaganza.

spectacles n. GLASSES, eyeglasses; informal specs.

spectacular adj. IMPRESSIVE, magnificent, splendid, eye-catching, breathtaking, glorious, dazzling, sensational, stunning, dramatic, exceptional, remarkable, unusual, picturesque; informal out of this world. ■ OPPOSITES unimpressive, dull.

spectator n. VIEWER, observer, onlooker, looker-on, watcher, beholder, witness, eyewitness, bystander; informal rubberneck. ■ OPPOSITES participant.

spectre n. APPARITION, ghost, phantom, wraith, spirit, shade, vision, revenant, manes; informal spook.

speculate v. **1** CONJECTURE, theorize, hypothesize, guess, take a guess, surmise, muse, reflect, meditate, deliberate, cogitate, consider, think. **2** GAMBLE, take a risk on, venture on; informal have a flutter on.

speculative adj. **1** CONJECTURAL, theoretical, hypothetical, suppositional, notional, academic, tentative, unproven, vague, indefinite. **2** RISKY, hazardous, gambling; informal chancy, dicey.

speech n. **1** COMMUNICATION, talk, conversation, discussion, dialogue, colloquy. **2** DICTION, articulation, enunciation, pronunciation. **3** TALK, lecture, address, discourse, oration, sermon, harangue, diatribe, tirade; literary philippic. **4** LANGUAGE, tongue, idiom, dialect, parlance; informal lingo.

dirt track.

speedy adj. (**speedier**, **speediest**) rapid. ■ **speedily** adv.

speleology /spee-li-ol-uh-ji/ n. the study or exploration of caves.

spell v. (**spelling**, **spelled** or **spelt**) **1** write or name the letters forming a word in correct order. **2** lead to or be a sign of. **3** (**spell out**) state explicitly. ▶n. **1** a form of words thought to have magical power. **2** a state of enchantment brought on by a spell. **3** a short period of time. □ **spellbound** entranced. ■ **spelling** n.

spend v. (**spending**, **spent**) **1** pay money to buy or hire goods or services. **2** use or use up. **3** pass time. □ **spendthrift** a person who spends money irresponsibly. ■ **spender** n.

sperm n. (pl. **sperm** or **sperms**) **1** semen. **2** a spermatozoon.

spermatozoon /sper-muh-tuh-zoh-on/ n. (pl. **spermatozoa**) the male sex cell of an animal, that fertilizes the egg.

spermicide n. a contraceptive substance that kills sperm.

spew v. **1** pour out in large quantities. **2** informal vomit.

sphere n. **1** a perfectly round solid figure. **2** an area of activity, interest, etc. ■ **spherical** adj. **spherically** adv.

sphincter n. a ring of muscle surrounding an opening in the body.

sphinx n. an ancient Egyptian stone figure with a lion's body and a human or animal head.

spice n. **1** a strong-tasting vegetable substance for flavouring food. **2** interest and excitement. ▶v. flavour with spice. ■ **spiciness** n. **spicy** adj.

spick and span adj. neat and clean.

spider n. an eight-legged insect-like animal. ■ **spidery** adj.

spiel /shpeel, speel/ n. informal an elaborate and insincere persuasive speech.

spigot n. a small peg or plug.

spike n. a thin, pointed piece of metal, wood, etc. ▶v. **1** impale on or pierce with a spike. **2** cover with spikes. **3** informal secretly add alcohol or a drug to drink or food. ■ **spiky** adj.

spill v. (**spilling**, **spilt** or **spilled**) **1** flow or cause to flow over the edge of a container. **2** move or empty out from a place. ▶n. **1** an amount spilt. **2** a fall from a horse or bicycle. **3** a thin strip of wood or paper used for lighting a fire. ■ **spillage** n.

Thesaurus

speechless adj. **1** STRUCK DUMB, dumbstruck, dumbfounded, astounded, thunderstruck. **2** SILENT, unspoken, unexpressed, unsaid, unvoiced, tacit.

speed n. RAPIDITY, swiftness, quickness, fastness, haste, hurry, hurriedness, expeditiousness, expedition, alacrity, promptness, fleetness, celerity, velocity. ▶v. **1** HURRY, hasten, make haste, rush, race, dash, sprint, scurry, tear, scamper, charge; informal scoot. **2** DRIVE TOO FAST, break the speed limit, exceed the speed limit; informal put one's foot down, step on it. **3** EXPEDITE, hasten, accelerate, advance, further, forward, facilitate, promote, boost, aid, assist. ■ OPPOSITES slow, hinder. □ **speed up** see ACCELERATE.

speedy adj. RAPID, swift, quick, fast, high-speed, expeditious, fleet, prompt, immediate, express. ■ OPPOSITES slow, leisurely.

spell[1] v. MEAN, signify, amount to, add up to, signal, denote, result in, cause, bespeak, portend, augur, presage. □ **spell out** SPECIFY, set out, itemize, detail, enumerate, particularize, stipulate, make clear, make plain, elucidate, clarify.

spell[2] n. **1** INCANTATION, conjuration, charm, abracadabra. **2** TRANCE, entrancement, enthralment, bewitchment.

spell[3] n. **1** PERIOD, interval, stretch, course, extent, span, patch. **2** TURN, stint, term, stretch, shift.

spellbound adj. RIVETED, entranced, enthralled, enraptured, transported, rapt, bewitched, fascinated, captivated, mesmerized, hypnotized; informal hooked.

spend v. **1** PAY OUT, lay out, expend, disburse, dish out; informal fork out, shell out, splash out, splurge. **2** OCCUPY, fill, take up, use up, pass, while away.

spendthrift n. SQUANDERER, prodigal, profligate, wastrel; informal big spender. ■ OPPOSITES miser.

spent adj. USED UP, consumed, exhausted, finished, depleted, drained, emptied; informal played out, burnt out.

sphere n. **1** GLOBE, ball, orb, globule. **2** AREA, field, range, scope, extent, compass, jurisdiction. **3** SOCIAL CLASS, station, rank, status, social circumstances, walk of life.

spherical adj. GLOBE-SHAPED, globular, globoid, round, orb-like, orbicular.

spice n. **1** FLAVOURING, seasoning, herb, condiment, relish. **2** EXCITEMENT, interest, colour, piquancy, zest, gusto, pep; informal zip, zing, zap.

spicy adj. **1** SPICED, seasoned, tangy,

spin v. (**spinning**, **spun**) **1** turn round quickly. **2** draw out and twist fibres to convert them into yarn. **3** (**spin out**) prolong. ▶ n. **1** a spinning motion. **2** informal a short drive for pleasure. **3** a favourable slant given to a news story. □ **spin doctor** informal a person employed by a political party or politician to give a favourable interpretation of events to the media. **spin-off** a product or benefit produced during or after the main activity. ■ **spinner** adj.

spina bifida n. a condition in which part of the spinal cord is exposed, often causing paralysis.

spinach n. a vegetable with large green leaves.

spinal adj. of the spine. □ **spinal cord** the nerve fibres in the spine connecting all parts of the body to the brain.

spindle n. **1** a rod with tapered ends, used in spinning wool etc. by hand. **2** a revolving pin or axis.

spindly adj. long or tall and thin.

spindrift n. sea spray.

spine n. **1** a series of bones extending from the skull to the small of the back, enclosing the spinal cord. **2** the part of a book enclosing the inner edges of the pages. **3** a hard pointed projection on certain plants and animals. ■ **spiny** adj.

spineless adj. **1** having no spine. **2** lacking determination.

spinet n. a small harpsichord.

spinnaker n. a large extra sail on a racing yacht.

spinney n. (pl. **spinneys**) a small wooded area.

spinster n. an unmarried woman.

spiral adj. forming a continuous curve around a central point or axis. ▶ n. **1** a spiral curve or shape. **2** a progressive rise or fall of prices, wages, etc. ▶ v. (**spiralling**, **spiralled**; US **spiraling**, **spiraled**) **1** follow a spiral course. **2** increase or decrease progressively. ■ **spirally** adv.

spire n. a tall pointed structure on the top of a church tower.

spirit n. **1** the character and feelings of a person rather than their body. **2** a supernatural being. **3** typical character, quality, or mood. **4** (**spirits**) a person's mood. **5** courage and determination. **6** the intended meaning of a law etc. **7** strong distilled alcoholic drink. ▶ v. (**spiriting**, **spirited**) take away rapidly and secretly. □ **spirit level** a sealed glass tube containing a bubble in liquid whose position shows whether a surface is level.

spirited adj. courageous and determined. ■ **spiritedly** adv.

spiritual adj. **1** of the human spirit. **2** of religion or religious belief. ▶ n. a religious song of a kind associated with black Christians of the southern US. ■ **spirituality** n. **spiritually** adv.

spiritualism n. the belief that it is possible to communicate with the spirits of the dead. ■ **spiritualist** n.

spirituous adj. old use strongly alcoholic.

Thesaurus

sharp, tart, hot, peppery, piquant, pungent. **2** LIVELY, spirited, suggestive, racy, off colour, improper, indecent, offensive; informal raunchy. ■ OPPOSITES bland, boring.

spill v. **1** POUR, pour out, flow, overflow, brim over, run over, slop over, well over. **2** REVEAL, disclose, divulge, leak, make known; informal let out, blab. ▶ n. FALL, tumble; informal header, nosedive.

spin v. **1** REVOLVE, rotate, turn, turn round, circle, whirl, gyrate. **2** WHIRL, reel, swim, be giddy. □ **spin out** see PROLONG.

spine n. **1** SPINAL COLUMN, vertebrae, vertebral column, backbone, dorsum. **2** NEEDLE, spike, barb, quill.

spiral adj. COILED, corkscrew, winding, twisting, whorled, helical, cochlear, cochleate, voluted. ▶ n. COIL, twist, whorl, corkscrew, wreath, curlicue, helix, volute. ▶ v. COIL, wind, twist, swirl, wreathe.

spirit n. **1** SOUL, psyche, inner self, ego. **2** BREATH OF LIFE, vital spark, animating principle, life force. **3** APPARITION, ghost, phantom, spectre, wraith, shade, revenant, manes; informal spook. **4** COURAGE, bravery, braveness, valour, mettle, pluck, grit, pluckiness, will power, motivation, backbone, determination, firmness of purpose, resoluteness; informal guts. **5** ATTITUDE, way, state of mind, mood, frame of mind, point of view, reaction, feeling, humour. **6** PREVAILING TENDENCY, animating principle, dominating characteristic, ethos, essence, quintessence, embodiment, personification. ■ OPPOSITES body, flesh.

spirited adj. **1** COURAGEOUS, brave, valiant, valorous, heroic, mettlesome, plucky, gritty, determined, resolute. **2** ANIMATED, lively, vivacious, enthusiastic, fervent, fiery, passionate, energetic. ■ OPPOSITES timid, lifeless.

spiritual adj. **1** NON-MATERIAL, incorpor-

spit v. (**spitting**, **spat** or **spit**) **1** forcibly eject saliva, food, or liquid from the mouth. **2** say in a hostile way. **3** rain lightly. ▶n. **1** saliva. **2** a metal rod for holding and turning roasting meat. **3** a narrow point of land projecting into the sea. □ **spitfire** a hot-tempered person.

spite n. a desire to hurt, annoy, or offend. ▶v. deliberately hurt, annoy, or offend. □ **in spite of** without being affected by. ■ **spiteful** adj. **spitefully** adv. **spitefulness** n.

spittle n. saliva.

splash v. **1** (of a liquid) fall in scattered drops. **2** wet with scattered drops. **3** move around in water, causing it to fly about. **4** display a story etc. prominently in a newspaper. **5** (**splash out**) informal spend money freely. ▶n. **1** an act of splashing. **2** a patch of colour.

splatter v. spatter.

splay v. spread out or further apart.

spleen n. **1** an abdominal organ involved in producing and removing blood cells. **2** bad temper.

splendid adj. **1** very impressive. **2** excellent. ■ **splendidly** adv.

splendour (US **splendor**) n. magnificent and impressive appearance.

splenetic adj. bad-tempered.

splice v. join by interweaving or overlapping the ends.

splint n. a rigid support for a broken bone.

splinter n. a small, thin, sharp piece of broken wood etc. ▶v. break into splinters. □ **splinter group** a small organization that has broken away from a larger one.

split v. (**splitting**, **split**) **1** break into parts by force. **2** divide into parts or groups. **3** end a relationship. ▶n. **1** a crack or split place. **2** an act of splitting. **3** (**the splits**) a gymnastic or dance position with the legs straight and at right angles to the body. □ **split infinitive** an infinitive with a word placed between *to* and the verb.

splodge n. informal a spot or smear.

splurge informal n. a sudden burst of extravagance. ▶v. spend extravagantly.

splutter v. **1** make a series of short explosive spitting sounds. **2** say incoherently. ▶n. a spluttering sound.

Thesaurus

eal, ethereal, intangible, other-worldly, unworldly. **2** RELIGIOUS, sacred, divine, holy, non-secular, churchly, ecclesiastic, devotional, devout. ■ OPPOSITES physical, secular.

spit v. EXPECTORATE, hawk. ▶n. SPITTLE, saliva, sputum.

spite n. MALICE, maliciousness, ill will, malevolence, venom, malignance, hostility, resentment, resentfulness, snideness, rancour, envy, hate, hatred, vengeance, vengefulness, vindictiveness. ■ OPPOSITES benevolence. □ **in spite of** DESPITE, despite the fact, notwithstanding, regardless of.

spiteful adj. MALICIOUS, ill-natured, malevolent, venomous, poisonous, malignant, malign, hostile, resentful, snide, rancorous, grudging, envious, vengeful, vindictive, splenetic; informal bitchy, catty. ■ OPPOSITES benevolent.

splash v. **1** SPATTER, sprinkle, spray, shower, splatter, squirt, slosh, slop; informal splodge. **2** PADDLE, wade, wallow, dabble. **3** BLAZON, display, exhibit, plaster, publicize, broadcast, headline, flaunt, trumpet.

splendid adj. **1** MAGNIFICENT, imposing, superb, grand, sumptuous, resplendent, opulent, luxurious, plush, de luxe, rich, costly, lavish, ornate, gorgeous, glorious, dazzling, brilliant, showy, elegant, handsome. **2** DISTINGUISHED, impressive, glorious, illustrious, brilliant, notable, noted, remarkable, outstanding, eminent, celebrated, renowned, noble, venerable. **3** EXCELLENT, fine, first-class, first-rate, marvellous, wonderful, great; informal fantastic, terrific, fabulous, fab. ■ OPPOSITES inferior, undistinguished.

splendour n. **1** MAGNIFICENCE, grandeur, sumptuousness, opulence, luxury, luxuriousness, richness, lavishness, gloriousness, elegance. **2** ILLUSTRIOUSNESS, brilliance, notability, eminence, renown, venerableness. **3** GLORIOUSNESS, brilliance, brightness, gleam, glow, lustre, radiance.

splice v. INTERWEAVE, braid, plait, intertwine, interlace, join, unite, connect, bind.

splinter n. SLIVER, fragment, shiver, shard, chip, shaving, shred, piece, bit. ▶v. SHATTER, fracture, split, disintegrate, crumble.

split v. **1** BREAK, chop, hew, lop, cleave, rend, rip, tear, slash, slit, splinter. **2** DIVIDE, separate, set apart, disunite. **3** SHARE, divide, halve, apportion, distribute, dole out, parcel out, allot, allocate; informal divvy. **4** BREAK UP WITH/FROM, separate from, part from, part company with, reach the parting of the ways, dissociate oneself from. ▶n. **1** BREAK, cut,

spoil v. (**spoiling**, **spoilt** or **spoiled**) **1** make something less good or enjoyable. **2** (of food) become unfit for eating. **3** harm the character of a child by being indulgent. **4** (**be spoiling for**) be very eager for. ▶ n. (**spoils**) stolen goods. ☐ **spoilsport** a person who spoils others' enjoyment.

spoiler n. **1** a flap on an aircraft wing which can be raised to create drag and so reduce speed. **2** a similar device on a vehicle to improve roadholding at speed.

spoke¹ n. each of the rods connecting the centre of a wheel to its rim.

spoke² past of SPEAK.

spoken past part. of SPEAK.

spokesman (or **spokeswoman** or **spokesperson**) n. a person who makes statements on behalf of a group.

sponge n. **1** an invertebrate water animal with a soft porous body. **2** a piece of a light, absorbent substance for washing, padding, etc. **3** a very light cake. ▶ v. (**sponging** or **spongeing**, **sponged**) **1** wipe or clean with a wet sponge. **2** informal live at the expense of other people. ■ **sponger** n. **spongy** adj.

spongiform adj. with a porous sponge-like texture.

sponsor n. **1** a person or organization that contributes to the costs of an event in return for advertising. **2** a person who pledges a sum of money to a charity after another person has taken part in a fund-raising event. **3** a person who introduces and supports a proposal for a new law. ▶ v. be a sponsor for. ■ **sponsorship** n.

✓ -or, not -er. sponsor.

spontaneous adj. done or occurring as a result of an unplanned impulse or without apparent external cause. ■ **spontaneity** n. **spontaneously** adv.

spoof n. informal a parody.

spook n. informal a ghost. ■ **spooky** adj.

spool n. a reel on which thread, film, etc. is wound. ▶ v. wind on to a spool.

spoon n. an eating and cooking utensil with a small, shallow bowl on a handle. ▶ v. transfer with a spoon. ☐ **spoonfeed** give excessive help to. ■ **spoonful** n.

spoonerism n. the accidental swapping round of the initial sounds or letters of two or more words, as in *you hissed the mystery lectures.*

spoor n. the track or scent of an animal.

sporadic adj. occurring at irregular intervals or only in a few places. ■ **sporadically** adv.

spore n. a tiny reproductive cell produced by ferns, fungi, etc.

sporran n. a pouch worn in front of a kilt.

sport n. **1** a competitive activity involving physical effort and skill. **2** informal a person who behaves well when teased or defeated. ▶ v. **1** wear a distinctive item. **2** play. ☐ **sports car** a low-built fast car. **sports jacket** a man's informal jacket. **sportsman** (or **sportswoman**) **1** a person who takes part in a sport. **2** a fair and generous person.

sporting adj. **1** connected with or inter-

Thesaurus

rent, rip, tear, slash, slit, crack, fissure, breach. **2** DIVISION, rift, schism, rupture, separation, break-up, alienation, estrangement. ■ OPPOSITES marriage.

spoil v. **1** DAMAGE, impair, mar, blemish, disfigure, deface, injure, harm, ruin, destroy, wreck. **2** UPSET, mess up, disorganize, ruin, destroy, wreck. **3** PAMPER, overindulge, mollycoddle, cosset, coddle, baby, spoon-feed, feather-bed, wait on hand and foot, kill with kindness. **4** GO BAD, go off, turn, go sour, become rotten, rot, become tainted, decompose, decay. ■ OPPOSITES improve, further.

spoilsport n. KILLJOY, damper, dog in the manger; *informal* wet blanket, party-pooper, misery.

spoken adj. ORAL, verbal, uttered, voiced, expressed, by word of mouth, unwritten. ■ OPPOSITES non-verbal,

written.

sponge v. CLEAN, wash, wipe, mop, rub, swab.

spongy adj. SOFT, cushiony, squashy, springy, resilient, elastic, porous, absorbent.

sponsor n. PATRON, backer, promoter, subsidizer, guarantor, supporter, angel. ▶ v. BE A PATRON OF, back, put up the money for, fund, finance, promote, subsidize, support, lend one's name to.

spontaneous adj. **1** VOLUNTARY, unforced, unconstrained, unprompted. **2** UNPLANNED, unpremeditated, unrehearsed, impromptu, extempore, spur-of-the-moment, extemporaneous; *informal* off-the-cuff. **3** NATURAL, instinctive, uninhibited, involuntary, automatic, impulsive, impetuous. ■ OPPOSITES conscious, voluntary.

ested in sport. **2** fair and generous. □ **sporting chance** a reasonable chance of success.

sportive adj. playful.

spot n. **1** a small round mark. **2** a pimple. **3** a place or position. ▶v. (**spotting, spotted**) **1** notice or perceive. **2** mark with spots. □ **on the spot 1** immediately. **2** at the scene of an action. **spot check** a random check. **spotlight 1** a lamp projecting a strong beam of light on a small area. **2** intense public attention. ■ **spotter** n. **spotty** adj.

spotless adj. absolutely clean or pure. ■ **spotlessly** adv.

spouse n. a husband or wife.

spout n. **1** a projecting tube or lip through or over which liquid can be poured. **2** a stream of liquid. ▶v. **1** send out or flow in a stream. **2** express in a lengthy or emphatic way.

sprain v. injure a joint by wrenching it violently. ▶n. such an injury.

sprang past of SPRING.

sprat n. a small edible sea fish.

sprawl v. **1** sit, lie, or fall with the arms and legs spread out awkwardly. **2** spread out irregularly. ▶n. a sprawling position or expanse.

spray n. **1** liquid sent through the air in tiny drops. **2** a liquid or device for spraying. **3** a stem or branch with flowers and leaves. **4** a bunch of cut flowers. ▶v. **1** apply liquid to something in tiny drops. **2** be sent out in tiny drops. □ **spray gun** a device for spraying paint etc.

spread v. (**spreading, spread**) **1** open out so as to be wider, longer, etc. **2** extend over a wide area or a period of time. **3** reach or cause to reach more and more people. **4** apply in an even layer. ▶n. **1** the act of spreading. **2** the extent covered by something. **3** a range. **4** a paste for spreading on bread. **5** an article etc. covering several pages of a newspaper. **6** informal a lavish meal. □ **spreadeagled** with the arms and legs extended. **spreadsheet** a computer program in which figures in a grid are used in calculations.

spree n. a short period of unrestrained

Thesaurus

sporadic adj. IRREGULAR, intermittent, scattered, random, infrequent, occasional, on and off, isolated, spasmodic. ■ OPPOSITES frequent, regular.

sport n. **1** PHYSICAL ACTIVITY, physical exercise, physical recreation, athletics, game, pastime. **2** AMUSEMENT, entertainment, diversion, play, fun, pleasure, enjoyment. ▶v. **1** PLAY, have fun, amuse oneself, entertain oneself, divert oneself, frolic, gambol, frisk, romp, cavort, caper, disport oneself. **2** WEAR, exhibit, display, have on show, show off.

sporting adj. SPORTSMANLIKE, fair, just, honourable, generous.

spot n. **1** MARK, dot, speck, fleck, smudge, stain, blotch, patch; informal splotch. **2** PIMPLE, pustule, papule, boil, whitehead, blackhead, blemish. **3** STAIN, taint, blemish, defect, flaw, brand, stigma. **4** AREA, place, site, location, scene, setting, situation. ▶v. **1** CATCH SIGHT OF, see, notice, observe, espy, discern, descry, detect, make out, pick out, recognize. **2** MARK, stain, dirty, soil, spatter; literary besmirch.

spotless adj. **1** CLEAN, snowy-white, whiter-than-white, spick and span, immaculate, shining, gleaming. **2** PURE, flawless, faultless, blameless, unstained, unsullied, untainted, unblemished, unimpeachable, above reproach. ■ OPPOSITES dirty, impure.

spotlight n. LIMELIGHT, public eye, glare of publicity, publicity, public attention, public interest.

spotted adj. DAPPLED, mottled, dotted, piebald, speckled.

spotty adj. **1** PIMPLY, acned. **2** see SPOTTED. **3** PATCHY, irregular, non-uniform.

spouse n. HUSBAND/WIFE, partner, mate, companion, consort, helpmate; informal better half, other half, old man/woman/lady, missis.

spout v. **1** SPURT, gush, spew, squirt, jet, spray, emit, erupt, disgorge, pour, stream, flow. **2** DECLAIM, orate, hold forth, ramble, rant, harangue, speechify, sermonize; informal gush.

sprawl v. **1** STRETCH OUT, lounge, lie around, repose, recline, slump, flop, loll, slouch. **2** SPREAD, stretch, spill over, ramble, straggle, trail.

spray[1] n. **1** SHOWER, jet, mist, drizzle, spindrift, foam, froth. **2** ATOMIZER, vaporizer, aerosol, sprinkler. ▶v. **1** SPRINKLE, shower, disperse, disseminate. **2** JET, spout, gush.

spray[2] n. SPRIG, posy, bouquet, nosegay, corsage, wreath, garland.

spread v. **1** STRETCH, extend, open out, unfurl, unroll. **2** ENLARGE, extend, stretch out, grow bigger, widen, broaden, grow, develop, branch out. **3** COVER, coat, layer, lay on, put on, apply, smear on; informal plaster on. **4** DISSEMINATE, ciractivity: *a shopping spree.*

sprig n. a small stem with leaves or flowers.

sprightly adj. (**sprightlier**, **sprightliest**) lively; energetic. ■ **sprightliness** n.

spring v. (**springing**, **sprang**; past part. **sprung**) 1 jump. 2 move, do, or appear suddenly. 3 appear or originate. 4 (**sprung**) having springs. ▶ n. 1 the season after winter and before summer. 2 a spiral coil that returns to its former shape after being pressed or pulled. 3 a jump. 4 a place where water flows from an underground source. 5 elasticity. □ **springboard** a flexible board from which a diver or gymnast jumps to gain more power. **spring-clean** clean thoroughly. **spring tide** a tide when there is the greatest difference between high and low water. ■ **springy** adj.

springbok n. a southern African gazelle.

sprinkle v. scatter small drops or particles over a surface.

sprinkler n. a device for watering lawns or putting out fires.

sprinkling n. a small, thinly distributed amount.

sprint v. run at full speed. ▶ n. 1 a fast run. 2 a short, fast race. ■ **sprinter** n.

sprite n. an elf or fairy.

spritzer n. a drink of white wine and soda water.

sprocket n. a projection on a wheel, engaging with links on a chain etc.

sprout v. 1 produce shoots. 2 grow hair. ▶ n. 1 a plant's shoot. 2 a Brussels sprout.

spruce adj. neat and smart. ▶ v. (**spruce up**) smarten. ▶ n. a coniferous tree.

sprung past part. of **SPRING**.

spry adj. lively.

spud n. informal a potato.

spume n. froth.

spun past & past part. of **SPIN**.

spur n. 1 a spiked device worn on a rider's heel for urging a horse on. 2 an encouragement. 3 a projection. ▶ v. (**spurring**, **spurred**) 1 urge a horse on with spurs. 2 encourage. □ **on the spur of the moment** on impulse.

spurious adj. false or fake. ■ **spuriously** adv.

spurn v. reject with contempt.

spurt v. 1 gush out in a stream. 2 move with a sudden burst of speed. ▶ n. 1 a gushing stream. 2 a sudden burst of ac-

Thesaurus

culate, transmit, make public, make known, broadcast, publicize, propagate, promulgate, bruit. ▶ n. 1 EXTENT, stretch, span, reach, compass, sweep. 2 EXPANSION, advance, increase, mushrooming, proliferation, escalation, diffusion. 3 BEDSPREAD, bedcover, cover, coverlet, counterpane, throw. 4 FEAST, banquet, repast; *informal* blowout.

spree n. OUTING, fling, revel, junket, orgy, debauch, bacchanal, bacchanalia; *informal* binge, bender, jag.

sprightly adj. SPRY, lively, energetic, active, agile, nimble, supple, animated, vivacious, spirited, brisk, vital, light-hearted, cheerful, merry, jolly, jaunty, perky, frisky, playful, sportive; *literary* frolicsome, blithe. ■ OPPOSITES inactive, lethargic.

spring v. JUMP, leap, bound, vault, hop. ▶ n. 1 JUMP, leap, bound, vault, hop. 2 BOUNCE, bounciness, liveliness, light-heartedness, merriment. □ **spring from** ORIGINATE, have its origins in, derive from, stem from, arise in, emanate from, proceed from, start from. **spring up** APPEAR, come into being, come into existence, shoot up, develop quickly, mushroom, burgeon.

springy adj. BOUNCY, elastic, resilient, flexible, stretchy, tensile. ■ OPPOSITES rigid.

sprinkle v. SPRAY, shower, splash, trickle, spatter, scatter, strew, dust, powder.

sprinkling n. 1 SCATTERING, dusting. 2 FEW, handful, trickle.

sprint v. RUN, race, rush, dash, put on a turn/burst of speed; *informal* scoot, tear, hare, hotfoot it.

sprout v. BUD, germinate, put forth shoots, shoot up, spring up, grow, develop, appear, mushroom, proliferate.

spruce adj. NEAT, well groomed, well turned out, smart, trim, dapper, elegant, chic; *informal* natty. ■ OPPOSITES dishevelled.

spur n. GOAD, prod, stimulus, stimulant, incentive, inducement, encouragement, impetus. ▶ v. PROD, goad, stimulate, give the incentive to, induce, encourage, motivate, prompt, urge, impel. ■ OPPOSITES discourage.

spurious adj. COUNTERFEIT, fraudulent, fake, bogus, sham, mock, feigned, pretended, pseudo, make-believe, imitation, contrived, fictitious, deceitful, specious; *informal* phoney. ■ OPPOSITES authentic, genuine.

spurn v. REJECT, turn away, repulse, retivity or speed.

sputter v. splutter.

sputum n. a mixture of saliva and mucus.

spy n. (pl. **spies**) a person who secretly collects information on an enemy or competitor. ▶v. (**spying**, **spied**) **1** be a spy. **2** watch secretly. **3** see.

sq abbrev. square.

squabble n. a noisy quarrel about a trivial matter. ▶v. have a squabble.

squad n. a group working together.

squadron n. **1** an operational unit in an air force. **2** a division of an armoured regiment. **3** a group of warships.

squalid adj. **1** dirty and unpleasant. **2** immoral or dishonest. ■ **squalor** n.

squall n. a sudden storm or wind. ■ **squally** adj.

squander v. waste money, time, etc.

square n. **1** a plane figure with four equal straight sides and four right angles. **2** an open area surrounded by buildings. **3** the product of a number multiplied by itself. **4** an instrument for testing right angles. ▶adj. **1** having the shape of a square. **2** right-angled. **3** equal to the area of a square whose side is of the unit specified. **4** level or parallel. **5** informal old-fashioned. ▶adv. directly; straight. ▶v. **1** make square.

2 (**squared**) marked out in squares. **3** multiply a number by itself. **4** make or be compatible. **5** settle a bill. □ **square dance** a dance in which four couples face one another in a square. **square meal** a large meal. **square root** a number which produces a specified quantity when multiplied by itself. **square up** take up the position of a person about to fight. ■ **squarely** adv.

squash v. **1** crush or squeeze so as to become flat, soft, or out of shape. **2** force into a restricted space. **3** suppress or reject. ▶n. **1** a state of being squashed. **2** a concentrated fruit-flavoured liquid, diluted to make a drink. **3** a game played with rackets and a small ball in a closed court. **4** a gourd eaten as a vegetable. ■ **squashy** adj.

squat v. (**squatting**, **squatted**) **1** crouch or sit on one's heels. **2** unlawfully occupy an uninhabited building. ▶adj. short and wide. ▶n. **1** a squatting position. **2** a building occupied unlawfully. ■ **squatter** n.

squawk v. & n. (make) a loud, harsh noise.

squeak n. a short, high-pitched sound or cry. ▶v. make or say with a squeak. ■ **squeaky** adj.

Thesaurus

buff, repudiate, snub, slight, cold-shoulder, disdain, look down one's nose at, scorn, despise, condemn; informal kick in the teeth, give the go-by. ■ OPPOSITES welcome, accept.

spurt v. GUSH, squirt, shoot, surge, well, jet, spring, pour, stream, flow, issue, emanate. ▶n. **1** GUSH, surge, jet, spray, outpouring. **2** BURST, outburst, fit, surge, access.

spy n. ENEMY AGENT, foreign agent, secret agent, undercover agent, intelligence agent, double agent, fifth columnist; informal mole, spook. ▶v. CATCH SIGHT OF, spot, see, notice, observe, glimpse, make out, discern, descry, espy. □ **spy on** KEEP UNDER SURVEILLANCE, watch, keep a watch on, keep an eye on, observe, keep under observation, follow, shadow, trail.

squabble n. DISPUTE, argument, wrangle, brawl; informal row, scrap, set-to, dust-up, run-in, spat, barney. ▶v. HAVE A DISPUTE, argue, bicker, have a difference of opinion, have words, wrangle, brawl; informal row, have a tiff.

squalid adj. **1** DIRTY, filthy, dingy, grubby, grimy, mucky, foul, vile, low,

wretched, mean, nasty, seedy, sordid, sleazy, slovenly, repulsive, disgusting, ramshackle, broken-down, tumble-down; informal grungy, grotty. **2** SORDID, vile, nasty, repulsive, horrible, disgraceful, shameful, abominable, odious, filthy, indecent, depraved. ■ OPPOSITES clean, decent.

squander v. WASTE, misspend, dissipate, fritter away, run through, lavish, splurge, be prodigal with, spend like water, pour down the drain; informal blow. ■ OPPOSITES save.

square n. PIAZZA, plaza, market square, marketplace, quadrangle. ▶adj. **1** EQUAL, even, level-pegging, drawn. **2** FAIR, just, equitable, honest, straight, upright, above board, ethical; informal on the level.

squash v. **1** CRUSH, squeeze, flatten, compress, press, smash, pulp, mash, pulverize, macerate. **2** CROWD, crush, cram, pack tight, jam, squeeze, wedge. **3** PUT DOWN, quash, quell, crush, suppress, scotch.

squashy adj. PULPY, mushy, spongy, squishy, oozy, pappy. ■ OPPOSITES firm.

squeal n. a long, high-pitched cry or sound. ▶v. **1** make or say with a squeal. **2** informal inform on.

squeamish adj. easily disgusted or made to feel sick.

squeeze v. **1** firmly press from opposite or all sides. **2** crush to extract liquid. **3** manage to get into or through a restricted space. ▶n. **1** an act of squeezing. **2** a hug. **3** a small amount of liquid produced by squeezing. **4** a strong financial demand or pressure.

squelch v. make a soft sucking sound, e.g. by treading in mud. ▶n. a squelching sound. ■ **squelchy** adj.

squib n. a small firework.

squid n. a sea animal with a long body and tentacles.

squiggle n. a short curly line. ■ **squiggly** adj.

squint v. **1** look at with partly closed eyes. **2** have a squint affecting one eye. ▶n. **1** a condition in which one eye does not look in the same direction as the other. **2** informal a quick look.

squire n. a country gentleman.

squirm v. **1** wriggle. **2** be embarrassed.

squirrel n. a tree-dwelling rodent with a bushy tail.

squirt v. **1** send out or be sent out in a thin jet from a small opening. **2** wet with a jet of liquid. ▶n. **1** a thin jet of liquid. **2** informal an insignificant person.

squish v. make a soft squelching sound.

■ **squishy** adj.

SS abbrev. **1** Saints. **2** steamship. ▶n. the Nazi special police force.

St abbrev. **1** Saint. **2** Street. **3** (**st**) stone (in weight).

stab v. (**stabbing**, **stabbed**) pierce, wound, or kill with a knife or other pointed object. ▶n. **1** an act of stabbing. **2** a sudden sharp feeling or pain. **3** informal an attempt.

stabilize (or **-ise**) v. make or become stable. ■ **stabilization** n. **stabilizer** n.

stable adj. **1** firmly fixed. **2** emotionally well-balanced. **3** not likely to change or fail. ▶n. **1** a building for housing horses. **2** an establishment where racehorses are kept and trained. ▶v. put or keep in a stable. ■ **stability** n. **stably** adv.

staccato adv. & adj. Music with each sound sharply distinct.

stack n. **1** a neat pile or heap. **2** informal a large quantity. **3** a chimney. ▶v. **1** arrange in a stack. **2** cause aircraft to fly at different altitudes while waiting to land. **3** arrange a pack of cards dishonestly.

stadium n. (pl. **stadiums** or **stadia**) a sports ground with tiers of seats for spectators.

staff n. **1** the employees of an organization. **2** a long stick used as a support, weapon, or sign of authority. **3** a stave in music. ▶v. provide with staff.

Thesaurus

squat adj. DUMPY, stubby, chunky, thickset, stocky, short.

squeak n. & v. SQUEAL, peep, pipe, yelp, whimper.

squeamish adj. **1** EASILY NAUSEATED, liable to be made to feel sick, easily put off, nervous, unable to stand the sight of. **2** SCRUPULOUS, particular, punctilious, finicky, fussy, fastidious.

squeeze v. **1** COMPRESS, crush, squash, mash, pulp. **2** GRIP, clutch, pinch, press, compress. **3** CROWD, crush, cram, pack tight, jam, squash, wedge. **4** PRESSURE, pressurize, strong-arm, blackmail; informal put the squeeze on, lean on, bleed, put the screws on, put the bite on.

squirm v. WRIGGLE, wiggle, writhe, twist, turn, shift.

squirt v. SPURT, spout, jet, stream, spray, gush, surge, pour, flow, issue, spew out.

stab v. KNIFE, pierce, puncture, run through, stick, skewer, gash, slash, wound, injure. ▶n. **1** PUNCTURE, gash, slash, incision, wound, injury. **2** PANG, twinge, ache, throb, spasm. **3** TRY, attempt, endeavour, essay, effort, venture; informal go, crack.

stability n. FIRMNESS, solidity, steadiness, secureness, strength, fastness, stoutness, sturdiness, sureness, durability, constancy, permanence, reliability, dependability. ■ OPPOSITES instability.

stable adj. **1** FIRM, solid, steady, secure, fixed, strong, fast, stout, sturdy, immovable. **2** SECURE, solid, strong, steady, firm, sure, steadfast, unwavering, unfaltering, unswerving, long-lasting, deep-rooted, well founded, well grounded, abiding, durable, enduring, lasting, constant, permanent. **3** WELL BALANCED, balanced, steady, reasonable, sensible, responsible, equable, self-controlled, sane. ■ OPPOSITES unstable.

stack n. **1** HEAP, pile, mass, accumulation, collection, hoard, store, stock, stockpile, mound, mountain. **2** ABUNDANCE, amplitude, a great deal, a lot; informal lots, bags, loads, heaps, tons, oodles, scads. ▶v. HEAP, pile, pile up,

stag n. a fully adult male deer. □ **stag night** an all-male celebration for a man about to be married.

stage n. **1** a point or step in a process. **2** a raised floor or platform on which actors, entertainers, etc. perform. **3** the acting profession. ▶ v. **1** present a performance of a play etc. **2** organize and carry out. □ **stagecoach** a horse-drawn vehicle formerly used to carry passengers along a regular route. **stage fright** nervousness before or during a performance. **stage whisper** a whisper intended to be overheard.

stagger v. **1** walk or move unsteadily. **2** astonish. **3** spread over a period of time. ▶ n. an act of staggering.

stagnant adj. **1** not flowing and having an unpleasant smell. **2** showing little activity.

stagnate v. become stagnant. ■ **stagnation** n.

staid adj. respectable and unadventurous.

stain v. **1** discolour; mark with dirty patches. **2** dye. ▶ n. **1** a discoloured patch or mark. **2** a thing that damages a person's reputation. **3** a dye. □ **stainless steel** a form of steel resistant to tarnishing and rust. ■ **stainless** adj.

stair n. **1** each of a set of fixed steps.

2 (**stairs**) a set of such steps. □ **staircase** (or **stairway**) a set of stairs and its surrounding structure. **stairwell** n. a shaft in which a staircase is built.

stake n. **1** a pointed post driven into the ground as a support, part of a fence, etc. **2** a sum of money gambled. **3** a share or interest in a business etc. ▶ v. **1** support with a stake. **2** mark an area with stakes. **3** (**stake out**) informal keep under secret observation. **4** wager. □ **at stake** at risk.

stalactite n. a deposit of calcium salts hanging from the roof of a cave.

stalagmite n. a deposit of calcium salts rising from the floor of a cave.

stale adj. **1** not fresh. **2** no longer new and interesting. **3** no longer interested or motivated. ▶ v. make or become stale. □ **stalemate 1** a position counting as a draw in chess. **2** a situation in which progress is impossible. ■ **staleness** n.

stalk n. a stem or other supporting part of a plant. ▶ v. **1** follow stealthily. **2** harass with unwanted and obsessive attention. **3** walk stiffly or proudly. □ **stalking horse** a person or thing used to disguise a real purpose. ■ **stalker** n.

stall n. **1** a stand or booth for the sale of

Thesaurus

....

amass, accumulate, collect, hoard, store, stockpile.

staff n. **1** STICK, cane, crook, rod, pole, baton, truncheon. **2** MACE, sceptre. **3** EMPLOYEES, workers, workforce, personnel. ▶ v. MAN, people, provide with staff.

stage n. **1** POINT, period, step, juncture, time, division, level. **2** LAP, leg, phase, step. **3** PLATFORM, dais, rostrum, podium. ▶ v. PUT ON, produce, direct, perform, mount, present.

stagger v. **1** REEL, sway, teeter, totter, wobble, lurch, pitch, roll. **2** AMAZE, astound, dumbfound, astonish, shock, shake, confound, nonplus, take aback, stun, strike dumb; informal flabbergast.

stagnant adj. **1** STILL, motionless, standing, foul, stale, dirty, filthy, brackish. **2** SLUGGISH, slow-moving, quiet, inactive, dull, static. ■ OPPOSITES fresh, active.

stagnate v. DO NOTHING, be sluggish, lie dormant, be inert, vegetate, idle, be idle, laze, loaf, hang about, languish.

staid adj. SEDATE, quiet, serious, grave, solemn, sombre, sober, proper, decorous, formal, demure, stiff, starchy;

informal stuffy. ■ OPPOSITES frivolous.

stain v. **1** SOIL, mark, discolour, stain, spot, blotch, blemish, smudge, smear, begrime; literary besmirch. **2** BLACKEN, tarnish, sully, blemish, damage, mar, injure, defame, denigrate, dishonour, besmirch, defile, taint, blot, slur. **3** VARNISH, dye, paint, colour. ▶ n. **1** MARK, spot, blotch, blemish, smudge, smear. **2** BLEMISH, damage, injury, taint, blot, slur, stigma. **3** VARNISH, dye, paint, colourant.

stake[1] n. POST, pole, stick, upright, rod, spike, pale. ▶ v. **1** SUPPORT, prop up, hold up, brace, tether. **2** ESTABLISH, declare, state, lay claim to.

stake[2] n. **1** WAGER, bet, ante. **2** FINANCIAL INTEREST, interest, share, investment, involvement, concern. ▶ v. WAGER, bet, put on, gamble, pledge, chance, venture, risk, hazard.

stale adj. **1** DRY, dried out, hard, hardened, mouldy, decayed. **2** STUFFY, close, musty, fusty, fuggy. **3** HACKNEYED, tired, worn out, threadbare, banal, trite, stock, stereotyped, run-of-the-mill, commonplace, unoriginal, unimaginative, uninspired, flat, insipid, vapid; informal goods in a market. **2** a stable or cow-shed, or a compartment in this. **3** (**stalls**) the ground-floor seats in a theatre. **4** a seat in the choir or chancel of a church. ▶v. **1** (of an engine) stop running. **2** (of an aircraft) be moving too slowly to be controlled effectively. **3** stop making progress. **4** delay by putting something off till later.

stallion n. an uncastrated adult male horse.

stalwart adj. loyal and hard-working. ▶n. a stalwart supporter.

stamen n. a male fertilizing organ of a flower.

stamina n. the ability to keep up physical or mental effort over a long period.

stammer v. speak with involuntary pauses and repetitions of the first letters of words. ▶n. a tendency to stammer.

stamp v. **1** bring down one's foot heavily on the ground or an object. **2** (**stamp out**) put an end to decisively. **3** impress a pattern or mark on a surface. ▶n. **1** a small piece of paper stuck to a posted item to show that postage has been paid. **2** an instrument for stamping a pattern or mark. **3** a mark made by this. **4** a distinctive quality. **5** an act of stamping the foot. □ **stamping ground** a place where one regularly spends time.

stampede n. a sudden rush of animals or people. ▶v. take part in or cause a stampede.

stance n. **1** the way in which someone stands. **2** a standpoint.

stanch US = STAUNCH.

stanchion n. an upright bar or post.

stand v. (**standing**, **stood**) **1** be or become upright, supported by one's feet. **2** place or be situated in a particular position. **3** remain valid or unchanged. **4** be in a specified condition. **5** tolerate. **6** be a candidate in an election. ▶n. **1** an attitude towards an issue. **2** a determined effort to resist attack etc. **3** a large tiered structure for spectators. **4** a platform. **5** a structure for holding or displaying something. **6** a stall or booth. □ **standby** **1** readiness for action. **2** a person or thing ready to be used in an emergency. **3** a system of selling certain tickets only at the last minute. **stand by 1** look on without interfering. **2** remain loyal to or abide by. **3** be ready for action. **stand down** resign or withdraw. **stand for 1** be an abbreviation of or symbol for. **2** tolerate. **stand-in** a substitute. **stand in** deputize. **stand-off** a deadlock between two equally matched opponents. **stand-offish** informal distant and cold in manner. **stand out** be noticeable. **standpipe** a vertical pipe extending from a water supply. **standpoint** an attitude towards an issue. **standstill** a situation without movement or activity. **stand up** informal fail to keep a date with someone. **stand up for** speak or act in support of.

---

old hat. ■ OPPOSITES fresh.

stalemate n. DEADLOCK, impasse, standstill, stand-off.

stalk[1] n. STEM, branch, shoot, twig.

stalk[2] v. **1** PURSUE, chase, follow, shadow, trail, track down, creep up on, hunt; *informal* tail. **2** STRIDE, march, flounce, strut, prance.

stall n. BOOTH, stand, table, counter. ▶v. **1** PLAY FOR TIME, use delaying tactics, delay, drag one's feet, beat about the bush, hum and haw. **2** HOLD OFF, stave off, keep at bay, keep at arm's length, evade, avoid.

stalwart adj. BRAVE, courageous, valiant, valorous, intrepid, fearless, manly, heroic, indomitable, bold, daring, plucky, spirited, adventurous; *informal* gutsy. *See also* BRAVE. ■ OPPOSITES timid.

stamina n. ENDURANCE, staying power, indefatigability, resilience, fortitude, strength, vigour, energy, staunchness,

robustness; *informal* grit, guts.

stammer v. STUTTER, stumble, mumble, splutter, hesitate, falter, pause.

stamp v. **1** TRAMPLE, step on, tread on, trample on, crush. **2** IMPRINT, inscribe, engrave, emboss, mark, sign. ▶n. MARK, hallmark, label, brand, tag, characteristics, quality. □ **stamp out** QUASH, suppress, put down, quell, crush, extinguish, scotch, put an end to, eradicate, eliminate.

stampede n. CHARGE, rush, flight, scattering. ▶v. CHARGE, rush, flee, take flight, dash, race, run.

stance n. STAND, standpoint, position, line, policy, attitude, angle, slant, viewpoint, point of view, opinion.

stand v. **1** BE UPRIGHT, be erect, rise, rise/get to one's feet, get up. **2** BE SITUATED, be located. **3** REMAIN/BE IN FORCE, remain/be valid, remain/be effective, hold, hold good, obtain, prevail, be the case. **4** PUT UP WITH, tolerate, bear, take,

standard n. **1** a level of quality or achievement. **2** a measure or model used to make comparisons. **3** (**standards**) principles of good behaviour. **4** a flag. ▸adj. used or accepted as normal or average. □ **standard lamp** a tall lamp placed on the floor.

standardize (or **-ise**) v. cause to conform to a standard. ∎ **standardization** n.

standing n. **1** status or reputation. **2** duration. □ **standing order** an instruction to a bank to make regular fixed payments to someone.

stank past of STINK.

stanza n. a verse of poetry.

staphylococcus n. (pl. **staphylococci**) a bacterium causing pus to be formed.

staple n. **1** a small piece of bent wire used to fasten papers together or to hold things in place. **2** a main item of trade or production. **3** a main or important element. ▸adj. main or important. ▸v. secure with a staple or staples. ∎ **stapler** n.

star n. **1** a huge mass of burning gas visible as a glowing point in the night sky. **2** a figure with rays or points representing a star. **3** a famous entertainer or sports player. ▸v. (**starring**, **starred**) **1** have as a leading performer. **2** have a leading role in a film etc. **3** mark with a star. □ **starfish** a star-shaped sea animal. **star sign** a sign of the zodiac. ∎ **stardom** n.

starboard n. the right-hand side of a ship or aircraft.

starch n. **1** a carbohydrate obtained from cereals and potatoes. **2** powder or spray made from this, used to stiffen fabric. ▸v. stiffen with starch. ∎ **starchy** adj.

stare v. look at with great concentration. ▸n. an act of staring.

stark adj. **1** desolate or bare. **2** sharply clear. **3** complete; sheer. ▸adv. completely.

starling n. a bird with dark shiny plumage.

starry adj. (**starrier, starriest**) full of or lit by stars. □ **starry-eyed** naively enthusiastic or idealistic.

start v. **1** begin to do, be, happen, or operate. **2** cause to happen or operate. **3** begin to move or travel. **4** jerk from surprise. ▸n. **1** an act of beginning or the point at which something begins. **2** an advantage given at the beginning of a race. **3** a jerk of surprise. ∎ **starter** n.

startle v. shock or surprise.

Thesaurus

endure, abide, countenance, stomach, brook, cope with, handle; *informal* wear; *old use* suffer. ▸n. **1** STANDSTILL, halt, stop, rest. **2** *see* STANCE. **3** PLATFORM, stage, staging, dais, rostrum. □ **stand out** BE NOTICEABLE, be noticed, be conspicuous, be striking, attract attention, catch the eye; *informal* stick out a mile, stick out like a sore thumb.

standard n. **1** YARDSTICK, benchmark, gauge, measure, criterion, guide, guideline, norm, touchstone, model, pattern, example, exemplar, paradigm, ideal, archetype, specification, requirement, rule, principle, law, canon. **2** LEVEL, grade, quality, worth, merit. **3** FLAG, banner, pennant, streamer, ensign, colours. **4** SUPPORT, prop, pole, cane, upright. ▸adj. **1** USUAL, ordinary, average, normal, habitual, common, regular, stock, set, fixed, conventional. **2** DEFINITIVE, established, classic, recognized, approved, accepted, authoritative, official. ∎ OPPOSITES unusual.

standardize v. MAKE UNIFORM, regulate, systematize, normalize, homogenize, regiment, bring into line.

standing n. STATUS, rank, social position, station, footing, place, circumstances.

stand-off n. DEADLOCK, impasse, stalemate.

standpoint n. POINT OF VIEW, viewpoint, opinion, perspective, angle, slant, frame of reference.

standstill n. HALT, stop, dead stop, stoppage, rest, pause, cessation, stand.

staple adj. CHIEF, primary, main, principal, basic, fundamental, essential, indispensable.

star n. **1** HEAVENLY BODY, celestial body. **2** HOROSCOPE, forecast, augury. **3** SUPERSTAR, name, lead, celebrity, dignitary, notable, somebody, VIP; *informal* bigwig, big shot, big cheese, big wheel.

stare v. GAZE, gape, goggle, look; *informal* gawp.

stark adj. **1** SHARP, sharply defined, obvious, evident, clear, clear-cut. **2** DESOLATE, bare, barren, arid, vacant, empty, forsaken, bleak, dreary, depressing, grim, harsh; *literary* drear. ∎ OPPOSITES indistinct, ornate.

start v. **1** BEGIN, commence, make a start, get going, go ahead, set things moving, buckle to/down, turn to, put one's

starve v. **1** suffer or die from hunger. **2** cause to do this. **3** informal feel very hungry. ■ **starvation** n.

stash informal v. store secretly. ▶ n. a secret store.

state n. **1** the condition that someone or something is in. **2** a country considered as an organized political community. **3** an area forming part of a federal republic. **4** the government of a country. **5** ceremony associated with monarchy or government. **6** informal an agitated condition. ▶ v. express in words. □ **stateroom 1** a room used on ceremonial occasions. **2** a private cabin on a ship. **statesman** (or **stateswoman**) an experienced and respected political leader or figure.

stateless adj. not recognized as a citizen of any country.

stately adj. (**statelier**, **stateliest**) dignified or grand.

statement n. **1** a clear expression of something in words. **2** a formal account of facts or events. **3** a written report of amounts paid into and out of a bank account.

static adj. **1** not moving or changing. **2** Physics of bodies at rest or forces in equilibrium. **3** (of an electric charge) acquired by objects that cannot conduct a current. ▶ n. **1** static electricity. **2** crackling on a telephone, radio, etc. ■ **statically** adv.

station n. **1** a place where trains stop on a railway line. **2** a place where a specified activity or service is based. **3** a broadcasting company. **4** the place where someone or something stands. **5** a person's social rank. ▶ v. assign to a station. □ **station wagon** US & Austral./NZ an estate car.

stationary adj. not moving or changing.

✓ Don't confuse the adjective **stationary** with the noun **stationery**.

stationer n. a seller of stationery.

stationery n. paper and other writing materials.

Thesaurus

shoulder to the wheel, put one's hand to the plough; informal get moving, start the ball rolling, get down to it, get down to business, get one's finger out, get the show on the road, take the plunge, kick off, pitch in, set off on one's backside. **2** START OUT, set out, set off, depart, leave, make a start; informal hit the road, push off, get the show on the road. **3** SET IN MOTION, set moving, turn on, activate. **4** BEGIN WORKING, start functioning, start operating. **5** JUMP, leap up, jerk, twitch, recoil, shrink, flinch, blench, wince, shy. ■ OPPOSITES finish. ▶ n. **1** BEGINNING, commencement, opening, inception, inauguration, dawn, birth; informal kick-off. **2** JUMP, leap, jerk, twitch, flinch, blench, wince, spasm, convulsion. ■ OPPOSITES end.

startle v. MAKE SOMEONE JUMP, disturb, agitate, perturb, unsettle, scare, frighten, alarm, surprise, astonish, shock; informal give someone a turn.

startling adj. DISTURBING, unsettling, alarming, surprising, unexpected, unforeseen, astonishing, amazing, staggering, shocking, stunning, extraordinary, remarkable. ■ OPPOSITES predictable, ordinary.

starvation n. EXTREME HUNGER, lack of food, fasting, famine, undernourishment, malnourishment.

starving adj. STARVED, famished, ravenous, very hungry; informal able to eat a horse; dated sharp set.

state¹ n. **1** CONDITION, shape, situation, circumstances, state of affairs, position, predicament, plight. **2** ANXIETY, nerves, panic, fluster; informal flap, tizzy. **3** COUNTRY, nation, land, realm, kingdom, republic.

state² v. EXPRESS, voice, utter, say, tell, declare, set out, lay down, affirm, assert, announce, make known, reveal, disclose, divulge, pronounce, articulate, proclaim, aver.

stately adj. CEREMONIAL, dignified, solemn, majestic, royal, regal, magnificent, grand, glorious, splendid, elegant, imposing, impressive, august, lofty, pompous.

statement n. DECLARATION, account, recitation, report, affirmation, assertion, announcement, revelation, disclosure, divulgence, pronouncement, articulation, proclamation, presentation, promulgation, averment.

static adj. UNMOVING, unvarying, undeviating, changeless, constant, stable, steady, stationary, motionless, at a standstill, frozen. ■ OPPOSITES mobile, variable.

station n. **1** STOP, stopping place, terminus, terminal, depot. **2** DEPOT, base, office, headquarters, seat. **3** POST, place, position, location, site. **4** CLASS, level, rank, grade, standing, status, caste.

stationary adj. **1** UNMOVING, motionless,

statistic n. **1** a fact or piece of data obtained by studying numerical data. **2** (**statistics**) the collection and analysis of numerical data. ■ **statistical** adj. **statistically** adv. **statistician** n.

statue n. a carved or cast figure of a person or animal.

statuesque adj. tall and graceful.

statuette n. a small statue.

stature n. **1** a person's height. **2** importance or reputation.

status n. **1** a person's social or professional position in relation to others. **2** high rank or social standing. **3** the situation at a particular time. □ **status quo** the existing state of affairs.

statute n. a written law.

statutory adj. required or permitted by law.

staunch adj. loyal and committed. ▶v. (US **stanch**) stop the flow of blood from a wound. ■ **staunchly** adv.

stave n. **1** any of the strips of wood forming the side of a barrel or tub. **2** a strong post. **3** a set of five horizontal lines on which musical notes are written. ▶v. (**staving, staved** or **stove**) **1** (**stave in**) dent or break a hole in. **2** (past & past part **staved**) (**stave off**)

stop or delay.

stay v. **1** remain in the same place or in a specified state. **2** live temporarily. **3** stop or delay. ▶n. **1** a period of staying somewhere. **2** a postponement.

stead n. (**in someone's** or **something's stead**) instead of someone or something. □ **stand in good stead** be useful to in the future.

steadfast adj. determined and firm. ■ **steadfastly** adv.

steady adj. (**steadier, steadiest**) **1** firmly fixed; not shaking. **2** not wavering. **3** sensible and reliable. **4** regular and continuous. ▶v. (**steadying, steadied**) make or become steady. ■ **steadily** adv. **steadiness** n.

steak n. a thick slice of meat (esp. beef) or fish.

steal v. (**stealing, stole**; past part. **stolen**) **1** take something without permission and without intending to return it. **2** move stealthily. □ **steal the show** attract the most attention and praise.

stealth n. cautious and secretive action or movement. ■ **stealthy** adj. **stealthily** adv.

steam n. **1** the hot vapour into which

Thesaurus

at a standstill, parked. **2** CHANGELESS, unchanging, constant, unvarying, invariable, undeviating. ■ OPPOSITES moving.

statue n. STATUETTE, sculpture, effigy, figure, figurine, bust, head.

statuesque adj. DIGNIFIED, stately, majestic, splendid, imposing, impressive, regal.

stature n. **1** HEIGHT, tallness, size. **2** STATUS, importance, import, standing, eminence, prominence, note, renown.

status n. STANDING, rank, level, grade, degree, position, importance, reputation, consequence.

staunch adj. LOYAL, faithful, dependable, reliable, steady, constant, stable, firm, steadfast, unswerving, unwavering, unhesitating, unfaltering. ■ OPPOSITES disloyal.

stay[1] v. **1** REMAIN, wait, stay put, continue, linger, pause, rest, delay; *old use* tarry. **2** LODGE, take a room, put up, be accommodated, sojourn, visit, reside, take up residence, dwell, live. **3** CHECK, curb, arrest, stop, delay, hold, prevent, hinder, impede, obstruct. ■ OPPOSITES leave. ▶n. **1** VISIT, sojourn, stop, stopover, holiday; *US* vacation. **2** POSTPONEMENT, suspension, adjournment, defer-

ment, delay.

stay[2] n. PROP, support, brace, bolster, buttress.

steadfast adj. **1** *see* STAUNCH. **2** FIRM, determined, resolute, unchanging, unwavering, unfaltering, unswerving, unyielding, inflexible, uncompromising, relentless, implacable. ■ OPPOSITES irresolute.

steady adj. **1** FIRM, fixed, stable, secure, immovable. **2** STILL, motionless, unmoving, sure. **3** STEADFAST, fixed, immovable, unwavering, unfaltering. **4** UNIFORM, even, regular, rhythmic, consistent. **5** WELL BALANCED, balanced, sensible, level-headed, rational, settled, down-to-earth, calm, equable, imperturbable, reliable, dependable, seriousminded, serious. ■ OPPOSITES unstable, shaky, fluctuating. ▶v. **1** MAKE STEADY, hold steady, stabilize, secure, balance, support. **2** CALM, calm down, settle, compose, tranquillize, control, get a grip on.

steal v. **1** THIEVE, take, appropriate, misappropriate, pilfer, purloin, walk off with, embezzle, pocket, abstract, shoplift; *informal* pinch, nick, filch, swipe, lift, rip off; *formal* peculate. **2** PLAGIARIZE, copy, pirate, appropriate; *informal* water is converted when heated. **2** power derived from this. **3** momentum. ▶v. **1** give off steam. **2** (**steam up**) mist over with steam. **3** cook or treat with steam. **4** move under steam power. **5** informal move quickly. □ **steamroller** a heavy, slow vehicle with a roller, used in road construction. ■ **steamy** adj.

steamer n. **1** a ship powered by steam. **2** a container in which food can be steamed.

steed n. literary a horse.

steel n. **1** a hard, strong alloy of iron with carbon. **2** strength and determination. ▶v. mentally prepare oneself to do something difficult. ■ **steely** adj.

steep adj. **1** rising or falling sharply. **2** informal (of a price) excessive. ▶v. **1** soak in liquid. **2** (**steeped in**) full of a particular quality. ■ **steeply** adv. **steepness** n.

steeple n. a church tower and spire. □ **steeplejack** a person who repairs tall structures such as chimneys or steeples.

steeplechase n. **1** a horse race with ditches and hedges as jumps. **2** a running race with hurdles and water jumps. ■ **steeplechaser** n.

steer v. **1** direct the course of a vehicle, ship, etc. **2** guide. ▶n. a bullock. □ **steer clear of** take care to avoid.

stellar adj. of a star or stars.

stem n. **1** the supporting part of a plant. **2** a long, thin supporting part. **3** the main part of a word, to which other elements are added. ▶v. (**stemming, stemmed**) **1** (**stem from**) be caused by. **2** stop the flow of.

stench n. a foul smell.

stencil n. a sheet of card etc. with a

cut-out design, painted over to produce a design on the surface below. ▶v. (**stencilling, stencilled**; US **stenciled, stenciling**) decorate with a stencil.

stenography n. US shorthand. ■ **stenographer** n.

stentorian adj. (of a voice) very loud.

step n. **1** an act of lifting and putting down the foot or feet in walking. **2** the distance covered by this. **3** a flat surface on which to place one's foot in moving from one level to another. **4** a position or grade in a scale. **5** a measure or action taken to achieve something. **6** (**steps**) a stepladder. ▶v. (**stepping, stepped**) lift and put down one's foot or feet. □ **step down** withdraw or resign. **step in** intervene.

stepladder n. a short free-standing folding ladder. **stepping stone 1** a raised stone on which to step when crossing a stream etc. **2** a stage in progress towards a goal. **step up** increase.

step- comb. form referring to a relationship resulting from a remarriage: *stepmother, stepsister*.

steppe n. a large grassy treeless plain in SE Europe or Siberia.

stereo n. (pl. **stereos**) **1** stereophonic sound. **2** a stereophonic CD player, record player, etc. ▶adj. stereophonic.

stereophonic adj. (of sound reproduction) using two or more channels so that the sound seems to come from more than one source.

stereoscope n. a device by which two photographs of the same object are viewed together to give an effect of depth. ■ **stereoscopic** adj.

stereotype n. an over-simplified idea of the typical characteristics of a person or thing. ▶v. view as a stereotype. ■ **stereotypical** adj.

Thesaurus s

lift, crib. **3** SLIP, slide, tiptoe, sneak, creep, slink, slither, flit, glide.

stealthy adj. SECRET, furtive, surreptitious, sly, sneaky, clandestine, covert, underhand, undercover; informal shady. ■ OPPOSITES above board, open.

steam n. VAPOUR, fume, smoke, exhalation.

steamy adj. **1** HUMID, muggy, sticky, moist, damp, sweltering, boiling. **2** EROTIC, sexy, passionate, tempestuous, sensuous, lustful, wanton.

steep adj. **1** SHEER, abrupt, precipitous, sudden, sharp, perpendicular, vertical, declivitous. **2** SHARP, rapid, sudden, precipitate. **3** see EXPENSIVE. ■ OPPOSITES

gentle, gradual.

steeple n. SPIRE, tower, campanile, turret, minaret.

steer v. **1** DRIVE, navigate, pilot, be at the wheel of. **2** GUIDE, lead, direct, conduct, usher.

stench n. STINK, foul smell/odour, reek; informal pong, whiff.

step n. **1** STRIDE, pace, footstep, footfall, tread, tramp. **2** WALK, gait, bearing, carriage. **3** RUNG, tread. **4** COURSE OF ACTION, move, act, action, deed, measure, manoeuvre, procedure, expedient, effort. **5** STAGE, level, grade, rank, degree. ▶v. WALK, tread, stride, pace, move, advance, proceed; informal hoof it.

sterile adj. **1** not able to produce children, young, or fruit. **2** free from bacteria etc. ■ **sterility** n. **sterilization** n. **sterilize** (or **-ise**) v.

sterling n. British money. ▶adj. excellent.

stern adj. severe or strict. ▶n. the rear of a ship or aircraft. ■ **sternly** adv. **sternness** n.

sternum n. (pl. **sternums** or **sterna**) the breastbone.

steroid n. any of a class of organic compounds including certain hormones.

stertorous adj. (of breathing) noisy and laboured.

stethoscope n. a medical instrument for listening to a person's heart or breathing.

stevedore n. a docker.

stew n. **1** a dish of meat and vegetables cooked slowly in a closed dish. **2** informal a state of anxiety. ▶v. **1** cook slowly in a closed dish. **2** (of tea) become strong.

steward n. **1** (fem. **stewardess**) an attendant on a ship or aircraft. **2** an official who supervises arrangements at a public event. **3** a person employed to manage an estate.

stick n. **1** a thin piece of wood. **2** an implement used to hit or direct the ball in hockey etc. **3** a long, thin object or piece. **4** informal criticism. ▶v. (**sticking**, **stuck**) **1** push a pointed object into or through something. **2** protrude or extend. **3** (**stick out**) be conspicuous. **4** informal put. **5** adhere or cause to adhere. **6** (**be stuck**) be fixed or unable to move, or unable to make progress. **7** (**stick to**) continue doing or using. **8** (**stick up for**) support.

sticker n. a sticky label or notice.

stickleback n. a small fish with spines along its back.

stickler n. a person who insists on a certain type of behaviour.

sticky adj. (**stickier**, **stickiest**) **1** tending or designed to stick. **2** humid.

stiff adj. **1** not easily bent. **2** unable to move easily. **3** not relaxed or friendly. **4** severe or strong. □ **stiff-necked** obstinate. ■ **stiffen** v. **stiffly** adv. **stiffness** n.

stifle v. **1** prevent from breathing freely. **2** suppress.

stigma n. **1** a mark of disgrace. **2** a part of a flower pistil.

Thesaurus

stereotype n. RECEIVED IDEA, standardized image, hackneyed conception, cliché. ▶v. TYPECAST, pigeonhole, conventionalize, standardize, label, tag, categorize.

sterile adj. **1** INFERTILE, barren, infecund. **2** UNFRUITFUL, unproductive, infertile, unyielding, arid, dry, barren. **3** STERILIZED, germ-free, antiseptic, disinfected, aseptic, uncontaminated, unpolluted, pure, clean. ■ OPPOSITES fertile, productive.

sterilize v. **1** DISINFECT, purify, fumigate. **2** MAKE INFERTILE, make barren, castrate, vasectomize, geld, neuter, spay, emasculate.

stern adj. **1** STRICT, harsh, hard, severe, rigorous, stringent, rigid, exacting, demanding, cruel, relentless, unsparing, inflexible, unyielding, authoritarian, tyrannical, despotic, Draconian. **2** SEVERE, forbidding, frowning, unsmiling, sombre, sober, austere. ■ OPPOSITES lax, genial.

stew v. SIMMER, boil, casserole, fricassee. ▶n. CASSEROLE, ragout, fricassee.

stick[1] n. PIECE OF WOOD, branch, twig, switch.

stick[2] v. **1** PUSH, insert, jab, poke. **2** GLUE, paste, gum, tape, sellotape, fasten, attach, fix, pin, tack. **3** BECOME

BOGGED DOWN, become embedded, become lodged, be unable to move.

sticky adj. **1** ADHESIVE, adherent, gummy, gluey, tacky. **2** GLUEY, glutinous, viscous; informal gooey. **3** CLOSE, humid, muggy, clammy, sultry, sweltering, oppressive. **4** AWKWARD, difficult, tricky, ticklish, delicate, thorny.

stiff adj. **1** RIGID, inflexible, unyielding, inelastic, firm, hard, hardened, brittle. **2** TIGHT, tense, taut, aching; informal creaky. **3** DIFFICULT, hard, arduous, tough, laborious, exacting, demanding, formidable, challenging, tiring, fatiguing, exhausting, Herculean. **4** SEVERE, harsh, hard, stringent, rigorous, drastic, strong, heavy, Draconian. **5** STRONG, vigorous, determined, resolute, dogged, tenacious, unflagging, stubborn, obdurate. **6** FORMAL, ceremonial, ceremonious, dignified, proper, decorous, pompous. ■ OPPOSITES soft.

stiffen v. **1** BECOME STIFF, thicken, set, gel, solidify, harden, congeal, coagulate. **2** STRENGTHEN, fortify, brace, steel, reinforce. ■ OPPOSITES soften, liquefy, weaken.

stifle v. **1** SMOTHER, check, restrain, keep back, hold back, hold in, withhold, choke back, muffle, suppress, curb. **2** SUPPRESS, quash, quell, put an end to,

stigmata pl. n. marks corresponding to the Crucifixion marks on Christ's body.

stigmatize (or **-ise**) v. regard or treat as shameful.

stile n. a set of steps in a fence or wall allowing people to climb over.

stiletto n. (pl. **stilettos**) **1** a thin, high heel. **2** a short, narrow dagger.

still adj. **1** not moving. **2** (of a drink) not fizzy. ▶ n. **1** deep, quiet calm. **2** a photograph or a single shot from a cinema film. **3** a distilling apparatus. ▶ adv. **1** even now or at a particular time. **2** nevertheless. **3** even: *better still*. ▶ v. make or become still. □ **stillborn** born dead. **still life** a painting or drawing of inanimate objects. ■ **stillness** n.

stilt n. **1** either of a pair of upright poles enabling the user to walk above the ground. **2** each of a set of posts supporting a building.

stilted adj. (of speech or writing) stiff and unnatural.

stimulant n. a substance that stimulates activity in the body.

stimulate v. **1** cause a reaction in an organ or tissue. **2** make more active or interested. ■ **stimulation** n.

stimulus n. (pl. **stimuli**) something that stimulates.

sting n. **1** a sharp part of an insect etc. able to wound by injecting poison. **2** a wound from this. **3** a sharp tingling sensation. ▶ v. (**stinging**, **stung**) **1** wound with a sting. **2** produce a stinging sensation.

stingy adj. (**stingier**, **stingiest**) informal mean.

stink v. (**stinking**, **stank** or **stunk**; past part. **stunk**) **1** have a foul smell. **2** informal be corrupt or bad. ▶ n. **1** a foul smell. **2** informal a row or fuss.

stint v. allow a limited or inadequate amount of. ▶ n. a period of work.

stipend /sty-pend/ n. a salary.

stipendiary adj. receiving a stipend.

stipple v. mark with many small dots.

stipulate v. demand or specify as part of an agreement. ■ **stipulation** n.

stir v. (**stirring**, **stirred**) **1** move an implement round in a liquid etc. to mix it. **2** move slightly or begin to be active. **3** wake or rise from sleep. **4** arouse a strong feeling. ▶ n. **1** an act of stirring. **2** a commotion.

stirrup n. each of a pair of loops at-

Thesaurus

put down, stop, extinguish, stamp out, crush, subdue, repress. **3** SUFFOCATE, smother, asphyxiate, choke.

stigma n. SHAME, disgrace, dishonour, slur, stain, taint. ■ OPPOSITES honour.

still adj. **1** MOTIONLESS, unmoving, without moving, immobile, unstirring, inert, lifeless, stock-still, stationary, static. **2** QUIET, silent, hushed, soundless, sound-free, noiseless, undisturbed. ■ OPPOSITES moving, noisy. ▶ n. QUIETNESS, quiet, silence, hush, soundlessness, noiselessness, calmness, calm, tranquillity, peace, peacefulness, serenity. ▶ adv. **1** AT THIS TIME, yet, up to this time, even now, until now. **2** NEVERTHELESS, however, in spite of that, notwithstanding, for all that.

stilted adj. STIFF, unnatural, wooden, forced, laboured, constrained, unrelaxed, awkward. ■ OPPOSITES natural.

stimulant n. **1** TONIC, restorative, reviver, energizer, analeptic; *informal* upper, pick-me-up, bracer. **2** STIMULUS, incentive, impetus, fillip, spur. ■ OPPOSITES sedative, deterrent.

stimulate v. ACT AS A STIMULUS/INCENTIVE TO, encourage, prompt, spur on, activate, stir up, excite, whip up, kindle, incite, instigate, foment, fan. ■ OPPOSITES discourage.

stimulating adj. **1** RESTORING, restorative, reviving, energizing, analeptic; *informal* pick-me-up. **2** INTERESTING, exciting, stirring, thought-provoking, inspiring, exhilarating, intriguing, provoking, provocative. ■ OPPOSITES sedative, boring.

stimulus n. STIMULANT, incentive, fillip, spur, push, drive, encouragement, inducement, incitement, goad, jog, jolt; *informal* shot in the arm.

sting n. IRRITATION, smarting, tingling, tingle, pain, hurt. ▶ v. **1** SMART, tingle, burn, be irritated. **2** HURT, wound, distress, grieve, vex, pain, anguish, torture, torment, harrow.

stingy adj. MEAN, miserly, parsimonious, niggardly, cheese-paring, penny-pinching; *informal* tight, tight-fisted; *US informal* cheap. ■ OPPOSITES generous.

stink v. SMELL BAD, give off a bad smell, reek; *informal* smell to high heaven. ▶ n. BAD SMELL, foul smell, stench, reek, malodour.

stint v. SKIMP ON, limit, restrict, hold back on, be sparing with, be economical with, be frugal with, be mean with, be parsimonious with, be niggardly with.

stipulate v. SPECIFY, set down, lay down, state clearly, demand, require, insist tached to a horse's saddle to support the rider's foot.

stitch n. **1** a loop of thread or yarn resulting from a single pass of the needle in sewing, knitting, etc. **2** a method of making a stitch. **3** a sudden pain in the side. ▶v. make or mend with stitches. □ **in stitches** informal laughing uncontrollably.

stoat n. a small brown mammal of the weasel family.

stock n. **1** a supply of goods or materials available for sale or use. **2** livestock. **3** money raised by selling shares in a company. **4** (**stocks**) shares in a company. **5** water in which bones, meat, etc. have been simmered. **6** ancestry. **7** the trunk or woody stem of a tree or shrub. **8** (**the stocks**) hist. a wooden structure with holes in which a criminal's feet and hands were locked as punishment. ▶adj. common or conventional. ▶v. **1** keep a stock of. **2** provide with a supply. □ **stockbroker** a broker who buys and sells shares for clients. **stock car** a car used in a type of racing in which cars collide with each other. **stock exchange** (or **stock market**) a market in which shares are bought and sold. **stock-in-trade** the typical thing a person or company uses or deals in. **stockpile** a large stock of goods accumulated for future use. **stock-still** completely still. **stocktaking** the recording of the amount of stock held by a business.

stockade n. an enclosure of wooden posts.

stocking n. a close-fitting covering for the foot and leg.

stockist n. a retailer stocking goods of a particular type.

stocky adj. (**stockier**, **stockiest**) short and sturdy. ■ **stockily** adv.

stodge n. informal heavy, filling food. ■ **stodgy** adj.

stoic n. a stoical person. ▶adj. stoical.

stoical adj. enduring pain and hardship without complaint. ■ **stoically** adv. **stoicism** n.

stoke v. tend and put fuel on a fire etc. ■ **stoker** n.

stole[1] n. a woman's wide scarf or shawl.

stole[2] past of STEAL.

stolen past part. of STEAL.

stolid adj. calm and dependable. ■ **stolidly** adv.

stomach n. **1** the internal organ in

Thesaurus

upon, make a condition of, make a point of.

stipulation n. SPECIFICATION, demand, requirement, condition, precondition, provision, proviso, prerequisite.

stir v. **1** MIX, blend, beat, whip. **2** DISTURB, move, agitate, rustle. **3** GET UP, get out of bed, rise, rouse oneself, bestir oneself, move about, be up and about, be active; informal shake a leg, look lively. **4** STIMULATE, excite, rouse, awaken, waken, kindle, quicken, inspire. **5** ROUSE, incite, provoke, inflame, goad, spur, egg on, urge, encourage, motivate, drive, impel. ▶n. EXCITEMENT, commotion, disturbance, fuss, uproar, to-do, flurry, ferment, brouhaha.

stirring adj. EXCITING, dramatic, thrilling, gripping, riveting, spirited, stimulating, moving, lively, animated, heady, passionate, impassioned. ■ OPPOSITES dull, unexciting.

stitch v. SEW, sew up, repair, mend, darn.

stock n. **1** STORE, supply, stockpile, reserve, reservoir, accumulation, pile, heap, load, hoard, cache. **2** SUPPLIES, goods, merchandise, wares, articles for sale, commodities. **3** FARM ANIMALS, livestock, cattle, beasts, herds, sheep, flocks. **4** DESCENT, line of descent, lineage, ancestry, extraction, family, parentage, relatives, pedigree, genealogy, strain, breed, background. ▶adj. **1** STANDARD, regular, average, readily available. **2** USUAL, routine, run-of-the-mill, commonplace, conventional, traditional, stereotyped, clichéd, hackneyed, overused, worn out, banal, trite. ▶v. **1** SELL, trade in, deal in, market, handle, supply, keep. **2** EQUIP, fit, outfit, kit out, furnish, supply, accoutre, provide.

stockpile v. COLLECT, gather, accumulate, amass, store, lay in, put away, put down, deposit; informal squirrel away, salt away, stash.

stocky adj. HEAVY-SET, thickset, dumpy, stubby, stumpy, squat, chunky, solid, sturdy, mesomorphic. ■ OPPOSITES slender.

stodgy adj. **1** HEAVY, solid, substantial, filling, starchy, leaden, indigestible. **2** DULL, uninteresting, boring, tedious, dry, wearisome, heavy-going, unimaginative, uninspired, monotonous, laboured, wooden, turgid. ■ OPPOSITES light, interesting.

stoical adj. IMPASSIVE, dispassionate, unimpassioned, unemotional, calm, selfwhich the first part of digestion occurs. **2** the belly. **3** appetite or desire. ▶ v. tolerate.

stomp v. tread heavily.

stone n. **1** the hard material of which rock is made. **2** a piece of stone. **3** a gem. **4** a hard seed in certain fruits. **5** (pl. **stone**) a unit of weight equal to 14 lb (6.35 kg). ▶ v. **1** throw stones at. **2** remove the stone from a fruit. □ **Stone Age** the prehistoric period when tools were made of stone. **stonewall** delay or block by giving evasive replies. **stonewashed** washed with small stones to give a faded appearance.

stony adj. (**stonier, stoniest**) **1** full of stones. **2** cold and unfeeling. ■ **stonily** adv.

stood past & past part. of STAND.

stooge n. **1** derog. a person doing routine or unpleasant work for another. **2** a performer who is the butt of a comedian's jokes.

stool n. **1** a seat without a back or arms. **2** a piece of faeces. □ **stool pigeon** a police informer.

stoop v. **1** bend forwards and down.

2 lower one's standards to do something wrong. ▶ n. a stooping posture.

stop v. (**stopping, stopped**) **1** come or bring to an end. **2** prevent from happening or from doing something. **3** cease moving. **4** block a hole. ▶ n. **1** an act of stopping. **2** a place where a bus or train stops regularly. **3** a thing preventing movement. **4** a set of organ pipes. □ **stopcock** a valve regulating the flow in a pipe. **stopgap** a temporary substitute. **stop press** late news added to a newspaper after printing has begun. **stopwatch** a watch that can be started and stopped, used to time races. ■ **stoppage** n.

stopper n. a plug for a bottle etc.

storage n. **1** the act of storing. **2** space for storing. □ **storage heater** an electric heater that stores up heat during the night.

store n. **1** a supply kept for use as needed. **2** a place to keep things for future use. **3** a large shop. ▶ v. keep for future use. □ **in store** about to happen. **set store by** consider important.

storey (US **story**) n. (pl. **storeys** or **stor-**

controlled, self-disciplined, forbearing, patient, long-suffering, resigned, philosophical, fatalistic, imperturbable, cool, unexcitable, unflappable, phlegmatic. ■ OPPOSITES excitable.

stolid adj. IMPASSIVE, unemotional, apathetic, uninterested, unimaginative, indifferent, dull, stupid, bovine, lumpish, wooden, doltish, thick, dense. ■ OPPOSITES lively, imaginative.

stomach n. ABDOMEN, belly, paunch, pot belly; informal tummy, gut, pot, breadbasket. ▶ v. STAND, put up with, bear, take, tolerate, abide, endure, swallow, submit to; old use suffer.

stone n. **1** PEBBLE, rock, boulder. **2** PRECIOUS STONE, jewel, gem, brilliant; informal rock. **3** TOMBSTONE, gravestone, headstone, memorial stone, monument. **4** KERNEL, pit, nut, seed, pip.

stony adj. **1** ROCKY, pebbly, gravelly, shingly, gritty, rough, hard. **2** COLD, chilly, frosty, icy, frigid, hard, stern, severe, rigid, fixed, expressionless, blank, poker-faced, deadpan. **3** UNFEELING, uncaring, unsympathetic, insensitive, callous, heartless, unmoved, unemotional, dispassionate, unresponsive, stern, severe, harsh, hard, cruel, cold-hearted, merciless, pitiless. ■ OPPOSITES sympathetic.

stooge n. UNDERLING, subordinate, assist-

ant, deputy; informal sidekick, dogsbody.

stoop v. **1** BEND DOWN, lean over, lean down, crouch down, duck, bow. **2** CONDESCEND, deign, lower oneself, humble oneself, demean oneself. **3** SINK TO, descend to, lower oneself to, demean oneself to, resort to.

stop v. **1** BRING TO A STOP, halt, bring to a halt, end, bring to an end, put an end to, finish, bring to a close, terminate, bring to a standstill, wind up, discontinue, cut short, interrupt, nip in the bud. **2** DISCONTINUE, cease from, refrain from, desist from, leave off, break off, forbear from, abandon; informal quit, knock off, pack in. **3** COME TO A STOP, come to a halt, end, come to an end, finish, come to a close, be over, cease, conclude, terminate, come to a standstill, pause. **4** PREVENT, hinder, obstruct, impede, block, check. **5** PLUG, seal, block, bung, staunch, stem. ■ OPPOSITES begin, start. ▶ n. **1** HALT, end, finish, close, cessation, conclusion, termination, standstill, stoppage, discontinuation, discontinuance. **2** STOPPING PLACE, station, halt, stage, terminus, terminal, depot. **3** BREAK, stop-off, stopover, stay, sojourn, overnight, rest.

stopgap n. TEMPORARY SUBSTITUTE, substitution, fill-in, makeshift, improvisation, expedient, last resort.

ies) each level of a building.

stork n. a large bird with a long bill and legs.

storm n. **1** a disturbance of the atmosphere with strong winds and rain or snow. **2** an uproar or outburst. ▶v. **1** move angrily and forcefully. **2** suddenly attack and capture. ■ **stormy** adj.

story n. (pl. **stories**) an account of imaginary or real events.

stout adj. **1** rather fat. **2** sturdy and thick. **3** brave and determined. ▶n. strong, dark beer. ■ **stoutly** adv.

stove[1] n. an apparatus for cooking or heating.

stove[2] past & past part. of STAVE.

stow v. **1** store tidily. **2** (**stow away**) hide oneself on a ship etc. so as to travel without paying. □ **stowaway** a person who stows away.

straddle v. **1** sit or stand with one leg on either side of. **2** extend across.

strafe v. attack with gunfire or bombs from the air.

straggle v. **1** lag behind. **2** grow or spread out in an irregular, untidy way.

■ **straggler** n. **straggly** adj.

straight adj. **1** extending in one direction only; without a curve or bend. **2** level or symmetrical. **3** tidy or ordered. **4** honest and direct. **5** clear and logical. **6** in continuous succession. **7** (of an alcoholic drink) undiluted. **8** informal heterosexual. ▶adv. **1** in a straight line or straight manner. **2** without delay. ▶n. the straight part of something. □ **straight away** immediately. **straight face** a serious expression. ■ **straighten** v.

straightforward adj. **1** easy to do or understand. **2** honest and open.

strain v. **1** make an unusually great effort. **2** injure by overexertion. **3** pull or push forcibly. **4** pour a liquid through a sieve to separate out any solid matter. ▶n. **1** a force pulling or stretching something. **2** an injury caused by straining. **3** a severe demand on strength or resources. **4** the sound of a piece of music. **5** a breed or variety of an animal or plant. **6** a tendency in a person's character. ■ **strainer** n.

Thesaurus

store n. **1** SUPPLY, stock, stockpile, reserve, accumulation, pile, heap, cache, deposit, reservoir. **2** STOREROOM, storehouse, warehouse, repository, depository. **3** SHOP, department store, supermarket, retail outlet, emporium. ▶v. STOCK UP WITH, get in supplies of, stockpile, collect, gather, accumulate, amass, lay in, put away, put down, deposit, hoard; informal squirrel away, salt away, stash.

storm n. GALE, hurricane, cyclone, tempest, squall, cloudburst, downpour, torrent. ▶v. ATTACK, charge, rush, make a raid/foray/sortie on, take by storm.

stormy adj. BLUSTERY, blustering, windy, gusty, squally, rainy, wild, tempestuous, turbulent. ■ OPPOSITES calm.

story n. **1** TALE, fairy tale, fable, myth, legend, anecdote, novel, novella, romance, narrative, chronicle; informal yarn. **2** NEWS ITEM, news report, article, feature, scoop.

stout adj. **1** FAT, fattish, plump, portly, tubby, obese, corpulent, rotund, big, heavy, thickset, overweight, bulky, burly, brawny, fleshy. **2** STRONG, heavy, solid, substantial, sturdy. **3** STOUT-HEARTED, brave, courageous, valiant, valorous, gallant, fearless, unafraid, intrepid, bold, plucky, heroic, lionhearted, daring, tough, doughty; informal gutsy, spunky. ■ OPPOSITES cowardly.

stow v. PLACE, deposit, put, put away, pack, store, load, bundle, stuff. ■ OPPOSITES unload.

straggle v. **1** WANDER, ramble, stray, roam, meander, rove, range, spread out. **2** TRAIL BEHIND, fall behind, lag, string out, linger, loiter. **3** GROW UNTIDILY, be messy, be dishevelled, be unkempt.

straight adj. **1** DIRECT, undeviating, unswerving, straight as an arrow. **2** SUCCESSIVE, consecutive, in a row, running, uninterrupted, solid, non-stop. **3** IN ORDER, orderly, neat, tidy, spruce, in place, organized, arranged, sorted out. **4** FORTHRIGHT, honest, faithful, sincere, frank, candid, direct, straightforward, plain-speaking, matter-of-fact, outspoken, straight from the shoulder, unequivocal, unambiguous, unqualified, unmodified. ■ OPPOSITES crooked, untidy, evasive.

straighten v. MAKE STRAIGHT, adjust, arrange, put in order, make tidy, tidy up, neaten, put to rights. □ **straighten out** PUT IN ORDER, put right, sort out, clear up, settle, resolve, regulate, rectify, disentangle, unsnarl.

straightforward adj. **1** STRAIGHT, direct, honest, frank, candid, forthright, plain-speaking, unambiguous, straight from the shoulder. **2** UNCOMPLICATED, easy, simple, elementary, effortless, un-

strained adj. **1** not relaxed. **2** not spontaneous.

strait n. **1** (also **straits**) a narrow stretch of water connecting two seas. **2** (**straits**) a difficult situation.

straitened adj. characterized by poverty.

straitjacket (or **straightjacket**) n. a strong garment with long sleeves for confining the arms of a violent person.

strait-laced (or **straight-laced**) adj. strictly moral.

strand v. **1** run aground. **2** leave unable to move from a place. ▶n. **1** a single length of thread etc. **2** an element in a complex whole. **3** literary a beach or shore.

strange adj. **1** unusual or odd. **2** not seen or met before. ■ **strangely** adv. **strangeness** n.

stranger n. **1** a person one does not know. **2** a person who does not know, or is not known in, a place.

strangle v. **1** kill or injure by squeezing the neck. **2** suppress or hinder. □ **stranglehold 1** a strangling grip. **2** complete control. ■ **strangler** n.

strangulation n. the act of strangling.

strap n. a strip of flexible material used for fastening, carrying, or holding on to. ▶v. (**strapping, strapped**) **1** fasten with a strap. **2** bind an injured part

with adhesive plaster.

strapping adj. big and strong.

strata pl. of STRATUM.

stratagem n. a plan intended to outwit an opponent.

strategic adj. **1** of strategy. **2** (of weapons) for use against enemy territory rather than in battle. ■ **strategically** adv.

strategy n. (pl. **strategies**) **1** a plan designed to achieve a long-term aim. **2** the planning and directing of military activity in a war or battle. ■ **strategist** n.

stratify v. (**stratifying, stratified**) form or arrange into strata. ■ **stratification** n.

stratosphere n. the layer of the atmosphere about 10–50 km above the earth's surface.

stratum n. (pl. **strata**) a layer or level in a series.

straw n. **1** dried stalks of corn etc. **2** a single dried stalk. **3** a thin hollow tube for sucking up a drink. □ **straw poll** an unofficial test of opinion.

strawberry n. a sweet red fruit.

stray v. **1** move from the right course or place. **2** move idly. ▶adj. **1** not in the right place. **2** (of a domestic animal) having no home. ▶n. a stray animal.

Thesaurus

demanding, routine; informal easy as falling off a log, easy as pie. ■ OPPOSITES complicated.

strain v. **1** DRAW TIGHT, tighten, make taut, tauten, stretch, extend, elongate, distend. **2** TAX, overtax, exert to the limit, overwork, push to the limit, fatigue, tire. **3** MAKE EVERY EFFORT, strive one's utmost, push/drive oneself to the limit, struggle, labour; informal pull out all the stops, go all out, give it one's all. **4** SIEVE, silt, screen, riddle, separate. ▶n. **1** TIGHTNESS, tautness, tension, distension. **2** STRESS, pressure, tension, overwork, exhaustion, anxiety.

strained adj. **1** FORCED, artificial, unnatural, false, constrained, laboured, wooden, stiff, self-conscious. **2** AWKWARD, embarrassed, uneasy, uncomfortable, tense, unrelaxed. **3** UNDER STRAIN, tense, troubled, uneasy, hostile. ■ OPPOSITES natural, relaxed.

strainer n. SIEVE, colander, filter, screen, riddle.

strand n. **1** THREAD, fibre, filament, length. **2** ELEMENT, component, theme.

stranded adj. **1** LEFT HELPLESS, left penniless, in dire straits, in difficulties, left

in the lurch, left high and dry, abandoned, forsaken. **2** GROUNDED, beached, shipwrecked, wrecked, marooned.

strange adj. **1** PECULIAR, odd, bizarre, unusual, atypical, abnormal, surprising, curious, weird, funny, unfamiliar. **2** UNKNOWN, unfamiliar. **3** INEXPLICABLE, anomalous, unexpected, extraordinary. ■ OPPOSITES ordinary, familiar.

stranger n. NEW PERSON, new arrival, newcomer, incomer, foreigner. □ **a stranger to** UNFAMILIAR WITH, unacquainted with, unaccustomed to, new to, fresh to, unused to, inexperienced in, unpractised in, unversed in, unconversant with.

strangle v. **1** THROTTLE, choke, strangulate, garrotte. **2** SUPPRESS, inhibit, repress, check, restrain, hold back, curb, stifle, gag.

strap n. BAND, belt, thong, cord, tie. ▶v. **1** FASTEN, secure, tie, bind, lash, truss, pinion. **2** BIND, bandage. **3** FLOG, lash, whip, scourge, beat; informal belt.

strategic adj. **1** CALCULATED, planned, plotted, tactical, diplomatic, politic, cunning, wily. **2** CRUCIAL, key, vital, critical, essential, important.

streak n. **1** a long, thin mark. **2** an element in someone's character. **3** a period of specified success or luck. ▸ v. **1** mark with streaks. **2** move very fast. **3** informal run naked in a public place. ■ **streaker** n. **streaky** adj.

stream n. **1** a small, narrow river. **2** a continuous flow of liquid, air, people, etc. **3** a group in which schoolchildren of the same age and ability are taught. ▸ v. **1** move in a continuous flow. **2** run with tears, sweat, etc. **3** float out in the wind. **4** put schoolchildren in streams. □ **on stream** in or into operation.

streamline 1 design or provide with a shape presenting little resistance to a flow of air or water. **2** make more efficient.

streamer n. a long, narrow strip of material used for decoration.

street n. a public road in a city, town, etc. □ **streetcar** US a tram.

strength n. **1** the quality of being strong. **2** a good or useful quality. **3** the number of people making up a group. □ **on the strength of** on the basis of. ■ **strengthen** v.

strenuous adj. requiring or using great effort. ■ **strenuously** adv.

streptococcus n. (pl. **streptococci**) a bacterium causing serious infections.

stress n. **1** pressure. **2** mental or emotional tension or exhaustion. **3** emphasis. **4** emphasis given to a syllable or word in speech. ▸ v. **1** emphasize. **2** subject to pressure, tension, or strain. ■ **stressful** adj.

stretch v. **1** be able to be made longer or wider without tearing or breaking. **2** pull out tightly or to a greater extent. **3** extend a part of the body to its full length. **4** extend over an area or period. **5** make demands on. ▸ n. **1** an act of stretching. **2** the capacity to stretch. **3** a continuous area or period. ■ **stretchy** adj.

Thesaurus

strategy n. POLICY, approach, programme, scheme, plan of action, master plan, schedule, blueprint, game plan.

stray v. **1** WANDER, roam, rove, go astray, ramble, meander, drift. **2** DIGRESS, wander, deviate, get off the subject, get sidetracked, go off at a tangent, lose the thread. ▸ adj. **1** STRAYED, gone astray, lost, homeless, wandering, vagrant, abandoned, unclaimed. **2** ODD, random, isolated, scattered, occasional, incidental, accidental, chance, freak.

streak n. **1** LINE, band, strip, bar, score, striation, vein, slash, smear. **2** STRAIN, vein, element, trace, touch, dash. **3** SMEAR, smudge, mark. **4** SPELL, period, course, stretch, series. ▸ v. **1** BAND, stripe, mark, slash, striate, fleck, daub, smear. **2** SMEAR, smudge, mark. **3** RACE, rush, speed, dash, sprint, hurtle, scurry, fly, flee, flash, whistle, zoom, zip; informal tear, whizz, go hell for leather.

stream n. **1** RIVER, brook, rivulet, rill, freshet; N. Engl. beck; Sc. & N. Engl. burn; US & Austral./NZ creek. **2** FLOW, rush, gush, surge, jet, outpouring, current, cascade. ▸ v. **1** FLOW, run, pour, course, spill, gush, surge, flood, cascade, well. **2** EMIT, issue, shed, spill. **3** FLUTTER, flap, swing, float, flow. **4** SURGE, pour, crowd.

streamlined adj. **1** SMOOTH, sleek, elegant. **2** EFFICIENT, smooth-running, well run, modernized, rationalized, slick.

street n. ROAD, thoroughfare, terrace, avenue, drive, row, crescent.

strength n. **1** POWER, might, force, brawn, muscle, muscularity, sturdiness, robustness, vigour, toughness, stamina. **2** FORTITUDE, courage, bravery, pluck, firmness, stamina, backbone; informal grit, guts. **3** ADVANTAGE, asset, strong point, forte. ■ OPPOSITES weakness.

strengthen v. **1** MAKE STRONG, make stronger, give strength to, nourish, build up. **2** GROW STRONG, grow stronger, gain strength, intensify, heighten. **3** REINFORCE, support, back up, bolster, authenticate, confirm, substantiate, corroborate. ■ OPPOSITES weaken.

strenuous adj. **1** ARDUOUS, laborious, taxing, demanding, difficult, hard, tough, uphill, heavy, weighty, burdensome, exhausting, tiring, fatiguing. **2** ENERGETIC, active, vigorous, forceful, strong, spirited, bold, determined, resolute, tenacious, earnest, keen, zealous. ■ OPPOSITES easy, half-hearted.

stress n. **1** STRAIN, pressure, tension, worry, anxiety. **2** EMPHASIS, priority, importance, weight, significance, value, worth, merit. **3** ACCENT, accentuation, emphasis. ▸ v. **1** LAY STRESS ON, emphasize, place emphasis on, give emphasis to, accentuate, underline, underscore, point up, highlight, spotlight, press home, dwell on, harp on, belabour. **2** LAY STRESS ON, place the accent on, accentuate, emphasize. **3** SUBJECT TO STRESS/STRAIN/TENSION, tax, overtax, pressurize, overwork, overstretch,

stretcher n. a framework for carrying sick, injured, or dead people.

strew v. (**strewing**, **strewed**; past part. **strewn** or **strewed**) **1** scatter over a surface or area. **2** cover with scattered things.

striation n. each of a series of ridges or grooves.

stricken adj. affected by something unpleasant.

strict adj. **1** demanding that rules are obeyed. **2** (of a rule) rigidly enforced. **3** following rules or beliefs exactly. ■ **strictly** adv. **strictness** n.

stricture n. **1** a restriction. **2** a critical remark.

stride v. (**striding**, **strode**) walk with long steps. ▶n. **1** a long step. **2** (**strides**) progress.

strident adj. **1** loud and harsh. **2** excessively forceful. ■ **stridency** n. **stridently** adv.

strife n. bitter disagreement.

strike v. (**striking**, **struck**) **1** hit. **2** make forcible contact with. **3** ignite a match by rubbing it against a rough surface. **4** occur or attack suddenly. **5** suddenly come into the mind of. **6** refuse to work as a form of organized protest. **7** find oil, gold, etc. **8** (**strike off**) officially expel from a professional group. **9** reach an agreement. **10** (of a clock) show the time by chiming. ▶n. **1** an act of striking by employees. **2** a sudden attack. □ **strike up 1** begin to play a piece of music. **2** begin a friendship or conversation.

striker n. **1** an employee on strike. **2** a forward in soccer.

striking adj. **1** noticeable. **2** very good-looking. ■ **strikingly** adv.

strimmer n. trademark a long-handled machine for cutting rough grass.

string n. **1** material consisting of threads twisted together to form a thin length. **2** a length of catgut or wire on a musical instrument, producing a note by vibration. **3** (**strings**) stringed instruments. **4** a set of things strung together. **5** a series. **6** (**strings**) informal conditions or restrictions. ▶v. (**stringing**, **strung**) **1** arrange on a string. **2** (**be strung out**) be spread out in a long line. **3** fit strings on a musical instrument etc. **4** (**string up**) kill by hanging.

stringent adj. strict and demanding. ■ **stringency** n. **stringently** adv.

Thesaurus

overburden, push to the limit, push too far. ■ OPPOSITES play down.

stretch v. **1** BE STRETCHY, be elastic, be tensile. **2** EXTEND, elongate, lengthen, expand, draw out, pull out, get larger, get bigger, enlarge, pull out of shape. **3** SPREAD, extend, unfold, cover, range. **4** BE A CHALLENGE TO, challenge, extend, tax, push to the limit. **5** STRAIN, overstrain, exaggerate, overdraw, push too far. ▶n. **1** EXPANSE, area, tract, extent, spread, sweep. **2** PERIOD, time, spell, term, space, run, stint.

strict adj. **1** PRECISE, exact, close, faithful, true, accurate, scrupulous, meticulous, conscientious, punctilious. **2** STRINGENT, rigorous, severe, harsh, hard, stern, authoritarian, inflexible, rigid, narrow, austere, illiberal, unyielding, uncompromising. **3** ABSOLUTE, utter, complete, total, perfect. ■ OPPOSITES flexible, easy-going.

stride v. STEP, pace, walk, stalk.

strident adj. HARSH, raucous, rough, grating, discordant, rasping, jarring, shrill, loud, screeching, unmelodious, unmusical. ■ OPPOSITES soft.

strife n. CONFLICT, friction, discord, disagreement, dissension, dispute, argument, quarrelling, wrangling, bickering, controversy, contention, ill feeling, hostility, animosity. ■ OPPOSITES peace, harmony.

strike v. **1** BANG, beat, hit, pound, batter. **2** HIT, slap, smack, beat, batter, thrash, thump, thwack, punch, cuff, box, rap, buffet, smite, cane, lash, whip; informal wallop, belt, clout, whack, bash, clobber, bop, biff, sock, plug. **3** RUN INTO, knock into, bang into, bump into, smash into, collide with, be in collision with, dash against. **4** ATTACK, charge, make an assault on, assault, storm, set upon, fall upon. **5** GO ON STRIKE, take industrial action, walk out; informal down tools. ▶n. **1** HIT, slap, smack, thump, thwack, punch, cuff, box, knock; informal wallop, clout, whack, bop, buffet, plug. **2** INDUSTRIAL ACTION, walkout. □ **strike out** DELETE, cross out, erase, rub out, obliterate.

striking adj. **1** NOTICEABLE, obvious, conspicuous, evident, visible, distinct, prominent, clear-cut, unmistakable, remarkable, extraordinary, incredible, amazing. **2** IMPRESSIVE, imposing, grand, splendid, magnificent, superb, marvellous, wonderful, dazzling; informal smashing. ■ OPPOSITES unremarkable.

string n. **1** TWINE, cord, yarn, rope, cable,

stringy adj. (**stringier**, **stringiest**) **1** like string. **2** tall and thin. **3** (of food) tough and fibrous.

strip v. (**stripping**, **stripped**) **1** remove covers or clothes from. **2** deprive of rank or property. ▶n. **1** an act of undressing. **2** the identifying outfit of a sports team. **3** a long, narrow piece or area. □ **strip light** a tubular fluorescent lamp. **striptease** an entertainment in which a performer gradually undresses.

stripe n. **1** a long narrow band differing in colour or texture from its surroundings. **2** a V-shaped stripe on a uniform showing rank. ■ **striped** adj. **stripy** adj.

stripling n. old use a young man.

stripper n. **1** a device or substance for removing paint etc. **2** a striptease performer.

strive v. (**striving**, **strove** or **strived**; past part. **striven** or **strived**) make great efforts.

strode past of STRIDE.

stroke n. **1** an act of hitting. **2** a sound of a striking clock. **3** an act of stroking. **4** a mark made by drawing a pen, paintbrush, etc. across a surface. **5** a style of swimming. **6** a sudden disabling attack caused by an interruption in the flow of blood to the brain. ▶v. gently move the hand over. □ **at a stroke** by a single action.

stroll v. walk in a leisurely way. ▶n. a leisurely walk.

strong adj. **1** physically powerful. **2** done with or exerting great force. **3** able to withstand pressure. **4** secure or stable. **5** great in power or ability. **6** intense. **7** full-flavoured. **8** containing much alcohol. **9** indicating the size of a group: *fifty strong*. □ **stronghold 1** a place strengthened against attack. **2** a place of strong support for a cause. **strong language** swearing. **strongroom** a room designed for safe storage of valuables. ■ **strongly** adv.

strontium n. a soft metallic element.

strop n. a leather strip used for sharpening razors.

stroppy adj. informal bad-tempered.

strove past of STRIVE.

struck past & past part. of STRIKE.

structure n. **1** the way a thing is constructed or organized. **2** a building or other constructed object. ▶v. give struc-

Thesaurus

line. **2** QUEUE, line, row, procession, file, column, stream, succession, sequence. ▶v. **1** HANG, suspend, sling. **2** STRETCH, sling, run, fasten, tie, secure together.

stringent adj. STRICT, firm, rigid, rigorous, severe, harsh, tough, tight, exacting, demanding, inflexible, hard and fast, uncompromising. ■ OPPOSITES easy.

stringy adj. **1** LANK, straggly, straggling. **2** TOUGH, fibrous, gristly, leathery.

strip[1] v. **1** STRIP NAKED, undress, take one's clothes off, remove one's clothes, disrobe. **2** PEEL, pare, skin, excoriate. **3** TAKE AWAY, dispossess of, deprive of, confiscate. **4** DISMANTLE, take to pieces, take to bits, take apart.

strip[2] n. PIECE, bit, band, belt, ribbon, stripe, bar, swathe, slip, fillet.

stripe n. STRIP, band, belt, bar.

striped adj. STRIPY, banded, barred, striated, variegated.

stripling n. YOUTH, adolescent, youngster, boy, lad, teenager, child, juvenile, minor, young man; informal kid, nipper, young 'un.

strive v. TRY, attempt, endeavour, make an effort, make every effort, exert oneself, do one's best, do all one can, do one's utmost, labour, toil, strain, struggle; informal go all out, give it one's best shot.

stroke n. **1** BLOW, hit, slap, smack, thump, thwack, punch, cuff, box, knock, rap, buffet, smite. **2** MOVEMENT, action, motion. **3** THROMBOSIS, embolism, cerebral vascular accident, CVA, seizure, shock, apoplexy. ▶v. CARESS, fondle, pat, touch, rub, massage, soothe.

stroll v. SAUNTER, amble, wander, meander, ramble, dawdle, promenade, go for a walk, take a walk, stretch one's legs, take the air; informal mosey along.

strong adj. **1** POWERFUL, mighty, brawny, muscular, well built, strapping, sturdy, burly, robust, vigorous, tough, hardy, lusty, Herculean, strong as an ox/horse/lion. **2** COURAGEOUS, brave, plucky, firm, resolute, strong-minded; informal gutsy. **3** DETERMINED, forceful, high-powered, assertive, tough, formidable, aggressive, redoubtable. **4** SOLID, well built, heavy, heavy-duty, hard-wearing, sturdy, durable, long-lasting, tough, secure. **5** KEEN, eager, enthusiastic, deep, acute, dedicated, passionate, fierce, loyal, fervent, zealous. **6** INTENSE, forceful, vehement, passionate, fervent. **7** COMPELLING, powerful, cogent, potent, weighty, convincing, plausible, effective, efficacious, sound, valid, well founded. **8** DEEP, intense, vivid, graphic.

ture to. ■ **structural** adj. **structurally** adv.

strudel n. flaky pastry rolled round a fruit filling.

struggle v. **1** make great efforts to get free. **2** make one's way or try to do with difficulty. ▶n. **1** an act of struggling. **2** a difficult task.

strum v. (**strumming**, **strummed**) play a guitar etc. by sweeping the thumb across the strings.

strumpet n. old use a promiscuous woman.

strung past & past part. of STRING.

strut n. **1** a bar supporting a structure. **2** a strutting walk. ▶v. (**strutting**, **strutted**) walk in a stiff, proud way.

strychnine /strik-neen/ n. a bitter, highly poisonous substance.

Stuart adj. of the royal family ruling Scotland 1371–1714, and Britain 1603–1649 and 1660–1714.

stub n. **1** the part of a pencil, cigarette, etc. remaining after use. **2** the counterfoil of a cheque, ticket, etc. ▶v. (**stubbing**, **stubbed**) **1** strike one's toe against something. **2** extinguish a cigarette by pressing it against something. ■ **stubby** adj.

stubble n. **1** the cut stalks of cereal plants left in the ground after harvesting. **2** short, stiff hairs growing after shaving. ■ **stubbly** adj.

stubborn adj. determined not to change one's attitude or position. ■ **stubborn-**

ly adv. **stubbornness** n.

stucco n. plaster for coating walls or moulding into decorations. ■ **stuccoed** adj.

stuck past part. of STICK. □ **stuck-up** informal arrogantly snobbish.

stud n. **1** a piece of metal with a large head projecting from a surface. **2** a fastener for clothes. **3** a small piece of jewellery for a pierced ear etc. **4** an establishment where horses are kept for breeding. **5** a stallion. ▶v. (**studding**, **studded**) decorate with studs or other small objects.

student n. a person studying at a university or college.

studio n. (pl. **studios**) **1** a room where an artist works or where dancers practise. **2** a room from which programmes are broadcast or recordings are made. □ **studio flat** a flat containing one main room.

studious adj. **1** spending a lot of time studying. **2** deliberate and careful. ■ **studiously** adv.

study n. (pl. **studies**) **1** time and effort spent in reading etc. to gain knowledge. **2** a detailed analysis of a subject or situation. **3** a room for reading and writing. **4** a piece of work done for practice or as an experiment. ▶v. (**studying**, **studied**) **1** make a study of; learn about. **2** look at closely. **3** (**studied**) done with careful effort.

stuff n. **1** matter, objects, etc. of a par-

Thesaurus

9 BRIGHT, brilliant, intense, radiant, gleaming, dazzling, glaring. **10** CONCENTRATED, undiluted, highly flavoured. ■ OPPOSITES weak.

structure n. **1** BUILDING, edifice, construction, erection, pile, complex. **2** CONSTRUCTION, form, configuration, conformation, shape, constitution, composition, make-up, organization, system, arrangement, design, frame, framework. ▶v. CONSTRUCT, build, form, put together, assemble, shape, design, organize, arrange, order.

struggle v. **1** STRIVE, try hard, endeavour, make every effort, exert oneself, do one's best, do all one can, do one's utmost, battle, labour, toil, strain; informal go all out. **2** FIGHT, grapple, wrestle, scuffle, brawl; informal scrap. ▶n. **1** STRIVING, battle, endeavour, effort, exertion, labour, toiling, pains. **2** FIGHT, scuffle, brawl, tussle; informal scrap, set-to, dust-up.

strut v. SWAGGER, prance, parade,

flounce; US sashay.

stubborn adj. OBSTINATE, headstrong, wilful, strong-willed, pig-headed, mulish, dogged, persistent, adamant, inflexible, uncompromising, unbending, unyielding, unmalleable, obdurate, intractable, refractory, recalcitrant. ■ OPPOSITES malleable.

stuck adj. **1** IMMOVABLE, immobile, fast, fixed, rooted. **2** BAFFLED, beaten, stumped, at a loss, perplexed, nonplussed, at one's wits' end; informal up against a brick wall.

student n. UNDERGRADUATE, pupil, schoolboy, schoolgirl, trainee, apprentice, probationer.

studied adj. DELIBERATE, wilful, conscious, calculated, purposeful, contrived, affected, forced, feigned, artificial. ■ OPPOSITES natural.

studious adj. SCHOLARLY, academic, intellectual, bookish, book-loving, serious, earnest.

study v. **1** APPLY ONESELF, revise, burn

S

ticular or unspecified kind. **2** basic constituents. ▶v. **1** fill tightly. **2** force into a confined space. **3** fill out the skin of a dead animal to restore the original appearance.

stuffing n. **1** a mixture put inside poultry before cooking. **2** padding used to stuff cushions etc.

stuffy adj. (**stuffier**, **stuffiest**) **1** lacking fresh air or ventilation. **2** narrow-minded.

stultify v. (**stultifying**, **stultified**) cause to feel bored or drained of energy.

stumble v. **1** trip and lose one's balance. **2** walk unsteadily. **3** make a mistake in speaking. **4** (**stumble across/on**) find by chance. ▶n. an act of stumbling. □ **stumbling block** an obstacle.

stump n. **1** the part of a tree trunk left in the ground after the rest has fallen or been cut down. **2** a remaining piece. **3** each of the uprights of a wicket in cricket. ▶v. **1** baffle. **2** (**stump up**) informal pay a sum of money. ■ **stumpy** adj.

stun v. (**stunning**, **stunned**) **1** knock unconscious. **2** astonish.

stung past & past part. of **STING**.

stunk past & past part. of **STINK**.

stunning adj. very attractive. ■ **stunningly** adv.

stunt v. **1** hinder the growth or development of. **2** an action displaying skill and daring. **3** something done to attract attention.

stupefy v. (**stupefying**, **stupefied**) make unable to think. ■ **stupefaction** n.

stupendous adj. very impressive. ■ **stupendously** adv.

stupid adj. **1** lacking intelligence. **2** dazed. ■ **stupidity** n. **stupidly** adv.

stupor n. a state of being nearly unconscious.

sturdy adj. (**sturdier**, **sturdiest**) strong-

Thesaurus

the midnight oil; informal cram, mug up, swot. **2** LEARN, read up, read, work at; informal mug up on. **3** INVESTIGATE, inquire into, research, look into, examine, analyse, review, survey, conduct a survey of, scrutinize.

stuff n. **1** MATERIAL, fabric, matter, substance. **2** THINGS, objects, articles, items, luggage, baggage, belongings, possessions, goods, paraphernalia. **3** FACTS, information, data, subject. ▶v. **1** FILL, pack, pad. **2** PACK, load, cram, squeeze, crowd, stow, press, force, compress, jam, wedge.

stuffy adj. **1** AIRLESS, close, muggy, stifling, suffocating, musty, stale; informal fuggy. **2** DULL, boring, dreary, staid, sedate, stiff, formal, pompous, starchy, prim, priggish, strait-laced, conventional, conservative, old-fashioned; informal fuddy-duddy, square. ■ OPPOSITES airy, exciting.

stumble v. **1** TRIP, slip, blunder, lumber, lurch, stagger, reel. **2** STAMMER, stutter, hesitate, falter; informal fluff one's lines.

stump n. END, stub, remnant, remains. ▶v. BAFFLE, be too much for, put at a loss, nonplus, mystify, foil, perplex, puzzle, confound, bewilder; informal flummox, discombobulate.

stun v. **1** DAZE, stupefy, knock senseless, knock out, lay out, knock stupid. **2** SHOCK, astound, dumbfound, stupefy, overwhelm, overcome, overpower, devastate, stagger, amaze, astonish, bewilder, confuse; informal flabbergast, knock sideways, knock for six.

stunning adj. SENSATIONAL, ravishing, dazzling, wonderful, marvellous, magnificent, glorious, exquisite, impressive, splendid, beautiful, lovely, gorgeous. ■ OPPOSITES ordinary.

stupendous adj. AMAZING, fantastic, astounding, astonishing, extraordinary, remarkable, wonderful, prodigious, phenomenal, staggering, breathtaking; informal mind-boggling, mind-blowing. ■ OPPOSITES ordinary.

stupid adj. **1** UNINTELLIGENT, foolish, dense, brainless, mindless, obtuse, dull-witted, dull, slow-witted, slow, dunce-like, doltish, simple-minded, half-witted, gullible, naive, moronic, imbecilic, cretinous; informal thick, dim, dumb, dopey, dozy. **2** FOOLISH, silly, idiotic, brainless, mindless, crackbrained, nonsensical, senseless, irresponsible, unthinking, ill-advised, ill-considered, inept, unwise, injudicious, indiscreet, shortsighted, inane, absurd, ludicrous, ridiculous, laughable, fatuous, asinine, pointless, meaningless, futile, fruitless, mad, insane, lunatic; informal cock-eyed. **3** DAZED, stupefied, unconscious. ■ OPPOSITES intelligent, sensible.

stupidity n. **1** LACK OF INTELLIGENCE, foolishness, denseness, brainlessness, mindlessness, dull-wittedness, dullness, slow-wittedness, slowness, doltishness; informal thickness, dimness, dumbness, dopiness, doziness. **2** FOOLISHNESS, folly, silliness, idiocy, brainlessness, senselessness, irresponsibility, injudiciousness, ineptitude, inaneness, inanity, ably built. ■ **sturdily** adv. **sturdiness** n.

sturgeon n. (pl. **sturgeon**) a large edible fish.

stutter v. stammer, esp. by repeating the first sound of a word. ▶n. a tendency to stutter.

sty n. (pl. **sties**) **1** a pigsty. **2** (also **stye**) an inflamed swelling on the edge of an eyelid.

style n. **1** a way of doing something. **2** a design or arrangement. **3** elegance. ▶v. design or arrange.

stylish adj. fashionably elegant. ■ **stylishly** adv. **stylishness** n.

stylist n. a person who designs fashionable clothes or cuts hair.

stylistic adj. of literary or artistic style. ■ **stylistically** adv.

stylized (or **-ised**) adj. represented in an artificial style.

stylus n. (pl. **styli**) **1** a pointed implement for scratching letters or engraving. **2** a hard point following a groove in a record.

stymie v. (**stymying** or **stymieing**, **stymied**) informal obstruct or thwart.

styptic adj. able to make bleeding stop.

styrene n. a liquid hydrocarbon used in plastics.

suave /swahv/ adj. charming, confident, and elegant. ■ **suavely** adv. **suavity** n.

sub informal n. **1** a submarine. **2** a substitute.

sub- prefix **1** under. **2** subordinate.

subaltern n. an army officer below the rank of captain.

subatomic adj. smaller than or occurring within an atom.

subconscious adj. & n. (of) the part of the mind of which one is not fully aware. ■ **subconsciously** adv.

subcontinent n. a large distinguishable part of a continent.

subcontract v. employ a firm or person outside one's company to do work. ■ **subcontractor** n.

subculture n. a cultural group within a larger culture.

subcutaneous adj. under the skin.

subdivide v. divide into smaller parts. ■ **subdivision** n.

subdue v. **1** quieten or make less intense. **2** bring under control.

subedit v. check and correct text before printing. ■ **subeditor** n.

subhuman adj. not behaving like or not fit for a human being.

subject n. **1** a person or thing that is being discussed or dealt with. **2** a branch of knowledge studied or taught. **3** the word in a sentence naming who or what performs the action of the verb. **4** a member of a state ruled by a monarch. ▶adj. (**subject to**) **1** likely or able to be affected by. **2** dependent on. **3** under the authority of. ▶v. (**subject to**) cause to undergo. ■ **subjection** n.

subjective adj. **1** based on personal

Thesaurus

surdity, ludicrousness, ridiculousness, fatuousness, fatuity, asininity, pointlessness, meaninglessness, futility, fruitlessness, madness, insanity, lunacy.

sturdy adj. **1** WELL BUILT, well made, muscular, athletic, strong, strapping, brawny, powerfully built, powerful, solid, substantial, robust, vigorous, tough, hardy, stalwart, mighty, lusty. **2** STRONG, vigorous, stalwart, firm, determined, resolute, tenacious, staunch, steadfast, unyielding, unwavering, uncompromising. **3** see STRONG (4). ■ OPPOSITES weak.

stutter v. STAMMER, stumble, hesitate, falter, splutter.

style n. **1** KIND, type, variety, sort, design, pattern, genre. **2** TECHNIQUE, method, methodology, approach, manner, way, mode, system. **3** STYLISHNESS, smartness, elegance, polish, suavity, urbanity, chic, flair, dash, panache, elan; informal pizzazz, ritziness. **4** FASHION, trend, vogue, mode.

stylish adj. FASHIONABLE, smart, elegant, chic, modish, à la mode, voguish, modern, up to date; informal trendy, dressy, natty, classy, nifty, ritzy, snazzy, snappy, with it. ■ OPPOSITES unfashionable.

subdue v. **1** CONQUER, defeat, vanquish, get the better of, overpower, overcome, overwhelm, subjugate, master, gain the upper hand, triumph over, crush, quash, quell, tame, humble, bring someone to their knees, hold in check. **2** CONTROL, curb, restrain, check, hold back, inhibit, rein in, repress, suppress, stifle. ■ OPPOSITES arouse.

subdued adj. **1** DIM, muted, toned down, softened, soft, lowered, shaded, low-key, subtle, unobtrusive. **2** LOW-SPIRITED, downcast, dejected, depressed, restrained, repressed, inactive, lifeless, dull, passive, unexcited, unresponsive; informal down in the mouth. ■ OPPOSITES bright, lively.

subject n. **1** TOPIC, theme, question, substance, gist, text, thesis. **2** BRANCH OF opinion. **2** of a case of nouns and pronouns used as the subject. ■ **subjectively** adv. **subjectivity** n.

sub judice /sub joo-di-si/ adj. being considered by a law court and so forbidden to be discussed elsewhere.

subjugate v. bring under control. ■ **subjugation** n.

subjunctive adj. (of a form of a verb) expressing what is imagined, wished, or possible.

sublet v. (**subletting**, **sublet**) let a property one is already renting oneself to another person.

sublimate v. transform into a purer or idealized form. ■ **sublimation** n.

sublime adj. of great beauty or excellence. ■ **sublimely** adv.

subliminal adj. affecting someone's mind without their being aware of it. ■ **subliminally** adv.

sub-machine gun n. a lightweight machine gun.

submarine n. a streamlined warship operating under the sea. ▶ adj. existing or done under the sea's surface. ■ **submariner** n.

submerge v. **1** push or go under water. **2** cover or hide.

submerse v. submerge.

submersible adj. designed to operate under water. ▶ n. a small boat that is submersible.

submission n. **1** the act of submitting. **2** a proposal submitted for consideration.

submissive adj. meek or obedient. ■ **submissively** adv.

submit v. (**submitting**, **submitted**) **1** give in to authority or greater power. **2** present for consideration.

subordinate adj. **1** lower in rank. **2** less important. ▶ n. a subordinate person. ▶ v. treat as less important. ■ **subordination** n.

suborn v. pay or persuade to commit an unlawful act.

subpoena /suh-pee-nuh/ n. a writ ordering a person to attend a court. ▶ v. (**subpoenaing**, **subpoenaed**) summon with a subpoena.

subscribe v. **1** arrange to receive something regularly by paying in advance. **2** contribute to a cause. **3** apply to take part in. **4** (**subscribe to**) agree with. ■ **subscriber** n. **subscription** n.

subscript adj. (of a letter, figure, etc.) written below the line.

subsequent adj. coming after in time. ■ **subsequently** adv.

Thesaurus

KNOWLEDGE, course of study, course, discipline. **3** CITIZEN, national. ▶ v. SUBMIT, put through, expose, lay open, treat. □ **subject to 1** CONDITIONAL UPON, contingent upon, dependent on. **2** SUSCEPTIBLE TO, liable to, prone to, in danger of, vulnerable to.

subjective adj. PERSONAL, personalized, individual, biased, prejudiced, bigoted. ■ OPPOSITES objective.

subjugate v. GAIN MASTERY OVER, gain control of, bring someone to their knees, bring to heel, bring under the yoke, conquer, vanquish, defeat, crush, quell, quash, overpower, overcome, subdue, tame, break, humble, tyrannize, oppress, enslave. ■ OPPOSITES liberate.

submerge v. **1** GO UNDER WATER, dive, sink, plummet. **2** IMMERSE, dip, plunge, duck dunk. **3** FLOOD, inundate, deluge, engulf, swamp, overflow.

submission n. **1** SURRENDER, yielding, capitulation, agreement, acceptance, consent, accession, compliance. **2** PRESENTATION, tender, proposal, suggestion. **3** ARGUMENT, assertion, contention, statement, claim, averment. ■ OPPOSITES defiance.

submissive adj. YIELDING, compliant, malleable, acquiescent, accommodating, tractable, manageable, unassertive, passive, obedient, biddable, dutiful, docile, meek, patient, resigned, subdued, humble, self-effacing, deferential, obsequious, servile, self-abasing; *informal* bootlicking. ■ OPPOSITES intractable.

submit v. **1** GIVE IN, yield, give way, capitulate, agree, accept, consent, accede, acquiesce, comply, conform. **2** PUT FORWARD, present, proffer, tender, advance, propose, suggest, table, introduce, move. ■ OPPOSITES resist, withdraw.

subordinate adj. LOWER-RANKING, junior, lower, lesser, inferior, minor, secondary, subsidiary, ancillary, auxiliary. ▶ n. JUNIOR, assistant, second, deputy, aide, subaltern, underling, inferior, second fiddle. ■ OPPOSITES superior.

subscribe v. (**subscribe to**) **1** PAY A SUBSCRIPTION TO, buy regularly, take regularly. **2** MAKE A DONATION TO, donate to, give to, give money to, make a contribution to, contribute towards; *informal* chip into. **3** AGREE WITH, accede to, consent to, accept, believe in, endorse, back, support.

subscription n. **1** FEE, membership fee,

subservient adj. **1** too willing to obey others. **2** less important. ■ **subservience** n.

subset n. a set of which all the elements are contained in another set.

subside v. **1** become less intense. **2** sink to a lower or the normal level. ■ **subsidence** n.

subsidiary adj. **1** related but less important. **2** (of a company) controlled by another. ▶ n. (pl. **subsidiaries**) a subsidiary company.

subsidize (or **-ise**) v. **1** pay part of the cost of producing. **2** support financially.

subsidy n. (pl. **subsidies**) a sum of money given to help keep the price of a product or service low.

subsist v. maintain or support oneself at a basic level. ■ **subsistence** n.

subsoil n. the soil lying immediately under the surface soil.

subsonic adj. of or flying at speeds less than that of sound.

substance n. **1** a particular kind of matter. **2** the physical matter of which a thing consists. **3** solid basis in reality. **4** importance. **5** the most important or essential part or meaning. **6** an intoxicating or narcotic drug.

substantial adj. **1** of considerable importance or size. **2** strongly built. ■ **substantially** adv.

substantiate v. support with evidence. ■ **substantiation** n.

substantive adj. existing in reality.

substitute n. a person or thing acting or used in place of another. ▶ v. use or act as a substitute. ■ **substitution** n.

subsume v. include in something else.

subterfuge n. a deception used to achieve a goal.

subterranean adj. underground.

subtext n. an underlying theme.

subtitle n. **1** (**subtitles**) captions at the bottom of a cinema or television screen that translate dialogue. **2** a secondary title. ▶ v. provide with subtitles.

subtle adj. **1** so delicate or precise as to be difficult to analyse or describe. **2** able to make fine distinctions. **3** using clever and indirect methods. ■ **subtlety** n. **subtly** adv.

subtotal n. the total of part of a group of figures.

subtract v. take away a number or amount from another. ■ **subtraction** n.

subtropical adj. of regions bordering on the tropics.

suburb n. an outlying residential part of a city. ■ **suburban** adj.

Thesaurus

dues, annual payment. **2** DONATION, contribution, offering.

subsequent adj. FOLLOWING, ensuing, succeeding, later, future, next, consequent. ■ OPPOSITES previous.

subservient adj. SERVILE, submissive, deferential, obsequious, sycophantic, grovelling, fawning, ingratiating, toadying, unctuous, truckling; *informal* bootlicking. ■ OPPOSITES domineering.

subside v. **1** ABATE, let up, moderate, quieten down, calm, slacken, die out, peter out, taper off, recede, lessen, diminish, dwindle. **2** GO DOWN, get lower, sink, settle, fall back, recede. ■ OPPOSITES strengthen, rise.

subsidize v. PAY A SUBSIDY TO, contribute to, give money to, back, support, invest in, sponsor, finance, fund, underwrite, foot the bill for; *informal* pick up the tab for.

subsidy n. GRANT, contribution, backing, support, investment, sponsorship, finance, funding, subvention.

subsist v. (**subsist on**) LIVE ON, exist on, eke out an existence on, survive on.

substance n. **1** MATTER, material, stuff, medium, mass, fabric. **2** SOLIDITY, body, corporeality, reality, actuality, materiality, concreteness, tangibility. **3** MEANINGFULNESS, significance, weight, power, soundness, validity. **4** WEALTH, affluence, prosperity, money, capital, means, resources, assets.

substantial adj. **1** REAL, material, weighty, sizeable, considerable, meaningful, significant, important, notable, major, marked, valuable, useful, worthwhile. **2** SOLID, sturdy, stout, strong, well built, durable, hard-wearing. **3** ESSENTIAL, basic, fundamental. ■ OPPOSITES insubstantial.

substitute n. REPLACEMENT, deputy, relief, proxy, reserve, surrogate, fill-in, stand-in, standby, locum, stopgap. ▶ v. **1** USE AS A REPLACEMENT, replace with, use instead of, exchange, switch, swap. **2** TAKE THE PLACE OF, replace, deputize for, act as deputy for, relieve, fill in for, act as stand-in for, cover for, take over from.

subterfuge n. TRICK, ruse, wile, ploy, stratagem, artifice, dodge, manoeuvre, pretext, expedient, intrigue, scheme, deception.

subtle adj. **1** DELICATE, faint, understated, low-key, muted, toned down. **2** FINE, fine-drawn, nice, slight, minute, tenu-

suburbia n. suburbs and suburban life.
subvention n. a subsidy.
subvert v. undermine the authority of. ■ **subversion** n. **subversive** adj.
subway n. **1** a tunnel under a road for use by pedestrians. **2** US an underground railway.
succeed v. **1** achieve an aim. **2** take over a role, title, etc., from someone. **3** come after and take the place of.
success n. **1** the achievement of an aim. **2** the gaining of wealth or status. **3** a successful person or thing.
successful adj. **1** having achieved an aim. **2** having achieved wealth or status. ■ **successfully** adv.
succession n. **1** a number of people or things following one after the other. **2** the act or right of inheriting a position, title, etc. □ **in succession** following one another. ■ **successor** n.
succinct adj. concise and clear. ■ **succinctly** adv.
succour (US **succor**) n. help.
succulent adj. **1** juicy. **2** having thick fleshy leaves. ▸n. a succulent plant. ■ **succulence** n.
succumb v. give in to pressure, temptation, etc.

such adj. & pron. **1** of the type previously mentioned or about to be mentioned. **2** to so high a degree. □ **as such** in the exact sense. **such as 1** for example. **2** of a kind that. **suchlike** things of the type mentioned.
suck v. **1** draw into the mouth by tightening the lips and breathing in. **2** hold in the mouth and pull at with the mouth muscles. **3** draw in a specified direction. **4** (**suck up to**) informal try to please to gain advantage. ▸n. an act of sucking.
sucker n. **1** an organ or device that can stick to a surface by suction. **2** informal a person who is easily fooled. **3** (**a sucker for**) informal a person very fond of or susceptible to. **4** a shoot springing from the base of a tree.
suckle v. feed from the breast or teat.
suckling n. a young child or animal that has not been weaned.
sucrose n. sugar.
suction n. the force produced when a partial vacuum is created by the removal of air.
sudden adj. occurring or done quickly and unexpectedly. ■ **suddenly** adv. **suddenness** n.

Thesaurus

ous, indistinct, indefinite. ■ OPPOSITES crude.
subtract v. TAKE AWAY, take from, deduct, remove, debit; informal knock off. ■ OPPOSITES add.
suburb n. OUTLYING DISTRICT, residential area, dormitory area, purlieus.
suburban adj. PROVINCIAL, unsophisticated, parochial, insular. ■ OPPOSITES cosmopolitan.
subversive adj. UNDERMINING, discrediting, destructive, disruptive, troublemaking, inflammatory, seditious, revolutionary, insurrectionary, treasonous, treacherous.
subvert v. OVERTHROW, overturn, wreak havoc on, sabotage, ruin, destroy, demolish, wreck, upset, disrupt, undermine, weaken.
subway n. UNDERGROUND RAILWAY, underground, metro, tube.
succeed v. **1** TRIUMPH, achieve success, be successful, do well, flourish, thrive; informal make it, make the grade, make a name for oneself. **2** BE SUCCESSFUL, turn out well, work, work out, come off; informal pan out, do the trick. **3** COME AFTER, follow, replace, take the place of, supplant, supersede. ■ OPPOSITES fail, precede.

success n. **1** ACCOMPLISHMENT, achievement, attainment, fulfilment, victory, triumph. **2** PROSPERITY, affluence, wealth, fame, eminence. **3** BEST-SELLER, winner, triumph; informal hit, smash hit, sensation. ■ OPPOSITES failure.
successful adj. **1** VICTORIOUS, triumphant. **2** PROSPEROUS, affluent, wealthy, well-to-do, famous, eminent, at the top, top. **3** FLOURISHING, thriving, booming, profitable, profit-making, moneymaking, lucrative. ■ OPPOSITES failing, unsuccessful.
succession n. SEQUENCE, series, progression, course, cycle, chain, train, run, continuation.
successor n. HEIR, heir apparent, next-in-line, replacement, supplanter. ■ OPPOSITES predecessor.
succinct adj. SHORT, brief, concise, compact, condensed, crisp, terse, tight, to the point, pithy, summary, short and sweet. ■ OPPOSITES lengthy.
succulent adj. JUICY, moist, luscious, mouth-watering. ■ OPPOSITES dry.
succumb v. GIVE IN, give way, yield, submit, surrender, capitulate, be overcome/overwhelmed, fall victim. ■ OPPOSITES resist.
suck v. SUCK UP, draw up, absorb, soak

sudorific adj. causing sweating.

suds pl. n. froth from soap and water.

sue v. take legal action against.

suede n. leather with a velvety nap on one side.

suet n. the hard white fat from round an animal's kidneys, used in cooking.

suffer v. **1** experience something bad. **2** be affected by a disease etc. **3** old use tolerate. ■ **sufferer** n.

sufferance n. toleration rather than actual approval.

suffice v. be enough.

sufficient adj. enough. ■ **sufficiency** n. **sufficiently** adv.

suffix n. a letter or letters added at the end of a word to form another word.

suffocate v. die or kill from lack of air. ■ **suffocation** n.

suffrage n. the right to vote in political elections.

suffragette n. hist. a woman who campaigned for the right to vote.

suffuse v. spread through or over. ■ **suffusion** n.

sugar n. a sweet crystalline substance obtained from various plants. ▶ v. **1** sweeten. **2** make more pleasant. □ **sugar beet** beet from which sugar is extracted. **sugar cane** a tropical grass from which sugar is extracted. **sugar**

soap an alkaline cleaning compound. ■ **sugary** adj.

suggest v. **1** put forward for consideration. **2** make one think of. **3** express indirectly.

suggestible adj. easily influenced.

suggestion n. **1** something suggested. **2** the act of suggesting. **3** a slight trace.

suggestive adj. **1** making one think of something. **2** hinting at sexual matters. ■ **suggestively** adv.

suicide n. **1** the act of killing oneself deliberately. **2** a person who does this. **3** an act which is extremely damaging to one's own interests. ■ **suicidal** adj. **suicidally** adv.

suit n. **1** a jacket and trousers or a jacket and skirt of the same fabric. **2** a set of clothes for a particular activity. **3** any of the sets into which a pack of playing cards is divided. **4** a lawsuit. ▶ v. **1** be convenient for or acceptable to. **2** (of clothes etc.) be right for the features or figure of. □ **suitcase** a case with a handle and a hinged lid for carrying clothes.

suitable adj. right for the purpose or occasion. ■ **suitability** n. **suitably** adv.

suite /sweet/ n. **1** a set of rooms or furniture. **2** a set of musical pieces.

suitor n. a man seeking to marry a

Thesaurus

up, blot up.

sudden adj. **1** IMMEDIATE, instantaneous, abrupt, unexpected, unforeseen, unanticipated, unlooked for, without warning. **2** RAPID, swift, speedy, fast, quick, meteoric. ■ OPPOSITES gradual.

suddenly adv. ALL OF A SUDDEN, all at once, instantaneously, abruptly, unexpectedly, without warning; informal out of the blue. ■ OPPOSITES gradually.

sue v. TAKE TO COURT, bring an action against, prefer/bring charges against, charge, prosecute, bring to trial, summons, indict; informal have the law on. □ **sue for** PETITION FOR, appeal for, solicit, request, ask for, beg for, plead for.

suffer v. **1** BE IN PAIN, feel pain, be racked with pain, hurt, ache. **2** BE DISTRESSED, be in distress, be upset, be miserable, be wretched, be hurt, hurt. **3** EXPERIENCE, undergo, sustain, encounter, meet with, endure. □ **suffer from** BE AFFECTED BY, be afflicted with, be troubled with.

suffice v. BE ENOUGH, be sufficient, do, serve, meet someone's needs; informal hit the spot.

sufficient adj. ENOUGH, adequate, plenty of, ample, plenty.

suffocate v. SMOTHER, stifle, asphyxiate, choke.

suffuse v. SPREAD OVER, cover, bathe, permeate, pervade, imbue.

suggest v. **1** PROPOSE, put forward, move, submit, recommend, advocate; informal throw out. **2** INDICATE, lead to believe, give the impression, give the idea, insinuate, hint, imply, intimate.

suggestion n. **1** PROPOSAL, proposition, plan, motion, submission, recommendation. **2** HINT, trace, touch, suspicion. **3** INSINUATION, hint, implication, intimation.

suggestive adj. PROVOCATIVE, titillating, sexual, sexy, indecent, indelicate, improper, off colour, smutty, ribald, risqué, lewd, salacious; informal blue.

suit n. **1** SET OF CLOTHES, outfit, costume, ensemble. **2** LAWSUIT, court case, action, proceedings, prosecution. ▶ v. **1** BECOME, look attractive on, go well with, look right on. **2** BE SUITABLE FOR, be convenient for, be acceptable to, meet someone's requirements, satisfy someone's demands.

suitable adj. **1** CONVENIENT, acceptable, satisfactory. **2** SUITED TO, befitting, apparticular woman.

sulk v. be silently bad-tempered or resentful. ▶ n. a period of sulking. ■ **sulkily** adv. **sulky** adj.

sullen adj. silently bad-tempered. ■ **sullenly** adv. **sullenness** n.

sully v. (**sullying, sullied**) stain.

sulphate (US **sulfate**) n. a salt of sulphuric acid.

sulphide (US **sulfide**) n. a compound of sulphur with another element.

sulphur (US **sulfur**) n. a yellow non-metallic element. □ **sulphuric acid** a strong corrosive acid. ■ **sulphurous** adj.

sultan n. a Muslim ruler. ■ **sultanate** n.

sultana n. 1 a seedless raisin. 2 the wife of a sultan.

sultry adj. 1 hot and humid. 2 suggesting sexual passion.

sum n. 1 an amount of money. 2 a total. 3 an arithmetical problem. ▶ v. (**summing, summed**) (**sum up**) summarize.

summarize (or **-ise**) v. give a brief account of.

summary n. (pl. **summaries**) a brief statement of the main points of something. ▶ adj. 1 brief and without unnecessary detail. 2 without the usual legal formalities. ■ **summarily** adv.

summation n. 1 the act of adding up. 2 a summary.

summer n. the season after spring and before autumn. ■ **summery** adj.

summit n. 1 the top of a mountain. 2 the highest level of achievement. 3 a meeting between heads of government.

summon v. 1 instruct to be present. 2 send for help. 3 arrange a meeting. 4 draw a quality or reaction from within oneself.

summons n. (pl. **summonses**) 1 an order to appear in a law court. 2 an act of summoning. ▶ v. order to appear in a law court.

sumo n. Japanese wrestling.

sump n. 1 a reservoir of oil in a petrol engine. 2 a hollow into which liquid drains.

sumptuous adj. splendid; lavish. ■ **sumptuously** adv.

sun n. 1 the star round which the earth orbits. 2 any similar star. 3 the light or warmth from the sun. ▶ v. (**sunning, sunned**) (**sun oneself**) sit or lie in the sun. □ **sunbathe** sit or lie in the sun to get a suntan. **sunbed** a device with ultraviolet lamps for acquiring an artificial suntan. **sunburn** skin inflammation caused by too much exposure to the sun. **sunburnt** (or **sunburned**) suffering from sunburn. **sundial** a device showing the time by the shadow cast by a pointer. **sundown** sunset. **sunflower** a tall plant with large yellow flowers. **sunrise** the time when the sun rises. **sunset** 1 the time when the sun sets. 2 the colours in the sky at sunset. **sun-**

Thesaurus

propriate to, relevant to, pertinent to, apposite to, in keeping with, in character with, tailor-made for. 3 RIGHT, appropriate, fitting, apt, well qualified, ideal. ■ OPPOSITES unsuitable.

sulk v. MOPE, pout, be sullen, be in a bad mood, be put out, be out of sorts, be grumpy; *informal* be in a huff.

sulky adj. MOPING, pouting, moody, sullen, piqued, disgruntled, ill-humoured, bad-tempered, grumpy. ■ OPPOSITES cheerful.

sullen adj. MOROSE, unresponsive, uncommunicative, unsociable, resentful, sulky, sour, glum, gloomy, surly, cross, angry, frowning, glowering, grumpy. ■ OPPOSITES cheerful.

sultry adj. 1 CLOSE, airless, stuffy, stifling, suffocating, oppressive, muggy, humid, sticky, hot, sweltering. 2 SENSUAL, sexy, voluptuous, seductive, provocative, alluring, tempting, passionate, erotic.

sum n. 1 SUM TOTAL, grand total, tally, aggregate, answer. 2 ARITHMETICAL PROB-

LEM, problem, calculation, reckoning, tally. □ **sum up** GIVE A SUMMARY OF, summarize, encapsulate, put in a nutshell.

summarize v. GIVE/MAKE A SUMMARY OF, sum up, give a synopsis of, precis, give a precis of, give a résumé of, give an abstract of, abridge, condense, epitomize, outline, sketch, give the main points of, give a rundown of, review, recap.

summary n. SYNOPSIS, precis, résumé, abstract, abridgement, digest, epitome, outline, sketch, rundown, review, summing-up, recap. ▶ adj. IMMEDIATE, instant, instantaneous, on the spot, direct, prompt, rapid, sudden, abrupt, peremptory.

summit n. 1 TOP, peak, crest, crown, apex, vertex, apogee. 2 PEAK, height, pinnacle, culmination, climax, crowning point, zenith, acme. ■ OPPOSITES base, nadir.

summon v. 1 SEND FOR, call for, bid, request someone's presence. 2 ORDER,

shine sunlight unbroken by cloud.
sunspot a dark patch on the sun's surface. **sunstroke** illness caused by excessive exposure to the sun. **suntan** a golden-brown skin colouring caused by exposure to the sun.

sundae n. a dish of ice cream with fruit, syrup, etc.

Sunday n. the day following Saturday. □ **Sunday school** a class held on Sundays to teach children about Christianity.

sunder v. literary split apart.

sundry adj. of various kinds. ▶ n. (**sundries**) various small items.

sung past part. of SING.

sunk past & past part. of SINK.

sunken past part. of SINK. ▶ adj. at a lower level than the surrounding area.

Sunni n. (pl. **Sunni** or **Sunnis**) a follower of one of the two main branches of Islam.

sunny adj. (**sunnier, sunniest**) **1** bright with or receiving much sunlight. **2** cheerful.

super adj. informal excellent.

superannuation n. regular payment made by an employee towards a future pension.

superb adj. **1** excellent. **2** magnificent. ■ **superbly** adv.

supercharger n. a device improving the efficiency of an engine by forcing more air or fuel into it. ■ **supercharged** adj.

supercilious adj. haughty and superior. ■ **superciliously** adv.

supercomputer n. a very powerful computer.

superficial adj. **1** of or on the surface. **2** not thorough or deep. ■ **superficiality** n. **superficially** adv.

superfluous adj. more than is needed. ■ **superfluity** n.

superhuman adj. having or showing exceptional ability or powers.

superimpose v. place or lay one thing over another.

superintend v. oversee.

superintendent n. **1** a supervisor. **2** a senior police officer.

superior adj. **1** higher in status, quality, or power. **2** thinking one is better than others. ▶ n. a person of superior rank. ■ **superiority** n.

superlative adj. **1** of the highest quality. **2** (of an adjective or adverb) expressing the highest degree of a quality.

Thesaurus

call, convene, assemble, muster, rally, convoke.

sumptuous adj. LAVISH, luxurious, de luxe, opulent, magnificent. ■ OPPOSITES plain.

sundry adj. SEVERAL, various, varied, miscellaneous, assorted, diverse.

sunken adj. **1** AT A LOWER LEVEL, below ground level, lowered. **2** HOLLOW, hollowed, concave, drawn, haggard.

sunlight n. SUN, sunshine, light, daylight, light of day.

sunny adj. **1** SUNLIT, bright, clear, cloudless, unclouded, without a cloud in the sky. **2** see CHEERFUL. ■ OPPOSITES dull.

sunrise n. DAWN, crack of dawn, daybreak, cockcrow; US sun-up.

sunset n. NIGHTFALL, close of day, twilight, dusk; US sundown.

sunshine n. see SUNLIGHT.

superb adj. SUPERLATIVE, excellent, first-rate, first-class, outstanding, remarkable, dazzling, marvellous, magnificent, wonderful, splendid, exquisite; informal fantastic, fabulous, brilliant. ■ OPPOSITES poor.

supercilious adj. ARROGANT, haughty, conceited, proud, vain, disdainful, scornful, condescending, superior, patronizing, imperious, overbearing, lofty,

lordly, snobbish, snobby; informal hoity-toity, uppity, snooty, stuck up.

superficial adj. **1** SURFACE, exterior, external, outer, outside, peripheral, slight. **2** CURSORY, perfunctory, hasty, hurried, casual, sketchy, desultory, slapdash. **3** SHALLOW, empty-headed, trivial, frivolous, silly, lightweight, insignificant. ■ OPPOSITES thorough, deep.

superfluous adj. SPARE, surplus, extra, unneeded, unrequired, excess, in excess, unnecessary, needless, inessential, uncalled for, unwarranted, gratuitous. ■ OPPOSITES necessary, essential.

superhuman adj. **1** HERCULEAN, phenomenal, prodigious, stupendous, heroic, extraordinary. **2** DIVINE, god-like, holy, supernatural, preternatural, paranormal, other-worldly. ■ OPPOSITES mundane.

superior adj. **1** BETTER, finer, higher-quality, higher-grade, greater, more expert, more skilful, more advanced, surpassing. **2** HIGHER, higher-ranking, higher up, senior. **3** HAUGHTY, disdainful, condescending, supercilious, patronizing, lofty, lordly, snobbish, snobby; informal high and mighty, hoity-toity, uppity, snooty, stuck up, toffee-nosed.

supermarket n. a large self-service shop selling food and household goods.

supernatural adj. not able to be explained by the laws of nature. ■ **supernaturally** adv.

supernova n. (pl. **supernovae** or **supernovas**) a star that suddenly becomes much brighter because of an explosion.

supernumerary adj. extra.

superpower n. an extremely powerful nation.

superscript adj. (of a letter, figure, etc.) written above the line.

supersede v. take the place of.

 -sede, not -cede.

supersonic adj. of or flying at a speed greater than that of sound.

superstition n. a belief in supernatural influences, or a practice based on this. ■ **superstitious** adj.

superstore n. a very large out-of-town supermarket.

superstructure n. 1 a structure built on top of something else. 2 the upper part of a building or ship.

supervene v. occur as an interruption or change. ■ **supervention** n.

supervise v. watch and direct the performance of a task or the work of a person. ■ **supervision** n. **supervisor** n. **supervisory** adj.

supine adj. 1 lying face upwards. 2 passive or lazy.

supper n. a light or informal evening meal.

supplant v. take the place of.

supple adj. bending easily. ■ **suppleness** n.

supplement n. 1 a thing added to improve or complete something. 2 a separate additional section of a newspaper. 3 an additional section for an extra facility. ▶ v. provide a supplement for. ■ **supplemental** adj. **supplementary** adj.

suppliant n. a person making a humble request.

supplicate v. humbly ask for something. ■ **supplicant** n. **supplication** n.

supply v. (**supplying**, **supplied**) make available to; provide. ▶ n. (pl. **supplies**) 1 a stock of something available. 2 the act of supplying. 3 (**supplies**) necessary provisions and equipment. ■ **supplier** n.

support v. 1 bear the weight of. 2 help,

Thesaurus

■ OPPOSITES inferior.

superlative adj. BEST, greatest, supreme, consummate, first-rate, first-class, of the first water, of the first order, brilliant, excellent, magnificent, outstanding, unsurpassed, unparalleled, unrivalled, peerless, matchless, transcendent. ■ OPPOSITES poor.

supernatural adj. OTHER-WORLDLY, unearthly, spectral, ghostly, phantom, magical, mystic, unreal, paranormal, supernormal, psychic, miraculous, extraordinary, uncanny.

supersede v. 1 TAKE THE PLACE OF, replace, take over from, displace, succeed, supplant, usurp. 2 DISCARD, cast aside, throw out, dispose of, abandon, jettison; informal chuck out.

supervise v. SUPERINTEND, be in charge of, direct, administer, manage, run, oversee, keep an eye on, watch, observe, inspect, be responsible for, guide.

supervision n. ADMINISTRATION, management, direction, control, charge, superintendence, observation, inspection, guidance.

supervisor n. OVERSEER, superintendent, inspector, controller, manager, director, administrator, chief, guide, adviser; informal boss.

supplant v. TAKE THE PLACE OF, take over from, replace, displace, supersede, oust, usurp, overthrow, remove, unseat.

supple adj. 1 LITHE, loose-limbed, limber. 2 PLIANT, pliable, flexible, bendable, stretchable, elastic. ■ OPPOSITES stiff.

supplement n. 1 ADDITION, supplementation, additive, extra, add-on. 2 PULL-OUT, insert, special-feature section, magazine section. ▶ v. ADD TO, augment, increase, top up, complement.

supplementary adj. 1 SUPPLEMENTAL, additional, extra, added, complementary. 2 ADDED, appended, attached, extra.

suppliant n. SUPPLICANT, petitioner, pleader, applicant, suitor, beggar, appellant.

supplicant n. see SUPPLIANT.

supplication n. PLEA, entreaty, begging, petition, appeal, solicitation, request, prayer, invocation; literary beseeching.

supplies n. PROVISIONS, stores, rations, food, provender; dated victuals.

supply v. 1 PROVIDE, give, furnish, contribute, donate, grant, come up with;

encourage, or approve of. **3** provide with the necessities of life. **4** confirm. ▶n. **1** a person or thing that supports. **2** the act of supporting. ■ **supporter** n. **supportive** adj.

suppose v. **1** assume. **2** require as a necessary condition. **3** (**be supposed to do**) be required or expected to do. ■ **supposedly** adv.

supposition n. an assumption.

suppository n. (pl. **suppositories**) a solid medical preparation designed to dissolve after being inserted in the rectum or vagina.

suppress v. **1** forcibly put an end to. **2** prevent from being expressed or pub-

lished. ■ **suppression** n.

suppurate v. form pus. ■ **suppuration** n.

supreme adj. **1** highest in authority or rank. **2** very great or greatest. ■ **supremacy** n. **supremely** adv.

surcharge n. an extra charge.

sure adj. **1** confident that one is right. **2** (**sure of/to do**) certain to get or do. **3** undoubtedly true. ▶adv. informal certainly. □ **sure-footed** not stumbling or slipping. ■ **sureness** n.

surely adv. **1** it must be true that. **2** certainly.

surety n. (pl. **sureties**) **1** a person who guarantees that someone will do some-

Thesaurus

informal fork out, shell out. **2** SATISFY, meet, fulfil. ▶n. **1** SUPPLYING, providing, provision, furnishing. **2** STOCK, store, reserve, reservoir, stockpile, heap, pile, mass, hoard, cache.

support v. **1** BEAR, carry, hold up, prop up, bolster up, brace, keep up, shore up, underpin, buttress. **2** MAINTAIN, provide for, sustain, take care of, look after. **3** GIVE MORAL SUPPORT TO, give strength to, comfort, help, sustain, encourage, buoy up, hearten, fortify; informal buck up. **4** BACK UP, substantiate, give force to, bear out, corroborate, confirm, verify, validate, authenticate, endorse, ratify. **5** BACK, champion, give help to, help, assist, aid, be on someone's side, side with, vote for, stand behind, stand up for, take up the cudgels for; informal stick up for. **6** ADVOCATE, promote, further, champion, be on someone's side, espouse, be in favour of, recommend, defend. ▶n. **1** BASE, foundations, pillar, post, prop, underprop, underpinning, substructure, brace, buttress, abutment, bolster, stay. **2** KEEP, maintenance, sustenance, food and accommodation, subsistence; old use aliment. **3** MORAL SUPPORT, friendship, strength, encouragement, buoying up, heartening, fortification; informal bucking up. **4** BACKING, contribution, donation, money, subsidy, funding, funds, finance, capital. **5** HELP, assistance, comfort, tower of strength, prop, backbone, mainstay.

supporter n. **1** SPONSOR, contributor, donor, backer, patron, friend, wellwisher. **2** CHAMPION, advocate, promoter, backer, defender, apologist, helper. **3** FAN, follower.

supportive adj. HELPFUL, encouraging, caring, sympathetic, understanding,

loyal, interested, positive, reassuring. ■ OPPOSITES unsympathetic.

suppose v. **1** ASSUME, take for granted, dare say, take as read, presume, expect, imagine, believe, think, fancy, suspect, guess, surmise, reckon, conjecture, theorize, opine. **2** TAKE AS A HYPOTHESIS, hypothesize, postulate, posit. **3** PRESUPPOSE, require, imply.

supposed adj. PRESUMED, assumed, believed, professed, so-called, alleged, putative, reputed.

supposition n. ASSUMPTION, presumption, suspicion, guess, surmise, conjecture, speculation, theory, hypothesis, postulation.

suppress v. **1** VANQUISH, put an end to, crush, quell, conquer, squash, stamp out, extinguish, put out, crack down on, clamp down on. **2** RESTRAIN, keep a rein on, hold back, control, keep under control, check, keep in check, curb, bottle up, choke back. **3** KEEP SECRET, conceal, hide, keep hidden, keep silent about, withhold, cover up, smother, stifle, muzzle. ■ OPPOSITES incite, reveal.

supremacy n. ASCENDANCY, dominance, superiority, predominance, paramountcy, dominion, sway, authority, mastery, control, power, rule, sovereignty, lordship.

supreme adj. **1** HIGHEST-RANKING, highest, leading, chief, foremost, principal. **2** EXTREME, greatest, utmost, uttermost, maximum, extraordinary, remarkable. **3** FINAL, last, ultimate. ■ OPPOSITES subordinate, minimal.

sure adj. **1** CERTAIN, definite, positive, convinced, confident, decided, assured, free from doubt, unhesitating, unwavering, unfaltering. **2** ASSURED, certain, guaranteed, inevitable, irrevocable. **3** RELIABLE, dependable, trustthing. **2** money given as a guarantee.

surf n. the mass or line of foam formed by breaking waves. ▶v. **1** stand on a surfboard and ride on the crest of a wave. **2** move from site to site on the Internet. □ **surfboard** a long, narrow board used in surfing. ■ **surfer** n.

surface n. **1** the outside or uppermost layer of something. **2** the upper limit of a body of liquid. **3** outward appearance. ▶adj. of or on the surface. ▶v. **1** come up to the surface. **2** become apparent. **3** provide with a particular surface.

surfeit n. an excess.

surge n. **1** a sudden powerful forward or upward movement. **2** a sudden increase. ▶v. **1** move in a surge. **2** increase suddenly.

surgeon n. a doctor qualified to practise surgery.

surgery n. (pl. **surgeries**) **1** medical treatment involving cutting open the body and removing or repairing parts. **2** a place where a doctor or nurse sees patients. **3** a time when an MP is available for consultation. ■ **surgical** adj. **surgically** adv.

surly adj. (**surlier**, **surliest**) bad-tempered and unfriendly. ■ **surliness** n.

surmise v. suppose or guess. ▶n. a guess.

surmount v. **1** overcome a difficulty. **2** be on top of. ■ **surmountable** adj.

surname n. a family name.

surpass v. be greater or better than.

surplice n. a white robe worn by clergy and choristers.

surplus n. an amount left over after what is needed has been used. ▶adj. more than what is needed or used.

surprise n. **1** a feeling caused by something sudden or unexpected. **2** something causing this. ▶v. **1** cause to feel surprise. **2** capture, attack, or find suddenly and unexpectedly.

....

✓ Don't forget the first *r*.

....

surreal adj. strange and dreamlike. ■ **surreally** adv.

surrealism n. an artistic movement combining normally unrelated images in a strange way. ■ **surrealist** n. **surrealistic** adj.

surrender v. **1** give in to an opponent. **2** give up a right or possession. ▶n. an act of surrendering.

Thesaurus

....

worthy, trusted, trusty, unfailing, infallible, never-failing, tested, true, foolproof, effective, efficacious; *informal* sure-fire. ■ OPPOSITES unsure, uncertain.

surface n. **1** OUTSIDE, exterior, top. **2** OUTWARD APPEARANCE, superficial appearance, facade. ▶adj. SUPERFICIAL, external, exterior, outward. ▶v. **1** COME TO THE SURFACE, come up, come to the top. **2** REAPPEAR, appear, come to light, come up, emerge, crop up. **3** GET UP, get out of bed, rise, wake, awaken.

surge n. GUSH, rush, outpouring, stream, flow, sweep, efflux. ▶v. **1** GUSH, rush, stream, flow. **2** RISE, swell, heave, billow, roll, eddy, swirl.

surly adj. BAD-TEMPERED, ill-natured, crabbed, grumpy, crotchety, grouchy, cantankerous, irascible, testy, crusty, gruff, abrupt, brusque, churlish, uncivil, morose, sullen, sulky. ■ OPPOSITES good-natured, friendly.

surmise v. GUESS, conjecture, suspect, deduce, assume, presume, gather, feel, be of the opinion, think, believe, imagine.

surmount v. GET OVER, overcome, conquer, triumph over, prevail over, get the better of, beat.

surname n. LAST NAME, family name, patronymic.

surpass v. BE GREATER THAN, be better than, beat, exceed, excel, transcend, outdo, outshine, outstrip, overshadow, eclipse.

surplus n. EXCESS, remainder, residue, surfeit. ■ OPPOSITES dearth, shortage. ▶adj. EXCESS, in excess, superfluous, leftover, unused, remaining, extra, spare.

surprise v. **1** ASTONISH, amaze, nonplus, take aback, startle, astound, stun, stagger, leave open-mouthed, take someone's breath away; *informal* flabbergast, bowl over, blow someone's mind. **2** TAKE BY SURPRISE, catch unawares, catch off guard, catch red-handed, catch in the act, catch out, burst in on, spring upon, catch someone with their trousers down; *informal* catch on the hop. ▶n. **1** ASTONISHMENT, amazement, incredulity, wonder. **2** SHOCK, bolt from the blue, bombshell, revelation; *informal* turn-up for the books.

surprised adj. ASTONISHED, amazed, nonplussed, startled, astounded, stunned, staggered, open-mouthed, speechless, thunderstruck; *informal* flabbergasted.

surprising adj. ASTONISHING, amazing, startling, astounding, staggering, in-

surreptitious adj. done secretly. ■ **surreptitiously** adv.

surrogate n. a deputy. □ **surrogate mother** a woman who bears a child on behalf of another. ■ **surrogacy** n.

surround v. be or place all round. ▶ n. a border.

surroundings pl. n. the conditions or area around a person or thing.

surtax n. an extra tax.

surveillance n. close observation.

survey v. **1** look carefully and thoroughly at. **2** record the features of an area of land to produce a map. **3** examine and report on the condition of a building. ▶ n. **1** a general examination or description. **2** a map or report obtained by surveying. ■ **surveyor** n.

survival n. **1** the state of surviving. **2** something that has survived from an earlier time.

survive v. **1** continue to live or exist, esp. in spite of an accident or ordeal. **2** remain alive after the death of.

■ **survivor** n.

susceptible adj. easily influenced or harmed by a particular thing. ■ **susceptibility** n.

sushi n. a Japanese dish of balls of cold rice served esp. with raw seafood.

suspect v. **1** believe to be likely or possible. **2** believe to be guilty without certain proof. **3** doubt the genuineness of. ▶ n. a person suspected of a crime. ▶ adj. possibly dangerous or false.

suspend v. **1** halt temporarily. **2** temporarily remove from a post. **3** (**suspended**) (of a sentence) not enforced as long as no further offence is committed within a specified period. **4** hang up.

suspender n. **1** a strap attached to a belt or garter and fastened to the top of a stocking to hold it up. **2** (**suspenders**) US braces for trousers.

suspense n. excited or anxious uncertainty about what may happen.

suspension n. **1** the suspending of something. **2** the mechanism by which

Thesaurus

credible, extraordinary, remarkable; *informal* mind-blowing. ■ OPPOSITES predictable.

surrender v. **1** GIVE IN, give oneself up, yield, submit, capitulate, lay down one's arms, raise/show the white flag, throw in the towel/sponge. **2** GIVE UP, relinquish, renounce, forgo, forsake, cede, abdicate, waive. **3** HAND OVER, give up, deliver up, part with, let go of, relinquish. ▶ n. **1** YIELDING, capitulation, submission. **2** RELINQUISHMENT, renunciation, resignation, ceding, cession, abdication.

surreptitious adj. STEALTHY, clandestine, secret, sneaky, sly, cunning, furtive, underhand, undercover, covert. ■ OPPOSITES open, blatant.

surround v. ENCIRCLE, enclose, go around, encompass, ring, gird, girdle, fence in, hem in, confine.

surrounding adj. NEIGHBOURING, nearby, adjacent, adjoining, bordering.

surroundings pl. n. ENVIRONMENT, setting, location, neighbourhood, vicinity, milieu, element, background.

surveillance n. OBSERVATION, watch, scrutiny, reconnaissance, espionage, spying.

survey v. **1** LOOK AT, look over, take a look at, observe, view, contemplate, regard, examine, inspect, scrutinize, scan, study, consider, review, take stock of; *informal* size up. **2** MAKE A SURVEY OF, value, carry out a valuation of, esti-

mate the value of, appraise, assess, prospect, triangulate. ▶ n. **1** STUDY, consideration, review, overview, examination, inspection, scrutinization, scrutiny. **2** VALUATION, appraisal. **3** INVESTIGATION, inquiry, research, study, review, probe, questionnaire.

survive v. **1** REMAIN ALIVE, live, hold out, pull through, cling to life. **2** LIVE ON, continue, remain, last, persist, endure, be extant, exist, be. **3** OUTLIVE, outlast, live after, remain alive after.

susceptible adj. IMPRESSIONABLE, credulous, gullible, innocent, defenceless, vulnerable, easily led, responsive, sensitive, thin-skinned. ■ OPPOSITES immune, resistant. □ **susceptible to** OPEN TO, responsive to, receptive to, vulnerable to, defenceless against.

suspect v. **1** FEEL, have a feeling, be inclined to think, fancy, surmise, guess, conjecture, have a suspicion that, speculate, have a hunch, suppose, believe, think, conclude. **2** DOUBT, have doubts about, harbour suspicions about, have misgivings about, be sceptical about, distrust, mistrust.

suspend v. **1** HANG, put up, swing, dangle, sling. **2** ADJOURN, interrupt, cut short, bring to an end, cease, discontinue, break off, arrest, put off, postpone, delay, defer, shelve, pigeonhole, table; *informal* put on ice. **3** DEBAR, shut out, exclude, keep out, remove.

suspense n. UNCERTAINTY, doubt, doubta vehicle is supported on its wheels. □ **suspension bridge** a bridge suspended from cables running between towers.

suspicion n. **1** a feeling that something is possible or that someone is guilty. **2** distrust. **3** a slight trace. ■ **suspicious** adj. **suspiciously** adv.

suss v. informal realize the true nature of.

sustain v. **1** give strength to. **2** support. **3** suffer an injury. **4** keep going over time. **5** uphold the validity of.

sustainable adj. (of industry etc.) avoiding using up natural resources. ■ **sustainability** n.

sustenance n. food and drink as needed to stay alive.

suture n. a stitch holding together the edges of a wound. ▶v. stitch with a suture.

suzerainty /soo-zuh-rayn-ty/ n. the right of one country to rule over another country that is not fully independent.

svelte adj. slender and elegant.

SW abbrev. south-west or south-western.

swab n. **1** a pad for cleaning wounds or taking specimens from the body. **2** a specimen taken with a swab. ▶v. (**swabbing**, **swabbed**) clean with a swab.

swaddle v. wrap in garments or cloth.

swag n. **1** a drooping ornamental arrangement of flowers, fabric, etc. **2** informal money or goods taken by a thief.

swagger v. walk or behave in a very confident manner. ▶n. a swaggering walk.

Swahili n. a Bantu language widely used in East Africa.

swain n. old use a young lover or suitor.

swallow v. **1** cause to pass down the throat. **2** move the throat muscles as if doing this. **3** engulf. **4** accept or believe. **5** resist expressing. ▶n. **1** an act of swallowing. **2** a swift-flying bird with a forked tail.

swam past of **swim**.

swamp n. a marsh. ▶v. **1** flood with water. **2** overwhelm with too much of something. ■ **swampy** adj.

swan n. a large white waterbird with a long neck. □ **swansong** the final performance or activity of a person's career.

swank v. informal show off.

swanky adj. (**swankier**, **swankiest**) informal luxurious and expensive.

swap (or **swop**) v. (**swapping**, **swapped**) exchange. ▶n. an act of exchanging.

sward n. an expanse of short grass.

swarm n. a large of group of people, flying insects, etc. ▶v. **1** move in a swarm. **2** be crowded. **3** (**swarm up**) climb by gripping with the hands and feet.

swarthy adj. (**swarthier**, **swarthiest**) having a dark skin.

Thesaurus

....

fulness, anticipation, expectation, expectancy, excitement, tension, anxiety, nervousness, apprehension, apprehensiveness.

suspicion n. **1** DOUBT, misgiving, qualm, wariness, chariness, scepticism, distrust, mistrust, funny feeling. **2** FEELING, surmise, guess, conjecture, speculation, hunch, supposition, belief, notion, idea, conclusion; informal gut feeling. **3** TRACE, touch, suggestion, hint, soupçon, tinge, shade.

suspicious adj. **1** DOUBTFUL, unsure, wary, chary, sceptical, distrustful, mistrustful, disbelieving. **2** GUILTY-LOOKING, dishonest-looking, suspect, strange-looking, funny-looking; informal shifty, shady. **3** QUESTIONABLE, doubtful, odd, strange, irregular, queer, funny; informal fishy, shady. ■ OPPOSITES trusting, innocent.

sustain v. **1** BEAR, support, carry, keep up, prop up, shore up. **2** SUPPORT, be a source of strength to, be a tower of strength to, comfort, help, assist, encourage, buoy up, cheer up, hearten; informal buck up. **3** KEEP ALIVE, keep going, maintain, preserve, feed, nourish.

sustained adj. CONTINUING, steady, continuous, constant, prolonged, perpetual, unremitting. ■ OPPOSITES intermittent.

sustenance n. FOOD, nourishment, provisions, comestibles, provender; informal grub, chow, scoff; dated victuals; old use aliment.

swagger v. STRUT, parade, prance.

swallow v. **1** GULP DOWN, eat, drink, consume, devour, ingest; informal swig, swill, scoff. **2** PUT UP WITH, tolerate, endure, stand, bear, abide, stomach, brook; old use suffer. **3** BELIEVE, accept; informal fall for, buy. **4** REPRESS, restrain, hold back, control, rein in.

swamp n. MARSH, bog, quagmire, mire, morass, fen, quag. ▶v. **1** FLOOD, inundate, deluge, wash out, soak, drench, saturate. **2** OVERWHELM, engulf, snow under, overload, overburden, weight down, besiege, beset.

swap v. EXCHANGE, interchange, trade,

swashbuckling adj. engaging in or full of flamboyant daring. ■ **swashbuckler** n.

swastika n. a symbol in the form of a cross with each arm bent at a right angle.

swat v. (**swatting**, **swatted**) hit hard with a flat object.

swatch n. a sample of fabric.

swathe n. (US **swath**) a strip cut in one sweep or passage of a mower etc. ▶ v. wrap in several layers of fabric.

sway v. 1 move gently to and fro. 2 cause someone to change their opinion. ▶ n. 1 a swaying movement. 2 power or influence.

swear v. (**swearing**, **swore**; past part. **sworn**) 1 promise solemnly or on oath. 2 use offensive or obscene language. □ **swear by** have great confidence in. **swear word** an offensive or obscene word.

sweat n. moisture given out through the pores of the skin. ▶ v. 1 give off sweat. 2 make a great effort. 3 be very anxious. □ **sweatshirt** a loose cotton sweater. **sweatshop** a place employing workers for long hours in poor conditions. ■ **sweaty** adj.

sweater n. a pullover with long sleeves.

swede n. a yellow root vegetable.

sweep v. (**sweeping**, **swept**) 1 clean by brushing away dirt or litter. 2 move swiftly or forcefully. 3 extend in a long, continuous curve. ▶ n. 1 an act of sweeping. 2 a long, swift, curving movement. 3 a long curved stretch of road etc. 4 a person whose job is cleaning soot from chimneys. □ **sweepstake** a form of gambling in which all the stakes are divided among the winners. ■ **sweeper** n.

sweeping adj. 1 wide in range or effect. 2 (of a statement) too general.

sweet adj. 1 having the pleasant taste of sugar. 2 having a pleasant smell. 3 delightful. 4 kind. 5 charming. ▶ n. 1 a small piece of confectionery made with sugar. 2 a sweet dish forming a course of a meal. □ **sweetbread** an animal's thymus gland or pancreas used as food. **sweetcorn** a variety of maize with sweet kernels eaten as a vegetable. **sweetheart** a girlfriend or boyfriend. **sweet tooth** a liking for sweet foods. ■ **sweeten** v. **sweetly** adv. **sweetness** n.

sweetener n. 1 a sweetening substance. 2 informal a bribe.

swell v. (**swelling**, **swelled**, past part.

Thesaurus

barter, switch.

swarm n. 1 HIVE, flight. 2 CROWD, multitude, horde, host, mob, throng, army, flock, herd, pack, drove. ▶ v. FLOCK, crowd, throng, stream, surge.

swarthy adj. DARK, dark-coloured, dark-skinned, dark-complexioned, dusky, tanned. ■ OPPOSITES pale, fair.

swashbuckling adj. DASHING, daring, adventurous, bold, gallant, swaggering. ■ OPPOSITES timid.

swathe v. WRAP, envelop, bind, swaddle, bandage, bundle up, cover, shroud, drape.

sway v. 1 SWING, shake, bend, lean, incline. 2 WAVER, hesitate, fluctuate, vacillate, oscillate. 3 INFLUENCE, affect, persuade, prevail on, bring round, win over, induce. ▶ n. 1 JURISDICTION, rule, government, sovereignty, dominion, control, command, power, authority, ascendancy, domination, mastery. 2 CONTROL, domination, power, authority, influence, guidance, direction.

swear v. 1 PROMISE, pledge, vow, give one's word, take an oath, swear on the Bible. 2 VOW, insist, declare, assert, maintain, contend, aver. 3 CURSE, blaspheme, utter profanities, be foul-mouthed, use bad language, swear like a trooper; informal cuss, turn the air blue, eff and blind.

sweat v. PERSPIRE, exude perspiration, drip with sweat, break out in a sweat.

sweaty adj. SWEATING, perspiring, clammy, sticky, moist, damp.

sweep v. BRUSH, clean, clean up, clear up. □ **sweep away/aside** CAST ASIDE, discard, disregard, ignore, take no notice of, dismiss.

sweet adj. 1 SWEETENED, sugary, sugared, honeyed, syrupy, saccharine. 2 SWEET-SMELLING, fragrant, aromatic, perfumed, scented, balmy. 3 SWEET-SOUNDING, musical, tuneful, dulcet, mellifluous, soft, harmonious, euphonious, silvery, silver-toned. 4 GOOD-NATURED, amiable, pleasant, agreeable, friendly, kindly, charming, likeable, appealing, engaging, winning, winsome, taking. 5 DEAR, dearest, darling, beloved, loved, cherished, precious, treasured. ■ OPPOSITES sour, savoury. ▶ n. 1 DESSERT, pudding; informal afters. 2 BONBON, sweetmeat; US candy; informal sweetie.

sweeten v. 1 MAKE SWEET, add sugar to, sugar. 2 SOFTEN, soften up, mellow, pacify, appease, mollify.

swollen or **swelled**) **1** become larger or more rounded. **2** increase in strength or amount. ▶ n. **1** a full or gently rounded form. **2** a gradual increase in strength or amount. **3** a slow, regular movement of the sea.

swelling n. a swollen place on the body.

swelter v. be uncomfortably hot.

swept past & past part. of SWEEP.

swerve v. abruptly go off from a straight course. ▶ n. an abrupt change of course.

swift adj. quick; fast. ▶ n. a fast-flying bird with slender wings. ■ **swiftly** adv. **swiftness** n.

swig v. (**swigging, swigged**) informal drink quickly.

swill v. **1** rinse out. **2** (of liquid) swirl round in a container. ▶ n. kitchen refuse mixed with water for feeding to pigs.

swim v. (**swimming, swam**; past part. **swum**) **1** propel oneself through water by moving one's arms and legs. **2** be covered with liquid. **3** experience a dizzy feeling. ▶ n. a period of swimming. ■ **swimmer** n.

swimmingly adv. informal smoothly and satisfactorily.

swindle v. cheat someone of money etc. ▶ n. a dishonest scheme to obtain money. ■ **swindler** n.

swine n. **1** (pl. **swine**) a pig. **2** (pl. **swine** or **swines**) informal an unpleasant person.

swing v. (**swinging, swung**) **1** move back and forth or from side to side while suspended. **2** move by grasping a support and leaping. **3** move in a smooth, curving line. **4** change from one opinion, mood, or state of affairs to another. **5** have a decisive influence on. ▶ n. **1** a hanging seat on which to sit and swing. **2** an act of swinging. **3** a change in public opinion. **4** a style of jazz music with an easy flowing rhythm. □ **in full swing** at the height of activity.

swingeing adj. severe; extreme.

swipe informal v. **1** hit with a swinging blow. **2** steal. **3** pass a swipe card through an electronic reader. ▶ n. a swinging blow. □ **swipe card** a plastic card carrying coded information which is read when the card is slid through an electronic device.

swirl v. move in a twisting pattern. ▶ n. a swirling movement or pattern.

swish v. move with a hissing sound. ▶ n. a swishing sound. ▶ adj. informal impressively smart.

Swiss adj. of Switzerland or its people. □ **Swiss roll** a thin sponge cake spread with jam etc. and rolled up.

switch n. **1** a device operated to turn electric current on or off. **2** a change or exchange. **3** a flexible shoot cut from a tree. ▶ v. **1** change in position or direction. **2** exchange. **3** (**switch off/on**) turn an electrical device off (or on).

Thesaurus

sweetheart n. GIRLFRIEND, boyfriend, lover, suitor, admirer, beau, inamorato, inamorata; literary swain; old use paramour.

swell v. **1** EXPAND, bulge, distend, become distended, inflate, become inflated, dilate, become bloated, blow up, puff up, balloon, intumesce. **2** INCREASE, grow larger, rise, mount, escalate, accelerate, step up, snowball, mushroom. **3** GROW LOUD, grow louder, intensify, heighten. ▶ adj. EXPENSIVE, luxurious, de luxe, fashionable, elegant, grand; informal plush, ritzy, posh.

swelling n. BUMP, lump, bulge, blister, inflammation, protuberance, tumescence.

swerve v. CHANGE DIRECTION, go off course, veer, turn aside, skew, deviate, sheer, twist.

swift adj. FAST, rapid, quick, speedy, fleet-footed, fleet, prompt, brisk, immediate, instantaneous; informal nippy. ■ OPPOSITES slow.

swill v. GULP DOWN, drink, quaff, swallow, down, drain, guzzle; informal swig. □ **swill out** SLUICE, wash down, wash out, clean out, flush out, rinse out.

swim v. GO SWIMMING, bathe, dive in; informal have a dip. □ **be swimming in** BE SATURATED IN, be drenched in, be soaked in, be steeped in, be immersed in.

swindle v. DEFRAUD, cheat, trick, fleece, dupe, deceive, rook, exploit; informal do, con, diddle, rip off, take for a ride, pull a fast one on, bilk. ▶ n. FRAUD, trick, deception, exploitation, sharp practice; informal con trick, con, diddle, rip-off, fiddle.

swindler n. FRAUDSTER, cheat, trickster, rogue, mountebank, exploiter; informal con man, con artist, shark, bilker.

swing v. **1** HANG, be suspended, dangle, be pendent. **2** MOVE BACK AND FORTH, sway, oscillate, wag. **3** CURVE, veer, turn, lean, incline, wind, twist. **4** CHANGE, fluctuate, oscillate, waver, see-saw, yo-yo. ▶ n. **1** SWAYING, oscilla-

□ **switchback** a road with alternate sharp ascents and descents. **switchboard** an installation for the manual control of telephone connections.

swivel n. a link or pivot enabling one part to revolve without turning the other. ▶v. (**swivelling**, **swivelled**; US **swiveling**, **swiveled**) turn round, or around a central point.

swollen past part. of SWELL.

swoon v. faint.

swoop v. **1** move rapidly downwards through the air. **2** carry out a sudden raid. ▶n. an act of swooping.

swop var. of SWAP.

sword n. a weapon with a long metal blade. □ **swordfish** an edible sea fish with a sword-like snout.

swore past of SWEAR.

sworn past part. of SWEAR. ▶adj. determined to remain the specified thing: *sworn enemies*.

swot informal v. (**swotting**, **swotted**) study hard. ▶n. a person who studies hard.

swum past part. of SWIM.

swung past & past part. of SWING.

sybarite n. a person fond of luxury and pleasure. ■ **sybaritic** adj.

sycamore n. a large tree of the maple family.

sycophant n. a person who tries to win favour by flattery. ■ **sycophancy** n. **sycophantic** adj.

syllable n. a unit of pronunciation in a word. ■ **syllabic** adj.

syllabub n. a dish of flavoured whipped cream.

syllabus n. (pl. **syllabuses** or **syllabi**) the topics in a course of study or teaching.

syllogism n. a form of reasoning in which a conclusion is drawn from two propositions.

sylph n. **1** an imaginary spirit of the air. **2** a slender woman or girl.

sylvan (or **silvan**) adj. literary of woods; wooded.

symbiosis n. (pl. **symbioses**) a situation in which two different organisms live with and are dependent on each other, to the advantage of both. ■ **symbiotic** adj.

symbol n. **1** a thing representing something else. **2** a mark or character used as a standard representation of something. ■ **symbolic** adj. **symbolically** adv.

symbolism n. **1** the use of symbols to represent ideas or qualities. **2** symbolic meaning. ■ **symbolist** n.

symbolize (or **-ise**) v. **1** be a symbol of. **2** represent by means of symbols.

symmetry n. (pl. **symmetries**) **1** the state of having exactly matching parts facing each other or round an axis. **2** the quality of being similar or equal. ■ **symmetrical** adj. **symmetrically** adv.

sympathetic adj. **1** feeling or showing sympathy. **2** showing or inspiring approval. ■ **sympathetically** adv.

sympathize (or **-ise**) v. feel or express

Thesaurus

. . . .

tion, wagging. **2** MOVE, change, variation, turnaround.

swirl v. WHIRL, eddy, circulate, revolve, spin, twist, churn, swish.

switch n. **1** CHANGE, change of direction, shift, reversal, turnaround, U-turn, about-turn. **2** EXCHANGE, trade, swap. ▶v. **1** CHANGE, shift, reverse. **2** EXCHANGE, interchange, trade, barter, swap.

swollen adj. EXPANDED, bulging, distended, inflated, dilated, bloated, blown up, puffed up, puffy, tumescent.

swoop v. POUNCE, dive, descend, sweep down on, drop down on.

sycophant n. TOADY, flatterer, truckler, Uriah Heep; informal bootlicker, yes-man.

sycophantic adj. SERVILE, subservient, obsequious, toadying, flattering, ingratiating, unctuous, truckling, Uriah Heepish; informal bootlicking.

symbol n. **1** EMBLEM, token, sign, badge, representation, figure, image, type.

2 SIGN, character, mark.

symbolic adj. **1** EMBLEMATIC, representative, typical. **2** REPRESENTATIVE, illustrative, emblematic, figurative, allegorical.

symbolize v. BE A SYMBOL OF, stand for, be a sign of, represent, personify, exemplify, typify, betoken, denote, epitomize, signify, mean.

symmetrical adj. BALANCED, well proportioned, proportional, in proportion, regular, even, harmonious, uniform, consistent, in agreement. ■ OPPOSITES asymmetrical.

sympathetic adj. **1** COMPASSIONATE, commiserating, commiserative, pitying, condoling, consoling, comforting, supportive, caring, concerned, solicitous, considerate, kindly, kind, kind-hearted, warm, warm-hearted, understanding, charitable, empathetic. **2** PLEASANT, agreeable, likeable, congenial, friendly, sociable, companionable, neighbourly, easy to get along with; informal simpatico.

sympathy. ■ **sympathizer** n.

sympathy n. (pl. **sympathies**) **1** the feeling of being sorry for someone. **2** understanding between people. **3** support or approval.

symphony n. (pl. **symphonies**) an elaborate musical composition for a full orchestra. ■ **symphonic** adj.

symposium n. (pl. **symposia** or **symposiums**) a conference or meeting to discuss a particular subject.

symptom n. **1** a change in the body or mind which is the sign of a disease. **2** a sign of an undesirable situation. ■ **symptomatic** adj.

synagogue n. a building where Jews meet for religious worship and teaching.

synapse n. a connection between two nerve cells.

synchronic adj. dealing with something as it exists at a particular time, not with its history.

synchronize (or **-ise**) v. cause to happen or operate at the same time or rate.

synchronous adj. existing or occurring at the same time.

syncopate v. alter the accents in music so that strong beats become weak and vice versa. ■ **syncopation** n.

syndicate n. a group of people or firms combining to achieve a common interest. ▶v. **1** control or manage by a syndicate. **2** publish or broadcast in a number of media at the same time. ■ **syndication** n.

syndrome n. a group of symptoms consistently occurring together.

synergy n. cooperation of two or more things to produce a combined effect greater than the sum of their separate effects.

synod n. an official meeting of Church ministers and members.

synonym n. a word or phrase meaning the same as another in the same language. ■ **synonymous** adj.

synopsis n. (pl. **synopses**) a brief summary or outline.

synovial adj. of or denoting a joint enclosed in a membrane containing a lubricating fluid.

syntax n. the arrangement of words and phrases to form sentences. ■ **syntactic** adj.

synthesis n. (pl. **syntheses**) **1** the combination of parts to form a connected whole. **2** the production of chemical compounds by reaction from simpler materials.

synthesize (or **-ise**) v. make by synthesis.

synthesizer n. an electronic musical instrument producing sounds by generating and combining signals of different frequencies.

synthetic adj. **1** made by chemical synthesis, esp. to imitate a natural product. **2** not genuine. ■ **synthetically** adv.

syphilis n. a serious sexually transmitted disease. ■ **syphilitic** adj.

syringe n. a tube with a nozzle and piston for sucking in and forcing out liquid. ▶v. spray liquid into or over with a syringe.

syrup (US **sirup**) n. a thick sweet liquid. ■ **syrupy** adj.

system n. **1** a set of things working together as a mechanism or network. **2** a person's or animal's body. **3** an organized scheme or method. **4** orderliness. ■ **systematize** (or **-ise**) v.

Thesaurus

3 IN SYMPATHY WITH, well disposed to, favourably disposed to, approving of, pro, on someone's side. ■ OPPOSITES unsympathetic.

sympathize v. SHOW/FEEL SYMPATHY FOR, be sympathetic towards, show compassion for, be compassionate towards, commiserate with, pity, offer condolences to, console, comfort, be supportive of, show understanding to, empathize with.

sympathy n. COMPASSION, commiseration, pity, condolence, consolation, comfort, solace, support, caring, concern, solicitude, solicitousness, consideration, kindness, kind-heartedness, warmth, warm-heartedness, charity, charitableness, understanding, empathy. ■ OPPOSITES indifference.

symptom n. SIGN, indication, signal, warning, mark, characteristic, feature, token, evidence, demonstration, display.

symptomatic adj. INDICATIVE OF, signalling, characteristic of, suggesting, suggestive of.

synthesis n. COMBINATION, combining, union, unification, blend, merging, amalgamation, fusion, coalescence, integration.

synthetic adj. MANUFACTURED, man-made, fake, artificial, mock, ersatz. ■ OPPOSITES real, natural.

system n. **1** STRUCTURE, organization, order, arrangement, set-up. **2** METHOD, methodology, technique, procedure,

systematic adj. done or acting according to a system. ■ **systematically** adv.

systemic adj. of or affecting an entire system.

Thesaurus

process, approach, practice, line, means, way, modus operandi, programme, policy, scheme, plan. **3** METHODICALNESS, systematization, orderliness, planning, logic, routine.

systematic adj. STRUCTURED, organized, methodical, orderly, well ordered, planned, systematized, logical, efficient, businesslike. ■ OPPOSITES unsystematic, chaotic.

Tt

T n. (**to a T**) informal to perfection. □ **T-bone** a piece of loin steak containing a T-shaped bone. **T-junction** a junction where one road joins another at right angles without crossing it. **T-shirt** a short-sleeved casual top. **T-square** a T-shaped instrument for drawing or testing right angles.

ta exclam. informal thank you.

tab n. a small projecting flap or strip. □ **keep tabs on** informal monitor the activities of.

tabard n. a short sleeveless tunic.

tabby n. (pl. **tabbies**) a grey or brown cat with dark stripes.

tabernacle n. **1** (in the Bible) a tent for the Ark of the Covenant. **2** (in the RC church) a container for the Eucharist. **3** a place of worship for some religions.

table n. **1** a piece of furniture with a flat top supported by legs. **2** a set of facts or figures displayed in rows or columns. ▶ v. present formally for discussion at a meeting. □ **tableland** a plateau of land. **tablespoon** a large spoon for serving food. **table tennis** a game played with bats and a light hollow ball on a table.

tableau /tab-loh/ n. (pl. **tableaux**) a group of models or motionless figures representing a scene.

table d'hôte /tah-bluh doht/ n. a restaurant meal at a fixed price and with limited choices.

tablet n. **1** a slab on which an inscription is written. **2** a disc-shaped or cylindrical pill.

tabloid n. a small-sized newspaper written in a popular style.

taboo n. (pl. **taboos**) a ban or restriction made by social custom. ▶ adj. banned or restricted by social custom.

tabular adj. arranged in columns or tables.

tabulate v. arrange in columns or tables. ■ **tabulation** n.

tachograph n. a tachometer recording engine speeds over a period of time.

tachometer /ta-kom-i-ter/ n. an instrument measuring the speed of an engine.

tachycardia /taki-kah-di-uh/ n. an abnormally rapid heart rate.

tacit adj. understood or meant without being stated. ■ **tacitly** adv.

taciturn adj. saying little. ■ **taciturnity** n.

tack n. **1** a small broad-headed nail. **2** a long stitch used to fasten fabrics together temporarily. **3** a course of action. **4** an act of tacking in sailing. **5** equipment used in horse riding. ▶ v. **1** fasten or fix with tacks. **2** (**tack on**) add as an extra. **3** change course by turning a sailing boat into the wind, esp. repeatedly.

tackle n. **1** the equipment needed for a task or sport. **2** a set of ropes and pulleys for lifting heavy objects. **3** an act of tackling in sport. ▶ v. **1** try to deal with a difficult task. **2** confront someone about a difficulty. **3** (in soccer, rugby, etc.) try to take the ball from or prevent the movement of an opponent.

Thesaurus

table n. **1** COUNTER, bar, buffet, bench, stand. **2** LIST, catalogue, tabulation, inventory, itemization, index. ▶ v. SUBMIT, put forward, propose, suggest, move, enter.

tablet n. **1** SLAB, panel, stone. **2** PILL, capsule, lozenge. **3** BAR, cake.

taboo adj. FORBIDDEN, prohibited, banned, proscribed, vetoed, ruled out, outlawed, not permitted, not acceptable, frowned on, beyond the pale. ▶ n. PROHIBITION, proscription, veto, interdiction, interdict, ban.

tacit adj. IMPLICIT, understood, implied, taken for granted, unstated, un-

declared, unspoken, silent, wordless. ■ OPPOSITES explicit.

taciturn adj. UNFORTHCOMING, uncommunicative, reticent, untalkative, tight-lipped, close-mouthed, quiet, silent. ■ OPPOSITES loquacious.

tack n. **1** DRAWING PIN, nail, pin, staple, rivet. **2** COURSE/LINE OF ACTION, method, approach, process, way, policy. ▶ v. NAIL, pin, staple, fix, fasten, affix, put up/down.

tackle n. EQUIPMENT, apparatus, outfit, tools, implements, accoutrements, paraphernalia, things, trappings; informal gear, stuff. ▶ v. **1** UNDERTAKE, attempt,

tacky adj. (**tackier**, **tackiest**) **1** (of glue etc.) not fully dry. **2** informal showing poor taste and quality.

taco n. (pl. **tacos**) a folded tortilla filled with spicy meat or beans.

tact n. sensitivity and skill in dealing with others. ■ **tactful** adj. **tactfully** adv. **tactless** adj. **tactlessly** adv.

tactic n. **1** an action intended to achieve something. **2** (**tactics**) the directing and organizing of armed forces and equipment during a war. ■ **tactician** n.

tactical adj. **1** planned to achieve a particular end. **2** (of weapons) for use in direct support of military operations. **3** (of voting) done to prevent the leading candidate from winning by supporting whoever is next strongest. ■ **tactically** adv.

tactile adj. **1** of the sense of touch. **2** liking to touch others.

tadpole n. the larva of a frog or toad etc. at the stage when it has gills and a tail.

taffeta n. a shiny silk or similar synthetic fabric.

tag n. **1** a label. **2** an electronic device attached to someone to monitor their movements. **3** a much repeated quotation or phrase. **4** the pointed end of a shoelace. ▶v. (**tagging**, **tagged**) **1** attach a tag to. **2** (**tag on**) add at the end. **3** (**tag along**) accompany someone without being invited.

tagliatelle /tal-yuh-tel-li/ pl. n. pasta in narrow ribbons.

t'ai chi /ty chee / n. a Chinese martial art and system of exercises.

tail n. **1** the part sticking out at the rear of an animal. **2** the rear part of an aircraft. **3** the final, more distant, or weaker part. **4** (**tails**) the side of a coin without the image of a head. **5** (**tails**) informal a tailcoat. ▶v. **1** secretly follow and observe. **2** (**tail off**) become smaller or weaker. □ **tailback** a long queue of traffic. **tailcoat** a man's formal coat with a long divided flap at the back. **tailgate 1** a hinged flap at the back of a truck. **2** the door at the back of an estate or hatchback car. **tail light** a light at the back of a vehicle. **tailplane** the horizontal part of an aircraft's tail. **tailspin** a spinning dive by an aircraft. **tailwind** a wind blowing from behind.

tailor n. a person who makes men's clothing for individual customers. ▶v. **1** make clothes to fit individual customers. **2** make or adapt for a particular purpose. □ **tailor-made** made for a particular purpose.

taint n. a trace of an undesirable quality. ▶v. make impure; contaminate.

take v. (**taking**, **took**; past part. **taken**) **1** reach for and hold. **2** occupy a place or position. **3** gain possession of by force. **4** carry or bring with one. **5** remove. **6** use. **7** accept. **8** require. **9** react to or interpret. **10** endure. **11** study or teach a subject. ▶n. **1** a sequence of sound or film recorded at one time. **2** an amount gained or acquired. □ **be taken with/by** find appealing. **take after** resemble a parent. **takeaway 1** a restaurant or shop selling cooked food to be eaten elsewhere. **2** a

Thesaurus

apply/address oneself to, get to grips with, set/go about, get to work at, embark on, set one's hand to, take on, engage in. **2** GRAPPLE WITH, seize, take hold of, confront, face up to; informal have a go at.

tacky[1] adj. STICKY, gluey, gummy; informal gooey.

tacky[2] adj. TAWDRY, tasteless, kitsch, vulgar, crude, garish, gaudy, flashy, trashy, cheap; informal flash, naff. ■ OPPOSITES tasteful.

tact n. DIPLOMACY, discretion, sensitivity, understanding, thoughtfulness, consideration, delicacy, subtlety, finesse, skill, perception, judgement, prudence, judiciousness.

tactful adj. DIPLOMATIC, politic, discreet, sensitive, understanding, thoughtful, considerate, delicate, subtle, perceptive, prudent, judicious.

tactic n. MANOEUVRE, expedient, device, stratagem, trick, scheme, plan, ploy, course/line of action, method, approach, tack, means.

tactical adj. STRATEGIC, politic, planned, shrewd, skilful, adroit, clever, cunning, artful; informal smart.

tactless adj. UNDIPLOMATIC, impolitic, indiscreet, insensitive, inconsiderate, indelicate, unsubtle, rough, crude, clumsy, awkward, inept, bungling, maladroit, gauche, undiscerning, imprudent, injudicious.

tag n. **1** LABEL, ticket, sticker, docket. **2** QUOTATION, stock phrase, platitude, cliché, epithet. ▶v. LABEL, put a ticket/sticker on, mark.

tail n. BRUSH, scut, dock. ▶v. FOLLOW, shadow, stalk, trail, track, dog, keep under surveillance.

tailor n. OUTFITTER, dressmaker, couturmeal of such food. **take back** retract a statement. **take in 1** deceive. **2** make a garment tighter. **3** understand. **take off 1** become airborne. **2** mimic. **3** depart hastily. **take-off** an act of taking off. **take on 1** employ. **2** undertake. **take over** assume control. **takeover** an act of taking over. **take to 1** fall into the habit of. **2** develop a liking or ability for. **3** go to a place to escape danger. **take up 1** adopt a pursuit. **2** occupy time or space. **3** pursue a matter. **4** accept an offer. **take up with** begin to associate with.

takings pl. n. money received for goods sold.

talc n. **1** talcum powder. **2** a soft mineral.

talcum powder n. a powder used to make the skin feel smooth and dry.

tale n. a story.

talent n. natural ability or skill. ■ **talented** adj.

talisman n. (pl. **talismans**) an object believed to bring good luck.

talk v. **1** speak in order to give information or express ideas or feelings. **2** have the power of speech. **3** (**talk back**) reply disrespectfully. ▶n. **1** conversation. **2** an address or lecture. **3** (**talks**) formal discussions. □ **talking-to** informal a reprimand.

talkative adj. fond of talking.

tall adj. of great or specified height. □ **a tall order** a difficult task. **a tall story** an implausible account.

tallow n. animal fat used to make candles and soap.

tally n. (pl. **tallies**) **1** a current score or amount. **2** a record of this. ▶v. (**tallying**, **tallied**) agree or correspond.

Talmud n. the ancient writings on Jewish law and legend. ■ **Talmudic** adj.

talon n. a claw of a bird of prey.

tambourine n. a percussion instrument with jingling metal discs.

tame adj. **1** (of an animal) not dangerous or frightened of people. **2** unexciting. ▶v. make tame or easier to control. ■ **tamely** adv.

Tamil n. **1** a member of a people of South India and Sri Lanka. **2** their language.

tamp v. pack down firmly.

tamper v. (**tamper with**) interfere with.

tampon n. a plug of soft material insert-

Thesaurus

ier, clothier, costumier. ▶v. FIT, suit, fashion, style, mould, shape, adapt, adjust, modify, convert, alter, accommodate.

take v. **1** GET/LAY HOLD OF, grasp, grip, clutch. **2** OBTAIN, receive, get, gain, acquire, secure, procure, come by, win. **3** SEIZE, catch, capture, arrest, carry off, abduct. **4** REMOVE, appropriate, make off with, steal, pilfer, purloin, pocket; informal filch, swipe, pinch, nick. **5** RESERVE, book, engage, rent, hire, lease. **6** TRAVEL BY/ON, use, make use of, utilize. **7** USE UP, require, call for, need, necessitate. **8** CARRY, fetch, bring, bear, transport, convey, cart, ferry. **9** ESCORT, accompany, conduct, guide, lead, usher, convoy. ■ OPPOSITES give. □ **take off** see IMITATE (2).

takings pl. n. PROCEEDS, returns, receipts, earnings, winnings, pickings, profit, gain, income, revenue.

tale n. STORY, narrative, anecdote, legend, fable, myth, parable, allegory, epic, saga; informal yarn.

talent n. FLAIR, aptitude, facility, knack, bent, ability, capacity, faculty, aptness, endowment, strong point, forte, genius.

talented adj. GIFTED, accomplished, able, capable, apt, deft, adept, proficient, bril-

liant, expert, artistic. ■ OPPOSITES incapable, inept.

talk v. **1** SPEAK, give voice/utterance, discourse, chat, chatter, gossip, prattle, prate, gibber, jabber, babble, rattle on, gabble; informal yak, gab, natter, rabbit. **2** COMMUNICATE, converse, speak to each other, discuss things, confer, consult each other, have negotiations, parley; informal chew the fat/rag, jaw, rap. ▶n. **1** TALKING, speaking, chatter, chatting, gossiping, prattling; informal nattering. **2** LECTURE, speech, address, discourse, oration, sermon, disquisition. **3** GOSSIP, rumour, hearsay, tittle-tattle.

talkative adj. LOQUACIOUS, garrulous, voluble, chatty, gossipy, conversational, long-winded, gushing, effusive; informal gabby, mouthy. ■ OPPOSITES taciturn.

tall adj. **1** BIG, colossal, gigantic, lanky, rangy, gangling. **2** HIGH, lofty, towering, soaring, sky-high. ■ OPPOSITES short.

tally n. COUNT, record, total, reckoning, enumeration, register, roll, census, poll. ▶v. AGREE, accord, concur, coincide, conform, correspond, match, fit, harmonize. ■ OPPOSITES disagree.

tame adj. **1** DOMESTICATED, gentle. **2** UNEXCITING, uninteresting, uninspired, dull, bland, flat, insipid, vapid, prosaic, humed into the vagina to absorb menstrual blood.

tan n. **1** a yellowish-brown colour. **2** a suntan. ▶v. (**tanning**, **tanned**) **1** develop a suntan. **2** convert animal skin into leather. ▶ abbrev. tangent.

tandem n. a bicycle for two riders, one behind the other. ▢ **in tandem 1** alongside each other. **2** one behind another.

tandoori adj. (of Indian food) cooked in a clay oven.

tang n. a strong taste or smell. ■ **tangy** adj.

tangent n. **1** a straight line that touches a curve but does not cross it. **2** the ratio of the sides (other than the hypotenuse) opposite and adjacent to an angle in a right-angled triangle. **3** a completely different line of thought or action. ■ **tangential** adj.

tangerine n. a small orange citrus fruit.

tangible adj. **1** able to be perceived by touch. **2** definite or real. ■ **tangibility** n. **tangibly** adv.

tangle v. **1** twist into a confused mass. **2** informal come into conflict. ▶n. a confused mass or muddle.

tango n. (pl. **tangos**) a ballroom dance.

tank n. **1** a large container for liquid or gas. **2** a heavy armoured fighting vehicle moving on a continuous metal track.

tankard n. a tall beer mug.

tanker n. a ship, vehicle, or aircraft for carrying liquid in bulk.

tannery n. (pl. **tanneries**) a place where animal skins are tanned.

tannin (or **tannic acid**) n. a bitter substance present in tea, grapes, etc.

tannoy n. trademark a public address system.

tantalize (or **-ise**) v. tease with the sight or promise of something unobtainable.

tantalum n. a hard metallic element.

tantamount adj. (**tantamount to**) equivalent in seriousness to.

tantra n. a Hindu or Buddhist text on mystical practices. ■ **tantric** adj.

tantrum n. an uncontrolled outburst of anger and frustration.

tap n. **1** a light blow. **2** a device for controlling a flow of liquid or gas from a pipe or container. **3** a device for listening secretly to telephone conversations. ▶v. (**tapping**, **tapped**) **1** knock gently. **2** draw liquid from a barrel, cask, etc. **3** take some of a supply. **4** connect a device to a telephone to listen secretly to conversations. ▢ **on tap** informal readily available. **tap dancing** a style of dancing performed in shoes fitted with metal pieces on the toes and heels. **taproot** a plant's chief root.

tapas pl. n. small Spanish savoury dishes.

tape n. **1** light, flexible material in a narrow strip, used to hold, fasten, or mark off something. **2** magnetic tape. **3** a cassette or reel containing magnetic tape. ▶v. **1** record on magnetic tape. **2** fasten, attach, or mark off with tape. ▢ **tape measure** a strip of tape marked for measuring length. **tape recorder** a device for recording and reproducing sounds on magnetic tape. **tapeworm** a ribbon-like worm living as a parasite in intestines.

taper v. **1** reduce in thickness towards one end. **2** (**taper off**) gradually lessen. ▶n. a thin candle.

tapestry n. (pl. **tapestries**) a piece of thick fabric with a design woven or

Thesaurus

drum, boring, tedious, wearisome. ■ OPPOSITES wild. ▶v. **1** DOMESTICATE, break, train. **2** SUBDUE, discipline, curb, control, master, overcome, suppress, repress, humble.

tamper v. MEDDLE, interfere, monkey around, mess about, tinker, fiddle.

tan v. BECOME SUNTANNED, suntan, take a suntan/tan, brown, go/turn brown, darken.

tangible adj. **1** TOUCHABLE, palpable, tactile, visible. **2** CONCRETE, real, actual, solid, substantial, hard, well documented, definite, clear. ■ OPPOSITES abstract.

tangled adj. **1** ENTANGLED, twisted, snarled, ravelled, knotted, knotty, matt-

ed, tousled, messy. **2** CONFUSED, jumbled, mixed up, messy, chaotic, complicated, involved, convoluted, complex. ■ OPPOSITES neat, straight, simple.

tank n. CONTAINER, receptacle, cistern, vat.

tantalize v. TEASE, torment, torture, frustrate, disappoint, thwart, lead on, entice, titillate, allure, beguile.

tantamount adj. (**tantamount to**) EQUIVALENT TO, equal to, as good as, synonymous with.

tape n. **1** BAND, strip, string, ribbon. **2** TAPE RECORDING, cassette, videotape, video cassette, video, audio tape, audio cassette. ▶v. **1** BIND, tie, fasten, stick, seal. **2** RECORD, tape-record, videoembroidered on it.

tapioca n. starchy grains used for puddings etc.

tapir /tay-peer/ n. a piglike animal with a flexible snout.

tappet n. a moving part in a machine which transmits motion from one part to another.

tar n. **1** a dark, thick liquid distilled from wood or coal. **2** a similar substance formed by burning tobacco. ▶v. (**tarring, tarred**) coat with tar.

taramasalata n. a creamy dip made from fish roe.

tarantella n. a fast whirling dance.

tarantula n. a large hairy spider.

tardy adj. (**tardier, tardiest**) **1** late. **2** slow to act or respond. ■ **tardily** adv. **tardiness** n.

tare n. **1** a weed. **2** the weight of a vehicle without its fuel or load.

target n. **1** a person or thing that is the aim of an attack. **2** a result which one aims to achieve. ▶v. (**targeting, targeted**) **1** select as an object of attack. **2** aim or direct.

tariff n. **1** a tax to be paid. **2** a list of fixed charges.

tarmac n. **1** trademark broken stone mixed with tar for surfacing roads etc. **2** an area surfaced with this. ▶v. (**tarmacking, tarmacked**) surface with tarmac.

tarn n. a small mountain lake.

tarnish v. **1** cause metal to lose its shine. **2** make less respected. ▶n. a dull film or stain.

tarot /ta-roh/ n. a set of cards for fortune-telling.

tarpaulin n. a sheet of heavy waterproof cloth.

tarragon n. a herb.

tarsus n. (pl. **tarsi**) the set of small bones in the ankle and upper foot.

tart n. **1** an open pastry case with a filling. **2** informal a prostitute. ▶v. (**tart up**) informal improve the appearance of. ▶adj. **1** sour. **2** (of a remark etc.) sharp or hurtful. ■ **tartly** adv. **tartness** n.

tartan n. a woollen cloth woven in a pattern of coloured checks and lines.

tartar n. **1** a hard deposit forming on teeth. **2** a deposit formed during the fermentation of wine.

tartare sauce n. mayonnaise mixed with gherkins and capers.

tartrazine n. a yellow dye used to colour food.

task n. a piece of work to be done. □ **take to task** reprimand. **task force** a group organized for a special task. **taskmaster** a person who makes others work hard.

tassel n. a decorative tuft of threads knotted at one end. ■ **tasselled** adj.

taste n. **1** the sensation perceived by the tongue on contact with a substance. **2** the ability to perceive this. **3** a small portion of food or drink tried as a sample. **4** a brief experience. **5** a liking. **6** the ability to judge what is good quality or appropriate behaviour. ▶v. **1** perceive or test the flavour of. **2** have a particular flavour. **3** have a brief experience of. ■ **taster** n.

tasteful adj. showing good judgement as to quality etc. ■ **tastefully** adv.

tasteless adj. **1** lacking flavour. **2** showing poor judgement as to quality etc. ■ **tastelessly** adv.

tasty adj. (**tastier, tastiest**) having a

Thesaurus

record, video.

taper v. NARROW, thin, become narrow/thinner, come to a point. ■ OPPOSITES thicken. □ **taper off** see DECREASE.

target n. **1** OBJECTIVE, goal, object, aim, end, intention. **2** BUTT, victim, scapegoat.

tariff n. **1** PRICE LIST/SCHEDULE, list of charges. **2** TAX, duty, toll, excise, levy, impost.

tarnish v. **1** DULL, dim, discolour, rust. **2** SULLY, besmirch, blacken, stain, blemish, blot, taint, befoul, drag through the mud. ■ OPPOSITES polish, enhance.

tart[1] n. PASTRY, flan, tartlet, quiche, pie.

tart[2] adj. SHARP, sour, tangy, piquant, pungent, bitter, acid, acidulous, vinegary. ■ OPPOSITES sweet.

task n. JOB, duty, chore, charge, assign-

ment, commission, mission, engagement, occupation, undertaking, exercise, errand, quest.

taste n. **1** FLAVOUR, savour, relish, tang. **2** MORSEL, bite, mouthful, spoonful, sample, sip, drop, swallow, touch, soupçon. **3** LIKING, love, fondness, fancy, desire, preference, penchant, predilection, inclination, partiality, leaning, bent, hankering, appetite, palate, thirst, hunger. **4** DISCRIMINATION, discernment, judgement, refinement, polish, finesse, elegance, grace, stylishness. ▶v. **1** SAMPLE, test, try, nibble, sip, sup. **2** MAKE OUT, perceive, discern, distinguish, differentiate.

tasteful adj. IN GOOD TASTE, aesthetic, artistic, harmonious, pleasing, elegant, graceful, beautiful, pretty, charming, pleasant flavour.

tat n. informal tasteless or badly made articles.

tattered adj. ragged.

tatters pl. n. torn pieces.

tattle n. & v. gossip.

tattoo n. (pl. **tattoos**) **1** a permanent design made on the skin with a needle and ink. **2** a military display with music and marching. **3** a rhythmic tapping. ▶v. mark the skin with a tattoo. ■ **tattooist** n.

tatty adj. (**tattier**, **tattiest**) informal worn and shabby.

taught past & past part. of **TEACH**.

taunt n. a jeering or mocking remark. ▶v. anger or upset with taunts.

taupe /tohp/ n. a greyish brown.

taut adj. stretched tight. ■ **tauten** v. **tautly** adv.

tautology n. (pl. **tautologies**) the saying of the same thing over again in different words. ■ **tautological** adj. **tautologous** adj.

tavern n. old use an inn or pub.

taverna n. a Greek restaurant.

tawdry adj. (**tawdrier**, **tawdriest**) showy but cheap and of poor quality. ■ **tawdriness** n.

tawny adj. of an orange-brown or yellowish-brown colour.

tax n. money that must be paid to the state. ▶v. **1** impose a tax on. **2** make heavy demands on. □ **tax return** a form on which a person states their income, used for tax assessment. ■ **taxable** adj. **taxation** n.

taxi n. (or **taxicab**) (pl. **taxis**) a car licensed to transport passengers in return for payment of a fare. ▶v. (**taxiing**, **taxied**) (of an aircraft) move slowly along the ground before take-off or after landing.

taxidermy n. the art of preparing and stuffing the skins of dead animals to make them look lifelike. ■ **taxidermist** n.

taxonomy n. the scientific classification of organisms. ■ **taxonomic** adj.

TB abbrev. tuberculosis.

tbsp (or **tbs**) abbrev. tablespoonful.

tea n. **1** a drink made by soaking the dried leaves of an Asian shrub in boiling water. **2** these leaves. **3** an afternoon or evening meal. □ **tea bag** a sachet of tea leaves on to which boiling water is poured to make tea. **teacake** a light, sweet currant bun. **tea towel** (or **tea cloth**) a cloth for drying washed crockery etc. **teaspoon** a small spoon for stirring tea etc.

teach v. (**teaching**, **taught**) **1** give lessons in a subject to a class or pupil. **2** show someone how to do something. ■ **teacher** n.

teak n. hard wood from a SE Asian tree.

team n. **1** a group of players forming one side in a competitive sport. **2** two or more people or animals working together. ▶v. **1** (**team up**) work together. **2** (**team with**) match with. □ **teamwork** organized effort as a group.

tear[1] v. (**tearing**, **tore**; past part. **torn**) **1** rip a hole in. **2** pull apart or to pieces. **3** informal move very quickly. ▶n. a hole or split caused by tearing. □ **tearaway** a wild or reckless person.

tear[2] n. a drop of clear salty liquid form-

Thesaurus

handsome, discriminating, refined, restrained. ■ OPPOSITES tasteless.

tasteless adj. **1** FLAVOURLESS, bland, insipid, watery, watered down, weak, thin, unappetizing, uninteresting, vapid. **2** VULGAR, crude, tawdry, garish, gaudy, loud, kitsch, flashy, showy, cheap, meretricious; informal tacky. ■ OPPOSITES tasteful.

tasty adj. FLAVOURSOME, full-flavoured, appetizing, palatable, toothsome, delectable, delicious, luscious, mouthwatering, piquant, pungent, spicy; informal scrumptious, yummy, fingerlicking. ■ OPPOSITES bland.

taunt v. GIBE AT, jeer at, sneer at, insult, chaff, tease, torment, provoke, ridicule, deride, mock, poke fun at.

taut adj. TIGHT, stretched, rigid, flexed, tensed. ■ OPPOSITES slack.

tawdry adj. SHOWY, gaudy, flashy, garish, loud, tasteless, cheap, cheapjack, shoddy, meretricious, Brummagem; informal flash, tatty, tacky, kitsch. ■ OPPOSITES tasteful.

tax n. LEVY, charge, duty, toll, excise, tariff, impost, tribute. ▶v. **1** LEVY A TAX ON, impose a toll on, charge duty on. **2** MAKE DEMANDS ON, weigh heavily on, weigh down, burden, load, encumber, overload, push, stretch, strain, try, wear out, exhaust, sap, drain, enervate, fatigue, tire, weary, weaken.

teach v. **1** GIVE LESSONS TO, instruct, educate, school, tutor, coach, train, drill, ground, enlighten. **2** GIVE LESSONS/INSTRUCTION IN, instil, inculcate, impart.

teacher n. SCHOOLTEACHER, schoolmaster, schoolmistress, master, mistress, instructor, educator, tutor, coach, training in and falling from a person's eye. □ **in tears** crying. **teardrop** a single tear. **tear gas** gas causing severe irritation to the eyes. ■ **tearful** adj. **tearfully** adv.

tease v. **1** playfully make fun of or attempt to provoke. **2** gently pull into separate strands. ▶ n. informal a person who teases.

teasel n. a plant with spiny flower heads.

teat n. **1** a nipple on a woman's breast or an animal's udder. **2** a plastic device through which milk can be sucked from a bottle.

technetium n. a radioactive metallic element.

technical adj. **1** of a particular subject, craft, etc. **2** of the practical use of machinery and methods in science and industry. **3** requiring specialized knowledge to be understood. **4** according to the law or rules when applied strictly. ■ **technically** adv.

technicality n. (pl. **technicalities**) a small formal detail in a set of rules.

technician n. **1** a person employed to look after technical equipment. **2** an expert in the techniques of a subject or craft.

Technicolor n. trademark a process of producing cinema films in colour.

technique n. **1** a way of doing something. **2** practical skill.

technocracy n. (pl. **technocracies**) a social or political system in which technical experts have great power. ■ **technocrat** n.

technology n. (pl. **technologies**) the application of scientific knowledge for practical purposes. ■ **technological**

adj. **technologically** adv. **technologist** n.

tectonic adj. of the earth's crust.

teddy (or **teddy bear**) n. (pl. **teddies**) a soft toy bear.

tedious adj. very long or boring. ■ **tediously** adv. **tedium** n.

tee n. **1** a space from which a golf ball is struck at the start of each hole. **2** a small peg for supporting a golf ball on a tee. ▶ v. (**teeing, teed**) **1** (**tee up**) place the ball on a tee. **2** (**tee off**) begin a round or hole in golf.

teem v. **1** (**teem with**) be full of or swarming with. **2** (of rain) fall heavily.

teenager n. a person aged between 13 and 19 years. ■ **teenage** (or **teenaged**) adj.

teens pl. n. the years of age from 13 to 19.

teeny adj. (**teenier, teeniest**) informal tiny.

teepee n. var. of TEPEE.

tee shirt n. a T-shirt.

teeter v. move or balance unsteadily.

teeth pl. of TOOTH.

teethe v. (of a baby) develop its first teeth. □ **teething troubles** short-term problems in the early stages of a project.

teetotal adj. choosing not to drink alcohol. ■ **teetotaller** n.

TEFL abbrev. teaching of English as a foreign language.

Teflon n. trademark a non-stick coating for saucepans etc.

telecommunications n. communication over a distance by cable, telephone, broadcasting, etc.

telegram n. a message sent by telegraph.

Thesaurus

er, lecturer, professor, don, pedagogue, guide, mentor, guru.

team n. GROUP, band, bunch, company, gang, crew, troupe, squad, side, line-up.

tear[1] n. RIP, split, hole, rent, run, rupture. ▶ v. RIP, split, rend, sever, rive, sunder, rupture.

tear[2] n. TEARDROP, drop, droplet, globule, bead.

tearful adj. IN TEARS, crying, weeping, weepy, sobbing, blubbering, snivelling, whimpering, wailing; informal blubbing. ■ OPPOSITES cheerful.

tease v. MOCK, ridicule, poke fun at, torment, provoke, badger, bait, goad, pest, bother, worry, vex, irritate, annoy, gibe; informal needle.

technical adj. **1** PRACTICAL, mechanical,

scientific, technological. **2** SPECIALIST, specialized, scientific.

technique n. **1** METHOD, system, procedure, style, manner, way, course of action, mode, fashion, means. **2** EXECUTION, skill, skilfulness, proficiency, expertise, expertness, mastery, artistry, art, craftsmanship, craft, ability.

tedious adj. WEARISOME, wearying, tiresome, tiring, fatiguing, soporific, overlong, long-winded, prolix, dull, deadly dull, boring, uninteresting, dry, dreary, drab, unexciting, lifeless, uninspired, flat, banal, vapid, insipid, monotonous, unvaried, prosaic, humdrum, run-of-the-mill, routine. ■ OPPOSITES exciting, interesting.

teem v. ABOUND, be abundant, be plenti-

telegraph n. a system or device for sending messages from a distance along a wire. ■ **telegraphic** adj. **telegraphy** n.

telekinesis n. the supposed ability to move objects by mental power.

telepathy n. supposed communication by means other than the senses. ■ **telepathic** adj.

telephone n. a device for transmitting speech over a distance using wire or radio. ▶v. call or speak to using the telephone. ■ **telephonic** adj. **telephonically** adv. **telephony** n.

telephonist n. an operator of a telephone switchboard.

telephoto lens n. a lens that produces a magnified image of a distant object.

teleprinter n. a device for transmitting telegraph messages as they are keyed.

telesales n. the selling of goods or services by telephone.

telescope n. an optical instrument for making distant objects appear nearer. ▶v. **1** (of an object made up of several tubes) slide into itself so as to become smaller. **2** condense. ■ **telescopic** adj.

teletext n. an information service transmitted to televisions.

televise v. show on television.

television n. **1** a system for transmitting visual images with sound and displaying them electronically on a screen. **2** a device with a screen for receiving television signals. **3** the activity or medium of broadcasting on television. ■ **televisual** adj.

telex n. **1** a system of telegraphy using teleprinters and the public telecommunications network. **2** a message sent by telex.

tell v. (**telling, told**) **1** communicate information to. **2** instruct to do something. **3** relate a story. **4** (**tell on**) informal report the wrongdoings of. **5** (**tell off**) informal reprimand. **6** determine or perceive. **7** distinguish. **8** have a noticeable or revealing effect. ■ **tellingly** adv.

teller n. **1** a bank cashier. **2** a person appointed to count votes. **3** a narrator.

telltale adj. revealing something. ▶n. a person who reports others' wrongdoings.

tellurium n. a silvery-white crystalline element.

telly n. (pl. **tellies**) informal a television.

temerity n. excessive confidence or boldness.

temp informal n. a temporary employee. ▶v. work as a temp.

temper n. **1** a state of mind as regards calmness or anger. **2** an angry state of mind. ▶v. **1** harden a metal by reheating and then cooling it. **2** moderate or neutralize. □ **keep** (or **lose**) **one's temper** manage (or fail to manage) to control one's anger.

tempera n. a method of painting using colours mixed with egg.

temperament n. a person's nature in terms of the effect it has on their behaviour.

temperamental adj. **1** of or caused by temperament. **2** tending to change mood in an unreasonable way. ■ **temperamentally** adv.

Thesaurus

ful, be copious, swarm, crawl, bristle, seethe, brim.

teetotaller n. ABSTAINER, non-drinker, Rechabite.

telephone n. PHONE, handset, receiver; informal blower. ▶v. CALL, call up, phone, ring up, ring; informal get on the blower to, buzz.

telescope v. CONCERTINA, crush, squash, squeeze, compress, compact. ■ OPPOSITES elongate.

television n. TV; informal telly, the box, goggle-box, small screen; US informal the tube, idiot box.

tell v. **1** MAKE KNOWN, impart, communicate, announce, proclaim, broadcast, divulge, reveal, disclose, declare, state, mention, utter, voice, say, speak. **2** INFORM, let know, make aware, apprise, notify. **3** INSTRUCT, order, give orders, command, direct, bid, charge, enjoin,

dictate to, call upon, require. **4** DISTINGUISH, differentiate, discriminate.

telling adj. MARKED, significant, substantial, considerable, important, striking, impressive, potent, powerful, forceful, effective, influential, decisive. ■ OPPOSITES insignificant.

temper n. **1** TEMPERAMENT, disposition, nature, humour, mood, character, frame of mind, mind, attitude, stamp. **2** BAD MOOD, ill humour, fury, rage, passion, fit of temper/pique, tantrum; informal paddy. ▶v. **1** TOUGHEN, anneal, harden, strengthen, fortify. **2** MODERATE, soften, tone down, modify, mitigate, alleviate, allay, palliate, mollify, assuage, lessen, weaken.

temperament n. DISPOSITION, nature, humour, mood, character, personality, make-up, constitution, complexion, temper, spirit, mettle, frame of mind,

temperance n. complete avoidance of alcohol.

temperate adj. **1** (of a climate) having mild temperatures. **2** showing self-control.

temperature n. **1** the degree of heat or cold. **2** a body temperature above normal.

tempest n. a violent storm.

tempestuous adj. **1** stormy. **2** full of strong and changeable emotion.

template n. a shaped piece of rigid material used as a pattern for cutting out etc.

temple n. **1** a building for the worship of a god or gods. **2** the flat part between the forehead and the ear.

tempo n. (pl. **tempos** or **tempi**) **1** the speed of a piece of music. **2** the pace of an activity or process.

temporal adj. **1** of time. **2** of worldly affairs. **3** of or situated in the temples of the head. ■ **temporally** adv.

temporary adj. lasting for a limited time. ■ **temporarily** adv.

temporize (or **-ise**) v. delay making a decision.

tempt v. entice someone to do some-

thing against their better judgement. ■ **temptation** n. **tempter** n. **tempting** adj. **temptress** n.

ten adj. & n. one more than nine; 10 or X. ■ **tenfold** adj. & adv.

tenable adj. able to be defended or upheld.

tenacious adj. holding firmly to something. ■ **tenaciously** adv. **tenacity** n.

tenancy n. (pl. **tenancies**) use of land or property as a tenant.

tenant n. a person who rents land or property from a landlord.

tend v. **1** frequently behave in a particular way or have a certain characteristic. **2** take care of.

tendency n. (pl. **tendencies**) an inclination to behave in a particular way.

tendentious adj. promoting a particular point of view.

tender adj. **1** gentle and kind. **2** easy to cut or chew. **3** painful to the touch. **4** easily damaged. ▶ v. **1** offer formally. **2** make a formal written offer to carry out work, supply goods, etc. for a stated fixed price. ▶ n. **1** a tendered offer. **2** a vehicle used by a fire service for carrying equipment. **3** a wagon attached to a

Thesaurus

cast of mind, mind, attitude, outlook stamp, quality.

temperamental adj. **1** CONSTITUTIONAL, inherent, innate, inborn, congenital, deep-rooted, ingrained. **2** EXCITABLE, emotional, volatile, mercurial, oversensitive, capricious, erratic, touchy, moody, hot-headed, explosive, impatient, petulant. ■ OPPOSITES calm.

temperance n. MODERATION, self-control, abstemiousness, continence, abstinence, self-denial. ■ OPPOSITES alcoholism.

temperate adj. MODERATE, mild, gentle, clement, balmy, pleasant, agreeable. ■ OPPOSITES extreme.

tempestuous adj. STORMY, turbulent, boisterous, violent, wild, uncontrolled, unrestrained, passionate, impassioned, emotional, intense, fierce. ■ OPPOSITES calm.

temple n. PLACE OF WORSHIP, holy place, shrine, sanctuary.

tempo n. BEAT, rhythm, cadence, throb, pulse.

temporal adj. SECULAR, non-spiritual, worldly, material, earthly, carnal. ■ OPPOSITES spiritual.

temporary adj. **1** SHORT-TERM, impermanent, interim, provisional, pro tem. **2** BRIEF, fleeting, passing, momentary,

short-lived, transient, transitory, ephemeral, fugitive, evanescent. ■ OPPOSITES permanent.

tempt v. ENTICE, lure, attract, appeal to, seduce, tantalize, incite, persuade, induce, egg on, urge, goad, prompt, sway, influence, cajole, coax. ■ OPPOSITES discourage, deter.

tempting adj. ALLURING, enticing, attractive, captivating, appealing, beguiling, fascinating, tantalizing, appetizing, mouth-watering. ■ OPPOSITES uninviting, off-putting.

tenable adj. JUSTIFIABLE, defensible, defendable, arguable, maintainable, supportable, plausible, credible, reasonable, rational, sound, viable. ■ OPPOSITES untenable.

tenacious adj. PERSISTENT, pertinacious, determined, dogged, resolute, firm, steadfast, purposeful, unshakeable, unswerving, relentless, inexorable, unyielding, inflexible, stubborn, obstinate, intransigent, obdurate, strong-willed.

tend[1] v. HAVE/SHOW A TENDENCY TO, incline towards, be apt/disposed/liable to, be likely to.

tend[2] v. LOOK AFTER, take care of, care for, attend to, minister to, see to, cater to, nurse, wait on, watch over, watch. ■ OPPOSITES neglect.

steam locomotive to carry fuel and water. ■ **tenderly** adv. **tenderness** n.

tendon n. a strong band of tissue attaching a muscle to a bone.

tendril n. **1** a thread-like part by which a climbing plant clings. **2** a slender curl of hair.

tenement n. a large house divided into flats.

tenet n. a central principle or belief.

tenner n. informal a ten-pound note.

tennis n. a game in which players use rackets to strike a ball over a net stretched across an open court.

tenon n. a projecting piece of wood shaped to fit into a mortise.

tenor n. **1** the highest ordinary adult male singing voice. **2** the general meaning or nature of something.

tense adj. **1** stretched tight. **2** anxious or nervous. ▶v. make or become tense. ▶n. a set of forms of a verb indicating the time of the action. ■ **tensely** adv.

tensile adj. **1** of tension. **2** able to be stretched.

tension n. **1** the state of being stretched tight. **2** mental or emotional strain. **3** a strained political or social state. **4** voltage of specified magnitude.

tent n. a portable fabric shelter supported by poles.

tentacle n. a long, thin, flexible part of certain animals, used for feeling or grasping.

tentative adj. **1** hesitant. **2** not certain. ■ **tentatively** adv.

tenterhook n. (**on tenterhooks**) in a state of nervous suspense.

tenth adj. & n. next after ninth; 10th.

tenuous adj. **1** very slight. **2** very thin. ■ **tenuously** adv.

tenure n. the holding of a job, or of land or buildings.

tepee (or **teepee**) n. a conical tent used by American Indians.

tepid adj. lukewarm.

tequila n. a Mexican alcoholic spirit.

tercentenary n. (pl. **tercentenaries**) a 300th anniversary.

tergiversation n. evasive or ambiguous language.

term n. **1** a word or phrase. **2** (**terms**) conditions laid down or agreed. **3** (**terms**) relations: *on good terms.* **4** a period for which something lasts. **5** each period in the year during which teaching is given in a school or college. **6** each quantity in a mathematical ratio, series, etc. ▶v. call by a specified term. □ **come to terms with** become able to accept or deal with. ■ **termly** adj. & adv.

termagant n. a bad-tempered or overbearing woman.

terminal adj. **1** of or situated at the end. **2** (of a disease) predicted to lead to death. ▶n. **1** the station at the end of a railway or bus route. **2** an airport building for passengers arriving and departing. **3** a point of connection in an electric circuit. **4** a keyboard and screen connected to a central computer system. ■ **terminally** adv.

terminate v. come or bring to an end. ■ **termination** n.

terminology n. (pl. **terminologies**) the

Thesaurus

tendency n. INCLINATION, disposition, predisposition, proclivity, propensity, proneness, aptness, bent, leaning, penchant, susceptibility, liability.

tender adj. **1** EASILY DAMAGED, breakable, fragile, frail, delicate, sensitive. **2** COMPASSIONATE, soft-hearted, kind, kindly, sympathetic, warm, caring, humane, gentle, solicitous, benevolent, sentimental. **3** LOVING, affectionate, warm, emotional, amorous. **4** SORE, painful, aching, smarting, throbbing, inflamed, irritated, red, raw, bruised. ■ OPPOSITES tough, hard-hearted.

tense adj. **1** TIGHT, taut, rigid, stretched, strained. **2** ANXIOUS, nervous, keyed up, worked up, overwrought, distraught, uneasy, worried, apprehensive, agitated, jumpy, edgy, on edge, restless, fidgety; *informal* uptight, wound up, jittery. ■ OPPOSITES relaxed.

tension n. **1** TIGHTNESS, tautness, rigidity. **2** ANXIETY, stress, stressfulness, suspense, pressure, strain, unease, disquiet, worry, apprehensiveness, agitation, jumpiness, edginess, restlessness.

tentative adj. **1** SPECULATIVE, conjectural, exploratory, trial, provisional, test, pilot, untried, unproven. **2** HESITANT, hesitating, faltering, wavering, uncertain, unsure, doubtful, cautious, diffident, timid. ■ OPPOSITES definite, confident.

tenuous adj. SLIGHT, flimsy, weak, insubstantial, shaky, sketchy, doubtful, dubious, nebulous, hazy, vague, unspecific, indefinite. ■ OPPOSITES definite.

term n. **1** WORD, expression, phrase, name, title, appellation, designation, denomination. **2** PERIOD, time, spell, interval, stretch, span, duration. ▶v. CALL, name, entitle, style, dub, label, tag, set of terms used in a subject. ■ **terminological** adj.

terminus n. (pl. **termini** or **terminuses**) a railway or bus terminal.

termite n. a small insect which eats wood.

tern n. a seabird.

ternary adj. composed of three parts.

terrace n. **1** a raised flat area, esp. forming part of a tier. **2** a patio. **3** a row of houses built in one block. ■ **terraced** adj.

terracotta n. **1** unglazed, brownish-red pottery. **2** a brownish-red colour.

terra firma n. dry land.

terrain n. land with regard to its physical features.

terrapin n. a freshwater turtle.

terrarium /ter-rair-i-uhm/ n. (pl. **terrariums** or **terraria**) an enclosed container in which small reptiles are kept or plants are grown.

terrestrial adj. **1** of the earth. **2** (of an animal or plant) living on or in the ground. **3** (of television broadcasting) not using a satellite.

terrible adj. very bad, serious, or unpleasant. ■ **terribly** adv.

terrier n. a small dog.

terrific adj. **1** very great or intense. **2** informal excellent. ■ **terrifically** adv.

terrify v. (**terrifying**, **terrified**) cause to feel terror.

terrine n. a mixture of chopped meat, fish, etc. pressed into a container and served cold.

territorial adj. of, having, or defending a territory. ■ **territorially** adv.

Territorial Army n. a voluntary military reserve force.

territory n. (pl. **territories**) **1** an area under the control of a ruler or state. **2** an area defended by an animal against others. **3** an area in which one has rights, responsibilities, or knowledge.

terror n. **1** extreme fear. **2** a cause of this. **3** informal a very annoying person.

terrorist n. a person who uses violence and intimidation to try to achieve political aims. ■ **terrorism** n.

terrorize (or **-ise**) v. threaten and frighten over a period of time.

terry n. a towelling fabric.

terse adj. using few words. ■ **tersely** adv. **terseness** n.

tertiary /ter-shuh-ri/ adj. third in order or level.

tessellated adj. decorated with mosaics. ■ **tessellation** n.

test n. **1** a procedure to establish the quality, performance, presence, etc. of something. **2** a short examination of skill or knowledge. **3** (also **test match**) an international cricket or rugby match. ▶v. subject to a test. □ **test tube** a thin glass tube closed at one end, used to hold material in laboratory tests. **test-tube baby** informal a baby conceived by in vitro fertilization. ■ **tester** n.

testament n. **1** a will. **2** evidence or

Thesaurus

designate, denominate.

terminal adj. FATAL, deadly, mortal, lethal, killing, incurable. ▶n. **1** TERMINUS, last stop, depot. **2** WORKSTATION, visual display unit, VDU.

terminate v. BRING TO A CLOSE/END/CONCLUSION, close, end, conclude, finish, stop, wind up, discontinue. ■ OPPOSITES commence.

terminology n. LANGUAGE, phraseology, vocabulary, nomenclature, jargon, terms, expressions, words; informal lingo.

terrible adj. **1** GREAT, extreme, incorrigible, outrageous, awful, dreadful, frightful, impossible. **2** BAD, poor, incompetent, useless, talentless; informal rotten, duff. **3** DREADFUL, terrifying, frightening, frightful, horrifying, horrible, horrific, horrendous, terrific, harrowing, hideous, grim, unspeakable, appalling, awful, gruesome.

terrific adj. **1** TREMENDOUS, great, very great, very big, huge, sizeable, considerable, intense, extreme, extraordinary, excessive. **2** VERY GOOD, excellent, superb, remarkable, magnificent, wonderful, marvellous, great, sensational; informal super, fantastic, fabulous, fab, A1, ace, unreal, awesome.

terrify v. FRIGHTEN, scare stiff, scare, petrify, make someone's hair stand on end, alarm, panic, intimidate.

territory n. **1** REGION, area, terrain, tract. **2** AREA, province, field, sector, department.

terror n. FRIGHT, dread, alarm, panic, intimidation, dismay, consternation, shock, horror; informal heebie-jeebies.

terrorize v. STRIKE TERROR IN/INTO, terrify, scare stiff, petrify, horrify.

terse adj. **1** CONCISE, succinct, compact, brief, short, to the point, crisp, pithy, elliptical, epigrammatic. **2** ABRUPT, curt, brusque, laconic, short, clipped, blunt. ■ OPPOSITES long-winded.

test n. **1** TRIAL, experiment, pilot study,

proof. **3 (Testament)** each of the two divisions of the Bible.

testate adj. having made a valid will before dying.

testator n. (fem. **testatrix**) a person who has made a will.

testicle n. either of the two organs producing sperm in male mammals. ■ **testicular** adj.

testify v. (pl. **testifying, testified**) **1** give evidence in a law court. **2** serve as evidence or proof.

testimonial n. **1** a formal statement of a person's good character and qualifications. **2** a public tribute.

testimony n. (pl. **testimonies**) **1** a formal statement, esp. one given in a law court. **2** evidence or proof.

testis n. (pl. **testes**) a testicle.

testosterone n. a male sex hormone.

testy adj. irritable. ■ **testily** adv.

tetanus n. a disease causing muscular spasms and rigidity.

tetchy adj. bad-tempered and irritable. ■ **tetchily** adv.

tête-à-tête /tet-ah-tet/ n. a private conversation between two people.

tether n. a rope or chain used to tie an animal to a post, fence, etc. ▶ v. tie with a tether.

tetrahedron n. (pl. **tetrahedra** or **tetrahedrons**) a solid with four triangular faces.

Teutonic adj. German.

text n. **1** a written or printed work. **2** the main body of a book as distinct from illustrations etc. **3** a passage from the Bible as the subject of a sermon. ▶ v. send someone a text message. □ **textbook** a book of information for use in studying a subject. **text message** an electronic message sent and received via mobile phone. ■ **textual** adj.

textile n. a woven or knitted fabric.

texture n. the feel or consistency of a substance. ▶ v. give a rough texture to. ■ **textural** adj.

thalidomide n. a sedative drug which was found to cause malformation of the fetus when taken during pregnancy.

thallium n. a toxic metallic element.

than conj. & prep. used to introduce the second part of a comparison.

thank v. express gratitude to. ▶ n. (**thanks**) **1** an expression of gratitude. **2** thank you. □ **thanksgiving** the expression of gratitude to God. **Thanksgiving** a national holiday held in the autumn in North America. **thank you** a polite expression of gratitude.

thankful adj. feeling or expressing gratitude. ■ **thankfulness** n.

Thesaurus

try-out, check, examination, assessment, evaluation, appraisal, investigation, inspection, analysis, scrutiny, study, probe, exploration, screening. **2** EXAM, examination; *US* quiz. ▶ v. **1** TRY OUT, trial, put through its paces, experiment with, pilot, check, examine, assess, evaluate, appraise, investigate, analyse, scrutinize, study, probe, explore, sample, screen. **2** PUT A STRAIN ON, tax, try, make demands on, stretch, challenge.

testament n. TESTIMONY, witness, evidence, proof, attestation, demonstration, indication, exemplification.

testify v. **1** GIVE EVIDENCE, bear witness, give one's testimony, attest. **2** ATTEST, swear, state on oath, declare, assert, affirm, allege, submit, claim. **3** BE EVIDENCE/PROOF OF, attest to, confirm, prove, corroborate, substantiate, bear out, show, demonstrate, bear witness to, indicate.

testimonial n. REFERENCE, character reference, recommendation, commendation, credential, endorsement.

testimony n. **1** EVIDENCE, sworn statement, attestation, affidavit, statement,

declaration, assertion, affirmation, allegation, submission, claim. **2** TESTAMENT, proof, evidence, attestation, witness, confirmation, corroboration, demonstration, indication.

testing adj. DIFFICULT, challenging, tough, hard, demanding, taxing, stressful. ■ OPPOSITES easy.

tetchy adj. IRRITABLE, cantankerous, irascible, bad-tempered, grumpy, grouchy, crotchety, crabby, testy, crusty, curmudgeonly, ill-tempered, ill-humoured, peevish, cross, fractious, pettish, crabbed, prickly, waspish; *informal* shirty, stroppy, narky, ratty; *US informal* cranky, ornery.

tether v. TIE (UP), hitch, rope, chain, fasten, secure. ▶ n. ROPE, chain, cord, lead, leash, restraint, halter.

text noun **1** TEXTBOOK, book, work. **2** THEME, subject, topic, motif, thesis, argument. **3** PASSAGE, extract, quotation, verse, line, reading.

texture n. FEEL, touch, appearance, surface, grain.

thank v. OFFER/EXTEND THANKS TO, express/show gratitude to, show appreciation to.

thankfully adv. **1** in a thankful way. **2** fortunately.

thankless adj. unpleasant and unlikely to be appreciated by others.

that pron. & adj. (pl. **those**) referring to a person or thing seen or heard or already mentioned or known, or to the more distant of two things. ▶ pron. introducing a clause defining or identifying something. ▶ adv. to such a degree. ▶ conj. introducing a statement or suggestion.

thatch n. a roof covering of straw, reeds, etc. ▶ v. cover with thatch. ■ **thatcher** n.

thaw v. **1** make or become unfrozen. **2** make or become friendlier. ▶ n. **1** a period of warmer weather that thaws ice and snow. **2** an increase in friendliness.

the adj. used to refer to one or more people or things already mentioned or understood; the definite article.

theatre (US **theater**) n. **1** a building in which plays etc. are performed. **2** the writing and production of plays. **3** a room for lectures with seats in tiers. **4** a room where surgical operations are performed.

theatrical adj. **1** of acting, actors, or the theatre. **2** exaggerated for effect. ▶ n. (**theatricals**) theatrical performances. ■ **theatricality** n. **theatrically** adv.

thee pron. old use you (as the singular object of a verb or preposition).

theft n. stealing.

their adj. of or belonging to them.

···
✓ Don't confuse **their** with **there**, which means 'in, at, or to that place or position'
···

theirs possess. pron. belonging to them.

···
✓ No apostrophe: thei**rs**.
···

theism /thee-i-z'm/ n. belief in a god or gods, esp. as creator of the universe. ■ **theist** n. **theistic** adj.

them pron. used as the object of a verb or preposition to refer to two or more people or things previously mentioned, or to a person of unspecified sex.

theme n. **1** a subject being discussed. **2** a prominent or frequently recurring melody in a musical piece. □ **theme park** an amusement park based around a particular idea. ■ **thematic** adj. **thematically** adv.

themselves pron. **1** used when a group of people or things or a person of unspecified sex performing an action are also affected by it. **2** they or them personally.

then adv. **1** at that time. **2** after that. **3** in that case.

thence adv. formal from that place or source. □ **thenceforth** from that time onward.

theocracy n. (pl. **theocracies**) a system of government by priests. ■ **theocratic** adj.

theodolite n. a surveying instrument for measuring angles.

theology n. (pl. **theologies**) **1** the study of God and religious belief. **2** a system of religious beliefs. ■ **theologian** n. **theological** adj. **theologist** n.

theorem n. a scientific or mathematical proposition that can be proved by reasoning.

theoretical adj. concerning or based on theory rather than practice. ■ **theoretically** adv.

theorize (or **-ise**) v. form a theory or theories about something. ■ **theorist** n.

Thesaurus

···

thankful adj. GRATEFUL, appreciative, pleased, indebted, obliged, under an obligation, beholden. ■ OPPOSITES ungrateful.

thankless adj. UNAPPRECIATED, unrewarded, unrewarding, unacknowledged, vain, in vain, fruitless, useless. ■ OPPOSITES rewarding.

thanks pl. n. GRATITUDE, gratefulness, appreciation, acknowledgement, recognition.

thaw v. DEFROST, unfreeze, melt, soften, liquefy. ■ OPPOSITES freeze.

theatre n. **1** DRAMA, dramaturgy, the stage, show business; informal show biz.

2 AUDITORIUM, hall, playhouse.

theatrical adj. **1** DRAMATIC, stage, dramaturgical, thespian. **2** OSTENTATIOUS, melodramatic, histrionic, emotional, exaggerated, overdone, dramatic, showy, affected, mannered, stilted; informal hammy.

theft n. STEALING, robbery, thieving, thievery, burglary, larceny, misappropriation, pilfering, purloining, shoplifting, embezzlement.

theme n. **1** TOPIC, subject, subject matter, matter, thesis, text, argument. **2** THEME SONG, melody, tune, air, leitmotif.

theory n. (pl. **theories**) **1** a set of ideas intended to explain something. **2** a set of principles on which an activity is based.

theosophy n. a philosophy believing that knowledge of God is achievable through intuition and meditation. ■ **theosophical** adj.

therapeutic adj. **1** of the curing of disease. **2** having a good effect on the body or mind. ■ **therapeutically** adv.

therapy n. (pl. **therapies**) treatment for a physical or mental disorder. ■ **therapist** n.

there adv. **1** in, at, or to that place or position. **2** on that issue. □ **thereabouts** near that place, time, or figure. **thereafter** after that time. **thereby** by that means. **therefore** for that reason. **therein** formal in that place, document, or respect. **thereof** formal of that. **thereupon** formal immediately after that.

....

☑ Don't confuse **there** with **their**, which means 'belonging to them'.

....

thermal adj. **1** of heat. **2** (of a garment) made of a fabric providing good insulation. ▶n. an upward current of warm air.

thermodynamics n. the study of the relations between heat and other forms of energy.

thermometer n. an instrument for measuring temperature.

thermonuclear adj. of or using nuclear reactions occurring at very high temperatures.

thermoplastic adj. (of a substance) becoming soft when heated and hardening when cooled.

Thermos n. trademark a vacuum flask.

thermosetting adj. (of a substance) setting permanently when heated.

thermostat n. a device that regulates temperature automatically. ■ **thermostatic** adj. **thermostatically** adv.

thesaurus n. (pl. **thesauri** or **thesauruses**) a book containing lists of synonyms.

these pl. of **THIS**.

thesis n. (pl. **theses**) **1** a theory put forward to be supported or proved. **2** a long essay written as part of a university degree.

thespian adj. of the theatre. ▶n. an actor or actress.

theta n. the eighth letter of the Greek alphabet (Θ, θ).

they pron. **1** the people or things or person of unspecified sex previously mentioned. **2** people in general.

thiamine (or **thiamin**) n. vitamin B$_1$, found in unrefined cereals, beans, and liver.

thick adj. **1** with opposite sides or surfaces relatively far apart. **2** made up of a large number of things close together. **3** dense or difficult to see through. **4** relatively firm in consistency. **5** informal stupid. **6** informal very friendly. ▶n. (**the thick**) the busiest or most intense part. □ **thickset** heavily or solidly built. **thick-skinned** not sensitive to criticism etc. ■ **thicken** v. **thickly** adv. **thickness** n.

thicket n. a dense group of bushes or trees.

thief n. (pl. **thieves**) a person who steals.

thieve v. steal. ■ **thievery** n.

thigh n. the part of the leg between the hip and the knee.

thimble n. a hard cap worn to protect the end of the finger in sewing.

thin adj. (**thinner, thinnest**) **1** not thick. **2** having little fat on the body. **3** (of a sound) faint and high-pitched. **4** weak and inadequate. ▶v. (**thinning, thinned**) make or become thinner. ■ **thinly** adv. **thinness** n.

Thesaurus

theoretical adj. HYPOTHETICAL, conjectural, suppositional, speculative, notional, postulatory, assumed, presumed. ■ OPPOSITES proven.

theory n. HYPOTHESIS, thesis, conjecture, supposition, speculation, guess, notion, postulation, assumption, presumption, opinion, view.

therapy n. **1** TREATMENT, remedy, cure. **2** PSYCHOTHERAPY, psychoanalysis.

thesis n. **1** THEORY, hypothesis, contention, argument, proposal, proposition, premise, postulation, idea. **2** DISSERTATION, paper, treatise, disquisition, essay, composition, monograph.

thick adj. **1** BROAD, wide, large, big, bulky, solid, substantial, fat; informal beefy. **2** DENSE, close-packed, concentrated, crowded, condensed. **3** OPAQUE, heavy, dense, soupy, murky, impenetrable. ■ OPPOSITES thin.

thicken v. SET, gel, solidify, congeal, clot, coagulate, cake.

thief n. ROBBER, burglar, housebreaker, larcenist, pilferer, shoplifter, pickpocket, embezzler, bandit, swindler, fraudster, mugger.

thieve v. STEAL, rob, pilfer, purloin, em-

thine possess. pron. & adj. old use your or yours.

thing n. **1** an inanimate object. **2** an unspecified object, activity, thought, etc. **3** (**things**) belongings. **4** (**the thing**) informal what is needed, acceptable, or fashionable.

think v. (**thinking, thought**) **1** have a particular opinion or belief. **2** use or direct one's mind. **3** (**think of/about**) take into account or consideration. **4** (**think up**) informal devise. ▶ n. an act of thinking. □ **think better of** reconsider and decide not to do. **think tank** a body of experts providing advice and ideas. ■ **thinker** n.

thinner n. a solvent used to thin paint etc.

third adj. & n. **1** next after second. **2** each of three equal parts. □ **third-degree** (of burns) affecting tissue below the skin. **the third degree** long and harsh questioning. **third party 1** a person or group besides the two main ones involved in a situation. **2** (of insurance) covering damage or injury suffered by a person other than the insured. **third-rate** of very poor quality. **Third World** the developing countries of Asia, Africa, and Latin America. ■ **thirdly** adv.

thirst n. **1** a feeling of needing or wanting to drink. **2** a strong desire. ▶ v.

(**thirst for/after**) have a strong desire for. ■ **thirstily** adv. **thirsty** adj.

thirteen adj. & n. one more than twelve; 13 or XIII. ■ **thirteenth** adj. & n.

thirty adj. & n. (pl. **thirties**) ten less than forty; 30 or XXX. ■ **thirtieth** adj. & n.

this pron. & adj. (pl. **these**) referring to the person or thing near, mentioned, or indicated. ▶ adv. to the degree or extent indicated.

thistle n. a prickly plant. □ **thistledown** the light fluff on thistle seeds.

thither adv. old use to or towards that place.

thong n. **1** a narrow strip of leather etc. used as a fastening. **2** a G-string.

thorax n. (pl. **thoraces** or **thoraxes**) the part of the body between the neck and the abdomen. ■ **thoracic** adj.

thorn n. **1** a stiff, sharp woody projection on a plant. **2** a thorny bush or tree. ■ **thorny** adj.

thorough adj. **1** complete with regard to every detail. **2** very careful and detailed. □ **thoroughbred** an animal of pure breed. **thoroughfare** a road or path between two places. ■ **thoroughly** adv. **thoroughness** n.

those pl. of THAT.

thou pron. old use singular form of 'you'.

though conj. despite the fact that. ▶ adv. however.

Thesaurus

bezzle, swindle; informal swipe, filch, rip off, nick, knock off.

thin adj. **1** SLIM, slender, lean, slight, svelte, light, skinny, spindly, scrawny, scraggy, bony, skeletal, wasted, emaciated, shrunken, anorexic, undernourished, underweight. **2** FINE, light, delicate, flimsy, diaphanous, gossamer, sheer, transparent, see-through, gauzy, filmy, translucent. **3** SPARSE, scarce, scanty, meagre, paltry, scattered. **4** FLIMSY, insubstantial, weak, feeble, lame, poor, shallow, unconvincing, inadequate, insufficient. ■ OPPOSITES fat. ▶ v. **1** DILUTE, water down, weaken. **2** REDUCE IN NUMBER, lessen, decrease, diminish, dwindle.

thing n. **1** OBJECT, article; informal whatchamacallit, whatsit, thingummy, thingamabob, thingamajig. **2** ACTION, act, deed, exploit, feat, undertaking, task, job, chore.

think v. **1** BELIEVE, suppose, expect, imagine, surmise, conjecture, guess, fancy. **2** CONSIDER, deem, hold, reckon, regard as, assume, presume, estimate. **3** PONDER, meditate, deliberate, contem-

plate, muse, cogitate, ruminate, concentrate, brood, rack one's brains, be lost in thought, be in a brown study.

thinker n. PHILOSOPHER, scholar, sage, theorist, intellect; informal brain.

thirst n. **1** THIRSTINESS, dryness, dehydration. **2** DESIRE, craving, longing, hankering, yearning, avidity, keenness, eagerness, hunger, lust, appetite, passion, covetousness; informal yen. □ **thirst for/after** DESIRE, crave, long for, hanker after, yearn for, hunger after, lust after, covet.

thirsty adj. **1** PARCHED, dehydrated, dry. **2** THIRSTING, avid, keen, eager, hungry, greedy, covetous.

thong n. STRIP, belt, strap, cord, lash, rope, tie, tether.

thorny adj. **1** PRICKLY, spiky, barbed, spiny, spined, spinose, bristly, sharp, pointed. **2** see DIFFICULT (2).

thorough adj. **1** IN-DEPTH, exhaustive, complete, comprehensive, intensive, extensive, widespread, sweeping, all-embracing, all-inclusive, detailed. **2** METICULOUS, scrupulous, assiduous, conscientious, painstaking, punctilious,

thought past & past part. of THINK. ▶ n.
1 an idea. **2** the process of thinking.
3 careful consideration.

thoughtful adj. **1** deep in thought.
2 thought out carefully. **3** considerate.
■ **thoughtfully** adv.

thoughtless adj. **1** inconsiderate.
2 without thinking of the consequences. ■ **thoughtlessly** adv.

thousand adj. & n. ten hundred; 1,000 or
M. ■ **thousandth** adj. & n.

thrall n. the state of being in another's
power.

thrash v. **1** beat repeatedly and violently. **2** move in a violent or uncontrolled
way. **3** informal defeat heavily. **4** (**thrash
out**) discuss thoroughly.

thread n. **1** a long, thin strand of cotton,
nylon, etc. **2** the spiral ridge of a screw
etc. **3** a theme running through a situation or piece of writing. ▶ v. **1** pass a
thread through. **2** move or weave in
and out of obstacles. □ **threadbare**
worn and tattered with age.

threat n. **1** a stated intention to harm
someone. **2** a person or thing likely to
cause harm or danger.

threaten v. **1** make a threat to or to do.

2 put at risk.

three adj. & n. one more than two; 3 or
III. □ **three-dimensional** having or appearing to have length, breadth, and
depth. **threesome** a group of three
people. ■ **threefold** adj. & adv.

thresh v. **1** separate grain from the
husks of corn etc. **2** move about wildly.

threshold n. **1** a strip of wood or stone
forming the bottom of a doorway. **2** a
level or point marking the start of
something.

> ✓ There is only one *h* in the middle:
> threshold.

threw past of THROW.

thrice adv. old use three times.

thrift n. economy in the use of resources.
■ **thrifty** adj.

thrill n. **1** a sudden feeling of excitement.
2 an exciting experience. **3** a wave of
emotion. ▶ v. have or cause to have a
thrill. ■ **thrilling** adj.

thriller n. an exciting novel, play, or
film, esp. involving crime.

thrive v. (**thriving**, **thrived** or **throve**;
past part. **thrived** or **thriven**) **1** grow or

Thesaurus

methodical, careful. **3** THOROUGHGOING,
out-and-out, utter, downright, sheer, absolute, unmitigated, unqualified, complete, total, perfect. ■ OPPOSITES cursory, careless.

thought n. **1** THINKING, reasoning, pondering, meditation, cogitation, rumination, musing, mulling, reflection,
introspection, contemplation, consideration, cerebration. **2** IDEA, notion, line
of thinking, theory, opinion.

thoughtful adj. **1** PENSIVE, reflective,
introspective, meditative, contemplative, ruminative, cogitative, absorbed,
rapt/lost in thought, in a brown study.
2 PROFOUND, deep, serious, pithy, meaty,
weighty. **3** CONSIDERATE, attentive, caring, solicitous, helpful, kind, kindly,
compassionate, tender, charitable.
■ OPPOSITES thoughtless.

thoughtless adj. **1** TACTLESS, undiplomatic, indiscreet, insensitive, inconsiderate, careless, selfish, impolite, rude.
2 UNTHINKING, heedless, careless, unmindful, absent-minded, injudicious,
ill-advised, ill-considered, imprudent,
unwise, foolish, silly, stupid, reckless,
rash, precipitate, negligent, remiss.
■ OPPOSITES thoughtful.

thrash v. BEAT, whip, horsewhip, flog,
lash, birch, cane, flagellate, scourge,

leather, spank, chastise, belt, wallop.

thread n. **1** YARN, cotton, filament, fibre.
2 STRAND, line, streak, strip, seam.

threadbare adj. WORN, frayed, tattered,
ragged, holey, shabby.

threat n. **1** THREATENING REMARK, warning,
ultimatum. **2** DANGER, peril, hazard,
menace, risk. **3** POSSIBILITY, chance,
probability, likelihood, risk.

threaten v. **1** MAKE THREATS, menace, intimidate, browbeat, bully, pressurize,
lean on. **2** BE IMMINENT, impend, hang
over, loom, foreshadow.

threatening adj. **1** MENACING, warning,
intimidating, bullying, minatory. **2** OM-
INOUS, inauspicious, foreboding.

threshold n. **1** DOORWAY, doorstep, entrance. **2** BEGINNING, commencement,
start, outset, inception, opening, dawn,
brink, verge, debut; informal kick-off.

thrifty adj. ECONOMICAL, careful, frugal,
sparing, scrimping, parsimonious,
penny-pinching, miserly. ■ OPPOSITES
spendthrift.

thrill n. **1** EXCITEMENT, sensation of joy,
wave of pleasure, glow, tingle; informal
buzz, charge, kick. **2** THROB, tremble,
tremor, quiver, flutter, shudder, vibration. ▶ v. EXCITE, stimulate, arouse, stir,
electrify, move, give joy/pleasure to;
informal give a buzz/charge/kick to.

develop well. **2** prosper.

throat n. **1** the passage from the back of the mouth to the oesophagus and lungs. **2** the front of the neck.

throaty adj. (of a voice) deep and husky. ■ **throatily** adv.

throb v. (**throbbing**, **throbbed**) **1** beat or sound with a strong rhythm. **2** feel regular bursts of pain. ▶n. a strong, regular beat or sound.

throes pl. n. severe or violent pains. □ **in the throes of** struggling in the midst of.

thrombosis n. (pl. **thromboses**) the formation of a blood clot in a blood vessel or the heart.

throne n. **1** a ceremonial chair for a monarch or bishop. **2** the power or rank of a monarch.

throng n. a densely packed crowd. ▶v. gather in large numbers in a place.

throttle n. a device controlling the flow of fuel or power to an engine. ▶v. strangle.

through prep. & adv. **1** from end to end or side to side of. **2** from start to finish. **3** by means of. ▶adj. **1** (of public transport) continuing to the final destination. **2** passing straight through a place. **3** having passed to the next stage of a competition. □ **throughout** all the way through. **throughput** the amount of material processed.

throve past of THRIVE.

throw v. (**throwing**, **threw**; past part. **thrown**) **1** send through the air from one's hand. **2** move or place hurriedly or roughly. **3** direct or cast light, a look, etc. somewhere. **4** send suddenly into a particular state. **5** confuse; put off. **6** form pottery on a wheel. ▶n. **1** an act of throwing, or the distance thrown. **2** a light cover for furniture. □ **throw**

away discard as useless. **throwback** a return to an earlier ancestral type or characteristic. **throw up** vomit.

thrum v. (**thrumming**, **thrummed**) make a rhythmic humming sound.

thrush n. **1** a brown songbird with spotted breast. **2** a fungal infection of the mouth and throat or the genitals.

thrust v. (**thrusting**, **thrust**) **1** push suddenly or violently. **2** make one's way forcibly. ▶n. **1** a thrusting force or movement. **2** the main point of an argument.

thud n. a dull, heavy sound. ▶v. (**thudding**, **thudded**) move or fall with a thud.

thug n. a violent man. ■ **thuggery** n. **thuggish** adj.

thumb n. the short, thick first digit of the hand. ▶v. **1** turn over pages with the thumb. **2** request a lift in a passing vehicle by signalling with the thumb. □ **under someone's thumb** completely under someone's control. **thumbnail** brief or concise.

thump v. **1** hit heavily. **2** (of the heart) beat rapidly. ▶n. a heavy blow or noise.

thunder n. **1** a loud rumbling or crashing noise heard after lightning. **2** a loud, deep noise. ▶v. **1** make the sound of thunder. **2** move noisily and forcefully. **3** speak loudly and angrily. □ **thunderbolt** a flash of lightning with a crash of thunder. **thunderclap** a crash of thunder. **thunderstorm** a storm with thunder and lightning. **thunderstruck** very surprised. ■ **thunderous** adj. **thundery** adj.

Thursday n. the day before Friday.

thus adv. formal **1** as a result of this. **2** in this way.

thwack v. strike with a heavy blow. ▶n. a heavy blow.

Thesaurus

■ OPPOSITES bore.

thrilling adj. EXCITING, stirring, electrifying, rousing, moving, gripping, riveting. ■ OPPOSITES boring.

thrive v. FLOURISH, prosper, do/go well, boom, burgeon, succeed, advance, get ahead, make progress. ■ OPPOSITES decline.

throb v. BEAT, pulse, pulsate, palpitate, pound, thump.

throng n. CROWD, horde, mob, mass, host, multitude, swarm, flock, pack, herd, drove, press, assemblage, gathering, congregation.

throttle v. CHOKE, strangle, strangulate, garrotte.

throw v. **1** HURL, toss, cast, sling, pitch, shy, lob, propel, launch, project, send; informal heave, chuck. **2** CAST, project, send.

thrust v. PUSH, shove, ram, drive, press, prod, propel.

thrusting adj. FORCEFUL, pushing, forward, pushy, energetic, assertive, aggressive, insistent, ambitious. ■ OPPOSITES meek.

thug n. RUFFIAN, rough, hoodlum, bully boy, hooligan, villain, gangster; informal heavy, bovver boy, tough.

thunder n. BOOM, booming, rumble, rumbling, outburst, roar, roaring. ▶v. BOOM, rumble, roar, blast, resound,

thwart v. prevent from accomplishing something.

thy adj. old use your.

thyme /tym/ n. a sweet-smelling herb.

thymus n. (pl. **thymi**) a gland in the neck producing white blood cells for the immune system.

thyroid n. a gland in the neck producing growth hormones.

thyself pron. old use yourself.

tiara n. a woman's jewelled semicircular headdress.

tibia n. (pl. **tibiae**) the inner of the two bones between the knee and the ankle.

tic n. a recurring spasm in the muscles of the face.

tick n. **1** a mark (✓) used to show that something is correct or has been chosen or checked. **2** a regular clicking sound, as made by a clock etc. **3** a bloodsucking insect-like animal. **4** informal a moment. ▶v. **1** mark with a tick. **2** make regular ticking sounds. **3** (**tick over**) (of an engine) run slowly in neutral. **4** (**tick off**) informal reprimand. □ **on tick** on credit.

ticket n. **1** a piece of paper or card entitling the holder to enter a place or to travel on public transport. **2** an official notice of a traffic offence. **3** a label showing the price, size, etc. of an item for sale. ▶v. (**ticketing**, **ticketed**) give a ticket to.

ticking n. a strong fabric used to cover mattresses.

tickle v. **1** lightly touch in a way that causes itching or twitching and often laughter. **2** appeal to or amuse. ▶n. an act of tickling or feeling of being tickled. ■ **tickly** adj.

ticklish adj. **1** sensitive to being tickled. **2** requiring care and tact.

tidal adj. of or affected by tides. □ **tidal wave** a very large ocean wave.

tiddler n. informal a small fish.

tiddly adj. informal **1** slightly drunk.
2 tiny. □ **tiddlywinks** a game involving flicking small counters into a cup.

tide n. **1** the regular alternate rise and fall of the sea. **2** a powerful surge of feeling or trend of events. ▶v. (**tide over**) help through a difficult period.

tidings pl. n. literary news.

tidy adj. (**tidier**, **tidiest**) neat and orderly. ▶v. (**tidying**, **tidied**) make tidy. ■ **tidily** adv. **tidiness** n.

tie v. (**tying**, **tied**) **1** attach or fasten with string etc. **2** form into a knot or bow. **3** restrict. **4** connect. **5** achieve the same score as another competitor. ▶n. (pl. **ties**) **1** a thing that ties. **2** a strip of material worn beneath a collar and knotted at the front. **3** an equal score in a game or match. **4** a sports match in which the winners proceed to the next round. □ **tiebreak** a means of deciding a winner when competitors have tied. **tie in** link or agree. **tie-up** a link. **tie up 1** bind someone's arms and legs. **2** conclude. **3** informal occupy fully.

tied adj. **1** (of a house) for occupation only by someone working for its owner. **2** (of a pub) owned and controlled by a brewery.

tier n. any of a series of rows or levels placed one above and behind the other. ■ **tiered** adj.

tiff n. informal a trivial quarrel.

tiger n. a large striped member of the cat family.

tight adj. **1** closed or fastened firmly. **2** close-fitting. **3** stretched so as to leave no slack. **4** allowing little room for movement. **5** strictly imposed. **6** (of money or time) limited. ▶pl. n. (**tights**) a close-fitting stretchy garment covering the legs, hips, and bottom. □ **tightrope** a rope or wire stretched high above the ground, on which acrobats balance. ■ **tighten** v. **tightly** adv. **tightness** n.

tigress n. a female tiger.

Thesaurus

reverberate.

thunderous adj. BOOMING, rumbling, roaring, resounding, reverberating, deafening, ear-splitting, loud, noisy, tumultuous.

thwart v. FRUSTRATE, foil, baulk, check, block, stop, prevent, defeat, impede, obstruct, hinder, hamper, stymie. ■ OPPOSITES assist.

tic n. TWITCH, spasm, jerk.

ticket n. **1** PASS, token, stub, coupon, card. **2** LABEL, tag, tally.

tickle v. **1** STROKE, pet, touch. **2** AMUSE,
entertain, divert, cheer, gladden.

tide n. TIDAL FLOW, tidewater, tide race, flow, ebb, current, stream.

tidy adj. **1** NEAT, trim, orderly, in order, in good order, well ordered, spruce, shipshape, well kept, clean, spick and span. **2** ORDERLY, organized, methodical, systematic, businesslike. ▶v. CLEAN, clean up, put to rights, put in order, straighten, make shipshape, spruce up, groom, smarten, neaten, brush down.

tie v. **1** TIE UP, fasten, attach, fix, bind, secure, tether, moor, lash, join, connect,

tilde /til-duh/ n. an accent (~) placed over a letter to mark a change in pronunciation.

tile n. a thin piece of baked clay etc. for covering roofs, floors, or walls. ▶v. cover with tiles. ■ **tiling** n.

till prep. & conj. until. ▶n. a cash register or drawer for money in a shop etc. ▶v. prepare land for crops.

tiller n. a horizontal bar fitted to a boat's rudder, used for steering.

tilt v. move into a sloping position. ▶n. a sloping position. □ **(at) full tilt** with maximum speed or force.

timber n. wood prepared for use in building and carpentry. ■ **timbered** adj.

timbre /tam-ber/ n. the quality of a voice or musical sound.

time n. **1** the continuing progress of existence and events in the past, present, and future. **2** a period of time. **3** a point of time measured in hours and minutes. **4** an instance of something happening or being done. **5** (**times**) expressing multiplication. **6** rhythm in music. ▶v. **1** arrange a time for. **2** do at a certain time. **3** measure the time taken by. □ **time bomb** a bomb designed to explode at a set time. **time-honoured** (of a custom) respected because of its long existence. **timepiece** a clock or watch. **timeshare** an arrangement in which joint owners use a property as a holiday home at different times. **timetable** a list of times at which events are scheduled to take place. ■ **timer** n. **timing** n.

timeless adj. not affected by the passage of time.

timely adj. done or occurring at a good time.

timid adj. lacking courage or confidence. ■ **timidity** n. **timidly** adv.

timorous adj. timid.

timpani (or **tympani**) pl. n. kettledrums. ■ **timpanist** n.

tin n. **1** a silvery-white metallic element. **2** a metal container. **3** a sealed metal container for preserving food. ▶v. (**tinning**, **tinned**) **1** coat with tin. **2** (**tinned**) preserved in a tin. □ **tinpot** informal of poor quality.

tincture n. a medicine made by dissolving a drug in alcohol.

tinder n. dry material which burns easily.

tine n. a prong or point, esp. of a fork.

tinge n. a slight trace of a colour or quality. ▶v. (**tinging** or **tingeing**, **tinged**) give a tinge to.

tingle n. a slight prickling or stinging sensation. ▶v. have or cause a tingle.

tinker n. a travelling mender of pots, kettles, etc. ▶v. fiddle with something in at attempt to repair it.

tinkle v. & n. (make) a light, clear ringing sound.

tinnitus n. ringing or buzzing in the ears.

tinny adj. **1** having a thin, metallic

Thesaurus

link, couple, rope, chain. **2** DRAW, be equal, be even, be neck and neck.

tier n. ROW, rank, bank, line, layer, level, storey.

tight adj. **1** FAST, secure, fixed, clenched, clenched. **2** TAUT, rigid, stiff, tense, stretched, strained. **3** CRAMPED, restricted, limited, constricted. **4** STRICT, rigorous, stringent, tough, rigid, uncompromising, exacting. ■ OPPOSITES loose, slack.

tighten v. **1** TAUTEN, make tight/taut, stretch, make rigid, rigidify, stiffen, tense. **2** INCREASE, make stricter, make rigorous/stringent/rigid. ■ OPPOSITES slacken.

till v. CULTIVATE, work, farm, plough, dig, turn over.

tilt v. LEAN, list, slope, slant, incline, tip, cant.

time n. **1** AGE, era, epoch, period. **2** WHILE, spell, stretch, span, period, term. **3** OCCASION, point, juncture. **4** MOMENT, point, instant, stage. **5** RHYTHM, measure, tempo, beat, metre. ▶v. **1** CLOCK, measure, calculate, regulate, count. **2** SCHEDULE, arrange, fix, set, timetable, programme.

timeless adj. AGELESS, enduring, lasting, permanent, abiding, unending, ceaseless, undying, deathless, eternal, everlasting, immortal, changeless. ■ OPPOSITES ephemeral.

timely adj. OPPORTUNE, well timed, convenient, appropriate, seasonable, felicitous. ■ OPPOSITES ill-timed.

timetable n. SCHEDULE, programme, calendar, list, agenda. ▶v. SCHEDULE, fix, set, programme.

timid adj. **1** FEARFUL, apprehensive, timorous, afraid, frightened, scared, fainthearted, cowardly, pusillanimous; informal chicken, yellow, lily-livered. **2** SHY, diffident, bashful, reticent, timorous, shrinking, retiring, coy, demure. ■ OPPOSITES bold.

tingle v. PRICKLE, prick, tickle, itch, sting, quiver, tremble. ▶n. TINGLING, prickling, sound. **2** made of thin or poor-quality metal.

tinsel n. a decoration made of thin strips of shiny metal foil.

tint n. **1** a shade of colour. **2** a dye for colouring the hair. ▶v. colour slightly.

tiny adj. (**tinier, tiniest**) very small.

tip n. **1** the end of something thin or tapering. **2** a place where rubbish is left. **3** a small sum of money given for good service in a restaurant, taxi, etc. **4** a piece of advice. **5** a prediction as to the likely winner of a race etc. ▶v. (**tipping, tipped**) **1** overbalance so as to fall over. **2** empty out the contents of a container by holding it at an angle. **3** cover the end of something thin or tapering with a material. **4** give a tip to someone for good service. **5** predict as likely to win or achieve something. **6** (**tip off**) informal give someone secret information. ◻ **tip-off** informal a piece of secret information.

tipple v. drink alcohol regularly. ▶n. an alcoholic drink. ■ **tippler** n.

tipster n. a person who gives tips as to the likely winner of a race etc.

tipsy adj. slightly drunk. ■ **tipsily** adv.

tiptoe v. (**tiptoeing, tiptoed**) walk quietly and carefully with one's heels raised.

tirade n. a long angry speech.

tire v. **1** make or become tired. **2** (**tire of**) become impatient or bored with.

▶n. US = TYRE.

tired adj. **1** in need of sleep or rest. **2** (**tired of**) impatient or bored with. ■ **tiredness** n.

tireless adj. having or showing great energy. ■ **tirelessly** adv.

tiresome adj. annoying or tedious.

tissue n. **1** any of the substances of which animals or plants are made. **2** a disposable paper handkerchief. ◻ **tissue paper** very thin, soft paper.

tit n. a small songbird.

titanic adj. of very great size or power.

titanium n. a silver-grey metallic element.

titbit n. **1** a small piece of tasty food. **2** an item of interesting information.

tit for tat n. a situation in which one takes retaliation for an insult or injury.

tithe n. one tenth of annual income or produce, formerly paid to the Church.

titillate v. excite or stimulate pleasantly. ■ **titillation** n.

> ☑ Don't confuse **titillate** with **titivate**.

titivate v. informal make smarter or more attractive. ■ **titivation** n.

title n. **1** the name of a book, piece of music, etc. **2** a word describing a position or job, or used in speaking to someone with a particular rank or job. **3** the position of champion in a sports

Thesaurus

pricking, tickle, itch, quiver, trembling, pins and needles.

tinker FIDDLE, play, toy, tamper, fool around, mess about.

tint n. SHADE, colour, tone, tinge, cast, tincture.

tiny adj. MINUTE, diminutive, miniature, mini, minuscule, infinitesimal, microscopic, dwarfish, midget, pocket-sized, Lilliputian, wee, small, little, insignificant, trifling, negligible, inconsequential; informal teeny, teeny-weeny, itsy-bitsy, pint-sized. ■ OPPOSITES huge.

tip[1] n. **1** POINT, peak, top, summit, apex, crown. **2** END, extremity, point. ▶v. CAP, top, crown.

tip[2] n. RUBBISH DUMP, dump, refuse dump, rubbish heap, midden. ▶v. **1** TILT, lean, list, cant, slant, topple, overturn, fall over, turn topsy-turvy, capsize. **2** POUR, empty, unload, dump.

tirade n. DIATRIBE, harangue, stream of abuse, verbal onslaught, lecture, upbraiding.

tire v. **1** FATIGUE, wear out, weary, exhaust, drain, enervate, debilitate, jade; informal take it out of, whack, fag out, knacker; US informal poop; Austral./NZ informal bush. **2** GET/GROW/BECOME TIRED, get fatigued, flag, droop.

tired adj. FATIGUED, worn out, weary, wearied, exhausted, drained, enervated, debilitated, jaded; informal done, done in, all in, dead beat, dog-tired, whacked, dead on one's feet, ready to drop, fagged out, knackered, bushed; US informal pooped. ■ OPPOSITES energetic, fresh.

tireless adj. UNTIRING, unflagging, indefatigable, energetic, industrious, vigorous, determined, resolute, dogged. ■ OPPOSITES lazy.

tiresome adj. **1** WEARISOME, laborious, wearing, tedious, boring, monotonous, dull, uninteresting, unexciting, humdrum, routine. **2** TROUBLESOME, irksome, vexatious, irritating, annoying, exasperating, trying. ■ OPPOSITES interesting, pleasant.

tiring adj. WEARYING, wearing, fatiguing, exhausting, draining, enervating, arducontest. **4** the legal right to ownership of property. □ **title role** the part in a play or film from which the title is taken.

titled adj. having a title indicating nobility or rank.

titter n. & v. (give) a short, quiet laugh.

tittle-tattle n. & v. gossip.

titular adj. holding a formal position or title but no real authority.

tizzy n. (pl. **tizzies**) informal a state of nervous excitement or worry.

TNT abbrev. trinitrotoluene, a high explosive.

to prep. **1** in the direction of. **2** so as to reach a state. **3** indicating the person or thing affected. **4** indicating that a verb is in the infinitive. ▶ adv. so as to be closed or nearly closed. □ **to and fro** backwards and forwards or from side to side. **to-do** informal a commotion or fuss.

toad n. a short, stout, tailless amphibian.

toadstool n. a fungus with a rounded cap on a stalk.

toady n. (pl. **toadies**) an ingratiating person. ▶ v. act in an ingratiating way.

toast n. **1** sliced bread heated until brown and crisp. **2** an act of raising glasses and drinking together in honour of a person or thing. **3** a respected or admired person. ▶ v. **1** make bread brown and crisp by heating it. **2** drink a toast to.

toaster n. an electrical device for making toast.

tobacco n. (pl. **tobaccos**) the dried leaves of an American plant which can be smoked or chewed.

tobacconist n. a shopkeeper selling cigarettes etc.

toboggan n. a small sledge for sliding downhill. ■ **tobogganing** n.

tocsin n. old use an alarm bell or signal.

today adv. **1** on this present day. **2** at the present time. ▶ n. **1** this present day. **2** the present time.

toddle v. (of a young child) move with short unsteady steps.

toddler n. a young child who is just beginning to walk.

toddy n. (pl. **toddies**) a hot drink of spirits, water, and sugar.

toe n. any of the digits at the end of the foot. ▶ v. push or touch with the toes. □ **toe the line** obey authority. **toehold** a small foothold.

toff n. informal a rich, upper-class person.

toffee n. a sweet made by boiling together sugar and butter. □ **toffee apple** a toffee-coated apple on a stick.

tofu n. a soft food made from mashed soya beans.

tog n. **1** (**togs**) informal clothes. **2** a unit for measuring the insulating properties of duvets. ▶ v. (**be togged out/up**) informal be dressed.

toga n. a loose outer garment worn by men in ancient Rome.

together adv. **1** in company. **2** so as to touch or combine. **3** regarded as a whole. **4** at the same time.

toggle n. **1** a narrow piece of wood etc. pushed through a loop to fasten a garment. **2** a switch or key turning a function on and off alternately.

toil v. work or move laboriously. ▶ n. laborious work. ■ **toilsome** adj.

toilet n. **1** a large bowl for urinating or defecating into. **2** old use the process of washing and dressing oneself. □ **toilet water** a light perfume.

toiletries pl. n. articles used in washing and grooming oneself.

token n. **1** a thing representing a fact, quality, or feeling. **2** a voucher that can be exchanged for goods. **3** a disc used to operate a machine. ▶ adj. done just for the sake of appearances.

told past & past part. of TELL.

Thesaurus

ous, laborious, strenuous, exacting, taxing.

titillate v. EXCITE, arouse, stimulate, provoke, thrill, interest, fascinate, tantalize, seduce; informal turn on.

title n. **1** NAME, designation, denomination, appellation, epithet, sobriquet; informal moniker, handle. **2** ENTITLEMENT, right, claim, ownership, proprietorship, possession, holding. ▶ v. ENTITLE, name, call, designate, label, tag, style, term.

titter n. SNICKER, snigger, giggle, laugh, chuckle, chortle.

toast v. **1** BROWN, crisp, warm up, heat,

heat up. **2** DRINK THE HEALTH OF, drink to, pledge, salute.

toddle v. TOTTER, teeter, wobble, falter, dodder.

together adv. WITH EACH OTHER, in conjunction, jointly, in cooperation, as one, in unison, side by side, hand in hand, hand in glove, shoulder to shoulder, cheek by jowl. ■ OPPOSITES separately.

toilet n. LAVATORY, WC, ladies' room, powder room, convenience, outhouse, urinal, latrine, privy; US washroom, bathroom; informal loo, bog; US informal john, can.

tolerable adj. **1** able to be tolerated. **2** fairly good. ■ **tolerably** adv.

tolerance n. **1** the ability to tolerate something. **2** an allowable variation in the size of a machine part. ■ **tolerant** adj.

tolerate v. **1** allow to exist or happen without protest. **2** endure patiently. ■ **toleration** n.

toll n. **1** a charge payable for the use of certain bridges or roads. **2** the number of casualties arising from a disaster etc. **3** a single ring of a bell. ▶ v. (of a bell) sound with slow strokes, esp. to mark a death.

tom (or **tomcat**) n. a male cat.

tomahawk n. a light axe formerly used by American Indians.

tomato n. (pl. **tomatoes**) a red fruit eaten as a vegetable.

....

☑ No *e* at the end in the singular: *tomato*.

....

tomb n. a stone structure forming a burial place. □ **tombstone** a flat inscribed stone marking a grave.

tombola n. a lottery in which tickets are drawn from a revolving drum.

tomboy n. a girl who enjoys rough, noisy activities.

tome n. a large book.

tomfoolery n. silly behaviour.

tomography n. a technique for displaying a cross section through the body using X-rays or ultrasound.

tomorrow adv. **1** on the day after today. **2** in the near future. ▶ n. **1** the day after today. **2** the near future.

tom-tom n. a drum beaten with the hands.

ton n. **1** a unit of weight equal to 2,240 lb or 1016.05 kg (**long ton**) or (especially in the US) 2,000 lb or 907.19 kg (**short ton**). **2** a metric ton. **3** a unit of measurement of a ship's weight equal to 2,240 lb or 35 cu. ft (0.99 cu. m). **4** informal a great weight or large number.

tone n. **1** the quality of a musical sound. **2** the feeling or mood expressed in a person's voice. **3** general character. **4** a basic interval in music, equal to two semitones. **5** a shade of colour. **6** firmness in a resting muscle. ▶ v. **1** give firmness to the body or a muscle. **2** (**tone down**) make less harsh or extreme. □ **tone-deaf** unable to perceive differences of musical pitch. ■ **tonal** adj. **tonality** n. **tonally** adv. **toneless** adj.

toner n. **1** a liquid applied to the skin to reduce oiliness. **2** a powder used in photocopiers.

tongs pl. n. an implement with two joined arms for picking up and holding things.

tongue n. **1** the muscular organ in the mouth, used in tasting and speech. **2** a language. **3** a strip of leather or fabric under a shoe's laces. □ **tongue in cheek** not seriously meaning what one is saying. **tongue-tied** too nervous to speak.

tonic n. **1** a medicinal drink taken to give energy etc. **2** (also **tonic water**) a carbonated drink with a bitter flavour.

tonight adv. on the present evening or night. ▶ n. the evening or night of the present day.

tonnage n. **1** weight in tons. **2** a ship's

Thesaurus

token n. **1** SYMBOL, sign, emblem, badge, representation, indication, mark, manifestation. **2** MEMENTO, souvenir, keepsake, remembrance, reminder, memorial. ▶ adj. PERFUNCTORY, superficial, nominal, slight, hollow.

tolerable adj. **1** ENDURABLE, bearable, sufferable, supportable, acceptable. **2** FAIRLY GOOD, fair, all right, passable, adequate, satisfactory, average, mediocre, ordinary, run-of-the-mill, indifferent, unexceptional; *informal* not bad, OK. ■ OPPOSITES intolerable.

tolerance n. **1** TOLERATION, openmindedness, lack of prejudice, broadmindedness, liberalism, forbearance, patience, magnanimity, understanding, charity, lenience. **2** ENDURANCE, sufferance, acceptance.

tolerant adj. OPEN-MINDED, unprejudiced, unbiased, broad-minded, liberal, catholic, forbearing, long-suffering, magnanimous, sympathetic, understanding, charitable, lenient, indulgent, permissive, free and easy, easy-going. ■ OPPOSITES intolerant.

tolerate v. **1** PERMIT, allow, sanction, accept, countenance, brook. **2** ENDURE, bear, suffer, take, stand, put up with, abide, accept, stomach, submit to.

toll n. **1** CHARGE, fee, payment, levy, tariff. **2** COST, damage, loss, inroads.

tomb n. GRAVE, burial place/chamber, sepulchre, vault, crypt, catacomb, mausoleum.

tone n. **1** SOUND, sound quality, colour, pitch, timbre, tonality. **2** TONE OF VOICE, expression, intonation, inflection, carrying capacity measured in tons.

tonne n. a metric ton.

tonsil n. either of two small masses of tissue in the throat.

tonsillitis n. inflammation of the tonsils.

tonsure n. a circular area on a monk's or priest's head where the hair is shaved off. ■ **tonsured** adj.

too adv. 1 more than is desirable or possible. 2 also.

took past of TAKE.

tool n. 1 a device or implement used for a particular task. 2 a person used by another. ▶ v. 1 impress a design on leather. 2 equip with tools. □ **toolbar** Computing a strip of icons used to perform certain functions.

toot n. a short, sharp sound made by a horn, trumpet, etc. ▶ v. make a toot.

tooth n. (pl. **teeth**) 1 each of a set of hard white structures in the jaws, used for biting and chewing. 2 a cog on a gearwheel or a point on a saw or comb. □ **toothpaste** a paste for cleaning the teeth. **toothpick** a thin, pointed piece of wood etc. for removing food stuck between the teeth. ■ **toothed** adj. **toothless** adj.

toothy adj. having or showing large teeth.

top n. 1 the highest or uppermost point, part, or surface. 2 a thing placed on or covering the upper part of something. 3 the utmost degree. 4 a garment for the upper part of the body. 5 a toy with a pointed base, that can be made to spin. ▶ adj. highest in position, rank, or degree. ▶ v. (**topping**, **topped**) 1 be more or better than. 2 be at the highest place or rank in. 3 reach the top of. 4 put a top or topping on. 5 (**top up**) fill up a partly full container. □ **topcoat**

1 an overcoat. 2 an outer coat of paint. **top-dress** apply fertilizer on the top of soil. **top hat** a man's formal black hat with a high crown. **top-heavy** unstable because too heavy at the top. **topknot** a knot of hair arranged on the top of the head. **topsoil** the top layer of soil. **top-spin** a fast forward spin given to a moving ball. ■ **topmost** adj.

topaz n. a colourless, yellow, or blue precious stone.

topiary n. the art of clipping shrubs or trees into attractive shapes.

topic n. a subject of a text, speech, etc.

topical adj. of or dealing with current affairs. ■ **topicality** n. **topically** adv.

topless adj. having the breasts uncovered.

topography n. the arrangement of the physical features of an area. ■ **topographical** adj.

topology n. the study of geometrical properties unaffected by changes in shape or size.

topping n. a layer of food poured or spread over another food.

topple v. overbalance or cause to overbalance and fall.

topsy-turvy adj. & adv. 1 upside down. 2 in disorder.

tor n. a hill or rocky peak.

Torah n. (in Judaism) the law of God as revealed to Moses.

torch n. 1 a portable electric lamp. 2 a burning piece of wood etc. carried as a light.

tore past of TEAR¹.

toreador n. a bullfighter.

torment n. 1 great physical or mental suffering. 2 a cause of this. ▶ v. 1 cause to suffer greatly. 2 annoy or tease unkindly. ■ **tormentor** n.

torn past part. of TEAR¹.

Thesaurus

modulation, accentuation. 3 MOOD, air, attitude, character, manner, spirit, temper, tenor, vein, drift.

tonic n. RESTORATIVE, stimulant, analeptic; *informal* pick-me-up.

tool n. IMPLEMENT, instrument, utensil, device, apparatus, gadget, appliance, machine, contrivance, contraption, aid.

top n. 1 HIGHEST POINT/PART, summit, peak, pinnacle, crest, crown, tip, apex, vertex, apogee. 2 UPPER PART, upper surface, upper layer. 3 CAP, lid, stopper, cork, cover. ■ OPPOSITES bottom. ▶ adj. 1 TOP-MOST, uppermost, highest. 2 FOREMOST, leading, principal, pre-eminent, greatest, finest. 3 MAXIMUM, maximal, great-

est, utmost. ■ OPPOSITES lowest, minimum. ▶ v. 1 CAP, cover, finish, garnish. 2 HEAD, lead, be first in. 3 SURPASS, exceed, go beyond, transcend, better, best, beat, excel, outstrip, outdo, outshine, eclipse.

topic n. SUBJECT, theme, issue, matter, question, argument, thesis.

topical adj. CURRENT, up to date, up to the minute, contemporary, popular. ■ OPPOSITES out of date.

topple v. 1 FALL OVER, tip over, keel over, overturn, overbalance, capsize. 2 OVERTHROW, oust, unseat, overturn, bring down, bring low.

torment n. AGONY, suffering, torture,

tornado n. (pl. **tornadoes** or **tornados**) a violent rotating wind storm.

torpedo n. (pl. **torpedoes**) a self-propelled underwater missile. ▶v. (**torpedoing, torpedoed**) attack or destroy with a torpedo.

torpid adj. sluggish and inactive. ■ **torpidity** n. **torpidly** adv. **torpor** n.

torque n. a force causing rotation.

torrent n. **1** a strong, fast-moving stream of liquid. **2** an outpouring. ■ **torrential** adj.

torrid adj. **1** very hot and dry. **2** passionate.

torsion n. the state of being twisted.

torso n. (pl. **torsos**) the trunk of the human body.

tort n. Law a wrongful act or a violation of a right for which damages may be claimed.

tortilla /tor-tee-yuh/ n. a thin, flat maize pancake.

tortoise n. a slow-moving reptile with a domed shell. ◻ **tortoiseshell 1** the mottled brown and yellow shell of certain turtles, used to make ornaments. **2** a cat with markings resembling tortoiseshell.

tortuous adj. **1** full of twists and turns. **2** lengthy and complex. ■ **tortuously** adv.

torture n. **1** the inflicting of severe pain as a punishment or means of coercion. **2** great suffering. ▶v. inflict torture on. ■ **torturer** n. **torturous** adj.

Tory n. (pl. **Tories**) a member or supporter of the British Conservative Party.

toss v. **1** throw lightly. **2** move from side to side. **3** throw a coin into the air to make a choice based on which side lands uppermost. **4** turn food in a liquid to coat it lightly. ▶n. an act of tossing.

tot n. **1** a very young child. **2** a small drink of spirits. ▶v. (**totting, totted**) (**tot up**) add up.

total adj. **1** comprising the whole number or amount. **2** complete. ▶n. a total number or amount. ▶v. (**totalling, totalled**; US **totaling, totaled**) **1** amount to. **2** find the total of. ■ **totality** n. **totally** adv.

totalitarian adj. (of government) consisting of only one leader or party and having complete control. ■ **totalitarianism** n.

totalizator (or **totalisator**) n. a device showing the number and amount of bets staked on a race.

tote informal n. a system of betting using the totalizator. ▶v. carry.

totem n. a natural object or animal believed to have spiritual significance and adopted as an emblem. ◻ **totem pole** a pole decorated with totems.

totter v. walk or rock unsteadily. ▶n. a tottering walk.

toucan n. a tropical American bird with a massive bill.

touch v. **1** come into or be in physical contact with. **2** bring the hand or another part of the body into contact with. **3** harm or interfere with. **4** affect. **5** (**be touched**) feel gratitude or sympathy. ▶n. **1** an act or way of touching. **2** the ability to perceive something through physical contact. **3** a small amount. **4** a detail or feature. **5** a way

Thesaurus

pain, excruciation, anguish, hell, misery, distress, affliction, wretchedness. ▶v. CAUSE AGONY/SUFFERING/PAIN TO, afflict, harrow, plague, torture, distress, worry, trouble.

torn adj. **1** RIPPED, split, slit, cut, lacerated, rent. **2** DIVIDED, wavering, vacillating, irresolute, uncertain, unsure, undecided.

torrent n. FLOOD, deluge, inundation, spate, cascade, rush, stream, current, downpour, rainstorm. ■ OPPOSITES trickle.

tortuous adj. TWISTING, winding, curving, curvy, sinuous, undulating, coiling, serpentine, snaking, snaky, zigzag, convoluted, meandering. ■ OPPOSITES straight.

torture n. **1** ABUSE, ill-treatment, punishment, torment. **2** AGONY, suffering, pain, excruciation, anguish, misery, distress. ▶v. **1** INFLICT PAIN/SUFFERING ON, abuse, ill-treat, punish, torment; informal work over. **2** TORMENT, afflict, harrow, plague, distress, worry, trouble.

toss v. **1** THROW, hurl, cast, sling, pitch, shy, lob, propel, launch, project; informal heave, chuck. **2** ROLL, sway, undulate, pitch, lurch, heave.

total n. SUM, sum total, aggregate, whole, entirety, totality. ▶adj. **1** COMPLETE, entire, whole, full, comprehensive, combined, aggregate, composite, integral. **2** THOROUGH, complete, utter, absolute, downright, out-and-out, outright, unmitigated, unqualified. ▶v. **1** ADD UP TO, come to, amount to. **2** ADD UP, count, reckon, tot up.

totalitarian adj. AUTOCRATIC, authoritarian, absolute, despotic, dictatorial, of dealing with something. □ **in touch** in communication. **lose touch** no longer be in communication. **touch-and-go** (of an outcome) uncertain. **touch down** (of an aircraft) land. **touchline** the boundary line on each side of a rugby or football field. **touch on** deal briefly with. **touchstone** a standard by which something is judged. **touch up** make small improvements to.

touché /too-shay/ exclam. used to acknowledge a good point made at one's expense.

touching adj. arousing sympathy or gratitude; moving.

touchy adj. (**touchier, touchiest**) quick to take offence.

tough adj. **1** strong enough to withstand wear and tear. **2** able to endure difficulty or pain. **3** strict. **4** involving difficulty or hardship. **5** (of a person) violent. ■ **toughen** v. **toughness** n.

toupee /too-pay/ n. a small wig.

tour n. **1** a journey for pleasure in which several places are visited. **2** a series of performances or matches in several places. ▶v. make a tour of. □ **tour de force** something accomplished with great skill.

tourism n. the commercial organization of holidays and services for tourists.

tourist n. a person visiting a place for pleasure.

tourmaline n. a mineral used as a gemstone and in electrical devices.

tournament n. a sporting contest consisting of a number of matches.

tourniquet /toor-ni-kay/ n. a bandage tied tightly round a limb to stop the flow of blood through an artery.

tousle v. make a person's hair untidy.

tout v. **1** try to sell. **2** resell a ticket for an event at a price higher than the official one. ▶n. a person who buys up tickets for an event to resell them at a profit.

tow v. pull along behind. ▶n. **1** an act of towing. **2** coarse fibres of flax or hemp. □ **towpath** a path beside a river or canal, originally for horses towing barges.

towards (or **toward**) prep. **1** in the direction of. **2** in relation to. **3** contributing to the cost of.

towel n. a piece of absorbent cloth or paper used for drying. ▶v. (**towelling, towelled**; US **toweling, toweled**) dry with a towel.

towelling (US **toweling**) n. absorbent cloth used for towels.

tower n. **1** a tall, narrow building or part of a building. **2** a tall structure. ▶v. be very tall. □ **tower block** a tall modern building with many storeys.

Thesaurus

tyrannical, undemocratic, oppressive. ■ OPPOSITES democratic.

totter v. TEETER, wobble, stagger, stumble, reel, sway, roll, lurch.

touch v. **1** BE IN CONTACT, come into contact, come together, meet, converge, be contiguous, adjoin, abut. **2** PRESS LIGHTLY, tap, brush, graze, feel, stroke, pat, fondle, caress. **3** AFFECT, move, make an impression on, influence, upset, disturb, make sad, arouse sympathy; *informal* get to. **4** REACH, attain, arrive at, come to. ▶n. **1** FEEL, feeling, sense of touch, tactile sense, tactility. **2** TEXTURE, feel, grain, finish, surface, coating. **3** BIT, trace, dash, taste, spot, drop, pinch, speck, smack, suggestion, hint, soupçon, tinge, whiff, suspicion; *informal* smidgen.

touching adj. MOVING, impressive, affecting, warming, heart-warming.

touchy adj. SENSITIVE, oversensitive, hypersensitive, thin-skinned, tetchy, testy, irascible, irritable, grouchy, grumpy, peevish, querulous, bad-tempered, captious, crabbed, cross, surly.

tough adj. **1** STRONG, durable, resistant, resilient, sturdy, firm, solid, hard, rigid, stiff. **2** CHEWY, leathery, gristly, stringy, fibrous, sinewy. **3** HARDY, strong, fit, sturdy, rugged, stalwart, vigorous, strapping, robust, resilient. **4** DIFFICULT, hard, arduous, onerous, laborious, strenuous, exacting, taxing, stressful. **5** FIRM, strict, stern, severe, harsh, hard-hitting, adamant, inflexible. **6** UNFORTUNATE, unlucky, hard, regrettable; *informal* too bad. ■ OPPOSITES tender, easy, lax.

toughen v. STRENGTHEN, fortify, reinforce, harden.

tour n. TRIP, excursion, journey, expedition, jaunt, outing, peregrination. ▶v. TRAVEL ROUND/THROUGH, explore, holiday in, go round, visit.

tourist n. VISITOR, sightseer, holiday-maker, tripper.

tournament n. COMPETITION, contest, series, meeting, event.

tout v. (**tout for**) ASK FOR, solicit, seek, petition for, appeal for, beg for.

tow v. PULL, draw, drag, haul, tug, trail, lug.

town n. **1** a settlement larger than a village. **2** the central business or shopping area of a town or city. □ **town hall** a building housing local government offices. **township** (in South Africa) a suburb or city mainly inhabited by black people.

toxaemia /tok-**see**-mi-uh/ (US **toxemia**) n. blood poisoning.

toxic adj. **1** poisonous. **2** of or caused by poison. ■ **toxicity** n.

toxicology n. the study of poisons. ■ **toxicologist** n.

toxin n. a poison produced by a living organism.

toy n. an object to play with. ▶v. (**toy with**) **1** consider casually. **2** move or touch idly or nervously. ▶adj. (of a breed of dog) very small.

trace v. **1** find or follow by careful investigation. **2** copy a design etc. by drawing over it on transparent paper. **3** draw an outline. ▶n. **1** a mark or other sign of the existence or passing of something. **2** a very small amount. **3** a slight indication. **4** each of the two straps by which a horse pulls a vehicle. □ **trace element** a chemical element present or required only in tiny amounts. ■ **traceable** adj.

tracery n. (pl. **traceries**) a decorative patten of interlacing lines, esp. in stone.

trachea /truh-kee-uh/ n. (pl. **tracheae** or **tracheas**) the windpipe.

tracheotomy n. (pl. **tracheotomies**) a surgical incision made in the windpipe.

tracing n. a copy of a drawing or map made by tracing.

track n. **1** a rough path or road. **2** a prepared course for racing. **3** a line of marks left by a person etc. in passing. **4** a railway line. **5** a section of a record, compact disc, etc. **6** a jointed metal band around the wheels of a heavy vehicle. ▶v. **1** follow the trail or course of. **2** (**track down**) find after a thorough search. □ **track record** a person's past achievements. **tracksuit** an outfit consisting of a loose sweatshirt and trousers. ■ **tracker** n.

tract n. **1** a large area of land. **2** a major passage in the body. **3** a pamphlet on a religious or political subject.

tractable adj. easy to deal with or control. ■ **tractability** n.

traction n. **1** the act of pulling a thing along a surface. **2** the exertion of a sustained pull on a limb to keep a broken bone in position. **3** the grip of a tyre on a road.

tractor n. a powerful vehicle for pulling farm equipment.

trade n. **1** the buying and selling of goods and services. **2** a job requiring manual skills and - training. **3** the people engaged in a particular business. ▶v. **1** buy and sell goods and services. **2** exchange. **3** (**trade in**) give a used article as partial payment for a new one. **4** (**trade on**) take advantage of. **5** (**trade off**) exchange as a compromise. □ **trademark** a symbol, word, or words chosen to represent a company or product. **tradesman** a person engaged in trading or a trade. **trade union** an organized association of workers formed to protect and promote their rights and interests. **trade wind** a wind blowing steadily towards the equator. ■ **trader** n.

tradition n. **1** the passing on of customs or beliefs from generation to generation. **2** a long-established custom. ■ **traditional** adj. **traditionally** adv.

traditionalism n. the upholding of

Thesaurus

towering adj. **1** HIGH, tall, lofty, elevated, sky-high. **2** OUTSTANDING, extraordinary, pre-eminent, superior, great, incomparable, unrivalled, peerless.

toxic adj. POISONOUS, venomous, virulent, noxious. ■ OPPOSITES harmless.

trace n. **1** MARK, sign, vestige, indication, evidence, remains, remnant. **2** BIT, hint, suggestion, suspicion, trifle, dash, tinge, jot, iota. ▶v. FIND, discover, detect, unearth, uncover, track down, turn up, ferret out, hunt down; *informal* dig up.

track n. **1** MARK, trace, impression, footprint, trail, spoor, scent. **2** COURSE, line, path, orbit, route, trajectory. **3** PATH,

trail, route, way. ▶v. FOLLOW, pursue, trail, trace, tail, shadow, stalk, dog.

trade n. **1** COMMERCE, buying and selling, dealing, trafficking, business, merchandising. **2** LINE OF WORK, line, occupation, job, career, profession, craft, vocation, calling, work, employment. ▶v. **1** BUY AND SELL, deal, traffic, market, merchandise. **2** SWAP, exchange, switch, barter.

trader n. MERCHANT, dealer, buyer, seller, marketer, merchandiser, broker, tradesman, tradeswoman.

tradition n. CUSTOM, belief, practice, convention, ritual, observance, habit, institution, usage, praxis.

traditional adj. CUSTOMARY, accustomed,

tradition, esp. to resist change. ■ **traditionalist** n. & adj.

traduce v. slander.

traffic n. **1** vehicles, ships, or aircraft moving along a route. **2** the act of trading in something illegal. ▶v. (**trafficking**, **trafficked**) trade in something illegal. □ **traffic warden** an official who locates and reports on vehicles breaking parking regulations. ■ **trafficker** n.

tragedian n. **1** an actor who plays tragic roles. **2** a writer of tragedies.

tragedy n. (pl. **tragedies**) **1** an event causing great sadness or suffering. **2** a serious play with an unhappy ending.

tragic adj. **1** extremely sad. **2** of dramatic tragedy. ■ **tragically** adv.

tragicomedy n. (pl. **tragicomedies**) a play or novel which contains elements of both comedy and tragedy. ■ **tragicomic** adj.

trail n. **1** a series of signs left behind by a person etc. in passing. **2** a long thin part stretching behind or hanging down. **3** a line of people or things. **4** a path. ▶v. **1** draw or be drawn along behind. **2** follow the trail of. **3** walk or move slowly or wearily. **4** (**trail away/off**) (of the voice) fade gradually. **5** be losing to an opponent in a contest.

trailer n. **1** an unpowered vehicle pulled by another. **2** an extract from a film etc. used to advertise it.

train v. **1** teach a particular skill to. **2** learn a particular skill. **3** become physically fit through exercise. **4** (**train on**) point at. **5** make a plant grow in a particular direction. ▶n. **1** a series of railway carriages or wagons moved by a locomotive. **2** a line of vehicles or pack animals. **3** a series of connected events or thoughts. **4** a long piece of trailing material at the back of a dress.

trainee n. a person being trained.

trainer n. **1** a person who trains people or animals. **2** a soft shoe for sports or casual wear.

traipse v. walk or move wearily.

trait n. a characteristic.

traitor n. a person who betrays their country or a cause. ■ **traitorous** adj.

trajectory n. (pl. **trajectories**) the path of an object moving through the air.

tram (or **tramcar**) n. a passenger vehicle powered by electricity and running on rails (**tramlines**) laid in a public road.

trammel v. (**trammelling**, **trammelled**; US **trammeling**, **trammeled**) hamper or restrict.

tramp v. **1** walk heavily or noisily. **2** walk wearily over a long distance. ▶n. **1** a homeless person who travels around and lives by begging. **2** the sound of heavy steps. **3** a long walk. **4** a cargo vessel that does not sail a fixed route.

trample v. tread on and crush.

trampoline n. a strong fabric sheet connected by springs to a frame, used for performing acrobatic leaps. ■ **trampolining** n.

trance n. a half-conscious state.

tranquil adj. free from disturbance; calm. ■ **tranquillity** n. **tranquilly** adv.

tranquillize (or **tranquillise**; US **tranquilize**) v. give a calming or sedative drug to.

tranquillizer (or **tranquilliser**; US

Thesaurus

conventional, established, ritual, ritualistic, habitual, set, fixed, routine, usual, old, time-honoured, historic, folk; *literary* wonted.

tragedy n. DISASTER, calamity, catastrophe, misfortune, misadventure, affliction, adversity.

tragic adj. **1** DISASTROUS, calamitous, catastrophic, fatal, terrible, dreadful, appalling, dire, awful, miserable, wretched, unfortunate. **2** SAD, unhappy, pathetic, moving, distressing, pitiful, piteous, melancholy, doleful, mournful, dismal, gloomy. ■ OPPOSITES fortunate, happy.

trail n. **1** TRACK, scent, spoor, traces, marks, signs, footprints. **2** PATH, pathway, footpath, track, road, route. ▶v. **1** DRAG, sweep, dangle, hang down, droop. **2** FOLLOW, pursue, track, trace, tail, shadow, stalk, dog. **3** LOSE, be down, be behind.

train n. **1** PROCESSION, line, file, column, convoy, caravan. **2** RETINUE, entourage, following, staff, household, followers, attendants. ▶v. **1** INSTRUCT, teach, coach, tutor, give lessons to, school, educate, drill, prepare, ground, guide. **2** EXERCISE, do exercises, work out, practise, prepare. **3** AIM, point, focus, direct, level, line up.

trait n. CHARACTERISTIC, attribute, feature, quality, property, idiosyncrasy, peculiarity, quirk.

traitor n. BETRAYER, turncoat, double-crosser, double-dealer, renegade, defector, deserter, apostate, Judas, quisling, fifth columnist.

trample v. TRAMP ON, tread on, walk over, stamp on, squash, crush, flatten.

tranquilizer) n. a drug used to reduce tension or anxiety.

transact v. conduct or carry out business. ∎ **transaction** n.

transatlantic adj. **1** crossing the Atlantic. **2** of or on the other side of the Atlantic.

transceiver n. a radio transmitter and receiver.

transcend v. **1** be or go beyond the range or limits of. **2** be better than. ∎ **transcendence** n. **transcendent** adj.

transcendental adj. of a spiritual or mystical realm.

transcontinental adj. crossing or extending across a continent.

transcribe v. **1** put into written form, or into a different written form. **2** arrange a piece of music for a different instrument. ∎ **transcription** n.

transcript n. a written version of material that was originally spoken or in another form.

transducer n. a device that converts variations in a physical medium into an electrical signal, or vice versa.

transept n. a part lying at right angles to the nave in a church.

transfer v. (**transferring**, **transferred**) **1** move from one place etc. to another. **2** pass property etc. to another person. ▶ n. **1** an act or the action of transferring. **2** a small picture which can be transferred to another surface by being pressed or heated. ∎ **transferable** adj. **transference** n.

transfigure v. transform into something more beautiful or spiritual. ∎ **transfiguration** n.

transfix v. **1** make motionless with fear or astonishment. **2** pierce with a sharp object.

transform v. **1** change in appearance or nature. **2** change the voltage of an electric current. ∎ **transformation** n.

transformer n. a device for changing the voltage of an electric current.

transfuse v. **1** give a transfusion of blood to someone. **2** permeate or imbue.

transfusion n. a medical process in which blood is transferred from one person or animal to another.

transgress v. break a rule or law. ∎ **transgression** n. **transgressor** n.

transient adj. lasting only for a short time. ∎ **transience** n.

transistor n. **1** a semiconductor device able to amplify or rectify an electric current. **2** a portable radio using circuits containing transistors.

transit n. **1** the carrying of people or things from one place to another. **2** an act of passing through a place.

transition n. the process of changing from one state or condition to another. ∎ **transitional** adj.

transitive adj. (of a verb) taking a direct object. ∎ **transitivity** n.

transitory adj. short-lived.

translate v. express or be expressed in another language. ∎ **translation** n. **translator** n.

transliterate v. write a letter or word using the letters of a different alphabet

Thesaurus

trance n. DAZE, stupor, hypnotic state, dream, reverie, brown study.

tranquil adj. PEACEFUL, restful, reposeful, calm, quiet, still, serene, placid, undisturbed.

tranquillizer n. SEDATIVE, opiate; *informal* downer. ∎ OPPOSITES stimulant.

transaction n. BUSINESS, deal, undertaking, affair, bargain, negotiation.

transcend v. GO BEYOND, exceed, overstep, rise above, surpass, excel, be superior to, outdo, outstrip.

transfer v. **1** CONVEY, move, shift, remove, take, carry, transport. **2** MAKE OVER, turn over, sign over, hand on, hand down, pass on, transmit, assign, delegate.

transform v. CHANGE, alter, convert, metamorphose, revolutionize, transfigure, transmogrify, remodel, redo, reconstruct, rebuild, reorganize, re-

arrange, renew, translate, transmute.

transformation n. CHANGE, alteration, conversion, metamorphosis, sea change, revolution, transfiguration, transmogrification, remodelling, reconstruction, reorganization, renewal, transmutation.

transgress v. GO BEYOND, overstep, exceed, infringe, breach, break, contravene, violate, defy, disobey.

transient adj. TRANSITORY, short-lived, short-term, impermanent, temporary, brief, short, ephemeral, evanescent, momentary, fleeting, flying, passing. ∎ OPPOSITES permanent.

transit n. MOVEMENT, transport, transportation, conveyance, haulage, travel, journeying, passage.

transition n. CHANGE, transformation, conversion, metamorphosis, shift, switch, jump, leap, progression, grad-

or language. ■ **transliteration** n.

translucent adj. allowing light to pass through partially. ■ **translucence** (or **translucency**) n.

transmigration n. the passing of the soul into another body after death.

transmission n. **1** the act of transmitting. **2** the mechanism transmitting power from an engine to the axle in a vehicle.

transmit v. (**transmitting, transmitted**) **1** cause to pass on from one place, person, or thing to another. **2** send out an electrical signal or a radio or television programme. ■ **transmissible** adj. **transmittable** adj. **transmitter** n.

transmogrify v. (**transmogrifying, transmogrified**) transform in a surprising or magical manner.

transmute v. change in form or substance. ■ **transmutation** n.

transom n. **1** the flat surface forming the stern of a boat. **2** a crossbar above a door or window.

transparency n. (pl. **transparencies**) **1** the condition of being transparent. **2** a photographic slide.

transparent adj. **1** able to be seen through. **2** obvious or evident. ■ **transparently** adv.

transpire v. **1** become known. **2** happen. **3** (of a plant) give off water vapour from the leaves. ■ **transpiration** n.

transplant v. **1** transfer to another place or situation. **2** take living tissue and put it in another body or part of the body. ▶ n. **1** an operation in which living tissue is transplanted. **2** something transplanted. ■ **transplantation** n.

transport v. carry people or goods from one place to another. ▶ n. **1** a system,

means, or the act of transporting. **2** (**transports**) strong emotions. ■ **transportation** n. **transporter** n.

transpose v. **1** cause two or more things to change places. **2** move to a different place or situation. **3** write or play music in a different key. ■ **transposition** n.

transsexual (or **transexual**) n. a person who emotionally and psychologically feels that they belong to the opposite sex.

transubstantiation n. the doctrine that the bread and wine of the Eucharist are converted by consecration into the body and blood of Christ.

transverse adj. placed or extending across something.

transvestite n. a person who derives pleasure from dressing in clothes worn by the opposite sex. ■ **transvestism** n.

trap n. **1** a device for catching and holding animals. **2** a scheme for tricking or catching someone. **3** a curve in a waste pipe that holds liquid to prevent gases from coming up. **4** a compartment from which a dog is released at the start of a race. **5** a two-wheeled horse-drawn carriage. ▶ v. (**trapping, trapped**) catch or hold in a trap. □ **trapdoor** a hinged or removable panel in a floor, ceiling, or roof.

trapeze n. a hanging horizontal bar used by circus acrobats.

trapezium n. (pl. **trapezia** or **trapeziums**) a quadrilateral with one pair of sides parallel.

trapezoid n. a quadrilateral with no sides parallel.

trapper n. a person who traps wild animals.

trappings pl. n. the signs or objects

Thesaurus

ation, development, evolution, transmutation.

translate v. RENDER, interpret, paraphrase, reword, convert, decipher, decode, explain, elucidate.

transmission n. **1** SENDING, conveyance, transport, dispatch, remission. **2** BROADCASTING, relaying, sending out. **3** BROADCAST, programme.

transmit v. **1** SEND, convey, transport, dispatch, forward, remit. **2** TRANSFER, pass on, hand on, communicate, impart, disseminate, spread, carry, diffuse. **3** BROADCAST, relay, send out, put on air.

transparent adj. **1** CLEAR, see-through, translucent, pellucid, crystal-clear,

crystalline, limpid, glassy, gauzy, diaphanous. **2** see OBVIOUS. ■ OPPOSITES opaque.

transpire v. COME ABOUT, take place, happen, occur, turn up, arise, chance; *literary* befall.

transport v. CONVEY, take, transfer, move, shift, bring, fetch, carry, bear, haul, cart, run, ship. ▶ n. TRANSPORTATION, conveyance, transit, carriage, freight.

transpose v. INTERCHANGE, exchange, switch, swap, transfer, reverse, invert, rearrange, reorder.

transverse adj. CROSSWISE, crossways, cross, athwart.

trap n. SNARE, net, mesh, gin, ambush,

associated with a particular status or role.

trash n. **1** US waste material. **2** poor-quality writing etc. ▶v. informal wreck or destroy. ■ **trashy** adj.

trattoria n. an Italian restaurant.

trauma n. **1** a deeply distressing experience. **2** physical injury. **3** emotional shock following a stressful event. ■ **traumatic** adj. **traumatize** (or **-ise**) v.

travail n. old use labour.

travel v. (**travelling**, **travelled**; US **traveling**, **traveled**) **1** go from one place to another. **2** journey along or through. ▶n. **1** the act of travelling. **2** (**travels**) journeys over a long distance.

traveller (US **traveler**) n. **1** a person who travels. **2** a Gypsy. □ **traveller's cheque** a cheque for a fixed amount that can be exchanged for cash in foreign countries.

travelogue n. a film, book, etc. about a person's travels.

traverse v. travel or extend across.

travesty n. (pl. **travesties**) an absurd or shocking misrepresentation.

trawl v. **1** catch fish with a trawl net. **2** search through thoroughly. ▶n. **1** an act of trawling. **2** (also **trawl net**) a large wide-mouthed fishing net.

trawler n. a boat used for trawling.

tray n. a shallow container with a rim for carrying things.

treacherous adj. **1** guilty of or involving betrayal. **2** having hidden dangers. ■ **treacherously** adv. **treachery** n.

treacle n. a thick sticky liquid produced when raw sugar is refined.

■ **treacly** adj.

tread v. (**treading**, **trod**; past part. **trodden** or **trod**) **1** walk in a specified way. **2** press down or crush with the feet. **3** walk on or along. ▶n. **1** a way or the sound of walking. **2** the top surface of a step or stair. **3** the part of a vehicle tyre that grips the road. □ **treadmill 1** a large wheel turned by the weight of people or animals treading on steps fitted into it, formerly used to drive machinery. **2** a tiring or boring job. **tread water** keep upright in deep water by making a walking movement.

treadle n. a lever worked by the foot to operate a machine.

treason n. the crime of betraying one's country. ■ **treasonable** adj.

treasure n. **1** a quantity of precious metals, gems, or other valuables. **2** a very valuable object. **3** informal a highly valued person. ▶v. **1** look after carefully. **2** value highly. □ **treasure trove** valuables of unknown ownership, found hidden.

treasurer n. a person in charge of the finances of a society etc.

treasury n. (pl. **treasuries**) **1** the funds or revenue of a state, society, etc. **2** (**Treasury**) the government department responsible for the overall management of the economy.

treat v. **1** behave towards or deal with in a certain way. **2** give medical care or attention to. **3** apply a process or a substance to. **4** (**treat to**) provide with food, drink, etc. at one's expense. ▶n. a surprise gift, event, etc. that gives great pleasure. ■ **treatment** n.

Thesaurus

pitfall, booby trap. ▶v. **1** SNARE, ensnare, enmesh, entrap, catch, corner. **2** TRICK, dupe, deceive, lure, inveigle, beguile.

trappings pl. n. ACCOUTREMENTS, appurtenances, appointments, trimmings, paraphernalia, fittings, equipment, apparatus, gear, adornment, ornamentation, decoration, finery, frippery, panoply.

trash n. **1** RUBBISH, waste, refuse, litter, garbage. **2** RIFF-RAFF, scum, rabble, vermin, good-for-nothings.

traumatic adj. PAINFUL, agonizing, shocking, scarring, disturbing, distressing, damaging, injurious, harmful.

travel v. JOURNEY, take a trip, tour, voyage, cross, traverse, cover, wander, ramble, roam, rove. ▶n. TRAVELLING, journeying, touring.

traveller n. TRIPPER, tourer, tourist, explorer, passenger, voyager, holiday-maker, sightseer, globetrotter.

traverse v. CROSS, go across, travel over, journey over, make one's way across, pass over, wander, roam, range.

treacherous adj. **1** see TRAITOROUS. **2** HAZARDOUS, dangerous, unsafe, flooded, icy, ice-covered, slippery.

tread v. WALK, step, go, pace, march, tramp.

treason n. BETRAYAL, treachery, disloyalty, faithlessness, sedition, subversion, mutiny, rebellion, lese-majesty.

treasure n. RICHES, valuables, wealth, fortune, hoard, jewels, gems, coins, gold. ▶v. VALUE, prize, set great store by, think highly of, hold dear.

treat n. SURPRISE, celebration, entertainment, amusement, diversion. ▶v. **1** ACT TOWARDS, behave towards, deal with,

treatise n. a formal written work on a subject.

treaty n. (pl. **treaties**) a formal agreement between states.

treble adj. three times as much or as many. ▶n. **1** an amount three times as large as usual. **2** a high-pitched voice, esp. a boy's singing voice. ▶v. make or become treble.

tree n. a tall woody perennial plant with a single thick stem and branches.

trefoil n. **1** a plant with three-lobed leaves. **2** a design in the form of three rounded lobes.

trek n. a long difficult journey, esp. on foot. ▶v. (**trekking, trekked**) go on a trek. ■ **trekker** n.

trellis n. a framework of bars used to support climbing plants.

tremble v. **1** shake uncontrollably from fear, excitement, etc. **2** be very frightened. ▶n. a trembling movement.

tremendous adj. **1** very great. **2** informal very good or impressive. ■ **tremendously** adv.

tremolo n. (pl. **tremolos**) a wavering effect in singing or music.

tremor n. **1** a trembling movement. **2** a slight earthquake. **3** a sudden feeling of fear or excitement.

tremulous adj. shaking slightly.

trench n. a deep ditch.

trenchant adj. (of speech or writing) expressed vigorously and clearly.

■ **trenchantly** adv.

trencher n. hist. a wooden platter or plate.

trend n. **1** a general tendency. **2** a fashion. □ **trendsetter** a person leading the way in fashion or ideas.

trendy adj. (**trendier, trendiest**) informal fashionable. ■ **trendily** adv. **trendiness** n.

trepidation n. nervousness.

trespass v. enter land or property without permission. ▶n. the act of trespassing. ■ **trespasser** n.

tress n. a lock of hair.

trestle n. a framework of a horizontal bar on sloping legs, used in pairs to support a surface such as a table top.

trews pl. n. trousers.

triad n. a group or set of three.

trial n. **1** an examination of evidence in a law court to decide if a person is guilty of a crime. **2** a test of performance or quality. **3** something that tries a person's patience. ▶v. (**trialling, trialled**; US **trialing, trialed**) test to assess performance etc. □ **on trial 1** being tried in a law court. **2** undergoing tests.

triangle n. **1** a figure with three straight sides and three angles. **2** a triangular steel rod used as a percussion instrument. ■ **triangular** adj.

triangulation n. the division of an area into a series of triangles to determine distances and relative positions.

Thesaurus

handle, cope with, contend with, manage, use. **2** REGARD, consider, view, look upon, deal with. **3** GIVE TREATMENT TO, medicate, doctor, nurse, care for, attend to, minister to, cure, heal. **4** APPLY TO, put on, use on, ply with. **5** PAY FOR, buy for, pay/foot the bill for, stand, finance, entertain, take out.

treatise n. DISCOURSE, exposition, disquisition, dissertation, thesis, study, essay, paper, monograph, pamphlet, tract.

treatment n. **1** ACTION, behaviour, conduct, handling, management, use, dealings. **2** MEDICAL CARE, medication, medicament, therapy, doctoring, nursing, first aid, care, ministration.

treaty n. AGREEMENT, pact, deal, compact, covenant, bargain, pledge, contract, alliance, concordat, convention, entente.

trek v. TRAMP, hike, trudge, march, slog, footslog, plod, walk, ramble, roam, range, rove, travel, journey; informal yomp. ▶n. EXPEDITION, trip, journey, trudge, tramp, hike, march, slog, walk,

odyssey.

tremble v. SHAKE, quiver, shudder, judder, teeter, totter, wobble, rock, vibrate, oscillate.

tremendous adj. **1** GREAT, huge, enormous, immense, massive, vast, colossal, prodigious, stupendous, gigantic, gargantuan, mammoth. **2** EXCELLENT, very good, great, marvellous, remarkable, extraordinary, exceptional, wonderful, incredible; informal super, fabulous, terrific, fantastic.

tremor n. TREMBLE, shake, shaking, shiver, quiver, twitch, judder, spasm, paroxysm.

trend n. **1** TENDENCY, drift, course, direction, bearing, current, inclination, bias, leaning, bent. **2** FASHION, vogue, style, mode, look, craze; informal fad.

trendy adj. see FASHIONABLE.

trespass v. INTRUDE, encroach, infringe, invade, obtrude.

trial n. **1** COURT CASE, case, hearing, inquiry, tribunal, litigation. **2** TEST, try-out, trial/test run, check, assay, experi-

triathlon n. an athletic contest involving three different events.

tribe n. a social group in a traditional society consisting of linked families. ■ **tribal** adj. **tribesman** n.

tribulation n. trouble or suffering.

tribunal n. a board of officials appointed to settle disputes.

tributary n. (pl. **tributaries**) a river flowing into a larger river or lake.

tribute n. **1** an act, statement, or gift intended to show gratitude or respect. **2** hist. a payment made by a state to a more powerful one.

trice n. (**in a trice**) in an instant.

triceps n. (pl. **triceps**) the large muscle at the back of the upper arm.

trichology /tri-**kol**-uh-ji/ n. the study of the hair and scalp and their diseases. ■ **trichologist** n.

trick n. **1** something done to deceive or outwit someone. **2** a skilful act performed for entertainment. **3** a mannerism. ▶v. deceive or outwit. ■ **trickery** n.

trickle v. **1** flow in a small stream. **2** come or go gradually. ▶n. a trickling flow.

tricky adj. (**trickier, trickiest**) **1** difficult or awkward. **2** deceitful.

tricolour /tri-**kuh**-ler/ (US **tricolor**) n. a flag with three bands of different colours.

tricycle n. a vehicle similar to a bicycle but with three wheels.

trident n. a three-pronged spear.

tried past & past part. of TRY.

triennial adj. taking place every three years.

trier n. a person who tries hard.

trifle n. **1** a thing of little value or importance. **2** a small amount. **3** a cold dessert of sponge cake and fruit covered with custard and jelly. ▶v. (**trifle with**) treat without seriousness or respect.

trifling adj. trivial.

trigger n. **1** a lever for releasing a spring or catch, esp. to fire a gun. **2** an event that causes something to happen. ▶v. **1** cause to function. **2** bring about. ◻ **trigger-happy** tending to shoot on the slightest provocation.

trigonometry n. the study of the relationships between the sides and angles of triangles.

trilateral adj. **1** involving three parties. **2** on or with three sides.

trilby n. (pl. **trilbies**) a soft felt hat with an indented crown.

trill n. & v. (make) a quavering sound or note.

trillion adj. & n. **1** a million million. **2** dated a million million million.

trilobite n. a fossil sea animal.

trilogy n. (pl. **trilogies**) a group of three related novels, plays, etc.

trim v. (**trimming, trimmed**) **1** cut away unwanted parts, esp. to neaten. **2** decorate along the edges. **3** adjust a sail. ▶n. **1** decoration along the edges. **2** an act of trimming. **3** good condition. ▶adj. (**trimmer, trimmest**) neat and smart.

trimaran /**try**-muh-ran/ n. a yacht with

Thesaurus

ment; informal dry run. **3** NUISANCE, pest, bother, worry, vexation, annoyance, irritant, irritation, bane, affliction, curse, burden, cross to bear; informal pain in the neck, hassle.

tribe n. ETHNIC GROUP, family, dynasty, clan, sect.

tribute n. ACCOLADE, commendation, testimonial, paean, eulogy, panegyric, encomium, applause, praise, homage, honour, exaltation, extolment, glorification, congratulations, compliments, bouquets; formal laudation.

trick n. **1** STRATAGEM, ploy, artifice, ruse, dodge, wile, device, manoeuvre, deceit, deception, subterfuge, swindle, fraud; informal con. **2** KNACK, art, gift, talent, technique, ability, skill, expertise; informal know-how. **3** HOAX, practical joke, joke, prank, jape, antic, caper, frolic, lark, gambol; informal leg-pull, gag, put-on. ▶v. DECEIVE, delude, mislead, take

in, cheat, hoodwink, fool, outwit, dupe, hoax, gull, defraud, swindle; informal con, pull a fast one on, put one over on; literary cozen.

trickery n. DECEIT, deception, cheating, subterfuge, guile, artifice, wiliness, craftiness, chicanery, dishonesty, fraud, swindling, imposture, double-dealing, duplicity; informal monkey/funny business, hanky-panky, jiggery-pokery. ■ OPPOSITES honesty.

trickle v. DRIP, dribble, leak, ooze, seep, exude, percolate. ■ OPPOSITES pour, gush.

tricky adj. **1** DIFFICULT, problematic, awkward, delicate, sensitive, ticklish, thorny, knotty, touchy, risky. **2** CUNNING, crafty, wily, artful, devious, scheming, sly, slippery, subtle, deceitful, deceptive; informal foxy. ■ OPPOSITES straightforward, honest.

trim adj. NEAT, tidy, neat and tidy, smart,

three hulls side by side.

trimming n. **1** (**trimmings**) small pieces trimmed off. **2** decoration.

trinity n. (pl. **trinities**) **1** (**the Trinity**) (in Christian belief) the three persons (Father, Son, and Holy Spirit) that together make up God. **2** a group of three.

trinket n. a small inexpensive ornament or item of jewellery.

trio n. (pl. **trios**) a set or group of three.

trip v. (**tripping**, **tripped**) **1** catch one's foot on something and stumble or fall. **2** (**trip up**) make a mistake. **3** move with quick light steps. **4** activate a mechanism. ▶ n. **1** a journey or excursion. **2** an act of stumbling. **3** informal a hallucinatory experience caused by taking a drug. **4** a device that trips a mechanism.

tripartite adj. **1** consisting of three parts. **2** involving three parties.

tripe n. **1** the stomach of a cow or sheep used as food. **2** informal nonsense.

triple adj. **1** having or involving three parts, things, or people. **2** having three times as much or as many. ▶ v. increase by three times the amount.

triplet n. **1** each of three children born at one birth. **2** a set of three.

triplicate adj. existing in three copies or examples.

tripod n. a three-legged stand.

triptych /trip-tik/ n. a picture or carving on three panels.

trite adj. unoriginal or overused.

tritium n. a radioactive isotope of hydrogen.

triumph n. **1** a great victory or achievement. **2** joy at this. ▶ v. achieve a triumph. ■ **triumphal** adj.

triumphant adj. **1** having won a battle or contest. **2** joyful after a victory or achievement. ■ **triumphantly** adv.

triumvirate n. a group of three power-

ful or notable people.

trivet n. a metal stand for a kettle or hot dish.

trivia pl. n. trivial details or pieces of information.

trivial adj. of little value or importance. ■ **triviality** n. **trivialize** (or **-ise**) v. **trivially** adv.

trod past & past part. of **TREAD**.

trodden past part. of **TREAD**.

troglodyte n. a person who lives in a cave.

troika n. **1** a Russian vehicle pulled by a team of three horses. **2** a group of three people working together.

troll n. (in folklore) an ugly giant or dwarf.

trolley n. (pl. **trolleys**) **1** a large metal basket on wheels, for transporting goods. **2** a small table on wheels.

trollop n. dated a promiscuous woman.

trombone n. a large brass wind instrument with a sliding tube. ■ **trombonist** n.

trompe l'œil /tromp loy/ n. a painting creating the illusion of a three-dimensional object or space.

troop n. **1** (**troops**) soldiers or armed forces. **2** a group of people or animals. ▶ v. come or go as a group.

trooper n. **1** a private soldier in a cavalry or armoured unit. **2** US a state police officer.

trophy n. (pl. **trophies**) **1** an object awarded as a prize. **2** a souvenir of an achievement.

tropic n. **1** a line of latitude 23°26′ north or south of the equator. **2** (**the tropics**) the region between these, with a hot climate. ■ **tropical** adj.

trot v. (**trotting**, **trotted**) **1** (of a horse) move at a pace faster than a walk. **2** run at a moderate pace with short steps. **3** (**trot out**) informal give an ac-

Thesaurus

spruce, well groomed, well dressed, well turned out, dapper, elegant; informal natty. ▶ v. CUT, clip, snip, shear, prune, pare, even up, neaten, tidy up.

trip n. **1** EXCURSION, tour, expedition, voyage, jaunt, outing, run. **2** HALLUCINATION, drug experience, vision. ▶ v. **1** STUMBLE, lose one's footing/balance, stagger, slip, slide, misstep, fall, tumble. **2** SKIP, dance, hop, prance, bound, spring, gambol, caper, frisk, cavort, waltz.

triumph n. **1** CONQUEST, victory, win, ascendancy, mastery, success; informal walkover. **2** EXULTATION, jubilation, jubilance, elation, rejoicing, joy, joyfulness,

pride. ■ OPPOSITES failure, despair. ▶ v. WIN, succeed, come first, be the victor, be victorious, gain a victory, carry the day, take the honours/prize/crown.

triumphant adj. **1** WINNING, victorious, successful, undefeated, unbeaten. **2** EXULTANT, jubilant, elated, rejoicing, joyful, joyous, proud, cock-a-hoop, gloating, boastful. ■ OPPOSITES unsuccessful, despondent.

trivial adj. UNIMPORTANT, insignificant, inconsequential, flimsy, insubstantial, petty, minor, of no account/matter, negligible, paltry, trifling, foolish, worthless; informal piddling, piffling. ■ OPPOScount that has been produced many times before. ▶ n. a trotting pace. ▢ **on the trot** informal one after another.

trotter n. a pig's foot.

troubadour /troo-buh-dor/ n. a medieval travelling poet.

trouble n. **1** difficulty or inconvenience. **2** a cause of this. **3** a situation likely to bring punishment or blame. **4** public disorder. ▶ v. **1** cause worry or inconvenience to. **2** make the effort to do something. ▢ **troubleshooter** a person who investigates and solves problems in an organization. ■ **troublesome** adj.

trough n. **1** a long, narrow open container for animals' food or drink. **2** a long region of low pressure.

trounce v. defeat heavily.

troupe n. a group of touring entertainers.

trouper n. **1** an entertainer with long experience. **2** a reliable person.

trousers pl. n. an outer garment for the body from the waist down, with a separate part for each leg.

trousseau /troo-soh/ n. (pl. **trousseaux** or **trousseaus**) the clothes etc. collected by a bride for her marriage.

trout n. (pl. **trout** or **trouts**) an edible fish of the salmon family.

trowel n. **1** a small hand-held tool for

digging. **2** a similar tool for applying and spreading mortar or plaster.

troy (or **troy weight**) n. a system of weights used for precious metals and gems.

truant n. a pupil who stays away from school without permission. ▶ v. (also **play truant**) stay away as a truant. ■ **truancy** n.

truce n. an agreement to stop fighting temporarily.

truck n. **1** a lorry. **2** an open railway wagon.

trucker n. a lorry driver.

truculent adj. quick to argue or fight. ■ **truculence** n. **truculently** adv.

trudge v. walk with slow, heavy steps. ▶ n. a long and tiring walk.

true adj. **1** in accordance with fact. **2** real or actual. **3** accurate. **4** loyal. ■ **truly** adv.

truffle n. **1** an underground fungus eaten as a delicacy. **2** a soft chocolate sweet.

trug n. a shallow oblong wooden basket.

truism n. a statement that is obviously true and says nothing new.

trump n. (in card games) a card of a suit chosen to rank above the others. ▶ v. **1** surpass by saying or doing something better. **2** (**trump up**) invent a false accusation or excuse.

Thesaurus

ITES significant.

troops pl. n. ARMED FORCES, army, military, services, soldiers, soldiery, fighting men/women.

trouble n. **1** PROBLEMS, worry, bother, anxiety, disquiet, unease, irritation, vexation, inconvenience, annoyance, agitation, harassment, difficulty, distress. **2** DIFFICULTY, misfortune, adversity, hardship, bad luck, distress, pain, suffering, affliction, torment, woe, grief, unhappiness, sadness, heartache. **3** BOTHER, inconvenience, disturbance, fuss, effort, exertion, work, labour, attention, care, thoughtfulness; informal hassle. **4** DISORDER, disease, illness, dysfunction. **5** DISTURBANCE, disorder, unrest, fighting, strife, conflict, tumult, commotion, turbulence, law-breaking. ▶ v. **1** WORRY, bother, disturb, annoy, irritate, vex, irk, fret, pester, torment, plague, inconvenience, upset, perturb, agitate, discompose, harass, distress; informal hassle. **2** TAKE THE TROUBLE/TIME, bother, make the effort, exert/disturb oneself, go out of one's way.

troublemaker n. MISCHIEF-MAKER, agita-

tor, instigator, rabble-rouser, demagogue.

troublesome adj. WORRYING, worrisome, bothersome, tiresome, disturbing, annoying, irritating, irksome, upsetting, perturbing, harassing, distressing, difficult, problematic, demanding, taxing.

truancy n. ABSENTEEISM, absence, French leave, shirking, malingering; informal bunking off, skiving.

truant n. ABSENTEE, dodger, malingerer, shirker, deserter; informal skiver. ▶ v. STAY AWAY FROM SCHOOL, play truant; informal skive (off), bunk off; US informal play hookey, goof off.

truce n. CEASE-FIRE, armistice, suspension/cessation of hostilities, peace, respite, moratorium.

true adj. **1** TRUTHFUL, accurate, correct, right, valid, factual, exact, precise, faithful, genuine, reliable, honest, veracious. **2** REAL, genuine, authentic, actual, bona fide, valid, legitimate; informal honest-to-goodness. **3** LOYAL, faithful, trustworthy, trusty, reliable, dependable, staunch, firm, fast, steady, constant, unswerving, unwavering, de-

trumpet n. a brass musical instrument with a flared end. ▸v. (**trumpeting**, **trumpeted**) 1 (of an elephant) make a loud sound through its trunk. 2 proclaim widely. ■ **trumpeter** n.

truncate v. shorten by cutting off the end. ■ **truncation** n.

truncheon n. a short thick stick carried as a weapon by a police officer.

trundle v. move or roll slowly.

trunk n. 1 the main woody stem of a tree. 2 the body apart from the limbs and head. 3 the long nose of an elephant. 4 a large box with a hinged lid for storing or transporting clothes etc. 5 US the boot of a car. 6 (**trunks**) men's shorts worn for swimming. □ **trunk road** an important main road.

truss n. 1 a framework supporting a roof etc. 2 a padded belt worn to support a hernia. ▸v. bind tightly.

trust n. 1 firm belief in the reliability, truth, or ability of someone or something. 2 responsibility for someone or something. 3 an arrangement whereby someone manages property for the benefit of another. 4 an organization managed by trustees. ▸v. 1 have trust in. 2 entrust. 3 hope. ■ **trustful** adj. **trustfully** adv. **trustworthiness** n. **trustworthy** adj.

trustee n. a person given legal powers to hold and manage property for the benefit of another.

trusty adj. old use reliable or faithful.

truth n. 1 the state of being true. 2 something which is true.

truthful adj. 1 telling or expressing the truth. 2 realistic. ■ **truthfully** adv. **truthfulness** n.

try v. (**trying**, **tried**) 1 attempt. 2 test by use. 3 (**try on**) put on a garment to see if it fits or suits one. 4 make severe demands on. 5 put on trial. ▸n. (pl. **tries**) 1 an attempt. 2 an act of testing by use. 3 Rugby an act of touching the ball down behind the opposing goal line to score points.

trying adj. annoying.

tryst /trist/ n. a meeting between lovers.

tsar (or **czar**) /zar/ n. an emperor of Russia before 1917. ■ **tsarist** adj.

tsetse /tet-si/ n. an African bloodsucking fly which transmits diseases.

tsp abbrev. teaspoonful.

tsunami /tsoo-nah-mi/ n. a tidal wave caused by an earthquake.

tub n. 1 a wide, open container. 2 a small container for food.

tuba n. a large low-pitched brass wind instrument.

tubby adj. (**tubbier**, **tubbiest**) informal short and fat.

tube n. 1 a long, hollow cylinder. 2 a flexible container sealed at one end and having a cap at the other. 3 (**the Tube**) trademark the underground railway in London.

tuber n. a thick underground part of the stem or root of some plants from which new plants grow. ■ **tuberous** adj.

tubercle n. a small rounded swelling.

Thesaurus

....

voted, sincere, dedicated, supportive, dutiful. ■ OPPOSITES untrue, false.

trump v. SURPASS, outperform, outdo, outshine. □ **trump up** INVENT, make up, fabricate, devise, concoct, hatch, contrive, fake; informal cook up.

trust n. 1 FAITH, confidence, belief, conviction, credence, assurance, certainty, reliance, hope, expectation. 2 RESPONSIBILITY, duty, obligation, commitment. ▸v. 1 PUT/PLACE ONE'S TRUST IN, have faith/confidence in, be convinced by, pin one's hopes on. 2 HOPE, assume, presume, expect, believe, suppose. ■ OPPOSITES distrust.

trustful adj. TRUSTING, unsuspicious, unguarded, unwary, unsuspecting, unquestioning, credulous, gullible, ingenuous, naive, innocent. ■ OPPOSITES suspicious.

trustworthy adj. RELIABLE, dependable, stable, staunch, loyal, faithful, trusty, responsible, sensible, level-headed, honest, honourable, upright, ethical, righteous, principled, virtuous. ■ OPPOSITES untrustworthy.

truth n. 1 TRUTHFULNESS, accuracy, correctness, rightness, validity, fact, factualness, factuality, genuineness, veracity, verity, honesty. 2 REALITY, actuality, factuality. ■ OPPOSITES falsehood, fiction.

truthful adj. 1 HONEST, trustworthy, candid, frank, open, forthright, straight, veracious. 2 TRUE, accurate, correct, right, valid, factual, exact, faithful, precise, genuine, reliable, honest, veracious. ■ OPPOSITES untruthful, inaccurate.

try v. 1 ATTEMPT, aim, endeavour, make an effort, exert oneself, undertake, strive, assay, seek, struggle, do one's best; informal have a go/shot/crack/stab. 2 TRY OUT, test, put to the test, experiment with, assay, investigate, examine, appraise, evaluate, assess, experience,

tuberculosis n. a serious infectious disease in which small swellings appear, esp. in the lungs. ■ **tubercular** adj.

tubing n. tubular pieces of plastic etc.

tubular adj. tube-shaped.

TUC abbrev. Trades Union Congress.

tuck v. **1** push, fold, or turn under or between two surfaces. **2** store in a safe or secret place. **3** (**tuck in**) informal eat heartily. ▶ n. **1** a flattened, stitched fold in a garment or material. **2** informal food eaten by schoolchildren as a snack.

Tudor adj. of the English royal dynasty which ruled 1485–1603.

Tuesday n. the day before Wednesday.

tufa n. a porous rock formed as a deposit from mineral springs.

tuft n. a bunch of threads, grass, or hair, held or growing together at the base. ■ **tufted** adj. **tufty** adj.

tug v. (**tugging**, **tugged**) pull hard or suddenly. ▶ n. **1** a hard or sudden pull. **2** a small, powerful boat for towing larger boats. □ **tug of war** a contest of strength in which two teams pull at opposite ends of a rope.

tuition n. teaching or instruction.

tulip n. a plant with bright cup-shaped flowers.

tulle /tyool/ n. a soft, fine net fabric.

tumble v. **1** fall suddenly, clumsily, or headlong. **2** move in a headlong way. ▶ n. **1** a fall. **2** an untidy mass or state. **3** an acrobatic feat. □ **tumbledown** dilapidated. **tumble dryer** a machine for drying washing in hot air inside a rotating drum.

tumbler n. **1** a drinking glass with no handle or stem. **2** an acrobat. **3** a part of a lock that holds the bolt until lifted by a key.

tumbril n. hist. an open cart used to take prisoners to the guillotine during the French Revolution.

tumescent adj. swollen. ■ **tumescence** n.

tummy n. (pl. **tummies**) informal the stomach or abdomen.

tumour (US **tumor**) n. a swelling of a part of the body caused by an abnormal growth of tissue.

tumult n. **1** a loud, confused noise. **2** confusion or disorder. ■ **tumultuous** adj.

tun n. a large cask.

tuna n. (pl. **tuna** or **tunas**) a large edible sea fish.

tundra n. a vast, flat, treeless Arctic region with permanently frozen subsoil.

tune n. a pleasant-sounding sequence of musical notes. ▶ v. **1** adjust a musical instrument to the correct pitch. **2** adjust a radio or television to the desired frequency. **3** adjust an engine to run smoothly. □ **in** (or **out of**) **tune** in (or not in) the correct musical pitch. ■ **tuneful** adj. **tunefully** adv. **tuneless** adj.

tuner n. **1** a person who tunes pianos etc. **2** a part of a stereo system that receives radio signals.

tungsten n. a hard grey metallic element.

tunic n. **1** a loose sleeveless garment reaching to the thigh or knees. **2** a close-fitting short coat worn as part of a uniform.

tunnel n. an underground passage. ▶ v. (**tunnelling**, **tunnelled**; US **tunneling**, **tunneled**) dig or force a passage underground or through something.

tunny n. (pl. **tunny** or **tunnies**) a tuna.

tup n. a ram.

turban n. a long length of material wound round a cap or the head, worn

Thesaurus

sample; informal check out.

trying adj. TROUBLESOME, bothersome, tiresome, irksome, vexatious, annoying, irritating, exasperating.

tuck v. GATHER, push, ease, insert, stuff.

tug v. PULL, jerk, yank, wrench, drag, draw.

tumble v. FALL OVER, fall down, fall headlong, topple, fall head over heels, fall end over end, lose one's footing/balance, stumble, stagger, trip up. ■ OPPOSITES rise.

tumbledown adj. DILAPIDATED, ramshackle, crumbling, disintegrating, falling to pieces/bits, decrepit, ruined, in ruins, rickety, tottering, teetering, shaky.

tumour n. LUMP, growth, cancer, cancerous growth, malignant growth, malignancy.

tumult n. DIN, uproar, commotion, racket, hubbub, hullabaloo, clamour, shouting, yelling, pandemonium, babel, bedlam, noise, ruckus. ■ OPPOSITES tranquillity.

tumultuous adj. LOUD, noisy, clamorous, ear-shattering, deafening, earpiercing, blaring, uproarious, unrestrained, boisterous, rowdy, unruly, disorderly, fierce, obstreperous, wild, violent.

tune n. MELODY, air, song, theme, strain,

by Muslim and Sikh men.

turbid adj. (of a liquid) cloudy or muddy.

turbine n. a machine in which a wheel or rotor is driven by a flow of water or gas.

turbocharger n. a supercharger driven by a turbine powered by the engine's exhaust gases. ■ **turbocharged** adj.

turbot n. (pl. **turbot** or **turbots**) a large edible flatfish.

turbulent adj. 1 involving much conflict, disorder, or confusion. 2 (of air or water) moving unsteadily or violently. ■ **turbulence** n. **turbulently** adv.

tureen n. a deep covered dish from which soup is served.

turf n. (pl. **turfs** or **turves**) 1 grass and the soil just below it. 2 a piece of turf. 3 (**the turf**) horse racing and racecourses. ▶ v. 1 (**turf off/out**) informal force to leave. 2 cover with turf. □ **turf accountant** a bookmaker.

turgid adj. 1 swollen or full. 2 (of language) pompous. ■ **turgidity** n.

Turk n. a person from Turkey.

turkey n. (pl. **turkeys**) a large bird bred for food.

Turkish n. the language of Turkey. ▶ adj. of Turkey or its language. □ **Turkish bath** a period of sitting in a room filled with very hot air or steam, followed by washing and massage. **Turkish delight** a sweet of flavoured gelatin coated in icing sugar.

turmeric n. a bright yellow spice.

turmoil n. a state of great disturbance or confusion.

turn v. 1 move around a central point. 2 move so as to face or go in a different direction. 3 make or become. 4 shape wood on a lathe. 5 twist or sprain an ankle. ▶ n. 1 an act of turning. 2 a bend or branch in a road, river, etc. 3 the time when a member of a group must or is allowed to do something. 4 a time when one period ends and another begins. 5 a change in circumstances. 6 a short walk. 7 a brief feeling of illness. 8 a short performance. □ **do someone a good turn** do something helpful for someone. **turn against** make or become hostile towards. **turncoat** a person who changes sides in a dispute etc. **turn down** reject. **turn in** hand over to the authorities. **turn off** switch off. **turn on** 1 switch on. 2 suddenly attack. 3 informal excite sexually. **turnout** the number of people attending or taking part in an event. **turn out** 1 switch off an electric light. 2 prove to be the case. 3 be present at an event. 4 (**be turned out**) be dressed in a particular way. **turnover** 1 the amount of money taken by a business. 2 the rate at which employees leave or goods are sold and are replaced. 3 a small pie made of pastry folded over a filling. **turnpike** hist. & US a road on which a toll is collected. **turnstile** a revolving gate allowing only one person at a time to pass through. **turntable** a circular revolving platform. **turn up** 1 increase the volume of. 2 be found. 3 appear. **turn-up** 1 the end of a trouser leg folded upwards on the outside. 2 informal an unexpected event.

turning n. a place where a road branches off another.

turnip n. a round root vegetable.

turpentine n. a liquid derived from cer-

Thesaurus

motif.

tunnel n. UNDERGROUND/SUBTERRANEAN PASSAGE, underpass, subway, burrow. ▶ v. DIG, excavate, burrow, mine, penetrate.

turbulent adj. 1 TEMPESTUOUS, stormy, raging, foaming, rough, choppy, agitated. 2 DISTURBED, agitated, unsettled, unstable, troubled, distraught, in turmoil. ■ OPPOSITES peaceful.

turgid adj. BOMBASTIC, high-flown, high-sounding, rhetorical, oratorical, grandiloquent, magniloquent, extravagant, pretentious, pompous, flowery, fulsome, orotund, fustian. ■ OPPOSITES simple.

turmoil n. AGITATION, ferment, confusion, disorder, disarray, upheaval, chaos, pandemonium, bedlam, tumult. ■ OPPOSITES peace.

turn v. 1 GO ROUND, rotate, revolve, circle, roll, spin, wheel, whirl, gyrate, swivel, pivot. 2 TURN ROUND, change direction/course, go back, return, reverse direction, make a U-turn. 3 TURN OVER, reverse, invert, flip over, turn topsy-turvy. 4 CHANGE, alter, transform, metamorphose, mutate. 5 BECOME, come to be, get, go. 6 GO/TURN SOUR, sour, curdle, become rancid, go bad, go off. ▶ n. 1 ROTATION, revolution, circle, spin, whirl, twirl, gyration, swivel. 2 TURNING, bend, curve, corner, twist, winding. 3 TIME, opportunity, chance, stint, chance, move, try, attempt; informal go, shot, crack. □ **turn down** see REJECT. **turn up** 1 INCREASE, raise, amplify, make louder, intensify. 2 ARRIVE, appear, put in an appearance, present oneself, be present;

tain trees, used to thin paint and clean brushes.

turpitude n. formal wickedness.

turps n. turpentine.

turquoise n. **1** a greenish-blue semi-precious stone. **2** a greenish-blue colour.

turret n. **1** a small tower. **2** an armoured tower for a gun on a ship, aircraft, or tank. ■ **turreted** adj.

turtle n. a sea reptile with a bony or leathery shell. □ **turn turtle** capsize. **turtle dove** a small dove with a soft call. **turtleneck** a high, round, close-fitting neckline.

turves pl. of TURF.

tusk n. a long, pointed tooth protruding from the mouth of an elephant, walrus, etc.

tussle n. a vigorous struggle. ▶v. engage in a tussle.

tussock n. a clump or tuft of grass.

tutelage /tyoo-ti-lij/ n. **1** protection or authority. **2** tuition.

tutor n. **1** a private teacher. **2** a university or college teacher. ▶v. act as a tutor to.

tutorial n. a period of tuition given by a university or college tutor. ▶adj. of a tutor.

tutu n. a female ballet dancer's short, stiff skirt that projects from the waist.

tuxedo /tuk-see-doh/ n. (pl. **tuxedos** or **tuxedoes**) a man's dinner jacket.

TV abbrev. television.

twaddle n. informal nonsense.

twang n. **1** a strong ringing sound made by the plucked string of a musical instrument. **2** a nasal way of speaking. ▶v. make or cause to make a twang.

tweak v. **1** twist or pull sharply. **2** informal improve by making fine adjustments. ▶n. an act of tweaking.

twee adj. excessively quaint, pretty, or sentimental.

tweed n. **1** a rough, flecked woollen cloth. **2** (**tweeds**) clothes made of

tweed. ■ **tweedy** adj.

tweet v. & n. (give) a chirp.

tweeter n. a loudspeaker designed to reproduce high frequencies.

tweezers pl. n. a small pair of pincers for plucking out hairs and picking up small objects.

twelve adj. & n. two more than ten; 12 or XII. ■ **twelfth** adj. & n.

twenty adj. & n. (pl. **twenties**) ten less than thirty; 20 or XX. ■ **twentieth** adj. & n.

twerp n. informal a silly person.

twice adv. **1** two times. **2** double in degree or quantity.

twiddle v. play or fiddle with idly. □ **twiddle one's thumbs** have nothing to do.

twig n. a slender woody shoot growing from a branch or stem. ▶v. (**twigging**, **twigged**) informal understand or realize.

twilight n. **1** the soft light from the sky when the sun is below the horizon. **2** the period of this.

twill n. a woven fabric with a surface of diagonal parallel ridges. ■ **twilled** adj.

twin n. **1** one of two children or animals born at one birth. **2** one of a pair that are exactly alike. ▶v. (**twinning**, **twinned**) **1** combine as a pair. **2** link a town with another in a different country for cultural exchange.

twine n. strong string. ▶v. wind or coil.

twinge n. a brief, sharp pain or pang.

twinkle v. shine with a flickering light. ▶n. a twinkling light.

twirl v. spin quickly and lightly round. ▶n. **1** an act of twirling. **2** a spiral shape.

twist v. **1** bend or curl. **2** force out of the natural position. **3** have a winding course. **4** deliberately change the meaning of. ▶n. **1** an act of twisting. **2** a spiral shape. **3** an unexpected development.

twit n. informal a silly person.

twitch v. make a short, sudden jerking

Thesaurus

informal show, show up.

turnover n. **1** (GROSS) REVENUE, income, volume of business, business, financial flow. **2** RATE OF REPLACEMENT, change, movement.

tutor v. TEACH, instruct, coach, educate, school, train, drill, direct, guide.

twig n. BRANCH, stick, offshoot, shoot, spray, stem.

twilight n. DUSK, late afternoon, early evening, gloaming; literary crepuscule.

twin n. DOUBLE, lookalike, image, dupli-

cate, clone; informal spitting image, spit, dead spit, dead ringer. ▶v. JOIN, link, couple, pair, yoke.

twinge n. STAB OF PAIN, spasm, pain, pang, ache, throb, tweak, tingle, cramp, stitch.

twist v. **1** BEND, warp, misshape, deform, contort, distort, wrench, wrest. **2** WRENCH, turn, sprain, rick. **3** WIND, curve, bend, twine, zigzag, meander, snake, worm. **4** DISTORT, pervert, warp, garble, misrepresent, falsify, misquote, movement. ▶n. a twitching movement.

twitter v. **1** (of a bird) make a series of short high sounds. **2** talk rapidly in a nervous or trivial way. ▶n. a twittering sound.

two adj. & n. one less than three; 2 or II. □ **two-dimensional** having or appearing to have length and breadth but no depth. **two-faced** insincere and deceitful. **twosome** a set of two people. **two-time** informal be unfaithful to a lover. ■ **twofold** adj. & adv.

tycoon n. a wealthy, powerful person in business or industry.

tying pres. part. of TIE.

tyke n. informal a mischievous child.

tympani var. of TIMPANI.

tympanum n. (pl. **tympanums** or **tympana**) the eardrum.

type n. **1** a kind or category. **2** informal a person of a specified nature. **3** printed characters or letters. ▶v. write using a typewriter or computer. □ **typecast** (of an actor) repeatedly cast in the same type of role. **typeface** a particular design of printed type. **typescript** a typed copy of a text. **typesetter** a person or machine that arranges or generates type for printing. **typewriter** a machine with keys for producing print-like characters. ■ **typist** n.

typhoid n. a serious infectious disease causing fever.

typhoon n. a tropical storm.

typhus n. an infectious disease causing a rash and fever.

typical adj. having the distinctive qualities of a particular type of person or thing. ■ **typically** adv.

typify v. (**typifying**, **typified**) be typical of.

typography n. the process or style of printing. ■ **typographer** n. **typographical** adj.

tyrannize (or **-ise**) v. dominate or treat cruelly.

tyrannosaurus rex n. a very large meat-eating dinosaur.

tyranny n. (pl. **tyrannies**) cruel and oppressive government or rule. ■ **tyrannical** adj. **tyrannically** adv. **tyrannous** adj.

tyrant n. a cruel and oppressive person, esp. a ruler.

tyre (US **tire**) n. a rubber covering, usu. inflated, that fits around a wheel.

tyro n. (pl. **tyros**) a beginner.

tzatziki /tsat-**see**-ki/ n. a Greek dish of yogurt with cucumber, garlic, and often mint.

Thesaurus

....

misreport, change, alter. ▶n. **1** BEND, warp, kink, deformity, contortion, distortion. **2** WRENCH, turn, sprain, rick. **3** DEVELOPMENT, turn, change, alteration, variation, slant.

twitch v. JERK, jump, quiver, shiver, quaver. ▶n. SPASM, jerk, jump, quiver, tremor, shiver, quaver.

type n. **1** KIND, sort, variety, form, class, classification, category, group, order, set, genre, strain, species, genus, ilk. **2** PRINT, fount, face, character.

typical adj. **1** REPRESENTATIVE, classic, standard, stock, orthodox, conventional, true to type, quintessential, archetypal. **2** NORMAL, average, ordinary, regular, general, customary, habitual, routine. **3** CHARACTERISTIC, in character, in keeping, to be expected. ■ OPPOSITES atypical.

typify v. EXEMPLIFY, characterize, personify, epitomize, symbolize, embody.

tyrannical adj. DESPOTIC, autocratic, dictatorial, authoritarian, high-handed, imperious, oppressive, coercive, domineering, bullying, harsh, strict, severe, cruel, brutal, unjust.

tyrant n. DESPOT, autocrat, dictator, absolute ruler, authoritarian, oppressor, martinet, slave-driver, bully.

Uu

ubiquitous /yoo-bi-kwi-tuhss/ adj. found everywhere. ■ **ubiquity** n.

udder n. the bag-like milk-producing organ of female cattle, sheep, goats, etc.

UFO n. (pl. **UFOs**) a mysterious object seen in the sky, believed by some to carry beings from outer space (short for *unidentified flying object*).

ugly adj. (**uglier**, **ugliest**) **1** unpleasant or unattractive in appearance. **2** hostile or threatening. ■ **ugliness** n.

UHF abbrev. ultra-high frequency, a radio frequency in the range 300 to 3,000 MHz.

UHT abbrev. ultra heat treated (esp. of milk).

UK abbrev. United Kingdom.

ukulele /yoo-kuh-lay-li/ n. a small four-stringed guitar.

ulcer n. an open sore. ■ **ulcerated** adj. **ulceration** n.

ulna n. (pl. **ulnae** or **ulnas**) the thinner, longer bone of the human forearm.

ulterior adj. other than what is obvious or admitted.

ultimate adj. **1** final. **2** best or most extreme. **3** fundamental. ■ **ultimately** adv.

ultimatum n. (pl. **ultimatums** or **ultimata**) a final warning that action will be taken unless one's demands are met.

ultra- prefix **1** beyond. **2** extremely.

ultramarine n. a brilliant deep blue.

ultrasonic adj. above the upper limit of human hearing.

ultrasound n. sound or other vibrations with an ultrasonic frequency, used in medical scans.

ultraviolet adj. of or using radiation with a wavelength just shorter than that of visible light rays.

ululate v. howl or wail. ■ **ululation** n.

umbel n. a broad flat flower cluster.

umber n. a brownish natural pigment.

umbilical adj. of the navel. □ **umbilical cord** a flexible tube by which a fetus is nourished while in the womb.

umbra n. (pl. **umbras** or **umbrae**) the dark central part of the shadow cast by the earth or the moon in an eclipse.

umbrage n. (**take umbrage**) take offence; become annoyed.

umbrella n. a folding dome-shaped device used as protection against rain.

umlaut /uum-lowt/ n. a mark (¨) placed over a vowel in some languages to indicate a change in pronunciation.

umpire n. (in certain sports) an official who supervises a game to ensure that the rules are observed. ▶ v. act as an umpire in.

umpteen adj. informal very many. ■ **umpteenth** adj.

UN abbrev. United Nations.

un- prefix **1** not. **2** reversing the action indicated by a verb.

unaccountable adj. **1** unable to be explained. **2** not responsible for results or consequences. ■ **unaccountably** adv.

unadulterated adj. not mixed with any different or extra elements.

ubiquitous adj. EVERYWHERE, omnipresent, ever-present, all-over, pervasive, universal. ■ OPPOSITES rare.

ugly adj. **1** UNATTRACTIVE, plain, homely, ill-favoured, unprepossessing, hideous, unlovely, unsightly, grotesque, horrible, horrid, frightful, vile, shocking, distasteful, disgusting, revolting; informal not much to look at. **2** THREATENING, menacing, ominous, sinister, dangerous, nasty, unpleasant, disagreeable. ■ OPPOSITES beautiful.

ulterior adj. HIDDEN, concealed, unrevealed, undisclosed, secret, covert, unapparent. ■ OPPOSITES overt.

ultimate adj. LAST, final, eventual, concluding, conclusive, terminal, end, furthest.

umpire n. ADJUDICATOR, arbitrator, arbiter, judge, moderator, referee; informal ref.

unable adj. NOT ABLE, incapable, powerless, impotent, not up/equal to, inadequate, ineffectual, incompetent.

unacceptable adj. UNSATISFACTORY, inadmissible, unsuitable, insupportable, intolerable, objectionable, offensive, obnoxious, undesirable, disagreeable, distasteful, improper.

unaccompanied adj. ALONE, on one's

unalloyed adj. **1** (of metal) pure. **2** complete; total.

unanimous /yoo-nan-i-muhss/ adj. **1** fully in agreement. **2** agreed by everyone involved. ■ **unanimity** n. **unanimously** adv.

unarmed adj. without weapons.

unassailable adj. unable to be attacked or defeated.

unassuming adj. not pretentious or arrogant.

unattended adj. not being supervised or looked after.

unavoidable adj. not able to be avoided or prevented. ■ **unavoidably** adv.

unaware adj. not aware of something. ▶ adv. (**unawares**) so as to surprise; unexpectedly.

unbalanced adj. emotionally or mentally disturbed.

unbeknown (or **unbeknownst**) adj. (**unbeknown to**) without the knowledge of.

unbelievable adj. **1** unlikely to be true. **2** extraordinary. ■ **unbelievably** adv.

unbend v. (**unbending**, **unbent**) **1** straighten. **2** become less formal or strict.

unbending adj. unwilling to change one's mind.

unbidden adj. without having been invited.

unborn adj. not yet born.

unbounded adj. having no limits.

unbridled adj. uncontrolled.

unburden v. (**unburden oneself**) confide in someone about a worry or problem.

uncalled adj. (**uncalled for**) undesirable and unnecessary.

uncanny adj. strange or mysterious. ■ **uncannily** adv.

unceremonious adj. impolite or abrupt. ■ **unceremoniously** adv.

uncertain adj. **1** not known, reliable, or definite. **2** not completely sure. ■ **uncertainly** adv. **uncertainty** n.

uncharitable adj. unkind or unsympathetic. ■ **uncharitably** adv.

uncharted adj. (of an area of land or sea) not mapped or surveyed.

uncle n. the brother of one's father or mother or the husband of one's aunt.

unclean adj. **1** dirty. **2** immoral. **3** (of food) forbidden by a religion.

uncommon adj. out of the ordinary;

Thesaurus

own, by oneself, solo, lone, solitary, single.

unaccustomed adj. UNUSED, not used, new, unpractised, unfamiliar, inexperienced, unversed.

unanimous adj. IN COMPLETE AGREEMENT/ACCORD, of one mind, like-minded, in harmony, at one, of a piece, with one voice, united, concordant. ■ OPPOSITES divided.

unassailable adj. IMPREGNABLE, invulnerable, invincible, secure, well defended. ■ OPPOSITES defenceless.

unassuming adj. see MODEST.

unattached adj. UNMARRIED, unwed, unwedded, uncommitted, free, available, single, on one's own, by oneself, unescorted. ■ OPPOSITES married.

unauthorized adj. UNOFFICIAL, unsanctioned, uncertified, unaccredited, unlicensed, unwarranted, unapproved, disallowed, prohibited, forbidden, illegal. ■ OPPOSITES official.

unavoidable adj. INESCAPABLE, inevitable, bound to happen, inexorable, ineluctable, certain, fated, predestined, necessary, compulsory, required, obligatory, mandatory.

unaware adj. UNKNOWING, unconscious, ignorant, heedless, unmindful, oblivious, uninformed, unenlightened; *informal*

in the dark. ■ OPPOSITES conscious.

unbelievable adj. BEYOND BELIEF, incredible, unconvincing, far-fetched, implausible, improbable, inconceivable, unthinkable, unimaginable, impossible, astonishing, astounding, staggering, preposterous. ■ OPPOSITES credible.

unbending adj. see INFLEXIBLE (3).

unbiased adj. IMPARTIAL, unprejudiced, non-partisan, neutral, objective, disinterested, dispassionate, detached, even-handed, open-minded, equitable, fair, just. ■ OPPOSITES prejudiced.

unbreakable adj. see INDESTRUCTIBLE.

uncertain adj. **1** UNKNOWN, undetermined, unsettled, in the balance, up in the air. **2** UNSURE, doubtful, dubious, undecided, unresolved, indecisive, irresolute, hesitant, wavering, vacillating, equivocating, vague, hazy, unclear, ambivalent, in two minds. **3** HESITANT, hesitating, tentative, halting, unsure, unconfident. ■ OPPOSITES predictable, sure, confident.

uncharted adj. UNMAPPED, unsurveyed, unexplored, unplumbed, unfamiliar, unknown, strange.

uncivilized adj. **1** BARBARIAN, barbarous, barbaric, primitive, savage, wild. **2** UNCOUTH, coarse, rough, boorish, vulgar, philistine, uneducated, uncultured, un-

unusual. ■ **uncommonly** adv.

uncompromising adj. unwilling to compromise.

unconcern n. a lack of worry or interest. ■ **unconcerned** adj.

unconditional adj. not subject to any conditions. ■ **unconditionally** adv.

unconscionable adj. not right or reasonable. ■ **unconscionably** adv.

unconscious adj. 1 not conscious. 2 done or existing without one realizing. 3 unaware. ■ **unconsciously** adv. **unconsciousness** n.

uncouth adj. lacking good manners.

uncover v. 1 remove a cover from. 2 discover something secret or unknown.

unction n. 1 the smearing of someone with oil as a religious ceremony. 2 excessive politeness.

unctuous adj. excessively polite or flattering. ■ **unctuously** adv.

undeceive v. tell someone that an idea or belief is mistaken.

undecided adj. 1 not having made a decision. 2 not settled or resolved.

undeniable adj. undoubtedly true. ■ **undeniably** adv.

under prep. 1 extending or directly below. 2 at a lower level or grade than. 3 controlled by. 4 according to the rules of. 5 undergoing. ▶ adv. extending or directly below something. □ **under**

way making progress.

under- prefix 1 below; beneath. 2 insufficiently.

underarm adj. & adv. done with the arm or hand below shoulder level.

undercarriage n. 1 an aircraft's landing wheels and supporting structure. 2 the supporting framework of a vehicle.

underclass n. the lowest and poorest social class in a country.

undercoat n. a layer of paint applied before the topcoat.

undercover adj. & adv. involving secret investigative work.

undercurrent n. 1 a current of water flowing below the surface. 2 an underlying feeling or influence.

undercut v. (**undercutting, undercut**) 1 offer goods or services at a lower price than a competitor. 2 cut or wear away the part under. 3 weaken; undermine.

underdog n. a competitor thought to have little chance of winning.

underdone adj. not cooked enough.

underestimate v. 1 estimate to be smaller or less important than in reality. 2 regard as less capable than in reality.

underfoot adv. 1 on the ground. 2 getting in one's way.

undergo v. (**undergoes, undergoing,**

Thesaurus

cultivated, unsophisticated, unrefined, unpolished.

unclean adj. *see* DIRTY.

uncomfortable adj. UNEASY, ill at ease, nervous, tense, edgy, self-conscious, awkward, embarrassed, discomfited, disturbed, troubled, worried, anxious, apprehensive. ■ OPPOSITES relaxed.

uncommon adj. *see* UNUSUAL.

uncompromising adj. INFLEXIBLE, unbending, unyielding, hard-line, tough, immovable, firm, determined, dogged, obstinate, obdurate, tenacious, relentless, implacable, inexorable, intransigent. ■ OPPOSITES flexible.

unconcerned adj. *see* INDIFFERENT.

unconditional adj. COMPLETE, total, entire, full, absolute, downright, utter, all-out, thoroughgoing, unequivocal, conclusive, definite, positive.

unconscious adj. 1 SENSELESS, insensible, comatose, knocked out, stunned, dazed; *informal* out like a light, out cold, out. 2 UNAWARE, heedless, ignorant, in ignorance, oblivious, insensible. 3 UNINTENTIONAL, unintended, accidental, un-

premeditated. ■ OPPOSITES aware.

unconventional adj. UNORTHODOX, irregular, unusual, uncommon, unwonted, rare, out of the ordinary, atypical, singular, individual, individualistic, different, original, idiosyncratic, nonconformist, bohemian, eccentric, odd. ■ OPPOSITES orthodox.

uncouth adj. ROUGH, coarse, uncivilized, uncultured, uncultivated, unrefined, unpolished, unsophisticated, crude, gross, loutish, boorish, oafish, rude, impolite, discourteous, unmannerly, bad-mannered, ill-bred, vulgar. ■ OPPOSITES refined.

uncover v. 1 EXPOSE, lay bare, bare, reveal, unwrap. 2 *see* DISCOVER.

undaunted adj. UNAFRAID, unflinching, indomitable, resolute, intrepid, bold, valiant, brave, courageous. ■ OPPOSITES fearful.

undemonstrative adj. UNEMOTIONAL, impassive, restrained, self-contained, reserved, uncommunicative, unresponsive, stiff.

thinking, unwitting, inadvertent, un-

u

underwent; past part. **undergone**) experience something unpleasant or difficult.

undergraduate n. a university student who has not yet taken a degree.

underground adj. & adv. **1** beneath the surface of the ground. **2** in secrecy or hiding. ▶ n. an underground railway.

undergrowth n. a dense growth of shrubs and other plants.

underhand adj. acting or done secretly or dishonestly.

underlay n. material laid under a carpet for support.

underlie v. (**underlying, underlay**; past part. **underlain**) be the cause or basis of.

underline v. **1** draw a line under. **2** emphasize.

underling n. a subordinate.

undermine v. **1** damage or weaken. **2** weaken the foundations of.

underneath prep. & adv. **1** situated directly below. **2** so as to be hidden by.

underpants pl. n. an article of underwear covering the lower part of the body and having two holes for the legs.

underpass n. a road or tunnel passing under another road or a railway.

underpin v. (**underpinning, underpinned**) **1** strengthen from below. **2** form the basis for an argument or theory.

underprivileged adj. not enjoying the same rights or standard of living as the majority.

underrate v. underestimate.

underscore v. underline.

undersell v. sell something at a lower price than a competitor.

undershoot v. (**undershooting, undershot**) **1** fall short of a target. **2** land short of a runway.

underside n. the bottom or lower side or surface.

undersigned n. the person or people who have signed the document in question.

underskirt n. a petticoat.

understaffed adj. having too few members of staff.

understand v. (**understanding, understood**) **1** know or realize the intended meaning or cause of. **2** interpret or view in a particular way. **3** believe to be the case from information received.

understandable adj. **1** able to be understood. **2** to be expected; normal or reasonable. ■ **understandably** adv.

understanding n. **1** the ability to understand. **2** sympathetic awareness or tolerance. **3** an agreement. ▶ adj. sympathetically aware of others' feelings. ■ **understandingly** adv.

understate v. represent as smaller or less important than in reality. ■ **understatement** n.

understated adj. pleasingly subtle.

understudy n. (pl. **understudies**) an actor who learns another's role in order to take their place if necessary.

undertake v. (**undertaking, under-**

Thesaurus

underestimate v. **1** MISCALCULATE, misjudge, set too low. **2** UNDERRATE, rate too low, undervalue, set little store by, not do justice to.

undergo v. GO THROUGH, experience, sustain, endure, bear, tolerate, stand, withstand, put up with, weather.

underground adj. **1** SUBTERRANEAN, below ground, buried, sunken. **2** SECRET, clandestine, surreptitious, covert, undercover, concealed, hidden.

underhand adj. DECEITFUL, devious, sneaky, furtive, surreptitious, covert, dishonest, dishonourable, unscrupulous, fraudulent. ■ OPPOSITES honest.

undermine v. WEAKEN, impair, damage, injure, sap, threaten, subvert, sabotage. **2** TUNNEL UNDER, dig under, burrow under, excavate. ■ OPPOSITES support.

underprivileged adj. DISADVANTAGED, deprived, in need, needy, in want, destitute, poor, impoverished, impecunious.

■ OPPOSITES wealthy.

understand v. **1** COMPREHEND, apprehend, grasp, see, take in, perceive, discern, make out, glean, recognize, appreciate, get to know, follow, fathom; *informal* get the hang/drift of, catch on, latch on to, tumble to, figure out, twig. **2** APPRECIATE, accept, commiserate with, feel compassionate towards, sympathize with, empathize with. **3** GATHER, hear, be informed, learn, believe, think, conclude. ■ OPPOSITES misunderstand.

understanding n. **1** COMPREHENSION, apprehension, grasp, perception, discernment, appreciation, interpretation. **2** INTELLIGENCE, intellect, mind, brainpower, brains, powers of reasoning; *informal* grey matter. **3** COMPASSION, sympathy, empathy, insight. **4** AGREEMENT, gentleman's agreement, arrangement, bargain, pact, compact, contract. ▶ adj. COMPASSIONATE, sympathetic, sensitive, considerate, kind, thoughtful, tolerant,

took; past part. **undertaken**) **1** begin an activity. **2** formally promise.

undertaker n. a person whose job is to prepare dead bodies for burial or cremation and to organize funerals.

undertaking n. **1** a formal promise. **2** a task.

undertone n. **1** a low or subdued tone. **2** an underlying quality or feeling.

undertow n. an undercurrent moving in the opposite direction to the surface water.

underwater adj. & adv. situated or occurring beneath the surface of the water.

underwear n. clothing worn under other clothes next to the skin.

underwent past of UNDERGO.

underworld n. **1** the world of criminals or of organized crime. **2** (in myths and legends) the home of the dead, imagined as being under the earth.

underwrite v. (**underwriting**, **underwrote**; past part. **underwritten**) **1** accept legal responsibility for an insurance policy. **2** finance. ▪ **underwriter** n.

undesirable adj. harmful or unpleasant.

undies pl. n. informal articles of underwear.

undo v. (**undoes**, **undoing**, **undid**; past part. **undone**) **1** unfasten or loosen.

2 cancel the effect of. **3** cause the ruin or downfall of.

undoing n. a person's ruin or downfall.

undone adj. **1** not tied or fastened. **2** not done or finished.

undoubted adj. not questioned or doubted. ▪ **undoubtedly** adv.

undreamed (or **undreamt**) adj. (**undreamed of**) not previously thought to be possible.

undress v. take clothes off. ▪ n. the state of being naked or only partially clothed.

undue adj. excessive. ▪ **unduly** adv.

undulate v. **1** move with a smooth wave-like motion. **2** have a wavy form or outline. ▪ **undulation** n.

undying adj. everlasting.

unearth v. **1** find in the ground by digging. **2** discover by searching.

unearthly adj. **1** supernatural or mysterious. **2** informal unreasonably early or inconvenient.

uneasy adj. (**uneasier**, **uneasiest**) troubled or uncomfortable. ▪ **unease** n. **uneasily** adv. **uneasiness** n.

uneatable adj. not fit to be eaten.

uneconomic adj. not profitable.

unemployable adj. not having enough skills or qualifications to get paid employment.

unemployed adj. **1** without a paid job.

Thesaurus

patient, forbearing.

understate v. DOWNPLAY, play down, make light of, minimize; informal soft-pedal. ▪ OPPOSITES exaggerate.

undertake v. TAKE ON, set about, tackle, shoulder, assume, enter upon, begin, start, commence, embark on, venture upon, attempt, try.

undertone n. **1** LOW TONE/VOICE, murmur, whisper. **2** UNDERCURRENT, hint, suggestion, intimation, insinuation, trace, tinge, touch, atmosphere, aura, tenor, flavour.

undervalue v. see UNDERESTIMATE (2).

underwear n. UNDERCLOTHES, undergarments, underclothing, lingerie; informal undies, unmentionables, smalls.

undesirable adj. UNWANTED, unwished for, unpleasant, disagreeable, nasty, unacceptable.

undisciplined adj. **1** UNRULY, disorderly, disobedient, obstreperous, recalcitrant, refractory, uncontrolled, unrestrained, wild, wilful, wayward. **2** UNSYSTEMATIC, unmethodical, disorganized, unorganized.

undisguised adj. OPEN, obvious, evi-

dent, patent, manifest, transparent, overt, unconcealed, unmistakable.

undistinguished adj. see ORDINARY (2).

undo v. **1** UNFASTEN, unhook, unbutton, untie, unlace, loosen, disentangle, release, free, open, unlock. **2** DESTROY, ruin, wreck, smash, shatter, annihilate, obliterate, overturn.

undoubted adj. UNDISPUTED, not in doubt, uncontested, unquestioned, not in question, certain, unquestionable, indubitable, incontrovertible, irrefutable.

undress v. TAKE OFF ONE'S CLOTHES, remove one's clothes, strip, disrobe; informal peel off.

undue adj. UNWARRANTED, unjustified, unreasonable, inappropriate, unsuitable, improper, ill-advised, excessive, immoderate. ▪ OPPOSITES appropriate.

undying adj. see ETERNAL.

uneasy adj. ILL AT EASE, troubled, worried, anxious, apprehensive, alarmed, disturbed, agitated, nervous, nervy, on edge, edgy, restive, restless, unsettled, discomposed, discomfited, perturbed, upset; informal jittery. ▪ OPPOSITES calm.

2 not in use. ∎ **unemployment** n.

unending adj. seeming to last for ever.

unequalled (US **unequaled**) adj. better or greater than all others.

unequivocal adj. leaving no doubt. ∎ **unequivocally** adv.

unerring adj. always right or accurate. ∎ **unerringly** adv.

uneven adj. **1** not level or smooth. **2** not regular. ∎ **unevenly** adv. **unevenness** n.

unexceptionable adj. not open to objection.

unexceptional adj. not out of the ordinary.

unexpected adj. not expected or thought likely to happen. ∎ **unexpectedly** adv.

unfailing adj. reliable or constant. ∎ **un-**

failingly adv.

unfair adj. not based on or showing fairness. ∎ **unfairly** adv. **unfairness** n.

unfaithful adj. **1** not faithful; disloyal. **2** having sex with a person other than one's regular partner. ∎ **unfaithfulness** n.

unfeeling adj. unsympathetic, harsh, or cruel.

unfit adj. **1** unsuitable. **2** not in good physical condition.

unflappable adj. informal calm in a crisis.

unfold v. **1** open or spread out. **2** reveal or be revealed.

unforeseen adj. not predicted.

unforgettable adj. highly memorable. ∎ **unforgettably** adv.

unfortunate adj. **1** unlucky. **2** regrettable. ∎ **unfortunately** adv.

Thesaurus

unemotional adj. UNDEMONSTRATIVE, passionless, cold, frigid, cool, reserved, restrained, unfeeling, unresponsive, unexcitable, unmoved, impassive, apathetic, indifferent, phlegmatic, detached.

unemployed adj. JOBLESS, out of work, out of a job, workless, redundant, laid off, idle; informal on the dole.

unequal adj. **1** DIFFERENT, differing, dissimilar, unlike, unalike, disparate, varying, variable. **2** UNEVEN, asymmetrical, unsymmetrical, unbalanced, lopsided, irregular, disproportionate. **3** UNFAIR, unjust, inequitable, uneven, one-sided, ill-matched. ∎ OPPOSITES fair, identical.

unequivocal adj. UNAMBIGUOUS, clear, clear-cut, plain, explicit, unqualified, categorical, direct, straightforward, blunt, point-blank, straight from the shoulder, positive, certain, decisive. ∎ OPPOSITES ambiguous.

unethical adj. see IMMORAL.

uneven adj. **1** ROUGH, bumpy, lumpy. **2** VARIABLE, varying, changeable, irregular, erratic, patchy. **3** UNEQUAL, asymmetrical, unsymmetrical, unbalanced, lopsided, irregular, disproportionate. ∎ OPPOSITES flat, regular, equal.

uneventful adj. UNEXCITING, uninteresting, monotonous, boring, dull, tedious, routine, ordinary, run-of-the-mill, pedestrian, commonplace, everyday, unexceptional, unremarkable. ∎ OPPOSITES exciting.

unexpected adj. UNFORESEEN, unanticipated, unpredicted, not bargained for, sudden, abrupt, surprising, startling, astonishing, out of the blue, chance, fortuitous. ∎ OPPOSITES predictable.

unfair adj. **1** UNJUST, inequitable, partial, partisan, prejudiced, biased, one-sided. **2** UNDESERVED, unmerited, uncalled for, unreasonable, unjustifiable, unwarrantable, out of proportion, disproportionate, excessive, extreme, immoderate. ∎ OPPOSITES just, justified.

unfaithful adj. **1** DISLOYAL, false-hearted, faithless, perfidious, treacherous, traitorous. **2** ADULTEROUS, fickle, untrue, inconstant; informal two-timing. ∎ OPPOSITES loyal.

unfamiliar adj. UNKNOWN, new, strange, alien, unaccustomed, uncommon.

unfashionable adj. OUT OF FASHION/DATE, old-fashioned, outmoded, outdated, dated, behind the times, passé, archaic, obsolete, antiquated.

unfasten v. see UNDO.

unfavourable adj. **1** ADVERSE, critical, hostile, inimical, unfriendly, negative, discouraging, poor, bad. **2** DISADVANTAGEOUS, adverse, unfortunate, unhappy, detrimental. ∎ OPPOSITES positive.

unfeeling adj. see CALLOUS.

unfit adj. **1** UNSUITED, ill-suited, unsuitable, unqualified, ineligible, unequipped, unprepared, untrained, incapable, inadequate, incompetent, not up to, not equal to. **2** OUT OF CONDITION, in poor condition/shape, flabby, unhealthy, debilitated, weak. ∎ OPPOSITES suitable.

unfold v. OPEN OUT, spread out, stretch out, flatten, straighten out, unfurl, unroll, unravel.

unforgivable adj. INEXCUSABLE, unpardonable, unjustifiable, indefensible, reprehensible, deplorable, despicable, contemptible, disgraceful, shameful.

unfounded adj. having no basis in fact.
unfrock v. defrock.
unfurl v. spread out or unroll.
ungainly adj. clumsy; awkward. ■ **ungainliness** n.
ungodly adj. **1** sinful or immoral. **2** informal unreasonably early or late.
ungovernable adj. uncontrollable.
ungrateful adj. not feeling or showing gratitude. ■ **ungratefully** adv.
unguarded adj. **1** not guarded. **2** not well considered; careless.
unguent /ung-gwuhnt/ n. an ointment or lubricant.
ungulate n. a mammal with hoofs.
unhand v. old use let go of.
unhappy adj. (**unhappier, unhappiest**) **1** not happy; sad. **2** unfortunate. ■ **unhappily** adv. **unhappiness** n.
unhealthy adj. (**unhealthier, unhealthiest**) **1** in poor health. **2** not

good for health. ■ **unhealthily** adv.
unheard adj. (**unheard of**) previously unknown.
unhinged adj. mentally unbalanced.
unholy adj. **1** wicked. **2** informal dreadful.
unicorn n. a mythical animal like a horse with a single horn on its forehead.
uniform adj. the same in all cases and at all times. ▶n. the distinctive clothing worn by members of the same organization or school. ■ **uniformed** adj. **uniformity** n. **uniformly** adv.
unify v. (**unifying, unified**) unite. ■ **unification** n.
unilateral adj. done by or affecting only one person, group, etc. ■ **unilaterally** adv.
unimpeachable adj. beyond doubt or criticism.
uninhabited adj. without inhabitants.

Thesaurus

■ OPPOSITES venial.
unfortunate adj. UNLUCKY, out of luck, luckless, ill-starred, star-crossed, hapless, wretched, miserable, unhappy, poor.
unfriendly adj. UNCONGENIAL, unsociable, inhospitable, unneighbourly, unsympathetic, aloof, cold, cool, distant, disagreeable, unpleasant, surly, sour, hostile, inimical, antagonistic, aggressive, quarrelsome.
ungainly adj. see AWKWARD.
ungrateful adj. UNTHANKFUL, unappreciative, impolite, uncivil, rude.
unhappy adj. **1** SAD, miserable, sorrowful, dejected, despondent, disconsolate, broken-hearted, down, downcast, dispirited, crestfallen, depressed, melancholy, blue, gloomy, glum, mournful, woebegone. **2** UNFORTUNATE, regrettable, inappropriate, unsuitable, inapt, tactless, ill-advised, injudicious.
unhealthy adj. **1** IN POOR HEALTH, unwell, ill, ailing, sick, sickly, poorly, indisposed, unsound, weak, feeble, frail, delicate, debilitated, infirm. **2** UNWHOLESOME, detrimental, injurious, damaging, deleterious, noxious.
unheard of adj. **1** UNPRECEDENTED, exceptional, extraordinary, undreamed of, unbelievable, inconceivable, unimaginable, unthinkable. **2** UNKNOWN, unfamiliar, new. ■ OPPOSITES common, well known.
unhurried adj. LEISURELY, leisured, easy, slow, slow-moving, deliberate, sedate. ■ OPPOSITES hasty.
unidentified adj. NAMELESS, unnamed,

unknown, anonymous, incognito, obscure, unmarked, undesignated, unclassified.
uniform adj. **1** CONSTANT, consistent, invariable, unvarying, unvaried, unchanging, undeviating, stable, regular, even, equal. **2** SAME, alike, like, selfsame, identical, similar, equal. ▶n. LIVERY, regalia, dress, regimentals.
unify v. UNITE, bring together, merge, fuse, amalgamate, coalesce, combine, blend, mix, bind, link up, consolidate. ■ OPPOSITES separate.
unimaginable adj. UNTHINKABLE, inconceivable, incredible, unbelievable, unheard of, unthought of, implausible, improbable, unlikely, impossible, undreamed of, fantastic; informal mindboggling, mind-blowing.
unimportant adj. OF LITTLE/NO IMPORTANCE, insignificant, of no consequence, inconsequential, of no account, immaterial, irrelevant, not worth mentioning, minor, slight, trivial, petty, paltry, insubstantial, inferior, worthless, nugatory; informal no great shakes; US informal dinky.
uninhabited adj. VACANT, empty, unoccupied, unpopulated, unpeopled, unsettled, abandoned, deserted, forsaken, barren, desert, desolate.
uninhibited adj. UNSELFCONSCIOUS, spontaneous, free and easy, informal, open, candid, outspoken, unrestrained, unrepressed, unconstrained, uncontrolled, uncurbed, unchecked, unbridled. ■ OPPOSITES repressed.
unintelligible adj. see INCOMPREHENSIBLE.

u

uninterested adj. not interested or concerned.

....

☑ Don't confuse **uninterested** with **disinterested**, which means 'impartial'.

....

uninviting adj. not attractive; unpleasant.

union n. **1** the act of uniting or the fact of being united. **2** a club or association. **3** a trade union. **4** (also **Union**) a political unit consisting of a number of states or provinces with the same central government. □ **Union Jack** the national flag of the UK.

unionist n. **1** a member or supporter of a trade union. **2** (**Unionist**) a person in Northern Ireland in favour of union with Great Britain.

unionize (or **-ise**) v. make or become members of a trade union. ■ **unionization** n.

unique adj. **1** being the only one of its kind. **2** (**unique to**) belonging only to one person, group, or place. **3** very special or unusual. ■ **uniquely** adv.

unisex adj. suitable for both sexes.

unison n. the fact of two or more things being said or happening at the same time.

unit n. **1** an individual thing, group, or person, esp. as part of a complex whole. **2** a device, item of furniture, or part of a building or organization with a specified function. **3** a fixed quantity that is used as a standard measurement. □ **unit trust** a company that invests money in a range of businesses on behalf of individuals, who can buy small units.

Unitarian n. a member of a Christian Church believing that God is one person and rejecting the idea of the Trinity.

unitary adj. **1** single. **2** of a unit or units.

unite v. come or bring together for a common purpose or to form a whole.

unity n. (pl. **unities**) **1** the state of being united. **2** a complex whole.

universal adj. of, for, or done by all. ■ **universally** adv.

universe n. all existing matter and space considered as a whole.

university n. (pl. **universities**) an educational institution where students study for a degree and where academic research is done.

Thesaurus

....

unintentional adj. UNINTENDED, accidental, inadvertent, unplanned, unpremeditated, chance, fortuitous, unconscious, involuntary, unwitting, unthinking. ■ OPPOSITES deliberate.

uninterested adj. INDIFFERENT, unconcerned, uninvolved, apathetic, unresponsive, impassive, dispassionate, aloof, detached, distant.

uninteresting adj. UNEXCITING, dull, boring, tiresome, wearisome, tedious, dreary, flat, monotonous, humdrum, commonplace, pedestrian, prosaic, hackneyed, stale.

uninterrupted adj. UNBROKEN, undisturbed, continuous, continual, constant, steady, sustained, non-stop, unending, endless, incessant, interminable, unremitting.

union n. **1** JOINING, junction, merger, fusion, amalgamation, blend, mixture, coalition, combining, combination, consolidation, confederation. **2** ASSOCIATION, alliance, league, coalition, consortium, syndicate, guild, confederation, federation, confederacy. **3** MARRIAGE, wedding, wedlock. ■ OPPOSITES separation.

unique adj. **1** ONLY, one and only, single, sole, lone, solitary, exclusive. **2** UNEQUALLED, without equal, unparalleled,

unmatched, matchless, peerless, unsurpassed, unexcelled, incomparable, inimitable, second to none.

unit n. **1** ENTITY, whole. **2** COMPONENT, part, section, element, constituent, subdivision, portion, segment, module, item, member.

unite v. **1** JOIN, link, connect, combine, amalgamate, fuse, weld. **2** COMBINE, mix, commix, blend, mingle, homogenize; *technical* admix. **3** JOIN TOGETHER, join forces, combine, amalgamate, band/club together, cooperate, work/pull together, pool resources. ■ OPPOSITES separate.

united adj. **1** COMBINED, amalgamated, allied, cooperative, concerted, collective, pooled. **2** IN AGREEMENT, agreed, in unison, of the same opinion/mind, of like mind, like-minded, at one, in accord, unanimous.

unity n. AGREEMENT, harmony, accord, concord, concurrence, unanimity, consensus, concert, togetherness, solidarity. ■ OPPOSITES disunity.

universal adj. GENERAL, all-embracing, all-inclusive, comprehensive, across the board, worldwide, global, widespread, common, predominant, preponderant, omnipresent, ubiquitous, catholic.

unkempt adj. having an untidy or disheveled appearance.

unkind adj. not caring or kind. ■ **unkindness** n.

unknown adj. not known. ▶n. an unknown person, thing, or place.

unleaded adj. (of petrol) without added lead.

unleash v. release; set loose.

unleavened adj. (of bread) made without yeast or other raising agent.

unless conj. except when; if not.

unlike prep. 1 not like. 2 uncharacteristic of. ▶adj. different.

unlikely adj. (**unlikelier**, **unlikeliest**) not likely to happen, be done, or be true. ■ **unlikelihood** n.

unlimited adj. not limited; infinite.

unload v. 1 remove goods from a vehicle, ship, etc. 2 informal get rid of.

unlooked adj. (**unlooked for**) unexpected; unforeseen.

unmanned adj. operated without a crew.

unmask v. reveal the true character of.

unmentionable adj. too shocking to be spoken about.

unmistakable (or **unmistakeable**) adj. not able to be mistaken for anything else. ■ **unmistakably** adv.

unmitigated adj. absolute.

unmoved adj. 1 not affected by emotion. 2 not changed in purpose.

unnatural adj. 1 different to what is found in nature. 2 different to what is normal or expected. ■ **unnaturally** adv.

unnecessary adj. not necessary or more than is necessary. ■ **unnecessarily** adv.

unnerve v. cause to feel nervous or frightened.

unnumbered adj. 1 not given a number. 2 countless.

unobtrusive adj. not conspicuous or attracting attention. ■ **unobtrusively** adv.

Thesaurus

■ OPPOSITES particular.

unjust adj. 1 UNFAIR, inequitable, prejudiced, biased, partisan, partial, one-sided. 2 UNDESERVED, unmerited, unwarranted, uncalled for, unreasonable, unjustifiable. ■ OPPOSITES fair.

unjustifiable adj. INDEFENSIBLE, inexcusable, unforgivable, unpardonable, uncalled for, unreasonable, blameworthy, culpable, unwarrantable. ■ OPPOSITES justifiable.

unkempt adj. UNTIDY, dishevelled, disordered, tousled, rumpled, windblown, scruffy, slovenly, sloppy. ■ OPPOSITES neat.

unkind adj. MEAN, cruel, vicious, spiteful, malicious, malevolent, harsh, pitiless, ruthless, unsympathetic, unfeeling, hard-hearted, heartless, cold-hearted, unfriendly, unkindly, unamiable, uncharitable, unchristian, inhospitable, ungenerous, nasty. ■ OPPOSITES kind.

unknown adj. 1 UNREVEALED, undisclosed, undetermined, unsettled, unascertained, in the balance, up in the air. 2 UNIDENTIFIED, unnamed, nameless, anonymous, incognito, unheard of, little known, obscure. 3 UNFAMILIAR, unexplored, uncharted, untravelled, undiscovered. ■ OPPOSITES familiar.

unlawful adj. see ILLEGAL.

unlikely adj. 1 IMPROBABLE, doubtful, dubious, faint, slight, remote. 2 IMPLAUSIBLE, questionable, improbable, unconvincing, incredible, unbelievable, inconceivable. ■ OPPOSITES probable, believable.

unlimited adj. 1 UNRESTRICTED, unconstrained, uncontrolled, unrestrained, unchecked, unhindered, unhampered, unimpeded, unfettered, untrammelled. 2 LIMITLESS, boundless, unbounded, immense, extensive, immeasurable, incalculable, untold, infinite. ■ OPPOSITES restricted, finite.

unloved adj. UNWANTED, unpopular, forsaken, rejected, jilted, disliked, hated, detested, loathed.

unlucky adj. 1 LUCKLESS, out of luck, down on one's luck, unfortunate, hapless, ill-starred. 2 UNSUCCESSFUL, failed, ill-fated. ■ OPPOSITES fortunate.

unmarried adj. SINGLE, unwed, unwedded, divorced, unattached, bachelor, celibate, husbandless, wifeless.

unmistakable adj. see OBVIOUS.

unmitigated adj. see ABSOLUTE.

unnatural adj. 1 UNUSUAL, uncommon, extraordinary, strange, queer, odd, bizarre, preternatural. 2 INHUMAN, heartless, uncaring, unconcerned, unfeeling, soulless, cold, hard, hard-hearted, callous, cruel, brutal, merciless, pitiless, remorseless, evil, wicked. 3 AFFECTED, artificial, feigned, false, self-conscious, contrived, forced, laboured, studied, strained, insincere, theatrical, stagy, mannered. ■ OPPOSITES natural.

unnecessary adj. NEEDLESS, unneeded, inessential, non-essential, uncalled for, gratuitous, useless, dispensable, expendable, redundant, superfluous.

u

unorthodox adj. different from what is usual, traditional, or accepted.

unpack v. open and remove the contents of a suitcase, container, etc.

unparalleled adj. having no equal; exceptional.

unpick v. undo the stitching of.

unplaced adj. not placed as one of the first three in a race.

unpleasant adj. 1 not pleasant. 2 not friendly or kind. ■ **unpleasantly** adv. **unpleasantness** n.

unpopular adj. not liked or popular. ■ **unpopularity** n.

unprecedented adj. never done or known before.

unprepared adj. not ready or able to deal with something.

unprepossessing adj. not attractive.

unprincipled adj. unscrupulous.

unprintable adj. too offensive to be published.

unprofessional adj. not in accordance with professional standards of behaviour. ■ **unprofessionally** adv.

unprompted adj. spontaneous.

unqualified adj. 1 not having the necessary qualifications or skills. 2 complete; absolute.

unquestionable adj. not able to be denied or doubted. ■ **unquestionably** adv.

unravel v. (**unravelling, unravelled**; US **unraveling, unraveled**) 1 undo twisted, knitted, or woven threads. 2 become undone. 3 solve a mystery.

unreasonable adj. 1 not based on good sense. 2 beyond what is acceptable or achievable. ■ **unreasonably** adv.

unrelenting adj. 1 not stopping or becoming less severe. 2 not giving in to requests. ■ **unrelentingly** adv.

Thesaurus

■ OPPOSITES necessary, essential.

unobtrusive adj. see INCONSPICUOUS.

unofficial adj. 1 INFORMAL, casual, unauthorized, unaccredited. 2 UNCONFIRMED, unauthenticated, uncorroborated, unsubstantiated.

unorthodox adj. see UNCONVENTIONAL.

unpalatable adj. UNSAVOURY, unappetizing, uneatable, inedible, nasty, disgusting, repugnant, revolting, nauseating, sickening, distasteful, disagreeable, unpleasant. ■ OPPOSITES tasty.

unparalleled adj. WITHOUT PARALLEL, unequalled, without equal, matchless, unmatched, peerless, unrivalled, unprecedented.

unpleasant adj. 1 DISGUSTING, unpalatable, unsavoury, unappetizing, repugnant, revolting, nauseating, sickening. 2 UNLIKEABLE, disagreeable, unlovable, unattractive, nasty, ill-natured, cross, bad-tempered. 3 DISAGREEABLE, irksome, troublesome, annoying, irritating, vexatious. ■ OPPOSITES agreeable, likable.

unpopular adj. DISLIKED, unliked, unloved, friendless, unwanted, unwelcome, avoided, ignored, rejected, shunned, out in the cold, cold-shouldered, unattractive, undesirable, out of favour.

unpredictable adj. ERRATIC, fickle, capricious, whimsical, mercurial, volatile, temperamental, unstable, undependable, unreliable.

unpremeditated adj. UNPLANNED, unintentional, extempore, impromptu, ad lib, spontaneous, spur of the moment, on the spot, impulsive, hasty; *informal* off

the cuff. ■ OPPOSITES planned.

unpretentious adj. SIMPLE, plain, ordinary, humble, unostentatious, unassuming, modest, unaffected, natural, straightforward, honest. ■ OPPOSITES pretentious.

unprofessional adj. AMATEUR, amateurish, unskilled, inexpert, untrained, unqualified, inexperienced, incompetent. ■ OPPOSITES professional.

unpromising adj. UNFAVOURABLE, adverse, unpropitious, inauspicious, gloomy, black, discouraging, portentous, ominous. ■ OPPOSITES auspicious.

unquestionable adj. BEYOND QUESTION/DOUBT, indubitable, undoubted, indisputable, undeniable, irrefutable, incontestable, incontrovertible, certain, sure, definite, positive, conclusive, self-evident, obvious.

unravel v. 1 UNTANGLE, disentangle, unwind, straighten out, separate out, unknot, undo. 2 SOLVE, resolve, work out, clear up, puzzle out, get to the bottom of, fathom; *informal* figure out. ■ OPPOSITES entangle.

unreal adj. IMAGINARY, make-believe, fictitious, mythical, fanciful, fantastic, fabulous, hypothetical, non-existent, illusory, chimerical, phantasmagoric.

unrealistic adj. IMPRACTICAL, impracticable, unworkable, unreasonable, irrational, illogical, improbable, foolish, wild, absurd, quixotic; *informal* half-baked. ■ OPPOSITES pragmatic.

unreasonable adj. 1 EXCESSIVE, immoderate, undue, inordinate, outrageous, extravagant, preposterous. 2 IRRATIONAL,

unremitting adj. not stopping or slackening.

unrequited adj. (of love) not returned.

unreserved adj. without doubts or reservations; complete. ■ **unreservedly** adv.

unrest n. **1** rebellious discontent and disorder. **2** uneasiness.

unrivalled (US **unrivaled**) adj. greater or better than all others.

unruly adj. (**unrulier, unruliest**) not easy to control. ■ **unruliness** n.

unsavoury (US **unsavory**) adj. **1** unpleasant to taste, smell, or look at. **2** not respectable.

unscathed adj. without suffering any injury.

unscrupulous adj. without moral principles; dishonest. ■ **unscrupulously** adv.

unseasonable adj. (of weather) unusual for the time of year. ■ **unseasonably** adv.

unseat v. **1** cause to fall from a saddle or seat. **2** remove from a position of power.

unselfish adj. putting other people's needs before one's own.

unsettle v. make uneasy; disturb.

unsettled adj. **1** changeable. **2** uneasy. **3** not yet resolved.

unshakeable (or **unshakable**) adj. (of a belief etc.) firm.

unsightly adj. unpleasant to look at. ■ **unsightliness** n.

unskilled adj. not having or needing special skill or training.

unsociable adj. not enjoying the company of others.

unsocial adj. **1** (of hours of work) falling outside the normal working day and so inconvenient. **2** antisocial.

unsolicited adj. not asked for.

unsound adj. **1** not safe or strong. **2** not based on reliable evidence or reasoning.

unsparing adj. **1** merciless; severe. **2** giving generously.

unspeakable adj. too bad or horrific to express in words. ■ **unspeakably** adv.

unstable adj. **1** not stable. **2** prone to mental health problems or sudden mood changes.

unstinting adj. given or giving freely or generously.

unstuck adj. (**come unstuck**) informal fail.

unstudied adj. natural and unaffected.

Thesaurus

illogical, blinkered, obstinate, obdurate, wilful, headstrong, temperamental, capricious. **3** UNACCEPTABLE, outrageous, ludicrous, absurd, irrational, illogical.

unreliable adj. **1** UNDEPENDABLE, irresponsible, untrustworthy, erratic, fickle, inconstant. **2** SUSPECT, questionable, open to question/doubt, doubtful, implausible, unconvincing, fallible, specious.

unrepentant adj. IMPENITENT, unremorseful, shameless, unregenerate, abandoned.

unrest n. DISSATISFACTION, discontent, unease, disquiet, dissent, discord, strife, protest, rebellion, agitation, turmoil, turbulence.

unrestricted adj. UNLIMITED, open, free, unhindered, unchecked, unbounded; *informal* free-for-all, with no holds barred.

unsavoury adj. UNPLEASANT, disagreeable, nasty, objectionable, offensive, obnoxious, repellent, repulsive, disreputable, degenerate, coarse, gross, vulgar, boorish, churlish, rude, uncouth.

unscrupulous adj. UNPRINCIPLED, unethical, amoral, immoral, conscienceless, shameless, corrupt, dishonest, dishonourable, deceitful, devious, exploitative, wrongdoing, bad, evil, wicked; *informal*

crooked. ■ OPPOSITES honest.

unselfish adj. ALTRUISTIC, self-sacrificing, selfless, kind, self-denying, openhanded, generous, liberal, unsparing, ungrudging, unstinting, charitable, philanthropic. ■ OPPOSITES selfish.

unshakeable adj. FIRM, steadfast, resolute, staunch, constant, unswerving, unwavering, unfaltering.

unsightly adj. *see* UGLY.

unskilled adj. UNTRAINED, unqualified, inexpert, inexperienced, amateurish, unprofessional.

unsophisticated adj. **1** UNWORLDLY, naive, simple, innocent, inexperienced, childlike, artless, guileless, ingenuous, natural, unaffected, unpretentious, unrefined, unpolished, gauche, provincial. **2** CRUDE, unrefined, basic, rudimentary, primitive.

unspeakable adj. INDESCRIBABLE, unmentionable, appalling, shocking, horrible, frightful, terrible, dreadful, deplorable, despicable, contemptible, repellent, loathsome, odious, monstrous.

unspoilt adj. PRESERVED, intact, perfect, unblemished, unimpaired, undamaged, untouched, unaffected, unchanged.

unstable adj. **1** UNSTEADY, infirm, rickety, shaky, wobbly, tottery, insecure,

unsung adj. not acknowledged or praised.

unsuspecting adj. not aware of the presence of danger.

unswerving adj. not changing or becoming weaker.

untenable adj. not able to be defended against criticism or attack.

unthinkable adj. too unlikely or unpleasant to be considered a possibility.

unthinking adj. without proper consideration.

untidy adj. (**untidier**, **untidiest**) **1** not arranged tidily. **2** not inclined to be neat. ■ **untidily** adv. **untidiness** n.

untie v. (**untying**, **untied**) unfasten something tied.

until prep. & conj. up to the point in time or the event mentioned.

untimely adj. **1** happening or done at an unsuitable time. **2** (of a death or end) premature. ■ **untimeliness** n.

unto prep. old use to.

untold adj. **1** too much or too many to be counted. **2** not told.

untouchable adj. **1** not able to be touched or affected. **2** unrivalled. ▶ n. offens. a member of the lowest Hindu social class.

untoward adj. unexpected and unwanted or inappropriate.

untried adj. not yet tested.

untruth n. (pl. **untruths**) **1** a lie. **2** the quality of being false. ■ **untruthful** adj. **untruthfully** adv.

unusual adj. **1** not often done or occurring. **2** exceptional. ■ **unusually** adv.

unutterable adj. too great or bad to describe. ■ **unutterably** adv.

unvarnished adj. **1** not varnished. **2** plain and straightforward.

unveil v. **1** remove a veil or covering from. **2** show or announce publicly for the first time.

unwaged adj. not doing paid work.

unwarranted adj. not justified.

unwell adj. ill.

unwieldy adj. hard to move or manage because of its size, shape, or weight.

unwilling adj. reluctant. ■ **unwillingly** adv. **unwillingness** n.

unwind v. (**unwinding**, **unwound**)

Thesaurus

precarious. **2** UNBALANCED, unhinged, irrational, deranged, mentally ill, insane, mad. ■ OPPOSITES stable.

unsuccessful adj. **1** WITHOUT SUCCESS, failed, vain, unavailing, futile, useless, worthless, abortive, nugatory, ineffective, ineffectual, inefficacious, fruitless, unproductive, unprofitable, baulked, frustrated. **2** FAILED, losing, unprosperous, unlucky, luckless, out of luck, unfortunate, ill-starred, ill-fated.

unsuitable adj. INAPPROPRIATE, inapt, inapposite, unfitting, incompatible, incongruous, out of place/keeping, ineligible, unacceptable, unbecoming, unseemly, indecorous, improper. ■ OPPOSITES appropriate.

unsure adj. see UNCERTAIN (2).

unsuspecting adj. UNSUSPICIOUS, unwary, off guard, trusting, gullible, credulous, ingenuous, naive, innocent. ■ OPPOSITES wary.

unsympathetic adj. UNCARING, unfeeling, insensitive, unconcerned, indifferent, unkind, unpitying, pitiless, unresponsive, apathetic, unmoved, untouched, heartless, cold, hard-hearted, stony-hearted, hard, harsh, callous. ■ OPPOSITES sympathetic.

untangle v. see UNRAVEL.

untenable adj. INDEFENSIBLE, insupportable, unsustainable, unsound, weak, flawed, defective, implausible, groundless, unfounded.

unthinkable adj. see INCONCEIVABLE.

unthinking adj. see THOUGHTLESS (2).

untidy adj. DISORDERED, disorderly, disarranged, disorganized, chaotic, confused, muddled, jumbled, topsy-turvy, at sixes and sevens; informal higgledy-piggledy, every which way, like a dog's breakfast. ■ OPPOSITES orderly.

untie v. see UNDO.

untiring adj. see TIRELESS.

untroubled adj. UNWORRIED, unruffled, unbothered, unconcerned, calm, cool, collected, composed, serene.

untrue adj. see FALSE.

unusual adj. **1** UNCOMMON, atypical, abnormal, rare, singular, odd, strange, curious, queer, bizarre, surprising, unexpected, different, unconventional, unwonted, unorthodox, irregular; informal weird. **2** EXTRAORDINARY, exceptional, singular, rare, remarkable, outstanding. ■ OPPOSITES common.

unwarranted adj. UNJUSTIFIABLE, unjustified, indefensible, inexcusable, unforgivable, unpardonable, uncalled for, gratuitous. ■ OPPOSITES justified.

unwelcome adj. **1** UNWANTED, undesired, uninvited, unpopular. **2** UNPLEASANT, disagreeable, unpalatable, displeasing, distasteful, undesirable.

unwell adj. see ILL.

unwieldy adj. CUMBERSOME, unmanage-

1 undo or become undone after winding. **2** relax after a period of work or tension.

unwise adj. foolish. ■ **unwisely** adv.

unwitting adj. **1** not aware of the full facts. **2** unintentional. ■ **unwittingly** adv.

unwonted adj. unaccustomed or unusual.

unworldly adj. having little awareness of the realities of life. ■ **unworldliness** n.

unworthy adj. not deserving attention, effort, or respect. ■ **unworthiness** n.

unwritten adj. (of a rule etc.) generally known about and accepted, although not made official.

up adv. **1** towards a higher place or position. **2** at or to a higher level or value. **3** into the desired condition or position. **4** out of bed. ▶ prep. from a lower to a higher point of. ▶ adj. **1** directed or moving towards a higher place or position. **2** at an end. ▶ v. (**upping**, **upped**) increase. □ **uphill** going or sloping upwards. **upstairs** on or to an upper floor. **upstream** in the direction opposite to that in which a stream or river flows. **up to date** using or aware of the latest developments and trends. **upwind** into the wind. ■ **upward** adj. & adv. **upwards** adv.

upbeat adj. cheerful.

upbraid v. scold.

update v. bring up to date.

upend v. set on its end or upside down.

upgrade v. raise to a higher standard or rank.

upheaval n. a violent or sudden disruption.

uphold v. (**upholding**, **upheld**) confirm or support.

upholster v. put a soft, padded covering on furniture.

upholstery n. material used to upholster furniture.

uplift v. **1** raise. **2** make more hopeful or happy. ▶ n. **1** an act of uplifting. **2** a feeling of hope or happiness.

upmarket adj. expensive and of high quality.

upon prep. formal on.

upper adj. higher in place, position, or status. ▶ n. the part of a boot or shoe above the sole. □ **have the upper hand** have an advantage or control. **upper case** capital letters. **upper class** the social group with the highest status. ■ **uppermost** adj. & adv.

uppity adj. informal self-important.

upright adj. **1** vertical; erect. **2** strictly honest or respectable. ▶ n. a vertical part or support.

uprising n. a rebellion.

uproar n. **1** a loud noise or disturbance. **2** a public expression of outrage.

uproarious adj. **1** very noisy. **2** very funny. ■ **uproariously** adv.

uproot v. **1** pull a plant, tree, etc. out of the ground. **2** move from home or a familiar location.

upset v. (**upsetting**, **upset**) **1** distress or worry. **2** knock over. **3** disrupt or disturb. **4** disturb the digestion of. ▶ n. a state of distress or disruption.

upshot n. an outcome.

Thesaurus

able, awkward, clumsy, massive, hefty, bulky, ponderous; informal hulking. ■ OPPOSITES manageable.

unwilling adj. RELUCTANT, disinclined, unenthusiastic, grudging, involuntary, averse, loth, opposed, not in the mood. ■ OPPOSITES willing.

unwind v. **1** see UNRAVEL. **2** see RELAX.

unwitting adj. UNKNOWING, unconscious, unintentional, unintended, inadvertent. ■ OPPOSITES deliberate.

unworthy adj. **1** NOT WORTHY, not good enough for, undeserving, ineligible for, unqualified for. **2** DISREPUTABLE, dishonourable, base, contemptible, reprehensible. ■ OPPOSITES deserving.

upgrade v. IMPROVE, better, ameliorate, enhance, rehabilitate, refurbish.

upheaval n. DISRUPTION, disturbance, disorder, confusion, turmoil, chaos.

uphill adj. ARDUOUS, difficult, laborious, strenuous, hard, tough, burdensome, onerous, taxing, punishing.

uphold v. SUPPORT, back up, back, stand by, champion, defend, endorse, maintain, sustain.

upkeep n. MAINTENANCE, running, preservation, conservation, repairs.

upper adj. **1** HIGHER, further up, loftier. **2** SUPERIOR, higher-ranking, elevated, greater. ■ OPPOSITES lower.

upright adj. **1** ERECT, on end, vertical, perpendicular, standing up, rampant. **2** HONEST, honourable, upstanding, decent, respectable, worthy, reputable, good, virtuous, righteous, law-abiding, ethical, moral. ■ OPPOSITES horizontal, dishonourable.

uproar n. TUMULT, turmoil, turbulence, disorder, confusion, commotion, mayhem, pandemonium, bedlam, din, noise, clamour, hubbub, racket. ■ OPPOSITES

upside down adv. & adj. **1** with the upper part where the lower part should be. **2** in or into total disorder.

upstage adv. & adj. at or towards the back of a stage. ▶v. divert attention from.

upstanding adj. honest and respectable.

upstart n. a person who has suddenly become important and behaves arrogantly.

upsurge n. an increase.

upswing n. an upward trend.

uptake (**quick/slow on the uptake**) informal quick (or slow) to understand something.

uptight adj. informal nervously tense or angry.

upturn n. an improvement or upward trend.

uranium n. a radioactive metallic element used as a fuel in nuclear reactors.

urban adj. of a town or city. ■ **urbanize** (or **-ise**) v.

urbane adj. confident, polite, and refined. ■ **urbanity** n.

urchin n. a poor child.

Urdu n. a language related to Hindi.

ureter /yuu-ree-ter/ n. the duct from the kidney to the bladder.

urethra /yuu-ree-thruh/ n. the duct which carries urine out of the body.

urge v. **1** encourage or earnestly ask to do something. **2** strongly recommend. ▶n. a strong desire or impulse.

urgent adj. requiring or calling for immediate action or attention. ■ **urgency** n. **urgently** adv.

urinal n. a receptacle in a public toilet into which men urinate.

urinate v. pass urine out of the body. ■ **urination** n.

urine n. a yellowish liquid containing waste substances, stored in the bladder before being passed out of the body. ■ **urinary** adj.

URL abbrev. uniform (or universal) resource locator, the address of a World Wide Web page.

urn n. **1** a vase, esp. one for holding a cremated person's ashes. **2** a large metal container with a tap, for keeping water or tea hot.

ursine adj. of bears.

US (or **USA**) abbrev. United States of America.

us pron. the form of 'we' used when the speaker or writer and another person or people are the object of a verb or preposition.

usable (or **useable**) adj. able to be used.

usage n. the using of something.

use v. **1** do something with an object or adopt a method. **2** (**use up**) consume the whole of. **3** treat in a particular way. **4** exploit unfairly. **5** (**used to**) did repeatedly, or existed or happened in the past. **6** (**be/get used to**) be or become familiar with through experience. **7** (**used**) second-hand. ▶n. **1** the using of something. **2** the ability to use something. **3** a purpose for which something is used. **4** value.

useful adj. able to be used for a practical

Thesaurus

calm.

upset v. **1** OVERTURN, knock over, push over, upend, tip over, topple, capsize. **2** DISTURB, discompose, unsettle, disconcert, dismay, disquiet, trouble, worry, bother, agitate, fluster, ruffle, frighten, alarm, anger, annoy, distress, hurt, grieve. **3** THROW INTO DISORDER/CONFUSION, disorganize, disarrange, mess up, mix up.

upshot n. RESULT, outcome, conclusion, issue, end, end result, denouement, effect, repercussion, reaction; informal payoff. ■ OPPOSITES cause.

upstart n. PARVENU/PARVENUE, social climber, nouveau riche, arriviste.

upward adj. RISING, climbing, mounting, ascending, on the rise. ■ OPPOSITES downward.

urbane adj. SUAVE, debonair, sophisticated, smooth, worldly, cultivated, cultured, civilized, polished. ■ OPPOSITES

uncouth.

urge v. **1** PUSH, drive, propel, impel, force, hasten, hurry, spur, incite, stir up, stimulate, prod, goad, egg on, encourage, prompt, entreat, exhort, implore, appeal, beg, plead; literary beseech. **2** ADVISE, counsel, advocate, recommend, suggest, support, endorse, back, champion. ■ OPPOSITES discourage. ▶n. DESIRE, need, compulsion, longing, yearning, wish, fancy, impulse.

urgent adj. **1** IMPERATIVE, vital, crucial, critical, essential, exigent, top-priority, high-priority, important, necessary, pressing, serious, grave. **2** IMPORTUNATE, insistent, clamorous, earnest, pleading, begging.

usable adj. FOR USE, to be used, utilizable, available, ready/fit for use, in working order, functional.

use v. **1** MAKE USE OF, utilize, employ, work, operate, wield, ply, avail oneself purpose. ■ **usefully** adv. **usefulness** n.

useless adj. **1** serving no purpose. **2** informal having little ability or skill. ■ **uselessly** adv.

user n. a person who uses something. □ **user-friendly** easy to use or understand.

usher n. a person who shows people to their seats in a cinema, theatre, or church. ▶ v. lead or guide.

usherette n. a woman who shows people to their seats in a cinema or theatre.

USSR abbrev. hist. Union of Soviet Socialist Republics.

usual adj. happening or done regularly or often. ■ **usually** adv.

usurp v. take a position of power illegally or by force. ■ **usurpation** n. **usurper** n.

usury n. the lending of money at unreasonably high rates of interest. ■ **usurer** n.

utensil n. a tool or container, esp. for household use.

uterus n. the womb. ■ **uterine** adj.

utilitarian adj. useful rather than decorative.

utilitarianism n. the belief that the greatest happiness of the majority

should be the guiding principle of behaviour.

utility n. (pl. **utilities**) **1** the state of being useful or profitable. **2** a company supplying water, electricity, gas, etc. to the public. □ **utility room** a room in which a washing machine and other domestic equipment is kept.

utilize (or **-ise**) v. make use of. ■ **utilization** n.

utmost adj. most extreme; greatest. ▶ n. (**the utmost**) the greatest or most extreme extent or amount.

Utopia n. an imagined perfect place. ■ **Utopian** adj.

utter[1] adj. complete; absolute. ■ **utterly** adv.

utter[2] v. make a sound or say something. ■ **utterance** n.

uttermost adj. & n. utmost.

U-turn n. **1** the turning of a vehicle in a U-shaped course so as to face the opposite way. **2** a reversal of policy.

UV abbrev. ultraviolet.

uvula /yoo-vyuu-luh/ n. (pl. **uvulae**) the fleshy projection hanging at the back of the throat.

uxorious adj. very or excessively fond of one's wife.

Thesaurus

of, put to use, put into service. **2** CON-SUME, get through, exhaust, deplete, expend, spend, waste, fritter away. ▶ n. **1** USEFULNESS, good, advantage, benefit, service, help, gain, profit, avail. **2** NEED, necessity, call, demand, requirement. □ **used to** ACCUSTOMED TO, familiar with, at home with, in the habit of, given to, prone to.

used adj. SECOND-HAND, nearly new, pre-owned, cast-off, hand-me-down. ■ OP-POSITES new.

useful adj. **1** OF USE, functional, utilitarian, of service, practical, convenient. **2** BENEFICIAL, advantageous, of help, helpful, worthwhile, profitable, rewarding, productive, valuable. ■ OPPOSITES useless.

useless adj. **1** VAIN, in vain, to no avail/purpose, unavailing, unsuccessful, futile, purposeless, fruitless, unprofitable, unproductive, abortive. **2** WORTHLESS, ineffective, ineffectual, incompetent, incapable, inadequate; informal no good. ■ OPPOSITES useful.

usual adj. **1** HABITUAL, customary, accus-

tomed, normal, regular, routine, everyday, established, set, familiar; literary wonted. **2** COMMON, typical, ordinary, average, run-of-the-mill, expected, standard, stock, regular. ■ OPPOSITES unusual.

usually adv. GENERALLY, as a rule, normally, by and large, in the main, mainly, mostly, for the most part, on the whole.

usurp v. TAKE OVER, seize, expropriate, appropriate, commandeer, assume.

utilitarian adj. PRACTICAL, functional, useful, to the purpose.

utter v. VOICE, say, pronounce, express, put into words, enunciate, articulate, verbalize, vocalize.

utterance n. **1** VOICE, expression, articulation, enunciation, verbalization, vocalization. **2** REMARK, word, comment, statement, opinion.

utterly adv. ABSOLUTELY, completely, totally, entirely, thoroughly, positively, extremely, categorically, perfectly, consummately, to the core, to the hilt, one hundred percent.

u

Vv

V (or **v**) n. the Roman numeral for five. ▶ abbrev. **1** volts. **2** versus. **3** very. □ **V-neck** a V-shaped neckline. **V-sign** a gesture of abuse made with the first two fingers pointing up and the back of the hand facing outwards.

vacancy n. (pl. **vacancies**) **1** an unoccupied position, job, or hotel room. **2** empty space.

vacant adj. **1** not occupied or filled. **2** showing no intelligence or interest. ■ **vacantly** adv.

vacate v. cease to occupy.

vacation n. **1** a holiday period between terms in universities etc. **2** US a holiday. **3** the act of vacating.

vaccinate v. inject with a vaccine. ■ **vaccination** n.

vaccine /vak-seen/ n. a substance that causes the production of antibodies in the body and so provides immunity against a disease.

vacillate /va-si-layt/ v. keep changing one's mind. ■ **vacillation** n.

vacuous adj. showing a lack of thought or intelligence. ■ **vacuity** n.

vacuum n. (pl. **vacuums** or **vacua**) **1** a space from which the air has been removed. **2** a gap. ▶ v. informal clean with a vacuum cleaner. □ **vacuum cleaner** an electrical device that collects dust by suction. **vacuum flask** a container to keep liquids hot or cold. **vacuum-packed** sealed in a pack with the air removed.

vagabond n. a vagrant.

vagary n. (pl. **vagaries**) an unpredictable change or action.

vagina /vuh-jy-nuh/ n. (pl. **vaginas**) the tube leading from the vulva to the womb. ■ **vaginal** adj.

vagrant n. a person without a settled home. ■ **vagrancy** n.

vague adj. **1** not certain or definite. **2** not thinking or expressing oneself clearly. ■ **vaguely** adv. **vagueness** n.

vain adj. **1** having a very high opinion of oneself. **2** useless or futile. □ **in vain** without success. ■ **vainly** adv.

vainglorious adj. literary boastful or vain.

valance n. a length of fabric around the base of a bed.

vale n. literary a valley.

valediction n. a farewell. ■ **valedictory** adj.

valency (or **valence**) n. (pl. **valencies**) the combining power of an element, as

Thesaurus

vacancy n. **1** OPENING, position, post, job, opportunity, slot. **2** BLANKNESS, lack of expression, lack of emotion/interest, vacuousness.

vacant adj. **1** EMPTY, void, without contents. **2** UNOCCUPIED, unfilled, free, empty, available, unengaged, uninhabited, untenanted, not in use, unused, abandoned, deserted; informal up for grabs. **3** BLANK, expressionless, inexpressive, deadpan, poker-faced, emotionless, uninterested, vacuous, inane. ■ OPPOSITES occupied.

vacate v. LEAVE, quit, depart from, evacuate, abandon, desert.

vacillate v. SHILLY-SHALLY, waver, dither, hesitate, equivocate, beat about the bush, hum and haw.

vacuous adj. VACANT, blank, expressionless, inane, unintelligent, brainless, stupid. ■ OPPOSITES intelligent.

vagrant n. TRAMP, beggar, person of no fixed address, itinerant, nomad, wanderer, vagabond; US hobo; US informal bum.

vague adj. **1** INDISTINCT, indeterminate, ill-defined, unclear, nebulous, amorphous, shadowy, hazy, fuzzy, blurry, bleary, out of focus. **2** IMPRECISE, inexact, inexplicit, non-specific, loose, generalized, ambiguous, equivocal, hazy, woolly. **3** ABSENT-MINDED, abstracted, dreamy, vacuous; informal with one's head in the clouds. ■ OPPOSITES clear, definite.

vaguely adv. **1** IN A GENERAL WAY, in a way, somehow, slightly, obscurely. **2** ABSENT-MINDEDLY, abstractedly, vacantly, vacuously.

vain adj. **1** CONCEITED, self-loving, narcissistic, self-admiring, egotistical, proud, haughty, arrogant, boastful, swaggering, imperious, overweening, cocky, affected. **2** UNSUCCESSFUL, futile, useless, measured by the number of hydrogen atoms it can displace or combine with.

valentine n. **1** a romantic card sent on St Valentine's Day (14 February). **2** a person to whom one sends such a card.

valet /va-lay/ n. a man's personal male attendant. ▶v. (**valeting, valeted**) **1** act as a valet to. **2** clean a car thoroughly.

valetudinarian /va-li-tyoo-di-**nair**-i-uhn/ n. a person in poor health or unduly anxious about their health.

valiant adj. brave. ■ **valiantly** adv.

valid adj. **1** (of a reason etc.) sound or logical. **2** legally or officially acceptable. ■ **validity** n.

validate v. **1** check the validity of. **2** make or declare valid. ■ **validation** n.

valise /vuh-**leez**/ n. a small suitcase.

valley n. (pl. **valleys**) a low area between hills.

valour (US **valor**) n. bravery. ■ **valorous** adj.

valuable adj. **1** worth a great deal of money. **2** very useful or important. ▶n. (**valuables**) valuable items.

value n. **1** the amount of money that something is worth. **2** the importance or usefulness of something. **3** (**values**) standards of behaviour. ▶v. **1** estimate the value of. **2** consider important or beneficial. ◻ **value added tax** a tax on the amount by which goods rise in value at each stage of production. ■ **valuation** n. **valuer** n.

valve n. **1** a device controlling flow through a pipe. **2** a structure allowing blood to flow in one direction only. **3** each half of the hinged shell of an oyster etc.

vamp n. informal a sexually attractive woman who exploits men. ▶v. (**vamp up**) repair or improve.

vampire n. a corpse supposed to leave its grave at night to drink the blood of the living. ◻ **vampire bat** a bloodsucking tropical bat.

van n. **1** a covered vehicle for transporting goods or people. **2** a railway carriage for luggage, mail, etc. **3** the leading part of an advancing group.

vanadium n. a hard grey metallic element.

vandal n. a person who deliberately destroys or damages property. ■ **vandalism** n.

vandalize (or **-ise**) v. deliberately destroy or damage.

vane n. a broad blade forming part of a windmill, propeller, etc.

vanguard n. the leading part of an advancing army.

vanilla n. a sweetish flavouring obtained from the pods of a tropical plant.

vanish v. disappear completely.

vanity n. (pl. **vanities**) **1** excessive pride in oneself. **2** futility.

vanquish v. defeat thoroughly.

vantage (or **vantage point**) n. a position giving a good view.

vapid adj. uninteresting; bland. ■ **vapidity** n.

vaporize (or **-ise**) v. convert into

Thesaurus

unavailing, to no avail, ineffective, inefficacious, fruitless, unproductive, abortive, unprofitable, profitless. ■ OPPOSITES modest, successful.

valiant adj. BRAVE, courageous, valorous, heroic, intrepid, fearless, undaunted, bold, daring, audacious, staunch, stalwart, indomitable, resolute, determined. ■ OPPOSITES cowardly.

valid adj. SOUND, well founded, well grounded, substantial, reasonable, logical, justifiable, defensible, vindicable, authentic, bona fide, effective, cogent, powerful, convincing, credible, forceful, weighty. ■ OPPOSITES invalid.

validate v. RATIFY, legalize, legitimize, authorize, sanction, warrant, license, approve, endorse, set one's seal to. ■ OPPOSITES invalidate.

valley n. DALE, dell, hollow, vale, dene, combe, depression; Sc. glen, strath.

valuable adj. **1** COSTLY, high-priced, expensive, priceless, precious. **2** USEFUL, helpful, beneficial, advantageous, worthwhile, worthy, important. ■ OPPOSITES worthless.

value n. **1** COST, face value, price, market price, worth. **2** WORTH, merit, usefulness, advantage, benefit, gain, profit, good, avail, importance, significance. ▶v. **1** SET A PRICE ON, price, evaluate, assess, appraise. **2** RATE HIGHLY, appreciate, esteem, hold in high regard, think highly of, set store by, respect, admire, prize, cherish, treasure.

vanguard n. ADVANCE GUARD, forefront, front, front line, front rank, leading position, van. ■ OPPOSITES rear.

vanish v. DISAPPEAR, be lost to sight/view, be/become invisible, evaporate, dissipate, disperse, fade, fade away, evanesce, melt away, recede from view, withdraw, depart, leave. ■ OPPOSITES appear.

vapour. ■ **vaporization** n.
vapour (US **vapor**) n. moisture suspended in the air.
variable adj. **1** liable to change. **2** able to be changed. ▸ n. a variable situation, feature, etc. ■ **variability** n. **variably** adv.
variance n. (**at variance**) disagreeing.
variant n. a form differing from other forms of the same thing.
variation n. **1** a change or slight difference. **2** a variant. **3** a new but still recognizable version of a musical theme.
varicose adj. (of a vein) swollen and twisted.
varied adj. involving a number of different types or elements.
variegated adj. having irregular patches of colour. ■ **variegation** n.
variety n. (pl. **varieties**) **1** the quality of being different or varied. **2** a range of things of the same type that are distinct in character. **3** a sort or kind. **4** a form of entertainment made up of a series of different acts.
various adj. **1** of different kinds. **2** several. ■ **variously** adv.
varlet n. old use a rogue or rascal.
varnish n. a liquid applied to give a hard, clear, shiny surface when dry. ▸ v. apply varnish to.
vary v. (**varying**, **varied**) make, be, or become different.
vascular adj. of or containing veins.
vase n. a decorative container for displaying cut flowers.

vasectomy n. (pl. **vasectomies**) the surgical cutting and sealing of part of the ducts carrying semen as a means of sterilization.
vaseline n. trademark a type of petroleum jelly used as an ointment and lubricant.
vassal n. **1** hist. a man given land by a king or lord in return for military service. **2** a subordinate person or country.
vast adj. of very great extent or quantity. ■ **vastly** adv. **vastness** n.
VAT abbrev. value added tax.
vat n. a large tank for liquids.
vaudeville n. a type of entertainment with a mixture of musical and comedy acts.
vault n. **1** a roof in the form of an arch. **2** a large storage room, esp. in a bank. **3** a burial chamber. **4** an act of vaulting. ▸ v. jump using one's hands or a pole to push oneself. ■ **vaulted** adj.
vaunted adj. praised or boasted about.
VC abbrev. Victoria Cross.
VCR abbrev. video cassette recorder.
VD abbrev. venereal disease.
VDU abbrev. visual display unit.
veal n. meat from a young calf.
vector n. **1** a quantity having direction as well as magnitude. **2** the carrier of a disease or infection.
veer v. change direction.
vegan n. a person who does not eat or use any animal products.
vegetable n. a plant used as food.
vegetarian n. a person who does not

Thesaurus

vanity n. CONCEIT, conceitedness, narcissism, egotism, pride, haughtiness, arrogance, boastfulness, braggadocio, pretension, affectation, ostentation, show, airs. ■ OPPOSITES modesty.

variable adj. VARYING, changeable, changing, mutable, protean, shifting, fluctuating, wavering, vacillating, inconstant, unsteady, unstable, fitful, capricious, fickle; informal blowing hot and cold. ■ OPPOSITES constant.

variation n. **1** CHANGE, alteration, modification, diversification. **2** VARIABILITY, changeability, fluctuation, vacillation, vicissitude. **3** DIFFERENCE, dissimilarity.

varied adj. DIVERSE, assorted, miscellaneous, mixed, motley, heterogeneous.

variety n. **1** VARIATION, diversification, diversity, multifariousness, many-sidedness, change, difference. **2** ASSORTMENT, miscellany, range, mixture, medley, motley, collection, multiplicity. **3** STRAIN, breed, kind, type, sort, class,

category, classification, brand, make. ■ OPPOSITES uniformity.

various adj. **1** VARYING, diverse, different, differing, dissimilar, disparate, assorted, mixed, miscellaneous, variegated, heterogeneous. **2** NUMEROUS, many, several, varied, sundry; literary divers.

varnish v. LACQUER, japan, shellac, enamel, glaze, veneer.

vary v. **1** DIFFER, be different, be dissimilar, be at variance, disagree, conflict, clash, be at odds. **2** CHANGE, be transformed, alter, metamorphose, suffer a sea change, vacillate, fluctuate.

vast adj. IMMENSE, huge, enormous, massive, bulky, tremendous, colossal, prodigious, gigantic, monumental, elephantine, Brobdingnagian, extensive, broad, wide, expansive, boundless, limitless, infinite; informal hulking. ■ OPPOSITES tiny.

vault[1] n. CELLAR, basement, underground chamber, tomb.

eat meat. ▶ **adj.** eating or including no meat. ■ **vegetarianism** n.

vegetate v. spend time in a dull, inactive way.

vegetation n. plants.

vegetative adj. **1** of vegetation. **2** of reproduction by asexual means. **3** alive but showing no sign of brain activity.

vehement adj. showing strong feeling. ■ **vehemence** n. **vehemently** adv.

vehicle n. **1** a car, lorry, or other machine for transporting people or goods on land. **2** a means of expressing something. ■ **vehicular** adj.

veil n. **1** a piece of fine fabric worn to protect or hide the face. **2** a thing that hides or disguises. ▶ v. **1** cover with a veil. **2** (**veiled**) partially hidden or disguised.

vein n. **1** any of the tubes by which blood is carried towards the heart. **2** (in plants) a structure carrying sap in a leaf. **3** a streak of a different colour. **4** a narrow deposit of a mineral or ore. ■ **veined** adj.

Velcro n. trademark a fastener made of two strips of fabric which cling together when pressed.

veld (or **veldt**) n. open grassland in southern Africa.

vellum n. fine parchment made from animal skin.

velocity n. (pl. **velocities**) speed.

velour n. a plush woven fabric resembling velvet.

velvet n. a fabric with a soft, short pile on one side. ■ **velvety** adj.

venal adj. open to bribery. ■ **venality** n.

vend v. sell. □ **vending machine** a machine that dispenses small articles when a coin is inserted.

vendetta n. a feud.

vendor n. a person selling something.

veneer n. **1** a thin covering of fine wood. **2** an outward show of a quality. ■ **veneered** adj.

venerable adj. worthy of great respect.

venerate v. respect greatly. ■ **veneration** n.

venereal disease n. a disease caught by having sex with a person already infected.

Venetian adj. of Venice. ▶ n. a person from Venice. □ **venetian blind** a window blind consisting of adjustable horizontal slats.

vengeance n. retaliation or revenge. □ **with a vengeance** with great intensity.

vengeful adj. wanting revenge.

venial adj. (of a fault or offence) slight and pardonable.

venison n. meat from a deer.

Venn diagram n. a diagram using overlapping circles to show relationships between mathematical sets.

venom n. **1** poisonous fluid produced by snakes, scorpions, etc. **2** hatred or bitterness. ■ **venomous** adj.

venous /vee-nuhss/ adj. of veins.

vent n. **1** an opening allowing air, gas, or liquid to pass through. **2** a slit in a garment. ▶ v. express a strong emotion freely.

ventilate v. cause air to enter and circulate freely in. ■ **ventilation** n.

ventilator n. **1** a machine or opening for ventilating a room etc. **2** a machine

Thesaurus

vault² v. JUMP, leap, jump over, leap over, spring over, bound over.

veer v. CHANGE COURSE/DIRECTION, turn, swerve, swing, sidestep, sheer, tack, be deflected.

vehemence n. FORCE, passion, forcefulness, emphasis, vigour, intensity, violence, earnestness, keenness, enthusiasm, zeal.

vehement adj. PASSIONATE, ardent, impassioned, fervent, fervid, strong, forceful, forcible, powerful, emphatic, vigorous, intense, earnest, keen, enthusiastic, zealous, spirited. ■ OPPOSITES mild.

vehicle n. **1** MEANS OF TRANSPORT, transportation, conveyance, car, bus, lorry. **2** CHANNEL, medium, means, agency, instrument, mechanism, organ, apparatus.

veil v. HIDE, conceal, cover up, disguise, camouflage, mask, screen.

vein n. **1** BLOOD VESSEL, artery, capillary. **2** LODE, seam, stratum. **3** STREAK, stripe, line, thread, marking.

veneer n. **1** FACING, covering, coat, finish. **2** FAÇADE, false front, show, outward display, appearance, semblance, guise, mask, pretence, camouflage.

venerable adj. VENERATED, respected, revered, reverenced, worshipped, honoured, esteemed, hallowed.

veneration n. RESPECT, reverence, worship, adoration, honour, esteem.

vengeance n. REVENGE, retribution, requital, retaliation, reprisal, an eye for an eye, quid pro quo; *informal* tit for tat.

venomous adj. **1** POISONOUS, toxic, lethal, deadly, fatal. **2** see SPITEFUL.

vent n. OPENING, outlet, aperture, hole, gap, duct, flue. ▶ v. GIVE VENT/EXPRESSION that pumps air in and out of a person's lungs to help them to breathe.

ventral adj. of or on the abdomen.

ventricle n. each of the two larger and lower cavities of the heart.

ventriloquist n. an entertainer who can make their voice seem to come from a puppet. ∎ **ventriloquism** n.

venture n. an undertaking involving risk. ▶ v. dare to do or say something. ∎ **venturesome** adj.

venue n. the place where an event or meeting is held.

veracious adj. truthful. ∎ **veracity** n.

veranda (or **verandah**) n. a roofed platform along the outside of a house.

verb n. a word used to describe an action, state, or occurrence.

verbal adj. **1** of or in the form of words. **2** spoken. **3** of a verb. ∎ **verbally** adv.

verbalize (or **-ise**) v. express in words.

verbatim /ver-bay-tim/ adv. & adj. in exactly the same words.

verbena n. a plant with bright showy flowers.

verbiage n. excessively long speech or writing.

verbose adj. using more words than are needed. ∎ **verbosity** n.

verdant adj. green with grass etc.

verdict n. **1** a decision made by a jury as to a person's innocence or guilt. **2** an opinion or judgement made after testing something.

verdigris /ver-di-gree/ n. a green substance formed on copper or brass by oxidation.

verdure n. green vegetation.

verge n. **1** a grass edging by the side of a road or path. **2** a limit beyond which something will happen. ▶ v. (**verge on**) be very close or similar to.

verger n. a church caretaker.

verify v. (**verifying**, **verified**) check the truth or correctness of. ∎ **verifiable** adj. **verification** n.

verily adv. old use truly; certainly.

verisimilitude n. the appearance of being true or real.

veritable adj. rightly so called.

vermicelli /ver-mi-**chel**-li/ pl. n. pasta made in long slender threads.

vermilion n. a brilliant red colour.

vermin n. wild animals and birds which carry disease or harm crops etc. ∎ **verminous** adj.

vermouth /ver-muhth/ n. a red or white wine flavoured with herbs.

vernacular n. the language spoken by the ordinary people of a country or region.

vernal adj. of or occurring in spring.

verruca /vuh-roo-kuh/ n. (pl. **verrucae** or **verrucas**) a contagious wart on the sole of the foot.

versatile adj. able to do or be used for many different things. ∎ **versatility** n.

verse n. **1** writing arranged with a regular rhythm. **2** a group of lines forming a unit in a poem or song. **3** a subdivision of a chapter of the Bible.

versed adj. (**versed in**) experienced or skilled in.

versify v. (**versifying**, **versified**) write verse or express in verse. ∎ **versification** n.

version n. **1** a form of something differing from other forms of the same type.

Thesaurus

TO, express, air, utter, voice, verbalize, let out, come out with.

ventilate v. AIR, aerate, oxygenate, freshen, cool, purify.

venture n. ENTERPRISE, undertaking, project, speculation, fling, plunge, gamble. ▶ v. DARE, take the liberty, make so bold as, presume to.

verbal adj. ORAL, spoken, said, uttered, articulated.

verbatim adj. WORD FOR WORD, literal, exact, faithful, precise.

verbose adj. WORDY, loquacious, garrulous, long-winded, prolix, diffuse, pleonastic, circumlocutory, periphrastic, tautological. ∎ OPPOSITES succinct.

verdict n. DECISION, judgement, adjudication, finding, conclusion, ruling, opinion, pronouncement.

verge n. EDGE, border, margin, rim, limit, boundary, end. ◻ **verge on** APPROACH, incline to/towards, tend towards, border on, come near.

verification n. CONFIRMATION, evidence, proof, substantiation, corroboration, attestation, validation, authentication, endorsement, accreditation, ratification.

verify v. CONFIRM, substantiate, prove, give credence to, corroborate, bear out, attest to, testify to, validate, authenticate, endorse, accredit, ratify. ∎ OPPOSITES refute.

vernacular n. EVERYDAY/SPOKEN LANGUAGE, colloquial/native speech, conversational language, common parlance, non-standard language, jargon, cant, patois; informal lingo, patter.

versatile adj. **1** RESOURCEFUL, flexible, all-round, multifaceted, adaptable, in-

2 an account of something told from a particular person's point of view.

verso n. (pl. **versos**) a left-hand page of an open book.

versus prep. against.

vertebra n. (pl. **vertebrae**) each of the small bones forming the backbone. ■ **vertebral** adj.

vertebrate n. an animal having a backbone.

vertex n. (pl. **vertices** or **vertexes**) **1** the highest point. **2** a meeting point of two lines that form an angle.

vertical adj. at right angles to a horizontal line or surface. ■ **vertically** adv.

vertiginous /ver-**tij**-i-nuhss/ adj. very high or steep.

vertigo n. giddiness caused by looking down from a great height.

verve n. vigour, spirit, and style.

very adv. in a high degree. ▶ adj. **1** actual; precise. **2** mere.

vesicle n. **1** a small fluid-filled sac. **2** a blister.

vespers n. a service of evening prayer.

vessel n. **1** a ship or large boat. **2** a hollow container for liquids. **3** a tube or duct carrying fluid in an animal or plant.

vest n. **1** a sleeveless undergarment worn on the upper part of the body. **2** US & Austral. a waistcoat. ▶ v. (**vest in**) give power, property, etc. to as a legal right. □ **vested interest** a personal

reason for wanting something to happen.

vestibule n. a small entrance hall.

vestige n. **1** a last remaining trace. **2** the smallest amount. ■ **vestigial** adj.

vestment n. a robe worn by the clergy or members of a choir during services.

vestry n. (pl. **vestries**) a room in a church, used as an office and for changing into ceremonial robes.

vet n. a veterinary surgeon. ▶ v. (**vetting, vetted**) make a careful and critical examination of.

veteran n. a person with long experience, esp. in the armed forces.

veterinarian n. US a veterinary surgeon.

veterinary /**vet**-ri-nuh-ri, **vet**-uhn-ri/ adj. of the treatment of injuries and diseases in animals. □ **veterinary surgeon** a person qualified to treat diseased or injured animals.

veto n. (pl. **vetoes**) **1** a right to reject a decision or proposal made by others. **2** such a rejection. ▶ v. (**vetoing, vetoed**) reject by veto.

vex v. annoy or worry. □ **vexed question** a widely discussed issue. ■ **vexation** n. **vexatious** adj.

VHF abbrev. very high frequency.

via prep. by way of; through.

viable adj. capable of working, surviving, or living successfully. ■ **viability** n.

viaduct n. a long bridge carrying a road

Thesaurus

genious, clever. **2** MULTI-PURPOSE, all-purpose, adjustable, adaptable, handy.

verse n. **1** STANZA, canto, couplet. **2** POEM, lyric, sonnet, ode, limerick, piece of doggerel, ditty, song, ballad.

version n. **1** ACCOUNT, report, story, rendering, interpretation, construction, understanding, reading, impression, side. **2** ADAPTATION, interpretation, translation. **3** VARIANT, variation, form, copy, reproduction.

vertical adj. UPRIGHT, erect, on end, perpendicular. ■ OPPOSITES horizontal.

vertigo n. DIZZINESS, giddiness, light-headedness, loss of balance; informal wooziness.

verve n. ENTHUSIASM, vigour, force, energy, vitality, vivacity, liveliness, animation, sparkle, spirit, life, dash, brio, fervour, gusto, passion, zeal, feeling, fire; informal zing, zip, vim, get-up-and-go, pizzazz.

very adv. EXTREMELY, exceedingly, to a great extent, exceptionally, uncommonly, unusually, decidedly, particularly,

eminently, remarkably, really, truly, terribly; informal awfully, jolly. ■ OPPOSITES slightly.

vessel n. **1** SHIP, boat, yacht, craft; literary barque. **2** CONTAINER, receptacle.

vet v. CHECK, check out, investigate, examine, appraise, look over, review, scrutinize; informal give the once-over, size up.

veteran n. OLD HAND, old-timer, old stager, past master; informal pro, old warhorse. ■ OPPOSITES novice. ▶ adj. LONG-SERVING, seasoned, old, adept, expert.

veto v. REJECT, turn down, prohibit, forbid, interdict, proscribe, disallow, outlaw, embargo, ban, bar, preclude, rule out; informal give the thumbs down to, put the kibosh on. ▶ n. REJECTION, prohibition, interdict, proscription, embargo, ban.

vex v. ANGER, annoy, irritate, incense, irk, enrage, infuriate, exasperate, pique, provoke, nettle, disturb, upset, perturb, discompose, put out, try or railway across a valley.

vial n. a small bottle.

viands pl. n. old use food.

vibe (or **vibes**) n. informal the atmosphere produced by a place or a mood passing between people.

vibrant adj. 1 full of energy and enthusiasm. 2 (of sound) resonant. 3 (of colour) bright. ■ **vibrancy** n. **vibrantly** adv.

vibraphone n. an electrical percussion instrument giving a vibrato effect.

vibrate v. 1 move with rapid small movements to and fro. 2 (of a sound) resonate. ■ **vibration** n.

vibrato n. (in music) a rapid, slight variation in pitch.

vibrator n. a vibrating device used for massage or sexual stimulation.

vicar n. (in the Church of England) a minister in charge of a parish.

vicarage n. the house of a vicar.

vicarious adj. experienced in one's imagination rather than directly. ■ **vicariously** adv.

vice n. 1 immoral or wicked behaviour. 2 criminal activities involving prostitution, pornography, or drugs. 3 a bad habit or characteristic. 4 a tool with movable jaws for holding an object firmly.

vice- comb. form next in rank to; deputy.

viceroy n. a person sent by a monarch to govern a colony. ■ **viceregal** adj.

vice versa adv. reversing the order of the items just mentioned.

vicinity n. (pl. **vicinities**) the surrounding area.

vicious adj. 1 cruel or violent. 2 savage and dangerous. □ **vicious circle** a situation in which one problem leads to another, which then makes the first one worse. ■ **viciously** adv. **viciousness** n.

vicissitudes /vi-siss-i-tyoodz/ pl. n. changes of circumstances or fortune.

victim n. a person harmed or killed.

victimize (or **-ise**) v. single out for cruel or unfair treatment. ■ **victimization** n.

victor n. a person who defeats an enemy or opponent.

Victorian adj. of the reign of Queen Victoria (1837–1901).

victorious adj. having won a victory. ■ **victoriously** adv.

victory n. (pl. **victories**) an act of defeating an opponent.

victualler /vi-t'l-er/ n. a person licensed to sell alcoholic drinks.

victuals /vi-t'lz/ n. dated food or provisions.

video n. (pl. **videos**) 1 a system of recording and reproducing moving images on magnetic tape. 2 a film on magnetic tape. ▶v. (**videoing**, **videoed**) make a video recording of. □ **video recorder** a machine for recording television programmes and playing video-

Thesaurus

someone's patience, try; informal peeve, miff, bug, hassle, aggravate, drive up the wall.

viable adj. WORKABLE, sound, feasible, practicable, applicable, usable. ■ OPPOSITES impractical.

vibrant adj. 1 LIVELY, energetic, spirited, vigorous, animated, sparkling, vivacious, dynamic, electrifying. 2 VIVID, bright, strong, striking. ■ OPPOSITES lifeless, pale.

vibrate v. SHAKE, oscillate, tremble, quiver, throb, pulsate, resonate, resound, reverberate, ring, echo.

vibration n. SHAKING, oscillation, throb, pulsation, resonance, reverberation, quivering, quiver.

vicarious adj. INDIRECT, second-hand, surrogate, by proxy, at one remove.

vice n. 1 SIN, sinfulness, wrong, wrongdoing, wickedness, badness, immorality, iniquity, evil, evil-doing, venality, corruption, depravity, degeneracy. 2 TRANSGRESSION, offence, misdeed, error, failing, flaw, defect, imperfection,

weakness, foible, shortcoming. ■ OPPOSITES virtue.

vicinity n. SURROUNDING DISTRICT, neighbourhood, locality, area, district, environs, precincts, purlieus; informal neck of the woods.

vicious adj. 1 FIERCE, ferocious, savage, dangerous, ill-natured, bad-tempered, hostile. 2 MALICIOUS, malevolent, malignant, spiteful, vindictive, venomous, backbiting, rancorous, caustic, mean, cruel; informal bitchy, catty. 3 VIOLENT, savage, brutal, fierce, ferocious, inhuman, barbarous, fiendish, sadistic. ■ OPPOSITES gentle.

vicissitude n. CHANGE, alteration, transformation, inconstancy, instability, uncertainty, unpredictability, chanciness, fickleness, ups and downs.

victim n. 1 INJURED PARTY, casualty, sufferer. 2 OFFERING, sacrifice, scapegoat.

victimize v. PERSECUTE, pick on, discriminate against, punish unfairly; informal have it in for, have a down on.

victor n. WINNER, champion, prizewinner,

tapes. **videotape 1** magnetic tape for recording moving images and sound. **2** a cassette of this.

vie v. (**vying, vied**) compete eagerly with others.

view n. **1** the ability to see something or to be seen from a particular position. **2** something seen from a particular position, esp. natural scenery. **3** an attitude or opinion. ▶ v. **1** look at or inspect. **2** regard in a particular way. **3** watch on television. □ **in view of** because or as a result of. **with a view to** with the hope or intention of. **viewfinder** a device on a camera showing what will appear in the picture. **viewpoint 1** a position giving a good view. **2** an opinion. ■ **viewer** n.

vigil n. a period of staying awake to keep watch or pray.

vigilant adj. keeping careful watch for danger or problems. ■ **vigilance** n. **vigilantly** adv.

vigilante /vi-ji-**lan**-ti/ n. a member of a self-appointed group undertaking crime prevention and punishment without legal authority.

vignette /vee-**nyet**/ n. a brief vivid description.

vigour (US **vigor**) n. **1** physical strength and good health. **2** energy and enthusiasm. ■ **vigorous** adj. **vigorously** adv.

Viking n. an ancient Scandinavian trader, pirate, and settler.

vile adj. very unpleasant or wicked. ■ **vilely** adv.

vilify v. (**vilifying, vilified**) speak or write about in abusive terms. ■ **vilification** n.

villa n. **1** a large country house. **2** a rented holiday home abroad.

village n. a small settlement in a country area. ■ **villager** n.

villain n. a wicked person. ■ **villainous** adj. **villainy** n.

villein n. hist. a feudal tenant entirely subject to a lord.

vim n. informal vigour.

vinaigrette n. salad dressing of oil and vinegar.

vindicate v. **1** clear of blame or suspicion. **2** show to be justified. ■ **vindication** n.

vindictive adj. having a strong or excessive desire for revenge. ■ **vindictively** adv. **vindictiveness** n.

Thesaurus

conquering hero; informal champ, top dog, number one. ■ OPPOSITES loser.

victorious adj. CONQUERING, vanquishing, triumphant, winning, champion, successful, prizewinning, top, first.

vie v. COMPETE, contend, contest, struggle, strive.

view n. **1** SIGHT, field/range of vision, vision, eyeshot. **2** OUTLOOK, prospect, scene, spectacle, vista, panorama, landscape, seascape. **3** POINT OF VIEW, viewpoint, opinion, belief, judgement, way of thinking, thinking, thought, notion, idea, conviction, persuasion, attitude, feeling, sentiment, impression. ▶ v. LOOK AT, watch, observe, contemplate, regard, behold, scan, survey, examine, scrutinize, see over.

viewpoint n. POINT OF VIEW, frame of reference, perspective, angle, slant, standpoint, position, stance, vantage point.

vigilant adj. WATCHFUL, on the lookout, observant, sharp-eyed, eagle-eyed, attentive, alert, on the alert, awake, wide awake, on one's guard, careful, cautious, wary, circumspect, heedful. ■ OPPOSITES inattentive.

vigorous adj. **1** ROBUST, healthy, in good health, hale and hearty, strong, sturdy, fit, in good condition/shape/kilter, tough. **2** ENERGETIC, lively, active, spry, sprightly, vivacious, animated, dynamic, full of life, sparkling. ■ OPPOSITES weak, feeble.

vigour n. ENERGY, activity, liveliness, spryness, sprightliness, vitality, vivacity, verve, animation, dynamism, sparkle, zest, dash, gusto, pep; informal zip, zing, oomph, vim. ■ OPPOSITES lethargy.

vile adj. FOUL, nasty, unpleasant, disagreeable, horrid, horrible, offensive, obnoxious, odious, repulsive, repellent, revolting, repugnant, disgusting, distasteful, loathsome, hateful, nauseating, sickening, base, low, mean, wretched, dreadful, ugly, abominable, monstrous. ■ OPPOSITES pleasant.

vilify v. DEFAME, run down, impugn, revile, berate, denigrate, disparage, drag through the mud, speak ill of, cast aspersions at, criticize, decry, denounce, fulminate against, malign, slander, libel, traduce, calumniate; informal badmouth, do a hatchet job on. ■ OPPOSITES commend.

villain n. ROGUE, scoundrel, wretch, cad, reprobate, evil-doer, wrongdoer, hoodlum, hooligan, miscreant; informal baddy, crook, rat, louse; old use blackguard.

vindicate v. ACQUIT, clear, absolve, free from blame, exonerate, exculpate.

vine n. a climbing plant producing grapes. □ **vineyard** a plantation of vines producing grapes used in wine-making.

vinegar n. a sour liquid made from wine, malt, etc. ■ **vinegary** adj.

vintage n. **1** the year in which a wine was produced. **2** a wine of high quality from a particular year. **3** the time that something was produced. ▶ adj. of high quality, esp. from the past.

vintner n. a wine merchant.

vinyl /vy-n'l/ n. a type of plastic.

viola[1] /vi-oh-luh/ n. an instrument like a violin but of lower pitch.

viola[2] /vy-uh-luh/ n. a plant of a group including pansies and violets.

violate v. **1** break a rule etc. **2** treat with disrespect. **3** rape. ■ **violation** n. **violator** n.

violence n. **1** actions using physical force intended to hurt, damage, or kill. **2** great force or intensity. ■ **violent** adj. **violently** adv.

violet n. **1** a small plant with purple or blue flowers. **2** a bluish-purple colour.

violin n. a musical instrument with four strings, played with a bow. ■ **violinist** n.

violoncello n. a cello.

VIP abbrev. very important person.

viper n. a type of poisonous snake.

virago n. (pl. **viragos** or **viragoes**) an aggressive woman.

viral adj. of a virus or viruses.

virgin n. **1** a person who has never had sex. **2** (**the Virgin**) Mary, the mother of Jesus. ▶ adj. **1** having had no sexual experience. **2** not yet used or spoilt. ■ **virginal** adj. **virginity** n.

virile adj. (of a man) having strength, energy, and a strong sex drive. ■ **virility** n.

virology n. the study of viruses. ■ **virologist** n.

virtual adj. **1** almost as described, but not completely. **2** of or using virtual reality. □ **virtual reality** an interactive system in which images that look like real objects are created by computer. ■ **virtually** adv.

virtue n. **1** behaviour showing high moral standards. **2** a good or desirable quality. **3** old use virginity or chastity. □ **by virtue of** as a result of.

virtuoso n. (pl. **virtuosi** or **virtuosos**) a person highly skilled in music or another art. ■ **virtuosity** n.

virtuous adj. having high moral standards. ■ **virtuously** adv.

virulent adj. **1** (of a disease or poison) extremely harmful. **2** bitterly hostile. ■ **virulence** n. **virulently** adv.

virus n. **1** a minute organism which can

Thesaurus

vindictive adj. VENGEFUL, revengeful, avenging, unforgiving, grudge-bearing, resentful, implacable, unrelenting, spiteful, rancorous, venomous, malicious, malevolent, malignant. ■ OPPOSITES forgiving.

vintage adj. CLASSIC, ageless, enduring, high-quality, quality, prime, choice, select, superior, best.

violate v. **1** BREAK, breach, infringe, contravene, infract, transgress, disobey, disregard, ignore. **2** DESECRATE, profane, defile, blaspheme. **3** DISTURB, disrupt, intrude on, interfere with, encroach on, invade. ■ OPPOSITES respect.

violence n. FORCE, brute force, roughness, ferocity, brutality, savagery; informal strong-arm tactics.

violent adj. **1** BRUTAL, vicious, destructive, savage, fierce, wild, intemperate, bloodthirsty, homicidal, murderous, maniacal. **2** UNCONTROLLABLE, powerful, uncontrolled, unrestrained, unbridled, ungovernable, wild, strong, passionate. **3** EXTREME, great, intense, strong, vehement, inordinate, excessive. ■ OPPOSITES gentle, weak.

virile adj. POTENT, manly, strong, vigorous, robust, muscular, rugged, strapping, sturdy, red-blooded; informal macho. ■ OPPOSITES effeminate.

virtue n. **1** GOODNESS, righteousness, morality, uprightness, integrity, rectitude, honesty, honourableness, honour, incorruptibility, probity, decency, respectability, worthiness, worth, trustworthiness. **2** GOOD QUALITY/POINT, merit, asset, credit, attribute, advantage, plus, benefit, strength. ■ OPPOSITES vice.

virtuoso adj. SKILFUL, masterly, impressive, outstanding, dazzling, bravura. ■ OPPOSITES incompetent.

virtuous adj. **1** GOOD, righteous, moral, ethical, upright, upstanding, honest, honourable, incorruptible, decent, respectable, worthy, trustworthy. **2** VIRGINAL, celibate, pure, chaste, innocent, modest. ■ OPPOSITES evil.

virulent adj. **1** POISONOUS, toxic, venomous, deadly, lethal, fatal, noxious, harmful. **2** SEVERE, extreme, violent, rapidly spreading, highly infectious/contagious, harmful, lethal. **3** HOSTILE, spiteful, venomous, vicious, vindictive,

v

cause disease. **2** a destructive code introduced secretly into a computer system.

visa n. a note on a passport permitting the holder to enter, leave, or stay in a country.

visage n. literary a person's face.

vis-à-vis /veez-ah-vee/ prep. in relation to.

viscera /viss-uh-ruh/ pl. n. the internal organs of the body. ■ **visceral** adj.

viscid /viss-id/ adj. sticky.

viscose n. a synthetic fabric made from cellulose.

viscount /vy-kownt/ n. a nobleman ranking between earl and baron.

viscountess n. **1** the wife or widow of a viscount. **2** a woman holding the rank of viscount.

viscous adj. thick and sticky. ■ **viscosity** n.

visibility n. **1** the state of being able to see or be seen. **2** the distance one can see under certain weather conditions.

visible adj. able to be seen or noticed. ■ **visibly** adv.

vision n. **1** the ability to see. **2** the ability to think about the future with imagination or wisdom. **3** a mental image. **4** a person of great beauty.

visionary adj. thinking about the future with imagination or wisdom. ▶ n. (pl. **visionaries**) a visionary person.

visit v. **1** go to see and spend time with

or in. **2** inflict harm on someone. ▶ n. an act of visiting. ■ **visitor** n.

visitation n. **1** an official or formal visit. **2** a disaster or difficulty seen as a divine punishment.

visor (or **vizor**) n. **1** a movable part of a helmet for covering the face. **2** a screen for shielding the eyes from light.

vista n. a pleasing view.

visual adj. of or used in seeing. □ **visual display unit** a device displaying information from a computer on a screen. ■ **visually** adv.

visualize (or **-ise**) v. form a mental image of. ■ **visualization** n.

vital adj. **1** absolutely necessary. **2** essential for life. **3** full of energy. ▶ n. (**vitals**) the body's important internal organs. □ **vital statistics** informal the measurements of a woman's bust, waist, and hips. ■ **vitally** adv.

vitality n. strength and activity.

vitamin n. an organic compound present in food and essential for normal nutrition.

vitiate v. make less good or effective.

viticulture n. the cultivation of grapevines.

vitreous adj. like or containing glass.

vitrify v. (**vitrifying**, **vitrified**) convert into glass or a glass-like substance.

vitriol n. **1** old use sulphuric acid. **2** extreme bitterness or malice. ■ **vitriolic** adj.

Thesaurus

malicious, malevolent, malignant, bitter, rancorous, acrimonious, abusive, aggressive, violent. ■ OPPOSITES harmless, amicable.

visible adj. **1** IN VIEW, perceptible, perceivable, discernible, detectable, seeable. **2** APPARENT, evident, noticeable, observable, detectable, recognizable, manifest, plain, clear, obvious, patent, palpable, unmistakable, unconcealed, undisguised, conspicuous, distinct, distinguishable. ■ OPPOSITES invisible.

vision n. **1** EYESIGHT, sight, power of seeing. **2** REVELATION, dream, hallucination, chimera, optical illusion, mirage, illusion, delusion, figment of the imagination. **3** FORESIGHT, far-sightedness, prescience, breadth of view, discernment.

visionary adj. **1** IDEALISTIC, impractical, unrealistic, utopian, romantic, quixotic, dreamy, dreaming; informal starry-eyed. **2** FAR-SIGHTED, discerning, wise. **3** IMPRACTICAL, unrealistic, unworkable, unfeasible, theoretical, hypothetical,

idealistic, utopian. ▶ n. MYSTIC, seer, prophet, dreamer, daydreamer, idealist, romantic, romanticist, fantasist, theorist, utopian.

visit v. PAY A VISIT TO, go/come to see, pay a call on, call on, call/look in on, stop by; informal pop/drop in on. ▶ n. CALL, social call, stay, sojourn, stopover.

visitation n. AFFLICTION, scourge, plague, pestilence, blight, disaster, tragedy, calamity, catastrophe, cataclysm.

visual adj. **1** OPTICAL, ocular. **2** TO BE SEEN, perceivable, discernible.

visualize v. CONJURE UP, envisage, picture, envision, imagine, conceive.

vital adj. **1** ESSENTIAL, necessary, needed, indispensable, key, important, significant, imperative, urgent, critical, crucial, life-and-death. **2** LIVELY, animated, spirited, vivacious, vibrant, zestful, dynamic, energetic, vigorous, forceful. ■ OPPOSITES unimportant, apathetic.

vitality n. LIFE, liveliness, animation, spirit, spiritedness, vivacity, vibrancy, zest, zestfulness, dynamism, energy,

vituperation n. bitter and abusive language. ■ **vituperative** adj.

viva[1] /vy-vuh/ (or **viva voce** /vy-vuh voh-chi/) n. an oral university examination.

viva[2] /vee-vuh/ exclam. long live!

vivacious adj. attractively lively. ■ **vivaciously** adv. **vivacity** n.

vivarium n. (pl. **vivaria**) a place for keeping animals in natural conditions.

vivid adj. **1** producing powerful feelings or clear images in the mind. **2** very deep or bright. ■ **vividly** adv. **vividness** n.

vivify v. (**vivifying**, **vivified**) enliven.

viviparous /vi-vip-uh-ruhss/ adj. giving birth to live young.

vivisection n. the performing of operations on live animals for scientific research.

vixen n. a female fox.

viz. adv. namely; in other words.

vizor var. of VISOR.

vocabulary n. (pl. **vocabularies**) **1** the words used in a particular language or activity or known to a person. **2** a list of words and their meanings.

vocal adj. **1** of or for the voice. **2** expressing opinions or feelings freely. ▶ n. a piece of sung music. □ **vocal cords** membranes in the throat that vibrate to produce the voice. ■ **vocally** adv.

vocalist n. a singer.

vocalize (or **-ise**) v. utter.

vocation n. **1** a strong feeling that one ought to pursue a particular career. **2** a

career. ■ **vocational** adj.

vociferate v. shout.

vociferous adj. vehement or loud. ■ **vociferously** adv.

vodka n. an alcoholic spirit made from rye, wheat, or potatoes.

vogue n. the current fashion or style.

voice n. **1** the sound produced in the larynx and uttered through the mouth, as speech or song. **2** an opinion, or the right to express an opinion. ▶ v. express in words. □ **voicemail** an electronic system for storing messages from telephone callers. **voice-over** a narration in a film etc. without an image of the speaker.

void adj. **1** not valid. **2** empty. ▶ n. an empty space. ▶ v. **1** declare to be no longer valid. **2** discharge water, gases, etc.

voile /voyl, vwahl/ n. a thin, semi-transparent fabric.

volatile adj. **1** easily evaporated. **2** liable to change unpredictably. ▶ n. a volatile substance. ■ **volatility** n.

vol-au-vent /vol-oh-von/ n. a small round case of puff pastry with a savoury filling.

volcano n. (pl. **volcanoes** or **volcanos**) a mountain with an opening through which lava is expelled. ■ **volcanic** adj.

vole n. a small mouse-like rodent.

volition n. the power of choosing and deciding oneself.

volley n. (pl. **volleys**) **1** a number of bullets, arrows, etc. fired at one time. **2** a

Thesaurus

vigour; *informal* zing, zip, pep, get-up-and-go.

vitriolic adj. CAUSTIC, mordant, acrimonious, bitter, acerbic, astringent, acid, acidulous, acrid, trenchant, virulent, spiteful, venomous, malicious, scathing, withering, sarcastic, sardonic; *informal* bitchy.

vivacious adj. LIVELY, full of life, animated, effervescent, bubbly, ebullient, sparkling, scintillating, light-hearted, spirited, high-spirited, merry, jolly, vibrant, vivid, dynamic, vital; *dated* gay. ■ OPPOSITES dull.

vivid adj. **1** STRONG, intense, colourful, rich, glowing, bright, brilliant, clear. **2** GRAPHIC, clear, lively, stirring, striking, powerful, highly coloured, dramatic, memorable, realistic, lifelike, true to life. ■ OPPOSITES dull.

vocal adj. **1** VOICED, vocalized, spoken, said, uttered, expressed, articulated, oral. **2** VOCIFEROUS, outspoken, forth-

right, plain-spoken, clamorous, strident, loud, noisy.

vocation n. PROFESSION, calling, occupation, walk of life, career, life's work, métier, trade, craft, job, work, employment, business, line, speciality.

vogue n. FASHION, mode, style, trend, taste, fad, craze, rage, latest thing.

voice n. **1** POWER OF SPEECH/ARTICULATION. **2** EXPRESSION, utterance, verbalization, vocalization, airing. ▶ v. PUT INTO WORDS, express, give utterance to, utter, articulate, enunciate, mention, talk of, communicate, declare, assert, divulge, air.

void adj. **1** EMPTY, emptied, vacant, bare, clear, free, unfilled, unoccupied, uninhabited, untenanted, tenantless. **2** NULL AND VOID, nullified, invalid, cancelled, inoperative, ineffective, non-viable, useless, worthless, nugatory. ■ OPPOSITES full, valid.

volatile adj. **1** MERCURIAL, changeable, variable, capricious, whimsical, fickle, series of questions, insults, etc. **3** (in sport) a strike of the ball made before it touches the ground. ▶v. strike the ball before it touches the ground. ▫ **volley-ball** a game for two teams in which a ball is hit by hand over a net.

volt n. a basic unit of electromotive force.

voltage n. electromotive force expressed in volts.

volte-face /volt-fass/ n. an abrupt and complete reversal of attitude or policy.

voluble adj. speaking fluently and at length. ■ **volubility** n. **volubly** adv.

volume n. **1** a book. **2** the amount of space occupied by something or enclosed within a container. **3** an amount or quantity. **4** degree of loudness.

voluminous adj. (of clothing) loose and full.

voluntary adj. **1** done or acting of one's own free will. **2** working or done without payment. ■ **voluntarily** adv.

volunteer n. **1** a person who offers to do something. **2** a person who works for no pay. **3** a person who freely joins the armed forces. ▶v. freely offer or offer to do something.

voluptuary n. (pl. **voluptuaries**) a person who loves luxury and pleasure.

voluptuous adj. **1** (of a woman) curvaceous and sexually attractive. **2** characterized by luxury and pleasure. ■ **voluptuously** adv.

vomit v. (**vomiting**, **vomited**) bring up matter from the stomach through the mouth. ▶n. vomited matter.

voodoo n. a religious cult involving sorcery and possession by spirits.

voracious adj. **1** wanting or eating great quantities of food. **2** eagerly consuming something. ■ **voraciously** adv. **voracity** n.

vortex n. (pl. **vortexes** or **vortices**) a whirling mass of water or air.

vote n. **1** a formal choice made between two or more candidates or courses of action. **2** (**the vote**) the right to participate in an election. ▶v. give or register a vote. ■ **voter** n.

votive adj. offered to a god as a sign of thanks.

vouch v. (**vouch for**) state or confirm the truth, accuracy, or honesty of.

voucher n. a piece of paper that may be exchanged for goods or services.

vouchsafe v. give or grant.

vow n. a solemn promise. ▶v. solemnly promise.

vowel n. a letter of the alphabet representing a spech sound in which the mouth is open and the tongue not touching the top of the mouth, the teeth, or the lips (e.g. *a* or *e*).

vox pop n. informal popular opinion represented by informal comments from the public.

voyage n. a long journey by sea or in space. ▶v. go on a voyage. ■ **voyager** n.

voyeur /vwa-yer/ n. a person who gets sexual pleasure from watching others when they are naked or having sex.

vs abbrev. versus.

VSO abbrev. Voluntary Service Overseas.

Thesaurus

flighty, giddy, inconstant, erratic, unstable. **2** EXPLOSIVE, eruptive, charged, inflammatory, tense, strained. ■ OPPOSITES stable.

voluble adj. TALKATIVE, loquacious, garrulous, chatty, gossipy, chattering, articulate, eloquent, forthcoming, fluent, glib. ■ OPPOSITES taciturn.

volume n. **1** BOOK, publication, tome. **2** SPACE, bulk, capacity. **3** LOUDNESS, sound, amplification.

voluminous adj. CAPACIOUS, roomy, commodious, ample, full, big, vast, billowing. ■ OPPOSITES small.

voluntary adj. OF ONE'S OWN FREE WILL, volitional, of one's own accord, optional, discretionary, at one's discretion, elective, non-compulsory. ■ OPPOSITES compulsory.

volunteer v. OFFER ONE'S SERVICES, present oneself, step forward.

voluptuous adj. **1** CURVY, shapely, full-

figured, ample, buxom, seductive, curvaceous. **2** HEDONISTIC, sybaritic, epicurean, self-indulgent, sensual, carnal, licentious, lascivious. ■ OPPOSITES scrawny, ascetic.

vomit v. **1** THROW UP, be sick; *informal* spew, puke. **2** BRING UP, regurgitate, spew up, spit up.

voracious adj. **1** GLUTTONOUS, greedy, ravenous, ravening, starving, hungry, insatiable. **2** COMPULSIVE, enthusiastic, eager.

vote n. BALLOT, poll, election, referendum, plebiscite. ▶v. CAST ONE'S VOTE, go to the polls, mark one's ballot paper.

vouch v. (**vouch for**) ATTEST TO, bear witness to, give assurance of, answer for, be responsible for, guarantee, go/stand bail for.

voucher n. COUPON, chit, slip, ticket, token.

vow v. SWEAR, state under oath, pledge,

vulcanite n. hard black vulcanized rubber.

vulcanize (or **-ise**) v. harden rubber by treating it with sulphur at a high temperature.

vulgar adj. **1** lacking sophistication or good taste. **2** referring inappropriately to sex or bodily functions. ◻ **vulgar fraction** a fraction shown by numbers above and below a line, not decimally. ∎ **vulgarity** n. **vulgarly** adv.

vulgarian n. a vulgar person.

vulgarism n. a vulgar word or expression.

vulnerable adj. exposed to being attacked or harmed. ∎ **vulnerability** n. **vulnerably** adv.

vulpine adj. of or like a fox.

vulture n. a large bird of prey that feeds on dead animals.

vulva n. the female external genitals.

vying pres. part. of **VIE**.

Thesaurus

promise, undertake, give one's word of honour.

voyage n. JOURNEY, trip, expedition, crossing, cruise, passage. ▶v. TRAVEL, journey, take a trip, sail, cruise.

vulgar adj. **1** RUDE, indecent, indecorous, indelicate, crude, unseemly, offensive, distasteful, obnoxious, suggestive, off colour, ribald, bawdy, obscene, lewd, salacious, licentious, concupiscent, smutty, dirty, filthy, pornographic, scatological; *informal* raunchy, blue. **2** TASTELESS, gross, crass, unrefined, tawdry, ostentatious, showy, flashy, gaudy, kitsch; *informal* tacky. ∎ OPPOSITES tasteful.

vulnerable adj. EXPOSED, unprotected, unguarded, open to attack, assailable, defenceless, weak, helpless, easily hurt/wounded/damaged, powerless, sensitive, thin-skinned. ∎ OPPOSITES invulnerable.

Ww

W abbrev. **1** watts. **2** West or Western.

wacky adj. (**wackier**, **wackiest**) informal odd but funny.

wad n. **1** a pad of soft material. **2** a bundle of papers or banknotes. ▶v. (**wadding**, **wadded**) line or pad. ■ **wadding** n.

waddle v. walk with short steps and a swaying motion. ▶n. a waddling walk.

wade v. **1** walk through water or mud. **2** read through with effort.

wader n. **1** a long-legged waterbird. **2** (**waders**) high waterproof boots.

wadi n. (pl. **wadis**) a valley or channel that is dry except in the rainy season.

wafer n. **1** a thin, light biscuit. **2** a very thin slice.

waffle v. informal speak or write at length in a vague or trivial way. ▶n. **1** informal lengthy but vague or trivial talk or writing. **2** a small crisp batter cake, eaten hot.

waft v. carry or move easily or gently through the air. ▶n. a gentle movement of air.

wag v. (**wagging**, **wagged**) move rapidly to and fro. ▶n. **1** a wagging movement. **2** informal a person fond of making jokes.

wage n. (also **wages**) a fixed regular payment for work. ▶v. carry on a war or campaign.

wager n. & v. (make) a bet.

waggle v. wag. ▶n. a waggling movement.

wagon (or **waggon**) n. **1** a vehicle, esp. a horse-drawn one, for transporting goods. **2** a railway vehicle for carrying goods in bulk.

waif n. a homeless child.

wail n. a long, high-pitched cry of pain or grief. ▶v. utter a wail.

wainscot (or **wainscoting**) n. wooden panelling on the lower part of the walls of a room.

waist n. **1** the part of the body between the ribs and hips. **2** a narrow middle part. □ **waistcoat** a close-fitting, waist-length garment with no sleeves or collar. **waistline** the measurement around a person's waist.

wait v. **1** stay where one is or delay action until a particular time or event. **2** be delayed or deferred. **3** (**wait on**) act as an attendant to. **4** act as a waiter or waitress. ▶n. a period of waiting.

waiter (or **waitress**) n. a person whose job is to serve customers in a restaurant.

waive v. refrain from insisting on a

Thesaurus

wad n. **1** LUMP, mass, chunk, hunk, bail, plug, block. **2** BUNDLE, roll.

waddle v. SWAY, wobble, totter, toddle, shuffle.

wade v. PADDLE, wallow. □ **wade in** SET TO, set to work, pitch in, buckle down, go to it, put one's shoulder to the wheel; *informal* get cracking, get stuck in.

waffle n. MEANINGLESS TALK/WRITING, padding, equivocation, prattle, jabbering, verbiage, logorrhoea; *informal* wittering. ▶v. RAMBLE, prattle, jabber, babble; *informal* rabbit, witter.

waft v. **1** FLOAT, glide, drift, be carried/borne/conveyed. **2** CARRY, bear, convey, transport, transmit.

wag[1] v. **1** SWING, sway, vibrate, quiver, shake, rock, twitch. **2** WAGGLE, wiggle, wobble, wave.

wag[2] n. WIT, humorist, jester, joker, jokester, comic, comedian, comedienne, wisecracker, punner, punster.

wage n. PAY, salary, earnings, payment, fee, remuneration, stipend, emolument. ▶v. CARRY ON, conduct, execute, engage in, pursue, undertake, devote oneself to, practise.

wager n. BET, gamble, stake, pledge, hazard; *informal* flutter. ▶v. LAY A WAGER, bet, place/make/lay a bet, lay odds, put money on, speculate.

wail n. CRY OF GRIEF/PAIN, lament, lamentation, weeping, sob, moan, groan, whine, complaint, howl, yowl, ululation. ▶v. CRY, lament, weep, sob, moan, groan, whine, howl, yowl, ululate.

wait v. **1** STAY, remain, rest, linger, abide; *old use* tarry. **2** BE PATIENT, hold back, stand by, bide one's time, hang fire, mark time; *informal* cool one's heels, sit tight, hold one's horses, sweat it out. ▶n. INTERVAL, stay, delay, hold-up.

W

right or claim. ■ **waiver** n.

wake v. (**waking**, **woke**; past part. **woken**) **1** stop sleeping. **2** cause to stir; rouse. ▶n. **1** a watch kept beside the body of someone who has died. **2** a party held after a funeral. **3** a trail of disturbed water left by a ship. □ **in the wake of** following as a result of.

wakeful adj. unable to sleep. ■ **wakefulness** n.

waken v. wake.

walk v. **1** move fairly slowly using one's legs. **2** travel over on foot. **3** accompany on foot. ▶n. **1** a journey on foot. **2** a way of walking. **3** a path for walking. □ **walk of life** social rank. **walking stick** a stick used for support when walking. **walkout** a sudden angry departure as a protest or strike. **walkover** an easy victory. ■ **walker** n.

walkie-talkie n. a portable two-way radio.

wall n. **1** a continuous upright structure forming a side of a building or room, or enclosing or dividing an area of land. **2** a barrier. **3** the outer layer or lining of a bodily organ or cavity. ▶v. enclose or block with a wall. □ **wallflower 1** a garden plant. **2** informal a girl who has no one to dance with at a party. **wall-**

paper decorative paper for covering the interior walls of a room.

wallaby n. (pl. **wallabies**) a marsupial like a small kangaroo.

wallet n. a small, flat, folding holder for money etc.

wallop informal v. (**walloping**, **walloped**) hit hard. ▶n. a heavy blow.

wallow v. **1** roll in mud or water. **2** (**wallow in**) indulge in.

wally n. (pl. **wallies**) informal a silly person.

walnut n. a wrinkled edible nut.

walrus n. a large, seal-like mammal with long tusks.

waltz n. **1** a ballroom dance. **2** music for this. ▶v. **1** dance a waltz. **2** move or act casually.

wan /won/ adj. pale and appearing ill. ■ **wanly** adv.

wand n. a slender rod, esp. one used in performing magic.

wander v. **1** walk or move in a leisurely or aimless way. **2** move slowly away from a fixed point. ▶n. an act of wandering. □ **wanderlust** a strong desire to travel. ■ **wanderer** n.

wane v. **1** (of the moon) show a gradually decreasing bright area after being full. **2** become weaker. □ **on the wane**

Thesaurus

□ **wait on** act as a waiter/waitress to, serve, attend to.

waiter, waitress n. steward, stewardess, server, attendant.

waive v. relinquish, renounce, give up, abandon, surrender, yield, cede, set aside, forgo, disregard, ignore.

wake v. **1** awake, awaken, waken, wake up, waken up, rouse, stir, come to, get up, arise. **2** rouse, stir up, activate, stimulate, spur, prod, galvanize, provoke. ■ opposites sleep. ▶n. vigil, death watch, watch.

wakeful adj. **1** unsleeping, restless, tossing and turning, insomniac. **2** alert, on the alert, vigilant, on the lookout, on one's guard, on the qui vive, watchful, observant, attentive, heedful, wary. ■ opposites asleep, inattentive.

walk v. **1** go by foot, travel on foot, foot it; informal hoof it. **2** stroll, saunter, amble, plod, trudge, hike, tramp, trek, march, stride, step out. **3** accompany, escort, convey. ▶n. **1** stroll, saunter, amble, promenade, ramble, hike, tramp, march, constitutional, airing. **2** manner of walking, gait, pace, step, stride. **3** road, avenue, drive, promenade, path, pathway, footpath, track,

lane, alley.

walkover n. easy victory; informal piece of cake, child's play, doddle, pushover.

wall n. **1** partition, room divider. **2** fortification, rampart, barricade, parapet, bulwark, stockade, breastwork.

wallet n. purse, pouch; US billfold, pocketbook; dated notecase.

wallow v. **1** roll, tumble about, lie around, splash around. **2** luxuriate in, bask in, take pleasure/satisfaction in, indulge oneself in, delight in, revel in, glory in, enjoy.

wan adj. pale, pallid, ashen, white, white as a sheet/ghost, anaemic, colourless, bloodless, waxen, pasty, peaky, tired-looking, washed out, sickly. ■ opposites ruddy.

wand n. baton, stick, staff, twig, sprig, withe, withy.

wander v. **1** ramble, roam, meander, rove, range, prowl, saunter, stroll, amble, peregrinate, drift; informal traipse, mooch. **2** stray, depart, diverge, veer, swerve, deviate. **3** be incoherent, ramble, babble, talk nonsense, rave, be delirious. ▶n. ramble, saunter, stroll, amble.

wanderer n. rambler, roamer, rover,

waning.

wangle v. informal obtain by trickery or persuasion.

want v. **1** desire to have or do. **2** (**wanted**) (of a suspected criminal) sought by the police. **3** lack or be short of. ▶n. **1** a desire. **2** lack or shortage.

wanting adj. **1** lacking. **2** absent.

wanton adj. **1** deliberate and unprovoked. **2** having many sexual partners. ■ **wantonly** adv.

WAP abbrev. Wireless Application Protocol, a means of enabling mobile phones to access the Internet and display data.

war n. a state or period of armed conflict between different nations or groups. ▶v. (**warring, warred**) engage in a war. □ **warfare** the activity of fighting a war. **warhead** the explosive head of a missile. **warlike** hostile. **warmonger** a person who seeks to bring about war.

warble v. **1** sing with trilling or quavering notes. ▶n. a warbling sound.

ward n. **1** a room with beds for patients in a hospital. **2** a division of a city or borough represented by a councillor. **3** a young person looked after by a guardian appointed by their parents or a court. ▶v. (**ward off**) keep at a distance or from doing harm.

warden n. an official with supervisory duties.

warder n. a prison guard.

wardrobe n. **1** a large, tall cupboard for hanging clothes in. **2** a collection of clothes.

ware n. **1** manufactured articles of a specified type. **2** (**wares**) articles offered for sale. □ **warehouse** a large building for storing goods.

warlock n. a man who practises witchcraft.

warm adj. **1** moderately hot. **2** helping the body to retain heat. **3** enthusiastic, affectionate, or kind. ▶v. **1** make or become warm. **2** (**warm to**) become more

Thesaurus

drifter, traveller, itinerant, wayfarer, nomad, bird of passage, rolling stone, gypsy, vagabond, vagrant, tramp, derelict, beggar.

wane v. DECREASE, decline, diminish, dwindle, shrink, contract, taper off, subside, sink, ebb, dim, fade away, vanish, die out, draw to a close, evanesce, peter out, wind down, be on the way out, abate, fail, deteriorate, degenerate. ■ OPPOSITES strengthen.

want v. **1** WISH, wish for, desire, demand, call for, long for, hope for, yearn for, pine for, fancy, crave, hanker after, hunger for, thirst for, lust after, covet, need; informal have a yen for. **2** NEED, be/stand in need of, require. **3** LACK, be lacking, be without, be devoid of, be bereft of, be short of, be deficient in, have insufficient of. ▶n. **1** LACK, absence, dearth, deficiency, inadequacy, insufficiency, shortness, paucity, shortage, scarcity, scarceness, scantiness. **2** WISH, desire, demand, longing, yearning, fancy, craving, hankering, hunger, thirst, lust, covetousness. **3** NEED, neediness, privation, poverty, destitution, penury, indigence.

wanting adj. LACKING, deficient, inadequate, imperfect, not up to standard/par, not good enough, disappointing, not acceptable, not up to expectations, flawed, faulty, defective, unsound, substandard, inferior, second-rate. ■ OPPOSITES sufficient.

wanton adj. **1** PROMISCUOUS, fast, immoral, loose, immodest, shameless, unchaste, of easy virtue, impure, abandoned, lustful, lecherous, lascivious, libidinous, licentious, libertine, dissolute, dissipated, debauched, degenerate. **2** WILFUL, malicious, malevolent, spiteful, wicked, evil, cruel, unmotivated, motiveless, arbitrary, groundless, unjustifiable, unjustified, needless, unnecessary, uncalled for, unprovoked, gratuitous, senseless, pointless, purposeless.

war n. WARFARE, conflict, hostilities, strife, combat, fighting, struggle, armed conflict, battle, fight, confrontation, skirmish. ■ OPPOSITES peace.

ward n. **1** ROOM, compartment, cubicle. **2** ADMINISTRATIVE DISTRICT, district, division, quarter, zone. **3** CHARGE, dependant, protégé/protégée, pupil. □ **ward off** FEND OFF, stave off, parry, avert, deflect, turn aside, drive back, repel, repulse, beat back, rout, put to flight, scatter, disperse.

warder n. PRISON OFFICER, guard, warden, jailer; informal screw.

warehouse n. STORE, storehouse, depot, depository, stockroom.

wares pl. n. GOODS, products, commodities, lines, merchandise, produce, stuff, stock.

warily adv. CAREFULLY, with care, cautiously, gingerly, circumspectly, guardedly, on one's guard, on the alert, watchfully, vigilantly, suspiciously, distrustfully, mistrustfully, charily.

interested in or enthusiastic about. □ **warm-blooded** (of animals) maintaining a constant body temperature. **warm up 1** prepare for exercise by doing gentle stretches. **2** heat or reheat. ■ **warmly** adv. **warmness** n. **warmth** n.

warn v. **1** inform of a possible danger or problem. **2** advise not to do something. **3** (**warn off**) order to keep away.

warning n. **1** something indicating a possible danger or problem. **2** advice against wrong or foolish actions. **3** advance notice.

warp v. **1** make or become bent or twisted as a result of heat or damp. **2** make abnormal or strange. ▶n. **1** a distortion. **2** the lengthwise threads on a loom.

warrant n. **1** an official authorization allowing the police to make an arrest, search premises, etc. **2** a voucher. **3** justification. ▶v. **1** justify. **2** guarantee.

warranty n. (pl. **warranties**) a written guarantee promising to repair or replace a purchased article.

warren n. a network of interconnecting rabbit burrows.

warrior n. a brave or experienced soldier or fighter.

wart n. a small, hard growth on the skin. □ **warthog** an African wild pig with warty lumps on its face. ■ **warty** adj.

wary adj. (**warier**, **wariest**) cautious. ■ **warily** adv. **wariness** n.

was see BE.

wash v. **1** clean with water and usu. soap or detergent. **2** (of flowing water) carry or move in a particular direction. **3** (**wash over**) occur without greatly affecting. **4** informal seem convincing or genuine. ▶n. **1** an act of washing. **2** clothes etc. to be washed. **3** the water or air disturbed by a moving boat or aircraft. **4** a cleansing solution. **5** a thin coating of paint. □ **washbasin** a basin for washing one's hands and face. **washout** informal a disappointing failure. **wash one's hands of** take no further responsibility for. **wash up** clean crockery and cutlery after use. ■ **washable** adj.

washer n. a small flat ring fixed between a nut and bolt.

washing n. clothes etc. to be washed or that have just been washed. □ **washing-up** crockery, cutlery, etc. to be washed.

wasp n. a stinging winged insect with a black and yellow striped body.

waspish adj. sharply irritable. ■ **waspishly** adv.

wassail old use n. lively festivities involving the drinking of much alcohol. ▶v. **1** celebrate in this way. **2** go carol singing.

wastage n. **1** the process of wasting. **2** an amount wasted. **3** the reduction in the size of a workforce by resignations or retirements.

Thesaurus

■ OPPOSITES trustingly.

warlike adj. AGGRESSIVE, belligerent, bellicose, pugnacious, combative, militaristic, militant, martial. ■ OPPOSITES peaceful, peaceable.

warm adj. **1** HEATED, tepid, lukewarm. **2** SUNNY, balmy. **3** KINDLY, friendly, affable, amiable, genial, cordial, sympathetic, affectionate, loving, tender, caring, charitable, sincere, genuine. **4** HEARTY, cordial, genial, friendly, hospitable, enthusiastic, eager, sincere, heartfelt, ardent, vehement, passionate, intense, fervent, effusive. ■ OPPOSITES cool, cold. ▶v. WARM UP, make warm, heat, heat up, reheat.

warn v. **1** INFORM, notify, give notice, give prior notice, tell, let know, acquaint, give fair warning, forewarn; informal tip off, put wise. **2** ADVISE, exhort, urge, counsel, caution, put on the alert, make aware. **3** GIVE A WARNING TO, admonish, remonstrate with.

warning n. **1** INFORMATION, notification, notice, word, forewarning; informal tip-off. **2** CAUTION, advice, exhortation, counselling. **3** ADMONITION, remonstrance. **4** OMEN, premonition, foretoken, token, augury, signal, sign, threat.

warrant n. **1** AUTHORIZATION, consent, sanction, permission, validation, licence, imprimatur, seal of approval. **2** OFFICIAL DOCUMENT, written order, papers. ▶v. JUSTIFY, vindicate, excuse, be a defence of, explain away, account for, be a reason for, offer grounds for, support.

wary adj. CAREFUL, cautious, circumspect, leery, chary, on one's guard, alert, wide awake, on one's toes, on the alert/lookout, on the qui vive, attentive, heedful, watchful, vigilant, observant. ■ OPPOSITES unwary.

wash v. **1** WASH ONESELF, have a wash, bath, shower, have a bath/shower. **2** CLEAN, cleanse, sponge, scrub, launder, shampoo. **3** SPLASH AGAINST, dash against, break against, beat against.

waste v. **1** use carelessly, extravagantly, or to no purpose. **2** fail to make use of. **3** become weaker and thinner. ▶ adj. **1** discarded because no longer required. **2** (of land) not used, cultivated, or built on. ▶ n. **1** an act of wasting. **2** waste material. **3** a large area of barren, uninhabited land. ▢ **lay waste to** completely destroy. ■ **waster** n.

wasteful adj. using something carelessly or extravagantly. ■ **wastefully** adv.

watch v. **1** look at attentively. **2** keep under careful observation. **3** be careful about. **4** (**watch out**) be careful. ▶ n. **1** a small timepiece usu. worn on the wrist. **2** an act of watching. **3** a shift worked by sailors, firefighters, or police officers. ▢ **watchdog 1** a dog kept to guard private property. **2** a group monitoring the practices of companies. **watchman** a man employed to guard an empty building. **watchtower** a tower built as a high observation point. **watchword** a word or phrase expressing a central aim or belief. ■ **watcher** n.

watchful adj. alert to possible difficulty or danger. ■ **watchfully** adv.

water n. **1** the liquid which forms the seas, lakes, rivers, and rain. **2** (**waters**) an area of sea under a particular country's authority. **3** urine. ▶ v. **1** pour water over. **2** give a drink of water to. **3** produce tears or saliva. **4** dilute with water. **5** (**water down**) make less forceful. ▢ **waterbed** a bed with a water-filled mattress. **water cannon** a device that ejects a powerful jet of water to disperse a crowd. **water chestnut** the crisp edible tuber of a tropical plant. **water closet** dated a flush toilet. **watercolour 1** artists' paint mixed with water rather than oil. **2** a picture painted with watercolours. **watercourse** a brook, stream, or artificial water channel. **watercress** a cress which grows in running water. **waterfall** a stream of water falling from a height. **waterfront** a part of a town alongside a body of water. **water ice** a frozen dessert of fruit juice in sugar syrup. **water lily** a plant that grows in water, with broad floating leaves. **waterline** the level normally reached by the water on the side of a ship. **waterlogged** saturated with water. **watermark** a faint design made in some paper, visible when held against the light. **water meadow** a meadow periodically flooded by a stream. **watermelon** a melon with watery red pulp. **watermill** a mill worked by a waterwheel. **waterproof** unable to be penetrated by water. **watershed 1** an area of land separating two river systems. **2** a turning point in a state of affairs. **waterskiing** the sport of skimming over water on skis while towed by a motor boat. **waterspout** a column of water formed by a whirlwind over the sea. **water table** the level below which the ground is saturated with water. **watertight 1** not allowing water to pass through. **2** unable to be called into question. **waterway** a river, canal, or other route for travel by water. **waterwheel** a wheel driven by flowing water to work machinery.

watery adj. **1** of or like water. **2** contain-

Thesaurus

4 BE ACCEPTED, be plausible, be convincing, hold up, hold water, stand up, bear scrutiny. ▶ n. CLEAN, cleaning, cleansing, bath, shower.

waste v. SQUANDER, dissipate, fritter away, misspend, misuse, spend recklessly, throw away, go through, run through; *informal* blow. ■ OPPOSITES conserve. ▶ n. **1** SQUANDERING, dissipation, frittering away, misspending, misuse, prodigality, unthriftiness. **2** RUBBISH, refuse, debris, dross, dregs, leavings, garbage, trash. ▶ adj. **1** LEFTOVER, unused, superfluous, supernumerary, unwanted, worthless, useless. **2** DESERT, barren, uncultivated, unproductive, arid, bare, desolate, solitary, lonely, empty, void, uninhabited, unpopulated, wild, bleak, cheerless. ▢ **waste away** GROW WEAK, wither, atrophy, become emaciated.

wasteful adj. PRODIGAL, profligate, thriftless, spendthrift, extravagant, lavish. ■ OPPOSITES thrifty.

watch v. **1** LOOK AT, observe, view, eye, gaze at, stare at, gape at, peer at, contemplate, behold, inspect, scrutinize, survey, scan, examine. **2** KEEP WATCH ON, keep an eye on, keep in sight, follow, spy on; *informal* keep tabs on. **3** MIND, take care of, look after, supervise, superintend, tend, guard, protect, keep an eye on. ▶ n. **1** WRISTWATCH, pocket watch, timepiece, chronometer. **2** GUARD, vigil.

watchful adj. OBSERVANT, alert, vigilant, attentive, heedful, sharp-eyed, eagle-eyed, wary, circumspect. *See also* WARY, ALERT.

watchman n. SECURITY GUARD/MAN,

ing too much water. **3** weak or pale.

watt n. a basic unit of electric power.

wattage n. an amount of electrical power expressed in watts.

wattle n. **1** interwoven sticks used to make fences, walls, etc. **2** a fleshy part hanging from the head or neck of a turkey etc.

wave v. **1** move one's hand to and fro as a greeting or signal. **2** move to and fro. ▶n. **1** a moving ridge of water. **2** a sudden increase in an emotion or type of event. **3** an act of waving. **4** a slightly curling lock of hair. **5** a regular to-and-fro motion of particles of matter involved in transmitting sound, light, heat, etc. □ **waveband** a range of wavelengths. **wavelength 1** the distance between successive crests of a wave of sound, light, etc. **2** a person's way of thinking.

waver v. **1** flicker. **2** begin to weaken; falter. **3** be indecisive.

wavy adj. (**wavier**, **waviest**) having a series of wave-like curves.

wax n. a soft solid substance that melts easily, used for making candles or polishes. ▶v. **1** polish or treat with wax. **2** remove hair from a part of the body by applying then peeling off wax. **3** (of the moon) show an increasingly large bright area until becoming full. **4** literary speak or write in the specified way. □ **waxwork** a lifelike dummy modelled in wax. ■ **waxen** adj. **waxy** adj.

way n. **1** a method or manner of doing something. **2** a road or path. **3** a route or means taken to reach, enter, or leave a place. **4** a direction. **5** a distance. **6** an aspect. ▶adv. informal by a great deal. □ **by the way** incidentally. **in the way** obstructing progress. **wayfarer** literary a traveller. **wayside** the edge of a road.

waylay v. (**waylaying**, **waylaid**) intercept someone in order to attack or question them.

wayward adj. self-willed and unpredictable. ■ **waywardness** n.

WC abbrev. water closet.

we pron. **1** used by a speaker to refer to himself or herself and one or more other people. **2** used in formal contexts

Thesaurus

guard, custodian, caretaker.

water n. SEA, river, lake, loch, pool, reservoir. ▶v. **1** SPRINKLE, moisten, dampen, wet, water down, douse, hose, spray, drench, saturate, flood. **2** EXUDE WATER, moisten, leak. □ **water down 1** ADD WATER TO, dilute, thin, weaken, adulterate. **2** PLAY DOWN, downplay, tone down, soft-pedal, understate, underemphasize.

waterfall n. FALLS, cascade, cataract.

watertight adj. **1** WATERPROOF, sound. **2** SOUND, flawless, incontrovertible, indisputable, foolproof, unassailable, impregnable. ■ OPPOSITES leaky, flawed.

watery adj. **1** AQUEOUS, liquid, liquefied, fluid, hydrous. **2** WET, damp, moist, sodden, soggy, squelchy, saturated, waterlogged, marshy, boggy, swampy, miry. **3** THIN, runny, weak, dilute, diluted, watered down, adulterated, tasteless, flavourless; informal wishy-washy. ■ OPPOSITES dry, thick.

wave v. **1** UNDULATE, ripple, stir, flutter, flap, sway, swing, shake, quiver, oscillate. **2** MOVE UP AND DOWN, move to and fro, wag, waggle, flutter. **3** GESTURE, gesticulate, signal, sign, beckon, indicate. ▶n. **1** BREAKER, roller, comber, ripple, billow, white horse, white cap, swell, surf. **2** STREAM, flow, rush, surge, flood. **3** UNDULATION, curl, kink. **4** SURGE, upsurge, groundswell, welling up, rush,

outbreak, rash. □ **wave aside** SET ASIDE, dismiss, reject, disregard, ignore.

waver v. **1** BECOME UNSTEADY, falter, wobble, hesitate. **2** BE IRRESOLUTE/INDECISIVE, hesitate, dither, equivocate, vacillate, shilly-shally, blow hot and cold, pussyfoot around, beat about the bush, hum and haw. **3** WEAVE, reel, totter, teeter, stagger, wobble.

wavy adj. UNDULATING, curvy, curling, squiggly, rippled, curving, winding. ■ OPPOSITES straight.

wax v. GET BIGGER, increase in size, enlarge, grow, develop, extend, widen, broaden, spread, mushroom. ■ OPPOSITES wane.

way n. **1** DIRECTION, route, course, road, roadway, street, thoroughfare, track, path, pathway, lane, avenue, drive. **2** METHOD, means, course of action, process, procedure, technique, system, plan, scheme, manner, modus operandi. **3** MANNER, style, fashion, mode. **4** DISTANCE, length, stretch, journey.

wayfarer n. TRAVELLER, walker, hiker, rambler, wanderer, roamer, rover, nomad, gypsy, vagabond, vagrant.

waylay v. LIE IN WAIT FOR, ambush, hold up, attack, accost, intercept, pounce on, swoop down on.

wayward adj. WILFUL, self-willed, headstrong, stubborn, obstinate, obdurate, perverse, contrary, uncooperative, reby a royal person instead of 'I'.

weak adj. **1** lacking strength and energy. **2** likely to break or give way. **3** not secure or stable. **4** lacking power, influence, or ability. **5** heavily diluted. **6** unconvincing. ■ **weaken** v. **weakly** adv.

weakling n. a weak person or animal.

weakness n. **1** the state or condition of being weak. **2** a disadvantage or fault. **3** a self-indulgent liking.

weal n. a red, swollen mark left on flesh by a blow or pressure.

wealth n. **1** a large amount of money and valuable possessions. **2** the state of being rich. **3** a large amount of something. ■ **wealthy** adj.

wean v. **1** make a young mammal used to food other than its mother's milk. **2** cause to give up a habit or addiction gradually.

weapon n. **1** a thing designed or used to inflict harm or damage. **2** a means of gaining an advantage or defending oneself. ■ **weaponry** n.

wear v. (**wearing**, **wore**; past part. **worn**) **1** have on one's body as clothing, decoration, or protection. **2** damage or suffer damage by friction or use. **3** withstand continued use. **4** (**wear off**) lose effectiveness or strength. **5** (**wear down**) overcome by persistence. **6** (**wear out**) exhaust. **7** (**wear on**) (of time) pass slowly. ▶ n. **1** clothing of a particular type. **2** damage from friction or use. ■ **wearable** adj. **wearer** n.

wearisome adj. causing weariness.

Thesaurus

fractory, recalcitrant, contumacious, unruly, ungovernable, unmanageable, incorrigible, intractable, difficult, fractious, disobedient, insubordinate. ■ OPPOSITES docile.

weak adj. **1** FRAIL, fragile, delicate, feeble, infirm, shaky, debilitated, incapacitated, ailing, indisposed, decrepit, puny, faint, enervated, tired, fatigued, exhausted, spent, worn out. **2** COWARDLY, pusillanimous, timorous, timid, spineless, ineffectual, useless, inept, effete, powerless, impotent, namby-pamby, soft; *informal* yellow, weak-kneed. **3** DEFECTIVE, faulty, poor, inadequate, deficient, imperfect, substandard, lacking, wanting. **4** UNSOUND, feeble, flimsy, lame, hollow, pathetic, unconvincing, untenable, implausible, unsatisfactory. **5** FAINT, low, muffled, stifled, muted, scarcely audible. **6** UNDER-STRENGTH, dilute, diluted, watery, thinned down, thin, adulterated, tasteless, flavourless, insipid; *informal* wishy-washy. ■ OPPOSITES strong.

weaken v. **1** ENFEEBLE, debilitate, incapacitate, sap someone's strength, enervate, tire, exhaust, wear out. **2** LESSEN, reduce, decrease, diminish, moderate, temper, sap, emasculate. **3** ABATE, lessen, decrease, dwindle, diminish, ease up, let up. ■ OPPOSITES strengthen.

weakling n. COWARD, mouse, milksop, namby-pamby; *informal* wimp, sissy, drip, wet, doormat, chicken, yellow-belly.

weakness n. **1** FRAILTY, fragility, delicateness, delicacy, feebleness, infirmity, debility, incapacity, indisposition, decrepitude, puniness, enervation, fatigue. **2** COWARDLINESS, timidity, spinelessness, ineffectuality, ineptness,

powerlessness, impotence. **3** DEFECTIVENESS, faultiness, inadequacy, deficiency. **4** UNSOUNDNESS, feebleness, flimsiness, lameness, untenability, implausibility. **5** FAINTNESS, low intensity, mutedness. **6** THINNESS, wateriness, tastelessness; *informal* wishy-washiness. **7** WEAK POINT, failing, foible, fault, flaw, defect, shortcoming, imperfection, blemish, Achilles' heel, chink in one's armour. ■ OPPOSITES strength.

wealth n. **1** MONEY, cash, capital, affluence, means, fortune, finance, property, riches, assets, possessions, resources, goods, funds. **2** MASS, abundance, profusion, copiousness, plenitude, amplitude, bounty, cornucopia. ■ OPPOSITES poverty, scarcity.

wealthy adj. RICH, well off, well-to-do, moneyed, affluent, prosperous, of means, of substance; *informal* well heeled, rolling in it/money, in the money, made of money, filthy/stinking rich, loaded, flush, on easy street, quids in. ■ OPPOSITES poor.

wear v. **1** BE DRESSED IN, dress in, be clothed in, clothe oneself in, have on, put on, don, sport. **2** HAVE, assume, present, show, display, exhibit. **3** ERODE, corrode, abrade, wash away, rub away, rub down, grind away, wear down. **4** BECOME WORN, wear thin, fray, become threadbare, go into holes. □ **wear off** LOSE EFFECTIVENESS, lose strength, fade, peter out, dwindle, decrease, diminish, disappear, subside, ebb, wane. **wear out** FATIGUE, tire, weary, exhaust, drain, strain, stress, weaken, enfeeble, prostrate, enervate; *informal* knacker; *US informal* poop.

weariness n. FATIGUE, tiredness, ex-

weary adj. (**wearier**, **weariest**) **1** tired. **2** tiring. ▶v. (**wearying**, **wearied**) make or become weary. ■ **wearily** adv. **weariness** n.

weasel n. a small, slender meat-eating mammal.

weather n. the state of the atmosphere in terms of temperature, wind, rain, etc. ▶v. **1** wear away or change by exposure to the weather. **2** come safely through. □ **under the weather** informal slightly unwell or depressed. **weather-beaten** damaged, worn, or tanned by exposure to the weather. **weathercock** a weathervane in the form of a cockerel. **weathervane** a revolving pointer to show the direction of the wind.

weave v. (**weaving**, **wove**; past part. **woven** or **wove**) **1** make fabric etc. by passing crosswise threads or strips under and over lengthwise ones. **2** make facts, events, etc. into a story. **3** (past & past part **weaved**) move from side to side to avoid obstructions. ▶n. a way in which fabric is woven. ■ **weaver** n.

web n. **1** a network of fine threads made by a spider. **2** a complex system of interconnected elements. **3** (**the Web**) the World Wide Web. **4** the skin between the toes of a duck, frog, etc. □ **web page** a document that can be accessed via the Internet. **website** a location on the Internet that maintains one or more web pages. ■ **webbed** adj.

webbing n. strong fabric used for straps and belts.

wed v. (**wedding**, **wedded** or **wed**) **1** formal marry. **2** combine or unite. □ **wedlock** the state of being married.

wedding n. a marriage ceremony.

wedge n. a piece of wood, metal, etc. thick at one end and tapering to a thin edge at the other. ▶v. **1** force apart or fix in position with a wedge. **2** force into a narrow space.

Wednesday n. the day before Thursday.

wee adj. Sc. little. ▶n. informal **1** an act of urinating. **2** urine. ▶v. informal urinate.

weed n. **1** a wild plant growing where it is not wanted. **2** informal a weak or thin person. ▶v. **1** remove weeds from. **2** (**weed out**) remove as inferior or unwanted. ■ **weedy** adj.

week n. **1** a period of seven days. **2** the five days from Monday to Friday, when many people work. □ **weekday** a day of the week other than Sunday or Saturday. **weekend** Saturday and Sunday. ■ **weekly** adj. & adv.

weeny adj. (**weenier**, **weeniest**) informal tiny.

weep v. (**weeping**, **wept**) **1** shed tears. **2** discharge liquid. **3** (**weeping**) (of a tree) having drooping branches. ▶n. a period of weeping.

weepy adj. (**weepier**, **weepiest**) informal **1** tearful. **2** sentimental.

weevil n. a small beetle that eats crops or stored foodstuffs.

weft n. the crosswise threads in weaving.

weigh v. **1** find out how heavy someone or something is. **2** have a specified weight. **3** (**weigh down**) be heavy and

Thesaurus

haustion, enervation, lassitude, languor, listlessness, lethargy.

wearisome adj. FATIGUING, tiring, exhausting, draining, wearing, trying, irksome, boring, tedious, dull, uninteresting, monotonous, humdrum, routine. ■ OPPOSITES refreshing.

weary adj. **1** FATIGUED, tired, exhausted, drained, worn, worn out, spent, careworn, wearied; informal dead tired/beat, dead on one's feet, dog-tired, all in, done in, whacked; fagged out, knackered, bushed; US informal pooped. **2** BORED, discontented, jaded, uninterested, listless, lethargic; informal browned off, fed up, sick and tired, cheesed off. ▶v. **1** FATIGUE, tire, exhaust, drain, wear out; informal wear to a frazzle, knacker. **2** BORE, irk; informal make fed up. **3** GROW WEARY, tire, get bored, have enough. ■ OPPOSITES refresh, interest.

weather v. **1** DRY, season, expose, expose to the elements. **2** COME/GET THROUGH, survive, withstand, live/pull through, bear up against, stand, endure, ride out, rise above, surmount, overcome, resist; informal stick out.

weave[1] v. **1** INTERLACE, intertwine, interwork, twist together, entwine, braid, plait. **2** MAKE UP, fabricate, put together, construct, invent, create, contrive.

weave[2] v. ZIGZAG, wind, criss-cross.

web n. LACEWORK, lattice, latticework, mesh, net, netting.

wed v. GET MARRIED, marry, become man and wife; informal get hitched/spliced, tie the knot, walk down the aisle. ■ OPPOSITES divorce, separate.

wedding n. WEDDING/MARRIAGE CEREMONY, marriage, nuptials.

wedge v. THRUST, stuff, pack, ram, force, cram, squeeze, jam.

troublesome to. **4** (often **weigh up**) assess the nature or importance of. **5** influence a decision or action. □ **weigh anchor** take up the anchor when ready to sail. **weighbridge** a machine for weighing vehicles, set in the ground to be driven on to.

weight n. **1** the heaviness of a person or thing. **2** a unit or system of units used for expressing this. **3** a piece of metal of known weight, used in weighing. **4** a heavy object. **5** ability to influence decisions etc. **6** importance. ▶v. **1** make heavier or keep in place with a weight. **2** attach importance to. **3** arrange so as to give one party an advantage. ■ **weightless** adj.

weighting n. additional wages paid to allow for a higher cost of living in a particular area.

weighty adj. (**weightier**, **weightiest**) **1** heavy. **2** serious and important. **3** influential.

weir n. a low dam built to regulate the flow of a river.

weird adj. strange; bizarre. ■ **weirdly** adv. **weirdness** n.

··

☑️ **weird** is an exception to the usual rule of *i* before *e* except after *c*.

··

welch var. of WELSH.

welcome n. **1** an instance or way of greeting someone. **2** an approving reaction. ▶v. **1** greet in a polite or friendly way. **2** be glad to receive or hear of. ▶adj. **1** gladly received. **2** much needed or desired. **3** allowed or invited to do

something.

weld v. **1** join metal parts by heating and pressing them together. **2** combine to form a whole. ▶n. a welded joint. ■ **welder** n.

welfare n. **1** well-being. **2** organized efforts to ensure the basic well-being of people in need. □ **welfare state** a system under which the state provides pensions, health care, etc.

well¹ adv. (**better**, **best**) **1** in a good way. **2** in an appropriate or right way. **3** in prosperity or comfort. **4** favourably. **5** to a great extent or degree. **6** very probably. ▶adj. (**better**, **best**) **1** in good health. **2** satisfactory. ▶exclam. expressing surprise, anger, resignation, etc. □ **as well 1** in addition. **2** with equal reason or an equally good result. **well advised** sensible; wise. **well appointed** well equipped or furnished. **well-being** comfort, good health, and happiness. **well disposed** having a sympathetic or friendly attitude. **well-heeled** informal wealthy. **well meaning** (or **well meant**) acting or done with good intentions. **well-nigh** almost. **well off 1** wealthy. **2** in a good situation. **well read** having read many literary works. **well spoken** having an educated and refined voice. **well-to-do** wealthy.

well² n. **1** a shaft sunk into the ground to obtain water, oil, etc. **2** an enclosed space in a building for stairs etc. or allowing in light. ▶v. (of a liquid) rise up to the surface.

wellington n. a knee-length waterproof

Thesaurus

··

weep v. CRY, shed tears, sob, blubber, snivel, whimper, whine, moan, lament, grieve, mourn, keen, wail; *informal* boohoo, blub.

weigh v. **1** MEASURE/GAUGE THE WEIGHT OF, put on the scales. **2** HAVE A WEIGHT OF, tip the scales at. **3** BALANCE, compare with, evaluate. □ **weigh up** CONSIDER, contemplate, think over, mull over, ponder, deliberate upon, meditate on, muse on, brood over, reflect on.

weight n. **1** HEAVINESS, load, quantity, poundage, tonnage, avoirdupois. **2** BURDEN, load, onus, millstone, albatross, oppression, trouble, worry, strain. **3** IMPORTANCE, significance, consequence, value, substance, force, influence; *informal* clout.

weird adj. **1** STRANGE, queer, uncanny, eerie, mysterious, mystifying, supernatural, preternatural, unnatural, unearth-

ly, ghostly; *informal* spooky, creepy. **2** ODD, eccentric, bizarre, outlandish, freakish, grotesque; *informal* offbeat, far out, way-out, out on a limb. ■ OPPOSITES normal, conventional.

welcome n. GREETING, salutation, reception, warm reception. ▶v. **1** BID WELCOME, greet, receive, embrace, receive with open arms, roll out the red carpet for, meet, usher in. **2** BE PLEASED BY, take pleasure in, feel satisfaction at. ▶adj. **1** WANTED, appreciated, popular, desirable. **2** GLADLY RECEIVED, pleasant, pleasing, agreeable, cheering, to one's liking, to one's taste. ■ OPPOSITES unwelcome.

welfare n. **1** WELL-BEING, health, good health, soundness, happiness, comfort, security, prosperity, success, fortune, good fortune. **2** STATE AID/BENEFIT, public assistance, social security, income rubber or plastic boot.

Welsh n. the language of Wales. ▶ adj. of Wales. ◻ **Welsh rarebit** (or **Welsh rabbit**) melted cheese on toast.

welsh (or **welch**) v. (**welsh on**) fail to honour a debt or obligation.

welt n. **1** a leather rim to which the sole of a shoe is attached. **2** a ribbed or reinforced border on a knitted garment. **3** a weal.

welter n. a confused mass.

welterweight n. a weight in boxing etc. intermediate between lightweight and middleweight.

wen n. a swelling or growth on the skin.

wench n. old use a girl or young woman.

wend v. (**wend one's way**) go slowly or by an indirect route.

went past of **GO**.

wept past & past part. of **WEEP**.

were see **BE**.

weren't contr. were not.

werewolf n. (pl. **werewolves**) (in folklore) a person who periodically changes into a wolf.

west n. **1** the direction in which the sun sets. **2** the western part of a place. ▶ adj. **1** lying towards or facing the west. **2** (of a wind) from the west. ▶ adv. towards the west. ■ **westerly** adj. & adv. **westward** adj. & adv. **westwards** adv.

western adj. situated in or facing the west. ▶ n. a film or novel about cowboys in the western US.

westerner n. a person from the west of a region.

westernize (or **-ise**) v. bring or come under the influence of Europe and North America.

wet adj. (**wetter**, **wettest**) **1** covered or saturated with liquid. **2** rainy. **3** (of paint etc.) not yet dry. **4** informal feeble or ineffective. ▶ v. (**wetting**, **wet** or **wetted**) make wet. ▶ n. **1** wetness. **2** rainy weather. ◻ **wet blanket** informal a person who spoils others' enjoyment by their lack of enthusiasm. **wet nurse** a woman employed to breastfeed another woman's child. **wetsuit** a rubber garment worn for warmth in water sports or diving. ■ **wetly** adv. **wetness** n.

wether n. a castrated ram.

whack informal v. **1** strike with a sharp blow. **2** (**whacked**) exhausted. ▶ n. **1** a sharp blow. **2** a share or contribution.

whale n. (pl. **whale** or **whales**) a very large sea mammal. ◻ **a whale of a time** informal a very enjoyable time. **whalebone** a horny substance from the upper jaw of whales, formerly used as stiffening in corsets etc.

whaler n. **1** a whaling ship. **2** a seaman engaged in whaling.

whaling n. the practice of hunting and killing whales.

wharf /worf/ n. (pl. **wharves** or **wharfs**) a level quayside area to which a ship

Thesaurus

support.

well[1] adj. **1** HEALTHY, in good health, fit, strong, robust, hale and hearty, able-bodied, up to par. **2** SATISFACTORY, all right, fine, good, thriving, flourishing; informal OK, fine and dandy.

well[2] n. **1** SPRING, fountain, waterhole, pool, borehole. **2** SOURCE, wellspring, fount, reservoir, repository, mine.

well advised adj. SENSIBLE, wise, prudent, judicious, circumspect, far-sighted, sagacious.

well balanced adj. **1** WELL ADJUSTED, sensible, reasonable, rational, level-headed, sound, practical, discerning, logical, sane, in one's right mind. **2** BALANCED, well proportioned, well ordered.

well built adj. STRONGLY BUILT, strong, muscular, brawny, sturdy, robust, strapping, husky, burly, big; informal hulking, hefty, beefy. ■ OPPOSITES puny.

well known adj. **1** KNOWN, widely known, familiar, common, usual, everyday. **2** FAMOUS, famed, renowned, celebrated, noted, notable, illustrious, eminent. ■ OPPOSITES unknown.

well-nigh adv. VIRTUALLY, next to, practically, all but, just about, almost, nearly, more or less.

well off adj. WEALTHY, rich, well-to-do, moneyed, affluent, prosperous, of means, of substance; informal well heeled, rolling in it/money, in the money, made of money, filthy/stinking rich, loaded, flush, on easy street, quids in. ■ OPPOSITES poor.

well spoken adj. ARTICULATE, nicely spoken, educated, polite, refined; informal posh.

wet adj. **1** DAMP, moist, moistened, wet through, soaked, drenched, saturated, sopping/dripping/wringing wet, sopping, dripping, soggy, waterlogged. **2** RAINY, raining, pouring, showery, drizzling, damp, humid, dank, misty. **3** FEEBLE, weak, inept, ineffective, ineffectual, effete, timid, timorous, cowardly, spineless, soft; informal namby-pamby, weedy. ▶ n. WETNESS, damp, dampness, may be moored to load and unload.

what pron. & adj. **1** asking for information about something. **2** whatever. **3** emphasizing a surprising or remarkable thing. ▶ pron. the thing or things that. ▶ adv. to what extent? □ **whatever 1** everything or anything that. **2** at all; of any kind. **whatnot** informal an unidentified or unspecified item or items. **whatsoever** whatever.

wheat n. a cereal crop whose grain is ground to make flour. □ **wheatmeal** wholemeal wheat flour.

wheaten adj. made of wheat.

wheedle v. coax or cajole.

wheel n. **1** a circular object that revolves on an axle, fixed below a vehicle to enable it to move or forming part of a machine. **2** a turn or rotation. ▶ v. **1** push or pull a vehicle with wheels. **2** move in a wide circle or curve. **3** turn round quickly. □ **wheel and deal** engage in commercial or political scheming. **wheelbarrow** a small cart with a single wheel at the front and two handles at the rear, used to move small loads. **wheelbase** the distance between a vehicle's front and rear axles. **wheelchair** a chair on wheels for an invalid or disabled person. **wheelwright** a person who makes or repairs wooden wheels.

wheeze v. breathe with a whistling or rattling sound in the chest. ▶ n. **1** a sound of wheezing. **2** informal a clever scheme. ■ **wheezy** adj.

whelk n. a shellfish with a spiral shell.

whelp n. a puppy. ▶ v. give birth to a puppy.

when adv. **1** at what time? **2** at which time or in which situation. ▶ conj. **1** at or during the time that. **2** whenever. **3** and just then. **4** although. □ **whenever 1** at whatever time. **2** every time that.

whence adv. formal from which or from where.

where adv. **1** in or to what place? **2** in

what direction or respect? **3** at, in, or to which. **4** in or to a place or situation in which. □ **whereabouts 1** where or approximately where? **2** the place where someone or something is. **whereas** in contrast with the fact that. **whereby** by which. **wherever 1** in or to whatever place. **2** in every case when. **whereupon** immediately after which. **wherewithal** the money etc. needed for a particular purpose.

wherry n. (pl. **wherries**) **1** a light rowing boat. **2** a large light barge.

whet v. (**whetting**, **whetted**) **1** sharpen a blade. **2** stimulate someone's interest or appetite. □ **whetstone** a fine-grained stone for sharpening blades.

whether conj. **1** expressing a choice between alternatives. **2** expressing an enquiry or investigation.

whey n. the watery part of milk remaining after curds have formed.

which pron. & adj. **1** asking for information specifying one or more members of a set. **2** introducing a clause giving further information about something previously mentioned. □ **whichever 1** any which; that or those which. **2** regardless of which.

whiff n. a smell smelt only briefly or faintly.

Whig n. hist. a member of a British political party that was succeeded by the Liberals.

while n. **1** (**a while**) a period of time. **2** (**the while**) meanwhile. ▶ conj. **1** at the same time as. **2** whereas. **3** although. ▶ v. (**while away**) pass time in a leisurely way. □ **worth (one's) while** worth the time or effort spent.

whilst conj. while.

whim n. a sudden desire or change of mind.

whimper v. make a series of low, feeble sounds. ▶ n. a whimpering sound.

whimsical adj. **1** quaint or fanciful. **2** capricious. ■ **whimsically** adv.

whine n. **1** a long, high-pitched com-

Thesaurus

moisture, moistness, condensation, humidity, water, liquid. ▶ v. DAMPEN, damp, moisten, sprinkle, spray, splash, water, irrigate, douse. ■ OPPOSITES dry.

wharf n. PIER, quay, jetty, dock, landing stage.

wheel v. TURN, go round, circle, rotate, revolve, spin, swivel round, pivot, whirl/twirl round, make a U-turn.

wheeze v. GASP, puff, pant, cough, rasp, whistle, hiss.

whereabouts n. LOCATION, site, position, situation, place, vicinity.

whet v. SHARPEN, put an edge on, edge, hone, strop, file, grind, rasp. ■ OPPOSITES blunt.

whim n. NOTION, fancy, idea, impulse, urge, caprice, vagary, craze, passion, inclination, bent.

whimper v. WHINE, cry, sniffle, snivel, moan, wail, groan.

plaining cry. **2** a similar shrill sound. **3** a petulant complaint. ▶v. **1** give or make a whine. **2** complain in a petulant way. ■ **whiny** adj.

whinge v. informal complain persistently.

whinny n. (pl. **whinnies**) a gentle neigh. ▶v. (**whinnying**, **whinnied**) neigh gently.

whip n. **1** a length of leather or cord on a handle, used to beat a person or urge on an animal. **2** an official maintaining discipline in a political party. **3** a written notice from a whip requesting attendance for voting. **4** a dessert made with whipped cream etc. ▶v. (**whipping**, **whipped**) **1** strike with a whip. **2** move rapidly. **3** beat into a froth. **4** (**whip up**) deliberately excite or provoke. □ **whipcord 1** thin, tightly twisted cord. **2** a closely woven ribbed fabric. **whiplash** injury caused by a severe jerk to the head. **whipping boy** a scapegoat. **whip-round** informal a collection of money from a group.

whippet n. a small dog resembling a greyhound.

whippy adj. flexible or springy.

whirl v. **1** move rapidly round and round. **2** (of the head etc.) seem to spin round. ▶n. **1** a whirling movement. **2** frantic activity. **3** a state of confusion. □ **whirlpool** a current of water whirling in a circle. **whirlwind** a column of air moving rapidly round and round.

whirr v. & n. (make) a low, continuous, regular sound.

whisk v. **1** move or take suddenly, quickly, and lightly. **2** beat with a light, rapid movement. ▶n. a utensil for whisking eggs etc.

whisker n. **1** each of the long hairs or bristles growing from the face of an animal. **2** (**whiskers**) the hair growing on a man's face.

whisky (Irish & US **whiskey**) n. (pl. **whiskies**) a spirit distilled from malted grain, esp. barley.

whisper v. speak very softly. ▶n. **1** a whispered remark. **2** a very soft voice.

whist n. a card game for two pairs of players.

whistle n. **1** a clear, high-pitched sound made by forcing breath between the lips or teeth. **2** any similar sound. **3** an instrument used to produce such a sound. ▶v. **1** give out a whistle. **2** blow a whistle. □ **whistle-stop** very fast and with only brief pauses.

Whit n. Whitsun. □ **Whit Sunday** a Christian festival held on the seventh Sunday after Easter.

white adj. **1** of the colour of milk or fresh snow. **2** very pale. **3** relating to people with light-coloured skin. **4** (of coffee or tea) served with milk. ▶n. **1** white colour. **2** the pale part of the eyeball around the iris. **3** the outer part around the yolk of an egg. **4** a white person. □ **white-collar** of work done in an office or other professional environment. **white elephant** a useless or unwanted possession. **white flag** a white flag waved as a symbol of surrender. **white-hot** so hot as to glow white. **white lie** a lie told to avoid hurting someone's feelings. **white noise** noise containing many frequencies with equal intensities. **White Paper** a government report giving information or proposals. **white spirit** a colourless liquid distilled from petroleum, used as a solvent. ■ **whiten** v. **whiteness** n.

whitebait n. the young of various sea

Thesaurus

whimsical adj. CAPRICIOUS, fanciful, fantastical, playful, mischievous, waggish, quaint, unusual, curious, droll, eccentric, peculiar, queer, bizarre, weird, freakish.

whine v. **1** WHIMPER, cry, wail, groan; informal grizzle. **2** see COMPLAIN (2).

whip v. **1** LASH, flog, scourge, flagellate, birch, switch, strap, cane, thrash, beat, strike, leather; informal belt, tan, give someone a hiding. **2** BEAT, whisk, mix. ▶n. LASH, scourge, horsewhip, bullwhip, cat-o'-nine-tails, knout, crop, riding crop.

whirl v. TURN ROUND, circle, spin, rotate, revolve, wheel, twirl, swirl, gyrate, reel, pirouette, pivot.

whirlpool n. VORTEX, maelstrom, eddy, whirl.

whirlwind n. TORNADO, hurricane, typhoon. ▶adj. SWIFT, rapid, quick, speedy, hasty, headlong.

whisk v. WHIP, beat, mix, stir. ▶n. MIXER, beater.

whisper v. MURMUR, mutter, speak softly, speak in muted/hushed tones. ▶n. **1** MURMUR, mutter, low voice, hushed tone, undertone. **2** RUMOUR, report, insinuation, suggestion, hint, gossip, word.

whit n. PARTICLE, bit, jot, iota, mite, little, trifle.

white adj. **1** PALE, wan, pallid, ashen, anaemic, colourless, bloodless, waxen, fish used as food.

whitewash n. **1** a solution of lime or chalk and water, used for painting walls white. **2** a deliberate concealment of mistakes. ▶ v. **1** paint with whitewash. **2** conceal mistakes.

whither adv. old use to what place or state?

whiting n. (pl. **whiting**) a small edible sea fish.

whitlow n. an inflammation near a nail.

Whitsun (or **Whitsuntide**) n. the weekend or week including Whit Sunday.

whittle v. **1** carve wood by cutting small slices from it. **2** (**whittle away/down**) gradually reduce.

whizz (or **whiz**) v. **1** move quickly through the air with a whistling sound. **2** move or go fast. ▶ n. a whizzing sound. □ **whizz-kid** informal a very successful or skilful young person.

who pron. **1** what or which person or people? **2** introducing a clause giving further information about a person or people previously mentioned. □ **whodunnit** (US **whodunit**) informal a detective story or play. **whoever 1** any person who. **2** regardless of who. **whosoever** formal whoever.

whole adj. **1** complete; entire. **2** in one piece. ▶ n. **1** a thing that is complete in itself. **2** all of something. □ **on the whole** taking everything into account; in general. **wholefood** food that has been processed as little as possible. **wholehearted** completely sincere and committed. **wholemeal** made from the whole grain of wheat. **whole number** a number without fractions.

wholesale n. the selling of goods in large quantities to be sold to the public by others. ▶ adv. & adj. **1** being sold in such a way. **2** on a large scale. ■ **wholesaler** n.

wholesome adj. good for health or well-being.

wholly adv. entirely; fully.

whom pron. used instead of 'who' as the object of a verb or preposition.

whoop n. a loud cry of joy or excitement. ▶ v. give a whoop. □ **whooping cough** a disease characterized by coughs followed by a rasping breath.

whopper n. informal **1** something very large. **2** a blatant lie.

whore n. a prostitute.

whorl /worl/ n. **1** each of the turns in a spiral or coil. **2** a ring of leaves or petals. **3** a complete circle in a fingerprint.

who's contr. **1** who is. **2** who has.

✓ Don't confuse **who's** with **whose**. **Who's** is short for **who is** or **who has**, as in *who's there* or *who's taken it?*; **whose** means 'belonging to which person' or 'of whom or which', as in *whose is this?* or *a man whose opinion I respect*.

whose adj. & pron. **1** belonging to which person. **2** of whom or which.

why adv. **1** for what reason or purpose? **2** on account of which. **3** the reason that.

wick n. a length of cord in a candle, lamp, etc. which carries liquid fuel to the flame.

wicked adj. **1** evil. **2** playfully mischievous. **3** informal excellent. ■ **wickedly** adv. **wickedness** n.

wicker n. thin canes interwoven to make furniture, baskets, etc. ■ **wicker-**

Thesaurus

pasty, peaky, whey-faced, grey. **2** GREY, silver, hoary, snowy-white, grizzled.

whiten v. MAKE WHITE, make pale, bleach, blanch, fade, wash out, etiolate.

whole adj. **1** ENTIRE, complete, full, total, solid, integral, unabridged, unreduced, undivided, uncut. **2** INTACT, sound, flawless, in one piece, unimpaired, undamaged, unharmed, unhurt, uninjured, unmutilated. ■ OPPOSITES incomplete.

wholehearted adj. UNRESERVED, unqualified, unstinting, complete, committed, hearty, emphatic, real, sincere, genuine. ■ OPPOSITES half-hearted.

wholesale adj. INDISCRIMINATE, mass, all-inclusive, total, comprehensive, extensive, wide-ranging, sweeping, broad. ■ OPPOSITES partial.

wholesome adj. **1** NUTRITIOUS, nourishing, health-giving, healthful, good, strengthening. **2** MORAL, ethical, uplifting, edifying, helpful, beneficial.

wholly adv. COMPLETELY, fully, entirely, totally, utterly, thoroughly, altogether, comprehensively, in every respect, perfectly, enthusiastically, with total commitment, unreservedly, heart and soul.

wicked adj. EVIL, sinful, bad, wrong, unrighteous, villainous, dastardly, black-hearted, iniquitous, heinous, monstrous, atrocious, abominable, base, gross, vile, foul, mean, vicious, hideous, dishonourable, unprincipled, nefarious, criminal, perverted, immoral, amoral, unethical, corrupt, dissolute, dissipated, degenerate, reprobate, de-

w

work n.

wicket n. either of the two sets of three stumps with two bails across the top that are defended by a cricket batsman.

wide adj. **1** of great or specified width. **2** including a great variety of people or things. **3** at a distance from a point or mark. ▶adv. **1** to the full extent. **2** far from a particular point or mark. □ **wide awake** fully awake. **widespread** spread among a large number or over a large area. ■ **widen** v. **widely** adv.

widow n. a woman whose husband has died and who has not remarried. ▶v. (**be widowed**) become a widow or widower.

widower n. a man whose wife has died and who has not remarried.

width n. **1** the measurement or extent of something from side to side. **2** a piece of something at its full extent from side to side.

wield v. **1** hold and use a weapon or tool. **2** have and use power.

wife n. (pl. **wives**) a married woman in relation to her husband. ■ **wifely** adj.

wig n. a covering of hair worn on the head.

wiggle v. move with short movements from side to side. ▶n. a wiggling movement. ■ **wiggly** adj.

wigwam n. a conical tent formerly lived in by some North American Indian peoples.

wild adj. **1** living or growing in the natural environment. **2** not civilized. **3** barren or uninhabited. **4** uncontrolled. **5** not based on reason or evidence. **6** informal very enthusiastic or excited. **7** informal very angry. ▶n. **1** (**the wild**) a natural environment. **2** (**the wilds**) a remote area. □ **spread like wildfire** spread with great speed. **wild card** a playing card that can have any value, suit, etc. that the player holding it requires. **wildcat** (of a strike) sudden and unofficial. **wildfowl** game birds. **wild goose chase** a hopeless search. **wildlife** the natural animals of a region. ■ **wildly** adv. **wildness** n.

wildebeest n. (pl. **wildebeest** or **wildebeests**) a gnu.

wilderness n. an uncultivated and uninhabited area.

wiles pl. n. cunning or trickery.

Thesaurus

bauched, depraved, unholy, impious, irreligious, ungodly, godless, devilish, demonic, diabolic; old use blackguardly. ■ OPPOSITES good, righteous.

wide adj. **1** BROAD, extensive, spacious. **2** BROAD, large, outspread, spread out, ample. **3** WIDE-RANGING, extensive, large, large-scale, vast, far-ranging, immense, broad, expansive, sweeping, encyclopedic, comprehensive, general, all-embracing, catholic, compendious. ■ OPPOSITES narrow.

wide-eyed adj. **1** SURPRISED, amazed, astonished, astounded. **2** NAIVE, impressionable, ingenuous, credulous, trusting, unsuspicious, innocent, simple, unsophisticated, inexperienced, green; informal wet behind the ears.

widen v. **1** MAKE WIDER, broaden, expand, extend, enlarge, increase, augment, add to, supplement. **2** OPEN WIDE, dilate.

widespread adj. UNIVERSAL, common, general, far-reaching, prevalent, rife, extensive, sweeping, pervasive, epidemic. ■ OPPOSITES limited.

width n. **1** WIDENESS, breadth, broadness, span, diameter. **2** RANGE, breadth, scope, span, extensiveness, vastness, immensity, expansiveness, comprehensiveness. ■ OPPOSITES length, narrowness.

wield v. **1** BRANDISH, flourish, wave, swing, use, employ, handle, ply, manipulate. **2** EXERCISE, exert, be possessed of, have, have at one's disposal, hold, maintain, command, control.

wild adj. **1** UNTAMED, undomesticated, unbroken, feral, savage, fierce, ferocious. **2** UNCULTIVATED, natural, native, indigenous. **3** UNCIVILIZED, primitive, ignorant, savage, barbaric, barbarous, brutish, ferocious, fierce. **4** STORMY, tempestuous, turbulent, blustery, howling, violent, raging, furious, rough. **5** UNDISCIPLINED, unrestrained, unconstrained, uncontrolled, out of control, unbridled, unchecked, chaotic, disorderly. **6** ROWDY, unruly, disorderly, turbulent, violent, lawless, riotous, out of control, unmanageable, ungovernable, unrestrained, excited, passionate, frantic. **7** CRAZY, beside oneself, berserk, frantic, frenzied, in a frenzy, hysterical, crazed, mad, distracted, distraught, irrational, deranged, demented, raving, maniacal, rabid. **8** EXTRAVAGANT, fantastical, impracticable, foolish, ill-advised, ill-considered, imprudent, unwise, madcap, impulsive, reckless, rash, outrageous, preposterous. ■ OPPOSITES tame, cultivated, calm, disciplined.

wilderness n. DESERT, wasteland,

wilful (US **willful**) adj. **1** intentional. **2** stubborn and determined. ■ **wilfully** adv. **wilfulness** n.

will¹ aux. v. (past **would**) **1** expressing the future tense. **2** expressing intention, ability, or a request.

will² n. **1** the faculty by which a person decides on and takes action. **2** (also **will power**) control or restraint deliberately exerted. **3** a desire or intention. **4** a legal document with instructions for the disposal of one's money and property after one's death. ▶ v. **1** intend or desire to happen. **2** bring about by one's mental powers. **3** leave in one's will. □ **at will** whenever one pleases.

willing adj. **1** ready or eager to do something. **2** given or done readily. ■ **willingly** adv. **willingness** n.

will-o'-the-wisp n. a dim, flickering light seen over marshy ground.

willow n. a tree with narrow leaves and catkins.

willowy adj. tall and slim.

willy (or **willie**) n. (pl. **willies**) informal a penis.

willy-nilly adv. whether one likes it or not.

wilt v. **1** (of a plant) become limp through lack of water. **2** lose one's energy.

wily adj. (**wilier**, **wiliest**) cunning. ■ **wiliness** n.

wimp n. informal a weak and cowardly person.

win v. (**winning**, **won**) **1** be the most successful in a contest etc. **2** gain as a result of success in a contest etc. **3** get by one's efforts. **4** (**win over**) gain the support of. ▶ n. a victory in a game or contest.

wince v. grimace or flinch due to pain or distress. ▶ n. an act of wincing.

winch n. a hauling or lifting device consisting of a cable winding round a horizontal rotating drum. ▶ v. hoist or pull with a winch.

wind¹ n. **1** a natural movement of the air. **2** breath as needed in exercise, playing an instrument, etc. **3** gas in the stomach and intestines. **4** meaningless talk. **5** wind instruments as a section of an orchestra. ▶ v. cause to be out of breath. □ **get wind of** informal hear a rumour of. **windbag** informal a person who talks at unnecessary length. **windbreak** a screen providing shelter from the wind. **windfall 1** fruit blown off a tree by the wind. **2** a piece of unexpected good fortune. **wind instrument** a musical instrument sounded by a current of air, esp. by the player blowing into it. **windmill** a building with sails or vanes that turn in the wind and generate power to grind corn etc. **windpipe** the tube carrying air down the throat to the lungs. **windscreen** (or US **windshield**) the glass screen at the front of a vehicle. **windsock** a light, flexible cone mounted on a mast to

Thesaurus

waste, the wilds, jungle, no-man's-land.

wiles pl. n. TRICKS, ruses, ploys, schemes, dodges, manoeuvres, subterfuges, artifices, guile, artfulness, cunning, craftiness.

wilful adj. **1** DELIBERATE, intentional, intended, conscious, purposeful, planned, premeditated, calculated. **2** HEADSTRONG, strong-willed, obstinate, stubborn, mulish, pig-headed, obdurate, intransigent, adamant, dogged, determined, unyielding, uncompromising, intractable, refractory, recalcitrant, disobedient, contrary, perverse, wayward, self-willed. ■ OPPOSITES accidental.

will n. **1** VOLITION, choice, option, decision, discretion, prerogative. **2** DESIRE, wish, preference, inclination, fancy, mind. **3** WILL POWER, determination, resolution, resolve, firmness of purpose, purposefulness, doggedness, single-mindedness, commitment, moral fibre, pluck, mettle, grit, nerve. **4** LAST WILL AND TESTAMENT, testament, last wishes.

willing adj. PREPARED, ready, game, disposed, content, happy, so-minded, consenting, agreeable, amenable, in the mood, compliant.

willingly adv. VOLUNTARILY, of one's own free will, of one's own accord, by choice, by volition, spontaneously, unforced.

wilt v. **1** DROOP, wither, shrivel, lose freshness, sag, flop. **2** DIMINISH, dwindle, lessen, grow less, flag, fade, melt away, ebb, wane, weaken, fail. ■ OPPOSITES flourish.

wily adj. CRAFTY, cunning, artful, sharp, astute, shrewd, scheming, intriguing, shifty, sly, guileful, deceitful, deceptive, fraudulent, cheating, underhand; informal crooked, foxy, fly. ■ OPPOSITES naive.

win v. **1** ACHIEVE, attain, earn, gain, receive, obtain, acquire, procure, get, secure, collect, pick up, come away with, net, bag. **2** BE VICTORIOUS, be the victor, gain the victory, overcome, achieve

w

show the direction and strength of the wind. **windswept** exposed to strong winds. **windsurfing** the sport of riding on water on a sailboard. **wind tunnel** a tunnel-like structure in which a strong current of air is created to test the effect of wind on objects. ▪ **windward** adj. & adv. **windy** adj.

wind² v. (**winding, wound**) **1** move in or take a twisting or spiral course. **2** pass repeatedly around a thing or person or itself. **3** make a clockwork device work by turning a key or handle. □ **wind down 1** draw or bring to a close. **2** informal relax. **wind up 1** bring or come to an end. **2** informal irritate.

windlass n. a winch, esp. on a ship or in a harbour.

window n. **1** an opening in a wall to let in light or air, usu. fitted with glass. **2** a framed area on a computer screen for viewing information. □ **window dressing 1** the arrangement of a display in a shop window. **2** the presentation of something to give a misleadingly favourable impression. **window-shopping** looking at goods displayed in shop windows without intending to buy.

wine n. **1** an alcoholic drink made from fermented grape juice. **2** a similar drink made from other fruits etc.

wing n. **1** a projecting part enabling a bird, bat, or insect to fly. **2** a structure projecting from both sides of an aircraft and supporting it in the air. **3** a part of a large building. **4** a group or faction within an organization. **5** (**the wings**) the sides of a stage out of view of the audience. **6** the part of a soccer, rugby, etc. field close to the sidelines. **7** an attacking player positioned near the sidelines. **8** the bodywork of a vehicle above the wheel. ▸ v. **1** fly, or move quickly as if flying. **2** wound in the wing or arm. □ **under one's wing** in or into one's protective care. **wingspan** the measurement from tip to tip of the wings of a bird etc. ▪ **winged** adj.

winger n. an attacking player on the wing in soccer etc.

wink v. **1** close and open one eye quickly as a signal. **2** shine or flash intermittently. ▸ n. an act of winking.

winkle n. a small edible shellfish. ▸ v. (**winkle out**) take out or obtain with difficulty.

winner n. **1** a person or thing that wins. **2** informal a successful thing.

winning adj. attractive. ▸ n. (**winnings**) money won by gambling. ▪ **winningly** adv.

winnow v. blow air through grain to remove the chaff.

winsome adj. charming.

winter n. the coldest season of the year, after autumn and before spring. ▸ v. spend the winter in a particular place. ▪ **wintry** adj.

wipe v. **1** clean or dry by rubbing with a cloth or one's hand. **2** erase data from a computer, video, etc. ▸ n. **1** an act of wiping. **2** a disposable cleaning cloth. □ **wipe out** completely destroy or eliminate. ▪ **wiper** n.

wire n. **1** metal drawn out into a thin,

Thesaurus

mastery, carry the day, carry all before one, finish first, come out ahead, come out on top, win out, succeed, triumph, prevail. ▪ OPPOSITES lose.

wind¹ n. **1** AIR CURRENT, breeze, gust, blast, gale, storm, hurricane; literary zephyr. **2** BREATH, respiration; informal puff. **3** FLATULENCE, gas; formal flatus.

wind² v. TWIST, twist and turn, curve, bend, loop, zigzag, snake, spiral, meander, ramble. □ **wind down** UNWIND, relax, become less tense, ease up, calm down, cool off. **wind up** BRING TO AN END/CONCLUSION, end, conclude, terminate, finish; informal wrap up.

windfall n. PIECE/STROKE OF GOOD LUCK, unexpected gain, godsend, manna from heaven, bonanza, jackpot.

windy adj. **1** BREEZY, blowy, blustery, blustering, gusty, gusting, boisterous, squally, stormy, wild, tempestuous, turbulent. **2** LONG-WINDED, loquacious, wordy, verbose, rambling, meandering, prolix, diffuse, turgid. **3** NERVOUS, scared, frightened, alarmed, fearful, timid, timorous, cowardly. ▪ OPPOSITES still.

wink v. **1** BLINK, flutter, bat; technical nictate. **2** FLASH, twinkle, sparkle, glitter, gleam.

winner n. CHAMPION, victor, vanquisher, conqueror, prizewinner. ▪ OPPOSITES loser.

winning adj. **1** VICTORIOUS, successful, triumphant, vanquishing, conquering. **2** CAPTIVATING, enchanting, bewitching, beguiling, disarming, taking, engaging, endearing, winsome, charming, attractive, fetching, alluring, sweet, lovely, delightful, darling, pleasing.

wintry adj. COLD, chilly, icy, frosty, freezing, frozen, snowy, arctic, glacial, bitflexible strand. **2** a length of this used for fencing, to carry an electric current, etc. ▶v. **1** install electric wires in. **2** fasten or reinforce with wire. □ **wiretapping** the secret tapping of telephone lines.

wireless n. dated **1** a radio. **2** broadcasting using radio signals.

wiring n. a system of electric wires in a device or building.

wiry adj. (**wirier, wiriest**) **1** like wire. **2** thin but strong.

wisdom n. **1** the quality of being wise. **2** a body of knowledge and experience. □ **wisdom tooth** each of the four hindmost molars in humans, usu. appearing around the age of 20.

wise adj. **1** having or showing experience, knowledge, and good judgement. **2** (**wise to**) informal aware of. □ **wiseacre** a person who pretends to be wise. **wisecrack** informal a joke or witty remark. ■ **wisely** adv.

wish v. **1** feel a strong desire for something. **2** hope or express a hope that someone has happiness, success, etc. ▶n. **1** a desire or hope. **2** (**wishes**) an expression of friendly feeling. **3** a thing wished for. □ **wishbone** a forked bone between the neck and breast of a bird.

wishful adj. based on impractical wishes rather than facts: *wishful thinking*.

wishy-washy adj. weak in colour,

character, etc.

wisp n. a small thin bunch or strand of something. ■ **wispy** adj.

wisteria n. a climbing shrub with bluish-lilac flowers.

wistful adj. having or showing sad or vague longing. ■ **wistfully** adv.

wit n. **1** (also **wits**) keen intelligence. **2** a natural talent for using words and ideas in a quick amusing way. **3** a person with this talent.

witch n. a woman believed to have evil magic powers. □ **witchcraft** the practice of magic. **witch doctor** a person believed to use magic powers to heal. **witch hazel** a lotion made from the bark and leaves of a plant. **witch-hunt** a campaign against a person with unpopular views.

with prep. **1** accompanied by. **2** in the same direction as. **3** having. **4** using. **5** in opposition to or competition with. **6** indicating manner or attitude. **7** in relation to. □ **with it** informal **1** fashionable. **2** alert.

withdraw v. (**withdrawing, withdrew;** past part. **withdrawn**) **1** remove or take away. **2** take money out of an account. **3** discontinue or retract. **4** leave or cause to leave a place. **5** stop taking part in an activity. **6** (**withdrawn**) very shy or reserved. ■ **withdrawal** n.

wither v. **1** become shrivelled and dry.

Thesaurus

ing, piercing, nippy. ■ OPPOSITES warm.

wipe v. RUB, brush, dust, mop, sponge, swab, clean, dry.

wiry adj. **1** LEAN, spare, sinewy, tough, strong. **2** BRISTLY, prickly, thorny, stiff, rigid.

wisdom n. **1** SAGENESS, sagacity, cleverness, intelligence, erudition, learning, education, knowledge, enlightenment, reason, discernment, perception, insight. **2** SENSE, common sense, prudence, judiciousness, judgement, shrewdness, astuteness, circumspection, strategy, foresight, reasonableness, rationality, logic, soundness, saneness; informal smartness. ■ OPPOSITES folly.

wise adj. **1** SAGE, sagacious, clever, intelligent, erudite, learned, educated, well read, knowledgeable, informed, enlightened, discerning, perceptive, experienced; formal sapient. **2** SENSIBLE, prudent, well advised, judicious, politic, shrewd, astute, reasonable, rational, logical, sound, sane; informal smart.

■ OPPOSITES unwise.

wish v. WANT, desire, long for, hope for, yearn for, pine for, have a fancy for, fancy, crave, hunger for, thirst for, lust after, covet, sigh for, set one's heart on, hanker after, have a yen for. ▶n. DESIRE, liking, fondness, longing, hope, yearning, want, fancy, aspiration, inclination, urge, whim, craving, hunger, thirst, lust, hankering, yen.

wistful adj. YEARNING, longing, forlorn, disconsolate, melancholy, sad, mournful, in a reverie, pensive, reflective, musing, contemplative, meditative.

wit n. **1** WITTINESS, humour, jocularity, funniness, facetiousness, drollery, waggishness, repartee, badinage, banter, raillery. **2** HUMORIST, wag, funny person, comic, jokester, banterer; informal card.

witch n. SORCERESS, enchantress, magician, necromancer, hex.

witchcraft n. WITCHERY, sorcery, black art/magic, magic, necromancy, wizardry, occultism, the occult, sortilege, thaumaturgy, wonder-working.

withdraw v. **1** TAKE BACK, pull back,

2 (withering) scornful.

withers pl. n. the highest part of a horse's back, at the base of the neck.

withhold v. (**withholding, withheld**) **1** refuse to give. **2** suppress a reaction etc.

within prep. **1** inside. **2** inside the range or bounds of. **3** in a time no longer than. ▶ adv. inside.

without prep. **1** not accompanied by or having. **2** not doing the action specified.

withstand v. (**withstanding, withstood**) remain undamaged or unaffected by.

witless adj. stupid.

witness n. **1** a person who sees an event take place. **2** a person giving evidence in a law court. **3** a person who is present at the signing of a document and signs to confirm this. ▶ v. be a witness to.

witter v. informal speak trivially and at length.

witticism n. a witty remark.

witty adj. (**wittier, wittiest**) quick, inventive, and amusing with words. ■ **wittily** adv. **wittiness** n.

wives pl. of WIFE.

wizard n. **1** a man with magical powers. **2** a person with great skill in a particular field. ■ **wizardry** n.

wizened adj. shrivelled or wrinkled with age.

woad n. a blue dye obtained from a plant.

wobble v. **1** move unsteadily from side to side. **2** (of the voice) tremble. ▶ n. a wobbling movement or sound. ■ **wobbly** adj.

wodge n. informal a large piece or amount.

woe n. **1** sorrow or distress. **2** trouble; misfortune. □ **woebegone** sad or miserable. ■ **woeful** adj. **woefully** adv.

wok n. a bowl-shaped frying pan used in Chinese cookery.

woke past of WAKE.

Thesaurus

take away, extract, remove. **2** RETRACT, take back, recall, unsay. **3** REVOKE, annul, nullify, declare void, rescind, repeal, abrogate. **4** PULL BACK, fall back, retire, retreat, disengage, back down, depart, go, leave; informal make oneself scarce. ■ OPPOSITES insert, enter.

withdrawn adj. RETIRING, reserved, uncommunicative, unforthcoming, unsociable, taciturn, silent, quiet, introverted, detached, aloof, self-contained, distant, private, shrinking, timid, timorous, shy, bashful, diffident. ■ OPPOSITES outgoing.

wither v. **1** DRY UP/OUT, shrivel, go limp, wilt, die. **2** DECLINE, fade, ebb, wane, disintegrate, die, perish. ■ OPPOSITES thrive.

withhold v. **1** HOLD BACK, keep back, restrain, hold/keep in check, check, curb, repress, suppress. **2** REFUSE TO GIVE/GRANT/ALLOW, refuse, decline, keep back.

withstand v. HOLD OUT AGAINST, stand up to, stand firm against, resist, fight, combat, oppose, endure, stand, tolerate, bear, put up with, take, cope with, weather, brave.

witness n. EYEWITNESS, observer, spectator, onlooker, looker-on, viewer, watcher, beholder, bystander. ▶ v. SEE, observe, view, watch, look on at, behold, perceive, be present at, attend.

witticism n. WITTY REMARK, clever saying, flash of wit, bon mot, quip, sally, pleasantry, riposte, joke, jest, epigram;

informal wisecrack, crack, one-liner.

witty adj. CLEVER, original, ingenious, sparkling, scintillating, humorous, amusing, jocular, funny, facetious, droll, waggish, comic.

wizard n. SORCERER, warlock, enchanter, witch, necromancer, magician, magus.

wizened adj. WITHERED, shrivelled, dried up, shrunken, wasted, wrinkled, lined, gnarled, worn.

wobble v. **1** ROCK, sway, see-saw, teeter, shake, vibrate. **2** TEETER, totter, stagger, waddle, waggle.

woe n. **1** MISERY, wretchedness, misfortune, disaster, grief, anguish, affliction, suffering, pain, agony, torment, sorrow, sadness, unhappiness, distress, heartache, heartbreak, despondency, desolation, dejection, depression, gloom, melancholy. **2** TROUBLE, misfortune, adversity, trial, tribulation, ordeal, burden, affliction, suffering, disaster, calamity, catastrophe. ■ OPPOSITES joy.

woebegone adj. MISERABLE, sad, unhappy, sorrowful, disconsolate, mournful, downcast, dejected, doleful, desolate, depressed, despairing, tearful. ■ OPPOSITES cheerful.

woeful adj. **1** SAD, saddening, unhappy, sorrowful, miserable, dismal, wretched, doleful, gloomy, tragic, pathetic, grievous, pitiful, plaintive, heart-rending, heartbreaking, distressing, anguished, agonizing, dreadful, terrible. **2** POOR, bad, inadequate, substandard, lament-

woken past part. of WAKE.

wold n. an area of high, open land or moor.

wolf n. (pl. **wolves**) a wild animal of the dog family. ▶ v. eat greedily. □ **cry wolf** raise false alarms. **wolf whistle** a whistle with a rising and falling pitch, expressing sexual admiration. ■ **wolfish** adj.

wolfram n. tungsten or its ore.

wolverine n. a meat-eating mammal found in cold northern regions.

woman n. (pl. **women**) an adult human female. □ **womankind** women as a group. ■ **womanhood** n. **womanly** adj.

womanize (or **-ise**) v. (of a man) have many casual affairs with women. ■ **womanizer** n.

womb n. the organ in a woman or female mammal in which offspring develop before birth.

wombat n. a burrowing Australian marsupial resembling a small bear.

won past & past part. of WIN.

wonder n. **1** a feeling of surprise and admiration. **2** a cause of wonder. ▶ v. **1** feel curiosity. **2** feel amazement and admiration. □ **wonderland** a place full of wonderful things. ■ **wonderment** n.

wonderful adj. very good, pleasant, or remarkable. ■ **wonderfully** adv.

wonky adj. (**wonkier**, **wonkiest**) informal **1** crooked. **2** unsteady or faulty.

wont /wohnt/ formal adj. accustomed. ▶ n. (**one's wont**) one's usual practice.

woo v. **1** try to gain the love of a woman. **2** seek the support or custom of.

wood n. **1** the hard fibrous material of a tree. **2** (also **woods**) a small forest. □ **woodbine** wild honeysuckle. **woodcut** a print made from a design cut in a block of wood. **woodland** land covered with trees. **woodlouse** a small insect-like animal with a segmented body. **woodpecker** a bird with a strong bill that pecks at tree trunks to find insects. **woodwind** wind instruments other than brass instruments. **woodwork** **1** the wooden parts of a room. **2** the activity of making things from wood. **woodworm** the larva of a kind of beetle, that bores into wood. ■ **woody** adj.

wooded adj. covered with trees.

wooden adj. **1** made of wood. **2** stiff and awkward. ■ **woodenly** adv.

woof n. the barking sound of a dog. ▶ v. bark.

woofer n. a loudspeaker for reproducing low frequencies.

wool n. **1** the soft hair forming the coat of a sheep. **2** yarn or fabric made from wool.

woollen (US **woolen**) adj. made of wool. ▶ n. (**woollens**) woollen garments.

woolly adj. **1** made of or like wool. **2** confused or unclear.

Thesaurus

able, deplorable, disgraceful, wretched, disappointing, feeble; *informal* rotten, lousy, shocking, duff. ■ OPPOSITES cheerful, excellent.

woman n. **1** FEMALE, lady, girl, member of the fair/gentle sex; *informal* chick, bird; *US informal* dame, broad. **2** GIRLFRIEND, lady-love, sweetheart, partner, lover, wife, spouse.

wonder n. **1** WONDERMENT, awe, surprise, astonishment, amazement, bewilderment, stupefaction, fascination, admiration. **2** MARVEL, phenomenon, miracle, prodigy, curiosity, rarity, nonpareil, sight, spectacle. ▶ v. **1** THINK, speculate, conjecture, ponder, meditate, reflect, deliberate, muse, ask oneself, puzzle, be curious about, be inquisitive about. **2** MARVEL, stand amazed, stand in awe, be dumbfounded, gape, stare, goggle, look agog; *informal* be flabbergasted, gawk, boggle.

wonderful adj. MARVELLOUS, awe-inspiring, awesome, remarkable, extraordinary, phenomenal, prodigious, miraculous, amazing, astonishing, as-

tounding, surprising, incredible, unprecedented, unparalleled, unheard of; *literary* wondrous. *See also* EXCELLENT. ■ OPPOSITES dreadful.

wonted adj. CUSTOMARY, accustomed, habitual, usual, normal, routine, regular, common, frequent, familiar, conventional.

woo v. **1** PAY COURT TO, seek someone's hand, pursue, chase after; *dated* court, set one's cap at. **2** IMPORTUNE, press, urge, entreat, beg, implore, supplicate, solicit, coax, wheedle.

wood n. **1** FOREST, woodland, copse, thicket, coppice, grove. **2** TIMBER, firewood, kindling; *US* lumber.

wooded adj. WOODY, forested, tree-covered, tree-clad, timbered, sylvan.

wooden adj. **1** MADE OF WOOD, wood, woody, timber. **2** STIFF, stolid, stodgy, expressionless, graceless, inelegant, ungainly, gauche, awkward, clumsy, maladroit. **3** EXPRESSIONLESS, inexpressive, blank, poker-faced, empty, vacant, vacuous, glassy, impassive, lifeless, spiritless, unanimated, emotionless,

w

woozy adj. informal dizzy or dazed. ▪ **woozily** adv.

word n. **1** a separate meaningful unit of language, used with others to form sentences. **2** a remark or statement. **3** (**words**) angry talk. **4** a command. **5** a promise. **6** news. ▶v. express in particular words. □ **word of mouth** spoken communication. **word-perfect** knowing one's part or speech by heart. **word processor** a computer or program for creating and printing a piece of text.

wording n. the way in which something is worded.

wore past of WEAR.

work n. **1** activity involving mental or physical effort. **2** such activity as a means of earning money. **3** a task to be done. **4** a thing or things done or made. **5** (**works**) a factory. **6** (**works**) the mechanism of a machine. **7** a defensive structure. ▶v. **1** do work as one's job. **2** (of a machine etc.) function. **3** have the desired result. **4** bring into a desired state. **5** produce or create. □ **get worked up** become stressed or angry. **workhouse** a former public institution in which poor people were housed and fed in return for work. **workout** a session of vigorous exercise. **work out 1** solve. **2** have a specified outcome. **3** plan in detail. **4** do vigorous exercise.

workshop 1 a room or building in which goods are made or repaired. **2** a meeting for discussion and activity on a particular subject or project. **workstation** a desktop computer that is part of a network. **worktop** a flat surface for working on in a kitchen. **work-to-rule** a form of industrial action in which workers refuse to do overtime or extra work.

workable adj. capable of producing the desired result.

workaday adj. ordinary.

worker n. **1** a person who works. **2** a neuter bee, wasp, ant, etc. that does the basic work of a colony.

working adj. **1** having paid employment. **2** doing manual work. **3** functioning. **4** used as the basis for work or discussion but likely to be changed later. ▶n. **1** a mine or part of a mine. **2** (**workings**) the way in which a system operates. □ **working class** the social group consisting largely of people who do manual or industrial work.

workman n. a man employed to do manual labour. □ **workmanlike** showing efficient skill. **workmanship** the skill with which a product is made or a job done.

world n. **1** the earth with all its countries and peoples. **2** all that belongs to a particular region, period, or area of ac-

Thesaurus

unemotional, unresponsive.

woolly adj. **1** WOOLLEN, made of wool, wool. **2** FLEECY, fluffy, shaggy, hairy, furry. **3** VAGUE, hazy, indefinite, muddled, confused, disorganized.

word n. **1** TERM, expression, name. **2** WORD OF HONOUR, promise, pledge, assurance, guarantee, undertaking, vow, oath. **3** NEWS, intimation, notice, communication, information, intelligence, message, report, account. ▶v. EXPRESS, phrase, couch, put, say, utter, state.

wordy adj. LONG-WINDED, verbose, loquacious, garrulous, voluble, prolix, protracted, discursive, diffuse, rambling, digressive, maundering, tautological, pleonastic.

work n. **1** EFFORT, exertion, labour, toil, slog, sweat, drudgery, trouble, industry; informal grind, elbow grease; literary travail. **2** TASK, job, chore, undertaking, duty, charge, assignment, commission, mission. **3** EMPLOYMENT, occupation, business, job, profession, career, trade, vocation, calling, craft, line, field, métier, pursuit. ▶v. **1** BE EMPLOYED, have a

job, hold down a job, earn one's living, do business, follow/ply one's trade. **2** EXERT ONESELF, put in effort, make efforts, labour, toil, slog, sweat, drudge, slave; informal grind, plug away, knock oneself out. **3** OPERATE, control, drive, manage, direct, use, handle, manipulate, manoeuvre, ply, wield. **4** GO, operate, function, perform, run. **5** SUCCEED, be successful, have success, go well, be effective, be effectual. ■ OPPOSITES rest, fail.

workable adj. PRACTICABLE, practical, viable, doable, feasible, possible. ■ OPPOSITES impracticable.

worker n. EMPLOYEE, hand, workman, working man/woman/person, blue-collar worker, white-collar worker, labourer, artisan, craftsman, craftswoman, wage-earner, proletarian.

working adj. **1** IN WORK, employed, in a job, waged. **2** FUNCTIONING, operating, going, running, in working order. ■ OPPOSITES unemployed, broken.

workmanship n. CRAFTSMANSHIP, craft, artistry, art, handicraft, handiwork, tivity. □ **worldwide** throughout the world. **World Wide Web** an information system on the Internet allowing documents to be connected to each other by hypertext links.

worldly adj. **1** of or concerned with material rather than spiritual things. **2** experienced and sophisticated.

worm n. **1** an animal with a long, soft body and no backbone or limbs. **2** (**worms**) intestinal parasites. **3** informal a weak or despicable person. ▶ v. **1** move by crawling or wriggling. **2** (**worm one's way into**) insinuate oneself into. **3** (**worm out of**) obtain information from someone by cunning persistence. **4** rid an animal of parasitic worms. □ **worm cast** a spiral mass of soil etc. thrown up by a burrowing worm. **wormwood** a woody shrub with a bitter taste.

worn past part. of WEAR. ▶ adj. **1** suffering from wear. **2** very tired. □ **worn out 1** exhausted. **2** damaged by wear and no longer usable.

worried adj. feeling or showing worry. ■ **worriedly** adv.

worry v. (**worrying**, **worried**) **1** feel or cause to feel anxiety. **2** annoy or disturb. **3** (of a dog) tear at with the teeth. **4** (of a dog) chase and attack sheep etc. ▶ n. (pl. **worries**) **1** anxiety. **2** a source of this. ■ **worrier** n.

worse adj. **1** less good or pleasing. **2** more serious or severe. **3** more ill or unhappy. ▶ adv. **1** less well. **2** more seriously or severely. ▶ n. something worse. ■ **worsen** v.

worship n. **1** deep respect paid to a god or goddess. **2** great admiration. ▶ v. (**worshipping, worshipped**; US **worshiping, worshiped**) **1** take part in an act of worship. **2** feel great admiration for. ■ **worshipper** n.

worst adj. most bad, severe, or serious. ▶ adv. **1** most severely or seriously. **2** least well. ▶ n. the worst part, event, etc. ▶ v. get the better of.

worsted /wuus-tid/ n. a smooth woollen yarn or fabric.

worth adj. **1** having a specified value. **2** deserving a particular treatment. ▶ n. **1** value or merit. **2** an amount of something equivalent to a particular sum. ■ **worthless** adj.

worthwhile adj. worth the time or

Thesaurus

expertise, skill, technique, work.

workshop n. **1** FACTORY, plant, mill, garage. **2** WORKROOM, studio, atelier, shop. **3** SEMINAR, study/discussion group, class.

world n. **1** EARTH, globe, sphere, planet. **2** SOCIETY, sector, section, group, division.

worldly adj. **1** EARTHLY, secular, temporal, material, materialistic, human, carnal, fleshly, corporeal, physical. **2** WORLDLY-WISE, experienced, knowing, sophisticated, cosmopolitan, urbane. ■ OPPOSITES spiritual, naive.

worldwide adj. UNIVERSAL, global, international, pandemic, general, ubiquitous, extensive, widespread, far-reaching, wide-ranging. ■ OPPOSITES local.

worn adj. **1** WORN OUT, threadbare, tattered, in tatters, ragged, frayed, shabby, shiny. **2** HAGGARD, drawn, strained, careworn; informal done in, dog-tired, dead on one's feet, fit to drop, played out, bushed, knackered; US informal pooped.

worried adj. ANXIOUS, disturbed, perturbed, troubled, bothered, distressed, concerned, upset, distraught, uneasy, ill at ease, disquieted, fretful, agitated, nervous, edgy, on edge, tense, over-wrought, worked up, apprehensive, fearful, afraid, frightened; informal uptight, a bundle of nerves; US informal antsy. ■ OPPOSITES carefree.

worry v. **1** BE WORRIED, be anxious, fret, brood. **2** MAKE ANXIOUS, disturb, trouble, distress, upset, concern, disquiet, discompose, fret, agitate, unsettle. ▶ n. **1** ANXIETY, disturbance, perturbation, trouble, bother, distress, concern, care, uneasiness, unease, disquiet, disquietude, fretfulness, agitation, edginess, tenseness, apprehension, fearfulness. **2** NUISANCE, pest, plague, trial, trouble, problem, irritation, irritant, vexation, thorn in one's flesh.

worsen v. **1** MAKE WORSE, aggravate, exacerbate, damage, intensify, increase, heighten. **2** GET/GROW/BECOME WORSE, take a turn for the worse, deteriorate, degenerate, retrogress, decline, sink, slip, slide, go downhill. ■ OPPOSITES improve.

worship n. REVERENCE, veneration, homage, respect, honour, adoration, devotion, praise, prayer, glorification, exaltation, extolment; formal laudation. ▶ v. **1** REVERE, venerate, pay homage to, honour, adore, praise, pray to, glorify, exalt, extol; formal laud. **2** ADORE, be devoted to, cherish, treasure, admire,

W

effort spent.

worthy adj. (**worthier, worthiest**) **1** deserving effort, attention, or respect. **2** (**worthy of**) deserving. ▶n. (pl. **worthies**) an important person. ■ **worthily** adv. **worthiness** n.

would aux. v. **1** past of WILL¹. **2** expressing possible consequence. **3** expressing a desire, polite request, or opinion. □ **would-be** wishing to be a particular type of person.

wouldn't contr. would not.

wound¹ n. **1** an injury caused by a cut, blow, or other impact. **2** an injury to a person's feelings. ▶v. inflict a wound on.

wound² past & past part. of WIND².

wove past of WEAVE.

woven past part. of WEAVE.

wow informal exclam. expressing astonishment or admiration. ▶v. impress and excite greatly.

WPC abbrev. woman police constable.

wrack n. a seaweed. ▶v. var. of RACK.

wraith n. a ghost.

wrangle n. a long dispute. ▶v. engage in a wrangle.

wrap v. (**wrapping, wrapped**) cover or enclose in paper or soft material. ▶n. a shawl. □ **wrap up 1** dress in warm clothes. **2** complete a meeting or deal.

3 (**wrapped up**) totally engrossed. ■ **wrapping** n. **wrapper** n.

wrasse n. a colourful sea fish.

wrath /roth/ n. extreme anger. ■ **wrathful** adj.

wreak v. **1** cause damage. **2** inflict vengeance.

wreath n. a decorative ring of flowers and leaves.

wreathe v. **1** encircle. **2** (of smoke) move with a curling motion.

wreck n. **1** the destruction of a ship at sea. **2** a ship destroyed at sea. **3** a badly damaged building, vehicle, etc. **4** a person in a very bad physical or mental state. ▶v. **1** cause a ship to sink or break up. **2** destroy or ruin.

wreckage n. the remains of something that has been wrecked.

wren n. **1** a very small bird. **2** a member of the former Women's Royal Naval Service.

wrench v. **1** pull or twist violently. **2** twist and injure a part of the body. ▶n. **1** a sudden violent twist or pull. **2** distress caused by parting. **3** an adjustable tool like a spanner.

wrest v. **1** forcibly pull from a person's grasp. **2** take power or control after a struggle.

wrestle v. **1** take part in a fight or con-

Thesaurus

adulate, idolize, hero-worship, lionize; *informal* be wild about.

worth n. **1** FINANCIAL VALUE, value, price, cost. **2** VALUE, use, usefulness, advantage, benefit, service, gain, avail, help, assistance, aid.

worthless adj. **1** VALUELESS, of little/no financial value; *informal* rubbishy, trashy. **2** USELESS, of no use, of no benefit, to no avail, futile, ineffective, ineffectual, pointless, nugatory. **3** GOOD-FOR-NOTHING, useless, despicable, contemptible, base, low, vile, corrupt, depraved; *informal* no-good, no-account. ■ OPPOSITES valuable, useful, worthwhile.

worthwhile adj. WORTH IT, worth the effort, valuable, of value, useful, of use, beneficial, advantageous, helpful, profitable, gainful, productive, constructive, justifiable.

worthy adj. VIRTUOUS, good, moral, upright, righteous, honest, decent, honourable, respectable, reputable, trustworthy, reliable, irreproachable, blameless, unimpeachable, admirable, deserving, meritorious, praiseworthy, laudable, commendable. ■ OPPOSITES disreputable.

wound n. INJURY, lesion, cut, graze, scratch, gash, laceration, tear, puncture, slash, sore. ▶v. CUT, graze, scratch, gash, lacerate, tear, puncture, pierce, stab, slash, injure, hurt, damage, harm.

wrap v. **1** ENVELOP, enfold, encase, enclose, cover, swathe, bundle up, swaddle. **2** WRAP UP, parcel up, package, do up, tie up, gift-wrap. ▶n. SHAWL, stole, cloak, cape, mantle.

wrath n. ANGER, rage, fury, annoyance, exasperation, high dudgeon, bad temper, ill humour, irritation, crossness, displeasure, irascibility; *literary* ire. ■ OPPOSITES happiness.

wreathe v. **1** COVER, envelop, festoon, garland, adorn, decorate. **2** TWIST, wind, coil, twine, entwine, curl, spiral, wrap.

wreck n. **1** SHIPWRECK, sunken ship/ vessel, derelict. **2** WRECKING, wreckage, destruction, devastation, ruination, ruin, demolition, smashing, shattering, disruption, disintegration, undoing. ▶v. **1** SMASH, demolish, ruin, damage; *informal* write off. **2** DESTROY, devastate, ruin, demolish, smash, shatter, disrupt, undo, spoil, mar, play havoc with. **3** SHIPtest involving close grappling with an opponent. **2** struggle with a task or problem. ■ **wrestler** n.

wretch n. **1** an unfortunate person. **2** informal a contemptible person.

wretched adj. **1** very unhappy or unfortunate. **2** infuriating. ■ **wretchedly** adv.

wriggle v. **1** move with quick twisting movements. **2** (**wriggle out of**) avoid by devious means. ▶n. a wriggling movement.

wring v. (**wringing, wrung**) **1** squeeze and twist, esp. to remove liquid. **2** squeeze someone's hand tightly. **3** (**wring from/out of**) obtain with difficulty or effort.

wrinkle n. a slight line or fold in fabric or the skin. ▶v. make or become covered with wrinkles. ■ **wrinkly** adj.

wrist n. the joint connecting the hand and forearm.

writ n. an official written command issued by a court or other legal authority.

write v. (**writing, wrote**; past part. **writ-**

ten) **1** mark letters, words, or other symbols on a surface with a pen, pencil, etc. **2** write and send a letter to someone. **3** compose a text or musical work. **4** be an author. **5** fill out a cheque etc. □ **write off 1** dismiss as insignificant. **2** decide not to pursue a debt. **write-off** a vehicle too badly damaged to be repaired. **write-up** a newspaper review of a recent performance etc. ■ **writer** n.

writhe v. twist or squirm in pain or embarrassment.

writing n. **1** a sequence of letters or symbols forming words. **2** handwriting. **3** (**writings**) books or other written works.

wrong adj. **1** not correct or true; mistaken. **2** unjust, dishonest, or immoral. **3** in a bad or abnormal condition. ▶adv. **1** mistakenly. **2** with an incorrect result. ▶n. an unjust or immoral action. ▶v. treat unjustly. □ **in the wrong** responsible for a mistake or offence. ■ **wrongly** adv.

wrongdoing n. illegal or dishonest

Thesaurus

WRECK, sink, capsize, run aground.

wreckage n. WRECK, debris, ruins, remains, remnants, fragments.

wrench v. TWIST, pull, tug, yank, wrest, jerk, tear, force.

wrest v. TWIST, wrench, pull, snatch, take away, remove.

wretch n. **1** POOR CREATURE/SOUL/THING, miserable creature, unfortunate, poor devil. **2** SCOUNDREL, villain, ruffian, rogue, rascal, reprobate, criminal, delinquent, miscreant; informal creep, jerk, louse, rat, swine, skunk; informal, dated rotter; old use blackguard.

wretched adj. **1** MISERABLE, unhappy, sad, broken-hearted, sorrowful, sorry, distressed, disconsolate, downcast, down, downhearted, dejected, crestfallen, cheerless, depressed, melancholy, gloomy, doleful, forlorn, woebegone, abject. **2** POOR, bad, substandard, low-quality, inferior, pathetic, worthless. ■ OPPOSITES cheerful, excellent.

wriggle v. TWIST, squirm, writhe, jiggle, wiggle, snake, crawl, slink.

wring v. **1** TWIST, squeeze. **2** EXTRACT, force, coerce, exact, extort, wrest, wrench, screw.

wrinkle n. CREASE, fold, pucker, gather, furrow, ridge, line, corrugation, crinkle, crumple, rumple. ▶v. CREASE, pucker, gather, furrow, line, corrugate, crumple, rumple.

write v. **1** WRITE DOWN, put in writing, put in black and white, commit to paper, jot down, note, set down, take down, record, register, list, inscribe, scribble, scrawl. **2** COMPOSE, draft, create, pen, dash off. □ **write off 1** FORGET ABOUT, disregard, give up for lost, cancel, annul, nullify, wipe out, cross out, score out. **2** DAMAGE BEYOND REPAIR, wreck, smash, crash, destroy, demolish; US informal total.

writer n. AUTHOR, wordsmith, penman, novelist, essayist, biographer, journalist, columnist, scriptwriter; informal scribbler, pen-pusher.

writhe v. TWIST ABOUT, twist and turn, roll about, squirm, wriggle, jerk, thrash, flail, toss, struggle.

writing n. **1** HANDWRITING, hand, penmanship, script, print, calligraphy, scribble, scrawl. **2** WORK, opus, book, volume, publication, composition.

wrong adj. **1** INCORRECT, inaccurate, in error, erroneous, wide of the mark, mistaken, inexact, imprecise, unsound, faulty, false; informal off beam, barking up the wrong tree, off target. **2** UNSUITABLE, inappropriate, inapt, inapposite, undesirable, infelicitous. **3** IMMORAL, bad, wicked, evil, unlawful, illegal, illicit, lawless, criminal, delinquent, felonious, dishonest, dishonourable, corrupt, unethical, sinful, iniquitous, behaviour. ∎ **wrongdoer** n.

wrongful adj. not fair, just, or legal. ∎ **wrongfully** adv.

wrote past of **write**.

wrought adj. (of metals) shaped by hammering. ▢ **wrought iron** a tough form of iron suitable for forging or rolling.

wrung past & past part. of **wring**.

wry adj. (**wryer**, **wryest** or **wrier**, **wriest**) **1** using or expressing dry, mocking humour. **2** (of the face) twisted in disgust or disappointment. ∎ **wryly** adv.

WWW abbrev. World Wide Web.

Thesaurus

blameworthy, culpable; *informal* crooked. **4** AMISS, awry, out of order, not right, faulty, defective. ▶n. **1** BADNESS, immorality, sin, sinfulness, wickedness, evil, iniquity, unlawfulness, crime, dishonesty, dishonour, injustice, transgression, abuse; *informal* crookedness. **2** MISDEED, offence, injury, crime, infringement, infraction, injustice, grievance, outrage, atrocity. ∎ OPPOSITES right. ▶v. **1** ABUSE, mistreat, maltreat, harm, hurt, do injury to. **2** MISREPRESENT, malign, dishonour, impugn, vilify, defame, slander, libel, denigrate, insult; *informal* bad-mouth.

wrongdoer n. LAWBREAKER, criminal, delinquent, culprit, offender, felon, villain, miscreant, evil-doer, sinner, transgressor, malefactor; *informal* wrong 'un, crook.

wrongful adj. UNFAIR, unjust, improper, unjustified, unwarranted, unlawful, illegal, illegitimate, illicit, groundless, indefensible, improper.

wry adj. **1** TWISTED, distorted, contorted, crooked, lopsided, askew. **2** IRONIC, sardonic, mocking, sarcastic, dry, droll, witty, humorous.

XxYyZz

X (or **x**) n. the Roman numeral for ten. □ **X chromosome** a sex chromosome, two of which are normally present in female cells and one in male cells.

xenon /zen-on/ n. an inert gaseous chemical element.

xenophobia /zen-uh-foh-bi-uh/ n. dislike or fear of people from other countries. ■ **xenophobic** adj.

Xerox /zeer-oks/ n. trademark **1** a machine for producing photocopies. **2** a photocopy. ▶v. (**xerox**) photocopy.

Xmas n. informal Christmas.

X-ray n. **1** an electromagnetic wave able to pass through solids. **2** an image of an object's internal structure produced by passing X-rays through it. ▶v. photograph or examine with X-rays.

xylophone /zy-loh-fohn/ n. a musical instrument played by striking a row of wooden bars with small hammers.

yacht /yot/ n. **1** a medium-sized sailing boat. **2** a powered boat equipped for cruising. ■ **yachting** n. **yachtsman** (or **yachtswoman**) n.

yak n. a large Asian ox with shaggy hair.

yam n. the tuber of a tropical plant, eaten as a vegetable.

yang n. (in Chinese philosophy) the active male principle of the universe.

Yank n. informal an American.

yank informal v. pull sharply. ▶n. a sharp pull.

yap v. (**yapping, yapped**) bark shrilly. ▶n. a shrill bark.

yard n. **1** a unit of length equal to 3 ft (0.9144 m). **2** a piece of enclosed ground next to a building. **3** a pole slung across a ship's mast for a sail to hang from. □ **yardstick** a standard for comparison. ■ **yardage** n.

yarmulke (or **yarmulka**) /yar-muul-kuh/ n. a skullcap worn by Jewish men.

yarn n. **1** spun thread. **2** informal a story.

yashmak n. a veil concealing all of the face except the eyes, worn by some Muslim women.

yaw v. (of a ship or aircraft) turn unsteadily from side to side. ▶n. yawing movement.

yawn v. **1** open the mouth wide and breathe in deeply due to tiredness or boredom. **2** (**yawning**) wide open. ▶n. an act of yawning.

Y chromosome n. a sex chromosome normally present only in male cells.

yd abbrev. yard.

year n. **1** the time taken by the earth to make one revolution around the sun. **2** (also **calendar year**) the period of 365 days (or 366 days in leap years) starting from the first of January. □ **yearbook** an annual publication listing events or aspects of the previous year. **yearling** an animal between one and two years old. ■ **yearly** adj. & adv.

yearn v. feel great longing.

yeast n. a fungus, or substance made from this, used as a fermenting agent and to make bread dough rise. ■ **yeasty** adv.

yell n. & v. (utter) a loud, sharp cry or call.

yellow adj. **1** of the colour of egg yolks or ripe lemons. **2** informal cowardly. ▶n. yellow colour. ▶v. turn yellow with age. ■ **yellowish** adj.

yelp n. & v. (utter) a short, sharp cry.

yen n. (pl. **yen**) **1** the basic unit of money of Japan. **2** informal a longing.

yeoman /yoh-muhn/ n. hist. a man owning a house and a small area of farmland.

yes exclam. **1** expressing agreement or consent. **2** used as a reply to a summons. □ **yes-man** informal a person who always agrees with their superiors.

yesterday adv. on the day before today.

Thesaurus

yank v. PULL, tug, jerk, wrench. ▶n. PULL, jerk, wrench.

yardstick n. MEASURE, standard, gauge, scale, guide, guideline, touchstone, criterion, benchmark, model, pattern.

yarn n. **1** THREAD, fibre, strand. **2** STORY, tale, anecdote, fable, traveller's tale; in-

formal tall tale/story, cock and bull story.

yawning adj. WIDE, wide open, gaping, cavernous.

yearly adj. ANNUAL, once a year, every year.

yearn v. LONG, pine, have a longing, crave, desire, want, wish for, hanker

▶ n. **1** the day before today. **2** the recent past.

yet adv. **1** up until now or then. **2** this soon. **3** from now into the future. **4** still; even. ▶ conj. but in spite of that.

yeti n. a large hairy manlike animal said to live in the Himalayas.

yew n. an evergreen tree with poisonous red berries.

Y-fronts pl. n. trademark men's or boys' underpants with a seam at the front in the shape of an upside-down Y.

Yiddish n. a language used by Jews from central and eastern Europe.

yield v. **1** produce or provide a natural or industrial product. **2** produce a result. **3** give way to demands or pressure. **4** give up possession of. ▶ n. an amount yielded.

yin n. (in Chinese philosophy) the passive female principle of the universe.

YMCA abbrev. Young Men's Christian Association.

yob n. informal a rude and aggressive young man. ■ **yobbish** adj.

yodel v. (**yodelling, yodelled**; US **yodeling, yodeled**) sing in a style that alternates rapidly between a normal voice and a high-pitched voice. ▶ n. a yodelling song or call. ■ **yodeller** n.

yoga n. a system involving simple meditation, breathing exercises, and the holding of particular body positions, based on Hindu philosophy.

yogurt (or **yoghurt**) n. a thick liquid food made from milk with bacteria added.

yoke n. **1** a piece of wood fastened over the necks of two animals pulling a plough etc. **2** a frame fitting over someone's shoulders, used to carry pails or baskets. **3** a burden or oppressive restriction. **4** a part of a garment fitting over the shoulders. ▶ v. join with a yoke.

yokel n. an unsophisticated country person.

yolk n. the yellow inner part of a bird's egg.

Yom Kippur n. an important day in the Jewish year, on which people pray and fast.

yonder adj. & adv. old use or dialect over there.

yonks pl. n. informal a very long time.

yore n. (**of yore**) literary long ago.

Yorkshire pudding n. a baked batter pudding eaten with roast beef or gravy.

you pron. **1** the person being addressed. **2** any person in general.

young adj. **1** having lived or existed for only a short time. **2** of or characteristic of young people. ▶ pl. n. young children or animals; offspring.

youngster n. a child or young person.

your adj. of or belonging to you.

> ☑ Don't confuse your meaning 'belonging to you' (as in *your daughter*) with the form **you're**, short for **you are** (as in *you're a good cook*).

yours possess. pron. belonging to you.

yourself pron. (pl. **yourselves**) **1** used when the person or people being addressed are affected by an action. **2** you personally.

youth n. (pl. **youths**) **1** the period between childhood and adult age. **2** the qualities associated with being young. **3** young people. **4** a young man. ▢ **youth club** a club providing leisure activities for young people. **youth hostel** a place providing cheap overnight accommodation, esp. for young people on holiday.

Thesaurus

after, covet, fancy, hunger for, thirst for; *informal* have a yen for.

yell v. SHOUT, cry out, howl, scream, shriek, screech, squeal, roar, bawl, whoop; *informal* holler.

yes adv. ALL RIGHT, of course, by all means, sure, certainly, in the affirmative; *informal* yeah, yah, yep, uh-huh, righto. ■ OPPOSITES no.

yield v. **1** GIVE, return, bring in, fetch, earn, net, produce, supply, provide, generate, furnish. **2** GIVE UP, surrender, relinquish, part with, deliver up, turn over, give over, remit, cede, renounce, resign, abdicate, forgo. **3** ADMIT/CONCEDE DEFEAT, surrender, capitulate, submit, lay down one's arms, give in, give up the struggle, succumb, raise/show the white flag, throw in the towel/sponge, cave in. ■ OPPOSITES withhold, resist.

yoke n. **1** HARNESS, collar, coupling. **2** OPPRESSION, tyranny, enslavement, slavery, servitude, bondage, thrall.

yokel n. RUSTIC, countryman, countrywoman, peasant, country bumpkin, provincial; *US informal* hayseed, hillbilly.

young adj. **1** YOUTHFUL, juvenile, junior, adolescent, in the springtime of life, in one's salad days. **2** NEW, recent, undeveloped, fledgling, in the making. ■ OPPOSITES old.

youngster n. YOUNG ADULT/PERSON,

youthful adj. **1** young or seeming young. **2** characteristic of young people. ■ **youthfully** adv. **youthfulness** n.

yowl n. & v. (make) a loud wailing cry.

yo-yo n. (pl. **yo-yos**) trademark a toy made of a pair of joined discs with a groove between them on which a string is wound, which can be spun down and up as the string unwinds and rewinds. ▶v. (**yo-yoing**, **yo-yoed**) move up and down repeatedly.

yuan n. (pl. **yuan**) the basic unit of money of China.

yucca n. a plant with sword-like leaves and spikes of white flowers.

yuck (or **yuk**) exclam. informal used to express disgust. ■ **yucky** adj.

Yule (or **Yuletide**) n. old use Christmas.

yummy adj. (**yummier**, **yummiest**) informal delicious.

yuppie (or **yuppy**) n. (pl. **yuppies**) informal a young middle-class professional person.

YWCA abbrev. Young Women's Christian Association.

zany adj. (**zanier**, **zaniest**) amusingly unconventional.

zap v. (**zapping**, **zapped**) informal **1** destroy. **2** move suddenly and rapidly. **3** use a remote control to change television channels.

zeal n. great energy or enthusiasm. ■ **zealous** adj. **zealously** adv.

zealot /zel-uht/ n. a fanatical follower of a religion or policy. ■ **zealotry** n.

zebra n. an African wild horse with black and white stripes. □ **zebra crossing** a pedestrian crossing marked with broad white stripes.

Zen n. a form of Buddhism.

zenith n. **1** the point in the sky directly overhead. **2** the highest or greatest point.

zephyr n. literary a gentle wind.

zero adj. & n. (pl. **zeros**) **1** the figure 0; nought. **2** a temperature of 0°C (32°F). ▶v. (**zeroing**, **zeroed**) (**zero in on**) take aim at or focus attention on. □ **zero hour** the time at which a military or other operation is set to begin.

zest n. **1** great enthusiasm and energy. **2** the outer coloured part of the peel of citrus fruit.

zigzag n. a line or course having sharp alternate right and left turns. ▶v. (**zigzagging**, **zigzagged**) move in a zigzag.

zilch n. informal nothing.

zinc n. a silvery-white metallic element.

zing n. informal energy or enthusiasm.

Zionism n. a movement for the development of a Jewish nation in Israel. ■ **Zionist** n. & adj.

zip n. **1** (also **zipper**) a fastener consisting of two flexible interlocking strips of metal or plastic, closed or opened by pulling a slide along them. **2** informal energy. ▶v. (**zipping**, **zipped**) **1** fasten with a zip. **2** informal move at high speed. □ **zip code** US a postcode.

zircon n. a brown or semi-transparent mineral.

zirconium n. a silver-grey metallic element.

zit n. informal a spot on the skin.

zither n. a stringed instrument played with the fingers and a plectrum.

zloty n. (pl. **zloty** or **zlotys**) the basic unit of money in Poland.

Thesaurus

youth, juvenile, teenager, adolescent, lad, boy, young man/woman, girl; *Sc. & N. Engl.* lass; *informal* kid, shaver, young 'un.

youth n. **1** YOUNG DAYS, early years, teens, early life, adolescence, boyhood, girlhood. **2** BOY, young man, lad, youngster, juvenile, teenager, adolescent; *informal* kid.

youthful adj. YOUNG, active, vigorous, spry, sprightly. ■ OPPOSITES old.

zany adj. ECCENTRIC, peculiar, odd, ridiculous, absurd, comic, clownish, madcap, funny, amusing, weird; *informal* screwy, wacky, daft; *US informal* kooky. ■ OPPOSITES conventional.

zeal n. **1** ARDOUR, fervour, fervency, passion, fire, devotion, vehemence, intensity, enthusiasm, eagerness, keenness, earnestness, vigour, energy, verve,

gusto, zest, fanaticism; *informal* zing. **2** ZEALOTRY, fanaticism, extremism. ■ OPPOSITES apathy.

zealot n. ENTHUSIAST, fanatic, extremist, radical, militant, bigot.

zealous adj. ARDENT, fervent, fervid, passionate, impassioned, devoted, intense, enthusiastic, eager, keen, earnest, vigorous, energetic, zestful, fanatical. ■ OPPOSITES apathetic.

zenith n. HIGHEST/HIGH POINT, crowning point, height, top, acme, peak, pinnacle, climax, prime, meridian, apex, apogee, vertex. ■ OPPOSITES nadir.

zero n. **1** NOUGHT, nothing, cipher. **2** NOTHING, naught, nil; *informal* zilch, not a sausage. □ **zero in on** FOCUS ON, centre on, concentrate on, home in on, pinpoint.

zest n. **1** RELISH, gusto, enthusiasm,

zodiac n. an area of the sky in which the sun, moon, and planets appear to lie, divided by astrologers into twelve equal parts or signs. ■ **zodiacal** adj.

zombie n. **1** a corpse supposedly brought back to life by witchcraft. **2** informal a completely unresponsive person.

zone n. an area with particular characteristics or a particular use. ▶v. divide into zones. ■ **zonal** adj.

zoo n. a place where wild animals are kept for study, conservation, or display to the public.

zoology n. the study of animals. ■ **zoological** adj. **zoologist** n.

zoom v. **1** move very quickly. **2** (of a camera) change smoothly from a long shot to a close-up or vice versa.

zucchini /zuu-kee-ni/ n. (pl. **zucchini** or **zucchinis**) US a courgette.

Zulu n. **1** a member of a South African people. **2** their language.

zygote n. a cell resulting from the joining of two gametes.

Thesaurus

eagerness, zeal, vigour, liveliness, energy, enjoyment, joy, delectation, appetite; *informal* zing, oomph. **2** PIQUANCY, spice, pungency, flavour, relish, tang, savour, interest.

zone n. AREA, sector, section, belt, district, region, province.

zoom v. FLY, buzz, rush, dash, pelt, race, tear, shoot, scurry, speed, hurry, hasten, whizz, hare, zip, zap.

z

Wordpower Guide

Vocabulary builder

This section gives a selection of words and phrases which are related to various keywords and which a conventional dictionary or thesaurus does not usually provide. It is designed as a means of enriching your vocabulary and also as a way of guiding you to a word or expression that may be on the tip of your tongue but that remains elusive.

acid ▶ alkali, base (*substances reacting with acid*), litmus test (*test for acid or alkali*), neutral (*neither acid nor alkaline*), pH (*scale of acidity or alkalinity*).

actor ▶ histrionic, thespian (*to do with actors or drama*); cast (*list of actors in a play or film*), ham (*a bad actor*).

aircraft ▶ aileron, flaps, fuselage, rudder, spoiler, stabilizer, tailplane, undercarriage (*parts of aircraft*); jet, piston engine, ramjet, turbofan, turbojet (*kinds of aircraft engine*); aerodynamics, aeronautics (*science of aircraft flight*), aviation (*business of operating aircraft*), avionics (*aircraft electronics*).

alcohol ▶ teetotalism, temperance (*refusal to drink alcohol*), alcoholism, dipsomania (*addiction to alcohol*), Dutch courage (*confidence gained from drinking alcohol*).

alloy ▶ *some common alloys:* amalgam (*mercury with other metals*), brass (*copper and zinc*), bronze (*copper and tin*), pewter (*tin with copper and antimony*), solder (*usually lead and tin*), steel (*iron with carbon and other metals*).

angle ▶ acute (*less than 90°*), obtuse (*more than 90° and less than 180°*), reflex (*more than 180°*), right angle (*exactly 90°*); trigonometry (*branch of mathematics concerned with angles*).

animal ▶ fauna (*animals of a particular region*), invertebrates (*animals without backbones*), vertebrates (*animals with backbones*), zoology (*scientific study of animals*).

Arab ▶ Bedouin (*an Arab nomad living in the desert*), sheikh (*the leader of an Arab tribe, family, or village*), souk (*an Arab market*).

architecture ▶ *some architectural styles:* baroque, classical, Gothic, neoclassical, Palladian, rococo, Romanesque.

art ▶ *some art schools and styles:* art deco, art nouveau, baroque, classicism, cubism, Dada, expressionism, Fauvism, Impressionism, Mannerism, Pre-Raphaelitism, surrealism.

atmosphere ▶ *layers of the earth's atmosphere (from lowest to highest):* troposphere, stratosphere, mesosphere, thermosphere, ionosphere.

back ▶ dorsal (*on the back or upper side*), lumbar (*of the lower back*), posterior (*further back in position*), supine (*lying on one's back*); lumbago (*back pain*).

bacteria ▶ bacillus (*rod-shaped bacterium*), coccus (*rounded bacterium*), sepsis, septicaemia (*presence of bacteria in tissues or blood*); *kinds of bacteria:* E. coli, legionella, listeria, meningococcus, pneumococcus, salmonella, staphylococcus, streptococcus.

ballet ▶ arabesque, entrechat, jeté, pirouette, plié (*ballet steps and movements*); barre (*bar used during exercises*), choreography (*design of dance movements*), pas de deux (*dance for two*), pointe (*tips of the toes*), tutu (*ballet dancer's dress*).

bankrupt ▶ insolvent (*relating to bankruptcy*), receiver (*official managing bankrupt business*), sequestrate (*take possession of property of bankrupt person*).

barrel ▶ cooper (*maker of barrels*), hogshead, keg, tun (*kinds of barrel*), hoop (*metal band around a barrel*), spigot (*plug for a barrel vent*), stave (*plank from which barrels are made*).

bee ▶ apiary (*place where bees are kept*), apiculture (*keeping of bees*), drone (*male bee*), royal jelly (*food for queen bee larvae*).

beetle ▶ *some common beetles:* Colorado beetle, death-watch beetle, ladybird, scarab, weevil.

bell ▶ belfry (*place in a bell tower where bells are kept*), campanile (*a bell tower*), campanology (*art of bell-ringing*), knell (*sound of a bell*), peal (*ringing of bells*); tocsin (*alarm bell*).

biology ▶ cytology (*biology of cells*), ecology (*study of interrelations of organisms*), morphology (*study of forms of organisms*), physiology (*study of normal functions of organisms*), taxonomy (*classification of living organisms*).

bird ▶ avian (*to do with birds*), aviary (*place where birds are kept*), ornithology (*study of birds*).

birth ▶ antenatal (*before birth*), Caesarean section (*operation to deliver baby*), congenital (*present from birth*), natal (*to do with the place and time of birth*), neonate (*newborn child*), obstetrics (*branch of medicine concerned with childbirth*), perinatal (*near to the time of birth*), postpartum (*following birth*).

blood ▶ *components of blood:* corpuscle, haemoglobin, plasma, platelet, rhesus factor, serum.

blue ▶ *shades of blue:* azure, cobalt, indigo, lavender, navy, sapphire, turquoise, ultramarine.

body ▶ corporal, corporeal, somatic (*having to do with the body*); metabolism (*the body's chemical processes*), posture (*a body position*).

bone ▶ marrow (*soft substance in the hollow of bones*), orthopaedics (*branch of medicine concerned with bone deformities*), osteoporosis (*brittleness of the bones*), osteoarthritis (*disease causing pain in joints*).

book ▶ appendix (*information at the end of a book*), bibliography (*list of books*), bibliophile (*collector or lover of books*); recto (*right-hand page of an open book*), verso (*left-hand page of an open book*).

brass ▶ *brass musical instruments:* bugle, cornet, euphonium, flugelhorn, French horn, horn, trombone, trumpet, tuba.

bridge ▶ aqueduct (*bridge carrying water*), drawbridge (*bridge that can be raised*), humpback bridge (*small road bridge with a steep curve*), span (*part of a bridge between supports*), suspension bridge (*bridge suspended from cables*).

brother ▶ confraternity (*a brotherhood*), fraternal (*of or like a brother*), fratricide (*murder of one's own brother or sister*), sibling (*brother or sister*).

brown ▶ *shades of brown:* auburn, bronze, chestnut, copper, dun, fawn, hazel, sepia, tan.

butterfly ▶ caterpillar (*butterfly larva*), chrysalis (*butterfly pupa*), lepidopteran (*to do with butterflies and moths*), metamorphosis (*transformation of butterfly larva to adult*).

camp ▶ billy (*cooking pot used when camping*), bivouac (*temporary camp without tents*), canteen (*small water bottle used when camping*), latrine (*communal toilet in a camp*).

cancer ▶ *types of cancer:* carcinoma, lymphoma, melanoma; *treatments for cancer:* chemotherapy, radiotherapy; carcinogen (*substance causing cancer*); oncology (*branch of medicine concerned with cancer*).

candle ▶ candelabrum (*branched candlestick*), chandelier (*hanging light with branches for several candles*), menorah (*Jewish branched candlestick*), sconce (*ornamental candle holder on wall*).

castle ▶ *parts of a castle:* bailey, barbican, battlement, drawbridge, dungeon, keep, moat, portcullis, rampart, turret.

cat ▶ feline (*of or like a cat or cats*); *wild cats:* bobcat, cheetah, cougar, jaguar, leopard, lion, lynx, ocelot, panther, puma, tiger, wildcat.

cave ▶ grotto (*small picturesque cave*), potholer (*explorer of caves*), stalactite, stalagmite (*rock formations within cave*), speleology (*study or exploration of caves*), troglodyte (*cave-dweller*).

cell ▶ *kinds of cell:* erythrocyte (*red blood cell*), gamete (*sex cell*), leucocyte (*white blood cell*), neuron (*nerve cell*), zygote (*cell formed by fusion of gametes*); meiosis, mitosis (*division of cells*).

child ▶ crèche (*a nursery*), infanticide (*murder of a child*), orphan (*child whose parents are dead*), paediatrics (*branch of medicine concerned with childhood diseases*).

Chinese ▶ *Chinese life and culture:* feng shui (*ancient Chinese system of designing and arranging buildings and objects*), kung fu, t'ai chi chuan (*Chinese martial arts*), Mandarin

(*official form of the Chinese language*), sinology (*study of Chinese language and culture*).

Christianity ▶ *dates in the Christian calendar:* Advent, Ascension, Christmas, Easter, Epiphany, Lent, Pentecost, Whit Sunday.

church ▶ *parts of a church:* aisle, apse, chancel, clerestory, crypt, nave, spire, steeple, transept, vestry.

circle ▶ *parts of a circle:* arc, circumference, diameter, radius, segment.

city ▶ civic, urban (*to do with a city*); citadel (*fortress protecting a city*), mayor (*elected head of a city*), metropolis (*main city of a region*), suburb (*district of private housing on the outskirts of a city*).

coal ▶ anthracite, lignite (*kinds of coal*); Carboniferous (*geological period when many coal deposits were laid down*), coke (*fuel made by heating coal in the absence of air*), colliery (*coal mine*).

coast ▶ littoral (*to do with a coast or shore*); corniche (*road running along a coast*), harbour (*place on coast where ships may moor*), riviera (*coastal region with subtropical climate*).

code ▶ cipher (*simple kind of code*), cryptogram (*a text written in code*), cryptography (*art of writing or solving codes*), decipher, decrypt (*convert code into normal language*), encipher, encrypt (*convert normal language into code*).

coffin ▶ bier (*movable platform supporting a coffin*), catafalque (*wooden framework supporting a coffin*), hearse (*vehicle carrying a coffin*), pall (*cloth spread over a coffin*), sarcophagus (*stone coffin*).

coin ▶ numismatics (*study or collection of coins*), obverse (*side of coin bearing head or main design*), reverse (*secondary side of coin*), mint (*place where money is coined*).

collector ▶ *collectors and the objects they collect:* antiquarian (*ancient objects*), bibliophile (*books*), deltiologist (*postcards*), lepidopterist (*butterflies and moths*), numismatist (*coins*), philatelist (*stamps*).

comedy ▶ *kinds of comedy:* burlesque, farce, satire, slapstick, stand-up, vaudeville.

computer ▶ *kinds of computer:* desktop, laptop, mainframe, notebook, palmtop, word processor, workstation; *parts of a computer:* disk drive, hard disk, hardware, keyboard, monitor, mouse, software, VDU.

country ▶ *to do with the country or the countryside:* bucolic, pastoral, rural, rustic.

cross ▶ *types of cross:* crucifix, St George's cross, saltire, swastika; cruciform (*cross-shaped*).

curve ▶ concave (*curving inwards*), convex (*curving outwards*); arc (*curve forming part of circumference of a circle*).

dance ▶ *some dances:* cancan, charleston, foxtrot, mambo, polka, rumba, salsa, tango, waltz; terpsichorean (*to do with dancing*).

death ▶ autopsy, post-mortem (*examinations of a corpse to discover cause of death*), inquest (*inquiry into the cause of a death*), memento mori (*object kept as a reminder of death*), rigor mortis (*stiffening of joints and muscles after death*), thanatology (*scientific study of death*).

devil ▶ diabolical (*of or like the Devil*); *names for the Devil:* Beelzebub, Lucifer, Old Nick, Satan.

dictionary ▶ gazetteer (*geographical dictionary*), lexicographer (*person who compiles dictionaries*), thesaurus (*book of synonyms*).

disease ▶ aetiology (*study of the causes of disease*), communicable, infectious (*referring to a disease which can be passed to others*), contagious (*referring to a disease spread by contact*), epidemic (*widespread occurrence of a disease*), epidemiology (*study of the spread of disease*), pathogen (*microorganism that can cause disease*), pathology (*branch of medicine concerned with diseases*).

doctor ▶ *doctors and their specialties:* cardiologist (*disorders of the heart*), dermatologist (*disorders of the skin*), gynaecologist (*female reproductive system*), obstetrician (*childbirth*), oncology (*tumours*), ophthalmologist (*disorders of the eye*), paediatrician (*childhood disorders*).

document ▶ archive (*collection of historical documents*), manuscript (*handwritten document*), pro forma (*standard document*), recto (*front of a loose document*), rubric (*heading on a document*), verso (*back of a loose document*).

dog ▶ canine (*of or like a dog or dogs*); *members of the dog family:* coyote, dingo, fox, jackal, wolf.

ear ▶ auditory (*to do with hearing*), aural (*to do with the ear*), tinnitus (*ringing in the ears*); *some parts of the ear:* auricle or pinna, cochlea, eardrum or tympanum.

earth ▶ circumnavigate (*travel around the earth*), geography (*study of physical features of the earth*), geology (*science of physical structure and substance of the earth*), terrestrial (*to do with the earth*).

earthquake ▶ aftershock (*smaller earthquake following larger one*), epicentre (*point on surface directly above focus*), focus (*point of origin of earthquake*), Richter scale (*measuring earthquake intensity*), seismic (*to do with earthquakes*), seismograph (*instrument for measuring earthquakes*), tsunami (*sea wave caused by earthquake*).

egg ▶ albumen (*egg white*), clutch (*set of eggs laid together*), incubate (*keep eggs warm for hatching*), ovate, oviform, ovoid (*egg-shaped*), oviparous (*egg-laying*), roe (*fish eggs*), spawn (*fish or amphibian eggs*).

eight ▶ octagon (*plane figure with eight straight sides and eight angles*), octahedron (*three-dimensional shape with eight faces*), octave (*series of eight musical notes between [and including] two notes*), octet (*group of eight musicians*).

election ▶ candidate (*person put forward for election*), canvass (*visit someone to seek their vote in an election*), hustings (*public political meetings before an election*), psephology (*statistical study of elections and voting*), suffrage (*the right to vote in political elections*).

element ▶ allotrope (*different form of a chemical element*), atom (*smallest particle of an element*), compound (*substance formed from two or more elements*), isotope (*form of the same element having different atomic mass*), periodic table (*table of the chemical elements*), valency (*combining power of an element*).

environment ▶ conservationist (*person dedicated to protecting the environment*), eco-friendly (*not harmful to the environment*), ecology (*study of organisms' relationships with each other and with the environment*), habitat (*natural environment of an organism*).

eye ▶ ocular (*to do with the eye*); ophthalmologist (*specialist in eye diseases*), ophthalmoscope (*instrument for inspecting eyes*); *parts of the eye:* conjunctiva, cornea, iris, pupil, retina; *eye defects or diseases:* astigmatism, cataract, conjunctivitis, glaucoma, myopia (*short-sightedness*).

feather ▶ down (*soft, fine feathers*), pinnate (*shaped like a feather*), plumage (*bird's feathers*), plume (*long, soft feather or arrangement of feathers*), preen (*of a bird: clean its feathers with its beak*); quill (*bird's main wing or tail feather*).

fetus ▶ amniotic fluid (*fluid surrounding a fetus*), placenta (*organ that nourishes the fetus*), umbilical cord (*cord attaching the fetus to the placenta*).

figure ▶ *plane figures:* triangle (*three sides*), quadrilateral (*four sides*), pentagon (*five sides*), hexagon (*six sides*), heptagon (*seven sides*), octagon (*eight sides*), nonagon (*nine sides*), decagon (*ten sides*).

fire ▶ arson (*act of deliberately setting fire to property*); combustible, flammable, inflammable (*able to catch fire easily*); ember (*piece of burning wood or coal in a dying fire*), ignite (*catch fire or set on fire*).

five ▶ pentagon (*plane figure with five straight sides and five angles*), pentathlon (*athletic event made up of five different events*), quintet (*group of five musicians*), quintuplet (*each of five children born at one birth*).

flower ▶ *parts of a flower:* anther, bract, calyx, carpel, corolla, pistil, sepal, stamen.

foot ▶ chiropody, podiatry (*medical treatment of the feet*); athlete's foot (*ringworm infection of the feet*), corn (*painful area of thickened skin on the toes or foot*), metatarsus (*bones of the foot*), pedicure (*cosmetic treatment of the feet*), verruca (*wart on the sole of the foot*).

four ▶ quadrilateral (*four-sided figure*), quadruped (*animal with four feet*), quadruplet (*each of four children born at one birth*), quartet (*group or set of four; group of four musicians*).

funeral ▶ cortège (*funeral procession*), hearse (*vehicle for* *conveying the coffin*), inter (*place a corpse in a grave or tomb*), obsequies (*funeral rites*), pall (*cloth spread over a coffin, hearse, or tomb*), wake (*party held after a funeral*).

gene ▶ chromosome (*thread-like structure in a cell carrying genetic information*), clone (*genetically identical individual*), dominant (*gene expressed in offspring when inherited from only one parent*), recessive (*gene expressed in offspring only when inherited from both parents*).

God ▶ atheism (*belief that God does not exist*), agnosticism (*belief that one cannot know whether or not God exists*), blasphemy (*irreverent talk about God*), divine (*to do with God or a god*), pantheon (*all the gods of a people or religion*), polytheism (*belief in more than one god*).

gold ▶ bullion (*gold or silver in bulk before coining*), carat (*measure of purity for gold*), gild (*cover with gold*), Midas touch (*power of turning everything into gold*), nugget (*small lump of gold found in the earth*).

green ▶ shades of green: aquamarine, emerald, jade, lime, olive; chlorophyll (*green pigment in leaves*), patina, verdigris (*green sheen or film*), verdure (*lush green vegetation*).

gun ▶ blunderbuss, cannon, carbine, howitzer, machine gun, mortar, musket, pistol, revolver, rifle, shotgun (*types of gun*); artillery (*large military guns*), ballistics (*the science of firearms*), firearm (*a portable gun*), emplacement (*a platform for a large gun*); barrage, broadside, cannonade, enfilade, fusillade, salvo, volley (*types of gunfire*).

hair ▶ alopecia (*abnormal hair loss*), depilate (*remove hair*), follicle (*sheath surrounding the root of a hair*), hirsute (*hairy*), toupee (*small wig worn to cover a bald spot*),

trichology (*branch of medicine concerned with the hair and scalp*).

hand ▶ ambidextrous (*able to use right or left hands equally well*), dexterity (*skill with the hands*), manicure (*cosmetic treatment of the hands*), manual (*involving the hands*), metacarpus (*bones of the hand*).

health ▶ convalesce (*gradually recover one's health after illness*), hypochondriac (*person abnormally anxious about their health*), salubrious (*health-giving or healthy*), sanitary (*to do with conditions affecting health*).

heart ▶ cardiac (*having to do with the heart*), cardiology (*branch of medicine concerned with the heart*), coronary (*having to do with the arteries that supply the heart*), pacemaker (*artificial device for regulating the heart muscle*); *parts of the heart:* aorta, atrium, mitral valve, vena cava, ventricle

heartbeat ▶ arrhythmia (*irregular heartbeat*), bradycardia (*abnormally slow heartbeat*), diastole (*phase when the heart muscle relaxes*), palpitation (*rapid, strong, or irregular heartbeat*), systole (*phase when the heart muscle contracts*), tachycardia (*abnormally rapid heart rate*).

heat ▶ *methods of transmitting heat:* conduction, convection, radiation; diathermy (*medical and surgical use of heat*), therm (*unit of heat*), thermal (*of heat*), thermodynamics (*science of heat and other forms of energy*).

Hinduism ▶ ashram (*Hindu religious retreat*), caste (*each of the hereditary classes of Hindu society*), guru (*Hindu spiritual teacher*), mahatma (*wise or holy Hindu teacher*).

horse ▶ equine (*of or like a horse or horses*); colt (*young uncastrated male horse*), foal (*young horse*), filly (*young female horse*), gelding *(castrated male horse)*, mare *(female horse)*, stallion *(uncastrated adult male horse)*.

illusion ▶ hallucination *(illusion experienced as real)*, mirage *(optical illusion caused by atmospheric conditions)*, special effects *(illusions created for film and television)*, trompe l'œil *(method of painting which creates an illusion)*.

imitation ▶ burlesque *(comically exaggerated imitation)*, ersatz *(referring to an inferior imitation of something)*, parody *(mocking imitation)*, pastiche *(imitation of artistic style)*.

Indian ▶ *Indian life and culture:* monsoon *(seasonal wind and accompanying rainy season)*, Raj *(period of British rule in India)*, sitar *(large Indian lute)*, tandoor *(clay oven)*; *Indian languages:* Sanskrit *(ancient language of India)*, Bengali, Gujarati, Hindi, Hindustani, Marathi, Tamil, Urdu.

injection ▶ ampoule *(glass capsule of liquid for injecting)*, hypodermic *(referring to injection beneath the skin)*, intravenous *(referring to injection into a vein)*, syringe *(instrument for making injections)*.

Irish ▶ *Irish life and culture:* Daíl *(lower House of Parliament in the Irish Republic)*, Hibernian *(of Ireland)*, hurling *(game resembling hockey)*, shamrock *(national emblem of Ireland)*, Taoiseach *(Prime Minister of the Irish Republic)*.

Islam ▶ ayatollah *(Shiite religious leader)*, hajj *(pilgrimage to Mecca)*, imam *(leader of prayers in a mosque)*, jihad *(war or struggle against unbelievers)*, mosque *(Muslim place of worship)*, minaret *(slender tower of a mosque)*, muezzin *(man who calls Muslims to prayer)*, Ramadan *(month of fasting)*, Shia, Sunni *(main branches of Islam)*.

island ▶ archipelago *(large group of islands)*, atoll *(ring-shaped chain of islands)*, insular *(relating to an island)*, key *(low-lying island)*.

Japanese ▶ *Japanese life and culture:* bonsai *(art of growing miniature trees)*, futon *(padded mattress)*, geisha *(hostess)*, haiku *(poem of 17 syllables)*, kabuki *(drama performed by men)*, kimono *(loose robe)*, manga *(fantasy cartoons and animation)*, Noh *(traditional masked drama)*, Shinto *(religion of spirit worship)*, sumo *(wrestling)*.

Judaism ▶ cantor *(person who leads prayers in a synagogue)*, kosher *(referring to food prepared in accordance with Jewish law)*, rabbi *(Jewish scholar, teacher, or religious leader)*, synagogue *(building used for Jewish worship)*.

kill ▶ euthanasia *(mercy killing)*, genocide *(killing of a whole people)*, homicide *(killing of another person)*, manslaughter *(unintentional killing)*, suicide *(killing of oneself)*.

knight ▶ charger *(horse ridden by a knight)*, chivalry *(medieval knights' code)*, dub *(make someone a knight by touching their shoulder with a sword)*, joust *(knights' mock combat)*, quest *(a knight's expedition)*.

language ▶ linguist *(person who studies language or languages)*, monolingual *(speaking or expressed in only one language)*, multilingual *(in or using several languages)*, polyglot *(person who knows several languages)*, vernacular *(language spoken by ordinary people)*.

leaf ▶ deciduous *(referring to trees that shed leaves annually)*, evergreen *(referring to trees that retain green leaves throughout the year)*, frond *(leaf of a palm or fern)*, vein *(slender rib running through a leaf)*.

light ▶ chiaroscuro (*treatment of light and shade in drawing and painting*); opaque (*not allowing light through*), translucent (*allowing light to pass through partially*), transparent (*allowing light to pass through so that objects behind can be clearly seen*).

lung ▶ pulmonary (*to do with the lungs*); alveoli (*tiny air sacs in the lungs*), bronchi (*air passages of the lungs*), pleura (*membranes enclosing the lungs*), pneumonia (*lung infection in which pus collects in the lungs*).

magic ▶ amulet, talisman (*objects thought to have magical powers*); elixir (*magic potion*), incantation (*words said as a magic spell*), necromancy (*black magic*), numerology (*magical power of numbers*).

-mania ▶ dipsomania (*alcoholism*), kleptomania (*uncontrollable need to steal*), megalomania (*obsession with power*), monomania (*obsession with one thing*), nymphomania (*uncontrollable sexual desire in a woman*), pyromania (*obsession with setting things on fire*).

map ▶ cartography (*science of map-making*), Ordnance Survey (*official UK map-making organization*), projection (*way of representing the earth's surface on a map*), relief map (*map showing contours by shading*).

marriage ▶ banns (*announcement in church of intended marriage*), dowry (*money or property brought by bride on her marriage*), maiden name (*surname of woman before her marriage*), spouse (*husband or wife*); monogamy (*practice of having only one spouse at at a time*), bigamy (*crime of having more than one spouse at one time*), polygamy (*custom of having several spouses at one time*).

mathematics ▶ *branches of mathematics:* algebra, arithmetic, calculus, geometry, statistics, trigonometry.

memory ▶ amnesia (*loss of memory*), flashback (*sudden vivid memory of past event*), keepsake (*small item kept in memory of person who gave or owned it*), memento (*item kept as a reminder*), mnemonic (*aid to memory*).

missile ▶ ballistic missile (*guided missile falling on to its target by gravity*), cruise missile (*flying bomb guided by an on-board computer*), heat-seeking missile (*able to home in on heat emitted by target*), silo (*underground launcher for missile*), torpedo (*underwater missile*).

moisture ▶ dehydrated, desiccated (*lacking moisture*), humidity (*amount of moisture in the air*), saturated (*full of moisture*).

monk ▶ cowl (*monk's hood*), habit (*monk's robe*), monastery (*religious house of monks*), novice, postulant (*beginner monk*), scapular (*monk's short cloak*), tonsure (*shaven part of monk's head*).

motion ▶ inertia (*tendency to remain in motion or motionless*), kinetic (*to do with motion*); impetus, momentum (*energy associated with motion*).

mountain ▶ alpine (*to do with high mountains*); arête (*sharp mountain ridge*), col (*high mountain pass*), peak (*pointed top of a mountain*), sierra (*long mountain chain*), summit (*highest point of a mountain*), tarn (*mountain lake*).

mouth ▶ oral, buccal (*to do with the mouth*); palate (*roof of the mouth*), saliva (*watery liquid produced in the mouth*), tonsil (*mass of tissue at the back of the mouth*).

music ▶ *some musical forms:* concerto, fantasia, fugue, march, opera, operetta, oratorio, prelude, rhapsody, requiem, sonata, song, symphony.

musician ▶ ensemble (*group of musicians performing together*), minstrel (*medieval musician*); maestro, virtuoso (*distinguished musician*).

name ▶ alias (*false name or identity*), anonymous (*not identified by name*), nom de plume (*pen name*), nomenclature (*body or system of names*), onomastics (*study of proper names*), pen name (*literary pseudonym*), pseudonym (*fictitious name*), toponym (*place name*).

number ▶ cardinal number (*number denoting quantity, e.g. five*), ordinal number (*number defining position in a series, e.g. fifth*), prime number (*number divisible only by itself and 1*), root (*number that when multiplied by itself gives a specified number*), square (*product of a number multiplied by itself*).

nun ▶ convent (*community of nuns*), nunnery (*religious house of nuns*), wimple (*nun's headdress*).

office ▶ depose (*remove from office forcefully*), impeach (*charge holder of public office with misconduct*), inaugurate (*admit formally to office*), incumbency (*period during which someone holds an office*), tenure (*holding of an office*).

old ▶ antiquarian (*person who collects or studies old things*), dotage (*period of life when one is old and weak*), geriatric (*of old people*), senile (*mentally weakened through age*).

opera ▶ aria (*song for a soloist in an opera*), diva (*celebrated female opera singer*), libretto (*words of an opera*), prima donna (*chief female singer in an opera company*).

operation ▶ *some operations:* amputation (*cutting off of a limb*), Caesarean section (*delivery of a baby by cutting through the mother's abdomen*), hysterectomy (*removal of all or part of the womb*), mastectomy (*removal of a breast*), tonsillectomy (*removal of the tonsils*).

page ▶ centrefold (*the two middle pages of a magazine*), flyleaf (*blank page at the start or end of a book*), footer (*line of text appearing at the bottom of each page of a document*), footnote (*piece of extra information printed at the bottom of a page*), header (*text printed at the top of each page of a document*), paginate (*number the pages of a book*).

pain ▶ anaesthetic (*drug making one unable to feel pain*), analgesic (*medicine relieving pain*), masochist (*person who enjoys experiencing pain*), neuralgia (*intense pain along a nerve*), sadist (*person who enjoys inflicting pain*).

parliament ▶ act (*law passed by parliament*), backbencher (*member of parliament who does not hold a government or opposition post*), bicameral (*referring to a parliament with two chambers*), bill (*draft of a proposed law presented to parliament*), Hansard (*record of UK parliamentary debates*), hung parliament (*with no party having a majority*), prorogue (*discontinue a session of parliament*).

people ▶ demotic, plebeian (*having to do with ordinary people*), hoi polloi (*a derogatory term for common people*), proletariat (*working-class people*), vernacular (*language spoken by ordinary people*).

percussion ▶ *percussion instruments:* bells, castanets, cymbals, drum, glockenspiel, gong, Jew's harp, maracas, piano, tambourine, xylophone.

phobia ▶ *examples of phobias:* acrophobia (*heights*), agoraphobia (*open or public places*), arachnophobia (*spiders*), claustrophobia (*confined places*), homophobia (*homosexuals*), technophobia (*new technology*), xenophobia (*foreigners or strangers*).

photograph ▶ daguerreotype (*early kind of photograph*), darkroom (*room for developing photographs*), paparazzi (*photographers who try to photograph celebrities*), slide (*small piece of film set in a frame, viewed with a projector*), transparency (*photograph printed on plastic or glass, viewed with a projector*).

plant ▶ botany (*study of plants*), chlorophyll (*green pigment of plants*), flora (*plants of a region*), herbivorous (*feeding on plants*), transpiration (*loss of water vapour from the leaves of a plant*); annual (*plant living one year*), biennial (*two years*), perennial (*three or more years*).

play ▶ denouement (*final part of a play in which all is resolved*), dialogue (*conversation between people in a play*), dramatize (*turn something into a play*), epilogue (*address to the audience at the end of a play*), prologue (*address to the audience at the start of a play*), soliloquy (*speech in which a character speaks their thoughts aloud*); comedy, farce, melodrama, pantomime, tragedy (*types of play*).

poem ▶ blank verse (*unrhymed poetry*), metre (*rhythmic pattern of a poem*), prosody (*study of forms and rhythms of poetry*), stanza (*group of lines forming basic unit of a poem*); forms of poem: ballad, elegy, epic, haiku, limerick, lyric, ode, sonnet; anthology (*collection of poems*).

pope ▶ papal, pontifical (*to do with popes*); bull (*papal edict*), encyclical (*letter from the pope to all Catholic bishops*), papacy (*the position or role of the pope*), Vatican (*official residence of the pope*).

population ▶ census (*official survey of a population*), demography (*study of human populations*), overspill (*part of the population moving from an overcrowded place to live elsewhere*).

power ▶ carte blanche (*power to do whatever one wishes*), megalomaniac (*person obsessed with exercising power*), omnipotence (*unlimited power*), usurp (*seize power unlawfully*).

pregnancy ▶ abortion (*deliberate bringing to an end of a pregnancy*), conceive (*become pregnant*), ectopic (*involving growth of the fetus outside the womb*), in vitro (*referring to conception achieved outside the body*); miscarriage (*birth of a fetus before it can survive independently*); progesterone (*hormone stimulating the uterus to prepare for pregnancy*).

pressure ▶ barometer (*device to measure pressure*), isobar (*line of equal pressure on a weather map*), pneumatic (*operated by air or gas under pressure*).

priest ▶ clerical (*having to do with priests*), neophyte (*newly ordained priest*), ordain (*make someone a priest*), presbytery (*house of a Roman Catholic parish priest*), seminary (*college for priests*).

prison ▶ custodial (*to do with prisons and imprisonment*), incarcerate (*lock someone up in prison*), parole (*release of a prisoner on promise of good behaviour*), remission (*reduction of a prison sentence*).

rabbit ▶ buck (*male rabbit*), doe (*female rabbit*), hutch (*box for housing rabbits*), kitten (*young rabbit*), myxomatosis (*disease of rabbits*), scut (*a rabbit's short tail*), warren (*network of rabbit burrows*).

read ▶ dyslexia (*reading disorder*), illegible (*not clear enough to be read*), illiterate (*unable to read or write*), literacy (*ability to read and write*).

red ▶ *shades of red:* burgundy, cerise, claret, crimson, maroon, puce, ruby, scarlet, vermilion.

religion ▶ denomination
(*recognized branch of a church or
religion*), divinity, theology (*study
of religion*), fundamentalism (*strict
following of the doctrines of a
religion*), scripture (*sacred writings
of a religion*); proselytize (*convert
from one religion to another*); *major
religions:* Buddhism, Christianity,
Hinduism, Islam, Judaism, Shinto,
Sikhism.

river ▶ backwater (*stretch of
stagnant water on a river*), basin
(*area drained by a river*), delta
(*triangular area where a river
branches at its mouth*),
embankment (*wall or bank built to
prevent a river flooding*), estuary
(*mouth of a large river*), fluvial (*to
do with a river*), tributary (*river or
stream flowing into a larger river*).

rock ▶ crevice (*narrow crack in
rock*), lava (*hot molten rock*),
pinnacle (*high pointed piece of
rock*), precipice (*tall, steep rock
face*); *types of rock:* igneous,
metamorphic, sedimentary.

Russian ▶ *Russian life and
culture:* dacha (*holiday home in the
country*), Duma (*lower chamber of
parliament*), glasnost (*policy of
more open government*), kremlin
(*citadel*), perestroika (*reforms
introduced in the former Soviet
Union in the 1980s*), samovar
(*decorated tea urn*), steppe (*large
area of flat grassland*).

sacred ▶ blaspheme (*speak
irreverently of sacred things*),
consecrate (*make or declare
something sacred*), desecrate (*treat
something holy with violent
disrespect*), sacrilege (*the treating of
something sacred with great
disrespect*), sanctum (*sacred place*).

saddle ▶ *parts of a saddle:* cantle,
crupper, girth, pommel, stirrup.

saint ▶ beatification (*the first step
towards making someone a saint*),
canonize (*officially declare someone

a saint*), hagiography (*the writing of
the lives of saints*).

salt ▶ brackish (*referring to water
that is slightly salty*), brine (*very
salty water*), desalinate (*remove salt
from seawater*), saline (*containing
salt*).

school ▶ alma mater (*the school
that one attended*), alumnus (*former
student of a school*), catchment
(*area from which a school's pupils
are drawn*), scholastic (*to do with
schools and education*).

Scottish ▶ *Scottish life and
culture:* Caledonian (*to do with
Scotland*), clan (*group of related
families*), claymore (*large sword*),
haggis (*dish consisting of offal and
suet or oatmeal*), Highland fling
(*vigorous dance*), Hogmanay (*New
Year's Eve*).

sea ▶ marine (*to do with the sea*),
maritime (*to do with shipping or the
sea*); oceanography (*scientific study
of the sea*), submarine (*existing or
happening under the surface of the
sea*).

seed ▶ seminal (*to do with a seed*);
dicotyledon (*plant whose seeds have
two seed leaves*), germinate (*of a
seed: begin to grow and put out
seeds*), monocotyledon (*plant whose
seeds have a single seed leaf*).

sense ▶ aural (*to do with the sense
of hearing*), olfactory (*to do with the
sense of smell*), sensory (*to do with
the senses*), tactile (*to do with the
sense of touch*), visual (*to do with
the sense of sight*).

sentence ▶ clause (*group of
words with a subject and verb,
forming a sentence or part of one*),
parse (*analyse structure of a
sentence*), syntax (*arrangement of
words to make well-formed
sentences*).

seven ▶ heptagon (*plane figure
with seven straight sides and seven
angles*), heptathlon (*athletic contest
made up of seven separate events*),
septet (*group of seven musicians*),

septuple (*made up of seven parts or elements*).

sew ▶ embroidery (*art of decorative sewing*), haberdasher (*seller of sewing materials*), needlewoman, seamstress (*woman skilled at sewing*); baste, tack (*sew loosely with long stitches*).

sex ▶ aphrodisiac (*arousing sexual desire*), celibate, chaste (*abstaining from sexual relations*), libido (*sexual desire*), Platonic (*referring to non-sexual love*), post-coital (*after sexual intercourse*).

sheep ▶ fleece (*wool coat of a sheep*), ovine (*of or like a sheep*); ewe (*female sheep*), mutton (*flesh of a mature sheep used as food*), ram (*male sheep*).

shell ▶ bivalve (*mollusc with two hinged shells*), carapace (*the hard upper shell of a tortoise or related animal*), crustacean (*animal with a hard shell, such as a crab*).

ship ▶ bow (*front end of a ship*), port (*side of a ship on the left when one is facing forward*), starboard (*side of a ship on the right when one is facing forward*), stern (*rearmost part of a ship*); load line, Plimsoll line (*line on ship's side showing legal limit of submersion*).

side ▶ lateral (*of or at the side*); equilateral (*having equal sides*), juxtapose (*place side by side*), polygon (*figure with many sides*).

sin ▶ absolve (*declare someone free from sin*), mortal (*referring to serious sin believed to deprive the soul of divine grace*), redeem (*save someone from sin*), venial (*referring to sin that does not deprive the soul of divine grace*).

sister ▶ sororal (*of or like a sister*), sorority (*sisterhood*), sibling (*brother or sister*).

six ▶ hexagon (*plane figure with six straight sides and six angles*), hexagram (*six-pointed star*), sextet (*group of six musicians*), sextuple (*made up of six parts or elements*),

sextuplet (*each of six children born at one birth*).

ski ▶ après-ski (*social activities following a day's skiing*), nursery slopes (*gentle ski slopes for beginners*), piste (*ski slope with compacted snow*), slalom (*ski race down a winding course*).

skin ▶ cutaneous (*to do with the skin*), dermatology (*branch of medicine concerned with the skin*), dermis, epidermis (*layers of the skin*), dermatitis, eczema (*inflammation of the skin*).

skull ▶ cranial (*of the skull*); cranium (*part of skull containing the brain*), fontanelle (*soft area of a baby's skull*), phrenology (*study of skull shape as supposed indicator of character*), trepan (*surgical saw to make holes in the skull*).

sleep ▶ dormant (*in or as if in a deep sleep*), hibernate (*of an animal: spend the winter in a state like deep sleep*), hypnotic, sedative (*causing sleep*), insomnia (*inability to sleep*), somnambulism (*sleepwalking*), somnolent, soporific (*tending to cause sleep*).

soil ▶ agronomy (*science of soil management and crop production*), humus (*organic component of soil*), loam (*soil of clay and sand containing humus*), marl (*soil consisting of clay and lime*).

song ▶ kinds of song: anthem, aria, ballad, calypso, carol, ditty, hymn, lullaby, madrigal, psalm, shanty, spiritual.

speech ▶ oral (*spoken rather than written*), oratory (*public speaking*), phonetic, phonic (*to do with speech sounds*), phonetics (*study and classification of speech sounds*).

speed ▶ Mach number (*indicating ratio of speed to the speed of sound*), supersonic (*faster than the speed of sound*), tachometer (*instrument measuring the working speed of an engine*), tempo (*speed at which a piece of music is played*).

star ▶ astral, stellar (*to do wih a star or stars*); constellation (*group of stars forming a pattern*), interstellar (*occurring or situated between stars*), magnitude (*degree of brightness of a star*), supernova (*exploding star*).

story ▶ allegory (*story with symbolic meaning*), fable, parable (*story illustrating moral lesson*), folklore, legend, mythology (*traditional stories in a culture*), narrator (*storyteller*), raconteur (*skilled storyteller*).

string ▶ *stringed instruments:* banjo, cello, double bass, guitar, harp, lute, lyre, mandolin, sitar, viola, violin.

surgery ▶ amputation (*surgical removal of a body part*), ligature (*cord used in surgery to tie an artery*), prosthetics (*surgical fitting of artificial body parts*), scalpel (*sharp knife used by a surgeon*).

swim ▶ aqualung, scuba (*swimmer's underwater breathing apparatus*), flume (*water slide at a swimming pool*), lido (*public open-air swimming pool*), natation (*technical word for swimming*).

sword ▶ fencing (*sport of fighting with blunted swords*), hilt (*sword handle*), pommel (*knob on sword's handle*), scabbard (*sheath for sword*).

tax ▶ black economy (*part of country's economy not taxed by government*), excise (*tax payable on alcohol etc.*), fiscal (*to do with taxes*), tariff (*tax to be paid on particular class of imports and exports*), tithe (*one tenth of income formerly paid as tax to support the Church*).

temperature ▶ absolute zero (*lowest temperature theoretically possible, equivalent to -273.15°C*), Celsius, centigrade (*referring to temperature scale on which water freezes at 0°*), Fahrenheit (*referring to temperature scale on which water freezes at 32°*).

ten ▶ decade (*period of ten years*), decagon (*plane figure with ten straight sides and ten angles*), decahedron (*solid figure with ten plane faces*), Decalogue (*the Ten Commandments*), decathlon (*athletic event in which each competitor takes part in the same ten events*), decimal (*referring to a number system based on the number ten*).

theatre ▶ thespian (*to do with the theatre*); impresario (*person who finances theatrical productions*), repertory (*performance of a theatre company's repertoire at regular intervals*); seats in a theatre, lowest to highest: stalls, dress circle, circle, gallery (or balcony).

three ▶ hat-trick (*three successes of the same kind*), triathlon (*athletic contest consisting of three different events*), triennial (*lasting for or recurring every three years*), trio (*group or set of three*), triumvirate (*group of three powerful people*).

tide ▶ ebb (*movement of the tide out to sea*), flood (*rising of the tide*), neap tide (*tide when there is least difference between high and low water*), spring tide (*tide when there is the greatest difference between high and low water*).

time ▶ anachronism (*something which seems to belong to another time period*), chronological (*of dates and time sequences*), horology (*study and measurement of time*), synchronous (*existing or occurring at the same time*), temporal (*to do with time*).

toe ▶ bunion (*painful swelling on the big toe*), corn (*painful area of thickened skin on the toes or foot*), hammer toe (*toe that is bent downwards*), pedicure (*cosmetic treatment of the feet and toenails*).

tomb ▶ catacomb (*underground cemetery*), cromlech, dolmen (*megalithic tombs*), inter (*place someone in a tomb*), mausoleum

(*building housing a tomb or tombs*),
sepulchre (*stone tomb or
monument*).

tooth ▶ dental (*of teeth*), dentist
(*person qualified to treat the teeth*),
dentition (*arrangement or condition
of the teeth*), enamel (*hard
substance covering the crown of a
tooth*), orthodontics (*treatment of
irregularities of the teeth*), plaque,
tartar (*deposits which form on the
teeth*); *human teeth:* bicuspids,
canines, incisors, molars,
premolars, tricuspids, wisdom
teeth.

touch ▶ palpable (*able to be touched
or felt*), tactile (*relating to the sense
of touch*), tangible (*perceptible by
touch*).

tower ▶ *types of tower:* belfry,
campanile, donjon, keep, minaret,
steeple, turret, watchtower,
ziggurat.

tree ▶ arboreal (*to do with trees*),
deciduous (*referring to trees that
shed their leaves annually*),
evergreen (*referring to trees that
retain green leaves throughout the
year*), silviculture (*growing and
cultivation of trees*), topiary (*art of
clipping shrubs or trees into
attractive shapes*).

triangle ▶ *types of triangle:*
equilateral (*having sides of equal
length*), isosceles (*having two sides
equal*), scalene (*having all sides
unequal*).

twelve ▶ dodecagon (*plane figure
with twelve straight sides and twelve
angles*), dodecahedron (*three-
dimensional shape with twelve
faces*), duodecimal (*of a counting
system based on twelve*), gross
(*twelve dozen, 144*).

twin ▶ fraternal, dizygotic
(*referring to twins derived from two
separate ova*); identical,
monozygotic (*referring to twins
derived from one ovum*); Siamese,
conjoined (*referring to twins whose
bodies are joined at birth*).

two ▶ biennial (*taking place every
two years*), binary (*composed of or
involving two things*), bisect (*divide
into two parts*), dichotomy
(*separation or contrast between two
things*), dual (*consisting of two
parts, elements, or aspects*).

unconscious ▶ coma (*state of
deep unconsciousness*), comatose
(*deeply unconscious*), narcosis
(*drug-induced unconsciousness*),
resuscitate (*revive someone from
unconsciousness*).

universe ▶ astronomy (*science of
stars, planets, and the universe*),
cosmic (*of the universe*), cosmology,
cosmogony (*science of the origin
and development of the universe*).

university ▶ alumnus (*former
student of a particular university*),
campus (*university site and
buildings*), don (*university teacher*),
fresher (*newly arrived first-year
student*), graduation (*the receiving
of a degree*), matriculation
(*enrolment in a university*).

valley ▶ *kinds of valley:* basin,
combe, dale, dene, dingle, glen,
gorge, strath, wadi.

verse ▶ blank verse (*verse without
rhyme*), couplet (*pair of successive
lines of verse*), doggerel (*badly
written verse*), scansion (*rhythm of
a line of verse*).

vitamin ▶ *diseases caused by lack
of a vitamin:* beriberi (*vitamin B_1*),
pernicious anaemia (*vitamin B_{12}*),
rickets (*vitamin D*), scurvy (*vitamin
C*).

voice ▶ cadence (*rise and fall in
pitch of the voice*), intonation (*rise
and fall of the voice in speaking*),
register (*particular part of the
range of a person's voice*), timbre
(*character of voice as distinct from
its pitch and strength*), vocal (*of the
human voice*).

vote ▶ abstain (*formally choose not
to vote*), disenfranchise (*deprive
someone of the right to vote*),
electoral roll (*official list of people

in a district entitled to vote),
electorate (*people in a district
entitled to vote*), enfranchise (*give
someone the right to vote*), floating
voter (*person who does not vote for
the same party all the time*),
franchise (*the right to
vote*), referendum (*general vote by
the electorate on a single political
question*).

walk ▶ ambulatory (*to do with
walking*), circumambulate (*walk
all the way round*), pedestrian
(*person walking on a road*),
perambulate (*walk from place to
place*), promenade (*place for public
walking*).

war ▶ ceasefire (*temporary period
in a war when fighting stops*),
martial (*having to do with war*),
neutral (*not supporting either side
in a war*), pacifism (*belief that
disputes should be settled through
peaceful means rather than war*).

watch ▶ analogue (*referring to a
watch with hands*), digital
(*referring to a watch with a
numerical display*), fob (*chain for a
watch*), horology (*art of making
clocks and watches*), synchronize
(*set a watch to the same time as
another*).

water ▶ aquatic (*living in water*),
aqueduct (*bridge carrying water*),
aqueous, hydrous (*containing
water*), dehydrate (*remove water
from something*), hydraulic
(*operated by water*), hydrolysis
(*chemical breakdown of substances
in water*).

wave ▶ crest (*the top of the ridge of
a wave*), spindrift (*spray blown
from waves*), spume (*froth on
waves*), tsunami (*tidal wave
produced by an earthquake*),
undulate (*move with a wave-like
motion*). ▶

wealth ▶ magnate, tycoon (*very
wealthy businessman*); arriviste,
nouveau riche, parvenu (*person
who has recently become wealthy*);
avarice (*excessive greed for wealth*),

Mammon (*wealth seen as an evil
influence*), plutocracy (*rule by rich
people*).

Welsh ▶ *Welsh life and culture:*
cromlech (*ancient stone tomb*),
Cymru (*Welsh word for Wales*),
eisteddfod (*competitive festival of
music and poetry*), hwyl (*stirring
emotional feeling associated with the
Welsh*).

whale ▶ ambergris (*substance
produced by sperm whales, used in
making perfume*), blubber (*the fat of
whales and other sea mammals*),
baleen whales (*whales having
plates of whalebone in the mouth for
feeding on plankton*), cetacean (*a
whale or related mammal, e.g. a
dolphin or porpoise*), krill (*shrimp-
like crustaceans eaten by whales*),
pod (*group of whales*).

wheel ▶ hub, nave (*centre of a
wheel*), linchpin (*pin through the
end of an axle keeping a wheel in
position*), sprocket (*projecting tooth
on a wheel*).

will ▶ codicil (*supplement to a will*),
executor (*person appointed to carry
out the terms of a will*), intestate
(*having left no will*), legacy
(*something left to someone in a will*),
testate (*having made a valid will*),
testator (*a person making a will*).

wind ▶ anemometer (*instrument
for measuring wind speed*),
Beaufort Scale (*scale of wind
speeds*), leeward (*on or towards the
side sheltered from the wind*),
windward (*on or towards the side
facing the wind*).

window ▶ *types of window:* bay,
casement, clerestory, dormer,
fanlight, oriel, sash window,
skylight.

wine ▶ bouquet, nose (*scent of a
wine*), carafe (*flask for serving
wine*), lees (*sediment in wine*),
oenology (*study of wines*), vinous
(*of or like wine*), vintage (*year or
place in which wine was produced*),
vintner (*wine merchant*); brut

(*referring to very dry sparkling wine*), demi-sec (*medium dry*), pétillant (*slightly sparkling*), sec (*dry*).

witch ▶ coven (*group of witches*), familiar (*spirit accompanying and obeying a witch*), warlock (*man who practises witchcraft*), Wicca (*pagan religion of modern witchcraft*).

wood ▶ ligneous (*made or consisting of wood*), marquetry (*furniture decoration of inlaid wood*), parquet (*flooring of wooden blocks*), veneer (*thin decorative covering of wood*), wainscot (*area of wooden panelling in a room*).

woodwind ▶ *woodwind instruments:* bassoon, clarinet, cor anglais, flute, oboe, piccolo, recorder.

word ▶ verbal (*of or in words*), lexical (*to do with the vocabulary of a language*); acronym (*word formed from initial letters*), anagram (*word formed from the letters of another*), malapropism (*the use of a similar-sounding but wrong word*), neologism (*newly invented word*), nonce word (*word invented for a particular occasion*), onomatopoeic (*referring to a word imitating the sound of what it refers to*), palindrome (*word or phrase spelled the same backwards as forwards*), verbatim (*in exactly the same words*).

writing ▶ calligraphy (*decorative handwriting*), cursive (*referring to joined-up writing*), epistolary (*of the writing of letters*), graphology (*study of handwriting*), palaeography (*study of ancient writing systems*).

X-ray ▶ barium meal (*mixture swallowed to allow X-rays to be made of the stomach or intestines*), mammography (*the use of X-rays to diagnose tumours of the breasts*), radiography (*the production of images by X-rays*), radiology (*the science of X-rays*), radiotherapy (*the treatment of disease using X-rays*).

year ▶ annals (*history of events year by year*), annual (*occurring once a year; covering a year*), annuity (*sum of money paid to someone each year*), biannual (*occurring twice a year*), biennial (*occurring every other year*), per annum (*for each year*), perennial (*lasting through a year or several years*).

yellow ▶ *shades of yellow:* amber, daffodil, flaxen, gold, lemon, mustard.

young ▶ juvenilia (*works produced by a writer or artist when young*), rejuvenate (*make someone younger or more energetic*), salad days (*period when one is young and inexperienced*), wunderkind (*very successful young person*).

zodiac ▶ *signs of the zodiac:* Aries (*Ram*), Taurus (*Bull*), Gemini (*Twins*), Cancer (*Crab*), Leo (*Lion*), Virgo (*Virgin*), Libra (*Scales*), Scorpio (*Scorpion*), Sagittarius (*Archer*), Capricorn (*Goat*), Aquarius (*Water Bearer*), Pisces (*Fish/Fishes*).

Foreign words and phrases

Over the centuries the English language has assimilated words and phrases from a variety of other languages and this process continues unabated. All the words and phrases listed here are likely to be encountered in British English, where they are often printed in italics. The illustrative examples provided are taken from a variety of sources including newspapers, magazines, journals, and books.

ab initio (Latin): from the beginning.

a cappella (Italian): sung without instrumental accompaniment: *an a cappella performance of a medieval mass.* [literally 'in chapel style']

à deux (French): for or involving two people: *dinner à deux.*

ad hoc (Latin): made or done for a particular purpose: *an ad hoc meeting of ministers and civil servants.* [literally 'to this']

ad infinitum (Latin): endlessly; forever. [literally 'to infinity']

ad interim (Latin): for the meantime.

ad nauseam (Latin): to a tiresomely excessive degree: *a phrase repeated ad nauseam in the media.* [literally 'to sickness']

a fortiori (Latin): more conclusively. [literally 'from stronger']

agent provocateur (French): a person who tempts a suspected criminal to commit a crime and so be caught and convicted. [literally 'provocative agent']

à huis clos (French): in private. [literally 'with closed doors']

al dente (Italian): (of food) cooked so as to be still firm when bitten. [literally 'to the tooth']

alfresco (Italian): in the open air: *lunch was served alfresco.*

amour propre (French): self-respect. [literally 'love of oneself']

annus mirabilis (Latin): a remarkable or auspicious year.

a posteriori (Latin): based on reasoning from known facts or past events rather than on assumptions or predictions. [literally 'from what comes after']

a priori (Latin): based on deduction rather than experience: *a priori assumptions about human nature.* [literally 'from what is before']

au courant (French): well informed; up to date: *they're not au courant with the Japanese literary scene.* [literally 'in the (regular) course']

au fait (French): having a good or detailed knowledge: *he's evidently au fait with the technology.* [literally 'to the point']

au fond (French): basically; in essence: *au fond, she's quite a reasonable woman.* [literally 'at the bottom']

au naturel (French): in the most simple or natural way.

beau geste (French): a noble and generous act. [literally 'splendid gesture']

beau idéal (French): the highest standard of excellence. [literally 'ideal beauty']

beau monde (French): fashionable society. [literally 'fine world']

beaux arts (French): the fine arts.

bête noire (French): a person or thing one particularly dislikes. [literally 'black beast']

belles-lettres (French): literary works written and read for their elegant style. [literally 'fine letters']

billet-doux (French): a love letter. [literally 'sweet note']

blitzkrieg (German): an intense, violent military campaign intended to bring about a swift victory. [literally 'lightning war']

bona fide (Latin): genuine; real: *a bona fide money-back guarantee.* [literally 'with good faith']

bon mot (French): a clever or witty remark. [literally 'good word']

bon vivant (French): a person with a sociable and luxurious lifestyle. [literally 'person living well']

brasserie (French): an informal or inexpensive restaurant. [literally 'brewery']

carpe diem (Latin): make the most of the present time. [literally 'seize the day!']

carte blanche (French): complete freedom to act as one wishes: *he was given carte blanche to make whatever changes he saw fit.* [literally 'blank paper']

cause célèbre (French): a controversial issue attracting much public attention. [literally 'famous case']

caveat emptor (Latin): the buyer is responsible for checking the quality of goods before purchasing them. [literally 'let the buyer beware']

c'est la guerre (French): used as an expression of resigned acceptance. [literally 'that's war']

chacun à son gout (French): everyone to their own taste.

chef-d'œuvre (French): a masterpiece. [literally 'chief work']

cherchez la femme (French): there is certain to be a woman at the bottom of a problem or mystery. [literally 'look for the woman']

comme il faut (French): correct in behaviour or etiquette. [literally 'as is necessary']

compos mentis (Latin): sane; in full control of one's mind.

cognoscenti (Italian): people who are well informed about something: *a man regarded by the cognoscenti as the greatest pianist in Europe.* [literally 'people who know']

cordon sanitaire (French): a guarded line placed around an area infected by disease to prevent anyone from leaving. [literally 'sanitary line']

Cosa Nostra (Italian): a US criminal organization related to the Mafia. [literally 'our thing']

coup de foudre (French): love at first sight. [literally 'stroke of lightning']

coup de grâce (French): a blow by which a mortally wounded person or thing is mercifully killed. [literally 'stroke of grace']

coup de main (French): a sudden surprise attack. [literally 'stroke of hand']

coup d'état (French): a sudden violent seizure of power. [literally 'blow of state']

cri de cœur (French): a passionate appeal or protest. [literally 'cry from the heart']

cui bono? (Latin): who stands to gain (implying that this person may have been responsible for a crime)? [literally 'to whom (is it) a benefit?']

de facto (Latin): in fact, whether by right or not: *the de facto president of the republic.*

Dei gratia (Latin): by the grace of God.

déjà vu (French): the sense of having experienced the present situation before. [literally 'already seen']

de jure (Latin): rightful; by right: *a de jure claim to the territory.* [literally 'of law']

de nos jours (French): contemporary: *a kind of Oscar Wilde de nos jours.* [literally 'of our days']

Deo gratias (Latin): thanks be to God.

Deo volente (Latin): God willing.

de profundis (Latin): expressing one's deepest feelings. [literally 'from the depths']

de rigueur (French): obligatory; required by etiquette or current fashion: *black tie was de rigueur on such occasions.* [literally 'in strictness']

dernier cri (French): the very latest fashion: *a dark suit in the cut that was the dernier cri of that time.* [literally 'the last cry']

de trop (French): not wanted; superfluous: *she hovered uncertainly in the doorway, feeling rather de trop.* [literally 'excessive']

deus ex machina (Latin): an unexpected event that saves an apparently hopeless situation. [literally 'god from the machinery']

dolce far niente (Italian): pleasant idleness. [literally 'sweet doing nothing']

dolce vita (Italian): a life of pleasure and luxury. [literally 'sweet life']

doppelgänger (German): an apparition or double of a living person. [literally 'double-goer']

double entendre (French): a word or phrase with two possible interpretations. [from obsolete French, 'double understanding']

dramatis personae (Latin): the characters in a play. [literally 'persons of the drama']

embarras de richesse (French): more options or resources than one knows what to do with. [literally 'embarrassment of riches']

éminence grise (French): a person who has power or influence without holding an official position. [literally 'grey eminence']

en famille (French): with one's family; in an informal way: *we ate en famille at the kitchen table.* [literally 'in family']

enfant terrible (French): a person whose behaviour is unconventional or controversial. [literally 'terrible child']

en masse (French): all together: *the cabinet resigned en masse.* [literally 'in a mass']

en passant (French): by the way: *what is interesting, en passant, is that it is a pre-war model.* [literally 'in passing']

entente cordiale (French): a friendly understanding between states.

entre nous (French): between ourselves: *entre nous, I'll be glad when he retires.*

esprit de corps (French): a feeling of pride and loyalty uniting the members of a group. [literally 'spirit of the body']

ex gratia (Latin): (of payment) given as a favour rather than because of any legal obligation. [literally 'from favour']

ex officio (Latin): by virtue of one's position or status: *an ex officio member of the committee.* [literally 'out of duty']

fait accompli (French): a thing that has been done or decided and cannot now be altered. [literally 'accomplished fact']

faute de mieux (French): for want of a better alternative.

faux pas (French): an embarrassing blunder or indiscretion. [literally 'false step']

femme fatale (French): a seductive woman. [literally 'disastrous woman']

fête champêtre (French): an outdoor entertainment; a garden party. [literally 'rural festival']

fin de siècle (French): relating to the end of a century.

force majeure (French): superior strength.

folie de grandeur (French): delusions of grandeur.

gîte (French): a small furnished holiday house in France.

grande dame (French): a woman who is influential within a particular sphere: *the grande dame of British sculpture*. [literally 'grand lady']

haute couture (French): the designing and making of clothes by leading fashion houses. [literally 'high dressmaking']

haute cuisine (French): high-quality cooking. [literally 'high cookery']

haut monde (French): fashionable society. [literally 'high world']

hors de combat (French): out of action due to injury or damage: *the juke box is currently hors de combat*. [literally 'out of the fight']

ideé fixe (French): an obsession. [literally 'fixed idea']

in absentia (Latin): while not present: *he was sentenced to death in absentia*. [literally 'in absence']

in camera (Latin): in private: *the meeting will be held in camera*. [literally 'in the chamber']

in extremis (Latin): in an extremely difficult situation; at the point of death. [literally 'in the most extreme or furthest']

in loco parentis (Latin): in the place of a parent: *the head teacher was acting in loco parentis*.

in medias res (Latin): in or into the middle of a sequence of events: *he began his story in medias res*. [literally 'in the middle of things']

in propria persona (Latin): in his or her own person.

in situ (Latin): in the original or appropriate position. [literally 'in place']

inter alia (Latin): among other things: *charges of, inter alia, insider dealing and stock manipulation*. [literally 'among others']

in toto (Latin): as a whole: *he rejected the proposals in toto*.

ipso facto (Latin): by that very fact or act: *the enemy of one's enemy may be ipso facto a friend*. [literally 'by the fact itself']

je ne sais quoi (French): a quality that is hard to describe: *an actor possessed of that certain je ne sais quoi that makes someone a star*. [literally 'I do not know what']

jeu d'esprit (French): a light-hearted display of wit. [literally 'game of the mind']

jeunesse dorée (French): wealthy, fashionable young people. [literally 'gilded youth']

joie de vivre (French): exuberant enjoyment of life. [literally 'joy of living']

laissez-faire (French): a non-interventionist policy. [literally 'allow to do']

locum tenens (Latin): a temporary deputy or stand-in. [literally 'one holding a place']

locus classicus (Latin): the best known or most authoritative passage on a subject. [literally 'classical place']

magnum opus (Latin): the most important work of an artist, writer, etc. [literally 'great work']

manqué (French): having failed to become what one might have been: *an artist manqué*. [from *manquer*, 'to lack']

mea culpa (Latin): an acknowledgement that something is one's fault. [literally 'by my fault']

memento mori (Latin): something kept as a reminder that death is inevitable. [literally 'remember (that you have) to die']

ménage à trois (French): an arrangement in which a married couple and the lover of one of them live together. [literally 'household of three']

modus operandi (Latin): a way of doing something. [literally 'way of operating']

modus vivendi (Latin): an arrangement that allows conflicting parties to coexist peacefully. [literally 'way of living']

mot juste (French): the most exact or appropriate word or expression.

ne plus ultra (Latin): the best example of something: *the ne plus ultra of decorative splendour.* [literally 'not further beyond']

nil desperandum (Latin): do not despair. [literally 'no need to despair']

noblesse oblige (French): privilege entails responsibility. [literally 'nobility obligates']

nolens volens (Latin): whether one wants or likes something or not. [from *nolens* 'not willing' + *volens* 'willing']

non sequitur (Latin): a conclusion or statement that does not logically follow from the previous statement. [literally 'it does not follow']

nouveau riche (French): people who have recently become rich and who display their wealth ostentatiously. [literally 'new rich']

objet d'art (French): a small decorative or artistic object.

on dit (French): a piece of gossip. [literally 'they say']

par excellence (French): better or more than all others of the same kind: *a singer-songwriter par excellence.* [literally 'by excellence']

parti pris (French): a preconceived view; a bias. [literally 'side taken']

per annum (Latin): for each year.

per capita (Latin): for each person. [literally 'by heads']

per se (Latin): by or in itself or themselves: *Jack had nothing against women per se, but she had alarmed him.*

persona non grata (Latin): a person who is not welcome somewhere.

pièce de résistance (French): the most important or impressive item: *the pièce de résistance was chocolate cake laced with brandy.* [literally 'piece (i.e. means) of resistance']

pied-à-terre (French): a small flat or house kept for occasional use. [literally 'foot to earth']

pis aller (French): a last resort. [from *pis* 'worse' + *aller* 'to go']

plat du jour (French): a special dish prepared by a restaurant on a particular day. [literally 'dish of the day']

plus ça change (French): used to express resigned acknowledgement of the fact that certain things never change. [from *plus ça change, plus c'est la même chose* 'the more it changes, the more it stays the same']

prima facie (Latin): accepted as so until proved otherwise: *a prima facie case of professional misconduct.* [from *primus* 'first' + *facies* 'face']

primus inter pares (Latin): the senior or representative member of a group. [literally 'first among equals']

pro rata (Latin): proportional; proportionally. [literally 'according to the rate']

proxime accessit (Latin): the person who comes second in an examination or is runner-up for an award. [literally 'came very near']

quid pro quo (Latin): a favour or advantage given in return for something. [literally 'something for something']

raison d'être (French): the most important reason for someone or something's existence: *football appeared to be his sole raison d'être.* [literally 'reason for being']

reductio ad absurdam (Latin): a method of disproving a premise by showing that its logical conclusion is absurd. [literally 'reduction to the absurd']

roman-à-clef (French): a novel in which real people or events appear with invented names. [literally 'novel with a key']

sangfroid (French): the ability to stay calm in difficult circumstances. [literally 'cold blood']

savoir faire (French): the ability to act appropriately in social situations. [literally 'know how to do']

sine die (Latin): (of proceedings) adjourned indefinitely. [literally 'without a day']

sine qua non (Latin): a thing that is absolutely essential: *tennis courts are a sine qua non for any summer camp.* [literally 'without which not']

soi-disant (French): self-styled; so-called: *a soi-disant novelist.* [from *soi* 'oneself' + *disant* 'saying']

sotto voce (Italian): in a quiet voice. [from *sotto* 'under' + *voce* 'voice']

sub judice (Latin): being considered by a court of law and therefore not to be publicly discussed elsewhere. [literally 'under a judge']

sub rosa (Latin): happening or done in secret: *the inspection must be sub rosa.* [literally 'under the rose']

sui generis (Latin): unique: *each of his novels is sui generis.* [literally 'of its own kind']

table d'hôte (French): a restaurant meal offered at a fixed price, with few if any choices. [literally 'host's table']

tant mieux (French): so much the better.

tant pis (French): so much the worse; too bad.

terra firma (Latin): dry land; the ground. [literally 'firm land']

terra incognita (Latin): unknown territory.

tête-à-tête (French): a private conversation. [literally 'head-to-head']

tour de force (French): a thing accomplished with great skill: *the aria is a musical tour de force.* [literally 'feat of strength']

tout de suite (French): at once. [literally 'quite in sequence']

verboten (German): forbidden.

via media (Latin): a compromise. [literally 'middle way']

victor ludorum (Latin): the overall champion in a sports competition. [literally 'victor of the games']

vis-à-vis (French): in relation to; as compared with: *the value of the dollar vis-à-vis other currencies.* [literally 'face-to-face']

vox populi (Latin): public opinion. [literally 'the people's voice']

zeitgeist (German): the characteristic spirit or mood of a particular historical period. [from *Zeit* 'time' + *Geist* 'spirit']

Commonly confused words

There are many words in the English language which look alike or sound alike but have quite different meanings. Such words are very easy to confuse and the following list explains the differences between the pairs (or trios) of words that commonly cause problems.

adopted, adoptive
children are **adopted**, but parents are **adoptive**.

accept, except
accept means 'agree', whereas **except** means 'not including'.

access, excess
access to somewhere is the means or opportunity to enter it or use it; an **excess** of something is more of it than is necessary or desirable.

adverse, averse
adverse means 'unfavourable, bad' whereas **averse** means 'strongly disliking or opposed to something' as in *I am not averse to helping out.*

affect, effect
affect means 'make a difference to someone or something', whereas **effect** means 'a result' or 'bring about a result'.

allusion, illusion
an **allusion** is an indirect reference to something; an **illusion** is a false idea or belief.

amoral, immoral
amoral means 'lacking any sense of morality', whereas **immoral** means 'not following accepted standards of morality'.

ante, anti
ante means 'before'; **anti** means 'against'.

appraise, apprise
to **appraise** something is to assess it, whereas to **apprise** someone of something is to inform them of it.

assent, ascent
assent means 'approval or agreement'; an **ascent** is an instance of going up something, as in *the first ascent of the Matterhorn.*

augur, auger
augur means 'be a sign of something in the future'; an **auger** is a tool used for boring holes in wood.

aural, oral
aural means 'relating to the ear or sense of hearing', whereas **oral** means 'relating to the mouth' or 'spoken rather than written'.

baited, bated
baited is an inflection of the verb 'to bait'; waiting for something with **bated** breath is to wait for it in a state of great suspense or excitement.

balmy, barmy
balmy means 'pleasantly warm', whereas **barmy** means 'mad, crazy'.

bass, base
bass denotes the lowest adult male singing voice; the **base** of something is its supporting part, foundation, or starting point.

biannual, biennial
biannual means 'occurring twice a year', whereas **biennial** means 'taking place every two years'.

breach, breech
a **breach** is a hole or gap, or an action that breaks a rule or agreement; the **breech** of a gun barrel is the back part of it.

cannon, canon
a **cannon** is a gun, whereas a **canon** is a clergyman, a rule or law, or a list of books or other works.

canvas, canvass

canvas is a kind of material; to **canvass** is to seek political support before an election or to seek people's opinions on something.

censure, censor, censer

to **censure** someone or something is to express strong disapproval of them, to **censor** a book or film is to suppress unacceptable parts of it, and a **censer** is a container in which incense is burnt.

chord, cord

a **chord** is group of musical notes sounded together; a **cord** is a length of string or an anatomical structure resembling this, as in *spinal cord* or *vocal cords*.

climactic, climatic

climactic means 'forming a climax', whereas **climatic** means 'relating to climate'.

complacent, complaisant

complacent means 'smug and self-satisfied'; **complaisant** means 'willing to please'.

complement, compliment

to **complement** something is to enhance it by adding extra features, whereas to **compliment** someone or something is to express praise or approval of them.

confidant, confident

a **confidant** (or **confidante** if the person is female) is a person in whom one confides; **confident** means 'self-assured' or 'certain'.

council, counsel

a **council** is an administrative or advisory body of people; **counsel** is advice or guidance.

councillor, counsellor

a **councillor** is a member of a council; a **counsellor** gives guidance on personal or psychological problems.

credible, creditable

credible means 'believable, convincing', whereas **creditable** means 'deserving praise'.

curb, kerb

a **curb** is a check or restraint, as in *curbs on public expenditure*; a **kerb** is the edge of a pavement.

currant, current

currants are dried fruits; a **current** is a flow of water, air, or electrically charged particles.

defuse, diffuse

defuse means 'remove the fuse from an explosive device' or 'reduce danger or tension in a difficult situation'; **diffuse** means 'spread over a wide area'.

desert, dessert

deserts are large waterless areas; **desserts** are puddings.

discreet, discrete

discreet means 'careful and judicious', whereas **discrete** means 'separate, distinct'.

draft, draught

in British English a **draft** means 'a preliminary version' or 'an order to pay a sum of money', while a **draught** means 'a current of air' or 'an act of drinking'; in American English the spelling **draft** is used for all senses.

elicit, illicit

elicit is a verb, meaning 'draw out a response or reaction'; **illicit** is an adjective meaning 'forbidden or unlawful'.

emigrate, immigrate

a person **emigrates** from their country and **immigrates** into another, leaving the first to settle permanently in the second.

envelop, envelope

to **envelop** something is to cover or surround it completely; an **envelope** encloses a letter or document.

equable, equitable

an **equable** person is calm and even-tempered; an **equitable** system is a fair one.

exceptionable, exceptional

exceptionable means 'causing disapproval or offence', whereas

exceptional means 'not typical' or 'unusually good'.

fawn, faun

a **fawn** is a young deer and also a light brown colour; a **faun** is a Roman god portrayed as part man, part goat.

flaunt, flout

to **flaunt** something is to display it ostentatiously; to **flout** a rule or law is to openly disregard it.

flounder, founder

flounder generally means 'have trouble doing or understanding something', whereas **founder** means 'fail or come to nothing'.

forbear, forebear

to **forbear** from something is to stop oneself doing it; a **forebear** is an ancestor.

foreword, forward

a **foreword** is a short introduction to a book; **forward** means 'onward' or 'ahead'.

fractious, factious

fractious means 'bad-tempered'; **factious** means 'having opposing or dissenting views'.

freeze, frieze

freeze denotes the process by which liquids turn into solids as a result of extreme cold; a **frieze** is a band of sculpted or painted decoration on a wall.

Gallic, Gaelic

Gallic means 'French'; **Gaelic** means 'Celtic'.

grisly, grizzly

grisly means 'horrific or revolting'; a **grizzly** is a bear.

hangar, hanger

a **hangar** is a large building for housing aircraft; a **hanger** is something to hang clothes on.

hoard, horde

a **hoard** is a store of something valuable, whereas **horde** is a disparaging term for a large group of people.

hummus, humus

hummus (or **houmous**) is a dip made from ground chickpeas; **humus** is an organic component of soil.

incredible, incredulous

incredible means 'impossible or hard to believe', whereas **incredulous** means 'unwilling or unable to believe something'.

interment, internment

interment means 'burial'; **internment** means 'imprisonment'.

lama, llama

a **lama** is a Buddhist monk; a **llama** is a South American animal.

loath, loathe

if you are **loath** to do something, you are reluctant or unwilling to do it; to **loathe** someone or something is to dislike them greatly.

loose, lose

as a verb **loose** means 'unfasten or set free'; **lose** means 'no longer have' or 'become unable to find'.

luxuriant, luxurious

luxuriant means 'rich and profuse in growth', whereas **luxurious** means 'very comfortable, elegant, and expensive'.

marital, martial

marital means 'to do with marriage', whereas **martial** means 'to do with war'.

meter, metre

a **meter** is a measuring device, whereas a **metre** is a metric unit; **metre** is also the rhythm of a piece of poetry.

militate, mitigate

to **militate** against something is to be a strong factor in preventing it; to **mitigate** something unpleasant or unwelcome is to make it less severe.

naturist, naturalist

a **naturist** is a nudist; a **naturalist** is an expert in natural history.

omit, emit

to **omit** something is to leave it out; to **emit** something is to discharge it, as in *factories which emit pollutants into rivers*.

ordinance, ordnance

an **ordinance** is an official order or a religious rite; **ordnance** is a term for guns or munitions.

palate, palette, pallet

a person's **palate** is the roof of their mouth, a **palette** is a small board on which an artist mixes colours, and a **pallet** is a portable platform on which goods can be stacked or transported; a **pallet** is also a straw mattress.

pedal, peddle

a **pedal** is a foot-operated lever, to **pedal** is to move by means of pedals; to **peddle** goods is to sell them.

pole, poll

a **pole** is a long thin piece of wood and also each of the two opposite points of a magnet; **poll** denotes the process of voting in an election.

pour, pore

liquids **pour** or are poured; to **pore** over a book is to read it attentively.

practice, practise

in British spelling **practice** is the noun and **practise** the verb.

principal, principle

principal means 'most important, main'; a **principle** is a general law or rule used as a basis for a system of belief or behaviour.

proscribe, prescribe

to **proscribe** something is to forbid or condemn it; to **prescribe** something is either to recommend the use of a medicine or treatment or to state officially that something should be done.

sceptic, septic

a **sceptic** is someone who questions accepted beliefs or statements; a **septic** wound is one that has become infected with bacteria.

shear, sheer

to **shear** a sheep is to cut off its wool; to **sheer** means 'swerve or change course quickly' or 'avoid an unpleasant topic', as in *her mind sheered away from these unwelcome images*.

sight, site

sight is the ability to see or something seen; a **site** is a place where something is located or happens.

stationary, stationery

the adjective **stationary** means 'not moving or changing'; **stationery** is a noun meaning 'paper and other writing materials'.

story, storey

a **story** is a tale or account; a **storey** is a floor of a building.

swat, swot

to **swat** a fly is to hit or crush it with a sharp blow; to **swot** for an exam is to study hard for it.

team, teem

a **team** is a group of sports players; **teem** means 'to be full of something' or 'to pour with rain'.

titillate, titivate

to **titillate** someone is to excite them; to **titivate** someone or something is to make them smarter or more attractive.

tortuous, torturous

tortuous means 'full of twists and turns' or 'excessively lengthy and complex'; **torturous** means 'characterized by pain and suffering', as in *a torturous and lingering death*.

turbid, turgid

turbid liquids are cloudy or muddy, whereas a **turgid** river is swollen or overflowing; **turgid** can also be used to describe language that is pompous and boring.

unsociable, unsocial, antisocial

unsociable means 'not enjoying or engaging in activities with others'; **unsocial** usually means 'socially inconvenient' and typically refers to a job's hours of work; **antisocial** means 'contrary to accepted social behaviour and therefore annoying'.

venal, venial

venal means 'susceptible to bribery'; in Christian theology a **venial** sin (in contrast to a mortal sin) is one that will not deprive the soul of divine grace.

wreath, wreathe

a **wreath** is an arrangement of flowers; to **wreathe** is to surround or encircle.

Countries of the world

country	related adjective/noun	currency unit
Afghanistan	Afghan	afghani = 100 puls
Albania	Albanian	lek = 100 qindarka
Algeria	Algerian	dinar = 100 centimes
America (*see* United States of America)		
Andorra	Andorran	euro = 100 cents (formerly French franc, Spanish peseta)
Angola	Angolan	kwanza = 100 lwei
Antigua and Barbuda	Antiguan, Barbudan	dollar = 100 cents
Argentina	Argentinian	peso = 10,000 centavos
Armenia	Armenian	dram = 100 luma
Australia	Australian	dollar = 100 cents
Austria	Austrian	euro = 100 cents (formerly schilling =100 groschen)
Azerbaijan	Azerbaijani	manat = 100 gopik
Bahamas	Bahamian	dollar = 100 cents
Bahrain	Bahraini	dinar = 1,000 fils
Bangladesh	Bangladeshi	taka = 100 poisha
Barbados	Barbadian	dollar = 100 cents
Belarus	Belorussian *or* Byelorussian	rouble
Belgium	Belgian	euro = 100 cents (formerly franc = 100 centimes)
Belize	Belizian	dollar = 100 cents
Benin	Beninese	African franc
Bhutan	Bhutanese	ngultrum = 100 chetrum
Bolivia	Bolivian	boliviano = 100 centavos
Bosnia–Herzegovina	Bosnian	dinar = 100 paras
Botswana	Botswanan / Tswana	pula = 100 thebe
Brazil	Brazilian	real = 100 centavos
Brunei	Bruneian	dollar = 100 sen
Bulgaria	Bulgarian	lev = 100 stotinki
Burkina Faso	Burkinese	African franc
Burma (officially called Myanmar)	Burmese	kyat = 100 pyas
Burundi	Burundian	franc = 100 centimes
Cambodia	Cambodian	riel = 100 sen
Cameroon	Cameroonian	African franc
Canada	Canadian	dollar = 100 cents
Cape Verde Islands	Cape Verdean	escudo = 100 centavos
Central African Republic	–	African franc
Chad	Chadian	African franc
Chile	Chilean	peso = 100 centavos
China	Chinese	yuan = 10 jiao or 100 fen
Colombia	Colombian	peso = 100 centavos
Comoros	Comoran	African franc
Congo	Congolese	African franc

country	related adjective/noun	currency unit
Congo, Democratic Republic of (Zaire)	Congolese	franc = 100 centimes
Costa Rica	Costa Rican	colón = 100 centimos
Croatia	Croat or Croatian	kuna = 100 lipa
Cuba	Cuban	peso = 100 centavos
Cyprus	Cypriot	pound = 100 cents
Czech Republic	Czech	koruna = 100 haleru
Denmark	Danish/Dane	krone = 100 øre
Djibouti	Djiboutian	franc = 100 centimes
Dominica	Dominican	dollar = 100 cents
Dominican Republic	Dominican	peso = 100 centavos
Ecuador	Ecuadorean	sucre = 100 centavos
Egypt	Egyptian	pound = 100 piastres or 1,000 milliemes
El Salvador	Salvadorean	colón = 100 centavos
Equatorial Guinea	Equatorial Guinean	African franc
Eritrea	Eritrean	nakfa = 100 cents
Estonia	Estonian	kroon = 100 sents
Ethiopia	Ethiopian	birr = 100 cents
Fiji	Fijian	dollar = 100 cents
Finland	Finnish / Finn	euro = 100 cents (formerly markka = 100 penniä)
France	French	euro = 100 cents (formerly franc = 100 centimes)
Gabon	Gabonese	African franc
Gambia, the	Gambian	dalasi = 100 butut
Georgia	Georgian	lari = 100 tetri
Germany	German	euro = 100 cents (formerly Deutschmark = 100 pfennigs)
Ghana	Ghanaian	cedi = 100 pesewas
Greece	Greek	euro = 100 cents (formerly drachma = 100 leptae)
Grenada	Grenadian	dollar = 100 cents
Guatemala	Guatemalan	quetzal = 100 centavos
Guinea	Guinean	franc = 100 centimes
Guinea-Bissau	–	peso = 100 centavos
Guyana	Guyanese	dollar = 100 cents
Haiti	Haitian	gourde = 100 centimes
Holland (see Netherlands)		
Honduras	Honduran	lempira = 100 centavos
Hungary	Hungarian	forint = 100 filler
Iceland	Icelandic / Icelander	krona = 100 aurar
India	Indian	rupee = 100 paisa
Indonesia	Indonesian	rupiah = 100 sen
Iran	Iranian	rial = 100 dinars
Iraq	Iraqi	dinar = 1,000 fils
Ireland, Republic of	Irish	euro = 100 cents (formerly pound [punt] = 100 pence)
Israel	Israeli	shekel = 100 agora
Italy	Italian	euro = 100 cents (formerly lira = 100 centesemos)

country	related adjective/noun	currency unit
Ivory Coast	Ivorian	African franc
Jamaica	Jamaican	dollar = 100 cents
Japan	Japanese	yen = 100 sen
Jordan	Jordanian	dinar = 1,000 fils
Kazakhstan	Kazakh	tenge = 100 teins
Kenya	Kenyan	shilling = 100 cents
Kiribati	–	dollar = 100 cents
Kuwait	Kuwaiti	dinar = 1,000 fils
Kyrgyzstan	Kyrgyz	som = 100 tiyin
Laos	Laotian	kip = 100 ats
Latvia	Latvian	lat = 100 santims
Lebanon	Lebanese	pound = 100 piastres
Lesotho	Lesothan / Mosotho, pl. Basotho	loti = 100 lisente
Liberia	Liberian	dollar = 100 cents
Libya	Libyan	dinar = 1,000 dirhams
Liechtenstein	– / Liechtensteiner	Swiss franc
Lithuania	Lithuanian	litas = 100 centas
Luxembourg	– / Luxembourger	euro = 100 cents (formerly franc = 100 centimes)
Macedonia	Macedonian	denar = 100 deni
Madagascar	Malagasay or Madagascan	franc = 100 centimes
Malawi	Malawian	kwacha = 100 tambala
Malaysia	Malaysian	ringgit = 100 sen
Maldives	Maldivian	rufiyaa = 100 laris
Mali	Malian	African franc
Malta	Maltese	lira = 100 cents
Marshall Islands	Marshallese	US dollar
Mauritania	Mauritanian	ouguiya = 5 khoums
Mauritius	Mauritian	rupee = 100 cents
Mexico	Mexican	peso = 100 centavos
Micronesia, Federated States of	Micronesian	US dollar
Moldova	Moldovan	leu = 100 bani
Monaco	Monegasque or Monacan	euro = 100 cents (formerly franc = 100 centimes)
Mongolia	Mongolian	tugrik = 100 mongos
Montenegro (see Union of Serbia and Montenegro)		
Morocco	Moroccan	dirham = 100 centimes
Mozambique	Mozambican	metical = 100 centavos
Myanmar (see Burma)		
Namibia	Namibian	rand = 100 cents
Nauru	Nauruan	Australian dollar
Nepal	Nepalese	rupee = 100 paisa
Netherlands, the	Dutch	euro = 100 cents (formerly guilder = 100 cents)
New Zealand	– / New Zealander	dollar = 100 cents
Nicaragua	Nicaraguan	cordoba = 100 centavos
Niger	Nigerien	African franc
Nigeria	Nigerian	naira = 100 kobo

country	related adjective/noun	currency unit
North Korea	North Korean	won = 100 jun
Norway	Norwegian	krone = 100 øre
Oman	Omani	rial = 1,000 baiza
Pakistan	Pakistani	rupee = 100 paisa
Panama	Panamanian	balboa = 100 centésimos
Papua New Guinea	Papua New Guinean *or* Guinean	kina = 100 toea
Paraguay	Paraguayan	guarani = 100 centimos
Peru	Peruvian	nuevo sol = 100 cents
Philippines	Filipino *or* Philippine	peso = 100 centavos
Poland	Polish / Pole	zloty = 100 groszy
Portugal	Portuguese	euro = 100 cents (formerly escudo = 100 centavos)
Qatar	Qatari	riyal = 100 dirhams
Romania	Romanian	leu = 100 bani
Russia	Russian	rouble = 100 copecks
Rwanda	Rwandan	franc = 100 centimes
St Kitts and Nevis	–	dollar = 100 cents
St Lucia	St Lucian	dollar = 100 cents
St Vincent and the Grenadines	Vincentian, Grenadian	dollar = 100 cents
Samoa	Samoan	tala = 100 sene
San Marino	–	euro = 100 cents (formerly Italian lira)
São Tomé and Principe	–	dobra = 100 centavos
Saudi Arabia	Saudi Arabian *or* Saudi	riyal = 20 qursh or 100 halalas
Senegal	Senegalese	African franc
Serbia (*see* Union of Serbia and Montenegro)		
Seychelles, the	Seychellois	rupee = 100 cents
Sierra Leone	Sierra Leonean	leone = 100 cents
Singapore	Singaporean	dollar = 100 cents
Slovakia	Slovak	koruna = 100 haleru
Slovenia	Slovene *or* Slovenian	tolar = 100 stotins
Solomon Islands	– / Solomon Islander	dollar = 100 cents
Somalia	Somali *or* Somalian	shilling = 100 cents
South Africa	South African	rand = 100 cents
South Korea	South Korean	won = 100 jeon
Spain	Spanish / Spaniard	euro = 100 cents (formerly peseta = 100 centimos)
Sri Lanka	Sri Lankan	rupee = 100 cents
Sudan	Sudanese	dinar = 10 pounds
Suriname	Surinamese	guilder = 100 cents
Swaziland	Swazi	lilangeni = 100 cents
Sweden	Swedish / Swede	krona = 100 öre
Switzerland	Swiss	franc = 100 centimes
Syria	Syrian	pound = 100 piastres
Taiwan	Taiwanese	New Taiwan dollar = 100 cents
Tajikistan	Tajik *or* Tadjik	somoni = 100 dirams
Tanzania	Tanzanian	shilling = 100 cents
Thailand	Thai	baht = 100 satangs
Togo	Togolese	African franc

country	related adjective/noun	currency unit
Tonga	Tongan	pa'anga = 100 seniti
Trinidad and Tobago	Trinidadian, Tobagonian	dollar = 100 cents
Tunisia	Tunisian	dinar = 1,000 milliemes
Turkey	Turkish / Turk	lira = 100 kurus
Turkmenistan	Turkmen *or* Turkoman	manat = 100 tenge
Tuvalu	Tuvaluan	dollar = 100 cents
Uganda	Ugandan	shilling = 100 cents
Ukraine	Ukrainian	hryvna = 100 kopiykas
Union of Serbia and Montenegro	Montenegrin, Serbian	dinar = 100 paras
United Arab Emirates	—	dirham = 100 fils
United Kingdom	British / Briton	pound = 100 pence
United States of America	American	dollar = 100 cents
Uruguay	Uruguayan	peso = 100 centésimos
Uzbekistan	Uzbek	som
Vanuatu	Vanuatuan	vatu = 100 centimes
Vatican City	—	euro = 100 cents (formerly Italian lira)
Venezuela	Venezuelan	bolivar = 100 centimos
Vietnam	Vietnamese	dong = 10 hao or 100 xu
Yemen	Yemeni	riyal = 100 fils
Zaire (*see* Congo, Democratic Republic of)		
Zambia	Zambian	kwacha = 100 ngwee
Zimbabwe	Zimbabwean	dollar = 100 cents

Chemical elements and symbols

actinium	Ac	hafnium	Hf	promethium	Pm
aluminium	Al	hassium	Hs	protactinium	Pa
americium	Am	helium	He	radium	Ra
antimony	Sb	holmium	Ho	radon	Rn
argon	Ar	hydrogen	H	rhenium	Re
arsenic	As	indium	In	rhodium	Rh
astatine	At	iodine	I	rubidium	Rb
barium	Ba	iridium	Ir	ruthenium	Ru
berkelium	Bk	iron	Fe	rutherfordium	Rf
beryllium	Be	krypton	Kr	samarium	Sm
bismuth	Bi	lanthanum	La	scandium	Sc
bohrium	Bh	lawrencium	Lr	seaborgium	Sg
boron	B	lead	Pb	selenium	Se
bromine	Br	lithium	Li	silicon	Si
cadmium	Cd	lutetium	Lu	silver	Ag
caesium	Cs	magnesium	Mg	sodium	Na
calcium	Ca	manganese	Mn	strontium	Sr
californium	Cf	meitnerium	Mt	sulphur	S
carbon	C	mendelevium	Md	tantalum	Ta
cerium	Ce	mercury	Hg	technetium	Tc
chlorine	Cl	molybdenum	Mo	tellurium	Te
chromium	Cr	neodymium	Nd	terbium	Tb
cobalt	Co	neon	Ne	thallium	Tl
copper	Cu	neptunium	Np	thorium	Th
curium	Cm	nickel	Ni	thulium	Tm
dubnium	Db	niobium	Nb	tin	Sn
dysprosium	Dy	nitrogen	N	titanium	Ti
einsteinium	Es	nobelium	Nb	tungsten	W
erbium	Er	osmium	Os	uranium	U
europium	Eu	oxygen	O	vanadium	V
fermium	Fm	palladium	Pd	xenon	Xe
fluorine	F	phosphorus	P	ytterbium	Yb
francium	Fr	platinum	Pt	yttrium	Y
gadolinium	Gd	plutonium	Pu	zinc	Zn
gallium	Ga	polonium	Po	zirconium	Zr
germanium	Ge	potassium	K		
gold	Au	praseodymium	Pr		

Collective names for animals and birds

Many of these names are humorous terms which were probably rarely if ever used: they were taken up by a writer called Joseph Strutt in 'Sports & Pastimes of England' (1801) and then by other antiquarian writers. The list is arranged in the alphabetical order of the birds and animals themselves.

a shrewdness of **apes**

a herd or pace of **asses**

a troop of **baboons**

a cete of **badgers**

a sloth of **bears**

a swarm, drift, hive, or erst of **bees**

a flock, flight, or pod of **birds**

a herd, gang, or obstinacy of **buffalo**

a bellowing of **bullfinches**

a drove of **bullocks**

a clowder or glaring of **cats**

an army of **caterpillars**

a herd or drove of **cattle**

a brood, clutch, or peep of **chickens**

a chattering of **choughs**

a rag or rake of **colts**

a covert of **coots**

a herd of **cranes**

a bask of **crocodiles**

a murder of **crows**

a litter of **cubs**

a herd of **curlew**

a herd or mob of **deer**

a pack or kennel of **dogs**

a school of **dolphins**

a trip of **dotterel**

a flight, dole, or piteousness of **doves**

a paddling of **ducks** (*on water*)

a safe of **ducks** (*on land*)

a fling of **dunlin**

a herd or parade of **elephants**

a herd or gang of **elk**

a busyness of **ferrets**

a charm of **finches**

a shoal or run of **fish**

a swarm or cloud of **flies**

a skulk of **foxes**

a gaggle of **geese** (*on land*)

a skein, team, or wedge of **geese** (*in flight*)

a herd of **giraffe**

a cloud of **gnats**

a flock, herd, or trip of **goats**

a band of **gorillas**

a pack or covey of **grouse**

a down, mute, or husk of **hares**

a cast of **hawks**

a siege of **herons**

a bloat of **hippopotami**

a drove, string, stud, or team of **horses**

a pack, cry, or kennel of **hounds**

a flight or swarm of **insects**

a fluther or smack of **jellyfish**

a mob or troop of **kangaroos**

a litter or kindle of **kittens**

a desert of **lapwings**

a bevy or exaltation of **larks**

a leap of **leopards**

a pride or sawt of **lions**

a tiding of **magpies**

a sord or suit of **mallard**

a stud of **mares**

a richesse of **martens**

a labour of **moles**

a troop of **monkeys**

a span or barren of **mules**

a watch of **nightingales**

a parliament or stare of **owls**

a yoke of **oxen**

a pandemonium of **parrots**

a covey of **partridges**

a muster of **peacocks**

a muster, parcel, or rookery of **penguins**

a bevy or head of **pheasants**

a litter or herd of **pigs**

a kit of **pigeons** (*in flight*)

a congregation, stand, or wing of **plovers**

a rush or flight of **pochards**

a pod, school, herd, or turmoil of **porpoises**

a covey of **ptarmigan**

a litter of **pups**

a bevy or drift of **quail**

a bury of **rabbits**

a string of **racehorses**

an unkindness of **ravens**

a crash of **rhinoceros**

a bevy of **roe deer**

a parliament, building, or rookery of **rooks**

a hill of **ruffs**

a pod, herd, or rookery of **seals**

a flock, herd, trip, or mob of **sheep**

a dopping of **sheldrake**

a wisp or walk of **snipe**

a host of **sparrows**

a murmuration of **starlings**

a flight of **swallows**

a game or herd of **swans** (*on land*)

a wedge of **swans** (*in flight*)

a drift, herd, or sounder of **swine**

a spring of **teal**

a knot of **toads**

a hover of **trout**

a rafter of **turkeys**

a bale or turn of **turtles**

a bunch or knob of **waterfowl**

a school, herd, pod, or gam of **whales**

a company or trip of **wigeon**

a sounder of **wild boar**

a dout or destruction of **wild cats**

a team of **wild ducks** (*in flight*)

a bunch, trip, plump, or knob of **wildfowl**

a pack or rout of **wolves**

a fall of **woodcock**

a descent of **woodpeckers**

a herd of **wrens**

a zeal of **zebras**